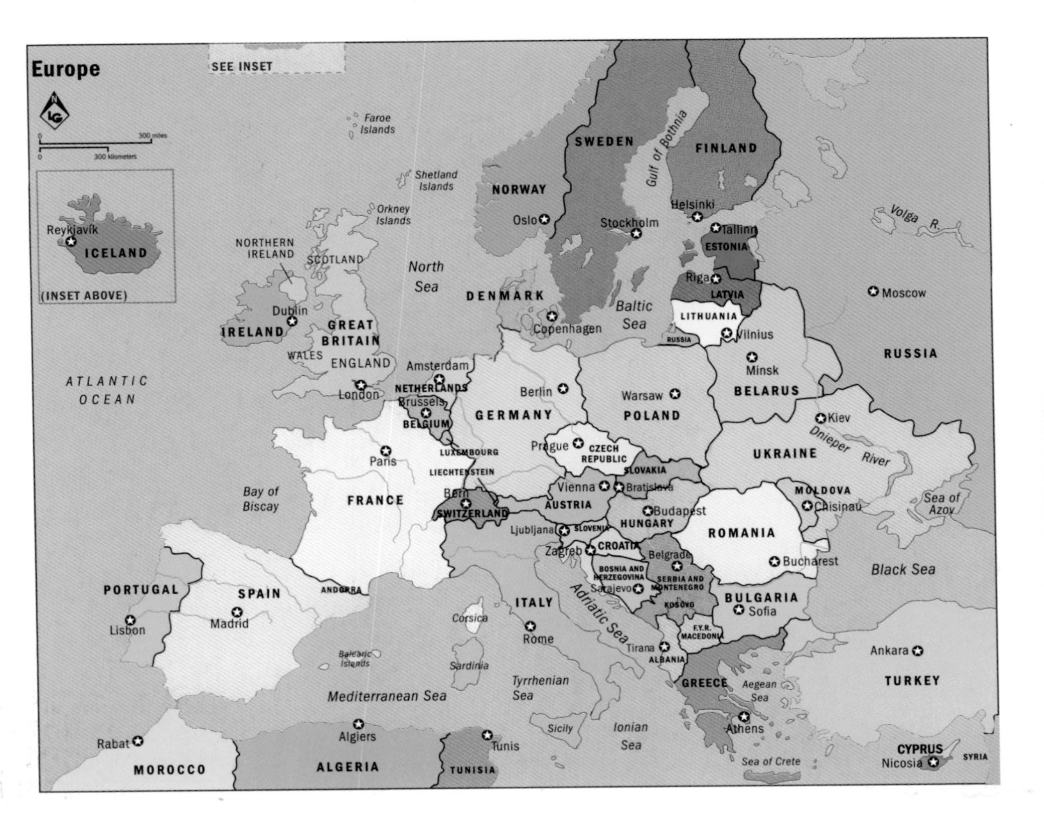
Europe
SEE INSET
0 300 miles
0 300 kilometers
Reykjavík
ICELAND
(INSET ABOVE)
Faroe Islands
Shetland Islands
Orkney Islands
NORTHERN IRELAND
SCOTLAND
North Sea
IRELAND
Dublin
GREAT BRITAIN
WALES
ENGLAND
London
ATLANTIC OCEAN
NORWAY
Oslo
SWEDEN
Stockholm
Gulf of Bothnia
FINLAND
Helsinki
Tallinn
ESTONIA
Riga
LATVIA
LITHUANIA
Vilnius
RUSSIA
DENMARK
Copenhagen
Baltic Sea
Volga R.
Moscow
RUSSIA
Minsk
BELARUS
Amsterdam
NETHERLANDS
Brussels
BELGIUM
LUXEMBOURG
LIECHTENSTEIN
Berlin
GERMANY
Warsaw
POLAND
Prague
CZECH REPUBLIC
SLOVAKIA
Kiev
Dnieper River
UKRAINE
Paris
FRANCE
Bay of Biscay
Bern
SWITZERLAND
Vienna
Bratislava
AUSTRIA
Budapest
HUNGARY
MOLDOVA
Chisinau
Sea of Azov
ROMANIA
Bucharest
Black Sea
Ljubljana
SLOVENIA
Zagreb
CROATIA
Belgrade
BOSNIA AND HERZEGOVINA
SERBIA AND MONTENEGRO
Sarajevo
KOSOVO
BULGARIA
Sofia
F.Y.R. MACEDONIA
Tirana
ALBANIA
PORTUGAL
Lisbon
SPAIN
Madrid
ANDORRA
Corsica
ITALY
Rome
Adriatic Sea
Balearic Islands
Sardinia
Tyrrhenian Sea
Mediterranean Sea
GREECE
Aegean Sea
Athens
Ankara
TURKEY
Sicily
Ionian Sea
Sea of Crete
CYPRUS
Nicosia
SYRIA
Rabat
MOROCCO
Algiers
ALGERIA
Tunis
TUNISIA

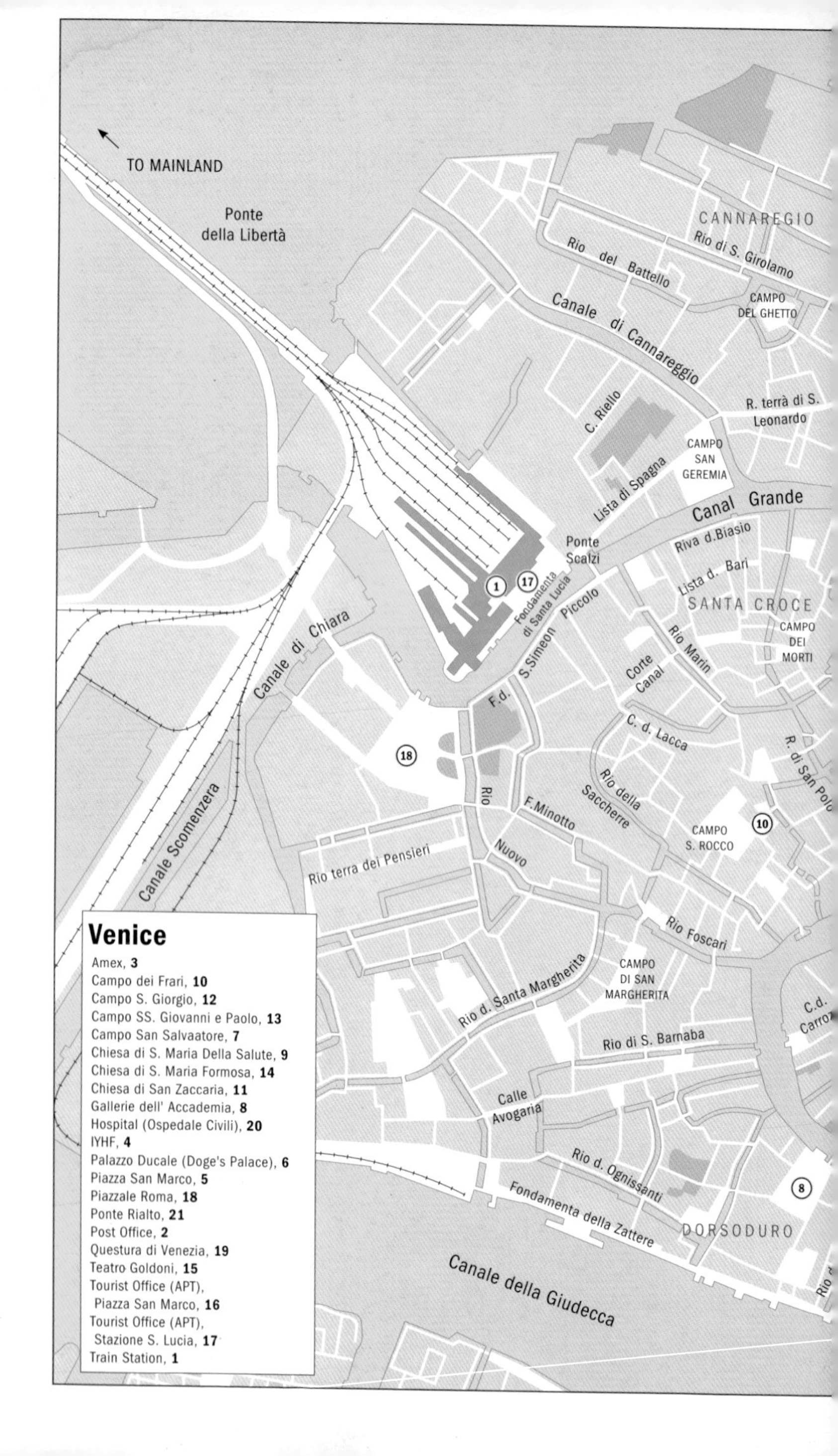
TO MAINLAND
Ponte della Libertà
CANNAREGIO
Rio di S. Girolamo
Rio del Battello
CAMPO DEL GHETTO
Canale di Cannareggio
R. terrà di S. Leonardo
C. Riello
CAMPO SAN GEREMIA
Lista di Spagna
Canal Grande
Ponte Scalzi
Riva d.Biasio
Lista d. Bari
SANTA CROCE
CAMPO DEI MORTI
Fondamenta di Santa Lucia
S.Simeon Piccolo
Rio Marin
Corte Canal
Canale di Chiara
F.d.
C. d. Lacca
R. di San Polo
Rio della Saccherre
CAMPO S. ROCCO
Canale Scomenzera
Rio Nuovo
F.Minotto
Rio terra dei Pensieri
Rio Foscari
CAMPO DI SAN MARGHERITA
Rio d. Santa Margherita
C.d. Carroz
Rio di S. Barnaba
Calle Avogaria
Rio d. Ognissanti
Fondamenta della Zattere
DORSODURO
Canale della Giudecca
Venice
Amex, 3
Campo dei Frari, 10
Campo S. Giorgio, 12
Campo SS. Giovanni e Paolo, 13
Campo San Salvaatore, 7
Chiesa di S. Maria Della Salute, 9
Chiesa di S. Maria Formosa, 14
Chiesa di San Zaccaria, 11
Gallerie dell' Accademia, 8
Hospital (Ospedale Civili), 20
IYHF, 4
Palazzo Ducale (Doge's Palace), 6
Piazza San Marco, 5
Piazzale Roma, 18
Ponte Rialto, 21
Post Office, 2
Questura di Venezia, 19
Teatro Goldoni, 15
Tourist Office (APT), Piazza San Marco, 16
Tourist Office (APT), Stazione S. Lucia, 17
Train Station, 1

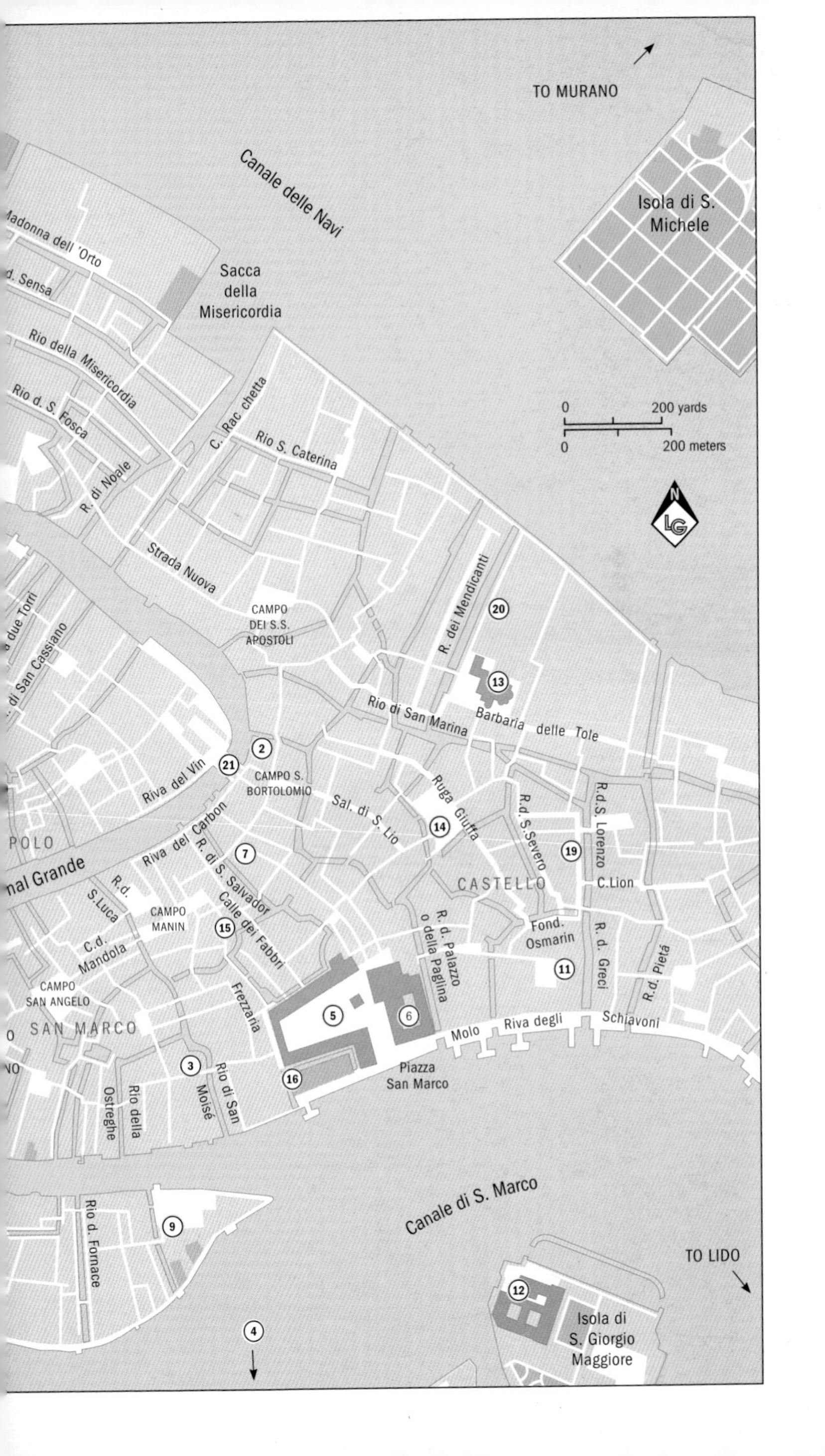

TO MURANO
Canale delle Navi
Isola di S. Michele
Madonna dell 'Orto
d. Sensa
Sacca della Misericordia
Rio della Misericordia
Rio d. S. Fosca
C. Racchetta
Rio S. Caterina
R. di Noale
Strada Nuova
0 200 yards
0 200 meters
CAMPO DEI S.S. APOSTOLI
R. dei Mendicanti
20
13
Rio di San Marina
Barbaria delle Tole
a due Torri
di San Cassiano
2
21
Riva del Vin
CAMPO S. BORTOLOMIO
Sal. di S. Lio
Ruga Giuffa
14
R.d. S.Severo
R.d.S. Lorenzo
19
POLO
nal Grande
Riva del Carbon
R. di S. Salvador
7
CASTELLO
C.Lion
R.d. S.Luca
CAMPO MANIN
Calle dei Fabbri
15
R. d. Palazzo o della Paglina
Fond. Osmarin
R. d. Greci
11
R.d. Pietá
C.d. Mandola
CAMPO SAN ANGELO
Frezzaria
5
6
SAN MARCO
Molo
Riva degli Schiavoni
3
Rio di San Moisé
16
Piazza San Marco
Ostreghe
Rio della
Canale di S. Marco
Rio d. Fornace
9
TO LIDO
12
Isola di S. Giorgio Maggiore
4

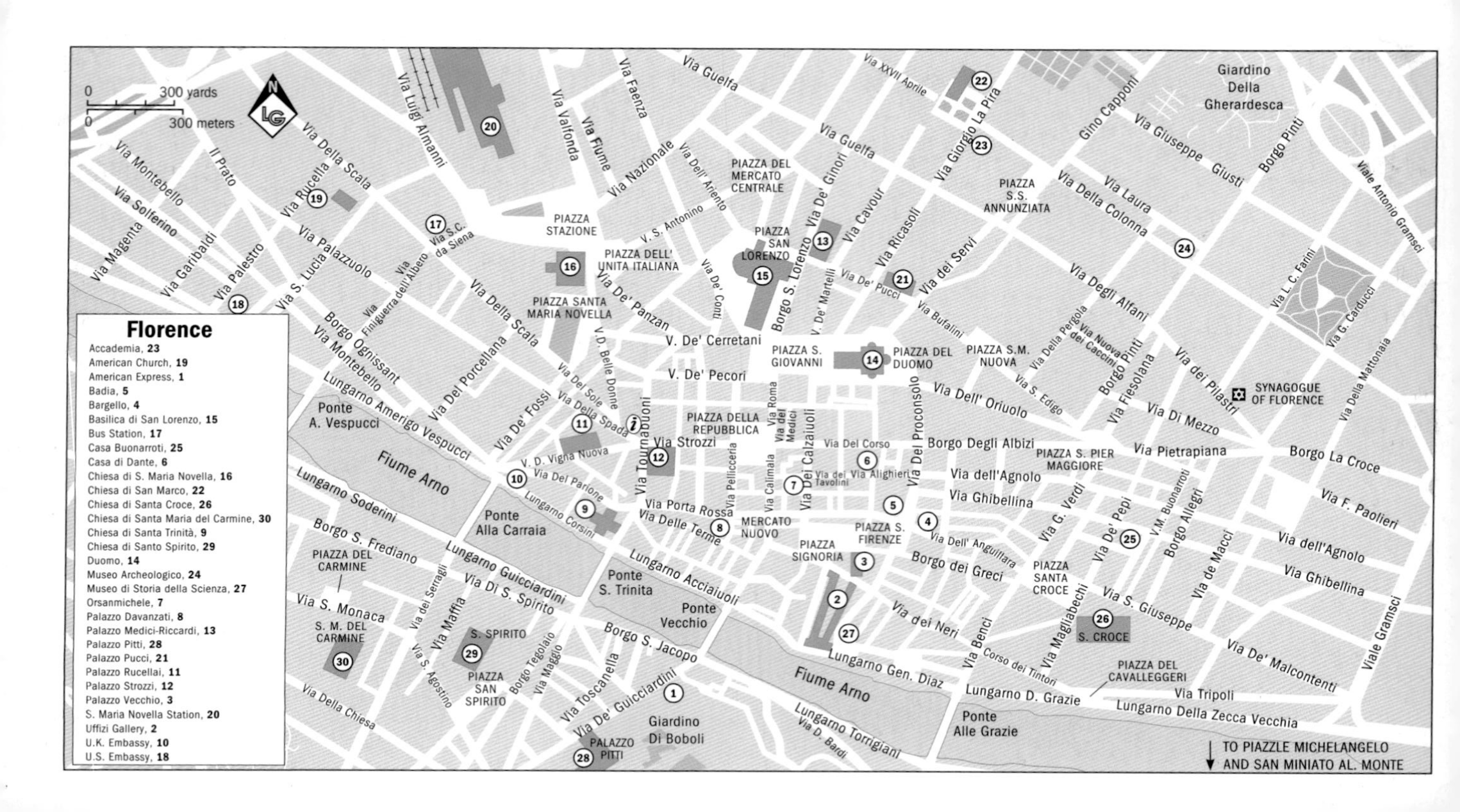
Florence
Accademia, 23
American Church, 19
American Express, 1
Badia, 5
Bargello, 4
Basilica di San Lorenzo, 15
Bus Station, 17
Casa Buonarroti, 25
Casa di Dante, 6
Chiesa di S. Maria Novella, 16
Chiesa di San Marco, 22
Chiesa di Santa Croce, 26
Chiesa di Santa Maria del Carmine, 30
Chiesa di Santa Trinità, 9
Chiesa di Santo Spirito, 29
Duomo, 14
Museo Archeologico, 24
Museo di Storia della Scienza, 27
Orsanmichele, 7
Palazzo Davanzati, 8
Palazzo Medici-Riccardi, 13
Palazzo Pitti, 28
Palazzo Pucci, 21
Palazzo Rucellai, 11
Palazzo Strozzi, 12
Palazzo Vecchio, 3
S. Maria Novella Station, 20
Uffizi Gallery, 2
U.K. Embassy, 10
U.S. Embassy, 18
0 300 yards
0 300 meters
N
LG
Via Guelfa
Via XXVII Aprile
Via Giorgio La Pira
Gino Capponi
Via Giuseppe Giusti
Giardino Della Gherardesca
Borgo Pinti
Viale Antonio Gramsci
Via Luigi Almanni
Via Valfonda
Via Fiume
Via Faenza
Via Nazionale
Via Dell' Ariento
PIAZZA DEL MERCATO CENTRALE
Via De' Ginori
Via Cavour
Via Ricasoli
Via dei Servi
PIAZZA S.S. ANNUNZIATA
Via Laura
Via Della Colonna
Via Degli Alfani
Via L. C. Farini
Via G. Carducci
Via Della Mattonaia
Via Montebello
Il Prato
Via Della Scala
Via Rucella
Via Solferino
Via Magenta
Via Garibaldi
Via Palestro
Via Palazzuolo
Via S. Lucia
Via S.C. da Siena
Via Finiguerra dell'Albero
PIAZZA STAZIONE
V. S. Antonino
PIAZZA DELL' UNITA ITALIANA
PIAZZA SAN LORENZO
Borgo S. Lorenzo
V. De' Martelli
Via De' Pucci
Via Bufalini
Via De' Conti
PIAZZA SANTA MARIA NOVELLA
Via De' Panzan
V. De' Cerretani
PIAZZA S. GIOVANNI
PIAZZA DEL DUOMO
PIAZZA S.M. NUOVA
Via Della Pergola
Via Nuova dei Caccini
Borgo Pinti
Via Fiesolana
Via dei Pilastri
SYNAGOGUE OF FLORENCE
Borgo Ognissant
Via Montebello
Lungarno Amerigo Vespucci
Via Del Porcellana
V. D. Belle Donne
V. De' Pecori
Via S. Edigo
Via Dell' Oriuolo
Via Di Mezzo
Ponte A. Vespucci
Via De' Fossi
Via Del Sole
Via Della Spada
Via Tornabuoni
Via Strozzi
PIAZZA DELLA REPUBBLICA
Via Roma
Via del Medici
Via Dei Calzaiuoli
Via Del Corso
Via Del Proconsolo
Borgo Degli Albizi
PIAZZA S. PIER MAGGIORE
Via Pietrapiana
Borgo La Croce
Fiume Arno
V. D. Vigna Nuova
Via Del Parione
Via Pellicceria
Via Calimala
Via dei Tavolini
Via Alighieri
Via dell'Agnolo
Via Ghibellina
Via F. Paolieri
Lungarno Soderini
Ponte Alla Carraia
Lungarno Corsini
Via Porta Rossa
Via Delle Terme
MERCATO NUOVO
PIAZZA SIGNORIA
PIAZZA S. FIRENZE
Via Dell' Anguillara
Via G. Verdi
Via De' Pepi
V.M. Buonarroti
Borgo Allegri
Via de Macci
Via dell'Agnolo
Borgo S. Frediano
PIAZZA DEL CARMINE
Lungarno Guicciardini
Via dei Serragli
Via Di S. Spirito
Ponte S. Trinita
Lungarno Acciaiuoli
Ponte Vecchio
Borgo dei Greci
PIAZZA SANTA CROCE
Via S. Giuseppe
Via Ghibellina
Via S. Monaca
S. M. DEL CARMINE
Via Maffia
S. SPIRITO
Via S. Agostino
Borgo Tegolaio
Via Maggio
PIAZZA SAN SPIRITO
Borgo S. Jacopo
Via dei Neri
Via Benci
Corso dei Tintori
Via Magliabechi
S. CROCE
Via De' Malcontenti
Viale Gramsci
Via Toscanella
Via De' Guicciardini
Lungarno Gen. Diaz
PIAZZA DEL CAVALLEGGERI
Via Tripoli
Lungarno D. Grazie
Lungarno Della Zecca Vecchia
Via Della Chiesa
Giardino Di Boboli
PALAZZO PITTI
Lungarno Torrigiani
Via D. Bardi
Ponte Alle Grazie
TO PIAZZLE MICHELANGELO AND SAN MINIATO AL. MONTE

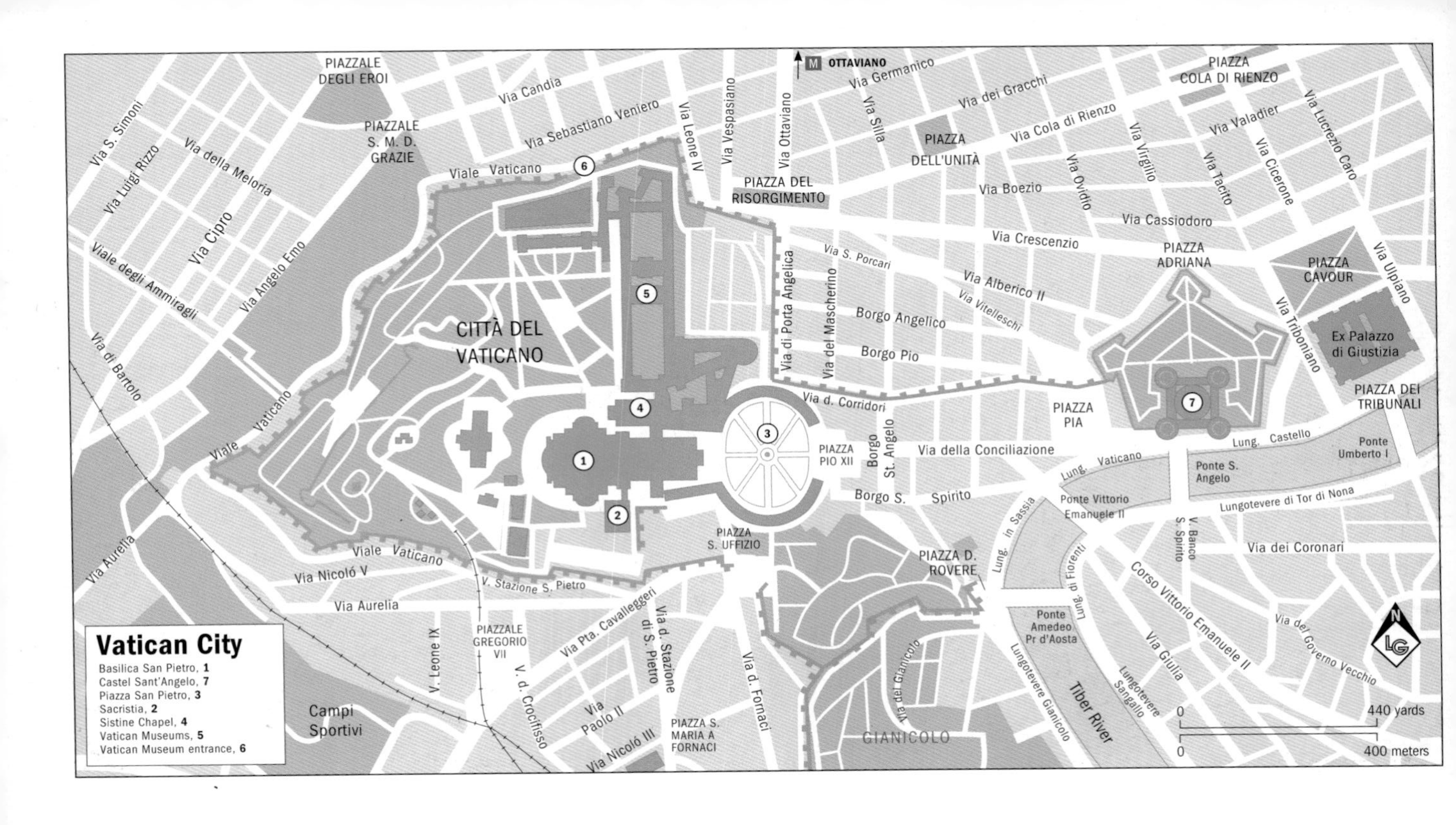
Vatican City
Basilica San Pietro, 1
Castel Sant'Angelo, 7
Piazza San Pietro, 3
Sacristia, 2
Sistine Chapel, 4
Vatican Museums, 5
Vatican Museum entrance, 6
OTTAVIANO
PIAZZALE DEGLI EROI
PIAZZALE S. M. D. GRAZIE
PIAZZA DEL RISORGIMENTO
PIAZZA DELL'UNITÀ
PIAZZA COLA DI RIENZO
PIAZZA ADRIANA
PIAZZA CAVOUR
Ex Palazzo di Giustizia
PIAZZA DEI TRIBUNALI
PIAZZA PIA
PIAZZA PIO XII
PIAZZA S. UFFIZIO
PIAZZA D. ROVERE
PIAZZALE GREGORIO VII
PIAZZA S. MARIA A FORNACI
CITTÀ DEL VATICANO
GIANICOLO
Campi Sportivi
Tiber River
Via S. Simoni
Via Luigi Rizzo
Via della Meloria
Via Cipro
Viale degli Ammiragli
Via Angelo Emo
Via di Bartolo
Via Aurelia
Via Candia
Via Sebastiano Veniero
Viale Vaticano
Via Leone IV
Via Vespasiano
Via Ottaviano
Via Germanico
Via Silla
Via dei Gracchi
Via Cola di Rienzo
Via Boezio
Via Ovidio
Via Virgilio
Via Tacito
Via Cicerone
Via Valadier
Via Lucrezio Caro
Via Ulpiano
Via Cassiodoro
Via Crescenzio
Via S. Porcari
Via Alberico II
Via Vitelleschi
Via di Porta Angelica
Via del Mascherino
Borgo Angelico
Borgo Pio
Via Tribonian
Via d. Corridori
Borgo St. Angelo
Via della Conciliazione
Borgo S. Spirito
Lung. Castello
Ponte Umberto I
Ponte S. Angelo
Lung. Vaticano
Ponte Vittorio Emanuele II
Lungotevere di Tor di Nona
V. Banco S. Spirito
Via dei Coronari
Lung. in Sassia
Lung. di Fiorenti
Corso Vittorio Emanuele II
Via del Governo Vecchio
Via Giulia
Ponte Amedeo Pr d'Aosta
Lungotevere Gianicolo
Lungotevere Sangallo
Via del Gianicolo
Via d. Fornaci
Via d. Stazione di S. Pietro
Via Pta. Cavalleggeri
Via Paolo II
Via Nicolò III
V. d. Crocifisso
V. Leone IX
V. Stazione S. Pietro
Via Nicolò V
Via Aurelia
0
440 yards
0
400 meters

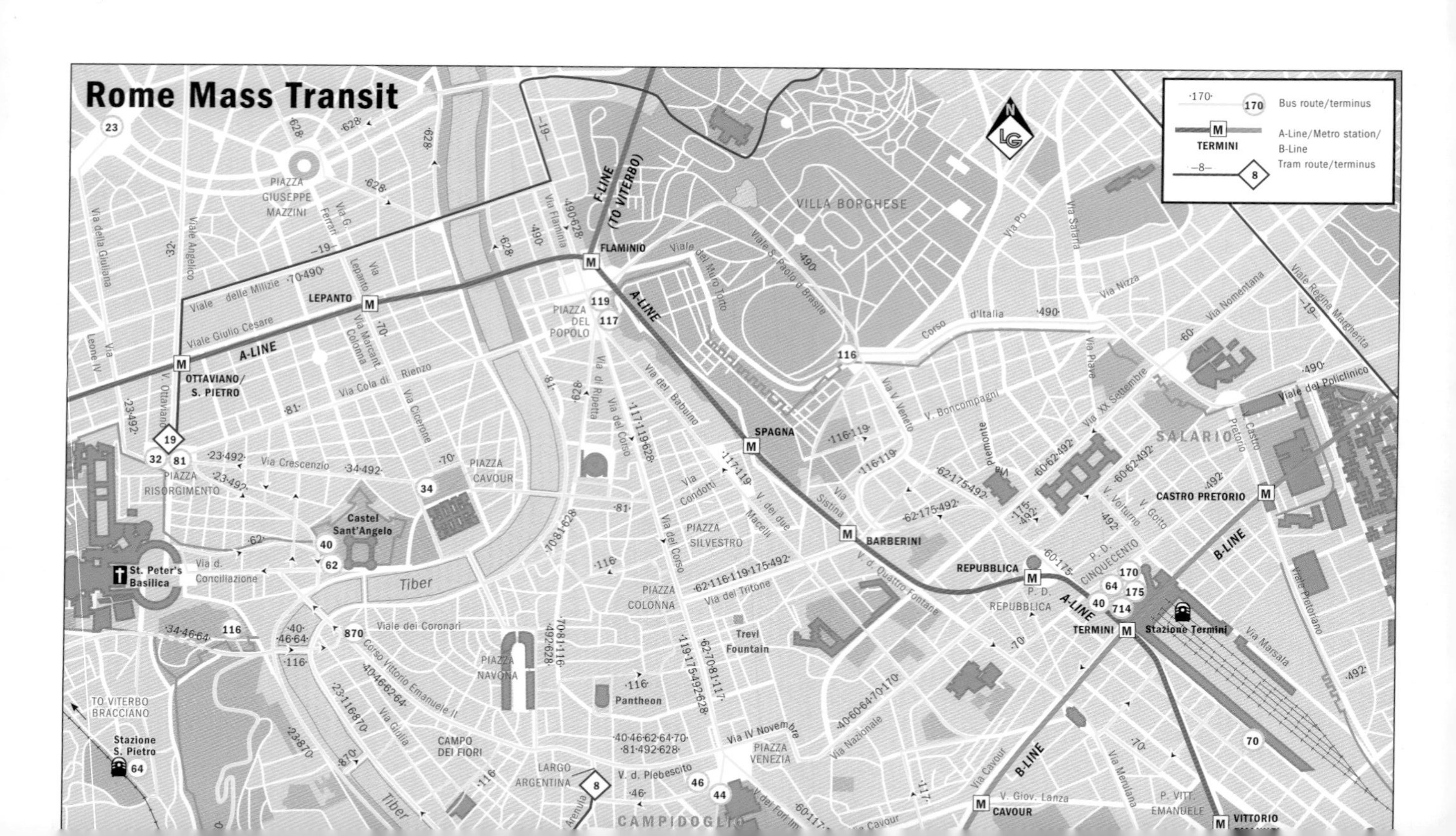

Rome Mass Transit
Bus route/terminus
A-Line/Metro station/
B-Line
Tram route/terminus
TERMINI
VILLA BORGHESE
SALARIO
CAMPIDOGLIO
F-LINE (TO VITERBO)
A-LINE
B-LINE
FLAMINIO
LEPANTO
OTTAVIANO/ S. PIETRO
SPAGNA
BARBERINI
REPUBBLICA
TERMINI
CASTRO PRETORIO
CAVOUR
VITTORIO
Stazione Termini
Stazione S. Pietro
TO VITERBO BRACCIANO
St. Peter's Basilica
Castel Sant'Angelo
Trevi Fountain
Pantheon
Tiber
PIAZZA GIUSEPPE MAZZINI
PIAZZA RISORGIMENTO
PIAZZA CAVOUR
PIAZZA DEL POPOLO
PIAZZA SILVESTRO
PIAZZA COLONNA
PIAZZA NAVONA
PIAZZA VENEZIA
CAMPO DEI FIORI
LARGO ARGENTINA
P. D. REPUBBLICA
P. D. CINQUECENTO
P. VITT. EMANUELE
Via della Giuliana
Viale Angelico
Via Leone IV
V. Ottaviano
Viale delle Milizie
Viale Giulio Cesare
Via Lepanto
Via G. Ferrari
Via Marcant. Colonna
Via Cola di Rienzo
Via Cicerone
Via Crescenzio
Via d. Conciliazione
Viale dei Coronari
Corso Vittorio Emanuele II
Via Giulia
Via Flaminia
Via di Ripetta
Via del Corso
Via del Babuino
Via Condotti
V. dei due Macelli
Via Sistina
Via del Tritone
V. d. Quattro Fontane
Via Nazionale
Via IV Novembre
V. d. Plebescito
V. dei Fori Im
Via Cavour
Arenula
Viale del Muro Torto
Viale S. Paolo d. Brasile
Via V. Veneto
V. Boncompagni
Via Piemonte
Corso d'Italia
Via Po
Via Salaria
Via Nizza
Via Piave
Via XX Settembre
Via Nomentana
Viale Regina Margherita
Viale del Policlinico
V. Castro Pretorio
V. Volturno
V. Goito
Viale Pretoriano
Via Marsala
Via Merulana
V. Giov. Lanza

BUS ROUTES
23, 32, 34, 40, 44, 46, 60, 62, 64, 70, 81, 116, 117, 119, 170, 175, 490, 492, 628, 673, 714, 870
TRAM ROUTES
3, 8, 19
0
500 meters
0
500 yards
COLOSSEO
Colosseum
MANZONI
S.Giovanni in Laterano
S. GIOVANNI
CIRCO MASSIMO
PIRAMIDE
Stazione Ostiense
Stazione Trastevere
Terme di Caracalla
B-LINE
Marcello
Forum
DEL GIANICOLO
TRASTEVERE
PIAZZA SONNINO
Isola Tiberina
PALATINO
CELIO
AVENTINO
TESTACCIO
Parco Testaccio
Porta Portese
Porta S. Sebastiano
Via Appia Antica
TO CATACOMBS
TO LAURENTINA
TO EUR
Via Labicana
Via di S. Giovanni in Laterano
Via di S. Stefano Rotondo
Via d. Laterani
Via dell'Amba Aradam
Via della Navicella
V. Claudia
Via di S. Gregorio
Via dei Cerchi
Via del Circo Massimo
Via di S. Prisca
Viale Aventino
Via Aventina
V. delle Terme
Viale di Terme di Caracalla
Viale Guido Baccelli
Viale Giotto
Via Druso
Viale Metronio
Via di Porta Latina
Via di Porta Sebastiano
Via Latina
Via Vetulonia
Via Satrico
Via Concordia
Via Etruria
Via Cerveteri
Via Magna Grecia
Via Gallia
V. Appia
Via Ostiense
Viale d. Piramide Cestia
Via Marmorata
Via Galvani
V. Giovanni Branca
Via Nicola Zabaglia
Viale di Trastevere
Viale Glorioso
V.Nicola Fabrizi
Via Dandolo
Via di S. Pancrazio
Via Giacinto Carini
Via G. Barrili
Via Alessandro Poerio
Via dei Quattro Venti
Viale di Villa Pamphili
Via di Donna Olimpia
Circonvallazione Gianicolense
Viale Guglielmo Marconi

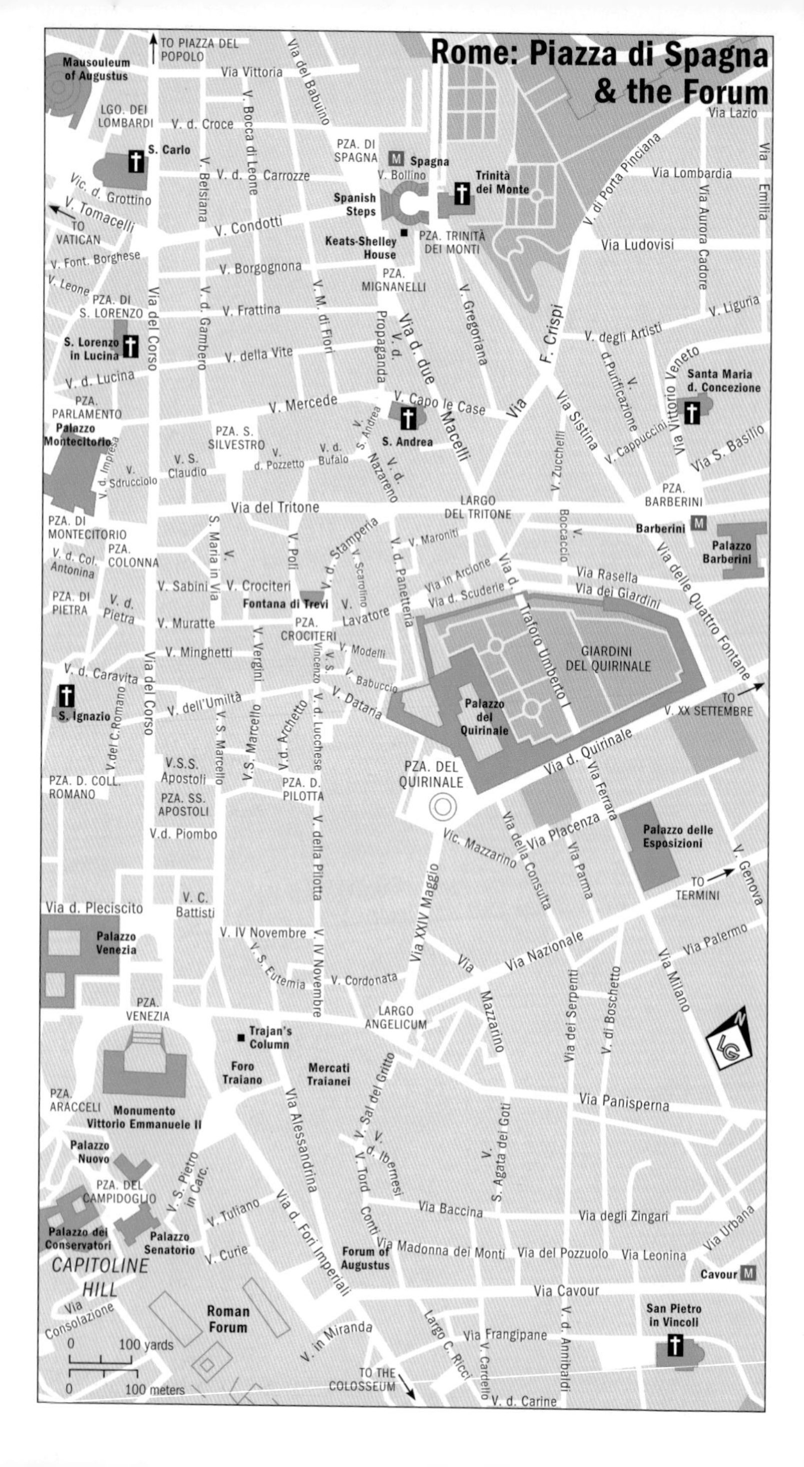

Rome: Piazza di Spagna & the Forum
TO PIAZZA DEL POPOLO
Mausouleum of Augustus
Via Vittoria
Via del Babuino
V. Bocca di Leone
LGO. DEI LOMBARDI
V. d. Croce
S. Carlo
V. Belsiana
V. d. Carrozze
PZA. DI SPAGNA
Spagna
V. Bollino
Trinità dei Monte
Via Lazio
V. di Porta Pinciana
Via Lombardia
Via Emilia
Vic. d. Grottino
V. Tomacelli
TO VATICAN
V. Condotti
Spanish Steps
Keats-Shelley House
PZA. TRINITÀ DEI MONTI
Via Ludovisi
Via Aurora
Cadore
V. Font. Borghese
V. Borgognona
PZA. MIGNANELLI
V. Leone
PZA. DI S. LORENZO
Via del Corso
V. d. Gambero
V. Frattina
V. M. di Fiori
V. d. Propaganda
Via d. due Macelli
V. Gregoriana
Via F. Crispi
V. degli Artisti
V. Liguria
S. Lorenzo in Lucina
V. della Vite
V. d. Purificazione
Via Vittorio Veneto
Santa Maria d. Concezione
V. d. Lucina
V. Mercede
V. Capo le Case
Via Sistina
PZA. PARLAMENTO
Palazzo Montecitorio
PZA. S. SILVESTRO
V. S. Andrea
S. Andrea
V. Cappuccini
Via S. Basilio
V. d. Impresa
V. Sdrucciolo
V. S. Claudio
V. d. Pozzetto
V. d. Bufalo
V. d. Nazareno
V. Zucchelli
PZA. BARBERINI
Via del Tritone
LARGO DEL TRITONE
PZA. DI MONTECITORIO
S. Maria in Via
V. Poli
V. d. Stamperia
V. Maroniti
V. Boccaccio
Barberini
Palazzo Barberini
V. d. Col. Antonina
PZA. COLONNA
V. Scarolino
V. d. Panetteria
Via in Arcione
Via d. Scuderie
Via d. Traforo Umberto I
Via Rasella
Via dei Giardini
Via delle Quattro Fontane
PZA. DI PIETRA
V. d. Pietra
V. Sabini
V. Crociteri
Fontana di Trevi
V. Lavatore
V. Muratte
PZA. CROCITERI
GIARDINI DEL QUIRINALE
V. Minghetti
V. Vergini
V. S. Vincenzo
V. Modelli
V. d. Caravita
V. Babuccio
TO V. XX SETTEMBRE
S. Ignazio
V. del C. Romano
V. dell'Umiltà
V. Dataria
Palazzo del Quirinale
V. S. Marcello
V. d. Archetto
V. d. Lucchese
Via d. Quirinale
V.S.S. Apostoli
PZA. DEL QUIRINALE
PZA. D. COLL. ROMANO
PZA. D. PILOTTA
Via Ferrara
PZA. SS. APOSTOLI
V. della Pilotta
Via della Consulta
Via Placenza
Palazzo delle Esposizioni
V.d. Piombo
Vic. Mazzarino
Via Parma
V. Genova
TO TERMINI
Via d. Pleciscito
V. C. Battisti
Via XXIV Maggio
Palazzo Venezia
V. IV Novembre
Via Nazionale
Via Palermo
V. S. Eutemia
V. Cordonata
Via Mazzarino
Via dei Serpenti
V. di Boschetto
Via Milano
PZA. VENEZIA
LARGO ANGELICUM
Trajan's Column
Foro Traiano
Mercati Traianei
PZA. ARACCELI
Monumento Vittorio Emmanuele II
Via Alessandrina
V. Sal del Gritto
Via Panisperna
Palazzo Nuovo
V. S. Pietro in Carc.
V. d. Ibernesi
V. Tor d. Conti
V. S. Agata dei Goti
PZA. DEL CAMPIDOGLIO
V. Tuliano
Via d. Fori Imperiali
Via Baccina
Via degli Zingari
Via Urbana
Palazzo dei Conservatori
Palazzo Senatorio
V. Curie
Forum of Augustus
Via Madonna dei Monti
Via del Pozzuolo
Via Leonina
Cavour
CAPITOLINE HILL
Via Cavour
Via Consolazione
Roman Forum
V. in Miranda
Largo C. Ricci
Via Frangipane
V. Cardello
V. d. Annibaldi
San Pietro in Vincoli
0 100 yards
0 100 meters
TO THE COLOSSEUM
V. d. Carine

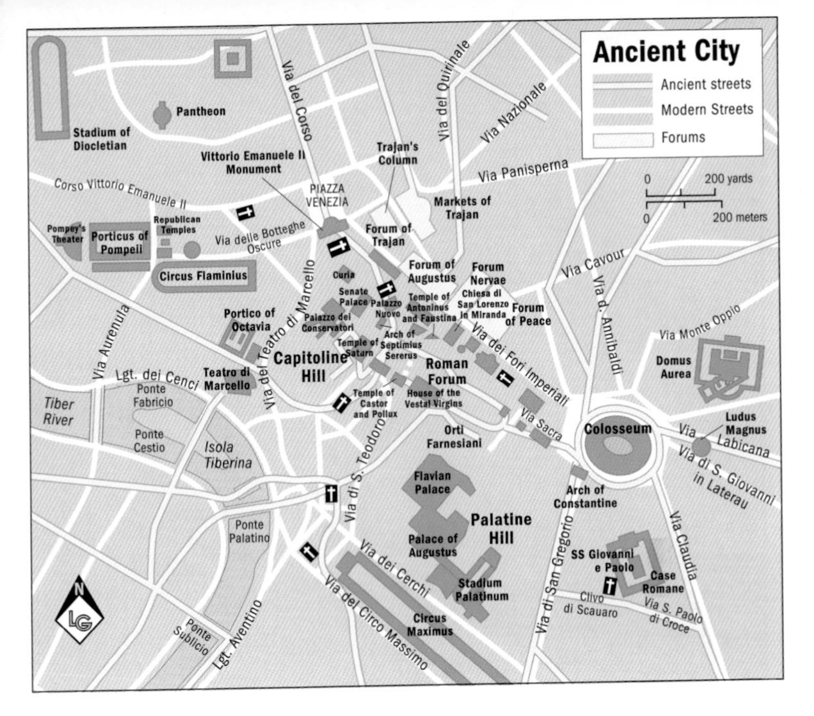
Ancient City
Ancient streets
Modern Streets
Forums
0
200 yards
0
200 meters
Pantheon
Stadium of Diocletian
Vittorio Emanuele II Monument
Trajan's Column
Via del Corso
Via del Quirinale
Via Nazionale
Via Panisperna
Corso Vittorio Emanuele II
PIAZZA VENEZIA
Markets of Trajan
Forum of Trajan
Pompey's Theater
Porticus of Pompeii
Republican Temples
Via delle Botteghe Oscure
Circus Flaminius
Curia
Forum of Augustus
Forum Nervae
Via Cavour
Senate Palace
Palazzo Nuovo
Temple of Antoninus and Faustina
Chiesa di San Lorenzo in Miranda
Forum of Peace
Portico of Octavia
Palazzo dei Conservatori
Arch of Septimius Sererus
Temple of Saturn
Via del Teatro di Marcello
Via Aurenula
Via d. Annibaldi
Via Monte Oppio
Domus Aurea
Capitoline Hill
Roman Forum
Via dei Fori Imperiali
Lgt. dei Cenci
Teatro di Marcello
Tiber River
Ponte Fabricio
Temple of Castor and Pollux
House of the Vestal Virgins
Via Sacra
Colosseum
Ludus Magnus
Via Labicana
Ponte Cestio
Isola Tiberina
Orti Farnesiani
Via di S. Giovanni in Laterau
Via di S. Teodoro
Flavian Palace
Arch of Constantine
Palatine Hill
Ponte Palatino
Palace of Augustus
Via dei Cerchi
Via di San Gregorio
SS Giovanni e Paolo
Via Claudia
Stadium Palatinum
Case Romane
Clivo di Scauaro
Via S. Paolo di Croce
Via del Circo Massimo
Circus Maximus
Ponte Sublicio
Lgt. Aventino
N
LG

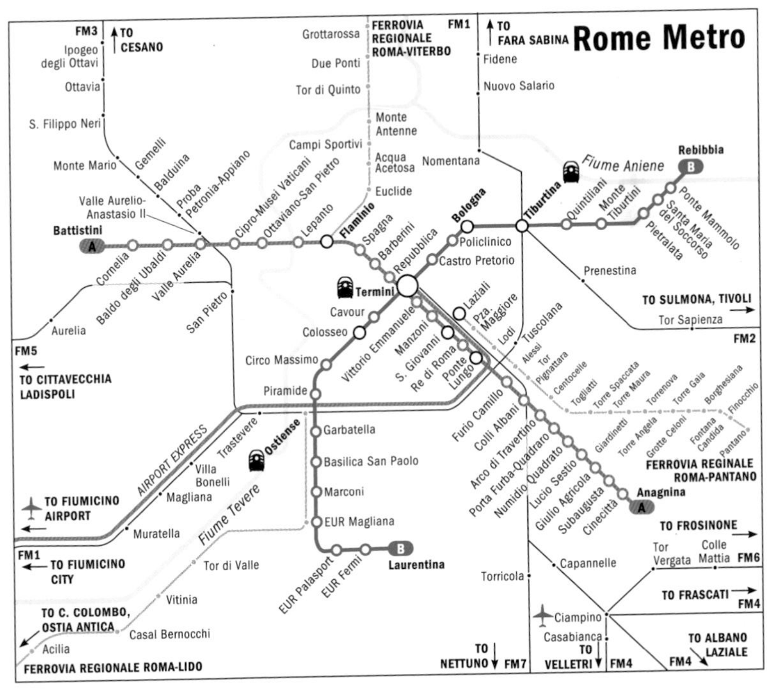
Rome Metro
FM3
TO CESANO
Ipogeo degli Ottavi
Ottavia
S. Filippo Neri
Monte Mario
Gemelli
Balduina
Proba Petronia-Appiano
Valle Aurelio-Anastasio II
Battistini
A
Cornelia
Baldo degli Ubaldi
Valle Aurelia
Cipro-Musei Vaticani
Ottaviano-San Pietro
Lepanto
Flaminio
Spagna
Barberini
Repubblica
Termini
San Pietro
Aurelia
Grottarossa
FERROVIA REGIONALE ROMA-VITERBO
Due Ponti
Tor di Quinto
Campi Sportivi
Monte Antenne
Acqua Acetosa
Euclide
FM1
TO FARA SABINA
Fidene
Nuovo Salario
Nomentana
Bologna
Policlinico
Castro Pretorio
Tiburtina
Fiume Aniene
Rebibbia
B
Quintiliani
Monte Tiburtini
Pietralata
Santa Maria del Soccorso
Ponte Mammolo
Prenestina
TO SULMONA, TIVOLI
Tor Sapienza
FM2
FM5
TO CITTAVECCHIA LADISPOLI
Cavour
Colosseo
Circo Massimo
Piramide
Vittorio Emanuele
Manzoni
S. Giovanni
Re di Roma
Ponte Lungo
Laziali
Pza. Maggiore
Lodi
Tuscolana
Alessi
Tor Pignattara
Centocelle
Togliatti
Torre Spaccata
Torre Maura
Torrenova
Torre Gaia
Borghesiana
Finocchio
Giardinetti
Torre Angela
Grotte Celoni
Fontana Candida
Pantano
FERROVIA REGINALE ROMA-PANTANO
Furio Camillo
Colli Albani
Arco di Travertino
Porta Furba-Quadraro
Numidio Quadrato
Lucio Sestio
Giulio Agricola
Subaugusta
Cinecittà
Anagnina
AIRPORT EXPRESS
Trastevere
Ostiense
Villa Bonelli
Magliana
Muratella
Fiume Tevere
TO FIUMICINO AIRPORT
Garbatella
Basilica San Paolo
Marconi
EUR Magliana
EUR Palasport
EUR Fermi
Laurentina
FM1
TO FIUMICINO CITY
Tor di Valle
Vitinia
TO C. COLOMBO, OSTIA ANTICA
Casal Bernocchi
Acilia
FERROVIA REGIONALE ROMA-LIDO
Torricola
Capannelle
Tor Vergata
Colle Mattia
FM6
TO FROSINONE
TO FRASCATI
FM4
Ciampino
Casabianca
TO NETTUNO
FM7
TO VELLETRI
TO ALBANO LAZIALE

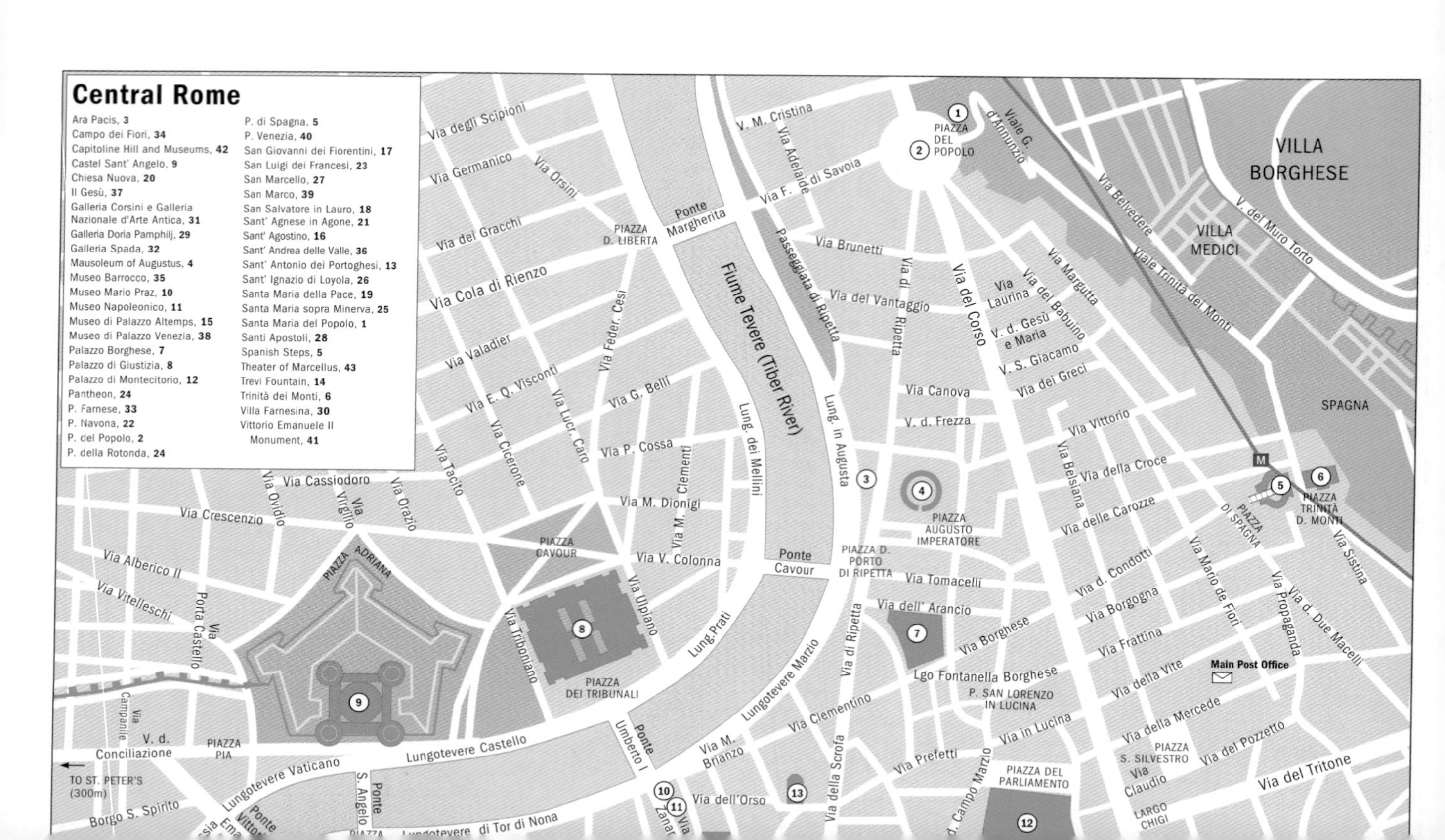
Central Rome
Ara Pacis, 3
Campo dei Fiori, 34
Capitoline Hill and Museums, 42
Castel Sant' Angelo, 9
Chiesa Nuova, 20
Il Gesù, 37
Galleria Corsini e Galleria Nazionale d'Arte Antica, 31
Galleria Doria Pamphilj, 29
Galleria Spada, 32
Mausoleum of Augustus, 4
Museo Barrocco, 35
Museo Mario Praz, 10
Museo Napoleonico, 11
Museo di Palazzo Altemps, 15
Museo di Palazzo Venezia, 38
Palazzo Borghese, 7
Palazzo di Giustizia, 8
Palazzo di Montecitorio, 12
Pantheon, 24
P. Farnese, 33
P. Navona, 22
P. del Popolo, 2
P. della Rotonda, 24
P. di Spagna, 5
P. Venezia, 40
San Giovanni dei Fiorentini, 17
San Luigi dei Francesi, 23
San Marcello, 27
San Marco, 39
San Salvatore in Lauro, 18
Sant' Agnese in Agone, 21
Sant' Agostino, 16
Sant' Andrea delle Valle, 36
Sant' Antonio dei Portoghesi, 13
Sant' Ignazio di Loyola, 26
Santa Maria della Pace, 19
Santa Maria sopra Minerva, 25
Santa Maria del Popolo, 1
Santi Apostoli, 28
Spanish Steps, 5
Theater of Marcellus, 43
Trevi Fountain, 14
Trinità dei Monti, 6
Villa Farnesina, 30
Vittorio Emanuele II Monument, 41
VILLA BORGHESE
VILLA MEDICI
SPAGNA
PIAZZA DEL POPOLO
PIAZZA TRINITÀ D. MONTI
PIAZZA DI SPAGNA
PIAZZA AUGUSTO IMPERATORE
PIAZZA D. PORTO DI RIPETTA
PIAZZA D. LIBERTA
PIAZZA CAVOUR
PIAZZA DEI TRIBUNALI
PIAZZA ADRIANA
PIAZZA PIA
P. SAN LORENZO IN LUCINA
PIAZZA S. SILVESTRO
PIAZZA DEL PARLIAMENTO
LARGO CHIGI
Fiume Tevere (Tiber River)
Main Post Office
Ponte Margherita
Ponte Cavour
Ponte Umberto I
Ponte S. Angelo
Via del Corso
Via di Ripetta
Via del Babuino
Via Margutta
Via Sistina
Via d. Due Macelli
Via Propaganda
Via Mario de Fiori
Via d. Condotti
Via Borgogna
Via Frattina
Via della Vite
Via della Mercede
Via del Pozzetto
Via del Tritone
Via Vittorio
Via della Croce
Via delle Carozze
Via Belsiana
Via dei Greci
V. S. Giacamo
V. d. Gesù e Maria
Via Laurina
Via Canova
V. d. Frezza
Via Tomacelli
Via dell' Arancio
Via Borghese
Lgo Fontanella Borghese
Via in Lucina
Via Prefetti
Via Clementino
Via della Scrofa
Via dell'Orso
Via M. Brianzo
Lungotevere Marzio
Lung. in Augusta
Passeggiata di Ripetta
Via Brunetti
Via del Vantaggio
Via F. di Savoia
Via Adelaide
V. M. Cristina
Viale G. d'Annunzio
Via Belvedere
Viale Trinità dei Monti
V. del Muro Torto
Lung. dei Mellini
Lung. Prati
Via degli Scipioni
Via Germanico
Via Orsini
Via dei Gracchi
Via Cola di Rienzo
Via Valadier
Via E. Q. Visconti
Via Feder. Cesi
Via G. Belli
Via P. Cossa
Via M. Clementi
Via M. Dionigi
Via V. Colonna
Via Ulpiano
Via Lucr. Caro
Via Cicerone
Via Tacito
Via Orazio
Via Virgilio
Via Cassiodoro
Via Ovidio
Via Crescenzio
Via Triboniano
Via Alberico II
Via Vitelleschi
Via Porta Castello
Via Campanile
V. d. Conciliazione
Lungotevere Castello
Lungotevere Vaticano
Borgo S. Spirito
TO ST. PETER'S (300m)

Ponte Principe Amadeo
PIAZZA D. ROVERE
Lungotevere Gianicolense
Lungotevere Sangallo
Corso Vittorio Emanuele II
V. dei Banchi Vecchi
Via d. Gonfalone
Via Scimia
Via Vetrina
Via del Governo Vecchio
V. d. Parione
Via Sora
V. Savelli
V. dell' Anima
PIAZZA NAVONA
Corso del Rinascimento
Dogana V
Via Giustiniani
PIAZZA DELLA ROTONDA
V. Pastini
V. Seminario
Via Colonnelle
PIAZZA S. EUSTACCHIO
Via Santa Chiara
V. Monterone
V. di Torre Argentina
V. Pie di Marmo
PZA. DEI COLLEGIO ROMANO
del Corso
V. Minghetti
Via dell'Umiltà
PIAZZA D. PILOTTA
Via dei Lucchesi
Via S.S. Apostoli
PIAZZA DEI S.S. APOSTOLI
Via Gatta
PIAZZA GRAZIOLI
Via del Gesù
V. C. Battisti
Via del Plebiscito
PIAZZA VENEZIA
TO THE FORUM AND THE PALATINE
PIAZZA D. GESÙ
LARGO DI TORRE ARGENTINA
LARGO TEATRO VALLE
PIAZZA SAN PANTALEO
V. Leutari
Via del Pellegrino
V. d. Cappellari
LARGO PEROSI
Via Giulia
Via del Monserrato
PZA. DEL PARADISO
LARGO DEI PALLARO
Via dei Chiavari
V. d. Monte d. Farina
Via d. Barbieri
LARGO ARENULA
LGO. DEI LIBRARI
Vic. d. Chiodaroli
V. d. Giubbonari
V. d. Botteghe Oscure
V.S. Marco
Via d'Aracoeli
Ponte Mazzini
Via S. Eligio
Via d. Armata
Lungotevere dei Tebaldi
Via d. Farnesi
Via Mascherone
V. Polverone
Via dei Pettinari
V. Paganica
V. Falegnami
V. d. Funari
V. M. Caetani
PIAZZA CAMPITELLI
Via di Orti di Albert
Via delle Mantellate
Via S. Francesco di Sales
Vic. di Penitenza
V. Penitenza
Via della Lungara
Lungotevere della Farnesina
Fiume Tevere (Tiber River)
PIAZZA V. PALLOTTI
Via del Zoccolette
V. Conservatorio
Via Arenula
PIAZZA CENCI
Via d. Portico d. Ottavia
Via Catalana
Via del Teatro di Marcello
MONTE CAPITOLINO
Via del Consolazione
Via di Riari
Via Corsini
PARCO GIANICOLENSE
Ponte Sisto
Lungotevere dei Vallati
Lung. dei Cenci
Via S. Dorotea
Lungotevere Sanzio
Ponte Garibaldi
PIAZZA G. G. BELLI
ISOLA TIBERINA
Ponte Fabricio
Lung. Pierleoni
V. Petroselli
Via Garibaldi
Via della Scala
PIAZZA DI SANT' EGIDIO
Via del Moro
Via d. Mattonato
PZA. DI S. MARIA IN TRASTEVERE
CORONARI
200 meters
200 yards

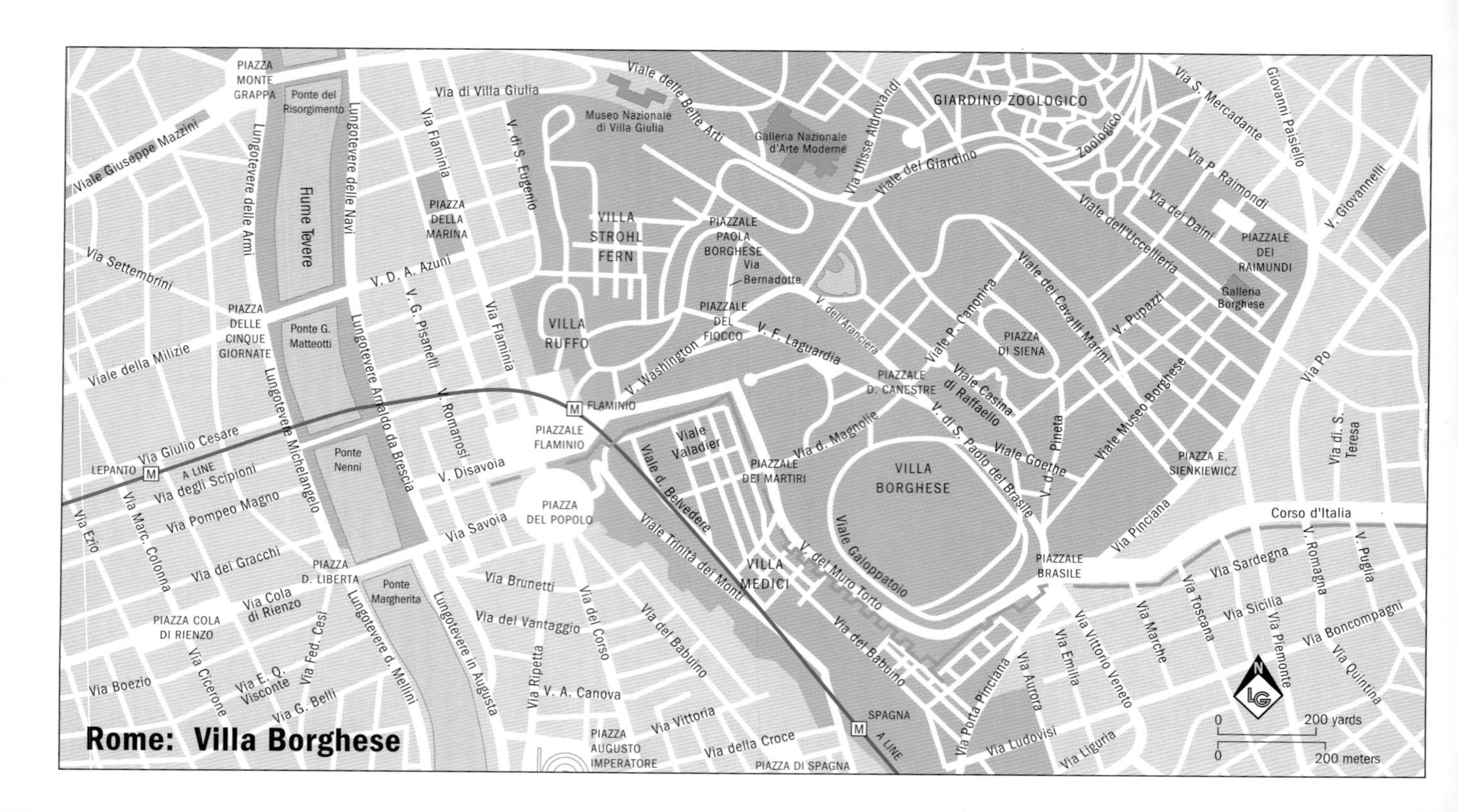
Rome: Villa Borghese
GIARDINO ZOOLOGICO
VILLA BORGHESE
VILLA STROHL FERN
VILLA RUFFO
VILLA MEDICI
Fiume Tevere
Museo Nazionale di Villa Giulia
Galleria Nazionale d'Arte Moderne
Galleria Borghese
PIAZZA MONTE GRAPPA
PIAZZA DELLA MARINA
PIAZZA DELLE CINQUE GIORNATE
PIAZZA D. LIBERTA
PIAZZA COLA DI RIENZO
PIAZZALE FLAMINIO
PIAZZA DEL POPOLO
PIAZZALE PAOLA BORGHESE
PIAZZALE DEL FIOCCO
PIAZZALE D. CANESTRE
PIAZZA DI SIENA
PIAZZALE DEI MARTIRI
PIAZZALE DEI RAIMUNDI
PIAZZA E. SIENKIEWICZ
PIAZZALE BRASILE
PIAZZA AUGUSTO IMPERATORE
PIAZZA DI SPAGNA
Ponte del Risorgimento
Ponte G. Matteotti
Ponte Nenni
Ponte Margherita
FLAMINIO
LEPANTO
SPAGNA
A LINE
Viale Giuseppe Mazzini
Lungotevere delle Armi
Lungotevere delle Navi
Via di Villa Giulia
Via Flaminia
V. di S. Eugenio
Viale delle Belle Arti
Via Ulisse Aldrovandi
Viale del Giardino
Zoologico
Via S. Mercadante
Giovanni Paisiello
Via P. Raimondi
Via dei Daini
V. Giovannelli
Viale dell'Uccelliera
Via Settembrini
V. D. A. Azuni
V. G. Pisanelli
Via Bernadotte
V. dell'Aranciera
Viale P. Canonica
Viale dei Cavalli Marini
V. Pupazzi
Viale della Milizie
Lungotevere Arnaldo da Brescia
Lungotevere Michelangelo
V. Romanosi
V. F. Laguardia
V. Washington
Viale Casina di Raffaello
Viale Museo Borghese
Via Po
Via di. S. Teresa
Via Giulio Cesare
Via degli Scipioni
Via Pompeo Magno
V. Disavoia
Via d. Magnolie
V. di S. Paolo del Brasile
Viale Goethe
V. d. Pineta
Via Ezio
Via Marc. Colonna
Via dei Gracchi
Via Savoia
Viale Valadier
Viale d. Belvedere
Viale Trinità dei Monti
Viale Galoppatoio
Via Pinciana
Corso d'Italia
V. Romagna
V. Puglia
Via Cola di Rienzo
Via Brunetti
Via del Corso
V. del Muro Torto
Via Sardegna
Via Sicilia
Via Toscana
Via Marche
Via del Vantaggio
Via del Babuino
Via Vittorio Veneto
Via Emilia
Via Aurora
Via Piemonte
Via Boncompagni
Via Quintina
Via Boezio
Via Cicerone
Via E. Q. Visconte
Via Fed. Cesi
Via G. Belli
Lungotevere d. Mellini
Lungotevere in Augusta
Via Ripetta
V. A. Canova
Via Vittoria
Via della Croce
Via Porta Pinciana
Via Ludovisi
Via Liguria
N
LG
0
200 yards
0
200 meters

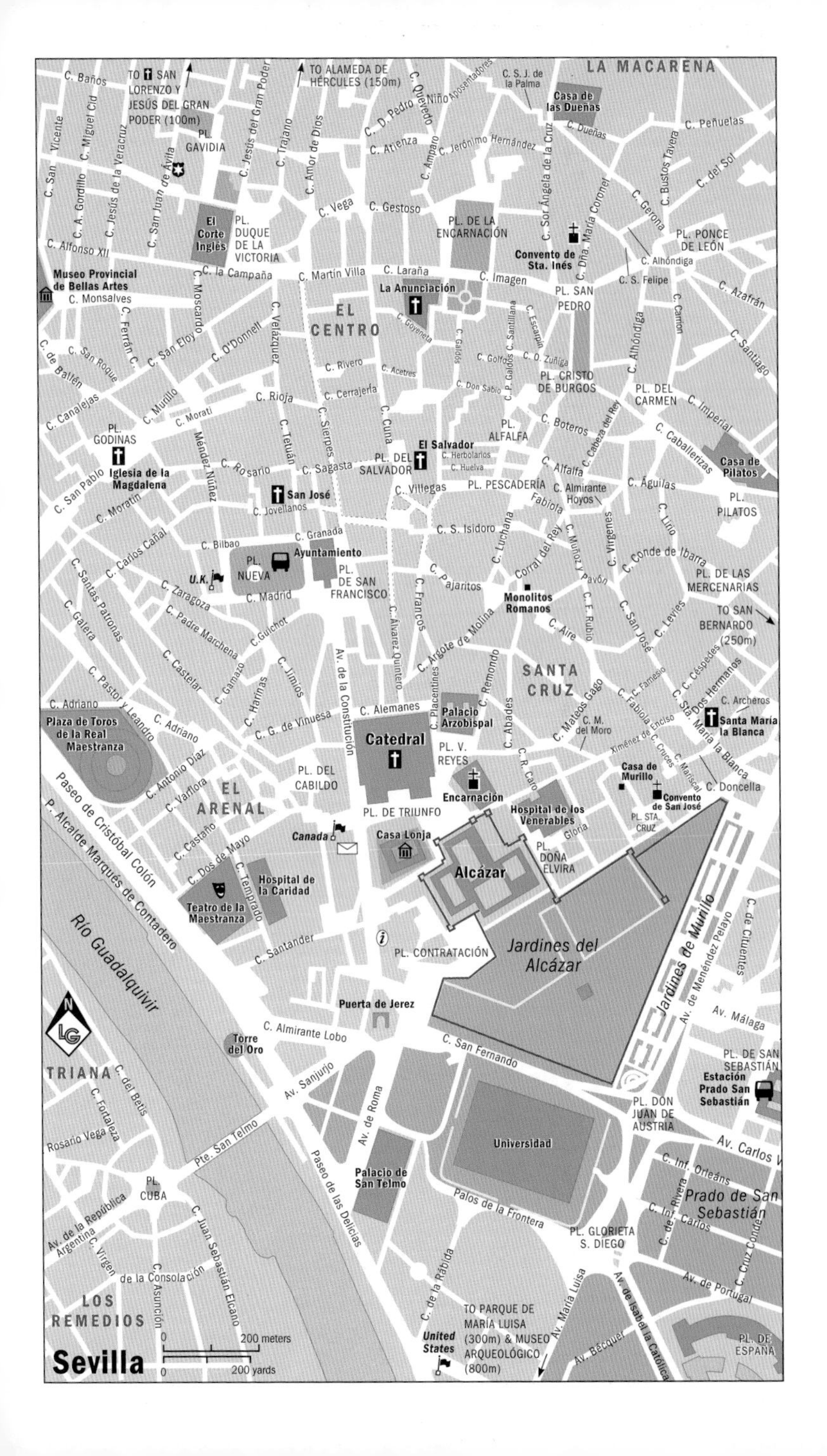

Sevilla
LA MACARENA
EL CENTRO
SANTA CRUZ
EL ARENAL
TRIANA
LOS REMEDIOS
Casa de las Dueñas
El Corte Inglés
Museo Provincial de Bellas Artes
La Anunciación
Convento de Sta. Inés
Iglesia de la Magdalena
San José
El Salvador
Ayuntamiento
Casa de Pilatos
Monolitos Romanos
Santa María la Blanca
Plaza de Toros de la Real Maestranza
Catedral
Palacio Arzobispal
Encarnación
Hospital de los Venerables
Casa de Murillo
Convento de San José
Casa Lonja
Alcázar
Hospital de la Caridad
Teatro de la Maestranza
Jardines del Alcázar
Jardines de Murillo
Puerta de Jerez
Torre del Oro
Río Guadalquivir
Universidad
Palacio de San Telmo
Estación Prado San Sebastián
Prado de San Sebastián
U.K.
Canada
United States
TO SAN LORENZO Y JESÚS DEL GRAN PODER (100m)
TO ALAMEDA DE HÉRCULES (150m)
TO SAN BERNARDO (250m)
TO PARQUE DE MARÍA LUISA (300m) & MUSEO ARQUEOLÓGICO (800m)
PL. GAVIDIA
PL. DUQUE DE LA VICTORIA
PL. DE LA ENCARNACIÓN
PL. SAN PEDRO
PL. PONCE DE LEÓN
PL. CRISTO DE BURGOS
PL. DEL CARMEN
PL. ALFALFA
PL. GODINAS
PL. DEL SALVADOR
PL. PESCADERÍA
PL. PILATOS
PL. NUEVA
PL. DE SAN FRANCISCO
PL. DE LAS MERCENARIAS
PL. DEL CABILDO
PL. V. REYES
PL. DE TRIUNFO
PL. STA. CRUZ
PL. DOÑA ELVIRA
PL. CONTRATACIÓN
PL. DE SAN SEBASTIÁN
PL. DON JUAN DE AUSTRIA
PL. CUBA
PL. GLORIETA S. DIEGO
PL. DE ESPAÑA
Av. de la Constitución
Paseo de Cristóbal Colón
P. Alcalde Marqués de Contadero
Paseo de las Delicias
Av. de Roma
Av. Carlos V
Av. de Portugal
Av. María Luisa
Av. de Isabel la Católica
Av. de Menéndez Pelayo
Av. Málaga
Av. Sanjurjo
Av. de la República Argentina
Pte. San Telmo
Palos de la Frontera
0 200 meters
0 200 yards

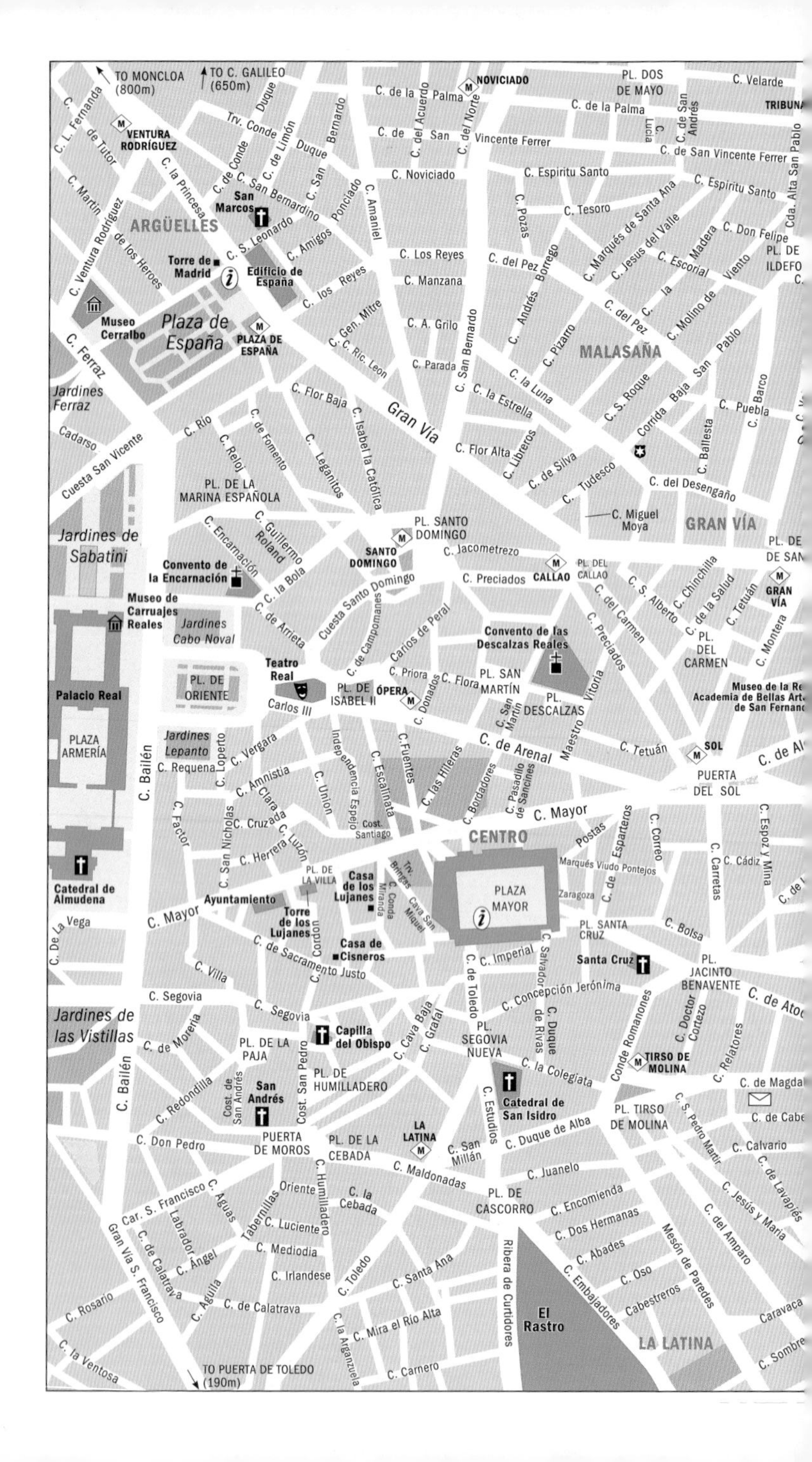

TO MONCLOA (800m)
TO C. GALILEO (650m)
VENTURA RODRÍGUEZ
NOVICIADO
PL. DOS DE MAYO
C. Velarde
TRIBUNA
C. de la Palma
C. de San Vincente Ferrer
C. Noviciado
C. Espiritu Santo
C. Tesoro
C. Pozas
C. Marqués de Santa Ana
C. Jesus del Valle
C. Escorial
C. Don Felipe
PL. DE ILDEFO
C. Madera
C. Molino de Viento
C. Los Reyes
C. del Pez
C. Manzana
C. Andrés Borrego
C. A. Grilo
C. Pizarro
MALASAÑA
C. Parada
C. San Bernardo
C. la Luna
C. la Estrella
C. S. Roque
Corrida Baja San Pablo
C. Barco
C. Puebla
C. Ballesta
C. Flor Alta
C. Libreros
C. de Silva
C. Tudesco
C. del Desengaño
C. Miguel Moya
GRAN VÍA
C. L. Fernanda de Tutor
C. Martin de los Heroes
C. Ventura Rodriguez
C. la Princesa
ARGÜELLES
San Marcos
Torre de Madrid
Edificio de España
Museo Cerralbo
Plaza de España
PLAZA DE ESPAÑA
C. Ferraz
Jardines Ferraz
Cadarso
Cuesta San Vicente
C. de Conde Duque
C. de Limón
Duque
Bernardo
C. San Bernardino
C. S. Leonardo
C. Amigos
Ponciado
C. Amaniel
C. los Reyes
C. Gen. Mitre
C. Ric. Leon
C. Flor Baja
C. Isabel la Católica
Gran Vía
C. Rio
C. Reloj
C. de Fomento
C. Leganitos
PL. DE LA MARINA ESPAÑOLA
Jardines de Sabatini
C. Encarnación
C. Guillermo Roland
Convento de la Encarnación
C. la Bola
SANTO DOMINGO
PL. SANTO DOMINGO
C. Jacometrezo
Cuesta Santo Domingo
C. Preciados
CALLAO
PL. DEL CALLAO
Museo de Carruajes Reales
Jardines Cabo Noval
C. de Arrieta
C. de Campomanes
Carlos de Peral
Convento de las Descalzas Reales
C. del Carmen
C. S. Alberto
C. Chinchilla
C. de la Salud
C. Tetuán
GRAN VÍA
PL. DEL CARMEN
C. Montera
PL. DE ORIENTE
Teatro Real
C. Priora
C. Flora
PL. SAN MARTÍN
PL. DE ISABEL II
ÓPERA
C. Donados
Carlos III
C. San Martín
PL. DESCALZAS
C. Maestro Vitoria
Museo de la Real Academia de Bellas Artes de San Fernando
Palacio Real
PLAZA ARMERÍA
Jardines Lepanto
C. Loperto
C. Vergara
Independencia Espejo
C. Escalinata
C. Fuentes
C. las Hileras
C. de Arenal
C. Tetuán
SOL
PUERTA DEL SOL
C. Bailén
C. Requena
C. Amnistia
C. Union
C. Bordadores
C. Pasadillo de Sancines
C. Mayor
C. Factor
C. San Nicholas
Clara
C. Cruzada
C. Luzón
Cost. Santiago
CENTRO
C. Esparteros
C. Correo
Postas
C. Carretas
C. Espoz y Mina
C. Cádiz
C. Herrera
PL. DE LA VILLA
Casa de los Lujanes
Trv. Bringas
C. Conde Miranda
Cava San Miguel
Marqués Viudo Pontejos
PLAZA MAYOR
Zaragoza
Catedral de Almudena
Ayuntamiento
Torre de los Lujanes
C. Mayor
C. De La Vega
C. Cordon
C. de Sacramento Justo
Casa de Cisneros
C. Imperial
C. Salvador
PL. SANTA CRUZ
C. Bolsa
Santa Cruz
PL. JACINTO BENAVENTE
C. de Atocha
C. Villa
C. Segovia
C. de Toledo
C. Concepción Jerónima
C. Duque de Rivas
Jardines de las Vistillas
C. de Morería
Capilla del Obispo
PL. DE LA PAJA
C. Cava Baja
C. Grafal
PL. SEGOVIA NUEVA
C. Conde Romanones
C. Doctor Cortezo
TIRSO DE MOLINA
C. Relatores
C. Redondilla
Cost. de San Andrés
San Andrés
Cost. San Pedro
PL. DE HUMILLADERO
C. la Colegiata
C. Estudios
Catedral de San Isidro
PL. TIRSO DE MOLINA
C. de Magdalena
C. de Cabestreros
C. Don Pedro
PUERTA DE MOROS
PL. DE LA CEBADA
LA LATINA
C. San Millán
C. Duque de Alba
C. S. Pedro Martir
C. Calvario
C. de Lavapiés
Car. S. Francisco
C. Aguas
C. Oriente
C. Humilladero
C. la Cebada
C. Maldonadas
C. Juanelo
PL. DE CASCORRO
C. Encomienda
C. Jesús y María
C. del Amparo
Gran Vía S. Francisco
C. de Calatrava
Labrador
C. Tabernillas
C. Luciente
C. Dos Hermanas
C. Ángel
C. Mediodia
C. Abades
Mesón de Paredes
C. Irlandese
C. Toledo
C. Santa Ana
C. Oso
C. Embajadores
Cabestreros
Ribera de Curtidores
C. Rosario
C. Aguila
C. de Calatrava
C. Mira el Río Alta
El Rastro
Caravaca
LA LATINA
C. la Ventosa
TO PUERTA DE TOLEDO (190m)
C. la Arganzuela
C. Carnero
C. Sombrerete

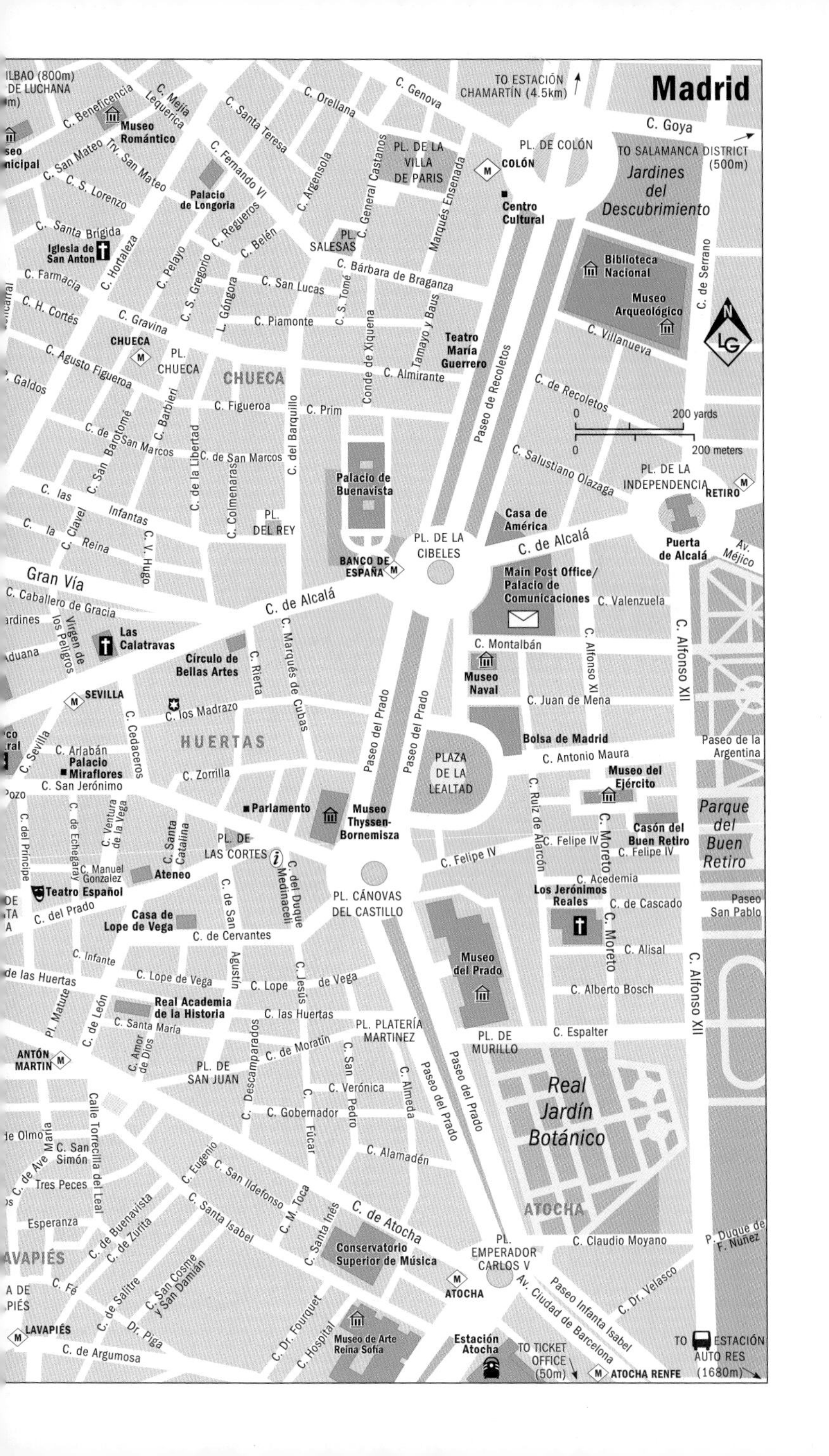
Madrid
TO ESTACIÓN CHAMARTÍN (4.5km)
TO SALAMANCA DISTRICT (500m)
Jardines del Descubrimiento
PL. DE COLÓN
COLÓN
Centro Cultural
Biblioteca Nacional
Museo Arqueológico
Museo Romántico
Palacio de Longoria
Iglesia de San Anton
CHUECA
PL. CHUECA
PL. DE LA VILLA DE PARIS
PL. SALESAS
Teatro María Guerrero
Palacio de Buenavista
PL. DEL REY
BANCO DE ESPAÑA
PL. DE LA CIBELES
Casa de América
PL. DE LA INDEPENDENCIA
RETIRO
Puerta de Alcalá
Main Post Office/ Palacio de Comunicaciones
Museo Naval
Bolsa de Madrid
PLAZA DE LA LEALTAD
Museo del Ejército
Casón del Buen Retiro
Parque del Buen Retiro
Las Calatravas
Círculo de Bellas Artes
SEVILLA
HUERTAS
Palacio Miraflores
Parlamento
Museo Thyssen-Bornemisza
PL. DE LAS CORTES
Ateneo
Teatro Español
Casa de Lope de Vega
PL. CÁNOVAS DEL CASTILLO
Los Jerónimos Reales
Museo del Prado
Real Academia de la Historia
PL. PLATERÍA MARTINEZ
PL. DE MURILLO
ANTÓN MARTIN
PL. DE SAN JUAN
Real Jardín Botánico
ATOCHA
LAVAPIÉS
Conservatorio Superior de Música
PL. EMPERADOR CARLOS V
Museo de Arte Reina Sofía
Estación Atocha
TO TICKET OFFICE (50m)
ATOCHA RENFE
TO ESTACIÓN AUTO RES (1680m)
0 200 yards
0 200 meters
C. Goya
C. Genova
C. Orellana
C. Santa Teresa
C. Fernando VI
C. Argensola
C. General Castanos
Marqués Ensenada
C. Bárbara de Braganza
C. San Lucas
C. Piamonte
C. Gravina
C. Almirante
C. Prim
C. Figueroa
Paseo de Recoletos
C. de Recoletos
C. Villanueva
C. de Serrano
C. Salustiano Olazaga
C. de Alcalá
Gran Vía
C. Caballero de Gracia
C. Valenzuela
C. Montalbán
C. Alfonso XI
C. Alfonso XII
C. Juan de Mena
C. Antonio Maura
Paseo del Prado
C. Felipe IV
C. Ruiz de Alarcón
C. Moreto
C. Acedemia
C. de Cascado
C. Alisal
C. Alberto Bosch
C. Espalter
C. Claudio Moyano
C. Dr. Velasco
Paseo Infanta Isabel
Av. Ciudad de Barcelona
C. de Atocha
C. Santa Isabel
C. San Ildefonso
C. de Argumosa
C. Lope de Vega
C. de Cervantes
C. del Prado
C. las Huertas
C. de Moratín
C. Zorrilla
C. San Jerónimo
C. los Madrazo
C. Marqués de Cubas
C. Infante
C. de León
C. Alamadén
C. Gobernador
C. Verónica
Paseo de la Argentina
Paseo San Pablo
Av. Méjico
P. Duque de F. Nuñez

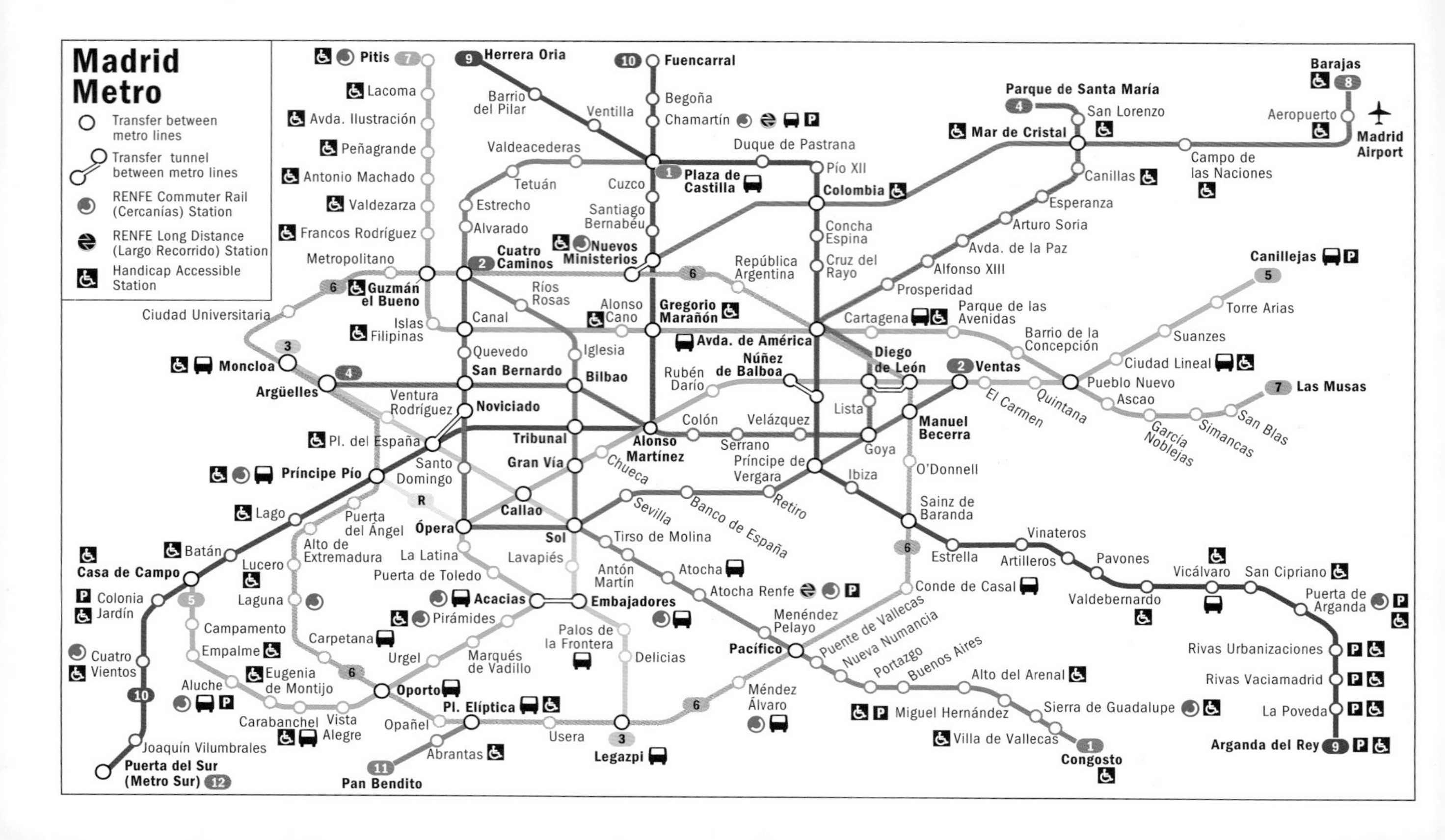

Madrid Metro
Transfer between metro lines
Transfer tunnel between metro lines
RENFE Commuter Rail (Cercanías) Station
RENFE Long Distance (Largo Recorrido) Station
Handicap Accessible Station
Pitis
Lacoma
Avda. Ilustración
Peñagrande
Antonio Machado
Valdezarza
Francos Rodríguez
Metropolitano
Guzmán el Bueno
Ciudad Universitaria
Islas Filipinas
Moncloa
Argüelles
Ventura Rodríguez
Pl. del España
Príncipe Pío
Lago
Batán
Casa de Campo
Colonia Jardín
Cuatro Vientos
Joaquín Vilumbrales
Puerta del Sur (Metro Sur)
Herrera Oria
Barrio del Pilar
Ventilla
Valdeacederas
Tetuán
Estrecho
Alvarado
Cuatro Caminos
Ríos Rosas
Canal
Quevedo
San Bernardo
Noviciado
Santo Domingo
Ópera
Callao
Gran Vía
Tribunal
Bilbao
Iglesia
Alonso Cano
Gregorio Marañón
Avda. de América
Fuencarral
Begoña
Chamartín
Duque de Pastrana
Plaza de Castilla
Cuzco
Santiago Bernabéu
Nuevos Ministerios
Pío XII
Colombia
Concha Espina
Cruz del Rayo
República Argentina
Rubén Darío
Núñez de Balboa
Colón
Velázquez
Serrano
Alonso Martínez
Chueca
Príncipe de Vergara
Lista
Goya
Diego de León
Manuel Becerra
Ventas
El Carmen
Quintana
Pueblo Nuevo
Ascao
García Noblejas
Simancas
San Blas
Las Musas
Ciudad Lineal
Suanzes
Torre Arias
Canillejas
Barrio de la Concepción
Parque de las Avenidas
Cartagena
Prosperidad
Alfonso XIII
Avda. de la Paz
Arturo Soria
Esperanza
Canillas
Mar de Cristal
San Lorenzo
Parque de Santa María
Campo de las Naciones
Aeropuerto
Madrid Airport
Barajas
Puerta del Ángel
Alto de Extremadura
Lucero
Laguna
Carpetana
Campamento
Empalme
Aluche
Eugenia de Montijo
Carabanchel
Vista Alegre
Oporto
Opañel
Urgel
Pirámides
Marqués de Vadillo
La Latina
Puerta de Toledo
Acacias
Embajadores
Lavapiés
Sol
Tirso de Molina
Antón Martín
Sevilla
Banco de España
Retiro
Ibiza
O'Donnell
Sainz de Baranda
Atocha
Atocha Renfe
Palos de la Frontera
Delicias
Menéndez Pelayo
Pacífico
Puente de Vallecas
Nueva Numancia
Portazgo
Buenos Aires
Alto del Arenal
Miguel Hernández
Sierra de Guadalupe
Villa de Vallecas
Congosto
Méndez Álvaro
Legazpi
Usera
Pl. Elíptica
Abrantas
Pan Bendito
Conde de Casal
Estrella
Vinateros
Artilleros
Pavones
Valdebernardo
Vicálvaro
San Cipriano
Puerta de Arganda
Rivas Urbanizaciones
Rivas Vaciamadrid
La Poveda
Arganda del Rey

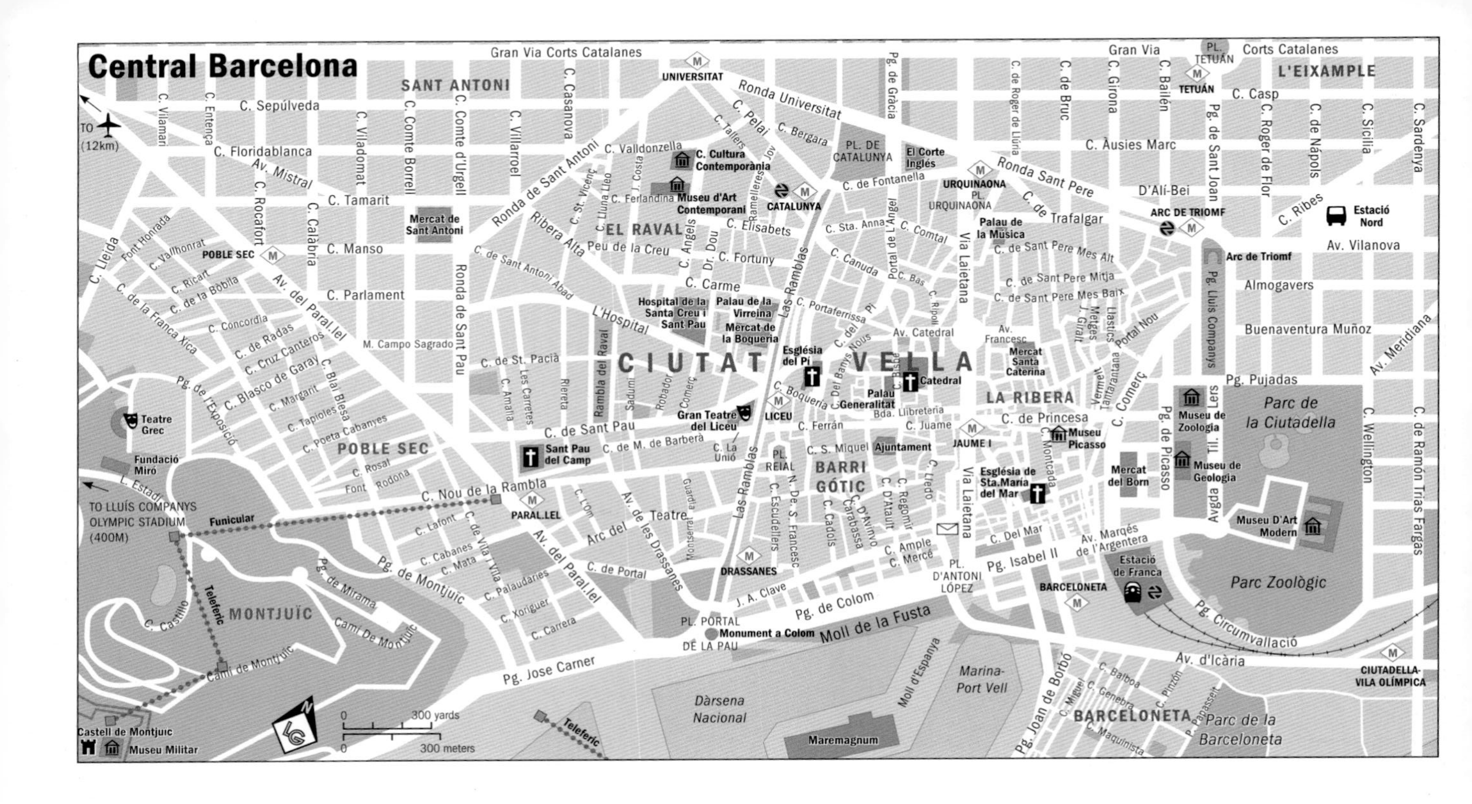
Central Barcelona
SANT ANTONI
EL RAVAL
CIUTAT VELLA
BARRI GÒTIC
LA RIBERA
L'EIXAMPLE
POBLE SEC
MONTJUÏC
BARCELONETA
Gran Via Corts Catalanes
Ronda Universitat
Ronda de Sant Antoni
Ronda de Sant Pau
Ronda Sant Pere
Las Ramblas
Via Laietana
Av. del Paral.lel
Pg. de Gràcia
Pg. de Sant Joan
Pg. Lluis Companys
Pg. de Picasso
Pg. de Colom
Pg. Isabel II
Pg. Jose Carner
Pg. de Montjuïc
Pg. Joan de Borbó
Moll de la Fusta
Moll d'Espanya
Av. d'Icària
Pg. Circumvallació
Av. Meridiana
Av. Vilanova
Av. Mistral
C. de Princesa
C. Ferrán
C. de Sant Pau
L'Hospital
C. Carme
Pl. de Catalunya
Pl. Reial
Pl. Portal de la Pau
Pl. Tetuán
Pl. Urquinaona
Pl. d'Antoni López
UNIVERSITAT
CATALUNYA
URQUINAONA
ARC DE TRIOMF
TETUÁN
JAUME I
LICEU
DRASSANES
PARAL.LEL
POBLE SEC
BARCELONETA
CIUTADELLA-VILA OLÍMPICA
Estació Nord
Estació de Franca
Arc de Triomf
Palau de la Música
Mercat Santa Caterina
Catedral
Palau Generalitat
Ajuntament
Església del Pi
Gran Teatre del Liceu
Mercat de la Boqueria
Palau de la Virreina
Hospital de la Santa Creu i Sant Pau
C. Cultura Contemporània
Museu d'Art Contemporani
Mercat de Sant Antoni
Sant Pau del Camp
El Corte Inglés
Museu Picasso
Església de Sta.Maria del Mar
Mercat del Born
Museu de Zoologia
Museu de Geologia
Museu D'Art Modern
Parc de la Ciutadella
Parc Zoològic
Parc de la Barceloneta
Marina-Port Vell
Dàrsena Nacional
Maremagnum
Monument a Colom
Teatre Grec
Fundació Miró
Castell de Montjuïc
Museu Militar
Funicular
Teleferic
TO LLUÍS COMPANYS OLYMPIC STADIUM (400M)
TO (12km)
0 300 yards
0 300 meters

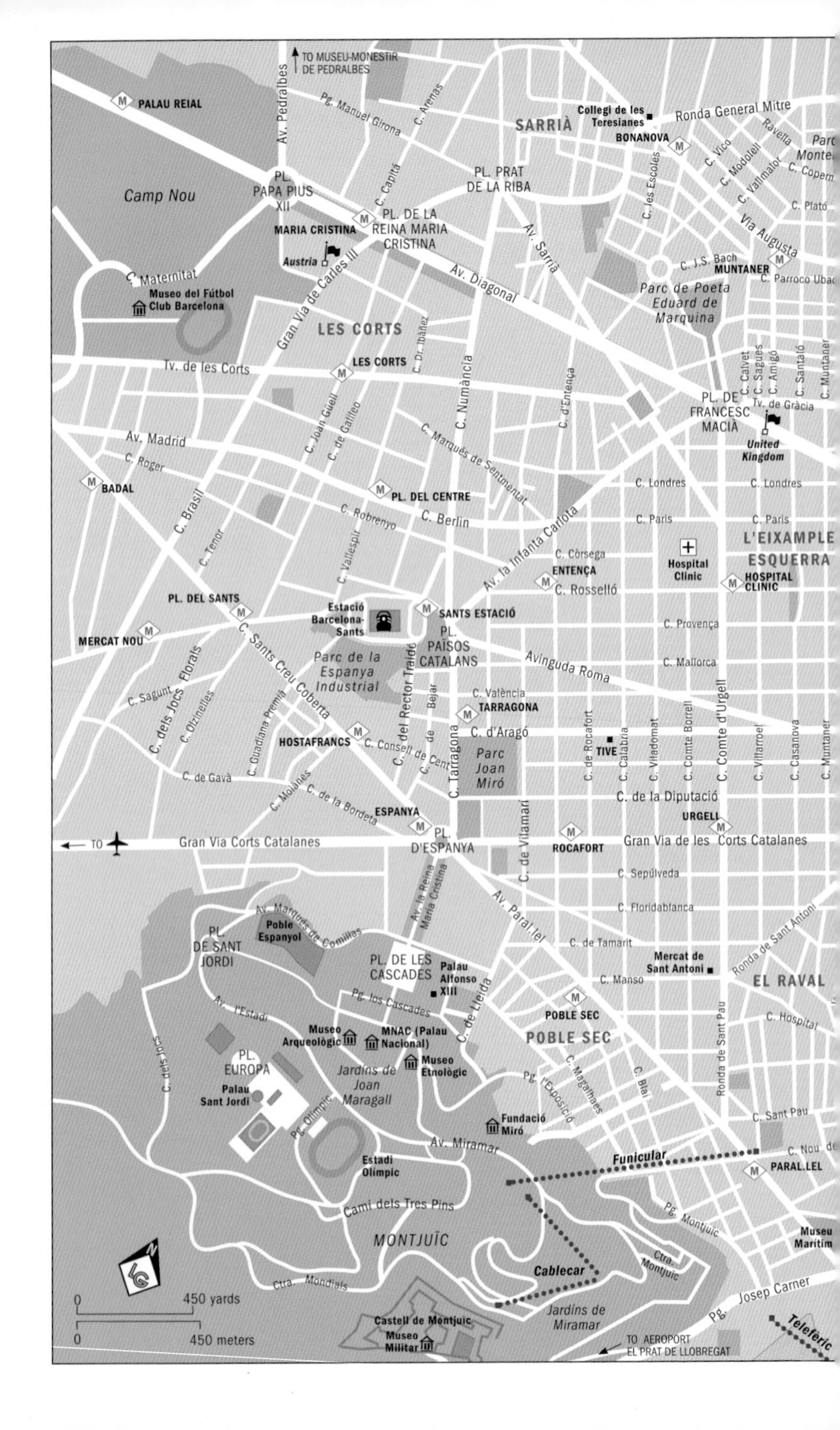
TO MUSEU-MONESTIR DE PEDRALBES
PALAU REIAL
Av. Pedralbes
Pg. Manuel Girona
C. Arenas
SARRIÀ
Collegi de les Teresianes
Ronda General Mitre
BONANOVA
Camp Nou
PL. PAPA PIUS XII
C. Capità
PL. PRAT DE LA RIBA
C. les Escoles
C. Vico
C. Modolell
Ravella
C. Vallmalor
C. Copernic
C. Plató
MARIA CRISTINA
PL. DE LA REINA MARIA CRISTINA
Av. Sarrià
Via Augusta
Austria
C. J.S. Bach
MUNTANER
C. Parroco Ubach
C. Maternitat
Museo del Fútbol Club Barcelona
Gran Via de Carles III
Av. Diagonal
Parc de Poeta Eduard de Marquina
LES CORTS
C. Dr. Ibáñez
Tv. de les Corts
LES CORTS
C. Numància
C. d'Entença
C. Calvet
C. Sagués
C. Amigó
C. Santaló
C. Muntaner
PL. DE FRANCESC MACIÀ
Tv. de Gràcia
United Kingdom
Av. Madrid
C. Joan Güell
C. de Galileo
C. Marqués de Sentmenat
C. Roger
BADAL
PL. DEL CENTRE
C. Londres
C. Brasil
C. Robrenyo
C. Berlin
C. Paris
L'EIXAMPLE ESQUERRA
C. Tenor
C. Vallespir
Av. la Infanta Carlota
C. Còrsega
ENTENÇA
Hospital Clinic
HOSPITAL CLINIC
C. Rosselló
PL. DEL SANTS
Estació Barcelona-Sants
SANTS ESTACIÓ
MERCAT NOU
C. Sants Creu Coberta
PL. PAÏSOS CATALANS
C. Provença
Parc de la Espanya Industrial
Avinguda Roma
C. Mallorca
C. dels Jocs Florals
C. Sagunt
C. Olzinelles
C. Guadiana Premià
C. del Rector Triadó
Bejar
C. València
TARRAGONA
C. d'Aragó
C. de Rocafort
C. Calabria
C. Viladomat
C. Comte Borrell
C. Comte d'Urgell
C. Villarroel
C. Casanova
HOSTAFRANCS
C. Consell de Cent
TIVE
Parc Joan Miró
C. Tarragona
C. de Gavà
C. Moianes
C. de la Bordeta
C. de la Diputació
ESPANYA
URGELL
TO
Gran Via Corts Catalanes
PL. D'ESPANYA
C. de Vilamarí
ROCAFORT
Gran Via de les Corts Catalanes
C. Sepúlveda
Av. la Reina Maria Cristina
Av. Paral.lel
C. Floridablanca
Av. Marquès de Comillas
Poble Espanyol
PL. DE SANT JORDI
PL. DE LES CASCADES
Palau Alfonso XIII
C. de Tamarit
Ronda de Sant Antoni
Mercat de Sant Antoni
C. Manso
EL RAVAL
Pg. los Cascades
C. de Lleida
Av. l'Estadi
POBLE SEC
POBLE SEC
C. Hospital
Museo Arqueològic
MNAC (Palau Nacional)
C. dels Jocs
PL. EUROPA
Museo Etnològic
Jardíns de Joan Maragall
Pg. l'Exposició
C. Magalhaes
C. Blai
Ronda de Sant Pau
Palau Sant Jordi
Pg. Olimpic
Fundació Miró
C. Sant Pau
Av. Miramar
Funicular
C. Nou de
Estadi Olímpic
PARAL.LEL
Camí dels Tres Pins
Pg. Montjuïc
MONTJUÏC
Museu Marítim
Cablecar
Ctra. Montjuïc
Ctra. Mondials
0
450 yards
450 meters
Pg. Josep Carner
Jardíns de Miramar
Castell de Montjuïc
Museo Militar
TO AEROPORT EL PRAT DE LLOBREGAT
Teleféric

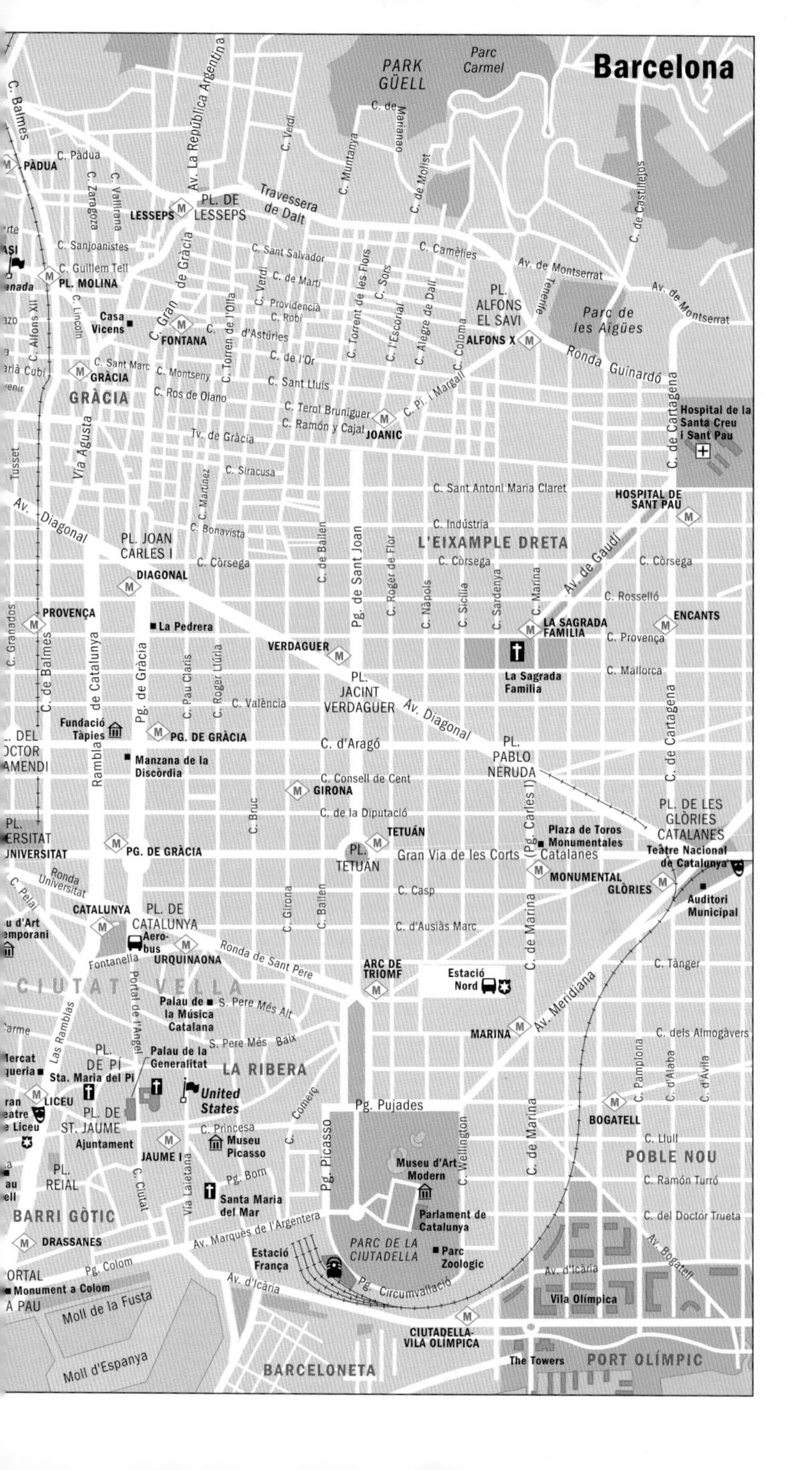

Barcelona
PARK GÜELL
Parc Carmel
Parc de les Aigües
L'EIXAMPLE DRETA
GRÀCIA
CIUTAT VELLA
LA RIBERA
BARRI GÒTIC
POBLE NOU
BARCELONETA
PORT OLÍMPIC
PARC DE LA CIUTADELLA
Travessera de Dalt
Av. Diagonal
Gran Via de les Corts Catalanes
Av. Meridiana
Ronda Guinardó
Av. de Montserrat
Av. de Gaudí
PÀDUA
LESSEPS
PL. DE LESSEPS
PL. MOLINA
FONTANA
GRÀCIA
JOANIC
ALFONS X
PL. ALFONS EL SAVI
HOSPITAL DE SANT PAU
Hospital de la Santa Creu i Sant Pau
DIAGONAL
PL. JOAN CARLES I
PROVENÇA
La Pedrera
VERDAGUER
PL. JACINT VERDAGUER
LA SAGRADA FAMILIA
La Sagrada Familia
ENCANTS
Fundació Tàpies
PG. DE GRÀCIA
Manzana de la Discòrdia
GIRONA
PL. PABLO NERUDA
TETUÁN
PL. TETUÁN
Plaza de Toros Monumentales
PL. DE LES GLÒRIES CATALANES
Teatre Nacional de Catalunya
MONUMENTAL
GLÒRIES
Auditori Municipal
CATALUNYA
PL. DE CATALUNYA
Aero-bus
URQUINAONA
ARC DE TRIOMF
Estació Nord
MARINA
Palau de la Música Catalana
Palau de la Generalitat
Sta. Maria del Pi
PL. DE PI
LICEU
PL. DE ST. JAUME
Ajuntament
United States
Museu Picasso
JAUME I
Santa Maria del Mar
PL. REIAL
DRASSANES
Museu d'Art Modern
Parlament de Catalunya
Parc Zoologic
Estació França
BOGATELL
Vila Olímpica
CIUTADELLA-VILA OLIMPICA
The Towers
Monument a Colom
Moll de la Fusta
Moll d'Espanya
Casa Vicens
C. Balmes
Av. La República Argentina
C. Verdi
C. Muntanya
C. de Marianao
C. de Molist
C. de Castillejos
C. Pàdua
C. Zaragoza
C. Vallirana
C. Sanjoanistes
C. Guillem Tell
C. Alfons XII
C. Lincoln
C. Gran de Gràcia
C. Sant Salvador
C. de Martí
C. Providència
C. Robí
C. d'Astúries
C. de l'Or
C. Sant Lluis
C. Torrent de l'Olla
C. Montseny
C. Ros de Olano
C. Sant Marc
C. Terol Bruniguer
C. Ramón y Cajal
C. Pi i Margall
C. Torrent de les Flors
C. Sors
C. l'Escorial
C. Alegre de Dalt
C. Coloma
C. Camèlies
Tenerife
C. de Cartagena
Via Augusta
Tusset
Tv. de Gràcia
C. Siracusa
C. Martínez
C. Bonavista
C. Còrsega
C. Sant Antoni Maria Claret
C. Indústria
C. de Bailén
Pg. de Sant Joan
C. Roger de Flor
C. Nàpols
C. Sicília
C. Sardenya
C. Marina
C. Rosselló
C. Provença
C. Mallorca
C. Granados
C. de Balmes
Rambla de Catalunya
Pg. de Gràcia
C. Pau Claris
C. Roger Llúria
C. València
C. d'Aragó
C. Consell de Cent
C. de la Diputació
C. Bruc
(Pg. Carles I)
C. Casp
C. d'Ausiàs Marc
C. Girona
C. Bailen
Ronda Universitat
C. Pelai
Ronda de Sant Pere
Fontanella
Portal de l'Àngel
Las Ramblas
S. Pere Més Alt
S. Pere Més Baix
C. Tànger
C. dels Almogàvers
C. Pamplona
C. d'Alaba
C. d'Àvila
C. de Marina
C. Llull
C. Ramón Turró
C. del Doctor Trueta
Av. Bogatell
Av. d'Icària
Pg. Pujades
Pg. Picasso
C. Wellington
C. Comerç
C. Princesa
Pg. Born
Via Laietana
C. Ciutat
Av. Marquès de l'Argentera
Pg. Circumvallació
Pg. Colom

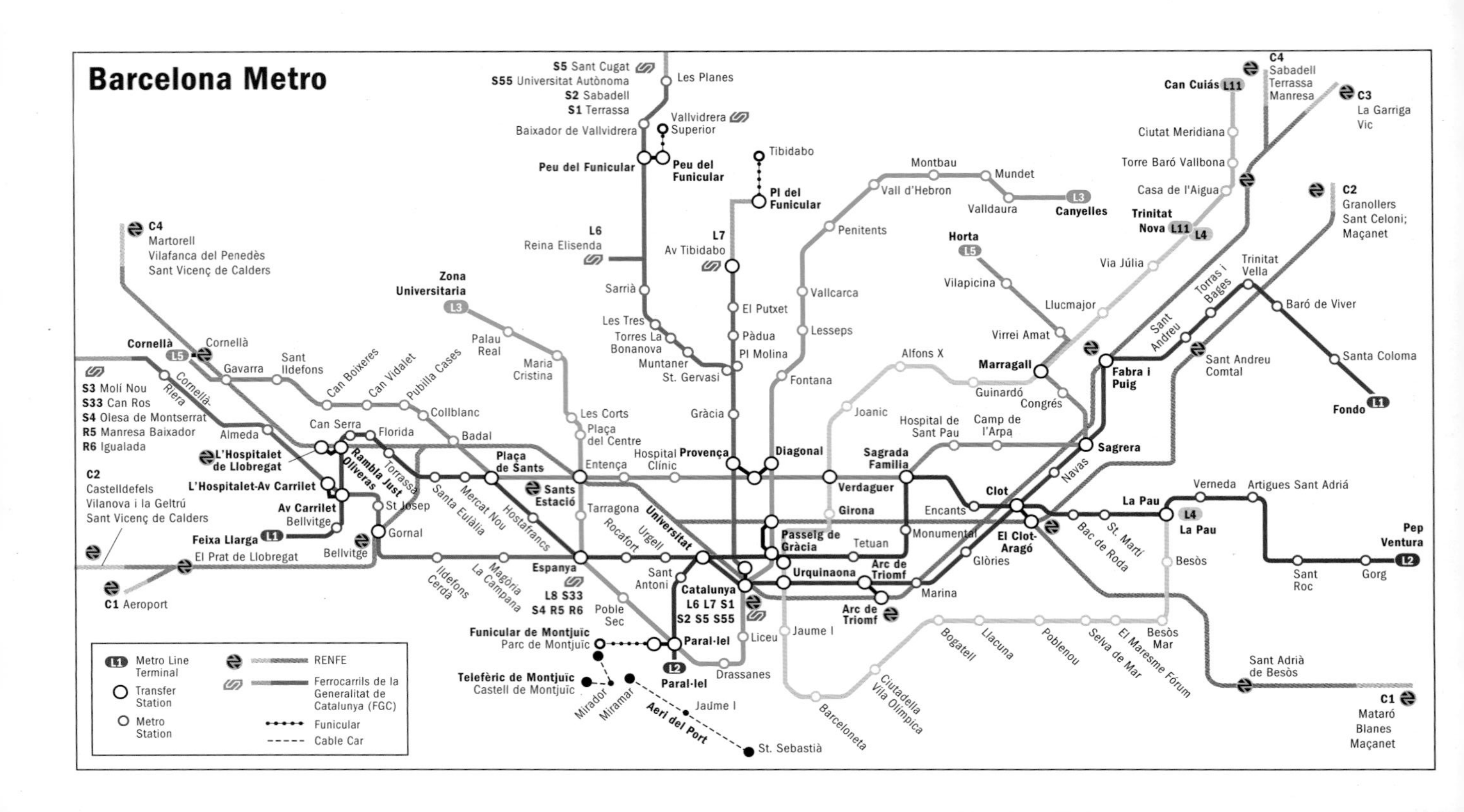
Barcelona Metro
S5 Sant Cugat
S55 Universitat Autònoma
S2 Sabadell
S1 Terrassa
Les Planes
Vallvidrera Superior
Baixador de Vallvidrera
Peu del Funicular
Peu del Funicular
Tibidabo
Pl del Funicular
L6
Reina Elisenda
L7
Av Tibidabo
Sarrià
Les Tres Torres
La Bonanova
Muntaner
St. Gervasi
El Putxet
Pàdua
Pl Molina
Gràcia
Montbau
Mundet
Vall d'Hebron
Valldaura
Canyelles
Penitents
Vallcarca
Lesseps
Fontana
C4
Sabadell
Terrassa
Manresa
Can Cuiás L11
C3
La Garriga
Vic
Ciutat Meridiana
Torre Baró Vallbona
Casa de l'Aigua
Trinitat Nova L11 L4
C2
Granollers
Sant Celoni;
Maçanet
Horta L5
Vilapicina
Llucmajor
Virrei Amat
Via Júlia
Trinitat Vella
Torras i Bages
Baró de Viver
Sant Andreu
Sant Andreu Comtal
Santa Coloma
Fondo L1
Fabra i Puig
Marragall
Alfons X
Guinardó
Congrés
Joanic
Hospital de Sant Pau
Camp de l'Arpa
Sagrera
Navas
Sagrada Familia
Verdaguer
Girona
Diagonal
Provença
Hospital Clínic
Clot
Encants
Monumental
El Clot-Aragó
Glòries
La Pau
L4
La Pau
Verneda
Artigues Sant Adriá
Bac de Roda
St. Martí
Besòs
Sant Roc
Gorg
Pep Ventura L2
C4
Martorell
Vilafanca del Penedès
Sant Vicenç de Calders
Zona Universitaria L3
Palau Real
Maria Cristina
Les Corts
Plaça del Centre
Entença
Cornellà L5
Cornellà
Gavarra
Sant Ildefons
Can Boixeres
Can Vidalet
Pubilla Cases
Collblanc
Badal
Cornellà-Riera
Almeda
S3 Molí Nou
S33 Can Ros
S4 Olesa de Montserrat
R5 Manresa Baixador
R6 Igualada
Can Serra
Florida
Torrassa
L'Hospitalet de Llobregat
Rambla Just Oliveras
L'Hospitalet-Av Carrilet
Av Carrilet
Bellvitge
St Josep
Gornal
Bellvitge
Feixa Llarga L1
C2
Castelldefels
Vilanova i la Geltrú
Sant Vicenç de Calders
El Prat de Llobregat
C1 Aeroport
Plaça de Sants
Santa Eulàlia
Mercat Nou
Hostafrancs
Sants Estació
Tarragona
Rocafort
Urgell
Universitat
Espanya
L8 S33
S4 R5 R6
Ildefons Cerdà
Magòria La Campana
Sant Antoni
Poble Sec
Catalunya
L6 L7 S1
S2 S5 S55
Passeig de Gràcia
Tetuan
Urquinaona
Arc de Triomf
Arc de Triomf
Marina
Liceu
Jaume I
Paral·lel
L2
Paral·lel
Drassanes
Funicular de Montjuïc
Parc de Montjuïc
Telefèric de Montjuïc
Castell de Montjuïc
Mirador
Miramar
Aeri del Port
Jaume I
St. Sebastià
Barceloneta
Ciutadella Vila Olímpica
Bogatell
Llacuna
Poblenou
Selva de Mar
El Maresme Fórum
Besòs Mar
Sant Adrià de Besòs
C1
Mataró
Blanes
Maçanet
L1 Metro Line Terminal
Transfer Station
Metro Station
RENFE
Ferrocarrils de la Generalitat de Catalunya (FGC)
Funicular
Cable Car

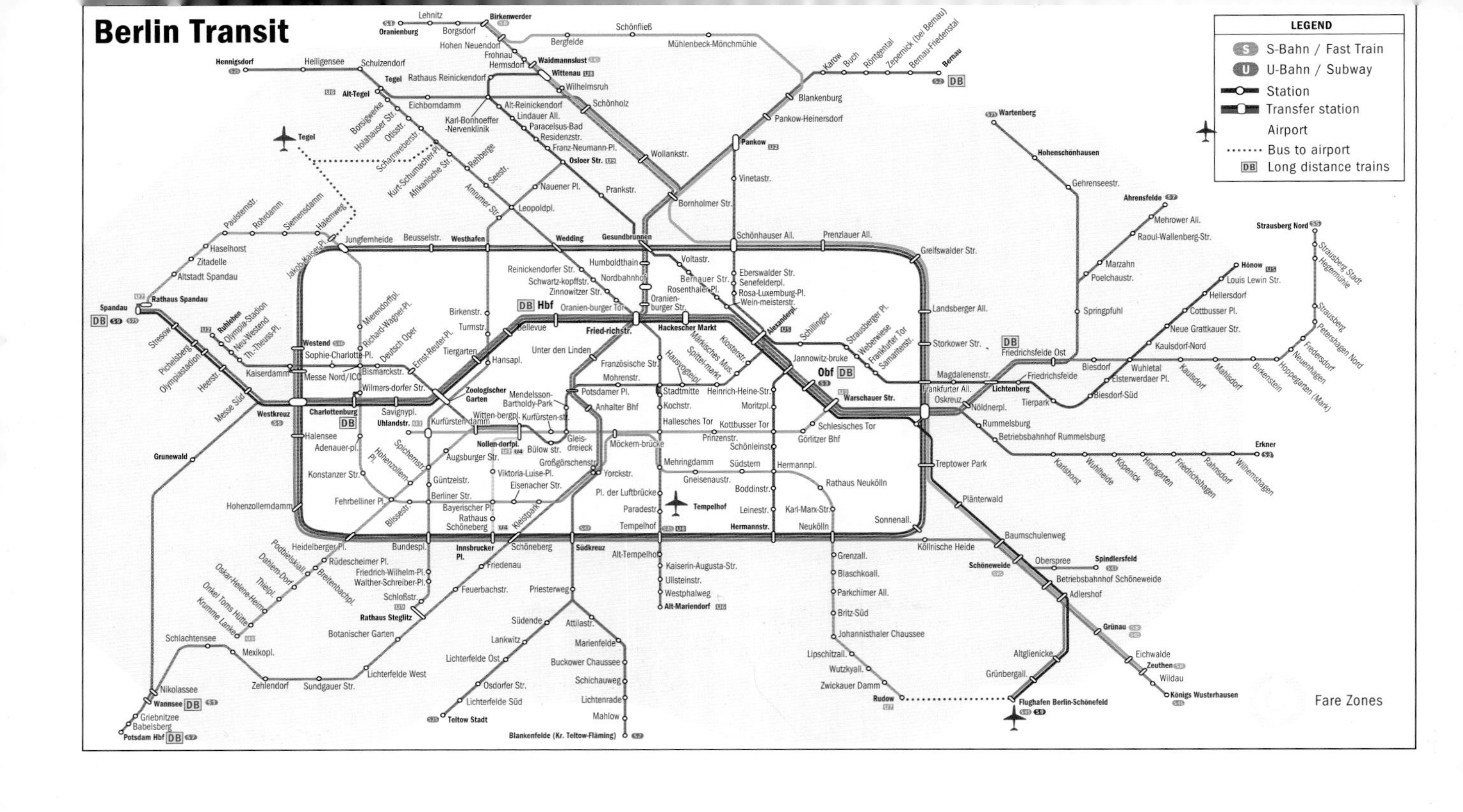

Berlin Transit
LEGEND
S-Bahn / Fast Train
U-Bahn / Subway
Station
Transfer station
Airport
Bus to airport
Long distance trains
Fare Zones
Oranienburg
Lehnitz
Borgsdorf
Birkenwerder
Hohen Neuendorf
Frohnau
Hermsdorf
Waidmannslust
Wittenau
Wilhelmsruh
Schönholz
Schönfließ
Bergfelde
Mühlenbeck-Mönchmühle
Hennigsdorf
Heiligensee
Schulzendorf
Tegel
Rathaus Reinickendorf
Alt-Tegel
Eichborndamm
Karl-Bonhoeffer-Nervenklinik
Alt-Reinickendorf
Lindauer All.
Paracelsus-Bad
Residenzstr.
Franz-Neumann-Pl.
Osloer Str.
Borsigwerke
Holzhauser Str.
Otisstr.
Scharnweberstr.
Kurt-Schumacher-Pl.
Afrikanische Str.
Rehberge
Seestr.
Amrumer Str.
Nauener Pl.
Leopoldpl.
Pankstr.
Wollankstr.
Bornholmer Str.
Karow
Buch
Röntgental
Zepernick (bei Bernau)
Bernau-Friedenstal
Bernau
Blankenburg
Pankow-Heinersdorf
Pankow
Vinetastr.
Wartenberg
Hohenschönhausen
Gehrenseestr.
Ahrensfelde
Mehrower All.
Raoul-Wallenberg-Str.
Marzahn
Poelchaustr.
Springpfuhl
Strausberg Nord
Strausberg Stadt
Hegermühle
Strausberg
Petershagen Nord
Fredersdorf
Neuenhagen
Hoppegarten (Mark)
Birkenstein
Hönow
Louis Lewin Str.
Hellersdorf
Cottbusser Pl.
Neue Grottkauer Str.
Kaulsdorf-Nord
Wuhletal
Kaulsdorf
Mahlsdorf
Biesdorf
Elsterwerdaer Pl.
Biesdorf-Süd
Spandau
Rathaus Spandau
Altstadt Spandau
Zitadelle
Haselhorst
Paulsternstr.
Rohrdamm
Siemensdamm
Halemweg
Jakob-Kaiser-Pl.
Jungfernheide
Beusselstr.
Westhafen
Wedding
Gesundbrunnen
Schönhauser All.
Prenzlauer All.
Greifswalder Str.
Landsberger All.
Storkower Str.
Frankfurter All.
Ostkreuz
Treptower Park
Sonnenall.
Neukölln
Hermannstr.
Tempelhof
Südkreuz
Schöneberg
Innsbrucker Pl.
Bundespl.
Heidelberger Pl.
Hohenzollerndamm
Halensee
Westkreuz
Messe Nord/ICC
Westend
Ruhleben
Olympia-Stadion
Neu-Westend
Th.-Theuss-Pl.
Stresow
Pichelsberg
Olympiastadion
Heerstr.
Messe Süd
Kaiserdamm
Sophie-Charlotte-Pl.
Mierendorffpl.
Richard-Wagner-Pl.
Deutsch Oper
Bismarckstr.
Wilmers-dorfer Str.
Charlottenburg
Savignypl.
Ernst-Reuter-Pl.
Zoologischer Garten
Tiergarten
Hansapl.
Bellevue
Birkenstr.
Turmstr.
Hbf
Reinickendorfer Str.
Schwartz-kopffstr.
Zinnowitzer Str.
Oranien-burger Tor
Humboldthain
Nordbahnhof
Oranien-burger Str.
Voltastr.
Bernauer Str.
Rosenthaler Pl.
Eberswalder Str.
Senefelderpl.
Rosa-Luxemburg-Pl.
Wein-meisterstr.
Fried-richstr.
Hackescher Markt
Alexanderpl.
Schillingstr.
Strausberger Pl.
Weberwiese
Frankfurter Tor
Samariterstr.
Jannowitz-bruke
Obf
Warschauer Str.
Unter den Linden
Französische Str.
Mohrenstr.
Hausvogteipl.
Märkisches Mus.
Spittel-markt
Klosterstr.
Stadtmitte
Heinrich-Heine-Str.
Potsdamer Pl.
Mendelsson-Bartholdy-Park
Anhalter Bhf
Kochstr.
Moritzpl.
Uhlandstr.
Kurfürstendamm
Witten-bergpl.
Kurfürsten-str.
Nollen-dorfpl.
Bülow str.
Gleis-dreieck
Möckern-brücke
Hallesches Tor
Kottbusser Tor
Prinzenstr.
Schönleinstr.
Schlesisches Tor
Görlitzer Bhf
Adenauer-pl.
Spichernstr.
Hohenzollern-Pl.
Augsburger Str.
Viktoria-Luise-Pl.
Großgörschenstr.
Yorckstr.
Mehringdamm
Südstern
Hermannpl.
Rathaus Neukölln
Konstanzer Str.
Güntzelstr.
Eisenacher Str.
Berliner Str.
Gneisenaustr.
Boddinstr.
Fehrbelliner Pl.
Blissestr.
Bayerischer Pl.
Rathaus Schöneberg
Kleistpark
Pl. der Luftbrücke
Paradestr.
Leinestr.
Karl-Marx-Str.
Magdalenenstr.
Lichtenberg
Friedrichsfelde
Friedrichsfelde Ost
Tierpark
Nöldnerpl.
Rummelsburg
Betriebsbahnhof Rummelsburg
Erkner
Karlshorst
Wuhlheide
Köpenick
Hirshgarten
Friedrichshagen
Rahnsdorf
Wilhemshagen
Plänterwald
Baumschulenweg
Köllnische Heide
Schöneweide
Oberspree
Spindlersfeld
Betriebsbahnhof Schöneweide
Adlershof
Grünau
Eichwalde
Zeuthen
Wildau
Königs Wusterhausen
Altglienicke
Grünbergall.
Flughafen Berlin-Schönefeld
Rudow
Zwickauer Damm
Wutzkyall.
Lipschitzall.
Johannisthaler Chaussee
Britz-Süd
Parkchimer All.
Blaschkoall.
Grenzall.
Alt-Tempelhof
Kaiserin-Augusta-Str.
Ullsteinstr.
Westphalweg
Alt-Mariendorf
Priesterweg
Südende
Attilastr.
Marienfelde
Buckower Chaussee
Schichauweg
Lichtenrade
Mahlow
Blankenfelde (Kr. Teltow-Fläming)
Lankwitz
Lichterfelde Ost
Osdorfer Str.
Lichterfelde Süd
Teltow Stadt
Friedenau
Feuerbachstr.
Rüdescheimer Pl.
Friedrich-Wilhelm-Pl.
Walther-Schreiber-Pl.
Schloßstr.
Rathaus Steglitz
Botanischer Garten
Lichterfelde West
Sundgauer Str.
Zehlendorf
Mexikopl.
Schlachtensee
Nikolassee
Wannsee
Griebnitzee
Babelsberg
Potsdam Hbf
Grunewald
Podbielskiall.
Dahlem-Dorf
Breitenbachpl.
Thielpl.
Oskar-Helene-Heim
Onkel Toms Hütte
Krumme Lanke
Tegel

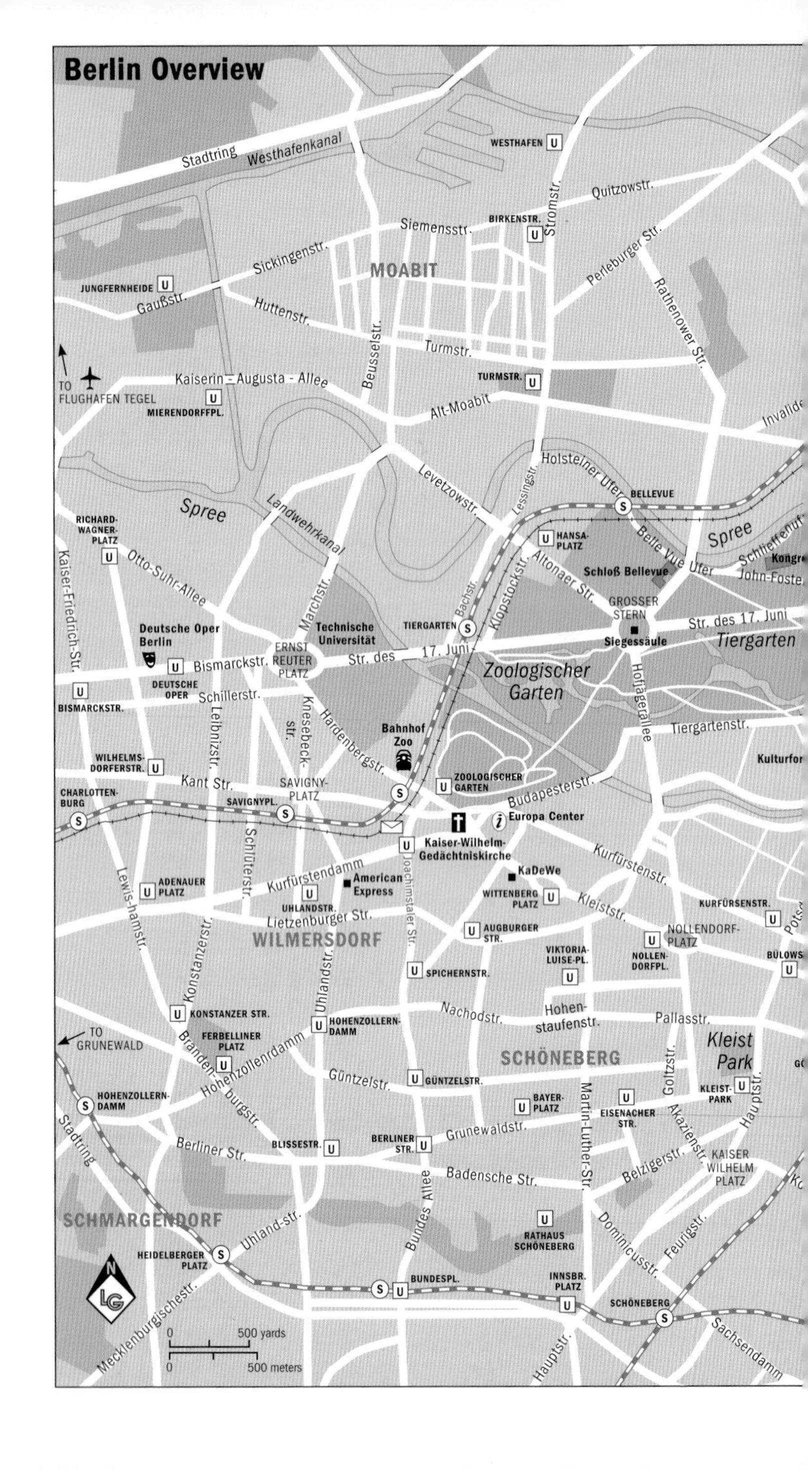
Berlin Overview
Stadtring
Westhafenkanal
WESTHAFEN
Quitzowstr.
Stromstr.
Siemensstr.
BIRKENSTR.
Perleburger Str.
Sickingenstr.
MOABIT
JUNGFERNHEIDE
Gaußstr.
Huttenstr.
Rathenower Str.
Beusselstr.
Turmstr.
TO FLUGHAFEN TEGEL
Kaiserin - Augusta - Allee
TURMSTR.
MIERENDORFFPL.
Alt-Moabit
Invalide
Holsteiner Ufer
Levetzowstr.
Lessingstr.
BELLEVUE
Spree
Landwehrkanal
RICHARD-WAGNER-PLATZ
HANSA-PLATZ
Spree
Otto-Suhr-Allee
Altonaer Str.
Belle Vue Ufer
Schloß Bellevue
John-Foste
Kaiser-Friedrich-Str.
Marchstr.
Bachstr.
Klopstockstr.
GROSSER STERN
Deutsche Oper Berlin
Technische Universität
TIERGARTEN
Siegessäule
Str. des 17. Juni
Tiergarten
ERNST REUTER PLATZ
Bismarckstr.
Str. des 17. Juni
Zoologischer Garten
DEUTSCHE OPER
BISMARCKSTR.
Schillerstr.
Hofjägerallee
Leibnizstr.
Knesebeckstr.
Hardenbergstr.
Bahnhof Zoo
Tiergartenstr.
WILHELMSDORFERSTR.
Kulturfor
Kant Str.
SAVIGNY-PLATZ
ZOOLOGISCHER GARTEN
CHARLOTTENBURG
SAVIGNYPL.
Budapesterstr.
Europa Center
Schlüterstr.
Kaiser-Wilhelm-Gedächtniskirche
Joachimstaler Str.
Kurfürstenstr.
Lewis-hamstr.
ADENAUER PLATZ
Kurfürstendamm
American Express
KaDeWe
UHLANDSTR.
WITTENBERG PLATZ
Kleiststr.
KURFÜRSENSTR.
Lietzenburger Str.
AUGBURGER STR.
NOLLENDORF-PLATZ
WILMERSDORF
VIKTORIA-LUISE-PL.
NOLLEN-DORFPL.
BULOWS
SPICHERNSTR.
Konstanzerstr.
Uhlandstr.
Nachodstr.
Hohenstaufenstr.
Pallasstr.
KONSTANZER STR.
HOHENZOLLERN-DAMM
Kleist Park
TO GRUNEWALD
FERBELLINER PLATZ
Hohenzollerndamm
SCHÖNEBERG
Brandenburgstr.
Güntzelstr.
GÜNTZELSTR.
Goltzstr.
KLEIST-PARK
HOHENZOLLERN-DAMM
BAYER-PLATZ
Martin-Luther-Str.
EISENACHER STR.
Akazienstr.
Hauptstr.
Stadtring
Berliner Str.
BLISSESTR.
BERLINER STR.
Grunewaldstr.
Belzigerstr.
KAISER WILHELM PLATZ
Badensche Str.
Bundes Allee
SCHMARGENDORF
Uhland-str.
RATHAUS SCHÖNEBERG
Dominicusstr.
Feurigstr.
HEIDELBERGER PLATZ
BUNDESPL.
INNSBR. PLATZ
SCHÖNEBERG
Mecklenburgischestr.
Hauptstr.
Sachsendamm
0 500 yards
0 500 meters
N
LG

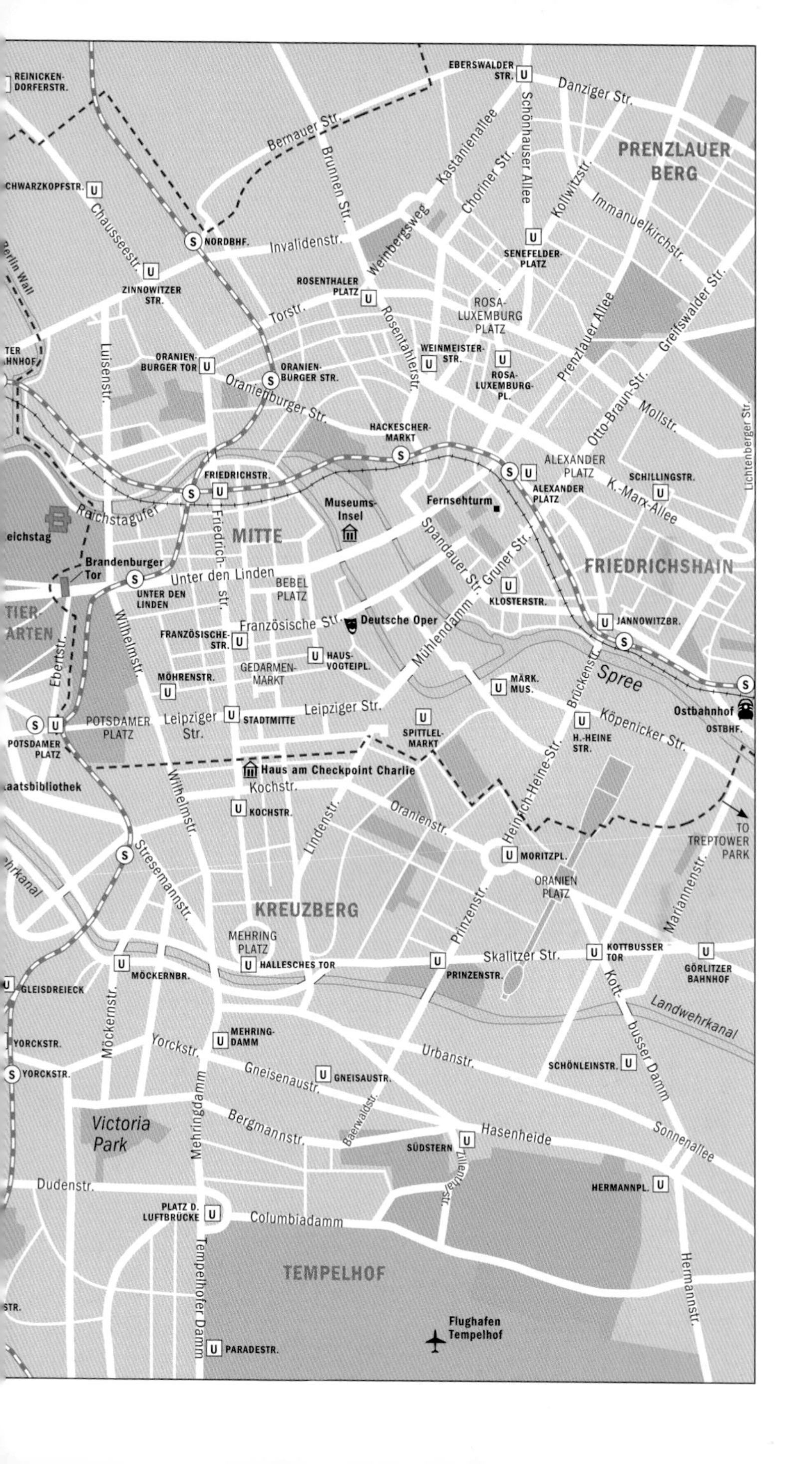

REINICKEN-DORFERSTR.
EBERSWALDER STR.
Danziger Str.
Bernauer Str.
Brunnen Str.
Kastanienallee
Schönhauser Allee
PRENZLAUER BERG
Choriner Str.
Kollwitzstr.
Immanuelkirchstr.
Chausseestr.
NORDBHF.
Invalidenstr.
Weinbergsweg
SENEFELDER-PLATZ
ZINNOWITZER STR.
ROSENTHALER PLATZ
Torstr.
Rosenthaler Str.
ROSA-LUXEMBURG PLATZ
Prenzlauer Allee
Greifswalder Str.
Luisenstr.
ORANIEN-BURGER TOR
ORANIEN-BURGER STR.
WEINMEISTER-STR.
ROSA-LUXEMBURG-PL.
Otto-Braun-Str.
Oranienburger Str.
Mollstr.
HACKESCHER MARKT
ALEXANDER PLATZ
Lichtenberger Str.
FRIEDRICHSTR.
SCHILLINGSTR.
Museums-Insel
Fernsehturm
K.-Marx-Allee
Reichstagufer
MITTE
Friedrich-str.
Spandauer Str.
Gruner Str.
FRIEDRICHSHAIN
Brandenburger Tor
Unter den Linden
UNTER DEN LINDEN
BEBEL PLATZ
KLOSTERSTR.
Französische Str.
Deutsche Oper
Mühlendamm
JANNOWITZBR.
FRANZÖSISCHE-STR.
HAUS-VOGTEIPL.
Ebertstr.
Wilhelmstr.
GEDARMEN-MARKT
MÖHRENSTR.
MÄRK. MUS.
Spree
Brückenstr.
POTSDAMER PLATZ
Leipziger Str.
STADTMITTE
Leipziger Str.
Ostbahnhof
OSTBHF.
Köpenicker Str.
SPITTEL-MARKT
H.-HEINE STR.
Heinrich-Heine-Str.
Haus am Checkpoint Charlie
Kochstr.
KOCHSTR.
Lindenstr.
Oranienstr.
TO TREPTOWER PARK
MORITZPL.
Stresemannstr.
ORANIEN PLATZ
Mariannenstr.
KREUZBERG
Prinzenstr.
MEHRING PLATZ
HALLESCHES TOR
Skalitzer Str.
KOTTBUSSER TOR
GÖRLITZER BAHNHOF
MÖCKERNBR.
PRINZENSTR.
GLEISDREIECK
Kott-busser Damm
Landwehrkanal
Möckernstr.
MEHRING-DAMM
YORCKSTR.
Yorckstr.
Urbanstr.
SCHÖNLEINSTR.
YORCKSTR.
Gneisenaustr.
GNEISAUSTR.
Victoria Park
Bergmannstr.
Baerwaldstr.
Hasenheide
SÜDSTERN
Zillestr.
Sonnenallee
Mehringdamm
Dudenstr.
HERMANNPL.
PLATZ D. LUFTBRÜCKE
Columbiadamm
Tempelhofer Damm
Hermannstr.
TEMPELHOF
Flughafen Tempelhof
PARADESTR.

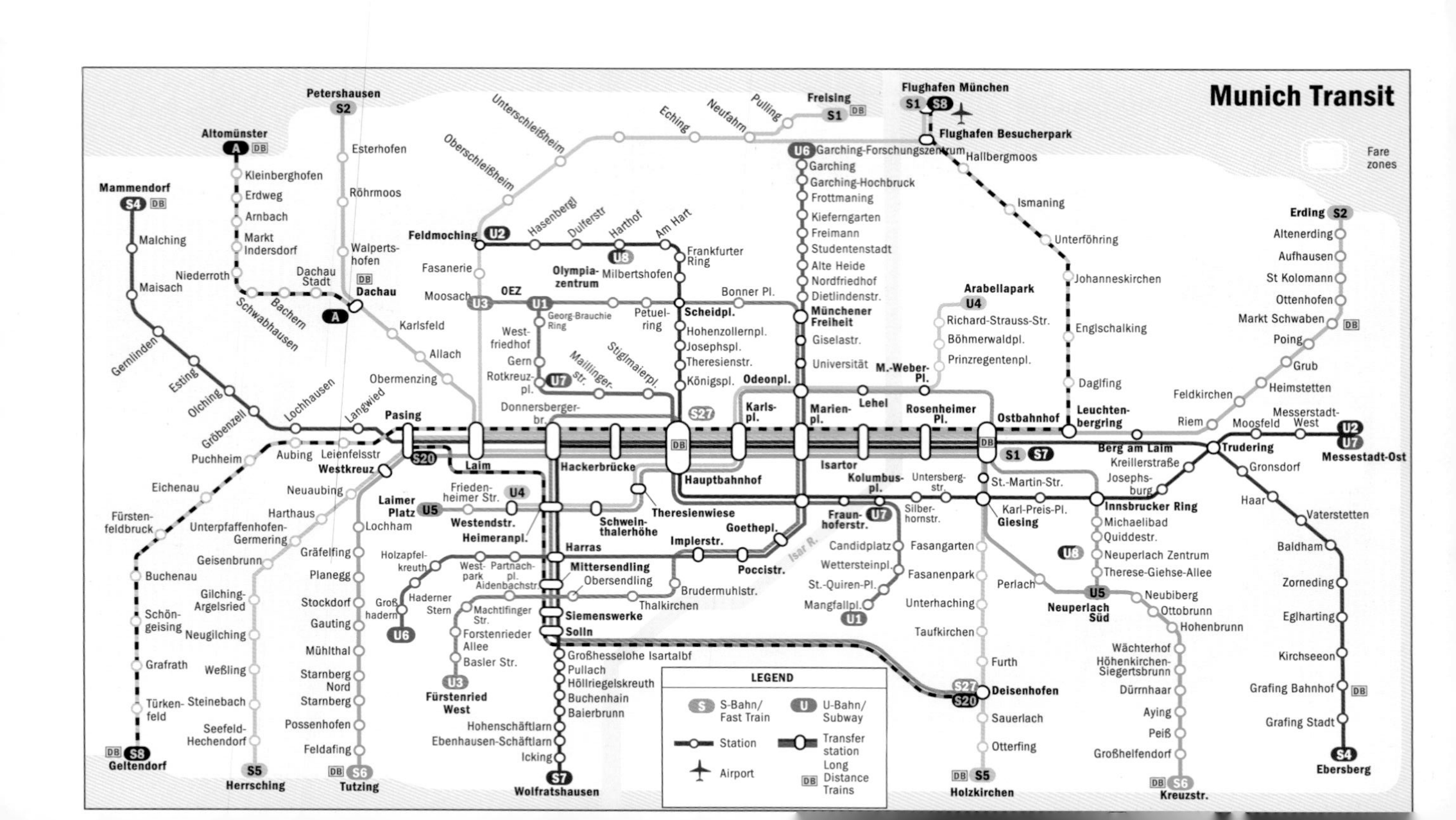

Munich Transit
Fare zones
LEGEND
S-Bahn/ Fast Train
U-Bahn/ Subway
Station
Transfer station
Airport
Long Distance Trains
Mammendorf
Malching
Maisach
Gernlinden
Esting
Olching
Gröbenzell
Lochhausen
Langwied
Pasing
Altomünster
Kleinberghofen
Erdweg
Arnbach
Markt Indersdorf
Niederroth
Schwabhausen
Bachern
Dachau Stadt
Dachau
Petershausen
Esterhofen
Röhrmoos
Walperts-hofen
Karlsfeld
Allach
Obermenzing
Unterschleißheim
Oberschleißheim
Feldmoching
Hasenbergl
Dülferstr
Harthof
Am Hart
Frankfurter Ring
Milbertshofen
Olympia-zentrum
Fasanerie
Moosach
OEZ
Georg-Brauchle Ring
West-friedhof
Gern
Rotkreuz-pl.
Maillinger-str.
Stiglmaierpl.
Petuel-ring
Scheidpl.
Bonner Pl.
Hohenzollernpl.
Josephspl.
Theresienstr.
Königspl.
Eching
Neufahrn
Pulling
Freising
Flughafen München
Flughafen Besucherpark
Garching-Forschungszentrum
Hallbergmoos
Garching
Garching-Hochbruck
Frottmaning
Kieferngarten
Freimann
Studentenstadt
Alte Heide
Nordfriedhof
Dietlindenstr.
Münchener Freiheit
Giselastr.
Universität
Ismaning
Unterföhring
Johanneskirchen
Englschalking
Daglfing
Arabellapark
Richard-Strauss-Str.
Böhmerwaldpl.
Prinzregentenpl.
M.-Weber-Pl.
Odeonpl.
Karls-pl.
Marien-pl.
Lehel
Rosenheimer Pl.
Ostbahnhof
Leuchten-bergring
Berg am Laim
Riem
Feldkirchen
Heimstetten
Grub
Poing
Markt Schwaben
Ottenhofen
St Kolomann
Aufhausen
Altenerding
Erding
Moosfeld
Messerstadt-West
Messestadt-Ost
Trudering
Gronsdorf
Haar
Vaterstetten
Baldham
Zorneding
Eglharting
Kirchseeon
Grafing Bahnhof
Grafing Stadt
Ebersberg
Kreillerstraße
Josephs-burg
Innsbrucker Ring
Michaelibad
Quiddestr.
Neuperlach Zentrum
Therese-Giehse-Allee
Neuperlach Süd
Neubiberg
Ottobrunn
Hohenbrunn
Wächterhof
Höhenkirchen-Siegertsbrunn
Dürrnhaar
Aying
Peiß
Großhelfendorf
Kreuzstr.
Perlach
St.-Martin-Str.
Karl-Preis-Pl.
Giesing
Untersberg-str.
Silber-hornstr.
Kolumbus-pl.
Isartor
Fraun-hoferstr.
Candidplatz
Wettersteinpl.
St.-Quirin-Pl.
Mangfallpl.
Fasangarten
Fasanenpark
Unterhaching
Taufkirchen
Furth
Deisenhofen
Sauerlach
Otterfing
Holzkirchen
Hauptbahnhof
Hackerbrücke
Donnersberger-br.
Laim
Theresienwiese
Schwein-thalerhöhe
Goethepl.
Implerstr.
Poccistr.
Isar R.
Westkreuz
Leienfelsstr
Aubing
Puchheim
Eichenau
Fürsten-feldbruck
Buchenau
Schön-geising
Grafrath
Türken-feld
Geltendorf
Neuaubing
Harthaus
Unterpfaffenhofen-Germering
Geisenbrunn
Gilching-Argelsried
Neugilching
Weßling
Steinebach
Seefeld-Hechendorf
Herrsching
Laimer Platz
Frieden-heimer Str.
Westendstr.
Heimeranpl.
Harras
Lochham
Gräfelfing
Planegg
Stockdorf
Gauting
Mühlthal
Starnberg Nord
Starnberg
Possenhofen
Feldafing
Tutzing
Holzapfel-kreuth
West-park
Partnach-pl.
Aidenbachstr.
Haderner Stern
Groß hadern
Machtlfinger Str.
Forstenrieder Allee
Basler Str.
Fürstenried West
Mittersendling
Obersendling
Thalkirchen
Brudermuhlstr.
Siemenswerke
Solln
Großhesselohe Isartalbf
Pullach
Höllriegelskreuth
Buchenhain
Baierbrunn
Hohenschäftlarn
Ebenhausen-Schäftlarn
Icking
Wolfratshausen

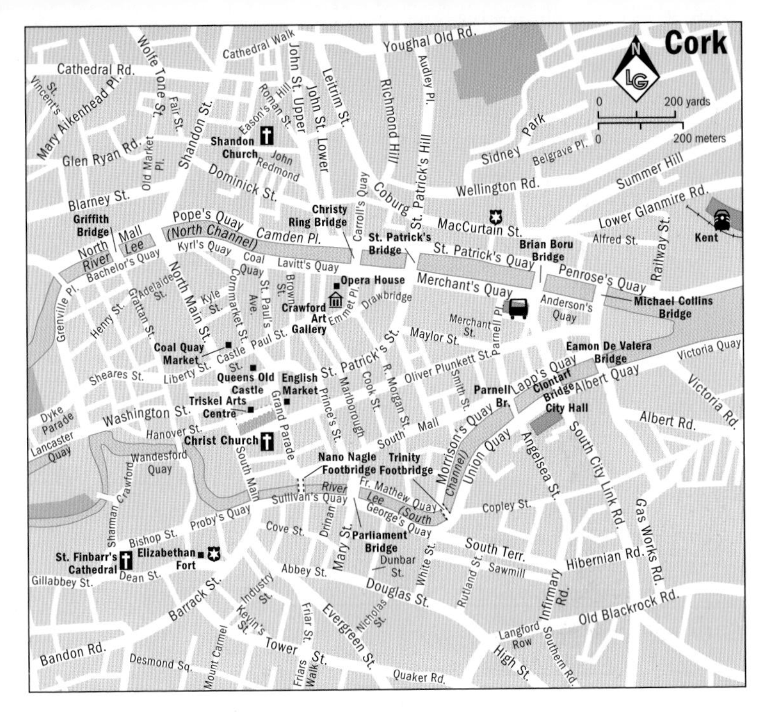
Cork
0
200 yards
0
200 meters
Cathedral Walk
Youghal Old Rd.
Cathedral Rd.
Wolfe Tone St.
John St. Upper
John St. Lower
Leitrim St.
Richmond Hill
Audley Pl.
St. Vincent's
Mary Aikenhead Pl.
Fair St.
Shandon St.
Eason's Hill
Roman St.
St. Patrick's Hill
Sidney Park
Belgrave Pl.
Shandon Church
John Redmond
Glen Ryan Rd.
Old Market Pl.
Dominick St.
Carroll's Quay
Coburg St.
Wellington Rd.
Summer Hill
Blarney St.
Christy Ring Bridge
MacCurtain St.
Lower Glanmire Rd.
Griffith Bridge
North Mall
Pope's Quay
(North Channel)
Camden Pl.
St. Patrick's Bridge
Brian Boru Bridge
Alfred St.
Railway St.
Kent
North River Lee
Kyrl's Quay
Bachelor's Quay
Coal Quay
Lavitt's Quay
St. Patrick's Quay
Penrose's Quay
Grenville Pl.
Adelaide St.
North Main St.
Cornmarket St.
Brown St.
Opera House
Merchant's Quay
Michael Collins Bridge
Henry St.
Grattan St.
Kyle St.
Ave.
St. Paul's
Crawford Art Gallery
Emmet Pl.
Drawbridge
Anderson's Quay
Merchant St.
Parnell Pl.
Coal Quay Market
Castle St.
Paul St.
St. Patrick's St.
Maylor St.
Eamon De Valera Bridge
Victoria Quay
Sheares St.
Liberty St.
Queens Old Castle
English Market
Cook St.
R. Morgan St.
Oliver Plunkett St.
Smith St.
Lapp's Quay
Clontarf Bridge
Albert Quay
Victoria Rd.
Dyke Parade
Washington St.
Triskel Arts Centre
Grand Parade
Prince's St.
Marlborough
Parnell Br.
City Hall
Albert Rd.
Lancaster Quay
Hanover St.
Christ Church
South Mall
Morrison's Quay
Union Quay
Angelsea St.
South City Link Rd.
Wandesford Quay
South Main
Nano Nagle Footbridge
Trinity Footbridge
(South Channel)
Sharman Crawford
Sullivan's Quay
River Lee (South
Fr. Mathew Quay
George's Quay
Copley St.
Gas Works Rd.
Proby's Quay
Cove St.
Drinan
Mary St.
Parliament Bridge
South Terr.
Bishop St.
St. Finbarr's Cathedral
Elizabethan Fort
Dunbar St.
White St.
Rutland St.
Sawmill
Hibernian Rd.
Gillabbey St.
Dean St.
Abbey St.
Infirmary Rd.
Barrack St.
Industry St.
Douglas St.
Old Blackrock Rd.
Nicholas St.
Kevin's St.
Friar St.
Evergreen St.
Langford Row
Bandon Rd.
Tower St.
Southern Rd.
High St.
Desmond Sq.
Mount Carmel
Friars Walk
Quaker Rd.

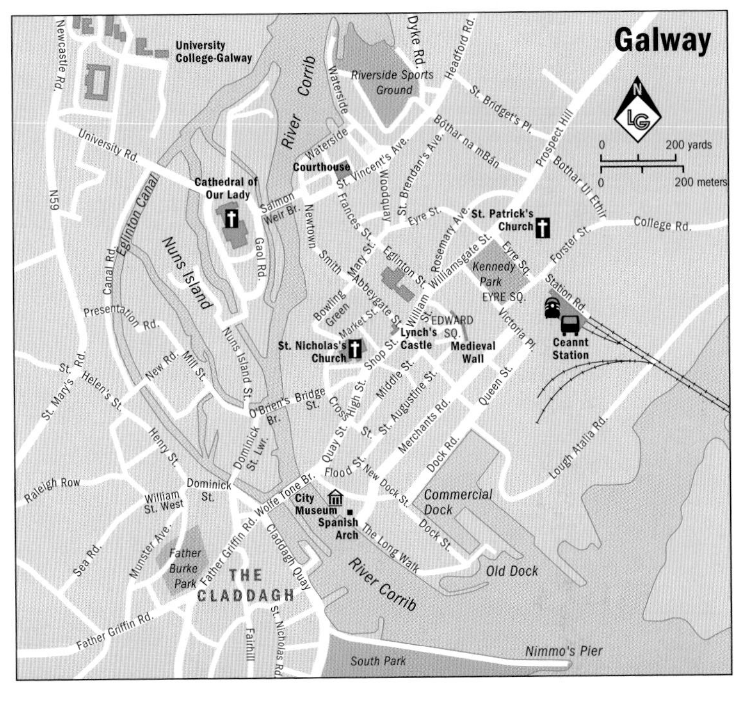
Galway
Newcastle Rd.
University College-Galway
Dyke Rd.
Headford Rd.
River Corrib
Waterside
Riverside Sports Ground
St. Bridget's Pl.
0
200 yards
0
200 meters
University Rd.
Bothar na mBán
St. Brendan's Ave.
Prospect Hill
Bothar Ui Ethir
Courthouse
St. Vincent's Ave.
Woodquay
N59
Eglinton Canal
Cathedral of Our Lady
Salmon Weir Br.
Newtown
Frances St.
Eyre St.
St. Patrick's Church
College Rd.
Nuns Island
Gaol Rd.
Canal Rd.
Smith
Mary St.
Eglinton St.
Rosemary Ave.
Williamsgate St.
Eyre Sq.
Forster St.
Kennedy Park
EYRE SQ.
Station Rd.
Abbeygate St.
Bowling Green
Presentation Rd.
Market St.
William St.
EDWARD SQ.
Victoria Pl.
Lynch's Castle
Ceannt Station
St. Nicholas's Church
Medieval Wall
New Rd.
Mill St.
Nuns Island St.
Shop St.
Middle St.
St. Mary's Rd.
St. Helen's St.
Queen St.
St. Augustine St.
O'Brien's Bridge
Br.
Cross St.
High St.
Merchants Rd.
Lough Atalia Rd.
Henry St.
Dominick St. Lwr.
Quay St.
Dock Rd.
Raleigh Row
Dominick St.
Flood St.
Wolfe Tone Br.
New Dock St.
Commercial Dock
William St. West
City Museum
Spanish Arch
Dock St.
Sea Rd.
Munster Ave.
Father Griffin Rd.
Claddagh Quay
The Long Walk
Father Burke Park
THE CLADDAGH
River Corrib
Old Dock
Father Griffin Rd.
Fairhill
St. Nicholas Rd.
Nimmo's Pier
South Park

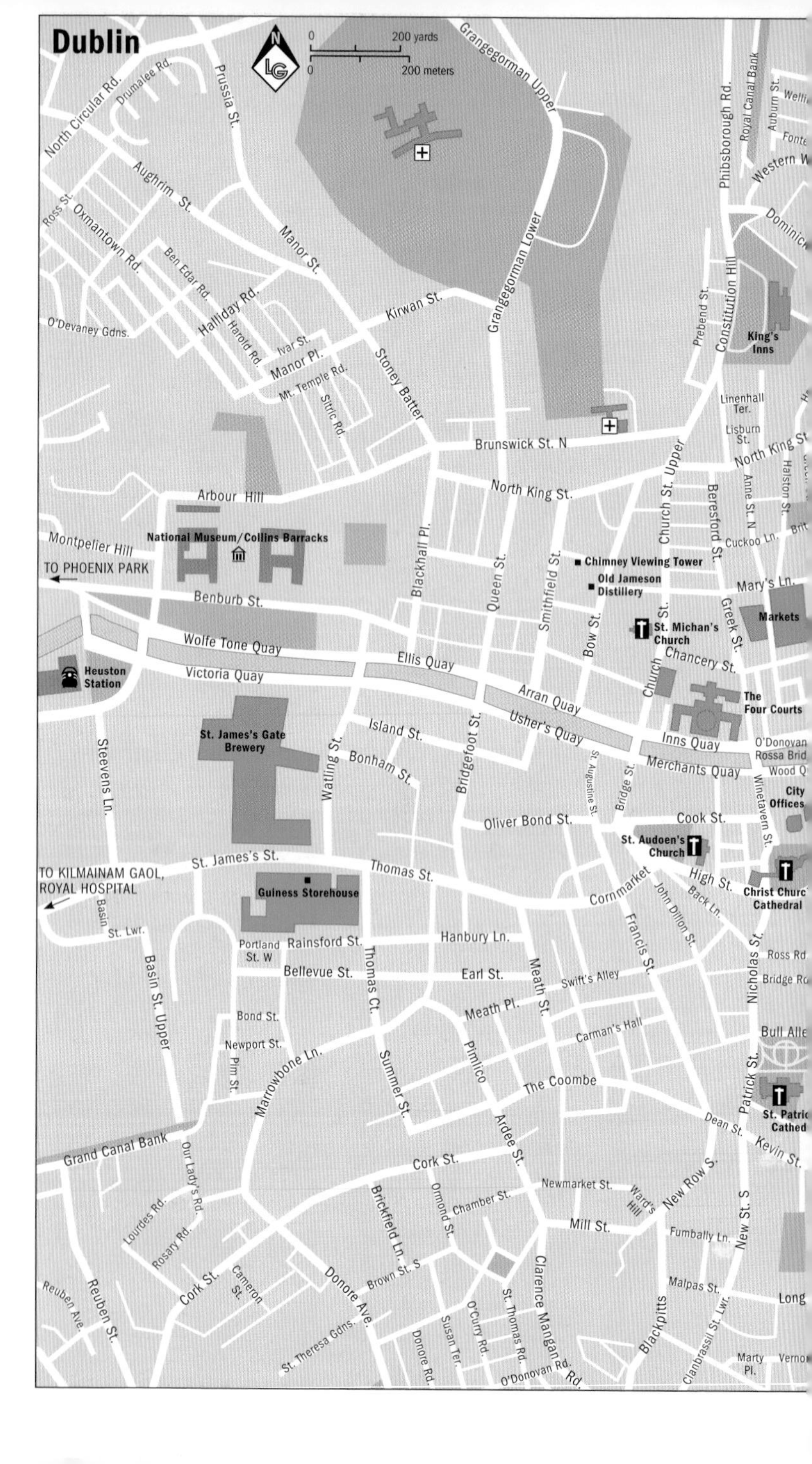
Dublin
0
200 yards
0
200 meters
TO PHOENIX PARK
TO KILMAINAM GAOL, ROYAL HOSPITAL
National Museum/Collins Barracks
Heuston Station
St. James's Gate Brewery
Guiness Storehouse
Chimney Viewing Tower
Old Jameson Distillery
St. Michan's Church
The Four Courts
Markets
King's Inns
City Offices
St. Audoen's Church
Christ Church Cathedral
North Circular Rd.
Drumalee Rd.
Prussia St.
Grangegorman Upper
Grangegorman Lower
Aughrim St.
Ross St.
Oxmantown Rd.
Manor St.
Ben Edar Rd.
Halliday Rd.
Harold Rd.
O'Devaney Gdns.
Kirwan St.
Ivar St.
Manor Pl.
Mt. Temple Rd.
Sitric Rd.
Stoney Batter
Brunswick St. N
Arbour Hill
North King St.
Montpelier Hill
Blackhall Pl.
Queen St.
Smithfield St.
Benburb St.
Wolfe Tone Quay
Victoria Quay
Ellis Quay
Arran Quay
Usher's Quay
Inns Quay
Merchants Quay
Bow St.
Church St.
Church St. Upper
Chancery St.
Greek St.
Beresford St.
Mary's Ln.
Cuckoo Ln.
Anne St. N
Halston St.
North King St.
Linenhall Ter.
Lisburn St.
Prebend St.
Constitution Hill
Phibsborough Rd.
Royal Canal Bank
Auburn St.
Western W
Dominic
O'Donovan Rossa Brid
Wood Q
Winetavern St.
Island St.
Bonham St.
Watling St.
Bridgefoot St.
St. Augustine St.
Bridge St.
Oliver Bond St.
Cook St.
Steevens Ln.
St. James's St.
Thomas St.
High St.
Back Ln.
Cornmarket
John Dillon St.
Francis St.
Basin St. Lwr.
Basin St. Upper
Portland St. W
Rainsford St.
Hanbury Ln.
Bellevue St.
Thomas Ct.
Earl St.
Meath St.
Swift's Alley
Nicholas St.
Ross Rd.
Bridge Rd
Bond St.
Newport St.
Pim St.
Meath Pl.
Carman's Hall
Bull Alle
Marrowbone Ln.
Summer St.
Pimlico
The Coombe
Patrick St.
St. Patric Cathed
Dean St.
Kevin St.
Grand Canal Bank
Our Lady's Rd.
Cork St.
Ardee St.
New Row S.
New St. S
Lourdes Rd.
Rosary Rd.
Brickfield Ln.
Ormond St.
Chamber St.
Newmarket St.
Ward's Hill
Mill St.
Fumbally Ln.
Cork St.
Cameron St.
Donore Ave.
Brown St. S
St. Thomas Rd.
Clarence Mangan Rd.
Malpas St.
Long
Reuben Ave.
Reuben St.
St. Theresa Gdns.
Donore Rd.
Susan Ter.
O'Curry Rd.
O'Donovan Rd.
Blackpitts
Clanbrassil St. Lwr.
Marty Pl.
Verno

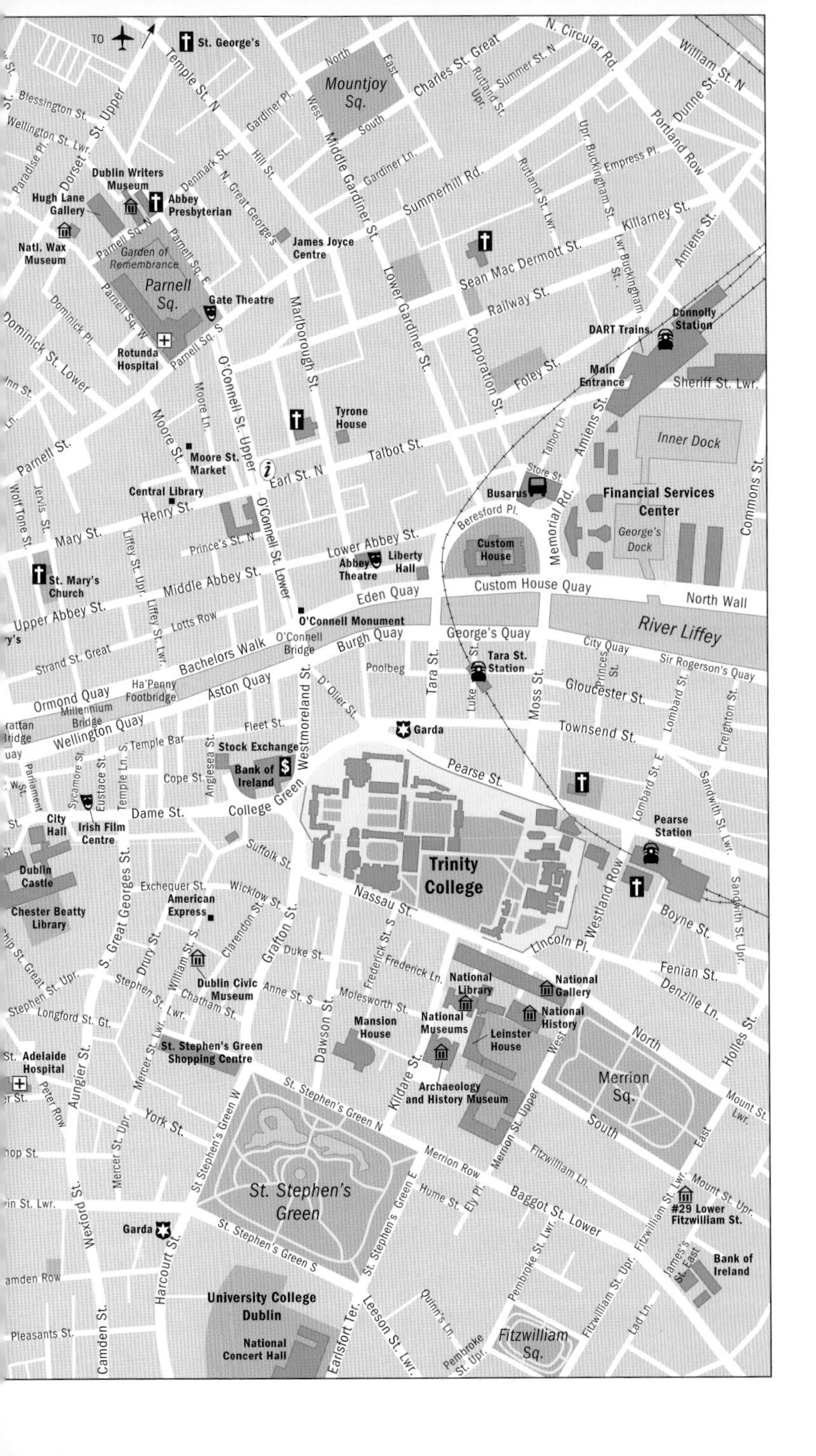

TO
St. George's
Temple St. N
Blessington St.
Wellington St. Lwr.
Dorset St. Upper
Paradise Pl.
Dublin Writers Museum
Hugh Lane Gallery
Abbey Presbyterian
Natl. Wax Museum
Garden of Remembrance
Parnell Sq.
Gate Theatre
Rotunda Hospital
Dominick Pl.
Dominick St. Lower
Parnell St.
Mountjoy Sq.
Charles St. Great
Gardiner Pl.
Hill St.
N. Great George's St.
Denmark St.
James Joyce Centre
Middle Gardiner St.
Gardiner Ln.
Summerhill Rd.
Rutland St. Upr.
Summer St. N
N. Circular Rd.
William St. N
Dunne St.
Portland Row
Upr. Buckingham St.
Empress Pl.
Rutland St. Lwr.
Killarney St.
Amiens St.
Sean Mac Dermott St.
Lwr Buckingham St.
Railway St.
Connolly Station
DART Trains
Main Entrance
Sheriff St. Lwr.
Foley St.
Corporation St.
Lower Gardiner St.
Marlborough St.
O'Connell St. Upper
Moore Ln.
Moore St.
Moore St. Market
Tyrone House
Talbot St.
Talbot Ln.
Inner Dock
Earl St. N
Central Library
Henry St.
Mary St.
Wolf Tone St.
Jervis St.
Liffey St. Upr.
Prince's St. N
O'Connell St. Lower
Store St.
Busaras
Beresford Pl.
Memorial Rd.
Financial Services Center
George's Dock
Commons St.
Custom House
Lower Abbey St.
Abbey Theatre
Liberty Hall
St. Mary's Church
Middle Abbey St.
Upper Abbey St.
Liffey St. Lwr.
Lotts Row
Eden Quay
Custom House Quay
North Wall
River Liffey
O'Connell Monument
O'Connell Bridge
Burgh Quay
George's Quay
City Quay
Sir Rogerson's Quay
Strand St. Great
Bachelors Walk
Poolbeg
Tara St.
Luke St.
Tara St. Station
Princes St.
Moss St.
Gloucester St.
Lombard St.
Creighton St.
Ormond Quay
Ha'Penny Footbridge
Millennium Bridge
Aston Quay
Westmoreland St.
D'Olier St.
Wellington Quay
Fleet St.
Temple Bar
Garda
Townsend St.
Stock Exchange
Bank of Ireland
Cope St.
Anglesea St.
Parliament St.
Sycamore St.
Eustace St.
Temple Ln. S
College Green
Pearse St.
Lombard St. E
Sandwith St. Lwr.
Dame St.
City Hall
Irish Film Centre
Pearse Station
Trinity College
Dublin Castle
Suffolk St.
Westland Row
Chester Beatty Library
S. Great Georges St.
Exchequer St.
American Express
Wicklow St.
Nassau St.
Boyne St.
Sandwith St. Upr.
Drury St.
William St. S
Clarendon St.
Grafton St.
Duke St.
Frederick St. S
Lincoln Pl.
Frederick Ln.
Fenian St.
Denzille Ln.
Stephen St. Upr.
Stephen St. Lwr.
Dublin Civic Museum
Chatham St.
Anne St. S
Molesworth St.
National Library
National Gallery
National History
Holles St.
Longford St. Gt.
Mansion House
National Museums
Leinster House
Dawson St.
Kildare St.
Mercer St. Lwr.
St. Stephen's Green Shopping Centre
St. Adelaide Hospital
Peter Row
Aungier St.
North
Merrion Sq.
West
Mount St. Lwr.
Archaeology and History Museum
St. Stephen's Green N
Merrion St. Upper
York St.
South
East
St. Stephen's Green W
Mercer St. Upr.
Merrion Row
Fitzwilliam Ln.
St. Stephen's Green
Hume St.
Ely Pl.
Baggot St. Lower
Mount St. Upr.
#29 Lower Fitzwilliam St.
Fitzwilliam St. Lwr.
Wexford St.
Garda
Harcourt St.
St. Stephen's Green S
St. Stephen's Green E
Pembroke St. Lwr.
James's St. East
Bank of Ireland
Camden Row
University College Dublin
Quinn's Ln.
Fitzwilliam St. Upr.
Lad Ln.
Camden St.
Pleasants St.
National Concert Hall
Earlsfort Ter.
Leeson St. Lwr.
Pembroke St. Upr.
Fitzwilliam Sq.

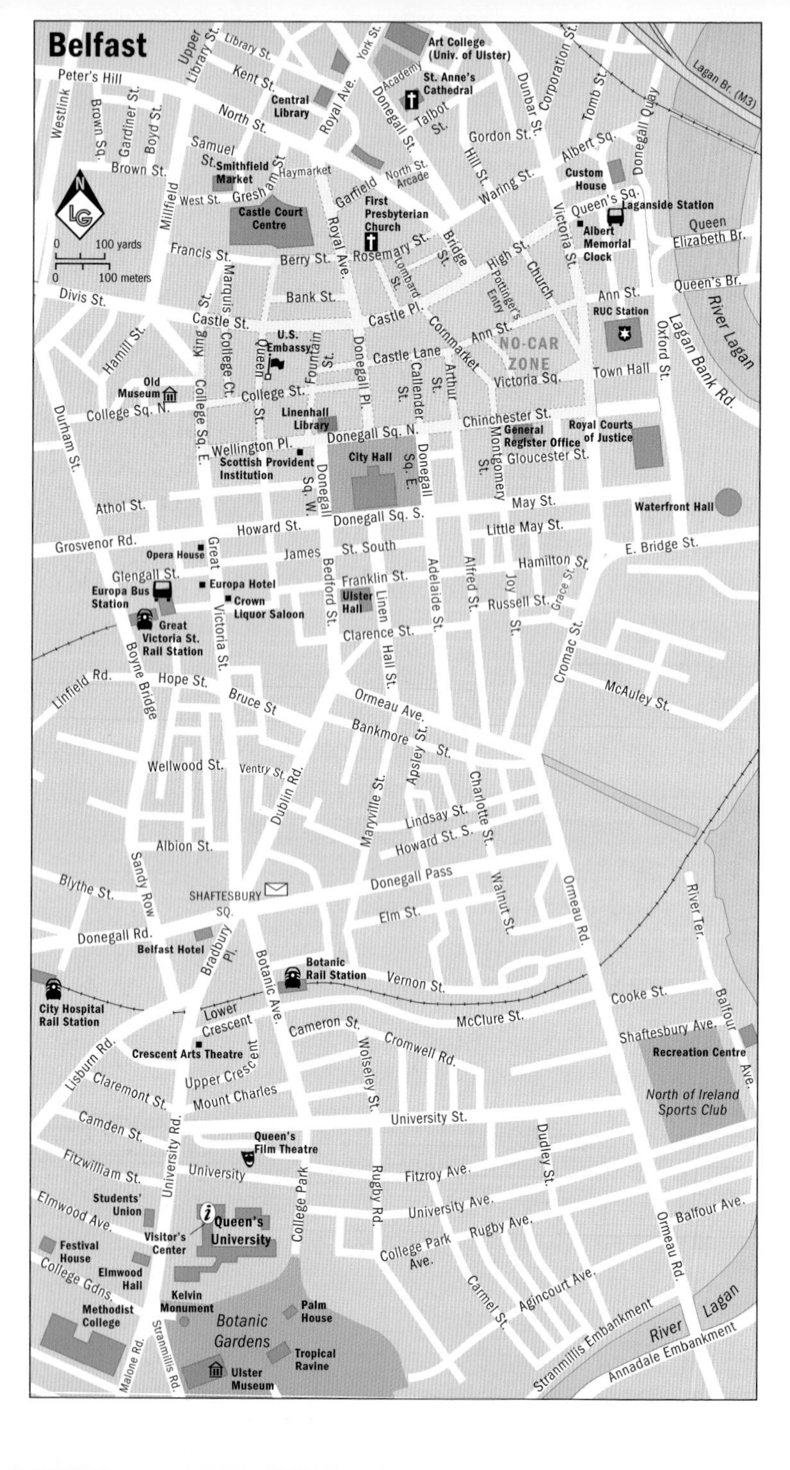
Belfast
Art College (Univ. of Ulster)
St. Anne's Cathedral
Central Library
Smithfield Market
Castle Court Centre
First Presbyterian Church
Custom House
Laganside Station
Albert Memorial Clock
RUC Station
NO-CAR ZONE
Town Hall
U.S. Embassy
Old Museum
Linenhall Library
General Register Office
Royal Courts of Justice
City Hall
Scottish Provident Institution
Waterfront Hall
Opera House
Europa Hotel
Crown Liquor Saloon
Europa Bus Station
Ulster Hall
Great Victoria St. Rail Station
SHAFTESBURY SQ.
Belfast Hotel
Botanic Rail Station
City Hospital Rail Station
Crescent Arts Theatre
Recreation Centre
North of Ireland Sports Club
Queen's Film Theatre
Students' Union
Queen's University
Visitor's Center
Festival House
Elmwood Hall
Methodist College
Kelvin Monument
Botanic Gardens
Palm House
Tropical Ravine
Ulster Museum
River Lagan
100 yards
100 meters

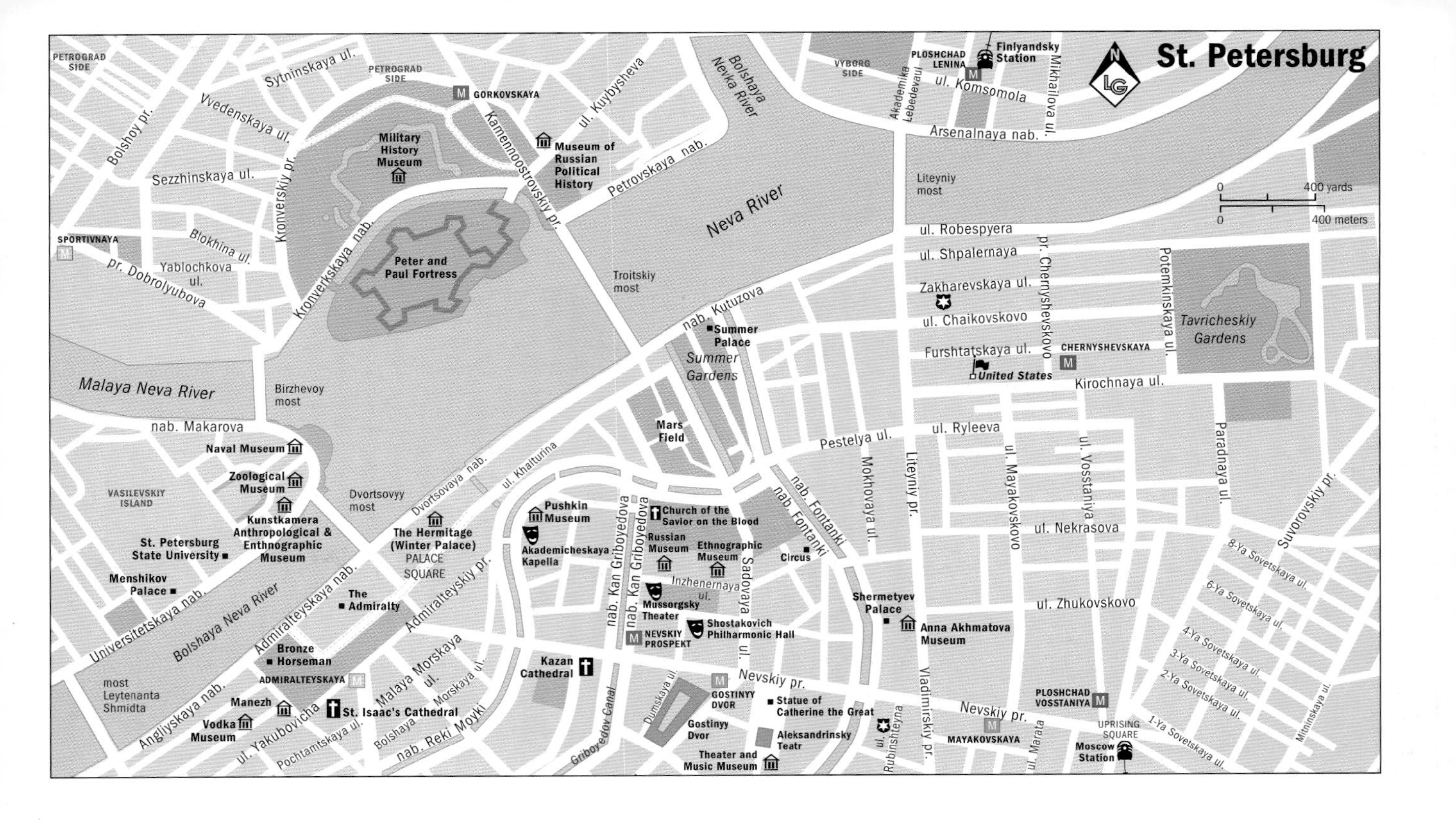

St. Petersburg
0
400 yards
400 meters
PETROGRAD SIDE
Sytninskaya ul.
Vvedenskaya ul.
Bolshoy pr.
Sezzhinskaya ul.
Kronverskiy pr.
Blokhina ul.
Yablochkova ul.
pr. Dobrolyubova
SPORTIVNAYA
GORKOVSKAYA
Military History Museum
Museum of Russian Political History
ul. Kuybysheva
Kamennoostrovskiy pr.
Petrovskaya nab.
Kronverkskaya nab.
Peter and Paul Fortress
Bolshaya Nevka River
Neva River
Troitskiy most
Malaya Neva River
Birzhevoy most
nab. Makarova
Naval Museum
Zoological Museum
VASILEVSKIY ISLAND
Kunstkamera Anthropological & Enthnographic Museum
St. Petersburg State University
Menshikov Palace
Universitetskaya nab.
Bolshaya Neva River
most Leytenanta Shmidta
Angliyskaya nab.
Manezh
Vodka Museum
ul. Yakubovicha
Pochtamtskaya ul.
Dvortsovyy most
Dvortsovaya nab.
The Hermitage (Winter Palace)
PALACE SQUARE
Admiralteyskaya nab.
The Admiralty
Admiralteyskiy pr.
Bronze Horseman
ADMIRALTEYSKAYA
St. Isaac's Cathedral
Malaya Morskaya ul.
Bolshaya Morskaya ul.
nab. Reki Moyki
ul. Khalturina
Pushkin Museum
Akademicheskaya Kapella
Kazan Cathedral
Griboyedov Canal
nab. Kan Griboyedova
nab. Kan Griboyedova
Church of the Savior on the Blood
Russian Museum
Ethnographic Museum
Inzhenernaya ul.
Mussorgsky Theater
NEVSKIY PROSPEKT
Shostakovich Philharmonic Hall
Dumskaya ul.
Gostinyy Dvor
GOSTINYY DVOR
Statue of Catherine the Great
Aleksandrinsky Teatr
Theater and Music Museum
Sadovaya ul.
Circus
nab. Fontanki
nab. Fontanki
Mars Field
Summer Palace
Summer Gardens
nab. Kutuzova
VYBORG SIDE
PLOSHCHAD LENINA
Finlyandsky Station
Akademika Lebedevaul
ul. Komsomola
Mikhailova ul.
Arsenalnaya nab.
Liteyniy most
ul. Robespyera
ul. Shpalernaya
Zakharevskaya ul.
ul. Chaikovskovo
Furshtatskaya ul.
United States
pr. Chernyshevskovo
CHERNYSHEVSKAYA
Kirochnaya ul.
Potemkinskaya ul.
Tavricheskiy Gardens
Paradnaya ul.
Pestelya ul.
ul. Ryleeva
Mokhovaya ul.
Liteyniy pr.
ul. Mayakovskovo
ul. Vosstaniya
ul. Nekrasova
ul. Zhukovskovo
Shermetyev Palace
Anna Akhmatova Museum
Nevskiy pr.
Nevskiy pr.
ul. Rubinshteyna
Vladimirskiy pr.
MAYAKOVSKAYA
ul. Marata
PLOSHCHAD VOSSTANIYA
UPRISING SQUARE
Moscow Station
Suvorovskiy pr.
8-Ya Sovetskaya ul.
6-Ya Sovetskaya ul.
4-Ya Sovetskaya ul.
3-Ya Sovetskaya ul.
2-Ya Sovetskaya ul.
1-Ya Sovetskaya ul.
Mitninskaya ul.

Moscow Center
Angliya Bookshops
MAYAKOVSKAYA
Tchaikovsky Halls
Mossoviet Theater
Stanislavskiy Theater
Young Spectators' Theater
Museum of Contemporary Russian History
PUSHKINSKAYA/ TVERSKAYA
PUSHKINSKAYA PL.
CHEKHOVSKAYA
Eliseevskiy Gastronom
Patriarch's Pond (Patriarshiye Prud)
European Medical Center
BARIKADNAYA
Patriarshy Domtours
Chekhov Museum-House
Stanislavskiy Museum-House
Ukraine
Gorky Museum House
US
New Zealand
THE ARBAT
ARBATSKAYA
ALEKSANDROVS SAD
SMOLENSKAYA
Pushkin Museum of Fine Arts
Canada
Cathedral of Chris the Savior (Khram Khrista Spasitelya)
KROPOTKINSKAYA
Pushkin Literary Museum
Tolstoy Museum
Gasheka
Zoologicheskaya u ul. Krasina
Bolshaya Sadovaya
Tverskaya-Yamskaya
Staropimenovskiy per.
Degtyarnyy per.
Mal. Dmitrovka
Ermolaevskiy per.
Mal. Kozin/nskaya per.
Spiridonovka
Spiridonevskiy per.
Bolshoy Kozikhinskiy per.
Bogoslovskiy per.
Bolshaya Bronnaya
Malaya Bronnaya
Sadovaya Kudrinskaya
Vspolnyy per.II
Granatnyy per.
Krasnaya Presnya
Tverskoy bul.
Leontevskiy per.
Voznesenskiy per.
Bryusov per.
Malaya Nikitskaya
Bolshaya Nikitskaya
Bol. Nikitskaya
Povarskaya
Ckaternyy per.
Khlebnyy per.
Merzlyakovskiy per.
Nikitskiy bul.
Kalashnyy per.
Trybnikovskiy per.
Borisoglebskiy pre.
Novinskiy bul.
Mal. Molchanovka
Bolshoy Kislovskiy per.
Novyy Arbat
Vozdvizhenka
Arbat
Znamenka
BOROVITS
Bolshoy Aphanacevskiy per.
Filipovskiy per.
Gogolevskiy bul.
Bolshoy Znamenskiy per.
Starokonyushennyy per.
per. Sivtsev Vrazhek
Plotnikov Per.
Smolenskiy bul.
Denezhyy per.
Gagarinskiy per.
Prechistenka
Ostozhenka
Volhonka
0
200 meters
200 yards
LG
N

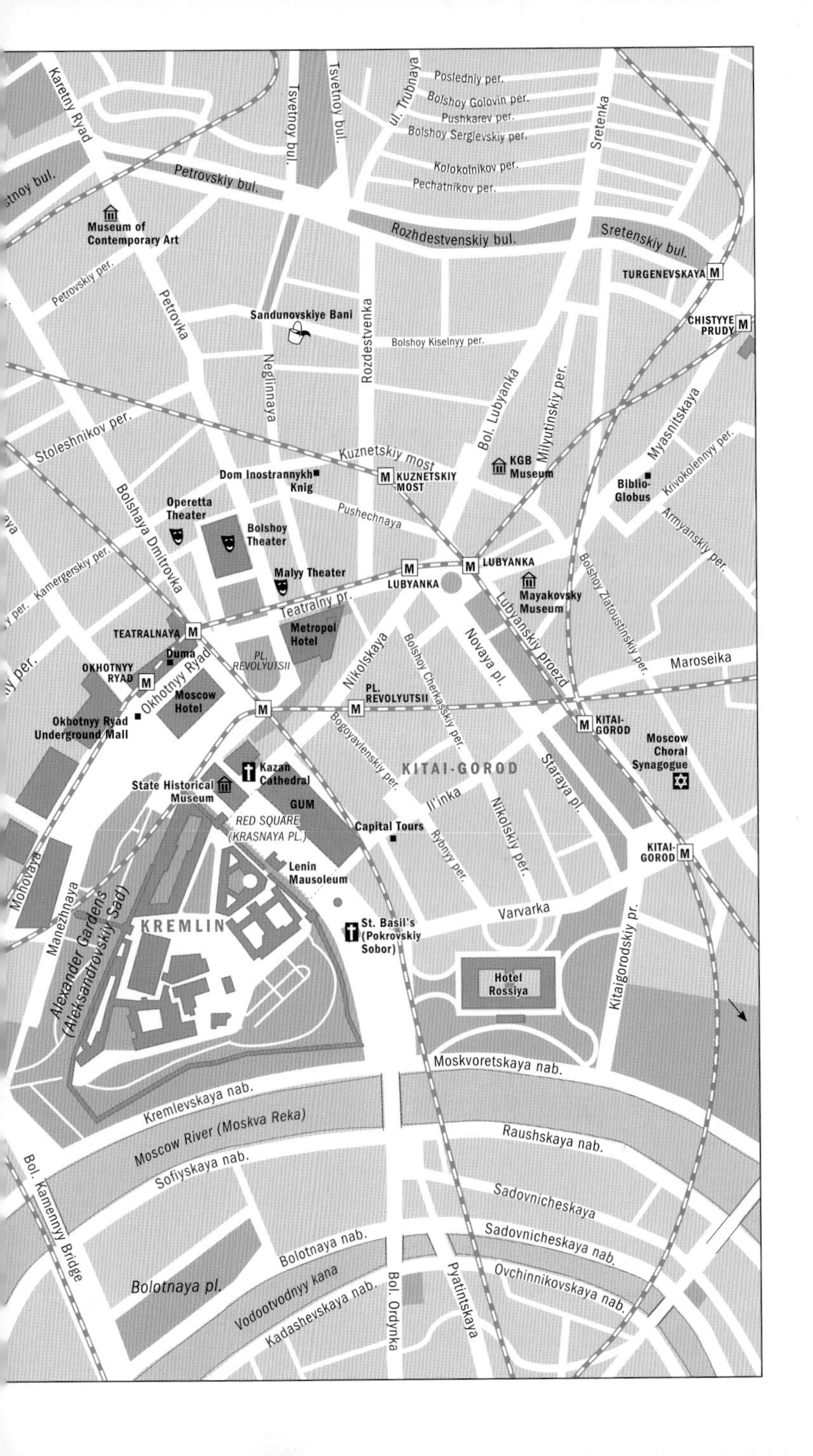

Karetny Ryad
Tsvetnoy bul.
ul. Trubnaya
Posledniy per.
Bolshoy Golovin per.
Pushkarev per.
Bolshoy Sergievskiy per.
Sretenka
Kolokolnikov per.
Pechatnikov per.
Petrovskiy bul.
Rozhdestvenskiy bul.
Sretenskiy bul.
Museum of Contemporary Art
Petrovskiy per.
Petrovka
TURGENEVSKAYA
CHISTYYE PRUDY
Sandunovskiye Bani
Rozdestvenka
Bolshoy Kiselnyy per.
Neglinnaya
Bol. Lubyanka
Milyutinskiy per.
Myasnitskaya
Stoleshnikov per.
Kuznetskiy most
KUZNETSKIY MOST
KGB Museum
Krivokolennyy per.
Dom Inostrannykh Knig
Biblio-Globus
Armyanskiy per.
Bolshaya Dmitrovka
Operetta Theater
Bolshoy Theater
Pushechnaya
Kamergerskiy per.
Malyy Theater
LUBYANKA
Mayakovsky Museum
Bolshoy Zlatoustinskiy per.
Teatralny pr.
Lubyanskiy proezd
TEATRALNAYA
Metropol Hotel
Nikolskaya
Bolshoy Cherkasskiy per.
Novaya pl.
Maroseika
Duma
OKHOTNYY RYAD
PL. REVOLYUTSII
Okhotnyy Ryad
Moscow Hotel
Okhotnyy Ryad Underground Mall
KITAI-GOROD
Moscow Choral Synagogue
Bogoyavlenskiy per.
Staraya pl.
Kazan Cathedral
State Historical Museum
GUM
Il'inka
Nikolskiy per.
RED SQUARE (KRASNAYA PL.)
Capital Tours
Rybnyy per.
Lenin Mausoleum
Mohovaya
Manezhnaya
Alexander Gardens (Aleksandrovskiy Sad)
KREMLIN
St. Basil's (Pokrovskiy Sobor)
Varvarka
Kitaigorodskiy pr.
Hotel Rossiya
Moskvoretskaya nab.
Kremlevskaya nab.
Moscow River (Moskva Reka)
Raushskaya nab.
Sofiyskaya nab.
Bol. Kamennyy Bridge
Sadovnicheskaya
Sadovnicheskaya nab.
Bolotnaya nab.
Ovchinnikovskaya nab.
Bolotnaya pl.
Vodootvodnyy kana
Kadashevskaya nab.
Bol. Ordynka
Pyatintskaya

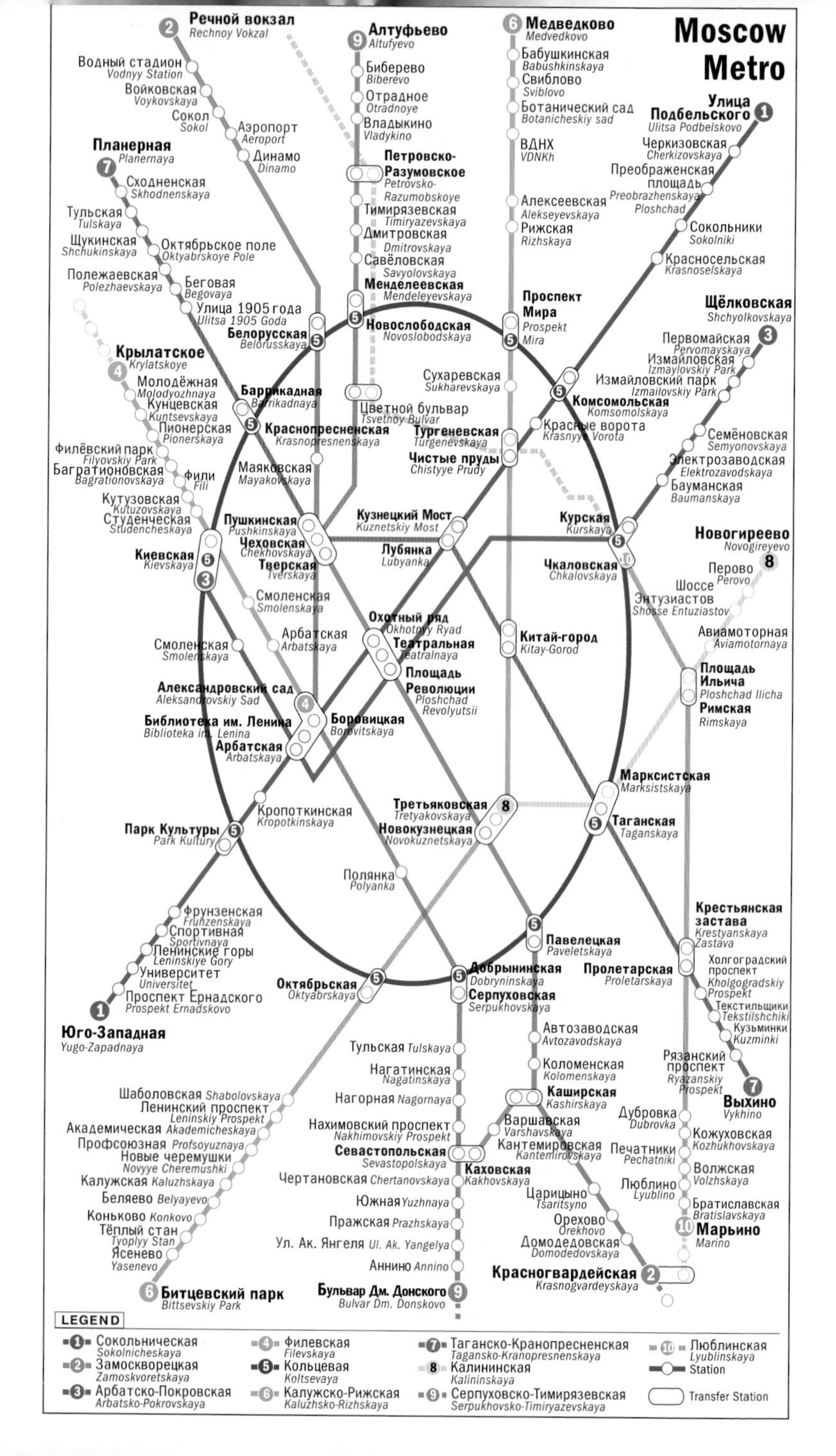

Moscow Metro
Речной вокзал
Rechnoy Vokzal
Водный стадион
Vodnyy Station
Войковская
Voykovskaya
Сокол
Sokol
Аэропорт
Aeroport
Динамо
Dinamo
Алтуфьево
Altufyevo
Бибирево
Biberevo
Отрадное
Otradnoye
Владыкино
Vladykino
Петровско-Разумовское
Petrovsko-Razumobskoye
Тимирязевская
Timiryazevskaya
Дмитровская
Dmitrovskaya
Савёловская
Savyolovskaya
Менделеевская
Mendeleyevskaya
Медведково
Medvedkovo
Бабушкинская
Babushkinskaya
Свиблово
Sviblovo
Ботанический сад
Botanicheskiy sad
ВДНХ
VDNKh
Алексеевская
Alekseyevskaya
Рижская
Rizhskaya
Улица Подбельского
Ulitsa Podbelskovo
Черкизовская
Cherkizovskaya
Преображенская площадь
Preobrazhenskaya Ploshchad
Сокольники
Sokolniki
Красносельская
Krasnoselskaya
Планерная
Planernaya
Сходненская
Skhodnenskaya
Тульская
Tulskaya
Щукинская
Shchukinskaya
Октябрьское поле
Oktyabrskoye Pole
Полежаевская
Polezhaevskaya
Беговая
Begovaya
Улица 1905 года
Ulitsa 1905 Goda
Белорусская
Belorusskaya
Новослободская
Novoslobodskaya
Проспект Мира
Prospekt Mira
Щёлковская
Shchyolkovskaya
Первомайская
Pervomayskaya
Измайловская
Izmaylovskiy Park
Измайловский парк
Izmailovskiy Park
Крылатское
Krylatskoye
Молодёжная
Molodyozhnaya
Кунцевская
Kuntsevskaya
Пионерская
Pionerskaya
Филёвский парк
Filyovskiy Park
Багратионовская
Bagrationovskaya
Фили
Fili
Кутузовская
Kutuzovskaya
Студенческая
Studencheskaya
Баррикадная
Barrikadnaya
Краснопресненская
Krasnopresnenskaya
Маяковская
Mayakovskaya
Цветной бульвар
Tsvetnoy Bulvar
Сухаревская
Sukharevskaya
Тургеневская
Turgenevskaya
Чистые пруды
Chistyye Prudy
Комсомольская
Komsomolskaya
Красные ворота
Krasnyye Vorota
Семёновская
Semyonovskaya
Электрозаводская
Elektrozavodskaya
Бауманская
Baumanskaya
Пушкинская
Pushkinskaya
Чеховская
Chekhovskaya
Тверская
Tverskaya
Кузнецкий Мост
Kuznetskiy Most
Лубянка
Lubyanka
Курская
Kurskaya
Чкаловская
Chkalovskaya
Новогиреево
Novogireyevo
Перово
Perovo
Шоссе Энтузиастов
Shosse Entuziastov
Авиамоторная
Aviamotornaya
Киевская
Kievskaya
Смоленская
Smolenskaya
Арбатская
Arbatskaya
Смоленская
Smolenskaya
Охотный ряд
Okhotnyy Ryad
Театральная
Teatralnaya
Площадь Революции
Ploshchad Revolyutsii
Китай-город
Kitay-Gorod
Площадь Ильича
Ploshchad Ilicha
Римская
Rimskaya
Александровский сад
Aleksandrovskiy Sad
Библиотека им. Ленина
Biblioteka im. Lenina
Арбатская
Arbatskaya
Боровицкая
Borovitskaya
Кропоткинская
Kropotkinskaya
Парк Культуры
Park Kultury
Третьяковская
Tretyakovskaya
Новокузнецкая
Novokuznetskaya
Марксистская
Marksistskaya
Таганская
Taganskaya
Полянка
Polyanka
Фрунзенская
Frunzenskaya
Спортивная
Sportivnaya
Ленинские горы
Leninskiye Gory
Университет
Universitet
Проспект Ернадского
Prospekt Ernadskovo
Юго-Западная
Yugo-Zapadnaya
Октябрьская
Oktyabrskaya
Добрынинская
Dobryninskaya
Серпуховская
Serpukhovskaya
Павелецкая
Paveletskaya
Пролетарская
Proletarskaya
Крестьянская застава
Krestyanskaya Zastava
Холгоградский проспект
Kholgogradskiy Prospekt
Текстильщики
Tekstilshchiki
Кузьминки
Kuzminki
Рязанский проспект
Ryazanskiy Prospekt
Выхино
Vykhino
Автозаводская
Avtozavodskaya
Коломенская
Kolomenskaya
Каширская
Kashirskaya
Варшавская
Varshavskaya
Кантемировская
Kantemirovskaya
Царицыно
Tsaritsyno
Орехово
Orekhovo
Домодедовская
Domodedovskaya
Красногвардейская
Krasnogvardeyskaya
Тульская Tulskaya
Нагатинская
Nagatinskaya
Нагорная Nagornaya
Нахимовский проспект
Nakhimovskiy Prospekt
Севастопольская
Sevastopolskaya
Каховская
Kakhovskaya
Чертановская Chertanovskaya
Южная Yuzhnaya
Пражская Prazhskaya
Ул. Ак. Янгеля Ul. Ak. Yangelya
Аннино Annino
Бульвар Дм. Донского
Bulvar Dm. Donskovo
Дубровка
Dubrovka
Кожуховская
Kozhukhovskaya
Печатники
Pechatniki
Волжская
Volzhskaya
Люблино
Lyublino
Братиславская
Bratislavskaya
Марьино
Marino
Шаболовская Shabolovskaya
Ленинский проспект
Leninskiy Prospekt
Академическая Akademicheskaya
Профсоюзная Profsoyuznaya
Новые черемушки
Novyye Cheremushki
Калужская Kaluzhskaya
Беляево Belyayevo
Коньково Konkovo
Тёплый стан
Tyoplyy Stan
Ясенево
Yasenevo
Битцевский парк
Bittsevskiy Park
LEGEND
1 Сокольническая
Sokolnicheskaya
2 Замоскворецкая
Zamoskvoretskaya
3 Арбатско-Покровская
Arbatsko-Pokrovskaya
4 Филевская
Filevskaya
5 Кольцевая
Koltsevaya
6 Калужско-Рижская
Kaluzhsko-Rizhskaya
7 Таганско-Кранопресненская
Tagansko-Kranopresnenskaya
8 Калининская
Kalininskaya
9 Серпуховско-Тимирязевская
Serpukhovsko-Timiryazevskaya
10 Люблинская
Lyublinskaya
Station
Transfer Station

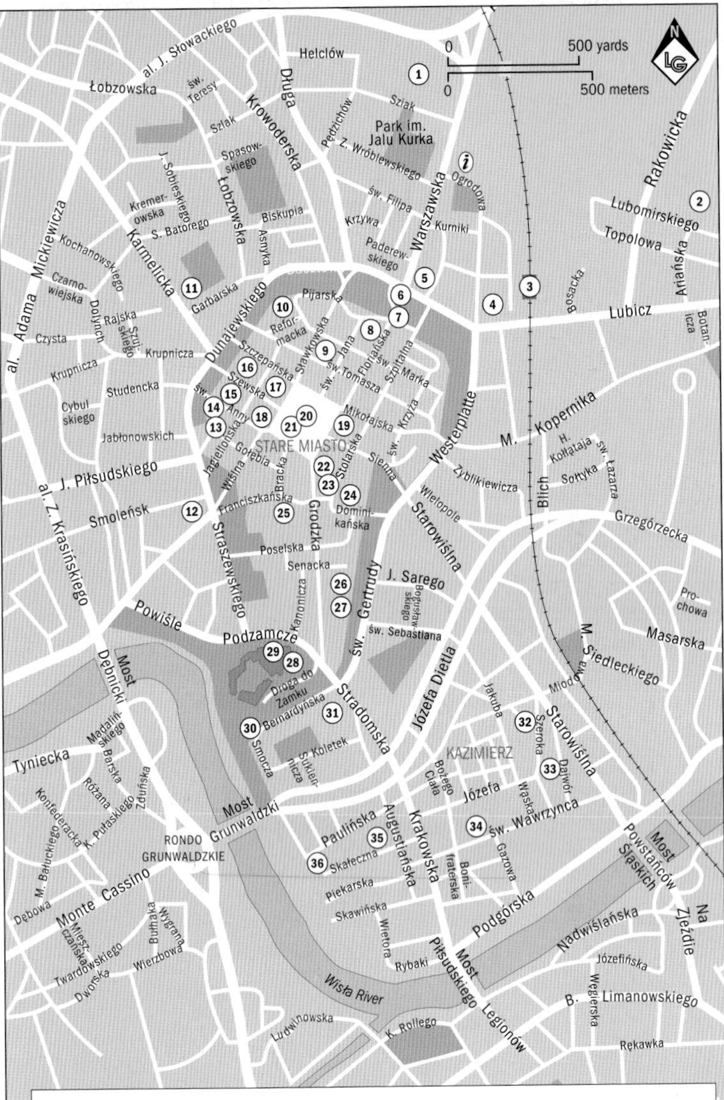

Central Kraków

Akademia Ekonomiczna, **2**
Almatur Office, **22**
Barbican, **6**
Bernardine Church, **31**
Bus Station, **4**
Carmelite Church, **11**
Cartoon Gallery, **9**
Collegium Maius, **14**
Corpus Christi Church, **34**
Czartoryski Art Museum, **8**
Dominican Church, **24**
Dragon Statue, **30**
Filharmonia, **12**
Franciscan Church, **25**
Grunwald Memorial, **5**
History Museum of Kraków, **17**
Jewish Cemetery, **32**
Jewish Museum, **33**
Kraków Główny Station, **3**
Monastery of the Reformed Franciscans, **10**
Pauline Church, **36**
Police Station, **18**
Politechnika Krakowska, **1**
St. Andrew's Church, **27**
St. Anne's Church, **15**
St. Catherine's Church, **35**
St. Florian's Gate, **7**
St. Mary's Church, **19**
St. Peter and Paul Church, **26**
Stary Teatr (Old Theater), **16**
Sukiennice (Cloth Hall), **20**
Town Hall, **21**
United States Embassy, **23**
University Museum, **13**
Wawel Castle, **28**
Wawel Cathedral, **29**

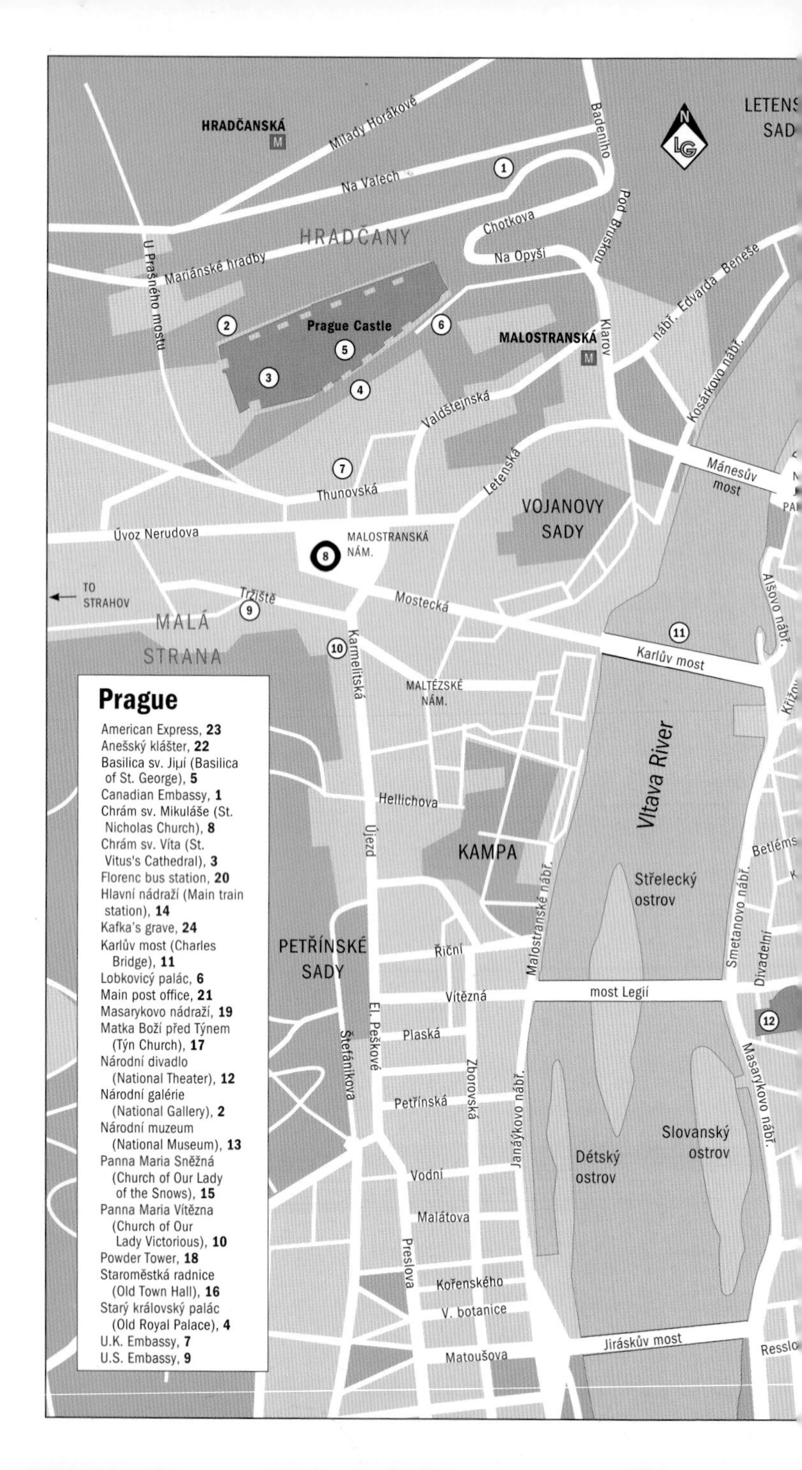

Prague

American Express, **23**
Anešský klášter, **22**
Basilica sv. Jiµí (Basilica of St. George), **5**
Canadian Embassy, **1**
Chrám sv. Mikuláše (St. Nicholas Church), **8**
Chrám sv. Víta (St. Vitus's Cathedral), **3**
Florenc bus station, **20**
Hlavní nádraží (Main train station), **14**
Kafka's grave, **24**
Karlův most (Charles Bridge), **11**
Lobkovicý palác, **6**
Main post office, **21**
Masarykovo nádraží, **19**
Matka Boží před Týnem (Týn Church), **17**
Národní divadlo (National Theater), **12**
Národní galérie (National Gallery), **2**
Národní muzeum (National Museum), **13**
Panna Maria Sněžná (Church of Our Lady of the Snows), **15**
Panna Maria Vítězna (Church of Our Lady Victorious), **10**
Powder Tower, **18**
Staroměstká radnice (Old Town Hall), **16**
Starý královský palác (Old Royal Palace), **4**
U.K. Embassy, **7**
U.S. Embassy, **9**

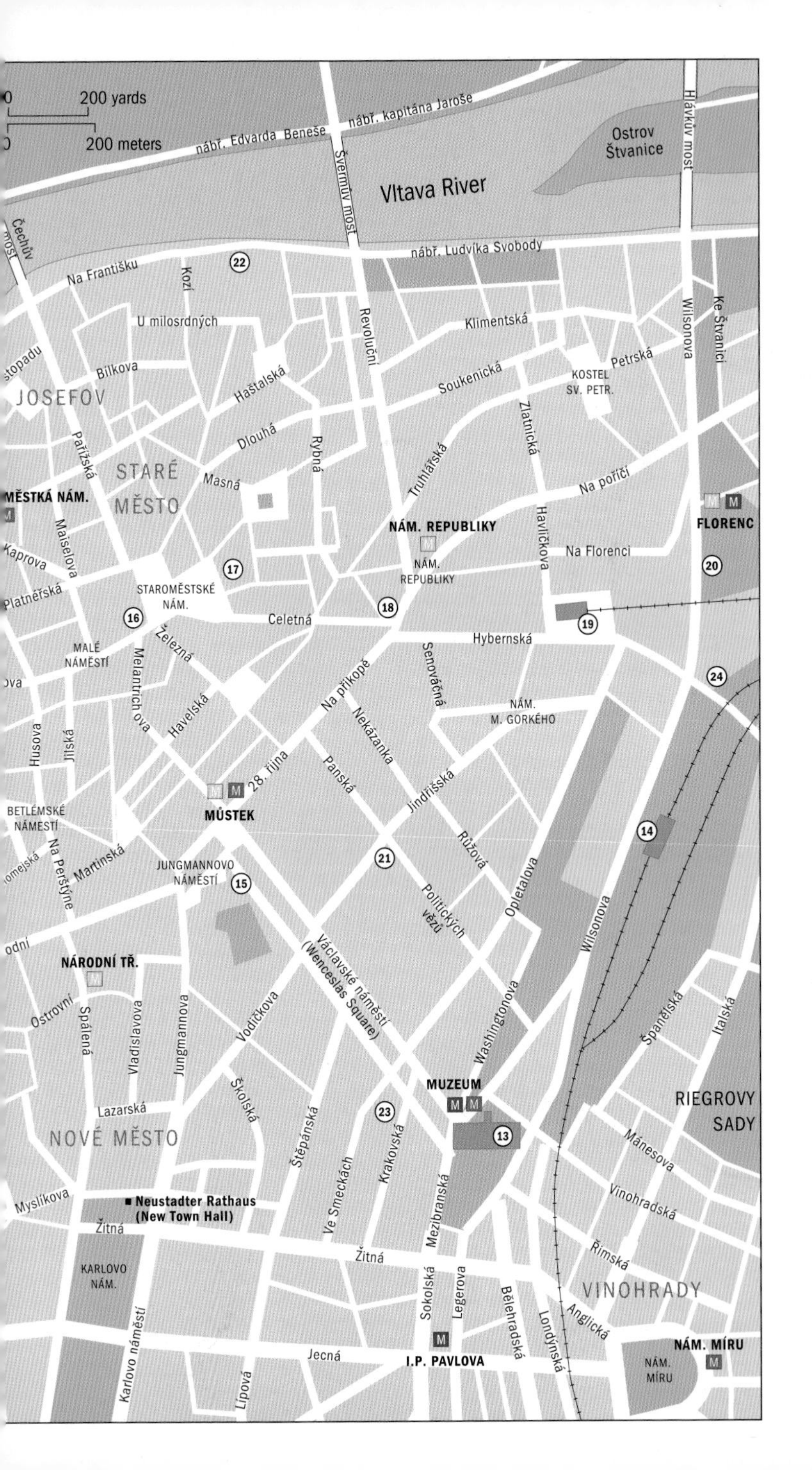

0 200 yards
0 200 meters
nábř. Edvarda Beneše
nábř. kapitána Jaroše
Švermův most
Hlávkův most
Ostrov Štvanice
Vltava River
Čechův most
nábř. Ludvíka Svobody
Na Františku
Kozí
U milosrdných
Revoluční
Klimentská
Wilsonova
Ke Štvanici
Bílkova
Haštalská
Soukenická
Petrská
KOSTEL SV. PETR.
JOSEFOV
Pařížská
Dlouhá
Rybná
Zlatnická
Truhlářská
STARÉ MĚSTO
Masná
Na poříčí
MĚSTKÁ NÁM.
Maiselova
NÁM. REPUBLIKY
Havlíčkova
FLORENC
Kaprova
Na Florenci
STAROMĚSTSKÉ NÁM.
Platnéřská
Celetná
Hybernská
MALÉ NÁMĚSTÍ
Železná
Melantrichova
Senovážná
Na příkopě
NÁM. M. GORKÉHO
Havelská
Nekázanka
Husova
Jilská
28. října
Panská
Jindřišská
MŮSTEK
BETLÉMSKÉ NÁMĚSTÍ
Na Perštýně
Martinská
JUNGMANNOVO NÁMĚSTÍ
Růžová
Politických vězňů
Opletalova
Wilsonova
NÁRODNÍ TŘ.
Ostrovní
Spálená
Vladislavova
Jungmannova
Vodičkova
Václavské náměstí (Wenceslas Square)
Washingtonova
Španělská
Italská
Školská
Štěpánská
MUZEUM
RIEGROVY SADY
Lazarská
NOVÉ MĚSTO
Krakovská
Ve Smečkách
Mezibranská
Mánesova
Vinohradská
Myslíkova
Neustadter Rathaus (New Town Hall)
Žitná
KARLOVO NÁM.
Sokolská
Legerova
Bělehradská
Londýnská
Římská
VINOHRADY
Anglická
Karlovo náměstí
Jecná
I.P. PAVLOVA
Lípová
NÁM. MÍRU
13
14
15
16
17
18
19
20
21
22
23
24

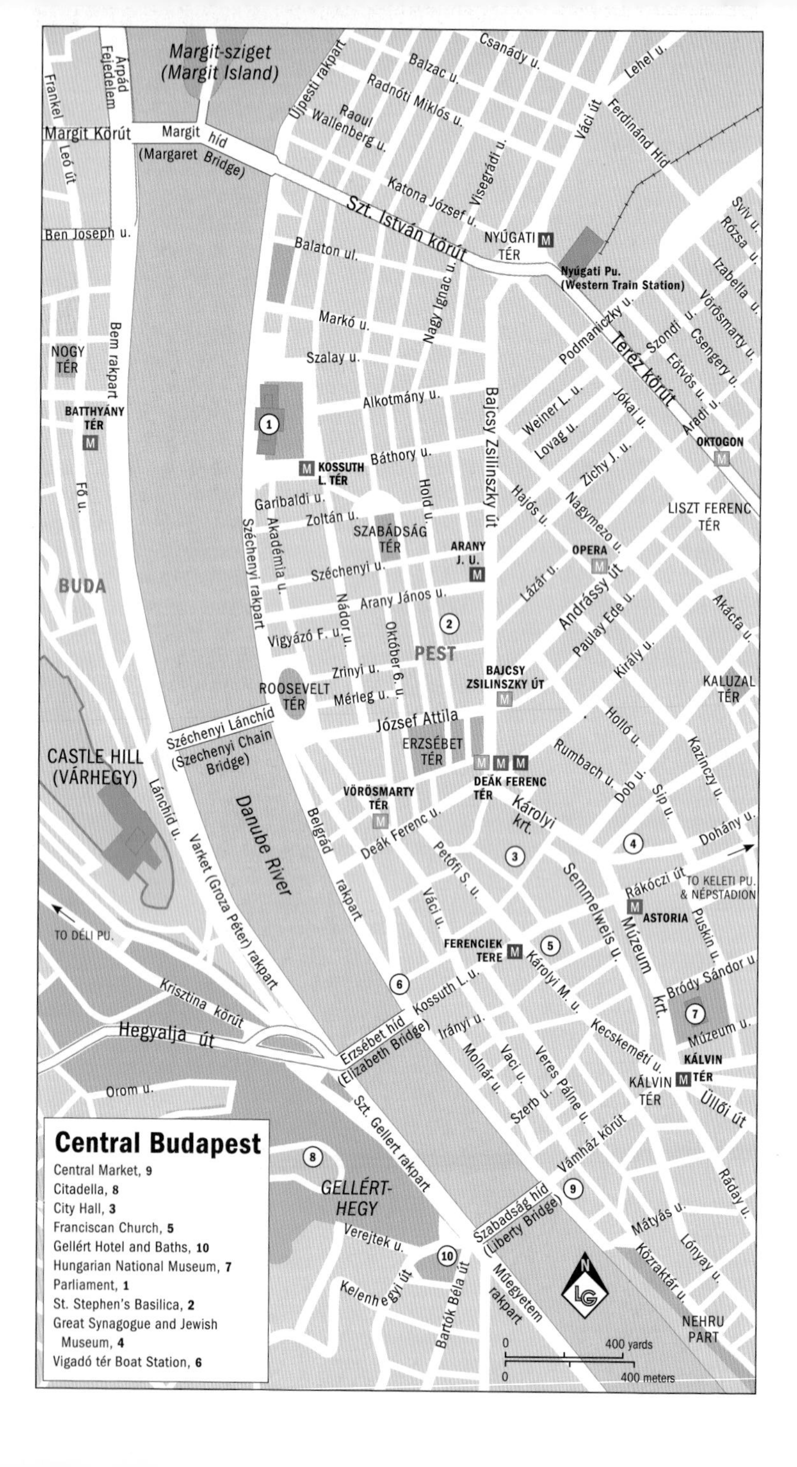

Central Budapest
Central Market, 9
Citadella, 8
City Hall, 3
Franciscan Church, 5
Gellért Hotel and Baths, 10
Hungarian National Museum, 7
Parliament, 1
St. Stephen's Basilica, 2
Great Synagogue and Jewish Museum, 4
Vigadó tér Boat Station, 6
Margit-sziget (Margit Island)
Margit híd (Margaret Bridge)
Szt. István körút
NYÚGATI TÉR
Nyúgati Pu. (Western Train Station)
Teréz körút
OKTOGON
LISZT FERENC TÉR
KOSSUTH L. TÉR
SZABÁDSÁG TÉR
ARANY J. U.
OPERA
Andrássy út
BUDA
PEST
ROOSEVELT TÉR
BAJCSY ZSILINSZKY ÚT
Széchenyi Lánchíd (Szechenyi Chain Bridge)
CASTLE HILL (VÁRHEGY)
Danube River
ERZSÉBET TÉR
DEÁK FERENC TÉR
VÖRÖSMARTY TÉR
KALUZAL TÉR
Károlyi krt.
TO KELETI PU. & NÉPSTADION
ASTORIA
FERENCIEK TERE
TO DÉLI PU.
Erzsébet híd (Elizabeth Bridge)
Hegyalja út
Krisztina körút
KÁLVIN TÉR
GELLÉRT-HEGY
Szabadság híd (Liberty Bridge)
NEHRU PART
BATTHYÁNY TÉR
NOGY TÉR
400 yards
400 meters

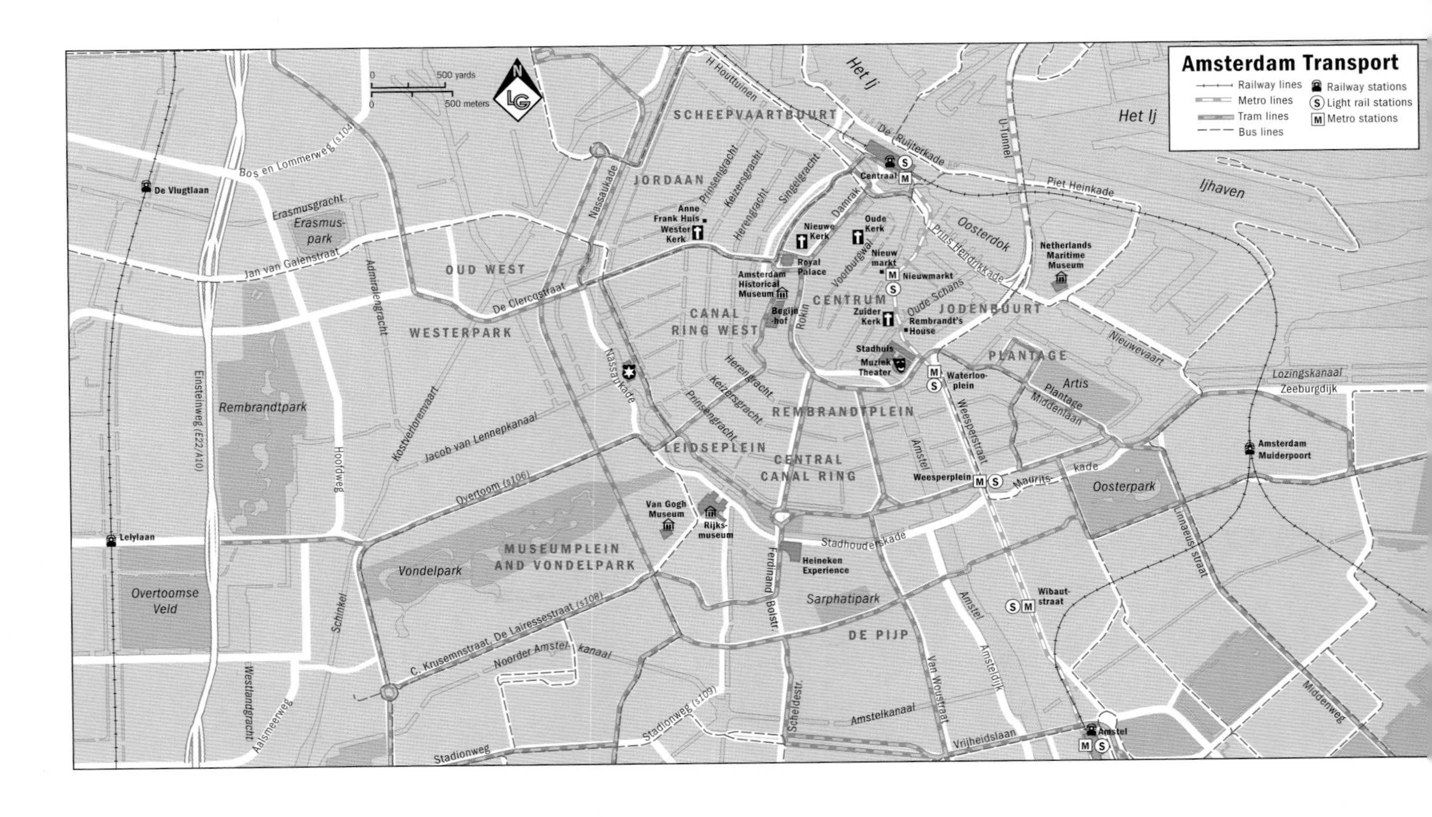
Amsterdam Transport
Railway lines
Metro lines
Tram lines
Bus lines
Railway stations
Light rail stations
Metro stations
0 500 yards
0 500 meters
Het Ij
Ijhaven
U-Tunnel
Piet Heinkade
De Ruijterkade
H Houttuinen
SCHEEPVAARTBUURT
JORDAAN
Centraal
Damrak
Prinsengracht
Keizersgracht
Herengracht
Singelgracht
Anne Frank Huis
Wester Kerk
Nieuwe Kerk
Oude Kerk
Royal Palace
Nieuw markt
Nieuwmarkt
Voorburgwal
Oosterdok
Prins Hendrikkade
Netherlands Maritime Museum
Amsterdam Historical Museum
Begijn -hof
Rokin
CENTRUM
Zuider Kerk
Oude Schans
Rembrandt's House
JODENBUURT
CANAL RING WEST
Stadhuis Muziek Theater
PLANTAGE
Nieuwevaart
Lozingskanaal
Zeeburgdijk
Waterloo-plein
Artis
Plantage Middenlaan
REMBRANDTPLEIN
LEIDSEPLEIN
CENTRAL CANAL RING
Amstel
Weesperstraat
Weesperplein
Maurits-kade
Oosterpark
Amsterdam Muiderpoort
Linnaeus straat
Van Gogh Museum
Rijks-museum
Stadhouderskade
Heineken Experience
Ferdinand Bolstr.
Sarphatipark
Wibaut-straat
DE PIJP
Van Woustraat
Amsteldijk
Amstelkanaal
Vrijheidslaan
Amstel
Middenweg
Scheldestr.
Stadionweg (s109)
Stadionweg
MUSEUMPLEIN AND VONDELPARK
Vondelpark
C. Krusemnstraat. De Lairessestraat (s108)
Noorder Amstel- kanaal
Overtoom (s106)
Nassaukade
Jacob van Lennepkanaal
Kostverlorenvaart
Admiralengracht
De Clercqstraat
OUD WEST
WESTERPARK
Jan van Galenstraat
Erasmusgracht
Erasmus-park
Bos en Lommerweg (s104)
De Vlugtlaan
Rembrandtpark
Hoofdweg
Einsteinweg (E22/A10)
Schinkel
Lelylaan
Overtoomse Veld
Westlandgracht
Aalsmeerweg

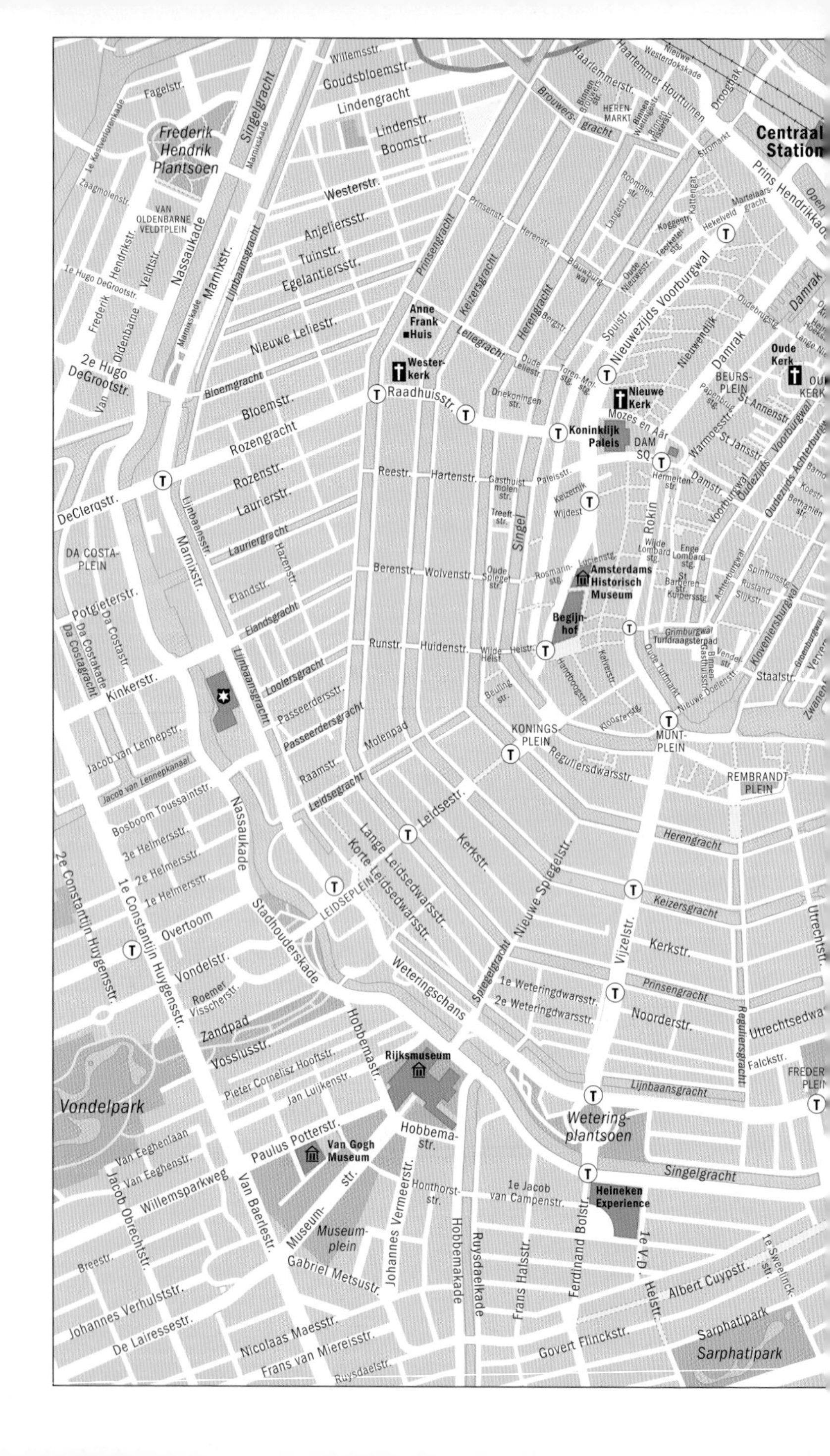

Centraal Station
Frederik Hendrik Plantsoen
Anne Frank Huis
Westerkerk
Nieuwe Kerk
Oude Kerk
Koninklijk Paleis
DAM SQ
Amsterdams Historisch Museum
Begijnhof
KONINGSPLEIN
MUNTPLEIN
REMBRANDTPLEIN
LEIDSEPLEIN
Rijksmuseum
Van Gogh Museum
Museumplein
Vondelpark
Weteringplantsoen
Heineken Experience
Sarphatipark
DA COSTAPLEIN
VAN OLDENBARNEVELDTPLEIN
BEURSPLEIN
Damrak
Rokin
Singel
Herengracht
Keizersgracht
Prinsengracht
Singelgracht
Lijnbaansgracht
Nassaukade
Marnixstr.
Stadhouderskade
Weteringschans
Raadhuisstr.
Rozengracht
Leidsestr.
Vijzelstr.
Nieuwezijds Voorburgwal
Overtoom
Ferdinand Bolstr.
Albert Cuypstr.
Hobbemakade
Van Baerlestr.

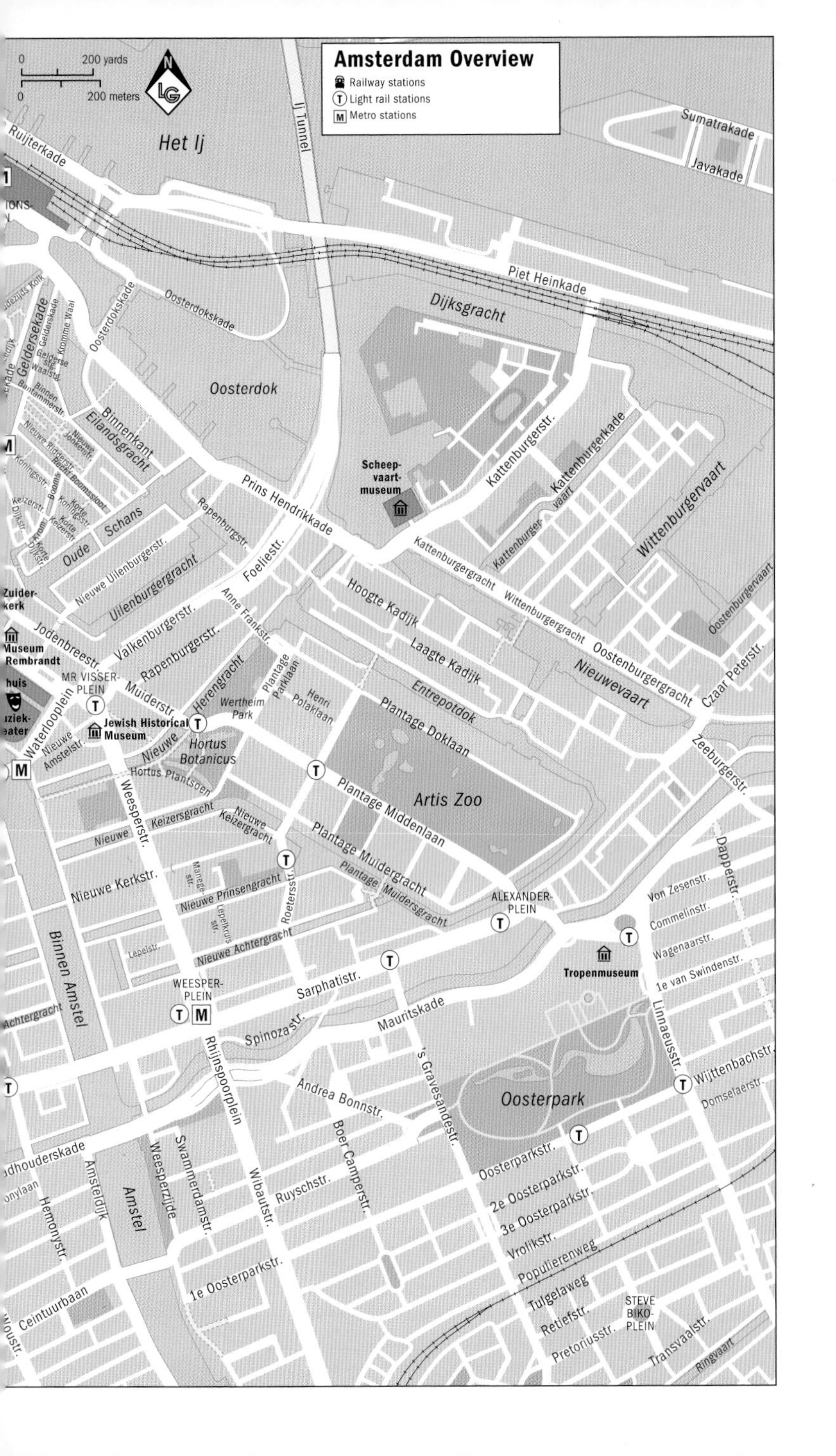

Amsterdam Overview
Railway stations
Light rail stations
Metro stations
0 200 yards
0 200 meters
Het Ij
Ij Tunnel
Ruijterkade
Sumatrakade
Javakade
Piet Heinkade
Dijksgracht
Oosterdokskade
Oosterdok
Binnenkant
Eilandsgracht
Prins Hendrikkade
Scheep-vaart-museum
Kattenburgerstr.
Kattenburgerkade
Kattenburgervaart
Wittenburgervaart
Kattenburgergracht
Wittenburgergracht
Oostenburgergracht
Oostenburgervaart
Nieuwevaart
Czaar Peterstr.
Rapenburgstr.
Schans
Oude
Nieuwe Uilenburgerstr.
Uilenburgergracht
Foeliestr.
Hoogte Kadijk
Laagte Kadijk
Entrepotdok
Anne Frankstr.
Valkenburgerstr.
Rapenburgerstr.
Zuider-kerk
Jodenbreestr.
Museum Rembrandt
MR VISSER-PLEIN
Muiderstr.
Herengracht
Wertheim Park
Plantage Parklaan
Henri Polaklaan
Plantage Doklaan
Jewish Historical Museum
Waterlooplein
Nieuwe Amstelstr.
Nieuwe
Hortus Botanicus
Hortus Plantsoen
Artis Zoo
Plantage Middenlaan
Zeeburgerstr.
Weesperstr.
Keizersgracht
Nieuwe Keizersgracht
Nieuwe
Plantage Muidergracht
Nieuwe Kerkstr.
Nieuwe Prinsengracht
Roetersstr.
ALEXANDER-PLEIN
Dapperstr.
Von Zesenstr.
Commelinstr.
Wagenaarstr.
1e van Swindenstr.
Binnen Amstel
Nieuwe Achtergracht
Lepelstr.
Tropenmuseum
WEESPER-PLEIN
Sarphatistr.
Achtergracht
Mauritskade
Spinozastr.
Linnaeusstr.
Rhijnspoorplein
's Gravesandestr.
Wittenbachstr.
Domselaerstr.
Andrea Bonnstr.
Oosterpark
Boer Camperstr.
Swammerdamstr.
Weesperzijde
Amsteldijk
Amstel
Hemonystr.
Wibautstr.
Ruyschstr.
Oosterparkstr.
2e Oosterparkstr.
3e Oosterparkstr.
Vrolikstr.
Populierenweg
1e Oosterparkstr.
Tugelaweg
Retiefstr.
Pretoriusstr.
STEVE BIKO-PLEIN
Transvaalstr.
Ringvaart
Ceintuurbaan

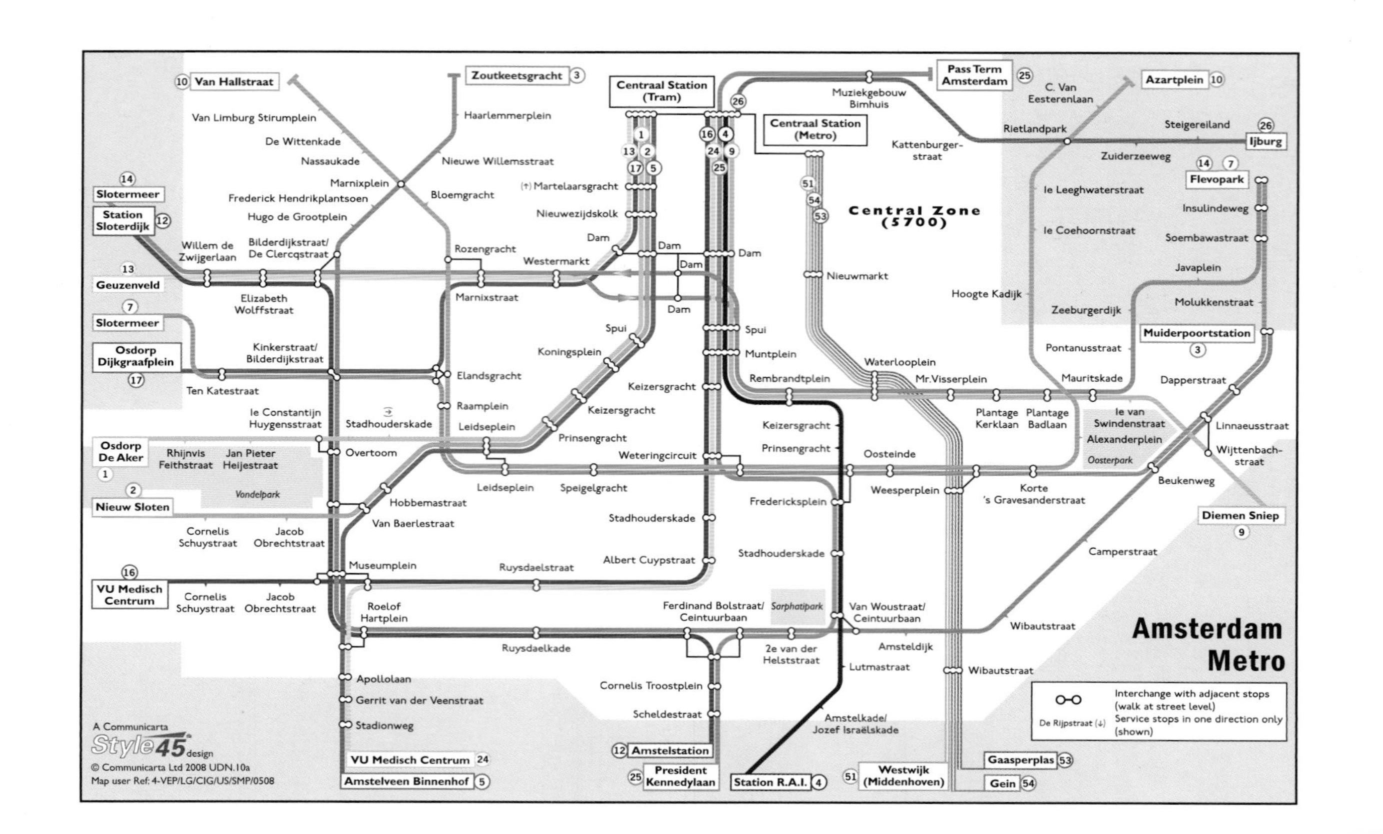
Amsterdam
Metro
Central Zone
(5700)
Centraal Station (Tram)
Centraal Station (Metro)
Pass Term Amsterdam
Van Hallstraat
Zoutkeetsgracht
Azartplein
Ijburg
Flevopark
Muiderpoortstation
Diemen Sniep
Slotermeer
Station Sloterdijk
Geuzenveld
Osdorp Dijkgraafplein
Osdorp De Aker
Nieuw Sloten
VU Medisch Centrum
Amstelveen Binnenhof
Amstelstation
President Kennedylaan
Station R.A.I.
Westwijk (Middenhoven)
Gaasperplas
Gein
Van Limburg Stirumplein
De Wittenkade
Nassaukade
Marnixplein
Frederick Hendrikplantsoen
Hugo de Grootplein
Bilderdijkstraat/ De Clercqstraat
Willem de Zwijgerlaan
Elizabeth Wolffstraat
Kinkerstraat/ Bilderdijkstraat
Ten Katestraat
Ie Constantijn Huygensstraat
Stadhouderskade
Overtoom
Rhijnvis Feithstraat
Jan Pieter Heijestraat
Vondelpark
Cornelis Schuystraat
Jacob Obrechtstraat
Haarlemmerplein
Nieuwe Willemsstraat
Bloemgracht
Rozengracht
Marnixstraat
Westermarkt
Elandsgracht
Raamplein
Leidseplein
Hobbemastraat
Van Baerlestraat
Museumplein
Roelof Hartplein
Apollolaan
Gerrit van der Veenstraat
Stadionweg
(↑) Martelaarsgracht
Nieuwezijdskolk
Dam
Spui
Koningsplein
Keizersgracht
Prinsengracht
Spiegelgracht
Weteringcircuit
Stadhouderskade
Albert Cuypstraat
Ruysdaelstraat
Ruysdaelkade
Ferdinand Bolstraat/ Ceintuurbaan
Sarphatipark
Cornelis Troostplein
Scheldestraat
Muntplein
Rembrandtplein
Frederiksplein
2e van der Helststraat
Van Woustraat/ Ceintuurbaan
Amsteldijk
Lutmastraat
Amstelkade/ Jozef Israëlskade
Muziekgebouw Bimhuis
Kattenburger- straat
Nieuwmarkt
Waterlooplein
Mr.Visserplein
Hoogte Kadijk
Plantage Kerklaan
Plantage Badlaan
Oosteinde
Weesperplein
Korte 's Gravesanderstraat
Wibautstraat
Camperstraat
C. Van Eesterenlaan
Rietlandpark
Steigereiland
Zuiderzeeweg
Ie Leeghwaterstraat
Ie Coehoornstraat
Zeeburgerdijk
Pontanusstraat
Mauritskade
Ie van Swindenstraat
Alexanderplein
Oosterpark
Insulindeweg
Soembawastraat
Javaplein
Molukkenstraat
Dapperstraat
Linnaeusstraat
Wijttenbach- straat
Beukenweg
Interchange with adjacent stops (walk at street level)
De Rijpstraat (↓) Service stops in one direction only (shown)
A Communicarta Style45 design
© Communicarta Ltd 2008 UDN.10a
Map user Ref: 4-VEP/LG/CIG/US/SMP/0508

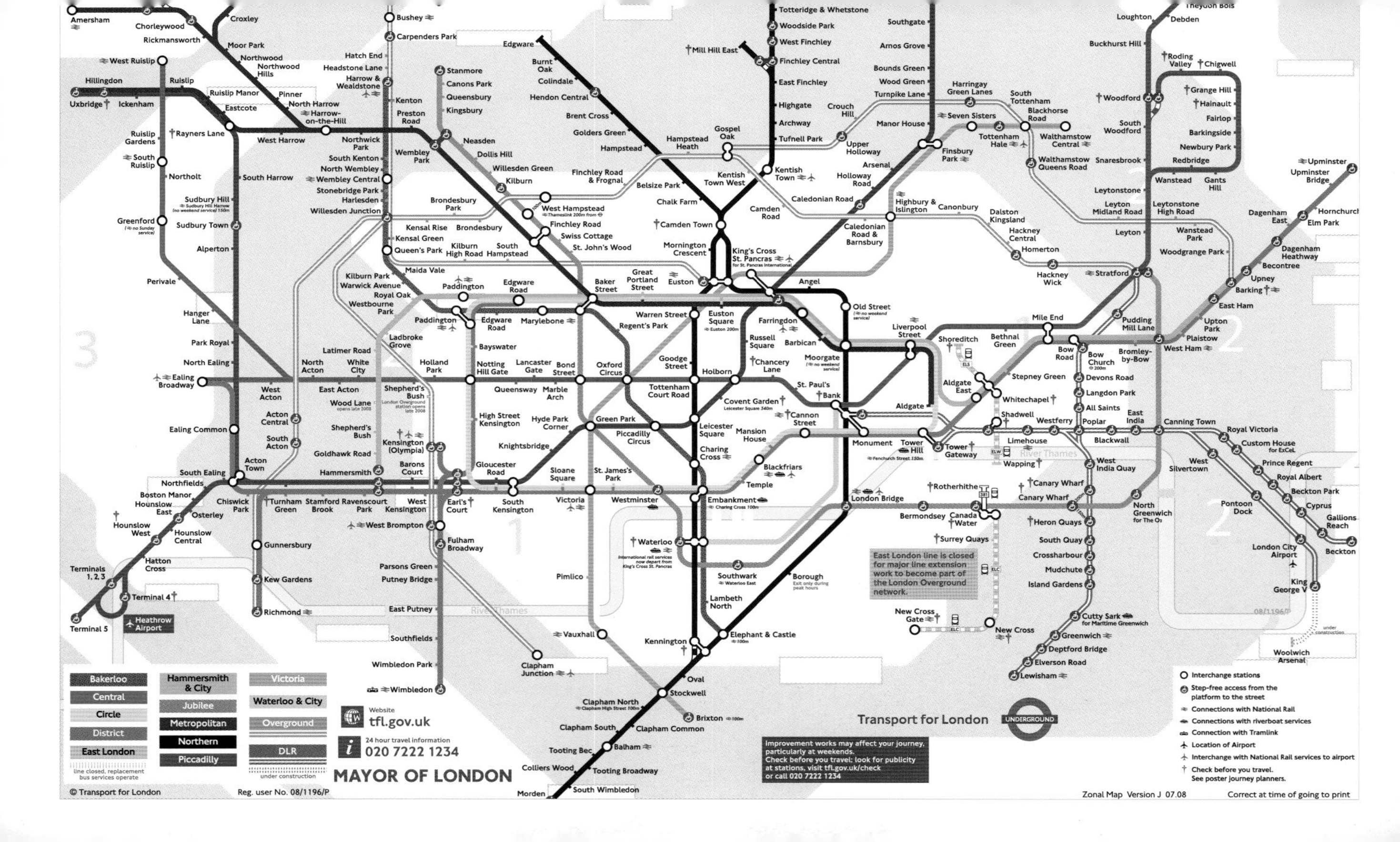

Amersham
Chorleywood
Rickmansworth
Croxley
Moor Park
Northwood
Northwood Hills
Pinner
North Harrow
Harrow-on-the-Hill
West Ruislip
Ruislip
Ruislip Manor
Eastcote
Hillingdon
Uxbridge
Ickenham
Rayners Lane
Ruislip Gardens
South Ruislip
West Harrow
Northolt
South Harrow
Sudbury Hill
Sudbury Town
Greenford
Alperton
Perivale
Hanger Lane
Park Royal
North Ealing
Ealing Broadway
Ealing Common
South Ealing
Acton Town
Northfields
Boston Manor
Osterley
Hounslow East
Hounslow Central
Hounslow West
Hatton Cross
Terminals 1, 2, 3
Terminal 4
Terminal 5
Heathrow Airport
Bushey
Carpenders Park
Hatch End
Headstone Lane
Harrow & Wealdstone
Kenton
Preston Road
Northwick Park
South Kenton
North Wembley
Wembley Central
Stonebridge Park
Harlesden
Willesden Junction
Wembley Park
Stanmore
Canons Park
Queensbury
Kingsbury
Neasden
Dollis Hill
Willesden Green
Kilburn
Edgware
Burnt Oak
Colindale
Hendon Central
Brent Cross
Golders Green
Hampstead
Mill Hill East
Totteridge & Whetstone
Woodside Park
West Finchley
Finchley Central
East Finchley
Highgate
Archway
Tufnell Park
Kentish Town
Camden Town
Chalk Farm
Belsize Park
Kentish Town West
Gospel Oak
Hampstead Heath
Finchley Road & Frognal
West Hampstead
Finchley Road
Swiss Cottage
St. John's Wood
Brondesbury Park
Brondesbury
Kensal Rise
Kensal Green
Queen's Park
Kilburn High Road
South Hampstead
Kilburn Park
Maida Vale
Warwick Avenue
Royal Oak
Westbourne Park
Paddington
Edgware Road
Marylebone
Baker Street
Great Portland Street
Euston
Euston Square
Warren Street
Regent's Park
Mornington Crescent
King's Cross St. Pancras
Angel
Old Street
Farringdon
Barbican
Russell Square
Chancery Lane
Moorgate
Liverpool Street
Bayswater
Notting Hill Gate
Lancaster Gate
Bond Street
Oxford Circus
Goodge Street
Tottenham Court Road
Holborn
St. Paul's
Bank
Queensway
Marble Arch
Covent Garden
Cannon Street
Holland Park
Ladbroke Grove
Latimer Road
North Acton
White City
East Acton
Shepherd's Bush
Wood Lane
Shepherd's Bush
Goldhawk Road
Hammersmith
West Acton
Acton Central
South Acton
Kensington (Olympia)
Barons Court
High Street Kensington
Hyde Park Corner
Green Park
Piccadilly Circus
Leicester Square
Mansion House
Monument
Tower Hill
Aldgate
Aldgate East
Knightsbridge
Gloucester Road
South Kensington
Sloane Square
Victoria
St. James's Park
Westminster
Embankment
Charing Cross
Temple
Blackfriars
London Bridge
Chiswick Park
Turnham Green
Stamford Brook
Ravenscourt Park
West Kensington
Earl's Court
West Brompton
Fulham Broadway
Parsons Green
Putney Bridge
East Putney
Southfields
Wimbledon Park
Wimbledon
Gunnersbury
Kew Gardens
Richmond
Pimlico
Vauxhall
Clapham Junction
Waterloo
Southwark
Lambeth North
Borough
Elephant & Castle
Kennington
Oval
Stockwell
Brixton
Clapham North
Clapham Common
Clapham South
Balham
Tooting Bec
Tooting Broadway
Colliers Wood
South Wimbledon
Morden
Southgate
Arnos Grove
Bounds Green
Wood Green
Turnpike Lane
Manor House
Crouch Hill
Upper Holloway
Harringay Green Lanes
South Tottenham
Seven Sisters
Tottenham Hale
Blackhorse Road
Walthamstow Central
Walthamstow Queens Road
Finsbury Park
Arsenal
Holloway Road
Caledonian Road
Camden Road
Caledonian Road & Barnsbury
Highbury & Islington
Canonbury
Dalston Kingsland
Hackney Central
Homerton
Hackney Wick
Stratford
Shoreditch
Bethnal Green
Mile End
Whitechapel
Stepney Green
Bow Road
Bow Church
Devons Road
Langdon Park
All Saints
Bromley-by-Bow
Pudding Mill Lane
West Ham
Plaistow
Upton Park
East Ham
Barking
Upney
Becontree
Dagenham Heathway
Dagenham East
Elm Park
Hornchurch
Upminster Bridge
Upminster
Loughton
Debden
Theydon Bois
Buckhurst Hill
Roding Valley
Chigwell
Woodford
Grange Hill
Hainault
Fairlop
Barkingside
Newbury Park
South Woodford
Snaresbrook
Redbridge
Gants Hill
Wanstead
Leytonstone
Leyton Midland Road
Leytonstone High Road
Leyton
Wanstead Park
Woodgrange Park
Shadwell
Limehouse
Westferry
Poplar
East India
Blackwall
Canning Town
Royal Victoria
Custom House for ExCeL
Prince Regent
Royal Albert
Beckton Park
Cyprus
Gallions Reach
Beckton
West Silvertown
Pontoon Dock
London City Airport
King George V
Woolwich Arsenal
North Greenwich for The O2
West India Quay
Canary Wharf
Heron Quays
South Quay
Crossharbour
Mudchute
Island Gardens
Cutty Sark for Maritime Greenwich
Greenwich
Deptford Bridge
Elverson Road
Lewisham
Tower Gateway
Wapping
Rotherhithe
Canada Water
Surrey Quays
Bermondsey
New Cross
New Cross Gate
River Thames
East London line is closed for major line extension work to become part of the London Overground network.
Improvement works may affect your journey, particularly at weekends. Check before you travel; look for publicity at stations, visit tfl.gov.uk/check or call 020 7222 1234
Bakerloo
Central
Circle
District
East London
line closed, replacement bus services operate
Hammersmith & City
Jubilee
Metropolitan
Northern
Piccadilly
Victoria
Waterloo & City
Overground
DLR
under construction
Website
tfl.gov.uk
24 hour travel information
020 7222 1234
MAYOR OF LONDON
Transport for London
UNDERGROUND
Interchange stations
Step-free access from the platform to the street
Connections with National Rail
Connections with riverboat services
Connection with Tramlink
Location of Airport
Interchange with National Rail services to airport
Check before you travel. See poster journey planners.
© Transport for London
Reg. user No. 08/1196/P
Zonal Map Version J 07.08
Correct at time of going to print

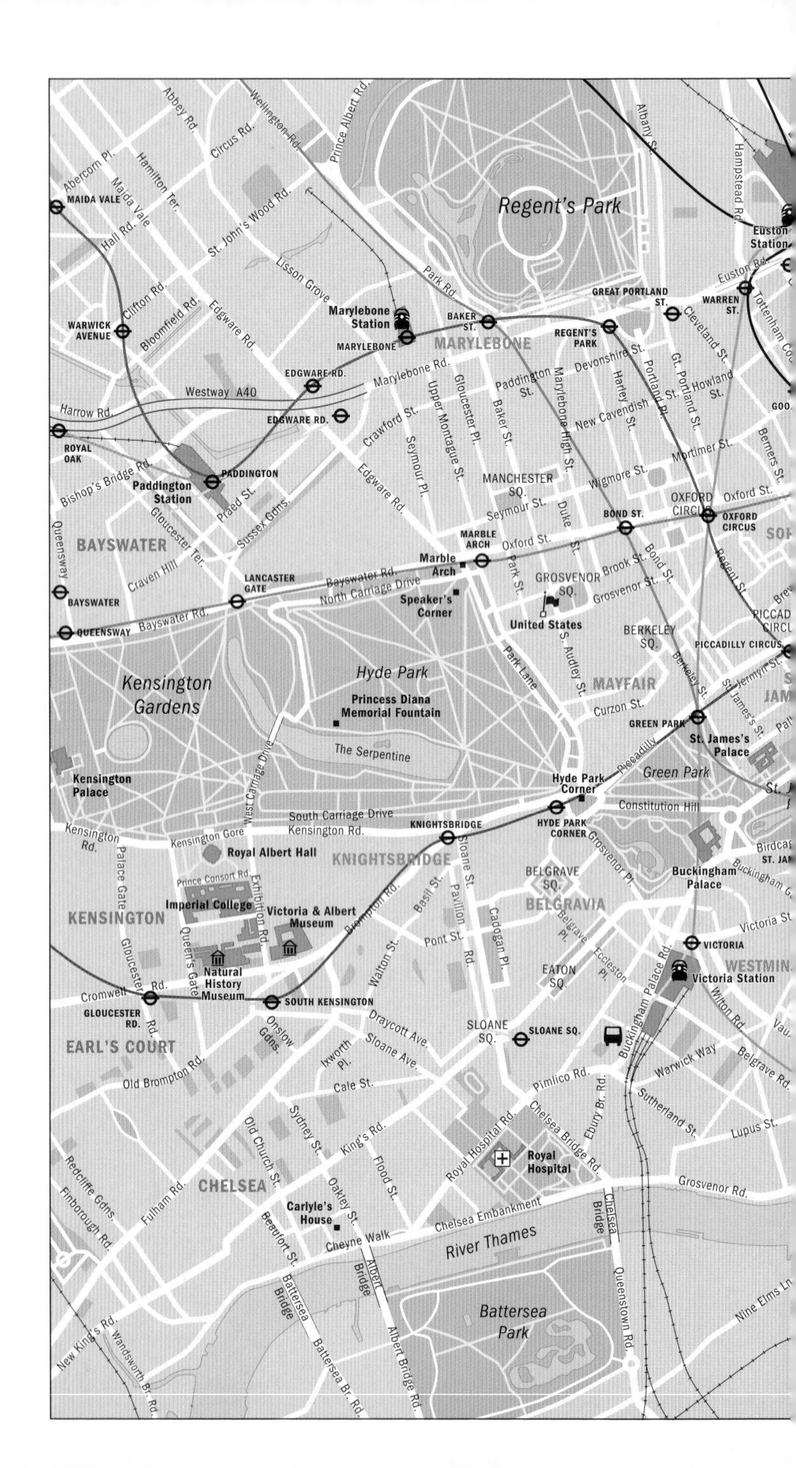

Regent's Park
Hyde Park
Kensington Gardens
Green Park
Battersea Park
River Thames
The Serpentine
MARYLEBONE
BAYSWATER
MAYFAIR
KNIGHTSBRIDGE
BELGRAVIA
KENSINGTON
EARL'S COURT
CHELSEA
Marylebone Station
Paddington Station
Euston Station
Victoria Station
Marble Arch
Speaker's Corner
United States
Princess Diana Memorial Fountain
Kensington Palace
Hyde Park Corner
St. James's Palace
Buckingham Palace
Royal Albert Hall
Imperial College
Victoria & Albert Museum
Natural History Museum
Royal Hospital
Carlyle's House
MAIDA VALE
WARWICK AVENUE
ROYAL OAK
PADDINGTON
EDGWARE RD.
MARYLEBONE
BAKER ST.
REGENT'S PARK
GREAT PORTLAND ST.
WARREN ST.
BOND ST.
OXFORD CIRCUS
LANCASTER GATE
BAYSWATER
QUEENSWAY
PICCADILLY CIRCUS
GREEN PARK
HYDE PARK CORNER
KNIGHTSBRIDGE
SOUTH KENSINGTON
GLOUCESTER RD.
SLOANE SQ.
VICTORIA
MANCHESTER SQ.
GROSVENOR SQ.
BERKELEY SQ.
BELGRAVE SQ.
EATON SQ.
SLOANE SQ.
Westway A40

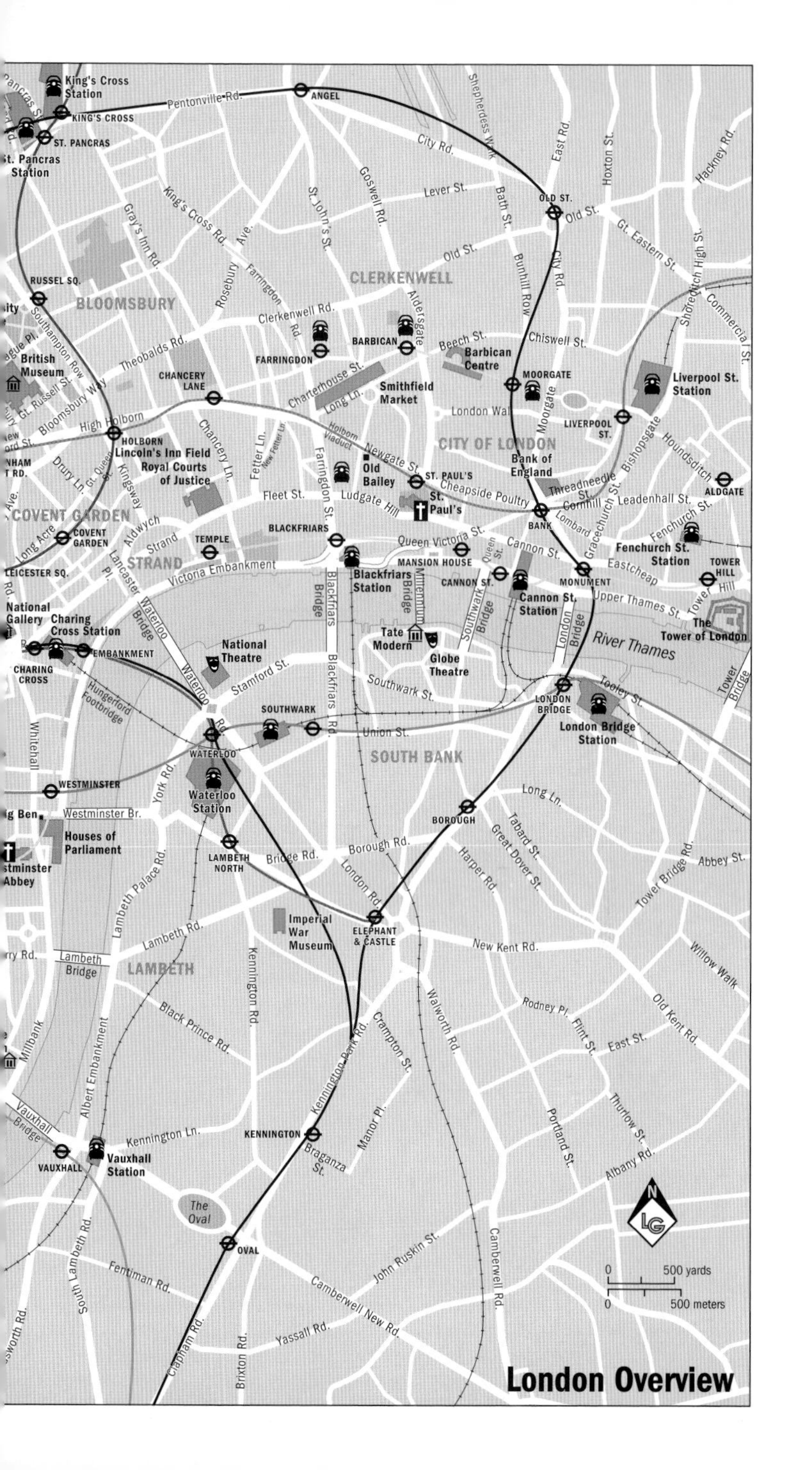
London Overview
King's Cross Station
King's Cross
St. Pancras
St. Pancras Station
Angel
Pentonville Rd.
City Rd.
Old St.
Bloomsbury
Clerkenwell
Russel Sq.
British Museum
Chancery Lane
Farringdon
Barbican
Barbican Centre
Moorgate
Liverpool St. Station
Liverpool St.
Smithfield Market
City of London
Bank of England
Holborn
Lincoln's Inn Field
Royal Courts of Justice
Old Bailey
St. Paul's
St. Paul's
Bank
Aldgate
Covent Garden
Temple
Blackfriars
Mansion House
Cannon St.
Fenchurch St. Station
Tower Hill
Strand
Leicester Sq.
Blackfriars Station
Cannon St. Station
Monument
National Gallery
Charing Cross Station
Tate Modern
Globe Theatre
The Tower of London
River Thames
Charing Cross
Embankment
National Theatre
Southwark
London Bridge
London Bridge Station
Waterloo
Waterloo Station
South Bank
Westminster
Big Ben
Houses of Parliament
Westminster Abbey
Borough
Lambeth North
Imperial War Museum
Elephant & Castle
Lambeth
Kennington
Vauxhall
Vauxhall Station
The Oval
Oval
0 500 yards
0 500 meters

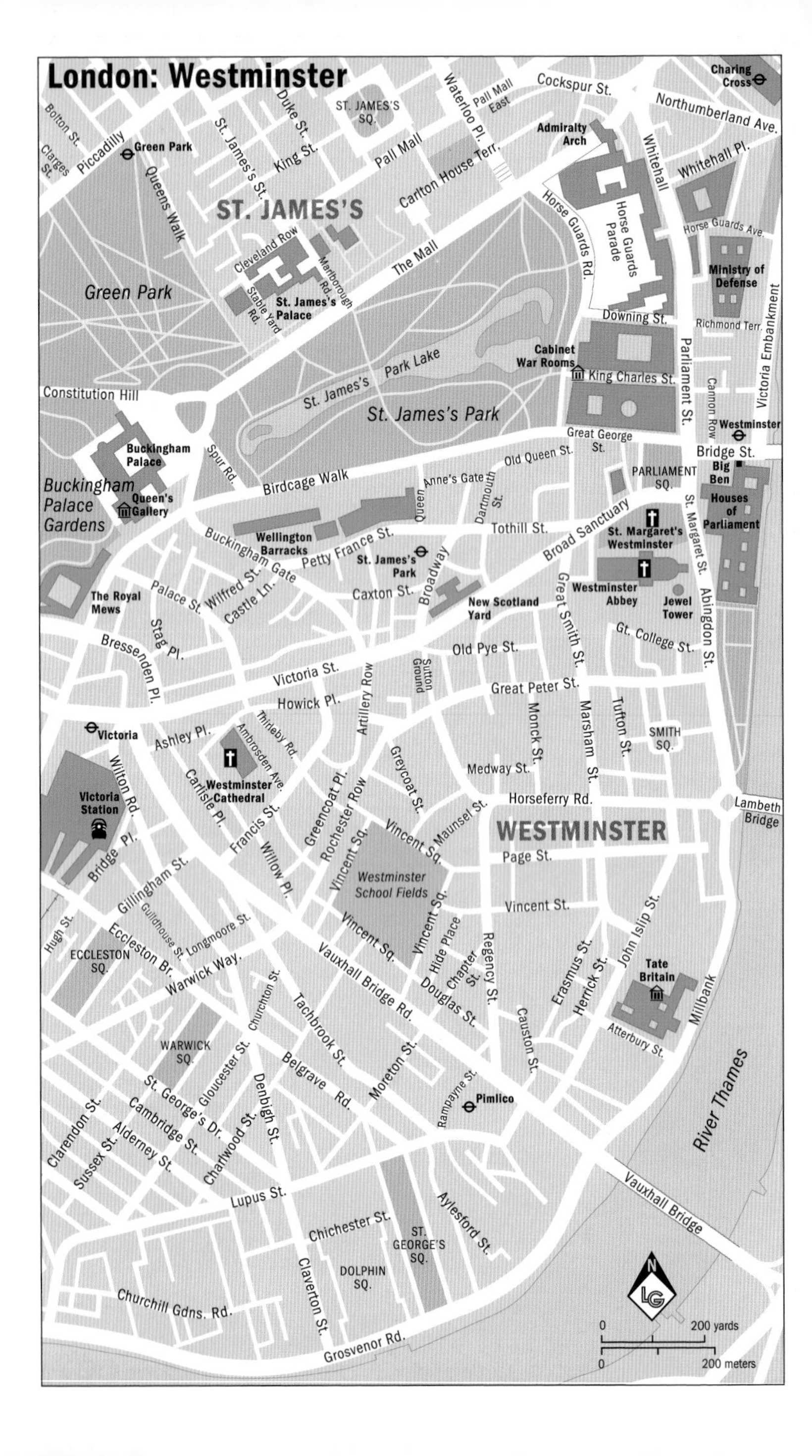
London: Westminster
ST. JAMES'S
WESTMINSTER
Green Park
St. James's Park
Buckingham Palace Gardens
Buckingham Palace
Queen's Gallery
The Royal Mews
Wellington Barracks
St. James's Palace
Admiralty Arch
Horse Guards Parade
Ministry of Defense
Cabinet War Rooms
Big Ben
Houses of Parliament
St. Margaret's Westminster
Westminster Abbey
Jewel Tower
New Scotland Yard
Westminster Cathedral
Victoria Station
Westminster School Fields
Tate Britain
River Thames
Charing Cross
Green Park
Westminster
St. James's Park
Victoria
Pimlico
Piccadilly
Constitution Hill
The Mall
Pall Mall
Birdcage Walk
Whitehall
Parliament St.
Victoria Embankment
Victoria St.
Horseferry Rd.
Vauxhall Bridge Rd.
Vauxhall Bridge
Lambeth Bridge
Millbank
Grosvenor Rd.
Lupus St.
Churchill Gdns. Rd.
Warwick Way
PARLIAMENT SQ.
SMITH SQ.
ECCLESTON SQ.
WARWICK SQ.
ST. GEORGE'S SQ.
DOLPHIN SQ.
ST. JAMES'S SQ.
0
200 yards
0
200 meters

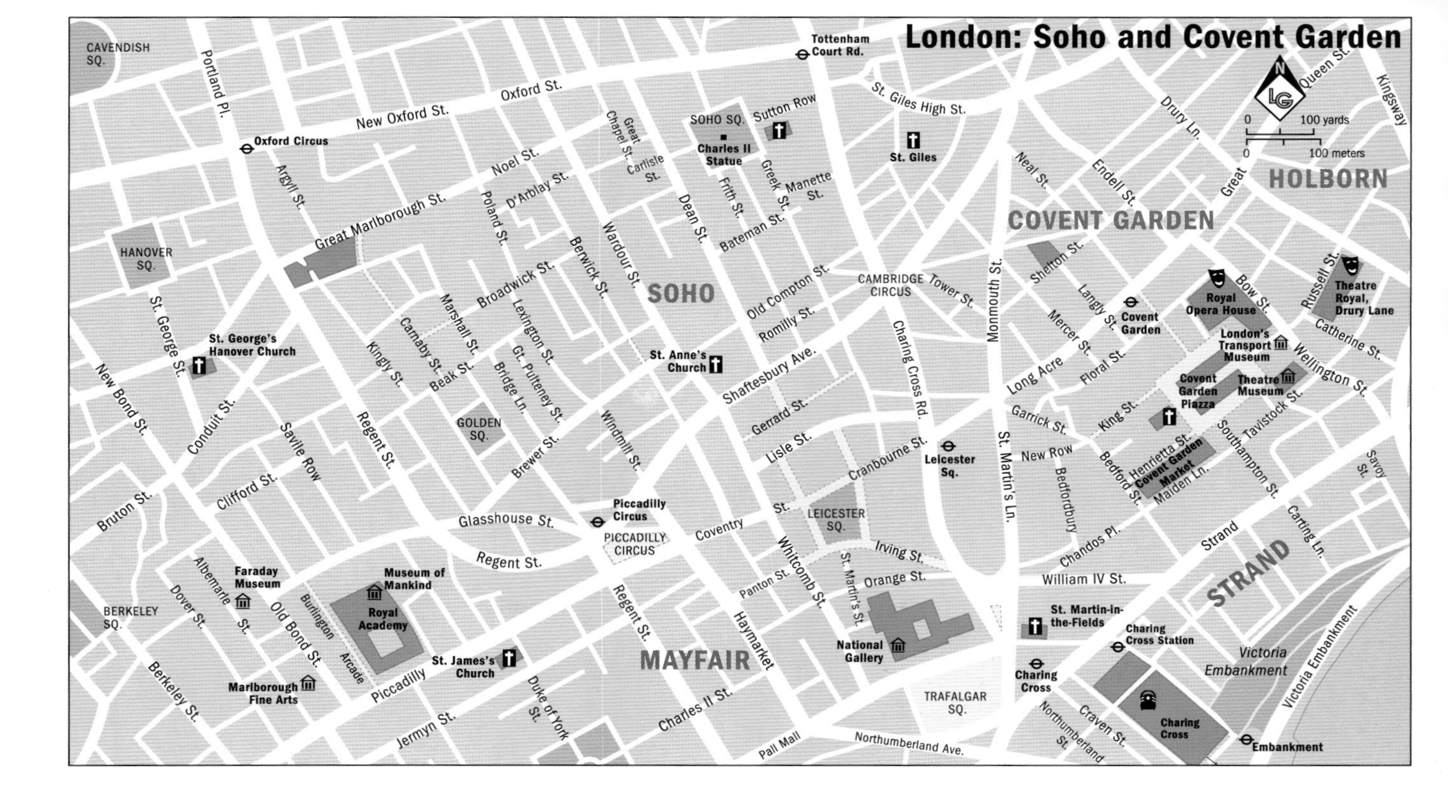
London: Soho and Covent Garden
0
100 yards
0
100 meters
LG
N
SOHO
COVENT GARDEN
HOLBORN
MAYFAIR
STRAND
CAVENDISH SQ.
HANOVER SQ.
SOHO SQ.
GOLDEN SQ.
LEICESTER SQ.
TRAFALGAR SQ.
BERKELEY SQ.
CAMBRIDGE CIRCUS
PICCADILLY CIRCUS
Tottenham Court Rd.
Oxford Circus
Covent Garden
Leicester Sq.
Piccadilly Circus
Charing Cross
Charing Cross Station
Embankment
Charles II Statue
St. Giles
St. Anne's Church
St. George's Hanover Church
St. James's Church
St. Martin-in-the-Fields
Royal Opera House
Theatre Royal, Drury Lane
London's Transport Museum
Theatre Museum
Covent Garden Piazza
Covent Garden Market
National Gallery
Museum of Mankind
Royal Academy
Faraday Museum
Marlborough Fine Arts
Charing Cross
Victoria Embankment
Portland Pl.
Oxford St.
New Oxford St.
St. Giles High St.
Sutton Row
Queen St.
Kingsway
Drury Ln.
Great Queen St.
Endell St.
Neal St.
Argyll St.
Noel St.
D'Arblay St.
Great Marlborough St.
Great Chapel St.
Carlisle St.
Frith St.
Greek St.
Manette St.
Dean St.
Bateman St.
Wardour St.
Berwick St.
Poland St.
Broadwick St.
Marshall St.
Carnaby St.
Kingly St.
Lexington St.
Gt. Pulteney St.
Bridge Ln.
Beak St.
Brewer St.
Windmill St.
Old Compton St.
Romilly St.
Shaftesbury Ave.
Gerrard St.
Lisle St.
Cranbourne St.
Charing Cross Rd.
Tower St.
Monmouth St.
Shelton St.
Langly St.
Mercer St.
Floral St.
Long Acre
Garrick St.
King St.
New Row
Bedfordbury
Bedford St.
Henrietta St.
Maiden Ln.
Southampton St.
Tavistock St.
Wellington St.
Catherine St.
Russell St.
Bow St.
Savoy St.
Carting Ln.
Strand
Chandos Pl.
William IV St.
St. Martin's Ln.
St. Martin's St.
Irving St.
Orange St.
Coventry St.
Panton St.
Whitcomb St.
Haymarket
Regent St.
Glasshouse St.
Piccadilly
Jermyn St.
Duke of York St.
Charles II St.
Pall Mall
Northumberland Ave.
Northumberland St.
Craven St.
St. George St.
New Bond St.
Conduit St.
Savile Row
Clifford St.
Bruton St.
Albemarle St.
Dover St.
Old Bond St.
Burlington Arcade
Berkeley St.

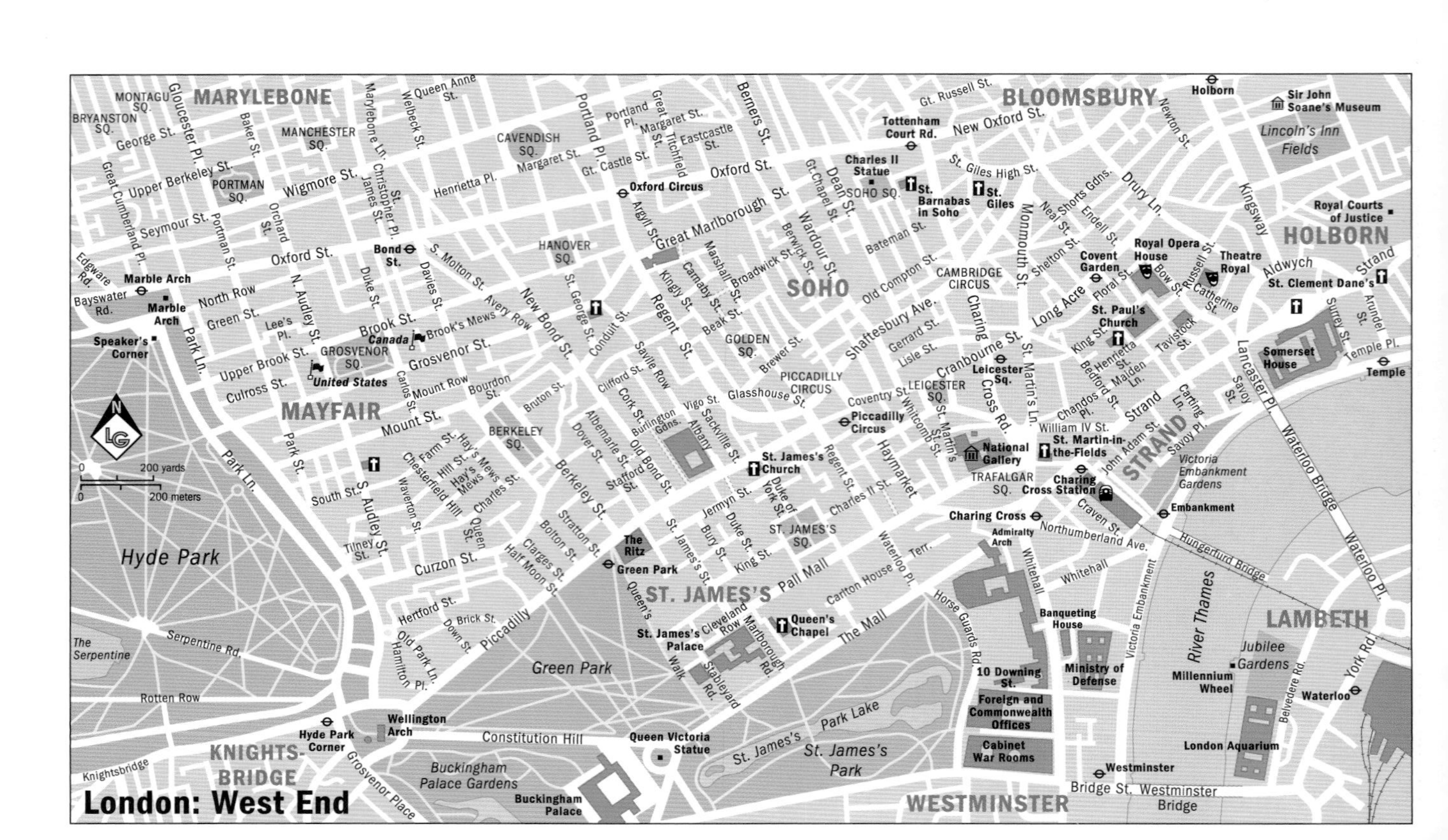
London: West End
MARYLEBONE
BLOOMSBURY
HOLBORN
SOHO
MAYFAIR
ST. JAMES'S
STRAND
LAMBETH
WESTMINSTER
KNIGHTS-BRIDGE
Hyde Park
Green Park
St. James's Park
Buckingham Palace Gardens
River Thames
Victoria Embankment Gardens
Lincoln's Inn Fields
Jubilee Gardens
The Serpentine
Park Lake
MONTAGU SQ.
BRYANSTON SQ.
MANCHESTER SQ.
PORTMAN SQ.
CAVENDISH SQ.
HANOVER SQ.
GROSVENOR SQ.
BERKELEY SQ.
GOLDEN SQ.
SOHO SQ.
CAMBRIDGE CIRCUS
PICCADILLY CIRCUS
LEICESTER SQ.
TRAFALGAR SQ.
ST. JAMES'S SQ.
Marble Arch
Bond St.
Oxford Circus
Tottenham Court Rd.
Holborn
Covent Garden
Leicester Sq.
Piccadilly Circus
Charing Cross
Embankment
Temple
Waterloo
Westminster
Green Park
Hyde Park Corner
Sir John Soane's Museum
Royal Courts of Justice
Theatre Royal
Royal Opera House
St. Clement Dane's
Somerset House
St. Paul's Church
Charles II Statue
St. Barnabas in Soho
St. Giles
Speaker's Corner
Canada
United States
National Gallery
St. Martin-in-the-Fields
Charing Cross Station
St. James's Church
The Ritz
Albany
Admiralty Arch
Banqueting House
Ministry of Defense
10 Downing St.
Foreign and Commonwealth Offices
Cabinet War Rooms
Millennium Wheel
London Aquarium
Queen's Chapel
St. James's Palace
Queen Victoria Statue
Buckingham Palace
Wellington Arch
Oxford St.
Regent St.
New Bond St.
Piccadilly
Pall Mall
The Mall
Whitehall
Strand
Haymarket
Charing Cross Rd.
Shaftesbury Ave.
Park Ln.
Constitution Hill
Waterloo Bridge
Hungerford Bridge
Westminster Bridge
Victoria Embankment
Northumberland Ave.
Horse Guards Rd.
Birdcage Walk
Queen's Walk
Long Acre
Kingsway
Aldwych
Drury Ln.
New Oxford St.
Wigmore St.
Great Marlborough St.
Wardour St.
Berwick St.
Dean St.
Old Compton St.
Monmouth St.
Brook St.
Grosvenor St.
Mount St.
Curzon St.
Berkeley St.
Jermyn St.
Savile Row
Carnaby St.
Baker St.
Gloucester Pl.
Portland Pl.
Serpentine Rd.
Rotten Row
Knightsbridge
Grosvenor Place
Bridge St.
200 yards
200 meters
0
0

London: Kensington

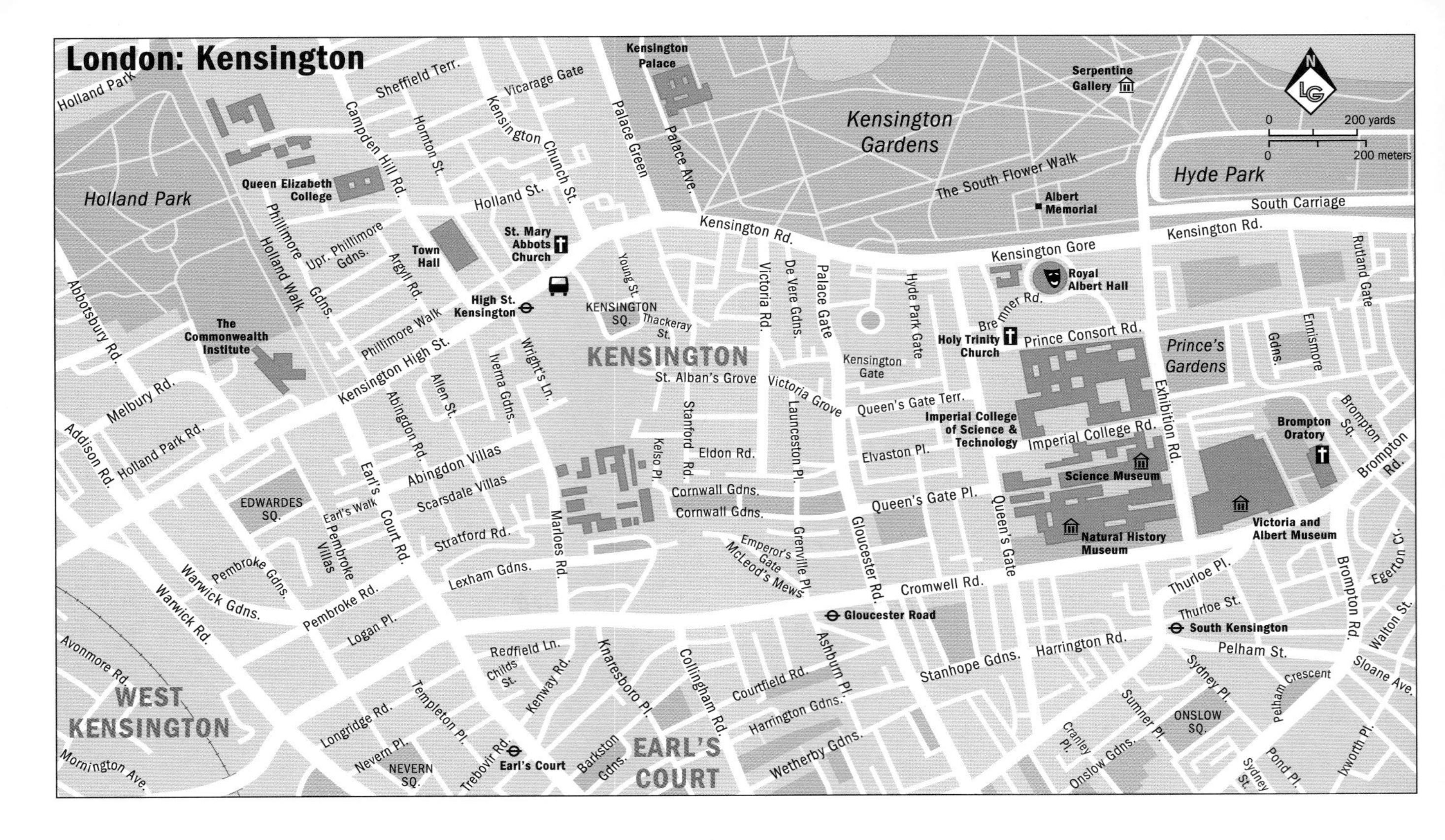

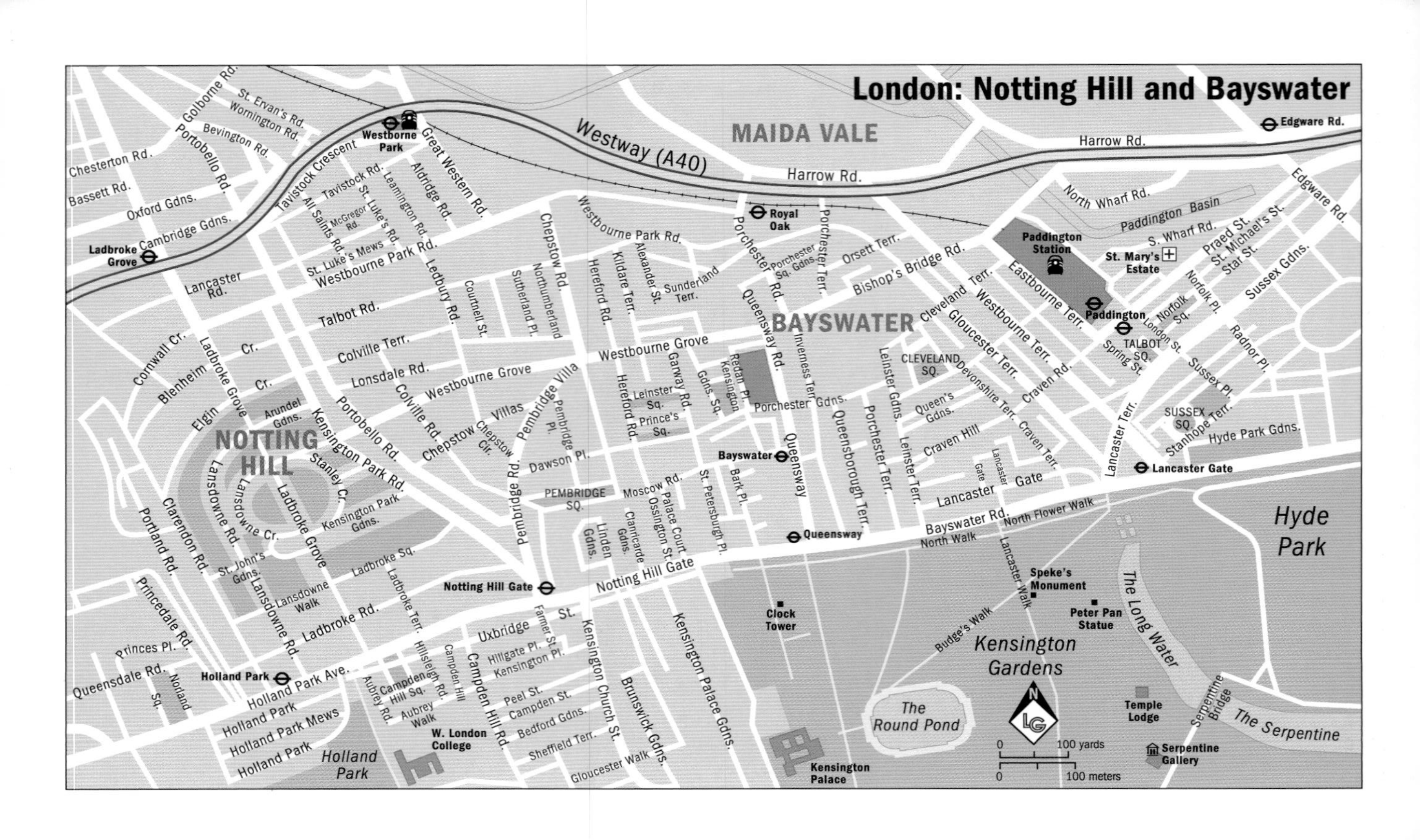
London: Notting Hill and Bayswater
MAIDA VALE
BAYSWATER
NOTTING HILL
Hyde Park
Kensington Gardens
Holland Park
Westway (A40)
Harrow Rd.
Edgware Rd.
Westbourne Park
Royal Oak
Paddington Station
Paddington
St. Mary's Estate
Ladbroke Grove
Lancaster Gate
Bayswater
Queensway
Notting Hill Gate
Holland Park
The Long Water
The Serpentine
Serpentine Bridge
Serpentine Gallery
Temple Lodge
Peter Pan Statue
Speke's Monument
The Round Pond
Clock Tower
Kensington Palace
W. London College
100 yards
100 meters
Westbourne Grove
Westbourne Park Rd.
Bishop's Bridge Rd.
Bayswater Rd.
Kensington Church St.
Kensington Palace Gdns.
Portobello Rd.
Ladbroke Grove
Kensington Park Rd.
Pembridge Rd.
Queensway Rd.
Porchester Rd.
Sussex Gdns.
Praed St.
Talbot Rd.
Ledbury Rd.
Chepstow Rd.
Uxbridge St.
Campden Hill Rd.
Holland Park Ave.

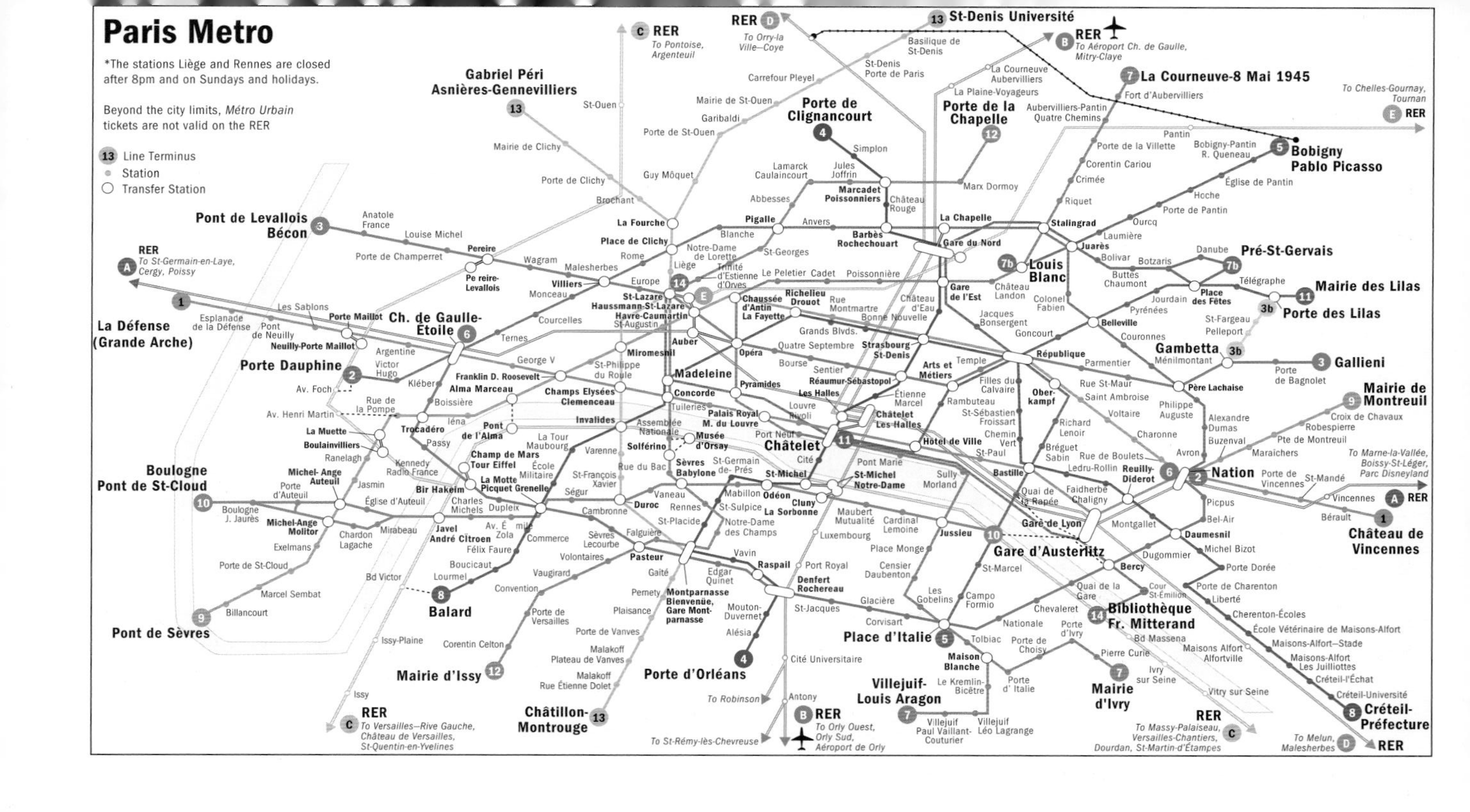
Paris Metro
*The stations Liège and Rennes are closed after 8pm and on Sundays and holidays.
Beyond the city limits, Métro Urbain tickets are not valid on the RER
13 Line Terminus
Station
Transfer Station
RER A To St-Germain-en-Laye, Cergy, Poissy
RER C To Pontoise, Argenteuil
RER D To Orry-la Ville—Coye
RER B To Aéroport Ch. de Gaulle, Mitry-Claye
To Chelles-Gournay, Tournan
E RER
To Marne-la-Vallée, Boissy-St-Léger, Parc Disneyland
A RER
To Melun, Malesherbes
RER
RER C To Massy-Palaiseau, Versailles-Chantiers, Dourdan, St-Martin-d'Étampes
RER B To Orly Ouest, Orly Sud, Aéroport de Orly
To St-Rémy-lès-Chevreuse
To Robinson
RER C To Versailles—Rive Gauche, Château de Versailles, St-Quentin-en-Yvelines
1 La Défense (Grande Arche)
1 Château de Vincennes
2 Porte Dauphine
2 Nation
3 Pont de Levallois Bécon
3 Gallieni
3b Gambetta
3b Porte des Lilas
4 Porte de Clignancourt
4 Porte d'Orléans
5 Bobigny Pablo Picasso
5 Place d'Italie
6 Ch. de Gaulle-Étoile
6 Nation
7 La Courneuve-8 Mai 1945
7 Villejuif-Louis Aragon
7 Mairie d'Ivry
7b Louis Blanc
7b Pré-St-Gervais
8 Balard
8 Créteil-Préfecture
9 Pont de Sèvres
9 Mairie de Montreuil
10 Boulogne Pont de St-Cloud
10 Gare d'Austerlitz
11 Châtelet
11 Mairie des Lilas
12 Porte de la Chapelle
12 Mairie d'Issy
13 Gabriel Péri Asnières-Gennevilliers
13 St-Denis Université
13 Châtillon-Montrouge
14 Bibliothèque Fr. Mitterand
Esplanade de la Défense
Pont de Neuilly
Les Sablons
Porte Maillot
Neuilly-Porte Maillot
Argentine
Victor Hugo
Av. Foch
Av. Henri Martin
Rue de la Pompe
Kléber
Boissière
Trocadéro
Iéna
La Muette
Boulainvilliers
Ranelagh
Passy
Kennedy Radio France
Jasmin
Michel-Ange Auteuil
Michel-Ange Molitor
Porte d'Auteuil
Boulogne J. Jaurès
Église d'Auteuil
Chardon Lagache
Mirabeau
Exelmans
Porte de St-Cloud
Marcel Sembat
Billancourt
Javel André Citroen
Bir Hakeim
Charles Michels
Av. Émile Zola
Félix Faure
Boucicaut
Lourmel
Bd Victor
Issy-Plaine
Issy
Corentin Celton
Porte de Versailles
Convention
Vaugirard
Volontaires
Commerce
La Motte Picquet Grenelle
Dupleix
Champ de Mars Tour Eiffel
École Militaire
La Tour Maubourg
Pont de l'Alma
Alma Marceau
Franklin D. Roosevelt
George V
Ternes
Courcelles
Monceau
Villiers
Malesherbes
Wagram
Pereire
Pereire-Levallois
Porte de Champerret
Louise Michel
Anatole France
Mairie de Clichy
Porte de Clichy
St-Ouen
Brochant
Guy Môquet
Porte de St-Ouen
Garibaldi
Mairie de St-Ouen
Carrefour Pleyel
St-Denis Porte de Paris
Basilique de St-Denis
La Fourche
Place de Clichy
Rome
Europe
Liège
St-Lazare
Haussmann-St-Lazare
Havre-Caumartin
St-Augustin
Miromesnil
St-Philippe du Roule
Champs Elysées Clemenceau
Invalides
Assemblée Nationale
Varenne
Solférino
Musée d'Orsay
Rue du Bac
Sèvres Babylone
St-François Xavier
Ségur
Cambronne
Duroc
Vaneau
Rennes
St-Placide
Falguière
Sèvres Lecourbe
Pasteur
Gaîté
Pernety
Plaisance
Porte de Vanves
Malakoff Plateau de Vanves
Malakoff Rue Étienne Dolet
Montparnasse Bienvenüe, Gare Montparnasse
Edgar Quinet
Vavin
Raspail
Denfert Rochereau
Mouton-Duvernet
Alésia
Cité Universitaire
Antony
St-Jacques
Glacière
Corvisart
Port Royal
Luxembourg
Notre-Dame des Champs
St-Sulpice
Mabillon
Odéon
Cluny La Sorbonne
St-Germain des Prés
St-Michel
St-Michel Notre-Dame
Maubert Mutualité
Cardinal Lemoine
Place Monge
Censier Daubenton
Les Gobelins
Campo Formio
St-Marcel
Jussieu
Madeleine
Concorde
Tuileries
Palais Royal M. du Louvre
Louvre Rivoli
Pont Neuf
Cité
Pyramides
Opéra
Auber
Chaussée d'Antin La Fayette
Richelieu Drouot
Quatre Septembre
Bourse
Sentier
Grands Blvds.
Rue Montmartre
Bonne Nouvelle
Réaumur-Sébastopol
Les Halles
Châtelet Les Halles
Étienne Marcel
Strasbourg St-Denis
Arts et Métiers
Rambuteau
Hôtel de Ville
Pont Marie
Sully Morland
St-Paul
Chemin Vert
St-Sébastien Froissart
Filles du Calvaire
Temple
République
Château d'Eau
Gare de l'Est
Jacques Bonsergent
Château Landon
Gare du Nord
La Chapelle
Barbès Rochechouart
Château Rouge
Marcadet Poissonniers
Simplon
Jules Joffrin
Marx Dormoy
Lamarck Caulaincourt
Abbesses
Pigalle
Anvers
Blanche
St-Georges
Notre-Dame de Lorette
Trinité d'Estienne d'Orves
Le Peletier
Cadet
Poissonnière
Stalingrad
Jaurès
Colonel Fabien
Belleville
Goncourt
Parmentier
Oberkampf
Richard Lenoir
Bréguet Sabin
Bastille
Ledru-Rollin
Faidherbe Chaligny
Reuilly-Diderot
Rue de Boulets
Quai de la Rapée
Gare de Lyon
Bercy
Quai de la Gare
Cour St-Émilion
Chevaleret
Nationale
Porte d'Ivry
Porte de Choisy
Bd Massena
Tolbiac
Maison Blanche
Porte d'Italie
Le Kremlin-Bicêtre
Villejuif Paul Vaillant-Couturier
Villejuif Léo Lagrange
Pierre Curie
Ivry sur Seine
Vitry sur Seine
Maisons Alfort Alfortville
Dugommier
Montgallet
Daumesnil
Michel Bizot
Porte Dorée
Porte de Charenton
Liberté
Charenton-Écoles
École Vétérinaire de Maisons-Alfort
Maisons-Alfort—Stade
Maisons-Alfort Les Juilliottes
Créteil-l'Échat
Créteil-Université
Picpus
Bel-Air
Porte de Vincennes
St-Mandé
Vincennes
Bérault
Avron
Alexandre Dumas
Buzenval
Maraichers
Pte de Montreuil
Robespierre
Croix de Chavaux
Charonne
Voltaire
Saint Ambroise
Rue St-Maur
Philippe Auguste
Père Lachaise
Ménilmontant
Couronnes
Porte de Bagnolet
St-Fargeau
Pelleport
Pyrénées
Jourdain
Place des Fêtes
Télégraphe
Danube
Botzaris
Buttes Chaumont
Bolivar
Laumière
Ourcq
Porte de Pantin
Hoche
Église de Pantin
Bobigny-Pantin R. Queneau
Pantin
Riquet
Crimée
Corentin Cariou
Porte de la Villette
Aubervilliers-Pantin Quatre Chemins
Fort d'Aubervilliers
La Plaine-Voyageurs
La Courneuve Aubervilliers

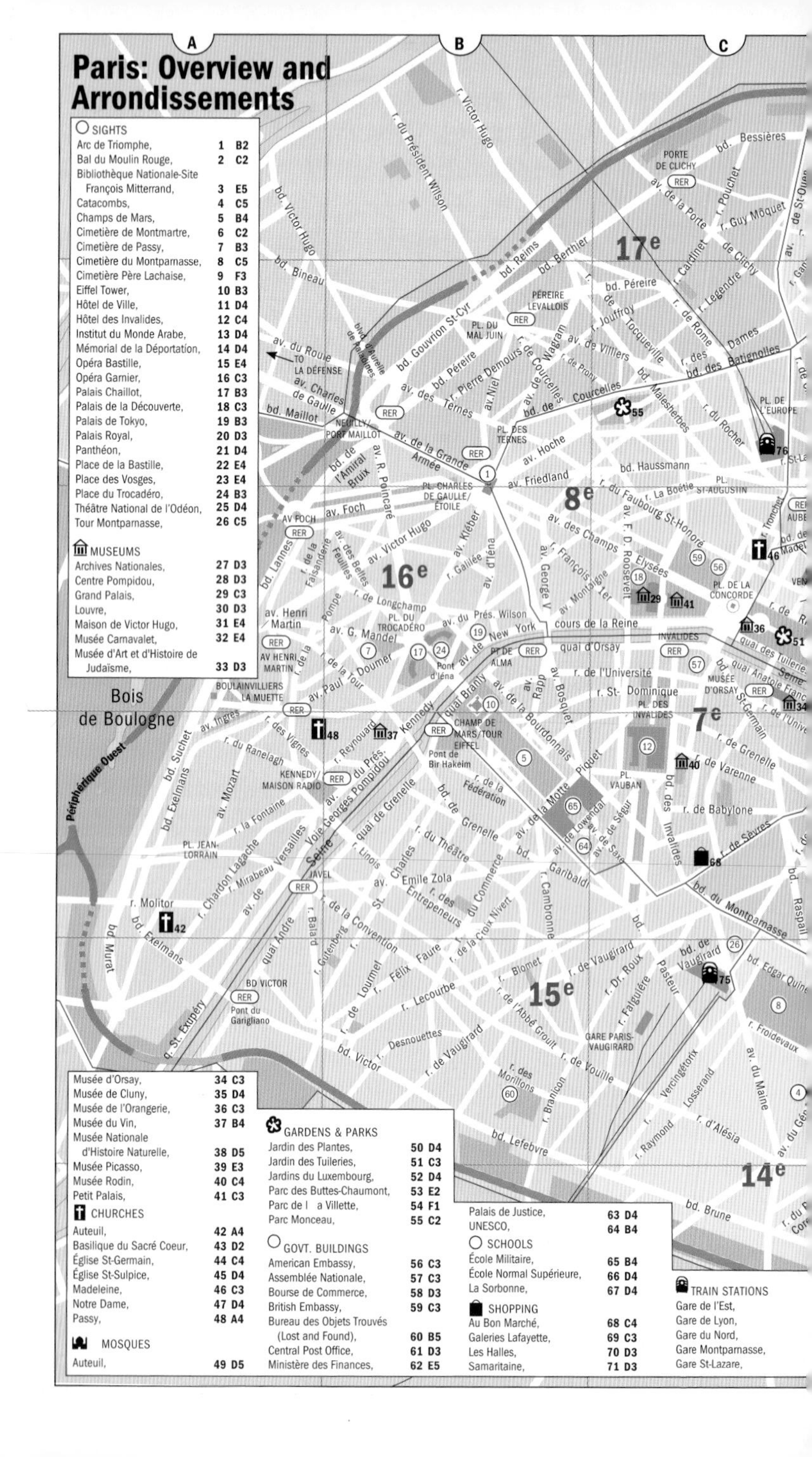

Paris: Overview and Arrondissements
A
B
C
SIGHTS
Arc de Triomphe, 1 B2
Bal du Moulin Rouge, 2 C2
Bibliothèque Nationale-Site François Mitterrand, 3 E5
Catacombs, 4 C5
Champs de Mars, 5 B4
Cimetière de Montmartre, 6 C2
Cimetière de Passy, 7 B3
Cimetière du Montparnasse, 8 C5
Cimetière Père Lachaise, 9 F3
Eiffel Tower, 10 B3
Hôtel de Ville, 11 D4
Hôtel des Invalides, 12 C4
Institut du Monde Arabe, 13 D4
Mémorial de la Déportation, 14 D4
Opéra Bastille, 15 E4
Opéra Garnier, 16 C3
Palais Chaillot, 17 B3
Palais de la Découverte, 18 C3
Palais de Tokyo, 19 B3
Palais Royal, 20 D3
Panthéon, 21 D4
Place de la Bastille, 22 E4
Place des Vosges, 23 E4
Place du Trocadéro, 24 B3
Théâtre National de l'Odéon, 25 D4
Tour Montparnasse, 26 C5
MUSEUMS
Archives Nationales, 27 D3
Centre Pompidou, 28 D3
Grand Palais, 29 C3
Louvre, 30 D3
Maison de Victor Hugo, 31 E4
Musée Carnavalet, 32 E4
Musée d'Art et d'Histoire de Judaïsme, 33 D3
Musée d'Orsay, 34 C3
Musée de Cluny, 35 D4
Musée de l'Orangerie, 36 C3
Musée du Vin, 37 B4
Musée Nationale d'Histoire Naturelle, 38 D5
Musée Picasso, 39 E3
Musée Rodin, 40 C4
Petit Palais, 41 C3
CHURCHES
Auteuil, 42 A4
Basilique du Sacré Coeur, 43 D2
Église St-Germain, 44 C4
Église St-Sulpice, 45 D4
Madeleine, 46 C3
Notre Dame, 47 D4
Passy, 48 A4
MOSQUES
Auteuil, 49 D5
GARDENS & PARKS
Jardin des Plantes, 50 D4
Jardin des Tuileries, 51 C3
Jardins du Luxembourg, 52 D4
Parc des Buttes-Chaumont, 53 E2
Parc de l a Villette, 54 F1
Parc Monceau, 55 C2
GOVT. BUILDINGS
American Embassy, 56 C3
Assemblée Nationale, 57 C3
Bourse de Commerce, 58 D3
British Embassy, 59 C3
Bureau des Objets Trouvés (Lost and Found), 60 B5
Central Post Office, 61 D3
Ministère des Finances, 62 E5
Palais de Justice, 63 D4
UNESCO, 64 B4
SCHOOLS
École Militaire, 65 B4
École Normal Supérieure, 66 D4
La Sorbonne, 67 D4
SHOPPING
Au Bon Marché, 68 C4
Galeries Lafayette, 69 C3
Les Halles, 70 D3
Samaritaine, 71 D3
TRAIN STATIONS
Gare de l'Est,
Gare de Lyon,
Gare du Nord,
Gare Montparnasse,
Gare St-Lazare,
17e
8e
16e
7e
15e
14e
Bois de Boulogne
Périphérique Ouest
Seine
PORTE DE CLICHY
PÉREIRE LEVALLOIS
PL. DU MAL JUIN
PL. DES TERNES
NEUILLY/PORT MAILLOT
PL. CHARLES DE GAULLE/ÉTOILE
AV FOCH
PL. DU TROCADÉRO
AV HENRI MARTIN
BOULAINVILLIERS
LA MUETTE
KENNEDY/MAISON RADIO
PL. JEAN-LORRAIN
JAVEL
BD VICTOR
Pont du Garigliano
CHAMP DE MARS/TOUR EIFFEL
Pont de Bir Hakeim
Pont d'Iéna
PT DE ALMA
INVALIDES
PL. DES INVALIDES
PL. VAUBAN
MUSÉE D'ORSAY
PL. DE LA CONCORDE
PL. ST-AUGUSTIN
PL. DE L'EUROPE
GARE PARIS-VAUGIRARD
TO LA DÉFENSE
RER
bd. Bessières
bd. Berthier
bd. Reims
bd. Péreire
bd. Gouvrion St-Cyr
bd. Victor Hugo
bd. Bineau
r. Victor Hugo
r. du Président Wilson
av. du Roule
av. Charles de Gaulle
bd. Maillot
av. de la Grande Armée
av. des Ternes
av. Niel
av. de Wagram
bd. de Courcelles
av. de Villiers
bd. des Batignolles
bd. Malesherbes
av. Hoche
av. Friedland
bd. Haussmann
r. du Faubourg St-Honoré
av. des Champs Elysées
av. Foch
av. Victor Hugo
av. Kléber
av. d'Iéna
av. George V
av. Montaigne
cours de la Reine
quai d'Orsay
r. de l'Université
r. St- Dominique
av. Henri Martin
av. G. Mandel
av. Paul Doumer
av. de New York
av. du Prés. Wilson
av. Rapp
av. Bosquet
av. de la Bourdonnais
av. de la Motte Piquet
av. de Lowendal
av. de Saxe
av. de Ségur
bd. des Invalides
r. de Grenelle
r. de Varenne
r. de Babylone
r. de Sèvres
bd. du Montparnasse
bd. Raspail
r. de Longchamp
av. Mozart
r. du Ranelagh
bd. Suchet
bd. Exelmans
r. Molitor
bd. Murat
Voie Georges Pompidou
quai de Grenelle
bd. de Grenelle
r. de la Fédération
r. du Théâtre
av. Emile Zola
r. de la Convention
r. Lecourbe
r. de Vaugirard
bd. Pasteur
bd. Garibaldi
r. Cambronne
bd. Victor
bd. Lefebvre
bd. Brune
r. d'Alésia
av. du Maine
r. Froidevaux
bd. Edgar Quinet

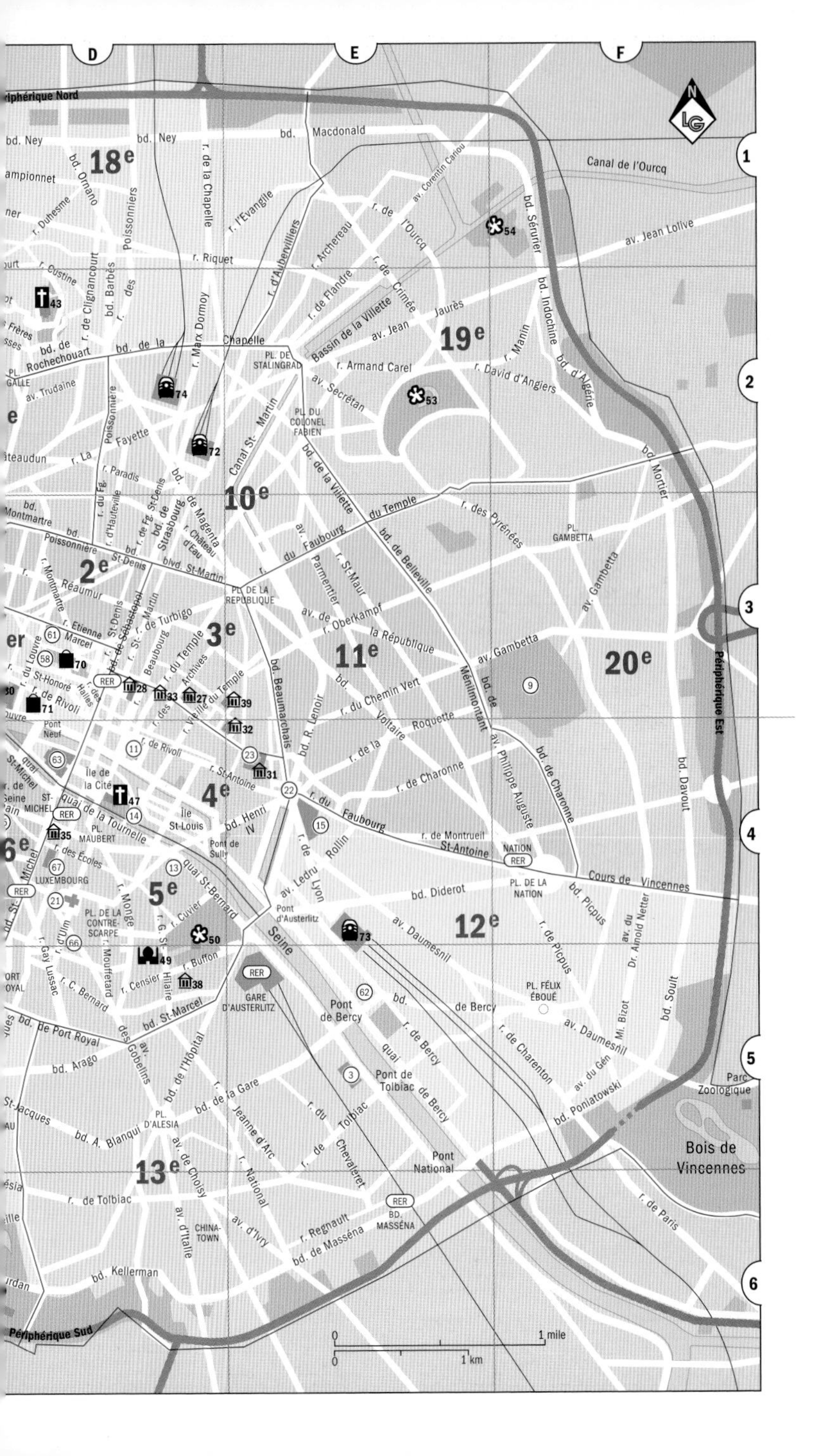

D
E
F
1
2
3
4
5
6
N
LG
Périphérique Nord
Périphérique Est
Périphérique Sud
18e
19e
10e
2e
3e
11e
20e
4e
5e
12e
13e
bd. Ney
bd. Macdonald
Canal de l'Ourcq
av. Jean Lolive
av. Corentin Cariou
r. de l'Ourcq
bd. Sérurier
r. de Crimée
av. Jean Jaurès
bd. Indochine
bd. d'Algérie
r. Manin
r. David d'Angiers
r. de Flandre
r. Archereau
Bassin de la Villette
r. Armand Carel
av. Secrétan
PL. DE STALINGRAD
PL. DU COLONEL FABIEN
bd. de la Villette
bd. Mortier
r. des Pyrénées
PL. GAMBETTA
av. Gambetta
r. du Faubourg du Temple
bd. de Belleville
av. Parmentier
r. St-Maur
av. de la République
r. Oberkampf
bd. Ménilmontant
r. du Chemin Vert
bd. Voltaire
r. de la Roquette
r. de Charonne
bd. de Charonne
av. Philippe Auguste
bd. Davout
r. du Faubourg St-Antoine
r. de Montreuil
NATION
PL. DE LA NATION
Cours de Vincennes
bd. Diderot
bd. Picpus
r. de Picpus
av. Daumesnil
av. du Dr. Arnold Netter
bd. Soult
PL. FÉLIX ÉBOUÉ
Mi. Bizot
av. du Gén
bd. Poniatowski
r. de Charenton
bd. de Bercy
r. de Bercy
quai de Bercy
Pont de Bercy
Pont de Tolbiac
Parc Zoologique
Bois de Vincennes
r. de Paris
Pont National
BD. MASSÉNA
bd. de Masséna
r. Regnault
r. du Chevaleret
r. de Tolbiac
r. National
r. Jeanne d'Arc
av. d'Ivry
av. de Choisy
av. d'Italie
CHINA-TOWN
bd. Kellerman
bd. A. Blanqui
PL. D'ALESIA
bd. de la Gare
bd. de l'Hôpital
av. des Gobelins
bd. Arago
bd. de Port Royal
bd. St-Marcel
r. Censier
r. G. St-Hilaire
r. Buffon
r. Cuvier
r. Monge
r. Mouffetard
r. C. Bernard
r. Gay Lussac
r. d'Ulm
PL. DE LA CONTRE-SCARPE
LUXEMBOURG
r. des Écoles
PL. MAUBERT
ST-MICHEL
quai de la Tournelle
quai St-Bernard
Seine
GARE D'AUSTERLITZ
Pont d'Austerlitz
av. Ledru Rollin
r. de Lyon
bd. Henri IV
Pont de Sully
Île St-Louis
Île de la Cité
Pont Neuf
r. de Rivoli
r. St-Antoine
bd. Beaumarchais
bd. R. Lenoir
r. Vieille du Temple
r. des Archives
r. du Temple
r. Beaubourg
r. St-Martin
r. de Turbigo
bd. de Sébastopol
r. St-Denis
r. Etienne Marcel
r. Réaumur
r. Montmartre
bd. Poissonnière
bd. Montmartre
bd. St-Denis
blvd. St-Martin
PL. DE LA RÉPUBLIQUE
r. Château d'Eau
bd. de Magenta
bd. de Strasbourg
r. du Fg. St-Denis
r. d'Hauteville
r. du Fg. Poissonnière
r. Paradis
r. La Fayette
Canal St-Martin
r. Marx Dormoy
r. de la Chapelle
r. d'Aubervilliers
r. l'Evangile
r. Riquet
bd. de la Chapelle
bd. de Rochechouart
av. Trudaine
r. des Poissonniers
bd. Barbès
r. de Clignancourt
r. Custine
r. Duhesme
bd. Ornano
r. du Louvre
r. St-Honoré
r. des Halles
RER
0
1 mile
1 km

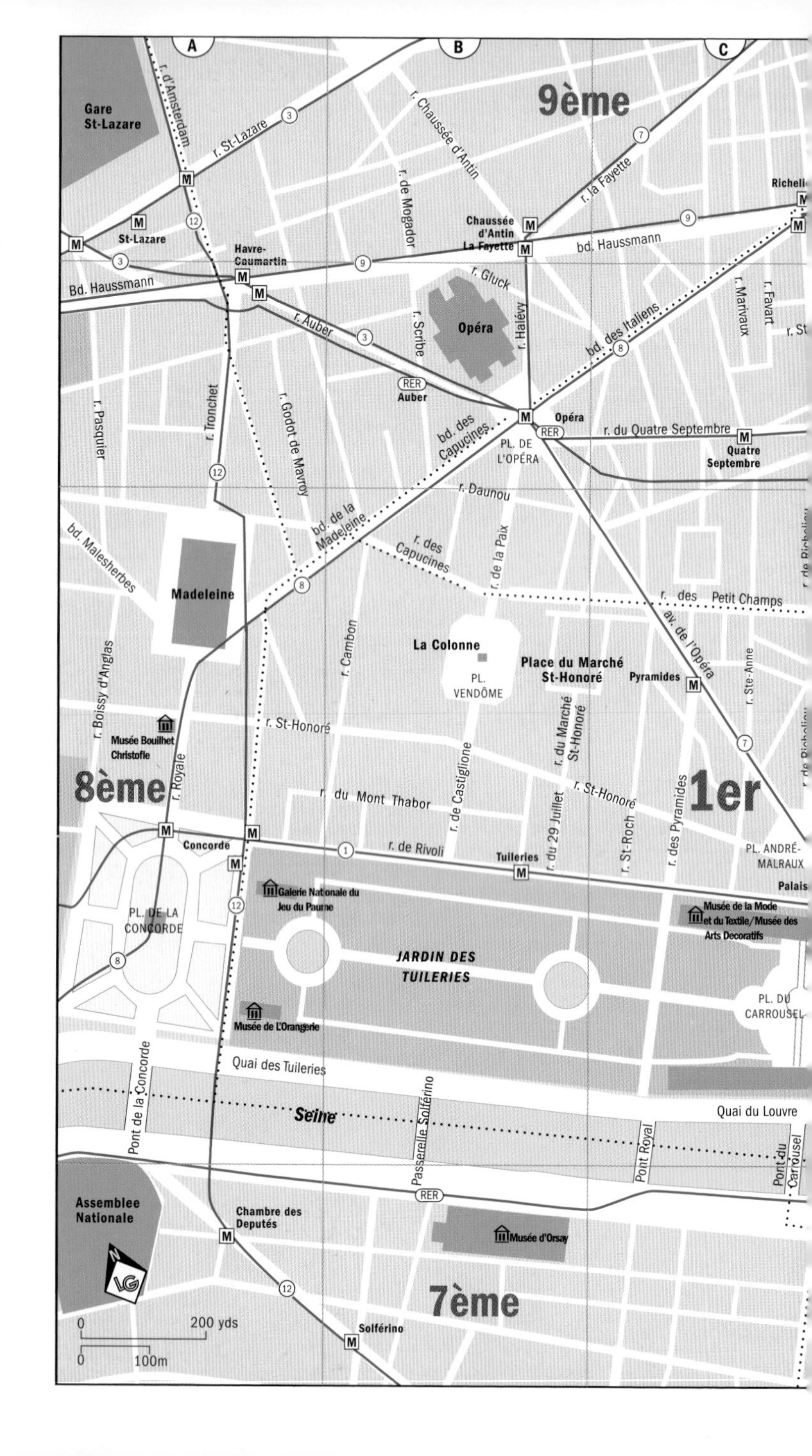

A
B
C
9ème
Gare St-Lazare
r. d'Amsterdam
r. St-Lazare
r. Chaussée d'Antin
r. de Mogador
r. la Fayette
St-Lazare
Havre-Caumartin
Chaussée d'Antin La Fayette
bd. Haussmann
Bd. Haussmann
r. Gluck
r. Auber
r. Scribe
Opéra
r. Halévy
bd. des Italiens
r. Marivaux
r. Favart
RER
Auber
r. Tronchet
r. Pasquier
r. Godot de Mavroy
bd. des Capucines
PL. DE L'OPÉRA
r. du Quatre Septembre
Quatre Septembre
r. Daunou
bd. Malesherbes
bd. de la Madeleine
r. des Capucines
r. de la Paix
Madeleine
r. des Petit Champs
av. de l'Opéra
La Colonne
PL. VENDÔME
Place du Marché St-Honoré
Pyramides
r. Cambon
r. Boissy d'Anglas
r. St-Honoré
Musée Bouilhet Christofle
r. Ste-Anne
8ème
r. Royale
r. du Mont Thabor
r. de Castiglione
r. du Marché St-Honoré
r. du 29 Juillet
r. St-Roch
r. des Pyramides
1er
Concorde
r. de Rivoli
Tuileries
PL. ANDRÉ-MALRAUX
Galerie Nationale du Jeu du Paume
PL. DE LA CONCORDE
Musée de la Mode et du Textile/Musée des Arts Decoratifs
JARDIN DES TUILERIES
PL. DU CARROUSEL
Musée de L'Orangerie
Quai des Tuileries
Pont de la Concorde
Seine
Passerelle Solférino
Pont Royal
Quai du Louvre
Pont du Carrousel
Assemblee Nationale
Chambre des Deputés
Musée d'Orsay
7ème
0
200 yds
100m
Solférino

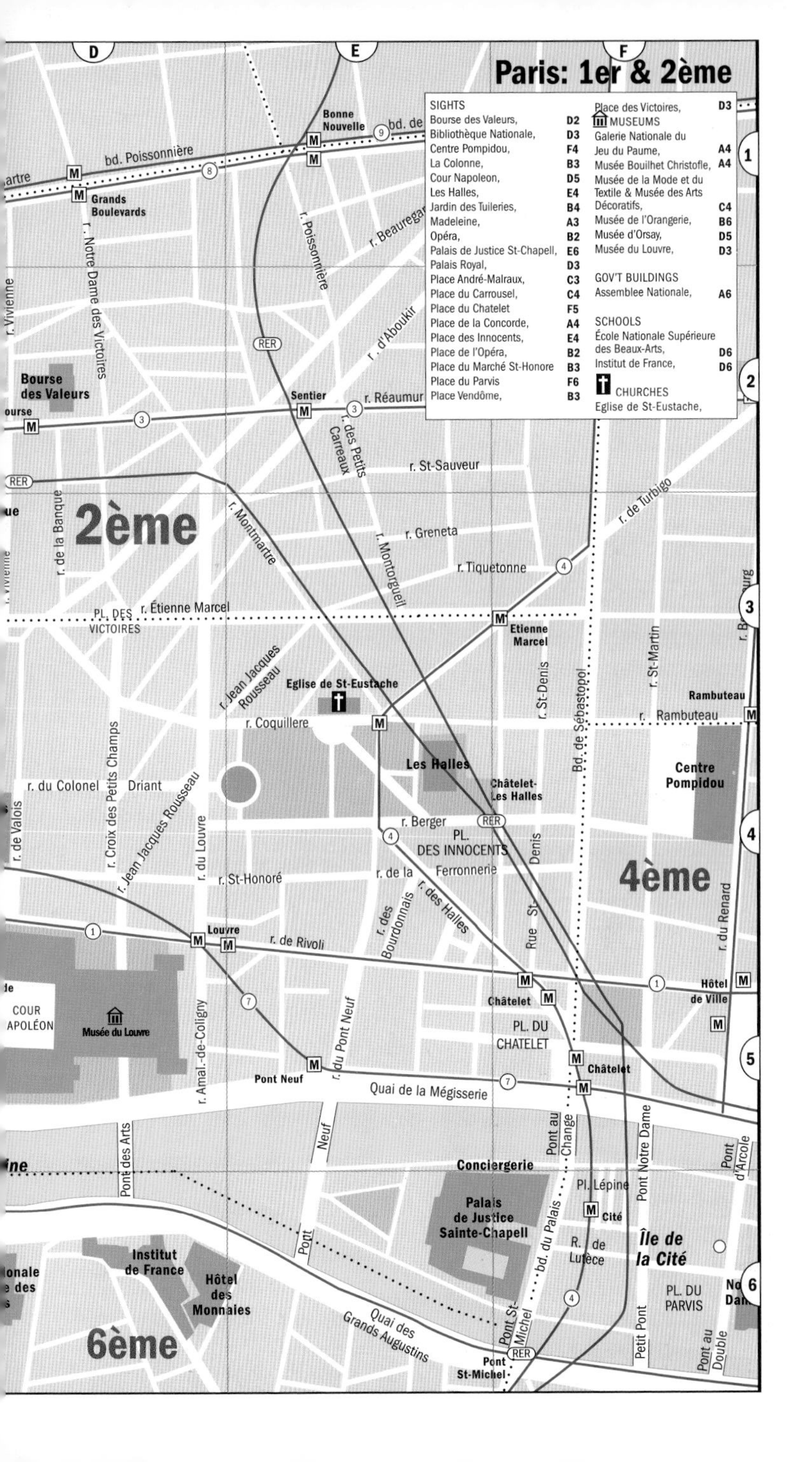
Paris: 1er & 2ème
SIGHTS
Bourse des Valeurs, D2
Bibliothèque Nationale, D3
Centre Pompidou, F4
La Colonne, B3
Cour Napoleon, D5
Les Halles, E4
Jardin des Tuileries, B4
Madeleine, A3
Opéra, B2
Palais de Justice St-Chapell, E6
Palais Royal, D3
Place André-Malraux, C3
Place du Carrousel, C4
Place du Chatelet F5
Place de la Concorde, A4
Place des Innocents, E4
Place de l'Opéra, B2
Place du Marché St-Honore B3
Place du Parvis F6
Place Vendôme, B3
Place des Victoires, D3
MUSEUMS
Galerie Nationale du Jeu du Paume, A4
Musée Bouilhet Christofle, A4
Musée de la Mode et du Textile & Musée des Arts Décoratifs, C4
Musée de l'Orangerie, B6
Musée d'Orsay, D5
Musée du Louvre, D3
GOV'T BUILDINGS
Assemblee Nationale, A6
SCHOOLS
École Nationale Supérieure des Beaux-Arts, D6
Institut de France, D6
CHURCHES
Eglise de St-Eustache,
D
E
F
1
2
3
4
5
6
bd. Poissonnière
Bonne Nouvelle
Grands Boulevards
r. Notre Dame des Victoires
r. Poissonnière
r. Beauregard
r. d'Aboukir
Bourse des Valeurs
Sentier
r. Réaumur
r. des Petits Carreaux
r. St-Sauveur
2ème
r. de la Banque
r. Montmartre
r. Greneta
r. Montorgueil
r. Tiquetonne
r. de Turbigo
PL. DES VICTOIRES
r. Étienne Marcel
Etienne Marcel
r. Jean Jacques Rousseau
Eglise de St-Eustache
r. St-Denis
Bd. de Sébastopol
r. St-Martin
Rambuteau
r. Rambuteau
r. Coquillere
Les Halles
Châtelet-Les Halles
Centre Pompidou
r. du Colonel Driant
r. Croix des Petits Champs
r. du Louvre
r. de Valois
r. Berger
PL. DES INNOCENTS
r. de la Ferronnerie
r. St-Honoré
4ème
r. du Renard
r. des Bourdonnais
r. des Halles
Rue St-Denis
Louvre
r. de Rivoli
Châtelet
Hôtel de Ville
COUR NAPOLÉON
Musée du Louvre
r. Amal.-de-Coligny
r. du Pont Neuf
PL. DU CHATELET
Pont Neuf
Quai de la Mégisserie
Pont des Arts
Pont Neuf
Conciergerie
Pont au Change
Pont Notre Dame
Pont d'Arcole
Pl. Lépine
Palais de Justice Sainte-Chapell
Cité
bd. du Palais
R. de Lutèce
Île de la Cité
Institut de France
Hôtel des Monnaies
PL. DU PARVIS
Quai des Grands Augustins
6ème
Pont St-Michel
Petit Pont
Pont au Double
RER

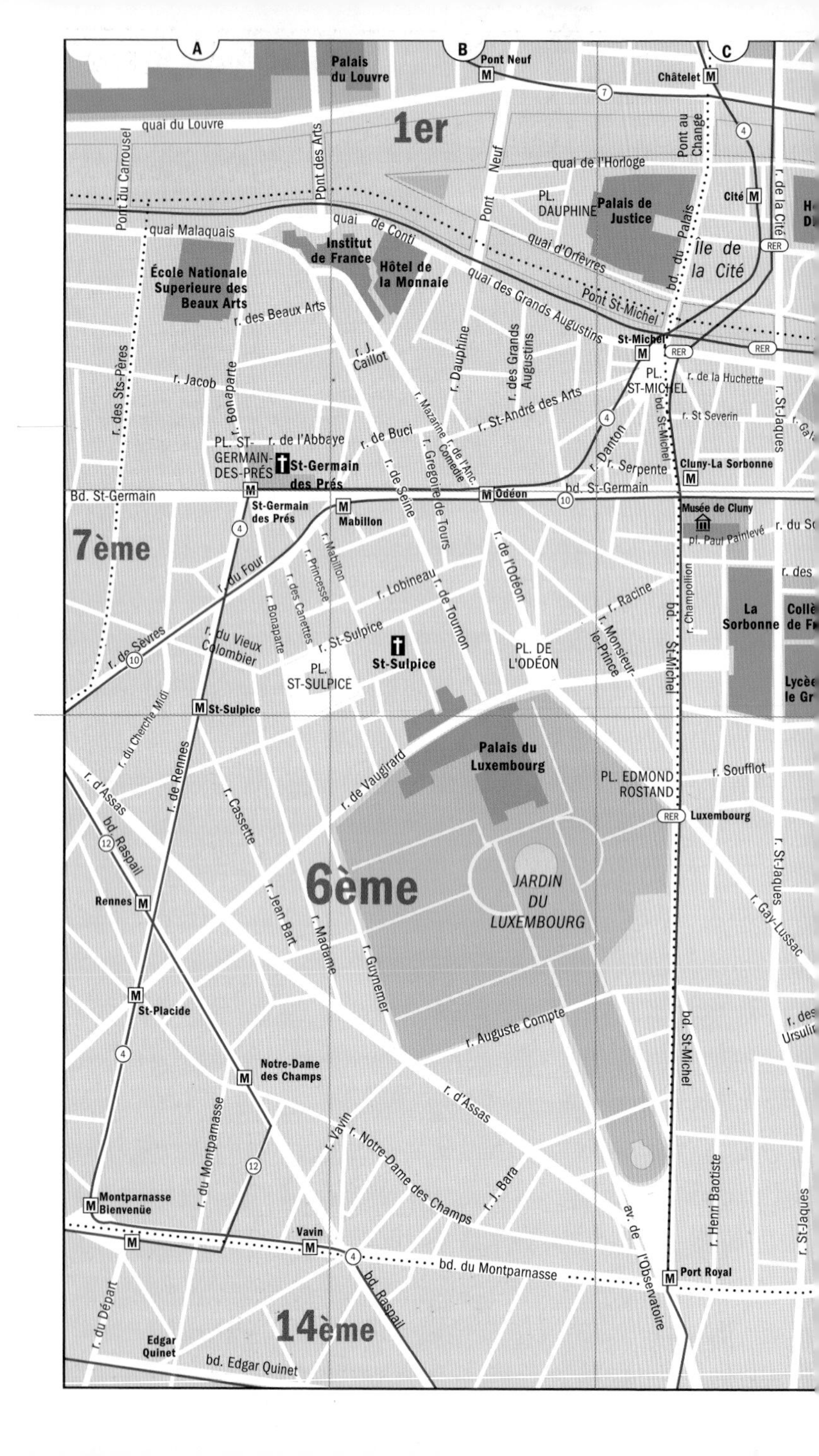

A
B
C
Palais du Louvre
Pont Neuf
Châtelet
1er
quai du Louvre
Pont du Carrousel
Pont des Arts
Pont Neuf
quai de l'Horloge
Pont au Change
PL. DAUPHINE
Palais de Justice
Cité
r. de la Cité
quai Malaquais
quai de Conti
Institut de France
Hôtel de la Monnaie
quai d'Orfèvres
Île de la Cité
bd. du Palais
École Nationale Superieure des Beaux Arts
quai des Grands Augustins
Pont St-Michel
r. des Beaux Arts
St-Michel
RER
r. J. Caillot
r. Dauphine
r. des Grands Augustins
r. des Sts-Pères
r. Jacob
r. Bonaparte
PL. ST-MICHEL
r. de la Huchette
r. St Severin
r. St-Jaques
r. St-André des Arts
r. Mazarine
r. de l'Anc. Comédie
bd. St-Michel
PL. ST-GERMAIN-DES-PRÉS
r. de l'Abbaye
r. de Buci
St-Germain des Prés
r. Danton
r. Serpente
Cluny-La Sorbonne
r. de Seine
r. Gregoire de Tours
Bd. St-Germain
Odéon
bd. St-Germain
Musée de Cluny
St-Germain des Prés
Mabillon
pl. Paul Painlevé
7ème
r. du Four
r. Mabillon
r. Princesse
r. de l'Odéon
r. Lobineau
r. de Tournon
r. des Canettes
r. Bonaparte
r. Racine
bd. St-Michel
r. Champollion
La Sorbonne
r. de Sèvres
r. du Vieux Colombier
r. St-Sulpice
St-Sulpice
PL. DE L'ODÉON
r. Monsieur-le-Prince
PL. ST-SULPICE
St-Sulpice
r. du Cherche Midi
Palais du Luxembourg
r. Soufflot
PL. EDMOND ROSTAND
r. de Vaugirard
r. d'Assas
r. de Rennes
r. Cassette
Luxembourg
bd. Raspail
r. St-Jaques
JARDIN DU LUXEMBOURG
6ème
Rennes
r. Jean Bart
r. Madame
r. Gay-Lussac
r. Guynemer
St-Placide
r. Auguste Compte
bd. St-Michel
Notre-Dame des Champs
r. d'Assas
r. du Montparnasse
r. Vavin
r. Notre-Dame des Champs
r. J. Bara
av. de l'Observatoire
r. Henri Baotiste
r. St-Jaques
Montparnasse Bienvenüe
Vavin
bd. du Montparnasse
Port Royal
bd. Raspail
r. du Départ
14ème
Edgar Quinet
bd. Edgar Quinet

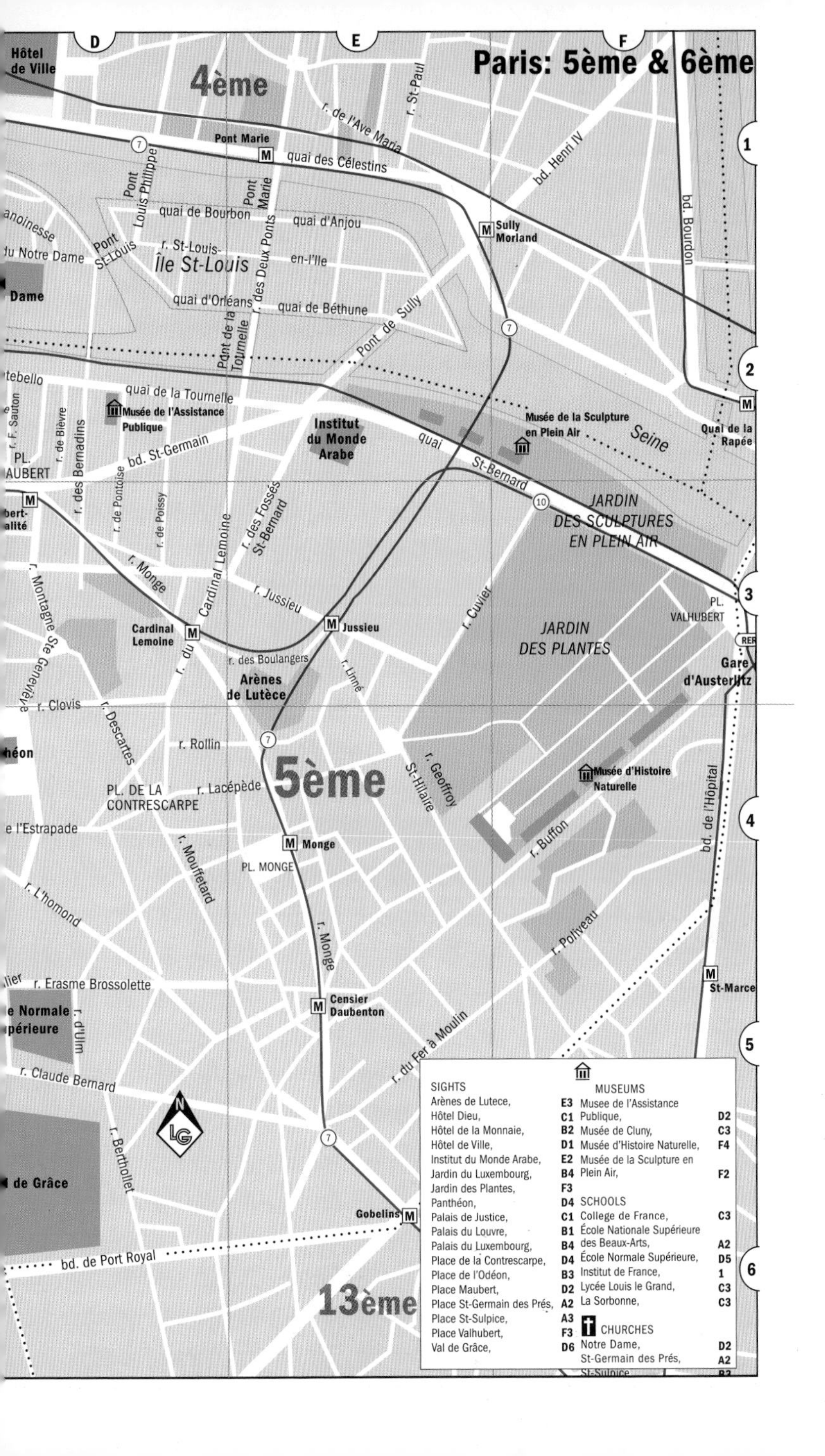
Paris: 5ème & 6ème
D
E
F
1
2
3
4
5
6
4ème
5ème
13ème
Hôtel de Ville
Pont Marie
quai des Célestins
r. de l'Ave Maria
r. St-Paul
bd. Henri IV
bd. Bourdon
Pont Louis Philippe
Pont Marie
quai de Bourbon
quai d'Anjou
Pont St-Louis
r. St-Louis-en-l'Ile
Île St-Louis
r. des Deux Ponts
quai d'Orléans
quai de Béthune
Pont de Sully
Pont de la Tournelle
Sully Morland
quai de la Tournelle
Musée de l'Assistance Publique
Institut du Monde Arabe
Musée de la Sculpture en Plein Air
Seine
Quai de la Rapée
quai St-Bernard
JARDIN DES SCULPTURES EN PLEIN AIR
bd. St-Germain
PL. MAUBERT
r. des Bernadins
r. de Bièvre
r. F. Sauton
r. de Pontoise
r. de Poissy
r. du Cardinal Lemoine
r. des Fossés St-Bernard
r. Monge
r. Jussieu
Jussieu
Cardinal Lemoine
r. Cuvier
JARDIN DES PLANTES
PL. VALHUBERT
Gare d'Austerlitz
r. des Boulangers
Arènes de Lutèce
r. Linné
r. Montagne Ste Geneviève
r. Clovis
r. Descartes
r. Rollin
PL. DE LA CONTRESCARPE
r. Lacépède
r. Geoffroy St-Hilaire
Musée d'Histoire Naturelle
r. Buffon
bd. de l'Hôpital
r. de l'Estrapade
r. Mouffetard
Monge
PL. MONGE
r. L'homond
r. Monge
r. Poliveau
St-Marcel
r. Erasme Brossolette
École Normale Supérieure
r. d'Ulm
Censier Daubenton
r. du Fer à Moulin
r. Claude Bernard
r. Berthollet
de Grâce
Gobelins
bd. de Port Royal
SIGHTS
Arènes de Lutece, E3
Hôtel Dieu, C1
Hôtel de la Monnaie, B2
Hôtel de Ville, D1
Institut du Monde Arabe, E2
Jardin du Luxembourg, B4
Jardin des Plantes, F3
Panthéon, D4
Palais de Justice, C1
Palais du Louvre, B1
Palais du Luxembourg, B4
Place de la Contrescarpe, D4
Place de l'Odéon, B3
Place Maubert, D2
Place St-Germain des Prés, A2
Place St-Sulpice, A3
Place Valhubert, F3
Val de Grâce, D6
MUSEUMS
Musee de l'Assistance Publique, D2
Musée de Cluny, C3
Musée d'Histoire Naturelle, F4
Musée de la Sculpture en Plein Air, F2
SCHOOLS
College de France, C3
École Nationale Supérieure des Beaux-Arts, A2
École Normale Supérieure, D5
Institut de France, 1
Lycée Louis le Grand, C3
La Sorbonne, C3
CHURCHES
Notre Dame, D2
St-Germain des Prés, A2

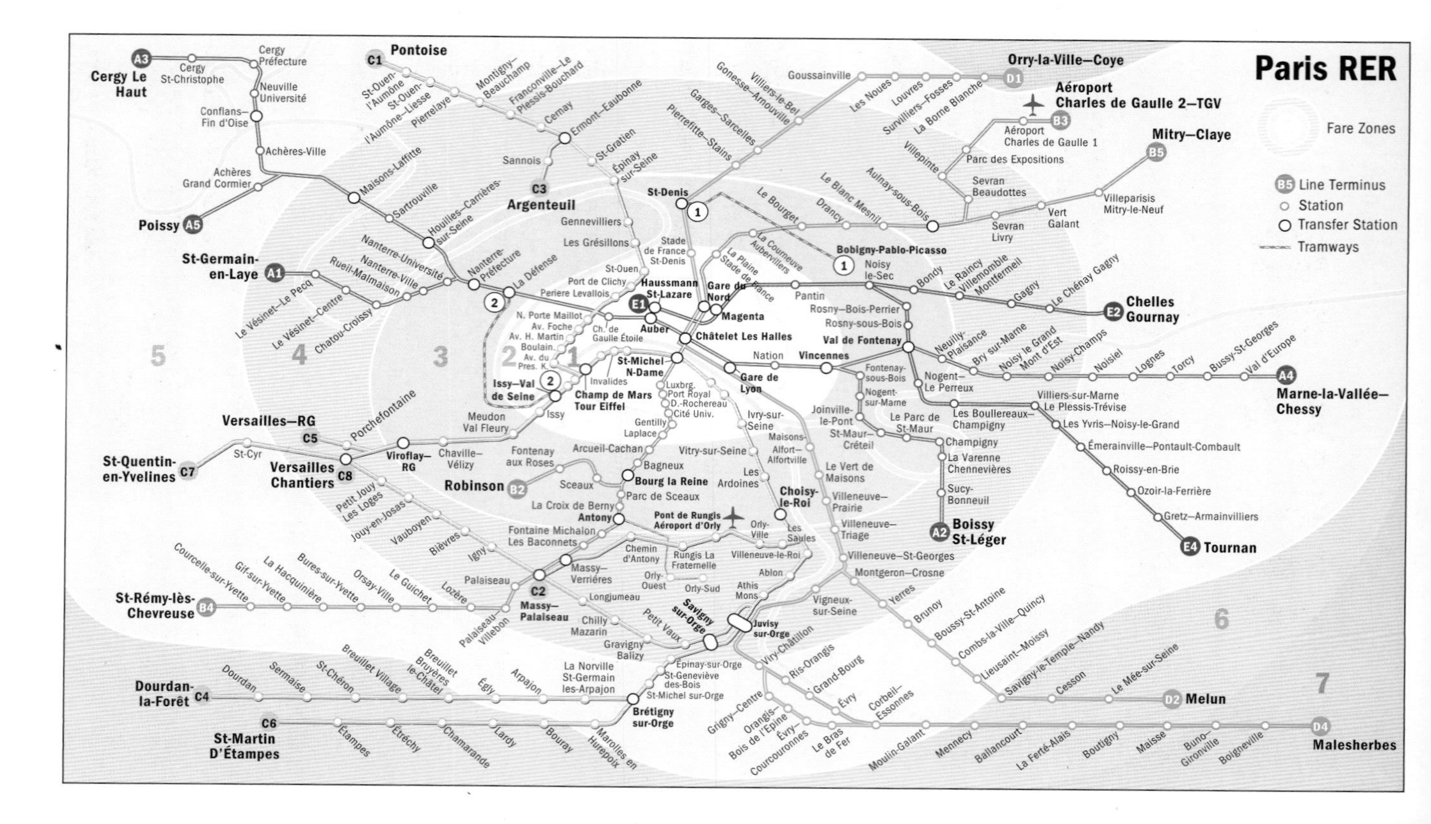

Paris RER
Fare Zones
B5 Line Terminus
Station
Transfer Station
Tramways
1
2
3
4
5
6
7
A3 Cergy Le Haut
Cergy St-Christophe
Cergy Préfecture
Neuville Université
Conflans–Fin d'Oise
Achères-Ville
Achères Grand Cormier
A5 Poissy
Maisons-Laffitte
Sartrouville
Houilles–Carrières-sur-Seine
A1 St-Germain-en-Laye
Le Vésinet–Le Pecq
Le Vésinet–Centre
Chatou-Croissy
Rueil-Malmaison
Nanterre-Ville
Nanterre-Université
Nanterre-Préfecture
La Défense
C1 Pontoise
St-Ouen-l'Aumône
St-Ouen-l'Aumône–Liesse
Pierrelaye
Montigny–Beauchamp
Franconville–Le Plessis-Bouchard
Cernay
Ermont-Eaubonne
Sannois
C3 Argenteuil
St-Gratien
Épinay sur-Seine
Gennevilliers
Les Grésillons
St-Ouen
Port de Clichy
Periere Levallois
N. Porte Maillot
Av. Foche
Av. H. Martin
Boulain.
Av. du Pres. K.
Ch. de Gaulle Étoile
Haussmann St-Lazare
E1
Auber
Gare du Nord
Magenta
Châtelet Les Halles
Stade de France St-Denis
St-Denis
Goussainville
Les Noues
Louvres
Survilliers–Fosses
La Borne Blanche
D1 Orry-la-Ville–Coye
Villiers-le-Bel Gonesse–Arnouville
Garges–Sarcelles
Pierrefitte–Stains
La Plaine Stade de France
La Courneuve Aubervilliers
Le Bourget
Drancy
Le Blanc Mesnil
Aulnay-sous-Bois
Villepinte
Parc des Expositions
Aéroport Charles de Gaulle 1
B3 Aéroport Charles de Gaulle 2–TGV
Sevran Beaudottes
Sevran Livry
Vert Galant
Villeparisis Mitry-le-Neuf
B5 Mitry–Claye
Bobigny-Pablo-Picasso
Noisy le-Sec
Pantin
Bondy
Le Raincy Villemomble Montfermeil
Gagny
Le Chénay Gagny
E2 Chelles Gournay
Rosny–Bois-Perrier
Rosny-sous-Bois
Val de Fontenay
Neuilly-Plaisance
Bry sur-Marne
Noisy le Grand Mont d'Est
Noisy-Champs
Noisiel
Lognes
Torcy
Bussy-St-Georges
Val d'Europe
A4 Marne-la-Vallée–Chessy
Nogent–Le Perreux
Les Boullereaux–Champigny
Villiers-sur-Marne Le Plessis-Trévise
Les Yvris–Noisy-le-Grand
Émerainville–Pontault-Combault
Roissy-en-Brie
Ozoir-la-Ferrière
Gretz–Armainvilliers
E4 Tournan
Nation
Vincennes
Fontenay-sous-Bois
Nogent-sur-Marne
Joinville-le-Pont
St-Maur–Créteil
Le Parc de St-Maur
Champigny
La Varenne Chennevières
Sucy-Bonneuil
A2 Boissy St-Léger
Gare de Lyon
St-Michel N-Dame
Invalides
Champ de Mars Tour Eiffel
Issy–Val de Seine
Issy
Meudon Val Fleury
Chaville–Vélizy
Viroflay–RG
Porchefontaine
C5 Versailles–RG
C8 Versailles Chantiers
St-Cyr
C7 St-Quentin-en-Yvelines
Luxbrg.
Port Royal
D.-Rochereau
Cité Univ.
Gentilly
Laplace
Arcueil-Cachan
Bagneux
Bourg la Reine
Parc de Sceaux
Fontenay aux Roses
Sceaux
B2 Robinson
La Croix de Berny
Antony
Fontaine Michalon
Les Baconnets
Massy–Verrières
C2 Massy–Palaiseau
Palaiseau
Palaiseau–Villebon
Lozère
Le Guichet
Orsay-Ville
Bures-sur-Yvette
La Hacquinière
Gif-sur-Yvette
Courcelle-sur-Yvette
B4 St-Rémy-lès-Chevreuse
Petit Jouy Les Loges
Jouy-en-Josas
Vauboyen
Bièvres
Igny
Ivry-sur-Seine
Vitry-sur-Seine
Les Ardoines
Maisons-Alfort–Alfortville
Choisy-le-Roi
Le Vert de Maisons
Villeneuve–Prairie
Villeneuve–Triage
Villeneuve–St-Georges
Montgeron–Crosne
Yerres
Brunoy
Boussy-St-Antoine
Combs-la-Ville–Quincy
Lieusaint–Moissy
Savigny-le-Temple–Nandy
Cesson
Le Mée-sur-Seine
D2 Melun
Pont de Rungis Aéroport d'Orly
Orly-Ville
Les Saules
Chemin d'Antony
Rungis La Fraternelle
Orly-Ouest
Orly-Sud
Villeneuve-le-Roi
Ablon
Athis Mons
Juvisy sur-Orge
Vigneux-sur-Seine
Savigny sur-Orge
Petit Vaux
Longjumeau
Chilly Mazarin
Gravigny Balizy
Épinay-sur-Orge
St-Geneviève des-Bois
St-Michel sur-Orge
Brétigny sur-Orge
La Norville St-Germain les-Arpajon
Arpajon
Égly
Breuillet Bruyères le-Châtel
Breuillet Village
St-Chéron
Sermaise
Dourdan
C4 Dourdan-la-Forêt
Marolles en Hurepoix
Bouray
Lardy
Chamarande
Étréchy
Étampes
C6 St-Martin D'Étampes
Viry-Châtillon
Ris-Orangis
Grand-Bourg
Évry
Corbeil-Essonnes
Grigny–Centre
Orangis–Bois de l'Epine
Évry–Courcouronnes
Le Bras de Fer
Moulin-Galant
Mennecy
Ballancourt
La Ferté-Alais
Boutigny
Maisse
Buno–Gironville
Boigneville
D4 Malesherbes

LET'S GO

PAGES PACKED WITH ESSENTIAL INFORMATION

"Value-packed, unbeatable, accurate, and comprehensive."

—The Los Angeles Times

"The guides are aimed not only at young budget travelers but at the independent traveler; a sort of streetwise cookbook for traveling alone."

—The New York Times

"Unbeatable; good sight-seeing advice; up-to-date info on restaurants, hotels, and inns; a commitment to money-saving travel; and a wry style that brightens nearly every page."

—The Washington Post

THE BEST TRAVEL BARGAINS IN YOUR BUDGET

"All the dirt, dirt cheap."

—People

"Let's Go follows the creed that you don't have to toss your life's savings to the wind to travel—unless you want to."

—The Salt Lake Tribune

REAL ADVICE FOR REAL EXPERIENCES

"The writers seem to have experienced every rooster-packed bus and lunar-surfaced mattress about which they write."

—The New York Times

"[Let's Go's] devoted updaters really walk the walk (and thumb the ride, and trek the trail). Learn how to fish, haggle, find work—anywhere."

—Food & Wine

"A world-wise traveling companion—always ready with friendly advice and helpful hints, all sprinkled with a bit of wit."

—The Philadelphia Inquirer

A GUIDE WITH A SPIRIT AND A SOCIAL CONSCIENCE

"Lighthearted and sophisticated, informative and fun to read. [Let's Go] helps the novice traveler navigate like a knowledgeable old hand."

—Atlanta Journal-Constitution

"The serious mission at the book's core reveals itself in exhortations to respect the culture and the environment—and, if possible, to visit as a volunteer, a student, or a teacher rather than a tourist."

—San Francisco Chronicle

LET'S GO PUBLICATIONS

TRAVEL GUIDES

Australia
Austria & Switzerland
Brazil
Britain
California
Central America
Chile
China
Costa Rica
Eastern Europe
Ecuador
Egypt
Europe
France
Germany
Greece
Hawaii
India & Nepal
Ireland
Israel
Italy
Japan
Mexico
New Zealand
Peru
Puerto Rico
Southeast Asia
Spain & Portugal with Morocco
Thailand
USA
Vietnam
Western Europe

ROADTRIP GUIDE

Roadtripping USA

ADVENTURE GUIDES

Alaska
Pacific Northwest
Southwest USA

CITY GUIDES

Amsterdam
Barcelona
Boston
Buenos Aires
London
New York City
Paris
Rome
San Francisco
Washington, DC

POCKET CITY GUIDES

Amsterdam
Berlin
Boston
Chicago
London
New York City
Paris
San Francisco
Venice
Washington, DC

LET'S GO

EUROPE

2009

JASON MEYER EDITOR

ASSOCIATE EDITORS

RONAN DEVLIN
JUN LI
KRYSTEN KECHES
LINGBO LI
NICKCLETTE IZUEGBU

RESEARCHER-WRITERS

RACHEL BANAY
ANDREW MOORE
AMANDA MANGASER
EMILY NAPHTAL
MEGHA MAJUMDAR
ALYSSA STACHOWSKI
ASHLEY MESSINA
CATHERINE ZIELINSKI

DEREK WETZEL MAP EDITOR
VANESSA DUBE MANAGING EDITOR

ST. MARTIN'S PRESS NEW YORK

HELPING LET'S GO. If you want to share your discoveries, suggestions, or corrections, please drop us a line. We appreciate every piece of correspondence, whether a postcard, a 10-page email, or a coconut. Visit Let's Go at **http://www.letsgo.com,** or send email to:

feedback@letsgo.com
Subject: "Let's Go: Europe"

Address mail to:

Let's Go: Europe
67 Mount Auburn St.
Cambridge, MA 02138
USA

In addition to the invaluable travel advice our readers share with us, many are kind enough to offer their services as researchers or editors. Unfortunately, our charter enables us to employ only currently enrolled Harvard students.

Distributed outside the USA and Canada by Macmillan.

ISBN-13: 978-0-312-38708-2
ISBN-10: 0-312-38708-3
First edition
10 9 8 7 6 5 4 3 2 1

Let's Go: Europe is written by Let's Go Publications, 67 Mount Auburn St., Cambridge, MA 02138, USA.

HOW TO USE THIS BOOK

Conquering the great continent that is **Europe** is no easy task. Yes, dear reader, there are many mysteries in this Old World. That is why you have come to us. We will be your Virgil, teaching you the art of budget travel. We will guide you through Genoa's labyrinthine *vicoli* and Vilnius's breakaway artists' republic. From old-school Parisian cafes to unexplored limestone karsts on Croatia's Dalmatian Coast, this continent—like a coffee shop in Amsterdam—has it. And our gritty, dutiful researchers have fanned out to Irish shoals and Russian *stolis*, between Norway's herring pickling factories and Austria's posh ski towns, to bring you the freshest, most comprehensive travel guide ever produced. Here's how to use it:

COVERING THE BASICS. The first chapter is **Discover** (p. 1). Its purpose is to help you find the best this Earth has to offer. If you prefer people telling you what to do (or just want some ideas), check out this chapter's **suggested itineraries.** The **Essentials** (p. 14) section gets down to the nitty-gritty, detailing the info you'll need to get around and stay safe on your journey. The **Transportation** (p. 46) section will help you get to and around Europe, while the **Beyond Tourism** (p. 60) chapter suggests ways to work and volunteer your way across the Continent. Then we get to the meat of the book: 34 **country chapters,** organized alphabetically. The **Appendix** (p. 1058) has a weather chart for major cities and a handy dandy phrasebook with nine languages to help you say "I'm lost," land a bed, or find your way to a bathroom no matter where you are.

TRANSPORTATION INFO. Because you've told *Let's Go* you're traveling on budget airlines, we've created a new transportation format to help you navigate getting to where you really want to go from that random town an hour away: **Regional Hubs,** listed in the Intercity Transportation section of major cities. We've also collected info on bus, ferry, and train routes; these range from solid Spanish AVE schedules to, well, any transportation in Romania.

RANKINGS AND FEATURES. Our researchers list establishments in order of value from best to worst, with absolute favorites denoted by the *Let's Go* thumbpick. Since the lowest price does not always mean the best value, we've incorporated a system of price ranges (❶-❺) for food and accommodations. Tipboxes come in a variety of flavors: warnings, helpful hints and resources, insider deals, cheap finds, and then a smattering of stuff you should know.

AWESOMENESS. From ☎ codes to avoiding scams, from the best borscht to the boldest brews, we'll guide you through the souvenir-cluttered jungle of the old-school Europa to the most authentic food, craziest nightlife, and most mind-bendingly beautiful landscapes around. Start in Brussels, in Stockholm, in Moscow. Open this bad boy up, and select your own adventure.

A NOTE TO OUR READERS. The information for this book was gathered by Let's Go researchers from May through August of 2008. Each listing is based on one researcher's opinion, formed during his or her visit at a particular time. Those traveling at other times may have different experiences since prices, dates, hours, and conditions are always subject to change. You are urged to check the facts presented in this book beforehand to avoid inconvenience and surprises.

CONTENTS

DISCOVER EUROPE 1
Tackling Europe 1
When to Go 1
What to Do 2
Suggested Itineraries 6

ESSENTIALS 14
Planning Your Trip 14
Safety and Health 23
Keeping in Touch 30
Accommodations 33
The Great Outdoors 37
Specific Concerns 40
Other Resources 44

TRANSPORTATION 46
Getting to Europe 46
Getting Around Europe 50

BEYOND TOURISM................60
A Philosophy for Travelers 60
Volunteering 60
Studying 62
Working 64

AUSTRIA 69
Vienna (Wien) 73
Linz 85
Salzburger Land and Hohe Tauern Region 85
Salzburg 86
Zell Am See 90
Hohe Tauern National Park 91
Tyrol (Tirol) 92
Innsbruck 92
Styria (Steiermark) 96
Graz 96

BELGIUM 98
Brussels (Bruxelles, Brussel) 102
Flanders (Vlaanderen) 107
Bruges (Brugge) 107
Antwerp (Antwerpen, Anvers) 111
Ghent (Gent) 112
Ypres (Ieper) 114
Wallonie 114
Liège (Luik) 114
Tournai (Doornik) 115
Namur 116
Dinant 116

GREAT BRITAIN 117
England 123
London 123
Southern England 150
Canterbury 150
Salisbury 151
Bath 152
Glastonbury 153
The Cornish Coast 154
Penzance 154
East Anglia and the Midlands 155
Oxford 155
Stratford-Upon-Avon 159
Birmingham 160
Cambridge 162
Northern England 165
Manchester 165
Liverpool 167
Peak District National Park 169
York 170
Newcastle-Upon-Tyne 173
Hadrian's Wall 174
Isle of Man 175
Douglas 176

WALES 178
Cardiff (Caerdydd) 178
Wye Valley 179
Chepstow 180
Tintern 180
Snowdonia National Park 180
Harlech 181
Caernarfon 181
Conwy 182

SCOTLAND........................182
Edinburgh 183
Glasgow 190
Stirling 193

The Trossachs 193
Loch Lomond 195
Inverness and Loch Ness 195
Fort William and Ben Nevis 196

BULGARIA 197
Sofia (София) 202
Plovdiv (Пловдив) 207
Veliko Turnovo (Велико Търново) 208
Varna (Варна) 208

CROATIA 210
Zagreb 215
Plitvice Lakes National Park 219
Northern Coast 220
Rijeka 220
Krk Town on Krk Island 221
Pula (Pola) 222
Rovinj 223
Dalmatian Coast 223
Zadar 224
Split 224
Brač Island: Bol 226
Dubrovnik 226

CZECH REPUBLIC 230
Prague (Praha) 235
West and South Bohemia 248
Karlovy Vary 248
České Budějovice 249
Český Krumlov 250
Moravia 251
Brno 251
Olomouc 252

DENMARK 253
Copenhagen (København) 258
Møn 267
Roskilde 267
Bornholm 268
Funen (Fyn) 269
Odense 269
Ærø 271
Jutland (Jylland) 271
Århus 271
Aalborg 273
Frederikshavn 273
Skagen 274

ESTONIA 275
Tallinn 279
Pärnu 283
Tartu 283
Estonian Islands 284
Saaremaa 284
Hiiumaa 285

FINLAND 286
Helsinki (Helsingfors) 290
Turku (Åbo) 298
Tampere 301
Savonlinna 302
Kuopio 303
Rovaniemi 304

FRANCE 305
Paris 311
Loire Valley (Val de Loire) 335
Orléans 335
Blois 336
Tours 337
Brittany (Bretagne) 338
Rennes 338
St-Malo 338
Dinan 339
Nantes 339
Normandy 340
Rouen 340
Caen 340
Bayeux 341
Mont-St-Michel 342
Flanders and Pas de Calais 342
Lille 343
Calais 343
Champagne and Burgundy 343
Reims 344
Épernay 344
Troyes 345
Dijon 345
Alsace-Lorraine and Franche-Comté 346
Strasbourg 346
La Route du Vin 347
Sélestat 348
Colmar 348
Nancy 349
Besançon 349
Rhône-Alpes and Massif Central 350
Lyon 350
Grenoble 355
Annecy 356

Chamonix 357
Le Mont-Dore 358
Dordogne and Limousin 358
Bourges 358
Périgueux 359
The Vézères Valley 359
Aquitaine and Pays Basque 360
Bordeaux 360
Bayonne 361
Parc National des Pyrénées 362
Cauterets 362
Languedoc-Roussillon 363
Toulouse 363
Carcassonne 364
Montpellier 365
Provence 365
Marseille 365
Aix-En-Provence 370
Avignon 371
Nîmes 371
French Riviera (Côte D'Azur) 372
Nice 372
Monaco and Monte-Carlo 377
Antibes 379
Cannes 379
St-Tropez 380
Corsica (La Corse) 380
Ajaccio (Aiacciu) 381
Bastia 381
Bonifacio (Bonifaziu) 382

GERMANY 383
Berlin 389
Northern Germany 409
Lübeck 410
Hamburg 410
Hanover (Hannover) 416
Central and Western Germany 417
Düsseldorf 417
Aachen 418
Cologne (Köln) 419
Bonn 423
Kassel 424
Frankfurt Am Main 425
Southwestern Germany 428
Trier 428
Rhine Valley (Rheintal) 429
Mainz 429
Lorelei Cliffs and Castles 430
Heidelberg 431
Stuttgart 434
Black Forest (Schwarzwald) 435
Constance (Konstanz) 435
Bavaria (Bayern) 436
Munich (München) 436
Nuremberg (Nürnberg) 442
Romantic Road 443
Füssen 444
Rothenburg Ob Der Tauber 444
Eastern Germany 445
Weimar 445
Eisenach 446
Wittenberg 447
Dresden 447
Leipzig 451

GREECE 453
Athens (Αθηνα) 458
The Peloponnese (Πελοπονησος) 466
Patras (Πατρα) 466
Olympia (Ολυμπια) 467
Sparta (Σπαρτη) 468
Monemvasia (Μονεμβασια) 468
Nafplion (Ναυπλιο) 469
Northern and Central Greece 470
Thessaloniki (Θεσσαλονικη) 470
Mount Olympus (Ολυμπος Ορος) 474
Meteora and Kalambaka (Μετεωρα and Καλαμπακα) 475
Delphi (Δελφοι) 475
Zagorohoria 476
Ioannina 477
Ionian Islands (Ιόνια Νησιά) 478
Corfu (Κέρκυρα) 478
ZaKynthos (Ζάκυνθος) 479
Cyclades (Κυκλάδες) 479
Mykonos (Μύκονος) 479
Paros (Πάρος) 480
Naxos (Νάξος) 482
Ios (Ίος) 482
Santorini (Σαντορίνη) 483
Crete (Kphth) 483
Heraklion (Ηρακλειο) 484
Knossos (Κνωσος) 485
Chania (Xania) 485
Rethymno (Ρεθυμνο) 486
Eastern Aegean Islands 487
Rhodes (Ρόδος) 487
Lesvos (Λέσβος) 487
Samothraki (Σαμοθράκη) 488

HUNGARY........................ 489
Budapest 494
Eger 506
Győr 508
Lake Balaton 509
Pécs 510

ICELAND.......................... 512
Reykjavík 518
Westman Islands (Vestmannaeyjar) 526
Landmannalaugar and Þórsmörk 528
Akureyri 528
Mývatn and Goðafoss 530
Húsavík 530
Jökulsárgljúfur National Park 531

IRELAND.......................... 532
Republic of Ireland 532
Dublin 537
Southeastern Ireland 546
The Wicklow Mountains 546
Kilkenny 547
Waterford 547
Cashel 548
Southwestern Ireland 548
Cork 549
Killarney and Killarney National Park 552
Ring of Kerry 554
Cahersiveen 554
Dingle Peninsula 554
Dingle Town 555
Slea Head, Ventry, and Dunquin 555
Western Ireland 555
The Cliffs of Moher and the Burren 556
Galway 557
Aran Islands (Oileáin Árann) 558
Connemara 558
Clifden and Connemara National Park 558
Sligo 559
Northwestern Ireland 560
Donegal Town (Dún Na Ngall) 560
Northern Ireland 561
Belfast (Béal Feirste) 561
Derry/Londonderry 567

ITALY.............................. 569
Rome 574
Lombardy (Lombardia) 596
Milan (Milano) 596
Bergamo 602
Mantua (Mantova) 602
The Lake Country 603
Italian Riviera (Liguria) 605
Genoa (Genova) 605
Finale Ligure 607
Camogli 607
Santa Margherita Ligure 607
Cinque Terre 608
Emilia-Romagna 609
Bologna 609
Parma 611
Ravenna 611
Rimini 612
Ferrara 613
Trentino-Alto Adige 614
Bolzano (Bozen) 614
Trent (Trento) 614
The Veneto 615
Venice (Venezia) 615
Padua (Padova) 626
Verona 626
Friuli-Venezia Giulia 628
Trieste (Triest) 628
Piedmont (Piemonte) 628
Turin (Torino) 628
Tuscany (Toscana) 630
Florence (Firenze) 630
Siena 640
Lucca 641
Pisa 641
Umbria 642
Perugia 642
Assisi 643
Orvieto 644
The Marches (Le Marche) 644
Urbino 644
Ancona 645
Campania 645
Naples (Napoli) 645
Bay Of Naples 650
Sorrento 650
Capri 651
The Amalfi Coast 651
Sicily (Sicilia) 653
Palermo 653

Syracuse (Siracusa) 654
Aeolian Islands (Isole Eolie) 654
Sardinia (Sardegna) 655
Cagliari 656
Alghero 656
Palau 656
La Maddalena Archipelago 657

LATVIA(LATVIJA)................ 658
Rīga 662

LIECHTENSTEIN................. 668
Vaduz and Lower Liechtenstein 669
Upper Liechtenstein 670

LITHUANIA....................... 671
Vilnius 675
Kaunas 679
Klaipėda 680
Nida 681
Palanga 681

LUXEMBOURG.................. 682
Luxembourg City 684
The Ardennes 689

MALTA............................. 691
Valletta 694

THE NETHERLANDS........... 700
Amsterdam 705
Haarlem 723
Leiden 724
The Hague (Den Haag) 725
Rotterdam 726
Utrecht 728
De Hoge Veluwe National Park 729
Groningen 729
Maastricht 730

NORWAY.......................... 731
Oslo 737
Lillehammer 745
Southern Norway 746
Kristiansand 746
Stavanger 747
The Fjords and West Norway 748
Bergen 748
The Oslo-Bergen Rail Line 753
Sognefjord 755
Nordfjord 757
Geirangerfjord 757
Geiranger 757
Lom, Jotunheimen, and Reinheimen 758
Romsdal and Trøndelag 759
Ålesund 759
Åndalsnes 760
Trondheim 761
Northern Norway 762
Tromsø 762
Lofoten Islands 764
Bodø 764
Moskenesøya 764
Vestvågøy 765
Svalbard Archipelago 766

POLAND.......................... 767
Warsaw (Warszawa) 772
Kraków 781
Lublin 788
Zakopane 789
Wrocław 790
Toruń 791
Łódź 793
Gdańsk 794
Sopot 798

PORTUGAL....................... 799
Lisbon (Lisboa) 804
Cascais 813
Sintra 813
Northern Portugal 814
Porto (Oporto) 814
Braga 816
Coimbra 817
Central Portugal 818
Évora 818
Algarve 819
Faro 819
Lagos 820

ROMANIA........................ 822
Bucharest (Bucureşti) 827
Sinaia 833
Transylvania (Transilvania) 834
Cluj-Napoca 834
Sighişoara 835
Braşov 835
Moldavia (Moldova) 836
Suceava 837
Constanţa 838

RUSSIA 839
Moscow (Москва) 846
St. Petersburg (Санкт-Петербург) 857

SLOVAKIA 867
Bratislava 871
The Tatra Mountains (Tatry) 876
Liptovský Mikuláš 876
Starý Smokovec 876
Košice 877

SLOVENIA 879
Ljubljana 882
Piran 885
Bled 886
Maribor 888

SPAIN 890
Madrid 896
Castilla la Mancha 907
Toledo 907
Castilla Y León 910
Segovia 910
Salamanca 911
Extremadura 913
Cáceres 913
Southern Spain 914
Córdoba 914
Seville (Sevilla) 917
Granada 924
Costa del Sol 928
Málaga 928
Tarifa 929
Gibraltar 930
Eastern Spain 931
Alicante (Alicant) 931
Valencia 932
Barcelona 934
Andorra 947
Andorra la Vella 948
Navarra 950
Pamplona (Iruña) 950
Basque Country (País Vasco) 952
San Sebastián (Donostia) 952
Bilbao (Bilbo) 955
Galicia (Galiza) 957
Santiago de Compostela 957
Balearic Islands 958
Mallorca 958
Ibiza 959

SWEDEN 960
Stockholm 965
Uppsala 976
Gotland 977
Southern Sweden (Skåne) 979
Kalmar and Öland 979
Malmö 980
Lund 981
Kåseberga 982
Ystad 983
Helsingborg 983
Gothenburg (Göteborg) 984
Central Sweden 988
Mora 989
Östersund 989
Åre 990
Gulf of Bothnia 990
Gävle 991
Örnsköldsvik 991
Umeå 992
Lappland (Sápmi) 993
Kiruna 993

SWITZERLAND.................. 995
German Switzerland 1000
Bernese Oberland 1000
Bern 1000
Jungfrau Region 1003
Interlaken 1003
Grindelwald 1006
Central Switzerland 1007
Zürich 1007
Luzern (Lucerne) 1012
St. Gallen 1014
Stein Am Rhein 1015
Northwestern Switzerland 1016
Basel (Bâle) 1016
Graubünden 1018
Davos 1018
Klosters 1018
Swiss National Park 1019
Valais 1020
Zermatt and the Matterhorn 1020
French Switzerland 1021

Geneva (Genève) 1021
Lausanne 1026
Italian Switzerland 1027
Lugano 1027

TURKEY **1028**
İstanbul 1034

UKRAINE **1046**
Kyiv (Київ) 1052
Lviv (Львів) 1056
Odessa (Одеса) 1057

APPENDIX **1058**
Climate 1058
Measurements 1058
Language Phrasebook 1059

INDEX **1071**

MAP INDEX **1082**

Europe
Reykjavík
ICELAND
300 miles
300 kilometers
Faroe Islands
Shetland Islands
Orkney Islands
North Sea
NORTHERN IRELAND
SCOTLAND
Glasgow
Edinburgh
Belfast
IRELAND
GREAT BRITAIN
Dublin
WALES
Cardiff
ENGLAND
London
NETHERLANDS
ATLANTIC OCEAN
Brussels
BELGIUM
LUXEMBOURG
Nantes
Paris
FRANCE
LIECHTENSTEIN
Zurich
SWITZERLAND
Bay of Biscay
Bordeaux
Lyon
Milan
Santiago de Compostela
Marseille
Nice
PORTUGAL
ANDORRA
MONACO
Madrid
Lisbon
Barcelona
Corsica (Fr.)
SPAIN
Valencia
Sardinia (It.)
Seville
Granada
Balearic Islands (Sp.)
Tangier
GIBRALTAR
Mediterranean Sea
Fez
Rabat
MOROCCO
ALGERIA
Algiers
Tunis
TUNISIA

Rovaniemi
Gulf of Bothnia
FINLAND
Oslo
SWEDEN
Helsinki
Tallinn
St. Petersburg
Stockholm
ESTONIA
Gothenburg
Riga
Moscow
LATVIA
Baltic Sea
LITHUANIA
Copenhagen
Vilnius
RUSSIA
RUSSIA
Gdansk
Minsk
Berlin
Warsaw
BELARUS
POLAND
Kiev
Prague
Kraków
CZECH REPUBLIC
Lviv
UKRAINE
SLOVAKIA
Bratislava
Vienna
MOLDOVA
Budapest
Sea of Azov
AUSTRIA
Chişinău
Ljubljana
Odessa
HUNGARY
SLOVENIA
ROMANIA
Yalta
Zagreb
CROATIA
Bucharest
BOSNIA AND HERZEGOVINA
Belgrade
Black Sea
Sarajevo
SERBIA AND MONTENEGRO
BULGARIA
Dubrovnik
KOSOVO
Sofia
Rome
Adriatic Sea
Istanbul
ITALY
Tirana
F.Y.R. MACEDONIA
Ankara
Thessaloniki
ALBANIA
TURKEY
GREECE
Aegean Sea
Izmir
Ionian Sea
Athens
Sicily
Nicosia
Sea
Sea of Crete
MALTA
LEBANON

RESEARCHER-WRITERS

Rachel Banay *Britain and Ireland*

After graduating from Harvard and hopping around Northern Ireland for *Let's Go: Britain*, Rachel joined the Europe team for a whirlwind tour of the Republic of Ireland. She impressed us with her ability to explore big cities within a single day and still have the time and energy to hit the pubs with new friends Guinness and Jameson.

Amanda Mangaser *Croatia, Greece, and Turkey*

While travelling the world, perhaps only in a swimsuit, Amanda's excitement about international exploration and vivid writing style left us anxiously waiting for more. Personal adversity, ferry schedules, cardboard box surprises, weeks in Athens... nothing fazed her wit or charm. Top prize for tales from the road on our most awesome route.

Megha Majumdar *Estonia, Latvia, Lithuania, Sweden, Malta*

A native of India, Megha joined *Let's Go* eager to begin researching her route. She covered a whopping five countries in just seven weeks, smiling through it all. Despite computer troubles and a rigorous itinerary, she added new coverage, savored blood sausage, climbed medieval towers, and even outwitted a swarm of vicious insects.

Ashley Messina *Czech Republic, Hungary, Poland, Slovakia*

Ashley fearlessly traversed four countries, expertly sampling local cuisines and always finding the top-shelf tea. Whether it was partying in Prague or finding the best *pierogi* in Poland, her excellent writing and timely, flawless copy kept the office running smoothly.

Andrew Moore *Finland, Iceland, Norway*

This accomplished skier was legendary for his crazy tales of roughin' it in Scandinavia—often choosing to forgo lodging expenses and sleep by the river and in a hotel lobby. Subsisting on mostly yogurt, he epitomized the B in budget. He'll soon be using his thrifty, hard-working charms as a US State Department employee.

Emily Naphtal *Austria, Switzerland, Liechtenstein, Slovenia*

Packing in four countries in two months, Emily proved to be quite the fighter. She biked through Slovenian castles and caves, experienced the Eurocup Fancamp in Salzburg, and even went skydiving after a computer meltdown in the Swiss Alps. Add a steaming cup of cappuccino and it was all in day's work for this determined researcher.

Alyssa Stachowski *Belgium, Denmark, Luxembourg, Netherlands*

Ridiculous, memorable moments filled the daily travels of Alyssa. Her tales never failed to amaze with their unique twists and turns, grooves and bumps. Ask about Copenhagen, Møn, and of course, Amsterdam—she may just leave you flabbergasted and hilariously entertained.

Catherine Zielinski *Bulgaria, Romania, Russia, Ukraine*

This researcher took on the Russian giants Moscow and St. Petersburg, mastering Cyrillic in the pursuit of perfect copy. A deadly time followed in Ukraine, while Romania and Bulgaria saw her hit her stride. Armed with charm and enthusiasm, she managed to wrangle a free Manu Chao concert. That's traveling like a true professional.

REGIONAL EDITORS AND RESEARCHER-WRITERS

LET'S GO: BRITAIN

Kimberly Hagan *Editor*
Charlie Riggs *Associate Editor*
Rachel Banay *Researcher-Writer*
Shoshanna Fine *Researcher-Writer*
Athena Jiang *Researcher-Writer*
Leslie Lee *Researcher-Writer*
Alanna Windsor *Researcher-Writer*
Diana Wise *Researcher-Writer*

LET'S GO: FRANCE

Colleen O'Brien *Editor*
Iya Megre *Associate Editor*
Mary Potter *Associate Editor*
Sarah Ashburn *Researcher-Writer*
Cicely Chen *Researcher-Writer*
Abigail Crutchfield *Researcher-Writer*
Edward-Michael Dussom *Researcher-Writer*
Vanda Gyuris *Researcher-Writer*
Joe Molimock *Researcher-Writer*

LET'S GO: GERMANY

Adam Estes	*Editor*
Arielle Fridson	*Associate Editor*
Aylin Erman	*Researcher-Writer*
Kayla Hammond	*Researcher-Writer*
Dana Kase	*Researcher-Writer*
Alexander McAdams	*Researcher-Writer*
Scott McKinney	*Researcher-Writer*
Leah Schwartz	*Researcher-Writer*

LET'S GO: ITALY

Raúl Carillo	*Editor*
Sara O'Rourke	*Associate Editor*
Matt Roller	*Associate Editor*
Mary Potter	*Associate Editor*
Mateo Corby	*Researcher-Writer*
Ashley Grand	*Researcher-Writer*
Paige Pavone	*Researcher-Writer*
Fabian Poliak	*Researcher-Writer*
Julia Rooney	*Researcher-Writer*
Ken Saathoff	*Researcher-Writer*

LET'S GO: PARIS

Samantha Gelfand	*Managing Editor*
Brianna Goodale	*Researcher-Editor*
Sara O'Rourke	*Researcher-Editor*

LET'S GO: SPAIN & PORTUGAL

Anna Kendrick	*Editor*
Meagan Michelson	*Associate Editor*
Daniel Barbero	*Associate Editor*
Jorge Alvarez	*Researcher-Writer*
Gabriela Bortolomedi	*Researcher-Writer*
Chimdimnma Esimai	*Researcher-Writer*
Jeffrey Phaneuf	*Researcher-Writer*
Russel Rennie	*Researcher-Writer*
Jessica Righthand	*Researcher-Writer*
Molly Strauss	*Researcher-Writer*

ACKNOWLEDGMENTS

TEAM EUROPE THANKS: Vanessa J. Dube for the edits, advice, and treats. Mr. Wetzel for providing clear direction and guidance. The digital saviors, InDesign tamers, and all-around playas PROD. Sam and Inés, leading the way with smiles and veteran wisdom. Laura Gordon for random fun and slosh ball. Pod-tastic award goes to Ricaloha, true audiophiles and brethren Mississippi-haters. Crunchalicious teams BRI/ITA/S&P/GER/FRA. The newly rebranded EUR Presents: Nick Traverse. Rachel, Amanda, Megha, Ashley, Andrew, Emily, Alyssa, and Catherine; thanks for blazing glorious trails of epic proportion through The Continent. Your coverage truly made this book possible, and your stories from the road kept us entertained all summer long.

JASON THANKS: RKJLN for a fantastic summer filled with tunes, red pens, and laughter. VDue-bee for sanity. Zen masters Alex and Jansen. Caroline for giving me mad people points. Daytrips, Alaskan salmon, and Costco. No thanks to Mississippi. Mom, Dad, the sisters, and tasty M&Ms. Uncle Pauly: rock on. Sori long ol jif mo bigbigman from ol rabis fasin. Presem masta Jisas Kraes.

RONAN THANKS: Thanks to Krysten for her sanity (a rare commodity), to Jun for laughing inappropriately, to Lingbo for being unique, to Nickclette for taking the piss out of us all. To Jason for being on the winning side, and Vanessa for baked goods. To Sanam for brightening the dullest of days, and to Mum, Dad and my siblings for always being there.

KRYSTEN THANKS: Jason, for fearlessly leading the Europod, ukulele in hand; Jun, for mango, strawberry-banana, and raspberry; Lingbo, for bus wisdom and crazy cooking; Nickclette, for Eurotrash and Riverdance; Ronan, for ladybirds, Spanish tortillas, and much-needed tunes; Vanessa, for delicious snacks and milkshake runs; Mom, Dad, Greg, and Tillie, for your love and support.

JUN THANKS: Dube, for her love of double-sided printing. Jason, for being the 007 of editors. Krysten, for being my index buddy. Lingbo, for reminding me of funny stories from our days in the Bestchester. Nickclette, for egging on our spazz-outs. Ronan, for putting up with my laughter. Austin, for everything, especially the weekend road trips. Tracy, Trang, and Sarah for keeping me in Paradise. Mom, Dad, Allison for the love, support, and riddles.

LINGBO THANKS: Jason for ukulele lessons. Ronan for being YouTube DJ. Nickclette for motherly wisdom. Krysten for being a sweet vegetarian harpist. Jun for unrelenting cheer (since 3rd grade). Mom and Dad for endless, loving support. Matt for BFFdom. Marianna for midnight Skype chats. And all the prisoners/homeless/bankers who made this the best summer. Ever.

NICKCLETTE THANKS: Europe for the laughs, music partays, and Spazz Thursdays. Jun, for being supa-dupa hardcore. Lingbo, for amazing quirkiness. Krysten, for Europod-pride and veggie reminders. DJ Ronan for encouraging a green office environment. Jason for ukelele inspiration. Dube, for being a phenomenal ME! Friends, for a great summer. And of course, THE FAM.

ABOUT LET'S GO

NOT YOUR PARENTS' TRAVEL GUIDE

At Let's Go, we see every trip as the chance of a lifetime. If your dream is to forge through the jungles of Costa Rica, we can take you there. If you'd rather bask in the Riviera sun at a beachside cafe, we'll set you a table. We write for readers who know that there's more to travel than sharing double deckers with other tourists. We'll show you just how far your money can go, and prove that the greatest limitation on your adventures is not your wallet but your imagination.

BEYOND THE TOURIST EXPERIENCE

Our fearless researchers scour the globe to give you the heads-up on both world-renowned and off-the-beaten-track attractions, sights, and destinations. They dive into the local scene to emerge with the freshest insights on everything from festivals to regional cuisine. We've opened our pages to scholars, and asked travelers to contribute their experience. Our Beyond Tourism chapter shares ideas about responsible travel and study abroad.

FORTY-NINE YEARS OF WISDOM

Let's Go got its start in 1960, when a group of creative and well-traveled students compiled their experience into a 20-page mimeographed pamphlet, which they gave to students on charter flights to Europe. Almost five decades later, we've expanded to cover all kinds of travel—while retaining our founders' adventurous attitude. Laced with witty prose and total candor, our guides are still researched and written entirely by students on shoestring budgets, experienced travelers who know that strikes, stolen luggage, food poisoning, and marriage proposals are all part of a day's work.

THE LET'S GO COMMUNITY

More than just a travel guide company, *Let's Go* is a community. Our small staff comes together because of our shared passion for travel and our desire to help other travelers see and enjoy the world. We love it when our readers become part of the Let's Go community as well—when you travel, drop us a postcard (67 Mt. Auburn St., Cambridge, MA 02138, USA) or send us an e-mail (feedback@letsgo.com).

For more information, visit us online: www.letsgo.com.

LET'S GO

Publishing Director
Inés C. Pacheco
Editor-in-Chief
Samantha Gelfand
Production Manager
Jansen A. S. Thurmer
Cartography Manager
R. Derek Wetzel
Editorial Managers
Dwight Livingstone Curtis, Vanessa J. Dube, Nathaniel Rakich
Financial Manager
Lauren Caruso
Publicity and Marketing Manager
Patrick McKiernan
Personnel Manager
Laura M. Gordon
Production Associate
C. Alexander Tremblay
Director of IT & E-Commerce
Lukáš Tóth
Website Manager
Ian Malott
Office Coordinators
Vinnie Chiappini, Jenny Wong
Director of Advertising Sales
Nicole J. Bass
Senior Advertising Associates
Kipyegon Kitur, Jeremy Siegfried, John B. Ulrich
Junior Advertising Associate
Edward C. Robinson Jr.
President
Timothy J.J. Creamer
General Manager
Jim McKellar
Editor
Jason Meyer
Associate Editors
Ronan Devlin, Nickclette Izuegbu, Krysten Keches, Lingbo Li, Jun Li
Managing Editor
Vanessa J. Dube
Map Editor
R. Derek Wetzel
Typesetter
Jansen A. S. Thurmer

PRICE RANGES ❶ ❷ ❸ ❹ ❺ EUROPE

Our researchers list establishments in order of value from best to worst, honoring our favorites with the Let's Go thumbs-up (☒). Because the best *value* is not always the cheapest *price*, we have incorporated a system of price ranges based on a rough expectation of what you will spend. For **accommodations,** we base our range on the cheapest price for which a single traveler can stay for one night. For **restaurants** and other dining establishments, we estimate the average amount one traveler will spend in one sitting. The table below tells you what you'll *typically* find in Europe at the corresponding price range, but keep in mind that no system can allow for the quirks of individual establishments. For country-specific information, a table at the beginning of each country chapter lists the price ranges for each bracket.

ACCOMMODATIONS	WHAT YOU'RE *LIKELY* TO FIND
❶	Campgrounds and dorm rooms, both in hostels and actual universities. Expect bunk beds and a communal bath. You may have to provide or rent towels and sheets. Be ready for things to go bump in the night.
❷	Upper-end hostels or lower-end hotels and pensions. You may have a private bathroom, or there may be a sink in your room and communal shower in the hall.
❸	A small room with a private bath or pension. Should have decent amenities, such as phone and TV. Breakfast may be included in the price of the room.
❹	Should have bigger rooms than a ❸, with more amenities or in a more convenient location. Breakfast probably included.
❺	Large hotels or upscale chains. Rooms should elicit an involuntary "wow." If it's a ❺ and it doesn't have the perks you want, you've paid too much.

FOOD	WHAT YOU'RE *LIKELY* TO FIND
❶	Street food, *gelateria*, milk bar, corner *crêperie*, or a fast-food joint, but also university cafeterias and bakeries. Soups, gyros, kebab, most *bliny* and other simple dishes in minimalist surroundings. Usually takeout, but you may have the option of sitting down.
❷	Sandwiches, *naleśniki*, *brocadillos*, appetizers at a bar, or low-priced entrees and *tapas*. Most *trattorie* or ethnic eateries are a ❷. Either takeout or a sit-down meal (sometimes with servers!), but only slightly more fashionable decor.
❸	Mid-priced entrees, pub fare, seafood, and exotic pasta dishes. A cheeseburger in Moscow. Many medieval-themed and hunting-lodge-decor establishments. Wild game. More upscale ethnic eateries. Since you'll have a waiter, tip will set you back a little extra.
❹	A somewhat fancy restaurant or *brasserie*. Entrees tend to be heartier or more elaborate, but you're really paying for decor and ambience. Few restaurants in this range have a dress code, but some may look down on T-shirts and sandals.
❺	Your meal might cost more than your room, but there's a reason—it's something fabulous, famous, or both. Slacks and dress shirts may be expected. Offers foreign-sounding food and a decent wine list.

DISCOVER EUROPE

Some things never change. Aspiring writers still spin romances in Parisian garrets; a glass of sangria at twilight on the Plaza Mayor tastes as sweet as ever; and iconic treasures, from the onion domes of St. Basil's cathedral to the behemoth slabs of Stonehenge, continue to inspire awe. But against this ancient backdrop, a freshly costumed continent takes the stage. As the European Union grows from a small clique of nations trading coal and steel to a 27-member commonwealth with a parliament and a central bank, Eastern and Western Europe find themselves more closely connected than ever before. Ease of travel between the two make it seem like the Continent is simultaneously shrinking and expanding. With improved transport links increasing the range of possible itineraries, determining the must-see destinations of 21st-century Europe has become even more difficult.

While Prague and Barcelona may have been the hot spots a few years ago, emerging cities like Kraków and Stockholm are poised to inherit the tourist money train. Newly minted cultural meccas like Bilbao's Guggenheim (p. 955) and London's Tate Modern (p. 141) have joined the ranks of timeless galleries like the Louvre (p. 327) and the Hermitage (p. 863), while a constant influx of students and DJs keep Europe's nightlife dependably hot. Whether it's Dublin's pubs, Lyon's upscale bistros, Sweden's frozen north country, Amsterdam's canals, or Croatia's dazzling beaches that call to you, *Let's Go: Europe 2009* will help to keep you informed and on-budget.

TACKLING EUROPE

Anyone who tells you that there is one "best way" to see Europe should be politely ignored. This book is designed to facilitate all varieties of travel, from a few days in Paris to a breathless, continent-wide summer sprint to a leisurely year (or two) abroad. This chapter is made up of tools to help you create your own itinerary: **themed categories** let you know where to find your museums, mountains, and madhouses, while **suggested itineraries** outline various paths across Europe. Look to chapter introductions for country-specific itineraries and for more detailed information.

WHEN TO GO

While summer sees the most tourist traffic in Europe, the best mix of value and accessibility comes in late spring and early fall. To the delight of skiing and ice-climbing enthusiasts, traveling during the low season (mid-Sept. to June) brings cheaper airfares and accommodations, in addition to freedom from hordes of fannypack-toting tourists. On the flip side, many attractions, hostels, and tourist offices close in the winter, and in some rural areas local transportation dwindles or shuts down altogether. Most of Europe's best **festivals** (p. 5) also take place in summer. For more advice on when to visit, see the **Weather Chart** on p. 1058 and the **Essentials** section at the beginning of each chapter.

WHAT TO DO

MUSEUMS

Europe has kept millennia worth of artistic masterpieces close to home in strongholds like the Louvre, the Prado, and the Vatican Museums. European museums do not merely house art, however. They also have exhibits on erotica, leprosy, marijuana, marzipan, puppets, and secret police—in short, whatever can be captioned. A trip across Europe qualifies as little more than a stopover without an afternoon spent among some of its paintings and artifacts—whether they include the pinnacles of Western culture, or more morbid or risqué fare.

THE SUBLIME	THE RIDICULOUS
BRITAIN: THE BRITISH MUSEUM (p. 142). Holding world artifacts like Egypt's Rosetta Stone or Iran's Oxus Treasure, the British Museum contains almost nothing British.	**DENMARK: LOUISIANA MUSEUM OF MODERN ART** (p. 267). This well-rounded museum's name honors the three wives of the estate's original owner—all of them were named Louisa.
BRITAIN: TATE MODERN (p. 141). Organized thematically, this former power station turned modern art powerhouse is as much a masterpiece as any of the works in its galleries.	**GERMANY: SCHOKOLADENMUSEUM** (p. 422). This chocolate museum, detailing the chocolate-making process, has gold fountains that spurt out samples and can be described only as magical.
FRANCE: THE LOUVRE (p. 327). Six million visitors come each year to see 35,000 works of art, including Da Vinci's surprisingly small painting of art's most famous face, the Mona Lisa.	**HUNGARY: SZAMOS MARZIPAN MUSEUM** (p. 505). Only one statuette on display at this museum is not composed of marzipan: an 80kg white chocolate effigy of Michael Jackson.
GERMANY: GEMÄLDEGALERIE (p. 405). With over 1000 works from 1200 to 1800 by the likes of Bruegel and Raphael, it's no wonder this is one of the most visited museums in Germany.	**ICELAND: PHALLOLOGICAL MUSEUM** (p. 530). With specimens from over 90 species, this museum—a mix of science and humor—is all about penises. We'll leave the puns up to you.
GREECE: NATIONAL ARCHAEOLOGICAL MUSEUM (p. 464). Athens itself may be museum enough for some, but this building collects artifacts of smaller dimensions.	**ITALY: PALERMO CATACOMBS** (p. 653). The withered faces and mostly empty eye sockets of 8000 posing corpses gaze enviously at living spectators in Europe's creepiest underground tomb.
ITALY: VATICAN MUSEUMS (p. 593). Look for the *School of Athens* here; the painting tops off a mindblowing amount of Renaissance and other art, including the incredible Raphael Rooms.	**THE NETHERLANDS: CANNABIS COLLEGE** (p. 716). Cannabis College is just like college, except there are no libraries, no lectures, no studying, no liquor, no dorms, and no full-time students.
THE NETHERLANDS: RIJKSMUSEUM (p. 717). Renovations shouldn't deter visitors who come to see the pinnacles of the Dutch Golden Age, including Rembrandts and Vermeers, that line the walls.	**NORWAY: VIGELANDPARKEN** (p. 741). Not quite a museum, but with enough art to be one, this park contains over 200 of Gustav Vigeland's controversial sculptures. Each depicts a stage of human life.
POLAND: NATIONAL MUSEUM (p. 797). In the vaults of a former Franciscan monastery, Gdank's National Museum has a large collection of 16th- to 20th-century art and furniture.	**PORTUGAL: OCEANÁRIO** (p. 811). Europe's largest oceanarium, with interactive exhibits exploring the four major oceans, allows visitors to get within a meter of sea otters and penguins.
SLOVAKIA: PRIMACÁLN PALÁC (p. 875). This pink- and-gold "Primate's Palace" was built in the 1700s for Hungarian religious leaders (not monkeys) and is now home to Bratislava's mayor.	**SPAIN: TEATRE-MUSEU DALÍ** (p. 947). Dalí's final resting place has works like *Napoleon's Nose Transformed into a Pregnant Woman Strolling Her Shadow with Melancholic amongst Original Ruins.*
SPAIN: MUSEO DEL PRADO (p. 905). It's an art-lover's heaven to see hell, as painted by Hieronymus Bosch. Velázquez's famous 10 by 9 ft. painting *Las Meninas* is as luminous as it is tall.	**SWITZERLAND: VERKEHRSHAUS DER SCHWEIZ** (p. 1013). The Swiss Transport Museum, with an IMAX theater and a wide array of cool contraptions, isn't nearly as dorky as its name implies.

ARCHITECTURE

European architecture is a huge part of the continent's appeal. Royal lines from the early Welsh dynasties and Greek ruling families to the Bourbons, Hapsburgs, and Romanovs have all been outlasted by the emblems of their magnificence—castles, palaces, and châteaux. Monarchs had loose purse strings and were jealous of each other; Louis XIV's palace at Versailles (p. 334), which has become a byword for opulence, whet the ambition of rival monarchs and spurred the construction of competing domiciles. No expense was spared for God, either, as the many splendid cathedrals, monasteries, synagogues, temples, and mosques rising skyward from their cityscapes attest. Córdoba's Mezquita (p. 916) and Budapest's Great Synagogue (p. 502) are among the finest of their kind, while Chartres's Cathédrale de Notre Dame (p. 321) and Cologne's Dom (p. 422) are pinnacles of Gothic style.

ROYAL REALTY	SACRED SITES
AUSTRIA: SCHLOß SCHÖNBRUNN (p. 82). If the palace isn't impressive enough, check out the classical gardens that extend behind for four times the length of the structure.	**BRITAIN: WESTMINSTER ABBEY** (p. 132). Royal weddings and coronations take place in the sanctuary; nearby, poets and politicians from the earliest kings to Winston Churchill rest in peace.
BRITAIN: BUCKINGHAM PALACE (p. 132). Britain's royal family has lived in Buckingham Palace since 1832, guarded by everybody's favorite stoic, puffy-hatted guards.	**FRANCE: CHARTRES CATHEDRAL** (p. 335). The world's finest example of early Gothic architecture has intact stained-glass windows from the 12th century and a crypt from the 9th.
DENMARK: EGESKOV SLOT (p. 270). This idyllic castle seems to be floating in a lake. Its moat is straight out of a fairy tale, with imaginative gardens and hedge mazes to match.	**GERMANY: KÖLNER DOM** (p. 422). With a 44m ceiling and 1350 sq. meters of stained glass illuminating the interior with particolored sunlight, Cologne's cathedral is Germany's greatest.
FRANCE: VERSAILLES (p. 334). Once home to the entire French court, the lavish palace, manicured gardens, and Hall of Mirrors epitomize Pre-Revolutionary France's regal extravagance.	**HUNGARY: THE GREAT SYNAGOGUE** (p. 502). Europe's largest synagogue can hold 3000. Inscribed leaves of a metal tree in the courtyard commemorate the victims of the Holocaust.
GERMANY: NEUSCHWANSTEIN (p. 444). A waterfall, an artificial grotto, a byzantine throne room, and a Wagnerian opera hall deck out the inspiration for Disney's Cinderella Castle.	**ITALY: SISTINE CHAPEL** (p. 591). Each fresco on its famous ceiling depicts a scene from Genesis. Michaelangelo painted himself as a flayed human skin hanging between heaven and hell.
ITALY: PALAZZO DUCALE (p. 622). The home of the Venetian *Doge* (mayor) could pass as a city unto itself, complete with on-site prisons that miscreants once entered via the Bridge of Sighs.	**RUSSIA: ST. BASIL'S CATHEDRAL** (p. 852). Commissioned by Ivan the Terrible to celebrate his victory over the Tatars, today its colorful, onion-shaped domes are instantly recognizable.
LUXEMBOURG: CHÂTEAU DE VIANDEN (p. 690). Though its displays of armor, furniture, and tapestries are run-of-the-mill, the expansive views from the hills make the castle a must-see.	**SPAIN: MEZQUITA** (p. 916). Córdoba's Mezquita, one of the West's most important Islamic monuments, is supported by 850 pink and blue marble and alabaster columns.
PORTUGAL: QUINTA DA REGALEIRA (p. 814). An eccentric millionaire owner turned this stunning palace into a fantasy land in the early 20th century, complete with "Dantesque" caves below.	**SPAIN: SAGRADA FAMILIA** (p. 943). Though it looks like it's already melting, Antoni Gaudí's cathedral isn't even finished. The world's most visited construction site should be completed in 2026.
SPAIN: THE ALHAMBRA (p. 927). The Spanish say, *"Si mueres sin ver la Alhambra, no has vivido."* ("If you die without seeing the Alhambra, you have not lived.") We agree.	**TURKEY: AYA SOFIA** (p. 1041). The gold-leafed mosaic dome of Byzantine emperor Justinian's masterful cathedral-turned-mosque appears to be floating on a bed of luminescent pearls.
SWEDEN: KUNGLIGA SLOTTET (p. 972). Still the official residence of the Swedish royal family, the *Kungliga Slottet* (Royal Palace) recently hosted lavish festivities for the Crown Princess's 30th birthday.	**UKRAINE: KYIV-CAVE MONASTERY** (p. 1055). Kyiv's oldest holy site houses the Refectory Church, the 12th-century Holy Trinity Gate Church, and caves where monks lie mummified.

OUTDOORS

Europe's museums and ruins tend be a stronger draw than its mountains and rivers. But for any traveler, budget or otherwise, solo or companioned, expert or neophyte, an excursion to the outdoors can round off (or salvage, as the case may be) any journey. Fjords, volcanoes, valleys, gorges, and plateaus mark the spots where the Earth's plates collide. Waters of innumerable shades of blue wash up on uninhabited shores of black-, white-, and red-sand beaches. Mountains, whether sprawling with trees or culminating in ice, continue to challenge mankind and dwarf the man-made, just as they did when civilization began.

JUST CHILLIN'	HARDCORE THRILL-SEEKIN'
AUSTRIA: THE HOHE TAUERN NATIONAL PARK (p. 91). Filled with glaciers, mountains, lakes, and endangered species, Europe's largest park offers mountain paths once trod by Celts and Romans.	**AUSTRIA: INNSBRUCK** (p. 92). The free Club Innsbruck membership is one of the best deals in Western Europe for avid skiers. When skiing becomes old hat, adventurers opt for paragliding.
BRITAIN: PEAK DISTRICT NATIONAL PARK (p. 169). Despite its name, this park doesn't have many mountains, but it does have some of Britain's finest scenery and it claims the title of the second most-visited national park in the world.	**FRANCE: MONT BLANC** (p. 357). The tallest mountain in Europe (4807m), Mont Blanc has vertigo-inducing slopes. It is a haven for international bikers, hikers, snowboarders, and skiers.
CROATIA: THE DALMATIAN COAST (p. 223). Touted as the new French Riviera, the Dalmatian Coast has some of the clearest waters in the Mediterranean. What it doesn't have is dalmations—at least no more than any other place.	**GERMANY: DER SCHWARZWALD** (p. 435). The eerie darkness pervading this tangled evergreen, once the inspiration Brothers Grimm, lures hikers and skiers (instead of red-caped little girls.)
DENMARK: ÆRØSKØBING (p. 271). Economic stagnation and recent conservation efforts have successfully fossilized the 19th-century lifestyle and charm of this tiny island town.	**ITALY: CINQUE TERRE** (p. 608). An outdoorsman's paradise, the hiking trails of Cinque Terre have opportunities for cliff diving, horseback riding, and kayaking between villages.
ESTONIA: HIIUMAA (p. 285). The Soviets unwittingly preserved rare species on this island by restricting access for 50 years. The Säärtirp peninsula's promontory is especially beautiful.	**NORWAY: FJÆRLAND** (p. 756). At the base of the Jostedalsbreen glacier, Fjærland provides a perfect rest from serious, year-round hiking and camping through Norway's fjords.
FRANCE: D-DAY BEACHES (p. 341). The heroism of the Allied forces is tastefully preserved on the beaches near Bayeux, where thousands of soldiers were killed or wounded over 60 years ago.	**NORWAY: SVALBARD ARCHIPELAGO** (p. 766). The northernmost town in the world also happens to be one of the most badass. Rifle skills are a must for solo trekking, but dog sledding is open to all.
GREECE: DELPHI (p. 475). Journey to the beautiful mountaintop of the Oracle of Delphi, where ancient citizens went to hear cryptic prophecies. Soak in the history, and prepare to know thyself.	**PORTUGAL: SAGRES** (p. 821). Once considered the edge of the world, the windy town of Sagres has dramatic cliffs and turquoise waters that now attract more windsurfers than navigators.
ICELAND: THERMAL POOLS (p. 523). Iceland may be expensive, but freeloaders can find naturally occurring "hotpots" outside of Reykjavík. Each thermal pool maintains its distinct character.	**SLOVAKIA: THE TATRA MOUNTAINS** (p. 876). Part of the Carpathian range and spanning the border between Slovakia and Poland, the Tatras make a great, if extremely demanding, hiking destination.
IRELAND: KILLARNEY NATIONAL PARK (p. 552). Glacial activity during the Ice Age shaped Ireland's best park, which has pristine lakes, forested mountains, and an elusive herd of 850 red deer.	**SPAIN: PAMPLONA** (p. 950). While not outdoorsy in the traditional sense, the Running of the Bulls in Pamplona attracts runners and adrenaline junkies from all over the world.
THE NETHERLANDS: HOGE VELUWE NATIONAL PARK (p. 729). Wild boars and red deer inhabit the 13,500 acres of forestry, while the park's museum houses works by Picasso and van Gogh.	**SWITZERLAND: INTERLAKEN** (p. 1003). Thanks to its mild climate and pristine landscape, Interlaken is Europe's adventure sports capital, with every adrenaline-inducing opportunity imaginable.

FESTIVALS

COUNTRIES	APR. - JUNE	JULY - AUG.	SEPT. - MAR.
AUSTRIA AND SWITZERLAND	**Vienna Festwochen** (early May to mid-June)	**Salzburger Festspiele** (late July-Aug.)	**Escalade** (Geneva; Dec. 11-13) **Fasnacht** (Basel; Mar. 2-4)
BELGIUM	**Festival of Fairground Arts** (Wallonie; late May)	**Gentse Feesten** (Ghent; mid- to late July)	**International French Language Film Festival** (Namur; late Sept.)
BRITAIN AND IRELAND	**Bloomsday** (Dublin; June 16) **Wimbledon** (London; late June-early July)	**Fringe Festival** (Edinburgh; Aug.) **Edinburgh Int'l Festival** (mid-Aug. to early Sept.)	**Matchmaking Festival** (Lisdoonvarna; Sept.) **St. Patrick's Day** (Mar. 17)
CZECH REPUBLIC	**Prague Spring Festival** (May-June)	**Int'l Film Festival** (Karlovy Vary; July)	**Int'l Organ Festival** (Olomouc; Sept.)
FRANCE	**Cannes Film Festival** (May 13-24)	**Festival d'Avignon** (July-Aug.) **Bastille Day** (July 14)	**Carnevale** (Nice, Nantes; Jan 25-Feb. 5)
GERMANY	**May Day** (Berlin; May 1) **Christopher St. Day** (late June)	**Rhine in Flames Festival** (various locations in the Rhine Valley; throughout summer)	**Oktoberfest** (Munich; Sept. 19-Oct. 4) **Fasching** (Munich; Feb. 1-5)
HUNGARY	**Danube Festival** (Budapest; June)	**Golden Shell Folklore** (Siófok; June) **Sziget Rock Festival** (Budapest; Aug.)	**Éger Vintage Days** (Sept.) **Festival of Wine Songs** (Pécs; Sept.)
ITALY	**Maggio Musicale** (Florence; May to mid-June)	**Il Palio** (Siena; July 2 and Aug. 16) **Umbria Jazz Festival** (July)	**Carnevale** (late Feb.) **Scoppio del Carro** (Florence; Easter Su)
THE NETHERLANDS	**Queen's Day** (Apr. 30) **Holland Festival** (June)	**Gay Pride Parade** (early Aug.)	**Flower Parade** (Aalsmeer; early Sept.)
PORTUGAL	**Burning of the Ribbons** (Coimbra; early May)	**Lisbon Beer Festival** (July)	**Carnaval** (early Mar.) **Semana Santa** (Apr. 5-12)
SCANDINAVIA	**Midsummer** (June 19-25)	**Savonlinna Opera Festival** (July) **Quart Music Festival** (Kristiansand; early July)	**Helsinki Festival** (late Aug.-early Sept.) **Tromsø Film Festival** (mid-Jan.)
SPAIN	**Feria de Abril** (Sevilla; mid-Apr.)	**San Fermines** (Pamplona; early to mid-July)	**Las Fallas** (Valencia; Mar.) **Carnaval** (Mar.)

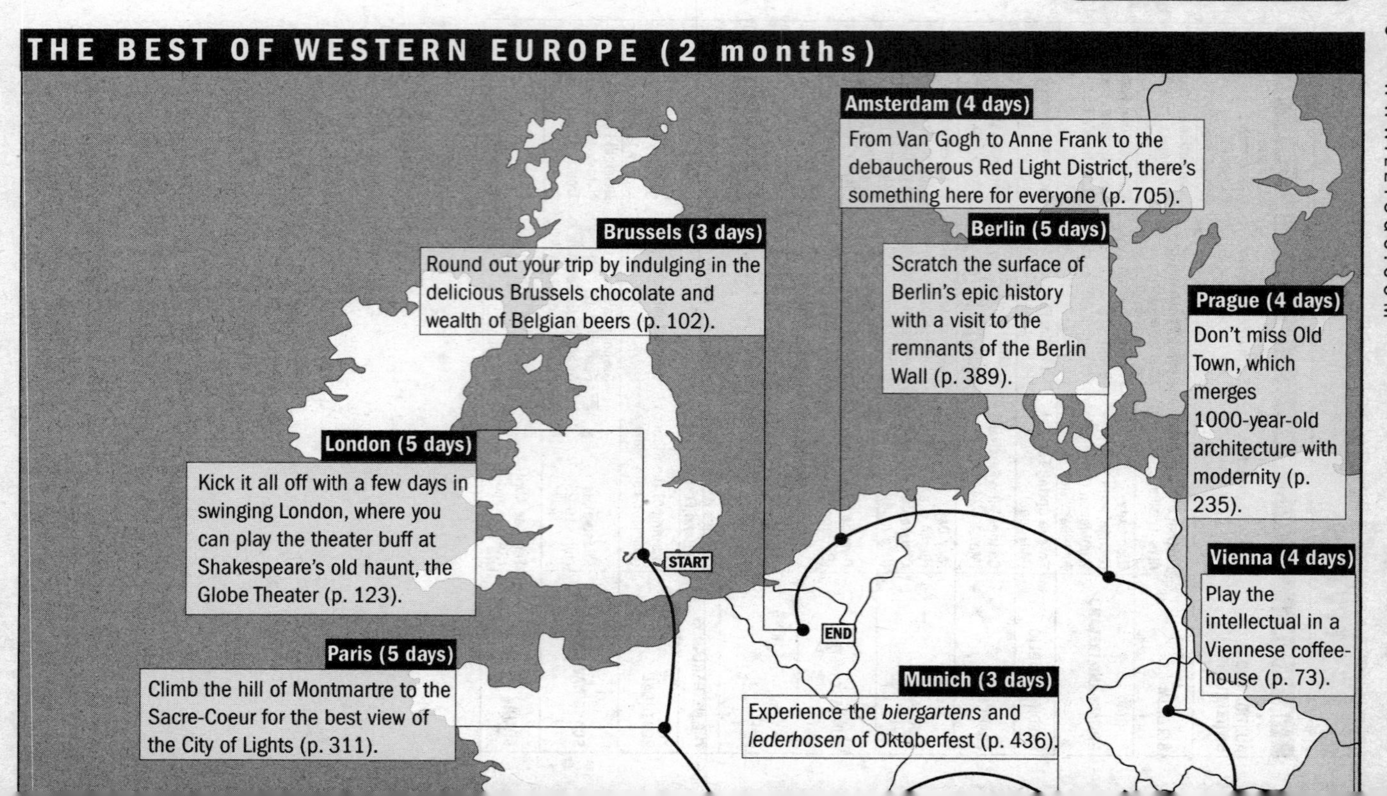
THE BEST OF WESTERN EUROPE (2 months)
London (5 days)
Kick it all off with a few days in swinging London, where you can play the theater buff at Shakespeare's old haunt, the Globe Theater (p. 123).
Paris (5 days)
Climb the hill of Montmartre to the Sacre-Coeur for the best view of the City of Lights (p. 311).
Brussels (3 days)
Round out your trip by indulging in the delicious Brussels chocolate and wealth of Belgian beers (p. 102).
Amsterdam (4 days)
From Van Gogh to Anne Frank to the debaucherous Red Light District, there's something here for everyone (p. 705).
Berlin (5 days)
Scratch the surface of Berlin's epic history with a visit to the remnants of the Berlin Wall (p. 389).
Prague (4 days)
Don't miss Old Town, which merges 1000-year-old architecture with modernity (p. 235).
Vienna (4 days)
Play the intellectual in a Viennese coffee-house (p. 73).
Munich (3 days)
Experience the biergartens and lederhosen of Oktoberfest (p. 436).
START
END

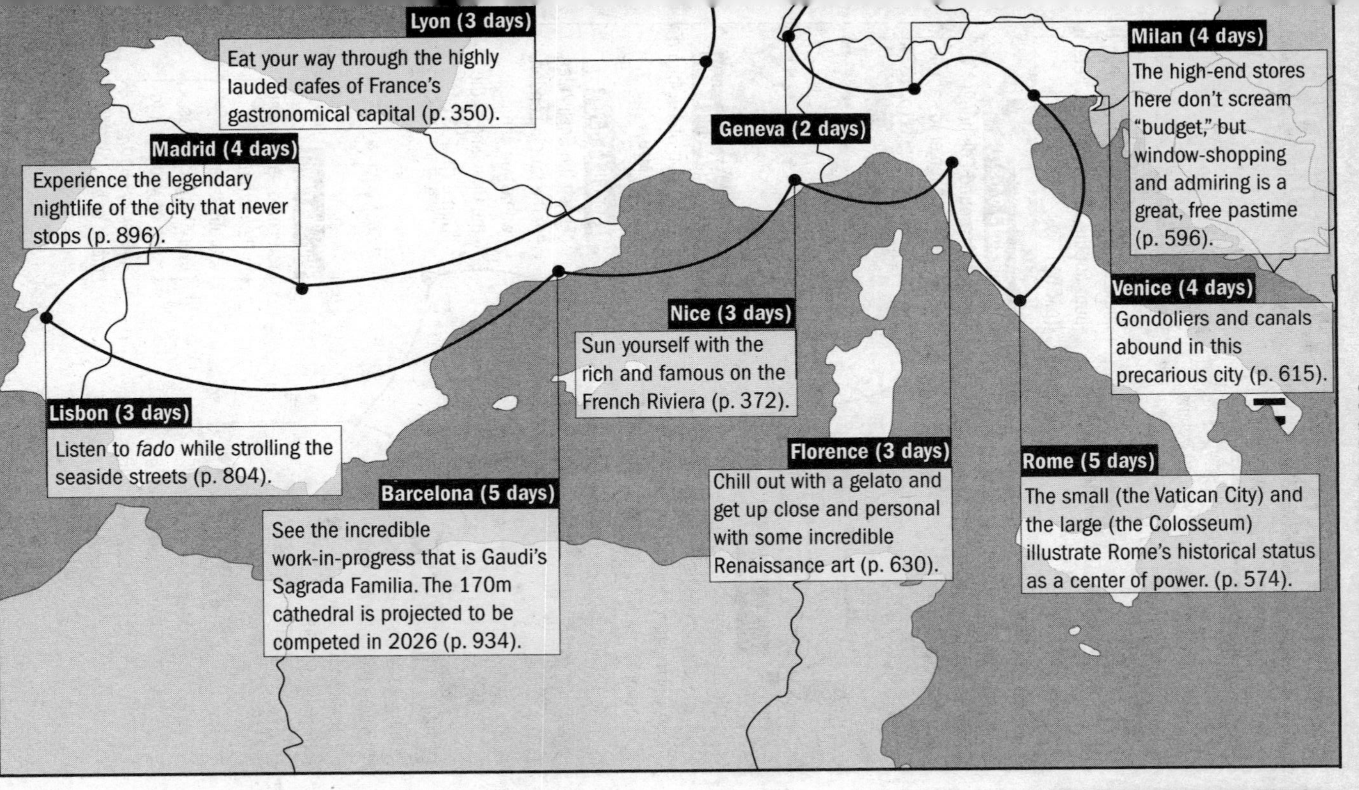
Lyon (3 days)
Eat your way through the highly lauded cafes of France's gastronomical capital (p. 350).
Madrid (4 days)
Experience the legendary nightlife of the city that never stops (p. 896).
Lisbon (3 days)
Listen to *fado* while strolling the seaside streets (p. 804).
Barcelona (5 days)
See the incredible work-in-progress that is Gaudí's Sagrada Familia. The 170m cathedral is projected to be competed in 2026 (p. 934).
Geneva (2 days)
Nice (3 days)
Sun yourself with the rich and famous on the French Riviera (p. 372).
Florence (3 days)
Chill out with a gelato and get up close and personal with some incredible Renaissance art (p. 630).
Milan (4 days)
The high-end stores here don't scream "budget," but window-shopping and admiring is a great, free pastime (p. 596).
Venice (4 days)
Gondoliers and canals abound in this precarious city (p. 615).
Rome (5 days)
The small (the Vatican City) and the large (the Colosseum) illustrate Rome's historical status as a center of power. (p. 574).

CHANNEL JUMPING (1 month)

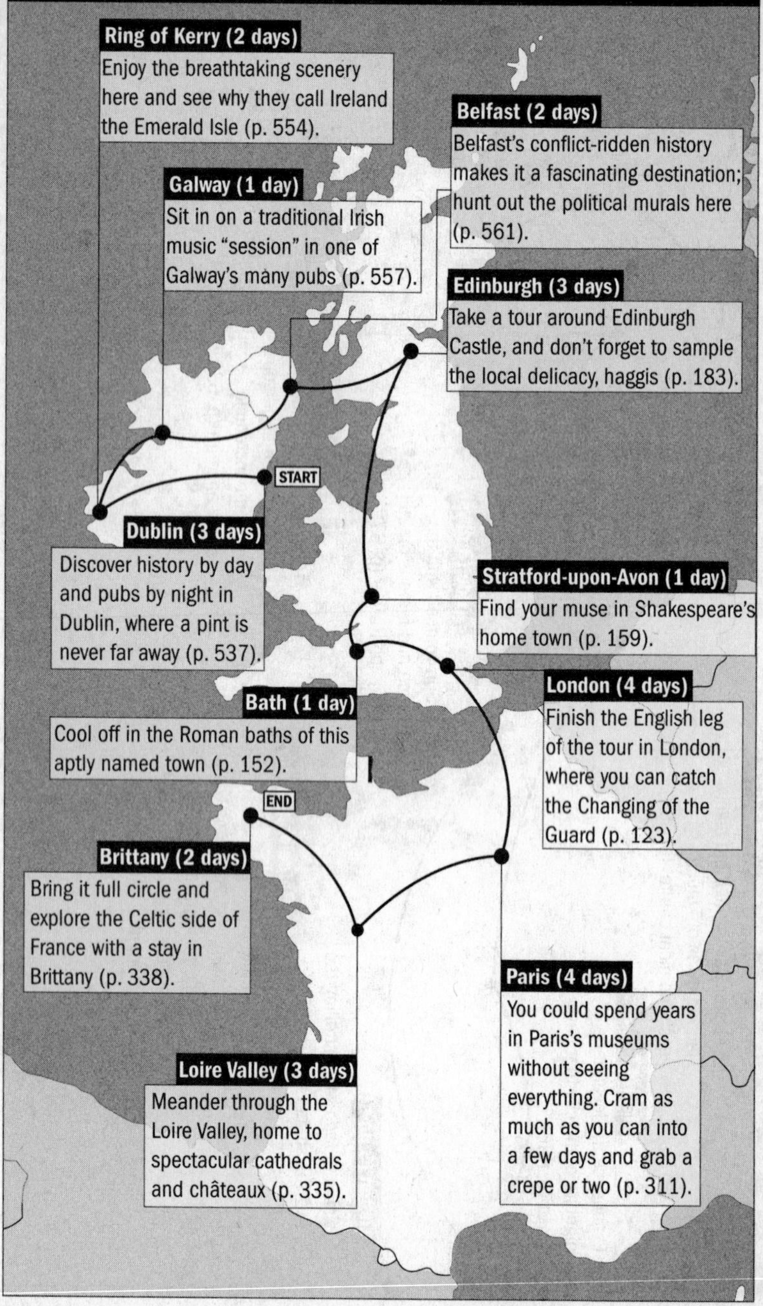

Ring of Kerry (2 days)
Enjoy the breathtaking scenery here and see why they call Ireland the Emerald Isle (p. 554).

Galway (1 day)
Sit in on a traditional Irish music "session" in one of Galway's many pubs (p. 557).

Belfast (2 days)
Belfast's conflict-ridden history makes it a fascinating destination; hunt out the political murals here (p. 561).

Edinburgh (3 days)
Take a tour around Edinburgh Castle, and don't forget to sample the local delicacy, haggis (p. 183).

START

Dublin (3 days)
Discover history by day and pubs by night in Dublin, where a pint is never far away (p. 537).

Stratford-upon-Avon (1 day)
Find your muse in Shakespeare's home town (p. 159).

London (4 days)
Finish the English leg of the tour in London, where you can catch the Changing of the Guard (p. 123).

Bath (1 day)
Cool off in the Roman baths of this aptly named town (p. 152).

END

Brittany (2 days)
Bring it full circle and explore the Celtic side of France with a stay in Brittany (p. 338).

Paris (4 days)
You could spend years in Paris's museums without seeing everything. Cram as much as you can into a few days and grab a crepe or two (p. 311).

Loire Valley (3 days)
Meander through the Loire Valley, home to spectacular cathedrals and châteaux (p. 335).

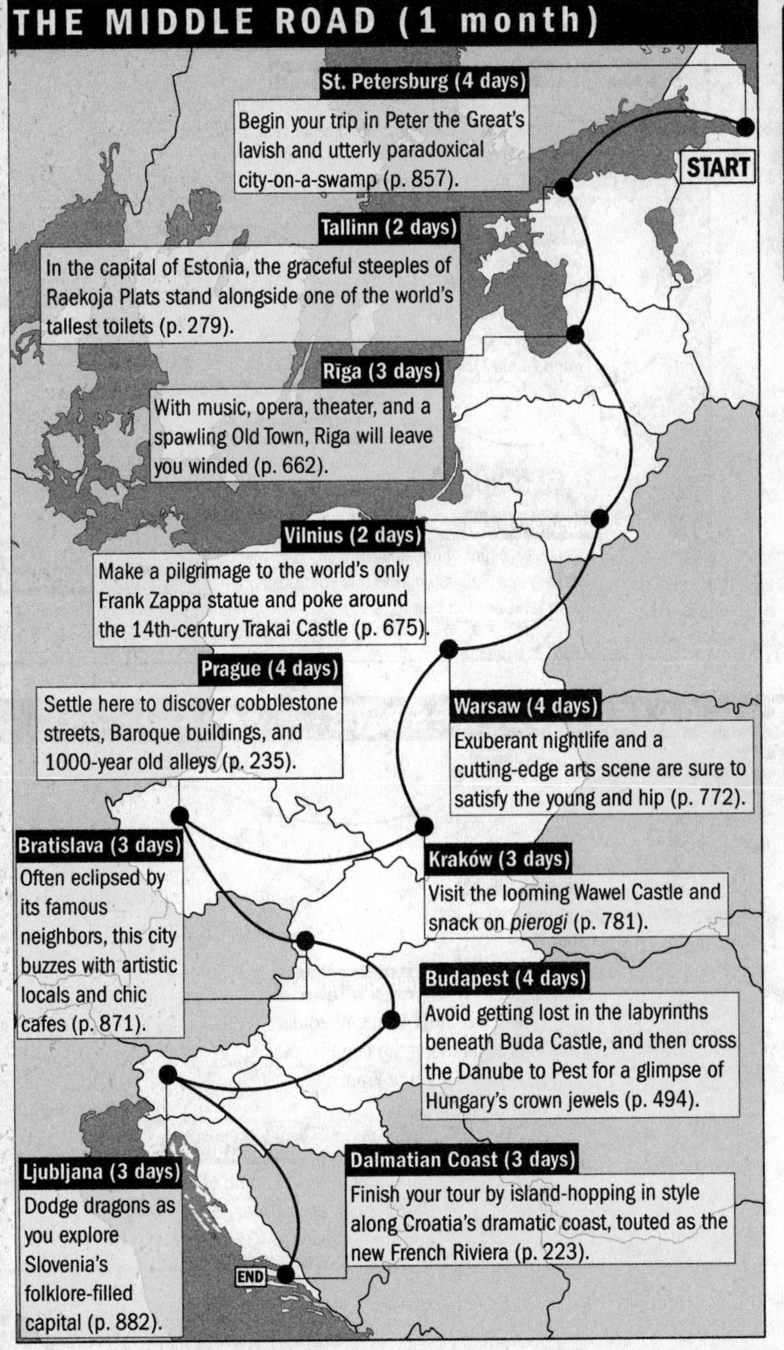
THE MIDDLE ROAD (1 month)
St. Petersburg (4 days)
Begin your trip in Peter the Great's lavish and utterly paradoxical city-on-a-swamp (p. 857).
START
Tallinn (2 days)
In the capital of Estonia, the graceful steeples of Raekoja Plats stand alongside one of the world's tallest toilets (p. 279).
Rīga (3 days)
With music, opera, theater, and a spawling Old Town, Riga will leave you winded (p. 662).
Vilnius (2 days)
Make a pilgrimage to the world's only Frank Zappa statue and poke around the 14th-century Trakai Castle (p. 675).
Prague (4 days)
Settle here to discover cobblestone streets, Baroque buildings, and 1000-year old alleys (p. 235).
Warsaw (4 days)
Exuberant nightlife and a cutting-edge arts scene are sure to satisfy the young and hip (p. 772).
Bratislava (3 days)
Often eclipsed by its famous neighbors, this city buzzes with artistic locals and chic cafes (p. 871).
Kraków (3 days)
Visit the looming Wawel Castle and snack on pierogi (p. 781).
Budapest (4 days)
Avoid getting lost in the labyrinths beneath Buda Castle, and then cross the Danube to Pest for a glimpse of Hungary's crown jewels (p. 494).
Dalmatian Coast (3 days)
Finish your tour by island-hopping in style along Croatia's dramatic coast, touted as the new French Riviera (p. 223).
Ljubljana (3 days)
Dodge dragons as you explore Slovenia's folklore-filled capital (p. 882).
END

BEST OF THE MEDITERRANEAN (6 weeks)

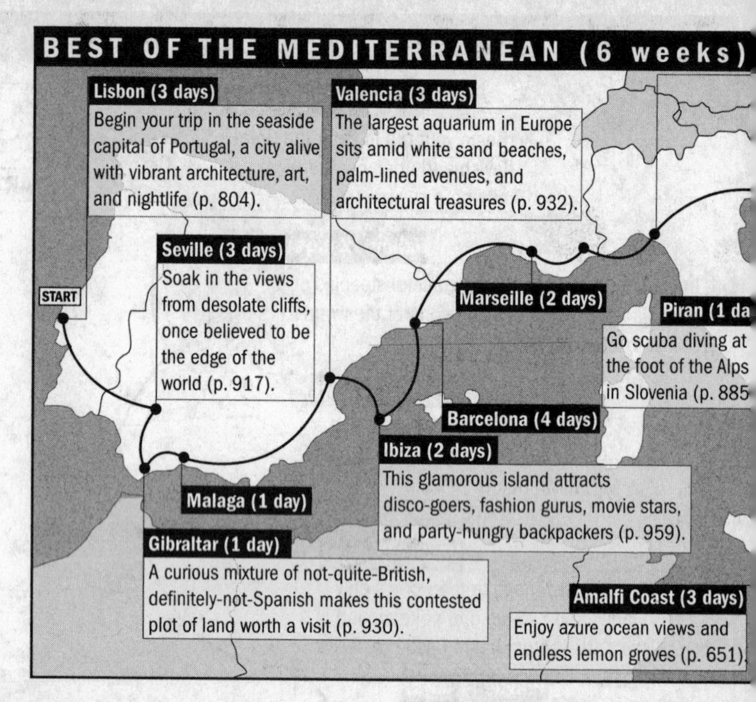
START
Lisbon (3 days)
Begin your trip in the seaside capital of Portugal, a city alive with vibrant architecture, art, and nightlife (p. 804).
Valencia (3 days)
The largest aquarium in Europe sits amid white sand beaches, palm-lined avenues, and architectural treasures (p. 932).
Seville (3 days)
Soak in the views from desolate cliffs, once believed to be the edge of the world (p. 917).
Marseille (2 days)
Piran (1 da
Go scuba diving at the foot of the Alps in Slovenia (p. 885
Barcelona (4 days)
Ibiza (2 days)
This glamorous island attracts disco-goers, fashion gurus, movie stars, and party-hungry backpackers (p. 959).
Malaga (1 day)
Gibraltar (1 day)
A curious mixture of not-quite-British, definitely-not-Spanish makes this contested plot of land worth a visit (p. 930).
Amalfi Coast (3 days)
Enjoy azure ocean views and endless lemon groves (p. 651).

THE ORIENT EXPRESS (3-4 weeks)

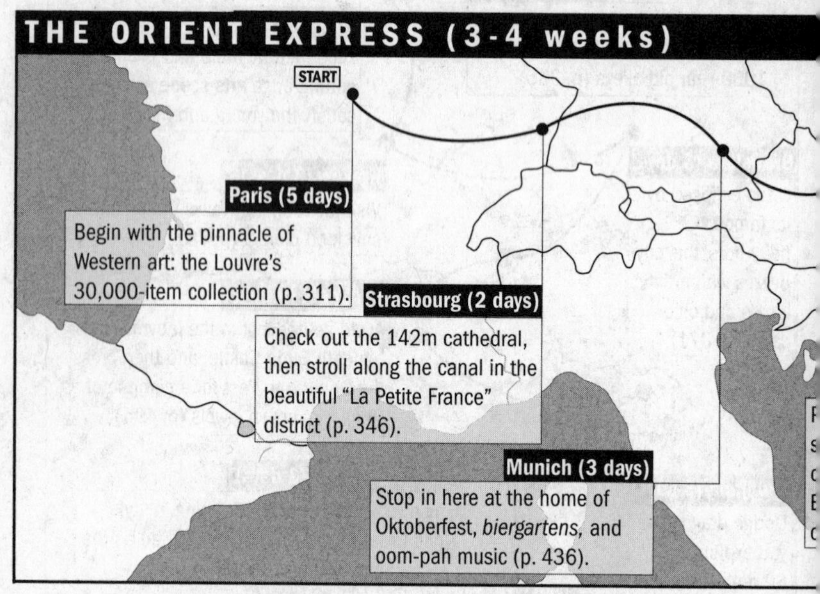
START
Paris (5 days)
Begin with the pinnacle of Western art: the Louvre's 30,000-item collection (p. 311).
Strasbourg (2 days)
Check out the 142m cathedral, then stroll along the canal in the beautiful "La Petite France" district (p. 346).
Munich (3 days)
Stop in here at the home of Oktoberfest, *biergartens,* and oom-pah music (p. 436).

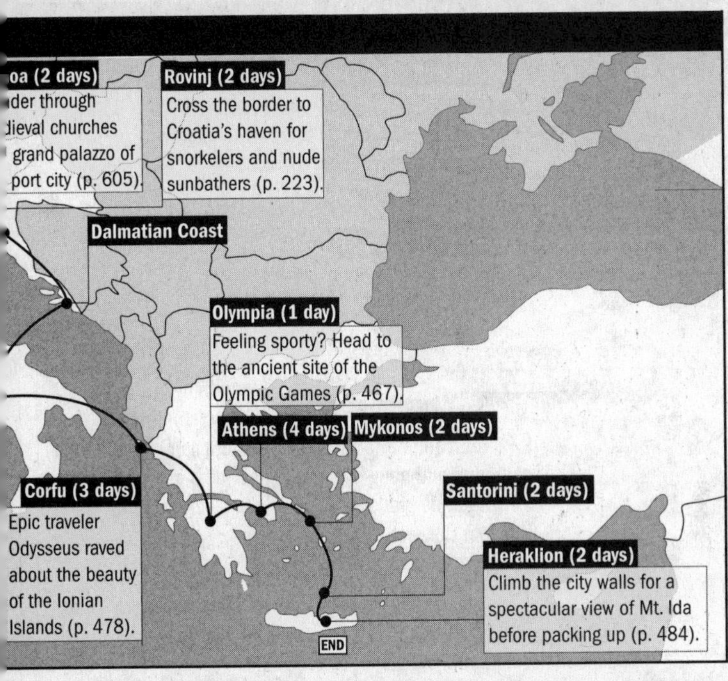
oa (2 days)
der through
dieval churches
grand palazzo of
port city (p. 605).
Rovinj (2 days)
Cross the border to Croatia's haven for snorkelers and nude sunbathers (p. 223).
Dalmatian Coast
Olympia (1 day)
Feeling sporty? Head to the ancient site of the Olympic Games (p. 467).
Athens (4 days)
Mykonos (2 days)
Corfu (3 days)
Epic traveler Odysseus raved about the beauty of the Ionian Islands (p. 478).
Santorini (2 days)
Heraklion (2 days)
Climb the city walls for a spectacular view of Mt. Ida before packing up (p. 484).
END

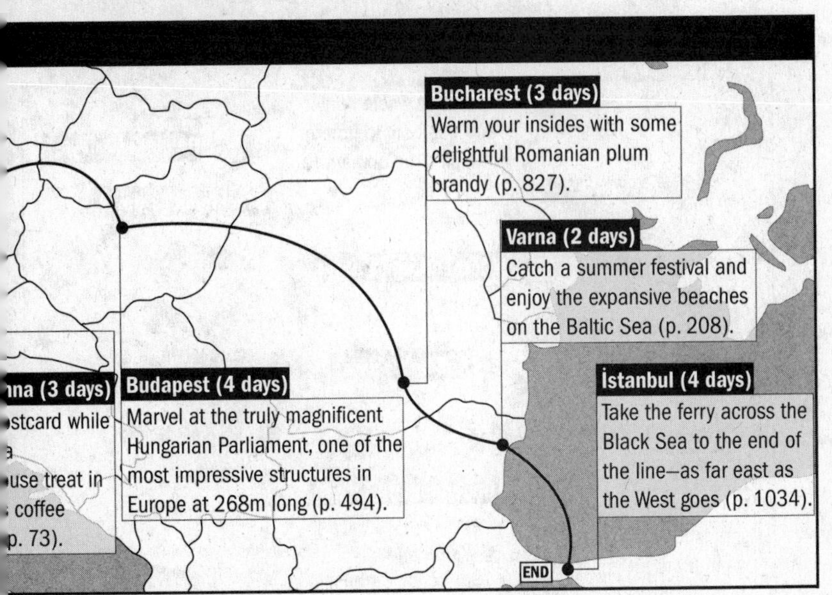
Bucharest (3 days)
Warm your insides with some delightful Romanian plum brandy (p. 827).
Varna (2 days)
Catch a summer festival and enjoy the expansive beaches on the Baltic Sea (p. 208).
İstanbul (4 days)
Take the ferry across the Black Sea to the end of the line—as far east as the West goes (p. 1034).
nna (3 days)
stcard while
use treat in
coffee
p. 73).
Budapest (4 days)
Marvel at the truly magnificent Hungarian Parliament, one of the most impressive structures in Europe at 268m long (p. 494).
END

BEST OF SCANDINAVIA (1 month)

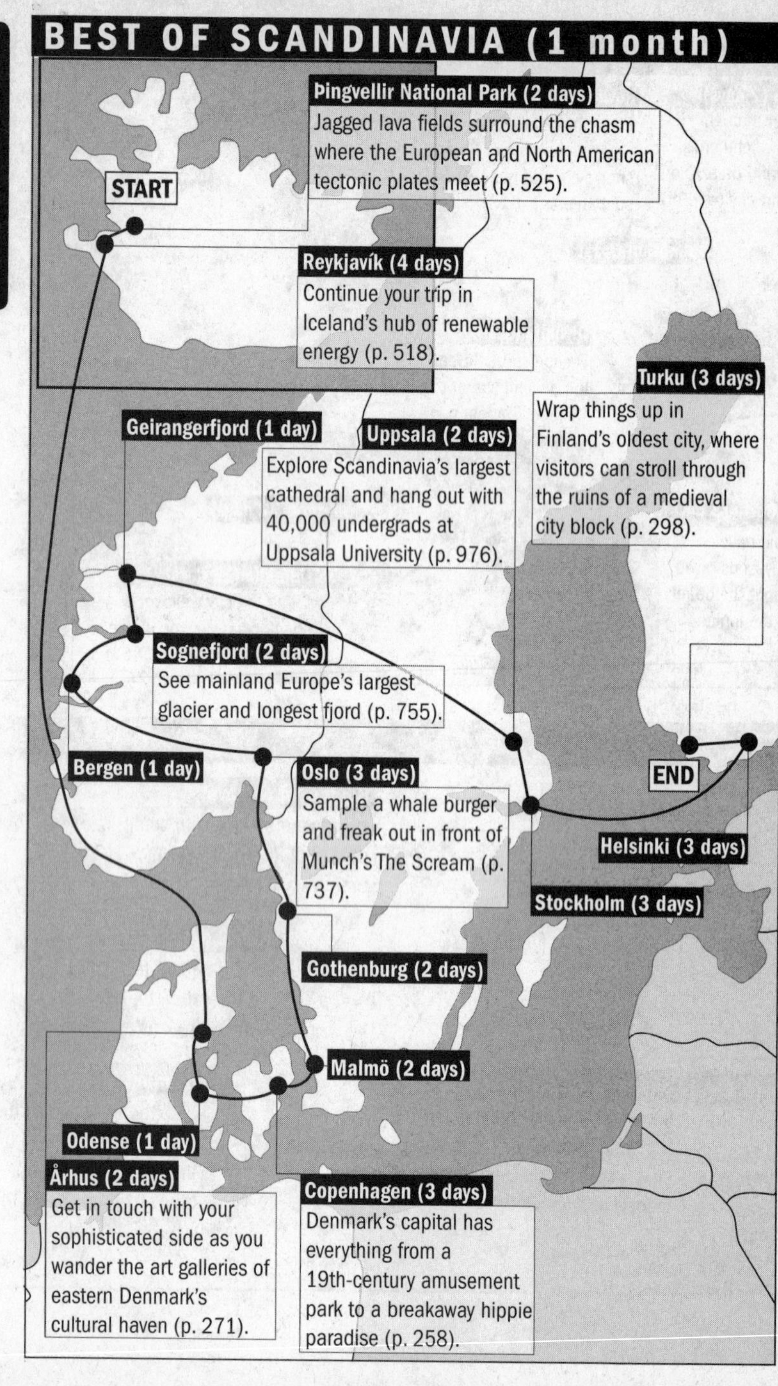
START
Þingvellir National Park (2 days)
Jagged lava fields surround the chasm where the European and North American tectonic plates meet (p. 525).
Reykjavík (4 days)
Continue your trip in Iceland's hub of renewable energy (p. 518).
Turku (3 days)
Wrap things up in Finland's oldest city, where visitors can stroll through the ruins of a medieval city block (p. 298).
Geirangerfjord (1 day)
Uppsala (2 days)
Explore Scandinavia's largest cathedral and hang out with 40,000 undergrads at Uppsala University (p. 976).
Sognefjord (2 days)
See mainland Europe's largest glacier and longest fjord (p. 755).
Bergen (1 day)
Oslo (3 days)
Sample a whale burger and freak out in front of Munch's The Scream (p. 737).
END
Helsinki (3 days)
Stockholm (3 days)
Gothenburg (2 days)
Malmö (2 days)
Odense (1 day)
Århus (2 days)
Get in touch with your sophisticated side as you wander the art galleries of eastern Denmark's cultural haven (p. 271).
Copenhagen (3 days)
Denmark's capital has everything from a 19th-century amusement park to a breakaway hippie paradise (p. 258).

FAR EAST (3-4 weeks)

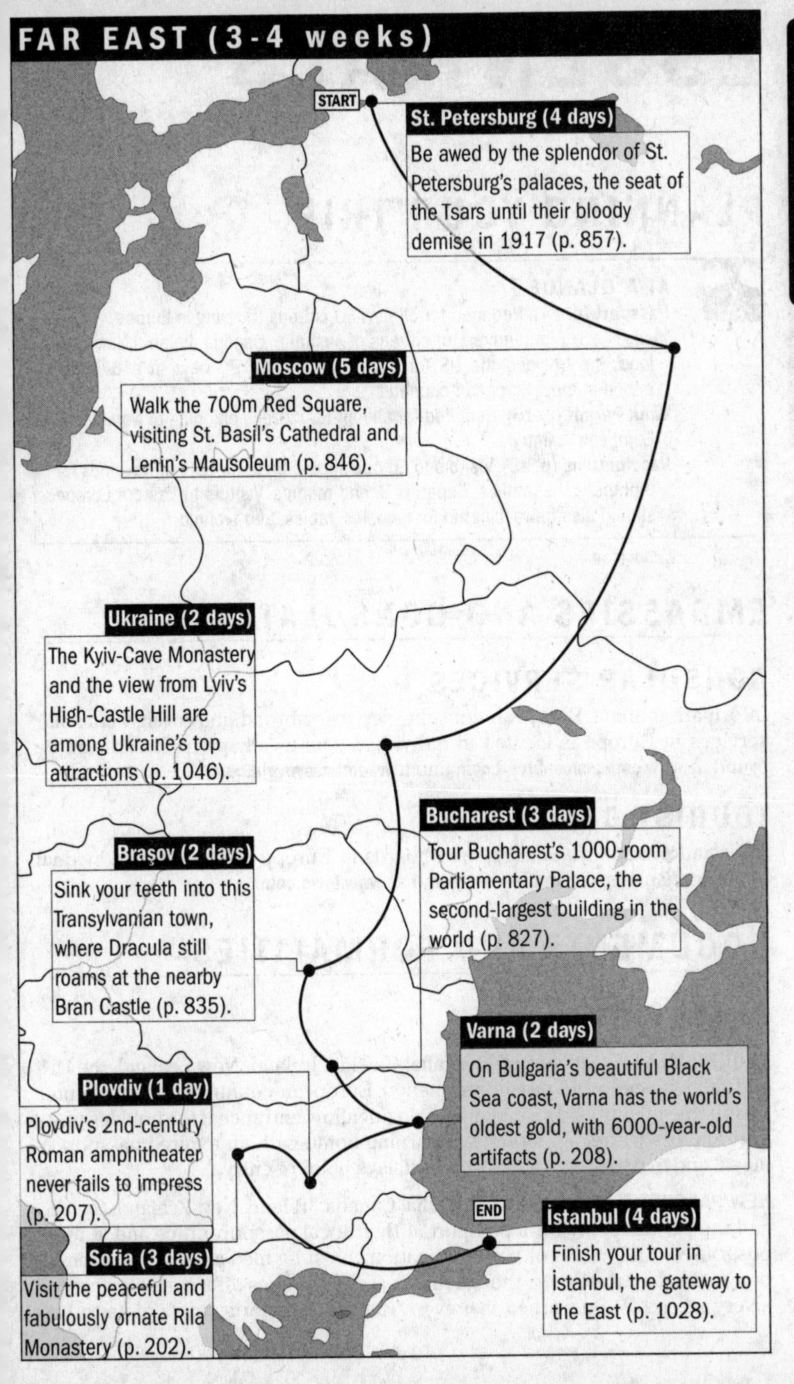
START
St. Petersburg (4 days)
Be awed by the splendor of St. Petersburg's palaces, the seat of the Tsars until their bloody demise in 1917 (p. 857).
Moscow (5 days)
Walk the 700m Red Square, visiting St. Basil's Cathedral and Lenin's Mausoleum (p. 846).
Ukraine (2 days)
The Kyiv-Cave Monastery and the view from Lviv's High-Castle Hill are among Ukraine's top attractions (p. 1046).
Bucharest (3 days)
Tour Bucharest's 1000-room Parliamentary Palace, the second-largest building in the world (p. 827).
Braşov (2 days)
Sink your teeth into this Transylvanian town, where Dracula still roams at the nearby Bran Castle (p. 835).
Varna (2 days)
On Bulgaria's beautiful Black Sea coast, Varna has the world's oldest gold, with 6000-year-old artifacts (p. 208).
Plovdiv (1 day)
Plovdiv's 2nd-century Roman amphitheater never fails to impress (p. 207).
END
İstanbul (4 days)
Finish your tour in İstanbul, the gateway to the East (p. 1028).
Sofia (3 days)
Visit the peaceful and fabulously ornate Rila Monastery (p. 202).

ESSENTIALS

PLANNING YOUR TRIP

AT A GLANCE

Passport (p. 14). Required for all non-EU citizens traveling in Europe.

Visa (p. 15). Not required for citizens of Australia, Canada, Ireland, New Zealand, the UK, and the US for stays shorter than 90 days in a 6-month period in most European countries.

Work Permit (p. 16). Required for all non-EU citizens planning to work in any European country.

Vaccinations (p. 25). Visitors to Europe should be up to date on vaccines for diphtheria, hepatitis A, hepatitis B, and mumps. Visitors to Eastern Europe should also be vaccinated for measles, rabies, and typhoid.

EMBASSIES AND CONSULATES

CONSULAR SERVICES

Information about European consular services abroad and foreign consular services in Europe is located in individual country chapters; it can also be found at **www.embassiesabroad.com** and **www.embassyworld.com.**

TOURIST OFFICES

Information about national tourist boards in Europe is located in individual country chapters; it can also be found at **www.towd.com.**

DOCUMENTS AND FORMALITIES

PASSPORTS

REQUIREMENTS. Citizens of Australia, Canada, Ireland, New Zealand, the UK, and the US need valid passports to enter European countries and to re-enter their home countries. Most countries do not allow entrance if the holder's passport expires within six months. Returning home with an expired passport is illegal and may result in a fine and/or delays upon re-entry.

NEW PASSPORTS. Citizens of Australia, Canada, Ireland, New Zealand, the UK, and the US can apply for a passport at their local passport office and at most post offices and courts of law. Applications must be filed at least two months before the departure date, though most passport offices offer rush services for a very steep fee. Be warned that even "rushed" passports can take up to two weeks to arrive. Citizens living abroad who need a passport or renewal should contact the nearest passport office or consulate of their home country.

PASSPORT MAINTENANCE. Photocopy the page of your passport with your photo, as well as your visas, traveler's check serial numbers, and any other important documents. Carry one set of copies in a safe place, apart from the originals, and leave another set at home. Consulates also recommend that you carry an expired passport or an official copy of your birth certificate in a part of your baggage separate from other documents.

If you lose your passport, immediately notify the local police and the nearest embassy or consulate of your home government. To expedite its replacement, you must show ID and proof of citizenship. It also helps to know all information previously recorded in the passport. In some cases, a replacement may take weeks to process, and it may be valid only for a limited time. Any visas stamped in your old passport will be lost. In an emergency, ask for temporary traveling papers that will permit you to re-enter your home country.

ONE EUROPE. European unity has come a long way since 1958, when the European Economic Community (EEC) was created to promote European solidarity and cooperation. Since then, the EEC has become the European Union (EU), a mighty political, legal, and economic institution. On May 1, 2004, 10 South, Central, and Eastern European countries—Cyprus, the Czech Republic, Estonia, Hungary, Latvia, Lithuania, Malta, Poland, Slovakia, and Slovenia—were admitted into the EU, joining 15 other member states: Austria, Belgium, Denmark, Finland, France, Germany, Greece, Ireland, Italy, Luxembourg, the Netherlands, Portugal, Spain, Sweden, and the UK. On January 1, 2007, two other countries, Bulgaria and Romania, came into the fold, bringing the tally of member states to 27.

What does this have to do with the average non-EU tourist? The EU's **freedom of movement** policy means that most border controls have been abolished and visa policies harmonized. Under this treaty, known as the **Schengen Agreement,** you're still required to carry a passport (or government-issued ID card for EU citizens) when crossing an internal border, but, once you've been admitted into one country, you're free to travel to other participating states. Most EU states are already members of Schengen (minus Bulgaria, Cyprus, Ireland, Romania, and the UK), as are Iceland and Norway. In 2009, Cyprus, Liechtenstein, and Switzerland will bring the number of Schengen countries to 27. Britain and Ireland have also formed a **common travel area,** abolishing passport controls between the UK and the Republic of Ireland.

For more information on the effects of EU policy for travelers, see **The Euro** (p. 19) and **Customs in the EU** (p. 17).

VISAS, INVITATIONS, AND WORK PERMITS

VISAS. As of August 2008, citizens of Australia, Canada, Ireland, New Zealand, the UK, or the US did not need a visa to visit the following countries for fewer than 90 days: Andorra, Austria, Belgium, Britain, Denmark, France, Germany, Greece, Ireland, Italy, Liechtenstein, Luxembourg, the Netherlands, Portugal, Spain, and Switzerland. For travelers planning to spend more than 90 days in any European country, visas cost US$35-200 and typically allow you six months in that country. Visas can usually be purchased at a consulate or at www.

itseasypassport.com/services/visas/visas.htm. Double-check entrance requirements at the nearest embassy or consulate of your destination for up-to-date info before departure. US citizens can consult http://travel.state.gov/travel.

WORK PERMITS. Admission as a visitor does not include the right to work, which is authorized only by a work permit. Entering a country in Europe to study typically requires a special study visa (which does not necessarily authorize employment), which can be fairly expensive, though many study-abroad programs are able to subsidize it. For more info, see **Beyond Tourism,** p. 60.

IDENTIFICATION

When you travel, always carry at least two forms of identification on your person, including a photo ID; a passport and a driver's license or birth certificate is usually adequate. Never carry all of your IDs together; split them up in case of theft or loss, and keep photocopies of them in your luggage and at home.

STUDENT, TEACHER, AND YOUTH IDENTIFICATION. The **International Student Identity Card** (ISIC), the most widely accepted form of student ID, provides discounts on some sights, accommodations, food, and transportation; access to a 24hr. emergency helpline; and insurance benefits for US cardholders (see **Insurance,** p. 25). Applicants must be full-time secondary or post-secondary school students. Because of the proliferation of fake ISICs, some services (particularly airlines) require additional proof of student identity.

The **International Teacher Identity Card** (ITIC) offers teachers the same insurance coverage as the ISIC and similar but limited discounts. For travelers who are under 26 years old but are not students, the **International Youth Travel Card** (IYTC) also offers many of the same benefits as the ISIC.

Each of these identity cards costs US$22. ISICs and ITICs are valid until the new year unless purchased between September and December, in which case they are valid until the beginning of the following new year. IYTCs are valid for one year from the date of issue. To learn more about ISICs, ITICs, and IYTCs, see www.myisic.com. Many travel agencies issue the cards; for more info, see the **International Student Travel Confederation** (ISTC) website (www.istc.org).

The **International Student Exchange Card** (ISE Card) is a similar identification card strictly available to students, faculty, and youths aged 12 to 26. The card provides discounts, medical benefits, access to a 24hr. emergency helpline, and the ability to purchase student airfares. An ISE Card generally costs US$25 and should be purchased well before your departure date; for more information, call in the US ☎800-255-8000, or visit online at www.isecard.com.

CUSTOMS

When you enter a European country, you must declare certain items from abroad and pay a duty on the value of those articles if they exceed a set allowance. Note that goods purchased at **duty-free** shops are not exempt from duty or sales tax; "duty-free" merely means that you need not pay a tax in the country of purchase. Duty-free allowances were abolished for travel between EU member states but still exist for those arriving from outside the EU. Upon returning home, you must likewise declare all goods and articles acquired abroad and pay a duty on the value of goods and articles in excess of your home country's allowance. In order to expedite your return, it is recommended to make a list of any valuables brought from home, and register them with customs before traveling abroad, and being sure to keep receipts for all goods acquired abroad.

CUSTOMS IN THE EU. As well as freedom of movement of people (p. 15), travelers in the European Union can also take advantage of the freedom of movement of goods. This means that there are no customs controls at internal EU borders (i.e., you can take the blue customs channel at the airport), and travelers are free to transport whatever legal substances they like as long as it is for their own personal (non-commercial) use—up to 800 cigarettes, 10L of spirits, 90L of wine (including up to 60L of sparkling wine), and 110L of beer. Duty-free allowances were abolished on June 30, 1999, for travel between the original 15 EU member states; this now also applies to Cyprus and Malta. However, travelers between the EU and the rest of the world still get a duty-free allowance when passing through customs.

MONEY

CURRENCY AND EXCHANGE

The currency chart on the next page is based on August 2008 exchange rates between euro and Australian dollars (AUS$), Canadian dollars (CDN$), New Zealand dollars (NZ$), British pounds (UK£), and US dollars (US$). Check the currency converter on websites like www.xe.com or www.bloomberg.com, or a large newspaper, for the latest exchange rates.

As a general rule, it's cheaper to convert money in Europe than in the United States. While currency exchange will probably be available in your arrival airport, it's wise to bring enough currency to last for the first 24-72hr. of your trip, since airport rates are generally less competitive.

EURO (€)		
	AUS$1 = €0.59	€1 = AUS$1.70
	CDN$1 = €0.62	€1 = CDN$1.62
	NZ$1 = €0.47	€1 = NZ$2.15
	UK£1 = €1.26	€1 = UK£0.79
	US$1 = €0.65	€1 = US$1.54

When exchanging money abroad, try to go only to banks or official exchange establishments that have at most a 5% margin between their buy and sell prices. Because you lose money with every transaction, convert large sums (unless the currency is depreciating rapidly), but no more than you'll need.

If you use traveler's checks or bills, carry some in small denominations (the equivalent of US$50 or less) for times when you are forced to exchange money at disadvantageous rates, but bring a range of denominations, as charges may be levied per check cashed. Store your money in a variety of forms; ideally, at any given time you will be carrying some cash, some traveler's checks, and an ATM and/or credit card. All travelers should also consider carrying some US dollars (about US$50 worth), which are often preferred by local tellers.

CREDIT, ATM, AND DEBIT CARDS

Where they are accepted, credit cards often offer superior exchange rates—up to 5% better than the retail rate used by banks and other currency exchange establishments. Credit cards may also offer services such as insurance or emergency help and are sometimes required to reserve hotel rooms or rental cars. **MasterCard** (a.k.a. **EuroCard** in Europe) and Visa (e.g., **Carte Bleue**) are the most frequently accepted; **American Express** cards work at some ATMs and at AmEx offices and major airports.

The use of ATM cards is widespread in Europe. Depending on the system that your home bank uses, you can most likely access your personal bank account from abroad. ATMs get the same wholesale exchange rate as credit cards, but there is often a limit on the amount of money you can withdraw per day. There is also typically a surcharge of US$1-5 per withdrawal.

Debit cards are as convenient as credit cards but withdraw money directly from the holder's checking account. A debit card can be used wherever its associated credit card company (usually MasterCard or Visa) is accepted. Debit cards often also function as ATM cards and can be used to withdraw cash from associated banks and ATMs throughout Europe.

The two major international money networks are **MasterCard/Maestro/Cirrus** (for ATM locations ☎+1-800-424-7787 or www.mastercard.com) and **Visa/PLUS** (for ATM locations ☎+1-800-847-2911 or www.visa.com). Most ATMs charge a transaction fee that is paid to the bank that owns the ATM.

PINS AND ATMS. To use a cash or credit card to withdraw money from a cash machine (ATM) in Europe, you must have a four-digit Personal Identification Number (PIN). If your PIN is longer than four digits, ask your bank whether you can just use the first four or whether you'll need a new one. Credit cards don't usually come with PINs, so, if you intend to hit up ATMs in Europe with a credit card to get cash advances, call your credit-card company before leaving to request one.

Travelers with alphabetic, rather than numerical, PINs may also be thrown off by the lack of letters on European cash machines. The following are the corresponding numbers to use: 1 = QZ; 2 = ABC; 3 = DEF; 4 = GHI; 5 = JKL; 6 = MNO; 7 = PRS; 8 = TUV; and 9 = WXY. Note that if you mistakenly punch the wrong code into the machine three times, it will swallow your card.

TRAVELER'S CHECKS

Traveler's checks are one of the safest means of carrying funds. American Express and Visa are the most recognized brands. Many banks and agencies sell them for a small commission. Check issuers provide refunds if the checks are lost or stolen, and many provide additional services, such as toll-free refund hotlines abroad, emergency message services, and assistance with lost and stolen credit cards or passports. Traveler's checks are readily accepted in most of Western Europe. Ask about toll-free refund hotlines and the location of refund centers when purchasing checks, and always carry emergency cash.

American Express: Checks available with commission at select banks, at all AmEx offices, and online (www.americanexpress.com; US residents only). Cardholders can also purchase checks by phone (☎800-528-4800).

Travelex: Thomas Cook MasterCard and Interpayment Visa traveler's checks available. For information about Thomas Cook MasterCard in Canada and the US call ☎800-223-7373, UK ☎0800 622 101; elsewhere, call UK collect ☎+44 1733 318 950. For Interpayment Visa in Canada and the US ☎800-223-7373, in the UK ☎0800 515 884; elsewhere, call UK collect ☎+44 1733 318 949. For more info, visit www.travelex.com.

Visa: Checks available (generally with commission) at banks worldwide. For office locations, call the Visa Travelers Cheque Global Refund and Assistance Center: in Australia ☎800-882-426, New Zealand ☎800-447-002, UK ☎0800 895 078, US

☎800-227-6811; elsewhere, call UK collect ☎+44 2079 378 091. Visa also offers TravelMoney, a pre-paid debit card that can be reloaded online or by phone. For more info on Visa travel services, see http://usa.visa.com/personal/using_visa/travel_with_visa.html.

THE EURO. As of January 1, 2009, the official currency of 16 members of the European Union—Austria, Belgium, Cyprus, Finland, France, Germany, Greece, Ireland, Italy, Luxembourg, Malta, the Netherlands, Portugal, Slovenia, and Spain—will be the euro.

The currency has some important—and positive—consequences for travelers hitting more than one euro-zone country. For one thing, money-changers across the euro-zone are obliged to exchange money at the official, fixed rate (below) and at no commission (though they may still charge a small service fee). Second, euro-denominated traveler's checks allow you to pay for goods and services across the euro-zone, again at the official rate and commission-free. At the time of printing, €1 = US$1.54 = CDN$1.62 = NZ$2.15. For more info, check an online currency converter or www.europa.eu.int.

GETTING MONEY FROM HOME

The easiest and cheapest solution for running out of money while traveling is to have someone back home make a deposit to the bank account linked to your credit card or ATM card. Failing that, consider one of the options below.

TOP TEN WAYS TO SAVE IN EUROPE

1. Always ask about discounts. If **under 26,** you should rarely go a full day without being rewarded for your youth and inexperience.
2. Be aware that room prices tend to shoot up and transportation is a hassle on **festival dates** and during local holidays.
3. Consider purchasing the combination transportation and sights **discount passes** offered by many city tourist offices; they often pay for themselves many times over.
4. Get **out** of the city. A day hiking or beach-lounging provides relief for both you and your wallet.
5. **Travel early;** trains, buses, and ferries leaving early in the day or on weekdays (as opposed to weekends) are generally cheaper than those leaving at other times.
6. Don't expect to eat out every meal in Europe. **Street markets** are excellent places to find cheap fruits and vegetables, and most hostels have kitchens.
7. In major cities, make your base on the **outskirts** of the town, where food and beds tend to be both cheaper and less touristed.
8. Bring a **sleepsack** to avoid the occasional linens rental charge.
9. Clubbing is expensive enough without depending on overpriced mojitos; start the night off with **market-purchased booze.**
10. Be your own tour guide; sightseeing is best—and free—on your own with your **Let's Go.**

WIRING MONEY

It is possible to arrange a **bank money transfer**, which means asking a bank back home to wire money to a bank in Europe. This is the cheapest way to transfer cash, but it's also the slowest, usually taking several days or more. Note that some banks may only release your funds in local currency, potentially sticking you with a poor exchange rate; inquire about this in advance. Money transfer services like **Western Union** are faster and more convenient than bank transfers, but also much pricier. Western Union has many locations worldwide. To find one, visit www.westernunion.com, or call: Australia ☎800 173 833, Canada and US ☎800-325-6000, UK ☎0800 833 833. To wire money using a credit card (Discover, MasterCard, or Visa), call in Canada and the US ☎800-225-5227, UK ☎0800 833 833. Money transfer services are also available to **American Express** cardholders and at selected **Thomas Cook** offices.

US STATE DEPARTMENT (US CITIZENS)

In serious emergencies only, the US State Department will forward money within hours to the nearest consular office or embassy, which will then disburse it according to internal instructions for a US$30 fee. If you wish to use this service, you must contact the Overseas Citizens Service division of the US State Department (from overseas ☎202-501-4444, toll-free 888-407-4747).

COSTS

The cost of your trip will vary depending on where you go, how you travel, and where you stay. The most significant expenses will probably be your round-trip (return) airfare to Europe (see **Getting to Europe: By Plane,** p. 46) and a rail pass or bus pass (see **Getting around Europe,** p. 50).

STAYING ON A BUDGET

Your daily budget will vary greatly from country to country. A bare-bones day in Europe would include camping or sleeping in hostels and buying food in supermarkets. A slightly more comfortable day would include sleeping in hostels or guesthouses and the occasional budget hotel, eating one meal per day at a restaurant, and going out at night. Be sure to factor in emergency reserve funds (at least US$200) when planning how much money you'll need.

TIPS FOR SAVING MONEY

Some simple ways to save include searching out free entertainment, splitting accommodation and food costs with trustworthy fellow travelers, and buying food in grocery stores. Full- or multi-day local transportation passes can also save you valuable pocket change. Bring a **sleepsack** (p. 22) to save at hostels that charge for linens, and do your **laundry** in the sink (unless you're explicitly prohibited from doing so). Museums often have certain days when admission is free. If you are eligible, consider getting an ISIC or an IYTC; many sights and museums offer reduced admission to students and youths. Renting a bike is cheaper than renting a moped or scooter. Drinking at bars and clubs quickly becomes expensive. It's cheaper to buy alcohol at a supermarket and imbibe before going out. That said, don't go overboard. Though staying within your budget is important, don't do so at the expense of your health.

TIPPING AND BARGAINING

In most European countries, a 5-10% gratuity is included in the food service bill. Additional tipping is not expected, but an extra 5-10% for good service is not unusual. Where gratuity is not included, 10-15% tips are standard and rounding up to the next unit of currency is common. Many countries have their own unique tipping practices with which you should familiarize yourself before visiting. In general, tipping in bars and pubs is unnecessary. For other services such as taxis or hairdressers, a 10-15% tip is usually recommended. Watch other customers to gauge what is appropriate. Bargaining is useful in Greece, and in outdoor markets across Europe.

TAXES

The EU imposes a value added tax (VAT) on goods and services, usually included in the sticker price. Non-EU citizens visiting Europe may obtain a refund for taxes paid on retail goods, but not for taxes paid on services. As the VAT is 15-25%, it might be worthwhile to file for a refund. To do so, you must obtain Tax-Free Shopping Cheques, available from shops sporting the Europe Tax-Free Shopping logo, and save your receipts. Upon leaving the EU, present your goods, invoices, and passport to customs and have your checks stamped. Then, go to an ETS cash refund office on site or file for a refund once back home. Keep in mind that goods must be taken out of the country within three months of purchase, and that most countries require minimum purchase amounts per store to become eligible for a refund. See www.globalrefund.com for more info and downloads of relevant forms.

PACKING

Pack lightly. Lay out only what you absolutely need, then take half the clothes and twice the money. The **Travelite FAQ** (www.travelite.org) is a good resource for tips on traveling light. The online **Universal Packing List** (http://upl.codeq.info) will generate a customized list of suggested items based on your trip length, the expected climate, your planned activities, and other factors. If you plan to do a lot of hiking, also consult **The Great Outdoors,** p. 37.

Luggage: If you plan to cover most of your itinerary by foot, a sturdy frame backpack is unbeatable. (For backpack basics, see p. 38.) Toting a suitcase or trunk is fine if you plan to live in 1 or 2 cities, but not if you plan to move around frequently. In addition to your main piece of luggage, a daypack (a small backpack or courier bag) is useful.

Clothing: No matter when you're traveling, it's a good idea to bring a warm jacket or wool sweater, a rain jacket (Gore-Tex® is both waterproof and breathable), sturdy shoes or hiking boots, and thick socks. Waterproof sandals are a must-have for grubby hostel showers. You may also want one outfit for going out, and maybe a nicer pair of shoes. If you plan to visit religious or cultural sites, remember to dress modestly.

DISPOSABLES. If you're tight on space and plan to give your clothes a good workout, consider buying a pack of simple cotton undershirts. A pack of plain t-shirts is cheap and light, and you won't feel bad throwing them away when they get covered in backpacker grime.

Sleepsack: Some hostels require that you either provide your own linens or rent linens from them. Save cash by making your own sleepsack: fold a full-size sheet in half the long way, then sew it closed along the long side and one of the short sides.

Adapters and Converters: In Europe, electricity is 230V AC, enough to fry any 120V North American appliance. Americans and Canadians should buy an adapter (changes the shape of the plug; US$10-30) and a converter (changes the voltage; US$10-30); don't use an adapter without a converter unless appliance instructions explicitly state otherwise. Australians and New Zealanders won't need a converter, but will need a set of adapters. For more on all things adaptable, check out http://kropla.com/electric.htm.

Toiletries: Toothbrushes, towels, soap, talcum powder (to keep feet dry), deodorant, razors, tampons, and condoms are available, but it may be difficult to find your preferred brand, so bring extras. Also, be sure to bring enough extra contact lenses and solution for your entire trip. Bring your glasses and a copy of your prescription, too, in case you need an emergency replacement. If you use heat disinfection, either switch temporarily to a chemical disinfection system (check first to make sure it's safe with your brand of lenses), or buy a converter to 220/240V. Pack minimal toiletries in your hand baggage to avoid confiscation at airport security checks.

KEEP IT CLEAN. Multi-purpose liquid soaps will save space and keep you from smelling like last night's fish and chips. Dr. Bronner's® and Campsuds® both make soap that you can use as toothpaste, shampoo, laundry detergent, dishwashing liquid, and more. Plus, they're biodegradable.

First Aid: For a basic first-aid kit, pack bandages, a pain reliever, antibiotic cream, a thermometer, a pocket knife, tweezers, moleskin, decongestant, motion-sickness remedy, diarrhea or upset-stomach medication (Pepto Bismol® or Imodium®), an antihistamine, sunscreen, insect repellent, and burn ointment. If you will be in remote regions of less-developed Eastern European countries, consider a syringe for emergencies (get an explanatory letter from your doctor). Leave all sharp objects in your checked luggage.

Film: Digital cameras can be a more economical option and less of a hassle than regular cameras, just be sure to bring along a large enough memory card and extra (or rechargeable) batteries. Less serious photographers may want to bring a disposable camera or two. Despite disclaimers, airport security X-rays can fog film, so buy a lead-lined pouch at a camera store or ask security to hand-inspect it. Always pack film in your carry-on luggage, as higher-intensity X-rays are used on checked luggage.

Other Useful Items: For safety, bring a **money belt** and a small **padlock.** Basic **outdoors equipment** (water bottle, compass, waterproof matches, pocketknife, sunglasses, sunscreen, hat) may also prove useful. Make quick repairs with a needle and thread; also consider electrical tape for patching tears. To do laundry by hand, bring detergent, a small rubber ball to stop up the sink, and string for a makeshift clothesline. Extra plastic bags are crucial for storing food, dirty shoes, and wet clothes, and for keeping liquids from exploding all over your clothes. Other items include an umbrella, a battery-powered alarm clock, safety pins, rubber bands, a flashlight, a utility pocketknife, earplugs, garbage bags, and a small calculator. A mobile phone can be a lifesaver on the road; see p. 32 for information on acquiring one that will work at your destination.

Important Documents: Don't forget your passport, traveler's checks, ATM and/or credit cards, adequate ID, and photocopies of all of the aforementioned. Other documents you may wish to have include: hosteling membership card (p. 33); a driver's license (p. 16); travel insurance forms (p. 25); an ISIC (p. 26); a rail or bus pass (p. 51).

ESSENTIALS

SAFETY AND HEALTH

GENERAL ADVICE

In any type of crisis situation, the most important thing to do is **stay calm.** Your country's embassy abroad is usually your best resource in an emergency; registering with that embassy upon arrival in the country is often a good idea. *Let's Go* lists consulates in the **Practical Information** section of large cities.

TRAVEL ADVISORIES. The following government offices provide travel information and advisories by telephone, by fax, or via the web:

Australian Department of Foreign Affairs and Trade: ☎+61 2 6261 1111; www.dfat.gov.au.

Canadian Department of Foreign Affairs and International Trade (DFAIT): ☎+1-800-267-8376; www.dfait-maeci.gc.ca. Visit the website for the booklet *Bon Voyage...But.*

Ireland Department of Foreign Affairs: ☎353 1 478 0822; www.foreignaffairs.gov.ie.

New Zealand Ministry of Foreign Affairs and Trade: ☎+64 4 439 8000; www.mfat.govt.nz.

United Kingdom Foreign and Commonwealth Office: ☎+44 20 7008 1500; www.fco.gov.uk.

US Department of State: ☎+1-888-407-4747; http://travel.state.gov. Visit the website for the booklet *A Safe Trip Abroad.*

DRUGS AND ALCOHOL. Drug and alcohol laws vary widely throughout Europe. "Soft" drugs are tolerated in the Netherlands, while in much of Eastern Europe drug possession may lead to a heavy prison sentence. If you carry **prescription drugs,** include both a copy of the prescriptions themselves and a note from a doctor, especially at border crossings. **Public drunkenness** is culturally unacceptable and against the law in many countries; it can also jeopardize your safety.

TERRORISM AND CIVIL UNREST. In the wake of September 11 and the war in Iraq, be vigilant near embassies and be wary of big crowds and demonstrations. Keep an eye on the news, pay attention to travel warnings, and comply with security measures. Overall, risks of civil unrest tend to be localized and rarely directed toward tourists. Tensions remain in Northern Ireland, especially around July "marching season," which reaches its height July 4-12. Notoriously violent separatist movements include the ETA, a Basque group that operates in southern France and Spain, and FLNC, a Corsican separatist group in France. The November 17 group in Greece is known for anti-Western acts, though they have not targeted tourists, to date. The box above lists offices to contact and webpages to visit to get the most updated list about travel advisories.

PERSONAL SAFETY

EXPLORING AND TRAVELING

To avoid unwanted attention, try to blend in. Respecting local customs (in many cases, dressing more conservatively than you would at home) may ward off would-be hecklers. Familiarize yourself with your surroundings before setting out, and carry yourself with confidence. Avoid checking maps on the street. If you are traveling alone, be sure someone at home knows your itinerary, and never tell anyone you meet that you're by yourself. When walking at night, stick to busy, well-lit streets and avoid dark alleyways. If you ever feel uncomfortable, leave the area as quickly and directly as you can.

There is no sure-fire way to avoid all the threatening situations you might encounter while traveling, but a good **self defense course** will give you concrete ways to react to unwanted advances. **Impact, Prepare,** and **Model Mugging** can refer you to local self defense courses in Australia, Canada, Switzerland and the US. Visit the website at www.modelmugging.org for more info.

If you are using a **car,** familiarize yourself with local driving signals and wear a seatbelt. Children under 40 lbs. should ride only in specially designed carseats, available for a small fee from most car rental agencies. Study route maps before you hit the road and, if you plan on spending a lot of time driving, consider bringing spare parts. For long drives in desolate areas, invest in a mobile phone (p. 32) and a roadside assistance program. Park your vehicle in a garage or well-traveled area and use a steering wheel locking device in larger cities. **Sleeping in your car** is very dangerous, and it's also illegal in many countries. For info on the perils of **hitchhiking,** see p. 59.

POSSESSIONS AND VALUABLES

Never leave your belongings unattended; crime occurs in even the most safe-looking hostels and hotels. Bring your own padlock for hostel lockers, and don't store valuables in a locker. Be particularly careful on **buses** and **trains;** horror stories abound about determined thieves who wait for travelers to fall asleep. Carry your bag or purse in front of you. When traveling with others, sleep in alternate shifts. When alone, use good judgment in selecting a train compartment: never stay in an empty one, and use a lock to secure your pack to the luggage rack. Use extra caution if traveling at night or on overnight trains. Try to sleep on top bunks with your luggage stored above you, and keep important documents and other valuables on you at all times.

There are a few steps you can take to minimize the financial risk associated with traveling. First, **bring as little with you as possible.** Second, buy a few combination **padlocks** to secure your belongings either in your pack or in a hostel or train station locker. Third, **carry as little cash as possible.** Keep your traveler's checks and ATM/credit cards in a **money belt**—not a "fanny pack"—along with your passport and ID cards. Fourth, **keep a small cash reserve separate from your primary stash.** This should be about US$50 (US$ or euro are best) sewn into or stored in the depths of your pack, along with your traveler's check numbers and photocopies of your passport and other important documents.

In large cities **con artists** often work in groups and may involve children. Beware of certain classics: sob stories that require money, rolls of bills "found" on the street, mustard spilled (or saliva spit) onto your shoulder to distract you while they snatch your bag. **Never let your passport and your bags out of your sight.** Hostel workers will sometimes stand at bus and train station arrival points to try to recruit tired and disoriented travelers to their hostel; never believe strangers who tell you that theirs is the only hostel open. Beware of **pickpockets** in city crowds, especially on public transportation. Also, be alert in public telephone booths: if you must say your calling card number, do so very quietly; if you punch it in, make sure no one can look over your shoulder.

If you will be traveling with electronic devices, check whether your homeowner's insurance covers loss, theft, or damage when you travel. If not, you might consider purchasing a low-cost separate insurance policy. **Safeware** (☎+1-800-800-1492; www.safeware.com) specializes in covering computers. State rates vary, but average US$200 for global coverage up to $4000.

PRE-DEPARTURE HEALTH

In your **passport,** write the names of any people you wish to be contacted in case of a medical emergency, and list any allergies or medical conditions. Matching a prescription to a foreign equivalent is not always easy, safe, or possible, so if you take prescription drugs, carry up-to-date prescriptions or a statement from your doctor stating the medication's trade name, manufacturer, chemical name, and dosage. While traveling, be sure to keep all medication in your carry-on luggage. For tips on packing a **first-aid kit,** see p. 22.

INSURANCE

Travel insurance covers four basic areas: medical/health problems, property loss, trip cancellation/interruption, and emergency evacuation. Though regular insurance policies may well extend to travel-related accidents, you may consider purchasing separate travel insurance if the cost of potential trip cancellation, interruption, or emergency medical evacuation is greater than you can absorb. Prices for independent travel insurance generally run about US$50 per week for full coverage, while trip cancellation/interruption may be purchased separately at a rate of US$3-5 per day, depending on length of stay.

Medical insurance (especially university policies) often covers costs incurred abroad; check with your provider. **Australians** traveling in Finland, Ireland, Italy, the Netherlands, Sweden, or the UK are entitled to many of the services that they would receive at home as part of the Reciprocal Health Care Agreement. **Homeowners' insurance** often covers theft during travel and loss of travel documents (passport, plane ticket, rail pass, etc.) up to US$500.

ISIC and **ITIC** (p. 16) provide basic insurance benefits to US cardholders, including US$100 per day of in-hospital sickness for up to 100 days and US$10,000 of accident-related medical reimbursement (see www.myisic.com for details). Cardholders have access to a toll-free 24hr. helpline for emergencies. **American Express** (☎+1-800-528-4800) grants most cardholders automatic collision and theft insurance on car rentals made with the card.

USEFUL ORGANIZATIONS AND PUBLICATIONS

The American **Centers for Disease Control and Prevention** (**CDC;** ☎+1-800-311-3435; www.cdc.gov/travel) maintains an international travelers' hotline and an informative website. Consult the appropriate government agency of your home country for consular information sheets on health, entry requirements, and other issues for various countries (see **Travel Advisories,** p. 23). For quick information on health and other travel warnings, call the **Overseas Citizens Services** (M-F 8am-8pm from US ☎+1-888-407-4747, from overseas ☎+1-202-501-4444), or contact a passport agency, embassy, or consulate abroad. For information on medical evacuation services and travel insurance firms, see the US government's website http://travel.state.gov/travel/abroad_health.html or the **British Foreign and Commonwealth Office** (www.fco.gov.uk). For general health information, contact the **American Red Cross** (☎+1-202-303-4498; www.redcross.org).

STAYING HEALTHY

Common sense is the simplest prescription for good health while you travel. Drink plenty of hydrating fluids to prevent dehydration and constipation, and wear sturdy, broken-in shoes and clean socks.

COMES IN HANDY. A small bottle of liquid hand cleanser, a stash of moist towelettes, or even a package of baby wipes can keep your hands and face germ-free and refreshed on the road. The hand cleanser should have an alcohol content of at least 70% to be effective.

ONCE IN WESTERN EUROPE

ENVIRONMENTAL HAZARDS

Heat exhaustion and dehydration: Heat exhaustion leads to nausea, excessive thirst, headaches, and dizziness. Avoid it by drinking plenty of fluids, eating salty foods (e.g., crackers), abstaining from dehydrating beverages (e.g., alcohol and caffeinated beverages), and wearing sunscreen. Continuous heat stress can eventually lead to heatstroke, characterized by a rising temperature, severe headache, delirium, and cessation of sweating. Victims should be cooled off with wet towels and taken to a doctor.

Sunburn: Always wear sunscreen (SPF 30 or higher) when spending time outdoors. If you get sunburned, drink more fluids than usual and apply an aloe-based lotion. Severe sunburns can lead to sun poisoning, a condition that can cause fever, chills, nausea, and vomiting. Sun poisoning should always be treated by a doctor.

Hypothermia and frostbite: A rapid drop in body temperature is the clearest sign of overexposure to cold. Victims may also shiver, feel exhausted, have poor coordination or slurred speech, hallucinate, or suffer amnesia. Do not let hypothermia victims fall asleep. To avoid hypothermia, keep dry, wear layers, and stay out of the wind. When the temperature is below freezing, watch out for frostbite. If skin turns white or blue, waxy, and cold, do not rub the area. Drink warm beverages, stay dry, and slowly warm the area with dry fabric or steady body contact until a doctor can be found.

High Altitude: Allow your body a couple of days to adjust to less oxygen before exerting yourself. Note that alcohol is more potent and UV rays are stronger at high elevations.

INSECT-BORNE DISEASES

Many diseases are transmitted by insects—mainly mosquitoes, fleas, ticks, and lice. Be aware of insects in wet or forested areas, especially while hiking and camping. Wear long pants and long sleeves, tuck your pants into your socks, and use a mosquito net. Use insect repellents such as DEET and soak or spray your gear with permethrin (licensed in the US only for use on clothing). **Ticks**—which can carry Lyme and other diseases—can be particularly dangerous in rural and forested regions.

Tick-borne encephalitis: A viral infection of the central nervous system transmitted during the summer by tick bites (primarily in wooded areas) or by consumption of unpasteurized dairy products. The risk of contracting the disease is relatively low, especially if precautions are taken against tick bites.

Lyme disease: A bacterial infection carried by ticks and marked by a circular bull's-eye rash of 2 in. or more. Later symptoms include fever, headache, fatigue, and aches and pains. Antibiotics are effective if administered early. Left untreated, Lyme disease can cause problems in joints, the heart, and the nervous system. If you find a tick attached to your skin, grasp the head with tweezers as close to your skin as possible and apply slow, steady traction. Removing a tick within 24hr. greatly reduces the risk of infection. Do not try to remove ticks with petroleum jelly, nail polish remover, or a hot match. Ticks usually inhabit moist, shaded environments and heavily wooded areas. If you are going to be hiking in these areas, wear long clothes and DEET.

Other insect-borne diseases: Lymphatic filariasis is a roundworm infestation transmitted by mosquitoes. Infection causes enlargement of extremities and has no vaccine. **Leishmaniasis,** a parasite transmitted by sand flies, can occur in rural areas of Western Europe. Common symptoms are fever, weakness, and swelling of the spleen, as well as skin sores. There is a treatment, but no vaccine.

FOOD- AND WATER-BORNE DISEASES

Prevention is the best cure: be sure that your food is properly cooked and the water you drink is clean. Watch out for food from markets or street vendors that may have been cooked in unhygienic conditions. Other culprits are raw shellfish, unpasteurized milk, and sauces containing raw eggs. If the region's tap water is known to be unsanitary, peel fruits and vegetables before eating them and avoid tap water (including ice cubes and anything washed in tap water). Buy bottled water, or purify your own water by bringing it to a rolling boil or treating it with **iodine tablets;** note that some parasites have exteriors that resist iodine treatment, so boiling is more reliable. Always wash your hands.

Giardiasis: Transmitted through parasites and acquired by drinking untreated water from streams or lakes. Symptoms include diarrhea, cramps, bloating, fatigue, weight loss, and nausea. If untreated, it can lead to severe dehydration. Giardiasis occurs worldwide.

Hepatitis A: A viral infection of the liver acquired through contaminated water or shellfish from contaminated water. Symptoms include fatigue, fever, loss of appetite, nausea, dark urine, jaundice, vomiting, aches and pains, and light stools. The risk is highest in rural areas and the countryside, but it is also present in urban areas. Ask your doctor about the Hepatitis A vaccine or an injection of immune globulin.

Traveler's diarrhea: Results from drinking fecally contaminated water or eating uncooked and contaminated foods. Symptoms include nausea, bloating, and urgency. Try quick-energy, non-sugary foods with protein and carbohydrates to keep your strength up. Over-the-counter anti-diarrheals (e.g., Imodium®) may counteract the problem. The most dangerous side effect is dehydration; drink 8 oz. of water with tsp. of sugar or honey and a pinch of salt, try uncaffeinated soft drinks, or eat salted crackers. If you develop a fever or your symptoms don't go away after 4-5 days, consult a doctor. Consult a doctor immediately for treatment of diarrhea in children.

Sexually transmitted infections (STIs): Gonorrhea, chlamydia, genital warts, syphilis, herpes, HPV, and other STIs are easier to catch than HIV and can be just as serious. Though condoms may protect you from some STIs, oral or even tactile contact can lead to transmission. If you think you may have contracted an STI, see a doctor immediately.

OTHER HEALTH CONCERNS

MEDICAL CARE ON THE ROAD

While healthcare systems in Western Europe tend to be quite accessible and of high quality, medical care varies greatly across Eastern and Southern Europe. Major cities such as Prague have English-speaking medical centers or hospitals for foreigners. In general, medical service in these regions is not up to Western standards; though basic supplies are usually there, specialized treatment is not. Tourist offices may have names of local doctors who speak English. In the event of a medical emergency, contact your embassy for aid and recommendations. All EU citizens can receive free or reduced-cost first aid and emergency services by presenting a **European Health Insurance Card.**

If you are concerned about obtaining medical assistance while traveling, you may wish to employ special support services. The **MedPass** from **GlobalCare, Inc.,** 6875 Shiloh Rd. East, Alpharetta, GA 30005, USA (☎800-860-1111; www.globalcare.net), provides 24hr. international medical assistance, support, and medical evacuation resources. The **International Association for Medical Assistance to Travelers** (**IAMAT;** US ☎+1-716-754-4883, Canada 519-836-0102; www.iamat.org) has free membership, lists English-speaking doctors worldwide, and offers detailed info on immunization requirements and sanitation. If your regular insurance policy does not cover travel abroad, you may wish to purchase additional coverage in case of emergency (see p. 25).

Those with medical conditions may want to obtain a **MedicAlert** membership (US$40 per year), which includes among other things a stainless steel ID tag and

a 24hr. collect-call number. Contact the MedicAlert Foundation International, 2323 Colorado Ave., Turlock, CA 95382, USA (☎+1-888-633-4298, outside US ☎+1-209-668-3333; www.medicalert.org).

WOMEN'S HEALTH

Women traveling in unsanitary conditions are vulnerable to urinary tract **infections.** Over-the-counter medicines can sometimes alleviate symptoms, but if they persist, see a doctor. Vaginal yeast infections may flare up in hot and humid climates. Wearing loose-fitting trousers or a skirt and cotton underwear will help, as will over-the-counter remedies. Bring supplies if you are prone to infection, as it may be difficult to find the brands you prefer on the road. **Tampons, pads,** and **contraceptive devices** are widely available in most of Western Europe, but can be hard to find in areas of Eastern Europe. **Abortion** laws also vary from country to country. In much of Western Europe, abortion is legal during at least the first 10-12 weeks of pregnancy, but remains illegal in Ireland, Monaco, and Spain, except in extreme circumstances.

KEEPING IN TOUCH

BY EMAIL AND INTERNET

Email is popular and easily accessible in most of Europe. Although in some places it's possible to forge a remote link with your home server, in most cases this is a much slower (and thus more expensive) option than taking advantage of free **web-based email accounts** (e.g., **www.gmail.com** and www.hotmail.com). **Internet cafes** and the occasional free Internet terminal at a public library or university are listed in the **Practical Information** sections of major cities. For lists of additional cybercafes in Europe, check out www.cybercaptive.com, www.netcafeguide.com, and www.cybercafe.com.

WARY WI-FI. Wireless hot spots make Internet access possible in public and remote places. Unfortunately, they also pose **security risks.** Hot spots are public, open networks that use unencrypted, unsecured connections. They are susceptible to hacks and "packet sniffing"—ways of stealing passwords and other private information. To prevent problems, disable ad hoc mode, turn off file sharing and network discovery, encrypt your email, turn on your firewall, beware of phony networks, and watch for over-the-shoulder creeps.

Travelers find that taking their **laptop computers** on the road with them can be a convenient option for staying connected. Laptop users can call an Internet service provider via a modem using long-distance phone cards specifically intended for such calls. Another option is **Voice over Internet Protocol (VoIP).** A particularly popular provider, **Skype,** allows users to contact other users for free, and to call landlines and mobile phones for an additional fee. Some Internet cafes allow travelers to connect their laptops to the Internet. Travelers with wireless-enabled computers may be able to take advantage of an increasing number of wireless "hot spots," where they can get online for free or for a small fee. Newer computers can detect these hot spots automatically; otherwise, websites like www.jiwire.com can help you find them. Bringing your laptop to a cafe can make you stand out as a (seemingly rich) tourist, so be wary of flashing that tech bling in sketchy neighborhoods.

BY TELEPHONE

CALLING HOME FROM EUROPE

Prepaid phone cards are a common and relatively inexpensive means of calling abroad. Each one comes with a Personal Identification Number (PIN) and a toll-free access number. Call the access number and then follow the directions for dialing your PIN. To purchase prepaid phone cards, check online for the best rates; www.callingcards.com is a good place to start. Online providers generally send your access number and PIN via email, with no actual "card" involved. You can also call home with prepaid phone cards purchased in Europe (see **Calling Within Europe,** p. 31).

PLACING INTERNATIONAL CALLS. All international dialing prefixes and country codes for Europe are shown in a chart on the **Inside Back Cover** of this book. To place international calls, dial:

1. The **international dialing prefix.** To call from **Australia,** dial 0011; **Canada** or the **US,** 011; **Ireland, New Zealand,** or the **UK,** 00.
2. The **country code** of the country you want to call. To call **Australia,** dial 61; **Canada** or the **US,** 1; **Ireland,** 353; **New Zealand,** 64; the **UK,** 44.
3. The **city/area code.** *Let's Go* lists the city/area codes for cities and towns in Europe opposite the city or town name, next to a ☎, as well as in every phone number. If the first digit is a zero (e.g., 020 for London), omit the zero when calling from abroad (e.g., dial 20 from **Canada** to reach **London**).
4. The **local number.**

Another option is to purchase a **calling card,** linked to a major national telecommunications service in your home country. Calls are billed collect or to your account. To obtain a calling card, contact the appropriate company listed below. Where available, there are often advantages to purchasing calling cards online, including better rates and immediate access to your account. Companies that offer calling cards include: **AT&T Direct** (US ☎800-364-9292; www.att.com); **Canada Direct** (☎800-561-8868; www.infocanadadirect.com); **MCI** (☎800-777-5000; www.minutepass.com); **Telecom New Zealand Direct** (www.telecom.co.nz); **Telstra Australia** (☎1800 676 638; www.telstra.com). To call home with a calling card, contact the operator for your service provider by dialing the appropriate toll-free access number. Placing a **collect call** through an international operator can be expensive but may be necessary in case of an emergency. You can frequently call collect without even possessing a company's calling card just by calling its access number and following the instructions. *Let's Go* lists access numbers in the **Essentials** sections of each chapter.

CALLING WITHIN EUROPE

The simplest way to call within a country is to use a public pay phone. However, much of Europe has switched to a **prepaid phone card** system, and in some countries you may have a hard time finding coin-operated phones. Prepaid phone cards (available at newspaper kiosks and tobacco stores), which carry a certain amount of phone time depending on the card's denomination, usually save time and money in the long run. Another kind of prepaid phone card comes with a PIN and a toll-free access number. Instead of inserting the card into the phone, you call the access number and follow the directions on the card. These cards can be used to make international as well as domestic calls.

ESSENTIALS

MOBILE PHONES

Mobile phones are an increasingly popular option for travelers calling within Europe. In addition to greater convenience and safety, mobile phones often provide an economical alternative to expensive landline calls. Virtually all of Western Europe has excellent coverage. The international standard for mobile phones is **Global System for Mobile Communication** (GSM). To make and receive calls in Europe, you need a **GSM-compatible phone** and a **subscriber identity module (SIM) card,** a country-specific, thumbnail-sized chip that gives you a local phone number and plugs you into the local network. Many SIM cards are prepaid, and incoming calls are free. When you use up the prepaid time, you can buy additional cards or vouchers (usually available at convenience stores) to "top up" your phone. For more info on GSM phones, check out www.telestial.com, www.orange.co.uk, www.roadpost.com, or www.planetomni.com. Companies like **Cellular Abroad** (www.cellularabroad.com) rent mobile phones that work in a variety of destinations around the world.

GSM PHONES. Just having a GSM phone doesn't mean you're necessarily good to go when you travel abroad. The majority of GSM phones sold in the United States operate on a different **frequency** (1900) than international phones (900/1800) and will not work abroad. Tri-band phones work on all three frequencies (900/1800/1900) and will operate through most of the world. Additionally, some GSM phones are **SIM-locked** and will only accept SIM cards from a single carrier. You'll need a **SIM-unlocked** phone to use a SIM card from a local carrier when you travel.

TIME DIFFERENCES

All of Europe falls within 3hr. of **Greenwich Mean Time (GMT).** For more info, consult the time zone chart on the **Inside Back Cover.** GMT is 5hr. ahead of New York time, 8hr. ahead of Vancouver time, 10hr. behind Sydney time, and 12hr. behind Auckland time. Iceland is the only country in Europe to ignore Daylight Saving Time; fall and spring switchover times vary in countries that do observe Daylight Saving. For more info, visit www.worldtimeserver.com.

BY MAIL

SENDING MAIL HOME FROM EUROPE

Airmail is the best way to send mail home from Europe. From Western Europe to North America, delivery time averages about seven days. **Aerogrammes,** printed sheets that fold into envelopes and travel via airmail, are available at post offices. Write "airmail" or "*par avion*" (or *por avión*, *mit Luftpost*, *via aerea*, etc.) on the front. Most post offices will charge exorbitant fees or simply refuse to send aerogrammes with enclosures. **Surface mail** is by far the cheapest and slowest way to send mail. It takes one to two months to cross the Atlantic and one to three to cross the Pacific—good for heavy items you won't need for a while, such as souvenirs that you've acquired along the way. Check the **Essentials** section of each chapter for country-specific postal info.

SENDING MAIL TO EUROPE

To ensure timely delivery, mark envelopes "airmail" in both English and the local language. In addition to standard postage systems, **Federal Express** (Australia ☎+61 13 26 10, Canada and the US +1-800-463-3339, Ireland +353 800 535 800, New Zealand +64 800 733 339, the UK +44 8456 070 809; www.fedex.com) handles express mail services from most countries to Europe.

There are several ways to arrange pick-up of letters sent to you while you are abroad. Mail can be sent via **Poste Restante** (General Delivery, *Lista de Correos*, *Fermo Posta*, *Postlagernde Briefe*, etc.) to almost any city or town in Europe with a post office, though it can be unreliable in Eastern Europe. See individual country chapters for more info on addressing Poste Restante letters. The mail will go to a special desk in a town's central post office, unless you specify a post office by street address or postal code. It's best to use the largest post office, since mail may be sent there regardless. It's usually safer and quicker, though more expensive, to send mail express or registered. Bring your passport for pick-up; there may be a small fee. If the clerks insist that there is nothing for you, ask them to check under your first name as well. *Let's Go* lists post offices in the **Practical Information** section for each city and most towns.

American Express's travel offices throughout the world offer a free **Client Letter Service** (mail held up to 30 days and forwarded upon request) for cardholders who contact them in advance. Some offices provide these services to non-cardholders (especially AmEx Travelers Cheque holders), but call ahead to make sure. *Let's Go* lists AmEx locations for most large cities in **Practical Information** sections; for a complete list, visit www.americanexpress.com/travel.

ACCOMMODATIONS

HOSTELS

Many hostels are laid out dorm-style, often with large single-sex rooms and bunk beds, although private rooms sleeping two to four are becoming more common. They sometimes have kitchens, bike or moped rentals, storage areas, airport transportation, breakfast and other meals, laundry facilities, and Internet. There can be drawbacks: some hostels close during certain daytime "lockout" hours, have a curfew, don't accept reservations, impose a maximum stay, or—less frequently—require that you do chores. In Western Europe, a hostel dorm bed will average around US$15-30 and a private room around US$30-50.

A HOSTELER'S BILL OF RIGHTS. There are certain standard features that we do not include in our hostel listings. Unless we state otherwise, you can expect that every hostel has free hot showers, no lockout, no curfew, some system of secure luggage storage, and no key deposit.

HOSTELLING INTERNATIONAL

Joining the youth hostel association in your own country (listed below) automatically grants you membership privileges in **Hostelling International (HI),** a federation of national hosteling associations. Non-HI members may be allowed to stay in some hostels but will have to pay extra. HI hostels are scattered throughout Western Europe and are typically less expensive than private hostels. HI's umbrella organization's website (www.hihostel.com), which lists the web addresses and phone numbers of all national associations, can be a great place to begin researching hosteling in a specific region. Other comprehensive hosteling websites include www.hostels.com and www.hostelplanet.com.

Most HI hostels also honor **guest memberships**—you'll get a blank card with space for six validation stamps. Each night you'll pay a nonmember supplement and earn one guest stamp; get six stamps and you're a member. In some countries you may need to remind the hostel reception. A new membership benefit is the **FreeNites program,** which allows hostelers to gain points toward free rooms. Most student travel agencies (see p. 46) sell HI cards, as do all of the national hosteling organizations listed below. All prices listed below are valid for **one-year memberships** unless otherwise noted.

BOOKING HOSTELS ONLINE. One of the easiest ways to ensure you've got a bed for the night is by reserving online. Click to the Hostelworld booking engine through www.letsgo.com, and you'll have access to bargain accommodations from Argentina to Zimbabwe with no added commission.

Australian Youth Hostels Association (YHA), 422 Kent St., Sydney, NSW 200 (☎02 9261 1111; www.yha.com.au). AUS$42, under 26 AUS$32.

Hostelling International-Canada (HI-C), 205 Catherine St. Ste. 400, Ottawa, ON K2P 1C3 (☎613-237-7884; www.hihostels.ca). CDN$35, under 18 free.

An Óige (Irish Youth Hostel Association), 61 Mountjoy St., Dublin 7 (☎01 830 4555; www.irelandyha.org). EUR€20, under 18 EUR€10.

Hostelling International Northern Ireland (HINI), 22-32 Donegall Rd., Belfast BT12 5JN (☎028 9032 4733; www.hini.org.uk). UK£15, under 25 UK£10.

Scottish Youth Hostels Association (SYHA), 7 Glebe Cres., Stirling FK8 2JA (☎01786 89 14 00; www.syha.org.uk). UK£8, under 16 free.

Youth Hostels Association (England and Wales), Trevelyan House, Dimple Rd., Matlock, Derbyshire DE4 3YH (☎01629 592 600; www.yha.org.uk). UK£16, under 26 UK£10.

Hostelling International-USA, 8401 Colesville Rd., Ste. 600, Silver Spring, MD 20910 (☎301-495-1240; www.hiayh.org). US$28, under 18 free.

OTHER TYPES OF ACCOMMODATIONS

YMCAS AND YWCAS

Young Men's Christian Association (YMCA) and **Young Women's Christian Association (YWCA)** lodgings are usually cheaper than a hotel but more expensive than a hostel. Not all locations offer lodging; those that do are often located in urban downtowns. Many YMCAs accept women and families; some will not lodge those under 18 without parental permission. **World Alliance of YMCAs,** 12 Clos Belmont, 1208 Geneva, SWI (☎41 22 849 5100; www.ymca.int), has more info and a register of Western European YMCAs with housing options.

YMCA of the USA, 101 North Wacker Dr., Chicago, IL 60606 (☎800-872-9622; www.ymca.net). Provides a listing of the nearly 1000 Ys across the US and Canada, as well as information on prices and services.

European Alliance of YMCAs (YMCA Europe), Na Porici 12, CZ-110 00 Prague 1, Czech Republic (☎420 224 872 020; www.ymcaeurope.com). Maintains listings of European Ys with opportunities to volunteer abroad.

HOTELS, GUESTHOUSES, AND PENSIONS

In Western Europe, **hotel singles** cost about US$30 (€20) per night, **doubles** US$40 (€26). You'll typically share a hall bathroom; a private bathroom and hot showers may cost extra. Some hotels offer "full pension" (all meals) and "half pension" (no lunch). Smaller **guesthouses** and **pensions** are often cheaper than hotels. If you make reservations in writing, note your night of arrival and the number of nights you plan to stay. After sending you a confirmation, the hotel may request payment for the first night. Often it's easiest to reserve over the phone with a credit card.

BED AND BREAKFASTS (B&BS)

For a cozy alternative to impersonal hotel rooms, **B&Bs** (private homes with rooms available to travelers) range from acceptable to sublime. Rooms generally cost about €35 for a single and €70 for a double in Western Europe, depending on the season and location. Any number of websites provide listings for B&Bs. Check out **InnFinder** (www.inncrawler.com), **InnSite** (www.innsite.com), or **BedandBreakfast.com** (www.bedandbreakfast.com).

UNIVERSITY DORMS

Many **colleges** and **universities** open their residence halls to travelers when school is not in session; some do so even during term-time. Getting a room may take a couple of phone calls and require advanced planning, but rates tend to be low and many offer free local calls and Internet. Where available, university dorms are listed in the **Accommodations** section of each city.

HOME EXCHANGES AND HOSPITALITY CLUBS

Home exchange offers the traveler various types of homes (houses, apartments, condominiums, villas, even castles), plus the opportunity to live like a native and to cut down on accommodation fees. For more info, contact **HomeExchange.com Inc.,** P.O. Box 787, Hermosa Beach, CA 90254, USA (☎310-798-3864 or toll free 800-877-8723; www.homeexchange.com), or **Intervac International Home Exchange** (www.intervac.com; see site for phone listings by country).

Hospitality clubs link their members with individuals or families abroad who are willing to host travelers for free or for a small fee to promote cultural exchange and general good karma. In exchange, members usually must be willing to host travelers in their own homes; a small membership fee may also be required. **The Hospitality Club** (www.hospitalityclub.org) is a good place to start. **Servas** (www.servas.org) is an established, more formal, peace-based organization, and requires a fee and an interview to join. As always, use common sense when planning to stay with or host someone you do not know.

LONG-TERM ACCOMMODATIONS

Travelers planning to stay in Western Europe for extended periods of time may find it most cost-effective to rent an **apartment.** Rent varies widely by region, season, and quality. Besides the rent itself, prospective tenants usually are also required to front a security deposit and the last month's rent. Generally, for stays shorter than three months, it is more feasible to **sublet** than lease your own apartment. Sublets are also more likely to be furnished. Out of session, it may be possible to arrange to sublet rooms from university students on summer break. It is far easier to find an apartment once you have arrived at your destination than to attempt to use the Internet or phone from home. By staying in a hostel for your first week or so, you can make local contacts and, more importantly, check out your new digs before you commit.

CAMPING

With Europe's vast terrain encompassing beaches, mountains, and plains, **camping** always has some new adventure to offer. Furthermore, you can explore nature for prices refreshingly easy on the wallet. Most towns have several campgrounds within walking distance, occasionally offering a cheap shuttle service to reach them. Even the most rudimentary campings (campgrounds) provide showers and laundry facilities, though almost all forbid campfires. In addition to tent camping, other patrons opt to drive RVs across Europe. Campgrounds usually charge a flat fee per person (usually around €4-6) plus a few euro extra for electricity, tents, cars, or running water. Most larger campgrounds also operate on-site general stores or cafes perfect for a quick, cheap bite. In some countries, it is illegal to pitch your tent or park your RV overnight along the road; look for designated camping areas within national parks, recognized campgrounds, or ask landowners permission before setting up residency on private property. In Sweden, Finland, and Norway, the **right of public access** permits travelers to tent one night in the forests and wilderness for free.

If planning on using campgrounds as your go-to accommodation, consider buying an **International Camping Carnet** (ICC, US$45). Available through the association of **Family Campers and RVers** (☎800-245-9755; www.fcrv.org), the card entitles holders to discounts at some campgrounds and may save travelers from having to leave their passport as a deposit. National tourist offices offer more info on country-specific camping. Additionally, check out **Interhike** (www.interhike.com) which lists campgrounds by region. First-time campers may also want to peruse **KarmaBum Cafe** (www.karmabum.com) for suggested itineraries, packing lists, blogs, and camping recipes. For more info on outdoor activities in Western Europe, see **The Great Outdoors,** below.

THE GREAT OUTDOORS

Camping can be a great way to see Europe on the cheap. There are organized **campgrounds** outside most cities. Showers, bathrooms, and a small restaurant or store are common; some sites have more elaborate facilities. Prices are low, usually US$5-15 per person plus additional charges for tents and cars. While camping is a cheaper option than hosteling, the cost of transportation to and from campgrounds can add up. Some public grounds allow **free camping,** but check local laws. Many areas have additional park-specific rules. **The Great Outdoor Recreation Pages** (www.gorp.com) provides excellent general info.

LEAVE NO TRACE. *Let's Go* encourages travelers to embrace the "Leave No Trace" ethic, minimizing their impact on natural environments. Trekkers should set up camp on durable surfaces, use cookstoves instead of campfires, bury human waste away from water supplies, bag trash and carry it out with them, and respect wildlife and natural objects. For more detailed information, contact the **Leave No Trace Center for Outdoor Ethics,** P.O. Box 997, Boulder, CO 80306 (☎800-332-4100 or 303-442-8222; www.lnt.org).

USEFUL RESOURCES

There are a variety of publishing companies that offer hiking guidebooks to meet the educational needs of the novice or the expert. For information about biking, camping, and hiking, write or call the publishers listed below to receive a free catalog. Campers heading to Europe should consider buying an **International Camping Carnet.** Similar to a hostel membership card, it's required at a few campgrounds in addition to providing discounts at others. It is available in North America from the **Family Campers and RVers Association** (www.fcrv.org) and in the UK from **The Caravan Club** (see below).

Automobile Association, Contact Centre, Carr Ellison House, William Armstrong Dr., Newcastle-upon-Tyne NE4 7YA, UK (☎08706 000 371; www.theaa.com). Publishes *Caravan and Camping Europe* and *Britain and Ireland* (UK£10) as well as road atlases for Europe as a whole and for Britain, France, Germany, Ireland, Italy, and Spain.

The Caravan Club, East Grinstead House, East Grinstead, West Sussex RH19 1UA, UK (☎01342 326 944; www.caravanclub.co.uk). For UK£36, members get access to campgrounds, insurance services, equipment discounts, maps, and a magazine.

Sierra Club Books, 85 2nd St., 2nd fl., San Francisco, CA 94105, USA (☎415-977-5500; www.sierraclub.org). Publishes general resource books on hiking and camping.

The Mountaineers Books, 1001 SW Klickitat Way, Ste. 201, Seattle, WA 98134, USA (☎206-223-6303; www.mountaineersbooks.org). Over 600 titles on hiking, biking, mountaineering, natural history, and conservation.

WILDERNESS SAFETY

Staying **warm, dry,** and **well hydrated** are the keys to a happy and safe wilderness experience. Before any hike, prepare yourself for an emergency by packing a first-aid kit, a reflector, a whistle, high-energy food, extra water, raingear, a hat, gloves, and several **extra pairs of socks.** For warmth, wear wool or insulating synthetic materials designed for the outdoors. Cotton is a bad choice as it takes a ridiculously long time to dry and loses its insulating effect when wet.

Check **weather forecasts** often and pay attention to the skies when hiking, as weather patterns can change suddenly, especially in mountainous areas. Always let someone—a friend, your hostel staff, a park ranger, or a local hiking organization—know when and where you are going. Know your physical limits and do not attempt a hike beyond your ability.

CAMPING AND HIKING EQUIPMENT

WHAT TO BUY

Good camping equipment is both sturdy and light. North American suppliers tend to offer the most competitive prices.

Sleeping Bags: Most sleeping bags are rated by season; "summer" means 30-40°F (around 0°C) at night; "four-season" or "winter" often means below 0°F (-17°C). Bags are made of down (warm and light, but expensive, and miserable when wet) or of synthetic material (heavy, durable, and warm when wet). Prices range US$50-250 for a summer synthetic and US$200-300 for a good down winter bag. Sleeping bag pads include foam pads (US$10-30), air mattresses (US$15-50), and self-inflating mats (US$30-120). Bring a stuff sack to store your bag and keep it dry.

Tents: The best tents are free-standing (with their own frames and suspension systems), set up quickly, and only require staking in high winds. Low-profile dome tents are the best all around. 2-person tents start at US$100, 4-person tents at US$160. Make sure your tent has a rain fly and seal its seams with waterproofer. Other useful accessories include a battery-operated lantern, a plastic groundcloth, and a nylon tarp.

Backpacks: Internal-frame packs mold to your back, keep a lower center of gravity, and flex to allow you to hike difficult trails, while external-frame packs are more comfortable for long hikes over even terrain, as they carry weight higher and distribute it more evenly. Make sure your pack has a hip-belt to transfer weight to your legs. Any serious backpacking requires a pack of at least 4000 cu. in., plus 500 cu. in. for sleeping bags in internal-frame packs. Sturdy backpacks cost anywhere from US$125 to US$420—your pack is an area where it doesn't pay to economize. On your hunt for the perfect pack, fill up each prospective model with something heavy, strap it on, and walk around the store to get a sense of how the model distributes weight. Either buy a rain cover (US$10-20) or store your belongings in plastic bags inside your pack.

Boots: Be sure to wear hiking boots with good ankle support. They should fit snugly and comfortably over 1-2 pairs of wool socks and a pair of thin liner socks. It is important to break in new boots over several weeks before you go to spare yourself from uncomfortable blisters. If this is your first pair of boots, get fitting advice from your local retailer.

Other Necessities: Synthetic layers, like those made of polypropylene or polyester, and a pile jacket will keep you warm even when wet. A space blanket (US$5-15) will help you to retain body heat and doubles as a groundcloth. Durable plastic water bottles are vital; however, you might want to take note of recent health concerns over the presence of BPA, used in the production of shatter- and leak-resistant bottles. Carry water-purification tablets for when you can't boil water. Virtually every organized campground in Europe forbids fires or the gathering of firewood, so you'll need a camp stove and a propane-filled fuel bottle to operate it. Keep in mind you may have to buy some equipment after you arrive because of airline restrictions. Also bring a first-aid kit, pocketknife, insect repellent, and waterproof matches or a lighter.

WHERE TO BUY IT

The online and mail-order companies listed below offer lower prices than many retail stores. A visit to a local camping or outdoors store will give you a good sense of the look and weight of certain items before you buy.

Campmor, 28 Parkway, P.O. Box 700, Upper Saddle River, NJ 07458, USA (☎800-525-4784; www.campmor.com). Wide selection of tents, packs, clothing, and other gear.

Cotswold Outdoor, Unit 11 Kemble Business Park, Crudwell, Malmesbury Wiltshire SN16 9SH, UK (☎08704 427 755; www.cotswoldoutdoor.com).

Discount Camping, 833 Main North Rd., Pooraka, SA 5095, Australia (☎08 8262 3399; www.discountcamping.com.au). Sells everything from tents to tools.

Eastern Mountain Sports (EMS), 1 Vose Farm Rd., Peterborough, NH 03458, USA (☎888-463-6367; www.ems.com). Offers GPS and electronic gear as well.

Gear-Zone, 17 Westlegate, Norwich, Norfolk NR1 3LT, UK (☎1603 410 108; www.gear-zone.co.uk) Comprehensive selection of clothing, tents, and bags.

Recreational Equipment, Inc. (REI), Sumner, WA 98352, USA (US and Canada ☎800-426-4840, elsewhere 253-891-2500; www.rei.com).

ORGANIZED ADVENTURE TRIPS

Organized adventure tours offer another way of exploring the wild. Activities include hiking, biking, skiing, canoeing, kayaking, rafting, climbing, photo safaris, and archaeological digs. Organizations that specialize in camping and outdoor equipment are also a good source for info. Some companies, like the ones below, list organized tour opportunities throughout Europe.

Specialty Travel Index, PO Box 458, San Anselmo, CA 94979, USA (US ☎888-624-4030, elsewhere 415-455-1643; www.specialtytravel.com).

Ecotravel (www.ecotravel.com). Online directory of various programs in Europe and throughout the world. Includes itineraries, guides, and articles.

NatureTrek, Cheriton Mill, Cheriton, Alresford, Hampshire, SO24 0NG (☎01962 733051; www.naturetrek.co.uk). Offers responsible travel opportunities all over the globe.

SPECIFIC CONCERNS

SUSTAINABLE TRAVEL

As the number of travelers on the road rises, the detrimental effect they can have on natural environments is an increasing concern. With this in mind, *Let's Go* promotes the philosophy of **sustainable travel.** Through sensitivity to issues of ecology and sustainability, today's travelers can be a powerful force in preserving as well as restoring the places they visit.

Ecotourism, a rising trend in sustainable travel, focuses on the conservation of natural habitats—mainly, on how to use them without exploitation or overdevelopment. Travelers can make a difference by doing advance research, by supporting organizations and establishments that pay attention to their carbon "footprint," and by patronizing establishments that strive to be environmentally friendly. **International Friends of Nature** (www.nfi.at) has info about sustainable travel options in Europe. For more info, see **Beyond Tourism,** p. 60.

ECOTOURISM RESOURCES. For more info on environmentally responsible tourism, contact one of the organizations below:

Conservation International, 2011 Crystal Dr., Ste. 500, Arlington, VA 22202, USA (☎+1-800-406-2306 or 703-341-2400; www.conservation.org).

Green Globe, Green Globe vof, Verbenalaan 1, 2111 ZL Aerdenhout, The Netherlands (☎+31 23 544 0306; www.greenglobe.com).

International Ecotourism Society, 1333 H St. NW, Ste. 300E, Washington, D.C. 20005, USA (☎+1-202-347-9203; www.ecotourism.org).

United Nations Environment Program, 39-43 Quai André Citroën, 75739 Paris Cedex 15, France (☎+33 1 44 37 14 50; www.uneptie.org/pc/tourism).

RESPONSIBLE TRAVEL

Your tourist dollars can make a big impact on the destinations you visit. The choices you make during your trip can have potent effects on local communities—for better or for worse. Travelers who care about the destinations they explore should become aware of the social, cultural, and political implications of their choices. Simple decisions such as buying local products, paying fair prices for products or services, and attempting to speak the local language can have a strong, positive effect on the community.

Community-based tourism aims to channel tourist money into the local economy by emphasizing tours and cultural programs run by members of the host community. This type of tourism also benefits the tourists themselves, as it often takes them beyond the traditional tours of the region. The *Ethical Travel Guide*, a project of **Tourism Concern** (☎+44 20 7133 3330; www.tourismconcern.org.uk), is an excellent resource for info on community-based travel, with a directory of 300 establishments in 60 countries.

TRAVELING ALONE

Traveling alone can be extremely beneficial, providing a sense of independence and a greater opportunity to connect with locals. On the other hand, solo travelers are more vulnerable targets of harassment and street theft. If you are traveling alone, look confident, try not to stand out as a tourist, and be especially careful in deserted or very crowded areas. If questioned, never admit that you are traveling alone. Maintain regular contact with someone at home who knows your itinerary, and always research your destination before traveling. For more tips, pick up *Traveling Solo* (6th ed.) by Eleanor Berman (Globe Pequot Press; 2008), visit www.travelaloneandloveit.com, or subscribe to **Connecting: Solo Travel Network,** 689 Park Rd., Unit 6, Gibsons, BC V0N 1V7, Canada (☎+1-604-886-9099; www.cstn.org; membership US$50).

WOMEN TRAVELERS

Women exploring on their own inevitably face some additional safety concerns. Single women can consider staying in hostels which offer single rooms that lock from the inside or in religious organizations with single-sex rooms. It's a good idea to stick to centrally located accommodations and to avoid solitary late-night treks or metro rides.

Always carry extra money for a phone call, bus, or taxi. **Hitchhiking** is never safe for lone women, or even for two women traveling together. Look as if you know where you're going, and approach older women or couples for directions if you're lost or uncomfortable. Generally, the less you look like a tourist, the better off you'll be. Dress conservatively, especially in rural areas. Wearing a conspicuous **wedding band** sometimes helps prevent unwanted advances.

Your best answer to verbal harassment is no answer at all; feigning deafness, pretending you don't understand the language, or staring straight ahead will usually do the trick. The extremely persistent can sometimes be dissuaded by a firm, loud "Go away!" in the appropriate language. Seek out a police officer or a passerby if you are being harassed. Memorize the emergency numbers in places you visit, and consider carrying a whistle on your keychain. A self defense course will both prepare you for a potential attack and raise your level of awareness of your surroundings (see recommendations on self defense, p. 24). Also, it might be a good idea to talk with your doctor about the health concerns that women face when traveling (p. 30).

GLBT TRAVELERS

Attitudes toward gay, lesbian, bisexual, and transgendered (GLBT) travelers are particular to each region in Europe. On the whole, countries in Northern and Western Europe tend to be queer-friendly, while Eastern Europe harbors enclaves of tolerance in cities amid stretches of cultural conservatism. Countries like Romania that outlawed homosexuality as recently as 2002 are becoming more liberal today, and can be considered viable destinations for GLBT travelers. Listed below are contact organizations that offer materials addressing some specific concerns. **Out and About** (www.planetout.com) offers a weekly newsletter addressing travel concerns and a comprehensive site addressing gay travel concerns. The online newspaper **365gay.com** has a travel section, and the French-language site **netgai.com** (http://netgai.com/international/Europe) includes links to country-specific resources.

Gay's the Word, 66 Marchmont St., London WC1N 1AB, UK (☎+44 20 7278 7654; http://freespace.virgin.net/gays.theword). The largest gay and lesbian bookshop in the UK, with both fiction and non-fiction titles. Mail-order service available.

Giovanni's Room, 345 S. 12th St., Philadelphia, PA 19107, USA (☎+1-215-923-2960; www.queerbooks.com). An international lesbian and gay bookstore with mail-order service (carries many of the publications listed below).

International Lesbian and Gay Association (ILGA), 17 Rue de la Charité, 1210 Brussels, BEL (☎+32 2 502 2471; www.ilga.org). Provides political information, such as homosexuality laws of individual countries.

ADDITIONAL RESOURCES.

Spartacus International Gay Guide 2008 (US$22).

The Damron Men's Travel Guide 2006. Gina M. Gatta, Damron Co. (US$22).

The Gay Vacation Guide: The Best Trips and How to Plan Them. Mark Chesnut, Kensington Books (US$15).

TRAVELERS WITH DISABILITIES

European countries vary in accessibility to travelers with disabilities. Some tourist boards, particularly in Western and Northern Europe, provide directories on the accessibility of various accommodations and transportation services. If these services are not available, contact establishments directly. Those with disabilities should inform airlines and hotels of their disabilities when making reservations; some time may be needed to prepare special accommodations. Call ahead to restaurants, museums, and other facilities to find out if they are wheelchair-accessible. **Guide dog owners** should inquire as to the quarantine policies of each destination country.

Rail is the most convenient form of travel for disabled travelers in Europe. Many stations have ramps, and some trains have wheelchair lifts, special seating areas, and special toilets. All Eurostar, some InterCity (IC), and some EuroCity (EC) trains are wheelchair-accessible. CityNightLine trains, French TGV (high speed), and Conrail trains feature special compartments. In general, the countries with the most **wheelchair-accessible rail networks** are: Denmark (IC and Lyn trains), France (TGVs and other long-distance trains), Germany (ICE, EC, IC, and IR trains), Ireland (most major trains), Italy (EC and IC trains), the Netherlands (most trains), Sweden (X2000s, most IC and IR trains), and Switzerland (all IC, most EC, and some regional trains). Austria, Poland, and the UK offer accessibility on selected routes. Bulgaria, the Czech Republic, Greece, Hungary, Slovakia, and Spain's rail systems have limited wheelchair accessibility. For those who wish to rent cars, some major **car rental** agencies (e.g., Hertz) offer hand-controlled vehicles.

USEFUL ORGANIZATIONS

Access Abroad, www.umabroad.umn.edu/access. A website devoted to making study abroad available to students with disabilities. The site is maintained by Disability Services, University of Minnesota, 230 Heller Hall, 271 19th Ave. S., Minneapolis, MN 55455, USA (☎+1-612-626-7379).

Accessible Journeys, 35 W. Sellers Ave., Ridley Park, PA 19078, USA (☎+1-800-846-4537; www.disabilitytravel.com). Designs tours for wheelchair users and slow walkers. The site has tips and forums for all travelers.

Flying Wheels, 143 W. Bridge St., Owatonna, MN 55060, USA (☎+1-507-451-5005; www.flyingwheelstravel.com). Specializes in escorted trips to Europe for people with physical disabilities. Plans custom trips worldwide.

The Guided Tour, Inc., 7900 Old York Rd., Ste. 114B, Elkins Park, PA 19027, USA (☎+1-800-783-5841; www.guidedtour.com). Organizes travel programs for persons with developmental and physical challenges in Ireland, Italy, Spain, and the UK.

Society for Accessible Travel and Hospitality (SATH), 347 5th Ave., Ste. 605, New York, NY 10016, USA (☎+1-212-447-7284; www.sath.org). An advocacy group that publishes free online travel information and the travel magazine *Open World*. Annual membership US$49, students and seniors US$29.

MINORITY TRAVELERS

In general, minority travelers will find a high level of tolerance in large cities; small towns and the countryside are less predictable. The increasingly mainstream reality of anti-immigrant sentiments means that travelers of African or Arab descent (regardless of their citizenship) may be the object of unwarranted assumptions and even hostility. Anti-Semitism remains a very real problem in many countries, especially in France, Austria, and much of Eastern Europe. Discrimination is particularly forceful against Roma (gypsies) throughout much of Eastern Europe. Jews, Muslims, and other minority travelers should keep an eye out for skinheads, who have been linked to racist violence in Central and Eastern Europe, and elsewhere. **The European Union Agency for Fundamental Rights (FRA),** Rahlgasse 3, 1060 Vienna, AUT (☎43 15 80 30; www.eumc.europa.eu), publishes a wealth of country-specific statistics and reports. Travelers can consult **United for Intercultural Action,** Postbus 413, NL-1000 AK, Amsterdam, NTH (☎31 20 683 4778; www.unitedagainstracism.org), for a list of over 500 country-specific organizations that work against racism and discrimination.

DIETARY CONCERNS

Vegetarians will find no shortage of meat-free dining options throughout most of Northern and Western Europe, although **vegans** may have a trickier time outside urban centers, where eggs and dairy can dominate traditional dishes. The cuisine of Eastern Europe still tends to be heavy on meat and gravy, although major cities often boast surprisingly inventive vegetarian and ethnic fare.

The travel section of **The Vegetarian Resource Group's** website, at www.vrg.org/travel, has a comprehensive list of organizations and websites that are geared toward helping vegetarians and vegans traveling abroad. The website for the

European Vegetarian Union (EVU), at www.europeanvegetarian.org, includes links to dozens of veggie-friendly organizations. For more info, consult *The Vegetarian Traveler: Where to Stay if You're Vegetarian, Vegan, Environmentally Sensitive*, by Jed and Susan Civic (Larson Publications; 1997), *Vegetarian Europe*, by Alex Bourke (Vegetarian Guides; 2000), and the indispensable, multilingual *Vegan Passport* (The Vegan Society; 2005), along with the websites www.vegdining.com, www.happycow.net, and www.vegetariansabroad.com.

Those looking to keep **kosher** will find abundant dining options across Europe; contact synagogues in larger cities for information, or consult www.kashrut.com/travel/Europe for country-specific resources. Your own synagogue or college Hillel should have access to lists of Jewish institutions across the nation. Hebrew College Online also offers a searchable database of kosher restaurants at www.shamash.org/kosher. Another good resource is the *Jewish Travel Guide*, edited by Michael Zaidner (Vallentine Mitchell; 2004). Travelers looking for **halal** groceries and restaurants will have the most success in France and Eastern European nations with substantial Muslim populations; consult www.zabihah.com for establishment reviews. Keep in mind that if you are strict in your observance, you may have to prepare your own food.

OTHER RESOURCES

TRAVEL PUBLISHERS AND BOOKSTORES

The Globe Corner Bookstore, 90 Mt. Auburn St., Cambridge, MA 02138 (☎617-497-6277; www.globecorner.com). Sponsors an Adventure Travel Lecture Series and carries a vast selection of guides and maps to every imaginable destination. Online catalog includes atlases and monthly staff picks of outstanding travel writing.

Hippocrene Books, 171 Madison Ave., New York, NY 10016 (☎718-454-2366; www.hippocrenebooks.com). Publishes foreign-language dictionaries and learning guides, along with ethnic cookbooks and a smattering of guidebooks.

WORLD WIDE WEB

Almost every aspect of budget travel is accessible via the web. In 10min. at the keyboard, you can make a hostel reservation, get advice on travel hot spots from other travelers, or find out how much a train ride costs. Listed here are some regional and travel-related sites to start off your surfing; other relevant websites are listed throughout the book. Because website turnover is high, use search engines (e.g., www.google.com) to strike out on your own.

LET'S GO ONLINE. Plan your next trip on our newly redesigned website, **www.letsgo.com.** It features the latest travel info on your favorite destinations, as well as tons of interactive features: make your own itinerary, read blogs from our trusty researcher-writers, browse our photo library, watch exclusive videos, check out our newsletter, find travel deals, and buy new guides. We're always updating and adding new features, so check back often!

Backpacker's Ultimate Guide: www.bugeurope.com. Tips on packing, transportation, and where to go. Also tons of country-specific travel information.

BootsnAll.com: www.bootsnall.com. Numerous resources for independent travelers, from planning your trip to reporting on it when you get back.

How to See the World: www.artoftravel.com. A compendium of great travel tips. Advice on everything from finding cheap flights to self defense.

Travel Intelligence: www.travelintelligence.net. A large collection of travel writing by distinguished travel writers.

Travel Library: www.travel-library.com. A fantastic set of links for general information and personal travelogues.

World Hum: www.worldhum.com. An independently produced collection of "travel dispatches from a shrinking planet."

INFORMATION ABOUT WESTERN EUROPE

BBC News: http://news.bbc.co.uk. The latest coverage from one of Europe's most reputable sources for English-language news, for free.

CIA World Factbook: www.odci.gov/cia/publications/factbook/index.html. Tons of vital statistics on countries' geography, government, economy, and people.

EUROPA: http://europa.eu/index_en.htm. English-language gateway to the European Union, featuring news articles and a citizen's guide to EU institutions.

TRANSPORTATION

GETTING TO EUROPE

BY PLANE

When it comes to airfare, a little effort can save you a bundle. Tickets sold by consolidators, couriers, and standby seating are good deals, but last-minute specials, airfare wars, and charter flights often beat these fares. The key is to hunt around, be flexible, and ask about discounts. Students, seniors, and those under 26 should never pay full price for a ticket.

AIRFARES

Airfares to Europe peak between mid-June and early September; holidays are also expensive. The cheapest times to travel are November to mid-December and January to March. Midweek (M-Th morning) round-trip flights run US$60-$120 cheaper than weekend flights, but they are generally more crowded and less likely to permit frequent-flier upgrades. Not fixing a return date ("open return") or arriving in and departing from different cities ("open jaw") is usually significantly pricier than buying a round-trip. Flights between Europe's capitals or regional hubs (Amsterdam, London, Paris, Prague, Warsaw, Zürich) tend to be cheaper than those to more rural areas.

If your European destinations are part of a more extensive globe-hop, consider a round-the-world (RTW) ticket. Tickets usually include at least five stops and are valid for about a year; prices range from US$1600-$5000. Try **Northwest Airlines/KLM** (☎800-225-2525; www.nwa.com) or **Star Alliance** (www.staralliance.com), a consortium of 16 airlines including United.

BUDGET AND STUDENT TRAVEL AGENCIES

While agents specializing in flights to Europe can make your life easy, they may not find you the lowest possible fare—they get paid on commission. Travelers holding **ISICs** and **IYTCs** (p. 16) qualify for big discounts from student travel agencies. Most flights from budget agencies are on major airlines, but in peak season some may sell seats on less reliable chartered aircrafts.

STA Travel, 9/89 5900 Wilshire Blvd., Ste. 900, Los Angeles, CA 90036, USA (24hr. reservations and info ☎800-781-4040; www.statravel.com). A student and youth travel organization with over 150 offices worldwide, including US offices in many college towns. Ticket booking, travel insurance, rail passes, and more.

The Adventure Travel Company, 124 McDougal St., New York, NY 10021, USA (☎1800 467 4594; www.theadventuretravelcompany.com). Offices across Canada and the US including Champaign, New York, San Francisco, Seattle, and San Diego.

FLIGHT PLANNING ON THE INTERNET. The Internet may be the budget traveler's dream when it comes to finding and booking bargain fares, but the array of options can be overwhelming. Many airline sites offer special last-minute deals online, though some require membership logins or email subscriptions. Try www.airfrance.com, www.britishairways.com, www.icelandair.com, and www.lufthansa.de. **STA** (www.sta.com) and **StudentUniverse** (www.studentuniverse.com) provide quotes on student tickets, while **Expedia** (www.expedia.com), **Orbitz** (www.orbitz.com), and **Travelocity** (www.travelocity.com) offer full travel services. **Priceline** (www.priceline.com) lets you specify a price, and obligates you to buy any ticket that meets or beats it; **Hotwire** (www.hotwire.com) offers bargain fares but won't reveal the airline or flight times until you buy. Other sites that compile deals include www.bestfares.com, www.flights.com, www.lowestfare.com, www.onetravel.com, and www.travelzoo.com. There are tools available to sift through multiple offers; **Booking Buddy** (www.bookingbuddy.com), **SideStep** (www.sidestep.com), and **Kayak** (www.kayak.com) let you enter your trip information once and search multiple sites. Spain-based **eDreams** (www.edreams.com) is convenient to book budget flights within Europe.

USIT, 19-21 Aston Quay, Dublin 2, Ireland (☎+353 1 602 1906; www.usit.ie). Ireland's leading student/budget travel agency has 20 offices throughout Northern Ireland and the Republic of Ireland. Offers programs to work, study, and volunteer worldwide.

COMMERCIAL AIRLINES

Commercial airlines' lowest regular offer is the **APEX** (Advance Purchase Excursion) fare, which provides confirmed reservations and allows "open-jaw" tickets. Generally, reservations must be made seven to 21 days ahead of departure, with seven- to 14-day minimum stay and 90-day maximum stay restrictions. These fares carry hefty cancellation and change penalties (fees rise in summer). Use **Expedia** or **Travelocity** to get an idea of the lowest published fares, then use the resources listed here to try to beat those fares. Low-season fares should be appreciably cheaper than the high-season ones listed here.

TRAVELING FROM NORTH AMERICA

Basic round-trip fares to **Europe** range from roughly US$400-1500: to **Frankfurt**, US$450-1250; **London**, US$250-550; **Paris**, US$600-1400. Standard commercial carriers like **American** (☎800-433-7300; www.aa.com), **United** (☎800-538-2929; www.united.com), and **Northwest** (☎800-225-2525; www.nwa.com) will probably offer the most convenient flights, but they may not be the cheapest. Check **Lufthansa** (☎800-399-5838; www.lufthansa.com), **British Airways** (☎800-247-9297; www.britishairways.com), **Air France** (☎800-237-2747; www.airfrance.us), and **Alitalia** (☎800-223-5730; www.alitaliausa.com) for cheap tickets from US destinations to all over Europe. You might find an even better deal on one of the following airlines if any of their limited departure points is convenient for you.

Icelandair: ☎800-223-5500; www.icelandair.com. Stopovers in Iceland for no extra cost on most flights. New York to Frankfurt Apr.-Aug. US$900-1000; Sept.-Oct. US$600-800; Dec.-Mar. US$500. For last-minute offers, subscribe to their "Lucky Fares" email list.

Finnair: ☎800-950-5000; www.finnair.com. Cheap round-trips from New York, San Francisco, and Toronto to Helsinki; connections throughout Europe. New York to Helsinki June-Sept. US$1250; Oct.-May US$830-1200.

BEFORE YOU BOOK. The emergence of no-frills airlines has made hopscotching around Europe by air increasingly affordable. Many budget airlines save money by flying out of smaller, regional airports. A flight billed as Paris to Barcelona might in fact be from Beauvais (80km north of Paris) to Girona (104km northeast of Barcelona). For a more detailed list of these airlines by country, check out www.whichbudget.com.

easyJet: UK ☎0871 244 2366; www.easyjet.com. 104 destinations including links to Eastern Europe. Also serves Egypt, Morocco, and Turkey.

Ryanair: Ireland ☎0818 303 030, UK 0871 246 00 00; www.ryanair.com. Serves 132 destinations in Austria, Belgium, the Czech Republic, France, Germany, Ireland, Italy, Latvia, the Netherlands, Poland, Portugal, Scandinavia, Spain, the UK, and Morocco.

SkyEurope: UK ☎0905 7222 747; www.skyeurope.com. 40 destinations in 19 countries around Central and Eastern Europe, including the Czech Republic and Slovakia.

Sterling: Denmark ☎70 10 84 84, UK ☎870 787 8038. www.sterling.dk. The first Scandinavian-based budget airline. Connects Denmark, Norway, and Sweden to 40 cities across Europe.

Wizz Air: Hungary ☎06 90 181 181, Poland ☎ 03 00 50 30 10; www.wizzair.com. 50 destinations in Belgium, Bulgaria, Croatia, France, Germany, Greece, Hungary, Ireland, Italy, the Netherlands, Norway, Poland, Romania, Slovenia, Spain, Sweden, and the UK.

You'll have to buy shuttle tickets to reach the airports of many of these airlines, and add an hour or so to your travel time. After round-trip shuttle tickets and fees for checked luggage or other services that might come standard on other airlines, that €0.01 sale fare can suddenly jump to €20-100. Be particularly aware of baggage allowances, which are generally small and strictly policed. Prices for no-frills airlines vary dramatically; shop around, book months ahead, pack light, and stay flexible to nab the best fares.

TRAVELING FROM THE UK AND IRELAND

Because of the many carriers flying from the British Isles to the continent, we only include discount airlines or those with cheap specials here. The **Air Travel Advisory Bureau** in London (www.atab.co.uk) provides referrals to travel agencies that offer discounted airfares. **Cheapflights** (www.cheapflights.co.uk) publishes bargains. For more info on budget airlines like Ryanair, see p. 48.

Aer Lingus: Ireland ☎08 18 36 50 00; www.aerlingus.com. Round-trip tickets from Cork, Dublin, and Shannon to destinations across Europe (€15-300).

bmibaby: UK ☎08 712 240 224; www.bmibaby.com. Departures from throughout the UK to destinations across Europe. Fares from UK£25.

TRAVELING FROM AUSTRALIA AND NEW ZEALAND

Air New Zealand: New Zealand ☎0800 73 70 00; www.airnz.co.nz. Flights from Auckland to London.

Qantas Air: Australia ☎13 13 13, New Zealand 0800 808 767; www.qantas.com.au. Flights from Australia to London for around AUS$2400.

Singapore Air: Australia ☎13 10 11, New Zealand 0800 808 909; www.singaporeair.com. Flies from Adelaide, Auckland, Brisbane, Christchurch, Melbourne, Perth, Sydney, and Wellington to Western Europe.

Thai Airways: Australia ☎13 00 65 19 60, New Zealand 09 377 3886; www.thaiair.com. Major cities in Australia and New Zealand to Frankfurt and London.

AIR COURIER FLIGHTS

Those who travel light should consider courier flights. Couriers help transport cargo on international flights by using their checked luggage space for freight. Generally, couriers are limited to carry-ons and must deal with complex flight restrictions. Most flights are round-trip only, with short fixed-length stays (usually one week) and a limit of one ticket per issue. Most of these flights also operate only out of major gateway cities. Round-trip courier fares from the US to Europe run about US$200-500. Most flights leave from L.A., Miami, New York, or San Francisco in the US, and from Montreal, Toronto, or Vancouver in Canada. Generally, you must be over 18 (in some cases 21). In summer, the most popular destinations require an advance reservation. Super-discounted fares are common for "last-minute" flights (3-14 days ahead).

Air Courier Association, 1767A Denver West Blvd., Golden, CO 80401, USA (☎800-461-8556; www.aircourier.org). Departure cities throughout Canada and the US to Western Europe (US$150-650). 1-year membership US$39, plus some monthly fees.

International Association of Air Travel Couriers (IAATC; www.courier.org). Courier and consolidator fares from North America to Europe. 1-year membership US$45.

Courier Travel (www.couriertravel.org). Searchable online database. 6 departure points in the US to various European destinations. Membership US$40 per household.

STANDBY FLIGHTS

Traveling standby requires considerable flexibility in arrival and departure dates and cities. Companies dealing in standby flights sell vouchers, along with the promise to get you to your destination (or near it) within a certain window of time (typically 1-5 days). You call in before your specific window of time to hear your flight options and the probability that you will be able to board each flight. You can then decide which flights you want to try to make, show up at the right airport at the appropriate time, present your voucher, and board if space is available. Vouchers can usually be bought for both one-way and round-trip travel. You may receive a refund only if every available flight within your date range is full; if you opt not to take an available (but less convenient) flight, you can only get credit toward future travel. Read agreements and contracts carefully, as tricky fine print abounds. To check on a company's service record in the US, contact the **Better Business Bureau** (☎703-276-0100; www.bbb.org). It is difficult to receive refunds, and clients' vouchers will not be honored when an airline fails to receive payment in time.

TICKET CONSOLIDATORS

Ticket consolidators, also known as **"bucket shops,"** buy unsold tickets in bulk from commercial airlines and sell them at discounted rates. Look for tiny advertisements in the Sunday travel section of any major newspaper; call quickly, as availability is extremely limited. Not all bucket shops are reliable, so insist on a receipt that gives full details of flight restrictions, refund policies, and tickets, and pay by credit card (in spite of the 2-5% fee).

GETTING AROUND EUROPE

GOING MY WAY, SAILOR? In Europe, fares are listed as either **single** (one-way) or **return** (round-trip). "Period returns" require you to return within a specific number of days; "day return" means you must return on the same day. Round-trip fares on trains and buses in Europe are simply twice the one-way fare. Unless stated otherwise, *Let's Go* always lists single fares.

BY PLANE

A number of European airlines offer discount coupon packets. Most are only available as add-ons for transatlantic passengers, but some are stand-alone offers. **Europe by Air's** FlightPass allows non-EU residents to country-hop to over 150 European cities for US$99 or $129 per flight, plus tax. (☎888-321-4737; www.europebyair.com.) **Iberia's** Europass allows passengers flying from the US to Spain to add a minimum of two additional destinations in Europe for $139 per trip. (US ☎800-772-4642; www.iberia.com.)

BY TRAIN

Trains in Europe are generally comfortable, convenient, and reasonably fast, although quality varies by country. Second-class compartments, which seat two to six, are great places to meet fellow travelers. However, trains can be unsafe, especially in Eastern Europe. For safety tips, see p. 24. For long trips, make sure you are on the correct car, as trains sometimes split at crossroads. Towns listed in parentheses on European train schedules require a switch at the town listed immediately before the parentheses.

You can either buy a **rail pass,** which allows you unlimited travel within a region for a given period of time, or rely on individual point-to-point tickets as you go. Almost all countries give students or youths (usually defined as anyone under 26) direct discounts on regular domestic rail tickets, and many also sell a student or youth card that provides 20-50% off all fares for up to a year.

RESERVATIONS. While seat reservations are required only for selected trains (usually on major lines), you are not guaranteed a seat without one (usually US$5-30). You should strongly consider reserving in advance during peak holiday and tourist seasons (at the very latest, a few hours ahead). You will also have to purchase a **supplement** (US$10-50) or special fare for high-speed or high-quality trains such as Spain's AVE, Switzerland's Cisalpino, Finland's Pendolino, Italy's ETR500 and Pendolino, Germany's ICE, and certain French TGVs. InterRail holders must also purchase supplements (US$3-20) for trains like EuroCity, InterCity, and many TGVs; supplements are often unnecessary for Eurail Pass and Europass holders.

OVERNIGHT TRAINS. On night trains, you won't waste valuable daylight hours traveling and you can avoid the hassle and expense of staying at a hotel. However, the main drawbacks include discomfort, sleepless nights, and the lack of scenery. The risk of theft also increases dramatically at night, particularly in Eastern Europe. **Sleeping accommodations** on trains differ from country to country. **Couchettes** (berths) typically have four to six seats per compartment (supplement about US$10-50 per person); **sleepers** (beds) in private sleeping cars offer more privacy, but are more expensive (supplement US$40-150). If you are using a rail pass valid only for a restricted number of days, inspect train schedules to maximize the use of your pass: an overnight train or boat journey often uses up only one of your travel days if it departs after 7pm.

SHOULD YOU BUY A RAIL PASS? Rail passes were designed to allow you to jump on any train in Europe, go wherever you want whenever you want, and change your plans at will. In practice, it's not so simple. You still must stand in line to validate your pass, pay for supplements, and fork over cash for seat and couchette reservations. More importantly, rail passes don't always pay off. Estimate the point-to-point cost of each leg of your journey; add them up and compare the total with the cost of a rail pass. If you are planning to spend a great deal time on trains, a rail pass will probably be worth it. But especially if you are under 26, point-to-point tickets may be cheaper.

A rail pass won't always pay for itself in the Balkans, Belgium, Eastern Europe, Greece, Iceland, Ireland, Italy, Luxembourg, the Netherlands, Portugal, or Spain, where train fares are reasonable, distances short, or buses preferable. If, however, the total cost of your trips nears the price of the pass, the convenience of avoiding ticket lines may be worth the difference.

MULTINATIONAL RAIL PASSES

EURAIL PASSES. Eurail is valid in most of Western Europe: Austria, Belgium, Denmark, Finland, France, Germany, Greece, Italy, Luxembourg, the Netherlands, Norway, Portugal, the Republic of Ireland, Spain, Sweden, and Switzerland. It is **not valid** in the UK. **Eurail Global Passes,** valid for a number of consecutive days, are best for those planning on spending extensive time on trains every few days. Other types of global passes are valid for any 10 or 15 (not necessarily consecutive) days within a two-month period, and are more cost-effective for those traveling longer distances less frequently. **Eurail Pass Saver** provides first-class travel for travelers in groups of two to five (prices are per person). **Eurail Pass Youth** provides parallel second-class perks for those under 26. Passholders receive a timetable for major routes and a map with details on bike rental, car rental, hotel, and museum discounts. Passholders also often receive reduced fares or free passage on many boat, bus, and private railroad lines. The **Eurail Select Pass** is a slimmed-down version of the Eurail Pass: it allows five to 10 days of unlimited travel in any two-month period within three, four, or five bordering European countries. **Eurail Select Passes** (for individuals) and **Eurail Select Pass Saver** (for people traveling in groups of two to five) range from US$505/429 per person (5 days) to US$765/645 (10 days). The **Eurail Select Pass Youth** (2nd class), for those ages 12-25, costs US$279-619. You are entitled to the same **freebies** afforded by the Eurail Pass, but only when they are within or between countries that you have purchased.

PICKY PASSES. In **Eastern Europe**, finding a pass is complicated. **Global passes** aren't accepted anywhere in Eastern Europe except Hungary and Romania; **Select passes** apply to Bulgaria, Croatia, and Slovenia, as well as Hungary and Romania; and **Regional passes** are available for all of those countries, with the exception of Bulgaria and the additions of the Czech Republic and Poland.

SHOPPING AROUND FOR A EURAIL. Eurail Passes can be bought only by non-Europeans from non-European distributors. These passes must be sold at uniform prices determined by the EU. However, some travel agents tack on a US$10 handling fee, and others offer certain bonuses with purchase, so shop around. Also, remember that pass prices rise annually, so if you're planning to travel early in the year, you can save cash by purchasing before January 1 (you have 3 months from the purchase date to validate your pass in Europe). It's best to buy a Eurail before leaving; only a few places in major cities sell them, and at a marked-up price. You can get a replacement for a lost pass only if you have purchased insurance on it under the **Pass Security Plan** (US$14). Eurail Passes are available through travel agents, student travel agencies like STA (p. 46), and **Rail Europe** (Canada ☎800-361-7245, US 888-382-7245; www.raileurope.com). It is also possible to buy directly from Eurail's website, www.eurail.com. Shipping is free to North America, Australia, and New Zealand.

OTHER MULTINATIONAL PASSES. If you have lived for at least six months in one of the European countries where **InterRail Passes** are valid, they are an economical option. The InterRail Pass allows travel within 30 European countries (excluding the passholder's country of residence). The **Global Pass** is valid for a given number of days (not necessarily consecutive) within a 10 day to one-month period. (5 days within 10 days, adult 1st class €329, adult 2nd class €249, youth €159; 10 days within 22 days €489/359/239; 1 month continuous €809/599/399.) The **One Country Pass** unsurprisingly limits travel to one country (€33 for 3 days). Passholders receive free admission to many museums, as well as **discounts** on accommodations, food, and many ferries to Ireland, Scandinavia, and the rest of Europe. Passes are available at www.interrailnet.com, as well as from travel agents, at major train stations throughout Europe, and through online vendors (www.railpassdirect.co.uk).

DOMESTIC RAIL PASSES

If you are planning to spend a significant amount of time within one country or region, a national pass—valid on all rail lines of a country's rail company—may be more cost-effective than a multinational pass. Many national passes are limited and don't provide the free or discounted travel on private railways and ferries that Eurail does. Some of these passes can be bought only in Europe, some only outside Europe; check with a rail agent or with national tourist offices.

NATIONAL RAIL PASSES. The domestic analogs of the Eurail pass, national rail passes are valid either for a given number of consecutive days or for a specific number of days within a given time period. Usually, they must be purchased before you leave. Though they will usually save travelers some money, the passes may actually be a more expensive alternative to point-to-point tickets, particularly in Eastern Europe. For more info, check out www.raileurope.com/us/rail/passes/single_country_index.htm.

RAIL-AND-DRIVE PASSES. Many countries (as well as Eurail) offer rail-and-drive passes, which combine car rental with rail travel—a good option for travelers who wish both to visit cities accessible by rail and to travel in the surrounding areas. Prices range US$300-2400. Children under 11 cost US$102-500, and adding more days costs US$72-105 per day (see **By Car**, p. 53).

FURTHER READING & RESOURCES ON TRAIN TRAVEL.

Info on rail travel and rail passes: www.raileurope.com or www.eurail.com.

Point-to-point fares and schedules: www.raileurope.com/us/rail/fares_schedules/index.htm. Allows you to calculate whether buying a rail pass would save you money.

Railsaver: www.railpass.com/new. Uses your itinerary to calculate the best rail pass for your trip.

European Railway Server: www.railfaneurope.net. Links to rail servers throughout Europe.

Thomas Cook European Timetable, updated monthly, covers all major and most minor train routes in Europe. Buy directly from Thomas Cook (www.thomascooktimetables.com).

BY BUS

In some cases, buses prove a better option than train travel. In Britain and Hungary, the bus and train systems are on par; in the Baltics, Greece, Ireland, Spain, and Portugal, bus networks are more extensive, efficient, and often more comfortable; in Iceland and parts of northern Scandinavia, bus service is the only ground transportation available. In the rest of Europe, bus travel is more of a gamble. Scattered offerings from private companies are often cheap, but sometimes unreliable. Amsterdam, Athens, London, Munich, and Oslo are centers for lines that offer long-distance rides across Europe. **International bus passes** allow unlimited travel on a hop-on, hop-off basis between major European cities, often at cheaper prices than rail passes.

Eurolines, offices in 19 countries (UK ☎8717 81 81 81; www.eurolines.co.uk or www.eurolines.com). The largest operator of Europe-wide coach services. Unlimited 15-day (high season €329, under 26 €279; low season €199/169) or 30-day (high season €439/359; low season €299/229) travel passes offer unlimited transit among 40 major European cities. Discount passes €29 or €39.

Busabout, 258 Vauxhall Bridge Rd., London, SW1V 1BS, UK (☎020 7950 1661; www.busabout.com). Offers 3 interconnecting bus circuits. 1 loop US$639; 2 loops US$1069; 3 loops US$1319. Flexipass with 6 stops $549; additional stops $59. Also sells discounted international SIM cards. (US$9; from US$0.29 per min.)

BY CAR

Cars offer speed, freedom, access to the countryside, and an escape from the town-to-town mentality of trains. Although a single traveler won't save by renting a car, four usually will. If you can't decide between train and car travel, you may benefit from a combination of the two; RailEurope and other rail pass vendors offer rail-and-drive packages. Fly-and-drive packages are also often available from travel agents or airline/rental agency partnerships. Before setting off, know the laws of the countries in which you'll be driving (e.g., both seat belts and headlights must be on at all times in **Scandinavia**, and remember to drive on the left in **Ireland and the UK**). For an informal primer on European road signs and conventions, check out www.travlang.com/signs. The **Association for Safe International Road Travel** (ASIRT) can provide more specific information about road conditions (☎301-983-5252; www.asirt.org). ASIRT considers road travel (by car or bus) to be relatively safe in Denmark, Ireland, the Netherlands, Norway, Sweden, Switzerland, and the UK, and relatively **unsafe** in Turkey and many parts of Eastern Europe. Western Europeans use **unleaded gas** almost exclusively, but it's not available in many gas stations in Eastern Europe.

RENTING A CAR

Cars can be rented from a US-based firm **(Alamo, Avis, Budget, or Hertz)** with European offices, from a European-based company with local representatives (Europcar), or from a tour operator (Auto Europe, Europe By Car, or Kemwel Holiday Autos) that will arrange a rental for you from a European company. Multinationals offer greater flexibility, but tour operators often strike better deals. Ask airlines about special fly-and-drive packages; you may get up to a week of free or discounted rental. See **Costs and Insurance**, p. 54, for more info. Minimum age requirements vary but tend to fall in the range of 21-25, with some as low as 18. There may be an additional insurance fee for drivers under 25. At most agencies, to rent a car, you'll need a driver's license from home with proof that you've had it for a year or an **International Driving Permit** (p. 56). Car rental in Europe is available through the following agencies:

Auto Europe (Canada and the US ☎888-223-5555; www.autoeurope.com).

Budget (Australia ☎1300 36 28 48, Canada ☎800-268-8900, New Zealand ☎0800 283 438, UK 87 01 56 56 56, US 800-527-0700; www.budget.com).

Europcar International (UK ☎18 70 607 5000; www.europcar.com).

Hertz (Canada and the US 800-654-3001; www.hertz.com).

COSTS AND INSURANCE

Expect to pay US$200-600 per week, plus tax (5-25%), for a tiny car with a manual transmission; automatics can double or triple the price. Larger vehicles and 4WD will also raise prices. Reserve and pay in advance if at all possible. It is less expensive to reserve a car from the US than from Europe. Rates are generally lowest in Belgium, Germany, the Netherlands, and the UK, higher in Ireland and Italy, and highest in Scandinavia and Eastern Europe. National chains often allow one-way rentals, with pick-up in one city and drop-off in another. There is usually a minimum hire period and sometimes an extra drop-off charge of several hundred dollars.

Many rental packages offer unlimited kilometers, while others offer a fixed distance per day with a per-kilometer surcharge after that. Be sure to ask whether the price includes **insurance** against theft and collision. Remember that if you are driving a conventional vehicle on an **unpaved road** in a rental car, you are almost never covered by insurance. Always check if prices quoted include tax and collision insurance; some credit cards provide insurance, allowing their customers to decline the collision damage waiver. Ask about discounts and check the terms of insurance, particularly the size of the deductible. Beware that cars rented on an **American Express or Visa/MasterCard Gold** or **Platinum** credit cards in Europe might not carry the automatic insurance that they would in some other countries. Check with your credit card company. Insurance plans almost always come with an **excess** (or deductible) for conventional vehicles; excess is usually higher for younger drivers and for 4WD. This provision means you pay for all damages up to the specified sum, unless they are the fault of another vehicle. The excess you will be quoted applies to collisions with other vehicles; other collisions ("single-vehicle collisions") will cost you even more. The excess can often be reduced or waived for an additional charge. Remember to return the car with a **full tank** of gas to avoid

high fuel charges. Gas prices are generally highest in Scandinavia. Throughout Europe, fuel tends to be cheaper in cities than in outlying areas.

LEASING A CAR

Leasing can be cheaper than renting, especially for more than 17 days. It is often the only option for those aged 18 to 21. The cheapest leases are agreements to buy the car and then sell it back to the manufacturer. Leases generally include insurance coverage and are not taxed. The most affordable ones usually originate in Belgium, France, or Germany. Expect to pay US$1000-2000 for 60 days. **Renault Eurodrive** leases new cars in a tax-free package to qualifying non-EU citizens (Australia ☎9299 33 44, Canada ☎450-461-1149, New Zealand ☎0800 807 778, US ☎212-730-0676; www.renault-eurodrive.com).

BUYING A CAR

If you're brave and know what you're doing, buying a used car or van in Europe and selling it just before you leave can provide the cheapest wheels for long trips. Check with consulates for import-export laws concerning used vehicles, registration, and safety and emission standards.

ON THE ROAD

Road conditions and **regional hazards** are variable throughout Europe. Steep, curvy mountain roads may be closed in winter. Road conditions in Eastern Europe are often poor as a result of maintenance issues and inadequately enforced traffic laws. Western European roads are generally excellent, but each area has its own dangers. In Scandinavia, for example, drivers should be on the lookout for moose and elk; on the Autobahn, the threat may come from cars speeding by at 150kph. In this book, region-specific hazards are listed in country introductions. Carry emergency equipment with you (see **Driving Precautions**, below) and know what to do in case of a breakdown. Car rental companies will often have phone numbers for emergency services.

DRIVING PERMITS AND CAR INSURANCE

INTERNATIONAL DRIVING PERMIT (IDP). To drive a car in **Europe**, you must **be over 18** and have an **International Driving Permit (IDP)**, though certain countries (such as the UK) allow travelers to drive with a valid American or Canadian license for a limited number of months. It may be a good idea to get an IDP anyway, in case you're in a situation (e.g., you get in an accident or become stranded in a small town) **where the police do not know English; information on the IDP is printed in 11 languages, including French, German, Italian, Portuguese, Russian, Spanish, and Swedish**. Your IDP must be issued in your home country before you depart. An application for an IDP usually requires a photo, a current license, an additional form of identification, and a fee of around US$20. To apply, contact your country's automobile association (i.e., the AAA in the US or the CAA in Canada). Be wary of buying IDPs from unauthorized online vendors.

CAR INSURANCE. If you rent, lease, or borrow a car, you will need an International Insurance Certificate, or Green Card, to certify that you have liability insurance and that it applies abroad. Green Cards can be obtained at car rental agencies, car dealerships (for those leasing cars), some travel agents, and some border crossings. Rental agencies may require you to purchase theft insurance in countries they consider to have a high risk of auto theft.

DRIVING PRECAUTIONS. When traveling in summer, bring substantial amounts of **water** (5L per person per day) for drinking and for the radiator. For long drives to unpopulated areas, register with police before beginning the trip, and again upon arrival at the destination. Check with the local automobile club for details. Make sure tires are in good repair and have enough air, and get good maps. A **compass** and a **car manual** can also be very useful. Always carry a **spare tire** and **jack, jumper cables,** extra **oil, flares,** a **flashlight** (torch), and **heavy blankets** (in case your car breaks down at night or in winter). A **mobile phone** may help in an emergency. If you don't know how to change a tire, learn, especially if you're traveling in deserted areas. Blowouts on dirt roads are very common. If the car breaks down, stay with your car to wait for help.

BY CHUNNEL FROM THE UK

Traversing 27 mi. under the sea, the Chunnel is undoubtedly the fastest, most convenient, and least scenic route from England to France.

BY TRAIN. Eurostar, Eurostar House, Waterloo Station, London SE1 8SE (UK ☎08 705 186 186; www.eurostar.com) runs frequent trains between London and the continent. Ten to 28 trains per day run to 100 destinations including Paris (4hr., US$75-400, 2nd class), Disneyland Paris, Brussels, Lille, and Calais. Book online, at major rail stations in the UK, or at the office above.

BY BUS. Eurolines provides bus-ferry combinations (see p. 53).

BY CAR. Eurotunnel, Customer relations, P.O. Box 2000, Folkestone, Kent CT18 8XY (UK ☎08 705 353 535; www.eurotunnel.co.uk) shuttles cars and passengers between Kent and Nord-Pas-de-Calais. Return fares for vehicle and all passengers range from UK£223-253 with car. One-way starts at UK£49, two- to five-day return for a car UK£165-298. Book online or via phone. Travelers with cars can also look into sea crossings by ferry (see below).

BY BOAT

Most long-distance ferries are quite comfortable; the cheapest ticket typically includes a reclining chair or couchette. Fares jump sharply in July and August. ISIC holders can often get student fares, and Eurail Pass holders get reductions and sometimes free trips. You'll occasionally have to pay a port tax (around US$10). The fares below are **one-way** for **adult foot passengers** unless otherwise noted. Though standard round-trip fares are usually twice the one-way fare, **fixed-period returns** (usually within 5 days) may be cheaper. Ferries run **year-round** unless otherwise noted. Bringing a **bike** costs up to US$15 in high season.

FERRIES FROM BRITAIN AND IRELAND

Ferries are frequent and dependable. The main route across the English Channel from Britain to France is Dover-Calais. The main ferry port on England's southern coast is Portsmouth, with connections to France and Spain. Ferries also cross the Irish Sea, connecting Northern Ireland with Scotland and England, and the Republic of Ireland with Wales. See the directory online at www.seaview.co.uk/ferries.html for schedules and more information.

Brittany Ferries: UK ☎0871 2440 744, France ☎825 828 828, Spain ☎942 360 611; www.brittany-ferries.com. **Cork** to **Roscoff, FRA** (14hr.); **Plymouth** to **Roscoff, FRA** (6hr.) and **Santander, SPA** (18hr.); **Poole** to **Cherbourg, FRA** (4hr.); **Portsmouth** to **St-Malo, FRA** (10hr.) and **Caen, FRA** (5hr.).

DFDS Seaways: UK ☎0871 522 9955; www.dfdsseaways.co.uk. **Harwich** to **Cuxhaven** (19hr.) and **Esbjerg, DEN** (18hr.); **Newcastle** to **Amsterdam, NTH** (16hr.), and **Haugesund, NOR** (18hr.); **Dover** to **Calais, FRA** (1-2hr.).

Irish Ferries: Northern Ireland ☎353 818 300 400; Republic of Ireland ☎08 18 30 04 00, Great Britain ☎87 05 17 17 17; www.irishferries.com. **Rosslare** to **Pembroke** (3hr.) and **Cherbourg** or **Roscoff, FRA** (18hr.). **Holyhead** to **Dublin, IRE** (2-3hr.).

P&O Ferries: UK ☎08 705 980 333; www.poferries.com. **Dover** to **Calais, FRA** (1hr., 25 per day, UK £14); **Hull** to **Rotterdam, NTH** (10hr.) and **Zeebrugge, BEL** (12hr.).

FERRIES IN SCANDINAVIA

Ferries run to many North Sea destinations. Booking ahead is not necessary for deck passage. Baltic Sea ferries sail between Poland and Scandinavia.

Color Line: Norway ☎0810 00 811; www.colorline.com. Ferries run from 6 cities and towns in Norway to **Frederikshavn** and **Hirtshal, DEN** (€24-80); **Strömsand, SWE** (€9-22); **Kiel, GER** (€98-108). Car packages from €137. Student discounts available.

Tallinksilja Line: Finland ☎09 180 41, Sweden ☎08 22 21 40; www.tallinksilja.com. Connects Helsinki and Turku to **Sweden** (€18-116) and **Stockholm, SWE** to **Tallinn, EST** (€20-33); **Rostock, GER** (€91-133); **Riga, LAT** (€22-32). Eurail passes accepted.

Viking Line: Finland ☎0600 415 77, Sweden ☎0452 40 00; www.vikingline.fi. Ferries run between **Helsinki** and **Turku, FIN** to destinations in **Estonia** and **Sweden**. M-Th and Su cruises min. age 18, F-Sa 21. One-way €33-59. Eurail discounts available.

MEDITERRANEAN AND AEGEAN FERRIES

Mediterranean ferries may be the most glamorous, but they can also be the most turbulent. Ferries run from Spain to Morocco, from Italy to Tunisia, and from France to both Morocco and Tunisia. Reservations are recommended, especially in July and August. Schedules are erratic, with varying prices for similar routes. Shop around, and beware of small companies that don't take reservations. Ferries traverse the Adriatic from Ancona, ITA to Split, CRO and from Bari, ITA to Dubrovnik, CRO. They also cross the Aegean, from Ancona, ITA to Patras, GCE and from Bari, ITA to Igoumenitsa and Patras, GCE. **Eurail** is valid on certain ferries between Brindisi, ITA and Corfu, Igoumenitsa, and Patras, GCE. Many ferry companies operate on these routes.

BY MOPED AND MOTORCYCLE

Motorized bikes and **mopeds** don't use much gas, can be put on trains and ferries, and are a good compromise between costly car travel and the limited range of bicycles. However, they're uncomfortable for long distances, dangerous in the rain, and unpredictable on rough roads. Always wear a helmet, and never ride with a backpack. If you've never ridden a moped before, a twisting Alpine road is not the place to start. Expect to pay about US$20-35 per day; try auto repair shops, and remember to bargain. **Motorcycles** are more expensive and normally require a license, but are better for long distances. Before renting, ask if the price includes tax and insurance. Avoid handing your passport over as a deposit; if you have an accident or mechanical failure you may not get it back until you cover all repairs. Pay ahead of time instead.

BY THUMB

WARNING. Let's Go strongly urges you to consider the risks before you choose to hitch. We do not recommend hitchhiking, and none of the information presented here is intended to do so.

No one should hitch without careful consideration of the risks involved. Hitching means entrusting your life to an unknown person and risking theft, assault, sexual harassment, and unsafe driving. However, some travelers report that hitchhiking in Europe allows them to meet locals and travel in areas where public transportation is sketchy. **Britain** and **Ireland** are probably the easiest places in Western Europe to get a lift. Hitching in **Scandinavia** is slow but steady. Long-distance hitching in the developed countries of northwestern Europe demands close attention to expressway junctions, rest stop locations, and destination signs. Hitching in southern Europe is generally mediocre. In some Eastern European countries, the line between hitching and taking a taxi is virtually nonexistent. Hitchhiking at night can be particularly dangerous; experienced hitchers stand in well-lit places. For women traveling alone or even two women traveling together, hitching is simply too dangerous. A man and a woman are a safer combination, two men will have a harder time, and three will go nowhere. Experienced hitchers pick a spot outside of built-up areas, where drivers can stop, return to the road without causing an accident, and have time to look over potential passengers as they approach. Hitching on super-highways is usually illegal: one may only thumb at rest stops or at the entrance ramps to highways. Finally, success often depends on appearance.

Most Western European countries have ride services that pair drivers with riders; fees vary according to destination. **Eurostop** (www.taxistop.be/index_ils.htm), Taxistop's ride service, is one of the largest in Europe. Also try **Allostop** in France (French-language website www.allostop.net) and **Verband der Deutschen Mitfahrzentralen** in Germany (German-language website www.mitfahrzentrale.de). Not all organizations screen drivers and riders; ask ahead.

BEYOND TOURISM

A PHILOSOPHY FOR TRAVELERS

BEYOND TOURISM HIGHLIGHTS
NURTURE endangered griffon vultures on the Cres Island in **Croatia** (p. 210).
RESTORE castles in **France** (p. 305) and **Germany** (p. 383).
POLITICK as an intern at NATO in **Belgium** (p. 98).
IMMERSE yourself in film production in the **Czech Republic** (p. 230).

As a tourist, you are always a foreigner. Sure, hostel-hopping and sightseeing can be great fun, but connecting with a foreign country through studying, volunteering, or working can extend your travels beyond tourist traps. Instead of feeling like a stranger in a strange land, you can understand Europe like a local. Instead of being that tourist asking for directions, you can be the one who gives them (and correctly!). All the while, you get the satisfaction of leaving Europe in better shape than you found it (after all, it's being nice enough to let you stay here). It's not wishful thinking—it's Beyond Tourism.

As a **volunteer** in Europe, you can unleash your inner superhero with projects from building homes in Ireland to digging up ancient treasures in Italy. This chapter is chock-full of ideas to get involved, whether you're looking to pitch in for a day or run away from home for a whole new life in European activism.

The powers of **studying** abroad are beyond comprehension: it actually makes you feel sorry for those poor tourists who don't get to do any homework while they're here; quite literally the perfect combo of academics and local culture.

Working abroad immerses you in a new culture and can bring some of the most meaningful relationships and experiences of your life. Yes, we know you're on vacation, but these aren't your normal desk jobs. (Plus, it doesn't hurt that it helps pay for more globetrotting.) If you're an EU citizen, work will be far easier to come by, but there are still options for those not so blessed.

SHARE YOUR EXPERIENCE. Have you had a particularly enjoyable volunteer, study, or work experience that you'd like to share with other travelers? Post it to our website, www.letsgo.com!

VOLUNTEERING

Feel like saving the world this week? Volunteering can be a powerful and fulfilling experience, especially when combined with the thrill of traveling in a new place. Europe offers an endless varieties of opportunities to volunteer, with exciting choices from teaching English to ecological conservation.

Most people who volunteer in Europe do so on a short-term basis at organizations that make use of drop-in or once-a-week volunteers. The best way to find opportunities that match your interests and schedule may be to check with local or national volunteer centers. As always, read up before heading out.

Those looking for longer, more intensive volunteer opportunities usually choose to go through a parent organization that takes care of logistical details and often provides a group environment and support system—for a fee. There are two main types of organizations—religious and secular—although there are rarely restrictions on participation for either. Websites like **www.volunteerabroad.com, www.servenet.org,** and **www.idealist.org** allow you to search for volunteer openings both in your country and abroad.

ONLINE DIRECTORIES: VOLUNTEERING

www.alliance-network.org. Various international service organizations.

www.idealist.org. Provides extensive listings of service opportunities.

www.worldvolunteerweb.org. Lists organizations and events around the world.

COMMUNITY DEVELOPMENT

If working closely with locals and helping in a hands-on fashion appeals to you, check out community development options. Many returning travelers report that working among locals was one of their most rewarding experiences.

Global Volunteers, 375 E. Little Canada Rd., St. Paul, MN 55109, USA (☎800-487-1074; www.globalvolunteers.org). A variety of 1- to 3-week volunteer programs throughout Europe. Fees range US$2000-3000, including room and board but not airfare.

Habitat for Humanity, 121 Habitat St., Americus, GA 31709, USA (☎800-422-4828; www.habitat.org). A Christian non-profit organization coordinating 9- to 14-day service trips in Britain, Germany, Greece, Hungary, Ireland, the Netherlands, Poland, Portugal, and Switzerland. Participants aid in building homes. Program around US$1000-2200.

Service Civil International Voluntary Service (SCI-IVS), 5505 Walnut Level Rd., Crozet, VA 22932, USA (☎206-350-6585; www.sci-ivs.org). Arranges placement in 2- to 3-week outdoor service camps (workcamps), or 3-month teaching opportunities throughout Europe. 18+. Registration fee US$235, including room and board.

Volunteer Abroad, 7800 Point Meadows Dr., Ste. 218 Jacksonville, FL 32256, USA (☎720-570-1702; www.volunteerabroad.com/search.cfm). Volunteer work in Europe.

CONSERVATION

As more people realize that long-cherished habitats and structures are in danger, diverse programs have stepped in to aid the concerned in lending a hand.

Club du Vieux Manoir, Ancienne Abbaye du Moncel, 60700 Pontpoint, FRA (☎33 03 44 72 33 98; http://cvmclubduvieuxmanoir.free.fr). Offers year-long and summer programs restoring castles and churches throughout France. €15 annual membership and insurance fee. Costs €14 per day, including food and tent.

Earthwatch Institute, 3 Clock Tower Pl., Ste. 100, P.O. Box 75, Maynard, MA, 01754, USA (☎978-461-0081; www.earthwatch.org). Arranges 2-day to 3-week programs promoting the conservation of natural resources. Fees vary based on program location and duration. Costs range US$400-4000, including room and board but not airfare.

The National Trust, P.O. Box 39, Warrington, WA5 7WD, UK (☎ 44 017 938 176 32; www.nationaltrust.org.uk/volunteers). Arranges numerous volunteer opportunities, including Working Holidays. From £60 per week, including room and board.

World-Wide Opportunities on Organic Farms (WWOOF), PO Box 2154, Winslow Buckingham, MK18 3WS England, UK (www.wwoof.org). Arranges volunteer work with organic and eco-conscious farms around the world. You become a member of WWOOF in the country in which you plan to work; prices vary by country.

HUMANITARIAN AND SOCIAL SERVICES

Europe's complex, war-torn history offers up opportunities to help rebuild. Numerous peace programs can prove to be fulfilling for volunteers.

Brethren Volunteer Service (BVS), 1451 Dundee Ave., Elgin, IL 60120, USA (☎800-323-8039; www.brethrenvolunteerservice.org). Peace and social justice based programs. Minimum commitment of 2 yr., must be 21 to serve overseas. US$75 fee for background check; US$500 fee for international volunteers.

Simon Wiesenthal Center, 1399 South Roxbury Dr., Los Angeles, CA 90035, USA (☎800-900-9036; www.wiesenthal.org). Fights anti-Semitism and Holocaust denial throughout Europe. Small, discretionary donation required for membership.

Volunteers for Peace, 1034 Tiffany Rd., Belmont, VT 05730, USA (☎802-259-2759; www.vfp.org). Arranges placement in camps throughout Europe. US$30 membership required for registration. Programs average US$250-500 for 2-3 weeks.

I HAVE TO PAY TO VOLUNTEER? Many volunteers are surprised to learn that some organizations require large fees or "donations," but don't go calling them scams just yet. While such fees may seem ridiculous at first, they often keep the organization afloat, covering airfare, room, board, and administrative expenses for the volunteers. If you're concerned about how a program spends its fees, request an annual report or finance account. A reputable organization won't refuse to inform you of how volunteer money is spent. Pay-to-volunteer programs might be a good idea for young travelers who are looking for more support and structure (such as pre-arranged transportation and housing) or anyone who would rather not deal with the uncertainty of creating a volunteer experience from scratch.

STUDYING

It's hard to dread the first day of school when London is your campus and exotic restaurants are your meal plan. A growing number of students report that studying abroad is the highlight of their learning careers. If you've never studied abroad, you don't know what you're missing—and, if you have studied abroad, you do know what you're missing.

Study-abroad programs range from basic language and culture courses to university-level classes, often for college credit (it's legit, Mom and Dad). In order to choose a program that best fits your needs, research as much as you can before making your decision—determine costs and duration as well as what kinds of students participate in the program and what sorts of accommodations are provided. (Since when was back-to-school shopping this fun?)

In programs that have large groups of students who speak the same language, there is a trade-off. You may feel more comfortable in the community, but you will not have the same opportunity to practice a foreign language or to befriend other international students. For accommodations, dorm life provides a better opportunity to mingle with fellow students, but there is less of a chance to experience the local scene. If you live with a family, you could potentially build lifelong friendships with natives and experience day-to-day life in more depth, but you might also get stuck sharing a room with their pet iguana. Conditions can vary greatly from family to family.

UNIVERSITIES

Most university-level study-abroad programs are conducted in the local language, although many programs offer classes in English as well as lower-level language courses. Savvy linguists may find it cheaper to enroll directly in a university abroad, although getting college credit may be more difficult. You can search online at **www.studyabroad.com** for various semester-abroad programs that meet your criteria, including your desired location and focus of study. If you're a college student, your friendly neighborhood study-abroad office is often a great resource, and the best place to start.

ONLINE DIRECTORIES: STUDY ABROAD

These websites are good resources for finding programs that cater to your particular interests. Each has links to various study-abroad programs broken down by a variety of criteria, including desired location and focus of study.

www.petersons.com/stdyabrd/sasector.html. Lists study-abroad programs at accredited institutions that usually offer cross credits.

www.studyabroad.com. A great starting point for finding college- or high-school-level programs in foreign languages or specific academic subjects. Also includes information for teaching and volunteering opportunities.

www.westudyabroad.com. Lists language courses and college-level programs.

AMERICAN PROGRAMS

The following is a list of organizations that can either help place students in university programs abroad or that have their own branch in Europe.

American Institute for Foreign Study, College Division, River Plaza, 9 W. Broad St., Stamford, CT 06902, USA (☎800-727-2437; www.aifsabroad.com). Organizes programs for high school and college study at universities in Austria, Britain, the Czech Republic, France, Hungary, Ireland, Italy, Russia, and Spain. Summer programs US$4900-6500; Semester-long programs US$11,000-16,000. Scholarships available.

Council on International Educational Exchange (CIEE), 7 Custom House St., 3rd fl., Portland, ME, 04101, USA (☎800-407-8839; www.ciee.org/study). Sponsors work, volunteer, academic, and internship programs in Belgium, Britain, the Czech Republic, France, Hungary, Ireland, Italy, the Netherlands, Spain, and Turkey for around US$14,000 per semester. Also offers volunteer opportunities. US$30 application fee.

International Association for the Exchange of Students for Technical Experience (IAESTE), 10400 Little Patuxent Pkwy. Ste. 250, Columbia, MD 21044, USA (☎410-997-3068; www.iaeste.org). Offers 8- to 12-week internships in Europe for college students who have completed 2 years study in a particular trade.

School for International Training, College Semester Abroad, Kipling Rd., P.O. Box 676, Brattleboro, VT 05302, USA (☎888-272-7881 or 802-258-7751; www.sit.edu/studyabroad). Programs in Europe cost around US$10,000-16,000. Also runs The Experiment in International Living (☎800-345-2929; fax 802-258-3428; www.usexperiment.org), 3- to 5-week summer programs that offer high school students homestays, community service, ecological adventure, and language training in Europe for US$5900-7000.

AUSTRALIAN PROGRAMS

The following organizations place Australian students in programs in Europe.

World Exchange Program Australia, (☎1 300 884 733; www.wep.org.au). Places Australian high school students for 3 months to 1 year in high schools abroad. Group study tours also available. Costs for one semester in Europe are AUS$8950-6290.

Innovative Universities European Union Centre (IUEU), (☎298 507 915 ; www.iueu.edu.au). Offers undergraduates from Flinders, La Trobe and Macquarie universities a chance to study abroad for one semester in their Global Citizenship program.

LANGUAGE SCHOOLS

Enrolling at a language school has two major perks: a slightly less rigorous courseload and the ability to learn exactly what those kids in Mainz are calling you under their breath. There can be great variety in language schools—independently run, affiliated with a large university, local, international—but one thing is constant: they rarely offer college credit. Their programs are also good for younger high-school students who might not feel comfortable with older students in a university program. Some worthwhile organizations include:

Association of Commonwealth Universities (ACU), Woburn House, 20-24 Tavistock Sq., London WC1H 9HF, UK (☎020 7380 6700; www.acu.ac.uk). Publishes information about Commonwealth Universities, including those in Cyprus and the UK.

Eurocentres, Seestr. 247, CH-8038 Zürich, SWI (☎41 1 485 50 40; www.eurocentres.com). Language programs for beginning to advanced students with homestays in Britain, France, Germany, Ireland, Italy, Spain, and Switzerland.

Language Immersion Institute, SCB 106, State University of New York at New Paltz, 1 Hawk Dr., New Paltz, NY 12561, USA (☎845-257-3500; www.newpaltz.edu/lii). 2-week summer language courses and some overseas courses in French, German, Greek, Hungarian, Italian, Polish, Portugese, Spanish, and Swedish. Around US$1000 for a 2-week course, not including accommodations.

Sprachcaffe Languages Plus, 413 Ontario St., Toronto, ON M5A 2V9, CAN (☎888-526-4758; www.sprachcaffe.com). Language classes in France, Germany, Italy, the Netherlands, and Spain for US$200-500 per week. Homestays available. Also offers French and Spanish language and travel programs for teenagers.

WORKING

Nowhere does money grow on trees (though *Let's Go*'s researchers aren't done looking), but there are still some pretty good opportunities to earn a living and travel at the same time. As with volunteering, work opportunities tend to fall into two categories. Some travelers want long-term jobs that allow them to integrate into a community, while others seek out short-term jobs to finance the next leg of their travels. In Europe, people who want to work long-term should look for jobs like teaching English, taking care of local children, and other opportunities that can be found through a bit of research and luck. People looking for short term work have options like picking fruit and working for summer programs abroad. **Transitions Abroad** (www.transitionsabroad.com) also offers updated online listings for work over any time span.

Employment opportunities for those who want short-term work may be more limited and are generally contingent upon the city or region's economic

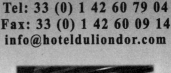

needs. In addition to local papers, international English-language newspapers, such as the International Herald Tribune (www.iht.com), often list job opportunities in their classified sections. If applicable, travelers should also consult federally run employment offices. Note that working abroad often requires a special work visa; see the box below for info about obtaining one.

VISA INFORMATION. EU Citizens: The EU's 2004 and 2007 enlargements led the 15 previous member states (EU-15) to fear that waves of Eastern European immigrants would flood their labor markets. This fear caused some members of the union to institute a transition period of up to seven years during which citizens of the new EU countries may still need a visa or permit to work. EU-15 citizens generally have the right to work in the pre-enlargement countries for up to three months without a visa; longer-term employment usually requires a work permit. By law, all EU-15 citizens are given equal consideration for jobs not directly related to national security. **Everyone else:** Getting a work visa in Europe is difficult for non-EU citizens. Different countries have varying policies for granting work permits to those from non-EU countries. It is possible for students to work part-time without a work permit in some countries. In 2007, the EU introduced the "blue card" program, aimed at long term, skilled workers, which requires an employment contract in place before immigration.

LONG-TERM WORK

If you're planning to spend more than three months working in Europe, search for a job well in advance. International placement agencies are often the easiest way to find employment abroad, especially for those interested in teaching English. Although often only available to college students, **internships** are a good way to segue into working abroad; although they are often un- or underpaid, many say the experience is well worth it. Be wary of advertisements for companies claiming to be able get you a job abroad for a fee—often the same listings are available online or in newspapers. Some organizations include:

Escapeartist.com (jobs.escapeartist.com). International employers post directly to this website; various jobs in European countries advertised.

International Cooperative Education, 15 Spiros Way, Menlo Park, CA, 94025, USA (☎650-323-4944; www.icemenlo.com). Finds summer jobs in Belgium, Britain, Germany, and Switzerland. $250 application fee and $700 placement fee.

StepStone (www.stepstone.com, branches across Europe listed at www.stepstone.com/EN/Company/Locations). Database covering international employment in Austria, Belgium, Britain, Denmark, France, Germany, Italy, the Netherlands, Norway, Portugal, and Sweden. Several search options and a list of openings.

TEACHING ENGLISH

While some elite private American schools offer competitive salaries, let's just say that teaching jobs abroad pay more in personal satisfaction and emotional fulfillment than in actual cash. Perhaps this is why volunteering as a teacher instead of getting paid is a popular option. Even then, teachers often receive some sort of a daily stipend to help with living expenses. For countries that have a low cost of living, even though salaries at private schools may be low compared to those in the US, the low cost of living makes it much more profitable. In almost all cases, you must have at least a bachelor's degree to be a full-fledged teacher, although college undergraduates can often get summer positions teaching or tutoring. Many schools require teachers to have a **Teaching English as a Foreign Language (TEFL)** certificate. You may still be able to find a teaching job without one, but certified teachers often find higher-paying jobs.

Those who can't speak the local language don't have to give up their dream of teaching, either. Private schools usually hire native English speakers for English-immersion classrooms where no local language is spoken. (Teachers in public schools will more likely work in both English and the local language.) Placement agencies or university fellowship programs are the best resources for finding teaching jobs. The alternative is to contact schools directly or to try your luck once you arrive in Europe. In the latter case, the best time to look is several weeks before the start of the school year. The following organizations are extremely helpful in placing teachers in Europe.

International Schools Services (ISS), 15 Roszel Rd., P.O. Box 5910, Princeton, NJ 08543, USA (☎609-452-0990; www.iss.edu). Hires teachers for more than 200 international and American schools around the world; candidates should have 2 years teaching experience and/or teacher certification. 2-year commitment expected.

Teaching English as a Foreign Language (TEFL), TEFL Professional Network Ltd., 72 Pentyla Baglan Rd., Port Talbot, SA12 8AD, UK (www.tefl.com). Maintains an extensive database of openings throughout Europe. Offers job training and certification.

AU PAIR WORK

Au pairs are typically women aged 18-27 who work as live-in nannies, caring for children and doing light housework in foreign countries in exchange for room, board, and a small spending allowance or stipend. One perk of the job is that it allows you to get to know Europe without the high expenses of traveling. Drawbacks, however, can include mediocre pay and long hours. Average weekly pay will vary depending on location. Much of the au pair experience depends on the family with which you are placed. The agencies below are a good starting point for looking for employment.

Childcare International, Ltd., Trafalgar House, Grenville Pl., London NW7 3SA (☎44 020 8906 3116; www.childint.co.uk). Offers au pair and nanny placement.

InterExchange, 161 6th Ave., New York, NY, 10013, USA (☎212-924-0446; www.interexchange.org). Au pair, internship, and short-term work placement in France, Germany, the Netherlands, and Spain. US$495-595 placement fee and US$75 application fee.

Sunny AuPairs (☎44 020 8144 1635, in US 503-616-3026; www.sunnyaupairs.com). Online, worldwide database connecting au pairs with families. No placement fee.

SHORT-TERM WORK

Believe it or not, traveling for long periods of time can be hard on the wallet. Many travelers try their hand at odd jobs for a few weeks at a time to help pay for another month or two of touring around. Work options vary across the continent, but work possibilities might include picking fruit, serving, or opportunities through keeping an ear out for wherever labor is needed. Another popular option is to work several hours a day at a hostel in exchange for free or discounted room and/or board. Most often, these short-term jobs are found by word of mouth or by expressing interest to the owner of a hostel or restaurant. Due to high turnover in the tourism industry, many places are eager for help, even if it is only temporary. Let's Go lists temporary jobs of this nature whenever possible, but recommends checking the work restrictions of your visa.

FURTHER READING ON BEYOND TOURISM

Alternatives to the Peace Corps: A Guide of Global Volunteer Opportunities, by Paul Backhurst. Food First Books, 2005.

The Back Door Guide to Short-Term Job Adventures: Internships, Summer Jobs, Seasonal Work, Volunteer Vacations, and Transitions Abroad, by Michael Landes. Ten Speed Press, 2005.

Green Volunteers: The World Guide to Voluntary Work in Nature Conservation, ed. Fabio Ausenda. Universe, 2007.

How to Get a Job in Europe, by Cheryl Matherly and Robert Sanborn. Planning Communications, 2003.

International Job Finder: Where the Jobs Are Worldwide, by Daniel Lauber and Kraig Rice. Planning Communications, 2002.

Live and Work Abroad: A Guide for Modern Nomads, by Huw Francis and Michelyne Callan. Vacation-Work Publications, 2001.

Short-Term Adventures That Will Benefit You and Others, by Doug Cutchins, Anne Geissinger, and Bill McMillon. Chicago Review Press, 2006.

Work Your Way Around the World, by Susan Griffith. Vacation-Work Publications, 2007.

AUSTRIA (ÖSTERREICH)

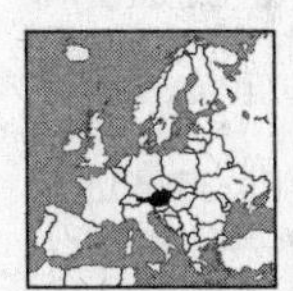

With Vienna's high culture and the Alps's high mountains, Austria offers different extremes of beauty. Many of the world's most famous composers and thinkers, including Mozart and Freud, called Austria home. Today, its small villages brim with locally brewed beer, jagged peaks draw hikers and skiers, and magnificent palaces, museums, and concerts are omnipresent. Stroll along the blue Danube River or relax in a Viennese coffeehouse and listen to a waltz.

DISCOVER AUSTRIA: SUGGESTED ITINERARIES

THREE DAYS Spend all three days in **Vienna** (p. 73). From the stately **Stephansdom** to the majestic **Hofburg Palace,** Vienna's many attractions will leave you with enough sensory stimulation to last you until your next trip.

ONE WEEK Begin in **Innsbruck** (1 day; p. 92) to take advantage of its skiing opportunities. Stop in **Salzburg** (2 days; p. 86) to see the home of Mozart and the **Salzburger Festspiele** (p. 73). Move on to **Linz** (1 day; p. 85) to try its famous Linzer torte. End your trip by basking in the glory of **Vienna** (3 days).

TWO WEEKS Start in **Innsbruck,** where museums and mountains meet (2 days; p. 92), then swing by **Zell am See** for more hiking (1 day; p. 90). Spend another two days wandering **Hohe Tauern National Park** (p. 91), visiting the **Pasterze Glacier** and **Großglockner Hochalpenstraße.** Visit the home of Kepler and see other magnificent architecture in **Linz** (1 day; p. 85). Follow your ears to **Salzburg** (3 days), then head to **Graz** (1 day; p. 96) for its throbbing nightlife. Finally, make your way to **Vienna** for a grand finale of romance, waltzes, and coffeehouse culture (4 days).

ESSENTIALS

FACTS AND FIGURES

OFFICIAL NAME: Republic of Austria.

CAPITAL: Vienna.

MAJOR CITIES: Graz, Innsbruck, Salzburg.

POPULATION: 8,205,000.

LAND AREA: 82,400 sq. km.

TIME ZONE: GMT +1.

LANGUAGE: German.

RELIGIONS: Roman Catholic 74%, Protestant 5%, Muslim 4%, Other/None 17%.

PERCENTAGE OF AUSTRIA'S LAND AREA COVERED BY THE ALPS: 62.

WHEN TO GO

Between November and March, prices in western Austria double and travelers need reservations months in advance. The situation reverses in the summer, when the eastern half of the country fills with tourists. Accommodations are cheaper and less crowded in the shoulder seasons (May-June and Sept.-Oct.).

Cultural opportunities also vary with the seasons: the Vienna State Opera, like many other theaters, has no shows in July or August, and the Vienna Boys' Choir only performs May-June and Sept.-Oct.

DOCUMENTS AND FORMALITIES

EMBASSIES. Foreign embassies in Austria are in Vienna (p. 77). Austrian embassies abroad include: **Australia,** 12 Talbot St., Forrest, Canberra, ACT, 2603 (☎02 6295 1533; www.austriaemb.org.au); **Canada,** 445 Wilbrod St., Ottawa, ON, K1N 6M7 (☎613-789-1444; www.austro.org); **Ireland,** 15 Ailesbury Ct., 93 Ailesbury Rd., Dublin, 4 (☎01 269 45 77); **New Zealand,** Level 2, Willbank House, 57 Willis St., Wellington, 6001 (☎04 499 63 93); **UK,** 18 Belgrave Mews West, London, SW1X 8HU (☎020 7344 3250; www.bmaa.gv.at/london); **US,** 3524 International Ct., NW, Washington, D.C., 20008 (☎202-895-6700; www.austria.org).

VISA AND ENTRY INFORMATION. EU citizens do not need a visa. Citizens of Australia, Canada, New Zealand, and the US do not need a visa for stays of up to 90 days, beginning upon entry into any of the countries in the EU's freedom-of-movement zone. For more info, see p. 15. For stays of longer than 90 days, all non-EU citizens need visas, available at Austrian embassies. For American citizens, visas are $80 or free of charge for students studying abroad.

TOURIST SERVICES AND MONEY

EMERGENCY	**Ambulance:** ☎144. **Fire:** ☎122. **Police:** ☎133.

TOURIST OFFICES. For general info, contact the **Austrian National Tourist Office,** Margaretenstr. 1, A-1040 Vienna (☎588 66 287; www.austria.info). All tourist offices are marked with a green "i"; most brochures are available in English.

MONEY. The **euro (€)** has replaced the **schilling** as the unit of currency in Austria. As a general rule, it's cheaper to exchange money in Austria than at home. Railroad stations, airports, hotels, and most travel agencies offer exchange services, as do banks. If you stay in hostels and prepare most of your own food, expect to spend €30-60 per day. Accommodations start at about €12 and a basic sit-down meal usually costs around €8. Menus will say whether service is included (*Preise inklusive* or *Bedienung inklusiv*); if it is, a tip is not expected. If not, 10% will do. Austrian restaurants expect you to seat yourself, and servers will not bring the bill until you ask them to do so. Say "*Zahlen bitte*" (TSAHL-en BIT-uh) to settle your accounts, and give tips directly to the server. Don't expect to bargain, except at street markets.

Austria has a **20% value added tax (VAT),** a sales tax applied to most purchased goods (p. 21). The prices given in *Let's Go* include VAT. In an airport upon exiting the EU, non-EU citizens can claim a refund on the tax paid for goods purchased at participating stores. In order to qualify for a refund in a store, you must spend at least €75; make sure to ask for a refund form when you pay. For more info on qualifying for a VAT refund, see p. 21.

TRANSPORTATION

BY PLANE. The only major international airport is Vienna's **Schwechat-Flughafen (VIE).** Other airports are in Innsbruck, Graz, Linz, and Salzburg. From London-Stansted, **Ryanair** (☎3531 249 7791; www.ryanair.com) flies to the latter three. For more info on flying to Austria, see p. 46.

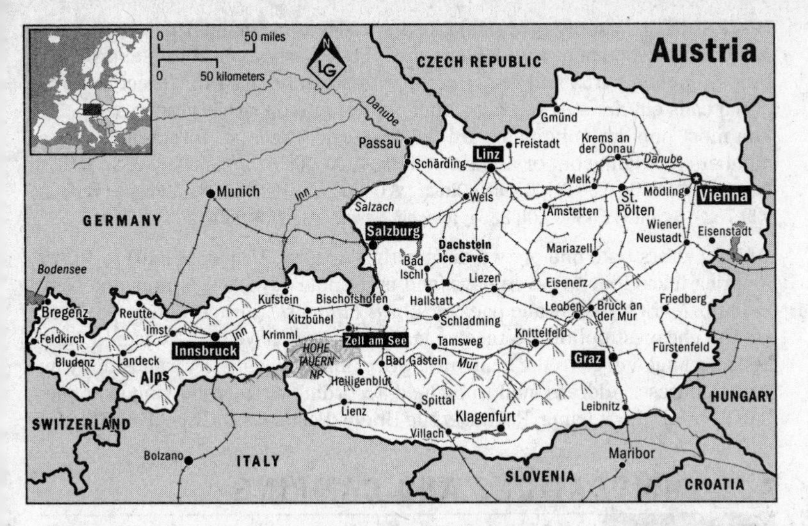

BY TRAIN. The **Österreichische Bundesbahn** (ÖBB; www.oebb.at), Austria's state railroad, operates an efficient system with fast and comfortable **trains.** Eurail and InterRail passes are valid in Austria, but they do not guarantee a seat without a reservation. The **Austria Rail** pass allows three to eight days of travel within any 15-day period on all rail lines. It also entitles holders to 40% off **bike rentals** at train stations (2nd-class US$148 for three days).

BY BUS. The Austrian **bus system** consists mainly of PostBuses, which cover areas inaccessible by train for comparably high prices. Buy tickets at the station or from the driver. For information, call ☎43 17 11 01 from abroad or ☎0810 222 333 within Austria from 7am-8pm.

BY CAR. Driving is a convenient way to see the more isolated parts of Austria, but gas is costly, an international license is required, and some small towns prohibit cars. The roads are well maintained and well marked, and Austrian drivers are quite careful. **Mitfahrzentralen** (ride-share services) in larger cities pair drivers with riders for a small fee. Riders then negotiate fares with the drivers. Be aware that not all organizations screen their participants; ask ahead.

BY BIKE. Bicycles are a great way to get around Austria, as roads in the country are generally smooth and safe. Many train stations rent **bikes** and allow you to return them to any participating station.

KEEPING IN TOUCH

PHONE CODES	**Country code:** 43. **International dialing prefix:** 00 (for Vienna, dial 00 431). For more info on how to place international calls, see **Inside Back Cover.**

EMAIL AND THE INTERNET. It's easy to find **Internet** cafes (€2-6 per hr.) in Austria, especially in larger cities. In small towns, however, cafes are less frequent and may charge more. Ask at a hostel or tourist office for suggestions.

TELEPHONES. Wherever possible, use a **calling card** for international phone calls, as long-distance rates for national phone services are often exorbitant. Prepaid phone cards and major credit cards can be used for direct international calls but are still less cost-efficient. For info on **mobile phones,** see p. 32. The most popular companies are A1, One, and T-mobile. Direct-dial access numbers for calling out of Austria include: **AT&T Direct** (☎0800 200 288); **British Telecom** (☎0800 890 043); **Canada Direct** (☎0800 200 217); **MCI WorldPhone** (☎0800 999 762); **Sprint** (☎0800 200 236); **Telecom New Zealand** (☎0800 200 222),

MAIL. Letters take one or two days within Austria. Airmail (€1.40) to North America takes four to seven days, and up to nine days to Australia and New Zealand. Mark all **letters** and packages "*mit Flugpost*" (airmail). Aerogrammes are the cheapest option. To receive mail in Austria, have mail delivered **Poste Restante.** Mail will go to the main post office unless you specify a subsidiary by street address. Address mail to be held according to the following example: LAST NAME, First name, Postlagernde Briefe, Postal code City, AUSTRIA.

ACCOMMODATIONS AND CAMPING

AUSTRIA	❶	❷	❸	❹	❺
ACCOMMODATIONS	under €16	€16-26	€27-34	€35-55	over €55

AUSTRIA

Always ask if your lodging provides a **guest card** *(Gästekarte)*, which grants discounts on activities, museums, and public transportation. The **Österreichischer Jugendherbergsverband-Hauptverband (ÖJH)** runs the over 80 **HI hostels** in Austria. Because of the rigorous standards of the national organization, these are usually very clean and orderly. Most charge €18-25 per night for dorms, with a €3-5 HI discount. **Independent hostels** vary in quality, but often have more personality and foster a lively backpacking culture. Slightly more expensive **Pensionen** are similar to American and British B&Bs. In small to mid-sized towns, singles will cost about €20-30, but expect to pay twice as much in big cities. **Hotels** are expensive (singles over €35; doubles over €48). Cheaper options have "Gasthof," "Gästehaus," or "Pension-Garni" in the name. Renting a **Privatzimmer** (room in a family home) is an inexpensive option. Contact the tourist office about rooms (€16-30). **Camping** in Austria is less about getting out into nature than having a cheap place to sleep; most sites are large plots glutted with RVs and are open in summer only. Prices run €10-15 per tent site and €5-8 per extra person. In the high Alps, hikers and mountaineers can retire to the well-maintained system of **Hütten** (mountain huts) where traditional Austrian fare and a good night's rest await them. Reserve ahead.

HIKING AND SKIING. Almost every town has hiking trails in its vicinity; consult the local tourist office. Trails are marked with either a red-white-red marker (only sturdy boots and hiking poles necessary) or a blue-white-blue marker (mountaineering equipment needed). Because of snow, most mountain hiking trails and mountain huts are open only from late June to early September. Western Austria is one of the world's best skiing regions; the area around Innsbruck is full of runs. High season is November to March.

FOOD AND DRINK

AUSTRIA	❶	❷	❸	❹	❺
FOOD AND DRINK	under €5	€5-10	€11-16	€17-25	over €25

Loaded with fat, salt, and cholesterol, traditional Austrian cuisine is bad for your skin, your heart, and your figure. *Wienerschnitzel* is a breaded meat cutlet (usually veal or pork) fried in butter. Natives nurse their sweet tooths with *Sacher Torte* (a rich chocolate cake layered with marmalade) and *Linzer Torte* (a light yellow cake with currant jam). Austrian beers are outstanding—try Stiegl, a Salzburg brew; Zipfer, from Upper Austria; and Styrian Gösser.

EAT YOUR VEGGIES. Vegetarians should look on the menu for Spätzle (noodles), Eierschwammerl (yellow mushrooms), or anything with "Vegi" in it.

HOLIDAYS AND FESTIVALS

Holidays: Just about everything closes on public holidays. New Year's Day (Jan. 1); Epiphany (Jan. 6); Easter (Apr. 13); Labor Day (May 1); Ascension (May 21); Corpus Christi (June 11); Assumption (Aug. 15); Austrian National Day (Oct. 26); All Saints' Day (Nov. 1); Immaculate Conception (Dec. 8); Christmas (Dec. 25); Boxing Day (Dec. 26).

Festivals: Vienna celebrates *Fasching* (Carnival) from New Year's until the start of Lent. Austria's most famous summer music festivals are the *Wiener Festwochen* (early May to mid-June; www.festwochen.at) and the *Salzburger Festspiele* (late July-late August; www.salzburgerfestspiele.at).

BEYOND TOURISM

Austria caters more to tourism than volunteerism; there are only limited opportunities to give back, so your best bet is to find them through a placement service. Short-term work abound at hotels, ski resorts, and farms. For more info on opportunities across Europe, see **Beyond Tourism**, p. 60.

Actilingua Academy, Glorietteg. 8, A-1130 Vienna (☎431 877 6701; www.actilingua.com). Study German in Vienna (from €419) for 2 to 4 weeks, with accommodation in dorms, apartments, or with a host family.

Bergwald Projekt/Mountain Forest Project, Hauptstr. 24, 7014 Trin (☎081 630 4145; www.bergwaldprojekt.ch). Organizes week-long conservation projects in the forests of Austria, Germany, and Switzerland.

Concordia, 19 North Street, Portslade, Brighton, BN41 1DH, UK (☎012 7342 2218; www.concordia-iye.org.uk). British volunteer organization that directs community projects in Austria, which have in the past included renovating historic buildings and parks and directing a youth drama project.

VIENNA (WIEN) ☎01

War, marriage, and Hapsburg maneuvering transformed Vienna (pop.1,700,000) from a Roman camp along the Danube into Europe's political linchpin. Beethoven and Mozart made Vienna an everlasting arbiter of high culture; the tradition continues today with the city's prestigious orchestras and world-class museums. Its dozens of coffeehouses radiate artistic and intellectual

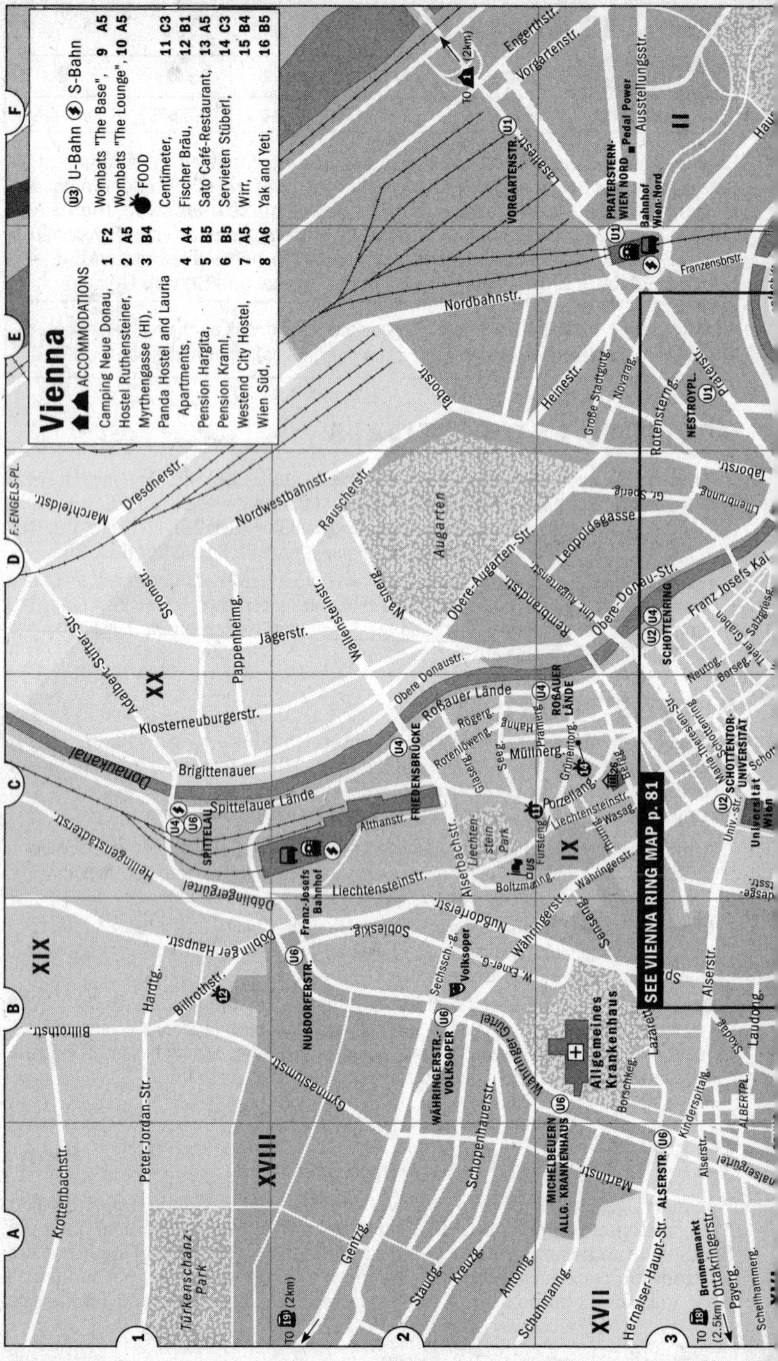

Vienna

ACCOMMODATIONS

Camping Neue Donau,	1	F2
Hostel Ruthensteiner,	2	A5
Myrthengasse (HI),	3	B4
Panda Hostel and Lauria Apartments,	4	A4
Pension Hargita,	5	B5
Pension Kraml,	6	B5
Westend City Hostel,	7	A5
Wien Süd,	8	A6
Wombats "The Base",	9	A5
Wombats "The Lounge",	10	A5

FOOD

Centimeter,	11	C3
Fischer Bräu,	12	B1
Sato Café-Restaurant,	13	A5
Servieten Stüberl,	14	C3
Wirr,	15	B4
Yak and Yeti,	16	B5

U3 U-Bahn S S-Bahn

SEE VIENNA RING MAP p. 81

COFFEEHOUSES		
Café Sperl,	17	C5
WINE TAVERNS		
10er Marie,	18	A3
Buschenschank Heinrich Nierscher,		A2
NIGHTLIFE		
Chelsea,	20	A4
Felixx,	21	C5
Mango,	22	C5
MUSEUMS		
Kunst Huas Wien,	23	E4
Österreichische Galerie: Oberes Belvedere,	24	D5
Österreichische Galerie: Unteres Belvedere,	25	E5
Freud Museum,	26	C3

energy—on any given afternoon, cafes turn the sidewalks into a sea of umbrellas while bars and clubs pulse with techno and indie rock until dawn.

INTERCITY TRANSPORTATION

Flights: The Wien-Schwechat Flughafen (**VIE;** ☎01 700 70; www.viennaairport.com), 18km from the city center, is home to Austrian Airlines (☎01 517 89; www.aua.com). The cheapest way to reach the city, the **S-Bahn** (☎65 17 17) stops at Wien Mitte (30min., 2-3 per hr., €3). The **Vienna Airport Lines bus** (☎930 00 23 00) takes 20min. to reach Südbahnhof and 40min. to Westbahnhof (2 per hr.; €6, round-trip €11). The **City Airport Train** (**CAT;** ☎01 25 250; www.cityairporttrain.com) takes only 16min. to reach Wien Mitte (2 per hr. 6:05am-11:35pm; purchased online €8, round-trip €15; from a ticket machine €9, round-trip €16; on board €10; Eurail not valid.)

Regional Hubs: The **M.R. Štefánik International Airport** (**BTS;** ☎48 57 11 11; www.letiskobratislava.sk) in Bratislava, Slovakia serves as a gateway to Western Europe. In addition to domestic flights from Slovakia, budget airlines **SkyEurope** (☎48 50 11 11; www.skyeurope.com) and **Ryanair** (www.ryanair.com; see Transportation, p. 48) run shuttle buses to and from Vienna (1-1½hr., 7-8 per day, 363Sk). Vienna-bound **trains** (☎20 29 11 11; www.zsr.sk) depart from **Bratislava Hlavná Stanica** hourly (1hr., round-trip 283Sk). **Buses** make a similar journey, leaving from **Mlynské nivy 31** (1hr., every hr., 400Sk). Another option is to sail to Vienna (1hr., 2 per day, 150Sk) with **Lodná osobná doprava,** Fajnorovo nábr. 2 (☎52 93 22 26; www.lod.sk; open daily 8:30am-5:30pm). For accommodations, food listings, and more info on Bratislava, see p. 871.

Trains: Vienna has 2 main train stations with international connections. Call ☎05 17 17 (24hr.) or check www.oebb.at for detailed train info. Credit cards accepted.

Westbahnhof, XV, Mariahilferstr. 132. Info counter open daily 7:30am-9pm. Trains go to: **Amsterdam, NTH** (12hr., 4 per day, €135); **Berlin, GER** (9-11hr., every 2hr., €100-130); **Budapest, HUN** (3hr., 17 per day, €36); **Hamburg, GER** (9-12hr., 6 per day, €80); **Innsbruck** (4-5hr., 7 per day, €54); **Munich, GER** (5hr., 10 per day, €72); **Paris, FRA** (14-24hr., 2 per day, €70-160); **Salzburg** (2-3hr., every hr., €43); **Zürich, SWI** (9hr., 3 per day, €88).

Südbahnhof, X, Wiener Gürtel 1a. Info counter open daily 7am-8pm. Trains go south and east to: **Graz** (2hr., every hr., €30); **Kraków, POL** (7hr., 4 per day, €46); **Prague, CZR** (4-5hr., 8 per day, €44); **Rome, ITA** (13-18hr., 6 per day, €75-100); **Venice, ITA** (7-11hr., 6 per day, €50-70).

Buses: Buses in Austria are rarely cheaper than trains; compare prices before buying a ticket. Postbus (☎0810 222 333; www.postbus.at) provides regional **bus** service and Eurolines (☎798 29 00; www.eurolines.at) connects to international destinations. Buses leave from the city stations at **Erdberg, Floridsdorf, Heiligenstadt, Hütteldorf, Kagran, Reumannpl.,** and **Wien Mitte/Landstr.**

ORIENTATION

Vienna is divided into 23 **Bezirke** (districts). District numbering begins in the city center, **Innenstadt.** Around the border of the city center, the **Ringstraße** (ring road) on three sides and the Danube Canal on the fourth, were originally the location of a wall that protected the city from invaders, most notably the Turks. At the center of the Innenstadt lies **Stephansplatz** and much of the pedestrian district. The best way to reach Innenstadt is to take the U-bahn to Stephanspl. (U1, U3) or **Karlsplatz** (U1, U2, U4); **Schwedenplatz** (U1, U4) is close to the city's nightlife. Tram lines #1 and 2 circle the Innenstadt on the Ringstr., with line 2 heading clockwise and 1 counterclockwise.

The **Ringstraße** consists of different segments, such as Opernring and Kärntner Ring. Many of Vienna's major attractions lie within District I and immediately around the Ringstr. Districts II-IX spread out from the city center following the clockwise traffic of the Ring. The remaining districts expand from yet another ring road, the **Gürtel** (Belt). Similar to the Ring, this major thoroughfare has numerous segments, including Margaretengürtel, Neubaugürtel, and Währinger Gürtel. Like Vienna's street signs, *Let's Go* indicates the district number in Roman or Arabic numerals before the street and number.

LOCAL TRANSPORTATION

Public Transportation: Wiener Linien (☎790 91 00; www.wienerlinien.at). The **U-Bahn** (subway), **Straßenbahn** (tram), **S-Bahn** (elevated tram), and **bus lines** operate on a 1-ticket system, so you can transfer between types of transportation without having to buy a new ticket. Purchase tickets at a counter, machine, on board, or at a tobacco shop *(trafik)*. A **single fare** (€1.70 in advance, €2.20 on board) lets you travel to any destination in the city and switch from bus to U-Bahn to tram to S-Bahn in any order, provided your travel is uninterrupted. Other ticket options include a **1-day pass** (€5.70), **3-day rover ticket** (€13.60), **7-day pass** (€14; valid M 9am to the next M 9am), and an **8-day pass** (€28; valid any 8 days, not necessarily consecutive; can be split between several people, but must be validated for each person). The **Vorteilscard** (Vienna Card; €18.50) allows for 72hr. of travel and discounts at museums and sights and can be purchased at the ticket office and hotels. To avoid a €60 fine from plainclothes inspectors, **validate your ticket** by punching it in the machine. Tickets need only be stamped once. Regular trams and subway cars do not run midnight-5am. **Night buses** run 2 per hr., 12:30-4:30am, along most routes; "N" signs designate night bus stops. A night bus schedule and **discount passes** are available from Wiener Linien information offices (open M-F 6:30am-6:30pm, Sa-Su 8:30am-4pm) in the Karlspl., Stephahnspl., Westbahnhof, and some other U-Bahn stations, and at the **tourist office** (p. 77).

Taxis: ☎313 00, ☎401 00, ☎601 60, or ☎814 00. Stands at Südbahnhof, Karlspl. in the city center, Westbahnhof, and by the Bermuda Dreieck. **Accredited taxis** have yellow-and-black signs on the roof. Base rate M-Sa €2.80, €0.20 per 0.2km; base rate Su 11pm-6am €3; holidays slightly more expensive. €2 surcharge for calling a taxi.

Car Rental: Hertz (☎700 73 26 61), at the airport. Open M-F 7am-11:30pm, Sa 8am-8pm, Su 7am-11:30pm. **Europcar** (☎700 73 26 99), at the airport. Open M-F 7:30am-11pm, Sa 8am-7pm, Su 7am-11pm.

Bike Rental: Pedal Power, II, Ausstellungsstr. 3 (☎01 729 72 34; www.pedalpower.at). €17 per 4hr., €27 per day, students €14/21. Delivery available. 2½hr. guided tours in English and German. €23, students €17. Open daily May-Sept. 8am-7pm; Mar.-Apr. and Oct. 8am-6pm. **Citybike** (www.citybikewien.at) has automated rental stations at 50 locations. Registration €1. €1 per 1st 2hr., then €4 per hr. thereafter. MC/V.

PRACTICAL INFORMATION

Main Tourist Office: I, Albertinapl. on the corner of Maysederg. (☎01 245 55; www.vienna.info). To find the office, follow Operng. up 1 block from the Opera House. Books rooms for a €2.90 fee. Open daily 9am-7pm.

Embassies and Consulates: Australia, IV, Mattiellistr. 2-4 (☎01 50 67 40). Open M-F 8:30am-4:30pm. **Canada,** I, Laurenzerberg 2 (☎01 531 38 30 00) M-F 8:30am-12:30pm and 1:30-3:30pm. **Ireland,** I, Rotenturmstr. 16-18, 5th fl. (☎01 715 42 46). Open M-F 9:30-11am and 1:30-4pm. **New Zealand,** III, Salesianerg. 15 (☎01 318 85 05). **UK,** III, Jaurèesg. 10 (☎01 716 13 53 33, after hours for UK nationals in emergencies only ☎0676 569 40 12). Open M-F 9:15am-12:30pm and 2-3:30pm. **US,** X, Boltzmanng. 16 (☎01 31 33 90). Open M-F 8-11:30am. 24hr. emergency services.

Luggage Storage: Lockers available at all train stations. €2-3.50 per 24hr.

GLBT Resources: Pick up the *Vienna Gay Guide* (www.gaynet.at/guide), *Coxx*, or *Xtra* from any tourist office or gay bar, cafe, or club. **Rosa Lila Tip,** VI, Linke Wienzeile 102 (lesbians ☎01 586 51 50, gay men ☎01 585 43 43; www.villa.at), is a knowledgeable resource and social center. English spoken. Take the U4 to Pilgramg. and look for the pink house on the left bank. Open M, W, F 5-8pm.

Emergency: ☎141.

24hr. Pharmacy: ☎15 50. Consulates have lists of English-speaking doctors.

Hospital: Allgemeines Krankenhaus, IX, Währinger Gürtel 18-20 (☎01 40 40 00).

Post Office: Hauptpostamt, I, Fleischmarkt 19 (☎01 0577 677 10 10). Open daily 6am-10pm. Branches throughout the city and at the train stations; look for yellow signs with trumpet logos. **Postal Codes:** A-1010 (1st district) through A-1230 (23rd district).

ACCOMMODATIONS AND CAMPING

Hostel Ruthensteiner, XV, Robert-Hamerlingg. 24 (☎01 893 42 02; www.hostelruthensteiner.com). Knowledgeable staff, spotless rooms, kitchen, and a secluded courtyard. Breakfast €2.50. Linens €2. Internet €2 per 40min. Key deposit €10. Reception 24hr. 32-bed summer dorm €16; 8-bed dorms €18; singles €32; doubles €50, with bath €54; quads €72/80. AmEx/MC/V; €0.40-0.80 per day surcharge. ❶

Wombats City Hostel, (☎01 897 23 36; www.wombats-hostels.com) offers 2 separate locations. **"The Lounge"** (XV, Mariahilferstr. 137). The bright walls and leather couches add a modern touch to the college dorm atmosphere. **"The Base"** (XV, Grang. 6). Farther from the train station and a quieter street, this wildly colorful hostel compensates with an in-house pub, guided tours, and nightly English-language movies. Internet €2 per hr. Dorms €21; doubles €50. MC/V. ❷

Westend City Hostel, VI, Fügerg. 3 (☎01 597 67 29; www.westendhostel.at), near Westbahnhof. A rose-filled courtyard and plain dorms provide a peaceful place to rest. Breakfast included. Free Wi-Fi. Reception 24hr. Lockout 10:30am-2pm. Open mid-Mar. to Nov. Dorms €20-23; singles €52-65; doubles €62-80. Cash only. ❷

Camping Neue Donau, XXII, Am Kleehäufel 119 (☎01 202 40 10; www.campingwien.at/nd). U1: Kaisermühlen. 4km from the city center and adjacent to Neue Donau beaches, though not directly on the water. Boat and bike rental available. Kitchen, showers, and supermarket. Laundry €4.50. Reception 8am-12:30pm and 3-6:15pm. Open Easter-Sept. €6-7 per person, €10-12 per tent. AmEx/MC/V. ❶

FOOD

Restaurants that call themselves *Stüberl* ("little sitting room") or advertise *Schmankerl* serve Viennese fare. Innenstadt restaurants are expensive. The neighborhood north of the university, where Universitätsstr. and Währingerstr. meet (U2: Schottentor), is more budget-friendly. Affordable restaurants line **Burggasse** in District VII and the area around Rechte and Linke Wienzeile near Naschmarkt (U4: Kettenbrückeng). The **Naschmarkt** itself hosts Vienna's biggest market of fresh (if pricey) produce. Its many eateries provide cheap, quick meals. (Open M-F 6am-6:30pm, Sa 6am-2pm.) The **Brunnenmarkt** (XVI, U6: Josefstädterstr.) has Turkish flair. A **kosher** supermarket is at II, Hollandstr. 10. (☎01 216 96 75. Open M-Th 8:30am-6:30pm, F 8am-2pm.)

Trzesniewski, I, Dorotheerg. 1 (☎01 512 32 91), from Stephansdom, 3 blocks down on the left side of the Graben. Once Kafka's favorite, this stand-up establishment has been serving delicious open-faced mini-sandwiches (€0.90) for over 100 years. Toppings are mainly egg- and cucumber-based, but can also include favorites such as salmon, onion, paprika, and herring. Open M-F 8:30am-7:30pm, Sa 9am-5pm. Cash only. ❶

Smutny, I, Elisabethstr. 8 (☎01 587 13 56; www.smutny.com), U6: Karlspl. A traditional Viennese restaurant serving *Wiener schnitzel* (€16.90) and *Fiakergulash* (goulash with beef, egg, potato, and sausage; €13.80). Open daily 10am-midnight. AmEx/MC/V. ❷

Centimeter, IX, Liechtensteinstr. 42 (☎01 470 060 643; www.centimeter.at). Tram D to Bauernfeldpl. This chain has huge portions of greasy, filling Austrian fare (€5.50-7) and hot or cold open-faced sandwiches for €0.10-0.15 per cm. Open M-Th 10am-midnight, F-Sa 11am-1am, Su 11am-midnight. MC/V. ❶

Yak and Yeti, VI, Hofmühlg. 21 (☎01 595 54 52; www.yakundyeti.at). U3: Zieglerg. This Himalayan restaurant serves tasty and filling *momos* (Nepalese dumplings; €8-10.50) and other ethnic specialties. Lunch buffet €6.50. Entrees €7-13. Special sampler platters €12-13. Open May-Sept. M-Sa 11:30am-10:30pm; Oct.-Apr. M-F 11:30am-2:30pm and 6-10:30pm, Sa 11:30am-10:30pm. Cash only. ❸

COFFEEHOUSES

For years these venerable establishments have been havens for artists, writers, and thinkers: Vienna's cafes watched Franz Kafka brood about solitude, Theodor Herzl plan a Zionist Israel, and Freud ponder the human mind. The most important dictate of coffeehouse etiquette is that you linger; the waiter *(Herr Ober)* will serve you when you sit down, then will leave you to sip your *Mélange* (coffee and steamed milk), read, and contemplate life's great questions. When you're ready to leave, ask to pay *("Zahlen bitte")*.

Kleines Café, I, Franziskanerpl. 3. Escape from the busy pedestrian streets with a *Mélange* (€3) and conversation on a leather couch in the relaxed interior, or by the fountain in the square. Sandwiches €3-5. Croissants, apple *(apfel)* strudel, and curd strudel €0.90. Eggs €7. Open daily 10am-2am. Cash only.

Café Central, I, Herreng. 14 (☎01 533 37 63; www.palaisevents.at), at the corner of Strauchg. With green-gold arches and live music, this luxurious coffeehouse well deserves its status as mecca of the cafe world.

COFFEE CULTURE

Vienna is the world's coffee capital, but for those used to *mocha lattes* or half-caff lite soys, understanding the jumble of German words on the *Kaffeehaus* menu can be daunting. Here's a cheat-sheet for deciphering the menu:

A **Mokka** or a **Schwarzer** is strong, pure black espresso and nothing more. The **Kleiner Brauner** ("small brown") lightens the espresso with milk or cream, while the **Verlängerter** lowers the stakes yet again with weaker coffee. The quintessential Viennese cafe drink, a **Mélange** melds black espresso with steamed milk, sometimes capping it with a dollop of whipped cream. The **Kapuziner** ("the monk") also consists of espresso with gently foamed milk but is more commonly known by its Italian name, "cappuccino." The **Einspanner** is a strong black coffee heaped with whipped cream and sometimes a dash of chocolate shavings. **Eiskaffee,** or hot coffee with vanilla ice cream, is refreshing on hot summer days.

Vienna's specialty coffee drinks combine espresso with a variety of liqueurs for caffeine with a punch. Some cafes serve the **Maria-Theresia,** with orange liqueur, or the **Pharisär,** with rum and sugar. Other liqueurs include **Marillen** (apricot) and **Kirsche** (cherry). Or, for a protein boost, try the milk-less mocha **Kaisermelange,** stirred with brandy and an egg yolk. Be prepared to shell out €6-7 for an indulgent delight.

House specialty: tempting coffee with apricot liqueur (€5.90). Open M-Th and Sa 7:30am-10pm, F and Su 10am-10pm. AmEx/MC/V.

Café Hawelka, I, Dorotheerg. 6 (☎01 512 82 30). A Viennese institution since 1939, this cafe has a long history as an artist's meeting place. The waiters move quickly between the tables and sofas, carrying plates of *Buchteln* (cake with plum marmalade; €3) and *mélange* (€3.20). Locals don't need menus to order, so come with an idea of what you want in mind. Open M and W-Sa 8am-2am, Su 10am-2am. Cash only.

WINE TAVERNS (HEURIGEN)

Marked by a hanging branch, *Heurigen* serve *Heuriger* (wine) and Austrian delicacies, often in a relaxed outdoors setting. The wine is from the most recent harvest; good *Heuriger* is white, fruity, and full-bodied. Open in summer, *Heurigen* cluster in the Viennese suburbs where the grapes grow. Tourist buses head to the most famous region, **Grinzing,** in District XIX; you'll find better atmosphere in the hills of **Sievering, Neustift am Walde** (both in District XIX), and **Neuwaldegg** (in XVII). True Heuriger devotees make the trip to **Gumpoldskirchen.**

Buschenschank Heinrich Nierscher, XIX, Strehlg. 21 (☎01 440 21 46). U6: Währingerstr. Enjoy a glass of *Heuriger* (€2.20) in the oversized country kitchen or the backyard overlooking the vineyards. Select a tray of meat, cheese, and bread for a light supper (€3-5). Open M and Th-Su 3pm-midnight. Cash only.

10er Marie, XVI, Ottakringerstr. 222-224 (☎01 489 46 47). U3: Ottakring, turn left on Thaliastr., then right onto Johannes-Krawarik. Locals frequent the large garden behind the yellow house. 0.25L of wine €2. Open M-Sa 3pm-midnight. MC/V.

SIGHTS

A stroll in District I, the social and geographical center, is a feast for the senses. Cafe tables spill into the streets and musicians attract onlookers as Romanesque arches, Jugendstil apartments, and the modern Haas Haus look on. Some of Vienna's most famous modern architecture is outside the Ring, where 20th-century designers found space to build. This area is also home to a number of Baroque palaces and parks that were once beyond the city limits.

STEPHANSDOM AND GRABEN. In the heart of the city, the massive **Stephansdom** is one of Vienna's most treasured landmarks. For a view of the old city, take the elevator up the North Tower or climb the 343 steps of the South Tower. *(☎01 515 52 35 26. North Tower open daily Apr.-June and Sept.-Oct. 8:30am-5:30pm; Nov.-Mar. 8:30am-5pm; July-Aug. 9am-5pm. South Tower open daily 9am-5:30pm. North Tower €4. South Tower €3.50.)* Downstairs, skeletons of plague victims fill the **catacombs.** The **Gruft** (vault) stores urns containing the Hapsburgs' innards. *(Tours in German M-Sa 2 per hr. 10-11:30am and 1:30-4:30pm, Su and holidays 1:30-4:30pm. €4.50. MC/V.)*

HOFBURG PALACE. Previously a medieval castle, this imperial palace was the Hapsburgs' home until 1918. Wing by wing, it was expanded over 800 years. Now containing the President's office and a few small museums, its grandest assets are in the **royal treasury.** *(☎01 533 75 70; www.hofburg-wien.at. U3: Herreng. Open daily Sept.-June 9am-5:30pm, July-Aug. 9am-8pm. €10, students €7.50.)*

HOHER MARKT AND STADTTEMPEL. Once both a market and an execution site, **Hoher Markt** was home to the Roman encampment, **Vindobona.** Roman ruins lie beneath the shopping arcade across from the fountain. *(Open Tu-Su 9am-1pm and 2-5pm. €4, students €3. MC/V.)* The biggest draw is the 1914 Jugendstil **Ankeruhr** (clock), whose figures—from Marcus Aurelius to Maria Theresa—rotate past

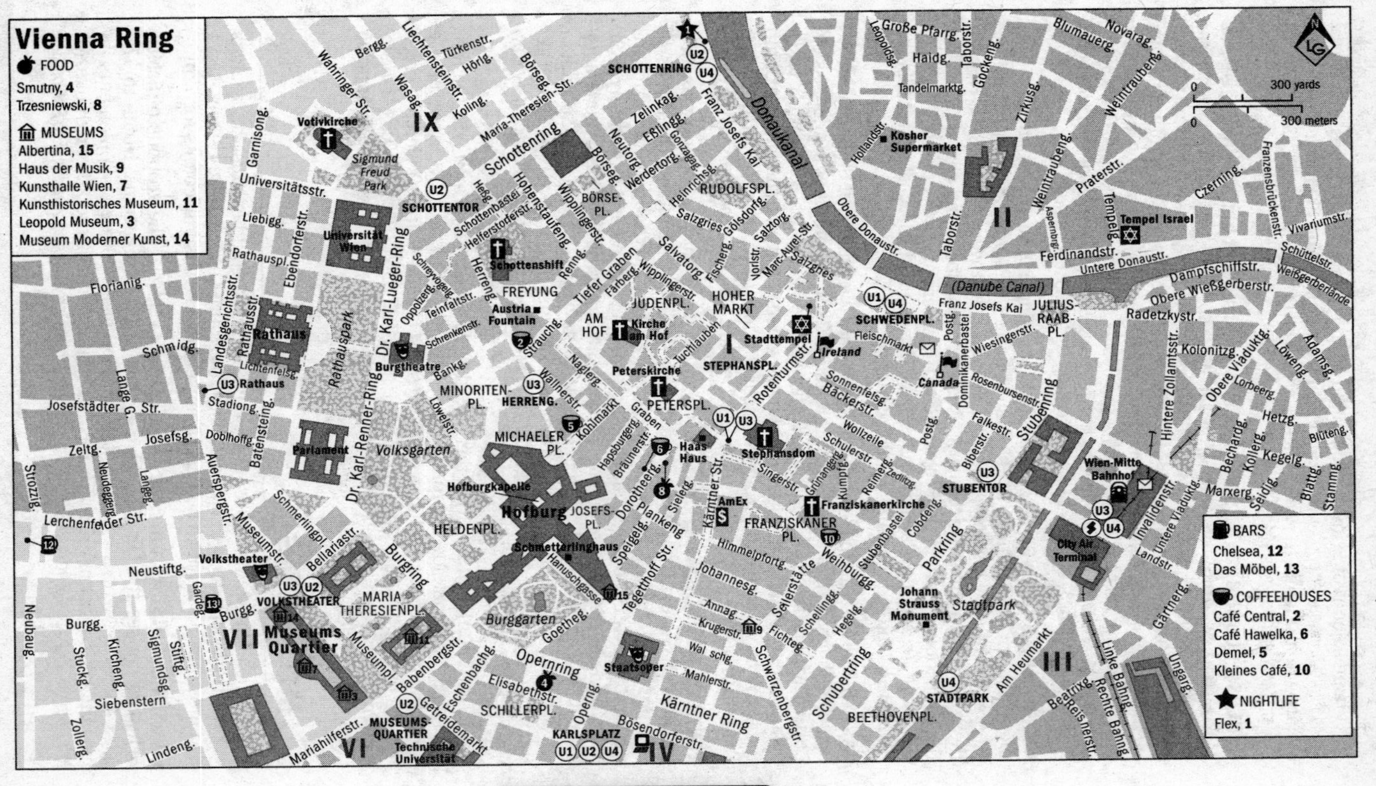
Vienna Ring
FOOD
Smutny, 4
Trzesniewski, 8
MUSEUMS
Albertina, 15
Haus der Musik, 9
Kunsthalle Wien, 7
Kunsthistorisches Museum, 11
Leopold Museum, 3
Museum Moderner Kunst, 14
BARS
Chelsea, 12
Das Möbel, 13
COFFEEHOUSES
Café Central, 2
Café Hawelka, 6
Demel, 5
Kleines Café, 10
NIGHTLIFE
Flex, 1
300 yards
300 meters
Donaukanal
(Danube Canal)
Stephansdom
Hofburg
Rathaus
Parlament
Volksgarten
Stadtpark
Burggarten
Staatsoper
Museums Quartier
Rathauspark
Schottenring
Dr. Karl-Lueger-Ring
Dr. Karl-Renner-Ring
Burgring
Opernring
Kärntner Ring
Schubertring
Stubenring

the Viennese coat of arms accompanied by the tunes of their times. (*1 figure per hr. All figures appear at noon.*) Hidden on Ruprechtspl. is the **Stadttempel,** the only synagogue in Vienna to escape destruction during Kristallnacht. (*Seitenstetteng. 4. Mandatory guided tours M and Th at 11:30am and 2pm. €2, students €1.*)

SCHLOSS SCHÖNBRUNN. Schönbrunn began as a humble hunting lodge, but Maria Theresa's ambition transformed it into a splendid palace. The **Imperial Tour** passes through the dazzling **Hall of Mirrors,** where six-year-old Mozart played. The longer **Grand Tour** also visits Maria Theresa's exquisite 18th-century rooms, including the ornate **Millions Room.** (*Schönbrunnerstr. 47. U4: Schönbrunn. ☎01 811 132 39; www.schoenbrunn.at. Open daily: July-Aug. 8:30am-6pm; Apr.-June and Sept.-Oct. 8:30am-5pm; Nov.-Mar. 8:30am-4:30pm. Imperial Tour 22 rooms; 35min.; €9.50, students €8.50. Grand Tour 40 rooms; 50min.; €12.90/11.40. English-language audio tour included.*)

AM HOF AND FREYUNG. Once a medieval jousting square, Am Hof now houses the **Kirche am Hof** (Church of the Nine Choirs of Angels) and **Collalto Palace,** where Mozart gave his first public performance. Just west of Am Hof is **Freyung,** the square with the **Austriabrunnen** (Austria Fountain) in the center. Medieval fugitives took asylum in the **Schottenstift** (Monastery of the Scots), giving rise to the name *Freyung* or "sanctuary." Today, the annual **Christkindl market** fills the plaza with baked goods and holiday cheer (Dec. 1-24).

KARLSKIRCHE. Situated in Karlspl., **Karlskirche** (the Church of St. Borromeo) is an eclectic masterpiece. Under restoration in 2007, it combines a Neoclassical portico with a Baroque dome and Trajan-inspired columns. An elevator takes visitors up to a platform with a dazzling new perspective on the church. Climb the stairs to view the city from the highest point. (*IV, Kreuzherreng. 1. U1, 2, or 4 to Karlspl. ☎01 504 61 87. Open M-Sa 9am-12:30pm and 1-7pm, Su 1-7pm. €6, students €4.*)

AUSTRIA

ZENTRALFRIEDHOF. The Viennese describe the Central Cemetery as half the size of Geneva but twice as lively. **Tor II** (Gate 2) contains the tombs of Beethoven, Brahms, Schubert, Strauss, and an honorary monument to Mozart, whose true resting place is an unmarked pauper's grave in the **Cemetery of St. Marx,** III, Leberstr. 6-8. **Tor I** (Gate 1) holds the old **Jewish Cemetery,** where many headstones are cracked and neglected. To navigate through the 2.5 million graves, pick up a **map** at the information desk just inside Tor II. (*XI, Simmeringer Hauptstr. 234. Tram #71 from Schwarzenbergpl. or Simmering. ☎01 76 04 10. Open daily May-Aug. 7am-7pm; Mar.-Apr. and Sept.-Oct. 7am-6pm; Nov.-Feb. 8am-5pm. Free.*)

PARKS AND GARDENS. Along the ring, the **Stadtpark** (City Park) was the first municipal park outside the former city walls. (*U4: Stadtpark.*) Clockwise up the Ring, the gorgeous greenhouses of **Burggarten** (Palace Garden) were reserved for the imperial family until only 1918. (*☎01 533 85 70. Open Apr.-Oct. M-F 10am-4:45pm, Sa-Su 10am-6:15pm; Nov.-Mar. M-Sa 10am-3:45pm.*) The romantic **Volksgarten** (People's Garden) is best viewed at sunset.

MUSEUMS

With a museum around almost every corner, Vienna could exhaust any zealous visitor. The **Vienna Card** (€19), available at the tourist office, large U-bahn stops, and most hostels, entitles holders to museum and transit discounts for 72hr.

ÖSTERREICHISCHE GALERIE (AUSTRIAN GALLERY). The grounds of **Schloß Belvedere** houses the Österreichische Galerie's two museums. Home to *The Kiss* and other works by Klimt, the **Oberes (Upper) Belvedere** supplements its magnificent collection of 19th- and 20th-century art with rotating exhibits. (*III, Prinz-Eugen-Str. 27. Walk from the Südbahnhof or take tram D from Schwarzenbergpl. to Schloß Bel-*

vedere, or take U1 to Suditorolerplatz. €9.50, students €6. MC/V.) The **Unteres (Lower) Belvedere** contains the Austrian Museum of Baroque Art and the Austrian Museum of Medieval Art. *(Unteres Belvedere, III, Rennweg 6. Tram #71 from Schwarzenbergpl. to Unteres Belvedere. €9.50, students €6. Both Belvederes ☎01 79 55 70; www.belvedere.at. Open M-Tu and Th-Su 10am-6pm, W 10am-9pm. Combo ticket €12.50, students €8.50.)*

KUNST HAUS WIEN. Artist-environmentalist Friedenreich Hundertwasser built this museum without straight lines—even the floor bends. Arboreal "tree tenants" grow from the windowsills and the top floor. *(III, Untere Weißgerberstr. 13. U1 or 4 to Schwedenpl., then tram N to Radetzkypl. ☎01 712 04 91; www.kunsthauswien.at. Open daily 10am-7pm. Each exhibit €9, both €12; students €7/9. MC/V.)*

ÖSTERREICHISCHES MUSEUM FÜR ANGEWANDTE KUNST (MAK). This intimate, eclectic museum is dedicated to design, examining Thonet bentwood chairs' smooth curves, Venetian glass' intricacies, and modern architecture's steel heights. *(I, Stubenring 5. U3: Stubentor. ☎01 71 13 60; www.mak.at. Open Tu 10am-midnight, W-Su 10am-6pm. €7.90, students €5.50. Sa and holidays free. MC/V.)*

HAUS DER MUSIK. At the **Haus der Musik,** science meets music. Relax in the prenatal listening room, experience the physics of sound, and have a go at conducting an orchestra. *(I, Seilerstätte 30, near the opera house. ☎01 51 64 80; www.hdm.at. Open daily 10am-10pm. €10, students €8.50. Half-price Tu after 5pm. MC/V.)*

KUNSTHISTORISCHES MUSEUM (MUSEUM OF FINE ARTS). One of the world's largest art collections features Italian paintings, Classical art, and an Egyptian burial chamber. The main building contains works by the Venetian and Flemish masters and across the street, in the Neue Burg wing of the Hofburg Palace, the **Ephesos Museum** exhibits findings from excavations in Turkey. The **Sammlung alter Musikinstrumente** includes Beethoven's harpsichord and Mozart's piano. *(U2: Museumsquartier. Across from the Burgring and Heldenpl., to the right of Maria Theresienpl. ☎01 525 24 41; www.khm.at. Main building open Tu-Th 10am-9pm, F-Su 10am-6pm; Ephesos and Sammlung open M and W-Su 10am-6pm. €10, students €7.50. Audio tour €3. AmEx/MC/V.)*

AUSTRIA

ALBERTINA MUSEUM. Treat your eyes to the beautiful paintings at the Albertina Museum. First an Augustinian monastery and then part of Hofburg Palace, it now houses the Collection of Graphic Arts. The *Prunkräume* (state rooms) richly display some of Albrecht Dürer's finest prints, including the famous praying hands. *(I, Albertinapl. 1. ☎01 534 835 40; www.albertina.at. Open M-Tu and Th-Su 10am-6pm, W 10am-9pm. €9, students €7. MC/V.)*

MUSEUMSQUARTIER. Central Europe's largest collection of modern art, the **Museum Moderner Kunst (MUMOK),** highlights Classical Modernism, Fluxus, Photo Realism, Pop Art, and Viennese Actionism in a building made from basalt lava. *(Open M-W and F-Su 10am-6pm, Th 10am-9pm. €9, students €6.50. AmEx/MC/V.)* The **Leopold Museum** has the world's largest Schiele collection, plus works by Egger-Lienz, Gerstl, and Klimt. *(Open M-W and F-Su 10am-7pm, Th 10am-9pm. €10, students €6.50. AmEx/MC/V.)* Themed exhibits of contemporary artists fill **Kunsthalle Wien.** *(U2: Museumsquartier. ☎01 52 57 00; www.mqw.at. Open M-W, F-Su 10am-7pm, Th 10am-10pm. Exhibition Hall 1 €7.50; students M €5, Tu-Su €6. Exhibition Hall 2 €6/3.50/4.50. Both €11/7/9.)*

ENTERTAINMENT

Many of classical music's greats lived, composed, and performed in Vienna. Beethoven, Haydn, and Mozart wrote their best-known masterpieces here; a century later, Berg, Schönberg, and Webern refreshed the music scene. Today, Vienna hosts many budget performances, though prices rise in the summer. The **Bundestheaterkasse,** I, Hanuschg. 3, sells tickets for the Staatsoper, the

Volksoper, and the Burgtheater. (☎01 514 44 78 80. Open June to mid-Aug. M-F 10am-2pm; mid-Aug. to June M-F 8am-6pm, Sa-Su 9am-noon.)

Staatsoper, I, Opernring 2 (☎01 514 44 22 50; www.wiener-staatsoper.at). Vienna's premier opera performs nearly every night Sept.-June. No shorts. Seats €3.50-254. 500 standing-room tickets go on sale 80min. before every show (every person; €2-3.50); arrive 2hr. before curtain. Box office in the foyer open M-F 9am until 1hr. before curtain, Sa 9am-noon; 1st Sa of each month and during Advent 9am-5pm. MC/V.

Wiener Philharmoniker Orchestra (Vienna Philharmonic Orchestra; ☎01 505 65 25; www.wienerphilharmoniker.at) plays in the Musikverein, Austria's premier concert hall. To purchase tickets, visit the box office, Bösendorferstr. 12, well in advance of performances. Tickets also available at Lothinringerstrasse 20. MC/V.

NIGHTLIFE

With one of the highest bar-to-cobblestone ratios in the world, Vienna is a great place to party. Take U1 or 4 to Schwedenpl., which will drop you within blocks of the **Bermuda Dreieck** (Bermuda Triangle), a hot clubbing area. If you make it out, head down **Rotenturmstraße** toward Stephansdom or walk around the areas bounded by the synagogue and Ruprechtskirche. Slightly outside the Ring, the streets off **Burggasse** and **Stiftgasse** in District VII and the **university quarter** in Districts XIII and IX have outdoor courtyards and hip bars. Viennese nightlife often starts after 11pm. For listings, pick up the indispensable *Falter* (€2.60).

Das Möbel, VII, Burgg. 10. U2 or 3: Volkstheater. (☎01 524 94 97; www.das-moebel.at). An artsy crowd chats amid metal couches and Swiss-army tables, all created by designers and available for sale. Don't leave without seeing the bathroom. Internet free for 1st 15min., €0.90 per 15min. thereafter. Open daily 10am-1am. Cash only.

Chelsea, VIII, Lerchenfeldergürtel 29-31. U6: Thaliastr. or Josefstädterstr. (☎01 407 93 09; www.chelsea.co.at), under the U-Bahn, between the two stops. Austrian and international bands rock this underground club twice a week, while weekend DJs spin techno-pop. Concerts start at 10pm. 0.5L beer €2.70. Cover €6-12 for performances, entrance to bar free. Happy hour 4-5pm. Open M-Sa 6pm-4am, Su 4pm-3am. Cash only.

Flex, I, Donaulände (☎01 533 75 89; www.flex.at), near the Schottenring U-Bahn station (U2 or U4) down by the Danube. Dance, grab a beer or bring your own, and sit by the river with everyone else. DJs start spinning techno, reggae, house, ska, or electronic at 11pm. Beer €4. Cover €2-10, free after 3:30am. Open daily 8pm-4am. Cash only.

FESTIVALS

Vienna hosts several important (mostly musical) festivals. The **Wiener Festwochen** (May 8-June 14, 2009) has a diverse program of concerts, exhibitions, and plays. (☎01 58 92 20; www.festwochen.or.at.) In May, over 4000 people attend **Lifeball,** Europe's largest AIDS charity event and Vienna's biggest gay celebration. With the Lifeball Style Police threatening to dispose of under-dressed guests (make-up and hair-styling are musts), come looking like you deserve to mix and mingle with Bill Clinton, Elton John, and other celebrities. (☎01 595 56 77; www.lifeball.org. €75-150). Democrats host the late-June **Danube Island Festival,** which celebrates with fireworks and concerts (☎01 535 35 35; www.donauinselfest.at; free). The *Staatsoper* and *Volkstheater* host the **Jazzfest Wien** (☎01 503 56 47; www.viennajazz.org) during the first weeks of July. Also in July, the annual **Film Festival** (www.wien-event.at), in Rathauspl., features nightly exhibitions of music films. From mid-July to mid-August, the **ImPulsTanz**

Festival (☎01 523 55 58; www.impulstanz.com) attracts some of the world's greatest dance troupes and offers seminars to enthusiasts. The city-wide film festival, **Viennale** (www.viennale.at), kicks off in mid-October.

LINZ ☎0732

Besides offering picturesque architecture, shopping, and views of the Danube, this home of Kepler, Hitler, and the world renowned Linzer torte, is currently preparing to be Europe's Cultural Capital for the year 2009 (www.linz09.at).

TRANSPORTATION AND PRACTICAL INFORMATION. **Trains** leave from the **Linz Main Station,** Bahnhofplatz 8 (☎0732 93000 3170), to Vienna (2hr., 2 per hr., €29), Salzburg (1½hr., 2 per hr., €21), and Munich (3½hr., 2 per hr., €56). An **Intercity Tram** is also available. Pay for a 24hr. pass (€3.40). The fine for not stamping your pass is €50. The **tourist office** is located at 1 Hauptplatz. (☎0732 7070 1777; www.linz.at/tourismus). English-speaking. Pick up **maps** and an incredibly helpful brochure with a self-tour of the city.

ACCOMMODATIONS AND FOOD. **Youth Hotel Linz ❷,** Wankmuellerhofstrasse 39, has free breakfast and city maps. (☎0732 34 23 61. Double rooms €36. Laundry €5, detergent €1. Internet €15 per 3hr.) **Kaffee Glockenspiel ❶,** Hauptplatz 18, is a stylish blue and white restaurant that serves Linz's own original Linzer torte (€2.90). (☎0732 795 339; www.kaffee-glockenspiel.at. Coffee €2.20-5.60 Open daily 8:30am-midnight.) **El Greco ❸,** 16 Hauptplatz, located outside in the main square, specializes in tasty Greek food. (☎0732 79 15 98. Entrees €8-14, vegetarian dishes €7-9, salads €3-7, fish €13-25. Open M-Th and Sa 11am-11pm, F and Su 11am-10pm. MC/V.) **Biobistro/Reformhaus,** Hauptplatz 2, is a grocery store that is perfect for eco-friendly, organic, or vegetarian cravings. (Open 8:30am-6:30pm M-Sa. MC/V.)

SIGHTS. You can't miss the 20m tall **Trinity Column,** Hauptplatz, in the center of the main square, built to protect the city from war, fire, and plague. **Mariedom,** at the corner of Stiftersrasse and Herrenstrasse, is Austria's largest church, with the capacity to hold 20,000 people. (☎0732 7778 850. Open M-Sa 7:30am-7:15pm, Su 8am-7:15pm. Free.) **Kepler's House,** Rathaugasse 5, is located right off Hauptplatz. Although it is currently closed for renovation, visitors can look at the exterior of the house where Johannes Kepler lived from 1612 to 1626 and formulated his famous **Laws of Planetary Motion** (☎0732 7070 177). The **Mauthausen-Gusen Concentration Camp,** Erinnerungsstrasse 1, in Mauthausen, lies 20km east of Linz. To get there, take the train from Linz to St. Valentin, and then switch trains to Mauthausen. In 1945, the camp contained about 85,000 inmates. After the war, the complex fell within the Soviet sector during the Austrian occupation. Today, visitors can pay tribute at the camp's memorial and museum. (☎072 382 2690. €3. Open 9am-5:30pm.)

SALZBURGER LAND AND HOHE TAUERN REGION

Salzburger Land's precious white gold, *Salz* (salt), first drew settlers more than 3000 years ago. Modern travelers instead prefer to seek the shining lakes and rolling hills of the Salzkammergut, making Salzburg an enticing destination.

SALZBURG

☎0662

As its Baroque architecture attests, Salzburg was Austria's ecclesiastical center in the 17th and 18th centuries. This golden age fostered a rich musical culture that lives on today in elaborate concert halls and impromptu folk performances. The city's love for its native genius, Mozart, climaxes in summer during the Salzburg Festival, when fans the world over come to pay their respects.

TRANSPORTATION

Trains leave from **Hauptbahnhof,** in Südtirolerpl. (☎05 17 17) for: Graz (4hr., every hr. 8am-6:30pm, €40); Innsbruck (2hr., 1 every day, €34); Munich, GER (2-3hr., 30 per day, €27); Vienna (3hr., 26 per day, €44); Zürich, SWI (6hr., 7 per day, €73). **Buses** depart from the depot in front of the train station. Single tickets (€1.80) available at automatic machines or from the drivers. Books of 5 tickets (€8), day passes (€4.20), and week passes (€11) are available at machines. Punch your ticket when you board or risk a €36 fine.

ORIENTATION AND PRACTICAL INFORMATION

Three hills and the **Salzach River** delineate Salzburg, located just a few kilometers from the German border. The **Neustadt** is north of the river, and the beautiful **Altstadt** squeezes between the southern bank and the **Mönchsberg** hill. The Hauptbahnhof is on the northern side of town beyond the Neustadt; bus #1 connects it to **Hanuschplatz,** the *Altstadt's* main public transportation hub, by the river near Griesg. and the Staatsbrücke. Buses #3, 5, and 6 run from the Hauptbahnof to Rathaus and Mozartsteg, also in the *Altstadt.* Neustadt hubs include **Mirabellplatz, Makartplatz,** and **Mozartsteg,** the pedestrian bridge leading across the Salzach to Mozartpl. To reach the *Altstadt* on foot, turn left from the station onto Rainerstr. and follow it straight under the tunnel and on to Mirabellpl.; continue to Makartplatz and turn right to cross the **Makartsteg** bridge.

Tourist Office: Mozartpl. 5 (☎0662 88 98 73 30), in the *Altstadt.* Books rooms (€2.20 fee and 10% deposit) and gives tours of the city (daily 12:15pm, €8). It also sells the **Salzburg Card,** which grants admission to all museums and sights and unlimited public transportation. 1-day pass €23, 2-day €31, 3-day €36. Open daily 9am-6pm.

Currency Exchange: Banks offer the best rates for cash but often charge higher commissions. Banking hours M-F 8am-12:30pm and 2-4:30pm.

Luggage Storage: 24hr. lockers at the train station €2-3.50.

GLBT Resources: Homosexual Initiative of Salzburg (HOSI), Müllner Hauptstr. 11 (☎0662 43 59 27; www.hosi.or.at), hosts workshops and offers a free guide to Salzburg. Open sporadically. The HOSI-run bar next door is open regularly W 7pm-midnight, F-Sa 8pm-midnight. Phone staffed F 7-9pm.

Post Office: At the train station (☎0662 88 30 30). Open M-F 7am-6pm, Sa 8am-2pm, Su 1-6pm. **Postal Code:** A-5020.

ACCOMMODATIONS

Within the city itself, budget hotels and hostels are few and far between. Instead, try looking for accommodations outside Salzburg that are still accessible by public transportation. For the best deal, check out *Privatzimmer* (rooms in a family home), usually located on the city's outskirts, with welcoming hosts and bargain prices. Reservations are recommended, especially in summer. For a complete list of *Privatzimmer* and booking help, see the tourist office.

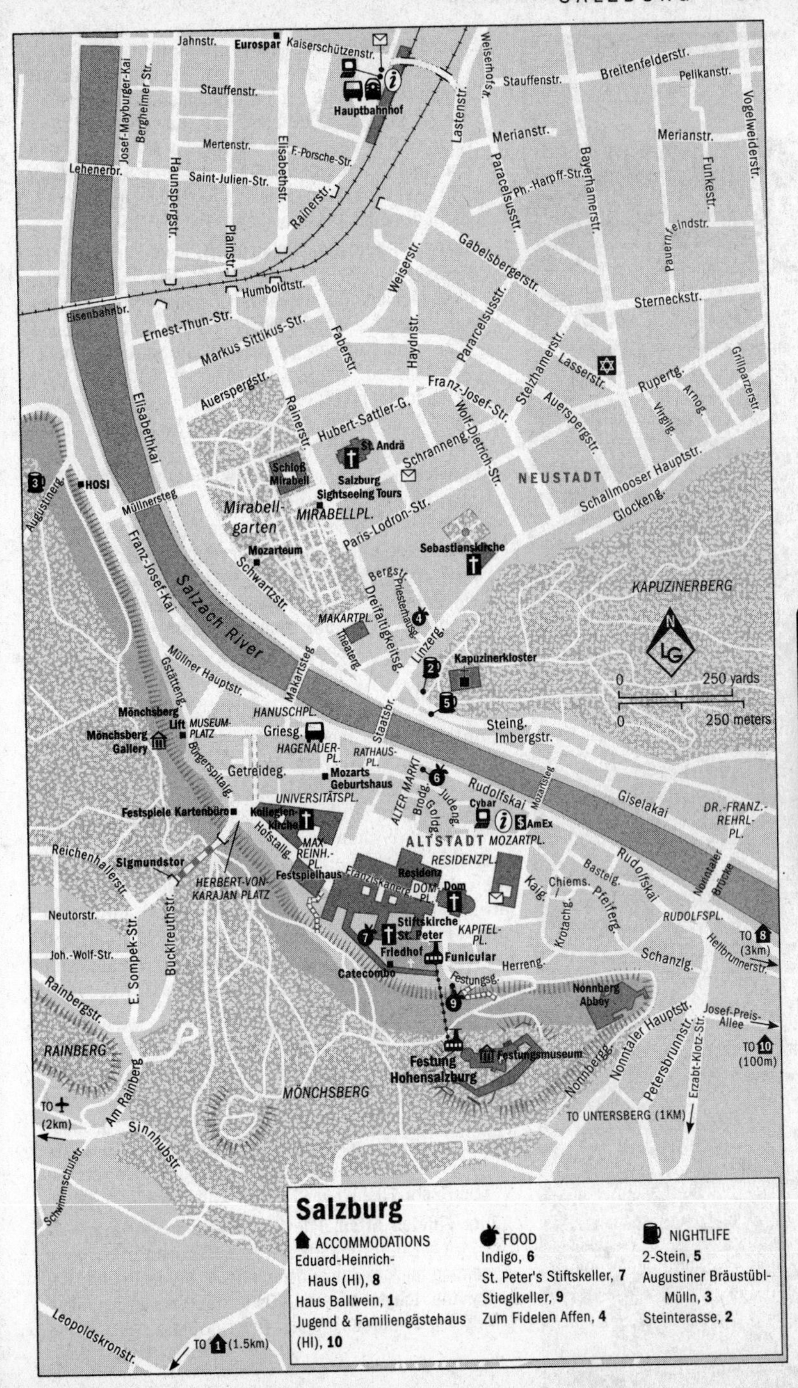
Salzburg
ACCOMMODATIONS
Eduard-Heinrich-Haus (HI), 8
Haus Ballwein, 1
Jugend & Familiengästehaus (HI), 10
FOOD
Indigo, 6
St. Peter's Stiftskeller, 7
Stieglkeller, 9
Zum Fidelen Affen, 4
NIGHTLIFE
2-Stein, 5
Augustiner Bräustübl-Mülln, 3
Steinterasse, 2
Hauptbahnhof
Eurospar
Jahnstr.
Kaiserschützenstr.
Stauffenstr.
Breitenfelderstr.
Pelikanstr.
Vogelweiderstr.
Josef-Mayburger-Kai
Bergheimer Str.
Mertenstr.
F.-Porsche-Str.
Elisabethstr.
Lastenstr.
Weiserhofstr.
Merianstr.
Paracelsusstr.
Bayerhamerstr.
Funkestr.
Lehenerbr.
Saint-Julien-Str.
Haunspergstr.
Plainstr.
Rainerstr.
Ph.-Harpff-Str.
Gabelsbergerstr.
Weiserstr.
Humboldtstr.
Sterneckstr.
Eisenbahnbr.
Ernest-Thun-Str.
Markus Sittikus-Str.
Faberstr.
Haydnstr.
Lasserstr.
Stelzhamerstr.
Grillparzerstr.
Auerspergstr.
Franz-Josef-Str.
Rupertg.
Arnog.
Virgilg.
Elisabethkai
Hubert-Sattler-G.
Wolf-Dietrich-Str.
St. Andrä
Schrenneng.
Schloß Mirabell
Salzburg Sightseeing Tours
NEUSTADT
Schallmooser Hauptstr.
Glockeng.
HOSI
Augustinerg.
Müllnersteg
Mirabellgarten
MIRABELLPL.
Paris-Lodron-Str.
Mozarteum
Sebastianskirche
Franz-Josef-Kai
Salzach River
Schwartzstr.
Bergstr.
Priesterhausg.
Dreifaltigkeitsg.
KAPUZINERBERG
MAKARTPL.
Theaterg.
Linzerg.
Kapuzinerkloster
Müllner Hauptstr.
Gstätteng.
Makartsteg
Staatsbr.
0 250 yards
0 250 meters
Mönchsberg Lift
MUSEUMPLATZ
HANUSCHPL.
Mönchsberg Gallery
Griesg.
Steing.
Imbergstr.
HAGENAUER-PL.
RATHAUS-PL.
Bürgerspitalg.
Getreideg.
Mozarts Geburtshaus
ALTER MARKT
Mozartsteg
UNIVERSITÄTSPL.
Brodg.
Goldg.
Judeng.
Rudolfskai
Giselakai
Festspiele Kartenbüro
Kollegienkirche
Cybar
AmEx
DR.-FRANZ.-REHRL-PL.
Hofstallg.
ALTSTADT
MOZARTPL.
Reichenhallerstr.
MAX REINH.-PL.
RESIDENZPL.
Sigmundstor
HERBERT-VON-KARAJAN PLATZ
Festspielhaus
Residenz
Franziskanerg.
DOM.-PL.
Dom
Kaig.
Chiems.
Basteig.
Pfeiferg.
Nonntaler Brücke
Neutorstr.
Stiftskirche St. Peter
KAPITEL-PL.
Krotachg.
RUDOLFSPL.
TO 8 (3km)
Hellbrunnerstr.
Joh.-Wolf-Str.
E. Sompek-Str.
Buckleuthstr.
Friedhof
Funicular
Herreng.
Schanzlg.
Catecombo
Festungsg.
Nonnberg Abbey
Rainbergstr.
Josef-Preis-Allee
TO 10 (100m)
RAINBERG
Festung Hohensalzburg
Festungsmuseum
Nonntaler Hauptstr.
Petersbrunnstr.
Erzabt-Klotz-Str.
Nonnberg.
MÖNCHSBERG
TO (2km)
Am Rainberg
TO UNTERSBERG (1KM)
Sinnhubstr.
Schwimmschulstr.
Leopoldskronstr.
TO 1 (1.5km)

AUSTRIA

LET THEM EAT CAKE

It comes as no surprise that the world's most famous cake-eating advocate, Marie Antoinette, came from Austria. A trip to this cake nation is not complete without indulging your sweet tooth on one of the following delicacies:

Linzer Torte: Named for the city of Linz, the Linzer Torte is allegedly "the oldest cake". Made from ground almonds, sugar, butter, flour, egg yolks, and either raspberry or red currant jam, the torte dates back to 1653. It might be surprising how late the "first cake" emerged, but the use of sugar cane did not become popular in Europe until well after Columbus reached America.

Sacher Torte: Made from chocolate, rum, and apricot preserves, the Sacher Torte has also stood the international taste-test of time. Created especially by sixteen year old Edouard Sacher, the royal pastry chef's apprentice, for Emperor Franz Josef in 1832, the torte can only be served in two pastry shops in Vienna: Sacher Café and Demels. Today, the Sacher Hotel sells around 360,000 of these tortes every year!

Strudel: introduced during the Hapsburg reign, the most popular two varieties, *Apfel* strudel and *Topfen* strudel, are made with apples and soft cheese, respectively. According to legend, the emperor's pastry chef decreed that the crust on a strudel should be so thin that a love letter could be read through it.

Eduard-Heinrich-Haus (HI), Eduard-Heinrich-Str. 2 (☎0662 62 59 76; www.hostel-ehh.at). Spacious rooms overlook the garden. Breakfast included. Laundry €6. Internet €2.60 per 20min. Key deposit €20 or ID. Reception M-F 7am-midnight, Sa-Su 7-10am and 5pm-midnight. Dorms €16-32; singles €29, with bath €33; doubles €41/47; triples €47/55; quads €62/78. €3 HI discount. Reserve ahead. AmEx/MC/V. ❶

Jugend & Familiengästehaus (HI), Josef-Preis-Allee 18 (☎0662 84 26 700; www.jfgh.at). Take bus #5 (dir.: Birkensiedlung) to Justizgebäude, close to the Altstadt. Kids pack this family-friendly hostel in May and June when school orchestras descend on Salzburg. Breakfast included. Laundry €3. Internet €3 per 40min. Reception 7am-12:30am. Dorms €15.50-35; doubles €54, with shower and toilet €86. €1.50 HI discount. €3 discount for 2 or more nights. AmEx/MC/V. ❷

Haus Ballwein, Moosstr. 69a (☎0662 82 40 29; www.haus-ballwein.at), south of the city. Take a bus to Makartpl., then south-bound bus #21 to Gsengerweg. Rooms are embellished with colorful curtains, natural wood paneling, and braided rugs. Bike rental €5 per day. Breakfast included. Singles €25, with shower €35; doubles €48/50-55; triples with bath €75; 4-person apartment €80. Cash only. ❷

FOOD

Countless beer gardens and pastry-shop patios make Salzburg a great place for outdoor dining. Local specialties include *Salzburger nockerl* (egg whites, sugar, and raspberry filling baked into three mounds that represent the hills of Salzburg) and the world-famous *Mozartkugel* (hazelnuts coated in pistachio marzipan, nougat, and chocolate). **Supermarkets** cluster on the Mirabellpl. side of the river. **Open-air markets** in Universitätspl. sell fresh fruits and veggies, giant pretzels, meats, and cheeses. (Open M-F 6am-7pm, Sa 6am-1pm.)

Indigo, Rudolfskai 8 (☎0662 84 34 80; www.indigo-food.com), is located along the river. This tiny eatery draws a local crowd with delicious salads, bowls of steaming Asian noodles, and sushi. Salads €1.35 per 100g. Noodles €5.50-7.50. Sushi €0.70-15.50, sandwiches (€3-4), curries (€4-5), and soup (€3.40-5.70). Open M-Th 10am-10pm, F-Sa 10am-midnight, Su noon-8pm. Free Wi-Fi 11:30am-2pm. Cash only. ❶

Zum Fidelen Affen, Priesterhausg. 8 (☎0662 87 73 61), off Linzerg. Hearty Austrian food keeps everyone coming back to Zum Fidelen Affen ("The Faithful Ape"). Try the toasted black bread with various toppings (€5-7), the farmer's salad (€9), or the Monkey Steak (roasted pork with bacon, mushrooms, and tomatoes; €10). Vegetarian options available. Open M-Sa 5pm-midnight. AmEx/MC/V. ❷

St. Peter's Stiftskeller, St-Peter-Bezirk 1-4 (☎0662 43 662 84 1268). At the foot of the cliffs next to St. Peter's Monastery. This place claims to be the oldest restaurant in Central Europe, established in AD 803. The innovative cuisine is anything but archaic. Entrees €10-23. Open M-F 11am-midnight. AmEx/MC/V. ❸

Stieglkeller, Festungsg. 10 (☎0662 84 2681). A short walk up the Festungsg. from the bottom of the Festungsbahn, near the cliffs and the entrance to Festung Hohensalzburg. A Salzburg favorite since 1492. Seating for 1600 outside under shady trees or inside under high ceilings and mounted antlers. Menu includes *Schweinsbraten* (roast pork with sauerkraut and dumplings; €11.20) and beef goulash with dumplings (€10.20). Open daily May-Sept. 10:30am-11pm. MC/V. ❸

SIGHTS

FESTUNG HOHENSALZBURG. Built between 1077 and 1681 by the ruling archbishops, the imposing Hohensalzburg Fortress, which looms over Salzburg from atop Mönchsberg, is the largest completely preserved castle in all of Europe—partly because it was never successfully attacked. The **Festungsmuseum** inside the fortress has side-by-side histories of Salzburg, the fortress, and the world. An audio tour (30min., 4 per hr.) leads visitors up the **watch-tower** for an unmatched panorama of the city and to an organ nicknamed the "Bull of Salzburg" for its off-key snorting. *(☎0662 8424 3011. Take the trail or the Festungsbahn funicular up to the fortress from Festungsg. Funicular May-Aug. 9am-10pm; Sept. 9am-9pm; Oct-Apr. 9am-5pm. Open daily July-Aug. 9am-7pm; Sept. and May-June 9am-6pm; Oct.-Apr. 9am-5pm. Last museum entry 30min. before closing. €10; includes round-trip funicular ride.)*

MOZARTS GEBURTSHAUS. Mozart's birthplace and childhood home holds a collection of the child genius' belongings, including his first violin and keyboard instruments. *(☎0662 084 4313. Getreideg. 9. Open daily July-Aug. 9am-7pm; Sept.-June 9am-6pm. Last entry 30min. before closing. €6.50, students €5.50. Cash only.)*

STIFTSKIRCHE, CATACOMBS, AND THE DOM. The **Monastery of St. Peter** rests against the Mönchsberg cliffs. **Stiftskirche St. Peter,** a church within the monastery, features a marble portal from 1244. In the 18th century, the building was remodeled in Rococo style. *(☎0662 844 5760. Open daily 9am-12:15pm and 2:30-6:30pm.)* To the right of the church's entrance is the monastery's **Friedhof** (cemetery). Tiger lilies, roses, and ivy embellish the fanciful curls of the wrought-iron crosses. The entrance to the **catacombs** is on the far right, against the Mönchsberg. *(Monastery open May-Sept. Tu-Su 10:30am-5pm; Oct.-Apr. W-Th 10:30am-3:30pm, F-Su 10:30am-4pm. €1, students €0.60. Cemetery open Apr.-Sept. 6:30am-7pm; Oct.-Mar. 6:30am-6pm. Free.)* The exit at the other end of the cemetery leads to the immense Baroque **Dom** (cathedral), where Mozart was christened in 1756 and later worked as concertmaster and court organist. The square in front of the cathedral, **Domplatz,** features a statue of the Virgin Mary and figures representing Wisdom, Faith, the Church, and the Devil.

RESIDENZ. Home of the later Salzburg princes, this palace once boasted 180 rooms of Renaissance, Baroque, and Classical art. Most of the building is now used by the University of Salzburg, but the second floor staterooms—the **Prunkräume**—still contain their original ornate furnishing. *(☎0662 804 226 90; www.salzburg-burgen.at. Residenzpl. 1. Open daily 9am-5pm. Last entry 4:30pm. €8.20, students €6.20; includes audio tour. Free with Salzburg Card.)*

KOLLEGIENKIRCHE. In Mozart's backyard stands one of the largest Baroque chapels on the continent. Sculpted clouds coat the nave, while pudgy cherubim frolic over the church's immense apse. *(Open daily 9am-5pm. Free.)*

MIRABELL PALACE AND GARDENS. Mirabellpl. holds the marvelous **Schloß Mirabell,** which the supposedly celibate Archbishop Wolf Dietrich built for his mistress and their 15 children in 1606. *(Open daily 7am-9pm. Free.)* However, the main attraction is the ornate maze of flowers beds and fountains behind the palace. The **Mirabellgarten** contains the moss-covered **Zauberflötenhäuschen** ("Magic Flute Little House") where Mozart purportedly composed *The Magic Flute.*

 FESTIVALS

During the **Salzburger Festspiele** (July-Aug.), operas, plays, films, concerts, and tourists overrun every available public space; expect room prices to rise accordingly and plan ahead. Info and tickets for Festspiele events are available through the *Festspiele Kartenbüro* (ticket office) and *Direkt Verkauf* (daily box office) at Karajanpl. 11, against the mountain and next to the tunnel. (☎0662 804 5500; www.salzburgfestival.at. Open mid-Mar. to June M-F 9:30am-3pm, through the end of Festspiele daily 9:30am-6pm. Tickets €15-360.) In other months, head to a concert organized by the Mozarteum. Their **Mozartwoche,** a week-long celebration of Mozart, during which his sacred works are performed, occurs at the end of January. (Jan. 25-Feb. 5. ☎0662 87 31 54; www.mozarteum.at.) The Dom has a concert program in July, August, and early October. (☎0662 88 46 23 45. €20, students €7.) From May to September, the Mirabell Gardens hosts outdoor performances including concerts, folk singing, and dancing. For more info, visit www.salzburg-festivals.com.

 BARS AND BEER GARDENS

Munich may be the world's beer capital, but much of its liquid gold flows south to Austria's pubs and *Biergärten* (beer gardens). These lager oases cluster in the city center along the Salzach River. The more boisterous revelers stick to Rudolfskai, between the *Staatsbrücke* and *Mozartsteg.* Elsewhere, especially along Chiemseegasse and around Anton-Neumayr-Platz, you can throw back a few drinks in a reserved *Beisl* (pub). Refined bars with middle-aged patrons can be found along Steingasse and Giselakai on the other side of the river.

Augustiner Bräustübl-Mülln, Augustinerg. 4 (☎0662 43 12 46). Although the monks are gone, the Bäukloster they founded in 1621 continues to turn out home-brewed beer by the barrel. Follow the long halls to the end to reach the Biergärten. Beer 0.3L €2.10, 0.5L €2.60. Open M-F 3-11pm, Sa-Su 2:30-11pm; last call 10:30pm. Cash only.

2-Stein, Giselakai 9 (☎0662 87 71 79). The go-to place for Salzburg's gay and lesbian scene. Mixed drinks from €5. Open M-W and Su 6pm-4am, Th-Sa 6pm-5am. MC/V.

Steinterrasse, Giselakai 3-5 (☎0662 874 34 60; www.hotelstein.at), on the 7th fl. of the Stein Hotel. This hip cafe-bar knows that a lofty rooftop panorama doesn't have to mean equally lofty prices. A young crowd comes to flirt while admiring the lights of the Altstadt. Beer €2.60-3.90. Mixed drinks €5-10. Open daily 9am-1am. AmEx/MC/V.

ZELL AM SEE ☎06542

Nestled among a ring of green and white mountains and cradling a turquoise glacial lake, Zell am See (pop. 10,000) serves year-round as a resort for mountain-happy European tourists. To reach the lift, walk 20min. up Schmittenstr. or take PostBus #661 (5min., every 1-2hr., €2). The moderately strenuous **Pinzgauer Spaziergang** begins at the top of the Schmittenhöhebahn and levels off high in the Kitzbüheler Alps. The trail is marked "Alpenvereinsweg" #19 or 719.

Most hikers devote an entire day to it, taking a side path to one of the valley towns west of Zell, where buses return to Zell am See. For a faster pace, **Outdo,** Schmittenstr. 8 (☎06542 701 65; www.outdoadventures.com) leads a variety of trips, including **rafting** (5hr., €45), **canyoning** (6hr., €50), and **mountain biking** (4-5hr., €29) tours. In winter, they offer group ski (3-day €125, 4-day €140, 5-day €150) and snowboarding classes (1-day €50, 3-day €110, 4-day €125).

Ask at your hostel or hotel for a free guest card, which provides discounts throughout the city. **Haus der Jugend (HI) ❷,** Seespitzstr. 13, equipped with a terrace on the lake, brings luxury to budget housing. From the station, take the exit facing the lake ("Zum See") and turn right on the lakeside footpath. When the path ends, turn left on Seespitzstr. Alternatively, take Post bus #660 or walk along Bundestrasse until reaching the train tracks once again. Then cross the tracks, take a left, and follow Seespitzstr. all the way to the lake. Note: the signs call the hostel "Jugendherberge." (☎06542 571 85; www.jungehotels.at/seespitzstrasse. Breakfast included. Lockers €1 deposit. Internet €1 per 12min. Reception 7:30-10am and 4-10pm. Dorms €18-22; doubles with bath €44. MC/V.) Closer to town, **Junges Hotel (HI) ❷,** Schmittenstr. 27, has enormous rooms and new facilities. From the train station, head left and up the hill. Take the first right on Brucker Bundesstr., then left on Schmittenstr. (☎06542 470 36; www.jungehotels.at/schmittenstrasse. Breakfast included. €21-24. AmEx/MC/V.) Near the train station, **Zum Casar ❷,** Schlossplatz 2, offers tasty Italian and Greek food. (☎06542 472 57; www.caesar.at. Meat entrees €5-7, pasta €6-8, pizza €5.60-8.60. Open daily 11am-2pm and 5pm-midnight. MC/V.)

Leaving the station at the intersection of Bahnhofstr. and Salzmannstr., **trains** run to: Innsbruck (1-2hr., every hr., €24); Kitzbühel (45min., every 2hr., €10); Vienna (5hr., €47) via Salzburg (1hr., every hr., €13). The **bus station** is right across the street from the train station, on Postpl. at Gartenstr. and Schulstr. Buy tickets on board or at the kiosk. (☎06542 54 44; www.postbus.at. Kiosk open M-F 7:45am-1:45pm.) Buses go to Haus de Jugend (see above, #660, €1.60), Franz-Josefs-Höhe (#651; mid-June to mid-Sept., every day at 9:25am, €13), Krimml (#670; 1hr., €8), and Salzburg (2hr., every 2hr., €11). The **tourist office,** Brucker Bundesstr. 1a, posts English-language **weather reports.** (☎06542 770; www.europasportregion.info. Open June-Sept. and Nov.-Apr. M-F 9am-6pm, Sa 9am-noon and 2-6pm, Su 9am-noon; May and Oct. M-F 8am-6pm, Sa 9am-noon.) For **mountain rescue,** call ☎140. **Postal Code:** A-5700.

AUSTRIA

HOHE TAUERN NATIONAL PARK

The enormous Hohe Tauern range, part of the Austrian Central Alps and the largest nature reserve in central Europe, encompasses 246 glaciers and 304 mountains over 3000m. Preservation is the park's primary goal, so no large campgrounds or recreation areas are permitted. *Experiencing Nature: Walking Destinations*, available at park centers and most area tourist offices, describes 54 different hikes, ranging from pleasant ambles to challenging mountain ascents. At the center of the park lies **Franz-Josefs-Höhe,** the most visited section, and the **Pasterze Glacier,** which hovers above the town of Heiligenblut.

TRANSPORTATION. Hohe Tauern National Park sits at the meeting point of the provinces of Salzburger Land, Tyrol, and Kärnten. The heart of the park is best reached by the highway, **Großglockner Hochalpenstraße.** As the zigzagging road climbs high into the mountains, it passes mesmerizing vistas of jagged peaks and plunging valleys, high Alpine meadows, and glacial waterfalls. **PostBus** #651 goes from Zell am See to Franz-Josefs-Höhe (1-2hr.; departs 9:25am, returns 3pm; €24.60). The road is open from May to mid-June and mid-

September to November 6am-8:30pm; mid-June to mid-September 5am-10pm. Snow chains are required in snow (car toll €28).

FRANZ-JOSEFS-HÖHE. An endless number of buses and cars climb the Großglockner Hochalpenstraße to this tourist mecca above the edge of the **Pasterze Glacier.** Once out of the parking area, the Panoramaweg affords a great view of **Großglockner** (3798m). Above the information center, the **Swarovski Observation Tower** provides free telescope use. (Open daily 10am-4pm.)

HIKING. Pick up a **free hiking map** from the National Park or tourist office. A detailed **topographic map** (€10-15) is necessary for prolonged hikes in the area. From the Franz-Josefs-Höhe parking lot, the initially steep **Pasterze Gletscherweg** (3hr.) descends to the edge of the retracting Pasterze Glacier and then continues through the valley and around the Stausee Margaritze to the **Glocknerhaus Alpine Center;** stay on the well-marked path. A **free shuttle bus** runs between Franz-Josefs-Höhe and Glocknerhaus—ask the staff to call for it.

Many hikes in the Großglockner area of the national park start at **Heiligenblut,** from the Retschitzbrücke parking area outside of town via Gemeindestr. The easy **Gößnitzfall-Kachlmoor trail** (round-trip 2hr.) leads through the Kachlmoor swamp to the Gößnitz Waterfalls at the head of the Gößnitz Valley. The rewarding but long **Gößnitztal-Langtalseen hike** (round-trip 10-12hr.) continues through Alpine pastures and valleys. Spend the night in the **Elberfelder Hütte ❶.** (Floor space €11; beds €21.) In the morning, pass three gleaming lakes before heading back to Heiligenblut via the Wirtsbauer Alm.

AUSTRIA

TYROL (TIROL)

With its celestial peaks, Tyrol has become a celebrated mountain playground for hikers and winter sports enthusiasts alike. Craggy summits in the northeast and south cradle the pristine Ötzal and Zillertal valleys while the mighty Hohe Tauern mountain range marches across eastern Tyrol. In the region's center, stylish Innsbruck flaunts bronze statues and Baroque facades.

INNSBRUCK ☎0512

After hosting the 1964 and 1976 winter Olympics, the mountain city of Innsbruck (pop. 118,000) rocketed to international recognition. Colorful architecture and relics from the Hapsburg Empire pepper the tiny cobblestone streets of the *Altstadt* (Old Town), while the nearby Alps await skiers and hikers

TRANSPORTATION AND PRACTICAL INFORMATION

Trains: Hauptbahnhof, Südtirolerpl. (☎0517 17). To: **Graz** (6hr., 2 per day, €49); **Salzburg** (2hr., every hr., €34); **Vienna** (5-6hr., every hr., €54); **Munich, GER** (2hr., every hr., €35); **Zürich, SWI** (4hr., 8 per day, €48).

Public Transportation: The **IVB** Office, Stainerstr. 2 (☎0512 530 70; www.ivb.at), off Marktgraben, has bus schedules and **route maps.** Open M-F 7:30am-6pm. Single fare €1.70, 24hr. pass €3.80, week €12. Discounts for students under 20. Most buses stop around 11:30pm; 4 Nachtbus **bus** lines run every hr. midnight-5am; most pass Maria-Theresien-Str., the train station, and Landesmuseum. IVB's Sightseer bus is the easiest way to visit Innsbruck's far-flung attractions. Single fare €2.80, round-trip €4.40, day pass €8.80. May-Oct. 2 per hr. 9am-6:30pm; Nov.-Apr. every hr. 10am-6pm. Tickets for all buses and **trams** can be bought on board, at a kiosk, or from the tourist office.

Bike Rental: Neuner Radsport, Maximilianstr. 23 (☎0512 56 15 01). Mountain bikes €16 per ½-day, €20 per day. Open M-F 9am-6pm, Sa 9am-noon. MC/V.

Tourist Office: Innsbruck Tourist Office, Burggraben 3 (☎0512 598 50; www.innsbruck.info), off Museumstr. Sells the **Innsbruck Card,** with unlimited public transport and entry to sights (1-day €25, 2-day €30, 3-day €35). Maps €1. Open daily 9am-6pm.

Laundromat: Bubblepoint Waschsalon, Brixnerstr. 1 (☎56 50 07 50; www.bubblepoint.at). Wash €4 per 7kg, soap included; dry €1 per 10min. Internet €1 per 10min. Open M-F 8am-10pm, Sa-Su 8am-8pm.

Mountain Rescue: ☎140.

Internet: International Telephone Discount, Südtirolerpl. 1 (☎0512 282 3690). Go right from the Hauptbahnhof. €0.07 per min. Open daily 9am-11pm.

Post Office: Maximilianstr. 2 (☎0577 677 6010). Open M-F 7am-9pm, Sa 7am-3pm, Su 10am-7:30pm. **Postal Code:** A-6010.

ACCOMMODATIONS

Options for budget accommodations are limited in June, when some hostels close, although student dorms are open to travelers in July and August. Request a free **Club Innsbruck** card from your hotel or hostel for discounts.

Hostel Fritz Prior-Schwedenhaus (HI), Rennweg 17b (☎0512 58 58 14; http://youth-hostel.aufbauwerk.com). From the station, take bus #4 to Handelsakademie, continue to the end and cross Rennweg. This hostel has comfortable rooms with bath. Breakfast €3.50. Laundry €5.40. Reception 7-9am and 5-10:30pm. Lockout 9am-5pm. Open July-Aug. Dorms €13; singles €23; doubles €38; triples €49. Cash only. ❶

Gasthof Innbrücke, Innstr. 1 (☎0512 28 19 34; www.gasthofinnbruecke.at). From the Altstadt, cross the Innbrücke. This 582-year-old inn, located in a narrow building, has a downstairs bar and restaurant. Breakfast included. Reserve ahead. Singles €33, with shower €41; doubles €57/72; triples €48/105. MC/V. ❸

Jugendherberge Innsbruck (HI), Reichenauer Str. 147 (☎0512 34 61 79; www.youth-hostel-innsbruck.at). From the train station, either take tram #3 to Museumstr., or just walk, and then take bus O to Jugendherberge. This former Olympic athlete housing-turned-hostel has clean rooms. Breakfast included. Laundry €3.30. Internet €1 per 10min. Reception July-Aug. 7am-1pm and 3-11pm; Sept.-June 7am-1pm and 5-11pm. Dorms €16-21 1st night, €14-16 thereafter; singles €33; doubles €50. Cash only. ❷

AUSTRIA

FOOD

The *Altstadt* cafes on Maria-Theresien-Str. are good but slightly overpriced. **M-Preis** supermarket is at Maximilianstr. 3 (☎0512 580 5110; open M-F 7:30am-7pm, Sa 8am-6pm) and inside the train station (☎05120 58 0730; open daily 6am-9pm). The chain restaurant **Baguette** sells sandwiches (€2-3) and salad served with bread (€5); it has a location on almost every corner of the city.

Theresienbräu, Maria-Theresien-Str. 51-53 (☎0512 587 580). This lively pub/restaurant is built around giant copper brewing kettles and fills up with young people at night. Try the golden brown house lager (0.5L €3.20) or Tyrolean specialties (€6-7). Open M-W 10am-1am, Th-Sa 10am-2am, Su 10am-midnight. MC/V. ❷

Noi Original Thaiküche, Kaiserjägerstr. 1 (☎0512 589 777). This tiny Thai kitchen packs a powerful punch with its spicy soups (€5-16) and noodles (€7-10). Lunch specials €8-9. Open M-F 11:30am-2:30pm and 6-11pm, Sa 6-11pm. Cash only. ❷

Kahlo's, Boznerpl. 6 (☎567 330; www.kahlos.com). Kahlo's will add a little more fiesta to your life with its spicy Mexican fare, drinks, strings of chilis, and sombreros. Enchiladas and burritos €10-12. Fajitas €12-15. Open daily 11:30am-11pm. AmEx/MC/V. ❷

SIGHTS

The greens and pinks of Innsbruck's *Altstadt* stand out brilliantly against the surrounding mountains. The Old Town centers around the **Goldenes Dachl** (Golden Roof), Herzog-Friedrich-Str. 15. The 16th-century gold balcony honors Maximilian I, Innsbruck's favorite Habsburg emperor. The nearby **Helbinghaus** is graced with pale-green floral detail and intricate stucco work. Church domes and shopping boutiques line Innsbruck's most distinctive street, **Maria-Theresien-Straße,** which runs south from the edge of the Altstadt. At its far end stands the **Triumphpforte** (Triumphal Arch), built in 1765 after the betrothal of Emperor Leopold II. In the middle, the **Annasäule** (Anna Column) commemorates the Tyroleans' 1703 victory over the Bavarians. Built from pink-and-white marble, **Dom St. Jakob,** 1 block behind the Goldenes Dachl, illustrates High Baroque ornamentation. Its prized possession is the small altar painting of Our Lady of Succor by Lukas Cranach the Elder. (1 block behind the Goldenes Dachl. Open Apr.-Sept. M-Sa 8am-7:30pm, Su 12:30-7:30pm; Oct.-Mar. M-Sa 10am-6:30pm, Su 12:30-6:30pm. Mass M-Sa 9:30am; Su 10 and 11:30am. Free.) In front of the Dom, Hofburg, the imperial palace, originally built in 1460, was completely remodeled under Maria Theresa. (Rennweg 1. In front of Dom St. Jakob. ☎58 71 8612; www.hofburg-innsbruck.at. Open daily 9am-5pm. Last entry 4:30pm. €5.50, students €4. English language guidebook €1.80.) Accessible by Sightseer bus or tram #3 and a short 15min. walk uphill, **Schloß Ambras** transformed from hunting lodge into elegant castle during Ferdinand II's reign. While the faces in the **Habsburg Portrait Gallery** may start to look identical, giant stuffed sharks and paintings of the incredibly hirsute Petrus and Madleine Gonzalez in the Kunst-und Wunderkammer (Cabinet of Curiosities) are guaranteed to stand out. (Schloßstr. 20. ☎431525 24 4802; www.khm.at/ambras. Sightseer bus or tram #3 stops at the bottom of the hill, leaving a 15min. walk. Open daily Aug. 10am-7pm; Sept.-Oct. and Dec.-July 10am-5pm. Portrait gallery open daily Aug. 10am-7pm; Sept.-Oct. and May-July 10am-5pm. May-Oct. €8, students €3; Dec.-Apr. €4.50/2.50. Tours €2; reservations required for English-language tours.)

HIKING AND SKIING

A **Club Innsbruck** membership (free; see **Accommodations**, p. 93) lets you in on one of Austria's best deals. The club's popular **hiking** program around Innsbruck and its surrounding villages provides free guides, transportation, and equipment. Moderate 3-5hr. group hikes from Innsbruck meet in front of the Congress Center (early June to early Oct. daily 9am; return around 4-5pm). Free 1hr. nighttime **lantern hikes** to Heiligwaßer near Igls leave Tuesday at 7:45pm and culminate in a hut party with traditional Austrian song and dance. For the early birds, the club also offers Friday **sunrise hikes** to Rangger Köpfl. leaving at 4:50am; reserve ahead. For self-guided hikes, take the J bus to **Patscherkofel Seilbahnen** (20min.). The lift provides access to moderately difficult 1-5hr. hikes near the 2246m bald summit of the Patscherkofel. (Open July-Aug. 9am-5pm; June and Sept. M-F 9am-4:30pm, Sa-Su 9am-5pm. €11, round-trip €17.) For more challenging climbs, ride the lifts up to the **Nordkette** mountains. Take the J bus to Hungerburg and catch the cable car to Seegrube (1905m) or continue on to Hafelekarspitze (2334m). Both stops lead to several hiking paths along jagged ridges and around rocky peaks, but be prepared: they are neither easy nor well-marked. (☎0512 293 344. Hungerburg to Seegrube €11, under 20 €9; to Hafelekar €12/10; Seegrube to Hafelekar €2.70/2.20.) To view Innsbruck from above, Mountain Fly offers a €95 tandem **paragliding** package, including transport and equipment (☎0664 282 8968).

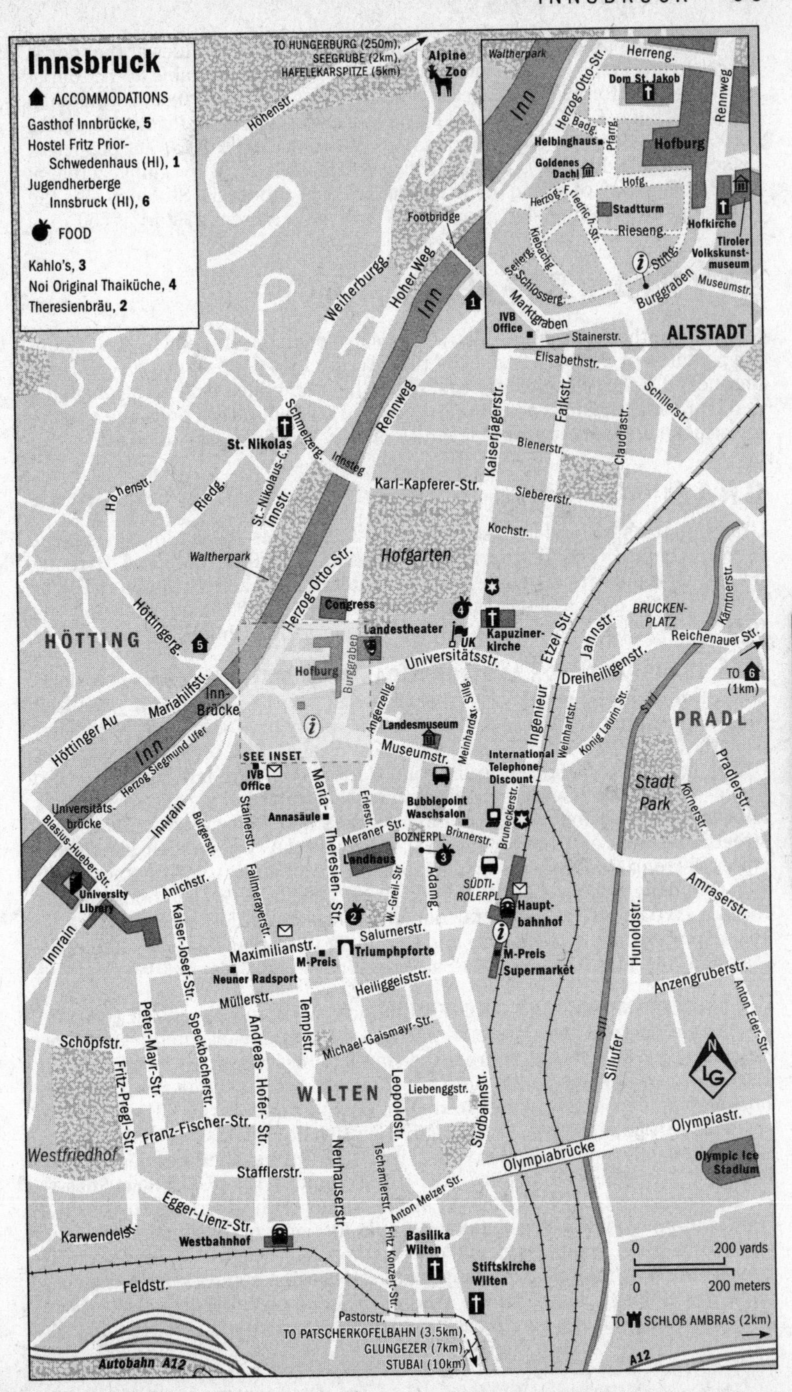
Innsbruck
ACCOMMODATIONS
Gasthof Innbrücke, 5
Hostel Fritz Prior-Schwedenhaus (HI), 1
Jugendherberge Innsbruck (HI), 6
FOOD
Kahlo's, 3
Noi Original Thaiküche, 4
Theresienbräu, 2
TO HUNGERBURG (250m), SEEGRUBE (2km), HAFELEKARSPITZE (5km)
Alpine Zoo
Waltherpark
Herreng.
Dom St. Jakob
Herzog-Otto-Str.
Rennweg
Inn
Badg.
Pfarrg.
Helbinghaus
Hofburg
Goldenes Dachl
Hofg.
Herzog-Friedrich-Str.
Stadtturm
Hofkirche
Riesеng.
Kiebachg.
Tiroler Volkskunst-museum
Seilerg.
Schlosserg.
Stiftg.
Burggraben
Museumstr.
Marktgraben
IVB Office
Stainerstr.
ALTSTADT
Höhenstr.
Footbridge
Weiherburgg.
Hoher Weg
Elisabethstr.
Schillerstr.
Rennweg
Kaiserjägerstr.
Falkstr.
Claudiastr.
Schmelzerg.
St. Nikolas
Innsteg
Bienerstr.
Karl-Kapferer-Str.
Siebererstr.
St.-Nikolaus-G.
Innstr.
Riedg.
Kochstr.
Hofgarten
Herzog-Otto-Str.
Congress
Landestheater
UK
Kapuziner-kirche
Höttingerg.
HÖTTING
BRUCKEN-PLATZ
Kärntnerstr.
Jahnstr.
Reichenauer Str.
Etzel Str.
Universitätsstr.
Dreiheiligenstr.
TO 6 (1km)
Burggraben
Mariahilfstr.
Inn-Brücke
Angerzellg.
Meinhardstr.
Sillg.
Ingenieur
Weinhartstr.
König Laurin Str.
Sill
PRADL
Höttinger Au
Landesmuseum
Herzog Siegmund Ufer
SEE INSET
Museumstr.
International Telephone Discount
Pradlerstr.
Stadt Park
IVB Office
Maria-Theresien-Str.
Erlerstr.
Körnerstr.
Universitäts-brücke
Innrain
Bürgerstr.
Bubblepoint Waschsalon
Annasäule
Meraner Str.
Brixnerstr.
Bruneckerstr.
BOZNERPL.
Blasius-Hueber-Str.
Landhaus
SÜDTI-ROLERPL.
Anichstr.
Fallmerayerstr.
Amraserstr.
University Library
W.-Greil-Str.
Adamg.
Haupt-bahnhof
Kaiser-Josef-Str.
Salurnerstr.
M-Preis Supermarket
Innrain
Maximilianstr.
M-Preis
Triumphpforte
Hunoldstr.
Neuner Radsport
Anzengruberstr.
Heiliggeiststr.
Anton Eder-Str.
Müllerstr.
Templstr.
Schöpfstr.
Peter-Mayr-Str.
Speckbacherstr.
Andreas-Hofer-Str.
Michael-Gaismayr-Str.
Sill
Sillufer
Fritz-Pregl-Str.
Leopoldstr.
Liebenggstr.
WILTEN
Südbahnstr.
Franz-Fischer-Str.
Olympiastr.
Westfriedhof
Neuhauserstr.
Tschamlerstr.
Olympiabrücke
Olympic Ice Stadium
Stafflerstr.
Anton Melzer Str.
Egger-Lienz-Str.
Karwendelst.
Westbahnhof
Basilika Wilten
Fritz Konzert-Str.
Stiftskirche Wilten
0 200 yards
0 200 meters
Feldstr.
TO SCHLOß AMBRAS (2km)
Pastorstr.
TO PATSCHERKOFELBAHN (3.5km), GLUNGEZER (7km), STUBAI (10km)
Autobahn A12
A12

For Club-led **ski excursions,** take the free ski shuttle (schedules at the tourist office) to any cable car. The **Innsbruck Gletscher Ski Pass** (available at the tourist office) is valid for all 60 lifts in the region (with Club Innsbruck membership: 3-day €95, 6-day €160). Individual lift passes are available for **Nordpark-Seegrube** (☎0512 293 344; www.nordpark.com), **Patscherkofel** (☎0512 598 50; www.patscherkofelbahnen.at), and **Glungezer** (☎0552 378 321; www.glungezerbahn.at; €21). One day of skiing on **Stubai glacier** costs about €35. Stubai is also the only slope for summer skiing; packages (bus, lift, and rental) start at €50.

STYRIA (STEIERMARK)

Many of southern Austria's folk traditions live on in the emerald hills and sloping pastures of Styria, where even the largest city—Graz—remains calm and untouched by large tourist crowds. While the crumbling medieval strongholds and Lipizzaner stallions are among the region's notable attractions, the easygoing atmosphere and Styrian vineyards convince many visitors to linger.

GRAZ ☎0316

Graz, Austria's second-largest city (pop. 250,000), is the nation's best-kept secret. *Altstadt* (Old Town), with picturesque red-tiled roofs and Baroque domes, feels unhurried: people lounge in outdoor cafes atop Schloßberg Hill or rock climb the cliffs along the Mur. Darkness rouses 45,000 university students from their books to participate in the city's energetic nightlife.

TRANSPORTATION AND PRACTICAL INFORMATION. **Trains** run to: **Innsbruck, SWI** (6-7hr., 7 per day, €48); **Munich, GER** (6hr., 3 per day, €72); **Salzburg** (4hr., every 2hr., €43); **Vienna Südbahnhof** (2hr., every hr., €30); **Zürich, SWI** (10hr., 3 per day, €83). To reach the city center, take tram #1, 3, 6, or 7 (€1.70, day pass €3.70). By foot, exit right from the train station, then turn left onto Annenstr. Follow it to the main bridge and cross to reach **Hauptplatz.** Five minutes away is **Jakominiplatz,** the public transportation system's hub. **Herrengasse,** a pedestrian street lined with cafes and boutiques, connects the two squares. The **tourist office,** Herreng. 16, gives an English-language walking tour of Altstadt (2hr.; Apr.-Oct. daily 2:30pm, Jan.-Mar. and Nov. Sa 2:30pm; €9.50) and books rooms for free. (☎0316 807 50; www.graztourismus.at. July-Aug. M-F 10am-7pm, Sa-Su 10am-6pm; Apr.-June, Sept.-Oct., and Dec. M-Sa 10am-6pm, Su 10am-4pm; Jan.-Mar. and Nov. M-F 10am-5pm, Sa-Su 10am-4pm.) **Postal Code:** A-8010.

ACCOMMODATIONS AND FOOD. Most accommodations in Graz are pricey and far from the city center. To reach the family-oriented **Jugendgästehaus Graz (HI)** ❷, Idlhofg. 74, from the station, cross the street, head right on Eggenberger Gürtel, turn left on Josef-Huber-G., then take the first right; the hostel complex is through the parking lot on your right. Buses #31, 32, and 33 run from Jakominipl. (☎0316 708 3210; www.jfgh.at. Breakfast included. Laundry €4. Free Internet. Reception 7am-11pm. Curfew 1am; night-key deposit €20. Dorms €22; singles €33; doubles €26. HI discount €1.10. MC/V.) **Hotel Strasser** ❹, Eggenberger Gürtel 11, fills its bright rooms with abstract art. Exit the train station, cross the street, and head right for 5min. on Eggenberger Gürtel. (☎0316 71 39 77. Breakfast included. Reception 24hr. Singles €45; doubles €70; triples €93. AmEx/MC/V.) On Hauptplatz, concession stands sell sandwiches and *Würstel* (€2-3). Situated in the shadow of Schloßberg, the cheery **Alte Münze** ❷, Schloßbergpl. 8, serves a local crowd Styrian specialties. (☎0316 82 91 51.

Entrees €7-15, vegetarian €7-12. Open mid-Mar. to Dec. Tu-Sa 8am-11:30pm; June-Sept. Tu-Sa 8am-11:30pm, Su 11am-10pm. Cash only.) The candle-lit **Continuum** ❶, Sporg. 29, dishes up pizza for €2-8. (☎0316 81 57 78. Sa-Su brunch buffet 10am-2pm €5. Open M-F 3pm-2am, Sa-Su 10am-2am. MC/V.) A **SPAR** supermarket is in the train station. (Open daily 6am-10pm.)

SIGHTS AND ENTERTAINMENT. North of Hauptpl., the wooded **Schloßberg** (Castle Hill) rises above Graz. Climb the zigzagging stone steps of the **Kriegsteig,** built by Russian prisoners during WWI, or take the elevator for €.60 per ride, to the city's emblem, the **Uhrturm** (clock tower), for sweeping views of Graz and the vast Styrian plain. The **Schloßbergbahn** (funicular), part of Graz's tram and bus network, runs from Kaiser-Franz-Josef-Kai to the **Glockenturm** (bell tower), where **Liesl,** a bell cast in 1587, chimes 101 times daily at 7am, noon, and 7pm, much to the consternation of late-risers and the hungover. The **Landhaushof** features architecture in the Lombard style, remodeled by architect Domenico dell'Allio in 1557. Most of Graz's museums are part of the **Landesmuseum Joanneum**—one ticket allows entrance into all participating museums. (☎80 17 96 60; www.museum-joanneum.at. 1-day pass €7, students €3; 2-day pass €12/5.) To the left of the tourist office, the **Landeszeughaus** (Provincial Armory), Herreng 16—the largest historical armory in the world—details the history of Ottoman attacks on the Hapsburgs and has enough spears, muskets, and armor to outfit 28,000 mercenaries. (☎80 17 98 10. Open Apr.-Oct. M-W and F-Su 10am-6pm, Th noon-8pm; Nov.-Mar. Tu-Su 10am-3pm.) The newest addition to the Graz riverscape is the futuristic "friendly alien ship" building of the modern art museum **Kunsthaus,** Lendkai 1, at the Hauptbrücke (☎80 17 92 00; www.kunsthausgraz.at. Open Tu-Su 10am-6pm.) A more popular part of Landesmuseum, **Joanneumis,** the mussel-shaped Murinsel in the center of the river, houses a chic cafe, open-air theater, and playground. Also included in a Landesmuseum Joanneum ticket is access to **Schloß Eggenberg,** a 17th-century castle built in the Spanish Escorial style, where the ornate **Planetensaal** (Planet Hall) is covered with paintings of the zodiac. (Tram #1 from Jakominipl. or Hauptpl. State rooms open by tour only Mar. 16-Nov. hourly 10am-4pm. Garden open May-Oct. daily 10am-6pm; Apr. and Nov.-Dec. daily 10am-4pm.) The palace also contains the **Alte Galerie,** a collection of Renaissance and Baroque art. (Open Apr.-Oct. Tu-Su 10am-6pm; Nov.-March Tu-Su 10am-5pm.) The modern steel sculpture at the corner of Opernring and Burgg. beckons to the magnificent **Opernhaus,** Franz-Josef-Pl. 10, which stages high-quality performances undeservedly overshadowed by those of Vienna.

The hub of after-hours activity is the so-called **Bermuda Triangle,** an area of the old city behind Hauptpl. and bordered by Mehlpl., Färberg., and Prokopig. Close to the university district, **Kulturhauskeller,** Elisabethstr. 30, is one of the many clubs where dance music beats all night. (Tu live bands. W karaoke. 19+. Cover €3 after 11pm. Open Tu-Sa 9pm-5am. MC/V.)

BELGIUM (BELGIQUE, BELGIË)

Surrounded by France, Germany, and The Netherlands, Belgium is a convergence of different cultures. Appropriately, the small country attracts an array of travelers: chocoholics, Europhiles, and art-lovers all come together in Belgium. Sweet-toothed foreigners flock to Brussels, the home of filled chocolate, to nibble confections from one of 2000 cocoa-oriented specialty shops and to brush shoulders with diplomats en route to European Union and NATO headquarters. In Flanders, Gothic towers surround cobblestone squares, while visitors below admire Old Masters' canvases and guzzle monk-brewed ale. Wallonie has less tourist infrastructure, but the caves of the Lesse Valley and the forested hills of the Ardennes compensate with their stunning natural beauty.

DISCOVER BELGIUM: SUGGESTED ITINERARY

WEEK. Plan for at least two days in **Brussels** (p. 102). Head north to the elegant boulevards of **Antwerp** (p. 111) and historic **Ghent** (p. 112). Finish by heading west to the winding streets and canals of Romantic Bruges (p. 107). Then, visit **Liège** (p. 114), a university town and transit hub, or spend some time exploring **Ypres** (p. 114) known for its military significance. Don't forget to bask in leafy Ardennes, using **Namur** (p. 116) as a base for hikes into Belgium's rural south.

ESSENTIALS

FACTS AND FIGURES

OFFICIAL NAME: Kingdom of Belgium.

CAPITAL: Brussels.

MAJOR CITIES: Antwerp, Ghent, Liège.

POPULATION: 10,584,534.

LAND AREA: 30,500 sq. km.

TIME ZONE: GMT +1.

HEAD OF STATE: King Albert II.

LANGUAGES: Dutch (60%), French (40%).

RELIGIONS: Roman Catholic (75%), Protestant (25%).

FRENCH FRIES: Invented in Belgium during the 18th century, despite what the name suggests. Served with mayonnaise.

VARIETIES OF BEER: Over 500!

WHEN TO GO

May, June, and September are the best months to visit with temperatures around 18-22°C (64-72°F) in Brussels and Antwerp, and about 6°C (10°F) higher in Liège and Ghent. July and August tend to be rainy and hot. Winters are cool, 2-7°C (36-45°F), and somewhat colder in the Ardennes.

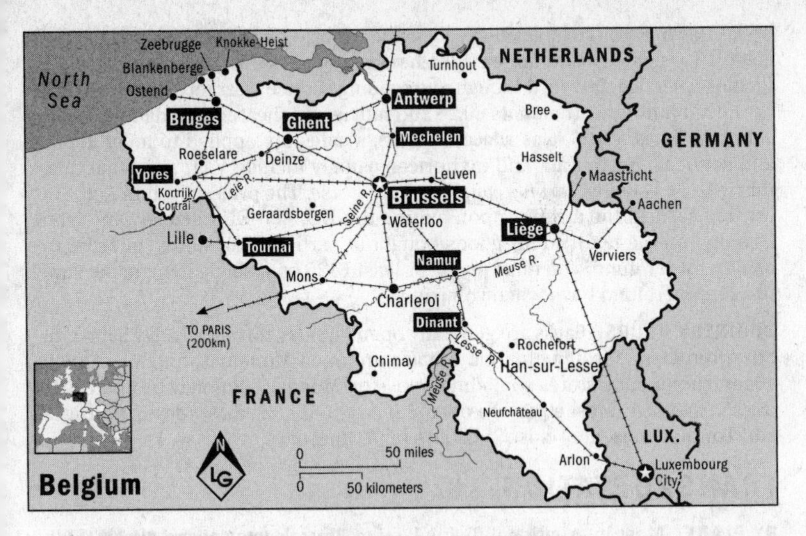

DOCUMENTS AND FORMALITIES

EMBASSIES AND CONSULATES. Foreign embassies in Belgium are in Brussels. Belgian embassies abroad include: **Australia** and **New Zealand,** 19 Arkana St., Yarralumla, ACT 2600 (☎02 62 73 25 02; www.diplomatie.be/canberra); **Canada,** 360 Albert St., Ste. 820, Ottawa, ON, K1R 7X7 (☎613-236-7267; www.diplomatie.be/ottawa); **Ireland,** 2 Shrewsbury Rd., Ballsbridge, Dublin 4 (☎01 205 71 00; www.diplomatie.be/dublin); **UK,** 17 Grosvenor Crescent, London, SW1X 7EE (☎020 7470 3700; www.diplomatie.be/london); **US,** 3330 Garfield St., NW, Washington, D.C., 20008 (☎202-333-6900; www.diplobel.us).

VISA AND ENTRY INFORMATION. EU citizens do not need a visa. Citizens of Australia, Canada, New Zealand, and the US do not need a visa for stays of up to 90 days, beginning upon entry into any of the countries in the EU's freedom-of-movement zone. For stays longer than 90 days, all non-EU citizens need visas (around US$85), available at Belgian consulates. Visit www.diplobel.us. US citizens' visas tend to be issued a few weeks after application submission.

BELGIUM

TOURIST SERVICES AND MONEY

EMERGENCY	**Ambulance:** ☎100. **Fire:** ☎100. **Police:** ☎101.

TOURIST OFFICES. Bureaux de Tourisme, marked by green-and-white or blue signs labeled "i," are supplemented by **Info Jeunes/Info-Jeugd,** info centers that help people find work and secure accommodations in Wallonie and Flanders, respectively. The **Belgian Tourist Information Center (BBB),** Grasmarkt 63, Brussels (☎025 04 03 90), has national tourist info. The weekly English-language *Bulletin* (www.thebulletin.be; €2.80 at newsstands) provides events and news info.

MONEY. The **euro (€)** has replaced the Belgian **franc** as the unit of currency in Belgium. **ATMs** generally offer the best exchange rates. **Credit cards** are used widely throughout Belgium, most notably in the country's major cities. A bare-bones day in Belgium might cost €35, while a more comfortable day runs about €50-65. Tipping is not common, though rounding up is. Restaurant bills usually include a service charge, although outstanding service warrants an extra 5-10% tip. Give bathroom attendants €0.25 and movie and theater attendants €0.50.

Belgium has a 21% **value added tax (VAT)**, a sales tax applied to most goods and services. Restaurant and taxi prices usually include VAT; at restaurants, this may be listed as *service comprise* or *incluse*. The prices given in *Let's Go* include VAT. In the airport, upon exiting the EU, non-EU citizens can claim a refund on the tax paid for goods bought at participating stores. In order to qualify for a refund, you must spend at least €125 on a single item; make sure to ask for a refund form when you pay.

BUSINESS HOURS. **Banks** are generally open Monday through Friday 9am-4pm but often close for lunch midday. **Stores** are open Monday through Saturday 10am-5pm or 6pm; stores sometimes close on Mondays, but may be open Sundays in summer. Most **sights** are open Sundays but closed Mondays; in Bruges and Tournai, museums close Tuesdays or Wednesdays.

TRANSPORTATION

BY PLANE. Most international flights land at **Brussels International Airport** (**BRU**; ☎27 53 87 98; www.brusselsairport.be), located roughly 20min. away from Brussels. Budget airlines, like **Ryanair** and **easyJet,** fly out of **Brussels South Charleroi Airport** (**CRL**; ☎71 25 12 11; www.charleroi-airport.com), about 1hr. south of Brussels, and Brussels International Airport. The Belgian national airline, **Brussels Airlines** (☎070 35 11 11, US ☎516-740-5200, UK ☎087 0735 2345; www.brusselsairlines.com), flies to Brussels from most major European cities.

BY TRAIN AND BUS. The extensive and reliable **Belgian Rail** (www.b-rail.be) network traverses the country. **Eurail** is valid in Belgium. A **Benelux Tourrail Pass** (US$210, under 26 US$160) allows five days of unlimited train travel in a one-month period in Belgium, the Netherlands, and Luxembourg. Travelers with time to explore Belgium's nooks and crannies might consider the **Rail Pass** (€70) or Go Pass (under 26 only; €45), both of which allow 10 single trips within the country over a one-year period and can be transferred among travelers. Because trains are widely available, buses are used primarily for local transport. Single tickets are €1.50, and are cheaper when bought in packs.

BY FERRY. **P&O Ferries** (☎070 70 77 71, UK ☎087 0598 03 33; www.poferries.com) from Hull, BRI to Zeebrugge, north of Bruges (12hr., 7pm, from €150).

BY CAR, BIKE, AND THUMB. Belgium honors drivers' licenses from Australia, Canada, the EU, and the US. New Zealanders must contact the New Zealand Automobile Association (☎0800 822 422; www.aa.co.nz) for an International Driving Permit. **Speed limits** are 120kph on motorways, 90kph on main roads, and 50kph elsewhere. **Biking** is popular; many roads in Flanders have bike lanes. **Hitchhiking** is illegal in Belgium. *Let's Go* does not recommend hitchhiking.

KEEPING IN TOUCH

PHONE CODES	**Country code:** 32. **International dialing prefix:** 00. For more info on how to place international calls, see **Inside Back Cover.**

EMAIL AND THE INTERNET. There are cybercafes in all of the larger towns and cities in Belgium. Expect to pay €2-3 per 30min. In smaller towns, Internet is generally available in hostels for €5-6 per hr.

TELEPHONE. Most pay phones require a **phone card** (from €5), available at post offices, supermarkets, and newsstands. Whenever possible, use a calling card for international phone calls, as long-distance rates for national phone services are often very high. Calls are cheapest 6:30pm-8am and weekends. **Mobile phones** are an increasingly popular and economical option. Major mobile carriers include Vodafone, Base, and Mobistar. When dialing within a city, the city code must still be dialed. For operator assistance within Belgium, dial ☎12 07; for international, dial ☎12 04 (€0.25). Direct-dial access numbers for calling out of Belgium include: **AT&T** (☎0800 100 10); **British Telecom** (☎0800 100 24); **Canada Direct** (☎0800 100 19); **Telecom New Zealand** (☎0800 100 64).

MAIL. Post offices are open Monday to Friday 9am-5pm, with a midday break. Sent within Belgium, a postcard or letter (up to 50g) costs €0.46 for non-priority and €0.52 for priority. Within the EU, costs are €0.70/0.80, and for the rest of the world €0.75/0.90. For info see www.post.be. **Poste Restante** available.

ACCOMMODATIONS AND CAMPING

BELGIUM	❶	❷	❸	❹	❺
ACCOMMODATIONS	under €10	€10-20	€21-30	€31-40	over €40

Hotels in Belgium are fairly expensive, with rock-bottom singles from €30 and doubles from €40-45. Belgium's 31 **HI youth hostels** are run by the **Flemish Youth Hostel Federation** (www.vjh.be) in Flanders and **Les Auberges de Jeunesses** (www.laj.be) in Wallonie. Expect to pay around €18 per night, including linen, for modern, basic hostels. Private hostels cost about the same but are usually nicer, although some charge separately for linen. **Hotels** are noticeably more expensive than the nicest hostel; make reservations in advance to secure accommodations. Most receptionists speak some English. Reservations are a good idea, particularly in summer and on weekends. **Campgrounds** charge about €4 per night and are common in Wallonie but not in Flanders. An International Camping Card is unnecessary in Belgium.

FOOD AND DRINK

BELGIUM	❶	❷	❸	❹	❺
FOOD	under €5	€5-9	€10-13	€14-18	over €18

Belgian cuisine, acclaimed but expensive, fuses French and German styles. An evening meal may cost as much as a night's accommodations. Fresh seafood appears in *moules* or *mosselen* (steamed mussels) and *moules frites* (steamed mussels with french fries), the national dishes, which are often tasty and reasonably affordable (€14-20). *Frites* (french fries) are ubiquitous and budget-friendly; Belgians eat them dipped in mayonnaise. Look for *friekots* ("french fry shacks") in Belgian towns. Belgian **beer** is a source of national pride, its consumption a national pastime. More varieties—over 500, ranging from ordinary pilsners (€1) to Trappist ales (€3) brewed by monks—are produced here than in any other country. Leave room for chocolate **pralines** from Leonidas or Neuhaus and Belgian **waffles** *(gaufres)*, sold on the street and in cafes.

BEYOND TOURISM

Volunteer *(benévolat)* and work opportunities in Belgium focus on its strong international offerings, especially in Brussels, which is home to both NATO and the EU. Private-sector short- and long-term employment is listed at www.jobsabroad.com/Belgium.cfm. A selection of public-sector job and volunteer opportunities is listed below. For more info on opportunities across Europe, see the Beyond Tourism chapter p. 60.

Amnesty International, r. Berckmans 9, 1060 Brussels (☎02 538 8177; www.amnesty-international.be). One of the world's foremost human rights organizations has offices in Brussels. Paid positions and volunteer work available.

The International School of Brussels, Kattenberg-Botisfort 19, Brussels (☎02 661 42 11; www.isb.be). The ISB hires teachers for positions lasting more than 1yr. Must have permission to work in Belgium.

North Atlantic Treaty Organization (NATO), bd. Leopold III, 1110 Brussels (www.nato.int). Current students and recent graduates (within 1yr.) who are nationals of a NATO member state and fluent in 1 official NATO language (English or French), with a working knowledge of the other, can apply for 6-month internships. Requirements and application details available at www.nato.int/structur/interns/index.html. Application deadlines are far ahead of start dates.

BRUSSELS (BRUXELLES, BRUSSEL) ☎02

The headquarters of NATO and the European Union, Brussels (pop. 1,200,000) is a population of officials. But, despite their number, these civil servants aren't the only ones with claims to Belgium's capital; beneath the drone of parliamentary procedure bustles the spirited clamor of local life. In a city that juxtaposes old and new, with skyscrapers and historic buildings on the same block, local voices echo throughout the city's intricate architecture.

TRANSPORTATION

Flights: Brussels Airport (BRU; ☎02 753 42 21, specific flight info 090 07 00 00, €0.45 per min.; www.brusselsairport.be) is 14km from the city and accessible by train. **South Charleroi Airport (CRL;** ☎02 71 25 12 11; www.charleroi-airport.com) is 46km outside the city, between Brussels and Charleroi, and services a number of European airlines, including **Ryanair.** From the airport, **Bus A** runs to the Charleroi-SUDT train station, where you can catch a train to Brussels. There is also a bus service which goes from the airport to Brussels's Gare du Midi (1hr., buy tickets on board).

Trains: (☎02 555 2555; www.sncb.be). All international trains stop at **Gare du Midi;** most also stop at **Gare Centrale** or **Gare du Nord.** Trains run to: **Amsterdam, NTH** (3hr.; €32, under 26 €24); **Antwerp** (45min., €6.10); **Bruges** (45min., €12); **Cologne, GER** (2hr.; €41, under 26 €29); **Liège** (1hr., €13); **Luxembourg City, LUX** (1hr., €28.80); **Paris, FRA** (1hr., €54). **Eurostar** goes to **London, BRI** (2hr., €79-224), with Eurail or Benelux pass from €75, under 26 from €60.

Public Transportation: The **Société des Transports Intercommunaux Bruxellois (STIB;** ☎090 01 03 10, €0.45 per min.; www.stib.irisnet.be) runs the **Métro (M), buses,** and **trams** daily from 5:30am-12:30am. 1hr. ticket €1.50, 1-day pass €4, 3-day pass €9, 5 trips €7, 10 trips €11.Check website for more info.

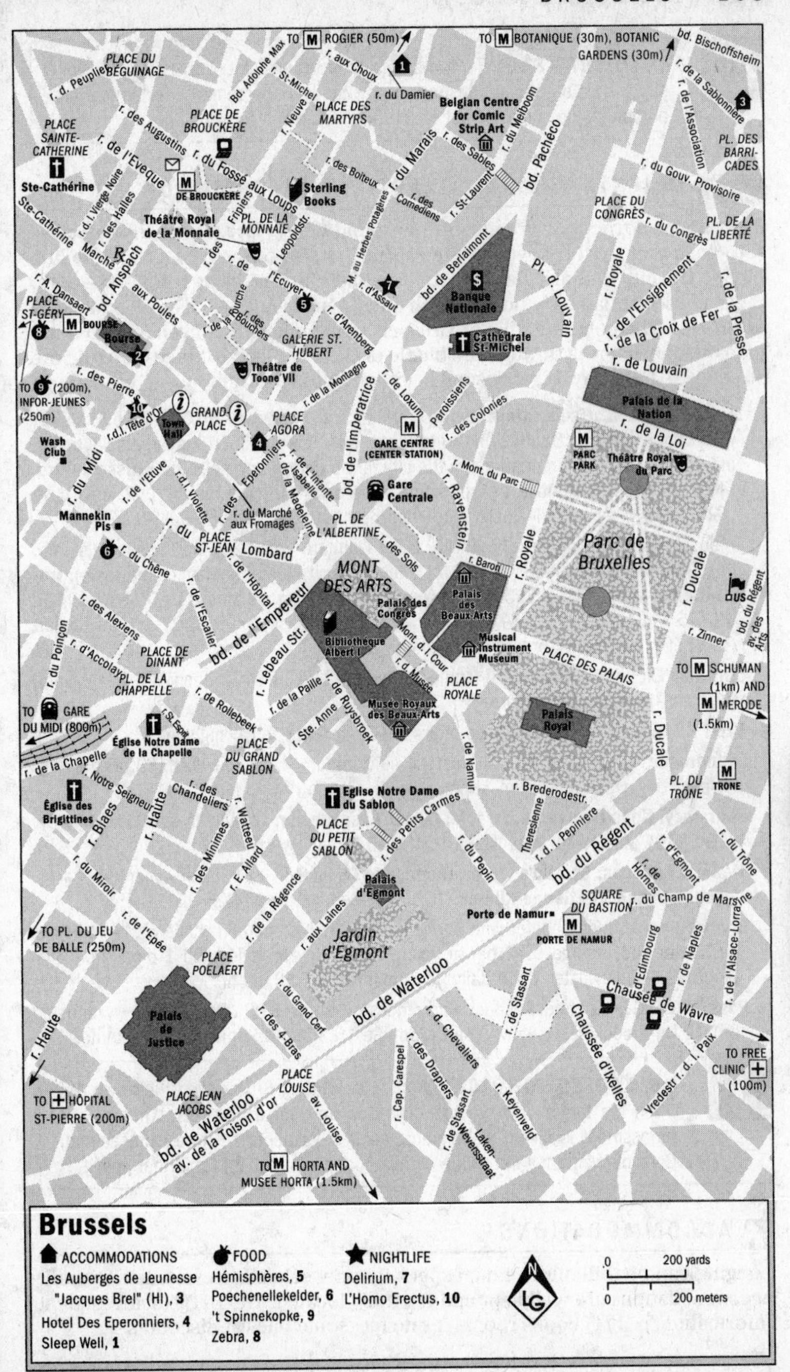
Brussels
ACCOMMODATIONS
Les Auberges de Jeunesse "Jacques Brel" (HI), 3
Hotel Des Eperonniers, 4
Sleep Well, 1
FOOD
Hémisphères, 5
Poechenellekelder, 6
't Spinnekopke, 9
Zebra, 8
NIGHTLIFE
Delirium, 7
L'Homo Erectus, 10
0 200 yards
0 200 meters
TO M ROGIER (50m)
TO M BOTANIQUE (30m), BOTANIC GARDENS (30m)
PLACE DU BÉGUINAGE
PLACE SAINTE-CATHERINE
Ste-Cathérine
PLACE DE BROUCKÈRE
DE BROUCKÈRE
PLACE DES MARTYRS
Belgian Centre for Comic Strip Art
Sterling Books
Théâtre Royal de la Monnaie
PL. DE LA MONNAIE
PLACE ST-GÉRY
BOURSE
Bourse
GALERIE ST. HUBERT
Théâtre de Toone VII
Banque Nationale
Cathédrale St-Michel
TO 9 (200m), INFOR-JEUNES (250m)
GRAND PLACE
Town Hall
PLACE AGORA
Wash Club
GARE CENTRE (CENTER STATION)
Gare Centrale
Mannekin Pis
PLACE ST-JEAN
PL. DE L'ALBERTINE
MONT DES ARTS
Palais des Congrès
Bibliothèque Albert I
Palais des Beaux-Arts
Musical Instrument Museum
Musée Royaux des Beaux-Arts
PLACE ROYALE
Palais de la Nation
PARC PARK
Théâtre Royal du Parc
Parc de Bruxelles
Palais Royal
PLACE DES PALAIS
US
TO M SCHUMAN (1km) AND M MERODE (1.5km)
PLACE DU CONGRÈS
PL. DE LA LIBERTÉ
PL. DES BARRICADES
PLACE DE DINANT
PL. DE LA CHAPPELLE
TO GARE DU MIDI (800m)
Église Notre Dame de la Chapelle
PLACE DU GRAND SABLON
Église des Brigittines
Eglise Notre Dame du Sabion
PLACE DU PETIT SABLON
Palais d'Egmont
Jardin d'Egmont
PL. DU TRÔNE
TRONE
SQUARE DU BASTION
Porte de Namur
PORTE DE NAMUR
TO PL. DU JEU DE BALLE (250m)
PLACE POELAERT
Palais de Justice
PLACE LOUISE
PLACE JEAN JACOBS
TO HÔPITAL ST-PIERRE (200m)
TO M HORTA AND MUSEE HORTA (1.5km)
TO FREE CLINIC (100m)
bd. Anspach
bd. de l'Empereur
bd. de l'Imperatrice
bd. de Berlaimont
bd. Pachéco
bd. du Régent
bd. de Waterloo
av. de la Toison d'or
av. Louise
r. Royale
r. Ducale
r. de la Loi
r. de Louvain
r. du Midi
r. Haute
r. Blaes
Chaussée de Wavre
Chaussée d'Ixelles

HOLD THAT STUB. Always hold on to your receipt or ticket stub to avoid steep fines on public transportation; although enforcement may appear lax, authorities do conduct spot checks and could charge you a fine.

ORIENTATION AND PRACTICAL INFORMATION

Most major attractions are clustered around **Grand-Place,** between the **Bourse** (Stock Market) to the west and the **Parc de Bruxelles** to the east. One **Métro** line circles the city and another bisects it, while efficient **trams** run north-south. Signs list street names in both French and Flemish; *Let's Go* lists all addresses in French. The concrete hills of Brussels make biking inconvenient, so don't plan on maneuvering through the bustle of the city by bike. Since cars rule the streets, the best way to get around is either by foot or tram.

Tourist Office: Brussels International Tourism and Congress (**BITC;** ☎02 513 8940; www.brures.com). M: Bourse. On Grand-Place in the Town Hall, BITC is the official tourist office. It books accommodations in the city for no charge and sells the **Brussels Card,** which provides free public transport and access to 30 museums for 1, 2, or 3 days (€20/28/33). Open daily Easter-Dec. 9am-6pm; Jan.-Easter M-Sa 9am-6pm.

Embassies and Consulates: Australia, 6-8 r. Guimard (☎02 286 0500; www.austemb.be). **Canada,** 2 av. Tervuren (☎02 741 0611; www.international.gc.ca/brussels). **Ireland,** 50 r. Wiertz (☎02 235 6676). **New Zealand,** 1 sq. de Meeus (☎02 512 1040). **UK,** 85 r. d'Arlon (☎02 287 6211; www.british-embassy.be). **US,** 27 bd. du Régent (☎02 508 2111; www.brussels.usembassy.gov).

Currency Exchange: Travelex, 4 Grand-Place (☎02 513 2845). Open M-F 10am-5pm, Sa 10am-7pm, Su 10am-4pm.

GLBT Resources: The tourist office offers the *Safer Guide* to gay nightlife.

Laundromat: Wash Club, 68 r. du Marché au Charbon. M: Bourse. Wash €3.50 per 8kg, €7 per 18kg. Open daily 7am-10pm.

Pharmacy: Neos-Bourse Pharmacie, 61 bd. Anspach at r. du Marché aux Poulets (☎02 218 0640). M: Bourse. Open M-Sa 8:30am-6:30pm.

Medical Services: St. Luc's, 10 av. Hippocrate (☎02 764 1111), convenient to Grand-Place. **Clinique St Etienne Kliniek,** 100 r. du Meridien (☎02 225 9111).

Internet: Some Internet cafes with phone booths can be found on ch. de Wavre. M: Porte de Namur. They charge €1-2 per hr. **Axen,** 179 r. Royale, is located 1 block from the Centre Van Gogh Hostel. Open daily 9am-midnight. €1.50 per hr.

Post Office: Corner of bd. Anspach and r. des Augustins (☎02 226 9700; www.laposte.be). M: De Brouckère. Open M-F 8am-7pm, Sa 10:30am-6:30pm. Poste Restante.

NO LADIES' CHOICE. Women navigating Brussels on their own are often the target of unwanted advances from male admirers. While sexual harassment is illegal in Belgium, isolated incidents are rarely prosecuted. Consider venturing out with a companion, and see p. 24 for further tips.

ACCOMMODATIONS

Lodging can be difficult to find, especially on weekends in summer. Overall, accommodations are well-kept and centrally located. The BITC (see Practical Information, p. 104) books rooms for no fee, sometimes at discounts.

Sleep Well, 23 r. du Damier (☎02 218 5050; www.sleepwell.be). M: Rogier. The bar, pool table, lounge, and colorful common spaces contribute to this accommodation's appeal. "Star" service is similar to staying in a hotel; visitors get rooms with private bath and TV, while "non-Star" service is like being in a hostel. Free storage is not locked. Laundry €2.50. Lockout for non-Star 11am-3pm. Non-star dorms €18-22.50; singles €29.50; doubles €54; triples €72. Star singles €42; doubles €60, triples €85. Varying discount after 1st night for all non-Star rooms except singles. MC/V. ❷

Les Auberges de Jeunesse "Jacques Brel" (HI), 30 r. de la Sablonnière (☎02 218 0187). M: Botanique. Spacious rooms surround a courtyard with a picturesque fountain. Breakfast and linens included. Bring lock for storage. Laundry €8. Free Internet 7pm-midnight. Reception 8am-1am. Lockout noon-3pm. Dorms €19-21; singles €34; doubles €52; triples and quads €63-84. €3 HI discount. MC/V. ❷

Hotel des Eperonniers, 1 r. des Eperonniers (☎02 513 5366). M: Gare Centrale. Choose between basic singles and spacious studios for up to 6 people. Just around the corner from Grand-Place. Prices vary depending on amenities. Breakfast €3.75. Reception 7am-midnight. Singles €27-57; doubles €45-73. AmEx/MC/V. ❹

FOOD

Inexpensive eateries cluster outside **Grand-Place.** Vendors along **Rue du Marché aux Fromages** to the south hawk cheap Greek and Middle Eastern food until late at night, while the smell of lobster and fresh seafood permeates the air on **Rue des Bouchers.** An **AD Delhaize** supermarket is on the corner of bd. Anspach and r. du Marché aux Poulets. (M: Bourse. Open M-Th and Sa 9am-8pm, F 9am-9pm, Su 9am-6pm.) **Grocery stores** are a great way to save while still getting quality Belgian treats like their famous chocolates and **waffles** (you can get about 10 for the price of one bought from vendors.)

Poechenellekelder, 5 r. du Chêne (☎02 511 9262). Across the street from *Manneken Pis*, enjoy a drink amid hanging marionettes in this tiny 3 story bar. Beer €1.90-8. Coffee (€2-6) is supplemented by a limited menu of *tartines* (open-faced sandwiches; €4-7) and pâté (€8). Open Tu-Su 11am-2am. Cash only. ❸

Hémisphères, 65 r. de l'Ecuyer (☎02 513 9370; www.hemispheres-resto.be). This restaurant, art gallery, and "intercultural space" serves Middle Eastern, Indian, and Asian fare. Delicious couscous with veggies or

WAFFLING THE ISSUE

At the base of the budget tour ist's food pyramid in Belgium lie an auspicious dietary group: th waffle (*gaufre* in French, *wafel* i Dutch). There are two types of Bel gian waffles, both made on such particular waffle irons that the can not be made well elsewhere.

Brussels waffles are flat an more or less rectangular. They'r light and airy, and bear som resemblance to ones eaten i the US (the kind served at dine brunches, not the ones tha emerge from the freezer, po out of the toaster, and beg to b drowned in high fructose cor syrup). Belgian recipes tend t use beaten egg whites and yeas as leavening agents, which giv them their light, crisp texture. **D Lièges** waffles, ubiquitous on Bel gian streets, are generally smalle sweeter, and denser than thei counterparts, and have a crunch caramelized-sugar crust.

Pause at a cafe for a Brussel waffle, and savor it with a knif and fork. Approach a street ven dor for a hand-held Liège waffl and continue to wander (in searc of your next waffle?). Both can b topped with chocolate, fruit, or ic cream, or dusted with powdere sugar. Waffles generally cost abou €1.50, though prices mount wit the toppings. Since you can't visi Belgium without sampling its waf fles, you might as well indulge!

meat (€11-15). Entrees €7-15. Concerts 1 Sa every month. Open M-F noon-3pm and 6-10:30pm, and Sa 6:30pm-late. MC/V. ❹

't Spinnekopke, 1 pl. du Jardin aux Fleurs (☎02 511 8695). M: Bourse. Locals "inside the spider's head" savor the authentically Belgian menu on the cozy yet elegant seating tucked away near a small square with a fountain. Entrees €15-25. Open M-F noon-3pm, 6pm-midnight, Sa 6pm-midnight. Kitchen closes at 11pm. AmEx/MC/V. ❺

Zebra, 31 pl. St-Géry. (☎02 513 5116). M: Bourse. Known for its mixed drinks, this centrally located cafe and bar also serves juices, milkshakes, and filling, light sandwiches (€3), salads (€6.50), and soups (€3.50). Open M-Th and Su 11:45am-1am, F-Sa 11:45am-2am. Kitchen closes at 11pm. MC/V. ❶

SIGHTS

GRAND-PLACE AND ENVIRONS. Three blocks behind the town hall, on the corner of r. de l'Étuve and r. du Chêne, is Brussels's most giggled-at sight, the **Mannekin Pis,** a tiny fountain shaped like a boy who seems to be peeing continuously. Legend claims it commemorates a young Belgian who defused a bomb destined for the Grand-Place. In reality, the fountain was installed to supply the neighborhood with water during the reign of Albert and Isabelle. Locals have created hundreds of outfits for him, each with a strategically placed hole. To even the gender gap, a statue of a squatting girl *(Jeanneken)* now pees down an alley off r. des Bouchers. Victor Hugo once called the statued and gilded Grand-Place "the most beautiful square in the world." During the day, be sure to visit **La Maison du Roi** (King's House), now the city museum whose most riveting exhibit is the collection of clothes worn by *Mannekin Pis*, and the town hall where 40min. guided tours reveal over-the-top decorations and an impressive collection of paintings. *(La Maison du Roi ☎02 279 4350. Open Tu-Su 10am-5pm. €3. Town Hall ☎02 548 0445. English-language tours Tu-W 3:15pm, Su 10:45am and 12:15pm; arrive early. €3, students €2.50.)* Nearby, the **Museum of Cocoa and Chocolate** tells of Belgium's other renowned edible export. Cacao fruits grow on display and the smell of chocolate permeates the air. *(11 r. de la Tête d'Or. ☎02 514 2048; www.mucc.be. Open July-Aug. and holidays daily 10am-4:30pm; Sept.-June Tu-Su 10am-4:30pm. €5, students €4.)* In the skylit **Galeries Royals St-Hubert arcade,** one block behind Grand-Place, a long covered walkway is lined with wide-ranging shops ranging shops.

MONT DES ARTS. The **Musées Royaux des Beaux-Arts** encompass the **Musée d'Art Ancien,** the **Musée d'Art Moderne,** several contemporary exhibits, and the **Musée Magritte.** The museums steward a huge collection of Belgian art, including Bruegel's famous *Landscape with the Fall of Icarus*, pieces by Rubens, and Brussels native René Magritte. Other masterpieces on display include David's *Death of Marat.* The great hall is itself a work of architectural beauty; the panoramic view of Brussels from the fourth floor of the 19th-century wing alone justifies the admission fee. *(3 r. de la Régence. M: Parc. ☎02 508 3211; www.fine-arts-museum.be. Open Tu-Su 10am-5pm. Some wings close noon-2pm. €9, students €3.50. 1st W of each month 1-5pm free. Audio tour €2.50.)* The **Musical Instrument Museum (MIM)** houses over 1500 instruments; stand in front of one and your headphones automatically play a sample of its music. *(2 r. Montagne de la Cour. ☎02 545 0130; www.mim.fgov.be. Open Tu-F 9:30am-4:45pm, Sa-Su 10am-5pm. €5, students €4. 1st W of each month 1-5pm free.)*

BELGIAN CENTER FOR COMIC STRIP ART. Comic strips *(les BD)* are serious business in Belgium. Today, a restored warehouse designed by famous architect Victor Horta pays tribute to what Belgians call the Ninth Art. Tintin and the Smurfs make several appearances, and displays document comic strip history. *(☎02 214 0140. R. des Sables. M: Rogier. Open Tu-Su 10am-6pm; students with ISIC €6.)*

ENTERTAINMENT AND NIGHTLIFE

The weekly *What's On*, part of the *Bulletin* newspaper and available free at the tourist office, contains info on cultural events. The **Théâtre Royal de la Monnaie,** on pl. de la Monnaie, is renowned for its opera and ballet. (M: De Brouckère. ☎02 229 1200, box office ☎02 70 39 39; www.lamonnaie.be. Tickets from €8, half-price tickets go on sale 20min. prior to the event.) The **Théâtre Royal de Toone VII,** 66 r. du Marché-aux-herbes, stages marionette performances, a distinctly Belgian art form. *(*☎02 513 5486; www.toone.be for show times and prices. F 8:30pm, Sa 4pm and 8:30pm; occasionally Tu-Th. €10, students €7.) On summer nights, live concerts on Grand-Place and the Bourse bring the streets to life. The *All the Fun* pamphlet, available at the tourist office, lists the newest clubs and bars. On **Place St-Géry,** patios are jammed with a laid-back crowd of students and backpackers. Choose from over 2000 beers at carefree **Delirium,** 4A impasse de la Fidélité. (☎02 251 4434; www.deliriumcafe.be. Jam session Th and Su 11pm. Open daily 10am-4am.) **GBLT nightlife** in Brussels primarily centers on r. des Pierres and r. du Marché au Charbon, next to Grand-Place. **L'Homo Erectus,** 57 r. des Pierres, is an extremely popular destination. (☎02 514 7493; www.lhomoerectus.com. Open daily 3pm-3am.)

DAYTRIP FROM BRUSSELS

MECHELEN (MALINES). Feel as if you are in a fairy tale amidst the potted flowers, old buildings, and impeccably clean streets in the tiny town of Mechelen (ME-kel-en). The residents (pop. 78,000) are nicknamed the "Moon Extinguishers" for once mistaking fog and a red moon for a fire in the tower of **St-Rombouts Tower and Cathedral.** Today, the tower holds two 49-bell carillons and is home to the world's foremost bell-ringing school. *(☎02 20 47 92; www.beiaardschool.be.)* A 1-2hr. **Cathedral tour** departs from the tourist office and heads up the 513 steps to the top to see the church's bells and an amazing view of the surrounding area. *(Tours Easter-Sept. Sa-Su 2:15pm, July-Aug. daily 2:15pm. €5.)* To reach St-Rombouts from Centraal station, walk down Hendrick Consciencestr., which becomes Graaf van Egmonstr., then Brul, to the pedestrian Grote Markt. *(Cathedral open daily Easter-Oct. 8:30am-5:30pm; Nov.-Easter 8:30am-4:30pm.)* Nearby, the 15th-century **St. John's Church** boasts Rubens' magnificent triptych *The Adoration of the Magi.* From the Grote Markt, walk down Fr. de Merodestr. and turn left onto St-Janstr. *(Open Tu-Su Easter-Oct. 1:30-5:30pm; Nov.-Easter 1:30-4:30pm.)* Just off Grote Markt is **Adagio ❸,** 16 Ijzerenleen, a cheaper alternative to Markt cafes. *(☎02 20 88 17. Entrees €7-12 Open M, Th-F 10am-10pm, Sa 8am-10pm, Su noon-10pm. AmEx/MC/V.)* **Trains** head to Antwerp (20min., 4 per hr., €3.70) and Brussels (20min., 4-5 per hr., €3.70). The **tourist office,** 2-6 Hallestr., is in the Grote Markt. *(☎070 22 28 00; www.inenuitmechelen.be. Open Apr.-Sept. M-F 9:30am-5:30pm, Sa-Su 10am-4:30pm; Oct.-Mar. M-F 9:30am-4:30pm, Sa-Su 10:30am-3:30pm.)*

BELGIUM

FLANDERS (VLAANDEREN)

BRUGES (BRUGGE) ☎050

Bruges (pop. 117,000) is arguably Belgium's most romantic city. Canals carve their way through rows of pointed brick houses and cobblestone streets en route to the breathtaking Gothic Markt. The city's buildings remain some of the best-preserved examples of Northern Renaissance architecture. Though a bit crowded, Bruges is a relaxing getaway to catch your breath.

TRANSPORTATION

Trains leave from the **Stationsplein,** a 10min. walk south of the city. (Open daily 4:30am-11pm. Info desk open daily 8am-7pm.) Trains head to: Antwerp (1hr., 2 per hr., €13); Brussels (1hr., 1-3 per hr., €12); Ghent (20min., 3 per hr., €5.60); Knokke (30min., 2 per hr., €3); Ostend (15min., 3 per hr., €3.30).

ORIENTATION AND PRACTICAL INFORMATION

Bruges is enclosed by a circular canal, with the train station, Stationsplein, just beyond its southern extreme. The historic district is entirely accessible by foot, while bikes are popular for countryside visits. The dizzying **Belfort** looms high over the center of town, presiding over the handsome **Markt.** On the easternmost edge of the city, the beautiful, windmill-lined **Kruisvestraat** and serene **Minnewater Park** have stretches of gorgeous green land, ideal for picnicking.

Tourist Office: In and Uit, 't Zand 34 (☎050 44 46 46; www.brugge.be). From the train station, head left to 't Zand and walk for 10min.; it's in the red concert hall. Books rooms for a €2.50 fee and €20 deposit, and sells **maps** (€0.50) and **info guides** for €1. (Open M-W and F-Su 10am-6pm, Th 10am-8pm).

Currency Exchange: Goffin, Steenstraat 2, is near the Markt and charges no commission on cash exchange (☎050 34 04 71.) Open M-Sa 9am-5:30pm.

Luggage Storage: At the train station. €2.60-3.60.

Laundromat: Belfort, Ezelstr. 51. Wash €3-6, dry €1. Open daily 7am-10pm.

Bike Rental: At the train station (☎050 30 23 28). Passport required. €6.50 per day.

Police: Hauwerstr. 7 (☎050 44 89 30).

Hospitals: A. Z. St-Jan (☎050 45 21 11; not Oud St-Janshospitaal, a museum). **St-Lucas** (☎050 36 91 11). **St-Franciscus Xaveriuskliniek** (☎050 47 04 70).

Internet: Teleboutique Brugge, Predikherenstr. 48, is one of the cheapest options. €2 per hour. Open daily 10am-10pm. Cash only.

Post Office: Markt 5. Open M and W-F 9am-6pm, Sa 9:30am-12:30pm.

ACCOMMODATIONS

Snuffel Backpacker Hostel, Ezelstr. 47-49 (☎050 33 31 33; www.snuffel.be). Take bus #3 or 13 (€1.30) from the station to the stop after Markt, then take the 1st left. Colorful rooms decorated by local artists. On-site bar Happy hour (9-10pm, beer €1) is a favorite among locals. Guests also get a free Bruges card, which gives access to museums and offers many discounts. Kitchen. Bike rental €6 per day. Breakfast €3. Lockers available; bring lock or rent one. Linens included. Free Wi-Fi. Key deposit €5. Reception 7:30am-midnight. Dorms €14; doubles €36; quads €60-64. AmEx/MC/V. ❷

Passage, Dweersstr. 26 (☎050 34 02 32; www.passagebruges.com). Old-world, refined hostel-hotel-cafe in an ideal location. Safes available. Breakfast €5; included in private rooms. Free beer at bar with purchase of dinner. Internet €4 per hr. Reception 9am-11pm; need code to get in after close. Open mid-Feb. to mid-Jan. Dorms €14; singles €25-45; doubles €45-60; triples and quads €75-90. AmEx/MC/V. ❷

Bauhaus International Youth Hostel and Hotel, Langestr. 133-137 (☎500 34 10 93; www.bauhaus.be). Take bus #6 or 16 from the station; ask to stop at the hostel. A giant candelabra and popular bar lead the way to airy rooms. Bike rental €9 per day. Break-

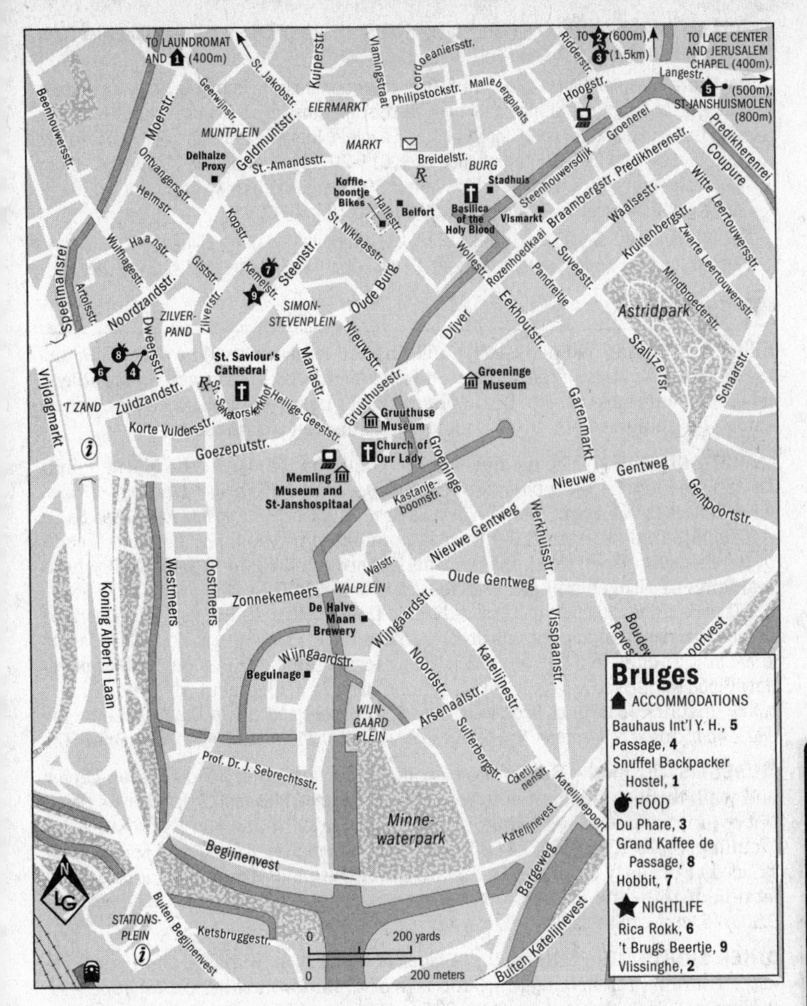

fast and linens included. Lockers €1.50. Internet €3 per hr. Reception 8am-midnight. Dorms €14-15; singles from €26; doubles from €40; triples from €57. AmEx/MC/V. ❷

FOOD

Inexpensive restaurants can be hard to find in Bruges. Seafood lovers should splurge at least once on the city's famous *mosselen* (mussels; €15-22) found at the **Vismarkt,** near the Burg. (Open Tu-Sa 8am-1pm.) Restaurants close early in Bruges (around 10pm); grab groceries at **Delhaize Proxy,** Noordzandstr. 4, near the Markt. (Open M-Sa 9am-7pm.)

Grand Kaffee de Passage, Dweersstr. 26-28 (☎050 34 02 32). Next to the Passage hostel. Traditional Belgian cuisine in a candlelit setting. Try the excellent Flemish stew

(€11). Desserts are cheap and tasty (€2-5). Entrees €8-15. Open daily 5-11pm. Closed from mid-Jan. to mid-Feb. AmEx/MC/V. ❸

Du Phare, Sasplein 2 (☎050 34 35 90; www.duphare.be). From the Burg, walk down Hoogstr. and turn left at the canal onto Verversdijk, crossing to the right side at the second bridge. Follow the canal for 20min. to Sasplein. Bus #4 stops right outside. This jazz and blues bistro serves international fare (€11-20). Open M and W 11:30am-2:30pm and 7pm-midnight, Tu and F-Sa 11:30am-2:30pm and 6:30pm-midnight, Su 11:30am-midnight. Reservations recommended F-Sa. AmEx/MC/V. ❸

Hobbit, Kemelstr. 8-10 (☎050 33 55 20; www.hobbitgrill.be). Try filling meats and pastas off funny newsprint menus. Entrees €7-11. Open daily 6pm-1am. AmEx/MC/V. ❷

SIGHTS

Filled with Gothic and neo-Gothic buildings and crisscrossed by canals, picturesque Bruges is best experienced on foot. Avoid visiting Bruges on Mondays, when museums are closed. If you plan to visit many museums, consider a cost-saving combination ticket (€15, includes admission to 5 museums).

MARKT AND BURG. The medieval **Belfort** (belfry) looms over the Markt; climb its 366 steep steps for a city view. *(Belfort open Tu-Su 9:30am-5pm. Last entry 4:15pm. €5. Bell concerts mid-June to Sept. M, W, and Sa 9pm, Su 2:15pm; Oct. to mid-June W and Sa-Su 2:15pm.)* Behind the Markt, the Burg is dominated by the finely detailed facade of the **Stadhuis** (Town Hall). Inside, wander through the gilded **Gothic Hall,** where residents of Bruges still get married. *(☎050 44 81 10. Open Tu-Su 9:30am-4:30pm. €2.50, under 26 €1.50. Audio tour included.)* This ticket will also get you into **Liberty of Bruges Museum,** which contains an ornate fireplace. *(Open M-Sa 9:30am-12:30pm and 1:30-5pm).* Tucked in a corner of the Burg next to the Stadhuis, the **Basilica of the Holy Blood** supposedly holds the blood of Christ in a spectacularly ornate sanctuary upstairs. *(Basilica open daily Apr.-Sept. 9:30am-noon and 2-6pm; Oct.-Mar. 10am-noon and 2-4pm; closed W afternoon. Holy Relic can be viewed at 11am and 2-4pm. Museum €1.50.)*

MUSEUMS. From the Burg, follow Wollestr. left and then head right on Dijver and walk through the garden to reach the **Groeninge Museum,** small for its price but overflowing with beautiful portraits and works by Jan van Eyck and Hans Memling. *(Dijver 12. ☎050 50 44 87. Open Tu-Su 9:30am-5pm. €8, under 26 €6. Audio tour included.)* Formerly a palace, the nearby **Gruuthuse Museum** houses a large collection of 16th- and 17th-century tapestries. *(Dijver 17. ☎050 44 87 62. Open Tu-Su 9:30am-5pm. €6, students €4. Audio tour included.)*

BELGIUM

OTHER SIGHTS. The 14th-century **Church of Our Lady,** at Mariastr. and Gruuthusestr., contains Michelangelo's famous work, *Madonna and Child. (Open Tu-F 9:30am-5pm, Sa 9:30am-4:45pm, Su 12:30-5pm; last entry 4:30pm. Church free. Tomb viewing €2.50, students €1.50. Ticket for the tomb included in Gruuthuse Museum ticket.)* Sophisticated beer aficionados will enjoy the accompanying samples at 150-year-old **De Halve Maan,** a beer museum and brewery. *(Welplein 26. ☎50 33 26 97; www.halvemaan.be. 45min. tours Apr.-Sept. 1 per hr. M-F 11am-4pm, Sa-Su 11am-5pm; Oct.-Mar. tours M-F 11am and 3pm, Sa-Su 1 per hr. 11am-4pm. €5, includes beer.)* For God-sanctioned fun, wander the grounds of the **Beguinage,** home to nuns who share their flower-covered yard with passersby. The Beguine's house displays furnishings typical of medieval Flemish households. *(From Simon Stevinplein, follow Mariastr., and turn right on Wijngaardstr.; at the canal, turn right and cross the footbridge. ☎050 33 00 11. Open Mar.-Nov. daily 10am-noon and 1:45-5pm; gate open 6:30am-6:30pm. Church and garden free; house €2, under 26 €1.)* Walk along the river to see the windmills; to enter, go down to 235-year-old windmill **St-Janshuismolen,** which still gives occasional flour-grinding demonstrations in summer when the wind is right. *(☎050 33 00 44. Open May-Sept. daily 9:30am-12:30pm and 1:30-5pm. €2, under 26 €1.)*

FESTIVALS AND NIGHTLIFE

Bruges plays host to the **Cactusfestival** (☎050 33 20 14; www.cactusfestival.be. €25 per day, €63 for 3 days), a series of alt-pop and hip-hop concerts the first full weekend in July. The city also sponsors **Klinkers,** an open-air music and film series that's free to the public during the months of July and August (☎50 33 20 14; www.klinkers-brugge.be).

At **'t Brugs Beertje,** Kemelstr. 5, off Steenstr., you can sample some of the 250 varieties of beer. (☎050 33 96 16. Open M, Th and Su 4pm-12:30am, F-Sa 4pm-2am.) Stop by Bruges's oldest pub, **Vlissinghe,** Blekersstr. 2, established in 1515. From the Burg, take Hoogstr. and turn left onto Verversdijk immediately before the canal. Cross the second bridge onto Blekersstr. (☎050 34 37 37. Open W-Sa 11am-midnight, Su 11am-7pm.) Steer clear of the pricey tourist-trap clubs behind the Markt. Belgian students tend to prefer the dance floor of **Rica Rokk,** 't Zand 6, where shots are €3 and a liter of beer starts at €19. (☎050 33 24 34; www.maricarokk.com. Open daily 9:30am-5am.) The tourist office has a limited list of **GLBT establishments.**

THE LONG ARM OF THE LAW. If you're wobbling back to your hostel with a bellyful of beer, think twice before yielding to nature's call en route. Police will fine you up to €152 if they catch you urinating in public. Keep €0.30 handy for the public toilets; many of these stalls close at 8pm.

ANTWERP (ANTWERPEN, ANVERS) ☎03

While Antwerp (pop. 466,000) was once known for its avant-garde fashion and jet-setting party hoppers, the hipster scene has since calmed down. But an afternoon of window-shopping in the city's diamond quarter or along the Meir reveals that Antwerp still holds an attraction for the backpaper fashionista.

TRANSPORTATION AND PRACTICAL INFORMATION. Antwerp has two train stations: **Berchem,** which handles most of the city's international traffic, and **Centraal,** the domestic-centered station. **Trains** leave from Berchem to: Amsterdam, NTH (2hr., 1 per hr., €21-29); Brussels (45min., 4 per hr., €6.10); and Rotterdam, NTH (1hr., 1 per hr., €13-18). Centraal ticket office is open daily 6am-10pm. Lockers are available in Centraal. The **tourist office** is downstairs. To reach Grote Markt from Berchem, take tram #8 (€1.20, €1.50 on board) to Groenpl. From Centraal take tram #2 (dir.: Linkeroever) or walk down Meir, the main pedestrian thoroughfare, to Groenpl. (☎03 232 0103. Open M-Sa 9am-5:45pm, Su 9am-4:45pm. English-language historical tour from Grote Markt 13 Sa-Su 11am. €5.) **Postal Code:** 2000.

ACCOMMODATIONS AND FOOD. The well-worn **New International Youth Hotel ❷,** Provinciestr. 256, is a 10min. walk from Centraal Station, on the corner of De Boeystr. and Provinciestr. Turn left out of the station onto Pelikaanstr., which becomes Simonsstr.; turn left Van Den Nestlei, walk under the bridge, then turn right onto De Boeystr. (☎03 230 0522; www.youthhotel.be. Breakfast included. Reception 8am-midnight. Dorms €19-21, under 26 with sleeping bag €15; singles €34; doubles €49-61; triples €70-79. MC/V.) Take the metro to Groenpl. for **Guesthouse 26 ❺,** Pelgrimsstr. 26, in the heart of the city. Inventive

BELGIUM

decor keeps guests returning. (☎03 289 3995; www.guesthouse26.be. Breakfast included. Reserve ahead. Singles €55-75; doubles €65-85. AmEx/MC/V.)

More than 400 religious figurines accompany your meal at **'t Elfde Gebod ❹**, Torfburg 10. (☎03 289 3466 Entrees €8-20. Open daily noon-2am. Kitchen open noon-10:30pm. MC/V.) **Da Giovanni ❷**, Jan Blomstr. 8, off Groenpl., serves hearty pizzas (€4-10) bringing Italy to Belgium with a traditional, rich decor of wine bottles and grapes hanging from the ceiling. (☎03 226 7450; www.dagiovanni.be. Pasta €7-13. Meat Entrees €13-18. Fish €13-20. Open daily 11am-midnight. 20% student discount. AmEx/MC/V.)

SIGHTS AND NIGHTLIFE. The main promenades, **De Keyserlei** and the **Meir,** draw crowds to their elegant department stores and avant-garde boutiques. On the western edge of the district, the **Cathedral of Our Lady,** Groenpl. 21, holds Rubens's *Descent from the Cross.* (www.dekathedraal.be. Open M-F 10am-5pm, Sa 10am-3pm, Su 1-4pm. Tours 1-3 per day. English tours at 3:45pm. €4, students €2, seniors and children €1.50.) A stroll by the Schelde River leads to the 13th-century **Steen Castle,** Steenplein 1. The **Museum Voor Schone Kunsten** (KMSKA; Royal Museum of Fine Arts), Leopold De Waelpl. 1-9, possesses one of the world's finest collections of Flemish paintings. (☎03 238 7809; www.kmska.be. Open Tu-Sa 10am-5pm, Su 10am-6pm. €6, under 19 free.)

Café d'Anvers, Verversrui 15, north of Grote Markt, used to be an old church but is now a palatial club located smack in the center of the red-light district. (☎03 226 3870; www.cafe-d-anvers.com. Cover: Th free; F €5, €8 after midnight; Sa free, €10 after midnight. Open Th 11pm-6am, F-Sa 11pm-7:30am). Bars behind the cathedral and in the trendy neighborhood around the Royal Museum of Fine Arts offer an alternative to the club scene. Step into the 15th-century cellars for a candlelit dinner at **Pelgrom,** Pelgrimstr. 15, before sampling the local *elixir d'Anvers* (strong herbal liqueur; €5) doled out by bartenders in traditional dress. (☎03 234 0809. Open daily noon-late.) **Gay nightlife** clusters around **Van Schoonhovenstraat,** north of Centraal Station. Head to the **Gay and Lesbian Center,** Dambruggestr. 204, for more info.

GHENT (GENT) ☎09

Once the heart of Flanders's textile industry, modern Ghent (pop. 233,000) still celebrates the memory of its medieval greatness, and its more recent industrial past, with awe-inspiring buildings in the city's main square. Ghent has yet to become a major tourist destination, so enjoy making new discoveries and blending in with locals on your trip.

TRANSPORTATION AND PRACTICAL INFORMATION. **Trains** run from St-Pietersstation (accessible by tram #1) to Antwerp (50min., 3per hr., €8.20), Bruges (25min., 3 per hr., €8), and Brussels (35min., 5 per hr., €7.40). The **tourist office,** Botermarkt 17A, in the crypt of the belfry, books rooms for no fee and leads walking tours. (☎09 266 5232; www.visitgent.be. Open daily Apr.-Oct. 9:30am-6:30pm; Nov.-Mar. 9:30am-4:30pm. Tours Nov.-Apr. daily 2:30pm; buy tickets by 2pm. €7.) The tourist office and most museums sell a pass for 15 museums and monuments in Ghent (€12.50). A great resource for young, budget-conscious backpackers, **Use-It,** St-Pietersnieuwstr. 21, has quirky **maps** for self-guided tours, free **Internet,** and free toilets. Search their website of rooms in town. (☎09 324 3906; www.use-it.be. Open M-F 1-6pm.) **Postal Code:** 9000.

ACCOMMODATIONS AND FOOD. If you must spend the night on a budget in Ghent, try **De Draecke (HI) ❷**, St-Widostr. 11. From the station, take tram

#1 (€1.20, €1.50 on board) to Gravensteen (15min.) Facing the castle, head left over the canal, then right on Gewad and right on St-Widostr. (☎09 233 7050; www.vjh.be. Breakfast and linens included. Internet €2 per 30min. Reception 7:30am-11pm. Dorms €20; doubles €50. €3 HI discount. AmEx/MC/V.) To get to **Camping Blaarmeersen ❶,** Zuiderlaan 12, take bus #9 from St-Pietersstation toward Mariakerke and to Europabrug (Watersportbaan); cross the street and hop on bus #38 or 39 to Blaarmeersen. Take the first street on the left to its end. (☎09 266 8160. Laundry restaurant. Open Mar. to mid-Oct. €4.50 per person, €4.50 per tent; low season €3.50/3.50.)

St-Pietersnieuwstraat, by the university, has cheap kebab and pita joints that stay open until around midnight. **Magazijn ❷,** Penitentenstr. 24, has filling fare (€8.50-16) and vegetarian options. (☎09 234 0708. Kitchen open Tu-F noon-2pm and 6-11pm, Sa 6-11pm. Bar open late. Cash only.) For groceries, stop by the **Contact GB** at Hoogpoort 42. (☎09 225 0592. Open M-Sa 8:30am-6pm. MC/V.)

SIGHTS. The **Leie canal** runs through the city and wraps around the **Gravensteen** (Castle of Counts), St-Veerlepl. 11, a partially restored medieval fortress. (☎09 225 9306. Open daily Apr.-Sept. 9am-6pm; Oct.-Mar. 9am-5pm. €6, under 26 €1.20.) Nearby is the historic **Partershol quarter,** with well-preserved 16th- to 18th-century houses. From Gravensteen, head down Geldmunt, make a right on Lange Steenst., and then turn right into the Old Town. From the Partershol, follow the river toward Groenten Markt and Korenmarkt. Walk across **St-Michielshelling** bridge for the best view of Ghent's skyline. From here, walk north on either of the two bridges, where you can take a 40min. boat tour (Mar.-Nov. 4 per hr., €5.50, students and over 60 €5, children €3). St-Michielshelling connects two majestic cathedrals. Facing the bridge with Graslei behind you, **St-Niklaaskerk** is on your right. The cathedral's unique interior is a true testament to the rich merchants who worshipped here from the 13th to the 15th centuries. (☎09 225 3700. Open M 2:30-5pm, Tu-Su 10am-5pm. Free.) On the left, on Limburgstr., the elaborately decorated **St-Baafskathedraal** holds Flemish brothers Hubert and Jan van Eyck's *Adoration of the Mystic Lamb* and Rubens's *St. Bavo's Entrance into the Monastery of Ghent.* (www.sintbaafskathedraal-gent.be. Cathedral and crypt open daily Apr.-Oct. 8:30am-6pm; Nov.-Mar. 8:30am-5pm. *The Ghent Alterpiece* exhibit open Apr.-Oct. M-Sa 9:30am-5pm, Su 1-5pm; Nov.-Mar. M-Sa 10:30am-4pm, Su 1-4pm. Cathedral and crypt free. The Ghent Alterpiece exhibit €3.) **Stedelijk Museum voor Actuele Kunst (SMAK),** in Citadel Park, a 30min. walk from the tourist office or a shorter ride on the #1 tram from Korenmarkt (dir.: Flanders Expo; €1.20, €1.50 on tram), regularly rotates its collection of cutting-edge modern art. (☎09 221 1703; www.smak.be. Open Tu-Su 10am-6pm. €5, students €3.80; free 1st F of each month 6-10pm.)

NIGHTLIFE AND FESTIVALS. **Korenmarkt** and **Vrijdagmarkt** are filled with restaurants and pubs. *Use-It's* (p. 112) guide to nightlife can direct you to live music options. One popular haunt is the dimly lit **Charlatan,** Vlasmarkt 6, which features a nightly DJ. (☎09 224 2457; www.charlatan.be. Live bands Th and Su. Open Tu-Su 7pm-late.) For **GLBT nightlife,** consult *Use-It's Ghent Gay Map* or head to the **Foyer Casa Rosa,** Kammerstr. 22/Belfortstr. 39, an info center and bar. (☎09 269 2812; www.casarosa.be. Bar open M-F 3pm-1am, Sa-Su 3pm-2am; info center open M 6-9pm, W 3-9pm, Sa 3-6pm.) The **Gentse Feesten** brings performers, carnival rides, and flowing *jenever* (flavored gin) to the city center. (Mid-July. ☎09 269 4600; www.gentsefeesten.be.)

YPRES (IEPER) ☎057

Famous for its fields of poppies and lined with tombstones of fallen soldiers, Ypres (EE-pruh; pop. 35,000) and its environs continue to bear witness to the city's role in WWI. It was here that the Germans realized that their anticipated quick victory would instead become an entrenched and bitter stalemate. Once a medieval textile center, Ypres was completely destroyed by four years of combat but was impressively rebuilt as a near-perfect replica of its former self. Today, the town is surrounded by over 150 **British cemeteries** and filled with memorial sites. The **In Flanders Field Museum,** Grote Markt 34, documents the gruesome history of the Great War. (☎057 23 92 20; www.inflandersfields.be. Open daily Apr.-Nov. 15 10am-6pm, last entry 5pm; Nov. 16.-Mar. Tu-Su 10am-5pm. €8. MC/V.) Behind the museum is **St. Martin's Cathedral,** rebuilt using pre-war plans and ornamented with a rose window given to Belgium by the British military. The cathedral itself is a testament to living history, with photographs on the altar that show the destruction of the church. (☎057 20 80 04. Open daily 9am-noon and 2-6pm. Free.) Across the Markt, the names of 54,896 of the 100,000 British soldiers whose bodies were never found are inscribed on the **Menin Gate.** Every night at 8pm, the **Last Post** bugle ceremony honors those who defended Ypres (www.lastpost.be). With Menin Gate behind you, go right and take the **Rose Coombs Walk** to visit **Ramparts Cemetery,** where tombstones line the river. **Bike** the 3-4km journey to the first cemetery or make a daytrip to the battlefields nearly 40km ride out of town.

B&Bs are the cheapest accommodations in Ypres; call ahead to ask about availability and arrival times. The old but comfortable **B&B Zonneweelde ❸,** Masscheleinlann 18, has TVs in every room and is only a 5min. walk from Grote Markt. (☎057 20 27 23. Singles €25; doubles €50; triples €75.) The quiet **B&B Nooit Gedacht ❸,** Ligywijk 129, is also a good bet. (☎057 20 84 00; www.nooit-gedacht-ieper.tk. Breakfast included. Free Internet. Singles €30; doubles €50; triples €70. Cash only.) Restaurants line the Grote Markt; the crowded **Au Miroir ❷,** Grote Markt 12, is a satisfactory option. (☎057 20 47 88. Entrees €6-20. Open daily 10am-midnight. AmEx/MC/V.)

Trains run to Bruges (2hr., 1 per hr., €11), Brussels (1hr., 1 per hr., €16), and Ghent (1hr., 1 per hr., €10). The **tourist office,** Grote Markt 34, is inside Cloth Hall; with the station behind you, head down Stationsstr., turn left on Tempelstr., then right on Boterstr. (☎057 23 92 20; www.ieper.be. Open Apr.-Sept. M-Sa 9am-6pm, Su 10am-6pm; Oct.-Mar. daily 9am-5pm.) **Postal Code:** 8900.

WALLONIE

LIÈGE (LUIK) ☎04

Located in the valley of the Maas River, Liège (lee-AJH; pop. 200,000), the largest city in Wallonie, is often dismissed as a mere transportation hub. However, its cutting-edge art scene and night-owl student hangouts temper the city's industrial character. By the river, you'll find the **Musée de L'Art Wallon,** 86 Féronstrée, a collection of Belgian art dating back to the Renaissance. (☎04 221 9231; www.museeartwallon.be. Open Tu-Sa 1-6pm, Su 11am-4:30pm. €5, students €3.) Turn onto r. de Bueren and climb (over 400 steps) to the **Montagne de Bueren** for an expansive view of the city. Take a right and climb a few more steps to find the peaceful gardens of the **Coteaux de la Citadelle.** From Féronstrée, turn left onto r. Léopold and right onto r. de la Cathédrale; after 10min. you will reach the Gothic naves and sparkling gold treasure of the **Cathédrale de St-Paul.** (☎04

232 6131. Cathedral open daily 8am-5pm. Treasure room open Tu-Su 2-5pm. Tour 3pm. Cathedral free. Treasure room €4, students €2.50.) In between the banks of the river, a large island makes up the working-class neighborhood of Outremeuse, which is home to the **Musée d'Art Moderne et d'Art Contemporain (MAMAC),** 3 Parc de la Boverie. The beautiful building and surrounding park are 20min. across the river and to the right from the Coeur Historique and St. Paul's. Take bus #17 (€1.30) to reach MAMAC from the station. (☎04 343 0403; www.mamac.be. Open Tu-Sa 1-6pm, Su 11am-4 :30pm. €5, students €3.) At night, students from the University of Liège pack **Le Carré,** a pedestrian area with narrow, bar-lined streets bisected by r. du Pot-d'Or.

To reach the commercial yet comfortable **Auberge Georges Simenon de Jeunesse de Liège (HI) ❷,** 2 r. Georges Simenon, walk across the Pont des Arches from the Coeur Historique, or take bus #4 and ask to get off at Auberge Simenon. (☎04 344 5689. Breakfast and linens included. Bikes €6 per day. Internet €0.60 per 15min. Reception M-Sa 7:30am-1am, Su 7:30am-11pm. Lockout 10am-3pm. Dorms €20; singles €32; doubles €48. €3 HI discount. MC/V.) Parallel to Féronstrée is **Hors Château,** a street lined with beautifully restored restaurants, cafes, and bars. **Newave à la Passerelle ❷,** 13 bd. Saucy, serves big paninis (€3.20-3.50) and couscous (€6-16) to a hungry crowd. (☎04 341 1566. Open Tu-Su noon-10pm. Cash only.) Down the road, **Chez Alberte ❶,** offers quick Belgian fare. (Fries €2-2.50, sandwiches €3-5).

Trains run to Brussels (1hr., 2-5 per hr., €13). The **tourist office,** 92 Féronstrée, is just a couple doors down from the Musée de L'Art Wallon. (☎04 221 9221; www.liege.be. Open M-F 9am-5pm, Sa 10am-4:30pm, Su 10am-2:30pm.) Across the Pont des Arches from the hostel, Cyberman, 48 r. Léopold, has **Internet.** (☎04 87 60 56 95. Open daily 10am-11pm. €1 per hr.)

TOURNAI (DOORNIK) ☎069

The first city liberated from the Nazis by Allied forces, Tournai (pop. 68,000) was once the capital of Gaul. The city's most spectacular sight is the world's only five-steepled cathedral, 800-year-old **Cathédrale Notre-Dame.** (Open daily June-Oct. 9:15am-noon and 2-6pm; Nov.-May 9:15am-noon and 2-5pm. Free, treasure room €1.) Climb the 257 steps of the nearby belfry, the oldest in Belgium, for a stunning view. The rooms you'll see along the climb served as prison cells until 1827. (Open Mar.-Oct. Tu-Su 10am-1pm and 2-6:30pm; Nov.-Feb. Tu-Su 10am-noon and 2-5pm. €2, under 20 €1.) Two blocks away, Victor Horta's **Musée des Beaux-Arts,** Enclos St-Martin, houses a small collection of Belgian and Dutch paintings. (☎069 33 23 45. Open Apr.-Oct. M and W-Su 9:30am-12:30pm and 2-5:30pm; Nov.-Mar. M and W-Sa 10am-noon and 2-5pm, Su 2-5pm. €3, first Su of each month free.) Continue up the hill from the tourist office to reach the convenient **Auberge de Jeunesse (HI) ❷,** 64 r. St-Martin, which has dormitory-style hallways and a full kitchen. (☎069 21 61 36; www.laj.be. Breakfast and linens included. Reception 8am-noon and 5-10pm; varies in low season. Hostel locked when reception closed. Reserve ahead. Open Feb.-Nov. Dorms €18-20; singles €34; doubles €50. €3 HI discount. MC/V.) Stop by the friendly, family-owned bakery **Boulangerie ❶,** just across the street from the hostel, for delicious fare including sizable sandwiches (€2), tasty pastries, and fresh breads. (Open daily 6am-5pm.) **Trains** leave pl. Crombez for Brussels (1hr., 1 per hr., €11.10) and Namur (2hr., 1 per hr., €15.20). The **tourist office** is at 14 Vieux Marché aux Poteries. (☎069 22 20 45; www.tournai.be. Open Apr.-Sept. M-F 8:30am-6pm, Sa 9:30am-noon and 2-5pm, Su 10am-noon and 2:30-6pm; Oct.-Mar. M-F 8:30am-5:30pm, Sa 10am-noon and 2-5pm, Su 2:30-6pm.) Inexpensive access to **Internet** is available at **CyberCenter,** 6 r. Soil de Morialme. (☎069 23 66 36. Open M-F 11am-11pm, Sa-Su 2pm-midnight. €3 per hr.) **Postal Code:** 7500.

NAMUR

☎081

Namur, capital of Wallonie (pop. 110,000), is the last sizable outpost before the wilderness of the Ardennes and a gateway for **hiking, biking, caving,** and **kayaking** in Belgium's mountainous regions. Houses atop the rolling hills and picturesque streets make this an ideal, moderately tourist-free getaway. In September, Namur hosts a multicultural crowd at the **International French Language Film Festival** (☎081 24 12 36; www.fiff.be). The town's foreboding **citadel** (☎081 65 45 00; www.citadelle.namur.be) remained an active Belgian military base until 1978. To get there take bus #3 (1 per hr., dir.: Citadel). The free *Storming the Citadel!*, at the tourist office, lists five historical walking tours (1-1½hr.). Trails thread through the surrounding **Parc de Champeau.** Flocks of geese dally near the homey **Auberge Félicien Rops (HI)** ❷, 8 av. Félicien Rops. Take bus # 4, 17, 30 or 31 from the train station. (☎081 22 36 88; www.laj.be. Breakfast and linens included. Kitchen available. Laundry €6.50. Free Internet. Reception 8am-11pm. Lockout 10am-4pm. Dorms €18-20.50; singles €34; doubles €50. €3 HI discount. MC/V.) To camp at **Les Trieux** ❶, 99 r. des Tris, 6km away, take bus #6. (☎081 44 55 83; www.campinglestrieux.be. Open Apr.-Oct. €3.50 per person, €4-6 per tent. Electricity €2.) **Trains** link Namur to Brussels (1hr., 2 per hr., €7.70) and Dinant (30min., 1 per hr., €4.10). The **tourist office** is on the Sq. de l'Europe Unie. (☎24 64 49; www.namurtourisme.be. Open daily 9:30am-6pm.) Rent **bikes** at La Maison des Cyclistes, 2B pl. de la Station. (☎081 81 38 48. Open M-W and F 10am-1pm and 2-4pm. €4 per hr., €9 per day.)

DINANT

☎082

Razed by the German army in 1914, Dinant (pop. 13,000) has managed to reinvent itself as a tourist destination because of its rich history and beautiful surrounding landscape. Dinant's **citadel** towers over the Meuse River. To see the spectacular view, you have to pay the €6.50 entrance fee and take a required 1hr. tour detailing Dinant's bloody history. Buy tickets at 3-5 pl. Reine Astrid. (☎082 22 36 70. Tour in German and French. Open Apr.-Oct. daily 10am-6pm; Nov.-Dec. and Feb.-Mar. M-Th and Sa-Su 10am-5pm; Jan. Sa-Su 10am-5pm.) Descend into the beautiful depths of the **Grotte Merveilleuse,** 142 rte. de Phillipeville, 600m from the train station, for a witty 50min. tour of the cave's limestone formations. With the train station behind you, take a right and follow signs to Phillipeville and La Grotte. Bring a jacket to avoid underground chills. (☎082 22 22 10; www.dinantourism.com. Open July-Aug. daily 10am-6pm; Apr.-June and Sept.-Oct. daily 11am-5pm; Dec.-Mar. Sa-Su 1-4pm. Tours 1 per hr., usually in English. €6.) Rooms in Dinant tend to be pricey, so try accommodations in nearby towns. **Café Leffe** ❸, 2 r. Sax, named after the famous beer originally brewed in an abbey in Dinant, is past the bridge from the tourist office, on the left (☎082 22 23 72; www.leffe.be. Entrees €7-13. Open daily 11am-11pm. Reserve in advance. AmEx/MC/V.) Get set up to **kayak** at the **Meuse at Anseremme.** (☎082 22 43 97; www.lessekayaks.be. Kayaks €17-26.) To get to the **tourist office** from the train station, turn right, take the first left, and take another immediate left by the river. (☎082 22 28 70; www.dinant-tourisme.be. Open M-F 8:30am-6pm, Sa 9:30am-5pm, Su 10am-4:30pm; low season reduced hours.) Rent bikes at **Raid Mountain-Bike,** 15 r. du Vélodrome (☎082 21 35 35. €16-20 per day. Passport required.). **Trains** run to Brussels (1hr., 1 per hr., €11.10) and Namur (30min., 1 per hr., €4.10). The **bike** ride from Namur is 28km.

CAVE MAN COURTESY. Small tips (€0.50-1) are considered courteous on cave tours, even though it is not customary to tip in restaurants.

BELGIUM

GREAT BRITAIN

After colonizing two-fifths of the globe, spearheading the Industrial Revolution, and winning every foreign war in its history but two, Britain seems intent on making the world forget its tiny size. It's hard to believe that the rolling farms of the south and the rugged cliffs of the north are only a day's train ride apart, or that people as diverse as clubbers, miners, and monks all occupy an area roughly the size of Oregon. Beyond the fairytale cottages and sheep farms of "Merry Olde England," today's Britain is a high-energy destination driven by international influence. Though the sun may have set on the British Empire, a colonial legacy survives in multicultural urban centers and a dynamic arts and theater scene. Brits now eat kebabs and curry as often as they do scones, and dance clubs in post-industrial settings draw as much attention as elegant country inns.

DISCOVER BRITAIN: SUGGESTED ITINERARIES

THREE DAYS. Spend it all in **London** (p. 123), the city of tea, royalty, and James Bond. After a stroll through **Hyde Park,** head to **Buckingham Palace** for the changing of the guard. Check out the renowned collections of the **British Museum** and the **Tate Modern.** Stop at famed **Westminster Abbey** and catch a play at Shakespeare's **Globe Theatre** before grabbing a drink in the **East End.**

ONE WEEK. Begin, of course, in **London** (3 days), then visit academia at the colleges of **Oxford** (1 day; p. 155.) Travel to **Scotland** for a day in the museums and galleries of **Glasgow** (p. 190) and finish off with pubs and parties in lively **Edinburgh** (2 days; p. 183).

THREE WEEKS. Start in **London** (4 days), to explore the museums, theaters, and clubs. Tour the smart college greens in **Cambridge** (2 days; p. 162) and **Oxford** (2 days), then amble through the capital of Wales, **Cardiff** (1 day; p. 178). Fie that you miss Shakespeare's hometown, **Stratford-upon-Avon** (1 day; p. 159), or that of The Beatles, **Liverpool** (1 day; p. 167). Head to **Manchester** for its infamous nightlife (1 day; p. 165) before moving on to **Glasgow** (1 day) and nearby scenic **Loch Lomond** (1 day; p. 195). Energetic **Edinburgh** (4 days) will keep you busy, especially during festival season. Finally, enjoy the beautiful **Peak District** (2 days; p. 169) and historic **York** (1 day; p. 170).

ESSENTIALS

FACTS AND FIGURES

OFFICIAL NAME: United Kingdom of Great Britain and Northern Ireland.

CAPITAL: London.

MAJOR CITIES: Cardiff, Edinburgh, Glasgow, Liverpool, Manchester.

POPULATION: 60,776,000.

LAND AREA: 244,800 sq. km.

TIME ZONE: GMT.

LANGUAGE: English; also Welsh and Scottish Gaelic.

RELIGIONS: Christian: Protestant and Catholic (72%), Muslim (3%).

TOTAL NUMBER OF HARRY POTTER BOOKS SOLD: 400,000,000.

WHEN TO GO

It's wise to plan around the high season (June-Aug.). Spring and fall are better times to visit; the weather is reasonable and flights are cheaper, though there may be less transportation to rural areas. If you plan to visit the cities, the low season (Nov.-Mar.) is most economical. Keep in mind, however, that sights and accommodations often close or have reduced hours. In Scotland, summer light lasts almost until midnight, but in winter, the sun may set as early as 3:45pm. Regardless of when you go, it will rain—always.

IT'S ALL BRITISH TO ME. The United Kingdom is a political union of England, Northern Ireland, Scotland, and Wales. This is also referred to as Britain, not to be confused with the island of Great Britain, which only includes England, Scotland, and Wales. *Let's Go* uses United Kingdom and Britain interchangeably. This chapter covers Great Britain. For Northern Ireland information and coverage, see p. 561.

DOCUMENTS AND FORMALITIES

EMBASSIES AND CONSULATES. Foreign embassies in Britain are in London (p. 125). British embassies abroad include: **Australia,** Commonwealth Ave., Yarralumla, ACT 2600 (☎02 6270 6666; http://bhc.britaus.net); **Canada,** 80 Elgin St., Ottawa, ON, K1P 5K7 (☎613-237-1530; www.britainincanada.org); **Ireland,** 29 Merrion Rd., Ballsbridge, Dublin 4 (☎01 205 3700; www.britishembassy.ie); **New Zealand,** 44 Hill St., Thorndon, Wellington, 6011 (☎04 924 2888; www.britain.org.nz); **US,** 3100 Mass. Ave. NW, Washington, D.C., 20008 (☎202-588-7800; www.britainusa.com).

VISA AND ENTRY INFORMATION. EU citizens do not need a visa. Citizens of Australia, Canada, New Zealand, and the US do not need a visa for stays of up to 6 months. Students planning to study in the UK for six months or more must obtain a student visa (around US$90). For a full list of countries whose citizens require visas, call your British embassy or visit www.ukvisas.gov.uk.

TOURIST SERVICES AND MONEY

EMERGENCY	**Ambulance, Fire,** and **Police:** ☎999.

TOURIST OFFICES. Formerly the British Tourist Authority, **Visit Britain** (☎020 8846 9000; www.visitbritain.com) is an umbrella organization for regional tourist boards. Tourist offices in Britain are listed under for each city and town. They stock maps and provide info on sights and accommodations.

IT'S JUST A TIC. Tourist offices in Britain are known as Tourist Information Centres, or TICs. Britain's National Parks also have National Park Information Centres, or NPICs. This chapter refers to all offices as TICs and NPICs.

MONEY. The British unit of currency is the **pound sterling** (£), plural pounds sterling. One pound is equal to 100 **pence,** with standard denominations of 1p, 2p, 5p, 10p, 20p, 50p, £1, and £2 in coins, and £5, £10, £20, and £50 in notes. **Quid** is slang for pounds. Scotland has its own bank notes, which can be used interchangeably with English currency, though you may have difficulty using Scottish £1 notes outside Scotland. As a rule, it's cheaper to exchange money in Britain than at home. ATMs offer the best exchange rates. Many British department stores, such as Marks & Spencer, also offer excellent exchange services. Tips in restaurants are often included in the bill, sometimes as a "service charge." If gratuity is not included, tip your server about 12.5%. A 10% tip is common for taxi drivers, and £1-3 is usual for bellhops and chambermaids. To the relief of budget travelers from the US, tipping is not expected at pubs and bars in Britain. Aside from open-air markets, don't expect to bargain. For more info on money in Europe, see p. 17.

The UK has a 17.5% **value added tax (VAT),** a sales tax applied to everything but food, books, medicine, and children's clothing. The tax is included in the amount indicated on the price tag. The prices stated in *Let's Go* include VAT. In the airport upon exiting the EU, non-EU citizens can claim a refund on the tax paid for goods purchased at participating stores. You can obtain refunds only for goods you take out of the country. To apply for a refund, fill out the form that you are given in the shop and present it with the goods and receipts at customs upon departure—look for the Tax-Free Refund Desk at the airport. At peak times, this process can take an hour. You must leave the UK within three months of your purchase to claim a refund, and you must apply for the refund before leaving. For more info on qualifying for a VAT refund, see p. 21. For VAT info specific to the UK, visit http://customs.hmrc.gov.uk.

BRITISH POUND (£)		
	AUS$1 = £0.47	£1 = AUS$2.14
	CDN$1 = £0.51	£1 = CDN$1.97
	EUR€1 = £0.79	£1 = EUR€1.27
	NZ$1 = £0.38	£1 = NZ$2.62
	US$1 = £0.54	£1 = US$1.86

TRANSPORTATION

BY PLANE. Most international flights land at **London's Heathrow (LHR;** ☎0870 000 0123; www.heathrowairport.com) or **Gatwick (WSX;** ☎0870 000 2468; www.gatwickairport.com) airports; **Manchester (MAN)** and **Edinburgh (EDI)** also have international airports. **Budget airlines,** like Ryanair and easyJet, fly out of many locales, including **Stansted Airport** and **Luton Airport,** (p. 124). The national airline, **British Airways** (☎0870 850 9850, US ☎800-247-9297; www.britishairways.com), offers discounted youth fares for those under 24. For more info on traveling by plane around Europe, see p. 50.

BY TRAIN. Britain's main carrier is **National Rail Enquiries** (☎08457 484 950). The country's train network is extensive, crisscrossing the length and breadth of the island. Prices and schedules often change; find up-to-date information from their website (www.nationalrail.co.uk/planmyjourney) or **Network Rail** (www.networkrail.co.uk; schedules only). **Eurostar** trains run to Britain from the Continent through the Chunnel (p. 57). The **BritRail Pass,** sold only outside Britain, allows unlimited travel in England, Scotland, and Wales (www.britrail.net). In Canada and the US, contact **Rail Europe** (Canada ☎800-361-7245, US ☎888-382-7245; www.raileurope.com). Eurail passes are not valid in Britain. Rail discount cards (£20), available at rail stations and through travel agents,

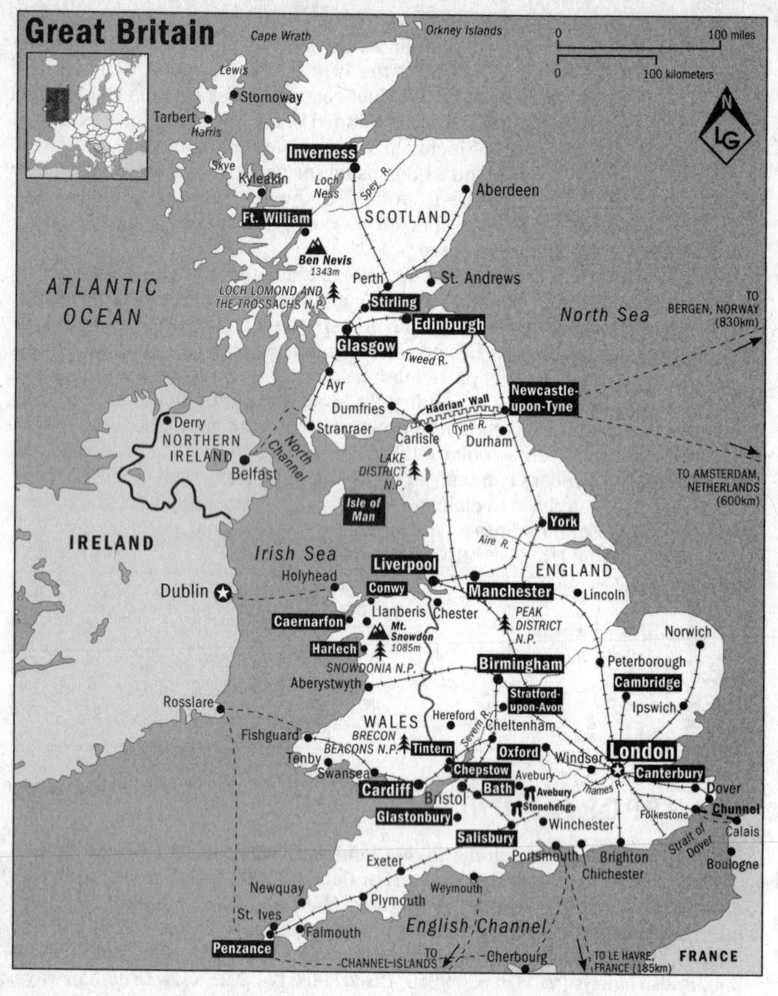

grant 33% off most point-to-point fares and are available to those ages 16-25 or over 60, full-time students, and families. In general, traveling by train costs more than by bus. For more info on train travel, see p. 50.

BY BUS. The British distinguish between **buses,** which cover short routes, and **coaches,** which cover long distances; *Let's Go* refers to both as buses. **National Express** (☎08705 808 080; www.nationalexpress.com) is the main operator of long-distance bus service in Britain, while **Scottish Citylink** (☎08705 505 050; www.citylink.co.uk) has the most extensive coverage in Scotland. The **Brit Xplorer Pass** offers unlimited travel on National Express buses (7-day £79, 14-day £139, 28-day £219). **NX2 cards** (£10), available online for ages 16-26, reduce fares by up to 30%. Plan ahead for the cheapest rides, National Express's **Fun Fares,** which are only sold online (limited number of tickets out of London from £1).

BY CAR. To drive, you must be 17 and have a valid license from your home country; to rent, you must be over 21. Britain is covered by a high-speed system of **motorways** (M-roads) that connect London to other major cities. Visitors should be able to handle **driving on the left side** of the road and driving **manual transmission** ("stick shift" is far more common than automatic). Roads are generally well maintained, but gasoline (petrol) prices are high. In London, driving is restricted during weekday working hours, with charges imposed in certain congestion zones; parking can be similarly nightmarish.

BY FERRY. Several ferry lines provide service between Britain and the Continent. Ask for discounts; ISIC holders can sometimes get student fares, and Eurail pass-holders are eligible for reductions and free trips. **Seaview Ferries** (www.seaview.co.uk/ferries.html) has a directory of UK ferries. Book ahead in summer. For more info on boats to Ireland and the Continent, see p. 57.

BY BIKE AND BY FOOT. Much of the British countryside is well suited to biking. Many cities and villages have rental shops and route maps. Large-scale *Ordnance Survey* maps, often available at TICs, detail the extensive system of long-distance hiking paths. TICs and NPICs can provide extra information.

BY THUMB. Hitchhiking or standing on M-roads is illegal; one may only thumb at rest stops or at the entrance ramps to highways. Despite this, hitchhiking is fairly common in rural parts of Scotland and Wales (England is tougher) where public transportation is spotty. *Let's Go* does not recommend hitchhiking.

KEEPING IN TOUCH

PHONE CODES	**Country code:** 44. **International dialing prefix:** 00. Within Britain, dial city code + local number, even when dialing inside the city. For more info on how to place international calls, see **Inside Back Cover.**

EMAIL AND THE INTERNET. Internet access is ubiquitous in big cities, common in towns, and sparse in rural areas. Internet cafes or public terminals can be found almost everywhere; they usually cost £2-6 per hour, but you often pay only for the time used. For more info, see www.cybercafes.com. Public libraries usually have free or inexpensive Internet access, but you might have to wait or make an advance reservation. Many coffee shops, particularly chains such as Caffe Nero and Starbucks, offer Wi-Fi for a fee.

TELEPHONE. Most public **pay phones** in Britain are run by British Telecom (BT). Public phones charge at least 30p and don't accept 1, 2, or 5p coins. A BT Chargecard bills calls to your credit card, but most pay phones now have readers where you can swipe credit cards directly (generally AmEx/MC/V). The number for the operator in Britain is ☎100, the international operator ☎155. Whenever possible, use a **calling card** for international phone calls, as long-distance rates for national phone services are often very high. **Mobile phones** are an increasingly popular and economical option. Major mobile carriers include T-Mobile, Vodafone, and O2. Direct-dial access numbers for calling out of Britain include: **AT&T Direct** (☎0800 890 011); **Canada Direct** (☎0800 096 0634 or 0800 559 3141); **Telecom New Zealand Direct** (☎0800 890 064); **Telstra Australia** (☎0800 890 061). For more info on calling home from Europe, see p. 31.

MAIL. Royal Mail has tried to standardize their rates around the world. Check shipment costs with the Postal Calculator at www.royalmail.com. **Airmail** is the best way to send mail home from Britain. Just write "Par Avión—Airmail" on the top left corner of your envelope or stop by any post office to get a free airmail label. Letters sent via Airmail should be delivered within three working days to European destinations and five working days to Australia, Canada, and the US. To receive mail in the UK, have mail delivered **Poste Restante.** Mail will go to the main post office unless you specify a subsidiary by street address. Address mail to be held according to the following example: First Name, Last Name, Poste Restante, post office address, Postal Code, UK. Bring a passport to pick up your mail; there may be a small fee.

ACCOMMODATIONS AND CAMPING

BRITAIN	❶	❷	❸	❹	❺
ACCOMMODATIONS	under £15	£15-20	£21-30	£31-40	over £40

Hostelling International (HI) hostels are prevalent throughout Britain. They are run by the **Youth Hostels Association of England and Wales (YHA;** ☎08707 708 868; www.yha.org.uk), the **Scottish Youth Hostels Association (SYHA;** ☎01786 891 400; www.syha.org.uk), and **Hostelling International Northern Ireland (HINI;** ☎028 9032 4733; www.hini.org.uk). Dorms cost around £12-15 in rural areas, £15-20 in larger cities, and £20-35 in London. Make reservations at least a week in advance, especially in more touristed areas on weekends and during the summer. You can book **B&Bs** by calling directly, or by asking the local TIC to help you. TICs usually charge a flat fee of £1-5 plus 10% deposit, deductible from the amount you pay the B&B proprietor. **Campgrounds** tend to be privately owned and cost £3-10 per person per night. It is illegal to camp in national parks.

FOOD AND DRINK

BRITAIN	❶	❷	❸	❹	❺
FOOD	under £6	£6-10	£11-15	£16-20	over £20

A pillar of traditional British fare, the cholesterol-filled, meat-anchored **full English breakfast** is still served in most B&Bs across the country. Beans on toast or toast smothered in Marmite (the most acquired of tastes—a salty, brown spread made from yeast) are breakfast staples. The best native dishes for lunch or dinner are roasts—beef, lamb, and Wiltshire hams—and **Yorkshire pudding,** a type of popover drizzled with meat juices. Despite their intriguing names, **bangers and mash** and **bubble and squeak** are just sausages and potatoes and cabbage and potatoes, respectively. Pubs serve savory meat pies like **Cornish pasties** (PASS-tees) or **ploughman's lunches** consisting of bread, cheese, and pickles. **Fish and chips** (french fries) are traditionally drowned in malt vinegar and salt. **Crisps,** or potato chips, come in an astonishing variety, with flavors like prawn cocktail. Britons make their desserts (often called "puddings" or "afters") exceedingly sweet and gloopy. **Sponges, trifles, tarts,** and the ill-named **spotted dick** (spongy currant cake) will satiate the sweetest tooth. To escape English food, try Chinese, Greek, or Indian cuisine. British **"tea"** refers to both a drink, served strong and milky, and to a social ritual. A high tea might include cooked meats, salad, sandwiches, and pastries, while the oft-stereotyped afternoon tea comes with finger sandwiches, scones with jam and **clotted cream** (a sinful cross between whipped cream and butter), and small cakes. **Cream tea,** a specialty of Cornwall and Devon, includes scones or crumpets, jam, and clotted cream.

HOLIDAYS AND FESTIVALS

Holidays: New Year's Day (Jan. 1, 2009); Epiphany (Jan. 6, 2009); Good Friday (Apr. 10, 2009); Easter (Apr. 13, 2009); Ascension (May 21, 2009); Pentecost (May 31, 2009); Corpus Christi (June 11, 2009); Bank Holidays (May 4, May 25, and Aug. 31, 2009); Assumption (Aug. 15, 2009); All Saints' Day (Nov. 1, 2009); Christmas (Dec. 25, 2009); Boxing Day (Dec. 28, 2009).

Festivals: Scotland's New Year's Eve celebration, *Hogmanay,* takes over the streets in Edinburgh and Glasgow. The *National Eisteddfod of Wales* (Aug. 1-8, 2009) has brought Welsh writers, musicians, and artists together since 1176. One of the largest music and theater festivals in the world is the *Edinburgh International Festival* (Aug. 14-Sept. 6, 2009); also highly recommended is the *Edinburgh Fringe Festival* (Aug. 2009). Manchester's Gay Village hosts *Manchester Pride* (www.manchesterpride.com) in August, and London throws a huge street party at the *Notting Hill Carnival* (Aug. 23-24, 2009). Bonfires and fireworks abound on England's *Guy Fawkes Day* (Nov. 5, 2009) in celebration of a conspirator's failed attempt to destroy the Houses of Parliament in 1605.

BEYOND TOURISM

There are many opportunities for volunteering, studying, and working in Britain. As a volunteer, you can participate in projects ranging from archaeological digs to lobbying for social change. Explore your academic passions at the country's prestigious institutions or pursue an independent research project. For more info on opportunities across Europe, see **Beyond Tourism,** p. 60.

The National Trust, Volunteering and Community Involvement Office, P.O. Box 39, Warrington WA5 7WD (☎0870 458 4000; www.nationaltrust.org.uk/volunteering). Arranges numerous volunteer opportunities, including volunteer work on holidays.

The Teacher Recruitment Company, Pennineway Offices (1), 87-89 Saffron Hill, London EC1N 8QU (☎0845 833 1934; www.teachers.eu.com). International recruitment agency that lists positions across the country and provides info on jobs in the UK.

University of Oxford, College Admissions Office, Wellington Sq., Oxford OX1 2JD (☎01865 288 000; www.ox.ac.uk). Large range of summer programs (£880-3780) and year-long courses (£8880-11,840).

ENGLAND

A land where the stately once prevailed, England is now a youthful, hip, and forward-looking nation on the cutting edge of art, music, and film. But traditionalists can rest easy; for all the moving and shaking in large cities, scores of ancient towns, opulent castles, and comforting cups of tea still abound.

LONDON ☎020

London offers visitors a bewildering array of choices: Leonardo at the National Gallery or Hirst at the Tate Modern; Rossini at the Royal Opera or Les Misérables at the Queen's; Bond Street couture or Camden cutting-edge—you could spend your entire stay just deciding what to do. London is not often described as a unified city but rather as a conglomeration of villages, whose heritage and traditions are still evolving. Thanks to the feisty independence and diversity of each area, the London "buzz" is continually on the move.

INTERCITY TRANSPORTATION

Flights: Heathrow (LON; ☎08700 000 123) is London's main airport. The **Piccadilly Line** leaves the airport to central London (1hr., 20 per hr., £4-10). **Heathrow Connect** runs to **Paddington** (20min., 2 per hr., £10), as does the more costly **Heathrow Express** (15min.; 4 per hr.; £15.50, round-trip £29). From **Gatwick Airport (LGW;** ☎08700 002 468), the **Gatwick Express** heads to **Victoria** (30min.; 4 per hr., round-trip £28.90).

Regional Hubs: London Luton Airport (LTN; ☎1582 405 100; www.london-luton.co.uk) serves as a hub for **easyJet, Ryanair,** and **Wizz Air.** First Capital Connect (☎0845 026 4700; www.firstcapitalconnect.co.uk) and Midland Mainline (☎0870 010 1296; www.midlandmainline.com) run **trains** between London King's Cross and Luton (30min.-1hr., 3-4 per hr., £10-20). Easybus (www.easybus.co.uk) and National Express (☎08705 808 080; www.nationalexpress.com) operate **buses** between London Victoria and Luton (1hr., 2-3 per hr., from £2). **London Stansted Airport (STN;** ☎0870 000 0303; www.stanstedairport.com) is the main hub for **Ryanair,** and also serves **easyJet** and **Wizz Air.** The Stansted Express (☎0845 600 7245; www.stanstedexpress.com) train shuttles between London Liverpool and Stansted (45min., 4 per hr., £15-24). Easybus runs **buses** between London Baker St. and Stansted and National Express runs **buses** from London Victoria (1hr., 3-6 per hr., from £2).

Trains: London has 8 major train stations: **Charing Cross** (southern England); **Euston** (the northwest); **King's Cross** (the northeast); **Liverpool Street** (East Anglia); **Paddington** (the west and south Wales); **St. Pancras** (the Midlands and the northwest); **Victoria** (the south); **Waterloo** (the south, the southwest, and the Continent). All stations are linked by the subway, referred to as the **Underground** or **Tube** (⊖). Itineraries involving a change of stations in London usually include a crosstown transfer by Tube. Get information from the **National Rail Enquiries Line** (☎08457 484 950; www.britrail.com).

Buses: Long-distance buses (coaches) arrive in London at **Victoria Coach Station,** 164 Buckingham Palace Rd. ⊖Victoria. **National Express** (☎08705 808 080; www.nationalexpress.com) is the largest operator of intercity services.

ORIENTATION

The **West End,** stretching east from Park Lane to Kingsway and south from Oxford St. to the River Thames, is the heart of London. In this area you'll find aristocratic **Mayfair,** the shopping near **Oxford Circus,** the clubs of **Soho,** and the boutiques of **Covent Garden.** Heading east of the West End, you'll pass legalistic **Holborn** before hitting the ancient **City of London** ("the City"), the site of the original Roman settlement and home to the Tower of London. The City's eastern border encompasses the ethnically diverse, working-class **East End.**

Westminster encompasses the grandeur of **Trafalgar Square** and extends south along the Thames; this is the location of both royal and political London, with the Houses of Parliament, Buckingham Palace, and Westminster Abbey. Farther west lies rich, snooty **Chelsea.** Across the river, the **South Bank** has an incredible variety of entertainment and museums. To the south, **Brixton** is one of the hottest nightlife spots in town, besides touristy Leicester Square and Piccadilly Circus. The huge expanse of **Hyde Park** lies west of the West End; along its southern border are chic **Knightsbridge** and posh **Kensington.** North of Hyde Park is the media-infested **Notting Hill** and the B&B- and hostel-filled **Bayswater.**

Bayswater, Mayfair, and **Marylebone** meet at Marble Arch, on Hyde Park's north-east corner; from there, Marylebone stretches west to meet academic **Bloomsbury,** north of Soho and Holborn. **Camden Town, Islington, Hampstead,** and **Highgate** lie to the north of Bloomsbury and the City. A good street atlas is essential. **London A to Z** (£10) is available at newsstands and bookstores.

LOCAL TRANSPORTATION

Public Transportation: Run by **Transport for London (TfL;** 24hr. info ☎020 7222 1234; www.thetube.com). The **Underground** or **Tube** (⊖) is divided into 6 concentric zones; fares depend on the number of zones crossed. Buy your ticket before you board and pass it through automatic gates at both ends of your journey. Runs approximately 5am-11:30pm. See Tube map in the front of this guide. **Buses** are divided into 4 zones. Zones 1-3 are identical to the Tube zones. Buses run 5:30am-midnight, after which a network of **Night Buses,** prefixed by "N," take over. Fares £2. **Travelcard** valid on all TfL services. 1-day Travelcard from £5.30 (Zones 1-2).

Licensed Taxicabs: An illuminated "taxi" sign on the roof of a black cab signals availability. Tip 10%. For pickup (min. £2 charge), call **Taxi One-Number** (☎08718 718 710).

Minicabs: Private cars. Cheaper but less reliable—stick to a reputable company. **London Radio Cars** (☎020 8905 0000; www.londonradiocars.com) offers 24hr. pickup.

PRACTICAL INFORMATION

Tourist Information Centre: Britain Visitor Centre, 1 Regent St. (www.visitbritain.com). ⊖Piccadilly Circus. Open M 9:30am-6:30pm, Tu-F 9am-6:30pm, Sa-Su 10am-4pm. **London Information Centre,** 1 Leicester Pl. (☎020 7930 6769; www.londoninformationcentre.com). ⊖Leicester Sq. Open M-F 8am-midnight, Sa-Su 9am-6pm.

Tours: The Big Bus Company, 35-37 Grosvenor Gardens (☎020 7233 7797; www.bigbus.co.uk). ⊖Victoria. Multiple routes and buses every 5-15min. 1hr. walking tours and Thames cruise. Buses start at central office and at hubs throughout the city. £20. £2 discount for online purchase. AmEx/MC/V. **Original London Walks** (☎020 7624 3978, recorded info ☎020 7624 9255; www.walks.com) offers themed walks, from "Haunted London" to "Slice of India." Most 2hr. £6, students £5, under 16 free.

Embassies: Australia, Australia House, Strand (☎020 7379 4334). ⊖Temple. Open M-F 9am-5pm. **Canada,** MacDonald House, 1 Grosvenor Sq. (☎020 7258 6600). ⊖Bond St. Open M-F 9am-5pm. **Ireland,** 17 Grosvenor Pl. (☎020 7235 2171). ⊖Hyde Park Corner. Open M-F 9:30am-1pm and 2:15-5pm. **New Zealand,** New Zealand House, 80 Haymarket (☎020 7930 8422). ⊖Piccadilly Circus. Open M-F 9am-5pm. **US,** 24 Grosvenor Sq. (☎020 7499 9000). ⊖Bond St. Open M-F 8:30am-5:30pm.

Currency Exchange: Banks, such as **Barclays, HSBC, Lloyd's,** and **National Westminster** (NatWest) have the best rates. Branches open M-F 9:30am-4:30pm. Call ☎0895 456 6524 for the nearest **American Express** location.

GLBT Resources: London Lesbian and Gay Switchboard (☎020 7837 7324; www.queery.org.uk). 24hr. helpline and information service.

Police: London is covered by 2 police forces: the **City of London Police** (☎020 7601 2222) and the **Metropolitan Police** (☎020 7230 1212) for the outskirts. At least 1 station in each of the boroughs is open 24hr. Call ☎020 7230 1212 for station list.

Pharmacies: Most pharmacies open M-Sa 9:30am-5:30pm; a "duty" chemist in each district opens Su; hours limited. **Zafash Pharmacy,** 233-235 Old Brompton Rd. (☎020 7373 2798), ⊖Earl's Ct., is 24hr. **Bliss Chemist,** 5-6 Marble Arch (☎020 7723 6116), ⊖Marble Arch, is open daily 9am-midnight.

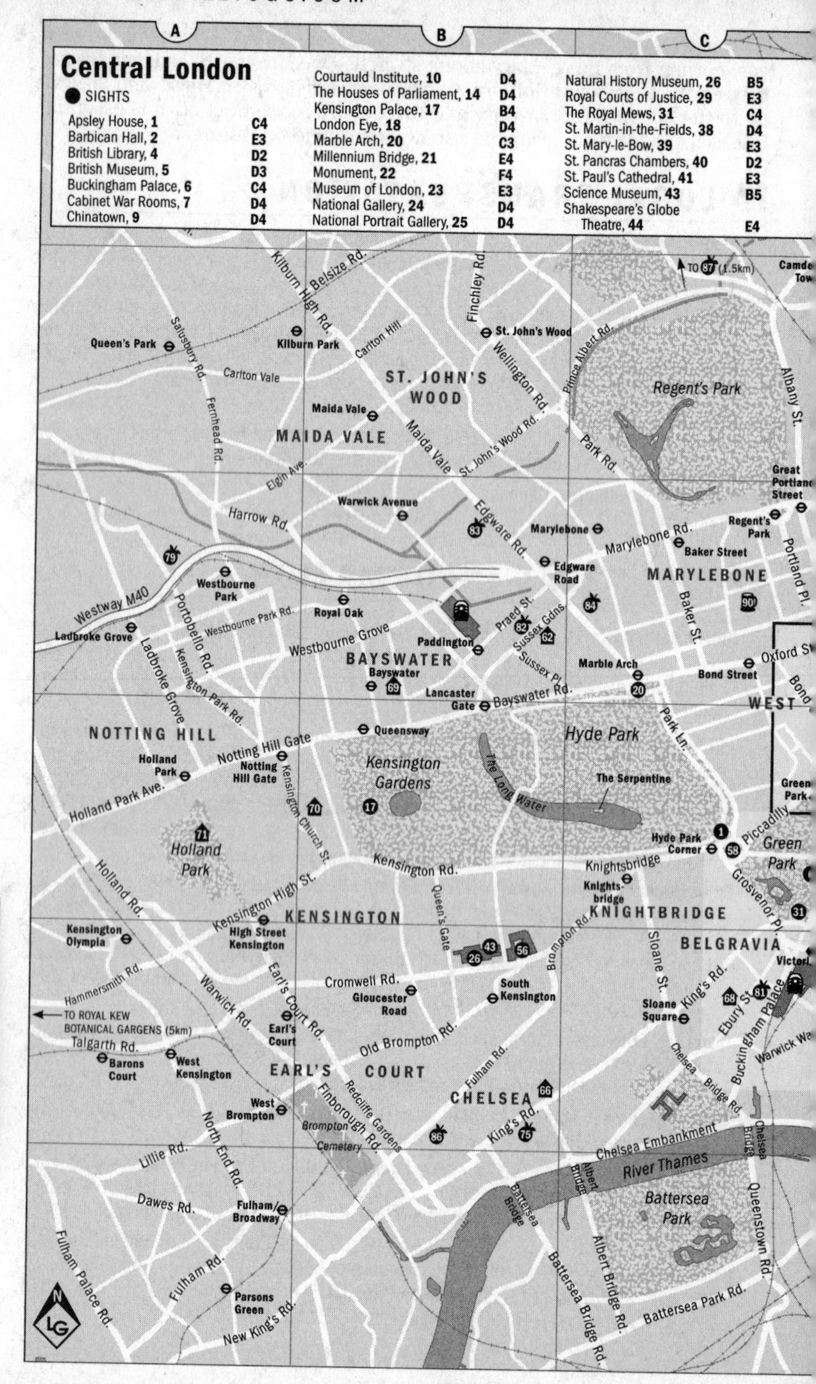

GREAT BRITAIN

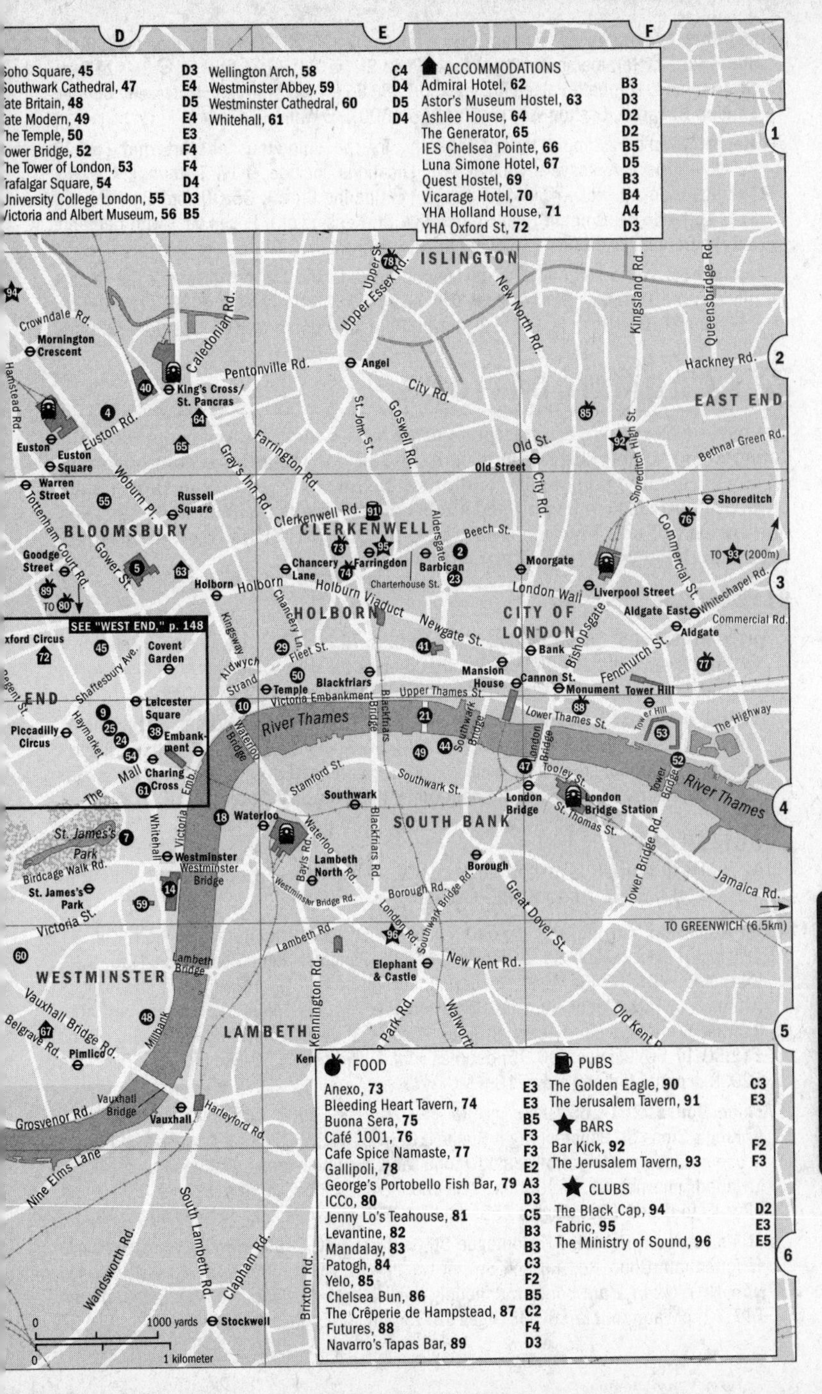
D
E
F
oho Square, 45 D3
outhwark Cathedral, 47 E4
ate Britain, 48 D5
ate Modern, 49 E4
he Temple, 50 E3
ower Bridge, 52 F4
he Tower of London, 53 F4
rafalgar Square, 54 D4
Jniversity College London, 55 D3
ictoria and Albert Museum, 56 B5
Wellington Arch, 58 C4
Westminster Abbey, 59 D4
Westminster Cathedral, 60 D5
Whitehall, 61 D4
ACCOMMODATIONS
Admiral Hotel, 62 B3
Astor's Museum Hostel, 63 D3
Ashlee House, 64 D2
The Generator, 65 D2
IES Chelsea Pointe, 66 B5
Luna Simone Hotel, 67 D5
Quest Hostel, 69 B3
Vicarage Hotel, 70 B4
YHA Holland House, 71 A4
YHA Oxford St, 72 D3
ISLINGTON
EAST END
BLOOMSBURY
CLERKENWELL
HOLBORN
CITY OF LONDON
SOUTH BANK
WESTMINSTER
LAMBETH
SEE "WEST END," p. 148
River Thames
TO GREENWICH (6.5km)
FOOD
Anexo, 73 E3
Bleeding Heart Tavern, 74 E3
Buona Sera, 75 B5
Café 1001, 76 F3
Cafe Spice Namaste, 77 F3
Gallipoli, 78 E2
George's Portobello Fish Bar, 79 A3
ICCo, 80 D3
Jenny Lo's Teahouse, 81 C5
Levantine, 82 B3
Mandalay, 83 B3
Patogh, 84 C3
Yelo, 85 F2
Chelsea Bun, 86 B5
The Crêperie de Hampstead, 87 C2
Futures, 88 F4
Navarro's Tapas Bar, 89 D3
PUBS
The Golden Eagle, 90 C3
The Jerusalem Tavern, 91 E3
BARS
Bar Kick, 92 F2
The Jerusalem Tavern, 93 F3
CLUBS
The Black Cap, 94 D2
Fabric, 95 E3
The Ministry of Sound, 96 E5
0 1000 yards
0 1 kilometer

GREAT BRITAIN

Hospitals: Charing Cross, Fulham Palace Rd. (☎020 8846 1234), entrance on St. Dunstan's Rd., ⊖Hammersmith. **Royal Free,** Pond St. (☎020 7794 0500), ⊖Belsize Park. **St. Thomas's,** Lambeth Palace Rd. (☎020 7188 7188), ⊖Waterloo. **University College London Hospital,** Grafton Way (☎08 4515 5500), ⊖Warren St.

Internet: Don't pay more than £2 per hr. Try the ubiquitous **easyInternet** (☎020 7241 9000; www.easyeverything.com). Locations include 9-16 Tottenham Ct. Rd. (⊖Tottenham Ct. Rd.); 456/459 Strand (⊖Charing Cross); 358 Oxford St. (⊖Bond St.); 160-166 Kensington High St. (⊖High St. Kensington). Prices vary with demand, but they're usually around £1.60 per hr. Min. 50p-£1.

Post Office: When sending mail to London, include the full postal code. The largest office is the **Trafalgar Square Post Office,** 24-28 William IV St. (☎020 7484 9305), ⊖Charing Cross. Open M, W-F 8:30am-6:30pm, Tu 9:15am-6:30pm, Sa 9am-5:30pm.

ACCOMMODATIONS

The best deals in town are **student residence halls,** which rent out rooms over the summer and sometimes Easter vacations. **B&B** encompasses accommodations of varying quality, personality, and price. Be aware that in-room showers are often prefabricated units jammed into a corner. Linens are included at all **YHAs,** but towels are not; buy one from reception (£3.50). YHAs also sell discount tickets to theaters and major attractions.

BAYSWATER

Quest Hostel, 45 Queensborough Terr. (☎020 7229 7782; www.astorhostels.com). ⊖Queensway. Night Bus #N15, 94, 148. Co-ed hostel with a chummy staff. Continental breakfast included. 4- to 9-person dorms £20-24; doubles £32. MC/V. ❶

Admiral Hotel, 143 Sussex Gardens (☎020 7723 7309; www.admiral-hotel.com). ⊖Paddington. Night Bus #N15, 94, 148. Beautifully kept B&B with a sleek bar. . English breakfast included. Free Wi-Fi. Singles £50-60; doubles £80; triples £90-100; quads £90-120; quints £110-140. Ask about winter and long-stay discounts. MC/V. ❸

BLOOMSBURY

Many B&Bs and hostels are on busy roads, so be wary of noise levels. The area becomes seedier closer to King's Cross.

The Generator, Compton Pl. (☎020 7388 7666; www.generatorhostels.com), off 37 Tavistock Pl. ⊖Russell Sq. or King's Cross St. Pancras. Night Bus #N19, N35, N38, N41, N55, N91, N243. Mixed-sex dorms, a hopping bar (6pm-2am), and cheap pints (6-9pm, £1.50). Continental breakfast included. Lockers, laundry, kitchen, and ATM. Internet 50p per 7min. Reception 24hr. Reserve 1 week in advance for Sa-Su. Dorms £12.50-17.50; singles £30-35; doubles with 2 twin beds £50-55; triples £20; quads £20. Discounts for long stays. 18+. MC/V. ❶

Ashlee House, 261-265 Gray's Inn Rd. (☎020 7833 9400; www.ashleehouse.co.uk). ⊖King's Cross St. Pancras. Night Bus #N10, N63, N73, N91, 390. A "designer" budget accommodation with retro-themed rooms and common areas. Continental breakfast included. Internet £1 per 30min. Reception 24hr. 16-bed dorms £18; 8- to 10-bed £20; 4- to 6-bed £22; singles £55; doubles £73. MC/V. Weekend prices higher. ❸

Astor's Museum Hostel, 27 Montague St. (☎020 7580 5360; www.astorhostels.com). ⊖Tottenham Court Rd., Russell Sq., or Goodge St. Night Bus #N19, N35, N38, N41, N55, N91, N243. Bare-bones but friendly. English breakfast and linens included. Dorms £17-22; private double £30-35. Ages 18-35 only. AmEx/MC/V. ❶

KENSINGTON AND EARL'S COURT

YHA Holland House, Holland Walk (☎020 7937 0748; www.yha.org.uk). ⊖High St. Kensington or Holland Park. Night Bus #27, 94, 148. One of the lovelier hostels in the city. Internet £1 per 50 min. Full English breakfast included; 3-course dinners £6.50. Reception 24hr. Book 2-3 weeks in advance for summer. Dorms £16.50-24.50, under 18 £12.50-18.50. £3 discount with student ID. AmEx/MC/V. ❶

Vicarage Hotel, 10 Vicarage Gate (☎020 7229 4030; www.londonvicaragehotel.com). ⊖High St. Kensington. Night Bus #27, N28, N31, N52. Walking on Kensington Church St. from Kensington High St., there are 2 streets marked Vicarage Gate; take the 2nd on your right. Victorian house with solid wood furnishings. Ensuite rooms with TV. Breakfast included. Reserve 2 months in advance with 1 night's deposit. Singles £52, with bath £88; doubles £88/114; triples £109/145; quads £112/160. MC/V. ❸

OTHER NEIGHBORHOODS

YHA Oxford Street (HI), 14 Noel St. (☎020 7734 5984; www.yha.org.uk). ⊖Oxford Cir. Night Bus: More than 10 Night Buses run along Oxford St., including #N7, N8, and N207. Small, clean, sunny rooms with limited facilities but an unbeatable location for nightlife. Spacious, comfy TV, smoking lounge, and bar. Towels £3.50. Internet and Wi-Fi £1 per 15 min. May-Sept. 3- to 4-person dorms £22-25, under 18 £16.50-19.50; 2-bed dorms £54-60. Oct.-Mar. £23.50/19/25.50. MC/V. ❶

Luna Simone Hotel, 47-49 Belgrave Rd. (☎020 7834 5897; www.lunasimonehotel.com). ⊖Victoria or Pimlico. Night Bus #N2, 24, N36. Sparkling, spacious showers, modern decor, and a staff that takes a keen interest in its guests. Singles without bath are cramped. Full English breakfast included. Free Internet. Singles £35-45, with bath £55-65; doubles with bath £75-95; triples with bath £95-115; quads with bath £100-140. 10-20% discount in low season. MC/V. ❸

IES Chelsea Pointe, (☎020 7808 9200; www.iesreshall.com), corner of Manresa Rd. and King's Rd., entrance on Manresa Rd. ⊖Sloane Sq., then Bus #11, 19, 22, 319; ⊖South Kensington, then Bus #49. Night Bus #N11, N19, N22. Brand-new university residence hall offers clean, spacious dorm rooms year-round. In the heart of trendy Chelsea, these prices are unheard of. All rooms have bath and free Internet. Laundry and 5 TV lounges available. Wheelchair-accessible. More availability during summer and winter school breaks. Singles £285 per week; doubles £342 per week. AmEx/MC/V. ❸

FOOD

Any restaurant charging under £10 for a main course is relatively inexpensive. For the best and cheapest ethnic restaurants, head to the source: Whitechapel for Bangladeshi baltis, Chinatown for dim sum, South Kensington for French pastries, Edgware Road for shawarma. The best places to get your own ingredients are street markets (see **Shopping,** p. 146). To buy groceries, try supermarket chains **Tesco, Safeway, Sainsbury's,** or **Marks & Spencer.**

BAYSWATER

Levantine, 26 London St. (☎020 7262 1111; www.levant.co.uk). ⊖Paddington. A Lebanese restaurant with the faint aroma of incense and rose petals. Indulge in Mezze offerings like falafel and homemade hummus (£4.25). Loads of vegetarian options. Belly-dancing and shisha (water pipe) nights. Open daily noon-12:30am. MC/V. ❷

Italian Ice Cream cart, near 122 Bayswater Rd. Luscious piles of creamy gelato are perfect to take on a stroll in the Kensington Gardens across the street. One scoop £1.50, two scoops £2.00. Open daily 11am-11pm. ❶

BLOOMSBURY

ICCo (Italiano Coffee Company), 46 Goodge St. (☎020 7580 9688). ⊖Goodge St. Delicious 11-inch pizzas made to order from £3 after noon. Pasta from £2. Buy any hot drink before noon and get a free freshly baked croissant. Sandwiches and baguettes ½-price after 4pm. Takeaway available. Open daily 7am-11pm. AmEx/MC/V. ❶

Navarro's Tapas Bar, 67 Charlotte St. (☎020 7637 7713; www.navarros.co.uk). ⊖Goodge St. Colorful, bustling tapas restaurant with tiled walls and flamenco music. . Tapas £3.50-11; 2-3 per person is plenty. £7.50 min. purchase. Set price menu £17. Open M-F noon-3pm and 6-10pm, Sa 6-10pm. AmEx/MC/V. ❸

CHELSEA

Buona Sera, at the Jam, 289a King's Rd. (☎020 7352 8827). ⊖Sloane Sq., then Bus #19 or 319. With "bunk" tables stacked high into the air, the treetop-esque dining experience alone justifies a visit. Pasta plates £8.20-10.80 and meat dishes £11.50-15. Open M 6pm-midnight, Tu-F noon-3pm and 6pm-midnight, Sa-Su noon-midnight. Reservations recommended. AmEx/MC/V. ❸

Chelsea Bun, 9a Limerston St. (☎020 7352 3635). ⊖Sloane Sq., then Bus #11 or 22. Spirited, casual Anglo-American diner that serves heaping portions of everything from the "Ultimate Breakfast" (£10.30) to Tijuana Benedict (eggs with chorizo sausage; £8). Sandwiches, pasta, and burgers £2.80-8. Early-bird specials available M-F 7am-noon (£2.20-3.20) and breakfast (from £4) served until 6pm. £3.50 min. per person lunch, £5.50 dinner. Open M-Sa 7am-11:30pm, Su 9am-7pm. MC/V. ❸

THE CITY OF LONDON

Cafe Spice Namaste, 16 Prescot St. (☎020 7488 9242; www.cafespice.co.uk). ⊖Tower Hill or DLR: Tower Gateway. The extensive menu of Goan and Parsi specialties explains each dish. Meat entrees are pricey (from £14.25), but vegetarian dishes (from £4.75) are more affordable. A varied wine list and excellent, expensive desserts. Open M-F noon-3pm and 6:15-10:30pm, Sa 6:30-10:30pm. AmEx/MC/V. ❸

Futures, 8 Botolph Alley (☎020 7623 4529; www.futures-vta.net), between Botolph Ln. and Lovat Ln. ⊖Monument. London's workforce besieges this tiny takeaway joint during lunch; come before noon. Variety of vegetarian soups, salads, and hot dishes (£2.50-5.20) all change weekly. Open M-F 8-10am and 11:30am-2:30pm. ❶

CLERKENWELL AND HOLBORN

Anexo, 61 Turnmill St. (☎020 7250 3401; www.anexo.co.uk). ⊖Farringdon. This Spanish restaurant and bar serves Iberian dishes in a colorful tiled interior. The large menu has authentic paella (£7.50-9), fajitas (£7.50-11.50), and tapas (from £3.50, most £4-5). Wheelchair-accessible. Happy hour M-Sa 5-7pm. Open M-F 11am-11pm, Sa 6-11pm, Su 4:30-11pm. Bar open 11am-2am. AmEx/MC/V. ❷

Bleeding Heart Tavern, corner of Greville St. and Bleeding Heart Yard (☎020 7404 0333). ⊖Farringdon. Turn right onto Greville Str. from Hatton Gardens. Seasonal menu features traditional British favorites like beef and ale sausages with colcannon potatoes (£8.95) and roast suckling pig with spiced apple slices (£12). Open M-F 7-10:30am, noon-2:30pm and 6-10:30pm. AmEx/MC/V. ❸

EAST LONDON

Café 1001, 91 Brick Lane, Dray Walk (☎020 7247 9679; www.cafe1001.co.uk), in an alley just off Brick Ln. ⊖Aldgate East. Bring your sketch pad to this artists' den, wedged among the various Bohemian hangouts of Brick Lane. Freshly baked cakes (£2 per slice), premade salads (£3), and sandwiches (£2.50). Nightly DJs 7pm-close, W live jazz. Open M-W and Su 7am-11:30pm, Th-Sa 6pm-midnight. ❶

Yelo, 8-9 Hoxton Sq. (☎020 7729 4626; www.yelothai.com). ⊖Old St. Pad thai, curry, and stir-fry (from £5.45) make for familiar fare, but the industrial lighting, exposed brick, and house music shake things up. Wheelchair-accessible. Takeaway and delivery available. Open daily 1-3pm and 6-11pm. ❶

MARYLEBONE AND REGENT'S PARK

Mandalay, 444 Edgware Rd. (☎020 7258 3696; www.mandalayway.com). ⊖Edgware Rd. A 5 min. walk north from the Tube. Looks ordinary, tastes extraordinary—one of the best deals around. Lunch specials offer great value (curry and rice £4; 3 courses £6). Entrees, including sizeable vegetarian selection, £4-8. Open M-Sa noon-2:30pm and 6-10:30pm. Dinner reservations recommended. MC/V. ❶

Patogh, 8 Crawford Pl. (☎020 7262 4015). ⊖Edgware Rd. With just 10 tables, this Persian restaurant gives new meaning to "hole in the wall." Generous portions of sesame-seed flatbread (£2). Takeaway available. Open daily noon-midnight. Cash only. ❷

NORTH LONDON

Gallipoli, 102 Upper St. (☎020 7359 0630), **Gallipoli Again,** 120 Upper St. (☎7359 1578), and **Gallipoli Bazaar,** 107 Upper St. (☎7226 5333). ⊖Angel. Dark walls and patterned blue tiles accompany Lebanese, North African, and Turkish delights like *iskender* kebab (grilled lamb with yogurt and marinated pita bread in secret sauce; £8.40) and the 2-course lunch (£8.95). Gallipoli Bazaar sits between the other 2 and serves up food, cocktails, and sheesha pipes. Open M-Th 10:30am-11pm, F-Sa 10am-midnight, Su 10:30am-11pm. Reservations recommended F-Sa. MC/V. ❷

The Crêperie de Hampstead, 77 Hampstead High St. (www.hampsteadcreperie.com), the metal stand on the side of the King William IV statue. ⊖Hampstead. Don't let the slow-moving line deter you; these crepes (£3-4) are worth the wait. Open M-Th 11:45am-11pm, F-Su 11:45am-11:30pm. ❶

THE WEST END

Masala Zone, 9 Marshall St. (☎020 7287 9966; www.realindianfood.com). ⊖Oxford Circus. Also in Islington at 80 Upper St. (☎020 7359 3399). Masala Zone oozes hipness with its softly lit interior and sunken dining room. The menu has typical favorites (£7-12) and "street food," which is served in small bowls (£4-6). The specialty is thalis, which are platters filled with healthy fare (£8-12). Open M-F noon-2:45pm and 5:30-11pm, Sa 12:30-11pm, Su 12:30-3:30pm and 6-10:30pm. MC/V. ❷

Rock and Sole Plaice, 47 Endell St. (☎020 7836 3785; www.rockandsoleplaice.com). ⊖Covent Garden. A self-proclaimed "master fryer" (qualifications unclear) turns out tasty haddock, cod, halibut, and sole filets (all with chips, £9-11). Packed during mealtime rushes. Open M-Sa 11:30am-11:30pm, Su 11:30am-10pm. MC/V. ❷

OTHER NEIGHBORHOODS

George's Portobello Fish Bar, 329 Portobello Rd. (☎020 8969 7895). ⊖Ladbroke Grove. Although this little space has lived through various incarnations, the fish and chips are a classic hit: cod, rockfish, and plaice come with huge servings of chunky chips (from £6.30). Open M-F 11am-11:45pm, Sa 11am-9pm, Su noon-9:30pm. ❷

Jenny Lo's Teahouse, 14 Eccleston St. (☎020 7259 0399). ⊖Victoria. Around the corner from Jenny's father's high-end restaurant (Ken Lo is one the UK's most famous chefs). The delicious pork noodle soup (£6.50) and the broad selection of Asian noodles (£6.50-8) make eating here worth the wait. Takeaway and delivery available (min. £5 per person). Open M-F noon-3:30pm and 6-10pm, Sa 6-9:30pm. Cash only. ❷

SIGHTS

WESTMINSTER

The City of Westminster, now a borough of London, has been the seat of British power for over 1000 years. William the Conqueror was crowned in Westminster Abbey on Christmas Day, AD 1066, and his successors built the Palace of Westminster, which today houses Parliament.

WESTMINSTER ABBEY. Founded as a Benedictine monastery, Westminster Abbey has evolved into a house of kings and queens both living and dead. Almost nothing remains of **St. Edward's Abbey:** Henry III's 13th-century Gothic reworking created most of the current grand structure. Britons buried or commemorated inside the Abbey include: **Henry VII; Mary, Queen of Scots; Elizabeth I;** and the scholars and artists honored in the **"Poet's Corner"** (Jane Austen, the Brontë sisters, Chaucer, Shakespeare, and Dylan Thomas). A door off the east cloister leads to the **Chapter House,** the original meeting place of the House of Commons. Next door to the Abbey (through the cloisters), the lackluster **Abbey Museum** is in the Norman undercroft. Just north of the Abbey, **St. Margaret's Church** enjoys a peculiar status: as a part of the Royal Peculiar, it is neither under the jurisdiction of the diocese of England nor the archbishop of Canterbury. *(Parliament Sq. Access Old Monastery, cloister, and garden from Dean's Yard, behind the Abbey. ⊖Westminster. Westminster. Abbey ☎020 7222 5152. Chapter House ☎020 7654 4840; www.westminster-abbey.org. Abbey open M-Tu and Th-F 9:30am-3:45pm, W 9:30am-7pm, Sa 9:30am-1:45pm, Su open for services only at 8, 10, and 11:15am and 3, 5:45, and 6:30pm. Museum open daily 10:30am-4pm. Partially wheelchair-accessible. Abbey and museum £12, students and children 11-17 £9, families of 4 £28. Services free. 1hr. tours £5 Apr.-Oct. M-F 10, 10:30, 11am, 2, 2:30pm, Sa 10, 10:30, 11am; Oct.-Mar. M-F 10:30, 11am, 2, 2:30pm, Sa 10:30, 11am. Audio tours £4 available M-F 9:30am-3pm, Sa 9:30am-1pm. AmEx/MC/V.)*

BUCKINGHAM PALACE. The Palace is open to visitors from the end of July to the end of September every year, but don't expect to meet the Queen—the State Rooms are the only rooms on view, and they are used only for formal occasions. "God Save the Queen" is the rallying cry at the **Queens Gallery,** dedicated to exhibits of absurdly valuable items from the Royal Collection. Detached from the palace and tour, the **Royal Mews** acts as a museum, stable, riding school, and working carriage house. The main attraction is the Queen's collection of coaches, including the Cinderella-like "Glass Coach" used to carry royal brides, including Princess Diana, to their weddings, and the State Coaches of Australia, Ireland, and Scotland. To witness the Palace for free, attend a session of the **Changing of the Guard.** Show up well before 11:30am and stand in front of the Palace in view of the morning guards, or use the steps of the Victoria Memorial as a vantage point. *(At the end of the Mall, between Westminster, Belgravia, and Mayfair. ⊖St. James's Park, Victoria, Green Park, or Hyde Park Corner. ☎020 7766 7324; www.the-royal-collection.com. Palace open late July to late Sept. daily 9:30am-6:30pm, last entry 4:15pm. £15, students £14, children 6-17 £8.50, under 5 free, families of 5 £67. Advance* *booking is recommended and required for disabled visitors. Queens Gallery open daily 10am-5:30pm, last entry 4:30pm. Wheelchair-accessible. £8, students £7, families £22. Royal Mews open late July to late Sept. daily 10am-5pm, last entry 4:15pm; Mar.-July and late Sept. to late Oct. M-Th and Sa-Su 11am-4pm, last entry 3:15pm. Wheelchair-accessible. £7, seniors £6, children under 17 £4.50, families £19. Changing of the Guard Apr. -late July daily, Aug.-Mar. every other day, excepting the Queen's absence, inclement weather, or pressing state functions. Free.)*

THE HOUSES OF PARLIAMENT. The Palace of Westminster has been home to both the House of Lords and the House of Commons (together known as Parliament) since the 11th century, when Edward the Confessor established his court here. Standing guard on the northern side of the building is the Clock Tower, nicknamed **Big Ben,** after the robustly proportioned Benjamin Hall, a former Commissioner of Works. **Victoria Tower,** at the south end of the palace building, contains copies of every Act of Parliament since 1497. A flag flying from the top signals that Parliament is in session. When the Queen is in the building, a special royal banner is flown instead. Visitors with enough patience or luck to make it inside the chambers can hear the occasional debates between members of both the Lords and the Commons. *(Parliament Sq., in Westminster. Queue for both Houses forms at St. Stephen's entrance, between Old and New Palace Yards. ⊖Westminster. ☎020 08709 063 773; www.parliament.uk/visiting/visiting.cfm. "Line of Route" Tour: includes both Houses. UK residents can contact their MPs for tours year-round, generally M-W mornings and F. Foreign visitors may tour Aug.-Sept. Book online, by phone, or in person at Abingdon Green ticket office (open mid-July) across from Palace of Westminster. Open Aug. M-Tu and F-Sa 9:15am-4:30pm, W-Th 1:15-4:30pm; Sept. M and F-Sa 9:15am-4:30pm, Tu-Th 1:15-4:30pm. 75min. tours depart every few min. £12, students £8, families of 4 £30. MC/V.)*

PARLIAMENTARY PROCEDURE. Arrive early in the afternoon to minimize waiting, which often exceeds 2hr. Keep in mind that the wait for Lords is generally shorter than the wait for Commons. To sit in on Parliament's "question time" (40min.; M-W 2:30pm, Th-F 11am) apply for tickets several weeks in advance through your embassy in London.

ST. JAMES'S PARK AND GREEN PARK. The streets leading up to Buckingham Palace are flanked by two expanses of greenery: St. James's Park and Green Park. In the middle of St. James's Park is the placid **St. James's Park Lake** and the pelicans who call it home—the lake and the grassy area surrounding it are an official waterfowl preserve. In the back corner, closest to the palace, is a children's playground in memory of Princess Diana. Across the Mall, the lush Green Park is the creation of Charles II; it connects Westminster and St. James's. *(The Mall. ⊖St. James's Park or Green Park. Open daily 5am-midnight. Lawn chairs available Apr-Sept. 10am-10pm or dawn-dusk; Mar. and Oct. 10am-6pm. £2 for 2hr., student deal £30 for the season. Last rental 2hr. before close. Tour behind the Guard Change every Th, £6. Summer walks in the park some M 1-2pm, including tour of Guard's Palace and Victoria Tower Gardens. Book in advance by calling ☎020 7930 1793.)*

WESTMINSTER CATHEDRAL. Following Henry VIII's divorce from the Catholic Church, London's Catholic community remained without a cathedral until 1884, when the Church purchased a derelict prison on what used to be a monastery site. The Neo-Byzantine church looks somewhat like a fortress and is now one of London's great religious landmarks. An elevator, well worth the minimal fee, carries visitors up the striped 273 ft. bell tower for an all-encompassing view of Westminster, the river, and Kensington. *(Cathedral Piazza, off Victoria St. ⊖Victoria. ☎020 7798 9055; www.westminstercathedral.org.uk. Open daily 8am-7pm. Bell tower open daily 9:30am-12:30pm and 1-5pm. Organ recitals Su 4:45pm. Free; suggested donation £2.)*

THE MILLENNIUM MILE

Time: 8-10hr.

Distance: 2½ mi. (4km)

When To Go: Begin at 8am.

Start: ⊖Tower Hill

Finish: ⊖Westminster

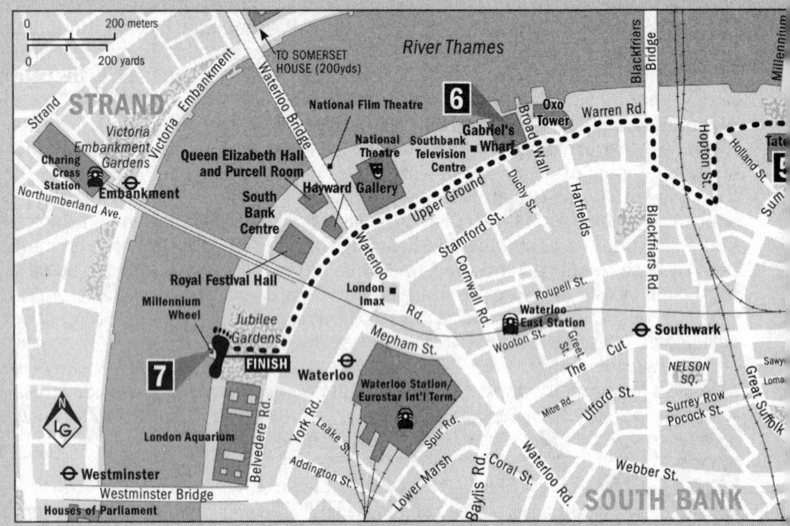

Stark, modern monuments to London's present—the round glass sphere of City Hall, the converted power station that is the Tate Modern—line your side of the river, while stately relics of a rich past—the Tower of London and St. Paul's Cathedral—stand on the opposite bank. Whether it's a search for Shakespeare and Picasso that brings you to the South Bank, or just a hankering for a nice walk, you will find yourself rewarded.

1. TOWER OF LONDON. Begin your trek to the Tower early to avoid the crowds. Tours given by the Yeomen Warders meet every 1½hr. near the entrance. Listen as they expertly recount tales of royal conspiracy, treason, and murder. See the **White Tower,** once a fortress and residence of kings. Shiver at the executioner's stone on the tower green and pay your respects at the Chapel of St. Peter ad Vinculum, which holds the remains of three queens. First, get the dirt on the gemstones at **Martin Tower,** then wait in line to see the **Crown Jewels.** The jewels include such glittering lovelies as the largest cut diamond in the world (p. 137). Time: 2hr.

2. TOWER BRIDGE. An engineering wonder that puts its plainer sibling, the London Bridge to shame. Marvel at its beauty, but skip the Tower Bridge Experience. Call in advance to inquire what times the Tower drawbridge is lifted (p. 137). Time: no need to stop walking; take in the mechanics as you head to the next sight.

3. DESIGN MUSEUM. On Butler's Wharf, let the Design Museum introduce you to the latest innovations in contemporary design. See what's to come in the forward-looking Review Gallery or hone in on individual designers and products in the Temporary Gallery. From the museum walk along the **Queen's Walk.** To your left you will find the *HMS Belfast,* which was launched in 1938 and then led the landing on D-Day in 1944. Time: 1hr.

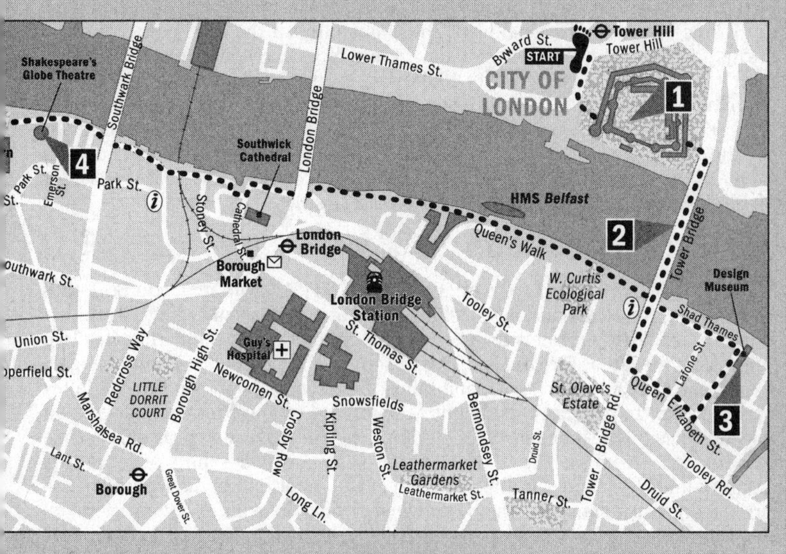

4. SHAKESPEARE'S GLOBE THEATRE. "I hope to see London once ere I die," says Shakespeare's Davy in *Henry IV*. In time, he may see it from the beautiful recreation of The Bard's most famous theater. Excellent exhibits detail the intracacies of costuming and stage effects in Shakespeare's day, as well as the more modern process of rebuilding of the theater almost 400 years after the original burned down (p. 137). You might be able to catch a matinee performance. Call in advance for tour and show times. Time: 1hr. for tour; 3hr. for performance.

5. TATE MODERN. It's hard to imagine anything casting a shadow over the Globe Theatre, but the massive former Bankside Power Station does just that. One of the world's premier modern art museums, the Tate promises a new spin on well-known favorites and works by emerging British artists. Be sure to catch one of the informative docent tours and don't forget to check out the rotating installation in the Turbine Room (p. 141). Time: 2hr.

6. GABRIEL'S WHARF. Check out the cafes, bars, and boutiques of colorful Gabriel's Wharf. If you missed the top floor of the Tate Modern, go to the public viewing gallery on the 8th floor of the **OXO Tower Wharf.** On your way to the London Eye, stop by the **South Bank Centre.** Established as a primary cultural center in 1951, it now exhibits a range of music from Philharmonic extravaganzas to low-key jazz. You may even catch one of the free lunchtime or afternoon events. Call in advance for dates and times. Time: 1½hr. for schmoozing and dinner.]

7. LONDON EYE. The London Eye, also known as the Millennium Wheel, has firmly established itself as one of London's top attractions, popular with locals and tourists alike. As Europe's tallest Ferris wheel, the Eye offers amazing 360° views from its glass pods; you may be able to see all of London lit up at sunset. Book in advance to minimize queue time (p. 137). Time: 1hr.

WHITEHALL. Synonymous with the British civil service, **Whitehall** refers to the stretch of road connecting Trafalgar Sq. with Parliament Sq. Toward the north end of Whitehall, **Great Scotland Yard** marks the former headquarters of the Metropolitan Police. Nearer Parliament Sq., heavily guarded steel gates mark the entrance to Downing Street. In 1735, No. 10 was made the official residence of the First Lord of the Treasury, a position now permanently identified with the Prime Minister. His neighbors, the Chancellor of the Exchequer, and the Parliamentary Chief Whip, live at No. 11 and No. 12, respectively. When Tony Blair's family was too big for No. 10, he switched houses with Gordon Brown, a move that proved convenient when Brown was appointed Prime Minister in 2007. The street is closed to visitors, but if you wait long enough, you might see the PM. South of Downing St., in the middle of Whitehall, Edward Lutyen's *Cenotaph* (1919) stands, a proud tribute to WWI dead. *(Between Trafalgar Sq. and Parliament Sq. ⊖Westminster, Embankment, or Charing Cross.)*

THE CITY OF LONDON

ST. PAUL'S CATHEDRAL. Originally built in 604 AD, the majestic St. Paul's is a cornerstone of London's architectural and historical legacy. Architect Christopher Wren's masterpiece is the fifth cathedral to occupy the site. Two years after the Great Fire of 1666, construction of the present cathedral began. Inside, the nave leads to the second-tallest freestanding dome in Europe (after St. Peter's in the Vatican), its height accentuated by the tricky perspective of the paintings on the inner surface. Climbing the 259 narrow steps is exhausting, but the views from the top of the dome are extraordinary and worth the trip: a panoramic cityscape. Circling the base of the inner dome, the **Whispering Gallery** is a perfect resounding chamber: whisper into the wall, and your friend on the other side will hear you—or, theoretically, he or she could if everyone else weren't trying the same thing. Far, far below the lofty dome, the **crypt** is packed wall-to-wall with plaques and tombs of great Britons and, of course, the ubiquitous gift shop. Lord Nelson commands a prime location, with radiating galleries of gravestones and tributes honoring other military heroes, from Epstein's bust of T.E. Lawrence (of Arabia) to a plaque commemorating the casualties of the Gulf War. The magnificently carved stone of the exterior is warmed and softened by the cathedral gardens which curve round the sides in a ramble of roses and clipped grass. *(St. Paul's Churchyard. ⊖St. Paul's. ☎020 7246 8350; www.stpauls.co.uk. Open M-Sa 8:30am-4pm; last admission 3:45pm. Dome and galleries open M-Sa 9:30am-4pm. Open for worship daily 7:15am-6pm. Partially wheelchair-accessible. Admission £10 concessions £8.50, children 7-16 £2.50; worshippers free. Group of 10 or more 50p discount per ticket. "Supertour" M-F 11, 11:30am, 1:30, 2pm; £3, concessions £2, children 7-16 £1; English only. Audio tour available in many languages daily 9am-3:30pm; £4 concessions £3.50)*

ST. PAUL'S FOR POCKET CHANGE. To gain access to the Cathedral's nave for free, attend an Evensong service (M-Sa 5pm, 45min). Arrive at 4:50pm to be admitted to seats in the choir.

GREAT BRITAIN

THE TOWER OF LONDON. The turrets of this multi-functional block—serving as palace, prison, royal mint, and museum over the past 900 years—are impressive not only for their appearance but also for their integral role in England's history. A popular way to get a feel for the Tower is to join one of the theatrical **Yeoman Warders' Tours.** Queen Anne Boleyn passed through Traitor's Gate just before her death, but entering the Tower is no longer as perilous as it used to be. **St. Thomas's Tower** begins the self-guided tour of the Medieval Palace. At the end of the **Wall Walk**—a series of eight towers—is **Martin Tower,** which houses an exhibit that traces the history of the British Crown and is now home to a fascinating collection of retired crowns (without the gemstones; those have been recycled into the current models); informative plaques are much better here than in the **Jewel House,** where the crown jewels are held. With the exception of the Coronation Spoon, everything dates from after 1660, since Cromwell melted down the original booty. The centerpiece of the fortress is White Tower, which begins with the first-floor **Chapel of St. John the Evangelist.** Outside, Tower Green is a lovely grassy area—not so lovely, though, for those once executed there. *(Tower Hill, next to Tower Bridge, within easy reach of the South Bank and the East End. ⊖Tower Hill or DLR: Tower Gateway. ☎0844 482 7777, ticket sales ☎0844 482 7799; www.hrp.org.uk. Open Mar.-Oct. M 10am-6:30pm, Tu-Sa 9am-6:30pm, Su 10am-6:30pm; buildings close at 5:30. Nov.-Feb. all closing times 1hr. earlier. Tower Green open only by Yeoman tours, after 4:30pm, or for daily services. Admission £16.50, concessions £14, children 5-15 £9.50, children under 5 free, families of 5 £46. Tickets also sold at Tube stations; buy them in advance to avoid long queues at the door. Tours: "Yeoman Warders' Tours" meet near entrance; 1hr., every 30min. M and Su 10am-3:30pm, Tu-Sa 9:30am-3:30pm. Audio tours £3.50, concessions £2.50.)*

TOWER BRIDGE. Not to be mistaken for its plainer sibling, **London Bridge,** Tower Bridge is featured in most movies set in London. A relatively new construction—built in 1894—its bright blue suspension cables connect the banks of the Thames, raising it above the cluster of other bridges in the area. Historians and technophiles will appreciate the **Tower Bridge Exhibition,** which combines scenic 140 ft. glass-enclosed walkways with videos presenting a history of the bridge. *(Entrance to the Tower Bridge Exhibition is through the west side upriver of the North Tower. ⊖Tower Hill or London Bridge. ☎020 7403 3761, for lifting schedule ☎020 7940 3984; www.towerbridge.org.uk. Open daily Apr.-Sept. 10am-6:30pm, last entry 5:30pm; Oct.-Mar. 9:30am-6pm, last entry 5pm. Wheelchair-accessible. £6, concessions £4.50, children 5-16 £3.)*

THE SOUTH BANK

SHAKESPEARE'S GLOBE THEATRE. This incarnation of the Globe is faithful to the first Globe, thatch roof and all. The original burned down in 1613 after a 14-year run as the Bard's preferred playhouse. Today's reconstruction stands as the cornerstone of the International Shakespeare Globe Centre. For information on performances, see p. 145. *(Bankside, close to Bankside pier. ⊖Southwark or London Bridge. ☎020 7902 1500; www.shakespeares-globe.org. Open daily Apr.-Sept. 9am-noon exhibit and tours, noon-5pm exhibit only; Oct.-Apr. 10am-5pm exhibit and tours. Wheelchair-accessible. £10.50 concessions £8.50, children 5-15 £6.50. To save money, buy a £5 groundling ticket, which includes access to the exhibits.)*

SOUTHWARK CATHEDRAL. A site of worship since AD 606, the cathedral has undergone numerous transformations in the last 1400 years: it was a convent in 606, a priory in 1106, a parish church in 1540, and finally, a cathedral since 1905. Shakespeare's brother Edmund is buried here. Near the center, the **archaeological gallery** is actually a small excavation by the cathedral wall, revealing a first-century Roman road. *(Montague Close. ⊖London Bridge. ☎020 7367 6700; www.southwark.anglican.org/cathedral. Open M-F 8am-6pm, Sa-Su 9am-6pm. Wheelchair-accessible. Admission free, suggested donation £4. Groups should book in advance; group rates available. Audio tours £5; concessions £4, children 5-15 £2.50. Camera permit £2; video permit £5.)*

LONDON EYE. At 135m (430 ft.), the British Airways London Eye, also known as the Millennium Wheel, is the biggest observational wheel in the world. The ellipsoidal glass "pods" give uninterrupted views from the top during each 30min. revolution. *(Jubilee Gardens, between County Hall and the Festival Hall. ⊖Waterloo. ☎087 990 8883, booking ☎0870 500 0600; www.ba-londoneye.com. Open daily Oct.-May*

10am-8pm, June 10am-9pm, July-Aug. 10am-9:30pm, Sept. 10am-9pm. Wheelchair-accessible. Buy tickets from box office at the corner of County Hall. Advance booking recommended, but check the weather. £15.50, concessions £12, children under 16 £7.75.

THE REAL DEAL. While the London Eye does offer magnificent views (particularly at night), the queues are long, and it's expensive. For equally impressive sights in a quieter setting, head to Hampstead Heath.

BLOOMSBURY AND MARYLEBONE

During the early 20th century, Gordon Sq. resounded with the philosophizing and womanizing of the **Bloomsbury Group,** a set of intellectuals including John Maynard Keynes, Bertrand Russell, Lytton Strachey, and Virginia Woolf. Marylebone's most famous resident (and address) never existed: 221b Baker St. was the fictional home of Sherlock Holmes, but 221 Baker St. is actually the headquarters of the Abbey National Bank.

REGENT'S PARK. When Crown Architect John Nash designed Regent's Park, he envisioned a residential development for the "wealthy and good." Fortunately for us commonfolk, Parliament opened the space to all in 1811, creating London's handsomest recreation area. *(⊖Regent's Park, Great Portland St., or Camden Town. ☎020 7486 7905; www.royalparks.org. Open daily 5am-dusk. Free.)*

BRITISH LIBRARY. The British Library is a paradox: the sleekest, most modern of buildings (finished in 1998) contains in its vast and comprehensive holdings some of the oldest and most precious English literary and historical documents. Most of the library is underground, with 12 million books on 200 miles of shelving; the above-ground brick building is home to cavernous reading rooms and a museum. Treasures of the **British Library Room** include Beethoven's tuning fork, Tudor documents, and original manuscripts of *Beowulf, Jane Eyre, and Tess of the D'Urbervilles*. *(96 Euston Rd.⊖Euston Sq. or King's Cross St. Pancras. ☎020 7412 7332; www.bl.uk. Open M 9:30am-6pm, Tu 9:30am-8pm, W-F 9:30am-6pm, Sa 9:30am-5pm, Su 11am-5pm. Tours of public areas M, W, F, 10:30am and 3pm. Tours including one of the reading rooms Su and bank holidays 11:30am and 3pm. Reservations recommended. Wheelchair-accessible. To use reading rooms, bring 2 forms of ID—1 with signature and 1 with home address. Free. Tours £8, concessions £6.50. Audio tours £3.50, concessions £2.50.)*

OTHER BLOOMSBURY SIGHTS. A co-founder and key advisor of **University College London,** social philosopher Jeremy Bentham still watches over his old haunts; his body has sat on display in the **South Cloister** since 1850, wax head and all, as requested in his will. *(Main entrance on Gower St. South Cloister entrance through the courtyard.⊖Euston. ☎020 7679 2000; www.ucl.ac.uk/Bentham-Project Quadrangle gates close at midnight; access to Jeremy Bentham ends at 6pm. Wheelchair-accessible. Free.)* Next to the British Library are the soaring Gothic spires of **St. Pancras Chambers.** Formerly the Midland Grand Hotel, the gorgeous red brick building is now a hollow shell being developed as apartments and a five-star hotel. *(Euston Rd. just west of the King's Cross St. Pancras Tube station. ⊖King's Cross St. Pancras.)*

CLERKENWELL AND HOLBORN

Clerkenwell buildings are beautiful from the outside but inaccessible to tourists; walk the **Clerkenwell Historic Trail** to see the exteriors. *(Free maps at the 3 Things Coffee Room, 53 Clerkenwell Close. ☎020 7125 37438. ⊖Farringdon. Open daily 8am-8pm.)*

THE TEMPLE. Named after the crusading Order of the Knights Templar, this complex of buildings houses legal and parliamentary offices, but it hasn't lost its clerical flavor: silent, suited barristers hurry by at all hours, clutching briefcases. The charming network of gardens and the medieval church remain open to the enterprising visitor. Make sure to see the **Inner Temple Gateway,** between 16 and 17 Fleet St., the 1681 fountain of **Fountain Court** (featured in Dickens's *Martin Chuzzlewit*), and Elm Court, tucked behind the church, a tiny yet exquisite garden ringed by massive stone structures. *(Between Essex St. and Temple Ave.; church courtyard off Middle Temple Ln. ⊖Temple or Blackfriars. Free.)*

ROYAL COURTS OF JUSTICE. Straddling the official division between the City of Westminster and the City of London, this neo-Gothic structure encloses courtrooms and the Great Hall (home to Europe's largest mosaic floor) amid elaborate passageways. All courtrooms are open to the public during trials. *(Where the Strand becomes Fleet St.; rear entrance on Carey St. ⊖Temple or Chancery Ln. ☎020 7947 6000, tours ☎020 7947 7684. Open M-F 9am-4:30pm; cases are heard 10:30am-1pm and 2-4pm. Wheelchair-accessible. Free. Tours £6.)*

KENSINGTON AND EARL'S COURT

Nobody took much notice of Kensington before 1689, when the newly crowned William III and Mary II moved into Kensington Palace. In 1851, the Great Exhibition brought in enough money to finance museums and colleges. Now that the neighborhood is home to expensive stores like Harrods and Harvey Nichols, it's hard to imagine the days when the area was known for taverns and highwaymen (robbers galloping on horseback).

HYDE PARK AND KENSINGTON GARDENS. Enclosed by London's wealthiest neighborhoods, **Hyde Park** has served as the model for city parks around the world, including Central Park in New York and Paris's Bois de Boulogne. **Kensington Gardens,** contiguous with Hyde Park and originally part of it, was created in the late 17th century when William and Mary set up house in Kensington Palace. *(Framed by Kensington Rd., Knightsbridge, Park Ln., and Bayswater Rd. ⊖Queensway, Lancaster Gate, Marble Arch, Hyde Park Corner, or High St. Kensington. ☎020 7298 2100; www.royalparks.org.uk. Open daily 6am-dusk. Admission free. "Liberty Drive" rides available Tu-F 10am-5pm for seniors and the disabled; call ☎077 6749 8096. A full program of music, performance, and children's activities takes place during summer; see park notice boards for details.)* In the middle of the park is the **Serpentine,** officially known as the "Long Water West of the Serpentine Bridge." Doggy-paddling tourists and boaters have made it London's busiest swimming hole. Nowhere near the water, the **Serpentine Gallery** holds contemporary art and is free and open to the public daily from 10am to 6pm. *(⊖Hyde Park Corner. Boating: ☎020 7262 1330. Open daily Apr.-Sept. 10am-6:30pm or later in fine weather. £6.50 per hour for up to four people (plus £5 deposit). Swimming at the Lido, south shore; ☎020 7706 3422. Open daily from June to early Sept. 10am-6pm. Lockers and sun lounges available. £4 after 4pm, students £3/2.50, children £1/80p, families £9.)* At the northeast corner of the park, near Marble Arch, you can see free speech in action as proselytizers, politicos, and flat-out crazies dispense wisdom to bemused tourists at **Speaker's Corner** on Sundays, the only place in London where demonstrators can assemble without a permit.

KENSINGTON PALACE. In 1689 William and Mary commissioned Christopher Wren to remodel Nottingham House into a palace. Kensington remained the principal royal residence until George III decamped to Kew in 1760, but it is still in use—Princess Diana lived here. Royalty fanatics can tour the rather underwhelming **Hanoverian State Apartments,** with *trompe l'œil* paintings by William Kent, or the **Royal Ceremonial Dress Collection,** a magnificent spread of tailored and embroidered garments. *(Western edge of Kensington Gardens; enter through the park. ⊖High St. Kensington, Notting Hill Gate, or Queensway. ☎020 7937 9561; www.hrp.*

org.uk/KensingtonPalace. Open daily 10am-6pm, last admission 1hr. before closing. Wheelchair-accessible. £12.30, students £10.75, children free, families of 5 £34. Combo passes with Tower of London or Hampton Court available. MC/V.)

KNIGHTSBRIDGE AND BELGRAVIA

APSLEY HOUSE AND WELLINGTON ARCH. Named for Baron Apsley, the house later known as "No. 1, London" was bought in 1817 by the Duke of Wellington, whose heirs still occupy a modest suite on the top floor. Most visitors come for Wellington's fine art collection, much of which was given to him by the crowned heads of Europe following the Battle of Waterloo. *(Hyde Park Corner. ⊖Hyde Park Corner. ☎020 7499 5676; www.english-heritage.org.uk/london. Open W-Su Apr.-Oct. 10 am-5pm; Nov.-Mar. 10am-4pm. Wheelchair-accessible. £5.50, students £4.40, children 5-18 £2.80 Joint ticket with Wellington Arch £6.90/5.20/3.50. Audio tour free. MC/V.)* Across from Apsley House, the Wellington Arch was ignored by tourists and Londoners alike until April 2001, when the completion of a restoration project revealed the interior to the public. *(Hyde Park Corner. ⊖Hyde Park Corner. ☎020 7930 2726; www.english-heritage.org.uk/london. Open W-Su Apr.-Oct. 10am-5pm, Nov.-Mar. 10am-4pm. Wheelchair-accessible. £3.30, students with ISIC £2.60, children 5-16 £1.70. MC/V.)*

THE WEST END

TRAFALGAR SQUARE. The square is named in commemoration of the defeat of Napoleon's navy at Trafalgar—England's greatest naval victory. It has traditionally been a site for public rallies and protest movements, but it is packed with tourists, pigeons, and the ever-ubiquitous black taxis on a daily basis. Towering over the square is the 170 ft. granite **Nelson's Column,** which until recently was one of the world's tallest displays of decades-old pigeon droppings. Now, thanks to a deep clean sponsored by the Mayor, this monument to naval hero Lord Nelson sparkles once again. *(⊖Charing Cross.)*

ST. MARTIN-IN-THE-FIELDS. The fourth church to stand here, James Gibbs's 1726 creation is instantly recognizable: the rectangular portico building supporting a soaring steeple has made it the model for countless Georgian churches in Ireland and America. Handel and Mozart both performed here, and today the church hosts frequent concerts with some of Europe's premier symphonies and conductors. In order to support the church's maintenance, a delicious cafe, book shop, and art gallery dwell in the Crypt. *(St. Martin's Ln., northeast corner of Trafalgar Sq.; crypt entrance on Duncannon St. ⊖Leicester Sq. or Charing Cross. ☎020 7766 1100; www.smitf.org. Call or visit website for hours and further information.)*

SOHO. Soho is one of the most diverse areas in central London. **Old Compton Street** is the center of London's GLBT culture. In the 1950s, immigrants from Hong Kong started moving en masse to the few blocks just north of Leicester Sq., around **Gerrard Street** and grittier **Lisle Street,** which now form **Chinatown.** Gaudy, brash, and world-famous, **Piccadilly Circus** is made up of four of the West End's major arteries (Piccadilly, Regent St., Shaftesbury Ave., and the Haymarket). In the middle of all the glitz and neon stands Gilbert's famous **Statue of Eros.** *(⊖Piccadilly Circus.)* Lined with tour buses, overpriced clubs, and generic cafes, **Leicester Sq.** is one destination that Londoners go out of their way to avoid due to throngs of tourists. *(⊖Piccadilly Circus or Leicester Sq.)* A calm in the midst of the storm, **Soho Square** is a rather scruffy patch of green space popular with picnickers. Its removed location makes the square more hospitable and less trafficked than Leicester. *(⊖Tottenham Ct. Rd. Park open daily 10am-dusk.)*

MUSEUMS AND GALLERIES

Centuries spent as the capital of an empire, together with a decidedly English penchant for collecting, have given London a spectacular set of museums. Art lovers, history buffs, and amateur ethnologists won't know which way to turn. Even better news for museum lovers: since 2002, admission to all major collections is free in celebration of the Queen's Golden Jubilee.

MAJOR COLLECTIONS

TATE MODERN. Sir Giles Gilbert Scott's mammoth building houses the second half of the national collection (the other set is held in the National Gallery). The Tate Modern is probably the most popular museum in London, as well as one of the most famous modern art museums in the world. The collection is enormous, but gallery space is limited—works rotate frequently. If you are dying to see a particular piece, head to the museum's computer station on the fifth floor to browse the entire collection. The seventh floor has unblemished views of the Thames and north and south of London. *(Main entrance on Bankside, on the South Bank; 2nd entrance on Queen's Walk. ⊖Southwark or Blackfriars. ☎020 7887 8888; www.tate.org.uk. Open M-Th and Su 10am-6pm, F-Sa 10am-10pm. Wheelchair-accessible on Holland St. Free tours (45 min) meet on the gallery concourses: 3rd level 11am and noon, 5th level 2 and 3pm. 5 types of audio tours; £2. Free; special exhibits up to £10. Free talks M-F 1pm; meet at the concourse on the appropriate level.)*

NATIONAL GALLERY. The National Gallery is an enormous gallery stuffed with masterpieces. Unless you have a few years, you will have to power past the magnificent collections of Titians, Botticellis, DaVincis, and medieval art. Don't miss the fabulously detailed *Arnolfini Wedding Portrait* by Van Eyck or Van Gogh's iconic *Sunflowers*. Founded by an Act of Parliament in 1824, the Gallery has grown to hold an enormous collection of Western European paintings, ranging from the 1200s to the 1900s. Numerous additions have been made, the most recent (and controversial) being the massive modern Sainsbury Wing, which holds almost all of the museum's large exhibitions as well as restaurants and lecture halls. If pressed for time, head to **Art Start** in the Sainsbury Wing, where you can design and print out a personalized tour of the paintings you want to see. Themed audio tours and family routes also available from the information desk. *(Main Portico entrance on north side of Trafalgar Sq. ⊖Charing Cross or Leicester Sq. ☎020 7747 2885; www.nationalgallery.org.uk. Open M-Tu and Th-Su 10am-6pm, W 10am-9pm. Special exhibitions in the Sainsbury Wing occasionally open until 10pm. 1hr. tours start at Sainsbury Wing information desk. Tours M-F and Su 11:30am and 2:30pm, Sa 11:30am, 12:30, 2:30, and 3:30pm. Wheelchair-accessible at Sainsbury Wing on Pall Mall East, Orange St., and Getty Entrance. Free; some temporary exhibitions £5-10, seniors £4-8, students and children ages 12-18 £2-5. Audio tours free, suggested donation £3.50. AmEx/MC/V.)*

NATIONAL PORTRAIT GALLERY. Take a vast and magnificent tour of the *Who's Who* in Great Britain, beginning with priceless portraits of the Tudors and ending with today's celebrities. Try to trace family resemblances through the royal families (the Stuarts' noses) or admire the centuries of changing costume: velvet, taffeta, fabulously-patterned brocade. The famous picture of Shakespeare with an earring hangs near the Queen Elizabeth portraits in the Tudor wing. New facilities include an IT Gallery, with computers to search for pictures and print out a personalized tour, and a third-floor restaurant offering an aerial view of London, although the inflated prices will limit most visitors to coffee. To see the paintings in chronological order, take the escalator in the Ondaatje Wing to the top floor. *(St. Martin's Pl., at the start of Charing Cross Rd., Trafalgar Sq. ⊖Leicester Sq. or*

Charing Cross. ☎020 7312 2463; www.npg.org.uk. Open M-W and Sa-Su 10am-6pm, Th-F 10am-9pm. Wheelchair-accessible on Orange St. Lectures Tu 3pm free. Popular events require tickets, available from the information desk. Evening talks Th 7pm free-£3. Talks on Sunday at 3pm. Live music F 6:30pm free. Gallery free; some special exhibitions free-£6. Audio tours £2.)

BRITISH MUSEUM. With 50,000 items from all corners of the globe, the magnificent collection is expansive and, although a bit difficult to navigate, definitely worth seeing. Most people don't even make it past the main floor, but they should—the galleries upstairs and downstairs are some of the best. Must-sees include the Rosetta stone, which was the key in deciphering ancient Egyptian hieroglyphics and the ancient mummies. *(Great Russell St. ⊖Tottenham Court Rd., Russell Sq., or Holborn. ☎020 7323 8299; www.britishmuseum.org. Great Court open M-W and Su 9am-6pm, Th-Sa 9am-11pm, 9pm in winter; galleries open daily 10am-5:30pm, selected galleries open Th-F 10am-8:30pm. Free 30-40min. tours daily starting at 11am from the Enlightenment Desk. "Highlights Tour" daily 10:30am, 1, and 3pm; advance booking recommended. Wheelchair-accessible. Free; £3 suggested donation. Temporary exhibitions around £5, concessions £3.50. "Highlights Tour" £8, concessions £5. Audio tours £3.50. MC/V.)*

VICTORIA AND ALBERT MUSEUM. As the largest museum of decorative (and not-so-decorative) art and design in the world, the V&A has over 9 mi. of corridors open to the public and is twice the size of the British Museum. It displays "the fine and applied arts of all countries, all styles, all periods." Unlike the British Museum, the V&A's documentation is consistently excellent and thorough. Highlights include the Glass Gallery, the Japanese and Korean areas with suits of armor and kimonos, and the Indian Gallery. Themed itineraries (£5) available at the desk can help streamline your visit, and **Family Trail** cards suggest kid-friendly routes. *(Main entrance on Cromwell Rd., wheelchair-accessible entrance on Exhibition Rd. ⊖South Kensington. ☎020 7942 2000; www.vam.ac.uk. Open M-Th and Sa-Su 10am-5:45pm, F 10am-10pm. Free tours meet at rear of main entrance. Introductory tours daily 10:30, 11:30am, 1:30, and 3:30pm, plus W 4:30pm. British gallery tours daily 12:30 and 2:30pm. Talks and events meet at rear of main entrance. Free gallery talks Th 1pm and Su 3pm, 45min.-1hr. Wheelchair-accessible. Admission free; additional charge for some special exhibits.)*

TATE BRITAIN. Tate Britain is the foremost collection on British art from 1500 to the present, including pieces from foreign artists working in Britain and Brits working abroad. There are four Tate Galleries in England; this is the original Tate, opened in 1897 to house Sir Henry Tate's collection of "modern" British art and later expanded to include a gift from famed British painter J.M.W. Turner. Turner's modest donation of 282 oils and 19,000 watercolors can make the museum feel like one big tribute to the man. In 2008, the exhibition moves temporarily to the Liverpool branch of the Tate (p. 168). *(Millbank, near Vauxhall Bridge, in Westminster. ⊖Pimlico. Information ☎020 7887 8888, exhibition booking ☎020 7887 8888; www.tate.org.uk. Open daily 10am-5:50pm, last admission 5pm. Open until 10pm on the first F of every month. Wheelchair-accessible via Clore Wing. Regular events include "Painting of the Month Lectures." 15min. M 1:15pm and Sa 2:30pm; occasional "Friday Lectures" F 1pm. Free; special exhibitions £7-11. Audio tours free. Free tours: "Art from 1500-1800" 11am, "1800-1900" M-F noon; "Turner" M-F 2pm; "1900-2005" M-F 3pm; "Collection Highlights" Sa-Su noon, 3pm.)*

OTHER MUSEUMS AND GALLERIES

Courtald Institute, Somerset House, Strand, just east of Waterloo Bridge (☎020 7420 9400; www.courtauld.ac.uk). ⊖Charing Cross or Temple. Small, outstanding collection ranges from 14th-century Italian icons to 20th-century abstractions. Manet's *A Bar at the Follies Bergères*, Van Gogh's *Self-Portrait with Bandaged Ear*, and a room devoted to Degas bronzes. Open daily 10am-6pm, last admission at 5:30pm. Wheelchair-accessible. £5, concessions £4, under 18 free.

Cabinet War Rooms, Clive Steps, far end of King Charles St. (☎020 7930 6961; www.iwm.org.uk). ⊖Westminster. Churchill and his strategists lived and worked underground here from 1939 to 1945. Highlights include the room with the top-secret transatlantic hotline—the official story was that it was Churchill's personal toilet. Open daily 9:30am-6pm; last admission 5pm. £12, students £9.50, under 16 free. MC/V.

British Library Galleries, 96 Euston Rd. (☎020 7412 7332; www.bl.uk). ⊖King's Cross St. Pancras. Stunning display of books, manuscripts, and related artifacts from around the world and throughout the ages. Highlights include the 2nd-century *Unknown Gospel,* The Beatles' hand-scrawled lyrics, a Gutenberg Bible, and pages from Leonardo da Vinci's notebooks. Open M and W-F 9:30am-6pm, Tu 9:30am-8pm, Sa 9:30am-5pm, Su 11am-5pm. Wheelchair-accessible. Free. Audio tours £3.50, concessions £2.50.

Science Museum, Exhibition Rd. (☎08708 704 868, IMAX ☎08708 704 771; www.sciencemuseum.org.uk). ⊖South Kensington. Dedicated to the Victorian ideal of progress, the museum focuses on the transformative power of technology in all its guises. Open daily 10am-6pm, except Dec. 24-26. Wheelchair-accessible. Free. MC/V.

Natural History Museum, Cromwell Rd. (☎020 7942 5000; www.nhm.ac.uk). ⊖South Kensington. Architecturally the most impressive of the South Kensington trio, this cathedral-like museum has been a favorite with Londoners since 1880. Open daily 10am-5:50pm; last admission 5:30pm. Closed Dec. 24-Dec. 30. Wheelchair-accessible. Admission free; special exhibits usually £5, children £3.50. MC/V.

Museum of London, London Wall, the City of London (☎0870 4444 3851; www.museumoflondon.org.uk). ⊖St. Paul's or Barbican. Enter through the Barbican or from Aldersgate. The collection's interactive exhibits trace the history of London from its Roman foundations to the present day, incorporating architectural history. However, the post-1660 exhibits are closed for renovation until 2010. Open M-Sa 10am-5:50pm, Su noon-5:50pm; last admission 5:30pm. Free. Audio tour £2.

Whitechapel Art Gallery, Whitechapel High St. (☎020 7522 7888; www.whitechapel.org). ⊖Aldgate East. Long the only artistic beacon in a culturally impoverished area, Whitechapel is now at the forefront of a buzzing art scene. Closed for expansion until 2009. Call for opening details. Wheelchair-accessible. Free.

ENTERTAINMENT

Although West End ticket prices are sky high and the quality of some shows questionable, the city that brought the world Shakespeare, the Sex Pistols, and Andrew Lloyd Webber still retains its theatrical edge. London is a city of immense talent, full of up-and-comers, experimenters, and undergrounders.

CINEMA

The heart of the celluloid monster is Leicester Square, where new releases premiere a day before hitting the city's chains. The dominant cinema chain is **Odeon** (ticket hotline ☎08712 244 007; www.odeon.co.uk). Tickets to West End cinemas cost £12-15.50; weekday matinees are cheaper. For the less mainstream, try **Electric Cinema,** 191 Portobello Rd., for the combination of baroque stage splendor and the big screen. For extra luxury, try viewing from one of the two-seat sofas. (⊖Ladbroke Grove. ☎020 7908 9696; www.the-electric.co.uk. Box office open M-Sa 9am-8:30pm, Su 10am-8:30pm. Front 3 rows M £7.50, Tu-Su £10; regular tickets M £12.50, Tu-Su £14.50; 2-seat sofa M £ 25 Tu-Su £30. Double bills Su 2pm £5-20. Wheelchair-accessible. MC/V.) **Riverside Studios,** Crisp Rd., shows a variety of excellent foreign and classic films. (⊖Hammersmith.

☎020 8237 1111; www.riversidestudios.co.uk. Double bills £7.50, concessions £6.50.) The **National Film Theatre (NFT)** screens a mind-boggling array of films—six movies hit the three screens every evening. (South Bank, under Waterloo Bridge. ⊖Waterloo, Embankment, or Temple. ☎020 7633 0274, booking ☎020 0870 787 2525; www.bfi.org.uk. £12.50, concessions £9.75, child £8.)

COMEDY

On any given night, you'll find at least 10 comedy clubs in operation: check listings in *Time Out* or in a newspaper. London comedians flee in August, when most head to Edinburgh to take part in the annual festivals (p. 189); consequently, plenty of comedians try out material in July. The UK's top comedy club, **Comedy Store,** founded in a strip club, sowed the seeds that gave rise to *Absolutely Fabulous* and *Whose Line is it Anyway?* All 400 seats have decent views of stage. Grab a £6 burger at the bar before the show. (1a Oxendon St, in Soho. ⊖Piccadilly Circus. Club inquiries ☎020 7839 6642, tickets ☎08700 602 340; www.thecomedystore.co.uk. Tu contemporary news-based satire; W and Su London's well-reviewed **Comedy Store Players** improv; Th-Sa standup. Shows Tu-Th and Su 8pm; F-Sa 8pm and midnight, sometimes only at midnight. Book in advance. 18+. Tu-W and F midnight shows and all Su shows £16; concessions £13; Th-F early show and all Sa shows £15. Happy hour 6:30-7:30pm. Box office open M-Th and Su 6:30-9:30pm, F-Sa 6:30pm-1:15am. AmEx/MC/V.) One of the few comedy venues to specialize in sketch comedy, the **Canal Cafe Theatre,** sits above the Bridge House pub; in North London. Cozy red velvet chairs and a raised rear balcony means that everyone gets a good view. Get dinner below and enjoy your drinks around the small tables. (Delamere Terr. ⊖Warwick Ave. ☎020 7289 6056; www.canalcafetheatre.com. Box office opens 30min. before performance. Weekly changing shows W-Sa 7:30 and 9:30pm; £5, concessions £4. "Newsrevue," Th-Sa 9:30pm and Su 9pm, is London's longest-running comedy sketch show, a satire of weekly current events; £9, concessions £7. £1.50 membership included in ticket price. MC/V.)

MUSIC

CLASSICAL

Barbican Hall, Silk St. (☎020 7638 4141; www.barbican.org.uk), in the City of London. ⊖Barbican or Moorgate. Recently refurbished, Barbican Hall is one of Europe's leading concert halls, with excellent acoustics and a nightly performance program. The resident **London Symphony Orchestra** plays here frequently. Many summer events sell out; it's worth checking what's going on early. Call in advance for tickets, especially for popular events. Otherwise, the online and phone box offices sometimes have good last-minute options. £6-35. Also includes the 2 venues below:

English National Opera, London Coliseum, St. Martin's Ln. (☎020 7632 8300; www.eno.org), in Covent Garden. ⊖Charing Cross or Leicester Sq. The Coliseum is staggering—huge, ornate, and complete with 500 balcony seats (£15-18) for sale every performance. Purchase best-available, standby student tickets (£12.50) and balcony tickets (£10) at box office 3hr. before show. ½-price tickets for children under 17. Regular tickets £16-87.Box office open M-Sa 10am-8pm. Wheelchair-accessible. AmEx/MC/V.

JAZZ

Jazz Café, 5 Parkway (☎020 7534 6955; www.jazzcafe.co.uk), in North London. ⊖Camden Town. Famous and popular. Shows can be pricey at this nightspot, but the top roster of jazz, hip-hop, funk, and Latin performers (£10-30) explains Jazz Café's popularity. DJs spin F-Sa following the show. Cover £5-10. Open daily 7pm-2am. Box office open M-Sa 10am-6pm, closed 2-3pm every day. MC/V.

Ronnie Scott's, 47 Frith St. (☎020 7439 0747; www.ronniescotts.co.uk), in Soho. ⊖Tottenham Court Rd. or Leicester Sq. London's oldest, most famous jazz club. Table reservations are essential for big-name acts; if it's sold out, try coming back at the end of the main act's 1st set, around midnight. Box office open M-F 11am-6pm, Sa noon-6pm. Club open M-Sa 6pm-3am, Su 6pm-midnight. Live music daily from 6:30pm. Tickets generally £26, after 11pm £10 M-Th. AmEx/MC/V.

POP AND ROCK

The Water Rats, 328 Grays Inn Rd. (☎020 7837 4412; www.themonto.com), in Bloomsbury. ⊖King's Cross St. Pancras. A hip pub-cafe by day, a stomping venue for top new talent by night. Cover £6 in advance, £8 at the door. Open for coffee M-F 8:30am-midnight. Music M-Sa 7pm-late (headliner 9:45pm). MC/V.

Carling Academy, Brixton, 211 Stockwell Rd. (☎020 7771 3000; www.brixton-academy.co.uk), in South London. ⊖Brixton. Art Deco ex-cinema with a sloping floor ensures a good view of the band. Named New Music Express's "Best Live Venue" in 2007. Box office open only on performance evenings; order online, by telephone, or at Carling Academy, Islington box office (16 Parkfield Street, Islington. Box office open M-Sa noon-4pm). Tickets £20-40, sometimes cheaper if booked online.

THEATER

London's West End is dominated by musicals and plays that run for years, if not decades. For a list of shows and discount tickets, head to the **tkts** booth in Leicester Sq. (⊖Leicester Sq. www.tkts.co.uk. Most shows £20-30; up to £2.50 booking fee per ticket. Open M-Sa 10am-7pm, Su noon-3pm. MC/V.)

REPERTORY

Shakespeare's Globe Theatre, 21 New Globe Walk (☎020 7401 9919; www.shakespeares-globe.org), in the South Bank. ⊖Southwark or London Bridge. Innovative, top-notch performances at this faithful reproduction of Shakespeare's original 16th-century playhouse. Choose among 3 covered tiers of hard, backless wooden benches (cushions £1 extra) or stand through a performance as a "groundling"; come 30min. before the show to get as close as you can. For tours of the Globe, see p. 137. Wheelchair-accessible. Performances from mid-May to late Sept. Tu-Sa 7:30pm, Su 6:30pm; June-Sept. also Tu-Sa 2pm, Su 1pm. Box office open M-Sa 10am-6pm, 8pm on performance days. Seats from £12, concessions from £10, yard (i.e., standing) £5. Raingear £2.50.

National Theatre, South Bank (info ☎020 7452 3400, box office 7452 3000; www.nationaltheatre.org.uk), in the South Bank. ⊖Waterloo or Embankment. Founded by Laurence Olivier, the National Theatre opened in 1976 and has been at the forefront of British theater ever since. Tickets typically start at £10. Complicated pricing scheme, which is liable to change from show to show; contact box office for details. Wheelchair-accessible. Box office open M-Sa 9:30am-8pm. AmEx/MC/V.

"OFF-WEST END"

The Almeida, Almeida St. (☎020 7359 4404; www.almeida.co.uk), in North London. ⊖Angel or Highbury and Islington. The top fringe theater in London. Shows M-Sa 7:30pm, Sa matinees 3pm. Tickets from £15. Box office open M-Sa 10am-6pm, 10am-7:30pm on performance evenings. Wheelchair-accessible. MC/V.

Donmar Warehouse, 41 Earlham St (☎08700 606 624; www.donmarwarehouse.com), in Covent Garden. ⊖Covent Garden. In the mid-90s, artistic director Sam Mendes (of *American Beauty* fame) transformed this gritty space into one of the most excellent theaters in the country. Tickets £13-29; under 18 and students standby 30min. before curtain £12; £7.50 standing room tickets available once performance sells out. Wheelchair-accessible. Box office open M-Sa 10am-7:30pm. AmEx/MC/V.

Royal Academy of Dramatic Arts (RADA), 62-64 Gower St. (☎020 7636 7076; www.rada.org), entrance on Malet St., in Bloomsbury. ⊖Goodge St. Britain's most famous drama school has 3 on-site theaters. Wheelchair-accessible. £3-11, concessions £2-7.50. Regular Foyer events during the school year M-Th 7 or 7:30pm (up to £6). Box office open M-F 10am-6pm, on performance nights 10am-7:30pm. AmEx/MC/V.

SHOPPING

London has long been considered one of the fashion capitals of the world. Unfortunately, the city features many underwhelming chain stores in addition to its one-of-a-kind boutiques. The truly budget-conscious should stick to window-shopping in Knightsbridge and on Regent Street. Vintage shopping in Notting Hill is also a viable alternative; steer clear of Oxford Street, where so-called vintage clothing was probably made in 2002 and marked up 200%.

DEPARTMENT STORES

Harrods, 87-135 Brompton Rd. (☎020 7730 1234; www.harrods.com). ⊖Knightsbridge. Given the sky-high prices, it's no wonder that only tourists and oil sheiks actually shop here. Do go, though; it's an iconic bit of London that even the cynical tourist shouldn't miss. Open M-Sa 10am-8pm, Su noon-6pm. Wheelchair-accessible. AmEx/MC/V.

Harvey Nichols, 109-125 Knightsbridge (☎020 7235 5000; www.harveynichols.com). ⊖Knightsbridge. Imagine Bond St., Rue St. Honoré, and 5th Ave. all rolled up into one store. 5 of its 7 floors are devoted to the sleekest fashion, from the biggest names to the hippest unknowns. Sales from late June to late July and from late Dec. to late Jan. Open M-F 10am-8pm, Sa 10am-8pm, Su noon-6pm. Wheelchair-accessible. AmEx/MC/V.

Selfridges, 400 Oxford St. (☎0870 837 7377; www.selfridges.com). ⊖Bond St. Tourists may flock to Harrods, but Londoners head to Selfridges. Fashion departments run the gamut from traditional tweeds to space-age clubwear. Open M-W 9:30am-8pm, Th 9:30am-9pm, F-Sa 9:30am-8pm, Su noon-6pm. Wheelchair-accessible. AmEx/MC/V.

STREET MARKETS

Better for people-watching than hardcore shopping, street markets may not bring you the big goods but they are a much better alternative to a day on Oxford Street. **Portobello Road Markets** (www.portobelloroad.co.uk) includes foods, antiques, secondhand clothing, and jewelry. In order to see it all, come Friday or Saturday when everything is sure to be open. (⊖Notting Hill Gate; also Westbourne Park and Ladroke Grove. Stalls set their own times.) **Camden Passage Market** (www.camdenpassageislington.co.uk) is more for looking than for buying—London's premier antique shops line these charming alleyways. (Islington High St., in North London. ⊖Angel. Turn right from the Tube; it's the alleyway that starts behind "The Mall" antiques gallery on Upper St. Stalls open W 7:30am-6pm and Sa 9am-6pm; some stores open daily, but W is the best day to go.) Its overrun sibling **Camden Markets** (☎020 7969 1500) mostly includes cheap clubbing gear and tourist trinkets; avoid the canal areas. The best bet is to stick with the **Stables Market,** farthest north from the Tube station. (Make a sharp right out of the Tube station to reach Camden High St., where most of the markets start. All stores are accessible from ⊖Camden Town. Many stores open daily 9:30am-6pm; Stables open F-Su.) **Brixton Market** has London's best selection of Afro-Caribbean fruits, vegetables, spices, and fish. It is unforgettably colorful, noisy, and fun. (Along Electric Ave., Pope's Rd., and Brixton Station Rd., and inside markets in Granville Arcade and Market Row; in South London. ⊖Brixton. Open M-Sa 10am-sunset.) Formerly a wholesale vegetable market, **Spitalfields** has become the best of the East End markets. On Sundays, food shares space with rows of clothing by 25-30 independent local designers. (Commercial St., in East London. ⊖Shoreditch (during rush hour), Liverpool St., or Aldgate East. Crafts market open M-F 10am-4pm, Su 9am-5pm. Antiques market open Th 9am-5pm.) **Petticoat Lane Market** is Spitalfield's little sister market, on Petticoat Ln., off of Commercial Street. It sells everything from clothes to crafts, and is open M-F 10am-2:30pm and Su 9am-2pm. Crowds can be overwhelming at times; head to the **Sunday (Up) Market** for similar items in a calmer environment. (☎020 7770 6100; www.bricklanemarket.com. Housed in a portion of the old Truman Brewery just off Hanbury St., in East London. ⊖Shoreditch or Aldgate East. Open Su 10am-5pm.)

NIGHTLIFE

From pubs to taverns to bars to clubs, London has all the nightlife that a person could want. First-time visitors may initially head to the **West End,** drawn by the flashy lights and pumping music of Leicester Sq. For a more authentic experience, head to the **East End** or **Brixton.** Soho's **Old Compton Street** is still the center of GLBT nightlife. Before heading out for the evening, make sure to plan out **Night Bus** travel. Listings open past 11pm include local Night Bus routes. Night Buses in the West End are ubiquitous—head to Trafalgar Sq., Oxford St., or Piccadilly Circus to catch buses to all destinations.

PUBS

Fitzroy Tavern, 16 Charlotte St. (☎020 7580 3714). ⊖Goodge St. Popular with artists and writers (Dylan Thomas was a regular), this pub now oozes with students. The center of Bloomsbury's "Fitzrovia" neighborhood (guess where the area's name came from). Umbrella-covered outdoor seating in summer. W 8:30pm comedy night (£5). Open M-Sa 11:30am-11pm, Su noon-10:30pm. MC/V.

The Jerusalem Tavern, 55 Britton St. (☎020 7490 4281; www.stpetersbrewery.co.uk). ⊖Farringdon. Showcase pub for St. Peter's Brewery with many nooks and crannies. Specialty ales (£2.65-2.85) like grapefruit or cinnamon, organic ales, Honey Porter, Summer

RULES OF THE PUB

British pubs are governed by a se[t] of complex and often unwritte[n] rules. Here's a primer to help you avoid some common mistakes:

1. If you expect someone to come around to your seat, you'll be waiting for some time. At most British pubs, you order at the bar.
2. So you've gotten up to go to the bar. But, before you go, check you[r] table number so that the serve[r] knows where to bring your food.
3. Get your wallet out right away most pubs require payment whe[n] you place your order.
4. In groups, it's common to buy drinks in rounds. One person goes to the bar and buys drinks for the whole table, someone else buy[s] the next round, and so on.
5. Put away that pack of cigarettes—as of 2007, it's illegal to smoke in enclosed public spaces.
6. Don't jump the invisible queue. Even if patrons aren't physically lining up to buy drinks, the bartender usually serves them in the order they come to the bar.
7. Don't tip as you leave. If you're impressed by the service, offer to buy the bartender a drink.
8. Pubs don't open before 11am before which time you probabl[y] shouldn't be drinking anyway.
9. You may have seen a pub called the "Red Lion" or the "White Horse" in several towns, but they're no[t] related to one another.
10. Keep your eyes on the clock. Licencing laws require most pubs to close by 11pm, so be sure to heed the call for "last orders" (sometimes indicated by a bell).

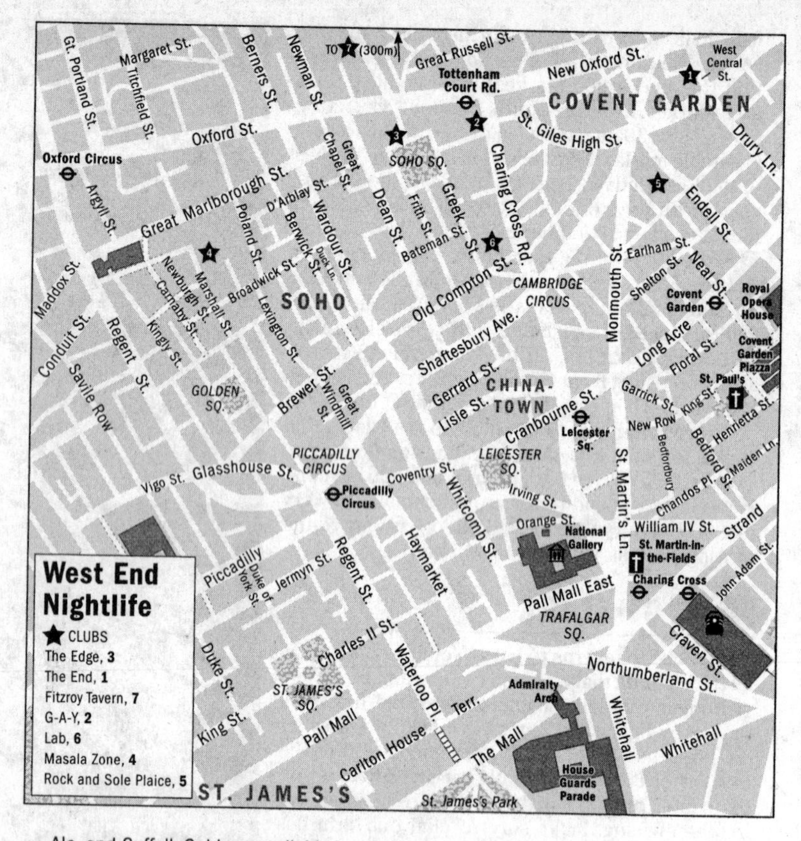

Ale, and Suffolk Gold are available in season. Pub grub £8-10. Open M-F 11am-11pm. Lunch daily noon-3pm, dinner Tu-Th 5-9:30pm. MC/V.

The Golden Eagle, 59 Marylebone Ln. (☎020 7935 3228). ⊖Bond St. The quintessence of "olde worlde"—both in clientele and in charm. Sidle up to this local-filled bar and enjoy authentic pub sing-alongs (Tu 8:30-10:30pm, Th-F 8:30-11pm) around the piano in the corner. Open M-Sa 11am-11pm, Su 11am-7pm. MC/V.

BARS

Lab, 12 Old Compton St. (☎020 7437 7820; www.lab-townhouse.com), in the West End. ⊖Leicester Sq. or Tottenham Court Rd. With restrooms for "bitches" and "bastards," the only thing this cocktail bar takes seriously is its stellar drink menu (cocktails £7). DJs play music nightly at 9pm. Open M-Sa 4pm-midnight, Su 4pm-10:30pm. AmEx/MC/V.

Bar Kick, 127 Shoreditch High St. (☎020 7739 8700), in East London. ⊖Old St. The flags on the ceiling add international flavor to the European-style food. Wheelchair-accessible. Open M-W and Su 11am-11pm, Th-Sa 11am-midnight. Kitchen open M-F 12:30-3:30pm and 6:30-10:30pm, Sa noon-11pm, Su noon-10:30pm. AmEx/MC/V.

Vibe Bar, 91-95 Brick Ln. (☎020 7247 3479; www.vibe-bar.co.uk), in East London. ⊖Aldgate East or Liverpool St. Night Bus: hub at Liverpool St. Station. Dance to hip-hop, soul, funk, and jazz. Pint £3. DJs spin daily from 7:30pm. Cover F-Sa after 8pm £4. Open M-Th and Su 10am-11:30pm, F-Sa 10am-1am. AmEx/MC/V.

CLUBS

Ministry of Sound, 103 Gaunt St. (☎087 0060 0010; www.ministryofsound.co.uk), in the South Bank. ⊖Elephant and Castle; take the exit for South Bank University. Night Bus #N35, 133, 343. Mecca for serious clubbers worldwide. Dress code casual, but famously unsmiling door staff make it prudent to err on the side of smartness. Cover F £12, Sa £15. Open F-Sa 11pm-7am.

The End, 16a West Central St. (☎020 7419 9199; www.endclub.com), in the West End. ⊖Tottenham Ct. Rd. Located just off High Holborn, behind New Oxford St., this is a cutting edge clubbers' Eden; theme nights online. Dress code is stylish casual, but no office wear allowed. Wheelchair-accessible. Cover varies; check website for prices. Open M 10pm-3am, W 10:30pm-3am, Th-F 10pm-4am, Sa 6pm-7am. AmEx/MC/V.

Fabric, 77a Charterhouse St. (☎020 7336 8898; www.fabriclondon.com), in Clerkenwell. ⊖Farringdon. Night Bus #242. This underground club has 5 bars and 3 rooms. Wheelchair-accessible. Get there before 11pm on Sa to avoid lines. Cover F £13; Sa after 11pm £16. Open F 10pm-6am, Sa 11pm-8am, Su 10pm-10am. AmEx/MC/V.

GLBT NIGHTLIFE

Many venues have Gay and Lesbian nights on a rotating basis. Check *TimeOut* and look for flyers/magazines floating around Soho: *The Pink Paper* (free from newsagents) and *Boyz* (www.boyz.co.uk; free at gay bars and clubs).

The Edge, 11 Soho Sq. (☎020 7439 1313; www.edgesoho.net), in the West End. ⊖Tottenham Court Rd. A friendly gay and lesbian drinking spot off Soho Sq. 4 floors of brick, silver, and hot pink interior feature a lounge bar on the 1st fl., a piano bar on the 2nd, and a newly refurbished disco dance bar at the top. Piano bar Tu-Sa, DJs and dancing Th-Sa. No cover. Open M-Sa noon-1am, Su noon-midnight. MC/V.

The Black Cap, 171 Camden High St. (☎020 7485 0538; www.theblackcap.com), in North London. ⊖Camden Town. North London's most popular gay bar and cabaret is always buzzing with a vivacious mixed crowd. Cover £2-4 T-Su after 10pm. Club open M-Th 10pm-2am, F-Sa 10pm-3am, Su 9pm-1am. Bar open M-Th noon-2am, F-Sa noon-3am, Su noon-1am. AmEx/MC/V.

G-A-Y, 157 Charing Cross Rd. (☎020 7434 9592; www.g-a-y.co.uk), in the West End. ⊖Tottenham Court Rd. G-A-Y (you spell it out when you say it) has become a Soho institution. Wheelchair-accessible. Cover varies by night and by week; free some nights with flyer or ad; Sa £10-16. Check website for event details. Open M and Th-F 11pm-4am, Sa 10:30pm-5am. Cash only.

DAYTRIP FROM LONDON

ROYAL BOTANICAL GARDENS, KEW.

Tube (1hr.) to ⊖Kew Gardens. Zone 3. Main entrance and Visitors Center are at Victoria Gate. Go up the white stairs that go above the station tracks, and walk straight down the road.

In the summer of 2003, UNESCO named the Royal Botanical Gardens a World Heritage site. The 250-year-old Royal Botanical Gardens extend in a verdant 300-acre swath along the Thames. The complimentary map and guide highlights which plants are in season. In the spring, wander through the woodland glades at the back of the park where thick English bluebells bloom knee-high.

In early summer, the rose gardens and azalea dells are at their peak. Take a walk through the autumn treetops on the new elevated walkway and appreciate the leaves from the vantage point of a squirrel (soon to be wheelchair-accessible). If English rain dampens the scenery, head to one of the three conservatories at the center to steam your clothes with the palms and potted plants. The **Princess of Wales Conservatory** houses 10 different climate zones, from rainforest to desert, including two devoted entirely to orchids. Close to the Thames in the northern part of the gardens, newly renovated **Kew Palace** is a modest red-brick affair used by royalty on garden visits, now open to the public for the first time in 200 years. On the hill behind and to the right of the palace, 17th-century medicinal plants flourish in the Queen's **Nosegay Garden.** *(☎020 8332 5000; www.kew.org. Open Apr.-Aug. M-F 9:30am-6:30pm, Sa-Su 9:30am-7:30pm; Sept.-Oct. daily 9:30am-6pm; Nov.-Jan. daily 9:30am-4:15pm. Last admission 30min. before close. Glasshouses open Apr.-Oct. 9:30am-5:30pm; Nov.-Feb. 9:30am-3:45pm. Free 1hr. walking tours daily 11am and 2pm start at Victoria Gate Visitors Center. £13, concessions £12, children under 17 free; 45min. before close £10.25. "Explorer" hop-on, hop-off shuttle makes 40min. rounds of the gardens; 1st shuttle daily 11am, last 4pm; £4, children under 17 £1. Free 1hr. "Discovery Bus" tours for mobility-impaired daily 11am and 2pm; booking required.)*

SOUTHERN ENGLAND

History and myth shroud Southern England. Cornwall, the alleged birthplace of King Arthur, was the last stronghold of the Celts in England, but traces of older Neolithic communities linger in the stone circles their builders left behind. In WWII, German bombings uncovered long-buried evidence of an invasion by Caesar, whose Romans dotted the countryside with settlements. William the Conqueror left his mark in the form of awe-inspiring castles and cathedrals. Apart from this pomp and circumstance lies a less palpable presence: the voices of British literati such as Jane Austen, Geoffrey Chaucer, Charles Dickens, and E.M. Forster echo above the sprawling pastures and seaside cliffs.

CANTERBURY ☎01227

Archbishop Thomas Becket met his demise at **Canterbury Cathedral** in 1170 after an irate Henry II asked, "Will no one rid me of this troublesome priest?" Later, in his famed *Canterbury Tales*, Chaucer caricatured the pilgrims who traveled the road from London to England's most famous execution site. The steps to the nave have been worn shallow by centuries of these plodding pilgrim feet. (☎01227 762 862; www.canterbury-cathedral.org. Cathedral open Easter-Sept. M-Sa 9am-5:30pm, Su 12:30-2:30pm; Oct.-Easter M-Sa 9am-5pm, Su 12:30-2:30 pm. 1hr. tours available, 3 per day M-Sa; check nave for times. Evensong M-F 5:30pm, Sa 3:15pm, Su 3:15 and 6:15pm. £7, concessions £5.50. Tours £3.50/3. Audio tour £3.50/2.50.) The skeletons of arches and crumbling walls are all that remain of **Saint Augustine's Abbey,** outside the city wall near the cathedral—St. Augustine himself is buried under a humble pile of rocks. (☎01227 767 345. Open July-Aug. daily 10am-6pm; Sept.-Mar. Sa-Su 11am-5pm; Jan.-Mar. W-Su 10am-5pm. £0.20, concessions £3.40, child £2.10, family £10.50.) England's first Franciscan friary, **Greyfriars,** 6A Stour St., has quiet riverside gardens. (☎01227 479 364. Gardens open daily 10am-5pm. Chapel open Easter-Sept. M-Sa 2-4pm. Free.) **The Canterbury Tales,** on St. Margaret's St., recreates Chaucer's medieval England in scenes complete with ambient lighting and wax characters. Audio tours take you through the scenes in a 45min. abbreviation of Chaucer's bawdy masterpiece. (☎01227 479 227; www.canterburytales.org.uk. Open daily July-Aug. 9:30am-5pm; Mar.-June and Sept.-Oct. 10am-5pm; Nov.-Feb. 10am-4:30pm. £7.75, students £6.75, child £5.75.)

B&Bs are around **High Street** and on **New Dover Road.** Ten minutes from the city center, **Kipps Independent Hostel ❶,** 40 Nunnery Fields, is a century-old townhouse with modern amenities. (☎01227 786 121. Kitchen available. Laundry £3. Internet £2 per hr. Free Wi-Fi. If there are no vacancies, ask to set up a tent in the garden. Key deposit £10. Dorms £15. Singles £20; doubles £34. MC/V.) Share sizzling steak fajitas (£27) and grab your own margarita (£6) at **Cafe des Amis du Mexique ❷,** St. Dunstan's St., home to inspired Mexican dishes in a funky cantina setting. (☎01227 464 390. Entrees £5-10. Open M-Th noon-10pm, F-Sa noon-10:30pm, Su noon-9:30pm AmEx/MC/V.) Right next door, **Cafè Belge ❸,** 89 St. Dunstans St., is an award-winning restaurant constantly packed with students. Try the famous "fifty ways to eat fresh mussels" (£13), served up in a big silver pail. (☎01227 768 222; www.cafebelge.co.uk. Entrees £9-14. Open M-Th 11am-3pm and 6pm-late, F 11am-3pm and 6pm-late, Sa 11am-late, Su 11am-4pm and 6-9pm.) **Coffee & Corks,** 13 Palace St., is a cafe-bar with a bohemian feel. (☎01227 457 707. Tea £1.50. Mixed drinks £4. Wine £10 per bottle. Free Wi-Fi. Open daily noon-midnight. MC/V.)

Trains run from East Station, off Castle St., to London Victoria (1hr., 2 per hr., £20.50) and Cambridge (3hr., 2 per hr., £33). Trains from West Station, Station Rd. W., off St. Dunstan's St., go to Central London (1hr., every hr., £12) and Brighton (3hr., 3 per hr., £6). National Express **buses** (☎08705 808 080) run from St. George's Ln. to London (2hr., 2 per hr., £14). The **TIC,** 12-13 Sun St., in the Buttermarket, books rooms for a £2.50 fee plus 10% deposit. (☎01227 378 100; www.canterbury.co.uk. Open Easter-Christmas M-Sa 9:30am-5pm, Su 10am-4pm; Christmas-Easter M-Sa 10am-4pm.) **Postal Code:** CT1 2BA.

SALISBURY ☎01722

Salisbury (pop. 37,000) centers on 13th-century **Salisbury Cathedral.** Its spire was the tallest in medieval England, and the bases of its marble pillars bend inward under 6400 tons of stone. If you hear a cracking sound, you should probably run as far away as possible. (☎01722 555 120. Open June-Aug. M-Sa 7:15am-8pm, Su 7:15am-6:15pm; Sept.-May daily 7:15am-6:15pm. Call ahead. Suggested donation £5, concessions £4.25. Roof and tower tour £5.50, concessions £4.50.) A well-preserved copy of the **Magna Carta** rests in the nearby **Chapter House.** (Open June-Aug. M-Sa 9:30am-5:30pm, Su noon-5:30pm; Sept.-May daily 9:30am-5:30pm. Free.) The **YHA Salisbury (HI) ❷,** Milford Hill House, on Milford Hill, offers basic, comfortable dorms with a TV lounge and kitchen. (☎01722 327 572. Breakfast included. Laundry £3. Reserve ahead. Dorms £15-17.50, under 18 £14. MC/V.) **Farthings B&B ❸,** 9 Swaynes Close, 10min. from the city center, is a comfortable, homey retreat. (☎01722 330 749; www.farthingsbandb.co.uk. Breakfast included. Singles £35; doubles £60. Oct.-Apr. £27/50. Cash only.) At **Harper's "Upstairs Restaurant" ❷,** 6-7 Ox Rd., Market Sq., inventive English dishes (£8-14) make hearty meals. (☎01722 333 118. 2-course special before 8pm £11.50. Open M-F noon-2pm and 6-9:30pm, Sa noon-2pm and 6-10pm; Oct.-May closed Su. AmEx/MC/V.) **Trains** run from South Western Rd., west of town across the River Avon, to London Waterloo (1hr., 2 per hr., £29.50), Portsmouth (1hr., 2 per hr., £14.40), and Winchester (1hr., 2 per hr., £12.20). National Express **buses** (☎08705 808 080) go from 8 Endless St. to London (3hr., 3 per day, £14). Wilts and Dorset buses (☎01722 336 855) run to Bath (X4; every hr., £4.50) and Winchester (#68; 1hr., 8 per day, £4.65). An **Explorer** ticket is good for one day of travel on Wilts and Dorset buses (£7.50, child £4.50). The **TIC** is on Fish Row, in back of the Guildhall in Market Sq.

(☎01722 334 956; www.visitsalisbury.com. Open June-Sept. M-Sa 9:30am-6pm, Su 10:30am-4:30pm; Oct.-May M-Sa 9:30am-5pm.) **Postal Code:** SP1 1AB.

DAYTRIP FROM SALISBURY: STONEHENGE AND AVEBURY. A ring of colossal stones amid swaying grass and indifferent sheep, Stonehenge has been battered for millennia by winds whipping at 80km per hour and visited by legions of people for over 5000 years. The monument, which has retained its present shape since about 1500 BC, was once a complete circle of 6.5m tall stones weighing up to 45 tons each. Sensationalized religious and scientific explanations for Stonehenge's purpose add to its intrigue. Some believe the stones are oriented as a calendar, with the position of the sun on the stones indicating the time of year. Admission to Stonehenge includes a 30min. audio tour. Ropes confine the throngs to a path around the outside of the monument. From the roadside or from Amesbury Hill, 2km up the A303, you can get a free view of the stones. There are also many walks and trails that pass by; ask at the Salisbury TIC. *(☎01980 624 715. Open daily June-Aug. 9am-7pm; mid-Mar. to May and Sept. to mid-Oct. 9:30am-6pm; mid-Oct. to mid-Mar. 9:30am-4pm. £6.50, students £5.20.)*

A question for the world: why is **Avebury's** stone circle, larger and older than its favored cousin Stonehenge, often so lonely during the day? Avebury gives an up-close and largely untouristed view of its 98 stones, dated to 2500 BC and standing in a circle with a 300m diameter. For the direct route, take the Stonehenge Tourbus, which leaves from the Salisbury train station. (Every hour, starting at 9:30am. £11 for tour, £17 with Stonehenge admission, students £14.) Wilts and Dorset **buses** (☎336 855) run daily service from the Salisbury train station and bus station (#3, 5, and 6; 30min.-2hr.; round-trip £4-8). The first bus leaves Salisbury at 9:45am, and the last leaves Stonehenge at 4:05pm. Check a schedule before you leave; intervals between drop-offs and pickups are at least 1hr. Wilts and Dorset also runs a tour bus from Salisbury (3 per day, £7.50-15). The closest lodgings are in **Salisbury** (see above).

BATH ☎01225

Perhaps the world's first tourist town, Bath (pop. 90,000) has been a must-see for travelers since AD 43, when the Romans built an elaborate complex of baths to house the town's curative waters. In 1701, Queen Anne's trip to the springs re-established the city as a prominent meeting place for artists, politicians, and intellectuals; it became an English social capital second only to London. No longer an upper-crust resort, today Bath plays host to crowds of tourists eager to appreciate its historic sites and well-preserved elegance.

TRANSPORTATION AND PRACTICAL INFORMATION. **Trains** leave from Dorchester St. for: Birmingham (2hr., 2 per hr., £36); Bristol (15min., every 10-15min., £6); London Paddington (1.5hr., 2 per hr., £47-66.50); London Waterloo (2hr., every hr., £28.20). National Express **buses** (☎08717 818 181) run from Bath Bus Station to London (3hr., every hr., £17.50) and Oxford (2hr., 1 per day, £9.50). The train and bus stations are near the south end of Manvers St. Walk toward the town center and turn left on York St. to reach the **TIC,** in Abbey Chambers, which books rooms for £3 and a 10% deposit. (☎9067 112 000; www.visitbath.co.uk. Open June-Sept. M-Sa 9:30am-6pm, Su 10am-4pm; Oct.-May M-Sa 9:30am-5pm, Su 10am-4pm.) **Postal Code:** BA1 1AJ.

ACCOMMODATIONS AND FOOD. B&Bs line Pulteney Rd. and Pulteney Gardens. Conveniently located **Bath Backpackers ❶,** 13 Pierrepont St., is a relaxed backpackers' lair with music-themed dorms, TV lounge, and "dungeon" bar. (☎01225 446 787; www.hostels.co.uk. Kitchen available. Internet £2 per hr. Luggage storage £2 per bag. Reception 8am-11pm. Check-out 10:30am. Reserve ahead in summer. 4-bed dorms £16-18, 8-bed £14-16, 10-bed £13-15. MC/V.) **St. Christopher's Inn ❷,** 16 Green St., has clean rooms and a downstairs pub. (☎01225 481 444; www.st-christophers.co.uk. Internet £3 per hr. Free Wi-Fi at the bar. Dorms £16-23.50. Discount for online booking. MC/V.)

Riverside Cafe ❶, below Pulteney Bridge, serves light dishes and delicious coffee. Patrons have a gorgeous view of the River Avon. (☎01225 480 532; www.riversidecafebar.co.uk. Sandwiches and soups £5-6. Open M-Sa 9am-9pm, Su 9am-5pm. MC/V.) Try the exotic vegetarian dishes, or the superb chocolate fudge cake (£5.25) at **Demuths Restaurant ❸,** 2 N. Parade Passage. (☎01225 446 059; www.demuths.co.uk. Entrees from £12. Open M-F and Su 10am-5pm and 6-10pm, Sa 9am-5pm and 6-10pm. Reserve ahead in summer. MC/V.) For groceries, head to the **Sainsbury's** supermarket on Green Park Rd. (☎01225 444 737. Open M-F 8am-10pm, Sa 7:30-10pm, Su 11am-5pm.)

SIGHTS. In 1880, sewer diggers uncovered the first glimpse of an extravagant feat of Roman engineering. For 400 years, the Romans harnessed Bath's bubbling springs, where nearly 1,000,000L of 47°C (115°F) water flow every day. The **Roman Baths Museum,** Abbey Church Yard, shows the complexity of Roman architecture and engineering, which included central heating and internal plumbing. (☎01225 447 785; www.romanbaths.co.uk. Open daily July-Aug. 9am-10pm; Sept.-Oct. and Mar.-June 9am-6pm; Nov.-Feb. 9am-5:30pm. £10.50, concessions £9, children £6.80, families £30. Joint ticket with Museum of Costume £14/12/8.30/38. Audio tour included.) Next to the baths, the towering **Bath Abbey** meets masons George and William Vertue's oath to build "the goodliest vault in all England and France." The Abbey's underground **Heritage Vaults,** built over medieval monk burial grounds, display the history of the abbey. (☎01225 422 462; www.bathabbey.org. Open M-Sa 9am-6pm, Su 1-2:30pm and 4:30-5:30pm. Vaults open daily 10am-4pm. Requested donation £2.50.) Walk up Gay St. to **The Circus,** a classic Georgian block where painter Thomas Gainsborough and 18th-century prime minister William Pitt lived. Near The Circus, the **Museum of Costume,** on Bennett St., has a dazzling parade of 400 years of fashions, from 17th-century silver tissue garments to J. Lo's racy Versace ensemble. (☎01225 477 785; www.fashionmuseum.co.uk. Open daily Mar.-Oct. 10:30am-6pm; Nov.-Feb. 10:30am-5pm. £7, concessions £6, children £5, family £20.)

GLASTONBURY ☎01458

The reputed birthplace of Christianity in England, an Arthurian hot spot, and home to England's biggest summer music festival, Glastonbury (pop. 8800) is a quirky intersection of mysticism and pop culture. Legend holds that Joseph of Arimathea founded **Glastonbury Abbey,** on Magdalene St., in AD 63. Though the abbey was destroyed during the English Reformation, the colossal pile of ruins and accompanying museum evoke the abbey's original grandeur. (☎01458 832 267; www.glastonburyabbey.com. Open daily June-Aug. 9am-6pm; Sept. and Apr.-May 9:30am-6pm; Oct. 9:30am-5pm; Nov. 9:30am-4:30pm; Dec.-Jan. 10am-4:30pm; Feb. 10am-5pm; Mar. 9:30am-5:30pm. £5, concessions £4.50, children £3, families £14.50.) For Arthurians, **Glastonbury Tor** (Glastonbury Hill) is a must-see. The 160m tower offers great views and is supposedly where King Arthur sleeps until his country needs him. To reach the Tor between April and October, take the bus from St. Dunstan's Car Park (£2.50), or turn right at the top of High St. onto Lambrook, which becomes Chilkwell St.; turn left on Wellhouse Ln. and follow the public footpath up the hill, looking out for cow dung. (Open year-round. Free.) The annual **Glastonbury Festival** (tickets ☎01458 834 596;

www.glastonburyfestivals.co.uk) is the biggest and best of Britain's summer music festivals. The weekend-long concert series has featured top bands, with recent headliners including Jay-Z, The Who, and Radiohead.

Glastonbury Backpackers ❶, 4 Market Pl., at the corner of Magdalene and High St., has spacious rooms in a superb central location. (☎01458 833 353; www.glastonburybackpackers.com. Kitchen available. Internet £1 per 20min. Free Wi-Fi at the downstairs pub. Reception until 11pm. Check-in 4pm. Check-out 11:30am. Dorms £14-16; twins £35-45, double ensuite £40-50. MC/V.) The vegetarian and whole-food menu at **Rainbow's End ❶,** 17a High St., includes soups, salads, and quiches for £3.25-3.65. (☎01458 833 896. Open daily 10am-4pm. Cash only.) **Heritage Fine Foods,** 32-34 High St., stocks groceries and discounted beer. (☎01458 831 003. Open M-Th 7am-9pm, F-Sa 7am-10pm, Su 8am-9pm.)

First Badgerline **buses** (☎08706 082 608, fare info ☎08456 064 446) run from town hall to Bristol (#375 or 376; 1.5hr., £5.10) via Wells. Travel to Yeovil on #376 (1hr., every hr.) to connect to destinations in the south, including Lyme Regis and Dorchester. From the bus stop, turn right on High St. to reach the **TIC,** the Tribunal, 9 High St. (☎01458 832 954; www.glastonburytic.co.uk. Open Apr.-Sept. M-Th and Su 10am-5pm, F-Sa 10am-5:30pm; Oct.-Mar. M-Th and Su 10am-4pm, F-Sa 10am-4:30pm.) **Postal Code:** BA6 9HG.

THE CORNISH COAST

With cliffsides stretching out into the Atlantic, Cornwall's terrain doesn't feel English. Years ago, the Celts fled westward in the face of Saxon conquest. Today, the migration to Cornwall continues in the form of artists, surfers, and vacationers. Though the Cornish language is no longer spoken, the area remains protective of its distinctive past and its ubiquitous pasties.

THAT'S EMBARRASSING. Cornwall's famous pasties (PAH-stees) are pie-like pastries usually filled with diced meat and vegetables. Not to be confused with the pasties (PAY-stees) you might find in a lingerie shop.

PENZANCE ☎01736

Penzance was once a model English pirate town; it appears, though, that Disney has since moved all the pirates to the Caribbean. The only ones here are in murals or made of wax. What Penzance lacks in swashbucklers it makes up for in galleries, quirky stores, and sunsets. A former Benedictine monastery, **Saint Michael's Mount** is on a hill that becomes an island at high tide—it marks the spot where St. Michael is believed to have appeared in AD 495. The interior has a champagne-cork model of the island and views from the top are well worth the 30-story climb. (☎01736 710 507, ferry and tide info ☎01736 710 265. Open mid-Mar. to June and Sept.-Nov. M-F and Su 10:30am-5pm; July-Aug. M-F and Su 10:30am-5:30pm. Last admission 45min. before close. £6.60, children £3.30, families £16.50. Garden only £3, children £1. Ferry £1.50.) Penzance contains an impressive number of art galleries; pick up the *Cornwall Galleries Guide* (£1) at the TIC. Walk 20min. from the train or bus station, or take First bus #5 or 6 from the bus station to the Pirate Pub and walk 10min. up Castle Horneck Rd. to reach the **YHA Penzance (HI) ❶,** Castle Horneck. Housed in an 18th-century mansion, this hostel has spacious dorms. (☎0870 770 5992. Internet £0.07 per min. Reception 8-10am and 5-10:30pm. Lockout 10am-noon. Dorms from £12, under 18 from £9. MC/V.) **Admiral Benbow,** 46 Chapel St., has the town's liveliest pub scene and is decorated with paraphernalia from local shipwrecks.

(☎01736 363 448. Open M-Sa 11am-1am, Su noon-midnight. Food served daily 12:30-2:30pm and 5:30-9:30pm.) **Trains** leave Wharf Rd. (☎08457 484 950), at the head of Albert Pier, for London (5hr., 7 per day, £74), Newquay (3hr., 4 per day, £7.40-13), and St. Ives via St. Erth (40-55min., every hr., £2.90-5). **Buses** also leave Wharf Rd. for London (8-9hr., 6 per day, £34.50) and Plymouth (3hr., 6 per day, £6.90). The **TIC** is between the train and bus stations on Station Rd. (☎01736 362 207; www.visit-westcornwall.com. Open May-Sept. M-F 9am-5pm, Sa 10am-4pm, Su 9am-2pm; Oct.-Apr. M-F 9am-5pm, Sa 10am-1pm.)

EAST ANGLIA AND THE MIDLANDS

The rich farmland and watery flats of East Anglia stretch northeast from London, cloaking the counties of Cambridgeshire, Norfolk, Suffolk, and parts of Essex. Mention of The Midlands inevitably evokes grim urban images, but there is a unique heritage and quiet grandeur to this smokestacked landscape. Even Birmingham, the region's much-maligned center, has its saving graces, among them a lively nightlife scene and the Cadbury chocolate empire.

OXFORD ☎01865

Sprawling college grounds and 12th-century spires mark this Holy Grail of British academia. Nearly a millennium of scholarship at Oxford (pop. 150,000) has educated world leaders, including 25 British prime ministers. Despite the tourist crowds, Oxford has irrepressible grandeur and pockets of tranquility.

TRANSPORTATION AND PRACTICAL INFORMATION. **Trains** (☎08457 000 125) run from Botley Rd., down Park End, to: Birmingham (1hr., 2 per hr., £23); Glasgow (5-7hr., every hr., £85.60); London Paddington (1hr., 2-4 per hr., £18.90-22.50); Manchester (3hr., every 2 hrs., £51.50). Stagecoach **buses** (☎08165 772 250; www.stagecoachbus.com) run to: Cambridge (3hr., 2 per hr., £9); London (1hr.; 3-4 per hr.; £12, students £9). National Express (☎08717 818 181) runs buses to: Birmingham (1hr., 5 per day, £11), Stratford-upon-Avon (1hr.; 2 per day; £9.80), Bath (1hr., 5 per day, £9.50), and Bristol (3hr., 2 per hr., £13.80). Oxford Bus Company (☎08165 785 400; www.oxfordbus.co.uk. Ticket office in Debenhams Department store, at the corner of George St. and Magdalen St.) runs to: London (1hr.; 3-5 per hr.; £12, students £10), Gatwick (2hr.; every hr. 8am-9pm; £20), and Heathrow (1hr.; 3 per hr.; £15). The **TIC,** 15-16 Broad St., books rooms for a £4 fee plus 10% deposit. (☎252 200; www.visitoxford.org. Open M-Sa 9:30am-5pm.) **Internet** is available at Oxford Central Library, Queen St. near the Westgate Shopping Center. (☎08165 815 549. Open M-Th and Sa 9am-7pm, F-Sa 9am-5:30pm. Free.) **Postal Code:** OX1 1ZZ.

ACCOMMODATIONS AND FOOD. Book at least a week ahead in summer, especially for singles. If it's late, call the **Oxford Association of Hotels and Guest Houses** (East Oxford ☎08165 721 561, West Oxford 08165 862 138, North Oxford 08165 244 691, South Oxford 08165 244 268). The newest hostel in town, **Central Backpackers ❷**, 13 Park End St., has spacious rooms and a popular rooftop terrace perfect for summertime barbecues. (☎08165 242 288. Kitchen available. Free luggage storage. Free Internet, including Wi-Fi. Reception 8am-11pm. Check-out 11am. 4-bed dorms £19; 6-bed dorms £18; 8-bed dorms £17; 12-bed dorms £16. Female dorms available. MC/V.) Turn right from the train

GREAT BRITAIN

GREAT BRITAIN

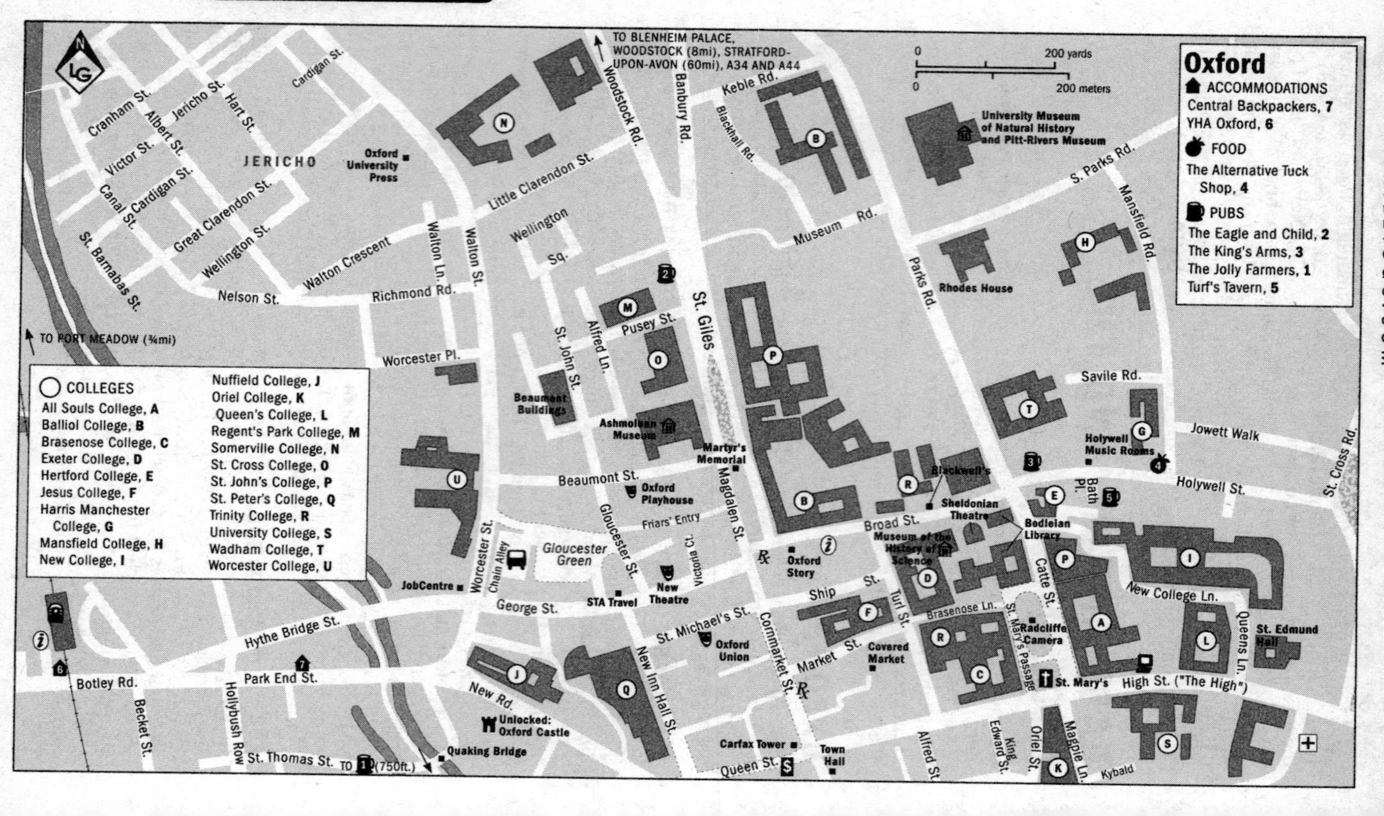

station to reach the superbly located **YHA Oxford (HI) ❷**, 2a Botley Rd., which offers more peaceful rooms and a kitchen. (☎08165 727 275. Full English breakfast included. Lockers £1. Laundry £3. Internet £1 for 15min. Wi-Fi £5 for 1hr. 4- and 6-bed dorms £16-27; twins £40-60. MC/V.) Students and residents alike flock to **The Alternative Tuck Shop ❶**, 24 Holywell St., for their famous panini and a slew of delicious made-to-order sandwiches, all for under £3. (☎08165 792 054. M-Sa 8:15am-6pm. Cash only.) Students fed up with college food and perpetual tourists are easily seduced by a bevy of budget options in Oxford. If you're cooking, try **Gloucester Green Market,** behind the bus station. (Open W 8am-3:30pm.) The **Covered Market** between Market St. and Carfax has fresh produce and deli goods. (Open M-Sa 8am-5:30pm.) Pick up groceries at the **Sainsbury's** on Magdalen St. (☎08165 204 969. Open M-Sa 7am-11pm, Su 11am-5pm.)

SIGHTS. The TIC sells a map (£1.25) and gives out the *Welcome to Oxford* guide, which lists the visiting hours of Oxford's colleges. Don't bother trying to sneak in after hours; even after hiding your pack and your copy of *Let's Go*, bouncers, affectionately known as "bulldogs," will squint and kick you out. Just down St. Aldate's St. from Carfax, **Christ Church College** has Oxford's grandest quad and most distinguished alumni, including 13 prime ministers. The dining hall (open 10:30am-noon and 2:30-4:30pm) and **Tom Quad** are also shooting locations for the **Harry Potter** movies. J.R.R. Tolkien lectured at **Merton College,** Merton St., whose library houses the first printed Welsh Bible. Nearby **St. Alban's Quad** has some of the university's best gargoyles. (☎08165 276 310; www.merton.ox.ac.uk. Open M-F 2-4pm, Sa-Su 10am-4pm. Free.) Soot-blackened **University College,** High St., was built in 1249 and vies with Merton for the title of oldest, claiming Alfred the Great as its founder. (☎08165 276 602; www.univ.ox.ac.uk. Open to tours only.)

South of Oriel, **Corpus Christi College,** the smallest of Oxford's colleges, surrounds a sundialed quad. The garden gate was built for visits between Charles I and his queen, who lived nearby during the Civil Wars. (☎08165 276 700; www.ccc.ox.ac.uk. Open daily 1:30-4:30pm. Free.) The prestigious **All Souls College,** at the corner of High and Cattle St., admits only the best scholars and stores only the best wine in its cellar. (☎08165 279 379; www.allsouls.ox.ac.uk. Open M-F 2-4pm. Closed in August. Free.) At **Queen's College,** High St., a boar's head graces the table at Christmas to honor a student who, attacked by a boar on the outskirts of Oxford,

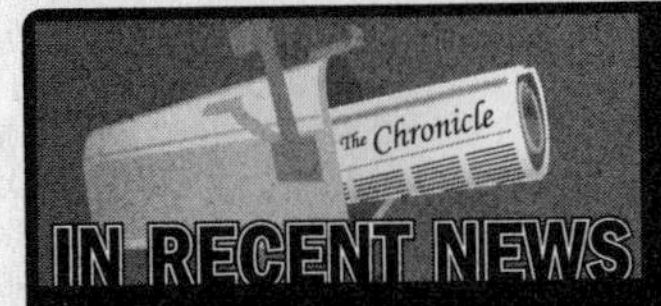

TRASHED AT OXFORD

It's summertime, the sun is shining, and you've just completed your final exam at the prestigious Oxford University. The first thing you can look forward to in your newfound freedom? A face-full of raw fish and custard.

Or, at least, a few years ago you could have. The tradition of "trashing," originating in the 1990s, refers to the practice of Oxford students throwing things at their friends upon completion of their final university exams. The items range from champagne to eggs, flour, liver, and dog food.

In 2005, the tradition started to get pretty out of hand. Street cleanups after trashing cost as much as £20,000, and one undergraduate even got an octopus thrown through his open window. Locals complained about food waste and foul-smelling streets.

As a result, the Oxford University Police clamped down on trashing. Knowing it would be impossible to eliminate the custom altogether, they cut back on the kinds of substances that could be thrown. Instead of liver and octopi, students throw much more harmless substances like confetti and glitter. So if you happen to be hit with a handful of glitter in the cobbled back alleys of Oxford in June—congratulations, you've just been trashed.

choked the animal to death with a volume of Aristotle. (☎08165 279 120; www.queens.ox.ac.uk. Open to tours only.) With extensive grounds, flower-edged quads, and a deer park, **Magdalen College** (MAUD-lin), on High St. near the Cherwell, is considered Oxford's handsomest. Oscar Wilde is among the distinguished alumni. (☎08165 276 000; www.magd.ox.ac.uk. Open daily Jun.-Oct. noon-6pm. £3, Nov.-May 1-6pm. £4, students £2.) Founded in 1555, **Trinity College,** Broad St., has a Baroque chapel with a limewood altarpiece, cedar lattices, and cherubim-spotted pediments. (☎08165 279 900; www.trinity.ox.ac.uk. Open M-F 10am-noon and 2-4pm, Sa-Su 2-4pm; during vacations also Sa-Su 10am-noon. £1.50, students £0.75.) Students at **Balliol College** preserve a semblance of tradition by hurling abuse over the wall at their conservative Trinity College rivals. Supposedly, the interior gates of the college bear lingering scorch marks from the executions of 16th-century Protestant martyrs. (☎08165 277 777; www.balliol.ox.ac.uk. Open daily 1:30-5pm. £1, students free.) Indira Gandhi and Margaret Thatcher attended **Somerville College,** Oxford's most famous former women's college. From Carfax, head down Cornmarket St., which becomes Magdalen St., St. Giles, and finally Woodstock Rd. (☎08165 270 600; www.some.ox.ac.uk. Open daily 9am-5pm. Free.)

The grand **Ashmolean Museum,** on Beaumont St., houses works by Leonardo da Vinci, Matisse, Monet, and van Gogh. Opened in 1683, the Ashmolean was Britain's first public museum and still holds one of the country's finest collections. The museum is undergoing extensive renovations until 2009, but continues to show an exhibit of "treasures"—more than 200 artifacts from its galleries—including the lantern carried by Guy Fawkes in the Gunpowder Plot of 1605 and the deerskin mantle of Powhatan, father of Pocahantas. (☎08165 278 000; www.ashmolean.org. Open Tu-Sa 10am-5pm, Su noon-5pm. Free. Tours £2.) **Bodleian Library,** on Broad St., is Oxford's main reading and research library with over five million books and 50,000 manuscripts. (☎08165 277 000; www.bodley.ox.ac.uk. Library open M-F 9am-10pm, Sa 9am-1pm; summer M-F 9am-7pm, Sa 9am-1pm. Tours leave from the Divinity School in the main quad M-Sa 2-4 times per day. Tours £6, audio tour £2.50.)

ENTERTAINMENT AND NIGHTLIFE. Punting on the River Thames, known in Oxford as the "Isis," or on the River Cherwell (CHAR-wul), is a traditional pastime. Punters propel their small wooden vessels using a tall pole and oar. Bring wine and rent a boat from the **Magdalen Bridge Boathouse,** just under Magdalen Bridge. (☎08165 202 643; www.oxfordpunting.co.uk. Open daily Mar.-Oct. 9:30am-dusk. £14 per hr. Cash only.) Music and drama at Oxford are cherished arts. *This Month in Oxford* and *Daily Information* (www.dailyinfo.co.uk), available for free at the TIC, list upcoming events.

Pubs outnumber colleges in Oxford. Many are so miniscule that a single band of students will squeeze out other patrons. Luckily, there's another place just around the corner, so be ready to crawl. **Turf's Tavern,** 4 Bath Pl., off Holywell St., is a popular 13th-century student pub tucked in an alley off of another alley. (☎08165 243 235. Open M-Sa 11am-11pm, Su noon-10:30pm. Kitchen closes 7:30pm. AmEx/MC/V.) Merry masses head to the back rooms at **The King's Arms,** 40 Holywell St., considered to be Oxford's unofficial student union. (☎08165 242 369. Open daily 10:30am-midnight. Food served 11:30am-9pm. MC/V.) *The Hobbit* and *The Chronicles of Narnia* were first read aloud at **The Eagle and Child,** 49 St. Giles, the favored haunt of their respective authors, J.R.R. Tolkien and C. S. Lewis. (☎08165 302 925. Open M-Th 10am-11pm, F-Sa 10am-11:30pm, Su 10am-10:30pm. Kitchen open noon-9pm.) **The Jolly Farmers,** 20 Paradise St., one of Oxfordshire's first gay and lesbian pubs, often finds itself crowded with twentysomethings. (☎08165 07771 561 848. Open daily noon-midnight.) After happy hour, head to **clubs** at Walton Street or Cowley Road.

STRATFORD-UPON-AVON ☎01789

Shakespeare was born here, and this fluke of fate has made Stratford-upon-Avon a major stop on the tourist superhighway. Proprietors tout the dozen-odd properties linked, however remotely, to the Bard and his extended family; shops and restaurants devotedly stencil his prose and poetry on their windows and walls. But, behind the sound and fury of rumbling tour buses and chaotic swarms of daytrippers, there lies a town worth seeing for the beauty of the Avon and for the riveting performances in the Royal Shakespeare Theatre.

THENCE, AWAY! Trains (☎08457 484 950) arrive at Station Rd., off Alcester Rd., and run to: Birmingham (50min., 2 per hr., £5.90); London Marlybone (2hr., 2 per hr., £45); and Warwick (25min., 9 per day, £4.50). National Express **buses** (☎08717 818 181) go to: London (3-4hr., 4 per day, £15.80) and Oxford (1hr., 1 per day, £8). Local Stratford Blue bus #X20 stops at Wood and Bridge St., and goes to Birmingham (1hr., every hr., £4). The TIC, **Bridgefoot,** is across Warwick Rd. (☎0870 160 7930; www.shakespeare-country.co.uk. Open Apr.-Oct. M-Sa 9am-5:30pm, Su 10am-4pm; Nov.-Mar. M-Sa 9am-5pm, Su 10am-3:30pm.) Surf the **Internet** at Cyber Junction, 28 Greenhill St. (☎263 400. £4 per hr. Open M-F 10am-6pm, Sa 10:30am-5:30pm.) **Postal Code:** CV37 6PU.

TO SLEEP, PERCHANCE TO DREAM. B&Bs line Evesham Place, Evesham Road, Grove Road, and Shipston Road, but reservations are a must, especially in the summer. **Carlton Guest House ❸,** 22 Evesham Pl., has spacious rooms and spectacular service. (☎293 548. Singles £24-30; doubles £52; triples £60-78. Cash only.) To reach **YHA Stratford (HI) ❷,** Wellsbourne Rd., follow B4086 from the town center (35min.), or take bus #X18 or 15 from Bridge St. (10min., every hr., £2.) This isolated hostel caters mostly to school groups and families and is a solid, inexpensive option for longer stays. (☎01789 297 093; www.stratfordyha.org.uk. Breakfast included. Internet £1 per 15min. Laundry £3. Dorms £20-25. £3 HI discount. MC/V.) Classy yet cozy, **The Oppo ❸,** 13 Sheep St., receives rave reviews from locals. (☎01789 269 980. Entrees from £9. M-Th noon-2pm and 5-9:30pm, F-Sa noon-2pm and 5-11pm, Su 6-9:30pm. MC/V.) **Hussain's ❷,** 6a Chapel St., a favorite of Ben Kingsley, offers Stratford's best Indian menu, featuring tandoori with handcrushed spices. (☎01789 276 506; www.hussainsindiancuisine.co.uk. Entrees from £6. Open daily 12:30-2:30pm and 5pm-midnight. AmEx/MC/V.) A **Somerfield** supermarket is in Town Sq. (☎292 604. Open M-Sa 8am-7pm, Su 10am-4pm.)

THE PLAY'S THE THING. Stratford's Will-centered sights are best seen before 11am, when daytrippers arrive, or after 4pm, when crowds disperse. Fans can buy an **All Five Houses ticket** for admission to all official Shakespeare properties: Anne Hathaway's Cottage, Mary Arden's House, Hall's Croft, New Place and Nash's House, and Shakespeare's Birthplace. (Tickets available at all houses. £14.50, concessions £12.50.) The **Three In-Town Houses** pass covers the latter three sights. (£10.60, concessions £9.30.) **Shakespeare's Birthplace,** on Henley St., is part period re-creation and part exhibit of Shakespeare's life and works. (☎01789 201 806. Open in summer M-Sa 9am-5pm, Su 9:30am-5pm; mid-season daily 10am-5pm; winter M-Sa 10am-4pm, Su 10:30am-4pm. £8, students £7.) **New Place,** on Chapel St., was Stratford's finest home when Shakespeare bought it in 1597; now only the foundation remains, the house itself destroyed

AKESPEAREAN DISSES

n Stratford-upon-Avon, you can ee where Shakespeare is buried, valk through the house where he grew up, and sit on a bench where ne kissed his sweetheart. But what no tour guide will tell you is how Will slung out insults. Any of the ollowing might come in handy, in Stratford and beyond:

. **Wipe thy ugly face, thou loggerheaded toad-spotted barnacle!** I'm sorry, you're just not hat attractive.
2. **Bathe thyself, thou rank reeling-ripe boar-pig!** One way to ell that guy in your hostel that he could use a shower.
3. **Thou puny milk-livered measel!** You're a coward!
4. **Thou dost intrude, thou infecious fat-kidneyed woldwarp!** Sometimes, you just need some personal space.
5. **Thou vain idle-headed strumpet!** You spend too much time in ront of that mirror.
6. **Clean thine ears, thou lumpish boil-brained lout!** What? You didn't hear me the first time?
7. **Thy breath stinks with eating toasted cheese.** Your breath is offensive. Brush your teeth.
8. **Remove thine ass hence, thou beslubbering beetle-headed clotpole!** For that drunkard in the club who just won't leave you alone.
9. **Thou droning boil-brained harpy!** To let your tour guide know hat you're not that interested.
10. **I'll see thee hang'd, thou villainous ill-breeding ratsbane!** Only use when you're truly furious.

by a disgruntled 19th-century owner to spite Bard tourists. (Summer M-Sa 9:30am-5pm, Su 10am-5pm; mid-season daily 11am-5pm; winter M-Sa 11am-4pm. £4, concessions £3.50.) New Place can be viewed from **Nash's House,** on Chapel St., which belonged to the first husband of Shakespeare's granddaughter. **Hall's Croft** and **Mary Arden's House** also capitalize on connections to Shakespeare's extended family and provide exhibits on Elizabethan daily life. (Open daily 9:30am-5pm in summer, 10am-5pm in mid-season, and 10am-4pm in winter. £7, concessions £6.) Pay homage to the Bard's grave in the **Holy Trinity Church,** Trinity St. (☎01789 266 316. Open daily 8:30am-6pm. Last admission 20min. before close. Requested donation £1.50.)

The **Royal Shakespeare Company** sells well over one million tickets each year. The Royal Shakespeare Theatre and the Swan Theatre, the RSC's more intimate neighbor, are currently undergoing a £100 million renovation and will re-open in 2010. The company will continue to perform shows down the road at **The Courtyard Theatre.** Visitors can get backstage tours and a glimpse at the high-tech stage to be installed at the Royal Shakespeare Theatre. Tickets are sold through the box office in the foyer of the Courtyard Theatre. (☎01789 0844 800 1110; www.rsc.org.uk. Open M and W-Sa 9:30am-8pm, Tu 10am-8pm. Tickets £10-48. Tickets £5 for ages 16-25. Standing room £5. Standby tickets in summer £15; winter £12. Disabled travelers should call ahead to advise the box office of their needs; some performances feature sign language interpretation or audio description.) The Shakespeare Birthplace Trust hosts a **Poetry Festival** every Sunday evening in July and August. Past participants include Seamus Heaney, Ted Hughes, and Derek Walcott. (☎01789 292 176. Tickets £7-15.) Theater crowds abound at the **Dirty Duck Pub,** 66 Waterside, where RSC actors make appearances almost nightly. (☎01789 297 312; www.dirtyduck.co.uk. Open daily 10am-midnight. AmEx/MC/V.)

BIRMINGHAM ☎0121

Birmingham (pop. 1,000,000), second in Britain only to London in population, is the hub of Midlands nightlife and offers a thriving arts scene. It is steadfastly defended by fun-loving "Brummies" as one of the UK's most lively cities.

TRANSPORTATION. **Trains** run from **New St. Station** (☎08457 484 950) to: Liverpool Lime Street (2hr., every hr., £23.60); London Euston (2hr, every 30min., £61.50); Manchester Piccadilly (2hr.,

2 per hr., £25.50); Oxford (1hr., at least every hr., £23). Book in advance for lower prices. Luggage storage £6 per day. National Express **buses** (☎08717 818 181; www.nationalexpress.com.) departs from **Digbeth Station** (temporarily on Oxford St.) for: Cardiff (1hr., 4 per day, £21.50), Liverpool (1hr., 5 per day, £10.80), London Heathrow (2hr., every hr., £28), Manchester (2hr., every 2 hrs., £12), Oxford (2hr., 5 per day., £11).

ORIENTATION AND PRACTICAL INFORMATION. Birmingham is at the center of train and bus lines between London, central Wales, southwest England, and all northern destinations. The TIC, **The Rotunda,** 150 New St., books rooms for free and offers listings and flyers for budget accommodations. (☎0844 888 3883; www.visitbirmingham.com. Branch at the junction of New and Corporation St. Open M, W-Sa 9:30am-5:30pm, Tu 10am-5:30pm, Su 10:30am-4:30pm.) **Postal Code:** B2 4TU.

ACCOMMODATIONS AND FOOD. Hagley Road has several budget B&Bs—the farther away from downtown, the lower the prices. Take bus #9, 109, 126, or 139 from Colomore Row to Hagley Rd. Near the bus stop, **Birmingham Central Backpackers ❷,** 58 Coventry St., has tidy ensuite rooms and a large comfortable common area with colorful pastel walls and a TV projection screen. The full bar also stocks plenty of snacks and simple items for dinner. (☎0121 643 0033; www.birminghambackpackers.com. Breakfast included. Internet 50p for 30min. Laundry £3.50. Beds from £16. MC/V.) **Canalside Cafe ❶,** 35 Worcester Bar, serves baguettes, chili, and vegetarian dishes. (☎0121 441 9862. Most sandwiches £4-5. Open M-F and Su noon-11pm, Sa noon-10pm. Cash only.) Get groceries from **Sainsbury's,** Martineau Pl., 17 Union St. (☎0121 236 6496. Open M-F 7am-9pm, Sa 7am-8pm, Su 11am-5pm.)

SIGHTS AND ENTERTAINMENT. Birmingham has a long-standing reputation as a grim, industrial metropolis. To counter this bleak stereotype, the city has revitalized its central district with a visitor magnet: shopping—and lots of it. The epic **Bullring,** Europe's largest retail establishment, is the foundation of Birmingham's material-world makeover. Recognizable by the wavy, scaled **Selfridges** department store, the center has more than 140 shops and cafes. (☎0121 632 1500; www.bullring.co.uk. Open M-F 9:30am-8pm, Sa 9am-8pm, Su 11am-5pm.) Twelve minutes south of town by rail or bus lies **Cadbury World,** a cavity-inducing celebration of the famed chocolate empire. Take a train from New St. to Bournville, or bus #84 from the city center. (☎0121 451 4159. Open Mar.-Oct. daily 10am-3pm; Nov.-Feb. Tu-Th and Sa-Su 10am-3pm. Reserve ahead. £13, students £10.) The **Birmingham International Jazz Festival** brings over 200 performers to town during the first two weeks of July. (☎0121 454 7020; www.birminghamjazzfestival.com.)

Broad Street, with trendy cafe-bars and clubs, gets rowdy on weekends; as always, exercise caution at night. Pick up the bi-monthly *What's On* to discover Birmingham's latest hot spots. **The Yardbird,** Paradise Pl., is an excellent alternative to the club scene. No dress code, no cover, no pretense—just good music, big couches, and drinks with friends. DJs spin beats on Friday, with live music on Saturdays. (☎0121 212 2524; www.myspace.com/theyardbirdbirmingham. M-W and Su noon-midnight, Th-Sa noon-2am. Cash only.) A popular bar at the heart of city nightlife, **Rococo Lounge,** 260 Broad St., has a large outdoor patio and red retro-modern furnishings. Half price on Friday. (☎0121 633 4260; www.rococolounge.com. M-Th noon-2am, Sa-Su noon-3am.)

CAMBRIDGE ☎01223

Unlike museum-oriented, metropolitan Oxford, Cambridge is a town for students before tourists. It was here that Newton's gravity, Watson and Crick's DNA model, Byron and Milton's poetry, and Milne's Winnie the Pooh were born. No longer exclusive to upper-class sons, the university develops the minds of female, international, and state-school pupils alike. At exams' end, Cambridge explodes in Pimm's-soaked glee, and May Week is a swirl of parties and balls.

TRANSPORTATION AND PRACTICAL INFORMATION. The **train** station is on Station Rd. Trains (☎08457 484 950) run to London King's Cross (45min., 3 per hr., £18) and Ely (20min., 3 per hr., round-trip £3.30). National Express (☎08705 808 080) **buses** and airport shuttles pick up at stands on Parkside St. along Parker's Piece Park. Buses go to: London Victoria (3hr., every hr., £11); Gatwick (4hr., every hr., £30.50); Heathrow (2½hr., 2 per hr., £26); Stansted (1hr., every hr., £10). Stagecoach Express (☎01604 676 060) runs to Oxford (3hr., every hr., from £6.50). **Bicycles** are the main mode of transportation in Cambridge. Rent at Mike's Bikes, 28 Mill Rd. (☎01223 312 591. £10 per day. £35 deposit. Lock and light included. Open M and F 9am-6pm, Sa 9am-5pm, Su 10am-4pm. MC/V.) The **TIC,** south of Market Sq. on Wheeler St., books rooms for £3 plus 10% deposit. (☎09065 268 006 www.visitcambridge.org. Open Easter-Oct. M-F 10am-5:30pm, Sa 10am-5pm, Su 11am-3pm; Nov.-Easter M-F 10am-5:30pm, Sa 10am-5pm.) **Postal Code:** CB2 3AA.

ACCOMMODATIONS AND FOOD. John Maynard Keynes, who studied and taught at Cambridge, tells us that low supply and high demand usually means one thing: high prices. **B&Bs** around **Portugal Street** and **Tenison Road** outside the city center demonstrate this theory. Book ahead in summer and check the guide to accommodations at the TIC. **YHA Cambridge ❷,** 97 Tenison Rd., close to the train station, has a relaxed, welcoming atmosphere that draws a diverse clientele with its well-equipped kitchen and two TV lounges. (☎01223 354 601. English breakfast included; other meals available. Lockers £1. Luggage storage £1-2. Internet £1 per 30 min. Reception 24hr. Dorms £20, under 18 £16. MC/V.) **Tenison Towers Guest House ❹,** 148 Tenison Rd., two blocks from the train station, has freshly baked muffins and impeccable rooms in a Victorian house. (☎01223 363 924; www.cambridgecitytenisontowers.com. No smoking. Singles £35-40; doubles £60. Cash only.)

South of town, **Hills Road** and **Mill Road** are full of budget restaurants popular with the college crowd. **Clown's ❶,** 54 King St., serves huge portions (£2.50-7) of pasta and dessert. (☎01223 355 711. Open M-Sa 8am-midnight, Su 8am-11pm. Cash only.) The walls are crammed with books at **CB1 ❶,** 32 Mill Rd., a decidedly chill student hangout and coffee shop. (☎01223 576 306. Free Wi-Fi. Coffee £1-2. Open M-Th 9am-8pm, F 9am-9pm, Sa-Su 10am-8pm.) **Market Square** has precarious pyramids of fruits and vegetables. (Open M-Sa 9:30am-5pm.) Students buy their Pimm's and baguettes at **Sainsbury's,** 44 Sidney St. (☎366 891. Open M-Sa 8am-10pm, Su 11am-5pm.)

SIGHTS. Cambridge is an architect's utopia, packing some of England's most magnificent monuments into less than one square mile. The soaring **King's College Chapel** and St. John's postcard-familiar **Bridge of Sighs** are sightseeing staples, while more obscure college quads open onto ornate courtyards and gardens. Most historic buildings are on the **east bank** of the Cam between Magdalene Bridge and Silver St. On the west bank, the meadowed **Backs** border the elegant **Fellows' Gardens,** giving the university a unique juxtaposition of cow and college. The **University of Cambridge** has three eight-week terms: Michaelmas (Oct.-Dec.), Lent (Jan.-Mar.), and Easter (Apr.-June). Visitors can access most of the 31 colleges daily, although times vary; call the TIC for hours. Porters (bowler-wearing ex-servicemen) maintain security. Travelers who look like undergrads (no backpack or camera) can often wander freely through the grounds after hours. The fastest way to blow your tourist cover is to trample the grass of the courtyards, a privilege reserved for the elite.

If you only have time for a few colleges, visit Trinity, King's, St. John's, and Queens'. Sir Isaac Newton originally measured the speed of sound by timing the echo in the cloisters along the north side of the Great Court at **Trinity College,** on Trinity St. Also the alma mater of Vladimir Nabokov, Ernest Rutherford, and Alfred Lord Tennyson, Trinity houses the stunning **Wren Library,** with A.A. Milne's handwritten manuscript of *Winnie the Pooh* and the original copy of Newton's *Principia*. (☎01223 338 400. Chapel and courtyard open daily 10am-5pm. Library open M-F noon-2pm. Easter-Oct. £2.50, concessions £1.30, children £1, families £4.40; Nov.-Easter free.) **King's College,** south of Trinity on King's Parade, is the alma mater of E.M. Forster and Salman Rushdie. Peter Paul Reubens's *Adoration of the Magi* hangs behind the altar of its Gothic chapel. (☎01223 331 100. Open M-Sa 9:30am-5pm, Su 10am-5pm. Tours arranged through the TIC. £5, students £3.50; with audio tour £7.50/6.) Established in 1511 by Henry VIII's mother, **Saint John's College,** on St. John's St., is one of seven colleges founded by women. It boasts the 12th-century School of Pythagoras, thought to be the oldest complete building in Cambridge, a replica of the Bridge of Sighs, and the longest room in the city—the Fellows' Room in Second Court spans 28m. (☎01223 338 600. Open M-F 10am-5:30pm, Sa-Su 9:30am-5:30pm. Evensong Tu-Su 6:30pm. £2.80, concessions £1.70, families £5.) **Queens' College,** Silver St., has the only unaltered Tudor courtyard in Cambridge. Despite rumors to the contrary, its **Mathematical Bridge** is supported by screws and bolts, not just by mathematical principle. (☎01223 335 511. Open Mar-Oct. M-F 10am-4:30pm, Sa-Su 9:30am-5pm. £2.) A break from academia, the **Fitzwilliam Museum,** on Trumpington St., elegantly displays Egyptian, Greek, and Asian treasures, as well as works by Brueghel, Monet, and Reubens. (☎01223 332 900. Open Tu-Sa 10am-5pm, Su noon-5pm. Suggested donation £3.)

ENTERTAINMENT AND NIGHTLIFE. **May Week** is, strangely enough, in June—you would think those bright Cambridge students could understand a calendar. An elaborate celebration of the end of the term, the week is crammed with concerts, plays, and balls followed by recuperative riverside breakfasts and 5am punting. **Punting** (p. 158) on the River Cam is a favorite pastime in Cambridge. Beware of punt-bombers: jumping from bridges into the river alongside a punt, thereby tipping its occupants into the Cam, has evolved into an art form. Scudamore's, Silver St. Bridge, rents **boats.** (☎01223 359 750; www.scudamores.com. M-F £18 per hr. plus a £70 deposit, Sa-Su £20 per hr. plus a £70 deposit. MC/V). Student-punted tours (£12, students £10) are another option. **King Street** has a diverse collection of pubs. **The Anchor,** Silver St., a jolly-looking pub overflowing with beer and good cheer, is located right on the Cam. Savor a pint in the same spot where Pink Floyd's Syd Barrett drew his inspiration or scoff at amateur punters colliding under Silver St. Bridge. (☎01223 353 554. Open M-W 11am-11pm, Th-Sa 11am-midnight, Su 11am-11pm. Food served M-Sa noon-10pm, Su noon-9pm.) Popular with locals, **The Free Press,** Prospect Row, has no pool table, no cell phones, and no loud music—just good beer and conversation. (☎01223 368 337. Open M-F noon-2:30pm and 6-11pm, Sa noon-3pm and 6-11pm, Su noon-3pm and 7-10:30pm.) When Watson and Crick ran into **The Eagle,** 8 Benet St., to announce their discovery of DNA, the barmaid insisted they settle their four-shilling tab before she'd serve them. Cambridge's oldest pub also has a Royal Airforce room,

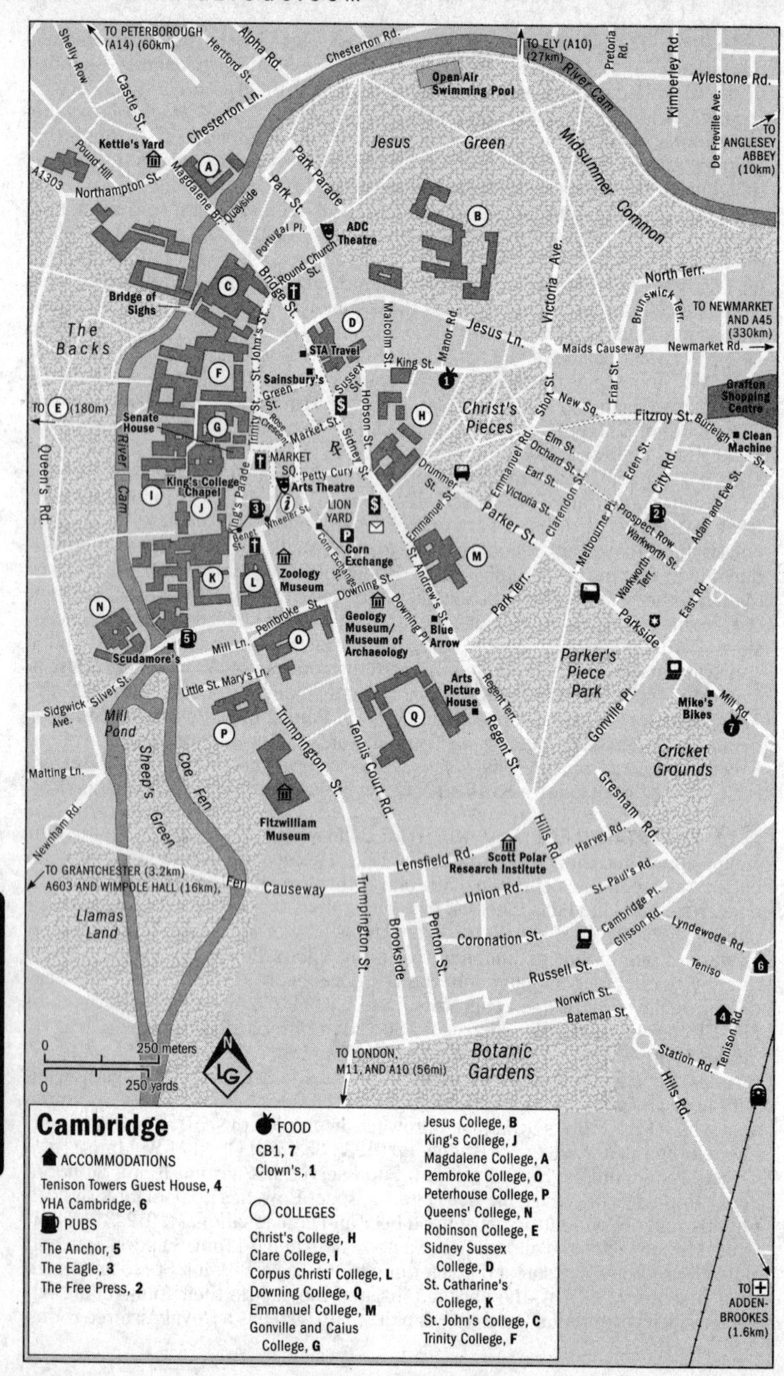
Cambridge
ACCOMMODATIONS
Tenison Towers Guest House, 4
YHA Cambridge, 6
PUBS
The Anchor, 5
The Eagle, 3
The Free Press, 2
FOOD
CB1, 7
Clown's, 1
COLLEGES
Christ's College, H
Clare College, I
Corpus Christi College, L
Downing College, Q
Emmanuel College, M
Gonville and Caius College, G
Jesus College, B
King's College, J
Magdalene College, A
Pembroke College, O
Peterhouse College, P
Queens' College, N
Robinson College, E
Sidney Sussex College, D
St. Catharine's College, K
St. John's College, C
Trinity College, F
TO PETERBOROUGH (A14) (60km)
TO ELY (A10) (27km)
TO ANGLESEY ABBEY (10km)
TO NEWMARKET AND A45 (330km)
TO E (180m)
TO GRANTCHESTER (3.2km) A603 AND WIMPOLE HALL (16km)
TO LONDON, M11, AND A10 (56mi)
TO ADDENBROOKES (1.6km)
Open Air Swimming Pool
Kettle's Yard
ADC Theatre
Bridge of Sighs
STA Travel
Sainsbury's
Senate House
King's College Chapel
MARKET SQ.
Arts Theatre
LION YARD
Corn Exchange
Zoology Museum
Geology Museum/ Museum of Archaeology
Blue Arrow
Scudamore's
Arts Picture House
Fitzwilliam Museum
Scott Polar Research Institute
Grafton Shopping Centre
Clean Machine
Mike's Bikes
Jesus Green
Midsummer Common
Christ's Pieces
Parker's Piece Park
Cricket Grounds
The Backs
Mill Pond
Sheep's Green
Coe Fen
Llamas Land
Botanic Gardens
River Cam
0 250 meters
0 250 yards
Chesterton Rd.
Chesterton Ln.
Castle St.
Northampton St.
Magdalene Br.
Quayside
Park Parade
Park St.
Portugal Pl.
Round Church St.
Bridge St.
St. John's St.
Trinity St.
Sidney St.
Sussex St.
Hobson St.
Malcolm St.
Jesus Ln.
King St.
Manor Rd.
Victoria Ave.
Maids Causeway
Newmarket Rd.
Market St.
Petty Cury
King's Parade
Benet St.
Wheeler St.
Corn Exchange St.
Downing St.
Pembroke St.
Mill Ln.
Little St. Mary's Ln.
Silver St.
Sidgwick Ave.
Trumpington St.
Tennis Court Rd.
St. Andrew's St.
Emmanuel St.
Drummer St.
Regent St.
Regent Terr.
Parker St.
Park Terr.
Parkside
Gonville Pl.
East Rd.
Mill Rd.
Fitzroy St.
Burleigh St.
City Rd.
Hills Rd.
Lensfield Rd.
Fen Causeway
Queen's Rd.
Newnham Rd.
Malting Ln.
Union Rd.
Coronation St.
Russell St.
Brookside
Penton St.
Station Rd.
Tenison Rd.
Gresham Rd.
Harvey Rd.
Aylestone Rd.
Kimberley Rd.
Pretoria Rd.
De Freville Ave.
North Terr.
Brunswick Terr.
Friar St.
New Sq.
Emmanuel Rd.
Clarendon St.
Melbourne Pl.
Prospect Row
Warkworth St.
Adam and Eve St.

where WWII pilots stood on each other's shoulders to burn their initials into the ceiling. (☎01223 505 020. Open M-Sa 11am-11pm, Su noon-10:30pm.)

NORTHERN ENGLAND

The north's major cities grew out of the wool and coal industries, but their reinvigorated city centers have embraced post-industrial attitude with fresh youth culture. The region's innovative music and arts scenes are world-famous: Liverpool and Manchester alone have produced four of *Q Magazine's* 10 biggest rock stars of the 20th century. When you need a break from city life, find respite in the Peak or Lake District.

MANCHESTER ☎0161

Teeming with electronic beats and post-industrial glitz, Manchester (pop. 440,000) has risen from factory soot to savor a reputation as one of England's hippest spots. In 1996, the IRA bombed the city center, a tragic event that sparked an urban renewal that has given Manchester a sleek modern look. The city is a hive of activity, from the shopping districts and museums to the wild nightlife and preeminent football team.

TRANSPORTATION AND PRACTICAL INFORMATION

Flights: Flights arrive at **Manchester International Airport** (**MAN;** ☎08712 710 711; www.manchesterairport.co.uk).

Trains: Piccadilly Station (☎08457 484 950) on London Rd., has trains that go to: **Birmingham** (1hr., every hr., £25.50); **Edinburgh** (4hr., 5 per day, £46.50); **London Euston** (2-3hr., every hr., £61.40 off-peak, £115 peak); **York** (40min., 2 per hr., £19.50). Luggage storage £6 for 24hr. Trains from Victoria Station on Victoria St. go to **Liverpool** (1 hr., every hour, £8.80) and **Leeds** (1.5 hours, every 30 min., £14.10).

Buses: National Express buses (☎08717 818 181; www.nationalexpress.com) go from Chorlton St. to Liverpool (1hr., every hr., £6), Birmingham (2-3hr., every hr., £12), and London (5-6hr., every hr., £22). Nearly 50 local bus routes stop at Piccadilly Gardens (1-day bus pass £4.30); route maps are available at the **visitor center.**

Tourist Office: Manchester Visitor Centre (☎0871 222 8223; www.visitmanchester.com), in the Town Hall Extension on Lloyd St., books rooms and offers a "Discover Manchester" tour—all for free. Open M-Sa 10am-5:30pm, Su 10:30am-5:30pm.

ACCOMMODATIONS

Browse the free *Where to Stay* guide (at the visitor center) for listings. Book ahead in summer, when large crowds flock to Manchester.

Hilton Chambers, 15 Hilton St. (☎0800 083 0236; www.hattersgroup.com/hiltonchambers). Helpful staff and large, clean rooms, topped off with a grill-equipped roof deck. Laundry £5. Free Wi-Fi. Reception 24hr. Dorms from £15; singles from £45. MC/V. ❷

The Hatters Hostel, 50 Newton St. (☎0800 083 3848; www.hattersgroup.com/hatters). Clean but crowded rooms and friendly service. Breakfast included. Laundry £5. Reception 24hr. Dorms £15-18; doubles £50; triples £61.50. MC/V. ❷

YHA Manchester (HI), Potato Wharf, Castlefield (☎0161 839 9960; www.yhamanchester.org.uk). Take the metro to G-Mex Station or bus #33 (dir.: Wigan) from Piccadilly Gardens to Deansgate. Breakfast included. Laundry £1.50. Internet £0.70 per min. Reception 24hr. Dorms £24.95; doubles £61.95. MC/V. ❸

FOOD

Restaurants in Chinatown can be pricey, but most offer a reasonable, multi-course "Businessman's Lunch" (M-F noon-2pm; £4-8). Better yet, visit Curry Mile, a stretch of affordable Asian restaurants on Wilmslow Rd.

Trof, 8 Thomas St. (☎0161 833 3197; www.trofnq.co.uk). Bohemian cafe, bar, and restaurant with delicious food and a unique character. Wash down ciabatta with melted goat cheese and roasted red pepper (£5.50) with one of the 40+ international beers. Open M-W 10am-midnight, Th-Sa 10am-1am, Su 9am-midnight. MC/V. ❷

Soup Kitchen, 31-33 Spear St. (☎0161 236 5100; www.soup-kitchen.co.uk). Offers large bowls of hearty homemade soups, salads, and sandwiches. Soup £2.50-2.95. Open M-F 10am-3pm, Sa-Su 10am-5pm. AmEx/MC/V. ❶

Tampopo Noodle House, 16 Albert Sq. (☎0161 819 1966; www.tampopo.co.uk). A Manchester favorite that serves noodles from all over Asia. Noodles £6.50-8.50. Open M-Sa noon-11pm, Su noon-10pm. AmEx/MC/V. ❷

SIGHTS

IN THE STILL OF THE NIGHT. Streets in the Northern Quarter are dimly lit at night. If you're crossing from Piccadilly to Swan St. or Great Ancoats St., use Oldham St., where the neon-lit clubs provide reassurance.

THE MANCHESTER ART GALLERY. Features 19th-century British painting, with a famous Pre-Raphaelite collection. They also have an interactive exhibit (try to make one of the paintings burp) and a gallery with recently restored paintings. *(Mosley St. ☎0161 235 888; www.manchestergalleries.org. Open Tu-Su 10am-5pm. Guided tours every Sa and Su at 2pm. Free.)*

URBIS MUSEUM. Don't miss the exploration of modern urban culture and art at this awe-inspiring museum, which is covered in 2200 plates of glass. *(Cathedral Gardens. ☎0161 605 8200; www.urbis.org.uk. Open daily 10am-6pm. Free.)*

THE MUSEUM OF SCIENCE AND INDUSTRY. Crawl through a Victorian sewer and look at working steam engines. *(Liverpool Rd., in Castlefield. ☎0161 832 2244; www.mosi.org.uk. Open daily 10am-5pm. Free. Admission for special exhibits varies.)*

CENTRAL LIBRARY. One of the largest municipal libraries in Europe, it holds a music and theater library, a literature library, and even a library devoted only to the history of the library itself. *(St. Peter's Sq. ☎0161 234 1900; www.manchester.gov.uk/libraries/central. Open M-Th 9am-8pm, F-Sa 9am-5pm. Free.)*

THE JOHN RYLANDS LIBRARY. See rare books and its most famous holding: the St. John Fragment, the earliest known part of the New Testament in any language. *(150 Deansgate. ☎0161 275 3751; www.library.manchester.ac.uk. Open M, W-Sa 10am-5m, Tu and Su noon-5pm. Free.)*

MANCHESTER UNITED MUSEUM AND TOUR CENTRE. Memorabilia from the club's 1878 inception to its recent trophy-hogging success may just convert you into a fanatic. *(North Stand, Old Trafford. From Old Trafford Metrolink stop, follow the signs up Warwick Rd. to the Sir Matt Busby Way, at the Old Trafford football stadium. ☎0870 442 1994; www.manutd.com. Open daily 9:30am-5pm. £6.50, student £3.75. Tours every 10min, except on match days. £10, student £6. Reserve ahead.)*

ROYAL EXCHANGE THEATRE. The glass-walled, circular theater stages traditional and Shakespearean plays and premiers original works. *(St. Ann's Sq. ☎0161 833 9833; www.royalexchange.co.uk. Box office open M-Sa 9:30am-7:30pm. Tickets £8.50-29.)*

NIGHTLIFE

At night, many of Manchester's lunchtime spots turn into pre-club drinking venues or become clubs themselves. Centered around Oldham St., the Northern Quarter is the city's youthful outlet for live music. Partiers head to Oxford St. for late-night clubbing. Gay and lesbian clubbers should check out the **Gay Village,** northeast of Princess St. Visit a number of festivals, most notably, **Manchester Pride** (Aug., ☎0161 236 7474; www.manchesterpride.com), which raises money for GLBT organizations and AIDS relief. Evening crowds fill the bars lining Canal St., but the area is also lively during the day.

Thirsty Scholar, 50 New Wakefield St. (☎0161 236 6071; www.thirstyscholar.co.uk). Students crowd into this small, dark bar underneath a railroad bridge. Tu-Th acoustic nights. DJs on the weekends. Happy hour M-F 4-8pm with selected beers for £2.20-2.50 a pint. Open M-Th, Su noon-midnight, F-Sa noon-2am.

The Temple, 100 Great Bridgewater, (☎0161 278 1817). Drinking German beer in this Victorian public-toilet-turned-pub makes for a one-of-a-kind experience. Voted best place for a first date. Open M-Th, Su noon-midnight, F-Sa noon-1am.

Cord, 8 Dorsey St. (☎0161 832 9494; www.cordbar.co.uk). This small venue is the perfect spot for a subdued, exclusive drink. 2 floors, with music in the basement. Open M-Th noon-11pm, F-Sa noon-1am, Su 3-10:30pm.

LIVERPOOL ☎0151

Many Brits still scoff at once-industrial Liverpool, but Scousers—as Liverpudlians are colloquially known, in reference to a local stew dish—have watched their metropolis undergo a cultural face-lift, trading in working-class grit for off-beat vitality. Several free museums, two deified football teams, and top-notch nightlife helped earn the city the title of European Capital of Culture 2008. And, of course, some fuss is made over The Beatles.

TICKET TO RIDE ON THE LONG AND WINDING ROAD. Trains (☎08457 484 950) leave **Lime Street Station** for: Birmingham (1½hr.; 2-3 per hr.; £9-22.80), London Euston (3hr., 2 perhr., £13-64), and Manchester Piccadilly (45min., 2-4 per hr., £8.80). National Express (☎08705 808 080) runs **buses** run from **Norton Street Station** to Birmingham (3hr., 4 per day, £10.20), London (5-6hr., 8 per day, £23), and Manchester (1-2hr., 2-3per hr., £6). The Isle of Man Steam Packet Company (☎08705 523 523; www.steam-packet.com) runs **ferries** from Princess Dock to the Isle of Man. P&O Irish Ferry service (☎0871 66 44 999; www.poirishsea.com) runs to Dublin. The **TICs,** at 08 Pl., Whitechapel, and Anchor Courtyard, Albert Dock, have the free, handy brochure *Visitor Guide to Liverpool, Merseyside, and England's Northwest*, and book rooms for a 10% fee. (☎233 2008; www.visitliverpool.com. Open M and W-Sa 9am-6pm, Tu 10am-6pm, Su 11am-4pm.) Expert guide Phil Hughes runs personalized 3-4hr. Beatles tours which include Strawberry Fields and Eleanor Rigby's grave. (☎0151 228 4565; touliverpool@hotmail.com. £14 per person for groups of 5-8, £70 total for groups less than 5.) Surf the **Internet** for free or peruse a helpful scale model of the city at the **Central Library** on William Brown St. (☎0151 233 5835. Open M-F 9am-6pm, Sa 9am-5pm, Su noon-4pm.) **Postal Code:** L1 1AA.

GOLDEN SLUMBERS AND STRAWBERRY FIELDS FOREVER. Budget hotels are located around Lord Nelson Street, next to the train station, and Mount Pleasant, one block from Brownlow Hill. Housed in a former Victorian warehouse, **International Inn ❷,** 4 South Hunter St., is clean and stylish, with a lounge and adjoining Internet cafe. (☎0151 709 8135; www.international-inn.co.uk. Free coffee, tea, and toast. Internet £3 per hr. Laundry £5. Dorms M-Th and Su £15, F-Sa £20; doubles £36/45. MC/V.) **Embassie Backpackers ❷,** 1 Falkner Square, is a former consulate with a family-like atmosphere, complete with kitchen and lounge. (☎0151 707 1089; www.embassie.com. Laundry £3. Free Wi-Fi. Free tea, coffee, and toast. Reception 24hr. Dorms M-Th and Su £15, F £17.50, Sa £20. Cash only.) **YHA Liverpool (HI) ❷,** 25 Tabley St., off The Wapping, is a tidy place with Beatles-themed rooms. (☎0870 7705 924. Kitchen available. Breakfast included. Laundry £2. Wheelchair-accessible. Dorms from £18, under 18 £16. £3 fee for non-members. MC/V.)

Trendy cafes and budget-friendly kebab stands line Bold and Hardman St. Many of the fast-food joints on Berry and Leece St. stay open late. Tucked into the basement of the Everyman Theatre, **Everyman Bistro ❷,** 5-9 Hope St., has a menu that changes twice daily, but always serves generous portions of tasty dishes from £6. (☎0151 708 9545. Open M-Th noon-midnight, F noon-2am, Sa 11am-2am. MC/V.) At **Tabac ❶,** 126 Bold St., sleek, trendy decor belies affordable food. Sandwiches (from £4.50) on freshly baked foccaccia are served until 9pm. (☎0151 709 9502. Breakfast from £2. Dinner specials £4.50-7.50. Open M-F 9am-11pm, Sa 9am-midnight, Su 10am-11pm. MC/V.) Pick up groceries at the **Tesco** in Clayton Sq., across from St. John's Shopping Centre. (Open M-F 6am-midnight, Sa 6am-10pm, Su 11am-5pm.)

MAGICAL MYSTERY TOUR. The TIC's *Beatles Map* (£3) leads visitors through the city's Beatles-themed sights including **Strawberry Fields** and **Penny Lane.** At Albert Dock, **The Beatles Story** traces the rise of the band through the Cavern Club, Beatlemania, and solo careers. (☎0151 709 1963; www.beatlesstory.com. Open daily 9am-7pm. £12.50, students £8.50.) The Liverpool branch of the **Tate Gallery,** also on Albert Dock, contains a collection of 19th- and 20th-century art. (☎0151 702 7400; www.tate.org.uk/liverpool. Open Tu-Su 10am-5:50pm. Suggested donation £2. Special exhibits £8, students £6.) The **Walker Art Gallery** focuses on British artists, from the 1700s to today. (☎0151 709 1963; www.liverpoolmuseums.iorg/walker. Open daily 10am-5pm. Free.) Completed in 1978, the **Anglican Liverpool Cathedral,** on Upper Duke St., boasts the highest Gothic arches, the largest organ in the UK, and the heaviest bells in the world. Climb the tower for a view that extends to Wales. (☎0151 709 6271; www.liverpoolcathedral.org.uk. Cathedral open daily 8am-6pm. Tower open daily Mar.-Oct. 10am-5pm; Nov.-Feb. 10am-4pm. Cathedral free, tower £4.25.) Neon-blue stained glass casts a glow over the controversially modern interior of the **Metropolitan Cathedral of Christ the King,** on Mt. Pleasant. (☎0151 709 9222. Open daily 8am-6pm, reduced hours in winter. Free.) The Liverpool and Everton **football clubs**—intense rivals—offer tours of their grounds. Bus #26 runs from the city center to Liverpool FC's Anfield. Bus #19 from the city center to **Everton's Goodison Park.** (Liverpool ☎0151 260 6677; tour £10, students £6. Everton ☎0151 330 2212. Tour £8.50, students £5. Reserve ahead.)

A HARD DAY'S NIGHT. Consult the *Liverpool Echo* (£0.35), sold daily by street vendors, for the most up-to-date information on city nightlife. The downtown **Ropewalks** area—especially Matthew, Church, and Bold St.—overflows with clubbers on weekends. **Mood,** 18-20 Fleet St., draws stylish crowds to its three stories of dance floors. (☎0151 709 8181; www.moodbars.com. Open M-F and Su 10pm-3am, Sa 9pm-3am. £2-5 cover after 11:30pm.) **The Cavern Club,** 10

Matthew St., where the Fab Four gained prominence, draws live bands who hope for history to repeat itself. (☎0151 236 9091. Cover £1 after 6pm Sa and Su. Pub open M-Sa from 11am, Su noon-11:30pm. Club open M-Tu 11am-7pm, W 11am-midnight, Th 11am-2am, F-Sa 11am-2:30am, Su 11am-12:30am.) **BaaBar,** 43-45 Fleet St., draws a stylish crowd and offers 35 varieties of shots (£1) with nearly nightly specials. (☎0151 708 8673. Cover varies with live music. Open M-Th 5pm-2am, F-Sa 2pm-3am, Su 3pm-1am. Cash only.)

PEAK DISTRICT NATIONAL PARK

The Peak District doesn't have any true mountains, but its more than 1400 sq. km offer almost everything else. Surrounded by industrial giants Manchester, Nottingham, and Sheffield, the Peak District is a sanctuary of deep gullies, green pastures, and rocky hillsides, with picturesque villages and manors set against some of Britain's best scenery. Transportation is easiest in the south and near outlying cities, but hikers should head north for a more isolated escape.

TRANSPORTATION AND PRACTICAL INFORMATION. The invaluable **Peak District Timetables** (£0.80), available at TICs, has accommodation and bike rental info, and maps. Two **train** lines (☎08457 48 49 50) start in Manchester and enter the park at New Mills. One stops at Buxton, near the park's edge (55min., at least every hr., £7.30); the other crosses the park via Edale (45min., M-F and Su 12 per day, Sa 18 per day, £8.40), Hope (45min., £8.50), and Hathersage (1hr., £8.50), ending in Sheffield (1¼hr., £6.50). **Buses** make a noble effort to connect scattered Peak towns; **Traveline** (☎0870 608 2608; www.traveline.org.uk) is a vital resource. The Transpeak **shuttle** makes the 3½hr. journey between Buxton, Bakewell, and Matlock (continuing to Manchester in one direction and Nottingham in the other). Bus #173 runs from Bakewell to Castleton (50min., 4 per day). Bus #200 runs from Castleton to Edale (20min., M-F 3 per day). The **Derbyshire Wayfarer** ticket, available at Manchester train stations and NPICs, allows one day of unlimited train and bus travel through the Peak District as far north as Sheffield and as far south as Derby (£8.30, students £4).

The NPICs at Bakewell, Buxton, Castleton, and Edale offer walking guides. **YHA Hostels** ❶ operates 15 locations (reserve ahead; dorms £15-19). For Buxton, Castleton, and Edale, see below. For the park's nine **YHA Camping Barns (HI)** ❶, book at the YHA Camping Barns Department, Trevelyan House, Dimple Rd., Matlock, Derbyshire, DE4 3YH. (☎0870 770 8868; £6 per person.) For **cyclists,** the park has three **Cycle Hire Centres** (£14 per day); the free *Cycle Derbyshire*, available at NPICs, includes contact info, hours, locations, and a trail map.

BAKEWELL AND EDALE. The town of Bakewell, 50km southeast of Manchester, is the largest village in the Peak District and the best base for exploring the region. Several scenic walks through the White Peaks begin nearby. **The Haven** ❹, Haddon Rd., is a 5min. walk from the town center. (☎01629 812113; www.visitbakewell.com. Doubles £55 during the week, £60 on weekends. Cash or check only.) A **Midlands Co-op** sells groceries at the corner of Granby Rd. and Market St. (Open M-Sa 8am-10pm, Su 10am-4pm.) Bakewell's **NPIC** is in Old Market Hall, on Bridge St. (☎01629 813227. Open daily Mar.-Oct. 9:30am-5:30pm; Nov.-Feb. 10am-5pm.) The northern **Dark Peak** area contains some of the wildest, most rugged hill country in England, including the spectacular peat marshes around Edale. For details on shorter trails nearby, check out the National Park Authority's *8 Walks Around Edale* (£1.40). Edale itself offers little more than a church, cafe, pub, school, and the nearby **YHA Edale (HI)** ❶, Rowland Cote. (☎0870 770 5808. Dorms £16, under 18 £12. MC/V.)

CASTLETON. Castleton's main attraction is the **Treak Cliff Cavern** and its purple seams of Blue John, a unique semi-precious mineral. (☎01433 62 05 71; www.bluejohnstone.com. Open daily Mar.-Oct. 10am-4:20pm; Nov.-Feb. 10am-3:20pm. 40min. tours 2-4 per hr. £7, students and YHA members £6.) The **NPIC** is on Buxton Rd. (☎01629 816 572. Open daily Easter-Oct. 9:30am-5:30pm; Nov.-Easter 10am-5pm.) **YHA Castleton (HI) ❷** is in the heart of town. It may be unavailable July-Aug., when it hosts children's camps. (☎01433 620 235. Kitchen available. Reserve 2-3 weeks ahead. Check-out 10am. Dorms £16, under 18 £12. MC/V.)

BUXTON. A main hub for Peak travel, the spa town of Buxton, highly reminiscent of Bath, is the picture of Georgian elegance. Just outside of town in the Buxton Country Park is the spectacular **Poole's Cavern,** a two-million-year-old limestone cave that has drawn tourists for centuries; legend has it that Mary, Queen of Scots, once visited. (☎01298 269 78; www.poolescavern.co.uk. Open daily Mar.-Nov. 9:30am-5pm, Dec.-Feb. Sa-Su 10am-4pm. 45min. tours every 20min. £7, students £5.50. Dress warmly.) The **TIC** is located in the Pavilion Gardens, St. Johns Rd. (☎01298 251 06; www.visitbuxton.com. Open daily 9:30am-5pm.) **Roseleigh Hotel ❸,** 19 Broad Walk overlooking Pavilion Gardens, has a reading parlor with shelves of travel and adventure books; the hosts are former tour guides. (☎01298 249 04; www.roseleighhotel.co.uk. Free Wi-Fi. Breakfast included. £33-38 per person. MC/V.) **Waitrose,** 33 Spring Gardens Centre, sells groceries (☎02198 767 469; open M-Tu 8:30am-7pm, W-F 8:30am-8pm, Sa 8am-7pm, Su 10am-4pm), while **The Slopes Bar ❶,** 10 Grove Parade, in the Grove Hotel, offers light meals and cafe fare in a swanky bistro setting. (☎01298 238 04. Open M-Th and Su 9:30am-7pm, F-Sa 9:30am-midnight; hot food served daily noon-5pm. Sandwiches £2-3. MC/V.)

YORK ☎01904

With a history rife with conflict, York (pop. 137,000) is known as the "most haunted city in the world." Despite the lore—or because of it—the city remains one of England's top destinations. Once impenetrable to outsiders, the crumbling medieval walls of York are now defenseless against hordes of travelers. Brandishing cameras in place of swords, visitors come to ogle Britain's largest Gothic cathedral and down a pint at one of the city's many pubs.

TRANSPORTATION AND PRACTICAL INFORMATION

Trains: York Station, Station Rd. (☎08457 484 950). Trains to: Edinburgh (2hr., 2 per hr., £67); London King's Cross (2hr., 2 per hr., £74); Manchester Piccadilly (1hr., 3 per hr., £18); Newcastle (1hr., 4 per hr., £21).

Buses: Stations at 20 Rougier St., Exhibition Sq., the train station, and on Piccadilly. Major bus stop on The Stonebow (Information ☎01904 551 400). National Express **buses** (☎08705 808 080) to: Edinburgh (6hr., 1 per day, £31); London (5hr., 15 per day, £23); and Manchester (3hr., 15 per day, £12).

Tourist Information Center: Exhibition Sq. (☎01904 550 099; www.visityork.org.) Take Station Rd. to Museum St., cross the bridge, and go left on St. Leonard's Pl. Open Apr.-Oct. M-Sa 9am-6pm, Su 10am-5pm; Nov.-Mar. M-Sa 9am-5pm, Su 10am-4pm.

Internet: York Central Library, Museum St., (☎01904 655 631). £1.50 per 15min.

Postal Code: YO1 8DA.

ACCOMMODATIONS

B&Bs (from £30) are usually outside the city walls and scattered along Blossom, Bootham, and Clifton St., and Bishopthorpe Rd. Reserve ahead in summer.

Foss Bank Guest House, 16 Huntington Rd., (☎01904 635 548). A 20min. walk from the train station or take bus #12 and get off on the 1st stop on Huntington Rd. Offers spacious, sun-lit rooms with shower and sink. Wi-Fi. Mention *Let's Go* when booking for a £1 discount. Singles £30; doubles £62. Cash only. ❸

YYHA York International, Water End (☎01904 653 147), Clifton, 2 mi. from train station. The long walk from the train station follows the river path "Dame Judi Dench," which connects to Water End. Caters to school groups but attracts guests of all ages. Breakfast included. Internet £1.50 per 15 min. Bike rental £1.50 per hr., £9.60 per day. Reserve in advance in summer. Dorms £20, under 18 £14.50; singles £27.50; doubles £52. £3 charge for non-YHA members. MC/V. ❷

FOOD

For authentic York grub, visit one of the city's pubs, or find cheap eats at the many Indian restaurants outside the city gates. Greengrocers have peddled for centuries at **Newgate Market** between Parliament St. and the Shambles. (Open Apr.-Dec. M-Sa 9am-5pm, Su 9am-4:30pm; Jan.-Mar. M-Sa 9am-5pm.) **Sainsbury's** grocery is at the intersection of Foss Bank and Heworth Green. (☎01904 643 801. Open M-Sa 8am-8pm, Su 11am-5pm.)

El Piano, 15 Grape Ln. (☎01904 610 676). Mexican flavors infuse the heart-healthy dishes served up in this laid-back and brightly painted establishment at the corner of the city center. Dishes served in 3 sizes: chica (£3), tapas (£4.25), and ración (£6). All food is vegan and gluten-free. Catch "cheap chow" M-W 10am-7pm, £6.95. Smaller dining rooms upstairs are aptly named the "Morrocan Room," adorned with floor pillows, and the bright "Sunshine Room." Open M-Sa 10am-midnight, Su noon-5pm. MC/V. ❷

Oscar's Wine Bar and Bistro, 8 Little Stonegate (☎01904 652 002), off Stonegate. Order at the bar and find a seat on the patio (if you can part the crowds) at this local favorite. Huge portions of delicious food like Oscar's special burger (£7.50), lasagna (£7.50), and a spicy bean burger (£6.95). Sandwiches £4-6. Happy hour M 4-11pm, Tu-F 5-7pm, Su 4-10:30pm. Open M-Sa 11:30am-11pm, Su noon-10:30pm. MC/V. ❷

Victor J's Artbar, 1 Finklestreet (☎01904 541 771). Hidden down an alley off Stonegate. This art-deco bar and bistro serves huge portions of toothsome sandwiches (brie, roasted veggies, and pesto ciabatta; £6) and burgers (£5-6). Open M-W and Sa 10am-midnight, Th-F 10am-1am, Su 11am-6pm. MC/V. ❷

SIGHTS

A 4km walk along the medieval walls is the best introduction to York. Beware the tourist stampede, which only wanes in the morning and just before the walls and gates close at dusk. The **Association of Voluntary Guides,** De Grey Rooms, Exhibition Square, offers free 2hr. walking tours. (☎01904 621 756; Tours daily Apr.-May and Sept.-Oct. 10:15am and 2:15pm; June-Aug. 10:15am, 2:15pm, and 6:45pm; Nov.-Mar. 10:15am.)

YORK MINSTER. It's estimated that half of the medieval stained glass in England lines this cathedral's walls, which is the largest outside Italy. The **Great East Window** depicts the beginning and end of the world in over 100 scenes. To get in for free, attended Evensong at 5:15pm. *(Deangate. ☎01904 557 216; www.yorkminster.org. Open daily 7am-6:30pm. Evensong M-Sa 5:15pm, Su 4pm. Free 1hr. guided tours from the entrance when volunteers are available Apr.-Sept. daily 9:30am-3:30pm; Oct.-Mar. 10am-2pm. £5.50, concessions £4.50. Combined ticket with Undercroft £7.50/5.)*

YORK CASTLE MUSEUM. Arguably Britain's premier museum of daily life, its rooms include **Kirkgate,** a reconstructed Victorian shopping street, and **Half**

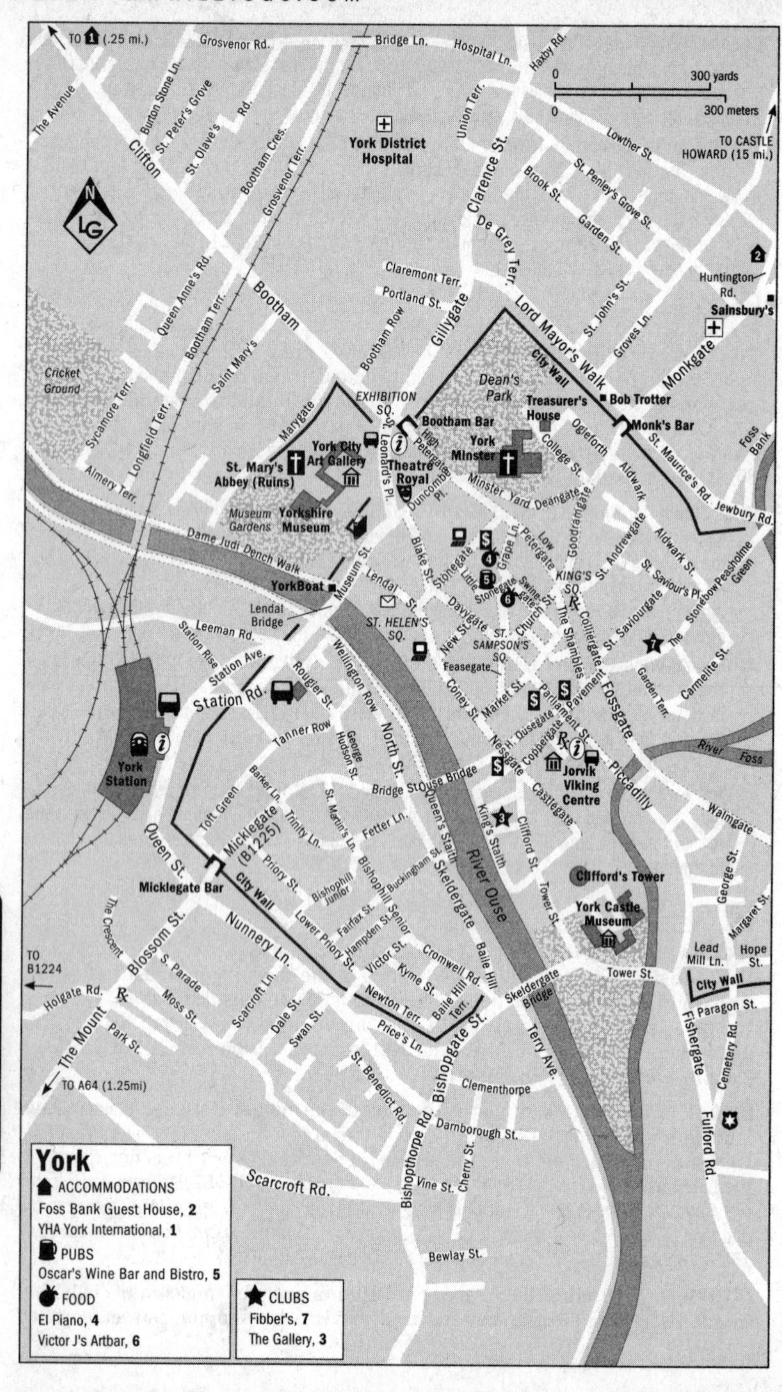
York
ACCOMMODATIONS
Foss Bank Guest House, 2
YHA York International, 1
PUBS
Oscar's Wine Bar and Bistro, 5
FOOD
El Piano, 4
Victor J's Artbar, 6
CLUBS
Fibber's, 7
The Gallery, 3
TO 1 (.25 mi.)
TO CASTLE HOWARD (15 mi.)
TO B1224
TO A64 (1.25mi)
300 yards
300 meters
York District Hospital
Cricket Ground
St. Mary's Abbey (Ruins)
York City Art Gallery
Yorkshire Museum
Museum Gardens
Theatre Royal
Bootham Bar
York Minster
Dean's Park
Treasurer's House
Bob Trotter
Monk's Bar
City Wall
YorkBoat
Lendal Bridge
York Station
Jorvik Viking Centre
Clifford's Tower
York Castle Museum
Micklegate Bar
River Ouse
River Foss
Huntington Rd.
Sainsbury's
EXHIBITION SQ.
ST. HELEN'S SQ.
ST. SAMPSON'S SQ.
KING'S SQ.
Lord Mayor's Walk
Bootham
Clifton
Gillygate
Monkgate
Micklegate (B1225)
Station Rd.
Fossgate
Piccadilly
Walmgate
Skeldergate
Bishopgate St.
Nunnery Ln.
Blossom St.
The Mount
Queen St.
Fishergate
Fulford Rd.
Scarcroft Rd.
Bishopthorpe Rd.
Terry Ave.
Tower St.
North St.

Moon Court, its Edwardian counterpart. *(Between Tower St. and Piccadilly. ☎01904 687 687; www.yorkcastlemuseum.org.uk. Open daily 9:30am-5pm. £7.50, concessions £6.50)*

CLIFFORD'S TOWER. One of the last remaining pieces of York Castle, the Tower serves as a chilling reminder of the worst outbreak of anti-Jewish violence in English history. In 1190, Christian merchants tried to erase their debts to Jewish bankers by annihilating York's Jewish community. One hundred and fifty Jews took refuge in the tower where, faced with the prospect of starvation or butchery, they committed mass suicide. *(Tower St. ☎01904 646 940. Open daily Apr.-Sept. 10am-6pm; Oct. 10am-5pm; Nov.-Mar. 10am-4pm. £3, concessions £2.40.)*

THE JORVIK VIKING CENTRE. This is one of the busiest attractions in York; arrive early or late to avoid lines, or reserve a day ahead. Visitors float in "time cars" through the York of AD 948, past artifacts, life-like mannequins, and painfully accurate smells. *(On Coppergate. ☎01904 615 555 for advance bookings; www.jorvik-viking-centre.co.uk. Open daily 10am-5pm. £7.75, students £6.60.)*

THE YORKSHIRE MUSEUM. Set on the 10 acres of the Museum Gardens, it houses Anglo-Saxon, Roman, and Viking artifacts, as well as the Middleham Jewel (c. 1450), an opulent sapphire set in gold. The eerie ruins of **St. Mary's Abbey,** once the most influential Benedictine monastery in northern England, are nearby. *(Enter from Museum St. or Marygate. ☎01904 687 687; www.yorkshiremuseum.org.uk. Open daily 10am-5pm. £5, students £4, families £14. Gardens and ruins free.)*

ENTERTAINMENT AND NIGHTLIFE

The Minster and area churches host a series of summer concerts, including the **York Early Music Festival.** (☎01904 658 338; www.ncem.co.uk. Mid-July.) The *What's On* guide, available at the TIC, publishes info on cultural events. In the evening, barbershop quartets, jugglers, and magicians fill King's Square and Stonegate There are more pubs in York than gargoyles on the Minster's wall.

The Gallery, 12 Clifford St., (☎01904 647 947), next door to the York Dungeon. This dressy club has two hot dance floors and six bars. Cover £3.50-10. Open M-Th and Su 10pm-2am, F-Sa 10pm-3am.

Fibber's, Stonebow House, the Stonebow (☎01904 651 250; www.fibbers.co.uk). Hear up-and-coming bands nightly here, followed by DJs after 10:30pm. Cover £5, students £3 before 11:30pm. Tickets sold daily 10:30am-4:30pm. Live music 8-10:30pm.

Tru, 3-5 Toft Green, (☎01904 620 203). Bring your glow sticks to rave in Tru's 3 rooms, which blast house music and chart toppers. Weekly student nights; discount with ID. No sneakers or sportswear F-Sa. Cover £2-7. Open M-Sa 10pm-3am.

NEWCASTLE-UPON-TYNE ☎0191

The largest city in the northeast, Newcastle (pop. 278,000) has taken many forms, from a medieval fortress to an industrial center. Today, the city is a frontrunner in architecture, fashion, music, and modern art.

TRANSPORTATION AND PRACTICAL INFORMATION. **Trains** leave from Central Station for Edinburgh (1hr., £40) and London King's Cross (3hr., 2 per hr., £103). National Express **buses** (☎08705 80 80 80) leave St. James Blvd. for Edinburgh (3hr., 4 per day, £15) and London (7hr., 4 per day, £27). The **TIC** is at 27 Market St. in the Central Arcade. (☎0191 277 8000. Open M-F 9:30am-5:30pm, Sa 9am-5:30pm.) **Postal Code:** NE1 7AB.

ACCOMMODATIONS AND FOOD. Book accommodations well ahead for weekends, when stag- and hen-night parties fill Newcastle's budget options. **Albatross Backpackers ❷,** 51 Grainger St., two minutes from the train station, has secure, modern facilities and is adjacent to major nightlife. (☎0191 233 1330; www.albatrossnewcastle.com. Reception 24hr. 2- to 10-bed dorms £17-23. MC/V.) To get to the small but welcoming **YHA Newcastle (HI) ❷,** 107 Jesmond Rd., take the metro to Jesmond and turn left on Jesmond Rd. (☎0870 770 5972. Internet £5 per hr. Reception 7-11pm. Curfew 11pm. Closed mid-Dec. to mid-Jan. £18, under 18 £13.50. AmEx/MC/V.) **University of Northumbria ❸,** Sandyford Rd., offers dorms conveniently located just outside the city center. Take the metro to Haymarket. (☎0191 227 3215; www.unn.ac.uk. Breakfast and linens included. Open mid-June to Aug. Singles M-Th £25, F-Su £30. MC/V.) **Pani's Cafe ❷,** 61 High Bridge St., has Italian dishes (£5-10) and a boisterous vibe. (☎0191 232 4366; www.paniscafe.com. Open M-Sa 10am-10pm. MC/V.)

SIGHTS AND NIGHTLIFE. The **BALTIC Centre for Contemporary Art,** housed in a renovated grain warehouse, showcases a cutting-edge collection. (☎0191 478 1810; www.balticmill.com. Open M and W-Su 10am-8pm, T 10:30am-8pm; last admission 15min. before closing. Free.) The BALTIC Centre is one of a trio of new buildings on the river, including the Norman Foster designed steel-and-glass Sage Gateshead, a complex of **concert halls,** and the **Gateshead Millennium Bridge,** a pedestrian and bicycle bridge that swivels upward once or twice per day to allow ships to pass. **Castle Garth Keep,** at the foot of St. Nicholas St., is all that remains of the 12th-century New Castle complex. (☎0191 232 7938. Open daily Apr.-Sept. 9:30am-5:30pm; Oct.-Mar. 9:30am-4:30pm. £1.50, students £0.50.) Theater buffs can enjoy an evening at the **Theatre Royal,** 100 Grey St., northern England's premier stage. (☎0844 811 2121; www.theatreroyal.co.uk. Student tickets half-price on performance day.)

As home of the nectar known as **brown ale,** Newcastle has a fittingly legendary party scene. *The Crack* (free at record stores) is the best source for nightlife listings. Rough and rowdy **Bigg Market** features the highest concentration of pubs in England, while neighboring **Quayside** attracts herds to its packed clubs. Catch up-and-coming bands nightly at **The Cluny,** 36 Lime St., Newcastle's premier underground music venue. (☎0191 230 4474. Open daily 11am-late, food served until 9pm.) **The Head of Steam,** 2 Neville St., near the train station, features funk, jazz, reggae, soul, and occasional local DJs. (☎0191 230 4236. Open M-Sa noon-1am, Su noon-midnight.)Newcastle's **Pink Triangle** of gay bars and clubs is just west of the Centre for Life along Westmoreland Rd., St. James Blvd. and Marlborough Cres. No matter what your plans are, be sure to finish the night Newcastle-style with a kebab and extra chili sauce.

HADRIAN'S WALL

In AD 122, Roman Emperor Hadrian ordered the construction of a wall to guard Britannia's border, hoping to prevent the blue-tattooed barbarians to the north from infiltrating his empire. The wall is Britain's most important Roman monument, stretching 117km from Carlisle in the west to Newcastle in the east.

TRANSPORTATION AND PRACTICAL INFORMATION. Although traveling by **car** is the easiest option, **Hadrian's Wall Bus AD122** (who knew public transportation had a sense of humor?) provides reliable service, with a guide on board twice a day. The bus runs between Carlisle and Newcastle, stopping at historical sights. Buy the **DayRover** ticket, available from TICs and bus drivers, to get the most out of AD122. (2hr., Apr.-Oct. 7-8 per day, £7.80.) Bus #685 runs between Newcastle and Carlisle via Greenhead, Hexham, and other wall towns. (2hr., every hr.) **Trains** (☎08457 484 950) run between Carlisle and Newcastle (1hr., every hr., £11). Stations are roughly 2km from the wall.

The Hexham **TIC** is at the bottom of the hill from the abbey on Hallgate Rd., and the **NPIC** is in **Once Brewed** hostel (see below) on Military Rd. (☎01434 344 396. Open Apr.-Oct. daily 9:30am-5pm; Nov.-Mar. Sa-Su 10am-3pm.) Pick up the free and invaluable *Hadrian's Wall Bus AD122 Bus & Rail Timetables*, available from any area TIC or bus. For general info, call the **Hadrian's Wall Information Line** (☎01434 322 002; www.hadrians-wall.org).

ACCOMMODATIONS. Carlisle and Hexham have many B&Bs and make good bases for trips to the wall. Two hostels lie along the Hadrian's Wall Bus route. **YHA Greenhead ❶**, 26km east of Carlisle near the Greenhead bus stop, is in a converted chapel near the wall. (☎08707 705 842. Kitchen available. Reception 8-10am and 5-10pm. Curfew 11pm. Dorms £15. MC/V.) The AD122 stops at the **YHA Once Brewed ❶,** Military Rd., Bardon Mill, 1km from the wall. (☎08707 705 980. Breakfast £4. Packed lunch £3.50-4.50. Dinner from £7. Laundry £1. Internet £2.50 per 30min. at the Twice Brewed pub next door. Reception 8-10am and 24pm-10pm. Open Feb.-Nov. Dorms £15, under 18 £10. MC/V.)

SIGHTS. West from Newcastle or north from Hexham, the **Chesters** cavalry fort is along the wall near Chollerford. The well-preserved **bath house** remains, showing how seriously the Romans took hygiene. (☎01434 681 379. Open daily Apr.-Sept. 10am-6pm; Oct. 10am-5pm; Nov.-Mar. 10am-4pm. £4.50, concessions £4.) Continuing west, **Housesteads,** on a scenic ridge 1km from the road, has one of the best-preserved wall sections. (☎01434 344 363. Open daily Apr.-Sept. 10am-6pm; Oct. 10am-5pm; Nov.-Mar. 10am-4pm. £4.50, concessions £3.80, children £2.60. Just 1.5km from Once Brewed Hostel (see above), archaeologists unearth artifacts daily at **Vindolanda Fort and Settlement.** An on-site museum displays finds from the area. (☎01434 344 277; www.vindolanda.com. Open daily Apr.-Sept. 10am-6pm; mid-Feb. to Mar. and Oct. to mid-Nov. 10am-5pm; mid-Nov. to mid-Feb. 10am-4pm. Last admission 45min. before closing. £5.20, concessions £4.30; Joint Saver tickets with Roman Army Museum £8/6.80.) Built from stones "borrowed" from the wall, the **Roman Army Museum** is at Carvoran, 1.5km northeast of Greenhead Hostel (see above) and five stops from Vindolanda on the AD122. (☎01697 747 485. Open daily Apr.-Sept. 10am-6pm; Feb.-Mar. and Oct.-Nov. 10am-5pm. Last admission 30min. before closing. £4.20, concessions £3.70. Joint Saver tickets with Vindolanda £8/6.80.)

Birdoswald Roman Fort, 25km east of Carlisle, offers views of walls, turrets, and milecastles. (☎01697 747 602. Open daily Apr.-Sept. 10am-5:30pm; Mar. and Oct. 10am-4pm. Last admission 30min. before closing. Museum and wall £4.50, concessions £3.60, children £3.30.) West of Carlisle, on the cliffs of Maryport, the **Senhouse Museum** houses Britain's oldest antiquarian collection, with exhibits on Roman religion and warfare. (☎01900 816 168; www.senhousemuseum.co.uk. Open July-Oct. daily 10am-5pm; Apr.-June Tu and Th-Su 10am-5pm; Nov.-Mar. F-Su 10:30am-4pm. £2.50.) **Hadrian's Wall National Trail** is an 135km, six-day route from coast to coast. Guides and information are available at TICs. The recently opened **Hadrian's Cycleway** provides access to all the wall's main attractions following minor roads and cycle paths.

ISLE OF MAN ☎01624

Wherever you go on this Irish Sea islet, you'll come across an emblem: three legs crossed like the spokes of a wheel. It's the **Three Legs of Man,** the symbol of

Manx pride and independence. Its accompanying motto translates to "Whichever Way You Throw Me, I Stand." This speaks to the predicament of the island over the last few millennia, during which it's been tossed around between the English, the Scots, and the Vikings. Today, Man controls its own affairs as a crown possession, although it is technically not part of the UK.

GETTING THERE

Ronaldsway Airport (**IOM;** ☎01624 821 600; www.gov.im/airport) is 16km southwest of Douglas on the coast road. Buses #1, 1C, 2A, and 2 connect to Douglas (25min., 1-3 per hr.), while others stop around the island. **Manx2** (☎0870 242 2226; www.manx2.com), **Flybe** (☎0871 522 6100; www.flybe.com), **Eastern Airways** (☎01652 680 600; www.easternairways.com), **Aer Arann** (☎0800 587 2324), **Loganair** (☎0870 850 9850), and **Euromanx** (☎0870 787 7879; www.euromanx.com) fly to the Isle. **Ferries** dock at the **Douglas Sea Terminal** at the southern end of town, where North Quay and the Promenade meet near the bus station. The Isle of Man Steam Packet Company (☎661 661 or 08705 523 523; www.steam-packet.com) runs ferries to: **Belfast** (2hr. 55min., up to 2 per week); **Dublin, IRE** (3hr.; Jun.-Aug. 2 per week, Sept.-May 1-2 per month); **Heysham, Lancashire** (3hr., 2 per day); **Liverpool** (2hr. 30min., 1-4 per day). Fares are highest in summer and on weekends (£15-36, round-trip £20-59). Book online for cheaper fares.

DOUGLAS

The Isle's capital and largest city, Douglas (pop. 27,000), a useful gateway for exploration, sprawls along the eastern side of Man. The city's promenade, bordered with pastel-colored rowhouses, makes it feel like a Victorian resort.

TRANSPORTATION. Isle of Man Transport (☎01624 662 525; www.iombusandrail.info) runs public **buses** and **trains.** The **TIC,** in the Sea Terminal, has bus maps and schedules. (☎01624 686 766; www.visitisleofman.com. Open Apr.-Aug. M-Sa 8am-7pm, Su 9am-3pm, Sept.-Mar. M-Sa 8am-6pm.) The TIC and all main tram and train stations sell **Island Explorer Tickets,** which provide unlimited travel on most buses, trains, and horse trams (1-day £13, 3-day £26, 7-day £40). Ask at the TIC about **tours** of the island. Try Eurocycles, 8A Victoria Rd., for **bike** rentals. (☎01624 624 909. £15 per day. ID deposit. Open M-Sa 9am-5pm.)

ORIENTATION AND PRACTICAL INFORMATION. Douglas stretches 3km along the shore, from Douglas Head to the Electric Railway terminal. Douglas Head is separated from town by the River Douglas. Ferry and bus terminals lie just north of the river. The **Promenade** curves from the ferry terminal to the Electric Railway terminal along the beach, dividing the coastline from the shopping district with a line of Victorian rowhouses. Shops and cafes line **The Strand,** a pedestrian thoroughfare that begins near the bus station and runs parallel to the Promenade, turning into Castle St. and ending near the Gaiety Theatre. **Internet** is at Feegan's Lounge, 8 Victoria St. (☎679 407; www.feegan.com; £1 per 20min.; open M-Sa 8:30am-6pm.) **Postal Code:** IM1 2EA.

AN UNSINKING ISLE. The Isle of Man sets itself apart from other, lesser isles. The island has its own Manx language (a cousin of Irish and Scottish Gaelic), tail-less Manx cat, multi-horned Manx Loghtan sheep, and a local delicacy–kipper (herring smoked over oak chips).

Manx currency is equivalent in value to British pounds, but it's not accepted outside the Isle. If you use an **ATM** on the island, it will likely give you Manx currency. Notes and coins from England, Scotland, and Northern Ireland can be used in Man. Some Manx shops accept the euro—look for signs. When preparing to leave, you will generally be successful asking for your change in UK tender. Post offices and newsstands sell Manx Telecom **phonecards.** Mobile phone users on plans from elsewhere in Britain will likely incur surcharges. The Isle shares Britain's international dialing code, ☎44. **In an emergency, dial ☎999.** It's wise to rely on phone cards and landlines for a short stay, although more long-term visitors should probably invest in a Manx **prepay SIM card,** available at the Manx Telecom shop, 41-43 Victoria St., Douglas. (£10-20. Open M-W and F, 8:30am-5pm, Th 9:30am-5pm, Sa 9am-5pm.) These allow access to the only official service, **Manx Pronto.**

ACCOMMODATIONS AND FOOD. Douglas is awash with B&Bs and hotels. For Tourist Trophy race weeks, they fill a year ahead and raise their rates. The **Devonian Hotel ❷,** 4 Sherwood Terr., on Broadway, is an immaculate Victorian-style townhouse just off the Promenade. (☎01624 674 676; www.thedevonian.co.uk. TV. Breakfast included. Singles £25-32; doubles from £55. Cash or check only.) Just up the Promenade, **Norley House ❸,** 3 Mona Dr., boasts simple but spacious non-ensuite rooms, a game room and bar, and friendly proprietors. (☎01624 623 301. Singles, doubles, and family rooms from £24, £20 without breakfast. Children £12, under 5 free. Laundry £7.50. MC/V).

Grill and chip shops line Duke, Strand, and Castle St., while many hotels along the Promenade have elegant restaurants. **Copperfield's Olde Tea Shoppe and Restaurant ❸,** 24 Castle St., holds Viking Feasts and Edwardian Extravaganzas, and serves classically British fare, such as spotted dick pudding with custard for £4.50. (☎01624 613 650. Open in summer M-Th and Sa 11am-6pm, F 11am-9pm; in winter M-Sa 11am-4pm. MC/V.) The **Food For Less** grocery is on Chester St., behind The Strand. (Open M-W and Sa 8am-8pm, Th-F 8am-9pm, Su 9am-6pm.) At the **Bay Room Restaurant ❶,** in the Manx Museum, diners enjoy hot lunches amid sculptures from the gallery collection. (☎01624 612 211. Sandwiches £4, cakes £2.50. Open M-Sa 10am-4:30pm. Cash only.)

SIGHTS AND HIKING. From the shopping district, signs point to the Chester St. parking garage next to Food For Less; an elevator ride to the 8th-floor roof leads to a footbridge to the **Manx Museum.** The museum covers the geology and history of Man, with the artistic side displayed at the **Manx National Gallery of Art.** Don't miss exhibits about the island's days as a Victorian getaway, when it was unofficially known as the Isle of Woman due to its attractive seasonal population. (☎01624 648 000. Open M-Sa 10am-5pm. Free.) The museum and gallery are part of the island-wide **Story of Mann,** a collection of museums and exhibits focused on island heritage, including sites in Ballasalla, the former capital Castletown, Peel, and Ramsey. A **Heritage Pass** (£11, child £5.50), available at all museums, grants admission to any four sites, which otherwise cost £3.30-5.50. (☎01624 648 000; www.storyofmann.com.)

Raad ny Foillan (Road of the Gull) is a 135km path around the island marked with blue seagull signs. The spectacular **Port Erin to Castletown Route** (12 mi.) offers views of the Isle's beaches, cliffs, fields of wildflowers, nesting birds, and bathing seals; a short detour toward Cregneash leads to Cronk Karran, a Neolithic-era stone burial circle. **Bayr ny Skeddan** (The Herring Road), once used by Manx fishermen, covers the 23km land route between Peel in the west and Castletown in the east. Appropriately, signs with herring pictures mark the trail. It overlaps with the **Millennium Way,** which covers the difficult and hilly

45km route from Castletown to Ramsey along the 14th-century Royal Highway, ending 1km from Ramsey's Parliament Sq. *Walks on the Isle of Man* (free), available at the TIC, gives a cursory description of 11 walks.

FESTIVALS AND NIGHTLIFE. TICs stock a calendar of events; ask for the free *What's On the Isle of Man* or check out www.isleofman.com or www.visitisleofman.com. During the two weeks from late May to early June, Man turns into a motorcycle mecca for the **Tourist Trophy (TT) Races** as the population doubles and 10,000 bikes flood the island (www.iomtt.com). The races were first held on Man in 1907 because restrictions on vehicle speed were less severe on the island than on mainland Britain. The circuit consists of 60km of hairpin turns that top racers navigate at speeds over 120 mph. The **World Tin Bath Championships**—a race across the harbor in tin tubs in August—and a **Darts Festival** in March invite Manx natives and visitors alike to revel in idiosyncrasy.

Pubs in Douglas are numerous and boisterous, especially during the TT Races. Pass through the turnstile at **Quids Inn,** 56 Loch Promenade, where drinks cost £1-1.50. Prepare to drink standing up on weekends. (☎01624 611 769. Open M-F 5pm-midnight, Sa-Su 3pm-midnight.) Most of the clubs in Douglas are 21+, and some have free entrance until 10 or 11pm, with a £2-5 cover thereafter. Relax at **Colours,** on Central Promenade, in the Hilton. A spacious sports bar gives way to live bands and dance music as the night goes on. (☎01624 662 662. Open M-W noon-2am, Th-Su noon-3:30am. £5 cover after 10pm.) At **Brendan O'Donnell's ❶**, 16-18 Strand St., Guinness posters and painted four-leafed clovers remind patrons of the Isle's proximity to Ireland. (☎01624 621 566. Guinness £3. Open M-Th and Su noon-11pm, F-Sa noon-midnight. Cash only.

WALES (CYMRU)

Known to early Anglo-Saxon settlers as *waleas* (foreigners), but self-identified as *cymry* (compatriots), the people of Wales (pop. 3,000,000) have always had a fraught relationship with their neighbors to the east. Wales clings to its Celtic heritage, and the Welsh language endures in conversation, commerce, and literature. After a technology boom in the 1970s, Wales turned its attention to tourism. Travelers today are lured by peaceful towns and imposing castles nestled among miles of beaches, cliffs, and mountains.

CARDIFF (CAERDYDD) ☎02920

Cardiff (pop. 318,000) calls itself "Europe's Youngest Capital" and seems eager to fulfill the title, mixing metropolitan renaissance with rich history. Next to traditional monuments are landmarks of a different tenor: a new stadium and cosmopolitan entertainment venues. At the same time, local pride, displayed through the red dragons on flags and in windows, remains as strong as ever.

TRANSPORTATION AND PRACTICAL INFORMATION. **Trains** (☎08457 484 950) leave Central Station, Central Sq., for: Bath (1hr., 1-3 per hr., £14.90); Birmingham (2hr., 3 per hr., £35); Edinburgh via Crewe or Bristol Parkway (6½-8hr., 2 per hr., £110.50); London Paddington (2hr., 2 per hr., £56). National Express **buses** (☎08705 808 080) leave from Wood St. for Birmingham (2½hr., 4 per day, £22.50), London (3hr., 17 per day, £21.30), and Manchester (5-8hr., 6 per day, £35.10). Pick up a free *Wales Bus, Rail, and Tourist Map and Guide* at the TIC. Cardiff Bus (Bws Caerdydd), St. David's House, Wood St. (☎02920 666 444), runs green and orange **city buses** in Cardiff and surrounding areas. (Service ends M-Sa 11:20pm, Su 11pm. £1.40-3.) The **TIC** is at Old Library, The Hayes. (☎02920 227 281; www.visitcardiff.com. Open M-Sa 9:30am-6pm, Su 10am-4pm.) The **public library,** on Bute St. just past the rail bridge, offers free **Internet.** In March 2009, it will move to The Hayes. (☎02920 382 116. Open M-W and F 9am-6pm, Th 9am-7pm, Sa 9am-5:30pm.) **Postal Code:** CF10 2SJ.

ACCOMMODATIONS AND FOOD. Budget lodgings are hard to find in Cardiff. The cheapest B&Bs (from £20) are on the city outskirts. **River House Backpackers ❷,** 59 Fitzhamon Embankment, is Cardiff's newest hostel, in a riverside Victorian villa outfitted with stylish, modern amenities. Run by a friendly brother-and-sister team, it has spotless bathrooms, kitchen, TV lounge, and BBQ terrace. (☎02920 399 810; www.riverhousebackpackers.com. Breakfast included. Free lockers. Internet £1 per 30min. Free Wi-Fi. Dorms £17.50-20; doubles £40. MC/V.) **Madame Fromage ❷,** 21-25 Castle Arcade, is a Francophile's dream, selling an array of cheeses, meats, and jams. Wash down the famous homemade lamb *cawl* (£6) or an overflowing grilled French goat cheese salad (£7.50) with a glass of wine. (☎02920 644 888. Open M-F 10am-5:30pm, Sa 9:30am-6pm, Su 11am-5pm. MC/V.) **10 Feet Tall ❷,** 11a-12 Church St., near the Queen's Arcade, serves North African and Mediterranean-inspired dishes in a wood-panelled lounge. Savor tapas like stuffed chili peppers or *patatas bravas* (£2.50), light lunches (£4-7), or hearty dishes like venison haunch (£12.50). It turns into a popular nighttime hangout, with live music every night and a house jazz band on F. (☎02920 228 883. Open M-Th and Su 11am-3am, F-Sa 11am-4am. Food served daily 11am-11pm. MC/V.) Budget travelers looking for food on the go can scavenge the stalls of **Central Market,** between St. Mary St. and Trinity St., for produce, bread, and raw meat. (Open M-Sa 8am-5:30pm.)

SIGHTS AND NIGHTLIFE. From a Roman legionary outpost to a Norman keep, medieval stronghold, and finally a Victorian neo-Gothic curiosity, extravagant **Cardiff Castle,** Castle St., has seen some drastic changes in its 2000-year existence. (☎02920 878 100. Open daily Mar.-Oct. 9am-6pm; Nov.-Feb. 9:30am-5pm. £8.95, concessions £7.50.) The **Civic Centre,** in Cathays Park, includes **Alexandra Gardens, City Hall,** and the **National Museum and Gallery.** The museum's exhibits range from a room of Celtic crosses to a display of Wales's indigenous flora and fauna. (☎02920 397 951. Open Tu-Su 10am-5pm. Free.)

After 11pm, many of Cardiff's downtown pubs stop serving alcohol and the action migrates to nearby clubs, most located on or around **St. Mary Street.** For nightlife info, check the free *Buzz* guide or the *Itchy Cardiff Guide* (£3.50), available at the TIC. Three worlds collide at **Clwb Ifor Bach,** 11 Womanby St. The ground floor plays cheesy pop (especially on W student nights), the middle floor bar has softer music, and the top rocks out to live bands or trance. (☎02920 232 199; www.clwb.net. Drink specials nightly. Cover £3-5, up to £10 for popular bands. Open W until 2am, Th-Sa until 3am.)

WYE VALLEY

William Wordsworth mused on the tranquility and pastoral majesty of the once-troubled Welsh-English border territory around Wye Valley. As the Afon Gwy (Wye River) winds through the surrounding abbeys, castles, and trails, much of the landscape seems untouched by human hands or the passage of time.

TRANSPORTATION. Chepstow is the best entrance to the valley. From Chepstow, **trains** (☎08457 484 950; www.nationalrail.com) go to Cardiff (1hr., 7 per day, £4.90) and London (3hr., 5 per day, £20.80). TICs offer the free *Monmouthshire Local Transport Guide* and *Discover the Wye Valley by Foot and by Bus.* **Hiking** is a great way to explore the region. The 220km Wye Valley Walk treks north from Chepstow, through Hay-on-Wye, and on to Prestatyn. Offa's Dyke Path has 285km of hiking and **biking** paths along the Welsh-English border. For info, call the Offa's Dyke Association (☎01547 528 753).

CHEPSTOW ☎01291

Chepstow's position at the mouth of the river and the base of the English border made it an important Norman fortification. Flowers spring from the ruins of **Castell Casgwent,** Britain's oldest dateable stone castle (c. 1070), which offers stunning views of the Wye. (☎01291 624 065. Open Apr.-Oct. daily 9am-5pm; Nov.-Mar. M-Sa 9:30am-4pm, Su 11am-4pm. £3.70, concessions £3.30.) **The First Hurdle Guest House ❹,** 9-10 Upper Church St., has comfortable rooms near the castle. (☎01291 622 189; www.thefirsthurdle.com. Singles £40; doubles £60. AmEx/MC/V; £1.50 surcharge.) An eclectic array of pubs and Chinese restaurants can be found near the town center. **Kreations ❶,** above Kreation Gift Shop, 12 St. Mary's St., offers traditional tea fare and hot sandwiches for around £2. (☎01291 621 711. Open M-Sa 9:30am-4:30pm, Su noon-6pm. Cash only.) Pick up groceries at **Tesco** on Station Rd. (Open M 8am-midnight, Tu-F 24hr., Sa midnight-10pm, Su 10am-4pm.) **Trains** arrive on Station Rd.; **buses** stop in front of Somerfield supermarket. Buy tickets at The Travel House, 9 Moor St. (☎01291 623 031. Open M-Sa 9am-5:30pm.) The **TIC** is in the Castle Car Park on Bridge St. (☎01291 623 772; www.chepstow.co.uk. Open daily Easter-Oct. 10am-5:30pm; Nov.-Easter 10am-3:30pm.) **Postal Code:** NP16 5DA.

TINTERN ☎01291

Eight kilometers north of Chepstow on A466, the Gothic arches of **Tintern Abbey** "connect the landscape with the quiet of the sky," according to Wordsworth. (☎01291 689 251. Apr.-Oct. daily 9am-5pm; Nov.-Mar. M-Sa 9:30am-4pm, Su 11am-4pm. £3.70, concessions £3.30.) A 3km hike along **Monk's Trail** leads to **Devil's Pulpit,** from which Satan is said to have tempted the monks as they worked in the fields. **YHA St. Briavel's Castle (HI) ❶,** 6km northeast of Tintern across the English border, occupies a 13th-century fortress. While a unique experience—it was formerly King John's hunting lodge—it's somewhat remote, and should only be booked by those prepared for a 2.5km uphill hike. From A466 (bus #69 from Chepstow; ask to be let off at Bigsweir Bridge) or Offa's Dyke, follow signs from the edge of the bridge. (☎0870 770 6040. Lockout 10am-5pm. Curfew 11:30pm. Dorms from £16. MC/V.) Campers can use the **field ❶** next to the old train station (£3). Try **The Moon and Sixpence ❷,** on Monmouth Rd., for classic pub grub (£6-8) with great views of the Wye. (☎02920 689 284. F nights live music. Open daily noon-midnight. Kitchen open M-Th noon-3pm and 6-9pm, F noon-3:30pm and 6-9:30pm, Sa-Su noon-midnight.)

SNOWDONIA NATIONAL PARK

Amid Edward I's impressive 13th-century manmade battlements in Northern Wales lies the 2175 sq. km natural fortress of Snowdonia National Park. The region's craggy peaks, the highest in England and Wales, yield diverse terrain—pristine blue lakes dot grasslands, while slate cliffs slope into wooded hills.

TRANSPORTATION AND PRACTICAL INFORMATION. Trains (☎08457 484 950) stop at larger towns on the park's outskirts, including Conwy (p. 182). The Conwy Valley Line runs across the park from Llandudno through Betws-y-Coed to Blaenau Ffestiniog (1hr., 3-7 per day). There, it connects with the Ffestiniog Railway, which runs through the mountains to Porthmadog, meeting the Cambrian Coast line to Barmouth and Aberystwyth. **Buses** run to the park interior from Conwy and Caernarfon; consult the *Gwynedd Public Transport Maps and Timetables* and *Conwy Public Transport Information*, free in all regional **TICs.** Six **NPICs** (www.eryri-npa.gov.uk) are scattered through Snowdonia, in Betws-y-Coed (☎01690 710 426), Dolgellau (☎01341 422 888), Harlech (☎01766 780 658), Aberdyfi (☎01654 767 321), Beddgelert (☎01766 890 615), and Blaenau Ffestiniog (☎01766 830 360).

HIKING. The highest peak in England and Wales, **Mount Snowdon** (1085m) is the park's most popular destination. Its Welsh name is *Yr Wyddfa* (the burial place)—local lore holds that Rhita Gawr, a giant cloaked with the beards of the kings he slaughtered, is buried here. Six paths of varying difficulty wind their way up Snowdon; pick up *Ordnance Survey Landranger Map #115* (£7) and *Outdoor Leisure Map #17* (£8), as well as individual trail guides, at TICs and NPICs. No matter how beautiful the weather is below, it will be cold, wet, and unpredictable high up—dress accordingly. Contact **Mountaincall Snowdonia** (☎09068 500 449) or visit an NPIC for local forecasts and ground conditions.

HARLECH ☎01766

Harlech Castle is part of the "iron ring" of fortresses built by Edward I to quell Welsh troublemakers, but it later served as the insurrection headquarters of Welsh rebel Owain Glyndwr. (☎01766 780 552. Open Apr.-Oct. daily 9am-5pm; Nov.-Mar. M-Sa 9:30am-4pm, Su 11am-4pm. £3.70, concessions £3.30.) Enjoy spacious rooms and castle views at **Arundel ❷,** High St.. If the steep climb from the train station isn't appealing, call ahead for a ride. (☎01766 780 637. Rooms £16. Cash only.) The charming **Cemlyn Tea Shop ❶,** High St., serves delicious sandwiches on homemade bread (£4.80-5.60). Gaze at the castle from the terrace in back and choose from over 30 different teas. (☎01766 780 425; www.cemlynrestaurant.co.uk. Open W-Su 10am-5pm. MC/V.) Harlech lies midway on the Cambrian Coast line; Arriva Cymru **train** T5 (☎08457 484 950) arrives from and runs to Porthmadog (20min., 2-9 per day, £2.50) and connects to other towns on the Llyn Peninsula. The **Day Ranger** pass allows unlimited travel on the Coaster line for one day (£7.70, children £3.85, families £15). The **TIC,** which is also an **NPIC,** is on High St. (☎01766 780 658. Open daily Easter-Oct. 9:30am-12:30pm and 1:30-5:30pm.) **Postal Code:** LL46 2YA.

CAERNARFON ☎01286

Majestic and fervently Welsh, the walled city of Caernarfon (car-NAR-von) has a world-famous castle at its prow and mountains in its wake. Edward I started building **Caernarfon Castle** in 1283 to intimidate the rebellious Welsh; its eagle-crowned turrets, colorful stones, and polygonal towers cost him the the Crown's annual budget and nearly 17% of his labor force. The castle is an architectural feat; its walls withstood a rebel siege in 1404 with only 28 defenders. (☎01286 677 617. Open Apr.-Oct. daily 9am-5pm; Nov.-Mar. M-Sa 9:30am-4pm, Su 11am-4pm. £5.10, concessions £4.70, families £15.) **Totter's Hostel ❶,** 2 High St., has spacious rooms and a 14th-century basement with stone arches. (☎01286 672 963; www.totters.co.uk. Dorms £15; doubles £45. Cash only.) Charming **Hole-in-the-Wall Street** offers bistros, cafes, and restaurants. Try Welsh lamb (£15) at **Stones Bistro ❸,** 4 Hole-in-the-Wall St. (☎01286 671 152. Open

Tu-Sa 6-10pm, Su noon-3pm. Reserve ahead. MC/V.) Arriva Cymru (☎08706 082 608) **buses** #5 and 5X leave the city center at Penllyn for Conwy. (1.5hr., 1-4 per hr.) National Express (☎08705 808 080) buses run to London (9hr., 1 per day, £28.50). The **TIC** is on Castle St. (☎01286 672 232. Open Easter-Oct. daily 9:30am-4:30pm; Nov.-Easter M-Sa 10am-4pm.) **Postal Code:** LL55 2ND.

CONWY ☎01492

The central attraction of this tourist mecca is the imposing 13th-century **Conwy Castle** and its impressive **town walls.** (☎01492 592 358. Open Apr.-Oct. daily 9am-5pm, Nov.-Mar. M-Sa 9:30am-4pm, Su 11am-4pm. £4.70, concessions £4.20. Guided tours £1; book ahead.) Enjoy comfortable rooms (some with quay views) at **Swan Cottage ❷,** 18 Berry St., a bed-and-breakfast in a renovated 16th-century building near the center of town. (☎01492 596 840; www.swancottage.net. Ensuite rooms with TVs. Singles £25; doubles £50. Cash only.) **Pen-y-Bryn Tea Rooms ❶,** on High St., offers great tea (Welsh tea including sandwiches; £7) and 16th-century timbered nooks. (☎01492 596 445. Sandwiches £4.50. Open daily 10am-5pm. Cash only.) Arriva Cymru **buses** (☎0871 200 22 33) #5 and 5X stop in Conwy on their way to Caernarfon from Llandudno (1hr. 15min.; M-Sa every 15min., Su every hr.; £2.10.) The **TIC** is at the castle entrance. (☎01492 592 248. Open daily Apr.-Oct. 9am-5pm; Nov.-Mar. M-Sa 9:30am-4pm, Su 11am-4pm.) **Postal Code:** LL32 8H7.

SCOTLAND

Half the size of England with only a tenth the population, Scotland possesses open spaces and wild natural splendor unrivaled by its neighbor to the south. The Scots revel in a distinct culture ranging from the fevered nightlife of Glasgow and the festival atmosphere of Edinburgh to the tight-knit communities of the Orkney and Shetland Islands. The Scots defended their independence for hundreds of years before reluctantly joining England to create Great Britain in 1707, and they only regained a separate parliament in 1999. The mock kilts and bagpipes of the big cities can grow tiresome: discover Scotland's true colors by venturing off the beaten path to find Gaelic-speaking B&B owners, peat-cutting crofters, and fishermen setting out in skiffs at dawn.

GETTING TO SCOTLAND

Buses from London (8-12hr.) are generally the cheapest option. National Express (☎08457 225 333; www.nationalexpress.com) **buses** connect England and Scotland via Edinburgh and Glasgow. Trains are faster (4-6hr.) but more expensive. National Express also runs **trains** (☎08457 225 333; www.nationalexpress.com) from London to Edinburgh and Glasgow. Fares vary depending on when you buy (£27-£100). A pricier option is the **Caledonian Sleeper,** run by First Scotrail (☎08456 015 929; www.firstgroup.com/scotrail), which leaves London Euston near midnight and gets to Edinburgh at 7am (£20-140). The cheapest airfares between England and Scotland are available from no-frills airlines. **easyJet** (☎0871 244 2366; www.easyjet.com) flies to Edinburgh and Glasgow from London Gatwick, Luton, and Stansted. The fares are web-only; book in advance and fly for as little as £5. **Ryanair** (☎08712 460 000; www.ryanair.com) flies to Edinburgh and to Glasgow Prestwick (1hr. from the city) from Dublin and London. **British Airways** (☎0844 493 0787; www.britishairways.com) sells round-trip tickets between England and Scotland from £85.

TRANSPORTATION

In the Lowlands (south of Stirling and north of the Borders), **trains** and buses run many routes frequently. In the Highlands, Scotrail and National Express trains run a few routes. Many stations are unstaffed—buy tickets on board. A great money-saver is the **Freedom of Scotland Travelpass,** which allows unlimited train travel and transportation on most Caledonian MacBrayne ("CalMac") ferries. Purchase the pass before traveling to Britain at any BritRail distributor. **Buses** tend to be the best and cheapest way to travel. **Traveline Scotland** has the best information on all routes and services (☎0871 200 2233; www.travelinescotland.com). **Scottish Citylink** (☎08705 505 050; www.citylink.co.uk) runs most intercity routes; **Postbuses** (Royal Mail customer service ☎08457 740 740) pick up passengers and mail once or twice a day in the most remote parts of the country, typically charging £2-5 (and sometimes nothing). Many travelers find that they can be a reliable way to get around the Highlands. **HAGGiS** (☎0131 557 9393; www.haggisadventures.com) and **MacBackpackers** (☎01315 589 900; www.macbackpackers.com) cater to the young and adventurous, with a number of tours departing from Edinburgh. Both run hop-on, hop-off excursions that let you travel Scotland at your own pace (usually under three months).

EDINBURGH ☎0131

A city of elegant stone amid rolling hills and ancient volcanoes, Edinburgh (ED-in-bur-ra; pop. 500,000) is the jewel of Scotland. Since David I granted it *burgh* (town) status in 1130, Edinburgh has been a haven for forward-thinking intellectuals and innovative artists. Today, world-class universities craft the next generation of Edinburgh's thinkers. Businessmen, students, and backpackers mix amidst the city's medieval architecture and mingle in lively pubs and clubs. In August, Edinburgh becomes a mecca for the arts, drawing talent and crowds from around the globe to its International and Fringe Festivals.

TRANSPORTATION

Flights: Edinburgh International Airport (EDI; ☎0870 040 0007) is 11km west of the city. Lothian Airlink (☎555 6363) **shuttles** go between the airport and Waverley Bridge (25min.; 4-6 per hr., every hr. after midnight; £3, round-trip £5, children £2/3.)

Trains: Waverley Station (☎08457 484 950), between Princes St., Market St., and Waverley Bridge. Trains to: **Aberdeen** (2hr.; M-Sa every hr., Su 8 per day; £34); **Glasgow** (1hr., 4 per hr., £10); **Inverness** (3hr., every 2hr., £32); **London King's Cross** (4hr., every hr., £103); **Stirling** (50min., 2 per hr., £6.10).

Buses: Edinburgh Bus Station, St. Andrew Sq. Open daily 6am-midnight. Ticket office open daily 8am-8pm. **National Express** (☎08705 808 080) to London (10hr., 4 per day, £30). **Scottish Citylink** (☎08705 505 050) to: Aberdeen (4hr., every hr., £18), Glasgow (1hr., 2-4 per hr., £4), and Inverness (4hr., 8-10 per day, £17). A **bus-ferry** route goes to Belfast (2 per day, £20) and Dublin, IRE (1 per day, £27).

Public Transportation: Lothian **buses** (☎555 6363; www.lothianbuses.com) provide most services. Exact change required (£1.10, children £70). Daysaver ticket (£2.50, children £2.20) available from any driver. **Night buses** cover select routes after midnight (£2). First Edinburgh (☎0870 872 7271) also operates buses locally. Traveline (☎0870 608 2608) has information on all **public transport.**

Bike Rental: Biketrax, 11 Lochrin Pl. (☎228 6633; www.biketrax.co.uk). Mountain bikes £12 per half-day, £16 per day. Open M-Sa 9:30am-5:30pm, Su noon-5pm.

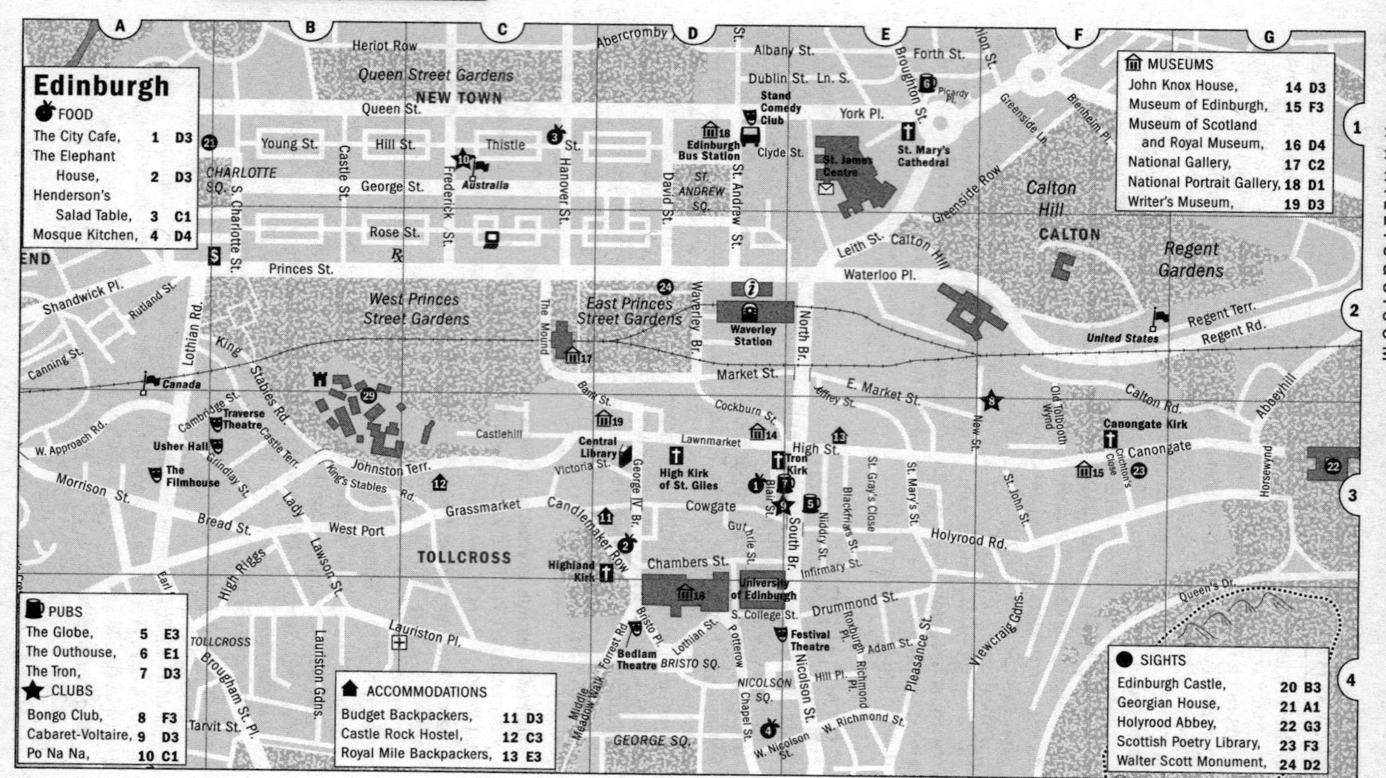
Edinburgh
FOOD
The City Cafe, 1 D3
The Elephant House, 2 D3
Henderson's Salad Table, 3 C1
Mosque Kitchen, 4 D4
PUBS
The Globe, 5 E3
The Outhouse, 6 E1
The Tron, 7 D3
CLUBS
Bongo Club, 8 F3
Cabaret-Voltaire, 9 D3
Po Na Na, 10 C1
ACCOMMODATIONS
Budget Backpackers, 11 D3
Castle Rock Hostel, 12 C3
Royal Mile Backpackers, 13 E3
MUSEUMS
John Knox House, 14 D3
Museum of Edinburgh, 15 F3
Museum of Scotland and Royal Museum, 16 D4
National Gallery, 17 C2
National Portrait Gallery, 18 D1
Writer's Museum, 19 D3
SIGHTS
Edinburgh Castle, 20 B3
Georgian House, 21 A1
Holyrood Abbey, 22 G3
Scottish Poetry Library, 23 F3
Walter Scott Monument, 24 D2
NEW TOWN
Queen Street Gardens
West Princes Street Gardens
East Princes Street Gardens
Calton Hill
CALTON
Regent Gardens
TOLLCROSS
Waverley Station
Edinburgh Bus Station
St. James Centre
St. Mary's Cathedral
Stand Comedy Club
High Kirk of St. Giles
Tron Kirk
Canongate Kirk
Highland Kirk
Central Library
University of Edinburgh
Festival Theatre
Bedlam Theatre
Traverse Theatre
Usher Hall
The Filmhouse
United States
Canada
Australia
Heriot Row
Queen St.
Young St.
Hill St.
Thistle St.
Castle St.
George St.
Frederick St.
Hanover St.
Rose St.
Princes St.
CHARLOTTE SQ.
S. Charlotte St.
Abercromby Pl.
Albany St.
Dublin St. Ln. S.
David St.
ST. ANDREW SQ.
St. Andrew St.
Clyde St.
York Pl.
Forth St.
Broughton St.
Picardy Pl.
Greenside Ln.
Blenheim Pl.
Greenside Row
Leith St.
Calton Hill
Waterloo Pl.
Regent Terr.
Regent Rd.
Shandwick Pl.
Rutland St.
Lothian Rd.
King Stables Rd.
Canning St.
The Mound
Waverley Br.
North Br.
Market St.
E. Market St.
Jeffrey St.
Calton Rd.
Old Tolbooth Wynd
Abbeyhill
Cambridge St.
Castle Terr.
W. Approach Rd.
Grindlay St.
Morrison St.
Johnston Terr.
King's Stables Rd.
Castlehill
Bank St.
Cockburn St.
Lawnmarket
Victoria St.
George IV Br.
High St.
New St.
Canongate
Crichton's Close
Horsewynd
Lady Lawson St.
Bread St.
West Port
Grassmarket
Candlemaker Row
Cowgate
Blair St.
South Br.
Niddry St.
Blackfriars St.
St. Gray's Close
St. Mary's St.
St. John St.
Holyrood Rd.
Guthrie St.
Chambers St.
Infirmary St.
Earl Grey St.
High Riggs
Lauriston Pl.
TOLLCROSS
Brougham St. Pl.
Tarvit St.
Lauriston Gdns.
Forrest Rd.
Bristo Pl.
Middle Meadow Walk
Lothian St.
BRISTO SQ.
Potterow
S. College St.
Drummond St.
Roxburgh Pl.
Adam St.
Hill Pl.
Richmond Pl.
NICOLSON SQ.
Chapel St.
Nicolson St.
W. Nicolson St.
W. Richmond St.
Pleasance St.
Viewcraig Gdns.
Queen's Dr.
GEORGE SQ.

ORIENTATION AND PRACTICAL INFORMATION

Edinburgh is a perfect city for walking. **Princes Street** is the main thoroughfare in **New Town,** the northern section of the city. From there you can view the impressive stone facade of the towering **Old Town** to the south. The **Royal Mile** (Castle Hill, Lawnmarket, High St., and Canongate) is the major road in the Old Town and connects **Edinburgh Castle** in the west to the **Palace of Holyroodhouse** in the east. **North Bridge, Waverley Bridge,** and **The Mound** connect Old and New Town. Two kilometers northeast, **Leith** is the city's seaport on the Firth of Forth.

Tourist Information Centre: Waverley Market, 3 Princes St. (☎0845 225 5121), on the north side of Waverley Station. Books rooms for £4 plus 10% deposit; sells bus, museum, theater, and tour tickets. Open July-Aug. M-Sa 9am-8pm, Su 10am-8pm; May-June and Sept. M-Sa 9am-7pm, Su 10am-7pm; Apr. and Oct. M-Sa 9am-6pm, Su 10am-6pm; Nov.-Mar. M-Sa 9am-5pm, Su 10am-5pm.

GLBT Services: Edinburgh Lesbian, Gay, and Bisexual Centre, 58a-60 Broughton St. (☎478 7069), inside Sala Cafe-Bar, or visit Gay Edinburgh at www.visitscotland.com.

Police: Headquarters at Fettes Ave. (☎0131 311 3901; www.lbp.police.uk).

Hospital: Royal Infirmary, 51 Little France Cr. (emergencies ☎536 6000.)

Internet: Free at the **Central Library** (☎0131 242 8000) on George IV Bridge. Open M-Th 10am-8pm, F 10am-5pm, Sa 9am-1pm. **easyInternet Cafe,** 58 Rose St. (☎0131 220 3577). £2 per hr. Open M-Sa 7am-10pm, Su 9am-10pm.

Post Office: In the St. James Centre beside the bus station (☎0131 556 9546). Open M-Sa 9am-5:30pm. **Postal Code:** EH1 3SR.

ACCOMMODATIONS

Edinburgh's accommodations cater to every kind of traveler. Hostels and hotels are the only city-center options, while B&Bs and guesthouses begin on the periphery. Reserve ahead for visits in the summer, New Year's and during festival season (late July-early September).

Budget Backpackers, 37-39 Cowgate (☎0131 226 2351; www.budgetbackpackers.co.uk). The most modern of the inner-city hostels. Spacious 2- to 12-bed rooms; female-only dorms available. Free city tour daily. Pub crawl M-Sa 9pm. Kitchen available. Breakfast £2. Key card access. Lockers free (bring your own padlock). Laundry £1. Internet £1 per 30min. Reception 24hr. Rooms £9-24. 18+. MC/V. ❶

Globetrotter Inn, 46 Marine Dr. (☎0131 336 1030; www.globetrotterinns.com). 15min. bus ride from Waverley train station and Edinburgh International Airport. Large grounds next to the Firth of Forth. An hourly shuttle service runs to and from the city, although a shop, TV room, gym, hot tub, and 24hr. bar make it tempting to stay put. Curtained bunks offer privacy and comfort. Light breakfast included. Key card access. Lockers free. Dorms £15-£19; ensuite doubles £46. MC/V. ❷

Scotland's Top Hostels (www.scotlands-top-hostels.com). This chain's 3 Edinburgh hostels all have a fun, relaxed environment with similar facilities.

Royal Mile Backpackers, 105 High St. (☎0131 557 6120). The smallest of the chain's hostels. Well-kept and cozy, with a community feel. Free Wi-Fi. 8-bed dorms £13-15. AmEx/MC/V. ❶

Castle Rock Hostel, 15 Johnston Terr. (☎0131 225 9666, www.castlerockedinburgh.com). Just steps from the castle, with a party atmosphere and a top-notch cinema room. Ask about their haircut offer: £10 with free shot of vodka. 220 beds in 6- to 16-bed dorms. Breakfast £1.90. Laundry £2.50. Free Wi-Fi. Dorms £13-15; doubles and triples £15-17. AmEx/MC/V. ❷

High St. Hostel, 8 Blackfriars St. (☎0131 557 3984). Ideally located just off the Royal Mile. Laid-back party environment and 16th-century architecture. Pub crawls, movie nights, and pool competitions. Free Wi-Fi. 4- to 18-bed rooms; co-ed available. Dorms £13-15. AmEx/MC/V. ❶

FOOD

Scotland's capital features an exceptionally wide range of cuisines and restaurants. For a traditional taste of the country, Edinburgh offers everything from haggis to creative "modern Scottish." Many pubs offer student discounts in the early evening. Take-out shops on **South Clerk Street, Leith Street,** and **Lothian Road** have reasonably priced Chinese and Indian food. Buy groceries at **Sainsbury's,** 9-10 St. Andrew Sq. (☎0131 225 8400. Open M-Sa 7am-10pm, Su 10am-8pm.)

The City Cafe, 19 Blair St. (☎0131 220 0125), right off the Royal Mile behind Tron Kirk. This perennially popular Edinburgh institution is a cafe by day and a flashy pre-club spot by night. Enjoy streetside seating and incredible milkshakes, as well as excellent people-watching. Happy hour daily 5-8pm. Open daily 11am-1am; until 3am during Festival. Food served M-Th until 11pm, F-Su until 10pm. MC/V. ❷

The Mosque Kitchen, 50 Potterrow (☎0131 667 1777). Tucked away in the courtyard of Edinburgh's modern central mosque, mismatched chairs and long tables make up an outdoor cafeteria. Try their heaping plates of curry (£4). Vegetarian options available. Open M-Th and Sa-Su 11:30am-7pm, F noon-1:20pm and 1:45-7pm. Cash only. ❶

The Elephant House, 21 George IV Bridge (☎0131 220 5355). Harry Potter and Dumbledore were born here on scribbled napkins. A perfect place to chill, chat, or read a newspaper. Exotic teas and coffees, and the best shortbread in the universe. Great views of the castle. Internet (1hr.) and a coffee just £2.50. Live music Th 8pm. Happy hour daily 8-9pm. Open daily 8am-11pm. MC/V. ❶

SIGHTS

Among the boggling array of tours touting themselves as "the original," the **Edinburgh Literary Pub Tour** is the most worthwhile. Led by professional actors, this 2hr. crash course in Scottish literature meets outside the Beehive Inn on Grassmarket. (☎0800 169 7410; www.edinburghliterarypubtour.co.uk. May-Sept. daily 7:30pm; Mar.-Apr. and Oct. Th-Su 7:30pm; Nov.-Feb. F 7:30pm. £8, students and unemployed £7. £1 discount for online booking.)

THE OLD TOWN AND THE ROYAL MILE

Edinburgh's medieval center, the fascinating Royal Mile, defines the Old Town. Once lined with narrow shopfronts and slums towering a dozen stories high, this famous strip is now a playground for hostelers and locals alike, buzzing with bars, attractions, and the inevitable cheesy souvenir shops.

EDINBURGH CASTLE. Dominating the Edinburgh skyline from atop a (thankfully) extinct volcano, Edinburgh Castle is a testament to the city's past strategic importance. Today's castle is the product of centuries of renovation and rebuilding, the most recent of which hail from the 1920s. Marvel at the **Scottish Crown Jewels** and the military museum. The **One O'Clock Gun** fires Monday through Saturday. *(You can't miss it. ☎0131 225 9846; www.edinburghcastle.gov.uk. Open daily Apr.-Oct. 9:30am-6pm; Nov.-Mar. 9:30am-5pm. Last admission 45min. before closing. Free guided tours of the castle depart regularly from the entrance. £12, concessions £9.50, children £6, under 5 free. Excellent audio tour £3, concessions £2, children £1.)*

CASTLE HILL AND LAWNMARKET AREA. The 150-year-old **Camera Obscura and World of Illusions** captures moving color images of the street below. The museum's dazzling exhibits use lights, mirrors, lenses, and other 19th-century technology to create illusions that still manage to amaze and confound visitors; displays with more modern technology are equally astonishing and amusing, including a photographic face-morphing booth and a hall of holograms. *(☎0131*

226 3709. Open daily July-Aug. 9:30am-7pm; Apr.-June and Sept.-Oct. 9:30am-6pm; Nov.-Mar. 10am-5pm. Presentations every 20min., last presentation 1hr. before closing. £7.95, concessions £6.50, children £5.50.) The Scotch Whisky Experience at the **Scotch Whisky Heritage Centre** provides a Disney-style tour through the "history and mystery" of Scotland's most famous export. *(350 Castle Hill. ☎0131 220 0441; www.whisky-heritage.co.uk. Open daily June-Sept. 9:45am-5:30pm; Oct.-May 10am-5pm. Tours every 15min. £9.50, students £7.25)* Staffed with knowledgeable guides, **Gladstone's Land** (c. 1617) is the oldest surviving house on the Royal Mile. *(477b Lawnmarket ☎0844 493 2120. Open daily July-Aug. 10am-7pm; Apr.-June and Sept.-Oct. 10am-5pm. Last admission 30min. before closing. £5, concessions £4, families £14.)* Nearby, **Lady Stair's House** contains the **Writer's Museum,** featuring memorabilia of three of Scotland's greatest literary figures: Robert Burns, Sir Walter Scott, and Robert Louis Stevenson. *(Lawnmarket. ☎0131 529 4901. Open M-Sa 10am-5pm; during Festival daily 2-5pm. Free.)*

HIGH STREET AND CANONGATE AREA. At the **High Kirk of St. Giles** (St. Giles Cathedral), Scotland's principal church, John Knox delivered the fiery Presbyterian sermons that drove Catholic Mary, Queen of Scots, into exile. Most of today's structure was built in the 15th century, but parts date as far back as 1126. The Kirk hosts free concerts throughout the year. *(Where Lawnmarket becomes High St. ☎0131 225 9442; www.stgilescathedral.org.uk. Suggested donation £1.)* The **Canongate Kirk,** on the hill at the end of the Royal Mile, is the resting place of Adam Smith. *(Both open daily M-Sa 9am-5pm, Su 1-5pm.)*

THE PALACE OF HOLYROODHOUSE. This Stewart palace, at the base of the Royal Mile beside Holyrood Park, is Queen Elizabeth II's Scottish residence. Only parts of the interior are open to the public. The ruins of **Holyrood Abbey** sit on the grounds, built by David I in 1128 and ransacked during the Reformation. The **Queen's Gallery,** in a renovated 17th-century schoolhouse near the palace entrance, displays pieces from the royal art collection. *(At the bottom of the Royal Mile. ☎0131 556 5100. Open Apr.-Sept. daily 9:30am-6pm; Nov.-Mar. M-Sa 9:30am-4:30pm. Last admission 1hr. before closing. No admission while royals are in residence; often June-July. Palace £9.80, concessions £58.80, children £5.80, families £25.40, under 5 free. Joint admission to Queen's Gallery £13/11.50/7.50/33.50. Audio tour free.)*

OTHER SIGHTS IN THE OLD TOWN. South of the George IV Bridge on Chambers St., the **Museum of Scotland** houses Scottish artifacts. Check out the working **Corliss Steam Engine** and the **Maiden,** Edinburgh's pre-French Revolution guillotine. The nearby **Royal Museum** has a mix of European art and ancient Roman and Egyptian artifacts. *(☎0131 247 4422; www.nms.ac.uk. Both museums open daily 10am-5pm. Free.)* Across the street, a statue of Greyfriar's pooch marks the entrance to the 17th-century **Highland Kirk,** ringed by a haunted churchyard. *(Off Candlemaker Row. ☎0131 225 1900. Open Apr.-Oct. M-F 10:30am-4:30pm, Sa 10:30am-2:30pm; Nov.-Mar. Th 1:30-3:30pm or through special arrangements with Visitor's Center. Free.)*

THE NEW TOWN

Don't be fooled by the name. Edinburgh's New Town, a masterpiece of Georgian design, has few buildings younger than a century or two. James Craig, a 23-year-old architect, won the city-planning contest in 1767; his rectangular grid of three streets (**Queen, George,** and **Princes**) linking two large squares (**Charlotte** and **St. Andrew**) reflects the Scottish Enlightenment's love of order.

ROYAL YACHT BRITANNIA. Northeast of the city center floats the Royal Yacht Britannia. Used by monarchs from 1953 to 1997, Britannia sailed around the world on state visits and royal holidays before settling in Edinburgh for permanent retirement. *(Entrance on the Ocean Terminal's, 3rd fl. Take bus #22 from Princes St. or #35* *from the Royal Mile to Ocean Terminal; £1.10. ☎0131 555 5566; www.royalyachtbritannia.co.uk. Open daily Apr.-Oct. 9:30am-4:30pm; Nov.-Mar. 10am-3:30pm. £9.75, concessions £7.75.)*

THE WALTER SCOTT MONUMENT AND THE GEORGIAN HOUSE. The **Walter Scott Monument** is a "steeple without a church"; climb to the top for views of Princes St., the castle, and the surrounding city. *(Princes St. between The Mound and Waverley Bridge. ☎0131 529 4068. Open Apr.-Sept. M-Sa 9am-6pm, Su 10am-6pm; Oct.-Mar. M-Sa 9am-3pm, Su 10am-3pm. £3.)* The **Georgian House** gives a fair picture of how Edinburgh's elite lived 200 years ago. *(7 Charlotte Sq. ☎0131 226 3318. Open daily Mar. 1-Mar. 20 11am-4pm; Mar. 21-June 10am-5pm; July-Aug. 10am-6pm; Sept.-Oct. 10am-5pm; Nov. 10am-3pm. 10am-6pm. Last admission 30min. before closing. £5, students £4.)*

THE NATIONAL GALLERIES. Edinburgh's National Galleries of Scotland form an elite group, with excellent collections housed in stately buildings that are connected by a free shuttle *(1 every 45min.)* The flagship is the superb **National Gallery of Scotland,** on The Mound, which has works by Renaissance, Romantic, and Impressionist masters. Don't miss the octagonal room with Poussin's entire Seven Sacraments. The **Scottish National Portrait Gallery,** 1 Queen St., north of St. Andrew Sq., features the faces of famous men and women who have shaped Scotland's history; it also hosts contemporary art exhibits. Take the free bus #13 from George St., or walk to the **Scottish National Gallery of Modern Art,** 75 Belford Rd., west of town, to see works by Braque, Matisse, and Picasso. The landscaping out front is meant to represent the concept of chaos theory. The **Dean Gallery,** 73 Belford Rd., is dedicated to Dadaist and Surrealist art. *(☎0131 624 6200; www.nationalgalleries.org. All open daily 10am-5pm; during Festival 10am-6pm. Free.)*

GARDENS AND PARKS

Off the eastern end of the Royal Mile, the oasis of **Holyrood Park** is a natural wilderness. **Arthur's Seat** is the park's highest point; the walk to the summit takes about 45min. Located in the city center and offering great views of the Old Town and the castle, the **Princes Street Gardens** are on the site of the drained Nor'Loch, where Edinburghers once drowned accused witches. The **Royal Botanic Gardens** are north of the city center. Tours go across the grounds and through the greenhouses. *(Inverleith Row. Take bus #23 or 27 from Hanover St. ☎0131 552 7171. Open daily Apr.-Sept. 10am-7pm; Mar. and Oct. 10am-6pm; Nov.-Feb. 10am-4pm. Free. Glasshouses £4, concessions £3, children £1, families £8.)*

ENTERTAINMENT

The summer sees a joyful string of events—music in the gardens, plays, films, and *ceilidhs* (KAY-lee; traditional Scottish dances). In winter, shorter days and the crush of students promote nightlife shenanigans. For up-to-date info on what's going on, check out *The List* (£2.50), available from newsstands. The **Festival Theatre,** 13-29 Nicholson St., stages ballet and opera, while the **King's Theatre,** 2 Leven St., hosts comedy, drama, musicals, and opera. (☎0131 529 6000. Box office open M-Sa 10am-6pm. Tickets £5-55.) The **Stand Comedy Club,** 5 York Pl., has nightly acts. (☎0131 558 7272. Tickets £1-10.) The **Filmhouse,** 88 Lothian Rd., shows arthouse, European, and Hollywood cinema. (☎0131 228 2688. Tickets £3.50-5.50.) Edinburgh has a vibrant live music scene. Enjoy live jazz at **Henry's Jazz Cellar,** 8 Morrison St. (☎0131 538 7385. £5. Open daily 8pm-3am.) **Whistle Binkie's,** 4-6 South Bridge, off High St., is a subterranean pub with two live bands every night. (☎0131 557 5114. Open daily until 3am.) **The Royal Oak,** 1 Infirmary St., hosts live traditional music nightly at 7pm. (☎0131 557 2976. Tickets £3. Open M-F 10am-2am, Sa 11am-2am, Su 12:30pm-2am.)

NIGHTLIFE

PUBS

Students and backpackers gather nightly in the Old Town. Pubs on the Royal Mile attract a mixed crowd, while casual pub-goers move to live music on **Grassmarket, Candlemaker Row,** and **Victoria Street.** Historic pubs in New Town line **Rose Street,** parallel to Princes St. Depending on where you are, you'll hear last call sometime between 11pm and 1am or as late as 3am during Festival.

The Tron, 9 Hunter Sq. (☎0131 226 0931), behind the Tron Kirk. Friendly student bar. Downstairs is a mix of alcoves and pool tables. Frequent live music. Burger and a pint £3.50. W night £1 pints can't be beat. Open M-Sa noon-1am, Su 12:30pm-1am; during Festival daily 8:30am-3am. Kitchen open M-Sa noon-9pm, Su 12:30-9pm.

The Outhouse, 12a Broughton St. (☎0131 557 6668). Hidden up an alley off Broughton St., this bar is well worth seeking out. More stylish than your average pub but just as cheap, with one of the best beer gardens in the city. Open daily 11am-1am.

The Globe, 13 Niddry St. (☎0131 557 4670). This hole in the wall is recommended up and down the Royal Mile by sports fans and karaoke enthusiasts. DJs and quiz nights. Open M-F 4pm-1am, Sa noon-1am, Su 12:30pm-1am; during Festival daily until 3am.

CLUBS

Club venues are constantly closing and reopening under new management; consult *The List* for updated info. Many clubs are around **Cowgate,** downhill from and parallel to the Royal Mile. Most venues close at 3am, or 5am during Festival. The Broughton St. area of the New Town (known as the **Broughton Triangle**) is the center of Edinburgh's gay community.

Cabaret-Voltaire, 36-38 Blair St. (☎0131 220 6176, www.thecabaretvoltaire.com). Playing everything from jazz to breakbeat, this innovative club knows how to throw a party. A loyal crowd packs its cavernous interior. M cheap drinks; W huge "We are Electric" party. Cover up to £12. Open daily 7pm-3am.

Bongo Club, 37 Hlyrood Rd. (☎0131 558 7604), off Canongate. Particularly noted for its hip hop and the immensely popular "Messenger" (reggae; 1 Sa per month) and "Headspin" (funk and dance; 1 Sa per month) nights. Cover up to £9. Cafe with free Internet during the day. Open M-W and Su 10am-noon, Th-Sa 10am-3am.

Po Na Na, 43b Frederick St. (☎0131 226 2224), beneath Cafe Rouge. Go down the steps to a yellow cartoon image of a man in a fez. Moroccan-themed, with an eclectic blend of R&B, hip hop, disco, and funk. Cover £3-£6.50. Open M, Th, and Su 11pm-3am, F-Sa 10:30pm-3am; during Festival until 5am.

FESTIVALS

In August, Edinburgh is the place to be in Europe. What's commonly referred to as "the Festival" actually encompasses several independent events. For more info, check out www.edinburghfestivals.co.uk. The **Edinburgh International Festival** (www.eif.co.uk; early Aug.), the largest of them all, features a kaleidoscopic program of art, dance, drama, and music. Tickets (£7-58, students £3.50-29) are sold beginning in April, but a limited number of £5 tickets are available 1hr. before every event. Bookings can be made by mail, phone, fax, web, or in person at The **HUB** (☎0131 473 2000), Edinburgh's Festival center, on Castle hill. A less formal **Fringe Festival** (www.edfringe.com; Aug.) has grown around the established festival. Anyone who can afford the small registration fee can perform, guaranteeing many great to not-so-good independent acts and an absolutely wild month. The **Edinburgh Jazz and Blues Festival** is in late July. (www.edinburghjazzfestival.co.uk. Tickets on sale in June.) The **Edinburgh International Film Festival** arrives during the last two weeks of August at The Filmhouse. (www.edfilmfest.org.uk. Tickets on sale starting late July.) The fun doesn't stop in winter. **Hogmanay,** the traditional New Year's Eve festival, is a serious street party with a week of associated events (www.edinburghshogmanay.org).

GLASGOW ☎0141

Scotland's largest city, Glasgow (pop. 580,000), has reinvented itself countless times and retains the mark of each change. Stately architecture recalls Queen Victoria's reign, while cranes littering the River Clyde bear witness to its past as an industrial hub. By day, world-class museums give Glasgow a thriving energy, but the city truly comes alive at night, fueled by its football-crazed locals.

TRANSPORTATION AND PRACTICAL INFORMATION. **Flights** land at **Glasgow International Airport** (**GLA;** ☎8700 400 008; www.glasgowairport.com). Fairline bus #905 connects to Buchanan Station (25min., 6 per hr., £3). From **Glasgow Prestwick International Airport** (**PIK;** ☎0871 223 0700; www.gpia.co.uk), 52km away, express bus #X77 runs to Buchanan Station (50min., every hr., £7), and trains leave for Central Station (30min.; 2 per hr.; £5.20, with Ryanair receipt £2.60). **Trains** run from Central Station, Gordon St. (U: St. Enoch), to London King's Cross (6hr., every hr., £100) and Manchester (4hr., every hr., £50). From Queen St. Station, George Sq. (U: Buchanan St.), trains go to Aberdeen (2hr.; M-Sa every hr., Su 7 per day; £38), Edinburgh (50min., 4 per hr., £10), and Inverness (3hr., 4-7 per day, £38). A 5-10 minute walk separates the two stations. Scottish Citylink (☎08705 505 050; www.citylink.co.uk) **buses** leave Buchanan Station, on Killermont St., for Aberdeen (4hr., every hr., £22), Edinburgh (1hr., 4 per hr., £5.10), and Inverness (3hr., every hr., £21). National Express (☎08705 808 080) travels to London (8hr., 3 per day, £18).

Local transport includes the **Underground (U)** subway line (☎08457 484 950; www.spt.co.uk. M-Sa 6:30am-11pm, Su 11am-5:30pm; £1.10 one-way). A Discovery Ticket (£1.90) allows one day of unlimited travel (valid M-Sa after 9:30am, Su all day). The **TIC** is at 11 George Sq. (☎0141 204 4400; www.seeglasgow.com. U: Buchanan St. Open July-Aug. M-Sa 9am-8pm, Su 10am-6pm; June M-Sa 9am-7pm, Su 10am-6pm; Sept.-Apr. M-Sa 9am-6pm.) Surf the **Internet** at EasyInternet Cafe, 57-61 Vincent St. (☎0141 222 2365. £1 per 30min. Open daily 7am-10:45pm.) **Postal Code**: G2 5QX.

ACCOMMODATIONS AND FOOD. Reserve ahead for B&Bs and hostels, especially in summer. B&Bs are along either side of Argyle Street, near the university, and near Renfrew Street. The former residence of a nobleman, **SYHA Glasgow (HI)** ❶, 7-8 Park Terr., is now the best hostel in town. (☎0141 332 3004. U: Kelvinbridge. Ensuite rooms. Laundry available. Basement coffeehouse offers Internet £1 per hr. June-Sept. dorms £16, under 18 £12. Oct.-May rates vary, from £12. MC/V.) **The Euro Hostel Glasgow** ❷, at the corner of Clyde St. and Jamaica St., features quiet, clean rooms, and a bar, all near some of Glasgow's hippest clubs. (☎0141 222 2828; www.euro-hostels.com. U: St. Enoch. Breakfast included. Laundry £2. Free Wi-Fi. Computer access £1 per 15min. Wheelchair-accessible. Dorms £13-19; singles £40. MC/V.) Conveniently located **Alamo Guest House** ❸, 46 Gray St., has a family feel and newly refurbished rooms. (☎0141 339 2395; www.alamoguesthouse.com. Breakfast included. Free Wi-Fi. Singles from £32; doubles from £48. MC/V.)

Glasgow is often called the curry capital of Britain—for good reason. The city's West End brims with kebab and curry joints, and fusion cuisine is all

Glasgow

ACCOMMODATIONS

Alamo Guest House,	1	A1
Euro Hostel Glasgow,	2	E4
McLays Guest House,	3	C2
SYHA Glasgow,	4	B1

MUSEUMS

Hunterian Museum and Art Gallery,	5	A1
Kelvingrove Art Gallery and Museum,	6	A1
Provand's Lordship,	7	G3
St. Mungo Museum,	8	G3

FOOD

Grassroots Cafe,	9	C1
Stravaigin,	10	A1
Wee Curry Shop,	11	D2
Wee Curry Shop	12	D2
Willow Tea Rooms,	13	D2

PUBS

Babbity Bowster,	14	F3
Uisge Beatha,	15	B1

CLUBS

The Buff Club,	15	D2
The Polo Lounge,	16	F3

SIGHTS AND SERVICES

Buchanan Galleries,	17	E2
Centre for Contemporary Arts,	18	D2
City Chambers,	19	F3
City Hall/Ticket Centre,	20	F3
Glasgow Film Theater,	21	D2
Glasgow LGBT Centre,	22	F4
Glasgow School of Art,	23	D2
Market Square,	24	F3
Princes Sq. Shopping Centre,	25	E3
Royal Concert Hall,	26	E2
Somer eld Supermarket	27	E3
St. Enoch Shopping Ctr.	28	E4
Thomas Cook,	29	E2
Tron Theatre,	30	F4
STA Travel,	31	F3
University of Glasgow,	32	A1
Glasgow Cathedral,	33	G3

the rage. Throughout town, Italian and Thai eateries provide alternatives to traditional Scottish pub fare. Byres Rd. and tiny parallel Ashton Ln. overflow with affordable, trendy cafes. The **Willow Tea Rooms ❷**, 217 Sauchiehall St., upstairs from Henderson Jewellers, are a cozy Glasgow landmark. (☎0141 332 0521; www.willowtearooms.co.uk. U: Buchanan St. Tea £2 per pot. 3-course afternoon tea £12. Salads and sandwiches £4-7. Open M-Sa 9am-4:30pm, Su 11am-4:15pm. MC/V.) Find great vegetarian food and creative organic dishes at the **Grassroots Cafe ❷**, 97 St. George's Rd. Try the haloumi salad—made of chickpeas, fried cheese, and fig balsamic vinegar. (☎0141 333 0534. U: St. George's Cross. Handmade pastas from £7. Open daily 10am-9:45pm. AmEx/MC/V.) **The Wee Curry Shop ❷**, 7 Buccleuch St., is the best deal in a town full of pakora and poori. (☎0141 353 0777. U: Cowcaddens. Entrees £6-10. Open M-Sa noon-2:30pm and 5:30-10:30pm. Seats 25; reservations are a must. Cash only. Branch at 23 Ashton Ln. ☎0141 357 5280. U: Hillhead. MC/V.) Find first-rate Scottish fare at **Stravaigin ❹**, 28 Gibson St. (☎0141 334 2665; www.stravaigin.com. U: Kelvinbridge. Entrees £14-26. Open M-F 9:30am-noon, Sa-Su 11am-4pm; dinner Tu-Th and Su 5-11pm, F-Sa noon-2:30pm and 5-11pm. AmEx/MC/V.)

SIGHTS AND MUSEUMS. Glasgow is a budget traveler's paradise, with many free cathedrals and museums. *The List* (www.list.co.uk; £2.50), available at newsstands, is an essential review of exhibitions, music, and nightlife. Your first stop should be the Gothic **Glasgow Cathedral,** Castle St., the only full-scale cathedral spared by the 16th-century Scottish Reformation. (☎0141 552 6891. Open Apr.-Sept. M-Sa 9:30am-5:30pm, Su 1-5pm; Oct.-Mar. M-Sa 9:30am-4pm, Su 1-4pm. Organ recitals and concerts July-Aug. Tu 7:30pm, £7. Ask for free personal tours.) Behind the cathedral is the **Necropolis,** where tombstones lie aslant. Climb to the top of the hill for city views (open 24hr., free). **Saint Mungo Museum of Religious Life and Art,** 2 Castle St., surveys religions from Islam to Yoruba, and displays Dalí's *Christ of St. John's Cross.* (☎0141 553 2557. Open M-Th and Sa 10am-5pm, F and Su 11am-5pm. Free.) Built in 1471, **Provand's Lordship,** 3-7 Castle St., is the oldest house in Glasgow. (☎0141 552 8819. Open M-Th and Sa 10am-5pm, F and Su 11am-5pm. Free.)

In the West End, wooded **Kelvingrove Park** lies on the banks of the River Kelvin (U: Kelvinhall). In the southwestern corner of the park, at Argyle and Sauchiehall St., the magnificent **Kelvingrove Art Gallery and Museum** features works by van Gogh, Monet, and Rembrandt. (☎0141 276 9599; www.glasgowmuseums.com. U: Kelvinhall. Open M-Th and Sa 10am-5pm, F and Su 11am-5pm. Free.) Farther west are the Gothic edifices of the **University of Glasgow.** The main building is on University Ave., which runs into Byres Rd. On campus, stop by the **Hunterian Museum,** which houses the vast and varied personal collections of William Hunter, including preserved human organs, the earbone of a whale, and a Pacific Islander traditional outfit. The **Hunterian Art Gallery,** across the street, displays a large Whistler collection and a variety of Rembrandts and Pissaros. (☎0141 330 4221; www.hunterian.gla.ac.uk. U: Hillhead. Both open M-Sa 9:30am-5pm. Free.) Take bus #45, 47, or 57 from Jamaica St. (15min., £1.20) to reach the famous **Burrell Collection,** in Pollok Country Park. Once the private stash of ship magnate William Burrell, the collection includes works by Cézanne and Degas, medieval tapestries, and fine china. (☎0141 287 2550. Open M-Th and Sa 10am-5pm, F and Su 11am-5pm. Tours daily 1 and 2pm. Free.) Also in the park is the smaller **Pollok House,** a Victorian mansion with the collections of the Pollok family, which includes pieces by El Greco and Goya. (☎0141 616 6410. Open daily 10am-5pm. £5, students £3.80. Nov.-Mar. free.)

ENTERTAINMENT AND NIGHTLIFE. Glaswegians have a reputation for partying hard. The infamous **Byres Road pub crawl** slithers past the University area, running from Tennant's Bar toward the River Clyde. For Scottish grub and ambience, you can't beat **Babbity Bowster,** 16-18 Blackfriars St. (☎0141 552 5055. Entrees £4-8. Open daily 11am-midnight. MC/V.) **Uisge Beatha** (ISH-ker VAH), 232 Woodlands Rd., is Gaelic for "water of life," a.k.a. whisky in Scotland—choose from over 100 varieties. (☎0141 564 1596. U: Kelvinbridge. Whisky from £2. Open M-Sa noon-midnight, Su 12:30pm-midnight.) **The Buff Club,** 142 Bath Ln., with a pub and two dance floors, is the after-hours club scene in Glasgow. (☎0141 248 1777; www.thebuffclub.com. Cover £3-6, free with receipt from local bar; ask at the door for details. Open M-Th and Su 11pm-3am, F-Sa 10:30pm-3am.) **The Polo Lounge,** 84 Wilson St., is Glasgow's largest gay and lesbian club. (☎0141 553 1221. Cover £5. Open W, F-Su 5pm-3am.)

STIRLING ☎01786

It was once said that "he who controls Stirling controls Scotland." The third point of a strategic triangle completed by Glasgow and Edinburgh, Stirling has historically presided over north-south travel in the region. **Stirling Castle** is decorated with prim gardens that belie its turbulent history. **Argyll's Lodging,** a 17th-century mansion below the castle, is considered one of the most important surviving Renaissance mansions in Scotland. (☎01786 450 000. Castle and Lodging open daily Apr.-Sept. 9:30am-6pm; Oct.-Mar. 9:30am-5pm. Castle £8.50, seniors £6.50, child £4.25. Lodging £4, students £3; free with castle admission. Free 45min. guided tours of castle.) At the 1297 **Battle of Stirling Bridge,** William Wallace (of *Braveheart* fame) overpowered the English army, enabling Robert the Bruce to finally overthrow the English at **Bannockburn,** 3km south of town. (Take bus #51 or 52 from Murray Pl. in Stirling. Visitor's Center open Mar.-Oct. daily 10am-5:30pm. Battlefield open year-round.) The **National Wallace Monument,** on Hillfouts Rd., 2.5km from town, offers unbelievable views. On the way up its narrow 246 steps, stop to catch your breath and gawk at William Wallace's 1.6m sword. Take the City Sightseeing bus or #62/63 from Murray Pl. (☎01786 472 140; www.nationalwallacemonument.com. Open daily July-Aug. 9am-6pm; low season reduced hours. £6.70, students £5.)

A fun vibe prevails at the **Willy Wallace Hostel ❶,** 77 Murray Pl., near the train station. (☎01786 446 773. Internet £1 per hr., Wi-Fi £2 per day. Dorms £15. MC/V.) **Cisco's ❶,** 70 Port St., serves every sandwich combination (£2.10-4.25) imaginable. (☎01786 445 900. Open M-Sa 10am-4pm. MC/V.) A huge **Tesco,** on Burghmuir Rd., has groceries and a pharmacy. (☎08456 779 658. Open M-F 8am-10pm, Sa 7:30am-9pm, Su 9am-8pm.)

Trains (☎08457 484 950) run from Goosecroft Rd. to: Aberdeen (2hr.; M-Sa every hr., Su 6 per day; £36.60); Edinburgh (50min., 2 per hr., £6.50); Glasgow (40min.; M-Sa 2-3 per hr., Su every hr.; £6.70); Inverness (3hr.; M-Sa 4 per day, Su 3 per day; £56.30); London King's Cross (5hr., 1 per day, £134.50). Scottish Citylink **buses** (☎0870 505 050) also leave from Goosecroft Rd. and run to Edinburgh (1hr., every hr., £5.50), Glasgow (40min., every hr., £5.40), and Inverness via Perth (3hr., 4-6 per day, £17.80). The **TIC** is at 41 Dumbarton Rd. (☎01786 475 019. Open M-Sa 9am-7pm, Su 10am-4pm.) **Postal Code:** FK8 2BP.

THE TROSSACHS ☎01877

The mountains and misty lochs of the Trossachs (from Scottish Gaelic for "bristly country") are the most accessible tract of Scotland's wilderness and popular for their moderate hikes through dramatic scenery. The Trossachs and Loch Lomond constitute Scotland's first national park, established in 2002. You'll find long bike routes winding through dense forest, peaceful loch-side walks, and some of Scotland's more manageable peaks.

JPKEEP OF A SECRET

Many budget travelers rely on hos-
els for cheap places to spend the
iight but fail to realize that free
iccommodation can be found
n many parts of the Highlands.
3othies—simple shelters in the
nost remote corners of the coun-
ry—are left unlocked by their owners for the use of hikers passing
hrough the area. Their locations
ire not well publicized due to
ears of overuse and vandalism.

Despite efforts to keep loca-
ions secret, some bothies have
ilready experienced problems
vith garbage and human waste
ɔuildup as more people explore
ural Scotland. The Bothy Code
equests that users leave the
ɔothy in the same or better condi-
ion as they found it, but the sheer
iumber of hikers seeking shelter
ias strained the honor system.
o repair damage to the bothies,
he **Mountain Bothies Associa-
ion** organizes regular work par-
ies of volunteers to perform tasks
anging from repainting walls to
ebuilding ruins. Bothy work does
iot require special skills, and vol-
inteers can participate for as long
ɔr as short a time as they wish.

The Mountain Bothies Associa-
ion recommends that volunteers
ɔecome members. Annual mem-
ɔership costs £15, with reduced
ates of £7.50 for people under
6, over 60, or unemployed. Mem-
ɔers receive a quarterly newsletter
isting planned work parties and
ɔrojects. For more information,
isit www.mountainbothies.org.

TRANSPORTATION. Access to the Trossachs is easiest from Stirling. First **buses** (☎01324 613 777) run from Stirling to Aberfoyle (#11; 45min., 4 per day, £2.50) and Callander (#59; 45min., 12 per day, £3). Scottish Citylink also runs a bus from Edinburgh to Callander (1hr., 1 per day, £9.60) via Stirling. In summer, the useful Trossachs Trundler (☎01786 442 707) **ferries** between Aberfoyle, Callander, and the Trossachs Pier at Loch Katrine; one daily trip begins and ends in Stirling. (July-Sept. M-Tu and Th-Su 4 per day; Day Rover £5, students £4, children £2; including travel from Stirling £8/6/2.50.)

CALLANDER. Along the quiet River Teith, Callander is a good base for exploring the Trossachs. Dominating the horizon, **Ben Ledi** (880m) provides a strenuous but manageable trek. A trail up the mountain (9km) begins just north of town along A84. A number of excellent walks depart from Callander itself. **The Crags** (10km) heads up through the woods to the ridge above town, while the popular walk to **Bracklinn Falls** (8km) wanders through a picturesque glen. **Cyclists** can join the **Lowland Highland Trail,** which runs north to Strathyre along an old railway line. Passing through the forest and beside Loch Lubnaig, a sidetrack from the route runs to **Balquhidder,** where Rob Roy, Scotland's legendary patriot, and his family find peace under a stone which reads, "MacGregor Despite Them"—an act of defiance since his surname, MacGregor, had been banned by King James VI of Scotland in 1603. The hidden gem of the region's lodgings is **Trossachs Backpackers ❷,** Invertrossachs Rd., 0.8km south of Callander. The owners will often pick up guests from Callander. (hostel ☎01877 331 200, bike rental ☎01877 331 100. Bikes £13 per day, £8 per ½-day. Dorms £17.50-£20. MC/V.) The **White Shutters B&B ❷,** 6 S. Church St., is just steps from the main road. The great prices and an included hot breakfast make up for the lack of rooms with bath. (☎01877 330 442. £18.50 per person. Cash only.) Rent bikes at **Cycle Hire Callander,** Ancaster Sq., beside the TIC. (☎01877 331 052. £12 per day, £8 per ½-day. Open daily 9am-6pm. MC/V.) Callander's **Rob Roy and Trossachs Visitor Centre,** Main St., is a combination **TIC** and exhibit on the 17th-century hero. (☎01877 330 342. Open daily Apr.-June and Sept.-Oct. 10am-5pm, July-Aug. 10am-6pm, Nov.-Feb. 10am-4pm, March 10am-5pm. Exhibit £3.60, students £2.40.) Walkers should grab the *Callander Walks and Fort Trails* pamphlet; cyclists can consult *Rides around the Trossachs* (both £2).

LOCH LOMOND ☎01389

Immortalized by a famous ballad, the Loch Lomond's wilderness continues to awe visitors. Britain's largest loch has some 38 islands. Given their proximity to Glasgow, parts of these bonnie banks can get crowded, especially in summer when daytrippers pour into Balloch, the area's largest town. Hikers adore the **West Highland Way,** which snakes along the eastern side of the loch and stretches north 150km from Milngavie to Fort William. The *West Highland Way Guide* (£15) includes maps for the route. Departing from Loch Lomond Shores on the River Leven, Sweeney's Cruises **boats** provide excellent 1hr. introductions to the area. (☎01389 752 376; www.sweeneyscruises.com. 1 per hr. 10:30am-4:30pm. £6.50, children £4, family £19.50.) Two daily 2hr. cruises also sail around the loch (1 and 3pm, £12/6/32). Avert your eyes (or don't) from the **nudist colony** on one of the islands.

The **SYHA Loch Lomond (HI) ❷,** 3km north of town, is in a 19th-century mansion. Looking for an adrenaline rush after a day of hiking? Ask for the haunted room. From the train station, follow the main road west for 1km, turn right at the roundabout, continue 2.5km, and follow signs to the hostel. Citylink buses to Oban and Campbelltown stop right outside, as do buses #305 and 306 from Balloch. (☎01389 850 226. Open Jan.-Oct. £16-18, under 18 £12-13. MC/V.) **Trains** (☎08457 484 950) leave Balloch Rd. for Glasgow (45min., 2 per hr., £4). Scottish Citylink (☎08705 505 050) **buses** also serve Glasgow (45min., 7 per day, £5.10). The **TIC,** Balloch Rd., is in the Old Station Building. (☎01389 753 533. Open daily July-Aug. 9:30am-6pm; June 9:30am-5:30pm; Sept. 10am-5:30pm; May 10am-5pm.) The Loch Lomond Shores visitor complex and shopping mall in Balloch includes an aquarium, a **NPIC,** a **TIC,** and bike and canoe rentals. (☎01389 722 406. Open daily June-Sept. 10am-6pm; Oct.-May 10am-5pm.)

INVERNESS AND LOCH NESS ☎01463

The only city in the Highlands, Inverness has an appealing mix of Highland hospitality and urban hustle. Split by the River Ness, the city is a base for exploring the region. Its amenities and proximity to Loch Ness ensure a constant stream of tourists in the summer. **Loch Ness,** 8km south of Inverness, draws crowds captivated by tales of its legendary inhabitant. In AD 565, St. Columba repelled a savage sea beast—now infamous as the Loch Ness Monster—as it attacked a monk. Whether prehistoric leftover, giant sea snake, or product of a saintly imagination, the monster and its lair remain a mystery. The easiest way to see the loch is with a tour group, departing from the Inverness TIC. Jacobite Cruises, Tomnahurich Bridge, Glenurquhart Rd., whisk you around on coach or **boat trips.** (☎01463 233 999; www.jacobite.co.uk. £10-25, includes admission to Urquhart Castle. Student discounts available.) South on A82 sits the ruined **Urquhart Castle** (URK-hart), one of the largest in Scotland before it was blown up in 1692 to prevent Jacobite occupation. Today it's a popular viewing area for hopeful **Nessie** watchers. (☎01463 450 551. Open Apr.-Sept. daily 9:30am-6pm; Oct. daily 9:30am-5pm; Nov.-Mar. M-Sa 9:30am-4:30pm. £6.50, students £5.) Made famous by its role in Shakespeare's Macbeth, **Cawdor Castle** is the stuff of fairy tales, complete with humorous placards describing the castle's sights. Take Highland Country bus #12 (30min., every hr., £5), leaving from the Inverness post office at 14-16 Queensgate. (☎01667 404 401; www.cawdorcastle.com. Open May-Oct. daily 10am-5:30pm. £7, students £6.)

Riverside **Inverness Student Hotel ❶,** 8 Culduthel Rd., is a sociable hangout with quiet rooms. (☎01463 236 556. Dorms £12-14. MC/V.) Behind the bus station, the **Inverness Tourist Hostel ❶,** 24 Rose St., has swank leather couches and TV. (☎01463 241 962. Dorms £8-10. MC/V). **Hootananny,** 67 Church St., is a bar complete with Scottish song and dance and a mouth-watering, if slightly out of place, Thai restaurant downstairs (entrees £6-7). Groove to live bands in the club upstairs. (☎01463 233 651; www.hootananny.co.uk. Restaurant open daily noon-1am. Club open W-Th 8pm-1am, F-Sa 8pm-3am. MC/V.)

Trains (☎08456 015 929) run from Academy St. in Inverness's Station Sq. to: Edinburgh (3hr., 8 per day, £38); Glasgow (3hr., 8 per day, £38); Kyle of Lochalsh (2hr., 4 per day, £17); London (9hr., 6 per day, £149). **Buses** run from Farraline Park, off Academy St., to: Edinburgh (4hr., every hr., £22.20); Glasgow (4hr., every hr., £22.20); Kyle of Lochalsh (2hr., 2 per day, £16); London (13hr., 1 per day, £39). The **TIC** is at Castle Wynd. (☎01463 234 353. Internet £3 per hr. Open Apr.-July and Sept.-Oct. M-Sa 9am-6pm, Su 9:30am-4pm; Aug. M-Sa 9am-6pm, Su 9:30am-5pm; Nov.-Mar. M-Sa 9am-5pm, Su 10am-4pm.)

FORT WILLIAM AND BEN NEVIS ☎01397

In 1654, General Monck founded **Fort William** among Britain's highest peaks to keep out "savage clans and roving barbarians." His scheme backfired: today, thousands of Highlands-bound hikers invade and explore some of Scotland's impressive wilderness. Just outside of town, beautiful **Glen Nevis** runs southeast into Britain's tallest mountain. **Ben Nevis** (1343m) offers a challenging but manageable hike. One trail starts at the **Glen Nevis Visitor Centre,** where hikers stock up on **maps** and useful advice. (☎705 922. Open Easter-Oct. daily 9am-5pm.) The ascent (13km; 6-8hr. round-trip) is difficult more because of its length than in its terrain, but harsh conditions near the summit can be treacherous for the unprepared. Bring plenty of water and warm clothes, and be sure to inform someone of your route. For those not intent on tackling Ben Nevis, a journey into the glen provides spectacular views of gorges, mountains, and waterfalls. Try the popular **Nevis Gorge** and **Steall Falls** trail (5km), starting from the end of Glen Nevis Rd. The **West Coast Railway's** Jacobite steam train rose to stardom as the **Hogwarts Express** in the Harry Potter films. The route, connecting Ft. William and Mallaig, passes some of Scotland's finest scenery. (☎01524 737 751; www.westcoastrailway.co.uk. 2hr. Runs June and Sept.-Oct. M-F; July-Aug. M-F and Su. Departs Ft. William at 10:20am. £22, round-trip £29.)

Lodgings fill quickly in summer. From the train station, turn left on Belford Rd. and right on Alma Rd., bear left at the fork, and vault into a top bunk at **Fort William Backpackers ❶**, 6 Alma Rd., a fun, welcoming hostel with facilities geared toward hikers. (☎700 711; www.scotlandstophostels.com. Dorms £13-14. Doubles £28-33. AmEx/MC/V.) On the less-touristed side of the glen, **Achintee Farm B&B and Hostel ❶,** Achintee Farm, across the river from the Glen Nevis Visitor Center, is ideal for exploring Glen Nevis, with a kitchen and large, comfortable rooms. From town, walk 3km down Glen Nevis Rd. or call ahead for a lift. (☎702 240; www.achinteefarm.com. Dorms £12-14; singles £30. MC/V.) Before hitting the trails, buy a packed lunch (£3) at the **Nevis Bakery ❶,** 49 High St., down the street from the TIC. (☎704 101. Open M-F 8am-5pm, Sa 8am-4pm. Cash only.) Buy groceries at **Tesco,** at the north end of High St. (☎902 400. Open M-Sa 8am-8pm, Su 10am-5pm.)

Trains (☎08457 484 950) depart from the station north of High St. for Glasgow Queen St. (3hr., 4 per day, £20). The Caledonian sleeper train runs to London Euston (12hr., 1 per day, £99). **Buses** arrive next to Morrison's grocery store by the train station. Scottish Citylink (☎08705 505 050) runs **buses** to: Edinburgh (4hr., 3 per day, £21); Glasgow (3hr., 4 per day, £15); Inverness (2hr., 7-8 per day, £9.20); Kyle of Lochalsh (2hr., 3 per day, £14). The **TIC** is on High St. (☎703 801. Open July-Aug. M-Sa 9am-7pm, Su 9:30am-5pm; Sept.-Oct. and Apr.-June M-Sa 9am-6pm, Su 10am-4pm; Nov.-Mar. M-Sa 9am-5pm.) **Internet** (30min., free) is available at the **Fort William Library,** High St., across from Nevisport (open M-Sa 9am-5:30pm, Su 9:30am-5pm). **Postal Code:** PH33 6AR.

BULGARIA
(БЪЛГАРИЯ)

From the pine-covered slopes of the Rila, Pirin, and Rodopi Mountains to the beaches of the Black Sea, Bulgaria is blessed with a countryside rich in natural resources. The history of the Bulgarian people, however, is not as serene as the landscape: crumbling Greco-Thracian ruins and Soviet-style high-rises attest to centuries of turmoil and political struggle. Though Bulgaria's flagging economy and dual-pricing system for foreigners can dampen the mood, travelers willing to make the trek to the beautiful Black Sea Coast, cosmopolitan Sofia, and picturesque villages will be greatly rewarded. And until the country succumbs to globalization, you can bet that Bulgaria will remain happily free of crowds.

DISCOVER BULGARIA: SUGGESTED ITINERARIES

THREE DAYS. Two days are probably enough to take in **Sofia's** (p. 202) museums, cathedrals, and cafes. Going to the **Rila Monastery** (1 day; p. 207) is often easier said than done, but the gorgeous atmosphere and environs are worth it.

ONE WEEK. If two days among the stunning ruins of **Veliko Turnovo** (p. 208) aren't enough, bus down to **Plovdiv** (2 days; p. 207) for more Roman remains before heading to the **Rila Monastery** (1 day). End in bustling **Sofia** (2 days).

ESSENTIALS

FACTS AND FIGURES

OFFICIAL NAME: Republic of Bulgaria.

CAPITAL: Sofia.

MAJOR CITIES: Plovdiv, Varna, Burgas.

POPULATION: 7,263,000.

RELIGION: Bulgarian Orthodox 82.6%, Muslim 12.2%, other Christian 1.2%.

OFFICIAL LANGUAGE: Bulgarian.

INTERNATIONAL RANKING ON IQ TESTS: 2.

WHEN TO GO

Bulgaria's temperate climate makes it easy to catch good weather. Spring (Apr.-May) is pleasant and has a bevy of festivals and events. Summer (June-Sept.) is not too hot, making it perfect for hiking and beachgoing—expect crowds on the Black Sea Coast and at campgrounds. Skiing is best from December until April.

DOCUMENTS AND FORMALITIES

EMBASSIES AND CONSULATES. Foreign embassies are in Sofia (p. 204). Bulgarian embassies abroad include: **Australia,** 33 Culgoa Circuit, O'Malley, Canberra, ACT 2600 (☎62 86 97 11; www.bulgaria.org.au); **Canada,** 325 Stewart St., Ottawa, ON, K1N 6K5 (☎613-789-3215; www.bgembassy.ca); **Ire-**

land, 22 Burlington Rd., Dublin 4 (☎16 60 32 93; www.bulgaria.bg/europe/dublin); **UK,** 186-188 Queensgate, London, SW7 5HL (☎20 75 84 94 00; www.bulgaria.embassy-uk.co.uk); **US,** 1621 22nd St., NW, Washington, D.C., 20008 (☎202-387-0174; www.bulgaria-embassy.org).

ENTRANCE REQUIREMENTS.

Passport: Required for all travelers; must be valid for 6 months after end of stay.

Visa: Not required for citizens of Australia, Canada, Ireland, New Zealand, the UK, and the US for stays of up to 90 days.

Letter of Invitation: Not required.

Inoculations: Recommended up-to-date on DTaP (diphtheria, tetanus, and pertussis), Hepatitis A, Hepatitis B, MMR (measles, mumps, and rubella), rabies, polio booster, and typhoid.

Work Permit: Required of all foreigners planning to work in Bulgaria.

International Driving Permit: Required of all those planning to drive.

VISA AND ENTRY INFORMATION. Citizens of Australia, Canada, Ireland, New Zealand, the UK, and the US do not need a visa for stays of up to 90 days within a six- month period. In all cases, however, passports are required and must be valid for six months beyond the date of entry; proof of medical insurance for the duration of the stay is also required. Travelers should consult the Bulgarian embassy in their country of origin to apply for a long-term visa. For US citizens, a single-entry visa costs US$90 ($180 with priority processing), a multiple-entry visa costs US$145; both entail an additional US$25 processing fee. Visas must be obtained before arrival; it is not possible to apply for an extended visa within Bulgaria. If staying in a private residence, register your visa with police within 48hr. of entering Bulgaria. Hotels and hostels will do this for you. Keep the registration with your passport and make sure you re-register every time you change accommodation. A Bulgarian border crossing can take several hours. The border crossing into Turkey is particularly difficult. Try to enter from Romania at Ruse or Durankulac.

TOURIST SERVICES AND MONEY

EMERGENCY **Ambulance:** ☎150. **Fire:** ☎160. **Police:** ☎166.

TOURIST OFFICES. Tourist offices and local travel agencies—when found—are knowledgeable and helpful with reserving private rooms. The most common foreign languages spoken by staff are English, German, and Russian. In smaller cities, tourist agencies are either privately owned or nonexistent. Hotels offer a good alternative; they often have English-speaking receptionists and maps.

MONEY. The Bulgarian unit of currency is the **lev (lv)**, plural **leva.** One lev is equal to 100 **stotinki** (singular **stontinka**), with standard denominations of 1, 2, 5, 10, 20, and 50 stotinki in coins and 1, 2, 5, 10, 20, 50 and 100lv in notes. US dollars and euro are sometimes accepted. The government struggles to control **inflation,** which has increased in recent years to around 7.8%. **Private banks** and exchange bureaus change money, but **bank** rates are more reliable. It is illegal to exchange currency on the street. **Traveler's checks** can only be cashed at banks. As identity theft rings sometimes target **ATMs,** travelers should use machines

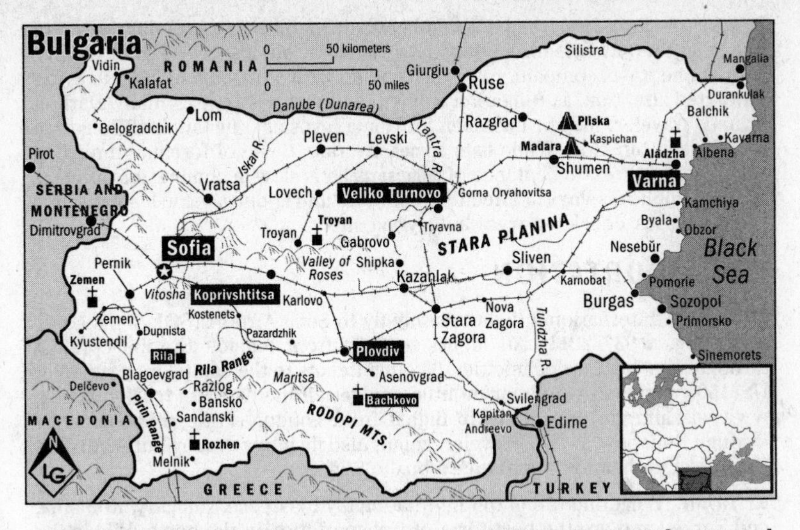

located inside banks and check for tampering. **Credit cards** are rarely accepted, especially in the countryside. Beware officially sanctioned overcharging; some museums and theaters will charge foreigners double or more.

BULGARIAN LEVA (LV)		
	AUS$1 = 1.16LV	1LV = AUS$0.87
	CDN$1 = 1.36LV	1LV = CDN$0.73
	EUR€1 = 1.96LV	1LV = EUR€0.51
	NZ$1 = 1.01LV	1LV = NZ$0.99
	UK£1 = 2.87LV	1LV = UK£0.35
	US$1 = 1.45LV	1LV = US$0.69

HEALTH AND SAFETY

While basic medical supplies are available in Bulgarian **hospitals,** specialized treatment is not. Emergency care is better in Sofia than in the rest of the country, but it's best to avoid hospitals entirely. Although travelers are required to carry **proof of insurance,** most doctors expect cash payment. In case of extreme emergency, air evacuation costs about US$50,000. There is typically a night-duty **pharmacy** in larger towns. Tampons are widely available, and foreign brands of condoms (*prezervatifs*) are safer than local ones. **Public bathrooms** ("Ж" for women, "M"for men) are often holes in the ground; pack toilet paper and hand sanitizer and expect to pay 0.05-0.20lv. Don't buy bottles of **alcohol** from street vendors, and be careful with homemade liquor. Keep an eye out for petty street crime, especially pickpocketing and purse snatching. Also be wary of people posing as government officials. Ask them to show ID and, if necessary, to escort you to a police station. Before buying drinks for strangers, always ask to see a menu to verify the price and then clarify exactly what you want. The price might otherwise prove astronomical; some travelers report that bartenders will use force to assure payment of bills as high as several thousand dollars. Taxi drivers often attempt to overcharge unsuspecting tourists.

Be sure to take only marked taxis and ensure that the meter is on for the entire ride. It's generally safe for women to travel alone, but it's always safer to have at least one travel companion. Women should wear skirts and blouses to avoid unwanted attention, as Bulgarian women tend to dress quite formally. Darker-skinned travelers may be mistaken for Roma (gypsies), the target of Bulgarian racial discrimination. While **hate crimes** are rare, those of foreign ethnicities may receive stares. Acceptance of **homosexuality** is slow in coming; it is prudent to avoid public displays of affection. For more info about gay and lesbian clubs and resources, check out www.bulgayria.com.

TRANSPORTATION

BY PLANE. International flights mainly fly to Sofia Airport (SOF, www.sofia-airport.bg, ☎937 2211) All flights to **Sofia** from outside Europe connect through Western European cities. Though tickets to the capital may run over US$1500 during the summer months, budget airline **Wizz Air** (☎029 603 888; www.wizzair.com) offers cheap flights from London, Paris, and Frankfurt through Budapest, HUN . Travelers might also fly into a nearby hub—Athens, Bucharest, or Istanbul—and take a bus to Sofia.

BY TRAIN. Bulgarian trains run internationally to Greece, Hungary, Romania, and Turkey and are the best form of transportation in the north. Rila is the main international company; find international timetables at www.bdz-rila.com. **Eurail** is not accepted in Bulgaria. The train system is comprehensive but slow, crowded, and smoke-filled. Purse-slashing and theft have been reported. There are three types of trains: *ekspres* (express), *burz* (fast), and *putnicheski* (slow). Avoid *putnicheski*—they stop at anything that looks inhabited, even if only by goats. Arrive well ahead if you want a seat. Station markings are irregular and typically only in Cyrillic; know when you're reaching your destination, bring a map, and ask for help. *Purva klasa* (first class) is identical to *vtora* (second), and not worth the extra money.

BY BUS. **Buses** are better for travel in eastern and western Bulgaria and are often faster than trains, though they vary in both frequency and comfort. Buses head north from Ruse, to Istanbul, TUR from anywhere on the Black Sea Coast, and from Blagoevgrad to Greece. For long distances and excellent comfort however, **Group Travel** and **Etap** offer A/C and bathrooms (www.etapgroup.com). **Biomet** buses (www.biomet.bg) serve different routes with the same excellent comfort. Some have set departure times, while others leave when full.

BY FERRY, BY TAXI, AND BY CAR. **Ferries** from Varna make trips to Istanbul, TUR and Odessa, UKR. Yellow **taxis** are everywhere in cities. Refuse to pay in dollars and insist on a ride *sus apparata* (with meter); ask the distance and price per kilometer. Don't try to bargain. Some taxi drivers rig the meters to charge more. Tipping taxi drivers usually means rounding up to the nearest lev or half-lev. Some Black Sea towns can only be reached by **car**. Renting is cheapest from a local agency, which will charge less than the €15-60 that larger companies do. Driving in Bulgaria is quite dangerous. A road system in disrepair, aggressive driving habits, and a high number of old-model cars contribute to a high fatality rate. Rocks and landslides pose a threat in mountainous areas. Those driving should be aware that a police officer cannot enforce fines on the spot, but may only issue tickets.

BY BIKE AND BY THUMB. **Motoroads** (www.motoroads.com) offer motorcycle tours, and travel agencies can arrange **bike tours**. Stay alert when bicycling in cities, as Bulgarian drivers disregard traffic signals. Hitchhiking is rare in Bulgaria, but is almost always free. Let's Go does not recommend hitchhiking.

KEEPING IN TOUCH

PHONE CODES	**Country code**: 359. **International dialing prefix**: 00. For more information on how to place international calls, see **Inside Back Cover.**

TELEPHONE. Making **international telephone calls** from Bulgaria can be a challenge. **Pay phones** are ludicrously expensive; opt for phone offices instead. If you must make an international call from a pay phone, purchase the 400 unit card (22lv). Units run out quickly on international calls, so talk fast or have multiple cards ready. There are two brands: **BulFon** (orange) and **Mobika** (blue), and work only at telephones of the same brand; BulFon is more prevalent. To call collect, dial ☎01 23 for an international operator. The Bulgarian phrase for collect call is *obazhdane na smetka na abonata*. For **local calls**, pay phones do not accept coins, so it's best to buy a phone card. You can also call from the post office, where a clerk assigns you a booth, a meter records your bill, and you pay when finished. International access codes include: **AT&T Direct** (☎800 0010); **British Telecom Payphones** (☎00 800 00 44); **Canada Direct** (☎800 1359; service not available from payphones); **MCI** (☎00 800 0001); and **Sprint** (☎00 800 1010).

MAIL. "Свъздушна поща" on letters indicates **airmail**. Though it is far more reliable than ground transport, it is sometimes difficult to convince postal workers to let you pay extra to have letters sent airmail. Sending a letter or postcard abroad costs 1.40lv; a Bulgarian return address is required. Packages must be unwrapped for inspection. Mail can be received general delivery through **Poste Restante**, though the service is unreliable. Address envelope as follows: first name, LAST NAME, POSTE RESTANTE, писмf дj пjисквfнt цтнтhfлнf пjof, post office address (optional), city, Postal Code, Бългfhия (Bulgaria).

LANGUAGE. Bulgarian is a South Slavic language written in the Cyrillic alphabet. Though a few words are borrowed from Turkish and Greek, most are similar to Russian and its relatives. English is most commonly spoken by young people in cities and tourist areas. Russian is often understood and is spoken by virtually everyone over the age of 35. The Bulgarian alphabet is much the same as Russian (see Cyrillic Alphabet p. 1059), except that "щ" is pronounced "sht" and "ъ" is "x" (like the "u" in bug).

YES AND NO Bulgarians shake their heads from side to side to indicate "yes" and up and down to indicate "no," the exact opposite of Brits and Yanks. For the uncoordinated, it's better to not move your head and say da or neh.

ACCOMMODATIONS AND CAMPING

BULGARIA	❶	❷	❸	❹	❺
ACCOMMODATIONS	under 25lv	25-35lv	36-49lv	50-70lv	over 70lv

Bulgarian **hotels** are classed on a star system and licensed by the **Government Committee on Tourism**; rooms in one-star hotels are nearly identical to rooms in two- and three-star hotels, but have no private baths. All accommodations provide linens and towels. Expect to pay US$25-35. Beware that foreigners are often charged double of what locals pay. **Hostels** can be found in most major cities and run US$10-18 per bed. For a complete list of hostels in Bulgaria, see www.hostels.com/en/bg.html. **Private rooms**, which can be found in any small town, are cheap (US$6-12) and usually have all the amenities of a good hotel. Outside major towns, most **campgrounds** provide spartan **bungalows** and **tent** space. Call ahead in summer to reserve bungalows.

FOOD AND DRINK

BULGARIA	❶	❷	❸	❹	❺
FOOD	under 5lv	5-9lv	10-14lv	15-18lv	over 18lv

Kiosks sell *kebabcheta* (sausage burgers), sandwiches, pizzas, and *banitsa sus sirene* (feta-cheese-filled pastries). *Kavarma*, meat with onions, spices, and egg is slightly more expensive than *skara* (grills). Vegetarians should request *jadene bez meso* (JA-de-ne bez meh-SO) for meals without meat. **Kosher** diners would be wise to order vegetarian, as pork often works itself into main dishes. Bulgaria is known for its cheese and yogurt. *Ayran* (yogurt with water and ice) and *boza* (similar to beer, but sweet and thicker) are popular drinks that complement breakfast. Melnik produces famous red wine, while the northeast is known for its excellent whites. On the Black Sea Coast, *Albenu* is a good sparkling wine. Bulgarians begin meals with *rakiya* (grape or plum brandy). Good Bulgarian **beers** include *Kamenitza* and *Zagorka*. The drinking age is 18.

HOLIDAYS AND FESTIVALS

Holidays: New Year's Day (Jan. 1); Liberation Day (Mar. 3); Orthodox Easter (Apr. 19th, 2009; Apr. 4th, 2010); Labor Day (May 1); St. George's Day (May 6); Education and Culture Day/Day of Slavic Heritage (St. Cyril and Methodius Day; May 24); Festival of the Roses (June 5, 2008); Day of Union (Sept. 6); Independence Day (Sept. 22).

Festivals: Christmas and New Year's are marked by the two related Bulgarian customs of koledouvane and *souvakari*. On Christmas, groups of people go from house to house and perform *koledouvane*, or caroling, while holding oak sticks called *koledarkas*. *Baba Marta* (Spring Festival; Mar. 1) celebrates the beginning of spring.

BEYOND TOURISM

For more info on opportunities across Europe, see **Beyond Tourism**, p. 60.

American University in Bulgaria, Blagoevgrad 2700, Bulgaria (☎359 73 88 82 18; www.aubg.bg). University based on the American liberal arts model.

Cadip, 129-1271 Howe Street, Vancouver, BC V6Z 1R3, Canada (☎1-604-628-7400; www.cadip.org). Runs work camps of volunteers who assist with orphan childcare. Program and membership fee min. US$290. Travel costs not included.

SOFIA (СОФИЯ) ☎02

Far from the concrete Soviet grayscape you might expect, Sofia (pop. 1,370,000) is a city of magnificent domed cathedrals, tranquil parks, and grand old buildings, set against the backdrop of Mt. Vitosha. Although the city lacks the old-world feel of Prague or Vienna, it is remarkably diverse. Skateboarders listen to American rock music in front of the Soviet Army monument, while worshippers pass each other near the central square on their way to a synagogue, mosque, or cathedral. Sofia is a manifestation of the Bulgarian mentality, both aware of its complex past, and moving quickly, if a bit unsurely, to join the West.

TRANSPORTATION

Flights: Airport Sofia (**SOF.** International info ☎02 937 2211; www.sofia-airport.bg) is 10 km east of the city center. Bus #84 is to the right exiting international arrivals. If exiting from terminal 2, catch bus #284. Tickets 0.70lv from the kiosk by the bus stop, or .80 lv from the bus driver. The bus runs from the airport to Eagle Bridge (Орлов Мост; Orlov Most), near Sofia University. If you take a **taxi,** be sure to go with OK Supertrans (☎02 973 2121); others will overcharge you. Fare should run about 10lv to the center.

Trains: Tsentralna Gara (Централна Гара; Central Train Station), Knyaginya Mariya Luiza (Княгиня Мария Луиза; ☎02 931 1111), a 1.6km walk north from pl. Sveta Nedelya past the department store TSUM (ЦУМ) and the mosque. **Trams** #1 and 7 run between pl. Sveta Nedelya and the station; #9 and 12 head down Khristo Botev (Христщ Бщтув) and bul. Vitosha (Витоша). Trains to: **Plovdiv** (2-3hr, 14 per day, 7.10lv), **Varna** (7.5-9hr, 7 per day, 25.20lv), and **Veliko Turnovo** (5-6hr, 8 per day, 16.30lv). **International tickets** available at the Rila Travel Agency. There is a branch at Gurko 5 (Гурко), off pl. Sveta Nedelya (☎02 987 0777; open M-Sa 7am-630pm). Destinations offered include: **Bucharest, ROM** (2 per day, 40lv); **Budapest, HUN** via Bucharest (1 per day, 105lv; sleeper car only); **İstanbul, TUR** (1 per day, 60lv; sleeping car only); **Thessaloniki, GCE** (2 per day, 30lv).

Buses: Private buses leave from either the **Central Bus Station** (Централна Автоара; Tsentralna Avtogara; ☎090 021 000; www.centralnaavtogara.bg); Maria Luiza 100 (Мария Луиза), down the street from the train station; or the parking lot across from the train station, the Trafik-Market (☎02 981 2979). Though pricier than trains, private buses are faster and more comfortable. **International** bus companies are across the train station entrance; **domestic** buses are more likely to leave from the bus station.

Public Transportation: Trams, trolleys, and **buses** cost 0.70lv per ride, 6lv for 10 rides, day pass 3lv, or 37lv for a month pass. Buy tickets from the driver (single rides only; 0.10lv extra) or at kiosks with "билети" (bileti) signs in the window; exact change only. Validate in the machines on board to avoid a 5lv fine. If you put your backpack on a seat, you may be required to buy a 2nd ticket, or pay a 7lv fine for an "unticketed passenger." This policy is observed much more stringently on routes to and from the airport. All transportation runs daily 5:00-11:30pm; after 9pm, service becomes less frequent.

Taxis: Some travelers relate horror stories about local taxi companies, but **OK Supertrans** (ОК Съпертранс; ☎02 973 2121) remains a reliable option. Always make sure the company's name and phone number are on the side of the car. Many drivers don't speak English, so learn to pronounce Bulgarian names for places and directions.0.50-0.60lv per km; slightly more expensive 10pm-6am.

ORIENTATION AND PRACTICAL INFORMATION

Sv. Nedelya Church is the locus of the city center, **ploshtad Sveta Nedelya** (Света Неделя). **Bulevard Knyaginya Mariya Luiza** (Княгиня Мария Луиза) connects pl. Sveta Nedelya to the train station. Trams #1 and 7 run from the train station through pl. Sveta Nedelya to **bul. Vitosha** (Витоша), one of the main thoroughfares, full of bars, restaurants, and Western clothing stores. Bul. Vitosha links pl. Sveta Nedelya to **ploshtad Bulgaria** and the concrete **Natsionalen Dvorets na Kulturata,** which serves as a large marketplace (Национален Дворец на Културата; NDK, National Palace of Culture). Historic **bulevard Tsar Osvoboditel** (Цар Освободител; Tsar the Liberator) runs by the Presidency building on the north, starting at ploshtad Nezavisimost (Незавbcbмост). Bul. Tsar Osvoboditel leads

to the former **Royal Palace,** the **Parliament building,** and **Sofia University.** The free *Insider's Guide* and *In Your Pocket Sofia* are indispensable. *The Program* (Програмата; Programata; www.programata.bg) is a weekly **city guide.** The print version is in Bulgarian; look online for the English version.

Tourist Office: Tourist Information Center, pl. Sveta Nedelya 1 (☎02 933 5826; www.bulgariatravel.org), next to Happy Bar and Grill. The English-speaking staff answers questions about Sofia and Bulgaria and hand out free **maps** and English-language publications about Sofia. Open M-F 9am-6pm.

Embassies: Australia, Trakiya 37 (Тракия; ☎02 946 1334; email austcon@mail.orbitel.bg). Consulate only. **Canada,** Moskovska 9 (Московска; ☎02 969 9710; consular@canada-bg.org). **UK,** Moskovska 9 (☎02 933 9222; www.british-embassy.bg). Open M-Th 9am-noon and 2-4pm, F 9am-noon. **Ireland,** Bacho Kiro 26-28 (Бао Киро; ☎02 985 3425; info@embassyofireland.org). Citizens of **New Zealand** should contact the UK embassy. **US,** Kozyak 16 (Козяк; ☎02937 5100; www.usembassy.bg). Open M-F 9am-noon, 2-4pm.

Medical Services: State-owned hospitals offer free 24hr. emergency aid to all; note that all staff may not speak English. **Pirogiv Hospital,** bul. Totieben 21, **emergency** ☎150, is open 24 hours. For dog bites or emergency tetanus shots (10lv), go to **First City Hospital** (Първа Градска Болница; Purva Gradska Bolnitsa), bul. Patriarkh Evtimiy 37 (Патриарх Евтимий; ☎02 988 3631).

Telephones: Telephone Center, General Gurko 4 (Гурко; ☎02 980 1010). Go right out of the post office on Vasil Levski (Васил Левски) and then left on Gurko. Local calls 0.09lv, international calls from 0.36lv per min. Internet 0.80lv per hr., 1.40lv per 2hr., 2lv per 3hr. Fastest connections in town.

Internet: Stargate, Pozitano 20 (Позитано), near Hostel Sofia. 1.20lv per hr. Open 24hr. Cash Only. Also at **Telephone Center** (see above).

Post Office: General Gurko 6 (Гурко; ☎02 949 6446; www.bgpost.bg). **Poste Restante** at window #12 in the 2nd hall; look for the signs in English. **Money transfers** at window #4 in the 1st hall. Open M-Sa 7am-8:30pm, Su 8am-1pm. **Postal Code:** 1000.

ACCOMMODATIONS

Hotels are rarely worth the exorbitant prices; hostels or private rooms are a much better option for a budget traveler.

Hostel Mostel, Makedonia Blvd 2 (Бул. Македония 2), occupies a past guesthouse meant for travelers on their way to Greece. Keeps a mediterranean feel; the gigantic common space downstairs draws travelers looking for a place to relax and mingle in the city. (☎0889 22 32 96; www.hostelmostel.com. Breakfast and dinner included. Free Internet and Wi-Fi. Reception 24hr. Kitchen. 6-8 bed dorms 20-26lv. Cash only). ❶

Hostel Sofia, Pozitano 16 (Позитано), has a great location and a homey feel. Though sociable, it's still quieter than some of the city's other, more party-oriented lodgings. From pl. Sv. Nedelya, walk down bul. Vitosha and turn right on Pozitano. (☎989 8582; www.hostelsofia.com. Common room with TV and DVD. Breakfast included. Laundry 5lv. Free Internet. Reception 24hr. 8-11 bed dorms 20lv for 1st and 2nd nights, 18lv thereafter. 10% discount per night Nov.-May. Cash only.) ❶

Art-Hostel, Angel Kunchev 21A (Ангел Кънев), draws an international crowd that stays up late at the bar and garden. From pl. Sv. Nedelya, walk down Vitosha and turn left on William Gladstone. Walk 2 blocks and turn right on Angel Kunchev. (☎987 0545; www.art-hostel.com. Kitchen, bar, and tea room. Breakfast included. Laundry 5lv. Free Internet. Reception 24hr. 10-bed dorms €10. Singles €26; doubles €36. Cash only.) ❶

FOOD

Cheap meals are a dime a dozen in Sofia. Across bul. Mariya Luiza from the TSUM shopping mall are two markets, the Women's Bazaar, and Central Hall.

Divaka, ul. William Gladstone 54, serves huge salads and sizzling veggie and meat dishes. Facing McDonald's in pl. Slaveikov, take the left side-street and continue right at the fork. Don't be afraid to share a table with strangers. (☎02 989 9543. English menu available. Beer 1.10lv. Entrees 6-12lv. Open 24hr. Cash only.) ❷

The Veggie Home, 10 Patriarch Evtimii, serves delectable vegetarian food, like falafels, specialty salads, and more, at fantastic prices in a cosy atmosphere. Delivery available as well. (☎02 981 56 77; entrees 4-12 lv; open daily 11am-midnight). ❶

Pri Yafata, ul. Solunska 28, serves traditional Bulgarian fare in a setting meant to take you back to the 19th century. The staff is friendly at this local fave. (☎02 980 17 27, entrees 6-12 lv. Free Wi-Fi. Open daily 10am-midnight, MC/V.) ❷

SIGHTS

BOYANA CHURCH (БОЯНСКА ЦЪРКВА; BOYANSKA TSURKVA). In the woods of the Boyana suburb, this UNESCO World Heritage site boasts some of the most striking religious artwork in the country. The tiny red-brick church houses two layers of religious murals painted by unknown medieval masters.

The church is in a little park with such a striking sense of tranquility that Queen Eleanor broke royal protocol and asked to be buried on the grounds. *(☎02 959 0939; www.boyanachurch.org. Ul Boyansko ezero 1-3, ул. Боянско езеро. Take bus #64 from Khladilnika (Хладилника), minibus #21, or a taxi from the center for 4-5lv. Open daily Nov.-Mar. 9am-5pm; Apr.-Oct. 9:30am-5:30pm; free M after 3pm. 10lv, students 5lv. Tour in English 5lv. English pamphlet 5lv. Combined ticket with the National History Museum 12lv.)*

NATIONAL HISTORY MUSEUM. The fortress-like Natural History Museum (Национален Историески Музей; Natsionalen Istoricheski Muzey) is communist architecture at its most imposing. The museum traces the evolution of Bulgarian culture from prehistoric times to the present; a period which spans roughly eight millennia. *(Residence Boyana, Palace 1. Take minibus #21, trolley #2, or bus #63 or 111 from the center, or tram #5 from Makedonya to Boyana. Even then, it's about a 15min. walk; it's best to hire a taxi, 5lv. ☎02 955 76 04; www.historymuseum.org. Open daily Nov.-Mar. 9am-5:30pm, Apr.-Oct. 9:30am-5:30pm. 10lv, students 5lv. Combined ticket with Boyana Church 12lv. English language tours 20lv, book in advance. Cash only.)*

CHURCHES. The huge gold- and green-domed Byzantine-style **St. Alexander Nevsky Cathedral** (Св. Александър Невски; Sv. Aleksandur Nevski), with architecture inspired by ancient Byzantium, dominates the Sofia skyline. It is the grandest edifice in all of Sofia, and houses over 400 frescoes by Russian and Bulgarian artists, illuminated only by candlelight. In a separate entrance to the left of the church, the crypt contains the **National Art Gallery's** spectacular array of painted icons and religious artifacts. *(In the center of pl. Aleksandur Nevski. English-language captions. Open daily 7am-7pm; crypt open Tu-Su 10am-6pm. Daily Liturgy 5pm, mass Sun 9:30am. Cathedral free. Crypt 4lv, students 2lv.)* From the main entrance of **St. Nicholas Russian Church** (Св. Николай; Sv. Nikolai) a path veering to the left leads to the crypt, the last resting place of the popular former head of the Russian church in Bulgaria, Archibishop Serafim. The Russian Orthodox come here to write prayers. *(On bul. Tsar Osvoboditel near pl. Sveta Nedelya. Open daily 8am-6:30pm. Liturgy W-Su 9am, W also 5pm, Sa also 5:30pm. Free.)*

SYNAGOGUE OF SOFIA (СОФИЙСКА СИНАГОГА; SOFIYSKA SINAGOGA). Sofia's only synagogue boasts a vast interior decorated with a star-spangled dome, marble columns, and the largest chandelier in Bulgaria. Recent renovations repaired damage done by a stray Allied bomb from WWII, which miraculously didn't explode. A museum upstairs outlines the history of Jews in Bulgaria. *(Ekzarkh Yosif 16, ☎02 983 5085; www.sophiasynagogue.com. English-language captions. Open daily 8:30am-4pm. Services daily 8am, also Sa 10am. Museum open M-F 8:30am-12:30pm, 1-3:30pm. Museum 2lv, students 1lv. Synagogue 2lv/1lv; includes English-language pamphlet.)*

BANYA BOSHI MOSQUE (БАНЯ БОШИ). Constructed in 1576 during the Ottoman occupation, this mosque escaped the fate suffered by the 26 other mosques in Sofia, which were shut down or destroyed during the communist era. The red brick building with minaret still intact has a sumptuous interior of red- and blue- floral tiled walls and a ceiling inscribed in golden calligraphy. *(Across from Central Hall, on Mariya Luiza (Мария Луиза). Open daily 3:30am-11:30pm. Entrance is free, but tourists are only allowed to enter only when prayer is not underway. Shoe removal required at door. Females must wear the provided hooded robe to cover knees, shoulders, and head.)*

ENTERTAINMENT AND NIGHTLIFE

Sofia's week-long **Beer Fest** takes place in late summer. Each night, different bands light up the crowd with traditional Bulgarian music, as well as pop and jazz. Fish and chips (1.50lv) complement beer (0.80lv). The event takes place in Alexander Batemberg. Theaters line **Rakovski** (аковски). From the town center, a left on Rakovski leads to the **National Opera and Ballet** (Национална

Опера и Балет; Natsionalna Opera i Balet), Vrabcha 1. (Враба; ☎02 987 1366; www.operasofia.com. Performances most days 6 or 7pm. Box office open M-F 9:30am-6:30pm, Sa-Su 10:30-6pm. Closed July-Aug. Tickets 5-15lv. Cash only.)

At night, Sofians fill the outdoor bars along **bulevard Vitosha** (Витоша) and the cafes around the **National Palace of Culture.** For the younger set, nightlife centers on **Sofia University,** at the intersection of **Vasil Levski** (Васил Левски) and **Tsar Osvoboditel** (Цар Освободител). **Apartment,** Neofit Rilski 68 (Неофит илски), is a relaxed hangout that achieves effortless artsiness. A DJ table remains open to daring guests. (☎08 86 65 50 93; www.apartment.org. Foreign films most nights at 10:30pm. Free Wi-Fi. Fresh squeezed juice 3lv. Beer from 1.50lv. No cover. Open daily noon-2am. Cash only.)

DAYTRIPS FROM SOFIA

RILA MONASTERY. Holy Ivan of Rila built the 10th-century Rila Monastery (илски Манастир; Rilski Manastir)—the largest and most famous in Bulgaria—as a refuge from worldly temptation. The **Nativity Church** is decorated with 1200 brilliantly colored frescoes. Modest clothing is necessary, especially for women. *(Monastery open daily approximately 7am-9pm.)* The **museum** in the monastery houses an intricate **wooden cross** that took 12 years to carve (with a needle) and left its creator, the monk Rafail, blind. *(Open daily 8:15am-4pm. 8lv, students 4lv. English lecture 20lv.)* Signs throughout the monastery show **hiking routes** in nearby **Rila National Park; Cyrillic/English maps** of the paths (7lv) are sold in the Manastirski Padarutsi (Манастирски Падаръци) shop.

Inquire at room #170 in the monastery about staying in a spartan but heated **monastic cell ❶**. *(☎070 54 22 08. Reception open from 2pm. 2-3 beds per room, single-sex. Doors lock at 10pm; ring the bell after that. Rooms 20lv.)* Behind the monastery are restaurants, cafes, and a mini-market. To get to the monastery, take **tram** #5 from pl. Sv. Nedelya to Ovcha Kupel Station (Ова Къпел) and take the bus to Rila Town (2hr., 6:25am and 10:20am, 5lv). From there, catch a **bus** to the monastery (30min., 3 per day, 1.50lv). A bus goes back from Rila to Sofia at 3pm (7lv).

PLOVDIV (ПЛОВДИВ)

Churches, galleries, Roman ruins, and 19th-century National Revival structures pack picturesque Plovdiv (pop. 350,000). The city's historical and cultural treasures are concentrated among the **Trimontium** (three hills) of **Stariya Grad** (Стария Град; Old Town). To reach the 2nd-century **Roman amphitheater** (Антиен Театър; Antichen Teatur) from pl. Tsentralen (Централен), take a right off Knyaz Aleksandr (Княз Александр) on Suborna (Съборна), then go right up the steps along Mitropolit Paisii. Built in the 2nd century at the order of Trajan the Roman Emperor, this marble masterpiece is the oldest Roman building in Bulgaria; it now hosts concerts and shows, such as the **Verdi Opera Festival** in June and July (☎032 63 23 48; 8-20lv) and the **Festival of the Arts** in late summer. (Amphitheater open daily 9am-7pm. 3lv.) At the end of ul. Suborna on Dr. Chomakov 2, the **Museum of Ethnography** (Етнографски Музей; Etnografski Muzey) exhibits artifacts like *kukerski maski* (masks used to scare away evil spirits). Concerts also take place in its courtyard throughout the summer. *(☎032 62 42 61. Open Tu, Th, Sa-Su 9am-noon and 2-5pm; W and F 2-5pm. 4lv, students 2lv. Cash only.)*

Plovdiv Guesthouse ❶, ul. Suborna 20, (Съборна), is worth staying at for its incredible breakfast alone. This beautiful guesthouse is a nice place to relax and is much calmer than most hostels. (☎032 622 432; www.plovdivguest.com. Dorms 20 lv. Laundry 2lv. Free Wi-Fi, Internet 2lv/hour. Cash only.) **Trains** run to Burgas (4-6hr., 7 per day, 13.40lv), Sofia (2-3hr., 15 per day, 8.10lv), and Varna (6.5-9hr., 5 per day, 17.40lv). Buy international tickets at Rila, bul. Khristo Botev

31A. (Христо Ботев. ☎032 64 31 20. Open M-F 8am-7:30pm, Sa 8am-2pm. Cash only.) **Buses** to Sofia (2hr., 1-3 per hr., 10lv) leave from the Yug (г) station, bul. Khristo Botev 47 (☎032 62 69 37), opposite the train station. **Internet** is available at Speed, Knyaz Aleksandr 12. (Княз Александр. 1lv per hr. Open 24hr.) The municipal **tourist information center** is at pl. Tsentralen 1. (☎032 65 67 94; tic@plovdiv.bg. Open daily 9am-7pm.) **Postal Code:** 4000.

DAYTRIP FROM PLOVDIV: BACHKOVO MONASTERY. In the Rodopi mountains 28km south of Plovdiv lies Bulgaria's second-largest monastery, Bachkovo Monastery *(Баковски Манастир; Bachkovski Manastir; ☎03 32 72 77)*. Built in 1083, the main church holds the **Icon of the Virgin Mary and Child** (Икона Света Богородица; Ikona Sveta Bogoroditsa), which is said to have miraculous healing powers. *(Open daily 8am-8pm. Free.)* **Hiking paths** lie uphill from the monastery; don't miss the **waterfall.** The Smolyan **bus** *(30min., 1-2 per hr., 4lv)* leaves from platform #1 at the Rodolpi station in Plovdiv; ask to go to Bachkovo. *(Kassa open 5:30am-8pm.)*

VELIKO TURNOVO (ВЕЛИКО ТЪРНОВО) ☎062

Veliko Turnovo (pop. 66,000), on the steep hills above the Yantra River, has watched over Bulgaria for more than 5000 years. The city's residents led the 1185 national uprising against Byzantine rule, and its revolutionaries wrote the country's first constitution in 1879. The ruins of the **Tsarevets** (Царевец), a fortress that was the main citadel and Second Bulgarian Kingdom's center of power (1185-1393), span a hillside right outside the city. (Open daily 8am-7pm, kassa closes 6pm. 4lv, students 2lv.) Once inside, climb uphill to the aptly named **Church of the Ascension** (Църква Възнесениегосподне; Tsurkva Vuzneseniyegospodne), which was restored in honor of the country's 1300th anniversary in 1981. For a foray into modern Bulgarian history, go to the **National Revival Museum** (Музей на Възраждането; Muzey na Vuzrazhdaneto; ☎062 62 98 21. Open M and W-Su 9am-6pm. 4lv, students 2lv.)

Hostel Mostel ❶, 10 Iordan Indjeto Str. (Ул. Йордан Инджето), is just a few steps from Tsarevets fortress and one of the best in the country. Breakfast is free, as is dinner, Internet, Wi-Fi and pickup from the station. The exceptional owners attract social travelers from all over. (☎897 859 359; www.hostelmostel.com. Dorms 20lv. Double 60lv. Cash only). Recommended by almost everyone in town, **Shtastlivetsa ❶,** 79 Stefan Stambalov, has an incredibly extensive menu serving massive portions of good food for low prices. (☎062 600 656, open daily 11am-11pm. Entrees 6lv-22lv. AmEx/MC/V.)

ETAP sends **buses** to Sofia (3hr., 13 per day, 40lv) and Varna (3hr., 10 per day, 40lv). Bus #10 leaves from Veliko Turnovo's main square for Gorna Oryakhovitsa (Горна Оряховица), the train station. **Trains** go to Burgas (6-7hr., 7 per day, 11lv), Sofia (5.5-7hr., 8 per day, 14.80lv), and Varna (4-7hr., 4 per day, 12.50lv). **Navigator Internet Club** (Yfdbufnjh), Nezavisimost 3 (Независимост), is open 24hr. (☎062 67 02 88. 1lv per hr. Cash only.) The **tourist office** is at bul. Hristo Botev 5. (Христо Ботев. ☎062 62 21 48. Open M-F 9am-6pm.) **Postal Code:** 5000.

VARNA (ВАРНА) ☎052

Expansive beaches, a Mediterranean climate, open-air nightlife, and frequent summer festivals draw visitors to Varna (pop. 312,000) on Bulgaria's Black Sea coast. Roman ruins and ancient gold artifacts are the chief attractions for those looking for sightseeing. From the train station, go right on bul. Primorski (Приморски) to reach the town's **beaches** and **seaside gardens.** The **Archaeological Museum** (Археологически Музей; Arheologicheski Muzey), bul. Maria Luiza 41, (in the park) has the **world's oldest gold artifacts,** dating from over 6000 years ago. (☎052 681 011; www.amvarna.com. Open Tu-Sa 10am-5pm. 10lv, students 2lv.) Cultural events include the **International Jazz Festival** in August (☎052 65 91 67; www.vsjf.com) and the **Varna Summer Festival** (☎052 60 35 04 or ☎052 65 91 59; www.varnasummerfest.org), a music, theater, and folk festival in late June-late July. For schedules and tickets, check the Festival and Congress Center, bul. Primorski; also the location of **Love is Folly,** a September film festival. (☎052 60 84 45. Box office open daily 10am-9pm.)

Gregory's Backpackers Hostel ❶, str. Fenix 82, in Zvezditsa 10km from Varna, has a bar, a fantastic movie selection, and free Wi-Fi; infamous for its fun-loving staff and guests. (☎052 37 99 09; www.hostelvarna.com. Free pickup 7am-10pm. Breakfast included. Kitchen available. Laundry 12lv. Internet 1.40lv per hr. Reserve ahead. Open Apr.-Oct. Dorms 22lv. Double 56lv. Camping in the backyard 10lv. Cash only.) Nightlife centers on the beach in **Primorski Park,** which features a strip of outdoor discos along Krabrezhna Aleya. A popular place along the strip is **Brilliantine,** ul. Slivnitsa 9 (☎052 614 346, open daily 9am-2am. Beer from 3lv, bottle of wine from 16lv).

Near the commercial harbor, **trains** depart for Plovdiv (6-7hr.,4 per day, 16.70lv), Veliko Turnovo (4 hr., 3 per day, 14.80lv), and Sofia (7.5-9.5hr., 7 per day, 25lv). **Buses** leave from ul. Vladislav Varenchik (Владислав Вареник). ETAP buses go to Sofia (6hr., 11 per day, 22lv) via Veliko Turnovo (3hr., 11lv) while Victory buses go to Burgas (2hr., 2 per day, 12lv). The **tourist office,** pl. Musala, will provide free brochures and help with accommodations and car rental (☎052 654 518, open M-F 9am-5pm). **Astra Tour,** near track #6 at the train station, finds private singles for 16-24lv and doubles for 25-40lv. (☎052 60 58 61; astratur@yahoo.com. Open May-Oct. daily 6am-9pm.) Access the **Internet** at Bitex.com, str. Zamenhof 1, 3rd fl., off pl. Nezavisimost. (☎052 63 17 65. 1.50lv per hr., 2lv 9am-2pm, 3lv midnight-8am. Open 24hr.) **Postal Code:** 9000.

CROATIA (HRVATSKA)

With attractions ranging from sun-drenched beaches and cliffs around Dubrovnik to the dense forests around Plitvice, Croatia's wonders and natural beauty never cease to amaze. Unfortunately, like so many treasures of great value, Croatia has been fought over time and time again, often finding itself in the middle of dangerous political divides and deadly ethnic tensions. It was only after the devastating 1991-1995 ethnic war that Croatia achieved full independence for the first time in 800 years. And while some marked-off areas still contain landmines, the biggest threats currently facing travelers to Croatia are the ever-rising prices and tides of tourists who clog the ferryways. Despite it all, this friendly and upbeat country demands to be seen at any cost.

DISCOVER CROATIA: SUGGESTED ITINERARIES

THREE DAYS: Spend a day poking around the bizarre and fascinating architecture of **Split** (p. 224) before ferrying down the coast to the beach paradise of **Brac** island (1 day; p. 226). Aftre recovering from your sunburn, make your way to former war-zone—and what some consider Eastern Europe's most beautiful city—**Dubrovnik** (1 day; p. 226).

BEST OF CROATIA, ONE WEEK. Enjoy the East-meets-West feel of **Zagreb** (1 day; p. 215) then head to busy **Rijeka** (1 day; p. 220). Relax in gorgeous **Krk Town** (1 day; p. 221) before stopping in **Zadar** (1 day; p. 224). Have a few hours' stop in gorgeous **Plitvice National Park** (p. 219), before **Brac** (1 day; p. 226). End your journey in **Dubrovnik** (2 days; p. 226).

ESSENTIALS

FACTS AND FIGURES

OFFICIAL NAME: Republic of Croatia.
CAPITAL: Zagreb.
MAJOR CITIES: Dubrovnik, Split.
POPULATION: 4,493,000.
TIME ZONE: GMT +1.
LANGUAGE: Croatian.
RELIGIONS: Roman Catholic (88%).
POPULATION GROWTH RATE: -0.04%.

WHEN TO GO

Croatia's best weather lasts from May to September, and crowds typically show up along the Adriatic coast in July and August. If you go in late August or September, you'll find fewer crowds, lower prices, and an abundance of seasonal fruits such as figs and grapes. Late autumn is wine season. While April and October may be too cool for camping, the weather is usually nice along the coast, and private rooms are plentiful and inexpensive. You can swim in the Adriatic sea from mid-June to late September.

DOCUMENTS AND FORMALITIES

EMBASSIES AND CONSULATES. All foreign embassies in Croatia are located in Zagreb (p. 215). Embassies abroad include: **Australia,** 14 Jindalee Crescent, O'Malley ACT 2606, Canberra (☎262 866 988; croemb@dynamite.com.au); **Canada,** 229 Chapel Street, Ottawa, ON K1N 7Y6 (☎613-562-7820; www.croatiaemb.net); **Ireland,** Adelaide Chambers, Peter St., Dublin 8 (☎01 476 7181; http://ie.mfa.hr); **New Zealand,** 291 Lincoln Rd., Henderson (☎9 836 5581; cro-consulate@xtra.co.nz), mail to: P.O. Box 83-200, Edmonton, Auckland; **UK,** 21 Conway Street, London, W1P 5HL. (☎020 7387 2022; http://croatia.embassy-homepage.com); **US,** 2343 Massachusetts Ave., NW, Washington, D.C. 20008 (☎202-588-5899; http://www.croatiaemb.org).

VISA AND ENTRY INFORMATION. Citizens of Australia, Canada, the EU, New Zealand, and the US do not need a visa for stays of up to 90 days. Visas cost US$26 (single-entry), US$33 (double-entry), and US$52 (multiple-entry). Apply for a **visa** at your nearest Croatian embassy or consulate at least one month before planned arrival. All visitors must **register with the police** within 48hr. of arrival—hotels, campsites, and accommodation agencies should automatically register you, but those staying with friends or in private rooms must do so themselves to avoid fines or expulsion. To register, go to room 103 on the 2nd floor of the **central police station** at Petrinjska 30, Zagreb. (☎456 3623, after hours 456 3111. Bring your passport and use form #14. Open M-F 8am-4pm.) Police may check foreigners' passports at any time and place. There is no entry fee. The easiest way of entering or exiting Croatia is by bus or train between Zagreb and a neighboring capital.

ENTRANCE REQUIREMENTS.

Passport: Required for all travelers.

Visa: see above.

Letter of Invitation: Not required for citizens of Australia, Canada, the EU, Ireland, New Zealand, the UK, and the US.

Inoculations: Recommended up-to-date DTaP (diphtheria, tetanus, and pertussis), Hepatitis A, Hepatitis B, MMR, polio booster, rabies, and typhoid.

Work Permit: Required for all foreigners planning to work in Croatia.

International Driving Permit: Required for those driving in Croatia.

TOURIST SERVICES AND MONEY

EMERGENCY	**Ambulance:** ☎94. **Fire:** ☎93. **Police:** ☎92. **General Emergency:** ☎112.

TOURIST OFFICES. Even the small towns have a branch of the resourceful **state-run tourist board** *(turistička zajednica)*. Their staff speak English and give out maps and booklets. **Private agencies** *(turistička* or *putnička agencija)*, such as **Atlas,** handle private accommodations. Local outfits are cheaper.

MONEY. The Croatian unit of currency is the **kuna (kn),** plural **kunas.** One kuna is equal to 100 **lipa. Inflation** hovers around 2.22%, so prices should stay relatively constant in the near future. Croatia became an official candidate for European Union membership in 2004, with admission projected for the end of the decade; travelers may occasionally find prices listed in euro (€), especially in heavily touristed areas like the Istrian Peninsula. Most tourist offices, hostels, and transportation stations exchange currency and traveler's checks; banks have the best rates. Some establishments charge a 1.5% commission to exchange **traveler's checks.** Most banks give MasterCard and Visa cash advances, and **credit cards** (namely American Express, MasterCard, and Visa) are widely accepted. Common **banks** include Zagrebačka Banka, Privredna Banka, and Splitska Banka. **ATMs** are everywhere. **Currency exchange** rate:

CROATIAN KUNA (KN)		
	AUS$1 = 4.27KN	1KN = AUS$0.24
	CDN$1 = 4.47KN	1KN = CDN$0.23
	EUR€1 = 7.20KN	1KN = EUR€0.14
	NZ$1 = 3.34KN	1KN = NZ$0.30
	UK£1 = 9.11KN	1KN = UK£0.11
	US$1 = 4.66KN	1KN = US$0.22

Expect to spend 300-470kn per day. Travel in Croatia is becoming more costly, with the bare minimum for accommodations, food, and transport costing 240kn. **Tipping** is not expected, although it is appropriate to round up when paying; some establishments will do it for you—check your change. Fancy restaurants often add a hefty service charge. **Bargaining** is reserved for informal transactions, such as hiring a boat for a day or renting a private room directly from an owner. Posted prices should usually be followed.

HEALTH AND SAFETY

Medical facilities in Croatia include public hospitals and clinics and private medical practitioners and pharmacies. Due to disparities in funding, private clinics and pharmacies tend to be better supplied. Both public and private facilities may demand cash payment for services; most do not accept credit cards.

Pharmacies sell Western products, including tampons and condoms *(prezervativi)*. UK citizens receive free medical care with a valid passport. **Tap water** is chlorinated; though it is relatively safe, it may cause mild abdominal discomfort. Croatia's **crime rate** is relatively low, but travelers should beware of pickpockets. Travel to the former conflict areas of **Slavonia** and **Krajina** remains dangerous due to **unexploded landmines,** which are not expected to be cleared until at least 2010. In 2005, a tourist was injured by a mine on the island of Vis, which inspectors had previously declared safe. Do not stray from known safe areas, and consult www.hcr.hr for detailed info. **Women** should go out in public with a companion to ward off unwanted attention. Although incidents of **hate crime** in Croatia are rare, **minority** travelers may experience stares. **Disabled** travelers should contact Savez Organizacija Invalida Hrvatske (☎1 4829 394), in Zagreb, as cobblestones and a lack of ramps render it a more difficult area. Although **homosexuality** is slowly becoming accepted, discretion is recommended.

TRANSPORTATION

BY PLANE AND TRAIN. Croatia Airlines flies to and from many cities, including Frankfurt, London, Paris, Zagreb, Dubrovnik, and Split. Budget airlines like **Ryanair** fly to Zadar and Pula. **Trains** (www.hznet.hr) are slow everywhere and nonexistent south of Split. Trains run to Zagreb from Budapest, HUN; Ljubljana, SLV; Venice, ITA; and Vienna, AUT; and continue on to other Croatian destinations. *Odlazak* means departures, *Odolazak* means arrivals.

BY BUS. Buses run faster and farther than trains at comparable or slightly higher prices and are the easiest way to get to many destinations, especially south of Split. Major companies include **Croatiabus** (www.croatiabus.hr), **Autotrans Croatia** (www.autotrans.hr), and **Austobusni Promet Varaždin** (www.ap.hr). The website of the main bus terminal in Zagreb (Austobusni Kolodvor Zagreb; www.akz.hr) provides info on timetables, although not in English.

BY BOAT. The **Jadrolinija** ferry company (www.jadrolinija.hr) sails the Rijeka-Split-Dubrovnik route, stopping at islands on the way. Ferries also go to Ancona, ITA from Split and Zadar and to Bari, ITA from Split and Dubrovnik. Though slower than buses and trains, ferries are more comfortable. A basic ticket grants only a place on the deck. Buy tickets in advance.

BY BIKE AND BY THUMB. Moped and **bike** rentals are an option in resort or urban areas. Hitchhiking is not recommended by *Let's Go.*

KEEPING IN TOUCH

PHONE CODES	**Country code:** 385. **International dialing** prefix: 00. For more info on how to place international calls, see **Inside Back Cover.**

EMAIL AND INTERNET. Most towns, no matter how small, have at least one Internet cafe. Connections on the islands are slower and less reliable than those on the mainland. Internet usage typically costs 20kn per hour.

TELEPHONE. Post offices usually have **public phones;** pay after you talk. All phones on the street require a country-specific **phone card** *(telekarta)*, sold at newsstands and post offices for 15-100kn. A Global Card allows calls for as cheap as 0.99kn per minute and provides the best international rates. For the international operator, dial ☎901. Croatia has two **mobile** phone networks, T-Mobile and VIP. If you bring or buy a phone compatible with the GSM 900/1800 network, SIM cards are widely available. Pressing the "L" button will cause the phone instructions to switch into English.

MAIL. The Croatian Postal Service is reliable. Mail from the US arrives within a week. Post office workers are generally helpful to foreigners. A postcard or letter to the US typically costs 3.50kn. *Avionski* and *zrakoplovom* both mean "airmail." Mail addressed to **Poste Restante** will be held for up to 30 days at the receiving post office. Address envelopes: First name LAST NAME, POSTE RESTANTE, Pt. Republike 28, post office address, Postal Code, city, CROATIA.

LANGUAGE. Croats speak **Croatian,** a South Slavic language written in Latin script. The language has fairly recently become differentiated from Serbo-Croatian. Only a few expressions differ from Serbian, but be careful not to use the Serbian phrases in Croatia—you'll make few friends. **German** and **Italian** are common second languages among the adult population. Most Croatians under 30 will speak and understand some English.

ACCOMMODATIONS AND CAMPING

CROATIA	❶	❷	❸	❹	❺
ACCOMMODATIONS	under 150kn	150-250Kn	251-350Kn	351-450Kn	over 450Kn

For info on Croatia's youth **hostels** (in Krk, Pula, Punat, Veli Losinj, Zadar, and Zagreb), contact the **Croatian Youth Hostel Association,** Savska 5/1, 10000 Zagreb (☎1 482 9294; www.hfhs.hr/home.php?lang=en). **Hotels** in Croatia can be expensive. If you opt for a hotel, call a few days ahead, especially in the summer along the coast. Those looking to stay in either hostels or hotels in the July-August tourist season should book early, as rooms fill up quickly. Apart from hostels, **private rooms** are the major budget option for accommodations. Look for signs, especially near transportation stations. English is rarely spoken by room owners. All accommodations are subject to a tourist tax of 5-10kn (one reason the police require foreigners to register). Croatia is also one of the top camping destinations in Europe—33% of travelers stay in **campgrounds.** Facilities are usually comfortable, and prices are among the cheapest along the Mediterranean. Camping outside of designated areas is illegal. For more info, contact the Croatian Camping Union, 8. Marta 1, P.O. Box 143, HR-52440 Poreč (☎52 45 13 24; www.camping.hr).

FOOD AND DRINK

CROATIA	❶	❷	❸	❹	❺
FOOD	under 30Kn	30-60Kn	61-90Kn	91-150Kn	over 150Kn

Croatian cuisine is defined by the country's varied geography. In continental Croatia in and to the east of Zagreb, heavy meals featuring meat and creamy sauces dominate. *Purica s mlincima* (turkey with pasta) is the regional dish near Zagreb. Also popular are *burek*, a layered pie made with meat or cheese, and the spicy Slavonian *kulen*, considered one of the world's best **sausages.** *Paticada* (slow-cooked meat) is also excellent. On the coast, textures and flavors change with the presence of **seafood** and Italian influence. Don't miss out on *lignje* (squid) or *Dalmatinski prut* (Dalmatian smoked ham). The **oysters** from Ston Bay have received a number of awards at international competitions. If your budget does not allow for such treats, *slane sardele* (salted sardines) are a tasty substitute. **Vegetarian** and **kosher** eating options can be diffcult to find in Croatia, albeit not impossible. In both cases, pizza and bakeries are safe and ubiquitous options. Mix red wine with tap water to make the popular *bevanda*, and white wine with carbonated water to get *gemišt*. Karlovačko and Ožujsko are the two most popular beers.

HOLIDAYS AND FESTIVALS

Holidays: New Year's Day (Jan. 1); Epiphany (Jan. 6); Easter Sunday and Monday Easter Sunday (Apr. 12-13, 2009; Apr. 4-5, 2010); May Day (May 1); Anti-Fascist Struggle Day (June 22); National Thanksgiving Day (Aug. 5); Independence Day (Oct. 8).

Festivals: In June, Zagreb holds the catch-all festival **Cest Is D'Best** ("The Streets are the Best"). Open-air concerts and theatrical performances make the **Dubrovnik Summer Festival** (Dubrovački Ljetni; from early July to late Aug.) the event of the summer. Zagreb's **International Puppet Festival** is from late Aug. to early Sept.

BEYOND TOURISM

Coalition for Work With Psychotrauma and Peace, M. Drzica 12, 32000 Vukovar, Croatia (☎385 32 45 09 91; www.cwwpp.org). Work in education and health care related to long-term conflict stress in Croatia.

Learning Enterprises, 2227 20th St. #304, NW, Washington, D.C. 20009, USA (☎001 20 23 09 34 53; www.learningenterprises.org). 6-week summer programs place 1st-time English teachers in rural Croatia, Hungary, Romania, and Slovakia. No-fee program includes orientation and room and board with a host family.

ZAGREB ☎01

More than the stopover en route to the Adriatic coast, Croatia's capital and largest city (pop. 779,000) possesses the grand architecture, wide boulevards, and sprawling parks of a major European city. In the old city center, smartly-dressed *Zagrebčani* outnumber visitors as both enjoy the sights and smells of outdoor cafes, flower markets, and fresh produce stalls. With its welcoming, English-speaking inhabitants, growing economy, impressive cultural offerings, and unspoiled surroundings, Zagreb is an enjoyable, laid-back, and worthwhile alternative to the sun-splattered coast.

TRANSPORTATION

Trains: Leave the **Glavni Kolodvor,** Trg Kralja Tomislava 12 (☎060 333 444, international info ☎378 2583; www.hznet.hr; AmEx/MC/V) for: **Ljubljana, SLN** (2 hr., 8 per day; 91kn, round-trip 235kn); **Rijeka** (4-6 hr., 3 per day, 105kn); **Split** (6-9 hr., 5 per day, 90kn); **Budapest, HUN** (7hr., 3 per day, 225kn); **Venice, ITA** (6hr., 1 per day, 320kn); **Vienna, AUT** (6hr., 2 per day, 355kn); **Zurich, SWI** (14hr., 1 per day, 647kn). There are no trains to Dubrovnik. To get to the station, take tram 2, 4, 6, 9, or 13 to the Glavni

Kolodvor stop. From the main square *(Trg Jelačića)*, take either tram 6 (toward Sopot) or tram 13 (toward Tržnica Gorica); the train station is two stops away. There are printed timetables (though not in English) for both domestic and international trains. The information booths' English-speaking staff is an extremely helpful resource.

Trams: The tram network, **Zagreb Electric Tram,** or **ZET,** covers most of the city and is the most convenient form of local transportation (☎01 356 1555; www.zet.hr). Trams are denoted by number (1-17) and run from 4am-11:20pm. **Night trams** run from 11:45pm-3:45am, but are unreliable. Buy tickets at newsstands or post offices (8kn) or from the driver (10kn). Day pass 25kn, under 6 free. Upon boarding, punch tickets in the boxes near the tram doors to avoid fines.

Buses: Leaving from the **Autobusni Kolodvor,** Avenija M. Držića bb (☎060 313 333; information and reservations from abroad ☎01 611 2789; www.akz.hr, click on "Vozni red" to search the timetables). Buses are often more efficient than trains. Trams 2, 5, 6, 7, and 8 stop at Autobusni Kolovdor. From Trg Jelačića, take tram 6 in the direction of Sopot; the bus station is six stops away. The ticketing area is upstairs. Timetables are displayed on screen in the main ticketing area and are also available online. Buses leave for: **Dubrovnik** (11hr., 8 per day, 125-253kn); **Plitvice** (2hr., 12 per day, 72-80kn); **Pula** (4hr., 17 per day, 162-216kn); **Rijeka** (3hr., 23 per day, 126-166kn); **Split** (7-9hr.; 38 per day, multiple buses every hour between 6am-midnight; 171-198kn); **Varaždin** (1.¾hr., 25 per day, 69kn); **Frankfurt, GER** (15hr., 2 per day, 660kn); **Ljubljana, SLN** (2½hr., 1 per day, 90kn); **Vienna, AUT** (7hr., 2 per day, 227kn). Large backpacks cost 7kn extra. The ticketing hall is upstairs; #14 is an information window staffed with English-speaking attendants. **Luggage storage** can be found in the *garderoba* up the staircase to the right of the ticketing hall (24hr.; 1.20kn per hr., 2.30kn per hr. for bags over 33 lbs.) **Restrooms** (3kn) are also upstairs from the ticketing hall in the waiting lounge.

PRACTICAL INFORMATION

Tourist Offices: The **Tourist Information Center (TIC),** Trg Jelačića 11, conveniently located in the main square, is a great resource for any traveler. There you'll find helpful attendants, free maps, and pamphlets the *Zagreb Info A-Z, Zagreb in Your Pocket,* and *Events and Performances.* Open M-F 8:30am-8pm, Sa 9am-5pm, Su and holidays 10am-2pm. (☎01 481 4051; www.zagreb-touristinfo.hr.) They also sell a **Zagreb Card** which covers all bus and tram rides and provides discounts in restaurants and museums (☎01 481 4052; www.zagrebcard.fivestars.hr. Valid for 1 or 3 days; 60/90kn.)

Internet: Get online at **Sublink,** Ulica Nikole Tesle (Teslina) 12 (☎481 9993; www.sublink.hr), where you'll find a friendly and welcoming English-speaking staff, cheap and fast connections, and printing and scanning services. (Open M-Sa 9am-10pm, Su and holidays 3pm-10pm. 0.245kn per min., 14.70kn per hr. 10% discount with ISIC/EURO under 26 card.) **Postal Code:** 10000.

ACCOMMODATIONS

Fulir Hostel, (☎01 483 0882; www.fulir-hostel.com), right outside of Zagreb's main square. Laidback hostel steps away from many of Zagreb's sights and nightlife. Communal kitchen. Linens and lockers included. Free Internet; Wi-Fi available. Mar.-Sept. 130kn per night, Oct.-Feb. 100kn per night. ❶

Ravnice Youth Hostel, 1 Ravnice 38d (☎01 233 2325; www.ravnice-youth-hostel.hr). Bright, clean, colorful rooms. Take tram 11 or 12 from Trg Jelačica, 4 from the train station, or 7 from the bus station to Dubrava or Dubec. The unmarked Ravnice stop is two stops past football stadium "Dinamo." Turn right on Ravnice St. and the hostel is on the second street on the left; look for a white sign marked "hostel." Laundry 50kn.

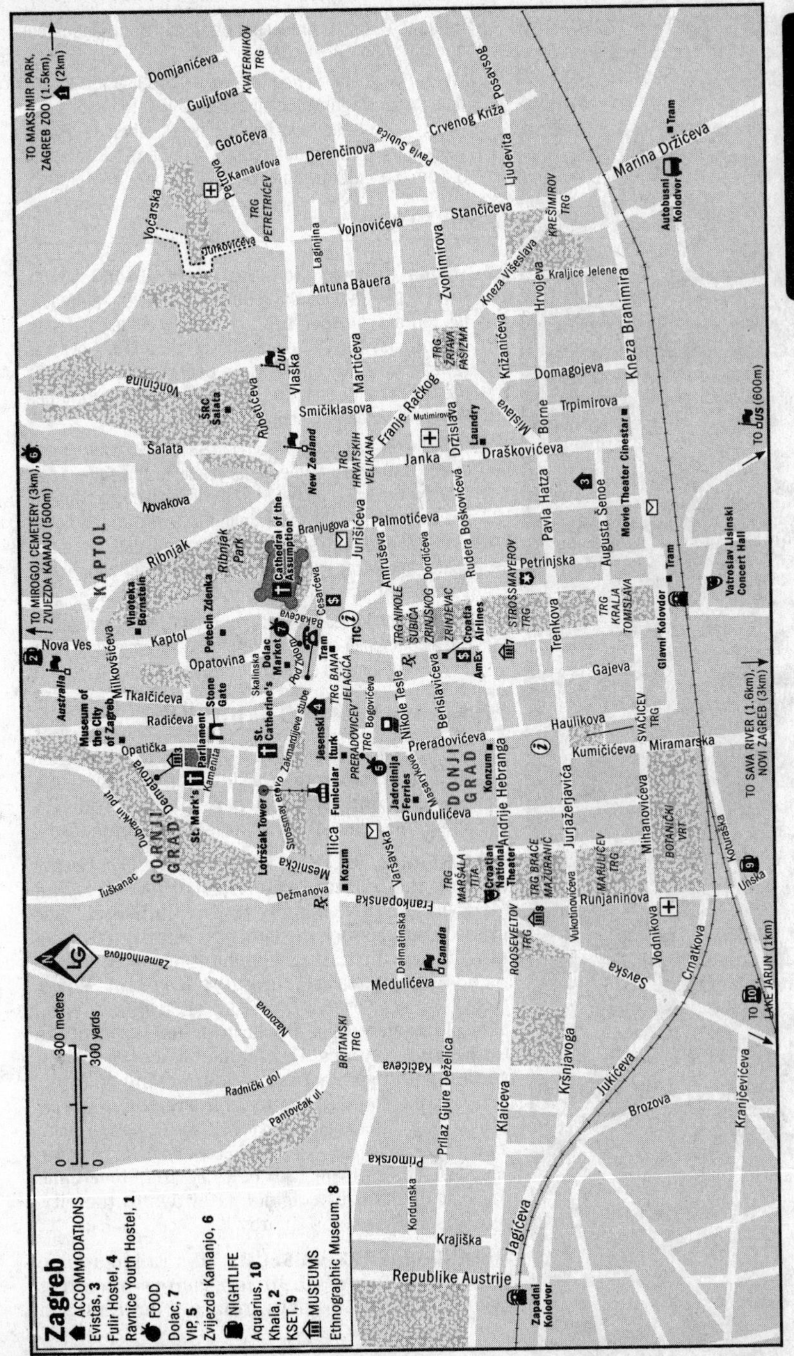
Zagreb
ACCOMMODATIONS
Evistas, 3
Fulir Hostel, 4
Ravnice Youth Hostel, 1
FOOD
Dolac, 7
VIP, 5
Zvijezda Kamanjo, 6
NIGHTLIFE
Aquarius, 10
Khala, 2
KSET, 9
MUSEUMS
Ethnographic Museum, 8
300 meters
300 yards
TO MAKSIMIR PARK, ZAGREB ZOO (1.5km), (2km)
TO MIROGOJ CEMETERY (3km), ZVIJEZDA KAMAJO (500m)
TO SAVA RIVER (1.6km), NOVI ZAGREB (3km)
TO LAKE JARUN (1km)
TO US (600m)
KAPTOL
GORNJI GRAD
DONJI GRAD
Cathedral of the Assumption
St. Mark's
Parliament
St. Catherine's
Stone Gate
Lotrščak Tower
Funicular
Museum of the City of Zagreb
Dolac Market
Jesenski
Jadrolinija Ferries
Croatian National Theater
Vatroslav Lisinski Concert Hall
Glavni Kolodvor
Autobusni Kolodvor
Zapadni Kolodvor
Movie Theater Cinestar
Croatia Airlines
AmEx
Konzum
Kozum
Laundry
Tram
TIC
SRC Šalata
Vinoteka Bornstein
Petecin Zdenka
Ribnjak Park
Australia
New Zealand
Canada
UK
TRG BANA JELAČIĆA
TRG KRALJA TOMISLAVA
TRG NIKOLE ŠUBIĆA ZRINJSKOG
TRG ŽRTAVA FAŠIZMA
TRG HRVATSKIH VELIKANA
TRG PETRETRIĆEV
KVATERNIKOV TRG
KREŠIMIROV TRG
STROSSMAYEROV TRG
TRG MARŠALA TITA
TRG BRAĆE MAŽURANIĆ
MARULIĆEV TRG
SVAČIĆEV TRG
ROOSEVELTOV TRG
BRITANSKI TRG
PRERADOVIĆEV TRG
BOTANIČKI VRT
Ilica
Vlaška
Jurišićeva
Praška
Gajeva
Kaptol
Tkalčićeva
Radićeva
Opatička
Opatovina
Ribnjak
Šalata
Novakova
Domjanićeva
Guljufova
Gotočeva
Petrova
Derenčinova
Vojnovićeva
Antuna Bauera
Martićeva
Smičiklasova
Franje Račkog
Zvonimirova
Stančičeva
Marina Držićeva
Kneza Branimira
Domagojeva
Trpimirova
Draškovićeva
Palmotićeva
Amruševa
Petrinjska
Augusta Šenoe
Pavla Hatza
Trenkova
Haulikova
Kumičićeva
Miramarska
Mihanovićeva
Preradovićeva
Gundulićeva
Andrije Hebranga
Jurjaževića
Masarykova
Varšavska
Frankopanska
Dežmanova
Mesnička
Runjaninova
Vodnikova
Savska
Crnatkova
Medulićeva
Kačićeva
Prilaz Gjure Deželića
Klaićeva
Kršnjavoga
Jukićeva
Brozova
Kranjčevićeva
Primorska
Kordunska
Krajiška
Republike Austrije
Jagićeva
Zamenhoffova
Nazorova
Radnički dol
Pantovčak ul.
Tuškanac
Demetrova
Dubravkin put
Strossmayerovo šetalište
Nova Ves
Milkovšićeva
Vončinina
Ribetićeva
Berislavićeva
Nikole Tesle
Bogovićeva
Pod Zidom
Bakačeva
Cesarčeva
Branjugova
Janka Držislava
Rudera Boškovićeva
Dordićeva
Hrvojeva
Kraljice Jelene
Kneza Višeslava
Križanićeva
Mislava
Borne
Ljudevita Posavskog
Crvenog Križa
Pavla Šubića
Kamaufova
Laginjina
Voćarska
Dalmatinska
Vukotinovićeva
Unska
Koturaška

ARNIVORE'S DILEMMA

Meat lovers are spoiled for choice n Croatia. Although Croatian cuisine varies by region, with strong talian influences in Istria and an emphasis on seafood in Dalmatia, visitors to Zagreb and its surrounding areas will find most Croatian menus dominated by meat—from amb to pork, from duck to veal. Here, *Let's Go* offers some guidance for your own meaty meal:

Pršut - Home-cured ham from he coastal highlands of Istria and Dalmatia. Try as a prelude to your meal—*pršut* served with cheese is a popular starter.

Sarma - Another starter, this dish consists of pickled cabbage leaves stuffed with minced meat.

Čevapčići - A grilled dish made with minced beef and spices, often served with onions and a paprika and eggplant relish *(ajvar)*.

Miješano meso - This mixed grill entrée includes a pork or veal cutlet, minced lamb or beef, and sausage, with *ajvar* on the side.

Pašticada - Served on special occasions, this Dalmatian dish consists of a beef joint cooked in wine, vinegar, and prunes.

Gulaš - Croatia's lighter take on Hungarian goulash, this stew may be made with beef, lamb, or veal.

Internet 16kn per hr. Reception 9am-10pm. Check-out noon. Dorms 125kn. Cash only. ❶

Evistas, Augusta Senoe 28 (☎01 483 9554), right outside of Zagreb's main square. When hostels are full, try a private room at this hotel, albeit less centrally located. Call ahead. Open M-F 9am-1:30pm and 3-8pm, Sa 9:30am-5pm. ❸

FOOD

Zvijezda Kamanjo, Nova Ves 84 (☎01 466 7171). Serves up traditional Croatian cuisine on a peaceful, private outdoor patio. From Trg Jelačića, follow Kaptol past the Cathedral until it turns into Nova Ves (20min. walk). Try the delicious beef stew *(Dalmatinska pašticada)* with gnocchi—a Croatian specialty. Entrees 35-80kn. Open daily noon-11pm. ❶

VIP, Trg P. Preradovića 5 (☎01 483 0089; www.vipres-toran.com). Head to the western side of the square and look for the white umbrellas. This lively bistro and internet cafe offers delectable Italian fare next to the flower market. Enjoy drinks *al fresco* with the locals, or pizza, pasta, and lasagna from 35-60kn. Internet connection 15kn per hr. Open 8am-11pm. ❶

Dolac, behind Trg Jelačića in *Gornji Grad* (Upper Town), along Pod Zidom. Open-air market selling a variety of goods. Open M-Sa 6am-3pm, Su 6am-1pm. Cash only. ❶

SIGHTS AND MUSEUMS

Zagreb is best seen on foot. Climb any of the streets extending north from Trg Jelačića to reach the historical Gornji Grad *(Upper Town)*. From Trg Jelačića, take Ilica, then turn right on Tomićeva.

CATHEDRAL OF THE ASSUMPTION. The Cathedral of the Assumption *(Katredrala Marijina Uznesnja)*, known simply as "the Cathedral," has graced Zagreb since the late 11th century. It's stunning during the day and enchanting when illuminated at night. *(Kaptol 1. Open daily 10am-5pm. Services M-Sa 7, 8, 9am, 6pm; Su 7, 8, 9, 10, 11:30am, 6pm. Free.)* **Mirogoj Cemetery,** Croatia's largest, just north of the Cathedral, contains 12 cream-colored towers, a garden with cypress trees, and touching epitaphs that tell the troubled history of the regions. *(Take the 106 "Mirogoj" bus from Kaptol in front of the Cathedral; 8min., 4 per hr. Open M-F 6am-8pm, Su 7:30am-6pm. No photography. Free)*. Built in the 13th century, the **Stone Gate,** the last of the four original gateways to the city, remains a site to stop to pray.

ETHNOGRAPHIC MUSEUM. The Ethnographic Museum *(Etnografski Muzej)*, across the street from the Mimara, displays artifacts from 19th- and

20th-century Croatian voyages to Africa, Asia, and South America, as well as a mix of traditional costumes, etchings and architecture native to Croatia. *(Mažuranicev Trg 14. ☎01 482 6220; www.etnografski-muzej.hr. English-language captions. Open Tu-Th 10am-6pm, F-Su 10am-1pm. 15kn, students and over 60 10kn; Th free. Cash only.)*

LOTRŠČAK TOWER. The 13th-century Lotrščak Tower, part of the original city wall, offers excited visitors the most breathtaking panoramic views of Zagreb. *(At the corner of Strossmayerovo and Dverce, right at the top of the funicular. Open Mar.-Nov. Tu-Su 11am-7pm. 10kn, students 5kn.)*

FESTIVALS AND NIGHTLIFE

In June, Zagreb's streets burst into life with performances for the annual Zagreb street festival **Cest is d'Best** ("The Streets are the Best,") and the **Eurokaz International Festival of New Theatre** (late June-early July). The huge **International Puppet Festival** occurs from late August to early September. In mid-December, locals flock to the colorful **Christmas Fair** for presents and holiday cheer

With a variety of clubs at **Lake Jarun** and many relaxed sidewalk cafes and bars lining lovely **Tkalčićeva,** Zagreb has an exceptional nightlife scene.

Aquarius, Mateja Ljubeka bb (☎01 364 0231. www.aquarius.hr), on Lake Jarun. Take tram #17 to Srednjaci, the third unmarked stop after Studenski dom S. Radic. Cross the street; once at the lake, turn left and continue along the boardwalk; Aquarius is the last building. Dance and swim at this lakeside cafe/club, Zagreb's hottest nightspot, with a diverse crowd and great music selection. Cafe open daily 9am-9pm. Club open M-F and Su 10pm-4am, Sa 10pm-6am. Cover 30-40kn. Cash only.

KSET, Unska 3 (☎01 612 9999). For tastes that veer toward the alternative, join the locals flocking to edgy KSET for an eclectic mix of music,which, depending on the night, ranges from jazz to punk to electronic. Open M-F 8-11:45pm, Sa 9pm-3am.

Khala, Nova Ves 17 (☎01 486 0241), is a chic but surprisingly affordable wine bar and peaceful lounge that morphs into a house music hotspot on the weekends. Open M-Th 8am-1am, F-Su 8am-4am. Cash only.

PLITVICE LAKES NATIONAL PARK

Though it's a trek from either Zagreb or Zadar, **Plitvice Lakes National Park** *(Nacionalni Park Plitvička Jezera)* is definitely worth the transportation hassle. Some 300 sq. km of forested hills, dappled with 16 lakes and hundreds of waterfalls, Croatia's oldest and largest national park is one of the country's most spectacular sights. Declared a national park in 1949, Plitvice was added to the UNESCO World Heritage list in 1979 for the unique evolution of its lakes and waterfalls, which formed through the interaction of water and petrified vegetation and continue to evolve as the water moves along new paths. There are eight main trails around the lake (lettered A-K), all of varying difficulties.

WATCH YOUR STEP. The takeover of Plitvice Lakes National Park by the Serbs in 1991 marked the beginning of Croatia's bloody war for independence. Throughout the 1991-95 conflict, the Serbs holding the area planted landmines in the ground. Both the park's premises and surrounding area have been officially cleared of mines, and the last mine-related accident dates back to 2002. However, do not stray from the trail for any reason.

Free **shuttles** drive around the lakes (3 per hr.), and a **boat** crosses Jezero Kozjak, the largest lake (2-3 per hr., 9:30am-6:30pm). At the main entrance, local women sell delicious **strudels,** bread-cakes stuffed with cheese, spinach, nuts, apples, peaches, or cherries (15kn). If you want to enjoy the peace of the lakes by yourself, go in the early morning or the late afternoon and avoid the shortest trails. Most tourists circulate around the four lower lakes *(Donja Jezera)* to get a shot of Plitvice's famous 78m waterfall, **Veliki Slap.**

Buses run to: Rijeka (3hr., 1 per day, 120kn); Split (3hr., 7 per day, 150kn); Zadar (2hr., 6 per day, 72kn); Zagreb (2hr., 9 per day, 70kn). Most bus drivers let passengers off at the park's main entrance. **Tourist offices** offer maps and exchange currency for a 1.5% commission at each of the three entrances. (☎023 751 026; www.np-plitvicka-jezera.hr. Open daily 7am-10pm. Park open daily July-Aug. 7am-8pm; May-June 7am-7pm; Apr.-Oct. 110kn, students 55kn; Nov.-Mar. 70kn/40kn. Tour guide 700kn, min. 4hr. for groups only. MC/V.) To get to the main info center from the bus stop, walk toward the pedestrian overpass; crossing the road can be dangerous.

NORTHERN COAST

Croatia's northern coast is surrounded by cold, crystal-clear waters; covered in wild forests and low coastal hills. Part of Italy until WWII, this region mixes Italian culture with Croatian sensibilities.

RIJEKA ☎051

Life moves at a fast pace in the bustling port city of Rijeka (pop. 144,000), a major transportation center that also serves as a base for island-hopping in the Kvarner Gulf. Though less idyllic than neighboring Opatija, Rijeka's dynamism and historical attractions make it a worthwhile stop.

TRANPORTATION AND PRACTICAL INFORMATION. The **bus** station, Trg Žabica 1, is located on the waterfront at the end of Krešimirova. (☎051 302 010. Open daily 5:30am-9:30pm.) Buses run to: Dubrovnik (12hr., 4 per day, 427kn); Krk Town (1½hr., 10-16 per day, 54kn); Pula (2.5hr, every hr., 91kn); Split (8hr., 12 per day, 236kn); Zagreb (2½hr., every hr., 140kn). To get to Korzo from the bus station, walk away from the water and turn right on Trpimirova. Cross the street to Jadranski trg and continue straight onto Korzo. The **tourist information center (TIC),** Korzo 33, has **maps** of Rijeka's main sights. (☎051 335 882; www.tz-rijeka.hr. Open mid-June to mid-Sept. M-Sa 8am-8pm, Su and holidays 8am-2pm; mid-Sept. to mid-June M-Sa 8am-8pm.) Rijeka's tourist board turns Korzo, the city's main street, into a **Wi-Fi** hotspot in the summer.

ORIENTATION AND SIGHTS. Daily life in Rijeka centers around **Korzo,** a wide pedestrian avenue with an abundance of stores and outdoor cafes. A stroll along Korzo takes you past the yellow **City Tower** *(Gradski toranj)*, which served as the main gate to the city when it was a Roman settlement. Behind the City Tower and through **Trg Ivana Koblera** is the **Roman Gate** *(Stara vrata)*, the oldest monument in Rijeka; through the arch are excavations with ancient Roman artifacts. Built in the 13th-century, the iconic **Trsat fortress** stands on a hill high above the city and offers unparalleled views of the city center and harbor. To reach Trsat, visitors can follow the footsteps of centuries of pilgrims by climbing the 16th-century *Petar Kružić* 538-step stairway, beginning at Titov trg on Križanićeva or hop on bus #1 or 1a.

ACCOMMODATIONS AND FOOD. Inexpensive accommodations in the city center are scarce, and no agencies officially book private rooms. **Youth**

Hostel Rijeka ❶, Šetalište XIII divizije 23, in a renovated villa overlooking the sea, has immaculate rooms and a friendly, helpful staff. From the bus station, walk to the waterfront and take the #2 bus toward Pećine Plumbum; the hostel is across the street from the fifth stop. (☎051 406 420; www.hfhs.hr. Breakfast included. Internet 5kn per 15min. Reception 24hr. Dorms €15.50; singles €28.40; doubles €18.90. HI non-members 10kn extra per night.) Those willing to pay a little extra opt for **Hotel Continental ❸**, a beautiful building along the river, a 2min. walk from the city center. The simply furnished rooms rest inside the grand exterior. (☎051 372 008; www.jadran-hoteli.hr. Breakfast included. Singles 397kn; doubles 469kn.)

A modern take on the traditional Croatian *konoba* (in coastal towns, a small inn or cellar), **Konoba Nebuloza ❷**, Titov trg 2b, serves up regional specialties like *žgvacet* (lamb stew) at affordable prices in an intimate dining space across from the stairway to Trsat. (☎051 372 294. Entrees 35-75kn. Open M-Sa 11am-midnight.) For a cheap meal along the waterfront, the meat dishes at **Mornar ❶**, Riva Boduli 5a, will satisfy hungry carnivores (☎051 313 257. Entrees 15-45kn. Open M-F 7am-6pm, Sa-Su 7am-3pm.) Enjoy a pastry or ice cream on the terrace at **Cont ❶**, Šetalište A. Kačića Miošića 1, in the Hotel Continental. (☎051 372 154; www.cont.hr. Pastries and cakes 8-13kn. Open daily 7am-10pm.)

ENTERTAINMENT AND NIGHTLIFE. Opened in 1885, the **Croatian National Theatre Ivan Zajc,** Uljarska 1, hosts performances during Rijeka's **Summer Nights Festival,** June and July. (☎051 355 900; www.hnk-zajc.hr.) A popular daytime café-bar **El Rio,** Jadranski trg 4c, comes to life when a young and hard-partying crowd flocks here for karaoke and dancing at night; DJs spin on the weekends. (☎051 214 428. Open M-W 7am-1am, Th-Sa 7am-5am, Su 9am-1am.) On the waterfront, catch up with Rijeka's most beautiful trendsetters under mood lighting in the Zen-inspired **Opium Buddha Bar,** Riva 12a. (☎051 336 397. Open M-W 7am-3am, Th-Su 7am-5am).

KRK TOWN ON KRK ISLAND ☎051

With its sun-drenched beach, narrow cobblestone streets, and mellow bars and cafes, peaceful Krk Town offers island charm without the crowds of nearby Baška. Along Ribarska, a well-preserved Roman **mosaic** among the ruins of thermal baths, Triton is depicted amongst dolphins and sea creatures. Next to the bus station, the travel agency **Autotrans ❶**, Šetalište Sv. Bernardina 3, books private accommodations, exchanges currency,

RUCKUS AND REVELR RIJEKA-STYLE

Though the mention of "Carniva may conjure images of Rio rathe than Rijeka, the Rijeka Carniva Croatia's largest, attracts thou sands of visitors every year with it own brand of glitz and spectacl From mid-January to early Febru ary, Rijeka bursts to life as local and visitors alike don costume and release their inhibitions a masked balls and glitzy parades.

2009 marks the 26th year tha the Carnival has been held i Rijeka, but today's celebration i in fact a modern incarnation of a Carnival tradition that began in th Middle Ages. Like other Carnival held around the world, the Rijek Carnival has Christian origins. Culminating on the day before Lent Shrove Tuesday (Mardis Gras o Fat Tuesday to American), th exuberant revelry serves as on last joyride before 40 days of self restraint leading up to Easter.

Though there's rarely a dul moment during the weeks of fes tivities, the International Parad along Korzo is the Carnival' crowning event. Replete with elab orately-crafted floats and som 10,000 extravagantly-costume revelers, the parade epitomize the chaotic excitement of this por city's unforgettable party.

The City of Rijeka Tourist Asso ciation organizes the carnival an may be contacted at ☎31 57 1 or www.ri-karneval.com.hr.

cashes travelers' checks commission-free, and offers bike rentals. (☎051 222 661; www.turizam.autotrans.hr. Jan.-June and Sept.-Dec. singles 77-88kn, doubles 126-187kn; July-Aug. singles 88-117kn, doubles 144-230kn. Stays under 4 days add 30%. Tourist tax 4.50-7kn. Registration 10kn. Bike rentals 20kn per hour, 90kn per day. Open M-Sa 9am-9pm, Su 9am-1:30pm). A 5min. walk from the bus station, **Autocamp Ježevac ❶,** Plavnička bb, offers tree-shaded campsites near the water. (☎051 21 081; jezevac@zlatni-otok.hr. Mar.-May and Sept.-Oct. 26kn per person, 17kn per tent; June 33/22.50kn; July-Aug. 36/24kn.) Across from the bus station is supermarket **Trgovina Krk ❶,** Šetalište Sv. Bernardina bb. (☎051 222 940. Open M-Sa 7am-9pm, Su 7am-1pm. AmEx/MC/V.) **Konoba Šime ❷**, A. Mahnića 1, literally in the city wall, serves up Adriatic specialties on a harborside terrace (☎222 042. Entrees 45-75kn). The **tourist information center,** Obala hrvatske mornarice bb, provides free **maps** with a tour of Krk and directory of accommodations and restaurants (☎051 220 226; www.tz-krk.hr). The **bus** station is at Šetalište Sv. Bernardina 1 (☎051 221 111). Ticketing open M-F 6:30am-2pm, Sa-Su 7:45am-1:30pm. Buy tickets onboard for later buses. Buses run between Rijeka and Krk Town (1½hr., 10-16 per day; 54kn Rijeka-Krk Town; 50kn Krk Town-Rijeka).

PULA (POLA) ☎52

Pula (pop. 62,000), the largest city on the Istrian Peninsula and a chaotic transportation hub, is Istria's unofficial capital. Home to some of the best-preserved Roman ruins in Croatia, Pula has a giant white-stone **Amphitheater**—the sixth-largest in the world—which is often used as a venue for summer performances. To get there from the bus station, walk straight toward the town center and take a left on Flavijevska. (Open daily 9am-9pm. 40kn, students 20kn.) From the amphitheater, walk down to the water and along the port to reach the **Forum** and **Temple of Augustus** *(Augustov hram)*, finished in the first century AD, and climb the narrow streets of the Old Town to the peaceful **Franciscan Monastery,** the **Fort** (hosting the **Historical Museum of Istria;** 10kn, students 7kn), and the ancient **Roman Theater.** From the Fort and Roman Theater on Castropola, walk down to Sergijevaca to the **Triumphal Arch of the Sergii** *(Slavoluk Sergijevaca)*. To reach the private coves of Pula's beaches, buy a bus ticket (11kn) from newsstands and take bus #1 to the Stoja campground.

Arenaturist ❶, Splitska 1, inside Hotel Riviera, arranges accommodations throughout Pula with no fee, and has a friendly, English-speaking staff. (☎52 529 400; www.arenaturist.hr. Open M-Sa 8am-8pm; also Su 8am-1pm in Aug. Accommodations 46-78kn.) If Pula's beaches are your priority, stay at the **Youth Hostel Pula (HI) ❶,** Zaljev Valsaline 4. Take bus #2 (dir.: Veruda; 11kn) to reach the hostel from the station. Get off at the second stop on Veruda (Veruda 2) and follow the HI sign; take a right off the road and walk straight, then take the first right and walk 3min. down the hill. Trampoline and pedalboats are available. (☎52 391 133; www.hfhs.hr. Breakfast included. Reception daily 8am-10pm. Reservations recommended. Bike rental 20kn per hr., 80kn per day. Internet 10am-10pm; 30kn per hr. Dorms July-Aug. 114kn; Sept. and June 93kn; Oct. and May 88kn; Nov. and Apr. 82kn.Tax 4.50-7kn.) **Pizzeria Jupiter ❶,** Castropola 42 (☎52 214 333), is the perfect spot for a bite before amphitheater concerts. From the bus station, walk past the amphitheater along Amfiteatarska, cross Sv. Ivana, and walk up Castropola, the street on the left. (Pizza 26-40kn. Open M-F 9am-11pm, Sa-Su 1-11pm. AmEx.)

Buses (☎52 502 997), the most convenient option for transport, run from Trg Istarske Brigade to Dubrovnik (15hr., 1 per day, 543kn); Zagreb (4-5hr.,18 per day, 200kn); Trieste, ITA (3hr., 4 per day, 100kn). There are no maps of the bus lines; buses #2 and #3 circle the town center in opposite directions. **Trains** (☎52

541 733) run from Kolodvorska 5 to Ljubljana, SLV (7hr., 2 per day, 138kn), and Zagreb (7hr., 3 per day, 148kn). The **tourist office** is at Forum 3 (☎52 212 987; www.pulainfo.hr. Open M-F 8am-9pm, Sa-Su 9am-9pm). **Postal Code:** 52100.

ROVINJ ☎052

The idyllic fishing port of Rovinj (ro-VEEN; pop. 14,000), with its mild climate and cool waters, was the favorite summer resort of Austro-Hungarian emperors. Today's vacationers still bask in this Mediterranean jewel's unspoiled beauty. Rovinj is the most Italian of Istria's towns: everybody here either is or speaks Italian, and all streets have names in both languages. The 18th-century **Church of Saint Euphemia** *(Crkva Sv. Eufemije)* houses the remains of St. Euphemia, the 15-year-old martyr who was killed by circus lions in AD 304. Inside, stairs lead visitors to the **bell tower** (61m) and panoramic views of this gorgeous, quintessential Mediteranean city and coast. (Open M-Sa 10am-6pm. Services M-Sa 7pm, Su 10:30am and 7pm. Free. Bell tower 10kn.) Rovinj's best beaches are on **St. Catherine's Island** *(Otok Sv. Katarine)* and **Red Island** *(Crveni Otok)*, two small islands right in front of town. To get there, take the ferry from the dock at the center of town to Sv. Katarine (round-trip 30kn) and Crveni Otok (round-trip 30kn). Head through the arch in the main square and follow the signs up Grisia toward the **Church of St. Euphemia** to check out an artists' colony.

Across the street from the bus station is **Natale,** Carducci 4, a travel agency which arranges private rooms in and around the center commission-free. (☎52 813 365; www.rovinj.com. Open July-Aug. daily 7:30am-10pm; Sept.-June M-Sa 7:30am-1:30pm and 4:30pm-7pm, Su 8am-noon. Doubles July-Aug. €76 for 1 night, €57 for 2 nights, €49 for 3 nights, €38 for 4+ nights; Sept.-June €64/€54/€42/€32. Apartments July-Aug. €48-76 for 4+ nights; Sept.-June €42-66 for 4+ nights.) **Camping Polari,** 2.5km east of town, has a supermarket, several bars, and a new pool. To get there, take one of the frequent buses (6min., 9kn) from the station (☎52 801 501. Mar. 26-May 23 and Sept. 6-Oct. 3 €12 per person; May 24-July 4 and Aug. 23-Sept. 5 €16.50 per person; July 5-Aug. 22 €20.80 per person. Residence tax June-Sept. €0.95 per person per day, Mar.-May and Oct. €0.75 per person per day. Notification fee €1.20 per person upon arrival. AmEx/MC/V.) Along the waterfront below the Church of St. Euphemia, **Valentino Bar,** Santa Croce 28, has elegant white tables right on the water. Patrons can also choose to to sit on comfortable smooth-surfaced rock ledges, dangling their legs in the ocean. (☎52 830 683. Open daily 6pm-1am.)

To reach the **tourist office,** walk along the water past the main square to Obala Pina Budicina 12. (☎52 811 566; www.tzgrovinj.hr, www.istria-rovinj.hr. Open daily mid-June to Sept. 8am-9pm; Oct. to mid-June 8am-3pm.) Rovinj is easily explored either on foot or by bike. **Bike rental** (70kn for 24hr., 50kn for half-day or 7hr.) is available at Bike Planet, Trg na Lokvi 3, which also has **maps.** (☎52 813 396. Open M-F 7:30am-12:30pm and 5-8pm, Sa 8:30am-1pm.) With no train station, Rovinj sends **buses** to Pula (45min., 20 per day, 33kn); Zagreb (5-6hr.; M-F 8 per day, Sa-Su 10 per day; 190kn); Ljubljana, SLV (5-6hr., 1 per day, 173kn). The bus station, in the center of town, is large, has an easily decipherable timetable, helpful attendants, and luggage storage. (☎52 811 453. 0.70 lipa per hr. 10kn per day, 15kn per day for items over 30kg.) **Postal Code:** 52210.

DALMATIAN COAST

Touted as the new French Riviera, the Dalmatian Coast offers a seascape of unfathomable beauty set against a backdrop of rugged mountains. With more than 1100 islands, Dalmatia is not only Croatia's largest archipelago, but also the cleanest and clearest waters in the Mediterranean.

ZADAR

☎023

Zadar (pop.71,000), crushed in WWII and the recent Balkan war, is now beautifully rejuvenated. In the *Stari Grad* (Old Town), surprisingly unaffected by earlier conflicts, time has stood still, leaving a wonderful old charm. The area's history is so well-preserved that Roman ruins serve as city benches. On the southern dock of the Old Town, concrete steps into the water form a 70m long **Sea Organ,** which plays notes as the seawater rushes in, producing a continuous and harmonious melody. In the **Roman Forum** in the center of the city, the pre-Romanesque **St. Donat's Church** *(Crkva Sv. Donata)*, a rare circular church, sits atop the ruins of an ancient Roman temple. (Open daily 9am-9pm. 10kn.)

At the entrance to the Old Town, coming from Obala Kralja Tomislava, **Miatours ❷,** on Vrata Sv. Krševana, books private rooms and transportation to nearby islands. (☎023 254 400; www.miatours.hr. Open daily July-Aug. 8am-8pm; Sept.-June 8am-2:30pm. Doubles 200-300kn. AmEx/MC/V.) A short bus ride from the city, in the Borik tourist area, the popular **Youth Hostel Zadar ❶,** Obala Kneza Trpimira 76, offers easy beach access and, apart from private accommodations, is the best bet for a bed on a budget. (☎023 331 145; www.hfhs.hr. Breakfast included. Online reservations recommended. Dorms Jan.-Apr., Nov.-Dec. €10.80-12.80, May and Oct. €12.20-14.20, June *and* Sept. €12.80-12.90, July-Aug €14.90-17.80. HI non-members 10kn extra per night. Tax €0.70-1.) **Trattoria Canzona ❷,** Stomorica 8, is popular with Zadarians of all ages. (☎023 212 081. Entrees 38-70kn. Open M-Sa 10am-11pm, Su noon-11pm. Cash only.)

Buses Ante Starčevića 1 (☎023 211 555) run to: Dubrovnik (8hr., 8 per day, 177-235kn); Pula (7hr., 3 per day, 235-241kn); Rijeka (4½hr., 12 per day, 153-196kn); Split (3½hr., 2 per hr., 77-128kn); Zagreb (3½-5½hr., 2 per hr., 107-140kn); Trieste, ITA (8hr., 1 per day, 182kn). **Luggage storage** is available at the bus station (1.20kn per hr. Open 6am-10pm.) Both the **train** and bus stations are only a 15min. walk from town, but trains are less convenient. To get to the Old Town, go through the pedestrian underpass and on to Zrinsko-Frankopanska to the water. Continue straight on to Obala Krajla Tomislava; the Old Town is on the left. Alternatively, to enter through the *Kopnena Vrata* (Mainland Gate) of the Old Town, take Kralja Dmitra Zvonimira and turn right on Ante Kuzmanića. To reach the main street, **Široka ulica,** walk through the gate and straight along Špire Brusine, then turn right on M. Klaića; Široka ulica is on the left. Buses #2 and 4 run from the bus station to the Old Town. The **tourist office,** M. Klaića bb, in the corner of Narodni trg, has free **maps** and an English-speaking staff. (☎023 316 166; www.visitzadar.net. Open daily July-Aug. 8am-midnight; Jan.-June, Sept.-Dec. 8am-8pm.) **Internet** can be accessed on Varoska 3. (☎023 311 265. 30kn per hr. Open daily 10am-11pm.) **Postal Code:** 23000.

SPLIT

☎021

With its rich history and rocking nightlife, the coastal city of Split (pop. 221,000) is more a cultural center than a beach resort. Here, centuries of history collide with modern life, making the city a fascinating labyrinth of perfectly preserved Roman monuments, medieval streets, and hip bars.

TRANSPORTATION AND PRACTICAL INFORMATION. Buses (☎021 327 777; www.ak-split.hr) run to: Dubrovnik (4hr.; 18 per day; 113-144kn, round-trip 179-228kn); Rijeka (7½-8hr., 12 per day, 246-318kn); Zadar (3hr., approx. 2 per hr., 100kn); Zagreb (5hr., 1-4 per hr., 175-203kn); Ljubljana, SLV (11hr., 1 per day, 307kn.) **Ferries** (☎021 338 333) depart from the dock right across from the bus station to: Supetar, Brač Island (45min., 14 per day, 30kn) and Stari Grad, Hvar Island (1hr., 6-7 per day, 42kn). Ferries also leave the international harbor to Ancona, ITA (10hr., 6 per wk., €40-55) and Bari, ITA (25hr., 4 per week, €45-62). Ask help from the assistants when deciphering the ferry schedules distributed at the **Jadrolinija** office. (Open daily 7am-9pm.) The **tourist information center,** Peristil bb, has a helpful staff and provides **free maps,** including one with a walking tour of Split. (☎021 345 606; www.visitsplit.com. Open Apr.-Oct. M-Sa 8am-9pm, Su/holidays 8am-1pm; Jan.-Mar., Nov.-Dec. M-F 8am-8pm, Sa 8am-1pm.) Those who stay in town for more than three days are entitled to a free **SplitCard** that gets big discounts for sightseeing, shopping, and sleeping. Bring a hostel receipt to any tourist office to prove your stay; otherwise purchase one for 60kn. **Postal Code:** 21000.

PASSPORT CHECK. Keep your passport handy when traveling between Split and Dubrovnik. Most buses pass through Bosnia and Herzegovina and there are passport checkpoints on your way in and out.

ACCOMMODATIONS AND FOOD. The small travel agency **Tour de Croatia,** Obala kneza domagoja 1, books private rooms, exchanges currency, and organizes excursions. (☎023 338 319; www.tourdecroatia.com. Open daily July-Aug. 8am-9pm; Sept.-June 9am-6pm.) At **Al's Place ❶,** Kružićeva 10, the city's first hostel, young-at-heart Al organizes daytrips and offers a wealth of expertise on Split and nearby islands. There are only 12 beds, which are usually full; reserve ahead. (☎098 918 2923; www.hostelsplit.com. Internet 5kn per 20min. Reception open daily 8:30am-1pm, 5pm-8:30pm. June-Aug.130kn; Sept.-May110kn. Cash only.) With its motto of "booze and snooze," **Split Hostel ❶,** Narodni Trg 8, is perfect for revelers. The friendly Australian staff lead nights out on the town. (☎021 342 787; www.splithostel.com. Free lockers and Wi-Fi. Reception daily 8am-10pm. Dorms Jan.-mid-Apr., Oct.-Dec. 110kn; mid-Apr.-May 125kn; June, Sept. 150kn; July-Aug. 180kn. 10% discount for pre-booking. Cash only.) Tucked away along the **narrow streets of the Old Town** are lots of snack bars and restaurants, as well as kiosks with pizzas (slices 8kn) and *bureks* (10kn). **Konoba Varos ❷,** adorned in fishnets, feeds hungry locals and curious visitors with delicious Croatian fare. Entrees 60kn-80kn (☎021 396 138).

SIGHTS. The *Stari Grad* (Old Town), wedged between a mountain range and a palm-lined waterfront, sprawls inside and around the ruins of a luxurious open-air **palace,** where the Roman emperor Diocletian summered when not persecuting Christians. The **basement halls** are near the palace entrance, at the beginning of the waterfront pedestrian street *Obala hrvatskog narodnog preporoda* (known to locals as the 'Riva'); take refuge from the midday heat in the cool relief of underground Split as you lose your way in this haunting maze sprinkled with imperial artifacts. (Open M-Sa 9am-9pm, Su and holidays 9am-6pm. 25kn, students 10kn.) The view of Split from the **bell tower** (60m) of **Cathedral of St. Domnius** *(Katedrala sv. Dujma)* is breathtaking, especially at dusk when you can see the seemingly glowing red rooftops and the Adriatic Sea sprawled around for miles; be sure to watch your head when climbing up. (Cathedral and tower open Mar.-Oct. daily 8am-8pm.10kn each.) The **Meštrović Gallery** *(Galerija Ivana Meštrovića)*, Šetalište Ivana Meštrovića 46, houses the splendid works of Croatia's most celebrated sculptor in a gorgeous villa facing the sea. To get there from the center of town, walk right facing the water, pass the marina, and follow the road up the hill; the gallery is right past the Archaeological Museum. (☎021 340 800. Open May-Sept. Tu-Sa 9am-9pm, Su noon-9pm; Oct.-Apr. Tu-Sa 9am-4pm, Su 10am-3pm. 30kn, students 15kn.)

NIGHTLIFE. Revelers flock to a string of bars and clubs on **Bačvice** beach. From the Old Town, walk past the train and bus stations, cross the bridge over the train tracks, and continue left down the hill toward the beach. Farther along the waterfront, beachside club **O'Hara,** Uvala Zenta 3, blasts techno on two floors and offers potent mixed drinks to its lively clientele. (☎021 364 262. Open M-Th 8pm-3am, F-Sa 8pm-4am.) Hidden on a narrow line of steps in the Old Town, **Puls,** Buvnina 1, is a popular bar with low tables, cushions directly on the pavement, and live music. DJs spin on the weekends. To get there from Obala Riva, enter Trg braće Radič, turn right at the corner snack bar, and continue straight. (Open M-F 7am-midnight, Sa 7am-1am, Su 4pm-midnight.)

BRAČ ISLAND: BOL ☎021

Central Dalmatia's largest island, Brač (pop. 13,000) is an ocean-lover's paradise. Most visitors come to Bol (pop. 1,500) for **Zlatni rat** (Golden horn), a beautiful peninsula of white-pebble beach surrounded by emerald waters and big waves perfect for windsurfing. If you prefer the "deserted island" environment, head for the less explored, calmer beaches to the east of town. The town itself is also pleasant, small enough to cross in 10min. On the eastern tip of Bol, the **Dominican monastery,** built in 1475, displays Tintoretto's altar painting *Madonna with Child* in its museum. (Museum open daily 10am-noon and 5-7pm. 10kn.) **Big Blue Sport,** Podan Glavice 2, offers windsurfing lessons and rentals, mountain bike rentals and excursions, and sea kayak rentals. (Shop ☎021 635 614, Sport Center ☎021 306 222; www.big-blue-sport.hr). There are seven **campgrounds** around Bol, three lie on Bračka cesta, the road into the western part of town. The largest is **Kito ❶**, Bračka cesta bb. (☎021 635 551; kamp_kito@inet.hr. Open May-Sept. €5 per person, tent and tax included.)

The **ferry** from Split docks at Supetar (45min., 14 per day, 30kn), the island's largest town. From there, take a **bus** to Bol (1hr.; 4-8 per day, last bus back to Supetar leaves M-Sa 4:35pm, Su 5:50pm; 35kn). The buses don't always coordinate with the ferries' arrivals; if you don't want to wait, you can take a slightly overpriced **taxi van** to Bol. (35min., 360kn, max. 7 people). Otherwise, enjoy the wait at the beach across the street. To reach Bol's **tourist information office,** Porad bolskih pomoraca bb, walk right from the bus station to the far side of the marina. (☎021 635 638; www.bol.hr. Open daily July-Aug. 8am-10pm; Jan.-June, Sept.-Dec. 8:30am-2pm, 4:30pm-8pm.) **Postal Code:** 21420.

DUBROVNIK ☎020

Lord Byron considered Dubrovnik (du-BROV-nik; pop. 43,800) "the pearl of the Adriatic," and George Bernard Shaw knew it as "Paradise on Earth." Although it's tough to live up to such adulation, a stroll through the torch-lit winding lanes of the *Stari Grad* (Old Town) and a sunset look into the sea from the city walls certainly justify Dubrovnik's reputation as Croatia's top destination.

TRANSPORTATION AND PRACTICAL INFORMATION. Jadrolinija **ferries** (☎020 41 80 00; www.jadrolinija.hr) depart opposite Obala S. Radića 40 for: Korčula (3hr., 5 per week, €10-12); Rijeka (21hr., 2 per week, €29-34); Split (8.5hr., 3 per wk., €14.50-17.50); Bari, ITA (8hr., 6 per week, €40-55). The **Jadrolinija** office is opposite the dock. (Open M, W 7am-11pm; T 8am-11pm; Th-F 8am-8pm; Sa 7am-8pm; Su 8am-2:30pm and 5pm-9pm.) **Buses** (☎020 30 50 70) run from Obala Pape Ivana Pavla II, 44A, to: Rijeka (12hr., 4 per day, 415kn);

Split (4hr., 1 per hr., 132kn); Zagreb (11hr., 9-10 per day, 234kn); Trieste, ITA (15hr., 1 per day, 370kn). There's **luggage storage** at the station (open daily 4:30am-10:30pm; 5kn per bag for 1hr.; after 1hr. 1.50kn per bag per hr).

If, like most budget travelers, you're staying in either Babin Kuk or Lapad, where a number of accommodations are located, a **daypass** will be your best bet for frequent shuttling back and forth from the Old Town. (8kn at kiosks, 10kn on board. Ticket valid for 1hr. after stamped. Daypass 25kn.) To get to the Old Town's central **tourist information office,** Široka 1, from the Pile Gate, walk straight along Placa (Stradun) and turn right on Široka. (☎020 32 35 87; www.tzdubrovnik.hr. Open daily 8am-8pm.) On the same street, **the post office,** Široka 8, has **ATMs** and public telephones; it also offers Western Union services. (☎020 32 34 27. Open M-F 7:30am-9pm, Sa 10am-5pm.) **Postal Code:** 20108.

ACCOMMODATIONS AND FOOD. A private room tends to be the cheapest and most comfortable option for two; arrange one through any of the indistinguishable agencies or bargain with locals at the station (doubles should go for 100-150kn per person). Take bus #6 from *Stari Grad* or #7 from the ferry and bus terminals, get off two stops past the Lapad post office, cross the street, walk uphill on Mostarska, and turn right at Dubravkina to reach **Apartmani Burum ❶**, Dubravkina 16, in Babin Kuk. This popular guesthouse has clean, comfortable rooms and apartments. (☎020 43 54 67; www.burumaccommodation.com. Kitchen available. Free pickup from bus station and rides to Old Town. Apr.-May 100kn; June-Sept. 150-250kn. Cash only.) **Begović Boarding House ❶,** Primorska 17, offers spacious doubles and apartments in a cozy villa. Call ahead and the owner will pick you up. (☎020 43 51 91; www.begovic-boarding-house.com. Private bathrooms. Internet first 30min. free, then 10kn per 30min. Reserve ahead July-Aug. June-Sept. singles 150-200kn; doubles 240-300kn; triples 300-360kn. Oct.-May 100-120kn, 200-240kn, 300-360kn. Cash.)

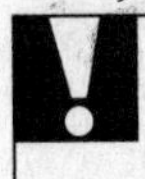

WELCOME! NOW, GET OUT!! Make sure to ask for a receipt when you pay for a private room. Without a receipt, your stay won't be registered, and the accommodation will be illegal.

Harborside favorite **Lokanda Peskarija ❷,** Na Ponti bb, has excellent, affordable seafood. From Placa, walk to the bell tower at the end of the street, turn right on Pred Dvorum, and take the first left out of the city walls. (☎020 32 47 50. Seafood 35-60kn. Open daily 8am-1am.) Exchange books, savor smoothies, and nosh on wraps at **Fresh ❷,** Vetranićeva 4. (Wraps 28kn. Smoothies 20kn. Open daily 10am-2am.) In the center of Old Town, self-service restaurant **Express ❷,** Marojice Kaboge 1, serves up inexpensive, filling meals of pastas, soups, and salads. (☎020 32 39 94. Entrees 25-50kn. Open daily 10am-10pm.)

SIGHTS. The entrance to the 2km limestone **City Walls** *(gradske zidine)* lies just inside the Pile Gate on the left, with a second entrance at the other end of Placa, next to the Old Port. (Open daily 8am-7:30pm. 50kn, students 20kn. Audio tour 40kn.) The baroque **Cathedral of the Assumption of the Virgin Mary** (Katedrala), Kneza Damjana Jude 1, is built on the site of a Romanesque cathedral and a 7th-century Byzantine cathedral. Its resplendent treasury (riznica) houses the "Diapers of Jesus," along with a host of golden reliquaries of St. Blaise. Above the altar, check out Titian's *Assumption of Our Lady.* (Cathedral open daily 8am-7pm; treasury open daily 8am-5pm. Cathedral free, treasury 10kn.) The 19th-century **Serbian Orthodox Church** (Srpska Pravoslavna Crkva) and its **Museum of Icons** (Muzej Ikona), Od Puča 8, together with the small yet intricate

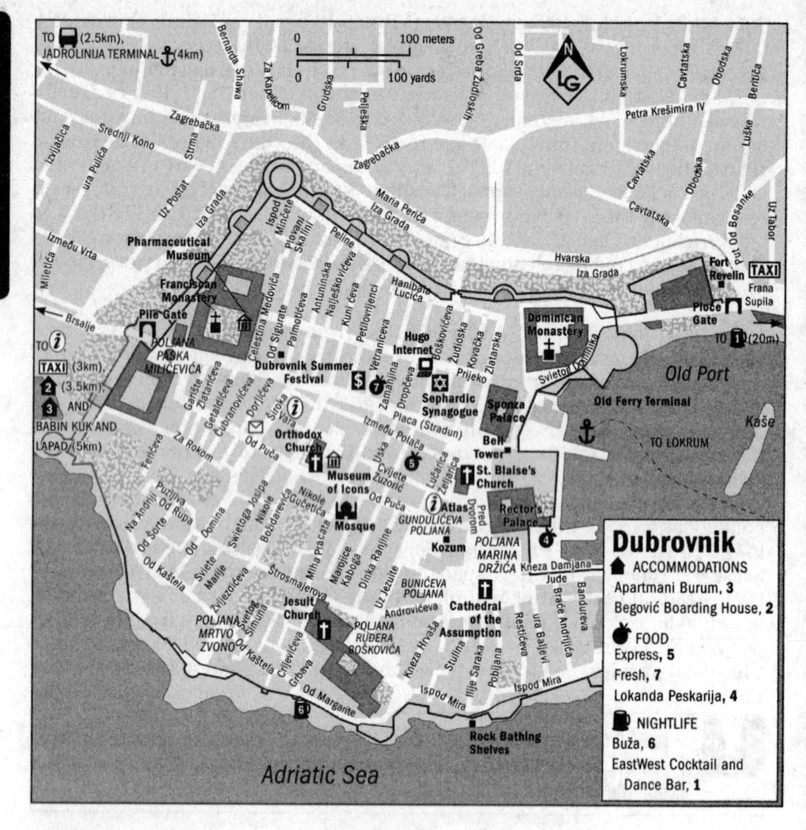

synagogue, Žudioska ulica 5, and **mosque,** Miha Pracata 3, stand as a symbol of Dubrovnik's tolerance. (Museum of Icons ☎020 32 32 83; open M-Sa 9am-2pm; 10kn. Synagogue and Jewish Museum ☎020 32 10 28; open May-Oct. M-F 10am-8pm; 15kn. Mosque open daily 10am-1pm and 8-9pm. Free.) Classical performances are held in many churches during summer.

BEACHES. Outside the fortifications of the Old Town are a number of **rock shelves** popular for sunning and swimming. To reach a beautiful but crowded **pebble beach** from the Placa's end, turn left on Svetog Dominika, bear right after the footbridge, and continue on Frana Supila. Hop on a ferry from the Old Port (daily service 9am-7pm, 10min., 2 per hr., 40kn return) to nearby **Lokrum,** which has great cliff jumping, a botanical garden, and a nude beach on its eastern end. More modest travelers can stroll (fully clothed) through the nature preserve to a smaller section of rock shelves found on the other side of the island.

HOPSCOTCH...KABOOM?! As tempting as it may be to stroll through the hills above Dubrovnik or wander the unpaved paths on Lopud, both may still be laced with **landmines.** Stick to paved paths and beaches.

FESTIVALS AND NIGHTLIFE. Dubrovnik becomes a party scene and cultural mecca from mid-July to late-August during the **Dubrovnik Summer Festival** (Dubrovački Ljetni Festival). The **festival office,** Od Sigurate 1, at the intersection of Placa and Od Sigurate, has schedules and tickets. (☎020 32 61 00; www.dubrovnik-festival.hr. Open daily during the festival 8:30am-9pm. 50-300kn.) By night, crowds gravitate to bars in *Stari Grad* and cafes on *Buničeva Poljana,* where live bands and street performers turn up in summer. From the open-air market, climb the stairs toward the Jesuit church, veer left, and follow the signs marked "Cool Drinks" along Od Margarite to **Buža,** Crijeviceva 9. Outside the city wall, perched on the rocks high above the bright blue Adriatic, this laid-back watering hole is the best place to enjoy spectacular sunsets and a midnight swim. (Beer 30-32kn. Mixed drinks 35kn. Open daily 9am-2am.) At posh **EastWest Cocktail and Dance Bar,** Frana Supila bb, a dressed-to-impress clientele reclines on white leather sofas and plush beds on the beach. (Beer 12-30kn. Mixed drinks 40-100kn. Thai massage 200kn per 30min., 300kn for 1hr. Open daily 8am-4am.)

DAYTRIPS FROM DUBROVNIK: LOPUD ISLAND

Jadrolinija's ferries (50min., June-Aug. 4 per day, round-trip 36kn) run to Lopud and the Elafiti Islands. Purchase tickets at the Jadrolinija office, Obala S. Radića 40, across from the dock (☎41 80 00; www.jadrolinija.hr). Šunj Beach: from the ferry dock, face the water and turn left. Walk along the water for 5min. until you reach Konoba Barbara. Take a left on the walkway and go uphill. Bear right at the fork and follow the path to steps leading to the beach.) Fortress: from the waterfront, turn left at the town museum and follow the signs until you reach it.

In the center of the Elafiti Islands, the island of Lopud boasts one of the Adriatic's most spectacular **beaches.** Unique among the region's beaches because of its fine sand, Šunj Beach *(Plaža Šunj)* stretches along the bay and features warm, shallow water. On the opposite side of the island, the picturesque village of Lopud lies on a bay and is easily traversed in 15min. On the other end of the waterfront, uphill from the cafés and restaurants and past most of the hotels, stands a gazebo with panoramic views of the town and nearby islands. For travelers with lots of energy (and sturdy shoes), a number of **trekking trails** traverse the island; winding through deserted vineyards and olive groves, different trails lead to the ruins of medieval churches with hilltop shrines, fortresses, and monasteries. The **Fortress** *(Kaštio)* has the most breathtaking vista; the **tourist office,** Obala Iva Kuljevana 12, is next to the dock and can provide maps of the island along with directions to Šunj and trekking information. (☎759 086. Open M, W, Sa-Su 8am-1pm and 5pm-7pm; T, Th 8am-3pm).

CZECH REPUBLIC (ČESKÁ REPUBLIKA)

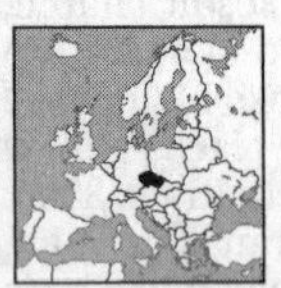

From the days of the Holy Roman Empire to reign of the USSR, the Czech people have stood at a crossroads of international affairs. Unlike many of their neighbors, however, the citizens of this small, landlocked country have rarely resisted as armies marched across their borders, often choosing to protest with words instead of weapons. As a result, Czech towns are among the best-preserved and the most beautiful in Europe. Today, the Czechs face another invasion, as tourists sweep in to savor the magnificent capital and some of the world's best beer.

DISCOVER CZECH REPUBLIC: SUGGESTED ITINERARIES

THREE DAYS. Voyage to the capital, **Prague** (p. 235). Stroll across the **Charles Bridge** to see **Prague Castle,** leave to explore areas like **Josefov.**

ONE WEEK. Keep exploring **Prague** (5 days; p. 235). Relax at the **Petřín Hill Gardens** and visit the impressive **Troja château.** Then head over to **Český Krumlov** (2 days; p. 250) for hiking, biking, and another stunning, ancient castle.

BEST OF CZECH REPUBLIC, THREE WEEKS. Begin in **Prague,** including a daytrip to the **Terezín concentration camp** (p. 247). Spend four days in UNESCO-protected **Český Krumlov** (p. 250) exploring the bike trails and floating down the **Vltava River** in an inner tube. Check out the weird **Revolving Theater** while you're at it. Wrap things up in **Olomouc** (p. 252), stronghold of old-fashioned Moravian culture.

ESSENTIALS

FACTS AND FIGURES

OFFICIAL NAME: Czech Republic.

CAPITAL: Prague.

MAJOR CITIES: Brno, Olomouc, Plzeň.

POPULATION: 10,221,000.

TIME ZONE: GMT +1.

LANGUAGE: Czech.

RELIGIONS: Atheist (49%) Roman Catholic (27%), Protestant (2%).

BEER CONSUMPTION PER CAPITA: 157L per year (largest in the world).

WHEN TO GO

The Czech Republic is the most touristed country in Eastern Europe, and Prague in particular is overrun. To beat the crowds, you may want to avoid the peak season (June-Aug.), though the weather is most pleasant then.

DOCUMENTS AND FORMALITIES

EMBASSIES AND CONSULATES. Foreign embassies are in Prague (p. 238). Czech consulates abroad include: **Australia,** 8 Culoga Circuit, O'Malley, Can-

berra, ACT 2606 (☎02 24 18 11 11; www.mzv.cz/canberra); **Canada,** 251 Cooper St., Ottawa, ON K2P 0G2 (☎613-562-3875; www.mzv.cz/Ottawa); **Ireland,** 57 Northumberland Rd., Ballsbridge, Dublin 4 (☎016 681 135; www.msz.cz/Dublin); **New Zealand,** Level 3, BMW Mini Centre, 11-15 Great South Road and corner of Margot Street, Newmarket, Auckland (☎9 522 8736; auckland@honorary.mvz.cz); **UK,** 6-30 Kensington Palace Gardens, Kensington, London W8 4QY (☎020 73 07 51 80; www.czechcentres.cz/london); **US,** 3900 Spring of Freedom St. NW, Washington, DC 20008 (☎202-274-9100; www.mzv.cz/washington).

ENTRANCE REQUIREMENTS.

Passport: Required of all travelers. Must be valid for 90 days after visiting.

Letter of Invitation: Not required of citizens of Australia, Canada, Ireland, New Zealand, the UK, and the US.

Inoculations: Recommended up-to-date on DTaP (diphtheria, tetanus, and pertussis) hepatitis A, hepatitis B, MMR (measles, mumps, and rubella), polio booster, rabies, and typhoid.

Work Permit: Required of foreigners planning to work in the Czech Republic.

International Driving Permit: Required of foreigners. For EU citizens, a national driver's license is sufficient.

VISA AND ENTRY INFORMATION. Citizens of Australia, Canada, New Zealand, and the US don't need a visa for stays of up to 90 days; UK citizens don't need visas for stays of up to 180 days. Visas for extended stays are available at embassies or consulates. Czech visas not available at the border. Processing is 14 days when the visa is submitted by mail, seven when submitted in person.

TOURIST SERVICES AND MONEY

EMERGENCY **Ambulance:** ☎155. **Fire:** ☎150. **Police:** ☎158.

TOURIST OFFICES. Municipal tourist offices in major cities provide info on sights and events, distribute lists of hostels and hotels, and often book rooms. **Tourist Information Centrum** is state-run. In Prague, these offices are often crowded and may be staffed by disgruntled employees. **CKM,** a national student tourist agency, books hostels and issues ISIC and HI cards. Most bookstores sell a national hiking map collection, *Soubor turistickch map*, with an English key.

MONEY. The Czech unit of currency is the **koruna** (**Kč;** crown), plural **koruny.** The government postponed its slated 2009 conversion to the euro and the earliest likely switch is in 2012. **Inflation** is around 2.6%. Relative to the rest of Eastern Europe, the Czech Republic's inflation rate is quite stable. **Banks** offer good exchange rates; **Komerční banka** is a common bank chain. **ATMs** are everywhere and offer the best exchange rates. **Bargaining** is usually acceptable, especially in heavily touristed areas, though not as much in formal indoor shops.

CZECH (KČ)		
	AUS$1 = 14.45KČ	10KČ = AUS$0.70
	CDN$1 = 15.61KČ	10KČ = CDN$0.64
	EUR€1 = 24.38KČ	10KČ = EUR€0.41
	NZ$1 = 11.76KČ	10KČ = NZ$0.85
	UK£1 = 30.83KČ	10KČ = UK£0.32
	US$1 = 16.59KČ	10KČ = US$0.61

HEALTH AND SAFETY

Medical facilities, especially in Prague, are of high quality, and sometimes employ English-speaking doctors. They often require cash payment, but some may accept credit cards. Travelers are urged to check with their insurance companies to see if they will cover emergency medical expenses. **Pharmacies** include *Lekarna*, and the most common chain is Droxi; pharmacies and supermarkets carry international brands of *náplast* (bandages), *tampóny* (tampons), and *kondomy* (condoms). The Czech Republic has a very low level of violent crime, but **petty crime** has increased with tourism; it is especially common in big cities, on public transportation, and near touristy areas, such as main squares in Prague. **Women** traveling alone should not experience many problems, but should exercise caution while riding public transportation, especially after dark. Hate crimes are rare in the Czech Republic, but **minorities** might experience some discrimination. This is especially true for travelers with darker skin. Travelers with **disabilities** might encounter trouble with the Czech Republic's accessibility, but there is a strong movement to make Prague's transportation system more wheelchair-friendly. Gay nightlife is taking off in Prague, and the country recently legalized registered partnerships for same-sex couples. Though tolerance is increasing, **GLBT travelers** are advised to avoid public displays of affection, especially in more rural areas.

TRANSPORTATION

BY PLANE. The main international airport is Ruzyně International Airport (**PRG;** ☎220 113 314; www.prg.aero). Many carriers, including **Air Canada, Air France, American Airlines, British Airways, CSA, Delta, KLM, Lufthansa,** and **SAS** fly into Prague. Direct flights are quite expensive; travelers might consider flying to a Western European capital and taking a train or discount airline into Prague.

BY TRAIN. The easiest and cheapest way to travel in the Czech Republic is by train. **Czech Railways** is the national train line. **Eurail** is accepted. The fastest international trains are **EuroCity** and **InterCity** (*expresní;* marked in blue on schedules). *Rychlík* trains are fast domestic trains (*zrychlený vlak;* marked in red on schedules). Avoid slow *osobni* trains, marked in white. *Odjezdy* (departures) are printed on yellow posters, *příjezdy* (arrivals) on white. Seat reservations (*mistenka,* 10Kč) are recommended on express and international trains.

BY BUS. Czech buses are often quicker and cheaper than trains in the countryside. **CSAD** runs national and international bus lines (www.ticketsbti.csad.cz), and many European companies operate international service. Consult the timetables or buy a bus schedule (25Kč) from kiosks.

BY CAR AND BY TAXI. Roads are generally well-kept, but side roads can be dangerous, and the number of fatal car accidents is increasing in the Czech Republic. **Roadside assistance** is usually available. To drive in the Czech Republic, an **International Driver's Permit** is required. **Taxis** are a safe way to travel, though many overcharge. Negotiate the fare beforehand and make sure the meter is running during the ride. Phoning a taxi service is generally more affordable than flagging down a cab on the street. *Let's Go* does not recommend **hitchhiking.**

KEEPING IN TOUCH

PHONE CODES	**Country code:** 420. **International dialing prefix:** 00. For more information on how to place international calls, see **Inside Back Cover.**

EMAIL AND THE INTERNET. Internet is readily available throughout the Czech Republic. Internet cafes offer fast connections for about 1-2Kč per minute. Wi-Fi access is becoming more prevalent.

TELEPHONE. Card-operated phones (175Kč per 50 units; 320Kč per 100 units) are simpler to use and easier to find than coin-operated phones. You can purchase phone cards (*telefonní karta*) at most *tábaks* and *trafika* (convenience stores). To make **domestic calls,** dial the entire number. City codes no longer exist in the Czech Republic, and dialing zero is not necessary. To make an **international call** to the Czech Republic, dial the country code followed by the entire phone number. Calls run 13Kč per minute to Australia, Canada, the UK, or the US and 12Kč per minute to New Zealand. Dial ☎1181 for English info, 0800 12 34 56 for the international operator. International access codes include: **AT&T** (☎00 800 222 55288); **British Telecom** (☎00 420); **Canada Direct** (☎800 001 115); **MCI** (☎800 001 112); and **Sprint** (☎800 001 187).

MAIL. The postal system is efficient, though finding English-speaking postal employees can be a challenge. A postcard to the US costs 18Kč, to Europe 17Kč. To send airmail, stress that you want it mailed by plane (*letecky*). Go to the customs office to send packages heavier than 2kg abroad. **Poste Restante** is generally available. Address envelopes with: First Name LAST NAME, POSTE RESTANTE, post office address, Postal Code, city, CZECH REPUBLIC.

LANGUAGE. Czech is a West Slavic language, closely related to Slovak and Polish. English is widely understood, mainly among young people, and German can be useful, especially in South Bohemia. In eastern regions, you're more likely to encounter Polish. Though Russian was taught to all school children under communism, the language is not always welcome. For basic Czech words and phrases, see **Phrasebook: Czech, p. 1060**.

ACCOMMODATIONS AND CAMPING

CZECH REPUBLIC	❶	❷	❸	❹	❺
ACCOMMODATIONS	under 320Kč	320-500Kč	501-800Kč	801-1200Kč	over 1200Kč

Hostels and **university dorms** are the cheapest options in July and August; two- to four-bed dorms cost 250-400Kč. **Hostels** are generally clean and safe throughout the country, but they are often rare in areas with few students. **Pensions** are the next most affordable option at 600-800Kč. **Hotels** (from 1000Kč) tend to be more luxurious and expensive. From June to September, reserve at least a week ahead in Prague, Český Krumlov, and Brno. Though staying in **private homes** is common in Eastern Europe, it is not very common in the Czech Republic. Scan train stations for *Zimmer frei* signs. Be cautious about paying in advance for this type of accomodation. There are many **campgrounds** scattered throughout the country; most are open only from mid-May to September.

FOOD AND DRINK

CZECH REPUBLIC	❶	❷	❸	❹	❺
FOOD	under 80Kč	80-110Kč	111-150Kč	151-200Kč	over 200Kč

Loving Czech cuisine starts with learning to pronounce *knedlíky* (KNED-lee-kee). These thick, wheat- or potato-based loaves of dough, feebly known in English as dumplings, are a staple. Meat, however, lies at the heart of almost all main dishes; the national meal (known as *vepřo-knedlo-zelo*) is *vepřové* (roast pork), *knedlíky*, and *zelí* (sauerkraut), frequently served with cabbage. If you're in a hurry, grab *párky* (frankfurters) or *sýr* (cheese) at a food stand. **Vegetarian** restaurants serving *bez masa* (meatless) specialties are uncommon outside Prague; traditional restaurants serve few options beyond *smaženy sýr* (fried cheese) and *saláty* (salads), and even these may contain meat products. Eating **kosher** is feasible, but beware—pork may sneak unnoticed into many dishes. *Jablkový závin* (apple strudel) and *ovocné knedlíky* (fruit dumplings) are favorite sweets, but the most beloved is *koláč*—a tart filled with poppy seeds or sweet cheese. *Vinárnas* (wine bars) serve Moravian wines and a variety of spirits, including *slivovice* (plum brandy) and *becherovka* (herbal bitter), the **national drink.** World-class local brews like *Plzeňský Prazdroj* (Pilsner Urquell), *Budvar*, and *Kruovice* dominate the drinking scene.

HOLIDAYS AND FESTIVALS

Holidays: New Year's Day (Jan. 1); Easter (Apr. 12, 2009; April 4th, 2010); May Day/ Labor Day (May 1); Liberation Day (May 8); Saints Cyril and Methodius Day (July 5); Jan Hus Day (July 6); St. Wencesclas Day (Sept. 28); Independence Day (Oct. 28); Struggle for Freedom and Democracy Day (Nov. 17); Christmas (Dec. 24-26).

Festivals: The Czech Republic hosts a number of internationally renowned festivals. If you are planning to attend, reserve tickets well in advance. In June, the **Five-Petaled Rose Festival,** a medieval festival in Český Krumlov (p. 250), features music, dance, and a jousting tournament. **Masopust,** the Moravian version of Mardi Gras, is celebrated in villages across the country from Epiphany to Ash Wednesday (Jan.-Mar.).

BEYOND TOURISM

For more info on opportunities across Europe, see Beyond Tourism, p. 60.

INEX—Association of Voluntary Service, Senovážné nám. 24, 116 47 Praha 1, Czech Republic (☎ 420 222 362 715; www.inexsda.cz/eng). Ecological and historical preservation efforts, as well as construction projects, in the Czech Republic.

The Prague Center for Further Education and Professional Development, Ptrossova 19, Nové Město, 110 00 Praha 1, Czech Republic (☎420 257 534 013; www.filmstudies.cz). Teaches courses on art, filmmaking, and design in Prague.

University of West Bohemia, Univerzitní 8, 306 14 Plzeň (☎420 377 631 111; www.zcu.cz). International university centrally located in a student-friendly brewery city.

PRAGUE (PRAHA)

Home to the stately Prague Castle and Old Town Square's pastel facades, Prague (pop. 1,200,000) retains small-town charm despite its size. In the 14th century, Holy Roman Emperor Charles IV refurbished Prague with stone bridges and lavish palaces still visible today. Since the lifting of the Iron Curtain in 1989, outsiders have flooded the Czech capital. In summer, most locals leave for the countryside when the foreigner-to-resident ratio soars above nine-to-one. Despite rising prices and a hyper-touristed Staré Město (Old Town), Prague still commands the awe of its visitors.

INTERCITY TRANSPORTATION

Flights: Ruzyně Airport (**PRG;** ☎220 111 111), 20km northwest of the city. Take bus #119 to Metro A: Dejvická (12Kč, luggage 6Kč per bag); buy tickets from kiosks or machines. Airport **buses** run by Cedaz (☎220 114 296; 20-45 min., 2 per hr.) collect travelers from nám. Republiky (120Kč); try to settle on a price before departing.

Trains: (☎221 111 122, international 224 615 249; www.vlak.cz). Prague has 4 main terminals. **Hlavní nádraží** (☎224 615 786; Metro C: Hlavní nádraží) and **Nádraží Holešovice** (☎224 624 632; Metro C: Nádraží Holešovice) are the largest and cover most international service. Domestic trains leave from **Masarykovo nádraží** (☎840 112 113; Metro B: nám. Republiky) and from **Smíchovské nádraží** (☎972 226 150; Metro B: Smíchovské nádraží). International trains run to: **Berlin, GER** (5hr., 6 per day, 1500Kč); **Bratislava, SLK** (5hr., 6 per day, 650Kč); **Budapest, HUN** (7-9hr., 5 per day, 1400Kč); **Kraków, POL** (7-8hr., 3 per day, 900Kč); **Moscow, RUS** (31hr., 1 per day, 3000Kč); **Munich, GER** (7hr., 3 per day, 1650Kč); **Vienna, AUT** (4-5hr., 7 per day, 1000Kč); **Warsaw, POL** (9hr., 2 per day, 1350Kč).

Buses: (☎900 144 444; www.vlak-bus.cz.) State-run **ČSAD** (☎257 319 016) has several terminals. The biggest is **Florenc,** Křižíkova 4 (☎900 149 044; Metro B or C: Florenc). Info office open daily 6am-9pm. To: **Berlin, GER** (7hr., 2 per day, 900Kč); **Budapest, HUN** (8hr., 3 per day, 1600Kč); **Paris, FRA** (15hr., 2 per day, 2200Kč); **Sofia, BUL** (24hr., 2 per day, 1600Kč); **Vienna, AUT** (5hr., 1 per day, 600Kč). 10% ISIC discount. **Tourbus** office (☎224 218 680; www.eurolines.cz), at the terminal, sells Eurolines and airport bus tickets. Open M-F 7am-7pm, Sa 8am-7pm, Su 9am-7pm.

ORIENTATION

Shouldering the river **Vltava,** greater Prague is a mess of suburbs and maze-like streets. All sightseeing destinations are in the compact downtown. The Vltava runs south to north through central Prague, separating **Staré Město** (Old Town) and **Nové Město** (New Town) from **Malá Strana** (Lesser Side). On the right bank, **Staroměstské náměstí** (Old Town Square) is Prague's focal point. From the square, the elegant **Pařížská ulice** (Paris Street) leads north into Josefov, the old Jewish quarter. South of Staré Město, the Nové Město houses **Václavské náměstí** (Wenceslas Square), the city's commercial core. West of Staroměstské nám., **Karlův Most** (Charles Bridge) spans the Vltava, connecting Staré Město with **Malostranské náměstí** (Lesser Town Square). **Pražský Hrad** (Prague Castle) overlooks Malostranské nám. from Hradčany hill. The train station and bus station lie northeast of Václavské nám. To reach Staroměstské nám., take Metro A line to Staroměstská and follow Kaprova away from the river.

LOCAL TRANSPORTATION

Public Transportation: Buy **interchangeable tickets** for the bus, Metro, and tram at newsstands, *tabák* kiosks, machines in stations, or the DP (Dopravní podnik; transport authority) kiosks. Validate tickets in machines above escalators to avoid fines issued by plainclothes inspectors who roam transport lines. 3 **Metro** lines run daily 5am-midnight: A is green on maps, B yellow, C red. **Night trams** #51-58 and **buses** #502-514 and 601 run after the last Metro and cover the same areas as day trams and buses (2 per hr. 12:30am-4:30am); look for dark blue signs with white letters at bus stops. 18Kč tickets are good for a 20min. ride or 5 stops. 26Kč tickets are valid for 1hr., with transfers, for all travel in the same direction. Large bags and baby carriages 6Kč. DP offices (☎296 191 817; www.dpp.cz; open daily 7am-9pm), in the Muzeum stop on Metro A and C lines, sells **multi-day passes** (1-day 100Kč, 3-day 330Kč, 5-day 500Kč).

Taxis: City Taxi (☎257 257 257) and **AAA** (☎140 14). 40Kč base, 25Kč per km, 5Kč per min. waiting. Hail a cab anywhere, but call ahead to avoid getting ripped off.

GOING THE DISTANCE. To avoid being scammed by taxis, always ask in advance for a receipt *(Prosím, dejte mi paragon;* please, give me a receipt) with distance traveled and price paid.

PRACTICAL INFORMATION

Tourist Offices: Green "i"s mark tourist offices. **Pražská Informační Služba** (**PIS;** Prague Information Service; ☎12 444; www.pis.cz) is in the **Staroměstské Radnice** (Old Town Hall). Open Apr.-Oct. daily 9am-7pm; Nov.-Mar. daily 9am-6pm. Branches at Na příkopě 20 and Hlavní nádraží. Open in summer M-F 9am-7pm, Sa-Su 9am-5pm; winter M-F 9am-6pm, Sa 9am-3pm. Branch in the tower by the Malá Strana side of the Charles Bridge. Open Apr.-Oct. daily 10am-6pm.

Budget Travel: CKM, Mánesova 77 (☎222 721 595; www.ckm-praha.cz). Metro A: Jiřího z Poděbrad. Sells budget airline tickets to those under 26. Also books accommodations in Prague from 350Kč. Open M-Th 10am-6pm, F 10am-4pm. **GTS,** Ve smečkách 27 (☎222 119 700; www.gtsint.cz). Metro A or C: Muzeum. Offers student discounts on airline tickets (225-2500Kč in Europe). Open M-F 8am-10pm, Sa 10am-5pm.

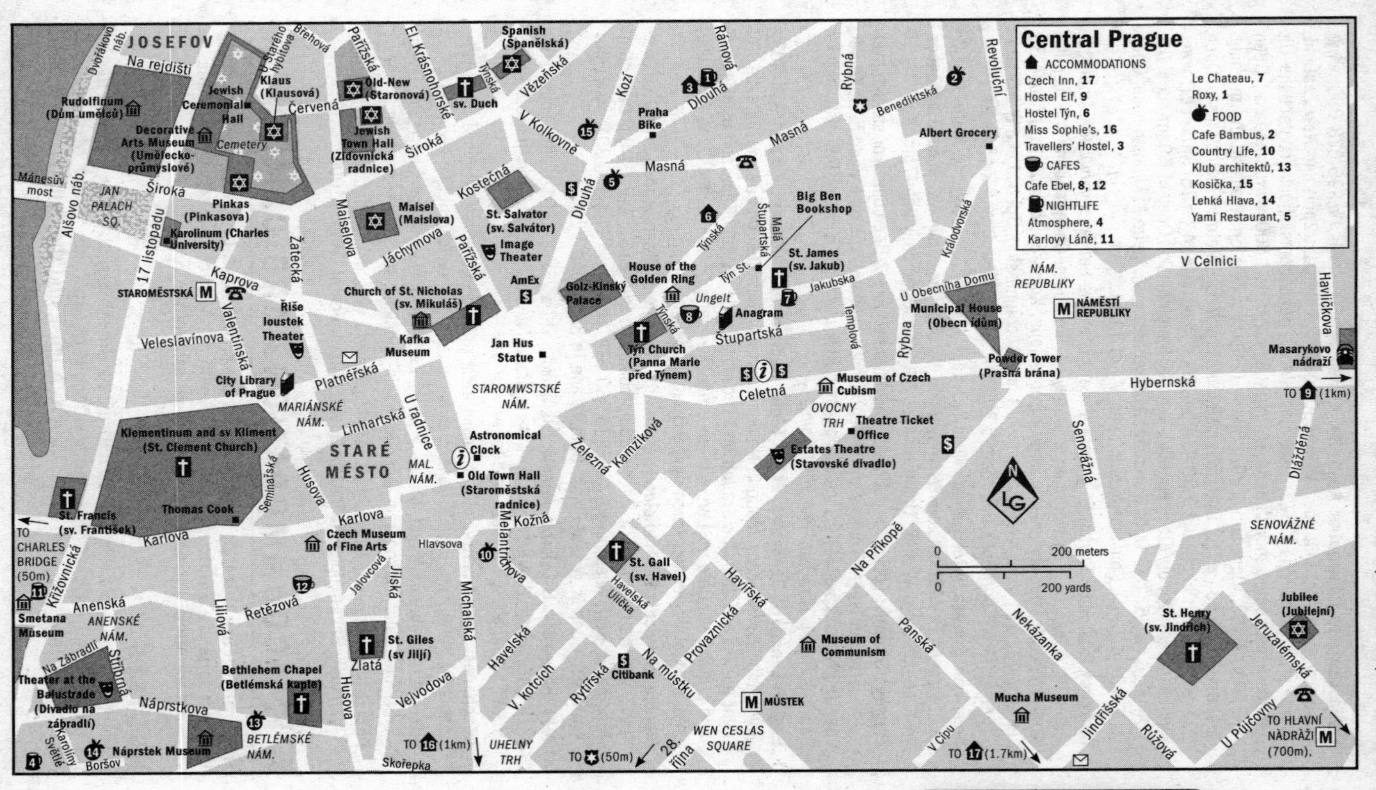
Central Prague
ACCOMMODATIONS
Czech Inn, 17
Hostel Elf, 9
Hostel Týn, 6
Miss Sophie's, 16
Travellers' Hostel, 3
CAFES
Cafe Ebel, 8, 12
NIGHTLIFE
Atmosphere, 4
Karlovy Lázně, 11
Le Chateau, 7
Roxy, 1
FOOD
Cafe Bambus, 2
Country Life, 10
Klub architektů, 13
Kosička, 15
Lehká Hlava, 14
Yami Restaurant, 5
0 200 meters
0 200 yards
JOSEFOV
STARÉ MĚSTO
STAROMWSTSKÉ NÁM.
NÁM. REPUBLIKY
NÁMĚSTÍ REPUBLIKY
MŮSTEK
STAROMĚSTSKÁ
WEN CESLAS SQUARE
Powder Tower (Prašná brána)
Municipal House (Obecní dům)
Museum of Czech Cubism
Estates Theatre (Stavovské divadlo)
Theatre Ticket Office
Museum of Communism
Mucha Museum
St. Henry (sv. Jindřich)
Jubilee (Jubilejní)
Masarykovo nádraží
TO 9 (1km)
TO HLAVNÍ NÁDRAŽÍ (700m)
TO 17 (1.7km)
TO (50m)
TO 16 (1km)
St. James (sv. Jakub)
Big Ben Bookshop
Anagram
Ungelt
House of the Golden Ring
Týn Church (Panna Marie před Týnem)
Golz-Kinský Palace
Jan Hus Statue
Astronomical Clock
Old Town Hall (Staroměstská radnice)
St. Gall (sv. Havel)
Havelská Ulička
Citibank
St. Giles (sv Jiljí)
Bethlehem Chapel (Betlémská kaple)
BETLÉMSKÉ NÁM.
Náprstek Museum
Theater at the Balustrade (Divadlo na zábradlí)
Smetana Museum
ANENSKÉ NÁM.
St. Francis (sv. František)
TO CHARLES BRIDGE (50m)
Klementinum and sv Kliment (St. Clement Church)
Thomas Cook
City Library of Prague
MARIÁNSKÉ NÁM.
MAL. NÁM.
Říše loustek Theater
Kafka Museum
Church of St. Nicholas (sv. Mikuláš)
Maisel (Maislova)
St. Salvator (sv. Salvátor)
Image Theater
AmEx
Spanish (Španělská)
sv. Duch
Old-New (Staronová)
Jewish Town Hall (Židovnická radnice)
Klaus (Klausová)
Jewish Ceremonial Hall
Cemetery
Pinkas (Pinkasova)
Karolinum (Charles University)
Decorative Arts Museum (Umělecko-průmyslové)
Rudolfinum (Dům umělců)
JAN PALACH SQ.
Czech Museum of Fine Arts
Praha Bike
Albert Grocery
OVOCNY TRH
UHELNY TRH
SENOVÁŽNÉ NÁM.
Na Příkopě
Celetná
Hybernská
Revoluční
V Celnici
Havlíčkova
Karlova
Husova
Pařížská
17 listopadu
Kaprova
Valentinská
Veleslavínova
Platnéřská
Linhartská
U radnice
Dlouhá
Masná
Rybná
Týnská
Štupartská
Železná
Kamzíková
Melantrichova
Michalská
Havelská
Na můstku
Senovážná
Jindřišská
Panská
Nekázanka
Jeruzalémská
Široká
Maiselova
Žatecká
Liliová
Řetězová
Náprstkova

Embassies and Consulates: Australia, Klimentská 10, 6th fl. (☎296 578 350; www.embassy.gov.au/cz.html; open M-Th 8:30am-5pm, F 8:30am-2pm) and **New Zealand,** Dykova 19 (☎222 514 672) have consulates, but citizens should contact the UK embassy in an emergency. **Canada,** Muchova 6 (☎272 101 800; www.canada.cz). Open M-F 8:30am-12:30pm and 1:30-4:30pm. Consular office open only in the morning. **Ireland,** Tržiště 13 (☎257 530 061; irishembassy@iol.cz). Metro A: Malostranská. Open M-F 9:30am-12:30pm and 2:30-4:30pm. **UK,** Thunovská 14 (☎257 402 111; www.britishembassy.gov.uk/czechrepublic). Metro A: Malostranská. Open M-F 9am-noon. **US,** Tržiště 15 (☎257 022 000; www.prague.usembassy.gov). Metro A: Malostranská. Open M-F 8am-4:30pm. Consular section open M-F 8:30-11:30am.

Currency Exchange: Exchange counters are everywhere but rates vary wildly. Train stations have high rates. Never change money on the street. **Chequepoints** are plentiful and open late, but can charge large commissions. **Komerční banka,** Na příkopě 33 (☎222 432 111), buys notes and checks for 2% commission. Open M and W 8:30am-5pm, Tu, Th 8:30am-5pm, F 8:30am-5:30pm. A 24hr. **Citibank** is at Rytířska 24.

American Express/Interchange: Václavské nám. 56 (☎222 800 224). Metro A or C: Muzeum. AmEx **ATM** outside. Western Union services available. MC/V **cash advances** (3% commission). Western Union services available. Open daily 9am-7pm.

Luggage Storage: Lockers in train and bus stations take 2 5Kč coins. For storage over 24hr., use the luggage offices to the left in the basement of Hlavní nádraží. 25Kč per day, bags over 15kg 40Kč. Fine for forgotten lock code 30Kč. Open 24hr. with breaks 5:30-6am, 11-11:30am, and 5:30-6pm.

English-Language Bookstore: The Globe Bookstore, Ptrossova 6 (☎224 934 203; www.globebookstore.cz). Metro B: Národní třída. Exit Metro left on Spálená, take the 1st right on Ostrovní, then the 3rd left on Pštrossova. Wide variety of new and used books and periodicals. Cafe upstairs with an expansive menu of teas, coffees, and cocktails. Internet 1.50Kč per min. Open daily 9:30am-midnight.

Medical Services: Na Homolce (Hospital for Foreigners), Roentgenova 2 (☎257 271 111, after hours 257 272 146; www.homolka.cz). Bus #167. Open 24hr. **Canadian Medical Center,** Velesavínská 1 (☎235 360 133, after hours 724 300 301; www.cmc.praha.cz). Open M, W, and F 8am-6pm, Tu and Th 8am-8pm.

24hr. Pharmacy: U Lékárna Anděla, Štefánikova 6 (☎257 320 918, after hours 257 324 686). Metro B: Anděl. If you are there after-hours, press the button marked "Pohotovost" to the left of the main door for service.

Telephones: Phone cards sold at kiosks, post offices, and some exchange establishments for 200Kč and 300Kč. Coins also accepted (local calls from 5Kč per min.).

Internet: Bohemia Bagel, Masná 2 (☎224 812 560; www.bohemiabagel.cz), Metro A: Staroměstská. 2Kč per min. Open M-F 7am-midnight, Sa, Su 8am-midnight.

Post Office: Jindřišská 14 (☎221 131 445). Metro A or B: Můstek. Internet 1Kč per min. Open daily 2am-midnight. Windows close 7:30pm. **Postal Code:** 11000.

ACCOMMODATIONS AND CAMPING

Hotel prices are through the roof in Prague, and hostel rates are on the rise. Reservations are a must at hotels and even at the nicer hostels in summer. A growing number of Prague residents rent affordable rooms.

HOSTELS

If you tote a backpack in Hlavní nádraží or Holešovice stations, you will likely be approached by hostel runners offering cheap beds. Many of these are university dorms vacated from June to August, and they often provide free transportation. However, more personal, well-appointed options can be had at similiar prices. Staff at hostels typically speak English.

STARÉ MĚSTO

Travellers' Hostel, Dlouhá 33 (☎224 826 662; www.travellers.cz). Metro B: nám. Republiky. Branches at Husova 3, Střelecký Ostrov 36, and U Lanové Dráhy 3. Social atmosphere, but neighboring nightclub and crowded facilities means it can get loud. Breakfast and linens included. Laundry 150Kč. Internet and Wi-Fi. Reserve ahead in summer. Reception 24hr. No curfew. Check-in 1pm, Check-out 10am. 16-bed dorms 400Kč; 6-bed 480Kč, 4-bed 500Kč; singles 1190Kč, with bath 1390Kč; doubles 690/800Kč per person. 40Kč ISIC discount. AmEx/MC/V. ❷

Hostel Týn, Týnská 19 (☎224 828 519; www.hostel-tyn.web2001.cz). Metro A: Staroměstská. In the heart of Staré Město, this hostel avoids the extremes of overcrowding and boredom: dorms may be small, but the crowd is social. Soft beds. Clean facilities. In-room lockers. Free Internet. Kitchen access. Reception 24hr. Check-out 10am. 5-bed dorms 350Kč; 4-bed dorm 470Kč; doubles 1240Kč. 200Kč deposit. ❷

NOVÉ MĚSTO AND VINOHRADY

Czech Inn, Francouzská 76 (☎267 267 600; www.czech-inn.com). Metro A: nám. Míru. From the Metro, take tram #4, 22, or 23 to Krymská and walk 50m uphill. This ultra-modern, fashionable hostel sets sky-high standards for budget accommodations. Swanky bar on ground fl. Breakfast 140Kč. Internet 50Kč per hr. Reserve ahead. Reception 24hr. Check-out noon. Dorms 429-545Kč; singles 1320-1450Kč; doubles 1540-1700Kč. Private room prices increase 200Kč on weekends. AmEx/MC/V. ❷

Miss Sophie's, Melounová 3 (☎296 303 530; www.missophies.com). Metro C: IP Pavlova. Take 1st left from subway platform, then follow Katerinská to 1st right onto Melounová. For the stylish budget traveler, a brick cellar lounge and artistic dorm decor make up for the bathroom shortage. Free Internet and Wi-Fi. Kitchen and linens included. Reception 24hr. Check-in 3pm. High-season dorms 560Kč; singles 1790Kč; doubles 2050Kč; triples 2400Kč; apartments 2290-2890Kč. Low-season 410/1150/1500/1700/1389-1990Kč. AmEx/MC/V. ❷

Hostel Elf, Husitská 11 (☎222 540 963; www.hostelelf.com). Metro B: Florenc. From the Metro, take bus #207 to U Památníku; the hostel is through the wooden gate. Despite noisy train tracks nearby, this graffiti-covered hostel is always packed. Party past dawn in the downstairs lounge. Reception 24hr. Breakfast and linens included. Free Internet. 8-bed dorms 340Kč; singles 980Kč, with bath 1230Kč; doubles 1160/1460Kč. ❷

OUTSIDE THE CENTER

Sir Toby's, Dělnická 24 (☎283 870 635; www.sirtobys.com). Metro C: Nádraží Holešovice. From the Metro, take the tram to Dělnická, walk to the corner of Dělnická, and turn left. Beautiful, classy hostel with a huge, fully equipped kitchen, a social cellar pub, and a welcoming staff. Reception 24hr. Check-in 2pm. Check-out 10am. Free Wi-Fi. Buffet breakfast 100 Kč. High-season dorms 360-500Kč; singles 1150Kč; doubles 3200Kč. Low-season 260-470/850/2600Kč. AmEx/MC/V. ❷

Hostel Boathouse, Lodnická 1 (☎241 770 051; www.hostelboathouse.com). Take tram #3, 17,or 52 from Karlovo nam. south toward Sídliště. Get off at Černý Kůň (20min.), go down the ramp to the left, and follow the yellow signs. Social atmosphere, caring staff, and home-cooked meals. Reception 24hr. Breakfast included. Dorms from 390Kč. ❶

OTHER ACCOMMODATIONS

Budget hotels are scarce, and generally the better hostel options offer more bang for your buck. Lower rates at hotels are often available if you call ahead.

Campgrounds can be found on the Vltava Islands as well as on the outskirts of Prague. **Bungalows** must be reserved ahead, but tent sites are generally available without prior notice. Tourist offices sell a **guide** to sites near the city (20Kč).

Dům U Krále Jiřího (Hotel King George), Liliová 10 (☎221 466 100; www.kinggeorge.cz). Metro A: Staroměstská. Elegant rooms with private bath. Breakfast included. Reception 7am-11pm. Check-in 2pm. Check-out 10am. Singles 2250Kč; doubles 3100Kč; triples 3900Kč; apartments 3100-7500Kč. Prices lower Jan.-Feb. and Nov.-Dec. ❺

Pension Museum, Mezibranská 15 (☎296 325 186; www.pension-museum.cz). Metro C: Muzeum. This ultra-modern B&B near Václavké nám. is well worth the splurge. Beautiful courtyard leads to plush and stylish rooms with TVs and spacious baths. Reserve 1-2 months ahead. Apr.-Dec. singles 2460Kč; doubles 2920Kč; apartments 3000-6000Kč. Jan.-Mar. 1580/1970/2000-5000Kč. AmEx/MC/V. ❺

Camp Sokol Troja, Trojská 171 (☎233 542 908), north of the center in the Troja district. From Metro C: Nádraží Holešovice, take bus #112 and ask for Kazanka. Clean facilities. July-Aug. and Dec. tent sites 120Kč per person, 100-170Kč per tent site. Singles 330Kč; doubles 660Kč. Low-season reduced rates. ❶

FOOD

The closer you are to the city center, the more you'll pay. You will be charged for everything the waiter brings to the table, so be sure to check your bill carefully. **Tesco,** Národní třída 26, has groceries. (Open M-F 7am-10pm, Sa 8am-8pm, Su 9am-8pm.) Look for the daily **market** in Staré Město where you can grab better deals. After a night out, grab a *párek v rohlíku* (hot dog) or a *smažený sýr* (fried cheese sandwich) from a Václavské nám. vendor.

RESTAURANTS

STARÉ MĚSTO

Klub architektů, Betlémské nám. 169/5A (☎224 401 214). Metro B: Národní třída. A 12th-century cellar with 21st-century ambience. Rub elbows with the locals in this intimate cavern of vaulted brick ceilings and low-hanging black lamps. The ostrich filet (320Kč) is a must for the adventurous diner. Veggie options 70-150Kč. Meat entrees 160-320Kč. Open daily 11:30am-midnight. AmEx/MC/V. ❸

Lehká Hlava (Clear Head), Borov 2 (☎222 220 665; www.lehkahlava.cz). Metro A: Staroměstská. Cooks up vegetarian and vegan cuisine that even devout carnivores will enjoy. Entrees 95-210Kč. Open M-F 11:30am-11:30pm; Sa and Su noon-11:30pm. Kitchen closed 2:30pm-5pm. Only cold food after 10pm. MC/V. ❷

Country Life, Melantrichova 15 (☎224 213 366). Metro A: Staroměstská. 3 extensive and fresh vegetarian buffets are a welcome respite from meat-heavy Czech cuisine. Buffet 20-50Kč per 100g. Soup 25Kč. Juices from 20Kč. Open M-Th 9am-8:30pm, F 8:30am-6pm, Su 11am-8:30pm. Cash only. ❷

Kozička, Kozí 1 (☎224 818 308; www.kozicka.cz). Metro A: Staroměstská. A relaxed Old Town restaurant with a unique goat theme. Metal statues of the frolicking creatures cover the walls and floor while diners select from a menu of Czech dishes like dumplings stuffed with spiced meat and spinach or the hearty goulash (both 160Kč). Entrees 120-350Kč. Open M-F noon-4am, Sa 6pm-4am, Su 6pm-3am. AmEx/MC/V. ❸

Yami Restaurant, Masná 3 (☎222 312 756) Metro A: Staroměstská. Japanese dishes in a relaxed, sleek Zen dining room. The courtyard out back holds 4 tables behind a screen where diners devour Yami's fusion rolls (205-335Kč per 8 pieces). Entrees 238-332Kč. Sushi 50-90Kč. Open daily noon-11pm. MC/V. ❸

Cafe Bambus, Benediktská 12 (☎224 828 110; www.cafebambus.com). Metro B: nám. Republiky. Patrons nosh on delicious Thai and Indian dishes (around 150Kč) and Czech *palančinky* (crepes; 75-110Kč) in a tropical setting. Beer from 48Kč. Open M-F 9am-2am, Sa 11am-2am, Su 11am-midnight. AmEx/MC/V. ❷

NOVÉ MĚSTO

Radost FX, Bělehradská 120 (☎224 254 776; www.radostfx.cz). Metro C: I.P. Pavlova. A stylish dance club and late-night cafe with an imaginative menu and great vegetarian food. Entrees 140-210Kč. Brunch Sa-Su 50-200Kč. Open daily 11am-late. ❸

Universal, V jirchářích 6 (☎224 934 416. www.universalrestaurant.cz). Metro B: Národní třída. Asian, French, and Mediterranean cuisines served in an eclectically decorated dining room. Huge salads 131-195Kč. Entrees 165-329Kč. Su brunch buffet 235-265Kč. Open M-Sa 11:30am-midnight, Su 11am-midnight. AmEx/MC/V; min. 500Kč. ❸

Ultramarin Grill, Ostrovní 32 (☎224 932 249; www.ultramarin.cz). Metro B: Národní třída. Classy decor without the prices to match. Young professionals feast on American dishes as well as Thai-inspired steak, duck, and lamb entrees 180-450Kč. Salads 100-198Kč. Open daily 10am-11pm. AmEx/MC/V. ❸

Velryba (The Whale), Opatovická 24. (☎ 224 931 444). Metro B: Národní třída. Relaxed Italian/Czech restaurant with gallery downstairs. The fish scales here will have you feeling like Jonah. Entrees 77-155Kč. Open daily 11am-midnight. Cash only. ❷

MALÁ STRANA

Bar bar, Všehrdova 17 (☎257 313 246; www.bar-bar.cz). Metro A: Malostranská. Reggae-inspired basement cafe with art shows. Lunch 120Kč. Entrees 125-275Kč. Beer from 20Kč. Open M-Th and Su noon-midnight, F-Sa noon-2am. MC/V. ❷

U Tří Černých Ruží, Zámecká 5 (☎257 530 019; www.u3cr.com). Metro A: Malostranská. At the foot of the New Castle steps. Intimate restaurant and bar with a local crowd. Large portions. Entrees 80-250Kč. Beer from 23Kč. Open daily 11am-midnight. ❷

CAFES AND TEAHOUSES

Cafe Rybka, Opatovická 7 (☎224 932 260). Metro B: Národní třída. Congenial corner cafe with an intellectual crowd, fantastic coffee, and a tiny bookstore. Espresso 25Kč. Tea 22Kč. Open daily 9:15am-10pm. Cash only.

Cafe Ebel, Řetězová 9 (☎222 222 018; www.ebelcoffee.cz). Metro A or B: Staroměstská. Ebel's espresso

ROLLING ON THE RIVER

Tourists flock to the Charles Bridge to take in the sights of the Vltava River, but why not enjoy the view from on the river? The **Prague Dinner River Cruise** operates year-round, and takes passengers along a slow, scenic route with prime views of the Charles Bridge, Prague Castle, Malá Strana, and Vysehrad Fortress, amongst others. Aside from the trip itself, this is an excursion that will feed and entertain you as well. Passengers nosh on an extensive buffet of classic Czech dishes whilst enjoying the repertoire of the live jazz band on deck. The cruise is an ideal location for a great date, and even better for a bad one, since your gentleman or lady friend can't desert you halfway through.

Travelers on a budget tend to avoid this sort of excursion as prices are usually quite high, but the river cruise comes at a surprisingly reasonable rate which includes the cruise, dinner buffet, and entertainment—a bargain when you consider the price of a meal in Old Town Square. Cocktail attire is appropriate, so leave your grungy backpacking clothes at home and spruce it up a bit for this worthwhile night on the town.

Cruises depart nightly at 7pm for 3hrs. Boarding point is the river embankment by the city center, near the Charles Bridge. Reservations can be made at the Prague Tourist Office in Old Town Square, online at www.pragueexperience.com. Cost is 790Kč per person.

(50-60Kč) is blended in-house by people who clearly know what they're doing. Small selection of sandwiches and pastries. English spoken. Branch at Týnská 2. Both open daily 9am-10pm. AmEx/MC/V.

Kavárna Medúza, Belgická 17 (☎222 515 107). Metro A: nám. Míru. Walk down Rumunská and turn left at Belgická. Local clientele by day, hipsters by night. Coffee 19-30Kč. Crepes 56-80Kč. Open M-F 10am-1am, Sa noon-1am, Su noon-midnight. MC/V.

U Zeleného Čaje, Nerudova 19 (☎225 730 027). Metro A: Malostranská. From Malostranské nám., go down Nerudova. This adorable shop at the foot of Prague Castle takes tea to new heights. Serves up several alcohol-infused teas and light vegetarian snacks. Tea 40-30Kč. Open daily 11am-10pm. Cash only.

SIGHTS

Escape the crowds that flock to Prague's downtown sights by venturing away from **Staroměstské náměstí**, the **Charles Bridge**, and **Václavské náměstí.** There are plenty of attractions for visitors hidden in the old Jewish quarter of Josefov, the hills of **Vyšehrad**, and the streets of **Malá Strana.**

STARÉ MĚSTO (OLD TOWN)

Navigating the 1000-year-old Staré Město—a jumble of narrow streets and alleys—can be difficult. Once the sun sets, the ancient labyrinth comes alive with the city's youth, who enliven its many bars and jazz clubs.

CHARLES BRIDGE. Thronged with tourists and the hawkers who feed on them, the Charles Bridge (Karlův Most) is Prague's most treasured landmark. The defense towers on each side offer splendid views. Five stars and a cross mark the spot where, according to legend, St. Jan Nepomuck was tossed over the side of the bridge for concealing the queen's extramarital secrets from a suspicious King Wenceslas IV in the 14th century. *(Metro A: Malostranská or Staroměstská.)*

OLD TOWN SQUARE. Staroměstské náměstí (Old Town Square) is the heart of Staré Město, surrounded by eight magnificent towers. *(Metro A: Staroměstská; Metro A or B: Můstek.)* Composed of several different architectural styles, the **Staroměstské Radnice** (Old Town Hall) has been missing a piece of its front facade since the Nazis partially demolished it in the final days of WWII. Crowds gather on the hour to watch the **astronomical clock** chime as skeletal Death empties his hourglass and a procession of apostles marches by. *(Exhibition hall open in summer M 10am-7pm, Tu-F 9am-7pm, Sa-Su 9am-6pm. Clock tower open M 11am-6pm, T-Su 9am-6pm; enter through 3rd fl. of Old Town Hall. Exhibition hall 20Kč, students 10Kč. Clock tower 60/40Kč.)* The spires of **Týn Church** (Chrám Matky Boží před Týnem) rise above a mass of baroque homes. Buried inside is astronomer Tycho Brahe, whose overindulgence at Emperor Rudolf's lavish dinner party in 1601 may have cost him his life. Since it was deemed improper to leave the table unless the emperor himself did so, Tycho had to remain in his chair until his bladder burst. He died 11 days later, though scholars believe mercury poisoning may have been the culprit. *(Open T-Sa 10am-1pm and 3pm-5pm. Mass T, F 5pm, W, Th 5pm, Sa 8am, Su 9:30am and 9pm. Free.)* The bronze statue of 15th-century theologian **Jan Hus,** the country's most famous martyr, stands in the middle of the square. Barely a surface in **St. James's Church** (Kostel sv. Jakuba) remains un-figured, un-marbleized, or unpainted. But keep your hands to yourself—legend has it that 500 years ago a thief tried to pilfer a gem from the Virgin Mary of Suffering, whereupon the figure sprang to life and yanked off his arm. *(Metro B: Staroměstská. On Malá Štupartská, behind Týn Church. Open M-Sa 10am-noon and 2-3:45pm. Mass Su 8, 9, and 10:30am.)*

NOVÉ MĚSTO (NEW TOWN)

Established in 1348 by Charles IV, Nové Město has become Prague's commercial center. The Franciscan Gardens offer an oasis from the bustling businesses.

WENCESLAS SQUARE. More a commercial boulevard than a square, **Václavské náměstí** (Wenceslas Square) owes its name to the statue of 10th-century Czech ruler and patron **Saint Wenceslas** (Václav) that stands in front of the National Museum. At his feet in solemn prayer kneel smaller statues of the country's other patron saints: St. Agnes, St. Adalbert (Vojtěch), St. Ludmila, and St. Prokop. The sculptor, Josef Václav Myslbek, took 25 years to complete the statue. The inscription under St. Wenceslas reads, "Do not let us and our descendants perish." *(Metro A or B: Můstek or Metro A or C: Muzeum.)*

FRANCISCAN GARDEN AND VELVET REVOLUTION MEMORIAL. Franciscan monks somehow manage to preserve this serene **rose garden** in the heart of Prague's commercial district. *(Metro A or B: Můstek. Enter through the arch to the left of Jungmannova and Národní, behind the statue. Open daily from mid-Apr. to mid-Sept. 7am-10pm; from mid-Sept. to mid-Oct. from7am-8pm; mid-Oct. to mid-Apr. 8am-7pm. Free.)* Down the street on Národní, a **plaque** under the arcades and across from the Black Theatre memorializes the citizens beaten by police in a 1989 protest. A subsequent wave of protests led to the collapse of communism in Czechoslovakia.

DANCING HOUSE. American architect Frank Gehry (of Guggenheim-Bilbao fame) built the gently swaying **Tančící dům** (Dancing House) at the corner of Resslova and Rašínovo nábřeží. Since its 1996 unveiling, it has been called an eyesore by some and a shining example of postmodern design by others. *(Metro B: Karlovo nám. As you walk down Resslova toward the river, the building is on the left.)*

JOSEFOV

Josefov, Central Europe's oldest Jewish settlement, lies north of Staroměstské nám., along Maiselova. In 1180, Prague's citizens built a 4m wall around the area. The closed neighborhood bred exotic tales, many of which centered around **Rabbi Loew ben Bezalel** (1512-1609) and his legendary Golem—a mud creature that supposedly came to life to protect Prague's Jews. The city's Jews remained clustered in Josefov until WWII, when the Nazis sent the residents to death camps. Ironically, Hitler's decision to create a "museum of an extinct race" sparked the preservation of Josefov's cemetery and synagogues.

SYNAGOGUES. The **Maiselova synagoga** (Maisel Synagogue) displays artifacts from the Jewish Museum's collections, returned to the community in 1994. *(On Maiselova, between Široká and Jáchymova.)* Turn left on Široká to reach the **Pinkasova** (Pinkas Synagogue). Drawings by children interred at the Terezín camp are upstairs. Some 80,000 names line the walls downstairs, a sobering requiem for Czech Jews persecuted in the Holocaust. Backtrack along Široká and go left on Maiselova to reach Europe's oldest operating synagogue, the 700-year-old **Staronová** (Old-New Synagogue), still the religious center of Prague's Jewish community. Up Široká at Dušní, the **Španělská** (Spanish Synagogue) has an ornate Moorish interior and was first in adopting the 1830s Reform movement. *(Metro A: Staroměstská. Men must cover their heads; yarmulke free. Synagogues open M-F and Su Apr.-Oct. 9am-6pm; Nov.-Mar. 9am-4:30pm. Closed Jewish holidays. Admission to all synagogues except Staronová 300Kč, students 200Kč. Staronová 200/150Kč.)*

OLD JEWISH CEMETERY. Filled with thousands of broken headstones, the Old Jewish Cemetery (Starý židovský hřbitov) stretches between the Pinkas Synagogue and the Ceremonial Hall. Between the 14th and 18th centuries, the graves were dug in layers. Rabbi Loew is buried by the wall opposite the entrance, found at the corner of Široká and Žatecká.

MALÁ STRANA

A criminals' and counter-revolutionaries' hangout for nearly a century, the streets of Malá Strana have become prized real estate. In **Malostranské Náměstí,** the towering dome of the Baroque **St. Nicholas's Cathedral** (Chrám sv. Mikuláše) is one of Prague's most prominent landmarks. Mozart played the organ here when he visited Prague, and the cathedral now hosts nightly classical music concerts. *(Metro A: Malostranská. Follow Letenská to Malostranské nám. ☎257 534 215. Open daily Mar.-Oct. 9am-5pm, Nov.-Feb. 9am-4pm. 60Kč, students 30Kč. Concerts 450/300Kč.)* Along Letenská, a wooden gate opens into the **Wallenstein Garden** (Valdštejnská zahrada). One of the city's best-kept secrets, a beautifully tended stretch of green and a bronze Venus fountain makes a beautiful sight. *(Letenská 10. Metro A: Malostranská. Open Apr.-Oct. daily 10am-6pm. Free.)* The **Church of Our Lady Victorious** (Kostel Panny Marie Vítězné) contains the famous wax statue of the **Infant Jesus of Prague,** said to bestow miracles on the faithful. *(Follow Letecká through Malostranské nám. and continue onto Karmelitská. ☎257 533 646. Open June-Sept. M-Sa 9:30am-9pm, Su 1pm-6pm, Oct.-May M-Sa 9:30am-5:30pm, Su 1pm-5pm. Catholic mass Su noon. Free.)* **Petřín Gardens and View Tower,** on the hill beside Malá Strana, provide a tranquil retreat with spectacular views. Climb the steep, serene footpath, or take the funicular from above the intersection of Vítězná and Újezd. *(Look for Lanovka Dráha signs. Funicular 4-6 per hr. 9am-11pm, 20Kč. Tower open May-Sept. daily 10am-10pm, Oct. 10am-6pm, Apr. 10am-7pm, Nov.-Mar. Sa-Su 10am-5pm. Tower 50Kč, students 40Kč.)* While in Mala Strana, take a detour down Velkopřevorské to check out the **John Lennon wall,** a previously ordinary structure that has been covered with Lennon-related graffiti including Beatles song lyrics, peace signs, and paintings of the singer.

PRAGUE CASTLE (PRAŽSKÝ HRAD)

Prague Castle, one of the world's biggest castles, has symbolized the Czech government for over 1000 years. Since the Bohemian royal family established their residence here, the castle has housed Holy Roman Emperors, the Communist Czechoslovak government, and now the Czech Republic's president. In the **Royal Gardens** (Královská zahrada), the **Singing Fountain** spouts its harp-like tune before the **Royal Summer Palace.** *(Trams #22 or 23 to Pražský Hrad and go down U Prašného Mostu. ☎224 373 368; www.hrad.cz. Castle open daily Apr.-Sept. 9am-6pm; Oct.-Mar. 9am-4pm. Royal Garden open Apr. and Oct. 10am-6pm, May and Sept. 9am-7pm, Aug. 9am-8pm, June and July 9am-9pm, Closed Oct.-Mar. Long tour 350Kč, students 175Kč, short tour 150/125Kč. Without guided tour, entrance to main Castle grounds and St. Vitus's Cathedral is free.)*

ST. VITUS'S CATHEDRAL. Inside the castle walls stands the beautiful Gothic St. Vitus's Cathedral (Katedrála sv. Víta) which was completed in 1929 after 600 years of construction. To the right of the altar stands the silver **tomb of St. Jan Nepomuck.** In the main church, precious stones and paintings telling the saint's story line the walls of **St. Wenceslas Chapel** (Svatováclavská kaple). Climb the 287 steps of the **Great South Tower** for an excellent view, or descend underground to the **Royal Crypt** (Královská hrobka), which holds the tomb of Charles IV.

OLD ROYAL PALACE. The Old Royal Palace (Starý královský palác), to the right of the cathedral, is one of the few Czech castles where visitors can wander largely unattended. The lengthy **Vladislav Hall** once hosted jousting competitions. Upstairs in the Chancellery of Bohemia, a Protestant assembly found two Catholic governors guilty of religious persecution and threw them out the window during the 1618 Second Defenestration of Prague.

ST. GEORGE'S BASILICA AND ENVIRONS. Across from the Old Royal Palace stands St. George's Basilica (Bazilika sv. Jiří), where the skeleton of St. Ludmila is on display. The convent next door houses the National Gallery of Bohemian Art. *(Open Tu-Su 10am-6pm. 100Kč, students 50Kč.)* To the right of the Basilica, follow Jiřská halfway down and take a right on **Golden Lane** (Zlatá ulička), a former workspace of alchemists. Franz Kafka had his workspace at #22.

OUTER PRAGUE

In the beautiful neighborhood of Troja, French architect J. B. Mathey's 17th-century **château** overlooks the Vltava. *(Metro C: Nádraží Holešovice, take bus #112 to Zoologická Zahrada. Open Apr.-Oct. Tu-Su 10am-6pm; Nov.-Mar. Sa-Su 10am-5pm. 100Kč, students 50Kč.)* Then venture next door to the **Prague Zoo.** *(Open daily June-Aug 9am-7pm, Apr.-May and Sept.-Oct. 9am-6pm, Mar. 9am-5pm, Nov.-Feb. 9am-4pm. 150 Kč, students 100Kč.)* Guided by a divine dream to build a monastery atop a bubbling stream, King Boleslav II and St. Adalbert founded **Břevnov Monastery,** Bohemia's oldest, in 993. To the right of **St. Margaret's Church** (Bazilika sv. Markéty), the stream leads to a pond. *(Metro A: Malostranská. Take tram #22 to Břevnovský klášter. Church open for mass M-Sa 7am and 6pm, Su 7:30, 9am, and 6pm. Tours Sa-Su 10am, 2, 4pm. 60Kč, students 30Kč.)*

MUSEUMS

MUCHA MUSEUM. The museum is devoted to the work of Alfons Mucha, the Czech's most celebrated artist. Mucha, an Art Nouveau pioneer, gained fame for his poster series of "la divine" Sarah Bernhardt. *(Panská 7. Metro A or B: Můstek. Walk up Václavské nám. toward the St. Wenceslas statue. Go left on Jindřišská and left again on Panská. ☎221 451 333; www.mucha.cz. Open daily 10am-6pm. 120Kč, students 60Kč.)*

FRANZ KAFKA MUSEUM. This fantastic multimedia exhibit of Kafka memorabilia uses photographs and original letters to bring visitors back to 19th-century Prague, as experienced by the renowned author. *(Cihelná 2b. Metro A: Malostranská. Go down Klárov toward the river, turn right on U. Luzické Semináré and left on Cilhená. ☎257 535 507; www.kafkamuseum.cz. Open daily 10am-6pm. 120Kč, students 60Kč.)*

CITY GALLERY PRAGUE. With seven locations throughout greater Prague, the City Gallery (Galerie Hlavního Města Prahy) offers an impressive variety of permanent and rotating collections. The **House of the Golden Ring** has an especially massive permanent collection of 19th- and 20th-century Czech art. *(Týnská 6. Metro A: Staroměstská. Behind and to the left of Týn Church. ☎222 327 677; www.citygallery-prague.cz. Call for hours. 50-120Kč, students 30-60Kč.)*

MUSEUM OF COMMUNISM. This gallery tries to expose the flaws of the Communist system that ruled over the Czech people. Nowhere will you find more pitchforks or more propaganda. *(Na Příkopě 10. Metro A: Můstek. ☎224 212 966; www.museumofcommunism.com. Open daily 9am-9pm. 180Kč, students 140Kč.)*

ENTERTAINMENT

To find info on Prague's concerts and performances, consult *The Prague Post*, *Threshold*, *Do mesta-Downtown*, or *The Pill* (all free at many cafes and restaurants). Most performances start at 7pm and offer standby tickets 30min. before curtain. Between mid-May and early June, the **Prague Spring Festival** draws musicians from around the world. June brings all things avant-garde with the **Prague Fringe Festival** (☎224 935 183; www.praguefringe.com), featuring dancers, comedians, performance artists, and—everyone's favorite—mimes. For tickets

ONE-CHILLING CHAPEL

n and around Prague, you'll find churches made of stone, brick, ron, glass—and one of bones. Kutná Hora, a small, picturesque village 1hr. from Prague, is infamous for its ossuary, a chapel illed with artistic and religious creations made entirely from parts of human skeletons. The village earned its fame from silver mining in the 14th century. Its morbid side only came out when ts graveyard gained a reputation as a sacred place to bury plague victims. Since the cemetery was overflowing with corpses, the Cisercian Order built a chapel to house the extra remains. In a fit of creativity (or possibly insanity), one monk began designing flowers from pelvises and crania. He never finished the ossuary, but he artist František Rint eventually completed the project in 1870, decorating the chapel from floor o ceiling with the bones of over 0,000 people.

rains run from Hlavní nádraži in Prague to Kutná Hora (1½hr., 1 per hr., one-way 62Kč). The ossuary is a 1km walk from the station. Turn right out of the station, then take a left, and go left again on the highway. Continue for 500m and go right at the church; the ossuary is at the end of the road. ☎728 125 488; www.kostnice.cz. Open daily 8am-6pm.

to the city's shows, try **Bohemia Ticket International,** Malé nám. 13, next to Čedok. (☎224 227 832; www.ticketsbti.cz. Open M-F 9am-5pm, Sa 9am-1pm.)

The majority of Prague's theaters close in July and August, but the selection is extensive during the rest of the year. The **National Theater** (Národní divadlo), Národní 2/4, stages ballet, drama, and opera. (☎224 901 487; www.narodni-divadlo.cz. Metro B: Národní třída. Box office open Sept.-June daily 10am-6pm and 45min. before performances. Tickets 50-1100Kč.) Every performance at the **Image Theatre,** Pařížská 4, is silent, conveying the message through dance, pantomime, and creative use of black light. (☎222 314 448; www.blacktheatreprague.cz. Performances daily 8pm. Box office open daily 9am-8pm. Tickets 440Kč, students 220Kč.) The **Marionette Theater** (Říše loutek), Žatecká 1, stages a hilarious version of *Don Giovanni*, now in its 16th season. (☎224 819 322. Metro A: Staroměstská. Performances June-July M-Tu and Th-Su 8pm. Box office open June-July daily, 10am-8pm. 490-600Kč, students 390-590Kč.)

NIGHTLIFE

With some of the world's best beer on tap, it's no surprise that pubs and beer halls are Prague's most popular nighttime hangouts. Tourists overrun the city center, so authentic pub experiences are largely restricted to the suburbs and outlying Metro stops. Locals prefer the many jazz and rock hangouts scattered throughout the city.

BARS

Vinárna U Sudu, Vodičkova 10 (☎222 232 207). Metro A or B: Můstek. Cross Václavské nám. to Vodičkova and follow the curve left. A labyrinth of 7 cavernous cellars playing a mix of house/techno for a lively alternative crowd. 1L red wine 125Kč. Open M-Th 8am-3am, F-Sa 8am-4am, Su 8am-2am. MC/V.

Vinárna Vinečko, Lodynská 135/2 (☎222 511 035; www.vineckopraha.cz). Metro A: Nám. Miru. Head west on Rumunská and turn left on Lodynská. A classy wine bar in the heart of the Vinohrady district brimming with thirsty locals and expats. Open M-F 11am-midnight, Sa-Su 2pm-midnight. Cash only.

Atmosphere, Karolíny Světlé 33 (☎222 222 114; www.atmoska.cz). Near the Charles Bridge. A friendly staff serves up surprisingly cheap entrees (99-230Kč) while night revelers sip on a wide range of affordable beers, wines, and cocktails in the enclosed courtyard. Cafe open 11am-1am, pub open noon-2am. MC/V.

Le Chateau, Jakubská 2 (☎222 316 328). From Metro B: nám. Republiky, walk through the Powder Tower to Celetná, then take a right on Templová. Seductive red walls and a youthful clientele keep this place overflowing onto the street until dawn. Nightly live music. Open M-Th noon-3am, F noon-6am, Sa 4pm-6am, Su 4pm-2am.

CLUBS AND DISCOS

Radost FX, Bělehradská 120 (☎224 254 776; www.radostfx.cz). Metro C: I.P. Pavlova. Radost is the best of Prague nightlife, playing only the hippest music from internationally renowned DJs. Creative drinks (Frozen Sex with an Alien; 140Kč) will expand your clubbing horizons. Cover from 100Kč. Open Th-Sa 10pm-5am.

Roxy, Dlouhá 33 (☎224 826 363; www.roxy.cz). Metro B: Nám. Republiky. Same building as the Travellers' Hostel (p. 239). Hip, youthful studio and club with experimental DJs and theme nights. Beer 25Kč. Cover Tu and Th-Sa 100-350Kč. Open daily 10pm-late.

Vagon, Národní třída 25 (www.vagon.cz). Metro B: Národní třída. Located down a flight of stairs near the station. There's no better way to sample Czech nightlife than to hit up this haunt of local musicians. Cover varies, about 75Kč on weekends. Open daily 5pm-late.

Mecca, U Průhonu 3 (☎283 870 522; www.mecca.cz). Metro C: Nádraží Holešovice. The place for Prague's beautiful and atypical, Mecca offers a packed house, with industrial-chic decoration. House music and some techno. Live DJs nightly. Open daily 9pm-late.

Karlovy Lázně, Novotného lávka 1 (☎222 220 502), next to the Charles Bridge. Popularly known as "Five Floors," this tourist magnet boasts 5 levels of sweaty, themed dance floors. Cover 150Kč, 50Kč before 10pm and after 4am. Open daily 9pm-5am.

GLBT NIGHTLIFE

All of the places below distribute *Amigo* (90Kč; www.amigo.cz), a thorough English-language guide to gay life in the Czech Republic. Check www.prague-gayguide.net or www.praguesaints.cz for a list of attractions and resources.

Friends, Bartolomejská 11 (☎224 236 272; www.friends-prague.cz). Metro B: Národní třída. From the station, turn right, head down Na Perštýně, and take a left on Bartolomejská. Rotating schedule features music videos and theme nights. Flecks of light from the disco ball overhead reflect off the eager faces of a stylish young crowd. Women and straight customers welcome but rare. Beer from 30Kč. Open daily 6pm-4am.

Valentino, Vinohradská ul. 40 (☎222 513 491; www.club-valentino.cz). Metro A or C: Muzeum. Czech's largest gay club draws a mixed crowd to its 4 bars and 3 levels. Rotating DJs spice it up. Relax downstairs or at the outside tables. Open daily 11am-late.

DAYTRIPS FROM PRAGUE

TEREZÍN (THERESIENSTADT)

Bus from Prague's Florenc station to the Terezín LT stop. The tourist office is at nám. CSA 179. ☎416 782 616; www.terezin.cz. Open M-Th 8am-5pm, F 8am-1:30pm, Su 9am-3pm.

In 1941, when the Nazis opened a concentration camp at Terezín, their propaganda films touted the area as a resort. In reality, over 30,000 Jews died there, while another 85,000 were transported to camps farther east. The **Ghetto Museum,** left of the bus stop, places Terezín in the wider context of WWII. Across the river, the **Small Fortress** was used as a Gestapo prison. (1hr., 70-80Kč. Museum and barracks open daily Apr.-Oct. 9am-6pm; Nov.-Mar. 9am-5:30pm. Fortress open daily Apr.-Oct. 8am-6pm; Nov.-Mar. 8am-4:30pm. Tour included in admission price for groups larger than 10; reserve ahead. Museum, barracks, and fortress 200Kč, students 150Kč.) Outside the walls lie the **cemetery** and

crematorium. Men should cover their heads before entering. (Open M-F and Su Apr.-Oct. 10am-6pm; Nov.-Mar. 10am-4pm. Free.)

ČESKÝ RÁJ NATIONAL PRESERVE

Buses run from Prague's Florenc station to Jičín. From there, buses go to Prachovské skály and other spots in Český Ráj. Buses can be unpredictable; you can walk along a 6km trail from Motel Rumcajs, Konwva 331, to the Preserve.

The sandstone pillars and gorges of **Prachovské skály** (Prachovské rocks) offer hikes with stunning views. Highlights include the **Pelíšek** rock pond and the ruins of the 14th-century **Pařez** castle. A network of trails cross the 588 acres of the park; green, blue, and yellow signs guide hikers to sights, while triangles indicate scenic vistas. Red signs mark the "Golden Trail," which connects Prachovské skály to **Hrubá Skála** (Rough Rock), a rock town surrounding a castle. From the castle, the trail leads up to the remains of **Valdštejnský Hrad** (Wallenstein Castle). Only the blue trail is suitable for biking.

WEST AND SOUTH BOHEMIA

West Bohemia overflows with curative springs; over the centuries, emperors and intellectuals alike have soaked in the waters of Karlovy Vary. Visitors seeking good beer head to the Pilsner Urquell brewery in Plzeň or the Budvar brewery in České Budějovice. Brooks, hills, and ruins mark rustic South Bohemia's landscape, making it a favorite among Czech cyclists and hikers.

KARLOVY VARY ☎353

The hot springs and enormous spas of Karlovy Vary (pop. 55,000) have drawn legendary Europeans including J.S. Bach, Sigmund Freud, Karl Marx, and Peter the Great. Today, frequent visitors are wealthy elderly Germans and Russians who sip from jugs filled with the therapeutic spring waters. Movie stars and fans also journey to the town for its International Film Festival each July.

TRANSPORTATION AND PRACTICAL INFORMATION. **Buses,** much more convenient than trains, run from Dolní nádraží, on Západní (☎353 504 516), to Plzeň (1hr., 10 per day, 84Kč) and Prague (2hr., 20 per day, 120Kč). To reach the town center from the station, turn left and take the left fork of the pedestrian underpass toward Lázně. Turn right at the next fork, follow the sign for the supermarket, and go up the stairs to reach T.G. Masaryka, which runs parallel to the main thoroughfare, Dr. Davida Bechera. **Centrum Taxi,** Zeyerova 9 (☎353 223 236), offers 24hr. service. **Infocentrum,** Lázeňská 1, next to the Mill Colonnade, has free **Internet,** books rooms (from 450Kč), and sells theater tickets (250-500Kč) and maps. (☎355 321 175; www.karlovyvary.cz. Open M-F 10am-6pm, Sa-Su 10am-4pm.) Another branch is in the bus station (☎353 232 838). The **post office,** T.G. Masaryka 1, has Western Union and Poste Restante. (Open M-F 7:30am-7pm, Sa 8am-1pm, Su 8am-noon.) **Postal Code:** 36001.

ACCOMMODATIONS AND FOOD. **Quest Hostel and Apartments ❷,** Moravská 42, is a winner, offering apartment-like rooms with spacious bathrooms and kitchens. Take bus #2, go past the market, down a hill, and then continue straight ahead uphill on Moravská. (☎353 820 030; www.hostel-karlovyvary.cz. Reception 8am-midnight. Check-out 11am. Breakfast included. 10-bed dorm 410Kč; 4- to 6-bed dorms 450Kč; doubles 500-500Kč.) Next to the post office, **Pension Romania ❹,** Zahradní 49, has huge, bright rooms overlooking the

Teplá River. All rooms equipped with TV, fridge, and private bath. (☎353 222 822. Breakfast included. Singles 950Kč, students 735Kč; doubles 1650-2530Kč; triples 2000Kč. Oct.-Mar. reduced rates.) Karlovy Vary is known for its sweet *oplatky* (spa wafers; from 5Kč). **E&T Bar ❷,** Zeyerova 3, is a haven of quality Czech food at reasonable prices. (☎353 226 022. Salads and entrees 75-225Kč. Open M-Sa 9am-2am, Su 10am-2am. Cash only.)

SIGHTS AND ENTERTAINMENT. The **spa district** starts at **Alžbětiny Lázně 5** (Elizabeth Bath 5), Smetanovy Sady 1, across from the post office. The spa offers water-based treatments. Reserve a few days ahead. (☎353 222 536; www.spa5.cz. Pool and sauna open M and F-Sa 9am-9pm, Tu-Th 6am-noon and 1pm-9pm, Su 9am-6pm. Treatments M-F 7am-3pm. Pool 100Kč. MC/V.) Follow the Teplá River to **Bath 3,** Mlynské nábř 5, which offers massages for 575Kč. (☎353 225 641. Treatments daily 7-11:30am and noon-3pm. Pool 100Kč.) Next door, the **Mlýnská kolonáda** (Mill Colonnade) hosts free concerts in the summer. Farther down is **Zawojski House,** Tržiště 9, an ornate Art Nouveau building that now houses Živnostenská Banka. Two doors down, **Vřídlo pramen** (Sprudel Spring), inside **Vřídelní kolonáda** (Sprudel Colonnade), is Karlovy Vary's hottest and highest-shooting spring. (Open daily 6am-7pm.) Follow Stará Louka to find signs for the **funicular,** which takes passengers up 127m to the **Diana Observatory** and its panoramic view of the city. (Funicular 4 per hr. June-Sept. 9:15am-6:45pm; Apr.-May and Oct. 9:15am-5:45pm; Feb.-Mar. and Nov.-Dec. 9:15am-4:45pm. Tower open daily 9am-7pm. Funicular 36Kč, round-trip 60Kč. Tower 12Kč.) *Promenáda*, a monthly booklet, is available for free at kiosks around town. It includes details on the popular **International Film Festival,** which screens independent films usually in the first week of July.

DAYTRIP FROM KARLOVY VARY: PLZEŇ. Recent attempts to clean up Plzeň (pop. 175,000) have left its buildings and gardens revived. But it's the world-famous beer, not the architecture, which lures so many visitors. A beer-lover's perfect day begins at legendary **Pilsner Urquell Brewery** (Měšťčanský Pivovar Plzeňský Prazdroj), where knowledgeable guides lead groups to the cellars for samples. *(☎377 062 888. Brewery open daily 10am-6pm. 1 hr. English tours daily June-Aug. 12:45, 2:15 and 4:15pm; Sept.-May 12:45pm. Tours 120Kč, students 50Kč. Brewery tap open M-Th 11am-11pm, F-Sa 11am-1am, Su 11am-10pm.)* Plzeň is also home to the world's third-largest **synagogue,** built in the Neoclassical style but with onion domes. *(From the southern end of nám. Republiky, go down Prešovská to Sady Pětatřicátníků and turn left; the synagogue is on the right. ☎377 223 558. Open Apr.-Oct. M-F and Su 11am-5pm, closed Jewish holidays. 50Kč, students 30Kč.)* Just when you think you've had enough of beer halls, the famous **U Salzmannů Restaurace ❸,** Pražská 8 (☎377 235 855), redeems their existence. Opened in 1637, the restaurant attracts local celebrities and specializes in old Czech standbys. *(Giant Pilsner Urquell 25Kč. Fries 35Kč. Open M-Th and Sa-Su 11am-11pm, F 11am-midnight. Su 11am-9pm MC/V.)* **Buses** leave from Husova 58 for Karlovy Vary (1hr., 16 per day, 70-80Kč) and Prague (2hr., 16 per day, 65-80Kč). To reach nám. Republiky, turn left on Husova, which becomes Smetanovy Sady, and turn left on Bedřicha Smetany, or take tram #2 (15Kč). The **tourist office** is at nám. Republiky 41. *(☎378 035 330; www.icpilsen.cz. Open Apr.-Sept. daily 9am-6pm; Oct.-Mar. M-F 10am-5pm, Sa-Su 10am-3:30pm.)* **Postal Code:** 30101.

ČESKÉ BUDĚJOVICE ☎38

České Budějovice (pop. 100,000), also known as Budweis, inspired the namesake pale American brew, which bears little resemblance to the thoroughly enjoyable, malty local Budvar. **Staré Město** centers on the main square, **Náměstí Přemysla Otakara II,** which is surrounded by colorful Renaissance and Baroque buildings. Animosity lingers between Anheuser-Busch and the **Budvar Brewery,** Karoliny Světlé 4. From the center, take bus #2 toward Borek, Točna. (☎387 705 341; www.budvar.cz. Tours for groups of 8 or more by reservation daily 9am-4pm. 100Kč, students 50Kč.) If you're looking for an interesting museum, **Jihočeské Motocylové Museum,** Piaristická nám., houses the private antiques collection of a motorcycle fanatic. (☎386 801 804. 40Kč, students 20Kč.)

Budget accommodation is scarce in České Budějovice, with most travelers opting to stay nearby in Český Krumlov. **Pension Minor ❸,** located in the town center at Školní 8, offers spacious and reasonably-priced rooms with private bath and satellite TV. (☎387 319 304; www.hotelminor.cz. Breakfast included. Singles 750Kč; doubles 1130Kč.) At **Restaurace Kněžská ❷,** Kněžská 1, a lively local crowd chats over heavy Czech dishes. The "Jagersteak" (sirloin, cream, and mushrooms; 265Kč) is a worthy splurge. (☎386 358 829. Entrees 25-265Kč. Open M-Th 10am-11pm, F 10am-midnight, Sa 11am-midnight. Cash only.)

Trains (☎387 854 490) leave from Nádražní 12 for: Brno (4hr., 5 per day, 274Kč); Český Krumlov (50min., 9 per day, 46Kč); Plzeň (2hr., 9 per day, 162Kč); Prague (2hr., 13 per day, 204Kč). **Buses** (☎386 354 444) go to Brno (4hr., 6 per day, 220Kč), Český Krumlov (45min., 22 per day, 32Kč), and Prague (2hr., 10 per day, 120-144Kč). To reach the town center from the station, go right on Nádražní, left at the first crosswalk, and follow Lannova třída (becomes Kanovnická). The **tourist office** is at nám. Otakara II 2. (☎386 801 413; www.c-budejovice.cz. Open May-Sept. M-F 8:30am-6pm, Sa 8:30am-5pm, Su 10am-4pm, Oct.-Apr. M and W 9am-5pm, Tu, Th, F 8am-4pm, Sa 9am-1pm.) **Postal Code:** 37001.

ČESKÝ KRUMLOV ☎38

This once-hidden gem of the Czech Republic has been discovered by tourists escaping Prague's overcrowded attractions. But when the sun goes down and the day-trippers leave, this fairy-tale town won't disappoint. The majestic **Zamek** (Castle), the second largest castle in the country, has been home to a succession of Bohemian and Bavarian nobles since the 1200s. Follow Radniční across the river to the entrance on Latrán. Climb the 162 steps of the tower for a fabulous view of the town. (☎380 704 711. Castle open June-Aug. Tu-Su 9am-6pm, Sept.-Oct. and Apr.-May Tu-Su 9am-5pm. Last tour 1hr. before closing. Tower open June-Aug. Tu-Su 9am-5:30pm, Sept.-Oct. and Apr.-May 9am-4:30pm. Castle tour 230Kč, students 130Kč. Tower 45Kč.) The enchanting castle **gardens** host the popular **Revolving South Bohemia Theater,** which has summer performances. (Gardens open May-Sept. Tu-Su 9am-7pm, Oct. and Apr. Tu-Su 8am-5pm. Free. Shows begin 8:30-9:30pm. Tickets 200-900Kč; available at the tourist office. Reserve ahead.) The **Egon Schiele Art Center,** Siroká 70-72, displays Schiele's works alongside those of other 20th-century Baltic artists. (☎380 704 011; www.schieleartcentrum.cz. Open daily 10am-6pm. 120Kč, students 70Kč.)

Cikánská Jizba (Gypsy Bar), Dlouhá 31, serves up Roma cuisine (80-180Kč) and music. (☎380 717 585. Open daily 3-11pm.) Every night is Halloween at the nearby **Nebeské pastviny** (Horror Bar) on the corner of Másna and Radniční. Costumed witches will bring over your drink. (☎775 234 214. Open daily 6pm-1am.) Most hostels provide free **inner tubes** so guests can ride down the Vltava River. **VLTAVA,** Kájovská 62, rents equipment, provides trips for rafting down the river, and rents bikes. (☎380 711 988; www.ckvltava.cz. Bike rental 320Kč per day. Open June-Sept. daily 9am-7pm, Oct.-May daily 9am-5pm.) Go **horseback riding** at **Jezdeck klub Slupenec,** Slupenec 1. Follow Horní to the highway, take the second left on Křížová, and follow the red trail to Slupenec. (☎380 711 052; www.jk-slupenec.cz. Open Tu-Su 9am-6pm. 300 Kč per hr.)

The laid-back **Krumlov House ❶,** Rooseveltova 68, has large, rustic rooms and a well-stocked common room. To get there from the bus station, walk to the end of the station toward the castle tower, take the pedestrian path on your left, cross the main street at the bottom of the hill, and take your first, sharp left onto Rooseveltova. (☎380 711 935; www.krumlovhostel.com. Reception 9am-8pm. Check-out 10am. No curfew. Linens and Wi-Fi included. Laundry 150Kč. Apr.-Oct. 14 dorms 300Kč; doubles 375Kč, with bath 400Kč; suites 450Kč. Oct. 15-Mar. dorms 250Kč; doubles 300Kč, with bath 350Kč; suites 400Kč.) **Hostel 99 ❷**, Věžní 99, has multi-level dorm rooms and a free keg every Wednesday night. From nám. Svornosti, take Radniční, which becomes Latrán; turn right on Věžní at the red-and-yellow gate. (☎380 712 812; www.hostel99.com. Reception 9am-9pm. Check-in noon, check-out 10am. Internet and kitchen access included. Dorms 250-300Kč; doubles 700-900Kč.) Just off Radniční, **Laibon ❶**, Parkán 105, serves excellent vegetarian cuisine and has a relaxing, river-front terrace. (Entrees 30-150Kč. Open daily 11am-11pm. Cash only.)

Trains run from Nádrazní 31 (☎755 1111) to České Budějovice (1hr., 8 per day, 46Kč) and Prague (2hr., 5 per day, 224Kč). A **bus** runs from the train station to the town center (5Kč). Buses run from the bus station to České Budějovice (45 min, 15 per day, 32Kč) and Prague (3 1/2 hr. 6 per day, 172Kč). The **tourist office** is at Nám. Svornosti 2. (☎380 704 622; www.ckrumlov.cz/infocentrum. Open Apr.-Oct. M-Sa 9am-1pm and 2-7pm.) **Postal Code:** 38101.

MORAVIA

The valleys and peaks of Moravia make up the easternmost third of the Czech Republic. Home to the country's two leading universities, the region is the birthplace of Tomáš G. Masaryk, first president of the former Czechoslovakia, psychoanalyst Sigmund Freud, and geneticist Johann Gregor Mendel.

BRNO

The two spires of St. Peter's Cathedral dominate the skyline of Brno (pop. 388,000), the second largest city in the country and an international market-place since the 13th century. Today, global corporations compete with family-owned produce stands, and churches soften the glare of casinos and clubs. **Špilberk Castle** (Hrad Špilberk) earned a reputation as the cruelest prison in Hapsburg Europe. Today the castle is a museum, and its cells house Baroque art. From Nám. Svobody, take Zámečnická and go right on Panenská; after Husova, head uphill. (www.spilberk.cz. Open May-Sept. Tu-Su 9am-6pm, Apr. and Oct. Tu-Su 9am-5pm, Nov.-Mar. 10am-5pm. 70Kč, students 50Kč.) The **Peter and Paul Cathedral** was allegedly saved from the Swedish siege of 1645 by the clever townspeople. The attacking general promised to retreat if his army didn't capture the city by noon; when the townsfolk learned of his claim, they struck the noon bells one hour early and the Swedes slunk away. The bells have been striking noon at 11am ever since. (On Petrov Hill. Climb Petrska from Zelný trh. Cathedral open M-Sa 8:15am-6:15pm. Su 7am-6pm. Chapel, tower, and crypt open M-Sa 11am-6pm, Su 1-6pm. Cathedral and chapel free. Tower 25Kč, students 20Kč. Crypt 25/10Kč.) Down Masarykova on the left is the **Capuchin Monastery Crypt** (Hrobka Kapucínského kláštera), where 18th-century monks developed a burial technique to allow bodies to dry naturally. (Open May-Sept. M-Sa 9am-noon and 2-4:30pm, Su 11-11:45am and 2-4:30pm, Oct.-Apr. Tu-Sa 9am-noon and 2-4:30pm, Su 11-11:45am and 2-4:30pm. 40Kč, students 20Kč.) The **Mendelianum,** Mendlovo nám. 1A, documents the life and work of Johann Gregor Mendel. (Open Apr.-Oct. Tu-Su10am-6pm; Nov.-Mar. Tu-Su 10am-5pm. 60Kč, students 30Kč.) English-speaking expats fill **Charlie's Hat,** Kobližná 12, a lively cellar bar with cheap beer and a loud pop/rock soundtrack. (☎542 210 557. Beer from 18Kč. Pub open daily 9pm-late.) The large **Klub Flěda,** Štefánikova 24, is Brno's prime music venue, hosting concerts and live DJs. Take tram #26 up Štefánikova to Hrncirska; Flěda is on the right. (www.fleda.cz. Open daily 2pm-midnight.) The free guide *Metropolis* lists upcoming events.

Get a good night's sleep at **Hotel Astorka ❸,** Novobranská 3. (☎542 592 370. Open July-Sept. Singles 580Kč; doubles 1160Kč; triples 1740Kč. 50% student discount. AmEx/MC/V.) **Hotel Avion ❸,** Česká 20, has comfortable rooms right in the center of town. From nam. Svobody, walk 100m down Česká, the hotel is on your right. (☎542 321 303; www.avion-hotel.cz. Breakfast included. Singles 650Kč; doubles 1300Kč. MC/V). Try the all-organic vegetarian buffet at **Rebio ❶,** Orlí 26. (☎542 211 130. Open M-F 8am-8pm, Sa 10am-3pm. Cash only.)

Trains (☎542 214 803) go to Prague (3-4hr., 22 per day, 300-400Kč); Bratislava, SLK (2hr., 12 per day, 200Kč); Budapest, HUN (4hr., 5 per day, 970Kč); Vienna, AUT (1hr., 5 per day, 540Kč). **Buses** (☎543 217 733) leave from Zvonařka and Plotní for Prague (2hr., 36 per day, 140Kč) and Vienna, AUT (2hr., 2 per day, 200Kč). Student Agency buses (☎542 4242) run to Prague (40 per day, 150Kč) down from the train station. For maps and information, the **tourist office,** Radnická 8, is in the town hall. (☎542 211 090; www.ticbrno.cz. Open M-F 8:30am-6pm, Sa-Su 9am-5:30pm.) **Postal Code:** 60100.

OLOMOUC ☎585

Formerly the capital of Moravia, the inviting university town of Olomouc (pop. 103,000) resembles Prague as it was before the city was totally overwhelmed by tourists. Find peace in a city wheres Baroque architecture that lines the paths in the town center, locals stroll outdoors during the day, and students keep the clubs thumping until dawn. Every May, the town plays host to the second-largest Oktoberfest celebration in Europe. The 1378 **radnice** (town hall) and its clock tower dominate the town center. The tourist office arranges trips up the tower (daily 11am and 3pm; 15Kč). An amusing **astronomical clock** is set in the town hall's north side. In 1955, Communist clockmakers replaced the attractive mechanical saints with archetypes of "the people." The 35m black-and-gold **Trinity Column** (Sloup Nejsvětější Trojice), the dolphin-shaped **Arion Fountain,** and the towering **St. Moritz Church** surround the square. A 10 minute walk from the main square, the three spires of 750-year-old **St. Wenceslas Cathedral** (Metropolitní Kostel sv. Václava) dominate the skyline. (Cathedral open Tu and Th-Sa 9am-5pm, W 9am-4pm, Su 11am-5pm. Donations requested.) Next door in the city's restored Přemyslid Castle, the newly opened **Archdiocesan Museum** holds the impressive remnants of the original castle in addition to a permanent collection of Moravian art. (☎585 514 111; www.olmuart.cz. Open Tu-Su 10am-6pm. Admission 50Kč, students 25Kč, W and Su free.)

The small **Poet's Corner Hostel ❶,** Sokolská 1, feels more like home than a hostel, with owners who cheerfully offer advice on attractions. (☎777 570 730; www.hostelolomouc.com. Laundry 100Kč. 7-bed dorms June-Aug. 350Kč; doubles 900Kč; triples 1200Kč.) **Hanácká Hospoda ❶,** Dolní nám. 38, is packed with locals devouring Czech fare. (☎777 721 171. Entrees 45-199Kč. Open M-Sa 10am-midnight, Su 10am-8pm. AmEx/MC/V.)

Trains (☎584 722 175) leave from Jeremenkova 23 for Brno (1hr., 5 per day, 120Kč) and Prague (3hr., 19 per day, 294Kč). **Buses** (☎585 313 917) leave from Rolsberská 66 for Brno (1hr., 10 per day, 75-95Kč) and Prague (4hr., 4 per day, 240-275Kč). The **tourist office,** Horní nám., is in the town hall. (☎585 513 385; www.olomoucko.cz. Open daily Mar.-Nov. 9am-7pm; Dec.-Feb. 9am-5pm.) Grab a terminal at **Internet u Dominika,** Slovenská 12. (☎777 181 857. 60Kč per hr. Open M-F 9am-9pm, Sa-Su 10am-9pm.) **Postal Code:** 77127.

DENMARK (DANMARK)

Straddling the border between Scandinavia and continental Europe, Denmark packs majestic castles, pristine beaches, and thriving nightlife onto the compact Jutland peninsula and its network of islands. Vibrant Copenhagen boasts the busy pedestrian thoroughfare of Strøget and the world's tallest carousel in Tivoli Gardens, while beyond the city, fairytale lovers can tour Hans Christian Andersen's home in rural Odense. In spite of the nation's historically homogenous population, its Viking past has given way to a dynamic multicultural society that draws in visitors as it turns out Legos and Skagen watches.

DISCOVER DENMARK: SUGGESTED ITINERARIES

THREE DAYS. Start off in the capital of **Copenhagen** (p. 258), soaking up some sun on a bike tour (p. 262) of the city or waiting out showers in the medieval ruins beneath **Christianborg Slot.** Channel the Bard at Kronborg Slot in **Helsingør** (p. 266), where the real-life Hamlet slept.

BEST OF DENMARK, 12 DAYS. Begin your journey in **Copenhagen** (3 days), then castle-hop to Frederiksborg Slot in nearby **Hillerød** (1 day; p. 266). The best way to explore the beautiful beaches, farmlands, and forests of **Bornholm** (2 days; p. 268) is to bike around the island. After returning to the mainland, head west to **Odense** (1 day; p. 269) for celebrations of Hans Christian Andersen's birth. Discover the museums and nightlife of little-known **Århus** (2 days; p. 271) before indulging your inner child at Legoland in **Billund** (1 day; p. 272). Finish your journey at the northern tip of Jutland, where the yellow houses of **Skagen** (2 days; p. 274) look out on the Baltic Sea.

ESSENTIALS

FACTS AND FIGURES

OFFICIAL NAME: Kingdom of Denmark.

CAPITAL: Copenhagen.

MAJOR CITIES: Aalborg, Århus, Odense.

POPULATION: 5,485,000.

LAND AREA: 42,400 sq. km.

TIME ZONE: GMT +1.

LANGUAGES: Danish. Pockets of Faroese, Greenlandic, and German. English is nearly universal as a second language.

TALLEST LEGO TOWER: Constructed in 2003 at Billund's Legoland; 27.22m.

WHEN TO GO

Denmark is best between May and September, when days are usually sunny and temperatures average 10-16°C (50-61°F). Winter temperatures average 0°C (32°F). Although temperate for its northern location, Denmark can turn rainy or cool at a moment's notice; always pack a sweater and an umbrella.

DOCUMENTS AND FORMALITIES

EMBASSIES AND CONSULATES. All foreign embassies are in Copenhagen (p. 259). Danish embassies abroad include: **Australia,** Gold Fields House, Level 14, 1 Alfred St., Circular Quay, Sydney, NSW, 2000 (☎02 92 47 22 24; www.gksydney.um.dk/en); **Canada,** 47 Clarence St., Ste. 450, Ottawa, ON, K1N 9K1 (☎613-562-1811; www.ambottawa.um.dk/en); **Ireland,** Harcourt Road, 7th floor, Block E, Iveagh Court, Dublin 2 (☎01 475 6404; www.ambdublin.um.dk/en); **New Zealand,** Forsyth Barr House, Level 7, 45 Johnston Street, P.O. Box 10-874, Wellington, 6036 (☎04 471 0520; www.danishconsulatesnz.org.nz); **UK,** 55 Sloane St., London, SW1X 9SR (☎020 73 33 02 00; www.amblondon.um.dk/en); **US,** 3200 Whitehaven St., NW, Washington, D.C., 20008 (☎202-234-4300; www.denmarkemb.org).

VISA AND ENTRY INFORMATION. EU citizens don't need visas. Citizens of Australia, Canada, New Zealand, and the US do not need a visa for stays of up to 90 days, beginning upon entry into any of the countries in the EU's freedom-of-movement zone. For stays longer than 90 days, non-EU citizens need a residence or work permit. For more info visit www.um.dk/en.

TOURIST SERVICES AND MONEY

EMERGENCY | **Ambulance, Fire,** and **Police:** ☎112.

TOURIST OFFICES. The **Danish Tourist Board** has offices in most cities throughout the country, with its main office in Copenhagen at Islands Brygge 43 (☎3288 9900; www.visitdenmark.dt.dk). The website offers a wealth of info as well as an online booking tool for accommodations.

MONEY. The Danish unit of currency is the **krone (kr),** plural **kroner.** One krone is equal to 100 **øre.** The easiest way to get cash is from **ATMs;** cash cards are widely accepted, and many machines give advances on **credit cards.** Money and **traveler's checks** can be exchanged at most **banks** for a 30kr fee. Denmark has a high cost of living, which it passes along to visitors; expect to pay 100-150kr for a hostel bed, 80-130kr for a day's groceries, and 50-90kr for a cheap restaurant meal. A bare-bones day might cost 250-350kr, and a slightly more comfortable one 400-600kr. There are no hard and fast rules for **tipping.** Service at restaurants is typically included in the bill, but it's always polite to round up to the nearest 10kr, and to leave an additional 10-20kr for good service.

Denmark has a 25% **value added tax (VAT),** a sales tax applied to most goods and services. The prices given in *Let's Go* include VAT. In the airport upon exiting the EU, non-EU citizens can claim a refund on the tax paid for goods purchased at participating stores. In order to qualify for a refund in a store, you must spend at least 300kr; make sure to ask for a refund form when you pay. For more info on qualifying for a VAT refund, see p. 21. Exchange rates:

DANISH KRONER (KR)		
	AUS$1 = 4.42KR	10KR = AUS$2.26
	CDN$1 = 4.63KR	10KR = CDN$2.16
	EUR€1 = 7.46KR	10KR = EUR€1.34
	NZ$1 = 3.49KR	10KR = NZ$2.86
	UK£1 = 9.42KR	10KR = UK£1.06
	US$1 = 4.82KR	10KR = US$2.08

BUSINESS HOURS. Shops are normally open Monday to Thursday from about 9 or 10am to 6pm and Friday until 7 or 8pm; they are always open Saturday mornings and in Copenhagen, they stay open all day Saturday. Regular banking hours are Monday to Wednesday and Friday 10am-4pm, Thursday 10am-6pm.

TRANSPORTATION

BY PLANE. International flights arrive at **Kastrup Airport** in Copenhagen (**CPH;** ☎3231 3231; www.cph.dk). Flights from Europe also arrive at **Billund Airport,** outside Århus (**BLL;** ☎7650 5050; www.billund-airport.dk). Smaller airports in Århus and Esbjerg serve as hubs for budget airline **Ryanair** (☎353 12 49 77 91; www.ryanair.com). **SAS** (Scandinavian Airlines; Denmark ☎70 10 20 00, UK 0870 60 72 77 27, US 800-221-2350; www.scandinavian.net), the national airline company, offers youth discounts to some destinations.

BY TRAIN AND BY BUS. The state-run rail line in Denmark is **DSB;** their helpful route planner is online at www.rejseplanen.dk. **Eurail** is valid on all state-run routes. The **ScanRail** pass is good for rail travel through Denmark, Finland, Norway, and Sweden, as well as many discounted ferry and bus rides. Remote towns are typically served by buses from the nearest train station. Buses are reliable and can be less expensive than trains.

RAIL SAVINGS. ScanRail passes purchased outside Scandinavia may be cheaper, depending on the exchange rate, and they are also more flexible. Travelers who purchase passes within Scandinavia can only use three travel days in the country of purchase. Check www.scanrail.com for more info.

BY FERRY. Several companies operate ferries to and from Denmark. **Scandlines** (☎33 15 15 15; www.scandlines.dk) arrives from Germany and Sweden and also operates domestic routes. **Color Line** (Norway ☎47 81 00 08 11; www.colorline.com) runs ferries between Denmark and Norway. **DFDS Seaways** (UK ☎08715 229 955; www.dfdsseaways.co.uk) sails from Harwich, BRI to Esbjerg and from Copenhagen to Oslo, NOR. For more info, check www.aferry.to/ferry-to-denmark-ferries.htm. Tourist offices help sort out the dozens of smaller ferries that serve Denmark's outlying islands. For more info on connections from Bornholm to Sweden, and from Jutland to Norway and Sweden, see p. 58.

BY BIKE AND BY THUMB. With its flat terrain and well-marked bike routes, Denmark is a cyclist's dream. You can rent bikes (50-80kr per day) from designated shops as well as from some tourist offices and train stations. The **Dansk Cyklist Forbund** (☎3332 3121; www.dcf.dk) provides info about cycling in Denmark and investing in long-term rentals. Pick up *Bikes and Trains* at any train station for info on bringing your bike on a train, which can cost up to 50kr. **Hitchhiking** on motorways is illegal. *Let's Go* does not recommend hitchhiking.

KEEPING IN TOUCH

PHONE CODES	**Country code:** 45. **International dialing prefix:** 00. For more info on how to place international calls, see **Inside Back Cover.**

EMAIL AND THE INTERNET. In Copenhagen and other cities, you can generally find at least one Internet cafe; expect to pay 15-30kr per hr. DSB, the national railroad, maintains Internet cafes in some stations as well. In smaller towns, access at public libraries is free; reserve a slot in advance.

TELEPHONE. **Pay phones** accept both coins and phone cards, available at post offices or kiosks in 100kr denominations. **Mobile phones** (p. 32) are a popular and economical alternative. For domestic directory info, dial ☎118; for international info, dial ☎113. International direct dial numbers include: **AT&T Direct** (☎8001 0010); **Canada Direct** (☎8001 0011); **MCI WorldPhone** (☎8001 0022); Sprint (☎8001 0877); **Telecom New Zealand** (☎8001 0064).

MAIL. Mailing a postcard or letter to Australia, Canada, New Zealand, or the US costs 8kr; to elsewhere in Europe it costs 7kr. Domestic mail costs 4.50kr.

ACCOMMODATIONS AND CAMPING

DENMARK	❶	❷	❸	❹	❺
ACCOMMODATIONS	under 100kr	100-160kr	161-220kr	221-350kr	over 350kr

Denmark's hotels are uniformly expensive, so **youth hostels** *(vandrehjem)* tend to be mobbed by budget travelers of all ages. HI-affiliated **Danhostels** are the most common and are often the only option in smaller towns. Facilities are clean, spacious, and comfortable, often attracting families as well as backpackers. Eco-conscious tourists can choose from one of the six Danhostels that have earned a **Green Key** (www.green-key.org) for their environmentally friendly practices. Room rates vary according to season and location; dorms range from 100 to 200kr per night, with a 35kr HI discount. Linens cost 40-60kr; sleeping bags are not permitted. Reserve ahead, especially in summer and near beaches. Danhostel check-in times are usually a non-negotiable 3-4hr. window. For more info, contact the **Danish Youth Hostel Association** (☎3331 3612; www.danhostel.dk). Independent hostels, found mostly in cities and larger towns, draw a younger crowd and tend to be more sociable, although their facilities are rarely as nice as those in Danhostels. Most tourist offices can book rooms for stays in **private homes** (150-250kr).

Denmark's 496 **campgrounds** (about 60kr per person) range from one star (toilets and drinking water) to three stars (showers and laundry) to five stars (swimming, restaurants, and stoves). Info is available at **DK-Camp** (☎7571 2962; www.dk-camp.dk). You'll need a **Camping Card Scandinavia** (125kr for 1yr. membership; available at www.camping.se; allow at least 3 weeks for delivery), valid across Scandinavia and sold at campgrounds as well as through the Danish Youth Hostel Association. Campsites affiliated with hostels generally do not require a card. If you plan to camp for only a night, you can buy a 24hr. pass (20kr). The **Danish Camping Council** *(Campingrådet)*, Mosedalvej 15, 2500 Valby (☎39 27 88 44; www.campingraadet.dk), sells passes and the *Camping Denmark* handbook (95kr). Sleeping in train stations, in parks, or anywhere on public property is illegal in Denmark.

DENMARK

FOOD AND DRINK

DENMARK	❶	❷	❸	❹	❺
FOOD	under 40kr	40-70kr	71-100kr	101-150kr	over 150kr

A "danish" in Denmark is a *wienerbrød* (Viennese bread), found in bakeries alongside other flaky treats. Traditionally, Danes have favored open-faced sandwiches called *smørrebrød* for a more substantial meal. For cheap eats, look for lunch specials *(dagens ret)* and all-you-can-eat buffets. National beers include Carlsberg and Tuborg; bottled brews tend to be cheaper than drafts. A popular alcohol is *snaps* (or *aquavit)*, a clear liquor flavored with fiery spices, usually served chilled and unmixed. Many vegetarian *(vegetarret)* options are the result of Indian and Mediterranean influences, and salads and veggies *(grønsager)* can be found on most menus. Expect to pay around 120kr for a sit-down meal at a restaurant and 40-80kr in cafes and ethnic takeouts.

HOLIDAYS AND FESTIVALS

Holidays: New Year's Day (Jan. 1); Easter (Apr. 12); Queen's Birthday (Apr. 16); Worker's Day (May 1); Whit Sunday and Monday (May 11-12); Constitution Day (June 5); Midsummer's Eve (June 23); Christmas (Dec. 24-26).

Festivals: In early Spring before the start of Lent, Danish children assault candy-filled barrels with birch branches on **Fastelavn** (Shrovetide), while adults take to the streets for carnivals. Guitar solos ring out over Roskilde during the **Roskilde Festival** (July 3-6), just before Copenhagen and Århus kick off their annual **jazz festivals,** mid-to-late July.

BEYOND TOURISM

For short-term employment in Denmark, check www.jobs-in-europe.net; For opportunities across Europe, see the **Beyond Tourism** chapter p. 60.

The American-Scandinavian Foundation (AMSCAN), 58 Park Ave., New York, NY, 10016, USA (☎212-879-9779; www.amscan.org/jobs/index.html). Volunteer and job opportunities throughout Scandinavia.

Vi Hjælper Hinanden (VHH), Aasenv. 35, 9881 Bindslev, DEN, c/o Inga Nielsen (☎98 93 86 07; www.wwoof.dk). For 50kr, the Danish branch of World-Wide Opportunities on Organic Farms (WWOOF) provides a list of farmers currently accepting volunteers.

COPENHAGEN (KØBENHAVN)

The center of Europe's oldest monarchy, Copenhagen (pop. 1,800,000) embodies a laid-back spirit. The Strøget, the city's famed pedestrian thoroughfare, now bustles with Middle Eastern restaurants and cybercafes, and neon signs glimmer next to angels in the architecture. The up-and-coming districts of Vesterbro and Nørrebro reverberate with some of Europe's wildest nightlife, while the hippie paradise of Christiania swings to a more downbeat vibe.

INTERCITY TRANSPORTATION

Flights: Kastrup Airport (CPH; ☎3231 3231; www.cph.dk). **Trains** connect the airport to København H (13min., 6 per hr., 20kr or 2 clips). Ryanair flies into nearby **Sturup Airport** in Malmö, SWE (**MMX;** ☎40 613 1000; www.sturup.com) at low rates.

Trains: København H (Hovedbanegården or Central Station; domestic travel ☎7013 1415, international 7013 1416; www.dsb.dk). Trains run to: **Berlin, GER** (8hr., 9 per day, 803kr); **Hamburg, GER** (5hr., 5 per day, 537kr); **Malmö, SWE** (25min., every 20min., 71kr); **Oslo, NOR** (8hr., 2 per day, 821kr); **Stockholm, SWE** (5hr., 1 per 1-2hr., 1040kr). For international trips, fares depend on seat availability and can drop to as low as 50% of the quotes listed above; **book at least 2 weeks in advance.**

ORIENTATION

Copenhagen lies on the east coast of the island of **Zealand** *(Sjælland)*, across the Øresund Sound from Malmö, Sweden. The 28km **Øresund Bridge,** which opened on July 1, 2000, established the first "fixed link" between the two countries. Copenhagen's main train station, København H, lies near the city center. Just north of the station, **Vesterbrogade** passes **Tivoli** and **Rådhuspladsen,** the main square, then cuts through the city center as **Strøget** (STROY-yet), the world's longest pedestrian thoroughfare. As it heads east, Strøget goes through a series of names: **Frederiksberggade, Nygade, Vimmelskaftet, Amagertorv,** and **Østergade.** The city center is bordered to the west by five **lakes,** outside of which are the less-touristy communities of **Vesterbro, Nørrebro,** and **Østerbro.** Vesterbro and Nørrebro are home to many of the region's immigrants, while some of Copenhagen's highest-income residents live on the wide streets of Østerbro.

LOCAL TRANSPORTATION

Public Transportation: Copenhagen has an extensive public transportation system. **Buses** (☎3313 1415; www.moviatrafik.dk) run daily 5:30am-12:30am; maps are available on any bus.

S-togs (subways and suburban trains; ☎3314 1701) run M-Sa 5am-12:30am, Su 6am-12:30am. S-tog tickets are covered by Eurail, ScanRail, and InterRail passes.

Metro (☎015 1615; www.m.dk) is small but efficient. All 3 types of public transportation operate on a zone system. To travel any distance, a 2-zone **ticket** is required (19kr; additional zones 9.50kr), which covers most of Copenhagen. For extended stays, the best deal is the **rabatkort** (rebate card; 120kr), available from supermarkets, corner stores, and kiosks, which offers 10 2-zone tickets at discount. The **24hr. pass** (115kr), available at train stations, grants unlimited bus and train transport in the Northern Zealand region, as does the **Copenhagen Card.**

Night buses, marked with an "N," run 12:30-5:30am on limited routes and charge double fare; they accept the 24hr. pass.

Taxis: Københavns Taxa (☎3535 3535) and **Hovedstadens Taxi** (☎3877 7777) charge a base fare of 19kr and then 11-16kr/km. København to Kastrup Airport costs 200kr.

Bike Rental: City Bike (☎3616 4233; www.bycyklen.dk) lends bikes mid-Apr. to Nov. from 110 racks all over the city for a 20kr deposit. Anyone can return your bike and claim your deposit, so keep an eye on it.

DENMARK

PRACTICAL INFORMATION

Tourist Offices: Copenhagen Right Now, Vesterbrog. 4A (☎7022 2442; www.visitcopenhagen.dk). From København H, cross Vesterbrog. toward the Axelrod building. Open M-F 9am-4pm, Sa 9am-2pm. Sells the **Copenhagen Card** (1-day 199kr; 3-day 429kr), which grants free or discounted admission to most sights and unlimited travel throughout Northern Zealand; however, cardholders will need to keep up an almost manic pace to justify the cost. **Use It,** Rådhusstr. 13 (☎3373 0620; www.useit.dk), has indispensable info and services for budget travelers. Offers *Playtime,* a comprehensive budget guide to the city. Provides daytime luggage storage, has free **Internet** (max. 20min.), holds mail, and finds lodgings for no charge. Open mid-June to mid-Sept. daily 9am-7pm; mid-Sept. to mid-June M-W 11am-4pm, Th 11am-6pm, F 11am-2pm.

Embassies and Consulates: Australia, Dampfærgev. 26, 2nd fl. (☎7026 3676). **Canada,** Kristen Bernikowsg. 1 (☎3348 3200). **Ireland,** Østbaneg. 21 (☎3542 3233). **New Zealand,** Store Strandst. 21, 2nd fl. (☎3337 7702). **UK,** Kastelsv. 36-40 (☎3544 5200). **US,** Dag Hammarskjölds Allé 24 (☎3555 3144). www.um.dk for complete list.

GLBT Resources: Landsforeningen for Bøsser og Lesbiske (LBL), Teglgårdstr. 13 (☎3313 1948; www.lbl.dk). Open M-F noon-2:30pm and 3-4:30pm. The monthly *Out and About,* which lists nightlife options, is available at gay clubs and the tourist office Other resources include www.copenhagen-gay-lfe.dk and www.gayguide.dk.

Police: Headquarters at Halmtorvet 20; Politigarden, Politiorvet 1 (☎3314 1448)

Medical Services: Doctors on Call (☎7013 0041 M-F 8am-4pm; ☎7020 1546 evenings/weekends; 400-600kr fee). Emergency rooms at **Amager Hospital,** Italiensv. 1 (☎3234 3234), **Frederiksberg Hospital,** Nordre Fasanv. 57 (☎3834 7711), and **Bispebjerg Hospital,** Bispebjerg Bakke 23 (☎3531 3531).

Internet: Free at **Use It** and **Copenhagen Hovedbibliotek (Central Library),** Krystalg. 15 (☎3373 6060). Coffee shop on 1st fl. Open M-F 10am-7pm, Sa 10am-2pm.

Post Office: In København H. Open M-F 8am-9pm, Sa-Su 10am-4pm. Address mail as follows: LAST NAME, First name, Post Denmark, Hovedbanegårdens Posthus, Hovedbanegården, 1570 Copenhagen V, DEN. **Use It** also holds mail for 2 months.

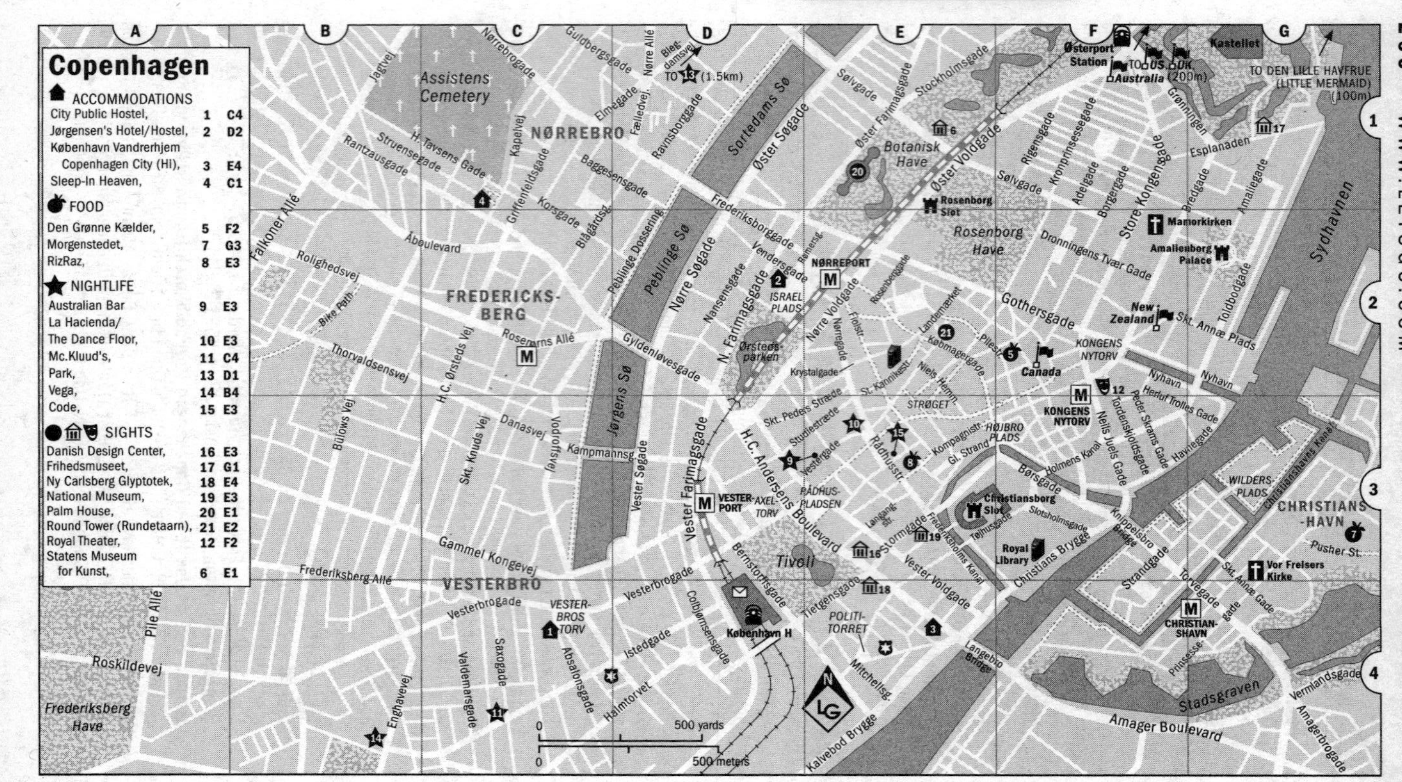
Copenhagen
ACCOMMODATIONS
City Public Hostel, 1 C4
Jørgensen's Hotel/Hostel, 2 D2
København Vandrerhjem Copenhagen City (HI), 3 E4
Sleep-In Heaven, 4 C1
FOOD
Den Grønne Kælder, 5 F2
Morgenstedet, 7 G3
RizRaz, 8 E3
NIGHTLIFE
Australian Bar 9 E3
La Hacienda/The Dance Floor, 10 E3
Mc.Kluud's, 11 C4
Park, 13 D1
Vega, 14 B4
Code, 15 E3
SIGHTS
Danish Design Center, 16 E3
Frihedsmuseet, 17 G1
Ny Carlsberg Glyptotek, 18 E4
National Museum, 19 E3
Palm House, 20 E1
Round Tower (Rundetaarn), 21 E2
Royal Theater, 12 F2
Statens Museum for Kunst, 6 E1
TO DEN LILLE HAVFRUE (LITTLE MERMAID) (100m)
500 yards
500 meters

ACCOMMODATIONS

Comfortable and inexpensive accommodations can be hard to find near the city center, but pedestrian-friendly streets and the great public transportation system ensure that travelers are never far from the action. Reserve well ahead in the summer. Be sure to check out early, as 10am is the standard.

Sleep-In Heaven, Struenseeg. 7 (☎3535 4648; www.sleepinheaven.com), in Nørrebro. M: Forum. Take bus 5A from the airport or from København H. (dir.: Husum; every 10-20min.) to Stengade. Go down Stengade and take your first right on Korsgade. Slight right to continue on Korsgade, left on Kapelvej, quick right onto HansTavsensGade and left into the alley. Laid-back hostel with friendly vibe with warm and helpful staff. Smoke-free. Breakfast 40kr. Linens 40kr. Lockers (refundable deposit). Free Wi-Fi. Max. 5-night stay. Reception and security guard 24hr. Dorms 145-160kr; doubles 500kr; triples 600kr. Ages 16-35. AmEx/MC/V; 5% surcharge. ❷

City Public Hostel, Absalonsg. 8 (☎3331 2070). Go down Vesterbrogade and take a left on Absalonsg.. Cheap rates and great location attracts a diverse crowd of travelers. Breakfast 30kr-40kr. Locks for storage 30kr. Linens and pillow 40kr, towel 10kr. Internet. Reception 24hr. Open May-Aug. Dorms 110-150kr. Cash only. ❷

Jørgensen's Hostel/Hotel Jørgensen, Rømersg. 11 (☎3313 8186; www.hoteljoergensen.dk). M: Nørreport. Small, comfortable rooms in a convenient location. Breakfast and linens included. Max. 5-night stay. Dorm lockout 11am-3pm. 6- to 14-bed dorms 150kr. Singles 475-625kr and doubles 575-750kr; both include TV and private en-suite bathrooms. Under age 35. Cash only for dorms; AmEx/MC/V for private rooms. ❷

Danhostel: København Vandrerhjem Copenhagen City (HI), H.C. Andersens Bvd. 50 (☎3311 8585; www.danhostel.dk/copenhagencity). A popular 15-story resting place, only 5min. from the city center. . Linens 60kr. Internet 14kr per 20min; 29kr per hr. Bike rental 100kr per day. Reception 24hr. Check-in 2-5pm. Reserve ahead.Single-sex-dorms 145-180kr; private rooms 580-720kr. 35kr HI discount. AmEx/MC/V. ❷

DENMARK

FOOD

Stylish cafes serving delectable dishes are plentiful throughout the streets of Copenhagen, but be prepared to spend some cash. For delicious, less expensive food, try local *Schawarma* and kebab shops that line **Strøget** (full meal 40-70kr). For less authentically Danish food, budget travelers stop by the many all-you-can-eat pizza, pasta, and ethnic buffets down **Vesterbrogade** (from 70kr). Traditional cuisine includes *smørebrød* (open-faced sandwiches) and can be found on any street in Copenhagen. Green grocers in **Vesterbro** along **Istedgade** provide fresh fruits and veggies (cash only.)

RizRaz, Kompagnistr. 20 (☎3315 0575; www.rizraz.dk). M: Kongens Nytorv. This relaxed restaurant has plenty of seating, an extensive Mediterranean and Middle Eastern influenced menu with a vegetarian lunch buffet (69kr), and beautiful paintings for sale. Dinner 79kr. Grill order (includes buffet) from 119kr. Open daily 11:30am-midnight. AmEx/MC/V. Also at Store Kannikestr. 19 (☎3332 3345). ❸

Den Grønne Kælder, Pilestr. 48 (☎3393 0140). M: Kongens Nytorv. Enjoy the vegetarian and vegan menu, rotated monthly and made from organic ingredients, in this cozy basement cafe. Try the local favorite "legendary hummus." Takeout 40-60kr. Lunch 50kr. Dinner starts at 105kr. Open M-Tu and Th-Sa 11am-10pm, W 1-10pm. Cash only. ❷

Morgenstedet, Langgaden, Bådsmandsstr. 43 (☎3295 7770; www.morgenstedet.dk), in Christiania. Walk down Pusher St. and take a left at the end, then take a right up the concrete ramp at the bike shop and a left before the bathrooms; it will be on your right.

A BIKING TOUR OF COPENHAGEN

TIME: 4hr. With visits to Rosenborg Slot and Christianborg Slot, 6hr.

DISTANCE: About 6km.

SEASON: Year-round, although Rosenborg Slot has reduced hours Nov.-Apr.

In Copenhagen, biking is the new black. From chic women in heels to businessmen in suits, biking is the European way to travel; not to mention a great way to burn off the delicious buffets you'll be devouring. Copenhagen's flat land makes the city an ideal spot for scenic cycling as you tour fine churches, museums, and of course, castles. Rentals from **City Bike** (p. 259) are a great way to explore Copenhagen, but be sure to stake one out early. Careful: the rules require that you only ride the bikes in the city center. The eastern banks of the five western lakes are fai game, but if you cross over to the other side of the lakes, you'll face a 1000kr fine. Don't ride at night with a City Bike—and make sure you keep an eye on your City Bike when exploring the castles and museums, as anyone can take your bike, not to mention your 20kr!

When biking through the city, you should bypass pedestrian thoroughfares like Strøget to avoid strolling couples and bedazzled tourists. If you want to ride out into the beautiful countryside, ask your hostel about rental bikes. They can be a great alternative and you may get a better quality bike. You can take your bike onto an S-tog for 10kr. In Denmark, you are legally required to use lights when riding at night, and police are not shy about handing out 400kr fines to enforce this law. Helmets are recommended, but not mandatory.

The tour starts and ends in **Rådhus-Pladsen.** Begin by carefully making your way down busy Hans Christian Andersens Boulevard.

1. BOTANISK HAVE. Take a right onto Nørre Voldg. and follow it until you see the gates leading into the University of Copenhagen's lush **Botanical Gardens** (p. 265). Wander along paths lined with more than 13,000 species of plants, or hone in on the **Palm House** to view its extravagant orchids, cycads, and other tropical rarities. Explore the grounds to the **Faculty of Science of the University of Copenhagen,** located just north of the Gardens atop a hill along Øster Voldg.

2. STATENS MUSEUM FOR KUNST AND ROSENBORG SLOT. Next, head back onto Øste Voldg. At the intersection with Sølvg., you'll see the gates of the **Statens Museum for Kunst** (State Museum of Fine Arts; p. 265) to the north and the spires of **Rosenborg Slot** (p. 265, to the south. The latter served as the 16th-century summer house of King Christian IV, and the royal family took refuge here in 1801 when the British navy was shelling Copenhagen. Lock up your bike and pop inside for a look at the Sculpture Street in the museum or Denmark's crowr jewels in the Slot's treasury, and don't forget to wander the King's Gardens.

3. ROUND TOWER. Backtrack down Øster Voldg. and turn left onto Gothersg. Make a righ onto Landemærket and then hop off again to scale the heights of the **Round Tower** (p. 264), a onetime royal observatory that still affords a sweeping view of the city.

4. AMALIENBORG PALACE. Head back up to Gothersg. and turn right. Pass by **Kongens Nytorv,** the 1670 "new square" that turns into a skating rink each winter, and take a left onto Bredg. Keep your eyes peeled for the gilded dome of the **Marmorkirken** (Marble Church) on your left, and then turn right to enter the octagonal plaza of **Amalienborg Palace** (p. 265), a se of four Rococo mansions that the queen and her family call home. Check out the Amalienborg Museum to admire the luxurious furnishings of 19th century King Frederik VII's room.

5. NYHAVN. Continue on through the plaza, turn right on Toldbodg., and then right before the bridge onto Nyhavn. Part of the city's old waterfront, Nyhavn was known for centuries as a seed strip for sailors to find grog, women, and a tattoo artist sober enough to wield a firm needle. Ove the past 30 years, Copenhagen has embarked on a clean-up campaign, and today you're mor likely to find an upscale deli serving smørrebrod than a tumbledown soup kitchen. Whenever a

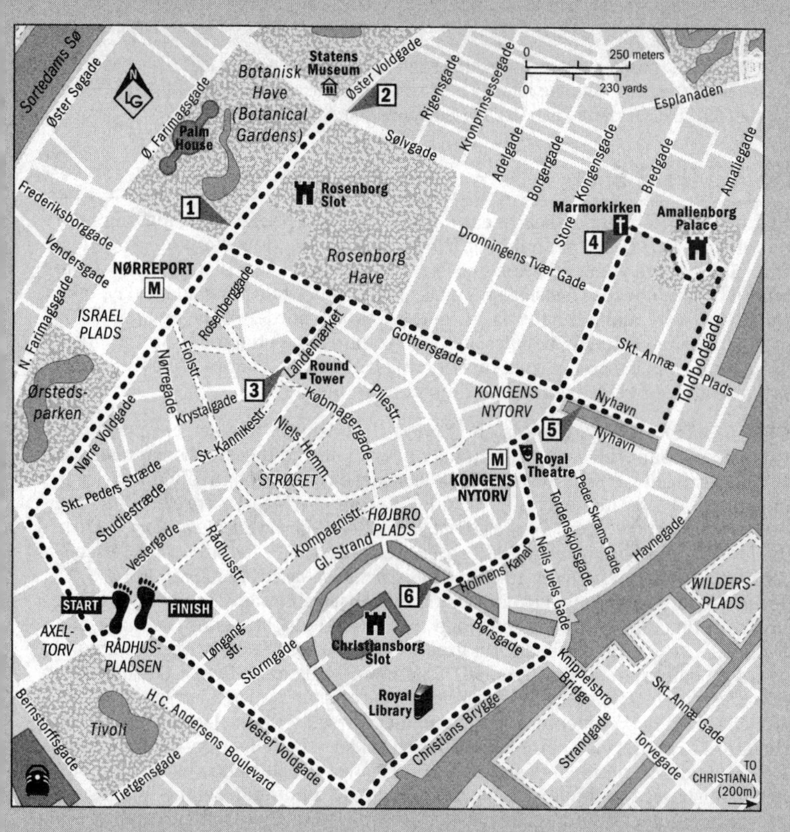

scrap of sunshine can be found, the good people of Copenhagen are soaking it up along the wharf, joined by Swedes from Malmö in search of cheap Danish beer.

6. CHRISTIANBORG SLOT. Walk your bike through Kongens Nytorv, and then thread your way between the **Royal Theater** (p. 265) and the metro station down Neils Juels G. Turn right onto Holmens Kanal and cross the bridge to reach **Christiansborg Slot** (p. 264), seat of the Danish Parliament. Look for the 103m tower; it's difficult to miss. If you arrive before 3:30pm, try to catch a tour of the **Royal Reception Rooms,** or head down into the ruins of the four previous castles underneath the present-day building. The first castle was demolished to make way for a larger one, the next two burned down in fires, and the Hanseatic League dismantled the fourth castle stone by stone after they captured the city in 1369.

7. SLIDING INTO HOME. You're in the home stretch. Head east toward the **Knippelsbro Bridge** and **Christiania** (p. 264), taking in the industrial skyline before lugging your bike down the steps to Christians Brygge below. Turn right and bike along the canal. Keep watch for the Black Diamond annex of the **Royal Library,** built in 1996 from black marble imported from Zimbabwe. Check your email at one of the free terminals inside. Make a right onto Vester Voldg. and coast back up to the Rådhus. The tour has ended; you've earned the right to call it a day. Now you can relax and watch the fireworks from Tivoli, while treating yourself to an ever--popular ice cream cone.

Sit in the enclosed outdoor dining area surrounded by lush bushes and flowerbeds and whet your appetite with the rotating menu of vegetarian cuisine. Soup with bread 45kr. Entrees 70kr. Desserts 25kr. Open Tu-Su noon-9pm. Cash only. ❷

SIGHTS

Flat Copenhagen lends itself to exploration by bike (p. 262). Walking tours are detailed in *Playtime* (available at **Use It**, p. 259). Window-shop down pedestrian **Strøget** until you reach Kongens Nytorv; opposite is the picturesque **Nyhavn,** where **Hans Christian Andersen** penned his first fairy tale. On a clear day, take the 6.4km walk along the five **lakes** on the western border of the city center or grab a bike and ride. Relax in the city hall square and listen to the street music as you enjoy an ice cream treat or a hot dog from local vendors. Most musuems are free and some have extended hours on Wednesdays.

CITY CENTER. **Tivoli Gardens,** the famed 19th-century amusement park, features newly-built rides, an aquarium, concert hall, and theatre. Located across the street from Central Station. **Tivoli Illuminations,** an evocative light show, is staged on Tivoli Lake each night 30min. before closing. *(Vesterbrogade 3 ☎3315 1001; www.tivoligardens.com. Open mid-Sept. to mid-Apr. M-Th and Su 11am-10pm, F 11am-12:30am, Sa 11am-midnight; mid-Aug. to mid-Sept. M-Th and Su 11am-midnight, F-Sa 11am-12:30am. Admission 85kr. Rides 10-60kr. Admission with unlimited rides 285kr. AmEx/MC/V.)* From Tivoli, cross Tietgensgade to find **Ny Carlsberg Glyptotek,** home to ancient art from the 19th and 20th centuries from the Mediterranean, Denmark and France. Also features a beautiful greenhouse garden. Tickets for free guided tours go quickly. *(Dantes Pl. 7. ☎3341 8141; www.glyptoteket.dk. Open Tu-Su 10am-4pm. 50kr, students and children free. Su free. Wheelchair-accessible. Tours mid-June to Aug. W 2pm. MC/V.)* Across H.C. Andersens Bvd., aquaint yourself with the latest trends from furniture to model cars at the **Danish Design Center,** which displays exhibitions of Danish and international design. The **Flow Market Exhibition** downstairs encourages consumers to think with sustainable growth in mind, selling items such as "inner calmness" and "clean air." *(H.C. Andersens Bvd. 27. ☎3369 3369; www.ddc.dk. Open M-Tu and Th-F 10am-5pm, W 10am-9pm, Sa-Su 11am-4pm. 50kr, seniors, youth ages 12-18 and students 25kr. W after 5pm free. AmEx/MC/V.)* The **National Museum's** vast collections include several large rune stones, ancient Viking art, and the permanent ethnographic exhibit, "People of the Earth." To reach the National Museum from H.C. Andersens Bvd., turn onto Stormg., take a right on Vester Volf., and go left on Ny Vesterg. *(Ny Vesterg. 10. ☎3313 4411. www.natmus.dk. Open Tu-Su 10am-5pm. Free. 1 hr. guided tours at noon, 1, 2pm on Sa, Sun, and holidays.)*

The home of Parliament *(Folketing)* and the royal reception rooms, **Christiansborg Slot** displays vivid, modernist tapestries that were designed by Bjørn Nørgård and presented to the Queen on her 50th birthday. *(Longangstraede 21. ☎3392 6300; www.ses.dk/christrainsborg. Ruins open daily May-Sept. 10am-4pm; Oct.-Apr. Tu-Su 10am-4pm. Ruins 40kr, students 30kr. Guided Castle tour daily Tu-Su at 11:30am and 1:30pm. Adults 65kr, students 55kr.)* Overlook the greater Copenhagen area from atop the impressive **Round Tower** *(Rundetaarn)*. *(Købmagerg. 52A. ☎3373 0373; www.rundetaarn.dk. Open daily May 20-Sept. 21. 10am-8pm, Sept. 21-May 20 10am-5pm. Observatory open mid-Oct.-mid-Mar. Tu, W 7-10pm. 25kr. AmEx/MC/V.)*

CHRISTIANSHAVN. In 1971, a few dozen flower children established the "free city" of **Christiania** in an abandoned Christianshavn fort. Today, the thousand-odd residents continue the tradition of artistic expression and an alternative lifestyle. Buildings surrounded by gorgeous bushes and flowerbeds are covered in ornate graffiti and murals. Vendors sell clothing and jewelry; nearby spots like **Woodstock Cafe** and **Cafe Nemoland** offer cheap beer and diverse crowds. Recent government crackdowns have driven Pusher Street's once open drug trade underground, and arrests for possession have become commonplace. It's a sensitive subject so don't ask; let local people do the talking. Be careful: do not take pictures on Pusher Sreet. *(Main entrance on Prinsesseg. Take bus #66 or 2A (runs every 5min.) from København H.)*

FREDERIKSTADEN. Northeast of the city center, Edvard Eriksen's tiny **Little Mermaid** *(Lille Havfrue)* statue honors Hans Christian Andersen's beloved tale. *(S-tog: Østerport. Turn left out of the station, go left on Folke Bernadottes Allé, bear right on the path bordering the canal, go left up the stairs, and then head right along the street.)* Head back along the canal and turn left across the moat to reach **Kastellet,** a rampart-enclosed 17th-century fortress that's now a park. *(Center of Churchill Park. ☎3311 2233. Open daily 6am-10pm.)* On the other side of Kastellet, the **Frihedsmuseet** (Museum of Danish Resistance) documents the German occupation from 1940-45, when the Danes helped over 7000 Jews escape to Sweden. *(At Churchillparken. ☎3313 7714. Open May-Sept. Tu-Su 10am-5pm; Oct.-Apr. Tu-Su 10am-3pm. English-language tours July-Sept. Tu and Th 11am. Free.)* Walk south down Amalieng. to reach **Amalienborg Palace,** a complex of four enormous mansions that serve as the winter residences of the royal family. Several apartments are open to the public, including the studies of 19th-century Danish kings. The changing of the guard takes place at noon on the vast plaza. *(☎3312 0808; www.rosenborgslot.dk. Open May-Oct. daily 10am-4pm; Nov.-Apr. Tu-Su 11am-4pm. 50kr, students 30kr. Combined ticket with Rosenborg Slot 80kr. MC/V.)*

About 13,000 plant species thrive in the beautiful gardens of **Botanisk Have.** *(Øster Farimagsgade 2B. ☎3532 2221 botanik.snm.ku.dk/english. Gardens open daily May-Sept. 8:30am-6pm; Oct.-Apr. daily Tu-Su 8:30am-4pm. Palm House open daily May-Dec. 10am-3pm; Jan.-Apr. daily Tu-Su 10am-3pm. Free.)* The **State Museum of Fine Arts** displays an eclectic collection of Danish and international art between its two buildings, which are linked by an impressive glass-roof gallery. *(Sølvg. 48-50. S-tog: Nørreport. Walk up Øster Voldg or take bus 6A ☎3374 8494; www.smk.dk. Open Tu and Th-Su 10am-5pm, W 10am-8pm. English-language tours July-Aug. Sa-Su 2pm. Permanent collection free. Special exhibits 80kr, students 50kr. W free. AmEx/MC/V.)*

FESTIVALS AND ENTERTAINMENT

Whether showcasing new cinematic pictures or entertaining musical acts, Copenhagen isn't short on summer festivals. During the world-class **Copenhagen Jazz Festival** (☎3393 2013; www.festival.jazz.dk), the city teems with free outodoor concerts. For more than your average film buff, the city truly comes alive for the **NatFilm Festival** (☎3312 0005; www.natfilm.dk) during late March and early April. International and domestic releases compete for Danish distribution deals. **Zulu Sommerbio** (Summer Cinema; www.zulu.dk) holds free screenings in parks and squares across the city throughout July and August. Movies are shown in their original languages with Danish subtitles.

Royal Theater, August Bournoville Pass. 1, (☎3369 6969) is home to the world-famous Royal Danish Ballet. The box office is just off the Konges Nytorv metro and sells same-day half-price tickets. Open M-Sa 10am-6pm. Tickets online at www.billetnet.dk.

Tivoli ticket office, Vesterbrog. 3, (☎3315 1012). Sells half-price tickets for the city's theaters. Open daily mid-Apr. to mid-Sept. 11am-8pm; mid-Sept. to mid-Apr. 9am-5pm.

NIGHTLIFE

In Copenhagen, the real parties begin on Thursday night; many bars and clubs have cheaper drinks and reduced covers. The streets near the **city center,** as well as of **Nørrebro** and **Vesterbro,** are lined with hip, crowded bars. Look for fancier options along **Nyhavn,** where laid-back Danes bring their own beer and sit on the pier; open containers are legal within the city limits. Copenhagen has a thriving gay and lesbian scene; check out *Playtime* or *Out and About* for listings.

PARTNER UP. The areas behind København H, the central train station, can be unsafe, especially at night. Explore with caution and bring a friend.

Vega, Enghavev. 40 (☎3325 7011; www.vega.dk), in Vesterbro. Bus 10. "Party time! Always crowded! Always a good time!" is what locals exclaim about this locale. One of Copenhagen's largest and most popular nightclubs, it showcases 4 floors, 5 dance rooms, 2 concert venues, and a popular bar. Dress well. Bar 18+; club 20+. Club cover after 1am 60kr. Bar open F-Sa 9pm-5am. Club open F-Sa 11pm-5am. MC/V.

Code, Radhusstraede 1 (☎3326 3626; www.code.dk), in Central Copenhagen. By day, an open cafe with a wide range of sandwiches. By night, a gay bar *and* lounge with an exotic cocktail selection. Shows 8pm-midnight. DJs on weekends 10pm-5am. MC/V.

The Australian Bar, Vesterg. 10 (☎2024 1411). M: Nørreport. Tucked away in the basement of an enclave, this relaxed bar has cheap drinks, pool tables, an arcade, and a dance-club playlist where you pick the music (8 songs/25kr). Beer 10-20kr. Mixed drinks 30kr. Reduced prices Th. Open M-W and Su 4pm-2am, Th-Sa 4pm-5am. MC/V.

La Hacienda/The Dance Floor, Gammel Torv 8 (☎3311 7478; www.la-hacienda.dk). M: Nørreport. Choose between **La Hacienda,** a laid-back lounge playing soul and hip hop, and **The Dance Floor,** a 2-story trance-driven club. Cover for men 150kr, women 130kr, 75kr before midnight; includes 1 champagne and 1 beer. Dress: Stylish and modern. 18+. Open F 11pm-8am, Sa 11pm-10am. AmEx/MC/V.

DAYTRIPS FROM COPENHAGEN

HILLERØD

At end of S-tog lines A and E. 40min., 6 per hr., 67kr or 4 clips. From train station, cross street onto Vibekev. and continue along the path until you can follow the sings; at the Torvet (main plaza), walk to the pond and bear left, following its perimeter to reach the castle entrance.

Hillerød is home to **Frederiksborg Slot,** one of Denmark's most impressive castles. Close to 90 rooms are open to the public, including the Chapel, the Rose Room, the Great Hall, and the Baroque gardens. *(☎4826 0439; www.frederiksborgmuseet.dk. Gardens open daily May-Aug. 10am-9pm; Sept.-Apr. reduced hours. Castle open daily Apr.-Oct. 10am-5pm, Nov.-Mar. 11am-3pm. Gardens free. Castle 60kr, students 50kr. AmEx/MC/V.*

HELSINGØR

At end of northern train line from Malmö, SWE via Copenhagen. 1hr., 3 per hr., 67kr or 4 clips.

Helsingør sits at a strategic entrance to the Baltic Sea, just 5km from Sweden. Originally built to levy taxes on passing ships, the majestic 16th-century **Kronborg Slot** is better known as **Elsinore,** the setting for Shakespeare's *Hamlet.* You'll feel like you were ttransplanted back to the 16th century. A statue of Viking chief Holger Danske sleeps in the dank, forbidding **dungeon;** legend holds that he will awake to defend Denmark in its darkest hour. The **tourist office,** Havnepl.

3, is in the Kulturhus, across from the station. (☎4921 3078; www.kronborg.dk. *Open daily May-Sept. 10:30am-5pm; Apr. and Oct. Tu-Su 11am-4pm; Nov.-Mar. Tu-Su 11am-3pm. 85kr. AmEx/MC/V. Festival: www.hamletsommer.dk. Tourist office: ☎4921 1333; www.visithelsingor.dk. Open July M-F 10am-5pm, Sa 10am-2pm; Aug.-Jun. M-F 10am-4pm, Sa 10am-1pm.)*

HUMLEBÆK AND RUNGSTED.

From Copenhagen, take a Helsingør-bound train. 45min., 3 per hr., 63kr or 4 clips. From Humlebæk Station, follow signs for 10min. or catch bus #388. From Copenhagen, take a Nivå-bound train. 30min., 3 per hr., 67kr or 4 clips. Follow the street leading out of the train station and turn right on Rungstedv., then right again on Rungsted Strandv., or take bus #388.

The gorgeous **Louisiana Museum of Modern Art,** 13 Gl. Strandv., honors the three wives (all named Louisa) of the estate's original owner. It rounds out its permanent collection—including works by Lichtenstein, Picasso, and Warhol—with several major exhibitions each year. Landscape architects have lavished attention on the seaside sculpture garden and the sloping lake garden. **The Karen Blixen Museum,** Rungsted Strandv. 111, provides a chronicle of the author's life. The grounds are home to 40 species of birds. *LMMA: ☎4919 0719; www.louisiana.dk. Open Tu-F 11am-10pm 90kr. AmEx/MC/V. KBM: ☎4557 1057. Open May-Sept. Tu-Su 10am-5pm; Oct.-Apr. W-F 1-4pm, Sa-Su 11am-4pm. 45kr. AmEx/MC/V.)*

DENMARK

MØN

Hans Christian Andersen once called the isle of Møn the most beautiful spot in Denmark. The sheer white **Møns Klint** (Chalk Cliffs), which plunge straight into calm blue waters, can be viewed from the rocky beaches below or the densely-forested hiking trails above. Walking away from the **Liselund Slot** (Doll Castle), you'll reach a path that becomes a **hiking trail,** which snakes 3km through a lush forest before arriving at the cliffs. Orchids line the trail of the 143m **Aborrebjerg** (Bass Mountain) near the island's youth hostel, lakeside **Møns Klint Vandrerhjem (HI) ❷,** Langebjergv. 1. Between late June and mid-August, take bus #632 from Stege to the campground stop, then continue in the direction of the bus and take the first right. In low-season, take bus #52 to Magleby and walk left 2.5km down the road. (☎5581 2030. Breakfast 60kr. Linens 60kr. Laundry 30kr. Reception 8-10:30am and 4-7pm. Open May-Sept. Dorms 150kr; singles and doubles 300kr. 35kr HI discount. MC/V; 5% surcharge.) To get to Møn, take the **train** from Copenhagen to Vordingborg (1hr., 139kr, Su closed), then bus #62 to Stege (45min., 42kr). **Buses** to Møn arrive in Stege, the island's largest town, across the island from the castle and cliffs. From Stege, take bus #52 to Busene (1 per 1-2hr., 13kr) and walk 10min. to the cliffs. Between mid-June and late August, bus #632 runs from Stege to the parking lots at the cliffs (30min., 3 per day, 13kr). Rent **bikes** in Klintholm Havn, the last stop on bus #52. The **info center,** Feriepartner Møn, Storeg. 2, is next to the Stege bus stop. (☎5586 0400; www.feriepartnermoen.dk. Open M-F 9:30am-4pm, Sa 9am-noon.)

ROSKILDE

Once the capital of the Danish Empire, Roskilde (pop. 53,000) is a short daytrip from Denmark's modern-day capital. Each summer in July, a diverse group of fans arrive to camp out and hear performances by music legends, contemporary stars, and up-and-comers. Since its debut in 1971, the **Roskilde Music Festival** (www.roskilde-festival.dk) has grown to be Northern Europe's largest outdoor concert. Stunning sarcophagi hold the remains of generations of Danish royalty in the red-brick church, **Roskilde Domkirke,** off the Stændertorvet. Head left out of the train station, go right on Herseg., and turn left onto Alg. (☎4635 1624; www.roskildedomkirke.dk. Open Apr.-Sept. M-Sa 9am-5pm, Su

12:30-5pm; Oct.-Mar. Tu-Sa 10am-4pm, Su 12:30-4pm. English-language tours mid-June to mid-Aug. M-F 11am and 2pm, Sa-Su 2pm, depending on church services. 25kr, students 15kr. Tours 20kr.) On the harbor next to the hostel, the **Viking Ship Museum,** Vindeboder 12, displays five ships that once protected the city of Roskilde. The museum also includes a shipyard where volunteers build vessels using Viking methods. Some of the ships are available for sailing. (☎M-F 4630 0200; Sa-Su 4630 0227; www.vikingeskibsmuseet.dk. Open daily 10am-5pm. For English-language tours call ☎4630 0253 or email booking@vikingeskibsmuseet.dk May-Sept. 95kr, students 75kr; Oct.-Apr. 55-45kr. Boat trips 60kr. Wheelchair-accessible. AmEx/MC/V.)

Roskilde Vandrerhjem (HI) ❷, Vindeboder 7, has comfy rooms. Reserve ahead during the music festival. (☎4635 2184; www.danhostel.dk/roskilde. Breakfast 45kr. Linens 60kr. Reception 7am-10pm. Dorms 185kr. 35kr HI discount. AmEx/MC/V.) To reach the rustic **Roskilde Camping** ❶, Baunehøjv. 7, take bus #603 (dir.: Veddelev; 15kr, 4km) to Veddelev Byg. (☎4675 7996; www.roskildecamping.dk. Electricity 30kr. Showers 6kr per 4min. Reception 8am-9pm. Open Apr. to mid-Sept. 71kr per tent site, 350-450kr per cabin. MC/V; 5% surcharge.) Restaurants line **Algade** and **Skomagergade** in the town center. **Memos** ❶, Jernbanegade 8, serves pita sandwiches (25-35kr) and has an **Internet** cafe (15kr per hr.) downstairs. (☎4632 7076. Open M-Th 11am-8pm, F-Sa 11am-4am.)

Trains depart for Copenhagen (25-30min., 4 per hr., 66kr) and Odense (1hr., 3 per hr., 181kr). The **tourist office,** Gullandsstr. 15, books rooms for a 25kr fee and 10-15% deposit. Walk through the Stændertorvet with the Domkirke on your right, turn left on Allehelgensgade, and follow the signs. (☎4631 6565; www.visitroskilde.dk. Open Apr. 1-Sept. 1 M-F 10am-5pm, Sa 10am-2pm.)

DENMARK

BORNHOLM

Residents of the island of Bornholm—which literally translates to "sunny island"—like to say that when Scandinavia was created, God saved the best piece for last and placed it in the Baltic Sea. The undulating farmlands of the south are ideal for bikers, while nature lovers will favor the dramatic, rocky landscape of the north. The central forest is one of the largest in Denmark, and the sandiest beaches are at Dueodde, on the island's southern tip.

TRANSPORTATION. The best way to get to Bornholm from Copenhagen is by a **bus** and **ferry** combination. Bornholmerbussen #866 leaves from København H for Ystad, SWE, where passengers can transfer to the ferry. (☎4468 4400; 3hr., 3 per day, 225kr.) A **train** and **ferry** combo runs from Copenhagen to Rønne by way of Ystad. (Train ☎7013 1415; www.dsb.dk; 2hr., 2-3per day. Ferry ☎5695 1866; www.bornholmferries.dk; 80min. Combination 200-251kr.) A discount **"red ticket"** (224kr, low-season 150kr) for the ferry is available online a week in advance, but the combo ticket is cheaper for travelers coming from Copenhagen. **Overnight ferries** from Køge (S-tog: A+, E, Ex), south of Copenhagen, leave at 11:30pm and arrive in Rønne at 6:30am (244kr, 281kr for a bed).

Bornholm has an efficient BAT **local bus** service; buses run less frequently on weekends. (☎5695 2121. 36-45kr, bikes 22kr; 24hr. pass 140kr.) Bus #1A/B makes a circuit of the coastline, heading from Rønne to Hammershus and stopping at most of the island's towns and attractions along the way. Bus #3 from Rønne passes by Østerlars Church on its way to Gudhejm, where the **ferry** departs for Christiansø, a small island to the north of Bornholm; check www.BAT.dk for more info. There are well-marked **bike** paths between all the major towns; pick up a guide (40kr) at Rønne's tourist office.

RØNNE. Rønne (pop. 14,000), on Bornholm's southwestern coast, is the principal port of entry to the island. **Rønne Vandrerhjem (HI) ❷**, Arsenalv. 12, is an area hostel located in a peaceful, wooded area. From the ferry, head toward the tourist office and turn right on Munch Petersens V. Stay left and onto Snellmark. Walk through the town and turn right on Sondre Alle. Pass the roundabout and Arsenalv. is 100m up on the right. (☎5695 1340; www.danhostel-roenne.dk. Breakfast 45kr. Linens 50kr. Laundry 80kr. Reception 8am-noon and 4-5pm. Open Apr.-Oct. Dorms 150kr; singles 300kr; doubles 400 kr. 35kr HI discount. Cash only.) **Sam's Corner ❷**, St. Torv 2, is a basic but popular burger and pizza joint with low prices (45-75kr) and large portions. (☎5695 1523. Open daily in summer 10am-10pm; in winter 10am-9pm. Cash only.) Get groceries at **Kvickly**, opposite the tourist office. (☎5694 8400. Open M-F 9am-8pm, Sa 9am-5pm, Su 10am-4pm. Cash only.) The **tourist office** is at Ndr. Kystv. 3. Turn right out of the ferry terminal, pass the BAT bus terminal, and cross toward the gas station; look for the giant sign. (☎5695 9500; www.bornholm.info. Open July-Aug. 9am-5:30pm; Sept.-June 9am-4pm. MC/V.)

ALLINGE AND SANDVIG. These seaside villages are excellent for snorkeling and serve as starting points for hikes and bike rides through Bornholm's northern coast. Many trails originate in Sandvig. The rocky area around Hammeren, northwest of the town, is a beautiful 2hr. walk that can be covered on foot. Just outside Sandvig is the lakeside **Sandvig Vandrerhjem (HI) ❷**, Hammershusv. 94. Get off the bus one stop past Sandvig Gl. Station and follow the signs. (☎5648 0362. Breakfast 50kr. Sheets and towels 70kr. Laundry 40kr. Reception 9-10am and 4-6pm. Open May-Sept. Dorms 150kr; singles 275kr; doubles 400kr. 35kr HI discount. Cash only.) **Riccos ❷**, Strandg. 8, in Sandvig, is a pleasant cafe in a private home near the sea with free Internet. (☎5648 0314. Open daily 7am-10pm. MC/V.) The Allinge **tourist office** is at Kirkeg. 4. (☎5648 0001. Open June-Aug. M-F 10am-4pm, Sa 10am-1pm; Oct.-May M-F 11am-4pm.) Rent **bikes** at the Sandvig Cykeludlejning, Strandvejen 121. (☎2145 6013. Open May-Sept. M-F 9am-3:30pm, Sa 9am-1pm, Su 10am-1pm. 60kr per day. Cash only.)

FUNEN (FYN)

Nestled between Zealand to the east and the Jutland Peninsula to the west, the island of Funen continually attracts excited travelers. Although this once-remote breadbasket has since been connected to Zealand by the magnificent Storebæltsbro bridge and tunnel, it still retains much of its isolated charm from the whimsical time of Hans Christian Andersen.

ODENSE

The regional capital of Funen, Odense (OH-den-suh, pop. 200,000) is a smaller, busy city by day or night. Take a break from the hustle and bustle of the pedestrian streets and relax among the many parks.

TRANSPORTATION AND PRACTICAL INFORMATION. **Trains** run to Copenhagen (1hr., 2 per hr., 224kr). **Buses** depart from behind the train station. The **tourist office**, in the Rådhuset, offers free **Internet** and useful guides. Turn left out of the train station and then take a right on Thomas B. Thriges Gade (the second light). The office will be on your right when you reach Vesterg. (☎66 12 75 20; www.visitodense.com. Open July-Aug. M-F 9:30am-4:30pm, Sa 10am-3pm, Su 11am-2pm; Sept. to mid-June M-F 9:30am-4:30pm, Sa 10am-1pm.)

DENMARK

The **library** in the station also has free **Internet.** (☎6551 4301; www.odenselib.dk). Open Apr.-Sept. M-Th 10am-7pm, F 10am-4pm, Sa 10am-2pm; low-season extended hours.) Rent **bikes** at **City Cykler,** Vesterbro 27. Continue down Vesterg. from the tourist office for 10min.; it will be on the right. (☎6612 9793; www.citycykler.dk. 125kr per day. Open M-F 10am-5:30pm, Sa 10am-1pm.)

ACCOMMODATIONS AND FOOD. **Danhostel Odense City (HI) ❷,** directly to the right of the train station, has a cafe and basement lounge area with TV and computer. Buy a snack at the cafe downstairs for free **Internet.** (☎63 11 04 25; www.cityhostel.dk. Breakfast 59kr. Linens 70kr. Laundry 45kr. Reception 8am-noon and 4-8pm. Dorms 150kr; singles 350kr; doubles 400kr; triples 420kr; quads 480kr. 35kr HI discount. MC/V; 4% surcharge.) To reach **DCU-Camping Odense ❶,** Odensev. 102, take bus #42 (dir.: Skt. Klemens; 14kr) 4km from town. (☎66 11 47 02; www.camping-odense.dk. Electricity 27kr. Wi-Fi. Reception high-season 7:30am-noon and 2-10pm; low-season 7:30am-noon and 4-10pm. Jan.-June 66kr; mid-June to mid-Aug. 70kr. Small cabins: high-season 420kr per day; 2940kr per week. low-season 335kr per day; 2345kr per week; blanket and pillow 60kr. Cabin prices include electricity. AmEx/MC/V.) **Vestergade** has a variety of restaurants and cafes offering traditional Turkish, Italian, and Danish cuisine. Don't overlook the alleys off Vesterg., including low-key **Vintapperstræde** and **Brandts Passage,** a hidden enclave with posh cafes. **Mamma's Pizzeria ❶,** Klaregade 4. is a take-away shop, deli, and restaurant that serves large portions of hearty home-cooked meals. (☎6614 5540; www.mammas.dk. Special takeout for two 90kr, deli paninis 42-48kr, entrees 80-90kr.)

SIGHTS AND NIGHTLIFE. Strategically built around the calm waters of the Odense River, Odense's parks lend themselves to great biking and leisurely walks.The **Hans Christian Andersen Hus,** Bangs Boder 29, takes visitors through a chronicle of the author's entire life from childhood jobs to love affairs. Enjoy free performances of his timeless stories in a mix of Danish, English, and German. From the tourist office, walk right on Vesterg., turn left on Thomas Thriges G., and go right on Hans Jensens Str. (☎65 51 46 01; www.museum.odense.dk. Open daily June-Aug. daily 9am-6pm; Sept.-May Tu-Su 10am-4pm. 60kr. Summer performances 11am, 1pm, 3pm.)

On weekend evenings, the area around Vesterg. is packed with people of all ages drinking and listening to live bands. After 11pm, the club and bar scene takes over. Head down **Skt. Knuds Plads** for fun, laid-back bars and a game of pool. For one of the best pub and disco experiences, locals swarm to **Boogie Dance Cafe**, Norreg. 21. (☎66 14 00 39; www.boogiedance.dk. Cover Th 20kr; F-Sa 40kr after midnight. Open Tu-W 11pm-4:30am, Th 11pm-5am, F 11pm-5:30am, Sa 11pm-6am. MC/V.) **Retro,** Overgaden 45, is an elite place to party: cocktails run about 85kr. This bustling nightclub, decked in awesome lighting and filled with young people, is strictly for dancing. There's a comfy bar downstairs with foosball and darts for more relaxed partygoers.

DAYTRIP FROM ODENSE: KVÆRNDRUP. Travelers young or old will find something of interest at the magical **Egeskov Slot,** Egeskov Gade 18, 25min. south of Odense in Kværndrup. More than just another castle, Egeskov has an assortment of attractions, including beautiful gardens and breathtaking views from the treetops. Get lost in the many hedge-mazes and tour the museums displaying old cars, motorcycles, airplanes, dolls, and more. Inside the castle itself, you will find traditional 18th-century artifacts among the various rooms, as well as an extensive hunting gallery. *(☎62 27 10 16; www.egeskov.com. Castle open Apr.-Sept. 10am-5pm, June 10am-6pm, July 1-Aug. 10 10am-8pm. Aug. 11-31 10am-6pm.*

Grounds, museum, maze 120kr; with castle 175kr. MC/V.) Take Svendborg-bound train (25min., 35min. past the hr., 52kr) from Odense. In Kværndrup, turn right out of the station, walk up to Bøjdenv. and catch bus #920 (every hr., 16kr), or turn right and walk 30min; there are no pedestrian walkways so be mindful of cars. Take a right on Egeskov and walk 350 meters to the castle. Take FynBus #801, Odense directly to the castle, mid-June to mid-Aug (1hr., 3-8 per day, 44kr).

ÆRØ

Literally translated, Ærø means "maple island," but there's more to it than just great tasting walnut and maple ice-cream. A charming getaway spot for those looking to cycle, hike, sail, or to take in clean air; Ærø is 80% self-sufficient in terms of renewable energy. Rent a bicycle at **Pilebaekkens Cykler,** Pilebækken 11, by walking down Vestergade and taking a left on Pilebaekken (☎6252 1110. Open M-F 9am-4 :30pm, Sa 9am-noon. Open mid-June-mid-July Su 10am-1pm). For overnight stays, sleep at the **Ærøskøbing Youthhostel ❷,** Smedevejen 15 (☎6252 1044; www.danhostel.dk/aeroskoebing. Dorms 150kr, singles 300kr. Open 3am-noon and 4-8pm). Just around the corner of the hostel is a long path leading to the water, where you will find a public playground with a barbeque area and wooden teepees. Ærøskøbing's helpful and friendly **tourist office,** Havnen 4, offers free **Internet** in low-season, but charges 20kr per 30min. in high-season. (☎6252 13 00; www.visitaeroe.dk. Open M-F 9am-4pm, Sa 11am-3pm, mid-June to Aug. Sa-Su 10am-6pm). Try the **Archipelago Trail,** a 36 km trail that stretches across the entire island through ancient burial chambers and beautiful fields. Several **trains** running from Odense to Svendborg are timed to meet the **ferry** to Ærøskøbing (2hr, 5-6per day, 158kr with ferry tax. Cash only.)

DENMARK

JUTLAND (JYLLAND)

Jutland's sandy beaches and historic houses complement its sleek wind turbines and contemporary art. Vikings once journeyed to the trading centers on the western half of the peninsula, but now the coast attracts windsurfers in search of prime waves. Cyclers and canoers enjoy the vast open spaces of the central lakes region, while the cities of Århus and Aalborg have emerged as major cultural havens in the east.

ÅRHUS

Pedestrian walkways wind through the impressive museums, crowded nightclubs, and well-developed art scene of Århus (OR-hoos; pop. 280,000). Denmark's second-largest city, Århus is an international melting pot, offering a variety of cultural events and cuisine. But don't let the upscale atmosphere in the city fool you. Just 10km south are beautiful beaches (yes, some are nude!) and extensive trails for biking, hiking, and running.

TRANSPORTATION AND PRACTICAL INFORMATION. **Flights** use Århus Airport (AAR; ☎8775 7000; www.aar.dk), 45km from the city center, as their base. **Airport buses** leave from the front of the main terminal building for Århus (45min., 90kr MC/V). The bus from Århus Station to the airport is 90kr one way. Accepts US currency. MC/V. Some budget airlines also fly to Billund (☎7650 5050; www.bll.dk). **Trains** run to Aalborg (1.5hr., 3 per hr., 118kr), Copenhagen (3.5hr., 2 per hr., 311kr), Odense (2.5hr., 2 per hr, 195kr), and Frederikshavn (2hr., every hr., 205kr). For **bus** service to Copenhagen and Berlin, check out www.abildskou.dk (☎7021 0888). Buses leave from outside the train station down the street to the right. From May to

October, free **bikes** are available to borrow from stands across the city with a 20kr deposit. MM Cykler Værksted, Mejlg. 41, rents bikes for 65kr per day. (☎8619 2927; www.mmcykler.dk. Open M-F 9am-5pm.)

To get to the **tourist office,** Banegårdspl. 20, head left after exiting the train station. The office sells the 24hr. **Tourist Ticket** (55kr), which offers unlimited use of the city's extensive bus system. The **Århus pass** (1-day 139kr, 2-day 169kr) includes admission to most museum and sights, as well as unlimited public transit. (☎8731 5010; www.visitaarhus.com. Open mid-June to early Sept. M-F 9:30am-6pm, Sa 9:30am-5pm, Su 9:30-1pm; low-season reduced hours.) The main public **library,** Mølleg. 1 in Mølleparken, offers free **Internet.** (☎8940 9255; www.aakb.dk. Open May-Sept. M-Th 10am-7pm, F 10am-2pm; Oct.-Apr. M-Th 10am-8pm, F10am-6pm, Sa-Su 10am-3pm.) **Postal code:** 8000.

ACCOMMODATIONS AND FOOD. **Århus City Sleep-In ❷,** Havneg. 20 is conveniently near the city nightlife. From the train station, turn right and follow Ny Banegårds., past the bus station and take a left at the light by the police station. Then turn left onto Haveng. where the street forks to either the train tracks or the harbour. Though surrounded by noisy nightlife, this popular hostel has a relaxed vibe. (☎8619 2055; www.citysleep-in.dk. Breakfast 55kr. Linens 50kr. Towels 20kr. Laundry 32kr. Internet 20kr per hr. Reception closed noon-12:45pm, 7-7:30pm, and 11pm-7am. Dorms 130kr; doubles 400-460kr. MC/V; 2% surcharge.) Quick and cheap takeout joints selling burgers, kebabs, and Asian-inspired meals line Skolegade, which becomes Mejlg. just behind City Sleep-In. Along **Aboulevarden** you'll find plenty of cafes. **Pinden's Restaurant,** Skoleg. 29 serves traditional Danish food. (☎8612 1102. Entrees 42-86kr. Open daily 11:30am-9pm. AmEx/MC/V.

SIGHTS. At **Den Gamle By,** watch actors bring to life a medieval village with authentic houses from all over Denmark. (Viborgvej 2. ☎8612 3188; www.dengamleby.dk. Open daily mid-June to mid-Sept. 9am-6pm; low-season M-Th 8:30-4pm, F 8:30am-3 :30pm.) The 3km **prehistoric trail** behind the museum, reconstructs Danish forests from different ages and leads to a popular beach. In the summer, bus #19 returns from the beach to the train station. (Take bus #1 north or bus #6 south.) **Århus Kunstmuseum (Aros)** features eight levels of galleries that hold multimedia exhibits and modern art. Highlights include Ron Mueck's *Boy*, a colossal 5m statue of a crouching boy. (Aros Alleé 2, off Vester Allé. ☎8730 6600; www.aros.dk. Open Tu-Su 10am-5pm, W 10am-10pm, 90kr, students 75kr.) If you're near the harbor, climb the **Århus Domikrke,** that nation's tallest cathedral. (Skoleg. 17. ☎8620 5400; www.aarhus-domkirke.dk. Open May-Sept. M-Sa 9:30am-4pm, Oct.-Apr. M-Sa 10am-3pm. Free.)

NIGHTLIFE AND FESTIVALS. **The Social Club,** Klosterg. 34, has three bars on two levels that bump loud music to dancing and mingling revelers. (☎8519 4250; www.socialclub.dk. All drinks 20kr. Cover after 2am Th 20kr; F-Sa 40kr. 11pm-midnight entrance only with student ID; one free beer and no cover. Open Th-Sa 11pm-6am.) **Train,** Tolbodg. 6, an old dockside warehouse, now acts as a club and concert hall. (☎8613 4722; www.train.dk. Concerts all ages, club 23+. Club open F-Sa 11pm-late.). The **Århus Festuge** is a rollicking 10-day celebration of theater, dance, and music held from late August through early September. The streets of Århus are lined with music venues, stages, and galleries. (☎8940 9191; www.aarhusfestuge.dk)

DAYTRIP FROM ÅRHUS: BILLUND. Dominating the city (and major transportation hub) of Billund, is one of the world's best toy fantasies. Release your inner child at the main attraction, **Legoland,** an amusement park with sprawling Lego sculptures made from over 50 million candy-colored blocks. The "Power Builder" ride allows you to design your own roller coaster. *Buses leave Billund Airport for Legoland (8-10min., 2-3 per hr., 16kr.) If not flying, take the train from Århus to Vejle (45min., 2 per hr., 90kr), then bus #244 (dir.: Grinsted; 61kr, 30 min.) Legoland: ☎7533 1333; www.legoland.dk. Open daily Mar. 15-Oct. 22 10am-6pm with extended hours during the summer; check website for details. Day pass 249kr. Free 30min. before rides close. MC/V.))*

AALBORG

A laid-back haven for university students by day, Aalborg (OLE-borg; pop. 162,000) heats up at night. At the corner of Alg. and Molleg., (Alg. 43), an **elevator** descends from outside the Salling Department Store to the half-excavated ruins of a **Franciscan friary.** (☎9631 7400. Open Tu-Su 10am-5pm; elevator closes at 4:30pm. Elevator 20kr up to 250kr.) North of town, the solemn grounds of **Lindholm Høje,** Vendilav. 11, hold 700 ancient Viking graves and a museum. Take bus #2C, which departs near the tourist office. (☎99 31 74 40; www.nordjyllandshistoriskemuseum.dk. Grounds open 24hr. Museum open daily 10am-5pm. English-language tours in July W 2pm. Grounds free. Museum 30kr, students 15kr. MC/V.) After a day of dusty antiquarianism, head to **Jomfru Ane Gade,** a pedestrian strip of bars and clubs that's packed with students. For an even wilder time, **Karneval i Aalborg** (last weekend in May; www.karnevaliaalborg.dk), Northern Europe's largest carnival, celebrates spring.

DENMARK

If you plan on spending the night in Aalborg, your only semi-budget option is the quite comfortable **Aalborg Vandrerhjen and Camping (HI) ❷,** Skydebanev. 50 alongside the Lim Fjord. Take bus #13 (dir.: Fjordparken, every 15 min., 16kr) to the end of the line. (☎9811 6044; www.BBBB.dk. Breakfast 50kr, Linens/towels 46kr. Laundry 40kr. Singles 490kr, doubles 520kr. Dorms open July-Sept. 270kr. Free Internet. Reception high-season 8am-11pm, low-season 8am-noon and 4-9pm. Campsite 75kr electricity 28kr. Reserve ahead online. MC/V; 4% surcharge.) Enjoy colorful street performances at the outdoor tables of **Café Ministeriet,** Møllesplads, which serves a lunch plate with three types of *smørrebrød* for 52kr. (☎98 19 40 50; www.cafeministeriet.dk. Open M-Th 10am-midnight, F-Sa 10am-2am, Su 10am-5pm. MC/V.)

Trains run to Århus (1hr., every hr., 157kr) and Copenhagen (5hr., 2 per hr., 338kr). Within the city, **buses** cost 16kr, including 1hr. transfers. Show the bus driver your train ticket and you won't have to pay a fare to the station. To find the **tourist office,** Østeråg. 8, head out of the train station, cross JFK Pl., and turn left on Boulevarden, which becomes Østeråg. (☎99 30 60 90; www.visitaalborg.com. Open July M-F 9am-5:30pm, Sa 10am-4pm; late June to Aug. M-F 9am-5:30pm, Sa 10am-1pm; Sept. to mid-June M-F 9am-4:30pm, Sa 10am-1pm.)

FREDERIKSHAVN

Since its days as a fishing village and naval base, Frederikshavn (fred-riks-HOW-n; pop. 35,000) has evolved into a transportation hub for Scandinavian ferry lines. Stena Line **ferries** (☎9620 0222; www.stenaline.com) leave for Gothenburg, SWE. Color Line (☎9956 1977; www.colorline.com) **boats/ferries** sail to Larvik, NOR. To get from the station to the **Frederikshavn Vandrerhjem (HI) ❶,** Buhlsv. 6, walk right on Skipperg. for 10min., turn left onto Nørreg., and take a right at the second light on Buhlsv. (☎9842 1475; www.danhostel.dk/frederikshavn. Breakfast 50kr. Linens 45kr. Laundry 40kr. Reception 8am-noon and 4-8pm. Dorms 120kr; singles 285kr; doubles 440kr. 35kr HI discount. Cash only.) Restaurants and shops cluster along **Søndergade** and **Havnegade;** Rådhus Allé has several grocery stores. To get to the commercial area from the train station, turn left and cross Skipperg. The **Frederikshavn Kirke,** a church with a huge anchor on its front lawn, will be on the left. Walk up one block to Danmarksg., the main pedestrian thoroughfare, and turn left. Danmarksg. becomes Sønderg. and intersects with Havneg. Head to Bangspo Park to take in a bit of lush. The **Powder Tower (Kruot Tarnet),** also in the park (☎9843 1919), showcases powder and cannon displays (open June-Aug. Tu-Su 10am-5pm, 15kr).

SKAGEN

Located on Denmark's northernmost tip, Skagen is a small fisherman's wharf. The picturesque town is framed by stunning ice-blue waters lined with sandy white beaches. The **Skagens Museum,** Brøndumsv. 4, features 19th- and 20th-century landscape paintings by local artists. From the train station, walk left down Sct. Laurentii V. and turn right on Brøndumsv. (☎9844 6444; www.skagensmuseum.dk. Open Apr.-Sept. Tu-Su 10am-5pm; Oct.-Mar. W-Su 10am-3pm. 70kr. AmEx/MC/V.) At nearby **Grenen,** tourists and locals alike have the unique opportunity to stand in two seas simultaneously and watch as the currents of the North and Baltic Seas collide in striking rhythm. Take the bus from the Skagen station (15kr; last return 7:30pm) or walk 5km down Fyrv. About 13km south of Skagen is the enormous **Råberg Mile** (ROH-bayrg MEE-leh), a sand dune formed by a 16th-century storm. The dune resembles a vast moonscape and migrates 15m east each year. Take bus #99 or the train from Skagen to Hulsig, then walk 4km down Kandestedv. Each July, the town welcomes Irish fiddlers and Scandinavian troubadours for the **Skagen Folk Music Festival** (☎9844 4094; www.skagenfestival.dk).

DENMARK

Reserve well ahead at the popular **Skagen Ny Vandrerhjem ❷,** Rolighedsv. 2. From the station, turn right on Chr. X's V., which becomes Frederikshavnv., then go left on Rolighedsv. They boast rooms that are unlike those of a typical hostel. (☎9844 2200; www.danhostelnord.dk/skagen. Breakfast 50kr. Linens 50kr. Reception 9am-noon and 4-6pm. Open Feb.-Nov. Dorms 185kr; singles 485kr; doubles 635kr. 35kr HI discount. Cash only.) To reach the campgrounds at **Poul Eeg Camping ❶,** Batterivej 21, turn left out of the train station, walk 3km straight down Sct. Laurentii V., and go left on Batterivej. (☎9844 1470. Bike rental 60kr per day. Tent sites 67-78kr. Cash only.) Turn right out of the station onto Sct. Laurentii V. to get to an area of restaurants near **Havnevej.** In the town center, **Orchid Thai Restaurant ❶,** Sct. Laurentii V. 60, offers authentic, cheap, and filling lunch boxes for 35kr. (☎9844 6044. Open daily 11am-10pm. MC/V.)

Trains run from Skagen to Frederikshavn (40min., weekdays every hr., weekends 4 per day, 48kr). Rent **bikes** at **Cykelhandler,** Kappelborgv. 23; around the corner from the tourist office (☎9844 2528. 20kr per hr., 60kr per day. Open M-F 8am-5:30pm, Sa 9:30am-noon. Cash only.) To get to the **tourist office,** Vestre Strandvej 10, turn right from the station onto Sct. Laurentii V., left on to Havnev., and right onto Havneplads. (☎9844 1377; www.skagen-tourist.dk. Open July M-Sa 9am-6pm, Su 10am-4pm; June and Aug. M-Sa 9am-5pm, Su 10am-2pm; low-season reduced hours.) The **library** to the left of the train station, Sct. Laurentii V. 23, has free **Internet.** (☎9844 2822; www.skagen.dk/skagbib. Open M and Th 10am-6pm, Tu-W and F 1-6pm, Sa 10am-1pm.) **Internet** is also available at **McCurdies,** Sct. Laurentii Vei 56, and **Jakobs Cafe og Bar,** Havnevei 4A.

ESTONIA (EESTI)

Eager to sever its Soviet bonds, Estonia has been quick to revive its historical and cultural ties to its Nordic neighbors, while Finnish tourism and investment are helping to revitalize the nation. The wealth that has reinvigorated Tallinn belies the poverty that still predominates outside of Estonia's big cities, as well as the discontent of its ethnically Russian minority, uneasy with Estonia's increasingly European leanings. Still, after successive centuries of domination by the Danes, Swedes, and Russians, most Estonians are now proud to take their place as members of modern Europe.

DISCOVER ESTONIA: SUGGESTED ITINERARIES

THREE DAYS. Spend a day exploring the streets and sights of **Old Town Tallinn** (p. 279)—don't miss the **Museum of Occupation.** During your second day, check out Peter the Great's sumptuous **Kadriorg Palace** and the **Art Museum of Estonia**, before heading down to **Pärnu** (p. 283). On your third day, relax on the beach climb the medieval **Red Tower.**

ONE WEEK. Begin in the south by visiting unique **Tartu** (2 days; p. 283). Then move west to **Pärnu** (1 day) and its **Museum of New Art.** Next, head out to the island of **Saaremaa** (2 days; p. 284). Rent a bicycle and take in the unspoiled beauty of the region. Don't miss the skeleton in **Bishopric Castle.** Spend your last 2 days among the medieval spires of seaside **Tallinn.**

ESSENTIALS

FACTS AND FIGURES

OFFICIAL NAME: Republic of Estonia.

CAPITAL: Tallinn.

MAJOR CITIES: Pärnu, Tartu.

POPULATION: 1,308,000.

TIME ZONE: GMT + 2.

DENSITY: 75 people per sq. mi.

LANGUAGE: Estonian.

CAN I BUY A VOWEL, PAT?: tööööööbik (nightingale or workaholic); hauaööõudused (horrors of the night in the grave).

WHEN TO GO

The best time to visit Estonia is in late spring (Apr.-May) and summer (June to early Sept.). Temperatures reach highs of 30°C (86°F) in July and August. Although winters can be cold (with limited hours of daylight), Estonia offers an abundance of skiing and skating. Beware that warm summer weather draws heavy crowds to Estonian beaches.

DOCUMENTS AND FORMALITIES

EMBASSIES AND CONSULATES. Foreign embassies to Estonia are in Tallinn (p. 280). Embassies and consulates abroad include: **Australia,** 86 Louisa Rd., Birchgrove, NSW 2041 (☎2 9810 7468; www.eesti.org.au/consulate); **Canada,** 260

Dalhousie St., Ste. 210, Ottawa, ON K1N 7E4 (☎613-789-4222; www.estemb.ca); **Ireland,** Riversdale House, St. Ann's, Ailesbury Rd., Dublin 4 (☎353 12 19 67 30; www.estemb.ie); **UK,** 16 Hyde Park Gate, London SW7 5DG (☎020 7589 3428; www.estonia.gov.uk); **US,** 2131 Massachusetts Ave., NW, Washington, D.C. 20008 (☎202-588-0101; www.estemb.org).

ENTRANCE REQUIREMENTS.

Passport: Required for all travelers.

Visa: Not required for citizens of EU countries, Australia, Canada, New Zealand, the US, and assorted other countries for stays under 90 days.

Letter of Invitation: Not required.

Inoculations: Recommended up-to-date on DTaP (diphtheria, tetanus, and pertussis), hepatitis A, hepatitis B, MMR (measles, mumps, and rubella), polio booster, tick-borne encephalitis, and typhoid.

Work Permit: Required of all those planning to work in Estonia.

International Driving Permit: Required of all those planning to drive.

TOURIST SERVICES AND MONEY

TOURIST OFFICES. Estonian Tourist Board offices, marked with a white "i" on a green background, are in most towns; they offer advice about accommodations and services. They keep extended hours in summer months, except on national holidays (June 23-24 and August 20), when they're open from 10am to 3pm.

MONEY. The Estonian unit of currency is the **kroon (EEK),** plural **krooni,** which is divided into 100 **senti.** Since its 2004 accession to the EU, however, Estonia has followed the path of economic integration and intends to switch to the euro between 2011 and 2013. Currently, the best foreign currencies to bring to Estonia are the euro and US dollar; travelers should stay attuned to economic developments over the coming months. Annual **inflation** averages 6%, although this has been decreasing over the last decade. A common bank in Estonia is **Hansabank,** which offers the most services, including **Western Union** transfers, currency exchanges and **travelers checks.** Hansabank also generally offers the best rates. **SEB Banks** are also widespread. **ATMs** are available everywhere, and offer acceptable exchange rates. Most **credit cards** are accepted throughout the country. **Tipping** is common; 10% is expected in restaurants. **Bargaining** is appropriate only at outdoor markets; written prices should be treated as fixed.

ESTONIAN KROONI (EEK)		
	AUS$1 = 9.24EEK	10EEK = AUS$1.08
	CDN$1 = 10.00EEK	10EEK = CDN$1.00
	EUR€1 = 15.65EEK	10EEK = EUR€0.64
	NZ$1 = 7.57EEK	10EEK = NZ$1.32
	UK£1 = 19.81EEK	10EEK = UK£0.50
	US$1 = 10.64EEK	10EEK = US$0.94

HEALTH AND SAFETY

Medical services for foreigners are few and far between, and usually require cash payments. There are two kinds of **pharmacies** *(apteek)*; some stock prescription medication, but most are chains that stock everything. **Public toilets**

(tasuline), marked with an "N" or a triangle pointing up for women and "M" or a triangle pointing down for men, usually cost 3EEK. While Tallinn's **tap water** is generally safe to drink, **bottled water** is necessary in the rest of the country. **Petty crime** is rare, though pickpocketing is common in Tallinn's Old Town, especially along Viru St. **Women** should not have a problem traveling alone, but may want to dress modestly. **Minorities** in Estonia are rare; they receive stares but generally experience little discrimination. For English-language help in an emergency, contact your embassy. **Homosexuality,** though not always tolerated, is legal and is generally treated with curiosity rather than suspicion.

EMERGENCY **Police:** ☎110. **Ambulance** and **Fire:** ☎112.

TRANSPORTATION

BY PLANE, TRAIN, AND FERRY. Several international airlines offer flights to Tallinn, the site of Estonia's major international airport (**TLL;** ☎605 8888; www.tallinn-airport.ee). Try **SAS** or **AirBaltic,** or consider the budget airline **easyJet** (p. 48). Some travelers find it convenient to fly into the larger international airport in Rīga, LAT. **Trains** in Estonia are mainly used for hauling freight. If you are traveling from Russia or another Baltic state, you may consider taking a **ferry,** but expect more red tape when crossing the border. **Tallinksilja** serves the entire Baltic Sea region (online at www.tallinksilja.com/en). Ferries also connect with Finland, Germany, and Sweden.

BY BUS. **Euroline buses** (www.eurolines.ee) run to Estonia from international cities. **Domestic buses** (www.bussireisid.ee) are cheaper and more efficient than trains, though service can be infrequent between smaller cities. Taking buses on the islands can be especially frustrating. Students receive half-price bus tickets from September to late June.

BY CAR, BIKE, AND THUMB. If entering Estonia by **car,** avoid routes through Kaliningrad and Belarus: both require visas. Although road conditions are steadily improving, the availability of roadside assistance remains poor. Check out the **Estonian Road Administration** (www.mnt.ee). **Taxis** (about 7EEK per km) are generally safe. **Bicycling** is common in Estonia. Those who want to **hitchhike** should stretch out an open hand. *Let's Go* does not recommend hitchhiking.

KEEPING IN TOUCH

PHONE CODES	**Country code:** 372. **International dialing prefix:** 800. For more info, see **Inside Back Cover.**

EMAIL AND INTERNET. Although Internet cafes are not as common as you might expect, Wi-Fi is widespread. Free Wi-Fi is available throughout Tallinn; check www.wifi.ee for more info or look for the "wifi.ee" sign.

TELEPHONE. **Public telephones,** which are very common at bus stations and shopping malls, require **magnetic cards,** available at any kiosk. These come in 20, 50, and 100 EEK denominations. **International calls** are expensive, usually costing around US$0.80 per minute. Tele2 cards offer the best rates. International direct dial numbers include: **AT&T Direct** (☎0 800 12 001); **Canada Direct** (☎0 800 12 011); **MCI** (☎0 800 12 122). If you bring a GSM **mobile phone,** SIM cards (around US$1) offer a convenient and sometimes cheap way to keep in touch. Tallinn, unlike other Estonian cities, has no city code; to call Tallinn from outside Estonia, dial Estonia's country code (372) and then the number. To call any city besides Tallinn from outside the country, dial the country code, the city code, and the number. The 0 before each city code only needs to be dialed when placing calls within Estonia.

MAIL. Estonia's state-run postal system is reliable, and mail from Estonia generally arrives in the US or Canada within 5-9 days. The standard rate for a letter to the US or Canada is 8EEK. Most postal workers speak English well. Mail can be received general delivery through **Poste Restante** to Tallinn, Pärnu, and Tartu. Address envelopes as follows: First name, LAST NAME, POSTE RESTANTE, post office address, 0001 (Postal Code) Tallinn (city), ESTONIA.

LANGUAGE. Estonian is a Finno-Ugric language, closely related to Finnish. Knowledge of English is widespread among Estonians, especially those of the younger generations. Many also know Finnish or Swedish, but German is more common among the older set and in resort towns. Russian was once mandatory, but Estonians in secluded areas have probably forgotten much of it.

ACCOMMODATIONS AND CAMPING

ESTONIA	❶	❷	❸	❹	❺
ACCOMMODATIONS	under 200EEK	200-400EEK	401-550EEK	551-600EEK	over 600EEK

Each tourist office has accommodations listings for its town and can often arrange a bed for visitors. There is little distinction between **hotels, hostels,** and **guesthouses;** some upscale hotels still have hall toilets and showers. The word *võõrastemaja* (guesthouse) in an establishment's name usually implies that it's less expensive. Some hostels are part of hotels, so be sure to ask for the cheaper rooms. **Homestays** are common and inexpensive. For info on hostels around Estonia, contact the **Estonian Youth Hostel Association,** Narva Mantee 16-25, 10120 Tallinn (☎372 6461 455; www.balticbookings.com/eyha). **Camping** is the best way to experience Estonia's islands; doing so outside of designated areas, however, is illegal and a threat to wildlife. **Farm stays** provide a great peek into local life. For more info visit **Rural Tourism** (www.maaturism.ee), or search for a variety of accommodations at www.visitestonia.com.

FOOD AND DRINK

ESTONIA	❶	❷	❸	❹	❺
FOOD	under 50EEK	50-80EEK	81-100EEK	101-140EEK	over 140EEK

Most cheap Estonian food is fried and doused with sour cream. Local specialties include *schnitzel* (breaded, fried pork fillet), *seljanka* (meat stew), *pelmenid* (dumplings), and smoked fish. Bread is usually dark and dense; a loaf of *Hiiumaa leib* easily weighs a kilo. Pancakes with cheese curd and berries are a delicious dessert. The national beer *Saku* and the darker *Saku Tume* are acquired tastes. Local beer, like Kuressaare's *Saaremaa*, is of inconsistent quality. *Värska*, a brand of carbonated mineral water, is particularly salty. It is difficult to keep a **vegetarian** or **kosher** diet in Estonia.

HOLIDAYS AND FESTIVALS

Holidays: New Year's Day (Jan. 1); Independence Day (Feb. 24); Good Friday (Apr. 10, 2009; Apr. 2, 2010); Easter Sunday (Apr. 12, 2009; Apr. 4, 2010); Labor Day (May 1); Pentecost (May 31, 2009; May 23, 2010); Victory Day (June 23); Midsummer's Day (June 24); Restoration of Independence (Aug. 20); Christmas (Dec. 25).

Festivals: Tallinn's **Beersummer** (p. 282), held in early July, is the kind of celebration its name leads you to expect. Tallinn also hosts the **Black Nights Film Festival** in December, featuring student and animation subfestivals in addition to showcasing international films. Pärnu's mid-June **Estonian Linedance Festival** culminates in a line dance the length of a city street. Check an updated list of cultural events at www.culture.ee.

BEYOND TOURISM

For more information on opportunities in Europe, see **Beyond Tourism,** p. 60.

Youth for Understanding USA (YFU), 6400 Goldsboro Rd., Ste. 100, Bethesda, MD 20817, USA (☎1-866-493-8872; www.yfu.org). Places US high school students in exchange programs. US$75 application fee plus $500 enrollment deposit.

TALLINN ☎0

Crisp sea air gusts over the medieval buildings and spires of Tallinn (pop. 401,000), the self-proclaimed "Heart of Northern Europe." The Old Town, though crowded with sightseers, hides quiet alleys and cafes. Visitors willing to venture beyond the compact center will be delighted by quirky cafes, lush parks, and the glorious seaside promenade.

TRANSPORTATION

Trains: Toompuiestee 35 (☎615 8610; www.evr.ee). Trams #1 and 2 run between the station and the Mere pst., just south of the town center, headed to **Pärnu** (2hr., 2 per day, 100-160EEK), **Tartu** (3-4hr., 4 per day, 80-130EEK), and **Moscow, RUS** (14hr.; 1 per day; 568EEK, sleeper car 898EEK).

Buses: Lastekodu 46 (☎680 0900), 1.5km southeast of Vanalinn. Trams #2 and 4 run on Tartu mnt. between Hotel Viru and the station. Buy tickets at the station (10EEK) or from the driver (15EEK). **Eurolines** (www.eurolines.ee) runs to **Rīga, LAT** (5-6hr., 9 per day, 200-250EEK), **St. Petersburg, RUS** (8-10hr., 6 per day, 190-270EEK), and **Vilnius, LIT** (10hr., 4 per day, 430EEK). 10% ISIC discount.

Ferries: At the end of Sadama (☎631 8550). Ferries cross to **Helsinki, FIN** (1-3hr., 47 per day, 350-755EEK). **Mainedd** travel agency, Raekoja pl. 18 (☎644 4744; mainedd@hot.ee), books ferry tickets with no commission. Student rates available. Open M-F 9:30am-5:30pm. MC/V.

Public Transportation: Buses, trams, minibuses, and **trolleys** run 6am-midnight. Buy tickets from kiosks (13EEK) or from drivers (20EEK). 10-ticket booklet 90EEK. Tickets valid on all but minibuses. Punch your ticket on board or face a 600EEK fine. 1hr., 2hr., and 1-day tickets are available from kiosks (15/20/45EEK). Cash only.

Taxi: Rate per km should be posted on your taxi's window. Call ahead and order a car to avoid a "waiting fee." Klubi Takso (☎638 0638; 14 200), 35EEK plus 7.50EEK per km. Silver Takso (☎627 8858; 15 222) 35EEK plus 7.50EEK per km. **Linnatakso** (☎644 2442), 7EEK per km, can provide taxis for disabled passengers. Another option Mar.-Oct. is a **bicycle taxi.** Velotaxi (☎508 8810) operates in Vanalinn. 35EEK per passenger.

ESTONIA

ORIENTATION

Even locals lose their way along the winding medieval streets of Tallinn's **Vanalinn** (Old Town), an egg-shaped maze ringed by five main streets: **Rannamäe tee, Mere puistee, Pärnu mantee, Kaarli puistee,** and **Toompuiestee.** Vanalinn has two sections: **All-linn** (Lower Town) and **Toompea,** a rocky, fortified hill west of All-linn. Only about 50% of the wall that once encircled Vanalinn is intact, but the best entrance is still through the 15th-century **Viru Gate,** across from Hotel Viru (unless you come from the ferry terminal, in which case it's best to go through the Great Coastal Gate, **Surr Rannavärav,** to the north). **Viru,** the main thoroughfare, leads directly to **Raekoja plats** (Town Hall Square), in the center of town.

PRACTICAL INFORMATION

Tourist Office: Kullassepa 4/Niguliste 2 (☎645 7777; www.tourism.tallinn.ee).Open July-Aug. M-F 9am-8pm, Sa-Su 10am-6pm; May-June M-F 9am-7pm, Sa-Su 10am-5pm; Sept. M-F 9am-6pm, Sa-Su 10am-5pm; Oct.-Apr. M-F 9am-5pm, Sa 10am-3pm.

Embassies: For more info, contact the Estonian Foreign Ministry (www.vm.ee). **Canada,** Toom-kooli 13 (☎627 3311; tallinn@canada.ee). Open M, W, F 9am-noon. **Ireland,** Vene 2 (☎681 1888; embassytallinn@eircom.net). Open M-F 10am-1pm and 2-3:30pm. **UK,** Wismari 6 (☎667 4700; www.britishembassy.ee). Open M-F 10am-noon and 2-4:30pm. **US,** Kentmanni 20 (☎668 8100; www.usemb.ee). Open M-F 9am-noon and 2-5pm. **Australian** citizens should contact the embassy in Stockholm, SWE. Citizens of **New Zealand** should contact the embassy in **The Hague, NTH.**

Currency Exchange: In general, banks have better rates than hotels and private exchange bureaus. Try **Eesti Uhispank,** Pärnu mnt. 12 (☎640 3614). Open M-F 9am-6pm, Sa 10am-3pm. There are **ATMs** throughout the city.

American Express: Suur-Karja 15 (☎626 6335; www.estravel.ee). Books hotels and tours, sells airline, ferry, and rail tickets, and provides visa services. Open June-Aug. M-F 9am-6pm, Sa 10am-5pm; Sept.-May M-F 9am-6pm, Sa 10am-3pm.

Pharmacy: Tõnismae Apteek, Tõniamagi 5 (☎644 2282). Open 24hr.

Laundry: Keemilin Pubastus, located on Uus 9. Full service 20EEK per kg. Open M-F 9am-6pm, Sa 10am-4pm. Cash only.

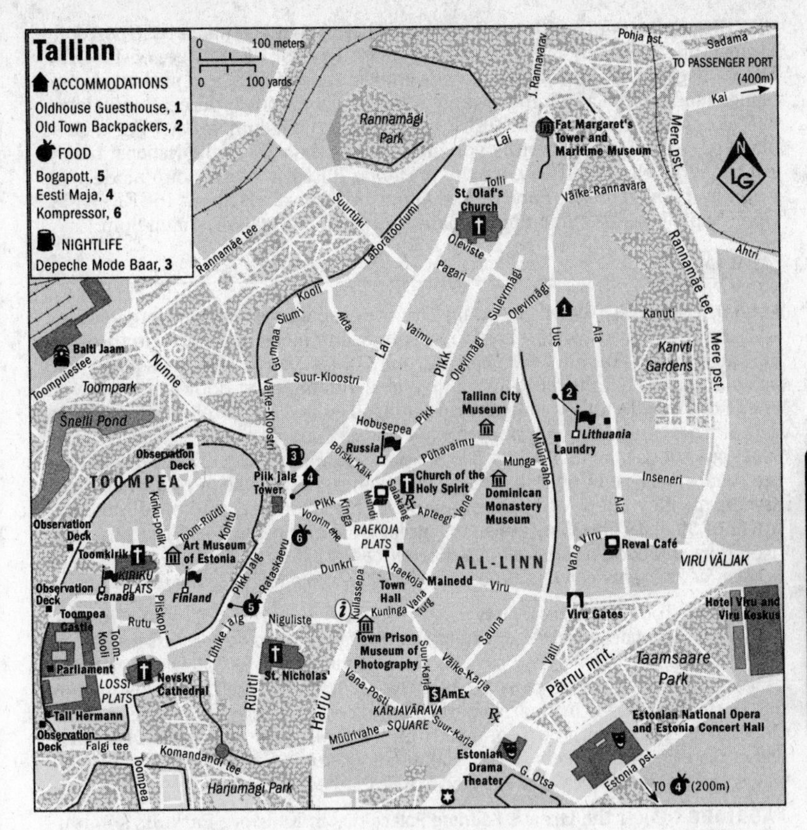

Internet: Public **Wi-Fi** networks are available at many cafes and hostels; look for the "wifi.ee" sign. **Metro,** Viru valjak 4 (☎610 1519), in the bus station below Viru keskus. 15EEK per 15min.; 35EEK per hr., students 15EEK. Open M-F 7am-11pm, Sa-Su 10am-11pm. MC/V; min. 50EEK. **Central Library,** Estonia pst. 8, 2nd fl. (☎683 0902). Free if you call ahead. Open M-F 11am-7pm, Sa 10am-5pm.

Post Office: Narva mnt. 1 (☎661 6616), opposite Hotel Viru. **Poste Restante** in basement. Open Tu-F 7:30am-8pm, Sa 8am-6pm. **Postal Code:** 10101.

ACCOMMODATIONS AND FOOD

Travel agencies are easy to find, but hostels fill up fast, so reserve ahead. **Oldhouse Guesthouse ❸,** Uus 22, offers cozy rooms in the Old Town. (☎641 1464; www.oldhouse.ee. Free Wi-Fi. 8-bed dorms 290EEK; singles 550EEK; doubles 650EEK. 10% ISIC discount. Cash only.) **Old Town Backpackers ❷,** Uus 14, has a bunch of beds in a cheerful room. (☎517 1337. www.balticbackpackers.com. Linens 25EEK. Internet 5EEK per 15min. Dorms 225EEK. MC/V.)

The secret is out about **Kompressor ❶,** Rataskaevu 3. This is the best place in town for Estonian pancakes, offering giant portions with fish, meat, and veggie fillings. (Pancakes 30-55EEK. Open daily 11am-midnight or 1am. Cash only.) **Eesti Maja ❷,** A. Lauteri 1, offers *sült* (jellied pig legs; 80EEK), blood sausages

(80EEK), and other traditional Estonian dishes. (www.eestimaja.ee. Open daily 11am-11pm. M-F 11am-3pm all-you-can-eat buffet 125EEK. Entrees 65-195EEK. MC/V.) **Bogapott** ❶, Pikk Jalg 9, serves crepes, sandwiches, and savory pies on dishes made in the adjoining ceramics studio. (www.bogapott.ee. Sandwiches 22EEK; crepes 40EEK; pies 10EEK. Open daily 10am-6pm. MC/V.) For a quiet place to read that novel while you eat, head to the cafe in the **National Library,** Tõnismägi 2. On a cold day, try the *puljong* (20EEK), a light soup made with water and boiled meat. (Sandwiches about 11EEK, salads about 16EEK. Wi-Fi. Open Sept.-June M-F 9am-8pm, Sa 11am-7pm; July-Aug. daily 10am-8pm.)

SIGHTS

ALL-LINN (LOWER TOWN). Head up Viru to reach **Raekoja plats,** where vendors sell everything from wizard hats to sweaters, and musicians perform throughout the summer. Tallinn's **town hall,** Europe's oldest, is right on the square. The museum inside details daily life in medieval Tallinn. Next door is a **tower** with one of the world's tallest toilets (77m), built so guards could relieve themselves without descending. *(Town hall open July-Aug. M-Sa 10am-4pm. 40EEK, students 25EEK. Tower open June-Aug. daily 11am-6pm. 30EEK, students 15EEK. Cash only.)* Take Mündi from the square, turn right on Pühavaimu, and then right on Vene to reach **Katariinan Käytävä,** an alley lined with galleries and cafes. At the north end of All-linn, the tower of **St. Olaf's Church** offers such a great view of the Old Town that the KGB used it as an observation post. *(Lai 50. Open daily Apr.-Oct. 10am-6pm. Services M and F 6:30pm, Su 10am and noon. Church free. Tower 30EEK, students 15EEK. Cash only.)*

TOOMPEA. Toompea's **Lossi plats** (Castle Square) is dominated by the Russian Orthodox **Alexander Nevsky Cathedral.** *(From Raekoja pl., head down Kullassepa, right on Niguliste, and uphill on Lühike jalg. Open daily 8am-6:30pm. Services 9am.)* **Dome Church,** the oldest in Estonia, towers over the hill. Over 300 barons are buried just inches below the floor; their intricately carved wooden family crests line the walls of the church. Walk south on Toompea from Lossi pl. to the **Museum of Occupation and of the Fight for Freedom,** which documents Estonia's repression by the Germans and Soviets. *(Open Tu-Su 11am-6pm. 10EEK, students 5EEK. Cash only.)*

KADRIORG. Peter the Great's **Kadriorg Palace** lies in Kadriorg Park. Its sumptuous grand hall is a stunning example of Baroque architecture, and the palace houses a lovely art collection. The **Mikkel Museum** is also on these grounds. The **Peter the Great House Museum** holds many of the tsar's original furnishings, as well as an imprint of his extremely large hand. *(Mäekalda 2. Palace open May-Sept. Tu-W and F-Su 10am-5pm, Th 10am-9pm; Oct.-Apr. W-Su 10am-5pm. 45EEK, students 35EEK. Mikkel Museum open May-Sept. W and F-Su 10am-9pm; Oct.-Apr. W-Su 10am-5pm. 25/10EEK. House Museum open mid-May to Sept. W-Su 10:30am-5pm. 15/10EEK. MC/V.)* At the opposite end of the park from the tram stop is the main branch of the **Art Museum of Estonia.** *(Weizenbergi 34. www.ekm.ee. Open May-Sept. Tu-Su 11am-6pm; Oct.-Apr. W-Su 11am-6pm. Contemporary art 30EEK, permanent exhibition 55EEK, combined ticket 75EEK. Free admission once a month; see website for specific dates. MC/V.)*

ENTERTAINMENT AND NIGHTLIFE

Pick up a free copy of *Tallinn This Week* at the tourist office. The **Estonia Concert Hall** and the **Estonian National Opera** (Rahvusooper Estonia) are both at Estonia pst. 4. (Opera ☎683 1260; www.opera.ee. Opera box office open daily 11am-7pm. Tickets 50-350EEK. MC/V.) Celebrate the power of barley in early July at **Beersummer** (www.ollesummer.ee). In the middle of December, the international **Dark Nights Film Festival** (www.poff.ee) showcases cinematic talent. **Depeche Mode Baar,** Nomme 4, plays all Depeche Mode, all day long and serves mixed drinks (40-80EEK) named after their songs. (www.edmfk.ee/dmbaar. 0.5L beer 45EEK. Open daily noon-4am. Cash only.)

PÄRNU ☎44

Famous for its mud baths, beaches, and festivals, Pärnu (pop. 45,000) is the summer capital of Estonia. Soak up some culture at Pärnu's **Museum of New Art,** Esplanaadi 10, where you will find all kinds of local contemporary art, from bold photographs to bewildering installations of imaginary animals. (☎443 0772. Open daily 9am-9pm. 25EEK, students 15EEK. MC/V.) Walk down Hommiku to the medieval **Red Tower,** used as a prison in the 17th century.

Hostel Lõuna ❷, Lõuna 2, offers comfortable rooms, as well as dorms with bedside tables and reading lamps. (☎443 0943; www.eliisabet.ee/hostel. Reception 24hr. Dorms 250-300EEK; doubles 500-900EEK; triples 750-900EEK.) **Kadri Kohvik ❷,** Nikolai 12, around the corner from the TIC, is a popular cafeteria that serves filling fish and meat dishes. (☎442 9782. Entrees 30-40EEK. Open M-F 7:30am-7pm, Sa-Su 9am-5pm.) Closer to the beach, **Lehe Kohvik ❶,** Lehe 5, offers light sandwiches, salads, and desserts. (Small entrees 30-50EEK. Open M-F 10am-11pm, F-Su 10am-11pm. MC/V.) **Onu Sam ❶,** Suvituse 11, satisfies late-night burger cravings. This booth on the way to the beach dishes out the goods 24hr. a day. (20-30EEK.) Head to **Veerev Olu** (The Rolling Beer), Uus 3A, for live rock and folk Saturday 9:30pm-1am. (☎442 9848. Beer 0.5L 30EEK. Food 35-80EEK. Open M-Th and Su 11am-midnight, F-Sa 11am-1am. MC/V.)

Eurolines **buses** (☎442 7841) go from Ringi 3 to Tallinn (2hr., 2 per hr., 100-110EEK), Tartu (2hr., 21 per day, 120-135EEK), and Rīga, LAT (3hr., 6-8 per day, 180-210EEK). Rent a **bike** from Rattarent, at the intersection of Ranna and Supeluse. (☎502 8269. 40EEK per hr., 150EEK per day.) The **tourist office,** Rüütli 16, books rooms for a 25EEK fee and hands out free maps. (☎447 3000; www.parnu.ee. Open mid-May to mid-Sept. M-F 9am-6pm, Sa 9am-4pm, Su 10am-3pm; mid-Sept. to mid-May M-F 9am-5pm. Cash only.) **Postal Code:** 80010.

ESTONIA

TARTU ☎7

The second largest city in Estonia, Tartu (pop. 100,000) is home to Tartu University (Tartu Ülikool). Historic spots like Raekoja Plats (Town Hall Square) and a population of bustling college students give Tartu its vibrant atmosphere.

TRANSPORTATION AND PRACTICAL INFORMATION. **Buses** (☎747 7227) leave from Turu 2, 300m southeast of Raekoja Plats, for Pärnu (2hr., 20 per day, 130EEK), Tallinn (2-3hr., 46 per day, 130-140EEK), and Rīga, LAT (5hr., 2 per day, 200EEK). **Trains** (☎761 56 851), generally less reliable than buses, depart from the intersection of Kuperjanovi and Vaksali for Tallinn (2-3hr., 3 per day, 95-140EEK). Exchange currency at **Tavid,** on Rüütli. The **tourist office,** located in the town hall, Raekoja Plats 14, offers free **Internet.** (☎744 2111; www.visittartu.com. Open mid-Sept. to mid-May M-F 9am-6pm, Sa 10am-5pm, Su 10am-3pm; mid-May to mid-Sept. M-F 9am-5pm, Sa-Su 10am-3pm.) **Postal Code:** 51001.

ACCOMMODATIONS AND FOOD. **Hostel Terviseks ❷,** Ülikooli 1, is barely a minute away from Raekoja Plats. The apartment style set-up, spacious bathroom, and light complimentary breakfast make this place comfortable and homey. (☎5353 1153. 6-bed and 8-bed mixed dorms 260EEK. Shared bath. Free Wi-Fi.) The university dorms at **Hostel Raatuse ❷,** Raatuse 22, are more luxurious than rooms in many hotels. (☎740 9958; www.tartucampus.eu. Free Wi-Fi in cafe. Singles 350EEK; doubles 600EEK. MC/V.) At the attic lounge **Maailm ❷,** Rüütli 12, slurp a Dostojevsky (vanilla ice cream and apple juice; 50EEK) while swaying on a swing. (☎742 9099; www.klubimaailm.ee. Entrees 70-85EEK. 21+ after 9pm. Open M-Sa noon-1am, Su noon-10pm. MC/V.) For pizza and zebra-themed decor, head to **Moka ❷,** Küütri 3. (☎744 2085. Pizza and other entrees 50-100EEK. Open M-F 9am-midnight, Sa 10am-1am, Su 11am-11pm.)

SIGHTS AND NIGHTLIFE. In **Raekoja Plats** (Town Hall Square), the building that houses the **Tartu Art Museum** (Tartu Kunstimuuseum) leans a little to the left—just like the student population. (Open W-Su 11am-6pm. 30EEK, students 12EEK. Ground floor 15/7EEK. F free. Cash only.) In the attic of Tartu University's main building, students were once held in a **lock-up** *(kartser)* for a list of offenses, including failing to return library books; their drawings and inscriptions are still visible. (Open M-F 11am-5pm. 5EEK. Cash only.) On Rüütli, Tartu's oldest street, waitresses zip about with beer mugs. Among the cafes and pubs, look for **Ruum** *and* **Raamat,** two linked shops with Indian crafts and used books. (Rüüstli 12. Open daily 10am-6pm.) Children and the young at heart will find the **Tartu Toy Museum,** 8 Lutsu, an engaging spot. The cheerful cottage displays dolls, puppets, and other toys from the 19th century to the present. (☎736 1550; www.mm.ee. Open W-Su 11am-6pm. 25EEK, students 20EEK.) Climb up the extremely narrow steeple of **Jaani Church** (Jaanir Kirik) for a decent view of the area, but be careful not to scrape your elbows in the process. (Tu-Sa 10am-7pm. Open Su only for service 11am-12:30pm. 25EEK, students 15EEK.) The dignified **Wilde Irish Pub,** Vallikraavi 4, attracts a middle-aged crowd. (Entrees 75-200EEK. Open M-Tu and Su noon-midnight, W-Th noon-1am, F-Sa noon-2am. Live bands F-Sa. Salsa night W. MC/V.)

DAYTRIP FROM TARTU: VILJANDI. A curious mesh of city malls and castle ruins, hilly Viljandi (pop. 19,900) is at its best in summer during the **Hansa Days.** Held in early June, this lively celebration commemorates Viljandi's days as a member of the medieval training guild, the **Hanseatic League.** Folk music concerts, open air markets, and people in traditional dress make the town pulse with earthy energy. The unrivalled highlight any time of year is the ruined **castle** built by the **Order of the Knights of the Sword.** The view of **Viljandi Lake** from the castle is a must-see—and it's free. Behind the castle, walk across the wooden bridge over a serene valley. In late July, keep an eye (and an ear) out for the **Viljandi Folk Music Festival,** which draws crowds from around the country.

Cheap beds are hard to come by, but buses to Tartu are fast and frequent, making Viljandi an excellent daytrip. If you'd like to stay the night, try **Hostel Ingeri ❷,** Pikk 2c, right by Vabaduse Plats. (☎5568 5369. Dorms 350-500EEK.) For a cheap bite, **Pappa Pizza ❶,** Tallinna 8, near the intersection of Tartu and Tallinna, may be your best bet. (☎43 33 906. Entrees 40-60EEK).

Buses run from Tartu to Viljandi (1hr., 1 per hr., 70EEK.) The **tourist information center** is at Vabaduse Plats 6. (☎43 30 442. Open in summer M-F 9am-6pm, Sa-Su 10am-3pm; in winter M-Sa 10am-5pm, Su 10am-2pm.) **Postal code:** 71020.

ESTONIAN ISLANDS

SAAREMAA ☎45

Windy **Kuressaare** (pop. 16,000) is the largest town on Saaremaa. The local accent and folklore distinguish the island from the mainland, although tourists seem to outnumber locals in summer months. Head south from Raekoja pl. (Town Hall Square) along Lossi to reach **Bishopric Castle.** Inside, hidden staircases and a skeleton share space with the **Saaremaa Museum,** which chronicles the island's history. (Open May-Aug. daily 10am-7pm; Sept.-Apr. W-Su 11am-6pm. 50EEK, students 25EEK. Cash only.)

SYG Hostel ❶, Kingu 6, is your best bet for clean and spacious budget rooms. (☎455 4388. Free Wi-Fi. Reception 24hr. Open June-Aug. Dorms 110-130EEK; singles 255EEK; doubles 300-350EEK; quads 480-580EEK. MC/V.) Grab traditional Estonian pancakes (25-40EEK), hotpots (60-70EEK), or non-traditional Estonian pizza (50-80EEK) at **Pannkoogikohvik ❶**, Kohtu 1. (☎453 3575. Open M-Th 9am-midnight, F-Sa 9am-2am, Su 10am-midnight. MC/V.)

Buses (☎453 1661) leave from Pihtla tee 2, at the corner with Tallinna, for Pärnu (3hr., 3-5 per day, 180-194EEK) and Tallinn (4-5hr., 9-11 per day, 190-200EEK.) Buses and ferries are not coordinated, so check schedules ahead of time. The **tourist office,** Tallinna 2, in the town hall, offers free **Internet** and arranges private rooms. (☎453 3120; www.saaremaa.ee. Open May to mid-Sept. M-F 9am-7pm, Sa 9am-5pm, Su 10am-3pm; mid-Sept. to Apr. M-F 9am-5pm.)

HIIUMAA ☎46

By restricting access to Hiiumaa (pop. 11,000) for 50 years, the Soviets unwittingly preserved the island's rare wildlife and scenery. Creek-laced **Kärdla** (pop. 4000) is Hiiumaa's biggest town. To explore the sights along the coast, rent a **bike** (150EEK per day) from Priit Tikka, which will deliver anywhere on the island (☎5660 6377. Cash only.) Bike west from Kärdla toward Kõrgessaare to the chilling **Hill of Crosses** (Ristimägi; 6km). About 2km past that, a right turn leads to the cast-iron **Tahkuna Lighthouse** (11km). Back on the main road, turn right again toward Kõrgessaare; continue 20km past the town to reach the impressive 16th-century **Kõpu Lighthouse.** (25EEK, students 15EEK. Cash only.) Local buses (3-4 per day, 14EEK) run to the town of Kaina, an ideal base for exploring the island of **Kassari,** attached to Hiiumaa by a land bridge. From Kaina, biking either east or west on Highway 83 will lead you to the 15km loop that runs through Kassari. On Kassari's southern tip is the **Sääretirp** peninsula, where pine and juniper bushes give way to a windswept rocky promontory.

Eesti Posti Hostel ❶, Posti 13, has comfy beds and clean baths. (☎5331 1860. Call for check-in. May-Sept. 255EEK per person; Oct.-Apr. 200EEK. Cash only.) In the town square, **Arteesia Kohvik ❶,** Keskväljak 5, is a local haunt. (Entrees 35-85EEK. Open daily 9am-9pm. Cash only.)

Direct **buses** run from Sadama 13 (☎463 2077), north of Kärdla's main square, Keskväljak, to Tallinn (4hr.; 2-3 per day; 160EEK,15% student discount, except in summer. Cash only). Public transportation on both Hiiumaa and Saaremaa is sparse; be sure to plan journeys ahead to avoid missing the few buses and ferries. There are two **tourist offices** on the island, one in Heltermaa (☎463 1001), and a bigger one in Kärdla. The Kärdla office, Hiiu 1, passes out free maps and bus schedules and sells **The Lighthouse Tour** (25EEK), a guide to sights with local legends. (☎462 2232; www.hiiumaa.ee. Open May to mid-Sept. M-F 9am-6pm, Sa-Su 10am-3pm; mid-Sept. to Apr. M-F 9am-5pm. Cash only.) The **cultural center,** Rookopli 18, has free **Internet,** and the town center has free Wi-Fi.

FINLAND (SUOMI)

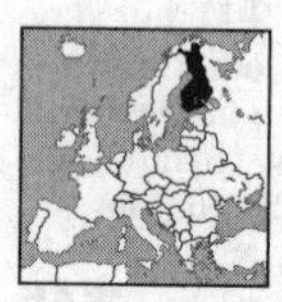

Caught in a territorial tug-of-war between Sweden and Russia since the 1400s, Finland finally secured autonomy in 1917, successfully defending its independence through both World Wars. Tarja Halonen, Finland's first female president, presides over the home of Nokia cell phones and hosts the annual World Sauna Championships. The country's lakes and boreal forest entice hikers while southern cities draw architecture students and art gurus. Finland—outside of stylish Helsinki—is more affordable than its Scandinavian neighbors.

DISCOVER FINLAND: SUGGESTED ITINERARY

THREE DAYS. Start off the first day in **Helsinki** (p. 290) by ambling along the tree-lined **Esplanadi** and checking out some of the city's great museums. Leave time for a thrilling bike ride down the Pellinge archipelago, south of **Porvoo** (p. 298). Afterwards, the venerable **Turku** (p. 298) is worth a look.

ONE WEEK. After three days in **Helsinki,** head off to **Tampere** (p. 301), with its lively music scene and museums in the shells of factories. Picnic on the islands of **Savonlinna** (p. 302) and daytrip out to the transcendent **Retretti Art Center.** From here, head back to **Helsinki** or embark on the trek north to **Rovaniemi** (p. 304).

ESSENTIALS

WHEN TO GO

The long days of Finnish summer are a tourist's dream, while the two-month polar night *(kaamos)* in the country's northern regions draws winter-sports fanatics. Ski season starts in early February, continuing well into March and April. Reindeer and snowmobile safaris, along with glimpses of the rare **aurora borealis,** reward travelers willing to brave winter temperatures, which regularly drop to -20°C (-4°F). Summer tourists, celebrating Midsummer *(Juhannus)* festivities (June 21-22), can expect average temperatures of 20-25°C (68-77°F).

DOCUMENTS AND FORMALITIES

EMBASSIES AND CONSULATES. Foreign embassies in Finland are in Helsinki (p. 292). Finnish embassies abroad include: **Australia** and **New Zealand,** 12 Darwin Ave., Yarralumla, ACT 2600 (☎26 273 38 00; www.finland.org.au); **Canada,** 55 Metcalfe St., Ste. 850, Ottawa, ON K1P 6L5 (☎613-288-2233; www.finland.ca/en); **Ireland,** Russell House, Stokes Pl., St. Stephen's Green, Dublin 2 (☎01 478 1344; www.finland.ie/en); **UK,** 38 Chesham Pl., London SW1X 8HW (☎020 78 38 62 00; www.finemb.org.uk/en); **US,** 3301 Massachusetts Ave. NW, Washington, D.C. 20008 (☎202-298-5800; www.finland.org).

FACTS AND FIGURES

OFFICIAL NAME: Republic of Finland.

CAPITAL: Helsinki.

MAJOR CITIES: Oulu, Tampere, Turku.

POPULATION: 5,245,000.

LAND AREA: 338,000 sq. km.

TIME ZONE: GMT +2.

LANGUAGES: Finnish, Swedish.

NATIONAL CELEBRITY: Father Christmas, or Santa Claus, rumored to live in a northern province (p. 304).

VISA AND ENTRY INFORMATION. EU citizens do not need a visa. Citizens of Australia, Canada, New Zealand, and the US do not need a visa for stays of up to 90 days, in any of the countries in the EU's freedom-of-movement zone. For more info, see p. 15. For stays longer than 90 days, all non-EU citizens need **Schengen** visas (around US$41), available at Finnish embassies and online at www.finland.org/en. Application processing takes about two weeks.

TOURIST SERVICES AND MONEY

EMERGENCY	**Ambulance, Police, and Fire:** ☎112.

TOURIST OFFICES. The **Finnish Tourist Board** (☎010 60 58 000; www.visitfinland.com) maintains an official online travel guide, which customizes its travel information and advice by home country.

MONEY. In 2002, the **euro** replaced the markka as the unit of currency in Finland. For more info, see p. 19. **Banks** exchange currency for a €2-5 commission, though **Forex** offices and **ATMs** offer the best exchange rates. Food from grocery stores runs €10-17 per day; meals cost around €8 for lunch and €12 for dinner. Although restaurant bills include a service charge, leaving small change for particularly good service is becoming more common. Finland has a 22% **value added tax (VAT),** a sales tax applied to services and imports. The nation has a reduced VAT of 17% for food products and 8% for public transportation, books, and medicines. The prices given in *Let's Go* include VAT. In the airport upon exiting the EU, non-EU citizens can claim a refund on the tax paid for goods purchased at participating stores. In order to qualify for a refund in a store, you must spend at least €40; make sure to ask for a refund form when you pay. For more info on qualifying for a VAT refund, see p. 21.

TRANSPORTATION

BY PLANE. Several airlines fly into Helsinki from Australia, Europe, and North America. The main airport is **Helsinki-Vantaa Airport (HEL;** ☎200 14636; www.helsinki-vantaa.fi). **Finnair** (Finland ☎0600 140 140, UK 087 0241 4411, US 800-950-5000; www.finnair.com) flies from 120 international cities and also covers the domestic market. The airline offers youth rates—inquire before purchasing. **AirÅland** (www.airaland.com) flies to Stockholm, SWE and the Åland Isles. **Ryanair** (☎353 12 49 77 91; www.ryanair.com) flies to **Tampere-Pirkkala Airport (TMP).**

BY TRAIN. The national rail company is **VR Ltd., Finnish Railways** (☎0600 41 900; www.vr.fi). Finnish rail is efficient and prices are high; seat reservations are required on **Pendolino** and recommended on **InterCity** trains (€6.40-12.60). **Eurail** is valid in Finland. A **Finnrailpass,** available only to foreigners, allows for three ($190), five ($251), or 10 travel days ($342) in a one-month period.

BY BUS. Buses are the only way to reach some smaller towns and points beyond the Arctic Circle. **Oy Matkahuolto Ab** (☎09 682 701; www.matkahuolto.fi) coordinates bus service. ISIC holders can buy a sticker (€6) for their **Matkahuolto Student Identity Card,** free from Matkahuoloto service outlets, agents, and VR (previously Suomen Valtion Rautatiet) ticket offices. The sticker gives students a 50% discount on one-way tickets purchased ahead for routes exceeding 80km. **Rail passes** are valid on buses when trains are not in service.

BY FERRY. Viking Line (Finland ☎09 123 51, Sweden 08 452 4000; www.vikingline.fi) and **Tallinksilja** (Finland ☎09 180 41, Sweden 08 666 33 30; www.tallinksilja.fi) sail from Stockholm, SWE to Helsinki, Mariehamn, and Turku. Travelers with both a **Eurail Pass** and a train ticket receive free passenger fare. Viking's "early bird" discounts are 15-50% off on ferry fares when booking trips within Finland or Sweden at least 30 days ahead. On Tallinksilja, Eurailer holders ride for free or lower rates, depending on the specific route and ticket type.

BY CAR. Finland honors foreign **driver's licenses** issued in the US, EU, and EEA countries for up to one year for drivers aged 18 years or older. Speed limits are 120kph on expressways, 30-40kph in densely populated areas, and 80-100kph on most major roads. Headlights must be used at all times. Finnish law requires all cars must have snow tires during the winter. Be wary of reindeer at night. For more info on car rental and driving in Europe, see p. 53.

BY BIKE AND BY THUMB. Finland has a well-developed network of cycling paths. **Fillari GT** route maps are available at bookstores (€10-16). Check www.visitfinland.com/cycling for pre-trip route planning. **Hitchhiking** is uncommon in Finland and illegal on highways. *Let's Go* does not recommend hitchhiking.

KEEPING IN TOUCH

PHONE CODES	**Country code:** 358. **International dialing prefix:** 00. For more info international calls, see **Inside Back Cover.**

EMAIL AND THE INTERNET. Internet cafes in Helsinki are relatively scarce compared to other European capitals, and in smaller towns they are virtually nonexistent. However, many **tourist offices** and **public libraries** offer short (15-30min.) slots of free Internet, and there is some free **Wi-Fi** access in Helsinki.

TELEPHONE. To make a long-distance call within Finland, dial 0 and then the number. **Pay phones** are rare but dependable. **Mobile phones** are extremely popular in the nation that gave the world Nokia, and prepaid mobile phone cards can be used to make international calls (cheapest 10pm-8am). For more info on mobile phones, see p. 32. For operator assistance, dial ☎118; for help with international calls, dial ☎92020. International direct dial numbers include: **ATandT Direct** (☎0800 1100 15); **Canada Direct** (☎0800 1100 11); **MCI** (☎08001 102 80); **Telecom New Zealand** (☎0800 1106 40).

MAIL. Finnish mail service is efficient. Postcards and letters under 50g cost €0.70 within Finland, €1 to the EU, and €1.40 to other destinations. International letters under 20g cost €0.70. Check www.posti.fi/english/index.html for more prices and mailing restrictions. To receive mail in Finland, have mail delivered **Poste Restante.** Mail will go to the main post office unless you specify a subsidiary by street address. Address mail according to the following format: First name, Last Name, Poste Restante, post office address, city, FINLAND.

LANGUAGES. **Finnish** is spoken by most of the population (92%), although children learn both **Swedish** and Finnish from the seventh grade. Three dialects of **Sámi** are also spoken by an ethnic minority in northern Finland. **English** is also widely spoken, with two-thirds of Finns reporting that they can speak at least some English; city-dwellers and those under 35 are generally the most proficient. For basic Finnish words and phrases, see **Phrasebook: Finnish,** p. 1061.

ACCOMMODATIONS AND CAMPING

FINLAND	❶	❷	❸	❹	❺
ACCOMMODATIONS	under €15	€15-28	€29-50	€51-75	over €75

Finland has over 100 youth hostels (*retkeilymaja;* RET-kay-loo-MAH-yah), although only half of them are open year-round. The **Finnish Youth Hostel Association** (Suomen Retkeilymajajärjestö; ☎09 565 7150; www.srmnet.org) is Finland's HI affiliate. Prices are generally around €23 per person for a dorm room, with a €2.50 HI discount. Most have laundry facilities and a kitchen; some have saunas and rent bikes or skis. **Hotels** are generally expensive (over €50 per night); *kesähotelli* (summer hotels) are usually student lodgings vacated from June to August, and cost about €25 per night. **Camping** is common; seventy campgrounds are open year-round (tent sites €10-25 per night; small cottages from €40). The **Camping Card Scandinavia** (€6) qualifies cardholders for discounts and includes limited accident insurance. For a guide or to purchase the Camping Card, contact the **Finnish Camping Site Association.** (☎09 477 407 40; www.camping.fi. Allow three weeks for delivery of the card.) Finland's **right of public access** *(jokamiehenoikeudet)* allows travelers to temporarily camp for free in the countryside, as long as they stay a reasonable distance (about 150m) from private homes. See p. 36 for more info.

FOOD AND DRINK

FINLAND	❶	❷	❸	❹	❺
FOOD	under €8	€8-15	€16-20	€21-30	over €30

Kebab and pizza joints are cheap and popular, but the local *Kauppatori* markets and *Kauppahalli* food courts are more likely to serve recognizably Finnish fare. Traditional diet slants toward breads and sausages. In summer, however, menus feature freshly caught trout, perch, pike, and herring; a new wave of five-star chefs in Helsinki are pairing French and Mediterranean ingredients with the bounty of local fisheries. To Santa's displeasure, bowls of **reindeer stew** are a staple of Lapland, while Kuopio is known for its pillowy rye pastries. Try the strawberries—Finland is their top European producer. A surprising number of adults drink milk with meals, followed by interminable pots of coffee. You must be 18 to purchase **beer** and **wine,** 20 or older to buy liquor; the minimum age in bars is usually 18, but can be as old as 25. Alcohol stronger than light beer must be bought at state-run **Alko** liquor stores, open weekdays until at least 6pm and Saturdays until at least 4pm.

HOLIDAYS AND FESTIVALS

Holidays: New Year's Day (Jan. 1); Epiphany (Jan. 6); Good Friday (Mar. 10, 2009; Mar. 2, 2010); Easter (Apr. 12, 2009; Apr. 4, 2010); May Day (May 1); Ascension (May 1); Pentecost (May 31, 2009; May 23, 2010); Corpus Christi (May 22); Midsummer (June 21-22); Assumption (Aug. 15); All Saints' Day (Nov. 1); Independence Day (Dec. 6); Christmas (Dec. 25); Boxing Day (Dec. 26).

Festivals: Flags fly high on **Midsummer's Eve** (June 21), when the Finnish desert their cities for seaside cabins. July is the festival high-season in Finland, with gays and lesbians celebrating **Helsinki Pride,** Turku's youth taking to the mosh pits of **Ruisrock,** and Pori's residents launching their **Jazz Festival.** Savonlinna's **Opera Festival** continues into early August, while the **Helsinki Festival,** Oulu's **Music Video Festival,** and Lahti's **Sibelius Festival** close out the summer. See www.festivals.fi for more info.

BEYOND TOURISM

It is relatively difficult for foreigners to secure full-time employment in Finland, but travelers may be able to obtain summer work. Check the CIMO website (see below) or www.igapyear.com for information on work placement. The organizations below coordinate limited work and volunteer opportunities. For more info on opportunities across Europe, see Beyond Tourism, p. 60.

The American-Scandinavian Foundation (AMSCAN), 58 Park Ave., New York, NY 10016, USA (☎212-879-9779; www.amscan.org/jobs/index.html). Volunteer and job opportunities throughout Scandinavia. There are a limited number of fellowships for study in Finland available to Americans.

Centre for International Mobility (CIMO), Säästöpankinranta 2A, P.O. Box 343, 00531 Helsinki (☎2069 0501; http://finland.cimo.fi). Provides information on youth exchange programs, technical and agricultural internships, Finnish language studies, and study abroad. CIMO also organizes **European Voluntary Service Programs** (www.4evs.net)for EU citizens, who can spend a fully funded year doing service in another EU country. EVS opportunities are largely in social work. Similarly, the EU offers the European Youth in Action Program, which also offers years abroad in Finland (ec.europa.eu/youth/youth-in-action-programme/doc126_en.htm).

HELSINKI (HELSINGFORS) ☎09

With all the appeal of a big city but without the grime, Helsinki's (pop. 570,000) attractive harbor, grand architecture, and parks make it a showcase of Northern Europe. A hub of the design world, the city also distinguishes itself with multicultural flair; here, youthful energy mingles with old-world charm.

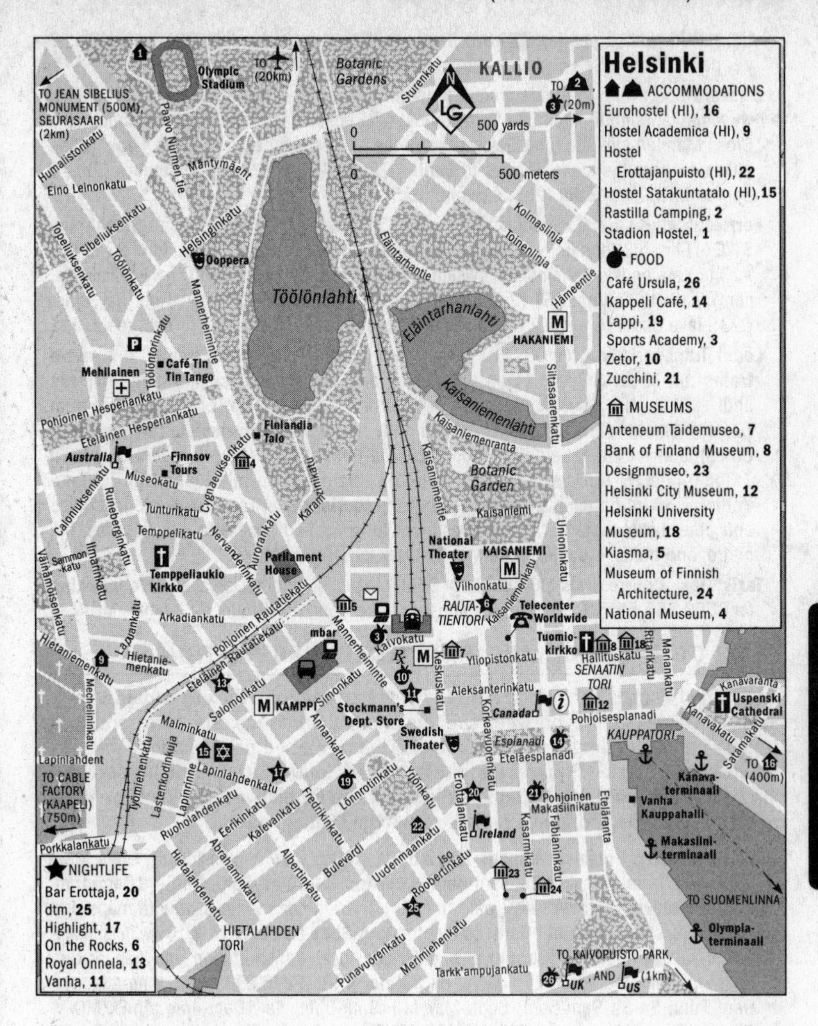

TRANSPORTATION

Flights: Helsinki-Vantaa Airport (**HEL;** ☎200 146 36; http://www.finavia.fi). Bus #615 runs from airport Platform 21 to and from the train station. (35min., buses depart roughly every 15min. weekdays 6am-9pm; every 30min. other times; from the airport M-F 6am-1am; to the airport M-F 5am-midnight. €3.80. Cash only.) A Finnair **bus** runs from airport platform 10 and from the Finnair building next to the train station (☎0600 140 140; www.finnair.com. 35min., about 3 per hr.; from the airport 5:45am-1:10am; to the airport 5am-midnight. €5.90. AmEx/MC/V.)

Trains: (☎030 072 0900, English-language info 231 999 02; www.vr.fi.) To: **Moscow, RUS** (13hr., 1 per day, from €92); **Rovaniemi** (10hr., 5 per day, from €75); **St. Peters-**

burg, RUS (5hr., 2 per day, €54.80); **Tampere** (2hr., 14 per day, €21-30); **Turku** (2hr., 7 per day, €23-34). See p. 840 for entrance requirements to Russia.

Buses: Depart from the underground Kamppi bus terminal, Narinkka 3 (☎0200 4000; www.matkahuolto.fi). From the train station, take Postik past the statue of Mannerheim. Cross Mannerheimintie onto Salomonkatu; the station will be on your left. Look for the blue sign near the stairs. Busses to **Lahti** (1-2hr., 1-2 per hr., €19), **Tampere** (2hr., 1 per hr., €22), and **Turku** (2hr., 2 per hr., €25).

Ferries: Viking Line, Lönnrotinkatu 2 (☎12 351; www.vikingline.fi), sails to **Stockholm, SWE** (16hr., 5:30pm, from €48) and **Tallinn, EST** (4hr., 11:30pm, €21). Tram #2 or bus #13 to Katajanokka terminal. Tallinksilja, Erottajankatu 19 (☎228 311; www.tallinksilja.com), sails to **Tallinn, EST** (2-3hr.; Apr.-Sept. 13 per day, Sept.-Dec. 6 per day; from €23). Take bus #15 to West terminal. For more info on Scandinavian ferries, see p. 58.

Local Transportation: (☎09 310 1071; www.hkl.fi). Most **buses, trams,** and **metro trains** run about 5:30am-11pm; major bus and tram lines, including tram #3T, run until 1:30am. Night **buses,** marked with "N," run M-Sa after 2am (€4). Single-fare tram €2; with 1hr. transfers to buses, trams, and the metro. **HKL Palvelupiste** (City Transport Office) is in the Rautatientori metro, below the train station. Open mid-June-July M-Th 7:30am-6pm, F 7:30am-5pm, Sa 10am-3pm; from Aug. to mid-June M-Th 7:30am-7pm, F 7:30am-5pm, Sa 10am-3pm. Sells the **tourist ticket** (as does the tourist office and other ticket kiosks), a good investment for unlimited access to buses, trams, the metro, and trains. 1-day €6, 3-day €12, 5-day €18. AmEx/MC/V.

Taxis: Taxi Centre Helsinki (☎0100 0700). Special airport fares with **Yellow Line** (☎0600 555 555). Reserve 1 day ahead, before 6pm. 30-55min. €22. AmEx/MC/V.

FINLAND

ORIENTATION AND PRACTICAL INFORMATION

Water and beaches surround Helsinki in every direction. The city's main street, **Mannerheimintie,** passes between the bus and train stations on its way south to the city center, ending at the Esplanadi. This tree-lined promenade leads east to **Kauppatori** (Market Square) and the beautiful South Harbor. Northeast of the city center lies **Kallio,** the bohemian district. Both Finnish and Swedish are used on all street signs and maps; *Let's Go* uses the Finnish names.

Tourist Offices: Pohjoisesplanadi 19 (☎3101 3300; www.visithelsinki.fi). Open May-Sept. M-F 9am-8pm, Sa-Su 9am-6pm; Oct.-Apr. M-F 9am-6pm, Sa-Su 10am-4pm. Representatives in green vests roam the city center in summer to distribute maps and answer questions. **Helsinki Card,** sold at the **Tour Shop** (☎2288 1500; www.helsinkiexpert.fi) in the tourist office, provides unlimited local transportation and free or discounted tours and admission. 1-day €33, 2-day €43, 3-day €53. Open June-Aug. M-F 9am-7pm, Sa-Su 9am-5pm; Sept.-May M-F 9am-5pm, Sa 10am-4pm. AmEx/MC/V. **Finnsov Tours,** Museokatu 15 (☎09 436 6960; www.finnsov.fi) arranges trips to Russia and expedites the visa process. Open M-F 9am-5pm. AmEx/MC/V.

Embassies: Canada, Pohjoisesplanadi 25B (☎619 228 530; www.canada.fi). Open June-Aug. M-Th 8am-noon and 1-4:30pm, F 8am-1:30pm; Sept.-May M-F 8:30am-noon and 1-4:30pm. **Ireland,** Erottajankatu 7A (☎09 646 006; helsinkiembassy@dfa.ie). Open M-F 9am-5pm. Consular division 9am-noon by appointment. **UK,** Itäinen Puistotie 17 (☎2286 5100; www.britishembassy.gov.uk/finland). Open mid-June-late August M-F 8:30am-3:30pm, from late Aug.-mid-June M-F 9am-5pm. By appointment. **US,** Itäinen Puistotie 14A (☎6162 5730; www.usembassy.fi). Open M-F 8:30am-5pm.

Luggage Storage: Lockers in the train station €3-4 per day. The Kiasma museum and the auditorium (lower entrance) of the National Museum (p. 296) provide free same day storage even if you don't pay admission.

GBLT Resources: Seta Ry, Mannerheimintie 170A 4, 5th fl. (☎09 681 2580; www.seta.fi). Tram #10. Organization with info on gay services. **QLife Traveler's Guide Finland** is available at the tourist office. See the www.qlife.fi for a plethora of information.

Laundromat: Café Tin Tin Tango, Töölöntorinkatu 7 (☎2709 0972; www.tintintango.info), an epic combination of bar, cafe, laundromat, and sauna. Wash €4, dry €2, detergent €1.20. Sandwiches €5-9. Open M-Th 7am-midnight, F 7am-2am, Sa 9am-2am, Su 10am-midnight. AmEx/MC/V.

General Emergency Number: ☎112

24 hr. Police: ☎189 4002 24hr. **Medical Hotline:** ☎100 23.

24hr. Pharmacy: Yliopiston Apteekki, Mannerheimintie 96 (☎0203 202 00).

Hospital: 24hr. clinic **Mehiläinen,** Pohjoinen Hesperiankatu 17 (☎010 414 4444).

Telephone: Telecenter Worldwide, Vuorikatu 8 (☎09 670 612; www.woodgong.com), offers reasonable rates. Open M-F 10am-9pm, Sa 11am-7pm, Su noon-7pm. MC/V.

Internet: Library 10, Elielinaukio 2G (☎3108 5000), upstairs in the main post office building. Free Wi-Fi, free 30min. slots of Internet. Open M-Th 10am-8pm, F-Su noon-6pm. Many **cafes** provide free Internet and Wi-Fi, including **mbar,** Mannerheimintie 22-24, (☎6124 5420) which offers free Wi-Fi and a DJ 3-5 times a week in the summer. M-Tu 9am-midnight, W-Th 9am-2am, F-Sa 9am-3am, Su noon-midnight. Visit www.hel.fi/en/wlan or check the tourist office for other Internet locations.

Post Office: Elielinaukio 2F (☎2007 1000). Open summer M-F 7am-9pm, Sa-Su 10am-6pm. **Postal Code:** 00100.

ACCOMMODATIONS AND CAMPING

Hostel Erottajanpuisto (HI), Uudenmaank. 9 (☎09 642 169; www.erottajanpuisto.com). Well-kept rooms in a central location. Breakfast €5. Lockers €1. Laundry €7. Free Internet and Wi-Fi. Reception 24hr. Summer dorms €23.50; singles €49; doubles €63. Low-season singles €48; doubles €64. €2.50 HI discount. AmEx/MC/V. ❷

Hostel Satakuntatalo (HI), Lapinrinne 1A (☎6958 5231; www.sodexho.fi/satakunta). M: Kamppi. Spacious, well-located rooms. Breakfast and sauna included. Lockers €2, free if you have a lock. Linens €5. Laundry €5.50, detergent €1.50. Free Internet and Wi-Fi. Reception 24hr. Open June-Aug. Dorms €19.5; singles from €41; doubles from €60; triples from €78; quads from €88. €2.50 HI discount. AmEx/MC/V. ❷

Hostel Academica (HI), Hietaniemenkatu 14 (☎1311 4334; www.hostelacademica.fi). M: Kamppi. Turn right onto Runeberginkatu and left after crossing the bridge. University housing transforms into a hostel in summer months. Rooms have kitchenettes and private bath. Sauna, linens, and towels included. Internet €2 per 30min, Wi-Fi €2 per hr., €5 per day. Reception 24hr. Open June-Aug. Dorms €23; singles €40-55; doubles €57-69. €2.50 HI discount. AmEx/MC/V. ❷

Stadion Hostel (HI), Pohjoinen Stadiontie 4 (☎09 477 8480; www.stadionhostel.com). Tram #3 or 7A to Auroran Sairaala and walk down Pohj. Cheap rooms and an active social scene. Breakfast €6. Linens included. Laundry €2.50. Free Internet. 24hr. reception. Dorms €19; singles €38; doubles €47. €2.50 HI discount. AmEx/MC/V. ❷

Eurohostel (HI), Linnankatu 9 (☎09622 0470; www.eurohostel.fi), near Katajanokka ferry terminal. Bright rooms and free sauna. Kitchen. Breakfast €7. Linens and towels included. Laundry €1. Internet €2 per 15min.; Wi-Fi €5 per day. Reception 24hr. Singles €40-44, dorms €24, family room €59-68. €2.50 HI discount. AmEx/MC/V. ❸

Rastila Camping, Karavaanikatu 4 (☎107 8517; www.hel.fi/rastila). M: Rastila. Change trains toward Vuosaari at Itäkeskus. A campground 12km from the city next to a beach. Electricity €4.50-7. Internet €1.50/15min. at reception, some free Wi-Fi access. Reception from mid-May to mid-Sept. 24hr.; from mid-Sept. to mid-May daily 8am-10pm. €5 per person; €10 per tent site in summer, €6 in winter; Cabins in summer €45-64. **Hostel** (☎3107 1441) (HI) open from mid-June to early August. Dorms €19. MC/V. ❶

FOOD

Restaurants and cafes are easy to find on Esplanadi and the streets branching off Mannerheimintie and Uudenmaankatu. Cheaper options surround the **Hietalahti flea market** at the southern end of Bulevardi. A **supermarket** is under the train station. (Open M-Sa 7am-10pm, Su 10am-10pm.) Helsinki has many budget restaurants that serve ethnic food. Get lunch at the open-air market **Kauppatori,** where stalls sell cooked fish and local produce; a meal from a cafe will cost about €6-8. (Open June-Aug. M-Sa 6:30am-6pm; Sept.-May M-F 7am-5pm.)

Zetor, Mannerheimintie 3-5 (☎010 766 4450; www.zetor.net), in the mall opposite the train station. Cheeky menu, cheekier farm-inspired decor, a trademark tractor, and ridiculously good Finnish food. Try some of their reindeer stew (€18). Homemade beer €4-7. Entrees €11-28. Attached bar 22+. Open M 1pm-2am, T 11am-3am, W-Sa 11am-4am, Su 1pm-1am. AmEx/MC/V. ❷

Kappeli Café, Eteläesplanadi 1 (☎(010 766 3880; www.kappeli.fi). This cafe has served the bohemian and the elite since 1867. Salads and sandwiches €6-9. Open from May to mid-Sept. M-Th 9am-midnight, F-Sa 9am-2am, Su 9am-11pm; from mid-Sept. to Apr. M-Sa 10am-midnight, Su 10am-11pm. Kitchen closes 1hr. earlier. AmEx/MC/V. ❶

Café Ursula, Ehrenströmintie 3 (☎09 652 817; www.ursula.fi). This upscale cafe also has delicious budget options and an idyllic setting on the Baltic Sea. Free Wi-Fi. Sandwiches €5-6. Salad bar 11am-6pm, €10-12. Lunch buffet €9-15. Open daily in summer 9am-midnight; in spring and fall 9am-10pm; in winter 9am-8pm. AmEx/MC/V. ❷

Zucchini, Fabianinkatu 4 (☎09 622 2907), south of the tourist office. Popular vegetarian and vegan fare made with mostly organic produce. Entrees €6-10. Open from late August to late July M-F 11am-4pm. AmEx/MC/V. ❷

Lappi, Annankatu 22 (☎09 645 550; www.lappires.com). Tourists splurge on specialties like reindeer, lingonberries, fresh salmon, and Arctic char in a rustic Finnish atmosphere. Entrees from €17. Reserve ahead. Open in summer M-F 5-10:30pm, Sa 1-10:30pm; in winter M-F noon-10:30pm, Sa 1-10:30pm. AmEx/MC/V. ❸

Sports Academy, Kaivokatu 8 (☎010 766 4300; www.sportsacademy.fi). A €15 burger should hold you to snacks and beer. But you're probably not here for the food. You're here to watch the game—as is everyone else. Beer €4-6. 1st fl. open daily 10am-3pm. 2nd fl. open M-Th 11am-1am, F-Sa 11am-3am, Su noon-10pm. ❸

SIGHTS

Helsinki's Neoclassical buildings and new forms reflect Finnish architect Alvar Aalto's joke: "Architecture is our form of expression because our language is so impossible." Helsinki's **Art Nouveau** (Jugendstil) and **Modernist** structures are home to a dynamic design community. Much of the architecture of the old center, however, is the brainchild of German Carl Engel, who modeled his design after St. Petersburg. Older buildings and public squares are adorned with interesting—and, at times, imposing statues. Most sights are in the city's compact center, making it ideal for **walking tours;** pick up a walking **guide** from the tourist office for routes. Trams 3B and 3T loop around the major sights in 1hr., providing a cheap alternative to tour buses. Helsinki has many **parks** that are perfect for an afternoon stroll, including Kaivopuisto in the south, Töölönlahti in the north, and Esplanadi and Tähtitorninvuori in the center of town.

SUOMENLINNA. This **military fortification,** spanning five islands, was built by Sweden to stave off the Russian Empire. It is one of the best examples of military engineering in the 18th century. The main island path, identified by the blue street signs, leads to the **visitors center,** home of the **Suomenlinna Museum,** which details the history of the fortress. *(☎4050 9691; www.suomenlinna.fi. Museum open daily May-Aug. 10am-6pm; Sept.-Apr. 11am-4pm. €5, students €4.30min. Film 2 per hr. AmEx/MC/V.)* The islands also feature the world's only combination **church and lighthouse** and Finland's only remaining WWII **submarine.** *(Submarine open from mid-May to Aug. 11am-6pm. €4, students €2. Cash only. English tours of the fortress leave from the museum June-Aug. daily 11am and 2pm; Sept. Sa-Su 1:30pm. €6.50, including admission to the Ehrensvard Museum, the Commander's residence. AmEx/MC/V.)* The **Toy Museum,** on the main island, has extensive exhibits on toys from the 19th century to today. *(☎668 417. Open July daily 11am-6pm; May-June and Aug. daily 11am-5pm; early Sept. daily 11am-4pm; Apr. Sa-Su 11am-4pm. €5. MC/V.)* Southern island's smooth **rocks** are popular with swimmers and sunbathers. *(City Transport ferries depart from Market St.; 15min., 1-3 per hr., round-trip €3.80. Combo ticket for military museum and submarine €6, students €3. Cash only.)*

SENAATIN TORI (SENATE SQUARE). The square and its gleaming white **Tuomiokirkko** (Dome Church) showcase Carl Engel's architecture and exemplify the splendor of Finland's 19th-century Russian period. The church's stunning marble reliefs house an interior so elegantly simple that every gilded detail becomes magnified. *(Unioninkatu 29. ☎2340 6120. Open June-Aug. M-Sa 9am-noon, Su noon-8pm; Sept.-May M-Sa 9am-6pm, Su noon-6pm. Organ concerts W and F at noon.)* Just south of Senate Sq., the **Helsinki City Museum** chronicles the city's 450-year history. The **City Museum** also has exhibits throughout Helsinki; pick up a list at the tourist office. *(Sofiankatu 4. ☎3103 6630. Open M-F 9am-5pm, Sa-Su 11am-5pm. Free.)* The red-brick **Uspenski Orthodox Cathedral** (Uspenskinkatedraadi), the largest Orthodox church in Northern and Western Europe, evokes images of Russia with its ornate interior and 13 golden cupolas. *(☎09 963 4267. Open M and W-F 9:30am-4pm, Tu 9:30am-6pm, Sa 9:30am-2pm Su noon-3pm. Closed M in winter.)*

ESPLANADI AND MANNERHEIMINTIE. A boulevard dotted with copper patina statues and fountains, Esplanadi is a great place to people-watch. The **Designmuseo** presents the work of designers like Aalto and Eliel Saarinen alongside creations by young artists and first-rate temporary exhibits. *(Korkeavuorenkatu 23. ☎622 0540; www.designmuseum.fi. Open June-Aug. daily 11am-6pm; Sept.-May Tu 11am-8pm, W-Su 11am-6pm. €7, students €3. AmEx/MC/V.)* On the same block, the small **Museum of Finnish Architecture** has temporary displays on the history and future of

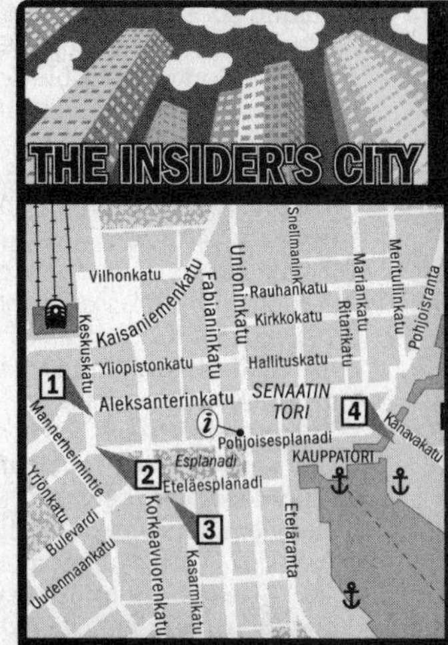

AALTO'S HELSINKI

Finlandia Hall may be architect Alvar Aalto's most recognizable gift to Helsinki, but a number of his other Modernist creations give visitors a sense of his aesthetic breadth.

1. Rautatalo (Iron House), Keskusk. 3. The stark facade conceals an airy atrium meant to recall an Italian *piazza,* one of Aalto's favorite motifs.

2. Academic Bookstore, Pohjoisesplanadi 39. Finland's largest bookstore named its upstairs cafe after Aalto, who designed the copper and marble building in 1969.

3. Savoy Restaurant, Eteläesplanadi 14. The €40 entrees are too pricey for the budget traveler, but the decor is all Aalto's work—right down to the trademark vases.

4. Stora Enso Headquarters, Kanavak. 1. This ultramodern "sugar cube" overlooks the South Harbor and provides a provocative contrast to the two magnificent churches that flank it.

building design. *(Kasarmikatu 24. ☎8567 5100; www.mfa.fi. Open Tu and Th-F 10am-4pm, W 10am-8pm, Sa-Su 11am-4pm. €3.50, students €1.70. Free F. AmEx/MC/V.)* Across from the train station, down a block on Kaivokatu lies the **Ateneum Art Museum** (Ateneum Taidemuseo), Finland's largest, with comprehensive exhibits on Finnish art. *(Kaivokatu 2. ☎1733 6401; www.ateneum.fi. Open Tu and F 9am-6pm, W-Th 9am-8pm, Sa-Su 11am-5pm. €6, students €4; €8/6.50 during special exhibits; first W of each month free 5-8pm. AmEx/MC/V.)* A couple blocks west of the train station on Mannerheimintie is **Kiasma** (Museum of Contemporary Art), a quirky warehouse that features top-flight modern art and even calibrates the width of its doors to Fibonacci's golden ratio. *(Mannerheimintie 2. ☎1733 6501; www.kiasma.fi. Open Tu 9am-5pm, W-Su 10am-8:30pm. €7, students €5; 1st W each month free 5-8pm. AmEx/MC/V.)* Farther down the road is the grand **Parliament House,** Mannerheimintie 30. *(☎09 432 2027. Only accessible by 1hr. tours to the Session Hall, Hall of State, and the Parliament cafeteria. Open Sa 11am and 2:30pm, Su noon and 1:30pm; July and Aug. also M-F 11am and 1pm. Free.)* The next building up Mannerheimintie is Saarinen's **National Museum of Finland** (Suomen Kansallismuseo), featuring a 1928 ceiling fresco by Gallen-Kallela and many exhibits on Finnish history. *(Mannerheimintie 34. ☎40 501; www.kansallismuseo.fi. Open Tu-W 11am-8pm, Th-Su 11am-6pm. €7, students €4, under 18 free, Tu 5:30-8pm free. AmEx/MC/V.)* Head back to the city center down Mannerheimintie, turn right on Arkadiankatu, and right again on Fredrikinkatu to reach the heavily touristed **Temppeliaukio Kirkko.** This striking church is hewn out of a hill of rock with only the domed roof visible from the outside. *(Lutherinkatu 3. ☎2340 5920. English-language services Su 2pm. Usually open in summer M, Tu, Th, F 10am-8pm, W 10am-6:45pm, Sa 10am-6pm, Su 11:45am-1:45pm and 3:30-6pm.)*

FINLAND

OTHER SIGHTS. The **Theater Museum** contains set models and costume designs from the National Theater. *(Tallberginkatu 1. M: Ruoholahti. After exiting, walk 5 blocks down Itämerenkatu Museums are in the G entrance. ☎4763 8300; www.teatterimuseo.fi. Open Tu-Su 11am-6pm. Theater Museum closed in July. Photography Museum €6, students €4; Hotel and Restaurant Museum €2/1; Theater Museum €6/3. MC/V.)* Near the Western Harbor, the crowded **Jean Sibelius Monument** pays homage to one of the 20th century's great composers. *(On Mechelininkatu in Sibelius Park. Take bus #24, dir.: Seurasaari to Rasjasaarentie. The monument will be behind you.)* The **Helsinki Zoo,** the country's largest, includes a menagerie of 200 animal species and a boat ride around the island. *(Korkeasaari. Take the ferry from Kauppatori or Hakaniemi, or the Zoo Line Bus from Herttoniemi metro station. ☎3103 7900; www.zoo.hel.fi Open daily May-Aug. 10am-8pm; Sept. and Apr. 10am-6pm; Oct.-Mar. 10am-4pm. €12, student €7.50. Catch the boat at dock 24.)*

ENTERTAINMENT AND FESTIVALS

Helsinki's parks are always animated. In the early evening, young people sit and drink in the downtown parks. A **concert** series enlivens the Esplanadi park all summer offering shows on most days throughout the summer. Highlights of the program are **Jazz Espa** in July, and **Ethno Espa** showcasing international music (www.kulttuuri.hel.fi/espanlava). Late June's **Helsinki Pride** celebration (www.helsinkipride.fi) is Finland's largest GLBT event and lasts for a week. The two week **Helsinki Festival** (www.helsinkifestival.fi), at the end of August, wraps up the summer with cultural events ranging from music and theater to film and visual arts. At the end of September, **Helsinki Design Week** (www.helsinkidesignweek.fi) reinforces the city's image as a style capital, while the **Love and Anarchy Film Festival** (www.hiff.fi) features works from across the globe. Throughout summer, concerts rock **Kaivopuisto** (on the corner of Puistokatu and Ehrenstromintie, in the southern part of town), the **Olympic Stadium,** and **Hietaniemi Beach** (down Hesperiankatu on the western shore). Check out the **Nordic Oddity** pamphlet series, with insider advice on sights, bars, and activities.

For high culture, try the **Helsinki Philharmonic and Radio Symphony Orchestra,** the **National Opera,** or the **National Theater.** Lippupiste and Lippupalvelu, Aleksanterinkatu 52 (☎0600 900 900), in the Stockmann department store, sell tickets for most of the big venues in the city(AmEx/MC/V).

NIGHTLIFE

Bars and summer beer terraces fill up in late afternoon; most clubs don't get going until midnight and stay crazy until 4am. Bars and clubs line Mannerheimintie, Uudenmaankatu, and Iso Roobertinkatu. East of the train station, nightlife centers around Yliopistonkatu and Kaisaniemenkatu, while in bohemian Kallio, the bars around Fleminginkatu have some of the cheapest **beer** in the city. A popular night activity is heavy-metal **karaoke;** check it out Wednesday and Sunday at **Hevimesta,** Hallituskatu 3.

Royal Onnela, Fredrikinkatu 46 (☎020 7759 460; www.ravintolaonnela.fi). Claims the title of biggest nightclub in Scandinavia. It has 9 dance rooms, suiting almost any musical taste from Finnish pop to disco and 80s/90s hits. Onnela dominates the Helsinki nightlife on Su. Beer €4.90, Su €1. €4 Silver card grants half-price on many drinks M,W, and Th. Sa 22+. Cover F €5 but free with Silver card, Sa €7. Club open M and W-Su 10pm-3:30am. Lapland Poro Bar open daily 6pm-4am. Karaoke bar open daily 8pm-4pm. Bars close early if not busy. AmEx/MC/V.

On the Rocks, Mikonkatu 15 (☎09 612 2030; www.ontherocks.fi). This legendary bar and club offers some of the best Finnish bands. M-Sa live music. 20+. Cover free-€12. Open daily in summer noon-4am; in winter 2pm-4am. AmEx/MC/V.

Bar Erottaja, Erottajankatu 13-17 (☎09 611 196). This art-student hangout is usually packed with people engaged in conversation while listening to music. Beer €3.20-580. F-Sa DJ. 22+ after 6pm. Open M-Tu and Su 2pm-1am, W-Sa 2pm-3am. AmEx/MC/V.

Vanha, Mannerheimintie 3 (☎1311 4368; www.vanha.fi). A lively student crowd occasionally rents the hall as a club to party in. Check website for performance schedule. Beer €5. Cover €5. Open F-Sa 10pm-4am. AmEx/MC/V.

Highlight, Fredrikinkatu 42 (☎050 409 0079). A dance club for the young and fit. 18+. Cover after 11pm €5. Open F-Sa 10pm-4am. AmEx/MC/V.

dtm, Iso Roobertinkatu 28 (☎09 676 314; www.dtm.fi). This popular club claims the title of largest gay club in Scandinavia. Occasional lesbian nights F-Sa. 22+ after 10pm. Cover €2.50, Sa €5, special events €5-10. M-Th beer, shots, cider €3 and Su pints €1 after 6pm. Open M-Sa 9am-4am, Su noon-4am. AmEx/MC/V.

OUTDOOR ACTIVITIES

TÖÖLÖNLAHTI AND ELÄINTARHANLAHTI. Just north of the train station are these two city lakes and accompanying parks, which offer great walks. Northwest of the Sibelius Monument across a bridge, the island of **Seurasaari** offers a retreat from the city. It is also home to an open-air museum of farmsteads and churches. *(Take bus #24 from Erottaja to the last stop. The island is always open for hiking. Museum ☎4050 9665. Open daily June-Aug. 11am-5pm; late May and early Sept. M-F 9am-3pm, Sa-Su 11am-5pm. Tours from mid-June to mid-August daily 3pm. €6, students €4. MC/V.)*

BEACHES. Many islands south of the city feature public beaches that are accessible by ferry, including a nude beach on Pihlajasaari Island. Beyond Espoo to the west is the **Nuuksio National Park,** where flying squirrels are a common sight. *(☎0205 64 4790; www.outdoors.fi/nuuksionp. Take the train to Espoo station and bus #85 from there to Kattila in Nuuksio in summer or Nuuksionpää in winter.)*

DAYTRIPS FROM HELSINKI

PORVOO (BORGÅ). Porvoo (pop. 47,000) is along Old King Road, 50km east of Helsinki. From the bus station, walk down Lundinkatu toward the river and turn right on Runeberginkatu, following it until you see the green signs of the **Tourist Information office,** Rihkamakatu 4 *(☎019 520 2316; www.porvoo.fi. Open from mid-June to Aug. M-F 9am-6pm, Sa-Su 10am-4pm; from Sept. to mid-June reduced hours.)* Porvoo is known for its medieval old town and its whitewashed **hilltop cathedral** where in 1809, Tsar Alexander I granted Finland autonomy. The cathedral fell victim to an attack in May 2006; it is being rebuilt and will reopen in December 2008. The house of Finland's national poet **Johan Ludvig Runeberg,** Aleksanterinkatu 3, looks just as it did when he called it home in the mid-1800s. *(☎019 581 330. Open May-Aug. daily 10am-4pm; Sept.-Apr. W-Su 10am-4pm. House and sculpture exhibit €5, students €2. Cash only.)* The **Historical Museum,** in the 1764 Town Hall in Old Market Sq., features an eclectic array of artifacts but is closed for renovation until sometime in 2009. *(☎019 574 7500. Check www.porvoomuseo.fi for more information.)* Charming, if overpriced, cafes line the streets of Old Town. Many, such as Cafe Helmi and Cafe Fanny, sell Runeberg cakes, which the poet himself enjoyed, for about €3. The small round cakes—with almonds and cinnamon topped off with raspberry jam and a squeeze of icing—are a delicious, regional favorite. *(Buses run from Helsinki (1hr., 3 per hr., €9-12). Harryn Pyörävarikko, Jokikatu 11, rents bikes to visitors heading as far south as Pellinki. ☎1965 4156.)* **Postal Code:** 06100.

FINLAND

LAHTI. World-class winter sports facilities make Lahti (pop. 100,000) a popular destination for outdoor enthusiasts and especially snow-lovers. For trail information, call **Lahti Sports Services** (☎03 816 816). The **Ski Museum** has ski-jump and slalom simulators and a simulated shooting range. *(☎038 144 523. Open M-F 10am-5pm, Sa-Su 11am-5pm. €5, students €3. MC/V.)* Towering 200m above the museum, the tallest of three **ski jumps,** accessible by a chairlift followed by an elevator, offers excellent views of the city. *(Open in summer daily 10am-5pm. €5, students €3; with Ski Museum €8/€5.)* The 100k of cross-country **ski trails** emanate out from the sports complex; the **tourist office** has info on the Ilvesvaellus Trail, a 30min. bus ride northwest. In Kariniemi Park, near the shore, the **Musical Fountains** combine water and music daily at 1 and 6pm in summer, 7pm in spring and fall. At the harbor, **Sibelius Hall** holds the **Sibelius Festival** in September, with performances of the composer's works. *(Trains head to Helsinki (1hr., 2 per hr., from €13.20), Savonlinna (3:30hr., 6 per day, from €41.50), and Tampere (1:45hr., 1 per hr., from €25). The tourist office is at Rautatienkatu 22. ☎020 728 1750; www.lahtitravel.fi. Open M-Th 9am-5pm, F 9am-4pm; also open from mid-July to mid-Aug. Sa 10am-2pm. AmEx/MC/V.)* **Postal Code:** 15110.

TURKU (ÅBO) ☎02

Finland's oldest city, Turku (pop. 175,000), has grown weatherbeaten with the passing of 775 years. It was the focal point of Swedish and Russian power struggles, the seat of Finnish governance until 1812, and then the victim of the worst fire in Scandinavian history in 1827. Yet Turku lives on as a cultural and academic center that remains one of the most important in Finland.

TRANSPORTATION. **Trains** run to and from Helsinki (2hr., 1 per hr., €24.60-32) and Tampere (2hr., 1 per 1-2hr., €22 or €24.30). Eurorail pass gets free trains except for Pendolino trains. Viking Line, Eenkinkatu 15 (☎3582 33311), **sails** to Stockholm, SWE (9hr., 2 per day, about €32). Many discounts available—see Viking Line office. AmEx/MC/V. **Tallinksilja Line** ferries also sail to Stockholm

(9hr., daily 8am and 8:15pm, around €20; MC/V). To get to the ferry terminal, catch bus #1 from the Kauppatori (€2.50) or walk to the end of Linnankatu, past the castle. **Buses** run from the bus station to Rauma (1.5 hr., 1-2 per hour, €15-18) and Pori (3hr., 1 every 2 hr., €22-26). A day pass costs €5.50.

ORIENTATION AND PRACTICAL INFORMATION. The **tourist office,** Aurakatu 4, sells the **TurkuCard** (24hr. €21, 48hr. €28), which provides entry to the city's museums and free bus rides. (☎262 7444; www.turkutouring.fi. Open M-F 8:30am-6pm, Sa-Su 9am-4pm. AmEx/MC/V.) **Cybercafes** are at Hämeenkatu 12 and Mariankatu 2. (Open M-F 9am-9pm, Sa-Su 10am-9pm. €0.04 per min. Coins only.) Free Internet is at the **public library,** located at Linnenkatu 2. (☎262 3611. Open 10am-8pm M-Th, F 10am-6pm, Sa 10am-3pm.) **Postal Code:** 20100.

ACCOMMODATIONS AND FOOD. To get to **Hostel Turku (HI) ❷,** Linnankatu 39, from the station, go west on Ratapihankatu, turn left on Puistokatu, and go right at the river and look for the blue sign. (☎02 262 7680; www.turku.fi/hostelturku. Bike rental available. Breakfast €5.20. Linens €4.70. Laundry €2 per hr. Internet €1 per 20min. Reception 6-10am and 3pm-midnight. Check-in 3-9pm. Dorms curfew 2am. Reserve ahead. Dorms €16; singles €36; doubles €42; quads €65. €2.50 HI discount, €1.50 ISIC discount. MC/V.) **Interpoint Hostel ❶,** Vähä Hämeenkatu 12A, offers what may well be the cheapest beds in Finland. (☎02 231 4011. Open from mid-July to mid-Aug. Dorms €10.) **Bridgettine Convent Guesthouse ❸**, Ursininkatu 15A, at Puutarhakatu, has peaceful, well-kept rooms. (☎02 250 1910; www.kolumbus.fi/birgitta/turku. Reception 8am-9pm, but 24hr. entrance with key. Singles €45; doubles €65; triples €90. Cash only.)

Produce fills the outdoor **Kauppatori** (open in summer M-F 7am-6pm, Sa until noon; in winter M-F 7am-5pm) and brown brick **Kauppahalli** (open M-F 7am-5:30pm, Sa 7am-3pm) on Eerikinkatu. **Sokos,** next to the Kauppatori, has a supermarket (Open M-F 9am-9pm, Sa 9am-6pm. MC/V.) Cheap eats line **Humalistonkatu.** Locals pack **Kerttu ❷,** Läntinen Pitkäkatu 35, where they feast on Jallupulla meatballs. (☎02 250 6990; www.kerttu.fi. Open mid-Aug. M-F 10:30am-midnight, Sa noon-midnight.) **Kasvisravintola Keidas ❷,** Itäinen Rantakatu 61, is a vegetarian boat-restaurant. €6 regular entree, €8.50 large. (Walk 20min. along the river, or take bus #3, 14, 15, or 55 from the Kauppatori. ☎02 535 3018; www.kasviskeidas.com. Open M-F 11am-4pm. MC/V.)

SIGHTS. At **Aboa Vetus and Ars Nova Museums** over a decade ago, during construction on a museum in a tobacco tycoon's riverside mansion, workers discovered a medieval city block beneath the house. Today, visitors can stroll through the ruins and view the accompanying modern art collection. (Itäinen Rantakatu 4-6. ☎02 250 0552; www.aboavetusarsnova.fi. Open Apr.-Aug. daily 11am-7pm; Sept.-Mar. Tu-Su 11am-7pm. Tours July-Aug. daily 10, 11:30am. €8, students €7. AmEx/MC/V.) The **Turku Cathedral** is the spiritual center of Finland's Lutheran Church. Finnish public radio has broadcast the cathedral's noontime bells since 1944. (Tuomiokirkkotori 20. ☎02 261 7100; www.turunseurakunnat.fi. Open daily from mid-Apr. to mid-Sept. 9am-8pm; from mid-Sept. to mid-Apr. 9am-7pm. Concerts June-Aug. Tu 8pm and W 2pm. English services Su 4pm. Free.) The **Sibelius Museum** presents the life of Finland's most famous composer, Jean Sibelius. (Piispankatu 17. ☎02 215 4494; www.sibeliusmuseum.abo.fi. Open Tu and Th-Su 11am-4pm, W 6-8pm. €3, students €1. 1hr. concerts in summer, fall, and spring W 7pm. Concerts in fall and spring €7/3, in summer included in admission. MC/V.) The 700-year-old **Turun Linna** (Turku Castle) has a historical museum with medieval artifacts. (Linnankatu 80. Catch bus #1 (€2) from Market Sq. or walk to the end of Linnankatu. ☎02 262 0322. Open from mid-Apr. to mid-Sept. daily 10am-6pm; from mid-Jan. to mid.Apr. and from mid-Sept. to late Nov. Tu and Th-F 10am-3pm and W, Sa, and Su 10am-6pm, and late Nov-Dec. Tu-F 10am-3pm and Sa 10am-5pm. €7, students €3.50. MC/V.)

 **FESTIVALS AND NIGHTLIFE.** The end of June brings the **Medieval Market Festival** to town, while power chords rock Ruissalo Island at July's **Ruisrock festival** (www.ruisrock.fi). The end of July brings the **Down By The Laituri** music festival on the river and in August, the annual **Turku Music Festival** (www.turkumusicfestival.fi) draws a range of artists to venues throughout the city. Pull up a stool at **Pub Uusi Apteekki,** Kaskenkatu 1, and have a beer at this old apothecary. (☎02 250 2595; www.uusiapteekki.fi. Open M-Th and Su 10am-2am and F-Sa 10am-3am. 20+. MC/V.) Finland's largest brewery restaurant, **Koulu,** Eerikinkatu 18, is a former girls' school and offers its own beers. (☎02 274 5757; www.panimoravintolakoulu.fi. Beer or cider about €5. F-Sa 22+. Open M-Th and Su 10am-2am, F-Sa 10am-3am. AmEx/MC/V.)

DAYTRIPS FROM TURKU

RAUMA

Buses run to Rauma from Turku (1.5hr., 1-2 per hr., €15-18). To reach the tourist office, Valtakatu 2, follow the street by the supermarket. (☎8378 7731; www.visitrauma.fi. Tourist office may be moving, check website for updated information.) All museums in Vahna Rauma can be seen with a combo ticket (€6; individual museums €3).

Farther north on the Baltic Coast, Rauma (pop. 42,500) is known for the well-preserved wooden buildings that make up the **Old Town,** the first UNESCO World Heritage Site in Finland. Just north of the outer edge of the old city, the Raumanjoki river, lies the frescoed **Church of the Holy Cross. Vahna Rauma,** as the old town is called, also offers several house museums. Besides its old town, Rauma is best known for its gorgeous **archipelago.** Many of the islands are great for **hiking.** Try the trails on Kuuskajaskari, a former fortress. **Ferries** leave from the marina to the northwest of the city. (Ferries 30min., in summer 3 per day, €8. MC/V.) Late August brings the **Blue Sea Film Festival** (www.blueseafilmfestival.com), which shows the best domestic films of the year. If you're interested in a great meal, **Ravintola Villa Tallbo ❷,** Petäjäksentie 178, has a €14 buffet lunch which has an incredible spread, including a variety of fish (☎02 822 0733).

PORI

Trains go to Helsinki (3.5hr., 6 per day, €38.60) and Tampere (1.5hr., 6 per day, around €15). Buses run to Tampere (2hr., 12 per day, €17), Turku (2-2.5hr., 1-2 per hour, €24), and Rauma (1hr., 1 per hr., €11.20). The tourist office, Yrjönkatu 17, offers 15min. of free Internet. The tourist office helps book rooms during festival time. (☎02 621 7900; www.maisa.fi. Open from June to mid-Aug. M-F 9am-6pm, Sa 10am-3pm; from mid-Aug. to May M-F 9am-4:30pm.)

Each July, crowds mob elegant Pori (pop. 76,000) for the renowned **Pori Jazz Festival** in mid-July. (☎02 626 2200; www.porijazz.fi. Tickets from €10; some concerts free. AmEx/MC/V.) The recently relocated **Finnish Rock Festival** (www.rmj.fi; late June) throws the biggest midsummer party in Finland. Book hotels in advance. For those seeking culture, check out the modern art exhibits of the **Pori Art Museum,** on the corner of Etelärantakatu and Raatihuonekatu. (☎02 621 1080; www.poriartmuseum.fi. Open Tu and Th-Su 11am-6pm, W 11am-8pm. Summer €5, students €2.50; in winter €3.50/1.50. MC/V.) Pori's best known attraction is located in a graveyard west of the town center on Maantiekatu. The **Juselius Mausoleum** is adorned with frescoes by native Akseli Gallén-Kallela. (☎02 623 8746. Open May-Aug. daily noon-3pm. Free.) Bus #32 (30min. €4.50) leads northwest to Yyteri Beach, home to windsurfers and those just relaxing.

TAMPERE ☎03

A striking example of successful urban renewal, the city of Tampere (pop. 205,000) has converted its old brick factories into innovative museums and attractive new spaces for restaurants and housing. As telecommunications and information technology edge out textile and metal plants, an attractive city has emerged to give Turku a run for its money as Finland's second capital.

TRANSPORTATION AND PRACTICAL INFORMATION. **Trains** go to Helsinki (2hr., 1-2 per hr., €26-32), Oulu (5hr., 9 per day, €55-65), and Turku (less than 2hr., 1 per 2hr., €22-25). Most city **buses** (€2) run through the main square on Hämeenkatu. Ryanair (☎0200 39000; www.ryanair.com) flies to **Tampere-Pirkkala Airport (TMP).** The **tourist office** is in the train station. (☎5656 6800; www.gotampere.fi. Open Jan.-May M-F 9am-5pm, June-Aug. M-F 9am-8pm and Sa-Su 9:30am-5pm, Sept. M-F 9am-5pm and Sa-Su 9:30am-5pm, and Oct.-Dec. M-F 9am-5pm and Sa-Su 11am-3pm.) **Postal Code:** 33100.

ACCOMMODATIONS AND FOOD. Newly renovated **Hostel Sofia (HI) ❷,** Tuomiokirkonkatu 12A, has comfortable, brightly colored dorms. (☎03 254 4020. Breakfast €6.50. Linens and towels included. Free Wi-Fi. Reception 8-10am and 4-11pm. Dorms €24-25; singles €45; doubles €65. €2.50 HI discount. MC/V.) Bus #1 (€2) goes to **Camping Härmälä ❶,** Leirintäkatu 8, where tightly packed cabins sit on the shore. (☎03 265 1355; www.lomaliitto.fi. Open from May to late Aug. €2-4 per person, €10-12 per tent site. Cabins €30-69. Electricity €5. In summer Härmälä also offers a hotel. MC/V.)

Restaurants fill the center of the city, lining **Hämeenkatu** and **Aleksanterinkatu.** The city's oldest and most lauded pizzeria, **Napoli ❶,** Aleksanterinkatu 31, serves 100 varieties in an Italian setting. (☎03 223 8887. Pizza €8-12. Open M-Th 11am-11pm, F 11am-midnight, Sa noon-midnight, Su 1-11pm. MC/V.) **Wok Wok ❶,** Verkatehtaankatu 7, serves customized stir-fry for under €9. (☎050 559 7483. Open M-Th 11am-9pm, F 11am-11pm, Sa noon-11pm, Su 1-9pm.)

SIGHTS. The delightfully haphazard **Vapriikki Museum Center,** Veturiaukio 4, has collections that run the gamut from shoe history to Finnish hockey. (☎5656 6966; www.tampere.fi/english/vapriikki. Open Tu and Th-Su 10am-6pm, W 11am-8pm. €5, students €1. Special exhibitions €6-8, students €2-3; includes museum admission. AmEx/MC/V.) The **Finlayson Complex,** named for Scottish cotton magnate James Finlayson, houses the **Media Museum Rupriikki,** with interesting exhibits on the history of mass communication and news. (☎5656 6411; www.tampere.fi/mediamuseo/english. Open Tu-Su 10am-6pm. €5, students €1. AmEx/MC/V.) The complex also houses the world's oldest **Spy Museum,** Satakunnankatu 18, where you can relish Cold War espionage. (☎03 212 3007; www.vakoilumuseo.fi. Open June-Aug. M-Sa 10am-6pm, Su 11am-5pm; Sept.-May daily 11am-5pm. €7, students €5.50. Cash only.) The frescoes of the **Tuomiokirkko,** Tuomiokirkonkatu 3 (open daily 9am-6pm), and its gorgeous stained glass windows, are unmatched in beauty across the city—except by the vaulted wood ceiling of the **Aleksanterinkirkko,** on Pyynikin kirkkopuisto. (Open daily June-Aug. 10am-5pm; Sept.-May 11am-3pm.) Take a short hike past Aleksanterinkirkko to Tampere's western edge and the **Pyynikki Observation Tower,** which offers views of the city and the surrounding nature preserve. Enjoy a traditional *munkki*, a doughnut-like pastry (€1.40), at its cafe. (☎212 3247. Open daily 9am-8pm. €1 to go to the top. Cash only.) The city's northern lakefront is home to **Särkänniemi theme park,** which has an observation tower of its own. (☎713 0200; www.sarkanniemi.fi. "Adventure Key" grants admission to all attractions, including rides €30, online €28 (winter €20). Hours vary; check website. MC/V.) Off the southern shore is **Viikinsaari Island,** a popular spot for picnics, short hikes, or just relaxing on the beach. **Ferries** depart from Laukontori harbor every hour on the hour (June-Aug. Tu-Th 10am-10:30pm, F-Sa 10am-12:30am, Su noon-7:30pm; some M in July 10am-10:30pm) and return every hour on the half-hour (20min., €8, students €7).

FESTIVALS AND NIGHTLIFE. Tampere's **Short Film Festival** draws international entries (www.tamperefilmfestival.fi; early March). Mid-July's **Tammerfest** (www.tammerfest.net) fills the city with music, while August's **International Theater Festival** puts on Finnish works (www.teatterikesa.fi). For nightlife, **Hämeenkatu, Aleksanterinkatu, Itsenäisyydenkatu,** and the surrounding streets bustle with energy. **Cafe Europa,** Aleksanterinkatu 29, is in a bohemian lounge. (☎223 5526; www.cafeeuropa.net. Beer €3.50-5.50. Cider €4.50-6. ISIC discount. Open M-Tu and Su noon-1am, W-Th noon-2am, F-Sa noon-3am. AmEx/MC/V.)

SAVONLINNA ☎015

The captivating town of Savonlinna (pop. 30,000) spans three islands in the heart of Finland's lake region, a popular summer destination. Tourists flock here to see the beautiful scenery and the medieval castle.

TRANSPORTATION AND PRACTICAL INFORMATION. **Trains** run to Helsinki (4-6hr., 7 per day, around €50). The Savonlinna-Kauppatori stop is in the center of town; Savonlinna Station is closer to the bus station. The **tourist office** and **travel agency**, Puistokatu 1, is across the bridge from the market. (☎517 510; www.savonlinnatravel.com. Open M-F 9am-5pm, extended hours July 4-Aug. 2 daily 9am-7pm. AmEx/MC/V.) **Postal Code:** 57100.

ACCOMMODATIONS AND FOOD. **Summer Hotel Vuorilinna (HI) ❸,** on Kylpylaitoksentie, shares its complex with the casino hotel. (☎03 739 5495; www.spahotelcasino.fi. Linens and laundry included. Free Internet and Wi-Fi in some buildings. Reception 7am-11pm. Open June-Aug.; call ahead for specific dates. Dorms from €28. €2.50 HI discount. AmEx/MC/V.) Bus #3 (€2.90) runs to **Vuohimäki Camping ❶,** on the Lake Pihlajavesi shore. (☎03 537 353. Bike rental €10 per day. Laundry €2.50, dry €1.50. Electricity €5. Showers €3. Reception 9am-midnight. Open mid-May-Aug. €25 per bed with linens, towels, and shower. Tent sites €12. 4- and 6-person cabins with bath €56-€84. MC/V.) The **Kauppatori** market sells local produce and pastries. (Open June and early Aug. M-F 6am-4pm, Sa 6am-3pm; July M-F 6am-8pm, Sa 6am-4pm, Su 9am-4pm; mid-Aug. to May M-F 7am-3pm, Sa 7am-2pm.)

SIGHTS. The town draws 60,000 people for July's month-long **Opera Festival,** which features stunning performances in **Olavinlinna Castle.** (www.operafestival.fi. Tickets, from €30, can be booked up to a year ahead. Check online.) The castle was built in 1475 to reinforce the eastern border against the tsars. (☎015 531 164. Open daily June to mid-Aug. 10am-6pm; mid-Aug.-May 10am-4pm. Tour departs on the hour. €5, students €3.50. MC/V.) Near the castle, Riihisaari, the **Provincial Museum** explores the history of the region, focusing on the shipping industry. (☎015 571 4712. Open June and Aug.-May Tu-Su 11am-5pm; July daily 11am-5pm. Ships open from mid-May to Aug. €4, students €2. Cash only.) The secluded northern island **Sulosaari** has several walking trails. From the Kauppatori, go under the train tracks, cross the footbridge, go through the parking lot, and pass the hotel to cross the next bridge. Daytrip to the **Retretti Art Center,**

where caves have contemporary art pieces that play off subterranean illumination and water reflections. (☎015 775 2200; www.retretti.fi. Open daily July 10am-6pm; June and Aug. 10am-5pm. €15, students €10. AmEx/MC/V.) **Trains** (4 per day, €3.60) make the 20min. trip from Savolinna. Walk along Punkaharju Ridge to reach **Lusto** (Finnish Forest Museum), which details environmental history of the area. (☎015 345 100; www.lusto.fi. Open daily June-Aug. 10am-7pm; Sept.-May reduced hours. €10, students €8. MC/V.)

KUOPIO ☎017

Eastern Finland's largest city, Kuopio (pop. 91,000) lies in the Kallavesi lake district. With most the city taken up by water and forests, it's no surprise that forestry is a major industry. In the summer months, visitors flock to Kuopio's most popular festivals of dance and wine.

TRANSPORTATION AND PRACTICAL INFORMATION. **Trains** go to Helsinki (4-5hr., as many as 10 per day, from €50-60) and Oulu (4-5hr., 5-7 per day, from €40). The **tourist office** is at Haapaniemenkatu 17. (☎017 182 584; www.kuopioinfo.fi. Open July M-F 9:30am-5pm, Sa 9:30am-3pm; June and Aug. M-F 9:30am-5pm; Sept.-May M-F 9:30am-4:30pm. AmEx/MC/V.) **Postal Code:** 70100.

BUG OFF! Mosquito-killing is a sport in Finland, but if going on a rampage doesn't appeal to you, carry a large supply of bug spray when heading into northern forests. You'll thank us.

ACCOMMODATIONS AND FOOD. At the **Virkkula Youth Hostel ❷**, Asemakatu 3, offers dorms in an elementary school. (☎040 418 2178. Linens €6. Internet €1 for first 30min. Reception 24hr. Open June-early Aug. Dorms €17. Cash only.) Rooms at **Rautatie Guest House ❸**, Asemakatu 1, have their own TVs; pricier rooms have baths. Reception is in the Asemagrilli restaurant in the train station. (☎017 580 0569. Breakfast and linens included. Reception M-F and Su 7:30am-8pm, Sa 7:30am-6pm. Singles €40-50; doubles €60-79; triples €97; quads €123. AmEx/MC/V.) The town center has many affordable eateries. Close to the train station, **Miramari ❶**, Puijonkatu 33, has good pizza. (☎017 282 8858. MC/V.) There's fresh produce at the Kauppatori market in the center of town and inside the **Kauppahalli market hall.** (www.kuopionkauppahalli.net. Kauppatori open M-Sa 8am-4pm. Kauppahalli open M-F 8am-5pm, Sa 8am-3pm.)

SIGHTS AND ENTERTAINMENT. Kuopio is the seat of the Finnish Orthodox Church, and the **Orthodox Church Museum,** 10min. from town at Karjalankatu. 1, showcases a collection of stunning textiles and icons. (☎017 206 100 266; www.ort.fi/kirkkomuseo. Open May-Aug. Tu and Th-Su 10am-4pm, W 10am-6pm; Sept.-Apr. Tu-F noon-3pm, Sa-Su noon-5pm. €5, students €3. Cash only.) The **Kuopio Museum,** Kauppakatu 23, holds both the Natural and Cultural History Museums, delights. (☎017 182 603; www.kuopionmuseo.fi. Open Tu and Th-F 10am-5pm, W 10am-7pm, Sa-Su 11am-5pm. €5, students €3. Cash only.) The 2km hike uphill to **Puijo Tower** culminates in a view of Kuopio, Lake Kallavesi, and the coniferous forests beyond. (☎017 255 5253; www.puijo.com. Open June-Aug. M-Sa 9am-10pm, Su 9am-9pm; Sept. daily 11am-6pm; Oct.-May Tu-Sa 11am-10pm. €4, students €3.50. AmEx/MC/V.) In mid-June, the **Kuopio Dance Festival** (www.kuopiodancefestival.fi) draws crowds to its performances. (☎017 0600 10800. Classes from €60. Book ahead. MC/V.) Kuopio is also home to an

International Wine Festival where happy oenophiles toast to a different country in early July (www.kuopiowinefestival.fi).

ROVANIEMI ☎016

Just south of the Arctic Circle, Rovaniemi (pop. 60,000) is the capital of Finnish Lapland and a gateway to the northern wilderness. In October 1944, architect **Alvar Aalto** orchestrated a construction scheme to rebuild the settlement in the shape of a reindeer's head. You can discern a head with antlers in a modern map of Rovaniemi with east facing up.

TRANSPORTATION AND PRACTICAL INFORMATION. **Trains** run to Helsinki (9-13hr., 5 per day, from €75) via Oulu (2.5hr., from €24.50) and Kuopio (7hr., 3 per day, about €60). **Buses** go to northern Finland and to Nordkapp, NOR (11hr., 3 per day, €119.4). The **tourist office,** Maakuntakatu 31 in Lordis Square, books Lapland wilderness safaris. (☎016 346 270; www.rovaniemi.fi. Internet and Wi-Fi. Open June-Aug. M-F 8am-6pm, Sa-Su 10am-4pm; Sept.-May M-F 9am-6pm; in Dec. also Sa-Su 10am-2pm. Safaris €22-122. AmEx/MC/V.) The **library,** Jorma Eton tie 6, an Aalto design, has free Internet. Open in summer M-Th 11am-7pm, F 11am-5pm, Sa 11am-3pm; in winter M-Th 11am-8pm, F 11am-5pm, Sa 11am-4pm.) **Postal Code:** 96200.

ACCOMMODATIONS AND FOOD. **Hostel Rudolf (HI) ❸,** Koskikatu 41-43, has well-furnished, recently renovated rooms with TV and bath. (☎016 321 321; www.rudolf.fi. Reception 24hr. at the Clarion Hotel Santa Claus, Korkalonkatu 29. Breakfast €8 at hotel. Apr. to mid-Nov. dorms €30; singles €41. Double €52. €2.50 HI discount. AmEx/MC/V.) **Koskikatu** is lined with cafes, bars, and a **K** supermarket. (Open M-F 8am-9pm, Sa 8am-6pm. MC/V.) Finnish "monster band" Lordi runs **Lordi's Rocktaurant ❷,** Koskikatu 25, good for salads, burgers, pizzas. (☎016 050 433 9811; www.rocktaurant.com. Open M-Tu 11am-6pm, W-Th 11am-9pm, F 11-10pm, Sa noon-10pm, Su noon-6pm. Open later in winter. MC/V.) A cheaper option is **Pizzeria Trocadero ❶,** Koskikatu 3. Pizza €6-8 with salad bar. (☎016 344 120. Open M-Th 12-10pm, F 12-10pm, Sa-Su 12-10pm.)

SIGHTS AND ENTERTAINMENT. The **Arktikum,** housed in a glass corridor at Pohjoisranta 4, has a cache of info on the Arctic and the history of Lapland's people and landscapes. (☎016 322 3260; www.arktikum.fi. Open daily from mid-June to mid-Aug. 9am-7pm; from mid-Aug. to mid-June daily 10am-6pm. €12, students €8. AmEx/MC/V.) If you've always wanted to visit Santa Claus at his supposed home in Finland, head to **Santa Claus Village,** 8km north of Rovaniemi. Here, the enterprising **Father Christmas** holds daily office hours while his band of elves runs an empire of gift shops. Send letters from Santa around the holidays for €6. After asking Santa why he lives in a gift shop, cross the white Arctic Circle line, which runs through the center of the village. (Take bus #8 (30min.; €3.40, round-trip €6.20) from the train station or the city center to Arctic Circle. ☎016 356 2096; www.santaclausvillage.info. Open daily May-Aug. 9am-6pm; Sept.-Nov. and Jan.-Apr. 10am-5pm; Dec. 9am-7pm.) For those more into swim than snow, take a dip in the **Vesihiisi** swimming hall, Nuortenkatu 11. (☎016 3222 592. www.rovaniemi.fi/uimahalli. Swim times M-F 6:30-8am, 2-8pm. Sa-Su 11am-5pm. €5.50, students €3.40. Morning swim €3.70/2.50.) **Doris Nightclub,** Koskikatu 4, is one of the clubs affiliated with the Sokos hotel. (☎020 1234 695. W-Th beer €1, F-Sa €3. Band nights €8-15. Open 10pm-4am W-Sa. Cover W-Th €3, F-Sa €5. 18+. AmEx/MC/V.)

FRANCE

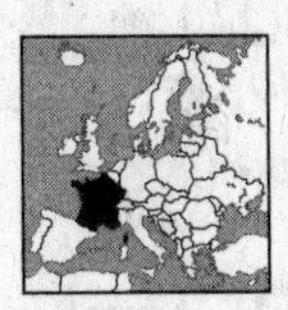

With its lavish châteaux, lavender fields, medieval streets, and sidewalk cafes, France conjures up any number of postcard-ready scenes. To the proud French, it is only natural that outsiders flock to their history-steeped homeland. Although France may no longer manipulate world events, the vineyards of Bordeaux, the museums of Paris, and the beaches of the Riviera draw more tourists than any other nation in the world. Centuries-old farms and churches share the landscape with inventive, modern architecture; street posters advertise jazz festivals as well as Baroque concerts. The country's rich culinary tradition rounds out a culture that cannot be sent home on a four-by-six.

DISCOVER FRANCE: SUGGESTED ITINERARIES

THREE DAYS. Don't even think of leaving **Paris,** the City of Light (p. 311). Explore the shops and cafes of the **Latin Quarter,** then cross the **Seine** to reach **Île de la Cité** to admire **Sainte-Chapelle** and the **Cathédrale de Notre Dame.** Visit the wacky **Centre National d'Art et de Culture Georges Pompidou** before swinging through **Marais** for food and fun. The next day, stroll down the **Champs-Élysées,** starting at the **Arc de Triomphe,** meander through the **Jardin des Tuileries,** and over to the **Musée d'Orsay.** See part of the **Louvre** the next morning, then spend the afternoon at **Versailles.**

ONE WEEK. After three days in **Paris,** go to **Tours** (1 day; p. 337), a great base for exploring the châteaux of the **Loire Valley** (1 day; p. 335). Head to **Rennes** for medieval sights and modern nightlife (1 day; p. 338), then to the dazzling island of **Mont-St-Michel** (1 day; p. 342).

BEST OF FRANCE, THREE WEEKS. Begin with three days in Paris, then daytrip to the royal residences at **Versailles.** Whirl through the **Loire Valley** (2 days) before traveling to the wine country of **Bordeaux** (1 day; p. 360). Check out the rose-colored architecture of **Toulouse** (1 day; p. 363) and the medieval streets of **Bourges** (1 day; p. 358) before sailing through **Avignon** (p. 371), **Aix-en-Provence** (p. 370), and **Nîmes** (p. 371) in sunny **Provence** (3 days). Let loose in **Marseille** (2 days; p. 365), and bask in the glitter of the Riviera in **Nice** (2 days; p. 372). Then show off your tan in the Alps as you travel **Lyon** (2 days; p. 350) to revel in their wild nightlife before heading off to **Chamonix** (1 day; p. 357). Spice it up with a mustard tour in **Dijon** (1 day; p. 345), and finish your trip with some German flavor in **Strasbourg** (1 day; p. 346), where trains will whisk you away to your next European adventure.

ESSENTIALS

WHEN TO GO

In July, Paris starts to shrink; by August it is devoid of Parisians, animated only by tourists and the pickpockets who love them. The French Riviera fills with Anglophones from June to September. During these months, French natives flee to other parts of the country, especially the Atlantic coast. Early summer and fall are the best times to visit Paris—the city has warmed up but not completely emptied out. The north and west have cool winters and mild summers,

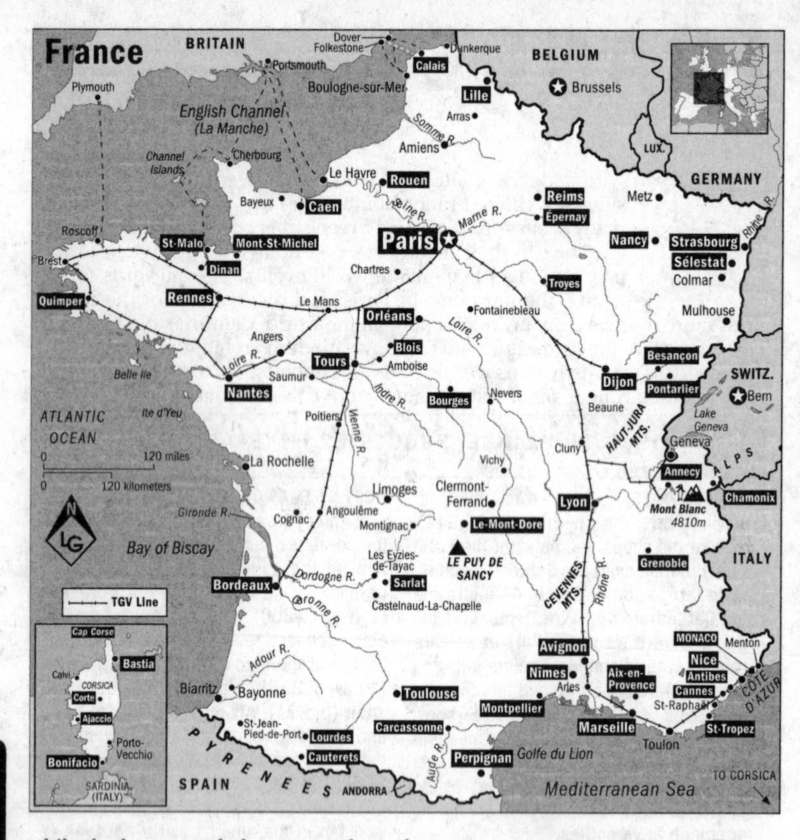

while the less-crowded center and east have a more temperate climate. From December through April, the Alps provide some of the world's best skiing, while the Pyrénées offer a calmer, if less climatically dependable, alternative.

FACTS AND FIGURES

OFFICIAL NAME: French Republic.

CAPITAL: Paris.

MAJOR CITIES: Lyon, Marseille, Nice.

POPULATION: 60,880,000.

LAND AREA: 547,000 sq. km.

TIME ZONE: GMT+1.

LANGUAGE: French.

RELIGION: Roman Catholic (88%), Muslim (9%), Protestant (2%), Jewish (1%).

CHEESE VARIETIES: Over 500.

DOCUMENTS AND FORMALITIES

EMBASSIES AND CONSULATES. Foreign embassies in France are in **Paris** (p. 312). French embassies abroad include: **Australia,** Level 26, St-Martins Tower, 31 Market St., Sydney NSW 2000 (☎+61 02 92 68 24 00; www.ambafrance-au.org); **Canada,** 1501, McGill College, Bureau 1000, Montréal, QC H3A 3M8 (☎+1-878-4385; www.consulfrance-montreal.org); **Ireland,** 36 Ailesbury Rd.,

Ballsbridge, Dublin, 4 (☎+353 1 227 5000; www.ambafrance.ie); **New Zealand,** 34-42 Manners St., Wellington (☎+64 384 25 55; www.ambafrance-nz.org); **UK,** 21 Cromwell Rd., London SW7 2EN (☎+44 207 073 1000; www.consulfrance-londres.org); **US,** 4101 Reservoir Rd., NW, Washington, D.C., 20007 (☎+1-202-944-6195; www.consulfrance-washington.org).

VISA AND ENTRY INFORMATION. EU citizens do not need a visa. Citizens of Australia, Canada, New Zealand, and the US do not need a visa for stays of up to 90 days, beginning upon entry into any of the countries in the EU's freedom-of-movement zone. For more info, see p. 14. For stays longer than 90 days, all non-EU citizens need Schengen visas (around US$81), available at French consulates and online at www.consulfrance-washington.org.

TOURIST SERVICES AND MONEY

EMERGENCY	**Ambulance:** ☎15. **Fire:** ☎18. **Police:** ☎17. **General Emergency:** ☎112.

TOURIST OFFICES. The **French Government Tourist Office** (**FGTO;** www.franceguide.com), also known as Maison de la France, runs tourist offices (called *syndicats d'initiative* or *offices de tourisme*) and offers tourist services to travelers abroad. In smaller towns, the **mairie** (town hall) may also distribute maps and pamphlets, help travelers find accommodations, and suggest excursions.

MONEY. The **euro (€)** has replaced the franc as the unit of currency in France. For more info, see p. 17. As a general rule, it's cheaper to exchange money in France than at home. Be prepared to spend at least €40-60 per day and considerably more in Paris. Tips are generally included in meal prices at restaurants and cafes, as well as in drink prices at bars and clubs; ask or look for the phrase *service compris* on the menu. If service is not included, tip 15-20%. Even when service is included, it is polite to leave a *pourboire* of up to 5% at a cafe, bistro, restaurant, or bar. Workers such as concierges may expect at least a €1.50 tip for services beyond the call of duty; taxi drivers expect 10-15% of the metered fare. Tipping tour guides and bus drivers €1.50-3 is customary.

France has a 19.6% **value added tax** (**VAT;** TVA in French), a sales tax applied to a wide range of goods and services. The prices included in *Let's Go* include VAT. In the airport upon exiting the EU, non-EU citizens can claim a refund on the tax paid for goods purchased at participating stores. In order to qualify for a refund in a store, you must spend at least €175; make sure to ask for a refund form when you pay. For more info on qualifying for a VAT refund, see p. 21.

TRANSPORTATION

BY PLANE. Most transatlantic flights to Paris land at **Roissy-Charles de Gaulle** (**CDG;** ☎01 48 62 22 80). Many continental and charter flights use **Orly** (**ORY;** ☎01 49 75 15 15). Aéroports de Paris (www.aeroportsdeparis.fr) has info about both. **Paris Beauvais Tillé** (**BVA;** ☎38 92 68 20 66; www.aeroportbeauvais.com) caters to budget travelers, servicing airlines like Ryanair (UK ☎0905 566 0000; www.ryanair.com). For more info on flying to France, see p. 46. Once in France, most people prefer other travel modes unless heading to **Corsica** (p. 380).

BY TRAIN. The French national railway company, **SNCF** (☎0892 35 35 35; www.sncf.fr), manages one of Europe's most efficient rail networks. Among the fastest in the world, **TGV** (www.tgv.com) trains (*train à grande vitesse;* high-speed) now link many major French cities, as well as some European destinations, including Brussels, Geneva, Lausanne, and Zürich. *Rapide* trains are slower. Local Express trains are actually the slowest option. French trains offer discounts of 25-50% on tickets for travelers under 26 with the **Carte 12-25** (€52; good for 1yr.). Locate the *guichets* (ticket counters), the *quais* (platforms), and the *voies* (tracks), and you will be ready to roll. Terminals can be divided into *banlieue* (suburb) and the bigger *grandes lignes* (intercity trains). While some select trains require reservations, you are not guaranteed a seat without one (usually US$5-30). Reserve ahead during holidays and high seasons.

If you are planning to spend a great deal of time on trains, a rail pass might be worthwhile, but in many cases—especially if you are under 26—point-to-point tickets may be cheaper. **Eurail** is valid in France. Standard **Eurail Passes,** valid for a given number of consecutive days, are best for those planning on traveling long distances. **Flexipasses,** valid for any 10 or 15 (not necessarily consecutive) days within a two-month period, are more cost-effective for those traveling longer distances less frequently. **Youth Passes** and **Youth Flexipasses** provide the same second-class perks for those under 26. It is best to purchase a pass before going to France. For prices and more info, contact student travel agencies, **Rail Europe** (Canada ☎800-361-7245, US 888-382-7245; www.raileurope.com), or **Flight Centre** (US ☎866-967-5351; www.flightcentre.com)

SELF-VALIDATE=GREAT. Validate *(composter)* your ticket! Orange validation boxes lie around every station, and you must have your ticket stamped with the date and time by the machine before boarding the train.

BY BUS. Within France, long-distance buses are a secondary transportation choice, as service is relatively infrequent. However, in some regions buses are indispensable for reaching out-of-the-way towns. Bus services operated by SNCF accept rail passes. *Gare routière* is French for "bus station."

BY FERRY. Ferries across the **English Channel** (La Manche) link France to England and Ireland. The shortest and most popular route is between Dover, BRI and Calais (1hr.) and is run by **P&O Stena Line** (☎08 25 12 01 56; www.posl.com) and **SeaFrance** (☎08 25 04 40 45; www.seafrance.com). **Norfolkline** (☎44 0870 870 1020; www.norfolkline-ferries.com) provides an alternative route from Dover, BRI to Dunkerque (1hr.). **Brittany Ferries** (France ☎0825 82 88 28, UK ☎0871 244 0744; www.brittany-ferries.com) travels from Portsmouth to Caen (5¾hr.), Cherbourg (4½hr.), and St-Malo (10¾hr.). For more info on English Channel ferries, see p. 57. For info on ferries to Corsica, see p. 380.

BY CAR. Drivers in France visiting for fewer than 90 days must be 18 years old and carry either an **International Driving Permit (IDP)** or a valid EU-issued or American driving license. You need to also have the vehicle's registration, national plate, and current insurance certificate on hand; French car rental agencies provide necessary documents. Agencies require renters to be 20, and most charge those aged 21-24 an additional insurance fee (€20-25 per day). If you don't know how to drive stick, you may have to pay a hefty premium for a car with automatic transmission. French law requires that both drivers and passengers wear seat belts. The almost 1,000,000km of French roads are usually in great condition, due in part to expensive tolls paid by travelers. Check www.francetourism.com/practicalinfo for more info on travel and car rentals.

BY BIKE AND BY THUMB. Of Europeans, the French alone may love **cycling** more than football. Renting a **bike** (€8-19 per day) beats bringing your own if you're only touring one or two regions. Hitchhiking is illegal on French highways, although some people describe the French's ready willingness to lend a ride. *Let's Go* does not recommend hitchhiking.

KEEPING IN TOUCH

PHONE CODES	**Country code:** 33. **International dialing prefix:** 00. When calling within a city, dial 0 + city code + local number. For more info on how to place international calls, see **Inside Back Cover.**

EMAIL AND THE INTERNET. Internet is readily available throughout France. Only the smallest villages lack Internet cafes, and in larger towns Internet cafes are well equipped and widespread, though often pricey. In addition to the locations suggested here, check out www.cybercaptive.com for more options.

TELEPHONE. Whenever possible, use a **calling card** for international phone calls, as long-distance rates for national phone services are often very high. Publicly owned **France Télécom** pay phones charge less than their privately owned counterparts. They accept *Télécartes* (phonecards), available in 50-unit (€7.50) and 120-unit (€15) denominations at newspaper kiosks and tabacs. **Mobile phones** are an increasingly popular and economical option. Major mobile carriers include Orange, Bouyges Telecom, and SFR. *Décrochez* means pick up; you'll then be asked to *patientez* (wait) to insert your card; at *numérotez* or *composez*, you can dial. The number for general info is ☎12; for an international operator, call ☎00 33 11. International direct dial numbers include: **AT&T Direct** ☎0 800 99 00 11; **Canada Direct** ☎0 800 99 00 16 or 99 02 16; **MCI WorldPhone** ☎0 800 99 00 19; **Telecom New Zealand** ☎0 800 99 00 64; **Telstra Australia** ☎0 800 99 00 61.

MAIL. Send mail from **La Poste** offices (www.laposte.net. Open M-F 9am-7pm, Sa 9am-noon). Airmail between France and North America takes five to 10 days; writing *"prioritaire"* on the envelope should ensure delivery in about five days at no extra charge. To send a 20g airmail letter or postcard within France or from France to another EU destination costs around €0.54, to a non-EU European country €0.75, and to Australia, Canada, New Zealand, or the US €0.90. To receive mail in France, have it delivered **Poste Restante.** Mail will go to the main post office unless you specify a subsidiary by street address. Address mail to be held as follows: Last name, First name, Poste Restante, postal code, city, France. Bring a passport to pick up your mail; there may be a small fee.

ACCOMMODATIONS AND CAMPING

FRANCE	❶	❷	❸	❹	❺
ACCOMMODATIONS	under €15	€15-27	€28-38	€39-55	over €55

The **French Hostelling International (HI)** affiliate, **Fédération Unie des Auberges de Jeunesse** (**FUAJ;** ☎01 44 89 87 27; www.fuaj.org), operates 150 hostels within France. A dorm bed in a hostel averages €10-15. Some hostels accept reservations through the **International Booking Network** (www.hostelbooking.com). Two or more people traveling together can save money by staying in cheap hotels rather than hostels. The French government employs a four-star hotel rating system. *Gîtes d'étapes* are rural accommodations for cyclists, hikers, and other amblers in less-populated areas. After 3000 years of settlement, true wilderness in France is hard to find, and it's illegal to **camp** in most public spaces, including national parks. Instead, look for organized *campings* (campgrounds), replete with vacationing families and programmed fun. Most have toilets, showers, and electrical outlets, though you may have to pay €2-5 extra for such luxuries; you'll often need to pay a fee for your car, too (€3-8).

FOOD AND DRINK

FRANCE	❶	❷	❸	❹	❺
FOOD	under €7	€7-12	€13-18	€19-33	over €33

French chefs cook for one of the world's most finicky clienteles. The largest meal of the day is *le déjeuner* (lunch), while a light croissant with or without *confiture* (jam) characterizes *le petit déjeuner* (breakfast). A complete French meal includes an *apéritif* (drink), an *entrée* (appetizer), a *plat* (main course), salad, cheese, dessert, fruit, coffee, and a *digestif* (after-dinner drink). The French drink **wine** with virtually every meal; *boisson comprise* entitles you to a free drink (usually wine) with your food. In France, the legal drinking age is 16. Most restaurants offer a *menu à prix fixe* (fixed-price meal) that costs less than ordering *à la carte*. The *formule* is a cheaper, two-course version for the hurried luncher. Odd-hour cravings between lunch and dinner can be satisfied at *brasseries* or creperies, the middle ground between cafes and restaurants. *Service compris* means the tip is included in *l'addition* (the check). It's easy to get a satisfying dinner for under €10 with staples such as cheese, pâté, wine, bread, and chocolate. For a budget-friendly **picnic,** get fresh produce at a *marché* (outdoor market) and then hop between specialty shops. Start with a *boulangerie* (bakery) for bread, proceed to a *charcuterie* (butcher) for meats, and then *pâtisseries* (pastry shops) and *confiseries* (candy shops) to satisfy a sweet tooth. When choosing a cafe, remember that major boulevards provide more expensive venues than smaller places on side streets. Prices are also cheaper at the *comptoir* (counter) than in the *salle* (seating area). For **supermarket** shopping, look for the chains **Carrefour, Casino,** and **Monoprix.**

HOLIDAYS AND FESTIVALS

Holidays: New Year's Day (Jan. 1); Good Friday (Apr. 10, 2009); Easter (Apr. 13, 2009); Labor Day (May 1); Ascension Day (May 21, 2009); Victory Day (May 8); Whit Monday (June1, 2009); Bastille Day (July 14); Assumption (Aug. 15); All Saints' Day (Nov. 1); Armistice Day (Nov. 11); Christmas (Dec. 25-26).

Festivals: Many cities celebrate a pre-Lenten Carnaval—for the most over-the-top festivities and partying, head to **Nice** (Jan. 25-Feb. 5). The **Cannes Film Festival** (May 13-24; www.festival-cannes.com) caters to the rich, famous, and creative. In 2009, the **Tour de France** will begin July 4. (www.letour.fr). The **Festival d'Avignon** (July-Aug.; www.festival-avignon.com) is famous for its theater productions.

BEYOND TOURISM

As the most visited nation in the world, France benefits economically from the tourism industry. Yet the country's popularity has adversely affected some French communities and their natural life. Throw off the *touriste* stigma and advocate for immigrant communities, restore a crumbling château, or educate others about the importance of environmental issues while exploring France. For more info on opportunities across Europe, see **Beyond Tourism,** p. 60.

Care France, CAP 19, 13 r. Georges Auric, 75019 Paris (☎01 53 19 89 89; www.carefrance.org). An international organization providing volunteer opportunities, ranging from combating AIDS to promoting education.

Club du Vieux Manoir, Ancienne Abbaye du Moncel, 60700 Pontpoint (☎03 44 72 33 98; cvmclubduvieuxmanoir.free.fr). Year-long and summer work restoring castles and churches. €14 membership and insurance fee; €12.50 per day, plus food and tent.

International Partnership for Service-Learning and Leadership, 815 2nd Ave., Ste. 315, New York, NY 10017, USA (☎212-986-0989; www.ipsl.org). An organization that matches volunteers with host families, provides intensive French classes, and requires 10-15hr. per week of service for a year, semester, or summer. Ages 18-30. Based in Montpellier. Costs range US$7200-US$23,600.

PARIS ☎01

Paris (pah-ree; pop. 2,153,600), a cultural and commercial center for over 2000 years, draws millions of visitors each year, from students who come to study to tourists who snap endless pictures of the Eiffel Tower. The City of Light, Paris is a source of inspiration unrivaled in beauty. Priceless art fills its world-class museums and history is found in its Roman ruins, medieval streets, Renaissance hotels, and 19th-century boulevards. A vibrant political center, Paris blends the spirit of revolution with a reverence for tradition, devoting as much energy to preserving conventions as it does to shattering them.

INTERCITY TRANSPORTATION

Flights: Some budget airlines fly into **Aéroport de Paris Beauvais Tillé (BVA),** 1hr. outside of Paris (p. 307). **Aéroport Roissy-Charles de Gaulle (CDG, Roissy;** ☎3950; www.adp.fr), 23km northeast of Paris, serves most transatlantic flights. 24hr. English-speaking info center. The **RER B** (a Parisian commuter rail line) runs to central Paris from Terminals 1 and 2. (35min.; every 15min. 5am-12:30am; €13). **Aéroport d'Orly (ORY;** ☎01 49 75 15 15), 18km south of Paris, is used by charters and continental flights.

Trains: Paris has 6 major train stations: **Gare d'Austerlitz** (to the Loire Valley, southwestern France, Portugal, and Spain); **Gare de l'Est** (to Austria, eastern France, Czech Republic, southern Germany, Hungary, Luxembourg, and Switzerland); **Gare de Lyon** (to southern and southeastern France, Greece, Italy, and Switzerland); **Gare du Nord** (to Belgium, Britain, Eastern Europe, northern France, northern Germany, the Netherlands, and Scandinavia); **Gare Montparnasse** (to Brittany and southwestern France on the TGV); **Gare St-Lazare** (to Normandy). All are accessible by Métro.

Buses: Gare Routière Internationale du Paris-Gallieni, 28 av. du Général de Gaulle, outside Paris. Ⓜ Gallieni. Eurolines (☎08 92 89 90 91, €0.34 per min.; www.eurolines.fr) sells tickets to most destinations in France and bordering countries.

ORIENTATION

The **Seine River** (SEHN) flows from east to west through Paris with two islands, **Île de la Cité** and **Île St-Louis,** situated in the city's geographical center. The Seine splits Paris in half: the **Rive Gauche** (REEV go-sh; Left Bank) to the south and the **Rive Droite** (REEV dwaht; Right Bank) to the north. Modern Paris is divided into 20 *arrondissements* (districts) that spiral clockwise outward from the center of the city. Each *arrondissement* is referred to by its number (e.g. the

Third, the Sixteenth). Sometimes it is helpful to orient yourself around central Paris's major monuments: on Rive Gauche, the sprawling **Jardin du Luxembourg** lies in the southeast; the **Eiffel Tower,** visible from many points in the city, stands in the southwest; moving clockwise and crossing the Seine to Rive Droite, the **Champs-Élysées** and **Arc de Triomphe** occupy the northwest, and the **Sacré-Coeur** stands high in the northeast. *Let's Go: Western Europe* splits Paris into five sections according to geographical grouping of *arrondissements*: the **city center** (*1er, 2ème, 3ème,* and *4ème*); **Left Bank East** (*5ème, 6ème,* and *13ème*); **Left Bank West** (*7ème, 14ème,* and *15ème*); **Right Bank East** (*10ème, 11ème, 12ème, 18ème, 19ème,* and *20ème*); **Right Bank West** (*8ème, 9ème, 16ème,* and *17ème*).

LOCAL TRANSPORTATION

Public Transportation: The **Métro** (Ⓜ) runs from 5:30am-1:20am. Lines are numbered and are referred to by their number and final destinations; connections are called *correspondances.* Single-fare tickets within the city cost €1.60; *carnet* of 10 €11.40. Buy extras for when ticket booths are closed (after 10pm) and hold onto your ticket until you exit. The **RER** (Réseau Express Régional), the commuter train to the suburbs, serves as an express subway within central Paris. Keep your ticket: changing to and getting off the RER requires sticking your validated ticket into a turnstile. Watch the signboards next to the RER tracks and check that your stop is lit up before riding. Buses use the same €1.40 tickets (validate in the machine by the driver). Buses run 7am-8:30pm, **Autobus de Nuit** until 1:30am, and **Noctambus** 1 per hr. 12:30am-5:30am at stops marked with a blue "N" inside a white circle, with a red star on the upper right-hand side. The **Mobilis pass** covers the Métro, RER, and buses (€5.80 for a 1-day pass in Zones 1 and 2). A **Carte Orange weekly pass** *(carte orange hebdomadaire)* costs €16.80 and expires on Su; photo required. Refer to the front of the book for maps of Paris's transit network.

CONSTANT VIGILANCE. The following stations can be dangerous at night: Anvers, Barbès-Rochechouart, Château d'Eau, Châtelet, Châtelet-Les-Halles, Gare de l'Est, Gare du Nord, and Pigalle. If concerned, take a taxi, or sit near the driver on a Noctilien bus.

Taxis: Alpha Taxis (☎01 53 60 63 50). **Taxi 75** (☎01 78 41 65 05). Taxis take 3 passengers (4th passenger €2-3 surcharge). **Tarif A,** daily 7am-7pm (€0.86 per km). **Tarif B,** M-Sa 7pm-7am, Su 24hr., and from the airports and immediate suburbs (€1.12 per km). **Tarif C,** from the airports 7pm-7am (€1.35 per km). In addition, there is a €2.20 base fee and min. €5.60 charge. It is customary to tip 15% and polite to add €1 extra.

Bike Rental: Vélib (www.en.velib.paris.fr). Self-service bike rental. Over 1450 terminals and 20,000 bikes in Paris. Buy a subscription (day €1, week €5, year €29) and rent bikes from any terminal in the city. Rentals under 30min. free. Available 24hr.

PRACTICAL INFORMATION

Tourist Office: Bureau Gare d'Austerlitz, 13*ème* (☎01 45 84 91 70). ⓂGare d'Austerlitz. Open M-Sa 8am-6pm. **Bureau Gare de Lyon,** 12ème (☎01 43 43 33 24). ⓂGare de Lyon. Open M-Sa 8am-6pm. **Montmartre Tourist Office,** 21 pl. du Tertre, 18ème (☎01 42 62 21 21). ⓂAnvers. Open daily 10am-7pm.

Embassies: Australia, 4 r. Jean-Rey, 15*ème* (☎0140 59 33 00; www.france.embassy.gov.au). Open M-F 9am-5pm. **Canada,** 35 av. Montaigne, 8*ème* (☎01 44 43 29 00; www.international.gc.ca/canada-europa/france). Open daily 9am-noon and 2-5pm.

Ireland, 12 av. Foch, 16*ème* (☎01 44 17 67 00; www.embassyofirelandparis.netfirms.com). Open M-F 9:30am-noon. **New Zealand,** 7ter r. Léonard de Vinci, 16*ème* (☎0145 01 43 43; www.nzembassy.com/france). Open July-Aug. M-Th 9am-1pm and 2-4:30pm, F 9am-2pm; Sept.-June M-Th 9am-1pm and 2-5:30pm, F 9am-1pm and 2-4pm. **UK,** 18bis r. d'Anjou, 8*ème* (☎44 51 31 02; www.amb-grandebretagne.fr). Open M-F 9:30am-12:30pm and 2:30-4:30pm. **US,** 2 av. Gabriel, 8*ème* (☎01 43 12 22 22; www.amb-usa.fr). Open M-F 9am-12:30pm.

Currency Exchange: American Express, 11 rue Scribe, 9*ème* (☎01 53 30 99 00; parisscribe.france@kanoofes.com). ⓂOpéra or RER: Auber. Exchange counters open M-Sa 9am-6:30pm; member services open M-F 9am-5pm, Sa 9am-noon and 1-5pm.

GLBT Resources: Centre Gai et Lesbien, 3 r. Keller, 11*ème* (☎0143 57 21 47; www.cglparis.org). ⓂLedru-Rollin or Bastille. Open M-F 4-8pm.

Laundromats: Laundromats are everywhere, especially in the 5*ème* and 6*ème*.

Crisis Lines: SOS Help!, ☎01 46 21 46 46. Confidential English-speaking crisis hotline. Open daily 3-11pm. **Rape: SOS Viol** (☎08 00 05 95 95). Open M-F 10am-7pm.

Pharmacies: Look for the neon green crosses that indicate pharmacies all over the city. Call the police for the *pharmacies de garde,* the rotating pharmacies in different *arrondissements* that handle emergencies.

Hospitals: American Hospital of Paris, 63 bd. Hugo, Neuilly (☎01 46 41 25 25; www.american-hospital.org). ⓂPort Maillot, then bus #82 to the end of the line. **Hertford British Hospital (Hôpital Franco-Britannique de Paris),** 3 rue Barbès, in the suburb of Levallois-Perret (☎01 46 39 22 22). ⓂAnatole France.

Post Office: Poste du Louvre, 52 rue du Louvre, 1er (☎01 40 28 20 40). ⓂLouvre. Open 24hr. Another office is **Paris Beaubourg,** 90 rue St-Denis. **Postal Codes:** 750xx, where "xx" is the *arrondissement* (e.g., 75003 for any address in the 3*ème*).

ACCOMMODATIONS

Accommodations in Paris are expensive. You don't need *Let's Go* to tell you that. Expect to pay at least €20 for a hostel dorm-style bed and €28 for a hotel single. Hostels are a better option for single travelers, whereas staying in a hotel is more economical for groups. Paris's hostels skip many standard restrictions (e.g., curfews) and tend to have flexible maximum stays. Rooms fill quickly after morning check-out; arrive early or reserve ahead. Most hostels and *foyers* include the *taxe de séjour* (€0.10-2 per person per day) in listed prices.

CITY CENTER

Hôtel des Jeunes (MIJE; ☎01 42 74 23 45; www.mije.com). 3 small hostels (below) in beautiful old Marais *hôtels particuliers* (mansions). Main welcome desk at Le Fourcy. Arranges airport pick-up and drop-off and reservations for sights, restaurants, and shows. Restaurant in a vaulted cellar in Le Fourcy. Breakfast, in-room shower, and linens included. Lockers free with €1 deposit. Internet access €0.10 per min. with €0.50 initial fee. 1-week max. stay. Reception 7am-1am. Lockout noon-3pm. Curfew 1am. Quiet hours after 10pm. Arrive before noon the first day of reservation. Reserve months ahead online and 2-3 weeks ahead by phone. MIJE membership required (€3). 4- to 9-bed dorms €29; singles €47; doubles €68; triples €90. Cash only. ❷

Maubuisson, 12, rue des Barres, 4*ème*. ⓂHôtel de Ville or Pont Marie. Half-timbered former convent on a silent street by a monastery. Accommodates more individual travelers than groups.

Le Fourcy, 6 rue de Fourcy, 4*ème*. ⓂSt-Paul or Pont Marie. Courtyard ideal for meeting travelers.

Le Fauconnier, 11 rue du Fauconnie, 4*ème*. ⓂSt-Paul or Pont Marie. Ivy-covered, sun-drenched building steps away from the Seine and Île St-Louis. All rooms have shower and sink.

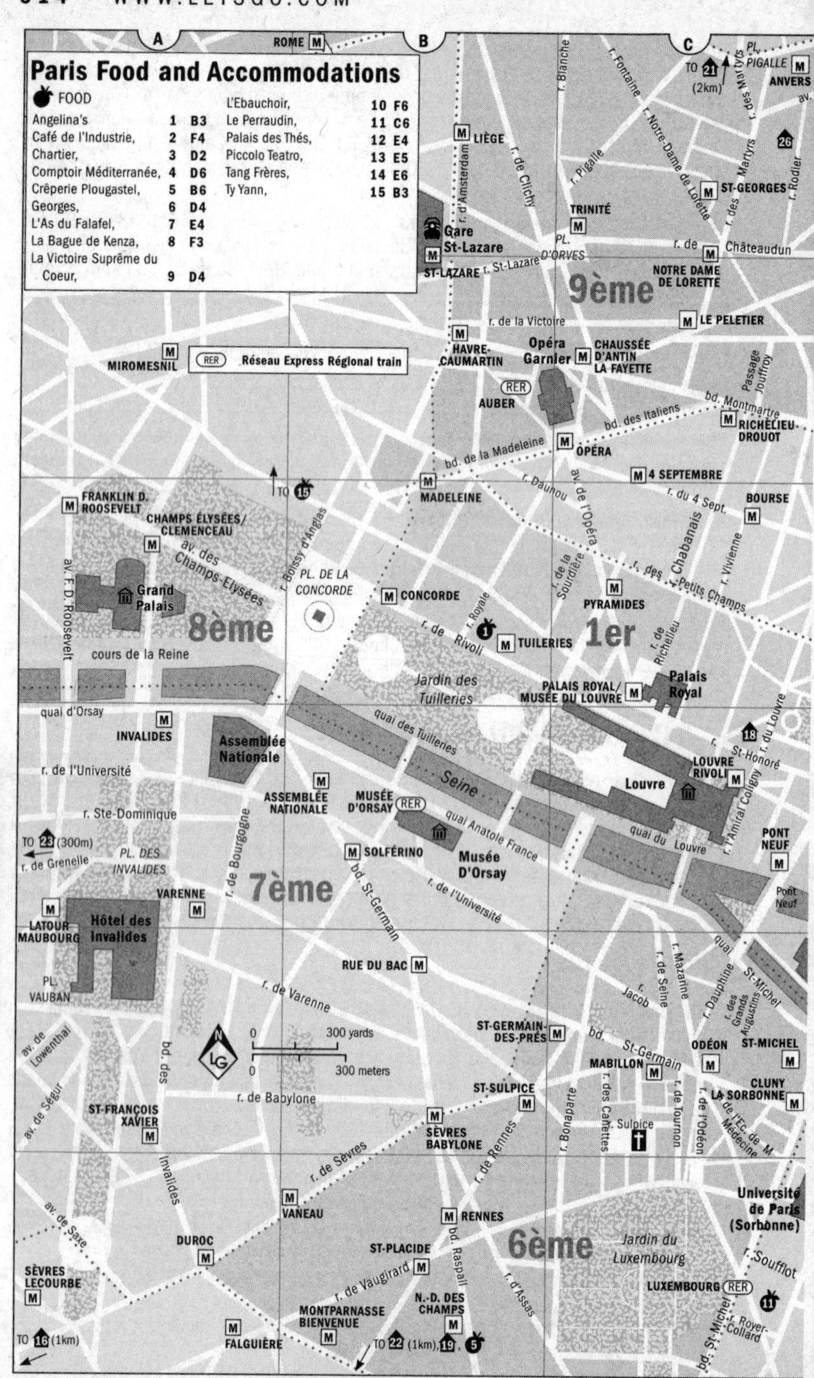
Paris Food and Accommodations
FOOD
Angelina's, 1 B3
Café de l'Industrie, 2 F4
Chartier, 3 D2
Comptoir Méditerranée, 4 D6
Crêperie Plougastel, 5 B6
Georges, 6 D4
L'As du Falafel, 7 E4
La Bague de Kenza, 8 F3
La Victoire Suprême du Coeur, 9 D4
L'Ebauchoir, 10 F6
Le Perraudin, 11 C6
Palais des Thés, 12 E4
Piccolo Teatro, 13 E5
Tang Frères, 14 E6
Ty Yann, 15 B3
RER Réseau Express Régional train
A
B
C
ROME
PL. PIGALLE
ANVERS
TO 21 (2km)
LIÈGE
r. Blanche
r. Fontaine
r. Notre-Dame de Lorette
r. des Martyrs
r. Rodier
r. d'Amsterdam
r. de Clichy
r. Pigalle
ST-GEORGES
TRINITÉ
Gare St-Lazare
ST-LAZARE
r. St-Lazare
PL. D'ORVES
r. de Châteaudun
NOTRE DAME DE LORETTE
9ème
LE PELETIER
r. de la Victoire
HAVRE-CAUMARTIN
Opéra Garnier
CHAUSSÉE D'ANTIN LA FAYETTE
Passage Jouffroy
MIROMESNIL
AUBER
bd. Montmartre
bd. des Italiens
RICHELIEU-DROUOT
bd. de la Madeleine
OPÉRA
4 SEPTEMBRE
MADELEINE
r. Daunou
av. de l'Opéra
r. du 4 Sept.
BOURSE
TO 15
FRANKLIN D. ROOSEVELT
CHAMPS ÉLYSÉES/ CLEMENCEAU
av. des Champs-Elysées
r. Boissy d'Anglas
r. Chabanais
r. Vivienne
r. de la Sourdière
r. des Petits Champs
PL. DE LA CONCORDE
CONCORDE
PYRAMIDES
av. F. D. Roosevelt
Grand Palais
8ème
r. Royale
r. de Rivoli
TUILERIES
1er
r. de Richelieu
cours de la Reine
Jardin des Tuilleries
PALAIS ROYAL/ MUSÉE DU LOUVRE
Palais Royal
quai d'Orsay
INVALIDES
Assemblée Nationale
quai des Tuilleries
r. du Louvre
r. St-Honoré
LOUVRE RIVOLI
Seine
Louvre
r. de l'Université
ASSEMBLÉE NATIONALE
MUSÉE D'ORSAY
r. Ste-Dominique
quai Anatole France
quai du Louvre
r. de l'Amiral Coligny
PONT NEUF
TO 23 (300m)
r. de Grenelle
PL. DES INVALIDES
r. de Bourgogne
SOLFÉRINO
Musée D'Orsay
VARENNE
7ème
bd. St-Germain
r. de l'Université
Pont Neuf
LATOUR MAUBOURG
Hôtel des Invalides
quai St-Michel
r. Mazarine
r. de Seine
RUE DU BAC
PL. VAUBAN
r. de Varenne
r. Jacob
r. Dauphine
r. des Grands Augustins
av. de Lowenthal
bd. des Invalides
ST-GERMAIN-DES-PRÉS
bd. St-Germain
ODÉON
ST-MICHEL
300 yards
300 meters
MABILLON
CLUNY LA SORBONNE
av. de Ségur
r. de Babylone
ST-SULPICE
r. Bonaparte
r. des Canettes
r. de Tournon
r. de l'Odéon
r. de l'Ec. de Médecine
ST-FRANÇOIS XAVIER
SÈVRES BABYLONE
Sulpice
r. de Sèvres
r. de Rennes
Université de Paris (Sorbonne)
VANEAU
RENNES
av. de Saxe
DUROC
ST-PLACIDE
bd. Raspail
6ème
Jardin du Luxembourg
r. Soufflot
SÈVRES LECOURBE
r. de Vaugirard
r. d'Assas
LUXEMBOURG
N.-D. DES CHAMPS
bd. St-Michel
r. Royer-Collard
MONTPARNASSE BIENVENUE
TO 16 (1km)
FALGUIÈRE
TO 22 (1km), 19
FRANCE

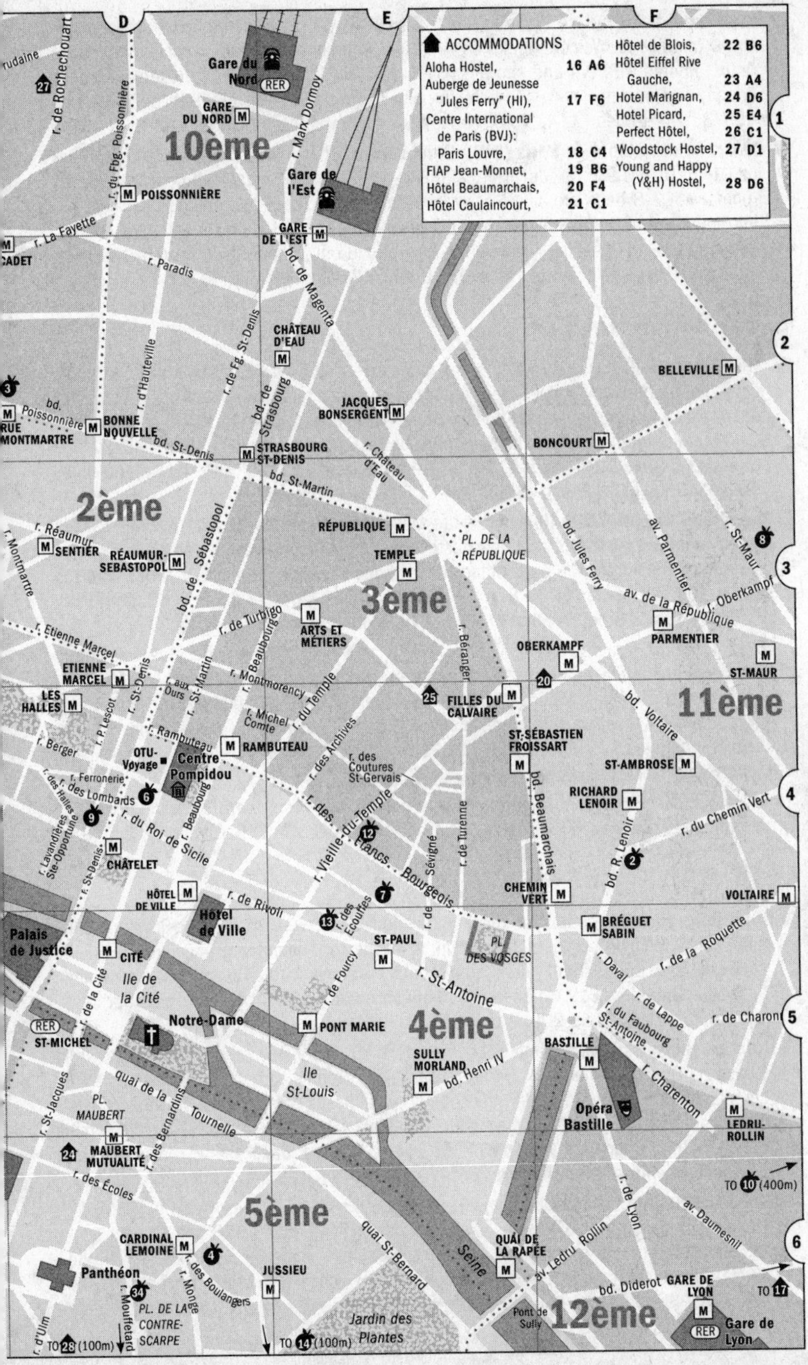

D E F

1 2 3 4 5 6

ACCOMMODATIONS

Name	No.	Grid
Aloha Hostel,	16	A6
Auberge de Jeunesse "Jules Ferry" (HI),	17	F6
Centre International de Paris (BVJ): Paris Louvre,	18	C4
FIAP Jean-Monnet,	19	B6
Hôtel Beaumarchais,	20	F4
Hôtel Caulaincourt,	21	C1
Hôtel de Blois,	22	B6
Hôtel Eiffel Rive Gauche,	23	A4
Hotel Marignan,	24	D6
Hotel Picard,	25	E4
Perfect Hôtel,	26	C1
Woodstock Hostel,	27	D1
Young and Happy (Y&H) Hostel,	28	D6

10ème
2ème
3ème
4ème
5ème
11ème
12ème

Gare du Nord RER
GARE DU NORD M
Gare de l'Est
GARE DE L'EST M
POISSONNIÈRE M
CADET
CHÂTEAU D'EAU M
JACQUES BONSERGENT M
BELLEVILLE M
BONCOURT M
BONNE NOUVELLE M
RUE MONTMARTRE
STRASBOURG ST-DENIS M
RÉPUBLIQUE M
PL. DE LA RÉPUBLIQUE
TEMPLE M
SENTIER M
RÉAUMUR-SEBASTOPOL M
ARTS ET MÉTIERS M
OBERKAMPF M
PARMENTIER M
ST-MAUR M
ETIENNE MARCEL M
LES HALLES M
FILLES DU CALVAIRE M
RAMBUTEAU M
OTU-Voyage
Centre Pompidou
ST-SÉBASTIEN FROISSART M
ST-AMBROSE M
RICHARD LENOIR M
CHÂTELET M
CHEMIN VERT M
VOLTAIRE M
HÔTEL DE VILLE M
Hôtel de Ville
BRÉGUET SABIN M
Palais de Justice
CITÉ M
ST-PAUL M
PL. DES VOSGES
Ile de la Cité
Notre-Dame
PONT MARIE M
RER ST-MICHEL
SULLY MORLAND M
BASTILLE M
Ile St-Louis
PL. MAUBERT
Opéra Bastille
LEDRU-ROLLIN M
MAUBERT MUTUALITÉ M
TO 10 (400m)
CARDINAL LEMOINE M
QUAI DE LA RAPÉE M
Panthéon
JUSSIEU M
GARE DE LYON M
TO 17
PL. DE LA CONTRE-SCARPE
Pont de Sully
Gare de Lyon RER
Jardin des Plantes
Seine
TO 28 (100m)
TO 14 (100m)

r. Trudaine
r. de Rochechouart
r. du Fbg. Poissonnière
r. Marx Dormoy
r. La Fayette
r. Paradis
bd. de Magenta
r. d'Hauteville
r. de Fg. St-Denis
bd. de Strasbourg
bd. Poissonnière
bd. St-Denis
r. Château d'Eau
bd. St-Martin
r. Réaumur
r. Montmartre
bd. de Sébastopol
bd. Jules Ferry
av. Parmentier
r. St-Maur
r. Oberkampf
av. de la République
r. Etienne Marcel
r. de Turbigo
r. Beaubourg
r. Béranger
r. Montmorency
r. du Temple
r. St-Denis
r. aux Ours
r. St-Martin
r. P. Lescot
r. Rambuteau
r. Michel Comte
bd. Voltaire
r. Berger
r. des Archives
r. des Coutures St-Gervais
r. Ferronerie
r. des Lombards
r. des Halles
r. du Roi de Sicile
r. Vieille-du-Temple
r. des Francs Bourgeois
r. de Turenne
bd. Beaumarchais
r. du Chemin Vert
r. Lavandières Ste-Opportune
r. Sévigné
bd. R. Lenoir
r. de Rivoli
r. des Ecouffes
r. de Sévigné
r. de la Roquette
r. Daval
r. de Fourcy
r. St-Antoine
r. de la Cité
r. de Lappe
r. du Faubourg St-Antoine
r. de Charonne
bd. Henri IV
r. Charenton
r. St-Jacques
quai de la Tournelle
r. des Bernardins
r. des Écoles
r. de Lyon
av. Daumesnil
av. Ledru Rollin
quai St-Bernard
r. Monge
r. des Boulangers
bd. Diderot
r. Mouffetard
r. d'Ulm

FRANCE

Hotel Picard, 26 rue de Picardie, 3*ème* (☎01 48 87 53 82; hotel.picard@wanadoo.fr). ⓂRépublique. Welcoming, family-run hotel with superb location. Lovely rooms have baths. Rooms with TVs and showers. Breakfast €5. Hall showers €3. Reserve 2 weeks ahead. Singles with sink €44, with sink and shower €65, with full bath €75; doubles €53/83/94; triples €114. 5% discount if you flash your *Let's Go*. MC/V. ❸

Centre International de Paris (BVJ): Paris Louvre, 20 rue Jean-Jacques Rousseau, 1*er* (☎01 53 00 90 90). ⓂLouvre or Palais-Royal. 3-building hostel with courtyard. Bright rooms with 2-8 beds are single sex except for groups. Breakfast included. Lockers €2. Internet €1 per 10min. 3 nights max. per reservation; extend the reservation once there. Reception 24hr. Reserve 1 week ahead; by phone only. Rooms held for only 5-10min. after check-in time; call if you'll be late. Dorms €28, doubles €30. ❷

LEFT BANK EAST

Hôtel Marignan, 13 rue du Sommerard, 5*ème* (☎01 43 54 63 81; www.hotel-marignan.com). ⓂMaubert-Mutualité. Clean, freshly decorated rooms can sleep up to 5. Hostel hospitality with hotel privacy. Kitchen. Breakfast included. Free Wi-Fi. Laundry. Singles €47-50, with toilet €55-60, with toilet and shower €75; doubles €60-68/69-80/82-90; triples €75-90/85-105/105-115; quads with toilet €100-125, with shower and toilet €120-140; quints with shower and toilet €105-155. AmEx/MC/V. ❹

Young and Happy (Y&H) Hostel, 80 rue Mouffetard, 5*ème* (☎01 47 07 47 07; www.youngandhappy.fr). ⓂMonge. Lively hostel with 21 clean, basic rooms, some with showers and toilets. Kitchen. Breakfast included. Linens €2.50; €5 deposit. Internet. Lockout 11am-4pm. Curfew 2am. 6-, 8-, or 10-person dorms €24; 3-, 4-, or 5-person dorms €26; doubles €28 per person. Jan.-Mar. €2 discount per night. MC/V. ❷

Hôtel de Nesle, 7 rue du Nesle, 6*ème* (☎01 43 54 62 41; www.hoteldenesleparis.com). ⓂOdéon. Absolutely sparkling. Every room represents a particular figure (e.g. Molière) or locale (e.g. Africa). Ceiling made of bouquets of dried flowers. Garden with duck pond. Laundry. Reserve by phone; confirm 2 days in advance of arrival time. Singles €55-65; doubles €75-100, extra bed €12. AmEx/MC/V. ❹

Hôtel Stella, 41 rue Monsieur-le-Prince, 6*ème* (☎01 40 51 00 25; http://site.voila.fr/hotel-stella). ⓂOdéon. Huge rooms with centuries-old woodwork. Reserve at least 1 month ahead. Singles €45; doubles €55; triples €75; quads €85. Cash only. ❹

LEFT BANK WEST

Hôtel Eiffel Rive Gauche, 6 rue du Gros Caillou, 7*ème* (☎01 45 51 24 56; www.hotel-eiffel.com). ⓂÉcole Militaire. Family-run. A favorite of Anglophone travelers. Spanish-style courtyard and tastefully decorated rooms. Flatscreen cable TVs, phones, safes, and full baths. Breakfast €12. Wi-Fi. Singles €95-155; doubles and twins €105-155; triples €115-175; quads €135-205. Extra bed €20. Prices vary seasonally. MC/V. ❺

Hôtel de Blois, 5 rue des Plantes, 14*ème* (☎01 45 40 99 48; www.hoteldeblois.com). ⓂMouton-Duvernet, Alésia, or Gaîté. Flowers adorn rooms with clean bathrooms, lush carpets, hair dryer, phone, and TV. Welcoming owner keeps scrapbook of previous guests' thank-you notes. 5 floors; no elevator. Breakfast €6.50. Reception 7am-10:30pm. Check-in 3pm. Check-out 11am. Wi-Fi €5 per hr., €26 per day. Reserve ahead. Singles and doubles with shower and toilet €55-70, with bath €75-85. AmEx/MC/V. ❹

FIAP Jean-Monnet, 30 rue Cabanis, 14*ème* (☎01 43 13 17 00, reservations 43 13 17 17; www.fiap.asso.fr). ⓂGlacière. Like a standard college dorm. 500-bed student center. Spotless rooms with bath and phone. 2 restaurants and *discothèque* every W and F night. Breakfast included. Internet €5 per hr. Wheelchair-accessible. Reception 24hr. Check-in 2:30pm. Check-out 9am. Curfew 2am. Reserve 2-4 weeks ahead; hostel often booked for summer before June. Be sure to specify if you want a dorm bed. 3- to 4-bed rooms €32; 5- to 6-bed rooms €25; singles €55; doubles €70. MC/V. ❷

Aloha Hostel, 1 rue Borromée, 15*ème* (☎01 42 73 03 03; www.aloha.fr). ⓂVolontaires. Frequented by lively international crowd. Varnished doors and cheery checkered sheets. Breakfast included. Linens €3, deposit €7; towels €3/6. Internet €2 per 30min.; free Wi-Fi. Reception 24hr. Lockout 11am-5pm. Curfew 2am. Reserve 1 week ahead. Apr.-Oct. dorms €23, doubles €50; Nov.-Mar. €19/46. Cash only. ❷

RIGHT BANK WEST

Perfect Hôtel, 39 rue Rodier, 9*ème* (☎01 42 81 18 86 or ☎42 81 26 19; www.paris-hostel.biz). ⓂAnvers. Lives up to its name. Rooms with balcony by request. Caring staff. Well-stocked kitchen, free coffee, and a beer vending machine (€1.50). Be careful in neighborhood after dark. Breakfast included. Reception 24hr. Reserve 1 month ahead. Singles €44, with toilet €60; doubles €50/60. Extra bed €19. Cash only. ❸

Woodstock Hostel, 48 rue Rodier, 9*ème* (☎01 48 78 87 76; www.woodstock.fr). ⓂAnvers. VW Bug adorns the lobby wall. Breakfast included. Linens €2.50 with €2.50 deposit. Internet and Wi-Fi €2 per 30min. Communal kitchen and hostel (not hostile) cat. Max. stay 2 weeks. Lockout 11am-3pm. Curfew 2am. Reserve ahead. High-season 4- or 6-person dorms €22; doubles €50. Low-season €19/22. Cash only. ❷

RIGHT BANK EAST

Auberge de Jeunesse "Jules Ferry" (HI), 8 bd. Jules Ferry, 11*ème* (☎01 43 57 55 60; paris.julesferry@fuaj.org). ⓂRépublique. 99 beds. Modern, clean, and bright rooms with sinks, mirrors, and tiled floors. Social atmosphere. Kitchen. Breakfast and linens included. Laundry €3. Lockers €2. Internet in lobby. 1-week max. stay. Reception and dining room 24hr. Lockout 10:30am-2pm. No reservations; arrive 8-11am to secure a bed. 4- to 6-bed dorms and doubles €22. MC/V. ❷

Hôtel Beaumarchais, 3 rue Oberkampf, 11*ème* (☎01 53 36 86 86; www.hotelbeaumarchais.com). ⓂOberkampf. Spacious hotel worth the money. Eye-popping decor. Each carpeted room with bath and safe. Suites include TV room with desk and breakfast table. A/C. Buffet breakfast €10. Reserve 2 weeks in advance. Singles €75-90; doubles €110-130; 2-person suites €150-170; triples €170-190. AmEx/MC/V. ❺

Le Village Hostel, 20 rue d'Orsel, 18*ème* (☎01 42 64 22 02; www.villagehostel.fr). ⓂAnvers. A quiet repose. All rooms with toilets and showers. Lovely views. Kitchen, stereo, telephones, and TV in lounge. Breakfast included. Internet and Wi-Fi €2 per 30min., €3.50 per hr. Reception 24hr. Lockout 11am-4pm. 1-week max. stay. Reserve online 1 month ahead. 4-, 6-, or 8-bed dorms €24; doubles €60; triples €81. MC/V. ❷

Hôtel Caulaincourt, 2 square Caulaincourt, 18*ème* (☎01 46 06 46 06; www.caulaincourt.com). ⓂLamarck-Caulaincourt. Formerly artists' studios. Wonderful skyline views. Breakfast included. Internet free 30min., €2 per hr. thereafter; free Wi-Fi. Lockout 11am-4pm. Curfew 2am. Towels €1. Reserve online 1 month ahead. 4- to 6-bed dorms €25; singles with shower €50, with shower and toilet €60; doubles €63/73; 2-bed doubles €66/76; triples with shower and toilet €89. Extra bed €10. MC/V. ❷

FOOD

When in doubt, spend your money on food in Paris. Skip the museum, sleep in the dingy hotel, but **eat well.** Paris's culinary scene has been famous for centuries, and eating in the City of Light remains as exciting today as it was when Sun King Louis XIV made feasts an everyday occurrence. The city also offers delicious international dishes in addition to traditional cuisine. As an alternative to a pricey sit-down meal, stop into an *épicerie* and create a picnic lunch for Luxembourg Gardens, Parc Buttes Chaumont, or on the steps at Sacré-Coeur. *Bon appetit!*

RESTAURANTS

CITY CENTER

Chez Janou, 2 rue Roger Verlomme, *3ème* (☎01 42 72 28 41). ⓂChemin-Vert. Food so good it induces desert-island hypotheticals: if you were stranded on a desert island, would you bring an endless supply of Chez Janou's *magret de canard* and *chevre au romarin,* or the best lover you've ever had? We're just not sure. Packed every night; reservations always recommended. Open M-F noon-3pm and 7:45pm-midnight, Sa-Su noon-4pm and 7:45pm-midnight. MC/V. ❸

La Victoire Suprême du Coeur, 29-31 rue du Bourg Tibourg, *1er* (☎01 40 41 95 03; www.vscoeur.com). ⓂHôtel de Ville. Run by the devotees of Sri Chinmoy. Classics like seitan "steak" with mushroom sauce (€14). Vegan options. 2-course *menu* €14. Open M-Tu and Th-F noon-3pm and 6:30-10:30pm, Sa noon-11pm, Su 11am-5:30pm. ❸

L'As du Falafel, 34 rue des Rosiers, *4ème* (☎01 48 87 63 60). ⓂSt-Paul or Hôtel de Ville. "The best falafel in the world," according to Lenny Kravitz. Also a Kosher stand. Falafel special €5. Open M-Th and Su noon-midnight, F noon-7pm. MC/V. ❶

Angelina's, 226 rue de Rivoli, *1er* (☎01 42 60 82 00). ⓂConcorde or Tuileries. RER: Neuilly-Porte Maillot. A favorite of Audrey Hepburn and Coco Chanel. Touristy, although the *chocolat à l'Ancienne dit 'l'africain'* (€7) is worth it. Pastries €5-7. Open daily 9am-7pm. AmEx/MC/V. Another location at 2 pl. de la Porte Maillot, *17ème* (☎01 42 60 82 00). ❷

Piccolo Teatro, 6 rue des Ecouffes, *4ème* (☎01 42 72 17 79). ⓂSt-Paul. Romantic vegetarian hideout. *Plats* €8-12. Open daily noon-3pm, 7-11pm. AmEx/MC/V. ❷

Georges, Centre Pompidou, 6th fl., *4ème* (☎01 44 78 47 99). ⓂRambuteau or Hôtel de Ville. A cafe almost more impressive than the museum. Unbeatable views. Splurge on a *plat* (king crab omelette €25). Champagne €8-12. *Gateau au chocolat de costes* €12. Dress to impress. Reserve for dinner. Open M and W-Su noon-2am. AmEx/MC/V. ❹

LEFT BANK EAST

Comptoir Méditerranée, 42 rue du Cardinal Lemoine, *5ème* (☎01 43 25 29 08; www.savannahcafe.fr).

WASTE NOT, WANT NOT

While contemporary French cuisine is renowned for its sophistication, the roots of French cooking can be found in some not-so-sophisticated parts of nature's most delicious creatures.

1. Pied de Porc (pig's feet): usually chopped, seasoned, and delicately fried.

2. Tête de Veau (calf's head): rolled up, sliced, and served to the applause of French diners everywhere. A national favorite.

3. L'Os à moelle (bone marrow): served on its own with salt, parsley, and eaten with a spoon.

4. Boudin (blood sausage): mentioned as far back as Homer's *Odyssey.* Now you too, sitting "beside a great fire," can "fill a sausage with fat and blood and turn it this way and that."

5. Foie Gras ("fatty" goose liver): some American cities have banned the sale of *foie gras* but the French hold fast to tradition.

6. Whole Fish: the best meat on any fish is behind the eye. So when the whole thing arrives on a plate, carpe diem!

7. Tripe (stomach): it's pretty meta—your intestines are digesting intestines.

8. Tail: can be eaten on its own, in a stew, or you name it.

9. Groin: in French, pigs say "groin," not "oink." So when you order this, you're also imitating it.

10. Filet (muscle): who knew?

Ⓜ Cardinal Lemoine. More Lebanese deli than restaurant. Colorful *plats* €6.50-12. Sandwiches €4.20. Open M-Sa 11am-10pm. MC/V. ❷

Tang Frères, 48 av. d'Ivry, 13*ème* (☎01 45 70 80 00). Ⓜ Porte d'Ivry. A sensory-overload, this huge shopping center in the heart of Chinatown contains a bakery, *charcuterie,* fish counter, flower shop, and grocery store. Exotic fruits (durian €7.80 per kg), cheap Asian beers (can of Kirin €0.85, 6-pack of Tsingtao €3.72), rice wines (€3.50 per 0.5-liter), and sake (€4.95-6.80). Noodles, rice, soups, spices, teas, and tofu in bulk. Also at 174 rue de Choisy. Ⓜ Place d'Italie. Open Tu-Sa 10am-8:30pm. MC/V. ❶

Le Perraudin, 157 rue St-Jacques, 5*ème* (☎01 46 33 15 75; www.restaurant-perraudin.com). RER: Luxembourg. Simple and elegant. Favorites like *boeuf bourguignon. Plats* €16-29. 3-course *menu* €30. Open M-F noon-2:30pm and 7-10:30pm. MC/V. ❸

LEFT BANK WEST

Crêperie Plougastel, 47 rue du Montparnasse, 14*ème* (01 42 79 90 63). Ⓜ Montparnasse-Bienvenue. Ambiance sets this cozy *crêperie* apart. Dessert *crêpes* feature homemade caramel. *Formule* (generous mixed salad and choice of 2 *galettes* and 5 dessert crepes) €14.50. *Cidre* €2.90. Open daily noon-11:30pm. MC/V. ❸

Bélisaire, 2 rue Marmontel, 15*ème* (☎01 48 28 62 24; m.garrel@free.fr). Ⓜ Vaugirard. Fit for aristocracy. Options on chalkboard menus rotate seasonally. Salmon and lobster ravioli are to die for. Packed daily; reservations are a must. 3-course lunch *menu* €22. 5-course dinner *menu* €40. Open daily noon-2pm and 8-10:30pm. MC/V. ❹

Aquarius Café, 40 rue de Gergovie, 14*ème* (☎01 45 41 36 88). Ⓜ Pernety. Celebrated local favorite. Protein-heavy vegetarian *plats.* Creative Middle Eastern cuisine. 3-course lunch *menu* €11. Open M-Sa noon-2:30pm and 7-10:30pm. MC/V. ❷

RIGHT BANK WEST

Ty Yann, 10 rue de Constantinople, 8*ème* (☎01 40 08 00 17). Ⓜ Europe. Breton chef and owner M. Yann cheerfully prepares outstanding *galettes* (€8-10) and crepes. Decorated with Yann's mother's pastoral paintings. Create your own crepe €6-7. Takeout 15% less. Open M-F noon-3:30pm and 7:30-10:30pm, Sa 7:30-10:30pm. MC/V. ❷

Chartier, 7 rue du Faubourg-Montmartre, 9*ème* (☎01 47 70 86 29; www.restaurant-chartier.com). Ⓜ Grands Boulevards. Parisian fixture since 1896; waitstaff still adds up the bill on each table's paper tablecloth. Enjoy *steak au poivre* (€8.50) and *langue de veau* (sheep's tongue; €9.80). Free Wi-Fi. Open daily 11:30am-10pm. AmEx/MC/V. ❷

La Fournée d'Augustine, 31 rue des Batignolles, 17*ème* (☎01 43 87 88 41). Ⓜ Rome. Lines out the door at lunch. Closet-sized patisserie bakes an absolutely fantastic baguette (€1). Fresh sandwiches (€3-4) range from light fare like goat cheese and cucumber to the more substantial grilled chicken and veggies. *Pain au chocolat* €1.10. Lunch *formule* €5.80-7. Open M-Sa 7:30am-8pm. AmEx/MC/V over €10. ❷

Chez Haynes, 3 rue Clauzel, 9*ème* (☎01 48 78 40 63). Ⓜ St-Georges. Paris's 1st African-American owned restaurant opened in 1949. Louis Armstrong, James Baldwin, and Richard Wright enjoyed the delicious New Orleans soul food. Ma Sutton's fried honey chicken €14. Sister Lena's BBQ spare ribs €16. Soul food Tu-Sa, Brazilian Su. Live music F-Sa nights; €5 cover. Open Tu-Su 7pm-midnight; hours vary. AmEx/MC/V. ❷

RIGHT BANK EAST

Ay, Caramba!, 59 rue de Mouzaïa, 19*ème* (☎01 42 41 23 80; http://restaurant-aycaramba.com). Ⓜ Pré-St-Gervais. Bright yellow Tex-Mex restaurant transforms chic Parisian dining into a home-grown fiesta. Patrons salsa to live latino singers F-Sa nights. Tacos

€18. Margaritas €7. Nachos rancheros €7. Open Su noon-3pm and 7:30pm-midnight, Tu-Th 7:30pm-midnight, F-Sa noon-3pm and 7:30pm-midnight. AmEx/MC/V. ❸

Le Bar à Soupes, 33 rue Charonne, 11*ème* (☎01 43 57 53 79; www.lebarasoupes.com). Ⓜ Bastille. Small, bright cafe. Big bowls of delicious, freshly-made soup (€5-6). 6 varieties change daily. €9.50 lunch *menu* is an astonishing deal; it comes with soup, a roll, wine or coffee, and cheese plate or dessert. Friendly staff will make your day. Gooey *gâteau chocolat* €4. Open M-Sa noon-3pm and 6:30-11pm. MC/V. ❷

SAVE YOUR WALLET, HAVE A PICNIC. As a major tourist attraction, Montmartre has inevitably high prices. Save a couple euro by avoiding its touristy cafes, and picnic in Paris. Buy a *croque monsieur* or ham sandwich *à emporter* and eat on the church's steps.

Le Cambodge, 10 av. Richerand, 10*ème* (☎01 44 84 37 70). Ⓜ République. Inexpensive and delicious Cambodian restaurant. Good vegetarian options. *Plats* €7-10. No reservations; wait up to 90min. M-Sa noon-2:30pm and 8-11:30pm. MC/V. ❷

L'Ébauchoir, 45 rue de Citeaux, 12*ème* (☎01 43 42 49 31; www.lebauchoir.com). Ⓜ Faidherbe-Chaligny. Funky, lively French restaurant. Daily-changing menu features delicious concoctions of seafood and meat. Vegetarian dishes upon request. Impressive wine list. Lunch *menu* €15. *Entrées* €8-15. *Plats* €17-25. Desserts €7. Open M 8-11pm and Tu-Sa noon-11pm. Kitchen open noon-2:30pm and 8-11pm. MC/V. ❸

Café de l'Industrie, 15-17 rue St-Sabin, 11*ème* (☎01 47 00 13 53). Ⓜ Breguet-Sabin. Happening cafe. Diverse menu. *Vin chaud* €4.50. Salads €8.50-9. Popular brunch platter (served Sa-Su; changes weekly) €12-15. Open daily 10am-2am. MC/V. ❷

Resto-Flash, 10 rue Lucien Sampaix, 10*ème* (☎01 42 45 03 30). Ⓜ Jacques Bonsergent. Kosher; regulated by the Beth-Din of Paris. Standards like *côte de veau* (€18) at slightly elevated prices. Open M-F 11:30am-3:30pm. MC/V. ❸

SALONS DU THÉ (TEA ROOMS)

Palais des Thés, 64 rue Vieille du Temple (☎01 48 87 80 60; www.palaisdesthes.com). Ⓜ St-Paul. Specialty shop sells over 200 organic teas (€8-135/100g) collected by the owners from 20 countries in Asia, Africa, and South America. Open M-Sa 10am-8pm. 4 other locations around the city. AmEx/MC/V. ❷

Ladurée, 16 rue Royale, 8*ème* (☎01 42 60 21 79; www.laduree.com). Ⓜ Concorde or FDR. Ever wanted to dine inside a Fabergé egg? Among the first Parisian *salons de thé.* Famous mini macaroons in 16 varieties €2. Boxes of *Chocolats Incomparables* from €18. Open M-Sa 8:30am-7pm and Su 10-7pm. Lunch served until 3pm. AmEx/MC/V. Also at 75 av. des Champs-Élysées, 8*ème* (☎01 40 75 08 75); 21 rue Bonaparte, 6*ème* (☎01 44 07 64 87); and 62 bd. Haussmann, 9*ème* (☎01 42 82 40 10). ❸

SPECIALTY SHOPS AND MARKETS

Food shops, particularly *boulangeries* (bakeries) and *pâtisseries* (pastry shops), are on virtually every street in Paris, or at least it seems like it. Your gustatory experiences, particularly when buying breads or pastries, will vary depending on how recently your food has left the oven.

La Bague de Kenza, 106 rue St-Maur, 11*ème* (☎01 43 14 93 15). Piles of creatively sweet Algerian pastries chock full of nuts, honey, and dried fruits (€1.50-2.20). Fruit-shaped marzipan €2.20. Algerian bread €2.10-3.50. Open M-Th and Sa-Su 9am-10pm, F 2-10pm. AmEx/MC/V over €16. Also at 173 rue du Faubourg St-Antoine, 11*ème*. ❶

Marché Monge, pl. Monge, 5*ème*. ⓂMonge. Busy but easy to navigate. Everything from cheese to jewelry and shoes in these stalls. Open W, F, and Su 8am-1pm. ❶

La Boulangerie par Véronique Mauclerc, 83 rue de Crimée, 19*ème* (☎01 42 40 64 55). ⓂLaumière. Bakes divine bread in 1 of France's 4 remaining wood-fire ovens. Organic ingredients. Paris's cheapest Su brunch (€11). Pastries, like amazing blueberry crumble, €3-4. Croissant €1.20. Open M and Th-Su 8am-8pm. MC/V over €15. ❷

Debauve et Gallais, 30 rue des Sts-Pères, 7*ème* (☎01 45 48 54 67; www.debauve-et-gallais.com). ⓂSt-Germaine des Prés or Sèvres-Babylone. Favorite of royals like Marie Antoinette. Chocolates produced without additives, dyes, or sweeteners. Open M-Sa 9:30am-7pm. Also at 33 rue Vivienne, 2*ème* (☎01 40 39 05 50). AmEx/MC/V. ❷

Marché Bastille, bd. Richard-Lenoir from pl. de la Bastille to rue St-Sabin., 11*ème*. ⓂBastille. Produce, cheese, mushrooms, bread, and meat. Popular Su morning outing. Open Th 7am-2:30pm, Su 7am-2:30pm. ❶

SIGHTS

While it would take weeks to see all of Paris's monuments, museums, and gardens, the city's small size makes sightseeing easy and enjoyable. In a few hours, you can walk from the Bastille in the east to the Eiffel Tower in the west, passing most major monuments along the way. A solid day of wandering will show you how close the medieval Notre Dame is to the modern Centre Pompidou and the funky *Latin Quarter* to the royal Louvre—the diversity of Paris is all the more amazing for the compact area in which it unfolds.

CITY CENTER

In the 3rd century BC, Paris consisted only of the **Île de la Cité,** inhabited by the Parisii, a Gallic tribe of merchants and fishermen. Today, all distance-points in France are measured from *kilomètre zéro*, a sundial in front of Notre Dame. On the far west side of the island is the **Pont Neuf** (New Bridge), actually Paris's oldest bridge—and now the city's most popular make-out spot. *(ⓂPont Neuf.)* To the east of Île de la Cité is the tiny **Île St-Louis. Rue St-Louis-en-l'Île** rolls down the center, and is a welcome distraction from busy Parisian life. There's a wealth of ice cream parlors, upscale shops, and boutique hotels, but not much to see. *(ⓂPont Marie.)* On the right bank, the **Marais** is home to some of Paris's best falafel (p. 318), museums, and bars, as well as much of Paris's Orthodox Jewish community. At the end of **rue des Francs-Bourgeois** sits the **place des Vosges,** Paris's oldest public square. Molière, Racine, and Voltaire filled the grand parlors with their *bon mots*, while Mozart played a concert here. Victor Hugo lived at no. 6, which is now a museum devoted to his life. *(ⓂChemin Vert or St-Paul.)*

CATHÉDRALE DE NOTRE DAME DE PARIS. This 12th- to 14th-century cathedral, begun under Bishop Maurice de Sully, is one of the world's most famous and beautiful examples of medieval architecture. After the Revolution, the building fell into disrepair—it was even used to shelter livestock—until Victor Hugo's 1831 novel *Notre Dame de Paris* (a.k.a. The Hunchback of Notre Dame) inspired citizens to lobby for the cathedral's restoration. The apocalyptic facade and seemingly weightless walls—effects produced by Gothic engineering and optical illusions—are inspiring even for the most church-weary. The cathedral's biggest draws are its enormous stained-glass rose windows that dominate the transept's northern and southern ends. A staircase inside the towers leads to a perch from which gargoyles survey the city. The best time to view the Cathedral is late at night, when you can see the full facade without mobs blocking the view. (*ⓂCité. ☎01 42 34 56 10; crypt ☎01 55 42 50 10; towers ☎01*

53 10 07 00. Cathedral open daily 7:45am-7pm. Towers open Jan.-Mar. and Oct.-Dec. 10am-5:30pm, Apr.-Sept. 10am-6:30pm; June-Aug. Sa-Su until 11pm. €8, ages 18-25 €5, under 18 free. In French M-F 2 and 3pm; call ☎ 01 44 54 19 30 for English, Russian, or Spanish tours. Free.)

STE-CHAPELLE, CONCIERGERIE, AND PALAIS DE JUSTICE. The Palais de la Cité contains three vastly different buildings. **Ste-Chapelle** remains the foremost example of flamboyant Gothic architecture and a tribute to the craft of medieval stained glass. On sunny days, light pours through the **Upper Chapel's** windows, illuminating frescoes of saints and martyrs. Around the corner is the Conciergerie, one of Paris's most famous prisons; Marie-Antoinette and Robespierre were incarcerated here during the Revolution. *(6 bd. du Palais, within Palais de la Cité. Ⓜ Cité. ☎ 01 53 40 60 97; www.monum.fr. Open daily Nov.-Feb. 9am-5pm and Mar.-Oct. 9:30am-6pm, last entry 30min. before closing. €8, seniors and ages 18-25 €5, under 18 free. Cash only.)* Built after the great fire of 1776, the **Palais de Justice** houses France's district courts. *(4 bd. du Palais, within the Palais de la Cité. Enter at 6 bd. du Palais. Ⓜ Cité. ☎ 01 44 32 51 51. Courtrooms open M-F 9am-noon and 1:30pm-end of last trial. Free.)*

MÉMORIAL DE LA DÉPORTATION. Commemorating the 200,000 French victims of Nazi concentration camps, the museum includes a tunnel lined with 200,000 quartz pebbles, honoring the Jewish custom of placing stones on graves. *(Ⓜ Cité. Open daily Apr.-Sept. 10am-noon and 2-7pm; Oct.-Mar. 10am-noon and 2-5pm. Free.)*

HÔTEL DE VILLE. Paris's grandiose city hall dominates a large square filled with fountains and Belle Époque lampposts. The present edifice is a 19th-century replica of the original medieval structure, a meeting hall for the cartel that controlled traffic on the Seine. *(Info office 29 rue de Rivoli. Ⓜ Hôtel de Ville. ☎ 01 42 76 43 43 or ☎ 42 76 50 49. Open M-F 9am-7pm when there is an exhibit; until 6pm otherwise.)*

LEFT BANK EAST

The Latin Quarter, named for the prestigious universities that taught in Latin until 1798, lives for its ever-vibrant student population. Since the student riots in May 1968, many artists and intellectuals have migrated to the cheaper outer *arrondissements*, and the haute bourgeoisie have moved in. The *5ème* still presents the most diverse array of bookstores, cinemas, and jazz clubs in the city. Shops and art galleries are found around **St-Germain-des-Prés** in the *6ème*. Farther east, the residential *13ème* doesn't have much to attract the typical tourist, but its diverse neighborhoods offer an authentic view of Parisian life.

JARDIN DU LUXEMBOURG. Parisian sunbathers flock to these formal gardens. The site of a medieval monastery, and later home to 17th-century French royalty, the gardens were liberated during the Revolution. *(6ème. Ⓜ Odéon or RER: Luxembourg. The main entrance is on bd. St-Michel. Open daily dawn-dusk.)*

ODÉON. The **Cour du Commerce St-André** is one of the most picturesque walking areas in the *6ème*, with cobblestone streets, centuries-old cafes (including Le Procope), and outdoor seating. Just south of bd. St-Germain, the Carrefour de l'Odéon, a favorite Parisian hangout, has more bistros and cafes. *(Ⓜ Odéon.)*

ÉGLISE ST-GERMAIN-DES-PRÉS. Paris's oldest standing church, **Église de St-Germain-des-Prés** was the centerpiece of the **Abbey of St-Germain-des-Prés,** the crux of Catholic intellectual life until it was disbanded during the Revolution. Worn away by fire and even a saltpetre explosion, the abbey's exterior looks appropriately world-weary. Its interior frescoes, redone in the 19th century, depict the life of Jesus in striking maroon, green, and gold. *(3 pl. St-Germain-des-Prés. Ⓜ St-Germain-des-Prés. ☎ 01 55 42 81 33. Open daily 8am-7:45pm. Info office open M 2:30-6:45pm, Tu-F 10:30am-noon and 2:30-6:45pm, Sa 3-6:45pm.)*

PLACE ST-MICHEL AND ENVIRONS. At the center of the Latin Quarter, bd. St-Michel, which divides the *5ème* and *6ème*, is filled with bookstores, boutiques, cafes, and restaurants. Tourists pack pl. St-Michel, where the 1871 Paris Commune and the 1968 student uprising began. You can find many traditional bistros on nearby r. Soufflot, the street connecting the Luxembourg Gardens to the Pantheon, and smaller restaurants on r. des Fossés St-Jacques. *(ⓂSt-Michel.)*

LA SORBONNE. The Sorbonne is one of Europe's oldest universities, founded in 1253 by Robert de Sorbon as a dormitory for 16 theology students. Nearby place de la Sorbonne, off bd. St-Michel, is flooded with cafes, bookstores, and during term-time, students. The **Chapelle de la Sorbonne,** which usually houses temporary exhibits on arts and letters, is undergoing renovations through 2009. *(45-47 r. des Écoles. ⓂCluny-La Sorbonne or RER: Luxembourg.)*

PANTHÉON. Though it looks like a religious monument, the Pantheon, occupying the Left Bank's highest point, celebrates France's great thinkers. The crypt houses the tombs of Marie and Pierre Curie, Victor Hugo, Jean Jaurès, Rousseau, Voltaire, and Émile Zola. On the main level, Foucault's Pendulum confirms the rotation of the earth. *(Pl. du Panthéon. ⓂCardinal Lemoine or RER: Luxembourg. ☎01 44 32 18 04. Open daily Apr.-Sept. 10am-6:30pm, Oct.-Mar. 10am-6pm. Last entry 45min. before closing. Crypt open daily 10am-6pm. €7.50, ages 18-25 €4.80, under 18 and 1st Su of the month Oct.-Mar. free. MC/V. Conservative dress required.)*

RUE MOUFFETARD. South of pl. de la Contrescarpe, r. Mouffetard plays host to one of Paris's busiest street markets, drawing a mix of Parisians and visitors. The stretch of r. Mouffetard past pl. de la Contrescarpe and onto r. Descartes and r. de la Montagne Ste-Geneviève is the quintessential Latin Quarter stroll. *(ⓂCardinal Lemoine, Pl. Monge, or Censier Daubenton.)*

JARDIN DES PLANTES. Opened in 1640 to grow medicinal plants for King Louis XIII, the garden now features science museums, rosaries, and a zoo, which Parisians raided for food during the Prussian siege of 1871. *(ⓂGare d'Austerlitz, Jussieu, or Censier-Daubenton. ☎01 40 79 37 94; www.mnhn.fr. Jardin des Plantes and Roserie open daily in summer 7:30am-7:45pm, in winter 7:30am-7:30pm. Free. Ménagerie Zoo, 3 quai St-Bernard and 57 rue Cuvier. Open Apr.-Sept. M-Sa 9am-6pm, Su and holidays 9am-6:30pm; Oct.-Mar. daily 10am-5pm. €7, students and ages 4-13 €5.)*

BIBLIOTHÈQUE NATIONALE DE FRANCE: SITE FRANÇOIS MITTERRAND. The complex that many Parisians refer to as "the ugliest building ever built" is the result of the last and most expensive of Mitterrand's Grands Projets. Its rotating art, literary, and photography exhibits are a welcome break from the city center's packed sights. *(Quai François Mauriac. ⓂQuai de la Gare or Bibliothèque François Mitterrand. ☎01 53 79 59 59; www.bnf.fr. Upper study library open Tu-Sa 10am-8pm, Su 1-7pm. Lower research library open M 2-8pm, Tu-Sa 9am-8pm, Su 1-7pm; closed 2 weeks in Sept. Ages 16+. €3.30. 15-day pass €20. Annual membership €35, students €18.)*

QUARTIER DE LA BUTTE-AUX-CAILLES. Historically a working-class neighborhood, the old-fashioned Butte-aux-Cailles (Quail Knoll) Quarter now attracts trend-setters, artists, and intellectuals. Funky new restaurants and galleries have cropped up in recent years. Rue de la Butte-aux-Cailles and rue des Cinq Diamants share duties as the *quartier's* main drags. *(ⓂCorvisart. Exit onto bd. Blanqui and turn onto r. Barrault, which will meet r. de la Butte-aux-Cailles.)*

LEFT BANK WEST

EIFFEL TOWER. Gustave Eiffel wrote of his tower: "France is the only country in the world with a 300m flagpole." Designed in 1889 as the tallest structure in the world, the Eiffel Tower was conceived as a modern monument to engineering that would surpass the Egyptian pyramids in size and notoriety. Critics dubbed it a "metal asparagus" and a "Parisian tower of Babel." Writer Guy de Maupassant ate lunch every day at its ground-floor restaurant—the only place in Paris, he claimed, from which he couldn't see the offensive thing. Nevertheless, when it was inaugurated in March 1889 as the centerpiece of the World's Fair, the tower earned Parisians' love: nearly two million people ascended it during the fair. Some still criticize its glut of tourists, trinkets, and vagrants, but don't believe the anti-hype—the tower is worth seeing. *(Ⓜ Bir-Hakeim or Trocadéro. ☎ 01 44 11 23 23; www.tour-eiffel.fr. Open daily from Jan. to mid-June and Sept.-Dec., elevator 9:30am-11:45pm (last access 11pm), stairs 9:30am-6:30pm (last access 6pm); from mid-June to Aug., elevator 9am-12:45am (last access 11pm), stairs 9am-12:45am (last access midnight). Elevator to 1st fl. €5, under 12 €2.50, under 3 free; 2nd fl. €8/4.50/free; summit €12/7/free. Stairs to 1st and 2nd fl. €4, under 25 €3, under 3 free.)*

PARC ANDRÉ CITROËN. The futuristic Parc André Citroën was created by landscapers Alain Provost and Gilles Clément in the 1990s. Hot-air balloon rides offer spectacular aerial views of Paris. *(Ⓜ Javel or Balard. ☎ 01 44 26 20 00; www.aeroparis.com. Open in summer M-F 8am-9:30pm, Sa-Su 9am-9:30pm; in winter M-F 8am-5:45pm, Sa-Su 9am-5:45pm. Guided tours leave from the Jardin Noir; €3-6.)*

INVALIDES. The gold-leaf dome of the **Hôtel des Invalides,** built by Napoleon as a hospital for crippled and ill soldiers, shines at the center of the *7ème*. The grassy **Esplanade des Invalides** runs from the hôtel to the Pont Alexandre III, a bridge with gilded lampposts from which you can catch a great view of the Invalides and the Seine. Both housed inside the Invalides complex, the **Musée de l'Armée** and **Musée de l'Ordre de la Libération,** documenting the Free France movement under General de Gaulle, are worth a look; the real star, however, is the **Musée des Plans-Reliefs,** which features dozens of enormous, detailed models of French fortresses and towns, all made around 1700. Napoleon's tomb is also here, resting in the Église St-Louis. *(127 r. de Grenelle. Ⓜ Invalides. Enter from either pl. des Invalides or pl. Vauban and av. de Tourville.)*

CATACOMBS. Originally excavated to provide stone for building Paris, the Catacombs were converted into a mass grave in 1785 when the stench of the city's public cemeteries became unbearable. Paris's "municipal ossuary" now has dozens of winding tunnels and hundreds of thousands of bones. *(1 av. du Colonel Henri Roi-Tanguy. Ⓜ Denfert-Rochereau; exit near Ⓜ Mouton Duvernet. ☎ 01 43 22 47 63. Open Tu-Su 10am-4pm. €7, over 60 €5.50, age 14-26 €3.50, under 14 free.)*

BOULEVARD DU MONTPARNASSE. In the early 20th century, avant-garde artists like Chagall, Duchamp, Léger, and Modigliani moved to Montparnasse. Soviet exiles Lenin and Trotsky talked strategy over cognac in cafes like Le Dôme, Le Sélect, and La Coupole. After WWI, Montparnasse attracted American expats like Calder, Hemingway, and Henry Miller. Chain restaurants and tourists crowd the now heavily commercialized street. Classic cafes like pricey La Coupole still hold their own, however, providing a wonderful place to sip coffee, read Apollinaire, and daydream away. *(Ⓜ Montparnasse-Bienvenüe or Vavin.)*

CHAMPS DE MARS. The Champs de Mars, an expanse stretching from the École Militaire to the Eiffel Tower, is named, appropriately enough, after the Roman god of war. Close to the *7ème*'s museums, the field was a drill ground for the École Militaire during Napoleon's reign. Today, despite frolicking children and a monument to international peace, the Champs can't quite hold a candle to Paris's many spectacular public parks and gardens. *(Ⓜ La Motte Picquet-Grenelle or École Militaire. From the av. de la Motte-Picquet, walk toward École Militaire.)*

RIGHT BANK WEST

ARC DE TRIOMPHE. Napoleon commissioned the Arc, at the western end of the Champs-Élysées, in 1806 to honor his Grande Armée. In 1940, Parisians were brought to tears by the sight of Nazis goose-stepping through the Arc. At the end of the German occupation, a sympathetic Allied army made sure that a French general would be the first to drive under the arch. The terrace at the top has a fabulous view. The **Tomb of the Unknown Soldier** has been under the Arc since November 11, 1920, and an eternal flame has been burning since 1921. *(Ⓜ Charles de Gaulle-Étoile. Open daily Apr.-Sept. 10am-11pm; Oct.-Mar. 10am-10:30pm. Last entry 30min. before closing. Wheelchair-accessible. €9, ages 18-25 €5.50, under 17 free.)*

LA DÉFENSE. Outside the city limits, west of the 16*ème*, the skyscrapers and modern architecture of La Défense make up Paris's newest (unofficial) *arrondissement*, a playground for many of Paris's biggest corporations. Its centerpiece is hard to miss: the Grande Arche de la Défense stretches 35 stories into the air and is shaped like a hollow cube. The roof of this unconventional office covers one hectare—Notre Dame could fit in its concave core. *(Ⓜ/RER La Défense or bus #73. If you take the RER, buy your ticket before going through the turnstile. Grande Arche open daily 10am-7pm; last ascent 6:30pm. €7.50; under 18, students, and seniors €6.)*

OPÉRA GARNIER. The exterior of the Opéra Garnier—with its newly restored multi-colored marble facade, sculpted golden goddesses, and ornate columns and friezes—is as impressive as it is kitschy. It's no wonder that Oscar Wilde once swore he saw an angel floating on the sidewalk. Inside, Chagall's whimsical ceiling design contrasts with the gold and red that dominate the theater. For shows, see **Entertainment,** p. 329. *(Ⓜ Opéra. ☎08 92 89 90 90; www.operadeparis.fr. Concert hall and museum open daily 10am-5pm. Last entry 30min. before closing. Concert hall closed during rehearsals; call ahead. €8, students and under 25 €4, under 10 free.)*

PLACE DE LA CONCORDE. Paris's most infamous public square, built between 1757 and 1777, is the eastern terminus of the Champs-Élysées at its intersection with the Jardin des Tuileries. During the Revolution and Reign of Terror, the area became known as the *place de la Révolution*, site of the guillotine that severed the heads of 1343 aristocrats, including Louis XVI, Marie Antoinette, and Robespierre. In 1830, the square was optimistically renamed *concorde* (peace) and the 3200-year-old Obélisque de Luxor, given to Charles X by the Viceroy of Egypt, replaced the guillotine. *(Ⓜ Concorde.)*

AVENUE DES CHAMPS-ÉLYSÉES. Extending from the Louvre, Paris's most famous thoroughfare was a piecemeal project begun under the reign of Louis XIV. The center of Parisian opulence in the early 20th century, with flashy mansions towering above exclusive cafes, the Champs has since undergone a bizarre kind of democratization. Shops along the avenue now range from designer fashion to cheap trinkets. While it may be an inelegant spectacle, the Champs offers some of the city's best people-watching—tourists, wealthy bar-hoppers, and even authentic Parisians crowd its broad sidewalks. *(Ⓜ Charles de Gaulle-Étoile. Runs from the pl. Charles de Gaulle-Étoile southeast to the pl. de la Concorde.)*

BOIS DE BOULOGNE. By day, this 2000-acre park, with several gardens and two lakes, is a popular picnicking, jogging, and bike-riding spot. By night, the *bois* becomes a bazaar of crime, drugs, and prostitution. *(On the western edge of the 16ème. Ⓜ Porte Maillot, Sablons, Pont de Neuilly, or Porte Dauphine or Porte d'Auteil.)*

RIGHT BANK EAST

CIMITIÈRE PÈRE LACHAISE. This cemetery holds the remains of such famous Frenchmen as Balzac, Bernhardt, Colette, David, Delacroix, Piaf, La Fontaine, Haussmann, Molière, Proust, and Seurat within its peaceful paths and elaborate sarcophagi. Foreigners buried here include Chopin, Modigliani, Gertrude Stein, and Oscar Wilde, though the most frequently visited grave is that of Jim Morrison. French Leftists make a ceremonial pilgrimage to the **Mur des Fédérés** (Wall of the Federals), where 147 *communards* were executed in 1871. *(16 rue du Repo. Ⓜ Père Lachaise. ☎ 01 55 25 82 10. Open from mid-Mar. to early Nov. M-F 8am-6pm, Sa 8:30am-6pm, Su and holidays 9am-6pm; from Nov. to mid-Mar. M-F 8am-5:30pm, Sa 8:30am-5:30pm, Su and holidays 9am-5:30pm. Free.)*

BASILIQUE DU SACRÉ-COEUR. This ethereal basilica, with its signature shining white onion domes, was commissioned to atone for France's war crimes in the Franco-Prussian War. During WWII, 13 bombs were dropped on Paris, all near the structure, but miraculously no one was killed. *(35 rue du Chevalier-de-la-Barre. Ⓜ Anvers, Abbesses, or Château-Rouge. ☎ 01 53 41 89 00; www.sacre-coeur-montmartre.fr. Basilica open daily 6am-11pm. Dome open daily 9am-6pm. Basilica free. Dome €5.)*

PLACE DE LA BASTILLE. This intersection was once home to the famous **Bastille Prison,** stormed on July 14, 1789, sparking the French Revolution. Two days later, the National Assembly ordered the prison demolished, but the ground plan of the prison's turrets remains embedded in the road near r. St-Antoine. At the center of the square is a monument of the winged Mercury holding a torch of freedom, symbolizing the movement towards democracy. *(Ⓜ Bastille.)*

OPÉRA DE LA BASTILLE. One of Mitterrand's Grands Projets, the Opéra opened in 1989 to loud protests over its unattractive design. It has been described as a huge toilet because of its resemblance to the city's coin-operated *pissoirs*. The opera has not struck a completely sour note, though; it has helped renew local interest in the arts. The guided tour offers a behind-the-scenes view of the world's largest theater. *(130 rue de Lyon. Ⓜ Bastille. ☎ 01 40 01 19 70; www.operadeparis. 1hr. tour almost every day, usually at 1 or 5pm; call ahead for schedule. €11, over 60 and students €9, under 18 €6. Open M-Sa 10:30am-6:30pm.)*

BAL DU MOULIN ROUGE. Along bd. de Clichy and bd. de Rochechouart, you'll find many Belle Époque cabarets, including the Bal du Moulin Rouge, immortalized by Toulouse-Lautrec's paintings, Offenbach's music, and Baz Luhrmann's 2001 blockbuster. The crowd consists of tourists out for an evening of sequins, tassels, and skin. The revues are still risqué, but the real shock is the price of admission. *(82 bd. de Clichy. Ⓜ Blanche. ☎ 01 53 09 82 82; www.moulin-rouge.com.)*

PARC DES BUTTES-CHAUMONT. In the south of the *19ème*, Parc des Buttes-Chaumont is a mix of manmade topography and transplanted vegetation; previously a lime quarry and gallows, Napoleon III commissioned Baron Haussman to redesign the space in 1862. Today's visitors walk the winding paths surrounded by lush greenery and dynamic hills, enjoying a great view of the *quartier* from the Roman temple atop cave-filled cliffs. *(Ⓜ Buttes-Chaumont or Botzaris. Open daily May-Sept. 7am-10:15pm; Oct.-Apr. 7am-8:15pm; some gates close early.)*

PARC DE LA VILLETTE. Previously a meatpacking district, La Villette is the product of a successful urban renewal project. Inaugurated by President Mitterrand in 1985 as "the place of intelligent leisure," it now contains museums, libraries, and concert halls in the Cité des Sciences and the Cité de la Musique. Every July and August, La Villette holds a free open-air film festival. The Zénith concert hall hosts major rock bands, and the **Trabendo** jazz and modern music club holds an extraordinarily popular annual jazz festival. *(211 av. Jean Jaurès. Ⓜ Porte de Pantin. General info ☎01 40 03 75 75, Trabendo 42 01 12 12, Zénith 42 08 60 00; www.villette.com. Info office open M-Sa 9:30am-6:30pm. Free.)*

MUSEUMS

No visitor should miss Paris's museums, which are universally considered to be among the world's best. Cost-effective for visiting more than three museums or sights daily, the **Carte Musées et Monuments** offers admission to 65 museums in greater Paris. It is available at major museums, tourist office kiosks, and many Métro stations. A pass for one day is €15, for three days €30, for five days €45. Students with art or art history ID can get into art museums free. Most museums, including the Musée d'Orsay, are closed on Mondays.

MUSÉE D'ORSAY. If only the *Académiciens* who turned the Impressionists away from the Louvre could see the Musée d'Orsay. Now considered masterpieces, these "rejects" are well worth the pilgrimage to this mecca of modernity. The collection, installed in a former railway station, includes painting, sculpture, decorative arts, and photography from 1848 until WWI. On the ground floor, Classical and Proto-Impressionist works are on display, including Manet's *Olympia*, a painting that caused scandal when it was unveiled in 1865. Other highlights include Monet's *Poppies*, Renoir's *Bal au moulin de la Galette*, Dégas's *La classe de danse*, and paintings by Cézanne, Gauguin, Seurat, and Van Gogh. The top floor offers one of the most comprehensive collections of Impressionist and Post-Impressionist art in the world. In addition, the exterior and interior balconies offer supreme views of the Seine and the jungle of sculptures below. Don't miss Rodin's imperious *Honoré de Balzac*. *(62 rue de Lille. Ⓜ Solférino or RER Musée d'Orsay. Access to visitors at entrance A of the square off 1 rue de la Légion d'Honneur. ☎01 40 49 48 14; www.musee-orsay.fr. Wheelchair-accessible; call ☎01 40 49 47 14 for info. Audioguides (2hr.; €5), available in English and other languages. Open Tu-W and F-Sa 9:30am-6pm (last ticket sales 5pm), Th 10am-9:45pm (last ticket sales 9:15pm); June 20-Sept. 20 Su 9am-6pm. €7.50, ages 18-25 €5, under 18 free; Su and after 4:15pm (after 8pm on Th) €5.50. 1hr. English-language tours usually Tu-Sa 11:30am and 2:30pm; call ahead to confirm. €6.50/5. Bookstore open Tu-Su 9:30am-6:30pm, Th until 9:30pm.)*

CROWDLESS CULTURE. Orsay's undeniably amazing collection draws massive crowds, marring an otherwise enjoyable museum. A Sunday morning or Thursday evening visit will avoid the tourist throngs.

FRANCE

MUSÉE DU LOUVRE. No visitor has ever allotted enough time to thoughtfully ponder every display at the Louvre, namely because it would take weeks to read every caption of the over 30,000 items in the museum. Its masterpieces include Hammurabi's Code, Jacques-Louis David's *The Oath of the Horatii* and *The Coronation of Napoleon*, Delacroix's *Liberty Leading the People*, Vermeer's *Lacemaker*, Leonardo da Vinci's *Mona Lisa*, the classically sculpted *Winged Victory of Samothrace*, and the *Venus de Milo*. Enter through I. M. Pei's stunning glass Pyramid in the Cour Napoléon, or skip the line by entering directly from the Métro. The Louvre is organized into three different wings: Denon, Richelieu, and Sully. Each is divided according to the artwork's date, national origin, and medium. *(Ⓜ Palais-Royal-Musée du Louvre. ☎01 40 20 53 17; www.louvre.fr. Open M, Th, and Sa 9am-6pm, W and F 9am-10pm. Last entry 45min. before closing; closure of rooms begins 30min. before closing. €9; W and F after 6pm €6; unemployed, under 18, and F after 6pm under 26 free; 1st Su of the month free.)*

CENTRE POMPIDOU. This inside-out building has inspired debate since its 1977 opening. Whatever its aesthetic merits, the exterior's chaotic colored piping provides an appropriate shell for the Cubist, Conceptual, Fauvist, and Pop works inside. The **Musée National d'Art Moderne** is the Centre Pompidou's main attraction. *(Pl. Georges-Pompidou. Ⓜ Rambuteau, Hôtel de Ville, or RER Châtelet-Les Halles. ☎ 01 44 78 12 33; www.centrepompidou.fr. Centre open M and W-Su 11am-10pm; museum open M, W, and F-Su 11am-9pm; Th 11am-11pm; last ticket sales 1 hr. before closing. €12, under 26 €9, under 18 free; 1st Su of the month free.)*

MUSÉE RODIN. The 18th-century Hôtel Biron holds hundreds of sculptures by Auguste Rodin, including the *The Thinker, Bourgeois de Calais*, and *La Porte d'Enfer*. Bring a book and relax amid the gracious gestures of bending flowers and flexing sculptures. *(79 rue de Varenne. Ⓜ Varenne. ☎ 01 44 18 61 10; www.musee-rodin.fr. Open Tu-Su Apr.-Sept. 9:30am-5:45pm; Oct.-Mar. 9:30am-4:45pm; last entry 30min. before closing. Gardens open Tu-Su Apr.-Sept. 9:30am-6:45pm Oct.-Mar. 9:30am-5pm. Café open Apr.-Sept. 9:30am- 5:30pm; Oct.-Mar. 9:30am-4:30pm. €6, seniors and ages 18-25 €4; special exhibits €7/5; 1st Su of the month and for under 18 free.)*

MUSÉE JACQUEMART-ANDRÉ. The 19th-century mansion of Nélie Jacquemart and her husband contains a world-class collection of Renaissance art, including *Madonna and Child* by Botticelli and *St. George and the Dragon* by Ucello. *(158 bd. Haussmann. ☎ 01 45 62 11 59. Ⓜ Miromesnil. Open daily 10am-6pm. Last entry 30min. before closing. €10, students and ages 7-17 €7.30, under 7 free. 1 free child ticket per 3 purchased tickets. English headsets included.)*

MUSÉE DE CLUNY. The Musée de Cluny, housed in a monastery built atop Roman baths, holds one of the world's finest collections of medieval art. Works include **La Dame et La Licorne** (The Lady and the Unicorn), a striking 15th-century tapestry series. *(6 pl. Paul-Painlevé. Ⓜ Cluny-La Sorbonne. Info ☎ 01 53 73 78 00, reception 53 73 78 16. Open M and W-Su 9:15am-5:45pm; last entry at 5:15pm. Closed Jan. 1, May 1, and Dec. 25. Temporarily free; prices TBD.)*

EXPLORA SCIENCE MUSEUM. Dedicated to bringing science to young people, the Explora Science Museum is the star attraction of La Villette, in the complex's Cité des Sciences et de l'Industrie. The building's futuristic architecture only hints at the close to 300 exhibits inside. *(30 av. Corentin-Cariou. Ⓜ Porte de la Villette. ☎ 01 40 05 80 00; www.cite-sciences.fr. Museum open Tu-Sa 10am-6pm, Su 10am-7pm. Last entry 30min. before closing. €8, under 25 or families of 5 or more €6, under 7 free.)*

MUSÉE CARNAVALET. Housed in Mme. de Sévigné's 16th-century *hôtel particulier*, this museum presents room after room of historical objects and curiosities from Paris's origins through the present day. *(23 rue de Sévigné. ☎ 01 44 59 58 58; www.paris.fr/musees/musee_carnavalet. Ⓜ Chemin Vert. Open Tu-Su 10am-6pm; last entry 5pm. Free. Special exhibits €7, under 26 €4, seniors €6, under 14 free.)*

MAISON DE BALZAC. Honoré de Balzac hid from bill collectors in this three-story hillside mansion, his home from 1840-1847. Here in this tranquil retreat, he wrote a substantial part of *La Comédie Humaine;* today's visitors can see his original manuscripts, along with his beautifully embroidered chair and desk at which he purportedly wrote and edited for 17hr. a day. *(47 rue Raynouard. Ⓜ Passy. ☎ 01 55 74 41 80; www.paris.fr/musees/balzac. Open Tu-Su 10am-6pm. Last entry 30min. before closing. Permanent collection free. Guided tours and temporary exhibits €4, families and seniors €3, students under 26 €2, under 12 free.)*

MUSÉE PICASSO. When Picasso died in 1973, his family paid the French inheritance tax in artwork. The French government put this collection, which includes work from his Cubist, Surrealist, and Neoclassical years, on display in

1985 in the 17th-century Hôtel Salé. *(30 av. Corentin-Cariou. Ⓜ Porte de la Villette. ☎ 01 40 05 80 00; www.cite-sciences.fr. Museum open Tu-Sa 10am-6pm, Su 10am-7pm. Last entry 30min. before closing. €8, under 25 or families of 5 or more €6, under 7 free.)*

INSTITUT DU MONDE ARABE (IMA). Housing 3rd- through 18th-century Arabesque art, the IMA building was designed to look like the ships that carried North African immigrants to France. Its southern face is comprised of **240 mechanized portals** which automatically open and close depending on how much light is needed to illuminate the interior. *(1 rue des Fossés St-Bernard. Ⓜ Jussieu. ☎ 01 40 51 38 38; www.imarabe.org. Museum open Tu-Su 10am-6pm. Closed May 1. €4, under 26 €3, under 12 free. Library open Sept.-June Tu-Sa 1-8pm; July-Aug. Tu-Sa 1-6pm. Free.)*

PALAIS DE TOKYO. Recently refurbished, this large warehouse contains the site *création contemporaine*, exhibiting today's hottest (and most controversial) art, as well as the **Musée d'Art Moderne de la Ville de Paris.** The museum's unrushed atmosphere and spacious architecture provide a welcome relief from the maelstrom of the Louvre and Musée d'Orsay. *(Palais de Tokyo, 11 av. du Président Wilson, 16ème. Ⓜ Iéna. ☎ 01 53 67 40 00; www.mam.paris.fr. Open Tu-Su 10am-6pm, last entrance 5:45pm. Permanent exhibitions free. Special exhibits €4.50-9; large families, seniors, under 27 €3-6; under 13 free.)* The **Palais** is outfitted to host prominent avant-garde sculptures, video displays, and multimedia installations. Exhibits change every two or three months; be on the lookout for each exhibit's *vernissage* (premiere party) for free entrance and refreshments. *(11 av. du Président Wilson. ☎ 01 47 23 54 01; www.palaisdetokyo.com. Ⓜ Iéna. Open Tu-Su noon-midnight. €6; seniors, under 25, and groups of 10 or more €4.50; artists and art students €1.)*

MUSÉE D'HISTOIRE NATURELLE. The Jardin des Plantes is home to the three-part Natural History museum, comprised of the modern **Grande Galerie de l'Évolution,** the **Musée de Minéralogie,** and the ghastly **Galeries de Paléontologie et d'Anatomie Comparée.** *(57 rue Cuvier, in the Jardin des Plantes. Ⓜ Gare d'Austerlitz or Jussieu. ☎ 01 40 79 30 00; www.mnhn.fr. Grande Galerie de l'Évolution open M and W-Su 10am-6pm. €8, age 4-13 and students under 26 €6. Musée de Minéralogie open Nov.-Mar. M and W-Su 10am-5pm; Apr.-Oct. M and W-F 10am-5pm, Sa-Su 10am-6pm. €7, students under 26 €5. Galéries d'Anatomie Comparée et de Paléontologie open Nov.-Mar. M and W-Su 10am-5pm; Apr.-Oct. M and W-F 10am-5pm, Sa-Su 10am-6pm. €6, students €4, under 4 free.)*

ENTERTAINMENT

Pick up one of the weekly bibles of Parisian entertainment, *Pariscope* (€0.40) and *Figaroscope* (€1), at any newsstand or *tabac*. *Pariscope* includes an English-language section. For concert listings, check the free magazine *Paris Selection*, available at tourist offices. Free concerts are often held in churches and parks, especially during summer festivals. They are extremely popular, so plan to arrive early. **FNAC** stores sell concert tickets.

OPERA AND THEATER

La Comédie Française, pl. Collette, 1er (☎ 08 25 10 16 80 or 44 58 14 00; www.comedie-francaise.fr). Ⓜ Palais-Royal. Founded by Molière; the granddaddy of all French theaters. Generally, you don't need to speak French to understand the jokes. Box office open daily 11am-6pm and 1hr. before shows. Tickets €11-35.

Opéra Comique, 5 rue Favart, 2ème (☎ 01 42 44 45 46 or 08 25 01 01 23; www.opera-comique.com). Ⓜ Richelieu-Drouot. Operas on a lighter scale. €6-95. MC/V.

Opéra Garnier, pl. de l'Opéra, 9*ème* (☎08 92 89 90 90; www.operadeparis.fr). Ⓜ Opéra. Mostly ballet, chamber music, and symphonies. Tickets usually available 2 weeks ahead. Box office open M-Sa 10:30am-6:30pm. Operas €7-160, ballets €6-80. AmEx/MC/V.

Opéra de la Bastille, pl. de la Bastille, 12*ème* (☎08 92 89 90 90; www.operadeparis.fr). Ⓜ Bastille. Opera and ballet with a modern spin. Subtitles in French. Check website for the season's events. Tickets can be purchased by Internet, mail, phone (M-Th 9am-6pm, Sa 9am-1pm), or in person (M-Sa 10:30am-6:30pm). Rush tickets 15min. before show for students under 25 and seniors. €7-196. AmEx/MC/V.

JAZZ AND CABARET

Au Duc des Lombards, 42 rue des Lombards (☎01 42 33 22 88; www.ducdeslombards.com). Ⓜ Châtelet. Murals of Ellington and Coltrane cover the exterior of this premier jazz joint. Still the best in French jazz. 3 sets each night Cover €19-25, students €12 if you call in advance. Couples €30 in advance. Beer €3.50-5. Mixed drinks €8; prices vary depending on show. Music 10pm-1:30am. Open M-Sa 5pm-2am. MC/V.

Le Baiser Salé, 58 rue des Lombards (☎01 42 33 37 71; www.lebaisersale.com). Ⓜ Châtelet. Cuban, African, and Antillean music featured together with modern jazz and funk in a welcoming, mellow space. African music festival in July. Jazz concerts start at 10pm, music until 2:30am (typically 3 sets). Cover around €20. Free M jam sessions at 10pm with 1-drink min. Beer €6.50-11.50. Mixed drinks €9.50; prices vary depending on show. Happy hour 5:30-8pm. Open daily 5pm-6am. AmEx/MC/V.

Bal du Moulin Rouge, 82 bd. de Clichy, 9*ème* (☎01 53 09 82 82; www.moulin-rouge.com). Ⓜ Blanche. World-famous cabaret. Reviews remain risqué. The late show may be cheaper, but can be crowded. Elegant attire required. Shows nightly 9, 11pm. Ticket for 9pm show €99, 11pm show €89; includes half-bottle of champagne. 7pm dinner and 9pm show €145-175. Occasional lunch shows €95-125; call for more info. MC/V.

SHOPPING

In a city where Hermès scarves serve as slings for broken arms and department store history stretches back to the mid-19th century, shopping is nothing less than an art form. Consumerism is as diverse as the citizens are, from the wild club wear sold near **rue Étienne-Marcel** to the off-the-beaten path boutiques in the **18ème** or the **Marais.** The great *soldes* (sales) of the year begin after New Year's and at the very end of June, with the best prices at the beginning of February and the end of July. If at any time of year you see the word *braderie* (clearance sale) in a store window, enter without hesitation.

A true gem, **Gabrielle Geppert,** 31-34 Galerie Montpensier, 1*er*, is a favorite of Sharon Stone. Find an assort of gold leather and snakeskin bags, rhine-studded sunglasses in all colors, fur purses, enormous necklaces and earrings—all by vintage designers: Chanel, Louis Vuitton, Prada, and Gucci. (☎01 42 61 53 52; www.gabriellegeppert.com. Ⓜ Palais-Royale. Open M-Sa 10am-7:30pm. MC/V.) **Abbey Bookshop,** 29 rue de la Parcheminerie, 5*ème*, is a laid-back shop overflows with new and used English-language titles, as well as Canadian pride courtesy of expat owner Brian. There's an impressive basement collection of anthropology, sociology, history, music, motherhood, and literary criticism titles. They're also happy to take special orders. (☎01 46 33 16 24; www.abbeybookshop.net. Ⓜ St-Michel or Cluny. Open M-Sa 10am-7pm, sometimes later.)

Paris's department stores are as much sights as they are shopping destination, especially in December, when the stores go all out to decorate their windows. **Galeries Lafayette,** 40 bd. Haussmann, 9*ème*, can be chaotic but carries it all. (☎01 42 82 34 56; www.galerieslafayette.com. Ⓜ Chaussée d'Antin-

Lafayette or Havre-Caumartin. Open M-W and F-Sa 9:30am-7:30pm, Th 9:30am-9pm. AmEx/V.) **Au Bon Marché,** 24, rue de Sèvres, *7ème*, is Paris's oldest, most exclusive, and most expensive, with items ranging from scarves to smoking accessories, *haute couture* to home furnishings. Across the street is **La Grande Épicerie de Paris** (38 rue de Sèvres), the celebrated gourmet food annex. (☎01 44 39 80 00. ⓂSèvres-Babylone. Store open M-W and F 9:30am-7pm, Th 10am-9pm, Sa 9:30am-8pm. *Épicerie* open M-Sa 8:30am-9pm. AmEx/MC/V.)

NIGHTLIFE

In the *5ème* and *6ème*, bars draw students, while Paris's young and hip, queer and straight swarm the **Marais,** the center of Paris's GLBT life. Great neighborhood spots are springing up in the Left Bank's outlying areas, particularly in the *13ème* and *14ème*. A slightly older crowd congregates around **Les Halles,** while the outer *arrondissements* cater to locals. The **Bastille,** another central party area, is more suited to pounding shots than sipping Bordeaux.

Clubbing in Paris is less about hip DJs' beats than about dressing up and getting in. Drinks are expensive, and clubbers consume little beyond the first round. Many clubs accept reservations, so come early to assure entry on busy nights. Bouncers like tourists because they generally spend more money, so speaking English might actually give you an edge. Clubs heat up between 2 and 4am. Tune in to Radio FG (98.2 FM) or Radio Nova (101.5 FM) to find out about upcoming events. Parisian GLBT life centers around the **Marais,** comprised of the *3ème* and *4ème*. Numerous bars and clubs line **rue du Temple, rue Ste-Croix de la Bretonnerie, rue des Archives,** and **rue Vieille du Temple,** while the *3ème* boasts a lively lesbian scene. For the most comprehensive listing of organizations, consult *Illico* (free at GLBT bars and restaurants) or Zurban's annual *Paris Gay and Lesbian Guide* (€5 at any kiosk).

buddha-bar, 8 rue Boissy d'Anglas, *8ème* (☎01 53 05 90 00; www.buddha-bar.com). ⓂMadeleine or Concorde. Too cool for capital letters. Perhaps the most glamorous and exclusive drinking hole in the city; Madonna drops by when she's in town. 2 dim, candlelit levels. 3-story Buddha. Creative mixed drinks €16-17. Beer €8-9. Sake €8. Wine €8-11. Open M-F noon-3pm and 6pm-2am, Sa-Su 6pm-2am. AmEx/MC/V.

Le Club des Poètes, 30 rue de Bourgogne, *7ème* (☎01 47 05 06 03; www.poesie.net). ⓂVarenne. Old-style and timbered. Restaurant by day, poetry club from 9-10pm each night. A troupe of readers and comedians bewitch the audience with poetry from Villon, Baudelaire, Rimbaud, and others. If you arrive after 10pm, wait to enter until you hear clapping or a break in the performance. Lunch *menu* €15. Wine €4-8. Open Sept.-July. Tu-Sa noon-3pm and 8pm-1am. Kitchen open until 10pm. MC/V.

Café Flèche d'Or, 102 bis rue Bagnolet, *20ème* (☎01 44 64 01 02; www.flechedor.fr). ⓂPorte de Bagnolet. Live concert venue. Cool, intense, and a little rough around the edges. Music ranges from reggae to hip-hop to electro pop to Celtic rock. DJ set Th-Sa midnight-6am. Free entry for concerts 8pm-2am. Beer €4-6. Mixed drinks €8-20. Open W-Sa 10am-3am, Th-Sa 10am-6am. MC/V.

Le 10 Bar, 10 rue de l'Odéon, *6ème* (☎01 43 26 66 83). ⓂOdéon. A classic student hangout where Parisian youth indulge in philosophical and political discussion. Either that or they're getting drunk and making inside jokes. Spiced sangria €3.50. Jukebox plays everything from Edith Piaf to Aretha Franklin. Open daily 6pm-2am. MC/V.

L'Estaminet, 39 rue de Bretagne, *3ème* (☎01 42 72 34 85), inside the Marché des Enfants Rouges. ⓂTemple. Tiny, clean-scrubbed, and airy wine bar is a place for relaxation. Delightful selection of inexpensive wines by the glass (€3-3.50) or bottle (€5-25). Traipse through the market and pick up something to munch on. MC/V.

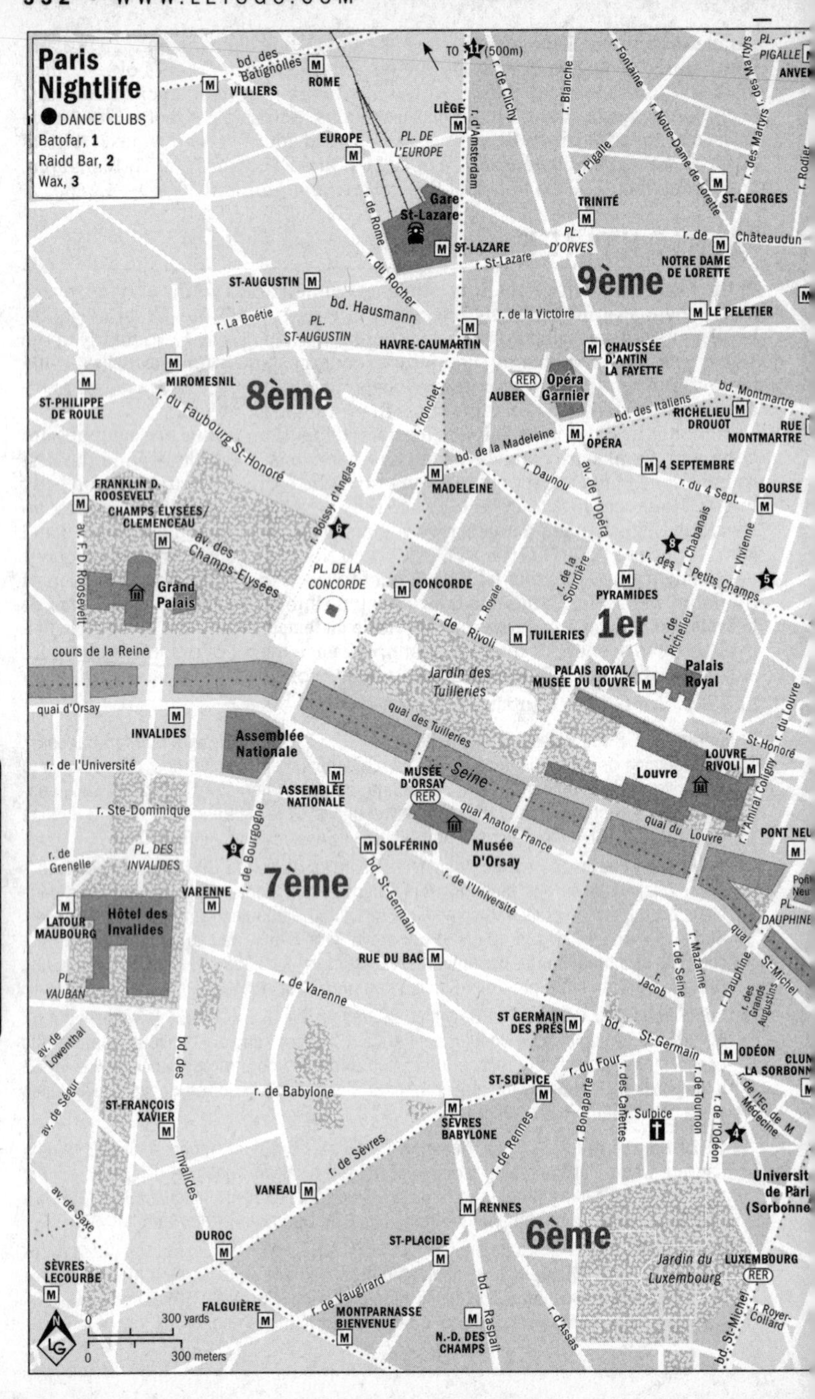
Paris Nightlife
DANCE CLUBS
Batofar, 1
Raidd Bar, 2
Wax, 3
8ème
9ème
1er
7ème
6ème
Gare St-Lazare
Opéra Garnier
Grand Palais
PL. DE LA CONCORDE
Jardin des Tuileries
Palais Royal
Louvre
Assemblée Nationale
Musée D'Orsay
Hôtel des Invalides
Seine
Jardin du Luxembourg
Université de Paris (Sorbonne)
300 yards
300 meters

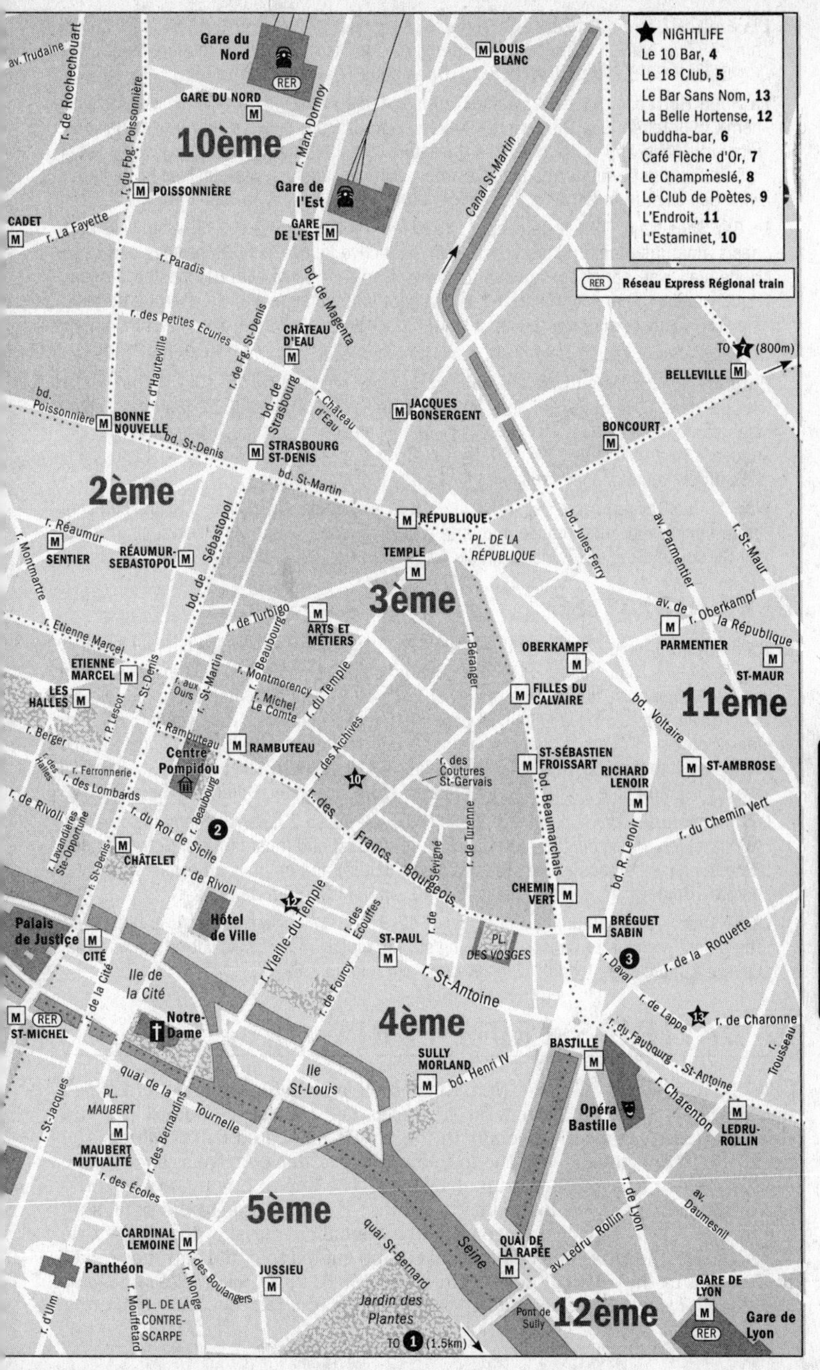

NIGHTLIFE
Le 10 Bar, 4
Le 18 Club, 5
Le Bar Sans Nom, 13
La Belle Hortense, 12
buddha-bar, 6
Café Flèche d'Or, 7
Le Champmeslé, 8
Le Club de Poètes, 9
L'Endroit, 11
L'Estaminet, 10
RER Réseau Express Régional train
10ème
2ème
3ème
4ème
5ème
11ème
12ème
Gare du Nord
GARE DU NORD
Gare de l'Est
GARE DE L'EST
LOUIS BLANC
POISSONNIÈRE
CADET
CHÂTEAU D'EAU
JACQUES BONSERGENT
BONNE NOUVELLE
STRASBOURG ST-DENIS
RÉPUBLIQUE
PL. DE LA RÉPUBLIQUE
TEMPLE
SENTIER
RÉAUMUR-SEBASTOPOL
ARTS ET MÉTIERS
BELLEVILLE
BONCOURT
TO 7 (800m)
PARMENTIER
OBERKAMPF
ST-MAUR
FILLES DU CALVAIRE
ETIENNE MARCEL
LES HALLES
RAMBUTEAU
Centre Pompidou
ST-SÉBASTIEN FROISSART
RICHARD LENOIR
ST-AMBROSE
CHÂTELET
CHEMIN VERT
BRÉGUET SABIN
Palais de Justice
CITÉ
Hôtel de Ville
ST-PAUL
PL. DES VOSGES
Ile de la Cité
ST-MICHEL
Notre-Dame
Ile St-Louis
SULLY MORLAND
BASTILLE
Opéra Bastille
LEDRU-ROLLIN
PL. MAUBERT
MAUBERT MUTUALITÉ
CARDINAL LEMOINE
Panthéon
JUSSIEU
QUAI DE LA RAPÉE
GARE DE LYON
Gare de Lyon
Jardin des Plantes
Pont de Sully
PL. DE LA CONTRE-SCARPE
TO 1 (1.5km)
Seine
Canal St-Martin
av. Trudaine
r. de Rochechouart
r. du Fbg. Poissonnière
r. Marx Dormoy
r. La Fayette
r. Paradis
bd. de Magenta
r. des Petites Ecuries
r. de Fg. St-Denis
r. d'Hauteville
bd. de Strasbourg
r. Château d'Eau
bd. Poissonnière
bd. St-Denis
bd. St-Martin
bd. de Sébastopol
r. Réaumur
r. Montmartre
r. de Turbigo
r. Etienne Marcel
r. Beaubourg
r. Montmorency
r. Michel Le Comte
r. du Temple
r. aux Ours
r. St-Martin
r. St-Denis
r. P. Lescot
r. Berger
r. Rambuteau
r. des Archives
r. des Coutures St-Gervais
r. Béranger
bd. Jules Ferry
av. Parmentier
r. St-Maur
av. de la République
r. Oberkampf
bd. Voltaire
r. Ferronnerie
r. des Lombards
r. des Halles
r. de Rivoli
r. Lavandières Ste-Opportune
r. du Roi de Sicile
r. des Francs Bourgeois
r. de Turenne
r. de Sévigné
bd. Beaumarchais
r. du Chemin Vert
bd. R. Lenoir
r. Vieille-du-Temple
r. des Ecouffes
r. de Fourcy
r. St-Antoine
r. Daval
r. de la Roquette
r. de Lappe
r. de Charonne
r. du Faubourg St-Antoine
r. Trousseau
r. Charenton
r. de la Cité
r. St-Jacques
quai de la Tournelle
r. des Bernardins
bd. Henri IV
r. des Écoles
r. de Lyon
av. Daumesnil
av. Ledru Rollin
quai St-Bernard
r. Monge
r. des Boulangers
r. Mouffetard
r. d'Ulm

FRANCE

L'Endroit, 67 pl. du Dr. Félix Lobligeois, 17*ème* (☎01 42 29 50 00). Ⓜ Rome. Snazzy diner-esque bar full of the hip and young. Alcohol kept on a giant rotating shelf. Wine €4-5. Beer €3-5. Mixed drinks €8-10. Open daily 10am-2am, often later F-Sa. MC/V.

La Belle Hortense, 31 rue Vieille du Temple, 4*ème* (☎01 48 04 71 60; www.cafeine.com). Ⓜ Hôtel de Ville. Literary bar/gallery/cafe draws a crowd of down-to-earth intellectuals. Walls and walls of books (literature, art, philosophy, children's) and mellow music. Frequent exhibits, readings, lectures, signings, and discussions. Free Wi-Fi. Varied wine selection from €4 per glass, €8 per bottle. Open daily 5pm-2am. MC/V.

Le Bar Sans Nom, 49 rue de Lappe, 11*ème* (☎01 48 05 59 36). Ⓜ Bastille. Laid-back oasis amid the clamor. Older crowd. Dim, seductive lounge with tall ceilings and huge, Bohemian wall hangings. Famous for creative mixed drinks (€9-10), posted on oversized wooden menus; don't leave Paris without trying their mojito. Free tarot-card reading (Tu 7-9pm, come early to grab a seat) has become something of an institution. Beer €5-6.50. Shots €6.50. Open Tu-Th 6pm-2am and F-Sa 6pm-4am. MC/V over €12.

Batofar, facing 11 quai François-Mauriac, 13*ème* (☎01 53 60 17 30; www.batofar.fr). Ⓜ Quai de la Gare or Bibliothèque Nationale de France. 45m long, 520-ton barge/bar/club made it big with a variety of music—mainly electronic, techno, hip hop, reggae, and house. Live artists daily. Cover €8-15; usually includes 1 drink. Open M-Th 11pm-6am, F-Sa later; hours change for special film and DJ events. MC/V.

Wax, 15 rue Daval, 11*ème* (☎01 40 21 16 18). Ⓜ Bastille. Always free and fun. In a concrete bunker with retro orange, red, and yellow couches. W and Su disco/funk, Th R&B, Sa-Su house. Beer €5-7. Mixed drinks €10. Open daily 9pm-dawn. MC/V over €15.

GLBT NIGHTLIFE

Raidd Bar, 23 rue du Temple, 4*ème*. Ⓜ Hotel de Ville. The Marais's most hip and happening GLBT club. Spinning disco globes cast undulating shadow and light in the intimate space, illuminating the topless torsos of the sexy bartenders. After 11pm, performers strip down in glass shower cubicles built into the wall showcase. Happy hour 5pm-9pm for all drinks, 5-11pm for beer; size doubles. Tu disco night, W 80s and house, Th "DJ VIP," F-Sa club, Su 90s. Beer €4. Mixed drinks €8. Notoriously strict door policy—women are not allowed unless with a greater ratio of (gorgeous) men. Open daily 5pm-5am. V.

Le Champmeslé, 4 rue Chabanais, 2*ème* (☎01 42 96 85 20; www.lachampmesle.com). Ⓜ Pyramides. Welcoming lesbian bar is Paris's oldest and most famous. Both men and women enjoy the popular cabaret shows (Sa 10pm) and monthly art exhibits. Beer €5 before 10pm, €7 after. Mixed drinks €8/10. Open M-Sa 3pm-dawn.

Le 18 Club, 18 rue Beaujolais, 1*er* (☎01 42 97 52 13; www.club18.fr). Ⓜ Pyramides. The oldest gay club in Paris is still going strong. Mostly male crowd. Mixed drinks €6-9. Cover €10; includes 1 drink. Open W and F-Sa midnight-6am.

DAYTRIPS FROM PARIS

VERSAILLES. Louis XIV, the Sun King, built and held court at Versailles's extraordinary palace, 12km west of Paris. The **château** embodies the Old Regime's extravagance, especially in the newly renovated **Hall of Mirrors,** the ornate State Apartments, and the fountain-filled gardens. Arrive as soon as the château opens to avoid horrendous crowds. The line to buy tickets is to the left of the courtyard, while the line to get into the château is to the right; skip the former line by buying a day pass at the Versailles tourist office, 2bis av. de Paris, or skip the latter line by buying a combo guided tour and entrance ticket to the right of the château ticket office. *(☎01 30 83 78 89; www.chateauversailles.fr. Château open Tu-Su Apr.-Oct. 9am-6:30pm; Nov.-Mar. 9am-5:30pm. Last entry 30min. before clos-*

ing. Admission to palace and self-guided tour through entrance A €8, after 3:30pm €6, under 18 free. Various other passes and guided tours also available. For group discounts and reservations call ☎08 10 81 16 14.) A shuttle (round-trip €6, 11-18 €4.50) runs through the gardens to Louis XIV's pink marble hideaway, the **Grand Trianon,** and Marie-Antoinette's **Petit Trianon,** including her pseudo-peasant Hameau, or hamlet. *(www.train-versailles.com. Both Trianons open daily Apr.-Oct. noon-6:30pm; Nov.-Mar. noon-5:30pm. Last entry 30min. before closing. Apr.-Oct. €9, 2hr. before closing €5, under 18 free; Nov.-Mar. €5, under 18 free.)* Take the RER C5 train from ⓂInvalides to the Versailles Rive Gauche station (30-40min., 4 per hr., round-trip €5.60). Make sure you keep your RER (not Métro) ticket to exit at the Versailles station.

CHARTRES. Chartres's phenomenal cathedral is one of the most beautiful surviving creations of the Middle Ages. Arguably the finest example of early Gothic architecture in Europe, the cathedral retains nearly all of its original 12th- and 13th-century stained-glass windows, many featuring the stunning "Chartres blue." Climb the spiral staircase to the top of the 16th-century Flamboyant Gothic left tower (Tour Jehan-de-Beauce), built 300 years after the rest of the cathedral, for dizzying views. *(☎02 37 21 75 02; www.cathedrale-chartres.com. Open daily 8:30am-7:30pm. No casual visits during mass. Mass M-F 11:45am and 6:15pm, Tu and F 9am and 6:15pm; Sa 11:45am and 6pm; Su 9:15 (Latin), 11am, 6pm (in the crypt). Call the tourist office for info on concerts in the cathedral. €10, students and children €5.)* **Trains** run from Paris's Gare Montparnasse (1hr., 1 per hr., round-trip €26). The cathedral towers are visible to the left from outside the station.

LOIRE VALLEY (VAL DE LOIRE)

The Loire, France's longest river, meanders toward the Atlantic through a valley containing vineyards that produce some of the nation's best wines. It's hardly surprising that a string of French (and English) kings chose to live in opulent châteaux by these waters rather than in the commotion of their capital cities.

TRANSPORTATION

Faced with widespread grandeur, many travelers plan overly ambitious itineraries—two châteaux per day is a reasonable goal. The city of Tours (p. 337) is the region's best rail hub. However, train schedules are inconvenient, and many châteaux aren't accessible by train. **Biking** is the best way to explore the region. Many stations distribute the invaluable *Châteaux pour Train et Vélo* booklet.

FRANCE

ORLÉANS ☎02 38

A gateway from Paris into the Loire, Orléans (pop. 200,000) cherishes its historical connection to **Joan of Arc,** who marched triumphantly past the **rue de Bourgogne** in 1429 after liberating the city from a British siege. Most of Orléans's highlights are near place Ste-Croix. With stained-glass windows that depict Joan's story, the **Cathédrale Sainte-Croix,** pl. Ste-Croix, is Orléans's crown jewel. (Open daily July-Aug. 9:15am-7pm; Sept.-June reduced hours.)

One block from the train station, **Hôtel de L'Abeille ❹,** 64 r. Alsace-Lorraine, has been owned by the same family since 1919. Twenty-nine comfortable rooms with antique furniture and fireplaces (albeit non-functional) are worth the price. (☎02 38 53 54 87; www.hoteldelabeille.com. Continental breakfast €8.50, in bed €9.50. Wi-Fi in lobby. Singles with shower €47, with full bath €51; doubles €62-66/69-79; triples and quads €95-110. AmEx/MC/V.) Rue de Bourgogne and rue Ste-Catherine have a variety of cheap buffets and a lively bar scene at night. At **Mijana ❸,** 175 r. de Bourgogne, a charming Lebanese

P 10 PLACES TO FIND THE "SENTIMENT DE L'EXISTENCE"

ean-Jacques Rousseau championed the phrase *"sentiment de 'existence,"* the fulfillment found iving in the moment. So kick back n Rousseau's stomping ground and enjoy the *dolce far niente*—he sweetness of doing nothing.

. Daydream atop of the **Denis Papin stairs** in Blois—the height nay just leave you lightheaded.
. Meditate beside the Loire from he raised **boardwalk** in Amboise.
. Take in a sea of wheat in solitude on the way to **Beauregard.**
. Feel on top of the world as you conquer the Loire and ascend to **Chaumont.**
. Gawk at Napoleon's magnificent cedar in the courtyard of the **Musée des Beaux-Arts** in Tours.
. Stroll the **quai Maynaud** and watch the sun slip behind Saumur's *château.*
. Sink into Cathédrale St-Louis's shadow in the **Jardin de l'Evêché** and lose your senses in the view of Blois's *vieille ville.*
. Let your desire for material goods melt away as you observe passersby in designer jeans in Le Mans's **place de la République.**
. Sit at the bank of the moat near Sully-sur-Loire's **château** and ponder your reflection in the water traversed by Jeanne d'Arc.
0. Contemplate yin and yang as he endless tension between good and evil unfolds before you under he Tapisserie de l'Apocalypse in he **Château d'Angers.**

couple prepares gourmet cuisine. (☎02 38 62 02 02; www.mijanaresto.com. Take-out sandwiches €4-6. Appetizers €7.20-8.50. *Plats* €14-17. Lunch specials, including *menu traditionel* €17.75. Open M-Sa noon-1:30pm, 7-10pm. Vegetarian options. Open M-Sa noon-1:30pm and 7-10pm. AmEx/MC/V over €15.) **Trains** leave from the Gare d'Orléans on pl. Albert I. to: Blois (40min.; at least 15 per day; €9.70 under 26 €7); Nantes (2hr.; M-F 3 per day, Sa-Su 2 per day; €35); Paris Austerlitz (1hr., every hr., €13); Tours (1hr., every 30min., €18). The **tourist office,** is located at 2 pl. de l'Étape. (☎02 38 24 05 05; www.tourisme-orleans.com. Open July-Aug. 9:30am-7pm; June 9:30am-1pm and 2-6:30pm; May and Sept. Tu-Sa 9:30am-1pm and 2-6pm; Oct.-Apr. reduced hours.) **Postal Code:** 45000.

BLOIS ☎02 54

Awash in a rich regal history, Blois (pop. 51,000) is one of the Loire's most charming, popular cities. Once home to monarchs Louis XII and François I, Blois's gold-trimmed **Château** was the Versailles of the late 15th and early 16th centuries. Housed within are well-preserved collections and historical museums with excellent temporary exhibits. While the royal apartments showcase extravagant and elegant pieces, the **Musée des Beaux-Arts** features a gallery of 16th- to 19th-century portraits, and the **Musée Lapidaire** exhibits sculptures from nearby châteaux. (☎02 54 90 33 33. Open daily Apr.-June. 9am-6:30pm; July and Aug. 9am-7pm; Sept 9am-6:30pm.; Oct.-Mar. 9am-noon and 2-5:30pm. Ticket booth closes 30min. before château. Admission including 2 museums €7.50, students under 25 €5, under 17 €3.) Bars and *boulangeries* on r. St-Lubin and r. des Trois Marchands tempt those en route to the 12th-century **Abbaye St-Laumer,** also called the **Église St-Nicolas.** (Open daily 9am-6:30pm. Su Mass 9:30am.) Five hundred years of expansions and additions to **Cathédrale St-Louis,** one of Blois's architectural jewels, have endowed it with an eclectic mix of styles. (Open daily 7:30am-6pm; crypt open June-Aug.) A spectacular view from the **Jardin de l'Evêché,** behind the cathedral, runs past the rooftops and winding alleys of the old quarter, stretching along the brilliant Loire.

Hôtel du Bellay ❷, 12 rue des Minimes, is a rustic old house, hidden away in a quiet, centrally located nook of the city, contains 12 clean but well-lived in rooms. (☎02 54 78 23 62; http://hoteldubellay.free.fr. Breakfast €5. Reception 24hr. Reservations recommended at least 3 weeks ahead. Singles and doubles with sink €25, with toilet €27, with shower €28, with bath €37; triples and quads €54-62. MC/V.)

Fragrant *pâtisseries* entice visitors on **rue Denis Papin,** while **rue St-Lubin, place Poids du Roi,** and **place de la Résistance** offer more dining options. At night, the château's "Son et Lumière" light show brightens Blois.

Trains leave pl. de la Gare for Amboise (20min., 15 per day, €6.20); Angers via Tours (1hr., 9-11 per day, €24); Orléans (30-50min., 14 per day, €9.70); Paris via Orléans (1hr., 8 per day, €26); Tours (40min., 8-13 per day 8am-7pm, €9.20). **Transports Loir-et-Cher (TLC;** ☎02 54 58 55 44; www.TLCinfo.net) sends **buses** from the station to nearby Chambord and Cheverny (3 per day mid-May to early Sept.; €12; students €9; reduced entry to châteaux with bus ticket). Rent a **bike** from Bike in Blois, 8 rue Henri Drussy, near pl. de la Résistance. (☎02 54 56 07 73; www.locationdevelos.com. €14 standard bike or €38 tandem bike per day; price reduction for extra days. Open M-F 9:15am-1pm and 3-6:30pm, Su 10:30am-1pm and 3-6:15pm. Cash only.) The **tourist office** is on pl. du Château. (☎02 54 90 41 41; www.bloispaysdechambord.com. Open Apr.-Sept. M-Sa 9am-7pm, Su 10am-7pm; Oct.-Mar. reduced hours.) **Postal Code:** 41000.

TOURS ☎02 47

On the surface, Tours (pop. 142,000) sparkles with the shops and bars of a modern metropolis. Yet behind its store-lined streets loom magnificent towers, ancient buildings, and majestic cathedrals. Home to 30,000 students, abundant restaurants, and booming nightlife, Balzac's birthplace is a comfortable base for château-hopping. The **Cathédrale St-Gatien,** off of r. Lavoisier, first erected in the fourth century AD, combines Romanesque columns, carvings, and two Renaissance spires into an intricate facade. (Cathedral open daily 9am-7pm. Cathedral free. Bimonthly free concerts throughout the year. Cloister open May-Sept. M-Sa 9:30am-12:30pm and 2-6pm; Apr. daily 10am-noon and 2-5:30pm; Oct.-Mar. Th-Sa 9:30am-12:30pm and 2-5pm. €3, students and under 18 €2.80.) Jutting up from modern commercial streets, the imposing **Tour de l'Horloge** and **Tour de Charlemagne,** on r. Descartes, are a ruinous testimony to the impressive proportions of the old *basilique*, destroyed after the 1789 Revolution. The **Nouvelle Basilique St-Martin** is an ornate church designed by Victor Laloux, architect of Paris's Musée d'Orsay (p. 327) and the Tours railway station. (Open daily 8am-8pm. Mass daily 11am.) **Musée des Compagnons,** 8 r. Nationale, showcases the masterpieces of France's best craftsmen and explains the decade-long traditional training of the Compagnonage—allegedly in place since King Solomon gathered workers to build the temple of Jerusalem. (☎02 47 21 62 20. Open mid-June to mid-Sept. M and W-Su 9am-12:30pm and 2-6pm; mid-Sept. to mid-June daily 9am-noon and 2-6pm. €5, students and seniors €3, under 12 €2.)

The **Association Jeunesse et Habitat ❷,** 16 r. Bernard Palissy, houses workers, students, and backpackers in spacious rooms with private baths. When exiting the tourist office, turn right on r. Bernard Palissy. (☎02 47 60 51 51. Free Internet. Singles with shower €18.50; doubles with bath €27.) Try **place Plumereau** and **rue Colbert** for bustling restaurants, cafes, and bars. At night, the elegant **place Plumereau** blossoms with animated bars. **Trains** leave pl. du Général Leclerc for Paris (3hr., every hr., €29), Poitiers (50min., 6 per day, €15.50), and Saumur (40min., 12 per day, €10.50) via St-Pierre-des-Corps. TGV runs to Bordeaux (4hr., every hr., €46), Paris (1hr., every hr., €54.50), and Poitiers (1hr., 13 per day, €18.90) via St-Pierre-des-Corps. To reach the **tourist office,** 78-82 r. Bernard Palissy, from the station, walk through pl. du Général Leclerc, the office is across the street. (☎02 47 70 37 37; www.ligeris.com. Open mid-Apr. to mid-Oct. M-Sa 8:30am-7pm, Su 10am-12:30pm and 2:30-5pm; mid-Oct. to mid-Apr. M-Sa 9am-12:30pm and 1:30-6pm, Su 10am-1pm.) **Postal Code:** 37000.

BRITTANY (BRETAGNE)

Despite superficially French *centre-villes*, châteaux, and *creperies*, Brittany reveres its pre-Roman Celtic roots. After 800 years of Breton settlement, the province became part of France when the duke's daughter married two successive French kings. Black-and-white *Breizh* (Breton) flags still decorate buildings, however, and the Celtic language Breton remains on street signs.

RENNES ☎02 99

The cultural capital of Brittany, Rennes (pop 212,000) flourishes from September to June because of its large, rowdy student population. Ethnic eateries, colorful nightspots, and crowds of university students enliven the cobblestone streets and half-timbered houses of the *vieille ville.* Medieval architecture peppers Rennes's *vieille ville*, particularly **rue de la Psalette** and **rue St-Guillaume.** At the end of r. St-Guillaume, turn left onto r. de la Monnaie to visit the **Cathédrale St-Pierre,** a 19th-century masterpiece with a solid, Neoclassical facade and frescoed, gilded interior. (Open daily 9:30am-noon and 3-6pm.) The **Musée des Beaux-Arts,** 20 q. Émile Zola, houses an excellent collection including Baroque and Breton masterpieces but few famous works. (☎02 23 62 17 45; www.mbar.org. Open Tu 10am-6pm, W-Su 10am-noon and 2-6pm. €4.30, students €2.20, under 18 free; with special exhibits €5.40/2.70/free.) Across the river and up r. Gambetta is the lush **Jardin du Thabor,** one of the most beautiful gardens in France. (☎02 99 28 56 62. Open daily June-Aug. 7:30am-8:30pm; Sept.-June 7:30am-6:30pm.) Rennes is a **partygoer's dream,** especially during term time. Look for action in **place Ste-Anne, place St-Michel,** and **place de Lices.** In a former prison, **Delicatessen,** 7 impasse Rallier du Baty, has swapped jailhouse bars for heavy beats. (Drinks €6-10. Cover €5-15. Open Tu-Sa midnight-5am.)

The **Auberge de Jeunesse (HI) ❶,** 10-12 Canal St-Martin, has simple dorms. Take the metro (dir.: Kennedy) to Ste-Anne. Follow r. de St-Malo to the right of the church downhill onto r. St-Martin; the hostel will be on the right after the bridge. (☎02 99 33 22 33; rennes@fuaj.org. Breakfast and linens included. Reception 7am-11pm. Dorms €17. MC/V.) **Rue St-Malo** has many ethnic restaurants, while the *vieille ville* contains traditional brasseries. **Le St-Germain des Champs (Restaurant Végétarien-Biologique) ❸,** 12 r. du Vau St-Germain, serves vegetarian *plats* for €10. (☎02 99 79 25 52. Open M-Sa noon-2:30pm. MC/V.)

Trains leave pl. de la Gare for: Caen (3hr., 4 per day, €33); Paris (2hr., 1 per hr., €53-65); St-Malo (1hr., 15 per day, €14.90); Tours (3hr., 4 per day, €37) via Le Mans. Buses go from 16 pl. de la Gare to Angers (2hr., 2 per day, €14) and Mont-St-Michel (1hr., 4 per day, €10). Local **buses** run Monday through Saturday 5:15am-12:30am and Sunday 7:25am-midnight. The metro line uses the same ticket (€1.10, day pass €4, carnet of 10 €11). To get from the train station to the **tourist office** is at 11 r. St-Yves. (☎02 99 67 11 11; www.tourisme-rennes.com. Open July-Aug. M-Sa 9am-7pm, Su 11am-1pm and 2-6pm; Sept.-June M 1-6pm, Tu-Sa 10am-6pm, Su 11am-1pm and 2-6pm.) **Postal Code:** 35000.

ST-MALO ☎02 99

St-Malo (pop. 52,000) combines all the best of northern France: sandy beaches, imposing ramparts, and cultural festivals. East of the walled city is **Grande Plage de Sillon,** the town's largest and longest beach. The slightly more sheltered **Plage de Bon Secours** lies to the west and features the curious (and free) **Piscine de Bon Secours,** three cement walls that hold in a deep pool of salt water even when the tide recedes. The best view of St-Malo is from the château's **watchtower,** part of the **Musée d'Histoire,** which houses artifacts from St-Malo's naval past. (☎02

99 40 71 57. Open Apr.-Sept. daily 10am-12:30pm and 2-6pm; Oct.-Mar. reduced hours. €5.20, students €2.60.) The **"Centre Patrick Varangot" (HI) ❶**, 37 av. du Révérend Père Umbricht, has 242 beds near the beach. From the train station, take bus #5 (dir.: Croix Désilles) or #10 (dir.: Cancale). By foot (30min.) from the station, turn right and go straight at the roundabout onto av. de Moka. Turn right on av. Pasteur, which becomes av. du Révérend Père Umbricht. (☎02 99 40 29 80; www.centrevarangot.com. Breakfast included. Linens included. Laundry €4. Free Internet and Wi-Fi. Reception daily 8am-11pm. Dorms €16.50-19; singles €25-29. MC/V.) The best eateries lie farther from the walls of the *vieille ville*. For scoops of gelato, head to **Le Sanchez ❶**, 9 r. de la Vieille Boucherie at pl. du Pilori. (☎02 99 56 67 17. 1 scoop €2, 2 scoops €3. Super Sanchez 3-scoop sundae €4.80. Open mid-June to mid-Sept. daily 8:30am-midnight; Apr. to mid-June daily 8:30am-7:30pm; mid-Sept to Mar. M-Tu and Th-Su 8:30am-7:30pm. MC/V min. €15 charge.) **Trains** run to Dinan (1hr., 5 per day, €8.50), Paris (4hr., 14 per day, €59.40-73.20), and Rennes (1hr., 14 per day, €12.40). The **tourist office** is in esplanade St-Vincent. (☎08 25 13 52 00. Open July-Aug. M-Sa 9am-7:30pm, Su 10am-6pm; Sept.-June reduced hours.) **Postal Code:** 35400.

DINAN ☎02 96

Perhaps the best-preserved medieval town in Brittany, Dinan (pop. 11,000) has cobblestone streets lined with 15th-century houses inhabited by traditional sculptors and painters. On the ramparts, the 13th-century **Porte du Guichet** is the original entrance to the **Château de Dinan.** Once a military stronghold, ducal residence, and prison, its two towers are now a museum. The *donjon* (keep) displays local art, while the **Tour de Coëtquen's** basement stores funerary sculptures. (Open June-Sept. daily 10am-6:30pm; Oct.-May reduced hours. €4.35, ages 12-18 €1.70.) To reach the **Auberge de Jeunesse (HI) ❶**, in Vallée de la Fontaine-des-Eaux, turn left from the station, cross the tracks, then turn right and head downhill for 2km before turning right again for another 2km. (☎02 96 39 10 83; dinan@fuaj.org. Breakfast €3.50. Linens included. Free Internet. Reception July-Aug. 8am-noon and 5-9pm; Sept.-June 9am-noon and 5-8pm. Dorms €12.40. MC/V.) Creperies, brasseries, and bars sit along **rue de la Cordonnerie** and **place des Merciers. Trains** run from pl. du 11 Novembre 1918 to Paris (3hr., 6 per day, €61.80) and Rennes (1hr., 8 per day, €12.70). The **tourist office** is at 9 r. du Château. (☎02 96 87 69 76. Open July-Aug. M-Sa 9am-7pm, Su 10am-12:30pm and 2:30-6pm; Sept.-June reduced hours.) **Postal Code:** 22100.

NANTES ☎02 40

With broad boulevards, relaxing public parks, and great bistros, Nantes (pop. 280,000) knows how to take life easy. The massive **Château des Ducs de Bretagne,** built to safeguard Breton independence in the late 15th century, now houses several exhibits detailing regional history. (Château grounds open daily mid-May to mid-Sept. 9am-8pm; mid-Sept. to mid-May 10am-7pm. Museum open mid-May to mid-Sept. 9:30am-7pm; mid-Sept. to mid-May 10am-6pm. Grounds free. Exhibits each €5, 18-26 €3; both €8/4.80.) Gothic vaults soar 39m in the bright **Cathédrale St-Pierre.** (Open daily Apr.-Oct. 8am-7pm, Nov.-Mar. 8am-6pm.) The **Musée des Beaux-Arts,** 10 r. Georges Clemenceau, features a wide range of European masterpieces on the second floor. (☎02 51 17 45 00. Open M, W, F-Su 10am-6pm, Th 10am-8pm. €3.50, students €2, under 18, Th 6-8pm, and 1st Su of each month free; €2 daily after 4:30pm.)

A 15min. walk from the train station, **Auberge de Jeunesse "La Manu" (HI) ❶**, 2 pl. de la Manu, once a tobacco factory, still has an industrial feel overshadowed by bright decor and a friendly staff. (☎02 40 29 29 20; nanteslamanu@fuaj.org. Breakfast and linens included. Luggage storage €1.50. Internet €1 per

40min. Reception daily July-Aug. 8am-noon and 3-11pm; Sept.-June 8am-noon and 5-11pm. Lockout July-Aug. 10am-4pm, Sept.-June 10am-5pm. Open Jan. to mid-Dec. 3- to 6-bed dorms €16.90. HI members only. MC/V.) Plenty of reasonably-priced eateries are between **place du Bouffay** and **place du Pilori.** One of France's most beautiful bistros, **Chez l'Huitre ❷,** 5 rue des Petites Écuries, has some of the freshest oysters. (☎51 82 02 02. 3-course *menu*, €8-12. Bucket of *huîtres* €3.50-13.60. Open daily noon-3pm and 6pm-10pm. MC/V.) For nightlife, the **Ste-Croix area,** near place du Bouffay, has bars and cafes in abundance. **Trains** leave from 27 bd. de Stalingrad for Bordeaux (4hr., 5 per day, €42), Paris (2-4hr., 1 per hr., €54-69), and Rennes (1hr., 7-15 per day, €21). The **tourist office** is at 3 cours Olivier de Clisson. (☎08 92 46 40 44; www.nantes-tourisme.com. Open M-W and F-Sa 10am-6pm, Tu 10:30am-6pm.) **Postal Code:** 44000.

NORMANDY

Rainy, fertile Normandy is a land of fields, fishing villages, and cathedrals. Invasions have twice secured the region's place in military history: in 1066, William of Normandy conquered England; on D-Day, June 6, 1944, Allied armies returned the favor, liberating France from Normandy's beaches.

ROUEN ☎02 35

Madame Bovary—literature's most famous desperate housewife—may have criticized Rouen (pop. 106,000), but Flaubert's hometown is no provincial hamlet. Historically important as the capital of Normandy and the city where **Joan of Arc** burned at the stake in 1431, Rouen today boasts splendid Gothic cathedrals and buzzing urban energy. The most famous of Rouen's "hundred spires" belong to the **Cathédrale de Notre-Dame,** pl. de la Cathédrale. The central spire, standing at 495 feet, is the tallest in France. Art lovers may also recognize the cathedral's facade from Monet's celebrated studies of light. (Open Apr.-Oct. M 2-7pm, Tu-Sa 7:30am-7pm, Su 8am-6pm; Nov.-Mar. M 2-7pm, Tu-Sa 7:30am-noon and 2-6pm, Su 8am-6pm.) The **Musée Flaubert et d'Histoire de la Médicine,** 51 r. de Lecat, down r. de Crosne from pl. de Vieux-Marché, houses a large collection of bizarre paraphernalia on both subjects. (☎02 35 15 59 95; www.chu-rouen.fr. Open Tu 10am-6pm, W-Sa 10am-noon and 2-6pm. €3, 18-25 €1.50, under 18 free.) **Hotel des Arcades ❸,** 52 r. de Carmes, is down the street from the cathedral. (☎02 35 70 10 30; www.hotel-des-arcades.fr. Breakfast €6.50. Singles €29-36, with shower €40-46; doubles €30-37/41-47; triples with shower €57. AmEx/MC/V.) Cheap eateries surround place du Vieux-Marché and the Gros Horloge area. **Chez Wam ❶,** 67 r. de la République, near l'Abbatiale St-Ouen, serves delicious *kebab-frites* (kebabs with fries; €4) ideal for picnics at the nearby **Jardins de l'Hôtel de Ville.** (☎02 35 15 97 51. Open daily 10am-2am. Cash only.) **Trains** leave r. Jeanne d'Arc, on pl. Bernard Tissot, for Lille (3hr., 3 per day, €30) and Paris (1hr., 1 per hr., €19.30). The **tourist office** is at 25 pl. de la Cathédrale. (☎02 32 08 32 40; www.rouentourisme.com. Open May-Sept. M-Sa 9am-7pm, Su 9:30am-12:30pm and 2-6pm; Oct.-Apr. M-Sa 9:30am-6:30pm.) **Postal Code:** 76000.

CAEN ☎02 31

Although Allied bombing leveled three-quarters of its buildings during WWII, Caen (pop. 114,000) has successfully rebuilt itself into an active university town. Caen's biggest (and priciest) draw is the **Mémorial de Caen,** which powerfully, tastefully, and creatively explores WWII, from the "failure of peace" to modern prospects for global harmony. (☎02 31 06 06 44; www.memorial-caen.fr. Open mid-Feb. to mid-Nov. daily 9am-7pm; mid-Nov. to mid-Feb. Tu-Su

9:30am-6pm. €17-18; students, seniors, and 10-18 €15-16, under 10 free. Prices vary by season.) The ruins of William the Conqueror's enormous **château** (ramparts free and open for visiting), sprawl above the center of town. The **Musée de Normandie,** within the château grounds on the left, traces the cultural evolution of people living on Norman soil from the beginning of civilization to the present. (☎02 31 30 47 60; www.musee-de-normandie.caen.fr. Open June-Sept. daily 9:30am-6pm; Oct.-May M and W-Su 9:30am-6pm. Free.) At night, Caen's already busy streets turn boisterous; well-attended bars and clubs pumping music populate the area around **rue de Bras, rue des Croisiers,** and **rue St-Pierre.**

The cheap and spacious four-bed dorms at **Auberge de Jeunesse (HI) ❶,** Résidence Robert Rème, 1 68 r. Eustache Restout, make its distance from town (3km) worth the trek. Take bus # 5, dir. Fleury Cimetière, to Lycée Fresnel (15min.); go back half a block in the direction the bus came from, then take a right on r. Restout, the hostel is on the left. (☎02 31 52 19 96; fax 02 31 84 29 49. Breakfast €2. Linens €2.50. Laundry wash €3, dry €1.50. Free Wi-Fi. Reception 5-9pm. Check-out 10am. Open daily June-Sept. Dorms €11. Cash only.) Eateries can be found near the château and around **Place Courtonne** and **Église St-Pierre.**

Trains run to: Paris (2hr., 11 per day, €29.80); Rennes (3hr., 2 per day, €31.10); Rouen (1hr., 9 per day, €22.30); Tours (3hr., 3 per day, €51). Bus Verts **buses** (☎08 10 21 42 14) cover the rest of Normandy. Twisto, operating **local buses** and **trams,** has schedules at its office on 15 r. de Gêole. (☎02 31 15 55 55; www.twisto.fr; €1.27, carnet of 10 €10.10.) The **tourist office** is in pl. St-Pierre. (☎02 31 27 14 14; www.caen.fr/tourisme. Open July-Aug. M-Sa 9am-7pm, Su 10am-1pm and 2-5pm; Mar.-June and Sept. M-Sa 9:30am-6:30pm, Su 10am-1pm; Oct.-Feb. M-Sa 9:30am-1pm and 2-6pm, Su 10am-1pm.) **Postal Code:** 14000.

BAYEUX ☎02 31

Escaping relatively unscathed from WWII, beautiful Bayeux (pop. 15,000) is an ideal base for exploring nearby D-Day beaches, especially in summer when more buses run. Visitors should not miss the 900-year-old **Tapisserie Bayeux,** 70m of embroidery depicting William the Conqueror's invasion of England. The tapestry is displayed in the **Centre Guillaume le Conquérant,** on r. de Nesmond. (Open daily May-Aug. 9am-7pm; mid-Mar. to Apr. and Sept.-mid-Nov. 9am-6-:30pm; mid-Nov. to mid-Mar. 9:30am-12:30pm and 2-6pm. €7.70, students €3.80, under 10 free.) Close by, **Cathédrale Notre-Dame** was the tapestry's original home. (Open daily July-Sept. 8:30am-7pm; Oct.-Dec. 8:30am-6pm; Jan.-Mar. 9am-5pm; Apr.-June 8am-6pm. French-language tours of the Old Town, including access to the labyrinth and treasury; 5 tours per day July-Aug., €4.) The **Musée de la Bataille de Normandie,** bd. Fabian Ware, recounts the D-Day landing and subsequent 76-day struggle for northern France. (☎02 31 51 46 90. Open daily May-Sept. 9:30am-6:30pm; Oct.-Apr. 10am-12:30pm and 2-6pm. English-language film about every 2hr. €6.50, students €3.80.) **Le Maupassant ❸,** 19 r. St-Martin, in the center of town, has cheerful rooms. (☎02 31 92 28 53; h.lemaupassant@orange.fr. Breakfast €5.95. Singles €29; doubles with shower €40; quads with bath €69. Extra bed €10. MC/V.) **Trains** leave pl. de la Gare for Caen (20min., 23 per day, €5.50) and Paris (2hr., 12per day, €32). The **tourist office** is at r. St-Jean. (☎02 31 51 28 28; www.bayeux-bessin-tourism.com. Open July-Aug. M-Sa 9am-7pm, Su 9am-1pm and 2-6pm; Sept.-June reduced hours.) **Postal Code:** 14400.

DAYTRIP FROM BAYEUX: D-DAY BEACHES. On June 6, 1944, more than a hundred thousand Allied soldiers invaded Normandy's beaches, leading to France's liberation and the downfall of Nazi Europe. Army Rangers scaled 30m cliffs under heavy fire at the **Pointe du Hoc,** between Utah and Omaha Beaches, to capture a strongly fortified German naval battery. Having achieved

FRANCE

their objective, the Army Rangers held the battery against counter attacks for two days past their anticipated relief. Of the 225 men in the division, only 90 survived. Often referred to as "Bloody Omaha," **Omaha Beach,** next to Colleville-sur-Mer and east of the Pointe du Hoc, is the most famous D-Day beach. On June 6, Allied preparatory bombings missed the German positions due to fog, while the full-strength German bunkers inflicted an 85% casualty rate on the first waves of Americans; ultimately, over 800 soldiers died on the beach. The 9387 graves at the **American Cemetery** stretch throughout expansive grounds on the cliffs overlooking the beach. *(Open daily 9am-6pm.)* To Omaha's east and just west of Gold Beach is **Arromanches,** a small town where the ruins of the Allies' temporary **Port Winston** lie in a giant semi-circle off the coast. The Arromanches **360° Cinéma** combines images of modern Normandy and 1944 D-Day. *(Open daily June-Aug. 9:40am-6:40pm; Sept.-May reduced hours. €4.20, students €3.70.)*

Reaching the beaches can be difficult without a car. Some sites are accessible by **Bus Verts** from Caen on lines #1, 3, and 4 and from Bayeux on lines 70 and 74; more buses run in July-Aug., including a special D-Day line from Bayeux and Caen to Omaha Beach (€1.55-10.20). Normandy Sightseeing Tours, based in Bayeux, runs **guided tours** with English-speaking guides. *(☎02 31 51 70 52; www.normandywebguide.com. Reservations required. ½-day tour €40-45, students €35-40; full-day tour €75/65. Pick-up at train station, pl. du Québec, or your hotel. MC/V.)*

MONT-ST-MICHEL ☎02 33

Once regarded as a paradise, the fortified island of Mont-St-Michel is a medieval wonder. Stone and half-timbering enclose the town's narrow main street which leads steeply up to the abbey's twisting stairs. Adjacent to the abbey church is **La Merveille** (the Marvel), a 13th-century Gothic monastery, while four crypts support the church and keep it balanced on the hilltop. (Open daily May-Aug. 9am-7pm; Sept.-Apr. 9:30am-6pm. €8.50, 18-25 €5.) Hotels on Mont-St-Michel are expensive, starting at €50 per night. Cheap beds are only 1.8km away at the **Camping du Mont-St-Michel ❶**, rte. du Mont-St-Michel (☎02 33 60 22 10; www.le-mont-St-michel.com. Laundry €6.10. Wi-Fi at adjoining Hôtel Motel Vert. Reception 24hr. Check-out 2pm. Gates closed 11pm-6am. Open from Feb. to mid-Nov. €4-5 per adult, €2-3 per child, €5-9 per tent site; dorms €8.60. MC/V). Courriers Bretons (☎02 99 19 70 70), runs **buses** from Mont-St-Michel to Rennes (1hr., 2-3 per week, €2.50). The **tourist office** is to the left of the entrance. (☎02 33 60 14 30; www.ot-mont-saintmichel.com. Open July-Aug. daily 9am-7pm; Apr.-June M-Sa 9am-12:30pm and 2-6:30pm, Su 9am-noon and 2-6pm; Oct.-Dec. and Jan.-Mar. M-Sa 9am-noon and 2-6pm, Su 10am-noon and 2-5pm; Sept. M-Sa 9am-6pm, Su 10am-noon and 2-6pm.) **Postal Code:** 50170.

FRANCE

DON'T BE CAUGHT ADRIFT. Those seeing the Mont illuminated at night should plan ahead. Evening transportation off the island doesn't exist, and walking across the 1km of sand during low tide is extremely dangerous.

FLANDERS AND PAS DE CALAIS

Every day, thousands of tourists pass through the channel ports of the Côte d'Opale on their way to Britain, yet few manage more than a glimpse at the surrounding regions, leaving Flanders, Picardy, and the coastal Pas de Calais undiscovered. When leaving from the ferry ports, don't miss the area's gems.

LILLE ☎03 20

A long-time international hub with rich Flemish ancestry and the best nightlife in the north, Lille (pop. 220,000) has abandoned its industrial days to become a stylish metropolis. The impressive **Palais des Beaux-Arts,** on pl. de la République (M: République), has the second-largest art collection in France, with a comprehensive display of 15th- to 20th-century French and Flemish masterpieces. (Open M 2-6pm, W-Su 10am-6pm. €10, students €7.) The aptly named **La Piscine,** 23 r. de L'Espérance (M: Gare Jean Lebas), has creative exhibits and a collection that includes works from the 19th and early 20th centuries displayed—where else?—around an indoor pool. (Open Tu-Th 11am-6pm, F 11am-8pm, Sa-Su 1-6pm. €3.50, F students free.) Dating from the 15th century, the **Vieille Bourse** (Old Stock Exchange), pl. Général de Gaulle, is now home to regular book markets. (Open Tu-Su 9:30am-7:30pm.)

To reach the affable **Auberge de Jeunesse (HI)** ❶, 12 r. Malpart, circle left around the train station, then turn right on r. du Molinel, left on r. de Paris, and right on r. Malpart. (☎03 20 57 08 94; lille@fuaj.org. Breakfast and linens included. Reception 24hr. Lockout 11am-3pm. Open late Jan. to mid-Dec. 3- to 6-bed dorms €18. €3 HI discount. MC/V.) **La Pâte Brisée** ❷, 65 r. de la Monnaie, in *vieux* Lille, is garden-themed. (☎03 20 74 29 00. *Menus* €8.50-19.90. Open M-F noon-10:30pm, Sa-Su noon-11pm. MC/V.) At night, students swarm the pubs on **rue Solférino** and **rue Masséna,** while *vieux* Lille has a trendier bar scene.

Trains leave from Gare Lille Flandres, on pl. de la Gare (M: Gare Lille Flandres), for Paris (1hr., 20 per day, €37-50) and Brussels, BEL (1hr., 1-3 per day, €18-24). Gare Lille Europe, on r. Le Corbusier (M: Gare Lille Europe), sends Eurostar trains to Brussels, BEL (40min., 15 per day, €18-24) and London, BRI (1hr., 15 per day, €110-175), and TGVs to Paris (1hr., 6 per day, €37-50). Eurolines **buses** (☎03 20 78 18 88) also leave there for Amsterdam, NTH (5hr., 2 per day, round-trip €47); Brussels, BEL (3 per day, 1hr., round-trip €22); London, BRI (5hr., 2 per day, round-trip €61). The **tourist office,** pl. Rihour (M: Rihour), is inside the Palais Rihour. (☎03 20 21 94 21; www.lilletourism.com. Open M-Sa 9:30am-6:30pm, Su 10am-noon and 2-5pm.) **Postal Code:** 59000.

CALAIS ☎03 21

Calais (pop. 80,000) is a relaxing Channel port where people speak English as often as French. Rodin's famous sculpture **The Burghers of Calais** stands in front of the Hôtel de Ville, at bd. Jacquard and r. Royale, though most come for the **beaches.** Clean and pleasant **Centre Européen de Séjour/Auberge de Jeunesse (HI)** ❶, av. Maréchal Delattre de Tassigny, is less than a block from the beach and offers a bar and library. (☎03 21 34 70 20; www.auberge-jeunesse-calais.com. Wi-Fi €1 per 2 hr. Singles €26; doubles €21. €3 HI discount. AmEx/MC/V.) Open-air morning **markets** are on pl. Crèvecoeur (Th and Sa) and pl. d'Armes (W and Sa). For more info on **ferries** to Dover, BRI see p. 57. During the day, free **buses** connect the ferry terminal and Gare Calais-Ville on bd. Jacquard, where **trains** leave for Boulogne (30min., 11 per day, €8), Lille (1hr., 16 per day, €16), and Paris (3hr., 6 per day, €30-60). The **tourist office** is at 12 bd. Clemenceau. (☎03 21 96 62 40; www.ot-calais.fr. Open June-Aug. M-Sa 10am-1pm and Su 10am-1pm and 2-6:30pm; Sept.-May 10am-1pm.) **Postal Code:** 62100.

CHAMPAGNE AND BURGUNDY

Legend has it that when Dom Perignon first tasted champagne, he exclaimed, "Come quickly! I am drinking stars!" Few modern-day visitors need further

FRANCE

convincing as they flock to the wine cellars in Reims and Épernay. To the east, Burgundy's abbeys and cathedrals bear witness to the Middle Ages's religious fervor. Today, the region draws epicureans with its fine wines and delectable dishes like *coq au vin* and *boeuf bourguignon*.

REIMS ☎03 26

From the 26 monarchs crowned in its cathedral to the bubbling champagne of its famed *caves* (cellars), everything Reims (pop. 191,000) touches turns to gold. The **Cathédrale de Notre-Dame,** built with golden limestone taken from the medieval city walls, features sea-blue stained-glass windows by Marc Chagall, hanging chandeliers, and an impressive royal history. (☎03 26 47 55 34. Open daily 7:30am-7:30pm. Free. English-language audio tour €5.) The adjacent **Palais du Tau,** 2 pl. du Cardinal Luçon, houses original statues from the cathedral's facade alongside majestic 16th-century tapestries. (☎03 26 47 81 79. Open May-Aug. Tu-Su 9:30am-6:30pm; Sept.-Apr. 9:30am-12:30pm and 2-5:30pm. €6.50, 18-25 €4.50, under 18 free.) **Champagne Pommery,** 5 pl. du Général Gouraud, gives the best tours of Reims's champagne caves. Its 75,000L *tonneau* (vat) is one of the largest in the world; it, along with the *maison*'s modern art exhibits, can be viewed in the lobby free of charge. (☎03 26 61 62 56; www.pommery.com. Reservations recommended, €10-17.)

STEER CLEAR. Many of the roads in Reims's *centre-ville* are under serious construction until 2010. If you plan to drive in the city, be prepared for confusing detours and bring an up-to-date road map. The sidewalks remain open, so if you are on foot, the inconveniences will be merely aesthetic.

The **Centre International de Séjour/Auberge de Jeunesse (HI) ❶,** chaussée Bocquaine, has clean rooms. (☎03 26 40 52 60. Breakfast included. Free Wi-Fi. Wheelchair-accessible. Reception 24hr. Dorms €19, with toilet and shower €22; singles €28/41; doubles €21/28; triples with shower €22. €3 HI discount. MC/V.) Restaurants, and bars crowd **place Drouet d'Erlon,** Reims's nightspot. **Trains** leave bd. Joffre for Épernay (20min., 11 per day, €4.80) and Paris (1hr., 11 per day, €21). The **tourist office** is at 2 r. Guillaume de Machault. (☎03 26 77 45 00; www.reims-tourisme.com. Open mid-Apr. to mid-Oct. M-Sa 9am-7pm, Su 10am-6pm; mid-Oct. to mid-Apr. M-Sa 9am-6pm, Su 11am-6pm.) **Postal Code:** 51100.

ÉPERNAY ☎03 26

Champagne's showcase town, Épernay (pop. 26,000) is rightly lavish and seductive. Palatial mansions, lush gardens, and champagne companies distinguish the aptly named **avenue de Champagne.** Here you'll find Moët & Chandon, 20 av. de Champagne, producers of the king of all champagnes: **Dom Perignon.** (☎03 26 51 20 20; www.moet.com. Reservations required. Open daily 9:30-11:30am and 2-4:30pm. Tours with several tasting options for those 18+ €13-25, 10-18 €8, under 10 free.) Ten minutes away is **Mercier,** 70 av. de Champagne, producers of the self-proclaimed "most popular champagne in France." Tours are in roller-coaster-style cars that tell the story of its Willy-Wonka-like founder, Eugène Mercier. (☎03 26 51 22 22. Open mid-Mar. to mid-Nov. daily 9:30-11:30am and 2-4:30pm; mid-Nov. to mid-Dec. and mid-Feb. to mid-Mar. M and Th-Su 9:30-11:30am and 2-4:30pm. Wheelchair-accessible. 30min. tour €8-15.) Budget hotels are rare in Épernay, but **Hôtel St-Pierre ❷,** 1 r. Jeanne d'Arc, offers spacious rooms at unbeatable prices. (☎03 26 54 40 80; fax 57 88 68. www.villasaintpierre.fr. Breakfast €6. Reception 7am-10pm. Singles €21, with shower €30; doubles €24/36. MC/V.) Ethnic food, as well as pricier Champagne-soaked cuisine, line **rue Gambetta,** near the tourist office. Bakeries and delis sporadically dot the area around **place des Arcades** and **place Hugues Plomb.**

Trains leave Cours de la Gare for Paris (1hr., 18 per day, €19) and Strasbourg (3hr., 3 per day, €40). From the station, walk through pl. Mendès France, head from r. Gambetta to pl. de la République, then turn left on av. de Champagne to reach the **tourist office,** 7 av. de Champagne. (☎03 26 53 33 00; www.ot-epernay.fr. Open Mar. 23 to mid-Oct. M-Sa 9:30am-12:30pm and 1:30-7pm, Su 11am-4pm; mid-Oct. to Easter M-Sa 9:30am-12:30pm and 1:30-5:30pm.) **Postal Code:** 51200.

TROYES ☎03 25

Although the city plan resembles a champagne cork, little else links Troyes (pop. 60,000) with its grape-crazy northern neighbors. Troyes features Gothic churches, 16th-century mansions, and an abundance of museums that complement an energy and social scene equal to cities many times its size. The enormous **Cathédrale St-Pierre et St-Paul,** pl. St-Pierre, down r. Clemençeau and past the town hall, is a flamboyant Gothic church with ornate detail and flying buttresses. Its stained glass, in the unique Troyes style, has miraculously survived several fires, bombings, and other disasters. (Open M-Sa 10am-1pm and 2-6pm, Su 10am-noon and 2-5pm. Free.) The **Musée d'Art Moderne,** just next door on pl. St-Pierre, houses over 2000 works by French artists, including Degas, Rodin, and Seurat, in a former Episcopal palace. (☎03 25 76 26 80. Open Tu-Su 10am-1pm and 2-6pm. €5, students and under 18 free. 1st Su of each month free.)

Les Comtes de Champagne ❸, 56 r. de la Monnaie, is in a 16th-century mansion with large, airy rooms. (☎03 25 73 11 70; www.comtesdechampagne.com. Reception 7am-10pm. Singles from €27; doubles from €33; triples from €61; quads from €67. AmEx/MC/V.) Creperies and inexpensive eateries lie near **rue Champeaux,** in **quartier St-Jean,** and on **rue Général Saussier,** in **quartier Vauluisant.** Lining **Champeaux** and **rue Molé** near **place Alexandre Israël,** cafes and taverns draw locals on warm nights. **Trains** run from av. Maréchal Joffre to Paris (1hr., 16 per day, €22). The **tourist office,** 16 bd. Carnot, is one block from the station. (☎03 25 82 62 70; www.ot-troyes.fr. Open Nov.-Mar. M-Sa 9am-12:30pm and 2-6:30pm, Su 10am-1pm; Apr.-Oct. M-Sa 9am-12:30pm and 2-6:30pm.) **Postal Code:** 10000.

DIJON ☎03 80

Dijon (pop. 150,000) isn't just about the mustard. The capital of Burgundy, once home to dukes who

SIPPING IN STYLE

Burgundy is known throughout the world for superb wines and country villages. The only downside of this stellar reputation is the sky-high cost of exploring these cultural treasures. However, Beaune's **Bourgogne Randonnées** offers tours of Burgundy's vineyards that—while far from cheap—are worth every penny.

Tours cost €69-250 per group, and comprehensively examine life in Beaune. The most affordable tour is a half-day extravaganza that includes a bike ride through the countryside, a tour through a local vineyard, and lunch with a *dégustation* (tasting) of six different wines. The most expensive tour is a half-day of driving, walking, or biking through a number of Côte de Beaune villages and vineyards, with a guide to explain everything from the history of the villages to how soil affects the wine's quality.

Sarah Bird, a fluent French and English speaker, leads all the tours with a contagious enthusiasm; she tailors each outing to suit travelers' particular interests. While the price tag on the tours could put quite a dent in the solo traveler's budget, the memorable day will be worth the euro, and you'll return from the vineyards with your thirsts—for wine or knowledge—quenched.

7 av. du 8 Septembre (☎03 80 22 06 03; www.bourgogne-randonnees.com).

wielded a power unmatched by the French monarchy, counters its historic grandeur with a modern irreverence. The diverse **Musée des Beaux-Arts** occupies the east wing of the colossal Palais des Ducs de Bourgogne, on pl. de la Libération, at the center of the *vieille ville.* (☎03 80 74 52 70. Open M and W-Su May-Oct. 9:30am-6pm; Nov.-Apr. 10am-5pm. Free. Temporary exhibits €2, students €1.) Built in only 20 years, the **Église Notre-Dame,** pl. Notre Dame, is one of France's most famous churches. Its 11th-century statue of the Black Virgin is credited with having liberated the city on two occasions: in 1513 from a Swiss siege and in 1944 from the German occupation (☎03 80 41 86 76; www.notre-dame-dijon.net). Dijon's **Estivade** (☎03 80 74 53 33; tickets under €8) brings dance, music, and theater to the city throughout July. In late summer, the week-long **Fêtes de la Vigne** and **Folkloriades Internationales** (☎03 80 30 37 95; www.fetesdelavigne.com; tickets €10-46) celebrate the grape harvest with dance and music from around the world. **Hotel Le Jacquemart ❸,** 32 r. Verrerie, offers florally decorated rooms and a gorgeous, old-fashioned staircase. (☎03 80 60 09 60. Breakfast €5.85. Reception 24hr. Singles €29-53; doubles €32-64. AmEx/MC/V.) **Rue Amiral Boussin** has charming cafes, while reasonably priced restaurants line **rue Berbisey, rue Monge, rue Musette,** and **place Émile Zola.** From the station at cours de la Gare, **trains** run to Lyon (2hr., 14 per day, €25), Nice (6-8hr., 6-8 per day, €88), and Paris (1-3hr., 15-19 per day, €52). The **tourist office** is at 34 r. des Forges. (☎08 92 70 05 58; www.dijon-tourism.com. Open daily May to mid-Oct. 9am-7pm; mid-Oct. to Apr. 10am-6pm.) **Postal Code:** 21000.

ALSACE-LORRAINE AND FRANCHE-COMTÉ

Influenced by its tumultuous past, the region's fascinating blend of French and German shows its dual heritage in local dialects, cuisine, and architecture. Alsatian towns display half-timbered Bavarian houses, while Lorraine's wheat fields are interspersed with elegant cities.

STRASBOURG ☎03 88

Just a few kilometers from the Franco-German border, Strasbourg (pop. 270,000) is a city with true international character. *Winstubs* (wine-bar restaurants specializing in local dishes) sit peacefully beside *pâtisseries* in the *vieille ville*, while German and French conversations mingle in the street.

BIG BUCKS FOR BIGWIGS. Prices rise during EU plenary sessions. To take in the city's sights without going broke, avoid visiting (during these dates in 2009) Jan. 12-15, Feb. 2-5, Mar. 9-12 and 23-26, Apr. 21-24, May 4-7, July 14-16, Sept. 14-17, Oct. 19-22, Nov. 23-26, and Dec. 14-17.

TRANSPORATION AND PRACTICAL INFORMATION. Trains leave from Pl. de la Gare. to Frankfurt, Germany (2-4hr., 13 per day, €52); Luxembourg (2-3hr., 10 per day, €33); Paris (4hr., 24 per day, €47; TGV 2hr., €63); Zurich, Switzerland (3hr., 4 per day, €40-47). SNCF **buses** run to surrounding towns from the station. The **Compagnie des Transports Strasbourgeois** (CTS), 14 rue de la Gare aux Marchandises (☎77 70 11, bus and tram info 77 70 70; www.cts-strasbourg.fr) has 5 tram lines which run 4:30am-12:30am. Find tickets (€1.30, round-trip €2.50) on board and *carnets* of 10 (€11.50) and day passes (€3.50) at **CTS,** 56 rue du Jeu des Enfants. Open M-F 8:30am-6:30pm, Sa 9am-5pm.) The **tourist office** is at 17 pl. de la Cathédrale. (☎03 88 52 28 28; www.ot-strasbourg.fr. Open daily 9am-7pm. There's also a branch at pl. de la Gare. (☎03 88 32 51 49. Open M-Sa 9am-12:30pm and 1:45-7pm.) **Postal Code:** 67000.

ACCOMMODATIONS AND FOOD. Great deals on hotels are all over the city, especially around the train station. Wherever you stay, make reservations early. Hotel prices often drop on weekends and when the EU Parliament is not in session. Near the train station, **Hôtel le Grillon ❷,** 2 r. Thiergarten, this offers the best value. (☎03 88 32 71 88; www.grillon.com. Breakfast €7.50. Internet €1 per 15min; free Wi-Fi. Reception 24hr. Singles €33, with shower €43-58; doubles €40/50-65. Extra bed €13. MC/V.) The scenic **La Petite France** neighborhood, especially along r. des Dentelles, is full of *winstubs* with Alsatian specialties.

SIGHTS. The **Cathédrale de Strasbourg** is a Gothic cathedral with a tower that stretches 142m skyward; young Goethe scaled its 332 steps to cure his fear of heights. Inside, the **Horloge Astronomique** demonstrates 16th-century Swiss clockmaking wizardry. Also check out the **Pilier des Anges** (Angels' Pillar), a depiction of the Last Judgment. (Cathedral open M-Sa 7-11:40am and 12:40-7pm, Su 12:45-6pm. Tower open daily July-Aug. 9am-7:15pm; Apr.-June and Sept. 9am-6pm; Mar. and Oct. 9am-5:30pm; Nov.-Feb. 9am-4:30pm. Clock tickets sold at the northern entrance; €1. Tower €4.60, students €2.30.) The Palais Rohan houses three excellent museums. The Musée des Beaux-Arts displays 14th- to 19th-century art, including works by Botticelli, Giotto, Goya, Raphaël, and Rubens. The **Musée des Arts Décoratifs,** refurbished for Napoleon in 1805, features pistachio-green rooms encrusted with gold and marble, including the emperor's bedroom and library. The **Musée Archéologique** illustrates Alsace's history through relics and a slew of skeletons. (2 pl. du Château. All open M and W-Su 10am-6pm. €6 each, students €3; free 1st Su of every month.)

NIGHTLIFE. Strasbourg specializes in friendly bars rather than throbbing clubs. **Place Kléber** attracts a student scene, while **rue des Frères** fills up quickly after 10pm with a diverse crowd. **Bar Exils,** 28 r. de l'Ail, boasts over 40 beers, leather couches, and an unflagging spirit that buzzes into the early morning. (☎03 88 35 52 70. Beer from €2; after 10pm €2.50. Open M-F noon-4am, Sa-Su 2pm-4am. MC/V min. €6.) Rock all night at **Le Tribord,** Ponts Couverts, a lively gay and lesbian club. (From pl. du Quartier Blanc, make a right onto the footpath by the canal in front of the Hotel du Départment, following it to the waterside. The club is the first boat on the right. ☎03 88 36 22 90. Beer from €2.50. Mixed drinks from €4. Open Th-Sa 10pm-4am.)

LA ROUTE DU VIN

The vineyards of Alsace flourish in a 150km corridor along the foothills of the Vosges from Strasbourg to Mulhouse—a region known as the Route du Vin. The Romans were the first to ferment Alsatian grapes, and today Alsatians sell over 150 million bottles annually. Consider staying in **Colmar** (p. 348) or **Sélestat** (p. 348), larger towns that anchor the southern Route, and daytripping to the smaller (and pricier) towns. The best source of info on regional *caves* is the **Centre d'Information du Vin d'Alsace,** 12 av. de la Foire aux Vins, at the Maison du Vin d'Alsace in Colmar. (☎03 89 20 16 20. Open M-F 9am-noon and 2-5pm.)

TRANSPORTATION

Buses, the cheapest option, run frequently from Colmar to surrounding towns, though smaller northern towns are difficult to reach. **Car rental** from Strasbourg or Colmar resolves transportation problems, albeit at a steep cost. Despite well marked trails, only those with stamina should bike the lengthy and often hilly roads from Colmar. **Trains** connect Sélestat, Molsheim, Barr, Colmar, and Mulhouse. Minimal sidewalks make country roads difficult to walk along.

SÉLESTAT ☎03 88

Sélestat (pop. 17,500), between Colmar and Strasbourg, is a haven of good wines and good vibes that is often overlooked by tourists on their way to more "authentic" Route cities. The **Maison du Pain,** on r. du Sel, reveals the history of breadmaking from 12,500 BC to the present. View models of ancient and modern bakeries before taking history into your own hands: a workshop in the ground-floor patisserie allows visitors to twist and bake their own **pretzels.** (Open Dec. daily 10am-7pm; Jan. and Mar.-Nov. Tu-F 9:30am-12:30pm and 2-6pm, Sa 9am-12:30pm and 2-6pm, Su 9am-12:30pm and 2:30-6pm. Closed Dec. 25-Jan. 7 and mid-Jan. to Feb. €4.60, students €3.80, ages 16-18 €1.60.) Founded in 1452, the **Bibliothèque Humaniste,** 1 r. de la Bibliothèque, contains a fascinating collection of illuminated manuscripts and meticulously handwritten books produced during Sélestat's 15th-century Humanist heyday. (Open July-Aug. M and W-F 9am-noon and 2-6pm, Sa 9am-noon and 2-5pm, Su 2-5pm; Sept.-June M-F 9am-noon and 2-6pm, Sa 9am-noon. €3.80, students €2.30.)

Hôtel de l'Ill ❸, 13 r. des Bateliers, has 15 rooms with shower and TV. (☎03 88 92 91 09. Breakfast €5. Reception 7am-9pm. Check-out 10am. Singles €33; doubles €42; triples €50. AmEx/MC/V.) **JP Kamm ❶,** 15 r. des Clefs, has outdoor dining and a large selection of mouthwatering desserts. (☎03 88 92 11 04. Pizzas and quiches €3.80-5.40. Ice cream from €4.60. Open Tu and Th-F 8am-7pm, W 8:30am-7pm, Sa 8am-6pm, Su 8am-1pm. Terrace service Tu-F until 6:30pm, Sa until 5:30pm. MC/V min. €8.) From pl. de la Gare, **trains** run to Colmar (15min., 38 per day, €4) and Strasbourg (30min., 54 per day, €7). (Ticket office open M 6am-7pm, Tu-F 7am-7pm, Sa 8:30am-5pm, Su 11:20am-6:50pm.) The **tourist office** is at bd. Général Leclerc. (☎03 89 58 87 20; www.selestat-tourisme.com. Open July-Aug. M-F 9:30am-12:30pm and 1:30-6:30pm, Sa 9am-12:30pm and 2-5pm, Su 10:30am-3pm; Sept.-June reduced hours.) **Postal Code:** 67600.

FRANCE

COLMAR ☎03 89

Colmar (pop. 68,000) is a great base for exploring smaller Route towns. The **Musée Unterlinden,** 1 r. d'Unterlinden has a collection ranging from Romanesque to Renaissance, including Grünewald's Issenheim Altarpiece, an Alsatian treasure. (Open May-Oct. daily 9am-6pm; Nov.-Apr. M and W-Su 9am-noon and 2-5pm. €7, students €5. MC/V min. €8.) The **Église des Dominicains,** pl. des Dominicains, is a bare-bones showroom for Colmar's other masterpiece, Schongauer's ornate *Virgin in the Rose Bower.* (Open June-Oct. M-Th and Su 10am-1pm and 3-6pm, F-Sa 10am-6pm; Apr.-May and Nov.-Dec. daily 10am-1pm and 3-6pm. €1.50, students €1.) The 10-day **Foire aux Vins d'Alsace** is the region's largest wine fair, with concerts, free tastings, and exhibitions. (Mid-Aug. ☎03 90 50 50 50; www.foire-colmar.com. 11:30am-1:30pm €1, 1:30pm-5pm €4, after 5pm €6. Concerts €20-43.) To reach the **Auberge de Jeunesse (HI) ❶,** 2 r. Pasteur, take bus #4 (dir.: Europe) to Pont Rouge. On Sundays take Bus B (dir.: Ingershiem) to Pont Rouge. (☎03 89 80 57 39. Breakfast included. Linens €4. Reception Nov. to mid-Dec. and mid-Jan. to Feb. 7-10am and 5-11pm; Apr.-Sept. 7-10am and 5pm-10:30pm. Lockout 10am-5pm. Curfew in summer midnight, in winter 11pm.

Open mid-Jan. to mid-Dec. Dorms €13; singles €17; doubles €26. HI discount €3. MC/V.) **Trains** depart pl. de la Gare for Lyon (4-5hr., 9 per day, €42), Paris (5hr., 2 per day, €52), and Strasbourg (30min., 12 per day, €10). The **tourist office** is at 4 r. d'Unterlinden. (☎03 89 20 68 92; www.ot-colmar.fr. Open July-Aug. M-Sa 9am-7pm, Su 10am-1pm; Sept.-June reduced hours.) **Postal Code:** 68000.

NANCY ☎03 83

Nancy (pop. 106,000) the intellectual heart of modern Lorraine with its many museums and beautiful architecture. The works on display at the **Musée de L'École de Nancy,** 36-38 r. du Sergent Blandan, reject straight lines, instead using organic forms to recreate aspects of the natural landscape. Take bus #122 (dir.: Villers Clairlieu) or 123 (dir.: Vandoeuvre Cheminots) to Painlevé. (☎03 83 40 14 86; www.ecole-de-nancy.com. Open W-Su 10:30am-6pm. €6, students €4. W students free. €8 pass to all museums.) The recently renovated **place Stanislas** houses three Neoclassical pavilions, including place de la Carrière, a former jousting ground that Stanislas Leszczynski—Duke of Lorraine from 1737 to 1766—refurbished with Baroque architecture, golden angel sculptures, and wrought-iron ornaments. The place's beauty can be absorbed over a large cup of coffee at one of its many cafes. **Rue Stanislas** and **Grand Rue** are great places to grab a drink. Suave, smoky **Blitz,** 76 r. St-Julien, is decorated in red velvet. (Beer from €2.30. Mixed drinks from €5. Open M 5:30pm-2am, Tu-Sa 2pm-2am. July-Aug. also open Su 5:30pm-1am. AmEx/MC/V min. €7 charge.)

Don't let the exterior of **Hôtel de L'Académie ❷,** 7 r. des Michottes, deter you; it has large, clean rooms in a convenient location. (☎03 83 35 52 31. Breakfast €3.50. Reception 7am-11pm. Singles €20-28; doubles €28-39. AmEx/MC/V.) Immerse yourself in the cheesy delights of **Le Bouche à Oreille ❷,** 42 r. des Carmes (☎03 83 35 17 17. Fondues €14-15. Lunch *menu* €11. Dinner *menu* €18. Open M, Sa 7-10:30pm, Tu-F noon-1:30pm and 7-10:30pm. AmEx/MC/V.). Restaurants also line **rue des Maréchaux, place Lafayette,** and **place St-Epvre.**

Trains depart from the station at 3 pl. Thiers for Paris (3 hr., 27 per day, €42-50) and Strasbourg (1hr., 20 per day, €23). The new **TGV** Est line also connects Nancy to Paris (1hr. To reach the **tourist office,** head through pl. Thiers, turn left on r. Mazagran, pass through a stone archway on the right, and continue straight. (☎03 83 35 22 41; www.ot-nancy.fr. Open Apr.-Oct. M-Sa 9am-7pm, Su 10am-5pm; Nov.-Mar. M-Sa 9am-6pm, Su 10am-1pm.) **Postal Code:** 54000.

BESANÇON ☎03 81

Bounded by the Doubs River on three sides and a steep bluff on the fourth, Besançon (pop. 123,000) hosts a slew of world-class museums and an active student population. Julius Caesar conquered the vulnerable city in 58 BC, unaware that Vauban's enormous 17th-century **citadelle** would one day make Besançon impenetrable. Besançon's mountaintop fortresses require an intense uphill climb to reach but reward visitors with breathtaking displays. Within the citadelle, the **Musée de la Résistance et de la Déportation** chronicles the Nazi rise to power and the events of WWII from a French perspective. (☎03 71 87 83 33; www.citadelle.com. Open daily July-Aug. 9am-7pm, Sept.-June reduced hours. In summer €7.80, students €6.50; in winter €7.20/6.) To reach the **Foyer Mixte de Jeunes Travailleurs (HI) ❷,** 48 r. des Cras, take a left from the train station onto r. de la Viotte, the first right onto r. de l'Industrie, then a right on r. de Belfort to pl. de la Liberté. Take bus #5 or night line A (dir.: Orchamps, 3-5 per hr., €1.15) to the Les Oiseaux stop. The hostel offers clean rooms with private bathrooms and Wi-Fi in the rooms. (☎03 81 40 32 00. Breakfast included. Open Apr.-Sept. Singles €23, 2nd night €18. AmEx/MC/V.) **Rue Claude-Pouillet** and **rue des Granges** have the cheapest eateries and the best nightlife.

Trains (☎08 36 35 35 35) leave av. de la Paix for Dijon (1hr., 34 per day, €13), Paris (2hr., 9 per day, €49), and Strasbourg (3hr., 9 per day, €30). Monts Jura **buses,** with an office in the train station (☎08 25 00 22 44), go to Pontarlier (1hr., 8 per day, €7.50). From the station, walk downhill; follow av. de la Paix as it turns into av. Maréchal Foch and continue to the left as it becomes av. de l'Helvétie before the river. Once you reach pl. de la 1ère Armée Française, the *vieille ville* is across the pont de la République. The **tourist office,** 2 pl. de la 1ère Armée Française, is in the park to the right. (☎03 81 80 92 55; www.besancon-tourisme.com. Open June-Sept. M 10am-7pm, Tu-Sa 9:30am-7pm, Su 10am-5pm; Oct.-May reduced hours.) **Postal Code:** 25000.

RHÔNE-ALPES AND MASSIF CENTRAL

Nature's architecture is the Alps' real attraction. The curves of the Chartreuse Valley rise to rugged crags in the Vercors range and crescendo at Europe's highest peak, Mont Blanc (4807m). From bases like Chamonix, winter skiers enjoy some of the world's most challenging slopes. In summer, hikers take over the mountains, seeking pristine vistas and clear air.

LYON ☎04 78

Ultra-modern, ultra-friendly, and undeniably gourmet, Lyon (pop. 453,000) elicits cries of "Forget Paris!" from backpackers. Its location—at the confluence of the Rhône and Saône rivers and along an Italian road—earned Lyon (then Lugdunum) its place as Roman Gaul's capital. A transportation hub, Lyon is now better known for its beautiful parks, modern financial center, well-preserved Renaissance quarter, and fantastic restaurants.

TRANSPORTATION

Flights: Aéroport Lyon-St-Exupéry (LYS; ☎08 26 80 08 26). Satobuses/Navette Aéroport (☎72 68 72 17) **shuttles** to Gare de la Part-Dieu, Gare de Perrache, and subway stops Grange-Blanche, Jean Macé, and Mermoz Pinel (every 20min., €8.60). **Air France,** 10 q. Jules Courmont, *2ème* (☎08 20 32 08 20), has 10 daily flights to Paris's **Orly** and **Charles de Gaulle airports** (from €118). Open M-Sa 9am-6pm.

Trains: The convenient **TGV,** which stops at the airport, is cheaper than daily flights to Paris. Trains passing through stop at **Gare de la Part-Dieu,** 5 pl. Béraudier (M: Part-Dieu), on the Rhône's east bank. Info desk open daily 5am-12:45am. Ticket window open M-Th and Sa 5:15am-11pm, F and Su 5:15am-midnight. Trains terminating in Lyon continue to Gare de Perrache, pl. Carnot (M: Perrache). Open daily 4:45am-12:30am. Ticket window open M 5am-10pm, Tu-Sa 5:30am-10pm, Su 7am-10pm. **SNCF trains** go from both stations to: **Dijon** (2hr., 1 per hr., €26); **Grenoble** (1hr., 1 per hr., €18); **Marseille** (1hr., 1 per hr., €44); **Nice** (6hr., 3 per day, €62); **Paris** (2hr., 17 per day, €60); **Strasbourg** (5hr., 6 per day, €49); **Geneva, SWI** (4hr., 6 per day, €23). The **SNCF Boutique** is at 2 pl. Bellecour. Open M-F 9am-6:45pm, Sa 10am-6:30pm.

Buses: On the Gare de Perrache's lowest level and at Gorge de Loup in the 9*ème* (☎72 61 72 61). It's almost always cheaper and faster to take the train. Domestic companies include **Philibert** (☎72 75 06 06). **Eurolines** (☎72 56 95 30; www.eurolines.fr) travels out of France; office on the main floor of Perrache open M-Sa 9am-9pm.

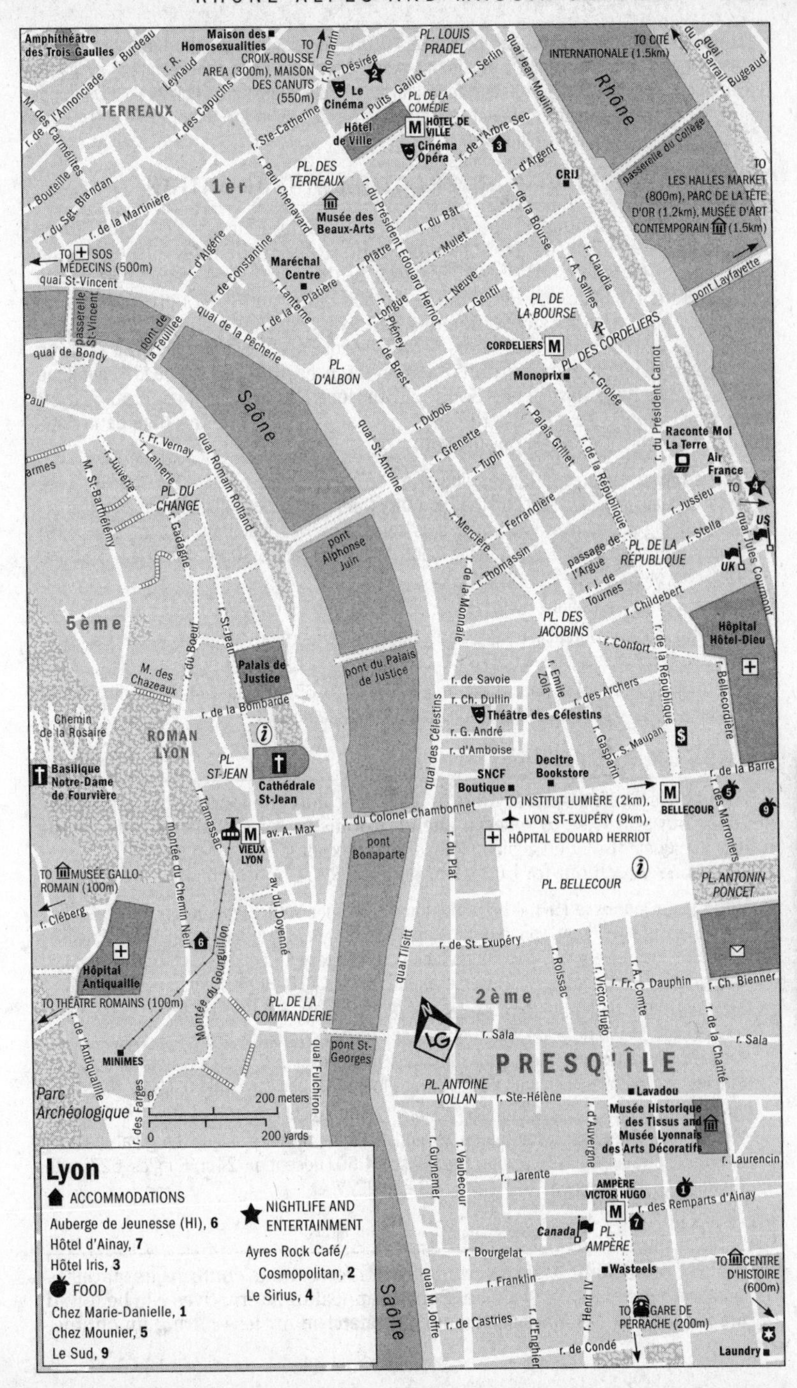
Lyon
ACCOMMODATIONS
Auberge de Jeunesse (HI), 6
Hôtel d'Ainay, 7
Hôtel Iris, 3
FOOD
Chez Marie-Danielle, 1
Chez Mounier, 5
Le Sud, 9
NIGHTLIFE AND ENTERTAINMENT
Ayres Rock Café/ Cosmopolitan, 2
Le Sirius, 4
Amphithéâtre des Trois Gaulles
Maison des Homosexualities
TO CROIX-ROUSSE AREA (300m), MAISON DES CANUTS (550m)
PL. LOUIS PRADEL
TO CITÉ INTERNATIONALE (1.5km)
Rhône
TERREAUX
Le Cinéma
Hôtel de Ville
HÔTEL DE VILLE
PL. DE LA COMÉDIE
Cinéma Opéra
PL. DES TERREAUX
Musée des Beaux-Arts
1èr
CRIJ
TO LES HALLES MARKET (800m), PARC DE LA TÊTE D'OR (1.2km), MUSÉE D'ART CONTEMPORAIN (1.5km)
TO SOS MÉDECINS (500m)
Maréchal Centre
quai St-Vincent
passerelle St-Vincent
pont de la Feuillée
quai de Bondy
quai de la Pêcherie
Saône
PL. D'ALBON
PL. DE LA BOURSE
CORDELIERS
PL. DES CORDELIERS
Monoprix
pont Lafayette
Raconte Moi La Terre
Air France
US
UK
PL. DU CHANGE
PL. DE LA RÉPUBLIQUE
PL. DES JACOBINS
pont Alphonse Juin
5ème
Palais de Justice
pont du Palais de Justice
Théâtre des Célestins
Hôpital Hôtel-Dieu
Chemin de la Rosaire
ROMAN LYON
PL. ST-JEAN
Cathédrale St-Jean
Basilique Notre-Dame de Fourvière
Decitre Bookstore
SNCF Boutique
BELLECOUR
TO INSTITUT LUMIÈRE (2km), LYON ST-EXUPÉRY (9km), HÔPITAL EDOUARD HERRIOT
VIEUX LYON
pont Bonaparte
PL. BELLECOUR
PL. ANTONIN PONCET
TO MUSÉE GALLO-ROMAIN (100m)
Hôpital Antiquaille
TO THÉÂTRE ROMAINS (100m)
MINIMES
2ème
PL. DE LA COMMANDERIE
pont St-Georges
PRESQ'ÎLE
Parc Archéologique
200 meters
200 yards
PL. ANTOINE VOLLAN
Lavadou
Musée Historique des Tissus and Musée Lyonnais des Arts Décoratifs
AMPÈRE VICTOR HUGO
Canada
PL. AMPÈRE
Wasteels
TO CENTRE D'HISTOIRE (600m)
TO GARE DE PERRACHE (200m)
Laundry
quai St-Antoine
quai Romain Rolland
quai des Célestins
quai Tilsitt
quai Fulchiron
quai M. Joffre
quai Jean Moulin
quai Jules Courmont
quai du G. Sarrail
passerelle du Collège
r. du Président Edouard Herriot
r. de la République
r. du Président Carnot
r. Victor Hugo
r. Sala
r. du Colonel Chambonnet
av. A. Max
montée du Chemin Neuf
Montée du Gourguillon
av. du Doyenné
r. St-Jean
r. du Boeuf
r. de la Bombarde
r. de St. Exupéry
r. Ste-Hélène
r. Franklin
r. de Castries
r. de Condé
r. Bourgelat
r. Jarente
r. des Remparts d'Ainay

Local Transportation: TCL (☎08 20 42 70 00; www.tcl.fr) has information offices at both bus stations and all major metro stops. *Plan de Poche* (pocket map) available from any TCL branch. Tickets valid for all forms of mass transport. (Tickets €1.60, carnet of 10 €12.80; student discount includes 10 passes valid for 1 month €11.10. Pass valid 1hr. in 1 dir., connections included.)

ORIENTATION AND PRACTICAL INFORMATION

Lyon is divided into nine *arrondissements* (districts). The 1*er*, 2*ème*, and 4*ème* lie on the *presqu'île* (peninsula), which juts toward the Saône River to the west and the Rhône to the east. Starting in the south, the 2*ème* (the centre ville) includes the Gare de Perrache and place Bellecour. The nocturnal **Terreaux** neighborhood, with its sidewalk cafes and lively, student-packed bars, makes up the 1*er*. Farther north, the *presqu'île* widens into the 4*ème* and the famous **Croix-Rousse.** The main pedestrian roads on the *presqu'île* are **rue de la République** and **rue Victor Hugo West** of the Saône, Fourvière Hill and its basilica overlook **Vieux Lyon** (5*ème*). East of the Rhône (3*ème* and 6-8*ème*) lie the **Gare de la Part-Dieu** and most of the city's population.

Tourist Office: Located in the Pavilion at pl. Bellecour, 2*ème* (☎04 72 77 69 69; www.lyon-france.com). M: Bellecour. The **Lyon City Card** authorizes unlimited public transportation along with admission to museums, tours, and river boat cruises. 1-day pass €19; 2-day €29; 3-day €39. Open June-Sept. M-Sa 9:30am-6:30pm, Su 10am-5:30pm; Oct.-May M-Sa 10am-5:30pm. MC/V.

Police: 47 r. de la Charité, ☎04 78 42 26 56. M: Perrache.

Hospital: Hôpital Hôtel-Dieu, 1 pl. de l'Hôpital, 2*ème*, near q. du Rhône, is the most central. City hospital line ☎04 78 08 20 69.

Post Office: pl. Antonin Poncet, 2*ème* (☎04 72 40 65 22), near pl. Bellecour. **Postal Code:** 69001-69009; last digit indicates *arrondissement.*

ACCOMMODATIONS

September is Lyon's busiest month; it's easier and cheaper to find a place in summer but still wise to reserve ahead. Rooms under €30 are rare. Low-end hotels are east of place Carnot. There are inexpensive options north of place des Terraux. Watch out for budget-breaking accommodations in *vieux* Lyon.

Auberge de Jeunesse (HI), 41-45 montée du Chemin Neuf, 5*ème* (☎04 78 15 05 50, www.fuaj.org). M: Vieux Lyon. A terrace and bar draw international backpackers. English-speaking staff. Breakfast and linens included. Laundry €4.05. Internet €5 per hr. Max. 6-night stay. Reception 24hr. Reserve ahead. Dorms €16. HI members only. MC/V. ❶

Hôtel Iris, 36 r. de l'Arbre Sec, 1er (☎04 78 39 93 80, ☎04 72 00 89 91; www.hoteliris.freesurf.fr). M: Hôtel de Ville. This tranquil former convent is in a prime location near Terreaux. Breakfast €5. Reception 8am-8:30pm. Reserve 2 weeks ahead in summer. Singles and doubles with sink €35-42, with toilet and shower €48-50. MC/V ❸

Hôtel d'Ainay, 14 r. des Remparts d'Ainay, 2*ème* (☎04 78 42 43 42). M: Ampère-Victor Hugo. Offers spacious rooms with private bath. Travelers enjoy the great location between Perrache and Bellecour. Breakfast €4.50. Reception 24hr. Singles €27, with shower €42; doubles €32/48. Extra bed €8. MC/V. ❸

FOOD

The galaxy of Michelin stars adorning Lyon's restaurants confirms its status as the gastronomic capital of France. Equally appealing alternatives can be found on **rue St-Jean, rue des Marronniers,** and **rue Mercière** for less during lunchtime.

Ethnic restaurants center on **rue de la République.** There are markets on the *quais* of the **Rhône** and **Saône** (open Tu-Su 8am-1pm).

THE PRIDE OF LYON

The pinnacle of the Lyonnais food scene is **Restaurant Paul Bocuse ❺,** 4km out of town, where the *menus* (€120-195) definitely cost more than your hotel room. (☎04 72 42 90 90; www.bocuse.fr. MC/V.) Some of these restaurants occasionally have more accessible weekend buffet brunches hovering around €30-40; check outside or call. However, gourmands need not sell their souls to enjoy Bocusian cuisine; the master has several **spin-off restaurants** in Lyon, themed around the four corners of the earth: Le Nord, Le Sud, L'Est and L'Ouest. Whether heading north, south, east, or west, reserve ahead.

Le Sud, 11 pl. Antonin Poncet, 2*ème* (☎04 72 77 80 00). M: Bellecour. Specializing in "la cuisine du soleil," Le Sud serves up Mediterranean fare in a casual dining room decorated with a huge metal sun. A seafood dish (from €15) is worth the splurge. Pasta dishes from €12. *Menus* €19-22. Open daily noon-2:30pm and 7-11pm, F-Sa noon-2-:30pm and 7pm-midnight. AmEx/MC/V. ❹

Chez Mounier, 3 r. des Marronniers, 2*ème* (☎04 78 37 79 26). M: Bellecour. Despite small portions, a friendly staff, top-notch cuisine, and great prices make this small restaurant a good choice. Afternoon *menu* €8. 4-course *menus* €11-20. Open Tu-Sa noon-2pm and 7-11pm, Su noon-1:30pm. MC/V. ❸

Chez Marie-Danielle, 29 r. des Remparts d'Ainay (☎04 78 37 65 60). M: Ampère-Victor Hugo. Award-winning chef Marie-Danielle makes guests feel at home as she whips up superb *lyonnais* fare in her intimate eatery. Lunch *menu* €15. Dinner *menu* €22. Open M-F noon-2pm and 7:30-10pm. MC/V. ❹

SIGHTS

VIEUX LYON

Stacked against the Saône at the foot of the Fourvière hill, *vieux* Lyon's narrow streets are home to lively cafes, hidden passageways, and magnificent medieval and Renaissance homes. The striking *hôtels particuliers*, with their delicate carvings and ornate turrets, sprang up between the 15th and 18th centuries when Lyon was the center of Europe's silk and printing industries.

TRABOULES. The distinguishing features of vieux Lyon townhouses are their *traboules*, tunnels connecting parallel streets through a maze of courtyards, often with vaulted ceilings and exquisite spiral staircases. Although their original purpose is debated, the *traboules* were often used to transport silk from looms to storage rooms. During WWII, the passageways proved invaluable as info-gathering and escape routes for the Resistance. Many are open to the public. A 2hr. tour beginning at the tourist office is the ideal way to see them. The tourist office has a list of open *traboules* and their addresses. *(English-language tours in summer every few days at 2:30pm; winter hours vary. €9, students €5.)*

CATHÉDRALE ST-JEAN. The cathedral's soaring columns dominate the southern end of *vieux* Lyon. It was here that Henri IV met and married Maria de Médici in 1600. Inside, every hour between noon and 4pm, mechanical angels pop out of the 14th-century **astronomical clock** in a reenactment of the Annunciation. *(Open M-F 8am-noon and 2-7:30pm, Sa-Su 8am-noon and 2-7pm. Free.)*

FRANCE

FOURVIÈRE AND ROMAN LYON

Fourvière Hill, the nucleus of Roman Lyon, is accessible via the rose-lined **Chemin de la Rosaire** (garden open daily 6am-9:30pm) and, for the more sedentary, *la ficelle* (funicular), which leaves from the *vieux* Lyon Metro station.

BASILIQUE NOTRE-DAME DE FOURVIÈRE. During the Franco-Prussian War, the people of Lyon prayed fervently to the Virgin Mary for protection; afterward, they erected this magnificent basilica in her honor. *(Behind the esplanade at the top of the hill. Chapel open daily 7am-7pm. Basilica open daily 8am-7pm.)*

MUSÉE GALLO-ROMAIN. Taking up five mostly underground floors, this expansive museum educates and fascinates. Both history buffs and novices will appreciate a collection of mosaics and statues. *(☎72 38 81 90; www.musees-gallo-romains.com. Open Tu-Su 10am-6pm. €3.80, students €2.30; under 18 and Th free.)*

PARC ARCHÉOLOGIQUE. While the Musée Gallo-Romain provides a wonderful collection of artifacts, the Roman experience in Lyon isn't complete without a walk through this ancient park. Next to the Minimes/Théâtre Romain funicular stop, the Parc holds the well-restored 2000-year-old **Théâtre Romain** and the **Odéon,** discovered when modern developers dug into the hill. On summer evenings, relax and enjoy the show; the **Nuits de Fourvière festival** plays in both venues. *(Open daily mid-Apr. to mid-Sept. 7am-9pm; mid-Sept. to mid-Apr. 7am-7pm. Free.)*

LA PRESQU'ÎLE AND LES TERREAUX

Monumental squares, statues, and fountains are the *presqu'île's* trademarks. At its heart, **place Bellecour** links Lyon's two main pedestrian arteries. Boutique-lined **rue Victor Hugo** runs south. To the north, crowded **rue de la République,** or "la Ré," is Lyon's urban aorta. It continues through **place de la République,** ending at **place Louis Pradel** in the 1*er*, at the tip of the **Terreaux district.** Once a marshy wasteland, it was filled with soil, creating a neighborhood of dry *terreaux* (terraces) where today chic bars keep things hopping long into the night.

MUSÉE HISTORIQUE DES TISSUS. Clothing and textile fanatics will enjoy the rows of extravagant 18th-century dresses and 4000-year-old Egyptian tunics displayed here. The neighboring **Musée des Arts Décoratifs,** housed in an 18th-century *hôtel* has rooms showcasing clocks and silverware from the Renaissance to the present. *(34 r. de la Charité, 2ème. M: Ampère Victor Hugo. ☎04 78 38 42 00, www.musee-des-tissus.com. Tissus open Tu-Su 10am-5:30pm. Arts Décoratifs open Tu-Su 10am-noon and 2-5:30pm. €5, students €3.50, under 18 free; includes both museums.)*

FRANCE

LA CROIX-ROUSSE AND THE SILK INDUSTRY

Though mass silk manufacturing is based elsewhere today, Lyon is proud of its historical dominance of the industry in Europe. The city's **Croix-Rousse district,** a steep, uphill walk from pl.Terreaux, houses the vestiges of its silk-weaving days; Lyon's few remaining silk workers still create delicate handiwork, reconstructing and replicating rare patterns for museum and château displays.

LA MAISON DES CANUTS. The silk industry lives on at this Croix-Rousse workshop, which provides the best intro to Lyon's *canuts* (silk weavers). Scarves cost €32 or more, but silk enthusiasts can purchase a handkerchief for €9. *(10-12 r. d'Ivry, 4ème. ☎04 78 28 62 04. Open Tu-Sa 10am-6:30pm. €5, students €2.50, under 12 free. English-language tours daily at 11am and 3:30pm.)*

EAST OF THE RHÔNE AND MODERN LYON

Lyon's newest train station and monstrous space-age mall form the core of the ultra-modern Part-Dieu district. Locals call the **Tour du Crédit Lyonnais** "le Crayon" for its unintentional resemblance to a giant pencil standing on end. Next to it, the shell-shaped **Auditorium Maurice Ravel** hosts major cultural events.

CENTRE D'HISTOIRE DE LA RÉSISTANCE ET DE LA DÉPORTATION. Housed in a building where Nazis tortured detainees during the Occupation, the museum presents documents, photos, and films about Lyon's role in the Resistance. *(14 av. Bertholet, 7ème. M: Jean Macé. ☎04 78 72 23 11. Open W-F 9am-5:30pm, Sa-Su 9:30am-6pm. €4, students €2, under 18 free; includes audio tour in 3 languages.)*

MUSÉE D'ART CONTEMPORAIN. This extensive mecca of modern art, video, and high-tech installations resides in the futuristic **Cité International de Lyon,** a super-modern complex with shops, theaters, and Interpol's world headquarters. All of its exhibits are temporary—even the walls are rebuilt for each display. *(Q. Charles de Gaulle, next to Parc de la Tête d'Or, 6ème. Take bus #4 from M: Foch. ☎04 72 69 17 17; www.moca-lyon.org. Open W-Su noon-7pm. €5, students €3 under 18 free.)*

NIGHTLIFE

At the end of June, the two-week **Festival Jazz à Vienne** welcomes jazz masters to Vienne, a sleepy river town south of Lyon, accessible by bus or train. (www.jazzavienne.com. Tickets free-€30.) In June and July, **Les Nuits de Fourvière** music festival features classical concerts, dance, movies, plays, and popular performers in the ancient Théâtre Romain and Odéon. (☎04 72 32 00 00; www.nuitsdefourviere.fr. Tickets and info at the Théâtre Romain and the FNAC shop on r. de la République. Tickets from €12.) Nightlife in Lyon is fast and furious; the city's vast array of pubs, **GLBT establishments,** riverboat nightclubs, and student bars make going out an adventure. The most accessible late-night spots are a strip of riverboat clubs docked by the east bank of the Rhône. Students buzz in and out of tiny, intimate bars on **rue Ste-Catherine** (*1er*) until 1am, before hitting up the clubs. For a more mellow (and more expensive) evening, head to the jazz and piano bars on the streets off **rue Mercerie.** *Lyon Libertin* (€2) lists hot nightlife venues. For superb tips about gay nightlife, pick up *Le Petit Paumé.*

Ayers Rock Café, 2 r. Désirée, 1er (☎08 20 32 02 03, www.ayersrockcafe.com). M: Hôtel de Ville. This Aussie bar is a cacophony of loud rock music and wild bartenders drumming on the hanging lights for 20-somethings. Open daily 6pm-3am, summer opens at 9pm, closes at 10pm on Su. Next door slightly more chic **Cosmopolitan,** 4 r. Désirée (☎08 20 32 02 03) serves New York-themed drinks. Tu student nights; happy hour 8pm-3am. Open M-Sa 8pm-3am, opens at 9pm in summer. MC/V.

Le Sirius, across from 4 q. Augagneur, *3ème* (☎04 78 71 78 71; www.lesirius.com). M: Guillotière. A young, international crowd packs the lower-level dance floor and bar of this cargo ship-themed riverboat. Open Tu-Sa 6pm-3am.

Q Boat, across from 17 q. Augagneur, 3*ème* (☎04 72 84 98 98, www.actunight.com). M: Guillotière. Formerly Le Fish, this club plays electronic and house music on a swanky boat. Chic Europeans crowd its 2 bars and top-floor deck. Dress well; admission at bouncer's discretion. Open W-Sa 5pm-5am, Su 2pm-5am. AmEx/MC/V.

GRENOBLE ☎04 76

Young scholars from all corners of the globe and sizable North and West African populations meet in Grenoble (pop. 168,000), a dynamic city whose surrounding snow-capped peaks are cherished by both athletes and aesthetes. *Téléphériques* (cable cars) depart from q. Stéphane-Jay every 10min. for the 16th-century **Bastille,** a fort perched 475m above the city. (Open July-Aug. M 11am-12:15am, Tu-Su 9:15am-12:15am; Sept.-June reduced hours. €4.15 one way, 6.10 round-trip; students €3.35/4.85.) After enjoying the views from the top, you can walk down the Parc Guy Pape, through the other end of the fortress, to the **Jardin des Dauphins** (1hr.). Cross the Pont St-Laurent and go up Montée Chalemont to reach the **Musée Dauphinois,** 30 r. Maurice Gignoux, which has exhibits on the history of skiing. (Open M and W-Su June-Sept. 10am-7pm; Oct.-May 10am-6pm. Free.) The **Musée de Grenoble,** 5 pl. de Lavelette, houses one of France's most prestigious art collections. (☎04 76 63 44 44; www.museedegrenoble.fr. Open M and W-Su 10am-6:30pm. €5, students €2, free under 18.) The biggest and most developed ski areas are to the east in Oisans; the **Alpe d'Huez** has 250km of trails. (Tourist office ☎04 76 11 44 44, ski area ☎04 76 80 30 30.) The **Belledonne region,** northeast of Grenoble, is at a lower altitude and lower prices; its most popular ski area is **Chamrousse.** Grenoble's funky night scene is found between **place St-André** and **place Notre-Dame.** International students and 20-somethings mix it up at **Le Couche-Tard,** 1 r. du Palais. (Mixed drinks €2.50. Student prices offered M-W. Open M-Sa 7pm-2am. AmEx/MC/V.)

From the tourist office, follow pl. Ste-Claire to pl. Notre-Dame and take r. du Vieux Temple on the right to reach **Le Foyer de l'Étudiante ❶,** 4 r. Ste-Ursule. This stately building serves as a student dorm during most of the year, but opens its large rooms to co-ed travelers from June to August, though the shortest stay offered is one week. (☎04 76 42 00 84. Laundry €2.20. Free Wi-Fi. Singles €118 per week; doubles €80 per week per person.) Grenoblaise restaurants cater to locals around **place de Gordes** and **pl. St. Andre,** while cheap pizzerias line **quai Perrière** across the river. Pâtisseries and North African joints center on **rue Chenoise** and **rue Lionne,** between the pedestrian area and the river. Cafes cluster around place **Notre-Dame** and place **St-André,** in the heart of the *vieille ville.*

Trains leave pl. de la Gare for: Lyon (1hr., 30 per day, €18); Marseille (4-5hr., 15 per day, €37); Nice (5-6hr., 5 per day, €57); Paris (3hr., 9 per day, €70). **Buses** leave from left of the train station for Geneva, SWI (3hr., 1 per day, €26). You can find the **tourist office** at 14 r. de la République. (☎04 76 42 41 41; www.grenoble-isere.info. Open Oct.-Apr. M-Sa 9am-6:30pm, Su 10am-1pm; May-Sept. M-Sa 9am-6:30pm, Su 10am-1pm and 2-5pm.) **Postal Code:** 38000.

ANNECY ☎04 50

With narrow cobblestone streets, romantic canals, and a turreted castle, Annecy (pop. 53,000), the "Venice of the Alps," seems more like a fairy tale than a modern city. A 13th-century château in the *vieille ville*, the **Palais de l'Isle** served as a prison for WWII Resistance fighters. (☎04 50 33 87 30. Open June-Sept. daily 10:30am-6pm; Oct.-May M, W-Su 10am-noon and 2-5pm. €3.40, students €1.) Award-winning floral displays in the **Jardin de l'Europe** are Annecy's pride and joy. In summer, the **lake** is a popular spot for windsurfing and kayaking, particularly along the **plage d'Albigny.** Annecy's **Alpine forests** have excellent hiking and biking trails. One of the best hikes begins within walking distance of the *vieille ville* at the **Basilique de la Visitation,** near the hostel, while a scenic 30km *piste cyclable* (bike route) hugs the lake's eastern shore.

Reach the clean **Auberge de Jeunesse "La Grande Jeanne" (HI) ❷,** rte. de Semnoz, via the ligne d'été bus in summer (dir.: Semnoz; €1) from the train station, or take bus #6 (dir.: Marquisats). From the station to Hôtel de Police, turn right on av. du Tresum, and follow signs to Semnoz. (☎04 50 45 33 19; annecy@fuaj.org. Breakfast and linens included. Internet €2 per 20min. Reception 7am-11pm. Open mid-Jan. to Nov. 4- and 5-bed dorms with showers starting from €17.60. MC/V.) Place Ste-Claire has morning **markets** (Tu, F, Su 8am-noon) and some of the city's most charming restaurants. **Trains** run from pl. de la Gare to: Chamonix (2hr., 7 per day, €20); Grenoble (1hr., 8 per day, €16); Lyon (2hr., 8 per day, €22); Nice (7-9hr., 6 per day, €86); Paris (4hr., 7 per day, €85). Next to the station, Autocars Frossard **buses** (☎04 50 45 73 90) leave for Geneva, SWI

(1hr., 2-3 per day, €10). **Tourist office,** 1 r. Jean Jaurès. (☎04 50 45 00 33; www.lac-annecy.com. Open June-Aug. M-Sa 9am-6:30pm, Su 9am-12:30pm and 1:45-6:30pm; Sept. to mid-Oct. and Mar.-May daily 9am-12:30pm and 1:45-6pm; late Oct.-Feb. M-Sa 9am-12:30pm and 1:45-6pm.) **Postal Code:** 74000.

CHAMONIX ☎04 50

The site of the first **Winter Olympics** in 1924 and home to Europe's highest peak (Mont Blanc; 4807m), Chamonix (pop. 10,000) draws outdoor enthusiasts from around the world. But be cautious—steep gradients and potential avalanches make the slopes challenging and dangerous. The pricey **Aiguille du Midi téléphérique** (cable car) offers a white knuckled ascent over snowy forests and cliffs to a needlepoint peak, revealing a fantastic panorama from 3842m. (☎08 92 68 00 67. Round-trip €38.) Bring your passport to continue via gondola to **Helbronner, ITA** for views of three countries, the Matterhorn and Mont Blanc. (Open May-Sept. Round-trip €55; includes Aiguille du Midi.) South of Chamonix, **Le Tour-Col de Balme** (☎04 50 54 00 58; day pass €37), above the village of Le Tour, attracts beginner and intermediate skiers, while Les Grands Montets (☎04 50 54 00 71; day pass €37), to the north, is the *grande dame* of Chamonix **skiing,** with advanced terrain and snowboarding facilities. The **tourist office** has a **map** (€4) with departure points and estimated duration of all trails, though some are accessible only by cable car.

Chamonix's *gîtes* (mountain hostels) are cheap, but fill up fast; call ahead. From the train station, walk down av. Michel Croz and turn on r. du Docteur Paccard for **Gîte le Vagabond ❶,** 365 av. Ravanel le Rouge, where a young group of Brits provide rustic bunk rooms with stone walls and a popular bar. (☎04 50 53 15 43; www.gitevagabond.com. Climbing wall and kitchen available. Breakfast €5. Linens €5. Free Wi-Fi. Dorms €15, *demi-pension* €15. Credit card deposit. MC/V.) Restaurants and nightlife center around **Rue du Docteur Paccard** and **Rue des Moulins. Trains** leave pl. de la Gare (☎35 36) and usually connect through St-Gervais to: Annecy (1hr., 8 per day, €13); Lyon (3hr., 7 per day, €29); Paris (5-8hr., 6 per day, €75-95); Geneva, SWI (4hr., 2 per day, €51). Société Alpes Transports **buses** (☎04 50 53 01 15) leave the train station for Geneva, SWI (1hr., 1-5 per day, €35). Local buses (€1.50) connect to ski slopes and hiking trails. The **tourist office** is at 85 pl. du Triangle de l'Amitié. (☎53 00 24; www.chamonix.com. Free Wi-Fi. Open daily 8:30am-7pm.) **Postal Code:** 74400.

LOST IN TRANSLATION

Hollywood movies and American television may have captivated a market in France, but there's often little rhyme or reason regulating the translation of their titles:

Lolita in Spite of Myself *(Mean Girls):* Vladimir Nabokov and Lindsay Lohan: the perfect pop-culture union.

The Counterattack of the Blondes *(Legally Blonde):* Perhaps a little aggressive for a movie about Reese Witherspoon and Harvard Law School.

The Little Champions *(Mighty Ducks):* From the Flying V to the quack chant, the *canard* is the heart and soul of this film.

Rambo *(Rambo):* Some words just transcend linguistic and cultural barriers.

The Man Who Would Murmur at the Ears of Horses *(The Horse Whisperer):* Just in case there was any ambiguity in the original title.

A Day with No End *(Groundhog Day):* If you don't get the Groundhog Day reference, this is going to be a long movie.

La Grande Évasion *(The Great Escape):* If they didn't translate this literally, Steve McQueen would've taken everyone down.

The Big Lebowski *(The Big Lebowski):* The French recognize that The Dude does not appreciate name changes.

Lost in Translation *(Lost in Translation):* Apparently one title that wasn't.

—Vinnie Chiappini

LE MONT-DORE ☎04 73

Le Mont-Dore (luh mohn dohr; pop. 1700), sits at the foot of a dormant volcano in an isolated valley. Le Puy de Sancy, Central France's highest peak, is only 3.5km from the centre ville, making the town a premier winter ski resort and hiking mecca. The **Établissement Thermal,** 1 pl. du Panthéon, today entertains *curistes* with a French-language tour of the *thermes*, providing a free *douche nasale gazeuse:* a tiny blast that effectively **clears sinuses.** (☎04 73 65 05 10, 04 73 65 09 37. Tours late Apr. to late Oct. M-Sa 4 per day; €3.20.)

Over 650km of trails lace the region's dormant volcanic mountains. Those planning an extended hike should review their route with the tourist office and leave a multi-day itinerary with the **peloton de montagne** (mountain police; ☎04 73 65 04 06, on r. des Chasseurs or at the base of Puy de Sancy.) Little more than dirt paths, some trails may be unmarked. Be sure to check weather reports—mist in the valley often signifies hail or snow in the peaks. For all the views without the exertion, the **téléphérique** runs from the base by a hostel on route de Sancy to a station just below the Puy de Sancy; a 10min. climb up steep stairs leads to the summit. (☎08 20 82 09 48. 5 per hr. €5.60, child €4.20; round-trip €7.30/5.70. MC/V.) The **funicular** departs from near the tourist office to **Salon des Capucins.** (3 per hr. €3.30, under 10 €2.70; round-trip €4.20/3.30. MC/V.) Both the funicular and the *téléphérique* can be used as departure points. A few hundred meters to the right of *téléphérique* #2, the path up **Puy de Sancy** (6.2km, 3hr., 555m vertical), culminates in a spectacular 360° view. Hikers should be careful, though, as the trail borders steep dropoffs. The hike to **La Grande Cascade** (4km, 2hr., 222m ascent) starts from the center of town and ends above the area's largest falls (30m). Call the central cross-country resort (☎04 73 21 54 32) or ask at the tourist office for info on **cross-country skiing** trails.

Hôtel Artense ❷, 19 av. de la Libération, near the tourist office, has clean, comfortable rooms. (☎04 73 65 03 43; www.artense-hotel.com. Breakfast €5. Reception 8am-7pm. Open Dec.-Oct. Singles and doubles €20-40; triples with bath €40-45; quads €43-53. MC/V.) You can find regional specialties at one of the street side shops between **place de la République** and **place du Pantheon. Trains** and SNCF **buses** (☎04 73 65 00 02) run from pl. de la Gare to Paris (6hr., 2 per day, €57). The **tourist office** is on av. de la Libération, near the ice-skating rink. (☎04 73 65 20 21. Open July-Aug. M-Sa 9am-7pm, Su 10am-noon and 2-6pm; May-June and Sept. M-Sa 9am-12:30pm and 2-6pm, Su 10am-noon and 2-6pm; Oct. M-Sa 9am-noon and 2-6pm.) **Postal Code:** 63240.

DORDOGNE AND LIMOUSIN

A lack of large population centers, waterfronts, and well-known attractions has kept this region from the fame it deserves. The Dordogne river cuts through the region's rolling hillsides, creating a spectacular backdrop for the many castles and hilltop cities. In nearby Périgord, green countryside is splashed with yellow sunflowers, chalky limestone cliffs, and ducks paddling down shady rivers.

BOURGES ☎02 48

Once France's capital, Bourges (pop. 75,000) attracts visitors with its Gothic architecture, half-timbered houses, shop-filled medieval streets, and its famous Printemps music festival in April. Bourges's wealth originated in 1433, when **Jacques Coeur,** Charles VII's financier, chose the humble city as the site for his palatial home. During the long French-language tour, you'll see more of the unfurnished **Palais Jacques Coeur,** 10bis r. Jacques Coeur, than Coeur ever did, since he was imprisoned for embezzlement before its completion. (Open July-Aug. 9:30am-noon and 2-7pm; Sept.-June reduced hours. Free.) Ask at the tourist office about excursions to 13 other châteaux along the **Route Jacques Coeur;** most are accessible only by car or bike. **Cathedral St-Étienne's** complex stained-glass scenes, tremendous size, and infinitely intricate facade make it Bourges's most impressive sight. (Open M-Sa Apr.-Sept. 8:30am-7:15pm; Oct.-Mar. 9am-5:45pm. Closed Su morning for mass. Free. Crypt and tower €7, students €4.50.) To get from the station to the well-kept **Auberge de Jeunesse (HI)** ❶, 22 r. Henri Sellier, bear right on r. du Commerce onto r. des Arènes, which becomes r. Fernault; and cross to r. René Ménard, then turn left onto r. Henri Sellier. (☎ 02 48 24 58 09. HI members only. Breakfast €3.50. Reception 8-10am and 6-10pm. Dorms €16. Cash only.) **Place Gordaine** and **rue des Beaux-Arts** are lined with cheap eateries, while the restaurants on rue Bourbonnoux and rue Girard feature regional menus in a more elegant atmosphere. **Trains** leave from pl. du Général Leclerc (☎08 92 35 35 35) for Paris (2hr., 8 per day, €28) and Tours (1hr., 4 per day, €20). From the station, follow av. H. Laudier as it turns into av. Jean Jaurès; bear left on r. du Commerce, which becomes r. Moyenne and leads to the **tourist office,** 21 r. Victor Hugo. (☎ 02 48 23 02 60. Open Apr.-Sept. M-Sa 9am-7pm, Su 10am-6pm; Oct.-Mar. reduced hours.) **Postal Code:** 18000.

PÉRIGUEUX ☎05 53

Périgueux (pop. 65,000) rests on the hills high above the Isle River. Rich with tradition and gourmet cuisine, the lovely old quarters of Périgueux preserve architecture from medieval and Gallo-Roman times. Périgueux's **Cathédrale St-Front,** the largest cathedral in southwestern France, is a massive Greek cross crowned by five immense Byzantine cupolas next to a belfry. (Open daily 8am-noon and 2:30-7pm.) Just down r. St-Front, the **Musée du Périgord,** 22 cours Tourny, houses one of France's most important collections of prehistoric artifacts, including a set of 2m mammoth tusks. (☎05 53 06 40 70. Open Apr.-Sept. M and W-F 10:30am-5:30pm, Sa-Su 1-6pm; Oct.-Mar. M and W-F 10am-5pm. €4, students €2, under 18 free.) The **Musée Gallo-Romain,** r. Claude Bertrand, has a walkway over the excavated ruins of the Domus de Vésone. (☎05 53 05 65 60. Open July 5-Sept. 2 daily 10am-7pm; Apr.-July 4 and Sept. 3-Nov. 11 Tu-Su 10am-12:30pm and 2-6pm; Nov.12-Jan. 6 and Feb.7-Mar. Tu-Su 10am-12:30pm and 2-5:30pm. Closed in January. €5.50, under 18 free. French, English, German, and Spanish-language tours daily July-Aug. €1.) Across from the train station, **Les Charentes** ❷, 16 rue Denis Papin, across from the station, offer clean rooms. (☎05 53 53 37 13. Breakfast €6. Reception 7am-10pm. Open late Jan. to early Dec. Reservations recommended in summer. Singles with shower €25, with TV €30, with toilet €35; doubles €30/35/40. Extra person €5. AmEx/MC/V.) **Au Bien Bon** ❷, 15 rue des Places, serves regional specialties. (☎05 53 09 69 94. Lunch *menu* €14. Open M-F noon-1:30pm, F-Sa 7:30-9:30pm. MC/V.) **Trains** leave r. Denis Papin for: Bordeaux (1hr., 12 per day, €18); Lyon (6-8hr., 2 per day, €51); Paris (4-6hr., 13 per day, €57); Toulouse (4hr., 12 per day, €32-44). The **tourist office** is at 26 pl. Francheville. (☎05 53 53 10 63; www.tourisme-perigueux.fr. Open June-Sept. M-Sa 9am-6pm, Su 10am-1pm and 2-6pm; Oct.-May M-Sa 9am-1pm and 2-6pm.) **Postal Code:** 24000.

THE VÉZÈRES VALLEY ☎05 53

Arguably the most spectacular cave paintings ever discovered line the **Caves of Lascaux,** "the Sistine Chapel of prehistory," near the town of Montignac, 25km north of Sarlat. Uncovered in 1940 by four teenagers, the caves were closed to the public in 1963 when algae and mineral deposits—nourished by the breathing of countless visitors per year—threatened to ruin the paintings. **Lascaux II**

FRANCE

replicates the original cave exactly: modern artists painted the designs with the same pigments used 17,000 years ago. (☎05 53 51 95 03; www.semitour.com. Ticket office open in summer 9am until tickets sell out. Tickets sold at the cave entrance during the winter. Open Jan. and Apr.-Oct. daily; Feb.-Mar. and Nov.-Dec. Tu-Su. Reservations recommended 1 week ahead July-Aug. €8.20, ages 6-12 €5.20, under 6 free.) The **train** station nearest Montignac is at Le Lardin, 10km away. From there, you can call a **taxi** (☎50 86 61). During the academic year, **CFTA** (☎05 55 59 01 48) runs **buses** from Périgueux and Sarlat; call or check the stations for times and prices. Numerous **campgrounds** dot the Vézères Valley near Montignac; the tourist office has a complete list. At the **Grotte de Font-de-Gaume,** 1km east of Les Eyzies-de-Tayac on D47, 15,000-year-old friezes are still open for viewing. (☎05 53 06 86 00; http://eyzies.monuments-nationaux.fr/fr/bdd/page/infospratiques. Open mid-May to mid-Sept. M-F and Su 9:30am-5:30pm; mid-Sept. to mid-May M-F and Su 9:30am-12:30pm and 2-5:30pm. Visit only by 1hr. tour; tours in French, in English based on demand; €6.50, ages 18-25 €4.50, under 18 free. Accessible to visually handicapped with a reservation.) Rooms tend to be expensive—consider staying in Périgueux or taking advantage of the nice camping options. Check out quiet, clean, and well-located **Demaison Chambre d'Hôte ❷,** rte. de Sarlat, 3min. outside of Les Eyzies-de-Tayac on the edge of the forest. From the train station, follow signs to Sarlat; the house is past the laundromat on the right. (☎05 53 06 91 43. Breakfast €5. Reserve ahead. Singles and doubles €25-36; triples and quads €48. Cash only.) The **tourist office** is on pl. de la Mairie in Les Eyzies-de-Tayac. (☎05 53 06 97 05; www.leseyzies.com. Open July-Aug. M-Sa 9am-7pm, Su 10am-noon and 2-6pm; Sept. and Apr.-June M-Sa 9am-noon and 2-6pm, Su 10am-noon and 2-5pm; Oct.-Mar. M-Sa 9am-noon and 2-6pm.) From Les Eyzies, **trains** go to Paris (4-6hr., 4 per day, €59), Périgueux (30min., 6 per day, €7), and Sarlat (1hr., 2 per day, €8).

AQUITAINE AND PAYS BASQUE

At the geographical edge of both France and Spain, Aquitaine (AH-kee-tenn) and the Pays Basque (PAY-ee bahss-kuh) are diverse in landscape and culture. In Aquitaine, sprawling vineyards abound and in Pays Basque, closer to the Spanish border, the clinking of cowbells mixes with the scent of seafood.

BORDEAUX ☎05 56

Though its name is synonymous with wine, the city of Bordeaux (bohr-doh; pop. 235,000) has more to offer than most lushes would expect. Everyone from punks to tourists gather on the elegant streets of the shop- and cafe-filled city center, while in the surrounding countryside, the vineyards of St-Émilion, Médoc, Sauternes, and Graves are internationally renowned.

TRANSPORTATION AND PRACTICAL INFORMATION. Trains leave Gare St-Jean, r. Charles Domercq, for: Lyon (8-10hr., 7 per day, €61-154); Marseille (6-7hr., 10 per day, €73); Nice (9-12hr., 2 per day, €105); Paris (3hr., 15-25 per day, €55); Toulouse (2-3hr., 10 per day, €32). From the train station, take tramway line C to pl. Quinconces (€1.30) and cross the street to reach the **tourist office,** 12 cours du 30 juillet, which arranges **winery tours.** (☎05 56 00 66 00; www.bordeaux-tourisme.com. Open July-Aug. M-Sa 9am-7:30pm, Su 9:30am-6:30pm; May-June and Sept.-Oct. M-Sa 9am-7pm, Su 9:30am-6:30pm; Nov.-Apr. M-Sa 9am-6:30pm, Su 9:45am-4:30pm.) **Postal Code:** 33000.

ACCOMMODATIONS AND FOOD. A favorite among backpackers, **Hôtel Studio ❷**, 26 r. Huguerie, has tiny, clean rooms with bath, phone, and TV. (☎05 56 48 00 14; www.hotel-bordeaux.com. Breakfast €5. Reserve ahead. Singles €19-29; doubles €25-35. AmEx/MC/V.) Find rooms decorated in metallic and bright colors at **Auberge de Jeunesse Barbey (HI) ❷**, 22 cours Barbey, four blocks from the Gare St-Jean in the run-down red light district. Visitors, especially those traveling alone, should exercise caution at night. (☎05 56 33 00 70; fax 33 00 71. Breakfast and linens included. Free Internet. Max. 3-night stay. Lockout 10am-4pm. Curfew 2am. 2- to 6-bed dorms €21. MC/V.)

The Bordelais's flair for food rivals their vineyard expertise. Hunt around rue St-Remi and place St-Pierre for regional specialties: oysters, *foie gras*, and *lamproie à la bordelaise* (eel braised in red wine). Busy **L'Ombrière ❸**, 13 pl. du Parlement, serves perfectly prepared French cuisine in one of the city's most beautiful squares. (Menu €15-23. Open daily noon-2pm and 7-11pm. MC/V.) Dine at **La Fromentine ❷**, 4 r. du Pas St-Georges, near pl. du Parlement, for galettes (€6-8) with imaginative names. (☎05 56 79 24 10. 3-course menu €10-15. Open M-F noon-2pm and 7-10pm, Sa 7-10pm. MC/V.)

SIGHTS AND ENTERTAINMENT. Nearly nine centuries after its consecration, the **Cathédrale St-André**, in pl. Pey-Berland, sits at the heart of Gothic Bordeaux. Its bell tower, the **Tour Pey-Berland**, rises 66m. (Cathedral open M 2-7pm, Tu-F 7:30am-6pm, Sa 9am-7pm, Su 9am-6pm. Tower open June-Sept. daily 10am-1:15pm and 2-6pm; Oct.-May Tu-Su 10am-12:30pm and 2-5:30pm. €5, 18-25 and seniors €3.50, under 18 with an adult free.) For the best cityscape of Bordeaux, look down from the 114m bell tower of the **Église St-Michel.** (Open June-Sept. daily 2-7pm. €2.50, under 12 free.) Back at ground level, a lively **flea market** sells anything from Syrian *narguilas* (hookahs) to African specialties. (Open daily 9am-1pm.) Note that this area, like around the train station, should not be frequented alone at night. On pl. de Quinconces, the elaborate **Monument aux Girondins** commemorates guillotined Revolutionary leaders from towns bordering the Gironde. Bordeaux's opera house, the **Grand Théâtre,** conceals a breathtaking interior behind its Neoclassical facade and houses concerts, operas, and plays in fall and winter. (☎05 56 00 85 95; www.opera-bordeaux.com. Tours M-Sa 11am-6pm. Concert tickets from €8. Opera tickets up to €80. 50% discount for students and under 26.)

Bordeaux has a varied, vibrant nightlife. For an overview, check out the free *Clubs and Concerts* brochure at the tourist office. Year-round, students and visitors pack the bars in **Place de la Victoire, Place Gambetta,** and **Place Camille Julian.** Popular but cheesy **El Bodegon,** on pl. de la Victoire, draws students with cheap drinks, theme nights, and weekend giveaways. (Beer €3. Happy hour 6-8pm. Open M-Sa 7am-2am, Su 2pm-2am.)

BAYONNE ☎05 59

In Bayonne (pop. 42,000), the self-proclaimed chocolate capital of France, visitors wander along the Nive River's banks and admire the small bridges, petite streets, and colorful shutters. The **Musée Bonnat,** 5 r. Jacques Laffitte, showcases works by Bayonnais painter Léon Bonnat alongside others by Degas, van Dyck, Goya, Rembrandt, and Rubens. (Nov.-Apr. daily 10am-12:30pm and 2-6pm; May-Oct. M and W-Su 10am-6:30pm; July-Aug., open Tu as well at the regular hours and W 10am-9:30pm for a free 'nocturne'. €5.50, students €3, under 18 free; Sept.-June 1st Su of the month and July-Aug. W 6:30-9:30pm free.) Starting the first Wednesday in August, let loose for five days during the **Fêtes Traditionnelles** (Aug. 5-9; www.fetes-de-bayonne.com).

The **Hôtel Paris-Madrid ❷**, pl. de la Gare, has clean rooms and knowledgeable proprietors at rock-bottom prices. (☎05 59 55 13 98. Breakfast €4. Reception daily from 6:30am-12:30am. Singles and doubles €20, with shower €28, with shower and toilet €35; triples and quads with bath €49-59. MC/V.) A **Monoprix** supermarket is at the corner of r. Pont Neuf and r. Orbe. (Open M-Sa 8:30am-8pm.) **Trains** depart from pl. de la Gare for: Biarritz (10min.; at least 15per day; €2.30, TGV €3); Bordeaux (2hr., at least 10 per day, € 22-28); Paris (5hr.,at least 8 per day, € 40-81); San Sebastián, SPA via Hendaye (30min., 15 per day, €8); Toulouse (4hr., 5 per day, €37). Local STAB buses (☎05 59 59 04 61) depart from the Hôtel de Ville for Biarritz (buses #1, 2, and 6 run M-Sa 6:30am-8pm, Lines A and B run Su 6:30am-7pm. €1.20). From the train station, take the middle fork onto pl. de la République, veer right over pont St-Esprit, pass through pl. Réduit, cross pont Mayou, and turn right on r. Bernède, which becomes av. Bonnat. The **tourist office,** pl. des Basques, is on the left. (☎05 59 42 64 64; www.bayonne-tourisme.com. Open July-Aug. M-Sa 9am-7pm, Su 10am-1pm; Sept.-June M-F 9am-6:30pm, Sa 10am-6pm.) **Postal Code:** 64100.

PARC NATIONAL DES PYRÉNÉES

Riddled with sulfurous springs and unattainable peaks, the Pyrénées change dramatically and impressively with the seasons. To get a full sense of the mountains' breadth, hikers should experience both the lush French and barren Spanish sides of the Pyrénées (a 4- to 5-day round-trip hike from Cauterets).

CAUTERETS ☎05 62

Nestled in a valley on the edge of the **Parc National des Pyrénées Occidentales** is Cauterets (pop. 1300). Its *sulfuric thermes* (hot springs) have long been instruments of healing. **Thermes de César,** av. du Docteur Domer, offers treatments. (☎05 62 92 51 60. Information/Reservation desk open M-Sa 8:30am-noon and 2-6pm and treatments available Open Sept.-June M-Sa 4-8pm and some Su; June-Sept. M-Sa 5-8pm. Hours may vary.) Most visitors come to ski and hike. **Hotel le Chantilly ❸,** 10 r. de la Raillère, one street away from the town center, is owned by a charming Irish couple. (☎05 62 92 52 77; www.hotel-cauterets.com. Breakfast €6. Reception 7am-10pm. Open late Dec. to Oct. July-Sept. Singles and doubles €34, with shower €42; triples from €52. Oct.-June €30/34/38. MC/V.) SNCF **buses** run from pl. de la Gare to Lourdes (1hr., 8 per day, €6.60). Rent **bikes** at Le Grenier, 4 av. du Mamelon Vert. (☎05 62 92 55 71. €23 per half day, €32 per day. Open daily 9am-7pm.) The **tourist office** is in pl. Foch. (☎05 62 92 50 50; www.cauterets.com. Open July-Aug. M-Sa 9am-12:30pm and 2-7pm, Su 9am-noon and 3-6pm; Sept.-June reduced hours.) **Postal Code:** 65110.

OUTDOOR ACTIVITIES

The **Parc National des Pyrénées Occidentales** shelters hundreds of endangered species in its snow-capped mountains and lush valleys. Touch base with the friendly **Parc National Office,** Maison du Parc, pl. de la Gare, in Cauterets, before braving the park's ski paths or 14 hiking trails. (☎05 62 92 52 56; www.parc-pyrenees.com. Open July-Aug. M-Sa 9:30am-noon and 2:30-7pm; Sept.-June M-F 9:30am-noon and 3-6pm. Maps €7-9.) Appropriate for a variety of skill levels, the trails begin and end in Cauterets. From there, the **GR10** (a.k.a. **circuit de Gavarnie**), which intersects most other hikes in the area, winds through Luz-St-Saveur, over the mountain, and then on to Gavarnie, another day's trek up the valley. One of the most spectacular trails follows the GR10 past the turquoise Lac de Gaube to the end of the glacial valley (2hr. past the lac), where you can spend the night at the **Refuge des Oulettes ❶.** (☎05 62 92 62 97. Open Mar.-Sept. Dorms €19.) Other *gîtes* (shelters) located in the park, usually located in towns along the GR10, cost about €11 per night.

LANGUEDOC-ROUSSILLON

With reasonable prices all over, Languedoc-Rousillon provides a great opportunity for travelers to see the south of France on a budget. Though it has been part of France since the 12th century, Languedoc preserves its rebellious spirit: its *joie de vivre* shows up in impromptu street performances and large neighborhood parties. Between the peaks of the Pyrénées, Roussillon inspired Matisse and Picasso and now attracts a mix of sunbathers and backpackers.

TOULOUSE ☎05 61

Vibrant, zany Toulouse (pop. 435,000) is known as *la ville en rose* (the pink city). It's the place to visit when all French towns begin to look alike. Exuberant yet laid-back, clean yet gritty, Toulouse is a university town whose graduating students don't want to leave. Its quality museums and concert halls makes it southwest France's cultural capital.

TRANSPORTATION AND PRACTICAL INFORMATION. **Trains** leave Gare Matabiau, 64 bd. Pierre Sémard, for: Bordeaux (2-3hr., at least 10 per day, €33); Lyon (4hr., at least 5 per day, €70); Marseille (4hr., at least 10 per day, €50); Paris (6hr., at least 10 per day, €90). The ticket office is open daily 7am-9:10pm. Eurolines, 68-70 bd. Pierre Sémard, sends **buses** to major cities. (☎05 61 26 40 04; www.eurolines.fr. Open M-F 9am-12:30pm and 1:30-6:30pm, Sa 9am-12-:30pm and 1:30-6pm.) Get map and information at the **tourist office,** r. Lafayette in pl. Charles de Gaulle. (☎05 61 11 02 22; www.ot-toulouse.fr. Open June-Sept. M-Sa 9am-7pm, Su 10:30am-12:30pm and 2-5:15pm; Oct.-May M-Sa 9am-6pm, Su 10:30am-12:30pm and 2-5pm.) **Postal Code:** 31000.

NOTHING TOU-LOUSE. Those visiting Toulouse for longer than a day or two should pick up a Carte Privilège at the tourist office. For a mere €13, cardholders get 30% discounts at museums and participating hotels. As a final bonus, cardholders receive free *apéritifs* at many Toulouse restaurants. The tourist office has a list of participating establishments.

ACCOMMODATIONS AND FOOD. A member of the French League of Youth Hostels, **Résidence Jolimont ❶,** 2 av. Yves Brunaud, doubles as a long-term *résidence sociale* for 18- to 25-year-olds. A basketball court and ping-pong tables bring excitement to large, plain double rooms. (☎05 34 30 42 80; www.residence-jolimont.com. Breakfast M-F €2.50. Dinner daily €7.90. Linens included. Reception 24hr. Doubles €16. €1 HI member discount. AmEx/MC/V.) **Hôtel Beauséjour ❷,** 4 r. Caffarelli, near the station, has clean, bright rooms with new beds, making it a great value. (☎/fax 05 61 62 77 59. Free Wi-Fi. Reception 7am-11pm. Singles €33, with bath €35; doubles €39/41; triples €44/46. MC/V.)

Cheap eateries on **rue du Taur,** in the student quarter. Markets (open Tu-Su 6am-1pm) line place des Carmes, place Victor Hugo, and place St-Cyprien. Neighborhood favorite **Jour de Fête ❷,** 43 r. du Taur, is a relaxed brasserie with tastes as creative as the local art decorating its brick walls. (☎05 61 23 36 48. *Plat* du jour €7. Open daily noon-midnight. Cash only.)

SIGHTS AND NIGHTLIFE. The **Capitole,** a brick palace next door to the tourist office, is Toulouse's most prominent monument. The building was home to the *bourgeois capitouls* (unofficial city magistrates) in the 12th century. (Open daily 9am-7pm in the summer. Free.) Rue du Taur leads to the **Basilique St-Sernin,** the longest Romanesque structure in the world. Its crypt houses holy relics from the time of Charlemagne. (☎05 61 21 80 45. Church open July-Sept. daily 8:30am-6:30pm; Oct.-June daily 8:30-noon and 2-6pm. Crypt open July-Sept. M-Sa 10am-5pm, Su 2:30am-5pm; Oct.-June M-Sa 10-11:30am and 2:30-5pm, Su 11:30-5pm. €2.) The 13th-century southern **Gothic Jacobin church,** 69 r. Pargaminières, entrance on r. Lakanal, houses the remains of St. Thomas Aquinas. (☎05 61 22 21 92; www.jacobins.mairie-toulouse.fr. Open daily 9am-7pm.) Across the river, **Les Abbatoirs,** 76 allées Charles-de-Fitte, previously an old slaughterhouse, presents intermittent exhibits by up-and-coming artists. (☎05 62 48 58 00. Open Tu-Su 11am-7pm. €6, students €3.)

Toulouse has something to please almost any nocturnal whim. Numerous cafes flank place **St-Georges, place St-Pierre,** and **place du Capitole,** and late-night bars line **rue de la Colombette** and **rue des Filatiers.** For cheap drinks and a rambunctious atmosphere, try **Café Populaire,** 9 r. de la Colombette, where you can polish off 13 glasses of beer for only €20, €13 on Mondays 9:30pm-12:45am. (☎05 61 63 07 00. Happy hour 7:30-8:30pm. Every 13th of the month beer €1. Open M-F 11am-2am, Sa 2pm-4am. Cash only.)

CARCASSONNE ☎04 68

Walking over the drawbridge and through the stone portals into Carcassonne's La Cité (pop. 46,000) is like stepping into a fairy tale: the clang of armor seems to haunt the first-century ramparts. However, the only battles raging today are between camera-wielding visitors vying for space on the narrow streets. Built as a palace in the 12th century, the **Château Comtal,** 1 r. Viollet-le-Duc, became a citadel after the royal takeover in 1226. (☎04 68 11 70 70. 45min. tours in English, French, and Spanish. Open daily Apr.-Sept. 10am-6:30pm; Oct.-Mar. 9:30am-5pm. €7.50, under 25 €4.80.) In the summer, Agglo'Bus runs **shuttles** from the bus stop from the train station to the citadel gates. (☎04 68 47 82 22. Daily mid-June to mid-Sept. 9:30am-noon and 1:30-7:30pm, 2-3 per hr., round-trip €1.50.) Converted into a fortress after the city was razed during the Hundred Years' War, the **Gothic Cathédrale St-Michel,** r. Voltaire, in the Bastide St-Louis, still has fortifications. (Open M-Sa 7am-noon and 2-7pm, Su 9am-1pm.)

Nestled in an alley in the heart of La Cité, the **Auberge de Jeunesse (HI) ❶,** r. de Vicomte Trencavel, offers the best lodging deal. (☎04 68 25 23 16; carcassonne@fuaj.org. Breakfast included. Laundry €6. Internet €2 per hr. Reception 24hr. Lockout 10am-3pm. Dorms €20.50. MC/V.) **Maison de la Blanquette de Limoux ❸,** pl. Marcou, is the best place to enjoy *cassoulet* (white bean stew; €11-13). (☎04 68 71 66 09. Open Apr. 2-June and Sept.-Nov. 14 daily noon-2:30pm and 7pm-midnight; July-Aug. M and W-Su noon-2:30pm and 7pm-midnight. Tu noon-2:30pm. MC/V). For dessert, shop around near **pl. Marcou.**

Trains (☎04 68 71 79 14) depart behind Jardin A. Chenier for: Marseille (3hr., 4 per day, €37-41); Nice (6hr., at least 4 per day, €63); Nîmes (2hr., at least 5 per day, €24-29); Toulouse (1hr., at least 5 per day, €14-16). Shops, hotels, the cathedral, and the train station are in the Bastide St-Louis, once known as the *basse ville* (lower city). The **tourist office** is at 28 r. de Verdun. (☎04 68 10 24 30; www.carcassonne-tourisme.com. Open July-Aug. daily 9am-7pm; Sept.-June M-Sa 9am-6pm, Su 9am-1pm.) **Postal Code:** 11000.

MONTPELLIER ☎04 67

Occasional live music brings each street corner to life in Montpellier (pop. 225,000), southern France's most lighthearted city. The gigantic, beautifully renovated **Musée Fabre,** 39 bd. Bonne Nouvelle, holds one of the largest collections of 17th- to 19th-century paintings outside Paris, with works by Delacroix, Ingres, and Poussin. (☎04 68 14 83 00. Open Tu, Th-F, and Su 10am-6pm, W 1-9pm, Sa 11am-6pm. €6, with temporary exhibits €7; students €4/5.)

The friendly owner of **Hôtel des Étuves ❷,** 24 r. des Étuves, keeps 13 plain, comfortable rooms, all with toilet and shower. (☎04 68 60 78 19; www.hoteldesetuves.fr. Breakfast €5. Reception M-Sa 6:30am-11pm, Su 7am-noon and 6-11pm. Reserve 1 week ahead. Singles €23, with TV €35; doubles €37; singles and doubles with bath €45. Cash only.) Standard French cuisine dominates Montpellier's *vieille ville,* while a number of Indian and Lebanese restaurants are on **rue des Écoles Laïques.** On pl. de la Comédie, **Crêperie le Kreisker ❶,** 3 passage Bruyas, serves 80 kinds of crepes (€1.90-6.80) topped with everything from buttered bananas to snails. (☎04 68 60 82 50. Open M-Sa 11:30am-3pm and 6:30-11pm. AmEx/MC/V.) At dusk, **rue de la Loge** fills with vendors, musicians, and stilt-walkers. The liveliest bars are in **place Jean Jaurès,** which lights up at night. **Le Rebuffy Pub,** 2 Rebuffy, is packed with local regulars and international students and always has something to do and someone to meet. (☎04 67 66 32 76. Beer €2.60-5.90. Open in summer M-F 9am-2am, Sa 11am-2am, Su 10pm-2am; in winter M-Sa 11am-1am, Su 10pm-1am. MC/V €8 min.) Gay nightlife is around **place du Marché aux Fleurs.**

Trains leave pl. Auguste Gibert (☎08 92 35 35 35) for: Avignon (2hr., at least 10 per day, €14.50-17.50); Marseille (2-3½hr., at least 10 per day, €24-28); Nice (4hr., 2 per day, €40-60); Paris (3hr., at least 10 per day, €66-130); Toulouse (2½ hr., at least 10 per day, €30-34). The **tourist office** is at 30 allée Jean de Lattre de Tassigny. (☎04 68 60 60 60; www.ot-montpellier.fr. Open July-Sept. M-F 9am-7:30pm, Sa 10am-6pm, Su 9:30am-1pm and 2:30-6pm; Oct.-June M-F 9am-6:30pm, Sa 10am-6pm, Su 10am-1pm and 2-5pm.) **Postal Code:** 34000.

PROVENCE

If Paris boasts world-class paintings, it's only because Provence inspired them. Mistral winds cut through olive groves in the north, while pink flamingoes, black bulls, and unicorn-like white horses gallop freely in the marshy south. From the Roman arena and cobblestone of Arles to Cézanne's lingering footsteps in Aix-en-Provence, Provence provides a taste of *La Vie en Rose.*

MARSEILLE ☎04 91

Dubbed "the meeting place of the entire world" by Alexandre Dumas, Marseille (pop. 821,000) is a jumble of color and commotion. A walk through its side streets is punctuated by the vibrant hues of West African fabrics, the sounds of Arabic music, and the smells of North African cuisine. A true immigrant city, Marseille offers visitors a taste of multiple cultures.

TRANSPORTATION

Flights: Aéroport Marseille-Provence (**MRS;** ☎04 42 14 14 14; www.marseille.aeroport.fr). Flights to **Corsica, ITA, Lyon,** and **Paris.** Shuttle **buses** run to **Gare St-Charles** (3 per hr.; €9). **Taxis** from the *centre-ville* to airport cost €40-50.

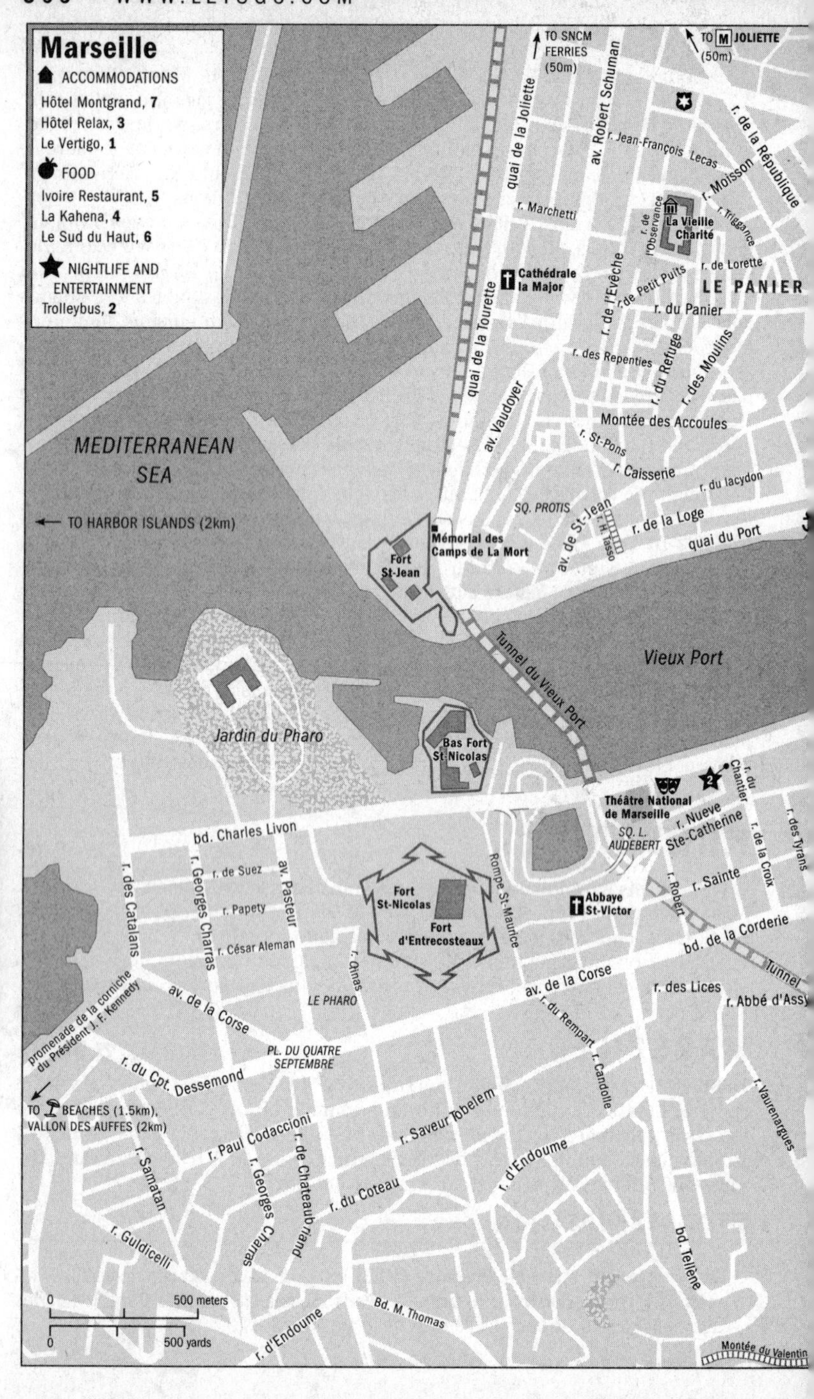

Marseille
ACCOMMODATIONS
Hôtel Montgrand, 7
Hôtel Relax, 3
Le Vertigo, 1
FOOD
Ivoire Restaurant, 5
La Kahena, 4
Le Sud du Haut, 6
NIGHTLIFE AND ENTERTAINMENT
Trolleybus, 2
MEDITERRANEAN SEA
TO HARBOR ISLANDS (2km)
TO SNCM FERRIES (50m)
TO M JOLIETTE (50m)
quai de la Joliette
av. Robert Schuman
r. Jean-François Lecas
r. de la République
r. Moisson
r. Marchetti
r. de l'Observance
La Vieille Charité
r. Triggance
r. de Lorette
Cathédrale la Major
quai de la Tourette
r. de l'Evêche
r. de Petit Puits
LE PANIER
r. du Panier
r. des Repenties
r. du Refuge
r. des Moulins
av. Vaudoyer
Montée des Accoules
r. St-Pons
r. Caisserie
r. du lacydon
SQ. PROTIS
av. de St-Jean
r. H. Tasso
r. de la Loge
quai du Port
Mémorial des Camps de La Mort
Fort St-Jean
Tunnel du Vieux Port
Vieux Port
Jardin du Pharo
Bas Fort St-Nicolas
Théâtre National de Marseille
r. du Chantier
bd. Charles Livon
SQ. L. AUDEBERT
r. Nueve Ste-Catherine
r. des Tyrans
r. de la Croix
r. des Catalans
r. Georges Charras
r. de Suez
av. Pasteur
r. Papety
r. César Aleman
Fort St-Nicolas
Fort d'Entrecosteaux
Rompe St-Maurice
Abbaye St-Victor
r. Robert
r. Sainte
bd. de la Corderie
Tunnel
r. des Lices
r. Abbé d'Ass
av. de la Corse
r. Oinas
LE PHARO
r. du Rempart
promenade de la corniche du Président J. F. Kennedy
PL. DU QUATRE SEPTEMBRE
r. Candolle
r. du Cpt. Dessemond
TO BEACHES (1.5km), VALLON DES AUFFES (2km)
r. Vaurenargues
r. Saveur Tobelem
r. Paul Codaccioni
r. Samatan
r. de Chateaubriand
r. d'Endoume
r. du Coteau
r. Georges Charras
r. Guldicelli
bd. Tellène
0
500 meters
0
500 yards
Bd. M. Thomas
r. d'Endoume
Montée du Valentin

FRANCE

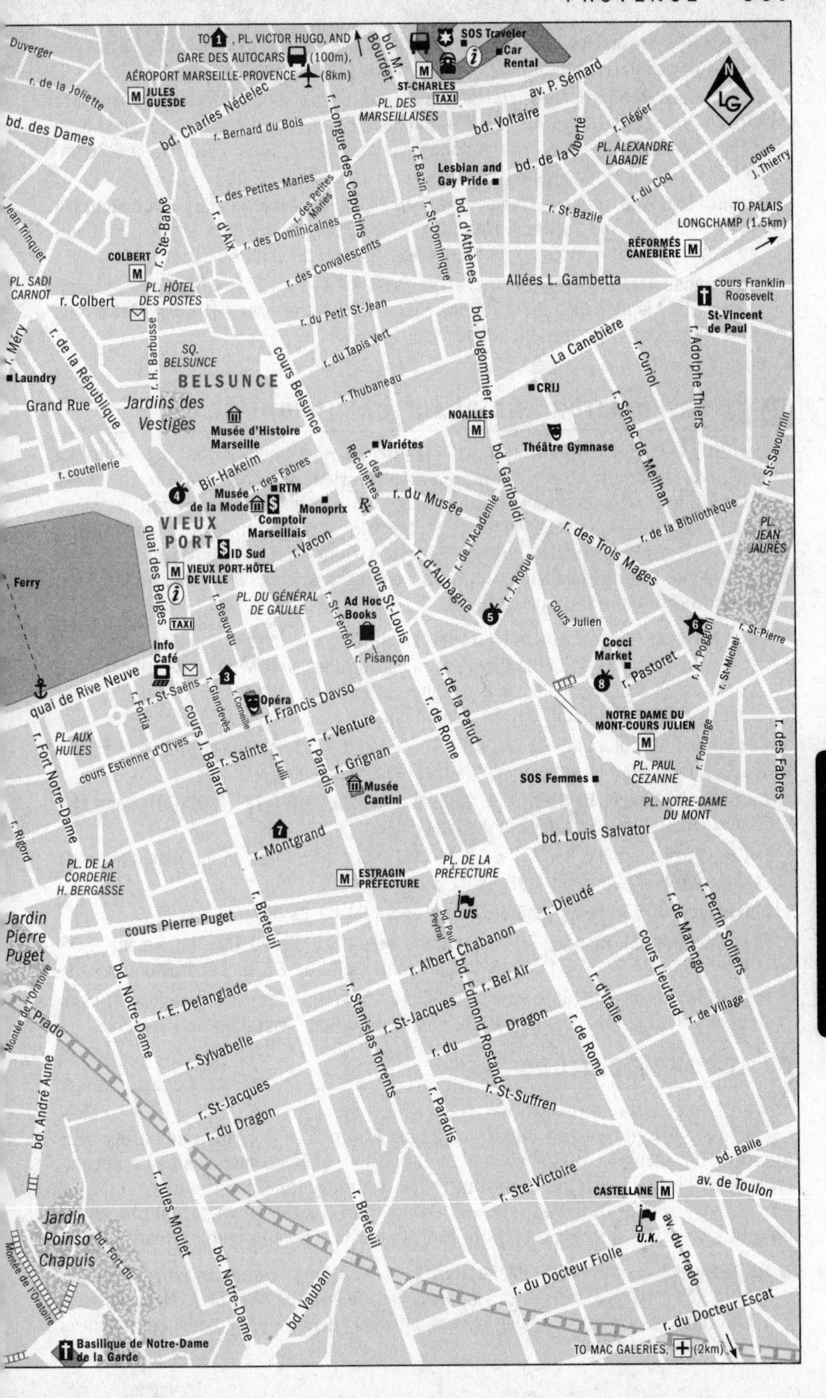
TO 1, PL. VICTOR HUGO, AND GARE DES AUTOCARS (100m), AÉROPORT MARSEILLE-PROVENCE (8km)
SOS Traveler
Car Rental
ST-CHARLES
TAXI
PL. DES MARSEILLAISES
JULES GUESDE
Duverger
r. de la Joliette
bd. des Dames
bd. Charles Nédelec
r. Bernard du Bois
r. Longue des Capucins
bd. M. Bourdet
av. P. Sémard
bd. Voltaire
r. Flégier
PL. ALEXANDRE LABADIE
cours J. Thierry
bd. de la Liberté
Lesbian and Gay Pride
r. du Coq
r. St-Bazile
TO PALAIS LONGCHAMP (1.5km)
RÉFORMÉS CANEBIÈRE
r. des Petites Maries
r. des Petites Maries
r. des Dominicaines
r. d'Aix
r. Ste-Barbe
Jean Trinquet
r. F. Bazin
r. St-Dominique
bd. d'Athènes
r. des Convalescents
COLBERT
PL. SADI CARNOT
r. Colbert
PL. HÔTEL DES POSTES
Allées L. Gambetta
cours Franklin Roosevelt
St-Vincent de Paul
r. du Petit St-Jean
r. du Tapis Vert
r. Méry
r. de la République
r. H. Barbusse
SQ. BELSUNCE
BELSUNCE
cours Belsunce
La Canebière
bd. Dugommier
r. Curiol
r. Adolphe Thiers
Laundry
Grand Rue
Jardins des Vestiges
r. Thubaneau
CRIJ
r. Sénac de Meilhan
Musée d'Histoire Marseille
NOAILLES
Théâtre Gymnase
r. St-Savournin
Variétés
r. coutellerie
Bir-Hakeim
r. des Fabres
RTM
r. des Recolettes
Musée de la Mode
Monoprix
r. du Musée
bd. Garibaldi
r. de la Bibliothèque
VIEUX PORT
Comptoir Marseillais
r. de l'Academie
r. des Trois Mages
PL. JEAN JAURÈS
ID Sud
r. Vacon
cours St-Louis
r. d'Aubagne
r. J. Roque
Ferry
quai des Belges
VIEUX PORT-HÔTEL DE VILLE
PL. DU GÉNÉRAL DE GAULLE
r. Beauvau
r. St-Ferréol
Ad Hoc Books
cours Julien
r. A. Poggioli
r. St-Pierre
TAXI
Info Café
r. Pisançon
Cocci Market
r. Pastoret
r. St-Michel
quai de Rive Neuve
r. St-Saëns
r. Glandevès
Opéra
r. Corneille
r. Francis Davso
r. de la Palud
r. de Rome
NOTRE DAME DU MONT-COURS JULIEN
r. Fortia
r. Venture
r. Fontange
r. des Fabres
PL. AUX HUILES
cours Estienne d'Orves
cours J. Ballard
r. Sainte
r. Lulli
r. Paradis
r. Grignan
Musée Cantini
SOS Femmes
PL. PAUL CEZANNE
PL. NOTRE-DAME DU MONT
r. Fort Notre-Dame
r. Rigord
r. Montgrand
bd. Louis Salvator
PL. DE LA CORDERIE H. BERGASSE
ESTRAGIN PRÉFECTURE
PL. DE LA PRÉFECTURE
r. Breteuil
r. Perrin Solliers
r. de Marengo
Jardin Pierre Puget
cours Pierre Puget
bd. Paul Peytral
US
r. Dieudé
cours Lieutaud
r. Albert Chabanon
bd. Edmond Rostand
r. Bel Air
r. d'Italie
Montée de l'Oratoire
Prado
bd. Notre-Dame
r. E. Delanglade
r. Stanislas Torrents
r. St-Jacques
r. du Dragon
r. de Rome
r. de Village
bd. André Aune
r. Sylvabelle
r. St-Suffren
r. St-Jacques
r. du Dragon
r. Paradis
bd. Baille
r. Ste-Victoire
CASTELLANE
av. de Toulon
Jardin Poinso Chapuis
bd. Fort du
r. Jules Moulet
r. Breteuil
U.K.
av. du Prado
r. du Docteur Fiolle
Montée de l'Oratoire
bd. Vauban
bd. Notre-Dame
r. du Docteur Escat
Basilique de Notre-Dame de la Garde
TO MAC GALERIES, (2km)
FRANCE

Trains: Gare St-Charles, pl. Victor Hugo (☎08 92 35 35 35). To **Lyon** (1hr., 21 per day, €54), **Nice** (2hr., 21 per day, €28.50), and **Paris** (3hr., 18 per day, €92.50).

Buses: Gare Routière, pl. Victor Hugo, near the train station. M: Gare St-Charles. To **Aix-en-Provence** (2-6 per hr., €4.80), **Cannes** (2-3hr., 4 per day, €19-26), and **Nice** (2hr., 1 per day, €19-27). Ticket windows are open M-F 6:15am-7:30pm, Sa 6:30am-6:30pm, Su 7:30am-noon and 12:45-6pm.

Ferries: SNCM, 61 bd. des Dames (☎08 25 88 80 88; www.sncm.fr). To **Corsica, ITA** (11hr.; €39-53) and **Sardinia, ITA** (14hr., €62-70). Open M-F 8am-6pm, Sa 8:30am-noon and 2-5:30pm. Prices higher June-Sept. Student discount €5-10.

Local Transportation: RTM, 6 r. des Fabres (☎04 91 91 92 10; www.rtm.fr). Tickets sold at bus and Metro stations (€1.70, day pass €4.50, 3-day pass €10). The **Metro** runs M-Th 5am-9pm, F-Su 5am-12:30am.

Taxis: Marseille Taxi (☎04 91 02 20 20). 24hr. €20-30 from Gare St-Charles.

ORIENTATION AND PRACTICAL INFORMATION

Marseille is divided along major streets into 16 *quartiers* (neighborhoods). **La Canebière** is the main artery, funneling into the **vieux port** (old port) to the west and becoming urban sprawl to the east. North of the *vieux port* and west of rue de la République lies **Le Panier,** the city's oldest neighborhood. Surrounding La Canebière are several *maghreb* (North African and Arabic communities), including the **Belsunce quartier,** which has many markets. The area around **rue Curiol** should be avoided late at night.

Tourist Office: 4 la Canebière (☎04 91 13 89 00; www.marseille-tourisme.com). M: Vieux Port. Sells the **Marseille City Pass,** which includes an RTM day pass, tourist office walking tours, the ferry to Île d'If, and admission to 14 museums (€20 for 1 day, €27 for 2 days). Open M-Sa 9am-7pm, Su 10am-5pm.

Consulates: UK, pl. Varian Fry (☎04 91 15 72 10). **US,** 12 bd. Paul Peytral (☎04 91 54 92 00). Both open by appointment M-F 9:30am-noon and 2-4:30pm.

Currency Exchange: ID SUD, 3 pl. Général de Gaulle (☎04 91 13 09 00). Open M-F 9am-6pm, Sa 9am-5pm. Also at the post office.

Police: 2 r. du Antoine Becker (☎04 91 39 80 00). Also found in the train station on esplanade St-Charles (☎04 96 13 01 88).

Emergency: SOS Traveler, Gare St-Charles (☎04 91 62 12 80).

Hospital: Hôpital Timone, 264 r. St-Pierre (☎04 91 38 00 00). M: Timone. SOS Médecins (☎04 91 52 91 52) and SOS Dentist (☎04 91 85 39 39). Doctors on call.

Post Office: 1 pl. Hôtel des Postes (☎04 91 15 47 00). Currency exchange at main branch only. Open M-F 9:30am-12:30pm and 1:30-6pm. **Postal Code:** 13001.

ACCOMMODATIONS

Marseille has a range of options, from pricey hotels in the *vieux port* to Belsunce's less reputable but cheap lodgings. Listings here prioritize safety and location. The tourist office also provides a list of **recommended safe accommodations.** The HI hostel is quiet but inconveniently far from the city center—particularly in light of infrequent bus service and early curfews. Most places fill up quickly on weekends and in summer; reserve at least a week ahead.

Le Vertigo, 42 r. des Petites Maries (☎04 91 91 07 11; www.hotelvertigo.fr). About 100m from the train station, this newcomer combines the best of youth hostel and small hotel. Its English-speaking owners, attractive decor, inviting beds, and spotless bathrooms make it worth every cent. Breakfast €5. Internet €1.50 per 30min.; free Wi-Fi. Reception 24hr. 2- to 6-bed dorms €23.90; doubles €55-65. MC/V. ❷

Hôtel Relax, 4 r. Corneille (☎04 91 33 15 87; www.hotelrelax.fr). M: Vieux Port. Just around the corner from the *vieux port,* this charming hotel offers clean rooms at fair prices. Amenities include A/C, bath, phone, TV, and soundproof windows. Breakfast €6. Free Wi-Fi. Reception 24hr. Singles €40; doubles €50-60; triples €70. AmEx/MC/V. ❷

Hôtel Montgrand, 50 r. Montgrand (☎04 91 00 35 20; www.hotel-montgrand-marseille.com). M: Estragin-Préfecture. Quiet, recently renovated rooms near the *vieux port.* A/C. Breakfast €5. Singles €52-59; family-size rooms €69. Extra person €8. MC/V. ❸

FOOD

Marseille's restaurants are as diverse as its inhabitants. African eateries and kebab stands line **cours St-Louis,** while outdoor cafes pack the streets around the **vieux port. Cours Julien** has a wonderful, eclectic collection of restaurants. Buy groceries at the **Monoprix** on bd. de la Canebière. (Open M-Sa 8:30am-9pm.)

Ivoire Restaurant, 57 r. d'Aubagne (☎04 91 33 75 33). M: Noailles. Loyal patrons come to this no-frills restaurant for authentic African cuisine and advice from its exuberant owner, Mama Africa. The Côte d'Ivoire specialties include *maffé* (a meat dish with peanut sauce; €7.50) and *jus de gingembre* (a refreshingly spicy ginger drink and West African aphrodisiac; €3.50). *Plats* €8.50-12. Open daily noon-4am. Cash only. ❷

Le Sud du Haut, 80 cours Julien (☎04 91 92 66 64). M: Cours Julien. Inviting, outdoor seating, and creative Provençal cuisine make this the ideal place for a leisurely meal. The **lunch formule** (€11.50) includes a *plat,* coffee, and dessert. Entrees €8-11. *Plats* €13-19. Open M-Sa noon-2:30pm and 8-10:30pm. MC/V. ❸

La Kahena, 2 r. de la République (☎04 91 90 61 93). M: Vieux Port. Offers tasty couscous dishes (€9-16) garnished with fresh fish and African ingredients, a blue-tiled interior, and speedy service. Open daily noon-2:30pm and 7-10:30pm. MC/V. ❸

SIGHTS

A walk through the city's streets tops any sights-oriented itinerary. Check www.museum-paca.org for info on museums. Unless otherwise noted, all the museums listed below have the same hours: from June to September Tuesday-Sunday 11am-6pm; from October to May Tuesday to Sunday 10am-5pm.

BASILIQUE DE NOTRE DAME DE LA GARDE. A stunning view of the city, surrounding mountains, and island-studded bay make this a must-see. During the WWII liberation, the Resistance fought to regain the basilica, which remains pocked with bullet holes and shrapnel scars. *(Take bus #60, dir.: Notre Dame. ☎04 91 13 40 80. Open daily in summer 7am-7pm; in winter 7:30am-5:30pm. Free.)*

HARBOR ISLANDS. Resembling a child's sandcastle, the **Château d'If** guards the city from its rocky perch outside the harbor. Its dungeon, immortalized in Dumas's *Count of Monte Cristo*, once held a number of hapless Huguenots. Nearby, the Île Frioul was only marginally successful in isolating plague victims when an outbreak in 1720 killed half of the city's 80,000 citizens. *(Boats depart from q. des Belges for numerous islands in the bay. ☎08 25 13 68 00. Round-trip 1½hr. Boats leave at 10, 11:30am, 1:30, 3, and 4:30pm. Adults €15, students €13.50.)*

ABBAYE ST-VICTOR. Fortified against invaders, this medieval abbey's **crypt**—still holding the remains of two martyrs—is one of Europe's oldest Christian sites. Its fifth-century construction brought Christianity to the pagan *Marseillais. (On r. Sainte at the end of q. de Rive Neuve. ☎04 96 11 22 60. Festival info ☎04 91 05 84 48. Open daily 9am-7pm. Crypt €2. Festival tickets €33, students €15.)*

MUSÉE CANTINI. This memorable museum chronicles the region's 20th-century artistic successes, with major Cubist, Fauvist, and Surrealist collections, including works by Matisse and Signac. *(19 r. Grignan. M: Estragin-Préfecture. ☎04 91 54 77 75. €2.50, students €1.50, over 65 and under 10 free.)*

MÉMORIAL DES CAMPS DE LA MORT. This small museum is located in a blockhouse built by the Germans during their occupation of Marseille. Sobering exhibits recall the death camps of WWII and the deportation of thousands of Jews from the *vieux port* in 1943. *(Q. de la Tourette. M: Vieux Port. ☎04 91 90 73 15. Open Tu-Su June-Aug. 11am-6pm; Sept.-May 10am-5pm. Free.)*

OTHER SIGHTS. The **Musée de la Mode**'s rotating exhibits feature international clothing from different eras. *(Espace Mode Méditerranée, 11 La Canebière. M: Vieux Port-Hôtel de Ville. ☎04 96 17 06 00. €3, students €1, seniors free.)* At the nearby **Musée d'Histoire de Marseille,** Greek, Phoenician, and modern artifacts reveal Marseille's rich past. A museum ticket also gives access to the **Jardin des Vestiges,** just next door. *(Enter through the Centre Bourse mall's lowest level. ☎04 91 90 42 22. Open Tu-Sa noon-7pm. €2, students €1, under 10 free.)* Bus #83 (dir.: Rond-Point du Prado) goes from the *vieux port* to Marseille's main **public beaches.** Get off the bus just after it rounds the David statue (20-30min.). Both the north and south **plages du Prado** offer views of Marseille's surrounding cliffs.

NIGHTLIFE

Late-night restaurants and a few nightclubs center around **place Thiers,** near the *vieux port.* On weekends, tables from the bars along the **quai de Rive Neuve** spill out into the sidewalk. A more counter-culture crowd unwinds along the **cours Julien.** Tourists should exercise caution at night, particularly in Panier and Belsunce, and near the Opera on the *vieux port.* Night buses are scarce, taxis are expensive, and the metro closes early (M-Th and Su 9pm, F-Sa 12:30am). **Trolleybus,** 24 q. de Rive Neuve (M: Vieux Port), is a mega-club in an 18th-century warehouse with three separate rooms for pop-rock, techno, and soul-funk-salsa. Prize-winning French and international DJs have been spinning here for 15 years. (Beer from €5. Mixed drinks €4-8. Cover Sa €10; includes 1 drink. Open July-Aug. W-Sa 11pm-6am; Sept.-June Th-Sa 11pm-6am. MC/V.)

AIX-EN-PROVENCE ☎04 42

Famous for festivals, fountains, and former residents Paul Cézanne and Émile Zola, Aix-en-Provence ("X"; pop. 141,000) caters to tourists without being ruined by them. The **chemin de Cézanne,** 9 av. Paul Cézanne, features a 2hr. self-guided tour that leads to the artist's birthplace and favorite cafes. (Open daily July-Aug. 10am-6pm; Apr.-June and Sept. 10am-noon and 2-6pm; Oct.-Mar. 10am-noon and 2-5pm. €5.50, ages 13-25 €2.) The **Fondation Vasarely,** av. Marcel-Pagnol, in nearby Jas-de-Bouffan, is a must-see for Op-Art fans. (Open Tu-Sa 10am-1pm and 2-6pm. €7, students €4.) The **Cathédrale St-Sauveur,** r. Gaston de Saporta, fell victim to misplaced violence during the Revolution; angry Aixois mistook the apostle statues for statues of royalty and defiantly chopped off their heads. The statues were re-capitated in the 19th century, but remain sans neck. (Open daily 8am-noon and 2-6pm.) In June and July, famous performers and rising stars descend on Aix for the **Festival d'Aix-en-Provence**. (☎04 42 16 11 70; www.festival-aix.com. Tickets from €8.)

July travelers should reserve rooms in March. **Hôtel Paul ❸,** 10 av. Pasteur, has relatively cheap, clean rooms and serves breakfast in a quiet garden. (☎04 42 23 23 89; hotel.paul@wanadoo.fr. Breakfast €5. Check-in before 6pm. Singles and doubles with bath €43, with garden-facing windows €53; triples €65; quads €76. Cash only.) Charming restaurants pack **rue Verrerie** and the roads north of **cours Mirabeau. Rue Verrerie,** off r. des Cordiliers, has bars and clubs.

Trains, at the end of av. Victor Hugo, run to Marseille (45min., 27 per day, €7), Nice (3-4hr., 25 per day, €35), and Paris (TGV 3hr., 10 per day, €77-131). **Buses** (☎08 91 02 40 25) leave av. de l'Europe for Marseille (30min., 6 per hr., €5). The **tourist office** is at 2 pl. du Général de Gaulle. (☎04 42 16 11 61; www.aixenprovencetourism.com. Open July-Aug. M-Sa 8:30am-9pm, Su 10am-8pm; Sept.-June M-Sa 8:30am-8pm, Su 10am-1pm and 2-6pm.) **Postal Code:** 13100.

AVIGNON ☎04 90

Temporary home to the papacy 700 years ago, Avignon (pop. 89,500) now hosts Europe's most prestigious theater festival. For three weeks in July, the **Festival d'Avignon** holds theatrical performances in over 20 venues, from cloisters to factories to palaces. (☎04 90 14 14 14; www.festival-avignon.com. Reservations accepted from mid-June. Tickets up to €45, under 25 receive discounted admission of €13 for all shows over €13.) The more experimental **Festival OFF,** also in July, is just as well established. (☎04 90 25 24 30; www.avignon-off.org. Tickets under €16. 30% discount with €10 Carte OFF.) The golden **Palais des Papes,** Europe's largest Gothic palace, is a reminder of the city's brief stint as the center of the Catholic Church. Although revolutionary looting stripped the interior of its lavish furnishings and fires erased its medieval murals, its vast chambers and few remaining frescoes are still remarkable. (☎04 90 27 50 00. Open daily Aug. 9am-9pm; July to mid Sept. 9am-8pm; mid-Sept. to Oct. and Apr.-June 9am-7pm; Nov.-Mar. 9:30am-5:45pm. €10.) The French children's song "Sur le pont d'Avigon" has immortalized the 12th-century bridge **Pont St-Bénézet.** Despite its supposedly divinely ordained location, the bridge has suffered from warfare and the once-turbulent Rhône. (☎04 90 27 51 16. €4. Free audio tour. Same hours as the Palais.) Farther downstream, **Pont Daladier** makes it all the way across, offering free views of the broken bridge and the Palais.

Avignon's accommodations fill up three to four months before festival season; reserve ahead or stay in Arles or Nîmes (p. 371). Rooms with many amenities, including A/C and TV, make **Hôtel Mignon ❸,** 12 r. Joseph Vernet, a good deal despite its small bathrooms. (☎04 90 82 17 30; www.hotel-mignon.com. Breakfast included. Free Internet and in-room Wi-Fi. Reception 7am-11pm. Singles €42-52, doubles €60-73, triples €72-83, quad €94. Prices increase 20% in festival season. AmEx/MC/V.) Restaurants group on **rue des Teinturiers.** Or try **Citron Pressé ❷,** 38 r. Carreterie. (☎04 90 86 09 29. 3-course *menu* with wine €12. *Plats* €3-7. Open M-Th noon-2:30pm, F-Sa noon-2pm and 7:30pm-11:30pm; during festival daily noon-2am. Cash only.) **Place des Corps Saints** has a few bars that remain busy year-round. **Trains** (☎04 90 27 81 89) run from bd. St-Roch to: Arles (20min., 1-2 per hr., €9); Lyon (2hr., 7 per day, €31); Marseille (1hr., 1 per hr., €28); Nîmes (30min., 14 per day, €9); Paris (TGV 3-4hr., 13 per day, €97). Exit the station, **buses** are on the right, going to Arles (1hr., 5 per day, €8) and Marseille (2hr., 1 per day, €19). The **tourist office** is at 41 cours Jean Jaurès. (☎04 32 74 32 74; www.avignon-tourisme.com. Open July M-Sa 9am-7pm, Su 9:45am-5pm; Apr.-June and Aug.-Oct. M-Sa 9am-6pm, Su 9:45am-5pm; Nov.-Mar. M-F 9am-6pm, Sa 9am-5pm, Su 10am-noon.) **Postal Code:** 84000.

NÎMES ☎04 66

Southern France flocks to Nîmes (pop. 145,000) for its *férias*, celebrations with bullfights, flamenco dancing, and other hot-blooded festivities. Every Thursday night in summer, art and musical performances fill the squares of the Old Town. **Les Arènes** is a well-preserved first-century Roman amphitheater that still holds bullfights and concerts. (☎04 66 21 82 56. Open daily June-Aug. 9am-7pm; Apr-May and Sept. 9am-6:30pm; Oct and March 9am-6pm; Nov.-Feb. 9:30am-5pm.

Closed during *férias* or concerts; call ahead. €7.70, students €5.90.) North of the arena stands the **Maison Carrée,** a rectangular temple built in the first century BC. Today, visitors can enjoy a 3D film retracing the town's Roman past. (Open daily June-Aug. 9.10am-7:30pm; Apr.-May and Sept. 10am-7pm; Mar. and Oct. 10am-6:30pm; Jan.-Feb. and Nov.-Dec. 10am-1pm and 2-5pm. Film 2 per hr. €4.50, students €3.60.) Across the square, the **Carrée d'Art** displays traveling exhibits of contemporary art. (Open Tu-Su 10am-6pm. Last entry at 5:30pm. €5, students €3.60.) To get to the newly renovated **Auberge de Jeunesse (HI) ❶,** 257 ch. de l'Auberge de Jeunesse, take bus I (dir.: Alès) from the train station to Stade, rte. d'Alès and follow the signs uphill. With jovial staff and a beautiful courtyard garden, this comfortable hostel is worth the 45min. trek from the train station. (☎04 66 68 03 20. Breakfast €4. Internet €1 per 15min. Free Wi-Fi. Reception 7:30am-1am. Open Mar.-Sept. Dorms €12.25 with HI card. Camping €8.90. MC/V.) **Trains** go from bd. Talabot to: Arles (25min., 8 per day, €10); Marseille (1hr., 9 per day, €22); Montpellier (30min., 31-46 per day, €9); Toulouse (3hr., 17 per day, €38). **Buses** (☎04 66 29 52 00) depart from behind the train station for Avignon (1hr., 3-5 per day, €8.30). The **tourist office,** is at 6 r. Auguste. (☎04 66 58 38 00; www.ot-nimes.fr. Open July-Aug. M 8:30am-8pm, Sa 9am-7pm, Su 10am-6pm; Sept.-June reduced hours.) **Postal Codes:** 30000; 30900.

FRENCH RIVIERA (CÔTE D'AZUR)

Between Marseille and the Italian border, sun-drenched beaches and warm Mediterranean waters combine to form the fabled playground of the rich and famous. Chagall, F. Scott Fitzgerald, Matisse, Picasso, and Renoir all flocked to the coast in its heyday. Now, the Riviera is a curious combination of high-rolling millionaires and low-budget tourists. In May, high society makes its yearly pilgrimage to the Cannes Film Festival and the Monte-Carlo Grand Prix, while Nice's February Carnaval and summer jazz festivals draw budget travelers.

NICE ☎04 93

Classy, colorful Nice (NIECE; pop. 340,000) is the Riviera's unofficial capital. Its non-stop nightlife, top-notch museums, and packed beaches are tourist magnets. During February Carnaval, visitors and *Niçois* alike ring in spring with revelry. When visiting Nice, prepare to have more fun than you'll remember.

TRANSPORTATION

Flights: Aéroport Nice-Côte d'Azur (NCE; ☎08 20 42 33 33). Air France, 10 av. de Verdun (☎08 02 80 28 02). To: **Bastia, Corsica** (€116; under 25 and couples €59) and **Paris** (€93/50). **Buses** on the Ligne d'Azur (€4, 3-4 per hr.) leave for the airport from the train station (#99), bus station (#98); before 8am, take bus #23 (€1, 3-4 per hr.).

Trains: Gare SNCF Nice-Ville, av. Thiers (☎14 82 12). Open daily 5am-12:00am. To: **Cannes** (40min., 3 per hr., €6.30); **Marseille** (2hr., 16 per day, €28.50); **Monaco** (15min., 2-6 per hr., €2.80-4); **Paris** (5hr., 9 per day, €136.10).

Buses: 5 bd. Jean Jaurès (☎04 93 85 61 81). Info booth open M-F 8:30am-5:30pm, Sa 9am-4pm. To **Cannes** (2hr., 2-3 per hr.) and **Monaco** (1hr., 3-6 per hr.). All ligne d'Azur buses are now €1 for any destination.

Ferries: Corsica Ferries (☎04 92 00 42 93; www.corsicaferries.com). Bus #1 or 2 (dir.: Port) from pl. Masséna. To **Corsica** (€20-40, bikes €10, cars €40-65). MC/V.

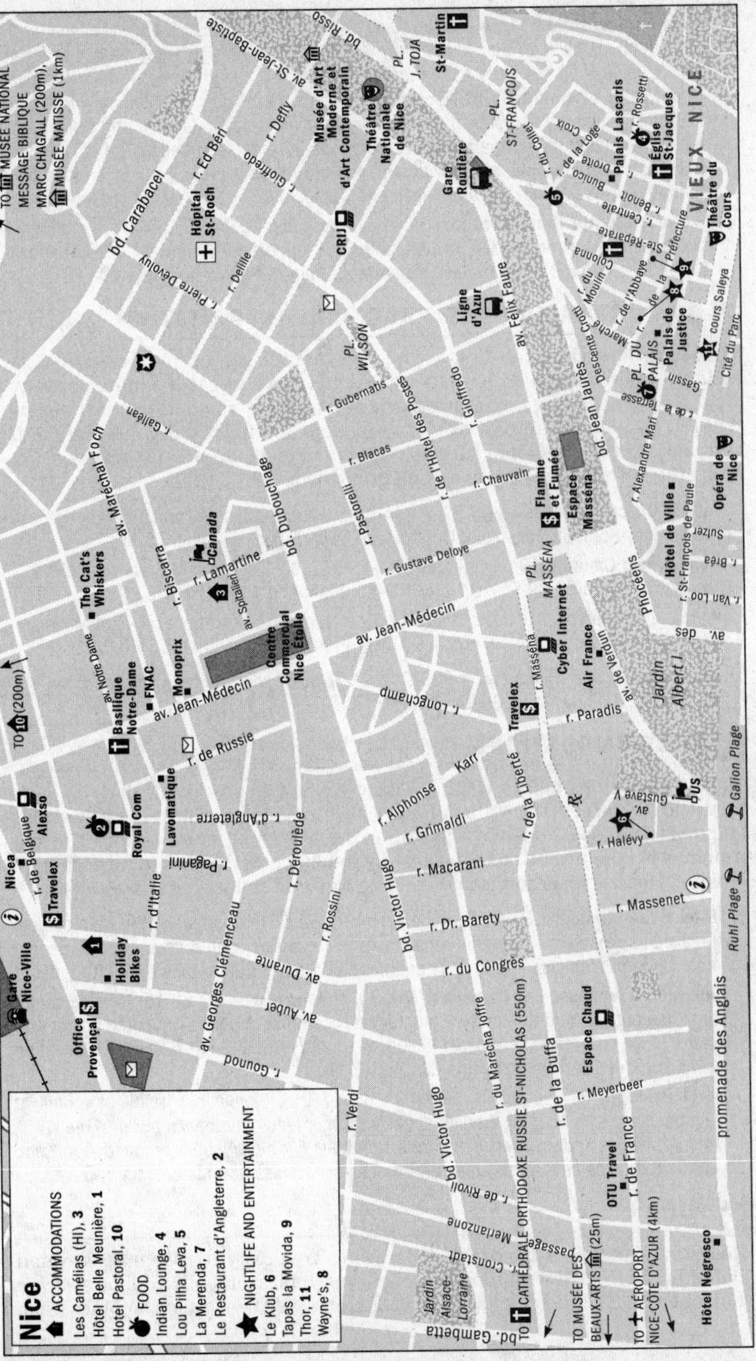

Nice

ACCOMMODATIONS
- Les Camélias (HI), 3
- Hôtel Belle Meunière, 1
- Hotel Pastoral, 10

FOOD
- Indian Lounge, 4
- Lou Pilha Leva, 5
- La Merenda, 7
- Le Restaurant d'Angleterre, 2

NIGHTLIFE AND ENTERTAINMENT
- Le Klub, 6
- Tapas la Movida, 9
- Thor, 11
- Wayne's, 8

Public Transportation: Ligne d'Azur, 10 av. Félix Faure (☎93 13 53 13; www.lignedazur.com), near pl. Leclerc. Buses run daily 7am-8pm. Tickets €1, 1-day pass €4, 7 day pass €15, and 10 trip pass €10. Purchase tickets and day passes on board the bus; *carnet* passes from the office. **Noctambus** (night service) runs 4 routes daily 9:10pm-1:10am. Completed in 2009, the Nice **tram** runs along Jean Médecin and Place Massena, connecting the northern reaches of the city to the eastern edge. The 8.7 km line is wheelchair-accessible, air-conditioned, and stops about every 5 minutes along its L shaped route from 6am to 2am. Prices and tickets are the same as the buses.

Bike and Scooter Rental: Holiday Bikes, 34 av. Auber (☎04 93 16 01 62; nice@holiday-bikes.com), near the train station. Bikes €18 per day, €75 per week; €230 deposit. Scooters €40/175; €500 deposit. Open M-Sa 9am-6:30pm. AmEx/MC/V.

ORIENTATION AND PRACTICAL INFORMATION

Avenue Jean Médecin, on the left as you exit the train station, and **boulevard Gambetta,** on the right, run directly to the beach. **Place Masséna** is 10min. down av. Jean Médecin. On the coast, **promenade des Anglais** is a people-watcher's paradise. To the southeast, past av. Jean Médecin and toward the bus station, is **vieux Nice.** Everyone should exercise caution at night, around the train station, along the port, in *vieux* Nice, and on promenade des Anglais.

Tourist Office: av. Thiers (☎08 92 70 74 07; www.nicetourisme.com). Open June-Sept. M-Sa 8am-8pm, Su 9am-7pm; Oct.-May M-Sa 8am-7pm, Su 9am-6pm.

Consulates: Canada, 10 r. Lamartine (☎04 93 92 93 22). Open M-F 9am-noon. **US,** 7 av. Gustave V (☎88 89 55). Open M-F 9-11:30am and 1:30-4:30pm.

Police: 1 av. Maréchal Foch (☎04 92 17 22 22), opposite end from bd. Jean Médecin.

Hospital: St-Roch, 5 r. Pierre Dévoluy (☎04 92 03 33 75).

Post Office: 23 av. Thiers (☎04 93 82 65 22), found near the train station. Open M-F 8am-7pm, Sa 8am-noon. **Postal Code:** 06033.

ACCOMMODATIONS

Make reservations before visiting Nice; beds are elusive particularly in summer. The city has two clusters of budget accommodations: near the **train station** and near **vieux Nice.** Those by the station are newer but more remote; the surrounding neighborhood has a deservedly rough reputation, so exercise caution at night. Hotels closer to *vieux* Nice are more convenient but less modern.

Hôtel Belle Meunière, 21 av. Durante (☎04 93 88 66 15), opposite the train station. Relaxed backpackers fill co-ed dorms in a former mansion. Laundry from €5.50. Reception 7:30am-midnight. Dorms €17; doubles €50; triples €60; quads €80. MC/V. ❷

Auberge de Jeunesse Les Camélias (HI), 3 r. Spitalieri (☎04 93 62 15 54; nice-camelias@fuaj.org), behind the Centre Commerical Nice Étoile. A centrally located hostel with plain, clean bathrooms. Breakfast included. Laundry €3. Internet €3 per hr. Reception 24hr. Lockout 11am-3pm. Dorms €21. MC/V. ❷

Hôtel Pastoral, 27 rue Assalit (☎04 93 85 17 22). Simple but well-kept rooms at reasonable prices. Helpful, English-speaking owner lends free beach towels. Free Wi-Fi, Internet, fridge, and microwave in dorms. Breakfast €3. Reservations required. Apr.-Sept. dorms €20; singles €30; doubles €45. Prices €5-10 less Oct.-March. MC/V. ❷

FOOD

Mediterranean spices flavor Niçois cuisine. Try crusty *pan bagnat,* a round loaf of bread topped with tuna, sardines, vegetables, and olive oil, or *socca,* a thin, olive-oil-flavored chickpea bread. Famous *salade niçoise* combines tuna, olives, eggs, potatoes, tomatoes, and a spicy mustard dressing. Save your euro for olives, cheese, and produce from the **markets** at cours Saleya and avenue Maché de la Libération (both open Tu-Su 7am-1pm). **Avenue Jean Médecin** features reasonable brasseries, panini vendors, and kebab stands.

La Merenda, 4 r. de la Terrasse. Behind a stained-glass exterior and a beaded curtain, this intimate restaurant serves some of the best regional dishes the city has to offer. Seatings at 7 and 9pm only; reserve in person in the morning for dinner. *Plats* €12-16. Open M-F noon-1:30pm and 7-9pm. Cash only. ❷

Lou Pilha Leva, 10-13 r. du Collet (☎04 93 13 99 08), in *vieux* Nice. The line of locals and tourists hungry for cheap Niçois fare extends around the corner. *Assortment Niçois* (€8) offers a sampling. Pizza €4.50. Open daily 9am-midnight. Cash only. ❶

Indian Lounge, 34 rue Droite (☎04 93 85 38 39; www.indianlounge.fr). Quick, spicy, and cheap Indian fare in a mesmerizing setting. Try the chicken biryani (€11.90), vegetable curry (€6), or a variety of Indian breads (€2-4). Meat dishes €10-12. Entrees €2-7.50. Open daily noon-2:30pm and 7pm-1:30am. MC/V. ❶

Le Restaurant d'Angleterre, 25 r. d'Angleterre (☎04 93 88 64 49), near the train station. Frequented by a loyal crowd of locals who come for traditional French and English favorites. The €15.50 *menu* includes salad, *plat,* side dish, and dessert. Open Tu-Sa 11:45am-2pm and 6:45-9:50pm, Su 11:45am-2pm. MC/V. ❸

SIGHTS

One look at Nice's waves and you may be tempted to spend your entire stay stretched out on the sand. As the city with the second-most museums in France, however, Nice offers more than azure waters and topless sunbathers.

MUSÉE NATIONAL MESSAGE BIBLIQUE MARC CHAGALL. Chagall founded this extraordinary museum to showcase an assortment of biblically themed pieces that he gave to the French State in 1966. Twelve of these colorful canvases illustrate the first two books of the Old Testament. The museum also includes an auditorium with stained-glass panels depicting the creation story. The auditorium hosts concerts; ask at the entrance for program info. *(Av. du Dr. Ménard. Walk 15min. north of the station, or take bus #22, dir.: Rimiez, to Musée Chagall. ☎04 93 53 87 20; www.musee-chagall.fr. Open M and W-Su July-Sept. 10am-6pm; Oct.-June 10am-5pm. €8.50, students 18-25 €6.50, under 18 and 1st and 3rd Su of each month free. MC/V.)*

MUSÉE MATISSE. Henri Matisse visited Nice in 1916 and never left. Housed in his 17th-century Genoese villa, this museum contains a small collection of paintings and a dazzling exhibit of Matisse's three-dimensional work, including dozens of cut paper tableaux. *(164 av. des Arènes de Cimiez. Bus #15, 17, 20, 22, or 25 to Arènes. Free bus between Musée Chagall and Musée Matisse. ☎04 93 81 08 08; www.musee-matisse-nice.org. Open M and W-Su 10am-6pm. Free admission. MC/V.)*

MUSÉE D'ART MODERNE ET D'ART CONTEMPORAIN. An impressive glass facade welcomes visitors to exhibits of French New Realists and American pop artists like Lichtenstein and Warhol. *(Promenade des Arts, at the intersection of av. St-Jean Baptiste and Traverse Garibaldi. Bus #5, dir.: St-Charles, to Musée Promenade des Arts. ☎04 93 62 61 62; www.mamac-nice.org. Open Tu-Su 10am-6pm. Free admission.)*

MUSÉE DES BEAUX-ARTS JULES CHARET. The former villa of Ukraine's Princess Kotschoubey has been converted into a celebration of French and Italian painting. Raoul Dufy, a local Fauvist painter, celebrated his city's spontaneity with sensational pictures of the town at rest and at play. *(33 av. Baumettes. Bus #38 to Musée Chéret or #12 to Grosso. ☎04 92 15 28 28; www.musee-beaux-arts-nice.org. Open M and W-Su 10am-6pm. Free admission.)*

FRENCH 101: A CRASH COURSE

raveling through France, you will ındoubtedly encounter familiar vords on signs and menus. Though hese cognates will appear to help ı your struggle to comprehend *le nonde francophone,* beware! Some can also lead you astray. Here are some *faux amis* (false cognates; literally, "false friends") o watch out for:

Blesser has nothing to do with spirituality (or sneezing). It means **o hurt,** not to bless.

Pain is anything but misery or the French: it's their word for **read.**

Bras is not a supportive undergarment, it's an **arm.**

Rage is not just regular anger, t's **rabies.**

Rabais, it follows, is not the disease you can catch from a dog, out a **discount.**

A *sale* is not an event with a lot of rabais; it means **dirty.**

Draguer means **to hit on,** not o drag, unless you encounter an overly aggressive flirt.

Balancer is **to swing,** not to steady oneself.

A *peste* is slightly more serious han a bothersome creature. It is ı **plague.**

Puéril is not grave danger, just **hildhood.**

Preservatif is not something ound in packaged food, but it can oe found close to packages, so to speak. This is the French word for **ondom.**

CATHÉDRALE ORTHODOXE RUSSE SAINT-NICOLAS. Also known as the **Église Russe,** the cathedral was commissioned by Empress Marie Feodorovna in memory of her husband, Tsar Nicholas Alexandrovich, who died in Nice in 1865. Soon after its 1912 dedication, the cathedral's tranquil gold interior became a haven for exiled Russian nobles. *(17 bd. du Tzarewitch, off bd. Gambetta. ☎04 93 96 88 02. Open M-Sa 9am-noon and 2:30-6pm, Su 2:30-5:30pm. Closed during mass. €3, students €2.)*

LE CHÂTEAU. At the eastern end of promenade des Anglais, the remains of an 11th-century fort mark the city's birthplace. The château itself was destroyed by Louis XIV in 1706, but it still provides a spectacular **view of Nice** and the sparkling Baie des Anges. In summer, an outdoor theater hosts orchestral and vocal musicians. Cool off in front of the waterfall after climbing the steep steps. *(☎04 93 85 62 33. Park open daily June-Aug. 9am-8pm; Sept. 10am-7pm; Oct.-Mar. 8am-6pm; Apr.-May 8am-7pm. Free walk to the top. Elevator daily June-Aug. 9am-8pm; Apr.-May and Sept. 10am-7pm; Oct.-Mar. 10am-6pm. €0.80, round-trip €1.)*

JARDIN ALBERT I. The city's oldest park, Jardin Albert I, below pl. Masséna, has plenty of benches and palm trees. The outdoor Théâtre de Verdure presents concerts in summer while an inflatable moonbounce entertains kids in the evenings. Unfortunately, the park is one of Nice's most dangerous spots after dark. Tourists should avoid crossing the park at night. *(Between av. Verdun and bd. Jean Jaurès, off promenade des Anglais. Box office open daily 10:30am-noon and 3:30-6:30pm. MC/V.)*

OTHER SIGHTS. Named by the rich English community that commissioned it, the **promenade des Anglais,** a palm-lined seaside boulevard, is filled with ice-cream eating tourists and jogging locals. **Hôtel Négresco** presents the best of *Belle Époque* luxury with coffered ceilings, crystal chandeliers, and a large collection of valuable artwork. The seashore between bd. Gambetta and the Opéra alternates private beaches with crowded public strands, but a large section west of bd. Gambetta is public. Many travelers are surprised to find that stretches of rock (not soft sand) line the **Baie des Anges;** make sure to bring your beach mat.

ENTERTAINMENT AND NIGHTLIFE

Nice's **Jazz Festival,** at the Parc et Arènes de Cimiez, attracts world-famous performers. (mid-July; ☎08 20 80 04 00; www.nicejazzfest.com. €31-51.) The **Carnaval** gives Rio a run for its money with three weeks of confetti, fireworks, parades, and parties.

(☎04 92 14 46 46; www.nicecarnaval.com.) Bars and nightclubs around **rue Masséna** and **vieux Nice** pulsate with dance and jazz but have a strict dress code. To experience Nice's nightlife without spending a euro, head down to the **promenade des Anglais,** where street performers, musicians, and pedestrians fill the beach and boardwalk. Hard to find *Le Pitchoun* provides the lowdown on trendy bars and clubs (in French; free; www.lepitchoun.com). Exercise caution after dark; men have a reputation for harassing lone women on the promenade, in the Jardin Albert I, and near the train station, while the beach sometimes becomes a gathering place for prostitutes and thugs.

BARS

Thor, 32 cours Saleya (☎04 93 62 49 90). Svelte bartenders pour pints for a youthful clientele amid war shields, long wooden oars, and glasses shaped like Viking horns in this raucous faux-Scandinavian pub. Daily live bands blare rock starting at 10:30pm. Happy hour 5:30-9pm; pints €4.50. Open daily 5:30pm-2:30am. MC/V.

Wayne's, 15 r. de la Préfecture (☎04 93 13 46 99; www.waynes.fr). A laid-back crowd drinks at tables by the bar while the rowdier crew finds its way downstairs to dance floor. Patrons dance on tables and each other. Pints €6. Mixed drinks €7. Happy hour noon-2pm, 5-9pm; all drinks €3.90. Open daily noon-2am. AmEx/MC/V.

Tapas la Movida, 3 r. de l'Abbaye (☎04 93 62 27 46). Attracts a young, alternative crowd. Prepare to crawl home if attempting the *bar-o-mètre* (a meter-long box of shots; €17). M-F live reggae, rock, and ska (€3). F-Sa DJ and theme parties. Open July-Aug. daily 9pm-12:30am; Sept.-June M-Sa 9pm-12:30am. Cash only.

Le Klub, 6 r. Halévy (☎04 93 16 87 26). Nice's most popular gay klub attracts a large krew of men and women to its sleek lounge, active dance floor, and lively stage. Mixed drinks €8-10. Cover €11-14; includes 1 drink. Open W-Su midnight-5am. AmEx/MC/V.

MONACO AND MONTE-CARLO ☎04 93

In 1297, François Grimaldi of Genoa established his family as Monaco's rulers, staging a coup aided by henchmen disguised as *monaco* (Italian for monk). The tiny principality jealously guarded its independence ever since. Monaco (pop. 7100) brashly displays its tax-free wealth with surveillance cameras, high-speed luxury cars, multi-million-dollar yachts, and Monte-Carlo's famous casino.

Crayon means **pencil,** not crayon, and gomme is not for chewing, unless you like the taste of rubber—it is an **eraser.**

An *extincteur* is not a bazooka. It is a **fire extinguisher.**

Fesses is not a colloquial term for "coming clean." It actually means **buttocks.**

As is not another way to say *fesses* or even an insult. This is a French compliment, meaning **ace** or **champion.**

Ranger is neither a woodsman nor a mighty morpher. This means **to tidy up.**

A *smoking* has little to do with tobacco (or any other substance). It is a **tuxedo** or **dinner suit.**

Raisins are juicy **grapes,** not the dried-up snack food. Try *raisins-secs* instead.

Prunes are **plums.** *Pruneaus* are the dried fruit.

Tampons are **stamps** (for documents), not the feminine care item. If you are looking for those, ask for a *tampon hygiénique* or *napkins.* To wipe your mouth, you would do better with a *serviette.*

The *patron* is not the customer, rather, it is the **boss.**

Glacier does translate literally; however, you are more likely to see it around town on signs for **ice cream vendors;** *glace* does not mean glass, but a frozen summer treat.

If the French language seems full of deception, think again. *Deception* in French actually means **disappointment.**

CALLING TO AND FROM MONACO	Monaco's country code is 377. To call Monaco from France, dial 00377, then the eight-digit Monaco number. To call France from Monaco, dial 0033 and drop the first zero of the French number.

TRANSPORTATION AND PRACTICAL INFORMATION. **Trains** run from Gare SNCF, pl. Ste-Dêvote, to Antibes (1hr., 2 per hr., €6.50), Cannes (1hr., 2 per hr., €8-8.40), and Nice (25min., 2 per hr., €3.10). **Buses** (☎04 93 85 64 44) leave bd. des Moulins and av. Princesse Alice for Nice (45min., 4 per hr., €1). The enormous **Rocher de Monaco** (Rock of Monaco) looms over the harbor. At the city's top, Monaco-Ville, the historical and legislative heart, is home to the **Palais Princier,** the **Cathédrale de Monaco,** and narrow cafe-lined pedestrian avenues. **La Condamine quarter,** Monaco's port, sits below Monaco-Ville, with a morning market, spirited bars, and lots of traffic. Monaco's famous glitz is concentrated in **Monte-Carlo,** whose casino draws international visitors. Bus #4 links the Ste-Dêvote train station entrance to the casino; buy tickets on board (€1). The **tourist office** is at 2A bd. des Moulins. (☎04 92 16 61 16. Open M-Sa 9am-7pm, Su and holidays 11am-1pm.) **Postal Code:** MC 98000 Monaco.

ACCOMMODATIONS AND FOOD. Rather than stay in expensive Monaco, the nearby town of **Beausoleil, FRA,** only a 10min. walk from the casino, offers several budget accommodations. The modest rooms at **Hôtel Diana ❸,** 17 bd. du Général Leclerc, come with A/C and TV. (☎04 93 78 47 58; www.monte-carlo.mc/hotel-diana-beausoleil. Singles €40-60; doubles €40-70; triples €75. Reservations recommended. AmEx/MC/V.) Unsurprisingly, Monaco has little in the way of cheap fare. Try the narrow streets behind the **place du Palais** for affordable sit-down meals, or, better yet, fill a picnic basket at the **market** on pl. d'Armes at the end of av. Prince Pierre. (Open daily 6am-1pm.)

SIGHTS AND ENTERTAINMENT. At the notorious **Monte-Carlo Casino,** pl. du Casino, Richard Burton wooed Elizabeth Taylor and Mata Hari shot a Russian spy. Optimists tempt fate at blackjack, roulette (daily from noon), and slot machines (July-Aug. daily from noon; Sept.-June M-F from 2pm, Sa-Su from noon). French games like *chemin de fer* and *trente et quarante* begin at noon in the exclusive salons privés (€20 extra cover). (Cover €10. Coat and tie required.) Next door, the relaxed **Café de Paris** opens at 10am and has no cover. All casinos have dress codes at night (no sandals, shorts, sneakers, or jeans). Guards are strict about the age requirement (18+); bring a passport as proof. On a seaside cliff, **Palais Princier** is the occasional home of Monaco's tabloid-darling royal family. Visitors can tour the small but lavish palace. (Open daily June-Sept. 10am-7pm; Oct. 10am-5:30pm. €7, students €3.50.) The venue for Prince Rainier and Grace Kelly's 1956 wedding, nearby **Cathédrale de Monaco,** pl. St-Martin, is the burial site for 35 generations of the Grimaldi family. Princess Grace lies behind the altar in a tomb marked with her Latinized name, "Patritia Gracia"; Prince Rainier is buried on her right. (Open daily Mar.-Oct. 8am-7pm; Nov.-Feb. 8am-6pm. Mass Sa 6pm, Su 10:30am. Free.) The **Private Collection of Antique Cars of His Serene Highness Prince Rainier III,** les Terraces de Fontvieille, showcases 100 sexy cars. (Open daily 10am-6pm. €6, students €3.)

Monaco's nightlife offers fashionistas a chance to see and be seen. Speckled with cheaper venues, **La Condamine,** near the port, caters to a young clientele while glitzy trust-funders frequent pricier spots near the casino. Vintage decor, video games, and the latest pop and techno beats draw young, international masses to **Stars N' Bars,** 6 q. Antoine 1. (☎04 97 97 95 95; www.starsnbars.com. Open June-Sept. daily 9:30am-3am; Oct.-May Tu-Su 11am-3am. AmEx/MC/V.)

ANTIBES ☎04 93

Blessed with beautiful beaches and a charming *vieille ville,* Antibes (pop. 80,000) is less touristy than Nice and more relaxed than St-Tropez. It provides much-needed middle ground on the glitterati-controlled coast. The **Musée Picasso,** in the Château Grimaldi on pl. Mariejol, displays works by the former Antibes resident and his contemporaries. The two main public beaches in Antibes, **plage du Ponteil** and neighboring **plage de la Salis,** are crowded all summer. Cleaner and slightly more secluded, the rocky beaches on Cap d'Antibes have white cliffs and blue water perfect for snorkeling.

For the cheapest accommodations in Antibes, grab a bunk at **The Crew House ❷,** 1 av. St-Roch. From the train station, walk down av. de la Libération; just after the roundabout, make a right onto av. St-Roch. (☎04 92 90 49 39; workstation_fr@yahoo.com. Luggage storage €1.50. Internet €4.80 per hr. Reception M-F 9am-8pm, Sa-Su 10am-6pm. Dorms Apr.-Oct. €25; Nov.-Mar. €20. MC/V.) A variety of restaurants set up outdoor tables along **boulevard d'Aguillon,** behind the *vieux port.* For cheaper eats, you're better off at **place Nationale,** a few blocks away. The **Marché Provençal,** on cours Masséna, is one of the best fresh produce markets on the Côte d'Azur. (Open Tu-Su 6am-1pm.)

Come summer, the hip neighboring town Juan-les-Pins is synonymous with wild nightlife. **Pam Pam Rhumerie,** 137 bd. Wilson, is a hot Brazilian sit-down bar. Bikinied showgirls take the stage at 9:30pm to dance and down flaming drinks. (☎04 93 61 11 05. Open daily mid-Mar. to early Nov. 2pm-5am. MC/V.) Brave long lines to attend one of the popular Mexican fiestas held in **Le Village.** (☎04 92 93 90 00. Ladies free M-Th midnight-12:30am. Cover €16; includes 1 drink. Open July-Aug. daily midnight-5am; Sept.-June F-Sa midnight-5am. MC/V.)

Frequent **buses** (10min., 2 per hr., €1) and **trains** (5min., 1-2 per hr., €1.20) run from Antibes, although walking between the two towns along bd. Wilson is also an option. Although touristy, the **petit train** (☎06 03 35 61 35) leaves r. de la République and serves as both a guided tour of Antibes and a means of transportation to Juan-les-Pins. (30min.; 1 per hr. July-Aug. 10am-10pm, May-Oct. 10am-7pm.; round-trip €8, 3-10 €3.50. Buy tickets on board. Cash only.) **Trains** leave pl. Pierre Semard in Antibes, off av. Robert Soleau, for Cannes (15min., 23 per day, €2.50), Marseille (2hr., 12 per day, €26.70), and Nice (15min., 25 per day, €4.40-5.40). RCA **buses** leave pl. de Gaulle for Cannes (20min.) and Nice (45min.). All buses depart every 20min. and cost €1. The **tourist office** is at 11 pl. de Gaulle. (☎04 97 23 11 11; www.antibes-juanlespins.com. Open July-Aug. daily 9am-7pm; Sept.-June M-F 9am-5pm.) **Postal Code:** 06600.

CANNES ☎04 93

Stars compete for camera time at Cannes's annual, world-famous and invite only **Festival International du Film** (May 15-26, 2009). During the rest of the year, Cannes (pop. 67,000) rolls up all but its most famous red carpet—leaving one at the Palais for your tacky photographic pleasure. During this downtime, it also becomes the most accessible of all the Riviera's glam towns. A palm-lined boardwalk, sandy beaches, and numerous boutiques draw the wealthy and the young. Of the town's three prestigious casinos, the least exclusive is **Le Casino Croisette,** 1 Lucien Barrière, next to the Palais des Festivals. (No shorts, jeans, or T-shirts. Jackets required for men in gaming rooms. 18+. Free entry. Open daily 10am-4am; table games 8pm-4am.)

Hotel Mimont ❸, 39 r. de Mimont, is Cannes's best budget hotel. English-speaking owners maintain basic, clean rooms two streets behind the train station.

(☎04 93 39 51 64; canneshotelmimont65@wanadoo.fr. Free Wi-Fi. Singles €34-40; doubles €40-47; triples €60. Prices about 15% higher July-Aug. Ask about €30 petites chambres for *Let's Go* readers. MC/V.) The zone around **rue Meynadier** has inexpensive restaurants. Cafes and bars near the waterfront stay open all night and are a great alternative to the expense of gambling and posh clubs. Nightlife thrives around **rue Dr. G. Monod.** Try **Morrison's,** 10 r. Teisseire, for casual company in a literary-themed pub. (☎04 92 98 16 17. Beer from €5.30. Happy hour 5-8pm. Open daily 5pm-2am. MC/V.) Coastal **trains** depart from 1 r. Jean Jaurès for: Antibes (15min., €2.50); Marseille (2hr., 6:30am-11:03pm, €25); Monaco (1hr., €8); Nice (40min., €5.80); St-Raphaël (25min., €6.10). **Buses** go to Nice (1hr., 3 per hr., €6) from the pl. de l'Hôtel de Ville (☎04 93 48 70 30) and Grasse (50min., 1 per hr., €1) from the train station. The **tourist office** is at 1 bd. de la Croisette. (☎04 93 39 24 53; www.cannes.fr. Open July-Aug. daily 9am-8pm; Sept.-June 9am-7pm.) Get Internet at **Cap Cyber,** 12 r. 24 Août. (€3 per hr. Open in summer 10am-11pm; in winter 10am-10pm. MC/V.) **Postal Code:** 06400.

ST-TROPEZ ☎04 94

Hollywood stars, corporate giants, and curious backpackers congregate on the spotless streets of St-Tropez (pop. 5400), where the Riviera's glitz and glamor shines brightest. The young, beautiful, and restless flock to this "Jewel of the Riviera" to flaunt tans and designer clothing on notorious beaches and in posh nightclubs. The best beaches are difficult to reach without a car, but the *navette municipale* (shuttle) leaves pl. des Lices for Les Salins, a secluded sunspot, and **plage Tahiti** (Capon-Pinet stop), the first of the famous plages des Pampelonne. (M-Sa 5 per day, €1. Tourist office has schedule.) Take a break from the sun at the **Musée de l'Annonciade,** pl. Grammont, which showcases Fauvist and neo-Impressionist paintings. (Open M and W-Su June-Sept. 10am-noon and 2-6pm; Oct.-May 10am-1pm and 4-7pm. €6, students €4.)

Budget hotels do not exist in St-Tropez. Camping is the cheapest option, but is only available outside the city. Prices remain shockingly high, especially in July and August. To reach **Les Prairies de la Mer ❸,** a social campground on the beach, take a *bateau vert* (☎04 94 49 29 39) from the *vieux* port to Port Grimaud (Apr. to early Oct., 5min., 1 per hr., round-trip €11). Bowling, supermarkets, tennis courts and other facilities are available. (☎04 94 79 09 09; www.riviera-villages.com. Open late Mar. to early Oct. July to mid-Aug. €8 per person, €45 per tent; Apr.-June and late Aug. €3/20; Sept. to mid-Oct. €3/20. Electricity €5. MC/V.) Pricey restaurants line the streets behind the waterfront and the *vieux* port. To eat cheap, stop by the snack stands and cafes near **place des Lices,** the center of St-Tropez's wild nightlife. Sodetrav **buses** (☎04 93 97 88 51) leave av. Général Leclerc for St-Raphaël (2hr., 10-12 per day, €11.30). **Ferries** (☎04 93 95 17 46; www.tmr-saintraphael.com), at the *vieux* port, serve St-Tropez from St-Raphaël (1hr., 4-5 per day, €13 one-way, 22 round-trip). The **tourist office** is on q. Jean Jaurès. (☎04 93 97 45 21. Open daily July-Sept. 9:30am-8pm; Sept.-Oct. and mid-Mar. to June 9:30am-12:30pm and 2-7pm; early Nov. to mid-Mar. 9:30am-12:30pm and 2-6pm.) **Postal Code:** 83990.

CORSICA (LA CORSE) ☎04 95

Bathed in turquoise Mediterranean waters, Corsica (COHR-sih-kuh; pop. 279,000) was dubbed *Kallysté* (the most beautiful) by the Greeks. The island guarded its culture during centuries of invasions by Phoenicia, Carthage, Rome, Pisa, and Genoa. Natives remain divided over the issue of allegiance to France, and often reject the French language in favor of Corse. Most of

Corsica's visitors come for its unspoiled landscapes and rich natural beauty, easily accessible from the major towns on the island.

TRANSPORTATION

Air France and its subsidiary **Compagnie Corse Méditerranée** (CCM) fly to Ajaccio and Bastia from Marseille. The Air France/CCM office is at 3 bd. du Roi Jérôme, Ajaccio (☎08 20 82 08 20). **Ferries** between the mainland and Corsica can be rough, and aren't much cheaper than planes. **Hydrofoils** (3hr.) run from Nice, while overnight ferries depart from Marseille (10hr.). The **Société National Maritime Corse Méditerranée** (SNCM; ☎08 91 70 18 01; www.sncm.fr) sends ferries from Marseille (€40-58, under 25 €25-45) and Nice (€35-47, under 25 €20-35) to Ajaccio and Bastia. **Corsica Ferries** (☎08 25 09 50 95; www.corsicaferries.com) has similar destinations and prices. **SAREMAR** (☎04 95 73 00 96) and **Moby Lines** (☎04 95 73 00 29) go from Santa Teresa, ITA to Bonifacio. (2-5 per day, €14-15, cars €26-52). Corsica Ferries (€16-32) and Moby Lines (€16-28) cross from Genoa and Livorno, ITA to Bastia. **Train** service in Corsica is slow, limited to destinations north of Ajaccio, and doesn't accept rail passes. Eurocorse Voyages **buses** (☎04 95 21 06 30) serve the whole island. **Hiking** is the best way to explore the mountainous interior. The GR20 is a difficult 12- to 15-day, 180km hiking trail that spans from Calenzana to Conca. The **Parc Naturel Régional de la Corse,** 2 Sargent Casalonga, in Ajaccio, has a guide to *gîtes d'étape* (rest houses) and **maps.** (☎04 95 51 79 00; www.parc-naturel-corse.com.)

AJACCIO (AIACCIU)

Napoleon must have insisted on the best from the very beginning: the little dictator couldn't have picked a better place to call home. Brimming with more energy than most Corsican towns, Ajaccio (pop. 60,000) has excellent museums and, in summer, nightlife to complement its palm-lined boulevards, sunlit buildings, and white-sand beaches. Inside the **Musée Fesch,** 50-52 r. Cardinal Fesch, cavernous rooms hold an impressive collection of 14th- to 19th-century Italian paintings however, it will be closed until the end of 2009. Also within the complex is the **Chapelle Impériale,** the final resting place of most of the Bonaparte family, though Napoleon himself is buried in Paris. (Open July-Aug. M 2-6pm, Tu-Th 10:30am-6pm, F 2-9:30pm, Sa-Su 10:30am-6pm; Sept.-June reduced hours. Museum €5.35, students €3.80. Chapel €1.50/0.75.) Although Ajaccio has many hotels, rates soar and vacancies plummet from June through August. The welcoming **Pension de Famille Tina Morelli ❹,** 1 r. Major Lambroschini, fills up quickly. (☎04 95 21 16 97. Breakfast included. Singles €50, with half-pension €72; doubles €70/124. Cash only.) Your best budget food option is the **morning market** on pl. du Marché. (Open Tu-Su 8am-1pm.) Pizzerias and bakeries can be found on **rue Cardinal Fesch. Boulevard Pascal Rossini,** near the casino, is home to Ajaccio's busiest bars. TCA **bus** #8 (€4.50) shuttles passengers from the bus station at q. l'Herminier to **Aéroport Campo dell'Oro** (**AJA;** ☎04 95 23 56 56), where flights serve Lyon, Marseille, Nice, and Paris. **Trains** (☎04 95 23 11 03) leave pl. de la Gare for Bastia (3-4hr., 4 per day M-Sa, €24) and Corte (2hr., 4 per day, M-Sa €13). Eurocorse Voyages **buses** (☎04 95 21 06 30) go to Bastia (3hr., 2 per day, €19), Bonifacio (3hr., 2 per day, €22), and Corte (1hr., 2 per day, €11). The **tourist office** is at 3 bd. du Roi Jérôme. (☎04 95 51 53 03; www.ajaccio-tourisme.com. Open July-Aug. M-Sa 8am-8:30pm, Su 9am-1pm and 4-7pm; Sept.-June reduced hours.) **Postal Code:** 20000.

BASTIA

Bastia (pop. 40,000), Corsica's second-largest city, is one of the island's most trampled gateways, with connections to the French mainland, remote villages, and vacation spots. Its 14th-century citadel, also called Terra Nova, is impressively intact, with ramparts reaching down the hill toward the vieux port, dwarfing nearby shops and bakeries. The tiny **Eco-Musée,** in the citadel's old powder *magazine* (ammunition storehouse), contains a detailed replica of a traditional Corsican village, complete with miniature houses and authentic vegetation. (Open Apr.-Oct. M-Sa 9am-noon and 2-6pm. €3.50, students €3.) On the other side of the *vieux* port, the 17th-century **Église St-Jean Baptiste,** pl. de l'Hôtel de Ville, is Corsica's largest church. Its gilded walls and ornate altars were constructed with funds raised by local fishermen. While there are no true budget hotels in Bastia, **Hôtel Posta Vecchia ❹,** 8 r. Posta-Vecchia, has a few small rooms that remain reasonably priced during high season. (☎04 95 32 32 38; www.hotel-postavecchia.com. Breakfast in bed €6.50. July-Sept. singles and doubles €50-80; triples €90; quads €100. Jan.-Mar. €40-55/65/75 (weekend prices during this season can be significantly less). April-June and Oct. €40-63/73/83. AmEx/MC/V.) Inexpensive cafes crowd **place St-Nicolas.**

Shuttle **buses** (€8) leave from the *préfecture*, across from the train station, for the **Bastia-Poretta Airport** (**BIA;** ☎04 95 54 54 54). Flights go to Marseille, Nice, and Paris. **Trains** (☎04 95 32 80 61) run to Ajaccio (4hr., 3-5 per day, €24) and Calvi (3hr., 2 per day, €19). Eurocorse **buses** (☎04 95 21 06 31) leave from rte. du Nouveau Port for Ajaccio (3hr., 1-2 per day, €20). The **tourist office** is in pl. St-Nicolas. (☎04 95 54 20 40; www.bastia-tourisme.com. Open daily July-Aug. 8am-8pm; Sept.-June 8:30am-noon and 2-6pm.) **Postal Code:** 20200.

BONIFACIO (BONIFAZIU)

At the southern tip of Corsica, the ramparts of Bonifacio (pop. 2660), atop 70m limestone cliffs, present an imposing visage to miles of turquoise sea. Bonifacio's boat tours reveal gorgeous natural sights. Ferries also run to the pristine sands of **Îles Lavezzi,** a nature reserve with beautiful reefs perfect for scuba diving. Book tours with Les Vedettes. (☎06 86 34 00 49. Grottes-Falaises-Calanques tour 1 per hr. 9am-6:30pm; €17. Îles Lavezzi tour 5 departures per day, last return 7pm; €32 Cash only.) To explore the haute ville, head up the steep, broad steps of the **montée Rastello,** located halfway down the port, from where excellent views of the hazy cliffs to the east can be seen. Affordable rooms are impossible to find in the summer; avoid visiting in August when prices soar. **Hôtel des Étrangers ❹,** av. Sylvère Bohn, offers spotless rooms, most with AC or fan; all with shower. (☎04 95 73 01 09. Breakfast €5. Reception 24hr. Reservations recommended July-Aug. Open early Apr. to early Sept. Mid-July to Sept. singles and doubles €48-70; triples €71-76; quads €78-86. Late May to early July €42-54/59-64/66-74. Apr. to mid-May €35-45/46-52/54-62. MC/V.) Eurocorse Voyages (☎04 95 21 06 30) sends **buses** to Ajaccio (3hr., 2 per day M-Sa, €22). To reach the main **tourist office,** at the corner of av. de Gaulle and r. F. Scamaroni, walk along the port and climb the stairs right before the *gare maritime*. (☎04 95 73 11 88. Open July-Aug. daily 9am-8pm; May-June and Sept. daily 9am-7pm; Oct.-Apr. M-F 9am-noon and 2-6pm.) **Postal Code:** 20169.

GERMANY (DEUTSCHLAND)

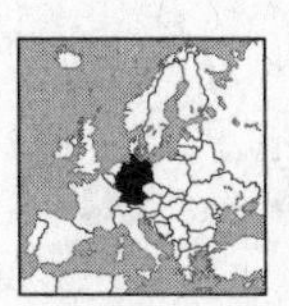

Encounters with history are unavoidable in Germany, as changes in outlook, policy, and culture are manifest in the country's architecture, landscape, and customs. Glass skyscrapers rise from concrete wastelands; towns crop up from fields and forests, interspersed with medieval castles and industrial structures. World-class music rings out from sophisticated city centers, while a grittier youth culture flourishes in quite different neighborhoods. Such divisions echo the entrenched Cold War separation between East and West. Today, nearly 20 years after the fall of the Berlin Wall, Germans have fashioned a new identity for themselves. Visitors will find flowing beer and wondrous sights from the darkest corners of the Black Forest to the shores of the Baltic Sea.

DISCOVER GERMANY: SUGGESTED ITINERARIES

THREE DAYS. Enjoy 2 days in **Berlin** (p. 389): stroll along **Unter den Linden** and the **Ku'damm,** gape at the **Brandenburger Tor** and the **Reichstag,** and explore the **Tiergarten.** Walk along the **East Side Gallery** and visit **Checkpoint Charlie** for a history of the **Berlin Wall.** Overnight it to **Munich** (p. 436) for a crazy stein-themed last day.

ONE WEEK. After scrambling through **Berlin** (3 days), head to **Hamburg** (1 day; p. 410). Take in the cathedral of **Cologne** (1 day; p. 419) before slowing down in the **Lorelei Cliffs** (1 day; p. 430). End your trip Bavarian-style in **Munich** (1 day).

THREE WEEKS. Begin in **Berlin** (3 days). Party in **Hamburg** (2 days), then zip to **Cologne** (1 day) and the former West German capital, **Bonn** (1 day; p. 423). Contrast the Roman ruins at **Trier** (1 day; p. 428) with glitzy **Frankfurt** (1 day; p. 425), then visit Germany's oldest university in **Heidelberg** (2 days; p. 431). Lose your way in the **Black Forest** (2 days; p. 435), before finding it again in **Munich** (2 days). See the beauty of the **Romantic Road** (2 days; p. 443). Get cultured in Goethe's **Weimar** (2 days; p. 445)—then dramatize your learnings in Faust's cellar in **Leipzig** (1 day; p. 451). End your trip in the reconstructed splendor of **Dresden** (1 day; p. 447).

ESSENTIALS

FACTS AND FIGURES

OFFICIAL NAME: Federal Republic of Germany.

CAPITAL: Berlin.

MAJOR CITIES: Cologne, Frankfurt, Hamburg, Munich.

POPULATION: 82,401,000.

LAND AREA: 349,200 sq. km.

TIME ZONE: GMT +1.

RELIGIONS: Protestant (34%), Roman Catholic (34%), Muslim (2%).

PERCENTAGE OF EUROPEAN BEER PRODUCTION: 26.5%.

BEER CONSUMED: 111.6L per capita (a whole lot of beer).

WHEN TO GO

Germany's climate is temperate. The mild months of May, June, and September are the best time to go, as there are fewer tourists and enjoyable weather. In July, Germans head en masse to summer spots. Winter sports gear up from November to April; ski season takes place from mid-December to March.

DOCUMENTS AND FORMALITIES

EMBASSIES. All foreign embassies are in Berlin (p. 393). German embassies abroad include: **Australia,** 119 Empire Circuit, Yarralumla, Canberra, ACT 2600 (☎02 6270 1911; www.germanembassy.org.au); **Canada,** 1 Waverly St., Ottawa, ON, K2P OT8 (☎613-232-1101; www.ottawa.diplo.de); **Ireland,** 31 Trimleston

Ave., Booterstown, Blackrock, Co. Dublin (☎01 269 3011; www.dublin.diplo.de); **New Zealand,** 90-92 Hobson St., Thorndon, Wellington 6001 (☎04 473 6063; www.wellington.diplo.de); **UK,** 23 Belgrave Sq., London, SW1X 8PZ (☎020 7824 1300; www.london.diplo.de); **US,** 4645 Reservoir Rd. NW, Washington, D.C., 20007 (☎202-298-4000; www.germany-info.org).

VISA AND ENTRY INFORMATION. EU citizens do not need a visa. Citizens of Australia, Canada, New Zealand, and the US do not need a visa for stays of up to 90 days, beginning upon entry into any of the countries in the EU's freedom-of-movement zone. For more info, see p. 14. For stays longer than 90 days, all non-EU citizens need visas (around €100), available at German consulates.

TOURIST SERVICES AND MONEY

EMERGENCY	**Ambulance** and **Fire:** ☎112. **Police:** ☎110.

TOURIST OFFICES. The **National Tourist Board** website (www.germany-tourism.de) links to regional info and provides dates of national and local festivals. Every city in Germany has a tourist office, usually near the *Hauptbahnhof* (main train station) or *Marktplatz* (central square). All are marked by a sign with a thick lowercase "i," and many book rooms for a small fee.

MONEY. The **euro (€)** has replaced the **Deutschmark (DM)** as the unit of currency in Germany. For more info, see p. 17. As a general rule, it's cheaper to exchange money in Germany than at home. Costs for those who stay in hostels and prepare their own food may range anywhere from €25-50 per person per day. **Tipping** is not practiced as liberally in Germany as elsewhere—most natives just round up €1. Tips are handed directly to the server with payment of the bill—if you don't want any change, say *"Das stimmt so"* (das SHTIMMT zo; "so it stands"). Germans rarely bargain except at flea markets. Germany has a 19% **value added tax (VAT),** a sales tax applied to most goods and services. The prices given in *Let's Go* include VAT. In the airport, non-EU citizens can claim a refund on the tax paid for goods purchased at participating stores. In order to qualify for a refund in a store, you must spend at least €25; make sure to ask for a refund form when you pay. For more info on VAT refunds, see p. 21.

BUSINESS HOURS. Offices and stores are open from 9am-6pm, Monday through Friday, often closing for an hour lunch break. Stores may be open on Saturday in cities or shopping centers. Banks are also open from approximately 9am-6pm and close briefly in the late afternoon, but they may stay open late on Thursday nights. Many museums are closed on Monday.

TRANSPORTATION

BY PLANE. Most international flights land at **Frankfurt Airport** (**FRA;** ☎069 6900; www.airportcity-frankfurt.com); **Berlin (BML), Munich (MUC),** and **Hamburg (HAM)** also have international airports. **Lufthansa,** the national airline, is not always the best-priced option. For cheaper domestic travel by plane than by train; check out **Air Berlin** (www.airberlin.com), among other options.

BY TRAIN. The **Deutsche Bahn** (**DB;** www.bahn.de) network is Europe's best—and one of its most expensive. Luckily, all trains have clean and comfy second-class compartments, and there are a wide variety of train lines to choose from. **RegionalBahn (RB)** trains include rail networks between neighboring cities and connects to **RegionalExpress (RE)** lines. **InterRegioExpress (IRE)** trains, covering larger networks between cities, are speedy and comfortable. **S-Bahn** trains run locally within large cities and high density areas. Some S-Bahn stops also service speedy **StadtExpress (SE)** trains, which directly connects city centers. **EuroCity (EC)** and **InterCity (IC)** trains zoom between major cities every 1-2hr. **InterCityExpress (ICE)** trains approach the luxury and kinetics of airplanes, barreling along the tracks at speeds up to 300kph, and service international destinations including Austria, Belgium, the Netherlands, and Switzerland. For overnight travel, choose between the first-class **DB Autozug** or cheaper **DB Nachtzug** lines.

Eurail is valid in Germany. The **German Rail Pass** allows unlimited travel for four to 10 days within a one-month period, including Basel, SWI and Salzburg, AUT. Non-EU citizens can purchase German Rail Passes at select major train stations in Germany (5- or 10-day passes only) or through travel agents (2nd class 4-day pass €169, 10-day €289; under 26 €139/199). A Schönes-Wochenende-Ticket (€33) gives up to five people unlimited travel on any of the slower trains (RE or RB) from 12:01am Saturday or Sunday until 3am the next day; single travelers often find larger groups who will share their ticket.

BY BUS. Bus service runs from the local **ZOB** *(Zentralomnibusbahnhof)*, usually close to the main train station. Buses are more expensive than trains. Rail passes are not valid on buses, except for a few run by Deutsche Bahn.

BY CAR AND BY BIKE. Given generally excellent road conditions, Germans drive fast. The rumors are true: the *Autobahn* does not have a speed limit, only a recommendation of 130kph (80 mph). Watch for signs indicating the right-of-way (usually a yellow triangle). Signs with an "A" denote the *Autobahn;* signs bearing a "B" accompany secondary highways, which typically have a 100kph (60mph) speed limit. In cities and towns, speed limits hover around 30-60kph (20-35 mph). For a small fee, **Mitfahrzentralen,** and their women-only counterparts, **Frauenmitfahrzentralen,** agencies pair up drivers and riders, who then negotiate trip payment between themselves. Seat belts are mandatory, and police strictly enforce driving laws. Germany has designated lanes for **bicycles**. .

BY THUMB. Hitchhiking (or even standing) on the Autobahn is illegal. *Let's Go* does not recommend hitchhiking.

KEEPING IN TOUCH

PHONE CODES	**Country code:** 49. **International dialing prefix:** 00. For more info on how to place international calls, see **Inside Back Cover.**

EMAIL AND THE INTERNET. Almost all German cities, as well as a surprising number of smaller towns, have at least one Internet cafe with web access for about €2-10 per hour. Wi-Fi is often available in bigger cities; in Berlin's new Sony Center (p. 399), the Wi-Fi is completely, blissfully free. Some German universities have Internet in their libraries, intended for student use.

TELEPHONE. Most public phones will accept only a phone card (Telefonkarte), available at post offices, kiosks, and some Deutsche Bahn counters. **Mobile phones** are an increasingly popular and economical alternative (p. 32). Phone numbers have no standard length. Direct-dial access numbers for calling out of Germany include: **AT&T USADirect** (☎0800 225 5288); **Canada Direct** (☎0800 888 0014); **MCI WorldPhone** (☎0800 888 8000); **Telecom New Zealand** (☎0800 080 0064);

and **Telstra Australia** (☎0800 080 0061); most of these services require a calling card or credit card. For more info, see p. 31.

MAIL. Airmail (*Luftpost* or *par avion*) usually takes three to six days to Ireland and the UK, and four to 10 days to Australia and North America. *Let's Go* lists addresses for mail to be held **Poste Restante** *(Postlagernde Briefe)* in the **Practical Information** sections of big cities. Mail will go to the main post office unless you specify a subsidiary by street address. Address mail to be held as follows: First name Last name, *Postlagernde Briefe*, Postal code, City, GERMANY.

ACCOMMODATIONS AND CAMPING

GERMANY	❶	❷	❸	❹	❺
ACCOMMODATIONS	under €15	€15-25	€26-33	€34-50	over €50

Germany currently has more than 600 **youth hostels**—more than any other nation. Official hostels in Germany are overseen by **DJH** *(Deutsches Jugendherbergswerk)*, Bismarckstr. 8, D 32756 Detmold, Germany (☎05231 740 10; www.jugendherberge.de). A growing number of **Jugendgästehäuser** (youth guesthouses) have more facilities than hostels and attract slightly older guests. DJH publishes *Jugendherbergen in Deutschland*, a guide to federated German hostels. Most charge €15-25 for dorms. The cheapest **hotel-style** accommodations are places with *Pension*, *Gasthof*, or *Gästehaus* in the name. Hotel rooms start at €20 for singles and €30 for doubles; in large cities, expect to pay nearly twice as much. *Frühstück* (breakfast) is almost always available, if not included. The best bet for a cheap bed is often a **Privatzimmer** (room in a family home), where a basic knowledge of German is very helpful. Prices can be as low as €15 per person. Reservations are made through the local tourist office or through a *Zimmervermittlung* (private booking office), sometimes for a small fee. Over 2500 **campsites** dot the German landscape. Bathrooms, a restaurant or store, and showers generally accompany a campground's well-maintained facilities. Camping costs €3-12 per tent site and €4-6 per extra person, with additional charges for tent and vehicle rental. Blue signs with a black tent on a white background indicate official sites.

FOOD AND DRINK

GERMANY	❶	❷	❸	❹	❺
FOOD AND DRINK	under €4	€4-8	€9-12	€13-20	over €20

A typical breakfast *(Frühstück)* consists of coffee or tea with **rolls** *(Brötchen)*, **cold sausage** *(Wurst)*, and **cheese** *(Käse)*. Germans' main meal, lunch *(Mittagessen)*, includes soup, broiled sausage or roasted meat, potatoes or dumplings, and a salad or vegetable. Dinner (*Abendessen* or *Abendbrot*) is a reprise of breakfast, with beer in place of coffee and a wider selection of meats and cheeses. Older Germans indulge in a daily ritual of coffee and cake *(Kaffee und Kuchen)* at 3 or 4pm. To eat cheaply, stick to a restaurant's daily menu *(Tagesmenü)*, buy food in supermarkets, or head to a **university cafeteria** *(Mensa)*. Fast-food stands *(Imbiß)* also offer cheap, often foreign eats. The average German beer is maltier and more "bread-like" than Czech or American beers; a common nickname for German brew is liquid bread *(flüßiges Brot)*.

BEYOND TOURISM

Germany's volunteering opportunities often involve environmental preservation—working on farms or in forests and educating people—though civil service and community building prospects still exist. For more info on opportunities across Europe, see the **Beyond Tourism** chapter p. 60

World-Wide Opportunities on Organic Farms (WWOOF), Postfach 210259, 01263 Dresden, Germany (www.wwoof.de). €18 membership in WWOOF gives you room and board at a variety of organic farms in Germany in exchange for chores.

Open Houses Network, Goethepl. 9B, D-99423 Weimar (☎03 643 502 390; www.openhouses.de). A group dedicated to restoring and sharing public space (mostly in Eastern Germany), providing lodging in return for work.

BERLIN ☎030

Dizzying and electric, this city of 3.4 million has such an increasingly diverse population that it can be difficult to keep track of which *Bezirk* (neighborhood) is currently the trendiest. Traces of the past century's Nazi and Communist regimes remain etched in residents' minds, and a psychological division between East and West Germany—the problem dubbed *Mauer im Kopf* ("wall in the head")—still exists nearly two decades after the Berlin Wall's destruction. Restless and contradictory, Germany's capital shows no signs of slowing down its self-motivated reinvention, and the Berlin of next year may be radically different from the Berlin of today.

INTERCITY TRANSPORTATION

Flights: The city is now transitioning from 3 airports to 1 (Flughafen Schönefeld will become the Berlin-Brandenburg International Airport, BBI), but at least until 2011, **Flughafen Tegel (TXL)** will remain West Berlin's main international airport. For info on all 3 of Berlin's airports, call ☎0180 500 0186 (www.berlin-airport.de). Take express bus #X9 from Bahnhof Zoo, bus #109 from Jakob-Kaiser-Pl. on U7, bus #128 from Kurt-Schumacher-Pl. on U6, or bus TXL from Potsdamer Pl. or Bahnhof Zoo. **Flughafen Schönefeld (BER),** southeast of Berlin, is used for intercontinental flights and travel to developing countries. Take S9 or 45 to Flughafen Berlin Schönefeld, or ride the Schönefeld Express train, which runs 2 per hr. through most major S-Bahn stations, including Alexanderpl., Bahnhof Zoo, Friedrichstr., Hauptbahnhof, and Ostbahnhof. **Flughafen Tempelhof (THF)** was slated to close October 31, 2008.

Trains: Berlin's massive new **Hauptbahnhof,** which opened in time for the 2006 World Cup, is the city's major transit hub, with many international and domestic trains continuing to **Ostbahnhof** in the East. Hauptbahnhof currently connects to the S-Bahn and a U55 line. **Bahnhof Zoologischer Garten** (a.k.a. Bahnhof Zoo), formerly the West's main station, now connects only to regional destinations. Many trains also connect to **Schönefeld Airport.** A number of U- and S-Bahn lines stop at **Oranienburg, Potsdam,** and **Spandau.** Trains in the Brandenburg regional transit system tend to stop at all major stations, as well as Alexanderpl. and Friedrichstr.

Buses: ZOB (☎030 301 03 80; www.zob-reisebuero.de), the "central" bus station, is actually at the western edge of town, by the Funkturm near Kaiserdamm. U2 to Kaiserdamm or S41/42 to Messe Nord/ICC. Open M-F 6am-9pm, Sa-Su 6am-3pm. **Gullivers,** at ZOB (☎030 890 660; www.gullivers.de), and **Berlin Linien Bus** (☎030 851 9331;

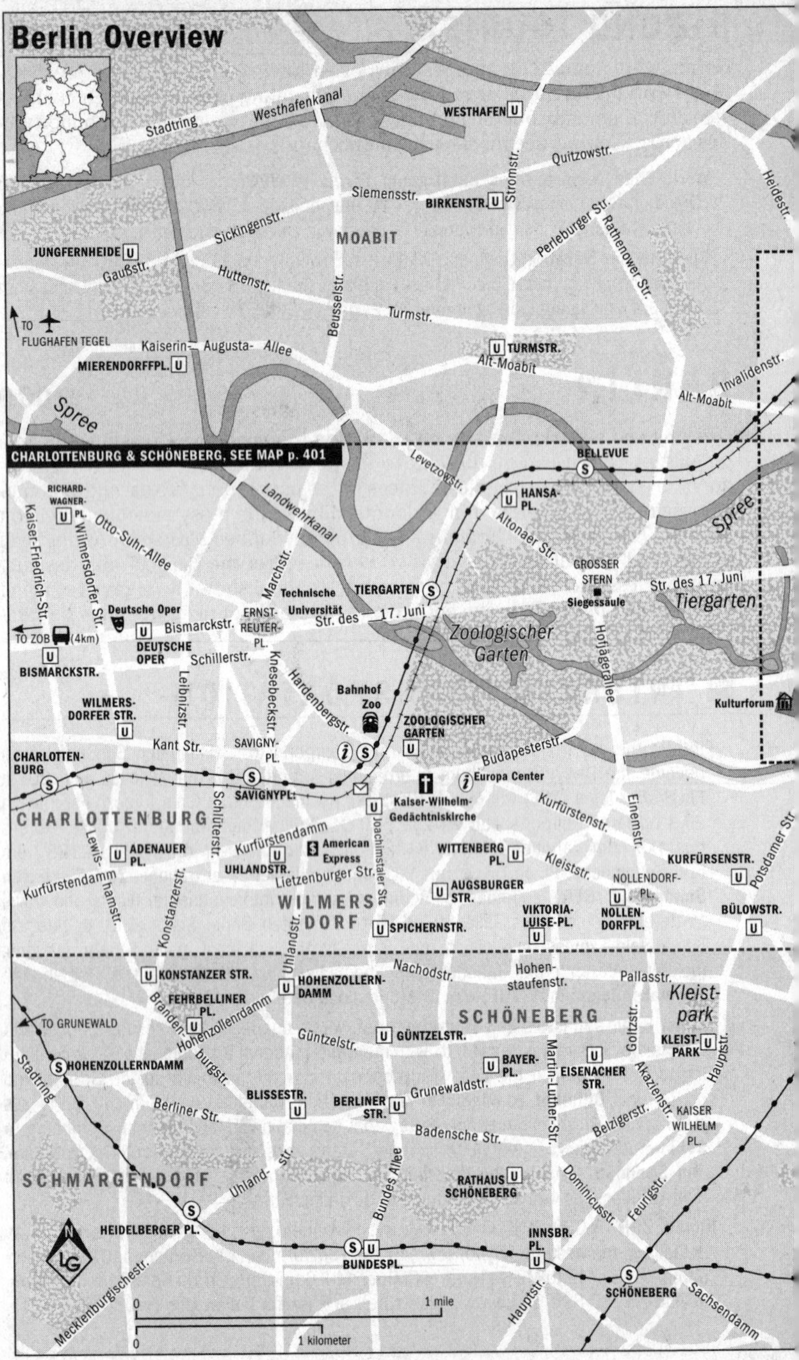

Berlin Overview

Stadtring
Westhafenkanal
WESTHAFEN U
Quitzowstr.
Heidestr.
Siemensstr.
BIRKENSTR. U
Stromstr.
Perleburger Str.
Rathenower Str.
Sickingenstr.
MOABIT
JUNGFERNHEIDE U
Gaußstr.
Huttenstr.
Beusselstr.
Turmstr.
TO FLUGHAFEN TEGEL
Kaiserin-Augusta-Allee
U TURMSTR.
MIERENDORFFPL. U
Alt-Moabit
Invalidenstr.
Spree

CHARLOTTENBURG & SCHÖNEBERG, SEE MAP p. 401

Levetzowstr.
BELLEVUE S
U HANSA-PL.
RICHARD-WAGNER-PL. U
Kaiser-Friedrich-Str.
Wilmersdorfer Str.
Otto-Suhr-Allee
Landwehrkanal
Altonaer Str.
Spree
Marchstr.
GROSSER STERN
Siegessäule
Str. des 17. Juni
Tiergarten
Technische Universität
TIERGARTEN S
ERNST-REUTER-PL.
Deutsche Oper
Bismarckstr.
TO ZOB (4km)
U DEUTSCHE OPER
Schillerstr.
U BISMARCKSTR.
Zoologischer Garten
Hofjägerallee
Leibnizstr.
Knesebeckstr.
Hardenbergstr.
Bahnhof Zoo
WILMERS-DORFER STR. U
ZOOLOGISCHER GARTEN U
Kulturforum
Kant Str.
SAVIGNY-PL.
CHARLOTTEN-BURG S
Budapesterstr.
S SAVIGNYPL.
Europa Center
Kaiser-Wilhelm-Gedächtniskirche
CHARLOTTENBURG
Schlüterstr.
Joachimstaler Str.
Kurfürstenstr.
Einemstr.
Potsdamer Str.
Lewis-hamstr.
U ADENAUER PL.
Kurfürstendamm
U UHLANDSTR.
American Express
WITTENBERG PL. U
Kleiststr.
KURFÜRSENSTR. U
Lietzenburger Str.
U AUGSBURGER STR.
NOLLENDORF-PL.
Kurfürstendamm
Konstanzerstr.
WILMERSDORF
Uhlandstr.
U SPICHERNSTR.
VIKTORIA-LUISE-PL. U
U NOLLEN-DORFPL.
BÜLOWSTR. U
Nachodstr.
Hohen-staufenstr.
Pallasstr.
U KONSTANZER STR.
U HOHENZOLLERN-DAMM
Kleistpark
FEHRBELLINER PL. U
Brandenburgstr.
Hohenzollerndamm
TO GRUNEWALD
SCHÖNEBERG
Goltzstr.
Güntzelstr.
U GÜNTZELSTR.
KLEIST-PARK U
Hauptstr.
Stadtring
S HOHENZOLLERNDAMM
Martin-Luther-Str.
U BAYER-PL.
U EISENACHER STR.
Akazienstr.
Grunewaldstr.
BLISSESTR. U
BERLINER STR. U
Berliner Str.
Belzigerstr.
KAISER WILHELM PL.
Badensche Str.
Bundes Allee
SCHMARGENDORF
Uhland-str.
RATHAUS SCHÖNEBERG U
Dominicusstr.
Feurigstr.
S HEIDELBERGER PL.
S U BUNDESPL.
INNSBR. PL. U
S SCHÖNEBERG
Sachsendamm
Mecklenburgischestr.
Hauptstr.
0 — 1 mile
0 — 1 kilometer

GERMANY

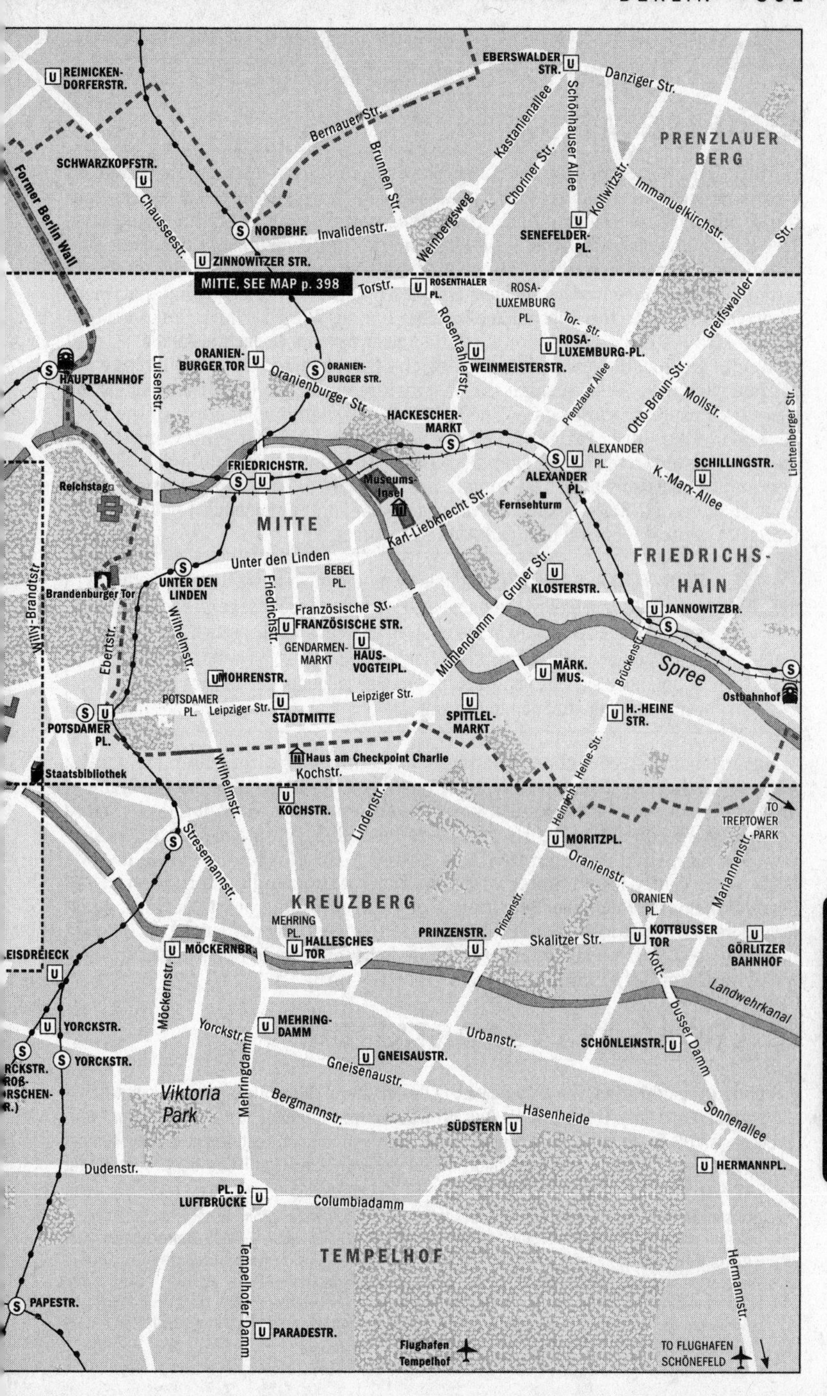

REINICKEN-DORFERSTR.
EBERSWALDER STR.
Danziger Str.
PRENZLAUER BERG
Bernauer Str.
Kastanienallee
Schönhauser Allee
Brunnen Str.
Choriner Str.
Kollwitzstr.
Immanuelkirchstr.
SCHWARZKOPFSTR.
Former Berlin Wall
Chausseestr.
Weinbergsweg
NORDBHF.
Invalidenstr.
SENEFELDER-PL.
ZINNOWITZER STR.
MITTE, SEE MAP p. 398
Torstr.
ROSENTHALER PL.
ROSA-LUXEMBURG PL.
Tor- str.
Greifswalder Str.
Rosenthalerstr.
ROSA-LUXEMBURG-PL.
ORANIEN-BURGER TOR
ORANIEN-BURGER STR.
WEINMEISTERSTR.
HAUPTBAHNHOF
Luisenstr.
Oranienburger Str.
Prenzlauer Allee
Otto-Braun-Str.
Mollstr.
Lichtenberger Str.
HACKESCHER-MARKT
ALEXANDER PL.
SCHILLINGSTR.
FRIEDRICHSTR.
Museums-insel
ALEXANDER PL.
K.-Marx-Allee
Reichstag
Fernsehturm
MITTE
Karl-Liebknecht Str.
FRIEDRICHS-HAIN
Unter den Linden
Gruner Str.
BEBEL PL.
Brandenburger Tor
UNTER DEN LINDEN
KLOSTERSTR.
Willy-Brandtstr.
Friedrichstr.
Französische Str.
JANNOWITZBR.
Wilhelmstr.
FRANZÖSISCHE STR.
Mühlendamm
GENDARMEN-MARKT
HAUS-VOGTEIPL.
Ebertstr.
MÄRK. MUS.
Brückenstr.
Spree
MOHRENSTR.
Leipziger Str.
Ostbahnhof
POTSDAMER PL.
Leipziger Str.
STADTMITTE
SPITTEL-MARKT
H.-HEINE STR.
POTSDAMER PL.
Haus am Checkpoint Charlie
Heine-Str.
Staatsbibliothek
Kochstr.
KOCHSTR.
Wilhelmstr.
Lindenstr.
Heinrich
TO TREPTOWER PARK
Stresemannstr.
MORITZPL.
Oranienstr.
Mariannenstr.
KREUZBERG
ORANIEN PL.
MEHRING PL.
PRINZENSTR.
Prinzenstr.
KOTTBUSSER TOR
Skalitzer Str.
HALLESCHES TOR
GÖRLITZER BAHNHOF
MÖCKERNBR.
EISDREIECK
Möckernstr.
Kott-busser Damm
Landwehrkanal
YORCKSTR.
MEHRING-DAMM
Yorckstr.
Urbanstr.
SCHÖNLEINSTR.
YORCKSTR.
GNEISAUSTR.
Gneisenaustr.
RCKSTR. ROß-RSCHEN-R.)
Viktoria Park
Mehringdamm
Bergmannstr.
Hasenheide
Sonnenallee
SÜDSTERN
Dudenstr.
HERMANNPL.
PL. D. LUFTBRÜCKE
Columbiadamm
TEMPELHOF
Hermannstr.
Tempelhofer Damm
PAPESTR.
PARADESTR.
Flughafen Tempelhof
TO FLUGHAFEN SCHÖNEFELD

www.berlinlinienbus.de) often have good deals on bus fares. Open in summer daily 8am-9pm; in winter reduced hours. Check website for more information.

ORIENTATION

Berlin's landmarks include the **Spree River,** which flows through the city from west to east, and the narrower **Landwehrkanal** that spills into the Spree from the south. The vast central park, **Tiergarten,** stretches between the waterways. Two radio towers loom above the city: the pointed **Funkturm,** in the west, and the globed **Fernsehturm,** rising above **Alexanderplatz** in the east. In the west, the major thoroughfare **Kurfürstendamm** (a.k.a. Ku'damm) is lined with department stores and leads to the **Bahnhof Zoologischer Garten,** West Berlin's transportation hub. Nearby is the elegant wreck of the **Kaiser-Wilhelm Gedächtniskirche,** as well as one of Berlin's few real skyscrapers, the **EuropaCenter.** Tree-lined **Straße des 17. Juni** runs east-west through the Tiergarten, ending at the **Brandenburger Tor,** the park's eastern border gate. The **Reichstag** (Parliament) is north of the gate; several blocks south, **Potsdamer Platz** bustles beneath the glittering Sony Center and the headquarters of the Deutsche Bahn. Heading east, Straße des 17. Juni becomes **Unter den Linden** and travels past most of Berlin's imperial architecture. In the east, **Karl-Marx-Allee, Prenzlauer Allee,** and **Schönhauser Allee** fan out from the central meeting point of Alexanderplatz.

FOR YOUR SAFETY. Berlin is by far the most tolerant city in Germany, with thriving minority communities. However, minorities, gays, and lesbians should exercise caution in the outlying eastern suburbs, especially at night. If you see people wearing dark combat boots (especially with white laces)—a potential sign of neo-Nazism—exercise caution but do not panic, and avoid drawing attention to yourself.

Berlin's short streets change names often; addresses often climb higher and higher and then wrap around to the other side of the street, placing the highest- and lowest-numbered buildings across from one another. Well-indexed **maps** are invaluable. Berlin is rightly considered a collection of towns, not a homogeneous city; each neighborhood has a strong sense of its individual history. **Mitte** is currently its commercial heart. The neighboring eastern districts of **Friedrichshain** and **Prenzlauer Berg** are the city's liveliest and most youthful, while **Kreuzberg** is the outpost of counterculture in the west. **Charlottenburg** in the west has a more staid, upscale character, while **Schöneberg** is in between Kreuzberg and Charlottenburg, both in geography and in spirit.

LOCAL TRANSPORTATION

Public Transportation: The **BVG** (www.bvg.de) is one of the world's most efficient transportation systems. The extensive **bus, Straßenbahn** (streetcar or tram), **U-Bahn** (subway), and **S-Bahn** (surface rail) networks will get you to your destination quickly. Almost all the reconstruction and expansion of the pre-war transit grid has been completed; service disruptions are rare, causing at most an extra 20min. wait.

Orientation and Basic Fares: Berlin is divided into 3 transit zones. **Zone A** encompasses central Berlin, including Flughafen Tempelhof. The rest of Berlin is in **Zone B,** while **Zone C** consists of the outlying areas, including Potsdam and Oranienburg. An AB ticket is the best deal, as you can buy extension tickets for the outlying areas. An **Einzelfahrausweis** (1-way ticket) is good for 2hr. after validation. Zones A and B €2.10; B and C €2.50; A, B, and C €2.80. Under 6 free with an adult; children under 14 reduced fare. Within the validation period, the ticket may be used on any

S-Bahn, U-Bahn, bus, or tram. A **Tageskarte** (1-day unlimited ticket; A and B €6.10; A, B, and C €6.50) is the best deal if you're planning to travel a lot in a single day.

Night Transport: U- and S-Bahn lines generally don't run M-F 1-4am. On F-Sa nights, all trains except for the U4, S45, and S85 continue but less frequently. An extensive system of **night buses** runs 2-3 per hr. and tends to follow major transit lines; pick up the free *Nachtliniennetz* map at a Fahrscheine und Mehr office. The letter N precedes night bus numbers. Trams run at night.

Taxis: (☎080 02 63 00 00). Call at least 15min. ahead. Women can request female drivers. Trips within the city cost up to €21. Request a *Kurzstrecke* to travel up to 2km in any direction for a flat €3 fee.

Bike Rental: Fahrradstation, Dorotheenstr. 30 (☎20 45 45 00; www.fahrradstation.de), near the Friedrichstr. S-Bahn station. Turn in at the parking lot next to STA. €15 per day for a bike. Open M-F 9am-8pm, Sa 10am-6pm, Su 10am-4pm.

PRACTICAL INFORMATION

Tourist Offices: Euraide (www.euraide.com), in the Hauptbahnhof. Sells phone cards, rail- and walking-tour tickets. Arrive early. Open June-Oct. daily 8am-noon and 1-6pm; Nov.-May M-F 8am-noon and 1-4:45pm.

City Tours: Terry Brewer's Best of Berlin (☎177 388 1537, www.brewersberlintours.com) is legendary. 8hr. tours €12. Shorter **free tours** leave daily at 10:30am from the Bandy Brooks shop on Friedrichstr. (S5, 7, 9, or 75 or U6 to Friedrichstr.)

Embassies and Consulates: Australia, Mitte, Wallstr. 76-79 (☎030 880 0880; www.australian-embassy.de). U2: "Märkisches Museum." Open M-Th 8:30am-5pm, F 8:30am- 4:15pm. **Canada,** Mitte, Leipziger Pl. 17 (☎030 20 31 20; www.canada.de). S1, 2 or U2: "Potsdamer Pl." Open M-F 8:30am-12:30pm and 1:30-5pm. **Ireland,** Mitte, Friedrichstr. 200 (☎030 22 07 20; www.embassyofireland.de). U2 or 6: "Stadtmitte." Open M-F 9:30am-12:30pm and 2:30-4:45pm. **NZ,** Mitte, Friedrichstr. 60 (☎030 20 62 10; www.nzembassy.com). U2 or 6: "Stadtmitte." Open M-Th 9am-1pm and 2-5:30pm, F 9am-1pm and 2-4:30pm. Summer hours M-Th 8:30am-1pm and 2-5:30pm, F 8:30am-1pm. **UK,** Mitte, Wilhelmstr. 70-71 (☎030 20 45 70; www.britischebotschaft.de). S1-3, 5, 7, 9, 25, or 75, or U6: Friedrichstr. Open M-F 9am-5:30pm. **US,** Clayallee 170 (☎030 832 9233; fax 83 05 12 15). U1: "Oskar-Helene-Heim." Telephone advice available M-F 2-4pm; after hours, call ☎830 50 for emergencies. Open M-F 8:30am-noon. The visiting address for the US Embassy is Pariser Pl. 2 (☎030 238 5174).

Currency Exchange: The best rates are usually found in large squares, at most major train stations, and at exchange offices with **Wechselstube** signs outside.

Luggage Storage: In **DB Gepack Center,** in the Hauptbahnhof, 1st floor, East Side. €4 per day. In **Bahnhof Zoo.** Lockers €3-5 per day. Max 72hr. Open daily 6am-10:30pm. 24hr. lockers also at **Ostbahnhof, Alexanderplatz** and bus station.

Crisis Lines: American Hotline (☎0177 814 1510). **Berliner Behindertenverband,** Jägerstr. 63D (☎030 204 3847), has advice for the disabled. **Frauenkrisentelefon** (☎030 615 42 43; www.frauenkrisentelefon.de) is a women's crisis line. Open M and Th 10am-noon, Tu-W and F 7-9pm, and Sa-Su 5-7pm.

Medical Services: The American and British embassies list English-speaking doctors. **Emergency doctor:** ☎31 00 31. **Emergency dentist:** ☎89 00 43 33. Both 24hr.

Internet: Cheap Internet cafes cluster on **Oranienstr.** in Kreuzberg and around U-Bahn stop **Ebeswalder Str.** in Prenzlauer Berg.

Post Offices: Joachimstaler Str. 7 (☎030 88 70 86 11), down Joachimstaler Str. from Bahnhof Zoo and near the Kantstr. intersection. Open M-Sa 9am-8pm. Branches: **Tegel Airport,** open M-F 8am-6pm, Sa 8am-noon; **Ostbahnhof,** open M-F 8am-8pm, Sa-Su 10am-6pm. **Postal Code:** 10001-14199.

ACCOMMODATIONS

Longer stays are most conveniently arranged through one of Berlin's many **Mitwohnzentrale,** which can set up house-sitting gigs or sublets (from €250 per month). **Home Company Mitwohnzentrale,** Joachimstaler Str. 17, has a useful placement website. (☎0421 792 6293; www.homecompany.de. U9 or 15 to Ku'damm. Open M-Th 9am-6pm, F 9am-5pm, Sa 11am-2pm. MC/V.)

MITTE

BaxPax Downtown Hostel/Hotel, Ziegelstr. 28 (☎030 28 77 48 80; www.baxpax.de). S1, S2, or S25 to "Oranienburger Str." or U6 to "Oranienbuger Tor." Bright dorms, outdoor lounge, and a rooftop bar. Internet €3 per hr. Breakfast €4.50. Laundry facilities. Quiet hours 10pm-7am. Dorms €17; singles €45; doubles €60-65; triples €70. MC/V. ❷

CityStay Hostel, Rosenstr. 16 (☎030 23 62 40 31; www.citystay.de). S5, S7, S9, or S75 to "Hackescher Markt" or U2, U5, or U8 to "Alexanderpl." Playful with ample amenities only steps from sights. Kitchen facilities. Free lockers. Women only dorms on request. Breakfast €4. Sheets €2.50. Laundry €5. Internet €3 per hr.; Wi-Fi free. Dorms €17-21; singles €40, with bath €55; doubles €50, with bath €64; quads €84. Cash only. ❷

Circus, Rosa-Luxemburg-Str. 39-41 (☎030 28 39 14 33; www.circus-berlin.de). U2 to "Rosa-Luxemburg-Pl." Close to Alexanderpl. Laundry, Internet (€0.05 per min.), a large bar with theme-nights. Wheelchair-accessible. Breakfast €2-5 until 1pm. 24hr. reception and bar. 4- to 8-bed dorms €19-23; singles €40, with bath €50; doubles €56, with bath €70; triples €75. Cheaper in winter. MC/V. ❷

CHARLOTTENBURG

Berolina Backpacker, Stuttgarter Pl. 17 (☎030 32 70 90 72; www.berolinabackpacker.de). S3, S5, S7, S9, or S75 to "Charlottenburg." Quiet hostel with bunk-free dorms. Communal (€1 per day) and private (€9.50) kitchens available. Internet €0.50 per 15 min. Breakfast €7. Reception closed 5am-7am. Check-out 11am. Singles €29-35; doubles €37-46; triples €37.50-49.50; quads €42-58; quints €38-54. AmEx/MC/V. ❶

Jugendgästehaus am Zoo, Hardenbergstr. 9a (☎030 312 94 10; www.jgh-zoo.de). Bus #245 to "Steinpl.," or walk from Bahnhof Zoo down Hardenbergstr. Clean hostel contains 85 beds in simple rooms. Reception 24hr. Check-out 10am. Lockout 10am-2pm. 4- to 8-bed dorms €18, over 27 €21; singles €26/29; doubles €46/52. Cash only. ❶

SCHÖNEBERG AND WILMERSDORF

Jugendhotel Berlincity, Crellestr. 22 (☎030 78 70 21 30; www.jugendhotel-berlin.de). U7 to "Kleistpark" or "Yorckstr." High ceilings and spacious accommodations. Breakfast and sheets included. Wi-Fi €1 per 20min., €5 per 24hr. Reception desk closed 7am-3am. Singles €39.50, with bath €58; doubles €64/84; triples €87/102; quads €112/126; quints €124/150, 6-person room €146/168. MC/V; cash preferred. ❸

Meininger City Hostel, Meininger Str. 10, Schöneberg (☎030 66 63 61 00 or 0800 634 64 64; www.meininger-hostels.de). U4, bus #146 or N46 to "Rathaus Schöneberg." Free linens, towels, and Wi-Fi. Breakfast €3.50. Free lockers available. Reception 24hr. Door locked at midnight, ring to enter. Book in advance. 5-6 bed dorms €19-26; 4-6 bed rooms €28-36; singles €52-69, doubles €35-49, triples €34-39. MC/V. ❶

KREUZBERG

Bax Pax, Skalitzer Str. 104 (☎030 69 51 83 22; www.baxpax-kreuzberg.de). U1 or U15 to "Görlitzer Bahnhof," across the street. Kitchen and an outdoor terrace. Internet €2 per

30min. Sheets €2.50. Breakfast €4.50. Reception 24hr. Big dorms €15; 7- to 8-bed dorms €17; 5-6 bed rooms €18; singles €31; doubles €48, with bath €60; triples €63; quads €76. Bike rental 1 day €12. AmEx/MC/V. ❷

Hostel X Berger, Schlesische Str. 22 (☎030 69 53 18 63; www.hostelxberger.com). U1 or U15 to "Schlesisches Tor," or night bus #N65 to "Taborstr." Social with roomy dorms. Some female-onl. Free Internet. Reception 24hr. Sheets €2, towel €1. Dorms €11-15; singles €28-32; doubles €36-40; triples €48-51; quads €60-64. Cash only. ❶

FRIEDRICHSHAIN

Sunflower Hostel, Helsingforser Str. 17 (☎030 44 04 42 50; www.sunflower-hostel.de). Spotless dorms, popular common areas. Breakfast €3 (8am-noon). Free Wi-Fi. Sheets and locks €3 deposit each. Laundry €4.50. Reception 24hr. Check out 11am. 7- to 8-bed €10-14.50; 5- to 6-bed dorms €12.50-16.50; singles €30-36.50; doubles €38-48; triples €51-61.50; quads €60-74. 7th night free. ISIC discount 5%. MC/V. ❶

Globetrotter Hostel Odyssee, Grünberger Str. 23 (☎030 29 00 00 81; www.globetrotterhostel.de). Convenient base for nightlife. Bar open until dawn. Internet access €0.50 per 10min. Breakfast €3. Sheets included with deposit. Reception 24hr. Check-in 4pm, check-out noon. Reserve ahead. 8-bed dorms €10-13; 6-bed dorms €12-15, doubles €39-45, with shower €46-52; triples €48-57; quads €56-68. MC/V. ❷

PRENZLAUER BERG

East Seven Hostel, Schwedter Str. 7 (☎030 93 62 22 40; www.eastseven.de). U2 to Senefelderpl. A new, relaxed hostel on a quiet street. Kitchen available. Free Wi-Fi. Internet €0.50 per 20min. Linen €3. Towels €1. Laundry €4. 6- to 8-bed dorms €13-17; singles €30 (Nov. 1-Feb 28), €37 (Mar. 1-Oct. 31); doubles €42/50; triples €52.50/63; quads €64/76. Reception 7am-midnight. Cash only. ❷

Lette'm Sleep Hostel, Lettestr. 7 (☎030 44 73 36 23; www.backpackers.de). U2 to "Eberswalder Str." 48-bed hostel with big social kitchen. Free Internet. Wheelchair-accessible. Reception 24 hours. Sheets €2. Apr.-Oct. 4- to 7-bed dorms €17-20. Nov.-Mar. €11-19. Doubles €40-49. Nov.-Mar. triples €60/63. AmEx/MC/V. ❷

FOOD

Perhaps the dearest culinary tradition is breakfast; Germans love to wake up late over a *Milchkaffee* (bowl of coffee with foamed milk) and a sprawling brunch buffet. Vendors of currywurst or bratwurst are perfect for a quick bite; or, find a 24hr. Turkish *Imbiß* (snack food stand) for late night cravings.

MITTE

The Sixties, Oranienburgerstr. 11 (☎030 28 59 90 41; www.sixtiesdiner.de). S3, S5, S7, S9, or S75 to "Hackescher Markt." Enjoy as you listen to the jukebox or gaze upon the Route 66 mural on the ceiling or the walls covered with iconic faces of the decade. Happy hour M-F noon-5pm. M-Th and Su 5pm-9pm. Open daily 10am-2am. ❷

am to pm, Am Zwirngraben 2 (☎ 030 24 08 53 01 or www.amtopm.de), directly next to the S-Bahn train station Hackescher Markt. Open 24 hours, am to pm has everything from croissants to cocktails (€4.50 5-9pm). Sit outside under their red tents and enjoy a quiet meal (€8.50-12.50), then head to the dance floor. ❸

Beth Café, Tucholskystr. 40 (☎030 281 31 35), just off Auguststr. S-Bahn to "Oranienburger Str." A perennial favorite among the local Jewish community. Dishes €2.50-8. Open M-Th and Sa-Su 11am-6pm. AmEx/MC. ❷

THE BEST WURST

So you're finally in Germany and itching to sink your teeth into your first authentic German Wurst. With over 1500 varieties, you'll have plenty of choices. All have one thing in common: German law mandates that sausages can only be made of meat and spices. If it has cereal filling, it's not wurst.

Bockwurst: This tasty sausage is commonly roasted or grilled at street stands, and is served dripping with ketchup and mustard in a *Brötchen* (roll). Although *Bock* means billy-goat, this wurst is made of ground veal with parsley and chives. Complement your *Bockwurst* with some *Bock* beer.

Thüringer Bratwurst: Similar to the *Bockwurst*, the *Bratwurst* has a little pork too, plus ginger and nutmeg.

Frankfurter: Unlike the American variety, the German *Frankfurter* can only have this name if made in Frankfurt. It's made of lean pork ground into a paste and then cold smoked, which gives it that orange-yellow coloring.

Knockwurst: Short and plump, this sausage is served with sauerkraut. It's made of lean pork and beef, with a healthy dose of garlic.

Weißwurst: Cream and eggs give this "white sausage" its pale coloring. *Weißwurst* goes with rye bread and mustard.

Currywurst: A great late-night snack, this pork *Bratwurst* is smothered in a tomato sauce and sprinkled with paprika and curry.

CHARLOTTENBURG

Orchidee, Stuttgarter Pl. 13 (☎030 31 99 74 67; www.restaurantorchidee.de). All-you-can eat sushi with free tea and miso soup all week (€14.95). Lunch special (11am-5pm) with sushi sets. Open M-Sa 11am-midnight, Su 3pm-midnight. Cash only. ❷

SCHÖNEBERG

Café Bilderbuch, Akazienstr. 28 (☎030 78 70 60 57; www.cafe-bilderbuch.de). U7 to "Eisenacher Str." Tasty brunch baskets, served around the clock, and sumptuous Sunday buffet (€8) continue to entice hungry patrons. Weekly dinner specials €5-8.50. Open M-Th 9am-1am, F-Sa 9am-2am, Su 10am-1am. Kitchen open 9am-11pm. Cash only. ❷

Café Berio, Maaßenstr. 7 (☎030 216 19 46; www.cafe-berio.de). U1, U2, U4, or U15 to "Nollendorfpl." 2-fl. Viennese-style cafe tempts passersby with its amazing breakfast menu (€3-11). Entrees €5-9. Happy hour cocktails 2 for 1 (M-Th and Su 7pm-9pm and F-Sa 7pm-midnight). Open M-Th and Su 8am-midnight, F-Sa 8am-1am. Kitchen closes at 11pm. Cash only. ❷

KREUZBERG

Café V, Lausitzer Pl. 12 (☎030 612 45 05). U1 or 15 to "Görlitzer Bahnhof." City's oldest vegetarian restaurant, featuring vegan and fish entrees. Dishes includespinach balls in cheese sauce (€9) and an array of specials (€4.80-7.80). Open daily 10am-2am. Cash only. ❸

Wirtshaus Henne, Leuschnerdamm 25 (☎030 614 77 30; www.henne-berlin.de). U1 or U15 to "Kottbusser Tor." Famous for its *Brathähnchen* (fried chicken). While it has a small beer garden, the real charm is in its dark wood interior. Reserve in advance. Open Tu-Sa from 7pm, Su from 5pm. Cash only. ❷

Restaurant Rissani, Spreewaldpl. 4 (☎030 61 62 49 33). U1 or 15 to "Görlitzer Bahnhof." Best Middle Eastern food in the neighborhood; conveniently near Görlitzer Park. Perfect pre-, post-, or mid-party stop. Open M-Th and Su noon-3am, F-Sa noon-5am. Cash only. ❶

FRIEDRICHSHAIN AND PRENZLAUER BERG

Babel, Kastanienallee 33 (☎030 44 03 13 18; www.babel-berlin.com). U2 to "Eberswalder Str." Locals are obsessed with Babel's falafel (€3-6). Grab your food to go, or lap up the gigantic portions. Open daily 11am-2am. Cash only. ❶

Prater Garten, Kastanienallee 7-9 (☎030 448 5688; www.pratergarten.de). U2 to "Eberswalder Str." Giant chestnut trees overhang sprawling picnic tables and umbrellas at Berlin's oldest beer garden. Outdoor theater and TV. *Bratwurst* €2.50. Beer €3-4. Open in good weather Apr.-Sept. daily from noon. Cash only. ❶

SIGHTS

MITTE

Mitte was once the heart of Berlin, but the Wall split it down the middle, and much of it languished in disrepair under the GDR. The wave of revitalization that swept Berlin after the collapse of communism started in Mitte and the area has become increasingly upscale ever since with glittering modern buildings and swank galleries. Designer boutiques are not shy about posting the hefty prices of ensembles in window displays, perhaps as a warning to those who enter this fashionable district hoping to find bargains.

UNTER DEN LINDEN

One of Europe's best-known boulevards, Unter den Linden was the spine of imperial Berlin. During the Cold War, it was known as the "Idiot's Mile" because it gave visitors to the East a limited view of the city. Beginning in Pariser Pl. in front of Brandenburger Tor, the street extends east through Bebelpl. and the Lustgarten, punctuated by dramatic squares. *(S1, 2, or 25 to Unter den Linden. Bus #100 runs the length of the boulevard; 10-15 per hr.)*

BRANDENBURGER TOR (BRANDENBURG GATE). Berlin's only remaining gate was built by Friedrich Wilhelm II in the 18th century as a symbol of victory. Later it was a symbol of the divided city; in the center of the city along the Wall, it was once a barricaded gateway. Today, it is the most powerful emblem of reunited Germany. The **Room of Silence** in the northern end of the gate, marked by the word 'peace' in various languages, provides a non-denominational place for meditation and reflection. *(Open daily 11am-6pm).*

RUSSIAN EMBASSY. Rebuilding the edifices of the rich and famous wasn't a big priority in the workers' state of the DDR. The exception was Berlin's largest embassy, a building which covers almost an entire city block. While the Palais reverted to being just another embassy at the end of the Cold War (the huge bust of Lenin that once graced its red star-shaped topiary was quietly removed in 1994), you can still marvel at the imposing building from behind the iron fencing. *(Unter den Linden 65. www.berlin.de.)*

BEBELPLATZ. It was here on May 10, 1933, Nazi students burned nearly 20,000 books by "subversive" authors such as Heinrich Heine and Sigmund Freud—both Jews. A plaque in the center of the square is engraved with Heine's eerily prescient 1820 German epigram: "Wherever they burn books, eventually they will burn people too." Underneath the square rests a memorial, visible through a glass window on the ground in the center, in the form of a stark white room lined with empty book shelves. On the west side of the Platz, the building with the curved facade is the **Alte Bibliothek.** Once the royal library, it is now home to Humboldt's law faculty. On the other side of the square is the **Deutsche Staatsoper,** one of Berlin's three opera houses. The distinctive blue dome at the end of the square belongs to the **St.-Hedwigs-Kathedrale.** Completed in 1773 as Berlin's first Catholic church built after the Reformation, it was destroyed by American bombers in 1943. Organ concerts draw visitors on Wednesday at 3pm. *(www.hedwigschor-berlin.de. Cathedral open M-F 10am-5pm, Su 1-5pm. Free.)*

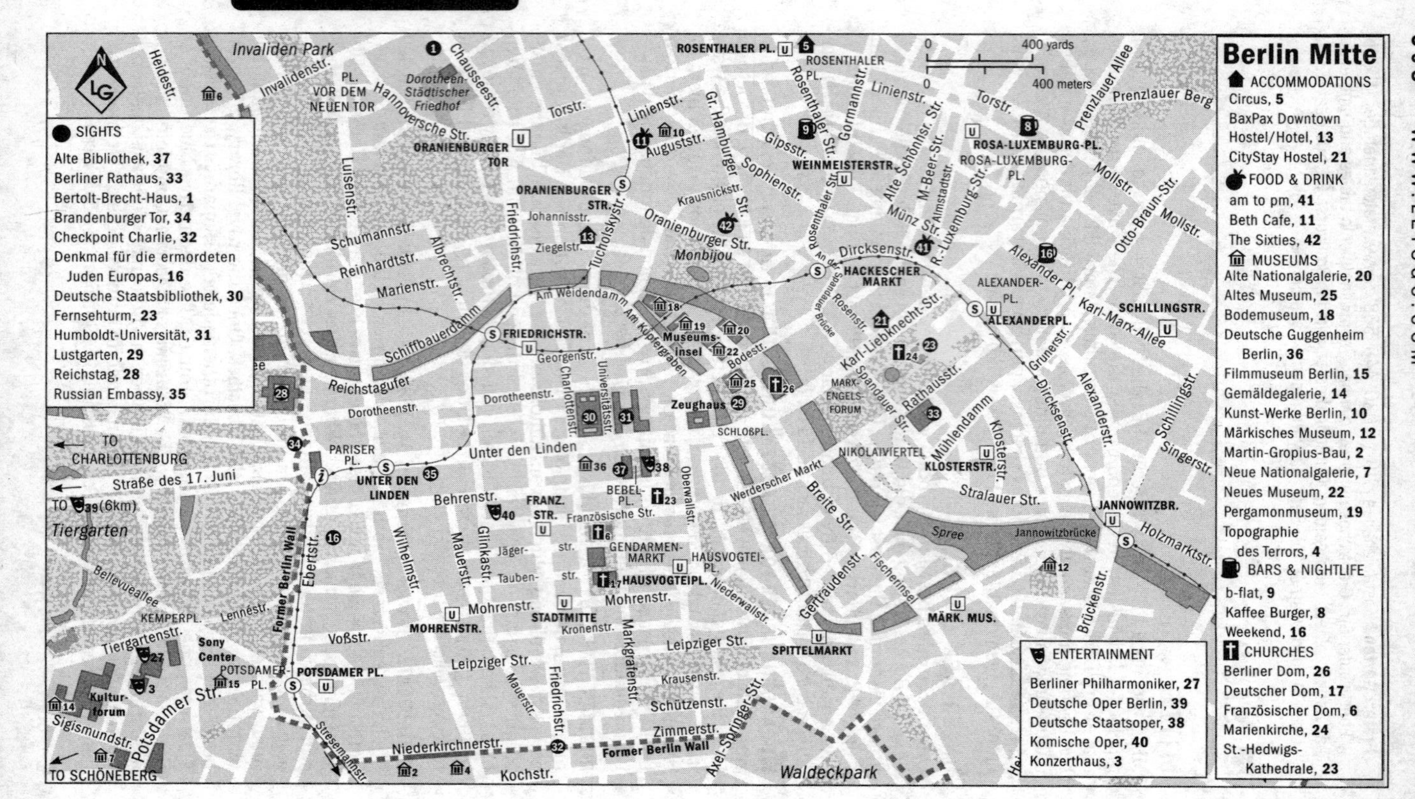
Berlin Mitte
ACCOMMODATIONS
Circus, 5
BaxPax Downtown Hostel/Hotel, 13
CityStay Hostel, 21
FOOD & DRINK
am to pm, 41
Beth Cafe, 11
The Sixties, 42
MUSEUMS
Alte Nationalgalerie, 20
Altes Museum, 25
Bodemuseum, 18
Deutsche Guggenheim Berlin, 36
Filmmuseum Berlin, 15
Gemäldegalerie, 14
Kunst-Werke Berlin, 10
Märkisches Museum, 12
Martin-Gropius-Bau, 2
Neue Nationalgalerie, 7
Neues Museum, 22
Pergamonmuseum, 19
Topographie des Terrors, 4
BARS & NIGHTLIFE
b-flat, 9
Kaffee Burger, 8
Weekend, 16
CHURCHES
Berliner Dom, 26
Deutscher Dom, 17
Französischer Dom, 6
Marienkirche, 24
St.-Hedwigs-Kathedrale, 23
SIGHTS
Alte Bibliothek, 37
Berliner Rathaus, 33
Bertolt-Brecht-Haus, 1
Brandenburger Tor, 34
Checkpoint Charlie, 32
Denkmal für die ermordeten Juden Europas, 16
Deutsche Staatsbibliothek, 30
Fernsehturm, 23
Humboldt-Universität, 31
Lustgarten, 29
Reichstag, 28
Russian Embassy, 35
ENTERTAINMENT
Berliner Philharmoniker, 27
Deutsche Oper Berlin, 39
Deutsche Staatsoper, 38
Komische Oper, 40
Konzerthaus, 3
0 400 yards
0 400 meters
TO CHARLOTTENBURG
TO 39 (6km)
TO SCHÖNEBERG
Former Berlin Wall

TIERGARTEN

In the center of Berlin, the lush Tiergarten provides welcome relief from the urban chaos around it. Stretching from Bahnhof Zoo to Brandenburg Gate, the vast, landscaped park was formerly used by Prussian monarchs as a hunting and parade ground. Today, it's frequented by strolling families, elderly couples, and, at night, cruising gay men. Straße des 17. Juni bisects the park from west to east, connecting Ernst-Reuter-Pl. to the Brandenburg Gate. The street is the site of many demonstrations and parades.

THE REICHSTAG. The current home of Germany's governing body, the *Bundestag*, the Reichstag has seen some critical moments in history. Here, in 1918, Philipp Scheidemann proclaimed "Es lebe die Deutsche Republik" ("Long live the German Republic"), and in 1933, Adolf Hitler used a fire here as an excuse to declare a state of emergency and seize power. Visitors enjoy panoramic views as they climb the spiral staircase inside the dome. *(☎030 22 73 21 52; www.bundestag.de. Open daily 8am-midnight; last entrance 10pm. Free.)*

SIEGESSÄULE (VICTORY COLUMN). In the heart of the Tiergarten, this slender 70m monument commemorates Prussia's crushing victory over France in 1870. The statue at the top—Victoria, the goddess of victory—is made of melted-down French cannons. In a less-than-subtle affront to the French, the Nazis moved the monument here in 1938 from its former spot in front of the Reichstag in order to increase its height and visibility. Climb the monument's 285 steps for a panorama of the city. *(Großer Stern. Take bus #100 or 187 to "Großer Stern" or S5, S7, or S9 to "Tiergarten." Accessible via the stairs at the West corners around the traffic circle. ☎030 391 29 61. Open Apr.-Nov. M-F 9:30am-6:30pm, Sa-Su 9:30am-7pm; Dec.-Mar. M-F 10am-5pm, Sa-Su 10am-5:30pm. €2.20, students €1.50.)*

POTSDAMER PLATZ. Built under Friedrich Wilhelm I as an approximation of Parisian boulevards, Potsdamer Pl. was designed for the primary purpose of mobilizing troops quickly. After reunification, Potsdamer Pl. became the new commercial center of a united Berlin, and achieved infamy as the city's largest construction site in the 1990s. Today its cutting-edge, ambitious architectural designs make for spectacular sightseeing. The complex of buildings overlooking Potsdamer Str. includes the glossy **Sony Center,** and an off-kilter glass recreation of Mt. Fuji that covers the courtyard enclosed by cafes, shops, and a movie theater. *(U2 or S1, S2, or S25 to "Potsdamer Pl.")*

FERNSEHTURM (TV TOWER). At 368m, this tremendous and bizarre tower, the tallest structure in Berlin, was originally intended to prove East Germany's technological capabilities 9though Swedish engineers were ultimately brought in when construction faltered. Look at the windows when the sun is out to see the cross-shaped glint pattern known as the Papsts Rache (Pope's Revenge), so named because it defied the Communist government's attempt to rid the city of religious symbols. An elevator whisks tourists up and away to the magnificent view from the spherical node (203m), and a slowly rotating cafe one floor up serves international meals for €8-16. *(☎030 242 33 33; www.berlinerfernsehturm.de. Open daily Mar.-Oct. 9am-midnight; Nov.-Feb. 10am-midnight. €9.50, under 16 €4.50.)*

MUSEUMSINSEL (MUSEUM ISLAND) AND ALEXANDERPLATZ

After crossing the Schloßbrücke over the Spree, Unter den Linden becomes Karl-Liebknecht-Str. and cuts through the Museumsinsel (Museum Island), home to five major museums and the **Berliner Dom.** Take S3, S5, S7, S9, or S75 to "Hackescher Markt" and walk toward the *Dom.* Or, pick up bus #100 along Unter den Linden and get off at "Lustgarten." Karl-Liebknecht-Str., which divides the Museumsinsel, leads into the Alexanderpl. Behind the Marx-Engels-Forum, the preserved streets of Nikolaiviertel (Nicholas' Quarter) stretch towards Mühlendamm. Take U2, U5, or U8, or S3, S5, S7, S9, or S75 to "Alexanderpl."

BERLINER DOM. This elegant, multi-domed cathedral is one of Berlin's most recognizable landmarks. Built during the reign of Kaiser Wilhelm II in a faux-Renaissance style, the cathedral suffered severe damage in a 1944 air raid. Today's church is the result of a 20-year process of reconstruction. Look for the Protestant icons (Calvin, Zwingli, and Luther) that adorn the decadent interior, or soak in a glorious view of Berlin from the top of the cupola. *(Open M-Sa 9am-8pm, Su noon-8pm, closed during services 6:30-7:30pm. Free organ recitals W-F 3pm. Frequent concerts in summer; buy tickets in the church or call. M-Sa 9am-8pm, Su 10am-8pm. Closes at 7pm Oct. 1- Mar 31. ☎030 202 69 119 or www.berlinerdom.de. Combined admission to Dom, crypt, tower, and galleries €5, students €3; audio guide €3 extra.)*

SCHEUNENVIERTEL. Northwest of Alexanderpl., near Oranienburger Str and Große Hamburger Str., is the Scheunenviertel (Barn Quarter), once the center of Berlin's Orthodox Jewish community. The neighborhood shows evidence of Jewish life back to the 13th century (though the Jews were expelled from the city several times before WWII). Today, the Scheunenviertel is known more for its teeming masses of outdoor cafes than for its historical significance, but the past few years have seen the opening of Judaica-oriented bookstores and kosher restaurants. *(S1, S2, or S25 to "Oranienburger Str." or U6 to "Oranienburger Tor.")*

NEUE SYNAGOGE. This huge building, modeled after the Alhambra, was used for worship until 1940, when the Nazis occupied it and used it for storage. Amazingly, the building survived *Kristallnacht*—the SS torched it, but a local police chief bluffed his way past SS officers to order the fire extinguished. The synagogue was later destroyed by bombing, but its restoration, largely financed by international Jewish organizations, began in 1988. The sanctuary's beautiful, gold-laced domes were opened to the public in 1995. *(Oranienburger Str. 29. ☎030 88 02 83 00. Open May-Aug. M and Su 10am-8pm, Tu-Th 10-am-6pm, F 10am-5pm; Sept.-Apr. M-Th and Su 10am-6pm, F 10am-6pm. Last admission 30min. before close. Closed Sat and Jewish holidays. A series of security checks is required to enter. Permanent exhibition "Open Ye the Gates" €3, students €2. Dome €1.50, students €1. Temporary exhibition: €3, students €2.)*

CHARLOTTENBURG

Charlottenburg is home to one of Berlin's main shopping streets, the Ku'damm. The area's sights can be expensive; budget travelers come mostly to explore the attractions near Bahnhof Zoo.

AROUND BAHNHOF ZOO. Former West Berlin centered on Bahnhof Zoo, the station that inspired U2's "Zoo TV" tour. In the surrounding area, peepshows mingle with department stores, souvenir shops, and other G-rated attractions.

GERMANY

Charlottenburg and Schöneberg

ACCOMMODATIONS
- A&O Hostel, **11**
- Berolina Backpacker, **8**
- Jugendgästehaus am Zoo, **4**

BARS AND NIGHTLIFE
- Connection, **1**
- Mister Hu, **7**
- Slumberland, **19**

FOOD & DRINK
- Baharat Falafel, **10**
- Cafe Berio, **20**
- Cafe Bilderbuch, **5**
- Damas Falafel, **3**
- Die Feinbäckerei, **22**
- Orchidee Sushi Restaurant, **9**
- Schwarzes Cafe, **15**
- Witty's, **18**

MUSEUMS
- Bauhaus-Archiv Museum Für Gestaltung, **13**
- Gemäldegalerie, **6**
- Neue Nationalgalerie, **14**
- Museum Berggruen, **2**

SIGHTS
- Aquarium, **12**
- Elefantentor, **16**
- Kaiser-Wilhelm-Gedächtiskirche, **17**

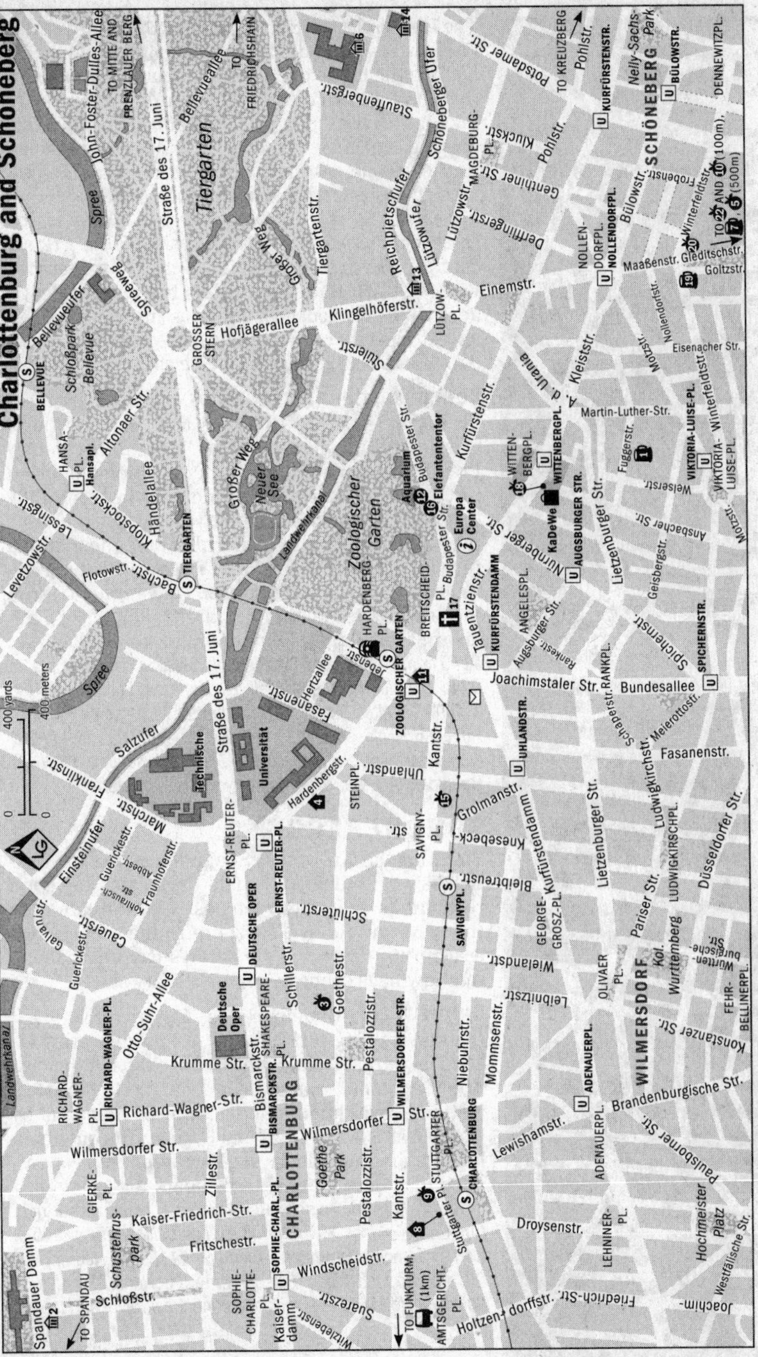
Charlottenburg and Schöneberg
Tiergarten
Zoologischer Garten
CHARLOTTENBURG
SCHÖNEBERG
WILMERSDORF
Spree
Landwehrkanal
Straße des 17. Juni
Großer Weg
Neuer See
Aquarium
Elefantentor
Europa Center
KaDeWe
Technische Universität
Deutsche Oper
Schloßpark Bellevue
GROSSER STERN
BELLEVUE
TIERGARTEN
ZOOLOGISCHER GARTEN
SAVIGNYPL.
CHARLOTTENBURG
KURFÜRSTENDAMM
UHLANDSTR.
WITTENBERGPL.
NOLLENDORFPL.
KURFÜRSTENSTR.
BÜLOWSTR.
VIKTORIA-LUISE-PL.
SPICHERNSTR.
AUGSBURGER STR.
ADENAUERPL.
WILMERSDORFER STR.
BISMARCKSTR.
DEUTSCHE OPER
ERNST-REUTER-PL.
RICHARD-WAGNER-PL.
SOPHIE-CHARL.-PL.
Hansapl.
Kantstr.
Kurfürstendamm
Hardenbergstr.
Budapester Str.
Tauentzienstr.
Bismarckstr.
Otto-Suhr-Allee
Kaiser-Friedrich-Str.
Wilmersdorfer Str.
Richard-Wagner-Str.
Krumme Str.
Goethestr.
Schillerstr.
Pestalozzistr.
Lietzenburger Str.
Bundesallee
Joachimstaler Str.
Nürnberger Str.
Kleiststr.
Martin-Luther-Str.
Motzstr.
Potsdamer Str.
Lützowufer
Reichpietschufer
Schöneberger Ufer
Hofjägerallee
Klingelhöferstr.
Tiergartenstr.
Bellevueallee
John-Foster-Dulles-Allee
Spreeweg
Altonaer Str.
Klopstockstr.
Händelallee
Bachstr.
Levetzowstr.
Lessingstr.
Salzufer
Franklinstr.
Marchstr.
Einsteinufer
Fasanenstr.
Uhlandstr.
Grolmanstr.
Knesebeckstr.
Bleibtreustr.
Wielandstr.
Leibnizstr.
Mommsenstr.
Niebuhrstr.
Lewishamstr.
Droysenstr.
Windscheidstr.
Schloßstr.
Spandauer Damm
Suarezstr.
Holtzendorffstr.
Brandenburgische Str.
Konstanzer Str.
Düsseldorfer Str.
Pariser Str.
Ludwigkirchstr.
Einemstr.
Winterfeldtstr.
Goltzstr.
Maaßenstr.
Hochmeister Platz
TO SPANDAU
TO FUNKTURM (1km)
TO KREUZBERG
TO MITTE AND PRENZLAUER BERG
TO FRIEDRICHSHAIN
0 400 yards
0 400 meters

GERMANY

ASTRY OR PRESIDENT?

"All free men, wherever they may ive, are citizens of Berlin. And herefore, as a free man, I take oride in the words: *Ich bin ein Berliner.*" Ending his speech with hese words on June 26, 1963, he 15th anniversary of the Berlin Airlift, John F. Kennedy assured a crowd of 1.5 million West Berlin-ers of the Allies' continued com-nitment to protect their city.

But JFK's final four words, the product of a last-minute decision o utter something in German, nave left some linguistic confu-sion in their historical wake. Some skeptics insist that Kennedy actu-ally called himself a jelly dough-nut (in German, *ein Berliner*). The difference between a citizen of Berlin and a pastry depends on he article *"ein"* (a), which a native German speaker would omit when expressing place of origin. Thus, a German from Hamburg would say, *"Ich bin Hamburger,"* while a hamburger, if it could talk, might ell you *"Ich bin ein Hamburger"* before disappearing down your esophagus. Natives point out that n Berlin the pastry is called a *Pfannkuchen*, and that Kennedy's version is grammatically valid.

The site of the speech now houses Berlin's municipal govern-ment and is open to tourists.

(John-F.-Kennedy-Pl. U4 to "Rathaus Schöneberg." ☎030 75 60 70 20. Open daily 10am-6pm.)

The **Zoologischer Garten,** one of the world's largest and oldest zoos, gained international attention in early 2007 as the home of celebrity polar bear **Knut.** Now that the fuss has died down, there's more room to take in the zoo's open-air habitats, attractive land-scaping, and large collection of endangered species. At the second entrance across from EuropaCenter is the famous **Elefantentor,** a pagoda of pachyderms. *(Budapester Str. 34. Park open daily 9am-7:30pm, animal houses open 9am-6pm, entrance closes at 6:30pm. €12, stu-dents €9, children €6. Combination ticket to zoo and aquarium €18/14/9.)* Within the zoo walls but independently accessible, an **aquarium** contains insects, reptiles, and kilometers of fish tanks. *(Budapester Str. 32. Open daily 9am-6pm. €12, students €9, children €6.)*

SCHLOSS CHARLOTTENBURG. This monumen-tal Baroque palace occupies a park in northern Charlottenburg and contains more 18th-century French paintings than any other location outside of France. Its pristine grounds include: the beautifully furnished **Altes Schloß;** the **Belvedere,** which houses the royal family's porcelain collection; the marbled receiving rooms of the **Neuer Flugel,** the **Neuer Pavil-lon,** and the palace **Mausoleum.** Leave time to stroll the **Schloßgarten** behind the main buildings, a para-dise of footbridges, fountains, and small lakes. *(Bus #145 from Bahnhof Zoo to "Luisenpl./Schloß Charlottenburg" or U2 to "Sophie-Charlottepl." Walk 10-15min. up Schloßstr. ☎030 320 92 75. Altes Schloß €10, students €7; closed on M. Neuer Flügel €6/5; closed on Tu. Open daily Apr.-Oct. 10am-6pm, Nov.-Mar. 10am-5pm. Belvedere €2/1.50, Mausoleum €2/1.50. Open daily Apr.-Oct. 10am-6pm, Nov.-Mar. noon-5pm.*

SCHÖNEBERG

South of the Ku'damm, Schöneberg is a residen-tial district notable for its laid-back cafes and good restaurants. It lies between posh Charlottenburg to the west and funky Kreuzberg to the east. In **Nol-lendorfplatz,** the nexus of Berlin's gay community, rainbow flags drape even the military store.

GRUNEWALD. In summer, this 745-acre birch forest, the dog-walking turf of many a Berliner, provides an ideal retreat from the heat and chaos of the city. About a kilometer into the woods, the **Jagdschloß,** a restored royal hunting lodge, houses paintings by German artists like Graff and Cranach. Its one-room hunting museum displays cabinets full of weapons, racks of antlers, mounted wild boars, and everything from goblets to tea sets adorned with hunting scenes. *(Am Grunewaldsee 29. U3 or U7 to "Fehrbelliner Pl.," or S45 or S46 to "Hohenzollerndamm," then bus #115, dir.: Neuruppiner Str. or Spanische Allee / Potsdamer to "Pücklerstr." Turn left on Pücklerstr. following the signs and continue straight into the for-*

est to reach the lodge. ☎030 813 35 97. www.spsg.de. Open May 15-Oct. 15 Tu-Su 10am-5pm; open for weekend tours Oct.16-May 14 11am, 1, 3pm. €2, students €1.50; with tour €3/2.50.)

KREUZBERG

Kreuzberg was once the most countercultural district in West Germany, home to artists, draft dodgers, and Turkish guest workers. While most of the punk *Hausbesetzer* (squatters) who occupied the area are now gone, the district still retains its distinctive spirit. Protests remain frequent and intense. The eastern end of the district, Kreuzberg 36, is the center of Berlin's Turkish population and fashionable nightlife (around Schlesische Str.), while the western end of the district, Kreuzberg 61, is more ritzy.

THE MAUERMUSEUM: HAUS AM CHECKPOINT CHARLIE. This museum at the famous border-crossing point has become one of Berlin's most popular attractions. The museum is a cluttered collection of artwork, newspaper clippings, photographs documenting the history of the wall, and displays of all types of devices used to get over, under, or through it. *(Friedrichstr. 43-45. U6 to "Kochstr." ☎030 253 72 50; www.mauer-museum.de. Museum open daily 9am-10pm. German-language films with English subtitles every 2hr. from 9:30am. €12.50, students €7.50. Audio tour €3.)*

ORANIENSTRASSE. This colorful mix of bars, cafes, and stores also plays host to a more radical element: May Day parades, which start on Oranienpl. and usually becomes riotous by nightfall. Revolutionaries jostle with Turkish families, while an anarchist punk faction and a boisterous gay and lesbian population shake things up after hours. *(U1 to "Kottbusser Tor" or "Görlitzer Bahnhof.")*

FRIEDRICHSHAIN AND LICHTENBERG

Friedrichshain is becoming the new hallowed ground of the unpretentiously hip. **Simon-Dach-Straße** is filled with outdoor cafes and a crowd of 20-somethings. The grungier area around **Rigaerstraße** is a stronghold of Berlin's legendary alternative scene, home to squatter bars, makeshift clubs, and lounging grounds.

EAST SIDE GALLERY. The longest remaining portion of the Berlin Wall, this 1.3km stretch also serves as the world's largest open-air art gallery, unsupervised and, on the Warschauer Str. side, open at all hours. The murals are remnants of the organized efforts of an international group of multi-national artists who gathered here in 1989 to celebrate the end of the city's division. *(Along Mühlenstr. Take U1 or U15 or S3, S5-S7, S9, or S75 to "Warschauer Str." or S5, S7, S9, or S75 to "Ostbahnhof" and walk back toward the river. www.eastsidegallery.com.)*

FORSCHUNGS- UND GEDENKSTÄTTE NORMANNENSTRASSE. The Lichtenberg suburb harbors perhaps the most hated and feared building of the DDR regime: the headquarters of the East German **secret police,** the *Staatssicherheit* or *Stasi*. During the Cold War, the Stasi kept dossiers on some six million of their own citizens, in a country of only 16 million people. Since a 1991 law returned the records to the people, the "Horror Files" have rocked Germany, exposing millions of informants—and wrecking careers, marriages, and friendships—at all levels of German society. The exhibit displays the extensive offices of Erich Mielke (the loathed Minister for State Security from 1957 to 1989), a large collection of tiny microphones and hidden cameras used for surveillance by the *Stasi*, and a replica of a Stasi prison cell. *(Ruschestr. 103, Haus 1. U5 to "Magdalenenstr." ☎030 553 68 54; www.stasimuseum.de. Exhibits in German. Recommended English-language info booklet €3. Open M-F 11am-6pm, Sa-Su 2-6pm. €4, students €3.)*

PRENZLAUER BERG

Everything in Prenzlauer Berg used to be something else. Brunches unfold in former butcher shops, furniture exhibits bring domestic grace to a former power plant, and kids cavort in breweries-turned-nightclubs. Relics of the area's past life are disappearing, but cafe owners know shabby chic when they see it—plenty of mismatched sofas remain, and old graffiti cover Prenzlauer Berg's increasingly trendy buildings. Now reputed to have the highest birth rate in Europe, Prenzlauer Berg is perhaps most striking for—no joke—the sheer number of fashionably dressed babies swarming its parks and sidewalks.

BERLINER MAUER DOKUMENTATIONSZENTRUM (BERLIN WALL DOCUMENTATION CENTER). A museum, chapel, and an entire city block of the preserved Berlin Wall—two concrete barriers separated by the open **Todesstreife** (death strip)—combine to form a controversial memorial to "victims of the communist tyranny." The museum assembles a comprehensive record of all things wall related. Climb up the spiral staircases to experience the full effect of the desolate scene below you. *(Bernauer Str. 111. ☎030 464 10 30; www.berliner-mauer-dokumentationszentrum.de. U8 to "Bernauer Str.," S1 and S2 to "Nordbahnhof." Open Apr.-Oct. Tu-Su 10am-6pm, Nov.-Mar. Tu-Su 10am-5pm. Free.)*

KOLLWITZPLATZ. This little triangle of greenery is a nexus of Prenzlauer Berg's cafe scene populated by young couples and, on Saturdays, an upscale **market** selling everything from handmade pasta to freshly pressed apple juice. The Platz centers on a statue of famed visual artist **Käthe Kollwitz**. The monument has been painted a number of times in past years in acts of affectionate vandalism, most notably with big pink polka-dots. *(U2 to "Senefelderpl.")*

MUSEUMS

With over 170 museums, Berlin is one of the world's great museum cities. Collections range from every epoch; the *Berlin Programm* (€1.60) lists them all.

SMB MUSEUMS

Staatliche Museen zu Berlin (SMB) runs over 20 museums in four major areas of Berlin—the **Museumsinsel, Tiergarten-Kulturforum, Charlottenburg,** and **Dahlem**—and elsewhere in Mitte and the Tiergarten. (www.smb.museum; ☎030 209 055 77.) All museums sell single-admission tickets (€8, students €4) and the three-day card (*Drei-Tage-Karte;* €19, students €9.50). Admission is free the first Sunday of every month and on Thursdays after 6pm. Unless otherwise noted, all SMB museums are open Tuesday through Sunday 10am-6pm and Thursday 10am-10pm. All offer free English-language audio tours.

MUSEUMSINSEL (MUSEUM ISLAND)

Declared a UNESCO world heritage site in 1999, Germany's greatest cultural treasures reside in five separate museums, separated from the rest of Mitte by two arms of the **Spree.** Currently, the **Neues Museum** is undergoing renovation: it is scheduled to reopen in late 2008, when the restoration of the Pergamonmuseum and the Altes Museum will begin. *(S3, 5, 7, 9, or 75 to "Hackescher Markt" or bus #100 to "Lustgarten." ☎030 20 90 55 55.)*

PERGAMONMUSEUM. Pergamonmuseum, one of the great ancient history museums, displays almost an entire ancient city reconstructed in Berlin. Named for the Turkish city from which the enormous **Altar of Zeus** (180 BC) was taken, the collection of artifacts from the ancient Near East includes the colossal blue **Ishtar Gate of Babylon** (575 BC) and the **Roman Market Gate of Miletus.** *(Bodestr. 1-3. ☎030 20 90 55 77. €8, students €4.)*

ALTE NATIONALGALERIE (OLD NATIONAL GALLERY). This museum of 19th-century art recently reopened after extensive renovations. The gallery presents everything from German Realism to French Impressionism; Manet, Monet, Degas, and Renoir are just a few names in an all-star cast. Enjoy a delicious drink at their outdoor **Sage Bar** under the columns overlooking the water. *(Lustgarten. ☎030 20 90 55 77. Open T-W and F-Su 10am-6pm, Th 10am-10pm. House ticket €8, student €4. Day ticket €12, student €6.)*

TIERGARTEN-KULTURFORUM

The Tiergarten-Kulturforum is a complex of museums at the eastern end of the Tiergarten, near the Staatsbibliothek and Potsdamer Pl. Students and local fine arts aficionados swarm throughout the buildings and on the multi-leveled courtyard in front. *(S1, S2, or S25 or U2 to "Potsdamer Pl." and walk down Potsdamer Str.; the museums will be on your right on Matthäikirchpl. ☎030 20 90 55 55.)*

GEMÄLDEGALERIE (PICTURE GALLERY). The Gemäldegalerie is one of Germany's most famous museums, and rightly so. It houses an enormous collection of 2700 13th- to 18th-century masterpieces by Italian, German, Dutch, and Flemish masters, including works by Dürer, Rembrandt, Rubens, Velazquez, Bruegel, Gainsborough, Raphael, Titian, and Botticelli. *(Stauffenbergstr. 40. ☎030 266 29 51. Open Tu-W and F-Su 10am-6pm, Th 10am-10pm.)*

HAMBURGER BAHNHOF: MUSEUM FÜR GEGENWART (MUSEUM FOR THE PRESENT). Berlin's foremost collection of contemporary art—with 10,000 square meters of exhibition space—lies in a converted train station. The museum features several whimsical works by Warhol, as well as pieces by Twombly and Kiefer. The vastness of the rooms and the stark white walls create excellent conditions for observation. *(Invalidenstr. 50-51. S3, S5, S7, S9, or S75 to "Hauptbahnhof" or U6 to "Zinnowitzer Str." ☎030 39 78 34 11; www.hamburgerbahnhof.de. Open Tu-F 10am-6pm, Sa 11am-8pm, Su 11am-6pm. €8, students €4, Th 2-6pm free.)*

CHARLOTTENBURG

Many excellent museums surround **Schloß Charlottenburg.** Take bus #145 from Bahnhof Zoo to Luisenpl./Schloß Charlottenburg, or take U2 to Sophie-Charlotte-Pl. and walk 10-15min. up the tree-lined Schloßstr.

MUSEUM BERGGRUEN. Subtitled "Picasso and His Time," the three-story Museum Berggruen explores the work of the groundbreaking 20th-century artist and the movements that sprung up around him. Picasso's influences, which include African masks and late paintings by Matisse, occupy the bottom floor. On the top floor are the elongated sculptures of Giacometti and paintings by Klee. *(Schloßstr. 1. ☎030 32 67 58 15. Open Tu-Su 10am-6pm. €6, students €3.)*

DAHLEM

SMB-PK DAHLEM. The **Museen Dahlem** consists of three museums, all housed in one building in the center of Dahlem's Freie Universität. The **Museum Europäischer Kulturen,** also part of the complex, is located a couple of blocks away. One ticket *(€6, students €3)* provides access to all three, which are also free on Thursdays 4hr. before closing. The **Ethnologisches Museum (Museum of Ethnology)** dominates the main building and richly rewards a trek to Dahlem. The exhibits are stunning, ranging from huge pieces of ancient Central American stonework to African elephant tusk statuettes. Most surprising are the enormous, authentic boats from the South Pacific and model huts that you can enter. *U3 to "Dahlem-Dork" and follow the "museen" signs to get to the main building. ☎ 030 83 01 44 38 Open Tu-F 10am-6pm, Sa-Su 11am-6pm. Th free 4hr. before closing.)*

INDEPENDENT (NON-SMB) MUSEUMS

JÜDISCHES MUSEUM BERLIN. The design for the zinc-plated Jewish Museum is fascinating even as an architectural experience. No two walls are parallel, creating a sensation of perpetual discomfort. Underground, three symbolic hallways—the Axis of the Holocaust, the Axis of Exile, and the Axis of Continuity—are intended to represent the trials of death, escape, and survival. The labyrinthine **Garden of Exile** replicates the dizzying effects of dislocation and the eerie **Holocaust Tower,** a giant, asymmetrical concrete room nearly devoid of light and sound encourages reflection. Exhibits feature works by contemporary artists, memorials to victims of the Holocaust, and a history of Jews in Germany. Enter at the top of the stairs from the Axis of Continuity. *(Lindenstr. 9-14. U6 to "Kochstr." or U1, U6, or U15 to "Hallesches Tor." ☎ 030 259 93 300. Open daily 10am-8pm, M until 10pm. Last entry 1hr. before close. €5, students €2.50. Special exhibits €4. Audio tour €2.)*

ENTERTAINMENT

Berlin has one of the world's most vibrant cultural scenes. Numerous festivals celebrating everything from Chinese film to West African music enrich the regular offerings; posters advertising special events plaster the city well in advance. Most theaters and concert halls offer up to 50% off for students who buy at the *Abendkasse* (evening box office), which generally opens 1hr. before shows. Other ticket outlets charge 15-18% commissions and do not offer student discounts. The **KaDeWe** **(see opposite page)** has a ticket counter. (☎030 217 7754. Open M-F 10am-8pm, Sa 10am-4pm.) Most theaters and operas close from mid-July to late August. The monthly pamphlets *Konzerte und Theater in Berlin und Brandenburg* (free) and *Berlin Programm* (€1.75) list concerts, film, and theater info, as do the biweekly *030*, *Kultur!news*, *Tip*, and *Zitty*.

CONCERTS, DANCE, AND OPERA

Berlin reaches its musical zenith in September, during the fabulous **Berliner Festwochen,** which draws the world's best orchestras and soloists. The **Berliner Jazztage** in November features top jazz musicians. For tickets (which sell out months ahead) and more info for both festivals, call **Berliner Festspiele** (☎030 25 48 90; www.berlinerfestspiele.de). In mid-July, the **Bachtage** features an intense week of classical music, while every Saturday night in August the **Sommer Festspiele** turns the Ku'damm into a multi-faceted concert hall with folk, punk, and steel-drum groups competing for attention.

THEATER AND FILM

Theater listings can be found on the yellow and blue posters in most U-Bahn stations. In addition to the world's best German-language theater, Berlin also has a strong English-language scene; look for listings in *Zitty* or *Tip* that say "*in englischer Sprache*" (in English). A number of privately run companies called Off-Theaters also occasionally feature English-language plays. As with concert halls, virtually all theaters are closed in July and August, indicated by the words *Theaterferien* or *Sommerpause.* On any given night you can choose from over 150 different films. O.F. next to a movie listing means original version; O.m.U. means original version with German subtitles. Mondays through Wednesdays are *Kinotage* days at most theaters, with reduced prices. In summer, *Freiluftkino* (open-air cinemas) show movies in the city's parks; winter brings the popular, international **Berlinale** film festival (early-mid Feb.).

SHOPPING

The high temple of consumerism is the dazzling, pricey, seven-story **KaDeWe department store** on Wittenbergpl. at Tauentzienstr. 21-24, continental Europe's largest department store. The name is a German abbreviation of *Kaufhaus des Westens* (Department Store of the West); for the tens of thousands of product-starved East Germans who flooded Berlin in the days after the Berlin Wall's fall, KaDeWe *was* the West. (☎030 212 10. Open M-F 10am-8pm, Sa 9:30am-8pm.) The sidewalks of the 3-kilometer-long **Kurfürstendamm,** near Bahnhof Zoo, have at least one big store from every mega-chain you can name. Upscale shopping also lines **Friedrichstraße** south of Unter den Linden. Near **Hackescher Markt** and **Alte Schönhauser Straße,** the art galleries of Mitte give way to clothing galleries with similar price tags. The flea market on **Straße des 17. Juni** has a better selection but higher prices than other markets. (Take S5, 7, 9, or 75 to "Tiergarten." Open Sa-Su 11am-5pm.) **Winterfeldtplatz,** near Nollendorfpl., overflows with food, flowers, and people crooning Bob Dylan tunes over acoustic guitars. (Open W and Sa 8am-1pm.) On Sundays a massive secondhand market takes over Prenzlauer Berg's **Mauerpark,** with everything from food to furniture.

NIGHTLIFE

Berlin's nightlife is absolute madness. Bars typically open around 6pm and get going around midnight, just as clubs begin opening their doors. The bar scene winds down anywhere between 1 and 6am; meanwhile, clubs fill up and don't empty until well after dawn, when they pass the baton to after-parties and 24hr. cafes. Between 1 and 4am, take advantage of the **night buses** and **U-Bahn** 9 and 12, which run all night on Friday and Saturday. Info about bands and dance venues can be found in the pamphlets *Tip* (€2.50) and *Zitty* (€2.30), available at newsstands, or in *030* (free), distributed in bars, cafes, and hostels.

BARS AND CLUBS

MITTE

Week-End, Alexanderstr. 7 (☎030 24 63 16 76; www.week-end-berlin.de), on the 12th fl. of the building with the neon "Sharp" sign. House music fuels the dance floor until morning. Wheelchair accessible. Cover €12. Open Th-Sa from 11pm. Cash only.

b-flat, Rosenthaler Str. 13 (☎030 28 38 68 35, tickets 030 283 31 23; www.b-flat-berlin.de). U8 to "Weinmeisterstr." or S3, S5, S7, S9, or S75 to "Hackescher Markt." Live jazz and acoustic nightly in a sleek, dimly-lit bar with pictures of musicians lining the walls. W free music. Cover €10, students €8. Open daily from 8pm. Cash only.

CHARLOTTENBURG

Quasimodo, Kantstr. 12a (☎030 312 80 86; www.quasimodo.de). U2, S5, S7, S9, or S75 to "Zoologischer Garten. Spacious venue showcases soul, R&B, and jazz. Cover for concerts €8-20. Tickets available F from 4:30pm or Sa-Sun from 11am at the cafe upstairs. Open 7pm; doors open 1hr. before concert. Drinks €2.50-4.50. Cash only.

A-Trane, Bleibtreustr. 1 (☎030 313 25 50; www.a-trane.de). S3, S5, S7, S9, or S75 to "Savignypl." Cozy tables litter the floor for serious jazz fans. Cover €7-15, student discount €2. Open M-Th and Su 9pm-2am, F-Sa 9pm-open end. Cash only.

SCHÖNEBERG

Slumberland, Goltzstr. 24 (☎030 216 53 49). U1-U4 to "Nollendorfpl." Palm trees, African art, and a sand floor transport you to the Bahamas. Listen to Bob Marley while drinking Hefeweizen (€3). The secret to the frappes (€2.30) is coffee crystals. Most drinks €2.50-4.50. Open M-F and Su 6pm-4am, Sa 11am-4am. Cash only.

Mister Hu, Goltzstr. 39 (☎030 217 21 11; www.misterhu-berlin.de). U1-U4 to "Nollendorfpl." Green bead lights and a bar made of rocky tiles with a bamboo forest backdrop give this energetic bar a cool mystique. Happy hour daily until 9pm (and all day Sun). All cocktails and longdrinks €5. Open M-Th and Su 6pm-3am, F and Sa 6pm-4am. Opens daily at 5pm in summer. Cash only.

KREUZBERG

Club der Visionaere, Am Flutgraben 1 (☎030 695 18 942; www.clubdervisionaererecords.com). U1 or U15 to "Schlesisches Tor" or night bus #N65 to "Heckmannufer." Multiple languages drift through the air to the people settled on ground-cushions. Beer €3. Open M-F 2pm-late, Sa-Su noon-late. Cash only.

Watergate, Falckensteinstr. 49 (☎030 61 28 03 94; www.water-gate.de). U1 or U15 to "Schlesisches Tor." One of the hippest clubs in Berlin. The view of the Spree from the "Water Floor" lounge is unbeatable. Crowds pick up at 2am. Cover W €6, F-Sa €10. Open W and F 11pm-late and Sa midnight-late. Cash only.

FRIEDRICHSHAIN

Berghain/Panorama Bar, Am Wriezener Bahnhof (☎030 29 00 05 97; www.berghain.de). S3, S5, S7, S9, or S75 to "Ostbahnhof." Heading up Str. der Pariser Kommune, take the third right into what looks like a parking lot. An "it" club where spaced-out techno fiends pulse to the music reverberating beneath the towering ceilings. Cover €12. Open Th-Sa from midnight. Check schedule online. Cash only.

PRENZLAUER BERG

Intersoup, Schliemannstr. 31 (☎030 23 27 3045; www.intersoup.de). U2 to "Eberswalder Str." This shabby bar eschews big name drink brands and popular music in favor of worn 70s furniture, soup specials (€4.50-5), and retro floral wallpaper. Downstairs, the small club **Undersoup** keeps things wild with live music dance parties (most W and Sa), karaoke, occasional films, and puppet theater (M and Tu). DJs most nights. Club cover max. €3. Open daily M-Sa 6pm-3am, Su 5pm-2am. Cash only.

TREPTOW

Insel, Alt-Treptow 6 (☎030 20 91 49 90; www.insel-berlin.net). S6, S8, S9, S41 of S42, to "Treptower Park," then bus #166, 167, 265 or N65 from Puschkinallee to "Rathaus Treptow." Enter through the park at the corner of Alt-Treptow. 3-story club crammed with gyrating bodies, multiple bars, and a cafe with hammocks. Club cover W free, Th-Sa €2.50-15. Club open W from 7:30pm; time varies Th-Sa, check the website. Cash only.

GLBT NIGHTLIFE

Berlin is one of Europe's most gay-friendly cities. In the gay mecca of **Schöneberg, Akazienstraße, Goltzstraße,** and **Winterfeldtstraße** have mixed bars and cafes, while the **"Bermuda Triangle"** of Eisenacherstr., Fuggerstr., and Motzstr. is more exclusively gay. *Gay-yellowpages*, *Sergej*, and *Siegessäule* have GLBT entertainment listings. **Mann-o-Meter,** Bülowstr. 106, at the corner of Else-Lasker-Schüler-Str., provides counseling, info on gay nightlife, and long-term accommodations, in addition to **Internet** access. (☎030 216 8008; www.mann-o-meter.de. Open M-F

5-10pm, Sa-Su 4-10pm.) **Spinnboden-Lesbenarchiv,** Anklamer Str. 38, has hip lesbian offerings, including exhibits, films, and other cultural info. Take U8 to "Bernauer Str." (☎030 448 5848. Open W and F 2-7pm.) The **Christopher Street Day (CSD)** parade, a 6hr. street party with ecstatic, champagne-soaked floats, draws over 250,000 participants annually in June. Nollendorfpl. hosts the **Lesbisch-schwules Stadtfest** (Lesbian-Gay City Fair) the weekend before the parade.

Das Haus B, Warschauer Pl. 18 (☎030 296 0800; www.dashausb.de). U1 or S3, 5-7, 9, or 75 to "Warschauer Str." East Berlin's most famous disco in the GDR era is a color-saturated haven for dancers, spinning techno, Top 40, and German *Schlager.* Cover W €3.50. F €5, Sa €6. Open W 10pm-5am, F-Sa 10pm-7am. Cash only.

Café Amsterdam, Gleimstr. 24 (☎030 448 07 92). S8, S41, S42, or S85 or U2 to "Schönhauser Allee." Romantic and quiet with gilt-framed paintings and sweet, creamy cocoa. Gay friendly. Free Wi-Fi. Food served M-Sa from 5:30pm. Breakfast buffet M-Sa from 8am, €5 per person. Open daily 8am-noon and 4pm-1am. Cash only.

Rose's, Oranienstr. 187 (☎030 615 65 70). U1 to "Görlitzer Bahnhof." Marked only by "Bar" over the door, a friendly, mixed gay and lesbian clientele packs this intense and claustrophobic party spot all night. The small menu covers all its bases with whiskey (€5) and Schnapps (€2). Open daily 11pm-6am, weekends 11pm-8am. Cash only.

Hafen, Motzstr. 19 (☎030 211 41 18; www.hafen-berlin.de). U1-U4 to "Nollendorfpl." Almost 20 years old, this spot is a gay cultural landmark. The mostly male clientele crowds the surrounding sidewalk in summer. "Weekly pub quiz" M at 10pm (1st M of the month in English). Drinks €2.50-7.50. Open daily 8am-4am. Cash only.

DAYTRIPS FROM BERLIN

KZ SACHSENHAUSEN. The small town of Oranienburg, just north of Berlin, was home to the Nazi concentration camp Sachsenhausen, where more than 100,000 Jews, communists, intellectuals, gypsies, and homosexuals were killed between 1936 and 1945. The **Gedenkstätte Sachsenhausen,** a memorial preserving the remains of the camp and recalling the imprisoned, was opened by the GDR in 1961. Some of the buildings have been preserved in their original forms, including sets of cramped barracks, the cell block where particularly "dangerous" prisoners were kept in solitary confinement and tortured daily, and a pathology department where Nazis performed medical experiments on inmates both dead and alive. However, only the foundations of **Station Z** (where prisoners were methodically exterminated) remain. A stone monolith commemorating the camp's victims stands sentinel over the wind-swept grounds. Barracks 38 and 39, the special "Jewish-only" barracks torched by neo-Nazis in 1992 and since reconstructed, feature displays on daily life in the camp during the Nazi period. The prison contains a museum housed in five original cells of the one remaining wing of the cell block. *(Str. der Nationen 22. S1 dir.: Oranienburg to the end 40min. Then either use the infrequent bus service on lines #804 and 821 to "Gedenkstätte," or take a 20min. walk from the station. Follow the signs from Stralsunder Str., turn right on Bernauer Str., left on Str. der Einheit, and right on Str. der Nationen. ☎030 301 20 00; www.gedenkstaette-sachsenhausen.de. Open daily Mar. 15-Oct. 14 8:30am-6pm; Oct. 15-Mar. 14 8:30am-4:30pm. Last entry 30min. before closing. Archive and library open Tu-F 9am-4:30pm. Visitor Information Service open M-F 8am-4:30pm. Museums closed M. Free. Audio guide €3.)*

NORTHERN GERMANY

Between the North Sea's western coast and the Baltic's eastern coast, the velvety plains are populated primarily by sheep and bales of hay. Farther south in

Lower Saxony, cities straddle rivers and sprawl through the countryside. Hamburg, notoriously rich and radical, trades in idyllic for exciting, while the small city of Hanover charms visitors with its gardens and flourishing culture.

LÜBECK ☎0451

Home to a notable college community, Lübeck (pop. 215,000) is easily one of areas most beautiful city. The city is a merchant of delicious *marzipan* and red-blond Dückstein beer, as well as a gateway to the Baltic. Between the station and the *Altstadt* stands the massive **Holstentor,** one of Lübeck's four 15th-century defensive gates and the city's symbol. (☎0451 122 41 29. Open daily Apr.-Dec. 10am-6pm; Jan.-Mar. Tu-Su 11am-5pm. €5, students and seniors €2, families €6.) The twin brick towers of the **Marienkirche,** a gigantic church housing the largest mechanical organ in the world, dominate the skyline. At the back of the church, two warped and splintered bronze bells lie on the church's shattered marble floor; the bells were dislodged by a 1942 British bomb raid. (☎0451 39 77 01 80. Open daily in summer 10am-6pm; in winter 10am-4pm. Suggested donation €1. Tours of church and tower June-Sept. W and Sa 3:15pm, Apr. and Oct. Sa only. €4, students €3.) The **Theaterfigurenmuseum,** Kolk 14, displays 1200 holdings from the world's largest private puppet collection. (☎0451 786 26; www.tfm-luebeck.com. Open daily Apr.-Sept. 10am-6pm; Oct. 10am-4pm; Nov.-Mar. 10am-3pm. €4, students €3, children €2.)

To reach **Rucksack Hotel ❷,** Kanalstr. 70, take bus #1, 11, 21, or 31 to "Katharineum," turn right at the church on Glockengießerstr, and continue until you reach the water. This popular hostel is a member of an eco-friendly shop collective housed within a former glass factory. (☎0451 70 68 92; www.rucksack-hotel-luebeck.de. Breakfast €3. Kitchen. Free Wi-Fi. Reception 10am-1pm and 5-9pm. 6- to 8-bed dorms €13; doubles €34, with bath €40; quads €60/68. Newly opened singles €35. Cash only.) Stop by the famous confectionery **I.G. Niederegger Marzipan Café ❷,** Breitestr. 89, for *marzipan*, a delicious treat made of almond paste, rosewater, and sugar. (☎0451 530 1126. Open M-F 9am-7pm, Sa 9am-6pm, Su 10am-6pm. AmEx/MC/V.) At vegetarian **Café Affenbrot ❷,** Kanalstr. 70, on the corner of Glockengießerstr., buy healthy indulgences for your *marzipan* (from €4.50-8.50) and surround yourself with students whose style is as unique as the decor. (☎0451 721 93; www.cafeaffenbrot.de. Open daily 9am-midnight; kitchen closes 11pm. Cash only.)

Trains run to Berlin (3½ hr., every hr., €40-57) and Hamburg (50min., every hr., €11-15.50). Lübeck's **tourist office,** Holstentorpl. 1, books rooms for no fee and sells the **Happy Day Card** (€6), which provides museum discounts and unlimited access to public transportation. The tourist office also leads German-language tours at 11am and 2pm for €6. (☎0451 88 22 33. Open June-Sept. M-F 9:30am-7pm, Sa 10am-3pm, Su 10am-2pm; Jan.-May and Oct.-Nov. M-F 9:30am-6pm, Sa 10am-3pm; Dec. M-F 9:30am-6pm, Sa 10am-3pm.) **Postal Code:** 23552.

HAMBURG ☎040

Germany's largest port city and the second largest city in Europe, Hamburg (pop. 1,800,000) radiates an inimitable recklessness. With a skyline punctuated by ancient church towers, modern skyscrapers, and masts of ships carrying millions of containers of cargo, Hamburg is a haven for artists, intellectuals, and revelers who live it up in Germany's self-declared capital of lust.

Hamburg

ACCOMMODATIONS
Jugendherberge auf dem Stintfang (HI), 2
Schanzenstern Altona, 3
Schanzenstern Übernachtungs- und Gasthaus, 5

FOOD
Oma's Apotheke, 4
La Sepia, 6
Unter den Linden, 9

NIGHTLIFE
Fabrik, 8
G-Bar, 7
Große Freiheit 36/ Kaiserkeller, 1

TRANSPORTATION

Trains: The **Hauptbahnhof** has connections every hour to: **Berlin** (1.5hr., €52); **Frankfurt** (5hr., €819); **Hanover** (1.5hr., €34); **Munich** (7hr., €108); **Copenhagen, DEN** (5hr., €72). DB Reisezentrum ticket office open M-F 5:30am-10pm, Sa-Su 7am-10pm; or purchase at ticket machines in the station anytime. The **Dammtor** train station is near the university; **Harburg** station is south of the Elbe; **Altona** station is to the west of the city's center; and **Bergedorf** is to the southeast.

Buses: The **ZOB** is on Steintorpl. across from the Hauptbahnhof, just past the Museum für Kunst und Gewerbe. Open M-Th and Su 5am-10pm, F-Sa 5am-midnight. **Autokraft** (☎40 280 8660) runs to **Berlin** (3hr., every 2hr. 7am-9pm, €25). **Touring Eurolines** (☎69 7903 501) runs to **Amsterdam, NTH** (8hr., M-Sa, €39); **London, UK** (daily, connecting in **Brussels,** €89); and **Paris, FRN** (11hr., daily, €69). Student discounts.

Public Transportation: HVV operates an efficient U-Bahn, S-Bahn, and bus network. One-way tickets within the downtown area €1.65; prices vary with distance and network. 1-day pass €5.10 (valid only after 9am); 3-day pass €15. Buy tickets at Automaten (machines), or consider buying a **Hamburg Card** (p. 412).

Bike Rental: Fahrradstation Dammtor/Rothebaum, Schlüterstr. 11 (☎41 46 82 77), rents bikes for just €3 per day. Open M-F 9am-6pm.

ORIENTATION AND PRACTICAL INFORMATION

Hamburg's city center sits between the **Elbe River** and two lakes: **Außenalster** and **Binnenalster.** The arc of the **Alsterfleet** canal, separating the *Altstadt* on the east from the *Neustadt* on the west, echoes the arch of the impressive system of parks and gardens just above it. Most major sights lie between the **St. Pauli Landungsbrücken** port area in the west and the *Hauptbahnhof* in the east. **Mönckebergstraße,** Hamburg's most famous shopping street, runs all the way to **Rathausmarkt,** the seat of the sumptuous town hall. North of downtown, the **university** dominates the **Dammtor** area, sustaining a community of students and intellectuals. To the west of the university, the **Schanzenviertel** hums with artists, squatters, and a sizeable Turkish population, similar to the atmosphere in Altona, still further west. At the south end of town, an entirely different atmosphere reigns in **St. Pauli,** where the raucous **Fischmarkt** (fish market) is surpassed only by the wilder **Reeperbahn,** home to Hamburg's best discos.

Tourist Office: The **St. Pauli Landungsbrücken** office (☎30 05 12 03) is between piers 4 and 5 (Open Oct.-Mar. daily 10am-5:30pm; Apr.-Sept. M, Su, and W 8am-6pm, Tu and Th-Sa 8am-7pm). Sells the **Hamburg Card,** which provides unlimited access to public transportation, reduced admission to museums, and discounts on restaurants, tickets, some hotels, and tours. 1-day card €8, 3-day €18, 5-day €33. The **Group Card** provides the same benefits for up to 5 people; 1-day €11.80, 3-day €29.80, 5-day €51.

Consulates: Canada, Ballindamm 35 (☎40 460 0270). S1 or 3 or U1 to Jungfernstieg; between Alstertor and Bergstr. Open M-F 9:30am-12:30pm. **Ireland,** Feldbrunnenstr. 43 (☎44 18 61 13). U1 to Hallerstr. Open M-F 9am-1pm. **New Zealand,** Domstr. 19, Zürich-Haus, block C, 3rd fl. (☎40 442 5550). U1 to Messberg. Open M-Th 9am-1pm and 2-5:30pm, F 9am-1pm and 2-4:30pm. **United Kingdom,** Harvestehuder Weg 8a (☎40 448 03 20). U1 to Hallerstr. Open M-Th 9am-4pm, F 9am-3pm. **US,** Alsterufer 27-28, 20354 Hamburg (☎40 4117 1422).

Currency Exchange: ReiseBank, on the 2nd fl. of the *Hauptbahnhof* near the Kirchenallee exit (☎40 32 34 83), has Western Union services, cashes traveler's checks, and exchanges currency. Open daily 7:30am-10pm. Watch out for steep hidden fees and consider trying one of the many exchange bureaus or banks downtown.

GLBT Resources: The neighborhood of St. Georg is the center of the gay community in the region. Pick up the free *Hinnerk* magazine and *Friends: The Gay Map* from **Cafe Gnosa** or from the tourist office. Organizations include **Hein und Fiete,** Pulverteich 21, which gives advice on health and entertainment in the area (☎40 24 03 33). Walk down Steindamm away from the *Hauptbahnhof,* turn right on Pulverteich; it's the building with the rainbow flag. Open M-F 4-9pm, Sa 4-7pm.

Internet: Internet Cafe, Adenauerallee 10 (☎28 00 38 98). €1.50 per hr. Open daily 10am-11:55pm. **Teletime,** Schulterblatt 39 (☎41 30 47 30). €0.50 per 15min. Open M-F 10am-10pm, Sa-Su 10am-7pm.

Post Office: At the Kirchenallee exit of the *Hauptbahnhof.* Open M-F 8am-6pm, Sa 8:30am-12:30pm. **Postal Code:** 20099.

ACCOMMODATIONS

Hamburg's dynamic **Schanzenviertel** area—filled with students, working-class Turks, and left-wing dissidents amid grafitti-splattered walls—houses two of the best backpacker hostels in the city. Small, relatively cheap *pensions* line **Steindamm** and the area around the *Hauptbahnhof*, where several safe hotels provide respite from the area's unsavory characters. **Lange Reihe** has equivalent lodging options in a cleaner neighborhood.

Schanzenstern Übernachtungs und Gasthaus, Bartelsstr. 12 (☎ 40 439 8441; www.schanzenstern.de). S21 or 31, or U3 to "Sternschanze." Bright, clean, and comfortable rooms. Breakfast €4-6. Reception 6:30am-2am. Free Internet between the reception area and the restaurant. Wheelchair-accessible. Laundry €4.50. Reserve ahead. Dorms €19; singles €37.50; doubles €53; triples €63; quads €77; quints €95. Cash only. ❷

Instant Sleep, Max-Brauer-Allee 277 (☎43 18 23 10; www.instantsleep.de). S21 or 31 or U3 to "Sternschanze." Helpful, bilingual staff, communal kitchen, and long-term stays. Lockers €5 deposit. Linens €3. Reception 8am-2am. Check-out 11am. Reserve ahead. Dorms €15.50; singles €30; doubles €44; triples €60. Cash only. ❷

Jugendherberge auf dem Stintfang (HI), Alfred-Wegener-Weg 5 (☎40 31 34 88, www.djh.de/jugendherbergen/hamburg-stintfang). S1, S3, or U3 to Landungsbrücke. Newly renovated. Breakfast and linens included. Reception 24hr. Check-out 10am. Lockout 2am-6:30am. Dorms €18.80-20.30, over 27 €3 extra per night. MC/V. ❷

FOOD

Seafood is common in the port city of Hamburg. In **Schanzenviertel,** avant-garde cafes and Turkish falafel and *döner* stands entice hungry passersby. **Schulterblatt, Susannenstraße,** and **Schanzenstraße** are packed with hip, unique cafes and restaurants, while cheaper establishments crowd the **university** area, especially along **Rentzelstraße, Grindelhof,** and **Grindelallee.** In **Altona,** the pedestrian zone approaching the train station is packed with food stands and produce shops.

La Sepia, Schulterblatt 36 (☎40 432 2484; www.lasepia.de). This Portuguese-Spanish restaurant serves delicious and reasonably-priced seafood. Lunch (11am-5pm) affords you a hearty €5 meal. Dinner €7.50-22. Open daily noon-3am. AmEx/MC/V. ❷

Unter den Linden, Juliusstr. 16 (☎40 43 81 40). Read complimentary German papers over *Milchkaffee* (coffee with foamed milk; €2.90-3.40), breakfast (€4.60-7.30). Salad or pasta (€3.70-6.90). Open daily 9:30am-1am. Cash only. ❷

Oma's Apotheke, Schanzenstr. 87 (☎40 43 66 20). Pub-like atmosphere popular with a mixed crowd. German, Italian, and American cuisine. Schnitzel €7.50. Hamburger with 1lb. fries €6.60. Open M-Th and Su 9am-1am, F-Sa 9am-2am. Cash only. ❷

WHAT'S THE PUNKT?

Germany has a well-earned reputation as one of the world's most environmentally friendly countries. Its system of charging *Pfand*, a monetary deposit on glass and plastic bottles—which applies not only at *Biergarten* but also in grocery stores and vending machines throughout the country—is only one manifestation of this heightened awareness.

In 1990, Germany instituted a system called *Der Grüne Punkt* (The Green Dot), which has become the most widely used recycling program in Europe. The system created incentives for manufacturers to use less packaging on all their materials. Essentially, retailers have to pay for a "Green Dot" on products: the more packaging, the higher the fee. The system has led to about one million tons less garbage being processed annually.

As of 2002, the German recycling initiative was expanded and deposits were added to many bottles sold in grocery and convenience stores. Don't just throw your bottle away when you've finished. Instead, do your part to help the environment (and your wallet) by returning your bottle to one of the big machines in the supermarket to get your euros back.

SIGHTS

ALTSTADT

RATHAUS. Built between 1886 and 1897, the town hall is one of *Altstadt's* most impressive buildings. The city and state governments both convene amid intricate mahogany carvings and spectacular chandeliers. In front, the **Rathausmarkt** hosts festivities ranging from demonstrations to medieval fairs. *(☎428 312 470. English-language tours every 2hrs. M-Th 10:15am-3:15pm, F 10:15am-1:15pm, Sa 10am-5pm, Su 10am-4pm. Building open daily 8am-6pm. Rooms accessible only through tours. €3, €2 with Hamburg Card.)*

GROßE MICHAELSKIRCHE. The 18th-century Michaelskirche, named after the archangel Michael, is arguably the best-recognized symbol of Hamburg. The church, battered repeatedly by lightning, fire, and allied bombs, was fully restored in 1996. A panoramic view of Hamburg awaits those who climb the 462 stairs of the spire (and those who opt for the elevator). There is daily organ music Apr.-Aug. at noon. *(U-Bahn to Baumwall, S-Bahn to Stadthausbrücke. ☎37 67 81 00. Church open daily May-Oct. 9am-8pm; Nov.-Apr. 10am-5pm. Crypt open June-Oct. daily 11am-4:30pm; Nov.-May Sa-Su 11am-4:30pm. Church suggested donation €2. Crypt and tower €2.50.)*

MÖNCKEBERGSTRAßE. Two spires punctuate Hamburg's glossiest shopping zone, which stretches from the *Rathaus* to the *Hauptbahnhof*. Closest to the Rathaus is **St. Petrikirche,** the oldest church in Hamburg, which also has the highest climbable tower, first dated back to 1195. *(☎40 325 7400. www.samlt-petri.de. Open M-Sa 10am-6:30pm, Su 9am-9pm. Tower €2, under 15 €1, under 10 free. Frequent free concerts.)* The other, **St. Jakobikirche,** is known for its 17th-century *arpschnittger* organ with almost 1000 pipes. *(☎40 303 7370. Open M-Sa 10am-5pm.)*

BEYOND THE ALTSTADT

PLANTEN UN BLOMEN. This huge expanse of manicured flower beds and trees includes the largest Japanese garden in Europe, complete with a teahouse built in Japan. *(S21 or 31 to Dammitor. www.plantenunblomen.hamburg.de. Open May-Sept. daily 7am-11pm, Oct.-Apr. 7am-8pm. Free.)* In summer, performers in the outdoor **Musikpavillon** range from Irish step-dancers to Hamburg's police choir. *(May-Sept. most performances 3pm. See garden website for performance listings)* At night, opt for the **Wasserlichtkonzerte,** a choreographed play of fountains and underwater lights set to music. *(Daily May-Aug. 10pm, Sept. 9pm.)*

KZ NEUENGAMME. An idyllic agricultural village east of Hamburg provided the backdrop for the Neuengamme concentration camp, where Nazis killed 55,000 prisoners through slave labor and imprisoned twice as many. Paths begin at the **Haus des Gedenkens,** a memorial house inscribed with the names and death dates of the victims, and winds through the camp's brick-making factory, barracks, and other memorials. *(Jean-Doldier-Weg 39. S21 to Bergedorf, then bus #227 or 327. About 1hr from city. Buses run from Bergedorf M-Sa 2-3 per hr., Su 1 per hr. ☎428 131 500; www.kz-gedenkstaette-neuengamme.de. Museum and memorial open Apr.-Sept. M-F 9:30am-4pm, Sa-Su noon-7pm; Oct.-Mar. M-F 9:30am-4pm, Sa-Su noon-5pm. Path open 24hr. Tours Su noon and 2pm.)*

GEDENKSTÄTTE BULLENHUSER DAMM UND ROSENGARTE. This schoolhouse is a memorial to 20 Jewish children who were subjected to extensive medical experimentation while in Auschwitz, then murdered by the SS in an attempt to destroy evidence hours before Allied troops arrived. Visitors are invited to plant a rose in the garden behind the school, where a row of memorial plaques line the fence. *(Bullenhuser Damm 92. S21 to Rothenburgsort. Follow the signs to Bullenhuser Damm along Ausschläger Bildeich, over the bridge. At the intersection with Grossmannstr, the garden is on the far left; the school is 200m farther. ☎428 131 0, www.kz-gedenkstaette-neuengamme.de. Exhibit open Th 2-8pm, Su 10am-5pm. Rose garden open 24hr. Free.)*

MUSEUMS

The **Hamburg Card** provides free or discounted access to nearly all museums. *Museumswelt Hamburg,* a free newspaper available at tourist offices, lists exhibits and events. Most museums are closed on Mondays and open 10am-6pm the rest of the week, and until 9pm on Thursdays.

HAMBURGER KUNSTHALLE. It would take days to fully appreciate every work in this sprawling fine arts museum. The oldest building presents the Old Masters and extensive special exhibits. In the connected four-level **Galerie der Gegenward,** contemporary art takes a stand in a mix of temporary and permanent exhibits. *(Glockengieberwall 1. Turn right from Spitalerstr. City exit to the Hauptbahnahof and cross the street. ☎428 131 200; www.hamburger.kunsthalle.de. Open Tu-W and F-Su 10am-6pm, Th 10am-9pm. €8.50, students €5, families €14.)*

DEICHTORHALLEN HAMBURG. Hamburg's contemporary art scene thrives inside these two airplane hangar-sized fruit markets. Inside you'll find painting and photography installations, as well as video displays. Exhibits rotate seasonally. *(Deichtorstr. 1-2. U1 to Steinstr. Follow signs from the U-Bahn. ☎32 10 20; www.deichtorhallen.de. Open Tu-Su 11am-6pm. Each building €7, students €5, families €9.50. Combo ticket to both halls €12/8/16.50. Under 18 free.)*

ENTERTAINMENT AND NIGHTLIFE

The **Staatsoper,** Große Theaterstr. 36, houses one of the premier **opera** companies in Germany; the associated John Neumeier **ballet** company is one of the nation's best. (U2 to Gänsemarkt. ☎40 35 68 68. Open M-Sa 10am-6:30pm and 90min. before performances.) **Orchestras** all perform at the **Musikhalle** on Johannes-Brahms-Pl. (U2 to Gänsemarkt. ☎40 34 69 20; www.musikhalle-hamburg.de. Box office open M-F 10am-4pm.)

Hamburg's unrestrained nightlife scene heats up in the **Schanzenviertel** and **St. Pauli** areas. The infamous **Reeperbahn** runs through the heart of St. Pauli; lined with sex shops, strip joints, and peep shows, it's also home to the city's best bars and clubs. Though the Reeperbahn is generally safe, it is unwise to stray alone into less crowded sidestreets. Parallel to the Reeperbahn lies **HerbertstraBe,** Hamburg's official prostitution strip, where licensed sex entrepreneurs flaunt their flesh (only over the age of 18 allowed.) Students head north to the streets of the **Schanzenviertel** and west to Altona, where cafes and trendy bars create an atmosphere more leftist than lustful. The **St. Georg** district, near Berliner Tor and along Lange Reihe, is the center of Hamburg's **gay scene.** In general, clubs open and close.

GroBe Freiheit 36/Kaiserkeller, GroBe Freiheit 36 (☎40 317 7780). Big names have performed upstairs, home to popular concerts and hip club music orchestrated by DJs. **Kaiserkeller,** downstairs, caters to the rock contingent. F-Sa club nights. Cover €5-6. Concerts 7-8pm, 10pm-5am. Frequent free entry until 11pm.

Fabrik, Barnerstr. 36 (☎40 39 10 70; www.fabrik.de). From Altona station, head toward Offenser Hauptstr. and go right on Bahrenfelderstr. Cranks out raging beats of an eclectic mix of names in music. Every 2nd Sa of the month, "Gay Factory" attracts a mixed crowd. Live DJ 10pm most Sa; cover €7-8. Cover for live music €18-30. Cash only.

Meanie Bar/Molotow, Spielbudenpl. 5 (☎40 31 08 45; www.molotowclub.com), parallel to the Reeperbahn. **Meanie Bar,** upstairs, has a more relaxed atmosphere. Open daily from 9pm. No cover. The **Molotow,** in the basement of the retro Meanie Bar, keeps it hip with fashionable crowds, live bands. Molotow cover for club nights and live bands €8-15. Open from 8pm for concerts, and from 11pm F-Sa for disco. Cash only.

HANOVER (HANNOVER) ☎0511

Despite its relatively small size, Hanover (pop. 523,000), is a major center in northern Germany known for hosting Oktoberfest Hannover, the second largest Oktoberfest in the world. Highlights are the three bountiful **Herrenhausen gardens.** The largest, **Großer Garten,** is one of Europe's most beautiful Baroque gardens, featuring geometric shrubbery and the **Große Fontäne,** one of Europe's highest-shooting fountains. It is also host to an annual international fireworks competition. To get there from the train station, walk to the far end of the lower shop level and take the U4 or 5 to Herrenhauser Garten. (Fountain spurts Apr.-Oct. M-F 11am-noon and 3-5pm, Sa-Su 11am-noon and 2-5pm. Garden open daily Apr. 9am-7pm; May-Aug. 9am-8pm; Sept. 9am-7pm; early Oct. 9am-6pm. Entrance €4, including admission to *Berggarten.* Concerts and performances June-Aug.; ☎0511 1684 1222 for schedule.) On the outskirts of the *Altstadt* is the **Neues Rathaus,** the impressive town hall built between 1901 and 1913. (Open May-Sept. M-F 9am-6pm, Sa-Su 10am-6pm. Free. Elevator M-F 9:30am-6pm, Sa-Su 10am-6pm. €2.50, students €2.) First-rate contemporary art museum, the **Sprengel Museum,** Kurt-Schwitters-Pl., hosts work from some of the 20th century's greatest artists. (Open Tu 10am-8pm, W-Su 10am-6pm. €7, students €4.) North of Friederikenplatz, is the **Sculpture Mile,** a 1.5km stretch of sculpture and art exhibits.

Hotel Flora ❶, Heinrichstr. 36, is in the center of town 10min. from the station. Take the back exit and continue straight ahead onto Berliner Allee, cross the street, then turn left on Heinrichstr, a quiet street close to the *Hauptbahnhof.* Rooms come with carpeting, framed Monet prints, and TVs. (☎0511 38 3910; www.hotel-flora-hannover.de. Breakfast included. Reception 8am-8pm. Singles €33-49, doubles €59-75, triples €72-96. Dogs €7.50. AmEx/MC/V.) **Jugendherberge Hannover (HI) ❶,** Ferdinand-Wilhelm-Fricke-Weg 1. Take the U3 or 7 to Fischerhof. From the stop, backtrack 10m, turn right, and cross the tracks; continue until the next stoplight at Lodemannweg, then turn right and follow the path as it curves and cross Stammestr. Turn right after going over the red footbridge. Balconies in the sun-filled rooms overlook a park. (☎0511 131 7674. Breakfast included. Internet €0.10 per min. Wheelchair-accessible. Reception 7:30am-1am. After 1am, doors open on the hr. Check-out 9am. Dorms €19.70-35.30. €3 discount under 27. MC/V.) Students fill the chic garden/bar at **The Loft,** Georg-str. 50a, off the main shopping road. (☎0511 363 1376. Happy hour M-Th, Su 9-10pm, F-Sa 8-9pm and midnight-1am. Open W-Sa from 8pm. Cash only.)

Trains leave at least every hour for: Berlin (2hr., €45-56); Frankfurt (3hr., €75); Hamburg (1hr., €38); Munich (4hr., €110); Amsterdam, NTH (4-5hr., €60-80). The **tourist office,** Ernst-August-Pl. 8, is in the Spardabank building across the street from the train station. (☎0511 1234 5111. Open Oct.-Mar. M-F 9am-7pm, Sa 9am-2pm; Apr.-Sept. also Su 9am-2pm.) The office leads **bus tours** of the city (2hr.; 1:30pm; €15) and sells the **Hannover Card** (1-day €9; 3-day €15; group ticket for up to 5 people €17/29), which covers transportation costs and reduces museum and sightseeing tour prices throughout the city. **Postal Code:** 30159.

CENTRAL AND WESTERN GERMANY

Niedersachsen (Lower Saxony), which stretches from the North Sea to the hills of central Germany, comprises agricultural plains and foggy marshland. Just south, North Rhine-Westphalia—the most economically powerful area in Germany—is so densely populated that it's nearly impossible to travel through the countryside without glimpsing the next hamlet, metropolis, or village ahead.

DÜSSELDORF ☎0211

Düsseldorf (pop. 582,000), the nation's *"Hautstadt"*—a pun on the German *"Hauptstadt"* (capital) and the French *"haute"*—is a stately metropolis with an *Altstadt* (Old Town) that features stellar nightlife and upscale shopping. In addition to glitz and glamour, Düsseldorf has an internationally recognized art school and top-notch museums that allure any creative mind.

TRANSPORTATION AND PRACTICAL INFORMATION. Trains run frequently to: Amsterdam, NTH (2hr., 1 per 2hr., €32-42); Berlin (4hr., 1-2 per hr., €100); Frankfurt (2hr., 4 per hr., €70); Hamburg (4hr., 4 per hr., €80); Munich (5-6hr., 3-4 per hr., €100-122). Düsseldorf's **S-Bahn** is well-integrated into the regional **VRR** *(Verkehrsverbund Rhein-Ruhr)* system, which links most nearby cities and is the cheapest way to travel between Aachen and Cologne. On the **public transportation system,** single tickets cost €1.10-2.10. *Tagestickets* (€5-21.20) allow up to five people to travel for 24hr. on any line. To reach the **tourist office,** Immermannstr. 65, head out of the train station and to the right; look for the Immermannhof building. It books rooms for free, except during trade fairs. (☎0211 172 0228. Open M-F 9:30am-1pm and 1:30-5:30pm, Sa 10am-1pm.) The **post office** is on Konrad-Adenauer-Pl. to the right of the tourist office. (Open M-F 8am-6pm, Sa 9am-2pm.) **Postal Code:** 40210.

ACCOMMODATIONS AND FOOD. Düsseldorf's hotels and hostels often double their prices during trade fairs, which take place from August to April. Clean, filled with friendly staff and patrons, and close to the center of town is **Backpackers Düsseldorf** ❷, Fürstenwall 180. Take bus #725 (dir.: Hafen/Lausward) from the station, and get off at Corneliusstr. (☎0211 302 0848; www.backpackers-duesseldorf.de. Kitchen available. Breakfast, lockers with mandatory deposit, linens, and towel included. Free Internet and Wi-Fi. Reception 8am-9pm. Reserve ahead F-Sa in summer. Dorms €22. MC/V.) The modern **Jugendgästehaus Düsseldorf (HI)** ❷, Düsseldorfer Str. 1, is conveniently located just over the Rheinkniebrücke from the *Altstadt.* Take U70 or 74-77 to

Luegpl., then walk 500m down Kaiser-Wilhelm-Ring. Or, get off at Belsenpl., and take bus #835 or 836 to the Jugendherberge stop. (☎0211 55 73 10; www.duesseldorf-jugendherberge.de. Breakfast and linen included. Reception 6am-1am. Curfew 1am. Dorms €24.80; singles €42; doubles €62; quads €93. €3.10 HI discount. Cash only.) The *Altstadt's* numerous options for cheap eats can't be beat; rows upon rows of pizzerias, Chinese diners, and Döner, waffle, and crepe stands reach from Heinrich-Heine-Allee to the banks of the Rhine. The local outlet of the Czech brewery **Pilsner Urquell ❷**, Grabenstr. 6, specializes in Eastern-European fare. (☎0211 868 1411. Entrees €5-15. Beer €2.50-4.10. Open M-Sa 11:30-1pm, Su 4pm-midnight. MC/V.)

SIGHTS. **Königsallee** ("the Kö"), just outside the *Altstadt*, embodies the vitality of wealthy Düsseldorf. The river running through it is serene and provides a lovely backdrop for the outdoor cafes. To reach the Kö from the train station, walk 10min. down Graf-Adolf-Str. Midway up the street is the upscale, marble-and-copper **Kö-Galerie.** Better deals in non-designer stores can be found along Flingerstr. in the *Altstadt.* To get to the Baroque **Schloß Benrath,** Benrather Schloßallee 104, in the suburbs of Düsseldorf, take tram #701. The Schloß's strategically placed mirrors and false exterior windows make the castle appear larger than it is. (☎0211 899 3832; www.schloss-benrath.de. Open Tu-Su mid-Apr. to Oct. 10am-6pm; Nov. to mid-Apr. 11am-5pm. Tours 1 per hr. €7, students €4.) At the upper end of the Kö is the beautiful **Hofgarten,** the oldest public park in Germany. To its west, the **K20 Kunstsammlung Nordrhein-Westfalen,** Grabbepl. 5, has various works by Expressionists, Surrealists, and former Düsseldorf resident Paul Klee. (U70 or 75-79 to Heinrich-Heine-Allee, and walk two blocks north. ☎838 1130; www.kunstsammlung.de. Open Tu-F 10am-6pm, Sa-Su 11am-6pm. Closed until fall 2009. €6.50, students €4.50.)

NIGHTLIFE. Rumor has it that Düsseldorf's 500 pubs make up the longest bar in the world. By nightfall, it's nearly impossible to see where one pub ends and the next begins in the crowded *Altstadt.* The newsletter *Prinz* (€3) gives tips on the entertainment scene; some youth hostels give it out for free. **Mad Wallstreet,** Kurzestr. 6, an economist's vision of heaven, is a play on the market economy, listing values on flatscreens to show fluctuating drink prices every 300 seconds throughout the night. The law of drunken supply and demand means prices of popular drinks soar as others plummet. (www.madwallstreet.de. Beer €0.90, shooters €1.90, mixed drinks €2.90. Open W-Sa 10pm-5am. Cash only.) **Zur Uel,** Ratinger Str. 16, is a restaurant by day and a rowdy German pub by night. (☎0211 32 53 69. Beer €2-3. M-Sa 9am-4am, Su 10am-1am. Food service M-Sa until 3pm, Su until 4pm.) **Stahlwerk,** Ronsdorfer Str. 134, located on the corner of Lierenfeldstr., is a classic 2 floor factory-turned-disco that packs in 1500 or more. Dress to impress and don't plan to leave before the city starts to wake up; most parties don't end until 7am. Take the U75 to "Ronsdorfer Str."(☎0211 73 03 50; www.stahlwerk.de. Cover €4-6. Open F-Sa and the last Su of the month from 11pm. Cash only.) **GLBT nightlife** clusters along Bismarckstr., at the intersection with Charlottenstr. *Facolte* (€2), a gay and lesbian nightlife magazine, is available at most newsstands in the city.

AACHEN ☎0241

Easygoing Aachen (pop. 259,000), Germany's westernmost city, was once "Roma secunda," the 8th-century capital of Charlemagne's enormous Gaulic empire. For a glimpse of Aachen's former splendor, visit the three-tiered dome, octagonal interior, and blue-gold mosaics of the **Dom** in the city center. Charlemagne's remains are housed in the ornate reliquary behind the altar.

(Open M-F 11am-7pm, Sa and Su 1-7pm, except during services. Services M-F 7am, 10am; Sa-Su 7, 8, and 10am; Su also 11:30am. Guided tours Sa and Su 2pm.) Aachen's earliest settlers were scared off by the natural springs that run through the area, believing that they came from hell. The Romans were indifferent to satanic connections and constructed the city's first **mineral baths.** These baths are now the luxurious **Carolus Thermen,** Passstr. 79. Take bus #51 from the Normaluhr stop on Theaterst. to Carolus Thermen. (☎0241 18 27 40; www.carolus-thermen.de. 2½hr. soak €10, with sauna €20; day-long soak €14.50, with sauna €29. Open daily 9am-11pm. Cash only.)

Located outside of the city center, **Hotel Cortis ❸,** Krefelderstr. 52, is a small B&B with cable TV in each room. Take bus #34 (dir.: Kohlscheid Banhof) from the Normaluhr stop to Carolus Thermen, then take bus #51 to Rolandstr. Turn left on Krefelderstr. (☎0241 997 4110; www.hotel-cortis.de. Breakfast included. Singles €28, with shower and bath €35; doubles €50, with bath €61. MC/V.) **Euroregionales Jugendgästehaus (HI) ❷,** Maria-Theresia-Allee 260, has spacious, bright rooms about a 10min. bus ride from the city center. Take bus #2 (dir.: Preusswald) from the Misereor stop to Ronheide. (☎0241 71 10 10; aachen.jugendherberge.de. Breakfast included. Curfew 1am. Dorms €23.20; singles €37; doubles €57.40. €3.10 HI discount. MC/V.) Centrally-located, **Tijuana ❸,** Markt 45-47, is a Mexican restaurant with a huge cocktail bar haunt for the young and trendy. (☎0241 234 9200. Entrees €6-14. Open M-Th and Su noon-1am, F-Sa noon-2am. Cash only.) The **pedestrian zone** and **Pontstraße,** off Marktpl., have a number of restaurants that are easy on the wallet.

Trains go to Brussels, BEL (2hr., 1 per hr., €25-30), Cologne (1hr., 2 per hr., €13-19), and Paris, FRA (3hr., 6-7 per day, €126). The **tourist office** is located at Friedrich-Wilhelm-Pl. in the Atrium Elisenbrunnen. From the station, head up Bahnhofstr., turn left onto Theaterstr., which becomes Theaterpl., and then turn right onto Kapuzinergraben, which becomes Friedrich-Wilhelm-Pl. (☎0241 180 2960. Open M-F 9am-6pm, Sa 9am-2pm, Su 10am-2pm; Closed Su Christmas-Easter.) **Postal Code:** 52062.

COLOGNE (KÖLN) ☎0221

Although 90% of historic Cologne (pop. 991,000) crumbled to the ground during WWII, the magnificent Gothic *Dom* amazingly survived 14 bombings and remains one of Germany's main attractions. Today, the city is the largest in North Rhine-Westphalia, offering first-rate museums, theaters, and nightlife.

TRANSPORTATION

Flights: Planes depart from **Köln-Bonn Flughafen (CGN).** Flight info ☎022 03 40 40 01 02; www.koeln-bonn-airport.de. Airport shuttle S13 leaves the train station M-F, 3-6 per hr.; Sa-Su, 2 per hr. Shuttle to Berlin, 24 per day, 6:30am-8:30pm.

Trains: Cologne's **Hauptbanhof** has trains that leave for **Berlin** (4-5hr., 1-2 per hr., €86-104); **Düsseldorf** (30min.-1hr., 5-7per hr., €10-18); **Frankfurt** (1-2hr., 2-3 per hr., €34-63); **Hamburg** (4hr., 2-3 per hr., €74-86); **Munich** (4-5hr., 2-3 per hr., €91-124); **Amsterdam, NTH** (2-3hr., 1-3 per hr., €40-56); **Paris, FRA** (4hr., 3 per hr., €87-120).

Public Transportation: KVB offices have free **maps** of the S- and U-Bahn, bus, and streetcar lines; branch downstairs in the *Hauptbahnhof.* Major terminals include the **Hauptbahnhof, Neumarkt,** and **Appellhofplatz.** Single-ride tickets from €1.50, depending on distance. Day pass from €5.20. The Minigruppen-Ticket (from €5.60) allows up to 4 people to ride M-F 9am-midnight and all day Sa-Su. Week tickets from €13.70. The

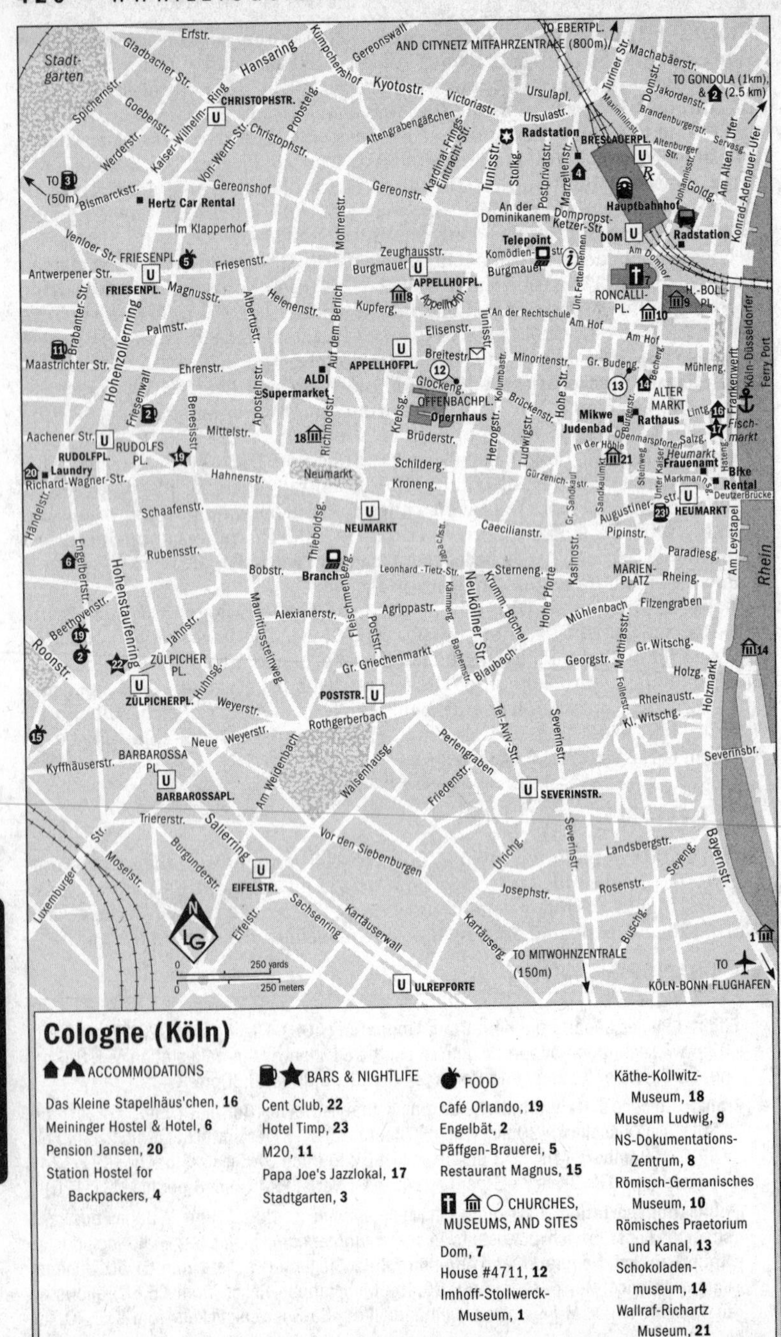

Cologne (Köln)
ACCOMMODATIONS
Das Kleine Stapelhäus'chen, 16
Meininger Hostel & Hotel, 6
Pension Jansen, 20
Station Hostel for Backpackers, 4
BARS & NIGHTLIFE
Cent Club, 22
Hotel Timp, 23
M20, 11
Papa Joe's Jazzlokal, 17
Stadtgarten, 3
FOOD
Café Orlando, 19
Engelbät, 2
Päffgen-Brauerei, 5
Restaurant Magnus, 15
CHURCHES, MUSEUMS, AND SITES
Dom, 7
House #4711, 12
Imhoff-Stollwerck-Museum, 1
Käthe-Kollwitz-Museum, 18
Museum Ludwig, 9
NS-Dokumentations-Zentrum, 8
Römisch-Germanisches Museum, 10
Römisches Praetorium und Kanal, 13
Schokoladen-museum, 14
Wallraf-Richartz Museum, 21
TO EBERTPL. AND CITYNETZ MITFAHRZENTRALE (800m)
TO GONDOLA (1km), & 2 (2.5 km)
TO 3 (50m)
Stadtgarten
Hertz Car Rental
Radstation
Hauptbahnhof
Telepoint
CHRISTOPHSTR.
BRESLAUERPL.
DOM
FRIESENPL.
APPELLHOFPL.
RUDOLFPL.
RUDOLFS PL.
Laundry
ALDI Supermarket
OFFENBACHPL.
Opernhaus
Neumarkt
NEUMARKT
Branch
ALTER MARKT
Rathaus
Mikwe Judenbad
Frauenamt
Bike Rental
HEUMARKT
MARIEN-PLATZ
ZÜLPICHER PL.
ZÜLPICHERPL.
POSTSTR.
BARBAROSSA PL.
BARBAROSSAPL.
SEVERINSTR.
EIFELSTR.
ULREPFORTE
Rhein
Ferry Port
Köln-Düsseldorfer
TO MITWOHNZENTRALE (150m)
TO KÖLN-BONN FLUGHAFEN
250 yards
250 meters
Hansaring
Kyotostr.
Hohenzollernring
Hohenstaufenring
Salierring
Sachsenring
Kartäuserwall
Neuköllner Str.
Tunisstr.
Severinstr.
Vor den Siebenburgen
Rothgerberbach
Blaubach
Mühlenbach
Caecilianstr.
Hahnenstr.
Ehrenstr.
Mittelstr.
Schildergasse
Gereonstr.
Venloer Str.
Aachener Str.
Richard-Wagner-Str.
Konrad-Adenauer-Ufer
Deutzer Brücke
Severinsbr.

WelcomeCard allows visitors to use all forms of public transportation in Cologne and Bonn (1-day €9, 2-day €14, 3-day €19).

Bike Rental: Kölner Fahrradverleih, Markmannsg. (☎0171 629 87 96), in the *Altstadt.* €2 per hr., €10 per day, €40 per wk.; €25 deposit. Open daily 10am-6pm.

ORIENTATION AND PRACTICAL INFORMATION

Cologne extends across the Rhine, but the city center and nearly all sights are located on the western side. The *Altstadt* splits into **Altstadt-Nord,** near the **Hauptbahnhof,** and **Altstadt-Süd,** just south of the **Severinsbrücke** bridge.

Tourist Office: KölnTourismus, Unter Fettenhennen 19 (☎0221 22 13 04 10; www.koelntourismus.de), across from the main entrance to the *Dom,* books rooms for a €3 fee and sells the **Welcome Card** (€9), which provides a day's worth of free public transportation and museum discounts. Open daily M-F 9am-10pm, Sa and Su 10am-5pm.

Post Office: At the corner of Breitestr. and Tunisstr. in the WDR-Arkaden shopping gallery. Open M-F 9am-7pm, Sa 9am-2pm. **Postal Code:** 50667.

ACCOMMODATIONS AND CAMPING

Conventions held in Cologne fill hotels in spring and fall, and the city's hostels often sell out during these times. If you're staying over a weekend in summer, reserve at least two weeks ahead.

Station Hostel for Backpackers, Marzellenstr. 44-56 (☎0221 912 5301; www.hostel-cologne.de). Large dorms without bunks and an ideal location attract crowds of backpackers. Breakfast price varies. Free Wi-Fi. Reception 24hr. 4- to 6-bed dorms €17-21; singles €30-37; doubles €45-52; triples €72. Cash only. ❷

Meininger City Hostel & Hotel, Engelbertst. 33-35 (☎0221 355 332 014; www.meininger-hostels.de). U1, 7, 12, 15, 16, or 18 to Rudolfpl., then turn left on Habsburgerst., right on Lindenst., and left on Engelbertst. Breakfast included. Reception 24hr. Free Wi-Fi, lockers, towels, and linen. Dorms €17-22; small dorms €20-24; multi-bed room (4-6) €24-32; twins €34-44; singles €43-56; triples €28-36. Cash only. ❷

Pension Jansen, Richard-Wagner-Str. 18 (☎0221 25 18 75; www.pensionjansen.de). U1, 6, 7, 15, 17, or 19 to Rudolfpl. Family-run with high-ceilinged rooms and colorful walls and decor. Breakfast included. Singles €45-80; doubles €65-90. Cash only. ❸

Das Kleine Stapelhäus'chen, Fischmarkt 1-3 (☎0221 272 7777; www.koeln-altstadt.de/stapelhaeuschen). From the Rathaus, cross the Altenmarkt and take Lintg. to the Fischmarkt. An old-fashioned, richly decorated inn overlooking the Rhine. Breakfast included. Singles €39-52, with bath €52-82; doubles €64-74/90-121. MC/V. ❹

FOOD

Cheap restaurants converge on **Zülpicherstraße** to the southeast and **Eigelstein** and **Weidengasse** in the Turkish district. Ethnic restaurants line the perimeter of the *Altstadt,* particularly from **Hohenzollernring** to **Hohenstaufenring.** German eateries surround **Domplatz.** An **open-air market** on Wilhelmspl. fills the Nippes neighborhood. (Open M-Sa 8am-1pm.)

Päffgen-Brauerei, Friesenstr. 64. Take U3-5, 12, 16, or 18 to Friesenpl. A local favorite since 1883. *Kölsch* (€1.40) is brewed on the premises, consumed in the 600-seat beer garden, and refilled until you put your coaster on top of your glass. Entrees €7-15. Open daily 10am-midnight. Sa and Su until 12:30am. Cash only. ❸

Café Orlando, Engelbertstr. 7 (☎0221 23 75 23; www.cafeorlando.de). U8 or 9 to "Zülpicher Pl." Free Wi-Fi and an assortment of newspapers create a Sunday morning atmosphere at this student popular cafe. Complete breakfasts (€3.10-6), omelettes, and salads (€5.50-8), and drinks (€3.50-4.80). Open daily 9am-11pm. Cash only. ❷

Restaurant Magnus, Zülpicherstr. 48 (☎0221 24 14 69). Take U8, 9, 12, 15, 16, or 18 to Zülpicher Pl. Locals steadily flock to this crowded cafe for funky tunes, artfully prepared meals (mostly Italian) from €4, and many delicious vegetarian options (€5-8). Open daily 8pm-3am. Cash only. ❷

Engelbät, Engelbertst. 7. (☎0221 24 69 14). U8 or 9 to Zülpicher Pl. The best place for plentiful crepes, vegetarian and otherwise (€5-8). Breakfast (€1.50-3.50) served daily until 3pm. Open daily 11am-midnight. Cash only. ❶

SIGHTS

DOM. Germany's greatest cathedral, the *Dom,* is a perfect realization of High Gothic style. Built over the course of six centuries, it was finally finished in 1880 and miraculously escaped destruction during WWII. A chapel on the inside right houses a 15th-century **triptych** depicting the city's five patron saints. Behind the altar in the center of the choir is the **Shrine of the Magi,** the cathedral's most sacred compartment, which allegedly holds the remains of the Three Kings and was once a pilgrimage site for monarchs. Before exiting the choir, stop in the **Chapel of the Cross** to admire the 10th-century **Gero crucifix,** which is the oldest intact sculpture of a crucified Christ. It takes about 15min. to scale the 509 steps of the **Südturm** (south tower); catch your breath at the **Glockenstube,** a chamber with the tower's nine bells, three-quarters of the way up. *(Cathedral open daily 6am-7:30pm. 45min. English-language tours M-Sa 10:30am and 2:30pm, Su 2:30pm. Tower open daily May-Sept. 9am-6pm; Nov.-Feb. 9am-4pm; Mar.-Apr. and Oct. 9am-5pm. Cathedral free. Tour €6, children €4. Tower €3.50, students €1.)*

MUSEUMS

Gourmands will want to head straight for the **Schokoladenmuseum,** which is best described as Willy Wonka's factory come to life. It presents every step of chocolate production, from the rainforests to the gold fountain that spurts streams of free samples. *(Rheinauhafen 1A, near the Severinsbrücke. ☎0221 931 8880; www.schokoladenmuseum.de. From the train station, head for the Rhine, and walk to the right along the river; go under the Deutzer Brücke, and take the 1st footbridge. Open Tu-Sa 10am-6pm, Su 11am-7pm. €6.50, students €4.)* Masterpieces from the Middle Ages to the Post-Impressionist period are gathered in the **Wallraf-Richartz Museum.** *(Martinstr. 39. From the Heumarkt, take Gürzenichtstr. 1 block to Martinstr. ☎0221 276 94; www.museenkoeln.de/wrm. Open Tu-W and F 10am-6pm, Th 10am-10pm, Sa-Su 11am-6pm. €7.50, students €5.)* The collection of the **Museum Ludwig** focuses on 20th-century and contemporary art. *(Bischofsgartenstr. 1, behind the Römisch-Germanisches Museum. ☎0221 22 12 61 65. Open Tu-Su 10am-6pm, 1st F of each month 10am-10pm. €9, students €6.)* The chilling **NS-Dokumentations-Zentrum,** Appellhofpl. 23-25, includes a former Gestapo prison with inmates' wall graffiti intact. *(☎0221 22 12 63 32. U3-6 or 19 to Appelhofpl. Open Tu-W and F 10am-4 pm, Th 10am-6pm. €3.60, students €1.50.)*

ENTERTAINMENT AND NIGHTLIFE

Cologne explodes in celebration during **Karneval** (late Jan. to early Feb.), a week-long pre-Lenten festival made up of 50 neighborhood processions. **Weiberfastnacht** (late Jan.) is the first major to-do: the mayor mounts the platform at Alter Markt and surrenders leadership to the city's women, who then hunt down their husbands at work and chop off their ties. The weekend builds to the out-of-control parade on **Rosenmontag** (Rose Monday; early Feb.), when thousands of merry participants sing and dance their way through the city center while exchanging *Bützchen* (kisses on the cheek). While most revelers nurse their hangovers on **Shrove Tuesday,** pubs and restaurants set fire to the straw scarecrows hanging out their windows.

Roman mosaics dating back to the 3rd century record the wild excesses of the city's early residents. The monthly *Kölner* (€1), sold at newsstands, lists clubs, parties, and concerts. The closer to the Rhine or *Dom* you venture, the faster your wallet will empty. After dark in **Hohenzollernring,** crowds of people move from theaters to clubs and finally to cafes in the early morning. The area around **Zülpicherpl.** is a favorite of students and the best option for an affordable good time. Radiating westward from Friesenpl., the **Belgisches Viertel** (Belgian Quarter) has slightly more expensive bars and cafes.

Papa Joe's Jazzlokal, Buttermarkt 37 (☎0221 257 7931). Papa Joe has a legendary reputation for providing good jazz and good times. *Kölsch* (€3.60) in 0.4L glasses. Live jazz M-Sa 10:30pm-12:30am. Su "4 o'clock Jazz"–8hours of, nonstop jazz from two bands starting at 3:30pm (not June-Sept.). Open daily 8pm-3am. Cash only.

Cent Club, Hohenstaufenring 25-27 (www.centclub.de). Near Zülpicher Pl. Take U8 or 9 to Zülpicher. This student disco features more dance (to R&B, pop, dance classics) and less talk, with the appeal of low-priced drinks. Shots €0.50. Beer €1-2. Mixed drinks from €3. Cover W-Sa €5. Open W-Sa 9pm-3am.

Hotel Timp, Heumarkt 25 (☎0221 258 1409; www.timp.de). Across from the Heumarkt U-Bahn stop. This club/hotel has become an institution in Cologne for travesty theater. Gay and straight crowds come for the glitter-filled cabarets. Drag shows daily 1-4am. No cover. 1st drink M-Th and Su €8, F-Sa €13. Open daily 10am-late. AmEx/MC/V.

M20, Maastrichterstr. 20 (☎0221 51 96 66; www.m20-koeln.de). U1, 6, or 7 to Rudolfpl. DJs deliver some of the city's best drum'n'bass and punk to a local crowd. Cocktails €5. Beer €1.50-3.20. Open from 8pm. Cash only.

Stadtgarten, Venloerstr. 40 (☎0221 95 29 94 33). Take U3, 5, 6, or 12 to Friesenpl. Downstairs hosts parties playing everything from soul to techno, while the upper concert hall is renowned for its jazz recordings and performances. Cover €6-15. Open M-Th 9pm-1am, F-Sa 9pm-3am. Cash only.

BONN ☎0228

While it was the residence of Chancellor Konrad Adenauer, Bonn (pop. 314,300) served as the West German capital—and was derided as "*Hauptdorf,*" or "capital village." The city also maintains notoriety from its most famous native—Beethoven. **Beethovenhaus,** Bonng. 20, Ludwig van Beethoven's birthplace, houses a fantastic collection of the composer's personal effects. The Digital Archives Studio offers recordings and scores of all of his works. (☎0228 981 7525; www.beethoven-haus-bonn.de. Open Apr.-Oct. M-Sa 10am-6pm, Su 11am-6pm; Nov.-Mar. M-Sa 10am-5pm, Su 11am-5pm. €5, students €4.) To reach Bonn's "other" palace, stroll down Poppelsdorfer Allee to **Poppelsdorfer Schloß,** which has a French facade, an Italian courtyard, and beautifully manicured botanical gardens; check out the world's largest water lilies in the greenhouses. (Gardens open Apr.-Oct. M-F and Su 9am-6pm; Oct.-Mar. M-F 9am-4pm.) Five museums line the *Museumsmeile* near the banks of the Rhine, though they're not within walking distance; take U16, 63, 66, 67, or 68 to the Heussallee/Museumsmeile stop. Around 7000 interactive exhibits examine post-WWII Germany at the **Haus der Geschichte,** Willy-Brandt-Allee 14. (☎0228 916 50. Open Tu-Su 9am-7pm. Free.) One block away, the immense **Kunstmuseum Bonn,** Friedrich-Ebert-Allee 2, houses a superb collection of 20th-century German art. (☎0228 77 62 60. Open Tu and Th-Su 11am-6pm, W 11am-9pm. €5, students €2.50.)

Deutsches Haus ❹, Kasernenstr. 19-21, is on a quiet residential street within easy walking distance of the *Altstadt* and serves a decadent included breakfast to its visitors. (☎0228 63 37 77; info@hotel-deutscheshaus.net. Reception 6am-11pm. Singles €35-38, with bath €65-75; doubles €65-67, with bath €83-90; triples €110-118. AmEx/MC/V.) For the spacious but distant **Jugendherberge Bonn (HI) ❷,** Haager Weg 42, take bus #621 (dir.: Ippendorf Altenheim) to Jugendgästehaus. (☎0228 28 99 70; bonn@jugendherberge.de. Reception 7am-1am. Wheelchair-accessible. Breakfast and linens included. Laundry €4. Curfew 1am. Dorms €24; singles €40.30; doubles €60.20. MC/V.) Take a break from meaty German fare at **Cassius-Garten ❷,** Maximilianstr. 28D, near the train station, which serves salad and whole-grain baked goods, all for €1.50 per 100g. (☎0228 65 24 29; www.cassiusgarten.de. Open M-Sa 8am-8pm.) *Schnüss* (€1), sold at newsstands, has club and concert listings. **The Jazz Galerie,** Oxfordstr. 24, is mostly jazz-less bar and disco popular with swanky youths. (☎0228 63 93 24. Cover €8.50; includes 2 drinks. Open Th from 9pm, F-Sa from 10pm. Cash only.)

Trains head to Berlin (5hr., 4 per day, €87-100) and Cologne (30min., 4-5 per hr., €9-15). The **tourist office** is located at Windeckstr. 1, off Münsterpl.; follow Poststr. from the station. (☎0228 77 50 00; www.bonn.de. Open M-F 9am-6:30pm, Sa 9am-4pm, Su 10am-2pm.) The **post office** is at Münsterpl. 17. (Open M-F 9am-8pm, Sa 9am-4pm.) **Postal Code:** 53111.

KASSEL ☎0561

Kassel's (pop. 198,000) park, the **Wilhelmshöhe,** is famed throughout Germany. To reach it, take tram #1 from Banhof Wilhelmshöhe (dir.: Wilhelmshöhe) to the last stop. Inside, **Schloß Wilhelmshöhe** is a dressed-down version of the Residenz in Würzburg; the palace houses art from the classical era to the 1700s. (☎0561 31 68 00. Open Tu-Su Mar.-Oct. 10am-5pm; Nov.-Feb. 10am-4pm. €6, students €2.) Wilhelm IX built **Schloß Löwenburg** in the 18th-century with stones deliberately missing so it would resemble a crumbling medieval castle—he was obsessed with the year 1495 and imagined himself a knight. (☎0561 31 68 02 44. Open Tu-Su Mar.-Oct. 10am-5pm; Nov.-Feb. 10am-4pm; Dec. 10am-4pm. Required tours 1 per hr.; €4, students €2, under 18 free.) Park paths lead to the statue of **Herkules** (Hercules), Kassel's emblem. A viewing pedestal provides stunning views of the park. (Pedestal open mid-Mar. to mid-Nov. Tu-Su 10am-5pm. €3, students €2.) To the east lies the city itself, whose historic sights were destroyed in WWII. The **Brüder-Grimm-Museum,** Schöne Aussicht 2, displays a handwritten copy of The Brothers Grimm's *Children's and Household Tales.* (☎0561 787 2033; www.grimms.de. Open daily 10am-5pm. €1.50, students €1.)

To reach the flower-filled **Jugendherberge und Bildungsstätte Kassel (HI) ❷,** Schenkendorfstr. 18, take streetcar #4 from the Wilhelmshöhe station to Querallee, then turn left on Querallee, which becomes Schenkendorfstr. (☎0561 77 64 55; www.djh-hessen.de/jh/kassel. Breakfast included. Internet €2 per hr., €15 per day. Reception 8am-11:30pm. Curfew 12:30am. Floor mattresses €15; dorms €20; singles €25; doubles €40. €3.10 HI discount. Cash only.) **Friedrich-Ebert-Straße,** the upper part of **Wilhelmshöher Allee,** and the area around **Königsplatz** have markets, takeout stands, and cafes scattered among clothing stores. **Limerick ❷,** Wilhelmshöher Allee 116, has a pan-European menu boasting 237 entrees and appetizers. The 25 beers on tap (€2-3) attract loyal crowds. (☎0561 77 66 49. Open M-Th 11am-1am, F-Sa 11am-2am, Su 11am-midnight. Cash only.)

Most trains stop only at Bahnhof Wilhelmshöhe. From Bahnhof Wilhelmshöhe to: Berlin (3hr., 2 per hr., €78); Düsseldorf (3hr., 1 per 2hrs., €44-80); Frankfurt (2hr., 3-4 per hr., €35-45); Hamburg (2hr., 3 per hr., €65); Munich (4hr., 2-3 per hr., €89). The **tourist offices** has two locations, one in the Bahnhof

Wilhelmshöhe and the another in the Rathaus. (☎0561 70 77 07; www.kassel-tourist.de. Both are open M-Sa 9am-6pm.) **Postal Code:** 34117.

FRANKFURT AM MAIN ☎069

International offices, shiny skyscrapers, and expensive cars can be found at every intersection in Frankfurt (pop. 660,000), best known as the home of the EU's Central Bank and a major international airport. Don't let Frankfurt's reputation as a transportation center fool you–from shopping to museums to great nightlife, there's always something to see and do in this international city.

TRANSPORTATION

Flights: The largest and busiest airport in Germany, Frankfurt's **Flughafen Rhein-Main** (**FRA;** ☎01805 37 24 36) is connected to the *Hauptbahnhof* by S-Bahn trains S8 and 9 (2-3 per hr.) Buy tickets (€3.60) from the green machines marked "Fahrkarten" before boarding. Taxis to the city center cost around €20.

Trains: Trains run from the **Hauptbahnhof** to: **Amsterdam, NTH** (4hr., 1 per 2hr., €150); **Berlin** (4hr., 2 per hr., €90-105); **Cologne** (1hr., 1 per hr., €38-60); **Hamburg** (3-5hr., 2 per hr., €78-98); **Munich** (3hr., 1 per hr., €64-81). For schedules, reservations, and info call ☎01805 19 41 95; www.bahn.de. Note: there is no English help option.

Public Transportation: Frankfurt's public transportation system runs daily 4am-1:30am. Single-ride tickets (€2.20; reduced fares available) are valid for 1hr. in 1 direction. **Eurail** is valid only on S-Bahn trains. The **Tageskarte** (day pass; €5.60) provides unlimited transportation on the S-Bahn, U-Bahn, streetcars, and buses, and can be purchased from machines in any station. S-Bahn trains leave the *Hauptbahnhof* from the lower level; U-Bahn trains are reached through the shopping passage *(Einkaufspassage).*

Taxis: ☎23 00 01, ☎23 00 33, or ☎25 00 01. From €1.40 per km.

Bike Rental: Deutsche Bahn (DB) runs the citywide service **Call a Bike** (☎0700 05 22 55 22; www.callabike.de). Bikes marked with the red DB logo can be found throughout the city for your immediate rental. To do so, call the service hotline or go online and set up an account. (€0.10 per min., €15 per day.)

ORIENTATION AND PRACTICAL INFORMATION

Frankfurt's *Hauptbahnhof* opens onto the city's red-light district; from the station, the *Altstadt* is a 20min. walk down Kaiserstr. or Münchenerstr. The tourist heavy **Römerberg** square is just north of the Main River, while most commercial stores lie farther north along **Zeil**, the city's commercial center. Cafes and services cluster near the university in **Bockenheim** (U6 or 7 to Bockenheimer Warte). Across the river, the **Sachsenhausen** area draws pub-crawlers and museum-goers (take U1, 2, or 3 to Schweizer Pl.).

Tourist Office: in the *Hauptbahnhof* (☎21 23 88 00; www.frankfurt-tourismus.de). Book rooms for a €3 fee or for free if you call ahead. Sells the **Frankfurt Card** (1-day €8, 2-day €12), which allows unlimited use of public transportation and provides discounts on many sights. Open M-F 8am-9pm, Sa-Su and holidays 9am-6pm. Branch in **Römerberg** square (open M-F 9:30am-5:30pm, Sa-Su 10am-4pm).

Currency Exchange: Cheaper exchange rates can be found outside the train station. Try **Deutsche Bank,** across the street. (Open M-F 9am-1pm, 2-5pm.)

Laundromat: SB Waschsalon, Wallstr. 8, near Haus der Jugend in Sachsenhausen. Wash €3.50 for a small machine (6 kg) or €5 for a large machine (12 kg). Dry €0.50 per 15min. Soap €0.50. Open M-Sa 6am-11pm.

Internet: In the basement of the train station. €2.50 per hr. Open M-Sa 8:30am-1am. Internet cafes are on Kaiserstr., across from the *Hauptbahnhof*.

Post Office: Goethe Pl. 7. Walk 10min. down Taunusstr. from the *Hauptbahnhof*, or take the U- or S-Bahn to Hauptwache and walk south to the square. Open M-F 7am-8pm, Sa 8am-2pm. **Postal Code:** 60313.

ACCOMMODATIONS AND CAMPING

Deals are rare and trade fairs make rooms scarce in Frankfurt; reserve several weeks ahead. The **Westend/University** area has a few cheap options.

Stay & Learn Hostel/Frankfurt Hostel, Kaiserstr. 74 (☎069 247 5130; www.frankfurt-hostel.com). Convenient, sociable hostel organizes free city tours and holds free bi-weekly dinners. 24-hr reception located on the 4th fl. Luggage storage included. Free breakfast. €2 beers at the bar. Internet €1 per hr. Free Wi-Fi. Dorms €17-20; singles €50; doubles €60; triples €66. Higher rates during trade fairs. MC/V. ❷

Haus der Jugend (HI), Deutschherrnufer 12 (☎069 610 0150; www.jugendherberge-frankfurt.de). Take bus #46 (dir.: Mühlberg) from the station to Frankensteiner Pl., or take tram #16 (dir.: Offenbach Stadtgrenze) to *Lokalbahnhof.* Great location along the Main and in front of Sachsenhausen's pubs and cafes. Breakfast and linens included. Check-in 1pm, check-out 9:30am; curfew 2am. Dorms from €21.50; under 27 from €17; singles €39-43; doubles €56-76. HI discount €3.10. MC/V. ❷

City Camp Frankfurt, An der Sandelmühle 35B (☎069 57 03 32; www.city-camp-frankfurt.de). An inexpensive option for all types of travelers. U1-3: Heddernheim. Take a left at the Kleingartnerverein sign and continue until you reach the Sandelmühle sign. Cross the stream, turn left, and follow signs to the campground. Reception M-F 9am-1pm, 4-8pm; Sa-Su 10am-1pm, 5-8pm. Campsites €6 per person, €2.50 per child under 14; €3.50 per tent. Showers €1 per 4min. Cash only. ❶

FOOD

The most reasonably priced meals can be found in **Sachsenhausen** or near the university in **Bockenheim. Kleinmarkthalle,** on Haseng. between Berlinerstr. and Töngesg., is a three-story warehouse with bakeries, butchers, fruits, nuts, cheese, and vegetable stands. (Open M-F 8am-6pm, Sa 8am-4pm.)

Cafe Laumer, Bockenheimer Landstr. 67 (☎069 72 79 12). U6 or U7 to "Westend." Dine like a local on the outdoor patio or in the backyard garden of this celebrated cafe in the Westend, only blocks from the Uni. Enjoy the special of the day (€6.70) or drink coffee (€2.20). Open M-F 8am-7pm, Sa 8:30am-7pm, Su 9:30am-7pm. AmEx/V/MC. ❷

Adolf Wagner, Schweizer Str. 71 (☎069 61 25 65). Saucy German dishes (€5-17) and some of the region's most renowned *Äpfelwein* (€1.40 per 0.3L) keep the patrons of this famous corner of Sachsenhausen jolly. Open daily 11am-midnight. Cash only. ❸

IMA Multibar, Klein Bockenheimer Str. 14 (☎069 90 02 56 65). This fast-paced and hip bar/cafe combo, on the back streets (off Zeil), offers hungry patrons delicious smoothies (€3.50) and wraps (€4-7.30) by day, and a great selection of beer, wine, and cocktails by night. Drinks from €7. MC/V. ❷

SIGHTS

Beneath the daunting skyscrapers that define the Frankfurt landscape are several historic sights, all of which have undergone some degree of reconstruction since the old city's destruction in 1944. The **Museumsufer** along the southern bank of the Main includes some of the city's most vital cultural institutions.

STÄDEL. The *Städel's* impressive collection comprises seven centuries of art and includes notable works by Old Masters, Impressionists, and Modernists. **Holbein's,** the first floor cafe, is a widely celebrated destination for visitors. *(Schaumainkai 63, between Dürerstr. and Holbeinstr. ☎605 0980; www.staedelmuseum.de. Open Tu and F-Su 10am-6pm, W-Th 10am-9pm. €10, students €8, under 12 and last Sa of each month free. English-language audio tour €4, students €3.)*

MUSEUM FÜR MODERNE KUNST. The modern architecture of this triangular "slice of cake" building complements the art within. This museum houses a permanent collection of European and American art from the 1960s to the present and stages large-scale temporary exhibitions. *(Domstr. 10. ☎21 23 04 47; www.mmk-frankfurt.de. Open Tu and Th-Su 10am-5pm, W 10am-8pm. €7, students €3.50.)*

RÖMERBERG. This plaza, at the heart of Frankfurt's *Altstadt*, is surrounded on all four sides by tons of things to see and do. With its picturesque **Fachwerkhaeuser** (half-timbered houses) and daunting **Statue of Justice** fountain at the center of the square, the Römerberg is justifiably the most heavily-touristed spot in Frankfurt. Across from the Römerberg, **Paulskirche** (St. Paul's Church), the birthplace of Germany's 19th-century attempt at constitutional government, now memorializes the trials of German democracy with an acclaimed mural. At the west end of the Römerberg, the gables of **Römer** have marked the site of Frankfurt's city hall since 1405. *(St. Paul's Church: ☎21 23 85 26. Open daily*

10am-5pm. Free. Römer enter from Limpurgerg. Open daily 10am-1pm and 2-5pm. €2. Gothic Dom: church open M-Th and Sa-Su 9am-noon and 2:30-6pm. Museum open Tu-F 10am-5pm and Sa-Su 11am-5pm. Church free. Museum €2, students €1.)

NIGHTLIFE

Though Frankfurt lacks a centralized nightlife scene, a number of techno clubs lie between **Zeil** and **Bleichstraße.** Wait until midnight or 1am for things to really heat up. Visit www.nachtleben.de for more info on Frankfurt's clubs. For drinks, head to the cobblestone streets of the **Sachsenhausen** district, between Brückenstr. and Dreieichstr., where there are rowdy pubs and beer gardens serving specialty *Aepfelwein.*

Odeon, Seilerstr. 34 (☎069 28 50 55). The party changes daily, with M night hip-hop, and Th-Sa house music. F 27+, Sa Wild Card. M and Th-F drinks half-price until midnight. Cover from €5, students €3 on Th only. Open M-Sa from 10pm. Cash only.

King Kamehameha Club, Hanauer Landstr. 192 (☎069 48 00 370; www.king-kamehameha.de). Take the U6 to "Ostbahnhof" and walk down Hanauer Landstr. With intricate timber rafters, exposed brick, and a raging dance floor. Partygoers drink vodka and Red Bull (€8). Open Th-Sa from 10pm. Cover from €10. Cash only.

SOUTHWESTERN GERMANY

The Rhine and Mosel River Valleys are filled with much to be seen and drunk. Along river banks, medieval castles loom over vineyards. Farther south, modern cities fade slowly into the beautiful hinterlands of the Black Forest.

TRIER ☎0651

Trier (pop. 103,500), the oldest town in Germany, has weathered more than two millennia in the western end of the Mosel Valley. An inscription at Trier's *Hauptmarkt* (Main Market) reads: "Trier stood one thousand and three hundred years before Rome." Trier reached its zenith in the early fourth century, when it served as the capital of the Western Roman Empire and was a major center of Christianity in Europe. Today, it hums with students pondering life's questions like the town's most famous son, Karl Marx. A one-day **combination ticket** (€6.20, students €3.10) provides access to all of the city's Roman monuments. The most famous is the massive second-century **Porta Nigra** (Black Gate), which travelers can climb for a breathtaking view of Trier's landscape. (Open daily Apr.-Sept. 9am-6pm; Oct. and Mar. 9am-5pm; Nov.-Feb. 9am-4pm. €2.10, students €1.60.) The enormous **Dom** nearby shelters the **Tunica Christi** (Holy Robe of Christ) and the tombs of archbishops. Amazingly, the original fourth-century church was four times larger than its current size. (Both open daily Apr.-Oct. 6:30am-6pm; Nov.-Mar. 6:30am-5:30pm. Free.) The 4th-century beautiful **Basilika,** originally Emperor Constantine's throne room, is the largest single room surviving from antiquity. (Open Easter-Oct. M-Sa 10am-6pm, Su noon-6pm; Nov.-Easter Tu-Sa 11am-noon and 3-4pm, Su noon-1pm. Free.) A 10min. walk uphill along Olewiger Str. leads to the **amphitheater.** (Open daily Apr.-Sept. 9am-6pm; Oct. and Mar. 9am-5pm; Nov.-Feb. 9am-4pm. Last entry 30min. before closing. Both €2.10, students €1.60.)

Hilles Hostel ❷, Gartenfeldstr. 7, is a lovely family-run hostel with bright, festive decor. (☎0651 710 27 85; www.hilles-hostel-trier.de. All rooms have bath. Fully stocked kitchen. Dorms from €15; doubles €32-38; quads €64; homestays from €400 a month. Laundry €2. Free Internet. MC/V.) With its large, comfortable beds and prime location, the joint hostel and guesthouse **Warsberger Hof** ❶, Dietrichstr. 42, is one of the best deals in town. Head straight through the Porta Nigra down Simeonst. to the *Hauptmarkt*, then turn right on Dietrichstr. (☎0651 97 52 50; www.warsberger-hof.de. Dorms €22.50; singles €27.50; doubles €24.50 per person. Reception 8am-11pm. Check-in 2:30pm. MC/V.) Restaurants line the pedestrian path along the river between the youth hostel and the Kaiser-Wilhelm-Brücke. **Astarix** ❷, Karl-Marx-Str. 11, attracts a young crowd with generous portions of pasta and pizza served in a relaxed environment. (Salads €2.60-6.40. Pasta and pizza €2.50-5. Open daily 1am-11pm.)

Trains run to Koblenz (2hr., 1-2 per hr., €8.50) and Luxembourg City, LUX (50min., 1 per hr., €14.40-17.40). From the station, walk down Theodor-Haus-Allee and turn left under the Porta Nigra to reach the **tourist office.** (☎0651 97 80 80; www.trier.de/tourismus. Open May-Oct. M-Th. 9am-6pm, F-Sa 9am-7pm, Su 10am-5pm; Nov.-Dec. M-Sa 9am-6pm, Su 10am-3pm; Jan.-Feb. M-Sa 10am-5pm, Su 10am-1pm. 2hr. English-language city tour Sa 1:30pm; 1hr. German- and English-language coach tour daily 1pm. Both tours €7, students €6.) A **Trier Card**, available at the tourist office, offers free intracity bus fare and discounts on sites over a three-day period (€9, students €6.50). **Postal Code:** 54290.

RHINE VALLEY (RHEINTAL)

The Rhine River carves its way through an 80km stretch of the Rhine Valley and flows north all the way from Mainz to Bonn. According to German folklore, this region of medieval castles and jagged cliffs is enchanted. Magical or not, it's certainly one of Germany's most stunning regions.

TRANSPORTATION

Two different **train** lines traverse the Rhine Valley, one on each bank; the line on the western side stays closer to the water and has better views. It's often tricky to switch banks, as train and ferry schedules don't always match up. A train crosses the river from Mainz to Wiesbaden. **Boats** are the best way to see the sights; the Köln-Düsseldorfer (KD) Line and Bingen Rüdesheim Line cover the Mainz-Koblenz stretch three to four times per day in summer (€20-40).

MAINZ ☎06131

The capital of Rheinland-Pfalz, and the proud birthplace of Johannes Gutenberg, Mainz is a small but lively city at the southern end of the Rheintal. Mainz was once the most powerful Catholic diocese in the world north of the Alps, and the **Martinsdom,** a colossal sandstone 10th-century cathedral, still stands as a relic of this legacy. (☎06131 25 34 12. Open Mar.-Oct. M-F 9am-6:30pm, Sa 9am-4pm, Su 1-2:45pm and 4-6:30pm; Nov.-Feb. M-F 9am-5pm, Sa 9am-4pm, Su 12:45-3pm and 4-5pm. Free.) On a hill south of the *Dom*, the **Gothic Stephanskirche** on Stephansberg is inlaid with stunning stained-glass windows by Russian exile Marc Chagall. (Open M-F 10am-noon and 2-5pm, Sa 2-5pm. Free.) The advent of movable type in 1455 is immortalized at the **Gutenberg Museum,** Liebfrauenpl. 5, across from the *Dom*, which has a replica of Gutenberg's original press. (Open Tu-Sa 9am-5pm, Su 11am-3pm. €5, students €3.)

To reach the plain but comfortable rooms and the surprisingly lively downstairs bistro of the **Jugendgästehaus (HI)** ❷, Otto-Brunfels-Schneise 4, take bus #62 (dir.: Weisenau) or 63 (dir.: Laubenheim) to Viktorstift/Jugendherberge, and follow the signs. (☎06131 853 32; www.diejugendherbergen.de. Breakfast included. Reception 7:30am-9:30pm. 4- to 6-bed dorms €18.40; singles and doubles add €10/5. MC/V.) Tucked along a tiny back street between the *Dom* and the Rhein, the **Weinstube Rote Kopf ❶,** Rotekopfg. 4, serves locally-produced wines and traditional regional dishes. The comfortable, welcoming ambiance comes at the right price; main dishes are €4.80 and up. (☎06131 23 10 13; www.rotekopf.de. Open M-Sa 11:30am-midnight.)

Trains run to Cologne (1hr., 2-3 per hr., €34-61); Frankfurt (40min., 4 per hr., €10-15); Hamburg (6hr., 1 per hr., €87-103); Koblenz (1hr., 3-5 per hr., €16.10-19.50). **KD ferries** (☎06131 23 28 00; www.k-d.com) depart from the wharfs on the other side of the *Rathaus* (City Hall). The **tourist office,** in Brückenturm by the river in the *Altstadt*, conducts English-language tours. From the station, walk straight down Schottstr., turn right onto Kaiserstr., and continue straight for 10min. until you reach Ludwigstr.; turn left and follow the green signs beginning at the cathedral. (☎06131 28 62 10; www.info-mainz.de/tourist. Open M-F 9am-6pm, Sa 10:30am-2pm. 2hr. English-language tours May-Oct. W and F-Sa 2pm; Nov.-Apr. Sa 2pm. €5.) **Postal Code:** 55001.

LORELEI CLIFFS AND CASTLES ☎067

The mythological Lorelei maiden once lured sailors to their deaths on the cliffs of the Rhine. Now it's tourists who come in spades, entranced by romantic villages, slanting vineyards, and dramatic castles. Tiny **St. Goarshausen** and larger **St. Goar,** towns on either side of the Rhine, host the spectacular **Rhein in Flammen** (Rhine in Flames) fireworks celebration in mid-September. St. Goarshausen, on the east bank, provides access (by foot) to a statue of the Lorelei and the cliffs. Directly above the town is the dark **Burg Katz** (Cat Castle), closed to visitors, and downstream, the smaller **Burg Maus** (Mouse Castle) provides a royal venue for daily falconry demonstrations at 11am and 2:30pm from May to early October. (Face the river, turn right, and follow the signs. ☎067 71 76 69. €8, children €6.) Towering over St. Goar, **Burg Rheinfels** is a sprawling castle with underground passage ruins. Take the "Rheinfels Express," a red trolley that leaves from St. Goar's center, or follow the red signs for Fußweg Burg Rheinfels up the hill. (Open mid-Mar. to mid-Oct. daily 9am-6pm; mid-Oct. to Nov. daily 9am-5pm; Dec. to mid-Mar. Sa-Su 11am-5pm. €5, children €2.50. Bring a flashlight, or buy a candle in the museum for €0.30.)

Comfortable St. Goar **Loreley-Jugendherberge (HI) ❶** sits directly beneath Burg Rheinfels. Follow the signs for Burg Rheinfels and the Jugendherberge from Heerstr. (☎067 413 88. Breakfast included. Reception 8am-8pm. Dorms €17.90; doubles €45. MC/V.) **Alla Fontana ❶,** Pumpeng. 5, is a local favorite that serves delicious homemade pizzas and pasta for €4.50-7.50. (☎067 96 117. Open Tu 5:30-10pm, W-Su 11:30am-2pm and 5:30-10pm.) For dessert, you've got to get a scoop of Rocco's homemade gelato at **Eis Café Milano ❶,** Heerstr. 103, where the jovial gentleman only charges €0.70 per scoop. (Open daily 11am-10pm).

Trains continuously run from St. Goarshausen to Koblenz (30min., 2 per hr., €6) and Mainz (1hr., 2 per hr., €10.60) and from St. Goar to Cologne (1.5hr., every hr., €24.50) and Mainz (1hr., 2 per hr., €9.90.) The Loreley VI **ferry** connects St. Goarshausen and St. Goar every 15 min. (M-F 6am-11pm, Sa-Su 8am-11pm. €1.30). To get to the Goarhausen's **tourist office,** Bahnhofstr. 8, make a left out of the train station and follow the signs. (☎067 71 91 00; www.loreley-touristik.de. Open M-F 9am-1pm and 2-5pm, Sa 10am-noon.) St. Goar's **tourist office,** Heerstr. 86, is a 5min. walk past the Marktpl. from the ferry dock. (☎067 413 83; www.st-goar.de. Open May-Sept. M-F 9am-12:30pm and 1:30-6pm, Apr. and Oct. M-F 9am-12:30pm and 1:30-5pm, Nov.-Mar. M-Th 9am-12:30pm and 1:30-5pm, F 9am-2pm.) **Postal Code:** 56329.

HEIDELBERG ☎06221

With its picturesque setting along the Neckar River and its crumbling castle looming high above the town, Heidelberg (pop. 142,000) has long been one of Germany's top tourist attractions. Today, legions of visitors fill the length of *Hauptstraß*. Fortunately, Heidelberg remains home to a large and prestigious university, which enables it to keep its youthful charm.

TRANSPORTATION AND PRACTICAL INFORMATION. **Trains** run to Frankfurt (1hr., 1-2 per hr., €14-24), Hamburg (7hr., 1 per hr., €87-101), and Stuttgart (1hr., 1-2 per hr., €18-33). Within Heidelberg, single-ride **bus** tickets cost €2.10; day passes (€5) are available on board. **Rhein-Neckar-Fahrgastschifffahrt** (☎06221 201 81; www.rnf-schifffahrt.de), in front of the *Kongresshaus*, runs **ferries** all over Germany and cruises up the Neckar to Neckarsteinach (3hr. round-trip, Easter-late Oct. 1 per hr., €10.50). Rent **bikes** at **Eldorado,** Neckarstaden 52, near the Alte Brücke. Take bus #41 or 42 from the *Hauptbahnhof* to Marstallstraße and continue for 100m. (☎06221 654 4460; www.eldorado-hd.de. Open Tu-F 9am-noon and 2-6pm, Sa 10am-6pm, Su 2-6pm. €5 per hr., €15 per day.)

Heidelberg's attractions lie mostly in the eastern part of the city, along the south bank of the Neckar. From the train station, take any bus or streetcar to Bismarckpl., then walk east down **Hauptstraße,** the city's main thoroughfare, to the *Altstadt*. The **tourist office,** in front of the station, books room for a €3 fee. (☎06221 138 8121. Open Apr.-Oct. M-Sa 9am-7pm, Su 10am-6pm; Nov.-Mar. M-Sa 9am-6pm.) The office sells the **Heidelberg Card,** which includes admission to many major sights. (1-day card €10, 2-day €14, 4-day €20.) The **post office** is at Sofienstr. 8-10. (Open M-F 9:30am-6pm, Sa 9:30am-1pm.) **Postal Code:** 69115.

ACCOMMODATIONS AND FOOD. **Sudpfanne Hostel ❶,** Haputstr. 223, offers the only cheap, dorm-style accommodations (from €20 per night) in the heart of town. Take bus #33 (dir.: Köpfel) from the *Hauptbahnhof* to "Nekcarmünzpl." (☎06221 163 636; www.heidelberger-sudpfanne.de. Check-in 3pm-midnight. Check-out noon. Free Internet. Cash only.) To get to the **Jugendherberge (HI) ❷,** Tiergartenstr. 5, take bus #32 from the *Hauptbanhof* to Chirurgische Klinik, then take bus #31 to Jugendherberge. Next to one of Europe's largest zoos, this hostel also teems with wild species, including *Schoolchildus germanus*, and features a discotheque in its basement. (☎65 11 90. Breakfast included. Reception until 2am. Reserve ahead. Dorms €24, under 27 €21; singles €29; doubles €34. MC/V.)

Historic student pubs outside the center have great dining options for hungry budget travelers. **T Falafel ❶,** Heug. 1., (☎06221 216 10 303) serves up delicious, piping hot Lebanese food from a small, hidden storefront in a side street off Hauptstr. Head to **Merlin ❷,** Bergheimer Str. 85, for calm cafe ambiance and a sorcery-themed breakfast for €4-10. (☎06221 65 78 56. Open M-Th and Su 10am-1am, F-Sa 10am-3:30am. AmEx/MC/V.)

SIGHTS. Every summer, droves of tourists lay siege to the **Heidelberg Castle.** The 14th-century castle has been destroyed twice by war (1622 and 1693) and once by lightning (1764), leaving it with a unique, battered beauty and a layered architectural history. The cool, musty wine cellar houses the **Großes Faß** (with a 221,726L capacity, it is the largest wine barrel ever used). The castle **gardens** offer great views of the city below; trek up at night to enjoy the city's lights. (☎06221 53 84 21. Grounds open daily 8am-6pm; last entry 5:30pm. English-language audio tour €3.50. English-language tours every hr. M-F 11:15am-4:15pm, Sa-Su 10:15am-4:15pm; €4, students €2. Schloß, Großes

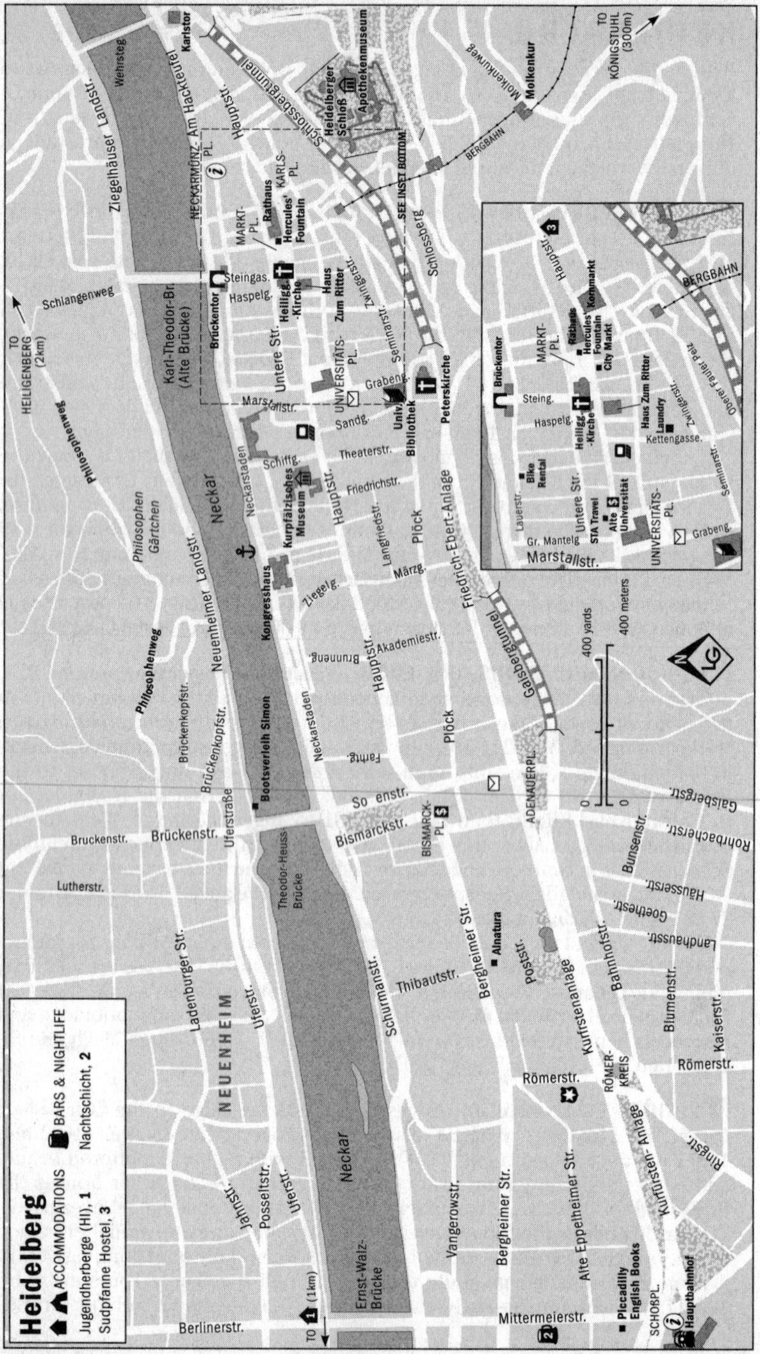

Heidelberg

ACCOMMODATIONS
Jugendherberge (HI), 1
Sudpfanne Hostel, 3

BARS & NIGHTLIFE
Nachtschicht, 2

Neckar
Karl-Theodor-Br. (Alte Brücke)
Theodor-Heuss Brücke
Ernst-Walz-Brücke
NEUENHEIM
Heidelberger Schloß
Apothekenmuseum
Molkenkur
Karlstor
Rathaus
Hercules' Fountain
Heiligg.-Kirche
Haus Zum Ritter
Brückentor
Univ. Bibliothek
Peterskirche
Kurpfälzisches Museum
Kongresshaus
Bootsverleih Simon
Alnatura
Piccadilly English Books
Hauptbahnhof
Philosophenweg
Philosophen Gärtchen
Schlossbergtunnel
Gaisbergtunnel
BERGBAHN
SEE INSET BOTTOM
TO HEILIGENBERG (2km)
TO KÖNIGSTUHL (300m)
TO 1 (1km)
400 yards
400 meters
Brückentor
Steing.
Haspelg.
Bike Rental
STA Travel
Alte Universität
Kornmarkt
City Markt
Laundry
Kettengasse.
Hauptstr.
Untere Str.
Marstallstr.
Gr. Mantelg
UNIVERSITÄTS-PL.
Grabeng.
Seminarstr.
Zwingerstr.
Lauerstr.
Oberer Fauler Pelz

Faß, and Pharmaceutical Museum €3, students €1.50.) Reach the castle by the uphill path (10min.) from the Kornmarkt or by the **Bergbahn,** one of Germany's oldest cable cars. (Take bus #33, dir.: Köpfel, to Rathaus/Bergbahn. Cable cars leave from the parking lot next to the bus stop daily Mar.-Oct. every 10min. 9am-8pm; Nov.-Feb. every 20 min. 9am-6pm. Round-trip €5.)

Heidelberg is also home to Germany's oldest (est. 1386) and most prestigious university. Over 20 Nobel laureates have been part of the faculty. Housed in the same building as the Museum der Universität Heidelberg is the **Alte Aula,** the school's oldest and most beautiful auditorium. *(Grabeng. 1. ☎06221 54 21 52.)* Before 1914, students were exempt from trials by civil authorities due to a code of academic freedom, so the faculty tried crimes from plagiarism to pig-chasing. View the irreverent, colorful graffiti of guilty students in the **Studentkarzer** jail. (Augustinerg. 2. ☎06221 54 35 54. Museum, auditorium, and jail open Apr.-Sept. Tu-Su 10am-6pm; Oct.-Mar. Tu-Sa 10am-4pm. €3, students €2.50.)

On the opposite side of the Neckar from the *Altstadt*, the steep **Philosophenweg** (Philosopher's Path), where famed thinkers Johann Wolfgang von Goethe, Ludwig Feuerbach, and Ernst Jünger once strolled, offers unbeatable views of the city. Follow signs to the top of **Heiligenberg** (Holy Mountain), where you'll find the ruins of the 9th-century **St. Michael Basilika,** the 11th-century **Stefanskloster,** and **Thingstätte,** an amphitheater built by the Nazis using forced labor, on the site of an ancient Celtic gathering place. (To get to the path, use the steep, stone-walled footpath 10m west of the Karl-Theodor-Brücke.) At the center of the **Altstadt** is the cobblestoned **Marktplatz,** where alleged witches and heretics were burned at the stake in the 15th century. Two of Heidelberg's oldest structures border the square. East of the Marktplatz, the **Kornmarkt** offers great views of the castle above and a beautiful central fountain. The twin domes of the **Brückentor** tower over the 18th-century Alte Brücke.

FESTIVALS AND NIGHTLIFE. A favorite event for both tourists and residents, the **Schlossbeleuchtung** (castle lighting) occurs annually on the first Saturday in June, the second Saturday in July, and the first Saturday in September. The ceremony begins after nightfall with the "burning" of the castle; meanwhile, fireworks are set off over the *Altstadt* from the Alte Brücke. Head to Neuenheim or the Philosophenweg for the best views.

TREASURE AND TRYSTS

If the *Nibelungenlied* (Song of the Nibelungs) can be trusted, budget-strained backpackers in Southwestern Germany need look no farther than the nearby Rhein to replenish their supply of cash: the medieval epic claims that the greatest treasure ever known is still buried beneath the river.

According to the legend, Worms, a town near Heidelberg, was home to the Burgundian princess Kriemhild and her older brother Günther. Several versions of the narrative exist, but most agree that Siegfried, slayer of the dragon Fafnir and owner of the *Nibelungenschatz* (a treasure of unsurpassed worth), set out to court Kriemhild after hearing of her unsurpassed beauty. Günther consented to the marriage only after Siegfried helped him beguile Brünhild, the Queen of Iceland.

Much later, when the two men, along with their wives, reunited, Brünhild learned that it was Siegfried, not Günther, who bested her in combat and won her hand. Afraid that his deception would become public knowledge, Günther had Siegfried assassinated. The *Nibelungenschatz* was thrown into the Rhein outside of Worms, and both Gunther and Kriemhild perished in subsequent attempts to recover it. The Nibelung story was later made famous in Wagner's *"Ring" cycle*, and also influenced Tolkien's *The Lord of the Rings*.

Popular nightspots fan out from the Marktpl. On the Neckar side of the Heiliggeistkirche, **Untere Straße** has the most expansive collection of bars in the city, and revelers fill the narrow way until 1 or 2am. **Steingasse,** off the Marktpl. toward the Neckar, is also lined with bars attracting excited late-night crowds. At **Nachtschicht,** in the Landfried-Komplex near the train station, university students dance in an old warehouse-turned nightclub. (☎06221 43 85 50; www.nachtschicht.com. Cover €8; M and F students €3.50. Open W 10pm-3am, Th-F 10pm-4am, Sa 10pm-5am. Cash only.)

STUTTGART ☎0711

Daimler-Benz, Porsche, and a host of other corporate thoroughbreds keep Stuttgart (pop. 591,000) speeding along in the fast lane. In the heart of the Stuttgart lies the **Schloßplatz,** a 19th-century grassy square framed by an ornate palace and graced by the "Jubilee Column." Because almost 20% of Stuttgart is under a land preservation order, the city is known for its urban green spaces, the crown jewel of which is the palatial **Schloßgarten.**. At the northern end of the gardens is Rosensteinpark, home to the **Wilhelma,** a must-see for every visitor to Stuttgart. The Wilhelma is a zoo, with over 8000 different animals, and botanical garden, boasting over 6000 species of plants, housed in the ornate buildings and manicured gardens that were built by King Wilhelm as a summer retreat. Take U14 (dir.: Remseck) to "Wilhelma." (☎0711 540 20; www.wilhelma.de. Open daily 8:15am-dusk. €11.40, after 4pm and Nov-Feb. €8; ages 6-17 €5.70/4.) The superb **Staatsgalerie Stuttgart,** Konrad-Adenauer-Str. 30-32, displays Dalí, Kandinsky, and Picasso in its new wing, as well as paintings from the Middle Ages to the 19th century in its old wing. (☎0711 47 04 00; www.staatsgalerie.de. Open Tu-W and F-Su 10am-6pm, Th 10am-9pm. €4.50, students €3; special exhibits add at least €2, W free.) The sleek, modern **Mercedes-Benz Museum,** Mercedesstr. 100, is a must for car-lovers. Take S1 (dir.: Plochingen) to Gottlieb-Daimler-Stadion and follow the signs. (☎0711 173 0000; www.mercedes-benz.com/museum. Open Tu-Su 9am-6pm. €8, students €4.) Stuttgart's club scene doesn't pick up until after midnight, but when it does, **Eberhardstraße, Rotebühlplatz,** and **Theodor-Heuss-Straße** are the most popular areas. **Bravo Charlie,** Lautenschlagerstr. 14, is a hip cafe and restaurant by day and Stuttgart's most popular bar and nightclub after dark. (☎0711 23 16 882, www.bravo-charlie.de. Open M 8:30am-1am, Tu-W 8:30am-2am, Th 8:30am-3am, F 8:30am-5am, Sa 10am-5am, Su noon-1am.) The monthly magazine *Schwulst* (www.schwulst.de) has info on **gay and lesbian nightlife.**

The comfortable **Jugendgästehaus Stuttgart (IB) ❶,** Richard-Wagner-Str. 2, is one of the most affordable places to stay in town. Take the U15 to "Bubenbad". Delicious breakfast buffet and sheets included. (☎0711 24 11 32; jgh-stuttgart@internationaler-bund.de. Dinner M-Th €7. Laundry facilities €1.50. Key deposit. Reception 24hr. Dorms €16.50; singles €21.50; doubles €19 per person. Bath add €5. 1-night stays add €2.50. Show your *Let's Go* for a 10% discount. AmEx/MC/V.) International clientele crash in hip rooms with funky wall paintings at **Alex 30 Hostel ❶,** Alexanderstr. 30. Take tram #15 (dir.: Ruhbank) to Olgaeck. (☎0711 838 8950; www.alex30-hostel.de. Breakfast €6. Linens €3. Dorms €22; singles €34; doubles €54, with shower €64. MC/V.) Look for mid-range restaurants in the pedestrian zone between Pfarrstr. and Charlottenstr. **San's Sandwich Bar ❶,** Eberhardstr. 47, serves sandwiches (€2.70-3.50) with plenty of vegetarian options and baked goodies. (☎0711 410 1118; www.sans-stuttgart.de. Open M-F 8:30am-10pm, Sa 10am-7pm. Cash only.)

Trains run to Berlin (6hr., 2 per hr., €122); Frankfurt (1-2hr., 2 per hr., €38-55); Munich (2-3hr., 2 per hr., €34-50); Paris, FRA (8hr., 4 per day, €95-111). **Tourist office,** Königstr. 1A, is across from the train station. (☎0711 222 80. Open M-F

9am-8pm, Sa 9am-6pm, Su 11am-6pm.) The **post office,** Arnulf-Klett-Pl. 2, is in the station. (Open M-F 8:30am-6pm, Sa 8:30am-12:30pm.) **Postal Code:** 70173.

BLACK FOREST (SCHWARZWALD)

Nestled in the southwest corner of Baden-Württemberg, with France to the west and Switzerland to the south, is the mysterious *Schwarzwald* (Black Forest), a web of small towns tucked between tree-covered hills. The eerie darkness of the Black Forest has inspired a host of German fairy tales, most notably Hansel and Gretel. Today, the trees lure hikers and skiers with their grim beauty. The gateway into the forest, tucked into its western edge, lies **Freiburg** (pop. 210,000) known for its **Münster,** a 13th- to 16th-century stone cathedral. (☎0761 298 5963. Open M-Sa 9:30am-5pm, Su 1-5pm. Tours M-F 2-3pm, Sa-Su 2:30-3:30pm. Tower €1.50, students €1.) Tourists flock in summer to the tiny village of **Triberg** (pop. 5000) to see the world's largest **cuckoo clocks** or hike around the breathtaking **Gutacher Wasserfall,** a series of cascades tumbling 163m down moss-covered rocks that attracts a half-million visitors each year. (Park open 24hr.; admission 9am-7pm. €2.50, under 18 €2. Free for anyone spending the night in town–be sure to get your *Gästekarte* when you check in.)

CONSTANCE (KONSTANZ) ☎07531

Situated between the **Bodensee** (Lake Constance) and the **Rhein,** Constance is the last German town before the Swiss and Austrian borders. Often said to be in the "German Riviera," this elegant university town was spared from destruction in WWII thanks to its proximity to non-German neighbors. Today, the city's *Altstadt* and large waterfront promenades are some of Germany's most beautiful. The **Münster** (Cathedral) in the town center displays ancient religious relics and dark tunnels beneath its soaring 76m Gothic spire. (Open M-F 10am-5pm, Sa-Su 12:30-5:30pm.) Wander down **Rheinsteig,** along the Rhine **Seestraße,** or near the yacht harbor on the lake. Constance also has a number of public **beaches;** all are free and open from May to September. Take bus #5 to **Freibad Horn,** which is the largest (and most crowded) of the beaches with a nude sunbathing section enclosed by hedges.

Though technically in Switzerland, the **Jugendherberge Kreuzlingen (HI) ❷,** Promenadenstr. 7, is only a 15-20 min. walk from downtown. With clean, comfortable rooms that overlook the lake, a stay there is worth the trek. From the train station, head to the harbor, turn right, and walk into Switzerland along Seestr. When the road curves under a bridge, take the gravel path that veers slightly to the right. Pass through the border checkpoint "Klein Venedig" until the road curves under the bridge. (from Germany ☎+41 71 688 26 63; from Switzerland ☎071 688 26 63), Breakfast included. Reception 8-10am and 5-9pm. Closed Dec.-Feb. €20 per person per room. AmEx/MC/V.) Fall asleep to the sound of lapping waves and RVs at **Campingplatz Brudehofer ❶,** Fohrenbühlweg 50. Take bus #1 to Staad and walk for 10min. keeping the lake to your left. The campground is on the waterfront. (☎07531 313 88; www.campingkonstanz.de. Showers €1. Reception closed 1-3pm. €4 per person, €2.30 per child, €3.80-5.80 per tent, €2.80 per car, €6-8 per RV, €0.50 per bike. Cash only.)

Trains run from Constance to most cities in southern Germany; access destinations in Switzerland by walking to the Kreuzlingen station. BSB **ferries** leave hourly for ports around the lake. You can purchase tickets on board or in the building behind the train station, Hafenstr. 6. (☎05731 364 0389; www.bsb-online.com. Open Apr.-Oct. M-Th 8am-noon and 1-4pm, F 8am-noon and 1-5pm.) The **tourist office,** Bahnhofspl. 13, to the right of the train station, can help you locate private rooms for a €2.50 fee. (☎07531 133 030; www.konstanz.

de. Open Apr.-Oct. M-F 9am-6:30pm, Sa 9am-4pm, Su 10am-1pm; Nov.-Mar. M-F 9:30am-12:30pm and 2-6pm.) **Postal Code:** 78462.

BAVARIA (BAYERN)

Bavaria is the Germany of Teutonic myth and Wagnerian opera. From the Baroque cities along the Danube to mad King Ludwig's castles high in the Alps, the region attracts more tourists than any other part of the country.

MUNICH (MÜNCHEN) ☎089

Bavaria's capital and cultural center, Munich (pop. 1,245,000) is a sprawling, liberal metropolis where world-class museums, handsome parks, colossal architecture, and a genial population create a thriving city.

TRANSPORTATION

Flights: Flughafen München (MUC; ☎089 97 52 13 13). **Buses** S1 and 8 run from the airport to the *Hauptbahnhof* and Marienpl. (40min., 3 per hr., €8.80 or 8 strips on the *Streifenkarte*). For all-day travel, buy a **Gesaskamtnetz** day pass that covers all zones (€10). The Lufthansa **shuttle bus** goes to the *Hauptbahnhof* (40min., 3 per hr., €10) but is slower and more expensive than taking the train.

Trains: Munich's **Hauptbahnhof** (☎118 61) is the hub of southern Germany with connections to: **Berlin** (6hr., 2 per hr., €110); **Cologne** (4½hr., 2 per hr., €122); **Frankfurt** (3hr., 2 per hr., €85); **Füssen** (2hr., 2 per hr., €20); **Hamburg** (6hr., 1 per hr., €115); **Amsterdam, NTH** (7-9hr., 17 per day, €140); **Budapest, HUN** (7-9hr., 8 per day, €98); **Copenhagen, DEN** (11-15hr., 8 per day, €156); **Paris, FRA** (8-10hr., 6 per day, €124-152); **Prague, CZR** (6-7hr., 4 per day, €55); **Rome, ITA** (10-11hr., 5 per day, €126); **Salzburg, AUT** (1-2hr., 1 per hr., €29); **Venice, ITA** (7-10hr., 6 per day, €92); **Vienna, AUT** (4-6hr., 1-2 per hr., €73); **Zürich, SWI** (4-5hr., 4-5 per day, €70). The train goes through Austria, so make sure you've included Austria in the list of countries the pass covers if you have a Eurail pass—otherwise pay a small nominal fee (under €10) before you board the train. Purchase a **Bayern-Ticket** (€21, 2-5 people €29) for unlimited train transit daily 9am-3am in Bavaria and to Salzburg. **EurAide,** in the station, sells tickets. **Reisezentrum** ticket counters at the station are open daily 7am-9:30pm. Purchase tickets at the ticket agent in the *Bahnhof.*

Public Transportation: MVV (☎089 41 42 43 44; www.mvv-muenchen.de) operates **buses**, **trains**, the **S-Bahn** (underground trains), and the **U-Bahn** (subway). Most run M-Th 5am-12:30am, F-Sa 5am-2am. S-Bahn trains run until 2 or 3am daily. Night buses and trams ("N") serve Munich's dedicated clubbers. Eurail, Inter Rail, and German rail passes are valid on the S-Bahn but not on buses, trams, or the U-Bahn.

Tickets: Buy tickets at the blue vending machines and validate them in the blue boxes before entering the platform; otherwise, risk a €40 fine.

Prices: Single-ride tickets €2.20 (valid 2hr.). **Kurzstrecke** (short-trip) tickets €1.10 (1hr. or 2 stops on the U- or S-Bahn, 4 stops on a tram or bus). A **Streifenkarte** (10-strip ticket; €10.50) can be used by more than 1 person. Cancel 2 strips per person for a normal ride, or 1 strip for a short trip; for rides beyond the city center, cancel 2 strips per zone. A **Single-Tageskarte** (single-day ticket; €5) for *Innenraum* (the city's central zone) is valid until 6am the next day; the **partner** day pass (€9) is valid for up to 5 people. **3-day** single pass €13; 5-person pass €21. The **XXL Ticket** (single €6.70, partner €12) gives day-long transit in Munich's 2 innermost zones, white and green. Single **Gesamtnetz** (day ticket for all zones) €10; 5-person pass €18.

Taxis: Taxi-München-Zentrale (☎089 216 10 or 089 194 10).

Munich (München)

ACCOMMODATIONS
- Euro Youth Hotel, **9**
- Jaegers, **8**
- Jugendherberge Pullach Burg Schwaneck (HI), **14**
- Jugendlager Kapuzinerhölzl (The Tent), **3**
- Wombat's, **7**

FOOD
- Buxs, **13**
- Café Ignaz, **4**
- Dean & David, **2**
- Mensa, **1**
- News Bar, **11**
- Poseidon, **21**
- Weisses Brauhaus, **12**

BEER GARDENS
- Augustinerkeller, **5**
- Hirschgarten, **6**

BARS AND BEERHALLS
- Bei Carla, **18**
- Café Am Hochhaus, **22**
- Café Selig, **15**
- Hofbräuhaus, **10**
- Sausalitos, **23**
- Trachtenvogl, **16**
- Zappeforster, **17**

CLUBS
- Atomic Cafe, **24**
- Kultfabrik, **19**
- Muffathalle, **20**

Bike Rental: Mike's Bike Tours, Bräuhausstr. 10 (☎089 25 54 39 87; after hours ☎0172 852 0660). €12 per 1st day; €9 per day thereafter. 50% discount with tour (below). Open daily mid.-Apr. to mid-Oct. 10am-8pm; Mar. to mid-Apr. and mid-Oct. to mid-Nov. 10:30am-1pm and 4:30-5:30pm.

ORIENTATION

Downtown Munich is split into quadrants by thoroughfares running east-west and north-south. These intersect at Munich's central square, **Marienplatz,** and link the traffic rings at **Karlsplatz** (called Stachus by locals) in the west, **Isartorplatz** in the east, **Odeonsplatz** in the north, and **Sendlinger Tor** in the south. In the east beyond the Isartor, the Isar River flows north-south. The *Hauptbahnhof* is beyond Karlspl., to the west of the ring. To get to Marienpl. from the station, take any eastbound S-Bahn or use the main exit and make a right on Bahnhofpl., a left on Bayerstr. heading east through Karlspl., and continue straight. The **university** is to the north amid the **Schwabing** district's budget restaurants; to the east of Schwabing is the **English Garden** and to the west, **Olympiapark.** South of downtown is the **Glockenbachviertel,** filled with nightlife hot spots and gay bars. Here, travelers can find many hostels and fast food options, although the area can be dimly lit at night. Oktoberfest takes place on the large, open **Theresienwiese,** southeast of the train station on the U4 and 5 lines.

PRACTICAL INFORMATION

The most comprehensive list of services, events, and museums can be found in the English-language monthly *Munich Found* for €3 at the tourist office.

Tourist Offices: Main office (☎089 23 39 65 55) on the front side of the *Hauptbahnhof,* next to Yorma's on Bahnhofpl. Books rooms for free with a 10-15% deposit, and sells English-language city **maps** (€0.30). Open M-Sa 9am-6pm, Su 10am-6pm. **Branch office,** on Marienpl. at the entrance to the Neues Rathaus tower, is open M-F 10am-8pm, Sa 10am-4pm, Su noon-4pm, and accepts MC/V.

Consulates: Canada, Tal 29 (☎089 219 9570). Open M-F 9am-noon; 2-4pm by appointment only. **Ireland,** Dennigerstr. 15 (☎089 20 80 59 90). Open M-F 9am-noon. **UK,** Möhlstr. 5 (☎089 21 10 90). Open M-Th 8:30am-noon and 1-5pm, F 8:30am-

Laundromat: SB Waschcenter, Lindwurmstr. 124. Wash €3.50, dry €0.60 per 10min. Soap €0.30. Open daily 7am-11pm. **Branch** at Untersbergstr. 8 (U2, 7, or 8 to Untersbergstraße) provides free Wi-Fi.

Medical Emergency: ☎112 or 192 22.

Post Office: Bahnhofpl. In the yellow building opposite the Hauptbahnhof exit. Open M-F 7:30am-8pm, Sa 9am-4pm. **Postal Code:** 80335.

GERMANY

ACCOMMODATIONS AND CAMPING

Lodgings in Munich tend to be either seedy, expensive, or booked solid. During mid-summer and Oktoberfest, book at least a week ahead or start calling before noon; rooms are hard to find and prices jump 10% or more.

Euro Youth Hotel, Senefelderstr. 5 (☎089 59 90 88 11; www.euro-youth-hotel.de), near the *Hauptbahnhof.* Laid-back hostel with an energetic atmosphere at night. Breakfast €3.90. Laundry €4.10. Internet €1 per 30min.; free Wi-Fi. Reception 24hr. In summer dorms €20; 3- to 5-bed dorms €24; singles €45; doubles €60, with breakfast, shower, and TV €75. In winter €10/13/45/60/75. Cheapest beds available online. MC/V. ❷

Jugendlager Kapuzinerhölzl (The Tent), In den Kirschen 30 (☎089 141 43 00; www.the-tent.de). Tram #17 from the *Hauptbahnhof* (dir.: Amalienburgstr.) to Botanischer

Garten (15min.). Follow the signs to the right. Join 250 international "campers" under a gigantic tent on a wood floor. Kitchen and laundry available. Free lockers; no lock provided. Internet €1 per 30min. Key deposit €25 or passport. Reception 24hr. Open June 15-Oct. 15. €7.50, includes breakfast, foam pad, and wool blankets; beds €11; camping €5.50 per person, €5.50 per tent. Cash only. ❶

Jaegers, Senefelderstr. 3 (☎089 55 52 82; www.jaegershostel.de). Modern, colorful hostel with a mellow lounge by day and a boisterous bar by night. Breakfast included. Internet €1 per 20min. Free Wi-Fi. Laundry €4. Reception 24hr. 40-bed dorms €20; smaller dorms €23-25; singles €55; doubles with bath €79. Rates may vary. AmEx/MC/V. ❷

FOOD

For a typical Bavarian lunch, spread a *Brez'n* (pretzel) with *Leberwurst* (liverwurst) or cheese. *Weißwürste* (white veal sausages) are a specialty, but are only eaten before noon. Don't eat the skin; slice them open instead. *Leberknödel* are liver dumplings. Just south of Marienpl., vendors gather in the **Viktualienmarkt** to sell meats, fresh veggies, and specialty dishes, but don't expect budget groceries. (Open M-F 10am-8pm, Sa 8am-4pm.) Off **Ludwigstraße,** the university district supplies students with inexpensive, filling meals. Many reasonably priced restaurants and cafes cluster on **Schellingstraße, Amalienstraße,** and **Türkenstraße** (U3 or 6 to Universität).

Dean & David, Schellingstr. 13 (☎089 33 09 83 18; www.deananddavid.com). U3 or U6 to Universität. Curries and fresh salads (from €3) in an airy, modern setting. Entrees €5-7. Free Wi-Fi. Open M-F 8am-10pm, Sa 10am-9pm. Cash only. ❷

Buxs, Frauenstr. 9 (☎089 291 9550). This vegetarian restaurant serves artful pastas, salads, and soups. Self-serve, with a weight-based charge (€2.30 per 100g). Takeout available. Open M-F 11am-6:45pm, Sa 11am-3pm. Cash only. ❷

Augustiner Beerhall and Restaurant, Neuhauser Str. 27 (☎089 23 18 32 57). This restaurant, between Marienpl. and the train station, offers Bavarian specialties and *Maß* (Augustiner brew; €6). Entrees €4-13.50. Open daily 9am-midnight. Cash only. ❸

BEER GARDENS (BIERGÄRTEN)

Munich has six great beer labels: *Augustiner, Hacker-Pschorr, Hofbraü, Löwenbraü, Paulaner,* and *Spaten-Franziskaner.* Most establishments only serve one brewery's beer, in four varieties:

TAP THAT

Although droves of tourists visi[t] Germany to guzzle its renowne[d] beer, few understand the intrica[...]cies of German *Bierkultur.* Bee[r] is typically served by the quar[t] (*Maß,* ask for *"Ein Maß, bitte,"*) and sometimes by the pint (Halb Maß). A *Helles* is a pale, ofte[n] Bavarian, lager. Those looking fo[r] a bitter, less malty beer with mor[e] alcohol order the foam-crowne[d] *Pilsener,* and often search far an[d] wide for the perfect head.

A *Radler* (Bikers Brew) i[s] a 50-50 blend of *Helles* an[d] sparkling lemonade, so name[d] because the inventor sought t[o] mitigate the inebriation of th[e] crazed cyclists passing throug[h] his pub. In the north, this sam[e] beverage is called an *Alster,* afte[r] the river. *Weißbier* is a cloud[y] strong beer made with malte[d] wheat (*Weizen*), while *Rauchbie[r]* acquires its distinctive smok[y] taste from malted barley.

Even the toasted, malty lage[r] *Dunkeles,* is not the stronges[t] beer. If you're in the mood fo[r] severe inebriation, try a Boc[k] (strong beer) or a *Doppelboc[k]* (even stronger). These beers ar[e] often brewed by monks becaus[e] they are rich enough to sustai[n] them through religious fasts. Piet[y] has never looked so enticing.

There are over 1000 Germa[n] breweries producing thousand[s] more brands of German bee[r] each year. With a liquor pool tha[t] big, you'll have more than enoug[h] opportunities to lift a glass an[d] shout *"Prost!"*

Helles (light), *Dunkles* (dark), *Weißbier* (cloudy blond wheat beer), and *Radler* ("biker's brew"; half beer, half lemon soda). For a *Maß* (1L; €5-7), you need only say, *"Ein Bier, bitte."* Specify for a *halb-Maß* (0.5L; €3-4) or a *Pils* (0.3L; €2-3).

Augustinerkeller, Arnulfstr. 52 (☎089 59 43 93), at Zirkus-Krone-Str. S1-8 to Hackerbrücke. From the station, make a right on Arnulfstr. Considered by many to be one of Munich's best *Biergärten.* Indulge in enormous *Brez'n* and soak up the dim lighting beneath 100-year-old chestnut trees. Open daily 10am-1am. Kitchen open 10:30am-10:30pm. AmEx/MC/V.

Hirschgarten, Hirschgarten 1 (☎089 17 25 91). Tram #17 (dir.: Amalienburgstr.) to Romanpl. Walk south to the end of Guntherstr. Europe's largest *Biergärten* (seats 8000) is boisterous and always crowded. Entrees €6-18. *Maß* €5.90. Open daily 9am-midnight. Kitchen open 9am-10pm. Cash only.

SIGHTS

RESIDENZ. Down the pedestrian zone from Odeonspl., the richly decorated state rooms and apartments of the Residenz, home to the Wittelsbach dynasty from 1623 to 1918, represent Neoclassical, Baroque, and Rococo styles. Highlights of the **Residenzmuseum** include the painting-packed **Antiquarium,** the royal **family portraits** in the ancestral gallery, and the lavish **papal chambers.** The adjacent **Schatzkammer** (treasury) contains crowns, crucifixes, reliquaries, and swords. Out back, the manicured **Hofgarten** shelters the lovely temple of Diana. *(Max-Joseph-Pl. 3. U3-6 to Odeonspl. ☎089 29 06 71. Open daily Apr. to mid-Oct. 9am-6pm; mid-Oct. to Mar. 10am-4pm. Half of the Residenz is open in the morning until 1:30pm and the other half is open after 1:30pm. Both parts are €6, students €5; both €9/8. Garden free. Free audio tour.)*

PETERSKIRCHE AND FRAUENKIRCHE. Across from the Neues Rathaus, the 12th-century **Peterskirche** is the city's oldest parish church. Scale over 300 steps up the tower for a grand view. *(Open M-Tu and Th-Su 7:30am-7pm. Tower €1.50, students €1.)* From Marienpl., take Kaufingerstr. toward the *Hauptbahnhof* to the onion-domed towers of the 15th-century **Frauenkirche**—one of Munich's most notable landmarks. *(Frauenpl. 1. Open daily 7am-7pm. Church free; towers €3.50, students €1.50.)*

ENGLISCHER GARTEN. More expansive than New York City's Central Park or London's Hyde Park, the Englischer Garten is Europe's largest metropolitan public park. On sunny days, the city turns out to bike, play badminton, or ride horses. The garden includes a Chinese pagoda, a classic *Biergärten,* a Greek temple, and a Japanese teahouse. FKK (*Frei Körper Kultur;* free body culture) on signs and park maps designates nude sunbathing areas. Daring *Müncheners* raft, surf, or swim the rapids of the Eisbach, which flows through the park.

SCHLOSS NYMPHENBURG. After a decade of trying for an heir, Ludwig I celebrated his son's 1662 birth by building an elaborate summer playground northwest of Munich. Modeled after Versailles, the palace's most unusual asset is its **Gallery of Beauties,** a collection of portraits of noblewomen and commoners whom the king fancied. In the gardens, the **Amalienburg, Badenburg,** and **Pagodenburg** manors housed exclusive parties. *(Tram #17, dir.: Amalienburgstr., to "Schloß Nymphenburg." ☎089 17 90 80. Complex open daily Apr. to mid-Oct. 9am-6pm; mid-Oct. to Mar. 10am-4pm. Badenburg and Pagodenburg closed mid-Oct. to Mar. Schloß €5, students €4; audio tour €3. Manors each €2/1. Marstallmuseum €4/3. Entire complex €10/8; in winter €8/6.)*

MUSEUMS

Many of Munich's museums would require days to explore completely. All state-owned museums, including the three **Pinakotheken,** are €1 on Sunday.

PINAKOTHEKEN. Designed by *Münchener* Stephan Braunfels, the beautiful **Pinakothek der Moderne** is four museums in one. Subgalleries display architecture, design, drawings, and paintings by artists ranging from Picasso to contemporary masters. *(Barerstr. 40. U2 to Königspl or tram #27 to Pinakotheken. ☎089 23 80 53 60. Open Tu-W and Sa-Su 10am-5pm, Th-F 10am-8pm. €9.50, students €6. Audio tour free.)* Commissioned in 1826 by King Ludwig I, the **Alte Pinakothek** houses 500 years of art, works by 19th- and 20th-century artists including works by Leonardo da Vinci, Rembrandt, and Rubens. *(Barerstr. 27. ☎089 23 80 52 16; www.alte-pinakothek.de. Open Tu 10am-8pm, W-Su 10am-6pm. €5.50, students €4.)* Next door, the **Neue Pinakothek** displays fascinating work of famous artists including Cézanne, Monet, and van Gogh. *(Barerstr. 29. ☎089 23 80 51 95; www.neue-pinakothek.de. Open M and Th-Su 10am-5pm, W 10am-8pm. €5.50, students €4; includes audio tour.)*

DEUTSCHES MUSEUM. If you don't know (or care) how engines power a Boeing 747, the Deutsches Museum's over 50 departments on science and technology will keep you entertained and educated. Exhibits include one of the first telephones, a recreated subterranean labyrinth of mining tunnels, and realistic models of medieval alchemist labs. *(Museuminsel 1. S1-8 to Isartor or tram #18 to Deutsches Museum. ☎089 217 91; www.deutsches-museum.de. Open daily 9am-5pm. €8.50, students €3. English-language guidebook €4.)*

BMW MUSEUM. This driving museum is a bit of a shrine to the company displaying past, present, and future BMW products. Illuminated frosted glass walls and touch-sensitive projections lead visitors past engines, chassis, and concept vehicles. *(Petuelring 130. U3 to Olympiazentrum, take the Olympiaturm exit, and walk a block up Lerchenauer Str.; the museum will be on your left. ☎089 180 211 88 22; www.bmw-museum.de. Open Tu-F 9am-6pm, Sa-Su 10am-8pm. €12, students €6.)*

ENTERTAINMENT

Munich deserves its reputation as a world-class cultural center. Sixty theaters are scattered generously throughout the city staging productions that range from dramatic classics at the **Residenztheater** and **Volkstheater** to comic opera at the **Staatstheater am Gärtnerplatz** to experimental works at the **Theater im Marstall.** Munich's numerous fringe theaters, cabaret stages, and art cinemas in **Schwabing** reveal its bohemian spirit. *Monatsprogramm* (free) and *Munich Found* (free at the tourist office) list schedules for festivals, museums, and performances. In July, a magnificent **opera festival** arrives at the **Bayerische Staatsoper** (Bavarian National Opera), Max-Joseph-Pl. 2. (☎089 21 85 01; www.bayerische.staatsoper.de. U3-6 to Odeonspl. or tram #19 to Nationaltheater.) For €8-10, students can buy tickets for performances marked "Young Audience Program" two weeks in advance. Snag leftover tickets—if there are any—at the **evening box office,** Max-Joseph-Pl. 2, near the theater, for €10. (Opens 1hr. before curtain.) Standing-room tickets are half-price and can be purchased at any time. The **daytime box** office is at Marstallpl. 5. (☎089 21 85 19 20. Open M-F 10am-6pm, Sa 10am-1pm. Performances Oct.-July).

FESTIVALS AND NIGHTLIFE

Müncheners party zealously during *Fasching* (Mardi Gras; Feb 19-25, 2009; Feb 11-17, 2010), shop with abandon during the *Christkindlmarkt* (Christ Child Market; Dec. 1-23), and chug unfathomable quantities of beer during the legendary **Oktoberfest** (Sept. 19-Oct. 4, 2009; Sept. 18-Oct. 3, 2010).

BARS AND BEER HALLS

Zappeforster, Corneliusstr. 16 (☎089 20 24 52 50). U1-3 or 6 to Sendlinger Tor. Students and young hipsters huddle around the tables on Gärtner Platz or bop along to the alternative beats in the no-frills interior. During the day, *Müncheners* lounge on cushions for coffee and conversation. Beer 0.5L €3. Open daily 11am-1am. Cash only.

Trachtenvogl, Reichenbachstr. 47 (☎089 201 5160; www.trachtenvogl.de). U1-2 or 7-8 to Frauenhofer. Enjoy 32 types of hot chocolate in a cozy living room with chic lamps. F live bands. Su chocolate fondue; reservations required in winter. Happy hour daily 6-7pm; Astra beer €1.60. Open M-Th and Su 10am-1am, F-Sa 10am-3am. Cash only.

Café Am Hochhaus, Blumenstr. 29 (☎089 05 81 52; www.cafeamhochhaus.de). U1-3 or 6 to Sendlinger Tor. Sometimes a dance party, sometimes a relaxed cafe, the mood at the popular Café Am Hochhaus changes nightly, with the crowd. Beer 0.5L €3.20. Mixed drinks €7-8. Open M-W and Su 8pm-3am, Th-Sa 8pm-5am. Cash only.

CLUBS

Kultfabrik, Grafingerstr. 6 (☎089 49 00 90 70; www.kultfabrik.info). Take U5 or S1-8 to Ostbahnhof, turn right on Friedenstr., then left on Grafingerstr. 23 clubs crammed into 1 complex. The Russian-themed **Club Kalinka** is one of the more rowdy spots, popular with young locals and backpackers. Doors open around 10pm and close late. MC/V.

Muffathalle, Zellstr. 4 (☎089 45 87 50 10; www.muffathalle.de), in Haidhausen. S1-8 to Rosenheimerpl. or tram #18 (dir.: St. Emmeram) to Deutsches Museum. Hip hop, jazz, spoken word, techno, and dance shows. Non traditional *Biergärten.* Open M-Th 5pm-late, F-Su noon-late. Buy tickets online or through München Ticket. Cash only.

OKTOBERFEST

From the penultimate Saturday of September through early October Every fall, hordes of tourists and locals make an unholy pilgrimage to Munich to drink and be merry in true Bavarian style. Participants chug five million liters of beer, but only on a full stomach of 200,000 *Würste.* What began in 1810 as a celebration of the wedding of Ludwig I has become the world's largest folk festival. Representatives from all over Bavaria met outside the city gates for a week of horse racing on fields they named **Theresienwiese** in honor of Ludwig's bride (U4 or U5 to Theresienwiese). The bash was such fun that Munich's citizens have repeated the revelry (minus the horses) ever since. Festivities begin with the "Grand Entry of the *Oktoberfest* Landlords and Breweries," a **parade** ending at noon with the ceremonial drinking of the first keg, to the cry of *"O'zapft is!"* or "It's tapped!" by the Lord Mayor of Munich. Other highlights include international folklore presentations, a costume and rifleman's parade, and an open-air concert. Each of Munich's breweries sets up a tent in the Theresienwiese. Arrive early (by 4:30pm) to get a table; you must have a seat to be served alcohol. Those sharing a love of alcohol with their kin will thoroughly appreciate the reduced prices of family days.

NUREMBERG (NÜRNBERG) ☎0911

Before it witnessed the fanaticism of Hitler's Nazi rallies, Nuremberg (pop. 501,000) hosted Imperial Diets (parliamentary meetings) in the first Reich. Today, the remnants of both regimes draw visitors to the city, which new generations have rechristened **Stadt der Menschenrechte** (City of Human Rights). Head up Königstr. for the real sights of the city. Take a detour to the left for the pillared **Straße der Menschenrechte** (Avenue of Human Rights) as well as the gleaming glass **Germanisches Nationalmuseum,** Kartäuserg. 1, which chronicles German art since prehistoric times. (☎0911 133 10. Open Tu and Th-Su 10am-6pm, W

10am-9pm. Last entry 1hr. before closing. €6, students €4, W 6-9pm free.) Hidden in the fence of the **Schöner Brunnen** (Beautiful Fountain), in the Hauptmarkt, is a seamless, spinning golden ring, thought to bring good luck. Atop the hill, the **Kaiserburg** (Fortress of the Holy Roman Emperor) looms symbolically over Nuremberg. Climb the **Sinwellturm** for the best views of the city. (Open daily 9am-6pm. €6, students €5; includes a tour of the castle and museum.). On the far side of the lake is the **Zeppelintribüne,** the grandstand where Hitler addressed the masses. The *Fascination and Terror* exhibit, in the **Kongresshalle** at the north end of the park, covers the Nazi era. (☎0911 231 5666. Open M-F 9am-6pm, Sa-Su 10am-6pm. €5, students €2.50; includes audio tour.) Tram #9 from the train station stops directly at the Kongresshalle *(Dokumentationszentrum)* stop. To reach the Zeppelintribüne, walk clockwise around the lake.

Jugendgästehaus (HI) ❶, Burg 2, sits in a castle above the city. From the tourist office, follow Königstr. over the bridge to the Hauptmarkt, head diagonally across to the fountain, and continue up Burgstr. (☎0911 230 9360. Reception 7am-1am. Curfew 1am. Dorms €21.40; singles €39.50; doubles €46. AmEx/MC/V.) The eccentricly-named and spacious rooms—like "Wrong Room" and "Right Room"—of **Lette'm Sleep ❶**, Frauentormauer 42, are only a short walk away from the train station. Take the first left after entering the *Altstadt* through Königpl. (☎0911 992 8128. Lockers available, bring your own lock. Linens €3. Free Internet. Reception 24hr. Dorms €16; singles €30; doubles €48-52. MC/V.) **Bratwursthäusle ❶**, Rathauspl. 1, has cheaper fare like three *Rostbratwurst* in a *Weckla* (bratwurst in a roll) for €1.80, six *Würste with kraut* for €6.20, and seasonal *Spargel* (white asparagus) for €4. (☎0911 22 76 95. Entrees €3-8. Open daily 10am-10:30pm. Cash only.) **Hauptmarkt vendors** sell cheese, sandwiches, pastries, and produce from early morning to dusk. Nuremberg's nightlife thrives in the *Altstadt*. **Hirsch,** Vogelweiherstr. 66, the city's most popular club, has multiple bars and a *Biergärten* out front. (Take nightbus #5 to Vogelweiherstr. ☎0911 429 414; www.der-hirsch.de. Mixed drinks €5.50. M-Th frequent concerts. Cover €3-15. Open M-Th 8pm-2am, F-Sa 10pm-5am. Cash only). **Cine Città,** Gewerbemuseumspl. 3, U-Bahn to Wöhrder Wiese, packs 16 bars and cafes, 17 German-language cinemas, an IMAX theater, and a disco inside one complex. (☎0911 20 66 60. Open M-Th and Su until 2am, F-Sa until 3am.) **Cartoon,** An der Sparkasse 6, is a popular gay bar near Lorenzpl. (☎0911 22 71 70. Shots €3.80. Mixed drinks €5-7.50. Open M-Th 11am-1am, F-Sa 11am-3am, Su 2pm-1am.)

Trains go to: Berlin (4½hr., every hr., €86); Frankfurt (2hr., 2 per hr., €46); Munich (1hr., 2 per hr., €47); Stuttgart (2-3hr., every hr., €30-36). Walk through the tunnel from the train station to the *Altstadt* and take a right to reach the **tourist office,** Königstr. 93. (☎0911 233 6132. Open M-Sa 9am-7pm, Su 10am-4pm.) A second office is in the Hauptmarkt. (Open M-Sa 9am-6pm.) **Internet** is available at the immaculate **Telepoint,** on the underground level of the train station. (€1.50 per hr. Open daily 8am-midnight.) **Postal Code:** 90402.

ROMANTIC ROAD

Groomed fields of sunflowers, vineyards, and hills checker the landscape between Würzburg and Füssen. Officially christened *Romantische Straße* (the Romantic Road) in 1950, the road is dotted with almost a hundred castles, helping to make it one of the most traversed routes in Germany.

TRANSPORTATION

Train travel is the most flexible, economical way to visit the Romantic Road. Deutsche Bahn operates a **bus** route along the Romantic Road, shuttling tourists from Frankfurt to Munich (13hr., €99), stopping in Würzburg (2hr., €22), Rothenburg (4hr., €35), and Füssen (11hr., €80). A Castle Road **bus** route connects Rothenburg with Nuremburg (3hr., €14). Both buses run once a day in each direction. For reservations and more detailed information, see www.romanticroadcoach.de. There is a 10% student and under 26 discount, and a 60% Eurail and German Rail Pass discount.

FÜSSEN ☎08362

Füssen ("feet") seems an apt name for a little town at the foot of the Bavarian Alps. Füssen is the ideal basecamp for some of Germany's best daytrips; the town is mere minutes from King Ludwig's famed **Königsschlößer,** one of the best hiking, biking, and boating regions in the country. Although Füssen's best accommodations are pensions, the tourist office keeps a list of *Privatzimmer* with vacant rooms. **Jugendherberge (HI)** ❷, Mariahilfer Str. 5, lies in a residential area 15min. from the town center. Turn right from the station and follow the railroad tracks. (☎08362 77 54. Laundry €1.60. Reception daily Mar.-Sept. 7am-noon and 5-10pm; Oct. and Dec.-Apr. 5-10pm. Lockout 11pm-6:30am; keycode available. Dorms €17.50. MC/V.) Bakeries, butcher shops, and *Imbiße* (snack bars) stand among the pricey cafes on **Reichenstraße,** particularly off the Luitpold Passage. The **Plus** supermarket is on the right toward the rotary from the station. (Open M-Sa 8:30am-8pm.) **Trains** run to Augsburg (1hr., every hr., €17) and Munich (2hr., every hr., €21). To get to the **tourist office,** Kaiser-Maximilian-Pl. 1, from the train station, walk the length of Bahnhofstr. and then head across the roundabout to the big yellow building on your left. (☎938 50; www.fuessen.de. Open June-Sept. M-F 9am-6pm, Sa 10am-2pm; Oct.-May M-F 9am-5pm, Sa 10am-noon.) **Postal Code:** 87629.

DAYTRIP FROM FÜSSEN: KÖNIGSSCHLÖßER. King Ludwig II, a frenzied visionary, built fantastic castles soaring into the alpine skies. In 1886, a band of nobles and bureaucrats deposed Ludwig, declared him insane, and imprisoned him; three days later, the king was mysteriously discovered dead in a lake. The fairy-tale castles that Ludwig created and the enigma of his death captivate tourists. The glitzy **Schloß Neuschwanstein** inspired Disney's Cinderella Castle, and is one of Germany's iconic attractions. Hike 10min. to the **Marienbrücke,** a bridge that spans the gorge behind the castle. Climb the mountain on the other side of the bridge for the enchantment without the crowds. Ludwig spent his summers in the bright yellow **Schloß Hohenschwangau** across the valley. Don't miss the night-sky frescoes in the king's bedroom. While you're there, spend the extra money to see both castles; seeing the pair of them makes the experience more memorable. From the Füssen train station, take **bus** #73 or 78, marked "Königsschlößer" (10min.; 1-2 per hr.; €1.70, round-trip €3.20) or **walk** the 4km along beautiful, winding roads. Tickets for both castles are sold at the **Ticket-Service Center,** about 100m uphill from the bus stop. Arrive before 10am to escape long lines. *(☎08362 93 08 30. Both castles open daily Apr.-Sept. 9am-6pm, ticket windows open 8am-5pm; Oct.-Mar. castles 10am-4pm, tickets 9am-3pm. Mandatory tours of each castle €9, students €8; 10 languages available. Combination ticket €17/15.)*

ROTHENBURG OB DER TAUBER ☎09861

Possibly the only walled medieval city without a single modern building, Rothenburg (pop. 12,000) is *the* Romantic Road stop. After the Thirty Years' War, without money to modernize, the town remained unchanged for 250 years. Tourism later brought economic stability and another reason to preserve the medieval *Altstadt.* The English-language tour led by the **night watchman** gives a fast-paced and entertaining introduction to Rothenburg history. (Starts at the

Rathaus on Marktpl. Easter-Dec. 25 daily 8pm. €6, students €4.) A long climb up the narrow stairs of the 60m **Rathaus Tower** leads to a panoramic view of the town's red roofs. (Open Apr.-Oct. daily 9:30am-12:30pm and 1-5pm; Dec. daily noon-3pm; Nov. and Jan.-Mar. Sa-Su noon-3pm. €2.) According to proud local lore, during the Thirty Years' War, the conquering Catholic general Johann Tilly offered to spare the town from destruction if any local could chug a keg containing 3.25L (almost a gallon) of wine. Mayor Nusch successfully met the challenge, passed out for several days, then lived to a ripe old age. His saving **Meistertrunk** (Master Draught) is reenacted with tremendous fanfare from the entire town each year (May 29-June 1, 2009).

For private rooms unregistered at the tourist office (€15-45), look for the *Zimmer frei* (free room) signs in restaurants and stores. The 500-year-old **Pension Raidel ❷,** Wengg. 3, will make you feel like you're sleeping in the past. (☎9861 31 15; www.romanticroad.com/raidel. Breakfast included. Singles €24, with bath €42; doubles €49/59. Cash only.) Dine on sinfully good food at **Zur Höll ❷,** Burgg. 8. Originally built as a home in AD 980, Zur Höll (To Hell) still serves Franconian fare (€4-18) by dim candlelight. (☎9861 42 29. Bratwurst with sauerkraut €6. Open daily 5pm-midnight. Cash only.)

Trains run to Steinach (15min., 1 per hr., €1.90), which has transfers to Munich (€32) and Würzburg (€12). The **Europabus** leaves from the *Busbahnhof* by the train station. The **tourist office,** Marktpl. 2, has great resources that will make your trip to Rothenburg much more organized, and offers 15min. of free **Internet**. From the train station, head left before taking a right on Ansbacherstr.. (☎9861 404 800. Open May-Oct. M-F 9am-6pm, Sa-Su 10am-3pm; Nov.-Apr. M-F 9am-noon and 1-5pm, Sa 10am-1pm.) **Postal Code**: 91541

EASTERN GERMANY

Saxony *(Sachsen)* and Thuringia *(Thüringen)*, the most interesting regions in eastern Germany outside of Berlin, encompass Dresden, Leipzig, and Weimar. Castles surrounding Dresden reveal Saxony's one-time wealth, while boxy GDR-era buildings recall the socialist aesthetic.

WEIMAR ☎03643

The writer Johann Wolfgang Goethe once said of Weimar (pop. 64,000), "Where else can you find so much that is good in a place that is so small?" Indeed, Weimar's diverse cultural attractions, lustrous parks, and rich history make the city a UNESCO World Heritage site and a worthwhile stop on any tour of eastern Germany. The **Goethehaus** and **Goethe-Nationalmuseum,** Frauenplan 1, preserve the chambers where the poet wrote, entertained guests, and, after a half-century in Weimar, died. The elegant abode is now stuffed with his art collection, and his fetching yellow buggy is parked under the house. (Open Apr.-Sept. Tu-F and Su 9am-6pm, Sa 9am-7pm; Oct. Tu-Su 9am-6pm; Nov.-Mar. Tu-Su 9am-4pm. €6.50, students €5. Museum only €3/2.50.) The multi-talented Goethe landscaped the vast and bushy **Park an der Ilm,** Corona-Schöfer-Str., which contains his quaint little **Gartenhaus,** a retreat he owned until his death. Take in the intense floral smell-scape, and see more of the poet's possessions. (Access from inside the park. Open daily Apr.-Oct. 10am-6pm; Nov.-Mar. 10am-4pm. €3.50, students €2.50.) With the Medieval Palace Tower out front, the **Schloßmuseum** (Palace Museum), Burgplatz 4, is one of the city's most impressive sites. (Open Apr.-Oct. Tu-Su 10am-6pm; Nov.-Mar. daily 10am-4pm. €5, students €4.)

Jugendherberge Germania (HI) ❷, Carl-August-Allee 13, is close to the train station but a 15min. walk from the city center. Small but comfortable beds at good prices make this hostel a deal. (☎03643 85 04 90; www.djh-thueringen.de. Breakfast included. First night €24, under 27 €21; €23/20 thereafter. Cash only.) Enjoy filling savory or sweet crêpes at **Crêperie du Palais ❶**, Am Palais 1, near Theaterpl. and down the street from the Hababusch hostel. (Open daily 11am-midnight. Cash only.) Both a cafe and a gallery, **ACC ❶**, Burgpl. 1-2, serves creative daily specials (€5-6.50), screens art films in the hallway, and offers free Wi-Fi to its clientele. (Open daily May-Sept. 10am-1am; Oct.-Apr. 11am-1am. AmEx/MC/V.) A **market** is on Marktpl. (Open M-Sa 6am-4pm.))

Trains run to Dresden (3hr., every hr., €43); Frankfurt (3hr., every hr., €53); and Leipzig (1hr., every hr., €24). To reach Goetheplatz, a **bus** hub at the center of the *Altstadt*, follow Carl-August-Allee downhill from the station to Karl-Liebknecht-Str. (15min.) The **Weimar Information Center,** Markt 10, is across from the *Rathaus*. (☎03643 85 74 50; www.weimar.de. Books rooms for free.) They sell **maps** (€0.20), city guides (€0.50), as well as the **Weimar Card,** which provides free admission to the *Goethehaus* and the *Schloßmuseum*, and discounts to most other sights in the city, as well as free public transportation within Weimar. Student admission is often still lower than the Weimar Card price. (72hr. €10, 72hr. extensions €5). Information center open Apr.-Oct. M-F 9:30am-6pm, Sa-Su 9:30am-3pm. Nov.-Mar. M-F 10am-6pm, Sa-Su 10am-2pm.)

EISENACH ☎03691

Birthplace of Johann Sebastian Bach, residence-in-exile of Martin Luther, and site of the famous Wartburg castle, Eisenach (pop. 44,000) has garnered national and international attention for almost a millenium. The picturesque city Martin Luther once called "my dear town," is best known as home to **Wartburg Fortress,** which protected Luther in 1521 after his excommunication. It was here, disguised as a bearded noble that Luther famously fought an apparition of the devil with an inkwell by translating the New Testament into German and growing a heretical mustache. Keep your eyes peeled for the view from the **southern tower** (entrance €0.50). To reach Wartburg, walk along Schloßberg and follow the signs, or catch one of the buses (every hr. 9am-5pm; €1.50, €1.10 at the tourist office) running between the train station and the castle parking lot that stops twice along the way. (Open daily Mar.-Oct. 8:30am-8pm, last tour 5pm; Nov.-Feb. 9am-5pm, last tour 3:30pm. Castle grounds free, but to see inside the palace, you must take a tour; every 15min in German, English tour 1:30pm; €7, students €4.) Eisenach is also the birthplace of composer **Johann Sebastian Bach**. Although his exact place of birth is unknown, historical records suggest that Bach was born in 1685 in the **Bachhaus,** Frauenplan 21. Roughly every hour, a guide deftly demonstrates Bach selections on five period keyboard instruments–house organ to clavichord–and provides historical context in German. (Open daily 10am-6pm. €6, students €3.50. English translations at exhibits.) Martin Luther served as a choir-boy and Bach was baptized at the 800-year-old **Georgenkirche,** where members of Bach's family were organists for 132 years. (Open M-Sa 10am-12:30pm and 2-5pm, Su 11:30am-12:30pm and 2-5pm.)

The **Residenz Haus ❶,** Auf der Esplanade, around the corner from the tourist office, offers clean, spacious rooms. (☎21 41 33; www.residenzhaus-eisenach.de. Shared baths. Breakfast €6. €20 per person in rooms of three or more; singles and doubles €25 per person. Cash only.) To reach the Mediterranean-inspired **Jugendherberge Arthur Becker (HI) ❶,** Mariental 24, take bus #3 or 10 (dir.: Mariental) to Liliengrund Parkpl., or call a taxi (€6). To make the 35min. walk, take Bahnhofstr. from the station and stay left before the tower for Wartburger Allee, which runs into Mariental. (☎74 32 59; ww.djh-thueringen.de. Breakfast included. Reception M-F 7am-10pm, Sa-Su 7-10am and 3-10pm. Dorms €21.50, under 27 €18.50. Cash only.) **La Fontana ❶,** Georgenstr. 22, with a large fountain in front, is the best deal in town. (☎74 35 39. Pizza and pasta €3-5. Open M-Th and Su 11:30am-10:30pm, F-Sa 11:30am-11pm. Cash only.) For groceries, head to **Edeka** on Johannispl. (Open M-F 7am-5pm, Sa 7am-4pm.)

Trains run to and from Weimar (1hr., 1 per hr., €13-17). The **tourist office**, is on Markt 9. (Apr.-Oct. M-F 10:30am and 2pm, Sa-Su 3-4 per day; Nov.-Mar. Sa-Su 10am and 2pm. 2hr. €5). From the station, follow Bahnhofstr. through the tunnel and veer left, then take a right onto Karlstr. (☎03691 792 30. Open M-F 10am-6pm, Sa 10am-4pm; Apr.-Oct. also Su 10am-4pm.) **Postal Code**: 99817.

WITTENBERG ☎03491

Martin Luther ignited the Protestant Reformation here in 1517 when he nailed his 95 Theses to the door of the **Schloßkirche;** Wittenberg (pop. 48,000) has celebrated its native heretic ever since. All major sights surround **Collegienstraße** (which becomes **Schloßstraße** toward the church). In the back of the old university courtyard, the **Lutherhaus,** Collegienstr. 54, chronicles the Reformation through art, artifacts, letters, and texts. Hundreds of early printed pamphlets, for and against Luther's ideas, show that the Reformation was also a media revolution. (☎03491 420 3118; www.martinluther.de. Open Apr.-Oct. daily 9am-6pm; Nov.-Mar. Tu-Su 10am-5pm. €5, students €3.) Wittenberg's elegant **Altes Rathaus,** Markt 26, dominates the *Markt* with its arctic facade. Inside, a sleek modern room displays a terrific collection of 20th-century Christian graphic art. The departure from classical oil paintings is stark. (☎03491 401 149 www.christlichekunst-wb.de. Open Tu-Su 10am-5pm. €3, students €2.)

The **Jugendherberge im Schloß (HI)** is next to the church, Schlossstr. 14-15; enter first through the archway. Medieval on the outside, modern on the inside, the hostel couldn't be more convenient. (☎0341 505 205. Breakfast included. Rooms have shower and toilet, some are wheelchair-accessible. Linens €3.50. Reception 8am-10pm. Check-out 9:30am. Curfew 10pm. Dorms €23, under 27 €20. HI members €3 discount. MC/V.) Look for cheap meals along the Collegienstr.-Schloßstr. strip. **Zum Schwarzen Bär ❷**, Schloßstr. 2, the Wittenberger Kartoffelhaus, serves spud-centric dishes with a sense of humor. (☎0341 411 200. Entrees €4-12. Open daily 11am-1am. Kitchen open until midnight. V.)

Trains leave for Berlin (45min., 1 per hr., €21) and Leipzig (1hr., every 2hr., €10). Follow the "City" and "Altstadt" signs out of the station to the red brick path, which leads to Collegienstr., the start of the pedestrian zone. The **tourist office,** Schloßpl. 2, opposite the church, supplies **maps** in a dozen languages, including English and German (€0.50), books rooms for free, and frequently gives tours in German. **Postal Code:** 06886.

DRESDEN ☎0351

Over the course of two nights in February 1945, Allied firebombs incinerated over three-quarters of Dresden, killing between 25,000 and 50,000 civilians. With most of the *Altstadt* in ruins, the surviving 19th-century *Neustadt* became Dresden's nerve center: today, it is still an energetic nexus of nightlife and alternative culture. Since the war, the *Altstadt* has resurrected its regal grandeur, .

TRANSPORTATION

Flights: Dresden Airport (DRS; ☎0351 881 3360; www.dresden-airport.de) is 9km from the city. S2 runs there from both train stations (13min. from *Neustadt,* 23min. from the *Hauptbahnhof;* 2 per hr. 4am-11:30pm; €1.80).

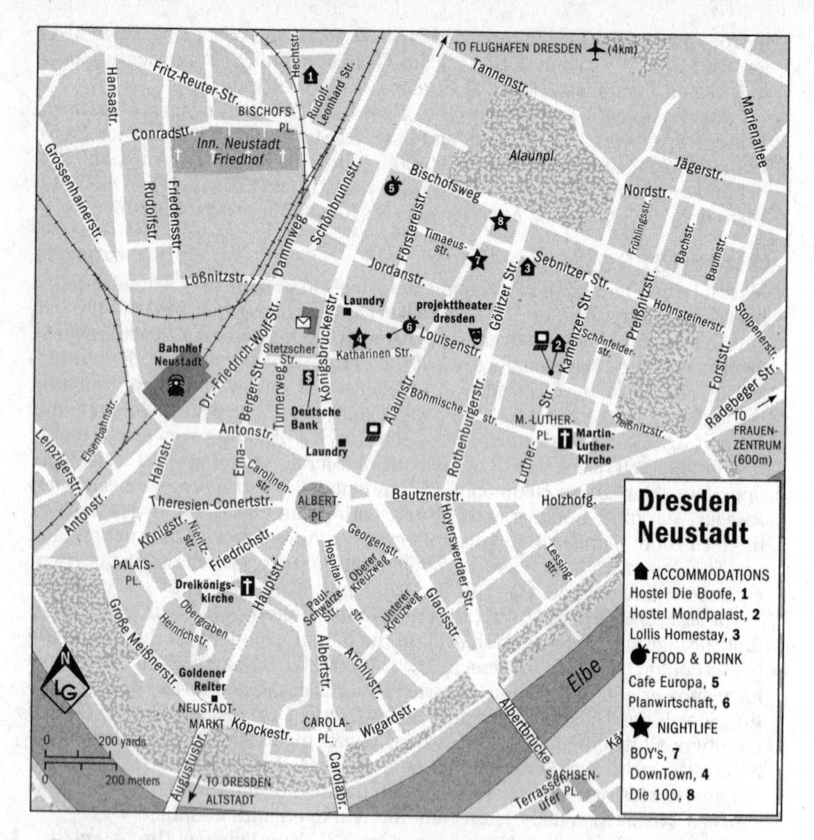

Trains: Nearly all trains stop at both the **Hauptbahnhof** in the *Altstadt* and **Bahnhof Dresden Neustadt** across the Elbe. Trains run to: **Berlin** (3hr., 1 per hr., €33-55); **Frankfurt am Main** (4hr., 1 per hr., €80); **Leipzig** (1hr., 1-2 per hr., €25); **Munich** (6hr., 1-2 per hr., €93); **Budapest, HUN** (11hr., 2 per day, €81); **Prague, CZR** (2hr., 9 per day, €20). Tickets are available at the *Reisezentrum* desk, but are cheaper at the machines located throughout the station's main hall.

Public Transportation: Much of Dresden is accessible on foot, but if jumping between districts, you may want to use **trams,** which cover the whole city. 1hr. ticket €1.80. Day pass €4.50. The €6 **Family Card,** good for 2 passengers until 4am, is probably the best deal. Weekly pass €17. Tickets are available from *Fahrkarte* dispensers at major stops and on **streetcars.** Validate on board. For info and **maps,** go to 1 of the **Service Punkt** stands in front of the *Hauptbahnhof* (open M-F 8am-7pm, Sa 8am-6pm, Su 9am-6pm) or at Postpl. (open M-F 8am-7pm, Sa 8am-6pm). Most major lines run hourly after midnight until 4am—look for the moon sign marked **Gute-Nacht-Linie.**

Taxis: ☎21 12 11 and ☎88 88 88 88 ("eight times eight"). Mercedes, BMW, and other fine German automobile taxis wait outside both train stations.

Bike Rental: Rent city bikes in either train station. In the *Hauptbahnhof,* look for **Gepaeck Center** (☎0351 461 32 62. Open daily 6:15am-9:30pm.) The **Fahrradverleih** is in the *Neustadt Bahnhof.* (☎0351 804 13 70. Open daily 6am-10pm.) €7 per day.

ORIENTATION AND PRACTICAL INFORMATION

A 60-degree hook in the **Elbe** bisects Dresden, 60km northwest of the Czech border, pointing toward the **Alsdadt** in the south and separating it from the **Neustadt** above. The **Hauptbahnhof** is at the southern foot of the city center. **Prager Str.,** a pedestrian zone lined with modern glass-window shops and fountains, leads from the train station to the **Altmarkt. Neumarkt,** the site of the famous **Frauenkirche,** and the **Zwinger palace,** which now extends into the rest of the city, border the Elbe and separate the Altmarkt from the river. The central walking bridge, **Augustusbrucke,** links the *Altstadt* city center with the *Neustadt's* pedestrian **Haupstr.,** at the Golden Rider statue. Haupstr, a tree-covered promenade, ends in the north at **Albertplatz,** a transportation hub that marks the effective end of the tourist zone. Thereafter, the city morphs into Dresden's residential youth headquarters. **Antonstr.** connects the **Dresden-Neustadt train station** to Albertpl. The Albertpl. pulse with the lively energy of Dresden's young alternative scene. Five romantic bridges—**Marienbrücke, Augustbrücke, Carolabrücke, Albertbrücke,** and the **"Blue Marvel" Loschwitzbrücke**—connect the city's two halves.

Tourist Office: 2 main branches: Prager Str. 2, near the *Hauptbahnhof* in the Prager Spitze shopping center (open M-Sa 10am-7pm), and Theaterpl. in the *Schinkelwache,* a small building directly in front of the Semper-Oper (open M-F 10am-6pm, Sa-Su 10am-4pm). 2 cards provide transportation and discounted rates to Dresden museums: the **Dresden City-Card,** valid for 48hr. of transport in the city-zone (€21), and the **Dresden Regio-Card,** good for 72hr. in the Oberelbe region, including Meißen and Saxon Switzerland (€32). Call the city hotlines for general info (☎0351 49 19 21 00), room reservations (☎0351 49 19 22 22), and tours and advance tickets (☎0351 49 19 22 33).

Luggage Storage: At all train stations. Lockers €2-2.50 for 24hr.

Laundromat: Eco-Express, Königsbrücker Str. 2. Wash €1.90 6-11am, €2.40 11am-11pm. Dry €0.50 per 10min. Powder soap €0.30. Open M-Sa 6am-11pm.

Post Office: The **Hauptpostamt,** Königsbrücker Str. 21/29 (☎0351 819 1373), in the *Neustadt.* Open M-F 9am-7pm, Sa 10am-1pm. Branch in the *Altstadt* on Wallstr. at the Altmarkt Galerie. Open M-F 8am-6pm, Sa 9am-noon. **Postal Code:** 01099.

ACCOMMODATIONS

The *Neustadt* is home to a number of independent hostels, close to the city's best nightlife. Quieter, though often larger, hostels are situated below the *Altstadt,* while pricier hotels are actually closer to many of the city sights.

Hostel Mondpalast, Louisenstr. 77 (☎0351 563 4050; www.mondpalast.de). Settle into comfy beds in large, clean rooms. Bike rental €5 per 3hr., €7 per day. Breakfast (until 2pm) €5. Linens €2. Internet €2 per hr. Reception 24hr. Check-out noon. 8- to 10- bed dorms Jan.-Mar. and Nov. €13, Apr.-Oct. and Dec. €13.50; 5- to 6-bed dorms €15/16; 3- to 4- bed dorms €16/17, with shower €18.50/19.50; singles €29/34, with shower €39/44; doubles €37/44, with shower €50/52. AmEx/MC/V. ❶

Hostel Die Boofe, Hechtstr. 10 (☎0351 801 3361; www.boofe.de). Focus of this hostel is the bar downstairs. Wheelchair-accessible. Breakfast €6. Internet €1 per hr. Reception 7am-midnight. Check-in 2pm. Check-out 11am. 4-bed dorm €15, with shower €18; singles €29/39; doubles €40/50. F-Sa add €1.50 per person, singles add €2.50. ❶

Lollis Homestay, Görlitzer Str. 34 (☎0351 8108 4558; www.lollishome.de). This hostel reproduces the relaxed feel of a student flat, with free coffee, tea, and a book exchange. Old bikes available to borrow. Breakfast €3. Linens €2. Laundry €3. Internet €2.50 per hr. Dorms €13-16; singles €27-38; doubles €36-42; triples €48-57; quads €60-72. 10% ISIC discount. MC/V; €2.50 surcharge. ❶

FOOD

It's difficult to find anything in the *Altstadt* that does not target tourists; the cheapest eats are at the *Imbiß* stands along **Prager Straße** and around **Postplatz.** The area in the *Neustadt* between **Albertplatz** and **Alaunpark** spawns a new bar every few weeks and is home to many quirky, student-friendly restaurants.

Cafe Aha, Kreuzstr. 7 (☎0351 496 0673; www.ladencafe.de), across the street from Kreuzkirche in the *Altstadt.* Ecologically sound foods and abundant vegetarian options. Store open M-F 10am-7pm, Sa 10am-6pm. Cafe open daily 10am-midnight; kitchen closes at 10:30pm. AmEx/MC/V; €10 min. ❷

Planwirtschaft, Louisenstr. 20 (☎0351 801 3187; www.planwirtschaft.de). Traditional and neo-German cuisine made with ingredients direct from local farms. Inventive soups, fresh salads (€3.50-7), entrees (€7-13), and "German tapas" (€6.80). Giant breakfast buffet (€9), daily 9am-3pm. Open M-Th and Su 9am-1am, F-Sa 9am-2am. MC/V. ❷

Cafe Europa, Königsbrücker Str. 68 (☎0351 804 4810; www.cafe-europa-dresden.de). Open 24hr. Draws a crowd of students and 20-somethings with 120 different drinks and a rack of 14 international newspapers. Breakfast menu with dishes from around the world €3.10-7.50, 6am-4pm. Pastas and more €6-10. Free Wi-Fi. AmEx/MC/V. ❶

SIGHTS

Saxony's electors once ruled nearly all of central Europe from the banks of the majestic Elbe. Destroyed during WWII and partially rebuilt during Communist times, Dresden's *Altstadt* is one of Europe's undisputed cultural centers.

KREUZKIRCHE. After it was leveled three times—by fire in 1669 and 1897 and then by the Seven Years' War in 1760—the Kreuzkirche survived WWII, despite the flames that ruined its interior. Its tower offers a bird's-eye view of downtown. *(An der Kreuzkirche 6. ☎0351 439 39 20; www.dresdner-kreuzkirche.de. Open Apr.-Oct. M-F 10am-5:30pm, Sa 10am-4:30pm, Su noon-5:30pm; Nov.-Mar. M-Sa 10am-3:30pm, Su noon-4:30pm. Church free. Tower €2.)* The world-class **Kreuzchor** boys' choir has sung here since the 13th century. *(☎0351 315 3560; www.kreuzchor.de. Vespers Sa 6pm , winter 5pm. For other concerts, pick up a schedule at the church.)*

FRAUENKIRCHE. The product of a legendary 10-year reconstruction effort after crumbling to the ground on February 13, 1945, the Frauenkirche re-opened on Oct. 31, 2005, completing Dresden's skyline with its regal silhouette. On weekends, the quickly moving line can curl around the Neumarkt. *(Neumarkt. ☎0351 498 11 31; www.frauenkirche-dresden.de. Open M-F 10am-noon and 1-6pm. Sa-Su hours vary, check the information center on Neumarkt for details or pick up a free copy of the German-language Leben in der Frauenkirche schedule at the tourist office and look for "Offene Kirche." Entry free. Audio guides €2.50, available in English. The church holds open masses M-F at noon and 6pm, except for Th 6pm. Afterward, a short tour in German is given. Cupola open daily 10am-1pm; Apr.-Oct. also 2-6pm, Nov.-Mar. 2-4pm. €8, students €5.)*

MUSEUMS

After several years of renovations, Dresden's museums are once again ready to compete with the best in Europe. Once home to several acquisitive Saxon kings, Dresden has accrued some formidable collections. If you plan on visiting more than one in a day, consider a **Tageskarte** (€12, students €7), which grants one-day admission to the Schloß, most of the Zwinger, and more. The **Dresden City-Card** and **Dresden Regio-Card** (see **Practical Information** above) include museum admission. Info about all museums is at www.skd-dresden.de.

ZWINGER. A glorious example of Baroque design, Zwinger narrowly escaped destruction in the 1945 bombings. The palace interior has been converted into museum space for the **Saxon State Art Collection.** Through the archway from the Semper-Oper, **Gemäldegalerie Alte Meister** has a world-class collection of Dutch and Italian paintings from 1400 to 1800, including Cranach the Elder's luminous *Adam and Eve*, Giorgione's *Sleeping Venus*, and Raphael's enchanting *Sistine Madonna*. *(☎0351 49 14 20 00. Open Tu-Su 10am-6pm. €6, students €3.50; includes entry to the Rüstkammer.)* The **Rüstkammer,** just across the archway, shows the deadly toys of the Wettin princes in one of the greatest collections of weaponry in Europe. *(Open Tu-Su 10am-6pm. €3, students €2.)*

ENTERTAINMENT

Dresden has long been a focal point for German music, opera, and theater. Most theaters break from mid-July to early September, but open-air festivals bridge the gap. Outdoor movies screen along the Elbe during **Filmnächte am Elbufer** in July and August. (Office at Alaunstr. 62. ☎0351 89 93 20; www.filmnaechte-am-elbufer.de. Most shows start at 8 or 9:30pm and cost €6.50.) The **Zwinger** has classical concerts in summer at 6:30pm.

Sächsische Staatsoper (Semper-Oper), Theaterpl. 2 (☎0351 491 10; www.semperoper.de). Home to amazing opera, the city's first class orchestra performs the German symphonic canon here as well. Tickets €4.50-160. Box office at Schinkelwache, across Theaterpl. Open M-F 10am-6pm, Sa-Su 10am-4pm, and 1hr. before performances.

projekttheater dresden, Louisenstr. 47 (☎0351 810 7610; www.projekttheater.de). Cutting-edge, international experimental theater. Tickets €11, students €9. Shows start 8 or 9pm, matinees at 10am or noon. Box office open 1hr. before all shows.

NIGHTLIFE

It's as if the entire *Neustadt* spends the day anticipating nightfall. A decade ago, the area north of Albertpl. was a maze of gray streets and crumbling buildings; since then, an alternative community has thrived in bars on **Louisenstraße, Goerlitzerstraße, Bischofsweg, Kamenzerstraße,** and **Albertplatz.** The German-language *Dresdener Kulturmagazin*, free at *Neustadt* hostels, describes every bar.

DownTown, Katharinenstr. 11-13 (☎0351 801 39 23; www.downtown-dresden.de). Constantly packed. Rotating pop, rock, and electronic music. Cover €4, students €3. Drinks €3-9. Open daily 7pm-5am. Club open Th-Sa 10pm-5am. Cash only.

Die 100, Alaunstr. 100 (☎0351 801 39 57; www.cafe100.de). Over 300 German, French, and Israeli wines (from €3.50 per glass, bottles from €13) on the menu. Unpolished, relaxed atmosphere in candlelit interior and intimate stone courtyard. In the cellar, there's often music. Salads and sandwiches €3-5. Open daily 5pm-3am. Cash only.

BOY's, Alaunstr. 80 (☎0351 796 88 24; www.boysdresden.de), just beyond the Kunsthof Passage. A half-naked devil mannequin guards this popular gay bar. The interior is a devilish/amorous red. Drinks €4-9. Open Tu-Th 8pm-3am, F-Su 8pm-5am. MC/V.

LEIPZIG ☎0341

Leipzig (pop. 500,000) is known as the city of music, and indeed, it's hard to walk more than a few blocks without being serenaded by a classical quartet, wooed by a Spanish guitar, or riveted by the choir music wafting from the Thomaskirche. Large enough to have a life outside its university but small enough to feel the influence of its students, Leipzig boasts world-class museums and corners packed with cafes, cabarets, and second-hand stores.

TRANSPORTATION AND PRACTICAL INFORMATION. Leipzig lies on the Berlin-Munich line. **Trains** run to: Berlin (2½hr., 2 per hr., €40); Dresden (1½hr, every hr., €28); Frankfurt (4hr., every hr., €67); Munich (5hr., every 2hr., €84). To find the **tourist office,** Richard-Wagner-Str. 1, walk across Willy-Brandt-Pl. and take Goethestr. toward the left; the office is on the first corner. (☎0341 710 4265. Open Mar.-Oct. M-F 9:30am-6pm, Sa 9:30am-4pm, Su 9:30am-3pm; Nov.-Feb. M-F 10am-6pm.) There you can buy the **Leipzig Card,** good for free tram and bus rides within the city, discounts on city tours, and reduced admission to museums. (1-day, until 4am, €8.90; 3-day €18.50, 3-day group ticket for 2 adults and 3 children up to 14 €34.) **Postal Code:** 04109.

ACCOMMODATIONS AND FOOD. To reach **Hostel Sleepy Lion ❶,** Käthe-Kollwitz-Str. 3, take streetcar #1 (dir.: Lausen) to Gottschedstr., or, from the station, turn right and walk along Trondlinring, then left on Goerdelering and continue straight on Käthe-Kollwitz-Str. Run by young locals and close to nightlife, the **Sleepy Lion ❶** draws an international crowd. In the lounge, pool balls crackle (€1 a game) and upbeat music blasts around the clock. (☎0341 993 9480; www.hostel-leipzig.de. All rooms with shower and toilet. Bike rental €5 per day. Breakfast €3.50. Linens €2.50. Internet €2 per hr. Reception 24hr. Dorms €14-16; singles €30; doubles €42; quads €68. Winter reduced rates. AmEx/MC/V.)

Imbiß stands, bistros, and bakeries line **Grimmaischestraße** in the Innenstadt. But life doesn't extinguish beyond the ring; the city extends a tentacle south, culminating in the student-populated Karl-Liebknecht-Str., (streetcar #10 or 11 to Südpl.), a funky refuge from downtown crowds and downtown prices. If you're itching to eat in the swarm of Barfussg. head to **Bellini's ❶,** Barfußgäßchen 3-7 (☎0341 961 7681), the most reasonably priced eatery on the row. (All dishes under €10. Crispy baguettes €4-5.50. Colorful salads and pastas €7.60-9.80. Open daily noon-late. MC/V.)

SIGHTS AND NIGHTLIFE. The heart of Leipzig is the **Marktplatz,** a cobblestone square guarded by the slanted 16th-century **Altes Rathaus** (old town hall). Head back to Thomasg., turn left, then turn right on Dittrichring to reach Leipzig's fascinating **Museum in der "Runden Ecke,"** Dittrichring 24. Situated in former Stasi headquarters, the museum carefully preserves and displays the tools the secret police used to play Big Brother. (☎0341 961 2443; www.runde-ecke-leipzig.de. Open daily 10am-6pm. Free.) Outside the city ring, the **Völkerschlachtdenkmal,** fashioned after a Mesopotamian temple in 1913, memorializes the centennial of the 1813 Battle of Nations, when the combined forces of Austria, Prussia, Russia, and Sweden defeated Napoleon near Leipzig. Climb the 364 steps for an impressive view of the city. (Tram #15 from the station to Völkerschlachtdenkmal. Open daily Apr.-Oct. 10am-6pm; Nov.-Mar. 10am-4pm. €5, students €3.) Leipzig's rounded, glass **Gewandhaus,** Augustuspl. 8, has housed a major international orchestra, once directed by Felix Mendelssohn, since 1843. (☎0341 127 0280; www.gewandhaus.de. Open M-F 10am-6pm, Su 10am-2pm, and 1hr. before performances. Tickets €9-26 and up.)

The free magazines *Frizz and Blitz* have nightlife info, as does *Kreuzer* (€2.50 at newsstands). **Barfußgäßchen,** a street off the *Markt,* is the place to see and be seen for younger people. Leipzig University students spent eight years excavating a series of medieval tunnels so they could get their groove on in the **Moritzbastei,** Universitätsstr. 9, a massive cave with bars, a cafe, and multi-level dance floors under vaulted brick ceilings. (☎0341 702 590; www.moritzbastei.de. Cover W €4, students €2.50; Sa €4.50/3. Free until 11pm. Cafe open M-F 10am-midnight, Sa noon-midnight, Su 9am-midnight. Club open W 10am-6am, Sa noon-6am. Cash only.)

GREECE (ΕΛΛΑΔΑ)

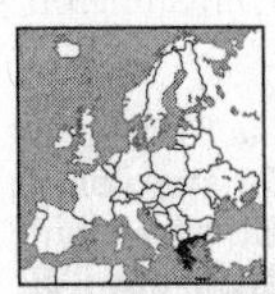

Greece is a land where sacred monasteries are mountainside fixtures, leisurely seaside siestas are standard issue, and circle-dancing and drinking until daybreak are summer rites. Visitors explore evidence of magnificent past civilizations, as well as Greece's island beaches, spectacular gorges, and famous hospitality. The Greek lifestyle is truly a unique mix of high speed and sun-inspired lounging, encouraging tourists to adopt the natives' go-with-the-flow attitude.

DISCOVER GREECE: SUGGESTED ITINERARIES

THREE DAYS. Spend it all in **Athens** (p. 458). Roam the **Acropolis,** gaze at innumerous treasures in the **National Archaeological Museum,** and pay homage at the **Parthenon.** Visit the ancient **Agora,** then take a trip down to **Poseidon's Temple,** long since dry, at Cape Sounion.

ONE WEEK. Begin your sojourn in **Athens** (3 days). Sprint to **Olympia** (1 day; p. 467) and see where the games began. Sail to **Corfu** (1 day; p. 478) and peer into Albania from atop Mt. Pantokrator. Lastly, soak up Byzantine history in **Thessaloniki** (2 days; p. 470).

BEST OF GREECE, THREE WEEKS. Explore **Athens** (4 days) before visiting the mansions of **Nafplion** (1 day; p. 469). Race west to **Olympia** (1 day) and take a ferry to the beaches of **Corfu** (2 days). Back on the mainland, wander **Thessaloniki** (2 days), then climb to the cliff-side monasteries of **Meteora** (1 day; p. 475). Consult the gods at **Mount Olympus** (1 day; p. 474) and the Oracle of **Delphi** (1 day). On Crete (3 days; p. 483), hike Europe's largest gorge. Seek rest on **Santorini** (1 day; p. 483), debauchery on **Ios** (1 day; p. 482), and sun on **Mykonos** (1 day; p. 479).

ESSENTIALS

FACTS AND FIGURES

OFFICIAL NAME: Hellenic Republic.

CAPITAL: Athens.

MAJOR CITIES: Thessaloniki, Patras.

POPULATION: 10,723,000.

LAND AREA: 131,900 sq. km.

TIME ZONE: GMT +2.

LANGUAGE: Greek.

RELIGION: Eastern Orthodox (98%).

HIGHEST PEAK: Mt. Olympus (2917m).

VERSES IN NATIONAL ANTHEM: 158.

WHEN TO GO

July through August is peak season; it is best to visit in May, early June, or September, when smaller crowds enjoy the gorgeous weather. Visiting during low season ensures lower prices, but many sights and accommodations have shorter hours or close altogether.

DOCUMENTS AND FORMALITIES

EMBASSIES. Foreign embassies in Greece are in Athens (p. 459). Greek embassies abroad include: **Australia,** 9 Turrana St., Yarralumla, Canberra, ACT, 2600 (☎62 7330 11); **Canada,** 80 MacLaren St., Ottawa, ON, K2P 0K6 (☎613-238-6271; www.greekembassy.ca); **Ireland,** 1 Upper Pembroke St., Dublin, 2 (☎31 676 7254, ext. 5); **New Zealand,** 5-7 Willeston St., 10th fl., Wellington (☎4 473 7775, ext. 6); **UK,** 1a Holland Park, London, W11 3TP (☎020 72 21 64 67; www.greekembassy.org.uk); **US,** 2217 Massachusetts Ave., NW, Washington, DC, 20008 (☎202-939-1300; www.greekembassy.org).

VISA AND ENTRY INFORMATION. EU citizens do not need a visa. Citizens of Australia, Canada, New Zealand, and the US do not need a visa for stays of up to 90 days, beginning upon entry into any of the countries in the EU's freedom-of-movement zone. For more info, see p. 15. For stays longer than 90 days, all non-EU citizens need Schengen visas, available at Greek embassies and online at www.greekembassy.org. Processing a tourist visa takes about 20 days.

TOURIST SERVICES AND MONEY

EMERGENCY	**Ambulance:** ☎166. **Fire:** ☎199. **Police:** ☎100. **General Emergency:** ☎112.

TOURIST OFFICES. Two national organizations oversee tourism in Greece: **Greek National Tourist Organization** (GNTO; known as the EOT in Greece) and the **tourist police** *(touristiki astinomia)*. The GNTO, Tsoha 7, Athens supplies general info about Grecian sights and accommodations. (☎2108 70 70 00; www.gnto.gr. Open M-F 8am-3pm.) In addition to the "Tourist Police" insignia decorating their uniforms, white belts, gloves, and cap bands help identify the tourist police. The **Tourist Police Service** and **General Police Directorate**, P. Kanellopoulou 4, Athens (☎2106 92 8510, 24hr. general emergency 171) deal with local and immediate problems concerning bus schedules, accommodations, and lost passports. Offices are willing to help, but their staff's English may be limited.

MONEY. The **euro (€)** has replaced the Greek **drachma** as the unit of currency in Greece. For more info, see p. 17. It's generally cheaper to change money in Greece than at home. When changing money in Greece, go to a bank with at most a 5% margin between its buy and sell prices. A bare-bones day in Greece costs €40-60. A day with more comforts runs €55-75. While all restaurant prices include a 15% gratuity, **tipping** an additional 5-10% for the assistant waiters and busboys is considered good form. Taxi drivers do not expect tips although patrons generally round their fare up to the nearest euro. Generally, **bargaining** is expected for street wares and at other informal venues, but when in doubt, wait and watch to avoid offending merchants. Bargaining for cheaper *domatia* (rooms to let), at small hotels, and for unmetered taxi rides is common.

Greece has a 19% **value added tax (VAT),** a sales tax applied to goods and services sold in mainland Greece and 13% VAT on the Aegean islands. Both are included in the listed price. The prices given in *Let's Go* include VAT. In the airport upon exiting the EU, non-EU citizens can claim a refund on the tax paid for goods purchased at participating stores. In order to qualify for a refund in a store, you must spend at least €120; make sure to ask for a refund form when you pay. For more info on qualifying for a VAT refund, see p. 21.

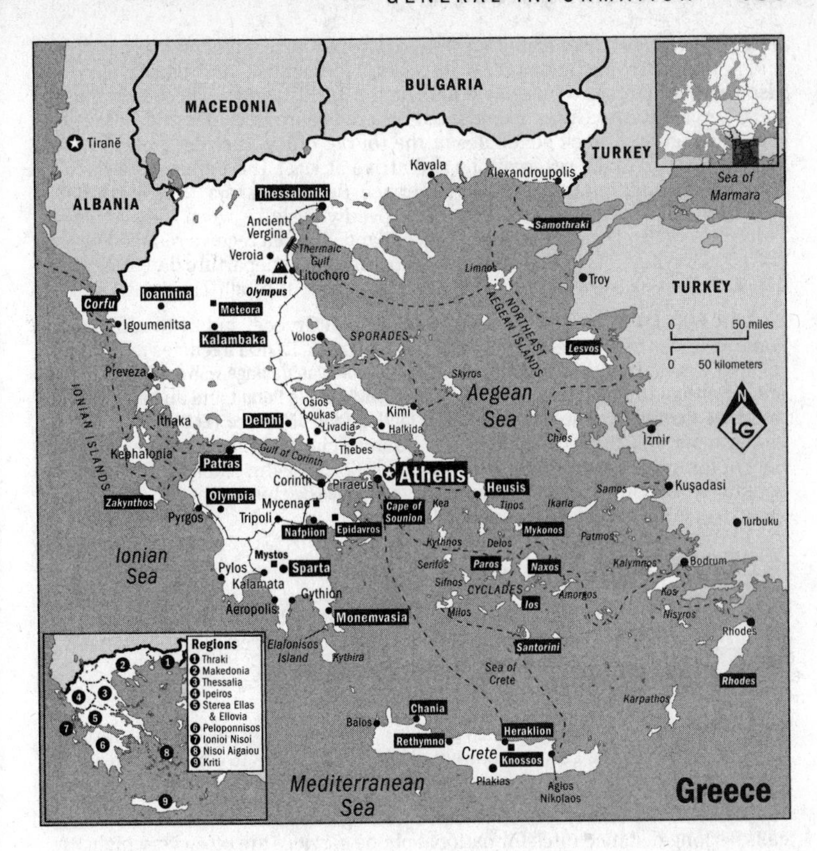

TRANSPORTATION

BY PLANE. International flights land in **Athens International Airport** (**ATH;** ☎21035 30 000; www.aia.gr); some also serve Corfu (CFU), Heraklion (HER), Kos (KSG), and Thessaloniki (SKG). **Olympic Airlines,** 96 Syngrou Ave., Athens, 11741 (☎21092 691 11; www.olympicairlines.com), offers domestic service. A 1hr. flight from Athens (€60-100) can get you to many Grecian island.

BY TRAIN. Greece is served by a number of international train routes that connect Athens and Thessaloniki to most European cities. Train service within Greece, however, is limited and sometimes uncomfortable. The new air-conditioned, intercity express trains, while a bit more expensive and less frequent, are worth the price. **Eurail** is valid on all Greek trains. **Hellenic Railways Organization** (**OSE;** ☎1110; www.osenet.gr) connects Athens to major Greek cities.

BY BUS. Few buses run directly from European cities to Greece, except for chartered tour buses. Domestic bus service is extensive and fares are cheap. **KTEL** (www.ktel.org) operates most domestic buses; check with an official source about scheduled departures, as posted schedules are often outdated.

BY FERRY. Boats travel from Bari, ITA, to Corfu, Durres, Igoumenitsa, Patras, and Sami and from Ancona, ITA, to Corfu, Igoumenitsa, and Patras. Ferries also run from Greece to various points on the Turkish coast. There is frequent ferry service to the Greek islands, but schedules are irregular and incorrect info is common. Check schedules at the tourist office, the port police, or at www.ferries.gr. Make reservations and arrive at least 1hr. before your departure time. In addition to conventional service, **Hellenic Seaways** (☎21041 99 000; www.hellenicseaways.gr) provides high-speed vessels between the islands at twice the cost and speed of ferries. Student and children receive reduced fares; travelers buying tickets up to 15 days before intended departure date receive a 15% **Early Booking Discount** on ferries leaving Tuesday through Thursday.

BY CAR AND MOPED. You must be 18 to drive in Greece, and 21 to rent a car; some agencies require renters to be at least 23 or 25. Rental agencies may quote low daily rates that exclude the 18% tax and **collision damage waiver (CDW)** insurance. Foreign drivers must have an **International Driving Permit** and an **International Insurance Certificate.** The **Automobile and Touring Club of Greece (ELPA),** Messogion 395, Athens, 15343, provides help and offers reciprocal membership to members of foreign auto clubs like AAA. (☎21060 68 800, 24hr. emergency roadside assistance 104, infoline 174; www.elpa.gr.) **Mopeds,** while great for exploring, are extremely dangerous—wear a helmet.

KEEPING IN TOUCH

PHONE CODES	**Country code:** 30. **International dialing prefix:** 00. For more info on how to place international calls, see **Inside Back Cover.**

EMAIL AND THE INTERNET. The availability of the Internet in Greece is rapidly expanding. In all big cities, most small cities and large towns, and on most islands, you'll be able to find Internet cafes. Expect to pay €2-6 per hr.

TELEPHONE. Whenever possible use a calling card for international phone calls, as long-distance rates for national phone services are often very high. **Pay phones** in Greece use prepaid **phone cards,** sold at *peripteros* (streetside kiosks) and OTE offices. **Mobile phones** are an increasingly popular, economical option. Major mobile carriers include Q-Telecom, Telestet, and Vodaphone. Direct-dial access numbers for calling out of Greece include: **AT&T Direct** (☎00 800 1311); **British Telecom** (☎00 800 4411); **Canada Direct** (☎00 800 1611); **Sprint** (☎00 800 1411); **NTL** (☎00 800 4422); For info on calling home from Europe, see p. 31.

MAIL. Airmail is the best way to send mail home from Greece. To send a letter (up to 20g) anywhere from Greece costs €0.65. To receive mail in Greece, have it delivered **Poste Restante.** Mail will go to the main post office unless you specify a subsidiary by street address. Address mail to be held as follows: First name LAST NAME, Town Post Office, Island, Greece, Postal Code, POSTE RESTANTE. Bring a passport to pick up your mail; there may be a small fee.

ACCOMMODATIONS AND CAMPING

GREECE	❶	❷	❸	❹	❺
ACCOMMODATIONS	under €19	€20-28	€29-38	€98-70	over €70

Local tourist offices usually have lists of inexpensive accommodations. A **hostel** bed averages €15-30. Those not endorsed by HI are usually still safe and reputable. In many areas, **domatia** are a good option; locals offering cheap lodging may approach you as you enter town, a common practice that is illegal. It's usually a better bet to go to an official tourist office. Prices vary; expect to pay €15-35 for a single and €25-45 for a double. Always see the room and negotiate with *domatia* owners before settling on a price; never pay more than you would to stay in a hotel. **Hotel** prices are regulated, but proprietors may push you to take the most expensive room. Budget hotels start at €20 for singles and €30 for doubles. Check your bill carefully, and threaten to contact the tourist police if you think you're being cheated. Greece has plenty of official **campgrounds,** which cost €2-3 per tent plus €4-8 per person. Though common in summer, camping on beaches—sometimes illegal—may not be the safest option.

FOOD AND DRINK

GREECE	❶	❷	❸	❹	❺
FOOD	under €5	€5-9	€10-15	€16-25	over €25

Penny-pinching carnivores will thank Zeus for lamb, chicken, or pork *souvlaki,* stuffed into a pita to make **gyros** (YEE-ros). **Vegetarians** can also find cheap eateries; options include *horiatiki* (Greek salad), savory pastries like *tiropita* (cheese pie) and *spanakopita* (spinach and feta pie). Frothy iced coffee milkshakes take the edge off the summer heat. **Ouzo** (a powerful licorice-flavored spirit) is served with *mezedes* (snacks of octopus, cheese, and sausage). Breakfast, served only in the early morning, is generally very simple: a piece of toast with *marmelada* or a pastry. Lunch, a hearty and leisurely meal, can begin as early as noon but is more likely eaten sometime between 2 and 5pm. Dinner is a drawn-out, relaxed affair served late. Greek restaurants are known as *tavernas* or *estiatorios;* a grill is a *psistaria.*

HOLIDAYS AND FESTIVALS

Holidays: Feast of St. Basil/New Year's Day (Jan. 1); Epiphany (Jan. 6); Clean Monday (Mar. 10); Independence Day (Mar. 25); St. George's Day (Apr. 23); Orthodox Good Friday (Apr. 17, 2009; Apr. 2, 2010); Orthodox Easter (Apr. 19-20, 2009; Apr. 4-5, 2010); Labor Day (May 1); Pentecost (May 11-12); Day of the Holy Spirit (June 16); Assumption (Aug. 15); Feast of St. Demetrius (Oct. 26); Okhi Day (Oct. 28); All Saints' Day (Nov. 1); Christmas (Dec. 25-26).

Festivals: Three weeks of **Carnival** feasting and dancing (mid Feb. to early Mar.) precede Lenten fasting. April 23 is **St. George's Day,** when Greece honors the dragon-slaying knight with horse races, wrestling matches, and dances. The **Feast of St. Demetrius** (Oct. 26) is celebrated with particular enthusiasm in Thessaloniki.

BEYOND TOURISM

Doing more than just sightseeing on a trip to Greece is as easy (and as challenging) as offering some of one's own time and energy. Though considered wealthy by international standards, Greece has an abundance of aid organizations to combat the nation's very real problems. For more information on opportunities across Europe, see **Beyond Tourism,** p. 60.

American School of Classical Studies at Athens (ASCSA), 54 Souidias St., GR-106 76 Athens (☎21072 36 313; www.ascsa.edu.gr). Provides study abroad opportunities in Greece for students interested in archaeology and the classics. US$2950-17,000 including tuition, room, and partial board.

Archelon Sea Turtle Protection Society, Solomou 57, 10432 Athens (☎/fax 21052 31 342; www.archelon.gr). Non-profit group devoted to studying and protecting sea turtles on the beaches of Zakynthos, Crete, and the Peloponnese. Opportunities for seasonal field work and year-round work at the rehabilitation center. €100 participation fee.

ATHENS (ΑΘΗΝΑ) ☎210

An illustrious past invigorates Athens. The ghosts of antiquity peer down from its hilltops, instilling residents with a sense of the city's historic importance. Home to 3.7 million people—a third of Greece's population—Athens is daring and modern; its patriotic citizens pushed their capital into the 21st century with massive clean-up and building projects before the 2004 Olympic Games. International menus, hipster bars, and large warehouse performance spaces crowd Byzantine churches, traditional *tavernas*, and toppled columns.

TRANSPORTATION

Flights: Eleftherios Venizelou (ATH; ☎210 353 0000; www.aia.gr). Greece's international airport operates as 1 massive yet navigable terminal. Arrivals are on the ground fl., departures on the 2nd. The **Suburban Rail** services the airport from the city center in 30min. 4 bus lines run to **Athens, Piraeus,** and **Rafina**. Budget airlines **SkyEurope** (www.skyeurope.com) and **Wizz Air** (www.wizzair.com) fly to Athens.

Trains: Hellenic Railways (OSE), Sina 6 (☎1110 362 7947; www.ose.gr). **Larisis Train Station** (☎210 529 8837) serves northern Greece. Ticket office open daily 5am-midnight. Trolley #1 from El. Venizelou in Pl. Syndagma (5 per hr., €1) or the Metro to Larisis Station. Trains go to **Thessaloniki** (7hr., 5 per day, €15; express 4¼hr., 2 per day, €48).

Buses: Terminal A, Kifissou 100 (☎210 512 4910). Take blue bus #051 from the corner of Zinonos and Menandrou near Pl. Omonia (4 per hr. from 5am-midnight, €0.80). Buses to: **Corfu** (9½hr., 2-3 per day, €39.50); **Corinth** (1½hr., 1 per hr., €7.50); **Patras** (3hr., 2 per hr., €17; express 2hr., 9 per day); **Thessaloniki** (6hr., 12-13 per day, €35). **Terminal B,** Liossion 260 (☎210 831 7153). Take blue bus #024 from Amalias, outside the National Gardens (45min., 3 per hr. 5:10am-11:40pm, €0.80). Buses to **Delphi** (3hr., 6 per day, €13.60).

THE WHEELS ON THE BUS GO... Getting to and from Athens by bus can be incredibly confusing as there are two intercity bus terminals (Terminal A and Terminal B) and yet another terminal (Mavromateon) serving destinations outside of Athens but within the prefecture of Attica (including Cape Sounion). The larger Terminal A is more difficult to reach than Terminal B, as the bus to the terminal departs from a random intersection in Omonia, but taking a local bus to the bus station is much cheaper than taking a taxi and is still the best bet.

Ferries: Most leave from the Piraeus port. Ferry schedule changes daily; check ahead at the tourist office (☎1440; www.openseas.gr or www.ferries.gr). Ferries sail directly to all major Greek **Islands** except for the Sporades and Ionians. To Crete: **Chania** (11hr., €30-33); **Heraklion** (11hr., €27-35); **Rethymno** (11hr., €21-29). Others to: **Ios** (7hr., €25.50-32); **Kos** (13hr., €36-45.50); **Lesvos** (12hr., €26); **Mykonos** (6hr., €21); **Naxos** (6hr., €24-30); **Paros** (5hr., €25-29); **Patmos** (8hr., €33-34); **Rhodes** (14hr., €43-53); **Santorini** (9hr., €27-34). International ferries head to **Turkey** (€30).

Public Transportation: Yellow **KTEL** buses travel all around Attica from orange bus stops throughout the city. Other buses in Athens and its suburbs are blue and designated by 3-digit numbers. Electrical antennae distinguish **trolleys** from buses. Public transport tickets (valid for bus, trolley, tram, and metro connections) are available at blue **OASA**

(Athens Urban Transport Organization) booths and some kiosks, and may be used for up to 90min. after validation. Travelers without validated tickets face a fine of 60 times the ticket price. A standard public transport ticket costs €0.80. 24hr. tickets (€3) and 7-day tickets (€10) are also available and convenient. The modern Athens **metro** consists of 3 lines running from 5:30am to midnight. The green **M1** line runs from northern Kifissia to Piraeus, the red **M2** from Ag. Antonios to Ag. Dimitrios, and the blue **M3** from Egaleo to the airport via Doukissis Plakentias. Buy tickets (€0.70 for trips in 1-2 successive zones of M1, €0.80 for trips in all 3 zones of M1 and for combined trips between M1, M2, and M3) in any station.

Taxis: Ikaros (☎210 515 2800); **Hermes** (☎210 411 5200); **Kosmos** (☎1300). Base fare €1; €0.34 per km, midnight-5am €0.65 per km. €3.20 surcharge from airport, €0.86 surcharge for trips from port, bus, and railway terminals, plus €0.32 for each piece of luggage over 10kg. Minimum fare €2.65. Call for pickup (€1.60-2.65 extra).

ORIENTATION AND PRACTICAL INFORMATION

Most travelers hang around the **Acropolis** and **Agoras,** while guide-bearing foreigners flood central **Plaka,** Athens's old town. Marked by the square and flea market, **Monastiraki** (Little Monastery) is a hectic, exciting neighborhood where crowded *tavernas* and Psiri's trendy bars keep pedestrian traffic flowing late into the night. In the heart of Athens, **Syntagma Square** is the transportation center. On the opposite side of Stadiou, bustling **Omonia Square** bursts with ethnic and ideological diversity. A short walk north on **Em. Benaki** leads to the hip, student-filled neighborhood of **Exarhia,** where a young, alternative vibe enlivens graffiti-painted streets lined with relaxed cafes, independent bookshops, and record stores. The **Larisis** train station is to the northwest of town, while most museums are on **Vas Sofias** to the east. The fashionable neighborhood of **Kolonaki** attracts a posh Athenian crowd and is situated below Lycavittos Hill. Take the M1 (green line) south to its end or bus #040 from Filellinon and Mitropoleos, in Syntagma (4 per hr.), to reach Athens's port city, **Piraeus.** The metro also travels east to several beaches. If you get lost, just look for Syntagma or the Acropolis, Athens's clearest reference points.

Tourist Office: Information Office, Amalias 26 (☎210 331 0392 or 210 331 0716; www.gnto.gr). Has tons of useful literature, up-to-date bus schedules, and the most detailed city map. Open M-F 9am-7pm, Sa-Su 10am-4pm.

Bank: National Bank, Karageorgi Servias 2 (☎210 334 0500), in Pl. Syntagma. Open M-Th 8am-2:30pm, F 8am-2pm; open for **currency exchange** M-F 3:30-5pm, Sa 9am-2pm, Su 9am-1pm. Commission about 5%. 24hr. currency exchange at the airport, but commissions there are usually exorbitant.

Emergencies: Poison control ☎210 779 3777. **AIDS Help Line** ☎210 722 2222.

Tourist Police: Dimitrakopoulou 77 (☎171). English spoken. Open 24hr.

Pharmacies: Check *Athens News* for a current list of 24hr. pharmacies.

Hospitals: Duty hospitals and **clinics** ☎1434. Free emergency health care for tourists. Geniko Kratiko; **Public General Hospital**, Mesogion 154 (☎210 777 8901). Near Kolonaki is the public hospital **Evangelismos,** Ypsilantou 45-47 (☎210 720 1000).

Internet: Athens has many Internet cafes. Expect to pay around €3 per hr. **Bits and Bytes,** Kapnikareas 19 (☎210 325 31; www.bnb.gr), in Plaka. 9am-midnight €5 per hr., midnight-9am €3 per hr. Open 24hr. Free city Wi-Fi at **Syntagma Square, Thesseion Square, Kotzia Square,** and across the Evangelismos Metro Station at the **National Hellenic Research Foundation** (SSID: athenswifi).

Post Office: Syntagma (☎210 323 7573 or 210 331 9501); corner of Mitropoleos. Open M-F 7:30am-8pm, Sa 7:30am-2pm, Su 9am-1:30pm. **Postal Code:** 10300.

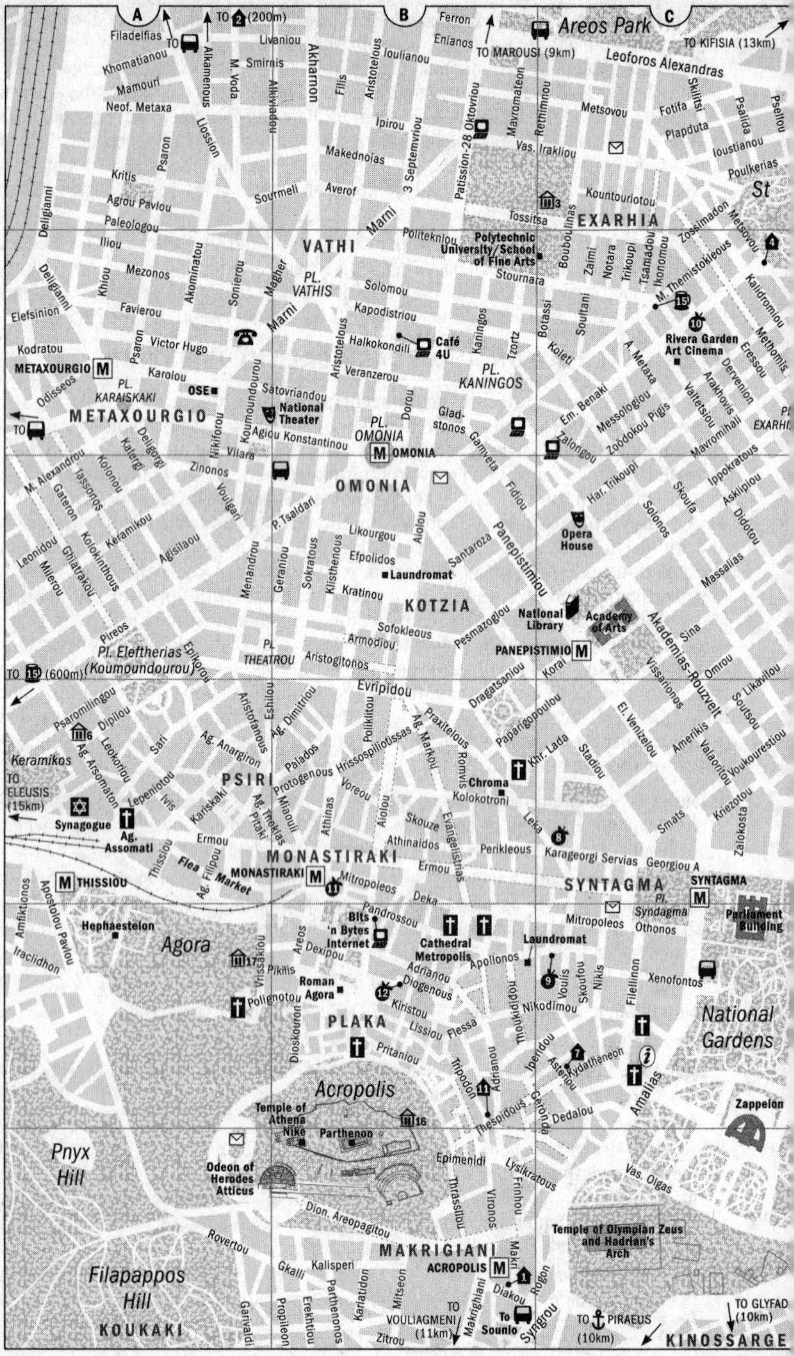
A
B
C
TO 2 (200m)
Filadelfias
TO
Alkamenous
Khomatianou
Mamouri
Neof. Metaxa
M. Voda
Smirnis
Livaniou
Akharnon
Alkiviadou
Filis
Aristotelous
Ioulianou
Ferron
Enianos
TO MAROUSI (9km)
Areos Park
TO KIFISIA (13km)
Leoforos Alexandras
Skilitsi
Psalida
Pseftou
Fotifa
Plapduta
Ioustianou
Poulkerias
Metsovou
Mavromateon
Rethimnou
Patission-28 Oktovriou
Ipirou
Liossion
Psaron
Makednoias
3 Septemvriou
Vas. Irakliou
Kritis
Agrou Pavlou
Sourmeli
Averof
Kountouriotou
Deligianni
Paleologou
Tossitsa
3
EXARHIA
Zossimadon
Metsovou
Marni
Politekniou
Polytechnic University/School of Fine Arts
Iliou
VATHI
Akominatou
Bouboulinas
Zaimi
Notara
Trikoupi
Tsamadou
Ikonomou
M. Themistokleous
4
Mezonos
Khiou
Sonierou
Magher
PL. VATHIS
Solomou
Stournara
Kalidromiou
Elefsinion
Favierou
Kapodistriou
Botassi
Soultani
15
Methonis
Kodratou
Psaron
Victor Hugo
Aristotelous
Halkokondili
Café 4U
Kaningos
Tzortz
Koleti
10
Rivera Garden Art Cinema
Eressou
METAXOURGIO
M
Karolou
Koumoundourou
Veranzerou
PL. KANINGOS
A. Metaxa
Arakhovis
Dervenion
Odisseos
PL. KARAISKAKI
OSE
Satovriandou
Dorou
Em. Benaki
Messologiou
Valtetsiou
METAXOURGIO
National Theater
PL. OMONIA
Glad-stonos
Zoodokou Pigis
Mavromihali
PL. EXARHI
TO
Deligiorgi
Kalergi
Nikiforou
Agiou Konstantinou
Gamveta
Zalongou
Vilara
M OMONIA
Ippokratous
M. Alexandrou
Kolonou
Zinonos
OMONIA
Har. Trikoupi
Skoufa
Asklipiou
Gateron
Iassonos
Voulgari
Fidiou
Solonos
Didotou
Keramikou
P. Tsaldari
Aiolou
Opera House
Leonidou
Kolokinthous
Agisilaou
Menandrou
Geraniou
Sokratous
Klisthenous
Likourgou
Efpolidos
Santaroza
Panepistimiou
Massalias
Milerou
Ghiatrakou
Laundromat
Kratinou
KOTZIA
Pesmazoglou
National Library
Academy of Arts
Akademias-Rouzvelt
Pireos
Sofokleous
Sina
Armodiou
PANEPISTIMIO M
Pl. Eleftherias (Koumoundourou)
Epikourou
PL. THEATROU
Aristogitonos
Korai
Vissarionou
Omrou
TO 15 (600m)
Evripidou
Dragatsaniou
Soutsou
Likavitou
Psaromilingou
Dipilou
Aristofanous
Eshilou
Ag. Dimitriou
Polikitou
Praxitelous
Paparigopoulou
El. Venizelou
Amerikis
Valaoritou
Voukourestiou
6
Sari
Ag. Anargiron
Hrissospiliotissas
Ag. Markou
Romvis
Khr. Lada
Stadiou
Keramikos
Leokoriou
Ag. Asomaton
PSIRI
Palados
Protogenous
Chroma
TO ELEUSIS (15km)
Lepeniotou
Kariskaki
Ag. Theklas
Voreou
Kolokotroni
Smats
Kriezotou
Ivis
Pitaki
Miaouli
Athinas
Aiolou
Skouze
Evangelistrias
Leka
Zalokosta
Synagogue
Ag. Assomati
Ermou
Athinaidos
8
Thissiou
Flea Market
Ag. Filippou
MONASTIRAKI
Perikleous
Karageorgi Servias
Georgiou A
Amfiktionos
Apostolou Pavlou
M THISSIOU
MONASTIRAKI M
Mitropoleos
Ermou
SYNTAGMA
SYNTAGMA M
11
Deka
Pl. Syndagma
Parliament Building
Hephaesteion
Pandrossou
Bits 'n Bytes Internet
Mitropoleos
Othonos
Areos
Dexipou
Cathedral Metropolis
Laundromat
Agora
17
Vrissakiou
Apollonos
Iraclidhon
Pikilis
Adrianou
Voulis
Skoufou
Nikis
Filellinon
Xenofontos
Roman Agora
Diogenous
9
Polignotou
12
Thoukididou
Nikodimou
Kiristou
National Gardens
PLAKA
Lissiou
Flessa
Dioskouron
Pritaniou
Tripodon
Adrianou
Ipeidou
7
Kydatheneon
Asteriou
Amalias
Acropolis
11
Temple of Athena Nike
16
Thespidous
Geronda
Dedalou
Zappeion
Parthenon
Pnyx Hill
Odeon of Herodes Atticus
Epimenidi
Lysikratous
Vas. Olgas
Thrassilou
Vironos
Frinhou
Dion. Areopagitou
Temple of Olympian Zeus and Hadrian's Arch
Rovertou
MAKRIGIANI
Makri
Filapappos Hill
Kalisperi
ACROPOLIS M
Rogon
Gkalli
1
Diakou
Karyatidon
Mitseon
Parthenonos
Erekhtiou
Propileon
Garivaldi
TO VOULIAGMENI (11km)
Makrighiani
To Sounio
Syngrou
TO PIRAEUS (10km)
TO GLYFADA (10km)
KOUKAKI
Zitrou
KINOSSARGE

GREECE

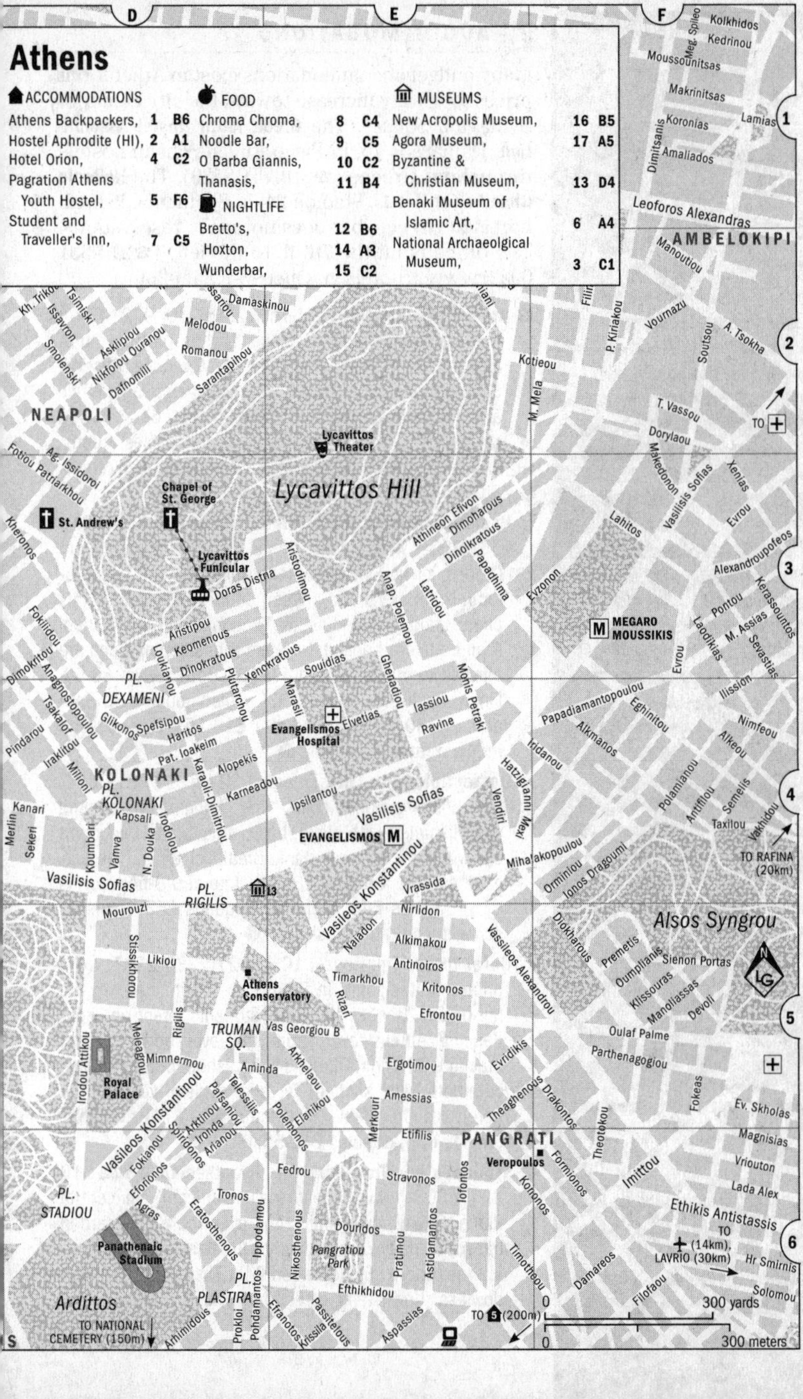

Athens

ACCOMMODATIONS

Athens Backpackers,	1	B6
Hostel Aphrodite (HI),	2	A1
Hotel Orion,	4	C2
Pagration Athens Youth Hostel,	5	F6
Student and Traveller's Inn,	7	C5

FOOD

Chroma Chroma,	8	C4
Noodle Bar,	9	C5
O Barba Giannis,	10	C2
Thanasis,	11	B4

NIGHTLIFE

Bretto's,	12	B6
Hoxton,	14	A3
Wunderbar,	15	C2

MUSEUMS

New Acropolis Museum,	16	B5
Agora Museum,	17	A5
Byzantine & Christian Museum,	13	D4
Benaki Museum of Islamic Art,	6	A4
National Archaeolgical Museum,	3	C1

ATHENS OFF THE BEATEN PATH

In a city packed with tourists, escaping the crowds may seem like an impossible feat. But there's much more to Athens than the Acropolis: arm yourself with a good map and a 24hr. public transportation ticket (€3), and explore this city on the cheap!

Antonis Tritsis Environmental Park: This expansive park in the western Athens area boasts many rare bird species. You don't need binoculars, however, to appreciate the natural beauty of this wildlife reserve and its mission to raise environmental awareness. Visitors can stock up on organic goodies at the park's shops. *(☎210 231 6977; 23 Spyrou Moustaki, Ilion park.www.ornithologiki.gr.)*

Fruit and vegetable markets: On any given day of the week, one or more of Athens's neighborhoods becomes a hotspot where locals stock up on fresh produce. For the best quality, go early—prices tend to drop as the selection dwindles. Try Xenokratous in Kolonaki on Friday and Kallidromiou St. in Exarhia on Saturday.

DESTE Foundation Centre for Contemporary Art: Check out the latest, hippest exhibition at this sleek building in one of Athens's northern suburbs. *Open W-Th 5pm-8pm. Free. (☎210 275 8490; Filellinon 11 & Em. Pappa St., Nea Ionia. www.deste.gr.)*

ACCOMMODATIONS

Many budget accommodations exist in Athens, but prices generally increase toward the city center at Syntagma Square. The **Greek Youth Hostel Association,** Damareos 75, in Pangrati, lists cheap hostels throughout Greece (☎210 751 9530). The **Hellenic Chamber of Hotels,** Stadiou 24, in Syntagma, lists all hotels in Greece, but does not make reservations. The office is on the 7th fl. to the left. (☎210 331 0022; www.grhotels.gr. Open M-F 8am-2pm.)

Athens Backpackers, Makri 12 (☎210 922 4044; www.backpackers.gr), in Plaka. Nightly party in summer at their rooftop bar under the Acropolis. Reserve ahead. Breakfast included. Free luggage storage, Wi-Fi, and fully-stocked kitchen. Laundry €5. 6- or 8-bed dorms €18-25. Other rooms such as doubles, quads, and 6-person studios are also available through Athens Studios (online at www.athensstudios.gr). ❷

Pagration Athens Youth Hostel, Damareos 75 (☎210 751 9530; www.athens-yhostel.com), in Pangrati. From Omonia or Pl. Syntagma, take trolley #2 or 11 to Filolaou. Number 75 and a green door—no sign—mark this cheery, family-owned hostel. TV lounge and full kitchen. If all beds are booked, travelers with sleeping bags are allowed to stay on the roof (€12). Hot showers €0.50. Linens included. Laundry €7. Quiet hours 2:30-5pm and 11:30pm-7am. Dorms €10-15. Low season reduced rates. Cash only. ❶

Hostel Aphrodite (HI), Einardou 12 (☎210 881 0589; www.hostelaphrodite.com), in Omonia. Welcoming establishment with clean, basic rooms, and basement bar with free welcome drink. Breakfast €4-5. Free luggage storage. Laundry €8. Free Internet. 8-bed dorms €15; doubles €44; triples €57; quads €68. Low season reduced rates. Cash only. ❶

Hotel Orion, Em. Benaki 105 (☎210 330 2387; www.orion-dryades.com), in Exarhia. A 10min. walk up the hill on Em. Benaki. University students intent on experiencing Athens away from the overtrodden tourist machine fill Orion. Offers fully furnished rooftop lounge, complete with kitchen, TV, and a clear view of the Acropolis. Breakfast €6. Laundry €3. Wi-Fi available. Singles €35; doubles €40-50. MC/V. ❷

Student's and Traveller's Inn, Kydatheneon 16 (☎210 324 4808; www.studenttravellersinn.com), in central Plaka. Clean hostel with 24hr. cyber cafe and garden bar (open daily 7am-midnight). Breakfast from €3. Free Internet and Wi-Fi. Reception 24hr. The "dungeon" (windowless, downstairs co-ed dorm) €18; co-ed dorms

€20-26, with bath €22-28; doubles €52-56, with bath €68-73; triples €72-78, with bath €84-90; quads €80-104, with bath €88-112. ❷

FOOD

Athens offers a mix of fast-food stands, open-air cafes, side-street *tavernas*, and upscale restaurants. On the streets, vendors sell dried fruits and nuts or fresh coconut (€1-2), and you can find a *spanakopita* (cheese and spinach pie) at any local bakery (€1.50-2). Diners on a budget can choose from the many *souvlaki* spots in **Monastiraki,** at the end of **Mitropoleos.** If you really want to eat like a local, head to the simple *tavernas* uphill on Em. Benaki in Exarhia.

O Barba Giannis, Em. Benaki 94 (☎210 382 4138), in Exarhia. With tall green doors, "Uncle John's" is an informal stop completely about the food and not the frills—just how the Athenian students, CEOs, and artists who consider themselves regulars like it. Entrees €5-10. Open M-F noon-1am, Sa-Su noon-6pm. Cash only. ❸

Thanasis, Mitropoleos 69 (☎210 324 4705), in Monastiraki. This legendary *souvlaki* joint serves up juicy lamb and beef kebabs. Try it in a pita with tomatoes, onions, and *tzatziki* (€1.70). Take-away pita €3. Open daily 9am-2am. ❶

ChromaChroma, Lekka 8 (☎210 331 7793), in Syntagma. Dine on colorful leather couches and listen to lounge music in this modern cafe. Entrees €6-14. Open M-Sa 8am-9pm. Kitchen open M-F noon-9pm, Sa 10am-6pm. MC/V. ❸

Noodle Bar, Apollonos 11 (☎210 331 8585), in Syntagma. Light fare includes the highly popular mango salad (€5) and Thai chicken coconut soup (€4.10). Open M-Sa 11am-midnight, Su 5:30pm-midnight. ❷

SIGHTS

ACROPOLIS

The Acropolis has stood over the heart of Athens since the fifth century BC. Although each Greek city-state had an *acropolis* (high point), the buildings atop Athens's peak outshine their imitators and continue to awe visitors. Visit as early or as late in the day as possible to avoid large crowds and the broiling midday sun. *(Enter on Dionissiou Areopagitou or Theorias. ☎210 321 0219. Open daily in summer 8am-7pm; in winter 8am-2:30pm. Admission price includes access to the Acropolis, the Agora, the Roman Agora, the Temple of Olympian Zeus, Keramikos, and the Theater of Dionysos, within a 4-day period; purchase tickets at any of the sights. €12, students and EU seniors over 65 €6, under 19 free. Cash only.)*

PARTHENON. The **Temple of Athena Parthenos** (Athena the Virgin), commonly known as the Parthenon, watches over Athens. Ancient Athenians saw their city as the capital of civilization; the **metopes** (scenes in the spaces above the columns) on the sides of the temple celebrate Athens's rise. The architect Iktinos successfully integrated the Golden Mean, about a four-to-nine ratio, in every aspect of the temple.

NEW ACROPOLIS MUSEUM. Recently completed after a protracted €130 million construction process, the New Acropolis Museum, 300m southeast of the Acropolis at 2-4 Makriyianni, houses a superb collection of statues, including five of the original **Caryatids** that supported the southern side of the Erechtheion. The carvings of a lion devouring a bull and of a wrestling match between Herakles and a sea monster display the ancient mastery of anatomical and emotional detail. Notice the empty space where room has been left for the British to return the missing Elgin Marbles. *(☎210 924 1043; www.newacropolismuseum.gr. Visitors can tour the ground floor 10am-noon. Expected to open early 2009.)*

TEMPLE OF ATHENA NIKE. Currently undergoing renovation, this tiny temple was first raised during the Peace of Nikias (421-415 BC), a respite from the Peloponnesian War. Ringed by eight miniature Ionic columns, it housed a winged statue of Nike, the goddess of victory. Athenians, afraid Nike might abandon them, clipped the statue's wings. The remains of the 5m thick **Cyclopean wall** that once circled the Acropolis now lie below the temple.

OTHER SIGHTS

AGORA. The Agora served as Athens's marketplace, administrative center, and focus of daily life from the sixth century BC to the AD sixth century. Many of Athenian democracy's greatest debates were held here; Socrates, Aristotle, Demosthenes, Xenophon, and St. Paul all lectured in the Agora. The 415 BC **Hephaesteion,** on a hill in the Agora's northwest corner, is Greece's best-preserved Classical temple, with friezes depicting Theseus's adventures. The **Stoa of Attalos,** an ancient shopping mall, played host to informal philosophers' plenteous gatherings. Reconstructed in the 1950s, it now houses the **Agora Museum.** *(Enter the Agora off Pl. Thission, from Adrianou, or as you descend from the Acropolis. ☎210 321 0185. Agora open daily 8am-7:30pm. Museum open Tu-Su 8am-7:20pm. €4, students and EU seniors €2, under 19 and with Acropolis ticket free.)*

ROMAN AGORA. Built between 19 and 11 BC with donations from Julius and Octavian Caesar, the Roman Agora served as the city's commercial hub. The ruined columns of the two surviving *prophylae* (halls), a nearly intact entrance gate, and the **gate of Athena Archgetis** stand as testaments to what was once a lively meeting place. Also nearby are the *vespasianae* (public toilets), constructed in the AD first century, as well as a 1456 mosque. By far the most intriguing structure on the site is the well-preserved (and restored) **Tower of the Winds,** with reliefs of the eight winds on each side of the octagonal clock tower. A weathervane crowned the original stone structure, built in the first century BC by the astronomer Andronikos. *(☎210 324 5220. Open daily 8am-7pm. €2; students €1; under 19, EU students, and with Acropolis ticket free.)*

TEMPLE OF OLYMPIAN ZEUS AND HADRIAN'S ARCH. On the edge of the National Gardens in Plaka, you can spot the massive remaining columns of the Temple of Olympian Zeus, the largest temple ever built in Greece. Shifts in power delayed the temple's completion until AD 131 under Roman emperor Hadrian, who added an arch to mark the boundary between the ancient city of Theseus and his new city. *(Vas. Olgas at Amalias. ☎210 922 6330. Open daily 8am-7pm. Temple €2, students €1, under 19, EU students, and with Acropolis ticket free. Arch free.)*

PANATHENAIC STADIUM. Also known as *Kallimarmaro* ("Beautiful Marble"), the horseshoe-shaped Panathenaic Stadium is wedged between the National Gardens and Pangrati. The site of the first modern Olympic Games in 1896, the stadium seats over 60,000 and served as the finish line of the marathon and the venue for archery during the 2004 Summer Olympic Games. It should be noted, visitors are no longer permitted to walk past the fence running along its open end. *(On Vas. Konstantinou. From Syntagma, walk down Amalias 10min. to Vas. Olgas, then follow it left. Or take trolley #2, 4, or 11 from Syntagma. Free.)*

MUSEUMS

NATIONAL ARCHAEOLOGICAL MUSEUM. Almost every artifact in this collection is a masterpiece. The museum's highlights include the **Mask of Agamemnon,** in fact excavated from the tomb of a king who lived at least three centuries before Agamemnon, as well as the colorful 16th-century BC "Spring

Fresco," from the Akrotiri settlement on Santorini (Thira), which depicts swallows floating above undulating red lilies. *(Patission 44. Take trolley #2, 4, 5, 9, 11, 15, or 18 across from the National Gardens in Syntagma, or trolley #3 or 13 from the north side of Vas. Sofias. The Metro stop is Victoria on the green line (M1). ☎210 821 7717. Open M 1-7:30pm, Tu-Su 8am-7:30pm. €7, students and EU seniors €3, EU students and under 19 free.)*

BENAKI MUSEUM OF ISLAMIC ART. Built on the ruins of ancient Athenian fortifications, the building's glass windows, marble staircases, and white walls showcase a collection of brilliant tiles, metalwork, and tapestries documenting the history of the Islamic world until the 19th-century. Its exhibits include an inlaid marble reception room brought from a 17th-century Cairo mansion and pottery with Kufic inscriptions. *(Ag. Asomaton 22 and Dipilou, in Psiri. M: Thisso. ☎210 325 1311; www.benaki.gr. Open Tu and Th-Su 9am-3pm, W 9am-9pm. €5, students free. W free.)*

BYZANTINE AND CHRISTIAN MUSEUM. Within its newly renovated interior, this well-organized museum documents the political, religious, and day-to-day aspects of life during the Byzantine Empire. Its collection of metalware, mosaics, sculpture, and icons presents Christianity in its earliest stages. *(Vas. Sofias 22. ☎210 721 1027 or 210 723 1570; www.byzantinemuseum.gr. Open Tu-Su 8:30am-6pm. €4; students and seniors €2; EU students, under 18, disabled, families with 3 or more children, military, and classicists free.)*

ENTERTAINMENT AND NIGHTLIFE

The weekly *Athens News* (€1) lists cultural events, as well as news and ferry info. Summertime performances are staged in venues throughout the city, including the ancient **Odeon of Herodes Atticus,** as part of the **Athens Festival** (May-Sept.; www.greekfestival.gr). Chic Athenians head to the seaside clubs in **Glyfada,** enjoying the breezy night air. **Psiri** and **Gazi** are the bar and club districts. Get started on **Miaouli,** where young crowds gather after dark. For an alternative to bar hopping, follow the guitar-playing local teens and couples that pack **Pavlou** at night. This serene promenade around the Acropolis is Athens's most romantic spot after sunset.

Bretto's, Kydatheneon 41 (☎210 232 2110), between Farmaki and Afroditis in Plaka. Prepare for a sensuous assault when entering this high-ceilinged, century-old wooden distillery. Glass of wine from €3. Cup of *ouzo* €3. Open daily 10am-3am.

Hoxton, Voutadon 42 (☎210 341 3395), in Gazi. With concrete walls and an industrial vibe, this über-trendy

ATHENS FOR FREE

Reeling from the €12 Acropoli admission fee? Though crowd of tourists have inflated the city' prices, there's still fun to be ha on a tight budget—or with no bud get at all. Save your Euros for *sou vlaki:* this is Athens for free.

Wi-Fi: Before ducking into a Internet cafe, take a look around— odds are you're within walkin distance of one of Athens's fre hotspots. Provided by the cit the hotspots are located in an around the city center: Syntagm Sq., Thesseion Sq., Kotzia Sq., an opposite the Evangelismos Metr Station at the National Helleni Research Foundation.

Escape the crowds: So, tha epic photo you took of the Parthe non on your visit to the Acropoli was marred by the head of a ran dom tourist? No worries! Leav the crowds behind and ascen Filopappou Hill, southwest o the Acropolis. Wander the hill' wooded paths and don't forge to stop for photos—the hill offer sweeping vistas of Attica, th Saronic Gulf and the Acropolis.

On guard: Members o the Greek Presidential Guar *evzones,* stand before the Tom of the Unknown Soldier, in fron of Parliament. Every hour, visitor can check out the changing of th guard. For the big show, head t the city center on Sunday at 11a to watch the *evzones* parade i traditional uniform toward Syn tagma Sq. Get there early, or b prepared to rub elbows with ever other tourist in Athens.

bar in a former warehouse is the place to be in Gazi, packing in crowds with Brit-pop, electro, and rock. No cover. Open daily 11pm-2am.

Wunderbar, Themistokleous 80 (☎210 381 8577), on Pl. Exarhia, plays pop and electronic music to relaxed martini-sippers. Late-night revelers lounge outside under large umbrellas. Beer €4. Mixed drinks €8. Open M-Th 9am-3am, F-Su 9am-5am.

DAYTRIPS FROM ATHENS

CAPE SOUNION PENINSULA (ΑΚΡΩΤΗΡΙΟ ΣΟΥΝΙΟ).

Orange-striped KTEL buses go to Cape Sounion from Athens. Bus #1 leaves from the Mavromateon 14 bus stop (near Aeros Park, on Alexandras and 28 Oktovriou-Patission) and stops at all points on the Apollo Coast (2hr., every hr. 6:30am-6pm, €5.70). The other follows a less scenic inland route that also stops at the port of Lavrio (2hr., every hr. 6am-6pm, €4). The last coastal bus leaves Sounion at 9pm (last inland at 9:30pm). Both temples ☎22560 39 363. Open daily 9:30am-sunset except on Jan. 1, Mar. 25, Easter, May 1, Dec. 25, Dec. 26. €4, students and EU seniors over 65 €2, EU students and children under 18 free. Nov.-Mar. Su free.

A tiny tourist colony rests atop the sharp cliff of Cape Sounion, where around 440 BC ancient Greeks built the enormous **Temple of Poseidon** in gleaming white marble. Legend holds that the surrounding Aegean Sea was named for King Aegeus of Athens, who leapt to his death from these cliffs when he saw his son Theseus's ship sporting a black sail—a sign of his son's demise. Unfortunately for Aegeus, Theseus was on board celebrating his triumph over the Minotaur and had forgotten to raise the victorious sail. Today, visitors flock to the site to see the 16 Doric columns that remain from Pericles's reconstruction. Hundreds of names have been carved into the monumental structure; look closely for Lord Byron's on the square column closest to the site entrance. Across the street 500m below is the somewhat deteriorated **Temple of Athena Sounias.**

THE PELOPONNESE (ΠΕΛΟΠΟΝΗΣΟΣ)

Stretching its fingers into the Mediterranean, the Peloponnese transports its visitors to another time and place. The achievements of ancient civilizations dot the peninsula's landscape, as most of Greece's significant archaeological sites—including Olympia, Mycenae, Messini, Corinth, Mystras, and Epidavros—rest in this former home of King Pelops. Away from urban transportation hubs, serene villages welcome visitors to traditional Greece.

PATRAS (ΠΑΤΡΑ) ☎2610

Located on the northwestern tip of the Peloponnese, sprawling Patras (pop. 172,000) operates as the region's primary transportation hub. Charter tourism often skips the city, favoring other nearby islands. During **Carnival** (end of Feb. to early Mar.; ☎2610 390 925; www.carnivalpatras.gr), however, Patras transforms into a gigantic dance floor of costumed, inebriated revelers consumed by pre-Lenten madness. The biggest European festival of its kind revives ancient celebrations in honor of Dionysus—god of wine and debauchery. Entirely covered in colorful frescoes, **Agios Andreas,** 199 Ag. Andreou, is Greece's largest Orthodox cathedral. Follow the waterfront with the town to your left to get there. (☎2610 321 184. Dress modestly. Open daily 7am-9pm.) Sweet black grapes are made into Mavrodaphne wine at the **Achaïa Clauss Winery.** Take bus #7 (30min., €1.20) toward Seravali from the intersection of Kanakari and Gerokostopoulou. (☎2610 368 100. Open daily 10am-5pm. Free.)

Across from the ferry terminal, lounge on the deck of **Rooms to Let Spyros Vazouras ❸,** Tofalou 2, where rooftop ocean views complement brightly tiled rooms with A/C and TV. (☎2610 452 157 or 2610 742 487; www.patrasrooms.gr. Singles €30; doubles €40; extra bed €10.) Centrally located **Pension Nicos ❷**, Patreos 3, sparkles with marble and inlaid stone decor while offering comfortable, pristine rooms at affordable prices. (☎2610 623 757. Reception 3rd fl. Curfew 4am. Singles €23; doubles €33, with bath €38; triples €43/48. MC/V.)

Trains (☎2610 639 108) leave from Amalias 27, right across the port, for Kalamata (5hr., 5 per day, €5) via Pirgos (2hr., 8 per day, €2-4), where you can catch a train to Olympia. A direct railway line between Patras and Athens is currently under construction. To reach Athens from Patras, go to Kiato (2 hr., 9 per day, €2-5), where you can transfer onto the **Suburban Rail** (Proastiakos; www.proastiakos.gr) to Athens (1½hr., 4 per day). KTEL **buses** (☎2610 623 886; www.ktel.org) leave from farther down on Amalias for: Athens (3hr., 2 per hr., €17); Ioannina (4hr., 2 per day, €20); Kalamata (3hr., 2 per day, €20); Thessaloniki (7hr., 4 per day, €39.40). **Ferries** go to Corfu (7hr., M-W and F-Su midnight, €30-33), Vathy on Ithaka (2-3hr.; M-F and Su 12:30, 8:30pm, Sa 12:30pm; €15), and Sami on Kephalonia (3hr.; M-F and Su 12:30, 8:30pm; €15). Six major ferry lines also travel to Italy: Ancona (21hr.); Bari (16hr.); Brindisi (14hr.); Venice (30hr.). The **tourist office,** Amalias 6, 50m past the bus station, provides a wealth of information about Patras, including 1-day, 3-day, and week-long itineraries, and offers free bike rental and short-term Internet access. (☎2610 461 740 or 2610 461 741; infocenterpatras.gr. Open daily 8am-10pm.) **Postal Code:** 26001.

OLYMPIA (ΟΛΥΜΠΙΑ) ☎26240

Every four years, ancient city-states would call a sacred truce and travel to Olympia for a pan-Hellenic assembly that showcased athletic ability and fostered peace and diplomacy. Modern Olympia, set among meadows and shaded by cypress and olive trees, is recognized as much for its pristine natural beauty as for its illustrious past. The ancient **Olympic site,** whose central sanctuary was called the **Altis,** draws hordes of tourists. Toward the entrance lie the ruins of the **Temple of Zeus.** Once home to master sculptor Phidias's awe-inspiring Statue of Zeus, one of the Seven Wonders of the Ancient World, the 27m sanctuary was the largest temple completed on the Greek mainland before the Parthenon. The **Temple of Hera,** dating from the seventh century BC, is better preserved than Zeus's temple; it sits to the left facing the hill, past the temples of Metroön and the Nymphaeum. Today, the **Olympic flame** lighting ceremony takes place here before the torch travels around the world to herald the Olympic Games' commencement. Facing away from the Temple of Hera, walk through the archway to reach the ancient **Olympic stadium.** (Open June-Sept. daily 8am- 7:30pm.) The **Archaeological Museum** has an impressive sculpture collection; check out the *Nike of Paeonius* and the *Hermes, carrying the infant Dionysus* by Praxiteles. (Open M 12:30-7:30pm, Tu-Su 8am-7:30pm. Temple and museum each €6, non-EU students €3, EU students free. Both €9/5/free.) Also onsite are the **Museum of the History of the Olympic Games** and the **Museum of the History of Excavations.** (Both museums open M 12:30-7:30pm, Tu-Su 8am-7:30pm. Free.)

The centrally located **Youth Hostel ❶**, Kondili 18, across from the main square, is a cheap place to meet international backpackers and has airy rooms with narrow balconies. (☎26240 22 580. Linens €1. Limited hot showers. Check-out 10am. Lockout 10am-12:30pm. Curfew 11:45pm. Open Feb.-Dec. Dorms €10; doubles €23. Cash only.) Mini-markets, bakeries, and fast food restaurants line **Kondili,** while a walk toward the railroad station or up the hill leads to inexpensive *tavernas*. A filling meal is as Greek as it gets at **Vasilakis Restaurant ❷**, on the corner of Karamanli and Spiliopoulou. Take a right off Kohili before the Youth Hostel, walking towards the ruins. (☎26240 22 104. *Souvlaki* pita €1.50. Chicken and fries €10. Open daily 11:30am-midnight.)

Trains leave the station in the lower part of town for Pirgos (25min., 5 per day, €1), as do **buses** (1hr., 7-15 per day, €1.90). The Town Hall **info center**, at the right end of Kondili, before the turn to the sights, serves as a tourist office. (☎26240 22 262. Open M-F 9:30am-3pm.) **Postal Code:** 27065.

SPARTA (ΣΠΑΡΤΗ) ☎27310

Though the Spartans of antiquity were renowned for their military strength and physical prowess (weak babies were abandoned on mountaintops), they left little of their fierce legacy behind. Modern Spartans, no longer producing Greek *hoplites*, make olive oil. A few stone fragments and a grove of olive trees comprise the meager ruins at **Ancient Sparta**, a 1km walk north along Paleologou from the town center. At the end of Paleologou, an imposing statue of King Leonidas stands heroically before the soccer stadium. Two blocks from the central *plateia* lies the city's **Archaeological Museum.** Opening into a garden of orange trees and headless statues, the museum displays votive masks, intricate mosaics, lead figures resembling a toy army, and Grecian vases. (☎27310 28 575. Closed indefinitely for renovations.)

Accommodations in Sparta rarely come cheap, and few attractions exist to assuage an empty wallet. **Hotel Cecil ❸**, Paleologou 125, on the corner of Thermopylon, has ordinary, spotless rooms with A/C, bath, phone, and TV in a recently renovated building. (☎27310 24 980. Reserve ahead. Singles €40; doubles €60; triples €75.) Family-run and popular with locals, **Diethnes ❷**, Paleologou 105, 2½ blocks to the right of the intersection of Lykourgou and Paleologou, serves tasty Greek food in an intimate garden with orange trees. Though it has a few vegetarian options (€5), the restaurant specializes in €7 lamb entrees. (☎27310 81 033. Open 8am-midnight.)

Buses go to Athens (3hr., 10 per day, €17) via Tripoli (1hr., €5) and Monemvasia (2hr., 3-4 per day, €9). Town center from the bus station: walk nine blocks uphill on Lykourgou; the **tourist office** is on the third floor of the glass building in the *plateia*. (☎ 27310 24 852. Open M-F 8am-2pm.) **Postal Code:** 23100.

DAYTRIP FROM SPARTA: MYSTRAS (ΜΥΣΤΡΑΣ). Once Byzantium's religious center and the locus of Constantinople's rule over the Peloponnese, Mystras, 6km from Sparta, is a well-preserved medieval town perched on a hillside. The **Agia Sophia** church, where the city's royalty lies buried, and the **Agios Theodoros** fresco contribute to Mystras's timelessness. Don't miss the **castle's** staggering panoramic views of the surrounding countryside. Modest dress is required to visit the functioning convent and its beautifully decorated Pantanassa Church. *(☎27310 83 377. Open daily Aug.-Sept. 8am-7:30pm; Oct.-July 8:30am-3pm. €5, students €3, EU students free.)* **Buses** to Mystras leave from the stop on Lykourgou before the intersection with Paleologou and from the corner of Lykourgou and Leonidou in Sparta for the ruins, returning 15min. later (20min., 4-9 per day, €1.40). **Taxis** go to Mystras from the corner of Paleologou and Lykourgou (€5).

MONEMVASIA (ΜΟΝΕΜΒΑΣΙΑ) ☎27320

On a monolithic rock that springs dramatically from the sea, Monemvasia is a Grecian treasure. No cars or bikes are allowed within the Old Town's walls, imbuing the flowered balconies and picturesque corners with a sense of medieval timelessness. Atop the rock, uphill from the *plateia* amidst the ruins of the upper town, is the beautiful **Agia Sofia**, a 12th-century Byzantine church. From Agia Sofia, paths continue uphill toward the old **citadel**, which affords sweeping views of the town and sea below. In the *plateia*, along the shop-lined main street, is the **Archaeological Collection.** (Open Tu-Su 8:30am-3pm. Free.) To get to the Old Town, cross the bridge from Gefyra and follow the road as it curves up the hill. It's an easy 20min. walk, but both the heat and crowds increase as the day wears on. It's better to go in the early morning or late evening, when the setting sun illuminates the panorama in breathtaking shades. A bus also shuttles people up and down the road and leaves from the bridge at the foot of the hill (2min., 4 per hr. 8am-midnight, €1).

Multiple pensions and waterfront *domatia* in **Gefyra** are a budget traveler's best option. Accommodation is available on the rock itself, but it's hardly "budget." With a unique, romantic ambience, dining in the Old Town is beautiful but expensive. On the main road to the right, just before the Archaeological Museum, is **Restaurant Matoula ❸,** with its vine-covered trellises and sweeping ocean views. The food is traditional, made from local ingredients, and the fresh fish is to die for. (☎27320 61 660. Entrees €8-14. *Moussaka* €8. Open daily noon-midnight. MC/V.) For those on a tight budget, there are many cheap Greek fast-food eateries and bakeries. Backpackers often picnic on the beach in New Town, soaking up the beautiful views for free. **Buses** leave from Spartis for Athens (4 per day, €26) and Sparta (2hr., €9). **Postal Code:** 23070.

NAFPLION (ΝΑΥΠΛΙΟ) ☎27520

A tiny Venetian town surrounded on three sides by sky-blue waters, Nafplion is one of the Peloponnese's most beautiful—and most popular—tourist destinations. In July and August, the town teems with more Americans and Italians than locals. After passing from the Venetians to Ottomans, Nafplion became Greece's first capital in 1821. The 18th-century **Palamidi fortress** crowns the city, offering spectacular views of the gulf. Climb the 999 steps from across the central *plateia*, right across from the bus station, or take a taxi up the 3km road. (☎27520 28 036. Open 8am-7pm. €4, students €2, EU students and under 18 free.) A small, pebbly beach, **Arvanitia,** is farther along Polizoidhou, past the Palamidi steps; if it's too crowded, follow the footpath to private coves, or take a taxi (€5) to sandy **Karathona** beach. To reach **Bouboulinas,** the waterfront promenade, go left from the bus station and follow Syngrou to the harbor; the **Old Town** is on your left. From Arvanitia, you can walk the short path around the promontory; keep the sea to your left and the town's walls to your right.

Old Town accommodations are often expensive, but **Dimitris Bekas's Domatia ❷,** Efthimiopoulou 26, is a great budget option for travelers spending the night. This small, central pension offers cozy rooms and a roof deck. The friendly manager steadfastly refuses to raise his prices during high season. From the bus station, walk right on Fotomara until you reach the small Catholic church, then turn right on Zygomala, and left up the first set of stairs. (☎27520 24 594. Reserve ahead July-Aug. Singles €22; doubles €28, with bath €30.) **Ellas ❷,** in Pl. Syntagma, has inexpensive Greek and Italian food. The cheerful staff serves people-watching patrons on the outdoor *plateia*. (☎27520 27 278. Entrees €5-7. Open daily noon-4pm and 7-11pm. MC/V.)

Buses, Syngrou 8 (☎27520 27 323; www.ktel-argolis.gr/en/index.htm), depart for: Athens (3hr., 1 per hr. 5am-8pm, €11.80); Epidavros (40min., 3-5 per day, €2.60); Mycenae (45min., 3 per day, €2.60). The **tourist office** is at 25 Martiou, located directly across from the bus station. (☎27520 24 444. Open daily 9am-1pm and 4-8pm.) **Postal Code:** 21100.

DAYTRIPS FROM NAFPLION: EPIDAVROS (ΕΠΙΔΑΥΡΟΣ). Like Olympia and Delphi, **Epidavros** was once both a town and a sanctuary—first to the ancient deity Maleatas and then to Apollo. Eventually, the energies of the sanctuary were directed toward the demigod-doctor Asclepius, the son of Apollo who caught Zeus's wrath (and fatal thunderbolt) when he began to raise people from the dead. Under the patronage of Asclepius, Epidavros became famous across the ancient world as a center of medicine. Today, visitors can explore the **sanctuary,** which is undergoing heavy restoration, and visit a small museum of ancient medical equipment and other artifacts. *(☎27530 22 009. Sanctuary open daily June-Sept. 8am-7pm; Oct.-May 8am-5pm. Museum open June-Sept. M noon-7pm, Tu-Su 8am-7pm; Oct.-May M noon-5pm, Tu-Su 8am-5pm. Both open during festival F-Sa 8am-8pm. €6, students €3, EU students and under 19 free.)* The best-known structure at the site, however, is the splendidly preserved fourth-century **theater,** renowned for its extraordinary acoustics: a match struck or a coin dropped in the center of the stage can be heard in the top rows. Fortunately for today's visitors, Greece's most famous ancient theater has come alive again after centuries of silence: during July and August it hosts the **Epidavros Theater Festival,** with performances by international artists and modern interpretations of classical plays. *(☎27530 22 026; www.greekfestival.gr/?lang=en. Performances begin at 9pm. Tickets at the site's box office: €10-50, the Athens Festival Box Office ☎210 32 72 000, or at Nafplion's bus station.* KTEL **buses** go to Nafplion (45min., 4 per day, €2.60) and make a special trip on performance nights (7:30pm, €6), returning spectators to Nafplion 20min. after the performance ends. Buses run from Ligurio to Athens (2½hr., 2 per day).

NORTHERN AND CENTRAL GREECE

Northern and central Greece offer an escape from tourist-packed Athens, with fantastic hiking and Byzantine and Hellenistic heritage. Scattered across the region, traditional villages host diverse attractions: the depths of the Vikos Gorge, the heights of Mount Olympus, and the serenity of Meteora's mountaintop monasteries. Greece's heartland boasts some of the country's great cities, including Thessaloniki and Ioannina. Connected to its Balkan neighbors, the north is where multicultural Greece emerges.

THESSALONIKI (ΘΕΣΣΑΛΟΝΙΚΗ) ☎2310

Thessaloniki (a.k.a. Salonica; pop. 364,000), the Balkans' trade center, has historically been one of the most diverse cities in Greece, and is second in size only to Athens. The city is an energetic bazaar of clothing shops and fashionable cafes, while its churches and mosques provide a material timeline of the region's restless past. Thessaloniki's current lack of tourism infrastructure and subway construction through 2012 may frustrate some travelers.

TRANSPORTATION

Flights: Macedonia Airport (SKG; ☎2310 985 000), 16km east of town. Take bus #78 from the KTEL station or Pl. Aristotelous (2 per hr.; €0.50 at kiosks, €0.60 onboard.) or taxi (€15). **Olympic Airlines,** Kountouriotou 3 (☎2310 368 311; www.olympicairlines.com; open M-F 8am-4pm), and **Aegean Airlines,** 1 Nikis, off Venizelou (☎2310 239 225; www.aegeanair.com; open M-F 8am-3pm, Sa 8am-2pm), fly to: **Athens** (1hr., 24 per day, €72); **Corfu** (1hr., 5 per week, €116); **Chania** (1hr., 9 per week, €144); **Ioannina** (35min., 4 per week, €130); **Heraklion** (1hr., 15 per week, €85); **Lesvos** (1hr., 15 per day, €96); **Rhodes** (2hr., 11 per week, €110).

Trains: To reach the **main terminal,** Monastiriou 28, (☎2310 517 517) in the western part of the city, take any bus down Egnatia (€0.50 at kiosks, €0.60 onboard). Trains go to: **Athens** (7hr., 3 per day, €15; express 5hr., 4 per day, €28); **Istanbul, TUR** (14hr., 1 per day, €25); **Skopje, MAC** (4hr., 2 per day, €11); **Sofia, BUL** (7hr., 2 per day, €16).

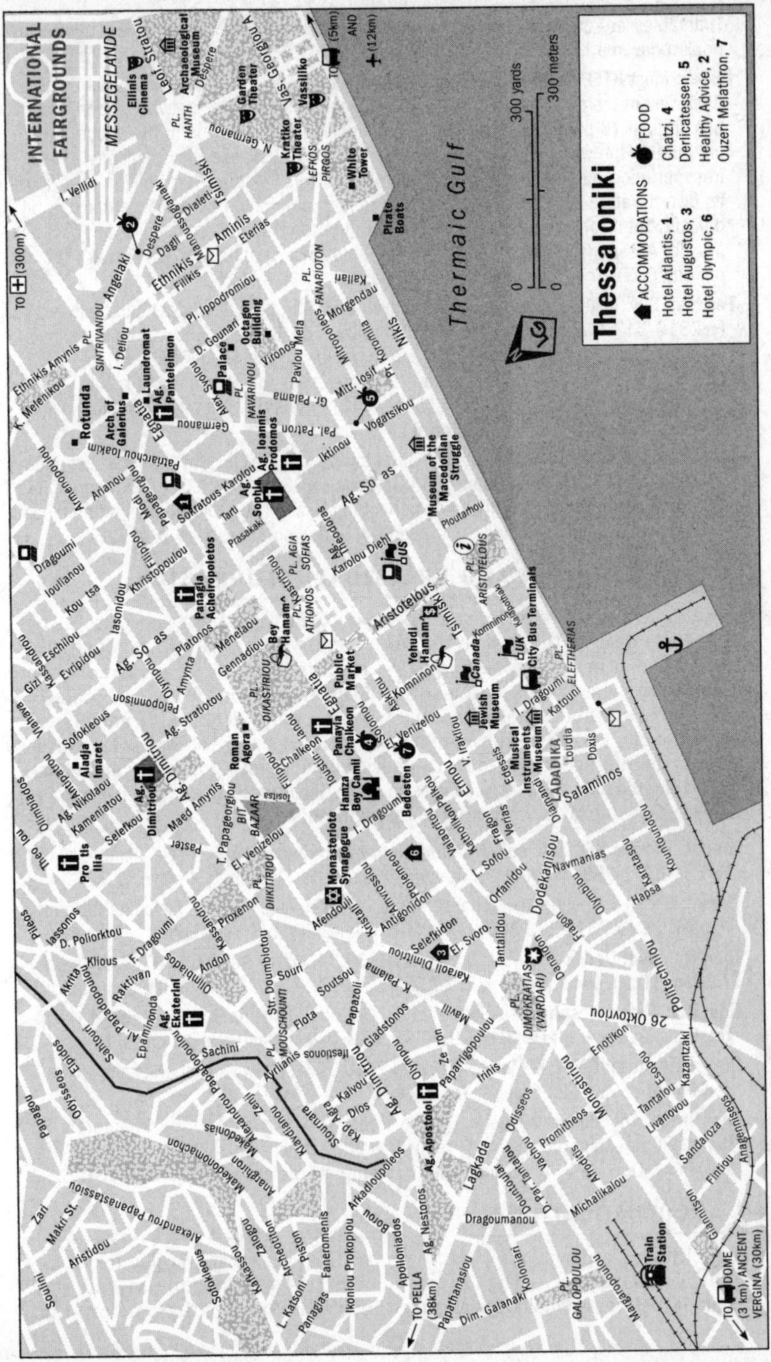

Thessaloniki

ACCOMMODATIONS
Hotel Atlantis, 1
Hotel Augustos, 3
Hotel Olympic, 6

FOOD
Chatzi, 4
Derlicatessen, 5
Healthy Advice, 2
Ouzeri Melathron, 7

300 yards
300 meters

Thermaic Gulf

INTERNATIONAL FAIRGROUNDS
MESSEGELANDE

Timetables are available online at www.ose.gr. All trains are run by OSE. It's wise to book a day in advance for trains to Athens.

Buses: Most **KTEL** buses leave from the central, dome-shaped **Macedonia Bus Station** 3km west of the city center (☎2310 595 408). Bus #1 shuttles between the train and bus stations (6 per hr., €0.50). Bus #78 connects the bus station to the airport, passing through the waterfront corridor (2 per hr., €0.50). Because Thessaloniki is a major transportation hub, each destination city has its own "platform" or parking spot, and its own ticketing booth. The absence of a central information desk makes things a bit difficult, but if you can locate the window for the town/city you are heading to, you'll be fine. To: **Athens** (6hr., 8 per day, €24); **Ioannina** (6hr., 6 per day, €28); **Patras** (7hr., 4 per day, €33). Schedules are subject to change.

Ferries: Buy tickets at **Karacharisis Travel and Shipping Agency,** Kountouriotou 8 (☎2310 513 005). Open M-F 8:30am-8:30pm, Sa 8:30am-2:30pm. Most destinations are pretty far from Thessaloniki (and more easily accessible via Athens), but if you must depart from this city, ferries leave once per week for: **Heraklion** (21-24hr., €38) via **Skiathos** (5hr., €19); **Mykonos** (13hr., €42); **Mytilini** (14 hr., €44); **Naxos** (14hr., €39) via **Syros** (12hr., €38); **Santorini** (17-18hr., €45).

Local Transportation: Local buses run often throughout the city. Buy tickets at *periptera* (newsstands; €0.50) or on board (€0.60). **Taxis** (☎2310 551 525) run down Egnatia, Mitropoleos, and Tsimiski with stands at Ag. Sophia and the intersection of Mitropoleos and Aristotelous. Rides should not exceed €4; phone orders cost an extra €1.50.

ORIENTATION AND PRACTICAL INFORMATION

Thessaloniki stretches along the Thermaic Gulf's northern shore from the iconic **White Tower** in the east to the prominent western **harbor.** Its rough grid layout makes it nearly impossible to get lost. Its most important arteries run parallel to the water. Closest to shore is **Nikis,** which goes from the harbor to the White Tower and is home to the city's main cafes. Farthest from shore is **Egnatia,** the city's busiest thoroughfare, a six-lane avenue; the Arch of Galerius stands at its intersection with D. Gounari. Inland from Egnatia are **Agios Dimitriou** and the **Old Town.** The city's main square, Aristotelous, has numerous banks, businesses, restaurants, and other establishments.

Tourist Offices: EOT (Greek National Tourist Organization), Plateia Aristotelous 8 (☎2310 271 888; www.eot.gr). Open M-F 8am-8pm, Sa 8am-1:30pm.

Banks: Banks with currency exchange and 24hr. **ATMs** line Tsimiski, including **Citibank,** Tsimiski 21 (☎2310 373 300). Open M-Th 8am-2:30pm, F 8am-2pm.

Tourist Police: Dodekanissou 4, 5th fl. (☎2310 554 870 or 2310 554 871). Open daily 7:30am-10pm. **Local police** ☎2310 553 800. Police booths also at the train station.

Hospital: Ahepa Hospital, Kiriakidi 1 (☎2310 993 111). **Hippokration General Hospital,** Papanastasiou 50 (☎2310 892 000). On weekends and at night call ☎1434.

Internet Access: GNET, K. Melenikoy 37 (☎2310 968 120; www.gnet.gr) is a cheap and convenient option. €2.20 per hr. Open 24 hr.

Post Office: Aristotelous 26, below Egnatia. Open M-F 7:30am-8pm, Sa 7:30am-2pm, Su 9am-1:30pm. Send parcels at the branch on Eth. Aminis near the White Tower (☎2310 227 604). Open M-F 7am-8pm. **Poste Restante** available. **Postal Code:** 54101.

ACCOMMODATIONS

Budget options are available, but be prepared to get what you pay for. Thessaloniki's less expensive, slightly run-down hotels are along the western end of **Egnatia** between **Plateia Dimokratias** (500m east of the train station) and

Aristotelous. Most face the chaotic road on one side and squalid back streets on the other. Hotels fill up quickly during high season, April through September.

Hotel Olympic, Egnatia 25 (☎2310 566 870; fax 2310 555 353). Simple, newly renovated rooms have A/C, bath, refrigerator, and TV. English-speaking staff eager to offer advice about Thessaloniki. Breakfast €5. Reception 24hr. Singles €40; doubles €50. €10 discount with *Let's Go* book Oct.-Aug. AmEx/MC/V. ❸

Hotel Augustos, El. Svoronou 4 (☎2310 522 955; www.augustos.gr). Better kept than most competitors. Comfortable rooms with frescoed ceilings and wooden floors. Singles €20, with bath and A/C €30; doubles €25/38; triples €50. Cash only. ❷

Hotel Atlantis, Egnatia 14 (☎2310 540 131; atlalej@otenet.gr). English-speaking management offers rooms with sinks and tiny balconies. Some newly renovated rooms with A/C. Singles €20, with bath €25; doubles €25/40; triples €30/45. Cash only. ❷

FOOD

The old city overflows with *tavernas* and restaurants providing sweeping views of the gulf, while the lovely **Bit Bazaar** has characteristic *ouzeries*. Thessaloniki's restaurants have a delightful custom of giving patrons free watermelon or sweets after a meal, but if you crave anything from dried fruits to apple-sized cherries, head to the bustling public **market,** right off Aristotelous.

Ouzou Melathron, Karypi 21-34 (☎2310 275 016; www.ouzoumelathron.gr). A student favorite for its great prices and pub atmosphere. Long, witty menu features chicken, snails, lamb, octopus, and cheese tapas. Entrees €4-14. Free round of drinks with ISIC. Open M-F 1:30pm-1:30am, Sa-Su 1:30pm-2am. D/MC/V. ❷

Healthy Advice, Alex Svolou 54 (☎2310 283 255). Canadian-run with Western-style sandwiches (€4-6). Salami straight from Italy, lean turkey and ham, and bread baked daily. English-, French-, and Arabic-speaking staff. Open daily 11:30am-2am. ❷

Derlicatessen, Kouskoura 7 (☎2310 226 367). Hands down most popular among locals for *souvlaki* (€2.20). Though it's a bit rough around the edges, Derlicatessen has its own charm—a real hole-in-the-wall neighborhood joint, covered in pictures of its patrons and owners. It's always busy. Open daily 11:30am-3am. ❶

Chatzi, El. Venizelou 50 (☎2310 279 058; www.chatzis.gr), now with 4 stores in town, might be better than Willy Wonka's. Row after row of olive-oil drenched, calorie-packed treats. The *kourkoumpinia* and *baklava* are phenomenal (€1.20 per 100g). Open M-F and Su 7am-3am, Sa 7am-4am. MC/V. ❶

SIGHTS

Reminders of Thessaloniki's Byzantine and Ottoman might pervade its streets. The **Roman Agora,** a second-century odeon and covered market, still rests at the top of Aristotelous. Its lower square once held eight *caryatids*, sculptures of women believed to have been magically petrified. (Open daily 8am-8pm. Free.) Originally a temple honoring Jupiter, the **Rotunda** (now **Agios Georgios**) was erected by the Roman Caesar Galerius at the beginning of the AD fourth century. It later became a church honoring martyred Christians, then a mosque under the Ottomans. (☎2310 968 860. Open Tu-F 8am-7pm, Sa-Su 8:30am-3pm. Free.) At D. Gounari and Egnatia stands the striking **Arch of Galerius,** known locally as *Kamara* (Arch), which constituted part of a larger gateway connecting the palace complex to the main city street. Erected by Galerius to commemorate his victory over the Persians, it now serves as a popular meeting spot for locals. Two blocks south of the arch, in Pl. Navarino, a small section of the once 150 sq. km **Palace of Galerius** is open for viewing. The weathered mosaic floors and octagonal hall, believed to have housed Galerius's throne, are particularly notable. The **Archaeological Museum,** M. Andronikou 6, features some of the area's most prized artifacts, including the Derveni krater and sculptures of Greek goddesses. (☎2310 830 538. Open M 10:30am-5pm, Tu-Su 8:30am-3pm. €6, students and seniors €3, EU students and children free.)

NIGHTLIFE

Thessaloniki is a city that lives outside, with citizens packing its bars, boardwalks, and cafes. The **Ladadika** district, a two-by-three-block rectangle of *tavernas* behind the port, was the city's red-light strip until the 80s, but has since transformed into a sea of dance clubs. The heart of the city's social life during the winter, it shuts down almost entirely in summer, when everyone moves to the open-air discos around the airport. As Thessaloniki's popular clubs change frequently, ask the locals for an update. The waterfront cafes and the **Aristotelous** promenade are always packed, as is the student-territory **Bit Bazaar,** a cobblestoned square of *ouzeries* and wine and tapas bars. For a unique experience, drink and dance to music on one of the three **pirate boats** that leave from behind the White Tower for 30min. harbor tours.

MOUNT OLYMPUS (ΟΛΥΜΠΟΣ ΟΡΟΣ) ☎23520

Erupting out of the Thermaic Gulf, the formidable slopes of Mt. Olympus, Greece's highest peak, mesmerized the ancient Greeks, who believed it to be their pantheon's divine dwelling place. Today, a network of well-maintained **hiking** trails makes the summit accessible to anyone with sturdy legs. Mt. Olympus has eight peaks: Ag. Andonios (2817m), Kalogeros (2701m), Mytikas (2917m), Profitis Ilias (2803m), Skala (2866m), Skolio (2911m), Stefani (the Throne of Zeus, 2909m), and Toumba (2801m). The region became Greece's first national park in 1938. From **Litochoro Town** (pop.7000, 300m), the easiest and most popular trail begins at **Prionia** (1100m), 18km from the village, and ascends 4km through a sheltered, forested ravine to **Zolotas refuge** (2100m), also known as Refuge A or—to the Greeks—as Spilios Agapitos. At the Zolotas refuge, you'll find reliable resources for all aspects of hiking: updates on weather and trail conditions, advice on routes, and reservations for any of the **Greek Alpine Club (EOS)** refuges. With years of knowledge and experience, the staff is happy to dispense info over the phone in English. (☎23520 84 544. Curfew 10pm. Open mid-May to Oct. Camping €5; dorms €10.)

To rest up before your big hike or race, head to **Hotel Park ❷,** Ag. Nikolaou 23, at the bottom of the hill after the park, which has large rooms with A/C, bath, fridge, phone, TV; a few balconies. (☎23520 81 252; hotelpark_litochoro@yahoo.gr. Breakfast €5. Reception 24hr. Singles €25; doubles €35; triples €45. Cash only.) For a meal with a view, try **Gastrodromio En Olympo ❸,** off the *plateia* by the church. (☎23520 21 300. Entrees €8-14. Open daily 10am-midnight. MC/V.) Those wisely seeking water and trail snacks for the arduous hike up Olympus should stay away from the expensive supermarkets above the *plateia* and head to **Arvanitides,** Perikliko Torba 14, at the end of Odos Ermi. (☎23520 21 195. Open M-F 8am-9pm, Sa-Su 8am-8pm.)

KTEL buses (☎23520 81 271) leave from the Litochoro station, Ag. Nikolaou 20, opposite the tourist office, for Athens (5hr., 3 per day, €30), Plaka (15min., 1 per hr., €2), and Thessaloniki (1hr., 16 per day, €8) via Katerini (30min., 1 per hr., €2). The **tourist office** is on Ag. Nikolaou by the park. (☎23520 83 100. Open daily 9am-2:30pm and 4:30-9:30pm.) **Postal Code:** 60200.

METEORA AND KALAMBAKA (ΜΕΤΕΩΡΑ AND ΚΑΛΑΜΠΑΚΑ) ☎24320

The monastic community of Meteora lies atop a series of awe-inspiring rock pinnacles. Inhabited by hermits since the 11th century, these summits were chosen as the location of a series of 21 frescoed Byzantine **monasteries** in the 14th century. Six monasteries remain in use and open to the public. Don't expect a hidden treasure—tour buses and sweaty faces are as common here as Byzantine icons, and the traditionally dressed monks drive Jeeps. For monastic silence rarely experienced during the day, visit the complex after hours, when the museums are closed. The largest, oldest, and most popular monastery, **Great Meteoron** houses a **folk and history museum** and the 16th-century **Church of the Transfiguration.** On the first level, visitors can peer through a door into the monastery's ossuary to see shelves upon shelves of deceased monks' skulls and other skeletal remains. The complex's second largest monastery, **Varlaam,** is 800m down the road. Take the right fork to reach the **Roussanou** convent, which was accessible only by rope ladder until 1897. (Modest dress required: no sleeveless shirts, long pants for men and long skirts for women. Tie-on skirts available at the monastery entrance. Hours vary by season and monastery. Great Meteoron, ☎24320 22 278 or 24320 75 398, open in summer M and W-Su 9am-5pm; Varlaam, ☎24320 22 277, open M-W and F-Su 9am-4pm; Roussanou, ☎24320 22 649, open daily 9am-6pm. Each monastery €2.) Meteora is accessible from the Kalambaka **bus** station (15min., 2-4 per day, €1.40), or visitors can walk 45min. up the hill along the **footpath** that begins at the end of Vlahava.

Meteora and Kalambaka's rocky landscapes create a **climber's** paradise; for info, equipment rental, guided excursions, and lessons, contact local climbing instructor **Kostas Liolios** (☎69725 67582; kliolios@kalampaka.com). Accommodation owners may approach you at the bus station offering lower prices for decent rooms; be aware that picking up people from the station is illegal here. At the base of Meteora, **Alsos House ❸**, Kanari 5, has rooms with A/C, balcony, bath, and gorgeous views. From the Town Hall and main square (Pl. Dimarhiou), follow Vlahava until it ends, then follow the signs. The owner sometimes hires students in summer in exchange for room and board. (☎24320 24 097; www.alsoshouse.gr. Breakfast included. Free Internet and Wi-Fi. Free parking. Reserve ahead. Singles €35-40; doubles €50-55; triples €70-75; 2-room apartment with kitchen €90. 10% *Let's Go* or ISIC discount. MC/V.) In the center of town, **Taverna Panellinion ❶**, Pl. Dimarhiou, serves up a wide range of traditional, delicious Greek fare on a lovely trellis-shaded patio. (☎24320 24 735. Entrees €5-8. Open daily noon-11pm.)

Trains (☎24320 22 451) leave Kalambaka for Athens (5hr., 2 per day, €21). **Buses** (☎24320 22 432) depart Kalambaka for: Athens (5hr., 7 per day, €25) via Trikala; Ioannina (3hr., 2 per day, €11.20); Patras (5hr.; Tu, Th-F, and Su 1 per day; €27.50); Thessaloniki (3hr., 6 per day, €17.50) via Trikala. Helpful staff provide maps and transportation information at the **municipal tourist office,** across the street from the fountain in Pl. Dimarhiou, at the beginning of Vlahava. (☎24320 77 734. Open M-F 8am-8pm, Sa 8am-2pm.) **Postal Code:** 42200.

DELPHI (ΔΕΛΦΟΙ) ☎22650

Troubled denizens of the ancient world journeyed to the stunning mountain-top of the **Oracle of Delphi,** where the priestess of Apollo conveyed the god's cryptic prophecies. Leading up the hillside along the **Sacred Way** are the remains of the legendary **Temple of Apollo,** followed by a perfectly preserved **theater** and a **stadium** that once hosted the holy **Delphic Games.** At the entrance to the site, the **archaeological museum** exhibits an extensive collection of artifacts found near the temple, including the **Sphinxes** (the oracle's guards). Head east from Delphi to reach the temple, but go early in the morning to avoid the nonstop flow of guided groups. (Archaeological site open daily 7:30am-7:30pm. Museum open M noon-6:30pm,Tu-Su 7:30am-7:30pm. Each €6, both €9; students €3/5; EU students free.) For overnight stays, the recently renovated **Hotel Sibylla ❷,** Pavlou 9, offers wonderful views and private baths at the best prices in town. (☎22650 82 335; www.sibylla-hotel.gr. No-commission currency exchange. Singles €20-24; doubles €26-30; triples €35-40. €2 *Let's Go* discount.) In July, Delphi springs to life with a series of musical and theatrical **performances** at its Cultural Center (☎22650 331 2781; www.eccd.gr). From Delphi, **buses** go to Athens (3hr., 6 per day, €13.60). Delphi's **tourist office,** Pavlou 12 or Friderikis 11, is right up to the stairs next to the town hall. (☎22650 82 900. Open M-F 8am-2:30pm.) **Postal Code:** 33054.

ZAGOROHORIA ☎26530

Between the Albanian border and the North Pindos mountain range, a string of 46 *horia* (little hamlets) show few signs of interference from modern society. Home to **Vikos Gorge**—the world's deepest canyon—and **Vikos-Aoös National Park,** the region is popular among nature enthusiasts. North of Vikos Gorge, the two **Papingo** villages, **Megalo** (large) and **Mikro** (small), have become vacation destinations for wealthy Greeks and serve as the start point for some beautiful hikes.

TRANSPORTATION AND PRACTICAL INFORMATION. **Buses** go to Ioannina from the Papingos (1hr., 2 per week, €5). Papingo visitors may consider hiking 3hr. to **Klidonia** to catch more frequent buses (1hr., 8 per day, €4). **Taxis** can take you to Ioannina or Konitsa (€35). The closest **banks** are in Kalpaki and Konitsa. Any trip should include a visit to the **Zagori Information Center** in the town of **Aspraggeli.** (☎26530 22 241. Open daily 9am-6pm.)

ACCOMMODATIONS AND FOOD. An increase in tourism has raised the region's lodging prices. If pensions and *domatia* are full or high-season prices are outrageous, backpackers may hike 3km to the **EOS Refuge ❶,** near Mt. Astraka. (☎26530 26 553. 60-bed dorm €10.) Freelance camping is illegal. **Pension Koulis ❸** has rooms reminiscent of an alpine ski lodge. Facing the town from where the cobblestoned road starts, take the first left after the church. The pension is on the corner of the next crossroads to the left. (☎26530 41 115. Breakfast included. Reception 24hr. Singles €35; doubles €50; triples €65. MC/V.) At **Tsoumanis Estiatorio ❷,** outside town on the road to Mikro Papingo, two brothers serve lamb from their father's flock and vegetables from their gardens. (☎26530 42 108. Entrees €5-9. Open daily 11am-1am.)

SIGHTS AND HIKING. **Vikos Gorge,** whose walls are 900m deep and only 110m apart, is the steepest on earth. In spring, the gorge's river rushes along the 15km stretch of canyon floor. By summer, all that is left is the occasional puddle in the dry riverbed. People have walked through the gorge's ravine since the 12th century BC, when early settlers took shelter in its caves. Today, hikers follow the well-marked **03 domestic trail** (red diamonds on white square backgrounds) section of the Greek National E4 route through the gorge. The path stretches from the village of Kipi in the south to Megalo Papingo at its northernmost tip, winding through Zagorohoria's center. The gorge can be accessed from Kipi, Monodendri, the Papingo villages, and Vikos Village.

Zagorohoria's most spectacular hikes begin in **Mikro Papingo,** from where visitors can climb **Mount Astraka** (2436m). Most ascents take about 4hr. and are appropriate for intermediate-level hikers. More advanced hikers climb 4hr. to the pristine **Drakolimni** (Dragon Lake; 2000m), an alpine pool filled with spotted newts. Both hikes can be paired with a stay in the **EOS Refuge** (1900m), on a nearby ridge. From the refuge, a path (3km, 1hr.) descends into the blossom-dotted valley, passes **Xeroloutsa**, a shallow alpine lake, and ends at Drakolimni. Multi-day treks deep into the Pindos are possible, using the EOS hut as a starting point. For easier hikes, the family-friendly **Papingo Natural Pools** are a great option. When the main road curves right before ascending to Mikro Papingo from Megalo, you'll see a small bridge and parking lot. Opposite the parking lot, the white-rock trail begins. The pools become warmer and cleaner as you climb along, but beware of the venomous snakes when taking a dip in the lower pools.

IOANNINA ☎26510

The capital of Epirus, Ioannina serves as the natural transportation hub for northern Greece. The city reached its height of fame after its 1788 capture by Ali Pasha, an Albanian-born visionary leader and womanizer. Legend has it that when Ali Pasha wasn't able to get the girl he wanted, he strangled all of his other lovers and threw their bodies into Ioannina's lake. The city is also the site of the **Frourio**, a monumental fortress built in the 14th century, where many of the city's residents live today. To reach the **Its-Kale** (inner citadel) from the Frourio's main entrance, veer left, and follow the signs. To the right along the wall are the remnants of Ali Pasha's **hamam** (baths). Catch a ferry from the waterfront (10min., 2 per hr. 7am-midnight, €2) to the island of **Nisi** to explore Byzantine monasteries and the **Ali Pasha Museum** (open daily 9am-9pm; €2). **Hotel Tourist ❸**, Kolleti 18, on the right a few blocks up G. Averof from the *kastro*, offers simple rooms with A/C, TV, bath, and phone. (☎26510 26443; www.hoteltourist.gr/en.htm. Singles €45; doubles €44; triples €66.) Portions are huge and prices reasonable at lakeside **Limni ❷**. (☎26510 78 988; www.limni-ioa.gr. Entrees €5-8.) **Buses**, Zossimadon 4, depart from the main terminal to: Athens (6hr., 7 per day, €34); Kalambaka (2hr., 2 per day, €11); Thessaloniki (5hr., 4 per day, €27). For info, call ☎26510 26 286. To reach the **tourist office**, walk down Dodonis; the office is located immediately after the school. (☎26510 46 662. Open M-F 7:30am-7:30pm.) **Postal Code:** 45110.

LOCAL LEGEND

THE WORLD'S BELLY BUTTON

As they make the ascent up the Sacred Way at Delphi, many visitors stride unknowingly past the center of the earth—or, more specifically, its belly button.

According to ancient Greek mythology, Zeus wished to find the center of the world—its *omphalos*, or "navel." The king of the gods sent two eagles, one from the west and one from the east, to fly across the earth until they met. The two eagles encountered one another at Delphi, and there an *omphalos* stone was erected to mark the center of the world. Of course, another legend holds that the stone marks the place where Apollo slayed the serpent Python.

The Archaeological Museum at Delphi houses an *omphalos* stone, a conical object representing the earth's navel. Though the marker at the actual site is less aesthetically evocative, visitors can place their hands on the stone and enjoy a glorious moment at the center of the world—or at least its belly button. Look for a concrete, egg-shaped stone set on a square base on the Sacred Way before the Temple of Apollo.

(p. 475. Delphi archaeological sites open daily 7:30am-7:30pm. Museum open M noon-6:30pm, Tu-Su 7:30am-7:30pm. Sites €6, museum €6, both €9; students €3/5; EU students free.)

IONIAN ISLANDS (ΙΟΝΙΑ ΝΗΣΙΑ)

West of mainland Greece, the Ionian Islands entice travelers with their lush vegetation and turquoise waters. Never conquered by the Ottomans, the islands reflect the influences of British, French, Russian, and Venetian occupants. Today, they are a favorite among Western Europeans and travelers seeking the truly unconventional Greece.

CORFU (ΚΕΡΚΥΡΑ) ☎26610

Ever since Homer's Odysseus raved about Corfu's beauty, the surrounding seas have brought a steady stream of conquerors, colonists, and tourists. There is something for everyone in Corfu, with archaeological sites, beautiful beaches, and rich nightlife. Situated between the New Fortress on the east and the Old Fortress on the west, **Corfu Town** (pop. 39,500) is a jumbled labyrinth of Venetian buildings. The winding streets and hidden plazas of the Old Town, though quaint and charming, are an urban planner's nightmares. Saunter along the serene, tree-shaded pathways of the grounds at **Mon Repos Estate,** which features a Doric temple, lovely gardens, and the **Museum of Paleopolis,** which displays the island's archaeological treasures. To reach the estate from the Old Town, walk away from the Old Fortress and follow Dimokratias along the waterfront to the end of the bay. Once you reach the hill, be careful walking up the road as there are no sidewalks and cars and motorcycles may emerge out of blind turns. (☎26610 30 680. Estate open daily 8am-7pm. Museum open Tu-Su 8:30am-3pm. Estate free. Museum €3, EU students €2.) **Paleokastritsa beach,** with caves perfect for exploring, lies west of Corfu Town. Take a KTEL bus to Paleokastritsa (45min., 4-7 per day, €2.10). Traditional villages encircle **Mt. Pantokrator** and its sunset panorama and views into Albania and Italy.

Finding cheap accommodations in Corfu Town is virtually impossible. Plan to stay in a nearby village only a bus ride away, or book months ahead. The **Federation of Owners of Tourist Accommodation of Corfu,** Polilas 2A, is more of a local service for hostel owners than a tourist office, but can be helpful in a crunch. (☎26610 26 133; www.holidaysincorfu.com. Open M-F 9am-3pm and 5-8pm.) KTEL buses run from Corfu Town to Ag. Gordios (45min., 3-7 per day, €2), home to an impressive beach and the backpacker's legend **Pink Palace Hotel ❷.** Patrons can partake in 24/7 bacchanalia with this quintessential party hostel. Lock up your valuables in the front desk's safety deposit box before enjoying the daily events. (☎26610 53 103; www.thepinkpalace.com. Bus service to Athens €55, mid-July to mid-Aug. €65. Scooter and kayak rentals €10 per day. Bar open 24hr. Breakfast, cafeteria-style dinner, and plane/bus/ferry pickup included. Laundry €9. Internet €2 per 35min. Dorms from €18; private rooms from €25.) For more mellow digs, take bus #11 to nearby Pelekas (20min., 7 per day, €1), where **Pension Martini ❷,** down the hill from the bus stop, on the left side of the street, offers sunny rooms with balconies and superb views. In the evening, join the family for wine or *ouzo* in the garden. (☎26610 94 326; www.pensionmartini.com. Singles and doubles €25-35.)

Olympic and **Aegean Airlines** connect Corfu's **Ioannis Kapodistrias Airport** (**CFU** or **LGKR;** ☎26610 39 040) to Athens (1hr., 2-3 per day, €64-121) and Thessaloniki (1hr., 3 per week, €85-142). **Ferries** run from Corfu Town to: Bari, ITA (10hr., 4 per week); Brindisi, ITA (8hr., 1-2 per day); Patras (8hr., 5 per week); Venice, ITA (24hr., 1 per day). Prices vary significantly. For more info, try any of the travel agencies that line the road to the port. **International Tours** (☎26610 39 007; www.intertourscorfu.com) and **Ionian Cruises** (☎26610 31 649; www.ionian-cruises.com), both across the street from the old port on El. Venizelou, book international ferries. Buy your ticket at least a day ahead and ask if it includes port tax. Green KTEL **buses** depart from the intercity bus station (☎26610 28 927) between I. Theotoki and the New Fortress for Athens (8hr., 3 per day, €40-47) and Thessaloniki (8hr., 2 per day, €38-45); prices include ferry. Blue municipal buses leave from Pl. San Rocco (☎26610 32 158; tickets €1) The **tourist office** is in Pl. San Rocco in a green kiosk. (☎26610 20 733. Open daily 9am-2pm and 6-9pm.) **Postal Code:** 49100.

ZAKYNTHOS (ΖΑΚΥΝΘΟΣ) ☎26950

Known as the greenest Ionian Island, Zakynthos is home to thousands of species of plants and flowers, as well as a large *Caretta caretta* (loggerhead sea turtle) population. **Zakynthos Town** maintains a romantic, nostalgic air. Boats leave Zakynthos Town for many of the island's spectacular sights, including the glowing **Blue Caves** on the northeastern shore past Skinari. Southwest of the Blue Caves is **Smuggler's Wreck.** A shipwrecked boat's remains have made the beach one of the most photographed in the world. **Keri Caves** and **Marathonisi** (also called Turtle Island because of its resemblance to a turtle) lie farther south. Agencies giving tours of Zakynthos advertise along Lomvardou; most excursions leave around 9:30am, return at 5:30pm, and cost €16-25. For a more intimate travel experience, skip the huge cruise ships and hire a small fishing boat from the docks in northern villages. A 10min. walk down the beach (with the water on your right) will take you to the deserted sands of **Kalamaki,** a turtle nesting site, and protected **National Marine Park** (www.nmp-zak.org). At night, the turtles inhabit some of Zakynthos's most picturesque beaches, like **Gerakas,** on the island's southeastern tip.

Athina Marouda Rooms for Rent ❶, on Tzoulati and Koutouzi, has simple, clean rooms with fans, large windows, and communal baths. (☎26950 45 194. June-Sept. singles €15; doubles €30. Oct.-May €10/20. Cash only.) Dining in the *plateias* and by the waterfront is a treat. **Village Inn ❸,** Lomvardou 20, at the right end of the waterfront before Pl. Solomou, feels more like a bayou lounge and has tables facing the water. (☎26950 26 991. Entrees €6-15. Th night live Greek music. Open daily 8am-midnight. MC/V.) Getting around the island can be frustrating—taxis can be terribly overpriced and tour operators may seem like glorified tourist babysitters. Dozens of places rent **scooters** (€15 per day), but driver's license requirements are strictly enforced. **Buses** go from the station, two blocks away from the water, to Kalamaki (20min., 12 per day, €1.20) and Laganas (20min., 15 per day, €1.20). Buses also board **ferries** to the mainland and continue to Athens (6hr., 5 per day, €23), Patras (3hr., 3 per day, €7), and Thessaloniki (10hr., M-Th and Su 1 per day, €43). **Postal Code:** 29100.

CYCLADES (ΚΥΚΛΑΔΕΣ)

Sun-drenched, winding stone streets, and trellis-covered *tavernas* define the Cycladic islands, but subtle quirks make each distinct. Orange and black sands coat Santorini's shoreline, and celebrated archaeological sites testify to Delos's mythical and historical significance. Naxos and Paros offer travelers peaceful mountains and villages, while notorious party spots Ios and Mykonos uncork some of the world's wildest nightlife.

MYKONOS (ΜΥΚΟΝΟΣ) ☎22890

Coveted by 18th-century pirates, Mykonos still attracts revelers and gluttons. Although Mykonos is a fundamentally chic sophisticates' playground, you don't have to break the bank to have a good time. Ambling down **Mykonos Town's** colorful alleyways at dawn or dusk, surrounded by tourist-friendly pelicans, is the cheapest, most exhilarating way to experience the island. Drinking and sunbathing are Mykonos's main forms of entertainment. While the island's beaches are nude, bathers' degree of bareness varies; in most places, people prefer to show off their designer bathing suits rather than their birthday suits. **Platis Yialos** and **Super Paradise** appeal to more brazen nudists, while **Elia** beach attracts a tamer crowd. The super-famous **Paradise** beach is so crowded with hungover Italians and overpriced sun beds that you can barely see its gorgeous water. The **Skandinavian Bar,** inland from the waterfront towards Little Venice, is a two-building party complex. (☎22890 22 669. Beer €4-6. Mixed drinks from €8. Open daily 9pm-5am.) After drinking all night, usher in a new day at **Cavo Paradiso,** on Paradise beach. Considered one of the world's top dance clubs, it hosts internationally renowned DJs and inebriated crowds. Take the bus to Paradise beach and follow the signs; it's a 10min. walk. (☎22890 27 205. Drinks from €10. Cover €25, after 2am €40; includes 1 drink. Open daily 3-11am.)

Like everything else on Mykonos, accommodations are prohibitively expensive. Camping is the best budget option. The popular **Paradise Beach Camping ❶,** 6km from Mykonos Town, has decent facilities, plenty of services, and proximity to the beach. (☎22890 22 129; www.paradisemykonos.com. Free pickup at port or airport. Safes available. Breakfast included. Internet €4.50 per hr. €5-10 per person, €2.50-4 per small tent, €4.50-7 per large tent; 1- to 2-person cabin €15-50. 3-person tent rental €8-18.) Cozy and colorful **Kalidonios ❸,** Dilou 1, off Kalogera, serves a range of Greek and Mediterranean dishes. (☎22890 27 606. Entrees €8-15. Open daily noon-12:30am. MC/V.) For a cheap meal, head to **Pasta Fresca ❶,** on Georgouli, near the Skandinavian Bar. Its streetside takeout window is the place to grab the best *gyros* (€2) and chicken pitas (€2) that Mykonos has to offer. (☎22890 22 563. Open daily 4pm-late.)

Ferries run from the New Port, west of town, to Naxos (3hr., 1 per week, €9.50), Paros (3hr., 1 per day, €8.40), and Piraeus (6hr., 1 per day, €26). The **tourist police** are at the ferry landing. (☎22890 22 482. Open daily 8am-9pm.) **Buses** run south from Mykonos Town to Platis Yialos and Paradise (20min., 2 per hr., €1.20-1.50) and to Elia (30min., 8 per day, €1.10). Windmills Travel, on Xenias, around the corner from South Station, has a number of **GLBT resources.** (☎22890 26 555; www.windmillstravel.com. Open daily 8am-10pm.) **Postal Code:** 84600.

PAROS (ΠΑΡΟΣ) ☎22840

Now a central transportation hub, Paros was once famed for its slabs of pure white marble, used to construct many of the ancient world's great statues and buildings. It's a favorite destination for families and older travelers, removed from the luxurious debauchery of Mykonos and the youth-filled streets of Ios. Behind the commercial surface of **Parikia,** Paros's port and largest city, flower-lined streets wind through archways to one of the world's most treasured Orthodox basilicas, the **Panagia Ekatontapiliani** (Church of Our Lady of 100 Doors). This white three-building complex is dedicated to St. Helen, mother of the Emperor Constantine, who reportedly had a vision of the True Cross here while traveling to the Holy Land. (Dress modestly. Open daily 7am-10pm. Mass M-Sa 7-7:30pm, Su 7-10am. Free.) About 8km north of town, **Naoussa beach** is the most popular and crowded destination on the island. On the opposite coast, **Aliki** beach is much quieter, but often windy.

Turn left at the dock and take a right after the cemetery ruins to reach the well-kept, cottage-like **Rena Rooms ❷.** (☎22840 22 220; www.cycladesnet.gr/rena. Free pickup and luggage storage. Reserve ahead. Singles €15-35; doubles €20-40; triples €30-55. 20% *Let's Go* discount. Additional discount if paid in cash. MC/V.) The funky **Happy Green Cow ❸,** a block off the *plateia* behind the National Bank, serves tasty vegetarian dinners. (☎22840 24 691. Entrees

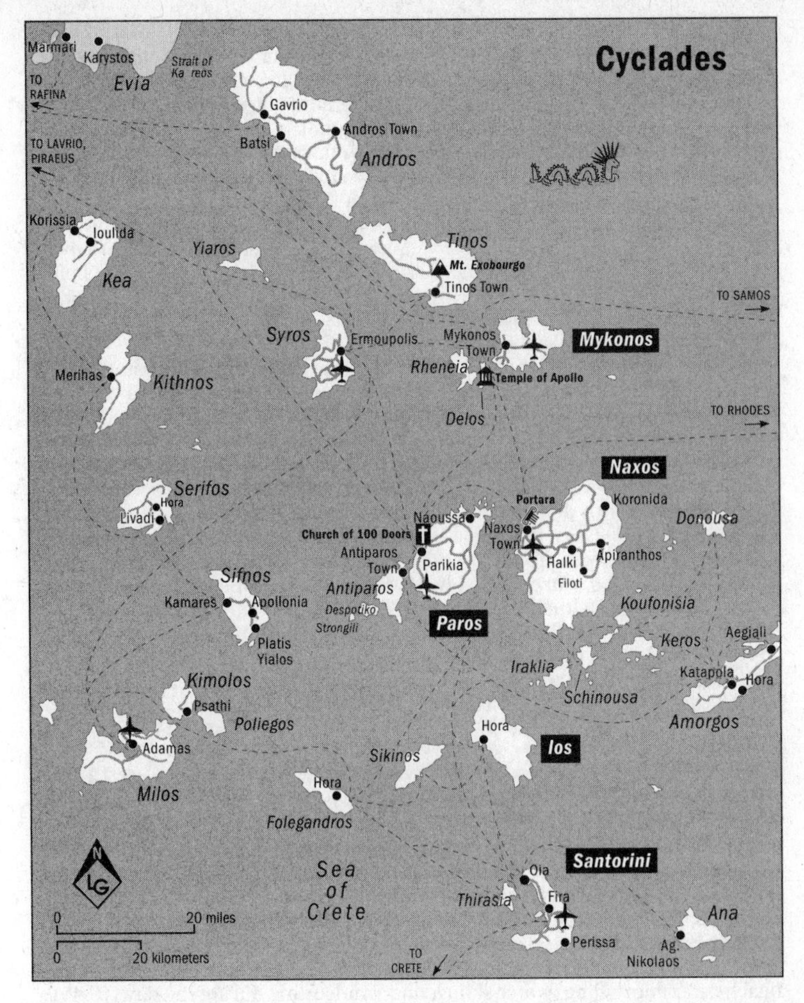

€12-15. Open Apr.-Nov. daily 7pm-midnight.) At the far end of the Old Town's waterfront, 5min. past the port and bus station, Paros's nightlife pulses late into the night. A central courtyard connects three themed bar areas: **The Dubliner,** an Irish pub, **Down Under,** an Aussie bar, and **Paros Rock Cafe,** decorated with bright colors and the appropriate flags. Follow the spotlight and crowds to the end of the harbor. (Beer €3-5. Mixed drinks €5-6. Cover €3; includes 1 drink.)

Ferries go to: Folegandros (5hr., 3 per week, €9); Ios (3hr., 5 per week, €13); Mykonos (5hr., 5 per week, €7); Naxos (1hr., 2 per day, €7); Thessaloniki (19hr., 2 per week, €38). Check with the budget travel office **Polos Tours** (☎22840 22 092; www.polostours.gr), 50m to the right of the ferry dock gate, for ferry schedules and departure times. The **tourist police** are on the *plateia* behind the telephone office. (☎22840 21 673. Open M-F 7am-2:30pm.) **Postal Code:** 84400.

NAXOS (ΝΑΞΟΣ) ☎22850

Ancient Greeks believed Dionysus, the god of wine and revelry, once lived on Naxos (pop. 20,000), the largest of the Cyclades. Olive groves, small villages, chalky ruins, silent monasteries, and unadulterated hikes fill its interior, while sandy beaches line its shores. **Naxos Town,** its capital, is a dense collection of labyrinthine streets, bustling *tavernas*, and tiny museums, crowned by the **Kastro,** an inhabited Venetian fortress, tranquil despite the tourists. At the Kastro's entrance, the **Domus Della Rocca-Barozzi** (a.k.a. the Venetian Museum) exhibits photographs, books, and furniture belonging to a local aristocratic family still living there. (☎22850 223 87; www.naxosisland.gr/venetianmuseum. Open daily in high season 10am-3pm and 7-11pm; low season 10am-3pm and 7-10pm. €5, students €3. Nightly summer concerts at 9:15pm. €10; reserve ahead at the museum reception.) The **Archaeological Museum** occupies the former Collège Français. (Open Tu-Su 8am-5pm. €3, students €2.)

Accommodations in Naxos are available in private rooms and studios on the street between the town's center and the nearby Ag. Giorgios beach, or in campsites by the island's many beaches. Though most campgrounds vary little in price (generally €4-8 per person, €2-3 per tent), **Naxos Camping** ❶ is the closest to Naxos Town (2km) and only 150m from **Ag. Giorgios** beach. (☎22850 235 00. Prices vary seasonally.) Nearby **Heavens Cafe Bar** ❷ serves scrumptious Belgian waffles with delicious fresh fruit for €5. (☎22850 227 47. Internet €3 per hr.; free Wi-Fi. Open daily 8am-2am.)

Ferries go from Naxos Town to: Crete (7hr., 1 per week, €21); Ios (1hr., 1 per day, €10); Mykonos (3hr., 1 per day, €9); Paros (1hr., 4 per day, €8); Piraeus (6hr., 4 per day, €28); Rhodes (13hr., 1 per week, €25); Santorini (3hr., 3 per day, €13). A bus goes from the port to the beaches of Ag. Giorgios, Ag. Prokopios, Ag. Anna, and Plaka (2 per hr. 7:30am-2am, €1.20). **Buses** (☎22850 222 91) also run from Naxos Town to **Apiranthos,** a beautiful village with narrow, marble paths (1hr., 5 per day, €2.30). The Naxos Town **tourist office** is located next to the bus station. (☎22850 229 93. Open daily 8am-11pm.) **Postal Code:** 84300.

IOS (ΙΟΣ) ☎22860

Despite recent concerted efforts to tone down its party-animal reputation, Ios remains the Greek debauchery heaven—or hell. Life on the island revolves around its insane and non-stop party scene: breakfast is served at 2pm, drinking begins at 3pm, people don't go out before midnight, and revelers dance madly in the streets until well after dawn. The **port** of Gialos is at one end of the island's sole paved road. The town of **Hora** sits above it on a hill, but most visitors spend their days at **Mylopotas beach,** a 25min. walk downhill from Hora or a short bus ride from town (3-6 per hr., €1.20). Establishments on the beach offer snorkeling, water-skiing, and windsurfing during the day (€9-45). Sunning is typically followed—or accompanied—by drinking; the afternoon bars are no less crowded than the nighttime ones. Head up from the *plateia* to reach the **Slammer Bar** for tequila slammers (€3), then stop by **Disco 69** for some dirty dancing (beer €5; cover €6 midnight-4am). Get lost in the street-side **Red Bull** (beer €3), dance on the tables at **Sweet Irish Dream** (beer €3; cover €5 2:30-4:30am), or grind to techno at **Scorpion Disco,** the island's largest club (cover €7 2-4:30am, includes a mixed drink and shot). Most clubs close between 4 and 7am, when the drunkenness and antics spill onto the streets. A few hours later, crowds begin to re-gather at the beach.

In addition to cheap dorms, **Francesco's** ❶ offers stunning sunset harbor views from its terrace. Take the steps up the hill to the left in the *plateia* and then the first left at the Diesel shop. (☎22860 91 223; www.francescos.net. Breakfast 9am-2pm €2.50-5. Internet €1 per 15min. Reception 9am-2pm and

6-10pm. Check-out 11am. Dorms €11-18; 2- to 4-person rooms with A/C and bath €15-28 per person.) Back in town, **Ali Baba's ❷**, next to Ios Gym, serves authentic Thai food. (☎22860 91 558. Entrees €6-12. Open Mar.-Oct. daily 6pm-1am.) Off the main church's *plateia*, **Old Byron's ❸** is an intimate wine bar and bistro with creative renditions of Greek staples. (☎697 819 2212. Entrees €9-15. Reserve ahead. Open M-Sa 6-11:30pm, Su noon-11:30pm. MC/V.) Greek fast food and creperies pack the central *plateia*. **Ferries** go to: Naxos (1hr., 1-3 per day, €9); Paros (3hr., 1-3 per day, €10); Piraeus (8hr., 2-3 per day, €35); Santorini (1hr., 3-5 per day, €7). **Postal Code:** 84001.

SANTORINI (ΣΑΝΤΟΡΙΝΗ) ☎22860

Whitewashed towns sitting delicately on cliffs, black-sand beaches, and deeply scarred hills make Santorini's landscape nearly as dramatic as the volcanic cataclysm that created it. Wander around the town's cobbled streets in **Fira** (pop. 2500), the island's capital. At Santorini's northern tip, the town of **Oia** (*EE-ah;* pop. 700) is the best place in Greece to watch the sunset, though its fame draws crowds hours in advance. To catch a glimpse of the sun, and not of someone taking a picture of it, walk down the hill from the village and settle alone near the many windmills and pebbled walls. To get to Oia, take a **bus** from Fira (25min., 23 per day, €1.20). **Red Beach,** and the impressive archaeological excavation site of the Minoan city **Akrotiri,** entirely preserved by lava (but currently closed for repairs), lie on Santorini's southwestern edge. Buses run to Akrotiri from Fira (30min., 15 per day, €1.60). Buses also leave Fira for the black-sand beaches of **Kamari** (20min., 32 per day, €1.20), **Perissa** (30min., 32 per day, €1.90), and **Perivolos** (20min., 21 per day, €1.90). The bus stops before Perissa in Pyrgos; from there, **hike** (2hr.) across a rocky mountain path to the ruins of **Ancient Thira.** Stop after 1hr. on a paved road at **Profitis Ilias Monastery,** whose lofty location provides an island panorama. (Open M and W 4-5pm, Sa 4:30-8:30pm. Dress modestly. Free.)

Close to Perissa's beach, **Youth Hostel Anna ❶** has colorful rooms and loads of backpackers hanging out on its streetside veranda. (☎22860 82 182. Port pickup and drop-off included. Reception 9am-5pm and 7-10pm. Check-out 11:30am. Reserve ahead. June-Aug. 10-bed dorms €12; 4-bed dorms €15; doubles €50; triples €60. Sept.-May €6/8/22/30. MC/V.) At night, head to **Murphy's** in Fira, which claims to be Greece's first Irish pub. (Beer €5. Mixed drinks €6.50. Cover €5 after 10pm. Open Mar.-Oct. daily 11:30am-late.)

Olympic Airways (☎22860 22 493) and **Aegean Airways** (☎22860 28 500) fly from Fira's airport to Athens (50min., 4-7 per day, €85-120) and Thessaloniki (1hr., 1-2 per day, €125). **Ferries** depart from Fira to: Crete (4hr., 4 per week, €16); Ios (1hr., 1-3 per day, €7); Naxos (3hr., 1-2 per day, €16); Paros (4hr., 1-4 per day, €17); Piraeus (10hr., 2-3 per day, €33). Most ferries depart from Athinios Harbor. Frequent **buses** (25min., €1.70) with changing daily schedules connect to Fira, but most hostels and hotels offer **shuttle** service as well. Check bus and ferry schedules at any travel agency for up-to-date information, and be aware that the self-proclaimed **tourist offices** at the port are actually for-profit agencies. **Postal Codes:** 84700 (Fira); 84702 (Oia).

CRETE (KPHTH)

According to a Greek saying, a Cretan's first loyalty is to his island, his second to his country. Since 3000 BC, when Minoan civilization flourished on the island, Crete has maintained an identity distinct from the rest of Greece; pride

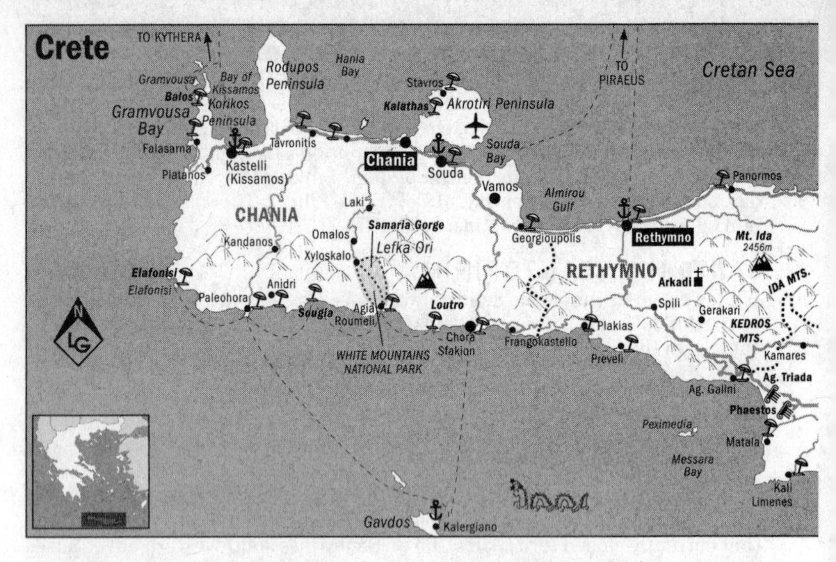

in the island proves well founded. Travelers will be drawn to Crete's warm hospitality and enticing beaches, gorges, monasteries, mosques, and villages.

HERAKLION (ΗΡΑΚΛΕΙΟ) ☎2810

Heraklion, also spelled Iraklion (pop. 138,000), Crete's capital and primary port, may not be particularly picturesque, but its importance as a transportation hub makes it a necessary stop on the way to Crete's more scenic destinations. Olympic Airways and Aegean Airlines **fly** domestically from the **Heraklion International Airport,** Nikos Kazantzakis (**HER;** ☎2810 397 129) to: Athens (50min., 4-7 per day, €80-100); Rhodes (1hr., 6 per week, €105-115); Thessaloniki (1hr., 2 per day, from €109). Budget airline Wizz Air also flies from Heraklion to Budapest, HUN (1-3hr., 1 per week, €145) and Katowice, POL (3hr., 1 per week, €280). From Terminal A, between the old city walls and the harbor, **buses** leave for Agios Nikolaos (1½hr., 19-21 per day, €6.20) and Chania (3hr., 16 per day, €12) via Rethymno (1-1½hr., €6.30). **Buses** leave across from Terminal B for Phaestos (1½hr., 1 per day, €5.70). **Ferries** also go to: Mykonos (8hr., 2 per week, €25); Naxos (8½hr., 3 per week, €23); Paros (7hr., 4 per week, €26); Santorini (4hr., 3 per week, €16). Check for travel delays online at **GNET,** Merambelou 14-16. (☎2810 221 622. Open daily 24hr.) Soothe the burn of a missed flight with drinks or a borrowed book atop the quiet rooftop garden at **Rent Rooms Hellas ❶,** Handakos 24. Walk east along the waterfront and turn left onto Handakos. (☎2810 288 851. Free luggage storage. Check-out 11am. Dorms €11; doubles €25-31; triples €42.) The open-air **market** on 1866, near Pl. Venizelou, sells cheese, meat, and produce. (Open M-Sa 8am-2pm.) **Ouzeri Tou Terzaki ❷,** Loch. Marineli 17, in the center of town, serves fresh Greek meals with complimentary raki liquor and fruit. (☎2810 221 444; www.en.terzakhs.gr. *Mezedhes* €5-10. Open M-Sa noon-midnight. MC/V.) Those looking to kill time between connections should check out the **Tomb of Nikos Kazantzakis,** on top of the city walls. Even visitors unfamiliar with his most famous novel, *Zorba the Greek*, should make the climb to catch a spectacular sunset over Mt. Ida. **Postal Code:** 71001.

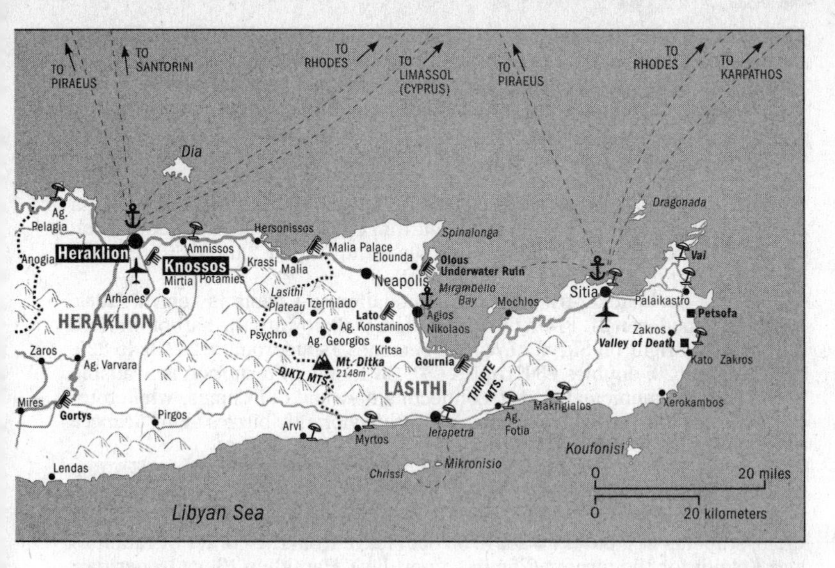

KNOSSOS (ΚΝΩΣΟΣ) ☎2810

Knossos, Crete's most famous archaeological site, is a must-see. Excavations have revealed the remains of the largest, most complicated of Crete's **Minoan palaces.** Legend and fact coexist at the palace of Knossos, the site of King Minos's machinations, the labyrinth with its monstrous Minotaur, and the imprisonment—and winged escape—of Daedalus and Icarus. The first palace was built around 1900 BC, but was destroyed by an earthquake around 1700 BC. Atop the ruins of the first structure was built a second, more magnificent palace, which was partially destroyed around 1450 BC and then wiped out by fire a century later. In the early 20th century, Sir Arthur Evans financed and supervised the excavations, restoring large parts of the second palace. His work often toed the line between preservation and tenuous interpretation, painting the palace's current form with controversy. Tourist crowds give the Minoan palace a Disneyland feel, but the sights are well worth navigating. Don't miss the **Dolphin Fresco** on the northern wall of the Queen's Hall. Walking north from the royal quarters, you'll stumble across the grand **pithoi**—storage jars so massive that, according to legend, Minos's son met a sticky demise by drowning in one filled with honey. (☎2810 231 940. Open daily 8am-7pm. €6, students €3.) To reach Knossos from Heraklion, take **bus** #2 from Terminal A (20min., 2 per hr., €1.30).

CHANIA (ΧΑΝΙΑ) ☎28210

Despite an avalanche of tourists, Chania (pop. 56,000), Crete's second largest city, retains a pleasantly relaxed seaside atmosphere. A day in idyllic Old Chania is easily whiled away people-watching from cafes or wandering along the waterfront. The **Venetian lighthouse** marks the entrance to the city's stunning architectural relic, the **Venetian Inner Harbor,** built in the 14th century. From the fortress's ruins, sunset views over the open sea dazzle tourists. The inlet has retained its original breakwater and Venetian arsenal, though the Nazis destroyed much of it during WWII. Nestled away on the northwestern tip of Crete, the heavenly **blue lagoon** of **Balos** is the island's uncontested best beach, where bright white sand, warm shallow water, and sky melt into one.

The most popular excursion from Chania is the 5-6hr. hike through **Samaria Gorge** (ΦΑΡΑΓΓΙ ΤΗΣ ΣΑΜΑΡΙΑΣ), a spectacular 16km ravine extending through the White Mountains. Sculpted by 14 million years of rainwater, the gorge is the longest in Europe. (Open daily May 1-Oct. 15. 7am-3pm. €5, under 15 free.) The trail starts at Xyloskalo and ends at **Agia Roumeli**, on the southern coast; take an early bus marked OMALOS from Chania to Xyloskalo (departures at 6:15am, 7:30am, and 8:30am, 1hr., €6.20) for a day's worth of hiking. To return to Chania on the same day, take a boat to Chora Sfakion from Agia Roumeli (departures at 3:45pm and 6pm, 1hr., €8). From Chora Sfakion, catch the bus back to Chania (departures at 5:30pm and 7:15pm, 2hr., €6.80). The bus doesn't depart until after the boat's arrival.

The only backpacker-friendly accommodation in Chania is central **Eftihis Rooms ❶**, Tsouderon 21. From the bus station, walk toward the harbor on Halidon and turn right on Skrydlof, which becomes Tsouderon. (☎28210 46 829. A/C. Singles €20; doubles €30; triples €30. Cash only.) Fresh food is available at the covered municipal **market**, connecting new and old Chania, while touristy *tavernas* line the harbor. Chania's nightlife vibrantly buzzes along **Sourmeli Street**, in the heart of the old harbor.

From the port of Souda, **ferries** go to Piraeus (9hr., 2 per day, €24). Bus #13 connects from the port of Souda to Chania's municipal market on Zymvrakakidon. (☎28210 27 044; www.chaniabus.gr/eng/index.html. 20-25min.; €1.30, students €1). **Buses** (☎28210 93 052) leave from the corner of Kidonias and Kelaidi for the airport (25min., 3 per day), Heraklion (3hr., 16 per day, €12), and Rethymno (1-1½hr., 16 per day, €6). **Taxis** to the airport cost €16-18. The **tourist information center**, Kidonias 29-31, is located next to the city hall. (☎28210 36 155; www.chaniacrete.gr. Open May-Sept. M-Sa 8:30am-7pm; Oct.-Apr. M-Sa 8:30am-2pm.) **Postal Code:** 73001.

RETHYMNO (ΡΕΘΥΜΝΟ) ☎28310

Rethymno has a reputation for bizarre power struggles. According to myth, **Zeus** was born to Rhea in the cave of Idaion Andron outside this regional capital. The titan Cronus, antsy about his infant son's approaching dominion, attempted to eat him; luckily for Greek mythological history, Rhea tricked Cronus into swallowing a stone instead, and Zeus grew up to be king of the gods. Warring humans followed Cronus's quest for power evident in Rethymno's skyline of minarets and ruined Venetian fortresses. The sprawling **Venetian Fortezza**, a fortress built in 1580, is the high point of the city, and provides magnificent views of the coast and surrounding towns. Explore the series of churches and crumbling facades that comprise the ruins. (☎28310 28 101. Open daily 8am-8pm, last entry 7:15pm. €4, students free.) On the corner of Pl. Martiron, the **public gardens** provide a much-needed oasis of shade in the scorching Greek sun. Rethymno's **Wine Festival** at the end of July is a crowded, all-you-can-drink celebration. **February Carnival** is the largest celebration in all of Crete.

The gardens and outdoor bar (beer and wine €1.50-2) buzz with backpackers at **Youth Hostel ❶**, Tombazi 41. Outdoor beds are available in the summer. From the bus station, walk down I. Gavriil and take the first left at Pl. Martiron through the Porta Megali; Tombazi is the second right. (☎28310 22 848; www.yhrethymno.com. Breakfast €2-4. Solar-powered showers during the day. Sheets €1. Internet €3 per hr. Wi-Fi €5 per day. Reception July-Aug. 8am-noon and 5-9pm. Check-out 10am. Dorms July-Aug. €10 per night, €60 per week; Sept.-June €9/54.) An **open-air market** on El. Venizelou by the New Town marina opens Thursdays at 7am and closes around 2:30pm, though the selection dwindles by 10am. For affordable nighttime eats, tourists and locals head to **Plateia Titou Petihaki.** The bar scene in Rethymno centers on **Ioulias Petichaki,**

Nearhou, and **Plateia Plasteira** near the western end of the harbor. **Rock Cafe Club,** I. Petihaki 6, is popular dancing locations. The patrons are unpretentious, the DJs are savvy, and the bars remain fully stocked. (☎23810 654 325. Beer €4. Mixed drinks €7. Open M-Th and Su 11pm-4am, F-Sa 11pm-morning.)

Buy **ferry** tickets to Piraeus (daily 8pm, €30) at any travel office. **Buses** run from the Rethymno station (☎28310 22 212), overlooking the water off I. Gavriil, to: Agia Galini (1hr., 4-5 per day, €5.60); Arkadi Monastery (1hr., 2-3 per day, €2.50); Chania (1hr., 17 per day 6:15am-10:30pm, €6); Heraklion (1½hr., 18 per day 6:30am-10:15pm, €6.30); Plakias (45min., 7 per day, €4.10). The **tourist office** (☎28310 29 148; www.rethymnon.gr) is located at the far eastern end of the waterfront on El. Venizelou. (Open 8:30am-8:30pm.) **Game Net Cafe,** Koundouriotou 8, in Pl. Martiron, has **Internet** at the best rates in town. (€2.50 per hr., €1.50 after midnight.) **Postal Code:** 74100.

EASTERN AEGEAN ISLANDS

Scattered along Turkey's coast, the islands of the **Dodecanese** are marked by a history of persistence in the face of countless invasions. The more isolated islands of the **Northeast Aegean** remain sheltered from creeping globalization. The palpable cultural authenticity here is a traveler's welcome and reward.

RHODES (ΡΟΔΟΣ) ☎22410

The undisputed tourism capital of the Dodecanese, the island of Rhodes has retained its sense of serenity in the sandy beaches along its eastern coast, the jagged cliffs skirting its western coast, and the green mountains dotted with villages in its interior. Beautiful ancient artifacts, remnants from a rich past, blanket the island. Rhodes is best known for a sight that no longer exists—the 33m **Colossus,** which was once one of the Seven Wonders of the Ancient World. The pebbled streets of the Old Town, constructed by the Knights of St. John, lend **Rhodes Town** a medieval flair. At the top of the hill, a tall, square tower marks the entrance to the **Palace of the Grandmaster,** which contains 300 rooms filled with intricate mosaic floorwork. (☎22410 25 500. €6, students €3.) The beautiful halls and courtyards of the **Archaeological Museum,** which dominates the **Plateia Argiokastrou,** shelter the exquisite first century BC statue of *Aphrodite Bathing.* (☎22410 31 048. Open Tu-Su 8:30am-3pm. €3, students €2.) On Rhodes's western shore, the ruins of **Kamiros** offer a glimpse of an ancient city grid. Daily **buses** run out of Rhodes Town. (☎22410 40 037. €4, students €2.) North of Kamiros, the Valley of Butterflies, or **Petaloudes,** attracts Jersey moths and nature enthusiasts alike. (☎22410 81 801. Open Easter-Oct. €5.) The vine-enclosed garden-bar of **Hotel Anastasia ❷,** 28 Oktovriou 46, complements bright, pastel rooms. (☎22410 28 007. Breakfast €4. Singles €35; doubles €50. V.) For cheap eateries, **Orfanidou** (popularly known as Bar St.) features venues with greasy food, while crepe stands (€2-5) line the streets of the Old Town. Nightlife in Rhodes's Old Town focuses around the street of **Militadou,** off Apelou. **Ferries** leave the eastern docks in Commercial Harbor, across from the Milon Gate into the Old Town, to: Halki (2hr., 2 per week, €8); Kos (2hr., 2 per day, €14); Patmos (7hr., i per day, €22); Sitia, Crete (10hr., 2 per week, €25). The Rhodes Town **tourist office** is at the intersection of Makariou and Papagou. (☎22410 44 333; www.ando.gr/eot. Open M-F 8am-2:45pm.) **Postal Code:** 8510.

LESVOS (ΛΕΣΒΟΣ) ☎22510

Olive groves, art colonies, and a petrified forest harmonize Lesvos, or Lesbos. Born on this island, the seventh-century lyrical poet Sappho garnered a large female following. Due to her much-debated homosexuality, the word "lesbian"—once describing a native islander—developed its modern connotation. Visitors can gaze upon **Sappho's statue** at **Mytilini,** the island's capital and central port city, or walk on preserved mosaic floors excavated from ancient Ag. Kyriaki at the **Archaeological Museum,** 8 Noemvriou. (Open Tu-Su 8am-3pm. €3, students €2, EU students and under 18 free.) Only 4km south of Mytilini, the village of **Varia** is home to the **Musée Tériade,** which displays lithographs by Chagall, Matisse, Miró, and Picasso, and the **Theophilos Museum,** which features work by neo-Primitivist Theophilos Hadzimichali. (☎22510 23 372. Musée Tériade open Tu-Su 9am-2pm and 5-8pm. Theophilos Museum open Tu-Su 10am-4pm. Each museum €2, students free.) Local **buses** (20min., 1 per hr.) leave Mytilini for Varia. Tell the driver you're going to the museums. **Molyvos,** a castle-crowned village, provides easy access to nearby **Eftalou's** hot springs and beaches. Abundant doubles at Mytilini *domatia* run €30-35 before July 15, and €35-50 during the high season. **Olympic** and **Aegean Airlines** fly out of the airport (**MJT;** ☎22510 61 590), 6km south of Mytilini, for Athens (1hr., 6 per day, €50-150) and Rhodes (1hr., 5 per week, €58). **Ferries** go from Mytilini to Thessaloniki (13hr., 1 per week, €35). Ticket can be purchased from **Zoumboulis Tours** (☎22510 37 755). **Postal Code:** 81100.

SAMOTHRAKI (ΣΑΜΟΘΡΑΚΗ) ☎22510

Samothraki (also called Samothrace) was once a pilgrimage site for Thracians who worshipped Anatolian gods. When the first colonists arrived in the 10th century BC, they saw the same vista still viewable from the ferry dock today: grassy fields at the base of the Aegean's tallest peak, **Fengari** (1670m). From **Kamariotissa,** Samothraki's port town, it is easy to reach the **Sanctuary of the Great Gods at Paleopolis,** where the famous *Winged Victory of Samothrace*, now a centerpiece in the Louvre, was found in 1863. (Open daily 8:30am-8:30pm. €3, students €2, EU students free.) Above the sanctuary rest the remains of the ancient Samothraki. Therma, a charming one-road village, has natural hot springs and hosts the trailhead for the 4hr. climb up Fengari. Unmarked **waterfalls** near **Therma** are also a worthwhile trip; check with the locals for hikes suiting your schedule and abilities. **Kaviros Hotel ❷,** to the left of the grocery store in Therma, has well-lit rooms with A/C, TV, and fridges. (☎25510 98 277. Singles and doubles €30-40 depending on season.) **Sinatisi ❷,** a few doors down from the national bank in Kamariotissa, is a local favorite for fresh fish. (☎25510 41 308. Open daily noon-5pm and 7pm-1am.) **Ferries** dock on the southern edge of Kamariotissa and run to Lesvos (7hr.). **Postal Code:** 68002

HUNGARY (MAGYARORSZÁG)

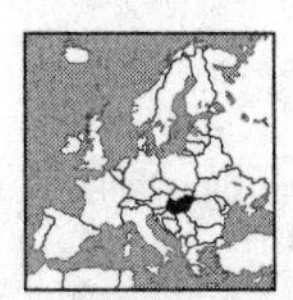

A country as unique as its language, Hungary has much more to offer than a profusion of wine, goulash, and thermal spas. Hip Budapest remains Hungary's ascendant social, economic, and political capital. Beyond the big-city rush are towns lined with cobblestone streets and wine valleys nestled in the northern hills, while beach resorts abound in the east. Though Hungary can be more expensive than some of its neighbors, it has a value all its own.

DISCOVER HUNGARY: SUGGESTED ITINERARIES

THREE DAYS. Three days is hardly enough time for **Budapest** (p. 494). Spend a day at the churches and museums of **Castle Hill** and an afternoon in the waters of the **Széchenyi Baths** before exploring the **City Park.** Get a lesson in Hungarian history at the **Parliament** before taking in the **Opera House.**

ONE WEEK. After four days in the capital, head up the Danube Bend to see the rustic side of Hungary in **Szentendre** (1 day; p. 505). Travel west to **Lake Balaton** (1 day; p. 509), a popular summer spot to swim and party. Next, visit **Eger** (1 day; p. 506) and sample the under-appreciated wines of the **Valley of the Beautiful Women.**

ESSENTIALS

FACTS AND FIGURES

OFFICIAL NAME: Hungary.

CAPITAL: Budapest.

MAJOR CITIES: Debrecen, Miskolc, Szeged.

POPULATION: 9,931,000.

TIME ZONE: GMT + 1.

LANGUAGE: Hungarian.

RELIGIONS: Roman Catholic (52%).

NUMBER OF MCDONALD'S RESTAURANTS: 94.

WHEN TO GO

Spring is the best time to visit; flowers are in bloom throughout the countryside and the tourists haven't yet arrived. July and August comprise Hungary's high-season, which means crowds, booked hostels, and sweltering summer weather. Autumn is beautiful, with mild, cooler weather through October. Avoid going in January and February, as temperatures average around freezing and many museums and tourist spots shut down or reduce their hours.

DOCUMENTS AND FORMALITIES

EMBASSIES AND CONSULATES. Foreign embassies are in Budapest (see p. 498). Hungary's embassies and consulates abroad include: **Australia,** 17 Beale Crescent, Deakin, ACT 2600 (☎62 82 32 26; www.matra.com.au/~hungemb);

Canada, 299 Waverley St., Ottawa, ON K2P 0V9 (☎613-230-2717; www.mfa.gov/emb/ottawa); **Ireland,** 2 Fitzwilliam Pl., Dublin 2 (☎661 2902; www.mfa.gov.hu/emb/dublin); **New Zealand,** Consulate-General, PO Box 29-039, Wellington 6443 (☎973 7507; www.hungarianconsulate.co.nz); **UK,** 35 Eaton Pl., London SW1X 8BY (☎20 72 35 52 18; www.mfa.gov/emb/london); **US,** 3910 Shoemaker St. NW, Washington, D.C. 20008 (☎202-362-6730; www.huembwas.org).

ENTRANCE REQUIREMENTS.

Passport: Required for all non-EU citizens.

Visa: See below.

Letter of Invitation: Not required.

Inoculations: Not required. Recommended up-to-date on DTaP (diphtheria, tetanus, and pertussis), hepatitis A, hepatitis B, MMR (measles, mumps, and rubella), polio booster, and typhoid.

Work Permit: Required for all foreigners planning to work in Hungary.

Driving Permit: International Driving Permits are recognized in Hungary, as are US and European licenses with Hungarian translations attached.

VISA AND ENTRY INFORMATION. Citizens of Australia, Canada, Ireland, New Zealand, and the US can visit Hungary without visas for up to 90 days; UK citizens can visit without a visa for up to 180 days. Consult your embassy for longer stays. Passports must be valid for six months after the end of the trip. There is no fee for crossing the Hungarian border. In general, border officials are efficient; plan on a 30min. crossing time.

TOURIST SERVICES AND MONEY

TOURIST OFFICES. **Tourinform** has branches in most cities and is a useful first-stop tourist service. Tourinform doesn't make accommodation reservations but will find vacancies, especially in university dorms and private *panzió*. Agencies also stock maps and provide local information; employees generally speak English and German. Most **IBUSZ** offices throughout the country book private rooms, exchange money, and sell train tickets, but they are generally better at assisting in travel plans than at providing info. Local agencies may be staffed only by Hungarian and German speakers, but they are often very helpful.

HUNGARIAN FORINTS (FT)	
AUS$1 = 138.90FT	1000FT = AUS$7.20
CDN$1 = 149.95FT	1000FT = CDN$6.67
EUR€1 = 235.32FT	1000FT = EUR€4.25
NZ$1 = 113.724FT	1000FT = NZ$8.80
UK£1 = 297.00FT	1000FT = UK£3.37
US$1 = 159.09FT	1000FT = US$6.29

MONEY. The national currency is the **forint (Ft).** One forint is divided into 100 **fillérs,** which have disappeared almost entirely from circulation. Hungary has a **Value Added Tax (VAT)** rate of 20%. **Inflation** is at 7.8%. Currency exchange machines are slow but offer good rates, though banks like **OTP Bank** and **Raiffensen** offer the best exchange rates for **traveler's checks.** It is illegal to change money on the street. Try to avoid extended-hour exchange offices, which have poor rates.

Watch for scams: the maximum legal commission for cash-to-cash exchange is 1%. 24 hr. **ATMs** are common throughout Hungary. Major **credit cards** are accepted in many hotels and restaurants in large cities, but they're very rarely accepted in the countryside. Service is not usually included in restaurant bills and while **tipping** is not mandatory, it's generally appropriate. Cab fares are standard: bargaining won't help, so be sure to set a price before getting in.

HEALTH AND SAFETY

In Budapest, **medical assistance** is easy to obtain and fairly inexpensive, but it may not always be up to Western standards. In an emergency, especially outside Budapest, one might be sent to Germany or Vienna. Most hospitals have English-speaking doctors on staff. **Tourist insurance** is useful—and necessary—for many medical services. In the event of an emergency, however, even non-insured foreigners are entitled to free medical services. **Tap water** is usually clean, but the water in Tokaj is poorly purified. **Bottled water** can be purchased at most food stores. **Public bathrooms** (*férfi* for men, *női* for women) vary in cleanliness: pack soap, a towel, and 30Ft as a tip for the attendant. Carry **toilet paper,** as many hostels do not provide it and public restrooms provide only a single square. Many **pharmacies** *(gyógyszertár)* stock Western brands of common items, including tampons *(betet)* and condoms *(ovszer)*.

Violent crime is rare. However, tourists are targets for petty theft and pickpocketing. Check prices before getting in taxis or ordering food or drinks; cab drivers and servers may attempt to overcharge unsuspecting tourists. **Women** traveling alone in Hungary should take the usual precautions. **Minorities** are generally accepted, though dark-skinned travelers may encounter prejudice. In an emergency, your embassy will likely be more helpful than the police. Though Hungary is known for being open-minded, **GLBT** travelers may face serious discrimination, especially outside Budapest.

EMERGENCY	**Police:** ☎107. **Ambulance:** ☎104 **Fire:** ☎105. **General Emergency:** ☎112.

TRANSPORTATION

BY PLANE. Many international airlines fly to Budapest. The national airline, **Malév,** flies to Budapest's airport, **Esterhazy,** from London, New York, and other major cities. Direct flights can be quite expensive, so flying to another European hub and taking a connecting plane or train may be the cheapest option. Other European airlines that fly to Hungary include **Sky Europe** (www.skyeurope.com) and **WizzAir** (www.wizzair.com).

BY TRAIN. Budapest is connected by train to most European capitals. Several types of **Eurail** passes are valid in Hungary. Check schedules and fares at www.elvira.hu. *Személyvonat* trains have many local stops and are excruciatingly slow; *gyorsvonat* trains, listed in red on schedules, move much faster for the same price. Large towns are connected by blue express lines; these air-conditioned **InterCity** trains are the fastest. A *pótjegy* (seat reservation) is required on trains labeled "R," and violators face a hefty fine.

The *peron* (platform) is rarely indicated until the train approaches the station and will sometimes be announced in Hungarian; look closely out the window as you approach a station. Many stations are not marked; ask the conductor what time the train will arrive (or simply point to your watch and say the town's name). Train reservations cost around US$5, and are recommended in summer and to get a sleeper compartment on night trains.

BY BUS AND BY FERRY. Buses tend to be efficient and well-priced. The major line is **Volanbusz,** a privately owned company. Purchase tickets on board, and arrive early for a seat. In larger cities, buy tickets at a kiosk, and punch them as you get on. Beware: plainclothes inspectors fine those caught without a ticket. A ferry runs down the Danube from Vienna and Bratislava to Budapest. For more info, contact **Utinform** (☎322 3600).

BY CAR AND BY TAXI. To **drive** in Hungary, carry your **International Driving Permit** and registration, and insurance papers. Car rental is available in most major cities but can be expensive. For 24hr. English assistance, contact the **Magyar Autóklub** (MAK; in Budapest, ☎345 1800). Taxi prices should not exceed the following: 6am-10pm base fare 200Ft per km, 60Ft per min. waiting; 10pm-6am 300Ft per km, 70Ft waiting. Beware of taxi scams. Before getting in, check that the meter works and ask how much the ride will cost. Taxis ordered by phone are more trustworthy than those hailed on the street.

BY BIKE AND BY THUMB. Biking terrain varies. Northeastern Hungary is topographically varied; the south is flat. **Bike rental** is sometimes difficult to find; tourist bureaus can help with locating rentals. Biking can be dangerous because cyclists do not have the right of way and drivers are not careful. Though it is fairly common in Hungary, *Let's Go* does not recommend **hitchhiking.**

KEEPING IN TOUCH

PHONE CODES	**Country code:** 36. **International dialing prefix:** 00. For more info on how to place international calls, see **Inside Back Cover.**

EMAIL AND THE INTERNET. Internet is available in major cities. Look for free Internet at hostels. Most Internet cafes charge 500-600Ft per hour. The Hungarian keyboard differs significantly from English-language keyboards.

TELEPHONE. For **intercity calls,** wait for the tone and dial slowly; "06" goes before the phone code. **International calls** require red or blue phones. The blue phones end calls after 3-9min. A 20Ft coin is required to start most calls. International calls cost around 9Ft, and you can make direct calls from Budapest's phone office. Phones often require *telefonkártya* (phone cards). International phone cards are sold by 2000Ft, and national cards are 800Ft. The best phone card for international calls is Barangolo. International access numbers include: **AT&T Direct** (☎06 800 01111); **Canada Direct** (☎06 800 01211); **MCI** (☎06 800 01411); **New Zealand Direct** (☎06 800 06411); and **Sprint** (☎06 800 01877). Mobile phones are common. Major vendors include Pannon GSM, T-Mobile, or Vodafone. Dialing a mobile from a public or private phone anywhere in Hungary is treated as a long-distance call, and it requires the entire 11-digit number.

MAIL. Hungarian mail is usually reliable; airmail *(légiposta)* takes one week to 10 days to the US and Europe. Mailing a letter costs about 36Ft domestically and 250Ft internationally. Those without permanent addresses can receive mail through **Poste Restante.** Address envelopes: First name, LAST NAME, POSTE RESTANTE, Post office address, Postal Code, city, HUNGARY.

LANGUAGE. Hungarian, a Finno-Ugric language, is distantly related to Turkish, Estonian, and Finnish. After Hungarian and German, English is Hungary's third most commonly spoken language. Almost all young people know some English. "Hello" is often used as an informal greeting. Coincidentally, "Szia!" (sounds like "see ya!") is another greeting—friends will often cry, "Hello, see ya!" For basic Hungarian words and phrases, see **Phrasebook: Hungarian,** p. 1064.

ACCOMMODATIONS AND CAMPING

HUNGARY	❶	❷	❸	❹	❺
ACCOMMODATIONS	under 2500Ft	2500-4000Ft	4001-7000Ft	7001-12,000Ft	over 12,000Ft

Tourism is developing rapidly, and rising prices make hostels attractive. Hostels are usually large enough to accommodate summer crowds. Many **hostels** can be booked through **Express** (in Budapest, ☎266 3277), a student travel agency, or through local tourist offices. From June to August, many university dorms become hostels. These may be the cheapest options in smaller towns, as hostels are less common outside Budapest. Locations change annually; inquire at Tourinform and call ahead. **Guesthouses** and **pensions** *(panzió)* are more common than hotels in small towns. Singles are scarce, though some guesthouses have a singles rate for double rooms; however, it can be worth finding a roommate, as solo travelers must often pay for doubles. Check prices; agencies may try to rent you their most expensive rooms. **Private rooms** *(zimmer frei)* booked through tourist agencies are sometimes cheap. After staying a few nights, make arrangements directly with the owner to save yourself the agency's 20-30% commission. Hungary has over 300 **campgrounds,** most open from May to September. For more info, consult *Camping Hungary*, a booklet available in most tourist offices, or contact Tourinform in Budapest (see **Tourist Services and Money,** p. 498).

FOOD AND DRINK

HUNGARY	❶	❷	❸	❹	❺
FOOD	under 400Ft	400-800Ft	801-1300Ft	1301-2800Ft	over 2800Ft

Hungarian food is more flavorful than many of its Eastern European culinary counterparts, with many spicy meat dishes. Paprika, Hungary's chief agricultural export, colors most dishes red. In Hungarian restaurants (*vendéglő* or *étterem*), *halászlé*, a spicy fish stew, is a traditional starter. Or, try *gyümölesleves*, a cold fruit soup with whipped cream. The Hungarian national dish is *bográcsgulyás*, a soup of beef, onions, green peppers, tomatoes, potatoes, dumplings, and plenty of paprika. *Borjúpaprikás* is veal with paprika and potato-dumpling pasta. For **vegetarians** there is tasty *rántott sajt* (fried cheese) and *gombapörkölt* (mushroom stew). Delicious Hungarian fruits and vegetables abound in summer. Vegetarians should also look for *salata* (salad) and *sajt* (cheese), as these will be the only options in many small-town restaurants. Keeping **kosher,** on the other hand, is fairly difficult. Avoid American food like hot dogs, which can cause food poisoning. The northeastern towns of Eger and Tokaj produce famous red and white **wines,** respectively. *Sör* (Hungarian beer) ranges from acceptable to first-rate. Lighter beers include *Dreher Pils, Szalon Sör*, and licensed versions of *Steffl*, *Gold Fassl*, and *Amstel*. Among the best-tasting *pálinka* (brandy-like liquor) are *barackpálinka* (an apricot schnapps) and *körtepálinka* (pear brandy). *Unicum*, advertised as the national drink, is an **herbal liqueur** containing over 40 herbs; legend has it that it was once used by the Hapsburgs to cure digestive ailments.

HOLIDAYS AND FESTIVALS

Holidays: New Year's Day (Jan. 1); National Day (Mar. 15); Labor Day (May 1); Pentecost (May 31, 2009; May 23, 2010); Constitution Day (St. Stephen's Day, Aug. 20); Republic Day (Oct. 23); All Saints' Day (Nov. 1); Christmas (Dec. 25-26).

Festivals: Central Europe's largest rock festival, **Sziget Festival,** hits Budapest for a week in late July or early August, featuring rollicking crowds and international superstar acts. Eger's fabulous **World Festival of Wine Songs** celebration kicks off in late September, bringing together boisterous choruses and world-famous vintage wines.

BEYOND TOURISM

Central European University, Nador u. 9, Budapest 1051, Hungary (☎36 13 27 30 09; www.ceu.hu). Affiliated with the Open Society Institute-Budapest. Offers international students the opportunity to take graduate-level courses. Tuition US$7775 per semester, not including personal expenses. Financial aid available.

Hungarian Dance Academy, Columbus u. 87-89, Budapest H-1145, Hungary (☎36 12 73 34 30; www.mtf.hu). Summer dance programs for students ages 11-24.

Central European Teaching Program, 3800 NE 72nd Ave., Portland, OR 97213, USA (☎503-287-4977; www.cetp.info). Places English teachers in state schools in Hungary and Romania for one semester (US$1700) or a full school year (US$2250).

BUDAPEST ☎01

While other parts of Hungary maintain a slow pace, Budapest (pop. 1.9 million) has seized upon cosmopolitan chic with a vengeance without giving up its old-time charms. Unlike in Prague, the sights of Budapest spread throughout the energetic city, giving it a life independent of the growing crowds of tourists; Turkish thermal baths and Roman ruins mix seamlessly with modern buildings and a legendary night scene. The area that constitutes Budapest was once two entities: the pasture-ruled city of Pest and the viticulture hills of Buda.

Although the city was ravaged by WWII, Hungarians rebuilt it, then weathered a Soviet invasion and 40 years of Communism. The resilient spirit of Budapest resonates as the city reassumes its place as a major European capital.

TRANSPORTATION

Flights: Ferihegy Airport (**BUD;** ☎01 296 9696). Malév (Hungarian Airlines; reservations ☎01 235 3888) flies to major cities. To the center, take bus #93 (20min., every 15min. 4:55am-11:20pm, 270Ft), then M3 to Kőbánya-Kispest (15min. to Deák tér, in downtown Budapest). Airport Minibus (☎01 296 8555) goes to lodgings (2990Ft).

Trains: Major stations are **Keleti Pályaudvar, Nyugati Pályaudvar,** and **Déli Pályaudvar.** (International and domestic information ☎40 49 49 49). Most **international trains** arrive at Keleti pu., but some from Prague go to Nyugati pu. For schedules, check www.elvira.hu. To: **Berlin, GER** (12hr.; 2 per day; 28,305Ft, reservation 765Ft); **Bucharest, ROM** (14hr., 5 per day, 19,482Ft); **Prague, CZR** (7-8hr., 5 per day, 11,700Ft); **Vienna, AUT** (3hr., 17 per day, 3315Ft); **Warsaw, POL** (11hr., 2 per day, 18,411Ft). The daily Orient Express stops on its way from **Paris, FRA** to **Istanbul, TUR.** Trains run to most major destinations in Hungary. Purchase tickets at an **International Ticket Office** (Keleti pu. open daily 8am-7pm; Nyugati pu. open M-Sa 5am-9pm; info desk 24hr.). Or try **MÁV Hungarian Railways,** VI, Andrássy út 35, with branches at all stations. (☎461 5500. Open Apr.-Sept. M-F 9am-6pm, Oct.-Mar. M-F 9am-5pm. Say "diák" for student or under 26 discounts.) The **HÉV commuter railway** station is at Batthyány tér, opposite Parliament. Trains head to **Szentendre** (45min., every 15min. 5am-9pm, 460Ft). Purchase tickets at the station for transport beyond the city limits.

Buses: Buses to international and some domestic destinations leave from the **Népliget station,** X, Ulloi u. 131. (M3: Népliget. ☎01 382 0888. Ticket window open M-F 6am-9pm, Sa-Su 6am-4pm.) To **Berlin, GER** (14hr., 6 per week, 18,000Ft); **Prague, CZR** (8hr., 6 per week, 9810Ft); **Vienna, AUT** (3-3.5hr., 5 per day, 2950Ft). Buses going east of Budapest are at the **Népstadion station,** XIV, Hungária körút 46-48. (M2: Népstadion. ☎01 252 4498. Open M-F 6am-6pm, Sa-Su 6am-4pm.) Buses to the **Danube Bend** and parts of the Uplands depart outside Árpád híd metro station on the M3 line. (☎01 329 1450. Cashier open 6am-8pm.) Check www.volanbusz.hu for schedules.

Public Transportation: Subways, buses, and **trams** are convenient. The **metro** has 3 lines: M1 (yellow), M2 (red), and M3 (blue). **Night transit** (É) buses run midnight-5am along major routes: #7É and 78É follow the M2 route; #6É follows the 4/6 tram line; #14É and 50É follow the M3 route. Single-fare tickets for public transport (one-way on 1 line; 270Ft, trams 230Ft) are sold in metro stations, in Trafik shops, and by sidewalk vendors. Punch them in the orange boxes at the gate of the metro or on buses and trams; punch a new ticket when you change lines, or face fines. Day pass 1350Ft, 3-day 3100Ft, 1-week 3600Ft, 2-week 4800Ft, 1-month 7350Ft.

Taxis: Beware of scams; check for yellow license plates and meter. **Budataxi** (☎01 233 3333) is cheaper for rides requested by phone. Also try **Főtaxi** (☎01 222 2222) and **6x6 Taxi** (☎01 466 6666). Base fare 300Ft, 350Ft per km, 60Ft per min. waiting.

ORIENTATION

Buda and Pest are separated by the **Danube River** (Duna), and the city preserves the distinctive character of each side. On the west bank, **Buda** has winding streets, beautiful vistas, a hilltop citadel, and the Castle District. Down the north slope of **Várhegy** (Castle Hill) is **Moszkva tér,** Buda's tram and local bus hub. On the east bank, **Pest,** the commercial center, is home to shopping boulevards, **Parliament** (Országház), and the **Opera House.** Metro lines converge in Pest at **Deák tér,** next to the main international bus terminal at **Erzsébet tér.** Two blocks west toward the river lies **Vörösmarty tér** and the pedestrian shopping zone

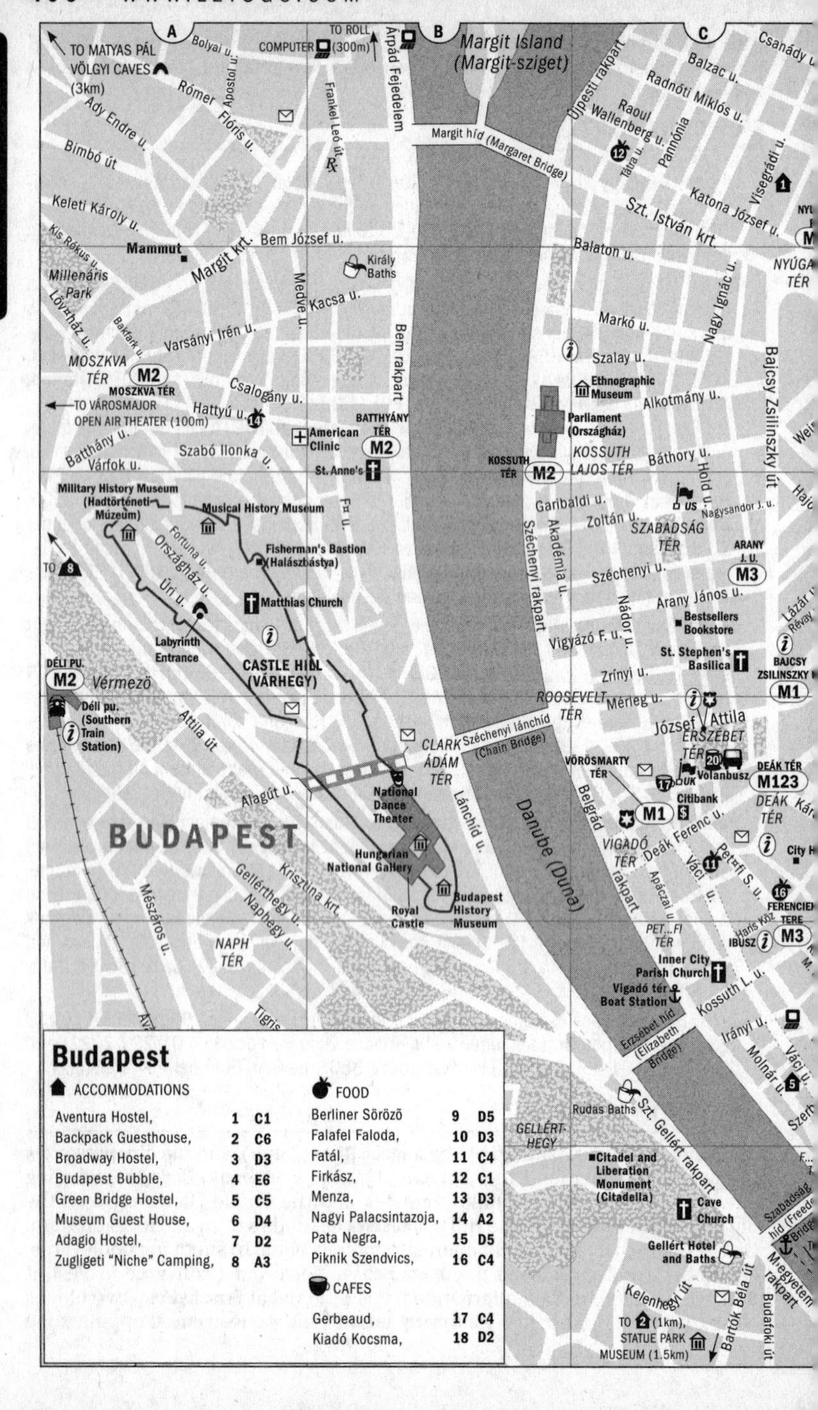
A
B
C
TO MATYAS PÁL VÖLGYI CAVES (3km)
COMPUTER (300m)
TO ROLL
Margit Island (Margit-sziget)
Margit híd (Margaret Bridge)
Bolyai u.
Apostol u.
Rómer Flóris u.
Ady Endre u.
Bimbó út
Frankel Leó út
Árpád Fejedelem
Keleti Károly u.
Kis Rókus u.
Mammut
Margit krt.
Bem József u.
Király Baths
Millenáris Park
Lövőház u.
Bakfark u.
Varsányi Irén u.
Kacsa u.
Medve u.
Bem rakpart
MOSZKVA TÉR
M2
MOSZKVA TÉR
TO VÁROSMAJOR OPEN AIR THEATER (100m)
Csalogány u.
Hattyú u.
Batthyány u.
Várfok u.
Szabó Ilonka u.
American Clinic
BATTHYÁNY TÉR
St. Anne's
Military History Museum (Hadtörténeti Múzeum)
Musical History Museum
Fisherman's Bastion (Halászbástya)
Fortuna u.
Országház u.
Úri u.
Matthias Church
Labyrinth Entrance
CASTLE HILL (VÁRHEGY)
TO 8
DÉLI PU.
Vérmező
Déli pu. (Southern Train Station)
Attila út
Alagút u.
CLARK ÁDÁM TÉR
Széchenyi lánchíd (Chain Bridge)
National Dance Theater
Hungarian National Gallery
Royal Castle
Budapest History Museum
Lánchíd u.
BUDAPEST
Gellérthegy u.
Krisztina krt.
Naphegy u.
NAPH TÉR
Mészáros u.
Tigris
Újpesti rakpart
Csanády u.
Balzac u.
Radnóti Miklós u.
Raoul Wallenberg u.
Pannónia
Tátra u.
Visegrádi u.
Katona József u.
Szt. István krt.
NYÚGATI TÉR
Balaton u.
Markó u.
Nagy Ignác u.
Szalay u.
Ethnographic Museum
Parliament (Országház)
Alkotmány u.
Bajcsy Zsilinszky út
KOSSUTH TÉR
KOSSUTH LAJOS TÉR
Báthory u.
Hold u.
Garibaldi u.
Zoltán u.
US
Nagysandor J. u.
SZABADSÁG TÉR
ARANY J. U.
M3
Széchenyi rakpart
Akadémia u.
Széchenyi u.
Arany János u.
Bestsellers Bookstore
Nádor u.
Vigyázó F. u.
St. Stephen's Basilica
BAJCSY ZSILINSZKY
M1
Zrínyi u.
ROOSEVELT TÉR
Mérleg u.
József Attila
ERZSÉBET TÉR
Volanbusz
VÖRÖSMARTY TÉR
UK
DEÁK TÉR
M123
Citibank
DEÁK TÉR
Belgrád rakpart
Danube (Duna)
VIGADÓ TÉR
Deák Ferenc u.
Váci u.
Petőfi S. u.
City H
FERENCIEK TERE
Apáczai
PETŐFI TÉR
IBUSZ
Haris Köz
Inner City Parish Church
Vigadó tér Boat Station
Kossuth L. u.
Irányi u.
Molnár u.
Erzsébet híd (Elizabeth Bridge)
Rudas Baths
Szt. Gellért rakpart
GELLÉRT-HEGY
Citadel and Liberation Monument (Citadella)
Cave Church
Gellért Hotel and Baths
Szabadság híd (Freedom Bridge)
Kelenhegyi út
TO 2 (1km), STATUE PARK MUSEUM (1.5km)
Bartók Béla út
Budafoki út
Megyetem rakpart
Budapest
ACCOMMODATIONS
Aventura Hostel, 1 C1
Backpack Guesthouse, 2 C6
Broadway Hostel, 3 D3
Budapest Bubble, 4 E6
Green Bridge Hostel, 5 C5
Museum Guest House, 6 D4
Adagio Hostel, 7 D2
Zugligeti "Niche" Camping, 8 A3
FOOD
Berliner Sörözõ 9 D5
Falafel Faloda, 10 D3
Fatál, 11 C4
Firkász, 12 C1
Menza, 13 D3
Nagyi Palacsintazoja, 14 A2
Pata Negra, 15 D5
Piknik Szendvics, 16 C4
CAFES
Gerbeaud, 17 C4
Kiadó Kocsma, 18 D2

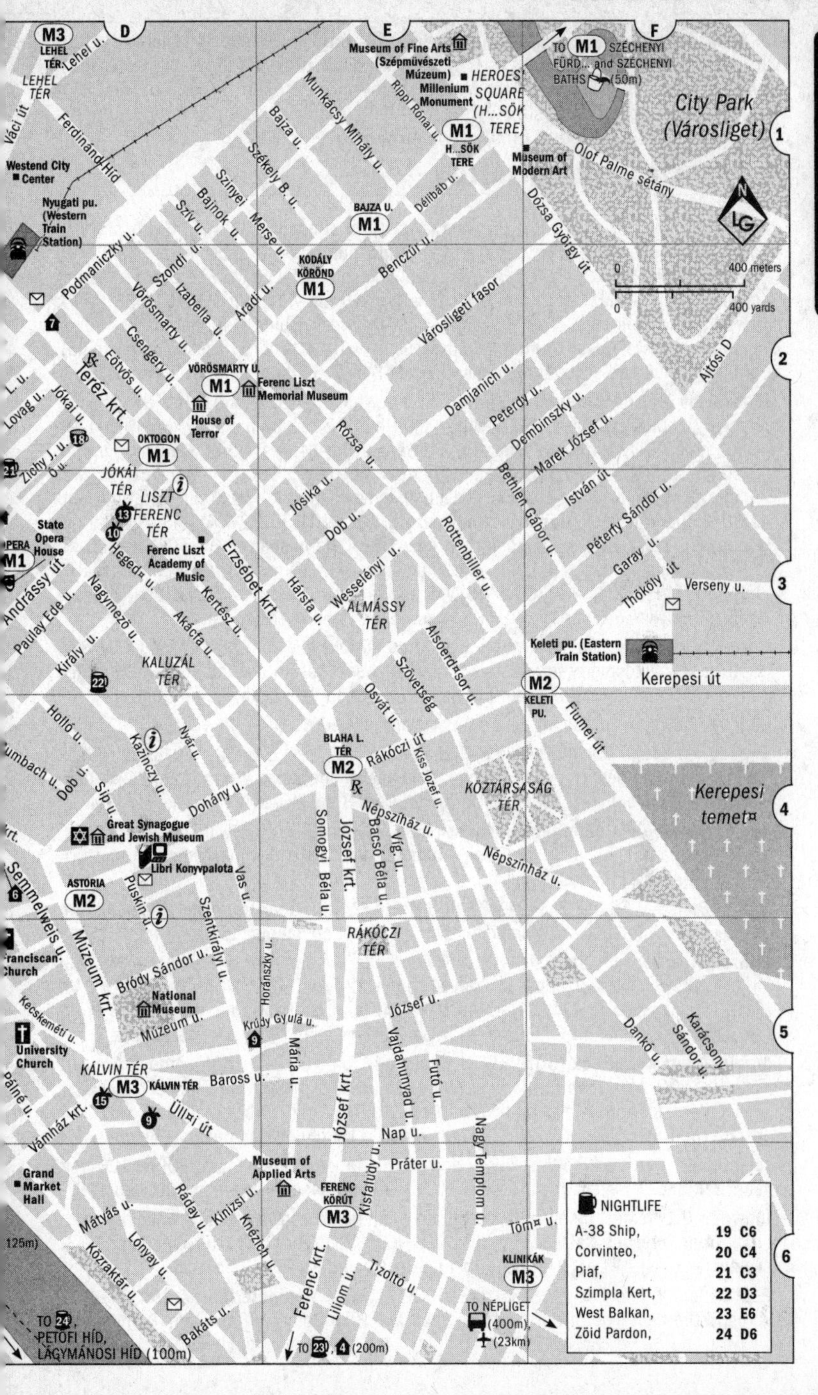
City Park (Városliget)
Museum of Fine Arts (Szépmüvészeti Múzeum)
Millenium Monument
HEROES' SQUARE (H...SÖK TERE)
TO M1 SZÉCHENYI FÜRD... and SZÉCHENYI BATHS (50m)
Museum of Modern Art
Olof Palme sétány
Westend City Center
Nyugati pu. (Western Train Station)
LEHEL TÉR
BAJZA U.
KODÁLY KÖRÖND
VÖRÖSMARTY U.
Ferenc Liszt Memorial Museum
House of Terror
OKTOGON
JÓKAI TÉR
LISZT FERENC TÉR
State Opera House
Ferenc Liszt Academy of Music
ALMÁSSY TÉR
KALUZÁL TÉR
Keleti pu. (Eastern Train Station)
Kerepesi út
KELETI PU.
BLAHA L. TÉR
KÖZTÁRSASÁG TÉR
Kerepesi temet¤
Great Synagogue and Jewish Museum
Libri Konyvpalota
ASTORIA
RÁKÓCZI TÉR
Franciscan Church
National Museum
University Church
KÁLVIN TÉR
Grand Market Hall
Museum of Applied Arts
FERENC KÖRÚT
KLINIKÁK
TO NÉPLIGET (400m), (23km)
TO 24, PETŐFI HÍD, LÁGYMÁNOSI HÍD (100m)
TO 23, 4 (200m)
0 400 meters
0 400 yards
NIGHTLIFE
A-38 Ship, 19 C6
Corvinteo, 20 C4
Piaf, 21 C3
Szimpla Kert, 22 D3
West Balkan, 23 E6
Zöid Pardon, 24 D6

Váci utca. Three main bridges join Budapest's halves: **Széchenyi Lánchíd** (Chain Bridge), **Erzsébet híd** (Elizabeth Bridge), and **Szabadság híd** (Freedom Bridge). Budapest addresses begin with a Roman numeral representing one of the city's 23 districts. Central Buda is I; central Pest is V. A **map** is essential for Budapest's confusing streets; pick one up at any tourist office or hostel.

PRACTICAL INFORMATION

Tourist Offices: All offices sell the **Budapest Card** (Budapest Kártya), which provides discounts, unlimited public transportation, and admission to most museums (2-day card 6500Ft, 3-day 8000Ft.). A great deal, except on Mondays when museums are closed. An excellent first stop in the city is **Tourinform,** V, Sütő u. 2 (☎01 438 8080; www.hungary.com). M1, 2, or 3: Deák tér. Off Deák tér behind McDonald's. Open daily 8am-8pm. **Vista Travel Center,** Andrássy út 1 (☎01 429 9751; incoming@vista.hu), arranges tours and accommodations. Open M-F 9am-6:30pm, Sa 9am-2:30pm.

Embassies and Consulates: Australia, XII, Királyhágó tér 8/9 (☎01 457 9777; www.hungary.embassy.gov.au). M2: Déli pu., then bus #21 or tram #59 to Királyhágó tér. Open M-F 8:30am-4:30pm. **Canada,** XII, Ganz u. 12-14 (☎01 392 3360). Open M-F 8:30am-12:30pm. **Ireland,** V, Szabadság tér 7 (☎01 302 9600), in Bank Center. M3: Arany János. Walk down Bank u. toward the river. Open M-F 9:30am-12:30pm and 2:30-4:30pm. **New Zealand,** VI, Nagymezo u. 50 (☎01 302 2484). M3: Nyugati pu. Open M-F 11am-4pm by appointment only. **UK,** V, Harmincad u. 6 (☎01 266 2888; www.ukinhungary.fco.gov.uk), near the intersection with Vörösmarty tér. M1: Vörösmarty tér. Open M-F 9:30am-12:30pm. **US,** V, Szabadság tér 12 (☎01 475 4400, after hours 475 4703; www.usembassy.hu). M2: Kossuth tér. Open M-F 8am-5pm.

Currency Exchange: Banks have the best rates. **Citibank,** V, Vörösmarty tér 4 (☎01 374 5000). M1: Vörösmarty tér. Cashes traveler's checks for no commission and provides MC/V cash advances. Bring your passport. Open M-Th 9am-5pm, F 9am-4pm.

Luggage Storage: Lockers at all 3 train stations. 150-600Ft.

English-Language Bookstore: Libri Könyvpalota, VII, Rákóczi u. 12 (☎01 267 4843). M2: Astoria. The best choice in the city; a multilevel bookstore, it has 1 fl. of up-to-date English titles. Open M-F 10am-7:30pm, Sa 10am-3pm. MC/V.

GLBT Hotline: GayGuide.net Budapest (☎06 30 93 23 334; www.budapest.gayguide.net). Posts an online guide and runs a hotline (daily 4-8pm) with information and reservations at GLBT-friendly lodgings.

Tourist Police: V, Sütő u. 2 (☎01 438 8080). M1, 2, or 3: Deák tér. Inside the Tourinform office. Open 24hr. Beware of impostors on the street demanding to see your passport.

Pharmacies: Look for green signs labeled Apotheke, Gyógyszertár, or Pharmacie. Minimal after-hours service fees apply. **II,** Frankel Leó út 22 (☎01 212 4406). AmEx/MC/V. **VI,** Teréz krt. 41 (☎01 311 4439). Open M-F 8am-8pm, Sa 8am-2pm. **VII,** Rákóczi út 39 (☎314 3695). Open M-F 7:30am-9pm, Sa 7:30am-2pm; no after-hours service.

Medical Services: Falck (SOS) KFT, II, Kapy út 49/b (☎01 275 1535). Ambulance service US$120. **American Clinic,** I, Hattyú u. 14 (☎01 224 9090; www.americanclinics.com). Open for appointments M-F 8am-8pm, Sa 8am-2pm. 24hr. emergency ☎01 224 9090. The US embassy (p. 498) also maintains a list of English-speaking doctors.

Telephones: Cards are sold at kiosks and metro stations. 50-unit card 800Ft, 120-unit card 1800Ft. Domestic operator and info ☎198 international operator 190, info 199.

Internet: Cybercafes are everywhere, but they can be expensive and long waits are common. **Ami Internet Coffee,** V, Váci u. 40 (☎01 267 1644; www.amicoffee.hu). M3: Ferenciek tér. 200Ft per 15min., 700Ft per hr. Open daily 9am-2am.

Post Office: V, Városház u. 18 (☎01 318 4811). **Poste Restante** (Postán Mar) in office around the right side of the building. Open M-F 8am-8pm, Sa 8am-2pm. Branches at

Nyugati pu.; VI, Teréz krt. 105/107; Keleti pu.; VIII, Baross tér 11/c; and elsewhere. Open M-F 7am-8pm, Sa 8am-2pm. **Postal Code:** Depends on the district—postal codes are 1XX2, where XX is the district number (1052 for post office listed above).

ACCOMMODATIONS AND CAMPING

Budapest's hostels are centers for the backpacker social scene, and their common rooms can be as exciting as many bars and clubs. Many hostels are run by the **Hungarian Youth Hostels Association (HI),** which operates from an office in Keleti pu. Representatives wearing Hostelling International shirts—and legions of competitors—accost travelers as they get off the train. Beware that they may provide inaccurate descriptions of other accommodations in order to sell their own. Private rooms are more expensive than hostels, but they do offer peace, quiet, and private showers. Arrive early, bring cash, and haggle. **Best Hotel Service,** V, Sütő u. 2, arranges apartment, hostel, and hotel reservations (6000Ft and up). Take M1, 2, or 3 to Deák tér. (☎318 4848; www.besthotelservice.hu. Open daily 8am-8pm.)

The Loft Hostel, V, Veres Palne 19, 4th fl., ring bell 44 (☎01 328 0916; www.lofthostel.hu). Enjoy the huge, rustic rooms and social common room of this newly-renovated hostel just steps away from the Danube. Internet and linen included. Reception 24hr. Flexible check-in and check-out. 8-bed dorms 3000Ft; 6-bed dorms 3500Ft; 4-bed dorms 4000; 500Ft price increase on weekends. Cash only. ❷

Carpe Noctem, VI, Szobi 5 (☎204 556 220; www.carpenoctemhostel.com). Take a left out of Nyugati pu. and another left at the second street; ring bell #13. A reputable party hostel with plenty of social space, the enthusiastic and welcoming staff of British expats make you feel more like friends than guests. 24hr. reception. Free Internet. Laundry 1000Ft. Dorms 3000Ft. Cash only. ❷

Budapest Bubble, VIII, Bródy Sándor 2, 1st fl. mezzanine (☎01 397 7974; budapestbubble@gmail.com). An intimate, inviting hostel near the National Museum with young, local hosts who are quick to provide information on the city. Internet and linen included. Reception 24hr. Flexible check-in and check-out. Dorms 3500-4500Ft, doubles 10,000-12,000Ft. Cash only. ❷

Backpack Guesthouse, XI, Takács Menyhért u. 33 (☎01 385 8946; www.backpackbudapest.hu), 12min. from central Pest. From Keleti pu., take bus #7 or 7a toward Buda. Get off at Tétényi u., then backtrack and turn left to go under the bridge. Take another left on Hamzsabégi út and continue to the 3rd right. A common room stocked with movies and a slew of hammocks in an inner garden make this neighborhood house a quiet, earthy hideaway from the traffic of the city. The 49E night bus runs here after trams stop. Laundry 1500Ft. Free Internet and Wi-Fi. Reception 24hr. Flexible check-in and check-out. Mattress in gazebo 2500Ft; 7- to 11-bed dorms 3000Ft, 4- to 5-bed dorms 3500Ft; doubles 9000Ft. MC/V. ❷

Aventura Hostel, XIII, Visegrádi u. 12 (☎01 239 0782; www.aventura.hu), in Pest. M3: Nyugati tér. Colorful, themed rooms (with no bunks!) and clean bathrooms. Provides info on special event and party listings around town. Breakfast included. Laundry 1500Ft. Free Internet and Wi-Fi. Reception 24hr. Flexible check-in and check-out. Dorms 3500-4500Ft; doubles 12,600Ft, with bath 15,000Ft. Cash only. ❸

Adagio Hostel, VII, Erzsebet krt. 25-27, 2nd floor, ring bell #15 (☎01 781 5144). A bargain on one of Pest's busiest streets, Adagio has a homey feel with its common room and clean facilities. Internet included. Laundry 1250Ft. Reception 24hr. Check-out 11am. 10-bed dorms 2500Ft; 4-bed dorms 4000Ft; doubles 12,000Ft. Cash only.

Green Bridge Hostel, V, Molnár u. 22-24 (☎01 266 6922; greenbridge@freemail.hu), in Pest's central district. Kick back and the enjoy the unbeatable location, friendly staff, and free snacks which make this a pleasant city retreat. Free Internet and Wi-Fi. Reception 24hr. Reserve ahead. Dorms 3900-4500Ft. Cash only. ❸

Broadway Hostel, VI, Ó u. 24-26 (☎01 688 1662; www.broadwayhostel.hu). M1: Opera. A new, luxurious alternative to the backpacking scene, with curtain partitions, fluffy comforters, and lockable closets. Inner courtyard with hammocks provides a laid-back hangout. Internet 250Ft per 30min. Reception 24hr. Check-out 10:30am. Dorms 3700Ft; singles 9150Ft; doubles 18,300Ft. Cash only. ❷

Museum Guest House, VIII, Mikszáth Kálmán tér 4, 1st fl. (☎01 318 9508; museumgh@freemail.c3.hu), in Pest. M3: Kálvin tér. Convenient location and loft beds. English spoken. Free Internet. Check-out 11am. Reserve ahead. Dorms 3000Ft. Cash only. ❸

Zugligeti "Niche" Camping, XII, Zugligeti út 101 (☎01 200 8346; www.campingniche.hu). Take bus #158 from above Moszkva tér to Laszállóhely, the last stop. Communal showers. Breakfast and Wi-Fi included. 1800Ft per person, 1500Ft per tent, 2000Ft per large tent, 1500Ft per car, 2550Ft per caravan. MC/V. ❶

HUNGARY?

Cafeterias with *"Önkiszolgáló Étterem"* signs serve cheap food (entrees 300-500Ft), and a neighborhood *kifőzés* (kiosk) or *vendéglő* (family-style restaurant) offers a real taste of Hungary. Corner markets, many open 24hr., stock the basics. The **Grand Market Hall,** IX, Fövam tér 1/3, next to Szabadság híd (M3: Kálvin tér), has acres of stalls, making it an attraction in itself. Ethnic restaurants populate the upper floor of **Mammut Plaza,** just outside the Moszkva tér metro in Buda, and **West End Plaza,** near the Nyugati metro in Pest.

RESTAURANTS

Fatál, V, Vácí u. 67 (☎01 266 2607), in Pest. M3: Ferenciek tér. Enormous portions of down-home, delicious Hungarian cuisine in a cool underground setting, off bustling Váci u. Entrees 590-2500Ft. Open daily 11:30am-2am. MC/V. ❷

Nagyi Palacsintazoja, II, Hattyu u. 16 (☎01 212 4866), in Buda. M2: Moszkva tér. Tiny, mirror-covered eatery dishes out sweet and savory crepes (130-400Ft) piled with toppings like cheese, fruit, or chocolate sauce. Enjoy your meal from the outdoor terrace for killer views of Parliament and Buda Castle. Limited space. Open 24hr. Cash only. ❶

Berliner Söröző, IX, Ráday u. 5 (☎01 217 6757; www.berliner.hu). An interesting mix of old-school Hungarian flavors and smooth Belgian drafts. Lively patio lets you enjoy warm summer nights and indulge in the chill atmosphere of Ráday utca. Entrees 1490-2950Ft. Beer from 400Ft. Open M-Sa noon-1am. Cash only. ❸

Firkász, XIII, Tátra u. 18 (☎01 450 1118; www.firkaszetterem.hu). The most traditional Hungarian restaurant in the city, from its paprika-infused dishes to its delicately embroidered table cloths. Entrees 1750-4500Ft. Open daily noon-midnight. MC/V. ❸

Pata Negra, IX, Kávin tér 8 (☎01 215 5616; www.patanegra.hu). This Spanish restaurant stands at the center of Kávin tér. Entrees (850-2200Ft) provide a refreshing, inventive break from typical Hungarian cuisine. Tapas (380-750Ft). Open M-W 11am-midnight, Th-F 11am-1am, Sa noon-1am, Su noon-midnight. Cash only. ❷

Parázs Presszó, VI, Szobi 4 (☎01 950 3770; www.parazspresszo.com). Diners browse the unusual but delicious Thai-Hungarian fusion menu from comfy cushions on the floor. English menu available. Entrees 750-2300Ft. Open daily noon-midnight. Cash only. ❷

Menza, Liszt Ferenc tér 2 (☎01 413 1482; www.menza.co.hu). Reminiscent of Communist-era *"menza,"* or canteens, this elegant eatery's decor offers a mix of 70s camp and modern chic. Menu boards list all manner of excellent Hungarian and international dishes on offer. Entrees 700-3500Ft. Open daily 10am-1am. AmEx/MC/V. ❷

Falafel Faloda, VI. Paulay Ede u. 53 (☎01 351 1243), in Pest. M1: Opera. Vegetarians come in droves for on-the-go falafel (750Ft) and the city's best salad bar. Salads 580-890Ft. Smoothies 320-380Ft and a wide selection of teas 200-230Ft. Open M-F 10am-8pm, Sa 10am-6pm. Cash only. ❶

Piknik Szendvics, V, Haris Köz 1 (☎01 318 3334; www.piknik-szendvics.hu), in Pest. M3: Ferenciek tér. Create a meal from inexpensive open-faced sandwiches (140-370Ft). Open M-F 9am-6pm, Sa 9am-2pm. Cash only. ❶

CAFES

Once the haunts of the literary, intellectual, and cultural elite—as well as political dissidents—the cafes boast mysterious histories and delicious pastries.

Altair, VIII, Puskin 26 (www.sirius-se.hu), in Pest. On the corner of Brody Sandor and Puskin, 1 block down from the National Museum. A true hidden gem, this Turkish-inspired teahouse has visitors take off their shoes to climb up to cozy, private lofts suspended in the air. Tea 530Ft. Open daily noon-10pm. Cash only.

Kiadó Kocsma, VI, Jókai tér 3 (☎01 331 1955), in Pest, next to Cafe Alhambra. M1: Oktogon. Playful atmosphere with a tranquil terrace, perfect for coffee (250Ft), tea (250Ft), or spirits (550-700Ft) as well as light, Hungarian-style snacks (390Ft-590Ft). Try the smoked salmon gnocchi (1500Ft). Open daily 10am-1am. MC/V.

Gerbeaud, V, Vörösmarty tér 7 (☎01 429 9020; www.gerbeaud.hu). M1: Vörösmarty tér. Hungary's most famous cafe and dessert shop has served delicious, homemade layer cakes (750Ft) and ice cream (330Ft) since 1858. Go for the tradition, but beware that sweets here cost at least double the price of any other dessert shop, and you'll be surrounded by double the tourists. Open daily 9am-9pm. AmEx/MC/V.

SIGHTS

In 1896, Hungary's millennial birthday bash prompted the construction of Budapest's most prominent sights. Among the works commissioned by the Hapsburgs were **Hősök tér** (Heroes' Square), **Szabadság híd** (Liberty Bridge), **Vajdahunyad Vár** (Vajdahunyad Castle), and continental Europe's first metro system. Slightly grayer for wear, war, and occupation, these monuments attest to the optimism of a capital on the verge of its Golden Age. See the sights with **Absolute Walking and Biking Tours.** (☎01 211 8861; www.absolutetours.com. 3½hr. tours 4000Ft, students 3500ft. Specialized tours 4000-7000Ft.) For the more independent sightseer, **The Walker's Guide** provides 18 hours of entertaining commentary on the city's sights. Available for rental at tourist offices throughout the city. 3000Ft for 3hr., 4000Ft for 6hr., and 5000Ft for all-day rental. (www.walkersguide.travel). **Boat tours** leave from Vigadó tér piers 6-7, near Elizabeth Bridge in Pest. The evening **Danube Legend** costs 4900Ft, students 3700; its day-time counterpart, the **Duna Bella,** costs 3900/2900Ft for 2hr.

BUDA

On the east bank of the Danube, Buda sprawls between the base of **Várhegy** (Castle Hill) and southern **Gellérthegy** and leads into the city's main residential areas. Older and more peaceful than Pest, Buda is filled with lush parks.

CASTLE DISTRICT. Towering above the Danube on Várhegy, the Castle District has been razed three times in its 800-year history. With its winding, statue-filled streets, impressive views, and hodgepodge of architectural styles, the UNESCO-protected district now appears much as it did under the Hapsburg reign. The reconstructed **Buda Castle** (Vár) houses fine museums (p. 504). Bullet holes in the facade recall the 1956 uprising. *(M1, 2, or 3: Deáktér. From the metro, take bus #16 across the Danube. Or, from M2: Moszkva tér, walk up to the hill on Várfok u. "Becsi kapu"* *marks the castle entrance.)* Beneath Buda Castle, the **Castle Labyrinths** (Budvári Labirinths) provide a spooky glimpse of the subterranean city. *(Úri u. 9. ☎01 212 0207; www.labirintus.com. Open daily 9:30am-7:30pm. 1500Ft, students 1100Ft.)*

MATTHIAS CHURCH. The colorful roof of **Matthias Church** (Mátyás templom) on Castle Hill is one of Budapest's most photographed sights. The church was converted into a mosque in 1541, then renovated again 145 years later when the Hapsburgs defeated the Turks. Ascend the spiral steps to view the exhibits of the **Museum of Ecclesiastical Art.** *(I, Szentháromság tér 2. www.matyas-templom.hu. Open M-F 9am-5pm, Sa 9am-1pm, Su 1-5pm. High mass daily 7, 8:30am, 6pm; Su and holidays also 10am and noon. Church and museum 700Ft, students 480Ft.)*

GELLÉRT HILL. After the coronation of King Stephen, the first Christian Hungarian monarch, in AD 1001, the Pope sent Bishop Gellért to convert the Magyars. After those unconvinced by the bishop's message hurled him to his death, the hill he was thrown from was named Gellérthegy in his honor. The **Liberation Monument** (Szabadság Szobor), on the hilltop, honors Soviet soldiers who died ridding Hungary of the Nazis. The adjoining Citadel was built as a symbol of Hapsburg power after the foiled 1848 revolution; the view from there is especially stunning at night. At the base of the hill is **Gellért** (p. 502), Budapest's most famous Turkish bath. *(XI. Take tram #18 or 19 or bus #7 to Hotel Gellért; follow Szabó Verjték u. to Jubileumi Park, continuing on marked paths to the summit. Citadel 1200Ft.)*

PEST

Constructed in the 19th century, the winding streets of Pest now link cafes, corporations, and monuments. The crowded Belváros (Inner City) is based around Vörösmarty tér and the swarming pedestrian boulevard Váci utca.

PARLIAMENT. The palatial Gothic Parliament (Országház) stands 96m tall, a number that symbolizes the date of Hungary's millennial anniversary. The building was modeled after the UK's, right down to the facade and the riverside location. *(M2: Kossuth tér. ☎01 441 4000. English-language tours daily 10am, noon, 2pm; arrive early. Min. 5 people. Ticket office at Gate X opens at 8am. Entrance with mandatory tour 2520Ft, students 1260Ft. Free with EU passport.)*

GREAT SYNAGOGUE. The largest synagogue in Europe and the second-largest in the world, Pest's Great Synagogue (Zsinagóga) was designed to hold 3000 worshippers. The enormous metal **Tree of Life,** a Holocaust memorial, sits in the garden above a mass grave for thousands of Jews killed near the end of the war. Each leaf bears the name of a family that perished. Next door, the **Jewish Museum** (Zsidó Múzeum) documents the storied past of Hungary's Jews. *(VII. At the corner of Dohány u. and Wesselényi u. M2: Astoria. Open May-Oct. M-Th 10am-5pm, F and Su 10am-2pm; Nov.-Apr. M-Th 10am-3pm, F and Su 10am-1pm. Services F 6pm. Admissions usually start at 10:30am. Covered shoulders required. Tours M-Th 10:30am-3:30pm on the half-hour, F and Su 10:30, 11:30am, 12:30pm. Admission 1400Ft, students 750Ft. Tours 1900Ft/1600Ft.)*

ST. STEPHEN'S BASILICA (SZ. ISTVÁN BAZILIKA). Though seriously damaged in WWII, the neo-Renaissance facade of the city's largest church has been mostly restored. The Panorama Tower offers an amazing 360° view of the city. A curious attraction is St. Stephen's mummified right hand, one of Hungary's most revered religious relics. A 100Ft donation dropped in the box will illuminate it for 2min. *(V. M1, 2, or 3: Deák tér. Church open daily 7am-7pm, Chapel May-Oct. M-Sa 9am-5pm, Su 1pm-5pm, Nov.-Apr. M-Sa 10am-4pm, Mass M-Sa 8am and 6pm, Su 8, 9, 10am, noon, 6, 7:30pm. Free. Tower open daily Apr.-Oct. M-Sa 10am-6pm. 500Ft, students 400Ft.)*

ANDRÁSSY ÚT AND HEROES' SQUARE. Hungary's grandest boulevard, Andrássy út extends from Erzsébet tér northeast to Heroes' Sq. (Hősök tér). The **State**

Opera House (Magyar Állami Operaház) is a vivid reminder of Budapest's Golden Age; its gilded interior glows on performance nights. *(Andrássy út 22. M1: Opera. ☎01 332 8197. 1hr. English-language tours daily 3 and 4pm. 2600Ft, students 1400Ft.)* At the Heroes' Sq. end of Andrássy út, the **Millennium Monument** (Millenniumi emlékm›) commemorates the nation's most prominent leaders.

CITY PARK (VÁROSLIGET). Budapest's park, located northeast of Heroes' Sq., is home to a zoo, a circus, an amusement park, and a castle. The castle's collage of Baroque, Gothic, and Romanesque styles chronicles the history of Hungarian design. Rent a rowboat or ice skates on the lake next to the castle. The park's main road is closed to automobiles on weekends. *(XIV. M1: Széchényi Fürdő. Zoo ☎01 273 4900; www.zoobudapest.com. Open May-Aug. M-Th 9am-6:30pm, F-Su 9am-7pm; Mar. and Oct. M-Th 9am-5pm, F-Su 9am-5:30pm; Apr. and Sept. M-Th 9am-5:30pm, F-Su 9am-6pm; Nov.-Jan. daily. 9am-4pm. 1700Ft, students 1200Ft. Park ☎01 363 8310. Open July-Aug. daily 10am-8pm; May-June and Sept. M-F 11am-7pm, Sa-Su 10am-8pm, Apr. and Oct. M-F noon-6pm, Sa-Su 10am-7pm. 3320Ft, children 213-Ft weekdays; weekends 3510Ft, kids 2250Ft.)*

MUSEUMS

MUSEUM OF APPLIED ARTS (IPARMÚVÉSZETI MÚZEUM). This collection of handcrafted pieces—including ceramics, furniture, metalwork, and Tiffany glass—deserves careful examination. Excellent temporary exhibits highlight specific crafts. Built for the 1896 millennium, the tiled Art Nouveau edifice is as intricate as the pieces within. *(IX. Üllői út 33-37. M3: Ferenc krt. ☎01 456 5100; www.imm.hu. Open Tu-Su 10am-6pm. 1600Ft, students 800Ft. Group tours available.)*

HOUSE OF TERROR. The Nazi and Soviet regimes housed prisoners in the basement of this building near Heroes' Sq. An acclaimed museum opened here in 2002 to document life under the two reigns of terror and memorialize the victims who were tortured and killed. *(VI. Andrássy Út 60. M1: Vörösmarty u. ☎01 374 2600; www.terrorhaza.hu. Open Tu-F 10am-6pm, Sa-Su 10am-7:30pm. 1500Ft, students 750Ft.)*

LUDWIG MUSEUM (LUDVIG MÚZEUM). Located on the outskirts of the city, the Ludwig Museum ("LuMu") displays cutting-edge Hungarian painting and sculpture. *(IX. Komor Marcell u. 1. Take tram #4 or 6 to Boráros tér, then take the HÉV commuter rail 1 stop to Lagymanyosi híd. ☎01 555 3444; www.ludwigmuseum.hu. Open Tu-Su 10am-8pm, last Sa. of the month 10am-10pm. Temporary exhibit 1200Ft, students 600Ft.)*

MUSEUM OF FINE ARTS (SZÉPMÚVÉSZETI MÚZEUM). A spectacular collection of European art is housed in this museum near Heroes' Sq. *(M1: Hősök tér. ☎01 469 7100; www.szepmuveszeti.hu.Open Tu-Su 10am-6pm, ticket booth until 5pm. Permanent exhibition 1200Ft, students 600Ft, temporary exhibitions 2600/1300Ft.)*

NATIONAL MUSEUM (NEMZETI MÚZEUM). An exhibit on the second floor chronicles the history of Hungary from the founding of the state through the 20th century; the first floor is reserved for temporary exhibits. *(VIII. Múzeum krt. 14/16. M3: Kálvin tér. ☎204 397 325; www.mng.hu. Open Tu-Su 10am-6pm. 800Ft, students 400Ft.)*

STATUE PARK MUSEUM. After the collapse of Soviet rule, the open-air Statue Park Museum (Szoborpark Múzeum) was created in Buda, south of Gellérthegy, to display Soviet statues removed from Budapest's parks and squares. The indispensable English-language guidebook (1000Ft) explains the statues' histories. *(XXII. On the corner of Balatoni út and Szabadkai út. Take express bus #7 from Keleti pu. to Étele tér, then take the yellow Volán bus from terminal #7 bound for Diósd 15min., every 15min., and get off at the Szoborpark stop. ☎01 424 7500; www.szoborpark.hu. 2-week passes for intercity transportation not accepted. Open daily 10am-dusk. 1500Ft, students 1000Ft.)*

BUDA CASTLE. Buda Castle houses several museums. Wings B-D hold the huge **Hungarian National Gallery** (Magyar Nemzeti Galéria), a definitive collection of Hungarian painting and sculpture. Its treasures include works by Realist Mihály Munkácsy and Impressionist Paál Lászlo, and medieval gold altarpieces. *(☎204 397 325; www.mng.hu. Open Tu-Su 10am-6pm. 800Ft, students 400Ft.)* In Wing E, the **Budapest History Museum** (Budapesti Törtenéti Múzeum) displays a collection of recently unearthed medieval artifacts. *(I. Szent György tér 2. ☎01 487 8800; www.btm.hu. Open Mar.-mid-Sept. daily 10am-6pm; mid-Sept.-Oct. 10am-6pm, closed Tu, Nov.-Feb. 10am-4pm, closed Tu. 1100Ft, students 550Ft.)*

FESTIVALS AND ENTERTAINMENT

The **Budapest Spring Festival** (www.fesztivalvaros.hu), March 13-29 in 2009, showcases Hungary's premier musicians and actors. In August, Óbudai Island hosts the **Sziget Festival** (www.sziget.hu), a rock festival. *Budapest Program, Budapest Panorama, Pesti Est,* and *Budapest in Your Pocket* are the best English-language entertainment guides, available at tourist offices and hotels. The "Style" section of the *Budapest Sun* (www.budapestsun.com; 300Ft) has film reviews and a 10-day calendar. For tickets, check Ticket Express Hungary, Andrássy u. 18. (☎01 303 0999; www.tex.hu. Open M-F 10am-6:30pm.)

The **State Opera House** (Magyar Állami Operaház), VI, Andrássy út 22, is one of Europe's leading performance centers. (M1: Opera. Box office ☎01 353 0170; www.opera.hu. Tickets 800-8700Ft. Box office open M-Sa 11am-7pm, Su 10am-1pm and 4-7pm. Closes at 5pm on non-performance days.) The **National Dance Theater** (Nemzetí Táncszínház), Szinház u. 1-3, on Castle Hill, hosts a variety of shows, but Hungarian folklore is the most popular. (☎01 201 4407, box office ☎01 375 8649; www.nemzetitancszinhaz.hu. Most shows 7pm. Tickets 1500-4000Ft. Box office open M-Th 10am-6pm, F 10am-5pm.) The lovely **Városmajor Open-Air Theater,** XII, Városmajor, in Buda, hosts musicals, operas, and ballets. (M1: Moszkva tér. ☎01 375 5922; www.szabadter.hu. Open June 27-Aug. 18. Box office open M-F 1-6pm, Sa 1-5pm, Su 10am-1pm.)

Both travelers and locals head to Budapest's thermal baths to soak away the grime. **Széchenyi,** XIV, Állatkerti u. 11/14, is one of Europe's largest baths. (M1: Hősök tér. ☎01 363 3210. Open daily 6am-10pm. 2400Ft; 400Ft returned if you leave within 2hr., 200Ft within 3hr.; **keep your receipt.** 15min. massage 2000Ft. Cash only.) The elegant **Gellért,** XI, Kelenhegyi út 4/6, has a rooftop sundeck and an outdoor wave pool. Take bus #7 or tram #47 or 49 to Hotel Gellért, at the base of Gellérthegy. (Open May-Sept. M-F 6am-7pm, Sa-Su 6am-5pm; Oct.-Apr. M-F 6am-7pm. 3100Ft, with scaled refund. 15min. massage 2500Ft. MC/V.)

NIGHTLIFE

Relaxing garden "cafe-clubs," elegant after-hours scenes, and nightly "freakin'" fests make up Budapest's nightlife scene. Pubs and bars stay busy until at least 4am and more club-like venues are alive past 5am. Upscale cafes near Pest's **Ferencz Liszt tér** (M2: Oktogon) attract Budapest's hip residents in their 20s and 30s, while less-apparent sidestreets house a more relaxed setting.

West Balkan, VIII, Tömő u. 2 (☎01 473 3651; www.west-balkan.com), in Pest. M3: Ferenc körút. 3 bars, indoor dance floor, and a whimsical outdoor garden keep Budapest's alternative scene grooving. Beer from 450Ft. Open daily 4pm-4am.

Szimpla Kert, VII, Kazinczy u. 14 (www.szimpla.hu). Graffiti designs on the walls, a random assortment of personal furniture, a movie screen and a concert stage give this garden/cafe/bar the most down-to-earth atmosphere in the city. Fresh crepes (100Ft) and a changing menu. Beer 250-300Ft. Open daily noon-2am. Cash only.

Corvintető, VII, Blaha Lujza tér 1-2 (☎01 772 2984; www.corvinteto.com), on the roof of Corvin Dept. Store, entry from Somogyi Béla street. Dance the night away with the city's hipsters at this popular summer rooftop party. Beer 300Ft. Open daily 6pm-5am.

A-38 Ship, XI (☎01 464 3940; www.a38.hu), anchored on the Buda side of the Danube, south of Petőfi Bridge. DJs spin on the decks of this revamped Ukrainian freighter. Also features frequent and varied live music. Beer 300Ft. Cover varies. Restaurant open M-Sa 11am-midnight. DJ nights open 11am-4am.

Zöld Pardon, XI (www.zp.hu), on the Buda side of Petőfi Bridge. This giant festival features a pool and 5 bars; 3 screens project the crowd on the dance floor. Concerts from 8pm, DJ from 10:30pm. Beer 250-400Ft. Open late Apr.-mid Sept. daily 9am-6am.

Piaf, VI, Nagymező u. 25, (☎01 312 3823), in Pest. M1: Opera. Knock on the inconspicuous door at this popular lounge near the bus station. The ground-level club hosts a sophisticated clientele, while the basement bar downstairs features a vastly different, alternative atmosphere. Cover 800Ft; includes 1 beer. Open daily 10pm-6am.

NIGHTLIFE SCAM. There have been reports of a scam involving Hungarian women who ask foreign men to buy them drinks. When the bill comes, accompanied by imposing men, it can be US$1000 per round. If victims claim to have no money, they are directed to an ATM in the bar. For a list of questionable establishments, check the US Embassy website at http://budapest.usembassy.gov/tourist_advisory.html. If you are taken in, call the police. You'll probably still have to pay, but get a receipt to file a complaint.

DAYTRIPS FROM BUDAPEST: THE DANUBE BEND

North of Budapest, the Danube sweeps in a dramatic arc called the **Dunakanyar** (Danube Bend), one of Hungary's most popular tourist attractions.

SZENTENDRE

HÉV trains go to Szentendre (45min., 3 per hr., 480Ft) from Budapest's Batthyány tér station. Buses run from Szentendre to Budapest's Árpád híd metro station (30min., 1-3 per hr., 280Ft), Esztergom (1hr., 1 per hr., 660Ft), and Visegrád (45min., 1 per hr., 375Ft). The stations are 10min. from Fő tér; descend the stairs past the HÉV tracks and through the underpass up Kossuth u. At the fork, bear right on Dumtsa Jenő u. Tourinform, Dumtsa Jenő u. 22, is between the center and the stations. (☎026 31 79 65. Open mid-Mar. to Oct. daily 9:30am-1pm and 1:30-4:30pm; Nov. to mid-Mar. M-F 9:30am-1pm and 1:30-4:30pm.)

The streets of Szentendre (pop. 23,000) brim with upscale galleries and restaurants. Head up **Templomdomb** (Church Hill) in Fő tér for a view from the 13th-century church. The **Czóbel Museum,** Templom tér 1, exhibits work by post-Impressionist artist Béla Czóbel, including his bikini-clad Venus of Szentendre. (Open from mid-Mar. to Sept. Tu-Su 9am-5pm, from Oct. to mid-Mar. W-Su 1pm-5pm. 500Ft, students 300Ft.) The popular **Kovács Margit Museum,** Vastagh György u. 1, off Görög u., displays whimsical ceramics by the 20th-century Hungarian artist. (Open June-Aug. Tu-Su 9am-7pm, Sept.-May Tu-Su 9am-5pm. 700Ft, students 350Ft.) The real "thriller" is at the **Szamos Marzipan Museum and Confectionery,** Dumtsa Jenő u. 12; an 80kg white-chocolate statue of Michael Jackson. (☎01 412 626; www.szamosmarcipan.hu. Open daily May-Oct. 10am-7pm; Nov.-Apr. 10am-6pm. 400Ft.) The **Nemzeti Bormúzeum** (National Wine Museum), Bogdányi u. 10, exhibits wines from across Hungary. (www.bor-kor.hu. Open daily 10am-10pm. Exhibit 200Ft, tasting and English-language tour 2000Ft.)

VISEGRÁD

Buses run to Visegrád from Budapest's Árpád híd metro station (1hr., 30 per day, 525Ft). The tourist office is at Rév út 15. (☎026 39 81 60; www.visegradtours.hu. Open Apr.-Oct. daily 8am-6pm; Nov.-Mar. M-F 10am-4pm.)

Host to the medieval royal court, Visegrád was devastated in 1702 when the Hapsburgs destroyed its 13th-century citadel. The **citadel,** a former Roman outpost, provides a dramatic view of the Danube and surrounding hills. To reach it, head north on Fő út, go right on Salamontorony u., and follow the path. In the foothills above Fő út are the ruins of King Matthias's **Királyi Palota** (Royal Palace), once considered just a myth. Exhibits include a computerized reconstruction of the original palace. At the end of Salamontorony u., the King Matthias Museum inside **Alsóvár Salamon Torony** (Solomon's Tower) displays artifacts from the ruins. (Palace open Tu-Su 9am-5pm. Museum open May-Oct. Tu-Su 9am-5pm. Free. 50min. English-language tours 9000Ft.) The palace grounds relive their glory days with parades, jousting, and music during the mid-July **Viségrad Palace Games.** (☎30 93 7749; www.palotajatekok.hu.)

ESZTERGOM

Trains go to Budapest (1.5hr., 25 per day, 620Ft). To reach the main square from the train station, turn left on Baross Gábor út, then right on Kiss János Altábornagy út (becomes Kossuth Lajos u.). MAHART boats (☎01 484 4013; www.mahartpassnave.hu) leave the pier at Gőzhajó u. on Primas Sziget Island for Budapest (5hr., 3 per day, 1990Ft). Grantours, Széchenyi tér 25, at the edge of Rákóczi tér, assists tourists. (☎033 41 70 52; grantour@mail.holop.hu. Open July-Aug. M-F 8am-6pm, Sa 9am-noon; Sept.-June M-F 8am-4pm.)

A millennium of religious history revolves around the **Basilica of Esztergom,** a hilltop cathedral now the seat of the Hungarian Catholic Church. Although pilgrims travel here to see the relics of saints, the **cupola** has a stunning view of the Danube Bend. (☎33 40 23 54; www.bazilika-esztergom.hu. Open Mar.-Oct. Tu-Su 9am-4:30pm; Nov.-Dec. Tu-F 9am-4:30pm, Sa-Su 10am-3:30pm. Cupola 200Ft.) The red marble **Bakócz Chapel,** to the left of the nave, is a Renaissance masterpiece. (Open daily Mar.-Oct. 6:30am-6pm; Nov.-Dec. 7am-4pm. Free.)

EGER ☎036

In the 16th century, Eger (EGG-air; pop. 57,000) was the site of Captain István Dobó's legendary struggles against Ottoman conquest. The spirited cellars of the **Valley of the Beautiful Women** lure travelers from Budapest who seek the alleged strengthening powers of *Egri Bikavér* (Bull's Blood) wine.

TRANSPORTATION AND PRACTICAL INFORMATION. **Trains** leave from the station on Vasút u. (☎036 31 42 64) for Budapest (2hr.; 21 per day, 4 direct; 2290Ft). Indirect trains run to Budapest via Füzesabony. Trains also go to: Aggtelek (3hr., 8 per day, 2040Ft); Debrecen (3hr., 12 per day, 1710Ft); Szeged (5hr., 12 per day, 3830Ft); Szilvásvárad (1hr., 6 per day., 525Ft). **Buses** (☎036 51 77 77; www.agriavolan.hu) head from the station on Barkóczy u. to Budapest (2hr., 25-30 per day, 1600Ft). City Taxi (☎036 55 55 55) runs **cabs. Dobó tér,** the main square, is a 15min. from the train station. Walk straight and turn right on Deák Ferenc út, right on Kossuth Lajos u., and left on Jókai u. To get to the center from the bus station, turn right on Barkóczy u. from terminal #10 and right again at Bródy u. Follow the stairs to end of street, turn right on Széchenyi u., and go left down Érsek u. **TourInform** is at Bajcsy-Zsilinszky u. 9. (☎036 51 77 15; www.ektf.hu/eger. Open M-F 9am-5pm, Sa 9am-1pm.) **Postal Code:** 3300.

ACCOMMODATIONS AND FOOD. Private rooms are the best budget option; look for *"Zimmer frei"* or *"szòba eladò"* signs, particularly on Almagyar u. and Mekcsey István u. near the castle. **Eger Tourist** ❷, Bajcsy-Zsilinszky u. 9, next to TourInform, arranges private rooms that cost about 3500Ft. (☎036 51 70 00. Open M-F 9am-5pm.) Family-run **Lukács Vendéghaz** ❸, Bárány u. 10, next to Eger Castle, has a lush garden, an outdoor patio, and large, comfortable rooms. (☎036 41 15 67. Singles 3000Ft; doubles 5000Ft. Tourist tax 340Ft. Cash only.) Centrally located **Hotel Minaret** ❹, Knézich K. u. 4, features a gym, restaurant, and swimming pool. (☎036 41 02 33; www.hotelminaret.hu. All rooms with satellite TV. Singles 11,600Ft; doubles 15,900Ft; triples 24,400Ft; quads 28,900Ft. Prices about 2000Ft lower Nov.-Mar. AmEx/MC/V.) From the Valley of the Beautiful Women, follow signs to **Tulipan Camping** ❶, Szépasszonyvölgy. (☎036 410 580. Open mid-Apr. to mid-Oct. 24hr. Office open daily 8-10am and again 7-8pm. 700Ft per person, 600Ft per tent site. Cash only.)

Széchenyi utca is lined with restaurants. In the Valley of the Beautiful Women, crowds fill the courtyard of **Kulacs Csárda Panzió** ❸. (☎036 31 13 75; www.kulacscsarda.hu. Entrees 1200-2500Ft. Open daily noon-10pm. AmEx/MC/V.) Near Eger Castle, **Palacsintavár Étterem** ❷, Dobó u. 9, lures a steady stream of crepe-craving customers. (☎036 41 39 80. Crepes 640-1550Ft. Open daily noon-11pm. MC/V.) **Dobos Cukrászda** ❶, Széchenyi u. 6, serves mouth-watering desserts. (Ice cream 150Ft. Desserts 350-900Ft. Open daily 9:30am-10pm.)

SIGHTS AND FESTIVALS. To sample Eger's renowned vintage, wander through the web of **wine cellars** in the Valley of the Beautiful Women (Szépasszonyvölgy). Walk down Széchenyi u. with Eger Cathedral to your right, turn right on Kossuth Lajos u., and left when it dead-ends into Vörösmarty u. Take a right on Király u. and keep walking (25min.). Built into the hillside, the valley contains 200 cellars. Most consist of only a few tables with benches, but each has its own personality; some are hushed while others burst with Hungarian and Gypsy sing-alongs. (Open from 9am, closing times vary; July-Aug. some open until midnight. 0.1L taste 75-150Ft, 1L 350Ft.) In summer, open-air **baths** offer a break from the sweltering heat. (www.egertermal.hu. Open May-Sept. M-F 6am-7pm, Sa-Su 8am-7pm; Oct.-Apr. daily 9am-7pm. 1100Ft, students 900Ft., seniors 450Ft.) From late July to mid-August, Eger resonates with opera and early court music at the **Baroque Festival.**

HABITAT FOR HUNGAR

Habitat Global Villagers, a branch of Habitat for Humanit leads volunteers on brief trips t various, less-touristed Hungarian regions. Travelers spend anywhere from 10-20 days in a host village, constructing houses for low income families and immersing themselves in the local culture In 2008, HGV organized two volunteer excursions to the village o Szarvas, about 120 miles southeast of Budapest, to build homes for struggling residents.

No previous construction experience is required; HGV group leaders ask only that you bring your enthusiasm. In addition to volunteering, participants are also scheduled for several days o sightseeing time to explore Budapest. Costs vary depending upon the length of the volunteer project, and all prices include lodging food, ground transportation, trave medical insurance, orientation materials, and a small donation to the local village.

All projects led by experienced Habitat for Humanity group leaders. The website, www.habitat.hu has updated information about upcoming volunteer trips. Fo more information, interested parties can contact the host office in Budapest at Podmaniczky u. 9 (☎354 1084; habitat@habitat.hu). 2008 prices ranged from $1,500-$2,000, plus the cost o round-trip airfare to Budapest.

DAYTRIP FROM EGER: BARADLA CAVES. On the Slovak-Hungarian border, **Aggtelek National Park** is home to more than 1000 caves, including the ever-popular **Baradla Cave.** Knowledgeable guides lead 1km **tours,** beginning in an ancient cave where skeletons from the Neolithic period were found. Various events are held in the music hall; calendars of events are available at TourInform (☎036 50 30 00). Services range from 1hr. basic tours (daily 9am,10am, noon, 1, 3, 5, 6pm; low-season daily 10am, 11:30am, 1pm, 3pm; 2100Ft, students 1300Ft.) to 5hr. guided hikes (6000/3600Ft). Arrange longer tours with TourInform. The temperature is 10°C year-round, so bring a jacket. The caves can be visited as a daytrip from Eger, but you'll miss the return bus if you take a longer hike. The bus leaves Eger daily at 8:45am and arrives in Aggtelek at 11:25am, returning from the stop across the street at 3pm. From the **bus,** cross the street and go down the path to the caves; the park entrance is on the right. (☎50 30 00; www.anp.hu. Open daily Apr.-Sept. 8am-6pm; Oct.-Mar. 8am-4pm.)

GYŐR ☎096

In the unspoiled western region of Őrség, Győr (DYUR; pop. 130,000) overflows with monuments, museums, and 17th- and 18th-century architecture. Turn right out of the train station, take a left before the underpass, and cross the street to reach the pedestrian-only **Baross Gábor utca.** Walk uphill on Czuczor Gergely u., one street to the right of Baross Gábor u., and turn left at Gutenberg tér to reach the **Ark of the Covenant statue** (Frigylada szobov) and **Chapter Hill** (Káptalandomb). At the top of the hill is the **Episcopal Cathedral** (Székesegyház) with its **Weeping Madonna of Győr.** The **Diocesan Library and Treasury** (Egyházmegyei Kincstár), Káptalandomb 26, in an alley off the cathedral square, displays 14th-century gold and silver. (☎096 31 21 53; www.egyhazmegyeikincstar.hu. Open Mar.-Oct. Tu-Su 10am-4pm. 700Ft, students 400Ft.) The **Imre Patkó collection,** Széchenyi tér 4, presents contemporary art; buy tickets in the **Xántus Janos Museum** next door and enter at Stelczera u. (☎096 31 05 88; www.gymsmuzeum.hu. Open May-Sept. Tu-Su 10am-6pm, Oct.-Apr. daily noon-4pm. 550Ft, students 300Ft.) Across the river is the huge **Rába Quelle water park,** Fürdő tér 1, supplied by thermal springs. From Bécsi Kapu tér, take the bridge over the small island and make the first right on the other side, then go right again on Cziráky tér. (☎096 51 49 00; www.gyortermal.hu. Open daily 9am-8:30pm. 3hr. ticket 1550Ft, students 1100Ft; full-day ticket 2100/1700Ft.)

In an alley off Bécsi Kapu tér, **Katalin Kert ❹,** Sarkantyú köz 3, has beautiful rooms with private baths. (☎096 54 20 88; katalinkert@axelero.hu. Singles 7100Ft; doubles 9900Ft. Tax 330Ft per person. MC/V.) **Matróz Restauran ❷,** Dunakapu tér 3, off Jedlik Ányos u., serves succulent dishes. (Entrees 600-1400Ft. Open M-Th and Su 9am-10pm, F-Sa 9am-11pm.)

Trains run from Budapest (2hr., 34 per day, 2040Ft) and Vienna, AUT (2hr., 13 per day, 5250Ft). **Buses** run to Budapest (2hr., 1 per hr., 2040Ft). The train station is 3min. from the city center. An underpass links the platforms and leads to the bus station, heading away from the town. The **TourInform** kiosk, Árpád u. 32, at the intersection with Baross Gábor u., arranges lodgings. (☎096 31 17 71. Open June-Aug. M-F 8am-8pm, Sa-Su 9am-6pm.) **Postal Code:** 9021.

DAYTRIP FROM GYŐR: ARCHABBEY OF PANNONHALMA. Visible on a clear day from Győr, the hilltop **Archabbey of Pannonhalma** (Pannonhalmi Főapátság) has seen a millennium of destruction and renovation since it was established by the Benedictine order in AD 996. It now houses a 360,000-volume library and a 13th-century basilica. TriCollis **Tourist Office** is to the left of the entrance. *(☎57 01 91; www.bences.hu. Hungarian-language tour of abbey with English text 1 per hr. 1750Ft, students 850Ft. English-language tours June-Sept. daily 11:20am, 1:20, 3:20pm; Oct.-May Tu-Su*

11:20am and 1:20pm. 2400/1500Ft.) Tours of the on-site winery provide insight into traditional monastic viticulture. *(Tours daily June-Sept. 12:30, 2:30, 4:30pm; Oct.-Nov. and Apr.-May 11:30am, 1:30, 3:30pm; Dec.-Mar. 11:30am and 1:30pm. 750Ft, with tasting 1600Ft.)* From Győr, take the **bus** from platform #11 (45min., 7 per day, 375Ft). Make sure to ask for Pannonhalma vár and get off at the large gates.

LAKE BALATON

A retreat since Roman times, Lake Balaton drew the European elite in the 19th century, but is now a budget paradise for German/Austrian students.

SIÓFOK. The sheer density of tourist offices reflects Siófok's popularity with summer vacationers. **The Strand** is a series of lawns running to the shore; entry is free to some sections, and about 500Ft to others. The largest **private beach** lies to the right of town as you face the water. (800Ft, children 450Ft. Open M-F 8am-3am.) Bars and clubs line the lakefront. **Renegade Pub,** Petőfi sétány 3, is a crowded bar and dance club. Dress to impress. (Open June-Aug. daily 8pm-4am.) Join the debauchery at **The Palace,** 8600 Siófok-Ezüstpart, the always busy (and always crazy) summer hot spot of Lake Balaton. Take the free **Palace-bus** that runs from the front of the water tower (Víztorony) in the city center. (Bus 1 per hr. from 9pm. ☎84 351 295; www.palace.hu. Open June to early Sept. daily 10pm-5am.) Take a 25min. bus or train ride to Balatonszéplak felsö to reach **Villa Benjamin Youth Hostel ❷,** Siófoki u. 9. (☎084 350 704. Free Internet. Singles 3000Ft; doubles 6000Ft; triples 9000Ft; 4- to 6-person apartments 14,000-21,000Ft; 8- to 10-person house 28,000-35,000Ft. Tax 300Ft. 10% HI discount. Cash only.) **Balaton Véndegló és Panzió ❷,** Kinizsi u. 3, is a conveniently located hotel and restaurant with in-room televisions and A/C. (☎084 31 13 13. 2-person dorms 5000-7600Ft. MC/V.) **Trains** run to Budapest (2hr., 7 per day, 1250Ft). **Buses** head to Budapest (1hr., 9 per day, 1480Ft) and Pécs (3hr., 4 per day, 2550Ft). **Tourinform,** Fő út. at Szabadság tér, is in the water tower opposite the train station. (☎084 315 355; www.tourinform.hu. Open mid-June to mid-Sept. M-Sa 8am-8pm, Sa-Su 9am-6pm; mid-Sept. to mid-June M-F 9am-4pm.)

KESZTHELY. At the lake's western tip, Keszthely (KEST-hay), once the playground of the powerful Austro-Hungarian Festetics family, is home to thermal springs. The **Helikon Palace Museum** (Helikon Kastélymúzeum) in the Festetics Palace, is a storybook Baroque setting with an immense 90,000-volume library, extravagant chambers, an

LOCAL LEGEND

TALES FROM THE CRYP

Perhaps the most picturesque village on Lake Balaton's sandy shores, Tihany is an ideal setting for a tranquil afternoon stroll. However, if you find your peaceful walk suddenly and rudely interrupted by a group of people shouting then you've probably stumbled upon the legendary Echo Hill.

Located near the Benedictine Abbey, locals say that if you shou in the direction of the abbey from the top of the hill on a quiet day you can hear up to 15 syllables of your voice echoed back. While the echo may seem merely coincidental, it is said that something (or someone) inside the church is responsible for the phenomenon.

Within the dark crypt of the abbey lies the tomb of Andrew I, the fourth King of Hungary. The remains of the early king have been stored here since the year 1060, the only Hungarian royal tomb to remain in its original location. Andrew I ruled over the country for nearly 14 years until his brother, Duke Béla, led an open revolt against the king which resulted in his flight from the country and premature death. Ever since, legend has it tha Andrew has made sure that his own voice, alongside the voices o others, continues to echo over the lake's expansive waters.

So if you find yourself up on Echo Hill on a particularly quie day, holler in the direction of the abbey and you just may hear a voice answering back - whether o not it's yours is the real mystery.

exotic arms collection, and a porcelain exhibit. From Fő tér, follow Kossuth Lajos u. toward Tourinform (see below) until it becomes Kastély u. (Open July-Aug. daily 9am-6pm., June Tu-Su 9am-5pm, Sept.-May Tu-Su 10am-5pm. 1650Ft, students 800Ft.) **The Strand** draws crowds drawn to its giant slide, paddle boats, and volleyball nets. From the center, walk down Erzsébet Királyné u. as it curves right into Vörösmarty u., then cut through the park, crossing the train tracks on the other side to get to the beach. (Open mid-May to mid-Sept. daily 8:30am-7pm. 800Ft, children 600Ft. 6:30-7pm free.)

Just past the castle, the new **Ambient Hostel ❷,** Sopron 10, has impeccably clean facilities and a stylish bar/cafe. (☎460 35 36. Dorms 3000Ft; doubles 7000Ft; triples 10050Ft.) **Central Kiss Máté Panzió ❸,** Katona J u. 27, has spacious, apartment-style rooms with kitchen and bath. (☎83 31 90 72. Singles 5600Ft; doubles 9000Ft; triples 13500Ft. 300Ft city tax.) **Donatello ❷,** Balaton u. 1/A, serves pizza and pasta in an open courtyard. Though the restaurant is named after the **Teenage Mutant Ninja Turtle,** the vittles are genuine Italian masterpieces. (☎83 31 59 89. Pasta 700-1040Ft. Pizza 570-1470Ft. Open daily noon-10pm.)

Trains run to Budapest (3hr.; 13 per day; 2780Ft, reservations 440Ft). **Buses** run from near the train station to Pécs (4hr., 5 per day, 2320Ft). From the station, take Mártirok u., ending in Kossuth Lajos u., and turn left to reach the main square, Fő tér. **Tourinform,** Kossuth Lajos u. 28, has free **maps** and checks for room availability. (☎83 31 41 44. Open daily 9am-7pm.)

TIHANY. Scenic hikes, charming cottages, and panoramic views grace the Tihany Peninsula. Though slightly creepy, the fascinating **Dolls' Museum,** Visszhang u. 4, packs an impressive collection of 19th-century toys into two rooms. (Open Jan.-Sept. daily 9am-7pm, Oct.-Dec. 10am-5pm. 500Ft, students 400Ft.) The **Benedictine Abbey** (Bencés Apátság) draws over one million visitors annually with its luminous frescoes and gilded Baroque altars. (Open daily Mar.-Oct. 9am-6pm; last entry 5:30pm. 600Ft, students 300Ft.) The well-marked **green line trail** runs past the **Hermit's Place** (Barátlakások), where the cells and chapel hollowed by 11th-century hermits are still visible. MAHART **ferries** run to Siófok (1hr.; 6-9 per day; 1200 Ft, students 800Ft). To reach the town from the ferry pier and neighboring Strand, walk underneath the elevated road and follow the Apátság signs up the steep hill to the abbey.

PÉCS ☎062

Pécs (PAYCH; pop. 180,000), at the foot of the Mecsek mountains, is an animated university town, rich in bookstores, museums, and sidewalk cafes.

TRANSPORTATION AND PRACTICAL INFORMATION. **Trains** run to: Budapest (3hr., 4 per day, 2220Ft). To reach the train station, just south of the historic district, take bus #30, 32, or 33 from town, or walk for about 20min. down Szabadsag or Irganasok. Be alert on Irgalmasok, which can feel unsafe at night. **Buses** go to Budapest (4hr., 5 per day, 3010Ft) and Siófok (3hr., 3 per day, 350Ft). The bus station is 15min. from the old city; from the center take Irgalmasok and turn right on Nagy Lajos Kiraly (☎062 52 01 55). Local bus tickets cost 280Ft, but most places in the city are walkable. Tourinform is at Széchenyi tér 9. (☎062 21 26 32. Open June-Aug. M-F 8am-6pm, Sa-Su 10am-8pm, Sept. M-F 8am-6pm, Sa 9am-2pm, Oct.-May M-F 8am-4pm.) There are pharmacies at Széchenyi tér. Internet Cafe **Kávézó,** Ferencesek 32, offers speedy connections (10Ft per min.). It is relatively easy to find English-speakers here; students are generally eager to help. **Postal Code:** 7621.

ACCOMMODATIONS AND FOOD. The brand-new **Nap Hostel Pécs ❷,** Király 23-25, pairs a lively, youthful atmosphere with an unbeatable location in the city's historical center. (Entrance on Szent Mor. ☎062 72 950 684; www.naphostel.com. Breakfast, linens, and Internet included. Dorms 3000-4000Ft. Cash only.) **Pollack Mihály Students' Hostel ❷,** Jokai u. 8, has small, comfortable singles with clean shared baths. (☎062 51 36 50. Singles 2300Ft.) Take bus #21 from the main bus terminal or #43 from the train station and get off at 48-as tér, or walk 20min. up the hill to Rákóczi út. and turn right to reach **Universitas Kollégium ❶,** Universitas u. 2, behind McDonald's. (☎062 31 19 66. Reception 24hr. Check-out 9am. Open July-Aug. 3-bed dorms 1300Ft. Cash only.)

Pécs's bars, cafes, and restaurants are among its biggest attractions. Chill with artists and students at **Dante Cafe ❶,** Janus Pannonis u. 11, in a courtyard of the Csontváry Museum. (☎062 72 210 361; www.cafedante.hu. Beer 240-450Ft. Live jazz Sa-Su. Open daily 10am-1am.) If you're feeling ambitious, make the uphill trek to the **Hotel Kikelet ❹,** Károlyi Mihály 1, whose restaurant prepares elegant and affordable dishes. The real attraction, however, is the outdoor terrace's stunning panoramic view of the city below. (From the main square, walk up Hunyadi, take a right on Kálvária, a left on Szőlő, and walk uphill for 15min. ☎062 51 29 00; www.hotelkikelet.hu. Entrees 1700-3600Ft.) **Cellarium Étterem ❸,** Hunyadi u. 2, is a prison-themed restaurant buried in a cellar. The menu promises that the house champagne is "equal with a good foreplay on a table (instead of a bed)." Here, you can live out your fantasy of eating Hungarian fare while being served by waiters in inmate costumes. (☎062 314 453. Entrees 1200-4000Ft. Live Hungarian music on weekends. AmEx/MC/V.)

SIGHTS. The *atelier* at the **Zsolnay Museum,** Káptalan u. 4, exhibits the Zsolnay family's world-famous porcelains. There is also a reconstruction of the family's elegant residence. To get there, walk up Szepessy I. u. and turn left on Káptalan u. (☎062 514 040. Open May-Oct. Tu-Su 10am-6pm, Nov.-Apr. Tu-Su 10am-5pm. 750Ft, students 350Ft; photography 350Ft.) Across the street, the **Vasarely Museum,** Káptalan u. 5, displays the works of Viktor Vasarely, a pioneer of Op-Art. (☎062 51 40 40, ext. 21. Open Apr.-Oct. Tu-Sa 10am-6pm, Su 10am-4pm. 600Ft, students 350Ft; photography 400Ft, video 800Ft.) In the same yard, the unusual **Mecksek Museum** reproduces a traditional mine in a 400m cellar. Staffed by actual mine workers, it impressively reproduces a mine's claustrophobic feel. (Open Apr.-Oct. Tu-Sa 10am-6pm, Su 10am-4pm; Nov.-Mar. Tu-Su 10am-4pm. 500Ft, students 300Ft.) At central Széchenyi tér stands the **Gázi Khasim Pasa Dzsámija** (Mosque of Ghazi Kassim), once a Turkish mosque built on the site of an earlier church. Its modern fusion of Christian and Muslim traditions has made it a city emblem. (Open mid-Apr. to mid-Oct. M-Sa 10am-4pm, Su 11:30am-4pm; mid-Oct. to mid-Apr. M-Sa 10am-noon, Su 11:30am-2pm. Free.) Walk downhill from Széchenyi tér on Irgalmasok u. to Kossuth tér to find the **1869 Synagogue.** Its intricate ceiling frescoes and stunning Ark of the Covenant give it a magical aura. Its entrance details the history of the Holocaust and names the 112 local children killed in concentration camps. (Yarmulkes provided; mandatory for men. Open May-Sept. daily 10am-5pm. 300Ft, students 200Ft.) Atop Pécs's hill on **Dóm tér** is the fourth-century Romanesque Cathedral, whose towers are visible from anywhere in the city. (☎062 51 30 30. Open Apr.-Oct. M-Sa 9am-5pm, Su 1-5pm; Nov.-Mar. M-Sa 10am-4pm, Su 1pm-4pm. Mass M-Sa 6pm; Su 8, 9:30, 11am, and 6pm. 800Ft, students 500Ft.)

ICELAND (ÍSLAND)

Created when the European and North American continents collided, Iceland's landscape is uniquely warped and contorted, marked by active volcanoes and the tortoise-like crawl of advancing and retreating glaciers. Nature is the country's greatest attraction, and visitors can pick their way through sunken ice kettles, bathe in natural hot springs, and bike through fishing villages on mountainous dirt roads. An emphasis on natural farming has made Icelandic produce and meat sought-after exports: Icelandic dining is a pleasure. Covered by more glaciers and highly dependent on and protective of its fishing industry, Iceland is quickly becoming a hot tourist and ecotourist destination.

DISCOVER ICELAND: SUGGESTED ITINERARY

THREE DAYS. Start off in **Reykjavík** (p. 518) and explore the city center and **Laugardalur** (p. 523) while munching on a lamb hot dog. Spend the next day hiking through a **bird reserve** (p. 524), followed by soaking it up in a **thermal pool** (p. 524). Cap it all off with a picnic in **Heiðmörk Reserve** (p. 524).

ONE WEEK. After three days in **Reykajavík,** spend a day at **Þingvellir National Park** (p. 525). Soothe your sore muscles with a day soaking in the **Blue Lagoon** (p. 526). Make sure to catch a free tour at **Nesjavelliri** (p. 526), a power plant driven by geothermal heat. Spend your last day exploring the **Westman Islands** (p. 526).

ESSENTIALS

FACTS AND FIGURES

OFFICIAL NAME: Republic of Iceland.

CAPITAL: Reykjavík.

MAJOR CITIES: Akureyri, Ísafjörður, Kópavogur, Hafnarfjörður.

POPULATION: 302,000.

TIME ZONE: GMT.

LANGUAGE: Icelandic.

PERCENTAGE OF ARABLE LAND: 0.07%.

EXPORT EARNINGS PROVIDED BY THE FISHING INDUSTRY: 70%.

WHEN TO GO

Visitors should brave peak-season crowds to enjoy all Iceland has to offer. From June through August, travelers will have the most accommodation and transportation options. The sky never quite gets dark in summer months, though the sun dips below the horizon for a few hours each night. July temperatures average around 11°C (52°F). December and January receive four or five hours of sunlight daily, but the nights are illuminated by **aurora borealis,** the famous Northern Lights. Winter in Reykjavík averages 0°C (32°F), making transportation slower and less reliable.

BURNING THE MIDNIGHT OIL. During the summer months, the sun never quite sets over Iceland. While the near 24hr. sunlight makes for easy all-night partying, it can take its toll on visitors. Bring a sleeping mask and over-the-counter, non-habit-forming sleep aids to avoid sleepless nights.

DOCUMENTS AND FORMALITIES

EMBASSIES AND CONSULATES. Foreign embassies in Iceland are in Reykjavík. Icelandic embassies and consulates abroad include: **Australia,** 16 Hann St., Griffith, Canberra (☎262 95 68 19; benefitfarm@bigpond.com.au); **Canada,** 360 Albert St., Ste. 710, Ottawa, ON K1R 7X7 (☎613-482-1944; www.iceland.org/ca); **Ireland,** Cavendish House, Smithfield, Dublin (☎1 872 9299; jgg@goregrimes.ie); **New Zealand,** Sanford Ltd., 22 Jellicoe St., Auckland (☎9 379 4720); **UK,** 2A Hans St., London SW1X 0JE (☎020 72 59 39 99; www.iceland.org/uk); **US,** 1156 15th St. NW, Ste. 1200, Washington, D.C. 20005 (☎202-265-6653; www.iceland.org/us).

VISA AND ENTRY INFORMATION. EU citizens do not need a visa. Citizens of Australia, Canada, New Zealand, and the US do not need a visa for stays of up to 90 days, beginning upon entry into any of the countries in the EU's freedom-of-movement zone. For more info, see p. 14. For stays longer than 90 days, all non-EU citizens need visas, available at embassies abroad; check www.utl.is/english/visas/apply to find the nearest location.

TOURIST SERVICES AND MONEY

EMERGENCY	**Ambulance, Fire,** and **Police:** ☎112.

MONEY. Iceland's unit of currency is the **króna (ISK),** plural **krónur.** One króna is equal to 100 **aurars,** with standard denominations of 1, 5, 10, 50, and 100kr in coins, and 500, 1000, and 5000kr in notes. For currency exchange, **ATMs** are located throughout the larger cities. **Banks** are usually open M-F 9:15am-4pm. Major Icelandic banks, such as Landsbankinn, do not have sister banks in other countries that allow lower exchange fees. In general, there's no way around the high costs in Iceland. On average, a night in a hostel will cost 1700ISK, a guesthouse 3000-4000ISK, and a meal's worth of groceries 700-1200ISK. Restaurants include a service charge on the bill. **Tipping** is discouraged.

ICELANDIC KRÓNUR (ISK)		
	AUS$1 = 54.36ISK	100ISK = AUS$1.84
	CDN$1 = 64.31ISK	100ISK = CDN$1.56
	EUR€1 = 91.84ISK	100ISK = EUR€1.09
	NZ$1 = 47.42ISK	100ISK = NZ$2.11
	UK£1 = 135.01ISK	100ISK = UK£0.74
	US$1 = 68.16ISK	100ISK = US$1.47

Iceland has a 24.5% **value added tax (VAT),** a sales tax on goods and services purchased within the **European Economic Area** (EEA: the EU plus Iceland, Liechtenstein, and Norway). The prices given in *Let's Go* include VAT. In the airport upon exiting the EEA, non-EEA citizens can claim a refund on the tax paid for goods at participating stores. In order to qualify for a refund in a store, you

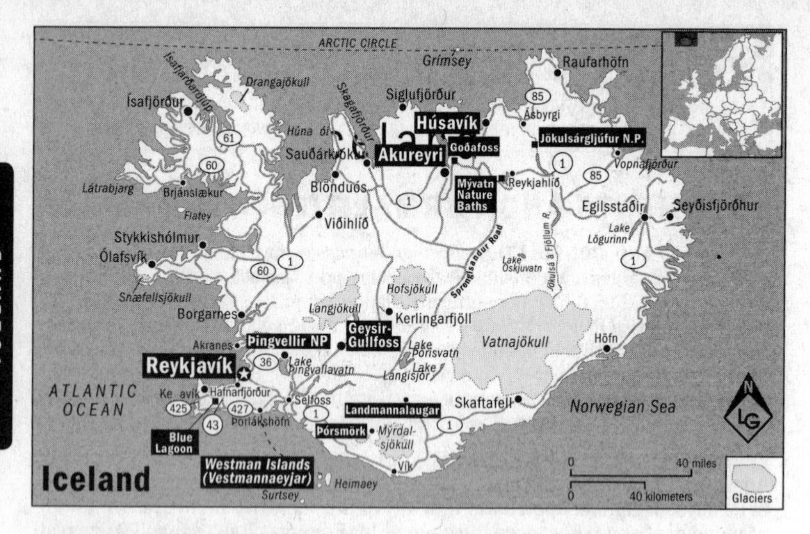

must spend at least 4000ISK; make sure to ask for a refund form when you pay. For more info on qualifying for a VAT refund, see p. 21.

TRANSPORTATION

BY PLANE. Iceland's main international airport is **Keflavik International Airport** (**KEF;** ☎ 425 6000; www.keflavikairport.com), which is 50km southwest of Reykjavík. **Icelandair** (Iceland ☎505 0700, UK 0870 787 4020, US and Canada 800-223-5500; www.icelandair.net) flies to Reykjavík year-round from Europe and the US. They also provide free stop-overs of up to seven days on flights to many European cities. No-frills **Iceland Express** (Iceland ☎550 0600, UK 0870 240 5600; www.icelandexpress.com) flies to nine Western European countries on the cheap. Icelandair's domestic counterpart, **Air Iceland** (☎570 3030; www.airiceland.is), flies from Reykjavík to most major towns in Iceland and Greenland.

SOARING PRICES. To get the most for your money, consider traveling by plane instead of bus. Discount airfare is often just as expensive, or cheaper, than terrestrial tickets. Check with Air Iceland for more info.

BY BUS. Several bus lines are organized by **Bifreiðastöð Íslands** (**BSÍ;** www.bsi.is); buses can be cheaper and more scenic than flights, although they run infrequently in the low-season. From mid-June to August, buses run daily on the **Ring Road (Route 1),** the highway that circles Iceland. Even then the going is slow; some unpaved stretches still exist in the east. The **Full Circle Passport** lets travelers circle the island at their own pace on the Ring Road (June-Aug.; 25,900ISK). However, it only allows travel in one direction, so travelers must move either clockwise or counter-clockwise around the country to get back to where they started. For an extra 19,200ISK, the pass provides access to the Westfjords in the extreme northwest. The **Omnibus Passport** is valid for periods of up to four weeks for unlimited travel on all scheduled bus routes, including non-Ring roads (1-week 26,900ISK, 2-week 42,000ISK, 3-week 50,000ISK; valid

May 15-Sept. 15). Travelers, especially those arriving in groups of two or more, should note that the inflexibility of the Full Circle Passport and the high cost of the Omnibus Passport make car rental a good idea for those planning on visiting rural parts of the country. Iceland has no intercity train service.

BY FERRY. The best way to see Iceland's gorgeous shoreline is on the **Norröna** ferry (☎983 5900; www.smyril-line.fo, website in Icelandic) that crosses the North Atlantic to Hanstholm, DEN; Tórshavn in the Faroe Islands; and Seyðisfjörður. From Tórshavn, you can either continue on to Bergen, NOR, or return to Seyðisfjörður. An **Eimskip Transport** liner leaves Reykjavík weekly and takes five days to get to continental ports at Thorshavn, Rotterdam, Hamburg, Fredrikstad, and Århus. (Reservations ☎525 7800; www.eimskip.com.)

BY CAR. Rental cars provide the most freedom for travelers and may even be the cheapest option for those who want to visit rural areas. Getting a car and touring Iceland's Ring Road (Rte. 1), which circles the entire island and passes many of the best destinations, is a popular way to explore the country. Book before you arrive for lower rates. Car rental *(bílaleiga)* companies charge 4000-8000ISK per day for a small car, and 10,000-25,000ISK for the **four-wheel-drive vehicles** that are imperative outside settled areas. On these routes, drivers should bring a container of extra gas, since some roads continue for 300km without a single gas station and strong headwinds can significantly affect the rate of fuel consumption. It is not uncommon for local drivers to **ford streams** in their vehicles; do not attempt this in a compact car, and cross in a convoy if possible. (24hr. reports on road conditions ☎800 6316, June-Aug. in English.) Drivers are required to wear seat belts and to keep their headlights on at all times. Iceland recognizes foreign driver's licenses, but you may need to purchase insurance for the rental vehicle (1500-3500ISK).

BY BIKE AND BY THUMB. Ferocious winds, driving rain, and gravel roads make long-distance cycling difficult. Hug the Ring Road if you prefer company; for less-traveled paths, branch out to the coastal roads that snake their way through the Eastfjords, or check **Cycling in Iceland** (http://home.wanadoo.nl/erens/icecycle.htm). Also check out the **Icelandic Mountain Bike Club,** Brekkustíg. 2, in Reykjavík, or drop by their clubhouse on the first Thursday night of each month after 8pm for some advice (☎562 0099; www.fjallahjolaklubburinn.is). Buses will carry bikes for a 500-900ISK fee, depending on the route. Hitchhikers try the roads in summer, but sparse traffic and harsh weather exacerbate the risks. Still, rides can be found with relative ease between Reykjavík and Akureyri; flagging down a ride is harder in the east and the south. *Let's Go* does not recommend hitchhiking.

KEEPING IN TOUCH

PHONE CODES	**Country code:** 354. **International dialing prefix:** 00. There are no city codes in Iceland. For more info on how to place international calls, see **Inside Back Cover.**

EMAIL AND INTERNET. Internet is widespread. Seek out libraries in small towns for Internet. At cafes, a connection will cost 200-300ISK per hour.

TELEPHONE. The state-owned telephone company, **Síminn,** usually has offices in post offices, where you can buy phone cards and get the best international call rates. **Pay phones** accept prepaid phone cards, credit cards (cheapest for calls to **mobile phones**), as well as 10ISK, 50ISK, and 100ISK coins. Iceland uses two different mobile phone networks: digital GSM phones service 98% of the country's population, but only a small fraction of its land area, so hikers, fishermen, and others who travel outside of settled areas rely on analog NMT phones. Prepaid GSM phone cards are available at gas stations and convenience stores. OG Vodafone generally offers the best prepaid rates. For operator assistance, dial ☎118; for international assistance, dial ☎1811. International direct dial numbers include: **AT&T Direct** (☎800 222 55 288); **British Telecom** (☎800 89 0354); **Canada Direct** (☎800 9010); **Telecom New Zealand** (☎800 9064).

MAIL. Mailing a letter or postcard (up to 20g) from Iceland costs from 60ISK within Iceland, from 70ISK to Europe, and from 80ISK outside of Europe. Post offices *(póstur)* are generally open M-F 9am-6pm in Reykjavík and 9am-4:30pm in the countryside. Check www.postur.is for additional info. To receive mail in Iceland, have mail delivered **Poste Restante.** Mail will go to the main post office unless you specify a subsidiary by street address. Address mail to be held according to the following example (Reykjavík): First name, Last name, Poste Restante, ÍSLANDSPÓSTUR, Posthússtr. 5, 101 Reykjavík, ICELAND.

LANGUAGE. Icelandic is a Nordic language which developed in 9th-century Norway and came into its present form in 12th-century Iceland. It is a very pure form of the old Norwegian language of the vikings. Most Icelanders, especially those under 35, speak at least some English.

ACCOMMODATIONS AND CAMPING

ICELAND	❶	❷	❸	❹	❺
ACCOMMODATIONS	under 2000ISK	2000-3000ISK	3001-5000ISK	5001-10,000ISK	over 10,000ISK

Iceland's **HI youth hostels** are clean and reasonably priced at roughly 1800-2300ISK for nonmembers. HI members receive a 150-400ISK discount. Visit **Hostelling International Iceland,** Sundlaugarvegur 34, 105 Reykjavík (☎553 8110; www.hostel.is), for locations and pricing as well as for info on Iceland's seven eco-friendly Green Hostels. Expect to pay around 2100ISK for sleeping bag accommodations (*svefnpokapláss;* beds with no linens or blankets) and another 650ISK for linens. **Guesthouses** and **farmhouses** (☎570 2700; www.farmholidays.is) are a cheap, homey option outside cities. Many remote lodgings will pick up tourists in the nearest town for a small fee. Campers can choose among Iceland's 125 designated **campsites** (usually open June-Aug.). Camping outside official sites is prohibited. Official campsites range from grassy areas with cold-water taps to sumptuous facilities around Reykjavík; listings can be found at www.camping.is. Most charge around 600-800ISK, and many don't allow open flames (so be sure to bring a camp stove). Visit www.infoiceland.is/infoiceland/accommodation/camping for tips.

FOOD AND DRINK

ICELAND	❶	❷	❸	❹	❺
FOOD	under 500ISK	500-1000ISK	1001-1400ISK	1401-2000ISK	over 2000ISK

Iceland is in the middle of a culinary explosion. A history of food shortages led Iceland to value all that was pickled, dried, or smoked. But now, with more exotic methods and flavors introduced by a trickle of Asian immigrants, not everything is simply boiled and salted. Fresh **fish** and gamey free-range

lamb—staples of Icelandic cuisine—remain essentials. But they're being mixed in new and delicious ways with vitamin-rich vegetables grown in greenhouse towns (such as Hveragerði) and a range of cheeses. Still, tradition is strong: *skyr*, a dairy product that tastes like a cross between yogurt and fresh cheese, and *hangikjot*, smoked lamb sandwiches, are more popular than ever. Food in Iceland is very expensive, and a cheap restaurant meal will cost at least 800ISK. **Grocery stores** are the way to go in virtually every town. **Alcohol** presents the same quandary: beer costs 500-600ISK for a large glass (0.5L, approx. 17 oz.) at pubs and cafes, while the price of hard liquor is even steeper. The country's national drink is *brennivín*, a schnapps made from potato, usually seasoned with caraway, and nicknamed "Black Death." Bootleggers in the countryside cook up batches of *landi*, a potent homemade moonshine, in protest against high liquor taxes. *Let's Go* does not recommend moonshine.

HOLIDAYS AND FESTIVALS

Holidays: New Year's Day (Jan. 1); Maundy Thursday (Apr. 9, 2009; Apr. 1, 2010); Good Friday (Apr. 10, 2009; Apr. 2, 2010); Easter (Apr. 12, 2009; Apr. 4, 2010); Sumardagurinn Fyrsti (1st day of summer; Apr. 24); Ascension (May 1); Pentecost (May 31, 2009; May 23, 2010); National Day (June 17); Tradesman's Day (Aug. 4); Christmas (Dec. 25); Boxing Day (Dec. 26).

Festivals: The month-long **Þorrablót festival** (during Feb.) is a holdover from the mid-winter feasts of past centuries. Icelanders eat *svi* (singed and boiled sheep's head), *hrútspungur* (pickled ram's testicles), and *hákarl* (shark meat that has been allowed to rot underground) in commemoration of their heritage. **"Beer Day,"** celebrated in bars and restaurants, celebrates the March 1st, 1989 lifting of a 75yr. prohibition. **Sumardagurinn Fyrsti** marks the 1st day of summer with a carnival. The Reykjanes Peninsula celebrates **Sjómannadagur** (Seamen's Day) on June 4 with boat races and tug-of-war. During the 1st weekend in August, Icelanders head to the country for **Verslunarmannahelgi** for barbecues, camping, and drinking.

BEYOND TOURISM

Travelers hoping to stay in Iceland may be able to secure summer work. Check www.eurojobs.com for info on job placement. Ecotourism opportunities abound; organizations run tours on horseback to hot springs and up mountains. For more info on opportunities across Europe, see **Beyond Tourism,** p. 60.

Earthwatch Institute, 3 Clock Tower Pl., Ste. 100, Box 75, Maynard, MA, 01754 (Canada and US ☎800-776-0188, UK 44 18 65 31 88 38, Australia 03 96 82 68 28; www.earthwatch.org). For a hefty fee (€2095), Earthwatch organizes volunteers, guided by scientists, to conduct geological fieldwork in the Icelandic glaciers. They also coordinate fundraising efforts to curtail the fee.

International Cultural Youth Exchange, Große Hamburger Str. 30, Berlin, GER (☎49 30 28 39 05 50; www.icye.org). ICYE brings together volunteers and host organizations on a variety of projects worldwide, including several in Iceland. ICYE also organizes European Voluntary Service programs (http://europa.eu.int/comm/youth/program/guide/action2_en.html) for EU citizens to serve for a fully funded year in another EU country.

Volunteers for Peace (☎802-259-2759; www.vfp.org). Runs 2800 "workcamps" throughout the world, including several in Iceland. $250 per 2- to 3-week workcamp, including room and board, plus $20 VFP membership fee.

REYKJAVÍK

Home of 60% of Icelanders, Reykjavík (pop. 200,000) is a modestly sized capital with an international clubbing reputation. Bold, modern architecture along with white painted concrete structures rise above the blue waters of the Faxaflói Bay. The city's refreshingly clear air complements the clean streets and well-kept gardens. The spring rain and the endless winter night force social life indoors for much of the year, where many locals sip espresso while arguing over environmental policy in this hub of renewable energy.

TRANSPORTATION

Flights: International flights arrive at **Keflavík Airport (KEF),** 55km from Reykjavík. From the main exit, catch a **Flybus** (☎562 1011; www.flybus.is) to **BSÍ Bus Terminal** (45min.; 1500ISK, round-trip 2700ISK). Flybus also offers free transport from the bus terminal to many hostels and hotels; ask or check website for more info. A public bus to the city center runs from Gamla-Hringbraut across the street from the bus terminal (M-F 7am-midnight, Sa-Su 10am-midnight; 280ISK). Flybus service to the airport departs from BSÍ; but most hostels and hotels can also arrange for bus pick-up. Nearby **Reykjavík Airport (RKV)** is the departure point for domestic flights. Take bus #15.

Buses: Umferðarmiðstöð BSÍ (BSÍ Bus Terminal), Vatnsmrarvegur 10 (☎562 1011; www.bsi.is), off Gamla-Hringbraut. Walk 15-20min. south along Tjörnin from the city center or take bus #1, 3, 5, or 14. (2-3 per hr., 280ISK). Open daily 4:30am-midnight.

Public Transportation: Bus service can be infrequent and roundabout; walking is often a speedier option. **Strætó** (☎540 2700; www.straeto.is) operates yellow city buses (280ISK). **Lækjartorg,** on Lækjargata, is the main bus station for the city center. Hlemmur, 1km east of Lækjartorg where Hverfisgata meets Laugavegur, is another major terminal, with more connections than Lækjartorg (open while buses run. After 8pm buy tickets at kiosk). Pick up a schedule at the terminal. Don't feel bad asking for navigational help at hostels and info desks—recent changes in the bus routes have confused even some drivers. Buy packages of 11 adult fares (2500ISK) or a day pass for 600kr, 3 day pass for 1500kr. Pay fare with coins; drivers do not give change. Ticket packages are sold at the terminal, city hall, and at swimming pools. If you need to change buses, ask the driver of the 1st bus for *skiptimiði* (free transfer ticket), valid for 1hr. after the fare has been paid. Most buses 2-3 per hr. M-Sa 7am-midnight, Su 10am-midnight.

Taxis: BSR (☎561 0000; www.bsr.is). 24hr. service. **Hreyfill** (☎588 5522; www.hreyfill.is/english). Also offers private tours for groups of 1-8.

Car Rental: Berg, Tangarhöfða 10 (☎577 6050; www.bergcar.is). Unlimited distance with insurance from 9000ISK per day; low-season reduced rates. Pick-up available at Keflavík and Reykjavík Airports. Berg is generally the cheapest option other than **Vaka** (567 6700, www.vakabilar.is. Reserve ahead). Fuel costs around 300ISK per L. Iceland can be a difficult country to drive in. Drivers should stick to the rim-road and exercise caution. See www.visitreykjavik.is for more information on car rental.

Bike Rental: Reykjavík Youth Hostel campground (p. 521). 1500ISK per 4hr., 2500ISK per day. Helmet included. **Borgarhjól,** Hverfisgata 50, is closer to the city center, down the road from Culture House. (☎551 5653; www.borgarhjol.net. Fees change frequently, though generally similar to those above.)

Hitchhiking: Many foreigners hitchhike outside of Reykjavík because of confusing bus routes, but it is never completely safe. *Let's Go* does not recommend hitchhiking.

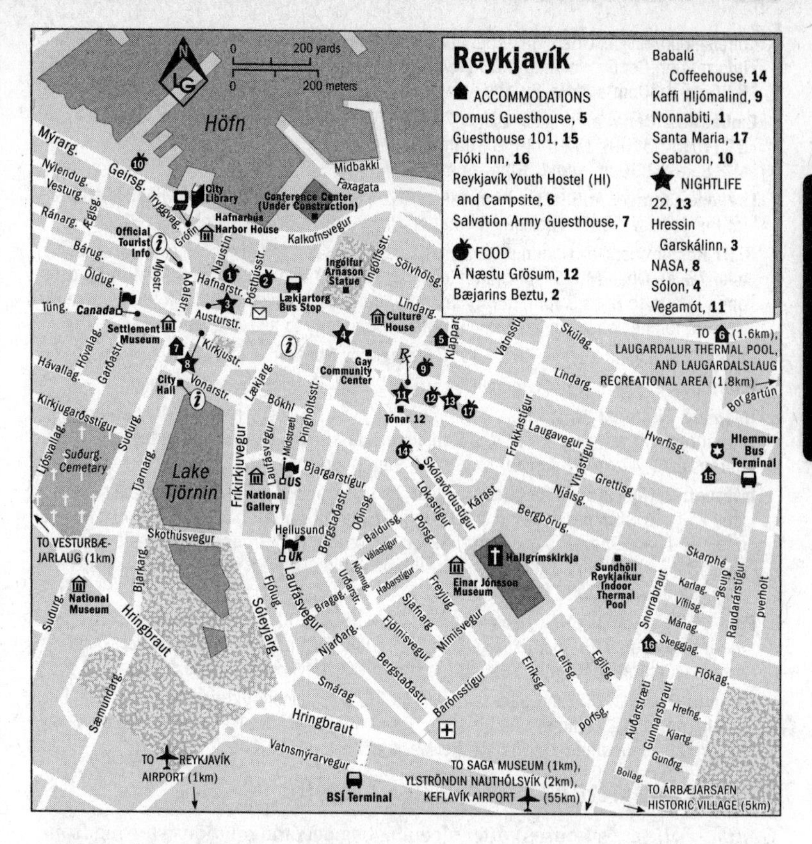

ORIENTATION AND PRACTICAL INFORMATION

Lækjartorg is Reykjavík's main square and a navigational base. Lækjargata, a main street, leads southwest from Lækjartorg and becomes **Fríkirkjuvegur** when it reaches **Lake Tjörnin** (the Pond), the southern limit of the city center. Reykjavík's main thoroughfare extends eastward from Lækjartorg, changing names from Austurstræti to Bankastræti and then to **Laugavegur,** as it is commonly known. Helpful publications, including *What's On in Reykjavík*, *Reykjavík City Guide*, and *The Reykjavík Grapevine*, are available for free at tourist offices and around the city. *The Grapevine*, published by American expatriates, includes opinionated local news coverage and comprehensive listings of current music and arts events as well as some helpful tips for travelers.

Tourist Offices: Upplsingamiðstöð Ferðamanna í Reykjavík, Adalstræti 2 (☎590 1550; www.visitreykjavik.is). Open from June to mid-Sept. daily 8:30am-7pm; Sept.-May M-F 9am-6pm, Sa 9am-4pm, Su 10am-2pm. Sells the Reykjavík Card (1-day 1200ISK, 2-day 1700ISK, 3-day 2200ISK), which allows unlimited public transportation, free entry to some sights and thermal pools (p. 523), and limited **Internet** at the tourist center. Several discount coupon books are also available at the center. Tourist Information Center, Bankastræti 2 (☎522 4979; www.itm.is) is just off of Laugavegur and offers solid advice. Open May-Aug. daily 8am-7pm; Sept.-May. M-F 10am-5pm. City Hall Information Center, Vonarstræti 3 (☎411 1005), is in the lobby of City Hall. Open M-F 8:30am-4:30pm and Sa-Su noon-4pm.

Embassies: Canada, Túngata 14 (☎575 6500). Open M-F 9am-noon. **UK,** Laufásvegur. 31 (☎550 5100). Open M-F 8:30am-noon. **US,** Laufásvegur 21 (☎562 9100). Open M-F 8am-12:30pm and 1:30pm-5pm.

Luggage Storage: At BSÍ Bus Terminal (☎562 1011), next to the ticket window. 400ISK for the 1st day, 200ISK per day thereafter. Open daily 4:30am-midnight.

GLBT Resources: Gay Community Center, Laugavegur 3, 4th fl. (☎552 7878; www.samtokin78.is). Open M-F 1-5pm (unofficially 9am-5pm) and Sa in winter 9am-5pm; cafe open M and Th 8-11:30pm; library open M and Th 8-11pm. More info at www.gayice.is. Be sure to check out the gay pride events in from early to mid-Aug. each year.

Police: Hverfisgata 113 (☎444 1000). **Emergency Number** ☎112.

Pharmacy: Lyfja Lágmúla, Lágmúla 5 (☎533 2300). Open daily 8am-midnight.

Hospital: National Hospital, on Hringbraut (☎543 1000), has a 24hr. emergency department. To save money try the **Heilsurverndarstödin**—the Health Center for Tourists Barónsstígur 47. (☎458 9060. Open M-F 9am-midnight.)

Internet: Reykjavík Public Library, Tryggvagur 15 (☎563 1705), is the cheapest option. Free Wi-Fi, 200ISK per hr. Open M-Th 10am-7pm, F 11am-7pm, Sa-Su 1-5pm. In winter, open M 10am-9pm, F 11am-7pm, Sa-Su 1-5pm. MC/V. **Ground Zero,** Vallarstræti 4 (☎562 7776), at Ingòlfstorg Sq. 300ISK per 30min., 500ISK per hr. Open M-F 11am-1am, Sa-Su noon-1am. AmEx/MC/V.

Post Office: Íslandspóstur, Pósthússtræti 5 (☎580 1000), in a big red building, is at the intersection with Austurstræti. Open M-F 9am-6:00pm. **Poste Restante** available; send to: Central Post Office Pósthússtræti 5 I5-101 Reykjavik, Iceland.

Alcohol: The legal drinking age in Iceland is 20. Most alcohol is not sold in stores but at **Vinbuð,** the government liquor store. Open M-Th, Sa-Su 11am-6pm, F 11am-7pm. MC/V. One is located in downtown Reykjavik at Austurstræti 10a.

ACCOMMODATIONS AND CAMPING

Gistiheimili (guesthouses) offer sleeping-bag accommodations starting from 2500ISK (bed and pillow in a small room; add 300-600ISK for linens). Hotels cost at least 6500ISK. Call ahead for reservations, especially in summer.

Reykjavík Youth Hostel (HI), Sundlaugarvegur 34 (☎553 8110). Bus #14 from Lækjargata. This popular, eco-friendly hostel is east of the city center, but it's adjacent to Reykjavík's largest thermal pool and has excellent facilities. The staff gives tips for exploring the city's less touristy sights. Breakfast 900ISK. Linens 700ISK. Laundry 350ISK per token. Free Wi-Fi; Internet 300ISK per 30min, 500ISK per hr. Reception 8am-midnight; ring bell after hours. Dorms 2300ISK, HI 1850ISK; doubles 4500/3800ISK. Pre-pitched tents 1450ISK per person. AmEx/MC/V. ❷

Domus Guesthouse, Hverfisgata 45 (☎561 1200). Take bus #13, 1, 3, or 6 and get off across from the Regnboginn movie theater on Hverfisgötu. Close to the city center, the guesthouse offers spacious rooms with TVs and couches. All sleeping-bag accommodations are located across the street. Breakfast included with private rooms. Open mid-May-Sept. Reception 2pm-midnight, ring doorbell after. Sleeping-bag accommodations 3900ISK; singles 9900ISK; doubles 11,900ISK. MC/V. ❸

Flóki Inn, Flókagata 1 (☎552 1155; www.innsoficeland.is), a 15min. walk from the city center. A relaxing, intimate guesthouse. Breakfast included. Reception 24hr. Free Wi-Fi, Internet 350ISK per. 15min. Some rooms have kitchen available. Singles 8800ISK; doubles 11,500ISK. Extra bed 2500ISK. Reduced prices Oct.-May. AmEx/MC/V. ❹

Salvation Army Guesthouse, Kirkjustræti 2 (☎561 3203; www.guesthouse.is). Located near City Hall in the heart of Reykjavík, this bright yellow hostel is cozy with modest accommodations. Its prime location makes it ideal for exploring the nightlife. 24hr. reception. Breakfast 800ISK. Sleeping-bag accommodations 3000ISK; singles 6600ISK; doubles 9600ISK. Reduced prices in winter. AmEx/MC/V. ❷

Guesthouse 101, Laugavegur 101 (☎562 6101; www.iceland101.com), off Snorrabraut (29) on the third fl. This converted office building east of the city center has small, bright, modern rooms. Wheelchair-accessible. Breakfast included. Singles 7600ISK; doubles 9900ISK. Reduced prices in winter. AmEx/MC/V. ❹

Reykjavík Youth Hostel Campsite (☎568 6944), next to the hostel. Helpful staff and a sociable character make this a good alternative. Luggage storage 300ISK. Reception 24hr. Open from mid-May to mid-Sept. Tent sites 850ISK. 4-person cabins 5000ISK. Showers. Electricity 400ISK. Can use hostel's facillties as well. AmEx/MC/V. ❶

FOOD

An Icelandic meal featuring *hákarl* (shark meat that has been allowed to rot underground), lamb, or puffin generally costs 1500ISK or more, but worth the splurge at least once. Check out the harbor area outside downtown for some affordable seafood. To maintain a leaner budget, check out the lunch specials throughout the city (www.restaurant.is) and cook for yourself in the evenings. Pick up groceries at **Bónus,** Laugavegur 59. (☎562 8200. Open M-F noon-6:30pm, Sa 10am-8pm.) Other restaurants are on **Austurstræti** and **Hverfisgata.**

Á Næstu Grösum, Laugavegur 20B (☎552 8410), entrance off Klapparstígur. This 2nd fl. all-vegetarian restaurant, the 1st in Iceland, uses fresh, seasonal ingredients in creative ways. The airy dining room showcases the work of up-and-coming local artists. Soup (800ISK) comes with free refills. Daily special 1490ISK. 3 items, rice and salad 1590ISK. Vegan options. Open M-F 11:30am-10pm, Su 5-10pm. MC/V. ❷

Santa Maria, Laugavegur 22A (☎552 7775). Recently opened, this authentic Mexican restaurant has gained popularity for a menu where nothing is over 1000ISK. MC/V. ❶

Babalú Coffeehouse, Skólavördustigur 22A (☎552 2278). Near the church, the second floor cafe is a perfect place to relax. Serves savory crepes (950ISK) and smaller, sweet crepes (650ISK). Enjoy a coffee (300ISK) on the patio. Free Wi-Fi. Open daily in summer 11am-10pm; in winter noon-7:30pm. AmEx/MC/V. ❷

Kaffi Hljómalind, Laugavegur 23 (☎517 1980), east of the city center. Organic, vegetarian-friendly cafe serves big portions of soup, with free refill and bread (700ISK). Breakfast combination 1050ISK. Free Wi-Fi, vocal patrons, a box of toys, and large windows make this a great place for people-watching or passing the time. Live music or poetry reading usually W 8pm. Open M-F 9am-10pm, Sa-Su 11am-10pm. MC/V. ❷

Shalimar, Austurstræti 4 (☎551 0292). Spice it up with this traditional Indian restaurant in the heart of downtown. Get some naan (300ISK) with your dinner special (1290ISK). Open M-F 11am-10pm, Sa 4pm-11pm, Su 4pm-10pm. AmEx/MC/V. ❸

Seabaron Restaurant, Geirsgata 8 (☎553 1500). Famous for its lobster soup (950ISK), it also offers fish and whale kabobs (1200ISK-1500ISK). Try it out for lunch. Open in summer daily 11:30am-10pm; in winter 11:30am-9pm. MC/V. ❸

Nonnabiti, Hafnarstræti 11 (☎551 2312), west of Lækjartorgata toward the main tourist office. This sandwich shop is good for cheap, tasty meals. Burgers 690-1000ISK. Hot sandwiches 500-830ISK. 100ISK discount on subs M-F 9:30am-1:30pm. Open M-Th 9am-2am, F 9am-5:30am, Sa 10am-5:30am, Su noon-midnight. AmEx/MC/V. ❶

Bæjarins Beztu, corner of Tryggvagur and Pósthússtræti. This tiny stand on the harbor serves the Icelandic hot dog (230ISK) by which all others are measured. The owner proudly displays a picture of Bill Clinton eating one of her hot dogs, served up with "the works." You know you've found it when you see the perpetual line outside the small red kiosk. Weekend crowds head here to satisfy late-night cravings, often singing while they wait. Open until 12:30am, or until crowds dissipate—sometimes past 6am. MC/V. ❶

SIGHTS

CITY CENTER. Reykjavík's City Hall, on the northern shore of Lake Tjörnin, houses an impressive **three-dimensional model** of Iceland that vividly renders the country's striking topography. *(Open in summer M-F 8am-7pm, Sa-Su 10-6pm; winter M-F 8am-7pm, Sa-Su noon-6pm. Free.)* Just beyond City Hall lies **Aðalstræti,** the oldest street in the city. The recently opened 871 +/- 2 **Settlement Museum,** 16 Aðalstræti, in the basement of Hotel Reykjavik Centrum, features the preserved foundation of a Viking longhouse, with interactive displays and artifacts. By dating surrounding volcanic deposits, archaeologists theorize that the structure was built around AD 869-873. *(☎411 6370. Open daily 10am-5pm. 600ISK. AmEx/MC/V.)* Nearby is the oldest house in the city, **Fogetastofur,** Aðalstræti 10, built in 1762, which offers exhibits, pictures, and maps describing Reykjavík's growth since the 18th century. *(Museum open M-F 9am-6pm, Sa-Su noon-5pm. Free.)* The **Hafnarhús** (Harbor House) is the most eclectic of the three divisions of the Reykjavík Art Museum. The museum, a renovated warehouse, holds a collection of paintings by Erro, Iceland's preeminent contemporary artist. *(Tryggvagata 17, off Aðalstræti. ☎590 1200; www.artmuseum.is. Open daily high-season 10am-5pm, Th 10am-10pm; low-season 1-4pm. Free.)* Follow Tryggvagata to the intersection of Lækjargata and Hverfisgata and look up on the hill to see the statue of **Ingólfur Arnason,** Iceland's first settler, and revel in the view of the mountains to the north. The **Culture House** has a detailed exhibit on Iceland's ancient history and mythology, including carefully preserved vellum manuscripts of Eddas and Sagas. *(Hverfisgata 15. ☎545 1400. Open daily 11am-5pm. 300ISK.)*

East of Lake Tjörnin, the **National Gallery of Iceland** presents contemporary Icelandic art. The toys and cushions on the bottom floor aren't an installment piece; they're for restless children. *(Fríkirkjuvegur 7. ☎515 9600. Open Tu-Su 10am-5pm. Free.)* Continue eastward to the **Hallgrímskirkja** landmark church on Skólavörðustígur, designed by Guðjón Samúelsson to look like it formed from a volcanic eruption. The church will be under construction until September 2009, but you can still go up to the tower for an unparalleled view of the city. *(☎510 1000; www.hallgrimskirkja.is. Open daily 9am-5pm; occasionally closes later in summer. Organ concerts Th at noon, in summer also Sa at noon. Elevator to the top 400ISK.)* Across from the church, the **Einar Jónsson Museum** on Njarðargata exhibits 300 of the sculptor's imposing, allegorical works inspired by Iceland's Christian and pagan heritage. Don't miss the free **sculpture garden** in the back. *(☎551 3797; www.skulptur.is. Open from June to mid-Sept. Tu-Su 2-5pm; mid-Sept.-May Sa-Su 2-5pm. 400ISK. Free with ISIC.)*

DON'T GET FLEECED. Visiting Reykjavík isn't cheap. Check out **Sirkus** (flea market) for deals on clothes, music, and jewelry. (In a large white building near the Harbor House on Tryggvagata. ☎562 5030. From noon to five on Saturdays and Sundays.) It's worth a stop just to try a free sample of the *hákarl*—rotten shark—a traditional Icelandic dish.

LAUGARDALUR. Sights cluster around Laugardalur, a large park east of the city center. The white dome of the **Ásmundarsafn** (Ásmundur Sveinsson Sculpture Museum), on Sigtún, houses works spanning Sveinsson's career in a building the artist lived in and designed. The sculpture garden around the museum features larger works, some of which are interactive pieces ideal for climbing or relaxing on. *(Take bus #14 to the Laugardalslaug thermal pools, turn left and walk down Reykjavegur to Sigtún. ☎553 2155. Open daily May-Sept. 10am-4pm; Oct.-Apr. 1-4pm. Free.)* Walking out of the museum, continue straight down Sigtún until it becomes Engjavegur and proceed to the **Reykjavík Botanic Garden,** one of the few forested areas in Iceland. *(Skúlatún 2. ☎553 8870. Garden open 24hr. Greenhouse and pavilion open daily Apr.-Sept. 10am-10pm; Oct.-Mar. 10am-5pm. Free.)* Just outside the garden, opposite the pavilion and greenhouse, a free outdoor exhibit outlines the history of the **Washing Springs,** Reykjavík's geothermal square, where the women of the city once came to do their cooking and their laundry. The Laugardalur region has a variety of sports facilities, but be sure to visit the city's largest thermal swimming pool, **Laugardalslaug** (see Thermal Pools, below).

OTHER SIGHTS. The **Saga Museum** rivals Madame Tussauds with its depiction of Icelandic history using life-size wax models. One figure shows a woman exposing her breast, which supposedly caused the Norwegian army to retreat during a bygone battle. *Let's Go* does not recommend flashing. *(Bus #18 south to Perlan. ☎511 1517; www.sagamuseum.is. Open Mar.-Oct. 10am-6pm; Nov.-Feb. noon-5pm. 1000ISK, students 800ISK.)* The renovated **National Museum** has a more comprehensive overview of Iceland's past with audio/visuals and interactive exhibits that let you try on Icelandic garb. *(Suðurgata 41. Bus #14, 1, 3, or 6 from Hlemmur station. ☎530 2200; www.natmus.is/english. Open May-Sept. 15 daily 10am-5pm; Sept 16-Apr. Tu-Su 11am-5pm. 600ISK, students 300ISK. W free. Free guided tours summer daily 11am, winter Sa 2pm. MC/V.)* From the National Museum, take bus #12 or 19 from Hlemmur to **Árbæjarsafn,** an open-air museum that chronicles the lives of past generations of Icelanders. Check for the website for summer weekend special events, like folk dances and Viking games. *(Kistuhylur 4. ☎411 6300; www.reykjavikmuseum.is. Open June-Aug. daily 10am-5pm. 600ISK, F Free. Low-season tours M, W, F 1pm-2pm; call ahead.)*

THERMAL POOLS

Reykjavík's thermal pools are all equipped with a hot pot (naturally occurring hot tub) and steam room or sauna, although each pool maintains a distinct character. Those searching for the cheapest option should seek out the city beach and its free hot pot at **Nauthólsvik.** Unless otherwise specified, all pools listed below charge 360ISK admission, with 10 visits for 2500ISK.

Laugardalslaug, Laugardalslaug-Sundlaugarvegur 105 (☎411 5100). Take bus #14 from the city center; entrance is on the right. The city's largest thermal pool features indoor and outdoor facilities, a water slide, 5 hot pots, and a sauna. Swimsuit or towel rental 350ISK, admission to all 3 750kr. Open Apr.-Sept. M-F 6:30am-10:30pm, Sa-Su 8am-10pm; Oct.-Mar. M-F 6:30am-10:30pm, Sa-Su 8am-8pm. MC/V.

Vesturbaejarlaug, Hofsvallagata (☎551 5004). This pool is often recommended by locals as it has far fewer tourists and a good ice cream store just outside. Outdoor pool, 3 hot tubs, steam bath. Open May-Aug. M-F 6:30am-10pm, Sa-Su 8am-8pm; Sept.-April M-F 6:30am-9:30pm, Sa-Su 8am-7pm.

Sundhöll Reykjavíkur, Barónsstígur 101 (☎411 5350). This centrally located pool is an easy walk from city center. It offers an indoor pool as well as sunbathing areas and hot pots. Open M-F 6:30am-9:30pm, Sa-Su 8am-7pm. AmEx/MC/V.

Sundlaug Seltjarnarness, Suðurströnd 170 (☎561 1551). Take bus #11 from Hlemmur station to Sundlaug stop and follow the signs. Swimsuit and towel rental 300ISK each. Open M-F 6:30am-10pm, Sa-Su 8am-8pm. AmEx/MC/V.

Ylströndin Nauthólsvík. Take bus #119 south until the last stop. Although not considered a classic thermal pool by locals, this remote city beach is worth it. Lockers 200ISK. Free. Open May-Sept. daily 10am-8pm. Closed in rainy weather.

HIKING

Reykjavík has a range of hikes for different experience levels. Take precaution when scaling heights—conditions on hilltops can be very different compared with weather at sea level and can change quickly. For a casual stroll, take bus #18 to the Perlan stop by the Saga Museum to reach trails on the forested hill around **Perlan,** one of which features a working model of the **Strokkur Geyser** (see Gullfoss and Geysir, p. 525). At the southwest corner of the park is **Nauthólsvík beach** (see Thermal Pools, above) and a scenic trail around the airport that leads back to the city. If you get tired, catch bus #12 on Skeljanes back to the center. Pick up **maps** at the tourist office. If basking in the midnight sun on a black lava beach is what you've always dreamed of, visit the **Grótta** bird reserve on the western tip of the peninsula. Take bus #11 out to Hofgarður and walk 15min. along the sea on Byggarðstangi. Although the Grótta itself is closed during nesting season (May-June), the bird-filled sky is still an amazing sight. Check out the **lighthouse** at the edge of the peninsula: high tides make it a temporary island. South of the city lies the **Heiðmörk Reserve,** a large park with picnic spots and beginner to intermediate hiking trails. Take bus #1 or 2 from Hlemmur to Hamraborg and transfer to bus #28. Ask the driver to let you off at Lake Elliðavatn; from there, walk 3-4km south to the reserve.

DOOR-TO-DOOR. Legs aching after a long hike? The BSÍ bus drivers will generally let you off anywhere along the route upon request. You can also flag buses down like taxis and they will often stop to pick you up. Pick up by excursion buses and flybus can be made though most hotels and hostels.

Secluded and slow-paced **Viðey Island,** home to Viking structures and Iceland's second-oldest church, has been inhabited since the 10th century. The island features several sculpture exhibitions and the new, playfully postmodern "Blind Pavilion." To Viðey take the ferry from the Reykjavík harbor Miðbakki. (☎533 5055; www.ferja.is. Ferry departs daily 1, 2, 3, 7, and 9pm; June 10-Aug. 12 also 8:30am. Round-trip 800ISK.) Across the bay from Reykjavík looms **Mt. Esja,** which you can ascend via a well-maintained trail (2-3hr.). The trail is not difficult, but hikers should be prepared for rain, hail, or even a brief but powerful snow squall. Arrive early in the morning in order to make the buses there and back; be especially mindful on Sundays. Take bus #15 to Háholt and transfer to bus #27 (once per 1-2 hr.) and exit at Esjuskáli or simply tell the bus driver you're heading to Esja and ask for an exchange ticket.

NIGHTLIFE

Despite being unnervingly quiet on weeknights, Reykjavík asserts its status as a wild party town each weekend. The city's thriving independent music scene centers at **12 Tónar,** Skólavörðustígur 12, a truly unique record store. After taking in the concerts, Icelanders hit the bars and clubs until the wee hours. Most bars do not have cover charges, but bouncers tend to regulate who enters, especially after 2am. Clubs have steep drink prices, so many locals drink at home or head to the **vínbuð** (government liquor store) before going out. Don't bother showing up before 12:30am and plan to be out until 4 or 5am. Boisterous crowds tend to bar-hop around **Austurstræti, Tryggvagata,** and **Laugavegur.** The establishments listed below are 20+, unless otherwise noted.

22, Laugavegur 22 (☎578 7800). With 3 floors, this bar, club, and lounge has a DJ Th-Su after midnight playing a variety of popular music. The top fl. is the conversation room, offering a deck for smokers. Beer 600ISK. Mixed drinks 750-1500ISK. Open M-Th and Su 11:30am-1am, F-Sa 11am-5:30am. AmEx/MC/V.

Sólon, Bankastræti 7A (☎562 3232). This trendy cafe morphs at night into a posh club bouncing with hip hop, pop, and electronica. Cafe downstairs, large dance floor and bar upstairs. Try Iceland's famous schnapps, *brennivín (*black death), used to stave off the dark, cold winters and chase the ammonia taste of *hákarl* (550ISK). Beer 700ISK. Th live music. Open M-Th 11am-1am, F-Sa 11am-5am, Su noon-midnight. Kitchen until 10pm. Club open midnight-late. AmEx/MC/V.

Hressingarskálinn, Austurstæti 20 (☎561 2240) Plays a variety of popular music. Th-Sa live music or other free entertainment. M-Th and Su 9am-1am, F-Sa 10am-5:30am. Kitchen open in summer until 11pm; in winter 10pm. AmEx/MC/V.

Vegamót, Vegamótarstígur 4 (☎511 3040), off Laugavegur. Students and professionals head to this posh bar to flaunt it and see others do the same. Beer 700ISK. 22+. Th-Sa live DJ. Open M-Th and Su 11:00am-1am, F-Sa 11:30am-4:30am. AmEx/MC/V.

NASA, Thorraldssenstræti 4 (☎511 1313; www.nasa.is), at Austurvollur Sq. The large central dance floor draws a varied crowd, depending on the evening's band. F-Sa live bands. Cover 500-1500ISK. Open F-Sa 11am-last customer. MC/V.

ICELAND

DAYTRIPS FROM REYKJAVÍK

Iceland's main attractions are its natural wonders. **Iceland Excursions** runs the popular "Golden Circle Classic" tour, which stops at Hveragerði, Kerið, Skálholt, Geysir, Gullfoss, and Þingvellir National Park. (☎540 1313; www.grayline.is. 9-10hr., 8773ISK.) Arctic Adventures is one company offering a variety of **adventure tours,** with the Golden Circle Rafting trip (13990ISK) a perennial favorite. (Laugavegur 11 in the Cintamani store. ☎562 7000; www.adventures.is. MC/V.) Also worth a look is a diving or **snorkeling tour** (see www.dive.is) as Iceland offers some of the best diving sights in the world. Highlanders offers exciting but pricey **off-road tours** in jeeps that can traverse rivers, crags, and glaciers. (☎588-9588; www.hl.is. From 13,900ISK.)

GULLFOSS AND GEYSIR. The glacial river Hvita plunges down 32m to create Gullfoss (Golden Falls). A dirt path passes along the falls, where many get soaked in the mist. The adjacent hill houses a small cafeteria and gift shop, and affords a stunning view of the surrounding mountains, plains, and cliffs. On the horizon you can see the tip of **Longjökull,** a glacier the size of Hong Kong. The Geysir (namesake of the word "geyser") area, 10km down the road, is a teeming bed of hot springs in a barren landscape. The **Strokkur Geyser** (the Churn) erupts around every 4min., spewing sulfurous water up to 35m. Exercise caution around the thermal pools—more than one tourist has fallen into the nearby Blesi pool and been badly scalded. The small, but excellent **museum** at the visitors center offers a multimedia show on the science behind these natural phenomena. The top portion of the museum is dedicated to **Aðalbjörg Egilsdottur,** who donated her collection of early 19th-century household Icelandic artifacts. *(Open daily 10am-5pm. BSÍ runs a round-trip bus to Gulfoss and Geysir with Iceland Excursions, departing from the BSÍ Terminal in Reykjavík June-Aug. daily 8:30am; 6hr., round-trip 5200ISK. Museum 800ISK, students 650ISK.)*

ÞINGVELLIR NATIONAL PARK. The European and North American tectonic plates meet at Þingvellir National Park, a place of both geologic and cultural significance for Iceland. The Öxará River, slicing through lava fields and jagged fissures, leads to the **Drekkingarhylur** (Drowning Pool), where adulterous women were once drowned, and on to Lake Þingvallavatn, Iceland's largest lake. This lake has exceptionally clear water, making for one of the best **diving**

and **snorkeling** sites in the world. *(For diving opportunities check out www.dive.is or call ☎663 2858.)* Not far from the Drekkingarhylur lies the site of the **Alþingi** (ancient parliament), where for almost nine centuries, starting in AD 930, Icelanders gathered annually in the shadow of the **Lögberg** (Law Rock) to discuss matters of law, economics, and justice. **Maps** are available at the **Þingvellir Visitors Center.** *(Info center ☎482 2660. Open June-Aug. daily 8:30am-8pm; May and Sept. daily 9am-5pm. BSÍ does not run buses to Þingvellir; the site can be reached only by taking a tour bus or driving. Check out Iceland on Your Own and Reykjavik Excursions opportunities.)*

BLUE LAGOON. The southwest corner of the Reykjanes Peninsula, only 15 minutes from Keflavík airport, harbors an oasis in the middle of a lava field: a vast pool of geothermally heated water. The lagoon has become a tourist magnet, but it's worth braving the crowds. The cloudy blue waters, rich in silica and other minerals, are famous for their healing powers. Bathers who have their fill of wading through the 36-39°C (97-102°F) waters can indulge in a steam bath, a silica facial, or an in-water massage (3600ISK for 10 min.). Stand under the waterfall for a free, all-natural **shoulder massage.** *(Open daily from mid-May to Aug. 8am-10pm; from Sept. to mid-May 9am-9pm. Towel rental 350ISK. Bathing suit rental 400ISK. Admission and locker 2300ISK. AmEx/MC/V.)* Try taking the **bus** to the Blue Lagoon on your way to or from Keflavík. Airport buses leave at 8:30am or 11am, spend a few hours at the lagoon and then take you back to the airport for the same 4400ISK fee. *(Buses run from BSÍ Bus Terminal in Reykjavík. 1hr., 6 per day 8:30am-6pm; round-trip 4400 ISK with Blue Lagoon admission. ☎420 8809; www.bluelagoon.com.)*

NESJAVELLIRI. This power plant provides Reykjavík with half of its hot water and electricity by capturing geothermal heat that escapes from the intersection of the North American and European tectonic plates. Pipes run 26km from Nesjavelliri to the capital city on rollers to avoid destruction by one of Iceland's frequent earthquakes. The geothermal energy hub is also fueled by three nearby volcanic systems. **Free tours** of the facilities are available and provide a detailed look at Iceland's latest strides in renewable energy. *(Accessible only by car or tour bus; see Iceland Excursions. ☎480 2408. Open June-Aug. M-Sa 9am-5pm, Su 1pm-6pm.)*

WESTMAN ISLANDS (VESTMANNAEYJAR)

The black cliffs of the Westman Islands (pop. 4000) are the most recent offerings of the volcanic fury that continues to shape Iceland. The archipelago is made up of 15 islands and many isolated rock pillars breaking through the waves; Heimaey is the only inhabited island, hosting Vestmannaeyjar.

TRANSPORTATION AND PRACTICAL INFORMATION. It's a good half-day of traveling to reach the islands by bus and ferry from Reykjavík. **Air Iceland** runs flights to the Westman Islands from Reykjavík's domestic airport. (☎481 3300; www.flugfelag.is. 20min. Check the website for the occasional steeply discounted net-rate tickets. Those under 25 can get stand-by discounts, often half-price, on all domestic flights.) To get to Vestmannaeyjar from the airport, exit and take a left down the main road—a 20min. downhill walk arrives at the center of town. The Herjólfur **ferry** departing from Þorlákshöfn is far slower but cheaper than flying. (☎481 2800. 2hr 45min.; departs daily noon and 7:30pm; returns daily 8:15am and 4pm. 2160ISK, student discount during school year.) **Buses** go from BSÍ Station to the **ferry** 1hr. before departure and return after landing (1200ISK). The **tourist office** is on the corner of Heiarðvegur and Standvegur, a block from the docks. (☎481 3322; www.vestmannaeyjar.is. Open May-Aug daily 10am-noon and 1pm-6pm. For other times, call ☎488 2000.)

ACCOMMODATIONS AND FOOD. Many islanders offer space, using their homes as guesthouses which creates an affordable and cozy accommodation option. The centrally located **Guesthouse Hreiðrið ❷**, Faxastígur 33, is just past the Volcanic Film Show theater on Heiðarvegur. (☎481 1045; http://tourist.eyjar.is. Reception 24hr. in summer. Sleeping-bag accommodations 1900ISK; singles 3800ISK; doubles 5800ISK. Low-season reduced rates. AmEx/MC/V.) **Guesthouse Sunnuhóll (HI) ❷**, Vestmannabraut 28B, has newly renovated rooms with ample space to stretch out after a hike around the island. The reception desk is in **Hotel Þórshamar,** Vestaunrabraut 28, near the center of town. (☎481 2900; www.hotelvestmannaeyjar.is. Breakfast 900ISK. Linens 700ISK. Free Wi-Fi. Internet 300ISK/30min. May-Sept. Sleeping bag accommodations 2300ISK, with HI discount 1800ISK; in winter 2100/1700. AmEx/MC/V.) Grab groceries at **Krónan** on Strandavegur. (Open M-Sa 11am-6pm.)

SIGHTS. In 1973, the volcano **Eldfell** (fire mountain) tore through the northern section of Heimaey, spewing lava and ash and forcing Vestmannaeyjar's population to evacuate overnight. The 1973 eruption and the destruction it wrought is memorialized in **Pompeii of the North,** a modern archeological site, which displays unearthed houses destroyed by Eldfell. The outdoor exhibit, which offers perspective on the natural disaster, is still growing as excavation continues. The **Volcanic Film Show,** on Heiðarvegur, runs a documentary about the eruption. (☎481 1045. 55min. shows daily mid-June to Aug. 11am, 2pm, 3:30pm, 9pm; mid-May-mid-June and Sept.-mid-Sept. 11am and 3:30pm. 700ISK, students 600ISK.) Across the street from the film show, the **Aquarium** and **Natural History Museum,** Heiðarvegur 12, feature exhibits on Westman's sea creatures, birds, and geology. A combined ticket (600ISK) grants access to both attractions, along with the **Folkmuseum,** on Ráðhúströ, and the medical museum at **Landlyst,** next to the harbor off Strandvegur. (Aquarium and Natural History Museum ☎481 1997; Folkmuseum ☎481 1184. Museums open May 15-Sept. 15 daily 11am-5pm; Sept. 16-May 14 Sa-Su 3-5pm. 400ISK per site. MC/V.)

OUTDOOR ACTIVITIES. Heimaey's 15 sq. km offer several spectacular hikes. The family run **Cafe Kró,** Tangagata 7, provides hiking advice, tour offers, Wi-Fi, and caffeine to fuel the journey. (☎488 4884. Coffee 290ISK. Soup 690ISK. Wi-Fi free with drink purchase. Open daily May-Aug 10:30am-9pm. Sept.-Apr. 5pm-9pm. 1½hr. boat and 2hr. bus tours twice

SURVIVING ICELAND

You might have the sixth sense—and no, not the one involving Bruce Willis and dead people. The Icelandic sixth sense allows you to see *huldufolk* (hidden people), magical creatures that 80% of Icelanders believe exist. Some *huldufolk* are friendly, upstanding citizens. Others are up to no damn good. To help you get through your trip to Iceland, *Let's Go* offers a brief survival guide:

Elves: Apparently, some look like humans, which makes picking them out a total crapshoot. **Strategy:** No cause for alarm. They're harmless and live in their Westman Islands (p. 526) village.

Faeries: A deceptive bunch. The beautiful faeries are known to lure you with soft, plaintive music. Then, BOOM—they'll carry you off. **Strategy:** Earplugs, or just run if you hear soft, plaintive music.

Gnomes: Small and subterranean. Strategy: Nothing to fear. Icelandic roads are often built around their settlements. They're that respected.

Trolls: Bad news if you run into one of these nocturnal beasts. Some live in Dimmuborgir, near Mývatn (p. 530). Strategy: Although they're ugly, trolls fuss over hygiene. Get them dirty, mess with their hair, etc. The power plant at Nesjavelliri (p. 526), for example, maintains a shower for the trolls to enjoy so they don't meddle with Reykjavík's water supply. An A+ tactic.

daily June-Aug. 3400ISK, students 3000ISK. AmEx/MC/V.) On the western side of the island, the cliff's edge at **Há** is a scenic spot. A popular, longer hike (2hr. round-trip) along **Ofanleitishamar** on the western coast passes two **puffin** colonies (nesting in mid-Aug.) and a black sand beach, **Klauf,** where brave swimmers tackle the 12°C (54°F) water in summer. **Surtsey** is the world's youngest island at 44 years old; look for it in the distance. After a steep climb, the best view awaits on the top of **Heimaklettur,** the island's highest point. Neighboring Eldfell can be scaled in an hour, but temperatures reach 180°C (356°F) in the caldera. Hidden in the northeast corner of the lava bed is **Gaujulundur,** a remote garden and **elf village** protected by a miniature fence (hint: some disbelievers can't see the elves). To get there, walk east along Strandvegur into the lava bed. Stay on the side of the road and continue until you hit a fork in the road. Take the left fork and walk until you see a sign for the garden. The three-day **People's Feast** (Þjóðhátíð) draws a young crowd of 10,000-12,000 to the island on the first weekend in August for bonfires, drinking, and related shenanigans. Reserve transportation and accommodations ahead. A smaller set of festivities during the first weekend of July celebrates the end of the Eldfell eruption.

LANDMANNALAUGAR AND ÞÓRSMÖRK

Wedged between two of southern Iceland's glaciers, Landmannalaugar and Þórsmörk are gateways to the diverse landscapes of the country, from jagged lava fields and mammoth volcanic craters to desert and pristine forests. The renowned four-day, 54km trek between the two regions is perhaps the best **hiking route** in the country, though it poses a number of challenges, among them variable weather conditions (trails open from mid-June to Aug.). More manageable hikes include a 2hr. loop through Landmannalaugar's multicolored volcanoes and bubbling hot springs, and the walk from Þórsmörk's **glacial valley** to the peak of **Valahnjukur,** which overlooks rivers and ash fields. Ferdafélag Íslands (Iceland Touring Association) offers **guided hikes** and general info on camping (☎568 2533; www.fi.is). Footsore travelers can soak away their aches and pains in Landmannalaugar's soothing **thermal brook.** Landmannalaugar has a **campsite** ❶ and **lodge** ❷ run by Ferðafélag Íslands. (Reserve online at www.fi.is/en. Open July-Sept. Camping 800ISK; mountain huts 2800ISK.) Reykjavik Excursions runs a bus that allows you to travel to either Þórsmörk or Landmannalaugar, hike to the other, and then return to Reykjavik. (www.re.is/home/thorsmork/laugavegur.) **Buses** run from the BSÍ terminal in Reykjavík to Landmannalaugar (4hr., from mid-June to mid-Sept. 2 per day, round-trip 10,000ISK) and Þorsmork (3hr., from June to mid-Sept. 1 per day, round-trip 6000ISK).

AKUREYRI

Although Akureyri (ah-KOO-rare-ee) has only 17,500 inhabitants, it claims the title "capital of the north." A college town with a few trendy hangouts, Akureyri also serves as an outpost for exploring the region's breathtaking highlands.

TRANSPORTATION AND PRACTICAL INFORMATION. Flights arrive from Reykjavík at **Akureyri Airport (AEY),** 3km south of the city along Drottningarbraut, the seaside road. Book online or fly standby—you may get rates cheaper than bus fares. See p. 514 for more info. **Buses** run from the Trex bus station, Hafnarstræti 77, to Reykjavík (6hr.; 8:30am, also 5pm in summer; 7900ISK). For **taxis,** try BSÓ, Strandgata. (☎461 1010. Open M-F 7am-2am, Sa-Su 24hr.)

Mountains and the harbor border Akureyri to the west, while the **Eyjafjörður fjord** lines the east. Within the city, follow **Hafnarstræti** to its end to reach Akureyri's main square, **Rádhústorg.** Most major services, including banks, can be found around Rádhústorg. The **police** station is at Þórunnarstræti 138 (☎464 7700).

The **hospital,** Eyrarlandsvegur (☎463 0100), on the south side of the botanical gardens, has a **24hr. emergency** department. The **tourist office** is in the fjord-side culture house at the corner of Glerárgata and Strandgata. (☎553 5999; www.nordurland.is and www.visitakureyri.is. Internet 300ISK per 30min. Open late June-Aug. daily M-F 7:30am-7pm; Sept.-May M-F 8:00am-4pm. Sept. and Oct. also weekends 9am-1pm. AmEx/MC/V.) **Postal Code:** 600.

ACCOMMODATIONS AND FOOD. Akureyri's only hostel, **Stórholt ❶,** Stórholt 1, draws an adventurous crowd. (☎894 4299; www.akureyrihostel.com. Linens 700ISK. Laundry 600ISK. Free Internet and Wi-Fi. Reception June-Aug. 8am-10pm; Sept.-May 9am-8pm. Dorms 2300ISK; singles 3500ISK; doubles 5600ISK. Cabins 7000-15,000. 200-400ISK HI discount. AmEx/MC/V.) **Guesthouse Sulur ❸,** Þórunnarstræti 93, is in a hilltop home just behind the main square. (☎461 1160. Free laundry and Wi-Fi. Reception 24hr. Sleeping bag accommodation 3600ISK; singles 5000ISK; doubles 5600ISK; triples 8100ISK. MC/V.)

The famous **Brynja ❶,** Adalstræti 3, has an Icelandic treat: frozen yogurt smothered in chocolate or caramel. (☎462 4478. Cones from 200ISK. Open M-F 9am-11:30pm, Sa-Su 10am-11:30pm; in winter daily 11am-11pm. AmEx/MC/V.) For other cheap food options, try the pedestrian alleys off **Rádhústorg.**

SIGHTS AND NIGHTLIFE. For a glimpse of late 19th-century life in Akureyri, walk down **Aðalstræti** and take a look at numbers 14 and 50, the city's oldest houses. Be sure to find **Laxdalshs,** the oldest building in the city at Hafnarstrti 11, which has a small museum. Back on Aðalstræti, **Nonnahús,** Aðalstræti 54., focuses on famous Icelandic author Jón Sveinsson, whose children's book *Nonni and Manni* has been translated into over 40 languages. (☎462 3555. Open from June to mid-Aug. daily 10am-5pm; call ahead in low-season. 500ISK. AmEx/MC/V.) Up the hill, **Akureyri Museum,** Aðalstræti 58, is marked by a well-kept garden at the entrance. The first floor chronicles Icelandic history, while the basement focuses on Akureyri. (☎462 4162. Open June-Sept. 15 daily 10am-5pm; Sept. 16-May Sa 2-4pm. 500ISK. 700ISK combination pass with Nonnahús. AmEx/MC/V.) Organ music emanates from **Akureyrarkirkja,** við Eyrarlandsvegen, the town's main church. The building looks similar to Reykjavík's Hallgrímskirkja—they were designed by the same architect, Guðjón Samúelsson. (☎462 7700. Open daily 10am-noon and 1pm-5pm and M-Tu and Th-F 5pm-10pm and W 5pm-8pm. Free.) Truly worth a visit are the northernmost **botanical gardens** in the world located at Hrafnagilstræti and Eyrarlandsvegen. (Open June-Sept. M-F 8am-10pm, Sa-Su 9am-10pm. Free.) Travelers can hike to **Mount Súlur** (1213m) along a trail that starts 5km out of town. More challenging hikes requiring glacier gear include Strýta (1456m) and Kerling (1536m). Visit the tourist office for maps (200-300ISK). A popular **swimming pool,** Þingvallastræti 21, is just 370ISK. Try the waterslide, sauna, or hot tub. (Towel 350ISK. Open M-F 7am-9pm, Sa-Su 7:30-6:30pm. MC/V.) The **Summer Arts Festival** (from mid-June to late Aug.) includes walks, concerts, and theater performances.

Many streets in Akureyri are deserted at night, but lines of cars circle one building in the town square in a tradition known as **Rúnturinn.** It's popular among high schoolers for passing time and flirting. Inside the circled central building, a well-dressed crowd spends hours at **Café Amour.** Beer starts at 700ISK, but look for deals on five bottles (1500ISK) during occasional Happy hours and student discounts (400ISK). Amour becomes a **techno dance hall** on the 2nd floor during weekends. (☎461 3030; www.cafeamour.is. Mixed drinks from 1350ISK. Open M-Th and Su 10am-1am, F-Sa 10am-4am. AmEx/MC/V.) **Kaffi Akureyri,** Strandgata 7, is a no-frills bar, with a crowd ranging from 20- to 60-year-olds. Knock down Opal and Topas shots with locals for 500ISK.

MÝVATN AND GOÐAFOSS

Like Þingvellir National Park to the south, Mývatn (MEE-va-ten) is a collision point of the European and North American tectonic plates, creating a volatile volcanic environment prone to eruption. The current landscape was shaped by 18th-century eruptions and, more recently, an eruption to the north that started in 1975 and didn't end until 1984. The focal point of the area is **Lake Mývatn,** a shallow body of water less than 4m deep, scarred by many small craters and surrounded by canyons, volcanoes, hot springs, and cooled lava sculpture gardens. Due to its depth, the lake is an ideal breeding ground for flies. Of note is the **myvargur fly,** whose name roughly translates to "tiny aggressive wolf." Heed locals' warnings and bring a mosquito mask to enjoy the scenery for any extended period of time. The freshwater **Mývatn Nature Baths** are a 4km hike from Reynihlíð, a small town on Lake Mývatn 99km east of Akureyri. Facing the lake, with the Verslun supermarket to your back, turn left, walk past the info office, and take your first right on Rte. 1. Walk for 20min. (☎464 4411; www.naturebaths.com. Open daily June-Aug. 9am-midnight; Sept.-May noon-10pm. 1400ISK. Towel and swimsuit rental 350ISK each. AmEx/MC/V.) **Hverfjall,** a massive 2000-year-old volcanic crater, is clearly visible from town. The caves at **Grotagja,** farther north along a circle hike, feature hot water baths. **Dimmuborgir,** south of Hverfjall, is a forest of fantastic natural lava formations, the most famous being **kirkja,** which resembles a Gothic church. According to legend, **Þorgeir,** a 10th-century Icelandic lawmaker, flung statues of pagan gods into a waterfall in AD 1000 to celebrate Iceland's conversion to Christianity. As a result of the event, the waterfall was named **Goðafoss** (Waterfall of the Gods). The waterfall is 50km from both Akureyri and Húsavík off Rte. 1.

The cheapest lodgings in Reynihlíð are clustered around the Verslun supermarket. **Guesthouse Elda ❹,** Helluhrauni 15, is conveniently located behind the market in a cozy home along Rte. 1. (☎464 4220. Singles 7400ISK; doubles 10,500ISK; triples 14,900ISK. Prices reduced in winter.) The campgrounds at **Blarg ❶,** in front of the tourist office at Rte. 1 and Rte. 8, have lake vistas. The **Blarg Guesthouse ❹** is also available here. (☎464 4240; ferdabjarg@simnet.is. Campground open mid-June to Aug. Campsites 850ISK; singles 5900ISK; doubles 8700ISK; triples 11,500ISK. AmEx/MC/V.) Pick up groceries or a snack for the trail at **Verslun,** at the bus stop in Reynihlíð.

Catch a **bus** from Akureyri to Reynihlíð (open June-Aug. daily 8:00am, 2500ISK). SBA buses run from Húsavík (45min., June-Aug. 1pm and 5pm, 1800ISK). The **tourist office** is located right at the bus stop in Reynihlíð. (Open Oct.-May M-F 10am-4pm.) The Reynihlíð **information office,** Hraunvegur 8, next to the supermarket, has **maps.** (☎464 4390; infomyvatn@est.is. Open daily mid-June to Aug. 9am-7pm; from Sept. to mid-June 9am-5pm. Maps 150ISK.)

HÚSAVÍK

Europe's premier whale-watching destination, Húsavík (WHO-saah-veek; pop. 2400) has attractions ranging from the majestic to the bizarre. Erected in 1974, **The Icelandic Phallological Museum,** Hédinsbraut 3A, is hard to miss with the giant phallus that greets passersby. The collection includes over 200 specimens and the penises of over 90 species—from the 2mm hamster specimen to the sperm whale's 70kg behemoth. Don't miss the folklore section, which displays a merman penis and two different types of ghost penises (yes, they are visible). See if you can spot the elusive elf member. (☎868 7966; www.phallus.is. Open from mid-May to mid-Sept. daily noon-6pm. Call in winter. 300ISK. Cash only.) Farther down Hédinsbraut, the **Húsavík Whale Museum,** next to the harbor, examines whales in a somewhat different way, with complete skeletons of different cetacean species. (☎464 2520; www.whalemuseum.is. Open daily June-Aug.

9am-7pm; May and Sept. 10am-5pm. 700ISK, students 600ISK. AmEx/MC/V.) **Safnahúsið,** Stórigarður 17, features natural history, folk, and maritime museums along with the city archives, library, and an art gallery. (☎464 1860. Open June-Aug. daily 10am-6pm. 500ISK; includes a cup of coffee or juice. Tours available in over 8 languages. Call ahead.) For **whale-watching,** book a 3hr. tour with Gentle Giants or North Sailing. (Gentle Giants ☎464 1500; www.gentlegiants.is. 4100ISK. AmEx/MC/V. North Sailing ☎464 7272; www.northsailing.is. 4200ISK. AmEx/MC/V. Both run tours May-Sept.; call for hours.)

Guesthouse options are available along **Baldursbrekka,** the second street on the left when heading north from the bus stop along the main harbor road. Emhild K. **Olsen ❷,** Baldursbrekka 17, caters to backpackers with large rooms in the basement of a home with spectacular views of the water. (☎464 1618. Free laundry. Sleeping-bag accommodations 2500ISK; singles 3500ISK; doubles 6000ISK. Cash only.) A **campground ❶,** 2min. further down Rte. 85, offers free indoor showers and a small kitchen. (☎464 4300. Open from mid-May to mid-Sept. Laundry 300ISK. Campsite 850ISK.) **Salka Restaurant ❷,** on the harbor, is famous for its shrimp and salmon dishes. (☎464 2551. Entrees from 1250ISK. Pizzas from 1450ISK. Open from mid-May to mid-Sept. 11:30am-11pm. In winter until 9pm. Bar open until 1am M-Th and Su and until 3am F-Sa. MC/V.)

Trex (☎461 1106; www.trex.is) **buses** run to Akureyri (1hr., 3 per day, 2300ISK) from the gas station at Hédinsbraut 2, on the main street north of the harbor. SBA (☎550 0700; www.sba.is) offers **bus tours** of the area. Buses leave the harbor for Reynihild on Lake Mývatn (45min., June-Aug. 2 per day, 1800ISK). The **tourist office,** Garðarsbraut 7, is next door to the Kasko supermarket. (☎464 4300. Open from mid-May to mid-Sept. M-F 9am-6pm, Sa-Su 10am-5pm.)

JÖKULSÁRGLJÚFUR NATIONAL PARK

The Jökulsa á Fjöllum River flows into Jökulsárgljúfur National Park from the Vatnajökull glacier to the south, creating astounding waterfalls throughout the region. Jökulsárgljúfur is a trek from any transport hub, but the park's magnificent **Dettifoss waterfall** amply compensates travelers who make the journey. Jökulsárgljúfur's third major waterfall, **Hafragilsfoss,** is 2km downstream from Dettifoss. The Hafragilsfoss parking area has a majestic view of both the waterfall and the canyon below. At the northernmost part of the park is **Ásbyrgi,** a gorgeous horseshoe shaped canyon. A rental **car** (p. 528), preferably four-wheel-drive, is often the cheapest and easiest way to reach Jökulsárgljúfur. Tour **buses** can bring you to the park, but often leave little time to see the sights, unless you camp overnight. The cheapest bus tours are run by SBA (☎550 0700; www.sba.is), partnered with Reykjavík Excursions, and leave at varying times from Akureyri and Húsavík. Check with the local **tourist offices** to book a trip. (Tours from mid-June to Aug. from 8700ISK.)

ICELAND

IRELAND

REPUBLIC OF IRELAND

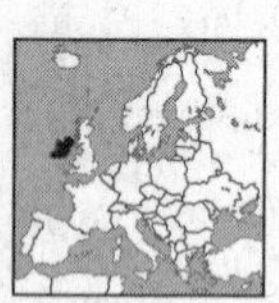

The green, rolling hills of Ireland, dotted with Celtic crosses, medieval monasteries, and Norman castles, have long inspired poets and musicians, from Yeats to U2. Today, the Emerald Isle's jagged coastal cliffs and untouched mountain ranges balance the country's thriving urban centers. Dublin pays tribute to the virtues of fine brews and the legacy of resisting British rule, while Galway offers a vibrant arts scene. In the past few decades, the computing and tourism industries have raised Ireland out of the economic doldrums, and current living standards are among the highest in Western Europe. Despite fears for the decline of traditional culture, the Irish language lives on in secluded areas known as the gaeltacht, and village pubs still echo with reels and jigs.

DISCOVER IRELAND: SUGGESTED ITINERARIES

THREE DAYS. Spend it all in **Dublin** (p. 537). Wander through **Trinity College,** admire the ancient **Book of Kells,** and sample the whiskey at the **Old Jameson Distillery.** Take a day to visit the **National Museums,** shop on **O'Connell Street** and get smart at the **James Joyce Cultural Centre.** Work up your pubbing potential by night in **Temple Bar.**

ONE WEEK. After visiting the sights and pubs of **Dublin** (3 days), enjoy the natural wonders of **Killarney** (1 day; p. 552) and the **Ring of Kerry** (1 day; p. 554). Return to the urban scene in the cultural center of **Galway** (2 days; p. 557).

BEST OF IRELAND, THREE WEEKS. Explore **Dublin** (4 days), then head to **Sligo** (3 days; p. 559) and visit the surrounding lakes and mountains. Continue on to **Galway** (3 days) and the **Aran Islands** (1 day; p. 558). After taking in the views from the **Cliffs of Moher** (1 day; p. 556), tour the scenic **Ring of Kerry** (2 days). Spend time in beautiful **Killarney** (2 days) and daytrip to **Blarney** to kiss the famous stone (1 day; p. 552) before hitting the big city of **Cork** (3 days; p. 549). On the way back to Dublin, stop by the beaches and the crystal factory in Ireland's oldest city, **Waterford** (1 day, p. 547).

ESSENTIALS

FACTS AND FIGURES

OFFICIAL NAME: Republic of Ireland.

CAPITAL: Dublin.

MAJOR CITIES: Cork, Galway, Limerick.

POPULATION: 4,109,000.

TIME ZONE: GMT.

LANGUAGES: English, Irish.

LONGEST LOCATION NAME IN IRELAND: Muckanaghederdauhaulia, in Galway County.

LEASE ON THE ORIGINAL GUINNESS BREWERY IN DUBLIN: 9000 years.

WHEN TO GO

Ireland has a consistently cool, wet climate, with average temperatures ranging from around 4°C (39°F) in winter to 16°C (61°F) in summer. Travelers should bring rain gear in any season. Don't be discouraged by cloudy, foggy mornings—the weather usually clears by noon. The southeastern coast is the driest and sunniest, while western Ireland is considerably wetter and cloudier. May and June offer the most sun; July and August are warmest. December and January have short, wet days, but temperatures rarely drop below freezing.

DOCUMENTS AND FORMALITIES

EMBASSIES AND CONSULATES. Foreign embassies in Ireland are in Dublin (p. 540). Irish embassies abroad include: **Australia,** 20 Arkana St., Yarralumla, Canberra, ACT 2600 (☎06 273 3022; irishemb@cyberone.com.au); **Canada,** Ste. 1105, 130 Albert St., Ottawa, ON K1P 5G4 (☎613-233-6281; www.irishembassyottawa.com); **UK,** 17 Grosvenor Pl., London SW1X 7HR (☎020 72 35 21 71; www.ireland.embassyhomepage.com); **US,** 2234 Massachusetts Ave., NW, Washington, D.C., 20008 (☎202-462-3939; www.irelandemb.org).

VISA AND ENTRY INFORMATION. EU citizens do not need a visa. Citizens of Australia, Canada, New Zealand, and the US do not need a visa for stays of up to 90 days, beginning upon entry into any of the countries in the EU's freedom-of-movement zone. For more info, see p. 15. For stays longer than 90 days, non-EU citizens must register with the **Garda National Immigration Bureau,** 13-14 Burgh Quay, Dublin, 2 (☎01 666 9100; www.garda.ie/gnib).

TOURIST SERVICES AND MONEY

EMERGENCY	Ambulance, Fire, and Police: ☎999. Emergency: ☎112.

TOURIST OFFICES. Bord Fáilte (Irish Tourist Board; ☎1850 23 03 30; www.ireland.ie) operates a nationwide network of offices. Most tourist offices book rooms for a small fee (around €4) and a 10% deposit, but many hostels and B&Bs are not on the board's central list.

MONEY. The **euro (€)** has replaced the **Irish pound (£)** as the unit of currency in the Republic of Ireland. For more info, p. 19. Northern Ireland uses the **pound sterling (£).** As a general rule, it is cheaper to exchange money in Ireland than at home. ATMs are the easiest way to retrieve money and are much more common than bureaux de change. MasterCard and Visa are almost universally accepted. If you stay in hostels and prepare your own food, expect to spend about €30 per person per day; a slightly more comfortable day (sleeping in B&Bs, eating one meal per day at a restaurant, going out at night) would cost €60. Most people working in restaurants do not expect a tip, unless the restaurant is targeted exclusively toward tourists. In that case, consider leaving 10-15%. Tipping is very uncommon for other services, such as taxis and hairdressers. In most cases, people are happy if you simply round up the bill to the nearest euro.

Ireland has a 21% **value added tax (VAT),** a sales tax applied to most goods and services, excluding food, health services, and children's clothing. The prices listed in *Let's Go* include VAT. In the airport upon exiting the EU, non-EU citizens can claim a refund on the tax paid for goods purchased at participating stores. While there is no minimum purchase amount to qualify for a refund, purchases greater than €250 must be approved at the customs desk before the refund can be issued. For more info on VAT refunds, see p. 21.

TRANSPORTATION

BY PLANE. A popular carrier to Ireland is national airline **Aer Lingus** (☎081 836 5000, US 800-474-7424; www.aerlingus.com), with direct flights to London, Paris, and the US. **Ryanair** (☎081 830 3030; www.ryanair.com) offers low fares from Cork, Dublin, and Shannon to destinations across Europe. **British Airways** (Ireland ☎890 626 747, UK 0844 493 0787, US 800-247-9297; www.ba.com) flies into most major Irish airports daily.

BY FERRY. Ferries run between Britain and Ireland many times per day. Fares for adults generally cost €15-30, with additional fees for cars. **Irish Ferries** (Ireland ☎01 818 300 400, UK 8705 17 17 17, US 772-563-2856; www.irishferries.com) and **Stena Line** (☎01 204 7777; www.stenaline.ie/ferry) typically offer discounts to students, seniors, and families. Ferries run from Dublin to Holyhead, BRI; from Cork to Roscoff, FRA (p. 57); and from Rosslare Harbour to Pembroke, Wales, Cherbourg, FRA, and Roscoff, FRA.

BY TRAIN. **Iarnród Éireann** (Irish Rail; www.irishrail.ie) is useful for travel to urban areas. The **Eurail Global** pass is accepted in the Republic but not in Northern Ireland. The **BritRail** pass does not cover travel in anywhere in Ireland, but the **BritRail+Ireland** pass (€289-504) offers five or 10 days of travel in a one-month period as well as ferry service between Britain and Ireland.

BY BUS. **Bus Éireann** (☎01 836 6111; www.buseireann.ie), Ireland's national bus company, operates Expressway buses that link larger cities as well as local buses that serve the countryside and smaller towns. One-way fares between cities generally range €5-25. Bus Éireann offers the **Irish Rover** pass, which also covers the Ulsterbus service in Northern Ireland (3 of 8 consecutive days €76, under 16 €44; 8 of 15 days €172/94; 15 of 30 days €255/138). The **Emerald Card,** also available through Bus Éireann, offers unlimited travel on Expressway and other buses, Ulsterbus, Northern Ireland Railways, and local services (8 of 15 consecutive days €248, under 16 €124; 15 of 30 days €426).

Bus Éireann works in conjunction with ferry services and the bus company **Eurolines** (www.eurolines.com) to connect Ireland with Britain and the Continent. Eurolines passes for unlimited travel between major cities range €199-439. Discounts are available in the low-season and for people under 26 or over 60. A major route runs between Dublin and Victoria Station in London; other stops include Birmingham, Bristol, Cardiff, Glasgow, and Liverpool, with services to Cork, Derry/Londonderry, Galway, Limerick, and Waterford.

BY CAR. Drivers in Ireland use the left side of the road. Gasoline (petrol) prices are high. Be particularly cautious at roundabouts—give way to traffic from the right. **Dan Dooley** (☎062 53103, UK 0800 282 189, US 800-331-9301; www.dandooley.com) and **Enterprise** (☎UK 0870 350 3000, US 800-261-7331; www.enterprise.ie) will rent to drivers between 21 and 24, though such drivers must pay an additional daily surcharge. Fares are €85-200 per week (plus VAT), including insurance and unlimited mileage. If you plan to drive a car in Ireland for longer than 90 days, you must have an **International Driving Permit (IDP).** If you rent, lease, or borrow a car, you will need a **green card** or an **International Insurance Certificate** to certify that you have insurance. It is always significantly less expensive to reserve a car from the US than from within Europe.

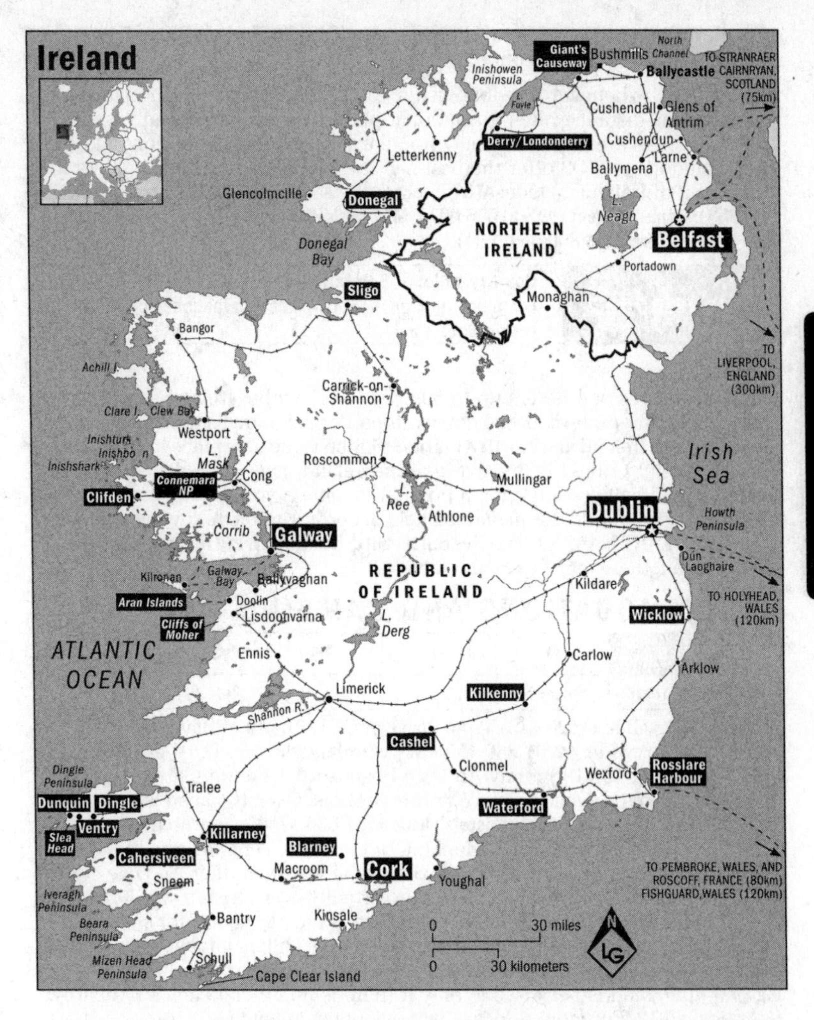

BY BIKE, FOOT, AND THUMB. Ireland's countryside is well suited to **biking,** as many roads are not heavily traveled. Single-digit "N" roads are more trafficked and should be avoided. Ireland's mountains, fields, and hills make **walking** and **hiking** arduous joys. The **Wicklow Way,** a 132km hiking trail in the mountains southeast of Dublin, has hostels within a day's walk of each other. Some locals caution against **hitchhiking** in County Dublin and the Midlands, where it is not very common. *Let's Go* does not recommend hitchhiking.

KEEPING IN TOUCH

EMAIL AND THE INTERNET. Internet access is available in most cafes, hostels, and libraries in cities and towns. One hour of web time costs about €3-6, though discounts are often available with an ISIC. Find listings of Internet cafes at www.cybercafes.com.

TELEPHONE. Whenever possible, use a calling card for international phone calls, as long-distance rates for national phone services are often very high. Mobile phones are an increasingly popular and economical option, and carriers Vodafone and O2 offer the best service. Direct-dial access numbers for calling out of Ireland include: **AT&T Direct** (☎800 550 000); **British Telecom** (☎800 890 353); **Canada Direct** (☎800 555 001); **MCI WorldPhone** (☎800 55 10 01); **Telecom New Zealand Direct** (☎800 55 00 64).

PHONE CODES	**Country code:** 353. **International dialing prefix:** 00. For more info on how to place international calls, see **Inside Back Cover.**

MAIL. Postcards and letters up to 50g cost €0.55 within Ireland and €0.82 to Europe and other international destinations. Airmail parcels take four to nine days between Ireland and North America. Dublin is the only place in the Republic with Postal Codes. To receive mail in Ireland, have mail delivered **Poste Restante.** Mail will go to the main post office unless you specify a subsidiary by street address. Address mail to be held according to the following example: First name LAST NAME, Poste Restante, City, Ireland. Bring a passport to pick up your mail; there may be a small fee.

ACCOMMODATIONS AND CAMPING

IRELAND	❶	❷	❸	❹	❺
ACCOMMODATIONS	under €17	€17-26	€27-40	€41-56	over €56

A **hostel** bed will average €13-20. **An Óige** (an OYJ), the **HI** affiliate, operates 27 hostels countrywide. (☎01 830 4555; www.irelandyha.org. One-year membership €20, under 18 €10.) Many An Óige hostels are in remote areas or small villages and are designed to serve nature-seekers. Over 100 hostels in Ireland belong to **Independent Holiday Hostels (IHH;** ☎01 836 4700; www.hostels-ireland.com). Most IHH hostels have no lockout or curfew, accept all ages, require no membership card, and have a less institutional feel than their An Óige counterparts; all are Bord Fáilte-approved. In virtually every Irish town, **B&Bs** can provide a luxurious break from hosteling. Expect to pay €30-35 for singles and €45-60 for doubles. "Full Irish breakfasts" are often filling enough to last until dinner. Camping in Irish State Forests and National Parks is not allowed. **Camping** on public land is permissible only if there is no official campsite nearby. Sites cost €5-13. For more info, see www.camping-ireland.ie.

FOOD AND DRINK

IRELAND	❶	❷	❸	❹	❺
FOOD	under €6	€6-10	€11-15	€16-20	over €20

Food in Ireland can be expensive, but the basics are simple and filling. Find quick and greasy staples at **chippers** (fish and chips shops) and **takeaways.** Most pubs serve Irish stew, burgers, soup, and sandwiches. Cafes and restaurants have begun to offer more vegetarian options to complement the typical meat-based entrees. **Soda bread** is delicious, and Irish **cheddars** are addictive. **Guinness,** a rich, dark stout, is revered with a zeal usually reserved for the Holy Trinity.

Known as "the dark stuff" or "the blonde in the black skirt," a proper pint has a head so thick that you can stand a match in it. **Irish whiskey,** which Queen Elizabeth once said was her only true Irish friend, is sweeter than its Scotch counterpart. "A big one" (a pint of Guinness) and "a small one" (a glass of whiskey) are often ordered alongside one another. When ordering at an Irish **pub,** one individual in a small group will usually approach the bar and buy a round of drinks for everyone. Once those drinks are downed, another individual will buy the next round. It's considered poor form to refuse someone's offer to buy you a drink. The legal age in Ireland to purchase alcohol is 18.

HOLIDAYS AND FESTIVALS

Holidays: New Year's Day (Jan. 1); St. Patrick's Day (Mar. 17); Good Friday and Easter Monday (Apr. 10, 2009 and Apr. 13, 2009); and Christmas (Dec. 25). There are 4 bank holidays, which will be observed on May 4, Jun. 8, Aug. 3, and Oct. 26 in 2009. Northern Ireland also observes Orangemen's Day (July 13).

Festivals: All of Ireland goes green for St. Patrick's Day (Mar. 17). On *Bloomsday* (June 16), Dublin celebrates James Joyce's Ulysses. In mid-July, the *Galway Arts Festival* offers theater, trad, rock, and film. Many return happy from the *Lisdoonvarna Matchmaking Festival* in the Burren in early Sept.

BEYOND TOURISM

To find opportunities that accommodate your interests and schedule, check with national agencies such as Volunteering Ireland (www.volunteeringireland.com). For more info on opportunities in Europe, see **Beyond Tourism,** p. 60.

L'Arche Ireland, "Seolta," Warrenhouse Rd., Baldoyle, Dublin, 13 (☎01 839 4356; www.larche.ie). Assistants can join residential communities in Cork, Dublin, or Kilkenny to live with, work with, and teach people with learning disabilities. Room, board, and small stipend provided. Commitment of 1-2yr. expected.

Sustainable Land Use Company, Doorian, Glenties, Co. Donegal (☎074 955 1286; www.donegalorganic.ie). Offers opportunities to assist with organic farming, forestry, habitat maintenance, and wildlife in the northern county of Donegal.

Focus Ireland, 9-12 High St., Dublin, 8 (☎01 881 5900; www.focusireland.ie). Advocacy and fundraising for the homeless in Dublin, Limerick, and Waterford.

DUBLIN ☎01

In a country known for its rural landscapes, the international flavor and frenetic pace of Dublin stick out like the 120m spire in the city's heart. Ireland's capital since the Middle Ages, Dublin offers all the amenities of other world-class cities on a more manageable scale, with all buildings topping off at five stories. Prestigious Trinity College holds treasures of Ireland's past, while Temple Bar has become one of Europe's hottest nightspots. The city's musical, cultural, and drinkable attractions continue to draw droves of visitors.

TRANSPORTATION

Flights: Dublin Airport (DUB; ☎01 814 1111; www.dublinairport.com). Dublin **buses** #41 and 41B run from the airport to Eden Quay in the city center (40-45min., every 10min., €1.80). Airlink **shuttle** (☎01 703 3092) runs nonstop to Busáras Central Bus

Station and O'Connell St. (20-25min., every 10-20min. 5:45am-11:30pm, €6), and to Heuston Station (50min., €6). A **taxi** to the city center costs roughly €25.

Trains: The **Irish Rail Travel Centre,** 35 Lower Abbey St. (☎01 836 6222; www.irishrail.ie), sells train tickets. Open M-F 8:30am-6pm, Sa 9:30am-6pm.

Pearse Station, Pearse St. (☎01 828 6000). Ticketing open M-Sa 7:30am-9:50pm, Su 9am-9:50pm. Receives southbound trains from Connolly Station and serves as a departure point for **Dublin Area Rapid Transit (DART)** trains serving the suburbs and coast (4-6 per hr., €2-6.70).

Connolly Station, Amiens St. (☎01 703 2358), north of the Liffey and close to Busáras. Bus #20b heads south of the river and #130 goes to the city center, while the DART runs to Tara Station on the south quay. Trains to: **Belfast** (2hr.; M-Sa 9 per day, Su 5 per day; €36), **Sligo** (3hr., M-Sa 8 per day, Su 6 per day per day, €29), and **Wexford and Rosslare** (3hr., 3 per day, €20.50).

Heuston Station (☎01 703 2132), south of Victoria Quay and west of the city center (a 25min. walk from Trinity College). Buses #78 and 79 run to the city center. Trains to: **Cork** (3hr., M-Sa 15 per day, Su 11 per day, €59.50); **Galway** (2hr.; M-Sa 7 per day, Su 6 per day; €31.50 M-Th and Sa, €44 F and Su); **Limerick** (2hr.; M-Sa 10, Su 7 per day; €45.50); **Waterford** (2hr.; M-Sa 6 per day, Su 4 per day; €24.50 M-Th and Sa, €31.50 F and Su).

Buses: Intercity buses to Dublin arrive at **Busáras Central Bus Station,** Store St. (☎01 836 6111; www.buseireann.ie), next to Connolly Station. Buses to: **Belfast** (3hr., 24 per day, €15); **Cork** (4½hr., 6 per day, €12); **Derry/Londonderry** (4hr., 9 per day, €20); **Donegal** (4hr., 10 per day, €18); **Galway** (3hr., 17 per day, €15); **Limerick** (3½hr., 13 per day, €10); **Rosslare** (3hr., 13 per day, €16.80); **Sligo** (4hr., 5-6 per day, €18); **Tralee** (6hr., 9 per day, €23); **Wexford** (2hr.; M-Sa 17 per day, Su 10 per day; €13.50).

Ferries: Irish Ferries, 2-4 Merrion Row, (☎0818 300 400; www.irishferries.com) off St. Stephen's Green. Open M-F 9am-5pm, Sa 9am-1pm. Stena Line ferries arrive from Holyhead at the **Dún Laoghaire** ferry terminal (☎01 204 7777; www.stenaline.com).

Public Transportation: Info on local buses available at **Dublin Bus Office,** 59 Upper O'Connell St. (☎01 873 4222; www.dublinbus.ie). Open M 8:30am-5:30pm, Tu-F 9am-5:30pm, Sa 9am-2pm, Su 9:30am-2pm. **Rambler** passes offer unlimited rides for a day (€6) or a week (€23). Dublin Bus runs the **NiteLink** service to the suburbs (M-Th 12:30 and 2am, F-Sa every 20min. 12:30-4:30am; €5; passes not valid). The **Luas** (☎01 461 4910 or ☎1800 300 604; www.luas.ie; phone line open M-F 7am-7pm, Sa 10am-2pm), Dublin's **Light Rail Tram System,** is the city's newest form of mass transit.

Taxis: Blue Cabs (☎01 802 2222), **ABC** (☎01 285 5444), and **City Cabs** (☎01 872 7272) have wheelchair-accessible cabs (call ahead). Available 24hr.

Car Rental: Europcar, Dublin Airport (☎01 812 0410; www.www.europcar.ie). Economy around €50 per day, €200 per wk. Ages 24-70.

Bike Rental: Cycle Ways, 185-6 Parnell St. (☎01 873 4748). Rents quality hybrid or mountain bikes. €20 per day, €80 per week with €200 deposit. Open M-W and F-Sa 9:30am-6pm, Th 9:30am-8pm, Su 11am-5pm. AmEx/MC/V.

ORIENTATION AND PRACTICAL INFORMATION

Although Dublin is compact, getting lost is not much of a challenge. Street signs, when posted, are located high up on the sides of buildings at most intersections. The essential *Dublin Visitor Map* is available for free at the Dublin Bus Office. The **Liffey River** forms a natural boundary between Dublin's North and South Sides. Heuston Station and the more famous sights, posh stores, and upscale restaurants are on the **South Side,** while Connolly Station, the majority of hostels, and the bus station are on the **North Side.** The North Side is less expensive than the more touristed South Side, but it also has a reputation for being rougher, especially after dark. The streets running alongside the Liffey are called **quays** (pronounced "keys"); the name of the quay changes with each bridge. **O'Connell Street,** three blocks west of the Busáras Central Bus Station,

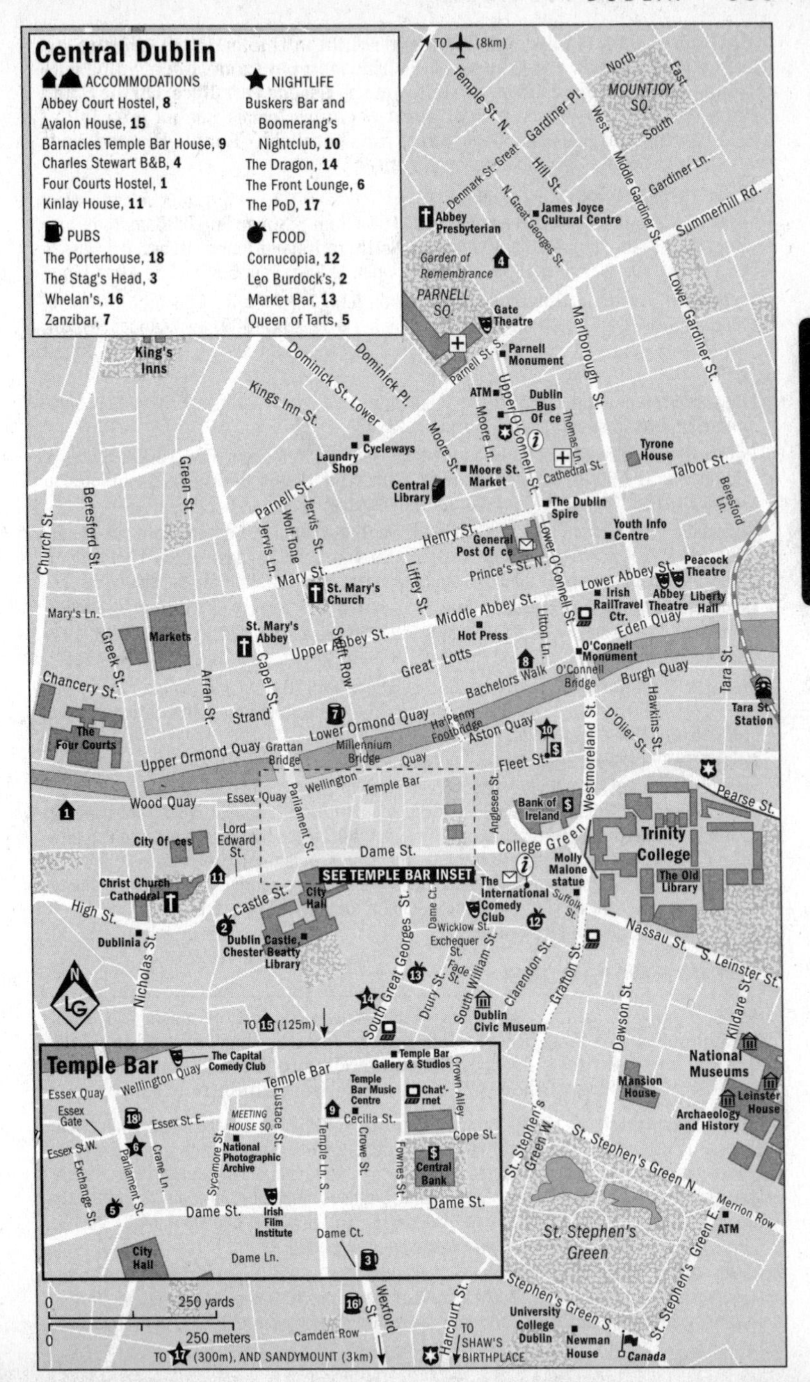
Central Dublin
ACCOMMODATIONS
Abbey Court Hostel, 8
Avalon House, 15
Barnacles Temple Bar House, 9
Charles Stewart B&B, 4
Four Courts Hostel, 1
Kinlay House, 11
NIGHTLIFE
Buskers Bar and Boomerang's Nightclub, 10
The Dragon, 14
The Front Lounge, 6
The PoD, 17
PUBS
The Porterhouse, 18
The Stag's Head, 3
Whelan's, 16
Zanzibar, 7
FOOD
Cornucopia, 12
Leo Burdock's, 2
Market Bar, 13
Queen of Tarts, 5
Temple Bar
The Capital Comedy Club
Temple Bar Gallery & Studios
Temple Bar Music Centre
Chat'-rnet
National Photographic Archive
Irish Film Institute
Central Bank
City Hall
SEE TEMPLE BAR INSET
Trinity College
The Old Library
St. Stephen's Green
National Museums
Leinster House
Archaeology and History
Mansion House
Dublin Civic Museum
University College Dublin
Newman House
Canada
Dublin Castle, Chester Beatty Library
Christ Church Cathedral
Dublinia
The Four Courts
Markets
General Post Office
Central Library
Abbey Presbyterian
James Joyce Cultural Centre
Gate Theatre
Parnell Monument
Dublin Bus Office
The Dublin Spire
Youth Info Centre
Peacock Theatre
Abbey Theatre
Liberty Hall
Irish RailTravel Ctr.
O'Connell Monument
Tara St. Station
Bank of Ireland
Molly Malone statue
The International Comedy Club
TO (8km)
TO 15 (125m)
TO 17 (300m), AND SANDYMOUNT (3km)
TO SHAW'S BIRTHPLACE
250 yards
250 meters

is the primary link between northern and southern Dublin. On the North Side, **Henry** and **Mary Streets** constitute a pedestrian shopping zone, intersecting with O'Connell St. two blocks from the Liffey at the **General Post Office.** On the South Side, a block from the river, **Fleet Street** becomes **Temple Bar,** an area full of music centers and galleries. **Dame Street** runs parallel to Temple Bar and leads east to **Trinity College,** Dublin's cultural center.

Tourist Office: Main Office, Suffolk St. (☎01 605 7700; www.visitdublin.com). Near Trinity College in a converted church. Open M-Sa 9am-5:30pm, Su 10:30am-3pm; July-Aug. M-Sa 9am-7pm; Su 10:30am-5pm. **Northern Ireland Tourist Board,** 16 Nassau St. (☎01 679 1977 or ☎1850 230 230). Open M-F 9:15am-5:30pm, Sa 10am-5pm.

Embassies: Australia, Fitzwilton House, Wilton Terr., 7th fl. (☎01 664 5300; www.ireland.embassy.gov.au); **Canada,** 7-8 Wilton Terr. (☎01 234 4000; www.canada.ie); **UK,** 29 Merrion Rd. (☎01 205 3700); www.britishembassy.ie); **US,** 42 Elgin Rd. (☎01 668 8777; http://dublin.usembassy.gov).

Luggage Storage: Connolly Station: Small lockers €4, large lockers €6. Open daily 5am-midnight. **Busáras:** Lockers €6/8. Open 24hr.

Police (Garda): Dublin Metro Headquarters, Harcourt Terr. (☎01 666 9500); Store St. Station (☎01 666 8000); Fitzgibbon St. Station (☎01 666 8400); Pearse St. Station (☎01 666 9000). **Police Confidential Report Line:** ☎800 666 111.

Pharmacy: Hickey's, 56 Lower O'Connell St. (☎01 873 0427). Convenient to bus routes. Open M-F 7:30am-10pm, Sa 8am-10pm, Su and bank holidays 10am-10pm. Other branches scattered about the city, including locations on Grafton St. and Henry St.

Hospital: St. James's Hospital, James St. (☎01 410 3000). Bus #123. **Mater Misericordiae Hospital,** Eccles St. (☎01 803 2000). Buses #3, 10, 11, 16, 22 36, 121. **Beaumont Hospital,** Beaumont Rd. (☎01 809 3000). Buses #103, 104, 27b, 42a.

Internet: The Internet Exchange at Cecilia St. (☎01 670 3000) in Temple Bar. €3 per hr. Open M-F 8am-2am, Sa-Su 10am-2am. There are numerous other Internet cafes with comparable rates around the city.

Post Office: General Post Office, O'Connell St. (☎01 705 7000). **Poste Restante** pickup at the Poste Restante window (see Mail, p. 32). Open M-Sa 8am-8pm. Smaller post offices, including one on Suffolk St. across from the tourist office, are typically open M-Tu and Th-F 9am-6pm, W 9:30am-6pm. **Postal Codes:** Dublin is the only place in the Republic that uses postal codes. The city is organized into regions numbered 1-18, 20, 22, and 24; even-numbered codes are for areas south of the Liffey, while odd-numbered ones are for the north. The numbers radiate out from the city center: North City Centre is 1, South City Centre is 2.

ACCOMMODATIONS

Because Dublin is an incredibly popular destination, it is necessary to book accommodations at least one week in advance, particularly around holidays and in the summer. If the following accommodations are full, consult Dublin Tourism's annual *Sleep!* Guide (€2.50), or ask hostel staff for referrals.

Four Courts Hostel, 15-17 Merchants Quay (☎01 672 5839). On the south bank of the river. Bus #748 from the airport stops next door. 230-bed hostel with pristine, well-lit rooms and hardwood floors. Quiet lounge and a combination TV/game room provide plenty of space to wind down. Continental breakfast included. In-room lockers. Free Wi-Fi; computer use €1 per 15min. Laundry €7.50. 8- to 16-bed dorms €17-21.50; 4- to 6-bed €25-38; doubles €64-72; triples around €90. ❶

Abbey Court Hostel, 29 Bachelor's Walk (☎01 878 0700; www.abbey-court.com). Corner of O'Connell St. and Bachelor's Walk near bridge. Hostel boasts clean, narrow rooms overlooking the Liffey. Hidden apartments each have lounge, TV, and courtyard.

IRELAND

Internet €1 per 15min., €2 per 40min. Continental breakfast at **NYStyle cafe** next door included. Free luggage storage; security box €1. Full-service laundry €8. 12-bed dorms €19-23; 6-bed €24-27; 4-bed €27-31; doubles €78-89. Long-term rate €108-126 per week includes breakfast. Apartments from €89 per night. ❷

Parkway Guest House, 5 Gardiner Pl. (☎01 874 0469; www.parkway-guesthouse.com). Sports fans bond with the proprietor, a former hurling star, while those less athletically inclined still appreciate his great eye for interior design, sound advice, and all-star breakfasts. Singles €40; doubles €60-80, €80-100 with bath. MC/V. ❸

Avalon House (IHH), 55 Aungier St. (☎01 475 0001; www.avalon-house.ie). Performers get free accommodation if they spend 1hr. teaching other guests. Wheelchair-accessible with elevator. Light continental breakfast included. Lockers and smaller lock boxes €1 per day; €8-10 deposit. Laundry €7. Free Wi-Fi. 24hr. reception. Large dorms €14-20; 4- to 6-bed dorms €24-31; singles €32-41; doubles €30-39. MC/V. ❶

Barnacles Temple Bar House, 19 Temple Ln. (☎01 671 6277). Patrons can nearly jump into bed from Temple Bar pubs, including the actual Temple Bar, next door. Spacious, sky-lit lounge with fireplace and TV. Breakfast included. Free luggage storage. Laundry €7. Free Wi-Fi; Internet on house computers €1 per 15min. 11-bed dorms €19-21; 6-bed €27-29.50; quads €28.50-31.50; doubles €80-87. ❶

Kinlay House (IHH), 2-12 Lord Edward St. (☎01 679 6644). Great location a few blocks from Temple Bar. If you don't get a room with a view of the Christ Church Cathedral, at least you can watch the plasma TV. Continental breakfast included. Lockers €1 with €5 deposit. Laundry €8. Free Internet. 4- to 6-bed dorms €22-33; 16- to 24-bed €18-24; doubles €30-38; triples €32-41. Min. stay 2 nights on weekend. ❶

IRELAND

FOOD

Dublin's many **open-air markets** sell fresh food at relatively cheap prices. The later in the week, the livelier the market. Bustling **Moore St. Market,** between Henry St. and Parnell St., is a great place to get fresh veggies. (Open M-Sa 10am-5pm.) The **Thomas Street Market,** along the continuation of Dame St., is a calmer alternative. (Generally open Th-Sa 11am-5pm, although some stalls are open during the week.) Produce can be found every day along Wexford Sreet. The best value for supermarkets around Dublin is in the **Dunnes Stores** chain, with full branches at St. Stephen's Green (☎01 478 0188; open M-W and F 8:30am-8pm, Th 8:30am-9pm, Sa 8:30am-7pm, Su 10am-7pm), the ILAC Centre off Henry St., and N. Earl St. off O'Connell.

Queen of Tarts, Dame St. (☎01 670 7499), across from City Hall (and new, bigger location on Cow's Lane, Temple Bar). Pastries, light meals, and coffee in a supremely feminine hideaway. Delectable tarts €10 (savory) and €5.50 (sweet). Breakfast €3.50-10. Sandwiches €8. Open M-F 7:30am-7pm, Sa-Su 9am-7pm. MC/V. ❶

Market Bar, Fade St. (☎01 613 9094; www.tapas.ie). Right off S. Great Georges after Lower Stephen St. Huge sausage factory given a classy makeover; now serves tapas in heaping portions. Small tapas €8; large tapas €12. Kitchen open M-Th noon-11:30pm, F-Sa noon-12:30am, Su 3-11pm. ❶

Cornucopia, 19 Wicklow St. (☎01 671 9449). If there's space, sit down in this cozy spot for a delicious meal (€11-12) or a cheaper salad smorgasbord (€4.25-9.25 for choice of 2, 4, or 6 salads). Accommodates many dietary restrictions. Open M-F 8:30am-9pm, Sa 8:30am-8pm, Su noon-7pm. ❷

Leo Burdock's, 2 Werburgh St. (☎01 454 0306), behind The Lord Edward Pub across from Christ Church Cathedral. Additional location on Lower Liffey St. Fish and chips served the right way—in brown paper. A nightly pilgrimage for many Dubliners. Takeaway only. Fish €4.50-7; chips €3. Open daily noon-midnight. ❶

SIGHTS

TRINITY COLLEGE. The British built **Trinity College** in 1592 as a Protestant seminary that would "civilize the Irish and cure them of Popery." The college became part of the path on which members of the Anglo-Irish elite trod on their way to high positions: it has educated such luminaries as Jonathan Swift, Robert Emmett, Thomas Moore, Oscar Wilde, and Samuel Beckett. The Catholic Church deemed it a cardinal sin to attend Trinity until the 1960s; when the Church lifted the ban, the size of the student body tripled. Today, it's a celebrated center of learning, located steps away from the teeming center of a cosmopolitan capital, and an unmissable stop on the tourist trail. *(Between Westmoreland and Grafton St., South Dublin. Main entrance fronts the traffic circle now called College Green. Pearse St. runs along the north edge of the college, Nassau St. the south. ☎01 608 1724; www.tcd.ie. Grounds always open. Free.)*

KILDARE STREET. Just southeast of Trinity College, the museums on Kildare St. offer scientific and artistic wonders. The **National Gallery's** extensive collection includes paintings by Brueghel, Goya, Caravaggio, Vermeer, and Rembrandt. *(Merrion Sq. W. ☎01 661 5133; www.nationalgallery.ie. Open M-W and F-Sa 9:30am-5:30pm, Th 9:30am-8:30pm, Su noon-5:30pm. Free guided tours Sa 3pm, Su 2, 3, 4pm; July also daily 3pm. Admission free. Temporary exhibits €10, students and seniors €6.)* The **National Museum of Archaeology and History,** Dublin's largest museum, has incredible artifacts spanning the last two millennia to illustrate the history of Ireland, including the **Tara Brooch.** *(Kildare St., next to Leinster House. ☎01 677 7444; www.museum.ie. Open Tu-Sa 10am-5pm, Su 2-5pm. Guided tours €2; call for times. Museum free.)*

DAME STREET AND THE CATHEDRALS. Norman King John built **Dublin Castle** in 1204 on top of the Viking settlement Dubh Linn ("black pool"); more recently, a series of structures from the 18th and 19th centuries has covered the site, culminating in an uninspired 20th-century office complex. Next door, the intricate inner dome of **Dublin City Hall** shelters statues of national heroes like **Daniel O'Connell.** *(Dame St., at the intersection of Parliament and Castle St. ☎01 677 7129; www.dublincastle.ie. State Apartments open M-F 10am-5pm, Sa-Su and holidays 2-4:45pm; closed during official functions. €4.50, students and seniors €3.50, children €2. Grounds free.)* At the **Chester Beatty Library,** behind Dublin Castle, visitors can see the treasures bequeathed to Ireland by American mining magnate Alfred Chester Beatty. *(☎01 407 0750; www.cbl.ie. 45min. tours W 1pm, Su 3 and 4pm. Open May-Sept. M-F 10am-5pm, Sa 11am-5pm, Su 1-5pm; Oct.-Apr. Tu-F 10am-5pm, Sa 11am-5pm, Su 1-5pm. Free.)* Across from the castle sits the historic **Christ Church Cathedral.** Stained glass sparkles above the raised crypts, one of which supposedly belongs to Strongbow. The entrance fee includes admission to the **"Treasure of Christ Church,"** a rotating exhibit that displays the church's hoard of medieval manuscripts, gleaming gold vessels, and funereal busts. *(At the end of Dame St., uphill and across from the Castle. A 10min. walk from O'Connell Bride, or take bus #50 from Eden Quay or 78A from Aston Quay. ☎01 677 8099. Open daily 9am-5pm except during services. €6, students and seniors €4.)* **St. Patrick's Cathedral,** Ireland's largest, dates back to the 12th century, although Sir Benjamin Guinness remodeled much of the building in 1864. Jonathan Swift spent his last years as Dean of St. Patrick's; his grave is marked on the floor of the south nave. *(From Christ Church, Nicholas St. runs south and downhill, eventually becoming Patrick St. Take bus #49, 49A, 50, 54A, 56A, 65, 65B, 77, or 77A from Eden Quay. ☎01 475 4817; www.stpatrickscathedral.ie. Open Mar.-Oct. daily 9am-6pm; Nov.-Feb. Sa 9am-5pm, Su 9am-3pm. Church closed to visitors Su half hr. before services which begin 8:30am, 11:15am, 3:15pm, although visitors are welcome to attend. €5.50, students and seniors €4.20.)*

GUINNESS BREWERY AND KILMAINHAM. Guinness brews its black magic at the St. James' Gate Brewery, right next door to the **Guinness Storehouse.** The abundance of stout-stamped paper bags hanging from the arms of tourists are a good indication of Ireland's number one tourist attraction. Forward-looking Arthur Guinness ensured the success of his original 1759 brewery by signing a 9000-year lease, which is dramatically set into the floor of the massive reception hall. The self-guided tour ends with a complimentary pint in the top floor's **Gravity Bar,** a modern, light-filled space that commands a stunning panoramic view of the city. *(St. James's Gate. From Christ Church Cathedral, follow High St. west through its name changes—Cornmarket, Thomas, and James. Or, take bus #51B or 78A from Aston Quay or #123 from O'Connell St. ☎01 408 4800; www.guinness-storehouse.com. Open daily July-Aug. 9:30am-7pm; Sept.-June 9:30am-5pm. €14, students over 18 and seniors €10, students under 18 €8, ages 6-12 €5, under 6 free.)* Almost all the rebels who fought in Ireland's struggle for independence between 1792 and 1921 spent time at **Kilmainham Gaol.** The ghastly, compelling stories of the prisoners are dealt out in two doses, first in the comprehensive museum that sets the jail in the context of its socio-political history, and then in a 1hr. tour of the dank chambers that ends in the haunting wasteland of an execution yard. *(Inchicore Rd. Take bus #51b, 51c, 78a, or 79 from Aston Quay. ☎01 453 5984. Open Apr.-Sept. daily 9:30am-6pm; Oct.-Mar. M-Sa 9:30am-5:30pm, Su 10am-6pm. Last admission hr. before close. Tours every 30min. €5.30, seniors €3.70, students €2.10, families €11.50. Small museum, separate from tour, is free of charge.)*

O'CONNELL STREET AND PARNELL SQUARE. Once Europe's widest street, O'Connell St. on the North Side now holds the less prestigious distinction of being Dublin's biggest shopping thoroughfare. The city's rich literary heritage comes to life at the **Dublin Writers' Museum,** which documents Dublin's rich literary heritage and the famous figures who played a part. Manuscripts, rare editions, and memorabilia of giants like Swift, Shaw, Wilde, Yeats, Beckett, Behan, Kavanagh, and O'Casey share space with caricatures and paintings. *(18 Parnell Sq. N. ☎01 872 2077; www.writersmuseum.com. Open June-Aug. M-F 10am-6pm, Sa 10am-5pm, Su 11am-5pm; Sept.-May M-Sa 10am-5pm, Su 11am-5pm. €7.25, students and seniors €6.10, children €4.55, families €21. Combined ticket with the Shaw birthplace €12.50, students and seniors €10.30.)* The **Irish Writers Centre,** adjacent to the museum, is the hub of Ireland's living community of writers, providing today's aspiring writers with frequent fiction and poetry readings. It is not a museum, but it does provide information about Dublin's literary happenings. *(19 Parnell Sq. N. ☎01 872 1302; www.writerscentre.ie. Open M-F 10am-5:30pm.)* Mock-ups at the **James Joyce Cultural Centre** reveal insight into Joyce's life, love, and labor, while intriguing items like the original door to his home at 7 Eccles St., a map tracing Stephen Daedalus' and Leopold Bloom's relative movements, and a 1921 Ulysses schema pique literary interest. *(35 N. Great Georges St., up Marlborough St. and past Parnell Sq. ☎01 878 8547; www.jamesjoyce.ie. Open year-round Tu-Sa 10am-5pm; Apr.-Oct. additionally Su noon-5pm. Guided tour every Sa 11am and 2pm; July-Aug. additionally Tu and Th 11am and 2pm; €10, students and seniors €8. Admission to the center €5, students and seniors €4.)*

OTHER SIGHTS. Dublin's greatest architectural triumph, the **Custom House** was designed and built in the 1780s by London-born James Gandon, who gave up the chance to be Russia's state architect so that he could settle in Dublin. The Roman and Venetian columns and domes give the cityscape a taste of what the city's 18th-century Anglo-Irish brahmins wanted Dublin to become. Carved heads along the frieze represent the rivers of Ireland; the sole woman is the Liffey. *(East of O'Connell St. at Custom House Quay, where Gardiner St. meets the river. ☎01 878 7660. Visitors Centre open mid-Mar.-Oct. M-F 10am-5pm, Sa-Su 2-5pm; Nov. to mid-Mar. W-F 10am-5pm, Su 2-5pm. €1, families €3, students free.)* The modest **St. Michan's Church,** dating back to 1095, is noteworthy for its ancient, creepy limestone vaults, which may have inspired Bram Stoker's *Dracula.* Everything in here is real, from the mummified corpses dating back 800 years to the grisly execution order of two 1798 rebels. *(Church St. ☎01 872 4154. Open Mar.-Oct. M-F 10am-12:45pm and 2-4:45pm, Sa 10am-12:45pm; Nov.-Mar. M-F 12:30-3:30pm, Sa 10am-12:45pm. Crypt tours €4, students and seniors €3.50, under 16 €3, families (2 adults, 2 children) €12. Church of Ireland services Su 10am.)* At the **Old Jameson Distillery,** learn how science, grain, and tradition come together to form liquid gold. The tour walks visitors through the creation of whiskey, although the stuff is really distilled in Co. Clare. Not to disappoint those hankering for a taste after all that talking, the tour ends at the bar with a free drink (or soft drinks for the uninitiated). Volunteer in the beginning to get the chance to taste-test a tray of six different whiskeys from around the world. *(Bow St. From O'Connell St., turn onto Henry St. and continue straight as the street narrows to Mary St., then Mary Ln.; the warehouse is on a cobblestone street on the left. Buses #68, 69, and 79 run from city center to Merchant's Quay. ☎01 807 2355. Tours daily 9:30am-6pm, typically every 45min. €12.50, students and seniors €9, children €6.)*

ENTERTAINMENT

Whether you seek poetry, punk, or something in between, Dublin is ready to entertain. The free *Event Guide* is available at music stores and hotels throughout the city. The glossier *In Dublin* (free at Tower Records, the tourist office) comes out every two weeks with feature articles and listings for music, theater, art exhibitions, comedy shows, clubs, museums, and movie theaters. Go to www.visitdublin.com for the latest hot spots.

Abbey Theatre, 26 Lower Abbey St. (☎01 878 7222; www.abbeytheatre.ie). The theater was founded by W.B. Yeats and Lady Gregory in 1904 to promote the Irish cultural revival and Modernist theater, a combination that didn't go over well with audiences. The Abbey's 1907 premiere of J.M. Synge's *Playboy of the Western World* led to storms of protest. Today, the Abbey (and Synge) have gained respectability. Ireland's National Theatre is on the cutting edge of international drama. Tickets €22-35; Sa 2:30pm matinee €18-22, students and seniors with ID €14. Box office open M-Sa 10:30am-7pm.

Peacock Theatre, 26 Lower Abbey St. (☎01 878 7222). The Abbey's experimental downstairs studio theater. Evening shows, plus occasional lunchtime plays, concerts, and poetry. Doors open M-Sa at 7:30pm. Tickets €15-22; Sa 2:30pm matinees €18, students/seniors €15. Available at Abbey box office.

Gate Theatre, 1 Cavendish Row (☎01 874 4045; www.gate-theatre.ie). Contemporary Irish and classic international dramas in intimate, elegant setting. Wheelchair-accessible. Box office open M-Sa 10am-7:30pm. Tickets €16-30; M-Th student ticket at curtain €15 with ID, subject to availability.

PUBLIN

James Joyce proposed that a "good puzzle would be to cross Dublin without passing a pub." When a local radio station once offered £100 to the first person to solve the puzzle, the winner explained that any route worked—you'd just have to stop in each one along the way. Dublin's pubs come in all shapes, sizes, and specialties. Ask around or check the publications *In Dublin*, *Hot Press*, or *Event Guide* for music listings. Normal pub hours in Ireland end at 11:30pm Sunday through Wednesday and 12:30am Thursday through Saturday. The laws that dictate these hours are subject to yearly changes—patrons often get about a half-hour after "closing" to finish off their drinks. An increasing number of pubs have late permits that allow them to remain open until at least 2am; drink prices tend to rise around midnight to cover the permit's cost (or so they claim). Bars that post their closing time as "late" mean after midnight and, sometimes, after what is legally mandated. ID-checking almost always happens at the door rather than at the bar. A growing number of bars are blurring the distinction between pub and club by hosting live music and staying open late into the night on weekdays.

The Stag's Head, 1 Dame Ct. (☎01 679 3687). Atmospheric Victorian pub with stained glass, marble-topped round tables, and evidence of deer decapitation front and center above the bar. Student crowd dons everything from T-shirts to tuxes. Pub grub, like bangers and mash, runs €6-12. Kitchen open M-Sa noon-4pm. Bar open M-Th 10:30am-11:30pm, F-Sa 10:30am-12:30am, Su 12:30-11pm.

The Porterhouse, 16-18 Parliament St. (☎01 679 8847). Way, way more than 99 bottles of beer on the wall, including 9 self-brewed porters, stouts, and ales. The Porterhouse Red is a must. 3 floors fill nightly with great crowd for trad, blues, and rock. Open M-W 11:30am-11:30pm, Th-F 11:30am-2am, Sa 11:30am-2:30am, Su 12:30-11pm.

Whelan's, 25 Wexford St. (☎01 478 0766; www.whelanslive.com). Pub hosts big-name trad, rock, and everything in between in attached music venue. Live music nightly starting at 8:30pm (doors open at 8pm). Th DJ takes the floor. Cover for shows next door €8-16. Open for lunch (€8-12) 12:30-2pm. Open M-W until 2am and Th-Sa until 3am.

Zanzibar, at the Ha'penny Bridge (☎01 878 7212). Dances between club and pub with explosive results. Unique private rooms on the balcony, one overlooking the Liffey. Th-Su DJ plays R&B, blues, and chart-toppers. Cover after 11pm F €5, Sa €7. Kitchen open until 10pm. 21+. Open Th-Sa 5pm-2:30am, Su noon-11:30pm.

CLUBLIN

As a rule, clubs open at 10 or 10:30pm, but they don't heat up until the pubs empty around 12:30am. Clubbing is an expensive end to the evening; covers run €5-20 and pints can surpass €5. To save some money, find a club with an expensive cover but cheap drink prices and stay all night. A handful of smaller clubs on Harcourt and Camden Streets are basic but fun. Most clubs close between 1:30 and 3am, but a few have been known to stay open until daybreak. To get home after 11:30pm, take the **NiteLink bus** (M-W 12:30am and 2am, Th-Sa every 20min. from 12:30am to 4:30am; €5), which runs designated routes from the corner of Westmoreland and College St. to Dublin's suburbs. Taxi stands are sprinkled throughout the city, the most central being in front of Trinity, at the top of Grafton St. Be prepared to wait 30-45min. on weekend nights. For the most up-to-date information on clubs, check the *Event Guide*.

The PoD, 35 Harcourt St. (☎01 476 3374; www.pod.ie), corner of Hatch St., in an old train station. Stylishly futuristic, orange interior. Serious about its music. Upstairs is **The Red Box** (☎478 0225), a huge, separate club with brain-crushing music and a crowd at the bar so deep it seems designed to winnow out the weak. Mellow train-station-turned-bar **Crawdaddy** hosts musical gigs, including some world stars. Cover €10-20; Th students €5; can rise fast when big-name DJs perform. Open until 2:30am on weekends.

The Mezz (The Hub), 21-25 Eustace St. (☎01 670 7655). Live bands rock nightly right inside the entrance of this poster-plastered, atmospheric club—try not to knock over a drum set as you make your way toward the bar. Quiet pub by afternoon (M-Sa 5pm-2:30am, Su 5pm-1am) transforms into a loud, live-music cauldron at night. No cover. It shares the building with **The Hub,** which, as one of the only 18+ clubs in Temple Bar, attracts the younger crowd. Cover at The Hub €5-10 or more, depending on the band—doors 8pm, dancing 11:30pm. Open Tu-Sa until 2:30am.

The Dragon, S. Great Georges St. (☎01 478 1590), a few doors down from The George. Opened in May 2005 as Dublin's newest gay club, although everyone is welcome. It's packed to its trendy rafters on weekend nights. Quieter lounge area in front gives way to a DJ spinning house by the dance floor in back. 18+. Open M and Th 5pm-2:30am, Tu-W 5-11:30pm, F-Sa 5pm-3:30am, Su 5-11pm. The upstairs bar is the drinking quarters for the Emerald Warriors, Ireland's gay rugby team.

The Village, 26 Wexford St. (☎01 475 8555). Posh ground-floor bar. Occasional live music below a popular upstairs weekend club. Th-Sa bands play 7-10:30pm (about €15), then DJs spin chill-out, jungle, and house downstairs. Tickets for live bands available next door. Club F €8, Sa €10. Bar open until 1:30am; club open Th-Sa until 3am.

SOUTHEASTERN IRELAND

Ireland's southeastern region is famous for its strawberries and oysters. Round towers, built by monks to defend against Viking attacks, litter the countryside from the medieval city of Kilkenny to the Rock of Cashel. The grassy fields and stunning mountain views provide a brilliant contrast to the trad and rock pumping through the pubs of Waterford, Kilkenny, and Wexford.

TRANSPORTATION

Rosslare Harbour is a useful departure point for ferries to Wales or France. Stena Line (☎01 204 7777; www.stenaline.ie) and Irish Ferries (☎818 300 400; www.irishferries.com) run **ferries** from Rosslare Harbour to Pembroke, BRI (3hr., 2 per day, €35) and to Roscoff and Cherbourg, FRA (18-19hr., 1 per 2 days, €69-78). From Rosslare Harbour, **trains** run to Dublin and Limerick via Waterford, while **buses** go to: Dublin (3hr., 13 per day, Su 10 per day, €16.80); Galway via Waterford (6hr., 3-4 per day, €24); Limerick (4hr., 4-5 per day, €13.50); Tralee (2-4 per day, € 23.40). Contact **Wexford Tourism** (☎053 916 1155) for more info.

THE WICKLOW MOUNTAINS ☎0404

Over 600m tall, carpeted in fragrant heather and pleated by sparkling rivers, the Wicklow summits provide a tranquil stop just outside Dublin. The **Wicklow Way,** a 125km hiking trail, winds past grazing sheep, scattered villages, and monastic ruins. The **National Park Information Office,** is the best source for hiking advice and **maps.** (☎0404 45425. Open May-Sept. daily 10am-5:30pm; Oct. Sa-Su 10am-5:30pm; Nov.-Jan. Sa-Su 10am-4pm; Feb.-Apr. Sa-Su 10am-5:30pm.) When the office is closed, call the duty **ranger line** (☎087 980 3899, 9am-5pm). The valley of **Glendalough** is home to St. Kevin's sixth-century monastery. A particularly good hike is the **Spinc and Glenealo Valley path** (3hr.), marked by white arrows. The trail ascends to a glorious lookout over Upper Lake, circles the valley where goats and deer wander, and passes old mining ruins before looping back. Bring a raincoat and water, and prepare for some moderate exertion.

At the secluded **Glendalough International Hostel (HI) ❷,** 5min. up the road from the Glendalough Visitor Centre, guests won't hear rambunctious travelers, just chirping birds. (☎0404 45342; www.anoige.ie. Breakfast €5-7.50; packed lunches €6; request the night before. Laundry €5. Single-sex dorms May-Sept. €23; Oct.-Apr. €19. €2 HI discount. AmEx/MC/V.) Just 1.5km up the road, tiny **Laragh** has food options and plenty of B&Bs. **St. Kevin's Bus Service** (☎01 281 8119; www.glendaloughbus.com) arrives at the Glendalough Visitor's Centre from the end of Dawson St. nearest to St. Stephen's Green in Dublin. (Buses run daily 2 per day, €13.) Public transportation in the mountains is extremely limited; buses or taxis are your best bet. **Glendalough Cabs** (☎087 972 9452; www.glendaloughcabs.com) offers 24hr. service.

KILKENNY ☎05677

Eight churches share the streets with 80 pubs in Kilkenny (pop. 30,000), Ireland's best-preserved medieval town. The13th-century **Kilkenny Castle,** complete with well-maintained public grounds, housed the Earls of Ormonde until 1932. (☎05677 04100. Open daily June-Aug. 9:30am-7pm; Sept. 10am-6:30pm; Oct.-Mar. 10:30am-12:45pm and 2-5pm; Apr.-May 10:30am-5pm. Required tour, 2-3 per hr., €5.30, students €2.10. MC/V.) Grab a free pint at **Smithwicks Brewery,** Parliament St. (☎05677 21014. Tours July-Aug. M-F 3pm. Pick up a free ticket in the morning at the security station on the right past the Watergate Theatre.) Climb the steep steps of the 30m tower of **St. Canice's Cathedral,** up the hill off Dean St., for a panoramic view. (☎05677 64971. Open June-Aug. M-Sa 9am-6pm, Su 2-6pm; Apr.-May and Sept. M-Sa 10am-1pm and 2-5pm, Su 2-5pm; Oct.-Mar. M-Sa 10am-1pm and 2-4pm, Su 2-4pm. €4, students €3. Tower €3/2.50.)

Most B&Bs are on **Waterford Road.** Conveniently located near the pubs on High St., the welcoming **Kilkenny Tourist Hostel ❶,** 35 Parliament St., offers clean, spacious rooms. (☎05677 63541. Laundry €5. Free Wi-Fi. Check-in 8:30am-11pm. Check-out 10am. Dorms €16-17; doubles €40-42; quads €72-76. Cash only.) **The Two Dames ❶,** 80 John St., serves creative sandwiches (€5-6) and stuffed baked potatoes (€6) that are as good as they smell. (☎05677 56841. Open M-F 8:30am-5pm, Sa 10am-4:30pm. Cash only.) Make a meal of free samples at the **SuperQuinn** grocery store in the Market Cross shopping center off High St. (☎05677 52444. Open M-Tu 8am-7pm, W-F 8am-9pm, Sa 8am-7pm, Su 8am-6pm.) Start your pub crawl at the end of **Parliament Street,** then work your way to the wilder bars on **John Street,** which stay open later. The best *craic* is at the **Pump House** (☎05677 63924), on Parliament St., **Tynan's Bridge House Bar** (☎05677 21291), by the river, and **Ryan's** (☎05677 087 633 0923), on Friary St. off High St.

Trains (☎05677 22024) leave from Dublin Rd. for Dublin (2hr., €23) and Waterford (45min., €13.50). **Buses** (☎05677 64933) depart from the same station for: Cork (3hr., 1-3 per day, €15.30); Dublin (2hr., 3-6 per day, €9.90); Galway (5hr., 5 per day, €19.40); Limerick (2hr., 4 per day, €15.20); Rosslare Harbour (2hr., 2 per day, €14.30); Waterford (1hr., 1-2 per day, €8.60). The **tourist office** is on Rose Inn St. (☎05677 51500; www.southeastireland.com. Open May-Sept. M-Sa 9am-6pm, Su 11am-5pm; Oct.-Apr. M-F 9:30am-5:30pm, Sa 10am-6pm.)

WATERFORD ☎051

Waterford is Ireland's oldest city, founded in AD 914 by the grandson of Viking Ivor the Boneless. Its location on a beautiful river attracts travelers looking to shop, club, and relax on its beaches. Waterford's real highlight, however, is the fully operational **Waterford Crystal Factory,** 3km away on N25. Tours allow you to watch experienced cutters transform sand into molten glass and, finally, into sparkling crystal. The showroom contains the largest collection of Waterford crystal in the world. To get there, catch the City Bus outside Dunnes on Michael St. (10-15min., M-Sa 3-4 per hr., €1.45) and request to stop at the factory. (☎051 332 500; www.waterfordvisitorcentre.com. Open daily Mar.-Oct. 8:30am-6pm; Nov.-Feb. 9am-5pm. Free. 1hr. tours 3-4 per hr. in high-season. €10, students €7.) **Waterford Treasures** at the granary has Viking artifacts and the only remaining item of Henry VIII's wardrobe, a velvet hat. (☎051 304 500; www.waterfordtreasures.com. Open Apr.-Sept. M-Sa 9:30am-6pm, Su 11am-6pm; Oct.-Mar. M-Sa 10am-5pm, Su 11am-5pm. Last admission 1 hr. before close. €7, students €5.) Stellar tour guide Jack Burtchaell keeps audiences entertained on his **Walking Tour of Historic Waterford.** (☎051 873 711. 1hr. tours depart from Waterford Treasures Mar.-Oct. daily 11:45am and 1:45pm. €7.)

Jane and Robert Hovenden provide clean, quiet accommodations at **Mayor's Walk B&B ❸,** 12 Mayor's Walk. From the bus station, walk down the quay to

IRELAND

the clock tower and turn right. Head up the main street and turn right at the traffic lights. Mayor's Walk is the second road on the left up the hill. A bus for the Waterford Crystal Factory stops across the street. (☎051 855 427; www.mayorswalk.com. Shared bathrooms. Singles €29; doubles €52. Cash only.) **Cafe Sumatra ❷**, 53 John St., is a good option for lunch or dinner. (☎051 876 404. Sandwiches €7-9. Entrees €9-10. Open M-Th 9am-7pm, F-Sa 9am-11pm, Su 11am-7pm. MC/V.) The quay is full of pubs. **T&H Doolan's,** 31-32 George's St., has been serving drinks in its dark wooden interior for 300 years. (☎051 841 504. Live music nightly 9:30pm. Open M-Th 10am-11:30pm, F-Sa 10am-12:30am, Su 12:30-11pm. MC/V.) A younger crowd flocks to the **"Golden Mile"** of late bars at the intersection of John, Manor, and Parnell St. Try **Geoff's,** 8 John St. (☎051 874 787) or **Ruby Lounge** (☎051 879 184) on the corner.

Trains (☎873 401; www.irishrail.ie) leave from the quay across the bridge for: Dublin (2hr., M-F 8 per day, €24.50); Kilkenny (50min., 4-6 per day, €13.50); Limerick (2hr., 4-6 per day, €18). **Buses** depart for: Cork (2hr., 13 per day, €15.50); Dublin (2hr., 5-10 per day, €11.30); Galway (5hr., 4-6 per day, €19.40); Limerick (2hr., 6-8 per day, €9.90). The **tourist office,** 41 the Quay, is across from the bus station. (☎875 823; www.southeastireland.com. Open in summer M-Sa 9am-6pm, Su 10am-6pm, Su 11am-5pm.)

IRELAND

CASHEL ☎062

Cashel (pop. 11,400) sits at the foot of the 90m **Rock of Cashel** (also called **St. Patrick's Rock** or **Cashel of the Kings**), a limestone outcropping topped by medieval buildings. (☎062 61437. Open daily mid-June to mid-Sept. 9am-7pm; mid-Mar. to mid-June and mid-Sept. to mid-Oct. 9am-5:30pm; mid-Oct. to mid-Mar. 9am-4:30pm. Tours every hr. €5.30, students €2.10.) Head down the cow path from the Rock to see the ruins of **Hore Abbey,** built by Cistercian monks and relatively free of tourist hordes. (Open 24hr. Free.) The internationally acclaimed **Brú Ború Heritage Centre,** at the base of the Rock, stages traditional music and dance performances. (☎062 61122; www.comhaltas.com. Mid-June to mid-Sept. Tu-Sa 9pm. €18, students €10.) The **Bolton Library,** on John St., houses rare manuscripts and what's reputed to be the world's smallest book. (☎062 61944. Open M-F 10am-4:30pm.) Enjoy a view of the Rock from the homey rooms and campsite at **O'Brien's Holiday Lodge ❷**, a 10min. walk out of town on Dundrum Rd. From the tourist office, walk down Main St. and turn right at the end. (☎062 61003; www.cashel-lodge.com. Laundry €10. Camping €8 per person. Dorms €18; doubles €65. MC/V.) **Spearman's ❶**, near the Friary St. end of Main St., has panini (€5.80) made from freshly baked bread. (☎062 61143. Open M-F 9am-5:45pm, Sa 9am-5pm. MC/V.) For groceries, go to the **SPAR** on Main St. (☎062 61527. Open daily 7:30am-9pm. AmEx/MC/V.) **Buses** (☎061 313 333) leave from Main St. near the tourist office for Cork (1hr., 6 per day, €10.80) and Dublin (3hr., 6 per day, €10.80). The **tourist office** is in City Hall on Main St. (☎062 62511; www.casheltouristoffice.com. Open daily 9:30am-5:30pm.)

SOUTHWESTERN IRELAND

The dramatic landscape of southwestern Ireland ranges from lakes and mountains to stark, ocean-battered cliffs. Rebels once hid among the coves and glens, but the region is now dominated by tourists taking in the stunning scenery of the Ring of Kerry and Cork's southern coast.

CORK ☎021

Cork (pop. 119,000) hosts most of the cultural activities in the southwest. The county gained the nickname "Rebel Cork" from its residents' early opposition to the British Crown and 20th-century support for Irish independence. Today, Cork's river quays and pub-lined streets reveal architecture both grand and grimy, evidence of the city's dual legacy of resistance and reconstruction.

TRANSPORTATION

Trains: Kent Station, Lower Glanmire Rd. (☎021 455 7277; www.irishrail.ie), across the North Channel from the city center. Open M-Sa 6am-8pm, Su 8am-8:50pm. To: **Dublin** (3hr., 10-15 per day, €59.50) via **Limerick** (1hr., 7-10 per day, €23.50); **Killarney** (2hr., 6-9 per day, €23.50); **Tralee** (2hr., 6-9 per day, €31).

Buses: Parnell Pl. (☎021 450 8188), on Merchant's Quay. Info desk open M-Sa 9am-6pm. Bus Éireann to: **Dublin** (4½hr., 6 per day, €10.80); **Galway** (4hr., 12 per day, €15.30); **Killarney** (2hr., 10-15 per day, €15.70); **Limerick** (2hr., 12 per day, €12.60); **Rosslare Harbour** (4hr., 3-4 per day, €19.40); **Sligo** (7hr., 3 per day, €23.40); **Tralee** (2hr., 12-15 per day, €15.20); **Waterford** (2hr., 13-14 per day, €15/50).

Ferries: Brittany Ferries, 42 Grand Parade, sails from Cork to Roscoff, FRA. (☎021 427 7801. 12hr., Sa only, from €117.)

Public Transportation: Downtown **buses** run 2-6 per hr. M-Sa 7:30am-11:15pm, with reduced service Su 10am-11:15pm. Fares from €1.20. Catch buses and pick up schedules along St. Patrick's St., across from the Father Matthew statue.

IRELAND

ORIENTATION AND PRACTICAL INFORMATION

The center of Cork is compact and pedestrian-friendly, framed by the North and South Channels of the River Lee. From the bus station along the North Channel, **Merchant's Quay** leads west to **Saint Patrick's Street,** which curves through the center of the city and becomes **Grand Parade.** On the other side of the North Channel, across St. Patrick's Bridge, **MacCurtain Street** runs east to **Lower Glanmire Road** before becoming the N8 to Dublin. Downtown shopping and nightlife concentrates on **Washington, Oliver Plunkett,** and St. Patrick's Streets.

Tourist Office: Tourist House, Grand Parade (☎021 425 5100; www.discoverireland.ie), near the corner of South Mall, books accommodations (10% deposit plus €4) and provides a free city guide and **map.** Open June-Aug. M-Sa 9am-6pm, Su 10am-4pm; Sept.-May M-Sa 9:15am-5pm.

Police (Garda): Anglesea St. (☎021 452 2000).

Pharmacies: Regional Late-Night Pharmacy, Wilton Rd. (☎021 434 4575), opposite the hospital. Bus #8. Open M-F 9am-10pm, Sa-Su 10am-10pm.

Hospital: Cork University Hospital, Wilton Rd. (☎021 454 6400). Bus #5 and #8.

Internet: Wired To The World Internet Cafe, 6 Thompson House, MacCurtain St., north of River Lee (☎021 453 0383; www.wiredtotheworld.ie). Internet €1 per hr. Cash only. Open M-Th 9am-midnight, F-Sa 9am-2am, Su 10am-midnight.

Post Office: Oliver Plunkett St. (☎021 485 1032). Open M, W-Sa 9am-5:30pm, Tu 9:30am-5:30pm.

ACCOMMODATIONS

Cork's fine array of busy hostels should put a smile on any budget traveler's face, but rooms go fast, so call ahead. For a full Irish breakfast and a little more privacy, head to one of the many B&Bs on **Western Road,** near the University.

Sheila's Budget Accommodation Centre (IHH), 4 Belgrave Pl. (☎021 450 5562; www.sheilashostel.ie). Friendly staff take great pride in ensuring their guests feel safe and have fun. 24hr. reception desk doubles as general store. Kitchen. Free luggage storage, small lock boxes €1 and staff hold valuables at desk for free. Free Wi-Fi. Breakfast €3. Laundry €6.50. Check-out 10:30am. Dorms €15-19; doubles €46-54. AmEx/MC/V. ❷

Kinlay House (IHH), Bob and Joan's Walk (☎021 450 8966; www.kinlayhousecork.ie), down the alley to the right of St. Anne's Church. Bright colors and warm atmosphere; some rooms have great views of the city. Plush lounge with TV and sunny Internet room. Kitchen. Continental breakfast included. Free valuables safe and luggage storage at reception. Laundry €8. Free Wi-Fi; Internet €4 per hr. Free parking. 8- to 15-bed dorms €13-16; doubles €44-48. Ensuite rooms available (additional €2). AmEx/MC/V. ❷

Brú Bar and Hostel, 57 MacCurtain St. (☎021 455 9667; www.bruhostel.com), north of the river. A lively place to stay up late and hang out at the attached bar (open 4pm-late). Continental breakfast included. Towels €2. Laundry €5. Free Internet. Check-in 1pm. Check-out 10am. 6-bed dorms €16.50-17.50; 4-bed dorms €21-22.50; doubles €50-60. MC/V. Book online for a discount. ❷

Cork International Hostel (An Óige/HI), 1-2 Redclyffe, Western Rd. (☎021 454 3289), near University College and a 20min. walk from Grand Parade. Offers clean, spacious rooms with bath. Kitchen and TV room. Continental breakfast €5. Luggage storage available. Internet €1 per 15min. Reception 8am-midnight. Check-in 1-10pm. Check-out 10:30am. Dorms €16-18.50; doubles €50-54. €2 HI discount. MC/V. ❶

IRELAND

FOOD

Cork's famous international flavor is reflected in its countless great eateries. For more traditional Irish cuisine, hit the small towns, or make your own with local ingredients in the expansive **English Market,** accessible from Grand Parade, Patrick, and Oliver Plunkett St. Get groceries at **Tesco,** on Paul St. inside the Paul St. Shopping Centre. (☎021 427 0781. Open M-Sa 8am-10pm, Su 8am-8pm.)

Ginos, 7 Winthrop St. (☎021 427 4485). Heaping scoops of heavenly gelato flavors like honeycomb and hazelnut could be an entire meal. Small pizza €5.50. Ice cream €1.40 per scoop. Open daily noon-10pm. MC/V. ❶

Tribes, 8 Tuckey St. (☎021 427 4446), off Oliver Plunkett St. Late-night, low-light java shop serves sandwiches, full meals and tea into the wee hours. Food served until 30min. before closing. 18+ after 8pm. Open M 10:30am-7:30pm, Tu-Th 10:30am-11pm, F-Sa 10:30am-3:30am, Su noon-11pm. Cash only. ❶

Amicus, St. Paul St. (☎021 427 6455), across from Tesco. Artistically presented dishes taste as delicious as they look. Lunch €8-12. Dinner €12-25. Open M-Th 8am-10pm, F-Sa 8am-11pm, Su 8am-9pm. AmEx/MC/V. ❸

Café Paradiso, 16 Lancaster Quay (☎021 427 7939), near the University campus. Celebrated chefs make the most of what Mother Earth has to offer, serving up award-winning vegetarian meals. Menu changes often. Lunch €8-16. Dinner €24-25. Open Tu-Sa noon-3pm and 6:30-10:30pm. MC/V. ❸

SIGHTS

Cork's sights are concentrated in three areas: the old town, the Shandon neighborhood to the north, and the university to the west. All sights can be reached by foot, although the university and gaol are farther. Hop on and off the **Cork City Tour,** a 1hr. bus ride that leaves from the tourist office and stops at locations all over town. (July-Aug. 2 per hr., Apr. and Oct. every hr.; €13, students and seniors €11. Cash only.) John Collins also begins his **Historic Walking Tour,** loaded with insider's tidbits, at the tourist office. (☎085 100 7300. Apr.-Sept. M-F 10am, 2, 4pm. €10, students and seniors €5. Cash only.)

THE OLD TOWN. In a city lacking greenery, the area around **Christ Church** provides a quiet refuge and is packed with sunbathers in summer. The site suffered a Protestant torch three times between its 1270 inception and final renovation in 1729. *(Off Grand Parade just north of Bishop Lucy Park. Free.)* Across the South Channel, there's a decent view of Cork from Keyser Hill. At the top of the stairs leading up the hill, **Elizabeth Fort** stands as an ivy-covered remnant of English domination. *(Follow S. Main St. away from the city center, cross the South Gate Bridge, turn right on Proby's Quay, and turn left on Keyser Hill. Free.)* Looming over nearby Proby's Quay, **St. Finbarr's Cathedral** is a testament to the Victorian obsession with the neo-Gothic and a trademark of the city. The cathedral houses art exhibits in the summer. *(Bishop St. ☎021 963 387. Open M-F 10am-12:45pm and 2-5pm. €3, students €1.50.)*

SHANDON AND EMMET PLACE. Like Christ Church, **St. Anne's Church** was ravaged by 17th-century English armies; the current church was built in 1722. The steeple houses the **Bells of Shandon,** which you can ring before climbing to the top. Its four clock faces are notoriously out of sync, earning the church its nickname, "the four-faced liar." *(Walk up John Redmond St. and take a right at the Craft Centre; St. Anne's is on the right. ☎021 450 5906; www.shandonbells.org. Easter-Nov. M-Sa 10am-5pm, Dec.-Easter M-Sa 10am-3pm. €6, students and seniors €5, families €12. Cash only.)* Across the North Channel, the giant brick-and-glass **Opera House** was erected two decades ago after the older, more elegant opera house went down in flames. *(Emmet Pl., near Lavitt's Quay. ☎021 427 0022.)* The nearby **Crawford Art Gallery** has impressive collections of Greek and Roman sculpture casts and 19th-century Irish art. *(Emmet Pl., off Paul St. ☎021 490 7855. Open M-Sa 10am-5pm. Free.)*

WESTERN CORK. Built in 1845, **University College Cork's** campus is a collection of Gothic buildings, manicured lawns, and sculpture-studded grounds. The classic Stone Corridor is lined with Oghan stones, ancient gravestones marked with inscriptions representing an early example of pagan Irish language. The campus is also home to the architecturally striking **Lewis Glucksman Gallery,** which draws innovative, must-see exhibits. *(Main gate on Western Rd. ☎021 490 3000; www.ucc.ie. Gallery open Tu-W and F-Sa 10am-5pm, Th 10am-8pm, Su noon-5pm.)* **Fitzgerald Park** has beautiful rose gardens, a pond, and art exhibits, courtesy of the Cork Public Museum. *(From the front gate of UCC, follow the signs across the street. ☎021 427 0679. Open M-F 11am-1pm and 2:15-5pm, Sa 11am-1pm and 2:15-4pm, Su 3-5pm. Free.)* Don't miss the **Cork City Gaol** across the river from the park. Furnished cells, sound effects, and videos illustrate the experience of inmates at the 19th-century prison. *(☎021 430 5022; www.corkcitygaol.com. Open daily Mar.-Oct. 9:30am-6pm; Nov.-Feb. 10am-5pm. €7, students €6. 1hr. audio tour.)*

NIGHTLIFE

Oliver Plunkett Street, Union Quay, Washington Street, and **South Main Street** have pubs, clubs, and live music. Check out the free *WhazOn?* Cork pamphlet or the Thursday "Downtown" section in the *Evening Echo* newspaper.

The Old Oak, 113 Oliver Plunkett St. (☎021 427 6165), across from the General Post Office. "Best Traditional Pub in Ireland" repeated winner. Huge, packed, and great for the 20- and 30-somethings. Pints around €4. Varied live music nightly from 10:30pm-close. Open M-W noon-1:30am, Th-Sa noon-1:45am, Su noon-1am. Kitchen open daily noon-

5:30pm. **Cyprus Avenue,** a music venue upstairs, is open nightly hosting various acts and a DJ on weekends. €10-20 cover for Cyprus Ave. Cash only.

An Spailpín Fánac (on spal-PEEN FAW-nuhk), 28 South Main St. (☎021 427 7949), across from Beamish Brewery. One of Cork's oldest (est. 1779) and favorite pubs. Visitors and locals come for live trad and bluegrass six nights a week. No cover. Cash only. Open M-Th noon-11:30pm, F-Sa noon-12:30am, Su 12:30-11pm.

An Brog, 72-73 Oliver Plunkett St. (☎021 427 0074), at the corner of Oliver Plunkett St. and Grand Parade. For those who crave good alternative rock and feel at home among students and eyebrow rings. Tends to get busy later. Pints €3 before 9pm, €4.50 after. Open M-Sa 11:30am-2am, Su 4pm-2am.

DAYTRIP FROM CORK

BLARNEY. Those impressed by the Irish way of speaking should head to Blarney Castle and its legendary Blarney Stone. The legend goes that the Earl of Blarney cooed and cajoled his way out of giving up his abode to Queen Elizabeth I, and his smooth-talking skills were imparted to the stone, which when kissed passes on the "gift of Irish gab." After stealing a smooch, enjoy the views from the top and take a walk around the dreamlike rock garden. *(Buses run from the bus station or Merchants Quay, Cork to Blarney. 13-22 per day, round-trip €5.10. Open May M-Sa 9am-6:30pm, Su 9:30am-5:30pm; June-Aug. M-Sa 9am-7pm, Su 9:30am-5:30pm; Sept. M-Sa 9am-6:30pm, Su 9:30am-sunset; Oct.-Apr. M-Sa 9am-sunset, Su 9:30am-sunset. Last entry 30min. before close. €10, €8 student.)*

KILLARNEY AND KILLARNEY NATIONAL PARK ☎064

Killarney is just minutes from some of Ireland's most beautiful natural scenery. Outside of town, forested mountains rise from the famous three Lakes of Killarney in the 95 sq. km national park.

TRANSPORTATION AND PRACTICAL INFORMATION. Trains (☎064 31067) leave from Killarney station, off E. Avenue Rd., for Cork (2hr., 6-9 per day, €23.50), Dublin (3hr., 7-9 per day, €62), and Limerick (3hr., 6-8 per day, €26). Book online for the best rates. **Buses** (☎064 30011) leave from Park Rd. for: Belfast, UK (5-6 per day, €33); Cork (2hr., 10-15 per day, €15.70); Dublin (6hr., 5-6 per day, €23). The bus station office is open M-F 1:30am-1pm and 2-5pm, Sa 8:30am-1pm and 2-4:30pm. O'Sullivan's, on Lower New St., rents **bikes.** (☎064 22389. Open daily 9am-6pm. €15 per 24hr., students €12.50 per 24hr., €85 per week. Cash only.) The **TIC** is on Beech Rd. (☎064 31633; www.discoverireland.ie. Open M-Sa 9am-8pm, Su 10am-5:45pm.) The **post office** is in Centra on Fair Hill. (☎185 057 5859. Open M-F 9am-5:30pm, Sa 9am-1pm.)

ACCOMMODATIONS AND FOOD. Neptune's Hostel (IHH) ❶, on Bishop's Ln. off New St., has a central location, clean dorms, and common spaces. Kitchen available. The front desk books discounted tours of the Ring of Kerry and the Gap of Dunloe. (☎064 35255; www.neptuneshostel.com. Breakfast €3. Lockers €1 per day, free valuables storage at reception. Free bike storage. Laundry €7. Free Wi-Fi. Check-in 7:30am-3am. Check-out 10am. Dorms €14-20; doubles €19-25. MC/V.) **Sugan Hostel ❶,** on Lewis Rd., basks in the glory of the luxurious Fairview hotel next door. It's a smaller and quieter option for those who won't feel restricted by quiet hours after midnight. On the upside, they book discounted tours to the Dingle Peninsula and Ring of Kerry and provide a kitchen for guests. (☎064 33104; www.killarneysuganhostel.com. Bike rental €12 per day for guests. Reception open 8am-10pm. Check-out 10am. Dorms €15-16, doubles €20. Cash only.)

For delectable meat, seafood, and vegetarian dishes, try **The Stonechat ❸**, 8 Fleming's Ln., the best restaurant in Killarney. (☎064 34295. Lunch €8-11. Dinner €14-24. Early-bird special nightly 6-7pm, 2 courses for €18 or 3 for €23. Open M-Sa 12:30-3pm and 6-9:30pm. AmEx/MC/V.) Live music wafts down Killarney's streets on summer nights. A trendy 20-something crowd gets down in the lounge-like **McSorley's,** 10 College St., which starts the night with the usual trad, but switches it up with rock, then switches again to a late-night DJ. (☎064 39770. Pints €4.60. Open M-Sa noon-2:30am, Su noon-1:30am. Nightclub upstairs open 11:30pm-2:30am. Cover for nightclub around €8 on weekend nights.) **Scott's Bar,** also on College St., is a bit more relaxed, keeping it simple with trad. (☎064 31060. Pints around €4. Pub food served daily 12:30-9pm. MC/V; only for purchases over €20.)

SIGHTS. It could take an entire day to explore **Muckross House,** 5km south of Killarney on Kenmare Rd., a 19th-century manor and garden. (☎064 31440; www.muckross-house.ie. Open daily Sept.-June 9am-5:30pm, July-Aug. 9am-6pm. €5.75, student €2.35.) A path leads to the 20m **Torc Waterfall,** the starting point for several short trails along beautiful **Torc Mountain.** It's a 3.5km stroll in the opposite direction to the **Meeting of the Waters,** a quiet spot where channels come together. Away from the paved path, the more secluded dirt trail through **Yew Woods** is inaccessible to bikes. To get to the 14th-century **Ross Castle,** the last stronghold in Munster to fall to Cromwell's army, take a right on Ross Rd. off Muckross Rd. when leaving town. The castle is 3km from Killarney. For a more scenic route, take the footpaths from Knockreer, outside of town along New St. (☎064 35851. Open daily June-Aug. 9am-6:30pm; mid-Mar. to May and Sept.-mid-Oct. 9:30am-5:30pm, mid-Oct.-mid-Nov. 9:30am-4:30pm. €5.30, students €2.10.) The best outdoor activity in the area is the biking around the **Gap of Dunloe,** which borders **Macgillycuddy's Reeks,** Ireland's highest mountain range, or hop on a boat from Ross Castle to the head of the Gap (1hr., €15; book at tourist office). From **Lord Brandon's Cottage,** head left over the stone bridge, continue 3km to the church, and then turn right onto a winding road. Climb 2km (well worth the effort) and enjoy an 11km stroll downhill with gorgeous views. The 13km trip back to Killarney passes the

GET DIRTY FOR A CLEAN PARK

For visitors who fall in love with Killarney National Park's beauty but find that Killarney's prices outpace their cash flow, the conservation organization **Groundwork** provides a happy solution. Groundwork hosts twelve work camps throughout the summer in Killarney National Park, during which time volunteers use hand tools to remove the invasive *Rhododendron Ponticum* species from remote areas of the Park, enjoying prime real estate on the shores of Lough Leane in a National Park hostel. The camps run Sunday to Sunday and incorporate evenings of merrymaking in Killarney and a day of leisurely exploration by boat. €35 covers room and board for one week (€50 for two weeks). Volunteers should be between 18 and 65 and in good health. The town of Killarney is accessible by Bus Eireann from many cities (www.buseireann.ie).

(Groundwork, Irish Wildlife Trust, Sigmund Business Centre, 93A Lagan Road, Dublin Industrial Estate, Glasnevin, Dublin 11. ☎353 1 8602839. www.groundwork.ie.)

ruins of **Dunloe Castle.** Bear right after Kate Kearney's Cottage, turn left on the road to Fossa, and finally turn right on Killorglin Rd.

RING OF KERRY

The Southwest's most celebrated peninsula offers picturesque villages, ancient forts, and rugged mountains. You'll have to brave congested roads hogged by tour buses, but rewards await those who explore on foot or by bike.

TRANSPORTATION

The term "Ring of Kerry" usually describes the entire **Iveragh Peninsula,** though it technically refers to the ring of roads circumnavigating it. Hop on the circuit run by **Bus Éireann** (☎064 30011), based in Killarney (mid-June to Sept. 1 per day, departs 1:15pm, returns 5:40pm; entire ring in 1 day €22.70). Or, book a **bus tour** with a private company; offices are scattered across town, and many accommodations will book a tour for you.

CAHERSIVEEN ☎066

Although best known as the birthplace of patriot Daniel O'Connell, Cahersiveen (CAH-her-sah-veen) also serves as a useful base for jaunts to Valentia Island, the Skelligs, and local archaeological sites. To see the ruins of **Ballycarbery Castle,** head past the barracks on Bridge St., turn left over the bridge, then left off the main road. About 200m past the castle turn-off stands a pair of Ireland's best-preserved stone forts, **Cahergall** and **Leacanabuaile Fort.** Enjoy views of the countryside and castle from the **Sive Hostel (IHH) ❶,** 15 East End, Church St. (☎066 947 2717; www.sivehostel.ie. Laundry €8. Dorms €13-15; doubles €36-44. Camping €8 per person.) The pubs on **Main Street** still retain the authentic feel of their former proprietors' main businesses, including a general store, a smithy, and a leather shop. The **Harp** bar and nightclub caters to local youth. (☎066 947 2436. 18+. Cover €10. Bar open daily 10:30am-midnight. Nightclub open Sa midnight-2:30am.) The Ring of Kerry **bus** stops behind the Great Gas petrol station (mid-June to Aug., 1 per day) and continues to Killarney (2hr., €12.60). The **tourist office** is across from the bus stop. (☎066 947 2589. Open late May to Sept. M-Sa 9:30am-5:15pm, Su 10am-5pm.)

Quiet, unspoiled **Valentia Island** makes a perfect daytrip, with roads ideal for biking or light hiking. Bridges on either end of the island connect it to the mainland, and a **ferry** runs from Reenard Point, 5km west of Cahersiveen (☎066 947 6141; Apr.-Sept. every 10min.; €2, cyclists €3, cars €5). Another ferry sails to the **Skellig Rocks,** about 13km off the shore of the Iveragh Peninsula. From the boat, Little Skellig may appear snow-capped, but it's actually covered with white birds. Climb 630 steps to reach a **monastery** built by 6th-century Christian monks, whose dwellings remain intact. The hostel in Cahersiveen can arrange the ferry ride (about 1hr.) for €40.

DINGLE PENINSULA

For decades, the Ring of Kerry's undertouristed counterpart, the Dingle Peninsula, has maintained a healthy ancient-site-to-tour-bus ratio. Only recently has the Ring's tourist blitz begun to encroach upon the spectacular cliffs and sweeping beaches of this Irish-speaking peninsula.

TRANSPORTATION

Dingle Town is most easily reached by **Bus Éirean** from Tralee (1hr., 4-6 per day, €9.60). The bus stop is behind the big SuperValu. There is no public transportation on the peninsula; many visitors chose to explore with **bikes.**

DINGLE TOWN ☎066

Dingle Town is the adopted home of **Fungi the Dolphin,** who has lived in the harbor for over two decades and is now a focus of the tourism industry. Boat tours leave from the pier daily 10am-5pm in summer; call ahead Sept.-June. (☎066 915 2626; www.dingledolphin.com. 1hr. tours leave every 30-45min. €16, 2-12 €8; free if Fungi gets the jitters and doesn't show.) **Sciúird Archaeology Tours** leave from the Dingle pier for bus tours of the area's ancient sites. (☎087 223 0436. Book ahead. 2hr., 2 per day, €20. Cash only.) **Moran's Tours** runs trips to Slea Head, passing through majestic scenery and stopping at historic sites. (☎915 1155. 2 per day, €20. Cash only.) At **Rainbow Hostel,** guests retire to clean rooms in a country house. From the pier, walk away from town and look for signs from the roundabout. A **free shuttle** meets buses to Dingle. (☎066 915 1044; www.rainbowhosteldingle.com. Internet €4 per hr. and free Wi-Fi. Check-in 1pm; check-out 10:30am. Dorms €16; doubles €40; singles €30. Cash only.) At **Out Of The Blue ❹,** opposite the pier, a sign on the brightly painted shack proclaims "Fresh Fish/Seafood Only"—and they mean it, shunning vegetarians and closing when no fresh fish is available. Inside, gratified customers enjoy dishes like monkfish with green mango puree and coriander butter. (☎066 915 0811. Entrees €24.50-35, and worth the splurge. Open M-Tu and Th-Su noon-3pm and 6-9:30pm. Call ahead for reservations. MC/V.) The **tourist office** is on Strand St. (☎066 915 1188. Open June M-Sa 9am-6pm, Su 10am-5pm; July-Aug. M-Sa 9:15am-7pm, Su 10am-5pm; Sept.-May daily 9:15am-1pm and 2-5pm.)

SLEA HEAD, VENTRY, AND DUNQUIN ☎066

The most rewarding way to see the cliffs and crashing waves of Dunquin and Slea Head is to **bike** along **Slea Head Drive.** Past Dingle Town toward Slea Head, the village of **Ventry** *(Ceann Trá)* is home to a **beach** and the **Celtic and Prehistoric Museum,** a collection that includes the largest intact woolly mammoth skull in the world. (☎066 915 9191; www.celticmuseum.com. Open Mar.-Nov. daily 10am-5:30pm; call ahead Dec.-Feb for opening information. €5.)

North of Slea Head and Ventry, the settlement of Dunquin *(Dún Chaoin)* consists of stone houses and little else. Past Dunquin on the road to Ballyferriter, the **Great Blasket Centre** has exhibits about the now-abandoned Blasket Islands. (☎066 915 6444. Open daily July-Aug. 10am-7pm; Easter-June and Sept.-Oct. 10am-6pm. €3.70, students €1.30.) At the **Dun Chaoin An Óige Hostel (HI) ❶,** in Ballyferriter, on Dingle Way across from the turn-off to the Blasket Centre, each bunk has a panoramic ocean view. (☎066 915 6121; mailbox@anoige.ie. Reception 9-10am and 5-10pm. Lockout 10am-5pm. Open Feb.-Nov. Dorms €13-17.50; doubles €36-38. €2 HI discount. MC/V.) **Kruger's,** Europe's westernmost pub, has great views. (☎066 915 6127. Live music F-Su around 9pm. Open M-Th 10:30am-midnight, F-Sa 10:30am-12:30am, Su noon-11:30pm.)

WESTERN IRELAND

Even Dubliners will say that the west is the "most Irish" part of Ireland; in remote areas you may hear Irish being spoken almost as often as English. The potato

IRELAND

SOWING THE SEEDS OF LOVE

What started as a pragmatic matchmaking service for country boys who did not get a chance to mingle with their sophisticated female counterparts is now sold as a six-week singles' bonanza. Every September through early October, Lisdoonvarna welcomes thousands of unattached partiers who come to partake in the live music, dancing, drinking, games and lovin' of the **Matchmaking Festival.** A far cry from its modest precursor over 150 years ago, during which bachelor farmers who had recently completed their harvests earnestly sought wives, the festival now attracts fun-loving strangers who indulge in daily dances starting at noon. Despite this shift, an official matchmaker still presides over the festival. Accordingly, events cater to those looking for flings, and something a bit more meaningful. Willie Daly inherited the tradition from his family, and he continues to make romantic matches part-time–he also runs an equestrian center outside of town.

Lisdoonvarna Matchmaking Festival; www.matchmakerireland.com. Six weeks, Sept.-mid-Oct. For more information or to book accommodations, call the Hydro Hotel (☎065 707 4005). Find cheaper dormitory beds at Sleepzone Burren (☎065 707 4036). Book early, as beds fill fast.

famine was most devastating in the west—entire villages emigrated or died—and the current population is still less than half of what it was in 1841.

THE CLIFFS OF MOHER AND THE BURREN ☎065

Plunging 213m straight down to the sea, the **Cliffs of Moher** provide incredible views of the Kerry Mountains, the Twelve Bens mountains, and the Aran Islands. Be careful of extremely strong winds; they blow a few tourists off every year, though new barriers offer more protection. *Let's Go* strongly discourages straying from the established paths onto privately owned land. The new **Visitors Centre** and **Atlantic Edge Exhibition** educate tourists on the cliffs. (☎065 708 6141; www.cliffsofmoher.ie. Open daily July-Aug. 8:30am-8:30pm, Sept.-Oct. 8:30am-7:30pm, Nov.-Feb. 9am-5pm, Mar.-May 8:30am-7pm. €4, students €3.50. MC/V.) To reach the cliffs, head 5km south of Doolin on R478, or hop on the Galway-Cliffs of Moher bus (#50; stops at Lisdoonvarna and Doolin; M-Sa 3-5 per day, Su 1-2 per day). From Liscannor, Cliffs of Moher Cruises (☎065 707 5949; www.cliffs-of-moher-cruises.com) sails **boats** under the cliffs (1hr., 1 per day, €20). Also run **ferries** to the cliffs from Doolin (1hr., 2-3 per day, €20).

The nearby **Burren** resembles an enchanted fairyland, with secluded coves, bright wildflowers, and 28 species of butterflies fluttering in the air. The old stone forts and isolated trees sprinkled around the countryside are supposedly home to leprechauns. The Burren town of **Lisdoonvarna** is known for its **Matchmaking Festival,** a six-week-long *craic*-and-snogging celebration that attracts over 10,000 singles each September. **Sleepzone Burren ❶,** past The Smokehouse restaurant on Doolin Rd., is an elegant hotel-turned-hostel perfect for launching into the Burren wild. (☎065 707 4036; www.sleepzone.ie. Kitchen. Free Wi-Fi and computer use. Dorms €16-20; singles €35-40; doubles €56-60. MC/V.) In the town of Ballyvaughan, guests at **O'Brien B&B ❸,** on Main St., enjoy the huge rooms and the fireplaces in the adjacent pub. The bus from Galway arrives in front of the B&B. (☎065 707 7003. Singles from €50. Doubles from €90. MC/V.) **Monk's Pub and Restaurant ❷,** sits on the pier with a view across the bay to Galway city. Tourists crowd around the huge stone fireplace for trad, while locals gravitate toward the bar. (☎065 707 7059. Famous seafood chowder €5. Music 2 nights per week, usually Th and Sa.) There are no **ATMs** in Ballyvaughan. **Bus** Eireann #50 and 423 (☎091 562 000) connects Galway to multiple towns in the Burren a few times a day in the summer and slightly less frequently in winter.

GALWAY ☎091

With its youthful, exuberant spirit, Galway (pop. 80,000) is one of the fastest growing cities in Europe. Performers dazzle crowds on the appropriately named Shop St., locals and tourists lounge in outdoor cafes, and hip crowds pack the pubs and clubs at night. In addition to its peaceful quay-side walks, Galway is only a short drive away from beautiful Connemara.

ORIENTATION AND PRACTICAL INFORMATION. Galway's train and bus stations are on a hill to the northeast of **Eyre Square,** a recently renovated block of lawns and monuments. A string of small, cheap B&Bs are north of the square along **Prospect Hill.** The western corner of the square is the gateway to the pedestrian center, filled with shoppers seeking cups of coffee or pints of stout. From the square, **Shop Street** becomes **High Street,** which then becomes **Quay Street.** The **Wolfe Tone Bridge** spans the River Corrib and connects the city center to the bohemian left bank. The **tourist office** is on Forster St. near the train and bus stations. (☎091 537 700; www.irelandwest.ie. Open Apr.-Oct. daily 9am-5:45pm; Nov.-Mar. M-Sa 9am-5:45pm.) For **Internet,** head to **Chat'rnet,** 5 Eyre St, across from The Hole in the Wall pub. (☎091 539 912. €4 per hr. Open M-Sa 9am-11pm, Su 10am-11pm. Cash only.) The **post office** is at 3 Eglinton St. (☎091 534 727. Open M and W-Sa 9am-5:30pm, Tu 9:30am-5:30pm.)

ACCOMMODATIONS AND FOOD. The number of accommodations in Galway has recently skyrocketed, but reservations are still necessary in summer. Most B&Bs are concentrated in **Salthill** or on **College Road.** **Barnacle's Quay Street House (IHH) ❶,** 10 Quay St., is the most conveniently located hostel in Galway. Its bright, spacious rooms are perfect for crashing after a night on the town. (☎091 568 644; www.barnacles.ie. Light breakfast included. Laundry €8. Kitchen. Free towels. Free Wi-Fi. Computer use €1 per 15min. Single-sex dorms available. Check-in 11am; check-out 10:30am. 4- to 12-bed dorms €13-20.50; doubles €56-68. MC/V.) **Sleepzone ❷,** Bóthar na mBán (BO-her na-MAHN), Woodquay, a left off Prospect Hill, has large rooms and top-notch facilities. (☎091 566 999; www.sleepzone.ie. Laundry €7. Free Wi-Fi. Single-sex dorms available. Dorms from €16-24; singles €30-55; doubles €50-76. Weekend and low-season rates vary. MC/V.) **Kinlay House ❶,** at the corner of Eyre Sq. and Merchant's Rd., has 220 beds in a convenient and clean location. From the bus station, walk down Station Rd. towards Square and turn left. (☎091 565 244; www.kinlaygalway.ie. Breakfast included. Free luggage room and safe. Towels €1. Free Wi-Fi; computer use €3 per hr. Reception 24hr. Check-out 10:30am. Dorms €15.50-22, doubles €56-63. MC/V.)

The cafes and pubs around Quay, High, and Shop Streets are good options for budget dining. An **open-air market** on Market St. sells fruit and ethnic foods. (Open Sa 8am-4pm.) How the stylish **Gourmet Tart Co. ❶,** 7 Lower Abbeygate St., manages to sell its sumptuous creations at such low prices remains a mystery, but be sure to take advantage of the best deal in Galway. (Sandwiches under €4, salad buffet €13 per kg., pastries €1-2. Open daily 7:30am-7pm. Cash only.) At **The Home Plate ❷,** on Mary St., diners enjoy large sandwiches (€7) and entrees (€7.50-10) on tiny wooden tables. (☎091 561 475. Open M-Sa noon-9pm, Su noon-6:30pm. Cash only.) **Zatsuma ❶,** 27 Shop St., produces delicious crepes (€3.25-6.75) with a skilled assembly line as salivating customers look on. (☎091 895 877; www.zatsuma.ie. Open daily 11am-3am. MC/V.)

SIGHTS AND ENTERTAINMENT. The best *craic* in Galway is people-watching: Eyre Sq. and Shop St. are full of street performers, some unknowing.

At the **Church of Saint. Nicholas** on Market St., a stone marks the spot where Columbus supposedly stopped to pray to the patron saint of travelers before sailing the ocean blue. (Open daily Apr.-Sept. 8:30am-8pm, Oct.-Mar. 9am-5pm. Free.) On Shop St., **Lynch's Castle** is a well-preserved 16th-century merchant's residence than now houses a bank. From Quay St., head across Wolfe Tone Bridge to the **Claddagh,** an area that was an Irish-speaking, thatch-roofed fishing village until the 1930s. The famous **Claddagh rings** are today's mass-produced reminders of yesteryear. The **Nora Barnacle House,** 8 Bowling Green, off Market St., has hardly changed since James Joyce's future wife Nora lived there with her family at the turn of the 20th century. Check out Joyce's love letters to his life-long companion. (☎091 564 743 www.norabarnacle.com. Open mid-May to mid-Sept. M-Sa 10am-1pm and 2-5pm, or by appointment. €2.50, students €2.) Hang with sea creatures for an afternoon at the **National Aquarium of Ireland,** on the Salt Hill Promenade. (☎091 585 100; www.nationalaquarium.ie. Open Apr.-Sept. M-F 9am-6pm, Sa-Su 9am-7pm; Oct.-Mar. M-F 9am-5pm, Sa-Su 9am-6pm. €9.75, students €7. MC/V.) Event listings are published in the free *Galway Advertiser,* available at the tourist office and most accommodations. In mid-July, the **Galway Arts Festival** (☎091 566 577) attracts droves of filmmakers, rock groups, theater troupes, and trad musicians.

IRELAND

ARAN ISLANDS (OILEÁIN ÁRANN) ☎099

The spectacular Aran Islands lie on the westernmost edge of Co. Galway, isolated by 32km of Atlantic Ocean. Churches, forts, ruins, and holy wells rise from the stony terrain of **Inishmore** (Inis Mór; pop. 800), the largest of the three islands. At the **Dún Aonghasa** ring fort, stones circle a sheer 100m drop. The **Inis Mór Way** is a mostly paved route that passes the majority of the island's sights. There are similar paths on **Inisheer** (Inis Oírr; pop. 250), the smallest island, and windswept **Inishmaan** (Inis Meáin; pop. 150). On Inishmore, the **Kilronan Hostel ❷,** next to the pier, offers a TV room and kitchen. (☎099 61255. Free Wi-Fi. Single-sex dorms available. Dorms from €20.) The SPAR supermarket in Kilronan has the island's only **ATM** (☎099 61203). Aran Island Ferries (☎091 568 903; www.aranislandferries.com) sends **boats** from Rossaveal, west of Galway, to Inishmore (45min., 2-4 per day, round-trip €25) and Inisheer (2 per day). Aran Direct (☎099 566 535) also leaves from Rossaveal for Inishmore (45min., 3 per day, round-trip €25) and runs **ferries.** Both companies run **buses** to Rossaveal (€7), which leave from Kinlay House, on Merchant St. in Galway, 1hr. before ferry departure. The **tourist office** on Inishmore stores luggage (€1 per item) and helps find accommodations. (☎099 61263. Open daily July-Aug. 10am-6:45pm; May-June and Sept. 10am-6pm, Oct.-Mar. 11am-5pm, Apr. 10am-5pm.)

CONNEMARA

The Connemara region in northwest County Galway is an outdoorsman's dream, comprised of a lacy net of inlets and islands that provide stunning views of two major mountain ranges: the Twelve Bens and the Maumturks.

CLIFDEN AND CONNEMARA NATIONAL PARK ☎095

English-speaking Clifden attracts crowds of tourists. For the best scenery, bike along **Sky Road,** a 20km loop that overlooks the coastline, castles, and the towering Bens. **Connemara National Park** occupies 12.5 sq. km of mountainous countryside. Bogs, often covered thinly with grass and flowers, constitute much of the park's terrain. The **Sruffaunboy Nature** and **Ellis Wood** trails are easy 20min. hikes. The newly constructed pathway up **Diamond Hill** is a more difficult journey, but it rewards climbers with views of the harbor and the spectacular Bens.

Experienced hikers head for the **Twelve Bens** (Na Beanna Beola; also called the Twelve Pins), a rugged mountain range that reaches heights of 2200m. A tour of six peaks takes a full day. Trails are scarce, so consult the Clifden tourist office before jumping into the bog. **Biking** the 65km circle through Clifden, Letterfrack, and the Inagh Valley is truly captivating, but only appropriate for fit bikers. The **Visitors Centre** provides help in planning hikes, but is confined by limited access points and trails. (☎095 41054. Open daily July-Aug. 9:30am-6pm; Mar.-June and Sept.-Oct. 10am-5:30pm.) Turn off from N59, 13km east of Clifden near Letterfrack, to reach the park.

The **White Heather House B&B ❸,** on the square, offers panoramic views. (☎095 21655. Singles €50 with bath; doubles €80. MC/V.) Near the pubs, **Clifden Town Hostel (IHH) ❶,** Market St., has a helpful owner and good facilities. (☎095 21076; www.clifdentownhostel.com. Open year-round, but call ahead Nov.-Mar. Dorms €16-18; doubles €38-40; triples €60-63; quads €72-76. Cash only.) **Shanaheever Campsite ❶** is 1.5km outside Clifden on Westport Rd. (☎095 22150; www.clifdencamping.com. Laundry €12. Tent or trailer sites €10 per person. Electricity €3. Free showers.) Most affordable restaurants in Clifden are attached to pubs. The family-run **Cullen's Bistro and Coffee Shop ❸,** Market St., cooks up hearty meals and delicious desserts. (☎095 21983. Irish stew €17.50. Open mid-Mar.-Oct. daily noon-7pm. Cash only.) **O'Connor's SuperValu,** on the square, sells groceries. (☎095 21182. Open M-Sa 8am-10pm, Su 8:30am-9pm.)

Bus Éireann runs **buses** from the library on Market St. to Galway via Oughterard (1hr., 2-4 per day, €10.40) and to Westport via Leenane (1hr., late June-Aug. M-Sa 1 per day, €11.70). **Bikes** are available at Mannion's, on Bridge St. (☎095 21160. €18 per day, €90 per week. €10 deposit. Open daily June-Aug. 9:30am-6pm, Sept.-May 10am-6pm. Cash only.) The **tourist office** is on Galway Rd. (☎095 21163; www.irelandwest.ie. Open M-Sa 10am-5:45pm, Su 10am-4:45pm.)

IRELAND

SLIGO ☎071

Since the beginning of the 20th century, William Butler Yeats devotees have made literary pilgrimages to Sligo (pop. 18,000); the poet spent summers in town as a child and set many of his works around Sligo Bay. Sligo Town is the commercial center and an excellent base for daytrips to local nature adventures. **Model Arts and Niland Gallery,** on the Mall, houses one of the country's finest collections of modern Irish art, but its closed for renovations until after summer 2009. (☎071 914 1405; www.modelart.ie. Open June-Oct. Tu-Sa 10am-5:30pm, Su 11am-4pm. Free. Check website for updates.) The two-room **Sligo County Museum,** Stephen St., showcases Yeats memorabilia, Sligo records and Celtic artifacts. (Open June-Aug. Tu-Sa 10-11:45am, 2-4:45pm; Sept.-May Tu-Sa 2-4:45pm. Free.) The well-preserved former Dominican friary, **Sligo Abbey,** is on Abbey St. (Open mid-Mar.-Oct. daily 10am-6pm, last entry 5:15pm; Nov.-mid-Dec. F-Su 9:30am-4:30pm; Jan.-Feb. reduced hours; call ahead for tours. €2.10, students €1.10.) Yeats is buried in **Drumcliffe Churchyard,** on the N15, 6.5km northwest of Sligo. To get there, catch the **bus** from Sligo to Derry, which stops at Drumcliffe (10min., 3-7 per day, €5.60). At 500m, **Ben Bulben's Peak** dominates the skyline and offers a challenging hike. From N15, follow the signs to Ben Bulben Farm. A dirt road breaks off to mark the beginning of the journey.

Most B&Bs are near Pearse Rd. Outside the center of town, the **Harbour House ❷,** Finisklin Rd., welcomes backpackers into comfortable bunks. From the bus station, turn left on Lord Edward St. and left on Union St., then take the first left on Finisklin Rd. (☎071 917 1547; www.harbourhousehostel.com Dorms €20; singles €22-25; doubles €44-50. MC/V.) **Pepper Alley ❶,** 1 Rockwood Parade by the river, serves sandwiches and pastries. (☎071 917 0720. Entrees

€3.60-8. Open M-Sa 8:30am-5pm. Cash only.) Grab groceries at the **Tesco** supermarket on O'Connell St. (☎071 916 2788. Open 24hr.) **Toffs,** along the river from Pepperwood Alley on J.F. Kennedy Parade, opens its doors to the young and trendy on the weekends. (☎071 916 1250. DJs Th-Su night. Pints €4.50. Th and Su 18+, F-Sa 19+. Th-Sa 11pm-2:30am, Su 11pm-1:30am. Cover €10.)

Trains (☎071 918 3311; www.irishrail.ie) leave from Lord Edward St. to Dublin (3hr., 6 per day, €29) via Carrick-on-Shannon and Mullingar. From the same station, **buses** (☎071 916 0066; www.buseireann.ie) head to: Belfast (4hr., 2 per day, €23.50); Derry/Londonderry (3hr., 3-7 per day, €17.20); Dublin (3-4hr., 5 per day, €16.20); Galway (2hr., 5-6 per day, €13.20). Turn left on Lord Edward St., then right on Adelaide St., and head around the corner to Temple St. to reach the **tourist office.** (☎071 916 1201; www.discoverireland.ie/northwest. Open July-Aug. M-Sa 9am-5pm, Su 10am-4pm; May-Sept. M-F 9am-5pm.)

NORTHWESTERN IRELAND

A sliver of land connects the mountains, lakes, and ancient monuments of Co. Sligo to Co. Donegal. Among Ireland's counties, Donegal (DUN-ee-gahl) is second only to Cork in size. Its *gaeltacht* is the largest sanctuary of the living Irish language in Ireland, and its geographic isolation and natural beauty embrace travelers sick of the tourist hordes farther south.

DONEGAL TOWN (DÚN NA NGALL) ☎074 97

A gateway for travelers heading to more isolated destinations in the north and northwest, the compact Donegal Town erupts with live music in pubs on weekends. The triangular center of town is called the **Diamond.** Six craftsmen and -women open their studios to the public around the pleasant courtyard of the **Donegal Craft Village,** 2km south of town on the Ballyshannon Rd. (☎074 97 22225. Open 10am-5pm, daily in summer, M-Sa spring and autumn, Tu-Sa winter. Admission free.) The Waterbus **shuttle** provides aquatic tours of Donegal Bay, departing from the quay next to the tourist office. (☎074 97 23666. Departure times depend on tides; call ahead. €15.) For two weeks in July, the **Earagail Arts Festival** celebrates the county's art scene (☎074 91 207777; www.eaf.ie; tickets free-€20), while the **Donegal Bluestacks Festival** features theater, arts, poetry, and music from late September to early October. (☎074 91 29186; www.donegalculture.com. Tickets free-€25.)

A 10min. walk from town, the family-run **Donegal Town Independent Hostel (IHH/IHO) ❶,** Killybegs Rd., welcomes backpackers with murals on the ceilings of the dorms and a comfortable TV lounge. (☎074 97 22805. Dorms €17; doubles €40, with bath €44. Tent sites €9 per person. Kitchen. MC/V.) The **Blueberry Tea Room ❷,** Castle St., buzzes with patrons enjoying breakfast (€3-7.50) and daily specials (€10-12). Check email at their Internet cafe on the second floor. (☎074 97 22933. Internet €2 for 30min. Open M-Sa 9am-7pm. Cash only.) For groceries, head to **SuperValu,** 2min. from the Diamond down Ballyshannon Rd. (☎074 97 22977. Open M-Sa 8:30am-9pm, Su 9am-7pm.) The **Reveller,** in the Diamond, caters to a young crowd with pool tables and loud music. (☎074 97 21201. F-Su live music 10:30pm-close. No cover. Open M-Th 10:30am-11:30pm, F-Sa 10:30am-12:30am, Su noon-11pm. Cash only.)

Bus Éireann (☎074 97 21101) **buses** leave from the Abbey Hotel on the Diamond for Derry/Londonderry (1hr., 3-8, €13.50) via Letterkenny (€8.10), Dublin (3hr., 6-8 per day, €16.20), and Galway (4hr., 3-4 per day, €17.10). To reach the **tourist office,** face away from the Abbey Hotel and turn right; it's outside the Diamond on the Ballyshannon/Sligo Rd. (☎074 97 21148; www.discoverdonegal.ie. Open May-Sept. M-Sa 9am-6pm, Su 10am-5pm; Oct.-Apr. M-Sa 9am-5pm.)

NORTHERN IRELAND

The calm tenor of everyday life in Northern Ireland has long been overshadowed by headlines about riots and bombs. While the violence has subdued, the divisions in civil society continue to some extent. Protestants and Catholics usually live in separate neighborhoods, attend separate schools, and patronize separate stores and pubs. The 1998 Good Friday Accord began a slow march toward peace, and all sides have renewed their efforts to make their country as peaceful as it is beautiful.

BELFAST (BÉAL FEIRSTE) ☎028

The second-largest city on the island, Belfast (pop. 276,000) is the center of Northern Ireland's cultural, commercial, and political activity. **Queen's University** testifies to the city's rich academic history—luminaries such as Nobel Laureate Seamus Heaney once roamed its halls, and Samuel Beckett taught the young men of **Campbell College.** The Belfast pub scene ranks among the best in the world, combining the historical appeal of old-fashioned watering holes with more modern bars and clubs. While Belfast has suffered from the stigma of its violent past, it has rebuilt itself, surprising most visitors with its neighborly, urbane feel. Progress is slow to take root in the still-divided West Belfast area, home to separate communities of Protestants and Catholics.

TRANSPORTATION

Flights: Belfast is served by 2 airports.

Belfast International Airport (☎028 9448 4848; www.belfastairport.com) in Aldergrove. **Aer Lingus** (☎087 0876 5000; www.aerlingus.com); **Air Transat** (☎028 9031 2312; www.airtransat.com); **BMI** (☎087 0264 2229; www.flybmi.com); **Continental** (☎012 9377 6464; www.continental.com); **easyJet** (☎087 1244 2366; www.easyjet.com); **Flyglobespan** (☎087 0556 1522; www.flyglobespan.com); **Jet2** (☎087 1226 1737; www.jet2.com); **Manx2** (☎087 0242 2226; www.manx2.com); **Wizz Air** (☎482 2351 9499; www.wizzair.com) operate from here. Translink Bus 300 has 24hr. **bus** service from the airport to Europa bus station in the city center M-F every 10min. 6:50am-6:15pm, every 15-40min. otherwise; Sa every 20min. 7:35am-6:40pm, at least once per hr. otherwise; Su every 30min. 8:15am-10:40pm, at least once per hr. otherwise. Call ☎9066 6630 or visit www.translink.co.uk for full timetables. £6, round-trip £9 if you return within 1 month. **Taxis** (☎028 9448 4353) get you there for £25-30.

Belfast City Airport (☎028 9093 9093; www.belfastcityairport.com), is located at the harbor. **Flybe** (☎087 1700 0535; www.flybe.com); **BMI** (☎087 0607 0555; www.flybmi.com); **Ryanair** (☎00353 1249 7791; www.ryanair.com); **Aer Arann** (☎080 0587 2324; www.aerarann.ie); **Manx2** (☎087 0242 2226; www.manx2.com) operate from here. To get from City Airport to Europa bus station, take **Translink Bus 600.** M-F every 20-30min., 8:35am-10:05pm, Sa every 20-30min. 8:05am-9:50pm, Su every 45min. 7:30am-9:50pm. Single £1.30, return £2.20.

Trains: For **train** and **bus** info, contact **Translink** (☎028 9066 6630; www.translink.co.uk; inquiries daily 7am-8pm). Trains depart from several of Belfast's stations **(Great Victoria Street, City Hospital, Botanic, Central)** for Derry/Londonderry (2hr.; M-F 9 per day, Sa 8 per day, Su 4 per day; £10.50 single, £15 return) and leave **Central Station,** E. Bridge St. to Dublin (2hr.; M-Sa 8 per day, Su 5 per day; £25 single, £36 return). The **Metro** buses are free with rail tickets.

Buses: Europa Bus Terminal, off Great Victoria St., (☎028 9043 4424; ticket office open M-Sa 7:35am-8:05pm, Su 9:15am-6:15pm). Buses to Derry/Londonderry (1hr.;

M-F 39 per day, Sa 20 per day, Su 11 per day; £10 single, £15 return) and Dublin (3hr.; 24 per day; buses at midnight, 1, 2, 3, 4, 5am depart Glengall St.; £10 single, £14 return). The **Centrelink bus** connects the station with the city center.

Ferries: Norfolk Ferries (☎01 819 2999; www.norfolkline-ferries.co.uk) operates out of the **SeaCat** terminal and runs to Liverpool, England (8hr., fares seasonal, starting at £99 with car and £20 without). Book online and before the day of travel to avoid a £10 booking fee. **Stena Line** (☎028 087 0570 7070; www.stenaline.com), up the Lagan River, has the quickest service to Scotland, docking in Stranraer (1hr.; book online, fares seasonal, starting at £55).

ORIENTATION

Buses arrive at the **Europa Bus Station** on Great Victoria Street. To the northeast is **City Hall** in Donegall Sq. Donegall Pl. turns into Royal Avenue and runs from Donegall Sq. through the shopping area. To the east, in Cornmarket, pubs in narrow entries (small alleyways) offer an escape. The stretch of Great Victoria St. between the bus station and Shaftesbury Sq. is known as the **Golden Mile** for its highbrow establishments and Victorian architecture. Botanic Avenue and Bradbury Pl. (which becomes University Road) extend south from Shaftesbury Sq. into **Queen's University** turf. The city center, Golden Mile, and the University are relatively safe areas. Although locals advise caution in the east and west, central Belfast is safer for tourists than most European cities.

Westlink Motorway divides working-class West Belfast, more politically volatile than the city center, from the rest of Belfast. The **Protestant district** stretches along Shankill Rd., just north of the **Catholic neighborhood,** centered around Falls Rd. The River Lagan splits industrial East Belfast from Belfast proper. The shipyards and docks extend north on both sides of the river as it grows into Belfast Lough. During the week, the area north of City Hall is essentially deserted after 6pm. Streets remain quiet even during the weekend, belying the boisterous pub/club scene. Although muggings are infrequent in Belfast, it's wise to use taxis after dark, particularly near pubs and clubs in the northeast.

PRACTICAL INFORMATION

Tourist Information Centre: Belfast Welcome Centre, 47 Donegall Pl. (☎028 9024 6609; www.gotobelfast.com). Offers comprehensive free booklet on Belfast and info on surrounding areas. Books reservations in Northern Ireland (£2) and the Republic (£3). Open M-Sa 9am-5:30pm, Su 11am-4pm, and June-Sept. M-Sa 9am-7pm.

Laundromat: Globe Drycleaners *and* **Launderers,** 37-39 Botanic Ave. (☎028 9024 3956). £5 per load. Open M-F 8am-9pm, Sa 8am-6pm, Su noon-6pm.

Police: 6-18 Donegall Pass and 65 Knock Rd. (☎028 9065 0222).

Hospital: Belfast City Hospital, 91 Lisburn Rd. (☎028 9032 9241). From Shaftesbury Sq., follow Bradbury Pl. and take a right at the fork for Lisburn Rd.

Internet: Belfast Central Library, 122 Royal Ave. (☎028 9050 9150). Open M-Th 9am-8pm, F 9am-5:30pm, Sa 9am-4:30pm. £1.50 per 30min. for nonmembers.

Post Office: Central Post Office, on the corner of High St. and Bridge St. (☎084 5722 3344). Open M-Sa 10am-5:30pm. **Postal Code:** BT2 7FD.

ACCOMMODATIONS

Despite fluctuating tourism and rising rents, Belfast provides a healthy selection of hostels for travelers. Almost all are near Queen's University, close to the city's pubs and restaurants, and a short walk or bus ride to the city center. Note that reservations are necessary during the summer.

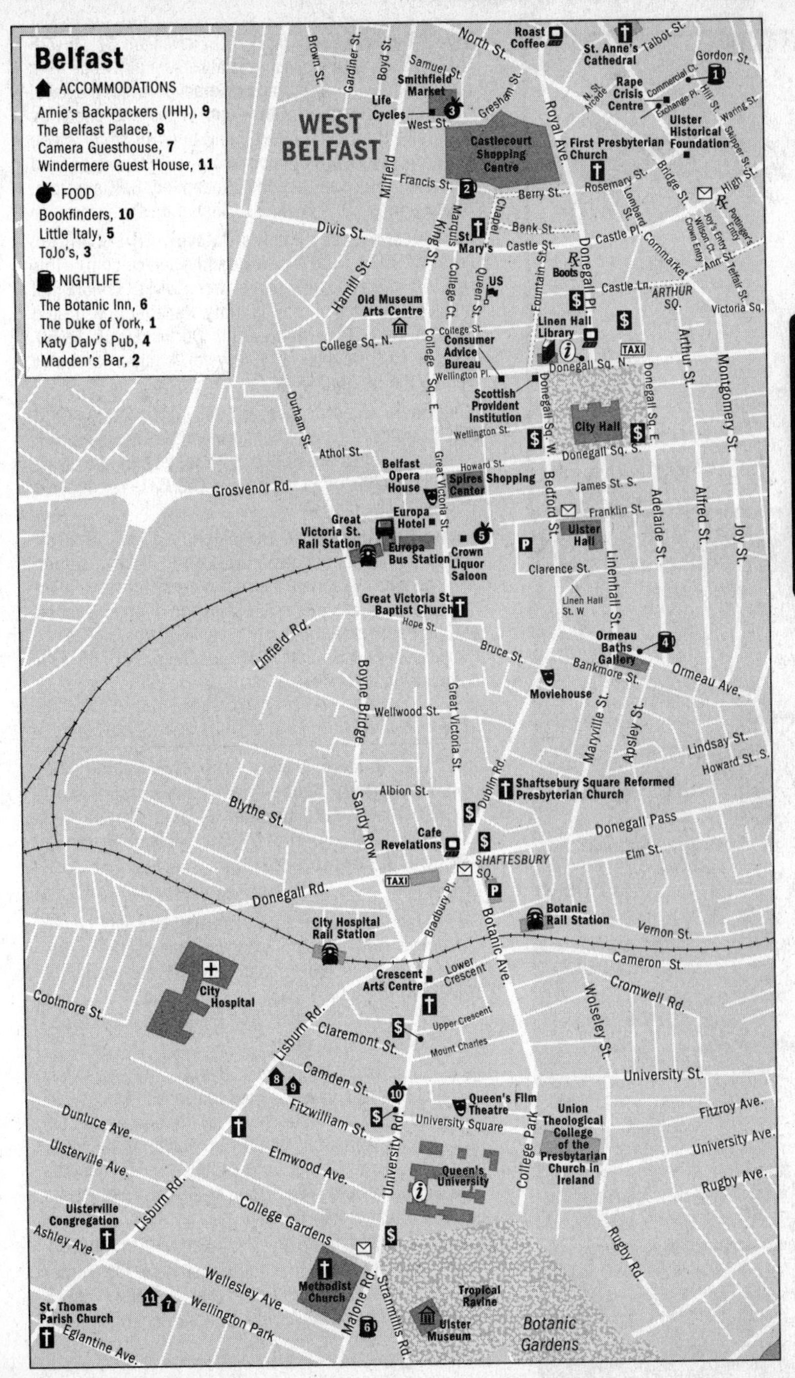
Belfast
ACCOMMODATIONS
Arnie's Backpackers (IHH), 9
The Belfast Palace, 8
Camera Guesthouse, 7
Windermere Guest House, 11
FOOD
Bookfinders, 10
Little Italy, 5
ToJo's, 3
NIGHTLIFE
The Botanic Inn, 6
The Duke of York, 1
Katy Daly's Pub, 4
Madden's Bar, 2
WEST BELFAST
Roast Coffee
St. Anne's Cathedral
Smithfield Market
Life Cycles
Rape Crisis Centre
Ulster Historical Foundation
Castlecourt Shopping Centre
First Presbyterian Church
St. Mary's
Boots
US
Old Museum Arts Centre
Linen Hall Library
Consumer Advice Bureau
Scottish Provident Institution
City Hall
Belfast Opera House
Spires Shopping Center
Great Victoria St. Rail Station
Europa Hotel
Europa Bus Station
Crown Liquor Saloon
Ulster Hall
Great Victoria St. Baptist Church
Ormeau Baths Gallery
Moviehouse
Shaftesbury Square Reformed Presbyterian Church
Cafe Revelations
SHAFTESBURY SQ.
ARTHUR SQ.
TAXI
Botanic Rail Station
City Hospital Rail Station
Crescent Arts Centre
City Hospital
Queen's Film Theatre
Union Theological College of the Presbytarian Church in Ireland
Queen's University
Ulsterville Congregation
Methodist Church
Tropical Ravine
Ulster Museum
Botanic Gardens
St. Thomas Parish Church
North St.
Talbot St.
Gordon St.
Brown St.
Gardiner St.
Boyd St.
Samuel St.
Gresham St.
Royal Ave.
N. St. Arcade
Commercial Ct.
Exchange Pl.
Hill St.
Waring St.
Skipper St.
West St.
Millfield
Francis St.
Berry St.
Rosemary St.
Bridge St.
High St.
Lombard St.
Pottinger's Entry
Joy's Entry
Wilson Ct.
Crown Entry
Marquis St.
Chapel
Bank St.
Castle Pl.
Cornmarket
Divis St.
King St.
Castle St.
Donegall Pl.
Ann St.
Telfair St.
Hamill St.
College Ct.
Queen St.
Fountain St.
Castle Ln.
Victoria Sq.
College St.
College Sq. N.
Donegall Sq. N.
Wellington Pl.
College Sq. E.
Donegall Sq. W.
Donegall Sq. E.
Arthur St.
Montgomery St.
Durham St.
Wellington St.
Donegall Sq. S.
Athol St.
Great Victoria St.
Howard St.
Grosvenor Rd.
James St. S.
Bedford St.
Franklin St.
Adelaide St.
Alfred St.
Joy St.
Clarence St.
Linenhall St.
Linen Hall St. W
Hope St.
Linfield Rd.
Bruce St.
Bankmore St.
Ormeau Ave.
Boyne Bridge
Wellwood St.
Maryville St.
Apsley St.
Lindsay St.
Howard St. S.
Dublin Rd.
Albion St.
Blythe St.
Sandy Row
Donegall Pass
Elm St.
Donegall Rd.
Bradbury Pl.
Botanic Ave.
Vernon St.
Cameron St.
Lower Crescent
Cromwell Rd.
Coolmore St.
Lisburn Rd.
Claremont St.
Upper Crescent
Mount Charles
Wolseley St.
Camden St.
University St.
Fitzwilliam St.
University Square
Fitzroy Ave.
Dunluce Ave.
Elmwood Ave.
University Rd.
College Park
University Ave.
Ulsterville Ave.
Rugby Ave.
College Gardens
Ashley Ave.
Rugby Rd.
Wellesley Ave.
Malone Rd.
Stranmillis Rd.
Wellington Park
Eglantine Ave.

IRELAND

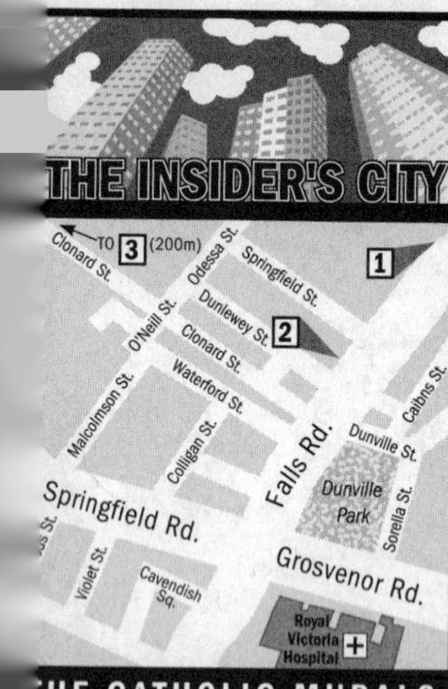

HE CATHOLIC MURALS

The murals of West Belfast are a powerful testament to the volatile past and fierce loyalties of the divided neighborhoods. Many of the most famous Catholic murals are on Falls Rd., an area that saw some of the worst of the Troubles.

1. Illustrations of protestors during the Hunger Strikes of 1981, during which they fasted for the right to be considered political prisoners.

2. Portrayal of Bobby Sands, the first hunger-striker to die, is located on the side of the Sinn Féin Office, Sevastopol St. Sands was elected as a member of the British Parliament under a "political prisoner" ticket during this time and is remembered as the North's most famous martyr.

3. Formerly operating as Northern Ireland's National RUC Headquarters, the most bombed of any police station in England, the Republic, or the North. Its fortified, barbed wire facade is on Springfield St.

Arnie's Backpackers (IHH), 63 Fitzwilliam St. (☎028 9024 2867; www.arniesbackpackers.co.uk). Look for a cutout sign of a sky-gazing backpacker. Arnie, the jovial owner, may greet you with a cup of tea and check on you daily. The hostel offers bunk beds in small, clean rooms, a kitchen, common room with television and fireplace, and back garden. Reception 8:30am-9pm. 8-bed dorms £9; 4-bed £11. Cash only. ❶

The Belfast Palace (Paddy's Palace), 68 Lisburn Rd. (☎028 9033 3367; www.paddyspalace.com). This sociable new hostel offers free Wi-Fi, continental breakfast, a kitchen, and laundry. Reception M-Th and Su 8am-8pm, F-Sa 8am-10pm. Dorms £9.50-13.50. Singles £27, doubles £37. Pay for 4 nights and stay free on the 5th. MC/V. ❶

Windermere Guest House, 60 Wellington Park (☎028 9066 2693; www.windermereguesthouse.co.uk). Leather couches provide comfy seating in the living room of this Victorian house. Singles £31-42; doubles £56-60. Cash only. ❸

Camera Guesthouse, 44 Wellington Park (☎028 9066 0026; www.cameraguesthouse.com). Quiet, serene and pristine Victorian house makes an appealing choice. Breakfasts offer wide selection of organic foods and herbal teas that cater to specific dietary concerns. Singles £34, with bath £48; doubles £45/52. 3% commission. MC/V. ❹

FOOD

Dublin Road, Botanic Avenue, and the **Golden Mile** around **Shaftesbury Square** have the most restaurants. The **Tesco** supermarket is at 2 Royal Ave. (☎028 9032 3270. Open M-W and Sa 8am-7pm, Th 8am-9pm, F 8am-8pm, Su 1-5pm.)

Little Italy, 13 Amelia St. (☎028 9031 4914). A little Mediterranean kitchen tucked in Belfast's city center. Customers watch at the brick counter as the industrious staff make their pizzas to order and savor the aromas of the Italiano, Vegetarian Special, Fabio, and Hawaiian pizzas. 9" £4-6, 10" £4-7, 12" £5-8. Open M-Sa 5pm-midnight. ❶

Tojo's, Smithfield Market (☎028 9032 4122). Offers some of Belfast's lowest prices for honest food. While it may look like a simple cafeteria, the chalkboard full of sandwich options, like the Tunatastic (tuna, corn, peppers; £3), fulfills its bold promise of "homemade food with a modern twist." Open M-F 8am-4pm and Sa 8am-5pm. Cash only. ❶

Bookfinders, 47 University Rd. (☎028 9032 8269). Find it one block from the University, on the corner of Camden St. A favorite with the University crowd because of its proximity, low prices, and disheveled character, Vegan soup and bread £3; sandwiches £3. Open M-Sa 10am-5:30pm. ❶

SIGHTS

DONEGALL SQUARE. The most dramatic and impressive piece of architecture in Belfast is also its administrative and geographic center. Dominating the grassy square that serves as the locus of downtown Belfast, **City Hall's** green copper dome is recognizable from nearly any point in the city. *(☎028 9027 0477. Free.)*

THE DOCKS AND EAST BELFAST. The poster child of Belfast's riverfront revival, the **Odyssey** packs five distinct sights into one entertainment center. *(2 Queen's Quay. ☎028 9045 1055; www.theodyssey.co.uk.)* The **W5 Discovery Centre** (short for "whowhatwherewhenwhy?") is a playground for curious minds and hyperactive schoolchildren. *(☎028 9046 7700; www.w5online.co.uk. Workshops run throughout the summer. Wheelchair-accessible. Open M-Sa 10am-6pm; closes at 5pm when school is in session, Su noon-6pm; last admission 1hr. before closing. £7, children £5. Family discounts available.)* Designed to accommodate the hordes of sinning sailors landing in Belfast port, the quirky **Sinclair Seaman's Church** does things its own way—the minister delivers his sermons from a pulpit carved in the shape of a ship's prow, collections are taken in miniature lifeboats, and the choir uses an organ from a Guinness barge with port and starboard lights. *(Corporation St., down from the SeaCat terminal. ☎028 9071 5997. Open W 2-5pm; Su service at 11:30am and 7pm.)*

CORNMARKET AND ST. ANNE'S. North of the city center, this shopping district consists of eight blocks around Castle Street and Royal Avenue. Relics of the old city remain in entries, or tiny alleys. Construction on **St. Anne's Cathedral,** also known as the Belfast Cathedral, was begun in 1899, but to keep from disturbing regular worship, it was built around a smaller church already on the site. Upon completion of the new exterior, builders extracted the earlier church brick by brick. *(Donegall St., a few blocks from the city center. Open M-Sa 10am-4pm, Su before and after services at 10am, 11am, 3:30pm.)*

GRAND OPERA HOUSE. The opera house was cyclically bombed by the IRA, restored to its original splendor at enormous cost, and then bombed again. Visitors today enjoy its grandeur, and tours offer a look behind the ornate facade and include a complimentary coffee and danish at the cafe, **Luciano's.** *(☎028 9023 1919; www.goh.co.uk. Office open*

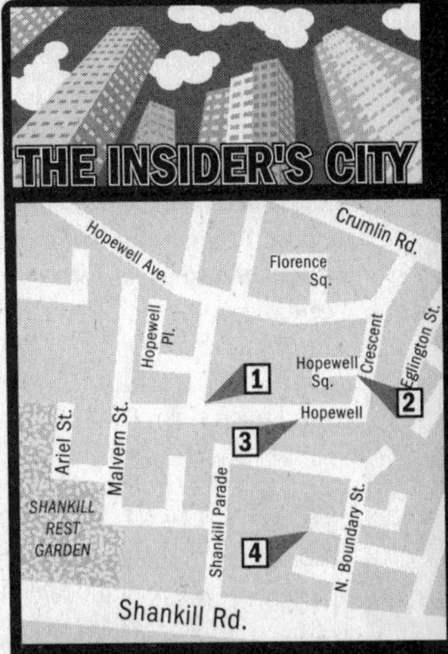

THE PROTESTANT MURALS

Many of the Protestant murals, in the Shankill area of West Belfast, are overtly militant. Most are found near Hopewell St. and Hopewell Cr., to the north of Shankill Rd., or down Shankill Parade, and are accessed by traveling south from Crumlin Rd.

1. Commemoration of the Red Hand Commando, a militant Loyalist group.
2. Painting of a Loyalist martyr, killed in prison in 1997.
3. Depiction of the Grim Reaper, with gun and British flag.
4. A collage of Loyalist militant groups including the UVF, UDU, and UDA.
5. Mural of the Battle of the Boyne, showing William of Orange's 1690 victory over James II.
6. The Marksman's gun seems to follow you as you pass by.
7. Portrait of the Top Gun, a man responsible for the deaths of many high-ranking Republicans.

M-F 8:30am-9pm, Sa 8:30am-6pm. Tours begin across the street at the office W-Sa 11am. Times vary, so call ahead. £3, seniors/students/children £2.)

WEST BELFAST. West Belfast is not a tourist site in the traditional sense, although the walls and houses along the streets display political murals which speak to Belfast's religious and political divide. Visitors should definitely take a **black cab tour** of the murals, easily booked at most hostels. **Black Taxi Tours** offer witty, objective presentations. *(☎077 2106 7752. 1hr. tour from £10 per person.)* The **Catholic neighborhood** is centered on **Falls Road,** where the Sinn Féin office is easily spotted: one side of it is covered with an advertisement for the Sinn Féin newspaper, An Phoblacht. On Divis St., **Divis Tower** was formerly an IRA stronghold. Farther north is Shankill Rd. and the **Protestant neighborhood.** Between the Falls and Shankill is the **Peace Line.** The side streets on the right guide you to the **Shankill Estate** and more murals. Crumlin Rd., through the estate, has the oldest Loyalist murals.

LIGHT TOURISM. It's safest to visit the Falls and Shankill during the day, when the neighborhoods are full of locals and the murals are visible. Do not visit the area during **Marching Season** (the weeks around July 12) when the parades are characterized by mutual antagonism.

ENTERTAINMENT AND NIGHTLIFE

Pubs in Belfast are the place to experience the city's *craic* and meet its colorful characters. Pubs were targets for sectarian violence at the height of the Troubles, so most are new or restored, although many retain their historic charm. Those in the city center and university area are now relatively safe. *Bushmills Irish Pub Guide*, by Sybil Taylor, relates the history of Belfast pubs (£7; available at local bookstores). For a full list of entertainment options, grab a free copy of *The Big List* or *Fate*, available in tourist centers, hostels, and certain restaurants and pubs.

The Duke of York, 7-11 Commercial Ct. (☎028 9024 1062). Take first left off Hill St. Rebuilt after it was bombed by the IRA in the 60s, today it is one of Belfast's favorite pubs. Serves the city's largest selection of Irish whiskeys and draws a diverse crowd with cheer and live music. Kitchen serves sandwiches and toasties daily until 2:30pm. Open M 11:30am-11pm, Tu-F 11:30am-1am, Sa 11:30am-2am, Su 2-9pm.

Madden's Bar, 74 Berry St. (☎028 9024 4114; www.maddensbarbelfast.com). You might hear Gaelic among the local crowd, and you'll definitely hear live music. W language class, 8:30pm, beginners' Irish step-dancing, 9:30pm. Th piping class followed by pipers' session and open mike. F folk night downstairs, trad upstairs. Sa blues, jazz, or electric folk downstairs, trad upstairs. Lunch M-F noon-2pm. Open daily 11am-1am.

Katy Daly's Pub, 17 Ormeau Ave. (☎028 9032 5942; www.the-limelight.co.uk). Behind City Hall, head toward Queen's, take a left on Ormeau Ave., and you'll find this stalwart of the Belfast music and nightlife scene. Students and young people, tourists included, congregate in this ultimate party spot (the Limelights, Spring, and Airbrake clubs are connected). Open M-Sa 3pm-1am, Su 8pm-midnight.

The Botanic Inn, 23 Malone Rd. (☎028 9050 9740). Standing in as the unofficial student union, the hugely popular "Bot" is packed nightly with raucous groups of friends and die-hard sports fans. Kitchen serves pub grub daily noon-8pm. Open M-Sa 11:30am-1am, Su noon-midnight. MC/V.

DERRY/LONDONDERRY ☎028

Modern Derry/Londonderry is trying to cast off the legacy of its political Troubles with much success. Although the landscape was razed by years of bombings, recent years have been relatively peaceful. Today's rebuilt city is beautiful and intimate with a cosmopolitan vibe.

WHAT'S IN A NAME? Originally christened Doire, meaning "oak grove," the city's name was anglicized to Derry and finally to Londonderry. The city's label remains a source of contention, as the minority Protestant population uses the official title while many Republican Northerners and some Protestants refer to the city as Derry. Even in the city center, some signs refer to Derry or Londonderry without any consistency.

TRANSPORTATION AND PRACTICAL INFORMATION. **Trains** (☎028 7134 2228) arrive on Duke St., Waterside, from Belfast (2hr., 4-9 per day, £10.50). A free Rail-Link bus connects the **train station** and the **bus station,** on Foyle St., between the walled city and the river; it leaves the bus station 15min. before each train is due to depart and connects with incoming trains. Ulsterbus **buses** (☎028 7126 2261) go to Belfast (1½hr., 10-36 per day, £9.40). The **Tourist Information Centre,** 44 Foyle St., has free copies of the Visitor's Guide to Derry. (☎028 7126 7284; www.derryvisitor.com. Open July-Sept. M-F 9am-7pm, Sa 10am-6pm, Su 10am-5pm; low-season reduced hours.) **Internet** is available at the central **library,** 35 Foyle St. (☎028 7127 2310. £3 per hr. Open M and Th 8:30am-8pm, Tu-W and F 8:30am-5:30pm, Sa 9:15am-5pm.) **Postal Code:** BT48 6AT.

ACCOMMODATIONS AND FOOD. Go down Strand Rd. and turn left up Great James St. to reach the social **Derry City Independent Hostel ❶,** 44 Great James St. (☎028 7137 7989; www.derryhostel.com. Breakfast included. Free Internet. Dorms £12-13; doubles £36. MC/V.) **The Saddler's House (No. 36) ❸,** 36 Great James St., offers elegant rooms in a lovely Victorian home. (☎028 7126 9691; www.thesaddlershouse.com. TV and tea/coffee facilities in all rooms. Free Internet. Breakfast included. Singles £30-45; doubles £50-60. MC/V.)

A **Tesco** supermarket is in the Quayside Shopping Centre, along Strand Rd. (☎028 7137 4400. Open M-F 9am-9pm, Sa 8:30am-8pm, Su 1-6pm.) **The Sandwich Co. ❶,** The Diamond, is perfect for cheap sandwiches. (☎028 7137 2500. Sandwiches £2.25-4.70. Open M-Sa 8:30am-5pm, Su 11am-5pm.) **The Ice Wharf/ Lloyd's No. 1 Bar ❷,** 22-24 Strand Rd., has almost every type of food imaginable at incredibly low prices. (☎028 7127 6610; www.lloydsno1.co.uk. Open M-W and Su 9am-midnight, Th-Sa 9am-1am.)

SIGHTS AND NIGHTLIFE. The **city walls,** 5.5m high and 6m thick, erected between 1614 and 1619, have never been breached—hence Derry's nickname "the Maiden City." The tower topping Derry's southeast wall past New Gate was built to protect **St. Columb's Cathedral,** on London St., the symbolic focus of the city's Protestant defenders. (☎028 7126 7313. Open M-Sa 9am-5pm. Tours 30-60min. £3.) The **Museum of Free Derry,** 55 Glenfada Pk., covers the Catholic civil rights struggle in Northern Ireland up until Bloody Sunday, chronicling civil rights marches, the Battle of the Bogside, internment, and Bloody Sunday in an eye-opening account. (☎028 7136 0880; www.museumoffreederry.org. Open M-F 9:30am-4:30pm; Apr.-Sept. additionally Sa 1-4pm; July-Sept. additionally Su 1-4pm. £3, students £2.) West of the city walls, Derry's residential neighborhoods—both the Protestant **Waterside** and **Fountain Estate,** as well as the Catholic **Bogside**—display murals.

After dark, check out **The Gweedore** or **Peadar O'Donnell's,** 53-60 Waterloo St., where Celtic paraphernalia hang and rock bands bang at night. Peadar O'Donnell's has live music Tu-Sa 11pm, trad Su night at 10pm, while The Gweedore has younger rock bands; both pubs are connected and owned by the same person, although they cater to different crowds. (☎028 7137 2318; www.peaderodonnells.com. Open M-Sa 11am-1am, Su 1pm-midnight.) **Sandino's Cafe Bar,** 1 Water St., is a good option for poetry readings or live music by local up-and-coming bands and international musicians. (☎028 7130 9297. M-Sa 11am-1am, Su 1pm-midnight.) A younger crowd chills out and enjoys live music on Tuesday and Thursday to Saturday at **Bound For Boston,** 27-31 Waterloo St. (☎028 7127 1315. Open M-Sa 11:30am-1am, Su 1pm-midnight.)

DAYTRIP FROM DERRY/LONDONDERRY: THE GIANT'S CAUSEWAY

To get to the Giant's Causeway from Derry, take the free shuttle from the city bus station across the river to the train station (it leaves 15min. before the train departs), and catch a train to Coleraine. From Coleraine, catch bus #172 or 252 to the Causeway. Ulsterbuses #172, 252 (the Antrim Coaster), and the Causeway Rambler drop visitors at the Giant's Causeway Visitors Centre. From there, a minibus runs to the most popular part of the Giant's Causeway (2min., 4 per hr., £1). ☎028 2073 1855; www.giantscausewaycentre.com. Centre open daily July-Aug. 10am-7pm; Sept.-Mar. 10am-4pm, June 10am-6pm. Free.

Geologists believe that the unique rock formations found at **Giant's Causeway** were created some 60 million years ago by lava outpourings that left curiously shaped cracks in their wake. Although locals have different ideas, everyone agrees that the Causeway is an awesome sight to behold. Comprising over 40,000 symmetrical hexagonal basalt columns, it resembles a descending staircase leading from the cliffs to the ocean's floor. Several other formations stand within the Causeway: **the Giant's Organ, the Wishing Chair, the Granny, the Camel,** and **the Giant's Boot.** Advertised as the 8th natural wonder of the world, the Giant's Causeway is Northern Ireland's most famous natural sight, so expect large crowds, or visit early in the morning or after the center closes.

Once travelers reach the Visitors Centre, they have two trail options: the more popular low road, which directly swoops down to the Causeway (20min.), or the more rewarding high road, which takes visitors 4 mi. up a sea cliff to the romantic Iron Age ruins of **Dunseverick Castle.** The trail is well-marked and easy to follow, but you can also consult the **free map** available at the Visitors Centre. The center also offers a 12min. film (£1) about the legend of Finn McCool and posits on the geological explanation for the formations.

ITALY (ITALIA)

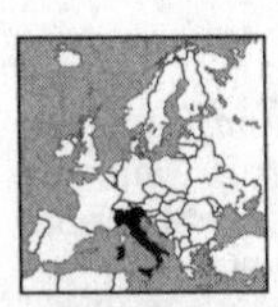

With offspring from Michelangelo to Armani, Italy has carved a distinct path through the centuries, consistently setting a world standard for innovation and elegance. Steep Alpine peaks in the north, lush olive trees in the interior, and aquamarine waters along the Riviera provide only a few of the country's breathtaking vistas. Indulging in daily *siestas* and frequently hosting leisurely feasts, Italians seem to possess a knowledge of and appreciation for life's pleasures, while their openness lets travelers ease into Italy's relaxed lifestyle.

DISCOVER ITALY: SUGGESTED ITINERARIES

THREE DAYS. Don't even think about leaving **Rome,** *La Città Eterna* (p. 574). Go back in time at the **Ancient City:** become a gladiator in the **Colosseum,** explore the **Roman Forum,** and stand in the well-preserved **Pantheon.** Spend a day to admiring the fine art in the **Capitoline Museums** and the **Galleria Borghese,** and then satiate your other senses in a *discoteca.* The next morning, redeem your debauched soul in **Vatican City,** gazing at the glorious ceiling of the **Sistine Chapel,** gaping at **St. Peter's Cathedral,** and enjoying the **Vatican Museums.**

ONE WEEK. Spend 3 days taking in the sights in **Rome** before heading north to **Florence** (2 days; p. 630) to immerse yourself in Italy's amazing Renaissance art at the Uffizi Gallery. Move to **Venice** (2 days; p. 615) to float along the canals.

BEST OF ITALY, 3 WEEKS. Begin by savoring the sights and history of **Rome** (3 days). Seek out the medieval houses of **Siena** (1 day; p. 640), and then move to **Florence** (3 days). Head up the coast to **Camogli** (1 day; p. 607), and the beautiful **Cinque Terre** (2 days; p. 608). Visit cosmopolitan **Milan** (2 days; p. 596) for shopping and **Lake Como** for hiking (1 day; p. 603). Join the star-crossed lovers Romeo and Juliet in **Verona** (1 day; p. 626). Paddle through labyrinthine canals and peer into delicate blown-glass in **Venice** (2 days) before flying south to **Naples** (2 days; p. 645). Be sure to check out the ash casts and preserved frescoes at ancient **Pompeii** (1 day; p. 650). Finally, hike and swim along the **Amalfi Coast** (1 day; p. 652) and revel in the shimmering waters of the Blue Grotto on the island of **Capri** (1 day; p. 651).

ESSENTIALS

FACTS AND FIGURES

OFFICIAL NAME: Italian Republic.

CAPITAL: Rome.

MAJOR CITIES: Florence, Milan, Naples, Venice.

POPULATION: 58,145,000.

TIME ZONE: GMT +1.

LANGUAGE: Italian; some German, French, and Slovene.

RELIGION: Roman Catholic (90%).

LONGEST SALAMI: Made by Rino Parenti in Zibello, displayed on Nov. 23, 2003; 486.8m in length.

WHEN TO GO

Traveling to Italy in late May or early September, when the temperature averages a comfortable 77°F (25°C), will ensure a calm, cool vacation. When planning, keep in mind festival schedules and weather patterns in northern and southern areas. Tourism goes into overdrive in June, July, and August: hotels are booked solid and prices know no limits. In August, Italians flock to the coast for vacationing, but northern cities are filled with tourists.

DOCUMENTS AND FORMALITIES

EMBASSIES AND CONSULATES. Foreign embassies in Italy are in Rome (p. 578). Italian embassies abroad include: **Australia,** 12 Grey St., Deakin, Canberra ACT 2600 (☎61 262 733 333; www.ambcanberra.esteri.it); **Canada,** 275 Slater St., 21st fl., Ottawa, ON K1P 5H9 (☎613-232-2401; www.ambottawa.esteri.it); **Ireland,** 63/65 Northumberland Rd., Dublin 4 (☎353 16 60 17 44; www.ambdublino.esteri.it); **New Zealand,** 34-38 Grant Rd., Wellington (☎64 44 735 339; www.ambwellington.esteri.it); **UK,** 14 Three Kings Yard, London, W1K 4EH (☎44 20 73 12 22 00; www.embitaly.org.uk); **US,** 3000 Whitehaven St., NW, Washington, DC 20008 (☎202-612-4400; www.ambwashingtondc.esteri.it).

VISA AND ENTRY INFORMATION. EU citizens do not need a visa. Citizens of Australia, Canada, New Zealand, and the US do not need a visa for stays of up to 90 days, beginning upon entry into any of the countries within the EU's freedom-of-movement zone. For more info, see p. 14. For stays longer than 90 days, all non-EU citizens need visas (around €60), available at Italian consulates. For more info on obtaining a visa visit www.esteri.it/visti/home_eng.asp.

TOURIST SERVICES AND MONEY

EMERGENCY	**Ambulance:** ☎118. **Fire:** ☎115. **Police:** ☎112. **General Emergency:** ☎113.

TOURIST OFFICES. The **Italian Government Tourist Board** (**ENIT;** www.italiantourism.com) provides useful info about many aspects of the country, including the arts, history, and activities. The main office in Rome (☎06 49 71 11; sedecentrale@cert.enit.it) can help locate any local office that is not listed online.

MONEY. The **euro (€)** has replaced the **lira** as the unit of currency in Italy. For more info, see p. 17. At many restaurants, a **service charge** *(servizio)* or **cover** *(coperto)* is included in the bill. Most locals do not tip, but it is appropriate for foreign visitors to leave an additional €1-2 at restaurants. Taxi drivers expect a 10-15% tip. Bargaining is common in Italy, but use discretion. It is appropriate at markets, with vendors, and unmetered taxi fares (settle the price before getting in). Haggling over prices elsewhere is usually inappropriate.

Italy has a 20% **value added tax** (**VAT,** or **IVA** in Italy), a sales tax applied to most goods and services. The prices given in *Let's Go* include VAT. In the airport upon exiting the EU, non-EU citizens can claim a refund on the tax paid for goods purchased at participating stores. In order to qualify for a refund in a store, you must spend at least €155; make sure to ask for a refund form when you pay. For more info on qualifying for a VAT refund, see p. 21.

BUSINESS HOURS. Nearly everything closes around 1-3pm for *siesta.* Most museums are open 9am-1pm and 3-6pm; some are open through lunch, however. Monday is often a *giorno di chiusura* (day of closure).

TRANSPORTATION

BY PLANE. Most international flights land at Rome's international airport, known as both **Fiumicino** and **Leonardo da Vinci** (**FCO;** ☎06 65 951; www.adr.it). Other hubs are Florence's **Amerigo Vespucci** airport **(FLR)** and Milan's **Malpensa (MXP)** and **Linate (LIN)** airports. **Alitalia** (☎800-223-5730; www.alitalia.com) is Italy's national airline. Budget airlines **Ryanair** (☎353 12 49 77 91; www.ryanair.com) and **easyJet** (☎0871 244 2366; www.easyjet.com) offer inexpensive fares to cities throughout the country; reserve ahead to get the best deals.

BY FERRY. Sicily, Sardinia, Corsica, and smaller islands along the coast are connected to the mainland by **ferries** *(traghetti)* and **hydrofoils** *(aliscafi)*. Italy's largest private ferry service, **Tirrenia** (www.tirrenia.it), runs ferries to Sardinia,

Sicily, and Tunisia. Other lines, such as the **SNAV** (tickets and special offers available online at www.aferry.to/snav-ferry.htm), have hydrofoil services from major ports such as Ancona, Bari, Brindisi, Genoa, La Spezia, Livorno, Naples, and Trapani. Ferry service is also prevalent in the Lake Country. Reserve well ahead, especially in July and August.

BY TRAIN. The Italian State Railway **Ferrovie dello Stato,** or **FS** (national info line ☎89 20 21; www.trenitalia.com), offers inexpensive, efficient service and Trenitalia passes, the domestic equivalent of the Eurail Pass. There are several types of trains: the *locale* stops at every station on a line, the *diretto* makes fewer stops than the *locale*, and the *espresso* stops only at major stations. The air-conditioned *rapido*, an **InterCity (IC)** train, zips along but costs more. Tickets for the fast, pricey **Eurostar** trains require reservations. **Eurail Passes** are valid without a supplement on all trains except Eurostar. Always validate your ticket in the orange or yellow machine before boarding to avoid a €120 fine.

BY BUS. Bus travel within Italy has its own benefits and disadvantages; in remote parts of the country private companies offer cheap fares and are often the only option, though schedules may be unreliable. Intercity buses serve points inaccessible by train. For city buses, buy tickets in *tabaccherie* or kiosks. Validate your ticket immediately after boarding to avoid a €120 fine. Websites www.bus.it and www.italybus.it are helpful resources for trip planning.

BY CAR. To drive in Italy, you must be 18 or older and hold an **International Driving Permit (IDP)** or an EU license. There are four kinds of roads: *autostrada* (superhighways; mostly toll roads; usually 130km per hr. speed limit); *strade statali* (state roads); *strade provinciali* (provincial); and *strade communali* (local). Driving in Italy is frightening; congested traffic is common in large cities and in the north. On three-lane roads, the center lane is for passing. **Mopeds** (€30-40 per day) can be a great way to see the more scenic areas but can be disastrous in the rain and on rough roads. Always exercise caution. Practice in empty streets and learn to keep up with traffic. Drivers in Italy—especially in the south—are notorious for ignoring traffic laws.

BY BIKE AND BY THUMB. While cycling is a popular sport in Italy, bike trails are rare. Rent bikes where you see a *noleggio* sign. Hitchhiking can be unsafe in Italy, especially in the south. *Let's Go* does not recommend hitchhiking.

KEEPING IN TOUCH

PHONE CODES	**Country code:** 39. **International dialing prefix:** 00. For more info on how to place international calls, see **Inside Back Cover.**

EMAIL AND THE INTERNET. While **Internet** is a relatively common amenity throughout Italy, **Wi-Fi** is not, and as a general rule, the prevalence of both decreases the further you travel from urban areas. A new Italian law requires a passport or driver's license to use an Internet cafe. Rates are €2-6 per hr. For free Internet access, try local universities and libraries.

TELEPHONE. Almost all **public phones** require a prepaid card *(scheda)*, sold at *tabaccherie*, Internet cafes, and post offices. Italy has no area codes, only regional prefixes that are incorporated into the number. **Mobile phones** are widely used in Italy; buying a prepaid SIM card for a GSM phone can be a good, inexpensive option. Of the service providers, **TIM** and **Vodafone** have the best networks. International direct dial numbers include: **AT&T Direct** (☎800 17 24 44); **Canada Direct** (☎800 17 22 13); **Telecom New Zealand Direct** (☎800 17 26 41); **Telstra Australia** (☎800 17 26 10).

MAIL. Airmail letters sent from Australia, North America, or the UK to Italy take anywhere from four to 15 days to arrive. Since Italian mail is notoriously unreliable, it is usually safer to send mail priority *(prioritaria)* or registered *(raccomandata)*. It costs €0.85 to send a letter worldwide. To receive mail in Italy, have mail delivered **Poste Restante.** Mail will go to the main post office unless you specify a subsidiary by street address. Address mail to be held according to the following example: First name LAST NAME, *Fermo Posta*, City, Italy. Bring a passport to pick up your mail; there may be a small fee.

ACCOMMODATIONS AND CAMPING

ITALY	❶	❷	❸	❹	❺
ACCOMMODATIONS	under €16	€16-25	€26-40	€41-60	over €60

Associazione Italiana Alberghi per la Gioventù (AIG), the Italian hostel federation, is a **Hostelling International (HI)** affiliate. A full list of AIG hostels is available online at www.ostellionline.org. Prices in Italy average around €15-25 per night for **dorms.** Hostels are the best option for solo travelers (single rooms are relatively scarce in hotels in the country), but curfews, lockouts, distant locations, and less-than-perfect security can detract from their appeal. Italian **hotel** rates are set by the state. A single room in a hotel *(camera singola)* usually starts at €25-50 per night, and a double *(camera doppia)* starts at €40-90 per room. A room with a private bath *(con bagno)* usually costs 30-50% more. Smaller **pensioni** are often cheaper than hotels. Be sure to confirm charges before checking in; Italian hotels are notorious for tacking on additional costs at check-out time. **Affittacamere** (rooms for rent in private houses) are an inexpensive option for longer stays. For more info, inquire at local tourist offices. There are over 1700 **campgrounds** in Italy; tent sites average €4.20. The **Federazione Italiana del Campeggio e del Caravaning** (www.federcampeggio.it) has a complete list of sites.

FOOD AND DRINK

ITALY	❶	❷	❸	❹	❺
FOOD	under €7	€7-15	€16-20	€21-25	over €25

Breakfast is the simplest meal in Italy: at most, *colazione* consists of coffee and a *cornetto* or *brioche* (croissant). For *pranzo* (lunch), locals grab panini or salads, or dine more calmly at an inexpensive *tavola calda* (cafeteria-style snack bar), *rosticceria* (grill), or *gastronomia* (snack bar with hot dishes for take-out). *Cena* (dinner) usually begins at 8pm or later. In Naples, it's not unusual to go for a midnight **pizza.** Traditionally, dinner is the longest meal of the day, usually lasting much of the evening and consisting of an *antipasto* (appetizer), a *primo piatto* (starch-based first course like pasta or risotto), a *secondo piatto* (meat or fish), and a *contorno* (vegetable side dish). Finally comes the *dolce* (dessert or fruit), then *caffè* (espresso), and often an after-dinner liqueur.

Lunch is usually the most important meal of the day in rural regions where daily work comes in two shifts and is separated by a long lunch and **siesta.** Many restaurants offer a fixed-price *menù turistico* including *primo*, *secondo*, bread, water, and wine. While food varies regionally, the importance of relaxing and having an extended meal does not. **La bella figura** (a good figure) is another social imperative, and the after-dinner **passeggiata** (walk) is as much a tradition as the meal itself. **Gelato** is a snack, a dessert, and even a meal in itself. **Coffee** and **wine** are their own institutions, each with their own devoted followers.

THE UGLY DUCKLING. Before shelling out the euro for a *piccolo cono* (small cone), assess the quality of an establishment by looking at the banana gelato: if it's bright yellow, it's been made from a mix. If it's slightly gray, real bananas were used. *Gelati* in metal bins also tend to be homemade, whereas plastic tubs indicate mass-production.

HOLIDAYS AND FESTIVALS

Holidays: New Year's Day (Jan. 1); Epiphany (Jan. 6); Good Friday (Apr. 10, 2009); Easter Sunday and Monday (Apr. 12-13, 2009); Liberation Day (Apr. 25); Labor Day (May 1); Feast of the Assumption (Aug. 15); All Saints' Day (Nov. 1); Immaculate Conception (Dec. 8); Christmas (Dec. 25); St. Stephen's Day (Dec. 26).

Festivals: The most common reason for a local festival in Italy is the celebration of a religious event—everything from a patron saint's holy day to the commemoration of a special miracle counts. **Carnevale,** a country-wide celebration, is held during the 10 days leading up to Lent. In Venice, costumed Carnevale revelers fill the streets and canals. During **Scoppio del Carro,** held in Florence's P. del Duomo on Easter Sunday, Florentines set off a cart of explosives in keeping with medieval tradition. The **Spoleto Festival** (known as the Festival dei Due Mondi, or Festival of Two Worlds) is one of the world's most prestigious international arts events. Each June and July it features concerts, operas, ballets, film screenings, and modern art shows (www.spoletofestival.it). For a complete list of festivals, contact the Italian Government Tourist Board (p. 570).

BEYOND TOURISM

From harvesting grapes on vineyards in Siena to restoring and protecting marine life in the Mediterranean, there are diverse options for working for a cause. Those in search of a more lucrative experience might consider working as an intern for the Italian press or teaching English in Italian schools. For more info on opportunities across Europe, see **Beyond Tourism,** p. 60.

Associazione Culturale Linguista Educational (ACLE), V. Roma 54, 18038 San Remo, Imperio (☎01 84 50 60 70; www.acle.org). Non-profit association that works to bring theater, arts, and English language instruction to Italian children. Employees create theater programs in schools and teach English at summer camps.

Cook Italy, (☎34 90 07 82 98; www.cookitaly.com). Region- or dish-specific cooking classes. Venues include Bologna, Cortona, Florence, Lucca, Rome, and Sicily. Courses 3- to 6- nights from €950. Housing, meals, and recipes included.

Aegean Center for the Fine Arts, Paros 84400, Cyclades, Greece (☎30 22 84 02 32 87; www.aegeancenter.org). Italian branch located in Pistoia. Instruction in arts, literature, creative writing, voice, and art history. Classes taught in English. Fees cover housing in 16th-century villa, meals, and excursions. 14-week program in the fall €8500.

ROME (ROMA) ☎06

Rome (pop. 2.8 million), *La Città Eterna,* is a concentrated expression of Italian spirit. Whether flaunting the Italian 2006 World Cup victory or retelling the mythical story of the city's founding, Romans exude a fierce pride for the Rome that was and the Rome that will be. Crumbling pagan ruins form the backdrop for the center of Christianity's largest denomination, and hip clubs and bars border grand cathedrals. Augustus once boasted that he found Rome a city of brick and left it a city of marble. No matter how you find it, you'll undoubtedly leave with plenty of memories and a new appreciation for *la dolce vita*.

INTERCITY TRANSPORTATION

Flights: Da Vinci International Airport (FCO; ☎06 65 21 01), known as **Fiumicino,** handles most flights. The **Termini** line runs nonstop to Rome's main station, **Stazione Termini** (30min., 2 per hr., €11). After hours, take the blue COTRAL **bus** (☎06 80 01 50 008) to Tiburtina from outside the main doors after customs (4 per day, €5). From Tiburtina, take bus #175 or 492, or metro B to Termini. A few domestic and budget flights, including Ryanair, arrive at **Ciampino (CIA;** ☎06 65 951). To get to Rome, take the COTRAL bus (2 per hr., €1) to **Anagnina** station, or the **Terravision Shuttle** (www.terravision.it) to V. Marsala at the Hotel Royal Santina (40min., €8).

Trains: Trains leave Stazione Termini for: **Bologna** (2-3hr., €33-42); **Florence** (1-3hr., €14-33); **Milan** (4-8hr., €30-50); **Naples** (1-2hr., €10-25); **Venice** (4-5hr., €33-50). Trains arriving in Rome between midnight and 5am arrive at **Stazione Tiburtina** or **Stazione Ostiense,** which are connected to Termini by bus #175.

ORIENTATION

Because Rome's winding streets are difficult to navigate, it's helpful to orient yourself to major landmarks and main streets. The **Tiber River,** which snakes north-south through the city, is also a useful reference point. Most trains arrive at Stazione Termini east of Rome's historical center. **Termini** and **San Lorenzo** to the east are home to the city's largest university and most of its budget accommodations. **Via Nazionale** originates two blocks northwest of Termini Station in **Piazza della Repubblica** and leads to **Piazza Venezia,** the focal point of the city, recognizable by the immense white **Vittorio Emanuele II monument.** From P. Venezia, **Via dei Fori Imperiali** runs southeast to the Ancient City, where the **Colosseum** and the **Roman Forum** attest to former glory. **Via del Corso** stretches north from P. Venezia to **Piazza del Popolo,** which has an obelisk in its center. The **Trevi Fountain, Piazza Barberini,** and the fashionable streets around **Piazza di Spagna** and the **Spanish Steps** lie to the east of V. del Corso. **Villa Borghese,** with its impressive gardens and museums, is northeast of the Spanish Steps. West of V. del Corso is the *centro storico*, the tangle of streets around the **Pantheon, Piazza Navona, Campo dei Fiori,** and the old **Jewish Ghetto.** West of P. Venezia, **Largo Argentina** marks the start of **Corso Vittorio Emanuele II,** which runs through the *centro storico* to the Tiber River. Across the river to the northwest is **Vatican City** and the **Borgo-Prati** neighborhood. South of the Vatican is **Trastevere** and residential **Testaccio.** Pick up a free color **map** in English at the tourist office.

LOCAL TRANSPORTATION

Public Transportation: The A and B **Metropolitana subway** lines (www.metroroma.it) meet at Termini and usually run 5:30am-11:30pm; however, due to construction on the forthcoming C line, the subway now closes at 10pm. **ATAC buses** (www.atac.roma.it) run 5am-midnight (with limited late-night routes); validate your ticket in the machine when you board. Buy tickets (€1) at *tabaccherie*, newsstands, and station machines;

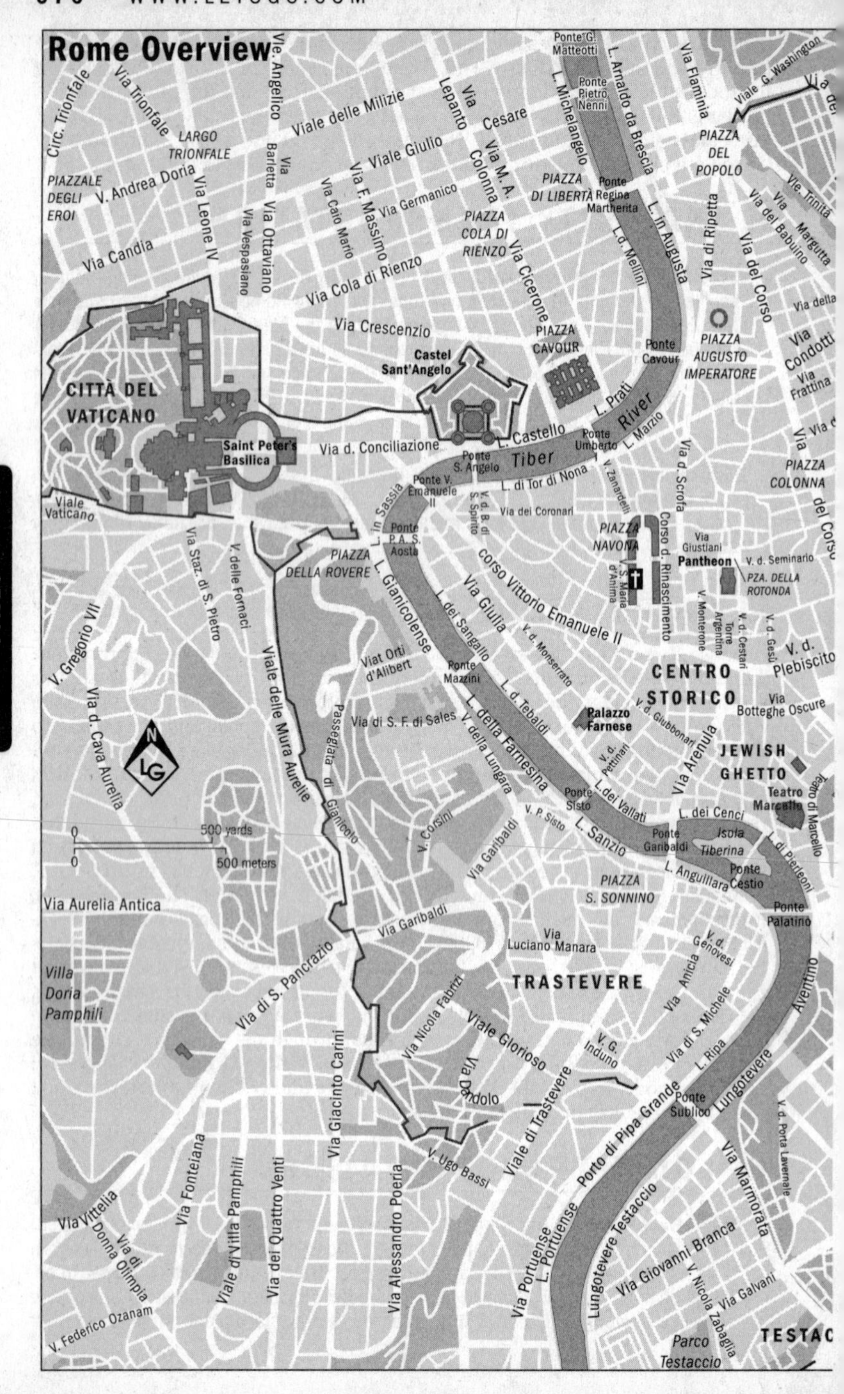
Rome Overview
CITTÀ DEL VATICANO
Saint Peter's Basilica
Castel Sant'Angelo
Tiber River
PIAZZA CAVOUR
PIAZZA DEL POPOLO
PIAZZA AUGUSTO IMPERATORE
PIAZZA COLONNA
PIAZZA NAVONA
Pantheon
PZA. DELLA ROTONDA
CENTRO STORICO
Palazzo Farnese
JEWISH GHETTO
Teatro Marcello
Isola Tiberina
PIAZZA S. SONNINO
TRASTEVERE
PIAZZA DELLA ROVERE
PIAZZA COLA DI RIENZO
PIAZZA DI LIBERTÀ
PIAZZALE DEGLI EROI
LARGO TRIONFALE
Villa Doria Pamphili
Parco Testaccio
TESTAC
Via Crescenzio
Via Cola di Rienzo
Viale delle Milizie
Viale Giulio Cesare
Via d. Conciliazione
Corso Vittorio Emanuele II
Via Giulia
Viale delle Mura Aurelie
Viale di Trastevere
Via Aurelia Antica
Via di S. Pancrazio
Via Garibaldi
Viale Glorioso
Via del Corso
Via Flaminia
Via di Ripetta
Lungotevere Testaccio
Via Marmorata
Via Portuense
0 500 yards
0 500 meters

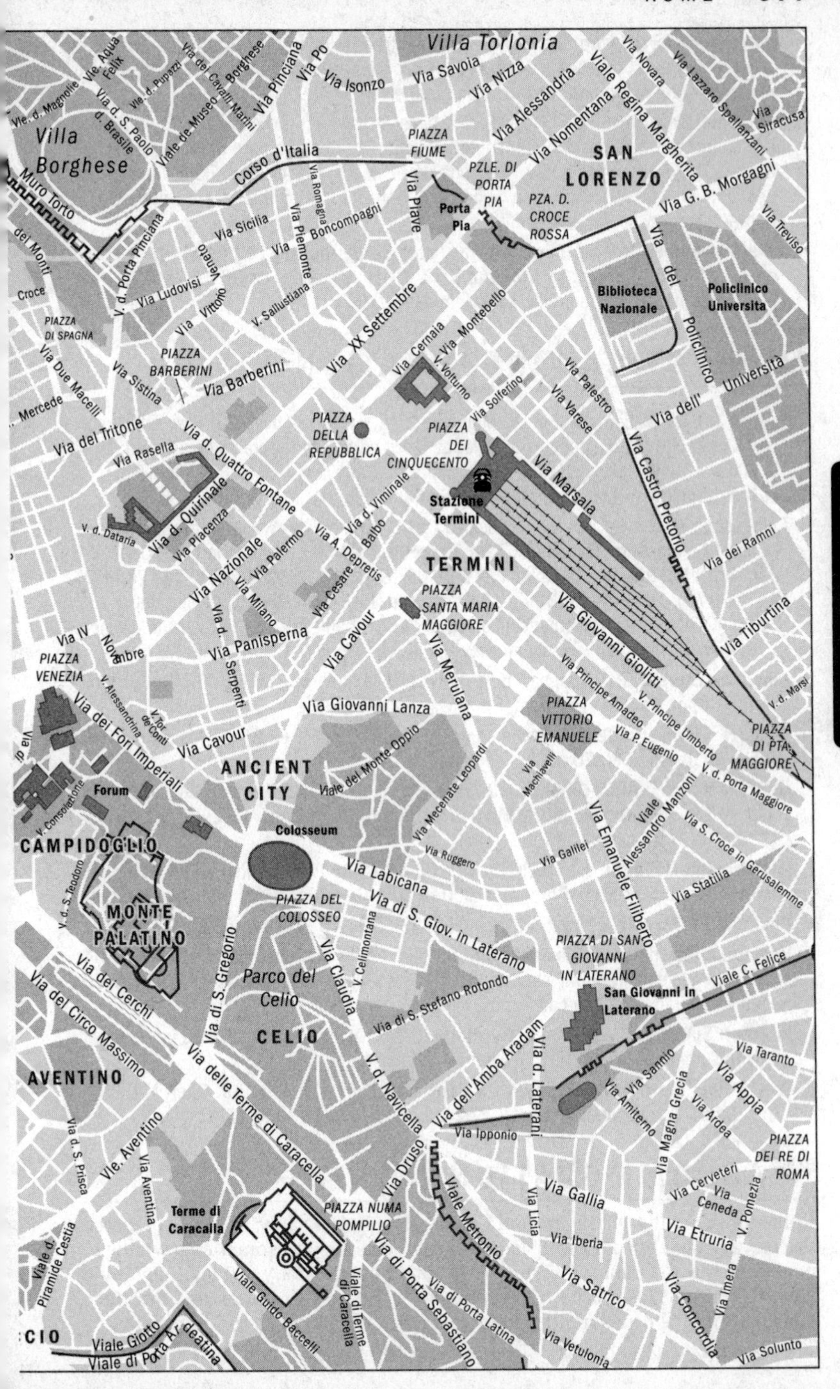
Villa Torlonia
Villa Borghese
PIAZZA FIUME
PZLE. DI PORTA PIA
Porta Pia
PZA. D. CROCE ROSSA
SAN LORENZO
Biblioteca Nazionale
Policlinico Universita
PIAZZA DI SPAGNA
PIAZZA BARBERINI
PIAZZA DELLA REPUBBLICA
PIAZZA DEI CINQUECENTO
Stazione Termini
TERMINI
PIAZZA SANTA MARIA MAGGIORE
PIAZZA VENEZIA
PIAZZA VITTORIO EMANUELE
PIAZZA DI PTA. MAGGIORE
ANCIENT CITY
Forum
Colosseum
CAMPIDOGLIO
MONTE PALATINO
PIAZZA DEL COLOSSEO
Parco del Celio
CELIO
PIAZZA DI SAN GIOVANNI IN LATERANO
San Giovanni in Laterano
AVENTINO
Terme di Caracalla
PIAZZA NUMA POMPILIO
PIAZZA DEI RE DI ROMA
Via Po
Via Pinciana
Via Isonzo
Via Savoia
Via Nizza
Via Alessandria
Via Nomentana
Viale Regina Margherita
Via Novara
Via Lazzaro Spallanzani
Via Siracusa
Corso d'Italia
Via Piave
Via G. B. Morgagni
Via Treviso
Muro Torto
Via Sicilia
Via Boncompagni
Via Piemonte
Via Romagna
V. d. Porta Pinciana
Via Ludovisi
Via Vittorio Veneto
V. Sallustiana
Via XX Settembre
Via Cernaia
Via Montebello
V. Volturno
Via Solferino
Via Palestro
Via Varese
Via del Policlinico
Via dell' Università
Via Castro Pretorio
Via Marsala
Via dei Ramni
Via Tiburtina
Via Due Macelli
Via Sistina
Via Barberini
Via del Tritone
Via Rasella
Via d. Quattro Fontane
Via d. Quirinale
V. d. Dataria
Via Piacenza
Via Nazionale
Via Palermo
Via Milano
Via A. Depretis
Via d. Viminale
Via Cesare Balbo
Via Cavour
Via Panisperna
Via IV Novembre
Via d. Serpenti
Via Merulana
Via Giovanni Giolitti
Via Principe Amadeo
V. Principe Umberto
Via P. Eugenio
V. d. Porta Maggiore
V. d. Marsi
Via Giovanni Lanza
V. Alessandrina
Via dei Fori Imperiali
V. Consolazione
Viale del Monte Oppio
Via Mecenate Leopardi
Via Machiavelli
Via Emanuele Filiberto
Viale Alessandro Manzoni
Via S. Croce in Gerusalemme
Via Ruggero
Via Galilei
Via Labicana
Via Statilia
Via di S. Giov. in Laterano
V. Celimontana
Via Claudia
Via di S. Gregorio
V. d. S. Teodoro
Via dei Cerchi
Via del Circo Massimo
Via di S. Stefano Rotondo
Viale C. Felice
Via delle Terme di Caracalla
V. d. Navicella
Via dell'Amba Aradam
Via d. Laterani
Via Sannio
Via Amiterno
Via Magna Grecia
Via Ardea
Via Appia
Via Taranto
Via Ipponio
Via Druso
Viale Metronio
Via Gallia
Via Licia
Via Iberia
Via Satrico
Via Cerveteri
Via Ceneda
V. Pomezia
Via Etruria
Via Concordia
Via Imera
Via Vetulonia
Via Solunto
Via d. S. Prisca
Vle. Aventino
Via Aventina
Viale d. Piramide Cestia
Viale Guido Baccelli
Viale di Terme di Caracella
Via di Porta Sebastiano
Via di Porta Latina
Viale Giotto
Viale di Porta Ardeatina

they're valid for 1 metro ride or unlimited bus travel within 1hr. of validation. **BIG daily tickets** (€4) and **CIS weekly tickets** (€16) allow for unlimited public transport. Beware: **pickpocketing** is rampant on buses and trains.

Taxis: Radiotaxi (☎06 35 70). Taxis are expensive. Ride only in yellow or white taxis, and make sure your taxi has a meter (if not, negotiate the price before riding). **Surcharges** apply at night (€2.60), on Su (€1), and when heading to or from Fiumicino (€7.25) or Ciampino (€5.50). Fares run about €11 from Termini to Vatican City, around €35 between the city center and Fiumicino.

Bike and Moped Rental: Bikes generally cost €5 per hr. or €10 per day while scooters cost €35-55 per day. Try **Bici and Baci,** V. del Viminale 5 (☎06 48 28 443; www.bicibaci.com). 16+. Open daily 8am-7pm. AmEx/MC/V.

PRACTICAL INFORMATION

Tourist Office: Enjoy Rome, V. Marghera 8/A (☎06 44 56 890; www.enjoyrome.com). From the middle concourse of Termini, exit right, with the trains behind you; cross V. Marsala and follow V. Marghera for 3 blocks. Open Apr.-Oct. M-F 8:30am-7pm, Sa 8:30am-2pm; Nov.-Mar. M-F 9am-6pm, Sa 9am-2pm.

Embassies: Australia, V. Antonio Bosio 5 (☎06 85 27 21; www.italy.embassy.gov.au). Open M-F 9am-5pm. **Canada,** V. Zara 30 (☎06 85 44 41; www.canada.it). Open M-F 9am-5pm. **Ireland,** P. di Campitelli 3 (☎06 69 79 121). **New Zealand,** V. Zara 28 (☎06 44 17 171). Open M-F 8:30am-12:45pm and 1:45-5pm. **UK,** V. XX Settembre 80a (☎06 42 20 00 01). Consular section open M-F 9:15am-1:30pm. **US,** V. Vittorio Veneto 119/A (☎06 46 741; www.usembassy.it/mission). Open M-F 8:30am-5:30pm.

American Express: P. di Spagna 38 (☎06 67 641; lost cards 800 87 20 00). Open M-F 9am-5:30pm, Sa 9am-12:30pm.

Luggage Storage: In Termini Station, underneath track #24. €3.80 for first 5hr., €0.60 per hr. up to 12hr., €0.20 per hr. thereafter.

GLBT Resources: ARCI-GAY, V. Goito 35/B (☎06 64 50 11 02; www.arcigayroma.it). Open M-F 4-8pm. **Circolo Mario Mieli di Cultura Omosessuale,** V. Efeso 2/A (☎06 54 13 985; www.mariomieli.org).

Laundromat: BollaBlu, V. Milazzo 20/B (☎06 44 70 30 96). Laundry about €10. Open daily 8am-midnight. **OndaBlu** (info ☎800 86 13 46). 17 locations throughout the city.

Pharmacies: Farmacia Piram, V. Nazionale 228 (☎06 48 80 754). Open 24hr. MC/V.

Hospitals: International Medical Center, V. Firenze 47 (☎06 48 82 371; www.imc84.com). Call ahead. Referral service to English-speaking doctors. General visit €100. Open M-Sa 9am-8pm; on-call 24hr.

Internet: Splashnet, V. Varese 33 (☎06 49 38 04 50), near Termini. €1.50 per hr. Open daily in summer 8:30am-1am; in winter 8:30am-11pm.

Post Office: Main Post Office (Posta Centrale), P. San Silvestro 19. Open M-F 8am-7pm, Sa 8am-1:15pm. Branch at V. d. Terme di Diocleziano 30, near Termini.

ACCOMMODATIONS

Rome swells with tourists around Easter, May through July, and in September. Prices vary widely with the seasons, and proprietors are sometimes willing to negotiate rates. Termini swarms with hotel scouts. Many are legitimate and have IDs issued by tourist offices; however, beware of impostors with fake badges directing travelers to run-down locations charging exorbitant rates.

CENTRO STORICO AND ANCIENT CITY

If being a bit closer to the sights is important to you, then choosing Rome's medieval center over the area near Termini may be worth the higher prices.

Pensione Rosetta, V. Cavour 295 (☎06 47 82 30 69; www.rosettahotel.com), a few blocks past the Fori Imperiali. 18 tidy rooms with bath, TV, and phone. A/C €10. Reserve 2 months ahead. Singles €60; doubles €85; triples €95; quads €110. AmEx/MC/V. ❹

Albergo del Sole, V. d. Biscione 76 (☎06 68 80 68 73; www.solealbiscione.it), off Campo dei Fiori. Comfortable rooms with phone, TV, and antique furniture. Reception 24hr. Check-in and check-out 11am. Reserve 2 months ahead in high-season. Singles €75, with bath €90-125; doubles €100-160; triples €200; quads €240. Cash only. ❺

Hotel Navona, V. d. Sediari 8, 1st fl. (☎06 68 64 203; www.hotelnavona.com). Owners have a nearby *residenza* with apartments to rent for longer stays. Breakfast, TV, A/C, and bath included. Reception 24hr. Singles €100-125; doubles €135-155; triples €180-210. Reservations with credit card and deposit. 5% *Let's Go* discount. MC/V. ❺

PIAZZA DI SPAGNA AND ENVIRONS

Though prices near P. di Spagna can be very steep, accommodations are often close to the metro and *centro storico*.

Pensione Panda, V. della Croce 35, 2nd fl. (☎06 67 80 179; www.hotelpanda.it). 28 renovated rooms with faux marble statues and frescoed ceilings. English spoken. A/C €6. Free Wi-Fi. Reserve ahead. Singles €65-75, with bath €68-80; doubles €75-98/78-108; triples €130/140; quads €180. 5% discount with cash payment. AmEx/MC/V. ❹

Hotel Boccaccio, V. del Boccaccio 25, 1st fl. (☎06 48 85 962; www.hotelboccaccio.com). M: A-Barberini, near P. Barberini. 8 basic, simply furnished rooms and a terrace. Singles €45; doubles €80, with bath €100; triples €108/135. AmEx/MC/V. ❸

BORGO AND PRATI (NEAR VATICAN CITY)

Pensioni near the Vatican offer some of the best deals in Rome and the sobriety one would expect from an area with this kind of nun-to-tourist ratio.

Colors, V. Boezio 31 (☎06 68 74 030; www.colorshotel.com). M: A-Ottaviano. This 3-fl. complex is part hostel, part hotel. Breakfast included. Internet €2 per hr. Hostel dorms €27; singles €90, with bath €105; doubles €100/130; triples €120. Hotel singles €90; doubles €120; triples €140. Low-season discount. Cash only. ❸

Hotel San Pietrino, V. G. Bettolo 43, 3rd fl. (☎06 37 00 132; www.sanpietrino.it). M: A-Ottaviano. Spacious rooms with free A/C, TV, and DVD. Laundry €8. Internet available. Reserve ahead in high-season. Singles €32-90; doubles €48-118; triples €72-148; family quads €92-166. Negotiable discounts and low-season specials. AmEx/MC/V. ❸

Hotel Lady, V. Germanico 198, 4th fl. (☎06 32 42 112; www.hoteladyroma.it). This cozy hotel's dimly lit hallways accentuate the ceiling's rich wooden beams. Rooms have antique furniture, sinks, desks, phones, and fans, but no A/C. Singles €50-90; doubles €70-111, with bath €90-150; triples €90-145. AmEx/MC/V. ❺

Ostello Per La Gioventù Foro Italico (HI), V. delle Olimpiadi 61 (☎06 32 36 267; www.hihostels.com). A barrack-style building holds massive dorm rooms, a cafeteria, and a common area. Breakfast, showers, and linens included. Internet access with phone card. Reception 7am-11pm. Curfew 1-1:30am. Dorms €18. €3 non-HI fee. AmEx/MC/V. ❷

SAN LORENZO AND EAST OF TERMINI

Welcome to budget traveler and backpacker central. Termini is chock-full of traveler's services, but be sure to use caution when walking in the area, especially at night: keep a close eye on your pockets and/or purse.

Hotel and Hostel Des Artistes, V. Villafranca 20, 5th fl. (☎06 44 54 365; www.hoteldesartistes.com). Houses a hotel and a renovated hostel with large dorms and private rooms. Hostel towels €1. Key deposit €10. 15min. free Internet. Reception 24hr. Check-out 10:30am. 4- to 10-bed dorms €12-23. Hostel cash only. Hotel AmEx/MC/V. ❷

Hotel Cervia, V. Palestro 55 (☎06 49 10 57; www.hotelcerviaroma.it). Clean rooms with fans. Breakfast €3, free for guests in rooms with bath. Reception 24hr. Singles €35-55, with bath €50-80; doubles €55-80/70-120; triples €75-110/90-150; quads €80-130/100-160. 5% *Let's Go* discount with cash payment. AmEx/MC/V. ❸

VIA XX SETTEMBRE AND NORTH OF TERMINI

Dominated by government ministries and private apartments, this area is less crowded and noisy than nearby Termini.

Hotel Papa Germano, V. Calatafimi 14/A (☎06 48 69 19; www.hotelpapagermano.com). Clean rooms with hair dryer, sink, and TV. Mini-fridge in rooms with bath. A/C €5. Breakfast, linens, and towels included. Internet €2 per hr. Dorms €25-30; singles €40-55; doubles €65-85, with bath €85-110; triples €75-95/95-125; quads €100-125/110-145. Discount with cash payment. AmEx/MC/V. ❷

Hotel Bolognese, V. Palestro 15, 2nd fl. (☎/fax 06 49 00 45; www.hotelbologneseinrome.com). The proud artist-owner's impressive paintings set this comfortable hotel apart. 14 newly renovated rooms, all with private bath. Breakfast included. Check-out 11am. Singles €30-60; doubles €50-90; triples €90-120. AmEx/MC/V. ❸

ESQUILINO AND WEST OF TERMINI

Esquilino, south of Termini, has tons of hotels close to major sights. The area west of Termini is more inviting than Esquilino, with busy, shop-lined streets.

Alessandro Palace, V. Vicenza 42 (☎06 44 61 958; www.hostelalessandropalace.com). Renovated dorms, all with bath and A/C. Fun, guests-only bar. Breakfast included. Lockers available. Linens included. Towels €2 in dorms. Internet €2 per hr. Reserve ahead. Dorms €25-30; doubles €90-100; triples €118-126; quads €140. AmEx/MC/V. ❷

Alessandro Downtown, V. C. Cattaneo 23 (☎06 44 34 01 47; www.hostelalessandrodowntown.com). Fewer amenities than the Palace, but similar in quality and communal feel. Breakfast and pasta party (M-F 7pm) included. Internet €2 per hr. Dorms €22.50-32.50; doubles €70, with bath €90; quads €120/140. AmEx/MC/V. ❷

Hotel Scott House, V. Gioberti 30 (☎06 44 65 379; www.scotthouse.com). Colorful, modern rooms have A/C, bath, phone, and satellite TV. Breakfast included. Internet available. Check-out 11am. Singles €35-68; doubles €63-93; triples €75-114; quads €88-129. €5 discount with cash payment. AmEx/MC/V. ❸

ALTERNATIVE HOUSING

RELIGIOUS HOUSING

Don't automatically think "Catholic" or even "inexpensive;" most rooms are open to people of all religions, and single rooms can run to €155. Don't expect quaint rooms in cloisters: religious housing has amenities similar to hotels. Do, however, consider the trade-offs: early curfews and/or chores are standard.

Domus Nova Bethlehem, V. Cavour 85/A (☎06 47 82 44 14). Rooms with A/C, bath, and TV. Breakfast included. Internet with phonecard. Curfew in summer 2am, in winter 1am. Singles €75; doubles €110; triples €140; quads €150. AmEx/MC/V. ❺

Santa Maria Alle Fornaci, P. S. Maria alle Fornaci 27 (☎06 39 36 76 32; www.trinitaridematha.it). All rooms have bath. Internet available. Breakfast included. Reception 24hr. Singles €60; doubles €90; triples €125. AmEx/MC/V. ❹

FOOD

Traditional Roman cuisine includes *spaghetti alla carbonara* (egg and cream sauce with bacon), *spaghetti all'amatriciana* (thin tomato sauce with chiles and bacon), *carciofi alla giudia* (deep-fried artichokes, common in the Jewish Ghetto), and *fiori di zucca* (stuffed, fried zucchini flowers). Pizza is often a good and inexpensive option. Try *pizza romana*, which is like foccaccia: a flat bread with olive oil, sea salt, rosemary, and sometimes more toppings. Lunch is typically the main meal of the day, though some Romans now enjoy panini on the go during the week. Restaurants tend to close between 3 and 6:30pm.

RESTAURANTS

ANCIENT CITY AND CENTRO STORICO

The *centro storico* can be frightfully expensive and generic, especially near famous landmarks. For authentic Roman food, head to side streets, which have an abundance of affordable and delicious options.

I Buoni Amici, V. Aleardo 4 (☎06 70 49 19 93). M: B-Colosseo. The owner's exceptional service complements the popular *linguine alle vongole* (with clams in the shell; €8) and the self-serve *antipasto* bar. *Primi* €7-8. *Secondi* €8-12. Wine €8-15. Homemade *dolci* €4. Cover €1. Open M-Sa 12:30-3pm and 7-11pm. AmEx/MC/V. ❷

L'Antica Birreria Peroni, V. San Marcello 19 (☎06 67 95 310). Wash down a *wurstel* (€6-7) with one of 4 well-priced beers on tap. Fantastic *fiori di zucca* (€1). *Primi* €5-7. Cover €1.50. Open M-Sa noon-midnight. AmEx/MC/V. ❷

Miscellanea, V. della Paste 110A (☎06 67 80 983). A favorite of students and locals. Free house wine included with meal. Salads (€6), *antipasti* (€6-7), and panini (€3) are the best values in town. Drinks €2-4. Desserts €2-3. Open daily 11am-2am. AmEx. ❶

Luzzi, V. S. Giovanni in Laterano 88 (☎06 70 96 332). Always packed with locals. The *penne con salmone* (€7) will leave you wanting more. *Primi* €5-7. *Secondi* €7-11. Open M-Tu and Th-Su noon-3pm and 7pm-midnight. AmEx/MC/V. ❷

JEWISH GHETTO

A 10min. walk south of the Campo, restaurants serve Roman specialties alongside traditional Jewish and kosher dishes. Many close on Saturdays.

Bar Da Benito, V. d. Falegnami 14 (☎06 68 61 508). A rare combination—*secondi* for less than €5 and a relaxing place to sit and enjoy your food. *Primi* €4.50. *Secondi* €4.50-7.50. *Dolci* €2-3.50. Open M-Sa 6:30am-7pm. Closed Aug. Cash only. ❷

Trattoria da Giggetto, V. d. Portico d'Ottavia 21-22 (☎06 68 61 105; www.giggettoalportico.com). Cavernous restaurant next to the ruins of the Portico d'Ottavia. *Primi* €8.50-14. *Secondi* €9-20. Cover €1.50. Open Tu-Su 12:30-3:30pm and 7:30-11pm. Closed the last 2 weeks of July. Reserve ahead for dinner. AmEx/MC/V. ❸

PIAZZA DI SPAGNA

The P. di Spagna and Trevi Fountain area, though busy at night and closer to tourist destinations, offers few high quality options at low prices. Head off the main drags (V. del Corso and V. dei Condotti) for worthy eateries.

Il Brillo Parlante, V. della Fontanella 12 (☎06 32 43 334; www.ilbrilloparlante.com). The wood-burning oven turns out pizza (€4.50-10). Handmade pasta and small plates, including *pecorino* cheese with honey and walnuts (€8.50), set this place apart. *Primi*

€8-9.50. *Secondi* €9.50-18. Open M 5pm-1am, Tu-Su 12:30-3:30pm lunch, 3:30-5pm pizza only, 5-7:30pm bar only, 7:30pm-1am dinner. Reserve ahead. MC/V. ❷

Trattoria da Settimio all'Arancio, V. dell'Arancio 50-52 (☎06 68 76 119). Decadent dishes with a subtle but pervasive orange theme. *Primi* €8-15. *Secondi* €8-20. Open M-Sa 12:30-3pm and 7:30-midnight. Reserve ahead. AmEx/MC/V. ❹

Vini e Buffet, V. della Torretta 60 (☎06 68 71 445), near P. di Spagna. A favorite of Romans with a penchant for regional wine, *pâtés* (€4-4.50), *crostini,* or *scamorze* (smoked mozzarella; €8-9). Salads €7.50-11. Wine €10-24. Open M-Sa 12:30-3pm and 7:30-11pm. Reservations recommended. Cash only. ❷

BORGO AND PRATI (NEAR VATICAN CITY)

The streets near the Vatican are paved with bars and pizzerias that serve mediocre sandwiches at inflated prices. For better, much cheaper food, venture down **Via Cola di Rienzo** several blocks toward P. Cavour and explore the side streets.

Paninoteca da Guido e Patrizia, Borgo Pio 13 (☎06 68 75 491), near Castel Sant'Angelo. Casual environment and decor make this place popular with locals. Guido holds court behind a well-stocked *tavola calda* (similar to a deli). Full meal (*primo, secondo,* and beverage) runs around €11. Open M-Sa 8am-6pm. Cash only. ❷

Franchi, V. Cola di Rienzo 200/204 (☎06 68 74 651; www.franchi.it). Benedetto Franchi ("Frankie") has been providing the citizens of Prati with mouth-watering picnic supplies for a half-century. Food is priced by the kilo. Open M-Sa 9am-8:30pm. AmEx/MC/V. ❷

Cacio e Pepe, V. Giuseppe Avezzana 11 (☎06 32 17 268). Dine outside and enjoy the namesake pasta, piled high with grated cheese and freshly ground pepper (€6). Full lunch €5-10. Open M-F 12:30-3pm and 7:30-11pm, Sa 12:30-3pm. Cash only. ❷

TRASTEVERE

The waits are long and the street-side tables are always cramped, but you can't get more Roman than Trastevere. The tiny cobblestone side streets winding in and out of the *piazzas* are crowded with shops, cafes, restaurants, and pubs.

Pizzeria San Callisto, P. S. Callisto 9/A (☎06 58 18 256), off P. S. Maria. Simply the best pizza (€4-8) in Rome. Thin-crust pizzas so large they hang off the plates. Order takeout to avoid waits. Open Tu-Su 6:30pm-midnight. AmEx/MC/V. ❷

Augusto, P. de' Renzi 15 (☎06 58 03 798), before P. S. Maria when coming from the river. Grab dinner here before hitting the clubs. Daily specials €5. *Secondi* €5.50-8. Open M-F 12:30-3pm and 8-11pm, Sa 12:30-3pm. Closed Aug. Cash only. ❶

SAN LORENZO AND TERMINI

Tourist traps proliferate in the Termini area. There is a well-stocked **CONAD** supermarket on the lower floor of the Termini Station, just inside the V. Marsala entrance. (☎06 87 40 60 55. Open daily 8am-midnight.) In San Lorenzo, inexpensive food options with local character cater to budget-conscious students with discriminating palates. At night, map your route and avoid walking alone.

Hostaria Romana da Dino, V. dei Mille, 10 (☎06 49 14 25). Look for the blue Pizzeria sign. This humble choice provides ample seating and delicious dishes at low prices. Delectable pizzas (€5-7) and pastas (€4.50-5). Try the house wine for a mere €1.10 per 0.25L. Open M-Tu and Th-Su noon-3pm and 6:30-10:30pm. MC/V. ❶

Africa, V. Gaeta 26-28 (☎06 49 41 077), near P. Indipendenza. Decked out in orange, yellow, and black, Africa has been serving Eritrean and Ethiopian food for 32 years. Meat-filled *sambusas* (€3) are a flavorful starter. Vegetarian menu available. *Secondi* €8-11. Cover €1. Open Tu-Su 8am-2am. AmEx/MC/V. ❷

SHOPPING

No trip to Italy is complete without a bit of shopping. Luckily, there are plenty of options for every budget. International chain stores like **Motivi, Mango, Stefanel, Intimissimi, Zara,** and the ubiquitous **United Colors of Benetton** are supplemented by techno-blasting teen stores in the city center, boutiques like **Ethic** and **Havana** in the *centro storico* and throughout the city, and designer shrines like **Cavalli, Dolce** *and* **Gabbana,** and **Prada,** with their sky-high prices.

Via del Corso, the main street connecting P. del Popolo and P. Venezia, offers a mix of high- and low-end leather goods, men's suits, silk ties, and women's clothing and accessories, but beware of high-priced tourist traps. Across the river from V. del Corso, **Via Cola di Rienzo** offers a more leisurely shopping approach—minus the tourists—with stores like **Diesel, Mandarina Duck, Mango, Stefanel,** and **Benetton.** Most of the upscale stores—**Armani, Bruno Magli, Dolce and Gabbana, Gianni Versace, Gucci, Prada, Salvatore Ferragamo**—can be found on **V. dei Condotti.** Authentic European clothing stores on **Via dei Giubbonari,** off Campo dei Fiori, will have you dressed to the nines before eight.

NIGHTLIFE

Though *enoteche* tend to be the primary destination for many locals, pubs are still a fun way to knock a few back without covers. The best Irish pubs are in Campo dei Fiori. Italian discos are flashy and fun, but keep in mind that many clubs close during the summer in favor of more distant destinations like Fregene or Frascati. Check *Roma C'è* or *Time Out* for info.

Caffé della Scala, P. della Scala 4 (☎06 58 03 610). In nice weather, the outdoor tables at this casual cafe-bar are filled day and night. The drinks menu uses unusual ingredients: Canadian whiskey, creme of cocoa, and cardamom pods are all mixed together in the potent "Christian Alexander." Open daily 5:30pm-2am. Cash only.

The Proud Lion Pub, Borgo Pio 36 (☎06 68 32 841). A tiny pub in the Vatican area whose Roman location belies its Scottish atmosphere. Beer €4. Open daily noon-2am.

Artu Café, Largo Fumasoni Biondi 5 (☎06 58 80 398), in P. San Egidio, behind Santa Maria. Patrons swear this bar/lounge is the best in Trastevere. Beer €2.50. Wine €3-6 per glass. Martinis €6.50-8. Free snack buffet 7:30-9pm. Open Tu-Su 6pm-2am. MC/V.

Distillerie Clandestine, V. Libetta 13 (☎06 57 30 51 02). Speakeasy-like nightspot with live music and DJ. Cover F-Sa €20. Open Sept. to mid-June W-Sa 8:30pm-3am.

Jungle, V. di Monte Testaccio 95 (☎06 33 37 20 86 94; www.jungleclubroma.com). A rock feel pervades on F; it becomes a smoky bar full of Italian goths on Sa. Extravagant yet disorienting light effects. Cover €10. Open F-Sa midnight-4am.

DAYTRIP FROM ROME: TIVOLI

From M: B-Rebibbia, exit the station, turn right, and follow signs for Tivoli through an underpass to reach the other side of V. Tiburtina. Take the blue COTRAL bus to Tivoli. Tickets (€1.60) are sold in the metro station or in the bar next door. Once the bus reaches Tivoli (35-45min.), get off at Ple. delle Nazioni Unite. The return bus to Rome stops across the street from the tourist office, which has maps and bus schedules. (☎07 74 31 12 49. Open Tu-Su 10am-6pm.) There is also an information kiosk in Ple. delle Nazioni Unite with free maps.

Tivoli is a beautifully preserved medieval town boasting villas once owned by Latin poets Horace, Catullus, and Propertius. The tourist office provides a **map** detailing sites such as a 15th-century castle and Gothic-style houses, all within walking distance of the bus stop. **Villa d'Este,** a castle with spectacular terraced

ITALY

gardens, was intended to recreate an ancient Roman *nymphaea* and pleasure palace. (☎07 74 31 20 70; www.villadestetivoli.info. Open Tu-Su May-Aug. 8:30am-6:45pm; Sept. 8:30am-6:15pm; Oct. 8:30am-5:30pm; Nov.-Jan. 8:30am-4pm; Feb. 8:30am-4:30pm; Mar. 8:30am-5:15pm; Apr. 8:30am-6:30pm. €9. Audio tour €4.) **Villa Gregoriana,** at the other end of town, is a park with extensive hiking trails and great views of Tivoli's well-preserved **Temple of Vesta.** (☎06 39 96 77 61. Open daily Apr. to mid-Oct. 10am-6:30pm; mid-Oct. to Nov. and Mar. 10am-2:30pm; Dec.-Feb. by reservation only. €4. Audio tour €4.) On the way back from Tivoli, visit the vast remains of **Villa Adriana,** the largest and most expensive villa built under the Roman Empire. (☎07 74 38 27 33. Take bus #4 from P. Garibaldi's newsstand next to the playground. Open daily 9am-7:30pm; last entry 6pm. €6.50. Archaeological tour €3.50, audio tour €4.)

LOMBARDY (LOMBARDIA)

Part of the industrial triangle that drives Italy's economy, home to fashion mecca Milan, and producer of rice fields as lush as China's, Lombardy is one of the most prosperous regions of Italy. The Lombards who ruled the area after the fall of the Romans had close relations with the Franks and the Bavarians, which explains why the region's modern culture has much in common with the traditions of its northern neighbors.

MILAN (MILANO) ☎02

Unlike Rome, Venice, or Florence, which wrap themselves in veils of historic allure, Milan (pop. 1,400,000), once the capital of the western half of the Roman Empire, presents itself simply as it is: rushed, refined, and cosmopolitan. This urban center also hides many artistic treasures, including Leonardo da Vinci's *Last Supper*. Milan owes much of its heritage to the medieval Visconti and Sforza families, and its culture to Austrian, French, and Spanish occupiers. Now that Italians run the show, the city flourishes as the country's producer of cutting-edge style, hearty risotto, and die-hard football fans.

TRANSPORTATION

Flights: Malpensa Airport (MXP), 48km from the city, handles intercontinental flights. **Malpensa Express** train leaves from Stazione Nord for the airport. Accessible via Cadorna Metro station (40min., onboard €11/13). **Linate Airport (LIN),** 7km away, covers domestic and European flights. From there, take **Starfly buses** (20min., €2.50) to Stazione Centrale, which is quicker than bus #73 (€1) to San Babila Metro station.

Regional Hubs: Orio al Serio Airport (BGY; ☎035 32 63 23; www.sacbo.it) in Bergamo (p. 602) is a hub for budget airlines **Ryanair, SkyEurope,** and **Wizz Air.**

Trains: Stazione Centrale (☎02 89 20 21; www.trenitalia.com), in P. Duca d'Aosta on M2. Trains run hourly to: **Bergamo** (1hr., €4.10); **Florence** (3hr., €15-36); **Rome** (7hr., €52-73); **Turin** (2hr., €8.75); **Venice** (2hr., €29.50).

Buses: Stazione Centrale. Intercity buses tend to be less convenient and more expensive than trains. **Autostradale, SAL, SIA,** and other carriers leave from P. Castello (M1: Cairoli) and Porta Garibaldi for **Bergamo,** the **Lake Country, Trieste,** and **Turin.**

Public Transportation: The **Metro** (Metropolitana Milanese, or **M**) runs 6am-midnight. Line #1 (red) stretches from the *pensioni* district east of Stazione Centrale through the

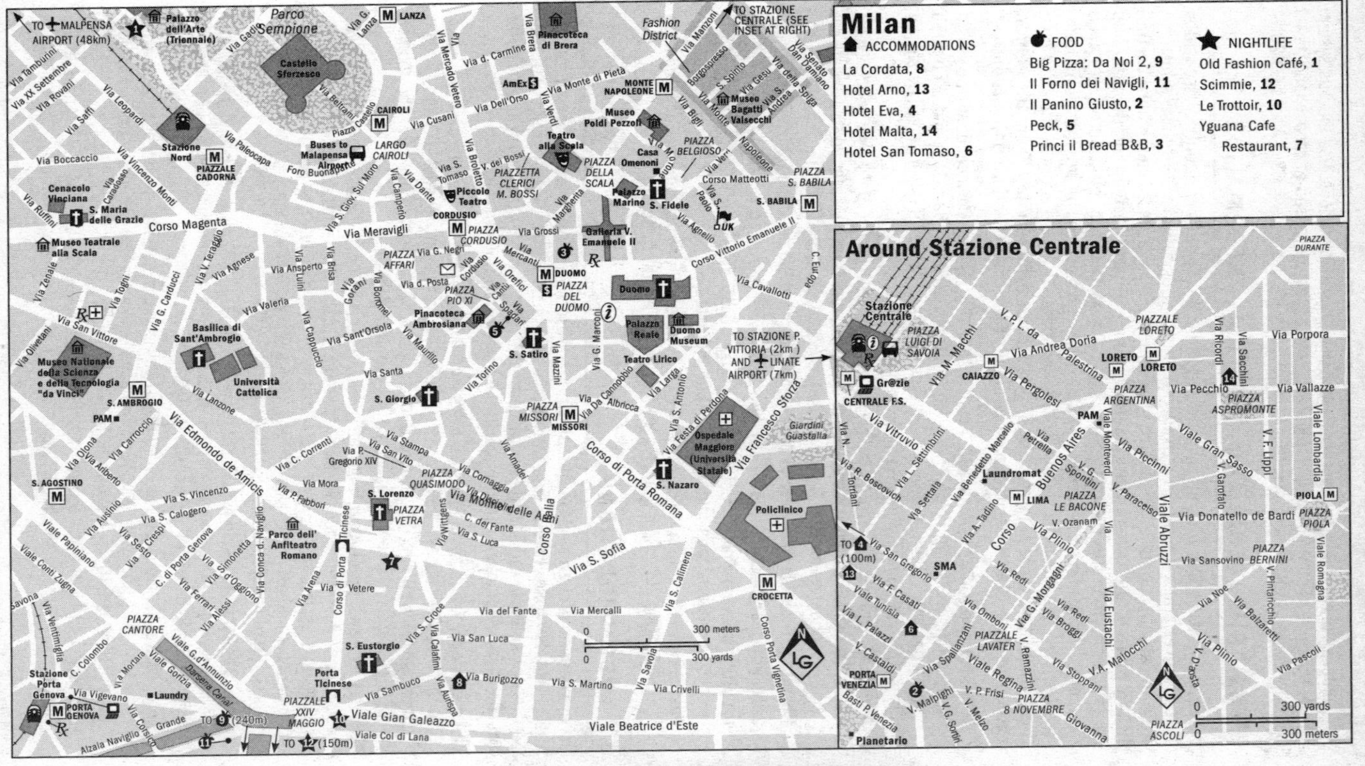
Milan
ACCOMMODATIONS
La Cordata, 8
Hotel Arno, 13
Hotel Eva, 4
Hotel Malta, 14
Hotel San Tomaso, 6
FOOD
Big Pizza: Da Noi 2, 9
Il Forno dei Navigli, 11
Il Panino Giusto, 2
Peck, 5
Princi il Bread B&B, 3
NIGHTLIFE
Old Fashion Café, 1
Scimmie, 12
Le Trottoir, 10
Yguana Cafe Restaurant, 7
Around Stazione Centrale
Stazione Centrale
CENTRALE F.S.
PIAZZA LUIGI DI SAVOIA
Viale Abruzzi
Corso Buenos Aires
TO STAZIONE CENTRALE (SEE INSET AT RIGHT)
TO MALPENSA AIRPORT (48km)
TO STAZIONE P. VITTORIA (2km) AND LINATE AIRPORT (7km)
Castello Sforzesco
Parco Sempione
Duomo
PIAZZA DEL DUOMO
Galleria V. Emanuele II
Teatro alla Scala
Pinacoteca di Brera
Pinacoteca Ambrosiana
Palazzo Reale
Duomo Museum
Ospedale Maggiore (Università Statale)
Policlinico
Basilica di Sant'Ambrogio
Università Cattolica
Museo Nazionale della Scienza e della Tecnologia "da Vinci"
Cenacolo Vinciano
S. Maria delle Grazie
Stazione Nord
Stazione Porta Genova
Porta Ticinese
Corso Magenta
Via Meravigli
Corso di Porta Romana
Via Francesco Sforza
Viale Beatrice d'Este
Via Edmondo de Amicis
Viale Gian Galeazzo
Darsena Canal
Fashion District
300 meters
300 yards

ITALY

center of town. Line #2 (green) connects Milan's 3 train stations. Use the **bus** system for trips outside the city proper. Metro tickets can be purchased at *tabaccherie,* ticket booths, and station machines. Single-fare tickets €1, 1-day pass €3, 10 trips €9.20.

ORIENTATION AND PRACTICAL INFORMATION

Milan resembles a giant bull's-eye, defined by its ancient concentric city walls. In the outer rings lie suburbs built during the 50s and 60s to house southern immigrants. In the inner circle are four squares: **Piazza del Duomo,** where **Via Orefici, Via Mazzini,** and **Corso Vittorio Emanuele II** meet; **Piazza Castello** and the attached **Largo Cairoli,** near the Castello Sforzesco; **Piazza Cordusio,** connected to Largo Cairoli by **Via Dante;** and **Piazza San Babila,** the entrance to the business and fashion district. The **duomo** and **Galleria Vittorio Emanuele** are roughly at the center of the circles. The **Giardini Pubblici** and the **Parco Sempione** radiate from the center. From the huge **Stazione Centrale,** northeast of the city, take M3 to the *duomo.*

Tourist Office: IAT, P. Duomo 19A. (☎02 72 52 43 01; www.milanoinfotourist.com), in P. del Duomo. Pick up helpful *Hello Milano*. Open M-Sa 8:45am-1pm and 2-6pm, Su 9am-1pm and 2-5pm. **Branch** in Stazione Centrale (☎02 77 40 43 18) has shorter lines. Open M-Sa 9am-6pm, Su 9am-1pm and 2-5pm.

American Express: V. Larga 4 (☎02 72 10 41), on the corner of V. Larga and S. Clemente. Exchanges currency, handles wire transfers, and holds mail for up to 1 month for AmEx cardholders for free. Open M-F 9am-5:30pm, Sa 9am-12:30pm.

Hospital: Ospedale Maggiore di Milano, V. Francesco Sforza 35 (☎02 55 031).

24hr. Pharmacy: (☎02 66 90 735). In Stazione Centrale's 2nd fl. *galleria.*

Internet: Internet Enjoy, Vle. Tunisia 11 (☎02 36 55 58 05). M1: Porta Venezia. €2-3 per hr. Open M-Sa 9am-midnight, Su 2pm-midnight.

Post Office: P. Cordusio 4 (☎02 72 48 21 26), near P. del Duomo. Currency exchange and **ATM.** Open M-F 8am-7pm, Sa 8:30am-noon. **Postal Code:** 20100.

ACCOMMODATIONS

Every season is high-season in fashionable Milan—except during August, when many hotels close. Prices rise in September, November, March, and April due to theater season and business conventions. For the best deals, try the hostels on the city periphery or in the areas east of Stazione Centrale.

La Cordata, V. Burigozzo 11 (☎02 58 31 46 75; www.ostellimilano.it). Common room with TV. Kitchen access. Laundry €3. Free Wi-Fi. Reception closed 1-2:30pm. 7-night max. stay. Closed Aug. 10-20 and Dec. 23-Jan. 2. Single-sex dorms €21-25; doubles €70-100; triples €90-110; quads €100-140. MC/V. ❷

Hotel Eva and Hotel Arno, both at V. Lazzaretto 17, 4th fl. (☎02 67 06 093; www.hotelevamilano.com and www.hotelarno.com). M1: Porta Venezia. This hostel has 18 large and inviting rooms with quirky decor, phone, and TV. Ring bell to enter. Clean shared bathroom. Free luggage storage. Free Internet (30min.) Singles €30-45; doubles €50-100; triples €65-90. AmEx/MC/V. ❸

Hotel San Tomaso, Vle. Tunisia 6, 3rd fl. (☎02 29 51 47 47; www.hotelsantomaso.com). M1: Porta Venezia. Sparkling rooms with fan, phone, and TV. Singles €35-65; doubles €50-100; triples €70-150. AmEx/MC/V. ❹

Hotel Malta, V. Ricordi 20 (☎02 20 49 615; www.hotelmalta.it). 15 bright, quiet rooms have bath, fan, hair dryer, and TV; some have balconies over the rose garden. Reserve ahead. Singles €40-75; doubles €55-120. MC/V. ❹

Campeggio Città di Milano, V. G. Airaghi 61 (☎02 48 20 01 34). M1: De Angeli, then bus #72 to S. Romanello Togni. Backtrack 10m and turn right on V. Togni. Campsite is a

10min. walk straight ahead. Enter at Aquatica water park. Electricity included. Laundry €5. Reserve ahead. Closed Dec.-Jan. €11 per person, €6.50-8.50 per tent. 2- to 6-person cabins €37-88; bungalows with bath and A/C €80-120. MC/V. ❶

FOOD

Trattorie still adhere to Milanese traditions by preparing *risotto alla Milanese* (rice with saffron), *cotoletta alla Milanese* (breaded veal cutlet with lemon), and *osso buco* (shank of lamb, beef, or veal). The Navigli district is home to all manner of cheap grub and the Saturday **Fiera di Sinigallia,** a bargaining extravaganza (on Darsena Banks, a canal near V. d'Annunzio). The area's bars have happy hour buffets of focaccia, pasta, and risotto with drinks.

Princi, V. Speronari 6, off P. del Duomo (☎02 87 47 97; www.princi.it). This combined bakery and deli with a modern zen vibe attracts a lunch crowd that comes for its cheap *primi* and *secondi* (€5) takeout. Fresh bread and pastries €1-4. Panini and pizza €3.50-5. Open M-Sa 7am-8pm. Cash only. ❶

Big Pizza: Da Noi 2, V. G. Borsi 1 (☎02 83 96 77), takes its name seriously. Epic pizzas (€4-9) emerge from the stone oven, and beer flows liberally. The house pizza has pasta on top (€8.50). Cover €1. Open M-Sa 10am-2:30pm and 7pm-midnight. Branches: Ple. XXIV Maggio 7 (M2: Porta Genova) and V. Buonarroti 16 (M1: Buonarroti). ❷

Il Forno dei Navigli, V. A. Naviglio Pavese 2. At the corner of Ripa di Porta Ticinese. Out of "the oven of Navigli" come the most elaborate pastries in the city. The *cestini* (pear tarts with Nutella; around €2.25) define decadence. Pastries and breads €0.50-6. Open M-Sa 7am-2pm and 6pm-1am, Su 6pm-1am. Cash only. ❶

Il Panino Giusto, V. Malpighi 3 (☎02 29 40 92 97). M1: Porta Venezia. If you believe sandwiches should contain goat cheese, truffled olive oil, veal *pâté,* or lard with honey and walnuts for under €8, welcome home. Panini €5-8. Beer €4-5. Open daily noon-1am. Branch on P. Beccaria near P. del Duomo. AmEx/MC/V. ❷

Peck, V. Spadari 9 (☎02 80 23 161; www.peck.it). Aromas from the ground floor spread throughout the wine cellar in the basement and the cafe/bar above. Open M 3:30-7:30pm, Tu-F 9:15am-7:30pm, Sa 8:45am-7:30pm. AmEx/MC/V. ❷

SIGHTS

NEAR THE DUOMO AND IN THE GIARDINI PUBBLICI

DUOMO. The geographical and spiritual center of Milan, the *duomo*—the third-largest church in the world—was begun in 1386 by **Gian Galeazzo Visconti,** who hoped to persuade the Virgin Mary to grant him a male heir. Work proceeded over the next centuries and was completed in 1809 at Napoleon's command. The marble tomb of **Giacomo de Médici** in the south transept was inspired by the work of Michelangelo. Climb (or ride) to the **roof walkway** for prime views of the city and the Alps. *(M1/3: Duomo. Cathedral open daily 7am-7pm. Modest dress required. Free. Roof open daily 9:30am-9:30pm. €5, elevator €7.)*

PINACOTECA AMBROSIANA. The 23 palatial rooms of the Ambrosiana display exquisite works from the 14th through 19th centuries, including Botticelli's circular *Madonna of the Canopy*, Caravaggio's *Basket of Fruit* (the first Italian still life), Raphael's wall-sized *School of Athens*, Titian's *Adoration of the Magi*, and Leonardo's *Portrait of a Musician.* The statue-filled courtyard is enchanting. *(P. Pio XI 2. M1/3: Duomo. Open Tu-Su 10am-5:30pm. €8, under 18 and over 65 €5.)*

CASTELLO SFORZESCO. The Castello Sforzesco was constructed in 1368 as a defense against Venice. Later, it was used as army barracks, a horse stall, and a storage house before Leonardo converted it into a studio. Restored after WWII damage, the complex houses 10 **Musei Civici** (Civic Museums). The **Museum of Ancient Art** contains Michelangelo's unfinished *Pietà Rondanini* (1564), his last work, and the **Museum of Decorative Art** has ornate furnishings and Murano glass. The underground level has a small Egyptian collection. *(M1: Cairoli or M2: Lanza. Open Tu-Su 9am-5:30pm. Combined admission €3, students €1.50, F 2-5:30pm free.)*

TEATRO ALLA SCALA. Founded in 1778, La Scala has established Milan as the opera capital of the world. Its understated Neoclassical facade and lavish interior set the stage for premieres of works by Mascagni, Puccini, Rossini, and Verdi, performed by virtuosos like Maria Callas and Enrico Caruso. Visitors can soak up La Scala's history at the **Museo Teatrale alla Scala.** *(Access through the Galleria Vittorio Emanuele from P. del Duomo. www.teatroallascala.org. Museum on left side of building. Open daily 9am-12:30pm and 1:30-5:30pm. €5, students €4.)*

BASILICA DI SANT'AMBROGIO. A prototype for Lombard-Romanesque churches throughout Italy, Sant'Ambrogio is the most influential medieval building in Milan. St. Ambrose presided over this church from AD 379 to 386, and his skeletal remains rest beside martyr St. Protasio. The 4th-century **Cappella di San Vittore in Ciel D'oro,** with exquisite mosaics adorning its cupola, is through the seventh chapel on the right. *(M2: S. Ambrogio. Walk up V. G. Carducci, and the church is on the right. Church open M-Sa 7:30am-noon and 2:30-7pm, Su 7:30am-1pm and 3-8pm. Free. Chapel open Tu-Su 9:30-11:45am and 2:30-7pm. €2, students €1.)*

CHIESA DI SANTA MARIA DELLA GRAZIE. The church's Gothic nave is dark and patterned with frescoes, contrasting the airy Renaissance tribune Bramante added in 1497. To the left of the church entrance is the **Cenacolo Vinciano** (Vinciano Refectory), home to Leonardo da Vinci's **Last Supper.** *(P di S. Maria della Grazie 2. M1: Conciliazione. From P. Conciliazione, take V. Boccaccio and then go right onto V. Ruffini for about 2 blocks. Reservations ☎02 89 42 11 46. Reservation fee €1.50. Church open M-Sa 7am-noon and 3-7pm, Su 7:30am-12:15pm and 3:30-9pm. Modest dress required. Refectory open Tu-Su 8:15am-6:45pm. €6.50, EU residents 18-25 €3.25, under 18 and over 65 free.)*

BASILICA DI SANT'EUSTORGIO. Founded in the 4th century to house the bones of the Magi, the church lost its original function when the dead sages were spirited off to Cologne in 1164. A great masterpiece of early Renaissance art is the **Portinari Chapel,** to the left of the entrance. Frescoes below the rainbow dome illustrate the life of St. Peter. The chapel stands on a **Paleochristian cemetery;** pagan and early Christian tombs are down the steps before the chapel entrance. *(P. S. Eustorgio 3. M2: S. Ambrogio. Basilica open M and W-Su 8:30am-noon and 3:30-6pm. Free. Cappella open Tu-Su 10am-6:30pm. €6, students and seniors €3.)*

SHOPPING AND ENTERTAINMENT

In a city where clothes really do make the man (or woman), fashionistas arrive in spring and summer to watch models dressed in the newest styles glide down the runway. When the music has faded and the designers have bowed, world-famous **saldi** (sales) in July and January usher the garb into the real world. The **Quadrilatero della Moda** (fashion district) has become a sanctuary in its own right. This posh land, where limos transport poodles dressed to impress and jean jackets can sell for €2000, is formed by **Via Monte Napoleone, Borgospresso, Via della Spiga,** and **Via Gesu.** Designer creations are available to mere mortals at the trendy boutiques along **Corso di Porta Ticinese.** Small shops and affordable staples from brand names can be found on **Via Torino** near the *duomo* and on **Corso Buenos Aires** near M1: Porta Venezia. Those who don't mind being a season behind can purchase famous designer wear from *blochisti* (stocks or wholesale clothing outlets), such as the well-known **Il Salvagente,** V. Bronzetti 16, off C. XXII Marzo (M1: S. Babila), or **Gruppo Italia Grandi Firme,** V. Montegani #7/A (M2: Famagosta). True bargain hunters cull the bazaars on **Via Faucé** (M2: Garibaldi; Tu and Sa) and **Viale Papinian** (M2: Agnostino; Sa mornings).

La Scala (p. 600) is one of the best places in the world to see an opera. (Infotel Scala ☎02 72 00 37 44; www.teatroallascala.org. Opera season runs Jan.-July and Sept.-Nov. Central box office located in the Metro station beneath P. del Duomo. Open daily noon-6pm. Tickets prices vary widely.) The **Milan Symphony Orchestra** plays from September to May at the **Auditorium di Milano.** (☎02 83 38 92 01; www.orchestrasinfonica.milano.it. Tickets €13-50, students €10-25.) The football clubs **Inter Milan** and **AC Milan** face off at their shared three-tiered stadium. **Ticket One,** located in FNAC stores, sells tickets for both teams as well as for concerts and other events (☎02 39 22 61; www.ticketone.it).

NIGHTLIFE

The nightlife in **Navigli** is popular with students and centers around V. Sforza. The **Brera** district invites tourists and Milanese to test their singing skills while sipping mixed drinks at one of its piano bars. **Corso di Porta Ticinese** is the sleek land of the all-night happy hour buffet, where the price of a mixed drink (€6-8) also buys dinner. A block of **Corso Como** near **Stazione Garibaldi** is home to the most exclusive clubs. Bars and clubs cluster around **Largo Cairoli,** where summer brings Milan's hottest outdoor dance venues. Southeast of **Stazione Centrale** is home to an eclectic mix of bars and much of Milan's gay and lesbian scene.

Le Trottoir, P. XXIV Maggio 1 (☎02 83 78 166; www.letrottoir.it). A young crowd comes for underground music downstairs and jazz or a DJ upstairs. Pizza and sandwiches €8, available until 2am. Mixed drinks €6-9. Cover €8, includes 1 drink. Happy hour daily 6-8pm; beer €4, mixed drinks €6. Open daily 3pm-3am. AmEx/MC/V.

Yguana Café Restaurant, V. P. Gregorio XIV 16 (☎02 89 40 41 95), just off P. Vetra. Lounge outside or groove to DJs spinning house and hip hop. Mixed drinks €8-10. The healthiest, most appealing, and most diverse happy hour buffet around! Happy hour M-Sa 5:30-9:30pm, Su 5:30-10pm. Lunch M-F 12:30-3pm. Su brunch noon-4pm. Open for drinks M-Th and Su 5:30pm-2am, F-Sa 5:30pm-3am. AmEx/MC/V.

Old Fashion Café, Vle. Alemagna 6 (☎02 80 56 231; www.oldfashion.it). M1/2: Cadorna F. N. Summer brings stylish clubgoers to couches encircling an outdoor dance

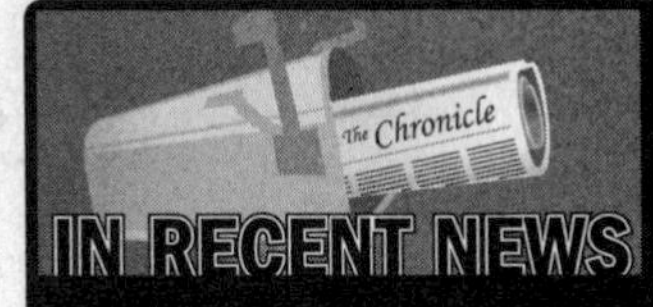

SLOW FOOD SPREADS FAST

The Slow Food movement sprung up in 1986 when Carlo Petrini of Bra, Italy decided enough was enough with grab-n-go fast-food chains. In a mere 22 years, his movement has grown to 80,000 members from all points of the globe who are attempting to counteract consumers' dwindling interest in the food they eat. Where is it from? What does it taste like? Sometimes we eat so quickly that we can't even remember.

Slow Food's requirements are three-fold; the food must be good, clean, and fair. In other words, it must taste good, not harm the environment, and food producers must receive fair compensation for their work. Ultimately, their view is that when you lift your fork to swirl that first bite of linguine, you are not just a consumer, but also an informed co-producer.

Keep an eye out for Slow Food's snail symbol on the doors of many restaurants in Italy for assured quality. They even opened a University of Gastronomical Sciences in 2004, offering Bachelor's and Master's degrees, along with many cultural seminars.

So before you grab that panini *"da portare via"* ("to go"), take a moment to step back and remember where your food is coming from. Even a little acknowledgement is a start.

floor with live music and DJ. Tu is the most popular night, with live music. F R&B. Cover varies; regular student discounts. Open daily 11pm-4:30am.

Scimmie, V. A. Sforza 49 (☎02 89 40 28 74; www.scimmie.it). Legendary nightclub offers nightly performances. Talented underground musicians play blues, fusion, jazz, and Italian swing. Mixed drinks €4-9. Concerts 7:30-9:30pm and 10:30pm-1:30am. Schedule posted online. Open daily until 2am. MC/V.

BERGAMO ☎035

Home to the **Orio al Serio International Airport** (**BGY;** ☎035 32 63 23; www.sacbo.it), Bergamo (pop. 120,000) is a hub for budget airlines **Ryanair, SkyEurope,** and **Wizz Air. Airport buses** go to the train station in Bergamo (10min., €1.60). **Trains** (☎035 24 79 50) run from Ple. Marconi to Milan (1hr., 1 per hr., €4.10). **Buses** run from the train station to Como (6 per day, €4.40) and Milan (2 per hr., €4.40).

For overnight layovers or missed flights, head to the art-filled **Ostello Città di Bergamo (HI) ❷,** V. G. Ferraris 1. From the airport, take bus 1C to Porta Nuova and change to bus #6; the hostel is at the next-to-last stop. (☎035 36 17 24; www.ostellodibergamo.it. 6- and 8-bed dorms €17; singles €30; doubles €42; 3-6 person rooms €18 per person. €3 HI discount.) Another option is the B&B **La Torretta Città Alta ❹,** Via Rocca 2. (☎035 57 61 59; www.latorrettabergamoalta.com. Singles €60-70; doubles €80-95; triples €90-110.) Dine at **Trattoria Casa Mia ❷,** V. S. Bernardino 20, which makes up for its out-of-the-way location with local flavor. (☎035 22 06 76. Lunch *menù* €10. Dinner *menù* €12. Open M-Sa noon-2pm and 7-10pm. Cash only.) Supermarket **Pellicano** is at Vle. V. Emanuele II 17; walk from the station past Ple. Repubblica. (Open M 8:30am-1:30pm, Tu-F 8:30am-1:30pm and 3:30-8pm, Sa 8:30am-8pm. MC/V.) **Postal Code:** 24122.

MANTUA (MANTOVA) ☎0376

Though Mantua (pop. 47,000) did not become a dynamic cultural haven until the Renaissance, the arts have shaped the city's history since the birth of the poet Virgil in 70 BC. Today, the huge **Festivaletteratura** brings writers from John Grisham to Salman Rushdie to the city in early September. Mantua's grand *palazzi*, including the opulent **Palazzo Ducale,** P. Sordello 40, were built by the powerful Gonzaga family, who ascended to power in 1328, ruled for 400 years, and commissioned well-known artists to leave their marks on the town's mansions and churches. The **New Gallery** houses dozens of locally produced altarpieces from the 16th-18th centuries, removed from monasteries during the Hapsburg and Napoleonic eras. (Open Tu-Su 8:45am-7:15pm. €6.50.) Music lovers first filled the balconies of the **Teatro Bibiena,** V. Accademia 4, when 14-year-old Mozart inaugurated the building in 1769. (Open Tu-Su 9:30am-12:30pm and 3-6pm. €2, under 18 €1.20.) In the southern part of the city, down V. P. Amedeo (which becomes V. Acrebi), through P. Veneto, and down Largo Parri, lies the **Palazzo del Te,** built by Giulio Romano in 1534 for Federico II Gonzaga. It is widely considered the finest building in the Mannerist style. The entirely frescoed **Room of Giants** depicts the demise of the rebellious Titans at the hands of Jupiter. The hidden garden and grotto at the far end are often overlooked. (Open M 1-6pm, Tu-Su 9am-6pm. €8, students €2.50.)

Hotel ABC ❹, P. D. Leoni 25-27, across from the train station, is a modern hotel with comfortable rooms. (☎0376 32 23 29; www.hotelabcmantova.it. Breakfast included. Reserve ahead. Singles €44-165; doubles €66-165; triples €77-222; quads €88-250.) **Ostello del Mincio ❷,** V. Porto 23/25, 10km from Mantua, is the only youth hostel in the area. (☎0376 65 39 24; www.ostellodelmincio.org. Dorms €16-18, with breakfast €17-22.) To get to **Trattoria con Pizza da Chiara ❸,** V. Corridoni 44/A, from P. Cavallotti, follow C. Libertà and turn left on V.

Roma, then right on the narrow V. Corridoni. Young professionals dine in this chic but unpretentious restaurant. (☎0376 22 35 68. Pizza and *primi* €4.50-9. *Secondi* €9-14.50. Cover €2. Open M and W-Su noon-2:30pm and 7-10:30pm. MC/V.) **Supermarket Sma,** V. Giustiziati 11, is behind the Rotonda di San Lorenzo on P. d'Erbe. (Open M-Sa 8:30am-7:30pm. AmEx/MC/V.)

Trains go from P. D. Leoni to Milan (2hr., 9 per day, €8.60) and Verona (40min., 20 per day, €2.60). From the train station, turn left on V. Solferino, then right on Via Bonomi to the main street, **Corso Vittorio Emanuele II.** Follow it to P. Cavallotti, across the river to C. Umberto I, which leads to P. Marconi, P. Mantegna, and the main *piazze,* **Piazza dell'Erbe** and **Piazza Sordello.** The **tourist office** is at P. Mantegna 6; follow V. Solferino until it becomes V. Fratelli Bandiera, then go right on V. Verdi. (☎0376 32 82 53; www.aptmantova.it. Open daily 9am-7pm.) **Internet** is available at Bit and Phone, V. Bertinelli 21. **Postal Code:** 46100.

THE LAKE COUNTRY

When Italy's monuments start blurring together, escape to the clear waters and green mountains of the northern Lake Country, which encompasses part of Piedmont and part of Lombardy. The mansion-spotted coast of Lake Como welcomes the rich and famous, palatial hotels dot Lake Maggiore's sleepy shores, and a young crowd descends upon Lake Garda for its watersports and bars.

ITALY

LAKE COMO (LAGO DI COMO)

As the numerous luxurious villas on the lake's shores attest, the well-to-do have been using Lake Como as a refuge since before the Roman Empire. Three lakes form the forked Lake Como, joined at the three central towns: Bellagio, Menaggio, and Varenna. These smaller towns offer a more relaxing stay than Como. For a taste of the Lake's true beauty, hop on a bus or ferry, and step off whenever a castle, villa, vineyard, or small town beckons.

TRANSPORTATION. The only towns on the lake accessible by **train** are Como and Varenna, though the latter has only a very small station with limited hours. Trains go from Stazione San Giovanni (☎031 89 20 21) to Milan (1hr., 1-2 per hr., €3.50) and Zürich, SWI (4hr., 5 per day, €46). From P. Matteotti, **bus** C46 goes to Bergamo (2hr., 5 per day, €4.40), and C10 goes to Menaggio (1hr., 1 per hr., €3.20). From the train station, bus C30 goes to Bellagio (1hr., 16 per day, €2.80). Spend the day zipping between the boutiques, gardens, villas, and wineries of the lake by **ferry** (day pass €20), leaving from the piers at P. Cavour.

COMO. Situated on the southwestern tip of the lake, vibrant Como (pop. 86,000) is the lake's largest town. **Ostello Villa Olmo (HI) ❷,** V. Bellinzona 2, has clean rooms and a friendly staff. From the train station, walk 20min. down V. Borgo Vico to V. Bellinzona. (☎031 57 38 00. Breakfast included. Reception 7-10am and 4pm-midnight. Lockout 10am-4pm. Strict curfew midnight. Open Mar.-Nov. Reserve ahead. Dorms €18. €3 HI discount. Cash only.) Chic cafes fill Como's historic center, south of Piazza Cavour. **Gran Mercato** supermarket is at P. Matteotti 3. (Open M and Su 8:30am-1pm, Tu-F 8:30am-1:30pm and 3:30-7:30pm, Sa 8am-7:30pm.) The **tourist office** is at P. Cavour 17. From the station, go left on V. Fratelli Recchi and right on Vle. Fratelli Rosselli, which turns into Lungo Lario Trento and leads to the *piazza.* (☎031 26 97 12. Open M-Sa 9am-1pm and 2:30-6pm, Su 9:30am-12:30pm.) **Postal Code:** 22100.

MENAGGIO. Halfway up Lake Como's western shore are the terra-cotta rooftops of Menaggio (pop. 3200). The town's beauty and excellent **ferry** connections make it the perfect base for exploring the lake. Daytrips by ferry to the gardens and villas of **Bellagio** and **Varenna** (both 10-15min., 1-2 per hr., €3.50) are extremely popular. The **Rifugio Menaggio** mountain station is the starting point for a 2hr. round-trip hike to **Monte Grona** (1736m) that offers views of the pre-Alps and the lakes. Alternatively, the 2hr. hike to **Chiesa di San Amate** (1623m) takes you over a mountain ridge to sneak a peak at alpine pastures. A number of shorter hikes start in Menaggio. **Vecchia Menaggio ❶**, V. al Lago 13, offers hotel rooms at great prices in a fantastic location right next to the *centro*. There is also an affordable Italian restaurant downstairs. (☎0344 32 082. Doubles €40, with bath €60.) Just up the street from the ferry dock, **Super Cappa Market**, V. IV Novembre 107, stocks groceries and hiking supplies. (Open M 8-12:30pm, Tu-Sa 8am-12:30pm and 3-7pm.) In the *centro* at P. Garibaldi 4, the helpful **tourist office** has info and maps on lake excursions. **Postal Code:** 22017.

LAKE MAGGIORE (LAGO MAGGIORE)

A translation of Stendhal reads: "If it should befall that you possess a heart and shirt, then sell the shirt and visit the shores of Lake Maggiore." Though writers have always been seduced by the lake's beauty, Lake Maggiore remains less touristed than its neighbors. **Stresa** is a perfect stepping-stone to the gorgeous **Borromean Islands.** Stay at the **Albergo Luina ❸**, V. Garibaldi 21, to the right past the ferry dock. (☎032 33 02 85. Breakfast €3.50. Reserve ahead in summer. Singles €35-52; doubles €55-80; triples €56-80. MC/V.) Daily excursion tickets allow you to travel between Stresa and the three islands. **Trains** run from Stresa to Milan (1hr., 2 per hr., €4.60). To reach the *centro* and the **IAT Tourist Office,** P. Marconi 16, from the ferry dock, exit the train station, turn right on V. P. d. Piemonte, take a left on Vle. D. d. Genova, and walk toward the water. Turn right at the water and walk 5-10min to reach P. Marconi and the tourist office.

THE BORROMEAN ISLANDS. Beckoning visitors with lush greenery and stately villas, the beauty of the Borromean Islands is one of the lake's major attractions. On **Isola Bella,** the opulent **Palazzo e Giardini Borromeo** showcases priceless tapestries and paintings. (Open Mar. 21-Oct. 21 daily 9am-5:30pm. €11.) From Isola Bella, ferries go to **Isola Superiore dei Pescatori,** which has a quaint fishing village with a rocky beach and ice-cold water. **Isola Madre** is the greenest island, most favored by the locals. The 16th-century **Villa Taranto** surprisingly houses several puppet theaters, and its gardens overflow with exotic flowers and white peacocks. (Open daily 8:30am-6:30pm. €8.50. Combined ticket with the Palazzo e Giardini Borromeo €16.)

LAKE GARDA (LAGO DI GARDA)

Garda has staggering mountains and breezy summers. **Desenzano,** the lake's southern transport hub, is only 1hr. from Milan and 2hr. from Venice. Sirmione and Limone are best explored as daytrips. **Riva del Garda,** at the lake's northern tip, has an affordable hostel to use as a base. Exploring **Sirmione's** 13th-century castle and Roman ruins can fill a leisurely day or busy afternoon. In **Limone,** windsurfing, swimming, and eating all revolve around the unbelievable view of the lake as it winds through the mountains. Uphill from the center near the water, **La Limonaia del Castèl,** V. IV Novembre 25, transports tourists into the world of a functioning 18th-century citrus house. Trees bearing clementines, grapefruits, lemons, and limes are spread over 1633 sq. yd. of terraces. (☎0365 95 40 08; www.limone-sulgarda.it. €1.) Riva del Garda's calm and beautiful pebble beaches are Lake Garda's restitution for the budget traveler put off by steep local prices. Sleep at backpacker hot spot **Ostello Benacus (HI) ❶**, P. Cavour 10.

(☎0464 55 49 11. Breakfast included. Laundry €4. Internet €2 per hr. Reception 7-9am and 3-11pm. Reserve ahead. Dorms €16. AmEx/MC/V.)

Sirmione's **tourist office** is at V. Guglilmo Marconi 6. (☎030 91 61 14; www.commune.sirmione.bs.it. Open Apr.-Oct. daily 8am-8pm; Nov.-Mar. M-F 9am-1pm and 2-6pm, Sa 9am-12:30pm.) Limone's tourist office is at V. IV Novembre 29. (☎0365 91 89 87. Open daily 8:30am-9pm.) Riva del Garda's tourist office is at Largo Medaglie d'Oro 5. (☎0464 55 44 44; www.gardatrentino.it. Open M-Sa 9am-noon and 3-6:30pm, Su 9am-noon and 3:30-6:30pm.) **Buses** run from Sirmione and Riva del Garda to Verona (1hr., 1 per hr., €4). **Ferries** (☎030 91 49 511; www.navigazionelaghi.it) run from Limone to Desenzano (4 per day, €10-13), Riva (17 per day, €3.40-5.20), and Sirmione (8 per day, €10-13). **Postal Codes:** 25019 (Sirmione), 25087 (Limone), 38066 (Riva del Garda).

ITALIAN RIVIERA (LIGURIA)

The Italian Riviera stretches 350km along the Mediterranean between France and Tuscany, forming the most touristed area of the Italian coastline. Genoa anchors the luminescent Ligurian coastal strip between the **Riviera di Levante** (rising sun) to the east and the **Riviera di Ponente** (setting sun) to the west. Lemon trees, almond blossoms, and turquoise waters greet visitors along the elegant coast, where glamor mixes with seaside relaxation. The **Cinque Terre** area (p. 608), just west of **La Spezia**, is especially worth the journey.

GENOA (GENOVA) ☎010

Genoa (pop. 640,000), a city of grit and grandeur, has little in common with its resort neighbors. As a Ligurian will tell you, *"si deve conoscerla per amarla"* (you have to know her to love her). Once home to Liguria's most noble families, Genoa's main streets are lined with *palazzi* and *piazze;* wander through medieval churches and maze-like pathways to discover this port city.

TRANSPORTATION. **Colombo Internazionale Airport** (**GOA;** ☎010 60 15 461), services European destinations. Volabus #100 runs to Stazione Brignole from the airport (3 per hr., €3.70). Most visitors arrive at one of Genoa's two train stations: **Stazione Principe,** in P. Acquaverde, or **Stazione Brignole,** in P. Verdi. **Trains** go to Rome (5-6hr., 12 per day, €27-50), Turin (2hr., 2-3 per hr., €8-12), and points along the Italian Riviera. AMT **buses** (☎010 55 82 414) run through the city (€1.60; day pass €4). **Ferries** to Olbia, Sardinia, and Palermo, Sicily depart from Terminal Traghetti in the Ponte Assereto section of the port.

ORIENTATION AND PRACTICAL INFORMATION. From Stazione Principe, take V. Balbi to V. Cairoli, which becomes V. Garibaldi. Turn right on V. XXV Aprile at P. delle Fontane Marose to get to **Piazza de Ferrari** in the center of town. From Stazione Brignole, turn right out of the station, then left on V. Fiume and right onto V. XX Settembre. Or, take bus #18, 19, or 30 from Stazione Principe, or bus #19 or 40 from Stazione Brignole. The **tourist office,** GenovaInforma, has several locations, including a kiosk in P. Matteotti. (☎010 86 87 452. Open daily 9am-1pm and 2-6pm.) **Internet** is available at **Number One Bar/Cafe,** P. Verdi 21R. (☎010 54 18 85. €4 per hr. Open M-Sa 7:30am-11:30pm.) **Postal Code:** 16121.

WATCH WHERE YOU WANDER. The shadowy streets of the *centro storico* are riddled with drug dealers and prostitutes. Avoid the area around Stazione Principe, as well as those around V. della Maddalena, V. Sottoripa, and V. di Prè when shops are closed and streets are empty.

ACCOMMODATIONS AND FOOD. Delight in views of the city below at **Ostello per la Gioventù (HI) ❶,** V. Costanzi 120. From Stazione Principe, take bus #35 to V. Napoli and transfer to #40, which runs to the hostel. From Stazione Brignole, take bus #40 (last bus 12:50am) all the way up the hill. (☎010 24 22 457. Breakfast included. Dorms €16. HI members only.) Conveniently located **Albergo Argentina ❷,** V. Gropallo 4, near Stazione Brignole, has nine large, clean, comfortable rooms. (☎010 83 93 722. Singles €30-40; doubles €50-65, with bath €60-75; triples €75-90; quads €85-100. MC/V.) For camping, try **Genova Est ❶,** on V. Marcon Loc Cassa. (☎010 34 72 053; www.camping-genova-est.it. Laundry €3.50. €5.90 per person, €5.60-8.60 per tent. Electricity €2.20.) **Trattoria da Maria ❷,** V. Testa d'Oro 14R, off V. XXV Aprile, has authentic Genovese specials. (☎010 58 10 80. 2-course *menù* €9. Open M-Sa 11:45am-3pm. MC/V.)

SIGHTS AND ENTERTAINMENT. **Centro storico,** the eerie and beautiful historical center bordered by Porto Antico, V. Garibaldi, and P. Ferrari, is a mass of winding streets. The area contains some of Genoa's most memorable sights, including the asymmetrical **San Lorenzo Duomo,** down V. San Lorenzo from P. Matteotti (open daily 9am-noon and 3-6pm; free), and the medieval **Torre Embraici.** Go down V. S. Lorenzo toward the water, turn left on V. Chiabrera, and left on V. di Mascherona to reach the **Chiesa Santa Maria di Castello,** in P. Caricamento, a labyrinth of chapels, courtyards, and crucifixes. (Open daily 9am-noon and 3:30-6:30pm. Closed to tourists during Su Mass. Free.) Don't miss the enigmatic **Palazzo Spinola di Pellicceria,** P. di Pellicceria 1, between V. Maddalena and P. San Luca, a late 16th-century palace which represents centuries of varying architectural styles. (☎010 27 05 300. Open Tu-Sa 8:30am-7:30pm, Su 1:30-7:30pm. €4, ages 18-25 €2.) From P. de Ferrari, take V. Boetto to P. Matteotti for a glimpse of the ornate interior and paintings by Rubens in **Chiesa di Gesù.** (Church open M-Sa 7am-12:45pm and 4-7:30pm, Su 8am-12:45pm and 5-9:45pm. Closed to tourists during Su Mass. Free.) Head past the church down V. di Porta Soprana to V. Ravecca to reach the **Porta Soprana,** one of the four gates into the city, near the boyhood home of **Christopher Columbus.** (Porta and Columbus' home open daily 10am-6pm. Combo ticket €7.) Genoa's multitude of *palazzi* were built by its merchant families. Follow V. Balbi through P. della Nunziata and continue to L. Zecca, where V. Cairoli leads to **Via Garibaldi,** called "Via Aurea" (Golden Street) after the wealthy families who inhabited it. The interior of the 17th-century **Palazzo Reale,** V. Balbi 10, west of V. Garibaldi, is bathed in gold. (Open Tu-W 9am-1:30pm, Th-Su 9am-7pm. €4, ages 18-25 €2.)

Corso Italia, an upscale promenade, is home to much of Genoa's nightlife. Most people drive to get to clubs, as they are difficult to reach on foot and the city streets can be dangerous. Italian and international students flock to bars in **Piazza Erbe** and along **Via San Bernardo.** The swanky bar **Al Parador,** P. della Vittoria 49R, is easy and fairly safe to reach from Stazione Brignole. It's in the northeast corner of P. Vittoria, near the intersection of V. Cadorna and V. B. Liguria. (☎010 58 17 71. Mixed drinks €4.50. Open M-Sa 24hr. Cash only.)

daily 9am-6pm. €3.) From V. Rizzoli, follow V. S. Stefano to P. S. Stefano, where the Romanesque **Chiesa Santo Stefano** contains the basin where Pontius Pilate absolved himself of responsibility for Christ's death. (☎051 22 32 56. Modest dress required. Open daily 7am-noon and 3:30-6:45pm. Free.)

Bologna's disproportionate number of bars, clubs, and pubs ensure raucous late night fun for hip students and travelers alike, especially around V. Zamboni. As its name implies, **College Bar,** Largo Resphigi 6/D, caters to a young crowd, with live music—ranging from jazz to techno—performed daily. (☎349 003 7366. 10am-5pm any 2 drinks €3.50. Open daily 10am-3am. Cash only.) **Cassero,** located in a 17th-century salt warehouse in the Porta Saragozza, is popular with the gay community, but all are welcome. (☎051 64 94 416. Drinks €3-7. ARCI-GAY card required, available at ARCI-GAY, V. Don Minzoni 18, €8 for 1 month. W, F and Sa nights feature special *discoteca* events. Open in summer daily 9pm-4/6am; in winter W-Sa/Su 9pm-4/6am.) Every year from mid-June to mid-September, the city commune sponsors a **festival** of art, cinema, dance, music, and theater. Many events are free, and few cost more than €5.

PARMA ☎0521

Though famous for its *parmigiano* cheese and *prosciutto*, Parma's (pop. 172,000) artistic excellence is not confined to the kitchen. Giuseppe Verdi composed some of his greatest works in Parma, and native artists Parmigianino and Correggio cultivated Mannerist painting here in the 16th century. The town centers around the 11th-century **duomo** where Correggio's *Virgin* ascends to a golden heaven, and the pink-and-white marble **baptistry** displays early medieval frescoes of enthroned saints and apostles. From P. Garibaldi, follow Str. Cavour and take the third right on Str. al Duomo. (*Duomo* open daily 9am-12:30pm and 3-6:30pm. Free. Baptistry open daily 9am-12:30pm and 3-6:30pm. €4, students €3.) Built in 1521 to house a miraculous picture of the Virgin Mary, the **Chiesa Magistrale di Santa Maria della Steccata,** up V. Garibaldi from P. Garibaldi, features frescoes by Parmigianino on the arch above the presbytery. Ask the priest to see the **Crypt of the Garnese Dukes.** (Open daily 7:30am-noon and 3-6:30pm. Free.) From P. del Duomo, follow Str. al Duomo across Str. Cavour, walk one block down Str. Piscane, and cross P. della Pace to reach the 17th-century **Palazzo della Pilotta,** with the **Galleria Nazionale** and the wooden **Teatro Farnese.**

Take bus #2, 2N, or 13 from the bus station to the brand new **Ostello della Gioventu (HI) ❷,** Via San Leonardo 86. The young staff and large common rooms make you feel right at home. (☎0521 19 17 547; www.ostelloparma.it. Reception 24hr. Dorms €18.50; doubles €41.) **Albergo Leon d'Oro ❸,** V. Fratti 4a, has clean, basic rooms with shared bath. (☎0521 77 31 82; www.leondoroparma.com. Singles €35-60; doubles €60-80. AmEx/MC/V.) Resist the urge to dine outside on one of Parma's many patios, and eat downstairs in the 16th-century stone building of **Ristorante Gallo d'Oro ❷,** Borgo della Salina 3. From P. Garibaldi, take Str. Farini and turn left. (☎0521 20 88 46. *Primi* €6.50-9. *Secondi* €6.50-10. Cover €2. Open M-Sa noon-2:30pm and 7:30-11pm. AmEx/MC/V.) **Dimeglio** supermarket is at Str. Ventidue Luglio 27/c. (Open daily 8:30am-1:30pm and 4:30-8pm.)

Trains go from P. Carlo Alberto della Chiesa to Bologna (1hr., 3 per hr., €5), Florence (2hr., 3 per day, €10), and Milan (1hr., 4 per hr., €7.40). The **tourist office** is at Str. Melloni 1/A. (☎0521 21 88 89; www.turismo.comune.parma.it. Open M 9am-1pm and 3-7pm, Tu-Sa 9am-7pm, Su 9am-1pm.) **Postal Code:** 43100.

RAVENNA ☎0544

Ravenna (pop. 150,000) enjoyed its 15 minutes of fame 14 centuries ago, when Emperor Justinian and Empress Theodora, rulers of the Byzantine Empire, made it the headquarters of their western campaign. Take V. Argentario from

V. Cavourto to reach the 6th-century **Basilica di San Vitale,** V. S. Vitale 17, whose thin windows let in enough light to make its mosaics glow. Across the courtyard is the tiny brick **Mausoleo di Galla Placidia,** where a single lamp illuminates 570 gold stars against a brilliant night sky. Around the sides are three stone sarcophagi. (☎0544 21 62 92. Open daily Apr.-Sept. 9am-7pm; Mar. and Oct. 9am-5:30pm; Nov.-Feb. 9:30am-5pm.) To see the pastoral mosaics in the **Basilica di Sant'Apollinare,** take bus #4 or 44 across from the train station (€1) to Classe. (Basilica open daily 8:30am-7:30pm. €3, under 18 and over 65 free.) Ravenna's most popular monument is the **Tomb of Dante Alighieri,** who was exiled from Florence in 1301 and died in Ravenna in 1321. The adjoining **Dante Museum** contains the fir chest that held **Dante's bones,** and 18,000 scholarly volumes on his works. From P. del Popolo, cut through P. Garibaldi to V. D. Alighieri. (☎0544 33 667. Tomb open daily Apr.-Sept. 9:30am-6:30pm. Free.)

From P. Farini, walk down Vle. Farini and make a left on V. Roma to get to a former orphanage that's now the luxurious **Ostello Galletti Abbiosi ❺,** V. Roma 140. (☎0544 31 313; www.galletti.ra.it. Breakfast included. Free Wi-Fi. Reception daily 7am-3am. Singles €55; doubles €90; triples €110; quads €125. AmEx/MC/V.) **Ostello Dante (HI) ❷,** V. Nicolodi 12, is a social hostel with a well-stocked common room. (☎0544 42 11 64. Breakfast included. Internet 1st 15min. free, €3 per hr. thereafter. Lockout 11am-2:30pm. Curfew 11:30pm; €1 key deposit. Dorms €14; singles €24; doubles €20. €3 HI discount. MC/V.) Drop by **Cupido ❶,** V. Cavour 43/A, a small eatery serving hearty plates of freshly made pasta and sandwiches. (☎0544 37 529. Pizza €2.70-6.30. *Primi* €5-5.50. *Crescioni* €3-4. Open Tu-F 11am-8pm, Sa 7am-8pm, Su 7am-3pm. AmEx/MC/V.)

Trains run from P. Farini to Bologna (1hr., 13 per day, €5) and Ferrara (1hr., 11 per day, €4.50), with connections to Florence and Venice. Follow V. Farini from the station to V. Diaz and the central P. del Popolo to find the **tourist office,** V. Salara 8. (☎0544 35 404; www.turismo.ravenna.it. Open Apr.-Sept. M-Th 8:30am-7pm, F 8:30am-11pm, Su 10am-6pm.) **Postal Code:** 48100.

ITALY

RIMINI ☎0541

The Ibiza of the Adriatic, Rimini is the party town of choice for young European fashionistas. Beaches, nightclubs, and boardwalks crammed with boutiques, fortune tellers, and artists characterize a city where it is perfectly acceptable—and admirable—to collapse into bed and bid the rising sun good night. Rimini's most treasured attraction is its remarkable **beach** with fine sand and mild Adriatic waves. Rimini's nightlife heats up around the **lungomare** in southern Rimini and near the port. Bus #11 fills with rowdy partygoers as it traverses the strip of clubs. At **Coconuts,** Lungomare Tintorin 5, a diverse crowd gathers until the wee hours for the tropical decor and two outdoor dance floors. (☎0541 52 325; www.coconuts.it. Mixed drinks €8. Open daily 6pm-5am.) *Discoteca* **T Life,** Vle. Regina Margherita 11, draws hoards of young partygoers to its bar and expansive dance floor. (☎0541 37 34 73. Shots €3-4. Mixed drinks €5-7.50. Cover €7-12, includes 1 drink. Open daily 11pm-4am. Cash only.)

Hostel Jammin' Rimini (HI) ❷, Vle. Derna 22, is at stop 13 on bus #11. Seconds from the beach, this hip hostel accommodates the Rimini partying lifestyle with a bar, no lockout, and breakfast until 10:30am. (Breakfast and linens included. Open Feb.-Dec. Dorms €21. AmEx/MC/V.) Stock up on groceries at the **STANDA** supermarket, V. Vespucci 13. (Open daily 8am-10:30pm. AmEx/MC/V.)

Trains (☎0541 89 20 21) run to Bologna (1hr., 44 per day, €6.80); Milan (3hr., 23 per day, €28); Ravenna (1hr., 23 per day, €3.10). The **tourist office** is at P. Fellini 3, stop 10 on bus #11. (Open in summer M-Sa 8:30am-7:15pm, Su 8:30am-2:15pm; in winter M-F 9am-1pm and 3:30-7pm, Sa 9am-1pm.) **Postal Code:** 47900.

FERRARA ☎0532

Rome has mopeds, Venice has gondolas, and Ferrara has *biciclette* (bicycles). In a city with 160,000 bicycles for 130,000 residents, bikers are a more common sight than pedestrians. The **medieval wall** supports a 9km bike path with views of the city. The 14th-century **Castello Estense** is surrounded by a fairytale moat. Inside, themed rooms, gardens, and dungeon tunnels wind through this former fortress. (☎0532 29 92 33. Open Tu-Su 9:30am-5:30pm. €10, under 18 and over 65 €8. Audio tour €5.) From the *castello*, take C. Martiri della Libertà to P. Cattedrale and the rose-windowed **Duomo San Romano,** across V. S. Romano from the **Museo della Cattedrale,** home to the church's precious works. (*Duomo* open M-Sa 7:30am-noon and 3-6:30pm, Su 7:30am-12:30pm and 3:30-7:30pm. Museum open Tu-Su 9am-1pm and 3-6pm. Closed last 2 weeks in July. €5, students €3, under 18 free.) Cross Largo Castello to C. Ercole I d'Este and walk to its intersection with C. Rossetti to reach the **Palazzo Diamanti,** whose facade is covered by white pyramid-shaped studs. Within, the **Pinacoteca Nazionale** holds works from the Ferrarese school of painting and panels by **El Greco.** (Open Tu-W and F-Su 9am-2pm, Th 9am-7pm. €4, students €2, over 65 and under 18 free.) Follow C. Ercole I d'Este behind the *castello* to find the **Palazzo Massari,** C. Porta Mare 9, home to **Padiglione d'Arte Contemporanea, Museo d'Arte Moderna e Contemporanea Filippo de Pisis,** and tapestry-adorned **Museo Ferrarese dell'Ottocentro/Museo Giovanni Boldini.** (All open Tu-Su 9am-1pm and 3-6pm. Filippo de Pisis €3, students €2. Ottocentro/Boldini €5/3. Combination ticket €8/3.)

Pensione Artisti ❷, V. Vittoria 66, near P. Lampronti, offers free bike use and a shared kitchen. (☎0532 76 10 38. Singles €28; doubles €48, with bath €60. Cash only.) **Pizzeria da Alice ❷,** Via G. Fabbri 476, located a short walk from the center, serves pies with especially generous toppings. (☎0532 67 477. Pizza €3-7. *Antipasti* €5-10. Cover €0.50. Open daily noon-3pm and 7pm-1am. Cash only.) Italy's oldest *osteria*, **Osteria Al Brindisi ❸,** V. G. degli Adelardi 11, has wined and dined the likes of Titian and Pope John Paul II since 1435. (☎0532 20 91 42. Cover €2. Open daily 9am-1am. MC/V.) For groceries, stop by **Supermercato Conad,** V. Garibaldi 53. (Open M-Sa 8:30am-8pm, Su 9am-1pm. MC/V.)

Trains go to: Bologna (30min., 43 per day, €3); Padua (1hr., 31 per day, €4.60); Ravenna (1hr., 14 per day, €4.50); Rome (3-4hr., 23 per day, €33.50); Venice (1hr., 30 per day, €6.15). ACFT (☎0532 59 94 11) and GGFP **buses** run from the train station to local beaches (1hr., 12 per day, €4.30) and Bologna

THE LOCAL STORY

THE ICEMAN COMETH

In September 1991, Erica and Helmut Simon were hiking through the Tyrolean region of northeastern Italy, enjoying the scenery and getting some exercise. In between their photo ops and trail mix stops, they discovered something a little out of the ordinary: a fully-clothed but completely frozen human being.

As it turned out, the body belonged to a man from the late Neolithic Age (3300-3100 BCE), whom bolzanini have nicknamed Ötzi and taken under their wing in Bolzano's South Tyrol Museum of Archaeology. Though some too-cool locals insist that only tourists are interested in this human artifcat, most take a sense of pride in the fact that Ötzi has made his way to their town.

In his real form, Ötzi isn't much to look at: he's a skeleton in a refrigerator. Plus, he's a little guy—at the time of his death, he stood only 5 feet, 2 inches tall and weighed only 132 pounds. His shoe size was 5½! (It turns out that this was about normal size in those days.)

But the museum has taken special care to portray him in a more flattering light, creating a replica on which a soft spotlight shines. Ötzi's no Prince Charming, but he's armed with a heavy coat, trusty tools, and a look of determination.

To see Ötzi, head to Bolazno's South Tyrol Museum of Archaeology *(p. 648).*

(1hr., 15 per day, €3.40). The **tourist office** is in Castello Estense. (☎0532 20 93 70. Open M-Sa 9am-1pm and 2-6pm, Su 9:30am-1pm and 2-5pm.) **Postal Code:** 44100.

TRENTINO-ALTO ADIGE

With its steep mountain trails and small towns, Trentino-Alto Adige appeals to outdoor enthusiasts. One glance at the lush conifers and snow-covered peaks of *Le Dolomiti* explains why backpackers and skiers still flock to the area. The near-impenetrable dolomitic rock has slowed major industrialization, preserving the jagged pink-purple cliffs of the Dolomites and evergreen forests that Le Corbusier once called "the most beautiful natural architecture in the world."

BOLZANO (BOZEN) ☎0471

A fusion of Italian and Austrian culture, Bolzano (pop. 100,000) has lots to offer year-round. Summer visitors bike along the crystal-green Talvera River and enjoy views of hills covered with rows of grape vines, while hikers climb to snowy peaks in the winter months. Gothic spires rise skyward from the Romanesque **duomo** in P. Walther. (Open M-F 10am-noon and 2-5pm, Sa 9:45am-noon. Free.) At the **South Tyrol Museum of Archaeology,** V. Museo 43, near Ponte Talvera, tourists file by the freezer holding **Ötzi,** a 5000-year-old frozen Neanderthal. (Open Tu-W and F-Su 10am-5pm, Th 10am-7pm. €8, students €6.) Take a right from the train station and walk 5min. to reach the **Youth Hostel Bolzano ❷,** V. Renon 23, where guests enjoy clean rooms and plenty of amenities. (☎30 08 65; www.ostello.bz. Breakfast included. Internet €2 per hr. Reception 8am-4am. Dorms €19.50; singles €22. AmEx/MC/V.) The markets of **Piazza delle Erbe** and the **wurst stand** at the intersection of V. Museo and P. delle Erbe allow visitors to sample Bolzano's Austrian-influenced fare. (Market open M-F 7am-7pm, Sa 7am-1pm; wurst stand open M-Sa 9am-8pm. Cash only.) The **tourist office,** P. Walther 8, is near the *duomo.* (☎30 70 00; www.bolzano-bozen.it. Open M-F 9am-1pm and 2-7pm, Sa 9am-2pm.) **Postal Code:** 39100.

TRENT (TRENTO) ☎0461

Between the Dolomites and the Veneto, Trent (pop. 105,000) offers a sampling of northern Italian life with festivals, delicious food, and spectacular scenery. The **Piazza del Duomo,** Trent's epicenter, is anchored by the massive **Fontana del Nettuno** in the center of the *piazza.* Nearby is the **Cattedrale di San Vigilio,** where the Council of Trent (1545-1563) met during the Counter-Reformation. (Open daily 7am-11:45am and 2:45-7pm. Free.) Walk down V. Belenzani and head right on V. Roma to reach the historic **Castello del Buonconsiglio,** the execution site of famed Trentino martyrs Cesare Battisti, Damiano Chiesa, and Fabio Filzi. (www.buonconsiglio.it. Open Tu-Su 9:30am-5pm. €6, students €3.) From the station, turn right on V. Pozzo, then right on V. Torre Vanga to get to the tidy rooms of **Ostello Giovane Europa ❶,** V. Torre Vanga 11. (☎26 34 84. Breakfast included. Reception 7:30am-11pm. Dorms €14-16; singles €25; doubles €42. AmEx/MC/V.) **Hotel Venezia ❹,** P. Duomo 45, offers rooms across from the *duomo.* (☎23 41 14; www.hotelveneziatn.it. Singles €50; doubles €70; triples €86. MC/V.) Head to the casual **Alla Grotta ❷,** Vico S. Marco 6, for huge pizzas piled high with delicious toppings. (☎98 71 97. Pizza €4.10-7.20. *Primi* €5.60-7.20. Open noon-2:30pm and 6:30pm-midnight. MC/V.) For advice on local trails, festivals, and guided tours, seek out the **tourist office,** V. Manci 2. Turn right from the train station and left on V. Roma, which becomes V. Manci. (☎21 60 00; www.apt.trento.it. Open daily 9am-7pm.) **Postal Code:** 38100.

THE VENETO

From the rocky foothills of the Dolomites to the fertile valleys of the Po River, the Veneto's geography is as diverse as its history. Once loosely united under the Venetian Empire, its towns have retained their cultural independence; in fact, visitors are more likely to hear regional dialects than standard Italian during neighborly exchanges. The tenacity of local culture and customs will come as a pleasant surprise for those expecting only mandolins and gondolas.

VENICE (VENEZIA) ☎041

In Venice (pop. 60,000), palaces stand tall on a steadily sinking network of wood, and the waters of age-old canals creep up the mossy steps of abandoned homes. People flock here year-round to float down labyrinthine canals, peer into delicate blown-glass, and gaze at the masterworks of Tintoretto and Titian. While dodging hoards of tourists and pigeons will prove inevitable, the city is nonetheless a worthwhile wonder.

ITALY

TRANSPORTATION

The **train station** is on the northwest edge of the city; be sure to get off at **Santa Lucia,** not at Mestre. Buses and boats arrive at **Piazzale Roma,** across the Canal Grande from the train station. To get from either station to **Piazza San Marco,** take *vaporetto* (water bus) #1, 2, 51, or 52 or follow signs for a 25-30min. walk.

Flights: Aeroporto Marco Polo (VCE; ☎041 26 09 260; www.veniceairport.it), 10km north of the city. Take the **ATVO shuttlebus** (☎042 13 83 671) from the airport to Ple. Roma on the main island (30min., 1 per hr. 8am-midnight, €3).

Trains: Stazione Santa Lucia (☎041 89 20 21). Ticket windows open M-F 8:30am-7:30pm, Sa-Su 9am-1:30pm and 2-5:30pm. **Information office** (☎041 89 20 21) to the left as you exit the platforms. Trains go to: **Bologna** (2hr., 32 per day, €8.20); **Florence** (3hr., 19 per day, €23.50); **Milan** (3hr., 26 per day, €13.75); **Rome** (4hr., 23 per day, €41.50). **Luggage storage** by track #14.

Buses: Local **ACTV** buses (☎041 24 24; www.hellovenezia.it), in Ple. Roma. Open daily 7:30am-8pm. **ACTV long-distance carrier** runs buses to **Padua** (1hr., 2 per hr., €4).

Public Transportation: The **Canal Grande** can be crossed on foot only at the Scalzi, Rialto, and Accademia *ponti* (bridges). **Traghetti** (gondola ferry boats) traverse the canals at 7 locations, including Ferrovia, San Marculola, Cà d'Oro, and Rialto (€0.50). **Vaporetti** (V; water buses) provide 24hr. service around the city, with reduced service midnight-5am (single-ride €6.50; 24hr. *biglietto turistico* pass €16, 3-day €31). Stock up on tickets by asking for a pass *non timbrato* (unvalidated), then validate before boarding by inserting tickets into one of the yellow boxes at each stop. **Lines #1** (slow) and **2** (fast) run from the station down Canal Grande and Canale della Giudecca; lines **#41** and **51** circumnavigate Venice from the station to Lido; **#42** and **52** do the reverse; line **LN** runs from F. Nuove to Burano, Murano, and Lido, and connects to Torcello.

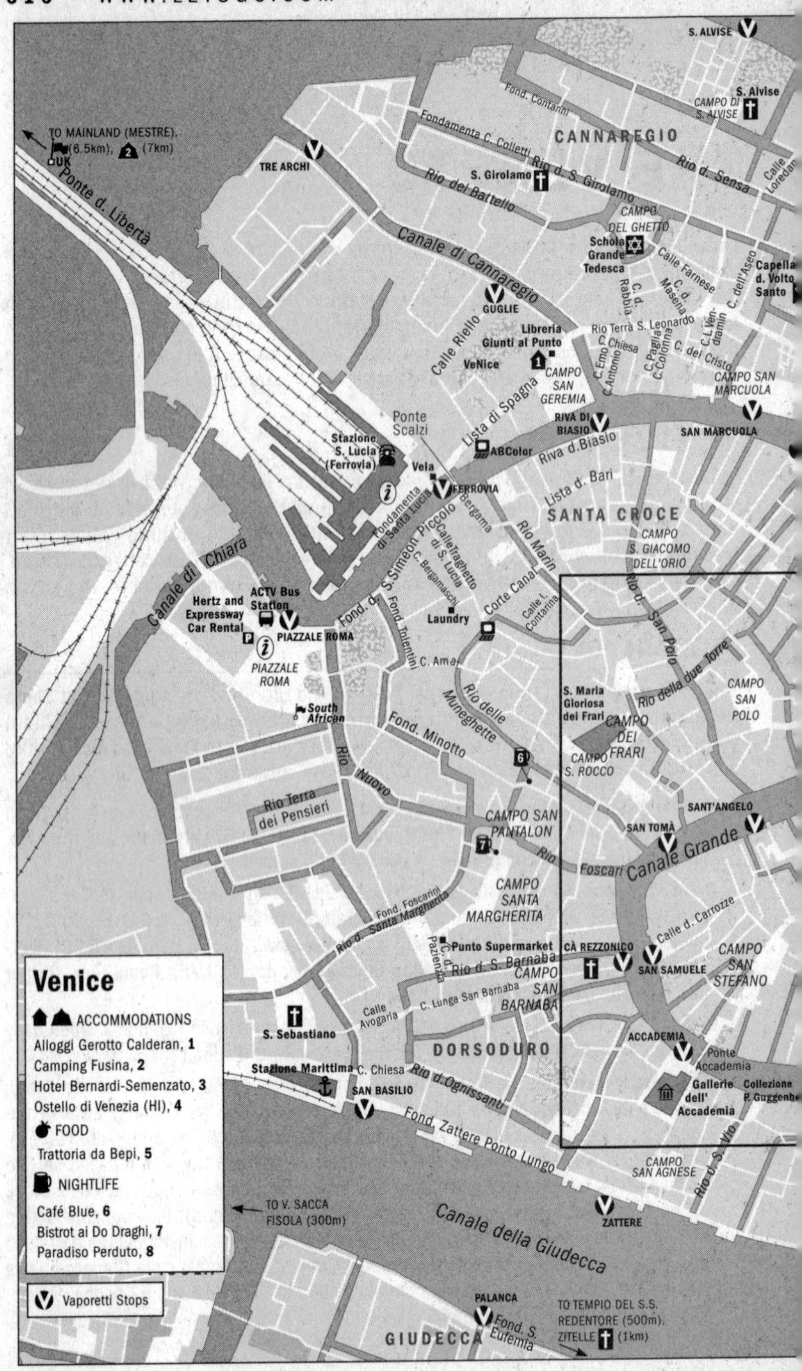

Venice
ACCOMMODATIONS
Alloggi Gerotto Calderan, 1
Camping Fusina, 2
Hotel Bernardi-Semenzato, 3
Ostello di Venezia (HI), 4
FOOD
Trattoria da Bepi, 5
NIGHTLIFE
Café Blue, 6
Bistrot ai Do Draghi, 7
Paradiso Perduto, 8
Vaporetti Stops
TO MAINLAND (MESTRE), (6.5km), 2 (7km)
UK
Ponte d. Libertà
TRE ARCHI
S. ALVISE
S. Alvise
CAMPO DI S. ALVISE
Fond. Contanni
Fondamenta C. Colletti
CANNAREGIO
Rio d. S. Girolamo
Rio d. Sensa
S. Girolamo
Rio del Battello
CAMPO DEL GHETTO
Schola Grande Tedesca
Calle Farnese
Capella d. Volto Santo
Canale di Cannaregio
GUGLIE
Libreria Giunti al Punto
Calle Riello
VeNice
CAMPO SAN GEREMIA
Lista di Spagna
Rio Terrà S. Leonardo
C. d. Rabbia
C. d. Masena
C. dell'Aseo
C. del Cristo
CAMPO SAN MARCUOLA
SAN MARCUOLA
RIVA DI BIASIO
Riva d. Biasio
Ponte Scalzi
Stazione S. Lucia (Ferrovia)
ABColor
Vela
FERROVIA
Lista d. Bari
SANTA CROCE
CAMPO S. GIACOMO DELL'ORIO
Fondamenta di Santa Lucia
Fond. d. S. Simeon Piccolo
Rio Marin
Corte Canal
Canale di Chiara
Hertz and Expressway Car Rental
ACTV Bus Station
PIAZZALE ROMA
Fond. Tolentini
Laundry
C. Amai
Rio d. San Polo
Rio della due Torre
S. Maria Gloriosa dei Frari
CAMPO DEI FRARI
CAMPO S. ROCCO
CAMPO SAN POLO
South African
Fond. Minotto
Rio delle Muneghette
Rio Nuovo
Rio Terra dei Pensieri
CAMPO SAN PANTALON
SANT'ANGELO
SAN TOMÀ
Canale Grande
Rio Foscari
CAMPO SANTA MARGHERITA
Fond. Foscarini
Rio d. Santa Margherita
Punto Supermarket
C. d. Pazienza
CÀ REZZONICO
SAN SAMUELE
Calle d. Carrozze
CAMPO SAN STEFANO
Rio d. S. Barnaba
CAMPO SAN BARNABA
C. Lunga San Barnaba
Calle Avogaria
S. Sebastiano
DORSODURO
ACCADEMIA
Ponte Accademia
Gallerie dell' Accademia
Collezione P. Guggenheim
Stazione Marittima
C. Chiesa
Rio d. Ognissanti
SAN BASILIO
Fond. Zattere Ponto Lungo
CAMPO SAN AGNESE
Rio d. S. Vio
TO V. SACCA FISOLA (300m)
ZATTERE
Canale della Giudecca
PALANCA
Fond. S. Eufemia
GIUDECCA
TO TEMPIO DEL S.S. REDENTORE (500m), ZITELLE (1km)

ITALY

TO MURANO (1.5km), TORCELLO (4km), BURANO (7km), AEROPORTO MARCO POLO (10km).
CIMITERO
Canale delle Fondamente Nuove
Isola di San Michele
ORTO
Chiesa della Madonna dell'Orto
Rio d. Madonna dell'Orto
Sacca della Misericordia
Campo dei Mori
S. Maria Valverde
Rio della Misericordia
Rio d. Noale
CAMPO SANTA FOSCA
Rio Trapolin
S. Fosca
Lunga Santa Catenna
Chiesa dei Gesuiti
CAMPO DEI GESUITI
FONDAMENTA NUOVE
Fondamenta Nuove
Calle Larga dei Botteri
0 200 meters
0 200 yards
Calle Rachetta
Calle delle Vele
Ruga Due Pozzi
C. del Fumo
Billa Supermarket
Strada Nuova
Cà d'Oro
CÀ D'ORO
Rio d. San Cassiano
S. del Pistor
CAMPO S.S. APOSTOLI
Internet Station
Calle dello Squero
Rio dei Mendicanti
OSPEDALE
Ospedale Civile
S.S. Giovanni e Paolo
C. d. Cappuccine
Rio d. San Marina
Barbaria delle Tole
CELESTIA
S. Francesco della Vigna
CAMPO D. CELESTIA
Ponte di Rialto
SAN POLO
CAMPO S. BARTOLOMEO
Riva del Vin
SAN SILVESTRO
RIALTO
Riva del Carbon
Sal. di S. Lio
CAMPO S. MARIA FORMOSA
Ruga Giuffa
S. Maria Formosa
Ponte Rosso
Famosa
Rio di S. Severo
C. di Mezzo
B. Lorenzo
C. Castello
C. Cappello
di S. Giorgio
Fondamenta
CAMPO SAN LORENZO
Scuola Dalmata San Giorgio degli Schiavoni
CASTELLO
Calle Lion
C. d. Furlani
Rio d. S. Salvador
Calle dei Fabbri
Rio d. S. Luca
CAMPO MANIN
Calle d. Mandola
CAMPO SANT'ANGELO
Rio del Palazzo
C. Corona
Fond. Osmarin
C. d. Madonna
S. S. Provolo
S. Zaccaria
CAMPO S. ZACCARIA
Calle della Pietà
C. Pietà
CAMPO BANDIERA E MORO
Rio d. Gorne
C. del Dose
C. del Forno
C. Crosera
TO ARSENALE (150m)
Frezzaria
PIAZZA SAN MARCO
San Marco
Palazzo Ducale
SAN MARCO
C. dei Vin
Riva degli Schiavoni
S. ZACCARIA
ARSENALE
Rio dell'Arsenale
Rio della Ostreghe
Rio d. San Mois
SAN MARCO
TO GIARDINI PUBLICI (250m)
Canale di San Marco
GIGLIO
SALUTE
S. Maria della Salute
SEE CENTRAL VENICE MAP p. 618
Rio d. Fornace
SAN GIORGIO
S. Giorgio Maggiore
Isola di S. Giorgio Maggiore
Fond. Zattere ai Saloni
Fond. delle Zitelle
ZITELLE
TO 31 (100m)
TO LIDO (2km)
ITALY

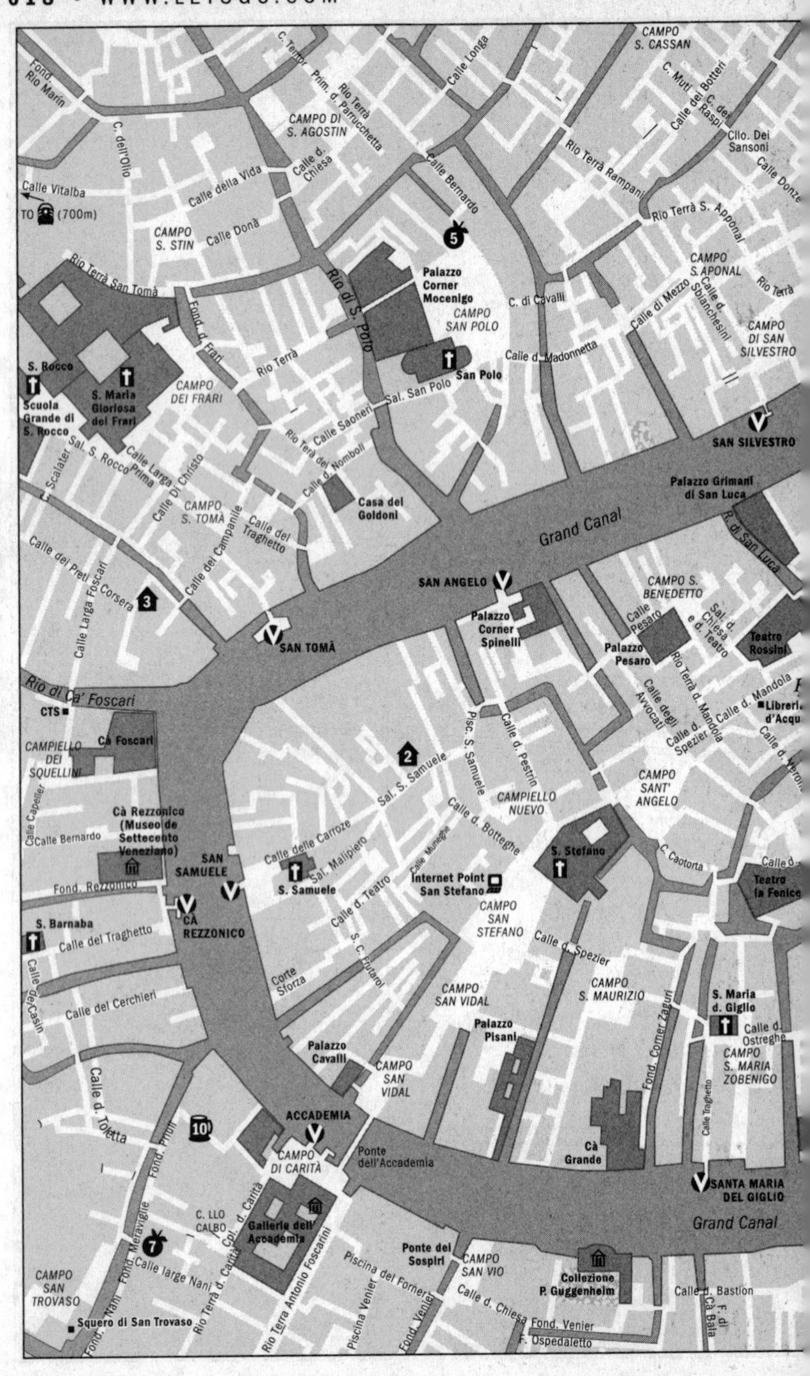

Grand Canal
Rio di Ca' Foscari
Rio di S. Polo
SAN SILVESTRO
SAN ANGELO
SAN TOMÀ
SAN SAMUELE
CÀ REZZONICO
ACCADEMIA
SANTA MARIA DEL GIGLIO
Palazzo Corner Mocenigo
CAMPO SAN POLO
San Polo
S. Rocco
Scuola Grande di S. Rocco
S. Maria Gloriosa dei Frari
CAMPO DEI FRARI
Casa del Goldoni
CAMPO S. TOMÀ
Palazzo Grimani di San Luca
Palazzo Corner Spinelli
Palazzo Pesaro
Teatro Rossini
CAMPO S. BENEDETTO
Cà Foscari
CTS
Cà Rezzonico (Museo de Settecento Veneziano)
S. Barnaba
S. Samuele
Internet Point San Stefano
S. Stefano
CAMPO SAN STEFANO
CAMPIELLO NUEVO
CAMPO SANT' ANGELO
Teatro la Fenice
CAMPO S. MAURIZIO
CAMPO SAN VIDAL
Palazzo Pisani
Palazzo Cavalli
S. Maria d. Giglio
CAMPO S. MARIA ZOBENIGO
Cà Grande
CAMPO DI CARITÀ
Ponte dell'Accademia
Gallerie dell' Accademia
Ponte del Sospiri
CAMPO SAN VIO
Collezione P. Guggenheim
CAMPO SAN TROVASO
Squero di San Trovaso
CAMPO S. CASSAN
CAMPO DI S. AGOSTIN
CAMPO S. STIN
CAMPO S. APONAL
CAMPO DI SAN SILVESTRO
CAMPIELLO DEI SQUELLINI
Calle Vitalba
TO (700m)

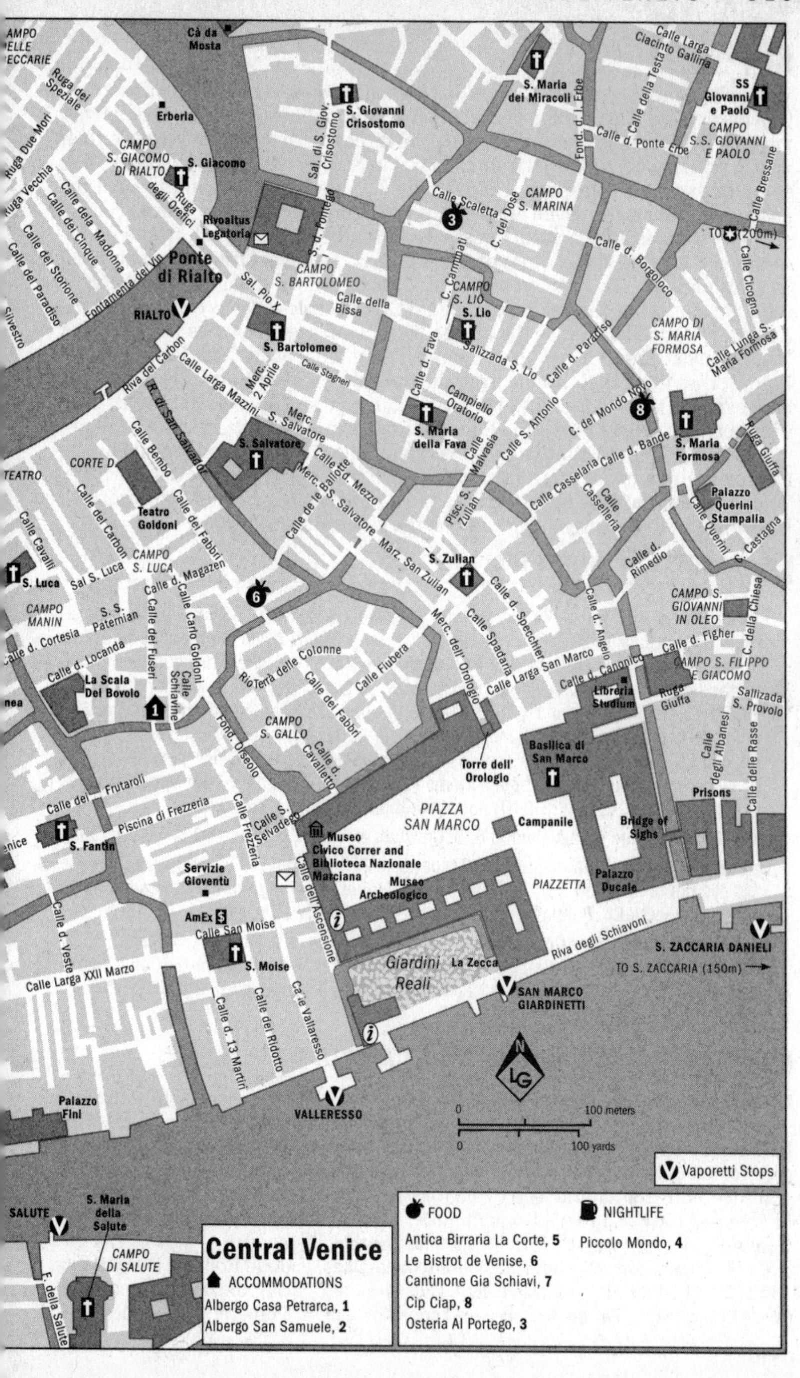
Central Venice
ACCOMMODATIONS
Albergo Casa Petrarca, 1
Albergo San Samuele, 2
FOOD
Antica Birraria La Corte, 5
Le Bistrot de Venise, 6
Cantinone Gia Schiavi, 7
Cip Ciap, 8
Osteria Al Portego, 3
NIGHTLIFE
Piccolo Mondo, 4
Vaporetti Stops
Cà da Mosta
Erberia
CAMPO S. GIACOMO DI RIALTO
S. Giacomo
Ruga degli Orefici
Rivoaltus Legatoria
Ponte di Rialto
RIALTO
Fontamenta del Vin
Riva del Carbon
S. Giovanni Crisostomo
Sal. di S. Giov. Crisostomo
S. Maria dei Miracoli
Calle Larga Ciacinto Gallina
SS Giovanni e Paolo
CAMPO S.S. GIOVANNI E PAOLO
Calle d. Ponte Erbe
Calle della Testa
Fond. d. l. Erbe
Calle Bressane
Calle Scaletta
CAMPO S. MARINA
C. del Dose
TO (200m)
Calle d. Borgoloco
Calle Cicogna
CAMPO S. BARTOLOMEO
Calle della Bissa
CAMPO S. LIO
S. Lio
Salizzada S. Lio
S. Bartolomeo
Calle Stagneri
Merc. 2 Aprile
Sal. Pio X
Calle Larga Mazzini
CAMPO DI S. MARIA FORMOSA
Calle Lunga S. Maria Formosa
Calle d. Paradiso
C. del Mondo Novo
S. Maria della Fava
Campiello Oratorio
Calle Malvasia
Calle S. Antonio
S. Maria Formosa
Calle d. Bande
Ruga Giuffa
Palazzo Querini Stampalia
Calle Querini
C. Castagna
Merc. S. Salvatore
S. Salvatore
R. di San Salvador
Calle Bembo
CORTE D.
TEATRO
Teatro Goldoni
Calle del Carbon
Calle dei Fabbri
Calle de le Ballotte
Calle d. Mezzo
Pisc. S. Zulian
Calle Casselaria
Calle d. Rimedio
S. Zulian
Marz. San Zulian
Calle d. Specchieri
Calle Spadaria
Merc. dell' Orologio
CAMPO S. GIOVANNI IN OLEO
C. della Chiesa
Calle d. Figher
CAMPO S. FILIPPO E GIACOMO
Calle Larga San Marco
Calle d. Canonica
Libreria Studium
Ruga Giuffa
Sallizada S. Provolo
S. Luca
CAMPO S. LUCA
Sal S. Luca
Calle Cavalli
CAMPO MANIN
S.S. Paternian
Calle d. Magazen
Calle Carlo Goldoni
Calle del Fuseri
Calle Schiavine
Calle d. Cortesia
Calle d. Locanda
La Scala Del Bovolo
Rio Terrà delle Colonne
Calle Fiubera
Calle dei Fabbri
CAMPO S. GALLO
Calle Cavalletto
Fond. Orseolo
Torre dell' Orologio
Basilica di San Marco
Calle degli Albanesi
Calle delle Rasse
Prisons
PIAZZA SAN MARCO
Campanile
Bridge of Sighs
Calle dei Frutaroli
Piscina di Frezzeria
Calle Frezzeria
Calle S. Selvadego
S. Fantin
Museo Civico Correr and Biblioteca Nazionale Marciana
Museo Archeologico
PIAZZETTA
Palazzo Ducale
Servizie Gioventù
AmEx
Calle San Moise
Calle dell'Ascensione
Calle d. Veste
S. Moise
Calle Larga XXII Marzo
Giardini Reali
La Zecca
Riva degli Schiavoni
S. ZACCARIA DANIELI
TO S. ZACCARIA (150m)
SAN MARCO GIARDINETTI
Calle d. 13 Martiri
Calle dei Ridotto
Calle Vallaresso
VALLERESSO
Palazzo Fini
0
100 meters
100 yards
SALUTE
S. Maria della Salute
CAMPO DI SALUTE
F. della Salute

ITALY

ORIENTATION

Venice is composed of 118 islands in a lagoon, connected to the mainland by a thin causeway. The city is a veritable labyrinth and can confuse even natives, most of whom simply set off in a general direction and patiently weave their way. If you unglue your eyes from the map and go with the flow, you'll discover some unexpected surprises. Yellow signs all over the city point toward the following landmarks: **Ponte di Rialto** (in the center), **Piazza San Marco** (central south), **Ponte Accademia** (southwest), **Ferrovia** (the train station, in the northwest), and **Piazzale Roma** (south of the station). The **Canal Grande** winds through the city, creating six *sestieri* (sections): **Cannaregio** is in the north and includes the train station, Jewish ghetto, and Cà d'Oro; **Castello** extends east toward the Arsenale; **Dorsoduro,** across the bridge from S. Marco, stretches the length of Canale della Giudecca and up to Campo S. Pantalon; **Santa Croce** lies west of S. Polo, across the Canal Grande from the train station; **San Marco** fills in the area between the Ponte di Rialto and Ponte Accademia; and **San Polo** runs north from Chiesa S. Maria dei Frari to the Ponte di Rialto. In each *sestiere*, addresses are not specific to a particular street—every building is given a number, and jumps between numbers are unpredictable. If *sestiere* boundaries prove too vague, Venice's **parrochie** (parishes) provide a more defined idea of where you are; *parrochia* signs, like *sestiere* signs, are on the sides of buildings.

ITALY

PRACTICAL INFORMATION

Tourist Office: APT, Cal. della Ascensione, S. Marco 71/F (☎041 52 98 740; www.doge.it), directly opposite the basilica. Open daily 9am-3:30pm. Avoid the mobbed branches at the train and bus stations. The **Rolling Venice Card** (€4) offers discounts on transportation and at over 200 restaurants, cafes, hotels, museums, and shops for ages 14-29. Cards are valid for 1 year from date of purchase and can be purchased at APT, which provides a list of participating vendors, or at the **ACTV VeLa** office (☎041 27 47 650) in Ple. Roma. Open daily 7am-8pm. **VeneziaSi** (☎800 84 30 06), next to the tourist office in the train station, books rooms for a €2 fee. Open daily 8am-9pm. Branches in Ple. Roma (☎041 52 28 640) and the airport (☎041 54 15 133).

Hospital: Ospedale Civile, Campo S. S. Giovanni e Paolo, Castello (☎041 52 94 111).

Internet: ABColor, Lista di Spagna, Cannaregio 220 (☎041 52 44 380). Look for the "@" symbol on a yellow sign, left off the main street heading from the train station. €6 per hr., students €4. Printing €0.15 per page. Open M-Sa 10am-8pm.

Post Office: Poste Venezia Centrale, Salizzada Fontego dei Tedeschi, S. Marco 5554 (☎041 27 17 111), off Campo S. Bartolomeo. Open M-Sa 8:30am-6:30pm. **Postal Codes:** 30121 (Cannaregio); 30122 (Castello); 30123 (Dorsoduro); 30135 (S. Croce); 30124 (S. Marco); 30125 (S. Polo).

ACCOMMODATIONS AND CAMPING

Hotels in Venice are often more expensive than those elsewhere in Italy, but savvy travelers can find cheap rooms if they sniff out options early in summer. Agree on a price before booking, and reserve one month ahead. **VeneziaSi** (see **Tourist Offices,** p. 620) finds rooms on the same day, but not cheap ones. If you're looking for a miracle, try religious institutions, which often offer rooms in summer for €25-110. Options include: **Casa Murialdo,** F. Madonna dell'Orto, Cannaregio 3512 (☎041 71 99 33); **Domus Cavanis,** Dorsoduro 896 (☎041 52 87 374), near the Ponte Accademia; **Istituto Canossiano,** F. delle Romite, Dorsoduro 1323 (☎041 24 09 713); **Istituto Ciliota,** Cal. Muneghe S. Stefano, San Marco 2976 (☎041 52 04 888); **Patronato Salesiano Leone XIII,** Cal. S. Domenico, Castello 1281

(☎041 52 8 9). For **camping,** plan on a 20min. boat ride from Venice. In addition to c ng options listed here, Litorale del Cavallino, on the Lido's Adriatic side, multiple beach campgrounds.

Alloggi Gerot lderan, Campo S. Geremia 283 (☎041 71 55 62; www.283.it). Half-hostel, half-h all good. Location makes it the best deal in Venice. Internet €4 per hr. Curfew 1a orms €25; singles €35-65; doubles €50-90; triples €75-105. 10% Rolling Venice unt; reduced prices for extended stays. Cash only. ❷

Ostello di Vene HI), F. Zitelle, Giudecca 87 (☎041 52 38 211). This hostel has sparkling baths weeping views of the city. Single-sex floors. Breakfast and linens included. Dinner Reception 7-9:30am and 1:30pm-midnight. Lockout 9:30am-1-:30pm. Curfew 1: Dorms €21. HI members only. MC/V. ❷

Hotel Bernardi-Sen to, Cal. dell'Oca, Cannaregio 4366 (☎041 52 27 257; www.hotelbernardi.com). hallways lead to large, elegantly furnished rooms—all with A/C and TV, some w ate bath. Breakfast included. Free Internet. Reception 7am-midnight. Check-out am. Singles with bath €35; doubles with bath €80-95; quads €120-130. 10 ng Venice discount on larger rooms. AmEx/MC/V. ❸

Albergo Casa Petrarca, hiavine, San Marco 4386 (☎041 52 00 430; www.casapetrarca.com). Cheerful eeps 7 sunny rooms, most with bath and A/C. Breakfast included. Singles €95; d €125-135. Extra bed €35. Cash only. ❺

Albergo San Samuele, S San Samuele, San Marco 3358 (☎041 52 28 045; www.albergosansamuele.i e white rooms on a quiet street, just 10min. from P. S. Marco. Free Wi-Fi. Re 4hr. Reserve 1-2 months ahead. Singles €45-65; doubles €65-85, with bath AmEx/MC/V. ❹

Camping Fusina, V. Moranza ☎041 54 70 055; www.camping-fusina.com), in Malcontenta. From Mestre, ta 11. ATM, Internet access, laundromat, restaurant, and TV on-site. Free hot showe ahead to reserve cabins. €8-9 per person, €8.50 per tent. Cabin singles €25; d 30. AmEx/MC/V. ❷

FOOD

With few exceptions, the best re nts lie in alleyways, not along the canals around San Marco. Venetian cu s dominated by fish, like *sarde in saor* (sardines in vinegar and onions), able only in Venice and sampled cheaply at most bars with other types of *etti* (tidbits of seafood, rice, and meat; €1-3). **Wines** of the Veneto and Fri ions include the whites *Prosecco della Marca*, *Bianco di Custoza*, and dr *ai*, as well as the red *Valpolicella*. Venice's renowned Rialto **markets** sprea tween the Canal Grande and the San Polo foot of the Rialto every Monda rough Saturday morning.

Le Bistrot de Venise, Cal. dei Fabbri, Marco 4685 (☎041 52 36 651; www.bistrotdevenise.com). Scrumptious dishes d on medieval and Renaissance recipes. *Enoteca: cichetti* €3-4, meat and chee ates €12-24. Restaurant: *primi* €18-22, *secondi* €28-32. Wine from €5 per glass. ce 12%. Open daily noon-3pm and 7pm-midnight. 10% Rolling Venice discount. MC ❺

Cantinone Gia Schiavi, F. Meraviglie, Dors ro 992 (☎041 52 30 034). In this old *enoteca,* customers choose from hundreds vines (glasses €2-5) and dozens of fresh *cichetti* (€1). Open M-Sa 8am-11pm, Su 8a noon. Cash only. ❶

Cip Ciap, Cal. del Mondo Novo 5799/A (☎04 52 36 621). Tiny pizzeria sells pizza by the gram (€1.20 per kg). Cheap, filling calzon s (€2.50). There's no seating, so find a bench in the nearby *campo.* Open M and W-Su 9am-9pm. Cash only. ❶

Antica Birraria La Corte, Campo S. Polo, San Polo 2168 (☎041 27 50 570; www.birrarialacorte.it). The expansive interior of this former brewery houses a restaurant and bar. Outdoor seating on the *campo.* Pizza €5.50-9. *Primi* €10-12. *Secondi* €13.50-19.

ITALY

Cover €2. Restaurant open daily noon-2:30pm and 7pm-10:30pm. Pizzeria open in summer 10am-midnight, in winter 10am-3pm and 9pm-midnight. AmEx/MC/V. ❸

Trattoria da Bepi, Cannaregio 4550 (☎041 52 85 031). This *trattoria* serves dishes like potato *tortelli* with ricotta (€9). *Primi* €7-12. *Secondi* €12.50-17. Cover €1.50. Reservations recommended. Open M-W and F-Su noon-3pm and 7-11pm. MC/V. ❸

Osteria al Portego, Cal. Malvasia 6015. Heading south on Salizzada S. Lio, turn left onto Cal. Malvasia, and left again toward Cte. Perina. This hidden *osteria,* filled with barrels of wine, is a favorite of students and locals. Dizzying array of *cicchetti* and wine. Open M-Sa 10:30am-3pm and 6-10pm. Cash only. ❶

SIGHTS

Venice's layout makes sightseeing a disorienting affair. Most sights center around the **Piazza San Marco.** Museum passes (€18, students €12), sold at participating museums, grant one-time admission to each of 10 museums over the course of six months. The Foundation for the Churches of Venice (☎041 27 50 462; www.chorusvenezia.org) sells the **Chorus Pass** (€9, students €6), which provides admission to all of Venice's churches.

ITALY

AROUND PIAZZA SAN MARCO

Venice's only official *piazza,* **Piazza San Marco** is an un-Venetian expanse of light, space, and architectural harmony. The 96m brick **campanile** (bell tower; open daily 9am-9pm, €6) provides one of the best views of the city; on clear days, the panorama spans Croatia and Slovenia.

BASILICA DI SAN MARCO. The symmetrical arches and incomparable mosaics of Venice's crown jewel grace Piazza San Marco. To avoid the long lines at Basilica di San Marco, visit early in the morning; still, late afternoon visits profit from the best natural light. Begun in the 9th century to house the remains of St. Mark, the church now sparkles with 13th-century Byzantine and 16th-century Renaissance mosaics. Behind the altar, the **Pala d'Oro** relief frames a parade of saints in gem-encrusted gold. Steep stairs in the atrium lead to the **Galleria della Basilica,** which affords views of the tiny golden tiles in the basilica's vast ceiling mosaics and the original bronze **Cavalli di San Marco** (Horses of St. Mark). A balcony overlooks the *piazza. (Basilica open M-Sa 9:45am-5pm, Su 2-4pm. Modest dress required. Free. Pala d'Oro and treasury open in summer M-F 9:45am-5pm, Sa-Su 2-4:30pm, in winter M-F 9:45am-4pm, Sa-Su 2-4pm. €3/2. Galleria open M-Sa 9:45am-4:45pm. €4.)*

PALAZZO DUCALE (DOGE'S PALACE). Once the home of Venice's *doge* (mayor), the Palazzo Ducale is now a museum. Veronese's *Rape of Europa* is among its spectacular works. In the courtyard, Sansovino's enormous sculptures, *Mars* and *Neptune,* flank the **Scala dei Giganti** (Stairs of the Giants), upon which new *doges* were crowned. The Council of Ten, the *doge*'s administrators, would drop the names of suspected criminals into the **Bocca di Leone** (Lion's Mouth), on the balcony. Climb the **Scala d'Oro** (Golden Staircase) to the **Sala delle Quattro Porte** (Room of the Four Doors) and the **Sala dell'Anticollegio** (Antechamber of the Senate), whose decorations depict myths about Venice. Courtrooms of the Council of Ten and the Council of Three lead to the **Sala del Maggior Consiglio** (Great Council Room), dominated by Tintoretto's *Paradise,* the largest oil painting in the world. Near the end, thick stone lattices line the **Ponte dei Sospiri** (Bridge of Sighs), named after the mournful groans of prisoners who walked it on their way to the prison's damp cells. *(Wheelchair-accessible. Open daily Apr.-Oct. 9am-7pm; Nov.-Mar. 9am-5pm. €16, students €10.)*

CHIESA DI SAN ZACCARIA. Designed in the late 1400s by Coducci and others, and dedicated to John the Baptist's father, this Gothic-Renaissance church holds S. Zaccaria's corpse in a sarcophagus along the nave's right wall. Nearby is Bellini's *Virgin and Child Enthroned with Four Saints*, a Renaissance masterpiece. *(S. Marco. V: S. Zaccaria. Open daily 10am-noon and 4-6pm. Free.)*

AROUND THE PONTE RIALTO

THE GRAND CANAL. The Grand Canal is Venice's "main street." Over 3km long and nearly 50m wide, it loops through the city and passes under three bridges: the **Ponte Scalzi, Rialto,** and **Accademia.** The *bricole*, candy-cane posts used for mooring boats on the canal, are painted with the colors of the family whose *palazzo* adjoins them. *(For great facade views, ride V. #1 or 2 from the train station to P. S. Marco. The facades are lit at night and produce dazzling reflections.)*

RIVOALTUS LEGATORIA. Step into the book-lined Rivoaltus shop on any given day and hear Wanda Scarpa greet you from the attic, where she has been sewing leatherbound, antique-style **journals** for an international cadre of customers and faithful locals for more than three decades. Though Venice is now littered with shops selling journals, Rivoaltus was the first and remains the best. *(Ponte di Rialto 11. Notebooks €19-39. Photo albums €37-79. Open daily 10am-7:30pm.)*

SAN POLO

The second-largest *campo* in Venice, **Campo San Polo** once hosted bloody bull-baiting matches during *Carnevale*. Today, the *campo* is dotted with elderly women and trees, and there is no blood spilled on the ground—only gelato.

BASILICA DI SANTA MARIA GLORIOSA DEI FRARI. Titian's corpse and two of his paintings reside within this Gothic church, known as *I Frari* and begun by Franciscans in 1340. **Assumption** (1516-18), on the high altar, marks the height of the Venetian Renaissance. The golden Florentine chapel, to the right of the high altar, frames Donatello's gaunt wooden sculpture, **St. John the Baptist.** Titian's tomb is an elaborate lion-topped triumphal arch with bas-relief scenes of Paradise. *(S. Polo. V: S. Tomà. Open M-Sa 9am-6pm, Su 1-6pm. €3.)*

CHIESA DI SAN GIACOMO DI RIALTO. Between the Rialto and nearby markets stands Venice's first church, diminutively called "San Giacometto." Across the *piazza*, a statue called *Il Gobbo* (The Hunchback) supports the steps, once used for announcements. At the foot of the statue, convicted thieves would

VENICE: IN HOT WATER?

It's hard to picture Venice without water. Images of drifting gondolas, glistening canals, and apartments on stilts lend as much flavor to the city as do its history and cuisine. But ironically, Venice's most essential element has recently become the bane of its existence, causing flooding and pollution in the now "sinking city."

While *la acqua alta* has always been a subject of Venetian concern, debate over how best to handle the situation erupted after a storm left parts of the city under six feet of water, permanently damaging historic buildings and priceless works of art.

The most significant preventative effort currently underway is the MOSE project (Experimental Electromechanical Module), a $5 billion endeavor to protect the city from tides higher than 50 in. By 2012, MOSE hopes to resolve water-related concerns. Meanwhile, it has created a controversy among Venetians, many of whom claim that the issue of flooding is greatly exaggerated. MOSE poses its own consequences for the city as well. The cost of the project has forced many to move out and has halted business growth, and MOSE may cause pollution, damage to biodiversity, and dangerous changes in tidal patterns.

Should the topic arise, try to keep your head above water and remain respectful; you will likely face a cascade of debate.

collapse after being forced to run naked from P. S. Marco. *(V: Rialto. Cross bridge and turn right. Church open M-Sa 10am-6pm. Free.)*

DORSODURO

COLLEZIONE PEGGY GUGGENHEIM. Guggenheim's Palazzo Venier dei Leoni displays works by Dalí, Duchamp, Kandinsky, Klee, Magritte, Picasso, and Pollock. The Marini sculpture *Angel in the City*, in front of the *palazzo*, was designed with a detachable penis so that Ms. Guggenheim could avoid offending her more prudish guests. *(F. Venier dei Leoni, Dorsoduro 701. V: Accademia. Turn left and follow the yellow signs. Open M and W-Su 10am-6pm. €10; students and Rolling Venice €5.)*

GALLERIE DELL'ACCADEMIA. The Accademia houses the world's most extensive collection of Venetian art. Among the enormous altarpieces in **Room II,** Giovanni Bellini's *Madonna Enthroned with Child, Saints, and Angels* stands out with its soothing serenity. In **Room VI,** three paintings by Tintoretto, *The Creation of the Animals*, *The Temptation of Adam and Eve*, and *Cain and Abel*, grow progressively darker with age. **Room X** displays Titian's last painting, a *Pietà* intended for his tomb. In **Room XX,** works by Bellini and Carpaccio depict Venetian processions and cityscapes so accurately that scholars use them as "photos" of Venice's past. *(V: Accademia. Open M 8:15am-2pm, Tu-Su 8:15am-7:15pm. €6.50. English-language tours F-Su 10am and 3:30pm, €7.)*

ITALY

CHIESA DI SANTA MARIA DELLA SALUTE. The *salute* (Italian for "health") is a hallmark of the Venetian skyline: perched on Dorsoduro's peninsula just southwest of San Marco, the church and its domes are visible from everywhere in the city. In 1631, the city had **Baldassarre Longhena** build the church for the Virgin, who they believed would end the current plague. Next to the *salute* stands the *dogana*, the customs house, where ships sailing into Venice were required to pay duties. *(Dorsoduro. V: Salute. ☎041 52 25 558. Open daily 9am-noon and 3-5:30pm. Free. Entrance to sacristy with donation. The inside of the dogana is closed to the public.)*

CASTELLO

CHIESA DI SANTISSIMI GIOVANNI E PAOLO. This structure is built primarily in the Gothic style but has a Renaissance portal and an arch supported by Greek columns. Inside, monumental walls and ceilings enclose the tombs and monuments of the *doges*. *(Castello. V: Fond. Nuove. Turn left, then right on Fond. dei Mendicanti. ☎041 52 35 913. Open M-Sa 9am-6:30pm, Su noon-6:30pm. €2.50, students €1.25.)*

CANNAREGIO

JEWISH GHETTO. In 1516, the *doge* forced Venice's Jewish population into the old cannon-foundry area, creating the first Jewish ghetto in Europe and coining the word "ghetto," the Venetian word for foundry. In the Campo del Ghetto Nuovo, the **Schola Grande Tedesca** (German Synagogue), the area's oldest synagogue, and the **Museo Ebraica di Venezia** (Hebrew Museum of Venice) now share a building. *(Cannaregio 2899/B. V: S. Marcuola. Museum open M-F and Su June-Sept. 10am-7pm; Oct.-May 10am-4:30pm. Enter synagogue by 40min. tour every hr. daily June-Sept. 10:30am-5:30pm; Oct.-May 10:30am-4:30pm. Museum €3, students €2. Museum and tour €8.50/7.)*

CÀ D'ORO. Delicate spires and interlocking arches make the Cà d'Oro's facade the most spectacular on the Canal Grande. Built between 1421 and 1440, it now houses the **Galleria Giorgio Franchetti.** For the best view of the palace, take a *traghetto* (ferry) across the canal to the Rialto Markets. *(V: Cà d'Oro. Open M 8:15am-2pm, Tu-Su 8:15am-7:15pm. €5, EU students 18-25 €2.50. Audio tour €4.)*

ISLANDS OF THE LAGOON

LIDO. The breezy resort island of Lido provided the setting for Thomas Mann's haunting novella, *Death in Venice*. Visonti's film version was also shot here at the Hotel des Bains, Lungomare Marconi 17. Today, people flock to Lido to enjoy the surf at the popular public beach. An impressive shipwreck looms at one end, while a casino, horseback riding, and the fine Alberoni Golf Club add to the island's charm. *(V #1 and 2: Lido. Beach open daily 9am-8pm. Free.)*

MURANO. Famous since 1292 for its glass, the six-island cluster of Murano affords visitors the opportunity to witness resident artisans blowing crystalline creations for free. For demonstrations, look for signs directing to the *fornace*, concentrated around the Colona, Faro, and Navagero *vaporetto* stops. The collection at the **Museo Vetrario** (Glass Museum) ranges from first-century funereal urns to a cartoonish, sea-green octopus presumably designed by Carlo Scarpa in 1930. *(V #DM, LN, 5, 13, 41, 42: Faro from either S. Zaccaria or F Nuove. Museo Vetrario, F. Giustian 8. Open M-Tu and Th-Su Apr.-Oct. 10am-6pm; Nov.-Mar. 10am-5pm. €5.50, students and Rolling Venice €3. Basilica open daily 8am-7pm. Modest dress required. Free.)*

ENTERTAINMENT AND FESTIVALS

Admire Venetian houses and *palazzi* via their original canal pathways. **Gondola** rides are most romantic about 50min. before sunset and most affordable if shared by six people. The rate that a gondolier quotes is negotiable, but expect to pay €80-100 for a 40min. ride. The most price-flexible gondoliers are those standing by themselves rather than those in groups at "taxi-stands."

Teatro Goldoni, Cal. del Teatro, S. Marco 4650/B (☎041 24 02 011), near the Ponte di Rialto, showcases live productions with seasonal themes. The **Mostra Internazionale di Cinema** (Venice International Film Festival), held annually from late August to early September, draws established names and rising stars from around the world. Movies are shown in their original language. (☎041 52 18 878. Tickets sold throughout the city; €20. Some late-night outdoor showings free.) The famed **Biennale di Venezia** (☎041 52 11 898; www.labiennale.org) is a contemporary exhibit of provocative art and architecture. The weekly *A Guest in Venice*, free at hotels and tourist offices or online (www.unospitedivenezia.it), lists current festivals, concerts, and art exhibits.

Banned by the church for several centuries, Venice's famous **Carnevale** was successfully reinstated in the early 1970s. During the 10 days preceding Ash Wednesday, masked figures jam the streets. For **Mardi Gras,** the population doubles; make arrangements well ahead. Venice's second-most colorful festival is the **Festa del Redentore** (3rd weekend in July), originally held to celebrate the end of the 16th-century plague.

NIGHTLIFE

Most residents would rather spend an evening sipping wine in a *piazza* than grinding in a disco. Establishments come and go with some regularity, though student nightlife is consistently concentrated around **Campo Santa Margherita,** in Dorsoduro, while that of tourists centers around the **Lista di Spagna.**

Café Blue, Dorsoduro 3778 (☎041 71 02 27). Grab a glass of wine (from €1.50) and a stool to watch the daytime coffee drinkers turn into a laid-back crowd as night falls. Free Wi-Fi. DJ W, live music in winter F. Open daily 10am-2am. MC/V.

Bistrot ai Do Draghi, Campo S. Margherita 3665 (☎041 52 89 731). The crowd at this tiny bistro is not as fierce as the name ("dragon") implies. Its wine selection has won accolades. Wine from €1.20 per glass. Open daily 7am-2am.

ITALY

Paradiso Perduto, F. della Misericordia, Cannaregio 2540 (☎041 09 94 540). Students flood this unassuming bar, which also serves *cicchetti* (mixed plate €11-15). Live jazz F. Open daily 11am-3pm and 6pm-1am.

Piccolo Mondo, Accademia, Dorsoduro 1056/A (☎041 52 00 371). Facing toward the Accademia, turn right. Ring bell to enter. Disco, hip hop, and vodka with Red Bull (€10) keep a full house at this small, popular *discoteca*, which heats up late behind its heavy, locked doors. Drinks from €7. Open daily 11pm-4am. AmEx/MC/V.

PADUA (PADOVA) ☎049

The oldest institutions in Padua (pop. 210,000) are the ones that still draw visitors: St Anthony's tomb, the looping Prato della Valle, and the university, founded in 1222. The starry blue ceiling of the **Cappella degli Scrovegni,** P. Eremitani 8, overlooks Giotto's epic 38-panel fresco cycle depicting Mary, Jesus, St. Anne, and St. Joachim in *Last Judgment*. Buy tickets at the attached **Musei Civici Eremitani,** whose art collection includes Giotto's beautiful crucifix, which once adorned the Scrovegni Chapel. (☎049 20 10 020; www.cappelladegliscrovegni.it. Entrance to the chapel only through the museum. Museum and chapel open M-F 9am-7pm; Nov.-Mar. chapel also open daily for evening visits 7-10pm. Reservations recommended by phone or website, €1. Museum €10, students €8, combined ticket €12. Evening visits to chapel €8. AmEx/MC/V.) Pilgrims flock to see St. Anthony's jawbone, tongue, and tomb displayed at the **Basilica di Sant'Antonio,** in P. del Santo. (☎049 82 42 811. Modest dress required. Open daily Apr.-Sept. 6:15am-7:45pm; Nov.-Mar. 6:15am-6:45pm. Free.) The university centers around the two interior courtyards of **Palazzo Bò,** as does the student-heavy nightlife. The chair of Galileo is preserved in the **Sala dei Quaranta,** where he once lectured. Next to the **duomo,** in P. Duomo, sits the tiny **Battistero.** Its interior walls are covered in frescoes depicting scenes from the New Testament. (*Duomo* open M-Sa 7:20am-noon and 4-7:30pm, Su 8am-1pm and 4-8:30pm. Free. *Battistero* open daily 10am-6pm. €2.50, students €1.50.)

ITALY

Belludi 37 ❹, whose name is also its address, has huge rooms with modern black and white decor, all with A/C, orthopedic beds, LCD TVs, free Internet, and private bathrooms. (☎049 66 56 33; www.belludi37.it. Breakfast included. Singles €50-70; doubles €90-110. AmEx/MC/V.) For cheap and simple accommodations, head to **Ostello Citta di Padova (HI) ❷,** V. Aleardi 30. (☎049 87 52 219; www.ostellopadova.it. Internet €5 per hr. Lockout 9:30am-4:30pm. Curfew 11:30pm. 6-bed dorms €18. MC/V.) Social Italians crowd the casual **Il Grottino ❷,** V. del Santo 21. (☎049 66 41 76. *Primi* €5-7. *Secondi* €10-18. Open in summer M-Tu and Th-Su 9am-3:30pm and 7pm-12:30am. Call ahead for winter hours. MC/V.) **Fly,** Galleria Tito Livio 4/6, between V. Roma and Riviera Tito Livio, is a cafe by day and a swinging hot spot by night. (☎049 87 52 892. Wine €2-3.50. Mixed drinks €3.50-4.50. Open daily 8am-1am.)

Trains run from P. Stazione to: Bologna (1hr., 32 per day, €6.40); Milan (2hr., 25 per day, €12.20); Venice (30min., 82 per day, €3); Verona (1hr., 44 per day, €5). SITA **buses** (☎82 06 834) leave from P. Boschetti for Venice (45min., 30 per day, €3). The **tourist office** is in the train station. (☎049 87 52 077. Open M-Sa 9am-2pm and 3pm-6:45pm.) To reach the *centro* from the station, take Corso del Popolo south, continuing as it becomes C. Garibaldi. **Postal Code:** 35100.

VERONA ☎045

Hopeless romantics delight in the bright gardens and lifelike sculptures of Verona (pop. 245,000). The setting of Shakespeare's drama Romeo and Juliet,

Verona is a popular spot for star-crossed lovers and lone travelers alike. From the winding river Adige to the city's dizzying towers, Verona offers the perks of a large city while maintaining a reputation for authentic local cuisine, rich wines, and an internationally renowned opera.

TRANSPORTATION AND PRACTICAL INFORMATION. **Trains** (☎89 20 21) go from P. XXV Aprile to: **Bologna** (2hr., 22 per day, €6); **Milan** (2hr., 34 per day, €7); **Trent** (1hr., 25 per day, €4.70); **Venice** (1hr., 41 per day, €8). From the station walk 20min. up **Corso Porta Nuova** or take bus #11, 12, 13, 51, 72, or 73 (Sa-Su take #91, 92, or 93) to Verona's center, the **Arena** in **P. Brà.** The **tourist office** is next to the *piazza* at V. d. Alpini 9. (☎806 86 80. Open M-Sa 9am-7pm, Su 9am-3pm.) Check email at **Internet Train,** V. Roma 17/A. (☎801 33 94. €2.50 per 30min. Open M-F 10am-11pm, Sa-Su 2-8pm. MC/V.) **Postal Code:** 37100.

ACCOMMODATIONS AND FOOD. Reserve hotel rooms ahead of time, especially during opera season (June-Aug.). The **Ostello della Gioventù ❶,** Villa Francescatti, Salita Fontana del Ferro 15, is in a renovated 16th-century villa with a central courtyard, located a ways from the heart of the city. From the station, take bus #73 or night bus #90 to P. Isolo, turn right, and follow the yellow signs uphill. (☎045 59 03 60. Breakfast included; dinner €8. Curfew 11:30pm; extended to 1:30am for opera-goers. Dorms €17; family rooms €19. Cash and traveler's checks only.) To get to the romantic, conveniently located **Bed and Breakfast Anfiteatro ❹,** V. Alberto Mario 5, follow V. Mazzini toward P. Brà until it branches to the right to become V. Alberto Mario. (☎347 24 88 462; www.anfiteatro-bedandbreakfast.com. TV and private bath. Breakfast buffet included. Singles €60-90; doubles €80-130; triples €100-150.) **Osteria al Duomo ❷,** V. Duomo 7/a, offers a small menu but serves authentic, simple cuisine like *tagliatelle* with shrimp and zucchini. (☎045 80 04 505. *Primi* €6.50-7. *Secondi* €7-15. Cover €1. Open M-Sa 11am-3pm and 7-11pm. MC/V.) A **PAM** supermarket is at V. dei Mutilati 3. (Open M-Sa 8am-8:30pm, Su 9am-8pm.)

SIGHTS AND ENTERTAINMENT. The heart of Verona is the first-century **Arena** in P. Brà. (☎045 80 03 204. Open M 1:30-7:30pm, Tu-Su 8:30am-7:30pm. Closes 4:30pm on opera night. Ticket office closes 1hr. before Arena. €4, students €3. Cash only.) From late June to early September, tourists and singers from around the world descend on the Arena for the city's annual **Opera Festival.** (☎045 80 05 151; www.arena.it. Box office open on opera night 10am-9pm, non-performance days 10am-5:45pm. General admission M-Th and Su €17-25, F-Sa €19-27. AmEx/MC/V.) From P. Brà, V. Mazzini leads to the bustling markets and impressive architecture of **Piazza delle Erbe.** The **Giardino Giusti,** V. Giardino Giusti 2, is a 16th-century garden with a thigh-high hedge maze, whose cypress-lined avenue gradually winds up to balconies with stunning views of Verona. (☎045 80 62 611. Open daily Apr.-Sept. 9am-8pm; Oct.-Mar. 9am-7pm. €5.) The della Scala family fortress, **Castelvecchio,** down V. Roma from P. Brà, boasts a courtyard garden and an art collection that includes Pisanello's *Madonna della Quaglia.* (☎045 80 62 611. Open M 1:30-7:30pm, Tu-Su 8:30am-7:30pm. €4, students €3. Cash only.) The balcony at **Casa di Giulietta** (Juliet's House), V. Cappello 23, overlooks a courtyard of couples waiting to rub the statue of Juliet and add their vows to the graffitied walls. The Capulets never lived here, so save your money for another scoop of gelato. (☎045 80 34 303. Open M 1:30-7:30pm, Tu-Su 8:30am-7:30pm. €4, students €3. Courtyard free.)

FRIULI-VENEZIA GIULIA

Bounded by the Veneto to the west and Slovenia to the east is the kaleidoscope that is Friuli-Venezia Giulia. Regional control has changed hands multiple times, resulting in a potpourri of cuisines, styles, and architecture.

TRIESTE (TRIEST) ☎040

After being volleyed among Italian, Austrian, and Slavic powers for hundreds of years, Trieste (pop. 241,000) celebrated its 50th anniversary as an Italian city in 2004. Subtle reminders of Trieste's Eastern European past are evident in its churches and cuisine—not to mention the portraits of smirking Hapsburg rulers found in its museums. The gridded streets of the **Città Nuova,** all lined with majestic Neoclassical palaces, center around the **Canale Grande.** Facing the canal from the south is the blue-domed Serbian Orthodox **Chiesa di San Spiridione.** (Open Tu-Sa 9am-noon and 5-8pm, Su 9am-noon. Modest dress required.) The ornate **Municipio** (Town Hall) is in the **P. dell'Unità d'Italia,** the largest waterfront *piazza* in Italy. P. della Cattedrale overlooks the town center. In the mid-19th century, Archduke Maximilian of Austria commissioned the lavish **Castello Miramare,** where each room is carefully preserved. Legend holds that visitors can still hear the wailing of Carlotta, Maximilian's wife, who went crazy after his murder. Take bus #36 (15min.; €1) to Ostello Tergeste and walk along the water for 15min. (☎040 22 41 43. Open M-Sa 9am-7pm, Su 8:30am-7pm. Ticket office open daily 9am-6:30pm. €4, ages 18-25 €2.)

Centrally located **Nuovo Albergo Centro ❸,** V. Roma 13, has sunny and spacious rooms. (☎040 34 78 790; www.hotelcentrotrieste.it. Breakfast included. Internet €4 per hr. Singles €37, with bath €52; doubles €54/74. 10% *Let's Go* discount. AmEx/MC/V.) On a shaded *piazza*, family-run **Buffet da Siora Rosa ❷,** P. Hortis 3, serves Triestini favorites like goulash and bread *gnocchi*. (☎040 30 14 60. Panini €3-4.50. Cover €1. Reserve ahead for outdoor seating. Open daily 8am-9:30pm. MC/V.) The covered **market** at V. Carducci 36/D has tables piled high with fruits and cheese. (Open M 8am-2pm, Tu-Sa 8am-5pm.) At night, trendsetters frequent **Via Roma Quattro,** whose name is also its address. (☎040 63 46 33. Open M-Sa 7:30am-11pm.) **Trains** leave P. della Libertà 8, down C. Cavour from the quay for Udine (1hr., 32 per day, €6.70) and Venice (2hr., 29 per day, €8.20). The APT **tourist office** is at P. dell'Unità d'Italia 4/E, near the harbor. (☎040 34 78 312. Open daily 9am-7pm.) **Postal Code:** 34100.

PIEDMONT (PIEMONTE)

More than just the source of the Po River, Piedmont has long been a fountainhead of nobility and fine cuisine. The area rose to prominence when the Savoys briefly named Turin capital of their reunited Italy in 1861. Today, European tourists escape Turin's whirlwind pace on the banks of Lake Maggiore, while hikers and skiers conquer Alpine mountaintops.

TURIN (TORINO) ☎011

A century and a half before Turin (pop. 910,000) was selected to host the **2006 Winter Olympics,** it served as the first capital of a unified Italy. Renowned for its chocolate and cafe culture, Turin also lays claim to numerous parks and contemporary art pieces, as well as some of the country's best nightlife offerings, all while avoiding the pollution and crime problems of a big city.

TRANSPORTATION AND PRACTICAL INFORMATION. **Trains** (☎011 66 53 098) run from **Porta Nuova,** in the center of the city, on C. V. Emanuele II to: Genoa (2hr., 1 per hr., €8.75); Milan (2hr., 1 per hr., €8.75); Rome (6-7hr., 26 per day, from €64); Venice (5hr., 20 per day, €21.50). A new **metro line** was recently installed and Turin's transportation system will continue to change in the next few years. Eventually, **Porta Susa** will be the main train station; for now, it is a departure point for trains to Paris via Lyon, FRA (5-6hr., 4 per day). Contact the **Turismo Torino,** P. Castello 161, for **brochures** with art, literary, and walking tours. (☎011 53 51 81; www.turismotorino.org. Open M-Sa 9:30am-7pm, Su 9:30am-3pm.) Unlike in other Italian cities, streets in Turin meet at right angles, so it's relatively easy to navigate. V. Roma is the major north-south thoroughfare. It runs to P. Castello, from which V. Pietro Micca extends southwest to the Olympic Atrium. **Postal Code:** 10100.

ACCOMMODATIONS AND FOOD. Turin's budget options are scattered around the city, though a few cluster near Stazione Porta Nuova. To get to comfortable **Ostello Torino (HI) ❶,** V. Alby 1, take bus #52 (#64 on Su) from Porta Nuova. After crossing the river, get off at the Lanza stop at V. Crimea and follow the "Ostello" signs to C. G. Lanza, before turning left at V. L. Gatti. (☎011 66 02 939; www.ostellotorino.it. Breakfast and linens included. Internet and Wi-Fi €1. Laundry €4. Reception M-Sa 7am-12:30pm and 3-11pm, Su 7-10am and 3-11pm. Lockout 10am-3pm. Curfew 11pm; ask for key if going out. Closed Dec. 21-Jan. 14. Single-sex or co-ed 3- to 8-bed dorms €15; doubles €31-38; triples €51; quads €68. MC/V.) The new **Open 011 ❷,** C. Venezia 11, near the V. Chiesa della Salute stop on bus #11, has a bar, library, restaurant, TV, and Wi-Fi. (☎011 51 62 038; www.openzero11.it. Dorms €16.50; singles €30; doubles €42.)

Spend the day at **Eataly,** via Nizza 224, Turin's new 10,000 sq. ft. culinary amusement park. Wine and beer tastings are just the beginning: classrooms feature cooking classes by famous guest chefs and museum-quality exhibits demonstrate various food preparation techniques. Take bus #1, 18 or 35 to the Biglieri stop, near the Lingotto Expo Center. (☎011 19 50 68 01; www.eataly.it. Reserve ahead for classes and wine tasting. Open daily 10am-10:30pm.) Chocolate has been the city's glory ever since Turin nobles began taking an evening cup of it in 1678. *Gianduiotto* (hazelnut chocolate) turns up in candies and gelato. Sample *bicerin* (Turin's hot coffee-chocolate-cream drink; €4), craved by Nietzsche and Dumas, at **Caffè Cioccolateria al Bicerin ❶,** Piazza della Consolata 5. (☎011 43 69 325. Open M-Tu and Th-F 8:30am-7:30pm, Sa-Su 8:30am-1pm and 3:30-7:30pm.) If Eataly doesn't have everything you need, head to **Porta Palazzo,** P. della Repubblica, perhaps Europe's largest open-air market. (M-F 7:30am-2pm, Sa 7:30am-sunset.)

SIGHTS AND NIGHTLIFE. The **Torino Card** (48hr. €18; 72hr. €20) is the best deal in the city: it provides entrance to more than 140 castles, monuments, museums, and royal residences in Turin, many of which are worth a visit. Once the largest structure in the world built using traditional masonry, the **Mole Antonelliana,** V. Montebello 20, a few blocks east of P. Castello, was originally a synagogue. It's home to the eccentric **Museo Nazionale del Cinema,** which plays hundreds of movie clips. (Museum open Tu-F and Su 9am-8pm, Sa 9am-11pm. €5.20, students €4.20.) The **Holy Shroud of Turin,** said to be Jesus' burial cloth, is housed in the **Cattedrale di San Giovanni,** behind the **Palazzo Reale.** With rare exceptions, a photograph of the shroud is as close as visitors will get. (Open daily 8am-noon and 3-6pm. Free.) The **Museo Egizio,** in the **Palazzo dell'Accademia delle Scienze,** V. dell'Accademia delle Scienze 6, has a world-class collection of Egyptian artifacts. (Open Tu-Su 8:30am-7:30pm. €6.50, ages 18-25 €3.)

I Murazzi is the center of Turin's social scene and consists of two stretches of boardwalk, one between Ponte V. Emanuele I and Ponte Umberto, and another smaller stretch downstream. Most people show up between 7:30 and 9:30pm and spend the next five hours sipping drinks, maneuvering among crowds at the waterfront, or dancing in the clubs. **The Beach,** V. Murazzi del Po 18-22, has the best dance floor in Turin. (☎011 88 87 77. Mixed drinks €6. Open W and Su 5-11pm, Th-Sa 11pm-5am.) **Quadrilatero Romano,** between P. della Repubblica and V. Garibaldi, attracts those who would rather sit, drink, and chat until 4am.

TUSCANY (TOSCANA)

ITALY

Recently, pop culture has glorified Tuscany as a sun-soaked sanctuary of art, nature, and civilization, and this time pop culture has it right. Every town claims a Renaissance master, every highway offers scenic vistas, every celebration culminates in parades, festivals, and galas, and every year brings more tourists to the already beaten Tuscan path.

FLORENCE (FIRENZE) ☎055

Florence (pop. 400,000) is the city of the Renaissance. By the 14th century, it had already become one of the most influential cities in Europe. In the 15th century, Florence overflowed with artistic excellence as the Medici family amassed a peerless collection, supporting masters like Botticelli, Donatello, and Michelangelo. These days, the tourists who flood the streets are captivated by Florence's distinctive character, creative spirit, and timeless beauty.

TRANSPORTATION

Flights: Amerigo Vespucci Airport (FLR; ☎30 61 300), in Peretola. **SITA** runs buses connecting the airport to the train station (€4.70).

Trains: Stazione Santa Maria Novella, across from S. Maria Novella. Trains run 1 per hr. to: **Bologna** (1hr., €4.70-6.80); **Milan** (3hr., €29); **Pisa** (1hr., €5.40; **Rome** (3hr., €32); **Siena** (1hr., €5.90); **Venice** (3hr., €18). For more info, visit www.trenitalia.it.

Buses: SITA, V. S. Caterina da Siena 17 (☎800 37 37 60; www.sita-on-line.it), runs buses to **San Gimignano** (1hr., 14 per day, €5.90) and **Siena** (1hr., 2 per day, €6.50). **LAZZI,** P. Adua 1-4R (☎35 10 61; www.lazzi.it), runs to **Pisa** (1 per hr., €6.30). Both offices are near S. Maria Novella.

Public Transportation: ATAF (☎800 42 45 00; www.ataf.net), outside the train station, runs orange city buses 6am-1am. Tickets 1hr. €1.30; 24hr. €5; 3-day €12. Buy them at any newsstand, *tabaccheria,* or ticket dispenser. You cannot purchase tickets on the bus. Validate your ticket using the orange machine on board or risk a €50 fine.

Taxis: ☎43 90, 47 98, or 42 42. Outside the train station.

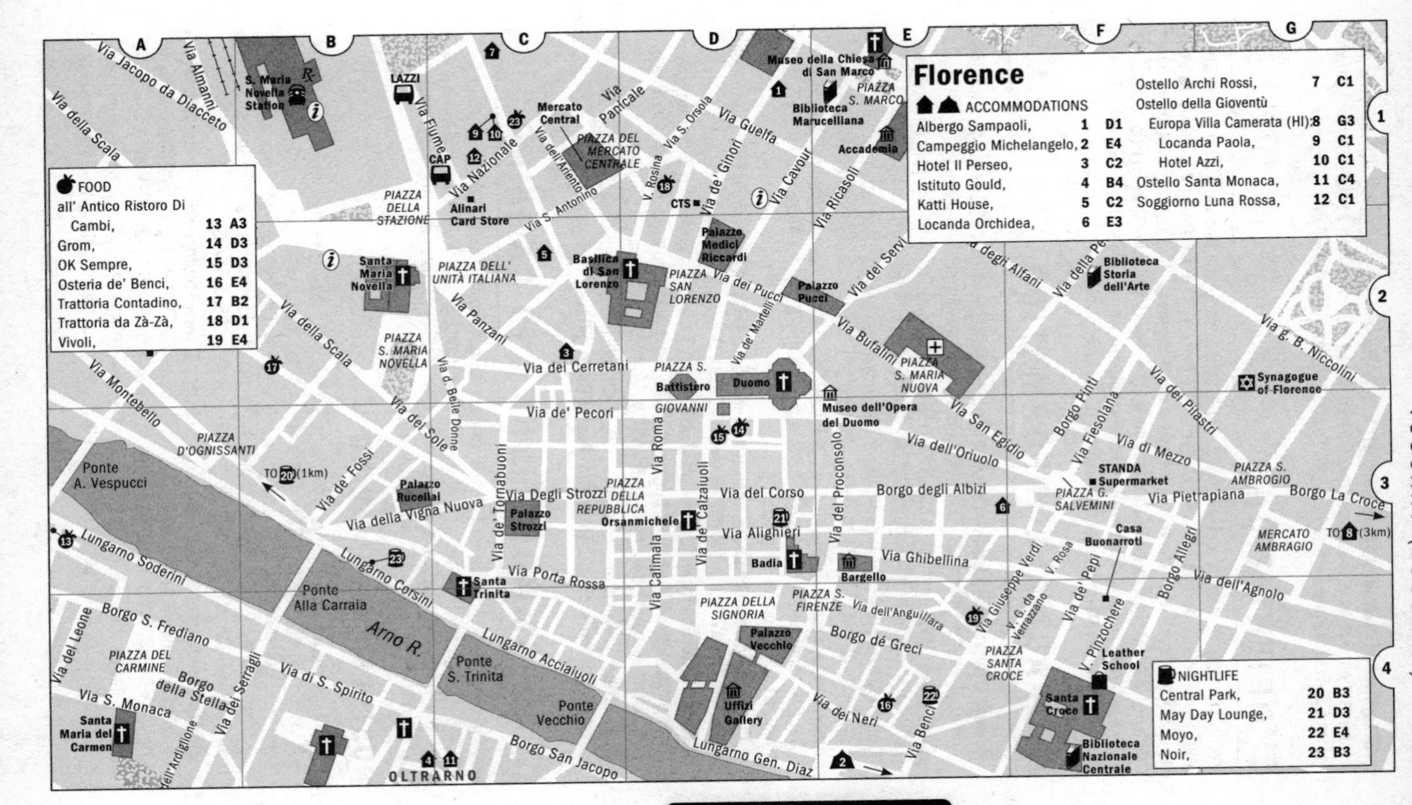
Florence
ACCOMMODATIONS
Albergo Sampaoli, 1 D1
Campeggio Michelangelo, 2 E4
Hotel Il Perseo, 3 C2
Istituto Gould, 4 B4
Katti House, 5 C2
Locanda Orchidea, 6 E3
Ostello Archi Rossi, 7 C1
Ostello della Gioventù
Europa Villa Camerata (HI):8 G3
Locanda Paola, 9 C1
Hotel Azzi, 10 C1
Ostello Santa Monaca, 11 C4
Soggiorno Luna Rossa, 12 C1
FOOD
all' Antico Ristoro Di Cambi, 13 A3
Grom, 14 D3
OK Sempre, 15 D3
Osteria de' Benci, 16 E4
Trattoria Contadino, 17 B2
Trattoria da Zà-Zà, 18 D1
Vivoli, 19 E4
NIGHTLIFE
Central Park, 20 B3
May Day Lounge, 21 D3
Moyo, 22 E4
Noir, 23 B3

Bike/Moped Rental: Alinari Noleggi, V. San Zanobi, 38r (☎28 05 00; www.alinarirental.com). Bikes €14-18 per day. Scooters €32 per day. Open M-Sa 9:30am-1:30pm and 2:45-7:30pm, Su and holidays 10am-1pm and 3-6pm. MC/V.

ORIENTATION

From the train station, a short walk on V. Panzani and a left on V. dei Cerretani leads you to the **duomo,** in the center of Florence. The bustling **Via dei Calzaiuoli** runs south from the *duomo* to **Piazza della Signoria.** V. Roma leads from the *duomo* through **Piazza della Repubblica** to the **Ponte Vecchio** (Old Bridge), which crosses from central Florence to **Oltrarno,** the district south of the **Arno River.** Note that most streets change names unpredictably.

PRACTICAL INFORMATION

Tourist Office: Informazione Turistica, P. della Stazione 4 (☎055 21 22 45). Info on cultural events. Free maps. Open M-Sa 8:30am-7pm, Su 8:30am-2pm.

Consulates: UK, Lungarno Corsini 2 (☎055 28 41 33). Open M-F 9am-1pm and 2-5pm. **US,** Lungarno Amerigo Vespucci 38 (☎055 26 69 51). Open M-F 9am-12:30pm.

Currency Exchange: Local banks have the best rates; beware of independent exchange services with high fees. Most banks are open M-F 8:20am-1:20pm and 2:45-3:45pm.

American Express: V. Dante Alighieri 22R (☎055 50 98). From the *duomo,* walk down V. dei Calzaiuoli and turn left on V. dei Tavolini. Mail held free for AmEx customers, otherwise €1.55. Open M-F 9am-5:30pm.

24hr. Pharmacies: Farmacia Comunale (☎055 28 94 35), at the train station by track #16. **Molteni,** V. dei Calzaiuoli 7R (☎055 28 94 90). AmEx/MC/V.

Internet: Internet Train, V. Guelfa 54/56R, has 15 locations in the city listed on www.internettrain.it. €4.30 per hr., students €3.20. Most branches open M-F 9am-midnight, Sa 10am-8pm, Su noon-9pm. AmEx/MC/V.

Post Office: V. Pellicceria (☎055 27 36 480), off P. della Repubblica. Poste Restante available. Open M-Sa 8:15am-7pm. **Postal Code:** 50100.

ACCOMMODATIONS AND CAMPING

Lodging in Florence doesn't come cheap. **Consorzio ITA,** in the train station by track #16, can find rooms for a €3-8.50 fee. (☎066 99 10 00. Open M-Sa 8am-8pm, Su 10am-7pm.) Make a *prenotazioni* (reservation) ahead, especially if you plan to visit during Easter or summer.

HOSTELS AND CAMPING

Ostello Archi Rossi, V. Faenza 94R (☎055 29 08 04; www.hostelarchirossi.com), near S. Maria Novella station. Rowdy Americans flood this well-known hostel throughout the year. Home-cooked breakfast included. Laundry €6. Free Internet. Lockout 11am-2:30pm. Curfew 2am. Reserve online 1 week ahead, especially in summer. 9-bed dorms €22; 6-bed dorms €24; 4-bed dorms €26; singles €35. MC/V. ❷

Istituto Gould, V. dei Serragli 49 (☎055 21 25 76; www.istitutogould.it), in the Oltrarno. Spotless rooms. Reception M-F 8:45am-1pm and 3-7:30pm, Sa 9am-1:30pm. 4-bed dorms €16-23, with bath €24; singles €36/43; doubles €52/62. MC/V. ❷

Ostello Santa Monaca, V. S. Monaca 6 (☎055 26 83 38; www.ostello.it). Breakfast €2.70-3.80. Laundry €6.50. Internet €3 per hr. June-Sept. 7-night max. stay. Lockout

10am-2pm. Curfew 2am. Reserve ahead. 16- to 22-bed dorms €17; 10-bed dorms €17.50; 8-bed dorms €18; 6-bed dorms €18.50; 4-bed dorms €19. AmEx/MC/V. ❷

Ostello della Gioventù Europa Villa Camerata (HI), V. Augusto Righi 2-4 (☎055 60 14 51). Despite its large size, much privacy can be found in this beautiful but remote villa. Arcade, bar, and TV with English-language movies. Breakfast included. Laundry €5.20. Lockout 10am-2pm. Curfew midnight. 3-night max. stay. Dorms €21.50; 4-bed rooms €20-22; 3-bed €23-25; 2-bed €30-32.50. HI members discount €3.50. MC/V. ❷

Campeggio Michelangelo, V. Michelangelo 80 (☎055 68 11 977; www.ecvacanze.it), beneath P. Michelangelo. Bus #13 from the bus station (15min.; last bus 11:25pm). Reception 7am-11pm. €11 per person, €16 per tent site. MC/V; min. €100. ❶

HOTELS

Locanda Orchidea, Borgo degli Albizi 11 (☎055 24 80 346; hotelorchidea@yahoo.it). Dante's wife was born in this 12th-century *palazzo*. Carefully decorated rooms with marble floors; some open onto a garden. Singles €55; doubles €75; triples with shower €100; quads with shower €120. Prices drop €20-35 in low-season. Cash only. ❹

Soggiorno Luna Rossa, V. Nazionale 7 (☎055 23 02 185). 3rd fl. Airy rooms have fans, TVs, and colorful stained-glass windows. Small shared baths. Breakfast included. Dorms €22. Singles €35; doubles €85; triples €100; quads €140. Cash only. ❷

Katti House/Soggiorno Annamaria, V. Faenza 21/24 (☎055 21 34 10). Lovingly kept lodgings with 400-year-old antiques and an attentive staff. Large, recently renovated rooms with A/C, bath, and TV. Singles €40-50; doubles €50-60; triples €60-75. Prices drop significantly Nov.-Mar. Call directly for best rates. Cash only. ❹

Albergo Sampaoli, V. S. Gallo 14 (☎055 28 48 34; www.hotelsampaoli.it). Helpful staff and a large common area with fridge access. All rooms have fans, Wi-Fi, and DVDs. Singles €30-60, with bath €35-74; doubles €44-55/45-84; triples €75-120; quads €90-140. Extra bed €25. 5% discount with advance reservation. MC/V. ❹

Hotel Il Perseo, V. Cerretani 1 (☎055 21 25 04; www.hotelperseo.it). Spotless rooms with satellite TVs and free Wi-Fi. Breakfast included. 2-night min. stay. Singles €110; doubles €110-125; triples €180; quads €210; suite €250. AmEx/MC/V. ❺

VIA FAENZA 56

Hotel Azzi (☎055 21 38 06; www.hotelazzi.com) has large rooms and a terrace. Styled as an artists' inn. Breakfast included. Dorms €25-35; singles €50-100; doubles €80-130; triples €105-165. Extra bed €25. AmEx/MC/V. ❹

Locanda Paola (☎055 21 36 82) has doubles with views of the surrounding hills. Breakfast included. Internet. Flexible 2am curfew. Dorms €33. MC/V. ❸

FOOD

Florentine specialties include *bruschetta* (grilled bread soaked in oil and garlic and topped with tomatoes, basil, and anchovy or liver paste) and *bistecca alla Fiorentina* (thick sirloin). The best local cheese is *pecorino*, made from sheep's milk. A liter of house wine usually costs €3.50-6 in a *trattoria*, but stores sell bottles of chianti for as little as €2.50. The local dessert is *cantuccini di prato* (almond cookies) dipped in *vinsanto* (a rich dessert wine). Florence's own Buontalenti family supposedly invented gelato; extensive sampling is a must. For lunch, visit a *rosticceria gastronomia*, peruse the city's pushcarts, or pick up fresh produce and meats at the **Mercato Centrale,** between V. Nazionale and S. Lorenzo. (Open June-Sept. M-Sa 7:30am-2pm; Oct.-May M-F 7am-2pm, Sa 7am-2pm and 4-8pm.) To get to **STANDA** supermarket, V. Pietrapiana 1R, turn

ITALY

right on V. del Proconsolo, take the first left on Borgo degli Albizi, and continue straight through P. G. Salvemini. (Open M-Sa 8am-9pm, Su 9am-9pm. MC/V.)

RESTAURANTS

Osteria de' Benci, V. de' Benci 13R (☎055 23 44 923), on the corner of V. dei Neri. Join locals for classics like *carpaccio* (thinly sliced beef; €15). *Primi* €9. *Secondi* €10-15. Cover €3.30. Open M-Sa 1-2:45pm and 7:30-11:45pm. AmEx/MC/V. ❹

all'Antico Ristoro Di' Cambi, V. S. Onofrio 1R (☎055 21 71 34). Near Ponte Vespucci. Prosciutto hangs from the restored 5th-century ceiling. Choose from over 100 types of wine (€10-300 per bottle). Knowledgeable waitstaff can help pick the best wine for each dish. The *sorbetto limone* (€4) is an ideal finish. *Primi* €6-8. *Secondi* €7-18. Cover €1. Open M-Sa noon-10:30pm. Closed 2 weeks in mid-Aug. AmEx/MC/V. ❹

Mamma Toscana, V. S. Antonino 34R (☎055 28 22 496). Try specialties like Risotto Michelangelo (buttery rice with tender shrimp surrounded by fresh mussels; €6) while the award-winning head chef encourages "Mangia, Mangia!" *Primi* €4-8. *Secondi* €6-10. Pizza €5-8. Cover 10%. Open daily noon-3:30pm and 6-10:30pm. AmEx/MC/V. ❷

Trattoria Contadino, V. Palazzuolo 71R (☎055 23 82 673). Filling, homestyle, fixed-price menu (€10) includes *primo, secondo,* side dish, bread, water, and 0.25L of wine. Open M-F noon-9:40pm. AmEx/MC/V. ❷

Trattoria Zà-Zà, P. del Mercato Centrale 26R (☎055 21 54 11). Brick archways inside, lively patio outside. Specializes in traditional Tuscan grilled meats. *Primi* €8-11. *Secondi* €10-22. Cover €2. Reserve ahead. Open daily 11am-11pm. AmEx/MC/V. ❸

Trattoria Anita, V. del Parlascio 2R (☎055 21 86 98), behind Palazzo Vecchio. American tourists pile into this casual Tuscan restaurant for the reasonable prices and authenticity of the food. Cover €1. *Primi* €5.50-7. *Secondi* €7-14. Generous lunch menu €7. Open M-Sa noon-2:30pm and 7-10pm. AmEx/MC/V. ❷

Dante, P. Nazario Sauro 12R (☎055 21 92 19; www.trattoria-dante.com). Artful plate settings and courteous service await in this local favorite. Choose from an extensive selection of pizza (€6.50-10) or treat yourself to a full-course meal. *Primi* €7-18. *Secondi* €16-28. Open M-Tu and Th-Su noon-3pm and 7-10:30pm. MC/V. ❹

GELATERIE

Florence's *gelaterie* get crowded. To avoid making salespeople cranky, follow protocol when ordering: first, pay at the register for the size you request, then—receipt in hand—choose a flavor. Most *gelaterie* also serve *granite*, flavored ices that are easier on the waistline but just as tasty.

Grom, V. del Campanile (☎055 21 61 58). The kind of gelato you'll be talking about in 50 years. As fresh as it gets. Sublimely balanced texture. Cups from €2. Open daily Apr.-Sept. 10:30am-midnight; Oct.-Mar. 10:30am-11pm.

Lorenzo il Magnifico, V. Sant'Antonino 37R (☎055 28 78 12). Choose from 60 homemade flavors ranging from fig sorbet to dark chili pepper chocolate and dine in an alcove adorned with plastic fruit and wooden ponies. €1.50-4. Open daily noon-11pm.

Vivoli, V. Isole della Stinche 7 (☎055 29 23 34), behind the Bargello. A renowned *gelateria* and long-time contender for the distinction of the best ice cream in Florence. Cups from €1.80. Open Tu-Sa 7:30am-1am, Su 9:30am-1am.

SIGHTS

For a list of museum openings, check out www.firenzeturismo.it. For museum reservations, call **Firenze Musei** (☎055 29 48 83; www.firenzemusei.it). There are **no student discounts** at museums and admission can be expensive. Choose destinations carefully and plan to spend a few hours at each landmark.

PIAZZA DEL DUOMO

DUOMO (CATTEDRALE DI SANTA MARIA DEL FIORE). In 1296, the city fathers commissioned Arnolfo di Cambio to erect a cathedral so magnificent that it would be "impossible to make it either better or more beautiful with the industry and power of man." Di Cambio succeeded, designing a massive nave with the confidence that by the time it was completed (1418), technology would have advanced enough to provide a solution to erect a dome. **Filippo Brunelleschi** was called in for this task: after studying long-neglected classical methods, he came up with his double-shelled, interlocking-brick construction. The *duomo* claims the world's third longest nave, trailing only St. Peter's in Rome and St. Paul's in London. *(Open M-W and F 10am-5pm, Th 10am-4pm, Sa 10am-4:45pm, Su 1:30-4:45pm. Mass daily 7am, 12:30, 5-7pm. Free.)* Climb the 463 steps inside the dome to **Michelangelo's lantern,** which offers an expansive view of the city from the 100m high external gallery. *(Open M-F 8:30am-7pm, Sa 8:30am-5:40pm. €6.)* The climb up the 82m **campanile** next to the *duomo*, also called "Giotto's Tower," reveals views of the *duomo*, the city, and the **battistero** (baptistry), whose bronze doors, forged by Ghiberti, are known as the **Gates of Paradise.** *(Campanile open daily 8:30am-7:30pm. €6. Baptistry open M-Sa noon-7pm, Su 8:30am-2pm. €3.)* Most of the *duomo*'s art resides behind the cathedral in the **Museo dell'Opera del Duomo.** Up the first flight of stairs is a late *Pietà* by Michelangelo. *(P. del Duomo 9, behind the duomo. ☎055 23 02 885. Open M-Sa 9am-6:50pm, Su 9am-1pm. €6.)*

ORSANMICHELE. Built in 1337 as a granary, the Orsanmichele became a church after a fire convinced officials to move grain operations outside the city. The ancient grain chutes are still visible outside. Within, tenacious visitors will discover Ghiberti's *St. John the Baptist* and *St. Stephen*, Donatello's *St. Peter and St. Mark*, and Giambologna's *St. Luke*. *(V. Arte della Lana, between the duomo and P. della Signoria. Open Tu-Su 10am-5pm. Free.)*

PIAZZA DELLA SIGNORIA AND ENVIRONS

From P. del Duomo, **Via dei Calzaiuoli,** one of the city's oldest streets, runs south past crowds, street vendors, *gelaterie*, and chic shops to **Piazza della Signoria,** a 13th-century *piazza* bordered by the Palazzo Vecchio and the Uffizi. With the construction of the Palazzo Vecchio in 1299, the square became Florence's civic and political center. In 1497, religious zealot Girolamo Savonarola lit the **Bonfire of the Vanities** here, barbecuing some of Florence's best art. Today P. della Signoria fills daily with photo-snapping tourists who later return for drinks and dessert in its upscale cafes. Monumental sculptures stand in front of the *palazzo* and inside the 14th-century **Loggia dei Lanzi.** *(Free.)*

THE UFFIZI. Giorgio Vasari designed this palace in 1554 for the offices *(uffizi)* of Duke Cosimo's administration; today, the gallery holds one of the world's finest art collections. Botticelli, Caravaggio, Cimabue, Fra Angelico, della Francesca, Giotto, Michelangelo, Raphael, Titian, Leonardo, even Dürer, Rembrandt, Rubens—you name it, it's here. Be sure to visit the **Cabinet of Drawings and Prints.** A few rooms are usually closed each day, and some works may be on loan. *(From P. B. S. Giovanni, take V. Roma past P. della Repubblica, where the street turns into V. Calimala. Continue until V. Vaccereccia and turn left. ☎055 23 88 651. Open Tu-Su 8:15am-6:35pm. €10; EU citizens 18-25 €5. Reserve ahead for €4 fee. Audio tour €4.70.)*

PALAZZO VECCHIO. Arnolfo del Cambio designed this fortress-like *palazzo* in the late 13th century to be the seat of government. It included apartments which functioned as living quarters for members of the city council while they served two-month terms. After the *palazzo* became the Medici's home in 1470, Michelozzo decorated the courtyard. The **Monumental Apartments,** which house the *palazzo*'s extensive art collections, are now an art and history museum. The worthwhile **Activities Tour** includes the "Secret Routes," which reveal hidden stairwells and chambers tucked behind exquisite oil paintings. The ceiling of the **Salone del Cinquecento,** where the Grand Council of the Republic met, is so elaborately decorated that the walls can hardly support its weight. The tiny **Studio di Francesco I** is a treasure trove of Mannerist art. *(☎055 27 68 224. Open M-W and F-Sa 9am-7pm, Su 9am-1pm. Palazzo and Monumental Apartments each €6, ages 18-25 €4.50. Activities tour €8/5.50. Courtyard free. Reserve ahead for tours.)*

THE BARGELLO AND ENVIRONS

BARGELLO. The heart of medieval Florence is in this 13th-century fortress, once the residence of the chief magistrate and later a brutal prison with public executions in its courtyard. It was restored in the 19th century and now houses the largely untouristed **Museo Nazionale.** Donatello's bronze *David*, the first free-standing nude since antiquity, stands opposite the two bronze panels of the *Sacrifice of Isaac*, submitted by Ghiberti and Brunelleschi in the baptistry door competition. Michelangelo's early works, including *Bacchus*, *Brutus*, and *Apollo*, are on the ground floor. *(V. del Proconsolo 4, between the duomo and P. della Signoria. ☎055 23 88 606. Open daily 8:15am-6pm. Closed 2nd and 4th M of each month. €7.)*

ITALY

BADIA. The site of medieval Florence's richest monastery, the Badia church is now buried in the interior of a residential block. Filippino Lippi's *Apparition of the Virgin to St. Bernard*, one of the most famous paintings of the 15th century, hangs in eerie gloom to the left of the church. Be sure to glance up at the intricately carved dark wood ceiling. Some say Dante may have first glimpsed his beloved Beatrice here. Visitors are asked to walk silently among the prostrate, white-robed worshippers. *(Entrance on V. Dante Alighieri, off V. Proconsolo. ☎055 26 44 02. Open to tourists M 3-6pm, but visitors can walk through at any time.)*

PIAZZA DELLA REPUBBLICA AND FARTHER WEST

The largest open space in Florence, the P. della Repubblica teems with crowds, overpriced cafes, restaurants, and *gelaterie*. In 1890, it replaced the Mercato Vecchio as the site of the city market, but has since traded stalls for more fashionable vendors. The inscription "*antico centro della città, da secolare squalore, a vita nuova restituito*" ("ancient center of the city, squalid for centuries, restored to new life") makes a derogatory reference to the *piazza*'s location in the old Jewish ghetto. The area around Mercato Nuovo and V. Tornabuoni was Florence's financial capital in the 1400s. Now it's residential, but still touristy.

CHIESA DI SANTA MARIA NOVELLA. The chapels of the wealthiest 13th- and 14th-century merchants are part of this church. Santa Maria Novella was home to an order of Dominicans, or *Domini canes* (Hounds of the Lord), who took a bite out of sin and corruption. The marble facade of the *chiesa* is considered one of the great masterpieces of early Renaissance architecture. The Medicis commissioned Vasari to paint new frescoes over the 13th-century ones on the walls, but the painter spared Masaccio's **Trinity,** the first painting to use geometric perspective. *(Open M-Th 9am-5pm, F-Su 1-5pm. €2.70.)*

CHIESA DI SANTA TRINITÀ. Hoping to spend eternity in elite company, the most fashionable *palazzo* owners commissioned family chapels in this church. The facade, designed by Bernardo Buontalenti in the 16th century, is almost Baroque in its elaborate ornamentation. Scenes from Ghirlandaio's *Life of St.*

Francis decorate the **Sassetti Chapel** in the right arm of the transept. The famous altarpiece, Ghirlandaio's *Adoration of the Shepherds*, resides in the Uffizi—this one is a copy. *(In P. S. Trinità. Open M-Sa 7am-noon and 4-7pm, Su 7-noon. Free.)*

SAN LORENZO AND FARTHER NORTH

ACCADEMIA. It doesn't matter how many pictures of him you've seen—when you come around the corner to see Michelangelo's triumphant **David**, you will be blown away. The statue's base was struck by lightning in 1512, the figure was damaged by anti-Medici riots in 1527, and David's left wrist was broken by a stone, after which he was moved here from P. della Signoria in 1873. In the hallway leading to *David* are Michelangelo's four *Slaves* and a *Pietà*. The master purposely left these statues unfinished, staying true to his theory of "releasing" figures from the living stone. Botticelli's Madonna paintings are also worth seeing. *(V. Ricasoli 60, between the churches of S. Marco and S. S. Annunziata. ☎ 055 23 88 609. Open Tu-Su 8:15am-6:50pm. Reserve ahead €4 extra. May-Sept. €10; Oct.-Apr. €7.)*

BASILICA DI SAN LORENZO. Because the Medicis lent the funds to build this church, they retained artistic control over its construction and decided to add Cosimo dei Medici's grave to Brunelleschi's spacious basilica. They cunningly placed it in front of the high altar to make the entire church his personal mausoleum. Michelangelo began the exterior, but, disgusted by Florentine politics, he abandoned the project, leaving the plain facade. *(Open M-Sa 10am-5pm, Mar.-Oct. also Su 1:30-5pm. €2.50.)* While the **Cappelle dei Medici** (Medici Chapels) offer a rare glimpse of the Baroque in Florence, the **Cappella dei Principi** (Princes' Chapel) emulates the baptistry in P. del Duomo. Michelangelo sculpted the **Sacrestia Nuova** (New Sacristy) to hold two Medici tombs. On the tomb of Lorenzo he placed the female Night and the muscular male Day; on Giuliano's sit the more androgynous Dawn and Dusk. *(Walk around to the back entrance in P. Madonna degli Aldobrandini. Open daily 8:15am-5pm. Closed 1st and 3rd M and 2nd and 4th Su. €6.)*

MUSEO DELLA CHIESA DI SAN MARCO. Remarkable works by Fra Angelico adorn this museum, once part of a convent complex and one of the most peaceful places in Florence. A large room to the right of the courtyard houses some of the painter's major works, including the church's altarpiece. The second floor displays Angelico's *Annunciation*. Every cell in the convent has its own Angelico fresco. To the right of the stairwell is Michelozzo's library, modeled on Michelangelo's work in S. Lorenzo. In cells 17 and 22, underground artwork, excavated from the medieval period, peeks through a glass floor. Near the exit, the two rooms of the **Museo di Firenze Antica** show Florence's ancient roots. Be sure to peek into the church itself, next to the museum, to admire the elaborate altar and vaulted ceiling. *(Enter at P.S. Marco 3. Open M-F 8:15am-1:50pm, Sa 8:15am-6:50pm, Su 8:15am-7pm. Closed 2nd and 4th M and 1st and 3rd Su of each month. €4.)*

PIAZZA SANTA CROCE AND ENVIRONS

CHIESA DI SANTA CROCE. The Franciscans built this church as far as possible from their Dominican rivals at S. Maria Novella. Ironically, the ascetic Franciscans produced what is arguably the most splendid church in the city. Luminaries buried here include Galileo, Machiavelli, Michelangelo (whose tomb was designed by Vasari), and humanist Leonardo Bruni. Check out Donatello's *Crucifix* (so irksome to Brunelleschi) in the Vernio Chapel, and his gilded *Annunciation*, by Bruni's tomb. At the end of the cloister next to the church is the perfectly proportioned **Cappella Pazzi**, whose decorations include Luca della Robbia's *tondi* of the apostles and Brunelleschi's moldings of the evangelists. *(Open M-Sa 9:30am-5:30pm, Su 1-5:30pm. €5.)*

ITALY

SYNAGOGUE OF FLORENCE. This synagogue, also known as the **Museo del Tempio Israelitico,** is resplendent with arches and Sephardic domes. David Levi, a wealthy Florentine Jewish businessman, donated his fortune in 1870 to build "a monumental temple worthy of Florence," recognizing the Jews' new freedom to live and worship outside the old Jewish ghetto. *(V. Farini 4, at V. Pilastri. ☎055 24 52 52. Free tours every hr.; reserve ahead. Open M-Th and Su 10am-6pm, F 10am-2pm. €4.)*

THE OLTRARNO

Historically disdained by downtown Florentines, the far side of the Arno remains a lively and unpretentious quarter, filled with students and relatively few tourists. Head back on Ponte S. Trinità after dallying in P. San Spirito.

PALAZZO PITTI. Luca Pitti, a 15th-century banker, built his *palazzo* east of P. S. Spirito against the Boboli hill. The Medicis acquired the *palazzo* in 1550 and expanded it in every way possible. Today, it houses six museums, including the **Galleria Palatina.** Florence's most important art collection after the Uffizi, the gallery has works by Caravaggio, Raphael, Rubens, and Titian. Other museums display Medici family costumes, porcelain, and **Royal Apartments**—reminders of the time when the *palazzo* was the living quarters of the royal House of Savoy. The **Galleria d'Arte Moderna** hides one of Italian art history's big surprises, the proto-Impressionist works of the Macchiaioli group. *(Open Tu-Su 8:15am-6:50pm. Ticket for Galleria Palatina, Royal Apartments, and Galleria d'Arte Moderna €8.50.)*

SAN MINIATO AL MONTE AND ENVIRONS

SAN MINIATO AL MONTE. An inlaid marble facade and 13th-century mosaics provide a prelude to the floor inside, patterned with doves, lions, and astrological signs. Visit at 5:40pm to hear the monks chant. *(Take bus #13 from the station or climb the stairs from Piazzale Michelangelo. ☎055 23 42 731. Open daily Mar.-Nov. 8am-7pm; Dec.-Feb. 8am-1pm and 2:30-6pm. Free.)*

PIAZZALE MICHELANGELO. A visit to Piazzale Michelangelo is a must. At sunset, waning light casts a warm glow over the city. Views from here are even better (and certainly cheaper) than those from the top of the *duomo.* Make the challenging uphill trek at around 8:30pm during the summer to arrive at the *piazzale* in time for sunset. Unfortunately, the *piazzale* doubles as a large parking lot, and is home to hordes of tour buses during summer days. *(Cross the Ponte Vecchio to the Oltrarno and turn left, walk through the piazza, and turn right up V. de Bardi. Follow it uphill as it becomes V. del Monte alle Croci. A staircase to the left heads to the piazzale.)*

ENTERTAINMENT

May starts the summer music festival season with the classical **Maggio Musicale.** The **Festa del Grillo** (Festival of the Cricket) is held on the first Sunday after Ascension Day, when crickets in tiny wooden cages are sold in the Cascine park to be released into the grass—Florentines believe the song of a cricket is good luck. In June, the *quartieri* of Florence turn out in costume to play their own medieval version of football, known as **calcio storico,** in which two teams face off over a wooden ball in one of the city's *piazze.* Their games so often end in riots that the festival was actually cancelled in 2007. The **Festival of San Giovanni Battista,** on June 24, features a tremendous fireworks display visible all along the Arno. The **Estate Fiesolana** (June-Aug.) fills the Roman theater in nearby Fiesole with concerts, opera, theater, ballet, and film events (☎800 41 42 40; www.estatefiesolana.it). In summer, the **Europa dei Sensi** program hosts **Rime Rampanti** (☎348 58 04 812; www.firenzenotte.

it), nightly cultural shows with music, poetry, and food from a chosen European country.

SHOPPING

For both the budget shopper and the big spender who's looking to make the splurge of a lifetime, Florence offers too many options and temptations. *Saldi* (sales) take over in January and July, even in V. Tornabuoni's swanky boutiques. The city's artisanal traditions thrive at its open markets. **San Lorenzo,** the largest, cheapest, and most touristed, sprawls for several blocks around P. S. Lorenzo. In front of the leather shops, vendors sell all kinds of goods—clothes, food, and toys. High prices are rare, but quality and honesty can be too. (Open daily 9am-twilight.) For everything from pot-holders to parakeets, shop at the market in **Parco delle Cascine,** which begins four bridges west of the Ponte Vecchio at P. V. Veneto and stretches along the Arno River each Tuesday morning. *Carta fiorentina*, paper covered in intricate floral designs, adorns books, journals, and paper goods, at **Alinari,** L. Alinari 15. (☎055 23 951. Open M 2:30-6:30pm, Tu-F 9am-1pm and 2:30-6:30pm, Sa 9am-1pm and 3-7pm. Closed 2 weeks in Aug. AmEx/MC/V.) Florentine **leatherwork** is renowned for its quality. Some of the best leather artisans in the city work around P. S. Croce and V. Porta S. Maria.

NIGHTLIFE

For reliable info, consult the city's entertainment monthly, *Firenze Spettacolo* (€2). **Piazza Santo Spirito** has live music in summer. When going to bars or clubs that are far from the *centro*, keep in mind that the last bus may leave before the fun winds down, and taxis are rare in the area with the most popular discos.

Moyo, V. dei Banchi 23R (☎055 24 79 738), near P. Santa Croce. A thriving lunch spot by day, hip bar by night, always crowded with young Italians. Lunch options from €7. Evening cocktails include free, self-serve snacks. Open daily 8am-3am. AmEx/MC/V.

Noir, Lungarno Corsini 12R (☎055 21 07 51). This bar mixes mojitos (€7) and other refreshing cocktails for locals. After paying, take your drink outside by the Arno. Best for smaller groups looking for a hip but tame evening. Beer from €3.50. Mixed drinks €6-7. Open daily 11am-1am. Closed 2 weeks in Aug. MC/V.

Central Park, in Parco della Cascinè (☎055 35 35 05). Open-air dance floor pulses with hip-hop, reggae,

WORD UP

You bought the bilingual dictionary, and you've probably got the Italian curse words down, but to *really* get in with locals, you've got to know some Tuscan slang. From picking up *una bella Italiana* in a club to respectfully telling street peddlers to scram, local lingo escapes translation and goes beyond clichéd idioms. Here are the top ten you'll need to fit in under the Tuscan sun.

1. **Ganzo/a!** (adj.) Cool. She/He is cool! *Lei é ganza!*
2. **Bono** (adj.) Hot. Zack/Kelly is hot! *Zack/Kelly é bono/a!*
3. **M'attizza** (v.) I'm hot for X. I'm hot for Lisa! *Lisa m'attizza.*
4. **Mannaggia!** (int.) Oh no. Oh no! I lost my *Let's Go!* Now I can't find that popular restaurant, The Max! *Mannaggia! Ho perso il mio* Let's Go! *Ora non posso vedere il ristorante popolare, The Max!*
5. **Secchione** (n.) Nerd. Screech is a nerd. *Screech è un secchione.*
6. **Accipicchia!** (int.) Wow. Wow, check out that dragon! *Accipicchia, che dragone!*
7. **Incasinato** (adj.) Screwed. I'm screwed. *Io sono incasinato(a).*
8. **Donnaiolo** (n.) Playboy. Slater is a playboy. *Slater è un donnaiolo.*
9. **Spettagolare** (v.) Gossip. Let's gossip about Skinner! *Spettagoliamo su Skinner!*
10. **Cicciobomba** (n.) Fatso. Jessie is a Fatso. *Jessie è un cicciobomba.*

and rock. Favored by Florentines, foreign teens, and college students. Mixed drinks €11; beer €9. Cover €20; no cover for foreign students before 1am. Open in summer Tu-Su 8pm-3am. AmEx/MC/V.

May Day Lounge, V. Dante Alighieri 16R (☎055 23 81 29). Artists display their work on the walls of this eclectic lounge that fills with offbeat Italians. Beer €3. Mixed drinks from €5. Happy hour 8-10pm. Open M-Sa 8pm-2am. Closed most of Aug. Cash only.

SIENA ☎0577

Siena's (pop. 49,000) vibrant character and local energy make it a distinctly Tuscan city. Locals are fiercely proud of their town's history, which dates back to the 13th century when the first Sienese began to craft a sophisticated metropolis, rich in wealth and culture. These days, the Sienese celebrate their heritage with festivals like the semi-annual *Palio*, a riotous display of pageantry in which jockeys race bareback horses around the central square.

TRANSPORTATION AND PRACTICAL INFORMATION. **Trains** run from P. Rosselli to Florence (1hr., 16 per day, €5.90) and Rome (3hr., 20 per day, €12.60) via Grosseto. TRA-IN/SITA **buses** (☎0577 20 42 46) run from P. Gramsci and the train station to Florence (1 per hr., €6.70) and San Gimignano (31 per day, €5.20). Across from the train station, take TRA-IN buses #3, 4, 7-10, 17, or 77 (€0.95) to Piazza del Sale or Piazza Gramsci, then follow signs to **Piazza del Campo,** Siena's *centro storico*, also known as **Il Campo.** The central **tourist office** is at P. del Campo 56. (☎0577 28 05 51; www.terresiena.it. Open mid-Mar. to mid-Nov. daily 9:30am-1pm and 2:30-6pm; mid-Nov. to mid-Mar. M-Sa 8:30am-1pm and 3-7pm, Su 9am-1pm.) Check email at **Cafe Internet,** Galleria Cecco Angiolieri 16. (€1.80 per hr. Open M-Sa 8:30am-11pm, Su 9am-11pm.) **Postal Code:** 53100.

ITALY

ACCOMMODATIONS AND FOOD. Finding a room in Siena can be difficult in July and August. Reserve at least a month ahead for *Il Palio*. **Prenotazioni Alberghi e Ristoranti,** in P. S. Domenico, finds rooms for a €2 fee. (☎0577 94 08 09. Open M-Sa 9am-7pm, Su 9am-noon.) **Casa Laura ❸,** V. Roma 3, is in the less touristy university area; sacrifice immediate access to downtown Siena for spacious, well-priced rooms. Ring the doorbell, labeled "Bencini Valentini." (☎0577 22 60 61. Kitchen available. Singles €35-40; doubles €65-67; triples €70; quads €75. MC/V.) Bus #10 and 15 from P. Gramsci stop at the spotless **Ostello della Gioventù "Guidoriccio" (HI) ❶,** V. Fiorentina 89, in Località Lo Stellino. (☎0577 52 212. Curfew midnight. Dorms €14.45. Cash only.)

Sienese bakeries prepare *panforte*, a confection of honey, almonds, and citron, sold at Bar/Pasticceria **Nannini ❶,** V. Banchi di Sopra 22-24, the oldest pasticceria in Siena. (€2.10 per 100g. Open M-Th 7:30am-9pm, F-Sa 7:30am-10pm, Su 8am-9pm.) **Osteria La Chiacchera ❷,** Costa di S. Antonio 4, has delicious pasta. (☎0577 28 06 31. *Primi* €5-6. *Secondi* €8-12. Open M and W-Su noon-3:30pm and 7pm-midnight. AmEx/MC/V.) A **CONAD** supermarket is in P. Matteoti. (Open M-Sa 8:30am-8:30pm, Su 9am-1pm and 4-8pm.)

SIGHTS AND ENTERTAINMENT. Siena radiates from **Piazza del Campo (Il Campo),** a shell-shaped brick square designed for civic events. At the top of the slope by Il Campo is the **Fonte Gaia,** a marble fountain that has refreshed Siena since the 1300s. At the bottom, the **Torre del Mangia** bell tower looms over the graceful **Palazzo Pubblico.** Inside the *palazzo* is the **Museo Civico,** best appreciated for its late medieval and early Renaissance collection of Sienese-style paintings. (*Palazzo*, museum, and tower open daily Mar.-Oct. 10am-6:15pm; Nov.-Feb. 10am-5:30pm. Museum €7, students €4.50. Tower €6. Combo with entrance to the *duomo*, the Museum, the Facciatone, the Crypt, the Baptistery, and the Oratory €10.) From the *palazzo* facing Il Campo, take the left stairs and cross V. di Città to get to Siena's hilltop **duomo.** To prevent the apse from being left hanging in mid-air, the lavish **baptistry** was constructed below. (Open daily Mar.-Sept. 9:30am-8pm; first two weeks in Mar. and all of Oct. 9:30am-7:30pm; Nov.-Feb. 10am-5pm. €3-5.50.) The decorated underground rooms of the **cripta** (crypt) were used by pilgrims about to enter the *duomo*. (Check hours at the *duomo*. €6, students €5.) The **Museo dell'Opera della Metropolitana,** to the right of the *duomo*, houses its overflow art. (Open daily Mar.-Sept. 9:30am-7:30pm; Oct. 9:30am-7pm; Nov.-Feb. 10am-4:30pm. €6.) Every year on July 2 and August 16, horses speed around the edge of the Campo as part of **Il Palio.** Arrive three days early to watch the trial runs and to pick a favorite *contrada* (team).

LUCCA ☎0583

Lucca (LOO-ka; pop. 9000) dabbles successfully in every area of tourist enjoyment: bikers rattle along the tree-lined promenade atop the town's medieval walls, fashionistas shop at trendy boutiques, and art lovers admire the architecture of the *centro*. No tour of the city is complete without seeing the perfectly intact city walls, or **baluardi** (battlements). The **Duomo di San Martino** was begun in the 6th century and finished in the 15th century. Nearby, the **Museo della Cattedrale** houses religious objects from the *duomo*. (*Duomo* open M-F 9:30am-5:45pm, Sa 9:30am-6:45pm, Su between masses. Free. *Museo* open Apr.-Oct. daily 10am-6pm; Nov.-Mar. M-F 10am-2pm, Sa-Su 10am-5pm. €4.) Climb the 227 stairs of the narrow **Torre Guinigi,** V. Sant'Andrea 41, for a view of the city and the hills beyond. (☎0583 31 68 46. Open daily June-Sept. 9am-11pm; Oct.-Jan. 9am-7pm; Feb.-May 10am-5pm. €5, students €3.50.) In the evening, *Lucchese* pack the **Piazza Napoleone.**

Family-run **Bed and Breakfast La Torre ❸,** V. del Carmine 11, offers large, bright rooms. (☎0583 95 70 44; www.roomslatorre.com. Breakfast included. Free Internet. Singles €35, with bath €50; doubles €50/80. MC/V.) From P. Napoleone, take V. Beccheria, then turn right on V. Roma and left on V. Fillungo. After six blocks, turn left into P. San Frediano and right on V. della Cavallerizza to reach the **Ostello per la Gioventù San Frediano (HI) ❶,** V. della Cavallerizza 12. (☎0583 46 99 57; www.ostellolucca.it. Breakfast €3. Dinner €10. Linens included. Towels €1.50. Laundry available. Reception 7:30-10am and 3:30pm-midnight. Lockout 10am-3:30pm. Dorms €18-19.50; 2- to 6-person rooms with bath €50-135. €3 HI discount. Cash only.) **Ristorante da Francesco ❷,** Corte Portici 13, off V. Calderia between P. San Salvatore and P. San Michele, offers patio seating and light meals. (☎0583 41 80 49. *Primi* €6. *Secondi* €7-11.50. 1L wine €7.20. Cover €1.50. Open Tu-Su noon-2:30pm and 8-10:30pm. MC/V.)

Trains (☎0583 89 20 21) run hourly from Ple. Ricasoli to Florence (1½hr., €5), Pisa (30min., €2.30), and Viareggio (20min., €2.30). **Buses** (☎0583 46 49 63) leave hourly from Ple. Verdi, next to the tourist office, for Florence (1hr., €4.70), Viareggio (30min., €2.20) and Pisa (50min., €2.50). The **tourist office** is in Ple. San Donato. (☎0583 58 31 50. Open daily 9am-7pm.) Rent bikes at **Cicli Bizzari,** P. Santa Maria 32. (☎0583 49 60 31. €2.50 per hr., €13 per day. Open daily 9am-7:30pm. Cash only.) **Postal Code:** 55100.

PISA ☎050

Millions of tourists arrive in Pisa (pop. 85,400) each year to marvel at the famous "Leaning Tower," forming a gelato-slurping, photo-snapping mire. Commanding a beautiful stretch of the Arno River, Pisa has a diverse array of cultural and artistic diversions, as well as three universities. The **Piazza del Duomo,** also known as the **Campo dei Miracoli** (Field of Miracles), is a grassy expanse that contrasts with the white stone of the tower, baptistry, *duomo*, and surrounding museums. Begun in 1173, the famous **Leaning Tower** began to tilt when the soil beneath it suddenly shifted. The tilt intensified after WWII, and thanks to the tourists who climb its steps daily, the tower slips 1-2m each year, though it's currently considered stable. Tours of 30 visitors are permitted to ascend the 294 steps once every 30min. (Tours depart daily June-Aug. 8:30am-11pm; Sept.-May 8:30am-7:30pm. Assemble next to info office 10min. before tour. €15. Cash only.) Also on the Campo is the **Battistero** (Baptistry), whose precise acoustics allow an unamplified choir to be heard 2km away. An acoustic demonstration occurs every 30min. (Open daily Apr.-Sept. 8am-7:30pm; Oct. 9am-5:30pm; Nov.-Feb. 9am-4:30pm; Mar. 9am-5:30pm. €5.) The dazzling **duomo** next door, considered one of the finest Romanesque cathedrals in the world, has a collection of splendid art, including a mosaic by Cimabue. (Open daily Apr.-Sept. 10am-8pm; Oct. and Mar. 10am-7pm; Nov.-Feb. 10am-1pm and 3-5pm. €2.) An **all-inclusive ticket** to the Campo's sights costs €10.50 and is available at the two *biglietterie* (ticket booths) on the Campo (at the Museo del Duomo and next to the tourist office adjacent to the tower).

Two minutes from the *duomo*, the **Albergo Helvetia ❸,** V. Don Gaefano Boschi 31, off P. Archivescovado, has large, clean rooms, small shared baths, a multilingual staff, and a welcoming downstairs bar. (☎050 55 30 84. Reception 8am-midnight. Reserve ahead. Singles €35, with bath €50; doubles €45-62. Cash only.) Steer clear of the countless touristy pizzerias near the tower and head to the river for a bite to eat, where the restaurants offer a more authentic ambience and consistently high quality. Try one of the many *primi* offerings, including various *sfogliate* (quiche) at **Il Paiolo ❶,** V. Curtatone e Montanara 9, near the university. (*Primi* and *secondi* €5-8. Open M-F 12:30-3pm and 8pm-1am, Sa-Su 8pm-2am. MC/V.) Get groceries at **Pam,** V. Giovanni Pascoli 8, just off C. Italia. (Open M-Sa 7:30am-8:30pm, Su 9am-1pm. Cash only.)

Trains (☎89 20 21) run from P. della Stazione, in the southern end of town, to Florence (75min., 2 per hr., €5.40), Genoa (2hr., 1 per hr., €8), and Rome (4hr., 1-2 per day, €23-29). To reach the **tourist office,** walk straight out of the train station and go left in P. Vittorio Emanuele. (☎050 42 291; www.turismo.toscana.it. Open M-F 9am-7pm, Sa 9am-1:30pm.) Take bus marked LAM ROSSA (€0.85) from the station to the Campo. **Postal Code:** 56100.

ITALY

UMBRIA

Umbria is known as the "green heart of Italy" due to its wild woods, fertile plains, craggy gorges, and gentle hills. Cobblestone streets and active international universities give the region a lively character rooted in tradition and history. Umbria holds Giotto's greatest masterpieces and was home to medieval master painters Perugino and Pinturicchio.

PERUGIA ☎075

In Perugia (pop. 160,000), visitors can experience the city's renowned jazz festival, digest its decadent chocolate, and meander through its two universities. The city's most popular sights frame **Piazza IV Novembre,** the heart of Perugia's social life. At its center, the **Fontana Maggiore** is adorned with sculptures and bas-reliefs by Nicolà and Giovanni Pisano. At the end of the *piazza* is the rugged, unfinished exterior of the Gothic **Cattedrale di San Lorenzo,** also known as the *duomo*, which houses the purported wedding ring of the Virgin Mary. (Open M-Sa 8am-12:45pm and 4-5:15pm, Su 4-5:45pm. Free.) The 13th-century **Palazzo dei Priori,** on the left when looking at the fountain, contains the impressive **Galleria Nazionale dell'Umbria,** C. Vannucci 19, which displays magnificent 13th- and 14th-century religious works. (Open Tu-Su 8:30am-7:30pm. €6.50.)

Ostello della Gioventù/Centro Internazionale di Accoglienza per la Gioventù ❶, V. Bontempi 13, is a welcoming and well-located hostel with kitchen access, a reading room, and a terrace. (☎075 57 22 880; www.ostello.perugia.it. Linens €2. Lockout 9:30am-4pm. Curfew 1am, midnight in winter. Closed mid-Dec. to mid-Jan. Dorms €15. AmEx/MC/V.) **Ostello Ponte Felcino ❷,** V. Maniconi 97, is located 5km from central Perugia but is easily accessible by bus #8. Set amongst gardens in a small town, this hostel has well-equipped common areas, a friendly staff, and complimentary breakfast. (☎075 59 13 991; www.ostellopontefelcino.com. Dinner €10. Dorms €16; double and triples €18; singles €22.) Locals flock to **Ferrari ❶,** V. Scura 1, off Corso Vannucci, for its variety of made-to-order pizzas large enough for two. (€5.50-7. Open daily 8am-2am.) Don't miss Perugia's famous chocolate store, **Perugina,** C. Vannucci 101. (Open M 2:30-7:45pm, Tu-Sa 9:30am-7:45pm, Su 10:30am-1:30pm and 3-8pm.)

Trains leave Perugia FS in P. Vittorio Veneto, Fontiveggio, for: Assisi (25min., 1 per hr., €2.05); Florence (2hr., 6 per day, from €8); Orvieto (1hr., 11 per day, €7); Rome (2hr., 7 per day, €11) via Terontola or Foligno. From the station, take the new **minimetro** (€1) to Pincetto off Piazza Mazeotti or take **bus** #6, 7, 9, 11, 13D, or 15 to the central P. Italia (€1); then walk down C. Vannucci, the main shopping street, to P. IV Novembre and the *duomo*. The **tourist office** is at P. Matteotti 18. Grab a *Perugia Little Blue*, a guide written in English with a student's perspective. (☎075 57 36 458. Open daily 8:30am-6:30pm.) **Postal Code:** 06100.

ITALY

ASSISI ☎075

Assisi owes its tranquil character to the legacy of St. Francis, patron saint of Italy and the town's favorite son. The undeniable jewel of Assisi (pop. 25,000) is the 13th-century **Basilica di San Francesco.** The subdued art of the lower church celebrates St. Francis's modest lifestyle, while Giotto's renowned fresco cycle in the upper church, the *Life of St. Francis*, pays tribute to the saint's consecration. (Lower basilica open daily 6am-6:45pm. Upper basilica open daily 8:30am-6:45pm. Modest dress required. Free.) Hike up to the looming fortress **Rocca Maggiore** for panoramic views of the countryside. From P. del Comune, follow V. S. Rufino to P. S. Rufino. Continue up V. Porta Perlici and take the first left up a narrow staircase. (Open daily 9am-8pm. €3.50, students €2.50.) On the way to Rocca Maggiore, explore the enchanting trails of **Colle del Paradiso,** V. della Rocca 3. (Open daily May-Oct. 10am-8pm. 6 tours per day. Free.) The pink-and-white **Basilica di Santa Chiara** houses the crucifix that is said to have spoken to St. Francis. It is surrounded by a dazzling courtyard with a fountain and lovely views of Umbrian scenery. (Open daily 6:30am-noon and 2-6pm.)

Camere Martini ❷, V. Antonio Cristofani 6, has sunny rooms with spectacular views and balconies surrounding a central courtyard. (☎075 81 35 36; camermartini@libero.it. Singles €25-27; doubles €40; triples €55; quads €65. Cash only.) **Ostello della Pace (HI) ❶,** V. d. Valecchi 177, offers bright rooms with two or three bunk beds and shared baths. From the train station, take the bus to P. Unità d'Italia; then walk downhill on V. Marconi, turn left at the sign, and walk for 500m. (☎075 81 67 67; www.assisihostel.com. Breakfast included. Laundry €3.50. Reception 7-9:30am and 3:30-11:30pm. Lockout 9:30am-3:30pm. Curfew 11pm. Reserve ahead. Dorms €16, singles with bath €18. HI card required; buy at hostel. MC/V.) Grab a personal pizza (€5-7) at **Pizzeria Otello ❶,** V. San Antonio 1. (Open daily noon-3pm and 7-10:30pm. AmEx/MC/V.)

From the station near the Basilica Santa Maria degli Angeli, **trains** go to Florence (2.5hr., 7 per day, €9), Perugia (30min., 1-2 per hr., €1.80), and Rome (2.5hr., 7 per day, €9). From P. Matteotti, follow V. del Torrione to Rufino, **Piazza del Commune,** the city center, and the **tourist office.** (☎81 25 34. Open M-Sa 8am-2pm and 3-6pm, Su 9am-1pm.) **Postal code:** 06081.

ORVIETO ☎0763

A city upon a city, Orvieto (pop. 20,700) was built in layers: medieval structures stand over ancient subterranean tunnels that Etruscans began burrowing into the hillside in the 8th century BC. **Underground City Excursions** offers the most complete tour of the city's twisted bowels. (☎0763 34 48 91. English-language tours leave the tourist office daily 11:15am and 4:15pm. €5.50, students €3.50.) It took 600 years, 152 sculptors, 68 painters, 90 mosaic artisans, and 33 architects to construct Orvieto's **duomo.** The **Capella della Madonna di San Brizio,** off the right transept, houses the dramatic apocalypse frescoes of Luca Signorelli. Opposite it, the **Cappella Corporale** holds the gold-encrusted chalice-cloth reputedly soaked with the blood of Christ. (Open M-Sa 7:30am-12:45pm and 2:30-7pm, Su 2:30-6:45pm. Modest dress required. *Duomo* free. *Capella* €5.) Two blocks down from the *duomo*, V. della Piazza del Popolo leads to the luxurious **Grand Hotel Reale ❸,** P. del Popolo 27, an opulent 13th-century palazzo with real old-world flair. (☎0763 34 12 47. Breakfast €8. Singles with bath €66; doubles €90; triples €117; quads €140. V.) **Nonnamelia ❸,** V. del Duomo 25, offers creative dishes and a wide variety of pizzas. (☎0763 34 24 02. Pizza €3.50-6. *Primi* €5.50-8. *Secondi* €7.50-14. Open daily 11:30am-3:30pm and 7-11pm. Cash only.) **Trains** run every hour to Florence (2hr., €11) and Rome (1hr., €7.10). The funicular travels up the hill from the train station to the center, **Piazza Cahen,** and a shuttle goes to the **tourist office,** P. del Duomo 24. (☎0763 34 17 72. Open M-F 8:15am-1:50pm and 4-7pm, Sa-Su 10am-1pm and 3-6pm.) **Postal Code:** 05018.

ITALY

THE MARCHES (LE MARCHE)

In the Marches, green foothills separate the shores of the Adriatic from Apennine peaks, and umbrella-dotted beaches from traditional hill towns. Inland villages, easily accessible by train, rely on agriculture and preserve the region's historical legacy in the architectural remains of the Gauls and Romans.

URBINO ☎0722

The birthplace of Raphael, Urbino (pop. 15,500) charms visitors with stone dwellings scattered along its steep streets. Most remarkable is the Renaissance **Palazzo Ducale,** in P. Rinascimento, a turreted palace that ornaments the skyline. Inside, a stairway leads to the **Galleria Nazionale delle Marche,** in the former residence of Duke Frederico da Montefeltro. Look for Raphael's *Portrait of a Lady*, and don't miss the servants' tunnels. (☎0722 32 26 25. Open M 8:30am-2pm, Tu-Su 8:30am-7:15pm. Ticket office closes 1hr. before museum. €8, EU students 18-25 €4, under 18 and over 65 free.) Walk back across P. della Repubblica onto V. Raffaello to the site of Raphael's 1483 birth, the **Casa Natale di Raffaello,** V. Raffaello 57, now a museum containing period furniture, works by local masters, and the *Madonna col Bambino*, attributed to Raphael himself. (☎0722 32 01 05. Open M-Sa 9am-1pm and 3-7pm, Su 10am-1pm. €3. Cash only.)

Just doors down from Raphael's home is **Pensione Fosca ❷.** (☎0722 32 96 22. Singles €21; doubles €35; triples €45. Cash only.) At **Pizzeria Le Tre Piante ❷**, V. Voltaccia della Vecchia 1, a cheery staff serves pizzas (€3.50-6.50) on a terrace overlooking the Apennines. (☎0722 48 63. *Primi* €6.80-7.50. *Secondi* €8-15. Open Tu-Su noon-3pm and 7-11:30pm. Cash only.) **Supermarket Margherita** is on V. Raffaello 37. (Open M-Sa 7:30am-2pm and 4:30-8pm. MC/V.)

Bucci **buses** (☎0721 32 401) run from Borgo Mercatale to Rome (4hr., 2 per day, €25). The **tourist office** is at V. Puccinotti 35. (☎0722 26 13. Open M and Sa 9am-1pm, Tu-F 9am-1pm and 3-6pm.)

ANCONA ☎071

Ancona (pop. 102,000) is the center of transportation for those heading to Croatia, Greece, and Slovenia. The P. del Duomo, a vigorous hike up a series of stairways, offers a view of the red rooftops and sapphire port below. Across the *piazza* is the **Cattedrale di San Ciriaco,** a Romanesque church with its namesake saint shrouded in velvet in the crypt. (☎071 52 688. Open in summer daily 8am-noon and 3-7pm; in winter daily 8am-noon and 3-6pm. Free.) **Pasetto Beach** seems far from the port's industrial clutter, though its "beach" is concrete.

From the train station, cross the *piazza*, turn left, take the first right, and then make a sharp right behind the newsstand to reach the **Ostello della Gioventù (HI) ❶**, V. Lamaticci 7. (☎071 42 257. Lockout 11am-4:30pm. Dorms €17. AmEx/MC/V.) **La Cantineta ❷**, V. Gramsci, offers specialties like *stoccafisso* (stockfish) at reasonable prices. (☎071 20 11 07. *Primi* €4-13. *Secondi* €5-15. Cover €1.50. Open Tu-Su noon-2:40pm and 7:30-midnight. AmEx/MC/V.)

Ferries leave Stazione Marittima for Croatia, Greece, and northern Italy. Jadrolinija (☎071 20 43 05; www.jadrolinija.hr) runs to Split, CRO (9hr., €48-53). ANEK (☎071 20 72 346; www.anekitalia.com) ferries go to Patras, GCE (22hr., €60-80). Schedules and tickets are available at the Stazione Marittima. Get up-to-date info at www.doricaportservices.it. **Trains** leave P. Rosselli for: Bologna (2hr., 36 per day, €11); Milan (4-5hr., 18 per day, €36); Rome (3-4hr., 11 per day, €14); Venice (5hr., 22 per day, €27.50). The train station is a 25min. walk from Stazione Marittima. **Buses** #1, 1/3, and 1/4 (€1) head up C. Stamira to P. Cavour, the city center. Ancona has no central tourist office, but brochures, maps, and accommodation listings can be found at Via Gramsci 2/A. (☎320 019 6321. Open May-Oct. daily 10am-1pm and 4-8pm.) **Postal Code:** 60100.

CAMPANIA

Sprung from the shadow of Mt. Vesuvius, Campania thrives in defiance of disaster. The submerged city at Baia, the relics at Pompeii, and the ruins at Cumae all attest to a land resigned to harsh natural outbursts. While Campania is one of Italy's poorest regions, often eclipsed by the prosperous North, the vibrant city of Naples and the emerald waters of the Amalfi Coast attract tourists.

NAPLES (NAPOLI) ☎081

Naples (pop. 1 million), Italy's third largest city, is also its most chaotic—Naples moves a million miles per minute. Locals spend their waking moments out on the town, eating, drinking, shouting, laughing, and pausing in the middle of busy streets to finish conversations. The birthplace of pizza and the modern-day home of tantalizing seafood, Naples boasts unbeatable cuisine. Once you submit to the city's rapid pulse, everywhere else will just seem slow.

TRANSPORTATION

Flights: Aeroporto Capodichino, V. Umberto Maddalena (**NAP;** ☎081 78 96 259; www.gesac.it). Connects to major Italian and European cities. **Alibus** (☎081 53 11 706) goes to P. Municipio and P. Garibaldi (20min., 6am-11:30pm, €3.10).

Trains: Trenitalia (www.trenitalia.it) goes from Stazione Centrale in P. Garibaldi to **Milan** (8hr., 15 per day, €39-50) and **Rome** (2hr., 31 per day, €11-38). **Circumvesuviana** (☎800 05 39 39) runs to **Herculaneum** (€1.80) and **Pompeii** (€2.40).

Ferries: Depart from **Stazione Marittima,** on Molo Angioino, and **Molo Beverello,** at the base of P. Municipio. From P. Garibaldi, take the R2, 152, 3S, or the Alibus to P. Municipio. **Caremar,** Molo Beverello (☎081 55 13 882), runs frequently to **Capri** and **Ischia** (both 1hr., €4.80-10). **Tirrenia Lines,** Molo Angioino (☎199 12 31 199), goes to **Cagliari** (16hr.) and **Palermo** (11hr.). **Hydrofoils** are generally faster and more expensive. The daily newspaper *Il Mattino* (€1) lists up-to-date ferry schedules.

Public Transportation: The **UnicoNapoli** (www.napolipass.it) ticket is valid on the buses, funicular, Metro, and trains in Naples (€1.10 per 90min., full-day €3.10). Route info for the **Metro** and funiculars is at www.metro.na.it.

Taxis: Consortaxi (☎081 20 20 20); **Napoli** (☎081 44 44 44). Only take metered taxis, and always ask about prices up front. Meter starts at €3; €0.05 per 65m thereafter. €2.50 surcharge added 10pm-7am.

ORIENTATION AND PRACTICAL INFORMATION

The main train and bus terminals are in the immense **Piazza Garibaldi** on the east side of Naples. From P. Garibaldi, a left on **Corso Garibaldi** leads to the waterfront district; **Piazza Guglielmo Pepe** is at the end of C. Garibaldi. Access **Piazza Plebiscito,** home to upscale little restaurants and shops, by walking down **Via Nuova Marina** with the water on your left. **Via Toledo,** a chic pedestrian shopping street, links the waterfront to the Plebiscito district, where the well-to-do hang out, and the maze-like **Spanish Quarter.** Along V. Toledo, **Piazza Dante** lies on the western extreme of the **Spaccanapoli** *(centro storico)* neighborhood. Walking away from the waterfront, a right on any of the streets leads to the historic district. While violent crime is rare, theft is fairly common, so exercise caution.

Tourist Offices: EPT (☎081 26 87 79; www.eptnapoli.info), at Stazione Centrale. Free maps. Grab **Qui Napoli,** a bimonthly publication full of listings and events. Open M-Sa 9am-7pm, Su 9am-1pm. **Branch** at P. Gesù Nuovo (☎081 55 12 701).

Consulates: Canada, V. Carducci 29 (☎081 40 13 38). **UK,** V. dei Mille 40 (☎081 42 38 911). **US,** P. della Repubblica (☎081 58 38 111, emergency 033 79 45 083).

Currency Exchange: Thomas Cook, at the airport and in P. Municipio 70 (☎081 55 18 399, branch 081 55 18 399). Open M-F 9:30am-1pm and 3-7pm.

Police: ☎113. **Ambulance:** ☎118.

Hospital: Incurabili (☎081 25 49 422). M: Cavour (Museo).

Post Office: P. Matteotti (☎081 552 42 33), at V. Diaz on the R2 line. Unreliable *fermo-posta.* Open M-F 8:15am-6pm, Sa 8:15am-noon. **Postal Code:** 80100.

ACCOMMODATIONS

Although Naples has some fantastic bargain accommodations, especially near **Piazza Garibaldi,** be cautious when choosing a room. Avoid hotels that solicit

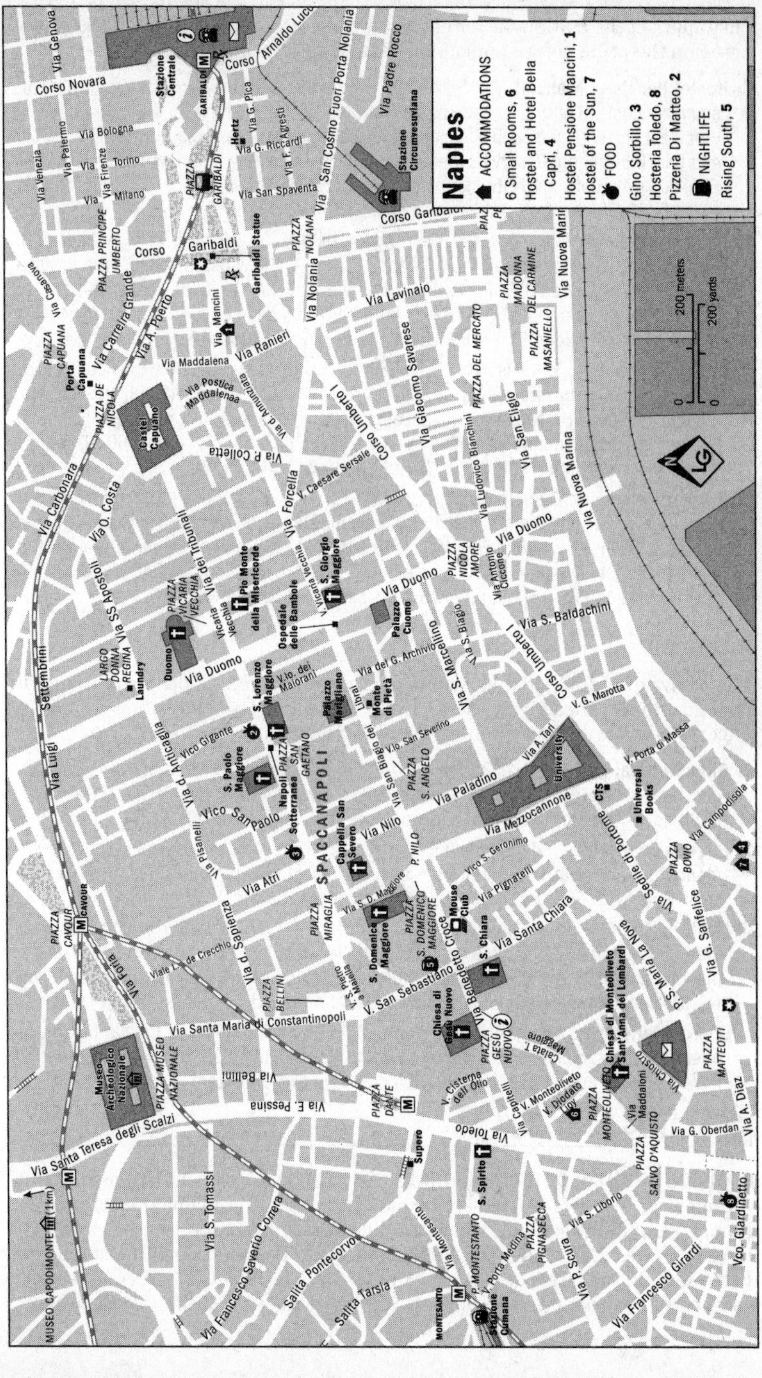

Naples

ACCOMMODATIONS
- 6 Small Rooms, 6
- Hostel and Hotel Bella Capri, 4
- Hostel Pensione Mancini, 1
- Hostel of the Sun, 7

FOOD
- Gino Sorbillo, 3
- Hosteria Toledo, 8
- Pizzeria Di Matteo, 2

NIGHTLIFE
- Rising South, 5

customers at the station, never give your passport until you've seen the room, agree on the price before unpacking, and be alert for hidden costs.

Hostel Pensione Mancini, V. P. S. Mancini, 33 (☎081 55 36 731; www.hostelpensionemancini.com). Bright, tidy, and spacious rooms, with new common room and kitchen. Breakfast and Wi-Fi included. Free luggage storage and lockers. Reception 24hr. Check-in and check-out noon. Reserve 1 week ahead. Mixed and female dorms €15-18; singles €30-40, with bath €45-55; doubles €45-55/50-65; triples €65-75/80-90; quads €72-80/80-90. 5% *Let's Go* discount. AmEx/MC/V. ❶

Hostel and Hotel Bella Capri, V. Melisurgo 4 (☎081 55 29 494; www.bellacapri.it). Top-notch hostel offers clean rooms with A/C and TV. Breakfast included. Free luggage storage, lockers, and Wi-Fi. Reception 24hr. With *Let's Go* discount, mixed and female dorms €15-19; singles €35-45, with bath €50-60; doubles €45-55/50-70; triples €60-70/70-90; quads €70-80/90-100; family rooms €100-140. AmEx/MC/V. ❸

Hostel of the Sun, V. Melisurgo 15 (☎081 42 06 393; www.hostelnapoli.com). Buzz #51. Dorms and private rooms are spacious, clean, and equipped with free lockers. Kitchen available. Breakfast included. Laundry €3, free load with 4-day stay. Free Wi-Fi. Reserve ahead in summer. Dorms €18-20; doubles €50-55, with bath €60-70; triples €75-80/70-90; quads €80-90. 10% *Let's Go* discount. MC/V. ❷

6 Small Rooms, V. Diodato Lioy 18 (☎081 79 01 378; www.6smallrooms.com). No sign; look for the call button. Friendly Australian owner and larger rooms than the name suggests. Kitchen available. Free lockers and Wi-Fi. Key (€5 deposit) for returning after midnight curfew. Dorms €18-20; singles with bath €30-40; doubles €40-45, with bath €55-60; triples €65-75; quad 85-95. 10% *Let's Go* discount. MC/V. ❷

FOOD

If you have ever doubted that Neapolitans invented pizza, Naples's *pizzerie* will take that doubt, knead it into a ball, throw it in the air, spin it on their collective finger, cover it with sauce and mozzarella, and serve it *alla margherita*.

Gino Sorbillo, V. dei Tribunali 32 (☎081 44 66 43; www.sorbillo.it). Basic *marinara* (€3), and *margherita* (€3.50) never tasted so good. Pizza €4.30-7.30. Service 10%. Open M-Sa noon-4pm and 7pm-1am. Closed 3 weeks in Aug. AmEx/MC/V. ❶

Pizzeria Di Matteo, V. dei Tribunali 94 (☎081 45 52 62), near V. Duomo. Pies, like the *marinara,* burst with flavor, while the building bursts with pizza aficionados. Expect a short wait. Pizza €2.50-6. Open M-Sa 9am-midnight. Cash only. ❶

Hosteria Toledo, Vicolo Giardinetto 78A (☎081 42 12 57), in the Spanish Quarter. Prepare yourself for Neopolitan comfort food. The *gnocchi* (€6) is hearty enough to be a meal on its own. If you're feeling adventurous or indecisive, try the chef's surprise. *Primi* €6-12. *Secondi* €5-10. Open M and Th-Su noon-4pm and 7pm-midnight. MC/V. ❷

Donna Margherita, Vico II Alabardieri 4/5/6 (☎081 40 01 29), in Chiaia. This place offers high quality food in a location close to city nightlife. Simple and elegant decor. Pizza €3.50-7. *Primi* €6-15. Open daily noon-4pm and 7pm-1am. MC/V. ❷

SIGHTS

MUSEO ARCHEOLOGICO NAZIONALE. Situated in a 16th-century *palazzo* and former military barracks, the archaeological museum contains treasures from Pompeii and Herculaneum. The mezzanine has a mosaic room; one design features a fearless Alexander the Great routing the Persian army. Check out the Farnese Bull, the largest extant ancient statue. The *Gabinetto Segreto* (secret cabinet) of Aphrodite grants glimpses into the goddess's life. *(M: P. Cavour. Turn right* *from the station and walk 2 blocks. ☎081 44 22 149. Open M and W-Su 9am-7:30pm. €6.50, EU students €3.25, under 18 and over 65 free. Audio tour in English, French, or Italian €4.)*

MUSEO AND GALLERIE DI CAPODIMONTE. Housed in another 16th-century *palazzo*, the museum resides inside a park often filled with locals. A plush royal apartment and the Italian National Picture Gallery lie within the palace. Among its impressive works are Bellini's *Transfiguration*, Masaccio's *Crucifixion*, and Titian's *Danae*. *(Take bus #178, C64, R4, M4, or M5 from the Archaeological Museum and exit at the gate to the park, on the right. 2 entrances: Porta Piccola and Porta Grande. ☎081 74 99 109. Open M-Tu and Th-Su 8:30am-7:30pm. €7.50, after 2pm €6.50.)*

PALAZZO REALE AND MASCHIO ANGIONO. The 17th-century Palazzo Reale contains opulent royal apartments, the **Museo di Palazzo Reale,** and a view from the terrace of the **Royal Chapel.** *(P. Plebescito 1. Take the R2 bus from P. Garibaldi to P. Trieste e Trento and walk around the palazzo to the entrance on P. Plebiscito. ☎081 40 05 47; www.pierreci.it. Open M-Tu and Th-Su 9am-7pm. €4, EU students €2, under 18 and over 65 free.)* The **Biblioteca Nazionale** stores 1½ million volumes. *(☎081 78 19 231. Open M-F 10am-1pm. Reservations required.)* The **Teatro San Carlo**'s acoustics are reputed to top those of Milan's La Scala. *(Theater entrance on P. Trieste e Trento. ☎081 79 72 331; www.teatrosancarlo.it. Open daily 9am-7pm.)* **Maschio Angiono's** five turrets shadow the bay. Built in 1284 by Charles II of Anjou as his royal residence, the fortress's most stunning feature is its entrance, with reliefs of Alphonse I of Aragon in 1443. *(P. Municipio. Take the R2 bus from P. Garibaldi. ☎081 42 01 241. Open M-Sa 9am-7pm. €5.)*

NAPOLI SOTTERRANEA (CATACOMBS AND THE UNDERGROUND). The catacombs of S. Gennaro, S. Gaudioso, and S. Severo all date back to the early centuries AD. Tours of the subterranean alleys beneath the city are fascinating: they involve crawling through narrow underground passageways, spotting Mussolini-era graffiti, and exploring Roman aqueducts. *(P. S. Gaetano 68. Take V. dei Tribunali and turn left right before S. Paolo Maggiore. ☎081 29 69 44; www.napolisotterranea.org. Tours every 2hr. M-F noon-4pm, Sa-Su 10am-6pm. €9.30, students €8.)*

DUOMO. Begun in 1315 by Robert of Anjou, the *duomo* has been redone over the centuries. Its main attraction is the **Capella del Tesoro di San Gennaro,** decorated with Baroque paintings. A 17th-century bronze grille protects the high altar, which houses the saint's head and two vials of his blood. Visitors can also view the newly opened underground **excavation site,** a tangle of Greek and Roman roads. *(Walk 3 blocks up V. Duomo from C. Umberto I or take bus #42 from P. Garibaldi. ☎081 44 90 97. Open M-Sa 8:30am-noon and 4:30-6:30pm. Free. Excavation site €3.)*

NIGHTLIFE

Content to groove at small clubs and discos during the winter, Neapolitans take to the streets and *piazze* in summer. **Piazza Vanvitelli** is accessible by the funicular from V. Toledo or the bus C28 from P. Vittoria. **Via Santa Maria La Nova** is another hot spot. Outdoor bars and cafes are a popular choice in **Piazza Bellini,** near P. Dante. **Rising South,** V.S. Sebastiono 19, nearby Gesù Nuovo, has everything from a bar to a cinema. (Drinks €2-6. Bar open daily Sept.-May 10pm-3am.) At **S'Move,** Vco. dei Sospiri 10, DJs spin techno nightly. (Beer from €3. Mixed drinks from €5. Open daily 6pm-4am. Closed 2 weeks in Aug.) **ARCI-GAY/Lesbica** (☎081 55 28 815) has info on gay and lesbian club nights.

DAYTRIPS FROM NAPLES

HERCULANEUM. Buried by volcanic ash, Herculaneum is less excavated than its famous neighbor, Pompeii. A modern city sits on the remains of the

TRASH TALK

fter nearly a decade of trash roblems, Naples may finally e cleaning up its act—and its treets. In 2008, the amount of ncollected garbage exceeded ,000 tons in the metropolitan egion around Naples, enough for he EU to finally put its foot down n the boot. Prime Minister Silvio erlusconi has made it a priority o rescue Naples's nearly defunct nunicipal waste disposal system rom the hands of the Camorra the Neapolitan Mafia) and to everse the dumping trend that ealth experts warned would breed nfectious diseases and rat infes-ations, and cause an increase in ancer and genetic defects.

As attempts to export the city's rash have yielded no sustainable olution, both citizens and politi-ians are pushing for the latest ut not last resort: a *termovaloriz-atore*, or incinerator. The chosen nodel would be located in a for-ner US military space in Agnano northwest of Naples). Engineers ffirm that the state-of-the-art echnology, which can burn up o 250,000 tons per year, would ose low risks for the area—and ven produce electricity from the ombustion process.

Meanwhile, Naples's tourist ndustry is less than healthy as a esult. World-renowned museums, athedrals, and pizza pies are ften skipped over by tourists who ear contact with the *immondizia* Italian for the trash problem), and ssume trash and pickpockets are ll that the city has to offer.

ancient town. Don't miss the **House of Deer.** (Open daily 8:30am-7:30pm. €11.) As its name suggests, the **House of the Mosaic of Neptune and Amphitrite** is famous for its mosaics. The **tourist office** (☎081 78 81 243) is at V. IV Novembre 84. *(Take the Circumvesuviana train, ☎081 77 22 444, from Naples to the Ercolano Scavi stop, dir.: Sorrento. 20min. The city is 500m downhill from the stop.)*

POMPEII. On the morning of August 24, AD 79, a deadly cloud of volcanic ash from Mt. Vesuvius settled over the Roman city of Pompeii, catching the 12,000 prosperous residents by surprise and engulfing the city in suffocating black clouds. Mere hours after the eruption, stately buildings, works of art, and human bodies were sealed in hardened casts of ash. These natural tombs would remain undisturbed until 1748, when excavations began to unearth a stunningly well-preserved picture of daily Roman life. Walk down V. della Marina to reach the colonnaded **Forum,** which was once the civic and religious center of the city. Exit the Forum through the upper end by the cafeteria and head right on V. della Fortuna to reach the **House of the Faun,** where a bronze dancing faun and the spectacular Alexander Mosaic (today in the Museo Archeologico Nazionale) were found. Continue on V. della Fortuna and turn left on V. dei Vettii to reach the **House of the Vettii** and the most vivid frescoes in Pompeii. Backtrack on V. dei Vettii, cross V. della Fortuna to V. Storto, turn left on V. degli Augustali, and take a quick right to reach a small frescoed brothel (the *Lupenare*). V. dei Teatri, across the street, leads to the oldest standing **amphitheater** in the world (80 BC). To get to the **Villa of the Mysteries,** the ancient city's best-preserved villa, head west on V. della Fortuna, right on V. Consolare, and all the way up Porta Ercolano and V. della Tombe. *(Take the Circumvesuviana train from Naples to the Pompeii Scavi stop, dir.: Sorrento. 40min., 2 per hr., round-trip €2.30. Archaeological site open daily Apr.-Oct. 8:30am-7:30pm; Nov.-Mar. 8:30am-5pm. €11.)*

BAY OF NAPLES

SORRENTO ☎081

Cliff-side Sorrento makes a convenient base for daytrips around the Bay of Naples. **Ostello Le Sirene ❷**, V. degli Aranci 160, is located near the train station. (☎081 80 72 925. Dorms €16-25; doubles €40-70. Cash only.) Seaside campground **Villaggio Campeggio Santa Fortunata ❶**, V. del Capo 39, has a private beach, pool, market, and restaurant. (☎081 80 73 579. €6-10 per person; tents €5-7.

Dorms €13-19.) Try the *gnocchi* (€5) or the *linguini al cartoccio* (linguini with mixed seafood; €7) at **Ristorante e Pizzeria Giardiniello ❷**, V. dell'Accademia 7. (☎081 87 84 616. Cover €1. Open Apr.-Nov. daily 11am-midnight; Dec.-Mar. M-W and F-Su 11am-midnight. AmEx/MC/V.) **Ferries** and **hydrofoils** depart for the Bay of Naples islands. Linee Marittime Partenopee (☎081 80 71 812) runs hydrofoils to Capri (20min., 17 per day, €14.50.) The **tourist office,** L. de Maio 35, is off P. Tasso, in the C. dei Forestieri compound. (☎081 80 74 033. Open M-Sa Apr.-Sept. 8:30am-6:30pm; Oct.-Mar. 8:30am-4:10pm.) **Postal Code:** 80067.

CAPRI ☎081

Augustus fell in love with Capri in 29 BC, and since then, the "pearl of the Mediterranean" has become a hot spot for the rich and famous. There are two towns on the island—**Capri** proper, near the ports, and **Anacapri,** high on the hills. The best times to visit are in late spring and early fall: crowds and prices increase in summer. Visitors flock to the **Blue Grotto,** a sea cave where the water shimmers a vivid neon blue. (Short boat ride from Marina Grande €10. Tickets at Grotta Azzurra Travel Office, V. Roma 53. Tours until 5pm.) **Buses** departing from V. Roma make the trip up the mountain to Anacapri every 15min. until 2am; buses leave Anacapri for most tourist attractions. Away from pricey Capri, Anacapri is home to less expensive hotels, lovely vistas, and quiet mountain paths. Upstairs from P. Vittoria in Anacapri, **Villa San Michele** has lush gardens, ancient sculptures, and summer concerts. (☎081 83 71 401. Open daily 9am-6pm. €6.) Take the chairlift up **Monte Solaro** from P. Vittoria for great views. (Chairlift open daily Mar.-Apr. and Oct. 9:30am-4:45pm; July-Sept. 9am-6pm. Round-trip €7.) For those who prefer cliff to coastline, walk 1hr. to the **Faraglioni,** three massive rocks, or undertake the steep 1hr. hike to the ruins of Emperor Tiberius's **Villa Jovis.** The view from the **Cappella di Santa Maria del Soccorso,** built onto the villa, is unrivaled. (Open daily 9am-6pm. €2.)

Hotel Bussola ❹, V. Traversa La Vigna 14, in Anacapri, is a new building with mythological statues and mosaics. Call from P. Vittoria in Anacapri for pickup. (☎081 83 82 010; www.bussolahermes.com. Reserve ahead. Doubles €70-130. MC/V.) For convenient access to the beach and Capri's center, stay at **Vuotto Antonio ❹**, V. Campo di Teste 2. The simple rooms are devoid of modern distractions like TV and A/C, leaving guests to contemplate the coastline from their terraces. (☎081 83 70 230. Doubles €70-105. Cash only.) **Al Nido D'Oro,** Vle. T. de Tommaso 32, in Anacapri, has fresh food at low prices. (☎081 83 72 148. *Primi* €5-8. Open M-Tu and Th-Su 11am-3:30pm and 7pm-midnight.) The **supermarket,** V.G. Orlandi 299, in Anacapri, is well-stocked. (Open M-Sa 8:30am-1:30pm and 5-8:30pm, Su 8:30am-noon.)

Caremar (☎081 83 70 700) **ferries** run from Marina Grande to Naples (1hr., 3 per day, €9.60). LineaJet (☎081 83 70 819) runs **hydrofoils** to Naples (40-50min., 11 per day, €17) and Sorrento (25min., 12 per day, €14.50). Boats to other destinations run less frequently. The Capri **tourist office** sits at the end of Marina Grande. (☎081 83 70 634; www.capritourism.com. Open June-Sept. daily 9am-1pm and 3:30-6:45pm; Oct.-May reduced hours.) In Anacapri, it's at V. Orlandi 59; turn right when leaving the bus stop. (☎081 83 71 524. Open M-Sa 9am-3pm; Oct.-May reduced hours.) **Postal Codes:** 80073 (Capri); 80071 (Anacapri).

THE AMALFI COAST ☎089

It happens almost imperceptibly: after the tumult of Naples and the grit of Sorrento, the highway narrows to a two-lane coastal road, and the horizon becomes illuminated with lemon groves and bright village pastels. Though the coastal towns combine simplicity and sophistication, the region's ultimate appeal rests in the tenuous balance it strikes between man and nature.

TRANSPORTATION. **Trains** run to Salerno from Naples (45min., 40 per day, €5-10). SITA **buses** (☎089 26 66 04) connect Salerno to Amalfi (1hr., 20 per day, €2). From Amalfi, buses also go to Positano (40min., 25 per day, €2) and Sorrento (1½hr., 1 per hr., €2). Travelmar (☎089 87 29 50) runs **hydrofoils** from Amalfi to Positano (25min., 7 per day, €6) and Salerno (35min., 6 per day, €6), and from Salerno to Positano (1hr., 6 per day, €6).

AMALFI AND ATRANI. Jagged rocks, azure waters, and bright lemons define Amalfi. Visitors crowd P. del Duomo to admire the elegant 9th-century **Duomo di Sant'Andrea** and the nearby **Fontana di Sant'Andrea.** The hostel **A'Scalinatella ❶,** P. Umberto 6, runs dorms, private rooms, and camps all over Amalfi and Atrani. (☎089 87 14 92; www.hostelscalinatella.com. Tent sites €5 per person. Dorms €21; doubles €50-60, with bath €73-83. Cash only.) Amalfi's many *paninoteche* (sandwich shops) are perfect for a tight budget. The **AAST Tourist Office** is at C. Repubbliche Marinare 27. On the same street, a tunnel leads to beach town Atrani, 750m down the coast. The 4hr. **Path of the Gods** follows the coast from **Bomerano** to **Positano,** with great views along the way. The hike from **Atrani** to **Ravello** (1-2hr.) runs through lemon groves and green valleys. **Postal Code:** 84011.

RAVELLO. Perched atop cliffs, Ravello has been claimed by artists and intellectuals and its natural beauty seeps into their works. The Moorish cloister and gardens of **Villa Rufolo,** off P. del Duomo, inspired Boccaccio's *Decameron* and Wagner's *Parsifal.* (Open daily in summer 9am-8pm. €5.) The villa puts on a **summer concert series** in the gardens; tickets are sold at the Ravello Festival box office, V. Roma 10-12 (☎089 85 84 22; www.ravellofestival.com). Don't miss Ravello's **duomo** and its bronze doors; follow V. S. Francesco out of P. Duomo to the impressive **Villa Cimbrone,** whose floral walkways and gardens hide temples, grottoes, and magnificent views. (Open daily 9am-sunset. €6.) **Palazzo della Marra ❸,** V. della Marra 3, offers four immaculate rooms with terraces and kitchen access. (☎089 85 83 02; www.palazzodellamarra.com. Breakfast included. Reserve ahead. Doubles €60-80. MC/V.) **Postal Code:** 84010.

POSITANO. Today, Positano's most frequent visitors are the wealthy few who can afford its high prices, but the town still has its charms for the budget traveler. To see the large *pertusione* (hole) in the mountain **Montepertuso,** hike 45min. uphill or take the bus from P. dei Mulini. The three **Isole dei Galli,** islands off Positano's coast, were allegedly home to Homer's mythical Sirens. The beach at **Fornillo** is a serene alternative to **Spiaggia Grande,** the area's main beach. Buses to Amalfi stop at nearby **Praiano beach,** a unique escape from commercial Positano. **Ostello Brikette ❷,** V. Marconi 358, with two large terraces and free Wi-Fi, is accessible by the orange Interno or SITA bus; exit at the Chiesa Nuova stop and walk 100m to the left of Bar Internazionale. (☎089 87 58 57. Dorms €22-25; doubles €65-100. MC/V.) A backpacker favorite, **C'era una volta ❶,** V. Marconi 127, serves a special daily pasta and €4 margherita pizza. (☎089 81 19 30. *Primi* €6-9. Open daily May-Jan. noon-2:30pm and 7pm-midnight. AmEx/MC/V.) The four small bars on the beach at Fornillo serve simple, fresh food. The **tourist office** is at V. del Saraceno 4. (☎089 87 50 67. Open M-Sa 8am-2pm and 3-8pm; low-season reduced hours.) **Postal Code:** 84017.

SICILY (SICILIA)

Sicily owes its cultural complexity to Phoenicians, Greeks, Romans, Arabs, and Normans, all of whom invaded and left their mark. Ancient Greeks lauded the golden island as the second home of the gods. Now, tourists seek it as the home of *The Godfather.* While the Mafia's presence lingers in Sicily, its power is waning. Active volcano Mt. Etna ominously shadows chic resorts, archaeological treasures, fast-paced cities, and sleepy towns.

TRANSPORTATION

From southern Italy, take a train to Reggio di Calabria, then a Trenitalia **hydrofoil** (25min., €2.80) to Messina, Sicily's transport hub. **Buses** (☎090 77 19 14) serve destinations throughout the island and also make the long trek to mainland cities. **Trains** head to Messina (via ferry) from Rome (9hr., 6 per day, €43), then connect to Palermo (3hr., 22 per day, €11) and Syracuse (3hr., 16 per day, €8.75).

PALERMO ☎091

In gritty Palermo (pop. 680,000), the shrinking shadow of organized crime hovers over the twisting streets lined with ruins. While poverty, bombings, and centuries of neglect have taken their toll on much of the city, Palermo is currently experiencing a revival. Operas and ballets are performed year-round at the **Teatro Massimo,** where the climactic opera scene of *The Godfather: Part III* was filmed. (Open Tu-Su 10am-3pm. Tours 25min., 2 per hr., €5.) The **Cappella Palatina,** full of incredible mosaics, is in **Palazzo dei Normanni.** (Open M-Sa 8:30am-noon and 2-5pm, Su 8:30am-12:30pm. €6.) At the haunting **Cappuccini Catacombs,** P. Cappuccini 1,8000 corpses in various states of decay line the underground tunnels. Take bus #109 or 318 from Stazione Centrale to P. Indipendenza, then transfer to bus #327. (Open daily 9am-noon and 1-5pm. €2.)

Homey **Hotel Regina ❷,** C. Vittorio Emanuele 316, is near the intersection of V. Maqueda and C. V. Emanuele. (☎091 61 14 216; www.hotelreginapalermo.it. Singles €28; doubles €54, with bath €64. AmEx/MC/V.) The best restaurants in town are between Teatro Massimo and the Politeama.

Trains leave Stazione Centrale in P. Giulio Cesare at the southern end of V. Roma and V. Maqueda, for Rome (12hr.; 3 per day; €42). All **bus** lines run from V. Balsamo, next to the train station. Pick up a combined metro and bus map from an **AMAT** or **metro** info booth. To reach the **tourist office,** P.

HOW DO YOU LIKE THEM LEMONS?

In the home of *limoncello, delizia limone,* and lemon gelato, no tourist can avoid sampling the famous limone Costa d'Amalfi (Amalfi Coast lemon). Far larger than the average supermarket variety, the ubiquitous citrus fruit resembles a grapefruit in size and in the thickness of its rind, but one bite reveals its lemony character through and through.

Lemon imagery in mosaics and frescoes at Pompeii and Herculaneum confirms the presence of these limone even in Roman times. The towns of Maiori and Minori have been famous producers of the *sfusato* lemon variety since the 11th century.

To make the cut as a *limone* Costa d'Amalfi, lemons must be grown on chestnut wood frames for at least two years, weigh more than 100 grams, and possess a thick and aromatic zest.

Given its lasting presence, the lemon has been absorbed into virtually every aspect of Amalfi cuisine. In cream for cakes, over seafood dishes, and in chocolates an confections, this sour citrus is a dear ingredient in the Amalfitano diet. So pucker up—you may be sweetly surprised.

Rigorous standards are upheld by the Consorzio Tutela Limone della Costa d'Amalfi IGP, Via Lama, Minori (☎089 87 32 11; www.igplimonecostadamalfi.it).

Castelnuovo 34, at the west end of the *piazza*, walk or take a bus from the station to P. Politeama, at the end of V. Maqueda. (☎091 60 58 351; www.palermotourism.com. Open M-F 8:30am-2pm and 2:30-6pm.) **Postal Code:** 90100.

SYRACUSE (SIRACUSA) ☎0931

With the glory of its Grecian golden days behind it, the city of Syracuse (pop. 125,000) takes pride in its extraordinary ruins and in the beauty of its offshore island, **Ortigia.** Syracuse's role as a Mediterranean superpower is still evident in the **Archaeological Park,** on the northern side of town. Aeschylus premiered his *Persians* before 16,000 spectators in the park's enormous **Greek theater.** (Open daily 9am-6pm; low-season 9am-2pm. €8.) On V. S. Giovanni is the **Catacomba di San Giovanni,** 20,000 now-empty tombs carved into the remains of a Greek aqueduct. (Open daily 9:30am-12:30pm and 2:30-5:30pm. Mandatory guided tours every 30 min. €5. AmEx/MC/V.) More ruins lie over the Ponte Umbertino on **Ortigia,** the serene island where the attacking Greeks first landed. The **Temple of Apollo** has a few columns still standing, but those of the **Temple of Athena** inside the *duomo* are much more impressive. For those who prefer tans to temples, take bus #21 or 22 to **Fontane Bianche,** a glitzy beach with soft sand and refreshing blue water. Recently opened **lolhostel ❶,** V. Francesco Crispi 94, is becoming a true Syracuse gem as the city's first youth hostel. (☎0931 46 50 88; www.lolhostel.com. A/C. Internet €3 per hr. Free Wi-Fi. Dorms €18-20; singles €35-40; doubles €60-64. Cash only.) **Ristorante Porta Marina ❸,** V. dei Candelai 35, offers a great selection of seafood in a sleek modern setting. (☎0931 22 553. *Primi* €7-16. *Secondi* €8-18. AmEx/MC/V.) Get the best deals on food around the station and Archaeological Park, or at Ortigia's **open-air market,** V. Trento, off P. Pancali. (Open M-Sa 8am-1pm.) On the mainland, C. Umberto links Ponte Umbertino to the train station, passing through P. Marconi, from which C. Gelone extends through town to the Archaeological Park. **Trains** leave V. Francesco Crispi for Messina (3hr., 9 per day, €9.50) and Rome (10-13hr., 2 per day, €44). To get from the train station to the **tourist office,** V. Malta 106, take V. Crispi to P. Marconi, then follow V. Malta towards Ortigia. (☎0931 46 88 69; www.provincia.siracusa.it. Open M-F 9am-1pm.) **Postal Code:** 96100.

AEOLIAN ISLANDS (ISOLE EOLIE) ☎090

Homer believed these islands to be a home of the gods, while residents consider them *Le Perle del Mare* (Pearls of the Sea). The rugged shores, pristine landscapes, volcanoes, and mud baths might as well be divinely inspired; however, living among the gods isn't cheap, and prices rise steeply in summer.

TRANSPORTATION. The archipelago lies off the Sicilian coast, north of **Milazzo,** the principal and least expensive departure point. **Trains** run from Milazzo to Messina (30min., 21 per day, €3.10) and Palermo (3hr., 12 per day, €11.60). An orange **AST bus** runs from Milazzo's train station to the port (10min., 2 per hr., €1). Ustica (☎0923 87 38 13; www.usticalines.it), Siremar (☎090 92 83 242; www.siremar.it), and Navigazione Generale Italiana (NGI; ☎090 92 84 091) **ferries** depart for Lipari (2hr., 3 per day, €7) and Vulcano (1hr., 3 per day, €6.50). **Hydrofoils** run twice as fast as ferries and more frequently, but for twice the price. Ticket offices are on V. dei Mille in Milazzo.

LIPARI. Lipari, the largest and most developed of the islands, is renowned for its beaches. Visitors descend upon its shores each summer, just as pirates did centuries ago. To reach the beaches of the **Spiaggia Bianca** and **Porticello,** take the Lipari-Cavedi **bus** to **Canneto.** Lipari's best sights—aside from its beautiful shores—are all in the hilltop *castello*, where a **fortress** with ancient Greek foundations dwarfs the surrounding town. Nearby is the **Museo Archeologico Eoliano,** whose collection includes Greek and Sicilian pottery. (Open May-Oct. M-Sa 9am-1pm and 3-6pm; Nov.-Apr. reduced hours. €6.) *Affittacamere* (private rooms) may be the best deals, but ask to see the room and get a price in writing before accepting. Relax on your private terrace away from the bustle in one of the eight rooms with bath and A/C at **Villa Rosa ❷**, V. Francesco Crispi 134. (☎090 98 12 217; www.liparivillarosa.it. Doubles €30-60.) Camp at **Baia Unci ❶,** V. Marina Garibaldi 2, at the entrance to the hamlet of Canneto, 2km from Lipari. (☎090 98 11 909. Open mid-Mar. to mid-Oct. €8-15 per person with tent. Cash only.) **Da Gilberto e Vera ❶,** V. Marina Garibaldi 22-24, is renowned for its sandwiches. (☎090 98 12 756; www.gilbertoevera.it. Panini €4.50. Open daily Mar.-Oct. 7am-4am; Nov.-Feb. 7am-2am. AmEx/MC/V.) Shop at **UPIM** supermarket, C. V. Emanuele 212. (Open M-Sa 8am-9:30pm, Su 8am-1:30pm. AmEx/MC/V.) The **tourist office,** C. V. Emanuele 202, is near the dock. (☎090 98 80 095; www.aasteolie.info. Open M-F 8:30am-1:30pm and 4:30-7:30pm; July-Aug. also open Sa 8am-2pm and 4-9pm.) **Postal Code:** 98055.

VULCANO. Black beaches, bubbling seas, and sulfuric mud spas attract international visitors to Vulcano. A steep 1hr. **hike** (€3) to the inactive **Gran Cratere** (Grand Crater), at the summit of Fossa di Volcane, snakes between the volcano's *fumaroli* (emissions of yellow, noxious smoke). On a clear day, you can see all the other islands from the top. The allegedly therapeutic **Laghetto di Fanghi** (mud pool) is up V. Provinciale to the right from the port (€2). This spa's pungent odor is impossible to miss. If murky gray-brown muck isn't your thing, step into the scalding waters of the **acquacalda,** where underwater volcanic outlets make the shoreline bubble like a hot tub, or visit the nearby black sands of **Sabbie Nere** (follow the signs off V. Ponente). To get to Vulcano, take the **hydrofoil** from the port at Lipari (10min., 17 per day, €5.80). Ferries and hydrofoils dock at **Porto di Levante,** on the eastern side of **Vulcanello,** the youngest volcano. V. Provinciale heads toward Fossa di Vulcane from the port. The **tourist office** is at V. Provinciale 41 (☎090 98 52 105. Open Aug. daily 8am-1:30pm and 3-5pm), or get info at the Lipari office. **Postal Code:** 98050.

SARDINIA (SARDEGNA)

An old Sardinian legend says that when God finished making the world, He had a handful of dirt left over, which He took, threw into the Mediterranean, stepped on, and—behold—created the island of Sardinia. African, Spanish, and Italian influences have shaped the architecture, language, and cuisine of this truly unique island, whose jewel-toned waters and ample beaches are widely considered some of the most beautiful in the world.

TRANSPORTATION

Alitalia **flights** link Alghero, Cagliari, and Olbia to major Italian cities; recently, Ryanair and easyJet have started to serve Sardinia's airports as well. Several **ferry** companies, among them Tirrenia ferries (☎89 21 23; www.tirrenia.it), run to Olbia from Civitavecchia, just north of Rome (5-7hr., 2 per day, €22-91), and Genoa (13hr., 6 per week, from €23-50), and to Cagliari from Civitavecchia (14hr., 1 per day, €29-44), Naples (16hr., 1 per week, €29-44), and Palermo

(13hr., 1 per week, €28-42). **Trains** run from Cagliari to Olbia (4hr., 1 per day, €15), Oristano (1hr., 17 per day, €5.20), and Sassari (4hr., 4 per day, €14). From Sassari, trains run to Alghero (35min., 11 per day, €2.20). **Buses** connect Cagliari to Oristano (1hr., 2 per day, €6.50) and run from Olbia to Palau (12 per day, €2.50), where ferries access the protected beaches of La Maddalena.

CAGLIARI ☎070

Exploring Cagliari, the charming and vibrant *capoluogo* of the region of Sardinia, will take you from fascinating Roman ruins to thoroughly modern resorts and clubs along endless stretches of beach. The **Roman amphitheater** comes alive with concerts, operas, and plays during the **arts festival** in July and August. Cross V. Roma from the train station or ARST station and turn right to get to the spacious rooms of **B&B Vittoria ❸**, V. Roma 75. (☎070 64 04 026; www.bbvittoria.com. Singles €48; doubles €78. Shared bath. 10% *Let's Go* discount. Cash only.) The B&B's owners also run **Hotel aer Bundes Jack ❹**, in the same building. (☎070 66 79 70; hotel.aerbundesjack@libero.it. Breakfast €7. Reserve ahead. Singles €48-58; doubles €70-88; triples €114. Cash only.) The **tourist office** is a kiosk in P. Matteotti facing V. Roma. (☎070 66 92 55. Open M-F 8:30am-1:30pm and 2-8pm, Sa-Su 8am-8pm; low-season reduced hours.) **Postal Code:** 09100.

ALGHERO ☎079

Vineyards, ruins, and horseback rides are just a short trip away from Alghero's parks and palms. Between massive white cliffs, 654 steps plunge downward at **Grotte di Nettuno,** 70-million-year-old, stalactite-filled caverns in Capo Caccia. Take the **bus** (50min., 3 per day, round-trip €3.50) or a **boat.** (1hr.; 3-8 per day; round trip €13, includes tour but not cave entrance. Caves open daily Apr.-Sept. 9am-7pm; Oct. 9am-5pm; Nov.-Mar. 9am-4pm. €10.) Outside of Alghero proper, **Hostal de l'Alguer ❶**, V. Parenzo 79, is the cheapest option in the area. (☎079 93 20 39. Breakfast included. Large dorms €18; 4- to 6-bed dorms €18-20; doubles €21-25. €3 HI discount.) Toward Fertilia, 2km from Alghero, **La Mariposa ❶** campground, V. Lido 22, has a bar, beach access, bikes, diving excursions, and a restaurant. (☎079 95 03 60; www.lamariposa.it. Hot showers €0.50. Mar.-Oct. €8-11 per person, €4-13 per tent; 4-person bungalows €47-78. Apr.-June no charge for tents and cars. AmEx/MC/V.) The **tourist office,** P. Porta Terra 9, is to the right of the bus stop. (☎079 97 90 54. Open Apr.-Oct. M-Sa 8am-8pm, Su 10am-1pm; Nov.-Mar. M-Sa 8am-8pm.) **Postal Code:** 07041.

PALAU ☎0789

Situated on the luminous waters of Sardinia's northern coast, Palau (pop. 4200) is both a gorgeous destination and a convenient base for exploring La Maddalena. Check out the **Roccia dell'Orso,** a rock that resembles a bear, from which you can enjoy stunning views of the countryside and port. (Buses to "Capo d'Orso"; 20min.; 4 per day 9:45am-6pm, last return 6:20pm; round-trip €1.50.) **Hotel La Roccia ❺**, V. dei Mille 15, has a lobby built around an enormous boulder and themed rooms, like *"Il Faro"* (the lighthouse). All 22 rooms have balcony, A/C, TV, and bath. (☎0789 70 95 28; www.hotellaroccia.com. Breakfast included. Singles €48-84; doubles €78-130. AmEx/MC/V.) Campgrounds on Palau provide a stellar budget option. **Baia Saraceno ❶**, Localit Puna Nera 1, offers three picturesque beaches 500m outside Palau. (☎0789 70 94 03; www.baiasaraceno.com. €8-17.50 per person, ages 4-12 €5.50-13. Electricity €3. 2-person bungalows €26-48, with bath €32-64. AmEx/MC/V.) After a day at the beach, try gelato or crepes at **Sicily Creperie ❶**, V. Nazionale 45. (☎33 16 44 67 72. Open 9:30am-1pm and 4-10:30pm. Cash only.) Palau's **tourist office,** P. Fresi, sits to the right of V. Nazionale when approaching from Stazione Maritime. (☎0789 70 70 25; www.palau.it. Open daily 9am-1pm and 4:30-7:30pm.) **Postal code:** 07020.

LA MADDALENA ARCHIPELAGO ☎078

An ancient land bridge that once connected Corsica and Sardinia, L'Arcipelago della Maddalena was declared Sardinia's first national park in 1996. The nearby island of **Razzoli** has magnificent swimming holes, and sightseers can set out by boat to islands like Santa Maria and Spargi. **Marinella IV** (☎0789 73 68 41; www.marinellagite.it) runs tour boats from Palau, located on Sardinia's northern coast. They make two or three stops at beaches and normally serve lunch. (Boats leave 10-11am and return 5-6pm. €35. Purchase tickets 1 day ahead.) **Panoramica Dei Comi** is a paved road circling the island—bike or motor along it for spectacular sea views, and then pause for a bit of sunbathing.

Charming **Hotel Arcipelago ❹**, V. Indipendenza 2, is a good deal but a 20min. walk from the *centro*. (☎0789 72 73 28. Breakfast included. Reservation required July-Aug. Singles €45-55; doubles €60-85. V.) Young locals flock to **Garden Bar ❸**, V. Garibaldi 65, for its tasty, varied cuisine and cool aquatic decor. (☎0787 73 88 25. Pizza €3.50-8. *Primi* €6-15. *Secondi* €6-20. Cover €1.50. Open daily 11:30am-3pm and 5-11pm. MC/V.)

EneRmaR and Saremar run **ferries** between Palau and La Maddalena (EneRmaR ☎0789 73 54 68 or 0789 70 84 84. www.enermar.it. 15min.; every 30min. 5:45am-11pm. Round-trip €10. Saremar ☎0789 70 92 70. 15min.; every 30min. 7am-7pm. €10.) Though there is no tourist office on the archipelago, Palau's **tourist office** usually has brochures on La Maddelena's attractions. (☎0789 70 70 25. www.palau.it. Open daily 9am-1pm and 4:30-7:30pm.) **Postal Code:** 07024.

LATVIA (LATVIJA)

The serenity and easy charm of Latvia belie centuries of suffering. The country has been conquered and reconquered so many times that the year 2008 was only the 39th year of Latvian independence—ever. These days, Latvia's vibrant capital, Rīga, is under siege by a new force: tourism. Cheap flights have brought so many Western visitors that Rīga's Old Town can feel like one big British bachelor party on summer weekends. You don't have to wander far from the beaten path, however, to discover the allure of Rīga's art nouveau elegance and student nightlife, its stunning seacoast, and the wild beauty of its Gaujas Valley National Park.

DISCOVER LATVIA: SUGGESTED ITINERARIES

THREE DAYS. Settle into **Rīga** (p. 662) to enjoy stunning **Art Nouveau** architecture, **cafe culture,** and the best **music and performing arts** scene in the Baltics. Don't miss the **Occupation Museum.**

ONE WEEK. Begin your tour in seaside **Ventspils** (2 days; p. 667). After three days in **Rīga**, head to **Cēsis** (2 days; p. 667) to enjoy **Cēsis Castle** and the wilds of **Gaujas Valley National Park.**

ESSENTIALS

FACTS AND FIGURES

OFFICIAL NAME: Republic of Latvia.

CAPITAL: Rīga.

MAJOR CITIES: Daugavpils, Rēzekne.

POPULATION: 2,245,000.

TIME ZONE: GMT +2.

LANGUAGE: Latvian.

RELIGIONS: Lutheran 55%, Roman Catholic 24%, Russian Orthodox 9%.

NATIONAL BIRD: White Wagtail.

NUMBER OF AIRPORTS: 42.

WHEN TO GO

Latvia is wet year-round, with cold, snowy winters and short, rainy summers. Tourism peaks in July and August; if you'd prefer not to experience central Rīga amid throngs of people, late spring or early fall is the best time to visit. Head to the beaches in summer, as much of the coast remains untouristed.

DOCUMENTS AND FORMALITIES

EMBASSIES AND CONSULATES. Foreign embassies and consulates to Latvia are in Rīga (p. 663). Latvian embassies and consulates abroad include: **Australia,** Honorary Consul, 2 Mackennel St., East Ivanhoe, VIC 3079 (☎613 94 99 69 20; latcon@ozemail.com.au); **Canada,** 350 Sparks St., Ste. 1200, Ottawa, ON K1R 7S8 (☎613-238-6014; www.am.gov.lv/en/ottawa); **Ireland,** 92 St. Stephen's

Green, Dublin, 2 (☎353 14 28 33 20; www.am.gov.lv/en/ireland); **New Zealand,** Honorary Consul, 162 Kilmore St., Amsterdam House, Level 3, Christchurch (☎640 33 65 35 05); **UK,** 45 Nottingham Place, London, W1U 5LY (☎442 073 120 040; www.london.am.gov.lv); **US,** 2306 Massachusetts Ave., NW, Washington, D.C., 20008 (☎202 328 2840; www.latvia-usa.org).

ENTRANCE REQUIREMENTS.

Passport: Required of all travelers.

Visa: Not required of citizens of Australia, Canada, Ireland, New Zealand, the UK, and the US for stays up to 90 days.

Letter of Invitation: Not required for countries listed above.

Inoculations: Recommended up-to-date on DTaP (diphtheria, tetanus, and pertussis), hepatitis A, hepatitis B, MMR (measles, mumps, and rubella), polio booster, tick-borne encephalitis, and typhoid.

Work Permit: Required of all foreigners planning to work in Latvia.

International Driving Permit: Required of all those planning to drive.

VISA AND ENTRY INFORMATION. Those wishing to stay for a longer period must submit an **Aim of Residence** form to the Foreigner's Service Center, Office of Citizenship and Migration Affairs, Alunāna iela 1, Rīga, LV-1050 (☎67 21 96 50; www.pmlp.gov.lv/en) to receive a visa for temporary or permanent residence. All travelers must display a passport valid for three months beyond the duration of their planned stay in Latvia, and must also be able to give proof of a valid insurance policy to cover potential health service needs while in Latvia.

TOURIST SERVICES AND MONEY

EMERGENCY

Ambulance: ☎03. **Fire:** ☎01. **Police:** ☎02. **General Emergency:** ☎112.

TOURIST OFFICES. Offices of the state-run tourist bureau, distinguished by a green "i" are scattered throughout the country. In Rīga, employees of such establishments speak fluent English, but elsewhere, they may not. Private tourist offices are more helpful outside the capital.

LATVIAN (LATI)	
AUS$1 = 0.42LS	1LS = AUS$2.41
CDN$1 = 0.45LS	1LS = CDN$2.23
EUR€1 = 0.70LS	1LS = EUR€1.42
NZ$1 = 0.34LS	1LS = NZ$2.94
UK£1 = 0.89LS	1LS = UK£1.12
US$1 = 0.48LS	1LS = US$2.09

MONEY. The Latvian unit of currency is the **lat (Ls),** plural **latu,** each of which is divided into 100 **santimu.** Although Latvia has been a member of the EU since 2004, persistent inflation has rendered it unlikely that it will switch to the euro until 2012 at the earliest. **Inflation** is around 10%. Most banks exchange currency for 1% commission, except for **Hansabanka,** which does not charge fees. **ATMs** are common in Rīga and may also be found in larger towns. Some restaurants and hotels accept MasterCard and Visa. **Traveler's checks** are harder to use, but

both AmEx and Thomas Cook checks can be converted in Rīga. It's often difficult to exchange non-Baltic currencies other than US dollars or euro.

HEALTH AND SAFETY

Although some private clinics provide adequate medical supplies and services, Latvian medical facilities generally fall below Western standards. Latvia has been hot-listed by the World Health Organization for periodic outbreaks of incurable strains of **tuberculosis.** As a precaution, drink **bottled water** (available at grocery stores and kiosks, and often carbonated) or boil tap water before drinking. **Pharmacies** *(aptieka)* in Latvia are generally privately owned and fairly well-stocked with antibiotics and prescription medication produced in Latvia or other Eastern European countries. Although violent **crime** in Latvia is rare, travelers should be on their guard for pickpockets and scam artists. A common scam is to dupe foreigners into ordering outrageously expensive drinks in bars; travelers should always verify the price of drinks in advance. Both men and women should avoid walking alone at night. If you feel threatened, say *"Ej prom"* (EY prawm), which means "go away"; *"Liec man miera"* (LEEtz mahn MEE-rah; "leave me alone") says it more forcefully, and *"Ej bekot"* (EY bek-oht; "go pick mushrooms"), is even ruder. **Women travelers** may be verbally hassled at any hour, especially if traveling alone, but usually such harassment does not escalate to physical action. **Minorities** in Latvia are rare; incidents of harassment have been known to occur, although generally there is little discrimination. Although **homosexuality** is legal in Latvia, public displays of affection may result in violence. Women walk down the street holding hands, but this is strictly an indication of friendship and does not mean that Latvia is gay-friendly. Safe options for GLBT travelers include gay and lesbian clubs, which advertise themselves freely in Rīga. Expect less tolerance outside the capital.

TRANSPORTATION

BY PLANE. Airlines flying to Latvia use Rīga International Airport (**RIX;** ☎6720 7009; www.riga-airport.com). **Air Baltic, Finnair, Lufthansa, SAS,** and others make the hop to Rīga from their hubs. Budget airlines **easyJet** (☎0871 244 2366; www.easyjet.com) and **Ryanair** (☎353 12 49 77 91; www.ryanair.com) offer inexpensive fares from a limited number of cities.

BY TRAIN AND BUS. **Trains** link Latvia to Berlin, GER; Lviv, UKR; Odessa, UKR; Moscow, RUS; St. Petersburg, RUS; Tallinn, EST; and Vilnius, LTU. Trains are cheap and efficient, and stations are clearly marked. Latvia is not covered by **Eurail.** The Rīga **commuter rail** is very good and provides extensive service. For daytrips from Rīga, it's best to take the **electric train.** The Latvian word for "departures" is *atiet;* "arrivals" is *pienāk.* **Buses** are faster, cheaper, and more comfortable than trains for travel within Latvia. The major bus company servicing Latvia is **Eurolines** (www.eurolines.lv). Some crowded trips may leave you standing for long hours without a seat.

BY CAR. Road conditions in Latvia are improving after years of deterioration. For more info, consult the **Latvian State Roads** (www.lad.lv). **Taxi** stands in front of hotels charge higher rates. **Hitchhiking** is common, but drivers may ask for a fee comparable to bus fares. *Let's Go* does not recommend hitchhiking.

KEEPING IN TOUCH

PHONE CODES	**Country code:** 371. **International dialing prefix:** 011. For more info on how to place international calls, see **Inside Back Cover.**

EMAIL AND INTERNET. Internet is readily available in Rīga but rarer elsewhere. Internet cafes typically offer a range of services including printing, laminating, and CD burning. Fees average 1Ls per hour; outside of Rīga service is somewhat cheaper. Many libraries and cafes offer free service.

TELEPHONE. To make local or **international calls,** you must purchase a **phone card,** which are come in 3, 5, and 10Ls denominations from post offices, telephone offices, kiosks, and state stores and have instructions in English. To operate a phone, dial 0, then press 1 or 2 for English and follow the instructions. For international calls, **Tele2** has the best rates. International direct dial numbers include: **AT&T Direct** (☎80 00 22 88); **MCI** (☎800 8888); **Telecom New Zealand** (☎800 2100). For domestic calls, if a number is six digits, dial a 2 before it.

MAIL. Latvia's postal system is reliable; it generally takes mail 10-12 days to reach the US or Canada from Latvia. All post offices have infodesks where English is spoken. Mail can be received through **Poste Restante,** though this is not widely available. Envelopes should be addressed as follows: First name LAST NAME, POSTE RESTANTE, post office address, Postal Code, city, LATVIA.

LANGUAGE. Influenced by German, Russian, Estonian, and Swedish, Latvian is one of two languages (the other is Lithuanian) in the Baltic language group. Russian is widely spoken, and many young Latvians study English.

ACCOMMODATIONS AND CAMPING

LATVIA	❶	❷	❸	❹	❺
ACCOMMODATIONS	under 9Ls	9-14Ls	15-19Ls	20-24Ls	over 24Ls

Hostels are common in Latvia, as are **hotel** chains, **bed and breakfasts,** and **family-run guesthouses.** Hostels are often overrun, especially on summer weekends.

The **Latvian Youth Hostel Association,** 17-2 Siguldas Pr., Rīga LV-1014 (☎921 8560; www.hostellinglatvia.com), is a useful resource for info on hostels in Rīga and elsewhere. **College dormitories** are often the cheapest option, but are open to travelers only in the summer. The majority of small towns outside the capital have at most one hotel in the budget range; expect to pay 3-15Ls per night. **Campgrounds** are in the countryside. Camping outside marked areas is illegal.

FOOD AND DRINK

LATVIA	❶	❷	❸	❹	❺
FOOD	under 2Ls	2-3Ls	4-5Ls	6-7Ls2	over 7Ls

Latvian food is heavy and starchy—and therefore, delicious. Dark rye bread is a staple. Try *speķa rauši*, a warm pastry, or *biezpienmaize*, bread with sweet curds. Dark-colored *kaņepju sviests* (hemp butter) is good but too diluted for "medicinal" purposes. A particularly good Latvian beer is *Porteris*, from the Aldaris brewery. Cities offer foreign, **kosher,** and **vegetarian** cuisine.

HOLIDAYS AND FESTIVALS

Holidays: New Year's Day (Jan. 1); Good Friday (Apr. 10, 2009; Apr. 2, 2010); Easter Sunday (Apr. 12, 2009; Apr. 4, 2010); Labor Day (May 1); Ligo Day (June 23); Midsummer's Day (June 24); Independence Day (Nov. 18); Christmas (Dec. 25).

Festivals: Midsummer's Eve is celebrated across the Baltic states every June 23-24. An updated calendar of cultural events is available at http://latviatourism.lv. **Dziesmu Svētki,** a national song and dance festival, packs the streets of Rīga once every five years. Check out their website for updated details: www.dziesmusvetki2008.lv.

LATVIA

BEYOND TOURISM

For more info on opportunities across Europe, see **Beyond Tourism,** p. 60.

American Field Service (AFS), 71 W. 23rd St., 17th fl., New York, NY 10010, USA (☎1-212-807-8686; www.afs.org). Offers summer-, semester-, and year-long homestay exchange programs. Community service programs also offered for young adults 18+. Teaching programs available for current and retired teachers. Financial aid available.

RĪGA ☎7

Rīga (pop. 750,000) is the center of Latvia's cultural and economic life, fusing a fascinating mix of Russian and Latvian influences. Medieval church spires dominate the Old Town, founded in 1201 by the German Bishop Albert, while early 20th-century Art Nouveau masterpieces line the city's newer streets. The recent boom in tourism has transformed large sections of the city, particularly the Old Town, but it's not hard to find unspoiled sections off the main drags.

TRANSPORTATION

Flights: Lidosta Rīga (**RIX;** ☎720 7009; www.riga-airport.com), 8km southwest of Vecrīga. Take bus #22 from Janvara iela 13 (30min., 2-6 per hr., 0.30Ls) to the Old Town. **Air Baltic** (☎720 7777; www.airbaltic.com) flies to many European cities.

Trains: Centrālā Stacija (Central Station), Stacijas laukums (☎723 3113; www.ldz.lv), next to the bus station south of the Old Town. International tickets are sold at counters

1-6; destinations include **Moscow, RUS** (17hr., 1 per day, 16Ls), **St. Petersburg, RUS** (14hr., 2 per day, 9Ls), and **Vilnius, LIT** (5hr., 1 per day, 10-17Ls).

Buses: Autoosta, Prāgas 1 (☎900 0009; www.autoosta.lv), 100m from the train station, across the canal from the Central Market. To: **Kaunas, LIT** (4-5hr., 2 per day, 7-8.30Ls); **Minsk, BLR** (10-12hr., 1 per day, 14-15Ls); **Tallinn, EST** (4-6hr., 11 per day, 7-10Ls); **Vilnius, LIT** (5-6hr., 4-6 per day, 7-9Ls).

ORIENTATION AND PRACTICAL INFORMATION

The city is divided in half by **Brīvības bulvāris,** which leads from the outskirts of town to the **Freedom Monument** in the center, becomes **Kaļķu iela,** and passes through **Vecrīga** (Old Rīga). To reach Vecrīga from the train station, turn left on Marijas iela and then right on any of the small streets beyond the canal.

Tourist Office: Rātslaukums 6 (☎703 4377; www.rigatourism.com), in the town square, next to the House of the Blackheads. Gives out free **maps,** arranges walking and bus tours (6-9Ls), books accommodation at no extra charge, and provides advice and brochures, including *Rīga in Your Pocket* (2Ls). Open daily in summer 9am-7pm; in low-season 10am-7pm. AmEx/MC/V.

Embassies and Consulates: Australia, Tomsona 33-1 (☎672 24251). Open Tu 10am-noon, Th 3-5pm. **Canada,** Baznīcas 20/22 (☎781 3945). Open M-F 9am-5:30pm. **Ireland,** Alberta iela 13 (☎67 03 93 70). Open M-Tu and Th-F 10am-noon. **UK,** Alunāna iela 5 (☎777 4700; www.britain.lv). Open M-F 9am-5pm. **US,** Raiņa bul. 7 (☎703 6200; www.usembassy.lv). Open M-Tu and Th 9-11:30am.

Currency Exchange: At any of the **Valutos Maiņa** kiosks. **Unibanka,** Pils iela 23, gives MC/V **cash advances** and cashes both AmEx and Thomas Cook **traveler's checks** without commission. Open M-F 9am-5pm.

24hr. Pharmacy: Vecpilsētas Aptieka, Audeju 20 (☎721 3340).

Internet: Many hostels and restaurants provide Wi-Fi. For dedicated kiosks, try **Planeta Internet Cafe,** Vailu iela 41 (☎672 200 30), near the Old Town Hostel. Open 10am-4pm daily. 0.30Ls for 30min., 1.10Ls for 2hr. **Lattlecom's** Wi-Fi networks blanket the Old Town. Look for establishments with the Lattlecom logo in the window and purchase an **access card** inside (0.94Ls per hr.)

Post Office: Stacijas laukumā 1 (☎701 8804; www.pasts.lv/en), near the train station. **Poste Restante** at window #9. Open M-F 7am-8pm, Sa 8am-6pm, Su 8am-4pm. Another branch at Brīvības bul. 19. **Postal Code:** LV-1050.

ACCOMMODATIONS

Make reservations well ahead during the high-season. Some tourist offices will arrange homestays and apartments for a small fee.

Old Town Hostel, Vaļņu iela 43 (☎722 3406; www.rigaoldtownhostel.lv). A friendly hostel equipped with a pub downstairs. Clean beds and bright, freshly painted dorms. Kitchen, sauna, free Internet, and Wi-Fi. English spoken. Safes in rooms. Check-in noon. 12-bed dorms from 8Ls; 6-bed 10Ls. MC/V. ❷

Friendly Fun Frank's, 11 Novembra krastmala 29, (☎599 0612; www.franks.lv). Walk toward the river and turn right on Novembra krastmala. This party hostel offers nightly outings (cover waived) to pubs and clubs in Rīga, as well as a free beer when you arrive. Fairly clean dorms and common room. Free Internet and spotty Wi-Fi. Dorms from 7Ls, online booking discount. Cash only. ❷

City Hostel, Elizabetes iela 101 (☎672 80124; www.cityhostel.lv). From the station, turn right and walk along Marijas; turn right on Elizabetes. Wooden bunks in a converted

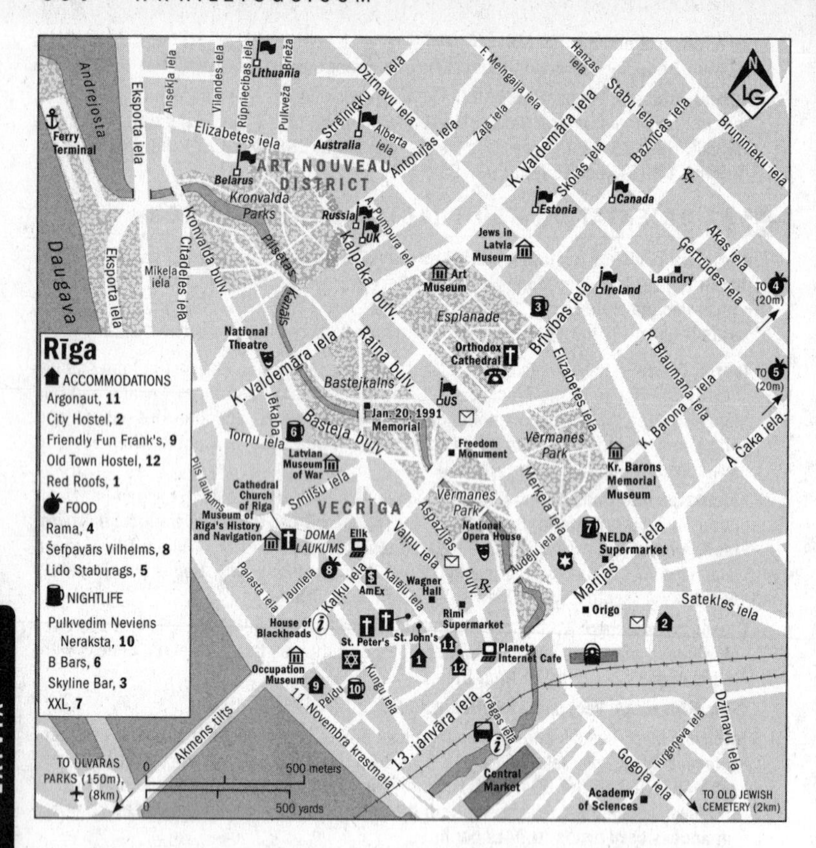

townhouse make for a quiet, comfy stay. Kitchen, common room, and free Internet. 10-bed dorms 5Ls; 8-bed 6Ls. Low-season discount. Cash only. ❶

Argonaut, Kalēju 50 (☎614 7214; www.argonauthostel.com). Key-card door access and gigantic lockers ensure security. Friendly staff. Basic kitchen, free Internet, and Wi-Fi in common room and kitchen. 10-bed dorms 8Ls; 4-bed dorms 12Ls. MC/V. ❷

Red Roofs, Jana 6 (☎673 50560; www.redroofs.lv). In the heart of the Old Town, this hostel provides clean, spacious rooms. Breakfast included. Free Wi-Fi. 8.50-12Ls. ❷

FOOD

Twenty-four hour food and liquor stores are at Marijas 5 (Nelda) and Brīvības bul. 68. **Centrālais Tirgus** (Central Market), in Zeppelin hangars behind the bus station, is one of the largest markets in Europe. (Open M and Su 8am-4pm, Tu-Sa 8am-5pm.) One fabulous Russian import that has stuck around is tea: tearooms dot the city and are perfect for an afternoon or evening snack.

Rama, K. Barona iela 56 (☎727 2490), between Gertrudes and Stabu iela. Eat well for about 2Ls at this Hare Krishna-run cafeteria, which serves hearty Indian-style vegetarian fare and donates profits to feed the poor. Open M-Sa 10am-7pm. Cash only. ❶

Šefpavārs Vilhelms, Škuņu iela 6. Look for the large chef statue outside this pancake house that offers meat, sweet, salty, and vegetarian pancakes. Slather on jam or sour cream and grab a glass of milk or yogurt: you'll be well fed for under 2Ls. Open M-Th 9am-10pm, Sa-Su 10am-10pm. Cash only. ❶

Lido Staburags, A. Čaka iela 55 (☎729 9787). Enormous portions of authentic Latvian cuisine served amid rustic decor. Try the unfiltered house beer (1.50Ls per 0.5L). Entrees 3-8Ls. Open daily noon-midnight. MC/V. ❷

SIGHTS

FREEDOM MONUMENT AND ENVIRONS. In the center of Vecrīga is the Freedom Monument (Brīvības Piemineklis), known as "Milda." *(At Raiņa bul. and Brīvības bul.)* Continuing along Kaļķu iela to the river, you'll see one of the few remaining Soviet monuments: the **Latvian Riflemen Monument** (Latviešu Strēlnieku Laukums) in the town square, honoring Lenin's famous bodyguards. Rising behind the statue is the **Occupation Museum** (Okupācijas muzejs), Strēlnieku laukums 1, which vividly depicts the Soviet and Nazi occupations. *(Open M-F 9am-7pm, Sa-Su 10am-7pm. Donations accepted.)* Next to the museum stands the **House of the Blackheads** (Melngalvju nams), Rātslaukums 7. Built in 1344 by a guild of unmarried merchants and then destroyed by the Nazis and Soviets, this unusual building was reconstructed in honor of Rīga's 800th birthday. The structure houses a museum and an assembly hall, and occasionally hosts concerts. *(Open May-Sept. Tu-Sa 10am-5pm, Oct.-Apr. Tu-Su 11am-5pm. 2Ls, students 1Ls. Cash only.)*

ELSEWHERE IN VECRĪGA. Follow Kaļķu iela from the Freedom Monument and turn right on Šķūņu iela to reach **Dome Square** (Doma laukums) and the **Cathedral Church of Rīga** (Doma baznīca). The organ boasts over 6700 pipes. *(Open daily June-Sept. 9am-6pm, Oct.-May 10am-5pm. Concerts in summer Su, W, F 7pm. Cathedral 2Ls, students 1.50Ls. Cash only.)* Next to the cathedral is the **Museum of Rīga's History and Navigation** (Rīgas Vēstures un Kugnie-cības Muzejs), Palasta iela 4. Established in 1773, this collection helped to rekindle Latvia's cultural heritage after Soviet efforts to suppress it. *(Open W-Su May-Sept. 10am-5pm; Oct.-Apr. 11am-5pm. 3Ls, students 1Ls. Tours in English, German, and Russian, 8Ls.)* From the top of the 123m spire of **St. Peter's Church** (Sv. Pētera baznīca), you can see much of the city. *(On Skāmu iela, off Kaļķu iela. Open Tu-Su in summer 10am-5:30pm; low-season 10am-5pm. Ticket office closes for lunch. Church 0.50Ls. Tower 2Ls. Cash only.)* The magnificent Neoclassical **State Museum of Art** (Latvjas nacionalais), Kr. Valdemāra iela 10A, has 18th- to 20th-century Latvian art and occasional concerts. *(www.vmm.lv. Open Oct.-Mar. Tu-Su 11am-5pm; Apr.-Sept. Tu 11am-5pm, W 11am-7pm, Th-Su 11am-5pm. 3Ls, students 1.50Ls.)* The newer areas of Rīga display **Art Nouveau** Jugendstil architecture; the style is most visible on Alberta iela, Elizabetes iela, and Strēlnieku laukums.

BASTEJKALNS. Rīga's central park, surrounded by the Old City moat (Pīlsētas kanāls), has ruins of the old city walls. Across and around the canal, five slabs of stone stand as **memorials** to the events of January 20, 1991, when Soviet forces stormed the Interior Ministry on Raiņa bul. At the northern end of Bastejkalns, on K. Valdemāra iela, sits the **National Theater,** where Latvia first declared its independence on November 18, 1918. *(Open daily 10am-7pm. Tickets 1-15Ls.)*

NIGHTLIFE

The nightlife scene is centered in Vecrīga, where there are a variety of options for those who want to dance until dawn.

Skyline Bar, Elizabetes iela 55. On the 26th fl. of the Reval Hotel Latvija. Has the best view in the city. Beer 2-3Ls. Mixed drinks 4-7Ls. F-Sa DJ from 9pm. 21+ after 11pm. Open M-Th and Su 3pm-2am, F-Sa 3pm-3am. AmEx/MC/V.

Pulkvedim Neviens Neraksta, Peldu 26/28 (www.pulkvedis.lv). The dark upstairs bar and dance floor contrast with the colorful basement lounge. Relaxed atmosphere. Great DJs. Beer 1.30-3Ls. F-Sa 3Ls. Open M-Th 8pm-3am, F-Sa 8pm-5am. AmEx/MC/V.

B Bars, Torņu iela 4, on the lane by Rīga Castle's Powder Tower. Try *balzams,* Latvia's national liquor—a mysterious herb-and-berry brew—in one of the dozen creative cocktails (3-5Ls.) Open M-W and Su 11am-midnight, Th-Sa 11am-1am. AmEx/MC/V.

XXL, A. Kalniņa iela 4 (☎728 2276; www.xxl.lv). Located off K. Barona iela. Gay bar, club, and sauna. Buzz to be let in. Mixed men and women F-Sa. Cover Tu-Sa 1-10Ls; 1Ls specials M. Open daily 6pm-7am. MC/V.

DAYTRIPS FROM RĪGA

JŪRMALA

The commuter rail runs from Rīga to Jūrmala (30min., 2 per hr., 0.50Ls). Alternatively, take one of the frequent trains from Rīga to Sloka, and get off at the Majori stop (1.25Ls round-trip). Public buses (0.30Ls) and microbuses (0.50Ls) also connect Jūrmala's towns.

Boardwalks and sun-bleached sand cover the narrow spit of Jūrmala. Visitors have come to this set of 13 small towns since the 19th century. The coastal towns between **Bulduri** and **Dubulti** are popular for sunning and swimming, but Jūrmala's social center is **Majori,** where trendy folk play volleyball or wander **Jomas iela,** a pedestrian street lined with cafes and shops. **Bicycles** are popular; rent one at **Picnic**, 21 Melluzu Prosp. (☎6776 7899. 2Ls per hr., 10Ls per day.)

Sue's Asia ❸, Jomas iela 74, offers Chinese, Indian, and Thai cuisine. Waitresses in saris serve the same fine fare that scored Rīga's branch a spot on *Condé Nast*'s list of the world's 100 best restaurants. (☎775 5900. Entrees 3-12Ls. Open daily noon-midnight. MC/V.) Head to **Dukats ❶,** Dubulti, Baznicas 12/14, for salads and cutlets under 3Ls. Look for the yellow "Bistro" sign. From the beach, exit at Stacija Dubulti. Don't forget to grab a delicious pastry on your way out. (☎776 0782. Open daily 8am-9pm. AmEx/MC/V.)

There are two **tourist offices** in Majori. The first, Lienes iela 5, by the train station, is run by the City Council and has free maps. Look for the white "i" on a green background. (☎714 7900; www.jurmala.lv. Open M-F 9am-7pm, Sa 10am-5pm, Su 10am-3pm.) The other, Jomas iela 42, is privately owned and offers similar services. Both offices can arrange accommodations at no extra charge. (☎776 4276; jurmalainfo@bkc.lv. Open in summer M-F 9am-7pm, Sa-Su 1-7pm; in winter M-F 9am-7pm. Cash only.) **Postal Code:** LV-2105.

SIGULDA

Trains run from Rīga on the Rīga-Lugaži commuter rail line (1hr., 9 per day, 0.97Ls). From the station, walk up Raiņa iela to the town center. Raiņa iela becomes Gaujas iela. After the bridge, the road turns into Turaidas iela and passes Turaida Castle. Buses run from Rīga hourly (1Ls). A bus labeled "Turaida" runs directly to Turaida Castle (7 per day, 0.30Ls).

The **Knights of the Sword,** Germanic crusaders who Christianized much of Latvia in the 13th century, made Segewald—modern-day Sigulda (pop. 10,000)—their base of operations. Today the Gauja National Park Administration has its headquarters in this town of well-tended gardens and hilly streets. 50km from Rīga, the area offers biking, bobsledding, bungee-jumping, horseback riding, hot-air ballooning, rafting, and skiing. **Makars Tourism Agency,** Peldu 1, arranges excursions and rents boats and camping equipment. (☎2924 4948; www.makars.lv.) The area's main sights lie along a 5km stretch of road. Farthest from town are the restored brick fortifications of the **Turaida Castle Complex** (Turaidas Muzejrezervats), Turaidas iela 10, visible throughout the Gauja Valley; climb the staircase in the main tower for a view of a carpet-like forest and a TV tower or two. (Tower open daily 9am-10pm. Admission free with ticket from Turaidas Museum Reserve. 3Ls, students 1Ls. Cash only.) Take Turaidas iela back down the hill to reach the famous **caves** of Sigulda. Inscriptions and coats of arms from as early as the 16th century cover the chiseled mouth of **Gutman's Cave** (Gūtmaņa ala). On a ridge to the right of Gaujas iela, on the same side of the river as town, is the **Sigulda Dome** palace, behind which lie the ruins of **Sigulda Castle** (Siguldas pilsdrupas). For a quick bite, head to the deli in supermarket **Elvi ❶,** Vidus iela 1, where you can fill up on 2-3Ls. (Open daily 8am-11pm.)

From the train station, 1km along Raiņa iela is the **Gauja National Park Visitor Centre,** Baznicas 7. (☎6780 0388; www.gnp.gov.lv. Open in summer M 9:30am-5pm, Tu-Su 9:30am-7pm; in winter daily 10am-4pm.) The **tourist information center** is at Valdemara 1a (open daily 9am-7pm). **Postal Code:** LV-2150.

CĒSIS

Cēsis is served by infrequent trains from Rīga via Sigulda (1-2hr., 1 per 4hr., 1.50Ls). Buses are more convenient (2hr., 2 per hr., 1.80Ls).

Sprawling medieval ruins and Cēsu, the local brew, make Cēsis (TSEY-sis; pop. 18,400) the classic Latvian town. Crusading Germans built the famous **Cēsis Castle** in 1209. Explore the old castle's dark interior with a hard-hat and your very own lantern. At the garden entrance, take a moment to view the fallen Lenin statue, complete with a wooden coffin. (☎412 1815. Open M-Th and Su 10am-7pm, F-Sa 10am-8pm. 2Ls, students 1Ls. Cash only.)

The **tourist office,** Pils laukums 1, across from the castle, offers free maps, has **Internet** (0.30Ls per 10min.), and arranges private rooms for a 1Ls fee. (☎412 1815; www.tourism.cesis.lv. Open in summer M and Su 9am-5pm, Tu-Sa 9am-7pm. AmEx/MC/V.) **Postal Code:** LV-4101.

VENTSPILS

Taking a bus is the most convenient way to travel to Ventspils. Buses run between Ventspils and Kuldiga (7 per day, 1.40Ls), Leipaja (8 per day, 2-4Ls), and Rīga (17 per day, 4Ls).

The colorful, cobblestone streets and perfectly manicured gardens of Ventspils (pop. 43,800) hardly convey the city's industrial past. Once a base for Russian oil exports, this wealthy port city is now home to the cleanest, most beautiful coastlines in Latvia. Stroll on the pebbled shore at **Blue Flag Beach,** internationally recognized for high water safety and cleanliness. Nearby, the **Seaside Open Air Museum,** Rinka iela 2, showcases the history of fishing in Ventspils, including an extensive exhibition of boats and a forest path dotted with the largest anchor collection in the world. (☎6362 4467. Open May-Oct. 10am-6pm; Nov.-Apr. M-F 11am-5pm. 1Ls, students 0.40Ls.) The **Livonian Order Castle,** Jana iela 17, is one of the oldest standing medieval fortresses. View tools, jewelry, and coins while the sounds of recorded dog barks and trumpets carry on in the background. Thankfully, silence reigns in the contemporary art displays on the upper floors. (☎6362 2031; www.ventspilsmuzejs.lv. 1.50Ls, students 0.75Ls.)

The **Guesthouse at Meza Street ❷,** Mezu iela 13, is a family-run guesthouse in a quiet neighborhood with clean rooms surrounded by tidy private gardens. (☎2942 2407. Shared baths. Breakfast 2Ls. Laundry 8Ls. Singles 8Ls; doubles 12Ls.) **Krodzins Don Basil ❷,** Annas iela 5, has enormous pasta plates (2-5Ls), salads, and excellent coffee. (☎6362 3434. Open daily 11am-11pm. MC/V.)

The **tourist information center** is at Darza iela 6. (☎362 2263; www.tourism.ventspils.lv. Open M-F 8am-7pm, Sa 10am-5pm, Su 10am-3pm.) The **post office** is at Platā iela 8. (Open M-F 8am-6pm, Sa 8am-4pm.) **Postal Code:** LV-3601.

LIECHTENSTEIN

Every year on Assumption Day (Aug. 15), which also happens to be Prince Hans-Adam II's birthday, all of Liechtenstein's citizens are invited to celebrate with the royal family at the Vaduz Palace. Luckily for him, only 35,000 people reside in the 160 sq. km nation. Despite its miniscule size and population, Europe's only absolute monarchy boasts imposing mountains with great biking, hiking, and skiing.

DISCOVER LIECHTENSTEIN: SUGGESTED ITINERARY

8AM. Wake-up. Shower.

8:15AM. Breakfast. Brush your teeth!

9AM. Spy on the royal family outside **Schloß Vaduz** (p. 669).

9:25AM. Debate the best hiking routes (p. 669) with the tourist office staff.

9:55AM. 5min. bathroom break.

10AM. Stampede the **Postmuseum.**

11AM. Lose track of time in **Liechtensteinisches Landesmuseum** (p. 670).

NOON. Nosh a pizza at **Brasserie Burg.**

12:30PM. Leave for Malbun.

1:15PM. Ride the chairlift and marvel at views of the **Silberhorn** and **Sareiserjoch.**

2PM. Become king of two mountains; trek the **Fürstin-Gina-Weg.**

3:22PM. 10min. hiking break. Eat trail mix and have a drink—water, preferably.

6:45PM. Shed your clothes (but don a swimsuit) for a refreshing dip in the **Alpenhotel** pool (p. 670).

7:45PM. If hiking smell persists, shower.

8PM. Dinner and bed. You're done!

ESSENTIALS

FACTS AND FIGURES

OFFICIAL NAME: Principality of Liechtenstein.

CAPITAL: Vaduz.

MAJOR TOWNS: Schaan, Triesen.

POPULATION: 35,000.

LAND AREA: 160 sq. km.

COASTLINE: 0km.

TIME ZONE: GMT +1

LANGUAGE: German (p. 1062).

RELIGIONS: Roman Catholic (79%), Protestant (8%).

FORM OF GOVERNMENT: Constitutional hereditary monarchy.

LITERACY: 100%

DOCUMENTS AND FORMALITIES. Citizens of Australia, Canada, New Zealand, the UK, the EU, and the US do not need a visa for stays of up to 90 days.

TRANSPORTATION. Catch a bus from Feldkirch in Austria (30min., 1 per hr., 3.80CHF), or from Buchs (25min., 4-5 per hr., 3.60CHF) or Sargans (30-40min. 4 per hr., 5.80CHF), across the border in Switzerland. Liechtenstein has no rail system. Its cheap, efficient **PostBus** (www.sbb.ch) system links all 11 towns. A **one-week bus ticket** (19CHF) covers the entire principality and buses to Swiss and Austrian border towns. You can buy all tickets and passes on board. The **Swiss Pass** (p. 997) and **Swiss Youth Pass** are valid in Liechtenstein.

EMERGENCY Ambulance, Fire, and Police: ☎112.

MONEY. The Liechtenstein unit of currency is the **Swiss franc (CHF),** plural Swiss francs. One Swiss franc is equal to 100 centimes, with standard denominations of 5, 10, 20, and 50 centimes and 1, 2, and 5CHF in coins, and 10, 20, 50, 100, 200, 500, and 1000CHF in notes. All major credit cards are widely accepted. As restaurant checks generally include a small service charge, most patrons round up the bill instead of leaving an additional tip. Switzerland has the best exchange rates. Conversion rates for the Swiss franc are listed on p. 997.

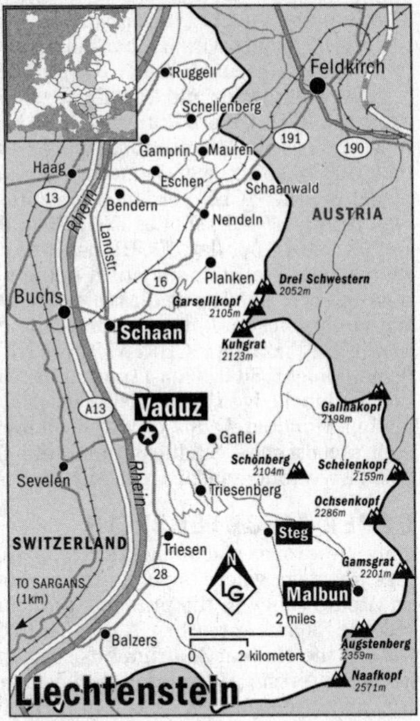

Liechtenstein has a 7.6% **value added tax (VAT),** a sales tax applied to national deliveries and services made in return for payments, in-house consumption, and importing services or objects. The prices given in *Let's Go* include VAT. In the airport upon exiting Liechtenstein and the EU, non-EU citizens can claim a refund on VAT paid for goods purchased at participating stores. In order to qualify for a refund, you must spend at least 400CHF: make sure to ask for a refund form. For more info on VAT refund, see p. 21.

BEYOND TOURISM. **European Voluntary Service** programs (http://ec.europa.eu/youth) enable EU citizens to spend a fully-funded year doing service in another European nation. Non-EU residents may visit local tourist offices to see about regional positions available. The **Special Olympics** (www.specialolympics.li) also provides travelers with volunteer opportunities. For more info on opportunities across Europe, see **Beyond Tourism**, p. 60.

VADUZ AND LOWER LIECHTENSTEIN ☎00423

As the capital, **Vaduz** (pop. 5000) attracts the most visitors of any part of Liechtenstein. Home to the ruling Prince, the 12th-century **Schloß Vaduz** (Vaduz Castle) stands as the principality's most recognizable icon. Visitors cannot see the interior where the royal family currently resides, but they can hike 20min. up to the castle for a closer look. The trail begins near the tourist office. Vaduz city train offers 35min tours (☎00423 777 3490; www.citytrain.li; 8CHF) of the old town, castle, and various other sights. Ask about it in the tourist office. For more art and culture, the **Kunstmuseum Liechtenstein** and **Postmuseum** reside in the same cube-shaped building diagonally across the street from the tourist office, Städtle 32. The Kunstmuseum hosts 7-week long, rotating, interactive, modern art exhibits. The curators are happy to assist in interpreting some of the peculiar modern art pieces. (☎00423 235 0300; www.kunstmuseum.li. Open Tu-W and F-Su 10am-5pm, Th 10am-8pm. Free.) The Postmuseum showcases almost every **stamp** the country has printed and has a video explaining the process of stamp making. (☎00423 239 6846. Open daily 10am-noon and 1-5pm. Free.) The **Liechtensteinisches Landesmuseum,** Städtle 43, chronicles the principality's history, beginning with its first inhabitants 8000 years ago. (☎00423 239 6820; www.landesmuseum.li. Open Tu and Th-Su 10am-5pm, W 10am-8pm.)

In between Vaduz and the village of Schaan sits Liechtenstein's sole **Jugendherberge (HI) ❷,** Untere Rüttig. 6. From Vaduz, take bus #11, 12, or 14 to Mühleholz, walk to the intersection, turn left on Marianumstr., and follow the signs. (☎00423 232 5022; www.youthhostel.ch/schaan. Breakfast included. Laundry 6CHF. Internet 1CHF per 5min. Reception 7:30-10am and 5-10pm. Open Mar.-Oct. Dorms 37CHF; singles 62CHF; doubles 94CHF. 6CHF HI discount. Bike rentals 22CHF per day, 15CHF per ½-day. AmEx/MC/V.) Finding cheap restaurants in Liechtenstein may turn into a never-ending quest. Either bring your own food, or splurge at **Brasserie Burg ❸,** Städtle 15, in the center of Vaduz, for sandwiches and burgers for 8CHF. (☎00423 232 2131. Salad buffet 9.50-14.50CHF. Pizza 14-18CHF. Wi-Fi 15CHF per 2hr. Open M-F 8:30am-11pm, Sa 9am-midnight, Su 9:30am-11pm. AmEx/MC/V.) Pick up a hiking **map** (16CHF), or an all-inclusive **Liechtenstein card** (25CHF for 2 days; includes bus system, Malbun Gondola, Vaduz Citytrain, all museum access, and more) at Liechtenstein's **tourist office,** Städtle 37, up the hill from the Vaduz bus stop. (☎00423 239 6300; www.tourismus.li. Open M-F 9am-noon and 1:30-5pm.)

UPPER LIECHTENSTEIN ☎00423

Only a few roads and hiking trails wind through the mountain villages of Upper Liechtenstein, where the country's real beauty lies. The city of **Malbun** rests in an Alpine valley in the principality's southeastern corner. Reach Malbun by bus #21 (30min., 2 per hr.). A popular hiking trail (4-5hr.) starts at the chairlift base at the Malbun Zentrum bus stop and follows **Fürstin-Gina-Weg** along two mountain crests. Be careful on the ridges above Malbun: the paths are narrow and often veer very close to cliffs. (Chairlift open July to mid-Oct. daily 8am-12:15pm and 1:15-4:50pm. 8CHF, students 6CHF; round-trip 13/10CHF.) In winter, skiers take to the slopes on the **Sareiserjoch** and the **Silberhorn.** (Chairlift open mid-Dec. to mid-Apr. 9am-4pm. Half-day passes 46CHF, students 35CHF; 1 day 68/55CHF; 2 days 123/98CHF.) **Hotel Steg ❶,** in the village of Steg, has the country's cheapest lodging. Take bus #21 to Steg Hotel. (☎00423 263 2146. Breakfast included. Linens included for private rooms. 10-bed dorms 25CHF; singles 45CHF; doubles 80CHF. MC/V.) **Alpenhotel Malbun ❸,** opposite the Malbun Jorabaoda bus stop, has an indoor pool. (☎00423 263 1181; www.alpenhotel.li. Reception 8am-10pm. Open mid-May to Oct. and mid-Dec. to Apr. Singles 70CHF; doubles 95CHF. AmEx/MC/V.) The **Schädler-Shop,** between the chairlift and the tourist office, has groceries. (Open M-F 8am-12:30pm and 1:30-5pm, Sa-Su 8am-6pm.) The **tourist office** is down the street from the Malbun Zentrum bus stop. (☎00423 263 6577; www.malbun.li. Open June-Oct. and mid-Dec. to mid-Apr. M-F 8am-6pm, Sa 9am-5pm, Su 8am-5pm.)

LITHUANIA (LIETUVA)

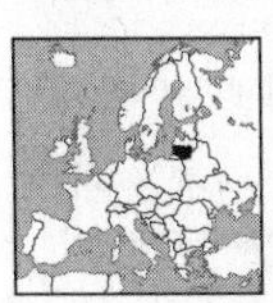

Lithuania has always been an offbeat place. Once the last pagan holdout in Christian Europe, the tiny country continues to forge an eccentric path, from the breakaway artists' republic and Frank Zappa statue in its capital, to drifting sand dunes, quirky folk art, and even a decaying Soviet missile base in the countryside. More conventional treats include the wild beauty of the coast and the Baroque architecture of Vilnius. Lithuania became the first Baltic nation to declare independence from the Soviet Union in 1990. Lithuania gained EU membership in 2004, and the country continues to push ahead with optimism.

DISCOVER LITHUANIA: SUGGESTED ITINERARIES

THREE DAYS. Head to the **Baltic Coast** to see the impressive **Drifting Dunes of Parnidis** in **Nida** (p. 681), then leave the **Curonian Spit** and go inland to the flourishing capital of **Vilnius** (p. 675).

ONE WEEK. After 4 days on the **Baltic Coast**, visit **Vilnius** (3 days), where you can explore the **Old Town,** wander through offbeat **Užupis,** and take a daytrip to **Trakai Castle,** the ancient capital.

ESSENTIALS

FACTS AND FIGURES

OFFICIAL NAME: Republic of Lithuania.

CAPITAL: Vilnius.

MAJOR CITIES: Kaunas, Klaipėda.

POPULATION: 3,565,000.

TIME ZONE: GMT +2.

LANGUAGE: Lithuanian.

NUMBER OF LAKES: 3000.

VEHICLE DENSITY: 18.5 per sq. km.

WHEN TO GO

Summers are brief but glorious in Lithuania, while winters are long and cold. Tourist season peaks between June and September, especially along the coast. A winter visit has its charms, especially if you're headed for Vilnius, but be aware that much of the coast closes in the low-season.

DOCUMENTS AND FORMALITIES

EMBASSIES AND CONSULATES. Foreign embassies to Lithuania are in Vilnius (p. 676). Lithuanian embassies and consulates abroad include: **Australia,** 40B Fiddens Wharf Rd., Killara, NSW 2071 (☎02 94 98 25 71); **Canada,** 130 Albert St., Ste. 204, Ottowa, ON K1P 5G4 (☎613-567-5458; www.lithuanianembassy.ca); **Ireland,** 90 Merrion Rd., Ballsbridge, Dublin 4 (☎1 668 8292); **New Zealand,** 17 Koraha St., Remuera, Auckland 1005 (☎9 524 9463); **UK,** 84 Gloucester Pl., London, W1U 6AU (☎20 74 86 64 01; www.lithuanianembassy.co.uk); **US,** 4590

MacArthur Blvd., NW, Ste. 200, Washington, D.C. 20007 (☎202-234-5860; www.ltembassyus.org). Check www.lithuania.embassyhomepage.com or http://lt.embassyinformation.com for more embassy info.

ENTRANCE REQUIREMENTS.

Passport: Required for all travelers.

Visa: Not required for stays under 90 days for citizens of Australia, Canada, Ireland, New Zealand, the UK, and the US.

Letter of Invitation: Not required for citizens of Australia, Canada, Ireland, New Zealand, the UK, and the US.

Inoculations: Recommended up-to-date on DTaP (diphtheria, tetanus, and pertussis), hepatitis A, hepatitis B, MMR (measles, mumps, and rubella), polio booster, tick-borne encephalitis, and typhoid.

Work Permit: Required of all those planning to work in Lithuania.

International Driving Permit: Required for all those planning to drive in Lithuania for periods of under 90 days except citizens of the US.

VISA AND ENTRY INFORMATION. Citizens of the EU do not need visas to travel to Lithuania. Citizens of Australia, Canada, New Zealand, and the US do not need a visa for stays of up to 90 days. Long-term visas (€60) can be purchased from the nearest embassy or consulate. Avoid crossing through Belarus to enter or exit Lithuania: not only do you need to obtain a transit visa (US$50) for Belarus in advance, but guards may also hassle you at the border.

TOURIST SERVICES AND MONEY

TOURIST OFFICES. Major cities have official tourist offices. **Litinterp** (Vilnius ☎5 212 38 50, Kaunas 37 22 87 18, Klaipėda 46 41 06 44; www.litinterp.lt) reserves accommodations and rents cars, usually without a surcharge. Most cities have an edition of the *In Your Pocket* series, available at kiosks and some hotels. Employees at tourist stations often speak English.

EMERGENCY	**Ambulance:** ☎033. **Fire:** ☎011. **Police:** ☎022. **General Emergency:** ☎112.

MONEY. The unit of currency is the **lita (Lt),** plural **litai** or **litų.** One lita is equal to 100 centų. The lita is fixed to the euro at €1 to 3.45Lt until the euro replaces the lita after 2010. The rapidly expanding economy has created **inflation** of about 5% in recent years. **Exchange bureaus** near the train station usually have worse rates than **banks.** Most banks cash **traveler's checks** for 2-3% commission. **Vilniaus Bankas** accepts major credit cards and traveler's checks for a small commission. Most places catering to locals don't take **credit cards.** Some establishments that claim to take MasterCard or Visa may not actually be able to do so.

LITHUANIAN LITAI (LT)		
	AUS$1 = 2.04LT	1LT = AUS$0.49
	CDN$1 = 2.21LT	1LT = CDN$0.45
	EUR€1 = 3.45LT	1LT = EUR€0.29
	NZ$1 = 1.67LT	1LT = NZ$0.60
	UK£1 = 4.38LT	1LT = UK£0.23
	US$1 = 2.35LT	1LT = US$0.43

HEALTH AND SAFETY

Lithuania's **medical facilities** are quickly catching up to Western standards. However, while most **hospitals** are stocked in basic medical supplies, there is a shortage of doctors. Many doctors expect immediate payment in cash. **Drink bottled mineral water,** and boil **tap water** for 10min. before drinking. Many **bathrooms** are nothing but a hole in the ground; carry toilet paper. Lithuania's **crime** rate is low; however, cab drivers think nothing of ripping you off, and petty crime is rampant. Nevertheless, Vilnius is one of the safer capitals in Europe.

Women traveling alone will be noticed but shouldn't encounter too much difficulty. Skirts, blouses, and heels are far more common than jeans, shorts, tank tops, or sneakers, but showing skin is acceptable at clubs. **Minorities** traveling to Lithuania may encounter unwanted attention or discrimination, though most is directed toward **Roma** (gypsies). Lithuania has made little effort to accommodate **disabled** travelers. **Homosexuality** is legal but not always tolerated.

TRANSPORTATION

BY PLANE. AirBaltic, Delta, Finnair, LOT, Lufthansa, SAS, and other airlines fly into Vilnius International Airport (**VNO;** ☎5 273 9305; www.vilnius-airport.lt). **Ryanair**

flies into Kaunas Airport (**KUN;** ☎37 399 307; www.kaunasair.lt). However, if you're already near the Baltic, trains and buses are the best option.

BY TRAIN. **Trains** are more popular for international and long-distance travel. Two major lines cross Lithuania: one runs north-south from Latvia through Šiauliai and Kaunas to Poland; the other runs east-west from Belarus through Vilnius and Kaunas to Kaliningrad, branching out around Vilnius and Klaipėda. Visit www.litrail.lt for more information.

BY BUS AND FERRY. Domestic **buses** are faster, more convenient, less crowded, and only slightly more expensive than trains. Whenever possible, try to catch an express bus; they're normally marked with an asterisk or an "E" on the timetable. They are direct, and can be up to twice as fast. Vilnius, Kaunas, and Klaipėda are easily reached by train or bus from Estonia, Latvia, Poland, and Russia. **Ferries** connect Klaipėda with Arhus and Aabenraa, DEN; Kiel, Zasnicas, and Mukran, GER; Baltijskas, RUS; and Ahus and Karlshamn, SWE.

BY CAR AND BY TAXI. All travelers planning to drive in Lithuania must purchase a **Liability Insurance Policy** at the Lithuanian border (79Lt for the 15-day min.) These policies may be purchased only with litas. There are inexpensive taxis in most cities. Agree on a price before getting in, or make sure that the meter is running. **Hitchhiking** is common; locals line up along major roads leaving large cities. Many drivers charge a fee comparable to local bus fares. *Let's Go* does not recommend hitchhiking.

KEEPING IN TOUCH

PHONE CODES	**Country code:** 370. **International dialing prefix:** 810. For more info on how to place international calls, see **Inside Back Cover.**

EMAIL AND INTERNET. Internet is widely available in Lithuania, though rarely for free. Most well-located Internet cafes charge 3-6Lt per hr.

TELEPHONE. There are two kinds of **public phones:** rectangular ones take magnetic strip cards, and rounded ones take chip cards. **Phone cards** are sold at phone offices and kiosks. Calls to Estonia and Latvia cost 1.65Lt per min.; Europe 5.80Lt; and the US 7.32Lt. Major **cell phone** operators include Bite, Omnitel, and Tele2. International access codes for calling out of Lithuania include: **Canada Direct** (☎8 800 900 04); **MCI** (☎8 800 900 26); **Sprint** (☎8 800 958 77).

MAIL. **Airmail** *(oro pastu)* letters abroad cost 1.70Lt (postcards 1.20Lt) and take about one week to reach the US. **Poste Restante** is available in Vilnius but hard to find elsewhere. Address the envelope as follows: first name LAST NAME, POSTE RESTANTE, post office address, Postal Code, city, LITHUANIA.

LANGUAGE. Lithuanian is one of only two Baltic languages (Latvian is the other). Polish is helpful in the south and German is spoken on the coast. Russian is also prevalent. Most Lithuanians understand basic English phrases. If someone seems to sneeze at you, he might be saying *ačiu* (ah-choo; thank you).

ACCOMMODATIONS AND CAMPING

LITHUANIA	❶	❷	❸	❹	❺
ACCOMMODATIONS	under 30Lt	31-80Lt	81-130Lt	131-180Lt	over 180Lt

Lithuania has many **youth hostels,** particularly in Vilnius and Klaipėda. HI membership is nominally required, but an **LJNN guest card** (10.50Lt at any of the hostels) will suffice. Their *Hostel Guide* has info on bike and car rentals and hotel reservations. **Hotels** across the price spectrum abound in Vilnius and most major towns. **Litinterp,** with offices in Vilnius, Kaunas, and Klaipėda, assists in finding **homestays** or **apartments** for rent. **Camping** is restricted by law to marked campgrounds; the law is well-enforced, particularly along the Curonian Spit.

FOOD AND DRINK

LITHUANIA	❶	❷	❸	❹	❺
FOOD	under 8Lt	8-17Lt	18-30Lt	31-40Lt	over 40Lt

Lithuanian cuisine is heavy and sometimes greasy. Keeping a **vegetarian** or **kosher** diet is difficult. Restaurants serve various types of *blynai* (pancakes) with *mėsa* (meat) or *varke* (cheese). *Cepelinai* ("zeppelins") are potato-dough missiles of meat, cheese, and mushrooms; *karbonadas* is breaded pork fillet; *saltibarščiai* is a beet-and-cucumber soup prevalent in the east; and *koldunai* are meat dumplings. Lithuanian **beer** flows freely. *Kalnapis* is popular in Vilnius and most of Lithuania, *Baltijos* reigns supreme around Klaipėda, and the award-winning *Utenos* is everywhere.

HOLIDAYS AND FESTIVALS

Holidays: New Year's Day and Flag Day (Jan. 1); Independence Day (Feb. 16); Restoration of Independence (Mar. 11); Easter Sunday (Apr. 12, 2009; Apr. 4, 2010); Labor Day (May 1); Midsummer's Day (June 24); Statehood Day (July 6); Assumption (Aug. 15); All Saints' Day (Nov. 1); Christmas (Dec. 25).

Festivals: Since the 17th century, regional craftsmen have gathered to display their wares each March in Vilnius at the **Kaziukas Fair.** The annual **Vilnius Festival,** held in June, attracts classical and jazz musicians from around the world and features performances at the Lithuanian National Philharmonic Hall.

BEYOND TOURISM

For more info on opportunities across Europe, see **Beyond Tourism,** p. 60.

Lithuanian Academy of Music and Theatre, Gedimino pr. 42, LT-01110 Vilnius, Lithuania (☎37 05 21 24 967; www.lmta.lt). Classes in music, art, and theater in Lithuania. Offers some music and multimedia arts classes in English.

VILNIUS ☎5

In 1323, an iron wolf on the top of Gediminas's Hill is said to have appeared to the Grand Duke in a dream and inspired him to found the city. The hill remains a good vantage point to take in the breadth of Lithuania's capital, which has turned its gaze resolutely toward modernity. The decaying ruins in the city are steadily giving way to stucco facades, Prada storefronts, and refurbished Baroque, Gothic, and Neoclassical architecture—reminders that Vilnius flourished for centuries before WWII and the grip of Soviet rule. Vilnius was chosen as one of the European Union's 2009 European Capitals of Culture.

TRANSPORTATION

Flights: Vilnius International Airport (**VNO;** Vilniaus oro uostas), Rodūnės Kelias 10a (☎05 230 6666; www.vilnius-airport.lt), 5km south of town. Buy a bus ticket (1.10Lt) from the Lietuvos Spauda kiosk on your right as you exit the hall. Take bus #1 to the Geležinkelio Stotis train station to reach the Old Town.

Trains: Geležinkelio Stotis, Geležinkelio 16 (☎05 233 0086, reservations in English 05 269 3722). Open daily 6-11am and noon-6pm. Trains run to: **Minsk, BLR** (5hr., 1 per day, 17Lt); **Moscow, RUS** (17hr., 1 per day, 138Lt); **St. Petersburg, RUS** (18hr., 1 per day, 126Lt); **Warsaw, POL** (8hr., Tu, Th, and Sa only, 85Lt).

Buses: Autobusų Stotis, Sodų 22 (☎05 290 1661, reservations 05 216 2977; www.toks.lt). **Eurolines Baltic International** (**EBI;** ☎05 215 1377; www.eurolines.lt) offers routes to **Berlin, GER** (17hr., 1 per day, 187Lt); **Rīga, LAT** (5hr., 4 per day, 45Lt); **St. Petersburg, RUS** (18hr., 4 per day, 129Lt); **Tallinn, EST** (9hr., 2 per day, 81Lt); **Warsaw, POL** (9-10hr., 3 per day, 105Lt); and other points west. Tickets in EBI kiosks to the right of the entrance to the bus station. For destinations within Lithuania, head to the *kasos* counters. ISIC discount. Open daily 6am-10pm.

Public Transportation: Buses and **trolleys** run daily 4am-midnight. Buy tickets at any **Lietuvos Spauda** kiosk (1.10Lt) or from the driver (1.40Lt). Tickets are checked frequently; punch them on board to avoid the 10Lt fine.

Taxis: Martono (☎05 240 0004). Cabbies are notorious for overcharging foreigners; get a local to hail one for you if possible. Make sure the meter is running before getting in.

ORIENTATION AND PRACTICAL INFORMATION

Geležinkelio runs east from the train and bus stations to **Aušros Vartų,** which leads downhill through the **Gates of Dawn** (Aušros Vartai) and into the **Old Town** (Senamiestis). Heading north, Aušros Vartų becomes **Didžioji** and then **Pilies** before reaching the base of Gediminas Hill. On the hill, the **Gediminas Tower** of the Higher Castle presides over **Cathedral Square** (Aikštė) and the banks of the River Neris. **Gedimino,** the main commercial artery, runs west from Aikštė.

Tourist Office: Vilniaus 22 (☎05 262 9660; www.vilnius.lt). Open M-F 9am-6pm, Sa 10am-4pm. Branches in the train station (☎05 269 2091) and town hall (☎05 262 6470). Open M-F 9am-6pm, Sa-Su 10am-4pm. **Laisvalaikis** card (100Lt) offers good deals for long-term visitors; card available at Respublika offices (☎05 852 123 344).

Embassies: Australia, Vilniaus 23 (☎05 212 3369; www.lithuania.embassy.gov.au/lt.html). Open Tu 10am-1pm, Th 2-5pm. **Canada,** Jogailos 4 (☎05 249 0950; www.canada.lt). Open daily 8:30am-5pm; consular services M, W, F 9am-noon. Open daily 8:30am-5pm. **UK,** Antakalnio 2 (☎05 246 2900; www.britain.lt). Open M-Th 8:30am-4:45pm, F 8:30am-3:30pm; consular services M-Th 9am-noon and 2-4:30pm, F 9am-noon. **US,** Akmenų 6 (☎05 266 5500; www.usembassy.lt). Open M-F 8am-5pm; consular services M-Th 8:30am-11:30am. Closed last W of each month.

Currency Exchange: Vilniaus Bankas, Vokiečių 9. Open M-Th 9am-6pm, F 9am-5pm. **Parex Bankas,** Geležinkelio 6, to the left of the train station. Open 24hr.

24hr. Pharmacy: Gedimino Vaistinė, Gedimino pr. 27 (☎05 261 0135). Open 24hr.

Hospital: Baltic-American Medical and Surgical Clinic, Nemenčinės 54A (☎05 234 2020 or 05 698 526 55; www.bak.lt). Accepts major American, British, and international insurance plans. Doctors on call 24hr.

Internet: Most hostels offer Wi-Fi or a computer with Internet, and many restaurants fall within wireless networks. Turn on your laptop while eating, or head to **Collegium,** Pilies 22 (☎05 261 8334). 6Lt per hr. Open M-F 8am-10pm, Sa-Su 11am-10pm.

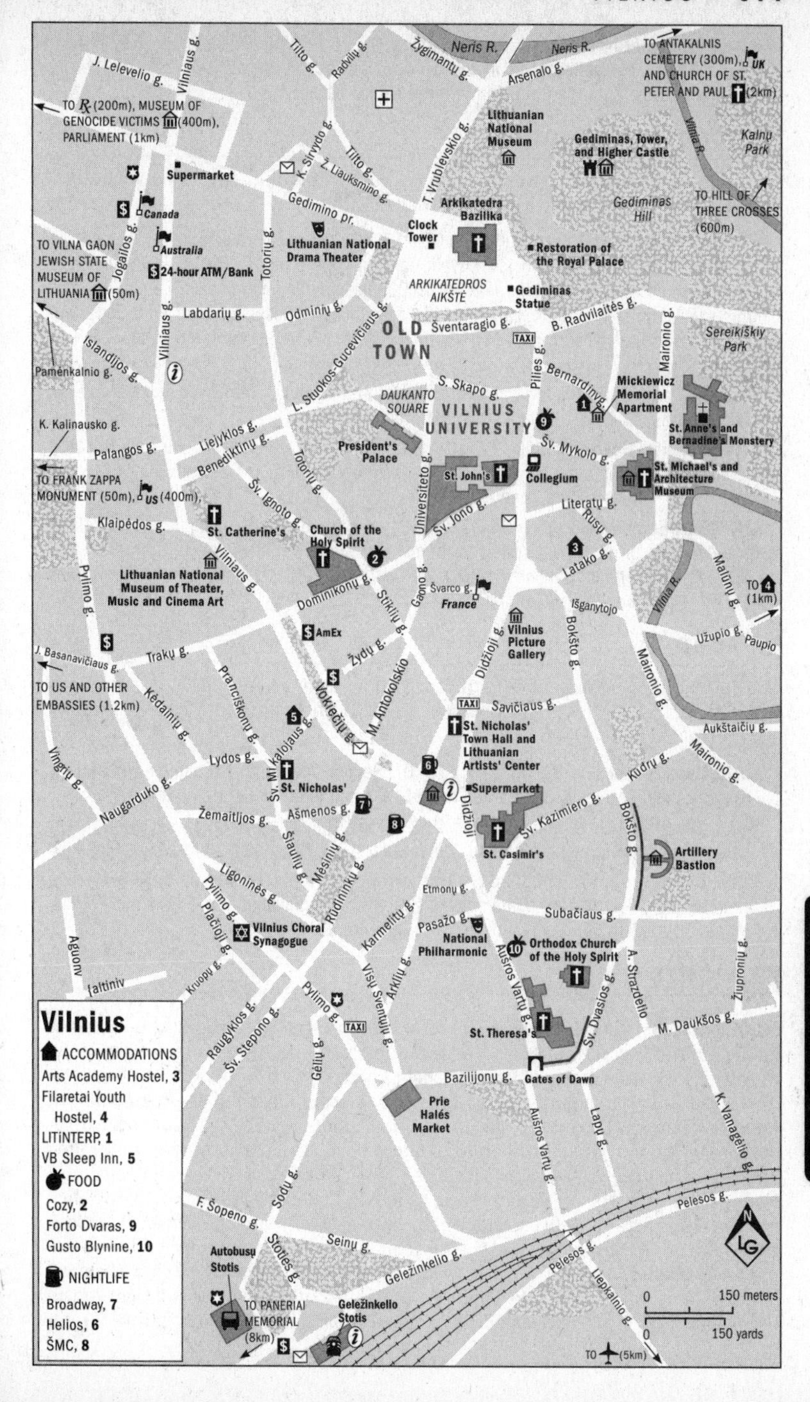
Vilnius
ACCOMMODATIONS
Arts Academy Hostel, 3
Filaretai Youth Hostel, 4
LITiNTERP, 1
VB Sleep Inn, 5
FOOD
Cozy, 2
Forto Dvaras, 9
Gusto Blynine, 10
NIGHTLIFE
Broadway, 7
Helios, 6
ŠMC, 8
OLD TOWN
VILNIUS UNIVERSITY
Neris R.
TO ANTAKALNIS CEMETERY (300m), UK AND CHURCH OF ST. PETER AND PAUL (2km)
TO (200m), MUSEUM OF GENOCIDE VICTIMS (400m), PARLIAMENT (1km)
Lithuanian National Museum
Gediminas Tower and Higher Castle
Kalnų Park
Gediminas Hill
TO HILL OF THREE CROSSES (600m)
Supermarket
Canada
Australia
24-hour ATM/Bank
TO VILNA GAON JEWISH STATE MUSEUM OF LITHUANIA (50m)
Lithuanian National Drama Theater
Clock Tower
Arkikatedra Bazilika
Restoration of the Royal Palace
ARKIKATEDROS AIKŠTĖ
Gediminas Statue
Sereikiškiy Park
Mickiewicz Memorial Apartment
St. Anne's and Bernadine's Monstery
DAUKANTO SQUARE
President's Palace
St. John's
Collegium
St. Michael's and Architecture Museum
TO FRANK ZAPPA MONUMENT (50m), US (400m)
St. Catherine's
Church of the Holy Spirit
Lithuanian National Museum of Theater, Music and Cinema Art
France
Vilnius Picture Gallery
TO (1km)
AmEx
TO US AND OTHER EMBASSIES (1.2km)
St. Nicholas' Town Hall and Lithuanian Artists' Center
St. Nicholas'
Supermarket
St. Casimir's
Artillery Bastion
Vilnius Choral Synagogue
National Philharmonic
Orthodox Church of the Holy Spirit
St. Theresa's
Gates of Dawn
Prie Halės Market
Autobusų Stotis
TO PANERIAI MEMORIAL (8km)
Geležinkelio Stotis
TO (5km)
0 150 meters
0 150 yards
J. Lelevelio g.
Vilniaus g.
Tilto g.
Radvilų g.
Žygimantų g.
Arsenalo g.
T. Vrublevskio g.
K. Sirvydo g.
Ž. Liauksmino g.
Gedimino pr.
Jogailos g.
Totorių g.
Labdarių g.
Odminių g.
Šventaragio g.
B. Radvilaitės g.
Maironio g.
Islandijos g.
Pamėnkalnio g.
L. Stuokos-Gucevičiaus g.
S. Skapo g.
Pilies g.
Bernardinų g.
K. Kalinausko g.
Liejyklos g.
Benediktinų g.
Palangos g.
Universiteto g.
Šv. Mykolo g.
Šv. Ignoto g.
Šv. Jono g.
Literatų g.
Rusų g.
Klaipėdos g.
Latako g.
Malūnų g.
Vilnia R.
Pylimo g.
Dominikonų g.
Gaono g.
Stiklių g.
Švarco g.
Išganytojo
Bokšto g.
Užupio g.
Paupio
J. Basanavičiaus g.
Trakų g.
Žydų g.
Didžioji g.
Pranciškonų g.
Kėdainių g.
M. Antokolskio
Vokiečių g.
Savičiaus g.
Aukštaičių g.
Šv. Mikalojaus g.
Lydos g.
Vingrių g.
Naugarduko g.
Kudrų g.
Žemaitljos g.
Ašmenos g.
Šv. Kazimiero g.
Šiaulių g.
Mėsinių g.
Ligoninės g.
Rūdininkų g.
Etmonų g.
Subačiaus g.
Plačioji g.
Karmelitų g.
Pasažo g.
Aguonų
Kruopų g.
Visų Šventųjų g.
Arklių g.
Aušros Vartų g.
A. Strazdelio
Žiupronių g.
Šv. Dvasios g.
M. Daukšos g.
Raugyklos g.
Šv. Stepono g.
Gėlių g.
Bazilijonų g.
Lapų g.
K. Vanagėlio g.
Sodų g.
F. Šopeno g.
Pelesos g.
Seinų g.
Stoties g.
Geležinkelio g.
Liepkalnio g.

LITHUANIA

Post Office: Lietuvos Paštas, Gedimino 7 (☎05 261 6759; www.post.lt), west of Katedros Aikštė. **Poste Restante** at the window labeled *"iki pareikalavimo"*; 0.50Lt fee. Open M-F 7am-7pm, Sa 9am-4pm. **Postal Code:** 01001.

ACCOMMODATIONS

Vilnius has a surprising number of youth hostels and inexpensive hotels. Reserve ahead, especially in the summer months.

Filaretai Youth Hostel, Filaretų 17 (☎05 215 4627; www.filaretaihostel.lt). Located in Užupis, 1km east of the Old Town. Walk east on Užupio across the Vilnia River. At the fork, bear left onto Krivių, then bear right onto Filaretų. Clean and friendly. Be aware that the area is dimly lit at night. Laundry 10Lt. Free Internet. Reserve ahead June-Sept. and weekends. Dorms 34Lt; triples and quads 42-52Lt. 5% HI discount. MC/V. ❷

VB Sleep Inn, Sv. Mikalojaus 3 (☎05 638 32818). Unbeatable location and laid-back social buzz. Look for the lane near the fountain on Vokieču. Free Wi-Fi. Pub crawl F-Sa, 20Lt. Dorms 39-45Lt; others 110-188Lt. Cash only. ❷

Arts Academy Hostel, Latako 2 (☎05 212 0102). Provides basic, centrally located rooms at unbeatable prices. Dorms only in summer. Dorms 20-22Lt; singles 60Lt; doubles 100Lt; triples 110Lt. Cash only. ❶

LITINTERP, Bernardinv 7/2 (☎05 212 3850; www.litinterp.lt). Places guests in B&Bs in the Old Town or in its own spacious rooms. Reception M-F 8:30am-5:30pm, Sa 9am-3pm. Reserve ahead. Singles 70-80Lt, with bath 90-100Lt; doubles 120-160Lt; triples 160-210Lt. 5% ISIC discount. MC/V. ❷

FOOD

Traditional *blynai* (pancakes) stuffed with meat or cheese are a great option for budget travelers. **Iki supermarkets** stock both local and Western brands. (Branch at Sodu 22. Open daily 8am-10pm.)

Forto Dvaras, Pilies 16 (☎05 526 11070). Serves traditional Lithuanian dishes in a rustic setting. Entrees 8-30Lt. Open daily 11am-midnight. AmEx/MC/V. ❷

Gusto Blynine, Ausros Vartu 6 (☎05 262 0056). Serves up a variety of stuffed pancakes. Vegetarian options available. Pancakes 2-10Lt. Open daily 9am-11pm. MC/V. ❶

Cozy, Dominikonų 10 (☎05 261 1137; www.cozy.lt). Meals are on the pricey side (entrees 18-36Lt), but try some snacks (10Lt) while emailing Mom. Free Wi-Fi. English menu. Open M-Th, Sa, Su 10am-2am, F 10am-4am. MC/V. ❶

SIGHTS

SENAMIESTIS. Facing the Old Town or Senamiestis, walk though the **Gates of Dawn** (Aušros Vartai) and enter the first door on the right to ascend worn steps to the 17th-century **Gates of Dawn Chapel** (Aušros Vartai Koplyčia). A few steps down Auros Vartų, a gateway leads to the **Orthodox Church of the Holy Spirit** (Šv. Dvasios bažnyčia), home to the remains of Saints Anthony, John, and Eustachio, beloved martyrs of Lithuania. Heading north, the street merges with Pilies and leads to **Vilnius University** (Vilniaus Universitetas), at Pilies and Šv. Jono. Founded in 1579, the university is the oldest in Eastern Europe. North on Pilies is **Cathedral Square** (Katedros Aikštė); its cathedral contains the **Chapel of St. Casimir** (v. Kazimiero koplyčia) and the royal mausoleum. Take the funicular up the hill to **Gediminas Tower** for a great view. Europe's most unexpected monument stands 50km west of the Old Town: a 4m steel shaft topped with a bust of the late freak rock legend **Frank Zappa** against a backdrop of wall graffiti. Zappa had no connection to Lithuania, but apparently he had fans there. *(Off Pylimo, between Kalinausko 1 and 3, on the right side of a parking lot.)*

OLD JEWISH QUARTER AND PANERIAI MEMORIAL. At the start of WWII, Vilnius had a thriving Jewish community of 100,000 (in a city of 230,000). Nazis left just 6000 survivors, and the **synagogue** at Pylimo 39 is the only of the former 105 synagogues still standing. The **Vilna Gaon Jewish State Museum of Lithuania** commemorates the city's Jewish heritage, providing an honest account of Lithuanians' persecution of their Jewish neighbors on the eve of the war. *(Pylimo 4. ☎05 262 9666; www.jmuseum.lt. Open M-Th 10am-5pm, F 10am-2pm. Donations requested.)* The **Paneriai Memorial** marks the spot in a forest where Nazis killed and buried 100,000 Lithuanians—70,000 of them Jews. The memorials are near pits that served as mass graves. *(Take the train to Kaunas from Platform 1, and get off at Paneriai, the first stop. 10min., but keep in mind trains may be spaced a few hours apart. 2.40Lt. round trip. From the station, walk in the direction of the train for about 20min. Free.)*

MUSEUM OF GENOCIDE VICTIMS. The horrors of the Soviet regime are exposed at this former KGB headquarters, which served as a Gestapo outpost during WWII. The basement has isolation rooms, torture chambers, and an execution cell, left untouched. With little in the way of touristy gimmicks, this grim building is chilling and memorable. *(Aukv 2a. Turn left after Gedimino 40, the building inscribed with names of KGB victims. ☎05 249 6264. Open every day 10am-5pm. English captions. Museum 4Lt; W free Sept.-June. 50% discount for students June-Sept. Guided tours in Lithuanian 15Lt, in English or Russian 30Lt. English-language audio tour 8Lt.)*

TRAKAI CASTLE. Built in the 14th century, Trakai Castle lies on an island 28km west of Vilnius and once served as a residence for the Grand Dukes of Lithuania. The palace, dungeon, and four defense towers are wonderfully preserved, and the castle currently displays priceless collections of porcelain, coins, weaponry, and artifacts. *(Buses leave for Trakai from Vilnius about every 30min. from platforms 5 and 6. 3.2Lt; pay on the bus. From Trakai station, walk toward the water in the direction that the bus was going and turn off the road onto a lakeside path after Karaimų 13. Open daily 10am-6:45pm. Closed M in winter. 12Lt, students 5Lt.)*

ENTERTAINMENT AND NIGHTLIFE

The National Philharmonic's **Vilnius Festival** starts in late May or early June (www.filharmonija.lt). Check *Vilnius in Your Pocket* and *Exploring Vilnius*, distributed at hotels, or the Lithuanian-language morning paper *Lietuvos Rytas* for event or festival listings. For info on GLBT nightlife, visit www.gayline.lt.

Broadway (Brodvėjus), Mėsinių 4. A loud, enormously popular club. Cover 10Lt, includes 2 drinks. Open M noon-3am, Tu noon-4am, W-Sa noon-5am, Su noon-2am. MC/V.

Helios, Didžioji 28. Ultra-modern style and an all-night sushi bar make this place the latest craze in Vilnius. Dress code enforced. 21+. Cover 15Lt. Open Tu-Sa 10pm-5am.

ŠMC (Contemporary Art Center), Vokiečiv 2. Popular with a young and artistic crowd. Beer 6Lt. Open M-F 11am-midnight, Sa 11am-3am, Su 11am-midnight. AmEx/MC/V.

KAUNAS ☎37

Kaunas (pop. 381,300) marked the Russian border in the late 17th century and served as the capital of Lithuania between WWI and WWII. Today, it is the nation's second-largest city. At the eastern end of **Laisvės,** the main pedestrian boulevard, the silver domes of the **Church of St. Michael the Archangel** sparkle over the city. (Open M-F 9am-3pm, Sa-Su 8:30am-2pm. Free.) Nearby, the **Antanas Zmuidzinavicius Works and Collections Museum,** V. Putvinskio 64, exhibits more than 2000 depictions of the devil, who was revered as a guardian in Lithuanian folklore until Christianity rained on the Satanic parade. (Open Tu-Su 11am-5pm. 5Lt, students 2.50Lt.) The western end of Laisvės merges with Vilniaus and leads to the well-preserved **Old Town.** Walk west from Old Town Square to reach the meeting of the Neris and Nemunas rivers and the beautiful **Santakos Park.** Take a microbus to the **Ninth Fort,** where the Nazis killed 50,000 prisoners, 30,000 of them Jews. Take microbus 30 (2Lt) and ask the driver for directions at the last stop, then walk about 20min. (☎37 37 77 15. Open M and W-Su 10am-6pm. Each museum 2Lt, students 1Lt.) Stumble through the dark catacombs of St. Michael the Archangel at the **Museum for the Blind,** guided only by smells and sounds. (Open W 11am-3:30pm, Sa 11am-1:30pm. 3Lt.)

Kaunas Archdiocese Guest House ❷, Rotuses 21, offers pristine rooms with private baths. (☎37 32 25 97. Singles 50Lt; doubles 80Lt; triples 140Lt; quads 130Lt. Cash only.) **Litinterp ❸,** Gedimino 28, arranges private rooms. (☎37 22 87 18; www.litinterp.lt. Open M-F 8:30am-5:30pm, Sa 9:30am-3pm. Singles 80-120Lt; doubles 140-160Lt. MC/V.) Tables quake and chairs levitate without warning at the wacky **Crazy House ❷,** Vilniaus 16. It's one of only two restaurants in the world where diners have to contend with moving furniture. (☎37 22 11 82. Entrees 6-26Lt. Open M-Th and Su 11am-midnight, F-Sa 11am-2am. MC/V.) Try the lunch special (main course and soup; 7Lt) at **Dviese ❶,** Vilniaus 8. (☎37 20 36 38. Open daily 10am-10pm. Cash only.) **Club Los Patrankos,** Savanoriv 124, is a nighttime hotspot. (☎37 33 82 28; www.lospatrankos.lt. Live DJ on weekends. Open Tu-Th 9pm-4am, F-Sa 9pm-6am, Su 1-5pm. MC/V.)

To reach Kaunas from Vilnius, take a **bus** (1hr., 2-3 per hr., 20Lt). Branches of the **tourist office** are at the bus stop and at Laisvės 36. (☎37 32 34 36; http://visit.kaunas.lt. Open M-F 9am-6pm, Sa-Su 9am-1pm and 2-6pm.) **Postal Code:** 3000.

KLAIPĖDA ☎46

Strategically located on the tip of the Neringa peninsula, Klaipėda (pop. 192,500) was briefly the capital of Prussia in the 19th century. As the northernmost Baltic harbor that doesn't freeze, Klaipėda's port still serves as a major shipping hub, and the city has a growing reputation as a jazz center. Follow Liepų eastward from the intersection with H. Manto to reach the **Clock Museum** (Laikrodžių Muziejus), Liepų 12, where elderly ladies let visitors peer at Egyptian sundials and Chinese fire clocks. (English-language pamphlet in each room. Open Tu-Sa noon-5:30pm, Su noon-4:30pm. 6Lt, students 3Lt.) The top of the 46m **Mary Queen of Peace Church Tower,** Rumpiškės 6A, offers a panoramic view, but is open only to groups. (2Lt, tickets available from the tourist office.) **Smiltynė,** across the lagoon, has deserted stretches of seashore. Would-be pirates will enjoy roaming the decks of the three Old Fishing Vessels on the road leading to the **Sea Museum** (Lietuvos Jūrų Muziejus) in Smiltynė. To reach the museum, purchase a ticket at the ferry terminal (2Lt) and ride a small yellow tram. (www.juru.muziejus.lt. Open June-Aug. Tu-Su 10:30am-6:30pm; May and Sept. W-Su 10:30am-6:30pm; Oct.-Apr. Sa-Su 10:30am-5pm. Tickets 4-8Lt.)

Klaipėda Traveler's Guesthouse (HI) ❷, Butkų Juzės 7-4, near the bus station, has sunny, clean dorms. (☎46 685 33140. Dorms June-Sept. 44Lt; Oct.-May 32Lt. HI nonmembers 2Lt extra. Cash only.) When it comes to food, head to **Péda ❷,** Targaus 10. While you wait for some smoked herring (8Lt), browse the gallery of metalworks by sculptor Vytautas Karčiauskas upstairs. (☎46 41 07 10. Open M-Th and Su 11am-11pm, F-Sa 11am-midnight. MC/V.) **Kebab stands** near the ferry terminal in Smiltynė sell cheap and satisfying fare (6-8Lt). The **central market** in Klaipėda is on Turgaus aikštė. (Open daily 8am-6pm.) The best bars line H. Manto on the mainland. "Save trees, eat beaver!" urges **Kurpiai,** Kurpių 1A. To aid you, this popular restaurant and jazz club serves beaver and ostrich.

(☎46 41 05 55; www.jazz.lt. Entrees 17-47Lt. Beer 5Lt. Live jazz nightly 9:30pm. Cover F-Sa 10-15Lt. Open M-Th noon-midnight, F, Sa, Su noon-3am. MC/V.)

Buses (☎46 41 15 47) go from Butkų Juzės 9 to Kaunas (3hr., 12 per day, 38Lt), Palanga (30-40min., 2 per hour, 4Lt), and Vilnius (4-5hr., 10-14 per day, 49Lt). **Ferries** (☎46 31 42 17) run from Old Port Ferry Terminal, Žvejų 8, to Smiltynė (7min., 2 per hr., 2Lt), with connections to Nida (1hr., 9Lt). From the International Ferry Terminal, take bus 1A or microbus 8A to the center (3Lt). The **tourist office,** Turgaus 7, offers **Internet.** (☎46 41 21 86; www.klaipedainfo.lt. Internet 4Lt per hr. Open in summer daily 9am-7pm.) **Postal Code:** 91247.

NIDA ☎469

Windswept sand dunes and quiet hiking trails have long drawn vacationers to the former fishing village of Nida (pop. 1500). One of four municipalities that make up the town of Neringa, Nida is the largest settlement on the **Curonian Spit,** one of the longest sea spits in the world. From the center, turn onto Naglių and head south to the **Drifting Dunes of Parnidis.** The remains of an enormous sundial sit atop the tallest dune (69m), marking a spot where beachgoers have the unique opportunity to look down on both the Curonian Lagoon and the Baltic Sea at once. Along Naglių on the way to the dunes, the **Fisherman's Ethnography Museum** provides a snapshot of one local fisherman's life (☎469 523 72). The **Neringa Museum of History** (Neringos Istorijos Muziejus), Pamario 53, presents a thought-provoking exhibit on Neringa's history and fishing community. (☎469 511 62. Open June-Sept. daily 10am-6pm; 2Lt, students 1Lt.) The regional specialty is *rūkyta žuvis* (smoked fish), served with bread. Stop by **Fischbrotchen ❶**, a yellow hut next to the bus station, for a 9Lt herring sandwich. (Open daily 11am-8pm.) From Naglių 18E, **buses** (☎469 524 72) run to Klaipėda/Smiltynė (1hr., 1 per hr., 9Lt). The **tourist office,** Taikos 4, opposite the bus station, arranges private rooms for a 5Lt fee. (☎469 523 45; www.visitneringa.com. Rooms from 30Lt. Open June-Aug. M-Sa 10am-6pm, Su 10am-3pm; Sept.-May M-F 10am-1pm and 2-6pm, Sa 10am-3pm.) **Postal Code:** 93121.

PALANGA ☎460

With the country's largest botanical park, over 20km of shoreline, and exuberant nightlife, Palanga (pop. 20,000) is the hottest summer spot in Lithuania. The beach and the pier are the main attractions, but Palanga's pride and joy is the **Amber Museum** (Gintaro Muziejus), housed in a mansion in the tranquil **Botanical Gardens.** The collection includes 15,000 pieces of the petrified resin—known as "Baltic Gold"—with primeval flora and fauna trapped inside. (☎460 51319; www.pgm.lt. Open daily June-Aug. 10am-12:30pm and 1:30-7pm; Sept.-May 11am-4:30pm. 5Lt, students 2.50Lt.) **Liukrena ❷,** Vytauto 93a, has a homey feel in a quiet neighborhood. (☎460 52521. Bike rentals available. Internet available for a fee. Singles May-June 75Lt, July-Aug. 110Lt; doubles 145/350Lt. Prices roughly half in winter.) Further down Vytauto, cafes and restaurants abound. The street runs parallel to the shore and passes the bus station, as well as the pedestrian thoroughfare **J. Basanavičiaus,** perpendicular to Vytauto. **Buses** (☎460 533 33) or **microbuses** from Klaipėda (30min., 2 per hr., 4-5Lt) arrive at Kretinjos 1. The **tourist office** to the right of the station books private rooms by email. (☎460 45005. Open M-F 9am-5pm, Sa 10am-2pm, Su 1-5pm.)

LUXEMBOURG

Tiny Luxembourg is often overlooked by travelers smitten with Dutch windmills or hungry for Belgian waffles. However, its castles rival those of the Rhineland, its villages are uncrowded and perfect for easy hikes, and Luxembourg City is a European financial powerhouse. It might be a stretch to call Luxembourg the "lux" of the Benelux countries, but the world's last grand duchy has considerable appeal.

DISCOVER LUXEMBOURG: SUGGESTED ITINERARY

ONE WEEK. Budget 2 days for **Luxembourg City** (p. 684), where you can explore the capital's maze of well-fortified tunnels by day and its lively nightlife after hours. The towns of **Echternach** (p. 689) and **Vianden** (p. 690) are notable stops, the former for its historic basilica and the latter for its hilltop château. From there, proceed south to discover **Ettelbrück** (p. 689), then west to the village of **Esch-sur-Sûre** (p. 690) for scenic hiking through wooded river valleys.

ESSENTIALS

FACTS AND FIGURES

OFFICIAL NAME: Grand Duchy of Luxembourg.

CAPITAL: Luxembourg City.

POPULATION: 486,000.

LAND AREA: 2,600 sq. km.

LANGUAGES: Luxembourgish, French, and German. English is widely spoken.

RELIGION: Roman Catholic 87%.

NO. OF CARS PER 1000 PEOPLE: Approx. 660, one of the highest rates in the world.

WHEN TO GO

The sea winds that douse Belgium with rain have usually shed their moisture by the time they reach Luxembourg; good weather prevails from May through October, although travelers leery of crowds may want to avoid July and August. Temperatures average 17°C (64°F) in summer and 1°C (34°F) in winter.

DOCUMENTS AND FORMALITIES

EMBASSIES AND CONSULATES. Foreign embassies and consulates are in Luxembourg City. Luxembourgian embassies and consulates abroad include: **Australia,** Level 4, Quay West, 111 Harrington St., Sydney, NSW, 2000 (☎02 9253 4708); **UK,** 27 Wilton Cres., London, SW1X 8SD (☎020 72 35 69 61); **US,** 2200 Massachusetts Ave., NW, Washington, DC, 20008 (☎202-265-4171; www.luxembourg-usa.org). Canadians should visit the Luxembourg embassy in Washington, DC; Irish citizens should go to the embassy in London.

VISA AND ENTRY INFORMATION. EU citizens do not need a visa. Citizens of Australia, Canada, New Zealand, and the US do not need a visa for stays of up to 90 days, beginning upon entry into any of the countries in the EU's freedom-of-movement zone. For more info, see p. 14.

TOURIST SERVICES AND MONEY

EMERGENCY	**Ambulance:** ☎112. **Fire:** ☎112. **Police:** ☎113.

TOURIST OFFICES. For general information, contact the **Luxembourg National Tourist Office,** Gare Centrale, P.O. Box 1001, L-1010 Luxembourg or check their website (☎42 82 821; www.visitluxembourg.lu).

MONEY. The **euro (€)** has replaced the **Luxembourg franc** as the unit of currency in Luxembourg. For more info, see p. 17. The cost of living in Luxembourg City is quite high, although the countryside is more reasonable. Restaurant bills usually include a service charge, although an extra 5-10% tip is a classy gesture. Tip taxi drivers 10%. Luxembourg has a 15% **value added tax (VAT),** a sales tax applied to most purchased goods. The prices given in *Let's Go* include VAT. In an airport upon exiting the EU, non-EU citizens can claim a refund on the tax paid for goods purchased at participating stores. In order to qualify for a refund in a store, you must spend at least €100; make sure to ask for a refund form when you pay. For more info on qualifying for a VAT refund, see p. 21.

TRANSPORTATION

BY PLANE. The national airline, **Luxair** (☎2456 4242; www.luxair.lu), and a slew of other European airlines fly to the **Luxembourg City airport (LUX).** Cheap last-minute flights on Luxair are often available online.

BY TRAIN AND BUS. A **Benelux Tourrail Pass** (€94 second-class, under 26 €71) allows five days of unlimited train travel in a one-month period in Belgium, Luxembourg, and the Netherlands. Within Luxembourg, the **Billet Réseau** (€5, book of 5 €20) is good for one day of unlimited bus and train travel. The **Luxembourg Card** (€10-24) includes one to three days of unlimited transportation along with free or discounted admission to more than 50 sights around the country.

BY BIKE AND THUMB. A 575km network of cycling paths already snakes its way through Luxembourg, and plans are in place to add another 325km to the network in the near future. Bikes aren't permitted on buses, but domestic trains will transport them for a small fee (€1.20). Service areas in Luxembourg are popular places to hitch rides into Belgium, France, and the Netherlands, as many motorists stop to take advantage of relatively low fuel prices. *Let's Go* does not recommend hitchhiking.

KEEPING IN TOUCH

PHONE CODES	**Country code:** 352. **International dialing prefix:** 00. Luxembourg has no city codes. For more info on how to place international calls, see **Inside Back Cover.**

TELEPHONES. There are no city codes in Luxembourg; from outside the country, dial 352 plus the local number. Public phones can only be operated with a phone card, available at post offices, train stations, and newspaper stands. Internet cafes are not abundant. Mobile phones are an increasingly popular and economical alternative (p. 31). International direct dial numbers include: AT&T

(☎8002 0111); **British Telecom** (☎8002 0044); **Canada Direct** (☎8002 0119); **MCI** (☎8002 0112); **Sprint** (☎8002 0115); **Telecom New Zealand** (☎8002 0064).

LANGUAGE. The official languages of Luxembourg are Luxembourgish, French, and German. While Luxembourgish, a West Germanic language, is used primarily in daily conversation, official documents are written in French, and the press is in German. English is spoken as a second, third, or fourth language.

ACCOMMODATIONS AND CAMPING

LUXEMBOURG	❶	❷	❸	❹	❺
ACCOMMODATIONS	under €18	€18-24	€25-34	€35-55	over €55

Luxembourg's nine **HI youth hostels** *(Auberges de Jeunesse)* are often booked solid during the summer; it's wise to reserve ahead. About half of the hostels close for several weeks in December. Beds are approximately €17-20. Contact **Centrale des Auberges de Jeunesse Luxembourgeoises** (☎26 27 66 40; www.youthhostels.lu) for more info. **Hotels** are expensive, costing upwards of €40 per night in the capital city. Luxembourg is a camper's paradise, and most towns have campsites. Contact **Camprilux** (www.camping.lu/gb/gbstart.htm) for more info.

FOOD AND DRINK

LUXEMBOURG	❶	❷	❸	❹	❺
FOOD AND DRINK	under €5	€5-9	€10-14	€15-22	over €22

Luxembourgish cuisine combines elements of French and German cooking. Specialties include *Judd mat Gaardenbou'nen* (smoked pork with beans), *Friture de la Moselle* (fried fish), and *Quetscheflued* (plum tart). Riesling wines, which show up most Chardonnays, are produced in the Moselle Valley.

HOLIDAYS AND FESTIVALS

Holidays: New Year's (Jan. 1); Maundy Thursday (Mar. 20); Easter (Apr. 12-13, 2009; Apr. 23-24, 2010); Labor Day (May 1); Ascension (May 1); May Day (May 1); Whit Sunday and Monday (May 11-12); Corpus Christi (May 22); National Day (June 23); Assumption (Aug. 15); All Saints' Day (Nov. 1); Christmas (Dec. 25); St. Stephen's Day (Dec. 26).

Festivals: The weeks leading up to Lent bring parades and masked balls under the guise of **Carnival.** Echternach hosts the **International Music Festival** in May and June, while **Riesling Open** wine festivals kick off during the 3rd weekend of September.

LUXEMBOURG CITY

As an international banking hot spot, Luxembourg City (pop. 76,000) has become one of the wealthiest cities in the world. Though small, the metropolis has a lot to offer, from the relics of its military history to the boons of its thriving economy. The majestic cliffs and gorgeous valleys make it an atypical city with great nature offerings and a fast paced urban lifestyle.

TRANSPORTATION

Flights: Findel International Airport (**LUX;** www.aeroport.public.lu), 6km from the city. Bus #16 (€1.50, 2-4 per hr.) runs to the train station. Taxis to city center are €17-25.

Trains: Gare CFL, pl. de la Gare (☎24 89 24 89; www.cfl.lu), a 15min. walk south of the city center. To: Amsterdam, NTH (6hr.; 1 per hr.; €52, under 26 €36); Brussels, BEL (2hr., 1 per hr., €30/16); Ettelbrück (25min., 3 per hr., €5); Frankfurt, GER (3hr., 1 per hr., €52); Paris, FRA (2-4hr., 1 per 2hr., €25-84).

Buses: For travel within the city, buy a **billet courte distance** (short-distance ticket; €1.50, book of 10 €10), valid for 1hr. A **billet réseau** (network pass; €4, book of 5 €20), also accepted on trains, allows for unlimited travel throughout the entire country for 1 day and is the most economical option for intercity travel. Most buses run until midnight. The **free night bus** (☎47 96 29 75) runs F-Sa 10pm-3:30am.

Taxis: €2.40/km. 10% more 10pm-6am; 25% more on Su. **Colux Taxis:** ☎48 22 33.

Bikes: Rent from **Vélo en Ville,** 8 r. Bisserwé (☎47 96 23 83), in the Grund. Open Apr.-Oct. M-Sa 10am-noon and 1-8pm. €5 per hr., €13 per half-day, €20 per day, €38 per weekend, €75 per week. Under 26 20% discount for full day and longer. MC/V.

ORIENTATION AND PRACTICAL INFORMATION

Five minutes by bus and 15min. by foot from the train station, Luxembourg City's historic center revolves around the **Place d'Armes.** From the train station, follow av. de la Gare or av. de la Liberté, then watch for signs with directions to the city's main sights. From the pl. d'Armes, walk down r. de Chimay; you will see the **Pétrusse Valley** in front of you, the **Place de la Constitution** on your right, and the **Pétrusse Casemates** to your left. Once there, the city's lower areas, the **Grund** and the **Clausen,** will be located diagonally to your right and left, 10min. and 15min. on foot, respectively. Between these areas are the **Bock Casemates.**

Tourist Offices: Grand Duchy National Tourist Office (☎42 82 82 20; www.ont.lu), in the train station. Open daily June-Sept. 8:30am-6:30pm; Oct.-May 9:15am-12:30pm and 1:45-6pm. **Centre Information Jeunes,** 26 pl. de la Gare (☎26 29 32 00; www.visitluxembourg.lu), across from the station inside Galerie Kons, provides young travelers with everything from tourist info to help on finding jobs. Open M-F 10am-6pm.

Embassies: Ireland, 28 rte. d'Arlon (☎45 06 10). Open M-F 9:30am-12:30pm. **UK,** 5 bd. Joseph II (☎22 98 64; www.britain.lu). Open M-F 9:30am-12:30pm. **US,** 22 bd. Emmanuel Servais (☎46 01 23; luxembourg.usembassy.gov). Open M-F 8:30am-5:30pm. **Australians, Canadians,** and **New Zealanders** should contact their embassies located in France or Belgium if necessary.

Currency Exchange: Banks are the only option for changing money or cashing traveler's checks. Most are open M-F 8:30am-4 or 4:30pm.

Luggage Storage: (☎49 90 55 74), in the train station. €3 per bag. 1-day storage during opening hours. Open daily 6am-9:30pm.

Laundromat: Quick Wash, 31 pl. de Strasbourg (☎26 19 65 42), near the station. Wash and dry €10. Open M-F 8:30am-6:30pm, Sa 8am-6pm.

Pharmacy: Pharmacies are marked with green crosses. Call ☎90 07 12 34 32 for a list of available of 24hr. pharmacies located throughout the city.

Hospital: Clinique St-Thérèse, 36 r. Ste-Zithe (☎49 77 61 or 49 77 65; www.zitha.lu). Call ☎90 07 12 34 32 for a schedule of 24hr. hospitals.

Internet: Centre Information Jeunes (see above) has limited free Internet for students.

Post Office: 38 pl. de la Gare, across the street and to the left of the station. Open M-F 6am-7pm, Sa 6am-noon. **Poste Restante.** Branch at 25 r. Aldringen, near pl. d'Armes. Open M-Sa 7am-7pm, Su 7am-5pm.

ACCOMMODATIONS AND CAMPING

Aside from camping, the city hostel is the only budget option in Luxembourg City. Hotels are cheaper near the train station than in the city center.

Auberge de Jeunesse (HI), 2 r. du Fort Olisy (☎22 68 89 20; www.youthhostels.lu). Walk 15 min. or take bus #9 (dir.: Neudorf) and get off at Plateau Altmuenster. From the bus stop, take the steep path down the bridge. This new, pristine hostel has river views and a restaurant. Breakfast and linens are included. In-room lockers; bring your own or rent a lock. Laundry €7.50. Internet €2.50 per hr. Bike rentals €8 per half-day, €15 per day. Reception 24hr. Call ahead to reserve shuttles straight to and from the airport (€3) or train station (€2), M-F 9am-5pm. Dorms €23; singles €35; doubles €55. €3 HI discount. AmEx/MC/V. ❷

Bella Napoli, 4 r. de Strasbourg (☎49 33 67). Hotel located above a pizza place. Simple rooms with hardwood floors and full bath. Breakfast included. Reception 8am-midnight. Singles €41; doubles €48; triples €60. AmEx/MC/V. ❹

Hotel Du Chemin De Fer, 4 r. Joseph Junck (☎49 35 28). Ordinary, clean rooms right across from the train station. Singles €45; doubles €65; triples €80. MC/V. ❸

Camping Kockelscheuer, 22 rte. de Bettembourg (☎47 18 15; www.camp-kockelscheuer.lu), 5km outside Luxembourg City. Take bus #5 from the station or city center to Kockelscheuer-Camping. Showers included. Laundry €4. Electricity €2.20. Open one week before Easter-Oct. Reception 7am-noon and 2-10:30pm; cars must arrive when reception is open. Tent sites €4.50, each additional adult €3.75. Cash only. ❶

DON'T LET THE BED BUGS BITE. Luxembourg mosquitoes seem to have an affinity for visiting tourists, so make sure to stock up on bug spray to prevent uncomfortable itching and infections during your stay.

FOOD

Although the area around the pl. d'Armes teems with a strange mix of fast-food joints and upscale restaurants, there are a few affordable and appealing alternatives. Stock up on groceries at **Supermarché Boon,** in Galerie Kons across from the train station. (Open M-F 8am-8pm, Sa 8am-6pm, Su 8am-noon.) Fancier cafes are centered primarily in the City Center, but can be very expensive.

Restaurant-Café Chiggeri, 15 r. du Nord (☎22 82 36). Serves traditional French food amid shimmering, night-sky decor in a jovial, yellow house with tons of semi-private seating. Wine list offers 2300 vintages. Dine more affordably at the cafe and bar downstairs. Entrees €17-24. Plate of the day €16. Gourmet Sunday buffet €17. Open M-Sa 10am-11pm, Su 11am-3pm. AmEx/MC/V. ❹

Apoteca, 12 r. de la Boucherie (☎26 73 77 77; www.apoteca.lu). Offers an innovative menu that changes weekly in cool, stone surroundings. Downstairs bar offers a less expensive, but limited menu (€8-10). Entrees €16-29. DJ's W-Sa evenings. Restaurant open Tu-Sa noon-2pm and 7:30-10pm; bar open Tu-Sa 5pm-1am. AmEx/MC/V. ❹

Auberge de Jeunesse Hostel Bar and Restaurant, 2 r. du Fort Olisy. The "Menu of the Day" includes a salad bar, desert, and entree for €9. So cheap that this is where the locals go to enjoy lunch. Order entrees de la carte (€5-15). Sandwiches €2-4. Good vegetarian selection. Open noon-3pm and 6-10pm. ❸

Mesa Verde, 11 r du St-Esprit (☎46 41 26), down the street from the pl. de Clairefontaine. A local favorite, this bright vegetarian restaurant features an ever-changing array of hand-painted murals and billowing fabrics decorating the walls. Entrees €19-25. Open Tu-Sa 6:30-11:30pm. Open for lunch W-F noon-2pm. MC/V. ❹

Namur, 27 r. des Capucins (☎22 34 08), down the street from pl. d'Armes. Marble floors, outdoor seating, and elegant ambience make the selection of pastries, chocolates, and sundaes (€5-6) even sweeter. Open M 2-6pm, Tu-Sa 8:30am-6pm. MC/V. ❷

SIGHTS

Luxembourg City is compact enough to be explored on foot. The most spectacular views of the city are from **Place de la Constitution** and from the bridge closest to the **Bock Casemates.** For guidance on your stroll, follow the signs pointing out the **Wenzel Walk.** It leads visitors through 1000 years of history as it winds around the old city, from the **Chemin de la Corniche** down into the casemates.

FORTRESSES AND THE OLD CITY. The city's first fortress, built in AD 963, saw its network of fortifications expand so far over the years that the city earned the nickname "Gibraltar of the North." The fortress contains the **casemates,** an intricate 17km network of tunnels through the fortress walls. First built to fortify the city's defenses, the casemates were partially dismantled when Luxembourg was declared a neutral state in 1867. Start at the **Bock Casemates** fortress, part of Luxembourg's original castle; the fortress looms over the Alzette River Valley and offers a fantastic view of the **Grund** and the **Clausen.** *(Entrance on r. Sigefroi, just past the bridge leading to the hostel. ☎22 28 09 or 22 67 53. Open Mar.-Oct. daily 10am-5pm. €1.75, students €1.50.)* A visit to the **Pétrusse Casemates,** built by the Spanish in the 1600s, takes explorers down 250 steps into historic chambers while providing views of the Pétrusse Valley. A tour is required, but it's interesting, short (30min.), and cheap. *(Pl. de la Constitution. English-language tours 1 per hr., July-Aug. 11am-4pm; intermittently in June. €2, students €1.50.)* The peaceful paths of the green Pétrusse Valley beckon for a stroll or an afternoon picnic in the shadow of the fortress walls. Double-decker **tourist buses** allow you to "hop on" and "hop off" at will; recordings play commentary in multiple languages. *(Info for train and buses ☎26 65 11; www.sightseeing.lu. 3 per hr. 9:40am-5:20 or 6:20pm from marked stops throughout the city. €12, students €10. Ticket valid for 24hr. Wheelchair-accessible.)*

MUSEUMS. The collection at the **Musée National d'Histoire et d'Art** includes both modern and ancient art and a chronicle of the conquering powers' influences on Luxembourg's art. *(Marché-aux-Poissons, at r. Boucherie and Sigefroi. ☎47 93 30; www.mnha.lu. Open Tu-Su 10am-5pm. Th 5-8pm free. €5, students and under 18 free.)* There's no gambling at **Casino Luxembourg,** only extensive contemporary art exhibits. *(41 r. Notre Dame, near pl. de la Constitution. ☎22 50 45; www.casino-luxembourg.lu. Open M, W, F 11am-7pm, Th 11am-8pm, Sa-Su 11am-6pm. €4, under 26 and students €3, under 18 free.)* The **Luxembourg Card** covers entrance to 55 museums and tourist attractions throughout the country. *(www.luxembourgcard.lu. Available at tourist offices and youth hostels. 1-day card €10, 2-day €17, 3-day €24.)*

ENTERTAINMENT AND NIGHTLIFE

There is no central location for nightlife in Luxembourg City, so an evening of barhopping also involves hopping on and off the city's night bus until bars close at 2am. In summer, the **Place d'Armes** comes to life with free concerts (www.summerinthecity.lu) and stand-up comedy. Pick up a copy of *UP FRONT* at the tourist office for a list of nightlife action and events.

Melusina, 145 r. de la Tour Jacob (☎43 59 22). Eat at the classy restaurant or dance all night at the club on weekends. Cover €8. 1 free drink 11pm-midnight. Restaurant open M-Sa noon-2pm and 7-11pm. Menu of the Day €10. Club open F-Sa 11pm-3am. Restaurant MC/V; club accepts cash only.

Urban, at the corner of r. de la Boucherie and r. du Marché-aux-Herbes (☎26 47 85 78; www.urban.lu). A friendly, crowded bar in the heart of downtown. Live DJ F and Sa nights. Beer €2-4. Mixed drinks €5-6. Open daily noon-1am. AmEx/MC/V.

Chocolate Elvis, (☎29 79 46; www.chocolate-elvis.lu), next door to club "The Complex," features party music at high decibels and beer (€2.20) that'll leave you feeling relaxed. Mixed drinks €6-6.50. Open M-F 5pm-1am, Sa-Su 6pm-1am.

VIP Room, 19 r. des Bains (☎26 18 78 67; www.viproom.lu), near the pl. du Théatre. Glitzy and exclusive with an atmosphere modeled after VIP clubs in Paris and St-Tropez. Open before 7pm for dinner. Club open Tu 7pm-midnight, W-Sa 7pm-late. AmEx/MC/V.

THE ARDENNES

In 1944, one of the bloodiest battles of World War II, the Battle of the Bulge, took place in these hills. Now quiet towns, imposing castles, and stunning scenery make the Ardennes an ideal tourist attraction. Carry raingear; the humidity here often breaks into short storms. Regardless, this area is ideal for anyone; for those looking to explore the great outdoors or to relax in a quiet town with cozy accommodations. Check transportations schedules thoroughly but you still may have to budget for extra waiting time.

ETTELBRÜCK. The main railway linking Luxembourg City to Liège, BEL, runs through Ettelbrück (pop. 7500), making the town the transportation hub for the Ardennes. History buffs waiting out a layover might investigate the **General Patton Memorial Museum,** 5 r. Dr. Klein, which commemorates Luxembourg's liberation during WWII. Take a right from the station, a left on r. de la Gare, a left on ave. J.F. Kennedy, and a right on r. Dr. Klein. (☎81 03 22; www.patton.lu. Open daily June-Sept. 15 10am-5pm; Sept. 16-May 30 Su 2-5pm. €2.50.) Near the train station is **Hotel Herckmans ❹,** 3 pl. de la Résistance, a small hotel above Stone's Steakhous with the most budget-friendly option in town. (☎81 74 28. Breakfast included. Singles €35-40; doubles €45-60; triples €80. AmEx/MC/V.) From the train station, turn left on Prince Henry, turn right when the road ends, and then take the first left onto the pedestrian-only Grande Rue, where much of commercial Ettelbrück is located. Grab a quick meal at **Bakes ❷,** 55 Grande Rue. (☎81 13 33. Sandwiches €3-4.50. Pastas €9. Open daily 7am-5:30pm. AmEx/MC/V.) **Trains** go to Clervaux (30min., 1 per hr., €5) and Luxembourg City (25min., 3 per hr., €4.50.) The station at Ettelbrück (open 5:50am-8:30pm) is the hub for **buses** throughout the Ardennes. Buy the **Oeko-Billjee** (€5) day pass for unlimited bus and train use for one day; validate the pass yourself at the orange booth on the platform. To reach the **tourist office,** walk to the end of Grande Rue and turn right onto r. de Bastogne. (☎81 20 68; www.sit-e.lu. Open M-F 9am-noon and 1:30-5pm; July-Sept. Sa 10am-noon and 2-4pm.)

ECHTERNACH. In the heart of the Little Switzerland region, Echternach (pop. 5200), the oldest town in Luxembourg, is also a charming tourist village and a paradise for the **hikers** and **bikers** who venture out into the surrounding woodlands. The turrets of the 15th-century town hall share the skyline with the towering **Basilica of St. Willibrord,** less interesting inside than out. To get there, go down r. de la Gare and take a left at pl. du Marché. (Open daily 9:30am-6:30pm. Free.) St. Willibrord draws thousands of pilgrims every Whit Tuesday (Pentecost) for the **Dancing Procession.** The basilica and the intimate Église Saints Pierre-et-Paul host Echternach's renowned **International Music Festival** from May to July. (☎72 83 47; www.echternachfestival.lu. Tickets free to €47.) The lakeside **Auberge de Jeunesse (HI) ❷,** 1 chemin vert Roudenhaff, a 30min. walk from the station, is equipped with a sports hall and an indoor 14m climbing wall. Walk past the Roman villa to get there. (☎72 01 58; www.youthhostels.lu. Wheelchair-accessible. Breakfast and linens included. Reception 8-10am and 5-11pm. Check-in 5-10pm. Bike rental €2.50 per hr., €8 per half-day, €16 per day. Reserve ahead in summer. Dorms €21.20; singles €33; doubles €26. €3 HI discount. MC/V.) Pick up groceries at **Match,** near pl. du Marché. (Open M-F 8am-7pm, Sa 8am-1pm.) **Buses** run to Ettelbrück (#500; 45min., 1 per hr.) and Luxembourg City (#111 or 110; 1hr., 2 per hr.) Rent **bikes** at Trisport, 31 rte. de Luxembourg. (☎72 00 86; www.trisport.lu. €15 per day. Open Tu-Th 9am-noon and 2-6pm, F 9am-noon and 2-7pm, Sa 9am-noon and 2-5pm. AmEx/MC/V.) The **tourist office,** 9-10 parvis de la Basilique, is in front of the Basilica. (☎72 02 30; www.echternach-tourist.lu. Open M-F 9:30am-5:30pm. Summer also open Sa-Su.)

VIANDEN. The village of Vianden (pop. 2000) is home to one of the most impressive castles in Western Europe. A patchwork of Carolingian, Gothic, and Renaissance architecture, the **Château de Vianden** holds displays of armor, furniture, and tapestries. Captions are mainly in German, but the main attraction is the view from the top of the hill, where you can look down at the castle towers and countryside. (☎84 92 91; www.castle-vianden.lu. Open daily Apr.-Sept. 10am-6pm; Oct. and Mar. 10am-5pm; Nov.-Feb. 10am-4pm. €5.50, students €4.50.) In August, the castle also hosts a **medieval festival,** where the Markt transforms into a scene from the 14th century with games, music, and entertainment. (Admission €7, students €6. Check castle website for more details.) The **Maison Victor Hugo,** 37 r. de la Gare, housed the author during his exile from France. (☎26 87 40 88; www.victor-hugo.lu. Open Tu-Su 11am-3:30pm. €4, ages 6-12 €2.50, ages 13-25 €3.50; reduced raters for large groups.) Take the **Chairlift** from 3 r. du Sanatorium up the mountain for thrilling views. (☎83 43 23. Open Easter-Oct. M-Sa 10am-5pm, Su 10am-6pm. €3, round-trip €4.50.) Vianden has hiking trails, and **bike paths** lead Echternach (30km). Rent bikes at the bus station. (Open mid-July to Aug. M-Sa 8am-noon and 1-5pm. €10 per half-day, €14 per day.) Modern, clean rooms await at the **Auberge de Jeunesse (HI) ❷,** 3 ru. du Château, near the foot of the castle. To get there, climb Grande Rue up the hill and toward the castle. The road changes to Montée du Château; the hostel is behind Hotel Oranienburg. (☎83 41 77; www.youthhostels.lu. Breakfast included. Reception 8-10am and 5-11pm. €3 HI discount. Dorms €19.20; singles €31.) **Hotel Petry's Restaurant ❸,** 15 r. de la Gare, serves filling dishes in a cozy atmosphere. (☎83 41 22. Meat entrees €6-19. Open May-Aug. daily 8am-9:30pm.) **Buses** head to Ettelbrück (#570; 30min., 2 per hr.) and Clervaux (#663; 45min., M-Sa 4 per day, Su 2 per day). From Luxembourg, take the train to Ettelbruck and the bus to Vianden. From the bus station, take r. de la Gare to the center of town; the **tourist office,** 1 r. du Vieux Marché, is over the bridge on the right. (☎83 42 571; www.tourist-info-vianden.lu. Internet €2 per hr. Open M-F 8am-noon and 1-5pm, Sa-Su 10am-2pm.)

ESCH-SUR-SÛRE. Cradled by the green Ardennes mountains and encircled by the ruins of Luxembourg's oldest castle, this village (pop. 320) is an ideal base for exploring the **Haute-Sûre Nature Reserve**, 15 rte. de Lultzhausen (☎89 93 311), or the area's 700km of nature trails. (Reserve open Mar.-Oct. M-Tu and Th-F 10am-noon and 2-6pm, Sa-Su 2-6pm; Nov.-Apr. closes 5pm.) **Hotel de la Sûre ❸,** 1 r. du Pont, the village's unofficial **tourist office,** is the best bet for lodgings. From the bus stop, walk up r. de l'Église (the street on the right closest to the tunnel) past the church. (☎83 91 10; www.hotel-de-la-sure.lu. Bike rental €5 per hr., €19-22 per day. Breakfast included. Free Internet. Reception 7am-midnight. Singles M-Th €27-70, F-Su €30-77. Discounts for longer stays. AmEx/MC/V.) **Camping im Aal ❶,** r. du Moulin, a 10min. walk from the bus drop-off point, is next to the Sûre river. To get there, cross the bridge and turn right past the playgrounds. (☎83 95 14; www.esch-sure.lu. Wash €3.50, dry €2.50. Open Feb.-Dec. Reception 8am-noon and 1-5pm. Tent sites €5 per person. Cash only.) **Buses** to Ettelbrück leave every hour, except on Sundays when they leave every two to four hours (#535; 25min.).

MALTA

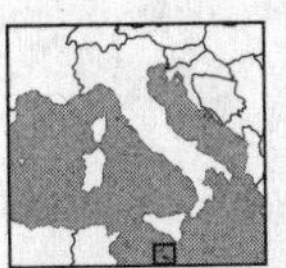

Don't be fooled by Malta's miniature size. Situated in the Mediterranean between Sicily and North Africa, this tiny country has a big personality. Malta won independence from the UK in 1964, and became a member of the EU in 2004. Today the three inhabited islands of Malta (Malta, Gozo, and Comino), attract divers, beachgoers, and history buffs alike. A country of diverse cultural influences, Malta boasts a variety of museums, cathedrals, and festivals.

DISCOVER MALTA: SUGGESTED ITINERARIES

THREE DAYS. Spend all three days in and around the sunny capital of **Valletta** (p. 694). Stroll along **Republic Street,** soak in the view from the **Upper Barakka Gardens,** and revel in the **Grand Master's Palace.** Take a daytrip to the charming towns of **Mdina** and **Rabat** (p. 698).

ONE WEEK. After exploring **Valletta** (2 days), take daytrips to nearby **Hypogeum** and **Birgu** (2 days, p. 698). Check out the flower-filled lanes of **Mdina** and **Rabat** (2 days), and end with a bang at **Sleima** and **St. Julian's** (1 day, p. 699), where you'll dance until the sun comes up.

ESSENTIALS

FACTS AND FIGURES

OFFICIAL NAME: Republic of Malta.

CAPITAL: Valletta.

MAJOR CITIES: Birkirkara, Mosta.

POPULATION: 404,000.

TIME ZONE: GMT +1.

LANGUAGES: Maltese, English.

RELIGION: 98% Roman Catholic.

LAND AREA: 316 sq. km.

WHEN TO GO

Malta is generally pleasant year-round. Accommodations often fill up during peak season, which runs May through September. Summers are hot and sunny, and beaches are usually crowded between the end of June and mid-September. July and August are particularly dry, with temperatures hovering around 30°C (86°F). Winters are mild and rainfall is relatively low. Those wishing to hike or bike should avoid the summer heat and travel to Malta in the fall or spring.

DOCUMENTS AND FORMALITIES

EMBASSIES AND CONSULATES. Foreign embassies to Malta are in Valletta (p. 695). Maltese embassies and consulates abroad include: **Australia,** 38 Culgoa Circuit, O'Malley, ACT 2606 (☎02 62 90 17 24); **Canada,** 3300 Bloor St., W. Ste. 300, Etobicoke, ON M8X 2X2 (☎416-207-0922; maltaconsulate.toronto@gov.mt); **Ireland,** 17 Earlsfort Terr., Dublin 2 (☎1 676 2340; maltaembassy.dublin@gov.mt); **New Zealand,** 20 Tanera Cres., Brooklyn, Wellington (☎4 463 5168; maltaconsul.wellington@gov.mt); **UK,** Malta House, 36-38 Piccadilly, London, W1U 0LE (☎20 72 92 48 00; maltahighcommission.london@gov.mt); **US,** 2017

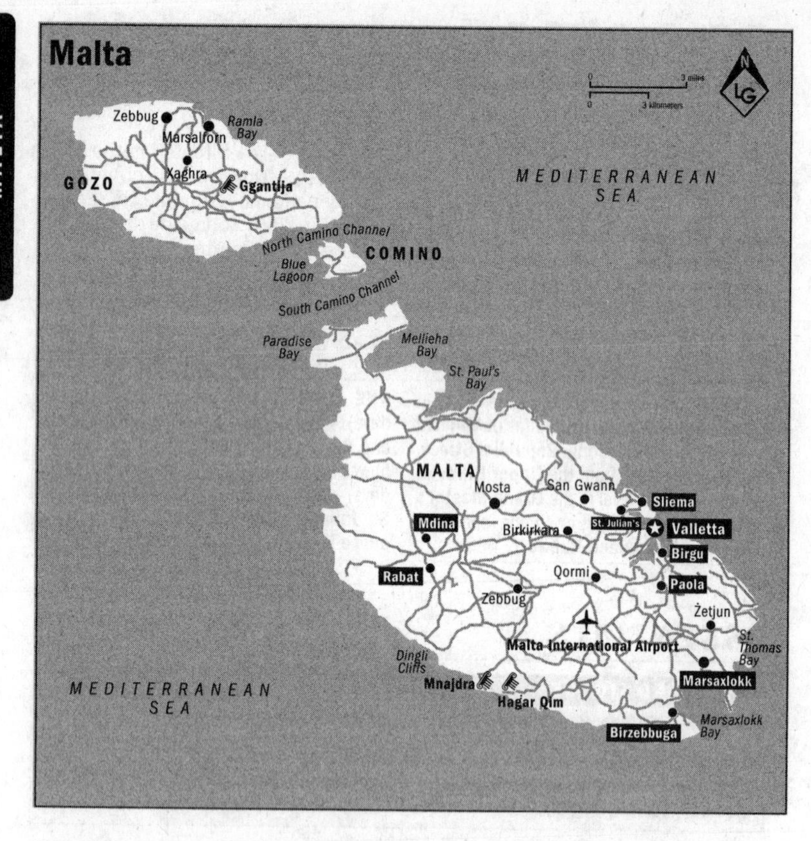

Connecticut Ave., NW, Washington, D.C. 20008 (☎202-462-3611; maltaembassy.washington@gov.mt). Check the Maltese Ministry of Foreign Affairs website (www.foreign.gov.mt) for more embassy info.

VISA AND ENTRY INFORMATION. Citizens of the EU do not need visas to travel to Malta. Citizens of Australia, Canada, New Zealand, the UK, and the US do not need a visa for stays of up to 90 days.

TOURIST SERVICES AND MONEY

EMERGENCY	General Emergency: ☎112.

TOURIST OFFICES. Major cities and towns in Malta, including Valletta, Luqa, and Victoria, have official tourist information centers run by the **Malta Tourism Authority (MTA).** Visit www.visitmalta.com for more information.

MONEY. The **euro (€)** replaced the Maltese **lira (Lm)** as Malta's unit of currency in January 2008. The lira is fixed to the euro at a permanent exchange rate of 0.4293 to 1. **Banks** include APS, Bank of Valletta, HSBC, and Lombard. When exchanging foreign currency, keep in mind that banks usually have better rates than hotels and shops. Major credit cards are widely accepted and **ATMs** are common. Adding a 10% **tip** is customary at restaurants and cafes.

TRANSPORTATION

BY PLANE. Many international airlines fly to Malta, including **Alitalia, Air France, British Airways, Finnair,** and **Lufthansa. Air Malta,** the Maltese national airline, flies to major cities in Europe, including Frankfurt, London, Rome, and Stockholm (☎2166 2211; www.airmalta.com). Budget airlines **easyJet** (☎0871 244 2366; www.easyjet.com), **Germanwings** (☎870 252 12 50; www.germanwings.com), and **Ryanair** (☎353 12 49 77 91; www.ryanair.com) offer inexpensive fares from a limited number of cities. Flights land at **Malta International Airport** in Luqa (**MLA;** ☎2124 9600; www.maltaairport.com).

BY BUS AND BY FERRY. The Malta Public Transportation Association (☎2125 0007; www.atp.com.mt.) runs **buses** throughout Malta and Gozo. A one-day bus travel ticket (€3.49) allows you to travel on all routes around Malta from 5:30am to 11pm. The main terminals are in Valletta and Victoria. The Gozo Channel Company (☎2158 0435; www.gozochannel.com) runs **ferries** between Malta and Gozo. Virtu Ferries operates high-speed vessels that travel from Sicily to Malta (☎2123 2522; www.virtuferries.com.)

BY CAR AND BY TAXI. **Rental cars** are available in most tourist areas. Traffic signage is generally good, and has improved a great deal over the last few years. **Taxis** are either white (no booking required) or black (booking required). Before getting into a taxi, make sure that the meter is running. **Hitchhiking** is rare in Malta. *Let's Go* does not recommend hitchhiking.

KEEPING IN TOUCH

PHONE CODES	**Country code:** 356. **International dialing prefix:** 00. For more info on how to place international calls, see **Inside Back Cover.**

EMAIL AND INTERNET. Internet access is widely available in Malta. Most Internet cafes charge around €2.50 per hr.

TELEPHONE. The most reliable **public phones** are card-operated. **Phone cards** may be purchased at souvenir shops and post offices. Easyline phone cards come in denominations of €5, 10, and 20. International access numbers include: **AT&T Direct** (☎800 901 10); **Canada Direct** (☎0 800 90 150); **MCI** (☎800 90120).

MAIL. Letters and postcards sent by airmail to Europe cost €0.37, to Canada and the US €0.51, and to Australia €0.63. To receive mail in Malta, have it delivered **Poste Restante.** Envelopes should be addressed as follows: First name, LAST NAME, POSTE RESTANTE, PO Boxes Department, Maltapost, Old Bakery Street, Valletta, MALTA. Mail can also be sent to Maltapost Head Office, Marsa, Malta. Be ready to present an ID or passport when picking up mail. For more info on postal service in Malta visit www.maltaposte.com.

LANGUAGE. The official languages of Malta are Maltese and English. Maltese, the only Semitic language written in the Latin alphabet, is closely related to Arabic and Italian (particularly Sicilian).

ACCOMMODATIONS AND CAMPING

MALTA	❶	❷	❸	❹	❺
ACCOMMODATIONS	under €16	€16-25	€26-40	€41-60	over €60

Malta is a small place, but there are a fair number of budget accommodations available. Unfortunately, most **hostels** and **guesthouses** do not have online booking options, so be sure to call ahead. Malta has only one designated **campground,** located on the northern tip of the main island (☎2152 1105; www.maltacampsite.com). Camping in other areas is allowed only if you obtain a permit from the **Malta Environment and Planning Authority (MEPA).**

FOOD AND DRINK

MALTA	❶	❷	❸	❹	❺
FOOD	under €5	€5-15	€16-20	€21-25	over €25

Maltese cuisine reflects a mixture of Mediterranean influences. Malta is particularly known for *fenkati*, traditional rabbit in red wine. *Pastizzi*, pastries filled with ricotta cheese or peas, are extremely popular. Fish dishes are also common. Menus are generally in English. For more information on restaurants in Malta, visit www.restaurantsmalta.com.

HOLIDAYS AND FESTIVALS

Holidays: New Year's Day (Jan. 1); Feast of St. Paul's Shipwreck (Feb. 10); Feast of St. Joseph (Mar. 19); Freedom Day (Mar. 31); Good Friday (Apr. 10, 2009; Apr. 2, 2010); Labor Day (May 1); Sette Guigno (June 7); Feast of St. Peter and St. Paul (June 29); Assumption (Aug. 15); Victory Day (Sept. 8); Independence Day (Sept. 21); Republic Day (Dec. 13); Christmas (Dec. 25).

Festivals: Many of the annual festivals in Malta revolve around religious holidays. Other celebrations include Carnival in February, the Malta Fireworks Festival in May, and arts and jazz festivals in July. Visit www.maltafestivals.com for an updated list of events.

BEYOND TOURISM

For more info on opportunities across Europe, see **Beyond Tourism,** p. 60.

Malta College of Arts, Science and Technology (MCAST), Kordin St., Paola PLA 9032, Malta (☎2398 7100; www.mcast.edu.mt). Courses in art and design, engineering, and agriculture. Foreign students should contact the International Office.

University of Malta, Msida MSD 2080, Malta (☎2133 3909; www.um.edu.mt). Student exchange programs with institutions in Australia, Canada, Japan, and the US.

VALLETTA

Valletta's ochre houses and sharply sloping streets cling to a narrow stretch of peninsula. Walking in this tiny city is ideal, and you'll be rewarded with grand views of the surrounding ocean. The rocky and fortified seaside means that the startlingly blue Mediterranean often remains out of reach. Instead, head to Valletta's atmospheric churches and museums in between strolling from souvenir shop to cafe. The city hides several worn neighborhoods in its folds, where cats watch you from corners and elderly men repair watches in the sun.

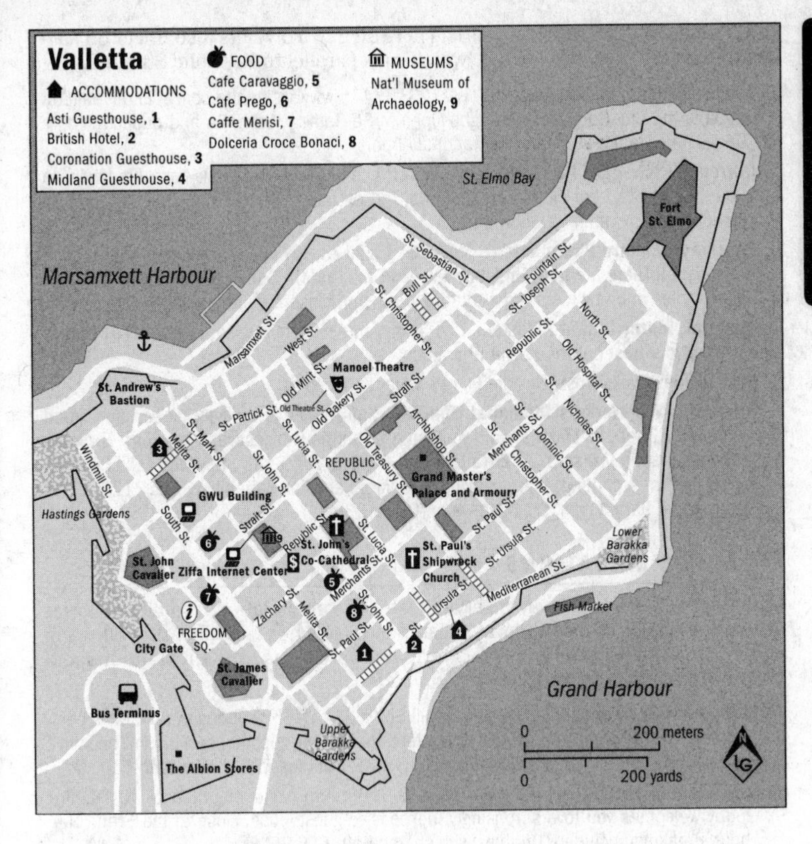

TRANSPORTATION

Flights: Malta International Airport (**MLA;** ☎2124 9600; www.maltaairport.com), in the town of Luqa, south of Valletta. Take bus #8 from outside the arrivals hall to Valletta. (30min., every 20-30min. 5:30am-8pm, €0.47.)

Buses: Main terminal located just outside the gates of Valletta. To: **Sliema** (bus #62, 67, 662, every 10min., €0.47); **Marsaxlokk** (bus #27, every 30min., €0.47); **Birzebbugia** (bus #11, every 10-20min., €0.47); **Rabat** (bus #80, every 10-20min., €0.47). Most routes run from 5:30am to at least 7pm, and many run until 9pm. From June 15 to Sept. 14, buses connect some cities from midnight until 3am. Pick up a free bus schedule from the tourist information office.

Taxis: City Cab (☎2133 3321, 7933 3327). **Boat taxis** leave for Birgu (Vittoriosa) and other cities from near the Customs House (about €4).

ORIENTATION AND PRACTICAL INFORMATION

Valletta's streets are laid out in a neat grid. The main avenue, **Republic Street** *(Triq ir-Repubblika)*, cuts across the city from the bus terminal to the sea at the other end. Several attractions, as well as plenty of shops and restaurants, draw sandal-and-shorts clad tourists here all day. Travelers also linger on **Merchants Street** *(Triq il-Merkanti)*, which runs parallel to Republic Street.

Tourist Office: 1 City Arcades (☎2123 7747; www.visitmalta.com). Enter Valletta through the City Gate and turn right. Open M-Sa 9am-5:30pm, Su and public holidays 9am-1pm. Branch at Malta International Airport.

Currency Exchange: HSBC, Bank of Valletta, and **Lombard Bank** have branches on Republic St., but are closed on Sundays. The exchange across from the City Gate, in Freedom Sq., is open on Sundays.

Pharmacy: Empire Pharmacy, 46 Melita St. (☎2123 8577; open M-Sa 9am-noon and 4pm-7pm). There are no 24hr. pharmacies in Valletta. On Sundays and public holidays, pharmacies open by roster on a rotating basis and close around noon.

Hospital: Mater Dei, in Birkirkara, is a 20min bus ride from Valletta (bus #75). It may also be your best bet for a 24hr pharmacy.

Post Office: Malta Post, Castille Pl. (www.maltapost.com).

Internet: GWU Workers Memorial Building, South St. This unlikely place offers good rates (€2.33 for 1hr 15mins), and you can use your time over several sessions. For more services, walk a few steps to **Ziffa Internet Center,** 194 Strait St., which sells CDs and DVDs and has printing, photocopying, scanning, and fax capabilities. (☎2122 4307. Open M-Sa 9am-11pm, Su 10am-4pm. €3 for 35min.)

ACCOMMODATIONS

Although Valletta has no dorm-style hostel accommodations, you'll find great prices for singles and doubles at guesthouses *(pensiones)*. All of the following are located fairly close to the bus terminus as well as to the restaurants and shops of Republic Street *(Triq ir-Repubblika)*.

Coronation Guesthouse, 10 Anton Vassalli St. (☎2123 7652). Though the paint is peeling and the flush may require skill to operate, this homey guesthouse with soft beds is a pleasant place to crash. Light breakfast included. Doubles with shared bath €14. ❷

Asti Guesthouse, 18 St. Ursula St. (☎2123 9506; http://mol.net.mt/asti). A gleaming lobby welcomes you to a surprisingly inexpensive guesthouse, close to the Grand Harbour. Breakfast included. Doubles with shared bath €16.30. ❷

Midland Guesthouse, 255 St. Ursula St. (☎2123 6024). Down the street from Asti is this quiet guesthouse with a cafe and a great view right around the corner. Breakfast included. Singles with shared bath €20. ❷

British Hotel, 40 Battery St. (☎2122 4730). For a view that'll make you stop and stare every time you cross the verandah, splurge on rooms here. Don't expect luxury, however; rooms are small and simple. Breakfast included. Singles with bath from €36. Internet access available for a small fee. Free Wi-Fi in bar and reception area. ❸

FOOD

Restaurants in Valletta can be expensive, but explore the streets leading off *Triq ir-Repubblika* to find cafes that won't have you eyeing your reserve cash supply. To grab the cheapest eats, follow local residents to the shops selling tasty *pastizzi* (pastry stuffed with cheese or peas; about €0.30 each) and *imqaret* (pastry stuffed with dates; about €0.20 each) near the bus terminus. Grocery stores aren't easy to come by. For a well-stocked shop, walk up Merchants Street to **The Albion Stores,** where crackers and lunch meat cost €1-2. (Walk toward the City Gates, just before St. Lucija St., to your right. Open daily 8:30am-7pm. Closes around 12:30pm for lunch.)

Dolceria Croce Bonaci, 24 St. John St. (☎2124 7933). Empty tables are hard to find at this popular, unpretentious cafe that dishes out filling snacks at the lowest prices. Try the fried pasta with ham and tomatoes (€1.75). Open daily 8:30am-4:30pm. Savory and sweet snacks €1.75-3.50. Cash only. ❶

Caffe Merisi, 11 South St. Savor deliciously cold milkshakes (€2.33) and pies (about €2) in an air-conditioned room, a welcome relief in Malta's burning summer heat. Free Wi-Fi sweetens the deal. Open M-F 7:30am-8pm, Sa 8am-3:30pm. MC/V. ❶

Cafe Prego, 58 South St. Elderly gentlemen serve sandwiches and pizzas (all €1-1.50) in the dim, hushed interior of this cafe. Open M-F 8am-7pm, Sa 8am-2pm. ❶

Cafe Caravaggio, 9 St. John Sq. (☎2123 6257). Listen to the bells of St. John's Co-Cathedral while sipping wine at this upscale restaurant with tables on the square. While you're in the mood to hand away those euros, try rabbit, cooked the traditional way (€11). Open daily 8am-around midnight. Entrees €4-15. AmEx/MC/V. ❷

SIGHTS AND ENTERTAINMENT

The city of Valletta is a sight in itself: it is listed as a World Heritage Site. Make sure you have ample time (that is, about an hour) to wander its lonely streets. Walk down *Triq ir-Repubblika* to the **National Museum of Archaeology** to view intriguing ancient art—including stone penises—dating from 5000BC onwards. *(☎2122 1623. Open daily 9am-7pm, last admission 6:30pm. €2.33, students €1.16. English explanations.)* For a great view of the Three Cities across the bay, don't miss the breezy **Upper Barakka Gardens.** *(Free.)* Queues form at **St. John's Co-Cathedral** for its grand Baroque interiors and art by Caravaggio. *(Entrance on Republic St. Open M-F 9:30am-4pm, Sa 9:30am-noon. €5.80, students €3.50. English audio guide included in entrance fee.)* For a more peaceful experience, head to **St. Paul's Shipwreck Church,** dedicated to the shipwreck of St. Paul on Maltese shores. The ornate interiors are packed with spiritual treasures, including part of the right wristbone of the apostle. *(St. Paul's St., entrance on St. Lucija. Open daily 10am-5pm, mass at 6pm. Free.)* More baroque splendor may be found at the 275-year-old **Manoel Theatre.** Catch a performance here, or take a guided tour. *(115 Old Theatre St. ☎2124 6389; www.teatrumanoel.com.mt. Tours Oct. 1-June 15 M-F every 45min. 10:15am-3:30pm, Sa 10:15am, 11am, 11:45am; June 16-Sept. 30 M-F every 45min. 10:15am-12:30pm, Sa 10:15am, 11am, 11:45am.)* The seat of government in Malta for centuries, the **Grand Master's Palace** and **Armoury** are worth a visit. *(Free. Open to the public every day except Th.)*

DAYTRIPS FROM VALLETTA

Most buses and ferries leave from Valletta, making the city the most convenient sight-seeing base in Malta. The rattling, yellow buses are frequent, cheap and fast—most towns are only about a 30min. ride away. Buy tickets on board.

HAL SAFLIENI HYPOGEUM AND TARXIEN TEMPLES (PAOLA)

Bus 11 goes to both sites (every 10-20mins., €0.47).

One of Malta's most popular historic sites, the **Hal Saflieni Hypogeum,** Burial St., consists of several levels of underground burial chambers and passages, the oldest of which dates back to 3600BC. Visitors marvel at the ancient paintings and visible evidence of early skilled workmanship. In order to ensure the preservation of the site, carbon dioxide levels must be kept in check—only a limited number of visitors are allowed in every day, so be sure to reserve a spot weeks in advance. (☎2180 5018. Required tours daily on the hour 9am-4pm, except noon. Book at www.heritagemaltashop.com, the Hypogeum, or at the Museum of Archaeology in Valletta. 10 people per tour. €9, students €4.70. Last minute tours at noon may be assembled depending on demand. Noon tours must be booked one day ahead. €20.) The **Tarxien Temples,** Neolithic Temples St., which date from 3600-2500BC, are a ten minute walk from the Hypogeum. (☎2169 5578. Open daily 9am-5pm, last admission 4:30pm. €2.30, students €1.16.)

RABAT AND MDINA

Bus 80 goes to Rabat and Mdina (every 10-20min., €0.47).

The neighboring cities of Rabat and Mdina hold historical intrigue and unforgettable charms. In Rabat, the **Wignacourt Museum,** just off Parish Square, houses eerie catacombs and a shelter from WWII. (Open M-Sa 10am-3pm. €2.50.) Follow the signs to **St. Paul's Catacombs,** a network of burial sites explained on the free audio guide. (Open daily 9am-5pm, last admission 4:30pm. €4.70, students €2.30.) **St. Paul's Church,** Parish Square, stands on the site where St. Paul is believed to have taken shelter after being shipwrecked. Inside is the grotto where the saint supposedly lived. (Free.) Friendly waitresses serve sandwiches (€1-4.50) and entrees like pasta and pizza (€5-13) at **La Piazza ❶,** Parish Square. (☎2145 0865. Open daily 8:30am-late. MC/V.)

Mdina's flower-filled balconies and sunlit lanes seem transported from another time. Just inside the city gate, the **National Museum of Natural History** houses specimens of animals and minerals. (☎2145 5951. €2.33, €1.16. Open daily 9am-4:30pm. Cash only.) Turn left from the square to reach popular strolling ground, **Villegaignon Street.** The richly decorated **St. Paul's Cathedral,** St. Paul's Square, is accompanied by a museum beside it. (Both cathedral and museum open M-F 9:30am-4:30pm, Sa 9:30am-3:30pm. Cathedral free, museum €2.50, students €1.75.) Walk all the way down Villegaignon Street to **Bastion Square** for a great view of the hazy sea. At **Fontanella Tea Garden ❶,** 1 Bastion St., dig into a cake while feasting on the view. (☎2145 0208. Cakes €2.20. Sandwiches €2-3. Pizza €7. Open in summer daily 10am-11pm, in winter 10am-6pm. Cash only.)

BIRZEBUGGA AND GHAR DALAM CAVE

Bus 11 goes to Birzebugga (€0.47). Ask the driver to let you off at Ghar Dalam, before Birzebugga on the way from Valletta.

Birzebugga's small, sandy beach draws families looking to play and bathe in the sun. However, Pretty Bay, as it's called by locals, is a rather wishful name—not far from the beach you can see heavy industrial equipment at work. If you're not into getting a tan, visit the **Ghar Dalam Cave and Museum.** The 144m long cave (not all of it open to the public) contains remains of Ice Age animals, as well as impressive stalagmites and stalactites. The museum houses rows of hippo toe bones and the like. (Open daily 9am-5pm. €3.50, students €1.75.)

MARSAXLOKK

Bus 27 goes to Marsaxlokk (€0.47).

On Sunday mornings, this small fishing village hosts a market selling everything from octopus to T-shirts. (Market closes around 12:30pm.) Shops line the harbor, where colorful *luzzu* (fishing boats) make for great photos. Linger afterwards for a cheap bite to eat at the **Malta Labour Party Club ❶** (Centru Laburista), Xatt is-Sajjieda, facing the harbour. (☎2165 1184. Open daily 8am-11pm. Sandwiches €0.70-6. Cash only.)

BIRGU (VITTORIOSA)

Buses 1, 4, and 6 go to Birgu (every 30min., €0.47). Boat taxis also run from Valletta (€4).

This bayside city, opposite Valletta, was crowned the capital of Malta by the Knights of St. John in the 16th century. Today, its quiet streets and boat-filled harbor appeal to those looking to escape the crowds of Valletta. The 17th-century **Inquisitor's Palace,** on Main Gate Street, houses a former prison, a chilling tribunal room, and religious artwork. (Open daily 9am-5pm. €4.66, students €2.33.) Amble down the street to Victory Square and turn left to reach the **Parish Museum,** where you can view the hat and sword of Grand Master La Vallette, after whom Valletta is named. (Open daily 9:30am-noon. Free.) Continue down the steps to the **Church of St. Lawrence** and cross the street to the long waterfront. Grab a drink at one of the pricey cafes on this strip, or walk by rows of swaying sailboats to bulky **Fort St. Angelo,** which is also clearly visible from Valletta's Grand Harbour. The **Maritime Museum** stands on this stretch as well. (Open daily 9am-5pm. €4.66, students €2.33.) Finally, head back toward the bus stop and follow signs to the **Malta at War Museum,** dedicated to the struggle of the Maltese during WWII. The chief draw is the underground air raid shelter. (☎2189 6617; www.maltaatwarmuseum.org. Open daily 10am-4pm. €7, 16 and under €6.)

SLIEMA AND ST. JULIAN'S

Bus 62 goes to Sliema and St. Julian's (€0.47). Nightbuses run midnight-3am during summer (€1.16). To reach St. Rita's Steps, get off at the last stop, walk up the road and turn right at the 'bus terminus' sign. Turn right again and you'll see (and hear) the clubs.

Embracing the coast, Sliema and St. Julian's pulse long after the capital calls it a day. Sliema is the calmer of the two—families stroll and children play along its seaside promenade. The shops and restaurants string their way to St. Julian's, where hip-hop spills onto the streets and the young and fashionable keep bartenders on their toes until the sun comes up. **Fuego Salsa Bar,** St. George's Bay, gets things swinging with free salsa lessons in a tropical themed setting. (Open daily 7:30pm-5am or later. M-W intermediate level salsa lessons, Th-F advanced. Lessons start 8:30pm. 18+. Cocktails €3.70-11.50.) The chief, though short, clubbing stretch is **St. Rita's Steps.** Youngsters run inside for cocktails while an older set relaxes at the outdoor tables at **Browns,** St. George's Road. (Cocktails €5-9.50.) Those looking for a tamer evening head to **Eden Cinemas,** only a short walk up St. George's Road. Fill your belly with tapas at nearby **Bar Coon,** St. George's Road. (Open daily 8am-late. €2-8. Cash only.) Groceries are available at **Arkadia Food Store,** Triq il-Knisja. (Open M-Sa 8am-8pm.)

THE NETHERLANDS (NEDERLAND)

The Dutch take great pride in their country, in part because they created vast stretches of it, claiming land from the ocean using dikes and canals. With most of the country's land below sea level, the task of keeping iconic tulips and windmills on dry ground has become something of a national pastime. Over the centuries, planners built dikes higher and higher to hold back the sea, culminating in a new "flexible coast" policy that depends on spillways and reservoirs to contain potentially disastrous flood waters. For a people whose land constantly threatens to become ocean, the staunch Dutch have a deeply grounded culture and down-to-earth friendliness. Time-tested art, ambitious architecture, and dynamic nightlife make the Netherlands a priority destination in Europe.

DISCOVER THE NETHERLANDS: SUGGESTED ITINERARIES

THREE DAYS. Go no farther than the canals and coffee shops of **Amsterdam** (p. 705). **Museumplein** is home to some of the finest art collections in Europe, while the houses of ill repute in the **Red Light District** are shockingly lurid.

ONE WEEK. Begin in **Amsterdam** (4 days). Take time to recover your energy among the stately monuments of **The Hague** (2 days; p. 725) and end the week in youthful **Rotterdam** (1 day; p. 726).

TWO WEEKS. You can't go wrong starting off in **Amsterdam** (5 days), especially if you detour to the flower trading in **Aalsmeer** (1 day; p. 722). The history of **Haarlem** (1 day; p. 723) is next, then to **The Hague** (2 days) and **Rotterdam** (1 day). Explore the museums in the college town of **Utrecht** (1 day; p. 728), then head to **Groningen** (1 day; p. 729) before enjoying the paths of **De Hoge Veluwe National Park** (1 day; p. 729) and **Maastricht** (1 day; p. 730).

ESSENTIALS

FACTS AND FIGURES

OFFICIAL NAME: Kingdom of the Netherlands.

MAJOR CITIES: The Hague, Rotterdam, Utrecht.

POPULATION: 6,571,000.

LAND AREA: 41,500 sq. km.

TIME ZONE: GMT +1.

LANGUAGE: Dutch; English is spoken almost universally.

RELIGIONS: Catholic (31%), Protestant (20%), Muslim (6%).

LAND BELOW SEA LEVEL: One-third of the country, kept dry by an extensive network of dikes 2400km (1500 miles) long.

WHEN TO GO

July and August are lovely for travel in the Netherlands, which results in crowded hostels and lengthy lines. If you fancy a bit more elbow room, you may prefer April, May, and early June, as tulips and fruit trees furiously bloom

and temperatures hover around 12-20°C (53-68°F). The Netherlands is famously drizzly year-round, so travelers should bring raingear.

DOCUMENTS AND FORMALITIES

EMBASSIES AND CONSULATES. Foreign embassies and consulates are in The Hague (p. 725). Both the UK and the US have consulates in Amsterdam (p. 706). Dutch embassies abroad include: **Australia,** 120 Empire Circuit, Yarralumla Canberra, ACT, 2600 (☎262 20 94 00; www.netherlands.org.au); **Canada,** 350 Albert St., Ste. 2020, Ottawa, ON, K1R 1A4 (☎613-237-5030; www.netherlandsembassy.ca); **Ireland,** 160 Merrion Rd., Dublin, 4 (☎12 69 34 44; www.netherlandsembassy.ie); **New Zealand,** P.O. Box 840, at Ballance and Featherston St., Wellington (☎044 71 63 90; www.netherlandsembassy.co.nz); **UK,** 38 Hyde Park Gate, London, SW7 5DP (☎20 75 90 32 00; www.netherlands-embassy.org.uk); **US,** 4200 Linnean Ave., NW, Washington, DC, 20008 (☎202-244-5300; www.netherlands-embassy.org).

VISA AND ENTRY INFORMATION. EU citizens do not need a visa. Citizens of Australia, Canada, New Zealand, and the US do not need a visa for stays of up to 90 days, beginning upon entry into any of the countries in the EU's freedom of movement zone. For more info, see p. 15. For stays longer than 90 days, all non-EU citizens need visas (around US$80), available at Dutch embassies and consulates or online at www.minbuza.nl/en/home, the website for the Dutch Ministry of Foreign Affairs. It will take approximately two weeks after application submission to receive a visa.

TOURIST SERVICES AND MONEY

EMERGENCY	**Ambulance, Fire,** and **Police:** ☎112.

TOURIST OFFICES. **VVV** (vay-vay-vay) tourist offices are marked by triangular blue signs. The website www.visitholland.com is also a useful resource. The **Holland Pass** (www.hollandpass.com, €25) grants free admission to five museums or sites of your choice and discounts at restaurants and attractions.

MONEY. The **euro (€)** has replaced the **guilder** as the unit of currency in the Netherlands. For more info, see p. 17. As a general rule, it's cheaper to exchange money in the Netherlands than at home. A bare-bones day in the Netherlands will cost €35-40; a slightly more comfortable day will run €50-60. Hotels and restaurants include a service charge in the bill; additional tips are appreciated but not necessary. Taxi drivers are generally tipped 10% of the fare.

The Netherlands has a 19% **value added tax (VAT),** a sales tax applied to retail goods. The prices given in *Let's Go* include VAT. In the airport upon exiting the EU, non-EU citizens who have stayed in the EU fewer than 180 days can claim a refund on the tax paid for purchases at participating stores. In order to qualify for a refund in a store, you must spend at least €130; make sure to ask for a refund form when you pay. For more info on VAT refunds, see p. 21.

TRANSPORTATION

BY PLANE. Most international flights land at **Schiphol Airport** in Amsterdam (**AMS;** ☎800 72 44 74 65, info ☎900 724 4746; www.schiphol.nl). Budget airlines, like **Ryanair** and **easyJet,** fly out of **Eindhoven Airport** (**EIN;** ☎314 02 91 98 18; www.eindhovenairport.com), 10min. away from Eindhoven, and **Schiphol Airport,** to locations around Europe. The Dutch national airline, **KLM** (☎020 474 7747, US ☎800-447-4747, UK ☎08705 074 074; www.klm.com), offers student discounts. For more info on traveling by plane around Europe, see p. 50.

BY TRAIN. The national rail company is the efficient **Nederlandse Spoorwegen** (**NS;** Netherlands Railways; www.ns.nl). **Sneltreinen** are the fastest, while **stoptreinen** make many local stops. One-way tickets are called *enkele reis*. Same-day, round-trip tickets *(dagretour)* are valid only on the day of purchase, but are roughly 15% cheaper than normal round-trip tickets. *Weekendretour* tickets are not quite as cheap, but are valid from 7pm Friday through 4pm Monday. A day pass *(dagkaart)* allows unlimited travel throughout the country for one day, for the price equivalent to the most expensive one-way fare across the country. **Eurail** and **InterRail** have passes that are valid in the Netherlands. **Holland Rail** passes are good for three or five travel days in any one-month period. The Holland Rail pass is cheaper in the Netherlands at DER Travel Service or RailEurope offices. Overall, train service tends to be faster than bus service.

BY BUS. With transportation largely covered by the extensive rail system, bus lines are limited to short trips and travel to areas without rail lines. A **nationalized fare system** covers city buses, trams, and long-distance buses. The country is divided into zones: a trip between destinations in the same zone costs two strips on a *strippenkaart* (strip card); a trip in two zones will set you back three strips. On buses, tell the driver your destination and he or she will cancel the correct number of **strips;** on trams and subways, stamp your own in either a yellow box at the back of the tram or in the subway station. Drivers sell cards with two, three, and eight strips, but it's cheaper to buy 15-strip or 45-strip cards at tourist offices, post offices, and some newsstands. Day passes *(dagkaarten)* are valid for travel throughout the country and are discounted as special summer tickets *(zomerzwerfkaarten)* June through August.

BY CAR. Normally, tourists with a driver's license valid in their home country can drive in the Netherlands for fewer than 185 days. The country has well-maintained roadways, although drivers may cringe at high fuel prices, traffic, and scarce parking near Amsterdam, The Hague, and Rotterdam. The yellow cars of the **Royal Dutch Touring Club** (**ANWB;** toll-free ☎08 00 08 88) patrol many major roads, and offer roadside assistance in the case of a breakdown.

BY BIKE AND BY THUMB. **Cycling** is the way to go in the Netherlands—distances between cities are short, the countryside is absolutely flat, and most streets have separate bike lanes. Bike rentals run €6-10 per day and €30-40 per week. For a database of bike rental shops and other cycling tips and information, visit www.holland.com/global/discover/active/cycling. **Hitchhiking** is illegal on motorways but common elsewhere. *Let's Go* does not recommend hitchhiking.

KEEPING IN TOUCH

EMAIL AND THE INTERNET. Internet cafes are plentiful throughout the Netherlands. Travelers with Wi-Fi-enabled computers may be able to take advantage of an increasing number of hot spots, which offer Wi-Fi for free or for a small fee. Websites like www.jiwire.com, www.wi-fihotspotlist.com, and www.locfinder.net can help locate hot spots.

PHONE CODES	**Country code:** 31. **International dialing prefix:** 00. For more info on how to place international calls, see **Inside Back Cover.**

TELEPHONE. Some pay phones still accept coins, but **phone cards** are the rule. KPT and Telfort are the most widely accepted varieties, the former available at post offices and the latter at train stations (from €5). Whenever possible, use a calling card for international phone calls, as long-distance rates for national phone services are often very high. **Mobile phones** are an increasingly popular and economical option. Major mobile carriers include Vodafone, KPN, T-Mobile, and Telfort. For directory assistance, dial ☎09 00 80 08, for collect calls ☎08 00 01 01. Direct-dial access numbers for calling out of the Netherlands include: **AT&T Direct** (☎0800 022 9111); **British Telecom** (☎0800 022 0444); **Canada Direct** (☎0800 022 9116); **Telecom New Zealand** (☎0800 022 4464). For more info on calling home from Europe, see p. 31.

MAIL. Post offices are generally open Monday through Friday 9am-5pm, Thursday or Friday nights, and Saturday mornings in some larger towns. Amsterdam and Rotterdam have 24hr. post offices. Mailing a postcard or letter within the EU costs €0.69 and up to €0.85 outside of Europe. To receive mail in the Netherlands, have mail delivered **Poste Restante.** Mail will go to the main post office unless you specify a subsidiary by street address. Address mail to be held according to the following example: First Name, Last Name, Poste Restante, followed by the address of the post office. Bring a passport to pick up your mail. There may be a small fee.

ACCOMMODATIONS AND CAMPING

NETHERLANDS	❶	❷	❸	❹	❺
ACCOMMODATIONS	under €36	€36-55	€56-77	€78-100	over €100

VVV offices around the country supply travelers with accommodation listings and can almost always reserve rooms for a €2-5 fee. **Private rooms** cost about two-thirds the price of a hotel, but are harder to find; check with the VVV. During July and August, many cities add a tourist tax (€1-2) to the price of all rooms. The country's 30 **Hostelling International (HI) youth hostels** are run by **Stayokay** (www.stayokay.com) and are dependably clean and modern. There is camping across the country, although sites tend to be crowded during the summer months; **CityCamps Holland** has a network of 17 well-maintained sites. The website www.strandheem.nl has camping information.

FOOD AND DRINK

NETHERLANDS	❶	❷	❸	❹	❺
FOOD	under €8	€8-12	€13-17	€18-22	over €22

Traditional Dutch cuisine is hearty, heavy, and meaty. Expect bread for breakfast and lunch, topped with melting *hagelslag* (flaked chocolate topping) in the morning and cheese later in the day. Generous portions of meat and fish make up dinner, traditionally the only hot meal of the day. Seafood, from various grilled fish and shellfish to fish stews and raw herring, is popular. For a truly authentic Dutch meal (most commonly available in May and June), ask for *spargel* (white asparagus), served with potatoes, ham, and eggs. Light snacks include *tostis* (hot grilled-cheese sandwiches, sometimes with ham) and *broodjes* (light, cold sandwiches). The Dutch colonial legacy has brought Surinamese and Indonesian cuisine to the Netherlands, bestowing cheaper and lighter dining options and a wealth of falafel stands in cities. Wash down meals with brimming glasses of Heineken or Amstel.

HOLIDAYS AND FESTIVALS

Holidays: New Year's Day (Jan. 1); Epiphany (Jan. 6); Good Friday (Apr. 11, 2009; Apr. 2, 2010); Easter (Apr. 4, 2009; Apr. 5, 2010); Queen's Day (Apr. 30); Ascension (May 1); WWII Remembrance Day (May 4); Liberation Day (May 5); Pentecost (May 11-12, 2009; May 23-24, 2010); Corpus Christi (May 22); Assumption (Aug. 15); All Saints' Day (Nov. 1); Saint Nicholas' Eve (December 5); Christmas (Dec. 25); Boxing Day (Dec. 26).

Festivals: Koninginnedag (Queen's Day; Apr. 30) turns the country into a huge carnival. The **Holland Festival** (June; www.hollandfestival.nl) has been celebrating performing arts in Amsterdam since 1948. In the **Bloemencorso** (Flower Parade; early Sept.), flower-covered floats crawl from Aalsmeer to Amsterdam. Historic canal houses and windmills are open to the public for **National Monument Day** (May 4). The **High Times Cannabis Cup** (late Nov.) celebrates pot.

BEYOND TOURISM

Volunteer and work opportunities often revolve around international politics or programs resulting from liberal social attitudes. Studying in the Netherlands can entail in-depth looks at sex and drugs. For more info on opportunities across Europe, see the **Beyond Tourism** chapter p. 60.

COC Amsterdam, Rozenstr. 14, Amsterdam (☎626 3087; www.cocamsterdam.nl). The world's oldest organization dedicated to the support of homosexuals and their families. Contact for involvement in support groups, gay pride activities, and publications.

University of Amsterdam, Spui 21, Amsterdam (☎525 8080 or 525 3333; www.uva.nl/english). Amsterdam's largest university offers a full range of degree programs in Dutch. Open to college and graduate students. Tuition €1445-10,000 per year, depending on the program. Discounts offered for EU citizens.

AMSTERDAM ☎020

Amsterdam's reputation precedes it—and what a reputation it is. Born out of a murky bog and cobbled together over eight centuries, the "Dam on the River Amstel" (pop. 743,000) coaxes visitors with an alluring blend of grandeur and decadence. Thick clouds of marijuana smoke waft from subdued coffee shops, and countless bicycles zip past blooming tulip markets. Against the legacy of Vincent van Gogh's thick swirls and Johannes Vermeer's luminous figures, gritty street artists spray graffiti in protest. Squatters sharpen the city's defiant edge, while politicians push the boundaries of progressive reform. GLBT citizens blend into a social landscape that defines acceptance but also faces difficult questions as the 21st century unfolds. At the same time, drug laws remain in a transient state as the constant push and pull of Netherlands government continues to test the levels of tolerance. With Muslim integration into Dutch secularism, the limits of liberal minds in an interdependent world, and the endless fight to fend off the encroaching seas, this city has its work cut out for it.

INTERCITY TRANSPORTATION

Flights: Schiphol Airport (AMS; ☎0800 72 447 465; www.schiphol.nl, flight info ☎0900 724 4746). **Sneltraihen** connects the airport to Centraal Station (20min., €3.80).

Trains: Centraal Station, Stationspl. 1 (☎0900 9292, €0.50 per min.; www.ns.nl). To: **Brussels, BEL** (2-3hr.; every hour; €32, under 26 €24); **Groningen** (2-3hr., 2 per hr., €27.80); **Haarlem** (20min., 6 per hr., €3.80); **The Hague** (50min., 1-6 per hr., €9.60); **Rotterdam** (1hr., 1-5 per hr., €13.20); **Utrecht** (30min., 3-6 per hr., €6.60).

ORIENTATION

Let the canals guide you through Amsterdam's cozy but confusing neighborhoods. In the city center, water runs in concentric half-circles, beginning at Centraal Station. The **Singel** runs around the **Centrum,** which includes the **Oude Zijd** (Old Side), the infamous **Red Light District,** and the **Nieuwe Zijd** (New Side), which, oddly enough, is older than the Oude Zijd. Barely a kilometer in diameter, the Centrum overflows with bars, brothels, clubs, and tourists wading through wafts of marijuana smoke. The next three canals—the **Herengracht,** the **Keizersgracht,** and the **Prinsengracht**—constitute the **Canal Ring.** Nearby **Rembrandtplein** and **Leidseplein** are full of classy nightlife, spanning from flashy bars to traditional *bruin cafes*. Just over the **Singelgracht, Museumplein** is home to the city's most renowned art museums. The verdant, sprawling **Vondelpark** also houses more of the city's reputable art museums. Farther out lie the more residential Amsterdam neighborhoods: to the north and west, the **Scheepvaartbuurt, Jordaan, Westerpark,** and **Oud-West;** to the south and east, **Jodenbuurt, Plantage, De Pijp,** and far-flung **Greater Amsterdam.** Though these districts are densely populated, they still boast excellent eateries and brilliant museums.

LOCAL TRANSPORTATION

Public Transportation: GVB (☎020 460 6060; www.gvb.nl), on Stationspl. in front of Centraal Station. Open M-F 7am-9pm, Sa-Su 10am-6pm. **Tram, metro,** and **bus** lines radiate from Centraal Station. Trams are the most convenient for city-center travel; the metro leads into the outlying neighborhoods. Runs daily 6am-12:30am. **Night buses** traverse the complex city roads 12:30-7:30am; pick up a schedule and map at the GVB (€3 per trip). Two strips (€1.60) gets you to nearly every sight within the city center and includes unlimited transfers for 1hr.

Buses: Trains are quicker, but the GVB will direct you to a bus stop for domestic destinations not included on a rail line. **Muiderpoort** (2 blocks east of Oosterpark) sends buses east; **Marnixstation** (at the corner of Marnixstr. and Kinkerstr.) west; and the **Stationsplein** head both north and south.

Bike Rental: Frédéric Rent a Bike, Brouwersgr. 78 (☎020 624 5509; www.frederic.nl), in the Scheepvaartbuurt. Bikes €10 per day, €40 per week. No deposit; leave passport or credit card. Lock and theft insurance included. **Maps** and advice liberally dispensed. Open daily 9am-6pm. Cash only.

PRACTICAL INFORMATION

Tourist Office: VVV, Stationspl. 10 (☎0900 400 4040; www.amsterdamtourist.nl), opposite Centraal Station. Books rooms and sells **maps** for €2. Internet €0.40 per min. Open daily 8am-9pm. Branches at Stadhouderskade 1, Schiphol Airport, and inside Centraal. Sells **I Amsterdam card,** which gives you free public transit, parking, boat trip, discounts. 24hr. pass €33, 48hr. pass €43, 72hr. pass €53.

Consulates: All foreign embassies are in **The Hague** (p. 725). **UK Consulate,** Koningslaan 44 (☎020 676 4343). Open M-F 8:30am-1:30pm. **US Consulate,** Museumpl. 19 (☎020 575 5309; http://amsterdam.usconsulate.gov). Open M-F 8:30-11:30am. Closed last W of every month.

Currency Exchange: American Express, Damrak 66 (☎020 504 8777), offers the best rates, no commission on American Express Traveler's Cheques, and a €4 flat fee for all non-Euro cash and non-AmEx traveler's checks. Open M-F 9am-5pm, Sa 9am-noon.

GLBT Resources: Pink Point (☎020 428 1070; www.pinkpoint.org), a kiosk located in front of the Westerkerk, provides info on GLBT life in Amsterdam. Open daily noon-6pm.

Police: Headquarters at Elandsgr. 117 (☎020 559 9111). The national non-emergency line, ☎0900 8844, connects you to the nearest station or the rape crisis department.

Crisis Lines: General counseling at **Telephone Helpline** (☎020 675 7575). Open 24hr. Rape crisis hotline (☎020 612 0245) staffed M-F 10:30am-11pm, Sa-Su 3:30-11pm. Drug counseling at the **Jellinek Clinic** (☎020 570 2378). Open M-F 9am-5pm.

Medical Services: For hospital care, **Academisch Medisch Centrum,**

Amsterdam

ACCOMMODATIONS
City Hotel, **1**
Durty Nelly's Hostel, **2**
Flying Pig Downtown, **3**
Frédéric Rent a Bike, **4**
Freeland, **5**
The Golden Bear, **6**
Hemp Hotel, **7**
Hotel Adolesce, **8**
Hotel Bema, **9**
Luckytravellers Fantasia Hotel, **10**
Shelter City, **11**
The Shelter Jordan, **12**
Stayokay Amsterdam Stadsdoelen, **13**
Stayokay Amsterdam Vondelpark, **14**
St. Christopher's Inn, **15**

BEST OF FOOD
Cafe-Restaurant Amsterdam, **16**
Cafe De Pijp, **17**
Cafe Latei, **18**
De Binnen Pret, **19**
In de Waag, **21**
Lanskroon, **22**
Loetje, **23**

BEST OF COFFEE SHOPS
Amnesia, **24**
Kadinsky, **25**

BEST OF NIGHTLIFE
Alto, **26**
Café de Jaren, **27**
Café Zool, **28**
Dulac, **29**
Kingfisher, **30**

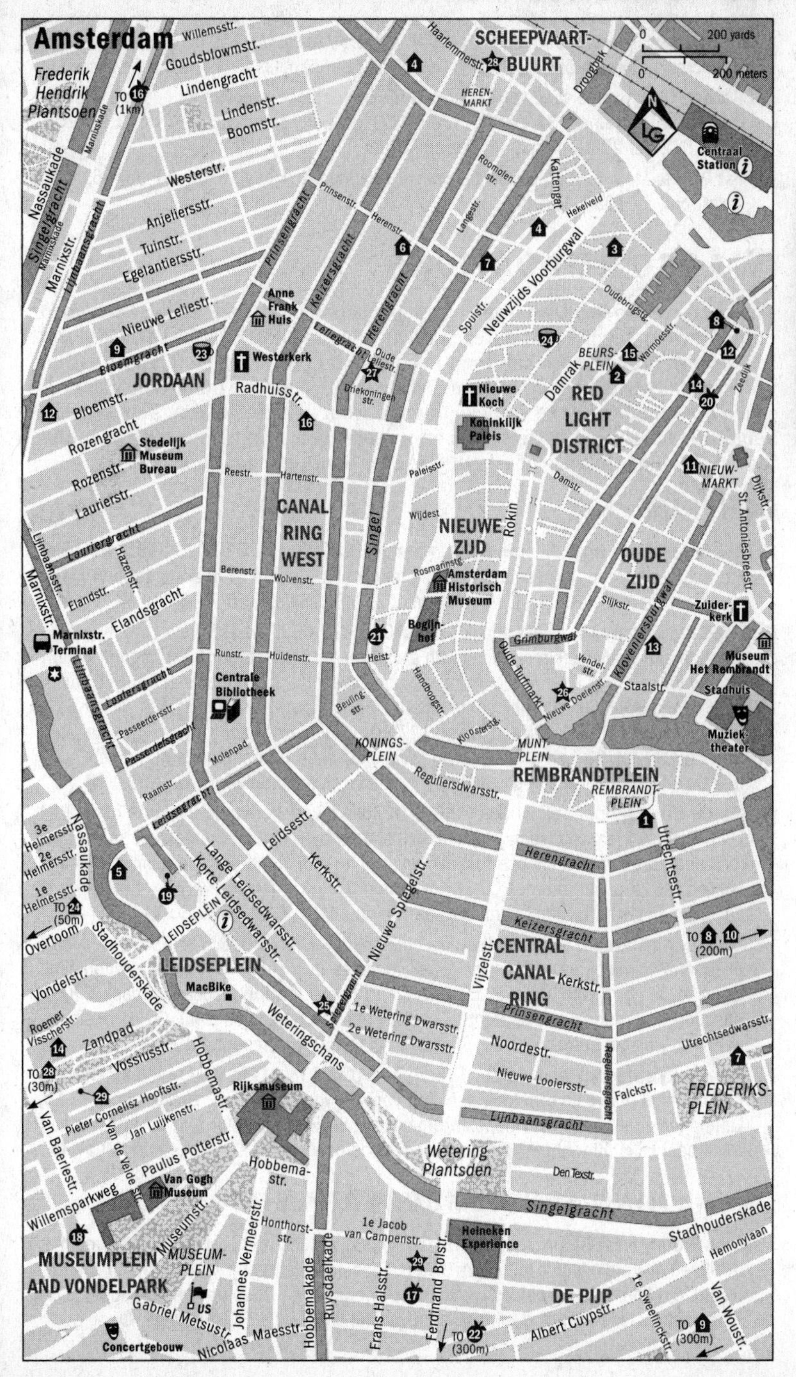
Amsterdam
SCHEEPVAART-BUURT
Centraal Station
JORDAAN
Anne Frank Huis
Westerkerk
Nieuwe Koch
Koninklijk Paleis
RED LIGHT DISTRICT
CANAL RING WEST
NIEUWE ZIJD
OUDE ZIJD
Stedelijk Museum Bureau
Amsterdam Historisch Museum
Begijnhof
Zuiderkerk
Museum Het Rembrandt
Stadhuis
Muziektheater
Marnixstr. Terminal
Centrale Bibliotheek
REMBRANDTPLEIN
LEIDSEPLEIN
MacBike
CENTRAL CANAL RING
FREDERIKSPLEIN
Rijksmuseum
Van Gogh Museum
Wetering Plantsden
Heineken Experience
MUSEUMPLEIN AND VONDELPARK
DE PIJP
Concertgebouw
US
Frederik Hendrik Plantsoen
NIEUWMARKT
KONINGSPLEIN
MUNTPLEIN
BEURSPLEIN
HERENMARKT
MUSEUMPLEIN
200 yards
200 meters
Damrak
Rokin
Singel
Herengracht
Keizersgracht
Prinsengracht
Singelgracht
Lijnbaansgracht
Leidsestr.
Vijzelstr.
Utrechtsestr.
Stadhouderskade
Weteringschans
Nieuwe Spiegelstr.
Hobbemastr.
Van Baerlestr.
Ferdinand Bolstr.
Albert Cuypstr.
Overtoom
Vondelstr.
Nassaukade
Marnixstr.
Radhuisstr.
Rozengracht
Bloemgracht
Egelantiersstr.
Westerstr.
Lindengracht
Goudsblowmstr.
Willemsstr.
Haarlemmerstr.
Kloveniersburgwal
Oudezijds Voorburgwal
Nieuwe Zijds Voorburgwal
Zeedijk
Reguliersdwarsstr.
Kerkstr.
Van Woustr.
Ruysdaelkade
Hobbemakade
Frans Halsstr.
Johannes Vermeerstr.
Paulus Potterstr.
Pieter Cornelisz Hooftstr.
Willemsparkweg
Gabriel Metsustr.
Nicolaas Maesstr.

Meibergdreef 9 (☎020 566 9111), is easily accessible on subway #50 or 54 (dir.: Gein; stop: Holendrecht). **Tourist Medical Service** (☎020 592 3355) offers 24hr. referrals for visitors.

Internet: Many coffee shops and hostels offer Internet for customers and guests. **easy-Internetcafé,** Damrak 33 (☎020 320 8082). €1 per 22min., €6 for 24hr., €10 per 1 week, €22 per 20 days. Open daily 9am-10pm.

Post Office: Main post office, Singel 250, at Raadhuisstr. Open M-W and F 9am-6pm, Th 9am-8pm, Sa 10am-1:30pm.

ACCOMMODATIONS

The chaos of the **Red Light District** prompts accommodations in the **Centrum** to enforce strong security measures, while hostels and hotels in the **Canal Ring** and the **Singelgracht** are more carefree. Accommodations in the Red Light District are often bars with beds over them. Before signing up for a bunk, consider how much noise and drug use you can tolerate from your neighbors. Amsterdam's canal-side hotels and hostels offer affordable accommodations with beautiful views, although they are often criticized for their tight quarters.

CENTRUM

St. Christopher's Inn/Winston Hotel, Warmoesstraat 129 (☎020 623 2380; www.winston.nl). Each room is decorated by different artist. Be sure to head to **Club Winston** next door for live music. Free Wi-Fi. Dorms €22-28. Singles €55-70. MC/V. ❶

Flying Pig Downtown, Nieuwendijk 100 (☎020 420 6822; www.flyingpig.nl). Knockout location and stylish decor matched with a welcoming, party environment. Stoner-friendly lounge in reception area and drinking matches every Su, Tu, Th that end with a DJ spinning tunes. Breakfast and linens included. Free Internet. Key deposit with locker €10. 32-bed dorm €26.90, 20-bed dorm €27.90. Queen-sized beds (holds two people): 32-bed €39.80, 20-bed dorm €41.80. Weekends extra €3 per night. ISIC holders get a free beer in summer and a 5% discount in winter. Online booking. AmEx/MC/V. ❶

Shelter City, Barndesteeg 21 (☎020 625 3230; www.shelter.nl). In the heart of the Red Light District, clean Christian youth hostel, staffed by volunteers. Breakfast and sheets included. Travelers can choose to clean on staff for one month for free room and board. Lockers €5 deposit. Internet €0.30 for 10min. Free live music every Th. Jazz every M 11pm-midnight (with drink purchase). Dorms June-Aug. €23.50-29.50. ❶

Stayokay Amsterdam Stadsdoelen, Kloveniersburgwal 97 (☎020 624 6832; www.stayokay.com/stadsdoelen). Clean, drug-free lodgings in a (relatively) quiet environment. Great for large groups. Breakfast, lockers, and linens included. Locker deposit €20 or passport. Internet €5 per hr. Rent bikes €10 per day. Reception 24hr. Co-ed or single-sex 8- to 20-bed dorms €25-27. Singles €74. €2.50 HI discount. MC/V. 1

Durty Nelly's Hostel, Warmoesstr. 115-117 (☎020 638 0125; www.xs4all.nl/~nellys). Clean hostel above its own Irish pub. Popular with young travelers. Locker deposit €10. Linens included. Towels €5 deposit. Breakfast €6. Reception 24hr. at bar; guests can drink beer (€3) after hours. Internet reservations only. Dorms €25-45. AmEx/MC/V. ❶

CANAL RING AND REMBRANDTPLEIN

Hemp Hotel, Frederikspl. 15 (☎020 625 4425; www.hemp-hotel.com). Each room is designed according to a different theme. Breakfast—featuring yummy hemp bread—included 11am-noon. Doubles with private shower €75. Doubles shared shower €70. Singles €60. Take tram line #4 to Frederiksplein. MC/V plus 5% surcharge. ❷

City Hotel, Utrechtsestr. 2 (☎020 627 2323; www.city-hotel.nl). Take tram #4 to Rembrandtplein. Clean, spacious, and above a pub on Rembrandtpl. Popular among young travelers. Breakfast included. Reception 24hr. 2- to 8-bed rooms €45 per person; 1- to 2 persons €100. 3 persons €135. AmEx/MC/V. ❷

The Golden Bear, Kerkstr. 37 (☎020 624 4785; www.goldenbear.nl). Amsterdam's oldest openly gay hotel. Rooms have a phone, fridge, TV, and DVD. Continental breakfast 8:30am-noon. Free Wi-Fi. Internet €2 per 30min. Singles from €60 (with double beds), with bath €105; doubles €62-132. Need key when reception closed 11pm-8am. ❸

WEST OF TOWN

Frédéric Rent a Bike, Brouwersgr. 78 (☎020 624 5509; www.frederic.nl). 3 cheerful rooms in the back of a bike shop—each named after a different painter. Another cheap option is to stay with Frédéric's parents in 1 of 2 rooms in their home. Bikes €10. Reception 9am-6pm. Chez Frédéric's parents €35; singles €40-50; doubles €60-100; houseboats for 2-4 people €100-160. Apartments available for short-term stays from €140 for 2 people to €225 for 6. Cash only; AmEx/MC/V required for reservation. ❶

The Shelter Jordan, Bloemstr. 179 (☎020 624 4717; www.shelter.nl). Well-run Christian hostel. No obligation to participate in any of the hostel's religious activities. Best suited for those under 35. No drugs or alcohol. Breakfast included (8-10:30am). Lockers with €5 key deposit and free storage for larger items. Linens €2. Cafe with Internet (€0.50 per 20min.) and a piano. Max. 1-month stay. June-Aug. €23.50-27.50, Nov.-Feb. €16.50-20.50, Sept.-Oct. and March-May €18.50-22.50. MC/V; 5% surcharge. ❶

LEIDSEPLEIN AND MUSEUMPLEIN

Freeland, Marnixstr. 386 (☎020 622 7511; www.hotelfreeland.com). Happy, fresh, clean and well-run establishment. Rooms have DVD player and private bath; most with A/C. Breakfast included. Free Internet in lobby; Wi-Fi throughout the hotel. Singles €60-70; doubles €80-120; triples €120-150. Book early. AmEx/MC/V. ❸

Stayokay Amsterdam Vondelpark, Zandpad 5 (☎020 589 8996; www.stayokay.com/vondelpark). Between music in the lobby, a pool table (€1), foosball (€0.50), and a bar this spotless hostel, in a quiet location, is more like a resort community. Well-suited for large groups. Breakfast and linens included; towels €3. Internet €1.50 per 15min. or €5 per hr. Reception 24hr. 12- to 14-bed dorms in high-season €24; 6- or 8-bed dorms €26; doubles €80; quads €116. €2.50 HI discount. MC/V. ❶

Hotel Bema, Concertgebouw 19B (☎020 679 1396; www.bemahotel.com). A luxury at an affordable price. Friendly staff and beautifully decorated, airy rooms. Breakfast included. Reception 8am-midnight. Singles €45; doubles and twins €70, with shower €90; triples €90/105; quads with shower €120. AmEx/MC/V; 5% surcharge. ❶

DE PIJP, JODENBUURT, AND PLANTAGE

Hotel Adolesce, Nieuwe Keizersgr. 26 (☎020 626 3959; www.adolesce.nl). Pristine, quiet, unique, and completely angst-free 10-room hotel in an old canal house. Drug-free. All rooms come with sink, TV, and phone; many have sofa and desk. Guests are welcome to coffee, tea, chocolate, fruit, biscuits; served all day. Reception 8:30am-1am. Singles €60-65; doubles €85-100; triples €120. MC/V. ❸

Luckytravellers Fantasia Hotel, Nieuwe Keizersgr. 16 (☎020 623 8259; www.fantasia-hotel.com). Younger, more laid-back feel than most hotels in the neighborhood. Rooms have eclectic decor and come with radio, phone, and safe. Breakfast included (8-10am). Singles €65-75; doubles €85-95; triples €120-130; quads and family rooms €150. AmEx/MC/V; 3% surcharge. ❸

MUNCHIES

Cheap restaurants cluster around **Leidseplein, Rembrandtplein,** and **De Pijp.** Cafes, especially in the **Jordaan,** serve inexpensive sandwiches (€2-5) and good Dutch fare (€6-10). Bakeries line **Utrechtsestraat,** south of **Prinsengracht.** Fruit, cheese, flowers, and even live chickens are sold at markets on **Albert Cuypstraat** in De Pijp (open M-Sa 9am-5pm).

CENTRUM

Cafe Latei, Zeedijk 143, (☎020 625 7485; www.latei.net) near Nieuw Markt. At this unique cafe and curiosity shop, everything is for sale—even your plate. Sandwiches around €3. All-day continental breakfast €6.40. From 6-10pm, vegetarian dishes €8, filling meaty meal €12. Open M-F 8am-6pm, Sa 9am-6pm, Su 11am-6pm. ❶

In de Waag, Nieuwmarkt 4 (☎020 452 7772; www.indewaag.nl). Eat by candlelight in this upscale restaurant—an old weigh house from 1488, complete with stone walls and long wooden tables. Comfortable outdoor seating available. Lunch sandwiches €5-10. Vegetarian dishes €19-21. Main courses €21-23. Complete three-course meal €32.50. Open daily 10am-1am. Kitchen closes at 10:30pm. ❹

Pannenkoekenhuis Upstairs Grimburgwal 2 (☎020 626 5603). Adorned with vintage photos of Dutch royalty. Traditional pancakes (€9), said to be among the best in Amsterdam, at one of 4 tables. Open M and F noon-7pm, Sa noon-6pm, Su noon-5pm. ❷

De Pannenkoekenboot, (☎020 636 8817; www.pannenkoekenboot.nl). Take the free NSDM Werf ferry outside of Centraal Station across the river. Enjoy a delicious buffet while touring the waters of Amsterdam. Reservations accepted. €16-25. ❹

CANAL RING AND REMBRANDTPLEIN

Lanskroon, Singel 385 (☎020 623 7743). Traditional Dutch pastries like *stroopwafels* (honey-filled cookies; €1.50), fresh fruit pies (€2.50), and exotically flavored sorbets, made on-site. Open Tu-F 8am-5:30pm, Sa 9am-6pm, Su 10am-6pm. Cash only. ❶

Foodism, Oude Leliestr. 8 (☎020 427 5103). Bright green walls, red tables, and an alternative air surround a warm and friendly staff that encourages customers to additional servings of healthy snacks and tasty smoothies (€4). Panini €5. Omelettes €6. Vegetarian and pasta platters €10-13. Breakfast all day €9.50. Open M-F noon-6pm. Weekends noon-10pm. Cash only. ❷

HE RED LIGHT SPECIAL

Prostitution has always been legal n the Netherlands, but brothels vere illegal for most of the 20th century. Since October 2000, it ias been legal for a business to employ men or women as prostiutes as long as they are over the egal age of consent (16) and work oluntarily. The owner of a brothel nust have a license from the govrnment and adhere to specific egulations, set by local authoriies. These require the payment of a tax by both prostitutes and employers, mandate the upkeep of a certain size workspace, and suggest that prostitutes get medial checkups four times per year.

The Netherlands has 12 red-light listricts with window prostitution, out the majority of prostitutes work n brothels and sex clubs; many also work as escorts. While previous statistics indicated a majority vere foreigners, the Dutch government has recently officially licensed prostitutes, making it legal for only Dutch citizens to rent rooms. Many oreigners who sold their services, particularly eastern European vomen, have resorted to underground clubs and escort agencies.

Windows are generally rented o prostitutes for 8hr. shifts which cost them €60-150; they make back the payment by charging €40-50 for 15-20min. of sex. Negotiations occur between prostitutes and potential customers hrough a propped-open door. Prostitutes have the final say about who gets admitted.

WEST OF TOWN

Cafe-Restaurant Amsterdam, Watertorenpl. 6 (☎020 682 2667; www.cradam.nl). A great lunch spot, this surprisingly casual and child-friendly restaurant, with high ceilings and a spacious dining room, has a continental menu of meat, fish, and vegetable choices (€11-18) that changes seasonally. Free Wi-Fi. Watch the game on the numerous TVs. Open M-Th 10:30am-midnight, F-Sa 10:30am-1am. Kitchen open M-Th until 10:30pm, F-Sa until 11:30pm. AmEx/MC/V. ❸

Harlem: Drinks and Soulfood, Haarlemmerstr. 77 (☎020 330 1498). American Southern soul food infused with Cajun and Caribbean flavors; the outdoor seating perfect for lazy Sundays. Dinner entrees €11-17. Open M-Th 10am-1am, F-Sa 10am-3am, Su 11am-1am. Kitchen closes 10pm. MC/V. ❸

THE NETHERLANDS

LEIDSEPLEIN AND MUSEUMPLEIN

De Binnen Pret, Amstelveenseweg 134 (☎020 679 0712; www.binnenpret.org). The menu changes everyday at this one-of-a-kind restaurant where it's all you can eat for €5. Plenty of vegetarian and vegan options. Serves only 30 at a time, so reserve in advance. Open Tu-F 7-9pm. Take tram 1 to end of Vondelpark. ❶

Loetje, Johannes Vermeerstraat 52 (☎020 662 8173). Known for the juiciest steak in all of Amsterdam. Typical Dutch decor with wood furnishings and chalkboard menus. Hamburger €5.50. Steaks €8-13. Frites €2. Beer €2. Open daily 11am-10pm. ❷

Bombay Inn, Lange Leidsedwarsstr. 46 (☎020 624 1784). Delicately spiced dishes at excellent value. Generous "tourist menu" includes 3 courses (chicken menu €8.50; lamb menu €9.50). Veggie sides come cheap as well (€5.50). Rice (€2.30) and other extras not included. Open daily 5-11pm. AmEx/MC/V. ❷

DE PIJP, JODENBUURT, AND PLANTAGE

Cafe De Pijp, Ferdinand Bolstr. 17-19 (☎020 670 4161). A hip and sociable restaurant in the heart of De Pijp with Mediterranean-influenced food complemented by even better company. Popular tapas starter for 2 €15. Entrees €13-15. Mixed drinks €5. Open M-Th 3:30pm-1am, F 3:30pm-3am, Sa noon-2am, Su noon-1am. Cash only. ❸

Bazar, Albert Cuypstr. 182 (☎020 664 7173). Extensive menu features inexpensive exotic cuisine from North Africa, Lebanon, and Turkey. Lunch special €10 per person (min. 2 people). Breakfast (Algerian pancakes and Turkish yogurt) and lunch start at €3.50. Reserve ahead for dinner. Open M-Th 9am-1am, F-Sa 9am-2am, Su 9am-midnight. ❷

SIGHTS

Amsterdam is not a city of traditional sights. But don't be fooled; this city—a collection of nearly 100 interlocking islands—is a sight in itself. Amsterdam is fairly compact, so tourists can easily explore the city on foot. When you get tired, the tram system will get you to any of the city's major sights within minutes. For a peaceful view of the city from the water, the Saint Nicolaas Boat Club (www.amsterdamboatclub.com) organizes canal tours.

CENTRUM

NIEUWMARKT. Nieuwmarkt is one of Amsterdam's most-beloved squares, lined with cafes, restaurants, markets, and coffee shops. On warm summer days, crowds pack the forum's endless terraces. Be sure to stop and take a look at the **Waag,** Amsterdam's largest surviving medieval building. Dating back to the 15th century, then known as *Sint Antoniespoort*, the Waag came into existence as one of Amsterdam's fortified city gates. As Amsterdam expanded, it was converted into a house for public weights and measures. At the end of the 17th century, the Surgeon's Guild built an amphitheater at the top of the central tower to house public dissections as well as private anatomy lessons—famously depicted by **Rembrandt van Rijn's** *The Anatomy Lesson of Dr. Tulp*. The Waag has also housed a number of other sites, including the Jewish Historical Museum and the Amsterdam Historical Museum. *(Metro to Nieuwmarkt.)*

BEGIJNHOF. Thankfully, you don't have to take vows to enter this secluded courtyard, located in the 14th-century home of the Beguines, a sect of free-thinking and religiously devoted laywomen. The casual visitor will be rewarded with access to one of the area's more attractive sights. The peaceful Begijnhof's rosy gardens, beautifully manicured lawns, gabled houses, and tree-lined walkways afford a much-needed respite from the excesses of the Nieuwe Zijd. While there, visit the court's two churches, the **Engelsekerk** and the **Begijnhofkapel.** *(From Dam, take Nieuwezijds Voorburgwal south 5min. to Spui, turn left, and then go left again on Gedempte Begijnensloot; the gardens are on the left. Alternatively, follow signs to Begijnhof from Spui. No guided tours, bikes, or pets. Open daily 9am-5pm. Free.)* One of the oldest houses in Amsterdam, **Het Houten Huys** (The Wooden House), can also be found on the premises. *(☎020 623 5554. Open M-F 10am-4pm.)*

RED LIGHT DISTRICT. No trip to Amsterdam would be complete without witnessing the notorious spectacle that is the Red Light District. After dark, the area actually glows red. Sex theaters and peep shows throw open their doors, and the streets are thick with people gawking at lingerie-clad prostitutes pressing themselves against windows. Wall-to-wall brothels crowd **Warmoesstraat** and **Oudezijds Achterburgwal.** There are also **sex shows,** in which actors perform strictly choreographed fantasies on stage; the most famous takes place at **Casa Rosso** *(Oudezijds Achterburgwal 106-108. ☎020 627 8954; www.janot.com. Open M-Th 8pm-2am, F-Sa 8pm-3am. €35, with 4 drinks €45.)*

FLESH PHOTOGRAPHY. As tempting as it may be, do not take pictures in the Red Light District, especially of prostitutes. Taking pictures is considered incredibly rude and can land the photographer in trouble.

OUDE KERK. Located right in the middle of the otherwise lurid Red Light District, the Old Church may be the only church in the world completely bounded by prostitution sites. Erected in 1306, the Oude Kerk was the earliest parish church built in Amsterdam, but it is now a center for cultural activities, hosting photography and modern art exhibits. At the head of the church is the massive **Vater-Müller organ,** built in 1724, and is still played for public concerts. The Gothic church has seen numerous hard times, including being stripped of its artwork and religious artifacts during the Alteration. The Protestant church has since served a number of functions: a home for vagrants, a theater, a market, and a space for fishermen to mend broken sails. *(Oudekerkspl. 23. ☎020 625 8284; www.oudekerk.nl. Open M-Sa 11am-5pm, Su 1-5pm. €5, students and over 65 €4, under 12 free. I Amsterdam cardholders free. Tower €5. Additional charge for exhibits.)*

SINT NICOLAASKERK. Above the impressive columned altar, a burst of color emanates from the stained-glass windows of this relatively new Roman Catholic church that may potentially bring any visitor to standstill. Completed in 1887 to honor the patron saint of sailors, it replaced a number of Amsterdam's secret Catholic churches from the era of the Alteration. The walls of the church are art themselves, lined with magnificent murals depicting the life and story of St. Nicolaas. Take time to admire its massive 2300-pipe organ. *(Prins Hendrikkade 73. ☎020 624 8749. Daily service 12:30pm; Su mass 10:30am Dutch, 1pm Spanish. Organ festival July-Sept. Sa 8:15pm. Contemporary and classical organ concerts occasionally Sa 3pm—call ahead. Open M 1-4pm, Tu-F 11am-4pm, Sa noon-3pm. Organ festival €6.)*

DAM SQUARE AND KONINKLIJK PALEIS. Next to the Nieuwe Kerk on Dam Sq. is the Koninklijk Paleis, one of Amsterdam's most impressive architectural feats. The palace is closed for renovations until 2009, but even the edifice's exterior bursts with architecture and history. It originally served as the town hall, but it was no ordinary municipal building. In a city at the center of burgeoning worldwide trade, governed by a group of magistrates, the town hall became the most important government building in the region. Its architect, Jacob van Campen, aimed to replace the entrenched Amsterdam Renaissance style with a more Classicist one. Across Dam Sq. is the Dutch **Nationaal Monument,** unveiled on May 4, 1956, to honor Dutch victims of WWII. Inside the 22m white stone obelisk is soil from all 12 of the Netherlands's provinces and the Dutch East Indies. Along the back of the monument, you'll find the provinces' crests bordered by the years 1940 and 1945. In addition to this reminder of Dutch suffering during the war, the monument is one of Amsterdam's central meeting and people-watching spots. *(Tram #5, 13, 17, or 20 to Dam.)*

SPUI. Pronounced "spow," this square was originally a body of water that constituted the southernmost point of the city. In 1882, the Spui was filled in and became the tree-lined, cobblestone square—perfect for quiet lounging on summer afternoons. The area, surrounded by bookstores, is home to an art market on Sundays and a book market on Fridays. Look out for **Het Lievertje** (The Little Urchin), a small bronze statue by Carel Kneulman that became a symbol for the Provos, a Dutch counter-culture movement, and was the site of many meetings and riots in the 1960s. *(Tram #1, 2, 4, 5, 9, 14, 16, 24, or 25 to Spui.)*

CANAL RING AND REMBRANDTPLEIN

WESTERKERK. This stunning Protestant church was designed by Roman Catholic architect Hendrick de Keyser and completed in 1631. The blue and yellow imperial crown of Maximilian of Austria—the Hapsburg ruler of the Holy Roman Empire in the late 15th century—rests atop the 85m tower, which has become a patriotic symbol for the citizens of Amsterdam. In contrast to the decorative exterior, the Protestant church remains properly sober and

BICYCLE BUILT FOR YOU

Even if you've experienced the Red Light District or clouded yourself in smoke at all of Amsterdam's coffeeshops, you can't say you've truly conquered this city unless you've ridden a bike here. The red bike lanes and special bike lights, as well as a multitude of cheap and convenient rental companies, permit tourists to whiz around as if they were locals.

A horseshoe-shaped path along any of the canals of the Central Canal Ring–Prinsengracht is prettiest–passes near the Anne Frank Huis, the Rijksmuseum, the van Gogh Museum, and the Heineken Brewery. Westerpark has wide-open biking lanes and smaller crowds than Vondelpark.

Take advantage of your mobility to explore farther afield. Leave Amsterdam to ride along the Amstel River, glimpsing windmills, houseboats, and quintessentially Dutch rolling hills. Cycle east along green trails to the seaside town of Spaarndam (20-25km). Or, use the canals as racetracks, leaving mellow locals in the dust.

MacBike, Weteringsschans 2 (☎528 76 88; www.macbike.nl), in Leidseplein, rents bikes and sells reliable bike-tour maps.

Holland-Rent-A-Bike, Damrak 247 (☎622 32 07), near Centraal Station, rents unmarked bikes to help you blend in with the locals.

plain inside; it is still used by a Presbyterian congregation. Make sure to climb the **Westerkerkstoren** as part of a 30min. guided tour for an awe-inspiring view of the city. *(Prinsengr. 281. ☎020 624 7766. Open Apr.-Sept. M-F 11am-3pm; July-Aug. M-Sa 11am-3pm. Tower closed Oct.-Mar. Tower tours Apr.-Sept. every 30min. 10am-5:30pm. €5.)*

HOMOMONUMENT. Since 1987, the Homomonument has stood a testament to the resilience of the homosexual community in Amsterdam. Its pale-pink granite triangles allude to the symbols homosexuals were required to wear in Nazi concentration camps. The raised triangle points to the **COC,** the oldest gay rights organization in the world; the ground-level triangle points to the **Anne Frank Huis;** the triangle with steps into the canal points to the **Nationaal Monument** on the Dam, a reminder that homosexuals were among those sent to concentration camps. On Queen's Day (Apr. 30) and Liberation Day (May 5), celebrations surround the monument. *(Next to Westerkerk. www.homomonument.nl.)*

CENTRAL CANAL RING. You haven't seen Amsterdam until you've spent some time wandering in the Central Canal Ring, the city's most expensive district and arguably its most beautiful. The **Prinsengracht** (Prince's Canal), **Keizersgracht** (Emperor's Canal), and **Herengracht** (Gentleman's Canal) are collectively known as the *grachtengordel* (canal girdle). In the 17th century, residents of Amsterdam were taxed according to the width of their homes, and houses could not be more than one plot (a few meters) wide. To encourage investment in construction, the city government allowed its elite to build homes that were twice as wide on a stretch now known as the **Golden Bend,** on Herengr. between Leidsegr. and Vijzelstr. Across the Amstel is the **Magere Brug** (Skinny Bridge), which sways precariously above the water. It is the oldest of the city's many pedestrian drawbridges and the only one still operated by hand.

REMBRANDTPLEIN. Rembrandtpl. proper is a grass rectangle surrounded by scattered flower beds, criss-crossed by pedestrian paths, and populated with half-dressed locals lazing about (when weather permits, of course). A bronze likeness of the famed master Rembrandt van Rijn and a 3D version of his famous painting *Night Watch* overlook the scene. By night, Rembrandtpl. competes with Leidsepl. for Amsterdam's hippest nightlife and partygoers, with a particularly rich concentration of GLBT hot spots in the area. South and west of the square lies **Reguliersdwarsstraat,** dubbed by locals "the gayest street in Amsterdam."*(In the northeast corner of the Canal Ring, just south of the Amstel.)*

LEIDSEPLEIN AND MUSEUMPLEIN

VONDELPARK. With meandering walkways, green meadows, and several ponds, this leafy park—the largest within the city center—is a lovely meeting place. In addition to a few good outdoor cafes, there's an open-air theater where visitors enjoy free music and dance concerts Thursday through Sunday during the summer. Try wandering around the hexagonally shaped, beautifully maintained rose gardens. *(In the southwestern corner of the city, outside the Singelgr. www.vondelpark.org. Theater ☎020 673 1499; www.openluchttheater.nl.)* If you get the munchies, try the pub-slash-restaurant **'t Blauwe Treehuis,** Vondelpark 5, a cylindrical tower situated inside the park, surrounded by trees and lush greenery *(☎020 662 0254. Lunch sandwiches €5. Dinner entrees €13. Finger food €4. Open 9am-1am. MC/V.)*

LEIDSEPLEIN. One of Amsterdam's more bizarre public spaces, Leidsepl. is a crush of cacophonous street musicians, blaring neon lights, and clanging trams. During the day, the square is packed; when night falls, tourists flock to the square. A slight respite is available just east of Leidsepl. along Weteringschans at **Max Euweplein.** The square sports a giant chess board with oversized pieces where older men hang out all day pondering the best moves.

DE PIJP, JODENBUURT, AND PLANTAGE

HORTUS BOTANICUS. With over 6000 plants and 4000 species, this outstanding botanical garden is a terrific place to get lost. Originally a medicinal garden founded in 1638, visitors can now wander past lush palms, flowering cacti, and working beehives. Take an enlightening stroll through simulated ecosystems, a rock garden, a rosarium, an herb garden, a three-climate greenhouse, and a butterfly room. *(Plantage Middenlaan 2A. ☎020 625 9021; www.dehortus.nl. Open M-F 9am-5pm; Sa-Su 10am-5pm. July-Aug. open until 7pm. Guided tours in English Su 2pm, €1. €7, ages 5-14, City card holders, and seniors €3.50. Cafe open M-F 10am-5pm, Sa-Su 11am-5pm; in summer also daily 6-9pm.)*

HEINEKEN EXPERIENCE. Since Heineken stopped producing here in 1988, it has turned the factory into an altar devoted to the green-bottled beer. Visitors guide themselves past holograms, virtual-reality machines, and other multimedia treats. A visit includes three beers (or soft drinks) and a souvenir, well worth the price of admission. To avoid the crowds, come before 11am and take your alcohol before noon like the real fans do. It will reopen after renovations in late October 2008. *(☎020 523 9666; www.heinekenexperience.com.)*

HOLLANDSCHE SCHOUWBURG. A poignant memorial to Amsterdam's Holocaust victims, Hollandsche Schouwburg opened at the end of the 19th century as a Dutch theater on the edge of the old Jewish quarter. A stone monument now occupies the space where the theater's stage once was. A memorial room reminds visitors of the extraordinary toll of WWII. *(Plantage Middenlaan 24. ☎020 531 0430; www.hollandscheschouwburg.nl. Open daily 11am-4pm; closed on Yom Kippur. Free.)*

PORTUGEES-ISRAELIETISCHE SYNAGOGE. Amsterdam's early Sephardic Jewish community, mainly refugees fleeing religious persecution in Spain, founded this large synagogue, known as the *Esnoga* (the Portuguese word for synagogue), in 1675. One of the few tangible remnants of Amsterdam's once-thriving Jewish community, the synagogue features a plain but beautiful *chuppah* (a Jewish wedding canopy). Visitors are free to walk through the large worship hall, which has massive brass candelabras and arches reminiscent of those of Amsterdam's canal houses. After you leave, take a look at **The Dockworker,** a bronze statue just behind the synagogue. *(Mr. Visserpl. 1-3. ☎020 624 5351; www.esnoga.com. Open Apr.-Oct M-F and Su 10am-4pm. Nov.-Mar. M-Th and Su 10am-4pm, F 10am-2pm. €6.50, students, seniors, and Museumjaarkaart holders €5, under 17 €4.)*

MUSEUMS

Whether you crave Rembrandts and van Goghs, cutting-edge photography, WWII history, or sexual oddities, Amsterdam has a museum for you. The useful www.amsterdammuseums.nl has plenty of info for easy planning.

CENTRUM

NIEUWE KERK. The New Church, an extravagant 15th-century brick-red cathedral at the heart of the Nieuwe Zijd, now serves a triple role as religious edifice, historical monument, and art museum. **Commemorative windows** are given to the church to honor royal inaugurations and other events. The church is still used for royal inaugurations and weddings. Check the website before you go; the church closes for two weeks between art exhibits. *(Adjacent to Dam Sq., beside*

Koninklijk Paleis. ☎638 6909; www.nieuwekerk.nl. Open daily 10am-5pm. Organ recitals June-Sept. Th 12:30pm, Su 8pm. Call ahead for exact times. €3, I Amsterdam Card, free.)

AMSTERDAMS HISTORISCH MUSEUM. Even though nothing beats a walk around the city itself, this archival museum offers an eclectic introduction to Amsterdam's historical development by way of ancient archaeological findings, medieval manuscripts, Baroque paintings, and multimedia displays. The section of the museum that features artistic accounts of gory Golden Age anatomy lessons is particularly interesting. Catch one of the Historical Museum's hidden surprises: in the covered passageway between the museum and the Begijnhof, there is an extensive collection of large 17th-century paintings of Amsterdam's civic guards. *(Kalverstr. 92 and Nieuwezijds Voorburgwal 357. ☎020 523 1822; www.ahm.nl. Open M-F 10am-5pm, Sa-Su 11am-5pm; closed Queen's Day. €8, seniors €6, ages 6-18 €4.)*

MUSEUM AMSTELKRING "ONS' LIEVE HEER OP SOLDER". The continued persecution of Catholics after the Alteration led Jan Hartmann, a wealthy Dutch merchant, to build this secret church in 1663. The chapel is housed in the attics of three separate canal houses and includes a fantastic 18th-century Baroque altar. The large antique organ, designed especially for this secret church's unique situation in 1794, is equally impressive. The church is still active, holding mass six times per year and performing marriages on request; check the website for information on either. *(Oudezijds Voorburgwal 40, at Heintje Hoeksstg. ☎020 624 6604; www.opsolder.nl. Open M-Sa 10am-5pm, Su and holidays 1-5pm. €7, students €5, 5-18 €1, under 5 and I Amsterdam Card free.)*

CANNABIS COLLEGE. If weed piques your interest, head to this staggeringly informative, non-academic think tank. The staff of volunteers is unbelievably friendly, knowledgeable, and eager to answer any questions. If you think you're enough of an expert and want to spread your reefer know-how, don't be afraid to ask about lending a hand. *(Oudezijds Achterburgwal 124. ☎020 423 4420; www.cannabiscollege.com. Open daily 11am-7pm. Free.)*

AMSTERDAM SEX MUSEUM. This almost requisite museum will disappoint those looking for a sophisticated examination of sexuality, but it does claim to be the first and oldest sex museum. The first of four floors features amusing life-size mannequins of pimps, prostitutes, and even a flasher. The museum also has ancient artifacts such as a stone phallus from the Roman age, but the exhibits are hardly informative; the majority is composed of photograph after photograph of sexual acts, some more familiar than others. *(Damrak 18. ☎020 622 8376; www.sexmuseumamsterdam.nl. Open daily 10am-11:30pm. €3.)*

CANAL RING AND WEST OF TOWN

ANNE FRANK HUIS. In 1942, the Nazis began deporting all Jews to ghettos and concentration camps, forcing Anne Frank's family and four other Dutch Jews to hide in the *achterhuis*, or annex, of this warehouse on the Prinsengracht. All eight refugees lived in this secret annex for two years, during which time Anne penned her diary. The endless line stretching around the corner attests to the popularity of the Anne Frank Huis, but it is not as long before 10am and after 7pm. *(Prinsengr. 267. ☎020 556 7100; www.annefrank.nl. Open daily Apr.-Aug. 9am-9pm; Sept.-Mar. 9am-7pm; closed on Yom Kippur. Last entry 30min. before closing. €7.50, 10-17 €3, under 10 free. Reservations can be made online. MC/V.)*

FOAM PHOTOGRAPHY MUSEUM. Housed in a traditional canal house, the Foam Photography Museum fearlessly explores every aspect of modern photography. All genres of the photographed image are welcome here, regardless of message or content. *(Keizersgr. 609. ☎020 551 6500; www.foam.nl. Open M-W, Sa-Su 10am-6pm. Th-F 10am-9pm. €7, students with ID €5, I Amsterdam Card and under 12 free.)*

BIJBELS MUSEUM. Inside two canal houses, this museum presents information on both the contents and history of the Bible and the cultural context in which it was written. Opened in 1851 with a display of the ancient Israeli Tabernacle, it includes the first Bible ever printed in the Netherlands. The house, a monument in itself, contains artistic designs that demonstrate the Bible's influence on culture and society. *(Herengr. 366-8. ☎020 624 2436; www.bijbelsmuseum.nl. Open M-Sa 10am-5pm, Su 11am-5pm. €7.50, students and ages 13-18 €4.50, under 13 free.)*

MUSEUMPLEIN

VAN GOGH MUSEUM. The Van Gogh Museum is one of Amsterdam's biggest cultural tourist attractions. Suffer the shortest wait and go around 10:30am or after 4pm. The permanent collection, including the Van Gogh masterpieces, is on the first floor. The second floor is home to a study area with web consoles and a small library, while the third floor holds a substantial collection of important 19th-century art by Impressionist, post-Impressionist, Realist, and Surrealist painters and sculptors. The partially subterranean exhibition wing is the venue for the museum's top-notch traveling exhibitions. *(Paulus Potterstr. 7 ☎020 570 5200; www.vangoghmuseum.nl. Open M-Th and Sa 10am-6pm, F 10am-10pm. €10, ages 13-17 €2.50, under 12 free. Audio tours €4. AmEx/MC/V; min. €25.)*

RIJKSMUSEUM AMSTERDAM. Even though the main building of the museum is closed for renovations, the Rijksmuseum is still a mandatory Amsterdam excursion. It houses masterpieces by Rembrandt van Rijn, Johannes Vermeer, Frans Hals, and Jan Steen. Of this tour-de-force collection, **Rembrandt's** gargantuan militia portrait *Night Watch* is a crowning, and deservedly famous, achievement. Equally astounding is the museum's collection of paintings by Vermeer, including *The Milkmaid.* Every Friday, you can stroll through the paintings while listening to the live opera and piano concerts that take place. *(Stadhouderskade 42. Visitors must enter instead through the Philips Wing, around the corner at the intersection of Hobbemastr. and Jan Luijkenstr. ☎020 674 7000; www.rijksmuseum.nl. Open M-Th and Sa-Su 9am-6pm, F 9am-8:30pm. Maps available at the ticket counters. €10, students and I Amsterdam Card Holders €8, under 18 free. Audio tour €4.)*

JODENBUURT AND PLANTAGE

STEDELIJK MUSEUM FOR MODERN AND CONTEMPORARY ART. As the Stedelijk's building on Museumpl. undergoes extensive renovations, its home until 2009 is a drab 11-story building to the east of Centraal Station. The museum has integrated its mission into the space admirably, filling two cavernous floors with exhibits of contemporary art that rotate every three months. . *(Oosterdokskade 5. ☎020 573 2745, recorded info 20 573 2911; www.stedelijk.nl. Open daily 11am-6pm. €9; ages 7-16, over 65, and groups of 15+ €4.50; under 7 free; families €23.)* Be sure to check out nearby hip **Club 11,** Oosterdokskade 3-5. Don't be fooled by its grafitti laden exterior—once you get up to the 11th floor, you'll be rewarded with an amazing view of the city and a nightclub and lounge. *(☎020 625 5999).*

JOODS HISTORISCH MUSEUM. In the heart of Amsterdam's traditional Jewish neighborhood, the Jewish Historical Museum links four different 17th- and 18th-century Ashkenazi synagogues with glass and steel connections. *(Jonas Daniel Meijerpl. 2-4. ☎020 531 0310; www.jhm.nl. Open M-W and F-Su 11am-5pm, Th 11am-9pm; closed on Yom Kippur. Free audio tour. €7.50; seniors, ages 7-16, ISIC holders €4.50; I Amsterdam Cardholders and under 13 free.)*

MUSEUM HET REMBRANDT. Dutch master Rembrandt van Rijn's house at Waterloopl. has become the happy home of the artist's impressive collection of 250 etchings. In the upstairs studio, Rembrandt produced some of his most important works. *(Jodenbreestr. 4, at the corner of Oude Schans. ☎020 520 0400; www.rembrandthuis.nl. Open daily 10am-5pm. €8, students €5.50, ages 6-15 €1.50, under 6 free.)*

GREATER AMSTERDAM

COBRA MUSEUM. This museum pays tribute to the 20th-century CoBrA art movement: the name is an abbreviation of the capital cities of the group's founding members (Copenhagen, Brussels, and Amsterdam). The beautiful, modern museum presents the movement's work from Karel Appel's experimentation with sculpture to Corneille's developing interest in color and non-Western worlds. *(Sandbergpl. 1-3, south of Amsterdam in Amstelveen. Tram #5 or bus #170, 171, or 172. The tram stop is a 10min. walk from the museum; after a 15min. ride, the bus will drop you off across the street. ☎020 547 5050, tour reservations ☎020 547 5045; www.cobra-museum.nl. Open Tu-Su 11am-5pm. €9.50, students, seniors, and 6-18 discounted prices. AmEx/MC/V.)*

COFFEE SHOPS AND SMART SHOPS

"Soft" drugs, including marijuana, are tolerated in the Netherlands. **Let's Go does not recommend drug use in any form.** Those who decide to partake should use common sense and remember that any experience with drugs can be dangerous. If you do choose to indulge in drug tourism, you must follow basic ground rules and take careful safety precautions. Never buy drugs from street dealers. If a friend is tripping, it is important never to leave his or her side. If there is a medical emergency, call **☎112 for an ambulance.**

KNOW THE LAW. On July 1, 2008, Amsterdam banned smoking indoors. At coffee shops, this means that you can only puff your stuff in designated smoking rooms. Amsterdam will also soon ban the sale of mushrooms.

COFFEE SHOPS

Amsterdam's coffee shops aren't really there to sell coffee. Places calling themselves coffee shops sell hashish, marijuana, and "space" goodies. As a general rule, the farther you travel from the touristed spots, the better value and higher quality the establishments you'll find. Look for the green-and-white **BCD** sticker that certifies a shop's credibility. When you move from one coffee shop to another, it is obligatory to buy a drink in the next shop, even if you already have weed. While it's all right to smoke on the outdoor patio of a coffee shop, don't go walking down the street smoking a joint: it's simply not done. Not only is this an easy way for pickpockets and con artists to pick out a tourist, but locals also consider it offensive.

Coffee-shop menus have more variety than most might assume. **Hashish** comes in three varieties: blonde (Moroccan), black (Indian), and Dutch (Ice-o-Lator), all of which can cost €4-35 per gram. Typically, cost is proportional to quality and strength. Black hash hits harder than blonde, and Ice-o-Lator can send even a seasoned smoker off his or her head. What separates hash from weed is that, while weed is the flower of the marijuana plant, hash is the extracted resin crystals—giving a different kind of high.

Marijuana is a dried, cured flower whose Dutch variety is incredibly strong. Take it easy so you don't pass out. The Dutch tend to mix tobacco with their pot as well, so joints are harsher on your lungs and throat if you're not a cigarette smoker. Pre-rolled joints are always rolled with tobacco; most coffee shops also offer pure joints at up to twice the cost. A coffee shop's staff is accustomed to explaining the different kinds of pot on the menu to tourists. It is recommended that you buy only a gram at a time. Most places will supply rolling papers and filter tips—Europeans smoke only **joints.** When pipes or bongs are provided, they are usually for tourists. Another popular way of getting high in Amsterdam is to use a **vaporizer.** These devices heat up cannabis products until the hallucinogenic substances like **THC** become gaseous, extracting more out of the product than regular burning via cigarettes. Beware that vaporizers are very strong, and those with copper piping may release nasty (and potentially **carcinogenic**) copper particles.

Space cakes, brownies, and all members of the baked-goods family are made with hash or weed, but the drugs take longer to affect a person, producing a "body stone" that can take up to two hours or longer to start. Start off with half a serving and see how you feel after an hour or two. It's always easier to eat more later than to wait out a higher dose than you can handle. The amount of pot or hash in baked goods cannot be standardized, and it is impossible to know what grade of drugs is in them. This makes ingesting this form of cannabis much more dangerous than smoking, with which you can monitor your intake more closely. Centrum coffeeshops are notorious for higher prices and poor quality product. Avoid these places and opt for smaller, cozier shops.

Amnesia, Herengr. 133 (☎020 638 3003). Slightly larger and significantly more elegant than other coffee shops. Wide selection of drinks, milkshakes, and snacks. Buy 5 joints (€3-5 each) and get 1 free. For an extra treat, try the Amnesia Haze (€11 per g), a 2004 Cannabis Cup winner. Open daily 9:30am-1am.

Kadinsky, Rosmarijnstg. 9 (☎020 624 7023; www.kadinsky.nl). One of the city's friendliest, hippest, and most comfortable stoneries. Joints €3.40-4. Weed €7-11 per g. 20% off 5g purchases. Open daily 9:30am-1am.

Yo Yo, 2e Jan van der Heijdenstr. 79 (☎020 664 7173). One of the few coffee shops where neighborhood non-smokers can relax. Apple pie (€1.80), *tostis,* soup, and (normal) brownies served. All weed is organic and sold in bags for €5 or €10, with a monthly €3.50 special. Joints €2.50. Open M-Sa noon-8pm.

Rusland, Rusland 16 (☎020 627 9468). Choose from over 40 varieties of herbal tea or refreshing yogurt shakes (€2.40). Admire the selection of handblown pipes while relaxing on the colorful pillowed benches in separate smoking rooms. Pre-rolled joints €2.50-4.50.

COFFEE ONLY?

Amsterdam is commonly identi- fied as the world capital of toler- ance. Chilled-out people puff thic clouds of smoke filling infamou coffeeshops, while popular smart shops sell everything from se stimulants to mushrooms. Recen governmental trends, howeve may soon dampen this interna tional perception.

Customers must be 18 to ente a coffeeshop and may only bu 5g per visit per shop. The shop themselves cannot advertise, se hard drugs, export soft drugs, o have more than 500g on stock. I April 2007, shops had to declar themselves a "bar" or a "coffee shop," forcing them to make choice between selling cannabi or alcohol. And, because of th ambiguity of how much THC is i smoothies and other food/drin items, the only legal "space" item available for purchase are cakes Most recently (July 2008), mush- rooms were banned by the govern ment, which was a huge blow t smartshop shelves.

This may not be the end to th controversial decrees being passe in the Netherlands. Rumors ove banning the purchase of cannab by foreigners have been widesprea ever since France, Germany, an other nearby countries have com plained of their citizens crossing th border predominantly to buy drug

Will Amsterdam's tolerant repu tation fade? Only time will tell, s puff away... for now.

Tasty Afghan bud €7 per g. Space muffins €5. Coffee and other drinks €1.70. Open M-Th and Su 10am-midnight, F-Sa 10am-1am. Cash only.

Grey Area, Oude Leliestr. 2 (☎020 420 4301; www.greyarea.nl). Last American-run coffee shop in Amsterdam. A single sticker-adorned room, this locale has a good reputation and a friendly staff more than happy to help beginners. Borrow a glass bong or vaporizer to smoke, or hit one of Amsterdam's cheapest pure marijuana joints (€3.50). Juice (€1.50) is also available. Open daily noon-8pm.

The Dolphins, Kerkstr. 39 (☎020 625 9162). Smoke with the fishes at this underwater-themed coffee shop, where an aquarium lights up the shop. Pre-rolled joints €7. Try the White Dolphin reefer (€10 per g; pure joint €5.50) for an uplifting high. Vaporizers and bongs available with a €10 deposit. Open M-Th and Su 10am-1am, F-Sa 10am-3am.

SMART SHOPS

Smart shops are scattered throughout Amsterdam and peddle a variety of "herbal enhancers" and hallucinogens. Do not take more than one dose at a time—many first-time users take too much because they don't feel anything immediately. A bad trip will occur if you mix hallucinogens with each other, marijuana, or alcohol. Don't be ashamed to tell someone if you have a bad trip. You won't be arrested, and locals have seen it all before.

Conscious Dreams, Kerkstr. 119 (☎020 626 6907; www.consciousdreams.nl). Offers an extensive variety of herbs, vitamins, "dream extracts," and herbal ecstasy. Don't hesitate to ask the staff for help. Herbal ecstasy €12 for 2 servings. Open daily 11am-10pm. AmEx/MC/V for purchases over €25.

Conscious Dreams Kokopelli, Warmoesstr. 12 (☎020 421 7000). Perhaps the best place to begin with psychedelic experimentation. Books, gifts, pipes, and lava lamps available alongside an overwhelming selection of oxygen drinks, fertility elixirs, vitamins, herbs, sex toys, cacti, aphrodisiacs, and chocolate body paint. A staff with background in neurobiology and botany on hand. Herbal XTC €9. Salvia €36 per g. NRG €10. Discuss all drugs' intensity and safety with the staff first. Open daily 11am-10pm.

Magic Valley, Spuistr. 60 (☎020 320 3001). Small, colorful shop vends sex stimulants. Ask for help from the well-versed staff. Small back section that sells bongs and souvenirs. Open M-Th and Su11am-10pm, F-Sa 10am-10pm. AmEx/MC/V.

ENTERTAINMENT

The **Amsterdams Uit Buro (AUB),** Leidsepl. 26, is stuffed with free monthly magazines, pamphlets, and tips to help you sift through seasonal offerings. It also sells tickets and makes reservations for just about any cultural event in the city for a commission. **Last Minute Ticket Shop,** part of the AUB, offers some of the best-deals for half-off tickets. Visit the office for a list of same-day performances at 50% off. (☎0900 0191; www.amsterdamsuitburo.nl or www.lastminuteticketshop.nl. AUB open M-Sa 10am-7:30pm, Su noon-7:30pm. Last Minute Ticket Shop begins selling tickets daily at noon.) The theater desk at the **VVV,** Stationspl. 10, can also make reservations for cultural events. (☎0900 400 4040, €0.40 per min.; www.amsterdamtourist.nl. Open F-Sa 9am-8pm.)

Filmmuseum, Vondelpark 3 (☎020 589 1400; www.filmmuseum.nl). At least 4 screenings per day, many of them older classics or organized around a special theme. Also houses an extensive information center, with 1900 periodicals and over 30,000 books on film theory, history, and screenplays. Box office open daily 9am-10:15pm.

NIGHTLIFE

Leidseplein and **Rembrandtplein** remain the busiest areas for nightlife, with coffeeshops, loud bars, and tacky clubs galore. Amsterdam's most traditional spots are the old, dark, wood-paneled *bruin cafes* (brown cafes). The concept of completely "straight" versus "gay" nightlife does not really apply; most establishments are gay-friendly and attract a mixed crowd. Rembrandtpl. is the hub for gay bars almost exclusively for men.

CENTRUM

Club NL, Nieuwezijds Voorburgwal 169 (☎020 622 7510; www.clubnl.nl). Enjoy posh seating under dim red lighting in this smoky club, reminiscent of the movie *Sin City*. Celebs like Kate Moss, P. Diddy, and Mick Jagger are regulars. Enjoy the pricey mixed drinks while listening to the lastest house music. Strict door policy to keep ratio of men to women equal. Gay friendly. 21+. Cover F-Su €5, includes coat check. Open M-Th and Su 10pm-3am, F-Sa 10pm-4am. AmEx/MC/V.

Café de Jaren, Nieuwe Doelenstr. 20-22 (☎020 625 5771). This fabulous 2-floor cafe's air of sophistication doesn't quite mesh with its budget-friendly prices. Its 2 impressive bars serve mixed drinks and beer (€1.80-3.10). Open M-Th and Su 10am-1am, F-Sa 10am-2am. Kitchen closes M-Th and Su at 10:30pm, F-Sa midnight. MC/V.

Absinthe, Nieuwezijds Voorburgwal 171 (☎020 320 6780). White-washed stone walls and cushioned niches bask in light from several disco balls. 17 varieties of absinthe available (€5-18). Open M-Th and Su 10pm-3am, F-Sa 10pm-4am. Cash only.

Cockring, Warmoesstr. 96 (☎020 623 9604; www.clubcockring.com). "Amsterdam's Premier Gay Disco." Straddles the line between a dance venue and a sex club. Live strip shows Th-Su from 1am. Men only. Cover M-W €2.50, Th-F and Su €3.50, Sa €5. Open M-Th and Su 11pm-4am, F-Sa 11pm-5am.

HARD SELL. In the Red Light District, it is not uncommon to be approached by drug pushers selling hard drugs. Remember, however, that the best way to avoid encounters is to not respond and never make eye contact.

CANAL RING AND REMBRANDTPLEIN

Café Zool, Oude Leliestr. 9 (☎020 131 8542; www.cafezool.nl). Neighborhood bar with a friendly clientele. Ask for Tim or Bas, both great sources of information about Amsterdam. Open M-Th and Su 4pm-1am, F 4pm-3am, Sa noon-3am. Cash only.

Bar Hoppe, Spui 18-20 (☎020 420 4420). Built in the 1670s, it serves up traditional Dutch drinks and a friendly owner who can talk about Amsterdam for hours. Open 8pm-1am, until 2am on weekends. Cash only.

Arc Bar, Reguliersdwarsstr. 44 (☎020 689 7070; www.bararc.com). Young, trendy crowd that overtakes the bar weekend nights. DJs spin nightly to a dancing-eager crowd that gets started around 6pm on the weekends. Mixed drinks €7.50-9. Open M-Th and Su 4pm-1am, F-Sa 4pm-3am. AmEx/MC/V.

Montmartre, Halvemaanstg. 17 (☎020 620 7622). Voted best gay bar by local gay mag *Gay Krant* 7 years in a row, but definitely straight-friendly. Trendy and popular with transgendered party revelers. Also known as "little brother" to Amsterdam's oldest gar bar, **Amstel Taveerne** (Amstel 54, ☎020 623 4254). Montmarte open M-Th and Su 5pm-1am, F-Sa 5pm-3am. Cash only.

WEST OF TOWN

Festina Lente, Looiersgr. 40 (☎020 638 1412; www.cafefestinalente.nl). Super-charming bar and cafe that attracts a young, fashionable, and friendly crowd. Multi-level indoor space filled with books. Ask the staff for board games on Sunday afternoons. Wine and beer from €2.50. Open M noon-1am, Tu-Th 10:30am-1am, F 10:30am-3am, Sa 11am-3am, Su noon-1am. Cash only.

Dulac, Haarlemmerstr. 118 (☎020 624 4265). Attracts locals and university students with its dimly-lit interior, pool table, booths and ample nooks. Entrees €7.50-17; half-price with student ID. Pint €3.50. Mixed drinks €7. DJ spins F-Sa 10pm-3am. Open M-Th and Su 4pm-1am, F-Sa 4pm-3am. Kitchen open daily until 10:30pm. AmEx/MC/V.

OT301, Overtoom 301 (www.squat.net/ot301). Frequent weekend nights fill the basement with young, open-minded people ready to dance and have fun. Cover never more than €5. Beer €2. Check the website in advance for events and opening hours.

LEIDSEPLEIN

Alto, Korte Leidsedwarsstr. 115. (☎020 626 3249). The vibe is subdued but the jazz is sizzling. Arrive early to get a table up front or listen from the bar. Free nightly jazz (and occasionally blues) M-Th and Su 10pm-2am, F-Sa 10pm-3am. Open M-Th and Su 9pm-3am, F-Sa 9pm-4am. Cash only.

Bourbon Street Jazz *and* **Blues Club,** Leidsekruisstr. 6-8 (☎020 623 3440; www.bourbonstreet.nl). A slightly older tourist crowd dances with abandon to blues, funk, rock, and soul bands. Beer €2.50. Cover Th and Su €3, F-Sa €5. Open F-Sa 10pm-5am, live music 11pm-4am; M-Th and Su 10pm-4am, live music 10:30pm-3am. AmEx/MC/V.

DE PIJP, JODENBUURT, AND PLANTAGE

Kingfisher, Ferdinand Bolstr. 24 (☎020 671 2395). A traditionally Dutch, low-key and unpretentious "brown cafe" that's hipper and more stylish than its neighbors. Use the terrace seating in summer, and listen to the hum of city while sipping one of their cocktails. Global beer selections €2-4. Mixed drinks €6. Frozen fruit smoothies €2. Club sandwiches €4. Open M-Th 11am-1am, F-Sa 11am-3am, Su noon-1am. Cash only.

Chocolate Bar, 1e Van Der Helststr. 62A (☎020 675 7672). In summer, 20-somethings relax on terrace sofas or enjoy DJs spinning lounge music indoors on the weekends. Mixed drinks €6-7. Open M-Th and Su 10am-1am, F-Sa 10am-3am. Cash only.

DAYTRIPS FROM AMSTERDAM

AALSMEER

Take bus #172 across from the Victoria Hotel near Centraal Station to the flower auction (Bloemenveiling Aalsmeer) and then on to the town of Aalsmeer. The first bus leaves at 5:midnight (45min.; every 15min.; 6 strips to the flower auction, 2 more to the town).

The primary reason to visit Aalsmeer is the **Bloemenveiling Aalsmeer** (Aalsmeer flower auction). This massive warehouse and trading floor hosts thousands of traders every day representing some of the world's largest flower-export companies. Nineteen million flowers and over two million plants are bought and sold daily, with an annual turnover of almost US$2 billion. . Since the flowers have to make it to their final destination by the end of the day, almost all the trading is finished by 11am. To see the most action, go between 7 and 9am. The trading floor is visible to tourists via a large catwalk along the ceiling. This self-guided tour takes approximately an hour to complete. *(Legmeerdijk 313, ☎020 739 2185; www.aalsmeer.com. Open M-F 7-11am. €5, ages 6-11 €3, €4 per person for groups of 15+. Guides available to hire for €75.)*

HAARLEM ☎023

Haarlem's (pop. 150,000) narrow cobblestone streets, rippling canals, and fields of tulips in spring make for a great escape from the urban frenzy of Amsterdam. Still, the city beats with a relaxed energy that befits its size.

TRANSPORTATION AND PRACTICAL INFORMATION. **Trains** depart for Amsterdam every few minutes (20min., €3.60). The **VVV,** Stationspl. 1, sells **maps** (€2) and finds accommodations for a €5 fee. It also sells discounted passes to museums. (☎0900 616 1600, €0.50 per min.; www.vvvzk.nl. Open Oct.-Mar. M-F 9:30am-5pm, Sa 10am-3pm; Apr.-Sept. M-F 9am-5:30pm, Sa 10am-4pm.)

ACCOMMODATIONS AND FOOD. The best place to stay is the **Stayokay Haarlem ❶,** Jan Gijzenpad 3, 3km from the train station. Rooms are spare (but cheery) and clean with bath. (☎023 537 1176; www.stayokay.com/haarlem. Breakfast included. Wheelchair-accessible. Dorms in high-season €29; doubles €102. €2.50 HI discount. AmEx/MC/V.) Ideally located right in the town square is **Hotel Carillon ❷,** Grote Markt 27. Bright, clean rooms all have TV, shower, and phone. (☎023 531 0591; www.hotelcarillon.com. Breakfast included. Reception and bar daily in summer 7:30am-1am; in winter daily 7:30am-midnight. Singles €40, with bath €60; doubles €65/80; triples €102; quads €110. MC/V.)

The Indonesian **Toko Nina ❶,** Koningstr. 48, has delicious prepared foods behind the deli counter. (☎023 531 7819; www.tokonina.nl. Combo meals €5.80-8.80. Open M 11am-7pm, Tu-F 9:30am-7pm, Sa 9:30am-6pm, Su 1-6pm. Cash only.) **Fortuyn ❶,** Grote Markt 23, one of the smaller grandcafes in Grote Markt, has more personal service. Sandwiches (€5-8) and snacks are served until 5pm, dinner (€18-23) until 10pm. (☎023 542 1899; www.grandcafefortuyn.nl. Open M-W and Su 10am-midnight, Th-Sa 10am-1am. Cash only.)

SIGHTS. The action in Haarlem centers on Grote Markt, its vibrant main square. Its main attraction is the **Grote Kerk,** whose interior glows with light from the enormous stained-glass windows and houses the splendid, mammoth **Müller organ,** once played by both Handel and Mozart. Also known as St. Bavo's, it holds many historical artifacts and the graves of Jacob van Ruisdael, Pieter Saenredam, and Frans Hals. (☎023 553 2040; www.bavo.nl. Open Nov.-Feb. M-Sa 10am-4pm, Mar.-Oct. Tu-Sa 10am-4pm. €2, children €1.30. Guided tours by appointment €0.50. Organ concerts Tu 8:15pm, June-Sept. also Th 3pm; www.organfestival.nl. €2.50.) These painters' masterpieces can be found in the **Frans Hals Museum,** Groot Heiligland 62. Spread through recreated period rooms, the paintings are displayed as they might have been in the Golden Age. Hals's work reveals casual brush strokes that are now understood as an early move toward Impressionism. (☎023 511 5775; www.franshalsmuseum.com. Wheelchair-accessible. Open Tu-Sa 11am-5pm, Su noon-5pm. €7, under 19 free, groups €5.30 per person.) The **Corrie ten Boomhuis,** Barteljorisstr. 19, served as a secret headquarters for the Dutch Resistance in WWII. It is estimated that Corrie ten Boom saved the lives of over 800 people by arranging to have them hidden in houses, including her own. (☎023 531 0823; www.corrietenboom.com. Open daily Apr.-Oct. 10am-4pm, last tour 3:30pm; Nov.-Mar. 11am-3pm, last tour 2:30pm. Tours every 30min., alternating between Dutch and English; call or check the clock outside for times. Free, but donations accepted.)

DAYTRIP FROM HAARLEM: ZANDVOORT AND BLOEMENDAAL AAN ZEE.

From Zandvoort, take a train to Amsterdam (30min., 3 per hr., €4.70) or Haarlem (10min., round-trip €3.20). Bloemendaal is a 30min. walk north of Zandvoort. You can also take bus #81 to Haarlem from both.

A mere 11km from Haarlem, the seaside town of Zandvoort aan Zee draws sun-starved Dutch and Germans to its miles of sandy beaches. You can stake out a spot on the sand for free, but most locals catch their rays through the comfort of beach clubs, wood pavilions that run along the shore with enclosed restaurants and outdoor patios. These clubs open early each morning, close at midnight, and are only in service during the summer. Nearby Bloemendaal aan Zee does not even qualify as a town; instead, it's a purely hedonistic collection of fashionable and fabulous beach clubs. Local club **Woodstock 69** is the granddaddy of them all, clocking in at almost 15 years old. There is a distinct hippie feel here with hammocks, tiki torches, and lots of loose clothing. *(☎023 573 8084.)* **Bloomingdale** tends to be the favorite of most locals. *(☎023 573 7580; www.bloomingdaleaanzee.com. Open daily 10am-midnight.)* Zandvoort's **VVV,** Schoolpl. 1, is about eight minutes from the beach and train station. The friendly staff can provide a guide to the beaches and accommodations, a map of hiking and biking trails in nearby **Kennemerland National Park,** and lots of information on the city. *(☎023 571 7947; www.vvzk.nl. Open Oct.-Mar. M-F 9am-12:30pm and 1:30-4:30pm, Sa 10am-2pm; Apr.-Sept. M-F 9am-12:30pm and 1:30-4:30pm, Sa 10am-4pm.)*

LEIDEN ☎071

Home to one of the oldest and most prestigious universities in Europe, Leiden (pop. 120,000) brims with bookstores, gated gardens, windmills, and some truly outstanding museums. The prized **Museum Naturalis,** Darwinweg 2, brings natural history to life through stunning exhibits of animals, plants, minerals, rocks, and fossils—all brilliantly explained in English and Dutch. (☎071 568 7600; www.naturalis.nl. Open July-Aug. daily 10am-6pm; Sept.-June Tu-F 10am-5pm, Sa-Su 10am-6pm. €9, ages 4-12 €5, ages 13-17 €6, under 4 free; after July 1 €11, ages 13-17 €9, ages 4-12 €7.) The **Rijksmuseum van Oudheden,** Rapenburg 28, focuses on the cultures of Ancient Egypt, Greece, and Rome, as well as the ancient beginnings of the Netherlands, showcasing everything from mummies and sarcophagi to outstanding Dutch artifacts from the Roman Empire. (☎071 516 3163; www.rmo.nl. Open Tu-F 10am-5pm, Sa-Su noon-5pm. €8.50, ages 4-17 €5.50, over 65 €7.50.) **Stedelijk Museum De Lakenhal Leiden,** Oude Singel 28-32, smaller than the national museums, is housed in the former cloth hall that was vital to Leiden's economic development as one of Europe's textile centers. It provides a glimpse into the history and development of the city through masterpieces by Rembrandt van Rijn, Lucas van Leyden, and Jan Steen. (☎071 516 5360; www.lakenhal.nl. Open Tu-F 10am-5pm, Sa-Su noon-5pm. €4, over 65 €2.50, under 18 free.) The collection of **Rijksmuseum voor Volkenkunde,** Steenstr. 1, holds more than 200,000 artifacts depicting the dress, customs, and artwork of myriad indigenous cultures. (☎071 516 8800; www.volkenkunde.nl. Open Tu-Su 10am-5pm. €7.50, ages 4-12 and over 65 €4.)

Your best bet for lodging is **Hotel Pension Witte Singel ❷,** Witte Singel 80. The guesthouse has a series of large, well-appointed, immaculate rooms with excellent views overlooking Leiden's gorgeous gardens and canals. (☎071 512 4592; www.pension-ws.demon.nl. Breakfast included. Free Wi-Fi. Singles €46; doubles €67-89. MC/V; 2% surcharge.) The restaurant and cafe **Annie's Verjaardag ❷,** Hoogstr. 1A, is a favorite with locals and students. (☎071 512 5737. Open M-Th and Su noon-1am, F noon-2am, Sa 11am-2am. MC/V.) Assiduously study the latest academic theories while sipping drinks at the popular student cafe **Einstein ❶,** Nieuwe Rijn 19 (☎071 512 5370).

Trains head to Leiden's slick, translucent Centraal Station from Amsterdam (35min., 8 per hr., €7.90) and The Hague (15min., 6 per hr., €3.20). To get to the **VVV,** the information center, Stationsweg 2D, walk for five minutes on Stationsweg from the train station's south exit toward the city center. The office sells **maps** and brochures (€2-5) and can help find hotel rooms (€2.30 fee for 1 person, €1.80 for each additional person). Ask about Leiden's walking tours. (☎071 516 1211; www.hollandrijnland.nl. Open M 11am-5:30pm, Tu-F 9:30am-5:30pm, Sa 10am-4:30pm; Apr.-Aug. also Su 11am-3pm.)

THE HAGUE (DEN HAAG) ☎070

Whereas Amsterdam is the cultural and commercial center of the Netherlands, The Hague (pop. 480,000) is without a doubt its political nucleus; all of the Netherlands's important governmental institutions are housed here. World-class art museums (the stunning Mauritshuis in particular), a happening city center, high-class shopping, and a tons of open green space combine to make this political hub anything but boring.

TRANSPORTATION AND PRACTICAL INFORMATION. **Trains** run from Amsterdam (55min., 1-6 per hr., €10) and Rotterdam (30min., 1-6 per hr., €4.30) to both of The Hague's major stations, Den Haag Centraal and Holland Spoor. The **VVV,** Hofweg 1, across from the Parliamentary buildings next to Dudok, has an extensive selection of city guides, bicycle **maps,** and guidebooks for sale in their shop, and the desk can arrange canal, carriage, and city tours. (☎070 340 3505; www.denhaag.com. Open M-F 10am-6pm, Sa 10am-5pm, Su noon-5pm.)

ACCOMMODATIONS AND FOOD. **Stayokay City Hostel Den Haag ❷,** Scheepmakerstr. 27, near Holland Spoor, is one of the best hostels in the Netherlands, with sparkling rooms, private baths, spacious lounging areas, and library. From Centraal Station take tram 1, 9, 12 or 16 to Spoor or tram 17 to Rijswijkseplein. Or walk 20 minutes down Lekstr., making a right on Schenkviaduct. The hostel is behind the pink building. (☎070 315 7888; www.stayokay.com/denhaag. Breakfast included 7:30-9:30am. Lockers €2 per 24hr. Linens included. Internet €5 per hr. Reception 7:30am-10:30pm. Wheelchair-accessible4- to 8-bed dorms €27.50; singles €56; doubles €67-78; quads €122. €2.50 HI discount. €2.50 weekend surcharge. MC/V.) **Hotel 't Centrum ❹,** Veenkade 5-6, has simple, airy, and elegant rooms. From either station take tram 17 (dir: Statenkwartier) to Noodrwal. (☎070 346 3657; www.hotelhetcentrum.nl. Check-in 2-11:30pm. Breakfast buffet €12.50; with champagne €15. Singles €49, Su €39, with bath €75/€65; doubles with bath €95/85; 1-person apartments including breakfast €90/85; 2-person €115/105; 3-person €125/115. AmEx/MC/V.) **HNM Café ❶,** Molenstr. 21A, has floor-to-ceiling windows, brightly colored chairs and walls, and a large bowl of Thai noodle soup (€7) on the menu. (☎070 365 6553. Salads €8.50. Dinner €10-14. Open M-W noon-midnight, Th-Sa noon-1am, Su noon-6pm. Cash only.) The excellent **Tapaskeuken Sally ❷,** Oude Molstr. 61, is great for tapas (☎070 345 1623. Open W-Sa 5:30-10:30pm. Cash only.)

SIGHTS AND ENTERTAINMENT. The opulent home of the International Court of Justice and the Permanent Court of Arbitration, the **Peace Palace,** Carnegiepl. 2, has served as the site of international arbitrations, peace-treaty negotiations, and high-profile conflict resolutions. Take a walk around the gardens and enjoy the magnificence of the Grand Hall. Although the Permanent Court of Arbitration is closed to the public, hearings of the International Court of Justice are free to attend (☎070 302 4242, guided tours ☎070 302 4137; www.vredespaleis.nl. Tours M-F 10, 11am, 2, 3, 4pm. Book one week ahead. No tours when the court is in session. €5, under 13 €3. Cash only.) With only two modest stories, the **Mauritshuis,** Korte Vijverberg 8, is one of the most beautiful small museums anywhere, with a near-perfect collection of Dutch Golden Age art. Not counting the precious selection of paintings by Peter Paul Rubens, Jacob van Ruisdael, and Jan Steen, the museum has several excellent

Rembrandts, including his famous *The Anatomy Lesson of Dr. Tulp.* Their showstopping pieces are *Girl with a Pearl Earring* and *View of Delft*, both by Johannes Vermeer. (☎070 302 3456; www.mauritshuis.nl. Open Tu-Sa 10am-5pm, Su 11am-5pm. Free audio tour. €9.50, under 18 and Museum Card holders free. AmEx/MC/V.) Show up at the **Binnenhof,** Binnenhof 8A, for a guided tour that covers both the historic **Ridderzaal** (Hall of Knights) and the **Second Chamber of the States-General,** the Netherlands's main legislative body. Tours don't run when Parliament is in session. The Binnenhof's courtyard is one of The Hague's best photo-ops. Take tram 2, 3, 6 or 10 to Binnenhof or walk about 15min. from Centraal; follow the signs. (☎070 364 6144; www.binnenhofbezoek.nl. Open M-Sa 10am-4pm. Last tour 3:45pm. Parliament is often in session Tu-Th. You can enter the Second Chamber only with a passport or driver's license. Entrance to courtyard free. Admission to Hall of Knights or Second Chamber €6; €8 for both. Tours €5, seniors and children €4.30. Cash only.)

In late June, the Hague hosts what the Dutch consider the largest free public pop concert in Europe, **Parkpop,** on 3 large stages in Zuiderpark with top big-name acts. (☎070 523 9064; www.parkpop.nl.) **De Paas,** Dunne Bierkade 16A, has 11 unusually good beers on tap, about 170 available in bottles, and nearly as many friendly faces around the bar. (☎070 360 0019; www.depaas.nl. Beer from €1.70. Open M-Th and Su 3pm-1am, F-Sa 3pm-1:30am. MC/V.)

DAYTRIP FROM THE HAGUE: DELFT. Lily-lined canals and stone footbridges still line the streets of picturesque Delft (pop. 100,000), the birthplace of the 17th-century Dutch painter **Johannes Vermeer** and the home of the famous blue-and-white ceramic pottery known as **Delftware.** The best of the three factories that produce it is **De Candelaer,** Kerkstr. 13, where everything is made from scratch, and visitors can listen to a free explanation of the process. *(☎070 213 1848; www.candelaer.nl. Open daily 9am-6pm. Will ship to the US. AmEx/MC/V.)* William of Orange, father of the Netherlands, used **Het Prinsenhof,** St. Agathapl. 1, as his headquarters during the Dutch resistance to Spain in the 16th century. The gorgeous old building now houses a museum chronicling his life as well as a collection of paintings, Delftware, and other artifacts from the Dutch Golden Age. *(☎070 260 2358; www.prinsenhof-delft.nl. Open Tu-Sa 10am-5pm, Su 1-5pm. €6, ages 12-16 €5, under 12 and Museum card holders free.)* A long stretch of a canal leads up to the 27 stained-glass windows at the monumental **Oude Kerk,** Heilige Geestkerkhof 25. The three antique organs are worth an examination, and the church is also Vermeer's final resting place. Its tower is about 75m high and leans a staggering—and slightly unnerving—1.96m out of line. *(☎070 212 3015; www.oudekerk-delft.nl. Open Apr.-Oct. M-Sa 9am-6pm; Nov.-Mar. M-F 11am-4pm, Sa 10am-5pm. Entrance to both Nieuwe Kerk and Oude Kerk €3, seniors €2, ages 3-12 €1.50.)* You can catch the **train** to either of the two train stations in The Hague (8min., 5 per hr., €2.30) or to Amsterdam (1hr., 5 per hr., €11.30) The **Tourist Information Point,** Hippolytusbuurt 4, has free **Internet** terminals as well as free **maps** and information on sights and events. You can also purchase a "hop-on, hop-off" city pass for the Hague and Delft, allowing you to use public transit. €13 for 24hr., €20 for 48hr. *(☎070 215 4051; www.delft.nl. Open M 10am-4pm, Tu-F 9am-6pm, Sa 10am-5pm, Su 10am-3pm.)*

ROTTERDAM ☎010

Marked by a razor-sharp skyline, countless steamships, and darting high-speed trains, Rotterdam (pop. 590,000) is the busiest port in Europe. It's also the country's most exciting multicultural capital, with the largest traditional immigrant population in the Netherlands. Festivals, art galleries, and an extremely dynamic nightlife make Rotterdam a busy center of cultural activity and the hippest, most up-and-coming city in the Netherlands.

TRANSPORTATION AND PRACTICAL INFORMATION. **Trains** roll out of Rotterdam Centraal to Amsterdam (1hr., 1-5 per hr., €13) and The Hague (30min., 1-5per hr., €4.30). Rotterdam has a network of **buses, trams,** and **two Metro lines** (**Calandlijn** and **Erasmuslijn**) that intersect in the center of the city at Beurs station. Metro tickets, equivalent to two strips, are valid for two hours. The **VVV,** Coolsingel 5, has free **maps** of public transportation as well as maps of the city. (☎0900 271 0120, €0.40 per min.; from abroad ☎010 414 0000; www.vvvrotterdam.nl. Open M-Th 9:30am-6pm, F 9:30am-9pm, Sa 9:30am-5pm.) Stop by the backpacker-oriented **Use-it Rotterdam,** Conradstr. 2, where you will find great money-saving tips and useful info. (☎010 240 9158; www.use-it.nl.)

ACCOMMODATIONS AND FOOD. For true backpackers, the clean, simple, and fun hostel **Sleep-in De Mafkees ❶,** Schaatsbaan 41-45, is a great place to stay. A "honeymoon suite" is available for guests in love and willing to kiss in public. (☎010 281 0459; www.only10euroanight.nl. Dorms available end of June-Aug. €10. Breakfast included. Personal locker €1 per day. Internet €0.80 per 15min. Must bring own sleeping bag or sheets; limited rentals. Reception closed 5:15pm-11:30am. Check-in at Use-It and store luggage in lockers.) Expect knowledgeable staff and clean, comfortable rooms at the commercial **Stayokay Rotterdam ❶,** Rochussenstr. 107-109, a hostel that's great for large groups. (☎010 436 5763; www.stayokay.com/rotterdam. Internet €5 per hr. Reception 24hr. Dorms €20-31; singles €40-45; doubles €56-65. €2.50 HI discount. AmEx/MC/V.) **Bazar ❷,** attracts nightly crowds with glittering colored lights, bright blue tables, and satisfying Mediterranean and Middle Eastern fusion cuisine. (☎010 206 5151. Sandwiches €4. Special dinner €8. Breakfast and lunch served all day. Reservations recommended for dinner. Open M-Th 8am-1am, F 8am-2am, Sa 10am-2am, Su 10am-midnight. AmEx/MC/V.) **Bagel Bakery ❶,** Schilderstr. 57A-59A, a popular stop for students, serves artfully-topped bagels in a well-lit, hip environment. Try their freshly-baked *liefdesbrood*, "true love bread." (☎010 412 1413. Open Tu-Th 9am-9pm, F-Sa 9am-10pm, Su 10am-9pm. Cash only).

SIGHTS AND ENTERTAINMENT. Only the extremely ambitious should attempt to see all of the **Museum Boijmans van Beuningen,** Museumpark 18-20, in one day. On the ground floor, you'll find post-war work by artists like Andy Warhol. The second floor is home to a large selection of Surrealist paintings as well as Expressionist pieces, plus several Monets and an impressive collection of Dutch and Flemish art by the like of Hans Memling, Anthony van Dyck, Jan Steen, Frans Hals, and Rembrandt van Rijn. (☎010 441 9400; www.boijmans.nl. Open Tu-Su 11am-5pm. €9, students €4.50, under 18 and Museum Card holders free. Wheelchair-accessible. Library open Tu-Su 11am-4:30pm; free with entrance ticket.) The **Nederlands Architectuurinstituut (NAI),** Museumpark 25, boasts one of the most extraordinary designs in all of Rotterdam. The multilevel glass and steel construction—which traverses a manmade pool and looks out onto Museumpark—is home to several exhibition spaces, a world-class archive, and 39,500 books. (☎010 440 1200; www.nai.nl. Open Tu-Sa 10am-5pm, Su 11am-5pm. Library and reading room open Tu-Sa 10am-5pm, Su 11am-5pm. €8, age 12-18, students, and seniors €5, ages 4-12 €1, Museum Card holders free.) Ascending the tallest structure in the Netherlands, the popular **Euromast,** Parkhaven 20, is the best way to take in a panoramic view of Rotterdam's jagged skyline. From the 112m viewing deck, you can take an elevator to the 185m mark, where you'll see all the way to Delft and The Hague. (☎010 436 4811; www.euromast.nl. Open daily Apr.-Sept. 9:30am-11pm; Oct.-Mar. 10am-11pm. Platforms open until 10pm. €8.30, ages 4-11 €5.40.)

Coffee shops line **Oude** and **Nieuwe Binnenweg.** At **Off_Corso,** Kruiskade 22, art exhibitions share the bill with regular dance parties and live DJs at this very popular club. (☎010 280 7359; www.offcorso.nl.) **Dizzy,** 's-Gravendijkwal 127, Rotterdam's premier jazz cafe for 25 years, hosts frequent jam sessions. (☎010 477 3014; www.dizzy.nl. Take tram 4 to Dijkzicht. Beer €1.80. Whiskey €5.20. Open M-Th noon-1am, F-Sa noon-2am, Su noon-midnight. AmEx/MC/V.)

UTRECHT ☎030

Smack-dab in the center of the Netherlands lies Utrecht (pop. 290,000), a mecca for history buffs, thesis writers, and student revelers. The swarms of fraternity boys that fill the city's outdoor cafes are a visible testament to Utrecht's status as the Netherlands's largest university town. Utrecht is also a cultural hub: visitors come here for action-packed festivals, nightlife, and tree-lined canals.

TRANSPORTATION AND PRACTICAL INFORMATION. Take **train** to Amsterdam (30min., 3-6 per hr., €6.60). The **VVV,** Dompl. 9, is in a building called the RonDom, a **visitor's center** for cultural history, across from the Domkerk. Pick up a free **map** of the city and a complete listing of museums and sights. (☎0900 128 8732, €0.50 per min.; www.utrechtyourway.nl. Open Apr.-Sept. M-Sa 10am-5pm, Su noon-5pm; Oct.-Mar. M-F and Su noon-5pm, Sa 10am-5pm.)

ACCOMMODATIONS AND FOOD. **Strowis Hostel ❶,** Boothstr. 8, has a laid-back staff, a convenient location, and unbeatable prices. This former squat feels more like a welcoming country villa. (☎030 238 0280; www.strowis.nl. Breakfast €6. Free lockers. Linens and blanket €1.25. Free Internet. Bike rental €6 per day. Curfew M-Th and Su 2am, F-Sa 3am. Max. 2-week stay. 14-bed dorms €15; 8-bed €16; 6-bed €17; 4-bed €18; singles/doubles €57.50; triples €69.) The three-story **B&B Utrecht City Centre ❶,** Lucasbolwerk 4, is geared towards free-spirited backpackers looking for a welcoming community. Hostel includes beds, a fully-stocked kitchen with edible food (open 24hr.), a music corner full of instruments, and an extensive movie collection. Take bus # 3, 4 or 11 to Stadsschouwburg or walk down Lange Viestr. for 10min.; it's to the left on the corner of Lucasbolwerk and Nobelstr. (☎065 043 4884; www.hostelutrecht.nl. Mandatory sheet rental €2.50. Towel €1. Free Wi-Fi and plenty of computers. Bike rental €5 per day. Private rooms located in separate building. Dorms €17.50; singles €55; doubles €65; triples €90; quads €120. MC/V.) **Het Nachtrestaurant ❷,** Oudegr. 158, has a decadent, pillow-lined cellar dining room, while the flashier clientele crowd the canal-side terrace. (☎030 230 3036. Tapas €3-6. Nightclub Sa 11pm-close. Open M-W 11am-midnight, Th-F 11am-1am, Sa 11am-10:30pm. Su noon-midnight. AmEx/MC/V.)

SIGHTS AND NIGHTLIFE. **Utrecht's Domtoren,** Achter de Dom 1, is impossible to ignore: the city's most beloved landmark is also the highest church tower in the Netherlands. The 112m tower presides over the province with magnificent spires and 26,000kg of bronze bells. The brick-red *Domkerk* was attached to the tower until an errant tornado blew away the nave in 1674. During the tour, you'll learn about the history of the church and get a glimpse of the church's bells. (☎030 231 0403. Open Oct.-Apr. M-F 11am-4:30pm, Sa 11am-3:30pm, Su 2-4pm; May-Sept. M-F 10am-5pm, Sa 10am-3:30pm, Su 2-4pm. Free concert every Sa 3:30pm. *Domtoren* accessible only through 1hr. tours daily Oct.-Mar. M-F noon, 2, 4pm, Sa 1 per hr. 10am-5pm, Su 1 per hr. noon-5pm; Apr.-Sept. M-Sa 1 per hr. 10am-5pm, Su 1 per hr. noon-5pm. Domkerk free. Domtoren €7.50, students and over 65 €6.50, ages 4-12 €4.50.) At the **Centraal Museum,** Nicolaaskerkhof 10, visitors enter a labyrinth of pavilions to experience Dutch art. The museum oversees the world's largest collection of work by De Stijl designer Gerrit Rietveld, but many of these objects have been transferred to the avant-garde **Rietveld Schroderhuis,** a UNESCO World Heritage Site.

The museum is accessible only by guided tour, so call ahead for reservations. (☎030 236 2362; 030 236 2310 for Rietveld Schroderhuis; www.centraalmuseum.nl. Open Tu-Su 11am-5pm, F noon-9pm. Audio tour free. €8, students, over age 65 and ages 13-17 €6, under 12 €2.)

At **'t Oude Pothuys,** Oudegr. 279, uninhibited patrons have been known to jump off the bar's terrace into the canal after a long night of festivities. (☎030 231 8970. Beer €2. Live music nightly 11pm. Open M-W and Su 3pm-2am, Th-Sa 3pm-3am. AmEx/MC.) A former squat turned political and cultural center, **ACU Politiek Cultureel Centrum,** Voorstr. 71, hosts live music (W, F cover €5-6), a political discussion group (M 8pm-2am), and a Su movie night. (☎030 231 4590; www.acu.nl. Beer €1.70. Vegetarian Tu, Th, Su 6pm-8:30pm. Organic and vegan dining W 3-5pm. Cash only. Open M-Th and Su 5pm-2am. F-Sa 9pm-4am.) Utrecht's theater school, **Hofman,** Janskerkhof 17A, is packed with students and twentysomethings throughout the week. Take advantage of student-friendly events and live music nights. (☎030 230 2470; www.hofman-cafe.nl. Beer €2. Open M-Th and Su 11am-2am, F-Sa 11am-3:30am. Cash only.)

DE HOGE VELUWE NATIONAL PARK ☎0318

At 13,565 acres, De Hoge Veluwe is the largest nature reserve in the Netherlands. The park's 36km of biking trails are its main attraction, and 1700 white bikes are available for free at five spots in the park. (Grounds open daily Apr. 8am-8pm; May and Aug. 8am-9pm; June-July 8am-10pm; Sept. 9am-8pm; Oct. 9am-7pm; Nov.-Mar. 9am-6pm. €7, ages 6-12 €3.50; 50% discount May-Sept. after 5pm. Cars €6. V.) Begin by picking up a **map** (€2.50) at any of the park entrances or at the De Hoge Veluwe Visitors Center, or **Bezoekerscentrum.** (☎0318 591 627; www.hogeveluwe.nl. Open daily Apr.-Oct. 9:30am-6pm, Nov.-Mar. 9:30am-5pm.) Deep within the park, the world-class **Kröller-Müller Museum** boasts an astounding 87 paintings and 180 drawings by **Vincent van Gogh**. The complex is also home to work by other early Modernist masters. (☎0318 591 241; www.kmm.nl. Open Tu-Su 10am-5pm; sculpture garden closes 4:30pm. €7, ages 6-12 €3.50, under 6 free.)

Arnhem is a good base for exploring the park. From its rail station, **trains** go to Amsterdam (1hr., 4 per hr., €14.40). From Arnhem, take bus #105 to Otterloo and transfer to bus #106, a **shuttle bus,** into De Hoge Veluwe. (M-F 10 per day 8:03am-4:02pm, Sa 9 per day 8:03am-4:02pm, Su 7 per day 10:03am-4:02pm; €4.80 or 6 strips). The exceptionally clean rooms of **Stayokay Arnhem ❶,** Diepenbrocklaan 27, appeal to a slightly older crowd. Take bus #3 to Ziekenhuis Rijnstate and follow signs to the hostel. (☎026 442 0114; www.stayokay.com/arnhem. Breakfast included. Laundry €3.50; dryer €2. Reception 8am-11pm. 6-bed dorms €23-32; 4-bed €25-35; doubles €63-90; singles €44.80. €2.50 HI discount. AmEx/MC/V.) The elegant and inviting **Zilli and Zilli ❸,** Marienburgstr. 1, is one of the more popular restaurants in Arnhem. (☎026 442 0288; www.zillizilli.nl. Sandwiches €4.50-8.50. Salads €7-12. Pasta €7.50-14. Meat entrees €16-22. Lunch served 11:30am-4:30pm. Dinner served after 5pm. Open M-Th and Su 11:30am-1am, F-Sa 11:30am-2am. AmEx/MC/V.)

GRONINGEN ☎050

Easily the most happening city in the northern Netherlands, Groningen (pop. 185,000) pulses with rejuvenated spirit. Heavily bombed in WWII, Groningen rebuilt itself completely; but unlike some other Dutch cities, Groningen managed to retain its Old World feel alongside its bland 1950s architecture. More than half of the city's inhabitants are under 35, due in no small part to its universities. As a result, Groningen is known throughout the Netherlands as a party city. **Vera,** Oosterstr. 44, bills itself as the "club for the international pop underground." This center for live music and cinema of all stripes is a not-to-be-missed party nearly every night. (☎050 313 4681; www.vera-groningen.nl. Events free-€11. Open daily

10pm-3am, sometimes later.) **Dee's Cafe,** Papengang 3, has rock music, foosball, and pool tables (both €0.50). Its weed and hash are grown and cut without chemicals or other additives. (☎050 313 2410; www.cafedees.nl. Weed €5-12. Space cakes €2.70. Internet €1 per 30min. Open M-W 11am-midnight, Th 11am-1am, F-Sa noon-3am.) The **Groninger Museum,** Museumeiland 1, presents modern art, traditional paintings, and ancient artifacts in steel-trimmed pavilions. (☎050 366 6555; www.groninger-museum.nl. Open Sept.-June Tu-Su 10am-5pm; July-Aug. M 1-5pm, Tu-Su 10am-5pm. €8, seniors €7, children €4.)

Simplon Jongerenhotel ❶, Boterdiep 73-2, pulls in fun, young residents with its clean lodgings and rock-bottom prices. (☎050 313 5221; www.simplon-jongerenhotel.nl. Breakfast and linens included with private rooms. Lockers free with €10 deposit. Laundry €4. Bike rental €6. Reception 24hr. Lockout noon-3pm. Large dorms €13; small dorms €18; singles €33-39; doubles €50-55; triples €70; quads €100; quints €120; 6-person rooms €132. Cash only.) **Ben'z ❸,** Peperstr. 17, serves dishes from North Africa, Europe, and the Middle East. (☎050 313 7917; www.restaurantbenz.nl. Appetizers €3-4. Entrees €10-17. 5-course menu €33. Open daily 4:30pm-midnight. Kitchen closes at 10pm. Cash only.)

The **train** to Amsterdam is one of the longer trips you can take in the Netherlands; make the transfer in Amersfoort (2hr., additional 30min. between trains; 2 per hr.; €27). The **VVV,** Grote Markt 25, gives guided walking tours throughout the year; reserve in advance. (☎900 202 3050; www.toerisme.groningen.nl. **Internet** €0.50 per min. Open M-F 9am-6pm, Sa 10am-5pm; June and -Aug. also Su 11am-3pm.)

MAASTRICHT ☎043

Maastricht's (pop. 120,000) strategic location has made it a hotbed of military conquest. The manmade **Caves of Mt. St. Pieter** were once a Roman limestone quarry; over centuries, the Dutch expanded them into the world's second largest underground complex, with over 20,000 passages totaling 240km. The most convenient starting point is Grotten Noord, Luikerweg 71. (☎043 325 2121; www.pietersberg.nl. €4.70, under 12 €3.70; combined entrance to Fort St. Pieter €8/5.50. 1hr. English-language tours Apr.-June and Sept.-Oct. Sa-Su 2pm, depending on demand.) The official seat of government for the province of Limburg, the **Province House,** Limburglaan 10, floats on water and has a collection of modern artwork by local artists. On February 7, 1992, the leaders of 12 European nations met to sign the **Maastricht Treaty,** which established the modern European Union, in the center of the Council Chamber. (☎043 389 9999; www.limburg.nl. Open M-F 9am-5pm.)

The brand-new **Stayokay Maastricht ❶,** Maasblvd. 101, is a quiet and comfortable place to stay with an older crowd. (☎043 750 1790; www.stayokay.com/maastricht. Breakfast and linens included. Towels €1.25. Internet €5 per hr. Bike rental €7.50 per day. Reception 7:30am-10:30pm. 6-bed dorms €21-30; 4-bed dorms €23-33; 2-bed dorms €28-40; singles €44.80. €2.50 HI discount. AmEx/MC/V.) Set sail and enjoy a night floating on the River Maas at the fun **Botel ❶,** Maasblvd. 95. This docked boat's tiny cabins are solid budget digs in this town. (☎043 321 9023; www.botel-maastricht.nl. Breakfast €6. Reception 24hr. Double cabin €44, with bath €48.)

Heaven 69 ❶, Brusselsestr. 146, doubles as a coffeeshop and serious restaurant. (☎043 325 3493; www.heaven69.nl. Marijuana and hash, €7-10 per g. Prerolled joints €4-5. Open daily 9am-midnight. Kitchen closes at 10pm.) Although Maastricht is not a huge party town, the best bars are run by fraternities at the University of Maastricht. **De Uni ❶,** Brusselsestr. 31, has evolved into an unbeatable local spot. (www.deuni.nl. Beer €1. Shots €1-1.50. Mixed drinks €2. Open W-Th 9:30pm-2am, F-Sa 9:30pm-3am. Closed mid-July to mid-Aug. Cash only.)

Trains to Amsterdam (2½hr., 2 per hr., €27.90) leave the station on the quieter, east side of Maastricht. The **VVV,** Kleine Staat 1, sells **maps** (€1.75) and hefty tourist booklets. (☎043 325 2121; www.vvvmaastricht.nl. Open May-Oct. M-Sa 9am-6pm, Su 11am-3pm; Nov.-Apr. M-Th 9am-6pm, Sa 9am-5pm.)

NORWAY
(NORGE)

Norway's rugged countryside and remote mountain farms gave birth to one of the most feared seafaring civilizations of pre-medieval Europe: the Vikings. Modern-day Norwegians have inherited their ancestors' independent streak, voting against joining the EU in 1994 and drawing the ire of environmental groups for their refusal to ban commercial whaling. Because of high revenues from petroleum exports, Norway enjoys one of the highest standards of living in the world. Its stunning fjords and miles of coastline make the country a truly worthwhile destination—but sky-high prices and limited public transportation in rural areas may challenge even the best-prepared budget traveler.

DISCOVER NORWAY: SUGGESTED ITINERARY

THREE DAYS. Oslo (p. 737) is the best jumping-off point. Enjoy the city's museums, like the **Munch Museum** (p. 741), and various ethnic eateries. After two days in Oslo, catch a westbound train for the scenic ride to **Bergen** (p. 748). En route, get sidetracked on the **Flåm Railway** (p. 753), or hike near **Eidfjord** (p. 754).

ONE WEEK. After exploring **Oslo** and the **Flåm Railway,** spend a day in **Bergen.** Linger, or make your way to the Art Nouveau architecture in **Ålesund** (1 day; p. 759) and the Nidaros Cathedral in **Trondheim** (1 day; p. 761). Then venture beyond the Arctic Circle to the fishing villages and scenery of the **Lofoten Islands** (1 day; p. 764).

ESSENTIALS

FACTS AND FIGURES

OFFICIAL NAME: Kingdom of Norway.

CAPITAL: Oslo.

MAJOR CITIES: Bergen, Stavanger, Tromsø, Trondheim.

POPULATION: 4,628,000.

LAND AREA: 307,500 sq. km.

TIME ZONE: GMT +1.

LANGUAGES: Bokmål and Nynorsk Norwegian; Sámi; Swedish and English are both widely spoken.

WINTER OLYMPIC MEDALS WON SINCE THE FIRST GAMES IN 1924: 280; more than any other nation.

WHEN TO GO

Oslo averages 18°C (63°F) in July and -4°C (24°F) in January. The north is the coldest and wettest region, though Bergen and the surrounding mountains to the south are also rainy. For a few weeks around the summer solstice (June 21), the area north of Bodø basks in the midnight sun. The **Northern Lights** are a top attraction—many come to see the spectacular nighttime displays formed when solar flares produce plasma clouds that run into atmospheric gases, which peak from November to February. Skiing is best just before Easter.

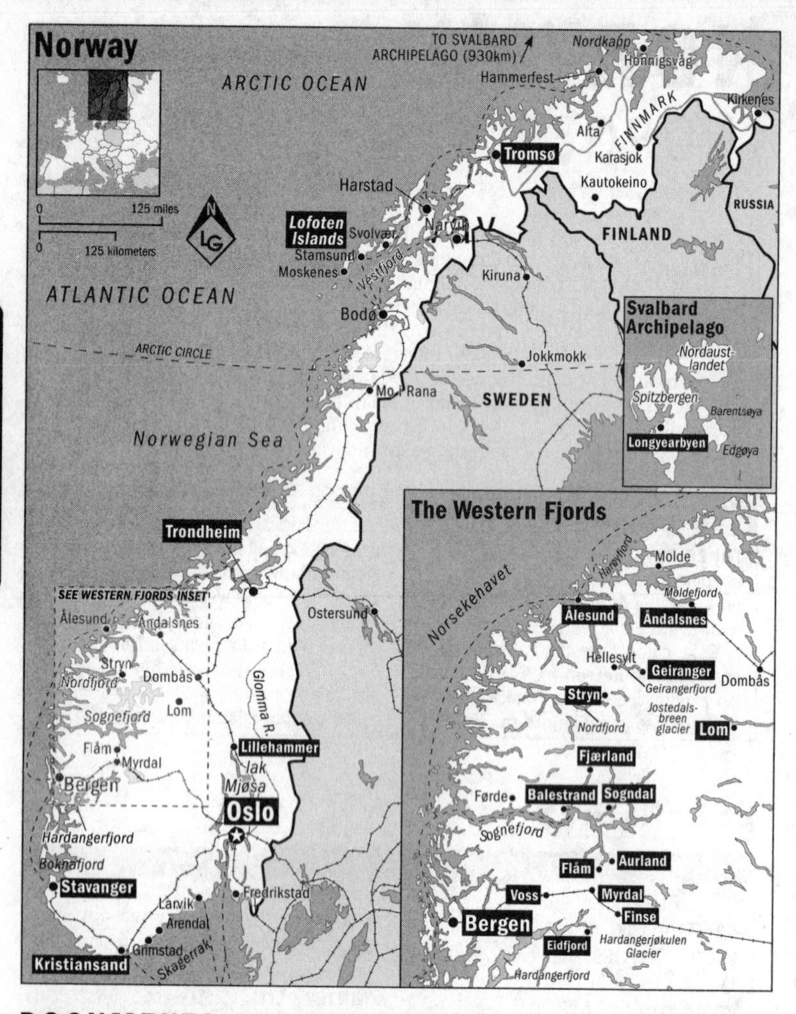

DOCUMENTS AND FORMALITIES

EMBASSIES AND CONSULATES. Foreign embassies in Norway are in Oslo. Norwegian embassies abroad include: **Australia,** 17 Hunter St., Yarralumla, ACT 2600 (☎262 73 34 44; www.norway.org.au); **Canada,** 90 Sparks St., Ste. 532, Ottawa, ON K1P 5B4 (☎613-238-6571; www.emb-norway.ca); **Ireland,** 34 Molesworth St., Dublin 2 (☎16 62 18 00; www.norway.ie); **UK,** 25 Belgrave Sq., London SW1X 8QD (☎20 75 91 55 00; www.norway.org.uk); **US,** 2720 34th St., NW, Washington, D.C., 20008 (☎202-333-6000; www.norway.org).

VISA AND ENTRY INFORMATION. EU citizens do not need a visa. Citizens of Australia, Canada, New Zealand, and the US do not need a visa for stays of up to 90 days, beginning upon entry into any of the countries within the EU's freedom of movement zone. For more info, see p. 14. For stays longer than 90 days, all non-EU citizens need visas, available at Norwegian consulates. For more info on obtaining a visa, go to www.norway.org/visas.

TOURIST SERVICES AND MONEY

EMERGENCY **Ambulance:** ☎113. **Fire:** ☎110. **Police:** ☎112.

TOURIST OFFICES. Virtually every town and village has a **Turistinformasjon** office; look for a white "i" on a square green sign. From the latter half of June through early August, most tourist offices are open daily; expect reduced hours at other times. Check www.visitnorway.com for a directory of local offices. More info on traveling in Norway is available at www.norway.no.

MONEY. The Norwegian unit of currency is the **krone (kr),** plural kroner. One krone is equal to 100 **øre.** Banks and large post offices change money, usually for a small commission. It's generally cheaper to exchange money in Norway than at home. **Tipping** is not expected, but an extra 5-10% is always welcome for good service. It is customary to leave coins on the counter or table rather than putting the tip on a credit card. Hotel bills often include a 15% service charge.

Norway has a 25% **value added tax (VAT),** a sales tax applied to goods and services. The prices given in *Let's Go* include VAT. Upon exiting the EU, non-EU citizens can claim a refund on the tax paid for goods purchased at participating stores. In order to qualify for a refund in a store, you must spend at least 315kr in a single store; be sure to ask for a refund form when you pay. For more info on qualifying for a VAT refund, see p. 21.

NORWEGIAN KRONER (KR)		
	AUS$1 = 4.74KR	10KR = AUS$2.11
	CDN$1 = 5.61KR	10KR = CDN$1.78
	EUR€1 = 8.01KR	10KR = EUR€1.25
	NZ$1 = 4.14KR	10KR = NZ$2.41
	UK£1 = 11.78KR	10KR = UK£0.85
	US$1 = 5.95KR	10KR = US$1.68

TRANSPORTATION

BY PLANE. The main international airport is **Oslo Airport Gardermoen (OSL;** ☎06 400; www.osl.no), though some flights land at **Bergen Airport Flesland (BGO;** ☎55 99 81 55) and **Trondheim Airport Værnes (TRD;** ☎74 84 30 00). **SAS** (Scandinavian Airlines; Norway ☎91 50 54 00, UK 08 71 52 12 772, US 800-221-2350; www.flysas.com), **Finnair,** and **Icelandair** fly to Norway. Students and those under 25 qualify for youth fares when flying domestically on SAS. Budget airlines **Norwegian** (☎21 49 00 15; www.norwegian.no) and **Widerøe** (☎75 11 11 11; www.wideroe.no) have internal fares under €100 and cheap prices to European destinations. **Ryanair** (☎353 12 49 77 91; www.ryanair.com) flies to **Sandefjord Airport Torp**, near Oslo, and **Haugesund,** near Bergen. Book early for the best fares on all airlines, or try your luck with SAS domestic standby tickets *(sjanse billetter)*, purchased at the airport on the day of travel for around 400kr.

BY TRAIN. Norway's train system includes a commuter network around Oslo and long-distance lines running from Oslo to Bergen and to Stavanger via

Kristiansand. Contact **Norwegian State Railways** (NSB) for timetables and tickets (☎81 50 08 88; www.nsb.no). The unguided **Norway in a Nutshell** tour combines a ride along the Flåm Railway, a cruise through Aurlandsfjord and Nærøyfjord to the port of Gudvangen, and a bus ride over the mountains to Voss. Tickets can be purchased from tourist offices or train stations in Bergen and Oslo. (☎81 56 82 22; www.norwaynutshell.com. Round-trip from Voss 595kr, from Bergen 895kr, from Oslo 1730kr.) Overnight trains may be the best option for travel as far north as Bodø and Trondheim; from there, you'll need buses or ferries to get farther north. **Eurail Passes** are valid in Norway. The **Norway Railpass,** available only outside Norway, allows three to five days of unlimited travel in a one-month period (from US$187).

RAIL SAVINGS. Booking rail tickets at least a day ahead is vital, saving you hundreds of krone. For rail travel within Norway, the **Minipris** offered by NSB is a great deal. A limited number of seats are made available on regional trains for 199kr and 299kr, including on expensive routes. Go to www.nsb.no to purchase tickets; when asked to choose the type of ticket, select Minipris. (If it is not on the menu, tickets are sold out.) Minipris tickets purchased outside Norway are 50kr cheaper than those purchased in the country.

BY BUS. Buses can be quite expensive but they are the only land travel option north of Bodø and in the fjords. **Nor-way Bussekspress** (☎81 54 44 44; www.nor-way.no) operates most of the bus routes and publishes a timetable *(Rutehefte)*, available at bus stations and on buses. Students with ISIC are eligible for a 25-50% discount—be insistent, and follow the rules listed in the *Nor-way Bussekspress* booklet. Bus passes, valid for 10 or 21 consecutive travel days (1300/2400kr), are good deals for those exploring the fjords or the north.

BY FERRY. Car ferries *(ferjer)* are usually cheaper (and slower) than the passenger express boats (*hurtigbåt* or *ekspressbåt*) cruising the coasts and fjords; both often have student and InterRail discounts. The **Hurtigruten** (☎81 03 00 00; www.hurtigruten.com) takes six to 11 days for the incredible cruise from Bergen to Kirkenes on the Russian border. Discounts for rail pass holders are limited to 50% off the Bergen-Stavanger route, but some lines also offer a 50% student discount. The common ports for international ferries are Oslo, Bergen, Kristiansand, and Stavanger. **DFDS Seaways** (☎21 62 13 40; www.dfdsseaways.com) sails from Oslo and Kristiansand to Copenhagen, DEN and Gothenburg, SWE. **Color Line** (☎22 94 42 00; www.colorline.com) runs ferries between Norway and Denmark, plus several domestic routes.

BY CAR. Citizens of Australia, Canada, the EU, New Zealand, and the US can drive in Norway for up to one year with a valid **driver's license** from their home country. Vehicles are required to keep **headlights** on at all times. Roads in Norway are in good condition, although blind curves are common and roads are narrow in some places. Drivers should be cautious, especially on mountain roads and in tunnels, as reindeer and sheep can make unexpected appearances. Driving around the fjords can be frustrating, as only Nordfjord has a road completely circumnavigating them. Insurance is required and usually included in the price of rental. Though expensive, renting a car can be more affordable than trains and buses when traveling in a group. There are numerous car ferries, so check schedules in advance. For more info on driving in Europe, see p. 53.

BY BIKE AND BY THUMB. The beautiful scenery around Norway is rewarding for **cyclists,** but the hilly terrain can be rough on bikes. Contact **Syklistenes Lands-**

forening (☎22 47 30 30; www.slf.no) for maps, suggested routes, and info. **Hitchhiking** is difficult in mainland Norway, but easier on the Lofoten and Svalbard Islands. Some travelers successfully hitchhike beyond the rail lines in northern Norway and the fjord areas of the west, while many others try for hours without success. Hitchhikers suggest bringing several layers of clothing, rain gear, and a warm sleeping bag. *Let's Go* does not recommend hitchhiking.

KEEPING IN TOUCH

PHONE CODES	**Country code:** 47. **International dialing prefix:** 095. For more info on how to place international calls, see **Inside Back Cover.**

EMAIL AND THE INTERNET. Oslo and Bergen have many Internet cafes. Expect to pay about 1kr per min. Smaller cities might have one or two Internet cafes, and most have a public library open on weekdays that offers 15-30min. of free Internet. Free **Wi-Fi** connections for travelers with laptops are also readily available. For more info on the Internet in Europe, seep. 30.

TELEPHONE. There are three types of **public phones:** black and gray phones accept 1, 5, 10, and 20kr coins; green phones accept only phone cards; red phones accept coins, phone cards, and major credit cards. **Phone cards** (*telekort;* 40, 90, or 140kr at post offices and Narvesen kiosks) are the cheapest option, especially when prices drop between 5pm and 8am. **Mobile phones** are increasingly popular and cheap in Norway; buying a prepaid SIM card for a GSM phone can be a good, inexpensive option. Of the service providers, **Netcom** and **Telenor** have the best networks. For help with domestic calls, dial ☎117. International direct access numbers include: **AT&T Direct** (☎80 01 90 11); **Canada Direct** (☎80 01 91 11); **MCI WorldPhone** (☎80 01 99 12); **Telecom New Zealand** (☎80 01 99 64).

MAIL. Mailing a first-class postcard or letter (under 20g) within Norway costs 7kr; outside Norway 9-11kr. To receive mail in Norway, have mail delivered **Poste Restante.** Mail will go to the main post office unless you specify a subsidiary by street address. Address mail to be held according to the following format: First name LAST NAME, Poste Restante, City, Norway. Bring a passport to pick up your mail; there may be a small fee.

LANGUAGE. Norwegian is universal; some people speak English and Swedish. The indigenous people of northern Norway speak different dialects of Sámi. For basic Norwegian words and phrases, see **Phrasebook: Norwegian** (p. 1065).

ACCOMMODATIONS AND CAMPING

NORWAY	❶	❷	❸	❹	❺
ACCOMMODATIONS	under 160kr	160-260kr	261-400kr	401-550kr	over 550kr

Norske Vandrerhjem (☎23 12 45 10; www.vandrerhjem.no) operates **HI youth hostels** *(vandrerhjem)*. Beds run 100-400kr, and HI members receive a 15% discount. Linens typically cost 45-60kr per stay, and sleeping bags are forbidden. Few hostels have curfews. Most hostels open in mid- to late June and close after the third week in August. Many **tourist offices** book private rooms and hotels for a fee (usually 30kr). Norwegian **right of public access** allows camping anywhere on public land for fewer than three nights, as long as you keep 150m from buildings and leave no trace. **Den Norske Turistforening** (**DNT;** Norwegian

Mountain Touring Association) sells maps (60-70kr), offers guided hiking trips, and maintains more than 350 mountain huts *(hytter)* throughout Norway. A one-year membership (465kr; under 26, 265kr) entitles the holder to discounts on DNT lodgings (☎40 00 18 68; www.dntoslo.no). The 42 staffed huts are open in summer; most have showers and serve dinner. Unstaffed huts are open mid-February to mid-October; a sizable minority have basic provisions for sale on the honor system. Members can leave a 100kr deposit at any tourist office to borrow a key. Prices vary according to age, season, and membership; official campgrounds ask 25-140kr for tent sites, 300-600kr for cabins. For more info on camping in Norway, visit www.camping.no.

FOOD AND DRINK

NORWAY	❶	❷	❸	❹	❺
FOOD	under 60kr	60-100kr	101-150kr	151-250kr	over 250kr

Many restaurants have an inexpensive *dagens ret* (dish of the day; 70-80kr). Otherwise, you'll rarely spend less than 150kr for a full meal. **Fish**—cod, herring, and salmon—is fresh and relatively inexpensive. Other specialties include cheese *(ost)*, Jarlsberg being the most popular; pork-and-veal meatballs *(kjøttkaker)* with boiled potatoes; and, for more adventurous carnivores, reindeer, ptarmigan, and whale meat *(hval)*. Christmas brings a meal of dried fish soaked in water and lye *(lutefisk)*. **Beer** is expensive in bars (45-60kr for ½L); purchase cheaper bottles from the supermarket. Try the local favorite, Frydenlund, or go rock-bottom with Danish Tuborg. You must be 18 to buy beer and wine, and 20 to buy liquor at the aptly named *Vinmonopolet* (wine monopoly) stores.

HOLIDAYS AND FESTIVALS

Holidays: New Year's Day (Jan. 1); Maundy Thursday (Apr. 9, 2009; Apr. 1, 2010)); Good Friday (Apr. 10, 2009; Apr. 2, 2010); Easter (Apr. 12, 2009; Apr. 4, 2010); Labor Day (May 1); Ascension (May 1); Pentecost (May 31, 2009; May 23, 2010); Constitution Day (May 17); Christmas (Dec. 25); Boxing Day (Dec. 26).

Festivals: Norway throws festivals virtually year-round, from the **Tromsø International Film Festival** (Jan. 15-20; www.tiff.no) to Bergen's operatic **Festpillene** (May 21-June 4; www.fib.no). The **Norwegian Wood Festival** in Frognerbadet (mid-June; www.norwegianwood.no) features pop, folk, and classic rock. Heavy metal enthusiasts flock to **Inferno,** held in Oslo on Easter weekend (www.infernofestival.net). For more info, check www.norwayfestivals.com.

BEYOND TOURISM

Citizens of the 40 signatory countries of the **Svalbard Treaty,** including Australia, Canada, New Zealand, the UK, and the US, can work on the Svalbard archipelago (p. 766), including at the **University Center in Svalbard (UNIS)** (☎02 33 00; www.unis.no). For more info on opportunities, see **Beyond Tourism,** p. 60.

The American-Scandinavian Foundation (AMSCAN), 58 Park Ave., New York, NY 10016, USA (☎212-879-9779; www.amscan.org/jobs). Volunteer and job opportunities throughout Scandinavia. Fellowships for study in Norway available to Americans.

Study in Norway (www.studyinnorway.no). Education and research opportunities throughout the country for summer and term-time study. Scholarships available.

OSLO ☎21, 22, 23

Scandinavian capitals consent to being urban without renouncing the landscape around them and Oslo (pop. 550,000) is no exception. The Nordmarka forest to the north and Oslofjord to the south bracket the city's cultural institutions, busy cafes, and expensive boutiques. While most of Norway remains homogeneous, Oslo has a vibrant immigrant community in its eastern and northern sections. But even as globalization moves Oslo towards greater cosmopolitanism, Norwegian history and folk traditions still shape the city. Olso is a rather pricey destination, but also an essential stop on any trip to Scandinavia.

TRANSPORTATION

Flights: Oslo Airport Gardermoen (**OSL;** ☎06 400; www.osl.no), 45km north of the center. The high-speed FlyToget train (☎81 50 07 77; www.flytoget.no) runs between the airport and downtown (20min.; 3-6 per hr.; 160kr, students 80kr). White SAS Flybussen run a similar route. (☎22 80 49 70; www.flybussen.no. 40min.; 2-3 per hr.; 140kr, students 75kr; round-trip 240kr) Some budget airlines fly into **Sandefjord Airport Torp,** south of Oslo as well as the newest airport, **Rygge.** Buses and trains (50 min. 131kr) leave from Oslo S daily. **Sandefjord Airport Torp (TRF;** ☎55 42 70 00; www.torp.no), 120km south of Oslo, is a budget airline hub for Ryanair, Widerøe, and Wizz Air. Trains (☎81 50 08 88) run to **Oslo** (1hr.; 1 per hr.). Buses (2 per hr.) and taxis shuttle between the train station and airport. Buses also go to **Oslo** (1-2 per hr., 180kr) and coordinate with Ryanair arrivals and departures. See www.torpekspressen.no.

Trains: Oslo Sentralstasjon (Oslo S), Jernbanetorget 1 (☎81 50 08 88). To: **Bergen** (6.5hr., 4 per day, 739kr); **Trondheim** (7hr., 4 per day, 813kr); **Copenhagen, DEN** via **Gothenburg, SWE** (8hr., 2 per day); **Stockholm, SWE** (6hr., 2 per day). Mandatory seat reservations for domestic trains 41-71kr. Check *mini pris* tickets and book ahead.

Buses: Nor-way Bussekspress, Schweigårds gt. 8 (☎81 54 44 44; www.nor-way.no). Follow the signs from the train station through the Oslo Galleri Mall to the Bussterminalen Galleriet. Student discounts (25-50%) on most long-distance trips.

Ferries: The **Stenaline** (stenaline.no) operates to **Frederikshavn, DEN** (12hr., 7:30pm, from 160kr one way). **Color Line** (☎55 81 00 08 11; www.colorline.com) runs to **Kiel, GER** (19hr., 2pm, from 1210kr). **DFDS Seaways** (☎21 62 13 40; www.dfds.com) runs to **Copenhagen, DEN** (16hr.) daily at 5pm (930kr, 25% student discount).

Public Transportation: Buses, ferries, subways, and **trams** cost 30kr per ride or 22kr in advance. Tickets include 1hr. of unlimited transfers. If you are caught traveling without a valid ticket, you can be fined up to 900kr. **Trafikanten** (☎177; www.trafikanten.no), in front of Oslo S, sells the Dagskort (day pass 60kr), Flexicard (8 trips 160kr), and 7-day Card (210kr). Open M-F 7am-8pm, Sa-Su 8am-6pm (same as tourist office). Tickets also at Narvesen kiosks and Automat machines in the metro. All **public transit** free with Oslo Pass. Pick up most buses outside Oslo S.

Bike Rental: The city's bike-share system allows visitors to borrow one of the 1000+ bikes available at racks throughout the city center. Both the main tourist office and the Oslo S branch sell system **enrollment cards** (70kr per day). Note that bikes must be returned to a rack every 3hr. and cards must be returned to the tourist office.

Hitchhiking: Hitchhiking is not common in this area of Norway because of the extensive transportation network—however, some travelers report hitching rides to major cities at truck terminals. *Let's Go* does not recommend hitchhiking.

ORIENTATION AND PRACTICAL INFORMATION

In Oslo center, the garden plaza **Slottsparken** (Castle Park) lies beside Oslo University and the **Nationaltheatret** (National Theater) and surrounds the Royal

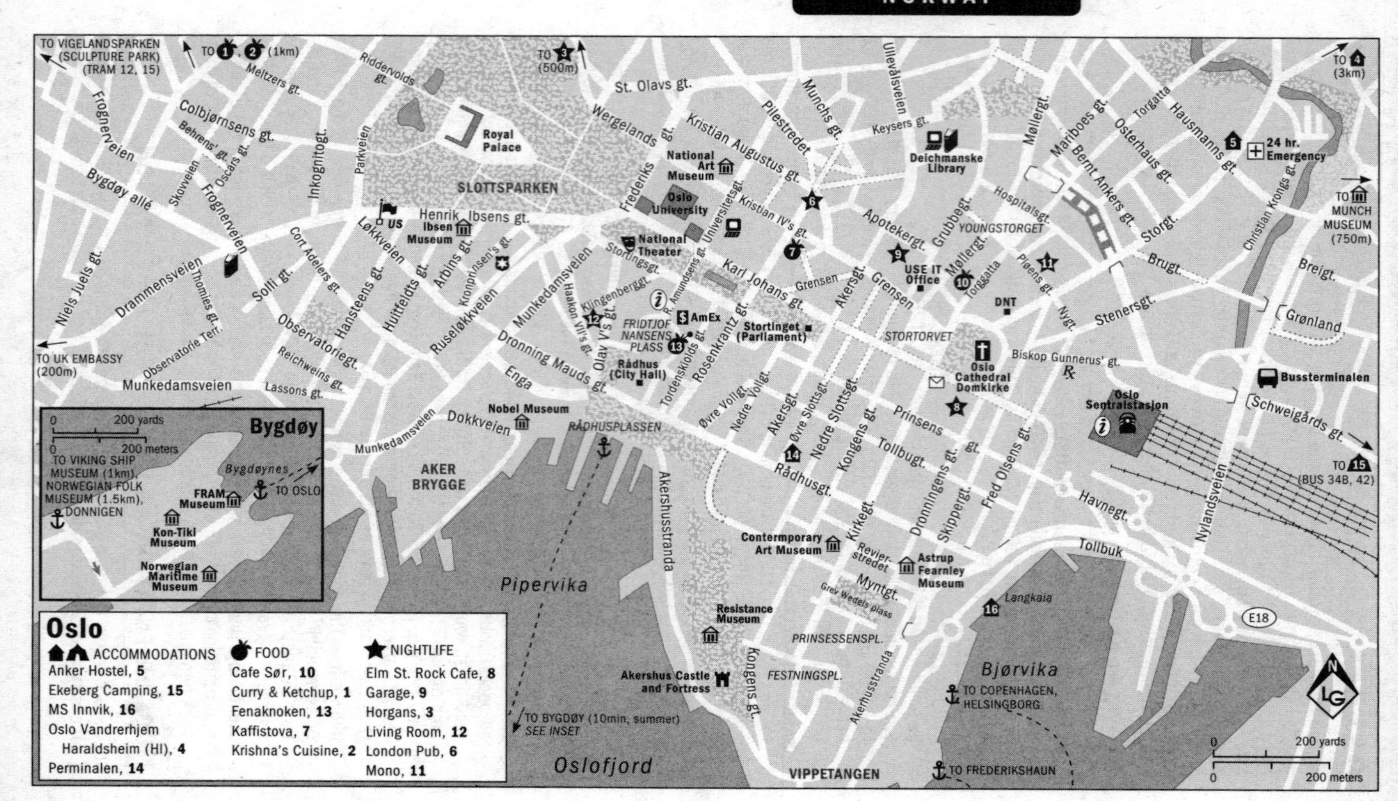
Oslo
ACCOMMODATIONS
Anker Hostel, 5
Ekeberg Camping, 15
MS Innvik, 16
Oslo Vandrerhjem Haraldsheim (HI), 4
Perminalen, 14
FOOD
Cafe Sør, 10
Curry & Ketchup, 1
Fenaknoken, 13
Kaffistova, 7
Krishna's Cuisine, 2
NIGHTLIFE
Elm St. Rock Cafe, 8
Garage, 9
Horgans, 3
Living Room, 12
London Pub, 6
Mono, 11
Bygdøy
0 200 yards
0 200 meters
TO VIKING SHIP MUSEUM (1km), NORWEGIAN FOLK MUSEUM (1.5km), DONNIGEN
Bygdøynes
TO OSLO
FRAM Museum
Kon-Tiki Museum
Norwegian Maritime Museum
TO VIGELANDSPARKEN (SCULPTURE PARK) (TRAM 12, 15)
TO 1, 2 (1km)
TO 3 (500m)
TO 4 (3km)
TO MUNCH MUSEUM (750m)
TO 15 (BUS 34B, 42)
TO UK EMBASSY (200m)
24 hr. Emergency
Bussterminalen
Oslo Sentralstasjon
Oslo Cathedral Domkirke
DNT
USE IT Office
Deichmanske Library
YOUNGSTORGET
STORTORVET
Stortinget (Parliament)
National Art Museum
Oslo University
National Theater
AmEx
FRIDTJOF NANSENS PLASS
Rådhus (City Hall)
RÅDHUSPLASSEN
Royal Palace
SLOTTSPARKEN
Henrik Ibsen Museum
US
Nobel Museum
AKER BRYGGE
Pipervika
Oslofjord
Akershus Castle and Fortress
Resistance Museum
Contermporary Art Museum
Astrup Fearnley Museum
Bjørvika
TO COPENHAGEN, HELSINGBORG
TO FREDERIKSHAUN
TO BYGDØY (10min, summer) SEE INSET
VIPPETANGEN
Langkaia
E18
0 200 yards
0 200 meters
Karl Johans gt.
Grensen
Akersgt.
Rosenkrantz gt.
Tordenskiolds gt.
Kongens gt.
Nedre Slottsgt.
Øvre Slottsgt.
Rådhusgt.
Tollbugt.
Prinsens gt.
Dronningens gt.
Skippergt.
Kirkegt.
Fred Olsens gt.
Havnegt.
Nylandsveien
Schweigårds gt.
Grønland
Brugt.
Storgt.
Stenersgt.
Biskop Gunnerus' gt.
Nygt.
Pløens gt.
Torggata
Møllergt.
Hausmanns gt.
Osterhaus gt.
Bernt Ankers gt.
Mariboes gt.
Christian Krohgs gt.
Breigt.
Ullevålsveien
Apotekergt.
Grubbegt.
Hospitalsgt.
Keysers gt.
Munchs gt.
Pilestredet
Kristian Augustus gt.
Kristian IV's gt.
Universitetsgt.
St. Olavs gt.
Wergelands gt.
Frederiks gt.
R. Amundsens gt.
Stortingsgt.
Klingenberggt.
Olav V's gt.
Haakon VII's gt.
Dronning Mauds gt.
Munkedamsveien
Ruseløkkveien
Kronprinsen's gt.
Arbins gt.
Huitfeldts gt.
Hansteens gt.
Observatoriegt.
Løkkveien
Parkveien
Inkognitogt.
Riddervolds gt.
Meltzers gt.
Colbjørnsens gt.
Oscars gt.
Behrens' gt.
Skovveien
Frognerveien
Bygdøy allé
Drammensveien
Thomies gt.
Observatorie Terr.
Solli gt.
Cort Adelers gt.
Reichweins gt.
Lassons gt.
Enga
Dokkveien
Niels Juels gt.
Akershusstranda
PRINSESSENSPL.
FESTNINGSPL.
Grev Wedels plass
Myntgt.
Revierstredet
Tollbuk
Nedre Vollgt.
Øvre Vollgt.

Palace. The city's main street, **Karl Johans gate,** runs through the heart of town from Slottsparken to the train station **Oslo Sentralstasjon** (Oslo S) at its eastern end. **Ferries** depart from the harbor, southwest of Oslo S near Akershus Castle. Many museums and beaches are southwest on the **Bygdøy peninsula.** Ferries to Bygdøy depart from the dock behind **Rådhus** (City Hall). Massive construction projects are currently reshaping the harbor, an initiative marked by the new opera house—its elaborate architecture and great fjord views from the roof make it worth a visit. **Parks** are scattered throughout Oslo, especially north of the Nationaltheatret. Of note is **Saint Hanshaugen,** a hilly park north of the city center up Akersgata as it becomes Ullevålsveien. A network of public trams, buses, and subways makes transit through the outskirts quick and easy. **Grünerløkka** to the north and **Grønland** to the east—home to many of Oslo immigrants—are often cheaper than the city's other neighborhoods, while their boutiques, cafes, and parks showcase some of the latest urban trends. Despite some concern, the area generally has few safety problems.

Tourist Offices: Fridtjof Nansenspl. 5 (☎81 53 05 55; www.visitoslo.com). Sells the **Oslo Pass,** offering unlimited public transport and admission to most museums. 1-day pass 220kr, 2-day 320kr, 3-day 410kr. Open June-Aug. daily 9am-7pm; Sept. and Apr.-May M-Sa 9am-5pm; Oct.-Mar. M-F 9am-4pm. **Oslo Central Station Tourist Info,** Jernbanetorget 1, outside Oslo S in the same building as the trafekanten. Open M-F 7am-8pm, Sa-Su 8am-6pm. **Use-It,** Møllergt. 3 (☎24 14 98 20; www.use-it.no), helps find beds for no fee, offers free Internet and baggage storage, supplies information on studying and working in Oslo, and publishes the invaluable *Streetwise Budget Guide to Oslo.* Open July-Aug. M-F 9am-6pm; Sept.-June M-F 11am-5pm. Check out http://use-it.unginfo.oslo.no/sider/practical.php.

HAPPENING OSLO. Use-It organizes summer events and "happenings" for youth and foreign travelers in Oslo. Check at the office for details.

Embassies and Consulates: Australia, contact the embassy in Denmark (p. 259). **Canada,** Wergelandsv. 7, 4th fl. (☎22 99 53 00; www.canada.no). Open June-Aug. M-F 8am-4pm; Sept.-May M-F 8:30am-4:30pm. **Ireland,** Haakon VII's gt. 1 (☎55 22 01 72 00; osloembassy@dfa.ie). Open M-F 8:30am-4:30pm. **UK,** Thomas Heftyes gt. 8 (☎23 13 27 00; www.britain.no). Open in M-F 9am-noon. **US,** Henrik Ibsens gt. 48 (☎22 44 85 50; www.usa.no). Open M-F 9am-5pm.

Currency Exchange: At any major bank: Christiania, Den Norske, Landsbanker, DnB NOR, and Forebu Oslo, the Post Office, or **Forex,** in Oslo S, which offers better deals.

Luggage Storage: Lockers at Oslo S and at the **Nationaltheatret station.** 20-45kr per 24hr. Max. 7 days. Available 4:30am-1:10am. Office open M-F 9am-3pm. You can leave bags in the Use-It office (see above) for an afternoon or night.

Library and Internet: Free terminals at the **Deichmanske Library,** Arne Garborgs pl., ☎23 43 29 00. Sign up for 1hr. or drop in for 15-30min. Open Sept.-May M-F 10am-7pm, Sa 11am-2pm; June-Aug. M-F 10am-6pm, Sa 11am-2pm. Or head to the National Library, Drammensveinen 42, www.nb.no. Open M-F 9am-7pm, Sa 9am-2pm. For Internet later in the evening, find places in **Storgata** north of the train station.

GLBT Resources: Landsforeningen for Lesbisk og Homofil fri gjøring (LLH), Kongensgt. 12 (☎55 23 10 39 39; www.llh.no). Also see tourist office and www.blikk.no.

Laundromat: Look for the word *"myntvaskeri."* **Selva AS,** Ullevålsveien 15 (☎41 64 08 33). Wash 40kr, dry 30kr. Open M-F 8am-9pm, Sa 10am-3pm.

Police: ☎02800 to bypass dispatch and connect directly.

24hr. Pharmacy: Jernbanetorvets Apotek (☎23 35 81 00), opposite Oslo S.

Hospital: Oslo Kommunale Legevakt, Storgt. 40 (☎22 93 22 93).

Post Office: Main branch at Dronningensgate 15 (☎23 35 86 90). Address **Poste Restante** mail to be held in the following format: First name, LAST NAME, Poste Restante, Oslo Central Post Office, N-0101 Oslo, NORWAY. Open M-F 9am-6pm, Sa 10am-3pm. The post office at Oslo S is open M-F 9am-8pm.

Alcohol: The drinking age is 18 but 20 for liquor, so nearly all bars are 20+ throughout the country. Vsit the state liquor store, **Vinmonopolet,** in Oslo S, for cheaper alcohol.

ACCOMMODATIONS AND CAMPING

Hostels in Oslo fill up in summer. Reservations are essential. The private rooms available through **Use-It** (see tourist offices) start from below 200kr. *Pensjonater* (pensions) are well-located but can be more expensive. Check with the tourist office for last-minute accommodation deals. Travelers can **camp** for free in the forest north of town; try the end of the **Sognsvann line #3.** Young Norwegians often drink at home before heading out because of high bar prices, but most hostels, including HI, prohibit alcohol consumption on their premises.

Perminalen, Øvre Slottsgt. 2 (☎23 09 30 81; www.perminalen.no). 15min. walk from Oslo S to Christianian Torv. Backpackers head to this central hotel/hostel. Spacious rooms equipped with A/C and cable TV. Breakfast included. Internet 5kr per 5min. Free Wi-Fi. Reception 24hr. Dorms 345kr; singles 595kr; doubles 795kr. AmEx/MC/V. ❸

Anker Hostel, Storgt. 55 (☎22 99 72 00; www.ankerhostel.no). It's an easy walk north from Oslo S, but if you're coming from elsewhere, take tram #11, 13, or 17 to Hausmanns gt. Rooms with kitchenettes and bath. Breakfast 85kr. Linens 50kr. Internet 10kr per 10min. Free Wi-Fi. Reception in summer 24hr., in winter 7am-11pm. Check in at the Best Western next door if you arrive late. Dorms 235kr; doubles 525kr. AmEx/MC/V. ❷

Oslo Vandrerhjem Haraldsheim (HI), Haraldsheimvn. 4 (☎22 22 29 65; www.haraldsheim.oslo.no). Take tram #17 toward Grefson to Sinsenkrysset and walk up the hill through the park. Standard bunk dorms in a quiet, residential neighborhood. Breakfast included. Free Wi-Fi. Internet 1kr per min. Linens 50kr. Reception 24hr. Dorms 235kr; singles 395kr, with bath 450kr; doubles 520/600kr. 15% HI discount. MC/V. ❷

MS Innvik, Langkaia 49 (☎22 41 95 00; www.msinnvik.no). From Oslo S, cross the highway E18 overpass and head right along the harbor. This theater boat and BandB is on Bjørvika Bay. Cabins come with bath. Breakfast included. Reception 24hr. No kitchen. Free Wi-Fi. Cafe. Concerts free for guests. Singles 425kr; doubles 750kr. MC/V. ❹

Ekeberg Camping, Ekebergveien 65 (☎22 19 85 68; www.ekebergcamping.no), 3km from town. Bus #34 or 74. 24hr. security. Grocery store open daily 8am-10pm. Showers 10kr per 6min. Laundry 40kr. Reception 7:30am-11pm. Open June-Aug. 2-person tent sites 170kr, 4-person 245kr; 55kr per extra person. AmEx/MC/V. ❶

FOOD

Visitors can choose between hearty, often bland Norwegian fare and a variety of ethnic dishes. Either way, they usually feel robbed blind once the check arrives. Smart backpackers stock up at the city's grocery stores perhaps even buying a very cheap grill and heading to one of Oslo's many parks (a popular Norwegian activity). Look for the chains **ICA, Kiwi,** and **Rema 1000** (generally open M-F 9am-9pm, Sa-Su 9am-6pm), or pick up fresh produce at the Youngstorget **open-air market** (M-Sa 7am-2pm). In the budget-friendly **Grønland district,** east of Oslo S, vendors hawk cheap kebabs, pizza, sushi, burgers, and falafel (from 40kr), while halal butchers can provide travelers with cooking meat.

Cafe Sør, Torggata 11 (☎41 46 30 47). This artsy, relaxing cafe attracts a young crowd with an array of teas and coffees (26-31kr). Sandwiches 93kr. At night, it's a popular hangout with nightly DJ's and weekly live acoustic performances. Beer 51kr. Free Wi-Fi. Open M-Th 11am-12:30am, F-Sa 11am-3am, Su 1pm-12:30am. AmEx/MC/V. ❷

Kaffistova, Rosenkrantz gt. 8 (☎23 21 41 00). Posh, airy eatery with modest portions of Norwegian fish, meat, and porridges. Vegetarian options. Lunch from 89kr. Dinner 123-173kr. Open M-F 10am-9pm, Sa-Su 11am-7pm. AmEx/MC/V. ❸

Krishna's Cuisine, Kirkeveien 59B (☎22 60 62 50), on the 2nd fl. Large plates of cheap Indian food. Exclusively vegetarian fare prepared with fresh seasonal ingredients. Lunch served all day 75kr. Entrees 50-110kr. Open M-Sa noon-8pm. Cash only. ❷

Curry and Ketchup, Kirkeveien 51 (☎22 69 05 22). A neighbor of Krishna's, this restaurant has a relaxed, sit-down feel. Generous helpings of Indian mainstays. Entrees 84-109kr. Open daily 2-10:30pm. Cash only. ❷

Fenaknoken, Matkultur i Tordenskidsgt. 12 (☎22 42 34 57). Gourmet Norwegian food store with seafood and free samples of delicacies like smoked elk or reindeer sausage. Fresh snack rolls 25kr, but this is mostly a shopping center, not an eatery. Open M-F 10am-5pm, Sa 10am-2pm. AmEx/MC/V. ❷

DINING FOR POCKET CHANGE. Oslo's sky-high food prices can bring travelers to tears. For a bite on the (relatively) cheap, be sure to steer clear of the west side and main drags and head instead to Gronland or elsewhere north or east of the city.

SIGHTS

VIGELANDSPARKEN. Sculptor **Gustav Vigeland** (1869-1943) designed this 80-acre expanse west of the city center. The park is home to over 200 of his mammoth works, depicting all stages of the human life cycle. His controversial, puzzling art is worth deciphering. **Monolith** is a towering granite column of intertwining bodies in the middle of the park. *(Entrance on Kirkeveien. Take bus #20 or tram #12 or 15 to Vigelandsparken. Open 24hr. Free.)* While wandering through the park, stop at the **Oslo Bymuseum** (Oslo City Museum) for art and photography collections, displays on the city's history, and restored pavilions. *(☎23 28 41 70; www.oslomuseum.no. Open Tu-Su 11am-4pm. Free.)* Next to the park, the **Vigelandmuseet** (Vigeland Museum) traces the artist's development from his early works to the monumental pieces of his later years. The museum is housed in the building Vigeland used as his apartment and studio. *(Nobelsgt. 32. ☎23 49 37 00. Open June-Aug. Tu-Su 10am-5pm; Sept.-May Tu-Su noon-4pm. 50kr, students 25kr. Oct.-Mar free. MC/V.)*

ART MUSEUMS. Renovations at **Munchmuseet** (Munch Museum) improved its security system after a 2004 theft of two paintings, including a version of *The Scream*, Munch's most famous work. The paintings have been recovered, albeit with some damage. The museum has a collection of Munch's other abstract works along with temporary Impressionist exhibits. *(Tøyengt. 53. Take the metro to Tøyen or bus #20 to Munchmuseet. ☎23 49 35 00; www.munch.museum.no. Open June-Aug. daily 10am-6pm, English tours 1pm; Sept.-May Tu-F 10am-4pm, Sa-Su 11am-5pm. 65kr, students 35kr; free with Oslo Pass. AmEx/MC/V.)* The definitive version of *The Scream* is at the **Nasjonalmuseet** (National Art Museum), which also has a collection of works by Cézanne, Gauguin, van Gogh, Matisse, and Picasso, as well as renowned Norwegians like Dahl and Sohlberg. *(Universitetsgt. 13. ☎21 98 20 00; www.nasjonalmuseet.no. Open Tu-W and F 10am-6pm, Th 10am-7pm, Sa-Su 10am-5pm. Free.)* Next door at Oslo University's **Aulaen** (Assembly Hall), several of Munch's dreamy, idealistic murals show his interest in bringing art to the masses. *(Enter through the door by the ionic columns off Karl Johans gt. Open June 27-Aug. 3 M-F 10am-4pm. Free.)*

The **Museet for Samtidskunst** (Contemporary Art Museum) displays works by Norwegian artists and rotates its collection frequently. If you can find it, check out Inner Space V, a steel staircase leading to a mysterious corridor with a true "light at the end of the tunnel." *(Bankplassen 4. Take bus #60 or tram #10, 12, 13, or 19 to Kongens gt. ☎22 86 22 10. Open Tu-W and F 11am-5pm, Th 11am-7pm, Sa-Su midnight-5pm. From June to early Sept. English tour Su 2pm. Free.)* Nearby, the private **Astrup Fearnly Museum** of Modern Art has a more international collection, with some striking installations and video pieces. *(Dronningens gt. 4. ☎22 93 60 60; www.afmuseet.no. Open Tu-W and F 11am-5pm, Th 11am-7pm, Sa-Su noon-5pm. Free.)*

AKERSHUS CASTLE AND FORTRESS. Originally constructed in 1299, this waterfront complex was rebuilt as a Renaissance palace after Oslo burned in 1624. Norway's infamous traitor, Vidkun Quisling, was imprisoned here prior to his execution for aiding the 1940 Nazi invasion. *(Tram #12 to Rådhusplassen. ☎23 09 39 17. Complex open daily 6am-9pm. Castle open May-Aug. M-Sa 10am-4pm, Su 12:30-4pm. Sept.-Oct. Th guided tours only in English at noon and 1pm. English and Norwegian guided tours from mid-June to early Aug. Sa-Su 3pm. Grounds free. Castle 65kr, students 45kr; free with Oslo Pass. MC/V.)* The castle grounds include the powerful **Resistance Museum,** which documents Norway's campaign against the Nazi occupation. *(☎23 09 31 38. Open June-Aug. M-F 10am-5pm, Sa-Su 11am-5pm; Sept.-May M-F 10am-4pm, Sa-Su 11am-4pm. 30kr, students 15kr; free to all military personnel. Free with Oslo Pass. MC/V.)* On the other side of the complex is the **Armed Forces Museum** which offers exhibits on the history of Norway's military from the Viking age on into the Cold War. A current temporary exhibit deals with Norwegian UN Peacekeeping. *(☎23 09 35 82. Open May-Aug. M-F 10am-5pm, Sa-Su 11am-5pm; Sept.-Apr. M-F 11am-4pm, Sa-Su 11am-5pm. Free.)*

BYGDØY. Bygdøy peninsula, across the inlet from central Oslo, is mainly residential, but its beaches and museums make it worth a visit. In summer, a public **ferry** leaves from Pier 3, Råhusbrygges, in front of City Hall. *(☎23 35 68 90; www.boatsightseeing.com. 10min.; Apr.-Sept. and from late May to mid-Aug. 2-3 per hr.; 22kr, 30kr on board. Or take bus #30 from Oslo S to Folkemuseet or Bygdøynes.)* The open-air **Norsk Folkemuseum,** near the ferry's first stop at Dronningen, recreates historical Norway, (especially that of the 18th century) with restored thatch huts, knowledgable actors in period costume, and special perfor-

JP FOR SOME KUBB?

A funny thing might happen walking through Oslo's parks. Out of nowhere, you may stumble upon people throwing wooden sticks at figurines. What's going on here? Are they vandalizing those poor, defenseless figurines?

Closer inspection reveals a whole world of fun you never knew existed—Kubb. No, not the obscure British band of the same name. Kubb is a game, nicknamed "Viking Chess," that combines bowling, chess, and horseshoes. The objective is to knock down your opponent's ten kubbs (rectangular wooden blocks). After taking these down, you move on to eliminate the king kubb—marked by a carved crown—for the win.

Kubb dates back to AD 1000 and was likely played by Vikings. It spread throughout Europe during the Norman conquests. Morbidly, some maintain that the Vikings played with the skulls and bones of their victims rather than wooden blocks. When rampant plundering and using your victims for games went out of fashion, the transition to wooden blocks began. Others believe that wooden blocks have always been used. They are common in Scandinavia, after all, and it would be unfortunate to postpone a game of kubb due to lack of skulls. Talk about a gathering gone badly wrong.

The game involves a surprising amount of strategy. Try your luck, but don't bet your life savings.

mances and demonstrations. *(Walk uphill from the dock and follow signs to the right for 10min., or take bus #30 from Nationaltheatret. ☎ 22 12 37 00; www.norskfolkemuseum.no. Open mid-May to mid-Sept. daily 10am-6pm; mid-Sept. to mid-May M-F 11am-3pm, Sa-Su 11am-4pm. Fold Dance show June-Aug. Su 2pm. In summer 95kr, students 70kr; in winter 70/50kr. MC/V.)* Down the road (5min.), the **Vikingskipshuset** (Viking Ship Museum) showcases the stunning remains of three well-preserved burial vessels. *(☎ 22 13 52 83; www.khm.uio.no..Open daily May-Sept. 9am-6pm; Oct.-Apr. 11am-4pm. 50kr, students 35kr; free with Oslo Pass. AmEx/MC/V.)* Then walk down to Bygdøynes, the ferry's second stop, and check out the **Kon-Tiki Museet,** named after a displayed balsa wood raft used on a journey from Lima, Peru to the Polynesian Islands, by Oscar-winning documentarian Thor Heyerdahl. The museum hold all sorts of artifacts from his journeys and efforts to demonstrate the potential for early cross-continental transportation. *(Bygdøynesveien 36. ☎ 23 08 67 67; www.kon-tiki.no. Open daily June-Aug. 9:30-5:30, April, May, and Sept. 10am-5pm, Mar. and Oct. 10:30am-4pm, and Nov-Feb. 10:30am-3:30pm. 50kr, students 35kr; free with Oslo Pass. AmEx/MC/V.)* Next door, the **Norsk Sjøfartsmuseum** (Norwegian Maritime Museum) is home to a video on Norway's stunning coastline and the country's oldest boat, among other nautical exhibits. Learn about the nation's seafaring history, from log canoes to cruise ships, and enjoy a view of Oslofjord. *(Bygdøynesveien 37. ☎ 24 11 41 50. Open mid-May to Aug. daily 10am-6pm; Sept. to mid-May M-W and Sa-Su 10:30am-4pm, Th 10:30am-6pm. 40kr, students 25kr. Free with Oslo Pass. MC/V.)* The Arctic exploration vessel **FRAM,** adjacent to the museum, was used on three expeditions in the early 20th century and has advanced farther north and south than any other vessel. Visitors can roam through the well-preserved interior. *(Bygdøynesveien 36. ☎ 23 28 29 50. Open daily June to Aug. 9am-6:00pm; May and Sept. daily 10am-5pm. Mar., Apr., Oct. daily 10am-4pm. Nov.-Feb. M-F 10am-3pm, Sa-Su 10am-4pm. 50kr, students 20kr; free with Oslo Pass. MC/V.)* The southwestern side of Bygdøy is home to two popular beaches: **Huk** appeals to a younger crowd, while **Paradisbukta** is more family-oriented. The shore between them is a **nude beach.** *(Take bus #30 or walk south for 25min. left along the shore from the Bygdøynes ferry stop.)*

OTHER SIGHTS. The **Royal Palace,** in Slottsparken, is open for guided tours, although tickets sell out ahead. Since it's not included in the Oslo pass, it may be enough just to view the daily changing of the guard at 1:30pm in front of the palace. *(Tram #12, 13, 19, or bus #30-32 to Slottsparken. Open from late June to mid-Aug. English-language tours M-Th, Sa noon, 2, 2:20pm; F and Su 2, 2:20, and 4pm. Buy tickets at post and tourist offices. 95kr, students 85kr.)* The nearby **Ibsenmuseet** (Henrik Ibsen Museum) documents the notoriously private playwright's life with a dramatic exhibition space and guided tours of his last apartment. *(Henrik Ibsens gt. 26. ☎ 22 12 35 50; www.ibsenmuseet.no. Open from mid-May to mid-Sept. Tu-Su 11am-6pm; from mid-Sept. to mid-May Tu-W and F-Su 11am-4pm, Th 11am-6pm. English- and Norwegian-language tours 7 per day; in winter 3 per day. 45kr; with tour 85kr, students 60kr; free with Oslo Pass. AmEx/MC/V.)* The **Domkirke,** next to Stortorvet in the city center, is hard to miss. The Lutheran cathedral has a colorful ceiling with biblical motifs. *(Karl Johans gt. 11. ☎ 23 31 46 00; www.oslodomkirke.no. Open M-Th 10am-4pm, F 10am-4pm and 10pm-midnight, Sa 10am-4pm and 9-11pm. Free.)* The **Nobel Peace Center,** by the harbor, features profiles on all laureates, information on the award and the ceremony, and traveling exhibitions on the main floor dealing with the issues of peace in the world. *(Brynjulf Bulls Plass 1. Tram #12 to Aker Brygge. ☎ 48 30 10 00; www.nobelpeacecenter.org. Open June-Aug. daily M-W and F-Su 10am-6pm, Th 10am-7pm; Sept.-May Tu, W, F 10am-4pm, Th 10am-7pm, Sa-Su 11am-5pm; 80kr, students 55kr; free with Oslo Pass. MC/V.)* For much of 2009, the facility will be closed for the construction of a new jump in time for trials before it hosts the 2011 World Championships. Take the 1st Subway line toward Frognerseteren to reach the world famous ski stadium **Holmenkollen.** The complex also features the world's oldest ski museum and special exhibitions on Arctic and Antarctic expeditions, A simulator recreates a leap off a ski jump and a blisteringly swift downhill run. *(Kongeveien 5. From the subway, follow the signs uphill 10min. ☎22 92 32 00; www.skiforeningen.no. Open daily June-Aug. 9am-8pm; Sept. and May 10am-5pm; Oct.-Apr. 10am-4pm. Museum and tower 70kr, students 60kr; free with Oslo Pass. Simulator 50kr, with Oslo Pass 40kr. AmEx/MC/V.)* **Historical Museum of the University of Oslo** has a variety of exhibits on the history of Norway. *(Frederiks Gate. ☎22 85 19 00; www.khm.uio.no. Open from mid-Sept. to mid-May daily 11am-6pm, from mid-May to mid-Sept. Tu-Su 10am-5pm. Free.)* Finally, for those weary of the city, there's the outdoors. **Bike trails** run through the city and along the river Akerelva. In winter, **skiing** (alpine and nordic) is a favorite activity. Supposedly, Norwegians are born with skis on their feet. Check the tourist office for the nearest trails and ski rental.

NORWAY

ENTERTAINMENT AND NIGHTLIFE

The monthly *What's On in Oslo*, free at tourist offices and most accommodations, follows the latest in opera, symphony, and theater. **Filmens Hus,** Dronningens gt. 16, is the center of Oslo's indie film scene. (☎22 47 45 00. Check schedule online at www.nfi.no/cinemateket. 75kr per movie, members 45kr; 6 month registration 100kr.) Jazz enthusiasts head to town for the **Oslo Jazz Festival** in mid-August. (☎22 42 91 20, booking ☎81 53 31 33; www.oslojazz.no). Buy tickets to this and other events online at billettservice.no and pick up at any post office. Countless bars along **Karl Johans gate** and in the **Aker Brygge harbor complex** attract a hard-partying crowd, while a mellow mood prevails at the cafe-by-day, bar-by-night lounges along **Thorvald Meyers gate** in Grüner Løkka. Alcohol tends to be expensive out on the town, so young Norwegians have taken to the custom of the *Vorspiel*—gathering at private homes to sip comparatively cheap, store-bought liquor before staggering out to the streets and then reconvening later for a little *nachspiel* (afterparty).

Mono, Pløens gt. 4 (☎22 41 41 66; www.cafemono.no). Jam to classic rock at this popular, funky club. Backyard area is a cafe for drinks during the day. Beer 56kr, 46kr before 6pm. M-Th and Su 20+, F-Sa 22+. 250 concerts a year (not on F). Cover for concerts 80-130kr. Frequent free concerts Sa at 6pm. Open M-Sa 11am-3:30am, Su 1pm-3:30am. Inside club opens around 6pm. MC/V.

Garage, Grensen 9 (☎22 42 37 44; www.garageoslo.no). Live music from across the globe. Rock F-Su. Beer 56kr at night, 46kr during the day. M-Th and Su 20+, F-Sa 22+. Cover for concerts 50-300kr. Open M-Sa 3pm-3:30am, Su 6pm-3:30am. MC/V.

Living Room, Olav V's gt. 1 (☎22 83 63 54; www.living-room.no). Popular lounge morphs into dance floor on weekends. Fairly strict dress code. Beer 61kr. 24+. Cover F-Sa 100kr. Open W-Su 11pm-3am. AmEx/MC/V.

Horgans, Hegdehaugsv. 24 (☎22 60 87 87). Sports bar with plenty of TVs showing the latest games, especially football matches. Also becomes a club on weekends. Beer 48kr Tu-F, 63kr after 9pm F and Sa. 23+. Cover 50kr Sa after midnight. Open Tu-Th 4pm-midnight, F-Sa 5pm-3am, Su 4pm-midnight. AmEx/MC/V.

London Pub, C.J. Hambros pl. 5 (☎22 70 87 00; www.londonpub.no). Entrance on Rosenkrantz gt. Oslo's "gay headquarters" since 1979. Large upstairs dance floor plays a mix of beats. Basement pool tables and bars draws an older crowd. Beer 36-56kr. 20+. Cover F-Sa 40kr. Open daily 3pm-3am. AmEx/MC/V.

Elm Street Rock Cafe, Dronningens gate 32 (☎22 42 14 27). Provides a good place to have a burger (84-136kr) with a lot of free sides and a beer (47kr) before a movie or concert in Oslo. Open M-Sa 11am-3:30am, Su 1pm-3:30am. Kitchen until 9pm. Live music most F and Sa in the summer. Concerts usually 50-100kr.

DAYTRIPS FROM OSLO

AROUND THE CITY. Harbor cruises visit the nearby islands of inner **Oslofjord.** The ruins of a **Cistercian Abbey,** as well as a picnic-friendly southern shore, lie on the island of Hovedøya, while Langøyene has Oslo's best **beach** and a free campground. *(Take bus #60 from City Hall to Vippetangen to catch ferry #92 or 93 to Hovedøya or ferry #94 to Langøyene.)* The well-preserved fortress town of **Fredrikstad** is less than 2hr. south of Oslo. The 28km **Glommastien** path winds through abandoned brickyards and timber mills along the Glomma River. **Ferries** travel to seaside resorts on the **Hvaler Islands.** The info office on the harbor, Toyhusgt. 98, has ferry schedules. *(☎69 30 46 00. Open June-Aug. M-F 9am-5pm, Sa-Su 11am-4pm; Sept.-May M-F 9am-4:30pm.Train to Fredrikstad 1hr.; 1 every 2hr.; 172kr, students 129kr.)*

LILLEHAMMER ☎61

Lillehammer (pop. 27,000) cherishes the laurels it earned as host of the **1994 Winter Olympics.** Travelers strap on their skis to hit the slopes here, as well as to indulge in the city's other outdoor adventures. The **Norwegian Olympic Museum** in Olympic Park traces the history of the Games. It's a 20min. walk from the train station; head two blocks uphill, turn left on Storgata, right on Tomtegata, go up the stairs, and follow the road uphill to the left. Or take bus #2 or 3 from the train station (5min., 28kr). The museum is in Håkons Hall, the 1994 hockey rink. (☎61 25 21 00; www.ol.museum.no. Open June-Aug. daily 10am-5pm; Sept.-May Tu-Su 11am-4pm. 75kr, students 60kr. AmEx/MC/V.) Climb the steps of the ski jump in Olympic Park for a view of **Lake Mjøsa** ("shining lake") Norway's largest, or simply take the **chairlift.** Give your spine a jolt on the **bobsled simulator** at the bottom of the hill and take time to view some summer ski jumping, daily from mid-June to mid-Aug. 10am-noon and 2-4pm. (☎61 05 42 00; www.olympiaparken.no. Open from early May to early June and from mid-Aug. to late Sept. 9am-5pm daily and from mid-June to mid Aug. 9am-8pm daily. Ski jump tower 15kr. Chairlift 45kr. Simulator 50kr. Combination ticket including chairlift 80kr.) The **Maihaugen** open-air museum chronicles rural Norwegian life over the past 300 years. From the train station, head up Jernbanegata and turn right onto Gågata. Turn left on Søndre gate., follow it to the end, and make a right on Sykenes. Travel uphill and make a left on Maihaugvegan. (☎61 28 89 00; www.maihaugen.no. Open June-Aug. daily 10am-5pm; Oct.-May Tu-Su 11am-4pm. Summer 100kr, students 80kr; low-season 80/70kr. Combination Ticket with the Ski Jump Tower and two local authors' homes 130kr, students 105kr. AmEx/MC/V.) To the north, **Hafjell,** Aaslettvegen 1, boasts some of the best ski slopes in the country. In summer, the trails are used for **mountain biking. Buses** to the complex leave from the train station. (☎61 27 47 00; www.hafjell.no. Bikes 750kr per day.) You can also travel to **Kvitfjell,** another ski resort, or **Hunderfossen,** the Olympic **bobsled** course 14km north of the city. Daring individuals may try the bobsled (or wheeled bobsled in the summer) with professional drivers.

Lillehammer Vandrerhjem Stasjon ❸, Jernbanetorget 2, a new hostel above the train station, features great rooms with bath and TV. (☎61 26 00 24; www.stasjonen.no. Breakfast, linens, and laundry included. Free Internet and Wi-Fi. Reception 7am-10pm. After 10pm check in at the Breiseth hotel across the street. Dorms 325kr, HI 275kr; singles 695kr/590kr; doubles 820kr. AmEx/MC/V.) Pizzerias and candy shops line Gågata, which runs north-south through the town center, changing names to Storgata at both ends. Picnic in **Søndre Park**

or relax with a beer in the **Bokhandel** park, which also serves small sandwiches and cakes. (☎61 25 08 85. Open May-Aug. daily 11am-3am. Beer 55kr.) Buy groceries at **Kiwi** on the end of Gågata, in the center of the city.

Trains run to Oslo (2hr., every hr. 4am-8pm, 322kr, student 242kr, can book online for *mini pris* tickets) and Trondheim (5hr., 4 per day, from 199kr if booked ahead). The **tourist office** and the **bus terminal** are both in the same station. (☎61 28 98 00; www.lillehammer.com. Open June and Aug. M-Sa 9am-6pm, Su noon-5pm; July M-Sa 9am-8pm, Su 11am-6pm; Sept.-May M-F 9am-4pm, Sa 10am-2pm.) If you're looking for free Internet, check out the attractive public **library** (☎61 24 71 40; www.biblioteket.lillehammer.kommune.no. Wiesesgata 2. Open from late June to mid-Aug M-Th 11am-5pm, F 11am-3pm; from late Aug. to mid-June M-Th 11am-6pm, F-Sa 11am-3pm.)

SOUTHERN NORWAY

Norway's southern coastline is a premier summer holiday destination. Its towns feature red-tiled bungalows and jetties full of boats. The nearby rocky archipelagos can be explored on the cheap by hopping on a local ferry.

KRISTIANSAND ☎38

Vacationers ferrying their way from Denmark to Oslo often stop in Kristiansand (pop. 80,000), Norway's fifth-largest city; home to some of the country's best beaches. **Hamresandsen,** accessible by the yellow city buses (#35 or 36, 27kr), is an especially popular beach to the north where temperatures often reach a sizzling 20°C (68°F). Also popular is the **Town Beach Bystranda** located near the downtown. The white wooden houses in the old town of **Posebyen,** northeast of the city center, quartered soldiers over the centuries and sheltered Jewish refugees during WWII. **Dyreparken,** a zoo 11km east of the city, is Kristiansand's main attraction. Catch bus #1 (dir.: Sørlandsparken; 27kr) from the bus station. (☎38 04 97 00. www.dyreparken.com. Open from June to late Aug. daily 10am-7pm; from late Aug. to May M-F 10am-3pm, Sa-Su 10am-5pm. 310kr, low-season from 120kr.) The first week in July, music fans take over the island of Odderøya for the **Quart Festival,** which features acts such as Death Cab for Cutie, Kanye West, and The Who. (☎38 14 69 69; www.quart.no.) Farther south, take in the view of the **skerries,** a string of small islands and coves, on a boat trip with the M/S Patricia. (☎90 76 14 53; www.pollen.as. 2hr. round-trip; leaves from Quay to West Harbor; July-Aug. 20 daily 11am, 1pm, 3:30pm; 150kr.) The tourist office offers free **walking tours** of the city (daily from mid-June to mid-Aug.), which ensure a view of the city's well known cathedral **Kristansand Domkirke.** (Kirkegata 38. ☎19 69 00. www.kristansand.kirken.no. Guided visits to the top 11am and 2pm, 20kr. Organ recital, Tu-Sa at 1pm. Open M-F 10am-4am, Sa 10am-3pm.) Walk down the center road Festningsgata to Baneheia park for an easy, 1.6km **hike** to another lush nature preserve in neighboring Ravnedalen.

Unfortunately, the Kristiansand Youth Hostel closed so budget lodgings are harder to find. There are plans to open a budget hotel, **123 Hotel,** in the summer of 2009 with prices under 600kr for a double room. Otherwise camping is the best option. For camping on the water, head to **Roligheden Camping ❶,** east of the city center across the Otra river. (☎38 09 67 22. 130kr, 50kr per extra person. 10kr showers. Open June-Aug. MC/V.) For cheap fare, head to the harbor **Fiskebrygga** (fish market), on Gravane near the intersection of Vestre Strandgt. and Østre Strandgt., between 11am and 4pm, when fishermen sell part of the morning's catch. **Rimi,** on the corner of Festningsgt. and Gyldenløvesgt., sells groceries. (☎38 02 95 16. Open M-F 8am-9pm, Sa 9am-6pm. Cash only.)

Trains run to Oslo (5hr.; 5 per day; 601kr, student 405kr), and Stavanger (3hr.; 6 per day; 405kr, student 304kr). Remember to check for *mini pris* tickets. Color Line **ferries** (☎81 00 08 11; www.colorline.com) sail to Hirsthals, DEN (3½hr.; 2 per day; in summer 440kr-480kr, low-season 280-320kr; 50% student discount in low-season). Fjordline also runs ferries (www.fjordline.no 81 53 35 00) up the coast and to Haugesund (2hr, 2-3 per day, 129kr round-trip.) Cheap **flights** can be found to and from the Kristansand airport. The flybus runs between the airport and bus station for 80kr one way, students 40kr (10 per day M-F, 5 Sa, 3 Su). The **tourist office,** Rådkusgata 6, off the marketplace, books rooms for a 50kr fee, offers Internet, shares a variety of information, and helps arrange local travel along the coast to locations like Grimstad. (☎12 13 14. Internet 1kr per min. Open mid-June to mid-Aug. M-F 8:30am-6pm, Sa 10am-6pm, Su noon-6pm; mid-Aug. to mid-June M-F 8:30am-3:30pm.) **Postal Code:** 4600.

STAVANGER ☎51

The harbor town of Stavanger (pop. 120,000) served as a 2008 European Capital of Culture, along with Liverpool, BRI (p. 167). Shedding the perception that it is merely a port city and a hub for the oil industry, Stavanger boasts a number of attractions, including the stunning Lysefjord to the east. On the western side of the harbor is **Gamle Stavanger** (Old Town), where lamp-lit, pedestrian walkways wind past well-preserved cottages. The 12th-century **Stavanger Domkirke** is one of Norway's oldest cathedrals. (☎65 33 60; www.kirken.stavanger.no. Open June-Aug. daily 11am-7pm; Sept.-May Tu-Th and Sa 11am-4pm. 11am Sunday Services. Free tours daily noon-5pm.) The sleek **Norwegian Petroleum Museum** (Norsk Oljemuseum), down Kirkegata from the church, explains drilling, refining, and life on oil platforms with high-tech displays. (☎93 93 00; www.norskolje.museum.no. Open June-Aug. daily 10am-7pm; Sept.-May M-Sa 10am-4pm, Su 10am-6pm. 80kr, students 40kr. AmEx/MC/V.) A popular attraction, **Pulpit Rock** (Preikestolen) offers magnificent views from an altitude of 600m. If the crowds and your nerves permit, lie flat and look into the abyss below. Take the **ferry** to Tau from Fiskepiren wharf in Stavanger, catch a bus, and **hike** up the well-marked trail (1-2hr.)

The best budget accommodations are around Lake Mosvatnet, south of the city, and near the airport (bus #5a or 5b, 2-4 per hr., 25kr). **Stavanger Hostel ❷,** Henrik Ibsens gt. 19, on the south shore of the lake, is a small red bungalow with quiet dorms. (☎54 36 36; www.vandrerhjem.no. Reception 7-10:30am and 4-10pm. Open from mid-June to mid-Aug. Dorms 280kr; singles 490kr; doubles 550kr. 15% HI discount. MC/V.) Bring your own tent and settle down at **Stavanger Camping ❶,** next door to the hostel. It offers stunning lake views. (☎53 29 71; www.stavangercamping.no. 140-150kr per tent site, 470-650kr per cabin. Showers 10kr. Electricity 40kr.) Sample native strawberries (from 25kr per bushel) at the **market** opposite the cathedral in the main square (open M-F 8am-5pm).

Trains run to Kristiansand (3hr., 7 per day, 405kr, students 304kr) and Oslo (8hr., 4 per day, 1006kr, students 755kr. Check *mini pris* tickets). **Buses** to Bergen (5-6hr., 2 per hr., 400kr, students 300kr) leave from Stavanger Byterminal. The Flaggruten express **boat** (4hr., 170-680kr) sails to Bergen. (☎055 05; http://eng.tide.no. 1-4 per day. 50% Eurail and Scanrail discount. 40% student discount.) The **tourist office,** Domkirkeplassen 3, books rooms (30kr). Check out its helpful website. (☎51 85 92 00; www.regionstavanger.com. Open June-Aug. daily 7am-8pm; Sept.-May M-F 9am-4pm, Sa 9am-2pm.) **Postal Code:** 4001.

WHAT THE FJUCK IS A FJORD? Fjords are long, narrow, U-shaped valleys flooded by the sea. Norway's formed from deep grooves cut into the ground by glacial erosion during the last Ice Age.

THE FJORDS AND WEST NORWAY

No trip to Norway is complete without seeing the Western Fjords. The region boasts a dramatic grandeur, from the depths of Sognefjord to the peaks of Jotunheimen National Park. Tourists come to Sogndal and Stryn to walk on the Jostedalsbreen glacier, continental Europe's largest, and to visit Balestrand and Geiranger. On the Atlantic coast, Bergen is the region's major port city.

TRANSPORTATION

Transportation around the Western Fjords can be tricky and often involves lengthy rides, but scenery-gazing is half the fun. **Trains** go to Åndalsnes in the north and Bergen in the south. **Buses** and boats run to locales in between these cities, including the main fjords and **national parks.** From Strandkaiterminalen in Bergen, Tide express **boats** (☎55 23 87 80; www.tide.no) run to Stavanger and points south of the city, while Fylkesbaatane (☎55 90 70 70 ; www.fjord1.no/fylkesbaatane) sails north into Nordfjord, Sognefjord, and Sunnfjord. Almost all destinations connect via bus to Bergen; check www.nor-way.no for schedules and fares. **Fjord1** (www.fjord1.no), a consortium of boat, bus, and ferry, companies, is an invaluable resource for planning regional trips. Schedules vary daily; call ☎177 for transportation info. **Tourist offices, boat terminals,** and **bus stations** can also help with itineraries. Plan your trip at least 2-3 days ahead.

BERGEN ☎55

Situated in a narrow valley between seven steep mountains and the waters of the Puddefjorden, Bergen (pop. 235,000) bills itself as the "Gateway to the Fjords." Norway's second-largest city has a walkable downtown, an active college scene, a well-preserved medieval district, and a thriving music scene.

TRANSPORTATION

Trains: The station is on Strømgtn. (☎55 96 69 00), 10min. southeast of the harbor. Trains run to: **Myrdal** (2hr., 8 per day, 240kr, students 180kr); **Oslo** (6-7hr., 4-5 per day, 739kr, student 554kr, *mini pris* 199kr); **Voss** (1hr., 1 per 1-2hr., 159, student 119kr).

Buses: Busstasjon, Strømgtn. 8 (☎177, outside Bergen ☎90 70), in the Storsenter mall. Buses run to: **Ålesund** (9-10hr., 1-2 per day, 596kr, student 447kr); **Oslo** (9-11hr., 3 per day, 490kr, students 487kr); **Sogndal** (4-5hr., 4-6 per day, 596kr, students 447kr); **Stryn** (6hr., 2 per day, 462kr, students 347kr); **Trondheim** (14hr., 1 per day, 490kr).

Domestic Ferries: The Hurtigruten **steamer** (☎55 81 03 00 00; www.hurtigruten.com) begins its coastal journey in Bergen and stops in **Ålesund, Trondheim,** the **Lofoten Islands,** and **Tromsø.** (From mid-Apr. to mid-Sept. daily 8pm; from mid-Sept. to mid-Apr. 10:30pm. 50% student discount.) Flaggruten **express boats** (☎55 055 05; www.flaggruten.no) head south to Stavanger (4hr., 1-2 per day, 680kr, student 340kr).

International Ferries: Depart from Skoltegrunnskaien, a 10min. walk past Bryggen along the right side of the harbor. Fjord Line (☎55 81 53 35 00; www.fjordline.co.uk) runs to **Hanstholm, DEN** (16hr.; 3 per week; from mid-June to mid-Aug. from 500kr, from mid-

Aug. to mid-June from 300kr) and **Newcastle, BRI** (25hr.; 2-3 per week; from mid-May to early Sept. from 800kr, from mid-Sept. to mid-May from 500kr). **Smyril Line** (☎55 59 65 20; www.smyril-line.com) goes to the **Faroe Islands** (24hr.; 360-685kr) and **Seyðisfjörður, ICE** (41hr.; 840-1495kr); check website for more on seasonal fares.

Public Transportation: Buses are 23kr within the city center, 31-38kr outside. The **Bergen Card** (1-day 190kr, 2-day 250kr), available at the train station, some hotels, and the tourist office, includes unlimited rides on city buses, free admission to most of the city's museums, and discounts at select shops and restaurants.

ORIENTATION AND PRACTICAL INFORMATION

The harborside *Torget* (fish market) is a central landmark. North of the *Torget*, **Bryggen** curves around the harbor to the old city. **Torgalmenningen,** the main pedestrian street, runs southwest from the *Torget.* Locals tend to stay farther down Torgalmenningen, near Håkons gaten and Nygårds gaten. South of the *Torget* is **Lille Lungegårdsvann,** a park-lined lake.

NORWAY

Tourist Office: Vågsalmenningen 1 (☎55 55 20 00; www.visitbergen.com), past the *Torget* in the Fresco Hall. Crowded in summer, with 30min. waits (or longer) not uncommon; visit early. Pick up a copy of the **city guide** and check out the daily events board. The staff helps plan fjord travel. Open June-Aug. daily 8:30am-10pm; May and Sept. daily 9am-8pm; Oct.-Apr. M-Sa 9am-4pm. **DNT** (Norwegian Mountain Touring Association), Tverrgt. 4-6 (☎55 33 58 10), off Marken, sells **maps** (94-119kr) and provides hiking info. Open M-W and F 10am-4pm, Th 10am-6pm, Sa 10am-2pm.

Budget Travel: Kilroy Travels, Vaskerelven 32 (☎55 30 79 25; www.kilroytravels.no). Sells student airline tickets and books rooms. Open M-F 10am-5pm. MC/V.

Currency Exchange: At banks near the harbor and at the post office. For small currency changes, go to the tourist office, which exchanges currency for less commission.

Luggage Storage: At train and bus stations. 20-40kr per day, depending on locker size. The same service is also available at the tourist office for 20kr per piece of luggage.

Laundromat: Jarlens Vaskoteque, Lille Øvregt. 17 (☎55 32 55 04; www.jarlens.no). Open M-Tu and F 10am-6pm, W-Th 10am-8pm, Sa 10am-3pm.

Hospital: 24-Hour Clinic, Vestre Strømkai 19 (☎55 56 87 00).

Internet: Get free Internet at the public **library,** Strømgt. 6 (☎55 55 56 85. Open from late June to early Aug. M 11am-6pm, Tu-Sa 10am-3pm; from mid May to late June and from early Aug. to mid Aug. M-Th 10am-6pm, F 10-4:30pm, Sa 10-3pm; from late-Aug. to mid-May M-Th 10am-7pm, F 10-3:30pm, Sa 10am-2pm.) Or try **Kong Oscar Billiards** for Internet. (☎55 32 68 01. Open M-Th and Su noon-1:30am, F-Sa noon-2:30am. Internet 40kr per hr. Beer 42-53kr. MC/V.)

Post Office: Småstrandgt. (☎81 00 07 10). Open M-F 9am-8pm, Sa 9am-6pm.

ACCOMMODATIONS

The tourist office books private rooms for a 30kr fee; you can nab doubles for as little as 300kr. You can camp for free on the far side of the hills above the city; walk 30min. up the slopes of Mount Fløyen or take the funicular.

Intermission, Kalfarveien 8 (☎55 30 04 00), near the train station. Students from a US Christian college staff this hostel with a homey vibe. Free waffle night M and Th. Free coffee, tea, and biscuits after 3pm everyday. Breakfast 25kr. Linens deposit 20kr. Laundry included, free detergent. Reception M-Th and Su 7-11am and 3pm-midnight, F-Sa until 1am. Lockout 11am-3pm. Curfew M-Th and Su midnight, F-Sa 1am. Open from mid-June to mid-Aug. Dorms 150kr. Cash only. ❶

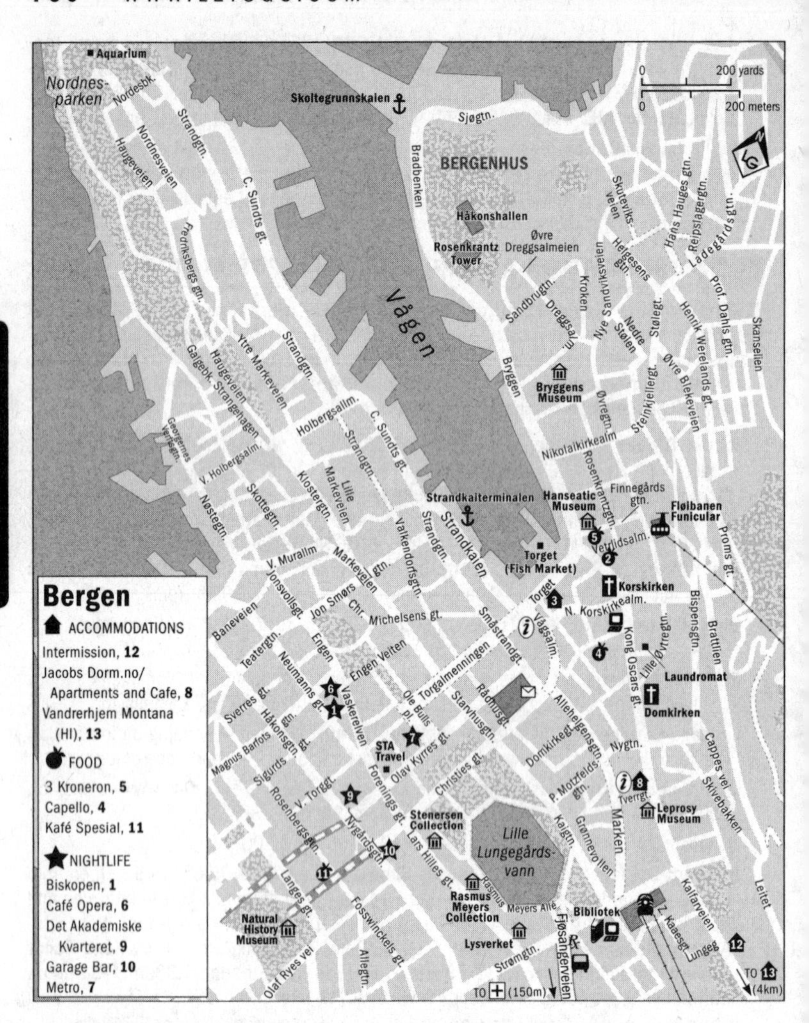

Jacobs Dorm.no/Apartments and Cafe, Kong Oscars gt. 44 (☎98 23 86 00; www.apartments.no). Bright, social, and tidy dorms. The outdoor patio becomes busy at night as guests get acquainted over beer (56kr). Free Internet and Wi-Fi. Reception 7am-2am. Lockout 11am-1pm. Dorms 220kr. AmEx/MC/V. ❷

YMCA InterRail Center (HI), Nedre Korskirkealm 4 (☎55 60 60 55), near the *Torget*. Socialize and make new friends in this lively hostel which is very popular with the backpacking crowd. The dorms resemble barracks. Breakfast 60kr. Free Wi-Fi. Internet 20kr per 30min. Reception 7-10:30am and 3:30pm-midnight. 30 person dorm 205kr (summer only); 4- to 6- bed rooms 260-280kr per person. Price includes mandatory 50kr 1st night linens. 15% HI discount. MC/V. ❶

Vandrerhjem Montana (HI), Johan Blyttsvei 30 (☎55 20 80 70; www.montana.no), is far from the center nearly 5km out of Bergen at the base of Mt. Ulriken. Head down

Kong Oscars gt. away from the center until you see a bus shelter next to a cemetery. From there, take bus #31 to Montana and follow the signs. Breakfast included. Linens and towel 70kr. Reception 24hr. May-Sept. dorms 200kr, Oct.-Apr. 180kr; singles 650/475kr; doubles 750/650kr. 15% HI discount. MC/V. ❷

FOOD

Bergen's **Torget** is a tourist's delight with colorful tents, fishmongers, and free samples of caviar, reindeer, salmon, and whale. (Open June-Aug. M-F and Su 7am-7pm, Sa 7am-7pm; Sept.-May M-Sa 7am-4pm.) Cheap restaurants focus around **Kong Oscar's Gate** and **Bergen's University Campus** near the museums. Plenty of Asian restaurants offer good lunch specials (55-70kr). For groceries, **Kiwi Mini Pris** is just next to the YMCA hostel by the *Torget.* (Open daily 9am-11pm. V.)

Kafé Spesial, Christiesgt. 13, off Nygårdsgtn. (☎92 81 27 36). This cheap eatery is popular with students. Pizza from 59kr. Heaping sandwiches 30-72kr. MC/V. ❶

Capello, Skosteredet 14 (☎55 96 12 11; www.capello.no). Take in the 60s Americana while eating pancakes stuffed with fresh ingredients (45-75kr). Open M-W noon-8pm, Th-Sa noon-1:30am. Kitchen open M-W noon-6pm, Th-Sa noon-10pm. MC/V. ❶

Vågen Fetevare, Kong Oscars gt. 10 (☎41 24 51 86). The plush chairs, wall trinkets, and colorful interior make this place a relaxing alternative to *Torget.* Sit outside if the weather is good. For lunch, try the open-faced sandwich (56kr) made from your choice of ingredients. Beer 55kr. Open June-Aug. M-Th 10am-10pm, F-Sa 10am-11pm, Su 11am-10pm; Sept.-May M-Th 9am-10pm, F-Sa 9am-11pm, Su 10am-10pm. Cash only. ❶

3 Kroneren, Kong Oscars gt. 1B (☎55 31 73 33). This kiosk has many options, from pork hot dogs (12kr) to gourmet reindeer sausages infused with cheese and chili (40kr), Santa's least favorite selection. Open daily 11am-6am. Cash only. ❶

SIGHTS

BRYGGEN AND BERGENHUS. The pointed gables of Bryggen line the right side of the harbor from the *Torget.* This row of medieval buildings serves as a reminder of the city's past status as the Hanseatic trading league's major Nordic port. Bryggen is home to galleries, restaurants, and a number of tourist shops. **Bryggens Museum** displays archaeological artifacts from the area and a 12min. film on the city's history. *(Dreggsalmenning 3, behind a small park at the end of the Bryggen houses. ☎55 58 80 10. Open mid-May-Aug. daily 10am-5pm; Sept.-mid-May. M-F 11am-3pm, Sa noon-3pm, Su noon-4pm. 50kr, students 25kr. AmEx/MC/V.)* From the museum, a 1½hr. walking tour (100kr) of the city leaves daily in English at 11am and noon and grants free admission to the **Hanseatic Museum,** in an old trading house near the Fløibanen funicular station. *(Finnegaardsgt. 1A. ☎55 54 46 90; www.hanseatisk.museum.no. Open June-Aug. daily 9am-5pm; Sept.-May Tu-Su 11am-2pm. From May to mid-Sept. 50kr, from mid-Sept. to Apr. 25kr. MC/V.)* Bergenhus, the city's harborside fortress, is home to **Rosenkrantz Tower,** which has splendid views of the city. The Håkonshallen contains the restored grand hall where Norwegian kings held court. *(Walk down Bryggen away from the Torget. ☎55 31 60 67. Hall and tower open from mid-May to Aug. daily 10am-4pm; from Sept. to mid-May hall open M-W and F-Su noon-3pm, Th 3-6pm; tower open Su noon-3pm only. 40kr, students 20kr. Separate admission for each building. Cash only.)*

MUSEUMS. Branches of the **Bergen Art Museum** are on the western side of Lille Lungegårdsvann. It showcases everything from 13th-century Russian icons to Norwegian painters. *(Rasmus Meyers allé 3, 7, and 9. ☎55 56 80 00; www.kunstmuseeneibergen.no. Open from mid-May to mid-Sept. daily 11am-5pm; from mid-Sept. to mid-May Tu-Su 11am-5pm. All 3 museums 50kr, students 35kr. AmEx/MC/V.)* The **Leprosy Museum,** Kong Oscars gt. 59, east of Lille Lungegårdsvann in St. Jørgens Hospital, is part of the Bergen City Museum system. *(☎55 96 11 55; www.bymuseet.no. Open from mid-May-Aug. daily 11am-4pm. 40kr, students 20kr.)* The **Edvard Grieg Museum** honors a Norwegian composer and pianist. *(Troldhaugveinen 65. ☎55 92 29 92. www.troldhaugen.com. Open May-Sept. daily 9am-6pm. Oct., Nov., and Apr. M-F 10am-2pm, Sa-Su noon-4pm. Jan-Mar. 10am-2pm. 60kr, student 20kr. Concerts every W and Su at 7:30pm and Sa 2pm. Free bus for concerts. Concert 220kr.)* The **Bergen Aquarium** offers three floors of sea critters. *(Take bus #11. Nordnesbakken 4. ☎55 55 71 71. www.akvariet.no. Open Sept.-Apr. daily 10am-6pm, May-Aug. daily 9am-7pm. May-Sept. 150kr, Oct.-Apr. 100kr, students 75kr.)*

HIKING

Seven **fjords** and seven mountains surround Bergen, a popular base for outdoor excursions. Visits to the waterways require careful planning and **guided tours,** but the peaks are easily accessible from the city center and have well-kept, marked hiking trails. If you're planning on the spending the night, or the weather is poor, invest in a detailed map. The four eastern mountains are the most popular, due to their proximity and relative ease. **Mount Fløyen** can be reached by the Fløibanen funicular or by hiking up a steep, paved road (45min.). Board the funicular 150m from the *Torget.* The road up the mountain begins nearby. *(☎55 33 68 00. Funicular open May-Aug. M-F 7:30am-midnight, Sa 8am-midnight, Su 9am-midnight; Sept.-May M-Th 7:30am-11pm, F 7:30-11:30pm, Sa 8am-11pm, Su 9am-11pm. One-way 35kr.)* At the summit, several relatively easy trails head into a forest with secluded ponds and stunning vistas (30min.-4hr.).

WATCH THE WEATHER. Even though the mountains are close to Bergen, they can still be dangerous, especially in inclement weather or thick fog. Always check with the tourist office or the DNT for up-to-date weather and safety info before departing for a hike.

A bus and **cable car** combination also runs from the city center to the top of **Mount Ulriken,** the highest of the eastern peaks. At 650m, the mountain provides a stellar panoramic view of the city, fjords, islands, and mountains. Take **bus** #31 to Haukeland Sykehus and walk up Haukelandsbakken until you reach the cable car. The cable car closed in 2008 but will most likely reopen in 2009 under new ownership. A 7hr. hike on fairly flat terrain between Floyen and Ulriken is possible. For the easiest trip, start at higher point of Ulriken.

ENTERTAINMENT AND NIGHTLIFE

Bergen hosts two festivals in late May and early June. **Festspillene** (☎55 21 06 30; www.festspillene.no), a two week international festival, explores all genres of art—from visual to theater to dance with some free concerts, others starting at 50kr. Since 1973, **Nattjazz** has attracted jazz acts big and small. (☎55 30 72 50; www.nattjazz.no. Day pass around 350kr.) Mid-October brings the up-and-coming **Bergen International Film Festival.** (☎55 30 08 40; www.biff.no). The city has an excellent live music scene, but nightlife rarely picks up until around 11:30pm on weekends; many locals throw back a round or two at home to avoid costly drinks at bars and clubs. Steer clear of pricey harborside tourist traps and head to the cafes and pubs on Nygårds gaten.

Biskopen, Neumanns Gate 18 (☎41 41 82 89). This student hangout offers a variety of reasonably priced single-malt whiskeys and beer (47kr) in a great atmosphere for conversation. Rock music plays upstairs with more tunes in the basement. 20+. Open M-Th and Su 6pm-3am, F 4pm-3am, Sa 1-3am. MC/V.

Café Opera, Aldersgrense 20 (☎55 23 03 15). Draws an eclectic clientele of artists and students. DJs around midnight transform the place into a nightclub W-Sa. Beer 49kr. F-Sa club nights pound a mix of styles. Open M 11am-12:30am, Tu-Th 11-3am. F-Sa 11am-3:30am, Su noon-12:30am. AmEx/MC/V.

Garage Bar, at the corner of Nygårdsgtn. and Christies gt. (☎55 32 02 10). Party at this lively alt-rock pub. 20+. Beer 44kr/53kr. Cover 40kr. Concerts free to 210kr. F-Sa after 12:30. Open M-Sa 1pm-3am, Su 3pm-3am. MC/V.

Metro, Ole Bulls pl. 4 (☎55 57 30 37; www.sincoas.no). This lounge/nightclub with hip-hop beats attracts posh, well-dressed patrons. Beer 62kr. M-Th and Su 20+, F-Sa 24+. Cover 100kr F-Sa. W 2-for-1 special. Open daily 11pm-3am. AmEx/MC/V.

Det Akademiske Kvarteret, Olav Kyrres gt. 49-53 (☎55 58 99 10). This complex, run by student volunteers from the University of Bergen, is home to the happening Grøhndals bar and sells some of the cheapest beer in town. Under renovation for 2008.

THE OSLO-BERGEN RAIL LINE

The 7hr. train journey from Oslo to Bergen is one of the world's most scenic rides, regardless of season. From Oslo, trains climb 1222m to remote Finse, stop in Myrdal for transfers to the Flåm railway, and then pass through Voss en route to Bergen. Purchase advance tickets at www.nsb.no. Note that hop-on, hop-off tickets are not available. You must plan each leg of the trip separately and choose your destinations ahead of time.

FINSE. Outdoor enthusiasts head to Finse, the highest point on the line, and hike north through the Aurlandsdalen Valley to **Aurland,** 53km from Flåm. Before setting out, ask about trail conditions at Finse's train station or at DNT offices in Oslo or Bergen; from early June to late September the trails are usually snow-free and accessible. You can sleep in DNT *hytte* (mountain huts), spaced one day's walk apart on the Aurland trails. Bikers can head down the rutted **Rallarvegen** trail, old Navvies road, which parallels the Oslo-Bergen train and extends 81km west to Voss. (www.rallarvegen.no.) Most of the bike ride is downhill; exercise extreme caution on the steep curves in the **Flåmdalen Valley.** Stay in a *hytte* in Hallingskeid (21km from Finse) or forge onward to Flåm (57km). Rent bikes at **Hotel Finse 1222.** (☎56 52 71 10. Bike rental M-W 420kr, Th-Su 520kr.) **Star Wars fans** will appreciate the nearby Hardangerjøkulen glacier (p. 754), which was a shooting location for Hoth, the ice planet scenes from *The Empire Strikes Back.* **Postal Code:** 5719

FLÅM AND THE FLÅM RAILWAY. The railway connecting Myrdal, a stop on the Oslo-Bergen line, with the tiny Sognefjord (p. 753) town of Flåm (pop. 400) is one of Norway's most celebrated attractions. It is an incredible feat of engineering; it has the steepest descent of any railway in the world. The highlight of the 55min. ride is a view of the thunderous **Kjosfossen waterfall,** where the train stops to allow photography. The scenic trip is heavily touristed. Make sure to call ahead. (☎57 63 21 00. www.flaamsbana.no or www.nsb.no. 55min., 10 per day, 210kr. 150kr for ScanRail or Eurail.) A 20km hike (4-5hr.) on the well-tended paths between Myrdal and Flåm more or less follows the train route and passes by smaller cascades and knoll campsites.

Flåm Camping and Youth Hostel (HI) ❶, a half-hostel, half-campground, is the best bet for cheap overnight stays in the area. (☎57 63 21 21. Showers 10kr per 5min. Linens 65kr. Laundry 60kr. Tent sites 1 person 90kr, 2 people 155kr; cabins 550-850kr. 15% HI discount. Dorms 175kr; singles 300kr; doubles 450-540kr. MC/V.) The **Coop Market,** right by the main complex, sells groceries. (☎57 63 21 08. Open M-F 9am-9pm, Sa 9am-6pm, Su noon-6pm. Reduced hours in winter.)

Fylkesbaatane **express boats** run daily to Aurland (15min.), Balestrand (1hr., 2 per day), and Bergen (5hr., 2 per day); check www.fjord1.no/fylkesbaatane for schedules. A popular, scenic sightseeing **ferry** route runs west through Sognefjord branches to Gudvangen (2hr., 4 per day, 225kr, student 130kr). From Gudvangen, you can take a **bus** south to Voss (45min., 74kr, student 64kr) and get back on the train (1hr., 5 per day, 70-90kr). Flåm's **tourist office** is next to the train station. (☎57 63 33 13; www.visitflam.com. Open daily June-Aug. 8:30am-8pm; Sept. 8:45am-4pm; May 8:30am-4pm.) Between October and April, direct questions about Flåm to the tourist office in nearby Aurland, 9km north. (☎55 57 63 33 13; www.alr.no. Internet 25kr per 15min. Bike rental 50kr per hr., 250kr per day. Open June-Sept.daily 8:30am-8pm. May 8:30am-4pm, Oct.-Apr. M-F 8:30am-3:30pm.) **Postal Code:** 5743.

VOSS. Voss (pop. 14,000) is an adventurer's dream. Deep powder and 40km of marked trails attract skiers in winter, while kayaking, paragliding, and parabungeeing (jumping from a flying parasail) draw summer thrillseekers. **Extreme Sports Week** (late June; www.ekstremsportveko.com) draws sports fanatics with a variety of daredevil feats. **Kayaking** trips to nearby Nærøyfjord allow beginners to visit otherwise inaccessible areas. Rental kayaks (1 day 495kr, 2 days 795kr, 3 days 1050kr, 275kr per day thereafter) are also available. (☎55 56 51 00 17; www.nordicventures.com. Open daily from mid-Apr. to mid-Oct. 9am-9pm or later. Kayaking daytrips 650-975kr; 2 days 2095kr; 3 days including hiking 2995kr. All trips fully catered. MC/V.) **Voss Rafting Center,** Nedkvitnesvegen 25, 4km from Voss off E16 in Skulestadmo, leads rafting trips at 10am and 3pm daily (from 490kr). Pickup from Voss can be arranged. (☎55 56 51 05 25; www.vossrafting.no. Open in summer daily 9am-5pm, phone bookings until 10pm; in winter M-F 9am-4pm. MC/V.) If you'd rather stay dry, take the 30min. hike from Voss to **Bordal Gorge.** From the tourist office, turn on the path marked Prestegardsalleen by the lake. Make the trek between July and August, when it is safest. Follow the signs for Bordalssjelet.

Turn right as you exit the train station and walk along E16 away from town for **Voss Vandrerhjem (HI) ❷.** If money is short, sleep on a foam mattress in the basement for 195kr. (☎56 51 20 17; www.vosshostel.com. Bike, canoe, and kayak rental all 100kr per 2hr. and 250kr per 12hr. Breakfast included. Linens 45kr. Sauna; laundry 40kr. Internet 1kr per min. Reception 24hr. Dorms 250kr; singles high-season 590kr, low-season 500kr; doubles 770/700kr. 15% HI discount. MC/V.) To reach **Voss Camping ❶,** behind the tourist office, head left from the train station, stick to the lake shore, and turn right onto the gravel path at the church. (☎56 51 15 97; www.vosscamping.no. Reception May-Sept. 8am-10pm. Reserve ahead. 140kr per tent site; 2 person cabin 500kr. Showers 10kr per 6min. MC/V.) Pick up the cheapest groceries at **Kiwi,** on the main street past the post office. (☎55 56 51 27 35. Open M-F 7am-11pm, Sa 7am-9pm.)

Trains leave for Bergen (1hr., 1 per 1-2hr., 159kr, students 119) and Oslo (5.5hr., 4 per day, 653kr, student 490). Book online ahead of time for *mini pris* tickets. To get to the **tourist office,** Uttrågata 9, turn left as you exit the train station, follow the main road and bear right at the fork by the church. (☎55 56 52 08 00; www.visitvoss.com. Free Internet. Bike rental 250kr/day. Open June-Aug. M-F daily 8am-7pm; Sept.-May M-F 8:30am-3:30pm. MC/V.) **Postal Code:** 5700.

EIDFJORD. In an eastern arm of Hardangerfjord accessible only by bus or car, Eidfjord (pop. 950) allows visitors to explore beyond the touristed Oslo-Bergen Line. The town draws hikers bound for the nearby **national park** and **Hardangervidda mountain plateau,** the largest of its kind in Europe. Inexperienced hikers should stick to the plateau's eastern half, while more seasoned adventurers can tackle the **Hardangerjøkulen glacier** in the north or, with a guide, its pristine southern tip. A 2hr. walk on a trail from the harbor leads to a **Viking burial ground** on top of a plateau in Haereid. Pick up a **trail map** from the tourist office and then head out along Simadalvegen. After passing the bridge, turn right and walk along the river; follow the path as it goes by the lake and winds uphill. A mini-tour from Voss whisks a mixed-age crowd to **Hardangervidda Nature Center,** which features interactive displays on the region's botany and zoology. (☎53 66 59 00; www.hardangervidda.org. Open daily June-Aug. 9am-8pm; Apr.-May and Sept.-Oct. 10am-6pm. Nature center 80kr. MC/V.) From there, the tour continues to the roaring **Vøringfossen Waterfall,** which plummets 182m into a serrated glacial valley. It's important to be careful; the stones are slippery, and safety rails are few and far between. (Mini-tour daily May-Sept. Departs from the harbor after ferry arrival. 195kr.) **Sæbø Camping ❶,** 6km from town near the Nature Center, has a spectacular lakeside location and a service building with a great array of amenities. (☎53 66 59 27; www.saebocamping.com. Kitchen available. Breakfast included. 110kr per tent site, 20kr per person; 4- to 8-bed cabins 360-920kr. Electricity 30kr. Showers included.) Eidfjord is best reached from Voss via Ulvik. **Buses** leave Voss at 8:45am (1 per day; 76kr, students 57kr) and arrive in Ulvik at 9:35am. From there, the **ferry** travels to Eidfjord (½hr, 100kr) from May to September, departing at 11:15 and returning at 2:40pm, allowing just enough time for a 200kr, 2hr. tour of the area. The **tourist office,** in the town center, will book accommodations for a 60kr fee. (☎53 67 34 00. www.eidfjord.kommune.no. Open from mid-June to mid-Aug. M-F 9am-7pm, Sa-Su 10-6pm; from May to mid-June and from mid-Aug. to Sept. M-Sa 9am-6pm, Su 11am-6pm; Oct.-Apr. M, W, and every other F 10am-4pm.) **Postal Code:** 5783.

SOGNEFJORD

The slender fingers of Sognefjord, Europe's longest fjord and the world's second longest, reach the foot of the Jotunheimen Mountains. Jostedalsbreen glacier, the largest in mainland Europe, lies just north of the region. The town of Sogndal is a gateway for glacier trips, while Balestrand and Fjærland are more charming villages ideal for sightseeing and exploring the fjord. Due to uncertain road conditions and limited bus routes, overland transportation is often more of a hassle than it's worth. For an alternative way to explore the area, try Fylkesbaatane **boats** (☎55 90 70 70; www.fylkesbaatane.no), which leave from Bergen on tours of Sognefjord and the Flåm valley. For tickets and more information, see the Balestand **tourist office,** which is across from the aquarium and just off the ship landing. (☎57 69 12 55; www.sognefjord.com. Bikes 40kr per hr., 160kr per day. Internet 15kr per 15min. Open from June to mid-Aug. M-Sa 7:30am-6pm; May and mid-Aug. to Sept. M-F 10am-5pm, Sa-Su 10am-3pm.)

BALESTRAND. Balestrand (pop. 1400) is known as a community for artists, who first flocked to the area in the 1800s, lured by the scenery. This legacy continues with the town's many free galleries. **Golden House,** in the same building as the tourist office, features a town history museum, Scandinavian art displays, a view out over the fjord, and works by local artists. (☎57 69 14 65. Open May-Sept. daily 10am-11pm. Free.) In front of Balestrand's docks, **Sognefjord Akvarium** has a small, very dark exhibit showcasing the rarely seen marine life of the fjords. To reach the **hiking trails** from the harbor, head uphill to the right, take the second left, and walk along the main road next to the youth hostel for 10min.; turn right on Sygna and follow the signs. **Moreld** leads 3hr. **kayak** tours (450kr) and day excursions (950-1050kr) on Sognefjord. It also rent kayaks. (☎40 46 71 00; www.moreld.net. Single kayaks 400kr per day; double 600kr per day.) Walk up the hill past the tourist office, follow the curve right and take the next left to reach **Kringsjå Hotel and Youth Hostel (HI) ❷.** (☎57 69 13 03; www.kringsja.no. Breakfast included. Linens 50kr. Open from late June to mid-Aug. Dorms 255kr; singles 600kr; doubles 720kr; triples 750kr. 15% HI discount. MC/V.) **Buses** run to Bergen (5-6hr., 1-3 per day), Oslo (8.5hr., 3 per day), and Sogndal (1hr., 5 per day). Fylkesbaatane express **boats** run to Bergen (from May-Sept. 4hr.; M-Sa 2 per day; 455kr, students 228kr), Flåm (2hr.; 1-2 per day; 215kr, students 108kr), and Fjaeland (1hr.; 3-4 per day; 185kr, students 93kr).

FJÆRLAND AND FJÆRLANDSFJORD. Fjærlandsfjord branches off Sognefjord in a thin northward line past Balestrand to Fjærland (pop. 300) at the base of Jostedalsbreen glacier. The town's preserved houses have largely been converted into secondhand bookstores set against stellar scenery. **Norwegian Book Town,** a network of 12 secondhand shops, holds over 250,000 volumes and sells novels for as little as 10kr. (☎57 69 22 10; www.bokbyen.no. Open May-Sept. daily 10am-6pm. MC/V.) The **Norsk Bremuseum** (Glacier Museum), 3km outside town on the only road, is famous throughout Norway for its eccentric geometric architecture and its exhibits. (☎57 69 32 88; www.bre.museum.no. Open June-Aug. daily 9am-7pm; Apr.-May and Sept.-Oct. 10am-4pm. 110kr, students 50kr. AmEx/MC/V.) Fjærland does not offer many winter activities because of inadequate bus transportation, but summer thaws out a dozen well-marked trails. One of the longer hikes runs up **Flatbreen** (2-3hr.) to the Flatbrehytta self-service cabin. The **hike** begins 5km northeast from the Norsk Bremuseum at the Østerdalenygard parking lot. (☎57 69 32 29. Limited availability June-Aug. Reserve ahead and bring a sleeping bag.) **Ferries** run to Balestrand (1hr.; 2 per day; 185kr, student 93kr.). The Glacier Bus provides a **guided tour** of the area. (2 per day; both glaciers 140kr, 1 glacier 110kr). From behind the Norsk Bremuseum, **buses** run to Ålesund (5½hr.; 3-5 per day; 349kr, students 277kr); Sogndal (30min.; M-Sa 3-7 per day; 131kr, students 86kr); and Stryn (2½hr., 4 per day, 250kr). There is one nice hotel in the town, but budget travelers would be better advised to go up by the glacier museum. (☎57 69 32 52. Cabins open all year, camping May-Oct. 9am-10pm.) The **tourist office** is near the harbor. (☎57 69 32 33; www.fjaerland.org. Open May-Sept. daily 10am-6pm.)

SOGNDAL. East of Balestrand, Sogndal (pop. 6700) is less charming than its neighbors but is an important base of operations for trips to Jostedalsbreen glacier and a transportation hub. Adventure companies like Jostedalen Breførarlag (☎57 68 32 50; www.bfl.no) run easy **glacier walks** (from 150kr) and offer courses in **rock climbing** (from 2050kr, not including equipment). Buy tickets at the glacier museum in Jostedalen. Icetroll (☎57 68 32 50; www.icetroll.com) runs **kayaking** trips on Jostedalsbreen's glacial lakes, some combined with hiking (from 750kr). Check out other options in the Sognefjord guide or the tourist office. **Sogndal Vandrerhjem (HI) ❷,** Helgheimsvegen 9, has some of the town's more affordable rooms in summer. (☎57 62 75 75. Breakfast included. Free laundry and Wi-Fi. Linens 50kr, towels 25kr. Open mid-June to mid-Aug. Reception 9-10am and 5-11pm. Dorms 200kr; singles 280kr; doubles 450-640kr. 15% HI discount.) **Buses** go to Gaupne (45min.) and Jostedal (2hr.) often. Buses also run from the west end of Gravensteinsgata in the town center to: Balestrand (1hr., 2-3 per day); Bergen (4-5hr.; 3-4 per day; 405kr, students 197kr); Fjærland (30min.; M-Sa 2-5 per day; 131kr, students 86kr); Oslo (7hr., 2-3 per day, 520kr); Stryn via Skei (2hr., 1 per day, 270kr). Fylkesbaatane express **boats** run to Bergen (4hr.; M-Sa 1 per day; 540kr, students 270kr) and stop at several destinations along Sognefjord. The **tourist office,** Hovevegen 2, is a couple of blocks up from the bus station. (☎97 60 04 43; www.sognefjord.no. Open from late June to Aug. M-F 9am-6pm, Sa 10am-4pm; from Sept. to late June M-F 9am-4pm.)

NORDFJORD

Nordfjord runs north of the ice-blue expanse of Jostedalsbreen glacier. The region was formerly less popular than Geirangerfjord and Sognefjord, but Jostedalsbreen National Park has attracted many visitors to the area in recent years. Although solo trips onto the glacier are tempting, it has dangerous soft spots and crevasses. Stryn serves as a major hub for essential guided tours.

STRYN. The Stryn municipality has three ideal base towns for exploring the area: **Stryn, Olden** and **Loen.** Stryn (pop. 2000) is a departure point for adventures around the Briksdalsbreen glacier and on the Bødal Glacier, both of which are branches of the Jostedalsbreen glacier. A **bus** (76kr) runs from Stryn's bus terminal to the base of Briksdalsbreen, via Olden (daily June-Aug. 9:30am, returning 1:40pm) and to Sande Camping, the starting point for Bødal Glacier exploration. **Briksdal Breføring AS Adventure** (☎57 87 68 00 www.briksdal-adventure.com) runs **raft trips** through the ice patches around the glacier. It also runs **glacier guiding trips** on Bødalsbreen (5-6hrs., 10:00am) and hikes on Lodalskapå.

Melkevoll Bretun ❶, is a well-positioned campground with a **tourist office** 45min. from Stryn, serving as the departure point for Briksdalsbreen glacier activities. Melkevoll Bretun also has stone age cave lodgings, where guests sleep on wooden slabs swaddled in reindeer skins. Bring an insulated sleeping bag. (☎57 87 38 64; www.melkevoll.no. Showers 10kr per 5min. Firewood 50kr. Electricity 30kr. Cabins 250-650kr. Cave dorms 110kr per person; min. 4 people. MC/V.) Glacier walks (500kr) on Bødalsbreen, another arm of Jostedalsbreen, leave from Loen. In town, the **Stryn Vertshus ❷** offers a clean and welcoming cafe at a bed and breakfast. (Tonningsgata 19. ☎57 87 05 30. Free Wi-Fi. Outdoor seating. 5 guest rooms, 750kr/double room with breakfast. Open June-Aug. M-F 9am-7pm, Sa 9am-1am, Su noon-7pm. MC/V.)

Buses run to: Ålesund (3½hr.; 1-4 per day; 255kr, students 191kr); Bergen (6hr.;l 3-4 per day; 462kr, students 347kr); Fjærland (2hr.; 1 per day; 250kr); Skei (2hr.; 3 per day; 140kr, student 105kr); Trondheim (7hr.; 1 per day; 490kr, students 409kr) via Lom (2hr.; 3 per day; 215kr, students 161kr). The public **library** is next to the bus station and offers free Internet. (M-F 10am-4pm June-Aug.; Sept.-May M, W, F 9am-5pm, Tu, Th 9am-6pm, Sa 10am-4pm.) Stryn's **tourist office** is at Tinggata 3. (☎57 87 40 54; www.nordfjord.no. Internet 15kr per 15min. Open July M-F 8:30am-8pm, Sa-Su 9:30am-7pm; June and Aug. M-F 8:30am-6pm, Sa 9:30am-5pm; Sept.-May M-F 8:30am-3:30pm.)

GEIRANGERFJORD

The 16km long Geirangerfjord, a UNESCO World Heritage Site, is lined with waterfalls that make it one of Norway's most spectacular—and touristed—destinations. While cruising through the icy water, watch for the **Seven Sisters waterfalls** and, across from them, the wooing **Suitor waterfall.** The suitor was rejected by all seven sisters and took to the bottle, which explains why the shape of a beer bottle is visible through the water, or so the story goes. Geirangerfjord can be reached from the north via the Trollstigen road from Åndalsnes, by bus from Ålesund, or for the most scenic route, via **ferry** from Hellesylt.

GEIRANGER ☎70

Geiranger (pop. 270), at the eastern end of Geirangerfjord, is a tourist mecca at the final point of the Trollstigen road. In summer, thousands overrun the town to take in the stunning views of the fjord. The surrounding, well-marked trails offer stunning views and some escape from the crowds.

TRANSPORTATION AND PRACTICAL INFORMATION. Pick up **buses** by the ferry station across from the troll statue. Buses run to Ålesund (3hr., 2-4 per day, 186kr). **Ferries** depart for Hellesylt (1hr., May and Oct. 4, June-Sept. 8 per day, 110kr). For info on **hiking** and rental bikes (75kr per hr., 300kr per day), visit the **tourist office,** up the path from the ferry landing. Internet 1kr/min. (☎70 26 30 99; www.visitgeirangerfjorden.com or www.dgt.no. Open daily from mid-June to Aug. 9am-7pm; from mid-May to mid-June and Sept. 11am-4pm.)

ACCOMMODATIONS AND FOOD. **Geiranger Camping,** 100m from the town center, is set at the mouth of the fjord. (☎70 26 31 20. Showers 10kr per 5min. Laundry 30kr wash, 30kr dry. Reception 8am-10pm. Open from mid-May to early Sept. 20kr per person, 70kr per tent site. 115kr with car. Electricity 35kr. MC/V.) The tentless should head on past Geiranger Camping on the road that loops around, following the fjord to the left. 1½ miles down the road: there are campsites renting cabins for as little as 200kr per person. **Villa Utsikten Hotel and Restaurant ❸,** 3½km from the town center, has affordable rooms. (☎70 26 96 60; www.villautsikten.no. Open from May to mid-Aug. Rooms from 300kr.)

SIGHTS. Nearby natural attractions include **Flydalsjuvet Cliff** (round-trip 2hr. on roads), **Storseter Waterfall** (2hr.), and views of the Seven Sisters waterfalls from **Skageflå Farm** (5hr.) or take a sightseeing boat to Skagehola and hike up a short ways. At **Langvaten,** hikers can climb into cloud cover that shrouds the top of **Dalsnibba Mountain Plateau** (1476m). To get there, take a bus from opposite the ferry docks (1hr., 3 per day, 180kr round trip). The **Geiranger Fjordsenter,** a 15min. walk from the tourist office on Rte. 63, explores the history of the region. Concerts and traditional **Norwegian music and folklore** performances are held throughout summer. (☎70 26 38 10; www.fjordsenter.info Open daily July 9am-10pm; June and Aug. 9am-6pm; May and Sept. 9am-4pm; 85kr.)

HELLESYLT. West of Geiranger at the intersection of Geirangerfjord and Sunnylvsfjord, Hellesylt (pop. 600), a base for seven well-marked **hikes,** is quieter than Geiranger. **Skaret** (2-3hr.) has a mountainside outlook with views of the town and fjord. From there, you can continue to **Steimnebba,** a nearby peak (4-6hr.). The **Stadheimfossen Campground ❶** has tent sites and cabins for groups. (☎70 26 50 79; www.stadheimfossen.no. Open Jan.-Sept. 50kr per tent site, from 350kr per cabin.) **Hellesylt Vandrerhjem (HI) ❷,** is a funky, 60s-style lodge above Hellesyltfossen waterfall. They'll pick you up at the harbor if you phone ahead. (☎70 26 51 28. Breakfast included. Linens and towels 45kr. Free Internet and Wi-Fi. Open from June to early Sept. Dorms 210kr; room for one or two 550kr. 15% HI discount.) When hunger strikes after mountain excursions, head to one of two grocery stores in town, **Spar** or **Coop. Buses** go to Ålesund (2hr.; 4 per day; 255kr, students 197kr) and Styrn (1hr.; 2 per day, last at 1:40pm; 98kr, students 74kr). **Ferries** depart for Geiranger (1hr.; May and Oct. 4, June-Sept. 8 per day; 110kr). The **tourist office** is by the docks. (☎94 81 13 32. Open early June M-F 10am-5pm, Sa-Su 11am-5pm; from mid-June to Aug. 9am-5pm daily.

LOM, JOTUNHEIMEN, AND REINHEIMEN

Near the last tributaries of the Western Fjords and the remote towns of the interior lies the pristine landscape of **Jotunheimen National Park** ("home of the giants"), the most visited in Norway. In 2006, **Reinheimen National Park** ("home of the reindeer") was established north of Jotunheimen. These enormous parks flank the village of Lom, with Breheimen, a glacier area that attained park status in 2007, to the west. Today, it is Scandinavia's top hiking destination.

LOM. The attraction of Lom (pop. 2500) is not what is to be found within the city, but what lies outside of it. The high-season for hiking usually runs from July to mid-August. In Jotunheimen, a popular trek leads to the summit of 2469m **Galhøpiggen,** northern Europe's tallest mountain. Ask at the tourist office for the best departure points, which vary according to skill level and weather conditions. The 6hr. trail from **Juvashytta** is a popular route, but it can only be completed with the help of paid guides (160kr) who navigate the perilous soft spots of the Jostedalsbreen glacier. Before guides were mandatory, several inexperienced tourists fell through crevasses. The complex at Juvashytta (accessible by toll road 80kr) also offers an summer alpine ski area and a nice **summer hotel** (250kr per. person for double rooms). A **bus** leaves from Lom for Juvashytta (from mid-June to mid-Aug. daily 8:40am; 76kr, students 57kr). From Krossbu, hikers can take a 4-6hr. glacier walk. Less experienced travelers without a guide should catch the bus to **Spiterstulen** (1 per day 8:45am, 76kr, students 57kr). From there, plan to hike 8-9hr., not on the glacier. **Nordal Turistsenter ❷,** in the city center, has cabins. Walk left as you exit the tourist office and cross the bridge to the main roundabout; take a left and follow the road until you see the cabins on your left. (☎61 21 93 00; www.nordalturistsenter.no. Laundry 25kr per machine. Reception 8am-11pm. Open Apr.-Dec. Tent sites 150kr per person, low-season 130kr; 200kr with car; 2- to 4-person cabins 395-440kr. Showers free.) Pick up groceries at **Kiwi,** off the main roundabout. (Open M-F 9am-9pm, Sa 9am-6pm. Cash only.) or the Coop across from the bus station. From Lom, **buses** run to: Bergen (8hr., 1 per day, 550kr); Oslo (6hr., 4 per day, 485kr); Sogndal (3hr., mid-June to mid-Sept. 2 per day, 220kr); Trondheim (6hr., 1 per day, 450kr). The **tourist office** is in the Fjellmuseum and National Park Center. From the bus station, turn left and cross the bridge. (☎61 21 29 90; www.visitjotunheimen.com. Open mid-May to mid-Aug. M-F 9am-7pm, Sa-Su 10am-7pm; from mid-Aug. to early May M-F 9am-4pm. Ring door bell. Museum www.fjell.museum.no. 50kr, students 30kr. AmEx/MC/V.)

ROMSDAL AND TRØNDELAG

Between the Western Fjords and the sparsely inhabited stretches of northern Norway, a group of coastal cities forms the third point of a triangle with Oslo and Bergen. Travelers are only beginning to discover this Norwegian heartland, hemmed in by the Trollstigen range and the valleys along Trondheimsfjord.

ÅLESUND ☎70

Seaside Ålesund (OH-less-oont; pop. 40,000) welcomes travelers with Art Nouveau architecture and attractive harbor views characteristic of the region. Climb up the 418 steps to the Aksla outlook in the city for views of the harbor. Head through the park across from Ålesund Vandrerhjem hostel and walk 20min. to the top. At the **Art Nouveau Center,** Apotekergata 16, a time machine exhibit transports visitors back to Ålesund's devastating 1904 fire and explains how the city got its artistic flair. For a glimpse of the past, visit the **Sunnmøre Museum,** which has reconstructed farmhouses and the remains of an 11th-century trading post. (Take bus #618 (10min., 24kr) to Sunnmøre. ☎70 17 40 00; www.sunnmore.museum.no. Open from late June to late Aug. M-Sa 11am-5pm, Su noon-5pm; late Aug.-late June M-Tu and F 11am-3pm, Su noon-3pm. Cruise

50kr. Museum 65kr, students 45kr. MC/V.) The 62° **Fjord Sightseeing Center,** in the tourist office, runs tours of Hjørundfjord and Geirangerfjord (p. 757). Tickets for its circular tours are good for a week of fjord sightseeing. (☎70 11 44 30; www.fjord-magic.com. Open from late-June to Aug. M-F 8am-7pm, Sa-Su 8am-6pm. Tours 490-1200kr; ask about cheaper one-way fares.) **Cruise Service AS,** Brunholmgata 10, offers excursions to otherwise inaccessible Trandal.

Ålesund Vandrerhjem (HI) ❷, Parkgata 14, has affordable rooms. From the bus station, walk east down Keiser Wilhelms gate, turn left on Radstugata and walk up the hill; it's on the corner with Parkgata. (☎70 11 58 30. Breakfast, linens, and laundry included. Free Internet and Wi-Fi. Reception May-Sept. 8:30-11am and 4pm-midnight; Sept.-May 4-6pm; 24hr. access. Dorms 245kr; singles 550kr; doubles 750kr. 15% HI discount. MC/V.) American-inspired food is found at **Let's Eat Deli ❷,** Keiser Wilhelms gate 37, half a block from Storgata. (☎70 13 13 07. Sandwiches 64-72kr. Open M-F 10:30am-5pm, Sa 10:30am-4pm. MC/V.)

Buses go to Stryn (3.5hr.; 3 per day; 255kr, students 196kr) and Trondheim (7hr.; 3 per day; 539kr, students 307kr); or catch a bus to Åndalsnes (2hr., 4 per day, 189kr), then catch a **train** to Trondheim (7-9hr., 535kr) that runs along the Rauma line to Dombås. Hurtigruten **boats** go to Trondheim (13hr.; 1 per day; 1003kr, students 502kr). The **tourist office** is at the Skateflukaia dock. (☎70 15 76 00; www.visitalesund.com. Internet 10kr per 10min. Open June-Aug. daily 8:30am-7pm; Sept.-May M-F 8:30am-4pm, Sa 10am-2pm.)

NORWAY

ÅNDALSNES ☎71

Åndalsnes (pop. 2500), on Romsdalsfjord, is a port on the edge of fjord country. Twenty kilometers out of town, accessible by bus or bike, hikes along the **Trollstigen** (Troll's Road) climb to over 1000m. The **Frokostplassen** path is suitable for both expert and casual hikers. The trail passes the 180m Stigfossen waterfall and approaches the sheer **Trollveggen** (Troll's Wall), a great place for serious climbers as it offers Europe's longest climbing route. The lip of the wall lured base-jumpers for years, until helicopter rescues drove the town into debt and the activity was outlawed. Thrill-seekers continue to make jumps on the sly and the surrounding area is now home to the World Base Race (www.worldbaserace.com). *Let's Go* does not recommend illegal activities. Head back to Åndalsnes on the **Kløvstien path** (5hr.), which was recently smoothed over for walkers but is still steep enough to require a handrail in some places. Bjorli is a hub for **skiing** in winter, especially at the end of January during the Romsdalsvinter festivals, with ski trips throughout the region. In mid-July, the paths between Åndalsnes and Bjorli fill for the **Norwegian Mountain Festival** (www.fjellfestivalen.no). During the first weekend of August, Åndalsnes hosts the **RaumaRock Festival** (www.raumarock.com; 3-day pass 990kr), which showcases Scandinavian artists. Just 2km from town, **Åndalsnes Vandrerhjem (HI) ❷,** Setnes, resembles a farmhouse with its grass roof and homey dorms. The Ålesund bus will stop at the hostel upon request. (☎71 22 13 82. www.aandalsnes-vandrerhjem.no.Breakfast included. Linens and towels 50kr. Free Wi-Fi. Lockable closets. Open from late May to Aug. Reception 4pm-10am. Dorms 260kr; singles 470kr; doubles 680kr. 15% HI discount. MC/V.) **Trains** run to Trondheim via the gorgeous Rauma line to Dombås and Oslo (6hr.; 2-4 per day; 717kr, student 538kr). **Buses** depart outside the train station for Ålesund (2hr.; 4 per day; 220kr, students 110kr.) and Geiranger (3hr., 2 per day via Trollstigen, 208kr). Find maps at the **tourist office,** located in the train station. (☎71 22 16 22; www.visitandalsnes.com. Free Internet. Open mid-June to mid-Aug. M-F 9am-6pm, Sa 10am-4pm, Su 11am-4pm. Early June and late Aug. M-F 8am-3:30pm.)

TRONDHEIM ☎73

More than a thousand years have passed since the Viking King Olav Tryggvason settled Trondheim (pop. 162,000) and made it Norway's seat of power. Today, despite several destructive fires, it retains some of its medieval charm and serves as a gateway to the north. Nearly 30,000 university students call Trondheim home, giving its canals and restored townhouses a youthful energy.

TRANSPORTATION AND PRACTICAL INFORMATION. **Trains** go to Bodø (11hr., 2 per day, 200-950kr) and Oslo (6hr., 4 per day, 200-900kr). **Buses** leave the train station for Ålesund (7-8hr.; 4 per day; 539kr, students 307kr) and Bergen (12hr.; 1 per day; night bus only; 751kr, students 563kr). The Hurtigruten **boat** departs daily at noon for Stamsund, in the Lofoten Islands (31hr.; 1997kr, 50% student discount). The **tourist office** is at Munkegata 19. The **Trondheim City Card** is also for sale (198kr), but offers mostly 2-for-1 discounts and is best for longer visits of two or more travelers. (☎73 80 76 60; www.visit-trondheim.com. Open June-Aug. M-F 8:30am-6pm, Sa-Su 10am-4pm; Sept-May 8:30am-4:00pm, Sa 10am-2pm.) **DNT** (Norwegian Mountain Touring Association), Sandgata 30, has **maps** and hiking info. (☎73 92 42 00; www.tt.no. Open March-Sept. M-W and F 8am-4pm, Th 10am-6pm. Oct.-Feb. M-W, F 8am-4pm, Th 10am-4pm.)

ACCOMMODATIONS AND FOOD. **Trondheim InterRail Center ❶,** Elgesetergata 1, in the Studentersamfundet (p. 762), has a fun-loving mood and the cheapest prices around. Cross the bridge from the train station, walk south along Søndregata, and go right on Kongens gate. Turn left on Prinsensgata and go across the bridge—the hostel is behind the red building on your left. (☎73 89 95 38; www.tirc.no. Breakfast included. Linens 50kr and 50kr deposit. Free Internet. Open July 1 to Aug. 10. Dorms 150kr. 39kr beer, dinner 45kr. MC/V.) For a tidy budget option, stay at **Lillegårdsbakken ❷,** off Øvre Bakklandet, uphill to Singsaker Sommerhotell, Rogertsgata 1. (☎73 89 31 00; http://sommerhotell.singsaker.no. Breakfast, linens, and towel included. 24hr. reception. Open mid-June to mid-Aug. Dorms 200kr; singles 410kr, private bath 520; doubles 620kr. 30kr bottle of beer. AmEx/MC/V.) If you're not visiting in the summer, try the **Trondheim Vandrerhjem ❷,** Weidemannsrei 41. Dorms 230kr; singles 490kr; doubles 620kr. 25kr student discount. Breakfast included. Towel 15kr, linens 65. Internet 2kr/min. Reception 7am-midnight, 24hr. key access.)

Gluttony may be one of the seven deadly sins, but that doesn't detract from the appeal of the all-you-can-eat **cake buffet** (Su 1-7pm; 62kr) at **Mormors Stue ❷,** off of Thomas Angells gate on Nedre Enkeltskillingsveita 2. After 5pm, beer is 34kr. (☎73 52 20 22. Open M-Sa 10am-11:30pm, Su 1-11:30pm. MC/V.) The early-bird dinner crowd snaps up fresh fish platters (125kr) at the riverside **Den Gode Nabo ❸,** Øvre Bakklandet 66, just over the Old Town Bridge in a basement to the right. (☎73 40 61 88 09; www.dengodenabo.as. Dinner special daily 4-7pm. Make your own pizza and salad bar 99kr. Open daily 1pm-1:30am. MC/V.) Nearby, **Cafe and Bar Bare Blåbær,** Innherredsveien 16, serves burgers and their special stone oven pizza (99-129kr) until midnight—then becomes a lounge and bar. (☎73 53 30 33. Beer 63kr. 20+ after 6pm. Open M-Th and Su 11am-1:30am, F-Sa 11am-3:30am. AmEx/MC/V.)

SIGHTS. Start in the north near the train station and head down Fjordgata to the *Ravnkloa* (fish market), where you can catch a **ferry** (June-Aug. daily 10am-6pm.10-15min. 50kr round-trip) to Munkholmen. The island is now popular for its attractive beaches. **Nidaros Cathedral,** in the southern end of the city, tops the list of churches to visit in Norway. The whole edifice sits on King Olof's (Norway's patron saint) tomb. (☎73 92 44 70; www.nidarosdomen.no. May-early June M-F 9-3pm, Sa 9-2pm, Su 1-4pm; early June-mid-Aug. M-F 9-6, Sa 9-2, Su 1-4; mid-Aug.-mid Sept. M-F 9-3, Sa 9-2, Su 1-4; mid-Sept.-Apr. M-F 12-2:30, Sa 11:30-2, Su 1-3. Organ concerts mid-June to mid-Aug. M-Sa 1; mid-Aug. to mid-June Sa 1pm. Music services mid-June to mid-Aug. M-F 5:40pm. Low-season free, otherwise 50kr. AmEx/MC/V.) Of all the museums in Trondheim, the **Kunstmuseum,** Bispegata 7B, is most worth a look. (☎73 53 81 80. www.tkm.museum.no. 50kr, 30kr students. late June-late Aug. Open daily 10am-5pm, Aug. 21- June 19 Tu-Su 11am-4pm. MC/V.) Across the scenic **Gamle Bybro** (Old Town Bridge) to the east, the weather-worn fishing houses of the old district are now chic galleries and cafes. The hill in this district is the site of the world's first bicycle elevator. Test your balance as you are shoved up the steep hill by an automated pulley. (Access card available at the tourist office for 100kr deposit.) The **Kristiansten Festning** (Kristiansten Fortress), overlooking Trondheim and the fjords, is one of the city's best picnic spots. (☎98 80 66 23; www.kristiansten-festning.no. Grounds open daily 8am-midnight, when the flag is raised. Interior open June-Aug. daily 11am-4pm. Museum 50kr.)

ENTERTAINMENT AND NIGHTLIFE. The **Olavsfestdagene Medieval Festival** (late July to early Aug.) fills the city with pop bands and pilgrims. (☎73 84 14 50; www.olavsfestdagene.no.) The **Studentersamfundet,** the student society's headquarters, houses a cafe with cheap food and beer next to the InterRail Center. There are 18 private bars in the maze-like building. (☎73 89 95 00; www.samfundet.no. Beer 24-48kr. Open daily Sept.-June until 2am and as late as 4am.) The Solsiden district is a waterfront promenade home to popular restaurants and lounges. The standout **Blæst,** TMV kaia 17, has three bars and a theater that hosts rock acts, DJs most weekends, and an improv comedy troupe on Saturdays. Wednesday is the day to go for 19kr beer and free concerts. (☎73 60 01 00; www.blaest.no. Concerts usually 100-200kr. 20+. Open M-Sa 11-3:30am, Su 12-1am. AmEx/MC/V.) When school is in session, the clubs and bars along **Brattorgata,** in the north near the train station, offer everything from tapas to fine malt whiskey. In summer, a stroll along **Carl Johans gate** or **Nordre gate** is the best bet for nightlife beyond Solsiden.

NORTHERN NORWAY

Visitors encounter everything from the city center of Tromsø to the natural wonders of the Lofoten Islands. Even farther north, the remote, frozen Svalbard Archipelago, where polar bears roam, sits on top of the world.

TROMSØ ☎77

Dubbed the "Paris of the Arctic" by explorers in awe of its cosmopolitan flair, Tromsø (pop. 63,500) exudes a worldliness that belies its chilly location. The town is a base for exploring Norway's northern mountains and lakes.

TRANSPORTATION AND PRACTICAL INFORMATION. Flights leave from **Tromso airport (TOS;** ☎67 03 46 00). The Hurtigruten **boat** travels to Stamsund, in the Lofoten Islands (20hr.; departs from Stamsund 7:30pm, from Tromsø 1:30am; 1074kr, students 537kr). **Buses** go to Narvik (4hr.; 2-3 per day; 370kr, students and Scanrail holders 185kr), a transportation hub for Finnish and Swedish destinations. The **tourist office,** Kirkegata 2, books dogsled, glacier, rafting, whale watching trips, and more. (☎77 61 00 00; www.visittromso.no.

Open mid-May-Aug. M-F 9am-7pm, Sa-Su 10am-5pm; Sept.-mid-May M-F 9am-4pm, Sa 10am-4pm.) The cheapest **tour** (495kr) goes by bus from behind the tourist office, through the Lyngen Alps to the island of Skjervøy. (In summer leaves 2:10pm and 4:00pm, both return at 11:45pm.) Most city buses leave from downtown along Havnegata and Fredrik Langes Gate. Get a **schedule** from the tourist office. (24kr). **Postal Code:** 9253.

ACCOMMODATIONS AND FOOD. **Fjellheim Sommerhotell ❶**, Mellomvegen 96, has the best lodging. The dorms are basic, but the hostel offers 24hr. make-your-own waffles. (Take bus #37 or walk along Mellomvegen. ☎77 75 55 60; www.fjellheimsommerhotell.no. Linens included. Internet 25kr per hr., Wi-Fi 100kr per stay. Laundry 25kr. Reception 24hr. Open mid-June to mid-Aug. Book ahead in late June. Dorms 250kr; singles 500kr, 600 w/bath; doubles 700kr, 900kr w/bath. AmEx/MC/V.) Head to the harbor for **Skarven ❷**, Strandtorget 1, which serves up ham or seal sandwiches. (☎77 60 07 43; www.skarven.no. Open M-Th and Su 11am-12:30am, F-Sa 11am-1am. AmEx/MC/V.) Or try **Le Mirage Cafe ❷**, Storgata 42, for a variety of cafe fare. (☎77 68 61 50. M-Th 12-1:30am, F-Sa 12-3:00am, Su 1-1:30am. AmEx/MC/V.) Stock up on groceries at **Spar**, Storgata 63 (☎77 62 84 00. Open M-F 9am-8pm, Sa 9am-7pm) or the larger Spar, open later (M-Sa until 11pm and Su until 8pm) further down Storengata.

SIGHTS AND HIKING. The tour at the **Mack Brewery** introduces visitors to beer-making with hilarious tour guides and samples of Mack beer. (Storgata 4-13. ☎77 62 45 80; www.mack.no. 45 min. English-language tours leave from Øllhallen at Storgata 4 June-Aug. M-Th 1 and 3:30pm; Sept.-May M-Th 1pm. 150kr; includes 1 beer.) If you like your sightseeing superheated, **Blåst,** a glass-blowing factory, gives free demonstrations. (Peder Hansens gt. 4. ☎77 68 34 60; www.blaast.no. Open M-F 9am-5pm, Sa 10am-3pm.) **Tromsø University Museum** delves into geology and the indigenous Sámi culture. (Take bus #37 from the city center or walk south along Mellomvegen for 30min. ☎77 64 50 00; www.tmu.uit.no. Open daily June-Aug. 9am-6pm; Sept.-May M-F 9-3:30, Sa 12-3pm, Su 11am-5pm. 30kr, students 15kr. MC/V.) The **Polaria** is a interactive museum and aquarium focused on Arctic ecosystems. (Hjarlmar Johansens gt. 12, right off Strandvegen Storgata transition. ☎77 75 01 11; www.polaria.no. Open daily mid-May to mid-Aug. 10am-7pm; mid-Aug. to mid-May noon-5pm. 95kr, students 60kr. AmEx/MC/V.) To see the midnight sun in June and early July, take the **Fjellheisen cable car,** Solliveien 12, a 10min. walk from the Arctic Cathedral, 420m to the top of Mt. Storsteinen. Bus 26 takes you to the cable car and offers you a discount if you buy your cable car ticket from the bus driver. (☎77 63 87 37; www.fjellheisen.no. Daily 2 per hr. 95kr., students 70kr.) The view from the top is spectacular and offers hiking trails around the mountain. Hikers looking for a challenge can trek to **Treriksrøysa,** and stand in Finland, Norway, and Sweden all at once—the **budget-friendly** way to say "I toured all of Scandinavia."

FESTIVALS AND NIGHTLIFE. The **Tromsø International Film Festival** is Norway's largest, attracting over 50,000 visitors annually (Jan. 13-18, 2009; ☎77 75 30 90; www.tiff.no). The following week, the **Northern Lights Festival** showcases classic music under the aurora borealis. **Sámi National Day** (Feb. 6) culminates in a **reindeer race** through the city center. Tromsø is a university town famous for its nightlife, which centers on Storgata and the side streets Strandskillet and Grønnegata. Drop in for tapas or a cappuccino at **Åpen Bar** (Open Bar), Grønnegata 81, a relaxed, candlelit lounge and bar. (☎77 68 46 00. Beer 61kr. Sept.-May F-Sa DJ. 20+, W 18+. Cover F 50kr., Sa 70kr. Restaurant open Tu-Th 4pm-midnight, F 3pm-3:30am, Sa 2pm-3:30am, kitchen closes at 10. Nightclub open W, F-Sa 10pm-3:30am. AmEx/MC/V.)

LOFOTEN ISLANDS ☎76

A jumble of emerald mountains, glassy waters, and colorful villages, the Lofoten Islands are some of the most strikingly gorgeous vistas in Scandinavia, proving that there is more to Norwegian beauty than fjords. The chain consists of four main islands (Moskenesøy, Flakstadøy, Vestågøy, and Austvågøy) but extends from Røst in the south to Austvågøy in the north.

TRANSPORTATION. The Hurtigruten express **boat** runs from Trondheim to Stamsund (31hr.; departs daily at noon, arrives at 7pm the next day; 1873kr). Another option is to take a **train** to Bodø (11hr., 2 per day, 200-940kr depending on the day and time. Book ahead if possible). From there, catch a **ferry,** departing from behind the train station, to Moskenes (3-4hr., 4-6 per day, 155kr, with car 561kr; buy ticket at ferry) or take the Hurtigruten (departs daily 3:00pm) to Svolvær (6hr., 425kr, student 1/2 price.) via Stamsund (4hr.; 397kr, students 1/2 price). **Flights** go from Bodø to **Leknes Airport,** Lufthavnveien 30 (**LKN;** ☎05 55 80), on Vestvågøy (45min., 5-6 per day, 783kr). Check www.wideroe.no for more info and discounts. Within the islands, local **buses** (☎76 11 11 11; www.nordtrafikk.no) are the main form of transport; pick up a schedule at a tourist office. In summer, buses #4-5 travel from Å to Leknes, where you can catch buses to the rest of the islands. Renting a **car** is the easiest way to see the island chain and visit locales off E10, the main highway. Agencies at Leknes Airport include: Avis (☎76 08 01 04) and Hertz (☎76 08 18 44). Berres Bil and Bât (☎76 09 32 40) is in Ramberg, southwest of Leknes on Flakstadøya.

NORWAY

BODØ

Bodø is a transportation hub for the Lofoten Islands. One housing option is **Opsahl Gjestegård ❹,** a small guesthouse just outside the city. (☎75 52 07 04. www.opsahlgjest.no. Breakfast included. 24hr. reception. Singles 530kr, doubles 690kr, triple 1050kr, quads 1400kr.) Eat affordably at the **Lovold Kafeteria ❸,** Tollbugata 9, located on the 2nd floor, which draws a mainly local clientele. (☎75 52 02 61. Open M-F 9am-6pm, Sa 9am-3pm. MC/V.) The **tourist office** is at Sjøgata 3. (Right by the water, in the same building as boat and bus ticketing. ☎75 54 80 00. www.visitbodo.com. Summer hours M-F 9am-8pm, Sa 10am-6pm, Su noon-8pm. Reduced hours in winter.)

MOSKENESØYA

Near the southern tip a highway, the quiet island of Moskenesøya (pop. 1200) houses both 19th-century fishing communities and eco-adventure tourism.

MOSKENES. Frequent **ferries** from Bodø make Moskenes a crossroads for tourists. **Moskenes Harbour Tourist Office,** in the red building at the ferry landing, helps with tour reservations. Pick up a guide to Lofoten. (☎76 09 15 99; www.lofoten-info.no. Internet 1kr per min. Open mid-June-mid-Aug. daily 9am-7pm; early May-mid-June and late Aug. M-F 10am-5pm. March, April, Sept. M-F 10am-noon.) Booking an adventure **boat tour** (☎90 77 07 41; 400-900kr), guided **hike** (contact tourist office), or **fishing trip** with locals (from Reine ☎91 34 55 99, from Å 97 75 60 21; 500kr) requires calling at least a few days ahead. A thrilling **boat safari** is well worth the expense (6hr.; 900kr). The trip takes 12 passengers through the **Maelstrom,** past the fishing hamlet of **Hell** (where Hell can actually freeze over), and into the ancient **Refsvikhula caves.** (☎98 01 75 64; www.

lofoten-info.no.) Although challenging and sparsely marked, mountain hikes are the primary attraction in the region; make sure you have the proper gear and pick up a **map** at the tourist office. A 3hr. trek heads to the DNT's (Norwegian Mountain Touring Association) **Munkebu cabin,** a good place to spend the night. DNT membership (p. 735) and a 300kr deposit are required for key rental. Members may bring guests. If you're not a member, go to **KIN Trykk,** Ramberg (☎76 09 34 20), where you pick up the key and try to convince the man who oversees the cabin that you're a reliable person; he may let you stay without membership. (200kr per night, under 25 100kr. Members 100/50kr.) Keys also available at **Sørvågen Handel** (☎76 09 12 15). If you brought a tent, pitch it just up the hill from the dock at **Moskenes Camping** (☎99 48 94 05).

Å. South of Moskenes, the fishing village of Å ("OH") takes great pride in being first alphabetically among world cities. Experienced hikers can tackle the 8hr. **Stokkvikka hike.** Bring a map and head down the southern bank of Lake Ågvatnet and up 400m to cross the Stokkvikskaret Pass. To relax on the region's sandy beaches, take the bus from Moskenesøya to Reine and catch a **ferry** (100kr) to Vinstad. An easy, well-marked trail follows the fjord to the water. The **Norsk Fiskeværsmuseum** has displays on the island's maritime mainstay—cod fishing—in six village buildings. (☎76 09 14 88. Open mid-June to mid-Aug. daily 10:30am-5:30pm; mid-Aug. to mid-June M-F 11am-3:30pm. 50kr, students 25kr. AmEx/MC/V.) Off the E10 highway is the **Stockfish Musuem,** a place to visit for its unique owner and a novel experience. (☎76 09 12 11. mid-June-mid-Aug. 10am-5pm, off season reduced hours. 40kr, student 25. Cash only.) Visitors can rent rooms in the private fishing lodges by the dock. **Å Hennvmgarden Independent Hostel ❶** has beds and small *rorbuer* cabins for groups of four or more. (☎76 09 12 11. Reception June-Sept. 10am-10pm; call ahead at other times. Cabins 490-1080kr. Summer hostel beds 110kr. 80kr towels and sheets. AmEx/MC/V.) **Å Dagligvarer A/S** sells groceries. (☎76 09 23 06. Open M-F 9am-7pm, Sa 9am-5pm, Su 4-7pm. MC/V.) **Buses** depart from behind the tourist office for Moskenes center (15min., 2-4 per day, 26kr).

VESTVÅGØY

Northeast of Moskenesøya, the island of Vestvågøy (pop. 11,000) is home to some of the chain's most striking scenery. Flights from Bodø and most buses arrive in **Leknes,** one of the largest towns in the island chain. Local favorite **Surprise Cafe ❶,**

APOCALYPSE NOW

We're a pessimistic bunch. Humans have envisioned many ways in which our species could be wiped out. Perhaps it will be a meteorite impact, or a worldwide nuclear war. Maybe super-intelligent machines will take over and enslave us. Whatever happens, let's just hope there's an underground shelter somewhere we can hide to ride things out, playing endless games of Monopoly and subsisting on canned soup until things on the surface improve.

Protection like this may not exist, but we can at least take solace knowing that there's a cave for the seeds. In 2008, construction finished on the Svalbard Global Seed Vault, a subterranean shelter built into a mountainside near Longyearbyen. The vault holds seeds for our most important crops, protecting them in the event of catastrophe so they can be reintroduced in the post-apocalyptic world. Remote Svalbard is an ideal location for the project. The thick rock above the vault and the bitter cold permafrost will keep the seeds frozen, preserving them indefinitely. There is the concern of how people will get to Svalbard (a.k.a. the middle of nowhere) after the world ends, but that's a problem for another day.

Who knows what will happen to the world and humanity? Whatever lies ahead, at least there will be apples and bananas waiting for us somewhere off the coast of mainland Norway.

Idrettgaten 27, offers a mix of American and Scandinavian cuisine and serves beer (45kr), as well as the ubiquitous hot baguette sandwich (41kr, large 75kr), stuffed with ham and cheese. (☎76 08 15 10. Open M-F 10am-5pm, Sa 11am-4pm. MC/V.) The **tourist office,** Storgata 31 in Leknes, helps travelers understand options for transportation, accommodation, and adventure. (☎76 05 60 70. vvak@online.no. Sept-mid-May M-F 9am-3:30pm, mid-May-mid-June M-F 9am-4pm, Sa 10am-2pm, mid-June-mid-Aug. M-F 9am-7pm, Sa-Su 10am-2pm.) The sparsely populated town of **Stamsund** is a port for the Hurtigruten steamer. **Stein Tinden** (500m) and **Justad Tinden** (732m), nearby peaks, are both 6hr. round-trip hikes and provide panoramic views. In June and early July, visitors can tan into the wee hours under the midnight sun, while clear nights in late autumn or early spring may reveal the **Northern Lights.** The comfy common rooms at **Stamsund Vandrerhjem (HI)** have kindled enough friendships between travelers to earn the hostel a national reputation. (☎76 08 93 34. Showers 5kr per 5min. Linens and towel 70kr or 40kr disposable linens. Laundry 30kr. Dryer 20kr. Bike rental 100kr per day. Fishing gear 100kr deposit. Free use of rowboats. Wheelchair-accessible. Open mid-Dec. to mid-Oct. Dorms 120kr; doubles 400kr; triples 480kr; cabins 400-700kr. 20kr HI discount. Cash only.) Given the sporadic bus schedules, a **rental car** may be the way to go. Rent from an agency at **Stamsund Hotel,** Postboks 89 (☎76 08 93 00; 300-800kr per day).

SVALBARD ARCHIPELAGO ☎79

Only 1000km south of the North Pole, the Svalbard archipelago is home to a breathtaking Arctic desert. The research and mining community of Longyearbyen (pop. 1800), the world's northernmost town, lies on the island of Spitsbergen. No activity in Svalbard is totally safe. Polar bears and glaciers make any trip possibly hazardous. Visit the Governor's Office website for safety information (www.sysselmannen.svalbard.no). Tours are the safest, most practical option, but they are also expensive. For a listing of tours, visit www.svalbard.net. A boat trip to the abandoned mining town of **Pyramiden** or the Russian mining settlement of **Barentsburg** is a must-see. Book ahead. Svalbard Wildlife Service lead trips to both. (☎79 02 56 60; www.wildlife.no. 1100-1200kr.) Budget lodgings cluster in Nybyen, 25min. north of Longyearbyen center. Try **Gjestehuset 102 ❸,** part of the Svalbard Wildlife Service. (☎79 02 56 60; 102@wildlife.no. Breakfast, linens, and towels included. Dorms 300kr; singles Mar.-Sept. 595kr, Oct.-Feb. 400kr; doubles 650kr. AmEx/MC/V.) **Svalbard Butikken** stocks groceries and duty-free goods. (☎02 25 20; www.svalbardbutikken.no. Open M-F 10am-8pm, Sa 10am-6pm, Su 3-6pm. AmEx/MC/V.)

Planes arrive at Svalbard Airport (LYR; ☎02 38 00) from Oslo (3hr., 1-3 per day in summer, from 1465kr) and Tromsø (1hr., 1-3 per day in summer, from 1310kr). **Flybus** goes from the airport directly to your lodging. The **tourist office,** in the UNIS building complex shared with the museum, is 500m north of Longyearbyen center. (☎79 02 55 50; www.svalbard.net. Open daily May-Sept. 10am-5pm, Oct-Apr. noon-5pm.) Two **taxi** companies are Longyearbyen Taxi (☎79 02 30 10) and Svalbard Maxi Taxi (☎79 02 13 05). One **car rental** agency is Hertz (☎02 11 88). **Bikes** are also a popular way to navigate the city. Visit Basecamp Spitsbergen in the town center for rentals (☎79 02 46 00).

POLAND
(POLSKA)

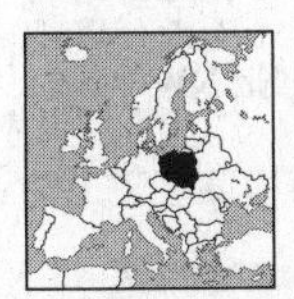

Poland is a sprawling country where history has cast a long shadow. Plains that stretch from the Tatras Mountains in the south to the Baltic Sea in the north have seen foreign invaders time and time again. Meanwhile, the contrast between Western cities like Wrocław and Eastern outposts like Bialystok is a remnant of Poland's subjection to competing empires. Ravaged during WWII, and later, viciously suppressed by the USSR, Poland is finally self-governed, and the change is marked. Today's Poland is a haven for budget travelers, where the rich cultural treasures of medieval Kraków and bustlin Warsaw are complemented by wide Baltic beaches, rugged Tatras peaks, and tranquil Mazury lakes.

DISCOVER POLAND: SUGGESTED ITINERARIES

THREE DAYS. In **Kraków** (p. 781), enjoy the stunning **Wawel Castle,** medieval **Stare Miasto,** and bohemian nightlife of the **Kazimierz area.** Daytrip to **Auschwitz-Birkenau** concentration camp (p. 787).

ONE WEEK. After three days in **Kraków,** go to **Warsaw** (2 days; p. 772), where the **Uprising Museum** and **Russian Market** shouldn't be missed; then head north to **Gdańsk** (2 days; p. 794) and soak up the sun on the beach at **Sopot** (p. 798).

BEST OF POLAND, THREE WEEKS. Begin with five days in **Kraków,** including a daytrip to **Auschwitz-Birkenau** or the **Wieliczka** salt mines. Spend two days in lovely **Wrocław** (p. 790), then enjoy the mountain air of **Zakopane** (1 day; p. 789). Head to dynamic **Warsaw** (7 days), then take a break in scenic **Toruń** (2 days; p. 791). In **Gdańsk** (4 days), don't miss the resort town of **Sopot** or **Malbork Castle.**

ESSENTIALS

FACTS AND FIGURES

OFFICIAL NAME: Republic of Poland.

CAPITAL: Warsaw.

MAJOR CITIES: Katowice, Kraków, Łódź.

POPULATION: 38,518,000.

TIME ZONE: GMT +1.

LANGUAGE: Polish.

ANNUAL PORK CONSUMPTION PER CAPITA: 83.2 lbs.

WHEN TO GO

Poland has snowy winters and warm summers, though all weather can be unpredictable. Tourist season runs from late May to early September, except in mountain areas, which also have a winter high-season (Dec.-Mar.). Though rain is a risk in the late spring and early autumn, these months are mild, so travelers may want to consider visiting in late April, September, or early October. Many attractions are closed from mid-autumn to mid-spring.

DOCUMENTS AND FORMALITIES

EMBASSIES AND CONSULATES. Foreign embassies to Poland are in Warsaw and Kraków. For Polish embassies and consulates abroad, contact: **Australia,** 7 Turrana St., Yarralumla, Canberra, ACT 2600 (☎02 62 73 12 08; www.poland.org.au); **Canada,** 443 Daly Ave., Ottawa, ON K1N 6H3 (☎613-789-0468; www.polishembassy.ca); **Ireland,** 5 Ailesbury Rd., Ballbridge, Dublin 4 (☎01 283 0855; www.dublin.polemb.net); **New Zealand,** 51 Granger Rd., Howick, Auckland 1705 (☎09 534 4670; www.polishheritage.co.nz); **UK,** 47 Portland Pl., London W1B 1JH (☎870 774 2700; www.polishembassy.org.uk); **US,** 2640 16th St. NW, Washington, D.C. 20009 (☎202-234-3800 ext. 2140; www.polandembassy.org).

ENTRANCE REQUIREMENTS.

Passport: Required for all travelers.

Visa: Not required for stays of under 90 days for citizens of Australia, Canada, New Zealand, and the US; not required for stays of under 180 days for citizens of the UK.

Letter of Invitation: Not required for most travelers.

Inoculations: Recommended up-to-date DTaP (diphtheria, tetanus, and pertussis), hepatitis A, hepatitis B, MMR, rabies, polio booster, and typhoid.

Work Permit: Required for all non-EU citizens planning to work in Poland.

International Driving Permit: Required for all non-EU citizens.

VISA AND ENTRY INFORMATION. Citizens of Australia, Canada, and the US need a visa for stays of over 90 days. EU citizens do not require a visa but will need to apply for temporary residence after 90 days. Visas for US citizens are free. Processing may take up to two weeks, but express visas can be processed within 24hr. You must be ready to present ample documentation concerning your stay, including verification of accommodation reservations, sufficient funds, and confirmation of health insurance coverage.

TOURIST SERVICES AND MONEY

TOURIST OFFICES. City-specific tourist offices are the most helpful and generally provide free info in English. Most have reliable free **maps** and sell more detailed ones. **Orbis,** the state-sponsored travel bureau, operates hotels in most cities and sells transportation tickets. **Almatur,** a student travel organization with offices in 15 major cities, offers ISICs. The state-sponsored **PTTK** and **IT** bureaus, found in nearly every city, are helpful for basic traveling needs. Try **Polish Pages,** a free guide available at hotels and tourist agencies.

POLISH ZŁOTYCH (ZŁ)	
AUS$1 = 2.29ZŁ	1ZŁ = AUS$0.44
CDN$1 = 2.77ZŁ	1ZŁ = CDN$0.36
EUR€1 = 3.96ZŁ	1ZŁ = EUR€0.25
NZ$1 = 1.94ZŁ	1ZŁ = NZ$0.52
UK£1 = 5.74ZŁ	1ZŁ = UK£0.17
US$1 = 3.09ZŁ	1ZŁ = US$0.32

MONEY. The Polish currency is the **złotych** (zł), plural is **złoty** (zwah-tee). **Inflation** is around 2%. **ATMs** *(bankomaty)* are common, and generally offer the best

rates; MasterCard and Visa are widely accepted at ATMs. Budget accommodations rarely accept **credit cards,** but some restaurants and upscale hotels do. **Tipping** varies, but generally a few additional złoty is acceptable.

HEALTH AND SAFETY

EMERGENCY	**Ambulance:** ☎999. **Fire:** ☎150. **Police:** ☎158. **General Emergency Number:** ☎112.

Medical clinics in major cities have private, **English-speaking doctors.** Expect to pay at least 50zł per visit. **Pharmacies** are well-stocked, and some stay open 24hr. Tap water is theoretically drinkable, but bottled mineral water will spare you from some unpleasant metals and chemicals. **Crime** rates are low, but tourists are sometimes targeted. Watch for muggers and pickpockets, especially on trains and in lower-priced hostels. Cab drivers may attempt to cheat those who do not speak Polish, and "friendly locals" looking to assist tourists are sometimes setting them up for scams. **Women** traveling alone should take the usual precautions. Those with darker skin may encounter discrimination due to long-standing prejudice against **Roma** (gypsies). There may be lingering prejudice against **Jews,**

ON THE BORDER

f you're traveling in Eastern Europe, chances are you're hitting nore than one country. Of course, rains and buses are plentiful and connect all of the major cities, but ravelers usually pay hefty prices or international tickets. Even if the distance between two cities isn't hat great, traveling across a border may mean a lot of extra fees and taxes. An increasing number of travelers on a budget are taking advantage of a lesser-known option: walking across borders.

Domestic train and bus lines n Eastern European countries are generally quite cheap and extensive. To save money on a dwindling budget, it is possible to ake a train or bus from your starting point to a city on the border of he country you're hoping to travel nto. The small German town of Zittau, for example, is a popular and convenient place to cross over into another country, as it is nestled on he site where the German, Polish, and Czech borders meet. After walking across, travelers can hop on a second domestic train within he new country and get to their inal destination. This may take slightly longer than a direct train, but walking can cut the cost of nternational travel in half.

Check domestic timetables and ares on-line. For travel in Poland, visit www.pkp.pl for an up-to-date schedule. www.vlak.cz has extensive timetables for travel within he Czech Republic and Slovakia.

despite governmental efforts; casual anti-Semitic remarks are often heard. Like many Eastern European nations, Poland is not widely **wheelchair-accessible** but special-interest groups, newly armed with EU funds, are working to change that. Warsaw in particular, with its many steep, winding steps, is difficult to access. **Homosexuality** is not widely accepted; discretion is advised. GLBT travelers might find www.gaypoland.pl a useful resource.

TRANSPORTATION

BY PLANE. Warsaw's modern **Okęcie Airport** (**WAW;** ☎22 650 4220; www.lotnisko-chopina.pl) is the hub for intl. flights. **LOT** (☎080 170 3703; www.lot.com), the national airline, flies to major cities in Poland.

BY TRAIN AND BUS. Trains are preferable to buses, since buses are slow and uncomfortable. For a timetable, see www.pkp.pl. *Odjazdy* (departures) are in yellow, *przyjazdy* (arrivals) in white. InterCity and *ekspresowy* (express) trains are listed in red with an "IC" or "Ex" in front of the train number. *Pośpieszny* (direct; in red) are almost as fast and a bit cheaper. Low-priced *osobowy* (in black) are the slowest and have no restrooms. If you see a boxed "R" on the schedule, ask the clerk for a *miejscówka* (reservation). Students and seniors should buy *ulgowy* (half-price) tickets instead of normal tickets. Beware: foreign travelers are not eligible for discounts on domestic buses and trains. **Eurail** is not valid in Poland. Look for **Wasteels** tickets and **Eurotrain** passes, sold at **Almatur** and **Orbis** for discounts. Stations are not announced and are often poorly marked. In the countryside, PKS markers (yellow steering wheels that look like upside-down Mercedes-Benz symbols) indicate stops. Buses have no luggage compartments. **Polski Express** (☎022 854 02 85; www.polskiexpress.pl), a private company, offers more luxurious service, but does not run to all cities.

Theft frequently occurs on overnight trains; avoid night trains, especially Kraków-Warsaw and Prague-Kraków.

BY CAR AND TAXI. **Rental cars** are readily available in Warsaw and Kraków. Road conditions are poor and drivers can be aggressive and reckless. For **taxis,** either arrange the price before getting in (in Polish, if possible) or be sure the driver turns on the meter. Arrange cabs by phone, if possible.

BY BIKE AND BY THUMB. Roads in Poland can be difficult for **bikes** to navigate. For more information on cycling, see www.rowery.org.pl. Though legal,

hitchhiking is rare and dangerous for foreigners. Hand-waving is the accepted sign. *Let's Go* does not recommend hitchhiking.

KEEPING IN TOUCH

PHONE CODES	**Country code:** 48. **International dialing prefix:** 00. For more information on how to place international calls, see **Inside Back Cover.**

EMAIL AND INTERNET. Internet access is available for about 5-15zł per hr.

TELEPHONE. You can purchase a long distance phone card at many places, including grocery stores. To operate the phone, start dialing the numbers you're given or insert the magnetic card. International access numbers include: **AT&T Direct** (☎00 800 111 111); **Canada Direct** (☎0 800 111 4118); **MCI** (☎00 800 111 2122); **Sprint** (☎00 800 11 3115).

MAIL. Mail in Poland is admirably efficient. Airmail *(lotnicza)* takes two to five days to Western Europe and seven to 10 days to Australia, New Zealand, and the US. Mail can be received via **Poste Restante.** Address mail as follows: First name, LAST NAME, POSTE RESTANTE, post office address, Postal Code, city, POLAND. Letters cost about 2.40zł. To pick up mail, show a passport.

LANGUAGE. Polish is a West Slavic language written in the Latin alphabet, and is closely related to **Czech** and **Slovak.** The language varies little across Poland. The two exceptions are in the region of **Kaszuby,** where the distinctive Germanized dialect is sometimes classified as a separate language, and in **Karpaty,** known for highlander accents. In western Poland and Mazury, **German** is the most common foreign language, although many Poles in big cities, especially young people, speak **English.** One more thing: the English word "no" means "yes" in Polish. For basic Polish words and phrases, see **Phrasebook: Polish,** p. 1066.

ACCOMMODATIONS AND CAMPING

POLAND	❶	❷	❸	❹	❺
ACCOMMODATIONS	under 45zł	45-65zł	66-80zł	81-120zł	over 120zł

Hostels *(schroniska młodzieżowe)* abound and cost 30-60zł per night. They are often booked solid by tour groups; call at least a week ahead. **PTSM** is the national hostel organization. **University dorms** become budget housing in July and August; these are an especially good option in Kraków. The **Almatur** office in Warsaw arranges stays throughout Poland. PTTK runs hotels called **Dom Turysty,** which have multi-bed rooms and budget singles and doubles. These hotels generally cost 80-180zł. **Pensions** are often the best deal: the owner's service more than makes up for the small sacrifice in privacy. **Private rooms** *(wolne pokoje)* are available most places, but be careful what you agree to; they should only cost 20-60zł. **Homestays** can be a great way to meet locals; inquire at the tourist office. **Campsites** average 10-15zł per person or 20zł with a car. Campgrounds may also rent out **bungalows;** a bed costs 20-30zł. *Polska Mapa Campingów,* available at tourist offices, lists campsites. Almatur runs a number of sites in summer; ask them for a list. Camping outside of official campsites is illegal.

FOOD AND DRINK

POLAND	❶	❷	❸	❹	❺
FOOD	under 8zł	8-17zł	18-30zł	31-45zł	over 45zł

Polish cuisine derives from French, Italian, and Slavic traditions. Meals begin with **soup,** usually *barszcz* (beet or rye), *chłodnik* (cold beets with buttermilk and eggs), *ogórkowa* (sour cucumbers), or *kapuśniak* (cabbage). Main courses include *gołąbki* (cabbage rolls with meat and rice), *kotlet schabowy* (pork cutlets), *naleśniki* (crepes), and *pierogi* (dumplings). **Kosher** eating is next to impossible, as most Jewish restaurants are not actually kosher. Poland offers a wealth of **beer, vodka,** and **spiced liquor. Żywiec** is the most popular beer. Even those who dislike beer will enjoy sweet **piwo z sokiem,** beer with raspberry syrup. *Wyborowa*, *Żytnia*, and *Polonez* are popular *wódka* (vodka) brands, while *Belweder* (Belvedere) is a major alcoholic export. *Żubrówka* vodka, also known as "Bison grass vodka," comes packaged with a blade of grass from the Bialowieża forest. It's often mixed with *z sokem jabłkowym* (apple juice). *Miód* (beer made with honey) and *krupnik* (mead) are old-fashioned favorites; as is *nalewka na porzeczce* (black currant vodka).

HOLIDAYS AND FESTIVALS

Holidays: Easter (Apr. 13, 2009; Apr. 4, 2010); May Day (May 1); Constitution Day (May 3); Pentecost (May 31, 2009; May 23, 2010); Corpus Christi (June 11, 2009; May 23, 2010); Assumption Day (Aug. 15); All Saints' Day (Nov. 1); Independence Day (Nov. 11); Christmas (Dec. 25).

Festivals: Unsurprisingly, many of the festivals revolve around Catholic holidays. Uniquely Polish festivals include all-night bonfire merrymaking before **St. John's Day** in June, also known as midsummer, as well as an annual August **folk festival** in Kraków.

BEYOND TOURISM

Auschwitz Jewish Center, Auschwitz Jewish Center Foundation, 36 Battery Pl., New York, NY 10280, USA (☎646-437-4276; www.ajcf.org). Offers fully paid 6-week programs for college graduates and graduate students in Oswiecim. Program focuses on cultural exchange and the study of pre-war Jewish life in Poland, with visits to the Auschwitz-Birkenau State Museum and other sites.

Jagiellonian University, Centre for European Studies, ul. Garbarska 7a, 31-131 Kraków, Poland (☎481 24 29 62 07; www.ces.uj.edu.pl). University founded in 1364 offers undergraduates summer- and semester-long programs in Central European studies and Polish language. One semester of tuition is US$3800. Scholarships available.

WARSAW (WARSZAWA) ☎022

Massive rebuilding is nothing new for Warsaw (pop. 1,700,000). At the end of World War II, two-thirds of its population had been killed and 83% of the city was destroyed by the Nazis as revenge for the 1944 Warsaw Uprising. Having weathered the further blow of a half-century of communist rule, Warsaw has sprung back to life as a dynamic center of business, politics, and culture—evidenced by the gleaming new skyscrapers popping up next to crumbling concrete. With Poland's recent accession into the European Union, the city is transforming its culture and landscape at an even faster pace. Now is the time to visit this compelling and underrated city.

TRANSPORTATION

Flights: Port Lotniczy Warszawa-Okęcie ("Terminal 1"), Żwirki i Wigury (info desk ☎022 650 4100, reservations ☎0 801 300 952). Take bus #175 to the city center (after 10:40pm, bus #611); buy tickets at the Ruch kiosk at the top of the escalator in the arrivals hall. (Open M-F 5:30am-10:30pm.) If you arrive past 10:30pm, buy tickets from the bus driver for a 3zł surcharge (students 1.50zł). The IT *(Informacja Turystyczna)* office is in the arrivals hall (see **Tourist Offices,** p. 775). Open M-F 8am-8pm.

Trains: Warszawa Centralna, al. Jerozolimskie 54 (☎022 94 36; www.intercity.pkp.pl), is the most convenient of Warsaw's 3 major train stations. Most trains also stop at **Warszawa Zachodnia (Western Station),** Towarowa 1, and **Warszawa Wschodnia (Eastern Station),** Lubelska 1, in Praga. Yellow signs list departures *(odjazdy);* white signs list arrivals *(przyjazdy).* English is rarely understood; write down when and where you want to go, then ask *"Który peron?"* ("Which platform?"). Prices listed are for IC (intercity) trains and normale (2nd class) fares. To: **Gdańsk** (4hr., 20 per day, 47-90zł); **Kraków** (3-5hr., 30 per day, 47-89zł); **Lódz** (1-2hr., 13 per day, 31zł); **Lublin** (2-3hr., 17 per day, 35zł); **Poznań** (2-3hr., 20 per day, 46-89zł); **Wrocław** (4-6hr., 12 per day, 50-96zł); **Berlin, GER** (6hr., 6 per day, €29-45); **Budapest, HUN** (10-13hr., 1 per day, 280zł); **Prague, CZR** (9-12hr., 2 per day, 270-310zł).

Buses: Both **Polski Express** and **PKS** buses run out of Warsaw.

Polski Express, al. Jana Pawła II (☎022 854 0285), in a kiosk next to Warszawa Centralna. Faster than PKS. Kiosk open daily 6:30am-10pm. To: **Gdansk** (6hr., 2 per day, 60zł); **Kraków** (8hr., 2 per day, 69zł); **Lódz** (2hr., 7 per day, 25zł); **Lublin** (3hr., 7 per day, 41zł).

PKS Warszawa Zachodnia, al. Jerozolimskie 144 (☎022 822 4811, domestic info ☎03 00 30 01 30, from cell phones ☎720 8383; www.pks.warszawa.pl), connected by tunnels to the Warszawa Zachodnia train station. Cross to far side al. Jerozolimskie and take bus #127, 130, 508, or E5 to the center. To: **Gdansk** (5-7hr., 18 per day, 35-51zł); **Kraków** (5-7hr., 8 per day, 40zł); **Lublin** (3hr., 9 per day, 22-30zł); **Torun** (4hr., 12 per day, 32zł); **Wrocław** (6-8hr., 4 per day, 43zł); **Kyiv, UKR** (14hr., 1 per day, 155zł); **Vilnius, LIT** (9hr., 3 per day, 115zł).

Centrum Podróży AURA, Jerozolimskie 144 (☎022 659 4785; www.aura.pl), at the Zachodnia station, left of the entrance. Books international buses to: **Amsterdam, NTH** (23hr., 2 per day, 209-279zł); **Geneva, SWI** (27hr., 2 per day, 269-320zł); **London, GBR** (27hr., 3 per day, 280-450zł); **Paris, FRA** (25hr., 1-3 per day, 220-334zł); **Prague, CZR** (28hr.; 3 per week; 115-145zł); **Rome, ITA** (28hr., 1 per day, 249-418zł).

Public Transportation: (info line ☎022 94 84; www.ztm.waw.pl). Warsaw's public transit is excellent. Daytime **trams** and **buses** 2.40zł, with ISIC 1.25zł; day pass 7.20/3.70zł; weekly pass 26/12zł. Punch the ticket in the yellow machines on board or face a 120zł fine. If you find that you're the only one validating your ticket, remember that many locals carry 90-day passes. Bus, tram, and subway lines share the same tickets, passes, and prices. There are also 2 **sightseeing bus routes:** #180 (M-F) and #100 (Sa-Su). Purchase an all-day ticket and you can hop on and off the bus. Night buses cost double, have "N" prefixes, and run 11:30pm-5:30am. If you need to use one, ask at a tourist bureau or accommodation to explain the system for ordering them; without an order, they won't stop. Warsaw's **Metro** is not particularly convenient for tourists.

Taxis: The government sets cab fare at 2zł per km; with privately run cabs, stated prices may be lower but the risk of overcharging is greater. State-run: **ME.RC. Taxi** (☎022 677 7777), **Wawa Taxi** (☎96 44). Privately run: **Euro Taxi** (☎96 62), **Halo Taxi** (☎96 23).

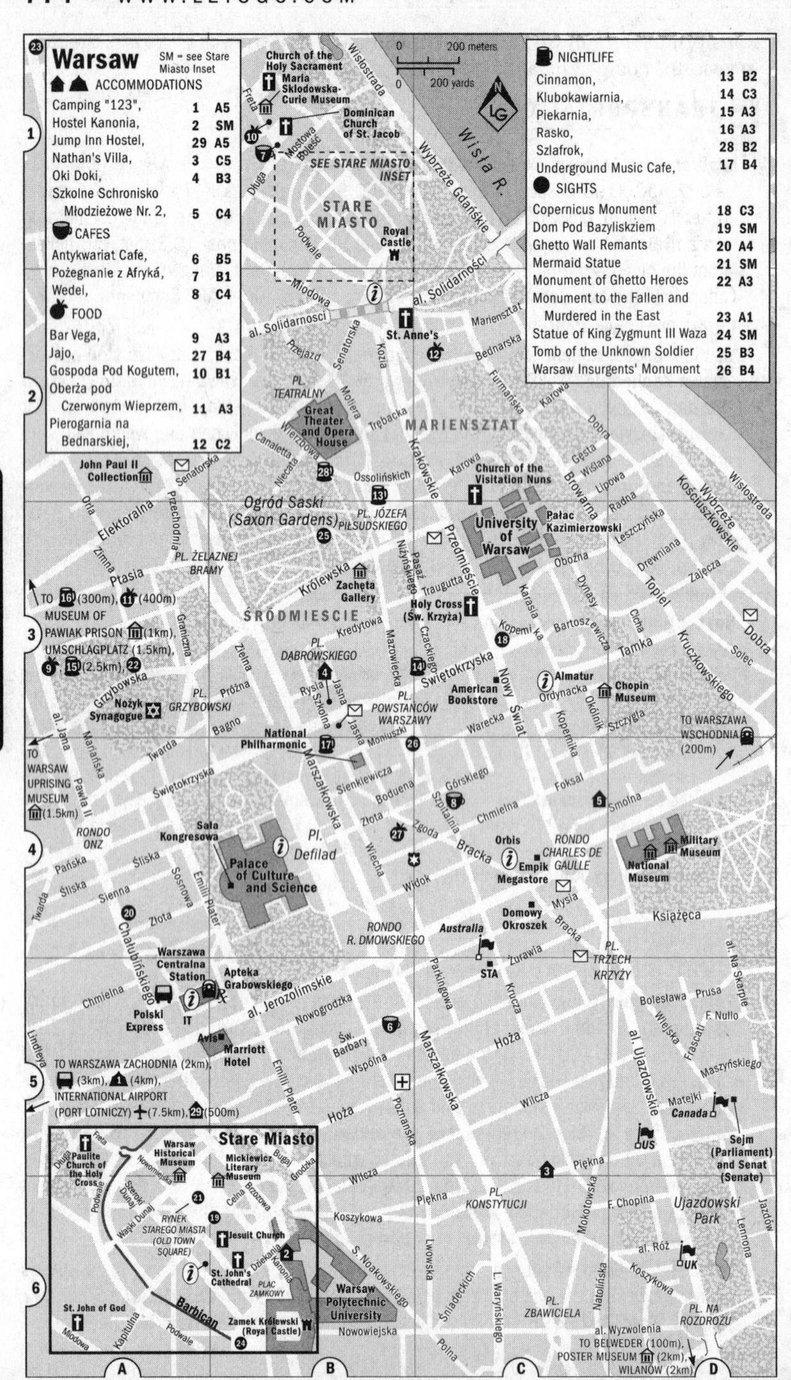
Warsaw
SM = see Stare Miasto Inset
ACCOMMODATIONS
Camping "123", 1 A5
Hostel Kanonia, 2 SM
Jump Inn Hostel, 29 A5
Nathan's Villa, 3 C5
Oki Doki, 4 B3
Szkolne Schronisko Młodzieżowe Nr. 2, 5 C4
CAFES
Antykwariat Cafe, 6 B5
Pożegnanie z Afryká, 7 B1
Wedel, 8 C4
FOOD
Bar Vega, 9 A3
Jajo, 27 B4
Gospoda Pod Kogutem, 10 B1
Oberża pod Czerwonym Wieprzem, 11 A3
Pierogarnia na Bednarskiej, 12 C2
NIGHTLIFE
Cinnamon, 13 B2
Klubokawiarnia, 14 C3
Piekarnia, 15 A3
Rasko, 16 A3
Szlafrok, 28 B2
Underground Music Cafe, 17 B4
SIGHTS
Copernicus Monument 18 C3
Dom Pod Bazyliskziem 19 SM
Ghetto Wall Remants 20 A4
Mermaid Statue 21 SM
Monument of Ghetto Heroes 22 A3
Monument to the Fallen and Murdered in the East 23 A1
Statue of King Zygmunt III Waza 24 SM
Tomb of the Unknown Soldier 25 B3
Warsaw Insurgents' Monument 26 B4
0 200 meters
0 200 yards
Wisła R.
SEE STARE MIASTO INSET
STARE MIASTO
Royal Castle
Church of the Holy Sacrament
Maria Sklodowska-Curie Museum
Dominican Church of St. Jacob
St. Anne's
Great Theater and Opera House
MARIENSZTAT
John Paul II Collection
Ogród Saski (Saxon Gardens)
Church of the Visitation Nuns
University of Warsaw
Pałac Kazimierzowski
Zachęta Gallery
Holy Cross (Św. Krzyża)
ŚRÓDMIEŚCIE
TO 16 (300m), 11 (400m) MUSEUM OF PAWIAK PRISON (1km), UMSCHLAGPLATZ (1.5km), 9, 15 (2.5km), 22
Nożyk Synagogue
American Bookstore
Almatur
Chopin Museum
TO WARSZAWA WSCHODNIA (200m)
TO WARSAW UPRISING MUSEUM (1.5km)
National Philharmonic
Sala Kongresowa
Palace of Culture and Science
Pl. Defilad
Orbis
Empik Megastore
RONDO CHARLES DE GAULLE
Military Museum
National Museum
Domowy Okroszek
Australia
STA
Warszawa Centralna Station
Apteka Grabowskiego
Polski Express
IT
Avis
Marriott Hotel
TO WARSZAWA ZACHODNIA (2km), (3km), (4km), INTERNATIONAL AIRPORT (PORT LOTNICZY) (7.5km), 29 (500m)
Canada
Sejm (Parliament) and Senat (Senate)
US
Ujazdowski Park
UK
TO BELWEDER (100m), POSTER MUSEUM (2km), WILANÓW (2km)
Stare Miasto
Paulite Church of the Holy Cross
Warsaw Historical Museum
Mickiewicz Literary Museum
RYNEK STAREGO MIASTA (OLD TOWN SQUARE)
Jesuit Church
St. John's Cathedral
PLAC ZAMKOWY
Warsaw Polytechnic University
St. John of God
Barbican
Zamek Królewski (Royal Castle)
A B C D
1 2 3 4 5 6

POLAND

ORIENTATION

The most prominent section of Warsaw lies west of the **Wisla River**. The city's grid layout and efficient public transportation make it very accessible. **Aleje Jerozolimskie** is the main east-west thoroughfare. **Warszawa Centralna,** the main train station, is at the intersection of al. Jerozolimskie and **al. Jana Pawla II,** the north-south street one block west of Marsza kowska. The northern boundary of pl. Defilad is **Świętokrzyska,** another east-west thoroughfare. Intersecting al. Jerozolimskie one city block east of Marsza kowska and the city center, the **Trakt Królewski (Royal Way)** takes different names as it runs north-south. This elegant promenade begins as **Nowy Swiat** in the city center and then turns into **Krakowskie Przedmiescie** as it leads into Stare Miasto (Old Town; just north of al. Solidarnosci overlooking the Wisla). Going south, the road becomes **al. Ujazdowskie** as it runs past embassy row, palaces, and Łazienki Park, all to the south the city center. **Praga,** the part of the city on the east bank of the Wisla, is accessible by tram via **al. Jerozolimskie** and **al. Solidarnosci.** In Praga, the two most trafficked north-south thoroughfares are **Targowa,** near the zoo, and **Francuska,** south of al. Jerozolimskie.

PRACTICAL INFORMATION

Tourist Offices: Informacji Turystyczna (IT), al. Jerozolimskie 54 (☎94 31; www.warsawtour.pl), inside Centralna train station. Provides **maps** and arranges accommodations (no fee). Their free booklets list popular restaurants and special events. Open daily May-Sept. 8am-8pm; Oct.-Apr. 8am-6pm. **Branches:** Krakowskie Przedmieście 39. Open daily, same hours. In the airport, open daily, same hours. Pl. Zamkowy 1/13 (outside the Stare Miasto). Open M-F 9am-6pm, Sa 10am-6pm, Su 11am-6pm.

Budget Travel: Almatur, Kopernika 23 (☎022 826 3512). ISIC 69zł. Open M-F 9am-7pm, Sa 10am-3pm. AmEx/MC/V. **Orbis,** Bracka 16 (☎022 827 7140), entrance on al. Jerozolimskie. Open M-F 9am-6pm, Sa 10am-6pm. MC/V.

Embassies: Most are near al. Ujazdowskie. **Australia,** Nowogrodzka 11 (☎022 521 3444; ambasada@australia.pl). Open M-F 9am-1pm and 2-5pm. **Canada,** ul. Jana Matejiki 1/5 (☎022 584 3100; wsaw@international.gc.ca). Open M-F 8:30am-4:30pm. **Ireland,** Mysia 5 (☎022 849 6633; ambasada@irlandial.pl). Open M-F 9am-1pm. **UK,** al. Róz (☎022 311 0000). Open M-F 8:30am-4:30pm. **US,** ul. Piękna 12 (☎022 625 1401 or ☎022 504 2784). Open M, W, F 9am-noon, Tu, Th 9am-3pm.

Currency Exchange: Except at tourist sights, *kantory* (exchange booths) have the best rates. 24hr. at Warszawa Centralna or at al. Jerozolimskie 61.

Luggage Storage (Kasa Bagażowa): At Warszawa Centralna train station. 7zł per item per day, plus 3zł per 50zł of declared value if you want insurance. To sidestep the language barrier and to retain more control over your bag, choose a locker (8zł). Open 24hr.

GLBT Resources: Lambda, (☎022 628 5222; www.lambda.org.pl), in English and Polish. Open Tu-W 6-9pm, F 4-10pm. Info at the English-language site http://warsaw.gayguide.net. The GLBT scene in Warsaw is discreet and lacks widespread political support.

24hr. Pharmacy: Apteka Grabowskiego "21" (☎022 825 6986), upstairs at the Warszawa Centralna train station. AmEx/MC/V.

Medical Services: Centrum Medyczyne LIM, al. Jerozolimskie 65/79, 9th fl. (24hr. **emergency line** ☎022 458 7000, 24hr. **ambulance** ☎430 3030; www.cm-lim.com.pl), at the Marriott. There are English-speaking doctors available. Open M-F 7am-9pm, Sa 8am-4pm, Su 9am-6pm, holidays 9am-1pm. Find another branch at **Domaniewski 41** (☎022 458 7000). Open M-F 7am-9pm, Sa 8am-8pm. **Central Emergency Station,** Hoża 56 (☎999) has a 24hr. ambulance on call.

Telephones: Directory assistance ☎022 118 913.

Post Office: Main branch, Świętokrzyska 31/33 (☎022 827 0052). Take a number at the entrance. For stamps and letters push "D"; for packages, "F." For **Poste Restante,** inquire at window #42. Open 24hr. *Kantor* open daily 8am-10pm. Most other branches open 8am-8pm. **Postal Code:** 00001.

ACCOMMODATIONS

Although accommodation options are rapidly improving, demand still outpaces supply, so reserve ahead, especially in summer. **Informacji Turystyczna** (IT; p. 775) maintains a list of accommodations in the city, including **private rooms,** and also arranges stays in **university dorms** (25-30zł) July through September.

Oki Doki, pl. Dabrowskiego 3 (☎022 826 5112; www.okidoki.pl). From Marszałkowska, turn right onto ul. Rysia, the hostel will be on your right.. Each room of this chic hostel was designed by a different Warsaw artist and has a unique theme. Beer (6zł) and breakfast (10zł) in the dining room/bar (open until 1am or later). Laundry 10zł. Free Internet and Wi-Fi. Bike rental 25zł per day, 6zł per hr. 24hr. reception. Check-in 3pm. Check-out 11am. Reserve ahead. May-Aug. dorms 45-60zł; singles 110zł; doubles 135zł, with baths 185zł. Sept.-Apr. prices tend to decrease by around 5zł. MC/V. ❷

Jump Inn Hostel, Prokuratorska 2 (☎022 825 1167; www.jumpinnhostel.com) From pl. Defilad, head south on Marszałkowska for 10 minutes, take a right on Wawelska, then a right on Prokuratorska—the hostel is on your right. Located in a peaceful residential area, Jump Inn provides a home away from home with its warm, spacious rooms and extensive amenities, including free Internet, laundry, and kitchen access. Hostel guests give particular props to the free afternoon soup. Breakfast and linens included. Reception 24hr. Dorms 40-65zł, singles 100-150zł. MC/V. ❷

POLAND

Nathan's Villa, Piękna 24/26 (☎050 935 8487; www.nathansvilla.com). From pl. Defilad, take any tram south on Marszałkowska to pl. Konstytucji. Go left on Piękna; the hostel is on the left. Nathan's matches a fun-loving, intimate atmosphere with unparalleled facilities and services. Though guests have been known to pass out on the lawn of this relentlessly hard-partying hostel, the rooms gleam with bright colors and brand-new furniture. Breakfast included. Free laundry. Free Internet and Wi-Fi. Reception 24hr. Dorms 40-60zł; private rooms 120-140zł. MC/V. ❷

Hostel Kanonia, ul. Jezuicka 2 (☎022 635 0676; www.kanonia.pl). Tucked into an alley right in the thick of Stare Miasto, this hostel's romantic decor and riverfront views soften the spartan rooms. Kitchen and common area. Breakfast 20zł. Free Internet and Wi-Fi. Check-in 2pm. Check-out 10am. Dorms 40-60zł; doubles 150zł. ISIC discount. ❷

Szkolne Schronisko Młodzieżowe nr. 2, Smolna 30 (☎022 827 8952), 2 blocks up Smolna from Nowy Swiat, on the left. From Centralna Station, take any tram east on al. Jerozolimskie and get off at Rondo Charles de Gaulle. The well-kept rooms of this sunny hostel exude respectability, and the central location can't be beat. Large kitchen. A/C. Free lockers and linen. Reception 24hr., but front doors locked midnight-6am. Lockout 10am-4pm. Curfew midnight. Dorms 36zł; singles 65zł. Cash only. ❶

Camping "123," Bitwy Warszawskiej 15/17 (☎022 823 3748). From Warszawa Centralna, take bus #127, 130, 508, or 517 to Zachodnia bus station. Cross to the far side of al. Jerozolimskie and take the pedestrian path west to Bitwy Warszawskiej; turn left. The campground is on the right. This tranquil campground is close to the center. Guarded 24hr. Open May-Sept. 12zł per person, 14zł per tent, 55.-65zł for campsites with electricity (labeled "stream," a literal translation of the Polish word for electricity). Singles 45zł; doubles 70zł; triples 100zł; quads 120zł. AmEx/MC/V. ❶

FOOD

At roadside stands, the food of choice is the *kebab turecki*, a pita with spicy meat, cabbage, and pickles (5-10zł). The **Kebab Bar,** ul. Nowy Świat 31, is a stand that serves up an excellent version. **MarcPol,** on ul. Marszałkowska, is a conveniently located grocery store (M-Sa 10am-7pm, Su 10am-5pm).

RESTAURANTS

Gospoda Pod Kogutem, Freta 48 (☎022 635 8282; www.gospodapodkogutem.pl). A rare find in touristy Stare Miasto: generous portions of delectable local food. The place to try something shamelessly traditional, like Polish-style *golonka* (pig's knuckle; 21zł) or *smalec*, surprisingly tasty fried bits of lard. Entrees 17-45zł. Open M noon-midnight, Tu-Su 11am-midnight. MC/V. ❷

Oberża pod Czerwonym Wieprzem, Żelazna 68 (☎022 850 3144; www.czerwonywieprz.pl). Donning a beret and a military-style mini-dress, an ironically cheerful hostess welcomes diners to this playful exploitation of Poland's communist past. The satire continues with a menu offering separate, cheaper dishes "for the proletariat" and more expensive selections "for dignitaries and the bourgeoisie." Entrees 11-24zł for the proletariat, 26-55zł for dignitaries and the bourgeoisie. Daily 11am-midnight. MC/V/AmEx. ❸

Jajo, ul. Zgoda 3 (☎022 826 4493). In the heart of Warsaw's commercial district, this Italian bistro combines an array of entrees (18-32zł) in a refreshingly sophisticated setting. The 3-course lunch menu, including a starter, entree, and a glass of wine, is a steal at just 20zł. Open M-Sa 10am-midnight, Su noon-9pm. AmEx/MC/V. ❷

Pierogarnia na Bednarskiej, ul. Bednarka 28/30 (☎022 828 0392), on a side street west of ul. Krakówscie Przedmiescie. Locals get their pierogi fix at this tiny, pleasant, and tavernesque shop; you don't even have to wait—they keep new pierogi boiling constantly. 3 pierogi 6zl. Open daily 11am-9pm. Cash only. ❶

Bar Vega, al. Jana Pawła II 36c (☎022 652 2754), near the former Ghetto. Secluded from the bustle of al. Jana Pawła II street vendors, the colorful Bar Vega serves a full vegetarian Indian meal for about the price of a coffee on Nowy Świat (small or big plate; 8 or 12zł, respectively). Bar Vega also funds a nonprofit to feed Warsaw's homeless children. Open M-F 11am-8pm, Sa-Su noon-7pm. Cash only. ❶

CAFES

Pożegnanie z Afryką (Out of Africa), Freta 4/6. (☎501 383 094). This Polish chain of cafes brews consistently incredible coffee (9-15zł). Perfect for artsy romancing. In warm weather, enjoy the Stare Miasto sidewalk seating and the iced coffee (9zł). Branches throughout the city. Open daily 8am-10pm. Cash only.

Antykwariat Cafe, Żurawia 45 (☎022 629 9929). Extending far into the courtyard beyond, Antykwariat ("Antiquarian") provides a coffee shop for all tastes. Each of its 4 rooms presents a different theme, from the "library room" with its shelves of rare books to the Japanese-inspired nook in the back. Delicate cups of coffee (5-17zł) and many varieties of tea (5zł) served with a wrapped chocolate. Also serves beer, wine, and desserts. Open M-Sa 4pm-11pm. Cash only.

Wedel, Szpitalna 17 (☎022 827 2916). The Emil Wedel house, built in 1893 for the Polish chocolate tycoon, was one of the few buildings in Warsaw to survive WWII. Its 1st fl. now houses an elegant dessert cafe. The glass chandeliers and dark marble columns of this chocolate-themed cafe offer a rare glimpse of pre-war Warsaw. Enjoy the suspicion that you've traveled back in time, along with a cup of miraculously rich hot chocolate (11zł) served alongside Wedel's selection of delectable cakes and ice cream concoctions. The adjacent **Wedel Chocolate** company store serves an array of brightly-wrapped truffles and chocolates. Open M-Sa 8am-10pm, Su 11am-8pm. AmEx/MC/V.

SIGHTS

To sightsee, trying using the bus. The bus routes #100 and 180 are convenient; they begin at pl. Zamkowy and run along pl. Teatralny, Marszalkowska, al. Ujazdowskie, and Lazienki Park. The routes then run back up the Royal Way, and go through Praga before returning to pl. Zamkowy.

STARE AND NOWE MIASTO. Warsaw's postwar reconstruction shows its finest face in Stare Miasto (Old Town), which features cobblestoned streets and colorful facades. *(Take bus #175 or E3 from the city center to Miodowa.)* The landmark **Statue of King Zygmunt III Waza,** constructed in 1644 to honor the king who moved the capital from Kraków to Warsaw, towers over the entrance. To its right stands the impressive **Royal Castle** *(Zamek Królewski)*, the royal residence from the 16th to 19th century. When the Nazis plundered and burned the castle in 1939, many Varsovians risked their lives hiding its priceless works. Today, the **Royal Castle Museum** houses these rescued treasures. It also has artifacts, paintings, and the stunning Royal Apartments. The massive spherical ballroom and the river-front courtyard are particularly beautiful. *(Pl. Zamkowy 4. ☎022 355 5170; www.zamek-krolewski.art.pl. Tickets and guides inside the courtyard. Open M and Su 11am-6pm, Tu-Sa 10am-6pm. 20zl, students 13zl. Free highlights tour Su 11am-6pm. English-language tour M-Sa, 85zl per group. AmEx/MC/V.)* Across Świętojańska sits Warsaw's oldest church, **St. John's Cathedral** *(Katedra św. Jana)*, which was destroyed in the 1944 Uprising but rebuilt after the war. *(Open daily 10am-1pm and 3-5:30pm. Crypts 1zl.)*

Świętojańska leads to the restored Renaissance and Baroque **Rynek Starego Miasta** (Old Town Square); the statue of the **Warsaw Mermaid** *(Warszawa Syrenka)* marks the center. According to legend, a greedy merchant kidnapped the mermaid from the Wisła River, but local fishermen valiantly rescued her. In return, she swore to defend the city, protecting it with a shield and raised sword. Ul. Krzywe Koło runs from the northeast corner of the Rynek to the restored **Barbican** (barbakan), a rare example of 16th-century Polish fortification. It's also popular spot to relax. The Barbican opens onto Freta, the edge of **Nowe Miasto** (New Town). Nobel Prize-winning physicist and chemist **Marie Curie** was born at Freta 16 in 1867. The house is now a museum. *(☎022 831 8092. Open Tu-Sa 10am-4pm, Su 10am-3pm. 6zl, students 3zl.)*

TRAKT KRÓLEWSKI. The Trakt Królewski (Royal Way) begins at the entrance to Stare Miasto on pl. Zamkowy and stretches 4km south toward Kraków, the former capital. On the left after pl. Zamkowy, the 15th-century **St. Anne's Church** *(Kościół św. Anny)* features a striking interior with its onyx statues, gilded chandeliers, and towering paintings. *(Open daily dawn-dusk.)* **Frederick Chopin** grew up near Krakówskie Przedmieście and gave his first public concert in **Pałac Radziwiłłów,** now the Polish presidential mansion guarded by four stone lions and the military police. A block down the road, set back from the street behind a grove of trees, the **Church of the Visitation Nuns** (Kościół Wizytówek) once rang with Chopin's Romantic chords. *(Open daily dawn-1pm and 3pm-dusk.)* Though the composer died abroad, his heart belongs to Poland; it now rests in an urn in **Holy Cross Church.** *(Kosciól sw. Krzyża. Krakówskie Przedmiescie 3. Open daily dawn-dusk.)*

The Royal Way continues down fashionable **Nowy Świat.** Turn left at Rondo Charles de Gaulle to reach Poland's largest museum, the **National Museum** (Muzeum Narodowe), which holds 16th- to 20th-century paintings in addition to a large collection of ancient and medieval artifacts. *(Al. Jerozolimskie 3. ☎022 022 629 3093, English-language tours 022 629 5060; www.mnw.art.pl. Open Tu-Su 10am-5pm.*

POLAND

Permanent exhibits 12zł, students 7zł. Special exhibits 17/10zł. English-language tours 50zł; call 1 week ahead. AmEx/MC/V.) Farther down, the Royal Way becomes al. Ujazdowskie and runs alongside **Łazienki Park** (Palac Łazienkowski), which houses the striking Neoclassical **Palace on Water** (Pałac na Wodzie). Buildings in the park feature rotating art exhibits. *(Bus #116, 180, or 195 from Nowy Świat or #119 from pl. Defilad to Bagatela. Park open daily dawn-dusk. Palace open Tu-Su 9am-4pm. 12zł, students 9zł.)* Just north of the park, off ul. Agrykola, the **Center of Contemporary Art** (Centrum Sztuki Wspólczesnej), al. Ujazdowskie 6, hosts multimedia exhibitions in the reconstructed 17th-century Ujazdowskie Castle. *(☎022 62 81 27 13; www.csw.art.pl. Open Tu-Th and Sa-Su 11am-7pm, F 11am-9pm. 12zł, students 6zł. Cash only.)*

FORMER GHETTO AND SYNAGOGUE. Walled **Muranów,** Warsaw's former ghetto, holds few traces of the nearly 400,000 Jews who made up one-third of the city's pre-war population. Built in the 1830s, the **Museum of Pawiak Prison** (Muzeum Więzienia Pawiaka) exhibits former inmates' photography and poetry. Over 100,000 Polish Jews were imprisoned here from 1939 to 1944. A dead tree outside bears the names of over 30,000 prisoners killed during WWII. *(Dzielna 24/26. ☎022 831 92 89. Open W 9am-5pm, Th and Sa 9am-4pm, F 10am-5pm, Su 10am-4pm. Donation requested.)* Follow al. Jana Pawła II, take a left on Anielewicza, and walk five blocks to reach the **Jewish Cemetery** (Cmentarz Żydowski). The thickly wooded cemetery holds the remains of socialist Ferdinand Lasalle, the families of physicist Max Born and chemist Fritz Haber, and writer Thomas Mann's wife. *(Ślężna 37/39. Tram #9 to Ślężna. ☎022 791 5904. Open Apr.-Oct. daily 9am-6pm. 5zł, students 3zł. Free English- and Polish-language tours Su noon.)* The restored **Nożyk Synagogue** (Synagoga Nożyka) was the city's only synagogue to survive WWII and now serves as the spiritual home for the 500 observant Jews remaining in Warsaw. *(Twarda 6. From the center, take any tram along al. Jana Pawła II to Rondo Onz. Turn right on Twarda and left at Teatr Żydowski, the Jewish Theater. ☎022 620 3496. Open M-F and Su Apr.-Oct. 10am-5pm; Nov.-Feb. 10am-3pm. Closed Jewish holidays. Morning and evening prayer daily. 5zł.)*

POLAND

ELSEWHERE IN WARSAW. Warsaw's commercial district, southwest of Stare Miasto, is dominated by the 52-story Stalinist **Palace of Culture and Science** (Pałac Kultury i Nauki, PKiN) on Marszałkowska, which contains a string of popular shops on the ground floor and offices on the higher floors. Locals claim the view from the top is the best in Warsaw—largely because you can't see the building itself. *(☎022 656 6000. Open daily 9am-8pm, with a special night viewing F-Sa from 8pm-11pm. Observation deck on 33rd fl. 20zł, students 15zł.)* Though a bit far from the city center, the new **Warsaw Uprising Museum** is a must-see. Educational without being pedantic and somber without being heavy-handed, it recounts the tragic 1944 Uprising with full-scale replica bunkers and ruins haunted by the sound of approaching bombs. *(Grzybowska 79, enter on Przyokopowa. From the center, take tram #12, 20, or 22 to Grzybowska; the museum is on the left. ☎022 539 79 01; www.1944.pl. Multimedia presentations have English-language subtitles. Open M, W, F 8am-6pm, Th 8am-8pm, Sa-Su10am-6pm. 4zł, students 2zł; Su free. Cash only.)*

PRAGA. Across the Wisla River from central Warsaw, the formerly run-down district of Praga is undergoing a renaissance and becoming increasingly more touristed. The gleaming onion domes and cupola of the **St. Mary Magdalene Cathedral** hint at the pre-Soviet Russian presence in Warsaw. *(Al. Solidarnosci 52. From Russian Market, take tram #2, 8, 12, or 25 to the intersection of Targowa and al.Solidarnosci; church is across the street on the left. ☎022 619 8467. Open M and Su 1-4pm, Tu-Sa 11am-3pm.)* With two tall spires, the pointed arches, and the long nave reconstructed in 1972, the **St. Michael** and **St. Florian Cathedral** is less restrained than Stare Miasto's churches. *(Florianska 3, 1 block from St. Mary Magdalene. ☎022 619 0960; www.*

katedra-floriana.wpraga.opoka.org.pl.) Across the street, **Praski Park** contains the **Island of Bears,** a manmade island on which bears have been kept since 1949. *(Free.)*

WILANÓW. In 1677, King Jan III Sobieski bought the sleepy village of Milanowo and rebuilt the existing mansion into a Baroque palace. Since 1805, **Pałac Wilanowski,** south of Warsaw, has served as a public museum and a residence for the Polish state's highest-ranking guests. Surrounded by elegant gardens, the palace is filled with frescoed rooms, portraits, and extravagant royal apartments. *(Take bus #180 from Krakówskie Przedmiesce, #516 or 519 from Marszałkowska south to Wilanów. From the bus stop, cross the highway and follow signs. ☎022 842 8101; www.wilanow-palac.art.pl. Open May 1 to mid-Sept. M,W, Sa 9:30am-6:30pm, Tu,Th, F 9:30am-4:30pm, and Su 10:30am-6:30pm; mid-Sept. to mid-Dec. and late Feb.-Apr. 30 M and W-Sa 9:30am-4:30pm, Su 10:30am-4:30pm. Last entry 1hr. before closing. Gardens open M and W-F 9:30am-dusk. Wilanów 23zł, students 15zł; Su free. Gardens 5/3zł. Cash only.)*

ENTERTAINMENT AND NIGHTLIFE

Warsaw offers a variety of live music options, and free outdoor concerts abound in summer. Classical music performances rarely sell out; standby tickets cost as little as 10zł. Inquire at the **Warsaw Music Society** (Warszawskie Towarzystwo Muzyczne), ul. Morskie Oko 2 (☎022 849 5651). Take tram #4, 18, 19, 35, or 36 to Morskie Oko from ul. Marszałkowska. Nearby Łazienki Park has free Sunday performances at the **Chopin Monument** (Pomnik Chopina; concerts mid-May to Sept. Su noon, 4pm). Jazz Klub **Tygmont** (☎022 828 3409; www.tygmont.com.pl. Open daily 4pm-4am.), ul. Mazowiecka 6/8, hosts free concerts on weekday evenings. From July through September, the Old Market Square of Stare Miasto swings with free jazz nightly at 7pm.

Teatr Dramatyczny, in the Pałac Kultury, has a stage for big productions and a theater for avant-garde works. (☎022 656 6865; www.teatrdramatyczny.pl. 20-40zł; standby tickets 12-18zł.) The **Montownia Artistic Theater,** ul. Konopnickiej 6, shows a number of independent productions and frequent plays in English. (☎022 339 0760; www.montownia.art.pl. **Kinoteka** (☎022 826 1961), in the Pałac Kultury, features Hollywood blockbusters. **Kino Lab,** ul. Ujazdowskie 6 (☎022 628 1271), shows independent films. See **Center for Contemporary Art,** p. 778.

Warsaw buzzes with activity during the evenings. *Kawiarnie* (cafes) around Stare Miasto and ul. Nowy Świat are open late, and pubs with live music attract crowds. In summer, outdoor beer gardens complement the pub scene. Several publications, including *Gazeta Wyborcza,* list gay nightlife.

Piekarnia, Młocinska 11 (☎022 636 4979; www.pieksa.pl). Take the #22 tram to Rondo Babka and backtrack on Okopowa. Make a right on Powiazkowska, a right on Burakowa, and a right on Mlocinska. The unmarked club will be down the road on your left. This Warsaw institution is so well-known that it needs neither a sign over the door nor a central location to woo the throngs of techno-lovers that flock here. Piekarnia was one of the first modern clubs in Poland and these days the so-hip-it-hurts scene picks up around 4am. If you can get past the selective bouncer and the swarm of youths outside, you're in for a fun night. Cover F 20zł, Sa 25zł. Open F-Sa 10pm-late.

Klubokawiarnia, Czeckiego 3 (www.klubo.pl). An authentic communist-era sign advertising "coffee, tea, and cold beverages" hangs over the bar, while portraits of Lenin gaze down from the bright red walls in this ironic imitation of the bad old days. Despite the nostalgic decor, Klubokawiarnia's DJs spin the hottest new tracks for a stylish young crowd. Special events on occasion, such as a "Pirate Night" or "Caribbean Night" with imported sand. Cover varies. Open daily 10pm-late. Cash only.

Underground Music Cafe, Marszałkowska 126/134 (☎022 826 7048; www.under.pl). Walk down the steps behind the large McDonald's. This 2-level dance club is a guaranteed weeknight party. A casual, young crowd of students and backpackers keep the smoky dance floor completely packed until 4am. M-Tu and Su old-school house; W and Sa hip-hop; Th 70s and 80s. Beer 5zł 11pm-midnight. Cover W-F 10zł, students 5zł; Sa 20/10zł. No cover M-Tu and Su. Open M-Sa 1pm-late, Su 4pm-late.

Szlafrok, Wierzbowa 9 (☎022 828 6477). From Marszałkowska, take a right on Senatorska, and another right on Wierzbowa; the club is on your right. This centrally-located club has all the class of a high-end establishment without the exclusivity. A sophisticated clientele mill about the gold and black columns whilst sipping from a selection of martinis and cosmopolitans. No sandals or sneakers. Cover varies. Open daily 5pm-4am.

Cinnamon, Pilsudskiego 1 (☎022 323 7600), in the Metropolitan Building across pl. Pilsudskiego from the National Opera. At this bar with attitude, one of Warsaw's strictest door policies ensures that Cinnamon is favored only by the hottest locals and expats. The lunar-themed interior and pink accents complement the suave and impeccably dressed staff who keep the martinis flowing all night long. Don't be surprised if you pop in for an elegant lunch and emerge at dawn the next day. Open daily 9am-late. MC/V.

Rasko, Krochmalna 32A (☎022 890 0299; www.rasko.pl). 1 block north of Grzybowska, turn left on Krochmalna; the bar is 2 blocks down on your right near a small sign and blue unmarked door. Rasko is a small, secluded, and artsy establishment that serves Warsaw's largely underground GLBT scene. Laid-back but cautious bouncer ensures that Warsaw's less tolerant elements stay out. The friendly staff are quick to mingle with clubgoers and even join in for a round of karaoke. Beer 7zł. Open daily 6pm-2am. MC/V.

POLAND

KRAKÓW ☎012

Although Kraków (KRAH-koof; pop 758,000) only recently emerged as a trendy international capital, it has long been Poland's darling. The regal architecture, cafe culture, and palpable sense of history that now bewitch throngs of visitors have drawn Polish kings, artists, and scholars for centuries. Unlike most Polish cities, Kraków emerged from WWII and years of socialist planning unscathed. The maze-like Old Town and the old Jewish quarter of Kazimierz hide scores of museums, galleries, cellar pubs, and clubs; 130,000 students add to the spirited nightlife. Still, the city's gloss and glamor can't completely hide the scars of the 20th century: the nearby Auschwitz-Birkenau Nazi death camps provide a sobering reminder of the atrocities committed in the not-so-distant past.

TRANSPORTATION

Flights: Balice Airport (John Paul II International Airport; Port Lotniczy im. Jana Pawła), Kapitana Medweckiego 1 (**KRK;** ☎012 411 1955; http://lotnisko-balice.pl/strona_en.html), 18km from the center. Connect to the main train station by bus #192 (40min.) or 208 (1hr.). Or take the **airport train** that leaves from the train platform #1 on W and F-Sa, at least once per hour. A taxi to the center costs 60-70zł. Carriers include British Airways, Central Wings, German Wings, LOT, Lufthansa, and Sky Europe. Open 24hr.

Trains: Kraków Główny, pl. Kolejowy 1 (☎012 393 5409, info ☎ 012 393 1580; www.pkp.pl). Ticket office open 5am-11pm. Go to Kasa Krajowej for domestic trains and Kasa Międzynardowa for international trains. AmEx/MC/V. To: **Gdańsk** ("Gdynia"; 7-10hr., 12 per day, 60-100zł); **Warsaw** (3-4hr., 15 per day, 81-127zł); **Zakopane** (3-5hr., 19 per day, 30-50zł); **Bratislava, SLK** (8hr., 1 per day, 188zł); **Budapest, HUN** (11hr., 1 per day, 159-208zł); **Kyiv, UKR** (22hr., 1 per day, 240zł); **Odessa, UKR** (21hr., 1 per day, 240zł); **Prague, CZR** (9hr., 2 per day, 128-165zł); **Vienna, AUT** (8hr., 2 per day, 157-194zł). *Let's Go* does not recommend traveling on night trains.

Buses: Bosacka 18 (☎300 300 150). Open daily 5am-11pm. To: **Lódz** (5hr., 5 per day, 50zł); **Warsaw** (6hr., 3 per day, 50zł); **Wrocław** (5hr., 2 per day, 43zł). AmEx/MC/V.

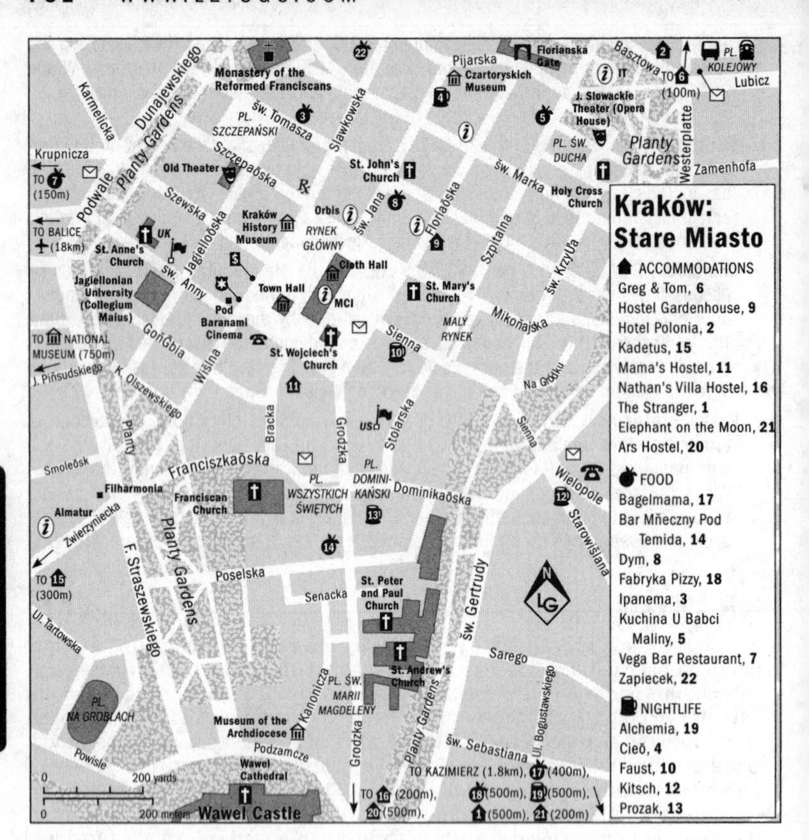

Public Transportation: Buy **bus** and **tram** tickets at Ruch kiosks (2.50zł) or from the automatic ticket machines throughout the city and punch them on board. Large packs need their own tickets. Night buses after 11pm 5zł; day pass 11zł; there is an 100zł fine if you or your bag are caught ticketless.

Taxis: Reliable taxi companies include: **Barbakan Taxi** (☎96 61, toll-free ☎08 00 40 04 00); **Euro Taxi** (☎96 64); **Radio Taxi** (☎919, toll-free ☎08 00 50 09 19); **Wawel Taxi** (☎96 66). It is up to 30% cheaper to call a taxi than to hail one.

ORIENTATION AND PRACTICAL INFORMATION

The heart of the city is the **Rynek Główny** (Main Marketplace), the center of **Stare Miasto** (Old Town). Stare Miasto is encircled by the Planty gardens and, a bit farther out, a broad ring road, which is confusingly divided into sections with different names: Basztowa, Dunajewskiego, Podwale, and Westerplatte. South of Rynek Główny looms the **Wawel Castle.** The **Wisła River** snakes past the castle and borders the old Jewish district of **Kazimierz.** The train station sits northeast of Stare Miasto. A well-marked underpass cuts beneath the ring road and into the Planty gardens; from there several paths lead into the Rynek (10min.).

Tourist Office: City Tourist Information, Szpitalna 25 (☎012 432 0110; www.krakow.pl/en). The official tourist office arranges accommodations, tours, and sells guides (7-12zł). English spoken. Open daily 9am-7pm. Private tourist offices throughout town.

Budget Travel: Orbis, Rynek Główny 41 (☎012 619 2447; www.orbis.krakow.pl). Sells train tickets and arranges trips to Wieliczka and Auschwitz (each 120zł, both 238zł; up to 50% ISIC discount). Also cashes **traveler's checks** and **exchanges currency.** Open M-F 9am-7pm, Sa 9am-5pm. There are many travel agencies in Stare Miasto.

Consulates: UK, sw. Anny 9 (☎012 421 5656 or ☎012 421 7030; ukconsul@bci.krakow.pl). Open M-F 9am-4pm. **US,** Stolarska 9 (☎012 424 5100; krakow.usconsulate.gov). Open M-F 9am-4:30pm; citizen services until 3pm.

Currency Exchange and Banks: ATMs, found all over the city, offer the best rates. Bank **BPH,** Rynek Główny 4, has **Western Union Services.** Many banks require those receiving money from abroad to change it into złotych at a bad rate. Open M-F 8am-6pm.

Bike Rental: Rentabike (☎888 029 792; www.rentabike.pl). Bikes 30zł for 5hr., 55zł for first day, 45zł for each additional day. Open 24hr.

Luggage Storage: At the train station. 1% of value per day plus 5zł for the 1st day and 3zł for each additional day. Lockers near the exit. Open 5am-11pm. Lockers also available at bus station. Small bag 4zł, large bag 8zł. Open 24hr.

English-Language Bookstore: Massolit, Felicjanek 4 (☎012 432 4150; www.massolit.com). Cozy atmosphere. Open mic night 3rd Su each month at 7pm. Open M-Th and Su 10am-8pm; F-Sa 10am-9pm.

Laundromat: Piastowska 47 (☎012 622 3181), in the basement of **Hotel Piast.** Take tram #4, 13, or 14 to WKS Wawel and turn left on Piastowska. Wash 15zł, dry 15zł, detergent 3zł. Open M-Sa 10am-7pm.

Pharmacy: Apteka Pod Zółtym Tygrysem, Szczepańska 1 (☎012 422 9293), off Rynek Główny. Posts list of 24hr. pharmacies. Open M-F 8am-8pm, Sa 8am-3pm. MC/V.

Medical Services: Medicover, Krótka 1 (☎012 616 1000). **Ambulance** services available. English spoken. Open M-F 7am-9pm, Sa 9am-2pm.

Telephones: At the post office and throughout the city.

Internet: Koffeina Internet Cafe, Rynek Główny 23. 2zł per 30min., 3zł per hr. Open 10am-10pm. **Klub Garinet,** Floriańska 18 (☎012 423 2233, ext 23). 4zł per hr. Open daily 9am-midnight. **Telekomunikacja Polska** offers free Internet.

Post Office: Westerplatte 20 (☎012 422 3991). **Poste Restante** at counter #1. Open M-F 7:30am-8:30pm, Sa 8am-2pm. **Postal Code:** 31075.

ACCOMMODATIONS

New hostels frequently open in Kraków to meet the growing demand, but budget accommodations fill up quickly in summer. Be sure to call ahead. University dorms open up in June, July and August; *Kraków in Your Pocket* has a list.

Nathan's Villa Hostel, ul. św. Agnieszki 1 (☎012 422 3545; www.nathansvilla.com), south of *Stare Miasto,* near the Jewish quarter. Famous for its social atmosphere, the hostel has spacious rooms and a lively cellar pub. Breakfast, laundry, and Wi-Fi included. Reception 24hr. Dorms 45-60zł. MC/V; 3% surcharge. ❷

Elephant on the Moon, ul. Biale Wzgorze 8 (☎ 695 949 604), a 15 min. walk or short tram ride from the center of town. Enjoy being fussed over at this extremely guest-oriented hostel, where the owners are friends first and staff second. Travelers cluster in the cozy living-room of this converted residential house and enjoy the hospitality—and baked goods—provided by the tight-knit staff. Breakfast and Internet included. Reception 24hr. Flexible check-in, check-out 10:30am. Dorms 45-60zł. Cash only. ❷

Ars Hostel, ul. Kolotek 7 (☎ 012 422 3659; www.arshostel.com), south of *Stare Miasto,* next to the Castle. A veritable haven for solo travelers, Ars not only offers a comfortable bed, but also provides nightly entertainment. The staff's seasoned travelers lead vodka tastings by night and mountain hikes by day, making for an extremely social crowd that parties on until the sun comes up. Breakfast and Internet included. Check-in 1:30pm, flexible check-out. Dorms 45-60zł. AmEx/MC/V. ❷

The Stranger, ul. Dietla 97/5 (☎ 012 432 0909; www.thestrangerhostel.com), situated in a new location near the Jewish Quarter. With its new digs comes more space, featuring large, newly-furbished dorm rooms, common area, and a bar/cafe downstairs. Breakfast included. Free Internet and laundry. Reception 24hr. Dorms 32-45zł. Cash only. ❷

Mama's Hostel, ul. Bracka 4 (☎ 012 429 5940; www.mamashostel.com.pl), off Rynek Główny. The most centrally located hostel in town, Mama's garners praise for its eager staff and clean facilities. Its party-friendly location, however, means it can get noisy. Breakfast, laundry and Internet included. Reception 24hr. Flexible check-in and check-out. 12-bed dorms 40zł; 6-bed dorms 60zł. MC/V; 3% surcharge. ❶

Hostel Gardenhouse, ul. Floriańska 5 (☎ 012 431 2824; www.gardenhousehostel.com), in a courtyard off Rynek Główny. Serene dorms decorated in floral. Breakfast, laundry, and Internet included. Reception 24hr. Dorms 55-65zł; doubles 160zł. AmEx/MC/V. ❷

POLAND

Hotel Polonia, Basztowa 25 (☎ 012 422 1233; www.hotel-polonia.com.pl), across from the train station. Neoclassical exterior, modern rooms, and see-through bathtubs. Breakfast 18zł, included for rooms with bath. Reception 24hr. Check-out noon. Singles 100zł, with bath 295zł; doubles 119/360zł; triples 139/429zł; suites 526zł. MC/V. ❹

Greg and Tom, ul. Pawia 12/17(☎ 012 422 4100; www.gregtomhostel.com). In addition to its convenient location near the center of Old Town, the hospitable staff and creature comforts of this hostel make it hard to leave. Breakfast, dinner, laundry, and Internet included. Reception 24hr. Dorms 50zł; doubles 75zł. AmEx/MC/V. ❷

Kadetus, ul. Zwierzyniecka 25 (☎ 012 422 3617; www.kadetus.com), southwest of Rynek Główny. Colorful dorms with modern furnishings. Breakfast, laundry, Internet, and Wi-Fi included. Reception 24hr. Dorms 40zł-45zł; doubles 65-70zł. Cash only. ❷

FOOD

Many restaurants, cafes, and grocery stores are located on and around Rynek Główny. More grocery stores surround the bus and train stations.

Bagelmama, ul. Podbrzezie 2 (☎ 012 431 1942; www.bagelmama.com), in Kazimierz, facing the Temple Synagogue. Poland is the mother of the bagel; here the blessed food returns home in triumph (3.50zł, with cream cheese or hummus 6-9zł). Strangely, it also has Kraków's best burritos (12-15zł). Open daily 10am-9pm. Cash only. ❶

Kuchina U Babci Maliny, ul. Szpitalna 38 (☎ 012 421 4818). Hearty Polish food served in quarters resembling a wooden stable upstairs and, incongruously, a Victorian drawing room below. Soup 5zł. Pierogi 8-15zł. Open daily 11am-10pm. AmEx/MC/V. ❶

Ipanema, św. Tomasza 28 (☎ 012 422 5323). Toucan figurines, bright paint, and hanging plants create a rainforest vibe to go along with the superb Brazilian cuisine. Entrees 16-50zł. Open M-Th and Su 1-11pm, F-Sa 1pm-midnight. AmEx/MC/V. ❸

Dym, św. Tomasza 13 (☎ 012 429 6661). A hub for sophisticated locals, Dym (meaning "smoke") earns high praise for its coffee (5zł), though many prefer to enjoy the relaxed vibe over beer (6-8zł). Open M-F 10am-midnight. Cash only. ❶

Fabryka Pizzy, Józefa 34 (☎ 012 433 8080). This popular Kazimierz pizza place lives up to its hype, preparing pizzas that are unusual and delicious. Browse from a menu of cleverly-named specials like the Donkey with a Sombrero (salami, red beans, hot pepper and tabasco) or the Diver's Party (shrimp, crab, mussels, olives and onions). Pizzas 15-30zł. Open M-Th and Su 11am-11pm, F-Sa noon-midnight. MC/V. ❷

Zapiecek, ul. Sławkowska 32 (☎ 012 422 7495). Every Polish city has its local pierogi institution, and Zapiecek is Kraków's. Combine the authentic yet affordable Polish fare (6-10zł) which will whet your appetite, add the Old Town location, and you've got the perfect afternoon lunch spot. Open daily 10am-9pm. Cash only. ❶

Vega Bar Restaurant, Krupnicza 22 (☎ 012 430 0846), also at św. Gertrudy 7 (☎422 3494). Fresh flowers and a colorful interior set the mood for delightful veggie cuisine—a rarity in Kraków. (4-12zł). 32 varieties of tea (2.50zł). Open daily 9am-9pm. MC/V. ❶

Bar Mleczny Pod Temida, ul. Grodzka 43 (☎ 012 422 0874). Conveniently located between Rynek Główny and Wawel Castle, this milk bar is dirt-cheap and a crowd-pleasing lunch spot. Entrees 2.50-10zł. Open daily 9am-8pm. ❶

SIGHTS

STARE MIASTO. At the center of *Stare Miasto* is the **Rynek Główny,** the largest market square in Europe, and at the heart of the *Rynek* stands the **Sukiennice** (Cloth Hall). Surrounded by multicolored row houses and cafes, it's a convenient center for exploring the nearby sights. The **Royal Road** (Droga Królewska), traversed by medieval royals on the way to coronations in Wawel, starts at St. **Florian's Church** (Kosciół św. Floriana), crosses pl. Matejki, passes the **Academy of Fine Arts** (Akademia Sztuk Pieknych), and crosses Basztowa to the **Barbakan.** The Gothic-style Barbakan, built in 1499, is the best preserved of the three such defensive fortifications surviving in Europe. *(Open daily 10:30am-6pm. 6zł, students 4zł.)* The royal road continues through **Floriańska Gate,** the old city entrance and the only remnant of the city's medieval walls. Inside *Stare Miasto*, the road runs down Floriańska, past the *Rynek* and along Grodzka. A map marking all the points can be found in front of Florianska Gate. Every hour at **St. Mary's Church** (Kościół Mariacki), the blaring Hejnał trumpet calls from the taller of St. Mary's two towers and cuts off abruptly to recall the near-destruction of Kraków in 1241, when invading Tatars shot down the trumpeter as he attempted to warn the city. A stunning interior encases the world's oldest Gothic altarpiece, a 500-year-old treasure dismantled, but not destroyed, by the Nazis. *(At the corner of the Rynek closest to the train station. Cover shoulders and knees. Church open daily 11:30am-6pm. Tower open Tu, Th, and Sa 9-11:30am and 1-5:30pm. Tower 6zł, students 4zł. Altar 4/2zł.)*

Collegium Maius of Kraków's Jagiellonian University (Uniwersytet Jagielloński) is the third-oldest university in Europe, established in 1364. Alumni include astronomer **Mikołaj Kopernik** (Copernicus). The Collegium became a museum in 1964 and now boasts an extensive collection of historical scientific instruments. *(ul. Jagiellońska 15. ☎012 663 1307; www.uj.edu.pl/muzeum. Open Apr.-Oct. M,W,F 10am-2:20pm, Tu, Th 10am-5:20pm, Sa 10am-1:20pm, Nov.-March M-F 10am-2:20pm, Sa 10am-1:20pm. Closed Sundays and holidays. Guided visits only; tours 3 per hr. English-language tour daily 1pm. 12zł, students 6zł, Sa free.)* **Ulica Floriańska** runs from the *Rynek* to the Barbakan and the Floriańska Gate, which formed the entrance to the old city; they are now the only remnants of the medieval fortifications. The **Czartoryskich Museum** has letters by Copernicus and paintings by Matejko, da Vinci, and Rembrandt. *(św. Jana 19. ☎012 422 5566. Open T-Sa 10am-6pm, Su 10am-4pm; closed last Su of each month. 10zł; students 5zł; Su free.)* From the *Rynek*, walk down Grodzka and turn right to reach the brightly colored **Franciscan Church** (Kosciól Franciscańska), decorated with vibrant colors and Stanisław Wyspiański's amazing stained-glass window *God the Father*. *(Pl. Wszystkich Swiętych 5. ☎012 422 5376. Open daily until 7:30pm. English-language tours free; donations requested.)*

POLAND

WAWEL CASTLE AND SURROUNDINGS. **Wawel Castle** (Zamek Wawelski), one of Poland's top attractions, is an architectural masterpiece overlooking the Wisła River. Begun in the 10th century and remodeled in the 16th, the castle contains 71 chambers, including the **Komnaty** (state rooms) and the **Apartamenty** (royal chambers). Among the treasures are a magnificent sequence of 16th-century tapestries commissioned by the royal family and a cache of armor, swords, spears, and ancient guns. The **Lost Wawel** exhibit traces Wawel Hill's evolution from the Stone Age, displaying archaeological fragments of ancient Wawel. You can also visit the **Oriental Collection** of Turkish military regalia and Asian porcelain. *(Open Apr.-Oct. M 9:30am-1pm, Tu-F 9:30am-5pm, Sa-Su 11am-6pm, Nov.-Mar. Tu-Sa 9:30am-4pm, Su 10am-4pm. Royal Private Apartments and Oriental Collection closed M. Wawel Castle Apr.-Oct. 15zł, students 8zł, Nov.-Mar. 14/7zł, M free. Lost Wawel and Oriental Collection 7/4zł each. Royal Apartments 22/17zł, Treasury and Armory 15/8zł.)* Next door is **Wawel Cathedral** (Katedra Wawelska), which once hosted the coronations and funerals of Polish monarchs. Famed poet Adam Mikiewicz lies entombed here, and Kraków native Karol Wojtyła served as archbishop before becoming Pope John Paul II. Steep stairs from the church lead to **Sigismund's Bell** (Dwon Zygmunta); the view of the city is worth the climb. *(Cathedral open M-Sa 9am-5pm, Su 12:30pm-5pm. Buy tickets at the kasa across the castle courtyard. 10zł, students 5zł.)* In the complex's southwest corner is the entrance to the **Dragon's Den** (Smocza Jama), a small cavern. The real treat is down the path that borders the castle walls: a wonderfully ugly metal statue of the fire-breathing dragon. *(Open daily Sept.-Apr. 10am-5pm, July-Aug. 10-6pm. 3zł.)*

POLAND

KAZIMIERZ. South of *Stare Miasto* lies Kazimierz, Kraków's 600-year-old **Jewish quarter.** On the eve of WWII, 68,000 Jews lived in the Kraków area, most of them in Kazimierz, but the occupying Nazis forced many out. The 15,000 remaining were deported to death camps by March 1943. Only about 100 practicing Jews now live here, but Kazimierz is a favorite haunt of Kraków's artists and intellectuals, and it is the center of a resurgence of Central European Jewish culture. *(From the Rynek, go down ul. Sienna, which turns into Starowiślana. After 1km, turn right onto Miodowa, then left onto Szeroka.)* The **Galicia Jewish Museum** documents the past and present of Galicia, a region in southern Poland that was once the heart of Ashkenazi Jewish culture. *(Dajwór 18. ☎012 421 6842; www.galiciajewishmuseum.org. Open daily 9am-7pm. 12zł, students 6zł.)* The tiny **Remuh Synagogue** is surrounded by **Remuh's Cemetery,** which has graves dating to the plague of 1551-1552 and a wall constructed from tombstones recovered after WWII. For centuries, the cemetery was covered with sand, protecting it from 19th-century Austrian invaders and from the Nazis, who used the area as a garbage dump. *(Szeroka 40. Open May-Oct. M-F and Su 9am-6pm, Nov.-Apr. M-F and Su 9am-4pm. Services F at sundown and Sa morning. 5zł, students 2zł.)* Also on Szeroka, the **Old Synagogue** is Poland's earliest example of Jewish religious architecture and now houses a museum of Jewish history and traditions. *(Szeroka 24. ☎012 422 0962. Open Apr.-Oct. M 10am-2pm, Tu-Su 10am-5pm; Nov.-Mar. M 10am-2pm, W-Th and Sa-Su 9am-4pm, F 10am-5pm. 7zł, students 5zł, M free.)* The **Center for Jewish Culture** organizes cultural events and arranges heritage tours. *(Meiselsa 17. ☎012 430 6449; www.judaica.pl. Open M-F 10am-6pm, Sa-Su 10am-2pm.)*

ENTERTAINMENT

The **Cultural Information Center,** św. Jana 2, sells the monthly guide *Karnet* (4zł) and directs visitors to box offices. (☎012 421 7787. Open M-Sa 10am-6pm.) The city jumps with jazz; check out **U Muniaka,** Florianska 3 (☎012 423 1205; open daily 7pm-2am) and **Harris Piano Jazz Bar,** Rynek Główny 28 (☎012 421 5741; shows 9pm-midnight; Tu-Sa and Su 1pm-2am.) Classical music-lovers will relish the **Sala Filharmonia** (Philharmonic Hall), Zwierzyniecka 1. (☎012 422 9477, ext. 31; www.filharmonia.krakow.pl. Box office open Tu-F 11am-7pm, Sa-Su 1hr. before curtain; closed June 20-Sept. 10.) The **opera** performs at the **Słowacki Theater,** sw. Ducha 1. (☎012 424 4525. Box office open M-Sa 9am-7pm, Su 4hr. before curtain. 30-50zł, students 25-35zł.) The **Stary Teatr** (Old Theater) has a few stages that host films, plays, and exhibits. (☎012 422 4040. Open Tu-Sa 10am-1pm and 5-7pm, Su 5-7pm. 30-60zł, students 20-35zł.)

NIGHTLIFE

Kraków in Your Pocket has up-to-date info on the hottest club and pub scenes, while the free monthly English-language *KrakOut* magazine has day-by-day listings of events. Most dance clubs are in Stare Miasto, while bohemian pubs and cafes cluster in Kazimierz. For tips on Kraków's **GLBT nightlife,** see www.gayeuro.com/krakow or www.cracow.gayguide.net.

Alchemia, Estery 5 (☎516 095 863; www.alchemia.com.pl). Candles twinkle in this pleasantly disheveled bar, which includes bizarre and fascinating decor—one of the many rooms is decorated to look like a 1950s kitchen. Frequented by artists, Brits, and students downing beer (*Żywiec;* 6.5zł) until dawn. During the day, this Kazimierz bar masquerades as a smoky cafe. Open daily 9am-4am.

Prozak, Dominikanska 6 (☎012 429 1128; www.prozak.pl). With a shisha bar, and more dance floors, bars, and intimate nooks than you'll be able to count, Prozak is one of the top clubs in town. Hipster students, porn star look-alikes, and music aficionados lounge on low-slung couches. Pass on the undersized mixed drinks (7-20zł) for pints of beer (7-10zł). No sneakers or sandals. Cover F-Sa 10zł. Open daily 7pm-late.

Kitsch, ul. Wielopole 15 (☎012 422 5299; www.kitsch.pl), located between the Rynek and Kazimierz. This gay-friendly establishment offers a great dancing atmosphere. 6-8zl beer, mixed drinks from 8zl. T Girls' night, W Boys' night, Th Student night, with beer at 5zl for women, men, and students, respectively. Open daily 7pm-late.

Cien, sw. Jana 15 (☎012 422 2177; www.cienklub.com). Posing becomes a spectator sport in the vaults of "Shadow," so dress to impress. The club plays house techno for Krakow's beautiful people, and party-goers take advantage of the red nooks along the walls to formulate a plan of approach. Mixed drinks 10-25zł. No sneakers or sandals. Open Tu-Th 8pm-5am, F-Sa 8pm-6am. MC/V.

Faust, Rynek Główny 6 (☎012 423 8300), entrance off of Sienna St. Sell your soul in this underground labyrinth, where a raucous, friendly crowd sits at massive wooden tables or dances unabashedly to pop and techno hits. Beer 4-8zł. Disco W-Sa. Open M-Th and Su noon-1am, F-Sa 3pm-4am. Cash only.

DAYTRIPS FROM KRAKÓW

AUSCHWITZ-BIRKENAU. An estimated 1½ million people, mostly Jews, were murdered and thousands more suffered unthinkable horrors in the Nazi concentration camps at **Auschwitz** (in Oświęcim) and **Birkenau** (in Brzezinka). The gates over the smaller *Konzentrationslager Auschwitz I* are inscribed with the ironic dictum "*Arbeit Macht Frei*" (Work Will Set You Free). Tours begin at the museum at Auschwitz. As you walk past the remainders of thousands of lives, the enormity of the atrocity becomes apparent. A 15min. English-language film, with footage shot by the Soviet Army that liberated the camp on January 27, 1945, is shown every 30 min. Children under 14 are strongly advised not to visit the museum. *(☎844 8102. Open daily June-Aug. 8am-7pm; Sept. and May 8am-6pm; Oct. and Apr. 8am-5pm; Nov. and Mar. 8am-4pm; Dec.-Feb. 8am-3pm. English-language tour 4 per day at 10am, 11am, 1pm, and 3pm. Museum free. Film 3.50zł. Guided 3hr. tour 39zł, students 30zł; film and bus included. English-language guidebook 3zł.)*

POLAND

The larger, starker **Konzentrationslager Auschwitz II-Birkenau** is in the countryside 3km from the original camp, a 30min. walk along a well-marked route or a short **shuttle** ride from the Auschwitz museum parking lot (1 per hr., free). Birkenau was built later in the war and hosted much of the apparati of mass extermination. Little is left of the camp today; most was destroyed by retreating Nazis to conceal the genocide. Reconstructed train tracks lead to the ruins of the crematoria and gas chambers. Near the monument lies a pond still gray from the ashes deposited there over 60 years ago. *(Open mid-Apr. to Oct. 8am-dusk. Free.)* **Auschwitz Jewish Center and Synagogue** features exhibits on pre-war Jewish life in the town of Oświęcim, films based on survivors' testimonies, genealogy resources, and a reading room. Take a **taxi** for about 20zł, or take **bus** #1, 3-6, or 8 from the train station in the town center, get off at the first stop after the bridge and backtrack. *(Pl. Ks. Jana Skarbka 3-5. ☎844 70 02; www.ajcf.pl. Open M-F and Su Apr.-Sept. 8:30am-8pm; Oct.-Mar. 8:30am-6pm. Donation requested.)*

Buses from Kraków's central station go to Oświęcim (1½-2hr., every 30 min., 7-10zł). Return buses leave frequently from the stop on the other side of the parking lot; turn right out of the museum. PKS buses depart from the stop outside the premises. Less convenient **trains** leave from Kraków Plaszów, south of the town center (10zł). Buses #2-5, 8-9, and 24-29 connect the Oświęcim train station to the Muzeum Oświęcim stop; or, walk a block to the right out of the station, turn left onto ul. Więźniów Oświęcimia, and continue 1.6km.

POLAND

WIELICZKA. The tiny town of Wieliczka, 13km southeast of Kraków, is home to a 700-year-old **salt mine.** Pious Poles carved the immense underground complex of chambers out of salt; in 1978, UNESCO declared the mine one of the world's 12 most priceless monuments. The most spectacular cavern is **St. Kinga's Chapel,** complete with an altar, relief works, and salt chandeliers. Most hostels and travel companies, including **Orbis** (p. 768), organize trips to the mines, but it's cheapest to take a private **minibus** like Contrabus that departs near the train and bus stations (30min., 4 per hr., 3.50zł). Look for "Wieliczka" marked on the door. In Wieliczka, head along the path of the former tracks, then follow signs marked *"do kopalni."* The only way to see the mines is by taking a lengthy **guided tour,** so allot at least 3hr. for the daytrip. *(ul. Daniłowicza 10. ☎278 73 02; www.kopalnia.pl. Wheelchair-accessible. Open daily Apr.-Oct. 7:30am-7:30pm; Nov.-Mar. 8am-4pm; closed holidays. Polish-language tours Apr.-June 47zł, students 32zł, July-Dec. 48/33zł, Jan.-Mar. 45/30zł. English-language tours June and Sept. 8 per day, July and Aug. every 35 people. 8:30am-6pm. Apr.-June 63zł, students 48zł, July-Dec. 64/49zł, Jan.-Mar. 61/46zł. MC/V.)*

LUBLIN ☎081

Unlike most Polish cities, Lublin (LOO-blin; pop. 400,000) survived WWII with its cobblestones intact. Its medieval Old Town is not a commercialized reconstruction like Warsaw's, but a more romantic and crumbling reality.

TRANSPORTATION AND PRACTICAL INFORMATION. **Trains** (☎94 36) run from pl. Dworcowy 1 to **Kraków** (4hr., 2 per day, 49zl), **Warsaw** (3hr., 10 per day, 34zl), and **Wroclaw** (9hr., 2 per day, 54zl). From the train station, take **bus** #1 to Stare Miasto (stop Khromelna) and the bus station. The **tourist office,** ul. Jezuica 1/3, near the Kraków Gate, has an English-speaking staff. (☎081 532 4412; infotur@loit.lublin.pl. Open M-F 9am-6pm, Sa 10am-4pm.)

ACCOMMODATIONS AND FOOD. From Stare Miasto's ul. Grodzka, walk through the gate at the end of the street and go down the flight of stairs on your right to reach **Domu Rekolekcyjnym ❶**, ul. Podwale 15, a rectory with simple rooms, friendly nuns, and an unbeatable location. (☎081 534 3085. Dorms 30-40zl, singles 60zl. Cash only.) **Szkolne Schronisko Mlodziezowe ❶**, ul. Dlugosza 6, is a quiet youth hostel located in a residential area. (☎081 533 0628. Lockout 10am-5pm. Flexible curfew 10pm. 10-bed dorms 25zl, students 19zl; triples 84/69zl. Cash only.)

Lublin's eateries cluster near ulica Krakówskie Przedmiescie; a dozen beer gardens can be found in Stare Miasto. **Nalesnikarnia Zadora ❷**, ul. Rynek 8, tucked in an alley on the northeast of the square, adds a creative touch to its savory and dessert crepes. (☎081 534 5534. Polish crepes 9-19zl. AmEx/MC/V.) The nearby "Jewish Pub" **Mandragora ❷**, Rynek 9, recalls the inside of your grandmother's living room with its antique lamps, decorative china, and white-knit tablecloths. Peruse the menu of traditional Jewish dishes and Israeli favorites whilst the owner's pet tabby cat slinks about your feet. (☎081 536 2020. Gefilte fish 15zl. Falafel 18zl. Kosher. Special Shabbat menu M-Th and Sa. Open M-Th and Su 10am-10pm, F-Sa 10am-midnight. MC/V.)

SIGHTS. The hill-top **Rynek** (main square) of Stare Miasto (Old Town) contains many of the city's historic sights. The 14th-century **Lublin Castle** (Zamek Lubelski) was used as a Gestapo jail during the Nazi occupation. The adjacent **Holy Trinity Chapel** has stunning Russo-Byzantine frescoes from the 15th century. (☎081 532 5001, ext. 35; www.zamek-lublin.pl. Open M-Sa 10am-5pm, Su 10am-6pm. Museum and chapel each 6.50zł, students 4.50zł; both 11zł/9zł.) Great views and seriously old art make the **Archdiocesan Museum of Sacred Art** (Muzeum Archidiecezjalne Sztuki Sakralnej), in the 17th-century Trinitarska Tower, worth a visit. (☎081 444 7450. Open Mar. 25-Nov. 15 daily 10am-5pm. 5zł, students 3zł.) Take eastbound bus #28 from the train station or trolley #153 or 156 from al. Raclawickie to reach **Majdanek**, the second largest Nazi concentration camp. The Nazis did not have time to destroy the camp as they retreated, so the disturbing original structures still stand. Visitors can walk from Lublin along **Droga Męczenników Majdanka** (Road of the Martyrs of Majdanek; 30min.) to Zamosc. (☎081 744 1955; www.majdanek.pl. Open Tu-Su 8am-4pm. Closed national holidays. Children under 14 not permitted. Free.)

POLAND

ZAKOPANE ☎018

The year-round resort of Zakopane (zah-ko-PAH-neh; pop. 28,000) lies in a valley surrounded by jagged peaks and alpine meadows. During vacation season (Jan.-Feb. and June-Sept.), the town fills with skiers or hikers headed for the **Tatra National Park** (Tatrzański Park Narodowy; 5zł, students 2.50zł).

TRANSPORTATION AND PRACTICAL INFORMATION. The **bus station** (☎018 201 4603) is located on the corner of ul. Kościuszki and ul. Jagiełłońska, facing the train station (☎018 201 4504). **Buses** run to Kraków (2-2hr., 3 per day, 10zł) and Warsaw (8hr., 4 per day, 55zł). A private express line runs between Zakopane and Kraków (2hr., 15 per day, 13zł), leaving from a stop on ul. Kościuszki, 50m toward the center from the station. **Trains** go to Kraków (3-4hr., 20 per day, 19zł) and Warsaw (8hr., 9 per day, 50zł). To reach the center from the station, walk down ul. Kościuszki, which intersects ul. Krupówki (15min.). The **tourist office,** ul. Kościuszki 17, has free maps of the town, sells hiking/skiing maps (5-9zł), helps locate rooms, and books English-language **rafting trips** (70-80zł) on the Dunajec. (☎018 201 2211. Open daily July-Sept. 8am-8pm; Oct.-June 9am-6pm.) **Postal Code:** 34500.

ACCOMMODATIONS AND FOOD. To find accommodations, look for signs marked *"pokój"* and *"noclegi"* that indicate private rooms; owners may greet you at the station. **Schronisko PISM "Szarotka" ❷,** ul. Notowarska 45G, has small, clean rooms with private baths. (☎018 201 3618; schroniskoptsm@pro.onet.pl. Linens 6zł. Lockout 11pm. Reserve ahead. Dorms 35-50zł, low-season 24-35zł. Cash only.) For a cozier night, head to the **Good Bye Lenin Hostel ❷,** 44 Chlabowka, just steps from the entrance to the National Park. While farther away from town, the welcoming staff, extensive amenities, and truly rustic atmosphere make the trip worthwhile. (☎018 200 1330; www.goodbyelenin.pl. Breakfast, laundry, linens and Internet included. Dorms 30-45zł, double room 100-110zł. MC/V.) Most restaurants and shops can be found along ul. Krupówki. The live music and regional fare at the kitschy **Gazdowo Kuznia ❸,** ul. Krupówki 1, always draw a crowd. (☎018 206 4111; www.gazdowokuznia.pl. Entrees 7-33zł. Open daily 11am until last customer.)

HIKING NEAR ZAKOPANE. Kuźnice, south of Zakopane, is a popular place to begin hikes. To get there, head uphill on ul. Krupówki to ul. Zamoyskiego; follow this road as it becomes ul. Chałubińskiego, which turns into ul. Przewodników Tatrzańskich and continues to the trailheads (1hr. from Zakopane center). You can also take a "mikro-bus" (3zł) from the stop in front of the **bus** station. From Kuźnice, the Kasprowy Wierch **cable car** takes passengers to the top of **Kasprowy Mountain** where Poland borders Slovakia.

Trails from Kuźnice are well marked. The **Tatrzański Park Narodowy** map (7zł), available at kiosks or bookstores, is a useful guide. The **Valley of the Five Polish Tarns** (Dolina Pięciu Stawów Polskich; 1 day) is an intense, beautiful hike. It starts at Kuźnice and follows the yellow trail through **Dolina Jaworzynka** (Jaworzynka Valley) to the steep blue trail, which leads to **Hala Gasienicowa** (2hr.). Crowds tend to gather on the steep final ascent to the peak of **Mount Giewont** (1894m; 6hr.). The mountain's silhouette resembles a man lying down; you'll envy him after the climb. From Kuźnice, the moderately difficult blue trail (7km) to the peak has a view of Zakopane, the Tatras, and Slovakia.

Morskie Oko (1406m) is a dazzling glacial lake. Take a bus from Zakopane (45min., 11 per day, 5zł) or a private minibus from opposite the station (30min., 5zł) to **Palenice Białczańska** or **Polona Palenica.** Hike the popular paved 18km loop (5-6hr.) or take the green trail to the blue trail (4hr.) for a majestic view. Donkey carts also take passengers to the lake (30min.; 30zł up, 20zł down).

WROCŁAW ☎071

Wrocław (VROTS-wahv), the capital of Lower Silesia (Dolny Śl ąsk), is a graceful city of Gothic spires and stone bridges. The tranquil main square was the last Nazi stronghold on the retreat to Berlin. Today, investment has rejuvenated the city, which enjoys one of the fastest development rates in Poland as tourism rises and cheap airlines turn it into a prime stag party destination.

TRANSPORTATION AND PRACTICAL INFORMATION. Trains run from Wrocław Główny, ul. Piłsudskiego 105 (☎071 367 5882), to: Kraków (4hr., 13 per day, 45-85zł); Poznań (2 ½—3 ½hr., 25 per day, 22-55zł); Warsaw (4-6hr., 8 per day, 50-90zł); Berlin, GER (5-6hr., 2 per day, 185zł). **Buses** leave from behind the train station. From the station, turn left on ul. Piłsudskiego, take a right on ul. Świdnicka, and go past Kosciuszki pl. over the Fosa River to reach the main square. The **tourist office,** Rynek 14, offers **maps** (6-16zł), bike rentals (10zł for 1st hr., 5zł per hr. thereafter, 50zł per day; 400zł deposit) and free Internet. (☎071 344 3111; www.itWrocław.pl. Open daily 9am-9pm.) **Postal Code:** 50-900.

ACCOMMODATIONS AND FOOD. Rooms are plentiful in Wrocław, but reserve ahead for rooms near the center. Check with the tourist office to make reservations in **student dorms,** which rent rooms June through August (20-50zł). **Mleczarnia Hostel ❷,** ul. Wodkowica 5, is less than a 5 min. walk from town square, right across the street from tram/bus stops. With more character than most hotels, Mleczarnia impresses with its handsome furniture, huge rooms, and innumerable antique decorations. (☎717 877 570. Free Internet and linens. Reception 24hr. Dorms 50-50zł. MC/V.) **The Stranger Hostel ❷,** ul. Kołłątaja 16/3, is opposite the train station on a road perpendicular to ul. Piłsudskiego, on the third floor of an unmarked building (ring buzzer #3). This hostel is a bit of a hike from town, but provides lots of social space and an "entertainment den" where people have been known to get rowdy. (☎071 634 1206. Free laundry, breakfast, and Internet. Reception 24hr. Dorms 50-60zł. AmEx/MC/V.)

La Havana ❷, Kuźnicza 12, (☎071 786 7071). The tongue-in-cheek presentation of Cuban communism here has made it wildly popular with the locals. (Open M-Th noon-3am, F noon-4am, Sa 1pm-4am, Su 1pm-2am. Reservations recommended on weekends. MC/V.) With its sleek, modern decor, **Bazylia ❶,** ul. Kuźnicza 42, is more posh than traditional milk bars but still serves reliably inexpensive fare. Prepare for a language barrier if you don't speak Polish. (Open M-F 7am-8pm, Sa-Su 7:30am-8pm. Entrees 3-9zł. Cash only.)

SIGHTS. The Gothic **Ratusz** (Town Hall) towers over the *Rynek* in the heart of the city. The beautiful central street **ulica Świdnicka** runs past the *Rynek*. The rotunda containing the 120-by-5m **Racławice Panorama,** ul. Purkyniego 11, was the site of an 18th-century peasant insurrection against the Russian occupation. To reach it, face away from the *Ratusz*, bear left onto ul. Kuźnicza, then turn right onto ul. Kotlarska, which becomes ul. Purkyniego. (☎071 344 2344. Shows 2 per hr. 9:30am-5pm. Commentary available in 5 languages at no extra charge. Open daily Apr.-Aug. 9am-5pm, Sept.-Oct. Tu-Su 9am-5pm, Nov.-Mar. Tu-Su 9am-4pm. 20zł, students 15zł.) The impressive Gothic buildings and winding roads of **Uniwersytet Wrocławski** (Wrocław University) form the cultural center of the city. **Aula Leopoldina,** an 18th-century frescoed lecture hall, is perhaps its most impressive sight.

NIGHTLIFE. For a lively night, head to **Bezennosc** (Insomnia), ul. Ruska 51, where a mannequin dressed as a grey-haired woman gazes eerily down onto patrons in upholstered chairs. Located in the newly-hip part of town and a playing a varied mix of music, this lively club attracts some of Wrocław's most fashionable. (Cover F-Sa 5zł. Beer 6-8zł. Open M-W and Su 6pm-2am, Th-Sa 6pm-4am. Cash only.) Stop by boisterous alt-rock hideout **Niebo Cafe** ul. Ruska 51, for a good drink. (☎071 342 9867. Beer 6zł. Open T-Su 1pm-last customer, M 5pm-last customer.) At relaxed bar-cafe **Kawiarnia "Pod Kalamburem,"** ul. Kuźnicza 29A, enjoy readings and film screenings. (Beer 5-15zł. Open M-Th 1pm-2am, F-Sa 1pm-late, Su 4pm-2am. Cash only.)

TORUŃ ☎056

Long known as "beautiful red Toruń" (pop. 210,000) for its impressive brick-and-stone architecture, this historic university town is the birthplace of Mikołaj Kopernik, better known as Copernicus. Five-hundred-year-old churches and the ruins of the local Teutonic castle dominate the skyline, while entertainers and pedestrians alike dominate the cobblestone pathways of Old Town.

TRANSPORTATION AND PRACTICAL INFORMATION

Trains leave from **Toruń Główny,** Kujawska 1 (☎056 94 36; open M-F 7am-5pm; Sa-Su 7am-2pm) for: Gdansk (3hr., 9 per day, 38zł); Łódź (3hr., 9 per day, 21-34zł); Poznań (21/2hr., 9 per day, 20-33zł); Warsaw (23/4hr., 8 per day, 40zł). **Buses** leave from **Dworzec PKS,** Dąbrowskiego 26 (☎056 655 5333; open 4am-midnight) for **Gdansk** (3hr., 2 per day, 34zł), Łódź (3hr., 13 per day, 27zł) and Warsaw (4hr., 6 per day, 32zł). Polski Express (☎228 445 555) runs **buses** from the Ruch kiosk north of pl. Teatralny to Łódź (3hr., 1 per day, 37/22zł) and Warsaw (3hr., 9 per day, 55/30zł). Most sights are in **Rynek Staromiejski** (Old Town Square). To get to there from the **train station,** take bus #22 or 27 across the Wisła River to plac Rapackiego. Head through the park, river on your right, to find the square. The **tourist office**, Rynek Staromiejski 25, has free **maps.** (☎056 621 0931; www.it.torun.pl. Open May-Aug. M and Sa 9am-4pm, Tu-F 9am-6pm, Su 9am-1pm; Sept.-Apr. M and Sa 9am-4pm, Tu-F 9am-6pm.) **Postal Code:** 87100.

ACCOMMODATIONS

POLAND

There are a number of reasonably priced accommodations in the center, but they fill up fast, so call ahead. Inexpensive hotels are often the best-situated option, but deal-seekers can check the tourist office for far-flung rooms in university dorms in July and August. (Singles 45zł; doubles 60zł.) **Orange Hostel ❶,** ul. Prosta 1, gets everything right, from its central location to laundry facilities that even include—amazingly—a dryer. (☎056 652 0033; www.hostelorange.pl. Kitchen. Breakfast included 7am-noon. Free laundry. Free Internet. Reception 24hr. Dorms 30zł; singles 50zł; doubles 80zł; triples 120zł.) It's a 20min. hike from town, but **Attic Hostel ❶,** ul. gen. Chłopickiego 4, offers beds in spacious, bright rooms. (☎056 659 8517; www.atticityhostel.noclegiw.pl. Breakfast included. Free Internet. Reception 7am-10pm. May-Aug. large dorms 30zł; singles 70zł; doubles 100zł; triples 120zł; quads 155zł. Sept.-Apr. 25/50/80/105/140zł. MC/V.)

FOOD

Manekin, Rynek Staromiejski 16 (☎056 652 2885). With an interior right out of the Wild Wild West, the popular Manekin serves massive yet artfully sweet and savory *nalesniki* (pancakes) for 4-13zł. The curry chicken and cheese (8.50zł) is a favorite. Open M-Th and Su 10am-11pm, F-Sa 10am-midnight. AmEx/MC/V. ❶

Cafe Relaks, Szewska 4. A cross between an ice cream parlour and an intimate cafe serves up cheap pierogi (8-14zł), but the gigantic sundaes (7-15zł) are the real reason people come here. Open daily 10am-8pm. Cash only. ❶

The Kopernik Factory, Żeglarska 24 (☎056 621 0337). This shop sells the most collectible dessert in town: gingerbread effigies of Polish kings, saints, and astronomers from 0.70zł for a small taste to 30zł for top-of-the-line historical figures. Open M-F 9am-7pm, Sa-Su 10am-6pm. MC/V. ❸

SIGHTS

STARE MIASTO (OLD TOWN). On the right bank of the Wisła River, Stare Miasto was constructed by the Teutonic Knights in the 13th century. Dom Kopernika, the probable birthplace of Copernicus, has been restored and showcases artifacts pertaining to the astronomer. *(Kopernika 15/17. ☎056 622 7038, ext.13. Open May-Sept. Tu-Su 10am-6pm, Oct.-Apr. Tu-Su 10am-4pm. 10zł students, 7zł. English-language captions available. Sound-and-light show 10/7zł. Both 18/12zł.)*

RATUSZ (TOWN HALL). The 14th-century town hall that dominates Rynek Staromiejski is a fine example of monumental burgher architecture. (☎*056 622 7038. Museum open daily May-Sept. 10am-8pm, Oct.-Mar. 10am-4pm, Apr. 10am-6pm. 10zł, students 6zł, Su free. Tower open May-Sept. Daily 10am-8pm. 10/6zł.)*

TEUTONIC KNIGHTS' CASTLE. A revolt in 1454 led to the destruction of the castle, but its ruins, on ul. Przedzamcze, are still standing. The remnants, despite the centuries, are an impressive sight. *(☎056 622 7039. Open daily 9am-8pm. Free.)*

KRZYWÁ WIEŻĄ (LEANING TOWER). The 15m tower was built in 1271 by a Teutonic Knight as punishment for breaking his order's rule of celibacy. The Cathedral of St. John the Baptist and St. John the Evangelist (Bazylika Katedralna pw. św. Janów), at the corner of ul. Zeglarska and św. Jana, is among the most impressive of churches in the area. *(ul. Krzywá Wieżą 17. At the corner of Zeglarska and Sw. Jana. Open Apr.-Oct. M-Sa 9am-5:30pm, Su 2-5:30pm. 3zł, students 2zł. Tower 6/4zł.)*

CHURCH OF THE VIRGIN MARY (KOŚCIÓŁ ŚW. MARII). Just across the Rynek Staromiejski are the stained-glass windows and intricate altars of the Church of the Virgin Mary. *(ul. Panny Marii. Open M-Sa 8am-5pm. Audio tour 2zł.)*

NIGHTLIFE

Piwnica pod Aniołami (Cellar Beneath the Angels), Rynek Staromiejski 1 (☎056 658 5482). Dance the night away at this club, an underground haven for Torun's alternative crowd with its vaulted ceilings and crimson-hued stone walls. Beer 3.50-5zł. Open M-F 10am-1am, Sa-Su 10am-4am. Cash only.

Niebo, Rynek Staromiejski 1 (☎056 621 0327). Its name translates to "heaven," but expect more than halos: instead, find an intimate Gothic cellar that boasts jazz and cabaret. Open M-Th and Su noon-midnight, F-Sa noon-2am.

Club Jazz God, Rabianska 17 (☎056 65 22 13 08; www.jazzgod.torun.com.pl). It lives up to its name with free live jazz Su 10pm; the rest of the week, students fill scattered seats for lively conversation and thunderous reggae, rock, and Polish pop starting around 8:30pm. Open M-Th and Su 5pm-2am, F-Sa 5pm-4am.

ŁÓDŹ ☎042

Poland's second largest city, Łódź (WOODGE; pop. 768,000) is home to some of the country's most interesting and least known sights and tastes. Łódź once housed the largest Jewish ghetto in Europe; today, residents are putting this plucky working-class city back on the map by hosting extraordinary art festivals and Jewish heritage exhibits.

TRANSPORTATION AND PRACTICAL INFORMATION. **Trains** run from Łódź Kaliska, al. Unii Lubelskiej 1 (☎41 02), to: Kraków (5hr., 6 per day, 49zł); Gdansk (7hr., 5 per day, 53zł); Warsaw (2hr.,7 per day, 33zł); Wrocław (4hr., 3 per day, 42zł). Polski Express **buses** (☎042 02 28 54 02 85; www.polskiexpress.org) depart from Łódź Fabryczna, pl. B. Salacinskiego 1, to Gdansk (4hr., 1 per day, 57zł) and Warsaw (2hr., 7 per day, 36zł). The IT **tourist office,** ul. Piotrkowska 87, books rooms, including university dorms in summer. (☎042 638 5955; www.cityoflodz.pl. Open May-Aug. M-F 8am-7pm, Sa-Su 10am-2pm, Sept.-Apr. M-F 8am-6pm, Su 10am-2pm.) **Postal Code:** 90-001.

ACCOMMODATIONS AND FOOD. The convenient **PTSM Youth Hostel (HI)** ❶, ul. Legionów 27, has quiet rooms with spacious bath and TV. Take tram #4 toward Helenówek from Fabryczna station to pl. Wolnosci; walk on

Legionów past Zachodnia. (☎630 6680; www.yhlodz.pl. Curfew 11pm. Reception 24hr. Singles 65zł; doubles 80zł; triples 120zł. MC/V.) **Anatewka ❸**, ul. 6 Sierpnia 2/4, serves phenomenal Jewish cuisine with flair. (☎042 630 3635. Entrees 17-45zł. Open daily 11am-midnight.) For cheaper eats, head to the **Zielony rynek** (the green market), a 5min. walk from Piotrkowska on Plac Barlickiego. This open-air market is open daily and features rows of fresh produce, bread, and various meats. Łódź's main thoroughfare, **ulica Piotrkowska,** is a bustling pedestrian shopping drag by day and a lively pub strip by night. Designed by an arts collective, the legendary bar and club **Łódź Kaliska,** ul. Piotrkowska 102, draws famous Polish actors and artists with its eccentric atmosphere and anything-goes decor. (☎042 630 6955; www.klub.lodzkaliska.pl. Beer 8zł. Open daily noon-late.)

SIGHTS. The eerily beautiful **Jewish Cemetery** (Cmentarz Żydowski), on ul. Zmienna, has over 200,000 graves. Near the entrance is a memorial to the Jews killed in the ghetto; signs lead to the **Ghetto Fields** (Pole Ghettowe), which are lined with faintly marked graves. Take tram #1 from ul. Kilinskiego or #6 from ul. Kościuszki or Zachodnia north to the end of the line (20min.); continue up the street, turn left on ul. Zmienna, and enter through the small gate on the right. (☎042 656 7019. Open May-Sept. M-Th and Su 9am-5pm, F 9am-3pm; Oct.-Apr. M-F and Su 8am-3pm. Closed Jewish holidays. 4zł, free for those visiting relatives' graves.) The **Jewish Community Center** (Gmina Wyznaniowa Żydowska), ul. Pomorska 18, in the town center, has information on those buried in the cemetery. (☎042 633 5156. Open M-F 10am-2pm. English spoken.)

GDAŃSK ☎058

At the mouth of the Wisła and Motlawa Rivers, Gdańsk (gh-DA-insk; pop. 458,000) has flourished for more than a millennium as a crossroads of art and commerce. This onetime Hanseatic trade city was treasured as the "gateway to the sea" during Poland's foreign occupation in the 18th and 19th centuries. Now, in its beautiful waterfront, cobblestone alleys, and sprawling construction, Gdansk displays both beauty and brawn.

TRANSPORTATION

Planes: Gdańsk Lech Wałesa Airport, (**GDN;** ☎058 348 11 11) 12km west of the city center. ZKMS **buses** run to Gdańsk Główny train station (30-40min., around 9zł). Budget airlines (p. 48) that fly to the city include **easyJet, Ryanair,** and **Wizz Air.**

Trains: Gdańsk Główny, Podwale Grodzkie 1 (☎058 94 36). To: **Kraków** (7-11hr., 14 per day, 59-105zł); **Łódź** 6-7hr., 8 per day, 49zł); **Lublin** (8hr., 5 per day, 54-98zł); **Malbork** (50min., 40 per day, 10-32zł); **Poznań** (4-5hr., 9 per day, 46zł); **Toruń** (3-4hr., 6 per day, 35-60zł); **Warsaw** (4hr., 22 per day, 50-82zł); **Wrocław** (6-7hr., 4 per day, 52zł). **SKM** (Fast City Trains; ☎058 628 5778) run to **Gdynia** (35min.; 4zł, students 2zł) and **Sopot** (20min.; 3.10/1.40zł) 6 per hr. during the day and less frequently at night. Buy tickets downstairs in the station's passageway, then punch it in a yellow *kasownik* machine.

Buses: 3 Maja 12 (☎058 302 1532), behind the train station, connected by an underground walkway. To: **Malbork** (1hr., 8 per day, 10-13zł); **Toruń** (2hr., 2 per day, 32zł); **Warsaw** (5hr., 9 per day, 45zł); **Kaliningrad, RUS** (6-7hr., 2 per day, 28zł). **Polski Express** buses run to **Warsaw** (4hr., 2 per day, 45zł).

Public Transportation: Gdańsk has an extensive **bus** and **tram** system. Buses run 6am-10pm. Tickets priced by the min. 10min. 1.40zł; 30min. 3.10zł; 1hr. 4.20zł; day pass 9zł. **Night buses,** marked "n," 10pm-6am. 3.30zł; night pass 5.50zł. Students ½-price.

Taxis: To avoid paying inflated tourist rates for **taxis,** book a cab by phone or over the **Internet** at the state-run **MPT** (☎058 96 33; www.artusmpt.gda.pl).

ORIENTATION AND PRACTICAL INFORMATION

Although Gdańsk sits on the Baltic Coast, its commercial center is 5km inland. From the train and bus stations, the center is a few blocks southeast, bordered by **Wały Jagiellońskie** and by the **Motława River.** Take the underpass in front of the station, go right, and turn left on Heweliusza. Turn right on Rajska and follow the signs to **Główne Miasto** (Main Town), turning left on Długa, also called **Trakt Królewski** (Royal Way). Długa becomes Długi Targ. Piwna and Sw. Ducha are Główne Miasto's other thoroughfare and parallel to Długa just to the north.

Tourist Offices: PTTK Gdańsk, Długa 45 (☎058 301 9151; www.pttk-gdansk.com.pl), in Główne Miasto, has free **maps** and **brochures.** Tours May-Sept. for groups of 3-10, 80zł per person. Open May-Sept. M-F 9am-5pm, Sa-Su 9am-3pm; Oct.-Apr. M-F 9am-6pm.

Budget Travel: Almatur, Długi Targ 11, 2nd fl. (☎058 301 2403; www.almatur.gda.pl). Sells **ISIC** (59zł) and air and **ferry** tickets. Open M-F 10am-6pm, Sa 10am-2pm.

Currency Exchange: Bank Pekao SA, Garncarska 23 (☎801 365 365). Cashes traveler's checks for 1% commission and provides MC/V cash advances for no commission. Open M-F 8am-6pm, Sa 10am-2pm.

English-Language Bookstore: Empik, Podwale Grodzkie 8 (☎058 301 6288, ext. 115). Sells maps. Open M-Sa 9am-9pm, Su 11am-8pm.

24hr. Pharmacy: Apteka Plus (☎058 763 1074), at train station. Ring bell at night.

Medical Services: For emergency care, go to Szpital Specjalistyczny im. M. Kopernika, Nowe Ogrody 5 (☎058 302 3031).

Internet: Jazz'n'Jive, Tkacka 17/18 (☎058 305 3616; www.cafe.jnj.pl), in the Old Town. 1zl per 10min., 3zł per 30min., 5zł per hr. Open daily 10am-10pm.

Post Office: Długa 23/28 (☎058 301 8853). For **Poste Restante,** use the entrance on Pocztowa. Open M-F 8am-8pm, Sa 9am-3pm. **Postal Code:** 80-801.

ACCOMMODATIONS

With Gdańsk's limited tourist infrastructure and increasing popularity among travelers, it's best to make accommodation arrangements ahead, especially in summer. **University dorms** are open to travelers in July and August; for further info, consult the PTTK tourist office (p. 768). **Private rooms** (30-80źł) can be arranged through either PTTK or **Grand-Tourist** ❷ (Biuro Podróży i Zakwaterowania), ul. Podwale Grodzkie 8, across from Empik. (☎058 301 2634; www.grand-tourist.pl. Open daily July-Aug. 8am-8pm; Sept.-June M-Sa 10am-6pm. Singles from 60-65zł; doubles 84-104zł; apartments 165-350zł. Cash only.)

Hostel Przy Targu Rybnym, ul.Grodzka 21 (☎058 301 5627; www.gdanskhostel.com), off Targ Rybny, across from the *baszta* (tower). This hostel feels more like a home with its eager staff and lively common area. Breakfast included. Free Internet. Reception 24hr. Dorms 45zł; doubles 200-250zł; quads and quints 240-350zł. Cash only. ❶

Baltic Hostel, 3 Maja 25 (☎058 721 9657; www.baltichostel.com), 5min. from the station. From the train station, take the KFC underpass to the bus station, then go right on 3 Maja and take the pedestrian path on the right–the hostel is all the way at the end. While its location at the end of a run-down alley is less than optimal, the renovated Baltic features bright, high-ceilinged rooms and buzzes with fellow backpackers. Breakfast and linens included. Free Internet. Free kayak use. Bike rental 20zl. Reception 24hr. Dorms 40zł; doubles 120zł. Cash only. ❷

POLAND

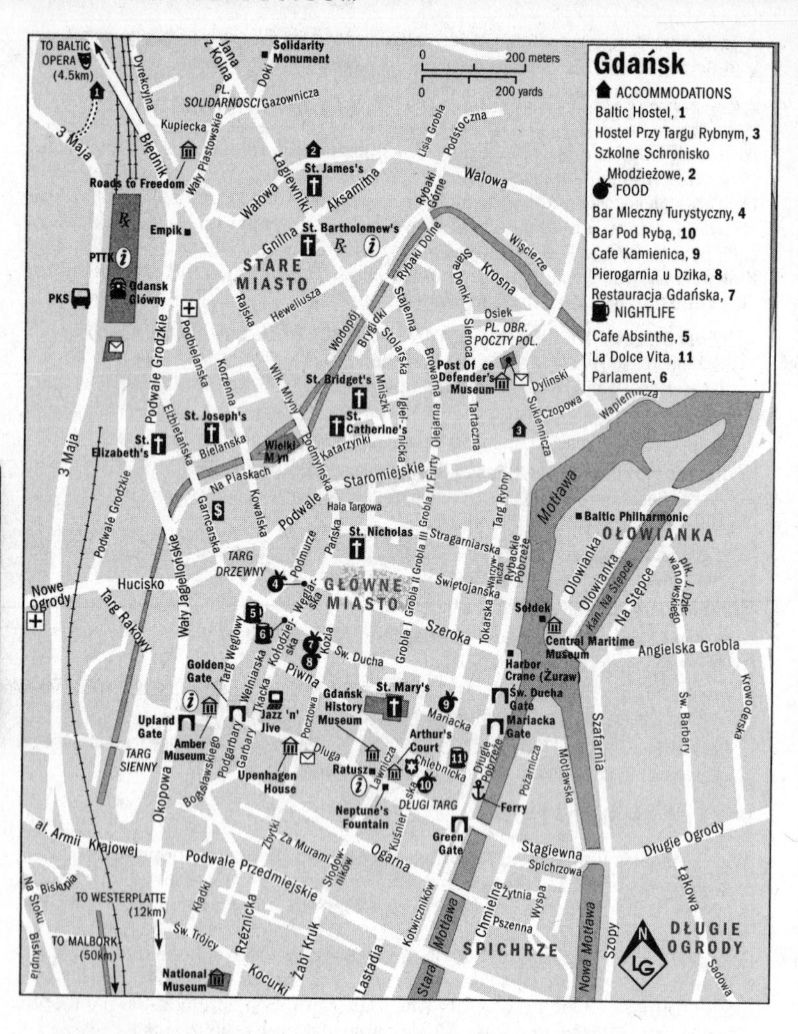

Szkolne Schronisko Młodzieżowe, Wałowa 21 (☎058 301 2313). From the train station, follow Karmelicka from City Forum; go left on Rajska and right on Wałowa. This hostel sports linoleum floors and metal doors; the rooms are spacious and feature well-kept furnishings. Full kitchen and common room set it a cut above most HI hostels, and the living is as clean as the rooms: there's a midnight curfew and no smoking or drinking. Reception 6am-midnight. Dorms 14-21zł; singles 27-31zł. Cash only. ❶

FOOD

Hala Targowa, on Pańska, in the shadow of Kościół św. Katarzyny, just off Podwale Staromiejskie, has rows of stands selling everything from raw meat to shoe soles. (Open May-Aug. M-F 9am-7pm, Sa 9am-5pm; Sept-Apr. M-F 9am-

6pm, Sa 9am-3pm.) An **Esta** supermarket is at Podwale Staromiejskie 109/112 in Targ Drzewny. (Open M-Sa 10am-10pm, Su noon-10pm.)

Cafe Kamienica, Mariacka 37/39 (☎058 301 1230), in St. Mary's shadow. Enjoy fresh, delicate entrees (arugula salad with sun-dried tomatoes; 18zł), next to antique couches and dark-wood furnishings. Tea 5zł. Superb coffee drinks 6-12zł. Light entrees 9-30zł. Open daily June-Sept. 9am-midnight; Oct.-May 10am-11pm. AmEx/MC/V. ❷

Bar Pod Rybą (Bar Under the Fish), Długi Targ 35/38/1 (☎058 305 1307). An unusual take on a Polish staple—huge baked potatoes with fillings (6-20zł). The Hungarian sausage topping comes highly recommended, while the eatery lives up to its fishy name with additives like fresh shrimp and mussels (5zl). Open daily July-Aug. 11am-10pm; Sept.-June 11am-7pm. AmEx/MC/V. ❶

Pierogarnia u Dzika (Wild Boar Pierogi Bar), Piwna 59/60 (☎058 305 2676). Locals swear by these pierogi (14-22zł) stuffed with everything from caviar to strawberries. The 35-piece platter (57zł) is terrific for large groups. Open daily 11am-11pm. MC/V. ❸

Restaurancja Gdańska, ul. Sw. Ducha 16/24, (☎058 305 7671). Clocks, antique mirrors, and oil paintings crowd the deep red walls of the restaurant's dramatic interior. The restaurant is a favorite of local celebrities, including former president Lech Wałesa. Entrees 25-70zł. Open daily 11am-midnight. AmEx/MC/V. ❷

Bar Mleczny Turystyczny, Szeroka 8/10 (☎058 301 60 13). With its huge windows thrown open upon one of Gdańsk's busiest areas, this milk bar is a bright, lively, and affordable lunch spot. Open M-F 7:30am-6pm, Sa-Su 9am-4pm. Cash only. ❶

SIGHTS

DŁUGI TARG. Długi Targ (Long Market) is a pedestrian thoroughfare at the heart of **Główne Miasto** (Main Town). The stone Upland Gate and the elegant blue-gray Golden Gate, emblazoned with gold leaf moldings and the shields of Poland, Prussia, and Germany, mark the western entrance to ul. Dluga. In the square, **Neptune's Fountain** (Fontanna Neptuna) faces the 16th-century facade of **Arthur's Court** (Dwór Artusa), a palace with a Renaissance interior and wood-carved spiral staircase that was restored in 1997. At the intersection of ul. Długa and Długi Targ, the 14th-century **Ratusz** (Town Hall) houses a branch of the **Gdańsk History Museum** (Muzeum Historii Gdanska), which covers the city's past from its first historical mention to the rubble left behind by WWII. *(Ratusz and Arthur's Court open June-Sept. M 11am-3pm, Tu-Sa 10am-6pm, Su 11am-6pm; Oct.-May Tu-Sa 10am-4pm, Su 11am-4pm. Each 8zł, students 5zł; combined ticket 20/7zł; T free.)*

ELSEWHERE IN GLÓWNE MIASTO. At the **Roads to Freedom** (Drogi do wolniści) across the street from the Gdańsk Shipyard (Stocznia Gdańska) where the movement was born, powerful multimedia depict the rise of the movement. *(From Podwale Grodzkie, veer right on Wały Piastowskie. The entrance is on the left. ☎058 308 4280. Open Tu-Su 10am-5pm. 6zl, students 4zł; W 2zł.)* In the vaults of a former Franciscan monastery, the **National Museum** (Muzeum Narodowe) hosts a large collection of gothic sculpture, art, and carved furniture. Hans Memling's *Last Judgment* is a must-see. *(Torunska 1. ☎058 301 7061; www.muzeum.narodowe.gda.pl. Open June-mid-Sept. Tu-F 9am-4pm, Sa-Su 10am-4pm; mid-Sept.-May Tu-Su 9am-4pm. 10zł, students 6zł; Sa free.)* The **Memorial to the Defenders of the Post Office Square** (Obronców Poczty) honors the postal workers' courageous stand against the invading Germans at the start of WWII. *(From Podwale Staromiejskie, go north on Tartaczna and turn right onto Obrońćów Polskiej Poczty1-2. ☎058 301 7611. Open Tu 10-3, W-Sa 10-4. 4zł, students 3zł.)* Ornate row houses line ul. sw. Ducha, ul. Mariacka, and ul. Chlebnicka, north of Długi Targ. Ul. Mariacka, with its stone porches and gaping dragon-head gutter spouts, leads to riverside ul. Długie Pobrzeże. To the left is the huge Gothic

POLAND

Harbor Crane (Zuraw) from the 13th century, part of the **Central Maritime Museum** (Centralne Muzeum Morskie). Two more branches of the museum lie across the river: one on land, the other on the ship **Sołdek.** *(☎058 301 8611. Open June-Aug. daily 10am-6pm; Sept.-May Tu-Su 10am-4pm. Crane 6zł, students 4zł. Museum 6/4zł. Sołdek 6/4zł. Shuttle boat round-trip 3/1.50zł.)* The flags of the Soviet bloc's first trade union, Lech Wałęsa's Solidarity (Solidarność), fly again at the **Solidarity Monument,** pl. Solidarności, north of the city center at the end of ul. Wały Piastowskie.

NIGHTLIFE

When the sun sets, crowds party in Długi Targ. *City* lists events in the Tri-City Area, and *Gdańsk in Your Pocket* offers updated club listings.

La Dolce Vita, Chlebnicka 2, (☎058 304 7887). This club is quickly becoming a Gdansk staple with its inventive cocktail menu and laid-back vibe. Open 2pm-2am.

Cafe Absinthe, ul. sw. Ducha 2, (☎058 320 3784), next to Teatr Wybreże. is one of the most popular clubs in town; attracting ruminating intellectuals by day and the city's most eccentric characters by night. Open daily 10am-4am.

Parlament, sw. Ducha 2, (☎058 302 1365). Popular Parlament entices a young crowd and frequent stag parties. Beer 5zł. 18+. Cover Th after 10pm 5zł; F-Sa before 10pm 5zł, 10zł after. Purchase drinks with non-refundable "prepaid cards," which are available at the entrance. Open Tu-Sa 8pm-late. Dance floor open Th-Sa 10pm-late.

POLAND

SOPOT ☎058

Poland's premier resort town, Sopot (pop. 50,000) draws visitors to its sandy beaches and renowned nightlife. Restaurants, shops, and street performers dot the pedestrian promenade ul. Bohaterów Monte Cassino. Europe's longest *molo* (wooden pier; 516m) provides sweeping views of the Baltic. (Open M-F. 3zł, Sa-Su 3.80zł.) During the summer months, the beachside **Copacabana** becomes the place to see and be seen, attracting hard-partying locals and tourists alike. (www.copacabanasopot.pl. 10zł after 10pm. Open 24hr.) **Soho clubogaleria,** ul. Monte Cassino 61, spins electropop, house, and lounge with attitude. (☎058 551 6527. Beer 7zł. Open daily noon-5am.) For a less-packed, more Bohemian feel, head over to **Sfinks** on Ul Mamuszki 1 (www.myspace.com/sfinks_sopot. Open Oct.-June Th-Sa 6pm-6am, July-Sept. M-Th and Su 4pm-4am, F-Sa 4pm-6am.) **Mandarynka**, ul. Bema 6, off ul. Monte Cassino, offers three tangerine-splashed floors of partying. (☎058 550 4563. Beer 7zł. Open M 1pm-2am, Tu-Th and Su midnight-2am, F-Sa noon-5am.)

Affordable **university dorms,** which can be arranged through the tourist office, are available, but only during the months of July and August. If visiting during the off-season, reserve a room in advance to get a reasonable price. A Sopot staple, **Bar Przystań ❶**, al. Wojska Polskiego 11, complements its beachside location with decorative fishing nets and an array of fresh seafood. (☎058 550 0241; www.barprzystan.pl. Fresh fish 6-9zł per 100g. Fish salads from 4zł per 100g. Open daily 11am-11pm. Cash only.)

The SKM **commuter rail** connects Sopot to Gdańsk (20min.; 1-6 per hr.; 3.10zł, students 1.40zł). Ulica Dworcowa begins at the station and leads to ul. Monte Cassino, which stretches out to the sea by the pier. **Ferries** (tramwaj wodny; ☎604 837 793) head from the end of the pier to Gdańsk (1hr.; 4 per day; 8zł, students 4zł) and Hel (1hr., 3 per day, 12/6zł). The IT **tourist office,** ul. Dworcowa 4, by the train station, sells **maps** (4-5zł) and arranges rooms. (☎058 550 3783. Open daily June to mid-Sept. 9am-8pm; mid-Sept. to May M-F 10am-6pm.)

PORTUGAL

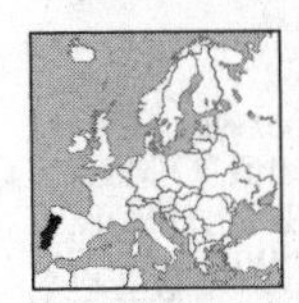

While Portugal is small, its imposing forests and mountains, scenic vineyards, and almost 2000km of coastline rival the attractions of Spain. Portugal's capital, Lisbon, offers marvelous museums, castles, and churches. The country experienced international glory and fabulous wealth 400 hundred years ago during the Golden Age of Vasco da Gama. Despite suffering under the dictatorship of Salazar for 30 years in the 20th century, Portugal has reemerged as a European cultural center with a growing economy. Extremes of fortune have contributed to the unique Portuguese concept of *saudade*, a yearning for the glories of the past and a dignified resignation to the fact that the future can never compete. Visitors may experience *saudade* through a *fado* singer's song or over a glass of port, but Portugal's attractions are more likely to inspire delight than nostalgia.

DISCOVER PORTUGAL: SUGGESTED ITINERARIES

THREE DAYS. Make your way through **Lisbon** (1 day; p. 804); venture through its famous Moorish district, the Alfama, Castelo de São Jorge, and the Parque das Nações. By night, listen to *fado* and hit the clubs in Bairro Alto. Daytrip to **Sintra's** fairy-tale castles (1 day; p. 813), then sip wine in **Porto** (1 day; p. 814).

ONE WEEK. After wandering the streets of **Lisbon** (2 days) and **Sintra** (1 day), lounge on the beaches of **Lagos** (1 day; p. 820) and admire the cliffs of **Sagres** (1 day; p. 821). Move on to the university town of **Coimbra** (1 day; p. 817) before ending your week in **Porto** (1 day).

BEST OF PORTUGAL, TWO WEEKS. After taking in the sights, sounds, and cafes of **Lisbon** (4 days), daytrip to enchanting **Sintra** (1 day). Head down to the infamous beaches and bars of **Lagos** (2 days), where hordes of visitors dance the night away. Take an afternoon in **Sagres** (1 day), once considered the edge of the world. Check out the macabre bone chapel in **Évora** (1 day; p. 818) before heading north to the vibrant university town of **Coimbra** (2 days). Be sure to sample the wide selection of port on offer in **Porto** (2 days). Finish your tour in the impressive gardens and plazas of **Braga** (1 day; p. 816).

ESSENTIALS

FACTS AND FIGURES

OFFICIAL NAME: The Portuguese Republic.

CAPITAL: Lisbon.

MAJOR CITIES: Coimbra, Porto.

POPULATION: 10,463,000.

TIME ZONE: GMT.

LANGUAGES: Portuguese, Mirandese.

RELIGION: Roman Catholic (85%).

NUMBER OF GRAPE VARIETALS AUTHORIZED FOR MAKING PORT: 48.

WHEN TO GO

Summer is high-season, but the southern coast draws tourists between March and November. In the low-season, many hostels slash their prices, and reservations are seldom necessary. While Lisbon and some of the larger towns (especially the university town of Coimbra) burst with vitality year-round, many smaller towns virtually shut down in winter, and sights reduce their hours.

DOCUMENTS AND FORMALITIES

EMBASSIES AND CONSULATES. Foreign embassies in Portugal are in Lisbon. Portuguese embassies abroad include: **Australia,** 23 Culgoa Circuit, O'Malley, Canberra, ACT 2606 (☎612 6290 1733); **Canada,** 645 Island Park Dr., Ottawa, ON K1Y 0B8 (☎613-729-2270); **Ireland,** Knocksinna Mews, 7 Willow Park, Foxrock, Dublin, 18 (☎353 289 4416); **UK,** 11 Belgrave Sq., London, SW1X 8PP (☎020 7235 5331); **US,** 2012 Massachusetts Ave. NW, Washington DC, 20036 (☎202-350-5400). **NZ** citizens should contact the embassy in Australia.

VISA AND ENTRY INFORMATION. EU citizens do not need a visa. Citizens of Australia, Canada, New Zealand, the UK, and the US do not need a visa for stays up to 90 days, beginning upon entry into any of the countries within the EU's freedom-of-movement zone. For more info, see p. 14. For stays longer than 90 days, all non-EU citizens need visas (around $100), available at Portuguese consulates.

TOURIST SERVICES AND MONEY

TOURIST OFFICES. For general info, contact the Portuguese Tourism Board, (☎+1 646 723 02 00; www.portugal.org). When in Portugal, stop by municipal and provincial tourist offices, listed in the Practical Information section of each city and town.

EMERGENCY	General Emergency: ☎112.

MONEY. The **euro (€)** has replaced the **escudo** as the unit of currency in Portugal. For more info on the euro, see p. 17. Generally, it's cheaper to exchange money in Portugal than at home. **ATMs** have the best exchange rates. Credit cards also offer good rates and may sometimes be required to reserve hotel rooms or rental cars; **MasterCard** (known in Portugal as **Eurocard**) and **Visa** are the most frequently accepted. Tips of 5-10% are customary only in fancy restaurants or hotels. Some cheaper restaurants include a 10% service charge; if they don't and you'd like to leave a tip, round up to the nearest euro and leave the change. Taxi drivers do not expect tips except for especially long trips. **Bargaining** is not customary in shops, but you can give it a shot at the local market *(mercado)* or when looking for a private room *(quarto)*. Portugal has a 21% **value added tax (VAT),** a sales tax applied to retail goods. The prices given in *Let's Go* include VAT. In the airport upon exiting the EU, non-EU citizens can claim a refund on the tax paid for goods purchased at participating stores. In order to qualify for a refund in a store, you must spend at least €50-100, depending on the shopkeeper; make sure to ask for a refund form when you pay. For more info on qualifying for a VAT refund, see (p. 21).

BUSINESS HOURS. Shops are open M-F from 9am to 6pm, although many close for a few hours in the afternoon. Restaurants serve lunch from noon to 3pm and dinner from 7 to 10pm—or later. Museums are often closed on Monday, and many shops are closed over the weekend. Banks usually open around 9am M-F and close in the afternoon.

TRANSPORTATION

BY PLANE. Most international flights land at **Portela Airport** in Lisbon (**LIS;** ☎218 41 35 00); some also land at **Faro** (**FAO;** ☎289 80 08 00) or **Porto** (**OPO;** 229 43 24 00). **TAP Air Portugal** (Canada and the US ☎800-221-7370, Portugal ☎707 20 57 00, UK ☎845 601 0932; www.tap.pt) is Portugal's national airline, serving domestic and international locations. **Portugália** (☎218 93 80 70; www.flypga.pt) is smaller and flies between Faro, Lisbon, Porto, major Spanish cities, and other Western European destinations. For more information, see p. 50.

BY TRAIN. Caminhos de Ferro Portugueses (☎213 18 59 90; www.cp.pt) is Portugal's national railway. Lines run to domestic destinations, Madrid, and Paris. For travel outside of the Braga-Porto-Coimbra-Lisbon line, buses are better. Lisbon, where local trains are fast and efficient, is the exception. Trains often leave at irregular hours, and posted schedules *(horários)* aren't always accurate; check ticket booths upon arrival. Fines for riding without a ticket *(sem bilhete)* are high. Those under 12 or over 65 get half-price tickets. Youth discounts are only available to Portuguese citizens. Train passes are usually not worth buying, as tickets are inexpensive. For more information on train travel, see p. 50.

BY BUS. Buses are cheap, frequent, and connect to just about every town in Portugal. **Rodoviária** (☎212 94 71 00), formerly the national bus company, has recently been privatized. Each company name corresponds to a particular region of the country, such as Rodoviária Alentejo or Minho e Douro, with a few exceptions such as EVA in the Algarve. Private regional companies, including **AVIC, Cabanelas,** and **Mafrense,** also operate buses. Beware of non-express buses in small regions like Estremadura and Alentejo, which stop every few minutes. Express service *(expressos)* between major cities is good, and inexpensive city buses often run to nearby villages. Portugal's main Euroline (p. 53) affiliates are Internorte, Intercentro, and Intersul. **Busabout** coaches stop in Portugal at Lisbon, Lagos, and Porto. Every coach has a guide on board to answer questions and to make travel arrangements en route.

BY CAR. A **driver's license** from one's home country is required to rent a car; no International Driving Permit is necessary. Portugal has the **highest automobile accident rate** per capita in Western Europe. The highway system *(itinerarios principais)* is easily accessible, but off the main arteries, the narrow roads are difficult to negotiate. Speed limits are ignored, recklessness is common, and lighting and road surfaces are often inadequate. Parking space in cities is nonexistent. In short, buses are safer. The national automobile association, the **Automóvel Clube de Portugal (ACP)**, (☎800 50 25 02; www.acp.pt), has breakdown and towing service, as well as first aid.

BY THUMB. In Portugal, **hitchhiking** is rare. Beach-bound locals occasionally hitchhike in summer, but more commonly stick to the inexpensive bus system. Rides are easiest to come by between smaller towns and at gas stations near highways and rest stops. *Let's Go* does not recommend hitchhiking.

KEEPING IN TOUCH

PHONE CODES	**Country code:** 351. **International dialing prefix:** 00. Within Portugal, dial city code and then the local number. For more info on placing international calls, see **Inside Back Cover.**

EMAIL AND THE INTERNET. Internet cafes in cities and most towns charge around €1.20-4 per hr. for Internet access. When in doubt, try a library, where there is often at least one computer equipped for Internet access.

TELEPHONE. Whenever possible, use a calling card for international phone calls, as long-distance rates for national phone services are often very high. Mobile phones are an increasingly popular and economical option. Major mobile carriers include: TMN, Optimus Telecom SA, and Vodafone. Direct-dial access numbers for calling out of Portugal include: **AT&T Direct** (☎800 80 01 28); **British Telecom** (☎800 80 04 40); **Canada Direct** (☎800 80 01 22); **Telecom New Zealand Direct** (☎800 80 06 40); **Telstra Australia** (☎800 80 06 10). For more info on calling home from Europe, see p. 31.

MAIL. Mail in Portugal is somewhat inefficient. **Airmail** *(via aerea)* takes one to two weeks to reach Canada or the US, and more to get to Australia and New Zealand. **Surface mail** *(superficie)*, for packages only, takes up to two months. **Registered** or blue mail takes five to eight business days for roughly three times the price of airmail. **EMS** or **Express Mail** will most likely arrive overseas in three to four days, though it costs more than double the blue mail price. To receive mail in Portugal, have mail delivered **Poste Restante.** Mail will go to the main post office unless you specify a subsidiary by street address. Address mail to be held according to the following example: Last Name, First Name, Posta Restante, Postal code City, PORTUGAL; AIRMAIL.

ACCOMMODATIONS AND CAMPING

PORTUGAL	❶	❷	❸	❹	❺
ACCOMMODATIONS	under €16	€16-20	€21-30	€31-40	over €40

Movijovem, R. Lúcio de Azevedo 27, 1600-146 Lisbon (☎707 20 30 30; www.pousadasjuventude.pt), the **Portuguese Hostelling International** affiliate, oversees the country's HI hostels. All bookings can be made through them. A bed in a *pousada da juventude* costs €9-15 per night, including breakfast and linens, slightly less in the low-season. Though often the cheapest option, hostels may lie far from the town center. To reserve rooms in the high-season, get an **International Booking Voucher** from Movijovem (or your country's HI affiliate) and send it to the desired hostel four to eight weeks in advance. In the low-season (Oct.-Apr.), double-check to see if the hostel is open. **Hotels** in Portugal tend to be pricey. Rates typically include breakfast and showers, and most rooms without bath or shower have a sink. When business is slow, try bargaining in advance—the "official price" is just the maximum. **Pensões,** also called **residencias,** are a budget traveler's mainstay, cheaper than hotels and only slightly more expensive (and much more common) than crowded youth hostels. Like hostels, *pensões* generally provide linens and towels. Many do not take reservations in high-season; for those that do, book ahead. **Quartos** are rooms in private residences, similar to Spain's casas particulares. These may be the the cheapest option in cities and the only option in town; tourist offices can help find one. Prices are flexible and bargaining expected. Portugal has 150 **official campgrounds** *(parques de campismo)*, often beach-accessible and equipped with grocery stores and cafes. Urban and coastal parks may require reservations. Police are cracking down on illegal camping, so don't try it. Tourist offices stock *Portugal: Camping and Caravan Sites*, a free guide to official campgrounds.

FOOD AND DRINK

PORTUGAL	❶	❷	❸	❹	❺
FOOD	under €6	€6-10	€11-15	€16-20	over €20

Portuguese dishes are seasoned with olive oil, garlic, herbs, and sea salt, but few spices. The fish selection includes *choco grelhado* (grilled cuttlefish), *linguado grelhado* (grilled sole), and *peixe espada* (swordfish). Portugal's renowned *queijos* (cheeses) are made from cow, goat, and sheep milk. For dessert, try *pudim flan* (egg custard). A hearty *almoço* (lunch) is eaten between noon and 2pm; *jantar* (dinner) is served between 8pm and midnight. *Meia dose* (half-portions) cost more than half-price but are often more than adequate. The *prato do dia* (special of the day) and the set *menú* of appetizer, bread, entree, and dessert, are also filling choices. Cheap, high-quality Portuguese *vinho* (wine) is astounding. Its delicious relative, *vinho do porto* (port), is a dessert in itself. Coffees include *bica* (black espresso), *galão* (with milk, in a glass), and *café com leite* (with milk, in a cup). *Mini-Preço* and *Pingo Doce* have cheap groceries.

NO SUCH THING AS A FREE LUNCH. Waiters in Portugal will put an assortment of snacks, ranging from simple bread and butter to sardine paste, cured ham, or herbed olives, on your table before the appetizer is served. But check the prices before you dig in: you nibble, you buy.

HOLIDAYS AND FESTIVALS

Holidays: New Year's Day (Jan. 1); Epiphany (Jan. 6); Good Friday (Apr. 10, 2009); Easter (Apr. 11-12); Liberation Day (Apr. 25); Ascension (May 21); Labor Day (May 1); Corpus Christi (Jun. 11, 2009); Portugal Day (June 10); Assumption (Aug. 15); Republic Day (Oct. 5); All Saints' Day (Nov. 1); Restoration of Independence Day (Dec. 1); Immaculate Conception (Dec. 8, 2009); Christmas (Dec. 25); New Year's Eve (Dec. 31).

Festivals: All of Portugal celebrates *Carnaval* (Feb. 24, 2009) and Holy Week (Apr. 5-12, 2009). Coimbra holds the *Queima das Fitas* (Burning of the Ribbons) festival in early May, celebrating the end of the university school year. In June, Batalha holds a *Feira International* celebrating the food, wine, and traditional handicrafts of the region, and Lisbon hosts the *Festas da Cidade*, honoring the birth of St. Anthony with music, games, parades, and street fairs. For more information on festivals, see www.portugal.org.

BEYOND TOURISM

As a volunteer in Portugal, you can contribute to efforts concerning environmental protection, social welfare, or political activism. While not many students think of studying abroad in Portugal, most Portuguese universities open their gates to foreign students. Being an au pair and teaching English are popular options for long-term work, though many people choose to seek more casual—and often illegal—jobs in resort areas. *Let's Go* does not recommend any type of illegal employment. For more info on opportunities across Europe, see **Beyond Tourism,** p. 60.

Volunteers for Peace, 1034 Tiffany Road, Belmont, VT 05730 USA (☎+1-801-259-2759; www.vfp.org). Organizes 2-3 week group projects in Spain, Portugal, and Morocco on a wide range of social and environmental issues. Average project cost $300.

Teach Abroad (www.teachabroad.com). Brings you to listings around the world for paid or stipend positions teaching English.

Universidade de Lisboa, Rectorate Al. da Universidade, Cidade Universitária, 1649-004 Lisbon, POR (☎217 96 76 24; www.ul.pt). Allows foreign students to enroll directly.

Volunteer Abroad (www.volunteer-abroad.com/Portugal.cfm). Offers opportunities to volunteer with conservation efforts around Portugal.

LISBON (LISBOA) ☎21

In 1755, a terrible earthquake destroyed much of Lisbon—a tragedy relived by the nostalgic ballads of *fado* singers. But today, Portugal's seaside capital thrives as a center of architecture, art, and nightlife. Romans and Arabs once called Lisbon home, and the city remains highly multicultural.

TRANSPORTATION

Flights: Aeroporto de Lisboa (LIS; ☎21 841 3500). From the terminal, turn right and follow the path to the bus stop. Take bus #44 or 45 to Pr. dos Restauradores, in front of the tourist office (15-20min., every 12-15min., €1.60). A **taxi** from downtown costs about €10 plus a €1.60 baggage fee. Ask at the tourist office (☎21 845 0660) inside the airport about buying prepaid vouchers for taxi rides from the airport. (M-F €15, Sa-Su €18. Open daily 7am-midnight.) Major airlines have offices at Pr. Marquês do Pombal and along Av. da Liberdade.

Trains: Caminhos de Ferro Portugueses (☎808 20 82 08; www.cp.pt). 5 main stations, each serving different destinations. Trains in Portugal–slow, inconsistent, and confusing–are the bane of every traveler's existence; buses, though more expensive and lacking toilets, are faster and more comfortable.

Estação Santa Apolónia, Av. Infante Dom Henrique, runs the international, northern, and eastern lines. All trains to Santa Apolónia also stop at **Estação Oriente** (M: Oriente) by the Parque das Nações. The international terminal has **currency exchange** and an info desk. To reach downtown, take **bus** #9, 46, or 59 to Pr. dos Restauradores. To: **Aveiro** (3-3hr., 16 per day, €24-35); **Braga** (5hr., 3 per day, €2-30); **Coimbra** (2hr., 24 per day, €15-20.15); **Madrid, SPA** (10hr., 10:05pm, €70); **Porto** (3-4hr., 20 per day, €19.50-27).

Estação do Barreiro, across the Rio Tejo. Travels south. Accessible by ferry from the Terreiro do Paço dock off Pr. do Comércio (30min., 2 per hr., €2.50). To get to **Évora** and **Lagos,** take a train to Pinhal Novo station and transfer. From Pinhal Novo, trains go to: **Lagos** (3hr., 5 per day 9:04am-8:04pm, €18) and **Évora** (1hr., per day, €8.50).

Estação Cais do Sodré, just beyond R. do Alecrim, near Baixa. M: Cais do Sodré. Take the metro or bus #36, 45, or 91 from Pr. dos Restauradores or tram #28 from Estação Santa Apolónia. To: the monastery in **Belém** (10min., 4 per hr., €1.15), **Cascais** and **Estoril** (30min., 2 per hr., €1.65), and the youth hostel in **Oeiras** (20min., 2 per hr., €1.30).

Estação Rossio, M: Rossio or Restauradores. Get off at M: Rossio and walk across the praça for two blocks until you see the station on your right. Alternatively, get off at M: Restauradores, and go down Av. da Liberdage, and the station will be on your right. The Estação de Sete Rios on the top fl. of M: Jardim Zoológico sends trains every 20min. to **Queluz** (€1.20) and **Sintra** (€1.65).

Buses: M: Jardim Zoológico. In the **metro** station, follow exit signs to Av. C. Bordalo Pinheiro, cross the street, and follow the path up the stairs. Look for autocarros signs. **Rede Expressos buses** (☎707 22 33 44; www.rede-expressos.pt) go to: **Braga** (5hr., 20 per day, €17.5); **Coimbra** (2hr., 25 per day, €12); **Faro** (4hr., 12per day, €17.50); **Lagos** (4-5hr., 13 per day, €17.50-18); **Porto** (3-4hr., 19 per day, €16) via **Leiria** (2hr., €9).

Public Transportation: CARRIS (☎21 361 3000; www.carris.pt) runs **buses, trams,** and **funiculars.** If you plan to stay in Lisbon for any length of time, consider a *passe turístico,* good for unlimited travel on all CARRIS transports. **Day passes** (€3.50) are sold in CARRIS booths in most train stations and busier metro stations. The 4 lines of the metro (☎21 350 0100; www.metrolisboa.pt) cover downtown and the modern business district. Single ride €0.75; book of 10 tickets €6.40. Trains run daily 6:30am-1am; some stations close earlier.)

Taxis: Rádio Táxis de Lisboa (☎21 811 9000), **Autocoope** (☎21 793 2756), and **Teletáxis** (☎21 811 1100). Along Av. da Liberdade and Rossio. Luggage €1.60.

PRACTICAL INFORMATION

The city center is made up of three neighborhoods: **Baixa** (low district), **Bairro Alto** (high district), and hilly **Alfama.** The suburbs extending in both directions along the river are some of the fastest-growing sections of the city. Several kilometers from downtown, **Belém** is a walk into Portugal's past. **Alcântara** is home to much of Lisbon's party scene as well as the Parque das Nações, site of the 1998 World Expo. Baixa's grid of mostly pedestrian streets is bordered to the north by **Rossio** (a.k.a. Praça Dom Pedro IV) and to the south by **Praça do Comércio,** on the Rio Tejo (River Tagus). East of Baixa is Alfama, Lisbon's oldest, labyrinthine district, and west of Baixa is Bairro Alto. Bairro Alto's upscale shopping district, the **Chiado,** is crossed by R. do Carmo and R. Garrett. **Avenida da Liberdade** runs north, uphill from Pr. dos Restauradores.

Tourist Office: Palácio da Foz, Pr. dos Restauradores (☎21 346 3314). M: Restauradores. Open daily 9am-8pm. The **Welcome Center,** Pr. do Comércio (☎21 031 2810), the city's main office, sells the **Lisbon Card,** which includes transportation and entrance to most sights (1-day €15, 2-day €26, 3-day €32). English spoken. Open daily 9am-8pm. Kiosks at Santa Apolónia, Belém, and other locations provide tourist info.

Embassies and Consulates: Australia, Av. da Liberdade 200 (☎21 310 1500; www.portugal.embassy.gov.au); **Canada,** Av. Liberdade 196 (☎21 444 3301; http://geo.international.gc.ca/canada-europa/portugal); **Ireland,** R. da Imprensa a Estrela 1-4 (☎21 392 9440); **New Zealand,** R. da Vista Alegre 10 (☎21 370 5787); **UK,** R. de São Bernardo 33 (☎21 392 4000; www.britishembassy.gov.uk/portugal); **US,** Av. das Forças Armadas (☎21 727 3300; www.american-embassy.pt).

Currency Exchange: Banks are generally open M-F 8:30am-3pm. **Cota Câmbios,** Pr. Dom Pedro IV 41 (☎21 322 0480), exchanges currency. Open daily 8am-10pm. The main post office, most banks, and travel agencies also change money.

Police: R. Capelo 13 (☎21 346 6141 or ☎21 342 1634). English spoken.

Late-Night Pharmacy: ☎118 (directory assistance). Look for the green cross at intersections, or try **Farmácia Azevedos,** Pr. Dom Pedro IV 31 (☎21 343 0482), at the base of Rossio in front of the metro.

Lisbon

ACCOMMODATIONS
Brasileira, **8**
Casa de Hospedes Globo, **15**
Easy Hostel, **11**
Goodnight Backpacker's Hostel, **10**
Lisbon Lounge Hostel, **12**
Luar Guest House, **14**
Oasis Backpackers Mansion, **6**
Pensão Beira Mar, **13**
Pensão Ninho das Águias, **9**

FOOD
Á Minha Maneira, **1**
Ali-a-papa, **2**
Calculta, **3**
Casa-Brasileira, **4**
Churrasqueira Gaúcha, **5**
Ristorante Pizzeria Valentino, **7**

TO (3km), COLOMBO SHOPPING CENTER AND ESTÁDIO DE LUZ (5km)
TO MUSEU GULBENIAN, CENTRE DE ARTE MODERNA
TO PRAÇA DE TOURA
TO HOSPITAL DONA ESTEFÂNIA (75m)
TO BELÉM (4.75km), MOSTEIRO DOS JERÓNIMOS, TORRE DE BELÉM
TO ESTACÃO SANTA APOLÓNIA (100m), PARQUE DAS NAÇÕES (5.5km), IGREJA DE SÃO VICENTE DE FORA, PANTEÃO NACIONAL, ESTACÃO DO BARREIRO

ESTRELA
BAIRRO ALTO
MOURARIA
BAIXA
ALFAMA
Jardim da Estrela
Jardim Botânico
Palácio da Assembléia Nacional
Livraría Británica
Elevador da Glória
São Roque
Web Cafe
Estação Rossio
RESTAURADORES
AVENIDA
MARTIM MONIZ
ROSSIO
BAIXA-CHIADO
Portugal Telecom
Teatro Nacional
Elevador de Santa Justa
Museu de Arquelógico Carmo
Teatro Nacional de São Carlos
Cyber.bica
Museu Nacional de Arte Contemporânea
Castelo de São Jorge
Igreja de São Vicente de Fora
Panteão Nacional
Fundação Espírito Santo Silva
Sé
Casa dos Bicos
Stock Exchange
Cruz Vermelha
Mercado de Ribeira
Estação Cais do Sodré
CAIS DO SODRÉ
Estação Santos
Ferry Terminal
Rio Tejo

PR. DAS FLORES
PR. DOM PEDRO IV
PR. DA FIGUEIRA
PR. DOCE
PR. LUIS DE CAMÕES
LG. DO CHIADO
PR. DO MUNICIPO
PR. DO COMÉRCIO

R. Nova
R. da Escola Politécnica
R. Imprensa Nacional
R. Luís Fernades
S. Jorge
R. de São Bernardo
R. do Santo Amaro
R. São Bento
R. N. Piedade
R. São Marçal
Cç. Estrela
R. B. Carneiro
R. A. Brandão
R. Meio
R. Garcia da Horta
R. d Franciscanas
Av. Dom Carlos I
R. Poiais de São Bento
R. Cruz Poiais
R. Eduardo Coelho
R. Academia Ciências
R. da Esperança
R. Poço Negros
R. da Boa Vista
R. de Dom Luís I
Av. 24 de Julho
R. da Conceiçãoda Glória
R. Dom Pedro V
R. Glória
Av. da Liberdade
Cç. da Glória
R. Teixeira
R. Rosa
R. Atalaia
R. Diário de Notícias
Tr. da Queimada
R. Século
Calçada do Combro
R. Nova da Trindade
R. Garrett
R. Flores
R. do Alecrim
R. de São Paulo
R. Ribeira Nova
R.A.M. Cardoso
R. Bragança
R. Serpa Pinto
R. Capelo
R. das Portas São Antão
R. Instituto Bacteriologico
R. S. Lázaro
R. da Palma
R. Benformoso
Calçada do Mon
R. Lagares
R. Cavaleiros
R. Carmo
R. Aurea
R. Augusta
R. Correeiros
R. Prata
R. Fanqueiros
R. Assunção
R. de Vitória
R. São Nicolau
R. Conceição
R. São Julião
R. do Comércio
R. do Crucifixo
R. Nova do Almada
R. da Madalena
R. do Arsenal
Av. Ribeira das Naus
Costa do Castelo
C. S. Vicente
R. A. Rosa
R. Remédios
R. Jardim do Tabaco
R. dos Bacalhoeiros
R. da Alfândega
R. Terreiro do Trigo
Av. Infante Dom Henrique

0 150 yards
0 150 meters

Hospital: Hospital de Saint Louis, R. Luz Soriano 182 (☎21 321 6500), Bairro Alto. Open daily 9am-8pm.

Internet: Web C@fé, R. Diário de Notícias 126 (☎21 342 1181). €0.75 per 15min. Open daily 4pm-2am. **Cyber.bica,** R. Duques de Bragança 7 (☎21 322 5004), in Bairro Alto. €0.75 per 15min. Open M-Sa 11am-midnight.

Post Office: Main office, Ctt. Correios, Pr. dos Restauradores (☎21 323 8971). Open M-F 8am-10pm, Sa-Su 9am-6pm. Often crowded. Branch at Pr. do Comércio (☎21 322 0920). Open M-F 8:30am-6:30pm. Cash only. Central Lisbon **Postal Code:** 1100.

ACCOMMODATIONS AND CAMPING

Hotels cluster on **Avenida da Liberdade,** while many convenient hostels are in Baixa along the Rossio and on **Rua da Prata, Rua dos Correeiros,** and **Rua do Ouro.** Most youth hostels are in Bairro Alto and around Santa Catarina. Lodgings near the **Castelo de São Jorge** are quiet and close to the sights. At night, be careful in Baixa, Bairro Alto, and especially Graça—many streets are poorly lit.

BAIRRO ALTO

Oasis Backpackers Mansion, R. de Santa Catarina 24 (☎21 347 8044; www.oasislisboa.com). M: Baixa-Chiado, exit Largo do Chiado. The Oasis is a backpacker's dream, located in a gorgeous building with a spacious living room. Enjoy an incredible dinner M-Sa for €5 and free Portuguese lessons. Breakfast included. Laundry €6. Free Internet. Co-ed dorms €20 if you book online; €18 if in person. AmEx/MC/V ❷

Luar Guest House, R. das Gáveas 101 (☎21 346 0949; www.pensaoluar.com). Follow the beautiful *azulejo* and wood staircase to bright rooms. Laundry €10 per 6kg. Singles €15, with shower €30; doubles €35-40; triples €45; quads €55-60. Cash only. ❷

Casa de Hóspedes Globo, R. Teixeira 37 (☎21 346 2279; www.pensaoglobo.com). Popular for its proximity to nightlife. Rooms with phone, TV, and often bath. English spoken. Laundry €10 per 6kg. Singles, doubles €25-40; triples with bath €40-50; quads with bath €50. Summer €10-15 higher. Cash only. ❷

BAIXA

Lisbon Lounge Hostel, R. de São Nicolau 41, 2nd fl. (☎21 346 2061). M: Rossio or Baixa-Chiado. This hostel with the look of a sleek resort has a common room, in addition to a lounge area on each floor. Perks include free Internet, Wi-Fi, and lockers. Breakfast included; dinner €6. Dorms €20; doubles with bath €50-60. Cash only. ❸

Easy Hostel, R. de São Nicolau 13, 4th fl. (☎21 888 5312). In the middle of Baixa, this hostel has spacious rooms, Internet, and free breakfast with freshly baked bread. Laundry is cheap, and fellow travelers hang out in the living room. Elevator makes life at Easy so much easier. Dorms M-F €18, Sa-Su €20. Cash only. ❷

Goodnight Backpacker's Hostel, R. dos Correeiros 113, 3rd fl. (☎21 343 0139). M: Rossio. To get to this brand-new hostel, walk through the storefront, go through the mirrored doors, and climb up the staircase. Bright colors splashed on the walls and whimsical Andy Warhol art make for a cheerful atmosphere. Free Internet, video games, and Wi-Fi in a smoke-free environment. Free lockers. Breakfast included. Dorms €19, 4-bed €20. Doubles €50. Cash only. ❷

ALFAMA

Pensão Ninho das Águias, Costa do Castelo 74 (☎21 885 4070). Climb the spiral staircase on the terrace to reach the reception desk. Among the best views Lisbon has to offer, especially from rooms #5, 6, and 12-14. English and French spoken. Reserve ahead in summer. May-Aug. singles €30; doubles €45, with bath €50; triples €60. Sept.-Apr. prices €10 lower. Cash only. ❸

Pensão Beira Mar, Lg. Terreiro do Trigo 16 (☎21 886 9933; beira@iol.pt), near the Sta. Apolonia train station. Close to the water, the Beira Mar is a calm getaway for budget travelers. Brightly decorated rooms include shower, television, and sink. Breakfast included. Free Internet and snacks. Living room and kitchen available. Reservations by email only. June-Aug. Singles €20-25; doubles €35-45; triples €60; quads €70. Oct.-May prices €5 lower. Cash only. ❷

OTHER AREAS

Pousada de Juventude de Lisboa (HI), R. Andrade Corvo 46 (☎21 353 2696). M: Picoas. Large, recently renovated rooms with a bar and reading room. Breakfast included. Reserve ahead. Dorms €16; doubles with bath €43. HI members only. MC/V. ❶

Lisboa Camping (☎21 762 82 00, www.lisboacamping.com, 6km northwest of Rossio) is inside the 900-acre *parque florestal.* Four-star camping area. (Children under 12 €3, adults €6, tents €6-7, car €4. Prices lower in winter. Bungalows available.)

FOOD

Lisbon has some of Europe's best wine and cheapest restaurants. Dinner costs €7-12 per person; the *prato do dia* (daily special) is often only €5. Head to **Rua dos Bacalhoeiros** and **Rua dos Correeiros** to find smaller and usually less expensive restaurants. The city's culinary specialties include *creme de mariscos* (seafood chowder with tomatoes) and *bacalhau cozido com grão e batatas* (cod with chickpeas and boiled potatoes). For cheap groceries, look for any **Mini-Preço** or **Pingo Doce** supermarket. (Most open M-Sa 8:30am-9pm.)

PORTUGAL

BAIRRO ALTO

A Brasileira, R. Garrett 120-122 (☎21 346 9541). M: Baixa-Chiado. A former stomping ground of early 20th-century poets and intellectuals. Sandwiches and croissants €2-5. Entrees €6-13. Open daily 8am-2am. AmEx/MC/V. ❷

Restaurante Calcuta, R. do Norte 17 (☎21 342 8295; www.calcuta1.pt), near Lg. Camões. Listen to soothing Indian music while you enjoy Calcutta favorites like the prawn masala (€9.50). Offers a wide selection of vegetarian options (€7.50-10). Open M-Sa 11:30am-3pm and 6:30-11:30pm; Su 6:30-11:30pm MC/V. ❷

Restaurante Ali-a-Papa, R. da Atalaia 95 (☎21 347 4143). Serves generous helpings of Moroccan food in a peaceful space; dishes include couscous and tangine. Vegetarian-friendly. Entrees €9-15. Open M-Tu and Th-Su, 7pm-12:30am. AmEx/MC/V. ❸

BAIXA AND ALFAMA

Minha Maneira, Lg. do Terreiro do Trigo 1 (☎21 886 1112; www.a-minha-maneira.pt). A former bank vault now serves as a wine cellar. Menu consists of various meat and fish dishes. Free Wi-Fi. Entrees €8-15. Open daily noon-3pm, 7-11:30pm. Cash only. ❷

Churrasqueira Gaúcha, R. dos Bacalhoeiros 26C-D (☎21 887 0609). Affordable Portuguese food cooked to perfection in a comfortable, cavernous setting. The best restaurant on a street already packed with great deals. Fresh meat, poultry, and fish. Entrees €8-12. Open M-Sa 10am-midnight. AmEx/MC/V. ❷

Ristorante-Pizzeria Valentino, R. Jardim do Regedor 37-45 (☎21 346 1727), in the Pr. do Restauradores. Watch the chefs prepare a variety of pizzas and pastas in an open kitchen. Try the popular *pizza hawaii* (€8) or *tagliatelle mare e monti* (pasta with seafood; €8). Pizzas €6-10. Entrees €7-19. Open daily noon-midnight. AmEx/MC/V. ❷

SIGHTS AND MUSEUMS

BAIXA

Though Baixa has few historic sights, the neighborhood's happening mood and dramatic history make it a destination in its own right.

AROUND THE ROSSIO. The **Rossio** (Pr. Dom Pedro IV) was once a cattle market, the site of public executions, a bull ring, and carnival ground. Now, the *praça* is the domain of ruthless local motorists who circle a statue of Dom Pedro IV. A statue of Gil Vicente, Portugal's first great dramatist, sits at the top of the **Teatro Nacional de Dona Maria II** at one end of the *praça*. Adjoining the Rossio is the elegant **Praça da Figueira,** on the border of Alfama.

AROUND PRAÇA DOS RESTAURADORES. Just past the Rossio train station, an obelisk and a bronze sculpture of the "Spirit of Independence" commemorate Portugal's break from Spain in 1640. Numerous shops line the praça and C. da Glória, the hill that leads to Bairro Alto. **Avenida da Liberdade,** Lisbon's most elegant promenade, also begins at Pr. dos Resaturadores. Modeled after the wide boulevards of Paris, this shady thoroughfare ends at **Praça do Marquês de Pombal,** where an 18th-century statue of the Marquês himself overlooks the city.

BAIRRO ALTO

Intellectuals mix with university students in the Bairro Alto. **Praça Luís de Camões,** in the neighborhood's center, is a nice place to rest while sightseeing.

MUSEU ARQUEOLÓGICO DO CARMO. Located under the skeletal arches of an old church destroyed in the 1755 earthquake, this partially outdoor museum allows visitors to get very close to historical relics like mummies. *(Lg. do Carmo. Open M-Sa winter 10am-6pm, summer 10am-7pm. €2.50, students €1.50, under 14 free.)*

BASÍLICA DA ESTRELA. Directly across from the Jardim da Estrela, the Basílica da Estrela dates back to 1796 and casts an imposing presence over the praça. Its dome, poised behind a pair of tall belfries, towers over surrounding buildings in the Lisbon skyline. Half-mad Dona Maria I promised God anything for a son. When she finally gave birth to a baby boy, she built this church in thanks. Ask to see the 10th-century nativity. *(Pr. da Estrela. Accessible by metro or tram #28 from Pr. do Comércio. ☎ 21 396 0915. Open daily 7:45am-8pm. Free.)*

ALFAMA

Alfama, Lisbon's medieval quarter, was the only neighborhood to survive the infamous 1755 earthquake. The area descends in tiers from the **Castelo de São Jorge** facing the Rio Tejo. Between Alfama and Baixa is the **Mouraria** (Moorish quarter), ironically established following the expulsion of the Moors in 1147. This labyrinth of *becos* (alleys), *escandinhas* (small stairways), and unmarked streets is a challenge to navigate, so be careful after nightfall.

CASTELO DE SÃO JORGE. Built by the Moors in the 11th century, the castle was conquered by Don Alfonso Enriquez, first king of Portugal. The castle was again improved and converted into the royal family's playground between the 14th and 16th centuries. Today, the Castelo consists of little more than stone ramparts, but the towers provide spectacular views of Lisbon. Wander around the ruins or explore the ponds. *(☎ 21 880 0620; www.egeac.pt. Open daily Mar.-Oct. 9am-9pm; Nov.-Feb. 9am-6pm. €5, students €2.50, under 10 and over 65 free.)*

LOWER ALFAMA. The small **Igreja de Santo António** was built in 1812 over the beloved saint's alleged birthplace. The construction was funded with money collected by the city's children, who fashioned miniature altars bearing saintly images to place on doorsteps—a custom reenacted annually on June 13, the saint's feast day and Lisbon's biggest holiday. *(Veer right when you see Igreja da Madalena in Lg. da Madalena on the right. Take R. de Santo António da Sé and follow the tram tracks. ☎21 886 9145. Open daily 8am-7pm. Mass daily 11am, 5, 7pm.)* In the square beyond the church is the 12th-century **Sé de Lisboa.** Although the cathedral's interior lacks the ornamentation of the city's other churches, its age and treasury make for an intriguing visit. The cloister includes an archaeological dig with ruins from the Iron Age, the Roman Empire, and the Muslim and Medieval Ages in Lisbon. *(☎21 886 6752. Open daily 9am-7pm except during Mass, held Tu-Sa 6:30pm and Su 11:30am and 7pm. Free. Treasury open M-Sa 10am-5pm. €2.50, students €1.50. Cloister open daily May-Sept. 2-7pm; Oct.-Apr. M-Sa 10am-6pm, Su 2-6pm. €2.50, students €1.30.)*

GRAÇA

Graça is one of Lisbon's oldest neighborhoods. In addition to views of the city and river, its impressive historical sights keep tourists trekking up its hilly streets. Graça is mainly a residential area, accessible by tram (#28; €1.30).

PANTEÃO NACIONAL. The massive building that is now the Panteão Nacional (National Pantheon) was originally meant to be the Igreja da Santa Engrácia. The citizens of Graça started building the church in 1680 to honor their patron saint, but their ambitions soon outstripped their finances. Salazar's military regime eventually took over construction, completing the project and dedicating it in 1966 as the Panteão Nacional, a burial ground for important statesmen. When democracy was restored in 1975, the new government relocated the remains of prominent anti-fascist opponents to this building. The building also houses the honorary tombs of explorers like Vasco da Gama and Pedro Cabral, as well as the remains of Portuguese artists. *(Take tram #28 from R. do Loreto or R. Garrett. ☎21 885 4820. Open Tu-Su 10am-5pm. €2.50, seniors €1.50.)*

PORTUGAL

IGREJA AND MOSTEIRO DE SÃO VICENTE DE FORA. The church, built between 1582 and 1692, is dedicated to Lisbon's patron saint, and has a great **view** from its tower. Ask to see the *sacristia* (chapel) with its fabulous inlaid walls of Sintra marble. *(Open daily 10am-6pm except during Mass, Tu and F-Sa 9:30am, Sa and Su 10:00am. Free. Chapel open Tu-Su 10am-5pm. €2.)*

SÃO SEBASTIÃO

Located north of Baixa, São Sebastião features busy avenues, department stores, and scores of strip malls. The area also houses two of the finest art museums in Portugal, legacies of oil tycoon Calouste Gulbenkian.

MUSEU CALOUSTE GULBENKIAN. When British citizen Calouste Gulbenkian died in 1955, he left his extensive art collection to Portugal, the country he chose to call home. The formidable collection includes Egyptian, European, Greek, Islamic, Mesopotamian, Oriental and Roman art from the 15th to 20th centuries. Highlights include works by Degas, Manet, Monet, Rembrandt, Renoir, and Rodin. *(Av. Berna 45. M: São Sebastião. ☎21 782 3000; www.gulbenkian.pt. Open Tu-Su 10am-5:45pm. €4; students, teachers, and seniors 50% discount.)*

CENTRO DE ARTE MODERNO. The Centro de Arte Moderno showcases Portuguese talent from the late 19th century to the present. The museum also has art from Portugal's former colonies. *(R. Dr. Nicolau Bettencourt. M: São Sebastião. ☎21 782 3474. Open Tu-Su 10am-5:45pm. €3; students, teachers, and seniors free; Su free.)*

BELÉM

The concentration of monuments and museums in Belém, a suburb of Lisbon, makes it a crucial stop on any tour of the capital. To reach Belém, take tram #15 from Pr. do Comércio (15min.) and get off at the Mosteiro dos Jerónimos stop, one stop beyond the regular Belém stop. Alternatively, take the train from Estação Cais do Sodré. Exit the station by the overpass near the Padrão dos Descobrimentos. To reach the Mosteiro dos Jerónimos, exit the overpass to the right, then go through the public gardens to R. de Belém.

MOSTEIRO DOS JERÓNIMOS. Established in 1502 to commemorate Vasco da Gama's expedition to India, the Mosteiro dos Jerónimos was granted UNESCO World Heritage status in the 1980s. The country's most refined celebration of the Age of Discovery, the monastery showcases Portugal's native Manueline style, combining Gothic forms with minute Renaissance detail. Note the anachronism on the main church door: Prince Henry the Navigator mingles with the Twelve Apostles on both sides of the central column. The symbolic tombs of Luís de Camões and navigator Vasco da Gama lie in opposing transepts. *(☎21 362 0034. Open May-Sept. Tu-Su 10am-6:30pm; Oct.-Apr. Tu-Su 10am-5:30pm. Church free. Cloister €6, over 65 €2, students free.)*

PADRÃO DOS DESCOBRIMENTOS. Directly across from the Mosteiro is the 52m Monument to the Discoveries, built in 1960 to commemorate the 500-year anniversary of Prince Henry the Navigator's death. The white monument is shaped like a narrow cross and depicts Henry and his celebrated compatriots, Vasco da Gama and Diogo Cão. An short film about the history of Lisbon is shown inside. *(Across the highway from the Mosteiro ☎21 303 1950. Open May-Sept. Tu-Su 10am-6:30pm; Oct.-Apr. 10am-5:30pm. €3, students and seniors €1.50.)*

PARQUE DAS NAÇÕES. The Parque das Nações (Park of Nations) lies on the site of the former Expo '98 grounds. Until the mid-1990s, the area was a muddy wasteland with a few run-down factories and warehouses along the banks of the Tejo. However, the government transformed it to prepare for the World Exposition and afterward spent millions converting the grounds into a park. The entrance leads through the Centro Vasco da Gama shopping mall to the center of the grounds, where kiosks provide maps. *(M: Oriente. Park ☎21 891 9333; www.parquedasnacoes.pt.)*

PORTUGAL

ENTERTAINMENT

Agenda Cultural and *Follow Me Lisboa*, free at the tourist office and at kiosks in the Rossio on R. Portas de Santo Antão, have information on concerts, *fado*, movies, plays, and bullfights.

FADO

Lisbon's trademark is **fado** (p. 811), an art combining singing and narrative poetry that expresses *saudade* (nostalgia). Numerous *fado* houses lie in the small streets of **Bairro Alto** and near **R. de São João da Praça** in Alfama. Some also offer folk-dancing performances. Popular *fado* houses have high minimum consumption requirements (usually €10-20). To avoid breaking the bank, explore nearby streets where various bars and small venues offer free shows with less notable performers. Arrive early if you don't have a reservation.

O Faia, R. Barroca 56 (☎21 342 6742). Performances by famous *fadistas* like Anita Guerreiro and Lenita Gentil and some of the finest Portuguese cuisine available make O

Faia worth your time and your money. Entrees €20-35. Min. consumption €20; includes 2 drinks. *Fado* 9:30, 11:30pm. Open M-Sa 8pm-2am. AmEx/MC/V.

Café Luso, Tv. da Queimada 10 (☎21 342 2281; www.cafeluso.pt). Pass below the club's yellow sign to reach *fado* nirvana. Lisbon's premier *fado* club combines the best of Portuguese music, cuisine, and atmosphere. *Fado* and folk dance, 5 singers per night. Set menu €25. Entrees €22-29. Min. consumption €25. *Fado* 8:30-10pm, then folklore dancing until 2am. Open M-Sa 7:30pm-2am. F-Su reserve ahead. AmEx/MC/V.

BULLFIGHTING

Portuguese bullfighting differs from its Spanish counterpart in that the bull is not killed in the ring, a tradition that dates back to the 18th century. These spectacles take place most Thursdays from late June to late September at **Praça de Touros de Lisboa,** Campo Pequeno. (☎21 793 2143. Open daily 10pm-2am.) The newly renovated *praça* is a shopping center during the day and a venue for the distinctly Portuguese *toureio equestre* (horseback bullfighting) at night.

FESTIVALS

In June, the people of Lisbon spill into the city for a summer's worth of revelry. Open-air *feiras* (fairs)—smorgasbords of food, drink, live music, and dance—fill the streets. On the night of June 12, the streets explode in song and dance during the **Festa de Santo António.** Banners are strung between streetlights, confetti coats Av. da Liberdade, crowds pack the streets of Alfama, and grilled *sardinhas* (sardines) and *ginginha* (wild cherry liqueur) are sold everywhere. Lisbon also has a number of commercial *feiras*. From late May to early June, bookworms burrow for three weeks in the outdoor **Feira do Livro** in the Parque Eduardo VII behind Pr. Marquês do Pombal. The **Feira Internacional de Lisboa** occurs every few months in the Parque das Nações, while in July and August the **Feira de Mar de Cascais** and the **Feira de Artesania de Estoril,** celebrating famous Portuguese pottery, take place near the casino. Year-round *feiras* include the **Feira de Oeiras** (antiques), on the fourth Sunday of every month, and the **Feira de Carcanelos** (clothes) in Rato (Th 8am-2pm). Packrats will enjoy the **Feira da Ladra** (flea market; literally "thieves' fair"), held behind the Igreja de São Vicente de Fora in Graça (Tu 7am-1pm, Sa 7am-3pm). To get there, take tram #28 (€1.30).

NIGHTLIFE

Bairro Alto, where small bars and clubs fill side streets, is the premier destination for nightlife in Lisbon. **Rua do Norte, Rua do Diário Notícias,** and **Rua da Atalaia** have many small clubs packed into three short blocks. Several gay and lesbian clubs are between **Praça de Camões** and **Travessa da Queimada,** as well as in the **Rato** area near the edge of Bairro Alto. The **Docas de Santo Amaro** hosts waterfront clubs and bars, while **Avenida 24 de Julho** and **Rua das Janelas Verdes** in the **Santos** area have the most popular clubs and discos. Another hot spot is the area along the river opposite the **Santa Apolónia** train station. Jeans, sandals, and sneakers are generally not allowed. Beer runs €3-5 at clubs. Crowds flow in around 2am and stay until dawn. The easiest option to reach most clubs is to take a taxi.

A Tasca Tequila Bar, Tr. da Queimada 13-15 (☎919 40 79 14). This always-full Mexican bar is a great place to go on a slow weeknight. Bartenders at the T-shaped counter serve potent beverages. Mixed drinks €5-6. Open M-Sa 6pm-2am.

Lux-Frágil, Av. Infante D. Henrique A, Cais da Pedra a Sta. Apolonia (☎21 882 0890). Described by many of its fans as the perfect nightclub, Lux has a high-tech lighting system and an amazing view of the water from its roof. Min. consumption is usually €15. Open Tu-Sa 10pm-6am. AmEx/MC/V.

Pavilhão Chinês, Dom Pedro V 89 (☎21 342 4729). Ring the doorbell and a red-vested waiter will let you in. Despite the thousands of collection pieces hanging from the ceiling, this bar manages to look classy. The place to play pool. Open daily 6pm-2am.

Dock's Club, R. da Cintura do Porto de Lisboa 226 (☎21 395 0856). This huge club plays hip hop, Latin, and house music; outdoor bar where you can cool down (or dry off). Famous Tu ladies nights, when women get in free and receive 4 free drinks. Open Tu and F-Sa midnight-5:30 am. AmEx/MC/V.

Jamaica, R. Nova do Carvalho 6 (☎21 342 1859). M: Cais do Sodre. This small club is famous for playing 80s music. Packed until the early morning. Women get in free, but men pay a €6 cover (includes 3 beers). Be careful when leaving the club; it's not the safest neighborhood late at night. Open Tu-Sa midnight-6am.

Kapital, Av. 24 de Julho 68 (☎21 395 7101). The classiest club in Lisbon has a ruthless door policy that makes admission a competitive sport. Three floors, with a terrace on the top level. Mixed drinks €5-8. Cover €10-20. Open M-Sa 11pm-6am. MC/V.

DAYTRIPS FROM LISBON

CASCAIS

Trains from Lisbon's Estação Cais do Sodré (☎213 42 48 93; M: Cais do Sodré) head to Cascais (30min., 3 per hr., €1.65). ScottURB has a bus terminal in downtown Cascais, To the left side of the blue glass tower of the shopping center behind the train station. Bus #418 (40min., 1 per hr.) and the more scenic #403 via Cabo da Roca (1hr., 1 per hr.) go from Cascais to Sintra for €3.35.

Cascais ("CASH-kise") is a beautiful beach town, serene during the low-season but full of vacationers in summer. **Praia da Ribeira, Praia da Rainha,** and **Praia da Conceição** are especially popular with sunbathers. To reach Praia da Ribeira, take a right upon leaving the tourist office and walk down Av. dos Combatantes de Grande Guerra until you see the water. Facing the water, Praia da Rainha and Praia da Conceição are to your left. Those in search of less crowded beaches should take advantage of the **free bike rentals** offered at two kiosks in Cascais. One is in front of the train station; the other is in the parking lot of the **Cidadela fortress,** up Av. dos Carlos I. Bring a legitimate photo ID and hotel information to use the bikes (8am to 6:30pm). Ride along the coast (to your right when facing the water) to reach the **Boca de Inferno** (Mouth of Hell), a stunning open cave where the crashing waves whisper the devil's words. Go on a rainy day and hear the cave roar. This natural wonder is 1km outside Cascais. When the sun sets, nightlife picks up on **Largo Luís de Camões,** the main pedestrian square. There are good restaurants on **Av. dos Combatantes de Grande Guerra,** between the tourist office and the ocean. The best is **Restaurante Dom Manolo ❷,** one of the only restaurants that cooks with a charcoal oven. Try the *sardinhas assadas*, mussels and grilled chicken. (☎214 83 11 26. Entrees €6.5-11. Open daily 10am-midnight.) To get to the **tourist office,** Av. dos Combatantes de Grande Guerra 25, exit the train station through the ticket office. To the right of McDonald's is Av. Valbom; the office is the yellow building at the end of the street. (☎214 86 82 04. Open M-Sa 9am-7pm, Su 10am-6pm.)

SINTRA

Trains (☎219 23 26 05) arrive at Av. Dr. Miguel Bombarda from Lisbon's Estação Sete Rios (40min., 3 per hr., €1.50). ScottURB buses (☎214 69 91 25; www.scotturb.com) leave Av. Dr. Miguel Bombarda for Cascais (#417; 40min., 1 per hr., €3.25) and Estoril (#418; 40min., 1 per hr., €3.25). Down the street, Mafrense buses go to Ericeira (50min., 1 per hr., €2.60).

For centuries, monarchs and the wealthiest of noblemen were drawn by the hypnotic beauty of Sintra (pop. 20,000). They left a trail of opulence and grandeur behind them. The must-see attraction is the UNESCO World Heritage Site **Quinta da Regaleira,** a stunning palace whose backyard was turned into a fantasy land by its eccentric millionaire owner at the turn of the 20th century. Statues, fountains, and ponds blanket the small park, which is surrounded by lush green trees and beautiful gardens. The **Poço Iniciático** (Initiatory Well) was inspired by secret Knights Templars rituals; bring a flashlight for exploring the "Dantesque" caves lurking beneath the main sights. To get to the palace, turn right out of the tourist office and follow R. Consiglieri Pedroso out of town as it turns into R.M.E.F. Navarro. (☎219 10 66 50. Open daily Apr.-Sept. 10am-8pm; Oct. and Feb.-Apr. 10am-6:30pm; Nov.-Jan. 10am-5:30pm. €6, students €4. Tours €10; 10:30am, 11am, noon, 2:30, 3:30pm.) The **Palácio de Pena** is equally elaborate—a colorful Bavarian palace resting atop a dark green mountain that features a lavish ballroom, fresco-covered "Arab Room," and a spectacular terrace view. (ScottURB bus #434 goes to the palace; €4. ☎219 10 53 40; www.parquesdesintra.pt. Open daily June-Aug. 9:45am-5:30pm; Oct.-May 10am-4pm. €11.45 children and seniors €9. Tours €5.) Other Sintra highlights include the **Palácio Nacional de Sintra** in the town center, and the 8th-century **Castelo dos Mouros,** downhill from the Palácio de Pena. Restaurants crowd the end of Rua João de Deus and Avenida Heliodoro Salgado. **Restaurante Apeadeiro ❷,** Av. Miguel Bombarda 3A, serves authentic Portuguese cuisine (read delicious meat and fish), for the cheapest prices in town (€7-13). **Tourist offices** are located in Pr. da República 23 (☎219 23 87 87) and in the train station (☎219 24 16 23. Both open daily June-Sept. 9am-8pm; Oct.-May 9am-7pm.)

PORTUGAL

NORTHERN PORTUGAL

The unspoiled Costa da Prata (Silver Coast), plush greenery of the interior, and rugged peaks of the Serra Estrela compose the Three Beiras region. To the north, port flows freely and *azulejo*-lined houses grace charming streets.

PORTO (OPORTO) ☎22

Porto (pop. 263,000) is famous for its namesake product—a strong, sugary wine developed by English merchants in the early 18th century. The port industry is at the root of the city's successful economy, but Porto has more to offer than fine alcohol. The city retains traditional charm with granite church towers, orange-tiled houses, and graceful bridges.

TRANSPORTATION AND PRACTICAL INFORMATION. Airlines including **TAP Air Portugal** (☎22 608 0231), Pr. Mouzinho de Albuquerque 105, fly to major European cities from **Aeroporto Francisco de Sá Carneiro** (**OPO;** ☎22 943 2400), 13km from downtown. The recently completed **metro E** (violet line) goes to the airport (25min., €1.35). The **aerobus** (☎22 507 10 54) runs from Av. dos Aliados near Pr. da Liberdade to OPO (40min., 2 per hr., €4). **Taxis** to Lisbon are €18-20 (15-20min.). Most **trains** (☎808 20 82 08; www.cp.pt) pass through Porto's main station, **Estação de Campanhã,** on R. da Estação. Trains run to: Aveiro (1hr., 47 per day, €2-13); Braga (1hr., 26 per day, €2-13); Coimbra (1-2hr., 24 per day, €12-16); Lisbon (3-4hr., 18 per day, €16-29); Madrid, SPA via Entroncamento (11-12hr., 1 per day, €64). **Estação São Bento,** Pr. Almeida Garrett, has local and regional trains. Internorte (☎22 605 2420), Pr. Galiza 96, sends **buses** to Madrid, SPA (10hr., 1-2 per day, €43) and other international hubs. Rede Expressos buses (☎22 200 6954; www.redeexpresso.pt), R. Alexandre Herculano 366, travel to: Braga (1hr., 10 per day, €5); Coimbra (1hr., 11 per day, €10); Lisbon (4hr., 11 per day, €16); Viana do Castelo (1hr., 4 per day, €6.40). Renex (☎22 200 3395), Campo Mártires da Pátria, has express service to Lagos (8hr., 6 per day, €23) via Lisbon (3hr., 12 per day, €16). Buy tickets for **local buses** and **trams** at kiosks or at the STCP office, located at Pr. Almeida Garrett 27, across from Estação São Bento (€1.80 for 2 trips, day-pass €5). The city's main **tourist office** is located at R. Clube dos Fenianos 25. (☎22 339 3470; www.portoturismo.pt. Open M-F 9am-6:30pm, Sa-Su 9:30am-6:30pm.) **OnWeb,** Pr. Gen. Humberto Delgado 291, has **Internet.** (Open M-Sa 10am-2am, Su 3pm-2am. Min. 1hr. €1.20 per hr., Wi-Fi €0.60 per hr.) The **post office** is located on Pr. Gen. Humberto Delgado. (☎22 340 0200. Open M-F 8:30am-7:30pm, Sa 9:30am-3pm.) **Postal Code:** 4000.

ACCOMMODATIONS AND FOOD. For good deals, look on **Praça Filipa de Lancastre** or near the *mercado* on **Rua Fernandes Tomás** and **Rua Formosa,** perpendicular to Av. dos Aliados. The **Pensão Duas Nações ❶,** Pr. Guilherme Gomes Fernandes 59, has the best combination of low price and high comfort. (☎22 208 1616. Reserve ahead or arrive well before noon. Laundry €7. Internet €1 per 30min. Singles €14, with bath €23-25; doubles €23-25; triples €36; quads €46. Cash only.) For a hip hostel, head up a few blocks from the S. Bento train station toward the tower. **Oporto Poets Hostel ❷,** Tv. da Ferraz 13, is just around the corner, with clean, bright rooms. (☎22 332 4209. Dorms €20; doubles €44. Low-season €18/40. Cash only.)

Quality budget meals can be found near Pr. da Batalha on **Rua Cimo de Vila** and **Rua do Cativo.** Places selling *bifanas* (small pork sandwiches) line R. Bomjardim. Ribeira is the place to go for a high-quality, affordable dinner. The **Café Majestic ❷,** R. de Santa Catarina 112, is a snapshot of 19th-century bourgeois opulence. (☎22 200 3887. Entrees €9-16. Open M-Sa 9:30am-midnight. AmEx/MC/V.) At the **Confeitaria Império ❶,** R. de Santa Catarina 149-151, choose from a huge selection of pastries and lunch specials. (☎22 200 5595. Open M-F 7:30am-8:30pm, Sa 7:30am-7pm.) The sprawling **Mercado de Bolhão** has a wide range of fresh food. Produce is on the upper level. (Open M-F 7am-5pm, Sa 7am-1pm.)

WINERIES. No visit to Porto is complete without one of the city's famous wine-tasting tours. They are cheap (€1-3) if not free, and take about 30min. Wine-tasting is most prevalent across the river, in **Vila**

I'LL TAKE TWO...

You've probably found yourself ogling the glass display case of Portugal's many *pastelarias* wondering which tempting treat to pick. Wonder no more—here's a guide to heaven:

Altreia. A sweet and simple treat from Northern Portugal made of pasta cooked with eggs and sugar topped with cinnamon.

Arroz-doce. Sweet rice. There are many variations of this rice pudding, so try it in different places.

Bolinhos. Little balls of cake filled with cream and/or dried fruit .

Bolinhos de Jerimu. Pumpkin, egg, and Port fried to sweet perfection. Yum.

Dolce de Ovos. Aveiro's small sweets made of egg yolks and sugar.

Pão-de-ló. The Portuguese version of sponge cake.

Pastel de Natas. Petit pastries filled with cinnamon cream, also known as *pastel de Belém.*

Pastel de Santa Clara. Star shaped puffs filled with almond flavored cream from the Northeast.

Rabanadas. Thick slices of bread soaked in milk or wine, tossed in sugar, and fried.

Pão de Deus. Sweet bread topped with a pineapple and coconut concoction. Add butter and the bread melts in your mouth while the shredded coconut gives a slight crunch. God's bread indeed.

Nova de Gaia, where there are 17 large port lodges. Tours often include visits to the wine cellars below. To get there, walk across the Ponte de D. Luiz I in Ribeira.

THE INSIDE SCOOP. To find the cheapest prices on port, avoid retail stores and check out the wineries and non-profit stores scattered around the city. If you are looking for a particular label, call before heading out.

SIGHTS AND ENTERTAINMENT. Your first brush with Porto's rich stock of fine artwork may be the celebrated collection of *azulejos* (painted tiles) in the **São Bento** train station. From the station, follow signs downhill on R. Mouzinho da Silveira to R. Ferreira Borges and the **Palácio da Bolsa** (Stock Exchange), the epitome of 19th-century Portuguese elegance. The most striking room of the *Palácio* is the extravagant **Sala Árabe** (Arabian Hall). Its gold and silver walls are covered with the juxtaposed inscriptions "Glory to Allah" and "Glory to Doña Maria II." (☎22 339 9000. Open daily Apr.-Oct. 9am-7pm; Nov.-Mar. 9am-1pm and 2-6pm. €5, students €3. Multilingual tours 2 per hr.) Nearby on R. Infante Dom Henrique, the Gothic **Igreja de São Francisco** glitters with an elaborately gilded wood interior. The neighboring museum houses religious art and artifacts; in the basement lies the **Ossário**, a labyrinth of cavernous catacombs with mass graves. (☎22 206 2100. Open daily Feb-May 9am-6pm June-Oct 9am-7pm July-Aug. 9am-8pm. €3, students €2.50.) On R. dos Clérigos rises the **Torre dos Clérigos** (Tower of Clerics), adjacent to the 18th-century **Igreja dos Clérigos.** (☎22 200 1729. Tower open daily Apr.-July, Sept, Oct. 9:30am-1pm and 2:30-7pm; Aug 9:30am-7pm Nov.-Mar. 10am-noon and 2-5pm. Tower €2, church free.) From there, head up R. da Restauração, turn right on R. Alberto Gouveia, and go left on R. Dom Manuel II to reach the **Museu Nacional de Soares dos Reis,** R. Dom Manuel II 44. This former royal residence houses a collection of 19th-century Portuguese art. (☎22 339 3770. Open Tu 2-6pm, W-Su 10am-6pm. €3, students and seniors €1.50. Su before 2pm free.) Porto is not a party city after hours—most people looking for a party congregate around the bar-restaurants of **Ribeira.**

BRAGA ☎253

The beautiful gardens, plazas, museums, and markets of Braga (pop. 166,000) have earned it the nickname "Portuguese Rome." Braga's most famous landmark, **Igreja do Bom Jesús,** is 5km outside of town. This 18th-century church was built in an effort to recreate Jerusalem in Braga, providing Iberian Christians with a pilgrimage site closer to home. Take the bus labeled "#02 Bom Jesús" at 10 or 40min. past the hour in front of Farmácia Cristal, Av. da Liberdade 571 (€1.40). At the site, either go on a 285m ride on the funicular (8am-8pm, 2 per hr., €1.50) or walk up the granite-paved pathway that leads to a 326-step zigzagging staircase (20-25min. walk). The treasury of the **Sé,** Portugal's oldest cathedral, showcases the archdiocese's most precious paintings and relics, including a collection of *cofres cranianos* (brain boxes), one of which contains the 6th-century cortex of Braga's first bishop. (☎253 26 33 17. Open Tu-Su 9am-noon and 2-5:30pm. Mass daily 5:30pm. Cathedral free. Treasury €3, chapels and choir €2.)

Take a taxi (€5 from the train station) to **Pousada da Juventude de Braga (HI) ❶**, R. Santa Margarida 6, which has a convenient location. (☎253 61 61 63. Reception 8am-noon and 6pm-midnight. Lockout noon-6pm. Dorms €9; doubles with bath €22.) Cafes on **Praça da República** are perfect for people-watching. Be sure to try *pudim do Abade de Priscos*, a pudding flavored with caramel and port wine. The **market** is in Pr. do Comércio. (Open M-Sa 7am-3pm.) A supermarket, **Pingo Doce,** is in the basement of the shopping mall. (Open daily 10am-11pm.)

Trains (☎808 20 82 08) pull into Estação da Braga, 1km from Pr. da República. Take R. do Souto; the station is 400m down on the left. Trains run to Lisbon (4-5hr., 3 per day, €22-30) and Porto (45-60min., M-F 26 per day €2-12.50). **Buses** leave Central de Camionagem (☎253 20 94 00) for: Coimbra (3hr., 6 per day, €13); Faro (12-15hr., 3-6 per day, €27); Lisbon (5hr., 10-11 per day, €18); Porto (1hr., 25 per day, €5). The **tourist office** is at Av. da Liberdade 1. (☎253 26 25 50. Open June-Sept. M-F 9am-7pm, Sa-Su 9am-12:30pm and 2-5:30pm; Oct.-May M-Sa 9am-12:30pm and 2-6:30pm.) **Postal Code:** 4700.

COIMBRA ☎239

For centuries, the Universidade de Coimbra was the only institute of higher education in Portugal, attracting young men from the country's elite. Today, tourists of all ages are drawn to the historic university district, but the large student population still dominates youthful Coimbra (pop. 200,000).

TRANSPORTATION AND PRACTICAL INFORMATION. Regional **trains** (☎808 20 82 08; www.cp.pt) stop at both **Estação Coimbra-B** (Velha) and **Estação Coimbra-A** (Nova), just two short blocks from the town center of Coimbra, while long-distance trains stop only at Coimbra-B station. A local train connects the two stations, departing after regional trains arrive (4min.; €1, free if transferring from another train). Trains run to Lisbon (2-3hr., 17 per day, €12-30) and Porto (1-2hr., 14 per day, €7-20). **Buses** (☎239 23 87 69) go from the end of Av. Fernão de Magalhães, 15min. past Coimbra-A, to Lisbon (2hr., 18 per day, €13) and Porto (1-2hr., 14 per day, €11). From the bus station, turn right, follow the avenue to Coimbra-A, then walk to Lg. da Portagem to reach the **tourist office.** (☎239 85 59 30; www.turismo-centro.pt. Open June 16-Sept. 14 M-F 9am-8pm, Sa-Su 9:30am-1pm and 2:30-6pm. Sept. 15-June 15 M-F 9am-5pm, Sa-Su 10am-1pm and 2:30-5pm.) Casa Aninhas, Pr. 8 de Maio, has free **Internet,** but you may have to wait in line due to high demand. (Passport or driver's license required. Open M-Sa 10am-midnight, Su 2pm-midnight.) **Postal Code:** 3000.

ACCOMMODATIONS AND FOOD. Residencial Vitória ❷, R. da Sota 11-19, has spacious, newly renovated rooms with bath, phone, cable TV, and A/C. Older rooms are cheaper, though still roomy

THE REAL CORPSE BRIDE

When Prince Dom Pedro took one look at his wife's lady-in-waiting, Inês de Castro, it was (forbidden) love at first sight. Upon discovering this illicit amor, Dom Pedro's father, King Alfonso, condemned the affair and had Inês exiled to a convent in Coimbra. The prince's wife soon died in childbirth, however, and Pedro and Inês continued their affair for the next decade. The prince's plans for a wedding were cut short: his father had Inês killed for fear that her children by Pedro would eventually claim the throne. Dom Pedro waged war against the king in retaliation until his mother convinced him to put the civil strife to an end.

Two years later, Dom Pedro took the throne; he had his lover's assassins tracked down and brought to the public courtyard. There, he watched as their hearts were torn from their living bodies. He then set about making his children rightful heirs to the throne. In a shocking announcement, Dom Pedro ordered a posthumous matrimonial ceremony to take place. Five years after her death, Inês was removed from her grave and dressed like a queen. Dom Pedro forced the court to kneel before her corpse and kiss her rotting hand. He had his own tomb built opposite hers, and on it reads *"Até ao fim do mundo"* (until the end of the world).

and quiet. (☎239 82 40 49. Breakfast €2.50. In summer, singles €15-30; doubles €30-45; triples €60. Winter €15-25/25-40/50. AmEx/MC/V.) **Restaurante Adega Paço do Conde ❶**, R. do Paço do Conde, is a local favorite. A budget oasis surrounded by tourist traps, the restaurant offers a variety of fish and meat options for only €5 and has outdoor seating. (☎239 82 56 05. Open M-Sa 11am-10pm MC/V.) Even cheaper fare can be found at the **UC Cantinas ❶**, the university student cafeterias, where full meals run under €2. One is on the right side of R. Oliveiro Matos, and the other is up the stairs in Lg. Dom Dinis. (ISIC required. Open daily for lunch at noon, for dinner at 7pm.) The **supermarket** Pingo Doce, R. João de Ruão 14, is 3min. up R. da Sofia from Pr. 8 de Maio. (☎239 85 29 30. Open daily 8:30am-9pm.)

SIGHTS AND ENTERTAINMENT. Take in the sights of the *cidade velha* (Old Town) by following the narrow stone steps from the river up to the university. Begin your ascent at the **Arco de Almedina,** a remnant of the Moorish town wall, one block uphill from Lg. da Portagem. The looming 12th-century **Romanesque Sé Velha** (Old Cathedral) is at the top. (Open M-Th and Sa 10am-1pm and 2-6pm, F 10am-1pm. Cloister €1, students €0.80.) Follow signs to the Jesuit-built **Sé Nova** (New Cathedral), with its blinding gold altar. (Open Tu-Sa 9am-noon and 2-6:30pm. Free.) Just a few blocks uphill is the 16th-century Universidade de Coimbra. Enter through the *Porta Férrea* (Iron Gate), off R. São Pedro, to the Pátio das Escolas, through which an excellent view of the rural outskirts of Coimbra stretches out to the horizon. The stairs to the right lead to the **Sala dos Capelos** (Graduates' Hall), which houses portraits of Portugal's kings, six of whom were born in Coimbra. The **Capela de São Miguel,** the university chapel, is adorned with magnificent *talha dourada* (gilded wood) carvings. The 18th-century **Biblioteca Joanina** (the university library) lies past the Baroque clock tower. Tickets to all university sights can be purchased outside the Porta Férrea, in the Biblioteca General. (☎239 85 98 00. Open daily Mar. 13-Oct. 8:30am-7pm; Nov.-Mar. M-F 9am-5pm Sa-Su 10am-4pm. Chapel and library €3.50, students and seniors €2.50; combined ticket €6/4.20.) Coimbra's nightlife is best from October to July, when students are in town. **A Capela,** R. Corpo de Deus, a former chapel converted into a small late-night cafe, is the best place to hear Coimbra-style *fado*, performed by both students and professionals. (☎239 83 39 85. Mixed drinks €4-5. *Fado* at 9:30, 10:30, 11:30pm. Cover €10; includes 1 drink. Open daily 9pm-3am.) Students run wild during the **Queima das Fitas** (Burning of the Ribbons), Coimbra's week-long festival during the second week of May. The festivities begin when graduates burn the narrow ribbons they got in first-year and receive wide ribbons to replace them.

CENTRAL PORTUGAL

Jagged cliffs and whitewashed fishing villages line the Costa de Prata of Estremadura, which has beaches that rival those of the Algarve. Lush greenery surrounds historic sights in the fertile region on the banks of the Rio Tejo.

ÉVORA ☎266

Évora (pop. 55,000) is the capital and largest city of the Alentejo region. Moorish arches line the streets of its historic center, which boasts a Roman temple, an imposing cathedral, and a 16th-century university. Attached to the **Igreja Real de São Francisco** in Pr. 1 de Mayo, the eerie **Capela dos Ossos** (Chapel of Bones) was built by three Franciscan monks—out of the bones of 5000 people—as a hallowed space to reflect on the profundity of life and death. From Pr. do

Giraldo, follow R. República; the church is on the right and the chapel is to the right of the main entrance. (☎266 70 45 21. Open May-Sept. M-Sa 9am-12:50pm and 2:30-5:45pm; Oct.-Apr. 9am-1pm and 2:30-5:15pm. €1.50; photos €0.50.) The 2nd-century **Templo Romano,** on Lg. Conde do Vila Flor, was built for the goddess Diana. Its large and well-preserved columns look spectacular at night. Facing the temple is the **Convento dos Loíos,** whose chapel interior is covered with dazzling *azulejos;* the actual monastery is now a luxury hotel. (Open Tu-Su 10am-12:30pm and 2-6pm. In winter it closes at 5pm. €3, €5 for church and next-door exhibition hall.) Around the corner is the colossal 12th-century **Basílica Catedral;** the 12 apostles on the doorway are masterpieces of medieval Portuguese sculpture. Climb the stairs of the cloister for an excellent view of the city. The **Museu de Arte Sacra,** above the nave, houses religious artifacts, including the sacred jewel-encrusted *Relicário do Santo Lenho,* a relic made from a piece of the cross on which Jesus was crucified. (Cathedral open daily in summer 9am-12:45pm and 2-4:45pm. Cloisters open daily 9am-noon and 2-4:30pm. Museum open Tu-Su in summer 9am-4:30pm; in winter 9am-12:30pm and 2-4:30pm. Cathedral €1. Cloisters and museum €3, students €2.50.)

Pensões cluster around **Praça do Giraldo.** From the tourist office, turn right onto R. Bernardo Matos to get to cozy **Casa Palma ❷,** R. Bernardo Matos 29A. (☎266 70 35 60. Singles €15-25; doubles €30-35. Cash only.) Budget restaurants can be found near the streets off Pr. do Giraldo, particularly **Rua Mercadores.** **Condestável ❶,** R. Diogo Câo, 3, is cheap and simple, but delicious. Enjoy a two-course meal for €5.90-7. It is also a nice place to have a drink at night. (☎266 70 20 08. Open daily 8am-noon. MC/V.) After sunset, head to **Praxis,** R. Valdevinos, the only club in town. From Pr. do Giraldo, take R. 5 de Outubro; the club will be on the right. (☎266 70 81 77. Beer €1.50. Mixed drinks €4-6. Min. consumption for men €7, for women €5. Open W-Su until 6am.)

Trains (☎266 70 21 25; www.cp.pt) run from Av. dos Combatentes de Grande Guerra to Faro (5hr., 2 per day, €13-20) and Lisbon (2hr., 4-6 per day, €11). **Buses** (☎266 76 94 10; www.rede-expressos.pt) go from Av. São Sebastião to: Faro (4hr., 3 per day, €14); Lisbon (2hr., 9 per day, €11); Porto (6-8hr., 6 per day, €19). The **tourist office** is at Pr. do Giraldo 73. (☎266 77 70 71. Open daily May-Oct. 9am-7pm; Nov.-Apr. 9am-6pm.) **Postal Code:** 7999.

PORTUGAL

ALGARVE

The Algarve, a desert on the sea, is a popular vacation spot, largely due to the nearly 3000 hours of sunshine it receives every year. In July and August, tourists mob the resorts and beaches, packing bars and clubs from sunset until long after sunrise. In low-season, the resorts become pleasantly depopulated.

FARO ☎289

Many Europeans begin their holidays in Faro (pop. 42,000), the Algarve's capital city. The **Vila Adentro** (Old Town)—a medley of museums, handicraft shops, and churches—begins at the **Arco da Vila,** a stone passageway. On Lg. do Carmo stands the **Igreja de Nossa Senhora do Carmo** and its chilling **Capela dos Ossos** (Chapel of Bones), built from the remains of monks buried in the church's cemetery. More than 1245 skulls and many other bones are arrayed in geometric designs on the walls and ceiling. (☎289 82 44 90. Open May-Sept. M-F 10am-1pm and 3-6pm; Oct.-Apr. M-F 10am-1pm and 3-5pm, Sa 10am-1pm. Su Mass 8:30am. Church free. Chapel €1.) To get to the sunny beach **Praia de Faro,** take bus #16 from the bus station or from the front of the tourist office (5-10min.; 5 per day, return 9 per day; €1.10). **Pousada da Juventude (HI) ❶,** R. Polícia de Segurança Pública, near the police station, is a bargain. (☎289 82 65 21; faro@

movijovem.pt. Breakfast included. July-Aug. dorms €13; doubles €28, with bath €38. Sept.-June €9/22/25. AmEx/MC/V.) Enjoy coffee and local marzipan at cafes along **Rua Conselheiro Bívar** and **Praça Dom Francisco Gomes.** A selection of fresh pastries and Portugal's famed port is available at **Supermercado Garrafeira Rui** on Praça Ferreira de Almeida. (☎289 82 15 86. Open 10am-1pm, 3pm-7pm.)

Trains (☎289 82 64 72) run from Lg. da Estação to Évora (4-6hr., 3-4 per day, €20) and Lagos (1hr., 9 per day, €6.15). EVA **buses** (☎289 89 97 00) go from Av. da República to Lagos (2hr., 8 per day, €5.25). Renex (☎289 81 29 80), across the street, sends buses to Porto (7hr., 6-13 per day, €26) via Lisbon (4hr., 9 per day, €18-19). Turn left past the garden on Av. República to reach the **tourist office,** R. da Misericórdia 8. (☎289 80 36 04. Open daily May-Sept. 9:30am-12:30pm and 2-7pm; Oct.-Apr. 9:30am-12:30pm and 2-5:30pm.) **Postal Code:** 8000.

LAGOS

Lagos resembles an exotic fraternity at night, swarming with surfers and college-aged students spilling out of bars into the stone streets. The city keeps you soaking in the ocean views, the sun on the beach, and the drinks at the bars.

TRANSPORTATION AND PRACTICAL INFORMATION. Trains (☎282 76 29 87) run from behind the marina to Évora (5hr., €14-22) and Lisbon (3-4hr., 7 per day, €16). The **bus station** (☎282 76 29 44), off Avenida dos Descobrimentos, is across the channel from the train station and marina. **Buses** run to Faro (2hr., 6 per day 7am-5:15pm, €5.35), Lisbon (5hr., 6 per day, €19), and Sagres (1hr., 16 per day, €3.40). Running along the channel, **Av. dos Descobrimentos** is the main road carrying traffic to and from Lagos. From the train station, walk through the marina and cross the pedestrian suspension bridge, then turn left onto Av. dos Descobrimentos. From the bus station, walk straight until you reach Av. dos Descobrimentos and turn right; after 15min., take another right onto R. Porta de Portugal to reach **Praça Gil Eanes,** the center of the Old Town. Praça Gil Eanes extends into Lg. Marquêz de Pombal, where the **tourist office** is located. (☎282 76 41 11. Open M-Sa 10am-6pm.) Get **Internet** at Snack Bar Ganha Pouco, the first right after the footbridge coming from the bus station. (Internet €2.50 per hr. Open M-Sa 8am-7:30pm.) **Postal Code:** 8600.

ACCOMMODATIONS AND FOOD. In summer, budget accommodations fill up quickly; reserve at least two weeks ahead. Locals renting rooms in their homes will greet you at the station. Though these rooms are often inconveniently located, they are frequently the best deals (€10-15 per person). Never agree to a room without first seeing it. It's hard not to have a good time at the **Rising Cock ❷**, Tv. do Forno 14. The hostel is a short walk from most of Lagos's bars and keeps up the city's famous party-town reputation with two patios, a common room, and a DVD library. (☎968 75 87 85; www.risingcock.com. Free Internet. High-season dorms €20, low-season €15; prices may vary. Cash only.) Follow Av. dos Descobrimentos toward Sagres to **Camping Trindade ❶,** just outside town. (☎289 76 38 93. €4 per tent site, €3.10 per person, €4.30 per car.)

Peruse multilingual tourist menus around **Praça Gil Eanes** and **Rua 25 de Abril.** A loyal following goes to **Casa Rosa ❶**, R. do Ferrador 22, which offers many vegetarian options, and free Internet. (☎282 18 02 38. All-you-can-eat spaghetti or vegetarian bolognaise €5. Open daily 5-11pm.) **Mediterraneo ❷,** R. Senhora da Graça 2, has great options for vegetarians with an extensive menu of Mediterranean and Thai cuisine. (☎282 18 31 00. Entrees €9-15. Open Tu-Sa 6-10:30pm.)

SIGHTS AND BEACHES. The few historical mementos that Lagos has to offer can be seen on a lazy afternoon walk back from the beach. The **Fortaleza da Ponta da Bandeira,** a 17th-century fortress with maritime exhibits and a tiled chapel, overlooks the marina. (☎282 76 14 10. Open Tu-Su 9:30am-12:30pm and 2-5pm. €2, students €1, under 13 free.) Also near the waterfront is the old **Mercado dos Escravos,** the site of the first sale of African slaves in Portugal in 1441. Opposite the Mercado dos Escravos is the gilded **Igreja de Santo António,** which houses a museum filled with artifacts from Lagos's past rulers. (Church and museum open Tu-Su 9:30am-12:30pm and 2-5pm. Church free. Museum €2.20, students and seniors €2.10.) The waterfront and marina offer jet ski rentals, scuba diving lessons, sailboat and dolphin-sighting trips, and motorboat tours of the **coastal rocks** and **grottoes.**

For a lazier day, head to one of Lagos's many **beaches.** A 4km blanket of sand marks **Meia Praia,** across the river from town. Take a 20min. walk over the footbridge or hop on the quick ferry near Pr. Infante Dom Henrique (€0.50). For a less crowded beach, follow Av. dos Descobrimentos toward Sagres to **Praia de Pinhão** (20min.). A bit farther down the coast, **Praia Dona Ana** features the sculpted cliffs and grottoes that grace many Algarve postcards. If you're up for more than lounging, Lagos has a wide variety of water sports, from scuba diving to surfing to (booze) cruising. Companies that offer tours of the grottoes line Av. dos Descobrimentos and the marina. **Surf Experience,** R. dos Ferreiros 21, offers one- and two-week surfing trips including lessons, transportation, and accommodations in Lagos. (☎282 76 19 43; www.surf-experience.com. Apr.-Nov. 1-week €525, 2-week €881; Dec.-Mar. €473/836.) The **Booze Cruise** is a 4hr., all-you-can-drink afternoon boat ride around Lagos's coast. (☎969 41 11 31; €35.) **Algarve Dolphins,** Marina de Lagos 10, organizes 1hr. dolphin-watching tours in high-speed boats. (☎282 08 75 87; www.algarve-dolphins.com. €30.)

DAYTRIP FROM LAGOS: SAGRES. Marooned atop a windy plateau at the southwesternmost point in Europe, desolate Sagres (pop. 2500) and its cape were once believed to be the edge of the world. Near the town stands the **Fortaleza de Sagres,** former home to Prince Henry the Navigator and his school of navigation. The pentagonal 15th-century fortress yields striking views of the cliffs and sea. *(Open daily May-Sept. 9:30am-8pm; Oct.-Apr. 9:30am-5:30pm. €3, under 25 €1.50.)* Six kilometers west lies the dramatic **Cabo de São Vicente,** where the second most powerful lighthouse in Europe shines over 100km out to sea. To get there on weekdays, take the **bus** from R. Comandante Matoso (10min., 2 per day, €1). EVA buses *(☎282 76 29 44)* run to Lagos (1hr., 14 per day, €3.10). From July to September, buses also run to Lisbon (1 per day, €15). The **tourist office** is on R. Comandante Matoso. *(☎282 62 48 73; www.visitalgarve.pt. Open Tu-Sa 9:30am-12:30pm and 1:30-5:30pm.)*

ROMANIA (ROMÂNIA)

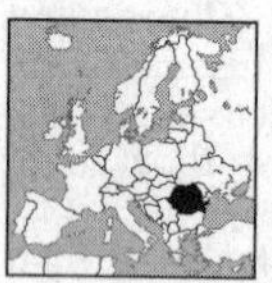

Devastated by the lengthy and oppressive reign of Nicolae Ceauşescu (in power 1965-1989), modern Romania remains in the midst of economic and political transition. This condition of flux, combined with a reputation for poverty and crime, sometimes discourages foreign visitors. But travelers who dismiss Romania do themselves a disservice—it is a budget traveler's paradise, rich in history, rustic beauty, and hospitality. Romania's fascinating legacy draws visitors to Dracula's dark castle and to the famous frescoes of the Bucovina monasteries. Meanwhile, Bucharest embodies modern Romania. Visitors to the capital can explore the imposing remnants of Ceauşescu's rule. Another Romanian treasure is the Black Sea Coast, whose resorts entice throngs of vacationers each summer.

DISCOVER ROMANIA: SUGGESTED ITINERARIES

THREE DAYS. Head for **Transylvania** (3 days; p. 834), a budget traveler's haven, to relax in the Gothic towns of **Sighişoara** (p. 835), **Sinaia** (p. 833), and the ruins of **Râşnov castle** (p. 836).

ONE WEEK. After three days in **Transylvania,** head to medieval **Bran** (1 day; p. 836) and stylish **Braşov** (1 day; p. 835), before ending in **Bucharest** (2 days; p. 827), the enigmatic capital.

ROMANIA

ESSENTIALS

FACTS AND FIGURES

OFFICIAL NAME: Romania.

MAJOR CITIES: Bucharest, Timişoara, Iaşi, Constanta.

POPULATION: 22,247,000.

LAND AREA: 230,340 sq. km.

TIME ZONE: GMT + 2.

LANGUAGE: Romanian.

RELIGIONS: Eastern Orthodox (87%).

FIRST EUROPEAN CITY WITH ELECTRIC STREETLAMPS: Timişoara.

WHEN TO GO

Romania's climate makes it a year-round destination. The south has hot summers and mild winters, while in the northern mountains, winters are harsher and summers are cooler. Tourist season peaks sharply in July and August only along the Black Sea Coast; elsewhere, travelers will find a refreshing lack of crowds even in mid-summer. Travelers would do well to remember, however, that summer can be brutally hot in much of Romania.

DOCUMENTS AND FORMALITIES

EMBASSIES AND CONSULATES. Foreign embassies are in Bucharest (p. 829). Romanian embassies abroad include: **Australia,** 4 Dalman Crescent, O'Malley,

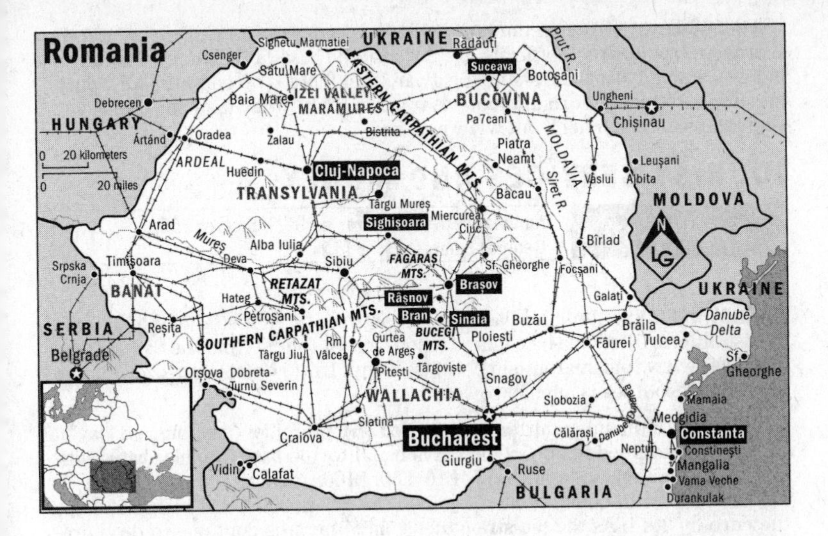

Canberra, ACT 2606 (☎262 862 343; www.canberra.mae.ro); **Canada,** 655 Rideau St., Ottawa, ON K1N 6A3 (☎613-789-3709; www.ottawa.mae.ro); **Ireland,** 26 Waterloo Rd., Ballsbridge, Dublin 4 (☎016 681 085; www.dublin.mae.ro); **UK,** 4 Palace Green, London W8 4QD (☎020 79 37 96 66; www.roemb.co.uk); **US,** 1607 23rd St., NW, Washington, D.C. 20008 (☎202-332-4846; www.roembus.org).

ENTRANCE REQUIREMENTS.

Passport: Required for all travelers.

Visa: Not required for stays under 90 days for citizens of Australia, Canada, the EU, Ireland, New Zealand, the UK, and the US.

Letter of Invitation: Not required for citizens of Australia, Canada, Ireland, New Zealand, the UK, and the US.

Inoculations: Recommended up-to-date on DTaP (diphtheria, tetanus, and pertussis), Hepatitis A, Hepatitis B, MMR (measles, mumps, and rubella), polio booster, rabies, and typhoid.

Work Permit: Required of all foreigners planning to work in Romania.

International Driving Permit: For stays longer than 90 days, all foreigners must obtain an International Driving Permit or a Romanian driver's license.

VISA AND ENTRY INFORMATION. Romanian visa regulations change frequently; check with your embassy or consulate for the most current information. Citizens of Australia, Canada, Ireland, New Zealand, the UK, and the US can visit Romania for up to 90 days without visas. In all cases, passports are required and must be valid for six months after the date of departure. Travelers should consult the Romanian embassy in their country of origin to apply for a long-term visa. For citizens of the US, a single-entry visa costs US$40; multiple-entry US$75. Visas are not available at the border. Romanian embassies estimate—but do not guarantee—a five-day processing time for most visas. Apply early to allow the bureaucratic process to run its slow, frustrating course. Visa extensions and related services are available at police headquarters in large cities or at Bucharest's Visas for Foreigners Office (Str. Luigi Cazzavillan 11, ☎01

650 3050). Long lines are common at the border for customs. Bags are rarely searched, but customs officials are strict about visa laws. In order to avoid being scammed, travelers should be aware that there is no entry tax for Romania. For additional information on visas and a list of Romanian embassies and consulates abroad, check out www.mae.ro.

TOURIST SERVICES AND MONEY

EMERGENCY	**Ambulance:** ☎961. **Fire:** ☎981. **Police:** ☎955. **General Emergency:** ☎112.

TOURIST OFFICES. Romania has limited resources for tourists, but the National tourist offices. Romania has limited resources for tourists, but the **National Tourist Office** (www.romaniatourism.com) is useful. Large hotels, however, can be excellent resources in smaller towns.

MONEY. The Romanian currency is the **leu** (L), plural **lei** (pronounced "lay"), which was revalued in 2005. One leu is equal to 100 **bani** (singular **ban**), with standard denominations of L1, L5, L10, L50, L100, and L500 in notes, and 1, 5, 10, and 50 bani in coins. Romania joined the EU in 2007, and plans to adopt the euro by 2014. As the leu strengthens, **inflation** rates continue to drop dramatically and now hover around 5%, though this statistic is liable to fluctuate. Romania has a 19% **value added tax** (VAT), a sales tax on goods and services. The prices given in *Let's Go* include VAT. **ATMs** generally accept MasterCard and Visa, and are the best way to withdraw money. **Private exchange bureaus,** which often offer better rates than banks, are everywhere. Many banks will cash **traveler's checks** in US dollars, then exchange them for lei, with high fees. Changing money on the street is both illegal and a surefire way to get cheated.

ROMANIAN LEI (L)		
	AUS$1 = L2.05	1L = AUS$0.49
	CDN$1 = L2.48	1L = CDN$0.40
	EUR€1 = L3.53	1L = EUR€0.28
	NZ$1 = L1.72	1L = NZ$0.58
	UK£1 = L5.14	1L = UK£0.19
	US$1 = L2.73	1L = US$0.37

HEALTH AND SAFETY

If possible, avoid Romanian **hospitals,** as the quality of health care is relatively low. Embassies can recommend good **private doctors** for emergencies. Some European medical clinics in Bucharest have English-speaking doctors and will require cash payments. *Farmacii* (pharmacies) stock basic medical supplies. **Public restrooms** are relatively uncommon in Romania and often lack soap, towels, and toilet paper. Though water in Romania is cleaner than it once was, avoid untreated **tap water** and do not use ice cubes; boil water before drinking it or drink imported **bottled water.** Beware of contaminated vendor food.

Violent crime is not a major concern, but **petty crime** against tourists is common. Be especially careful on public transport and night trains. Pickpocketing, is prevalent in Romania, and taxis and money-exchange services sometimes swindle tourists. Beware of distracting children and con artists dressed as policemen who ask for your passport or wallet. If someone shows a badge and claims to be a plain-clothes policeman, he may be lying and trying to scam you. No police officer would ask to see credit cards or cash. When in doubt, ask the officer to escort you to the nearest police station. The **drinking age,** which is 18, is reportedly not strictly enforced, but if you smoke marijuana, be prepared to spend the next seven years in a Romanian prison. Solo **female travelers** should say they are traveling with a male, dress conservatively, and avoid going out alone after dark. **Sexual harassment** can be a problem in Bucharest. **Minorities,** and especially those with dark skin, may encounter unwanted attention, as they may be mistaken for **Roma** (gypsies), who face discrimination in Romania. Practitioners of **religions** other than Orthodox Christianity may feel uncomfortable in the province of Moldavia. Though homosexuality is now legal, Most Romanians hold conservative attitudes toward sexuality, which may translate into harassment of **GLBT** travelers and often manifests itself in the form of anti-gay propaganda in major cities. For more information about gay and lesbian clubs and resources, check out www.accept-romania.ro.

TRANSPORTATION

BY PLANE. Many international airlines fly into **Bucharest Henri Coanda International Airport** (**OTP;** ☎021 204 1000; www.otp-airport.ro), although flights from locations outside of Europe tend to be very expensive. It is often cheaper to fly into another major European city, such as Budapest or Prague, and then to catch a train to Bucharest. **Romanian Airlines** (TAROM; www.tarom.ro) and **CarpatAir** (www.carpatair.com) fly to a number of European and Middle Eastern destinations and smaller airports within Romania, including Cluj-Napoca, Constanţa, Suceava, and Timişoara.

BY TRAIN. Trains are fast and efficient for international travel and less expensive than flights. **Eurail** is accepted within the Romanian rail network. To buy tickets for the national railway, go to the **CFR** (Che-Fe-Re) office in larger towns. You must buy **international tickets** ahead. Train stations sell domestic tickets 1hr. in advance. The English-language timetable *Mersul Trenurilor* (hardcopy L12; www.cfr.ro) is very useful. There are four types of trains: *InterCity* (indicated by an "IC"); *rapid* (in green); *accelerat* (red); and *personal* (black). International trains (blue) are indicated with an "i." *InterCity* trains stop only at major cities. *Rapid* trains are the next fastest; *accelerat* trains are slower and dirtier. The sluggish and decrepit *personal* trains stop at every station. The difference between **first class** (clasa întâi; 6 people per compartment) and **2nd class** (clasa doua; 8 people) is small, except on personal trains. In an **overnight train,** shell out for a *vagon de dormit* (sleeper car) and buy both compartment tickets if you don't want to share.

ROMANIA

BY BUS. Traveling to Romania by **bus** is often cheaper than entering by plane or train, but not as fast. Tourist agencies may sell tickets, but buying tickets from the carrier saves commission and is often cheaper. Use the slow local bus system only when trains are unavailable. **Local buses** can be cheaper than trains but are packed and poorly ventilated. Minibuses are a good option for short distances, as they are often cheaper, faster, and cleaner than trains. Rates are posted inside.

BY FERRY AND BY TAXI. In the Danube Delta, boats are the best mode of transport. A **ferry** runs down the new European riverway from Rotterdam, NTH to Constanta, and in the Black Sea between İstanbul, TUR, and Constanta. **Taxis** should be avoided if possible, as scams are very, very common. If it is necessary to take a taxi, particularly an intercity taxi, definitely call for a taxi, verify that the meter is operational, and agree on a price beforehand. Your ride should cost no more than L6 per km plus a L7 flat fee.

BY THUMB. Some travelers report that hitchhiking is very common in rural Romania and, in some places, that it is the only way to get around without a car. Hitchhikers stand on the side of the road and put out their palm, as if waving. Drivers generally expect a payment similar to the price of a train or bus ticket for the distance traveled; L1 for every 10km is a fair price. *Let's Go* does not recommend hitchhiking.

KEEPING IN TOUCH

PHONE CODES	**Country code:** 40. **International dialing prefix:** 00. For more information on how to place international calls, see **inside back cover.**

INTERNET AND TELEPHONE **Internet cafes** are relatively common—though not always easy to find—in cities and larger towns and cost L3 per hr. They are typically open late and sometimes 24hr. Most **public phones** are orange and only accept **phone cards,** sold at telephone offices, Metro stops, and some post offices and kiosks. These cards are only accepted at telephones of the same brand; the most prevalent is Romtelecom. Rates run around L1.20 per min. to neighboring countries, L1.60 per min. to most of Europe, and L2 per min. to the US. Phones operate in English if you press "i." At an **analog phone,** dial ☎971 for international calls. People with **European cell phones** can avoid roaming charges by buying a SIM card at Connex, Dialog, or CosmoRom. International access codes include: **AT&T** (☎0808 03 4288); **British Telecom** (☎02 18 00 44 44); **MCI WorldPhone** (☎02 18 00 18 00); **Canada Direct** (☎02 18 00 50 00).

MAIL. At the post office, request *par avion* for airmail, which takes two weeks for delivery. For postcards or letters, it costs L3 to mail within Europe and L5 to mail to the rest of the world. Mail can be received through **Poste Restante** (mail is held at the post office for collection), though you may run into problems picking up your package. Address envelopes as follows: LAST NAME, first name, Oficiul Postal nr. 1 (post office address), city - POSTE RESTANTE, Romania, Postal Code. Major cities have UPS and Federal Express.

LANGUAGE. Romanian is a Romance language, but differs from other Romance tongues in its Slavic-influenced vocabulary. German and Hungarian are widely spoken in Transylvania. French is a common second language for the older generation, while English is common among the younger. Avoid Russian, which is often understood but disliked. For basic Romanian words and phrases, see **Phrasebook,** p. 1067.

ACCOMMODATIONS AND CAMPING

ROMANIA	❶	❷	❸	❹	❺
ACCOMMODATIONS	under L40	L40-70	L71-100	L101-200	over L200

Many **hostels** are fairly pleasant, and some have perks like breakfast and free beer. While some **hotels** charge foreigners 50-100% more, lodging is still inexpensive (US$7-20). **Guesthouses** and **pensions** are simple and comfortable but rare. In summer, many towns rent low-priced rooms in **university dorms.** Consult the tourist office. **Private rooms** and **homestays** are a great option, but hosts rarely speak English. Rooms run L50-80. Look at the room and fix a price before accepting. **Bungalows** are often full in summer; reserve far ahead. Hotels and hostels often provide the best info for tourists.

FOOD AND DRINK

ROMANIA	❶	❷	❸	❹	❺
FOOD	under L7	L7-11	L12-15	L16-20	over L20

A complete Romanian meal includes an appetizer, soup, fish, an entree, and dessert. Lunch includes soup, called *supă* or *ciorbă* (the former has noodles or dumplings, the latter is saltier and with vegetables), an entree, and dessert. *Clătite* (crepes), *papanaşi* (doughnuts with jam and sour cream), and *torts* (creamy cakes) are all delicious. In the west, you'll find as much Hungarian food as Romanian. Some restaurants **charge by weight** rather than by portion. Although prices may be listed per 50 or 100 grams, the actual serving can be up to 300 grams. Some servers will attempt to charge unsuspecting tourists extra. If the menu is not specific, always ask. *Garnituri*, the extras that come with a meal, are usually charged separately. This means you're paying for everything, even a bit of butter or a dollop of mustard. Pork rules in Romania, so keeping **kosher** is difficult. Local drinks include *ţuică*, a brandy made from plums and apples, and double-distilled *palincă*, which approaches 70% alcohol. *Vişinată* liqueur is made from wild cherries. Always verify that the server brings the exact vintage that was ordered, since some will attempt to substitute a more expensive wine and claim that they ran out of the one you ordered.

HOLIDAYS AND FESTIVALS

Holidays: New Year's (Jan. 1-2); Epiphany (Jan. 6); Martisor (Mar. 1); Orthodox Easter Holiday (Apr. 19-20, 2009, Apr. 4-5, 2010); Labor Day (May 1); National Unity Day/Romania Day (Dec. 1); Christmas (Dec. 25-26).

Festivals: Dragobete (Feb. 24), known as "the day when the birds are getting engaged," is a traditional Romanian fertility festival. For **Martisor** (Mar. 1), locals wear porte-boneurs (good-luck charms) and give flowers to friends and lovers. **Romania Day** (Dec. 1), commemorates the day in 1918 that Transylvania became a part of Romania.

BEYOND TOURISM

For more info on opportunities across Europe, see **Beyond Tourism, p. 60.**

Volunteerabroad.com, http://www.volunteerabroad.com/Romania.cfm. Listed projects are diverse, ranging from work with orphanages to teaching English through drama.

University of Bucharest, 36-46, M. Kogalniceanu Bd., Sector 5, 70709 Bucharest, Romania (☎402 13 07 73 00; www.unibuc.ro). Accepts international students, although proficiency in Romanian is a prerequisite.

BUCHAREST (BUCUREŞTI) ☎021

Once a storied stop on the Orient Express, Bucharest (booh-kooh-RESHT; pop. 2,100,000) is now infamous for its heavy-handed transformation under dictator Nicolae Ceauşescu. During his 25-year reign, he nearly ruined the city's splendor by replacing historic neighborhoods, boulevards, and Ottoman ruins with concrete blocks, highways, and communist monuments. Since the

1989 revolution citizens have since endured a mix of communist nostalgia and break-neck capitalism. Though it retains only glimmers of the sophisticated city it once was, life here is now as fascinating as it is frustrating.

TRANSPORTATION

Flights: Henri Coanda (Otopeni) Airport (**OTP;** ☎021 204 1200; www.otp-airport.ro). Avoid pricey taxis outside the terminal. Call a cab (**Euro Taxi**; ☎9851 or **Taxi Alfa** ☎9488) or buy a bus ticket (L5 for 2 trips) from the corner kiosk at the exit from the airport, open 6am-9pm. Bus #783 runs from the airport to Pţa. Unirii. (60min., M-F 4 per hr. 5:30am-8pm, every 30 min. 8:30pm-11pm, every 30 min. Sa-Su 5:30am-11pm.) Flying into Bucharest can be expensive; it is often a better idea to fly into Budapest or Zagreb and enter Romania via train or bus.

Trains: Gara de Nord (☎021 223 0880, info 95 21). M1: Gara de Nord. to: **Braşov** (2.5-4hr., 18 per day, L26); **Constanta** (5hr., 9 per day, L41); **Sighişoara** (4-5hr., 10 per day, L49); **Budapest, HUN** (14hr., 3 per day, L172); **Kraków, POL** (27hr., 1 per day, L299); **Prague, CZR** (36hr., 1 per day, L360); **Sofia, BUL** (11hr., 2 per day, L95). **CFR,** Str. Domniţa Anastasia 10-14 (☎021 313 2643; www.cfr.ro), books domestic and international tickets. Open M-F 7am-8pm, Sa 9am-1:30pm. Cash only. **Wasteels** (☎021 317 0369; www.wasteels.ro), inside Gara de Nord, books international tickets. English spoken. Open M-F 8am-7pm, Sa 8am-2pm. AmEx/MC/V.

Buses: The profusion of bus services can make taking a bus difficult; **trains** are preferable for domestic travel. Although both trains and buses are notoriously late, buses have been known to be capricious and run on a schedule of their own. There are 6 official bus stations in Bucharest, each serving different directions. Internationally, however, buses are the best way to reach **Athens, GCE** and **İstanbul, TUR.** Multiple companies near the train station sell tickets to most of Europe. **Toros,** Calea Griviţei 134 (☎021 223 1898), sends buses to İstanbul (10hr., 2 per day, L125). Open daily 7am-5pm. Cash only. Next door at Calea Griviţei 136-138, **Transcontinental** (☎021 331 1600; www.tci.ro) goes to Athens (2 per week, €80). They also sell **Eurolines** bus tickets, which cover most of Western Europe, but tend to cost upward of €150, so a plane may be a better deal for a similar price. English spoken. Open daily 9am-5pm. Cash only.

Public Transportation: Buses, trolleys, and **trams** cost L2.60 and run daily 5:30am-11:30pm. To avoid a L30 fine, validate tickets by sliding them into the small boxes and then pushing hard on the black button outside the box. The transportation system is invaluable, but figuring out how it works is a chore. **Express buses** take only magnetic cards (L5 per 2 trips, L20 per 10 trips). Tickets and magnetic cards are sold at RATB kiosks, often near bus stops. Pickpocketing can be a problem during peak hours. The **Metro** offers reliable, less-crowded service (L2 per 2 trips, L7 per 10). Runs 5am-11:30pm. **Maps** of the public transportation system, which include a detailed city map, can be purchased from kiosks.

Taxis: Taxi drivers will cheerfully rip off foreigners and locals alike—often preferring to sit around in their taxis rather than drive you for a reasonable price. Drivers rarely speak English. Normal rates should be around L1.50 base fee and L1.4-L1.8 per km. The base fee is often posted; look for the "tarif." Fake taxis are a problem; avoid taxis that post the number "9403," as this is a commonly used fake number. Reliable companies include **Meridien** (☎94 44), **ChrisTaxi** (☎94 61), and **Taxi2000** (☎94 94).

ORIENTATION AND PRACTICAL INFORMATION

Bucharest's main street changes its name from **Bulevard Lascăr Catargiu** to **Bulevard General Magheru** to **Bulevard Nicolae Bălcescu** to **Bulevard I.C. Brătianu** as it runs north-south through the city's four main squares: **Piaţa Victoriei, Piaţa Romầna, Piaţa Universităţii,** and **Piaţa Unirii.** Another thoroughfare, running parallel, is

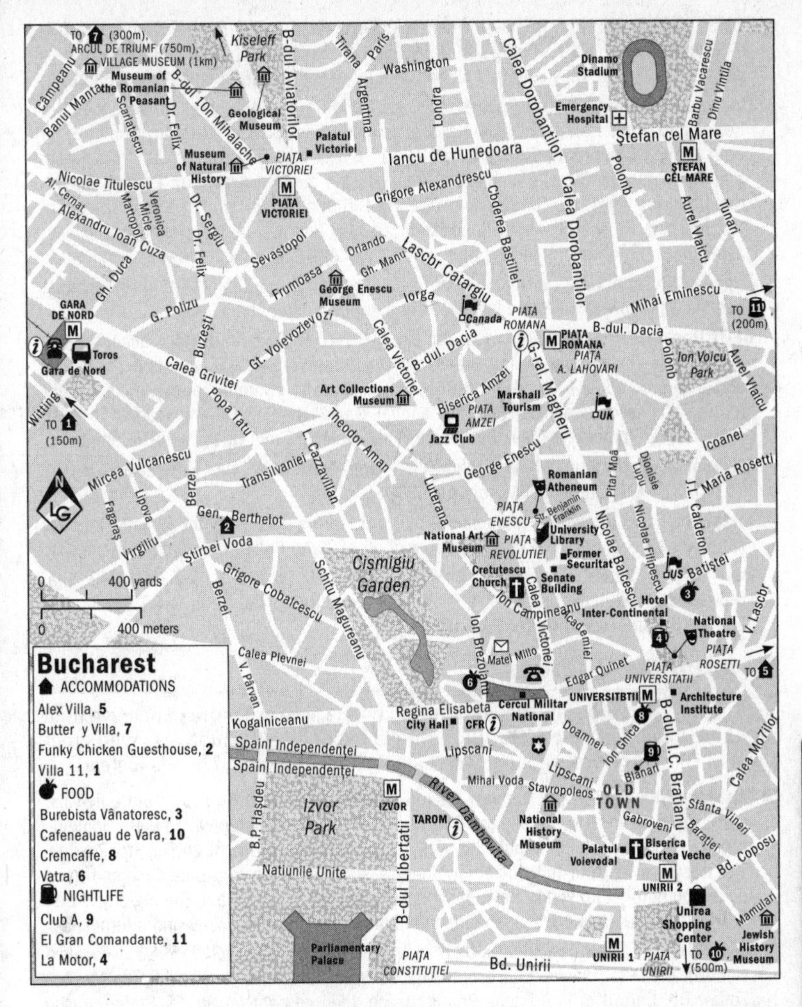

Calea Victoriei, which crosses **Piaţa Revoluţiei.** To reach the center from Gara de Nord, take M1 to Pţa. Victoriei, then change to M2 in the direction of Depoul IMGB. Go one stop to Pţa. Româna, two stops to Pţa. Universităţii, or three stops to Pţa. Unirii. It's a 15min. walk between each of squares.

Tourist Office: No municipal office. Hotels are a good resource. The staff speaks English and many hotels have free **maps** handy.

Embassies and Consulates: Australia, Pţa. Montreal 10, World Trade Center, entrance F, 1st fl. (☎021 316 7553). M4: 1 Mai. Open M-Th 9am-5:30pm, F 9am-2:30pm. **Canada,** Str. Tuberozelor 1-3 (☎021 307 5000). M1 or 2: Pţa. Victoriei. Open M-Th 8:30am-5pm, F 8:30am-2pm. **Ireland,** Str. Buzeşti 50-52, 3rd fl. (☎021 310 2131). M2: Pţa. Victoriei. Open M-F 10am-noon and 2-4pm. Citizens of **New Zealand** should contact the UK embassy. **UK,** Str. Jules Michelet 24 (☎021 201 7279, www.britshembassy.gov.uk). M2: Pţa. Romană. Open M-Th 9am-noon and 2-6pm, F 9am-noon. **US,** 7-9, Tudor Arghezi Street (☎021 200 3300, after hours ☎021 200 3433; www.usembassy.ro). M2: Pţa. Universităţii. Behind Hotel Intercontinental. Open M-F 8am-5pm.

Currency Exchange: Exchange agencies and **ATMs** are everywhere. Stock up before heading to remote areas, but don't exchange more than you'll need—many won't buy lei back. **Banca Comerciala Româna** (☎021 312 6185; www.bcr.com), in Pţa. Universităţii and on Ştefan cel Mare, exchanges currency for no fee and **American Express Travelers Cheques** for 1.5% commission. Open M-F 8:30am-5:30pm. The Pţa. Universităţii location, Bd. Regina Elisabeta 5, has both an **ATM** and a currency exchange machine, available 24hr. Changing money on the street is illegal and almost always a scam.

Luggage Storage: Gara de Nord. L3 per bag, L6 per large bag. Open 24hr. However, most hostels will allow you to store luggage with them even after check-out.

GLBT Resources: Accept Romania, Str. Lirei 10 (☎021 252 5620; www.accept-romania.ro). English-speaking staff has a wealth of information on GLBT events in the center and organizes counseling services, support groups, and informal get-togethers. Accept Romania is also responsible for the annual **Gay-Fest,** a week-long festival to raise awareness of minority issues, the 1st and 2nd weeks of June. Open M-F 9:30am-5pm.

Medical Services: Spitalul de Urgenţă (Emergency Hospital), Calea Floreasca 8 (☎021 317 0121). M1: Ştefan cel Mare. Open 24hr.

Telephones and Internet: Phone cards (L10 or L15) are necessary for all calls. Internet cafes are everywhere. Free Wi-Fi available at all KFC and Pizza Hut locations in the city.

Post Office: Central Post Office, Str. Matei Millo 10 (☎021 315 8793). M2: Pţa. Universităţii. Like most branches, this one has **Poste Restante.** Open M-F 7:30am-1pm and 1:30-8pm. **Postal Code:** 014700.

ACCOMMODATIONS

Renting private rooms is uncommon, and hotels here are more expensive than in other Romanian cities. Travelers should avoid "representatives" who greet them at Gara de Nord, sticking with established hostels and hotels instead.

Butterfly Villa Hostel, Str. Dumitru Zosima 82 (☎40 747 032 644, www.butterfly-villa.com). From Gara de Nord, take bus 282 and get off at the 6th stop called Piata Domenii. Cross the boulevard, Ion Mihalache, walk to the left, and turn right on Dumitru Zosima. The hostel is on your left. Incredibly friendly staff, fantastic free breakfast and good prices bring together young fresh backpackers looking for a home in the big city. 8-bed dorm €12; doubles €16. Call ahead in summer. Cash only. Free Wi-Fi and internet. ❷

Alex Villa, Str. Avram Iancu 5 (☎021 313 3198 or cell ☎072 351 5088, www.alexvilla.ro). M2: Pţa. Universităţii. From Gara de Nord, take trolley #85 to Calea Moşilor. Follow Bd. Carol I to Pţa. Pache Protopopescu, then go right on Str. Sf. Ştefan. At the playground, take a left on Avram Iancu. Central location, yet relaxed neighborhood. Multilingual owner, Alex, is incredibly inviting and helpful. Breakfast, and Internet included. 4-bed dorms L40, L100 for a double room. Laundry L10. Cash only. ❶

Funky Chicken Guesthouse, Str. General Berthelot 63 (☎021 312 1425, www.funkychickenhostel.com), near Cişmigiu Park and Pţa. Revolutiei. The cheapest prices in town mean only the basics provided. The outside terrace is a nice place to relax and drink a beer with other broke backpackers. Small kitchen available. Laundry and free cigarettes included, but no Internet. 4- to 8-bed dorms €8. Call ahead in summer. Cash only. ❶

Villa 11, Str. Institut Medico Militar 11 (☎07 22 49 59 00). M1 or M4: Gara de Nord. From the train station, take a right on Bd. Dinicu Golescu and left on Str. Vespasian. A little far from the hubbub of the city center, a quiet hostel with home-cooked breakfast daily. English spoken. Shared baths. 3- to 8-bed dorms L55; singles L90; Cash only. ❷

FOOD

The **open-air market** at Pţa. Amzei, near Pţa. Romană, has cheese, meat, and produce. (Open M-F 6am-9pm, Sa 6am-7pm, Su 6am-3pm. Cash only.) A large **La Fourmi Supermarket** is in the basement of the Unirea Shopping Center on Pţa. Unirii. (Open M-F 8am-9:30pm, Sa 8:30am-9pm, Su 10am-6pm. MC/V.)

Cafeneaua Actorilor de vara ❷, Parcul Tineretull, Bd. Nicolae Balcescu (☎0724 14 74 32; www.cafeneauaactorilor.ro). Open only during the summer months, usually from June-Aug., this restaurant sits right in the middle of Bucharest's Tineretului Park, surrounded by beautiful lakes and greenery in the middle of the city. The pizzas are fantastic, but expect a bit of a wait at night. Spontaneous karaoke known to occur. Beer L5-9. Entrees L10-30. Open daily noon-1am.

Burebista Vânatoresc, Str. Batiştei 14, off B-dul. Nicolae Bălcescu (☎021 211 8929; www.restaurantburebista.ro). M2: Pţa. Universităţii. Complete with a stuffed bear, hunting trophies, and a live folk band daily after 8pm. Menu features game, including wild boar. English-language menu. Entrees L20-70. Open daily noon-midnight. MC/V. ❸

Cremcaffe, Str. Toma Caragiu 3 (☎021 313 9740; www.cremcaffe.ro). M2: Pţa. Universităţii. Off B-dul. Regina Elisabeta, find Str. Toma Caragiu behind the statues, 1 block from Pţa. Universităţii. Established in 1950, this elegant Italian coffeehouse specializes in desserts. Also features delicious focaccia and ciabatta sandwiches (from L14), with a good vegetarian selection. Coffee and liqueur blends L13-20. English-language menu. Open M-F 7:30am-midnight, Sa-Su 9am-midnight. Cash only. ❸

Vatra, Ion Brezoianu 23-25 (☎021 315 8375; www.vatra.ro). M2: Pţa. Universităţii. From Pţa. Universităţii, head down B-dul. Regina Elisabeta. A block before Cişmigiu Park, turn right down Brezoianu. Traditionally attired waitstaff serves relatively cheap, authentic Romanian cuisine in a lively dining room with rough-hewn wooden tables. English-language menu. Beer L4-6. Entrees L9-24. Open daily noon-midnight. Cash only. ❷

SIGHTS

CIVIC CENTER. To create his ideal Socialist capital, Ceauşescu destroyed five sq. km of Bucharest's historical center, demolishing over 9000 19th-century houses and displacing more than 40,000 people. The Civic Center (Centru Civic) that he built lies at the end of the 6km B-dul. Unirii, and is 1m wider than its inspiration, the Champs-Élysées. Its centerpiece, the 1000-room **Parliamentary Palace** (Palatul Parlamentului), is the world's second-largest building after the Pentagon in Washington, D.C. As much as 80% of Romania's GDP was consumed by the project during its construction. *(☎021 311 36 11 M1 or 3: Izvor. M2: Unirii. Visitors' entrance on the north side of the building by the river. Open daily 10am-4pm. L15. 40min. English-language tours L15. Cash only.)*

CIŞMIGIU GARDEN. One of Bucharest's oldest gardens; the peaceful, tree-filled eye of central Bucharest's storm of gray modernity. Join the locals and stroll among the carefully tended flower gardens, statues, cobblestone pathways, and fountains that surround the small lake. *(M2: Pţa. Universităţii. Bus #61 or 336. Open 24hr. Rowboats and pedal boats L10 per hr. Open M-Th 11am-9pm, F 11am-midnight, Sa 10am-midnight, Su 10am-9pm. Cash only.)*

SIGHTS OF THE REVOLUTION. Crosses and plaques throughout the city commemorate the *eroii revoluţiei Române*, "heroes of the revolution," and the year 1989; many of Romania's streets are named after iconic dates from the revolution. The first shots of the Revolution were fired at Piaţa Revoluţiei on December 21, 1989. The square holds the **University Library,** the **National Art**

THE LOCAL STORY

SON OF A...

'es, Dracula did exist—sort of. He was not the ruler of Transylvania, but of Wallachia; he was not a count, but a *voivode* (a local governor or "prince"); and he was not a vampire. Still, the truth about Vlad Ţepeş (1431-1476) is enough to make anyone lock the id to his coffin at night.

Dracula's story begins with his ather, the ruthless Vlad Basarab, who became known as **Vlad Dracul** (dragon) for his membership in the Order of the Dragon. Drac" in Romanian can be transated as either dragon or, fittingly, devil. In a diplomatic move, Dracul sent his 10-year-old son, Dracula Son of the Dragon), to the Ottonan Empire as a hostage in 1442. There, Vlad learned his preferred method of torture: impalement. Victims of impalement—which nvolved the insertion of a large wooden stake into the victim's body, avoiding piercing the vital organs—begged for a swift death hroughout the slow, agonizing process of blood loss and exposure to the elements.

Known as Vlad the Impaler, Dracula impaled not only murderers, thieves, and political rivals but also the destitute and the crippled n a bid to rid his territory of poverty. His crowning achievement, however, was in turning the Turks' gruesome practice against them. n 1462, the invading Turks turned ail at Wallachia's border—which had been decorated with 20,000 of their impaled countrymen—and Vlad's legacy was born.

Museum, and the **Senate Building** (former Communist Party Headquarters) where Ceauşescu delivered his final speech. Afterward, he fled the roof by helicopter but didn't get very far; shortly thereafter, he was captured by his pursuers and executed on national television. A white marble triangle with the inscription *Glorie martirilor noştri* ("glory to our martyrs") commemorates the rioters who overthrew the dictator. **Piaţa Universităţii** overlooks memorials to victims of the revolution and the 1990 protests against the new government. Crosses line Bd. Nicolae Bălcescu; the black cross lies where the first victim died. *(M2: Pţa. Universitatii. Turn right on Bd. Regina Elisabeta and then right on Calea Victoriei.)*

MUSEUMS. **The Village Museum** (Muzeul Satului), Sos. Kiseleff 28-30, sits on the shores of Lake Herastrau and is an excellently designed open-air replica of traditional rural village life in different Romanian regions. Each exhibit bears a plaque showing exactly where it is from and when it was transferred. *(M2: Aviatorilor. ☎021 317 91 10; www.muzeul-satului.ro. English-lang. captions. Open M 9am-5pm, Tu-Su 9am-7pm. L6, students L3. Cash only.)* The massive **National Art Museum** (Muzeul National de Arta) centers around three main exhibitions—Medieval Romanian Art, Modern Romanian Art, and European paintings and sculptures. The modern Romanian exhibition is a definite highlight, with works from all of Romania's best artists, including Aman and Tattarescu. *(B/C5, Calea Victoriei 49-53, in Pţa. Revolutiei. M2: Pţa. Universitatii. ☎021 313 3030; www.mnar.arts.ro. Open W-Su May-Sept. 11am-7pm; Oct.-Apr. 10am-6pm. Each wing L8, students L5; both wings L15/7.50; free 1st W of each month. Cash only.)* The **Museum of the Romanian Peasant** (Muzeul Tbranului Român) captures Romanian rural life and is considered one of the best museums in the city. Built almost 100 years ago, it houses everything from clothing to ages-old handmade pottery. Don't miss the small, fascinating collection of Communist memorabilia, tucked downstairs near the restrooms—it has one of the few remaining publicly exhibited portraits of Nicolae Ceauşescu. *(Şos. Kiseleff 3. M2 or 3: Pţa. Victoriei or bus #300. ☎021 317 9660; www.muzeultaranuluiroman.ro. Some English captions. Open Tu-Su 10am-6pm. L6, students L2. Cash only.)* The **National History Museum** (Muzeul National de Istorie al României), has extensive jewel collections and countless artifacts from all over the country. *(Calea Victoriei 12. M1 or 2: Pţa. Unirii. ☎021 315 8207 www.mnir.ro. Open W-Su 10am-6pm from June-August. Sept.-May 9am-5pm. L7, students L2. Cash only.)*

OTHER SIGHTS. Several of modern Bucharest's most fashionable streets, including **Calea Victoriei,**

Şoseauna Kiseleff, Bulevardul Aviatorilor, and **Bulevardul Magheru,** are sights in themselves. Side streets just off Pţa. Victoriei and Pţa. Dorobanţilor are lined with villas and houses typical of beautiful 19th-century Bucharest. **Herăstrău Park** is a popular place for people of all ages to stroll; it also contains rides for people of all ages. At the head of Kiseleff street is Romania's **Arcul de Triumf,** commemorating Romania's WWI casualties. The **old center** lies west of B-dul. Brbtianu and south of B-dul. Regina Elisabeta. On **Str. Lipscani** (open only to pedestrians and taxis) cafes, art galleries, and quaint cobblestone streets abound. The ruins of one of Dracula's actual palaces, **Curtea Veche** (Old Court), can be seen on Str. Franceza. With access from both Lipscani and Blănari streets, **Hanul cu Tei** hosts a myriad of eclectic specialty shops and art gallerys. Once an inn, it retains its original 19th century structure. *(Open M-F 9am-6pm, Sa-Su 9am-2pm.)*

ENTERTAINMENT AND NIGHTLIFE

For the best deals on already cheap **opera, symphony,** and **theater** tickets, stop by the box office about a week before a show. There are no summer performances. (Opera at B-dul. Mihail Kogalniceanu 70-72; ☎021 313 18 57; www.operanb.ro.) At night, pack a map and cab fare, but expect to be frustrated by unreasonable cab drivers demanding sky high rates. At night, streets are poorly lit and public transportation stops at midnight.

El Gran Comandante, Str. Vlitorului 26. (☎0728 55 60 43). Newly opened and dedicated to Che, but you don't have to be a fan of his to enjoy the cheap drinks and relaxed rock that is a welcome break from Eastern Europe's love of house music. Beer L2-5, Drinks from L5. Open Tu-Sa 7pm-6am.

Club A, Str. Blănari 14 (☎021 315 5592; www.cluba.ro). M2: Pţa. Universităţii. Bucharest's most famous hot spot, with cheap drinks and loud music. Live music also available most weekends. Beer from L2.40. Cover M-W and Su men L3; Th men L4; F-Sa men L5, women L2. Open M-W 10am-5am, Th-F and Su 9pm-5am, Sa 9pm-6am.Cash only.

La Motor/Laptaria, B-dul. Balcescu 1-3, is a student bar with a huge terrace. (M2: Pţa. Universităţii. Beer L3-5. Open M-Th and Su noon-2am, F-Sa noon-4am. Cash only.)

SINAIA ☎0244

Sinaia (sih-NYE-uh; pop. 15,000) first made its mark in the late 1880s as an alpine getaway for Romania's royal family, and it draws visitors back today with absolutely fantastic hiking. Carol I, king of the newly independent country, oversaw construction of the fantastically opulent **Peleş Castle** (Castelul Peleş), completed in 1914. The more modest, nearby **Pelişor Castle,** built in 1902, was furnished in the Art Nouveau style. Pelişor is a bit of a walk up a hill, but the surrounding river and scenery make up for the climb. After visiting the castles, go and barter at one of the countless artisan stands at below the entrance. (☎02 44 31 09 18; www.peles.ro. Both castles open Tu 11am-5pm, W-Su 9am-5pm; low-season closed Tu. Tours in Romanian required at Peleş (L15, students L5. Pelişor L10/3.) The nearby **Bucegi Mountains** are good for hiking in summer and skiing in winter. A **telecabina** (cable car) to the mountains leaves from B-dul. Carol I 26; to reach it, turn up the hill across from the tourist office on Str. Cuza Voda. There are two stops, one at 1400m and the other at 2000m. (☎0244 31 19 39. Cable cars run Tu-Su 9am-5pm; Dec.-Feb. and June-Aug. L12 to 1400m, L21 to 2000m; round-trip L20/40. Cash only).

The **Cabana Miorita ❶,** at the Cota 2000 station, with a bar and restaurant, is the queen of the mountain cabin system. (☎02 44 31 22 99. 12-bed dorms L20; 7-bed dorms L30; private rooms L40-50. Cash only.) **Hostel Blue Silver ❷,** Str. Libertatii 18-20, has a kitchen and walls covered with Michael Jordan posters.

(☎02 44 313 341. Doubles 100L; triples 150L.) For traditional fare, head to **Restaurant Bucegi ❶**, on Sinaia's main street, Bd. Carol I, near Hotel New Montana. (Entrees L9-35. Open daily 9:15am-11:30pm. MC/V.) Two levels, bear skins, and a large terrace draw locals and tourists alike. Grab a beer and pizza with locals at **Old Nick's Pub ❶**, B-dul. Carol I 8, by Hotel Sinaia. (☎02 44 31 24 91; www.oldnickpub.ro. Beer L5-12. Entrees L10-18. Open daily 9am-2am. Cash only.)

Trains (☎02 44 31 00 40) run to Braşov (2hr., 33 per day, L18), Bucharest (2-3hr., 20 per day, L40), and Cluj-Napoca (6hr., 6 per day, L60). To get to the center of town from the train station, climb the steps across from the station, and at the top go left on Bd. Carol I. The staff at the **tourist office,** B-dul. Carol I 47, speaks English. (☎02 44 31 56 56; www.infosinaia.ro. Open M-F 8:30am-4:30pm.) **ATM, telephone office** and **post office are** in the same building. (Post office open M-F 7am-8pm, Sa 8am-1pm.) **Postal Code:** 106100.

TRANSYLVANIA (TRANSILVANIA)

The name evokes images of an evil land of black magic and vampires, but Transylvania (also known as Ardeal)—with a history of Saxon settlement dating back to the 12th century—is a relatively Westernized region. The vampire legends do, however, resonate with the region's architecture: Transylvanian buildings are tilted, jagged, and more sternly Gothic than anywhere else in Europe. Medieval cities make this a travelers' favorite, while hikers revel in the untamed wilderness of the misty Făgăraş Mountains.

CLUJ-NAPOCA ☎0264

Cluj-Napoca (KLOOZH nah-POH-kah; pop. 350,000) is Transylvania's student center and its unofficial capital. In the center of town, the 80m Gothic steeple of the 14th-century Catholic **Church of St. Michael** (Biserica Sf. Mihail) rises from **Piaţa Unirii.** In front of the cathedral stands the monument to 15th-century ruler Matthias Corvinus. Take Str. Regele Ferdinand across the river, turn left on Str. Drbgblina, and climb the stairs to your right for a dazzling city view from **Cetătuie Hill.** Over 12,000 plant species grow in the **Botanical Garden** (Grădina Botanica), Str. Republicii 42, off Str. Napoca. (Gardens open daily in summer 9am-8pm, fall-spring 9am-5:45pm; greenhouses daily 9am-5:45pm; museum Tu-Th 10am-1pm. L4, students L2. Photography L20.) The **National History Museum of Transylvania,** on the corner of Str. Constantin Daicoviciu and Str. Roosevelt, has over 400,000 displays, tracing the history of the region since the Paleolithic era, though there are no english subtitles on captions. (☎004 0264. Open Tu-Su 10am-4pm. L6, students L3; photography L5. Cash only.) The **Transylvanian International Film Festival** takes place in early June; most films are subtitled or in English. There is live music in town every night during the festival. (Films L5-10; student discounts available.) Hotels distribute the free pamphlet *Zile si Nopţi?* (Days and Nights?), which lists the latest nightlife.

Retro Youth Hostel ❷, Str. Potaissa 13, has clean dorm rooms, Wi-Fi, common space, and kitchen. The staff arranges excursions for groups to nearby ice caves and salt mines. (☎02 64 45 04 52; www.retro.ro. Breakfast L14. Laundry L10. Dorms L44. HI and ISIC discount 5%. MC/V.) **Roata ❷**, Str. Alexandru Ciura 6A, off Str. Emil Isac, is a traditional Romanian restaurant that serves excellent food in big portions. (☎02 64 19 20 22. Appetizers L5-15. Entrees L11-30. Open M and Su 1pm-midnight, Tu-Sa noon-midnight. Cash only.) **Diesel ❸**, situated right in the center of town in Piaţa Unirii 17, is a busy cafe that attracts beautiful people on weekends. (☎0264 43 90 43. Dress code at club and lounge. Cafe open daily 8am-late. Club open daily 9pm-late. Lounge open Th-Sa. Live music or DJs Th-Sa. Beer L7-15. Mixed drinks L7-20. Cash only.)

Trains go to: Bucharest (8-12hr., 6 per day, L60) via Braşov (5-7hr., L42); Sibiu (4hr., 1 per day, L38); Timişoara (5-7hr., 6 per day, L41); Budapest, HUN (6-7hr., 2 per day, L114). Local **buses** and **trams** run 5am-10pm; tickets (L1.30) are sold at **RATUC** kiosks (open 5am). Validate your ticket on board. **ATMs** line B-dul. Ferdinand. **Internet** cafe Total Net Soft is at Str. Emil Isac 2. (7am-11pm L1.60 per hr., 11pm-7am L1 per hour. Open 24hr. Cash only.) **Postal Code:** 400110.

SIGHIŞOARA ☎0265

With only 30,000 people and a large gypsy population, this sleepy town seems almost untouched by the whirlwind of tourism that has swept through Transylvania in the last 10 years. Narrow streets wind across the town's rivers, and the hills enclosing it only add to the sense of seclusion and detachment. Though small, many backpackers do pass through to relax and see the birthplace of Vlad Ţepeş, the inspiration for Bram Stoker's *Dracula* (see **Bran,** p. 836). Its gilded steeples and old clock tower have survived centuries of assault, fires, and floods. The **Cetatea** (Citadel), built by the Saxons in 1191, is now a medieval city within a city. Enter through the **turnul cu ceas** (clock tower), off Str. O. Goga, passing the **History Museum** on the way up. To your left as you ascend the tower, the **torture room** offers a gruesome glimpse into the methods used centuries ago. (Open M-F, 10am-5pm. L10, L3 for students). Central **Piaţa Cetăţii** was historically used for markets, executions, and impalings, which enlivened the dullest of Saturday afternoons. The nearby church, **Biserica Mănăstirii,** holds organ concerts Fridays at 6pm. (Open Tu-Sa 10am-5pm, Su 11:15am-3pm. L2, students L1. Concerts L4. Cash only.)

Turn right from the station to reach **Nathan's Villa Hostel ❶**, Str. Libertăţii 8. Known as a party hostel, Nathan's still provides weary travelers with a comfortable place to rest. The vivacious staff organizes daytrips. (☎0265 77 25 46; www.nathansvilla.com. Breakfast included. Free laundry. Kitchen available. Reception 24hr. 12-bed dorms L35; doubles L80. Cash only.) **Casa Vlad Dracul ❷,** where Vlad Ţepeş was born, is now a comfortable classy restaurant and bar, dimly lit by candles as it tries to preserve Vlad's vibe. (☎0265 77 15 96. Beer from L4. Entrees L11-41. Vegetarian options available. Open 10am-midnight. AmEx/MC/V.) **Trains** go to Bucharest (4hr., 10 per day, L48) via Braşov (2hr., 8 per day, L29-37) and Cluj-Napoca (3hr., 8 per day, L40). To reach the city center from the station, turn right on Str. Libertăţii and left on Str. Gării. Veer left at the Russian cemetery, then turn right on the footbridge over Târana Mare, and walk down Str. Morii. The **Associatia Turistică Sighişoara** (tourist office) is at Str. Octavian Goga 8. (☎0265 77 04 15. Open M-Sa 10am-5pm.) Culture Cafe, attached to the Burg Hostel, has free **Wi-Fi.** (☎0265 77 84 89. Open daily 7am-late. L3.50 per hr. MC/V.) **Postal Code:** 545400.

ROMANIA

BRAŞOV ☎0268

Braşov (pop. 284,000) is a picturesque town with a lively German heritage. It serves as an ideal departure point for mountain trips. A **telecabina** goes up **Muntele Tâmpa** (behind a giant Hollywood-esque sign that reads "BRAŞOV."); to reach it from **Piaţa Sfatului,** the main square, walk down Apollonia Hirscher, make a left on Str. Castelui, take a right on Suisul Castelui, and climb the stairs to the beige building on the right. (Cable car runs M noon-5:45pm, Tu-F 9:30am-6pm, Sa-Su 9:30am-7pm. L6, round-trip L10. Cash only.) Alternatively, follow the red triangle markings to hike to the top (1-2hr.). **Strada Republicii** is the city's main pedestrian avenue, while beyond the square and along Str. Gh. Bariţiu is Romania's most celebrated Gothic edifice, the Lutheran **Black Church** (Biserica

Neagră). Built in 1383, it received its name after being charred by a 1689 fire. (Open M-Sa 10am-5pm. Organ concerts June and Sept. Tu 6pm; July-Aug. Tu, Th, Sa 6pm. L5. Cash only.) In August and September, Pţa. Sfatului hosts the **Golden Stag Festival** (Cerbul de Aur), which attracts international musicians. The **International Chamber Music Festival** is in September.

Locals offer private rooms at the train station; expect to pay around L20 per night. Alternatively, try **Kismet Dao Villa Hostel ❷**, at Str. Democraţiei 2B. From Pţa. Unirii, walk up Str. Balea and turn right onto Str. Democraţiei. This hostel has a big common room, great views of the hills from the balconies, and lots of free perks, like breakfast, Internet, Wi-Fi, one complimentary drink per day, and laundry. (☎0268 51 42 96, www.kismetdao.com. Check-out noon. 6-10 bed dorms L40-45; doubles L130. MC/V; 4% surcharge.) Romantic, candlelit **Bella Muzica ❷**, downstairs at Str. G. Baritiu 2, has an eclectic Mexican-Romanian menu, as well as free tortilla chips and free shots of *pălincă*. (☎0268 47 69 46. English menu. Beer L4-8. Entrees L9-45. Open daily noon-midnight. MC/V.)

Trains run to Bucharest (2-3hr., over 20 per day, L37-42), Cluj-Napoca (5hr., 2 per day, L59-64), and Sibiu (2-3hr., 6 per day, L35). Buy tickets at **CFR**, B-dul. 15 Noiembrie 43. (☎0268 47 06 96. Open M-F 7am-8pm. Cash only.) From the station, either take bus #4 to Pţa. Sfatului (10min.) and get off in front of Black Church, or take bus #51 to Pţa. Unirii. The **tourist office**, located inside the museum in Pta. Sfatului, has an English-speaking staff. (☎0268 41 90 78; www.brasovcity.ro. Open daily 9am-5pm.) Get **Internet** at Non-stop Internet Cafe, G. Baritsiu 8. (☎0268 741 01 85. L2 per hr. Open 24hr.) **Postal Code:** 500001.

DAYTRIPS FROM BRAŞOV: BRAN CASTLE. Vlad Ţepeş, the model for the hero-villain of Bram Stoker's novel Dracula, probably never lived in Bran, the inspiration for his fictional castle, though he may have been a prisoner here. In fact, Stoker, an **Irishman**, never even visited Romania. But Dracula's fictional exploits pale in comparison with Ţepeş's actual ones: as a local prince of the Wallachia region, he protected the area from the encroaching Turks of the Ottoman Empire, garnering infamy for impaling not only his enemies, but even some of his own people. The ticket to the castle includes a visit to the **Bran Village Museum**, which recreates a traditional Romanian village. *(Open May-Oct M 10am-7pm, Tu-Su 9am-7pm. Nov-Mar M closed, Tu-Su 9am-5pm. L12, students L6. To reach Bran from Braşov, take a taxi or city bus #12 to Autogară 2 (45min., 2 per hr., L3.50). Get off at the souvenir market or at the sign marked "Cabana Bran Castle 500m.")*

RÂSNOV FORTRESS. On a windswept hill in Râşnov sits a ruined **fortress** topped by an immense wooden crucifix. Much of the castle has been renovated recently, but work continues on the topmost portion, which shows every one of its nearly 800 years. Drop a coin down the spectacularly deep well (146m), dug in 17 years by two Turkish prisoners in exchange for their freedom. The small museum houses a collection of the weapons used to protect the fortress over the ages The fortress is less touristy than Bran, and the 360° panoramic view from the top is breathtaking. *(☎0268 23 02 55 English-language captions. Open daily 9am-7pm. L10. Cash only. Most buses to Bran stop in Râșnov (25min.), and direct buses to Râșnov depart from the Autogara (4 per hr., L2.50). From the bus stop, follow Str. Republicii past an open-air market. Following the signs for Muzeu Cetate, go right and then left through an arch.)*

MOLDAVIA (MOLDOVA)

Northeastern Romania, known as Moldavia, extends from the Carpathian Mountains to the Prut River. Starker than Transylvania but more developed than Maramureş, Moldavia is home to the painted monasteries of Bucovina, which combine Moldavian and Byzantine architecture with Romanian Orthodox Christian images. Dress modestly; no shorts or uncovered shoulders.

WHAT'S IN A NAME? Quite a lot, apparently. Moldavia and Moldova are not the same place. While Moldavia is the northeastern part of Romania, Moldova is a separate country between Russia and Romania. The distinction is further confused because the region of Moldavia is known as "Moldova" in Romanian. Although as of 2007, US citizens no longer need a visa to enter Moldova (the country), Australians and New Zealanders still do. Make sure you don't accidentally book a bus that passes through Moldova unless you have proper documentation.

SUCEAVA ☎0230

Once Moldavia's capital, Suceava is home to the grand **Citadel of the Throne** (Cetatea de Scaun), built in 1388. Climb up and walk along the ramparts for a spectacular view of the city and surrounding park. Taxis (5min., L4) can be arranged from the main square, Pţa. 22 Decembrie, though the 10min. hike uphill following the forest path is pleasant. (Open daily high-season 8am-8pm; low-season 10am-6pm. L2, students L1; photography L5.) The pretty **Village Museum of Bucovina** immortalizes traditional life. (Open M-F 10am-6pm, Sa-Su 10am-8pm. L2, students L1.) From Str. Ana Ipatescu, walk past the bus shelter and turn left to find the **Biserica St. Dumitru,** built in 1535 and decorated inside with frescoes. It is a functioning church, so visiting hours vary.

The delightful **High Class Hostel ❷,** Str. Mihai Eminescu 19, has exceptional service and a central location. (☎723 78 23 28; www.classhostel.ro. Breakfast L10. Dinner L25. Laundry L10 per 3kg. Free Internet and Wi-Fi. 4- to 6-bed dorms L50. MC/V.) **Pub Chagall ❷,** is in a courtyard off the pedestrian part of Str. Ştefan cel Mare—take a left after entering the arch. Tasty thin-crust pizzas and filling pub food are available in a red brick cellar. (☎02 30 53 06 21. Entrees L9-20. Open M-Sa 10am-midnight, Su 11am-midnight. Cash only.)

Trains run to: Braşov (8hr., 1 per day, L54); Bucharest (6-7hr., 6 per day, L35-74); Cluj-Napoca (6-7hr., 4per day, L44); Gura Humorului (1hr., 6 per day, L7.80). Buy tickets at **CFR**, Str. N. Balcescu 4. (☎02 30 21 43 35. Open M-F 7:30am-8:30pm. Cash only.) Turn right off Str. N. Balcescu for **buses** (☎0230 52 43 40) that run from the station on Str. V. Alecsandri (open 5am-9pm) to Bucharest (8hr., 5 per day, L25), Cluj-Napoca (6hr., 2 per day, L 37), and Gura Humorului (1hr., 12 per day, L4.50). **Taxis** around town charge about L1.70 per km. **Bilco Agentia de Turism,** Str. N. Balcescu 2, organizes car tours to the monasteries and sells maps of Bucovina for L8. (☎0230 52 24 60. €60-100 per car. Private guides available. Open in summer M-Sa 8:30am-7pm; in winter M-F 9:30am-5pm, Sa 9:30am-3pm. MC/V.) **Libraria Lidana,** on Str. C. Porumbescu behind the theater in the main square, sells maps of Suceava. (☎0230 37 73 24. Open M-F 9am-6pm, Sa 9am-3pm.) **Postal Code:** 720290.

DAYTRIP FROM SUCEAVA: BUCOVINA MONASTERIES. Hidden in rural Romania in the Carpathian foothills, Bucovina's painted monasteries are a source of national pride. They offer perfect examples of Moldavian architecture, a unique mix of Byzantine, Roman, and Gothic styles. Suceava can serve as an ideal base for monastery tours. A half-day trip from Suceava leads to **Moldoviţa,** which houses a small, vibrant community of 40 nuns and some of the best-preserved frescoes in Romania. *(Open in summer daily 8am-7pm; in winter*

8am-5pm. L4, students L2. Take a train from Suceava to Vama (1hr., 8 per day, L7) and continue to Vatra Moldovitei (40min., 3 per day, L2.70.) **Sucevița,** for its part, is as much a fortress as a convent. After passing 4m thick walls and a watchtower, visitors enter through a tiny door meant to hinder mounted attackers. The frescoes that cover the church's outside walls are in miraculous condition. *(Public transportation to Sucevița is unavailable, but many car tours run out of Suceava. Church open daily 7am-8pm. L4, students L2.)* Ștefan cel Mare built **Voroneț** in 1488 in three months, three weeks, and three days. Almost 40 years later, in 1524, his son Petru Rareș added its famous frescoes. The monastery is accessible by foot from Gura Humorului. *(Walk left from the train station on Ștefan cel Mare, turn left on Cartierul Voroneț, and follow the signs for a scenic 5km. Open daily in summer 9am-7pm; otherwise 8am-5pm. L5, students L2.)*

CONSTANŢA ☎0241

Inhabited since 700 BC, Constanţa (pop. 308,000) is both an industrial city and a beach resort. Mamaia and other nearby resort towns may have a more singular purpose, but Constanţa draws thousands of Romanians beyond its beaches to its retro discos and esplanades.

The **Museum of Folk Art,** B-dul. Tomis 32, highlights 19th- and 20th-century Romanian art, including costumes and interior decorations. (☎0241 61 80 19. Open in high-season daily 9am-7:30pm; Oct.-May W-Su 9am-5pm. L9, students L5, English tour guides available.) The site of the Forum from the 4th to the 6th century, the **Museum of National History and Archaeology,** Pţa. Ovidiu 12, celebrates Constanţa's Roman heritage. (☎0241 618 763. Open daily in high-season 9am-8pm; Oct-May 9am-5pm. L10, students L5.) The impressive **Great Mahmudiy Mosque** stands at Str. Arhiepiscopiei 5 (Ovidiu Sq.). The 47m minaret has the best view of the city, and the criers climb 140 steps to the top five times a day to call the people to prayer. (Open daily 9:30am-9:30pm. L4, students L2.)

When the sun sets, **Oscar,** Str. Sarmisegetusa 15, rocks out to older tunes, while dancing continues into the wee hours at **Club "No Problem,"** Complex Dacia on B-dul. Tomis, a street littered with clubs of all sizes and musical styles. (☎0241 51 33 77. Cover L10 for live music. Open Th-Sa 10pm-5am.)

Since Constanţa is a resort town without hostels, accommodations do not come cheap. At the train station, countless grandmas will greet you, offering private rooms for about L30 a night; they are usually trustworthy, but be wary. **Hotel Turist,** bl. Mamaia 288, is a 15 minute walk from Mamaia beach with A/C, Wi-Fi and breakfast. (☎0241 831 006; www.turistct.com. Doubles L100.) **Casa Ana ❸,** Bd. Tomis 17, serves traditional Romanian food as well as delectable international fare. (☎0241 553 999. Appetizers L3-7. Entrees L15-30. Open daily 10am-midnight. Cash only.) **Trains** run to Bucharest, (4-6hr., 7 per day, L44). Buy tickets at **CFR,** Vasile Canarache 4. (☎0241 61 49 50. Open M-F 7:30am-7:30pm, Sa 8am-2pm. International booth open M-F 9am-4pm. Cash only.) **Condor, Niş-Tur,** and **Ozlem** (☎0241 63 83 43), run **buses** to İstanbul, TUR (L100) via Varna, BUL (L40), although each bus usually only sends one per day so check times in advance. The bus station is open daily 5am-11pm. **Taxis** (☎0241 55 55 55) are easily waved down, but agree on a price before embarking on the trip. Public transit (L1.20 per ride) consists of **buses, trams,** and **trolleys** run 5am-11:30pm. For information try the Litoral s.a. **tourist office,** B-dul. Tomis 133. (☎0241 83 11 63; www.litoral.info.ro. Open M-F 9am-5pm.) The **post office** is at B-dul. Tomis 79-81. (☎0241 66 46 34. Open M-F 8am-8pm, Sa 8am-1pm.)

RUSSIA (РОССИЯ)

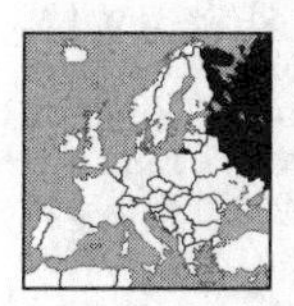

Over a decade after the fall of the USSR, mammoth Russia still struggles to redefine itself. Between fierce, worldly Moscow and graceful, majestic St. Petersburg lies a gulf as wide as any in Europe—and a swath of provincial towns that seem frozen in time. Mysterious and inexpensive, with good public transportation and scores of breathtaking sights, Russia is in many ways ideal for the adventurous budget traveler. While the legacy of Communism endures in bureaucratic headaches and the political situation in Chechnya raises tensions, Russia remains the epitome of Eastern European grandeur.

DISCOVER RUSSIA: SUGGESTED ITINERARIES

BEST OF MOSCOW, ONE WEEK. Queue up for the **Lenin Mausoleum** (p. 852) in the morning, then visit Russia's most recognizable landmark, **St. Basil's Cathedral** (p. 852). Check out the minarets and armory inside the **Kremlin** (p. 851) and play spy on a private tour through the old **KGB Building** (p. 855). Don't miss the collections of Russian art at the **State and New Tretyakov Galleries** (p. 854), or the shrines to literary success at museums for **Pushkin, Gorky, Tolstoy, and Mayakovsky** (p. 855).

BEST OF ST. PETERSBURG, ONE WEEK. Begin with a stroll down **Nevskiy Prospect** (p. 864), St. Petersburg's main drag, then stop at the city's most famous church, the **Church of Our Savior on Spilled Blood** (p. 863). Head to the bell tower of **St. Isaac's Cathedral** (p. 863) for an incomparable view of the city. Visit an attic of aristocracy, the **Hermitage** (p. 863), where the riches are displayed in unthinkable abundance. Then wander the **canals** that make St. Petersburg "the Venice of the North."

ESSENTIALS

FACTS AND FIGURES

OFFICIAL NAME: Russian Federation.

CAPITAL: Moscow.

MAJOR CITIES: St. Petersburg, Nizhniy Novgorod, Novosibirsk, Yekatarinburg.

POPULATION: 140,702,000.

TIME ZONE (WEST RUSSIA): GMT +3.

LANGUAGE: Russian.

CHESS GRANDMASTERS: 194.

OIL EXPORTS: 5,080,000 bbl. per day (213,360,000 gallons).

WHEN TO GO

It may be wise to plan around the peak season (June-Aug.). Fall and spring (Sept.-Oct. and Apr.-May) are more appealing times to visit, since the weather is mild and flights are cheaper. If you intend to visit the large cities and linger indoors at museums and theaters, the bitter winter (Nov.-Mar.) is most economical. Keep in mind, however, that some sights and accommodations close or run reduced hours. Another factor to consider is the number of hours of daylight—in St. Petersburg, summer light lasts almost to midnight, but in winter the sun sets at around 3:45pm.

DOCUMENTS AND FORMALITIES

EMBASSIES AND CONSULATES. Foreign embassies are in Moscow (p. 849); consulates are in St. Petersburg (p. 860). Russian embassies abroad include: **Australia,** 78 Canberra Ave., Griffith, ACT 2603 (☎662 959 033; www.australia.mid.ru); **Canada,** 285 Charlotte St., Ottawa, ON K1N 8L5 (☎613-235-4341; www.rusembcanada.mid.ru); **Ireland,** 184-186 Orwell Rd., Rathgar, Dublin 14 (☎14 92 20 48; www.ireland.mid.ru); **New Zealand,** 57 Messines Rd., Karori, Wellington (☎44 76 61 13, visas 476 9548; www.russianembassy.co.nz); **UK,** 6/7 Kensington Palace Gardens, London W8 4QP (☎20 72 29 64 12), visa 229 8027; www.great-britain.mid.ru); **US,** 2650 Wisconsin Ave., NW, Washington, D.C. 20007 (☎202-298-5700; www.russianembassy.org).

ENTRANCE REQUIREMENTS.

Passport: Required for all travelers.

Visa: Required for all travelers.

Letter of Invitation: Required for all travelers.

Inoculations: Recommended up-to-date on DTaP (diphtheria, tetanus, and pertussis), Hepatitis A, Hepatitis B, MMR (measles, mumps, and rubella), polio booster, rabies, and typhoid.

Work Permit: Required of all foreigners planning to work in Russia.

International Driving Permit: Required of those planning to drive in Russia.

VISA AND ENTRY INFORMATION. Almost every visitor to Russia needs a **visa.** The standard tourist visa is valid for 30 days, while a business visa is valid for up to three months. Both come in single-entry and double-entry varieties. All applications for Russian visas require an **invitation** stating dates of travel. If you have an invitation from an authorized travel agency or Russian organization and want to get a visa on your own, apply for the visa in person or by mail at a Russian embassy or consulate. For same-day processing you must apply in person. Download an application form at www.ruscon.org. (Single-entry visas US$131-300; double-entry US$131-350, except on 10-day processing; multiple-entry US$131-450. Prices change constantly, so check with the embassy) **Visa services** and **travel agencies** can also provide visa invitations (US$30-80), as well as secure visas in a matter of days (from US$160). Some agencies can obtain visas overnight (up to US$450-700). **Host Families Association** (www.hofa.ru), arranges homestays, meals, and transport. Visa invitations for Russia, Ukraine, and Belarus cost US$30-40; www.travelcentre.com.au provides invitations to Russia, sells rail tickets, and arranges tours. **VISAtoRUSSIA.com,** 2502 North Clark Street, Suite 216, Chicago, IL 60614, USA (☎800-339-2118, in Europe ☎749 59 56 44 22), provides invitations from US$30. Students and employees may be able to obtain student visas from their school or host organization.

The best way to cross the **border** is to fly directly into Moscow or St. Petersburg. Another option is to take a train or bus into one of the major cities. Expect delays and red tape. Upon arrival, travelers must fill out an **immigration card** (part of which must be kept until departure from Russia) and to **register** their visa within three working days. Registration can be done at your hostel or hotel, or for a fee at a travel agency. As a last resort, head to the central **OVIR** (ОВИ) office to register. Do not skip this nuisance, as taking care of it will leave one less thing for bribe-seeking authorities to hassle you about—fines for visa

non-registration run about US$150. When in Russia, carry your passport at all times; give it to no one except hotel or OVIR staff during registration.

TOURIST SERVICES AND MONEY

EMERGENCY	**Ambulance:** ☎03. **Fire:** ☎01 **Police:** ☎02.

TOURIST OFFICES. There are two types of Russian tourist offices—those that only arrange tours and those that offer general travel assistance. Offices of the former type are often unhelpful with general questions, but general information offices are usually eager to assist, particularly with visa registration. Big hotels often house tourist agencies with English-speaking staff. The most accurate maps are sold by street kiosks. A great web resource is www.waytorussia.net.

MONEY. The Russian unit of currency is the рубль (ruble; R), plural рубли (ru-BLEE). One ruble is equal to 100 копейки (kopecks; k), singular копейка, which comes in denominations of 1, 5, 10 and 50. Rubles have banknote denominations of 5, 10, 50, 100, 500, and 1000 and coin denominations of 1, 2, and 5. Government regulations require that you show your passport when you exchange money. Find an Обмен Валта (Obmen Valyuta), hand over your currency—most will only exchange US dollars and euro—and receive your rubles. **Inflation** runs around 12%. Do not exchange money on the street. **Banks** offer the best combination of good rates and security. ATMs (банкоматы; bankomaty) linked to major networks can be found in most cities. Banks, large restaurants, and currency exchanges often accept major **credit cards,** especially Visa. Main branches of banks will usually accept **traveler's checks** and give **cash advances** on credit cards. It's wise to keep a small amount of money (US$20 or less) on hand. Most establishments don't accept torn, written-on, or crumpled bills, and old bills are often declined. Keep in mind, however, that establishments that display prices in dollars or euro also tend to be much more expensive.

RUSSIAN RUBLES (R)		
	AUS$1 = 21.72R	10R = AUS$0.46
	CDN$1 = 24.07R	10R = CDN$0.42
	EUR€1 = 34.85R	10R = EUR€0.29
	NZ$1 = 19.27R	10R = NZ$0.52
	UK£1 = 51.57R	10R = UK£0.19
	US$1 = 25.45R	10R = US$0.39

HEALTH AND SAFETY

In a medical emergency, either leave the country or go to the American or European Medical Centers in Moscow or St. Petersburg; these clinics have English-speaking, Western doctors. Water is drinkable in much of Russia, but not in Moscow or St. Petersburg, so use **bottled water.** The 0.5-5R charge for **public toilets** generally gets you a hole in the ground and maybe some toilet paper.

Crimes against foreigners are on the rise, particularly in Moscow and St. Petersburg. Although it is often difficult to blend in, try not to flaunt your nationality. Seeming Russian may increase your chances of police attention, but keeps you safer among the citizenry. It is unwise to take pictures of anything related to the military or to act in a way that might attract the attention of anyone in uniform. Avoid interaction with the police unless an emergency necessitates it. It is legal for police to stop anyone on the street (including foreigners) to ask for documentation, so **carry your passport and visa with you at all times.** If you do not (and sometimes even if you do), expect to be taken to a police station and/or to be asked to pay a fine. *Let's Go* does not endorse bribery, but some travelers report that such "fines" are negotiable and, for minor infractions, should not amount to more than 500-1000R. Do not let officials go through your possessions, as travelers have reported incidences of police theft. If police try to detain you, threaten to call your embassy ("*ya pozvonyu svoyu posolstvu*"). It may be simpler and safer to go ahead and pay.

Sexual harassment can still be a problem in Russia. Local men will try to pick up lone **women** and will get away with offensive language and actions. The routine starts with an innocent-sounding "*Devushka...*" (young lady); say "*Nyet*" (No) or simply walk away. Women in Russia tend to dress quite formally. Those who do not speak Russian will also find themselves the target of unwanted attention. The authorities on the Metro and police on the street will frequently stop dark-skinned individuals, who may also receive rude treatment in shops and restaurants. Although **violent crime** against foreigners is generally rare, anti-Semitic and racist hate crimes—including murder—are on the rise. **Homosexuality** is still taboo even in the larger cities; it is best to be discreet.

TRANSPORTATION

BY PLANE. Most major international carriers fly into **Domodedovo** (DME, ☎095 933 6666, www.domodedovo.ru/en) in Moscow or **Pulkovo-2** (LED, ☎812 572 1272, www.pulkovoairport.ru/eng) in St. Petersburg. **Aeroflot**, (Leningradskiy Prospect 37, Building 9, Moscow 125167 ☎495 753 5555; www.aeroflot.org) is the most popular domestic carrier. Aeroflot has come a long way since the fall of communism, and its much-maligned safety record in fact bears comparison with most European airlines. From London, Aeroflot offers cheap flights into Russia. A number of European budget airlines land in **Tallinn, EST; Riga, LAT;** or **Helsinki, FIN,** from which you can reach Russia by bus or train.

BY TRAIN AND BY BUS. In a perfect world, all travelers would fly into St. Petersburg or Moscow, skipping customs officials who tear packs apart and demand bribes, and avoiding Belarus entirely. Nevertheless, many travelers find themselves headed to Russia on an eastbound train. If that train is passing through **Belarus,** you will need a **US$100 transit visa** to pass through the country. If you wait until you reach the Belarusian border to get one, you'll likely pay more and risk being pulled off the train for an unexpected weekend getaway in Minsk. **Trains,** however, are a cheap and relatively comfortable way to travel to Russia from **Tallinn, EST; Riga LAT;** and **Vilnius, LIT.** Domestically, trains are generally the best option. Weekend or holiday trains between St. Petersburg and Moscow sometimes sell out a week in advance. The best class is *lyuks*, with two beds, while the 2nd-class *kupeyny* has four bunks. The next class down is *platskartny*, an open car with 52 shorter, harder bunks. Aim for bunks 1-33; they're farthest from the bathroom. Day trains sometimes have a very cheap fourth class, "*opshiya*," which typically only provides hard wooden benches. Hotels and tourist offices are invaluable resources for those who don't speak Russian; almost no train station officials speak English, and train schedules are impossibly complicated. **Women** traveling alone can try to buy out a *lyuks* compartment or can travel *platskartny* and depend on the crowds to shame would-be harassers. *Platskartny* is a better idea on the theft-ridden St. Petersburg-Moscow line, as you are less likely to be targeted in that class. Try to board trains on time; changing your ticket carries a fee of up to 25%.

BY BUS. Buses, cheaper than trains, are better for very short distances. Russian roads are in poor condition, making for bumpy trips. They are often crowded and overbooked. Be assertive in ousting people who try to sit in your seat.

BY BOAT. Cruise ships stop in the main Russian ports: St. Petersburg, Murmansk, and Vladivostok. However, they usually allow travelers less than 48hr. in the city. **Ferries** run from Vladivostok to both Japan and Korea, while Kaliningrad is served by links to Sweden and Lithuania. A river cruise runs between Moscow and St. Petersburg.

BY CAR AND BY TAXI. Although it is sometimes necessary to reach Russia's more remote regions, **renting a car** is both expensive and difficult; poor road conditions, the necessity of bribing traffic inspectors, dangerous driving practices, and the frequency of automobile crime make the experience particularly stressful. If you must drive, however, remember to bring your **International Driv-**

ing Permit. Avis, Budget, and **Hertz** rent cars in Russia. Hailing a **taxi** is indistinguishable from **hitchhiking,** and should be treated with equal caution. Though it is technically illegal, most drivers who stop will be private citizens trying to make a little extra cash; even cars labeled taxis may not be official. Those seeking a ride should stand off the curb and hold out a hand into the street, palm down; when a car stops, riders tell the driver the destination before getting in; he will either refuse altogether or ask "Сколько?" (Skolko?; How much?), leading to negotiations. Non-Russian speakers will get ripped off unless they manage a firm agreement and are well-aware of the fair price—if the driver agrees without asking for a price, you must ask "*skolko*?" yourself (sign language works too). Never get into a car that has more than one person in it. *Let's Go* does not recommend hitchhiking.

KEEPING IN TOUCH

PHONE CODES	**Country code:** 7. **International dialing prefix:** 8, await a second tone, then 10. For more information on placing international calls, see **inside back cover.**

EMAIL AND INTERNET. Internet cafes are prevalent throughout St. Petersburg and Moscow, but aren't as popular elsewhere, where connections are slower. Internet typically costs 35-70R per hr. Many Internet cafes are open 24hr.

TELEPHONE. Most public telephones take **phonecards**, which are sold at central telephone offices, Metro stations, and newspaper kiosks. When you are purchasing phonecards from a telephone office or Metro station, the attendant will often ask, "На улицу?" (Na ulitsu?; On the street?) to find out whether you want a card for the phones in the station or for outdoor public phones. Be careful: phone cards in Russia are very specific, and it is easy to purchase the wrong kind. For five-digit numbers, insert a "2" between the dialing code and the phone number. Make direct **international calls** from telephone offices in St. Petersburg and Moscow: calls to Europe run US$1-1.50 per min., to the US and Australia about US$1.50-2. **Mobile phones** have become a popular accessory among Russians and are a comforting safety blanket for visitors. Most new phones are compatible with Russian networks and cell phone shops are common, but service can be costly. On average, a minute costs US$0.20 and users are charged for incoming calls. For longer stays consider purchasing a SIM card ($10), but take care that your phone is not locked before buying. Major providers Megafon, BeeLine GSM, and MTS have stores throughout the cities, as do rental chains like Euroset and Svyaznoy. International access codes include: **AT&T** (which varies by region: see www.usa.att.com/traveler/access_numbers/index.jsp for specific info); **British Telecom** (http://www.thephonebook.bt.com); **Canada Direct** (www.infocanadadirect.com); **Sprint** (www.sprint.com/traveler).

MAIL. Mail service is more reliable leaving the country than coming in. Letters to the US arrive one to two weeks after mailing, while letters to other destinations take two to three weeks. Airmail is "авиа" (aviya). Send mail "заказное" (zakaznoye; certified; 40R) to reduce the chance of it being lost. Since most post office employees do not speak English it can be helpful to say "*banderoley*," which signifies international mail, and to know the Russian name of the country of destination. **Poste Restante** (mail held for collection at the post office) is Pismo Do Vostrebovaniya. Address envelopes: LAST NAME, first name, Postal Code, city, Письмо До Востребования, оссия.

LANGUAGE. Russian is an East Slavic language written in the Cyrillic alphabet. Once you get the hang of the Cyrillic alphabet, you can pronounce just about any Russian word, even if you sound like an idiot. Although English is increasingly common among young people, learn at least a few helpful Russian phrases. For basic Russian words and phrases see **Phrasebook: Russian,** p. 1068.

ACCOMMODATIONS AND CAMPING

RUSSIA	❶	❷	❸	❹	❺
ACCOMMODATIONS	under 500R	501-750R	751-1200R	1201-2000R	over 2000R

The **hostel** scene in Russia is limited mostly to St. Petersburg and Moscow and averages US$18-25 per night. Some hostels, particularly those in smaller towns, will only accept Russian guests. Reserve in advance. **Hotels** offer several classes of rooms. "Лкс" (Lyux), usually two-room doubles with TV, phone, fridge, and bath, are the most expensive. "Поли-лкс" (Polu-lyux) rooms are singles or doubles with TV, phone, and bath. The lowest-priced rooms are "без удобств" (bez udobstv), which means one room with a sink. Expect to pay 300-450R for a single in a budget hotel. As a rule, only cash is accepted. In many hotels, **hot water**—and sometimes all water—is only turned on for a few hours each day.

University dorms offer cheap rooms; some accept foreign students for about US$5-10 per night. The rooms are livable, but don't expect sparkling bathrooms or reliable hot water. Make arrangements through an educational institute from home. In the larger cities, private rooms and apartments can often be found for very reasonable prices (about 200R per night). Outside major train stations, there are usually women offering **private rooms** to rent—bargain with them and ask to see the room before agreeing. **Camping** is very rare in Russia.

FOOD AND DRINK

RUSSIA	❶	❷	❸	❹	❺
FOOD	under 80R	81-150R	151-300R	301-500R	over 500R

Russian cuisine is a medley of dishes both delectable and unpleasant; tasty борщ (borshch; beet soup) can come in the same meal as сало (salo; pig fat). The largest meal of the day, обед (obed; lunch), includes: салат (salat; salad), usually cucumbers and tomatoes or beets and potatoes with mayonnaise or sour cream; суп (sup; soup); and курица (kuritsa; chicken) or мясо (myaso; meat), often called котлеты (kotlety; cutlets). Other common foods include щи (shchi; cabbage soup) and блины (bliny; potato pancakes). Vegetarians and kosher diners traveling in Russia will probably find it easiest to avoid rural cuisine and to eat in foreign restaurants. On the streets, you'll see a lot of шашлики (shashliki; barbecued meat on a stick) and квас (kvas), a slightly alcoholic dark-brown drink. Beware of any meat products hawked by sidewalk vendors; they may be several days old. Kiosks often carry alcohol such as imported cans of beer, which are warm but safe. Beware makeshift labels in Russian—you have no way of knowing what's really in the bottle. Усский Стандарт (Russkiy Standart) and Флагман (Flagman) are the best vodkas; the much-touted Stolichnaya is made mostly for export. Among local beers, Балтика (Baltika; numbered 1-7 according to brew and alcohol content) is the most popular and arguably the best. *Baltika 1* is the weakest (5%), *Baltika 7* the strongest (7%). *Baltikas 4* and *6* are dark; the rest are lagers.

HOLIDAYS AND FESTIVALS

Holidays: New Year's (Jan. 1-2); Orthodox Christmas (Jan. 7); Orthodox New Year (Jan. 14); Defenders of the Motherland Day (Feb. 23); Orthodox Easter Holiday (Apr. 19th, 2009; April 4th 2010); Labor Day (May 1); Victory Day (May 9); Independence Day (June Accord and Reconciliation Day; Nov. 7); Constitution Day (Dec. 12).

Festivals: The country that perfected the "workers' rally" may have lost Communism but still knows how to Party. Come April, St. Petersburg celebrates **Music Spring**, an international classical music festival, with a twin festival in Moscow. In June, the city stays up late to celebrate the sunlight of **White Nights** (Beliye Nochi; mid-June to early July). The **Russian Winter Festival** is celebrated in major cities from late Dec. to early Jan. with folklore exhibitions and vodka. People eat pancakes covered in honey, caviar, fresh cream, and butter during **Maslyanitsa** (Butter Festival; end of Feb.).

BEYOND TOURISM

For more info on opportunities across Europe see **Beyond Tourism,** p. 60

Kitezh Children's Community (http://atschool.eduweb.co.uk/ecoliza/files/kitezh.html). Teach English to Russian orphans in a rural setting. Young people taking a "gap year" between high school and college are especially common as volunteers.

The School of Russian and Asian Studies, 175 E. 74th St. 21B, New York, NY 10021 (☎1-800-557-8774; www.sras.org). Provides study-abroad opportunities at language schools and degree programs at universities. Also arranges work, internship, and volunteer programs throughout Russia.

MOSCOW (МОСКВА) ☎(8)495

On the 16th-century sidestreets of Moscow (pop. 12,600,000) it is still possible to glimpse centuries-old golden domes squeezed between drab Soviet housing complexes and countless Lenin statues. Visiting Europe's largest city is a thrilling, intense experience, flashier and costlier than St. Petersburg, and undeniably rougher too. Very slowly, Moscow is re-creating itself as one of the world's most urbane capitals, embracing innovation with the same sense of enterprise that helped it command and then survive history's most ambitious social experiment.

TRANSPORTATION

Flights: International flights arrive at **Sheremetyevo-2** (Шереметыево-2; ☎495 956 4666). Take the **van** under the "автолайн" sign in front of the station to M2: Rechnoy Vokzal (еной Вокзал), or take bus #851 to M2: Rechnoy Vokzal or bus #517 to M8: Planyornaya. **Taxis** to the center of town tend to be overpriced; bargain down to at most 1000R. Yellow Taxi (☎495 940 8888) has fixed prices (base fare usually 400R). **Cars** outside the departures level charge 500-800R; agree on a price before getting in.

Trains: Moscow has 8 train stations arranged around the M5 (circle) line. Tickets for longer trips are sold at the **Moskovskoye Zheleznodorozhnoye Agenstvo** (Московскоыe Железнодорожноыe Агенство; Moscow Train Agency; Russian destinations ☎495 266 9333, international ☎495 262 0604; www.mza.ru; MC/V), on the far side of Yaroslavskiy Vokzal from the Metro station. **Train** schedules and station names are posted in Cyrillic on both sides of the hall. (Tickets available at the *kassa,* open M-F 8am-1pm and 2-7pm, Sa 8am-1pm and 2-6pm. 24hr. service available at the stations.)

Belorusskiy Vokzal (Белорусский), pl. Tverskoy Zastavy 7 (Тверской Заставы; ☎495 266 0300). M2: Belorusskaya (Белорусская). To: **Berlin, GER** (27hr., 1 per day, 5,550R); **Prague, CZR** (32hr., 1 per day, 3800R); **Vilnius, LIT** (14hr., 1 per day, 1360-2240R); **Warsaw, POL** (21hr., 8 per day, 4 direct, 2200R).

Kazanskiy Vokzal (Казанский), Komsomolskaya pl. 2 (Комсомольская; ☎495 266 2300). M5: Komsomolskaya. Opposite Leningradskiy Vokzal. To **Kazan** (10-12hr., 9 per day, 2 direct, 750-1800R).

Leningradskiy Vokzal (Ленинградский), Komsomolskaya pl. 3 (☎495 262 9143). M1 or 5: Komsomolskaya. To **St. Petersburg** (8hr., 10-20per day, 500-2100R); **Helsinki, FIN** (14hr., 1 per day, 3500R); and **Tallinn, EST** (16hr., 1 per day, 1300-2300R).

Rizhskiy Vokzal (Рижский), pr. Mira 79/3 (пр. Мира; ☎495 631 1588). M6: Rizhskaya (ижская). To **Riga, LAT** (16hr., 2 per day, 1000-4500R) and destinations in **Estonia**.

Yaroslavskiy Vokzal (Ярославский), Komsomolskaya pl. 5a (☎495 921 5914). M1 or 5: Komsomolskaya. Starting point for the **Trans-Siberian Railroad**. To Novosibirsk (48hr-72 hours., every other day, 1900-4900R), **Yaroslavl** (4hr., 1-2 per day, 220-500R), **Siberia**, and the **Far East.**

Public Transportation: The **Metro** (Метро) is fast, clean, and efficient. Metro **trains** and **buses** run daily 5:30am-1am. A station serving multiple lines may have multiple names. Buy token-cards fare cards (19R; 5 trips 75R, 10 trips 180R) from the kassy in stations. Buy **bus** and **trolley tickets** from kiosks labeled "проездные билеты" (15R) or from the driver (25R). Punch your ticket when you get on, or risk a fine.

METRO MADNESS. *Let's Go* has tried to simplify navigation by numbering each Metro line; for a key, see this guide's color map of the Moscow Metro. When speaking to Russians, use the color or name, not our number.

Taxis: Most **taxis** do not use meters and tend to overcharge. Agree on a price before getting in (150-200R across town). **Yellow Taxis** (☎495 940 8888) have fixed rates (base fare 400R). It is common and cheaper to hail a **private car** (called gypsy cabs; частники; chastniki), done by holding your arm out horizontally. Never get into a taxi or car with more than 1 person already in it. Let's Go does not recommend hitchhiking.

ORIENTATION AND PRACTICAL INFORMATION

A series of concentric rings spread outward from the **Kremlin** (Кремль; Kreml) and **Red Square** (Красная Площадь; Krasnaya Ploshchad). The outermost **Moscow Ring Road** marks the city limits, but most sights lie within the **Garden Ring** (Садовое Кольцо; Sadovoe Koltso). Main streets include **Tverskaya Ulitsa** (Тверская), which extends north along the Metro's green line, as well as the **Arbat** (Арбат) and **Novyy Arbat** (Новый Арбат), which run west, parallel to the blue lines. Some kiosks sell English-language and Cyrillic maps; hostels and hotels also have English tourist **maps.** Be careful when crossing streets, as drivers are oblivious to pedestrians; for safety's sake, most major streets have an underpass (переход; perekhod).

RUSSIA

Tours: Tourist Information Centre, Ilyinka 4. Enter through the door on the western-most side. (☎495 232 5657; www.moscow-city.ru). M: Gostinyy Dvor. Open daily 10am-7pm. **Capital Tours,** ul. Ilyinka 4 (☎495 232 2442; www.capitaltours.ru), in Gostinyy Dvor. Offers 3hr. English-language bus tours of the city. Tours daily 11am and 2:30pm; 750R. 3hr. tours of the Kremlin and armory M-W, F-Su 10:30am and 230pm (1400R). **Patriarshy Dom Tours**, Vspolny per. 6 (Вспольный; from the US ☎650 678 7076, in Russia ☎495 795 0927; www.russiatravel-pdtours.netfirms.com). M5 or 7: Barrikadnaya (Баррикадная). English-language tours (510-2380R) include "Stalin's Moscow" and "Retrace the Steps of Dr. Zhivago." Open M-F 9am-6pm. No tours Th.

Budget Travel: Student Travel Agency Russia (STAR), located at Baltiyskaya 9, 3rd fl. (Балтийская; ☎495 797 9555; www.startravel.ru). M2: Sokol (Сокол). Offers dis-

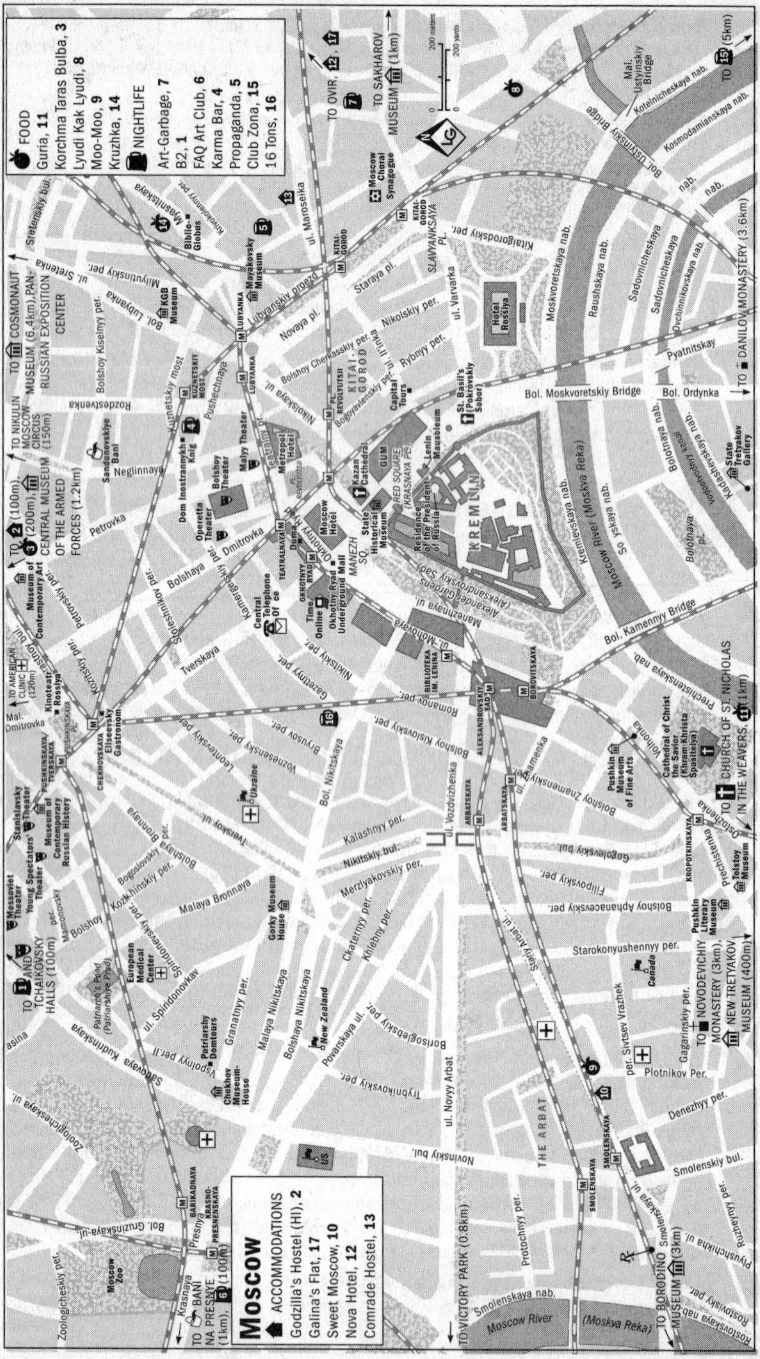

Moscow

ACCOMMODATIONS
Godzilla's Hostel (HI), 2
Galina's Flat, 17
Sweet Moscow, 10
Nova Hotel, 12
Comrade Hostel, 13

FOOD
Guria, 11
Korchma Taras Bulba, 3
Lyudi Kak Lyudi, 8
Moo-Moo, 9
Kruzhka, 14

NIGHTLIFE
Art-Garbage, 7
B2, 1
FAQ Art Club, 6
Karma Bar, 4
Propaganda, 5
Club Zona, 15
16 Tons, 16

count plane tickets, ISICs, and worldwide hostel booking. Branch at Mokhovaya 9 (Моховая), near the Kremlin. Open M-F 10am-7pm, Sa 11am-4pm; June-Aug. also Su 11am-4pm.

Embassies: Australia, Podkolokolnyy per. 10/2 (Подколокольный; ☎495 956 6070; www.australianembassy.ru). M6: Kitai Gorod (Китай Город). Open M-F 9am-12:30pm and 1:10-5pm. **Canada**, Starokonyushennyy per. 23 (Староконшенный; ☎495 105 6000; www.canadianembassy.ru). M1: Kropotkinskaya (Кропоткинская) or M4: Arbatskaya (Арбатская). Open daily 9am-3pm. **Ireland**, Grokholskiy per. 5 (Грохольский; ☎495 937 5911). M5 or 6: Prospect Mira (Проспект Мира). Open M-F 9:30am-5:30pm. **New Zealand**, Povarskaya 44 (Поварская; ☎495 956 3579). M7: Barikadnaya (Барикадная). Open M-F 9am-12:30pm and 1:30-5:30pm. **UK**, Smolenskaya nab. 10 (Смоленская; ☎495 956 7200; www.britemb.msk.ru). M3: Smolenskaya. Open M-F 9am-1pm, 2-5pm. **US,** Novinskiy 21 (Новинскийj ☎495 728 5000; www.usembassy.ru). M5: Krasnopresnenskaya (Краснопресненская). Open M-F 9am-6pm. American Citizen Services (☎495 728 5577, after hours ☎495 728 5000) lists English-speaking establishments. Open M-F 9am-noon and 2-4pm.

Currency Exchange: **Banks** are everywhere. Typically only main branches cash **traveler's checks** or issue **cash advances**. Many banks and hotels have **ATMs**. Avoid withdrawing cash from machines on busy streets, as it may make you a target for muggers. The majority of ATMs dispense only ruble.

American Express: ul. Usacheva 33 (☎495 933 8400). M1: Sportivnaya. Exit at the front of train, turn right, and then right again on Usacheva. Open M-F 9am-5pm.

English-Language Bookstore: **Anglia British Bookshop**, Vorotnikovskiy per. 6 (Воротникщвский; ☎495 699 7766; www.anglophile.ru). M2: Mayakovskaya. Open M-F 10am-7pm, Sa 10am-6pm; Su 11am-5pm. AmEx/MC/V.

24hr. Pharmacies: Look for signs marked "круглосутоно" (kruglosutochno; always open). Locations include: Tverskaya 17 (Тверская; ☎495 629 6333), M2: Tverskaya and Zemlyanoy Val 1/4 (Земляной Вал; ☎495 917 0434), M5: Kurskaya (Курская).Новослободская; M9: Novoslobodskaya). 24-100R per hr. Open 24hr. MC/V.

Medical Services: American Clinic, Grokholskiy per. 31 (☎495 937 5757; www.americanclinic.ru). M5 or 6: Prospect Mira (Проспект Мира). American board-certified doctors that practice family and internal medicine. Consultations US$120. Open 24hr., including house calls. AmEx/MC/V. **European Medical Center**, Spiridonievsky per. 5 (☎495 933 6655; www.emcmos.ru). M3: Smolenskaya. Consultations 4320R.

A NEW SORT OF CHEMISTRY CLASS

If you have an extra several thousand rubles handy, you also have the chance to try the newest and perhaps strangest gastronomic experience to hit Moscow since the creation of *okroshka*, a soup flavored with *kvas* (a weakly alcoholic drink). These days, chef Anatoly Komm has introduced Russians—the people of hearty meals—to tiny creations in the newest fad: molecular cuisine.

With four high-class restaurants in Moscow, Komm holds tasting events with such suggestive titles as "The Alchemy of Taste" and "Frost and Sea Molecular Spectacle." Diners are asked to turn off their cell phones, to leave cigarettes behind, and to keep their minds open before being presented with between 10 and 20 courses of visionary taste treasures.

The basic principle behind Komm's meals is purely scientific: by breaking food down into its smallest components, one can later put these particles back together in combinations that will excite the tastebuds in new ways. For a fistfull of rubles, you can try a Russkaya Zakuska (Russian Appetizer), a liquid combining the tastes of every traditional Russian appetizer—a thought that is at once disturbing and intriguing.

Check out www.anatolykomm.ru.

Telephones: Local calls require **phone cards,** sold at kiosks and some Metro stops.

Internet: **Timeonline** (☎495 223 9687), at the bottom of the Okhotnyy Ryad (Охотный Ряд) underground mall. M1: Okhotnyy Ryad. At night, enter through the Metro underpass. Wi-Fi 50-90R per hr. Open 24hr. Cash only. **Cafemax** (www.cafemax.ru) has 4 locations: Pyatnitskaya 25/1 (Пятницкая; M2: Novokuznetskaya); Akademika Khokhlova 3 (Академика Хохлова; M1: Universitet), on the territory of MGU; Volokolamskoye shosse 10 (Волоколамское шоссе; M2: Sokol); and Novoslobodskaya 3 (Новослободская; M9: Novoslobodskaya). 24-100R per hr. Open 24hr. MC/V.

Post Office: **Moscow Central Telegraph**, Tverskaya ul. 7 (Тверская), uphill from the Kremlin. M1: Okhotnyy Ryad (Охотный яд). **International mail** at window #23. Faxes at #11. Bring packages unwrapped; they will be wrapped and mailed for you. Open M-F 8am-2pm and 3-8pm, Sa-Su 7am-2pm and 3-7pm. **Postal Code:** 125009.

ACCOMMODATIONS

Nova House, 4 Devyatkin pereulok. (Девяткин переулок; ☎495 623 4659. Apt. 6 M1: Kitai Gorod. Go down Maroseika from Kitai Gorod, past McDonald's, and turn left onto Devyatkin Pereulok. Go 30m, and the door will be under an arch. No signs are displayed; ring buzzer 6. This guesthouse has an incredibly hospitable owner named Alex who will make you feel at home in the big city. Only 7min. from Red Square, you can take advantage of free Internet, Wi-Fi, laundry, and a kitchen before relaxing in the living room and watching a soccer game after a hectic day in the city. English spoken. Reception 24hr. Dorms 680R. Cash only. ❷

Godzilla's Hostel (HI), Bolshoy Karetniy 6/5 (Большой Каретний; ☎495 699 4223; www.godzillashostel.com). M9: Tsvetnoy Bulvar (Цветной Бульвар). Fun, social hostel with great location, 7min. from Pushkin Square and 20min. from the Kremlin. English spoken. Female-only dorm available. Kitchen available. Free Internet. Reception 24hr. Check-out noon. Dorms 725R; doubles 1740R. ❷

Sweet Moscow, Stariy Arbat ul. 51, 8th fl. #31 (☎495 241 1446; www.sweetmoscow.com). M4: Smolenskaya. Turn right on Smolenskaya pl., then left at the McDonald's onto the Stariy Arbat. The hostel is located across from Hard Rock Cafe; no signs are displayed, so ring the buzzer. In the middle of the city's most famous pedestrian street. Laundry 150R. Free Internet. Extremely helpful English-speaking reception 24hr. 6-, 8-, and 10-bed dorms US$25. Cash only. ❶

Galina's Flat, 8 Chaplygina St, apt. 35, 5th fl. (☎495 621 6038; email galinas.flat@mtu-net.ru.) One of the best locations for one of the cheapest prices in all of Moscow, Galina owns the apartment and rents out dorm beds to guests. The kitchen is open to all guests, and since there are only 6 beds email Galina in advance. English spoken. Reception 24hr. Dorms 400R. Cash only. ❶

Comrade Hostel, Maroseyka 11/4. Enter the courtyard, go left to building 5 and up to the third floor. (☎495 628 3126.) This centrally located hostel has a friendly, young, English-speaking staff and a calm atmosphere. Free Wi-Fi. 24hr check-in. 5-bed mixed dorm May-Sept. 840R, Oct.-Apr. 690R Laundry 200R. ❸

FOOD

Many restaurants offer "business lunch" specials (бизнес ланч; typically noon-4pm; US$5-10). For fresh produce, head to a **market.** Some of the best are by the **Turgenevskaya** and **Kuznetskiy Most** Metro stations. (Open daily 10am-8pm.) To find grocery stores, look for "продукты" (produkty) signs or look for big pictures of produce, bread, and sausages on the walls of buildings.

Lyudi Kak Lyudi (Люди как Люди; "People like People"), Solyanskiy Tupik 1/4 (☎495 921 1201). M1: Kitai Gorod. Enter from Solyanka. Fun, dimly-lit cafe is a favorite of young Russians. Business lunch 130R. Sandwiches 100R. English menu. Open M-Th 8am-11pm, F 8am-6am, Sa 11am-6am, Su 11am-10pm. Cash only. ❶

Korchma Taras Bulba (Корма Тарас Бульба), Sadovaya-Samotechnaya 13 (Садовая-Самотуоная; ☎495 694 0056, 24hr. 778 3430; www.tarasbulba.ru). M9: Tsvetnoy Bulvar (Цветной Бульвар). From the Metro, turn left and walk up Tsvetnoy bul. Delicious Ukrainian specialities served by waitresses in folk dress. English-language menu with pictures for extra guidance. Entrees 50-550R. Open 24hr. 12 locations. MC/V. ❸

Kruzhka. Over 20 locations, including 13/1 Myasnitskaya street. Visit www.kruzhka.com for all locations (☎495 411 9445). This bargain chain saves many a poor Muscovite student from starvation. With illustrated menus to help guide your order, sit back and enjoy a pint as you dine on cheap shawarma or chicken kebabs. Entrees 80-230R. Beer from 50R. Open M-Th and Su noon-midnight. F-Sa noon-4pm. Cash only. ❷

Guria (Гуриа), Komsomolskiy pr. 7/3 (Комсомольский; ☎495 246 0378), opposite St. Nicholas of the Weavers. M1 or 5: Park Kultury (Парк Культуры). Walk behind 7/3 until you reach the restaurant. Near Gorky Park and art galleries. Classy and traditional restaurant serves authentic Georgian fare at some of the city's lowest prices. Locals prefer the private, green-roofed gazebo tables in the garden. Enjoy the company of stuffed bears and moose heads if you choose to dine indoors. English-language menu. Entrees 150-500R. Open daily noon-midnight. MC/V. ❸

Moo-Moo (Му-Му), Koroviy Val 1 (Коровый Вал; ☎495 237 2900), M5: Dobryninskaya (Добрынинская); and Arbat 45/42 (Арбат; ☎495 241 1364), M4: Smolenskaya (Смоленская). Look for the signature cow statue outside. Moo-Moo's many locations offer cheap continental and Russian home cooking, served cafeteria-style inside leaf-covered walls. English-language menu. Salads 30-60R. Entrees 80-130R. Beer from 35R. Open daily 10am-11pm. Cash only. ❶

SIGHTS

Moscow's sights reflect the city's interrupted history; because St. Petersburg was the seat of the tsardom for 200 years, there are 16th-century churches and Soviet-era museums, but little in between. Though Moscow has no grand palaces and 80% of its pre-revolutionary splendor was demolished by the Soviet regime, the city's museums house the very best of Russian art and history.

THE KREMLIN. The Kremlin (Кремль; Kreml) is the geographical and historical center of Moscow, with origins that date back to the 12th century. In the Kremlin's Armory and its magnificent churches, the glory and the riches of the Russian Empire are on display. Besides the sights listed below, the only other place in the triangular complex visitors may enter is the **Kremlin Palace of Congresses,** the white marble behemoth built by Khrushchev in 1961 for the Communist Party, and since converted into a theater. Tourists were banned from entering the Kremlin until the 1960s; now English-speaking guides offer **tours** of the complex starting at around 1200R. Consider a prearranged tour through **Capital Tours** (see **Tours**, p. 847) or haggle to reduce the price. *(☎495 202 3776; www.kreml.ru. M1, 3, 4, or 9: Aleksandrovskiy Sad (Александровский Сад). Open M-W and F-Su 10am-5pm. Buy tickets at the kassa in the Alexander Gardens 9:30am-4:00pm. Kassa closed Th. No large bags. 300R, students 150R. Audio tour 220R. MC/V.)*

ARMORY MUSEUM AND DIAMOND FUND. At the southwest corner of the Kremlin, the Armory Museum (Оружейная Палата; Oruzheynaya Palata) shows the opulence of the Russian court and includes coronation gowns, crowns, and the best collection of carriages in the world. Each of the **Fabergé Eggs** in Room 2 reveals an intricate jeweled miniature. The **Diamond Fund** (Выставка Алмазного Фонда; Vystavka Almaznovo Fonda) has even more glitter, including the world's largest chunks of platinum. Consider hiring a guide, as most exhibits are in Russian. (☎495 921 4720. *Open M-W and F-Su. Armory lets in groups for 1hr. visits at 10am, noon, 2:30, 4:30pm. 350R, students 70R. Diamond Fund lets in groups every 20min. 10am-1pm and 2-6pm. 350R, students 250R. Bags and cameras must be checked.*)

CATHEDRAL SQUARE. A plethora of golden domes from nine different cathedrals fills the skyline of this square. The church closest to the Armory is the **Annunciation Cathedral** (Благовещенский Собор; Blagoveshchenskiy Sobor), the former private church of the tsars, which guards luminous **icons** by Andrei Rublev and Theophanes the Greek. The square **Archangel Michael Cathedral** (Архангельский Собор; Arkhangelskiy Sobor), which gleams with metallic coffins, is the final resting place for many tsars who ruled before Peter the Great, including Ivans III (the Great) and IV (the Terrible), and Mikhail Romanov. The colorful 15th-century **Assumption Cathedral** (Успенский Собор; Uspenskiy Sobor), located in the center of the square, was used to host tsars' coronations and weddings. It also housed Napoleon's cavalry in 1812. To the right lies the **Ivan the Great Bell Tower** (Колокольная Ивана Великого; Kolokolnaya Ivana Velikovo), once the highest point in Moscow; the tower is currently under renovation. Directly behind it is the 200-ton **Tsar Bell** (Царь-колокол; Tsar-kolokol), the world's largest bell. It has never rung and probably never will—a 1737 fire caused an 11-ton piece to break off.

RED SQUARE. The 700m long Red Square (Красная Площадь; Krasnaya Ploshchad) has hosted everything from farmer's markets to public hangings, from Communist parades to renegade Cessna landings. Across Red Square, northeast of the Kremlin, is **GUM,** once the world's largest purveyor of Soviet "consumer goods," now an upscale shopping mall fit to satisfy the shopping needs of the Russian elite. Also flanking the square are the **Lenin Mausoleum, Saint Basil's Cathedral,** the **State Historical Museum,** and the pink-and-green **Kazan Cathedral.** (*Combo ticket for St. Basil's and Historical museum available at either location. 230R, students 115R.*)

LENIN'S MAUSOLEUM. Lenin's likeness can be seen in bronze all over the city, but he appears in the eerily luminescent flesh in Lenin's Mausoleum (Мавзолей В.И. Ленина; Mavzoley V. I. Lenina). In the Soviet era, this squat red structure was guarded fiercely, with a long wait. Today's line is still long, and the guards remain stone-faced, allowing only a short glimpse of the former ruler as they move people along briskly. Exit along the **Kremlin wall,** where Stalin, Brezhnev, and John Reed, founder of the American Communist Party, are buried. The line to see Lenin forms between the Historical Museum and the Kremlin wall; arrive by noon to have a chance of making it through. (*Open Tu-Th and Sa-Su 10am-1pm. Free. No cameras or cell phones; check them at the bag check in the Alexander Gardens.*)

SAINT BASIL'S CATHEDRAL. Moscow has no more familiar symbol than the colorful onion-shaped domes of St. Basil's Cathedral (Собор Василия Блаженного; Sobor Vasiliya Blazhennovo). Ivan the Terrible built it to celebrate his victory over the Tatars in Kazan in 1552, and it was completed in 1561. "Basil" is the English equivalent of Vasily, the name of a fool who correctly predicted that Ivan would murder his own son. St. Basil's labyrinthine interior is filled with decorative and religious frescoes. Listen out for the choral groups that often perform in the upper chambers. (*M3: Ploshchad Revolyutsii (Плщщфдь Зувщлщи).* ☎*495 698 3304. Open daily 11am-6pm; kassa closes 5:30pm. 100R, students 50R. English-language audio tour 120R. Tours 1000R; call 2 weeks ahead. Photo 100R, video 130R.*)

NORTH OF RED SQUARE

Just outside the main gate to Red Square is an elaborate gold circle marking **Kilometer 0,** the spot from which all distances from Moscow are measured. Don't be fooled by this tourist attraction—the real Kilometer 0 lies underneath the Lenin Mausoleum. Just a few steps away, the **Alexander Gardens** (Александровский Сад; Aleksandrovskiy Sad) are a respite from the pollution of central Moscow. At the northern end of the gardens is the **Tomb of the Unknown Soldier** (Могила Неизвестного Солдата; Mogila Neizvestnovo Soldata), where an eternal flame burns in memory of the losses suffered in the "Great Patriotic War" (WWII). To the west is **Manezh Square** (Манежная Площадь; Manezhnaya Ploshchad), a recently converted pedestrian area; nearby lies the smaller **Revolution Square** (Площадь Революции; Здщырсрфв Кумщднгеышш). Both squares are connected in the north by **Okhotnyy Ryad** (Охотный Ряд; Hunters' Row), once a market for wild game, now an underground mall. Across Okhotnyy Ryad is the **Duma,** the lower house of Parliament. Opposite Revolution Square is **Theater Square** (Театральная Площадь; Teatralnaya Ploshchad), home of the **Bolshoi Theatre** (see **Entertainment**, p. 855). More posh hotels, chic stores, and government buildings line Tverskaya Ulitsa, Moscow's main thoroughfare.

CHURCHES, MONASTERIES, AND SYNAGOGUES

CATHEDRAL OF CHRIST THE SAVIOR. Moscow's most controversial landmark is the enormous gold-domed Cathedral of Christ the Savior (Храм Христа Спасителz; Khram Khrista Spasitelya). Stalin demolished Nicholas I's original cathedral (built in 1839 to commemorate Russia's 1812 victory in the Patriotic War), on this site to make way for a gigantic Palace of the Soviets, but Khrushchev abandoned the project and built a heated outdoor pool instead. In 1995, after the pool's vapors damaged paintings in the nearby Pushkin Museum; Mayor Yury Luzhkov and the Orthodox Church won a renewed battle for the site and built the US $250 million cathedral in only five years. *(Volkhonka 15 (Волхонка), near the Moscow River. M1: Kropotkinskaya (Кропоткинская; ☎495 202 4734). www.xxc.ru. Open M-Sa 10am-6pm, Su 8:30am-6pm. Closed last M of the month. Cathedral and museum free. No cameras, shorts, or hats.)*

NOVODEVICHY MONASTERY AND CEMETERY. A serene escape from the city, Moscow's most famous monastery (Новодевиий Монастырь; Novodevichiy Monastyr) is hard to miss thanks to its high brick walls, golden domes, and tourist buses. In the center, the **Smolensk Cathedral** (Смоленский Собор; Smolenskiy Sobor) displays icons and frescoes. The cemetery (кладбище; kladbishche) is a pilgrimage site that holds the graves of such famous figures as Khrushchev, Chekhov, and Shostakovich. *(M1: Sportivnaya (Спортивная) ☎495 246 8526. Open M and W-Su 10am-5:30pm; kassa closes 4:45pm; closed 1st M of month. Cathedral closed on rainy and humid days. Cemetery ☎495 246 0832. Open daily 10am-5:30pm. Cathedral and special exhibits each 150R, students 60R. Photo 80R, video 170R.)*

MOSCOW CHORAL SYNAGOGUE. Over 100 years old, the synagogue provides a break from the city's ubiquitous onion domes. Though the synagogue remained open during Soviet rule, all but the bravest Jews were deterred by KGB agents who photographed anyone who entered. More than 200,000 Jews now live in Moscow, and services are increasingly well attended, but the occasional graffiti is a sad reminder that anti-Semitism is not dead in Russia. *(M6 or 7: Kitai-Gorod (Китай-Город). Go north on Solyanskiy Proyezd (Солянский Проезд) and take the 1st left. Open M-F 10am-6pm for visitors. Services M-F 8:30am, Sa-Su 9am; evening services daily at 7pm.)*

CHURCH OF ST. NICHOLAS IN KHAMOVNIKI. (Церковь Николая в Хамовниках; ul. Lva Tolstogo) This small late 17th-century church makes you feel like you've stumbled into a fairytale from the hub-bub of Moscow's busy streets. The church is free to enter, and was built by a community of Muscovite weavers. Its glowing candles cast shadows upon the intricate artwork that lines the walls. Former parishoners include Leo Tolstoy. *(M1: Sportinavya.)*

AREAS TO EXPLORE

MOSCOW METRO. Most cities put their marble above ground and their cement below, but Moscow's love of opulence means the glitz and glamour extends hundreds of feet underground. The metro (Московское Метро) is worth a tour of its own. See the Baroque elegance of **Komsomolskaya,** the stained glass of **Novoslobodskaya,** and the statues of revolutionary archetypes from farmer to factory worker in **Ploshchad Revolyutsii**—all for the price of a metro ticket.

THE ARBAT. Now a pedestrian shopping arcade, the Arbat was once a showpiece of *glasnost* and a haven for political radicals, Hare Krishnas, street poets, and *metallisty* (heavy metal rockers). Some of that eccentric flavor remains, thanks to street performers and guitar-playing teenagers. Nearby runs the bigger, newer, and uglier **Novyy Arbat,** lined with gray high-rises and massive modern stores. *(M3: Arbatskaya; Арбатская.)*

VICTORY PARK. On the left past the **Triumphal Arch,** which celebrates the 1812 defeat of Napoleon, lies Victory Park (Парк Победы; Park Pobedy), a monument to WWII. It includes the **Museum of the Great Patriotic War** *(Музей Отеественной Войны; Muzey Otechestvennoy Voyny; open Tu-Su 10am-7pm, closed last Th of each month),* the **Victory Monument,** and the gold-domed **Church of St. George the Victorious** (Храм Георгия Победаносного; Khram Georgiya Pobedonosnovo), which honors the 27 million Russians who died in battle during WWII. *(M3: Park Pobedy.)*

MUSEUMS

Moscow's museums are by far the most patriotic part of the city. Government museums and small galleries alike proudly display Russian art, and dozens of historical and literary museums are devoted to the nation's past.

STATE TRETYAKOV GALLERY. With over 130,000 works of 11th- to early 20th-century Russian art, the Tretyakov Gallery (Государственная Третьяковская Галерея; Gosudarstvennaya Tretyakovskaya Galereya) could absorb an art lover for quite some time. A superb collection of **icons,** including works by Andrei Rublev and Theophanes the Greek is also on display. *(Lavrushinskiy per. 10 (Лаврушинский). ☎495 230 7788; www.tretyakov.ru. M8: Tretyakovskaya. Turn left out of the Metro, left again, then take a right on Bolshoy Tolmachevskiy per.; turn right after 2 blocks onto Lavrushinskiy per. Open Tu-Su 10am-7:30pm; kassa closes 6:30pm. 250R, students 150R.)*

NEW TRETYAKOV GALLERY. Where the first Tretyakov chronologically leaves off, this new gallery (Новая Третьяковская Галерея; Novaya Tretyakovskaya Galereya) begins. The collection starts on the third floor with early 20th-century art and moves through the neo-Primitivist, Futurist, Suprematist, Cubist, and Social Realist schools. The second floor holds temporary exhibits; go on weekday mornings to avoid crowds. Leaving the front door, turn left to find a statue gallery that is a real gem. The dumping ground for decapitated Lenins and Stalins and other Soviet-era statues, it now also contains sculptures of Gandhi, Einstein, Niels Bohr, and Dzerzhinsky, the founder of the Soviet secret police. *(Krymskiy Val 10 (Крымский Вал). ☎495 283 1378; www.tretyakov.ru. M5: Oktyabraskaya (Октябрьская). Open Tu-Su 10am-7:30pm; kassa closes at 6:30pm. 250R, students 150R. Sculpture garden open daily 9am-10pm. 100R.)*

PUSHKIN MUSEUM OF FINE ARTS. Moscow's most important collection of non-Russian art, the Pushkin Museum (Музей Личннх Колечцц. А.С. Пушкина; Muzey Izobrazitelnykh Iskusstv im. A.S. Pushkina) contains major Classical, Egyptian, and Renaissance works, boasting originals from Botticelli, Monet, Cezanne and Van Gogh. *(Volkhonka 12 (Волхонка). ☎495 203 9578; www.gmii.com. M1: Kropotkinskaya (Кропоткинская). Open Tu-Su 10am-6pm; kassa closes 6pm. 60R, students 30R.)* The building to the right (Volkhonka 10) of the entrance houses the **Museum of Private Collections** (Vезтй Линых Rјллtций; Muzey Lichnych Kolletsiy), with artwork by Kandinsky, Rodchenko, and Stepanov. *(Open W-Su noon-7pm; kassa closes 6pm. 100R, students 50R.)*

STATE HISTORICAL MUSEUM. This English-language exhibit (Государственный Историеский Музей; Пщыгвфкыемуттнн Шыещкшсруылшн Ьгяун) on Russian history runs from the Neanderthals through Kyivan Rus to modern Russia. Each hall's decoration reflects the era it houses. *(Krasnaya pl. 1/2. M1: Okhotnyy Ryad (Охотный Ряд). ☎495 692 3731; www.shm.ru. Open M and W-Sa 10am-6pm, Su 11am-8pm; kassa closes 1hr. earlier; closed 1st M of month. 150R, students 60R.)*

KGB MUSEUM. Documenting the history and strategies of Russian secret intelligence from Ivan the Terrible to Putin, the KGB Museum (Музей КГБ; Muzey KGB) gives punters the chance to quiz a current FSB agent. *(Bul. Lubyanka 12 (Лубянка). M1: Lubyanka. ☎495 299 6724 . By pre-arranged tour only. Patriarshy Dom Tours, p. 847, leads 2hr. group tours; 550R per person.)*

HOMES OF THE LITERARY AND FAMOUS. The **Mayakovsky Museum** (Музей им. В. В. Маяковского; Muzey im. V. V. Mayakovskovo) is a biographical walk-through of the futurist poet's life and art. Mayakovsky lived and died in a communal apartment on the fourth floor of this building. *(Lubyanskiy pr. 3/6 (Лубянский). M1: Lubyanka. ☎495 921 9560 Open M-Tu and F-Su 10am-6pm, Th 1-9pm; kassa closes 1hr. earlier; closed last F of month. 90R, students 50R.)* If you've never seen Pushkin-worship first-hand, the **Pushkin Literary Museum** (Литературный Музей Пушкина; Literaturnyy Muzey Pushkina) with its large collection of Pushkin memorabilia, will either convert or frighten you. Either way, the sheer amount of Pushkinalia merits the small entrance price. *(Prechistenka 12/2 (Преис тенка). Entrance on Khrushchevskiy per (Хрущевский). M1: Kropotkinskaya (Кропоткинская). Open Tu-Su 10am-6pm; kassa closes 5:30pm; closed last F of month. 60R.)* The **Tolstoy Museum** (Музей Толстого; Muzey Tolstovo), in the author's first Moscow neighborhood, displays original texts, paintings, and letters related to his masterpieces. *(Prechistenka 11 (Пречис тенка). M1: Kropotkinskaya (Кропоткинская). ☎495 637 7410; www.tolstoymuseum.ru. Open Tu-Su 10am-6pm; kassa closes 30min. earlier; closed last F of month. 150R, students 50R.)*

ENTERTAINMENT

From September through June, Moscow boasts some of the world's best **ballet, opera,** and **theater** performances. Tickets are often cheap (from 130R) if purchased ahead and can be bought from the theater *kassa* or from kiosks in town. **Bolshoi Theater** (Большой Театр), Teatralnaya pl. 1, is home to the opera and the ballet company. Though the main stage is under renovation, and not due to reopen until November 2009, performances continue on the secondary stage. (Театральная; ☎495 250 7317; www.bolshoi.ru. M2: Teatralnaya. *Kassa* on Petrovska ul., open daily 11am-3pm and 4-8pm. Performances Sept.-June daily 7pm, occasional matinees. 50-5000R. AmEx/MC/V.) The **Moscow Operetta Theater,** Bolshaya Dmitrovka 6, stages operettas. (Большая Дмитровка; ☎495 692 1237; www.mosoperetta.ru. *Kassa* open daily 11am-3pm and 4-7:30pm. Performances daily, 6 or 7pm. 300-1500R.)

NIGHTLIFE

Moscow's nightlife is the most varied, expensive, and debaucherous in Eastern Europe. Many clubs flaunt their exclusivity, but the city's incessant insomnia and love of house music make finding a full dance floor easy. Check the weekend editions of *The Moscow Times* or *The Moscow Tribune* for club reviews, music listings, and information on upcoming concerts.

SAVE FACE. When navigating the hostile, exclusive world of Moscow nightlife, our researchers have found that there is only one proven technique to ensure that "face control" (the bouncer) doesn't ruin the night before it starts: become a wealthy, tall, waifish, blonde model in high Russian style. More realistically, try to find friends with connections, dress up, go early, and get ready to have your face controlled.

Propaganda, (Пропаганда), Bolshoy Zlatoustinskiy per. 7 (Большой Златоустинский; ☎495 624 5732; www.propogandamoscow.com). M6 or 7: Kitai Gorod (Китай-Город). Exiting the Metro, walk down Maroseyka and take a left on Bolshoy Zlatoustinsky per. Come before midnight to sip on reasonably priced drinks, then go downstairs for some quality house music and dance until dawn. Go early to eat (and avoid strict face control). Dancing after midnight. Th DJ night. Beer from 80R, after 11pm from 60R. Open daily noon-6am.

FAQ Art Club, Gozetniy per. 9/2 (☎495 629 0827; www.faqclub.ru). M2: Teatralnaya. Chill with Moscow's young, alternative crowd on the tented patio or in 1 of 4 house-themed rooms—drawings for the pre-school playhouse are appreciated. Jazz concerts Su 8pm, 300R. Call to reserve a table. Entrees 115-420R. Beer from 115R. Mixed drinks from 130R. Hookahs from 500R. Free Wi-Fi available. Open daily 7pm-6am.

Karma Bar, Pushechnaya 3 (Пушечная; ☎495 624 5633; www.karma-bar.ru). M1 or 7: Kuznetzkiy Most (Кузнетский Мост). With your back to the Metro, walk through the arch on your left and turn right on Pushechnaya. Crowd-pleasing Latin beats keep the party alive. English spoken. Beer 110-170R. Vodka 150-160R. Mixed drinks 260-320R. Su hiphop. Cover F-Sa after 11pm men 240R, women 200R. Open Th-Sa 9pm-6am, Su 11pm-6am. Sportswear strictly prohibited.

Art-Garbage, Starosadskiy per. 5/6 (Старосадский; ☎495 628 8745; www.art-garbage.ru). M6 or 7: Kitai Gorod (Китай-Город). Art gallery, club, and restaurant, Art-Garbage is refreshingly more laid-back than many of the chic and trendy Moscow establishments. Better for drinking on the inviting patio than for dancing. Hard liquor from 60R. Beer from 70R. Cover F-Sa 150-500R. Open F-Su 11am-6am.

B2, Bolshaya Sadovaya 8 (Большая Садовая; ☎495 209 9918; www.b2club.ru). M5: Mayakovskaya. This multi-story complex has it all, and without the face control: a quiet beer garden, billiard room, several dance floors, jazz club, karaoke, restaurant, sushi bar, and weekend disco. Beer 80-180R. Hard liquor from 100R. F-Sa Concerts from 200R; some free with ISIC; check website. Open daily noon-6am. MC/V.

Club Zona (Зона), ul. Leninskaya sloboda, 19/2. (ул. Ленинская слобода; ☎495 675 6975; www.zonaclub.ru.) M3: Avtozavodskaya. Dance until dawn with Moscow's young and restless in the city's largest nightclub. Once you get past the barbed wires and steel gates of this prison-themed club, you'll be faced with a feast of spectacles aimed to surprise even those who have seen it all. 5 floors. Come early to eat and avoid strict face control. English spoken. Dress to impress. Beer from 90R. Mixed drinks 120-250R. Cover 500-1,000R. F-Sa 11pm-7am.

Sixteen Tons, Presnensky Val 6/1. (☎495 253 0530; www.16tons.ru.) M2: Ulitsa 1905 Goda. Resembles an English pub on the main floor with a quirky dance floor upstairs.

This pub/restaraunt/club hosts local Russian acts. Great for getting to know some Muskovites gnoshing on pub grub. Cover Th-Sa. 100-400R. Open daily 11am-6am.

ST. PETERSBURG (САНКТ-ПЕТЕРБУРГ) ☎(8)812

Saint Petersburg combines the Russian high-life with a strong literary intellectual vibe. Peter the Great's penchant for gilded facades and the legacy of Russian literary giants ensure that splendor and culture are never far away. However, due to its location and Russian visa requirements, this majestic city serves more as a shrine to Russia's superb architecture, art, and literature than as an international tourist hotspot. Take advantage of this during the winter, when the snow-covered city still has many cultural events, or during the summer, when the city's white nights are truly worth losing some sleep over.

TRANSPORTATION

Flights: The main airport, **Pulkovo** (Пулково), 18/4 Pilotov str. (www.pulkovo.ru) has 2 terminals: Pulkovo-1 (☎812 704 3822) for domestic flights and Pulkovo-2 (☎812 704 3444) for international flights. To get to the town center from the airport, go to the 1st bus stop on your left when exiting the airport, and grab **bus** #13 to Movskovskaya metro station. Go 7 stops over on the **metro** to Nevskiy Pr. to land in the center of town. Alternatively, hostels can also arrange **taxis** for about US$35-40. To get to the airport from the Moskovskaya (Московская) train station: take bus #13 to Pulkovo-1 (20min.) or to Pulkovo-2 (25min.).

Trains: Tsentralnye Zheleznodorozhny Kassy (Центральные Железнодорожные Кассы; Central Railroad Ticket Offices), Canal Griboyedova 24 (Грибоедовфа; ☎067).Bring cash and expect about a 20 minute wait to buy tickets from any of the open tickets windows (marked *kassy*) on your left and right.

Finlyandskiy Vokzal (Финляндский; Finland Station.), 6 Lenina pl. (Пл. Ленина; ☎812 768 7539). M1: Pl. Lenina. Sells tickets to destinations in the suburbs of St. Petersburg. Ticket counters #9 and #10 also sell tickets to **Helsinki, FIN**, (6hr., 2 per day, 2000-6000R). Luggage storage; look for signs. Also sells domestic airline tickets. Interesting fact! Lenin arrived here from Finland disguised as a railway worker on April 3rd, 1917 to start the October Revolution.

Moskovskiy Vokzal (Московский; Moscow Station), 2 Vosstaniya pl. (Восстания; ☎812 168 4597). M1: Pl. Vosstaniya. 24hr. luggage storage; look for signs. From 50R. To: **Moscow** (5-9hr., 15-20 per day, 515-2500R); **Novgorod** (electrichka 3-4hr., 1 per day, 320R); **Siberia,** and **Sevastopol, UKR** (35hr., 1 per day, 1520-2700R).

Vitebskiy Vokzal (Витебский; Vitebsky Station; ☎812 168 5939 ☎812 168 3918). M1: Pushkinskaya. To: **Kyiv, UKR** (24hr., 1 per day, 990-1450R); **Odessa, UKR** (36hr.; June-Sept. 1 per day, Oct.-May 4 per week; 1100-2330R); **Riga, LAT** (13hr., 1 per day, 1700-2600R); **Tallinn, EST** (8hr., 1 per day, 640-1600R); **Vilnius, LIT** (14hr., 1 every other day, 1070-1790R); **Warsaw, POL** (1 day, 9 hr., 1 per day, 1100-1900 R). Luggage storage 51R per day.

Buses: Автовокзал (Bus Station), nab. Obvodnogo Kanala 36 (Обводного Канала; ☎812 766 5777; www.avokzal.ru). M4: Ligovsky Prospect. Take bus #3, 24, 34, 74 or trolleybus #42 to the canal. Facing the canal, turn right and walk 2 long blocks. The station will be on your right. 10R surcharge for advance tickets. Domestic and international desinations. Ticket office open daily 8am-8pm.

Local Transportation: St. Petersburg's **Metro** (Метро) is the deepest in the world and runs daily 5:45am-12:30am. You need a **zheton** (жетон; token) to enter, which costs 17R. Passes available for 7, 15, 30, or 90 days. 4 lines cover much of the city. **Buses, trams, and trolleys** (14R) run fairly frequently (6am-midnight). Licensed **private mini-**

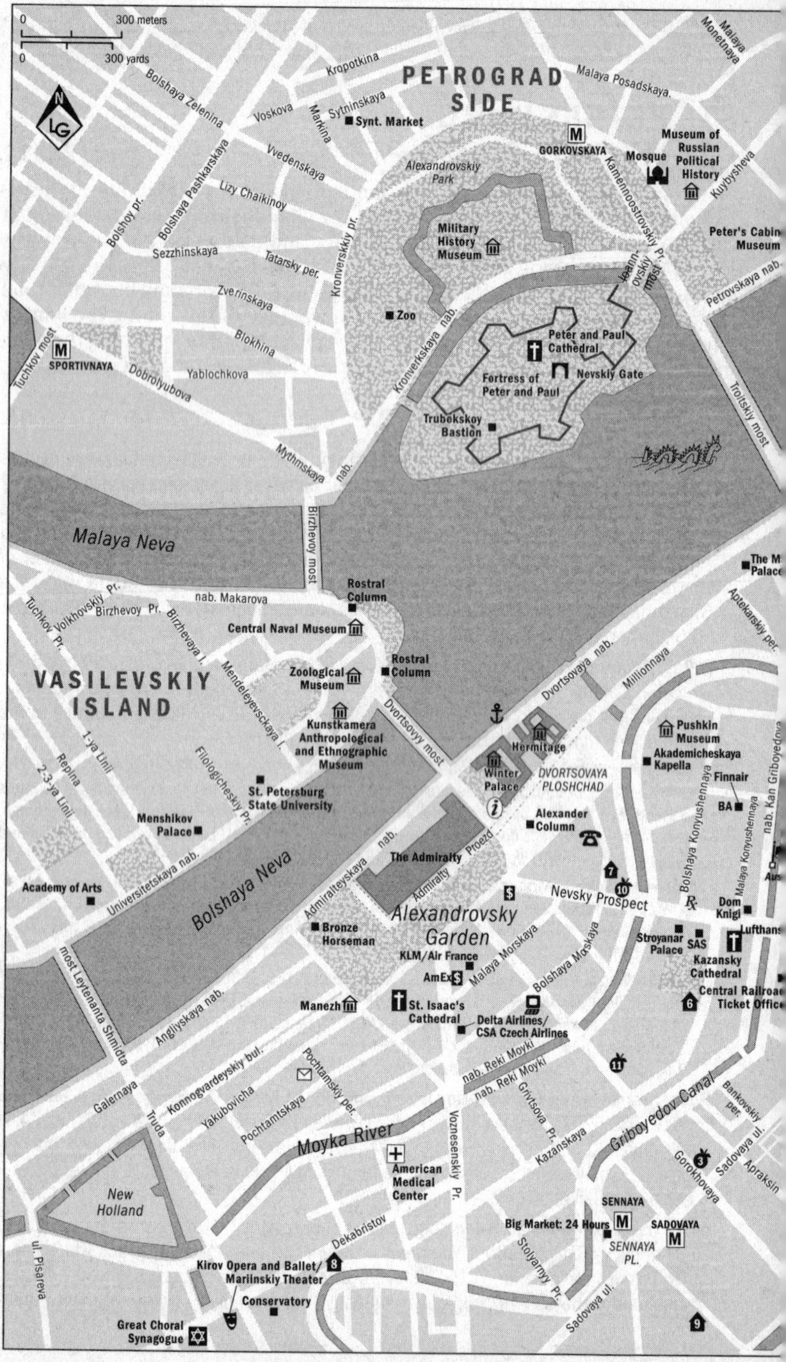

0 300 meters
0 300 yards
PETROGRAD SIDE
VASILEVSKIY ISLAND
Malaya Neva
Bolshaya Neva
Moyka River
Griboyedov Canal
Kropotkina
Malaya Posadskaya
Malaya Monetnaya
Bolshaya Zelenina
Voskova
Sytninskaya
Markina
Synt. Market
Vvedenskaya
Bolshaya Pashkarskaya
Lizy Chaikinoy
Bolshoy pr.
Sezzhinskaya
Tatarsky per.
Zverinskaya
Blokhina
Yablochkova
Dobrolyubova
Tuchkov most
SPORTIVNAYA
Mythmskaya
nab.
Kronverskiy pr.
Kronverkskaya nab.
Alexandrovskiy Park
Military History Museum
Zoo
GORKOVSKAYA
Kamennoostrovskiy Pr.
Mosque
Museum of Russian Political History
Kuybysheva
Peter's Cabin Museum
Petrovskaya nab.
Ioann-ovskiy most
Peter and Paul Cathedral
Nevskiy Gate
Fortress of Peter and Paul
Trubekskoy Bastion
Troitskiy most
Birzhevoy most
The M Palace
Aptekarskiy per.
Rostral Column
nab. Makarova
Volkhovskiy Pr.
Birzhevoy Pr.
Tuchkov Pr.
Birzhevaya l.
Central Naval Museum
Rostral Column
Zoological Museum
Mendeleyevsckaya l.
Kunstkamera Anthropological and Ethnographic Museum
Dvortsovyy most
Dvortsovaya nab.
Millionnaya
Hermitage
Winter Palace
DVORTSOVAYA PLOSHCHAD
Pushkin Museum
Akademicheskaya Kapella
Finnair
BA
1-ya Linii
Repina
2-3-ya Linii
Filologicheskiy Pr.
St. Petersburg State University
Menshikov Palace
Universitetskaya nab.
Academy of Arts
Alexander Column
Bolshaya Konyushennaya
Malaya Konyushennaya
nab. Kan Griboyedova
The Admiralty
Admiralty Proezd
Admiralteyskaya nab.
Nevsky Prospect
Dom Knigi
Lufthansa
Alexandrovsky Garden
Bronze Horseman
KLM/Air France
AmEx
Malaya Morskaya
Bolshaya Morskaya
Stroyanar Palace
SAS
Kazansky Cathedral
Central Railroad Ticket Office
most Leytenanta Shmidta
Angliyskaya nab.
Manezh
St. Isaac's Cathedral
Delta Airlines/ CSA Czech Airlines
nab. Reki Moyki
nab. Reki Moyki
Galernaya
Konnogvardeyskiy bul.
Yakubovicha
Pochtamtskiy per.
Pochtamtskaya
Truda
Grivtsova Pr.
Kazanskaya
Bankovskiy per.
Sadovaya ul.
Apraksin
Gorokhovaya
Voznesenskiy Pr.
American Medical Center
New Holland
SENNAYA
Big Market: 24 Hours
SADOVAYA
SENNAYA PL.
Dekabristov
Stolyarnyy Pr.
Sadovaya ul.
ul. Pisareva
Kirov Opera and Ballet/ Mariinskiy Theater
Conservatory
Great Choral Synagogue

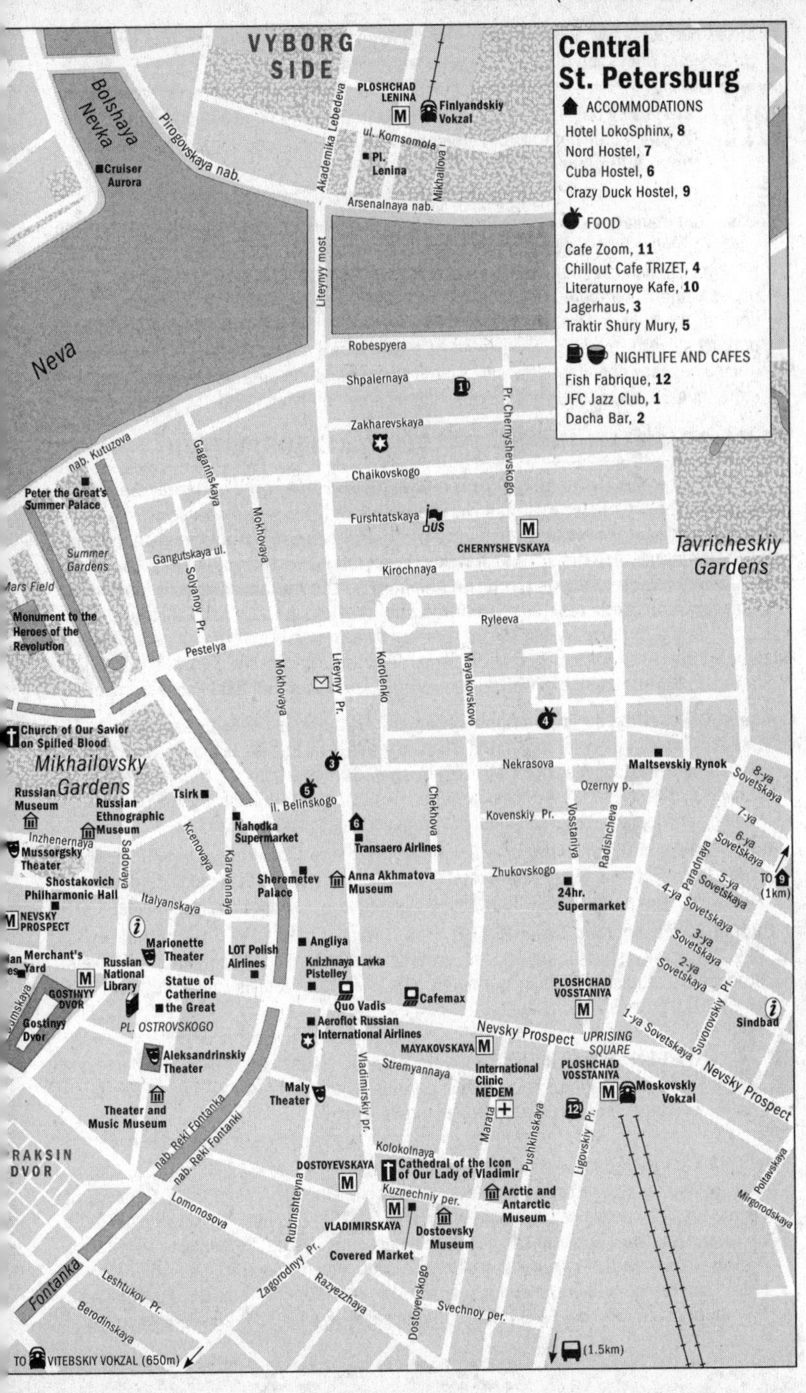
Central St. Petersburg
ACCOMMODATIONS
Hotel LokoSphinx, 8
Nord Hostel, 7
Cuba Hostel, 6
Crazy Duck Hostel, 9
FOOD
Cafe Zoom, 11
Chillout Cafe TRIZET, 4
Literaturnoye Kafe, 10
Jagerhaus, 3
Traktir Shury Mury, 5
NIGHTLIFE AND CAFES
Fish Fabrique, 12
JFC Jazz Club, 1
Dacha Bar, 2
VYBORG SIDE
PLOSHCHAD LENINA
Finlyandskiy Vokzal
ul. Komsomola
Pl. Lenina
Akademika Lebedeva
Mikhailova
Bolshaya Nevka
Pirogovskaya nab.
Cruiser Aurora
Arsenalnaya nab.
Liteynyy most
Neva
Robespyera
Shpalernaya
Zakharevskaya
Pr. Chernyshevskogo
Chaikovskogo
nab. Kutuzova
Gagarinskaya
Peter the Great's Summer Palace
Furshtatskaya
US
CHERNYSHEVSKAYA
Tavricheskiy Gardens
Mokhovaya
Summer Gardens
Gangutskaya ul.
Solyanoy Pr.
Mars Field
Kirochnaya
Monument to the Heroes of the Revolution
Ryleeva
Pestelya
Liteynyy Pr.
Korolenko
Mayakovskovo
Church of Our Savior on Spilled Blood
Mikhailovsky Gardens
Nekrasova
Maltsevskiy Rynok
Tsirk
il. Belinskogo
Ozernyy p.
8-ya Sovetskaya
Russian Museum
Russian Ethnographic Museum
Nahodka Supermarket
Chekhova
Kovenskiy Pr.
Vosstaniya
Radishcheva
7-ya
Inzhenernaya
Kcenovaya
Transaero Airlines
6-ya Sovetskaya
Mussorgsky Theater
Sadovaya
Karavannaya
Sheremetev Palace
Anna Akhmatova Museum
Zhukovskogo
Paradnaya
5-ya Sovetskaya
TO 9 (1km)
Shostakovich Philharmonic Hall
24hr. Supermarket
4-ya Sovetskaya
Italyanskaya
NEVSKY PROSPECT
Marionette Theater
Angliya
3-ya Sovetskaya
Merchant's Yard
Russian National Library
LOT Polish Airlines
Knizhnaya Lavka Pistelley
2-ya Sovetskaya
GOSTINYY DVOR
Statue of Catherine the Great
PLOSHCHAD VOSSTANIYA
Suvorovskiy Pr.
Gostinyy Dvor
Quo Vadis
Cafemax
PL. OSTROVSKOGO
Aeroflot Russian International Airlines
Nevsky Prospect
UPRISING SQUARE
1-ya Sovetskaya
Sindbad
MAYAKOVSKAYA
Aleksandrinskiy Theater
Vladimirskiy pr.
Stremyannaya
International Clinic MEDEM
PLOSHCHAD VOSSTANIYA
Moskovskiy Vokzal
Nevsky Prospect
Maly Theater
Marata
Pushkinskaya
Ligovskiy Pr.
Theater and Music Museum
nab. Reki Fontanka
nab. Reki Fontanki
RAKSIN DVOR
Kolokolnaya
DOSTOYEVSKAYA
Cathedral of the Icon of Our Lady of Vladimir
Kuznechniy per.
Arctic and Antarctic Museum
Poltavskaya
Lomonosova
Rubinshteyna
VLADIMIRSKAYA
Dostoevsky Museum
Mirgorodskaya
Zagorodnyy Pr.
Covered Market
Fontanka
Leshtukov Pr.
Razyezzhaya
Dostoyevskogo
Svechnoy per.
Berodinskaya
TO VITEBSKIY VOKZAL (650m)
(1.5km)

RUSSIA

buses (маршзутки; ьфкыркгелш; 15-17R) move more quickly and stop on request (routes and prices are displayed on windows in Cyrillic).

SMILE FOR THE POLICE: Beware of taking photos in the metro! This is prohibited both in St. Petersburg and Moscow, and will result in fines of up to 300 ruble.

Taxis: Both marked and private cabs operate in St. Petersburg. **St. Petersburg Taxi** is the city's umbrella service. (☎068 from a land line, ☎324 7777 from a mobile phone; 20R per km.) Marked cabs have a metered rate of 15-20R per km but most cabs want to set prices without the meter. Because taxis are notorious for overcharging tourists, always confirm the price before your trip. Ask "*skolka*?" which means "how much," and always barter below the given price. Instead of taking a taxi, many locals hail **private cars,** which is usually cheaper but unsafe for travelers new to the area. Never get in a car with more than 1 person in it. *Let's Go* does not recommend hitchhiking.

ORIENTATION AND PRACTICAL INFORMATION

St. Petersburg sits at the mouth of the **Neva River** (Нева) on 44 islands among 50 canals. The heart of the city lies on the mainland, between the south bank of the Neva and the **Fontanka River.** Many of St. Petersburg's major sights, including the **Hermitage,** are on or near **Nevskiy Prospect** (Невский проспект), the city's main street, which extends from the **Admiralty** to the **Alexander Nevskiy Monastery;** the **Moscow Train Station** is near the midpoint. Trolleys #1, 5, 7, 10, 17, and 22 run along Nevskiy Pr. northwest of the center and across the Neva lies **Vasilevskiy Island** (Vasilevskiy Ostrov), the city's largest island. On the north side of the Neva is the **Petrograd Side** archipelago, where the **Peter and Paul Fortress** stands.

Tourist Office: City Tourist Information Center, ul. Sadovaya 14 (Садовая; ☎812 310 2822; www.saintpetersburgvisit.ru). M3: Gostinyy Dvor. English-language advice, brochures, and guidebooks. Open M-F 10am-7pm, Sa noon-8pm. *St. Petersburg in Your Pocket* and *St. Petersburg Times* (www.sptimes.ru), free in tourist offices, hotels, and hostels, provide culture, entertainment, and nightlife listings.

Tours: Peter's Walking Tours, 3-ya Sovyetskaya 28 (3-я Советская; www.peterswalk.com), in the International Youth Hostel. Tours, including the "Dostoevsky Murder Route Pub Crawl," (June-Sept.) 430-800R. Specialty tours (4-6hr.) available on request.

Budget Travel: Sindbad Travel (FIYTO), 2-ya Sovetskaya 12 (2-я Советская; ☎812 332 2020; www.sindbad.ru). M1: pl. Vostanniya. Books plane, train, and bus tickets. Student discounts on flights, partnered with STA Travel. English spoken. Open M-F 10am-10pm, Sa-Su 10am-6pm.

WATER WATER EVERYWHERE. St. Petersburg lacks an effective water purification system, making exposure to giardia (p. 28) very likely, so boil tap water, buy bottled water, or use iodine.

Consulates: Australia, Italyanskaya 1 (Итальянская; ☎/fax 812 325 7333; http://www.russia.embassy.gov.au). M2: Nevskiy Prospect. Open M-F 9am-6pm. **Canada,** St Petersburg, Malodetskoselsky prosp. #32. (☎812 275 0502.) In an emergency, citizens of **Ireland** and **New Zealand** can call the UK consulate. **UK,** Pl. Proletarskoy Diktatury 5 (Пролетарской Диктатурыж ☎812 320 3200, emergency ☎812 937 6377; www.britain.spb.ru). M1: Chernyshevskaya. Open M-F 9am-1pm, 2-5pm. **US,** Furshtatskaya 15 (Фурштатская; ☎812 331 2600, emergency ☎812 331 2888; www.stpetersburg-usconsulate.ru). M1: Chernyshevskaya. M-F 9am-5:30 pm. Closed US and Russian holidays. Phone inquiries M-Tu, Th-F 10am-1pm, W 3-5pm.

Currency Exchange: ATMs are ubiquitous downtown and occasionally dispense dollars or euros. For **exchange booths** look for "обмен валуты" (obmen valyuti) signs everywhere, and don't forget your passport.

English-Language Bookstore: **Angliya British Bookshop** (Англия), nab. Reki Fontanka 38 (Реки Фонтанки; ☎812 579 8284). M2: Nevskiy Prospect. Open daily 10am-8pm. MC/V. **Dom Knigi** (Дом Книги; House of Books), Nevskiy pr. 28 (☎812 448 2355; www.spbdk.ru). M2: Nevskiy Prospect. Open daily 9am-midnight. MC/V.

Emergency: **Police**: ☎02. **Ambulance**: ☎03. **Fire**: ☎01. **Police Services for Foreigners**: ☎812 702 2177.

24hr. Pharmacy: PetroFarm, Nevskiy pr. 22 (☎812 314 5401), stocks Western medicines and toiletries. Pharmacist daily 9am-10pm. MC/V. Pharmacies are ubiquitous throughout the city, just look for an "*Аптека*" sign—many are open until late at night.

Medical Services: American Medical Center, nab. Reki Moyki 78 (Реки Мойки; ☎812 740 2090; www.amclinic.com). M2: Sennaya Pl. English-speaking doctors provide comprehensive services, including house calls and a helicopter ambulance. Insurance billing available. Consultation US$75. Open 24hr. AmEx/MC/V.

Internet Access: Quo Vadis, Nevskiy pr. 76 (☎812 333 0708; www.quovadis.ru). Enter from Liteynyy pr. and go to the 2nd fl.; it's the door on the left. Internet and Wi-Fi 70R per 30min., with ISIC 50R; 130R per hr., with ISIC 90R. Open 9am-11pm. MC/V. **Cafe-Max,** Nevskiy pr. 90 (☎812 273 6655), 2nd fl. Internet 65-150R per hr. Open 24hr. **F.M. Club,** ul. Dostoyevskogo 6 (Достоевского ул.; ☎812 764 3673; www.fmclub.spb.ru). With a full bar inside, grab a drink and surf the net. 60R per hr. Open 24hr.

Post Office: Почта оссии (Pochta Rossii). Main branch at Pochtamtskaya 9 (Почтамтская; ☎812 312 3954). From Nevskiy pr., turn onto Malaya Morskaya (Малая Морская), which becomes Pochtamtskaya. Currency exchange at window 1, information at window 2. Telephone service. Internet 50R per 30min. International mail at windows 8 and 9. Open 24hr. **Postal Code:** 190 000.

ACCOMMODATIONS

Travelers can choose from a variety of hostels, hotels, and private apartments, though hotels tend to be outrageously expensive. Hotels and hostels will register your visa upon arrival and in most cases can provide you with the necessary invitation for a fee, usually about 1000-2000R (see p. 840).

Crazy Duck Hostel, Moskovsky pr 4 (Московский проспект; ☎812 310 1304; www.crazyduck.ru). M1: Sennaya Ploschad (Сенная площадь). Take a left coming out of the metro and take a left on Moskovsky Pr. Go to the door by the "ФОТО" (photo) sign and ring apt. 7. This new hostel is a perfect mix of a clean, homey atmosphere and a great social vibe. Living room has comfy couches and a large TV, while the impressive kitchen comes stocked with free tea and coffee. Check-in 2pm. May-Oct. 550-750R. Jan.-Apr. 500-700 R. Free kitchen, Internet, and Wi-Fi. Cash only. ❷

Hotel LokoSphinx, (Локосфинкс), Canal Griboyedova 101 (Грибоедовфа; ☎812 314 8890; www.lokosphinxhotel.ru). Overlooking the canal, this 18th century building is the former cottage of Prince DeKonde. Offers a lot of privacy. Regal furnishings. Make reservations well in advance during the summer. All rooms equipped with phone and TV. English spoken. Sauna free for guests. Breakfast included. Laundry US$1-2 per item. Free Wi-Fi. Check-in 2pm. Singles 3000R; doubles 2400-3000R; apartments 2760-5640R. MC/V. ❹

Cuba Hostel, Kazanskaya 5,(☎812 921 7115; www.cubahostel.ru). M2: Nevskiy Prospect. This Latin-themed hostel sits right off Nevskiy Prospect and offers basic dorms ranging from 4 to 10 beds. What it lacks in glamor, however, is more than made up for by its vivacious ambiance. Many guests gather in the common room at night to drink, mingle, and be merry. English spoken. Check-in noon. May-Oct 550-700R. Nov.-Apr. 500-650R. Free lockers, kitchen, luggage storage, and Internet. Cash only. ❷

Nord Hostel, Bolshaya Morskaya 10 (Большая Морская; ☎812 571 0342; www.nordhostel.com). M2: Nevskiy Prospect. Centrally located in a beautiful building, Nord Hostel has much to offer: kitchen, lounge, TV, and even a piano. Staff and many of the guests speak English. Some small but airy dorms, usually co-ed. Breakfast included. Free luggage storage and laundry. Free Internet. Check-out 11am. 6- or 10-bed dorms Apr.-Jan. €24; Feb.-Mar. €18. Cash only. ❸

FOOD

The **covered market,** Kuznechnyy per. 3, just around the corner from M1: Vladimirskaya (Владимирская; open M-Sa 8am-8pm, Su 8am-7pm) and the **Maltsevskiy Rynok** (Мальцевский Рынок), Nekrasova 52 (Некрасова), at the top of Ligovskiy pr. (Лиговский; M1: Pl. Vosstaniya; open daily 9am-8pm), are St. Petersburg's largest outdoor markets. The cheapest supermarkets are **Dixie,** indicated by orange and yellow square signs, but **Nakhodka** (Находка) supermarkets, nab. Reki Fontanki 5 (Реки Фонтанки), are considered the best. There are **24hr convenience stores** on the side streets off Nevskiy pr. Look for "24 часа" signs.

Cafe Zoom, Gorokhovaya 22 (Гороховая; ☎812 448 5001; www.cafezoom.ru). "Tell me what you're reading and I'll tell you where you are," read the placemats of this chic literary themed cafe, popular with the young intelligentsia. English-language menu. Vegetarian options. Entrees 100-300R. Open M-Sa 11am-midnight, Su 1pm-midnight. Kitchen open M-Sa 11am-10:30pm, Su 1-10:30pm. 20% lunch discount. MC/V. ❷

Literaturnoye Kafe (Литературное Кафе), 18 Nevskiy pr. (☎812 312 6057). M2: Nevskiy Prospect. In its former incarnation as a confectioner's shop, this cafe attracted luminaries from Dostoevsky to Pushkin (who came here the night before his fatal duel with Dantes). Now caters to tourists, serving traditional Russian fare. English-language menu. Entrees 250-500R. Open daily 11am-11pm. AmEx/MC/V. ❸

Chillout Cafe TRIZET (Уилайт Кафе ТИЗЕТ), ul. Vosstaniya 30/7 (Восстания; ☎812 579 9315). M1: Cherneshevskaya. Perfect for a relaxing lunch, a good evening spent with friends, or a nighttime sortie. Helpful staff serve European and Middle Eastern food to patrons lounging on the wall-to-wall couches. Business lunch noon-6pm 160R. Entrees 200-350R. Beer and liquor from 80R. Hookah (pronounced "kal-yan") 300-500R. DJ F-Su 9pm-2am, F-Su 9pm-5am. Open M-Th 11am-2am, F-Su 11am-5am. ❸

Traktir Shury Mury (Трактир Шуры Муры), ul. Belinskogo 8 (Белинского; ☎812 279 8550). M2: Gostinyy Dvor. Russian and European cuisine served to locals in a traditional *dacha* (countryhouse) by traditionally costumed waitresses. English-language menu. Entrees 140-300R. Open 11am-4am. MC/V.

Kneipe Jager Haus, ul. Gorozovya 24 ул. (Гороховая, д.34 ☎812 310 8270. M1: Sennaya Ploschad (Сенная площадь). Remniscent of a dark alpine cabin, this fun young restaurant, popular with the locals, is lit by candles made out of Jager bottles sitting at every table. Flowing bread baskets and a live accordion player are free perks. English-language menu. Entrees 120-340R. Beer and liquor from 80R. Hookah from 300R. Open 24 hours. MC/V.

SIGHTS

Museums and sights often charge foreigners several times more than Russians. Avoid paying the higher price by handing the cashier the exact amount for a Russian ticket and saying "adeen" (one). Walk with confidence, as if you know where you are going, and do not keep your map, camera, or *Let's Go* in plain sight.

THE HERMITAGE. Originally a collection of 255 paintings bought by Catherine the Great in 1764, the State Hermitage Museum (Зрмитаж; Ermitazh) houses the world's largest art collection; it rivals the Louvre and the Prado in architectural, historical, and artistic significance. The collection is housed in the **Winter Palace** (Зимний дворец; Zimniy Dvorets), commissioned in 1762. Tsars lived in the complex until 1917, when the museum was nationalized. Only 5% of the 3 million-piece collection is on display at a time; even so, a full tour would cover a distance of 24 mi. English-language floor plans are available at the info desk. Arrive early during the summer, when lines can be over two hours long. Also, avoid paying the photography fee by keeping your camera in your bag when buying your entrance—once inside no one checks if you've paid for the photo privileges. *(Nab. Dvortsovaya 36 (Дворцовая). ☎812 571 3420; www.hermitagemuseum.org. M2: Nevskiy pr. Open Tu-Sa 10:30am-6pm, Su 10:30am-5pm. 350R, students free. English-language tours 200R. Audio tour 300R. Photography 100R. Free entrance 1st Th of month.)*

ST. ISAAC'S CATHEDRAL. Intricately carved masterpieces of iconography are housed under the awesome 19th-century dome of St. Isaac's Cathedral (Исаакиевский Со,ор; Isaakievskiy Sobor). On a sunny day, the 100kg of gold that coats the dome is visible for miles. The 360° view of the city from atop the **colonnade** is worth the 260-step climb. *(☎812 315 9732. M2: Nevskiy pr. Turn left on Nevskiy pr., then left on ul. Malaya Morskaya. Cathedral open M-Tu and Th-Su in summer 10am-7pm; in winter 11am-7pm. Colonnade open M-Tu and Th-Su 10am-4am in summer; 11am-3pm in winter. Cathedral 300R, students 170R; colonnade 150/100R. Photography 50R museum, 30R colonnade.)*

CHURCH OF OUR SAVIOR ON SPILLED BLOOD. This church's colorful forest of elaborate "onion" domes was built between 1883 and 1907 over the site of Tsar Alexander II's 1881 assassination. Also known as the Church of Christ's Resurrection and the Church of the Bleeding Savior, the cathedral (Спас На Крови; Spas Na Krovi) took 27 years to restore after it was used as a vegetable warehouse and morgue during the Communist crackdown on religion. It is equally impressive on the inside, housing the largest display of tile mosaic in the world, with each wall depicting a particular theme from the bible. *(☎812 315 1636; www.cathedral.ru; Open M-Tu and Th-Su 11am-7pm. Kassa closes 1hr. earlier. 300R, students 170R. Photography 50R.)*

THE CATS THAT SAVED ART HISTORY

While cats have historically served as popular pets for Russians, they served as something else during the 900-day siege of Leningrad in World War II. As food supplies dwindled and growing numbers of citizens died of starvation, cats suffered the brutal indignity of being added to the menus of the desperate.

The obliteration of cats led to a revitalization of the city's rodent population. Any naturalist will tell you that such an upset to the ecological balance has disastrous results. The colossal vermin population infiltrated the Hermitage and began to nosh on the paintings that had been stored in its basement to protect them from the relentless German bombing. When the siege finally ended, hundreds of furry felines were purchased by the state and set free in the Hermitage to help eliminate the rats. The program was successful, and it is said that today, there are still 150 cats on staff at the Hermitage patrolling the storage areas.

This legend accounts in part for cats' ubiquitous presence in the city. In fact, the pedestrian stretch of Mikhailovskaya ul. beside Eliseevskiy is lined with small cat statues paying tribute to the rodent-hunters. For good luck, throw a coin up on these figurines, many of which are located on platforms one story above street-level.

SMOLNY CATHEDRAL. In striking blue and gold, this 94m high cathedral is over 200 years old. Said to be the perfect architectural fusion of European and Russian architectural styles, the cathedral is surrounded by four other blue-and-white churches that form a cross. Many symphonic and chamber orchestras give **concerts** here, making the church a significant venue for the classical music scene of the city. During the summer the breathtaking **view** from the belfry is worth the climb. *(3 Rastrelli Pl., M3 Chernyshevskaya. ☎812 314 2186; open Th-Tu 11am-6pm in the winter, 10am-6pm in the summer. Kassa closes 1 hr. earlier. 200R, students 100R.)*

PALACE SQUARE. (Дворцовая Площадь; Dvortsovaya Ploshchad) This huge, windswept expanse in front of the Winter Palace has witnessed many turning points in Russia's history. Catherine took the crown here after overthrowing her husband, Tsar Peter III. Much later, Nicholas II's guards fired into a crowd of protestors on "Bloody Sunday," precipitating the 1905 revolution. Finally, Lenin's Bolsheviks seized power from the provisional government during the storming of the Winter Palace in October 1917. The 700-ton **Alexander Column** took two years to cut from a cliff. At 47m it is the largest freestanding monument in the world, commemorating Russia's defeat of Napoleon in 1812.

PETER AND PAUL FORTRESS. Across the river from the Hermitage stand the walls and golden spire of St. Petersburg's first settlement, the Peter and Paul Fortress (Петропавловская Крепость; Petropavlovskaya Krepost). Originally built as a defense against the Swedes in 1703, the fortress was later used as a prison for political dissidents. Inside, the **Peter and Paul Cathedral** (Петропавловский Собор; Petropavlovskiy Sobor) glows with rosy marble walls and a Baroque partition covered with intricate iconography. The cathedral holds the remains of Peter the Great and his successors. Turn right upon entering to view the **Chapel of St. Catherine the Martyr.** The remains of the last Romanovs—Tsar Nicholas II and his family—were moved here from the Artists' Necropolis on July 17, 1998, the 80th anniversary of their murder by the Bolsheviks. Condemned prisoners awaited their fate at **Trubetskoy Bastion** (Трубецкой Бастон), where Peter the Great tortured his son, Aleksei. Dostoevsky and Trotsky served time here. *(M2: Gorkovskaya. ☎812 230 6431; www.spbmuseum.ru. Fortress open M and W-Su 6am-10pm, Tu 11am-4pm. Cathedral open daily 10am-10pm. Roof walk across the Nevskaya panorama 10am-6pm 70R students 3R. A single ticket covers most sights. Purchase at the central kassa or in the smaller one inside the main entrance. 250R, students 130R.)*

ALEXANDER NEVSKIY MONASTERY. Alexander Nevskiy Monastery (Александро-Невская Лавра; Aleksandro-Nevskaya Lavra) is a major pilgrimage site and peaceful strolling ground. The **Artists' Necropolis** (Некрапол Мастеров Искусств; Nekropol Masterov Iskusstv) is the resting place of Dostoevsky and composers Mussorgsky, Rimsky-Korsakov, Glinka, and Tchaikovsky. The **Church of the Annunciation** (Благовещенская Церков; Blagoveshchenskaya Tserkov), along the stone path on the left, holds the remains of war heroes. At the end of the path is the **Holy Trinity Cathedral** (Свято-Тройтский СоБор; Svyato-Troytskiy Sobor), teeming with devout *babushki* kissing Orthodox icons. This is an active monastery, so there is a **strict dress code** in the cathedral: no shorts, and women must cover their shoulders and heads. *(M3/4: Pl. Aleksandra Nevskovo. ☎812 2741612. Grounds open daily 6am-11pm. Artists' Necropolis open daily 11am-7pm. Cathedral open daily 6am-9pm. Kassa closes 5pm. Cemetery 100R, students 50R; cathedral grounds 100/50R.)*

ALONG NEVSKIY PROSPECT. Many sights are clustered around the western end of bustling Nevskiy pr., the city's 5km main thoroughfare. Unfortunately, there is no metro station immediately nearby; one was built, but after the station was completed, construction of an entrance or exit connecting it to the surface was not approved, due to concerns about crime and vagrancy. The

Admiralty (Адмиралтейство; Admiralteystvo), across the street from the Winter Palace, towers over the surrounding gardens and most of Nevskiy pr. Originally intended for shipbuilding by Peter the Great, it was a naval headquarters until recently, when it became a naval college. In the park to the left of the Admiralty stands the **Bronze Horseman** statue of Peter the Great, one of the most widely recognized symbols of the city. *(M2: Nevskiy pr.)* Walking east on Nevskiy pr., the enormous, Roman-style **Kazansky Cathedral** (Казанский Собор; Kazanskiy Sobor) looms to the right. It houses the remains of General Kutuzov, commander of the Russian army in the war against Napoleon. *(☎812 314 4663. M2: Nevskiy pr. Open daily 8:30am-7:30pm. Free.)* The 220-year-old **Merchants' Yard** (Гостиный Двор; Gostinyy Dvor), one of the world's oldest indoor shopping malls, is to the right *(M3: Gostinyy Dvor. Open M-Sa 10am-10pm, Su 10am-9pm).* Nearby **Ostrovskovo Square** (Островского) houses the Aleksandrinskiy Theater (see **Festivals and Entertainment,** p. 865), a massive statue of Catherine the Great, and the **public library,** which contains Voltaire's private library, purchased in its entirety by Catherine the Great. *(Foreigners can obtain a library card for free; bring passport, visa, and 2 photographs. Library open daily 9am-9pm.)* Turn left before the Fontanka canal on nab. Reki Fontanka and look down before crossing the bridge at ul. Pestelya to find the **Smallest Monument in the World.** According to lore, landing a coin on the platform of the tiny bird statue brings good luck.

SUMMER GARDENS AND PALACE. Trezzini built the long, shady paths of the Summer Gardens and Palace (Летний Сад и Дворец; Letniy Sad i Dvorets) for Peter the Great in 1710. Peter's modest **Summer Palace,** in the northeast corner, reflects his cosmopolitan taste, with furnishings ranging from Spanish and Portuguese chairs to Dutch tile and German clocks. **Mars Field** (Марсово Поле; Marsovo Pole), a memorial to the victims of the Revolution and Civil War (1917-19), extends out from the Summer Gardens. *(M2: Nevskiy pr. Turn right on nab. Kanala Griboyedova (Канала Грибоедова), cross the Moyka, and turn right on ul. Pestelya (Пестеля). ☎812 314 0374. Garden open W-Su 10am-6pm, free. Palace open M 10am-4pm, Tu-Su 10am-6pm; closed last M of the month; kassa closes 5pm. Palace 300R, students 150R.)*

OTHER MUSEUMS. Spread over several buildings, the **State Russian Museum** (усский Музей; Russkiy Muzey) boasts the world's second-largest collection of Russian art. Exhibits are displayed in three other locations throughout the city. *(M3: Nevskiy Prospect;. ☎812 595 4248; www.rusmuseum.ru. Open M 10am-5pm, W-Su 10am-6pm. 300R, students 150R. Tickets to all museum sites 600R/300R. Photography 100R.)* **Dostoevsky's House** (Дом Достоевского; Dom Dostoevskovo) is where the author penned *The Brothers Karamazov* and spent the last two years of his life. *(Kuznechnyy per. 5/2 (Кузненый). M1: Vladimirskaya. On the corner of ul. Dostoevskovo. ☎812 311 4031. Open Tu-Su 11am-5pm. 120R, students 70R. Photography 40 R.)*

RUSSIA

FESTIVALS AND ENTERTAINMENT

From mid-May to mid-July, the city holds a series of outdoor concerts as part of the **White Nights Festival,** celebrating the long summer nights. Bridges over the Neva River go up at 1:30am and don't come back down until 4:30 or 5:30am, so be wary of partying on one side if your hostel is on the other. The home of Tchaikovsky, Prokofiev, and Stravinsky still lives up to its reputation as a mecca for the performing arts. The **Mariinskiy Theater** (Марийнский; or Kirov), Teatralnaya pl. 1 (Театральная), M4: Sadovaya, houses perhaps the world's most famous ballet company. Tchaikovsky's *Nutcracker* and *The Sleeping Beauty,* along with works by Baryshnikov and Nijinsky premiered here. Tickets can be purchased in Gostinyy Dvor or at the theatre's box office at 1 Theatre Square from 11am-7pm. (☎812 326 4141; www.mariinsky.ru; tickets 320-4800R. *Kassa* open Tu-Su 10am-7pm.) **Aleksandrinskiy Teatr**

(Александринский Театр), pl. Ostrovskovo 6, M3: Gostinyy Dvor, attracts famous Russian actors and companies. (☎812 312 1546. Tickets 100-2500R.) **Mussorgsky Opera and Ballet Theater** (Театр Имени Муссоргского; Еуфек Шьутш Ьгыыщкпылщмщ), pl. Iskusstv, is open all summer, whereas the Mariinskiy closes for several weeks. (☎812 595 4284; www.mikhailovsky.ru. Bring your passport. Tickets 300-1500R. *Kassa* open 11am-3pm, 4-7pm.) **Shostakovich Philharmonic Hall,** ul. Mikhailovskaya 2, M3: Gostinyy Dvor, opposite the Russian Museum, is over 200 years old, and was the site of some Beethoven premieres. (☎812 312 9871; www.philharmonia.spb.ru. Tickets 750-2000R. *Kassa* open daily 11am-3pm and 4-7pm.) The Mussorgsky and Shostakovich theaters both lie around the **Square of the Arts.** The Friday issue of the *St. Petersburg Times* has comprehensive listings of entertainment and nightlife. Book tickets to various performances online in English at **www.kassir.ru.**

NIGHTLIFE

Griboedov, Ul. Voronezhskaya 2 (Воронежская; ☎812 764 4355; www.griboedovclub.ru). M3: Ligovsky Pr. Dance the night away underground in a former Soviet bomb shelter. Famous for its themed celebrations, Griboedov has more of a house-party feel than giant club glamor. Cheap vodka and low ceilings create a genuine retro-Soviet feel. Open daily 9pm-6am. Cover free-400R. Beer from 70R. Cash only.

Fish Fabrique, Ligovskiy 53 (Лиговский; ☎812 764 4857; www.fishfabrique.spb.ru). M1: pl. Vosstaniya. Walk in through the courtyard, into the black door directly in front, and follow the corridor and stairs to the bar. An almost hidden location and a tight-knit, young clientele make this the perfect chill hangout. Fried bread called *grenki* is perfect at 3am. Th-Sa concerts 11pm. Beer 50-90R. Hard liquor 40-130R. Cover 150-250R. Open M-Th and Su 5pm-6am. F-Sa 5pm-8:30pm and 9pm-6am. Cash only.

Dacha, (Дача), Dumskaya ul. 9 (Думская). M2: Gostiny Dvor. Cheap beer contributes to a cheerful vibe in this bar with leather couches and young university students. Right next to two other similar bars, young people come here in search of a place to relax and socialize. Open daily 6pm-6am. Beer from 70R, hard liquor from 60R. DJ every night from 11pm-6am. Cover F-Sa 100R, includes a free drink. Cash only.

JFC Jazz Club, Shpalernaya 33 (Шпалерная; ☎812 272 9850; www.jfc.sp.ru). M1: Chernyshevskaya. This friendly club offers a wide variety of quality jazz and holds occasional classical, folk, and funk concerts. Beer from 100R. Hard liquor from 50R. Live music nightly 8-10pm. Cover 200-700R. Reserve table ahead. Open daily 7-11pm.

DAYTRIP FROM ST. PETERSBURG

PETERHOF. Bent on creating his own Versailles, Peter started building the **Grand Palace** (Большой Дворец; Bolshoy Dvorets) in 1709. Catherine the Great later expanded and remodeled it, creating an absolutely stunning palace surrounded by hundreds of fountains and golden statues. Though Peterhof was burned to the ground during the Nazi retreat, it was reconstructed from various maps and photographs, and lost none of its former splendor. Today, the **Lower Gardens** are a perfect place for a picnic along the shores of the Gulf of Finland. *(Open daily 11am-6pm, 300R, students 150R. Grand Palace ☎812 450 6223. Open Tu-Su 10:30am-6pm; closed last Tu of month. 500R, students 250R. Fountains operate May-Oct. 11am-5pm.)* There are 17 museums on the grounds. Roaming the nearby **Upper Gardens** is free. *(Upon exiting, go across the street and catch bus #424, whose final destination is Peterhof. 45R.)*

SLOVAKIA (SLOVENSKO)

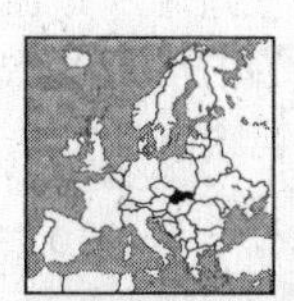

Slovakia is a nation of dualities. Known for its beautiful mountain ranges, vibrant folk culture, and generous hospitality, Slovakia appeals to hikers and lovers of rural life. But the country also enjoys rapid industrialization and one of the fastest-growing economies in the former Eastern Bloc. Many scenic villages lie only hours away from the sophisticated, up-and-coming capital.

DISCOVER SLOVAKIA: SUGGESTED ITINERARIES

THREE DAYS. Devote your stay to a leisurely exploration of **Bratislava.** Make sure to check out **Primate's Palace** (no monkeys, unfortunately; p. 875). Also stop by the **UFO,** atop New Bridge, to see if there's a party going on (p. 874).

ONE WEEK. From **Bratislava** (2 days), head to **Starý Smokovec** (5 days, p. 876). There you can mountain bike, hike, or ski the grand **High Tatras.** Leave time for a daytrip to **Štrbské Pleso** (p. 877), with its waterfalls and rigorous hikes.

ESSENTIALS

FACTS AND FIGURES

OFFICIAL NAME: Slovak Republic.

MAJOR CITIES: Bratislava.

POPULATION: 5,445,000.

TIME ZONE: GMT +2.

LANGUAGES: Slovak-84%, Hungarian-11%

CAR PRODUCTION PER CAPITA: 106 vehicles per 1000 inhabitants, the most in the world.

WHEN TO GO

Slovakia is blissfully free of massive crowds. The Tatras draw the most tourists during peak season from July to August, and for good reason: cold winter weather makes the summer a much more pleasant (and safe) time for hiking the beautiful mountain range. To avoid any crowds at all, explore the Tatras in the two months before or after high-season.

DOCUMENTS AND FORMALITIES

EMBASSIES AND CONSULATES. Foreign embassies to Slovakia are in Bratislava (p. 873). Slovak embassies abroad include: **Australia,** 47 Culgoa Circuit, O'Malley, Canberra, ACT 2606 (☎262 901 516; www.slovakemb-aust.org); **Canada,** 50 Rideau Terr., Ottawa, ON K1M 2A1 (☎613-749-4442); **Ireland,** 20 Clyde Rd., Ballsbridge, Dublin 4 (☎33 56 60 00 12; www.mfa.sk/zu/index); **UK,** 25 Kensington Palace Gardens, London W8 4QY (☎020 73 1364 70; www.slovakembassy.co.uk); **US,** 3523 International Ct. NW, Washington, D.C. 20008 (☎202-237-1054; www.slovakembassy-us.org).

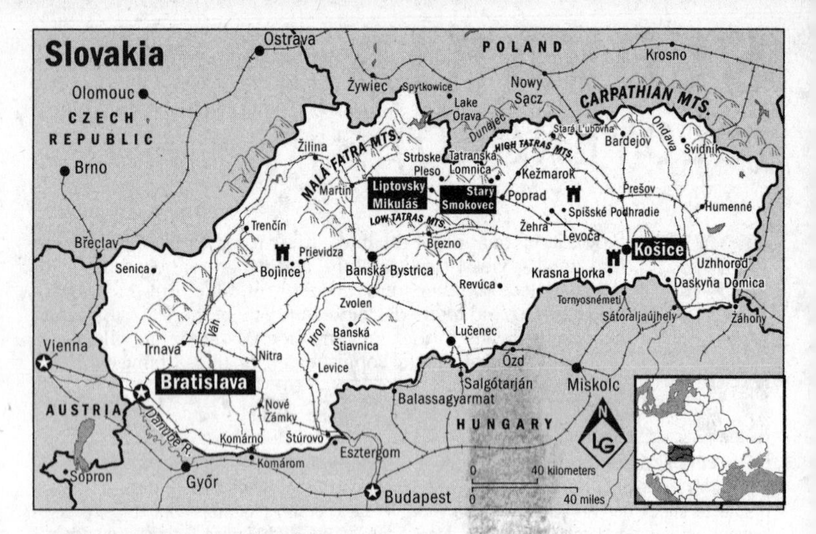

VISA AND ENTRY INFORMATION. Citizens of Australia, Canada, Ireland, New Zealand, the UK, and the US can travel to Slovakia without a visa for up to 90 days. Those traveling for business, employment, or study must obtain a temporary residence permit. Types of visas include single- and multiple-entry, as well as long-term. For more information, see www.slovakia.org/visainfo.htm.

ENTRANCE REQUIREMENTS.

Passport: Required for all travelers.

Letter of Invitation: Not required for citizens of Australia, Canada, Ireland, New Zealand, the UK, and the US.

Inoculations: Recommended up-to-date on DTaP (Diphtheria, tetanus, and pertussis) hepatitis A, hepatitis B, MMR (measles, mumps, and rubella), polio booster, rabies, and typhoid.

Work Permit: Required for foreigners planning to work in Slovakia.

International Driving Permit: Required for all those planning to drive in Slovakia except for UK citizens, who only need an IDP to rent cars.

TOURIST SERVICES AND MONEY

TOURIST OFFICES. The **Slovak Tourist Board** (☎484 136 146; www.sacr.sk) provides useful information. The tourist office, **SlovakoTourist,** and other tourist agencies usually can help. Public tourist offices are marked by a white "i" inside a green square. Slovakia has few **hostels,** most of which are found in and around Bratislava. English is often spoken at tourist offices, which usually provide maps and information about transportation. If booking accommodations at an office, be wary of handing over cash on the spot.

MONEY. Although Slovakia is now a member state of the EU, the **Slovak koruna (Sk),** plural **koruny,** remains the main unit of currency and comes in denominations of 20, 50, 100, 200, 500, 1000, and 5000 koruny. Slovakia's transition to the euro is slated for early 2009. The koruna is divided into 100 **halier,** issued in standard denominations of 50 halier. Bear in mind that smaller establishments may not be able to break 5000Sk bills. **Credit cards** are not accepted in many Slovak establishments, but MasterCard and Visa are the most useful, followed by American Express. **Inflation** is down to about 4.5%, which means prices are relatively stable. **ATMs** are plentiful and give the best exchange rates, but also tend to charge a flat service fee; it is most economical to withdraw large amounts at once. Banks **Slovenská-Sporitelňa** and **Unibank** handle MC/V cash advances. Banks require that you present your passport for most transactions.

SLOVAKIAN KORUNY (SK)		
	AUS$1 = 22.26SK	10SK = AUS$0.45
	CDN$1 = 27.00SK	10SK = CDN$0.37
	EUR€1 = 38.07SK	10SK = EUR€0.26
	NZ$1 = 18.73SK	10SK = NZ$0.53
	UK£1 = 55.77SK	10SK = UK£0.18
	US$1 = 30.15SK	10SK = US$0.33

HEALTH AND SAFETY

Medical care varies a great deal in Slovakia. **Tap water** varies in quality and appearance but is probably safe, though bottled water is always safest. If water comes out of the faucet cloudy, let it sit for 5min.; air bubbles may be to blame. *Drogerii* (drugstores) stock Western brands. **Petty crime** is common; be wary in crowded areas. Violent crimes are not unheard of, but tourists are rarely targets. Accommodations for **disabled** travelers are rare. **Women** traveling alone are rarely harassed, but may encounter stares. Dress modestly and avoid walking or riding public transportation at night. **Minority** travelers with darker skin may encounter discrimination and should exercise caution. Homosexuality is not accepted by all Slovaks; **GLBT** couples may experience stares or insults.

EMERGENCY	**Ambulance and General Emergency:** ☎112. **Fire:** ☎150. **Police:** ☎158.

TRANSPORTATION

BY PLANE AND TRAIN. **Bratislava** (**BTS;** ☎233 033 353; www.airportbratislava.sk) is a large hub for budget airlines. Many travelers fly to Bratislava and then take a shuttle to Vienna, AUT. For more info on budget airlines, see p. 47. If you are flying from outside Europe, it's best to fly to another budget hub and then connect to Bratislava. For train info, check the national company's website (**ŽSR;** www.zsr.sk). **EastPass** is valid in Slovakia, but **Eurail** is not. **InterCity** or **EuroCity** trains are faster but cost more. A boxed R on the timetable means that a *miestenka* (reservation) is required. Reservations are often required for *expresný* (express) trains and first-class seats, but are not necessary for *rychlík* (fast), *spešný* (semi-fast), or *osobný* (local) trains. Both first and second class are relatively comfortable and considered safe. Buy tickets before boarding the train, except in small towns. Master schedules *(cestovný poriadoký)* are sold at info desks and are posted in most stations.

BY BUS. In hilly regions, **ČSAD** or **Slovak Lines** buses are the best and sometimes the only option. Except for very long trips, buy tickets on board. The following footnotes on schedules are important: x (crossed hammers) means weekdays only; **a** is Saturday and Sunday; **b** means Monday through Saturday; **n** is Sunday; and **r** and **k** mean excluding holidays. *Premava* means including; *nepremava* is except; following those words are often lists of dates. Check www.slovaklines.sk for updated schedules.

BY BIKE AND BY THUMB. Rambling wilds and ruined castles inspire great bike tours, and renting a **bike** in Bratislava is becoming easier. Biking is very popular, especially in the Tatras. *Let's Go* does not recommend hitchhiking, but it is common and considered somewhat safe in Slovakia.

KEEPING IN TOUCH

PHONE CODES	**Country code:** 421. **International dialing prefix:** 00. For more info on placing international calls, see **Inside Back Cover.**

EMAIL AND INTERNET. Internet access is common in Slovakia, even in smaller towns. Internet cafes usually offer cheap (1Sk per min.), fast access.

TELEPHONE. Recent modernization of the Slovak **phone** system has required many businesses and individuals to switch phone numbers. The phone system is still unreliable; try multiple times if you don't get through. International and national phones exist in each city, but there is no good way to distinguish between them. **Card phones** are common and are usually better than the coin-operated variety. Purchase cards (100-500Sk) at the post office. Be sure to buy the "Global Phone" card if you plan to make international calls. International direct dial numbers include: **AT&T Direct** (☎0800 000 101); **Canada Direct** (☎ 0800 0001 151); **MCI** (☎08000 00112); **Telecom New Zealand** (☎0800 00 64 00).

MAIL. Mail service is generally efficient. Letters abroad take two to three weeks to arrive. Letters to Europe cost 11-14Sk; letters to the US cost 21Sk. Almost every *pošta* (post office) provides express mail services. To send a package abroad, go to a *colnice* (customs office). Mail can be received via **Poste Restante.** Address mail as follows: First name LAST NAME, POSTE RESTANTE, post office address, Postal Code, city, Slovakia.

LANGUAGE. Slovak is a West Slavic language written in the Latin alphabet. It is closely related to the other languages in this group—Czech and Polish—and speakers of one will understand the others. Older people speak a little Polish. Attempts to speak Slovak will be appreciated. English is common among Bratislava's youth, but German is more prevalent outside the capital. Russian is occasionally understood but unwelcome. The golden rules of speaking Slovak are to pronounce every letter and stress the first syllable.

ACCOMMODATIONS AND CAMPING

SLOVAKIA	❶	❷	❸	❹	❺
ACCOMMODATIONS	under 250Sk	250-500Sk	501-800Sk	801-1000Sk	over 1000Sk

Foreigners are often charged much more than Slovaks for accommodations. Finding cheap rooms in Bratislava before **student dorms** open in July is very difficult, especially in Slovensk Raj and the Tatras. In other regions, finding a bed is easy if you call ahead. The national tourist office, **SlovakoTourist,** and other tourist agencies usually can help. Slovakia has few **hostels,** most of which are found in and around Bratislava. These usually provide few amenities. **Juniorhotels (HI)** tend to be a bit nicer than hostels. **Hotel** prices are dramatically lower outside Bratislava and the Tatras, with budget hotels running 300-600Sk. **Pensions** *(penzióny)* are smaller and less expensive than hotels. **Campgrounds** are on the outskirts of most towns and usually rent bungalows to travelers. Camping in national parks is illegal. In the mountains, *chaty* (mountain huts) range from plush quarters (around 600Sk) to bunks with outhouses (about 200Sk).

FOOD AND DRINK

SLOVAKIA	❶	❷	❸	❹	❺
FOOD	under 120Sk	120-190Sk	191-270Sk	271-330Sk	over 330Sk

The national dish, *bryndzové haluky* (small dumplings in sauce), is a godsend for vegetarians and those sticking to a **kosher** diet. Pork products, however, are central to many traditional meals. *Knedliky* (dumplings) or *zemiaky* (potatoes) frequently accompany entrees. Enjoy *kolačky* (pastry), baked with cheese, jam, or poppy seeds, and honey, for dessert. *Pivo* (beer) is served at a *pivnica* or *piváreň* (tavern). The favorite Slovak beer is the slightly bitter *Spis*. Another popular alcohol is *Slivovica*, a plum brandy with an alcoholic content of well over 50%; it is so concentrated that some say it won't cause hangovers.

HOLIDAYS AND FESTIVALS

Holidays: Independence Day of Slovakia (Jan. 1); Epiphany (Jan. 6); Good Friday (Apr. 10, 2009; Apr. 2, 2010); Easter (Apr. 13, 2009; Apr. 4, 2010); May Day (May 1); Sts. Cyril and Methodius Day (July 5); Anniversary of Slovak National Uprising (Aug. 29); Constitution Day (Sept. 1); Our Lady of the 7 Sorrows (Sept. 15); All Saints' Day (Nov. 1); Day of Freedom and Democracy (Nov. 17); Christmas (Dec. 24-26).

Festivals: Bojnice's **Festival of Ghosts and Spirits,** in late spring, is a celebration of the dead and the ghosts that are said to haunt the castle. Bratislava hosts **Junifest,** a 10-day beer festival that includes hundreds of performances by artists, in early June. Near Poprad, the **Vychod Folk Festival** occurs in mid-summer.

BEYOND TOURISM

For more info on opportunities across Europe, see **Beyond Tourism,** p. 60.

Brethren Volunteer Service, 1451 Dundee Ave., Elgin, IL 60120 USA (☎800-323-8039, ext. 410; www.brethrenvolunteerservice.org). Christian organization places volunteers with civic and environmental groups in Slovakia.

The British Trust for Conservation Volunteers (BTCV), 163 Balby Rd., Balby, Doncaster DN4 ORH, UK (☎013 02 38 88 83; www2.btcv.org.uk). Works in concert with the Slovak Wildlife Society (www.slovakwildlife.org) to give volunteers the opportunity to assist in monitoring bear and wolf populations in the Tatras Mountains.

BRATISLAVA ☎02

Often eclipsed by its famous neighboring capitals, sophisticated Bratislava (pop. 450,000) is finally stepping into the limelight. Each night of the week, the city's artfully lit streets buzz with activity. During the day, both locals and visitors can be found sipping coffee at the hundreds of chic cafes dotting the cobblestone Staré Mešto (Old Town), sauntering along the Danube River, or exploring the well-kept castle that shines over the city.

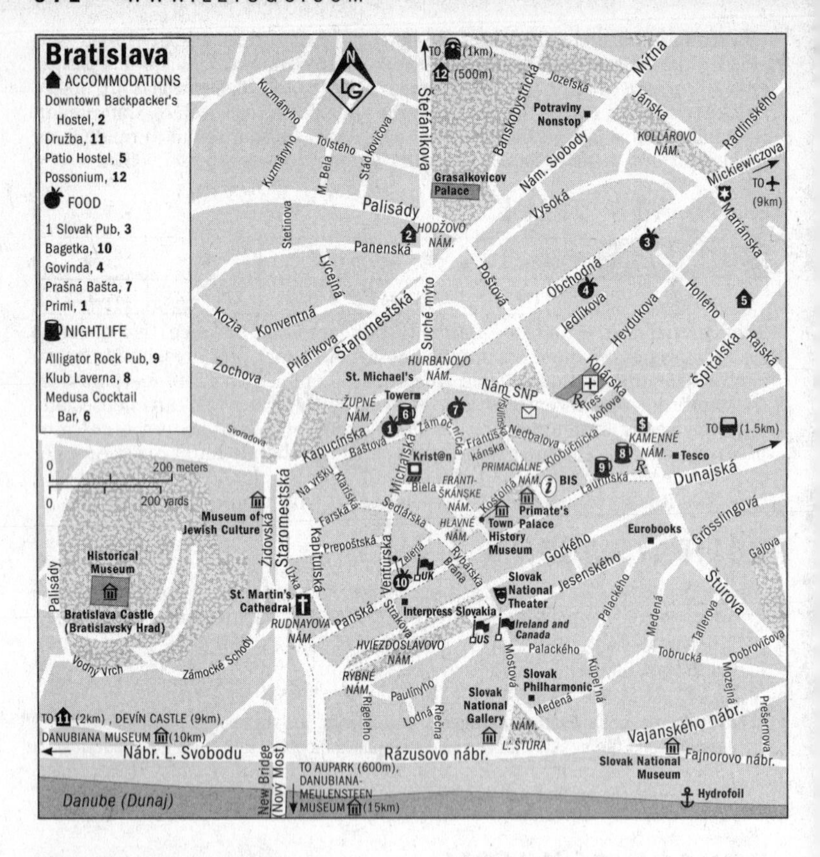

TRANSPORTATION

Flights: M.R. Štefánik International Airport (**BTS;** ☎02 48 57 11 11; www.letiskobratislava.sk), 9km northeast of town. Often used as a hub to reach **Vienna, AUT**. To reach the center of Bratislava, take bus #61 (1hr.) to the train station and then take tram #1 to Potová on nám. SNP.

Trains: Bratislava Hlavná Stanica, at the end of Predstaničné nám., off Šancová. Železnice Slovenskej republiky (☎02 20 29 11 11; www.zsr.sk), posts schedules on its website. To **Košice** (5-6hr., 10 per day, 518Sk), **Prague, CZR** (4-5hr., 3 per day, 450Sk), and **Vienna, AUT** (1hr., 1 per hr., round-trip 283Sk). Get off at Hlavná Stanica, the main train station. To reach the center from the station, take tram #2 to the 6th stop or walk downhill, take a right, then an immediate left, and walk down Stefanikova (15-20min).

Buses: Mlynské nivy 31 (☎02 55 42 16 67, info 09 84 22 22 22). Bus #210 runs between the train and bus stations. Check your ticket for the bus number (č. aut.), as several depart from the same stand. **Eurolines** has a 10% discount for those under 26. To: **Banská Bystrica** (3-4hr., 2-3 per hr., 250-300Sk); **Budapest, HUN** (4hr., 3 per day, 610Sk); **Prague, CZR** (4hr., 5 per day, 520Sk); **Vienna, AUT** (1hr., 1 per hr., 400Sk). From the station, take trolley #202, or turn right on Mlynské nivy and walk to Dunajská, which leads to Kamenné nám. (Stone Sq.) and the center of town (15-20min).

Local Transportation: Tram and **bus** tickets (10min. 14Sk, 30min. 18Sk, 1hr. 22Sk) are sold at kiosks and at the orange *automaty* in bus stations. Use an *automat* only if its light is on. Stamp your ticket when you board; the fine for riding ticketless is 1200Sk. Trams and buses run 4am-11pm. **Night buses,** marked with blue-and-yellow numbers with an "N" in front of them, run midnight-4am. Some kiosks and ticket machines sell passes (1-day 90Sk, 2-day 170Sk, 3-day 210Sk).

Taxis: BP (☎169 99); **FunTaxi** (☎167 77); **Profi Taxi** (☎162 22).

ORIENTATION AND PRACTICAL INFORMATION

The **Dunaj** (Danube) flows eastward across Bratislava. Four bridges span the river; the main **Nový Most** (New Bridge) connects Bratislava's center, **Staromestská** (Old Town) in the north, to the commercial and entertainment district on the river's southern bank. **Bratislavský Hrad** (Bratislava Castle) towers on a hill to the west, while the city center sits between the river and **námestie Slovenského Národného Povstania** (nám. SNP; Slovak National Uprising Sq.).

Tourist Office: Bratislava Culture and Information Center (BKIS), Klobúčnicka 2 (☎161 86; www.bkis.sk). Books private rooms and hotels (1000-4800Sk plus 50Sk fee); sells **maps** (free-120Sk) and books tours (400 per person). Open June-Oct. 15 M-F 8:30am-7pm, Sa 9am-5pm, Su 9:30am-5pm; May M-F 8:30am-6pm, Sa 9am-4pm, Su 10am-3pm. **Branch** in train station annex open M-F 8am-2pm and 2:30-7pm, Sa-Su 8am-2pm and 2:30-5pm.

Embassies: Citizens of **Australia** and **New Zealand** should contact the UK embassy in an emergency. **Canada,** Mostová 2 (☎02 59 20 40 31; www.canada.cz). Open M-F 8:30am-noon and 1:30pm-4:30pm. **Ireland,** Mostová 2 (☎02 59 30 96 11; www.dfa.ie). Open M-F 9am-12:30pm. **UK,** Panská 16 (☎02 59 98 20 00; www.britishembassy.sk). Open M-Th 8:30am-12:30pm and 1:30pm-5pm, F 8:30am-2pm. **US,** Hviezdoslavovo nám. 4 (☎02 54 43 08 61, emergency 09 03 70 36 66; www.slovakia.usembassy.gov). Open M-F 8am-noon and 2-3:30pm.

Currency Exchange: Ludová Banka, nám. SNP 15 (☎02 59 21 17 63, ext. 760; www.luba.sk) cashes American Express **Travelers Cheques** for 1% commission and offers MC/V cash advances. Open M-F 8am-8pm.

Luggage Storage: At the train station. 30-40Sk. Open daily 5:30am-midnight.

Internet: There are Internet cafes all over central Bratislava, especially along Michalská and Obchodná. **Megainet,** Šancová 25. 1Sk per min. Open daily 9am-10pm.

Post Office: Nám. SNP 34 (☎02 59 39 31 11). Offers fax service. **Poste Restante** and phone cards at counters #2-4. Poste restante M-F 7am-8pm, Sa 9am-2pm. Open M-F 7am-8pm, Sa 9am-6pm, Su 9am-2pm. **Postal Code:** 81000 Bratislava 1.

ACCOMMODATIONS

In July and August, several **university dorms** open as hostels (from 150Sk). **Pensions** and **private rooms** are cheap alternatives. Most places add a 50Sk tourist tax. **BKIS** (see **Orientation and Practical Information,** p. 873) has more info.

Patio Hostel, Špitálska 35 (☎02 52 92 57 97; www.patiohostel.com), near the bus station. From the train station, take tram #13 to the arch. The entrance is tucked behind a dimly lit, run-down archway, but the hostel itself is clean and comfortable, with sunny rooms, a friendly staff, and a colorful common area. Free Internet and laundry. Reception 24hr. Check-in 2pm. Check-out 11am. 6- to 12-bed dorms 500-700Sk; doubles 950-1000Sk; triples 850-900Sk. AmEx/MC/V. ❸

Downtown Backpacker's Hostel, Panenská 31 (☎54 64 11 91; www.backpackers.sk). From the train station, turn left on Stefánikova and right on Panenská, or take bus

SLOVAKIA

OUT OF THIS WORLD - LITERALLY

Visitors to Bratislava can't help but notice the towering, futuristic structure which straddles the New Bridge (Nový Most) over the Danube River. Constructed between the years 1967-1972 as a symbol of Communist modernism, the 850m tower has earned the name "The UFO". While the observation deck is open to visitors, there is a far more pleasurable way to enjoy the view from the top.

Taste would be an extremely appealing restaurant anywhere, but its location (in the tower) and decor make it downright spectacular. Combining futuristic touches with an overriding elegance, the dining room features clear high-backed chairs, tall crystal flowers, and floor-to-ceiling glass windows with spectacular views of the city and the Bratislava Castle. While enjoying the scenery, diners choose from an inventive Mediterranean/Asian fusion menu. The dinner menu is served in 6 courses, featuring such dishes like Seared Royal pigeon with shiitake mushrooms and Monkfish loin in pimento crust. Food this good comes at a price, of course, but Taste provides a dining experience that visitors won't forget.

Entrance on the Nový Most Bridge. ☎62 52 03 00; www.u-f-o.sk. Reservations recommended. Dinner menu 3000Sk; vegetarian 2800Sk; lunch 1800 -2200Sk.

#81, 91, or 93 for 2 stops. Swanky 19th-century building, with backpackers relaxing under a bust of Lenin and enjoying beers from the downstairs bar. Laundry 200Sk. Free Internet. Reception 24hr. Reserve ahead. Check-out 11am. Check-in 2pm. Dorms 500-600Sk; doubles 800Sk, with bath 1000Sk. 10% HI discount. Tourist tax 50Sk. MC/V. ❸

Possonium, Šancová 20. (☎220 720 007; www.possonium.sk) From the train station, walk straight down the hill, cross the main street, and turn left. The hostel is on the right. The new Possonium is a social hostel with friendly staffers and a quirky, horror-themed bar. Free Internet. Dorms 450-600Sk; doubles 850-950Sk. Tourist Tax 50Sk. MC/V. ❸

Družba, Botanická 25 (☎02 65 42 00 65; www.hotel-druzba.sk). Take bus #32 (dir.: Pri Kríži) or tram #1 or 5 to Botanická Záhrada. Cross the pedestrian overpass and go to the 2nd of the 2 concrete buildings. The university dorm is far from the Old Town, but its spacious dorms are bright and well-equipped. Dorms open early July to late Aug. Hotel open year-round. Reception M-Th 7am-3:30pm, F 7am-1pm. Dorms 190Sk; singles 790Sk; doubles 1400Sk. Tourist tax 50Sk. MC/V. ❶

FOOD

Buy groceries at **Tesco Potraviny,** Kamenné nám. 1. (Open M-F 8am-10pm, Sa 8am-8pm, Su 9am-8pm.) Try the indoor **fruit market** at Stará Trznícá, Kamenné nám. (Open M-F 7am-6pm, Sa 7am-1pm.)

1 Slovak Pub, Obchodná 62 (☎02 52 92 63 67; www.slovakpub.sk). Join the crowd at one of Bratislava's largest and cheapest traditional Slovak restaurants. Each room has a theme, including "country cottage" and "Room of Poets." Lunch until 5pm; 35-99Sk. Dinner entrees 79-300Sk. 10% discount for Patio Hostel guests. Open M-Th 10am-midnight, F-Sa 10am-2am, Su noon-midnight. MC/V. ❷

Govinda, Obchodná 30 (☎02 52 96 23 66). Venture into this colorful, underground nook to sample the heavenly veggie fare. Combination plate 104-124Sk. Open M-F 11am-8pm, Sa 11:30am-5pm. Cash only. ❶

Primi, Michalská 19 (☎02 54 43 15 42; www.primi.sk). This outdoor restaurant/bar is the pre-party spot for Bratislava's youth. Diners enjoy the garden atmosphere while choosing from an extensive menu of international entrees (179-450Sk) and gourmet pizzas (129-239Sk). Open M-Th 11am-1am, F-Su 11am-3am. MC/V. ❸

Prasná Bašta, Zámočnícka 11 (☎02 54 43 49 57; www.prasnabasta.sk). This hidden eatery's pleasant outdoor terrace and frequent live music draw crowds for generous portions of Slovak cuisine. Entrees 105-379Sk. Open daily 11am-11pm. MC/V. ❸

Bagetka, Zelená 8 (☎02 54 41 94 36). Tucked in an inconspicuous alley off of the main town square, this sandwich bar is a fast, cheap, and satisfying option. Entrees 50-90Sk. Open M-F 9:30am-9pm, Sa noon-9pm, Su 2pm-9pm. Cash only. ❶

SIGHTS

NÁMESTIE SNP AND ENVIRONS. Most of the city's major attractions are in the **Staré Mešto** (Old Town). From Nám. SNP, which commemorates the bloody 1944 Slovak National Uprising, walk down Urulínska to the pink-and-gold **Primate's Palace** (Primaciálný Palác), built in the 1700s for Hungary's religious leaders and now home to Bratislava's mayor. *(Primaciálné nám. 1. Buy tickets on 2nd fl. Open Tu-Su 10am-5pm. 40Sk, students free.)* Established in September 2000, the contemporary **Danubiana-Meulensteen Art Museum** is a piece of modern art in itself. On a small peninsula near the Hungarian border, the museum is surrounded by a small sculpture park. *(Take bus #91 from beneath Nový Most to the last stop, Cunovo; 35min., 20Sk. Follow the signs 3.5km to the museum. ☎09 03 60 55 05; www.danubiana.sk. Open Tu-Su May-Sept. 10am-8pm; Oct.-Apr. 10am-6pm. 80Sk, students 40Sk. MC/V.)* **Hviezdoslavovo námestie** is home to the gorgeous 1886 **Slovak National Theater** (Slovenské Národné Divadlo). With the Danube on your left, walk along the waterfront to the **Nový Most** (New Bridge), designed by the Communist government in the 70s. *(☎625 203 00; www.u-f-o.sk. Deck open daily 10am-11pm. 200Sk, students 100Sk.)* The **Museum of Jewish Culture** holds artifacts from Slovak Jews. *(Židovská 17. ☎02 59 34 91 42; www.slovak-jewish-heritage.org. Open M-F and Su 11am-5pm. 200Sk, students 60Sk.)*

CASTLES. On an imposing cliff 9km west of the center, the stunning **Devín Castle** (Hrad Devín) ruins overlook the confluence of the mighty Danube and Morava rivers. *(Bus #29 from Nový Most to the last stop. ☎65 73 01 05. English-language info 35Sk. Open May-Sept. Tu-F 10am-5pm, Sa-Su 10am-7pm; Apr. and Oct.-Nov. Tu-Su 10am-5pm; last entry 30min. before closing. Museum 130Sk, students 70Sk.)* Visible from Danube Banks, the **Bratislava Castle** (Bratislavský Hrad) is Bratislava's defining landmark.

ENTERTAINMENT AND NIGHTLIFE

The weekly English newspaper, *Slovak Spectator*, also has current events info. **Slovenské Národné Divadlo** (Slovak National Theater), Hviezdoslavovo nám. 1, puts on ballets and operas. (☎02 57 78 25 34; www.snd.sk. Buy tickets at Pribinova 17. Box office open Sept.-June M-F 8am-7pm, Sa 9am-1pm. 100-300Sk.) The **Slovenská Filharmonia** (Slovak Philharmonic), Medená 3, has two to three performances per week in fall and winter. The box office, Palackého 2, is around the corner. (☎02 59 20 82 33; www.filharm.sk. Open M-Tu and Th-F 1-7pm, W 8am-2pm. 100-200Sk.)

By night, Old Town is filled with young people preparing for a night out. At the packed, techno-infused hot spot **Klub Laverna,** Laurinská 19, a slide transports drunken clubbers from the upper level to the floor. (☎02 54 43 31 65; www.lavernaklub.sk, entrance on SNP street. Mixed drinks 85-250Sk. Cover F-Sa 100Sk. Open daily 9pm-6am.) Nearby at Laurinská 7, the underground **Aligator Pub** is the spot for Bratislava's tattoo-covered, alternative crowd. (☎02 43 19 10 94. Beer from 30Sk. Open Tu-Sa 5pm-3am.) For a less-crazed evening, head to **Medusa Cocktail Bar,** Michalská 21, which defines chic with its posh decor and huge selection of mixed drinks. (Cocktails 149-399SK). Open M-Th 11am-1am, Sa 11am-3am, Su 11am-midnight. AmEx/MC/V.) For info on GLBT nightlife, pick up a copy of *Atribut* at any kiosk.

THE TATRA MOUNTAINS (TATRY)

The mesmerizing Tatras, spanning the border between Slovakia and Poland, form the highest part of the Carpathian mountain range. The High Tatras feature sky-scraping hikes, glacial lakes, and deep snows. Sadly, many of the lower slopes on the Slovak side of the High Tatras were devastated by freak storms and mudslides in the fall of 2004, and vast swaths of the formerly lush pine forest are now brown fields of broken trees. Recent forest fires further scarred the landscape, though the upper regions escaped largely unscathed. To the south, the separate Low Tatras have ski resorts and tree-covered mountains.

LIPTOVSKÝ MIKULÁŠ ☎044

Liptovský Mikuláš (pop. 33,000) is a springboard for hikes in the **Low Tatras** (Nízke Tatry). To scale **Mount Ďumbier** (2043m), the region's tallest peak, catch an early bus to Liptovský Ján (25-30min., 1-2 per 2hr., 25Sk), then follow the blue trail up the Štiavnica River toward the **Svidovské Sedlo.** Go right at the red trail (2hr.), then begin the 1hr. climb up Sedlo Javorie. Head left on the yellow trail to the summit of Mt. Ďumbier (2hr.). Descend the ridge and follow the red sign to Chopok (2024m), the second-highest peak. From **Chopok,** it's a walk down the blue trail to the bus stop behind the Hotel Grand at Otupné (1hr.).

A worthwhile visit from Liptovský Mikuláš is the **Demänovská Jaskyňa Slobody** (Demänov Cave of Liberty). To get to the cave, take the **bus** from platform #3 in Liptovský Mikuláš to Demänovská Dolina, get off at Demänovská Jaskyňa Slobody (20-35min., 1 per hr., 25Sk), and walk to the cave on the blue trail toward Pusté Sedlo Machnate (1hr.). Tours are mandatory, with two lengths offered. Bring a sweater. (☎044 559 1673; www.ssj.sk. Open June-Aug. Tu-Su 9am-4pm, entrance every hr.; Sept. to mid-Nov. and mid-Dec. to May 9:30am-2pm, entrance 1 per 2hr. 45min. Tour 200Sk, with ISIC 180Sk. 2hr. tour 420/380Sk.)

Hotel Kriváň ❷, Štúrova 5, opposite the tourist office, has centrally located rooms. (☎044 552 2414. Singles 400Sk, with bath 500Sk; doubles 600/800Sk. Cash only.) The local favorite **Liptovská Izba Reštaurácia ❶,** nám. Osloboditemov 22, serves Slovak dishes in a rustic setting. (☎044 551 4853. Entrees 40-150Sk. Open M-Sa 10am-10pm, Su noon-10pm. Cash only.) Check out the **open-air market** to the right of the tourist office. (Open M-F 8am-4pm, Sa 8am-noon.)

Trains from Liptovský Mikuláš to Bratislava (4-5hr., 12 per day, 364Sk) are cheaper than **buses.** To reach the town center, follow Štefánikova toward the gas station at the far end of the lot, go right on Hodžu, and take a left on Štúrova. The **tourist office,** nám. Mieru 1, in the Dom Služieb complex, books private rooms and sells **maps.** (☎044 552 2418; www.mikulas.sk. Open July-Aug. M-F 9am-7pm, Sa 9am-1pm, Su 10am-7pm; Sept. to mid-Dec. and Apr.-June M-F 9am-5pm, Sa 9am-1pm; mid Dec. to March M-F 9am-6pm, Sa 9am-1pm.)

STARÝ SMOKOVEC ☎052

Spectacular trails begin at Starý Smokovec, the central resort in the **High Tatras.** A **funicular** picks up passengers behind the train station and takes them to Hrebienok (1285m), the starting point for many hikes. (Open daily 7:30am-7pm. Ascent July-Aug. 170Sk, Sept.-June 140Sk; descent 60/50Sk; round-trip 190/160Sk.) Alternatively, from the funicular station, hike 55min. up the green trail to Hrebienok. The green trail then continues 20min. north to the foaming **Cold Stream Waterfalls** (Volopáday studeného potoka). From the falls, take the red trail, which connects with the eastward blue trail (1-2hr.) to **Tatranská Lomnica**. The hike to **Little Cold Valley** (Malá studená dolina) is fairly relaxed.

Many chalets along the trails provide lodging for travelers. **Zamkovského chata ❷,** (☎052 442 2636) is on the red trail (40min.) from Hrebienok. The green trail (2hr.) climbs above the treeline to a high lake and another chalet, **Téryho chata ❷.** (☎052 442 5245. Dorms 300Sk.) Inexpensive accommodations in town are scarce; inquire at the tourist office. *Penzión* runners greeting backpackers at the station often offer the cheapest beds (500-600Sk per person. **Penzión Tatra ❸** offers tidy rooms and extensive ammenities. Turn right out of the train station; the pension is on the right just before the bus station. (☎903 650 802; www.tatraski.sk. All rooms equipped with private bathrooms, TV, and Wi-Fi. Private rooms 750Sk; apartments 950Sk.) For a relaxed, less touristed atmosphere, take a 25min. bus to the newly opened **Ginger Monkey Hostel ❷,** 294 High St., in the quaint village of Ždiar. Easy access to hiking trails, two entertaining hosts, a fun-loving crowd, and unbelievable views combine to make this a mountain haven that you'll never want to leave. (☎524 498 084; www.thegingermonkey.eu. Flexible check-in and check-out. Breakfast, linens, and Internet included. Dorms 400Sk; singles 450Sk; twins 900Sk. Cash only.) The classy **Reštaurácia Cukráreň ❸,** serves up an extensive array of entrees (129-289SK). Diners can enjoy mountain views from the pleasant outdoor patio. (In the shopping complex opposite the bus station. Open daily 8am-9pm.)

TEŽ trains run to Poprad (30min., 1 per hr., 20Sk). **Buses** run to Bratislava (6hr., 2 per day, 440Sk) and Levoča (20-50min., 2-4 per day, 60Sk). The **Tatranská Informačná Kanceléria (TIK)**, in the mall above the train station, provides weather forecasts, sells **maps,** including the useful VKÚ map #113 (125Sk), and arranges accommodations. (☎052 442 3440; www.zcrvt.szm.sk. Pensions 500Sk; hotels 700-900Sk. Open daily June-Sept. 8am-8pm; Oct.-May 8am-5pm.)

HIKING NEAR STARÝ SMOKOVEC. The town of **Štrbské Pleso** is the base for many beautiful hikes. From the tourist office, pass the souvenir lot and go left at the junction. Head uphill to reach the lift that goes 1840m up to **Chata pod Soliskom,** a chalet overlooking the lakes and valleys. (☎905 652 036. Dorms 250Sk. Lift open daily May-Sept. and Dec.-Mar. 8:30am-4pm. Last lift up 3:30pm. 150Sk, students 90Sk; round-trip 230/120Sk.) Or, continue on the challenging yellow trail and along **Mlynická dolina** past several mountain lakes and the dramatic **Vodopády Skok** waterfalls. The path (6-7hr.) involves strenuous ascents on **Bystré Sedlo** (2314m) and **Velké Solisko** (2412m). At the end of the yellow trail, turn left onto the red trail to complete the loop and return to Štrbské Pleso (30min.). The **grocery store** is opposite the train station (open 7am-10pm). TEŽ **trains** run to Štrbské Pleso from Starý Smokovec (45min., 1-2 per hr., 30Sk). The **tourist office** is across from the station. (☎052 449 2391. Open M-Sa 8-11:30am and noon-4pm; low-season reduced hours.)

KOŠICE ☎055

Established nearly 900 years ago, Košice (KO-shih-tseh; pop. 236,000) is Slovakia's second-largest city. Every October, athletes from around the world converge at the Košice Peace Marathon, Europe's oldest marathon. The city's enchanting **Staré Mešto** (Old Town) is home to peaceful fountains, shady parks, and Slovakia's largest church, the magnificent Cathedral of St. Elizabeth. Outside the center, towering concrete housing blocks surround the city for miles, providing a stark reminder of Košice's Communist past.

TRANSPORTATION AND PRACTICAL INFORMATION. Trains (☎181 88) run from the station on Predstaničné nám. to Bratislava (5-6hr., 13 per day, 518Sk), Budapest, HUN (4hr., 3 per day, 662Sk), and Kraków, POL (6-7hr., 3 per day, 756Sk). **Buses** (☎055 625 1445), slightly cheaper and slower, depart to the left of the train station. To reach the city center, exit the train station and follow the "Centrum" signs across the park. Walk down **Mlynská** to reach **Hlavná námestie,** the main square, or take tram #6 to nám. Osloboditemov and turn right to find the **tourist office,** Hlavná nám. 59. (☎055 625 8888; www.kosice.sk/icmk. Open June-Sept. M-F 9am-6pm, Sa 9am-1pm, Su 1pm-5pm, Oct.-May M-F 9am-6pm, Sa 9am-1pm.) Check email at **Internet Cafe,** Hlavná nám. 9. (50Sk per hr. Open daily 9am-10pm.) Košice's **post office,** Poštová 20, has Poste Restante. (☎055 617 1401. Open M-F 7am-7pm, Sa 8am-noon.) **Postal Code:** 04001.

ACCOMMODATIONS AND FOOD. Hotels and pensions add a 20Sk tax per person per night. **K2 Tourist Hotel ❷,** Štúrova 32, a bargain near Staré Mešto, provides comfortable and attractive rooms. From Hlavná nám., turn right on Štúrova. (☎055 625 5948. Reception 24hr. Check-in and check-out noon. 3- to 4-bed dorms 375Sk. MC/V; 50sk surcharge.) The friendly staff at central **Gazdovská Pension ❸,** Cajkovského 4, helps visitors navigate the city. (☎055 625 0143. Reserve ahead. Singles 800Sk; doubles 1600Sk. Cash only.)

Reštaurácia Ajvega ❶, Orlia 10, offers organic Slovak and Mexican food, including vegetarian options, in a trendy, eccentric setting. (☎055 622 0452. Soups 30-40Sk. Entrees 89-155Sk. Open M-Th 8am-10pm, F 8am-midnight, Sa-Su 11am-10pm. Cash only.) The popular **Reštaurácia Veverička** (Squirrel Restaurant) **❷,** Hlavná nám. 95, serves local dishes on its sun-drenched patio. (☎055 622 3360. English menu. Entrees 65-300Sk. Open daily 9am-10pm. Cash only.) A **Tesco** supermarket is located at Hlavná nám. 109. (☎055 670 4810. Open M-F 7am-10pm, Sa 7am-6pm, Su 8am-6pm. MC/V.)

SIGHTS AND NIGHTLIFE. The **Cathedral of St. Elizabeth** (Dom sv. Alžbety), in Hlavná nám., was constructed in high Gothic style in 1378. (Tower open M-F 9am-5pm, Sa 9am-1pm. Cathedral 30Sk, students 15Sk. Tower 35/20Sk. Both 70/15Sk.) The **East Slovak Museum** (Východoslovenské Múzeum), Hviezdoslavova 3, includes Ferenc Rakóczi's House, an exhibit on a rebellion leader and an exposé on jail life from the 17th to 19th centuries. From Hlavná nám., take a right at the State Theatre onto Univerzitná. (☎055 622 0309; www.vsmuzeum.sk. Open Tu-Sa 9am-5pm, Su 9am-1pm. Mandatory Slovak-language tours 30Sk, students 15Sk. Prison exhibit 30/15Sk.)

The busy and stylish **Jazz Club,** Kováčska 39, houses a disco and pub. (☎055 622 4237. Beer 30-60Sk. Tu and Th-Sa disco nights; cover 50Sk. Open Tu-W 8pm-3am, Th-Sa 8pm-4am. Cash only.) **Irish Pub Diesel,** Hlavná nám. 92, has cheap beer, a casual atmosphere, and a disco party every Th night. (☎055 622 2186; www.irishpubkosice.com. Cover 50Sk on Th. Open M-W 11am-midnight, Th 11am-2:30am, F 11am-1:30am, Sa 3pm-1am, Su 3pm-midnight.)

DAYTRIP FROM KOŠICE: JASKYŇA DOMICA. **Jaskyňa Domica,** a challenge to reach, has breathtaking caverns. Stalactites and stalagmites jut out from three-million-year-old UNESCO-protected walls. The largest cave measures 48 million L. When underground water levels permit, the longer tour includes a boat ride covering 1.5km of the cave. The shorter tour covers a mere 780m. Only 5km of the 23km cave lie on the Slovak side—the rest is accessible from **Hungary.** To see more, travel 1km (10min. on foot above ground) to the border and find the Hungarian entrance. **Buses** from Košice go to Plešivec (1hr., 7-10 per day, 128Sk) where a connecting bus (1 per 1-2hr., 3Sk) leaves for Jaskyňa Domica. Check the timetable across from the cave entrance or at the **TIC** for bus schedules. *(☎055 788 2010; www.ssj.sk. Cave open June-Aug. 9am-4pm, Sept.-Dec. and Feb.-May 9:30am-2pm. Mandatory tours June-Aug. Tu-Su 1 per hr.; Sept.-Dec. and Feb.-May 4 per day. 45min. tour 170Sk, students 150Sk; 1hr. tour 200/180Sk. Cash only.)*

SLOVENIA (SLOVENIJA)

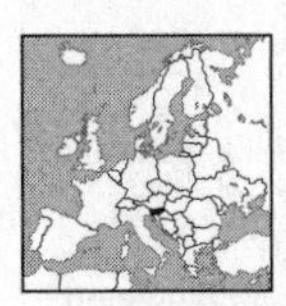

The first and most prosperous of Yugoslavia's breakaway republics, tiny Slovenia revels in republicanism, peace, and independence. With a historically westward gaze, Slovenia's liberal politics and high GDP helped it gain early entry into the European Union, further eroding its weak relationship with Eastern Europe. Fortunately, modernization has not adversely affected the tiny country's natural beauty and diversity: it is still possible to go skiing, explore Slovenia's stunning caves, bathe under the Mediterranean sun, and catch an opera—all in a single day.

DISCOVER SLOVENIA: SUGGESTED ITINERARIES

THREE DAYS. In **Ljubljana** (p. 882), the charming cafe culture and nightlife—especially in eclectic, Soviet-chic Metelkova—is worth at least two days. Then relax in tranquil, fairytale **Bled** (1 day; p. 886).

ONE WEEK. After 3 days in the capital city **Ljubljana,** enjoy **Bled** (1 day) and its cousin **Bohinj** (1 day; p. 887). Head down the coast to the mini-Venice of **Piran** (2 days; p. 885).

ESSENTIALS

FACTS AND FIGURES

OFFICIAL NAME: Republic of Slovenia.
CAPITAL: Ljubljana.
MAJOR CITIES: Maribor, Celje, Kranj.
POPULATION: 2,009,000.
TIME ZONE: GMT + 1.
LANGUAGE: Slovenian.
RELIGION: Roman Catholic (58%).
TRACTORS PER 100 PEOPLE: 6.

WHEN TO GO

July and August are the peak months in Slovenia; tourists flood the coast, and prices for accommodations rise. Go in spring or early autumn, and you will be blessed with a dearth of crowds and great weather for hiking and exploring the countryside. Skiing is popular from December to March.

DOCUMENTS AND FORMALITIES

EMBASSIES AND CONSULATES. Foreign embassies to Slovenia are in Ljubljana (p. 883). Embassies and consulates abroad include: **Australia,** Level 6, 60 Marcus Clarke St., Canberra, ACT 2601 (☎262 434 830; vca@gov.si); **Canada,** 150 Metcalfe St., Ste. 2101, Ottawa, ON K2P 1P1 (☎613-565-5781; www.gov.si/mzz-dkp/veleposlanistva/eng/ottawa/embassy.shtml); **Ireland,** Morrison Chambers, 2nd fl., 32 Nassau St., Dublin 2 (☎1 670 5240; vdb@mzz-dkp.gov.si); **UK,** 10 Little College St., London SW1P 3SJ (☎020 72 22 57 00; www.gov.si/mzz-dkp/veleposlanistva/eng/london/events.shtml); **US,** 1525 New Hampshire Ave. NW, Washington, DC 20036 (☎202-667-5363; www.gov.si/mzz-dkp/veleposlanistva/eng/washington). Citizens of **New Zealand** should contact the embassy in Australia.

VISA AND ENTRY INFORMATION. Citizens of the European Union, Australia, Canada, Ireland, New Zealand, the UK, and the US do not need **visas** for stays of up to 90 days. Visas take from four to seven business days to process and are not available at the border.

ENTRANCE REQUIREMENTS.

Passport: Required for all travelers (except EU citizens).

Visa: Not required for stays of under 90 days for citizens of Australia, Canada, Ireland, New Zealand, the UK, and the US.

Letter of Invitation: Not required.

Inoculations: Recommended up-to-date on DTaP (diphtheria, tetanus, and pertussis), hepatitis A, hepatitis B, MMR (measles, mumps, and rubella), polio booster, rabies, and typhoid.

Work Permit: Required of all foreigners planning to work in Slovenia.

International Driving Permit: Required of those driving in Slovenia.

TOURIST SERVICES AND MONEY

EMERGENCY Ambulance and Fire: ☎112. Police: ☎113.

There are **tourist offices** in most major cities and tourist destinations. Staff members generally speak English or German and, on the coast, perfect Italian. They can usually find accommodations for a small fee and generally give advice and maps for free. Kompas is the main tourist organization.

The **euro (€)** has replaced the **tolar** in Slovenia. SKB Banka, Ljubljanska Banka, and Gorenjska Banka are common **banks.** American Express Travelers Cheques and Eurocheques are accepted almost everywhere, but major credit cards are not consistently accepted. MasterCard and Visa **ATMs** are everywhere.

HEALTH AND SAFETY

Medical facilities are of high quality, and most have English-speaking doctors. EU citizens receive free medical care with a valid passport; other foreigners must pay cash. **Pharmacies** are stocked according to Western standards; ask for *obliž* (band-aids), *tamponi* (tampons), and *vložki* (sanitary pads). **Tap water** is safe to drink. **Crime** is rare in Slovenia. **Women** should, as always, exercise caution and avoid being out alone after dark. There are few **minorities** in Slovenia, but minorities generally just receive curious glances. Navigating Slovenia with a **wheelchair** can be difficult and requires patience and caution on slippery cobblestones. **Homosexuality** is legal, but may elicit unfriendly reactions.

TRANSPORTATION

BY PLANE. Flights arrive at **Ljubljana Airport (LJU).** Most major airlines offer connections to the national carrier, **Adria Airways** (www.adria-airways.com). To save money, consider flying into Vienna, AUT, and taking a train to Ljubljana.

BY TRAIN AND BUS. First and second class differ little on **trains.** Those under 26 get a 20% discount on most international fares. ISIC holders should ask for the 30% *popust* (discount) off domestic tickets. Schedules often list trains

by direction. *Prihodi vlakov* means arrivals; *odhodi vlakov* is departures; *dnevno* is daily. **Eurail** is not accepted in Slovenia. Though usually more expensive than trains, **buses** may be the only option in mountainous regions. The bus is also a better choice than the train to Bled, as the train station is far from town. Buy tickets at stations or on board.

BY CAR, FERRY, BIKE, AND THUMB. **Car** rental agencies in Ljubljana offer reasonable rates, and Slovenia's roads are in good condition. A regular **ferry** service connects Portorož to Venice, ITA, in summer. Nearly every town in Slovenia has a bike rental office. While those who hitchhike insist that it is safe and widespread in the countryside, hitchhiking is not recommended by *Let's Go*.

KEEPING IN TOUCH

PHONE CODES	**Country code:** 386. **International dialing prefix:** 00. For more info on placing international calls, see **Inside Back Cover.**

EMAIL AND INTERNET. Internet access is fast and common. Though free Internet is hard to find anywhere but in the biggest cities, there are Internet cafes in most major tourist destinations. Expect to pay approximately €2-4 per hour.

TELEPHONE. All phones take **phone cards,** sold at post offices, kiosks, and gas stations. Dial ☎115 for collect calls and ☎1180 for the international operator. Calling abroad is expensive without a phone card (over US$6 per min. to the US). Use the phones at the post office and pay when you're finished.

MAIL. Airmail *(letalsko)* takes from one to two weeks to reach Australia, New Zealand, and the US. Address **Poste Restante** as follows: first name, LAST NAME, Poste Restante, post office address, Postal Code, city, SLOVENIA.

LANGUAGE. Slovenian is a South Slavic language written in the Latin alphabet. Most young Slovenes speak at least some English, but the older generations are more likely to understand German or Italian. The tourist industry is generally geared toward Germans, but most tourist office employees speak English.

ACCOMMODATIONS AND CAMPING

SLOVENIA	❶	❷	❸	❹	❺
ACCOMMODATIONS	under €15	€15-21	€22-27	€28-33	over €33

All establishments charge a nightly tourist tax. Youth hostels and student dormitories are cheap (€15-20), but generally open only in summer (June 25-Aug. 30). Hotels fall into five categories (L, deluxe; A; B; C; and D) and are expensive. Pensions are the most common form of accommodation; usually they have private singles as well as inexpensive dorms. Private rooms are the only cheap option on the coast and at Lake Bohinj. Prices vary, but rarely exceed US$30. Campgrounds can be crowded, but most are in excellent condition. Camp in designated areas to avoid fines.

FOOD AND DRINK

SLOVENIA	❶	❷	❸	❹	❺
FOOD	under €3	€3-5	€6-8	€9-10	over €10

For homestyle cooking, try a *gostilna* or *gostišče* (country-style inn or restaurant). Traditional meals begin with *jota*, a soup with potatoes, beans, and sauerkraut. Pork is the basis for many dishes, such as *Svinjska pečenka* (roast pork). **Kosher** and **vegetarian** eating is therefore very difficult within the confines of Slovenian cuisine. Those with such dietary restrictions might find pizza and bakery items their best options. Slovenia's **winemaking** tradition dates from antiquity. Renski, Rizling, and Šipon are popular whites, while Cviček and Teran are favorite reds. Brewing is also centuries old; Lako and Union are good beers. For something stronger, try *žganje*, a fruit brandy, or Viljamovka, distilled by monks who guard the secret of getting a whole pear inside the bottle.

HOLIDAYS AND FESTIVALS

Holidays: New Year's Day (Jan. 1); Culture Day (Prešeren Day; Feb. 8); Easter Holiday (Apr. 12-13); National Resistance Day (Apr. 27); Labor Day (May 1-2); Independence Day (June 25); Reformation Day (Oct. 31); Christmas Day (Dec. 25).

Festivals: Slovenia embraces its alternative artistic culture as much as its folk heritage. Hitting Ljubljana in July and Aug., the International Summer Festival is the nation's most famous. The Peasant's Wedding Day *(Kmecka ohcet)*, a presentation of ancient wedding customs held in Bohinj at the end of July, and the Cow's Ball *(Kravji Bal)* in mid-Sept., which celebrates the return of the cows to the valleys from higher pastures, are a couple of the country's many summertime folk exhibitions.

LJUBLJANA ☎01

The average traveler only stops in Ljubljana (loob-lee-AH-na; pop. 275,000) for an hour en route from Venice to Zagreb, but those who stay longer become enchanted by Slovenia's lively capital city. Bridges guarded by **dragons** span the graceful canals, while street performances liven up summer nights. Its fortified castles, frescoed churches, and modern high-rises, reveals the city's richly layered history. It has persevered through medieval existence and communism and soon aspires to be the seat of the EU presidency.

TRANSPORTATION

Trains: Trg OF 6 (☎01 291 3332). To: **Bled** (1hr., 12 per day, €4.12); **Koper** (2hr., 3 per day, €9); **Budapest, HUN** (9hr., 6 per day, €29); **Sarajevo, BOS** (11hr., 3 per day, €840) via **Zagreb, CRO** (2hr., 8 per day, €12); **Venice, ITA** (5hr., 5 per day, €25).

Buses: Trg OF 4 (☎01 090 4230; www.ap-ljubljana.si). To: **Bled** (1hr., hourly until 9pm, €6.40); **Koper** (2hr., 5-10 per day, €12); **Maribor** (3hr., 10 per day, €12); **Zagreb, CRO** (3hr., 1 per day, €14).

Public Transportation: Buses run until 10:30pm. Drop €1 (exact change only) in the box beside the driver or buy cheaper €0.80 *žetoni* (tickets) at post offices, kiosks, or the main bus terminal. Day passes (€3.80) sold at **Ljubljanski Potniški Promet,** Celovška c. 160 (☎01 582 2426 or ☎01 205 6045). Open M-F 6:45am-7pm, Sa 6:45am-1pm. Pick up a bus map at the **Tourist Information Center (TIC).**

ORIENTATION AND PRACTICAL INFORMATION

The train and bus stations are side-by-side on **Trg Osvobodilne Fronte** (Trg OF or OF Sq.). To reach the center, turn right on Masarykova and left on Miklošičeva c.; continue to **Prešernov trg,** the main square. After crossing the **Tromostovje** (Triple Bridge), you'll see Stare Miasto at the base of Castle Hill. The tourist office is on the left at the corner of Stritarjeva and Adamič-Lundrovo nab.

Tourist Office: Tourist Information Center (TIC), Stritarjeva 1 (☎01 306 1215, 24hr. English-language info ☎090 939 881; www.ljubljana.si). Helpful staff speak excellent English. Pick up **free maps** and the free, useful *Ljubljana from A to Z.* Open daily June-Sept. 8am-10pm; Oct.-May 9am-7pm. Box office in TIC open M-F 9am-6pm, Sa-Su 9am-1pm. AmEx/MC/V.

Embassies: Australia, Durajska c. 50 (☎01 588 3108). Open M-F 9am-1pm. **Canada,** Durajska c. 22 (☎01 430 3570). Open M-F 9am-1pm. **Ireland,** Poljanski nasip 6 (☎01 300 8970). Open M-F 9am-noon. **UK,** Trg Republike 3 (☎01 200 3910). Open M-F 9am-noon. **US,** Prešernova 31 (☎01 200 5500). Open M-F 9am-noon and 2-4pm.

Currency Exchange: Menjalnice (private exchange) booths abound. **Ljubljanska banka** branches throughout town exchange currency for no commission and cash **traveler's checks** for a 1.5% commission. Open M-F 9am-noon and 2-7pm, Sa 9am-noon.

Luggage Storage: *Garderoba* (lockers) at train station. Luggage €2-3 per day.

Pharmacy: Lekarna Mikloišič, Miklošičeva 24. Open 7:30am-5:30pm most days, 7:30am-1pm on Sat. (☎01 230 6252).

Internet: Most hostels in town offer free Internet. **Cyber Cafe Xplorer,** Petkovško nab. 23 (☎01 430 1991; www.sisky.com), has Wi-Fi. €2.50 per 30min., students €2.38. 20% discount 10am-noon. Open M-F 10am-10pm, Sa-Su 2-10pm.

Post Office: Trg OF 5 (☎01 433 0605). Open M-F 7am-midnight, Sa 7am-6pm, Su 9am-noon. **Poste Restante,** Slovenska 32 (☎01 426 4668), *atizročitev pošiljk* (outgoing mail) counter. Open M-F 7am-8pm, Sa 7am-1pm. **Postal Code:** 1000.

ACCOMMODATIONS

In the busier months of July and August, **Hostelling International Slovenia** (PZS; ☎01 231 2156) helps travelers easily find accommodations. The **TIC** finds private rooms (singles €27-45; doubles €40-75). There is a daily **tourist tax** (€0.62-1.25) at all establishments.

Fluxus, Tomšičeva 4 (☎01 251 5760; www.fluxus-hostel.com). In addition to having a strategic main square location and funky decor, this small gem offers travelers a real sense of community. 1 bath for 16 beds. Kitchen and laundry. Free Internet and printer. Reception 24hr. Reserve ahead. Dorms €21; double €63. Cash only. ❷

Hotel/Hostel Park, Tabor 9 (☎01 300 2500; www.hotelpark.si). The large size and central location of Hotel/Hostel Park makes finding a room easy even if booking on short notice. Rooms are cleaned daily. Towels and sheets included. Free Internet. Breakfast provided for hotel guests only. Dorms €18. ❶

Celica, Metelkova 8 (☎01 230 9700; www.hostelcelica.com). With your back to the train station, walk left down Masarykova, then right on Metelkova; blue signs lead the way. Local and foreign artists transformed this former prison into modern art. Bar, cafe, free Internet, and cultural arts programs. Breakfast included. Reception 24hr. Reserve ahead. Dorms €16-20; cells €18-25. Cash-only deposit €10 per person. MC/V. ❷

Ljubljana Resort: Hotel *and* **Camping,** Dunajska 270 (☎01 568 3913; www.ljubljanaresort.si). Take bus #6 or 8 to Ježica. From bus stop, continue down road, turn right into the resort's long drive way, and follow signs. Both campground and spacious rooms with TVs and showers are available. Reception 24hr. Flexible check out 1pm. Pool and snack bar. Reservations recommended. June 20-Aug. 20 camping €13 per person; Aug. 21-June 19 €9. Singles €90-110; doubles €130-150. Tourist tax €1.02. MC/V. ❶

FOOD

Maximarket, Trg Republike 1, has a **Mercator** in the basement. (Open M-Th 9am-8pm, F 9am-10pm, Sa 8am-3pm.) There is an **open-air market** next to St. Nicholas's Cathedral. (Open June-Aug. M-Sa 6am-6pm; Sept.-May 6am-4pm.)

Zvezda Cafe, Wolfova 14 (☎01 421 9090). This small cafe has fantastic gelato with flavors like chocolate hazelnut and jaffa. Even Mozart has his own flavor, based on chocolates with pistachio candies from Salzburg (€2-3). Sip one of the 38 specialty teas (€2), or try a cake or sandwich. Cash only for gelato, MC/V in cafe. ❷

POMF, 40 Trubarjeva cesta (☎04 186 8582). This small restaurant features indoor and outdoor seating and a variety of flavorful Slovenian favorites for low prices. Vegetarian options available. Entrees €2-6. Open M-Th 10am-11pm, F 10am-noon, Sa noon-midnight, Su noon-11pm. MC/V. ❶

Cafe Romeo, Stari trg 6. Popular with local hipsters, this is one of the few places in town that serves food on Su. Riverside outdoor seating supplements a fashionable black-and-red leather interior. Snack-oriented menu features burritos (€4.50), nachos (€3.50), and dessert crepes (€3.50). Open daily 10am-1am. Kitchen open M-Sa 11am-midnight, Su 11am-11pm. Cash only. ❷

SIGHTS

A good way to see the sights is a walking tour, which departs from the *rotovž* (city hall), Mestni trg 1. (2hr. July-Aug. M-F 10am, Su 11am; May-Sept. daily 10am; Oct.-Apr. F-Su 11am. €10. Buy tickets at the tour or at the TIC.)

SAINT NICHOLAS' CATHEDRAL (STOLNICA SV. NIKOLAIA). This dazzling cathedral's beautifully preserved frescoes are a must-see. *(Dolničarjeva 1. ☎01 231 0684. Open daily 6am-noon and 3-7pm. Free.)*

NATIONAL MUSEUM (NARODNI MUSEI). Contains exhibits on archaeology, culture, and local history from the prehistoric era to the present. Upstairs, the Natural History Museum features an impressive taxidermy collection. *(Muzejska 1. ☎01 241 4400. Open M-W, F, and Su 10am-6pm, Th 10am-8pm. National Museum and National History Museum each €3, students €2. Both €4/3. 1st Su of month free.)*

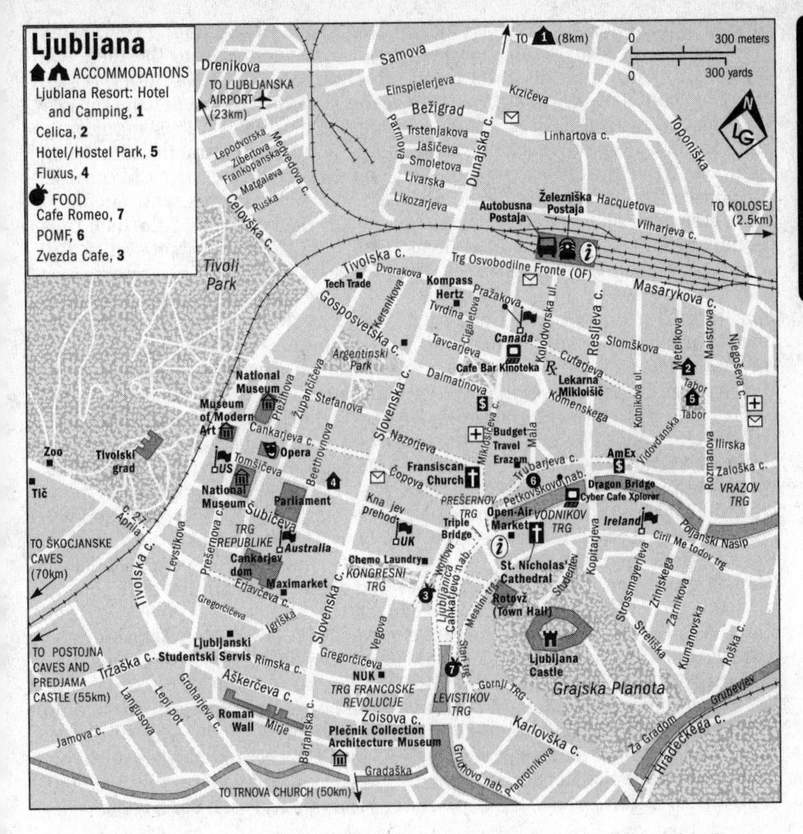

DRAGON BRIDGE (ZMAJSKI MOST). Head to Vodnikov trg, where this famous dragon-guarded bridge stretches across the Ljubljanica River.

PREŠERNOV TRG. Close to city hall, down Stritarjeva, and across the *Tromostovje* (Triple Bridge) is the central square of Ljubljana, with its pink 17th-century Franciscan church. *(Prešernov trg 4. ☎01 242 9300. Free.)*

LJUBLJANA CASTLE (LJUBLJANSKI GRAD). The narrow Studentovska leads uphill to the Ljubljana Castle, which has a breathtaking view. A trolley leaves every hour from 9am to 7pm for €3 from Stritarjeva ul. near the tourist office. However, the walk is only 10min. and offers more views. *(Grajska planota 1. ☎01 232 9994. Open daily May-Oct. 10am-6pm; Nov.-Apr. 10am-6pm. Access to the top tour and 20min. presentations are offered every 30min. 9am-9pm. €3.)*

PIRAN ☎05

Unlike more modern towns on the Istrian Peninsula, Piran—chartered in 1384—has retained its Venetian charm with beautiful churches, winding cobblestone streets, and dilapidated medieval architecture. A short walk uphill from behind the red building at **Tartinijev trg,** the town's central square, leads to the Gothic **Church of Saint George** (Cerkev sv. Jurija) and the 17th-century **Saint George's Tower,** with a view of Piran and the Adriatic. (Open daily mid-

June to Sept. 10am-1pm and 4-7pm; Oct. to mid-June 11am-5pm. Free.) From the tower, head away from the church and continue uphill to the medieval **city walls** to see Piran, in all its red-tile-roofed, Mediterranean glory. (Open Apr.-Oct. 8am-9pm; Nov.-Mar. 9am-5pm. Free.) On the way down from the city walls and St. George's Church, take a left and explore St. Francis' monastery. The central gallery now features art exhibits. Piran's real attraction, however, is the **sea.** While the closest sand beach is in the neighboring town of Portorož, it's possible to go swimming off Piran's own rocky shores, and excellent **scuba diving** can be arranged through Sub-net, Prešemovo nab. 24, which runs certification classes and guided dives. (☎05 673 2218; www.sub-net.si. €30 guided dive, €40 to explore a wreck. €60 per rental piece. €220 beginner's open water dive. Open Tu-Su 9am-7pm. Cash only.) The **Maritime Museum** (Pomorski Muzej), off Tartinijev trg on Cankarjevo nab., has three stories of exhibits on marine archaeology and seamanship, and an impressive collection of scuba diving suits as well as ship replicas. (☎05 671 0040. English captions. Open in the summer Tu-Su 9am-noon and 6-9pm, in the winter 3-6pm. €3.50, students €2.50.) July welcomes the **Primorska Summer Festival,** featuring outdoor plays, ballets, and concerts. Inquire at the tourist office for schedules.

Youth Hostel Val (HI), Gregorčičeva 38A, has spotless two- to four-bed suites. From the bus station, follow the coast past Tartinijev trg as it curves away from the harbor; the hostel is three blocks up. (☎05 673 2555; www.hostel-val.com. Breakfast included. Reception 8am-6pm. Dorms mid-May to mid-Sept. €25; mid-Sept. to mid-May €20.) Waterfront cafes line Prešemovo nab., but **Tri Vdove ❸** stands out for its seafood dishes and sophisticated interior. Try one of the value meals (€12-14) with soup, salad, entree, and dessert. (☎05 673 0290. Entrees €5-38. Open daily 11am-midnight. AmEx/MC/V.) A **Mercator** supermarket, Levstikova 5, is a short walk behind the tourist office. (Open M-F 7am-8pm, Sa 7am-1pm, Su 8am-noon. AmEx/MC/V.) **Buses** go to Ljubljana (7-8 per day; €12). A **minibus** runs the length of Obala, from Lucija through Portorož and on to Piran (3 per hr., 5:30am-midnight, €1). Alternatively, a 25min. walk takes you from Piran to Portorož; facing the sea, head left. The friendly, English-speaking staff at the **tourist office,** Tartinijev trg 2., in the central square, provides bus schedules. (☎05 673 4440. 9am-5pm; later in summer.) **Postal Code:** 6330.

BLED ☎04

Snow-covered peaks, a turquoise lake, and a stately medieval castle make Bled (pop. 11,000) one of Slovenia's most striking, visited destinations. But its beauty is only slightly diminished by popularity: more crowds show up each summer to swim, hike, paraglide, shop, or just enjoy the air.

ORIENTATION AND PRACTICAL INFORMATION. **Trains** leave from the Lesce-Bled station, about 4km from Bled, for Ljubljana. (1hr., 7 per day, €4.) **Buses,** a more convenient option, go from Bled to Bohinjsko Jezero (45min., every hr. 7:20am-8:20pm, €3.60), Ljubljana (1hr., every hr. 5am-9:30pm, €6.30), and Vintgar (1 per day June 14-Sept. 30; €2.50). The lakeside **tourist office,** on the corner of the c. Svobode 10 building, gives out free maps of Bled and sells hiking **maps** (€4-10) of the region. (☎04 574 1122; www.bled.si. Open June-Sept. M-Sa 8am-7pm; Mar.-May 9am-7pm; Nov.-Feb. 9am-5pm.) **Internet** is available at the **Apropo Cocktail Bar/Internet Cafe,** Ljubljanska c. 4. (☎04 574 4044. €2 for 30min. Free Wi-Fi. Open daily 8am-midnight.) **Postal Code:** 4260.

ACCOMMODATIONS AND FOOD. The spotless new **Traveller's Haven ❷,** Riklijeva c. 1. offers a great experience with a kitchen, free laundry, free

Internet, free DVD rental, and free bike rental. (☎04 139 6545; travellershaven@t2.net. Dorms €19. Cash only.) The comfortable dorm beds, spotless private baths, and filling breakfast at **Bledec Youth Hostel (HI)** ❷, Grajska c. 17, make it feel more like a pension. Turn left from the bus station and follow the street to the top, bearing left at the fork. (☎04 574 5250; www.mlino.si. Breakfast included. Laundry €8. Internet €2 per 30min. Reception 24hr. Check-out 10am. Restaurant and common room available. Reserve ahead. Dorms €21, members €20; doubles €25; tourist tax €0.10. AmEx/MC/V.)

Big portions, high-quality regional food, and excellent service distinguish **Gostilna pri Planincu** ❶, Grajska c. 8, near the bus station. Try the flavorful beef goulash (€3.80) or choose from the wide selection of meat and fish dishes. (☎04 574 1613. Dessert crepes €2.50-3.50. Open daily 9am-11pm.) **Pizzeria Rustika** ❷, Riklijeva c., offers a variety of gourmet pizzas (€5.40-7.90), sandwiches (€2.50-6.60), and salads (€3-6). For dessert, guests can try one of their creative ice cream desserts (€2.10-3.80). (☎04 576 8900. Open M 3-11pm, Tu-Su noon-11pm.) Pick up some groceries at the various **Mercator** locations. One is located in the central area Ljubljanska c. 4; another is across from Traveller's Haven hostel on Riklijeva c. (Open M-F 7am-7pm, Sa 7am-3pm, Su 8am-noon.)

SIGHTS AND ENTERTAINMENT. The **Church of the Assumption** *(Cerkev Marijinega Vnebovzetja)* rises from the only Slovenian island in the center of the lake. To get there, either rent a boat (1st hr. €12, €6.30 per hr. thereafter), hop on a gondola (round-trip €12), or just swim (500m from the west side of the lake, next to the campground). Entrance to the church and museum costs €3. Built in 1011, **Bled Castle** *(Blejski Grad)* rules the lake from atop a huge rock face cliff on its shores. The fastest way to ascend is from the small marked path branching off to the right of Riklijeva c., near St. Martin's Church. Learn about the geological and archaeological history of the region at the castle's **museum,** and snap fantastic photos of **Bled Lake** and the surrounding mountains. (☎04 578 0525. Open daily May-Oct. 8am-8pm; Nov.-Apr. 8am-5pm. €7, students €6. MC.) **Soteska Vintgar,** a 1.6km gorge carved by the waterfalls and rapids of the Radovna River, winds through the rocks of the **Triglav National Park** *(Triglavski Narodni)* and culminates with the 16m **Šum Waterfall** (down the stairs behind the second ticket booth). Walk the 4km instead of taking the bus to the trailhead, and you'll pass small towns and open fields. Bring food; a picnic bench tucked neatly into a nook lies halfway along the hike. The **park info office** is at Kidričeva c. 2. (☎04 574 1188. €4, students €3.) To get there, go over the hill on Grajska c., away from the town center, and take a right at the bottom of the hill. Turn left after 100m and follow signs for Vintgar. Alternatively, hop on one of the frequent buses to Podhom (10min., M-Sa 10 per day, €1.30) and follow the 1.5km route. From mid-June through September, **Alpetour** (☎04 532 0440) runs a bus to the trailhead (15min., 10am; one-way €2.50, round-trip €4.50). **Agency Kompas,** Ljubljanska c. 4, rents **bikes** (€3.50 per hr., €11 per day) and offers whitewater rafting trips. (☎00386 04 572 7500; www.kompas-bled.si. Rafting €25. Open M-Sa 8am-7pm, Su 8am-noon and 4-7pm. AmEx/MC/V.)

DAYTRIPS FROM BLED: LAKE BOHINJ (BOHINJSKO JEZERO). Although it is only 26km southwest of Bled, Bohinjsko Jezero (BOH-heen-sko YEH-zeh-roh) surpasses its famous neighbor in its largely untouched natural beauty. Protected by the borders of **Triglav National Park,** the larger glacial lake draws aquatic adventurers with its pristine waters, and the towering mountains rising out of the lake attract hikers who yearn to scale the summits. Trails are marked with a white circle inside a red circle; trail maps are available at the **tourist bureau,** Ribčev Laz 48 (☎574 6010; www.bohinj.si. Open July-Aug. M-Sa

A NATIONAL SAINT

The Slovenian people are not strangers to tumultuous change. Residents of Maribor watched Hitler speak in their main square during World War II, and they labored long hours in factories during their time as Yugoslavia's second most industrial city. Today, older residents struggle to adjust to capitalism, as tourists from around the world lounge in outdoor cafes. But through all the turbulence, Mariboreans have clung to two things: religion and national pride.

A son of Maribor and a national hero, Anton Slomšek (Slohmshek, 1800-62), speaks to both of these values. Catholics, who make up 70% of Maribor's current population, memorialized this first Slovenian bishop in Slomšek Square, the religious center of Maribor. In 1999, Pope John Paul II broke with tradition and canonized him not in Rome, but in his hometown–Maribor.

However, St. Slomšek's influence stretches far beyond church walls. He opened the first Slovenian-language school, produced textbooks, and strengthened national Slovenian education. In addition, he co-founded The Hermagoras Society, the oldest Slovene publishing house.

Pause and reflect on this man's memorial in Slomšek Square. By tirelessly advocating for his country and his faith, he has anchored Slovenians and helped them flourish, despite the unstable political landscape of the last centuries.

8am-8pm, Su 8am-7pm; Sept.-June M-Sa 8am-6pm, Su 9am-3pm), in Bohinjska Bistrica, a bigger town 6km east of the lake. A **Mercator** supermarket neighbors the tourist office. (☎572 9534. Open M-F 7am-8pm, Su 7am-5pm.) See the beautiful **Savica Waterfall** *(Slap Savica)*, at the Ukanc end of the lake. It is a 6km walk from the bus station up to the waterfall. If the hiking spirit compels you, head to the stunning **Black Lake** *(Črno Jezero)* at the base of the Julian Alps' highest peaks (1hr.). Although this is a fun climb, be aware that the hike is extremely steep; avoid going alone or bringing a heavy pack. Facing the small lake's shore, a trail to the right *(Dol Pod Stadorjem)* leads to **Mount Viševnik,** a grassy hillside that overlooks the small peaks. (*Buses run to Bohinjska Bistrica, the largest town in the area, 6km from the lake; from there, trains head to Ljubljana (2hr., 8 per day, €5.30) via Jesenice. Buses also run from Hotel Zlatorog in Ukanc to Ribčev Laz (10min., every hr., €1.30) and from Ribčev Laz to Bled (35min., 11-16 per day, €3.60), Bohinjska Bistrica (15min., every hr., €1.60), and Ljubljana (2hr., every hr., €8.30). Buses going to Bohinjsko Jezero (Lake Bohinj) stop at Hotel Jezero in Ribčev Laz or at Hotel Zlatorog in Ukanc.*)

MARIBOR ☎02

Surrounded by the wine-growing Piramida Hill, the slow Drava River, and the adventuresome ski haven of Pohorje, Maribor (MAHR-ee-bohr; pop. 110,000) brims with youthful energy, despite its deep history. Although second in size to Ljubljana, this 700-year-old university town exudes a provincial feel.

TRANSPORTATION. From the train station, Partizanska c. 50 (☎02 292 2100), **trains** run to Ljubljana (2½ hr., 12 per day; €7.47-8.91) and Ptuj (1hr., 9 per day, €2.71). The bus station, Mlinska 1, sends **buses** to Ljubljana (2½-3hr., 10 per day, €12) and Ptuj (40min., 2 per hr. until 9pm, €3.60).

ORIENTATION AND PRACTICAL INFORMATION. The majority of Maribor's sights lie in the city center, on the north shore of the Drava River; this makes it easy to explore the town by foot. Pick up a map from the train station or at the **tourist office** on Partizanska c. 6a. It's stocked with **maps** and brochures, and staff will help you book the cheapest sleeping option. (☎02 234 6611; www.maribor-tourism.si. Rooms €25-35. 90min. city tours W and F 10am, Su 11am; €5. Open M-F 9am-7pm, Sa 9am-5pm, Su 9am-noon.) From the train station, turn left and follow Partizanska past the large Franciscan **Church of Saint Mary** to Grajski trg, where you'll see the **Florian Column.** Turn left down

Vetrinska, and then turn right on Koroska c. to reach Glavni trg. From the main bus station turn right on Mlinska, follow it to Partizanska, and take a left. Try not to arrive on a Sunday; few businesses are open.

Banka Koper, located in the mall complex, Ulica Vita Kraigherja 5, has a 24hr. cash machine that accepts MC/V. The exchange office is open M-F 8am-4pm. Next door, the **post office** is open M-F 8am-7pm, Sa 8am-noon. For free **Internet,** head to **Kibla Multimedia Center,** ul. Kneza Koclja 9. Enter Narodni Dom and go through the large art space on the left (☎02 229 4012; www.kibla.org. Open July 15-Aug 15). The main square near the river, **Glavni Trg,** has Wi-Fi.

ACCOMMODATIONS AND FOOD. Across the river from the old town, about a 15 minute walk from the center lays **Dijaški Dom (HI) ❶,** 26 Junij, Železnikova 12. From the local bus station in front of the train staion, take bus #3 *(Brezje)* to the "Pokopališče" stop. Cross the street and walk a few paces to the right, then take the first left and follow the road as it curves. Past the Mercator supermarket, you'll see a building with "12" painted on the side. Tidy rooms and quiet environs make this the best deal in town. (☎02 480 1710. Free Internet. Open June 25-Aug. 25. Singles €15, doubles €25.) **Lollipop Hostel ❷,** Maistrova ul. 17, is a very small, homey hostel conveniently located in the center. The staff also offers tours of the city. (☎02 024 3160. Dorms €20. Free Wi-Fi. Breakfast included.) For traditional fare, head towards the old town. **Toti Rotov ❷,** Glavni trg 14, has savory set meals (€7) and a variety of international dishes—all served in a lovely 16th century townhouse. (☎02 228 7650; Entrees €3-15. Open M-Th 8am-midnight, F-Sa 8am-2pm. AmEx/MC/V.)

SIGHTS. As an important trade post between Vienna and the Adriatic, Maribor saw lots of international traffic during the middle ages. With a keen eye, observers can spot remnants of its complicated history. At various times, the locals lived underneath the Romans, Franciscan monks, the Hapsburgs, the Third Reich, communism, and finally capitalism. Starting from the tourist office, glance down Partizanska/Slovenska c., the key merchant road beginning in the Middle Ages. Next, behold the **Franciscan Church,** Maribor's one and only basilica. Fun fact: the bells which ring every hour were transformed into cannons during both world wars. Continuing down Partizanska c., enter the old town and visit **Maribor Castle** and its corresponding museum. Unfortunately, the castle is under renovation until 2015. Stop just before the castle and turn to the right to see the former location of Maribor's first castle, destroyed by lightning. In its place are **Freedom Square** *(Trg svobode)* and **Castle Square** *(Grajski Trg).* From Grajski Trg, continue down Slovenska ul. and make a left onto Gledaliska ul. This will lead to **Slomskov Trg.** Make sure to peek inside the beautiful **Maribor Cathedral,** Slomškov trg 20. (Open daily 6:30am-7pm. Free.) After leaving the church, look across the square to the opera house, Miklosiceva c. Opera aficionados from all over come here every year to watch traditionally performed operas. Take Postna ul. down towards the river to reach Maribor's main square, **Glavni Trg,** seat of the government buildings and the perfect place for a photo. Finally, continue down to the **Drava River.** Don't miss the oldest vine in the world *(Stara trta)*—400 years old and still bearing fruit. Finish up at the **museum,** Vojašniška 8, behind the vine to learn more about Maribor's wine making traditions. (☎02 251 5100. Open Tu-Su 10am-6pm. Free.)

SPAIN (ESPAÑA)

SPAIN

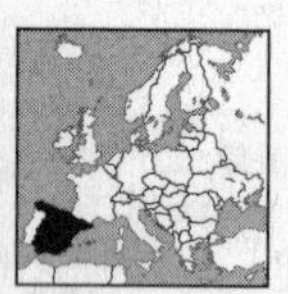

The fiery spirit of flamenco; the energy of artistic genius; the explosive merging of urban style and archaic tradition—this is Spain. Here, dry golden plains give way to rugged coastline, and modern architectural feats rise from ancient plazas. Explore winding medieval alleyways that lead to bustling city centers, or watch from a cafe as mulleted youths pass by. In Spain, there is always a reason to stay up late, and there is always time for an afternoon *siesta*.

DISCOVER SPAIN: SUGGESTED ITINERARIES

THREE DAYS. Soak in **Madrid's** (p. 896) art and culture as you walk through the **Retiro's** gardens and peruse the halls of the **Prado, Thyssen-Bornemisza,** and **Nacional Centro de Arte Reina Sofía.** By night, move from the *tapas* bars of Santa Ana to Malasaña and Chueca. Daytrip to **Segovia** (p. 910) or **El Escorial** (p. 907).

ONE WEEK. Begin in southern Spain, exploring the **Alhambra's** Moorish palaces in **Granada** (1 day; p. 924) and the mosque in **Córdoba** (1 day; p. 914). After two days in **Madrid,** travel northeast to **Barcelona** (2 days) and the beaches of **Costa Brava** (1 day; p. 947).

THREE WEEKS. Head to **Madrid** (3 days), with daytrips to **El Escorial** (1 day) and **Segovia** (1 day). Travel to **Córdoba** (2 days), and on to **Seville** (3 days; p. 917). Catch the bus to **Arcos de la Frontera** (1 day; p. 923) before heading south to charming **Málaga** (1 day; p. 928). Head inland to **Granada** (2 days), then seaward again to **Valencia** (1 day; p. 932) before traveling up the coast to **Barcelona** (3 days). Daytrip to the **Costa Brava** (1 day), taking in the **Teatre-Museu Dalí** and the **Casa-Museu Salvador Dalí.** End from Barcelona, heading to the beaches and tapas bars of **San Sebastián** (1 day; p. 952)

ESSENTIALS

FACTS AND FIGURES

OFFICIAL NAME: Kingdom of Spain.

CAPITAL: Madrid.

GOVERNMENT: Parliamentary monarchy.

MAJOR CITIES: Barcelona, Granada, Seville, Valencia.

POPULATION: 40,448,000.

LAND AREA: 500,500 sq. km.

TIME ZONE: GMT +1.

LANGUAGES: Spanish (Castilian), Basque, Catalan, Galician.

RELIGION: Roman Catholic (94%).

LARGEST PAELLA EVER MADE: 20m in diameter, this giant *paella* fed 100,000 people in 1992.

WHEN TO GO

Summer is high season in Spain, though in many parts of the country, *Semana Santa* and other festivals are particularly busy. Tourism peaks in August, when

the coastal regions overflow while inland cities empty out. Winter travel has the advantage of lighter crowds and lower prices, but sights reduce their hours.

DOCUMENTS AND FORMALITIES

EMBASSIES. Foreign embassies in Spain are in Madrid. Spanish embassies abroad include: **Australia:** 15 Arkana St., Yarralumla, ACT 2600; mailing address: P.O. Box 9076, Deakin ACT 2600 (☎+612 6273 35 55; www.mae.es/Embajadas/Canberra/es/Home). **Canada:** 74 Stanley Ave., Ottawa, ON K1M 1P4 (☎+1-613-747-2252; www.embaspain.ca). **Ireland:** 17 Merlyn Park, Ballsbridge, Dublin 4 (☎+353 1 269 1640; www.mae.es/embajadas/dublin). **New Zealand:** 56 Victoria Street, P.O.B. 24-150, Wellington 6142 (☎+64 4 913 1167; emb.wellington@maec.es). **UK:** 39 Chesham Pl., London SW1X 8SB (☎ +44 207 235 5555; embaspuk@mail.mae.es). **US:** 2375 Pennsylvania Ave. NW, Washington, D.C. 20037 (☎+1-202-728-2330; www.spainemb.org).

VISA AND ENTRY INFORMATION. EU citizens do not need a visa. Citizens of Australia, Canada, New Zealand, the US, and many Latin American countries do not need a visa for stays of up to 90 days, beginning upon entry into the EU's freedom-of-movement zone. For more info, see p. 14. For stays over 90 days, all non-EU citizens need visas, available at Spanish consulates (€100).

TOURIST SERVICES AND MONEY

TOURIST OFFICES. For general info, contact the **Instituto de Turismo de España,** Jose Lazaro Galdiano 6, 28071 Madrid (☎913 433 500; www.tourspain.es).

EMERGENCY	**Ambulance:** ☎061. **Fire:** ☎080. **Local Police:** ☎092. **National Police:** ☎091. **General Emergency:** ☎112.

SPAIN

MONEY. The **euro (€)** has replaced the **peseta** as the unit of currency in Spain. For more info, see p. 17. As a general rule, it's cheaper to exchange money in Spain than at home. **ATMs** usually have good exchange rates. In restaurants, all prices include a service charge. Satisfied customers occasionally toss in some spare change—usually no more than 5%—and while it is purely optional, **tipping** is becoming increasingly widespread in restaurants and other places that cater to tourists. Many people give train, airport, and hotel porters €1 per bag, while taxi drivers sometimes get 5-10%. **Bargaining** is only common at flea markets and with street vendors.

Spain has a 7% **value added tax** (**VAT;** in Spain, **IVA**) on restaurant meals and accommodations and a 16% VAT on retail goods. The prices listed in *Let's Go* include VAT. In an airport upon exiting the EU, non-EU citizens can claim a refund on the tax paid for goods purchased at participating stores. In order to qualify for a refund in a store, you must spend at least €50-100, depending on the shop; make sure to ask for a refund form when you pay. For more info on qualifying for a VAT refund, see p. 21.

BUSINESS HOURS. Almost all museums, shops, and churches close from 2-4pm or longer for an afternoon **siesta.** Most Spaniards eat lunch during their *siesta* (as well as nap), so restaurants open in the late afternoon. Shops and sights reopen at 3pm, and some may stay open until 8pm. Most restaurants will start serving dinner by 9pm, although eating close to midnight is very common in Spain. After midnight, the clubhopping commences. Increasingly, some large chains and offices are open all day, in large part due to an effort by the Spanish government to encourage a stronger economy and more "normal" business hours. It's still a safe bet that nearly every store will be closed on Sundays.

TRANSPORTATION

BY PLANE. Flights land mainly at **Barajas Airport** in Madrid (**MAD;** ☎913 93 60 00) and the **Barcelona International Airport** (**BCN;** ☎932 98 39 25). Contact AENA (☎902 40 47 04; www.aena.es) for info on flight times at most airports. See p. 46 for info on flying to Spain.

BY FERRY. Spain's islands are accessible by ferry; see the **Balearic Islands** (p. 958). Ferries are the least expensive way of traveling between Spain and Tangier or the Spanish enclave of **Ceuta** in Morocco. For more info see p. 57

BY TRAIN. Direct trains are available to Madrid and Barcelona from several European cities, including Geneva, CHE; Lisbon, POR; and Paris, FRA. Spanish trains are clean, relatively punctual, and reasonably priced. However, most train routes do tend to bypass small towns. Spain's national railway is **RENFE** (☎902 24 02 02; www.renfe.es). When possible, avoid *transvía*, *semi-directo*, or *correo* trains, as they are very slow. *Estrellas* are slow night trains with bunks and showers. *Cercanías* (commuter trains) go from cities to suburbs and nearby towns. There is no reason to buy a Eurail Pass if you plan to travel only within Spain. Trains are cheap, so a pass saves little money; moreover, buses are the most efficient means of traveling around Spain. Several Rail Europe passes cover travel within Spain. See www.raileurope.com for more info on the following passes. The **Spain Flexipass** ($186) offers three days of unlimited travel in a two-month period. The **Spain Rail 'n' Drive Pass** ($343) is good for three days of unlimited first-class train travel and two days of unlimited mileage in a rental car. The **Spain-Portugal Pass** offers three days or more of unlimited first-class travel in Spain and Portugal over a two-month period (from $341). For more info, see p. 50.

JUST SAY NO. If you are planning on traveling only within Spain (and Portugal), do not buy a **Eurail Pass.** Bus travel is usually the best option, and trains are less expensive than in the rest of Europe. A Eurail Pass makes sense only for those planning to travel in other European countries as well.

BY BUS. In Spain, buses are cheaper and have far more comprehensive routes than trains. Buses provide the only public transportation to many isolated areas. For those traveling primarily within one region, **buses are the best method of transportation.** Spain has numerous private companies and the lack of a centralized bus company may make itinerary planning difficult. Companies' routes rarely overlap, so it is unlikely that more than one will serve your intended destination. **Alsa** (☎913 27 05 40; www.alsa.es) serves Asturias, Castilla y León, Galicia, and Madrid, as well as international destinations including France, Germany, Italy, and Portugal. **Auto-Res** (☎902 02 00 52; www.auto-res.net) serves Castilla y León, Extremadura, Galicia, Valencia, and Portugal.

BY CAR. Spain's highway system connects major cities by four-lane *autopistas.* Speeders beware: police can "photograph" the speed and license plate of your car and issue a ticket without pulling you over. If you are pulled over, fines must be paid on the spot. **Gas** prices, €0.80-1.10 per liter, are lower than in many European countries but high by North American standards. Renting a car is cheaper than elsewhere in Europe. Spain accepts Canadian, EU, and US driver's licenses; otherwise, an International Driving Permit (IDP) is required. Try **Atesa** (☎902 10 01 01; www.atesa.es), Spain's largest rental agency. The automobile association is **Real Automóvil Club de España** (RACE; ☎902 40 45 45; www.race.es). For more on renting and driving a car, see p. 54.

BY THUMB. Hitchhikers report that Castilla and Andalucía are long, hot waits, and hitchhiking out of Madrid is virtually impossible. The Mediterranean coast and the islands are more promising; remote areas in the Balearics, Catalonia, or Galicia may be best accessible by hitchhiking. Although approaching people for rides at gas stations near highways and rest stops purportedly gets results, *Let's Go* does not recommend hitchhiking.

KEEPING IN TOUCH

PHONE CODES

Country code: 34. **International dialing prefix:** 00. Within Spain, dial city code + local number, even when dialing inside the city. For more info on how to place international calls, see **Inside Back Cover.**

EMAIL AND THE INTERNET. Email is easily accessible within Spain. Internet cafes are listed in most towns and all cities, and generally charge as little as €2 per hr. In small towns, if Internet is not listed, check the library or the tourist office for listings. For a list of internet cafes in Spain, consult www.cybercafes.com.

TELEPHONE. Whenever possible, use a prepaid phone card for international phone calls, as long-distance rates for national phone service are often very high. Find them at tobacconists. However, some public phones will only accept change. Mobile phones are an increasingly popular and economical option, costing as little as €30 (not including minutes). Major mobile carriers include **Movistar** and **Vodafone.** Direct-dial access numbers for calling out of Spain include: **AT&T Direct** (☎900 990 011); **British Telecom** (☎900 96 4495); **Canada Direct** (☎900 990 015); **Telecom New Zealand Direct** (☎900 990 064).

MAIL. Airmail *(por avión)* takes five to eight business days to reach Canada or the US; service is faster to the UK and Ireland and slower to Australia and New Zealand. Standard postage is €0.78 to North America. Surface mail *(por barco)* can take over a month, and packages take two to three months. Certified mail *(certificado)* is the most reliable way to send a letter or parcel and takes four to seven business days. Spain's overnight mail is not actually overnight, not worth the expense. To receive mail in Spain, have it delivered **Poste Restante.** Mail will go to the main post office unless you specify a subsidiary by street address. Address mail to be held according to the following example: Last Name, First Name; *Lista de Correos;* City; Postal Code; SPAIN; AIRMAIL.

ACCOMMODATIONS AND CAMPING

SPAIN	❶	❷	❸	❹	❺
ACCOMMODATIONS	under €18	€18-24	€25-34	€35-45	over €45

The cheapest and most basic options are *refugios*, *casas de huéspedes*, and *hospedajes*, while *pensiones* and *fondas* tend to be a bit nicer. All are essentially boarding houses with basic rooms, shared bath, and no A/C. Higher up the ladder but not necessarily more expensive, *hostales* generally have sinks in bedrooms and provide linens and lockers, while *hostal-residencias* are similar to hotels in overall quality. The government rates **hostales** on a two-star system; even establishments receiving one star are typically quite comfortable. The system also fixes **hostal** prices, posted in the lounge or main entrance. Prices invariably dip below the official rates in the low season (Sept.-May), so bargain away. **Red Española de Albergues Juveniles** (REAJ; www.reaj.com), the Spanish **Hostelling International** (HI) affiliate, runs more than 200 hostels year-round. Prices vary, but are generally €9-15 for guests under 26 and higher for those 26 and over. Breakfast is usually included; lunch and dinner are occasionally offered at an additional charge. Hostels usually have lockouts around 11am and have curfews between midnight and 3am. As a rule, don't expect much privacy—rooms typically have 4-20 beds in them. To reserve a bed in the high season (July-Aug. and during festivals), call at least a few weeks in advance. **Campgrounds** are generally the cheapest choice for two or more people. Most charge separate fees per person, per tent, and per car; others charge for a *parcela* (a small plot of land), plus per-person fees. Tourist offices can provide more info; pick up the *Guía de Campings* for a comprehensive guide.

FOOD AND DRINK

SPAIN	❶	❷	❸	❹	❺
FOOD	under €6	€6-10	€11-15	€16-20	over €20

Fresh, local ingredients are still an integral part of Spanish cuisine, varying according to each region's climate, geography, and history. The old Spanish saying holds true: "*Que comer es muy importante, porque de la panza, ¡nace la danza!*" (Eating is very important, because from the belly, dance is born!)

Spaniards start the day with a light breakfast *(desayuno)* of coffee or thick hot chocolate and a pastry. The main meal of the day *(comida)* consists of several courses and is typically eaten around 2 or 3pm. Dinner at home *(cena)* tends to be light. Dining out begins anywhere between 8pm and midnight. Bar-hopping for *tapas* is an integral part of the Spanish lifestyle. Some restaurants are "open" from 8am until 1 or 2am, but most serve meals only from 1pm or 2pm to 4pm and 8pm to midnight. Many restaurants offer a *plato combinado* (main course, side dish, bread, and sometimes a beverage) or a *menú del día* (two or three set dishes, bread, beverage, and dessert) for roughly €5-9. If you ask for a *menú*, this is what you may receive; *carta* is the word for menu.

Tapas (small dishes of savory meats and vegetables cooked according to local recipes) are quite tasty, and in most regions they are paired with beer or wine. *Raciones* are large *tapas* served as entrees; *bocadillos* are sandwiches. Spanish specialties include *tortilla de patata* (potato omelet), *jamón serrano* (smoked ham), *calamares fritos* (fried squid), *arroz* (rice), *chorizo* (spicy sausage), *gambas* (shrimp), *lomo de cerdo* (pork loin), *paella* (steamed saffron rice with seafood, chicken, and vegetables), and *gazpacho* (cold tomato-based soup). Vegetarians should learn the phrase "*yo soy vegetariano*" (I am a vegetarian) and specify this means no *jamón* (ham) or *atún* (tuna). A normal-sized draft beer is a *caña de cerveza;* a *tubo* is a little bigger. A *calimocho* is a mix of Coca-Cola and red wine, while *sangria* is a drink of red wine, sugar, brandy, and fruit. *Tinto de verano* is a lighter version of *sangria:* red wine and Fanta. *Café solo* means black coffee; add a touch of milk for a *nube;* a little more and it's a *café cortado;* half milk and half coffee makes a *café con leche.*

HOLIDAYS AND FESTIVALS

Holidays: New Year's Day (Jan. 1); Epiphany (Jan. 6); Maundy Thursday (Apr. 9, 2009); Good Friday (Apr. 10, 2009); Easter (Apr. 11-12); Labor Day (May 1); Assumption (Aug. 15); National Day (Oct. 12); All Saints' Day (Nov. 1); Constitution Day (Dec. 6); Feast of the Immaculate Conception (Dec. 8); Christmas (Dec. 25); New Year's Eve (Dec. 31).

Festivals: Almost every town in Spain has several festivals. In total, there are more than 3000. Nearly everything closes during festivals. All of Spain celebrates *Carnaval* the week before Ash Wednesday (Feb. 25, 2009); the biggest parties are in Catalonia and Cádiz. During the annual festival of *Las Fallas* in mid-Mar., Valencia honors St. Joseph with parades, fireworks, and the burning of effigies. The entire country honors the Holy Week, or *Semana Santa* (Mar. 16-22). Seville's *Feria de Abril* has events showcasing many different Andalusian traditions, including bullfighting and flamenco (Apr. 28-May 3, 2009). *San Fermín* (The Running of the Bulls) takes over Pamplona July 6-14 (see p. 950). For more information, see www.tourspain.es or www.gospain.org/fiestas.

BEYOND TOURISM

Spain offers volunteer opportunities from protecting dolphins on the Costa del Sol to fighting for immigrants' rights. Those seeking long-term work in Spain should consider teaching English. Short-term jobs are available in the restaurant, hotel, and tourism industries, and are typically held by those without permits. For info on opportunities across Europe, see **Beyond Tourism**, p. 60.

Enforex, Alberto Aguilera, 26, 28015 Madrid, Spain (☎915 943 776; www.enforex.com). Offers 20 Spanish programs in Spain, ranging from 1 week to a year in duration. Opportunities in 12 Spanish cities, including Granada, Sevilla, Barcelona, and Madrid.

Ecoforest, Apdo. 29, Coin 29100 Málaga, Spain (☎661 07 99 50; www.ecoforest.org). Fruit farm and vegan community in southern Spain that uses environmental education to develop a sustainable lifestyle for residents. Visitors are welcome to stay, contributing €5-15 per day towards operating costs.

MADRID ☎91

After Franco's death in 1975, young *Madrileños* celebrated their liberation from totalitarian repression with raging all-night parties across the city. This revelry became so widespread that it defined an era, and *la Movida* (the Movement) is now recognized as a world-famous nightlife renaissance. The newest generation has kept the spirit of *la Movida* alive—Madrid is truly a city that never sleeps. While neither as funky as Barcelona nor as charming as Seville, Madrid is the political, intellectual, and cultural capital of Spain, balancing its history and heritage with the festive insomnia it has come to embrace.

INTERCITY TRANSPORTATION

Flights: All flights land at **Aeropuerto Internacional de Barajas** (**MAD;** ☎902 40 47 04), 20min. northeast of Madrid. The **Barajas metro line** connects the airport to all of Madrid (€2). **Bus-Aeropuerto** #200 (look for "EMT" signs) runs to the city center (☎902 50 78 50. 4-6 per hr., €1.) and stops in the metro station **Avenida de América.**

Trains: 2 *largo recorrido* (long distance) **RENFE** stations, **Atocha** and **Chamartín,** connect Madrid to the rest of Europe. Call RENFE (☎902 24 02 02; www.renfe.es).

Estación Chamartín (☎91 300 6969). M: Chamartín. Bus #5 runs to and from Puerta del Sol (45min.). Alternatively, take a red Cercanías train (15min., 6 per hr., €1.05) from M: Atocha Renfe. Chamartín services both international and domestic destinations in the northeast and south. Major destinations include: **Barcelona** (9hr., 10pm, €40-53); **Bilbao** (6hr., 2 per day, €40-53); **Lisbon, POR** (9hr., 10:45pm, €54); **Paris, FRA** (13hr., 7pm, €115-130). Chamartín offers services, including a **tourist office,** Vestíbulo, Puerta 14 (☎91 315 9976; open M-Sa 8am-8pm, Su 8am-2pm), accommodations service, car rental, currency exchange, luggage storage (*consignas;* €2.40-4.50; open daily 7am-11pm), **police,** and **post office.**

Estación de Atocha (☎91 506 6137). M: Atocha Renfe. Domestic service only. AVE (☎91 506 6137) has high-speed service to southern Spain, including **Seville** (2hr., 22 per day, €67-74) via **Córdoba** (1hr., €55-61) and **Barcelona** (3hr., 20 per day, €105-124).

Buses: Many private companies, each with its own station and set of destinations, serve Madrid. Most pass through the Estación Sur de Autobuses.

Estación Sur de Autobuses: C. Méndez Álvaro (☎91 468 4200; www.estaciondeautobuses.com). M: Méndez Álvaro. Info booth open daily 6am-1am. **ATMs** and **luggage storage** (€1.30 per bag per day) available. Serves over 40 bus companies, with destinations all over Spain, including **Alicante, Santiago de Compostela, Cuenca, Badajoz, Valencia,** and **Toledo.**

LOCAL TRANSPORTATION

Metro: Madrid's metro is safe, speedy, and spotless (☎902 44 44 03; www.metromadrid.es). Metro **tickets** cost €1; a metrobus (ticket of 10 rides valid for the metro and bus) is €6.70. Buy them at machines in any metro stop, *estanco* (tobacco shop), or newsstand. Also available are 1-, 2-, 3-, 5-, and 7-day **unlimited ride** tickets (*abono turístico;* €4-40). Hold onto your ticket until you leave the metro or face a fine. Spanish-language **bus** info ☎91 406 8810. Buses run 6am-11pm. Bus fares are the same as metro fares and tickets are interchangeable. *Búho* (owl) is the **night bus** service (2 buses per hr. midnight-3am, 1 per hr. 3-6am. Look for buses N1-N24.)

Taxis: Call **Radio Taxi Independiente** (☎91 405 5500), **Radio Taxi Madrid** (☎91 782 0091), or **Teletaxi** (☎91 371 3711). A *libre* sign in the window or a green light indicates availability. Base fare is €1.85 (€2.90 after 10pm), plus €0.87-1 per km from 6am-10pm and €1-1.10 per km from 10pm-6am. Teletaxi charges a flat rate of €1 per km.

SPAIN

ORIENTATION

Marking the epicenter of both Madrid and Spain, **Kilómetro 0** in **Puerta del Sol** ("Sol" for short) is within walking distance of most sights. To the west are the **Plaza Mayor,** the **Palacio Real,** and the **Ópera district.** East of Sol lies **Huertas,** the heart of cafe, museum, and theater life. The area north of Sol is bordered by **Gran Vía,** which runs northwest to **Plaza de España.** North of Gran Vía are three club- and bar-hopping districts, linked by Calle de Fuencarral: **Malasaña, Bilbao,** and **Chueca.** Modern Madrid is beyond Gran Vía and east of Malasaña and Chueca. East of Sol, the tree-lined thoroughfares **Paseo de la Castellana, Paseo de Recoletos,** and **Paseo del Prado** split Madrid in two, running from **Atocha** in the south to **Plaza Castilla** in the north, passing the Prado, the fountains of **Plaza de Cibeles,** and **Plaza de Colón.** Madrid is safer than many European cities, but Sol, Pl. de España, Pl. Chueca, and Pl. Dos de Mayo are still intimidating at night. Travel in groups, avoid the parks and quiet streets after dark, and watch for thieves and pickpockets in crowds.

PRACTICAL INFORMATION

Tourist Offices: Madrid Tourism Centre, Pl. Mayor 27 (☎91 588 1636; www.esmadrid.com). M: Sol. **Branches** at Estación Chamartín, Estación de Atocha, and the airport. English and French usually spoken. All open daily 9:30am-8pm. Regional office of the **Comunidad de Madrid,** C. del Duque de Medinaceli 2 (☎91 429 4951; www.madrid.org). M: Banco de España. Open M-Sa 8am-8pm, Su 9am-2pm. Pick up the *Guia del Ocio* (€1) or *In Madrid* for info on city events and establishments.

Embassies: Australia, Pl. del Descubridor Diego de Ordás 3, 2nd fl. (☎91 353 6600; www.spain.embassy.gov.au). **Canada,** Núñez de Balboa 35 (☎91 423 3250; www.canada-es.org). **Ireland,** Po. Castellana 46, 4th fl. (☎91 436 4093). **New Zealand,** Pl. de la Lealtad 2, 3rd fl. (☎91 523 0226). **UK,** Po. de Recoletos 7-9 (☎91 524 9700; www.ukinspain.com). **US,** C. Serrano 75 (☎91 587 2200; www.embusa.es).

Currency Exchange: In general, credit and ATM cards offer the best exchange rates. Avoid changing money at airport and train station counters; they tend to charge exorbitant commissions. **Banco Santander Central Hispano** charges no commission on **AmEx Travelers Cheques** up to €300. Main branch, Po. Castellana 7 (☎91 558 1111). M: Sol. Follow C. San Jerónimo to Pl. Canalejas. Open Apr.-Sept. M-F 8:30am-2pm; Oct.-Mar. M-F 8:30am-2pm, Sa 8:30am-1pm. **Banks** usually charge 1-2% commission (min.

A
B
C
Centro Cultural Conde Duque
TO C. GALILEO (650m)
TO MONCLOA, MUSEO DE AMERICA (1.4km), AND EL PARDO
VENTURA RODRÍGUEZ
Motocicletas Antonio Castro
Iglesia de San Marcos
Princesa
ARGÜELLES
Torre de Madrid
Edificio de España
Museo Cerralbo
TO TEMPLO DE DEBOD (225m)
PL. DE ESPAÑA
PLAZA DE ESPAÑA
Atesa Car Rental
Jardines Ferraz
TO CAMPO DEL MORO (400m)
Jardines de Sabatini
Convento de la Encarnación
Jardines Cabo Noval
Palacio Real
PL. DEL ORIENTE
Teatro Real
Catedral de Ntra. Sra. de la Almudena
Jardines Lepanto
TO HOSPITAL DE MADRID (600m)
PL. DEL DOS DE MAYO
NOVICIADO
MALASAÑA
Gran Vía
GRAN VÍA
SANTO DOMINGO
PL. DE SANTO DOMINGO
CALLAO
PL. DEL CALLAO
Casa del Libro
Convento de las Descalzas Reales
PL. SAN MARTÍN
PL. DE LAS DESCALZAS
ÓPERA
PL. DE ISABEL II
El Corte Inglés
SOL
PUERTA DEL SOL
CENTRO
PL. MAYOR
Torre de los Lujanes
Ayuntamiento
PL. DE LA VILLA
PL. DE SAN MIGUEL
Casa de los Lujanes
Casa de Cisneros
Santa Cruz
PL. DE SANTA CRUZ
PL. JACINTO BENAVENTE
Jardines de las Vistillas
PL. DE LA PAJA
Iglesia de San Pedro
San Andrés
Museo de San Isidro
Champion Supermarket
Catedral de San Isidro
PL. SEGOVIA NUEVA
LA LATINA
PL. DE HUMILLADERO
PL. DE LA CEBADA
TIRSO DE MOLINA
PL. TIRSO DE MOLINA
Filmoteca Española
PL. DE CASCORRO
LA LATINA
PL. DEL GENERAL VARA DEL RAY
El Rastro
TO GLORIETA PUERTA DE TOLEDO (190m), ESTADIO VICENTE CALDERON (1.6km)
C. Mayor
C. de Arenal
C. de Bailén
C. de Toledo
C. de Segovia
Gran Vía de San Francisco
C. de San Bernardo
Cuesta de San Vicente
C. de la Princesa
C. de Preciados
C. de la Montera
C. de Atocha
C. de Embajadores
C. de la Ribera de Curtidores
C. del Duque de Alba
C. de Fuencarral
C. de Hortaleza

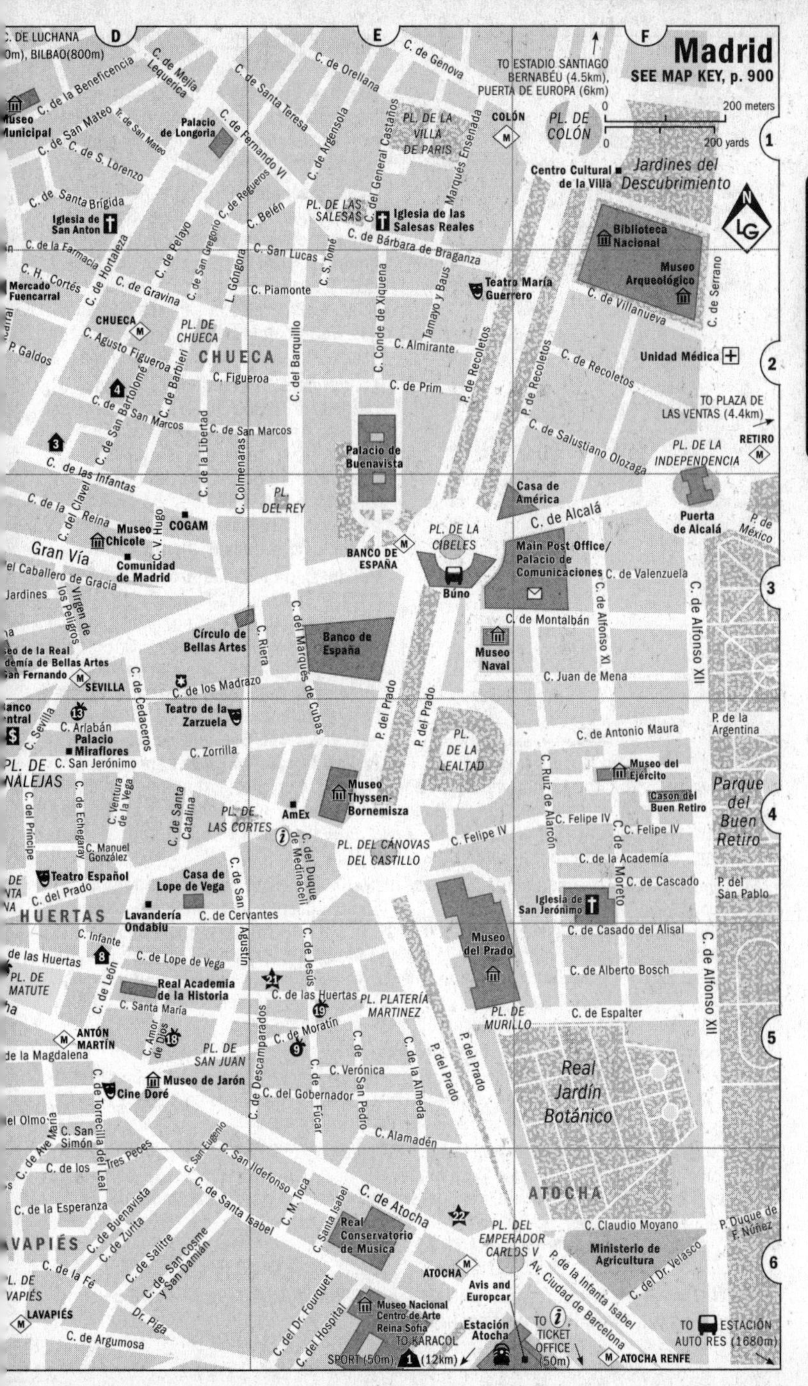
Madrid
SEE MAP KEY, p. 900
D
E
F
1
2
3
4
5
6
200 meters
200 yards
TO ESTADIO SANTIAGO BERNABÉU (4.5km), PUERTA DE EUROPA (6km)
C. DE LUCHANA
0m), BILBAO(800m)
TO PLAZA DE LAS VENTAS (4.4km)
COLÓN
PL. DE COLÓN
Jardines del Descubrimiento
Centro Cultural de la Villa
Biblioteca Nacional
Museo Arqueológico
Unidad Médica
RETIRO
PL. DE LA INDEPENDENCIA
Puerta de Alcalá
Museo Municipal
Palacio de Longoria
Iglesia de San Anton
Mercado Fuencarral
CHUECA
PL. DE CHUECA
CHUECA
PL. DE LA VILLA DE PARIS
PL. DE LAS SALESAS
Iglesia de las Salesas Reales
Teatro María Guerrero
Palacio de Buenavista
PL. DEL REY
COGAM
Museo Chicole
Comunidad de Madrid
Gran Vía
PL. DE LA CIBELES
BANCO DE ESPAÑA
Búho
Casa de América
Main Post Office/ Palacio de Comunicaciones
Círculo de Bellas Artes
Banco de España
Museo Naval
Museo de la Real Academia de Bellas Artes San Fernando
SEVILLA
Teatro de la Zarzuela
Palacio Miraflores
PL. DE LA LEALTAD
Museo del Ejército
Casón del Buen Retiro
Parque del Buen Retiro
PL. DE CANALEJAS
PL. DE LAS CORTES
AmEx
Museo Thyssen-Bornemisza
PL. DEL CÁNOVAS DEL CASTILLO
Teatro Español
Casa de Lope de Vega
HUERTAS
Lavandería Ondablu
Iglesia de San Jerónimo
Museo del Prado
PL. DE MATUTE
Real Academia de la Historia
PL. PLATERÍA MARTINEZ
ANTÓN MARTÍN
PL. DE SAN JUAN
PL. DE MURILLO
Real Jardín Botánico
Museo de Jarón
Cine Doré
ATOCHA
LAVAPIÉS
PL. DE LAVAPIÉS
LAVAPIÉS
Real Conservatorio de Música
PL. DEL EMPERADOR CARLOS V
ATOCHA
Avis and Europcar
Ministerio de Agricultura
Museo Nacional Centro de Arte Reina Sofía
Estación Atocha
TO KARACOL SPORT (50m)
(12km)
TO TICKET OFFICE (50m)
ATOCHA RENFE
TO ESTACIÓN AUTO RES (1680m)
C. de Génova
C. de Orellana
C. de Santa Teresa
C. de Fernando VI
C. de Argensola
C. del General Castaños
Marqués Ensenada
C. de la Beneficencia
C. de Mejía Lequerica
C. de San Mateo
C. de S. Lorenzo
C. de Santa Brígida
C. de Regueros
C. Belén
C. de Bárbara de Braganza
C. de la Farmacia
C. de Hortaleza
C. de Pelayo
C. de San Gregorio
L. Góngora
C. San Lucas
C. S. Tomé
C. H. Cortés
C. de Gravina
C. Piamonte
C. Conde de Xiquena
Tamayo y Baus
P. de Recoletos
C. de Villanueva
C. de Serrano
C. Almirante
C. de Recoletos
C. Agusto Figueroa
C. de Barbieri
C. Figueroa
C. del Barquillo
C. de Prim
P. Galdos
C. de San Bartolomé
C. de San Marcos
C. de la Libertad
C. Colmenaras
C. de Salustiano Olozaga
C. de las Infantas
C. del Clavel
C. de la Reina
C. V. Hugo
C. de Alcalá
P. de México
C. de Valenzuela
C. de Alfonso XI
C. de Alfonso XII
C. Caballero de Gracia
Virgen de los Peligros
C. Riera
C. del Marqués de Cubas
C. de Montalbán
C. de Cedaceros
C. de los Madrazo
C. Juan de Mena
P. del Prado
C. Sevilla
C. Arlabán
C. Zorrilla
C. de Antonio Maura
P. de la Argentina
C. San Jerónimo
C. Ruiz de Alarcón
C. del Príncipe
C. de Echegaray
C. Ventura de la Vega
C. de Santa Catalina
C. Manuel González
C. de San Agustín
C. del Duque de Medinaceli
C. Felipe IV
C. de Moreto
C. de la Academía
C. de Cascado
P. del San Pablo
C. del Prado
C. de Cervantes
C. de Casado del Alisal
C. Infante
C. de las Huertas
C. de Lope de Vega
C. de Jesús
C. de Alberto Bosch
C. de León
C. Santa María
C. de las Huertas
C. de Moratín
C. Amor de Dios
C. de Descamparados
C. de Espalter
C. de la Magdalena
C. Verónica
C. de San Pedro
C. de la Almeda
C. de Torrecilla del Leal
C. del Gobernador
C. de Fúcar
C. Alamadén
C. San Simón
C. de Ave María
C. del Olmo
C. de los Tres Peces
C. San Eugenio
C. San Ildefonso
C. M. Toca
C. de Santa Isabel
C. de Atocha
C. Santa Isabel
C. de la Esperanza
C. de Buenavista
C. de Zurita
C. de Salitre
C. de San Cosme y San Damián
C. de la Fé
Dr. Piga
C. de Argumosa
C. del Dr. Fourquet
C. del Hospital
C. Claudio Moyano
P. de la Infanta Isabel
Av. Ciudad de Barcelona
C. del Dr. Velasco
P. Duque de F. Núñez

SPAIN

SPAIN

Madrid
SEE MAP, p. XXX

ACCOMMODATIONS

Camping Alpha,	1	E6
Cat's Hostel,	2	C5
Hostal Don Juan,	3	D2
Hostal R. Arantza,	4	D2
Hostal Oriente,	5	B3
Hostal Santillan,	6	B2
Hostel Miguel Ángela,	7	C4
La Posada de Huertas,	8	D5

FOOD

Arrocería Gala,	9	E5
Café-Botillería Manuela,	10	C1
Casa Alberto,	11	D5
El Estragón Vegetariano,	12	A5
La Finca de Susana,	13	D4
La Granja de Said,	14	C1
Inshala,	15	A4
El Mejillón de Madrid,	16	C4
Restaurante Casa Granada,	17	C5
La Sanabresa,	18	D5
Taberna Maceira,	19	E5

NIGHTLIFE

Joy Eslava,	20	B4
Teatro Kapital,	21	E5
Trocha,	22	E6

charge €3). Booths in Sol and Gran Vía are not a good deal.

Luggage Storage: At the airport (€3.70 for the first day, €4.78 per day for the next two weeks) and bus and train stations (€2.75 per bag per day).

GLBT Resources: Pick up a free guide to gay nightlife in Spain called *Shanguide*. The **Colectivo de Gais y Lesbianas de Madrid (COGAM),** C. Puebla, 9 (☎91 522 4517; www.cogam.org), M: Callao, provides a wide range of services and activities. Reception M-Sa 5-10pm. Open M-Th 10am-2pm and 5-8pm, F 10am-2pm.

Laundromat: Lavandería Ondablu, C. León, 3 (☎91 369 50 71). M: Antón Martín, Sol, or Sevilla. Wash €3.50, dry €1. Also in most hostels; wash and dry €5. Open M-F 9:30am-10pm, Sa 10:30am-7pm. Also at C. Hortaleza, 84 (☎91 531 28 73). M: Chueca. €4.50 each for wash and dry. Open daily 9:30am-10:30pm.

Police: C. de los Madrazos 9 (☎91 322 1160). M: Sevilla. From C. de Alcalá, take a right onto C. Cedacneros and a left onto C. de los Madrazos. Open daily 9am-2pm. To report crimes committed in the **metro,** go to the office in the Sol station. **Policía Municipal,** C. Montera 18, has staff 24hr. **Servicio de Atención al Turista Extranjero (SATE)** are police who deal exclusively with tourists; help with administrative formalities, reporting the crime, canceling credit cards, contacting embassies and family members, and finding lost objects. (C. Leganitos, 19. ☎91 548 85 37 for the office or ☎902 102 112 to report a crime. M: Plaza de España. Open daily 9am-10pm.)

Medical Services: In a medical emergency, dial ☎061 or 112. **Hospital de Madrid,** Pl. del Conde del Valle Suchil 16 (☎91 447 6600; www.hospitaldemadrid.com). **Hospital Ramón y Cajal,** Ctra. Colmenar Viejo, km 9100 (☎91 336 8000). Bus #135 from Pl. de Castilla. For non-emergencies, go to **Unidad Médica,** C. del Conde de Aranda 1, 1st fl. (☎91 435 1823; www.unidadmedica.com). M: Serrano or Retiro. Regular personnel on duty M-F 9am-8pm, Sa 10am-1pm. Initial visit €110, students €75. AmEx/MC/V. Embassies and consulates keep lists of English-speaking doctors.

Internet Access: Internet cafes are everywhere. While the average is €2 per hr., small shops in apartments charge even less, so keep a lookout. Internet is often free in hostels. **Kioscocity,** C. Montera 47, above the Argentine bar/convenience store. €1 for 15 min., €1.50 for 30 min., €2 per hour. Open daily 9am-2am.

Post Office: Palacio de Comunicaciones, C. Alcalá 51, on Pl. de Cibeles (☎902 19 71 97; www.correos.es). M: Banco de España. Fax and *Lista de Correos*. Windows open M-Sa 8:30am-9:30pm, Su 8:30am-2pm for stamp purchases. **Postal Code:** 28080.

ACCOMMODATIONS

Make reservations for summer visits. Expect to pay €15-50 per person, depending on location, amenities, and season.

EL CENTRO: SOL, ÓPERA, AND PLAZA MAYOR

Hostel Miguel Ángel, Pl. Celenque, 1, 4th fl. (☎91 522 23 55; www.hostelmiguelangel.com), one block up off C. Arenal. M: Sol or Callao. The cleanest "backpacker hostel" around and the best deal in the centro. Immaculate rooms have clean, toy-like blue and yellow beds with bright curtains and comforters. Communal bathrooms are big and very clean. Sheets, safe, and breakfast included. Wi-Fi available. English spoken. Make reservations. Beds €18-21; triple €70. ❷

Hostal Oriente, C. de Arenal, 23, 1st fl. (☎91 548 03 14). M: Ópera. Elegance at a low price. Rooms have magnificently clean white tile; creamy peach walls and linens. Glass-enclosed balconies add breeze but an uninspiring view. 17 rooms have TV, phone, A/C, and bath. Reserve ahead of time. Singles €43; doubles €60; triples €82. MC/V. ❹

HUERTAS

Cat's Hostel, C. Cañizares, 6 (☎91 369 28 07; www.catshostel.com). M: Antón Martín. This renovated 18th-century palace features clean dorms (2-16 beds), small doubles with private baths, a patio area with a fountain and a stained-glass skylight, bar, and cafe. Great community and awesome cave-like bar in the basement. Breakfast, luggage storage, and Internet access included. Laundry €5 wash and dry. Reserve ahead—it fills up quickly. Dorms €20; doubles with bath €44. MC/V. ❷

La Posada de Huertas, C. Huertas, 21 (☎91 429 55 26; www.posadadehuertas.com). M: Antón Martín or Sol. Rooms for 4 or 8 are well kept with comfortable beds. Spotless bathrooms. Kitchen, Wi-Fi, and breakfast included. €5 wash and dry. Check-out 10:30am. Luggage storage. Beds from €18; singles €50; doubles €70. MC/V. ❷

GRAN VÍA AND CAMPING

Hostal Santillan, Gran Vía, 64, 8th fl. (☎91 548 23 28; www.hostalsantillan.com) M: Pl. de España. Take the elevator to the top of this gorgeous building. Leaf-patterned curtains and wooden furniture give rooms a warm feel. All have shower, sink, TV, and fan. A little more can get you a bath and much bigger room (by half); explore the options. Singles €30-€35; doubles €55; triples €72. MC/V. ❸

Camping Alpha (☎91 695 80 69; www.campingalpha.com). On a tree-lined site 12½km down Ctra. de Andalucía in Getafe. M: Legazpi. From the metro, walk down Vado Santa Catalina, cross the bridge, and bear right. Take the green bus #447, which stops across from the Museo de Jamón (10min., every 20-30min. 6am-10pm, €1.25). Ask for the Camp Alpha stop. Cross the footbridge and walk 1½km back toward Madrid along the busy highway; follow signs. Welcoming reception, paved roads, pool, tennis courts, showers, and laundry. Oct-May €5.44 per person; June-Sept. €6.80 per person. €7 per tent and per car. Seasonally (see dates above), bungalows for 1-2 €52/63; for 3-4 €79/94; for 5 €85-100. IVA not included. ❶

MALASAÑA AND CHUECA

Hostal Don Juan, Pl. Vasquez de Mella, 1, 2nd fl. (☎91 522 31 01). M: Chueca. Luxury fit for its romancing namesake. Chinese vases, wall tapestries, and old wooden chests fill the lobby, adjacent to a modern Art Deco common room with sofas and chandeliers. Rooms come with beautiful wooden flooring and hand-carved wooden furniture, A/C, TV, and gleaming bath. Singles €38; doubles €53; triples €70. MC/V. ❹

Hostal R. Arantza, C. San Bartolomé, 7. 1st fl. M: Chueca. Dark wooden doors and brown leather everywhere give the feeling of a classy old professor's study. Airy rooms with pink sheets and leafy newly-tiled balconies. Communal showers and private showers are very clean. Singles €35, with shower €40; doubles €40/45. Cash only. ❸

SPAIN

FOOD

In Madrid, it's not hard to fork it down without forking over too much. Most restaurants offer a *menú del día* (€9-11), which includes bread, one drink, and a choice of appetizer, main course, and dessert. Many small eateries cluster on **Calles Echegaray, Ventura de la Vega,** and **Manuel Fernández González** in Huertas. **Chueca** is filled with *bars de cañas* (small beer from the tap), which serve complimentary *tapas*. The streets west of **Calle Fuencarral** in Gran Vía are lined with cheap restaurants, while **Bilbao** has affordable ethnic cuisine. Linger in Madrid's cafes to absorb the sights of the city; you won't be bothered with the check until you ask. Keep in mind the following words for quick, cheap *madrileño* fare: *bocadillo* (a sandwich on half a baguette; €2-3); *ración* (a large *tapa* served with bread; €3-6); and *empanada* (a puff pastry with meat fillings; €1.30-2). The *Guía del Ocio* has a complete listing of Madrid's vegetarian options under the section "Otras Cocinas." **Dia%** and **Champion** are the cheapest supermarket chains; smaller markets are open later but are more expensive.

Arrocería Gala, C. de Moratín, 22 (☎91 429 25 62; www.paellas-gala.com). M: Antón Martín. Pastoral Spanish scenes of bulls on hillsides are gracefully overlaid in vine and shadows from the gorgeous chandeliers. The specialty *paellas* (€10 per person) are second to none. Quality *sangria* €10 per pitcher. Reserve ahead on weekends. Open Tu-Su 1-5pm and 9pm-1:30am. Cash only. ❸

La Finca de Susana, C. Arlaban (☎91 369 35 57; lafinca-restaurant.com). M: Sevilla. Simple but very elegant dining at shockingly low prices. The beef and arugula sushi (€7.80) is one of countless top-notch plates. Arrive early to avoid the line that forms down the street. Also runs Bazaar Restaurante in Malasana y Chueca. Open daily 1-3:45pm and 8:30-11:45pm. AmEx/MC/V. ❷

La Granja de Said, C. de San Andrés, 11 (☎91 532 87 93). M: Tribunal or Bilbao. Moorish tracery in the doorways, beautiful tiling, and the dim glow of light through lamps and coverings brings the Middle East to Chueca. Gorge, then puff peacefully on hookah (€8). Tabbouleh salad €6. Falafel plate €7. Open daily 1pm-2am. MC/V. ❷

El Estragón Vegetariano, Pl. de la Paja, 10 (☎91 365 89 82; www.guiadelocio.com/estragonvegetariano). M: La Latina. This unobtrusive restaurant, with its quiet decor and patio feel, would blush at any superlatives we could give it, but its vegetarian delights could convince even the most die-hard carnivores to switch teams. *Menús* (M-F €10, Sa-Su and evenings €25). Open daily 1:30-4pm and 8pm-midnight. AmEx/MC/V. ❸

La Sanabresa, C. Amor de Dios, 12 (☎91 429 03 38). M: Antón Martín. Cheap dishes ensure there's a loud line of locals out the door. The *carnes* (€5) and enormous vegetable plates (€2.50) are good deals. Open Tu-Su 1-4pm and 8:30-11pm. MC/V. ❶

El Mejillón de Madrid, Pasaje de Matheu, 4, just off Espoz y Mina. No-frills seafood under umbrellas in the street on Madrid's shellfish row. Try the heaping plate of mussels (€8), the restaurant's namesake, or the plate of *paella* (€25) for two or more. Four orders of *raciones* (€4-8) bring a free jug of *sangría* for up to 4 people—a sweet deal. Open M-Th and Su 11:30am-12:30am, Th-Sa 11:30am-1:30am. Cash only. ❷

Taberna Maceira, C. de Jesús, 7 (☎91 429 15 84), also C. Huertas, 66 (☎914 29 58 18). M: Antón Martín. The yellow-green walls, wooden panelling and grog barrels make this funky seafood place feel like a psychedelic pirate ship. Try the *mejillones Maceira* (mussels in cream sauce; €5). Open M 8pm-12:45am, Tu-F 1-4:15pm and 8:30pm-12:45am, Sa-Su 1-4:45pm and 8:30pm-1:30am. Cash only. ❸

Inshala, C. de la Amnistía, 10 (☎91 548 26 32). M: Ópera. Perfect for a fancy date, but cheap enough for a backpacker's meal. Moroccan decor, but decidedly eclectic international fare, ranging from Japanese to Mexican. Weekday lunch *menú* €9. Dinner €12-20. Reservations strongly recommended. Open in summer M-Th noon-5pm and 8pm-1am, F-Sa noon-5pm and 8pm-2am; in winter M-Sa noon-2am. MC/V. ❸

TAPAS

Not long ago, bartenders in Madrid covered *(tapar)* drinks with saucers to keep away the flies. Later, servers began putting little sandwiches on top of the saucers, which became known as "*tapas.*" Hopping from bar to bar gobbling *tapas* is an alternative to a full sit-down meal. Most *tapas* bars (*tascas* or *tabernas*) are open noon-4pm and 8pm-midnight; many are on **Plaza Santa Ana** and **Plaza Mayor** as well as north of Gran Vía in Chueca.

Casa Alberto, C. de las Huertas, 18 (☎91 429 93 56; www.casaalberto.es). M: Antón Martín. The manual-wash bar and the shanks hanging from the walls are throwbacks in one of Madrid's oldest establishments, founded in 1827. It's the place to be, so getting a table during the bar's bustling meal hours can be difficult. Sweet vermouth (€1.45) is served with original house tapas. Try the delicious *gambas al ajillo* (shrimp with garlic) or the *patatas ali-oli* (€4.50). Open Tu-Sa noon-5:30pm and 8pm-1:30am. MC/V. ❷

Restaurante Casa Granada, C. Doctor Cortezo, 17, 6th fl. (☎91 420 08 25). The unmarked door on the left side of C. Doctor Cortezo as you head downhill is easy to miss, but the experience of the rooftop *tapas* terrace at the top is hard to forget. Come around 8pm and stay for the sunset, but don't forget to put your name on the outdoor seating list when you arrive. *Cañas* of beer (€2.20) come with *tapas. Raciones* €6.50-€8. Open M-Sa noon-midnight, Su noon-9pm. MC/V. ❷

Café-Botillería Manuela, C. de San Vicente Ferrer, 29 (☎91 531 70 37; www.manuelacafe.com). M: Tribunal. Old-world Parisian café with gold taps and golden trim with a delicious modern touch–the player piano is stacked with everyone's favorite board games. Enjoy the conversation over your *caña* (€2.50). *Tapas* €3-8. Cocktails €6. Live music last Sa of every month, 9:30pm. Open June-Aug. M-Th 6pm-2am, F-Su 4pm-3am; Sept.-May daily 4pm-2am. ❶

TAPAS A TO Z

Food on toothpicks and in small bowls? The restaurant isn't being stingy, and your food isn't shrinking; you're experiencing an integral part of the Spanish lifestyle. The *tapas* tradition is one of the oldest in Spain. These tasty little dishes are Spain's answer to hors d'oeuvres, but they have more taste, less pretension, and they're eaten instead of meals.

To the untrained tourist, *tapas* menus are often indecipherable, if the bar has even bothered to print any. In order to avoid awkward encounters with tentacles or parts of the horse you rode in on, keep the following things in mind before *tapeando* (eating tapas).

Servings come in three sizes: *pinchos* (eaten with toothpicks), *tapas* (small plate), and *raciónes* (meal portion). On any basic menu you'll find: *Aceitunas* (olives), *albóndigas* (meatballs), *callos* (tripe), *chorizo* (sausage), *gambas* (shrimp), *jamón* (ham), *patatas bravas* (fried potatoes with spicy sauce), *pimientos* (peppers), *pulpo* (octopus), and *tortilla española* (onion and potato omelette). The more adventurous should try *morcilla* (blood sausage), or *sesos* (cow's brains). Often, bartenders will offer tastes of *tapas* with your drink and strike up a conversation. Ask for a *caña* (glass) of the house *cerveza* (beer) to guarantee the full respect of the establishment.

SIGHTS

Madrid, large as it may seem, is a walking city. Its public transportation should only be used for longer distances or between the day's starting and ending points; you don't want to miss the sights above ground. Whether soothing tired feet after perusing the **Avenida del Arte** or seeking shelter from the sweltering heat, there's nothing better than a shaded sidewalk cafe or a romantic park.

EL CENTRO

El Centro, spreading out from Puerta del Sol (Gate of the Sun), is the gateway to historical Madrid. Although several rulers carved the winding streets, the Hapsburgs and the Bourbons built El Centro's most celebrated monuments. As a result, the easily navigable area is divided into two major sections: Hapsburg Madrid and Bourbon Madrid. Unless otherwise specified, Hapsburg directions are given from Puerta del Sol and Bourbon directions from Ópera. *(M: Sol).*

HAPSBURG MADRID

PLAZA MAYOR. Juan de Herrera, the architect of **El Escorial** (p. 907), also designed this plaza. Its elegant arcades, spindly towers, and open verandas, built for Felipe III in 1620, are defining elements of the "Madrid style," which inspired architects nationwide. Toward evening, Pl. Mayor awakens as *Madrileños* resurface, tourists multiply, and cafes fill up. Live *flamenco* performances are a common treat. While the cafes are a nice spot for a drink, food is overpriced. *(M: Sol. Walk down C. Mayor. The plaza is on the left.)*

CATEDRAL DE SAN ISIDRO. Though Isidro—patron saint of crops, farmers, and Madrid—was humble, his final resting place is anything but. Designed in the Jesuit Baroque style at the beginning of the 17th century, the cathedral received San Isidro's remains in 1769. Rebuilt after rioting workers tried to burn it down in the 30s, it served as the cathedral of Madrid until 1993. *(M: Latina. From Pta. del Sol, take C. Mayor to Pl. Mayor, cross the plaza, and exit on C. de Toledo. Open daily in summer 7:30am-1:30pm and 5:30-9pm; in winter 7:30am-1pm and 5:30-8:30pm. Free.)*

PLAZA DE LA VILLA. Plaza de la Villa marks the heart of what was once Old Madrid. The horseshoe-shaped door on C. Codo is one of the few examples of the Gothic-*mudéjar* style left in Madrid. Across the plaza is the 17th-century Ayuntamiento, originally both the mayor's home and the city jail. Inside is Goya's *Allegory of the City of Madrid. (M: Sol. Go down C. Mayor and past Pl. Mayor.)*

BOURBON MADRID

PALACIO REAL. The luxurious Palacio Real lies at the western tip of central Madrid, overlooking the Río Manzanares. Felipe V commissioned Giovanni Sachetti to replace the Alcázar, which burned down in 1734, with a palace that would dwarf all others—he succeeded. Today, King Juan Carlos and Queen Sofía use the palace only on special occasions. The **Salón del Trono** (Throne Room) contains the two magnificent Spanish thrones, supported by golden lions. The room also features a ceiling fresco painted by Tiepolo, outlining the qualities of the ideal ruler. The **Salón de Gasparini,** site of the king's ceremonial dressing before the court, houses Goya's portrait of Carlos IV. Perhaps most beautiful is the **Chinese Room,** whose walls swirl with green tendril patterns. The **Real Oficina de Farmacia** (Royal Pharmacy) has crystal and china receptacles used to hold royal medicine. Also open to the public is the **Real Armería** (Armory), which has an entire floor devoted to knights' armor. *(From Pl. de Isabel II, head toward the Teatro Real. M: Ópera. ☎91 454 87 88. Open Apr.-Sept. M-Sa 9am-6pm, Su 9am-3pm; Oct.-Mar. M-Sa 9:30am-5pm, Su 9am-2pm. Arrive early to avoid lines. €8, with tour €10; students €3.50/6. Under 5 free. EU citizens free W.)*

OTHER SIGHTS

PARQUE DEL BUEN RETIRO. Join an array of vendors, palm-readers, football players, and sunbathers in the area Felipe IV converted from a hunting ground into a *buen retiro* (nice retreat). The 300-acre park is centered around a magnificent monument to King Alfonso XII and a lake, the **Estanque Grande.** *(Rowboats* *for 4, €4.40 per 45min.)* Around the lake, all manner of mimes, puppeteers, and street performers show off for the benefit of the crowd (and a few coins).

EL RASTRO (FLEA MARKET). For hundreds of years, *El Rastro* has been a Sunday-morning tradition in Madrid. The market begins in La Latina at Pl. Cascorro off C. Toledo and ends at the bottom of C. Ribera de Cortidores. El Rastro sells everything from zebra hides to jeans to antique tools to pet birds. Whatever price you're thinking (or being offered), it can probably be bargained in half. The flea market is a pickpocket's paradise, so leave your camera behind, bust out the money belt, and turn that backpack into a frontpack. Police (p. 900) are available if you need them. (Open Sundays and holidays 9am-3pm.)

SPAIN

MUSEUMS

Considered to be among the world's best art galleries, the Museo del Prado, Museo Thyssen-Bornemisza, and the Museo Nacional Centro de Arte Reina Sofía form the impressive "Avenida del Arte."

MUSEO DEL PRADO. One of Europe's finest centers for 12th- to 17th-century art, the Prado is Spain's most prestigious museumhome to the world's greatest collection of Spanish paintings. Its 7000 pieces are the result of hundreds of years of collecting by the Hapsburgs and Bourbons. The museum provides an indispensable guide for each room. English-language **audio tours** are available for €3. On the first floor, keep an eye out for the unforgiving realism of **Diego Velázquez** (1599-1660). His technique of "illusionism" is on display in the magnificent **Las Meninas,** considered by some art historians to be the best painting ever made. Deaf and alone, **Goya** painted the *Pinturas Negras* (Black Paintings), so named for the darkness of both their color and their subject matter. The Prado also displays many of **El Greco's** religious paintings, characterized by luminous colors, elongated figures, and mystical subjects. On the second floor are works by other Spanish artists, including **Murillo** and **Ribera.** *(Po. del Prado at Pl. Cánovas del Castillo. M: Banco de España or Atocha. ☎ 91 330 2800; www.museoprado.es. Open Tu-Su 9am-8pm €6, students €3, under 18 and over 65 free. Tu-Sa 6-8pm and Su 5-8pm free.)*

MUSEO NACIONAL CENTRO DE ARTE REINA SOFÍA. Since Juan Carlos I decreed this renovated hospital a national museum in 1988, the Reina Sofía's collection of **twentieth-century art** has grown steadily. Rooms dedicated to **Salvador Dalí, Juan Gris,** and **Joan Miró** display Spain's vital contributions to the Surrealist movement. **Picasso's** masterpiece, **Guernica,** is the highlight. *(Pl. Santa Isabel 52. ☎ 91 774 1000; www.museoreinasofia.es. M: Atocha. Open M and W-Sa 10am-9pm, Su 10am-2:30pm. €3, students €1.50. Sa after 2:30pm, Su, holidays, under 18, over 65 free.)*

MUSEO THYSSEN-BORNEMISZA. The Thyssen-Bornemisza exhibits works ranging from 14th-century paintings to 20th-century sculptures. The museum's collection constitutes the world's most extensive private showcase. The top floor is dedicated to the **Old Masters** collection, which includes such notables as Hans Holbein's austere *Portrait of Henry VIII* and El Greco's *Annunciation.* The Thyssen-Bornemisza's Baroque collection, with pieces by Caravaggio, Claude Lorraine, and Ribera, rivals the Prado's. The **Impressionist** and **Post-Impressionist** collections demonstrate the evolution toward modern art forms. The ground floor of the museum houses the extensive **twentieth-century** collection. The showcased artists include Chagall, Dalí, Hopper, O'Keeffe, Picasso, Pollock, and Rothko. *(Paseo del Prado, 8, on the corner of Po. del Prado and C. Manuel González. M: Banco de España or Atocha. ☎ 91 369 0151; www.museothyssen.org. Open Tu-Su 10am-7pm. Last entry 6:30pm. €6, students with ISIC and seniors €4, under 12 free. Audio guides €4.)*

NAKED TRUTH

Civil liberties have come a long way in Spain since Franco died; a fact that became clear to me as I walked through the Plaza de Oriente one day.

Traffic stopped, and a din arose from down C. Bailén, which runs in front of the Palacio Real. Then hundreds—perhaps thousands—of naked protesters rode by slowly on bicycles. What they wanted was unclear at first. Some chanted *"Gasolina es asesina"* (gas is an assassin), others merely *"Coches = mierda"* (cars are shit). Whatever it was, they were out in force, with their children, wives, and coworkers, drinking beer and taking pictures as they rode.

I stopped and talked to a few of the unclad riders. "We're protesting for urban transport," one said, patting his bicycle. He told me that riding your bicycle in Madrid is often dangerous because drivers don't care about cyclists. The protestors rode on, followed by a police escort, ostensibly protecting the group from traffic.

Enjoying the irony, I paused and saw the mass of naked riders being escorted past one of the most beautiful royal palaces in the world, an image that will stay with me. Riding naked in my puritanical country, much less past the Capitol or the home of the President, would not be tolerated. *Madrileños* cherish their rights, and that's the naked truth.

- Russell Rennie

ENTERTAINMENT

FÚTBOL

Every Sunday and some Saturdays between September and June, one of the two big local teams plays at home. **Real Madrid** plays at Estadio Santiago Bernabéu, Av. Cochina Espina, 1. (☎91 457 11 12. M: Santiago Bernabéu. Summer tours 10:30am-6:30pm; ☎90 229 17 09; www.realmadrid.com) **Atlético de Madrid** plays at Estadio Vicente Calderón, Po. de la Virgen del Puerto, 67. (☎91 364 22 34; www.clubatleticodemadrid.com. M: Pirámides or Marqués de Vadillos.)

BULLFIGHTS

Some call it animal cruelty, others tradition; either way, the **Plaza de Ventas** remains the most important bullfighting arena in the world since its opening in 1931. From early May to early June, the **Fiestas de San Isidro** stage a daily *corrida* (bullfight) with top *matadores* and the fiercest bulls in the largest ring in Spain, Plaza de las Ventas, C. Alcalá, 237. (☎91 356 22 00; www.las-ventas.com or www.taquillatoros.com. M: Ventas.) A seat costs €2-115, depending on its location in the oppressive *sol* (sun) or *sombra* (shade). Wherever you sit, bring a cushion—the concrete is not comfortable. Tickets are available, in person only, the Friday and Saturday before and Sunday of a bullfight. Advance tickets are recommended for the Fiestas de San Isidro. There are also bullfights every Sunday from March to October and less frequently the rest of the year. Look for posters in bars and cafes for upcoming *corridas* (especially on C. Victoria, off C. San Jerónimo). **Plaza de Toros Palacio de Vistalegre** also hosts bullfights and cultural events. (☎91 422 07 80. M: Vista Alegre.)

NIGHTLIFE

Madrileños start in the tapas bars of Huertas, move to the youthful scene in Malasaña, and end at the wild parties of Chueca or late-night clubs of Gran Vía. Students fill the streets of Bilbao and Moncloa, where *terrazas* and *chiringuitos* (outdoor cafe-bars) line the sidewalks. Madrid's fantastic gay scene centers on Plaza Chueca. Bouncers on power trips love to make examples; dress well to avoid being overcharged or denied. Women may not be charged at all.

Joy Eslava, C. Arenal, 11 (☎91 366 54 39; www.joy-madrid.com). M: Sol. Madrid's sexy, rich, and famous come here to dance to R&B and club hits under artsy projections and frenetic strobing. This is the place to be—dress well and come early so you don't stand outside as the young and gorgeous head through the VIP entrance. Drinks €15. Cover M-Th and Su €12-15, F-Sa €18, includes one drink; look for drink coupons to ease the pain. Open daily midnight-6am.

Trocha, C. Huertas, 55 (☎91 429 78 61; www.trochabar.com). M: Antón Martín. Watch the barman squeeze the lemons and limes into your *caipirinha* (€6-7), the house specialty, as you sit back and take in the smooth jazz and art prints on the walls. The ultimate place to relax. Other drinks €4-7. Open daily 4:30pm-2:30am.

Teatro Kapital, C. de Atocha, 125 (☎91 420 29 06). M: Atocha. 7 fl. of renowned *discoteca* insanity. From hip-hop to house, open *terrazas* to cinemas, karaoke to climbing stairs, it is easy to lose yourself, your dignity, and all your money in the madness. Drinks €9-12. Cover €12-18 includes 1 drink, but look for people handing out cards that will get you 2 drinks included if you head in before 1:30am. Open Th-Su midnight-6am.

SPAIN

DAYTRIP FROM MADRID

EL ESCORIAL

(Autocares Herranz buses run between El Escorial and Moncloa Metro.; 50min., 2-6 per hr., €3.20. Complex ☎918 90 59 03. Open Apr.-Sept. Tu-Su 10am-7pm; Oct.-Mar.10am-6pm. Last entry 1hr. before closing. Monastery €7, with guide €9; students and seniors €3.50.)

This enormous complex was described by Felipe II as "majesty without ostentation." The Monasterio de San Lorenzo del Escorial was a gift from Felipe II to God, the people, and himself, commemorating his victory over the French at the battle of San Quintín in 1557. Near the town of San Lorenzo, El Escorial is filled with artistic treasures, a church, a magnificent library, two palaces, and two pantheons. To avoid crowds, enter via the gate on C. Floridablanca, on the western side. The adjacent **Museo de Arquitectura y Pintura** has an exhibit comparing El Escorial's construction to that of similar structures. The **Palacio Real** is lined with 16th-century *azulejo* tiles and includes the majestic **Salón del Trono**.

CASTILLA LA MANCHA

Land of austere plains and miles of empty landscapes, Castilla La Mancha has played host to bloody conflicts and epic heroes both real and imaginary. The region is one of Spain's least developed and provokes the imagination with its solitary crags, gloomy medieval fortresses, and whirling windmills.

TOLEDO ☎925

Cervantes called Toledo (pop. 75,000) "the glory of Spain and light of her cities." The city is a former capital of the Holy Roman, Visigoth, and Muslim Empires, and its churches, synagogues, and mosques share twisting alleyways. Toledo is known as the "City of Three Cultures," symbol of a time when Spain's three religions coexisted peacefully, although as one might expect, locals will tell you the history is somewhat romanticized.

TRANSPORTATION AND PRACTICAL INFORMATION. From the station on Po. de la Rosa, just over Puente de Azarquiel, **trains** (RENFE info ☎902 24 02 02) run to Madrid (30min., 9-11 per day, €9). **Buses** run from Av. Castilla

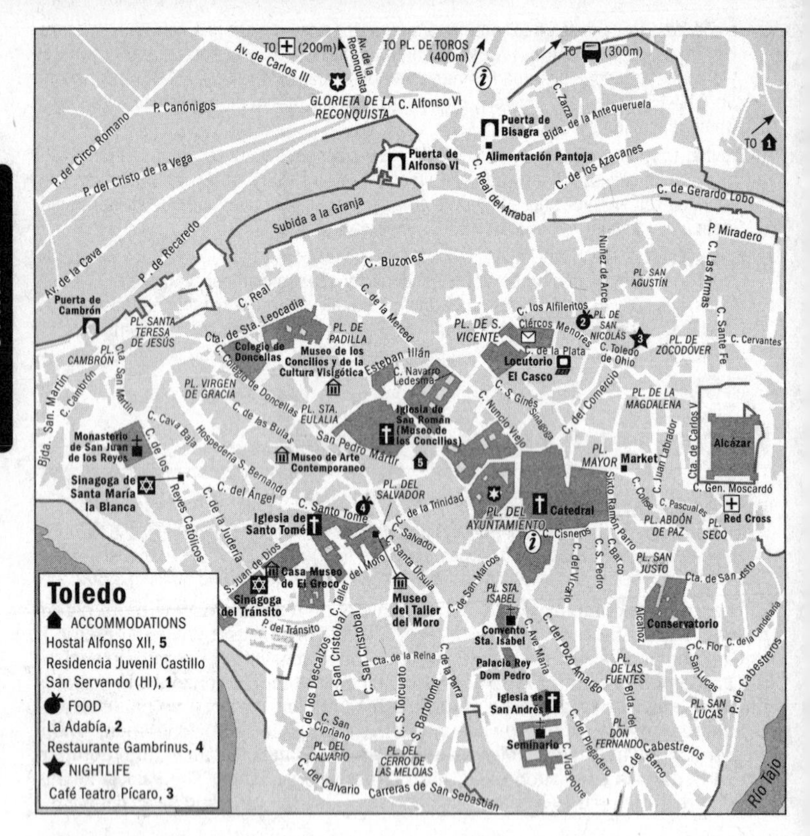

La Mancha (☎925 21 58 50), 10min. from **Puerta de Bisagra** (the city gate), to Madrid (1hr., 2 per hr., €4.53) and Valencia (5hr., 1 per day, €25). Within the city, buses #8.1 and #8.2 serve the bus station and buses #1-7 run from the Pl. de Zocodóver to points outside the old city. Buses (€1; at night €1.30) stop to the right of the train station, underneath and across the street from the bus station. Though Toledo's streets are well labeled, it's easy to get lost; pick up a map at the **tourist office,** at Pta. de Bisagra. (☎925 22 08 43. Open July-Sept. M-F 9am-7pm, Sa 10am-6pm, Su 10am-2pm; Oct.-June M-F 9am-6pm, Sa 10am-6pm, Su 10am-2pm.) **Postal Code:** 45001.

ACCOMMODATIONS AND FOOD. Toledo is full of accommodations, but finding a bed in summer can be a hassle, especially on weekends. Reservations are strongly recommended. Spacious rooms among suits of armor await at the **Residencia Juvenil San Servando (HI) ❶,** Castillo San Servando, uphill on Subida del Hospital from the train station, in a 14th-century castle with a pool, TV room, and Internet. (☎925 22 45 54. Dorms €11, with breakfast €15; under 30 €9.20/11. MC/V.) To get to **Hostal Alfonso XII ❹,** C. Alfonso XII, 18 (☎925 25 25 09; www.hostal-alfonso12.com), turn off C. Santo Tomé up Campana and follow it to C. Alfonso XII. Scented herbs and flowers fill the halls and rooms with good aromas. Wooden beams traverse the ceilings and add the finishing note to an elegant, deceptively rustic place with modern amenities. Rooms have TV, A/C, and Wi-Fi. (Singles €40; doubles €55; triples €70. MC/V.) *Pastelería* windows beckon with *mazapán* (marzipan) of every shape and size. For the widest array, stop by the **market** in Pl. Mayor, behind the cathedral. (Open M-Sa 9am-8pm.) To reach **La Abadía ❷,** Pl. de San Nicolás 3, bear left when C. de la Sillería splits; Pl. de San Nicolás is on the right. Dine on the regional lunch *menú* (€10) in a maze of underground rooms. Combo *tapas* plates €5-10.(☎925 25 11 40. Open daily 8am-midnight. AmEx/MC/V.) **Restaurante Gambrinus ❷,** C. Santo Tomé, 10 offers the shadiest outdoor seating in the old city, which is perfect for people-watching as you slowly conquer a hearty traditional Spanish plate. There are big soups (€6) for the hungry. (☎925 21 44 40. Meat dishes €10-11. Open daily 11am-4pm and 8pm-midnight. MC/V.)

SIGHTS AND NIGHTLIFE. At Arco de Palacio, up C. del Comercio from Pl. de Zocodóver, Toledo's **cathedral** boasts five naves, delicate stained glass, and unapologetic ostentation. The **sacristía** holds 18 works by *El Greco* (including *El Espolio*), as well as paintings by other notable Spanish and European masters. (☎925 22 22 41. Open M-Sa 10am-6:30pm, Su 2-6:30pm. €8, students €6. Audio tour €3. Dress modestly.) Greek painter Doménikos Theotokópoulos, better known as **El Greco,** spent most of his life in Toledo. A great introduction to his work is the **Casa Museo de El Greco,** on C. Samuel Leví 2, which contains 19 of his works. (☎925 22 44 05. Open in summer Tu-Sa 10am-2pm and 4-9pm, Su 10am-2pm; in winter Tu-Sa 10am-2pm and 4-6pm, Su 10am-2pm. €2.40; students, under 18, Sa afternoon, and Su free. Closed for renovations until at least 2009.) Up the hill and to the right is the **Iglesia de Santo Tomé,** which still houses one of his most famous and recognized works, **El Entierro del Conde de Orgaz** (The Burial of Count Orgaz). Arrive early to beat the tour groups. Pl. del Conde, 4. (☎925 25 60 98; www.santotome.org. Open daily Mar.-Oct. 15 10am-7pm; Oct.16-Feb. 10am-6pm. €2.30, students and over 65 €1.80.)

On the same street as Museo El Greco is the **Sinagoga del Tránsito,** one of two remaining synagogues in Toledo's *judería* (Jewish quarter). Inside, the **Museo Sefardí** documents early Jewish history in Spain. Look up at the Hebrew letters carved into the *mudéjar* plasterwork and a stunning coffered wood ceiling. (☎711 35 52 30; www.museosefardi.net. Open Mar.-Nov. Tu-Sa 10am-2pm and 4-9pm, Su 10am-2pm; Dec.-Feb. Tu-Sa 10am-2pm and 4-6pm, Su 10am-2pm. €2.40, students, seniors, and under 18 free. Sa after 4pm and Su free.) Nestling in the middle of the city, the **Iglesia de Los Jesuitas** is a Jesuit church that has **amazing views** from its towers. Located at one of the highest points in the city, the roof offers a panorama of all the towers and tiled roofs in the old city and the hills for miles around. It's breezy, so hold on to your hat. (Pl. Padre Juan de Mariana, 1, up C. Nuncio Viejo from the Cathedral, and then a left on Alfonso X El Sabio. ☎925 25 15 07. Open daily Apr.-Sept. 10am-6:45pm; Oct.-March 10am-5:45pm. €2.30.) For nightlife, head through the arch and to the left from Pl. de Zocodóver to **Calle Santa Fé,** which brims with beer and local youth. For upscale bars and clubs, try **Calle de la Sillería** and **Calle los Alfileritos,** west of Pl. de Zocodóver. To escape the raucous noise, check out the chill **Café Teatro Pícaro,** C. Cadenas, 6, where lights play on abstract art, and *batidos* (milkshakes €3, with Baileys €4) and mixed drinks abound. (☎925 22 13 01; www.picarocafeteatro.com. Mixed drinks €5. Beer €1.50-2.50. Open M-F 4pm-3am, Sa-Su 4pm-5am.)

CASTILLA Y LEÓN

Well before Fernando of Aragón and Isabel of Castilla were joined in world-shaking matrimony, Castilla was the political and military powerhouse of Spain. Castellano became the dominant language of the nation in the High Middle Ages. The aqueduct of Segovia, the Gothic cathedrals of León, and the sandstone of Salamanca continue to stand out as national images. Castilla's comrade in arms, León, though chagrined to be lumped with Castilla in a 1970s provincial reorganization, is very culturally similar to its co-province.

SEGOVIA ☎921

Legend has it that the devil built Segovia's (pop. 56,000) famed aqueduct in an effort to win the soul of a Segovian water-seller named Juanilla. With or without Lucifer's help, Segovia's attractions draw their share of eager tourists.

TRANSPORTATION AND PRACTICAL INFORMATION. **Trains** (RENFE; ☎902 24 02 02) run from Po. Obispo Quesada, rather far from town, to Madrid (2hr., 7-9 per day, €5.90). La Sepulvedana buses (☎921 42 77 07) run from Estación Municipal de Autobuses, Po. Ezequiel González 12, to Madrid (1hr., 2 per hr., €6.43) and Valladolid (2hr., 12 per day, €6.85). From the train station, bus #8 stops near the **Plaza Mayor,** the city's historic center and site of the regional **tourist office.** Maps are crucial in Segovia, so pick one up. (☎921 46 03 34. Open July-Sept. 15 M-Th and Su 9am-8pm, F-Sa 9am-9pm; Sept. 16-June 9am-2pm and 5-8pm.) Access the **Internet** for free at the **public library,** C. Juan Bravo 11. (☎921 46 35 33. Passport required. Limit 30min. Open Sept.-June M-F 9am-9pm, Sa 9am-2pm; July-Aug. M-F 9am-3pm, Sa 9am-2pm.) **Postal Code:** 40001.

ACCOMMODATIONS AND FOOD. Reservations are a must for any of Segovia's hotels, especially those near major plazas. Arrive early to ensure space and expect to pay €21 or more for a single. *Pensiones* are significantly cheaper, with basic rooms and shared bathrooms. **Natura La Hosteria ❹**, C. Colón 5 and 7, is located just outside the Plaza Mayor with big and beautiful—though pricey—rooms, each decorated differently. (☎921 46 67 10; www.naturadesegovia.com. Free Wi-Fi. Prices vary, so call ahead. Generally, singles €35-40; doubles as low as €50-60, high as €70-80. MC/V.) **Hotel San Miguel ❸,** C. Infanta Isabel, 4 is a contrast to Segovia's stone and more "antique" lodgings. This hotel is full of bright, modern amenities. Huge full bath is sparkling, and big beds have downy, quilt-like patched comforters. The balcony has good views over the street. (☎921 46 36 57; www.sanmiguel-hotel.com. Rooms come with TV, A/C, and phone. Singles €35; doubles €60. MC/V.)

Sample Segovia's famed lamb, *cochinillo asado* (roast suckling pig), or *sopa castellana* (soup with bread, eggs, and garlic), but steer clear of expensive Pl. Mayor and Pl. del Azoguejo. For eclectic and scrumptious dishes (€4-11), try **Restaurante La Almuzara ❷**, C. Marqués del Arco 3, past the cathedral. (☎921 46 06 22. Salads €4-11. Soups €6.50-9. Lunch *menú* €10. Open Tu 8-11:30pm, W-Su 12:45-4pm and 8-11:30pm. MC/V.) At the casual but classy **Bar-Mesón Cueva de San Estéban ❸,** C. Vadeláguila 15, off Pl. Esteban and C. Escuderos, the owner knows his wines and the food is excellent. (☎921 46 09 82. Lunch *menú* M-F €9, Sa-Su €10. Meat dishes €12-20. Open daily 11am-midnight. MC/V.) Buy groceries at **Día,** C. Gobernador Fernández Jiménez, 3, off Av. de Fernández Ladreda. (Open M-Th 9:30am-2pm and 5:30-8:30pm, F-Sa 9am-9pm.)

SIGHTS AND ENTERTAINMENT. The serpentine **Roman aqueduct**, built in 50 BC and spanning 813m, commands the entrance to the Old Town. Some 20,000 blocks of granite were used in the construction—without a drop of mortar. This spectacular feat of engineering, restored by the monarchy in the 15th century, can transport 30L of water per second and was used until the late 1940s. With its spiraling towers and smooth, pointed turrets, Segovia's **Alcázar**, a late-medieval castle and site of Isabel's coronation in 1474, would be at home in a fairy tale—it was reportedly a model for the castle in Disney's Cinderella. The mystifying message in the throne room, *tanto monta*, signifies that Fernando and Isabel had equal authority as sovereigns. The **Torre de Juan II** (80m), 152 steps up a nausea-inducing spiral staircase, provides a view of Segovia and the surrounding plains. (Pl. de la Reina Victoria Eugenia. ☎921 46 07 59. Alcázar open daily Apr.-Sept. 10am-7pm; Oct.-Mar. 10am-6pm. Tower closed Tu. Palace €4, seniors and students €2.50. Tower €2. English-language audio tour €3.) The 23 chapels of the **cathedral,** towering over Pl. Mayor, earned it the nickname "The Lady of all Cathedrals." The interior may look less impressive than the facade, but its vastness will make you feel truly small. (☎921 46 22 05. Open daily Apr.-Oct. 9am-6:30pm; Nov.-Mar. 9:30am-5:30pm. Mass M-Sa 10am, Su 11am and 12:30pm. €3, under 14 free.)

Though the city isn't particularly known for its sleepless nights, *segovianos* know how to party. Packed with bars and cafes, the **Plaza Mayor** is the center of it all. Head for **Calle Infanta Isabel,** appropriately nicknamed *calle de los bares* (street of the bars). Find drinks and plastic tchotchkes in the fun techno club **Toys,** C. Infanta Isabel 13. (☎609 65 41 42. Beer €1. Mixed drinks €4.50-5.50. Open daily 10pm-4am.) Continuing in the doll vein is **Geographic Chic,** C. Infanta Isabel, 13. Small dressed mannequins line the windows and cherubs sit smilingly on the bar and light fixtures. A mixed crowd sips mixed drinks and dances for fun as the lights sweep the bar. (☎921 46 30 38. Beer €3. Cocktails €5. Open W-Sa 10:30pm-4am.) From June 23 to 29, Segovia holds a **fiesta** in honor of San Juan and San Pedro, with free open-air concerts on Pl. del Azoguejo and dances and fireworks on June 29.

SALAMANCA ☎923

Salamanca "la blanca" (pop. 163,000), city of royals, saints, and scholars, glows with the yellow stones of Spanish Plateresque architecture by day and a vivacious club scene by night. The prestigious Universidad de Salamanca, grouped in medieval times with Bologna, Oxford, and Paris as one of the "four leading lights of the world," continues to add youthful energy to the city.

TRANSPORTATION AND PRACTICAL INFORMATION. **Trains** go from Po. de la Estación (☎923 24 02 02) to Madrid (2hr., 6-7 per day, €15) and Lisbon, POR (6hr., 1 per day, €47). **Buses** leave from the station (☎923 23 67 17) on Av. Filiberto Villalobos 71-85 for: Barcelona (11hr., 2 per day, €47); León (2hr., 4-7 per day, €13); Madrid (2hr., 16 per day, €12-17); Segovia (2hr., 2 per day, €10). Majestic **Plaza Mayor** is the center of Salamanca. From the train station, catch bus #1 (€0.80) to Gran Vía and ask to be let off at Pl. San Julián, a block from Pl. Mayor. The **tourist office** is at Pl. Mayor 32. (☎923 21 83 42. Open June-Sept. M-F 9am-2pm and 4:30-8pm, Sa 10am-8pm, Su 10am-2pm; Oct.-May M-F 9am-2pm and 4:30-6:30pm, Sa 10am-6:30pm, Su 10am-2pm.) *DGratis*, a free weekly newspaper about events in Salamanca, is available from newsstands, tourist offices, and around Pl. Mayor. Free **Internet** is available at the **public**

library, C. Compañía 2, in Casa de las Conchas. (☎923 26 93 17. Limit 30min. Open July to mid-Sept. M-F 9am-3pm, Sa 9am-2pm; mid-Sept. to June M-F 9am-9pm, Sa 9am-2pm.) **Postal Code:** 37001.

ACCOMMODATIONS AND FOOD. Reasonably priced *hostales* and *pensiones* cater to the floods of student visitors, especially off Pl. Mayor and C. Meléndez. **Hostal Las Vegas Centro ❷,** C. Meléndez 13, 1st fl., has friendly owners and spotless rooms with terrace and TV. (☎923 21 87 49; www.lasvegascentro.com. Singles €20, with bath €24; doubles €30. MC/V.) At nearby **Pensión Barez ❶,** C. Meléndez 19, 1st fl., clean rooms overlook the street. (☎923 21 74 95. Rooms €14. Cash only.) Many cafes and restaurants are in Pl. Mayor. Pork is the city's speciality, with dishes ranging from *chorizo* (spicy sausage) to *cochinillo* (suckling pig). Funky **Restaurante Delicatessen Café ❷,** C. Meléndez 25, serves a wide variety of *platos combinados* (€10.50-11) and a lunch *menú* (€11) in a colorful solarium. (☎923 28 03 09. Open daily 1:30-4pm and 9pm-midnight. MC/V.) *Salamantinos* crowd **El Patio Chico ❷,** C. Meléndez 13, but the hefty portions are worth the wait. (☎923 26 51 03. Entrees €5.50-17. *Menú* €14. Open daily 1-4pm and 8pm-midnight. MC/V). At **El Ave Café ❷,** C. Libreros 24, enjoy your lunch (*menú* €11) on the terrace or take a peek at the colorful murals inside. (☎923 26 45 11. Open daily 8am-midnight. MC/V). **Carrefour,** C. Toro 82, is a central supermarket. (☎923 21 22 08. Open M-Sa 9:30am-9:30pm.)

SIGHTS AND NIGHTLIFE. From Pl. Mayor, follow R. Mayor, veer right onto T. Antigua, and left onto C. Libreros to reach **La Universidad de Salamanca** (est. 1218), the city's focal point. Hidden in the delicate Plateresque filigree of the entryway is a tiny frog perched on a skull. According to legend, those who can spot him without assistance will be blessed with good luck. The old lecture halls inside are open to the public, but to get into the library you'll need to befriend a professor. The 15th-century classroom **Aula Fray Luis de León** has been left in its original state more or less. Located on the second floor atop a Plateresque staircase is the **Biblioteca Antigua,** one of Europe's oldest libraries. The staircase is thought to represent the ascent of the scholar through careless youth, love, and adventure on the perilous path to true knowledge. Don't miss the 800-year-old scrawlings on the walls of the **Capilla del Estudiante** and the benches of the **Sala Fray Luis de Leon.** Across the street and through the hall on the left corner of the patio is the **University Museum.** The reconstructed **Cielo de Salamanca,** the library's famous 15th-century ceiling fresco of the zodiac, is preserved here. (University ☎923 29 45 00, ext. 1225, museum ext 1150. Museum open Mon-Sa 10am-2pm and 4pm-8pm, Su 10am-2pm. University open M-F 9:30am-1:30pm and 4-7:30pm, Sa 9:30am-1:30pm and 4-7pm, Su 10am-1:30pm. €4, students and seniors €2). It's not surprising it took 220 years to build the stunning **Catedral Nueva,** in Pl. de Anaya. Be sure to climb the tower to get a spectacular **view** from above. (Open daily Apr.-Sept. 9am-8pm; Oct.-Mar. 9am-1pm and 4-6pm. Tower open daily 10am-8pm, last entry 7:45pm. Cathedral free. Tower €3; see www.ieronimus.com) According to *salamantinos*, Salamanca is the best place in Spain to party. Nightlife centers on **Plaza Mayor,** where troubadours serenade women, then spreads out to **Gran Vía, Calle Bordadores,** and side streets. **Calle Prior** and **Rúa Mayor** are also full of bars, while intense partying occurs off **Calle Varillas.** After a few shots (€1-2) at **Bar La Chupitería,** Pl. de Monterrey, wander from club to club on C. Prior and C. Compañía.

EXTREMADURA

Arid plains bake under the intense summer sun, relieved only by scattered patches of golden sunflowers. This land of harsh beauty and cruel extremes hardened New World conquistadors such as Cortés and Pizarro. The region is only now drawing tourists looking for the "classic" Spanish countryside.

CÁCERES ☎927

Stepping into Cáceres's (pop. 90,000) *barrio antiguo* (old city) is like walking into a time-warp. The bustle of the modern city is silenced by an overwhelming wave of medieval antiquity. Built between the 14th and 16th centuries, the *barrio antiguo* is comprised of miniature palaces once used to show off rival families' power and wealth.

TRANSPORTATION AND PRACTICAL INFORMATION. RENFE **trains** (☎927 23 37 61) run from on Av. de Alemania, 3km from the Old Town, to Lisbon, POR (6hr., 2 per day, €35), Madrid (4hr., 6 per day, €16-35), and Seville (4hr., 1 per day, €15). **Buses** (☎927 23 25 50) go from Av. de la Hispanidad to Madrid (4-5hr., 7-9 per day, €19), Salamanca (4hr., 7-28 per day, €13), and Seville (4hr., 8-14 per day, €16). From the bus or train station, the best way to get to the center of Cáceres is via bus #1 (€0.75 per ride, 10 rides for €5.50). From the station, walk out the exit opposite the buses, turn left uphill, then turn right at the intersection. The **tourist office** is at Pl. Mayor 9-10 (☎927 01 08 34; otcaceres@eco.juntaex.es), in the outer wall of the *ciudad monumental*. (Open July-Sept. M-F 8am-3pm, Sa-Su 10am-2pm; Oct.-June M-F 9am-2pm, Sa-Su 9:45am-2pm.) The **post office** is on Av. Miguel Primo de Rivera. (☎927 62 66 81. Open M-F 8:30am-8:30pm, Sa 9:30am-2pm.) **Postal Code:** 10071.

ACCOMMODATIONS AND FOOD. Hostels are scattered throughout the new city and line Pl. Mayor in the Old Town. Reserve ahead on summer weekends. **Albergue Turistico "Las Veletas,"** C. Margallo, 36, has a beautiful garden, free Wi-Fi, and simple rooms that open to great views. (☎927 21 12 10). **Pensión Carretero ❷,** Pl. Mayor 22, has spacious rooms with painted tile floors. (☎927 24 74 82; pens_carretero@yahoo.es. June-Aug. singles €25; doubles €30; triples €40; Sept.-May €15/20/35. AmEx/MC/V.) **Plaza Mayor** overflows with restaurants and cafes serving up *bocadillos*, *raciones*, and *extremeño* specialties. Take in the stork-covered walls of the ciudad monumental while the friendly staff of **Cafetería El Pato ❸,** in the Pl. Mayor, dishes out everything from ham and eggs to ewe's milk cheese sandwiches. (☎927 24 67 36. Entrees €6.60-15. *Menú* €10-13. Open Tu-Sa noon-4pm and 8pm-midnight. AmEx/MC/V.)

SIGHTS. Cáceres's **ciudad monumental** (Old Town) comprises miniature palaces once used to show off each family's power and wealth. It is a melting pot of architectural influences: wealthy Spanish families incorporated Arabic, Gothic, Incan, Renaissance, and Roman influences into their palaces. From the Pl. Mayor, take the stairs from the left of the tourist office to the Arco de la Estrella, the entrance to the walled city. The 16th-century **Casa del Sol** is the most famous of Cáceres's numerous mansions; its crest is the city's emblem. The **Palacio y Torre de Carvajal,** on the corner of C. Amargura, is one of the few *palacios* in the city open to the public. (Open M-F 8am-8pm, Sa-Su 10am-2pm. Free.) The **Casa de las Veletas** (House of Weather Vanes) displays ethnographic/archeological pieces about Cáceres's early history, Celtiberian stone animals, Visigothic tombstones, and an astonishing **Muslim cistern.** Through a garden adjoining the main building, morning visitors can access the must-see **Casa de los Caballos.** Inside is the fine arts collection of the **Museo de Cáceres,** which houses a tiny but brilliant Who's Who of Spanish art. It features originals by El Greco, Picasso, Miró, along with rotating exhibits. (Pl. de las Veletas, 1. ☎927 01 08 77. Open Apr.-Sept. Tu-Sa 9am-2:30pm and 5-8:15pm, Su 10:15am-2:30pm; Oct.-Apr. Tu-Sa 9am-2:30pm and 4-7:15pm, Su 10:15am-2:30pm. €1.20; students, seniors, and EU citizens free. Free on Su.)

SOUTHERN SPAIN

Southern Spain (Andalucía) is all that you expect of Spanish culture—flamenco, bullfighting, tall pitchers of sangria, and streets lined with orange trees. The Moors arrived in AD 711 and bequeathed to the region far more than flamenco music and gypsy ballads. The cities of Seville and Granada reached the pinnacle of Islamic arts, while Córdoba matured into the most culturally influential city in medieval Islam. Andalucía's *festivales*, *ferias*, and *carnavales* are world-famous for their extravagance.

CÓRDOBA ☎957

Captivating Córdoba (pop. 324,000), located on the south bank of the Río Guadalquivir, was Western Europe's largest city in the 10th century. Remnants of the city's hey-day survive in its well-preserved Roman, Jewish, Islamic, and Catholic monuments. Today, lively festivals and nonstop nightlife make Córdoba one of Spain's most beloved cities.

TRANSPORTATION. RENFE **trains** (☎957 40 02 02; www.renfe.es) run from Pl. de las Tres Culturas, off Av. de América, to: Barcelona (10-11hr., 4 per day, €55-90.80); Cádiz (2hr., 5 per day, €18-55); Madrid (2-4hr., 21-33 per day, €48-61); Málaga (2-3hr., 5 per day, €19-41); Seville (45min., 4-8 per day, €8.20-14.40). **Buses** (☎957 40 40 40) leave from Estación de Autobuses, on Glorieta de las Tres Culturas across from the train station. Alsina Graells Sur (☎957 27 81 00) sends buses to Cádiz (4-5hr., 1-2 per day, €21), Granada (3-4hr., 9-11 per day, €12), and Málaga (2-3hr., 5 per day, €12). Bacoma (☎902 42 22 42) runs to Barcelona (10hr., 3 per day, €64). Secorbus (☎902 22 92 92) has cheap buses to Madrid (4hr., 3-6 per day, €14.40).

ORIENTATION AND PRACTICAL INFORMATION. Córdoba is split into two cities: the old and the new. The modern and commercial northern half extends from the train station on Av. de América down to **Plaza de las Tendillas,** the city center. The old section in the south includes a medieval maze known as the **Judería** (Jewish quarter). The easiest way to reach the old city from the train station is to take either bus #3 or #4 (€1) to the Pl. de Tendillas. To get to the **tourist office,** C. Torrijos 10, from the train station, take bus #3 along the river to the Puente Romano. Walk under the stone arch; the office is on the left. (☎957 35 51 79. Open July-Aug. M-F 9:30am-7:30pm, Sa 10am-7:30pm, Su 10am-2pm; Sept.-June M-Sa 9am-7:30pm, Su 10am-2pm.) **Tele-Click,** C. Eduardo Dato 9, has **Internet.** (☎957 94 06 15. €1.80 per hr. Open M-F 10am-3pm and 5:30-10:30pm, Sa-Su noon-11pm.) The **post office** is at C. José Cruz Conde 15. (☎957 47 97 96. Open M-F 8:30am-8:30pm, Sa-Su 9:30am-2pm.) **Postal Code:** 14070.

ACCOMMODATIONS AND FOOD. Most accommodations can be found around the whitewashed walls of the Judería and in Old Córdoba, a more

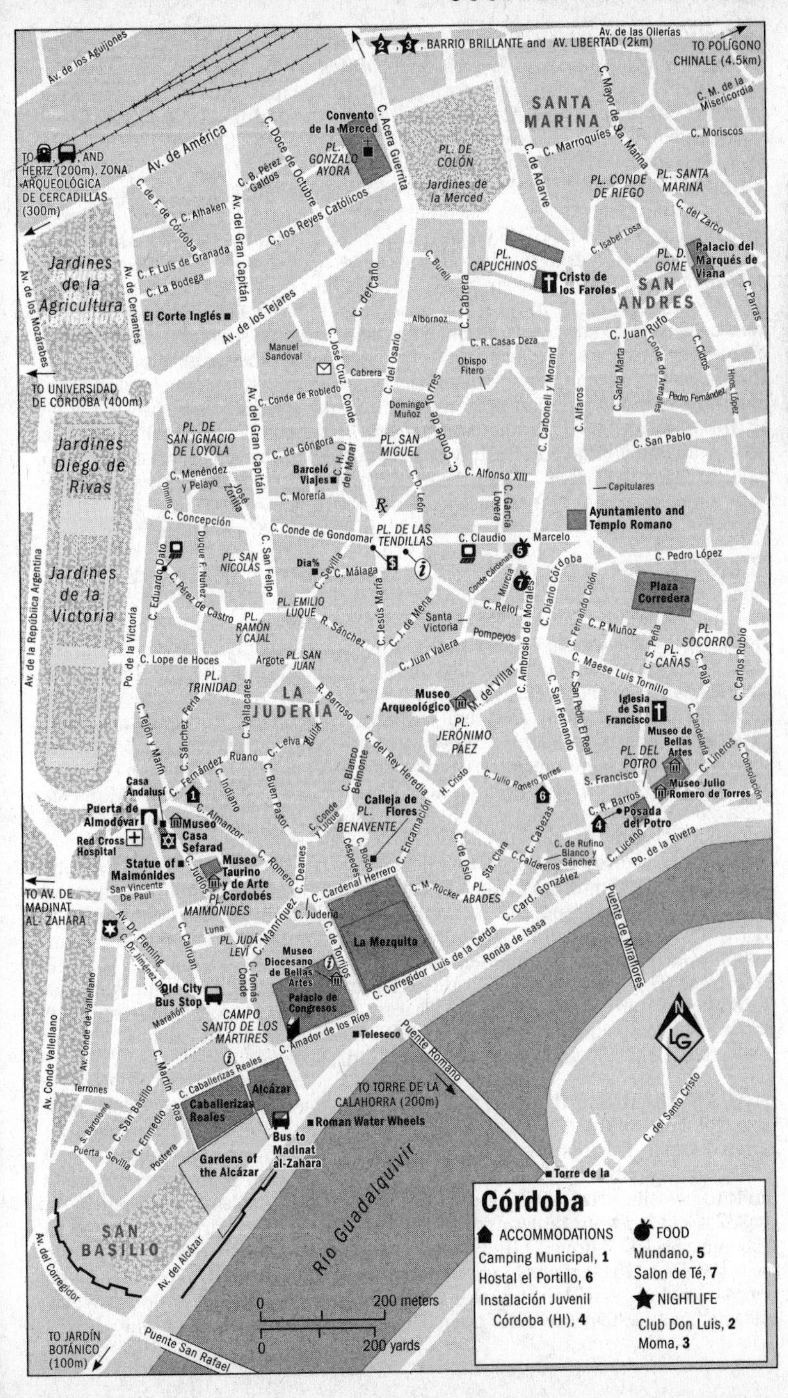
Córdoba
ACCOMMODATIONS
Camping Municipal, 1
Hostal el Portillo, 6
Instalación Juvenil Córdoba (HI), 4
FOOD
Mundano, 5
Salon de Té, 7
NIGHTLIFE
Club Don Luis, 2
Moma, 3
2, 3, BARRIO BRILLANTE and AV. LIBERTAD (2km)
TO POLÍGONO CHINALE (4.5km)
TO, AND HERTZ (200m), ZONA ARQUEOLÓGICA DE CERCADILLAS (300m)
TO UNIVERSIDAD DE CÓRDOBA (400m)
TO AV. DE MADINAT AL-ZAHARA
TO TORRE DE LA CALAHORRA (200m)
TO JARDÍN BOTÁNICO (100m)
SANTA MARINA
SAN ANDRES
LA JUDERÍA
SAN BASILIO
Jardines de la Agricultura
Jardines Diego de Rivas
Jardines de la Victoria
Convento de la Merced
PL. GONZALO AYORA
PL. DE COLÓN
Jardines de la Merced
PL. CONDE DE RIEGO
PL. SANTA MARINA
PL. CAPUCHINOS
Cristo de los Faroles
Palacio del Marqués de Viana
PL. D. GOME
El Corte Inglés
PL. DE SAN IGNACIO DE LOYOLA
PL. SAN MIGUEL
Barceló Viajes
PL. DE LAS TENDILLAS
Ayuntamiento and Templo Romano
PL. SAN NICOLÁS
Dia%
PL. EMILIO LUQUE
PL. RAMÓN Y CAJAL
Plaza Corredera
PL. SOCORRO
PL. CAÑAS
PL. TRINIDAD
PL. SAN JUAN
Museo Arqueológico
PL. JERÓNIMO PÁEZ
Iglesia de San Francisco
Museo de Bellas Artes
PL. DEL POTRO
Museo Julio Romero de Torres
Posada del Potro
Casa Andalusí
Puerta de Almodóvar
Museo Casa Sefarad
Red Cross Hospital
Statue of Maimónides
Museo Taurino y de Arte Cordobés
PL. MAIMÓNIDES
Calleja de Flores
PL. BENAVENTE
PL. ABADES
La Mezquita
PL. JUDÁ LEVÍ
Museo Diocesano de Bellas Artes
Palacio de Congresos
Old City Bus Stop
CAMPO SANTO DE LOS MÁRTIRES
Teleseco
Alcázar
Caballerizas Reales
Roman Water Wheels
Bus to Madinat al-Zahara
Gardens of the Alcázar
Torre de la
Río Guadalquivir
Puente Romano
Puente de Miraflores
Puente San Rafael
Av. de América
Av. de los Tejares
Av. del Gran Capitán
Av. de Cervantes
Av. de los Mozárabes
Av. de la República Argentina
Av. Conde Vallellano
Av. del Corregidor
Av. del Alcázar
Po. de la Victoria
Po. de la Ribera
Ronda de Isasa
C. Corregidor Luis de la Cerda
C. Cardenal Herrero
C. Los Reyes Católicos
C. Concepción
C. Conde de Gondomar
C. Claudio Marcelo
C. Alfonso XIII
C. San Pablo
C. San Fernando
C. del Santo Cristo
C. Amador de los Ríos
200 meters
200 yards

residential area between the Mezquita and C. de San Fernando. Reserve ahead during *Semana Santa* and May through June. Popular **Instalación Juvenil Córdoba (HI) ❷**, Pl. Judá Leví, is a former mental asylum converted into a backpacker's paradise. The large rooms all have A/C and bath. (☎957 29 01 66. Wheelchair-accessible. Breakfast included; dinner €5.50. Linens €1.20. Laundry €4. Reception 24hr. Private rooms available. Mar.-Oct. dorms €20, under 26 €19; Nov.-Feb. €18/17. €3.50 HI discount. MC/V.) **Hostal el Portillo ❷**, C. Cabezas 2, is a traditional Andalusian house in a quiet area. Rooms are spacious and equipped with bath and A/C. (☎957 47 20 91. Singles €18-20; doubles €30-35. MC/V.)

Córdobeses converge on the outdoor *terrazas* between **Calle Doctor Severo Ochoa** and **Calle Doctor Jiménez Díaz** for drinks and *tapas* before dinner. Cheap restaurants are farther away from the Judería in **Barrio Cruz Conde** and around **Avenida Menéndez Pidal** and **Plaza de las Tendillas.** Regional specialties include *salmorejo* (cream soup) and *rabo de toro* (bull's tail simmered in tomato sauce). **Mundano ❶**, C. Conde de Cárdenas 3, combines delicious home style food—including many vegetarian options—with funky style and art shows. (☎957 47 37 85. Entrees €3-5. *Tapas* €2-4.70. Open M-F 10am-5pm and 10pm-2am, Sa noon-6pm and 10pm-2am. Cash only.) For a taste of the old Moorish Córdoba, head to **Salon de Té ❶**, C. Buen Pastor 13, a recreated 12th-century teahouse with a huge variety of Arab pastries, juices, and teas. (☎957 48 79 84. Beverages €2-4. Pastries €1.50-3. Open daily 11am-10:30pm. Cash only.)

SIGHTS. Built in AD 784, Córdoba's **La Mezquita** mosque is considered the most important Islamic monument in the Western world. Inside, 850 granite and marble columns support hundreds of striped arches. At the far end of the Mezquita lies the **Capilla Villaviciosa,** the first Christian chapel to be built in the mosque. In the center, pink-and-blue marble Byzantine mosaics shimmer across the arches of the **Mihrab** (prayer niche), which is covered in Kufic inscriptions of the 99 names of Allah. Although the town rallied violently against the construction of a **cathedral** in the center of the mosque, the towering *crucero* (transept) and *coro* (choir dome) were built after the Crusaders conquered Córdoba in 1236. (☎957 47 91 70. Strict silence. Wheelchair-accessible. Open Mar.-Oct. M-Sa 8:30am-7pm, Su 8:30-10:30am and 2-7pm. €8, ages 10-14 €4, under 10 free. Admission free during mass M-Sa 8:30-10am, Su 11am and 1pm.)

Along the river on the left of the Mezquita is the **Alcázar,** built for Catholic monarchs in 1328 during the Reconquista. Fernando and Isabel bade Columbus *adiós* here; the building later served as Inquisition headquarters. (☎957 42 01 51. Open Tu-Sa 8:30am-2:30pm and 4:30-6:30pm, Su and holidays 9:30am-2:30pm. Gardens open summer 8pm-midnight. Alcázar €4, students €2; gardens €2; F free.) The **Judería** is the historic area northwest of the Mezquita. Just past the statue of Maimonides, the small **Sinagoga,** C. Judíos 20, is a solemn reminder of the 1492 expulsion of the Jews. (☎957 20 29 28. Open Tu-Sa 9:30am-2pm and 3:30-5:30pm, Su 9:30am-1:30pm. €0.30, EU citizens free.)

ENTERTAINMENT AND FESTIVALS. For the latest cultural events, pick up a free copy of the *Guía del Ocio* or *Los Noches del Embrujo* at the tourist office. Flamenco is not cheap in Córdoba, but the shows are high quality and a bargain compared to similar shows in Seville and Madrid. Hordes of tourists flock to see the prize-winning dancers at the **Tablao Cardenal,** C. Torrijos 10. (☎957 48 33 20; www.tablaocardenal.com. €18, includes 1 drink. Shows M-Sa 10:30pm.) **Soul**, C. Alfonso XIII 3, is a hip bar with an older crowd and deafening bass. (☎957 49 15 80; www.bar-soul.com. Beer €2.10. Mixed drinks €4.50. Open Sept.-June daily 9am-4am.) A string of popular nightclubs runs along **Avenida Brillante,** such as **Club Don Luis** (open Th-Sa midnight-4:30am; cash only). Pubs with crowded *terrazas* line **Avenida Libertad,** including chic, African-influenced **Moma.** (☎957 76 84 77. Beer €2-2.50. Mixed drinks from €5. Open M-W and Su 9am-3am, Th-Sa 9am-5am. AmEx/MC/V.) An alternative to partying is a nighttime stroll along the **walk-through fountains** and falling sheets of water that line Av. de América directly between Pl. de Colón and the train station.

Of Córdoba's festivals, floats, and parades, **Semana Santa** (Holy Week; Apr. 5-12, 2009) is the most extravagant. The first few days of May are dedicated to the **Festival de las Cruces,** during which residents make crosses decorated with flowers. In the first two weeks of May, during the **Festival de los Patios,** the city erupts with concerts, flamenco, and a city-wide patio-decorating contest. Late May brings the **Feria de Nuestra Señora de Salud** (La Feria de Córdoba), a week of colorful garb, dancing, music, and wine-drinking. Every July, Córdoba hosts a **guitar festival,** attracting talented strummers from all over the world.

SEVILLE (SEVILLA) ☎954

Site of a Roman acropolis, capital of the Moorish empire, focal point of the Spanish Renaissance, and guardian of traditional Andalusian culture, romantic Seville (pop. 700,000) represents a fusion of cultures. Bullfighting, flamenco, and tapas are at their best here, and Seville's cathedral is among the most impressive in Spain. The city offers more than historical sights: its **Semana Santa** and **Feria de Abril** celebrations are among the most elaborate in Europe.

TRANSPORTATION

Flights: All flights arrive at **Aeropuerto San Pablo** (**SVQ;** ☎954 44 90 00), 12km out of town on Ctra. de Madrid. A taxi ride to the town center costs about €25. **Los Amarillos** (☎954 98 91 84) buses run to the airport from Prado de San Sebástian stop (1-2 per hr., €2.10). **Iberia,** C. Guadaira 8 (☎954 22 89 01), flies to **Barcelona** (1hr., 6 per day) and **Madrid** (45min., 6 per day).

Trains: Estación Santa Justa, on Av. de Kansas City (☎902 24 02 02). Near Pl. Nueva is the **RENFE** office, C. Zaragoza 29. (☎954 54 02 02. Open M-F 9am-1:15pm and 4-7pm.) Altaria and Talgo trains run to: **Barcelona** (9-13hr., 3 per day, €57-94); **Córdoba** (1hr., 6 per day, €15); **Valencia** (9hr., 1 per day, €49). AVE trains go to **Córdoba** (45min., 15-20 per day, €25-28) and **Madrid** (2hr., 15-21 per day, €67-75).

Buses: The bus station at Prado de San Sebastián, C. Manuel Vázquez Sagastizabal, serves most of Andalucía. (☎954 41 71 11. Open daily 5:30am-1am.) **Estación Plaza de Armas** (☎954 90 80 40) primarily serves areas outside of Andalucía.

Los Amarillos, Estación Prado de San Sebastián (☎954 98 91 84). To **Arcos de la Frontera** (2hr., 2-3 per day, €7), **Marbella** (3hr., 2-3 per day, €16), and **Ronda** (2hr., 3-5 per day, €11).

Alsa, Estación Pl. de Armas (☎954 90 78 00 or 902 42 22 42). To: **Cáceres** (4hr., 9 per day, €17); **León** (11hr., 3 per day, €42); **Salamanca** (8hr., 5 per day, €30); **Valencia** (9-11hr., 4 per day, €48-55). Seniors 50% discount. MC/V.

Alsina Graells, Estación Prado de San Sebastián (☎954 41 88 11). To **Córdoba** (2hr., 7-9 per day, €10), **Granada** (3hr., 10 per day, €19), and **Málaga** (2hr., 10-12 per day, €15).

Damas, Estación Pl. de Armas (☎954 90 77 37). To **Faro, POR** (4hr, 4 per day, €16), **Lagos, POR** (7hr., 4 per day, €19), and **Lisbon, POR** (6hr., 3 per day, €30).

Socibus, Estación Pl. de Armas (☎902 22 92 92). To **Madrid** (6hr., 14 per day, €19).

Public Transportation: TUSSAM (☎900 71 01 71; www.tussam.es) is the city bus network. Most lines run daily 6 per hr. (6am-11:15pm) and converge on Pl. Nueva, Pl. de la Encarnación, and in front of the cathedral. C-3 and C-4 circle the city center, and #34 hits the youth hostel, university, cathedral, and Pl. Nueva. **Night service** departs from

SPAIN

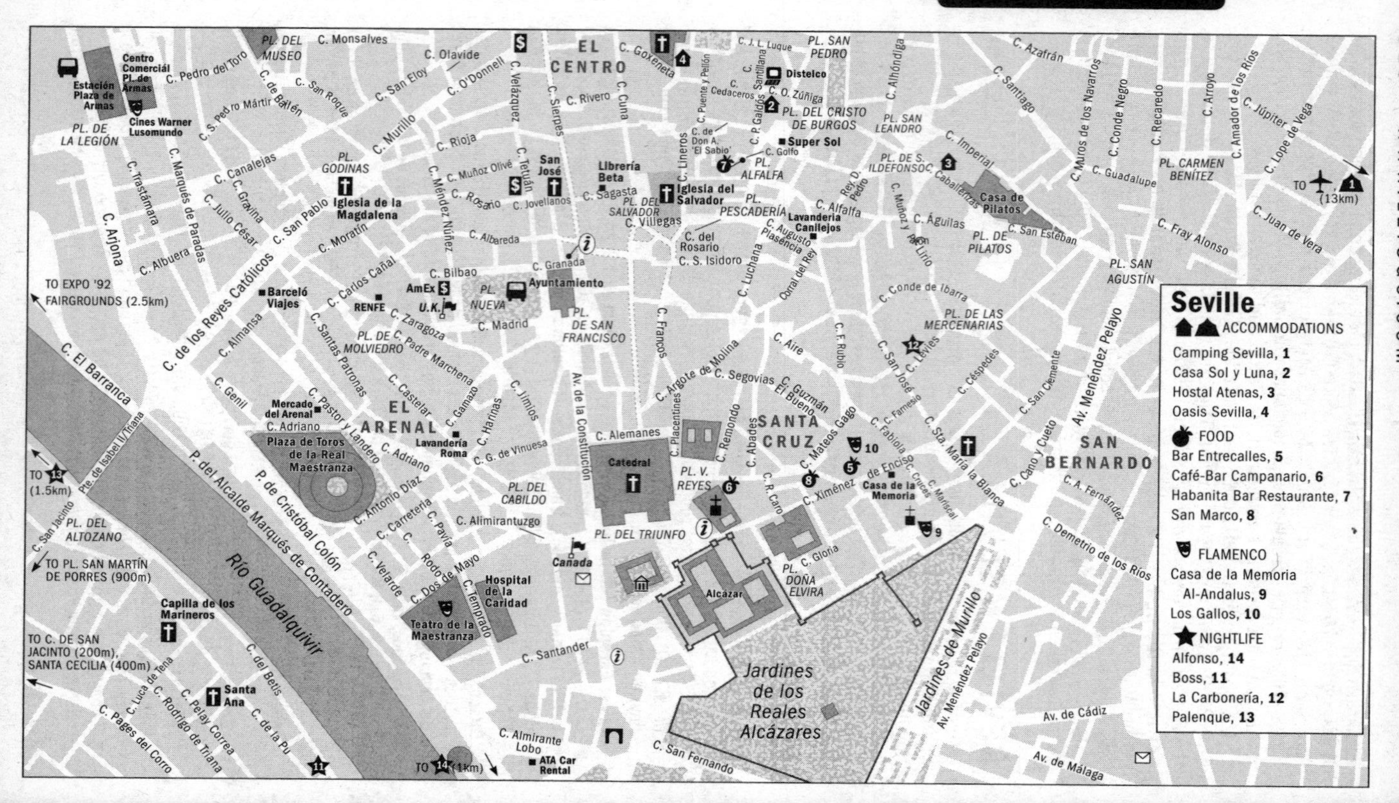
Seville
ACCOMMODATIONS
Camping Sevilla, 1
Casa Sol y Luna, 2
Hostal Atenas, 3
Oasis Sevilla, 4
FOOD
Bar Entrecalles, 5
Café-Bar Campanario, 6
Habanita Bar Restaurante, 7
San Marco, 8
FLAMENCO
Casa de la Memoria
Al-Andalus, 9
Los Gallos, 10
NIGHTLIFE
Alfonso, 14
Boss, 11
La Carbonería, 12
Palenque, 13
EL CENTRO
SANTA CRUZ
SAN BERNARDO
EL ARENAL
Estación Plaza de Armas
Centro Comercial Pl. de Armas
Cines Warner Lusomundo
PL. DE LA LEGIÓN
PL. DEL MUSEO
PL. GODINAS
Iglesia de la Magdalena
San José
Librería Beta
Iglesia del Salvador
PL. DEL SALVADOR
PL. ALFALFA
PL. PESCADERÍA
Lavandería Canilejos
Distelco
Super Sol
PL. DEL CRISTO DE BURGOS
PL. SAN PEDRO
PL. SAN LEANDRO
PL. DE S. ILDEFONSO
Casa de Pilatos
PL. DE PILATOS
PL. CARMEN BENÍTEZ
PL. SAN AGUSTÍN
PL. DE LAS MERCENARIAS
Barceló Viajes
RENFE
AmEx
U.K.
PL. NUEVA
Ayuntamiento
PL. DE SAN FRANCISCO
PL. DE MOLVIEDRO
Mercado del Arenal
Lavandería Roma
Plaza de Toros de la Real Maestranza
PL. DEL CABILDO
Catedral
PL. V. REYES
Casa de la Memoria
PL. DEL TRIUNFO
Canada
Alcázar
PL. DOÑA ELVIRA
Hospital de la Caridad
Teatro de la Maestranza
Jardines de los Reales Alcázares
Jardines de Murillo
Río Guadalquivir
PL. DEL ALTOZANO
Capilla de los Marineros
Santa Ana
ATA Car Rental
Av. de la Constitución
Av. Menéndez Pelayo
Av. de Cádiz
Av. de Málaga
P. de Cristóbal Colón
P. del Alcalde Marqués de Contadero
C. de los Reyes Católicos
C. El Barranca
Pte. de Isabel II/Triana
C. Sierpes
C. Tetuán
TO EXPO '92 FAIRGROUNDS (2.5km)
TO (13km)
TO (1.5km)
TO (1km)
TO PL. SAN MARTÍN DE PORRES (900m)
TO C. DE SAN JACINTO (200m), SANTA CECILIA (400m)

Pl. Nueva (M-Th and Su 1 per hr. midnight-2am, F-Sa 1 per hr. all night). Fare €1.10, 10-ride *bonobús* ticket €5, 30-day pass €30.

Taxis: Radio Taxi (☎954 58 00 00). Base rate €1.25, €0.40 per km, Su 25% surcharge. Extra charge for luggage and night taxis.

ORIENTATION AND PRACTICAL INFORMATION

The **Río Guadalquivir** flows roughly north to south through the city. Most of the touristed areas of Seville, including **Santa Cruz** and **El Arenal,** are on the east bank. The *barrios* of **Triana, Santa Cecilia,** and **Los Remedios,** as well as the **Expo '92 fairgrounds,** occupy the west bank. The **cathedral,** next to Santa Cruz, is Seville's centerpiece. **Avenida de la Constitución** runs alongside it. **El Centro,** a commercial pedestrian zone, lies north of the cathedral, starting where Av. Constitución hits **Plaza Nueva** and **Plaza de San Francisco,** site of the *Ayuntamiento*. **Calle Tetuán,** a popular shopping street, runs north from Pl. Nueva through El Centro.

Tourist Offices: Centro de Información de Sevilla Laredo, Pl. de San Francisco 19 (☎954 59 01 88; www.turismo.sevilla.org). Free Internet, max. 1hr. Open M-F 8am-3pm. **Turismo Andaluz,** Av. de la Constitución 21B (☎954 22 14 04). Info on all of Andalucía from helpful English-speaking staff. Open M-F 9am-7pm, Sa 10am-2pm and 3-7pm, Su 10am-2pm.

Luggage Storage: Estación Prado de San Sebastián (€1 per bag per day; open 6:30am-10pm), Estación Plaza de Armas (€3 per day), and train station (€3 per day).

Laundromat: Lavandería y Tintorería Roma, C. Castelar 2C (☎954 21 05 35). Wash, dry, and fold €6 per load. Open M-F 9:30am-2pm, 5:30-8:30pm, Sa 9am-2pm.

24hr. Pharmacy: Check list posted at any pharmacy for those open 24hr.

Medical Services: Red Cross (☎913 35 45 45). **Ambulatorio Esperanza Macarena** (☎954 42 01 05). **Hospital Virgen Macarena,** Av. Dr. Fedriani 56 (☎955 00 80 00).

Internet: Sevilla Internet Center, C. Almirantazgo, 1-2 (☎954 50 02 75). Ring bell. €3/hr.

Post Office: Av. de la Constitución 32 (☎954 21 64 76), opposite the cathedral. **Lista de Correos** and fax. Open M-F 8:30am-8:30pm, Sa 9:30am-2pm. **Postal Code:** 41080.

ACCOMMODATIONS AND CAMPING

Rooms vanish and prices soar during *Semana Santa* and the *Feria de Abril;* reserve several months ahead. In Santa Cruz, the streets around Calle Santa María la Blanca are full of cheap, centrally located hostels. Hostels by the Plaza de Armas bus station are close to El Centro and Calle del Betis.

Hostal Atenas, C. Caballerizas 1 (☎954 21 80 47; www.hostal-atenas.com), near Pl. Pilatos. Slightly pricier than other options but with good reason—everything about this hostel is appealing, from ivy arches leading to an old-fashioned indoor patio to cheerful rooms. All rooms with A/C and bath. Singles €35; doubles €54; triples €75. MC/V. ❸

Casa Sol y Luna, C. Pérez Galdós 1A (☎954 21 06 82; www.casasolyluna1.com). Beautiful hostel with a marble staircase and themed rooms. Laundry €10. Min. 2-night stay. Singles €22; doubles €38, with bath €45; triples €60; quads €80. Cash only. ❷

Oasis Sevilla, reception at Pl. Encarnación, 29 1/2, rooms above reception and at C. Alonso el Sabio 1A (☎954 29 37 77; www.hostelsoasis.com). Dorms on Pl. Encarnación crowded but centrally located; 2- and 4-bed dorms on C. Alonso are quieter. Breakfast, Internet, and a pool. Reserve ahead. Dorms €18; doubles €46. MC/V. ❷

Camping Sevilla, Ctra. Madrid-Cádiz km 534 (☎954 51 43 79), near the airport. From Pr. San Sebastián, take bus #70 (stops 800m away at Parque Alcosa). Hot showers, supermarket, and pool. €3.80 per tent, €3.30 per car. MC/V. ❶

FOOD

Seville, which claims to be the birthplace of *tapas*, keeps its cuisine light. *Tapas* bars cluster around **Plaza San Martín** and along **Calle San Jacinto.** Popular venues for *el tapeo* (tapas barhopping) include **Barrio de Santa Cruz** and **El Arenal.** Find produce at **Mercado de la Encarnación,** near the bullring in Pl. de la Encarnación. (Open M-Sa 9am-2pm.) There is a supermarket below **El Corte Inglés,** in Pl. del Duque de la Victoria. (☎954 27 93 97. Open M-Sa 9am-10pm. AmEx/MC/V.)

Habanita Bar Restaurant, C. Golfo 3 (☎606 71 64 56; www.andalunet.com/habanita), on a tiny street off C. Pérez Galdós, next to Pl. Alfalfa. Exquisite Cuban fare, including *yucca* (yam) and *ropa vieja* ("old clothes"; shredded beef and rice). Entrees €6-16. Open M-Sa 12:30-4:30pm and 8pm-12:30am, Su 12:30-4:30pm. MC/V. ❷

Café-Bar Campanario, C. Mateos Gago 8 (☎954 56 41 89). This clean-cut, modern cafe-bar is more vegetarian-friendly than most *tapas* bars. Sip some of the strongest *sangria* in town (0.5L €12, 1L €15). *Tapas* €2.50-3.40. *Raciones* €10-14. Crepes and sandwiches €3.60-5.80. Open daily 11am-midnight. AmEx/MC/V. ❷

Bar Entrecalles, C. Ximenez de Enciso 14 (☎617 86 77 52). Situated at the center of the tourist buzz, but retains a local following. *Tapas* €2. Generous portions of delicious *gazpacho* (€2). Open daily 1pm-2am. Cash only. ❶

San Marco, C. Mesón del Moro 6 (☎954 56 43 90), in Santa Cruz's *casco antiguo.* Pizza, pasta, and dessert in an 18th-century house with 17th-century Arab baths. Other San Marco locations around town are in equally impressive settings. Entrees €5-10; salads €4-9. Open daily 1:15-4:30pm and 8:15pm-12:30am. MC/V. ❷

SIGHTS

CATEDRAL. Legend has it that 15th-century *reconquistadores* wished to demonstrate their religious fervor by constructing a church so great that "those who come after us will take us for madmen." With 44 chapels, the cathedral of Seville is the third largest in the world (after St. Peter's Basilica in Rome and St. Paul's Cathedral in London) and the biggest Gothic edifice ever constructed. The cathedral took more than a century to complete. *(☎954 21 49 71. Entrance by the Pl. de la Virgen de los Reyes. Open M-Sa 9:30am-4pm, Su 2:30-6pm. €7.50, seniors and students €2, under 16 free. Audio tour €3. Mass in the Capilla Real M-Sa 8:30, 10am, noon, 5pm; Su 8:30, 10, 11am, noon, 1, 5, 6pm.)*

ALCÁZAR. The oldest European palace still used as a private residence for royals, Seville's Alcázar epitomizes extravagance. Though the Alhambra in Granada gets more press, the Alcázar features equally impressive architecture. Built by the Moors in the 7th century, the palace was embellished greatly during the 17th century. It displays an interesting mix of Moorish, Gothic, Renaissance, and Baroque architecture, most prominently on display in the *mudéjar* style of many of the arches, tiles, and ceilings. Catholic monarchs Fernando and Isabel are the palace's best-known former residents; their grandson Carlos V also lived here and married his cousin, Isabel of Portugal, in the **Salón Carlos V.** Visitors enter through the **Patio de la Montería,** across from the Almohad facade of the Moorish palace. Through the archway lie the Arabic residences, including the **Patio del Yeso** (Patio of Mortar) and the **Patio de las Muñecas** (Patio of the Dolls), so named because of the miniature faces carved into the bottom of one of the room's pillars. Of the Christian additions, the most notable is the **Patio de las Doncellas** (Patio of the Maids). Court life in the Alcázar revolved around this columned quadrangle. The golden-domed **Salón de los Embajadores** (Ambassadors' Room) is allegedly the site where Fernando and Isabel welcomed Columbus back from the New World.

The upstairs **private residences,** the official home of the king and queen of Spain, have been renovated and redecorated throughout the centuries; most of the furniture today dates from the 18th and 19th centuries. These residences are accessible only by 25min. tours. Gardens adorned with fountains and exotic flowers stretch in all directions from the residential quarters. *(Pl. del Triunfo 7. ☎954 50 23 23. Open Tu-Sa 9:30am-7pm, Su 9:30am-5pm. Tours of the upper palace living quarters 2 per hr. Aug.-May 10am-1:30pm and 3:30-5:30pm; June-July 10am-1:30pm; max. 15 people per tour. Buy tickets in advance. €7; students and over 65 free. Tours €4. Audio tours €3.)*

PLAZA DE TOROS DE LA REAL MAESTRANZA. Home to one of the two great bullfighting schools (the other is in **Ronda,** p. 923), Plaza de Toros de la Real Maestranza fills to capacity (13,800) for weekly fights and the 13 *corridas* of the *Feria de Abril.* Visitors must follow the multilingual tours through the small **Museo Taurino de la Real Maestranza;** tours also go behind the ring to the chapel where matadores pray before fights and to the medical emergency room, used when their prayers go unanswered. *(☎954 22 45 77; www.realmaestranza.com. Open May-Oct. 9:30am-8pm; Nov.-Apr. 9:30am-7pm. Tours 3 per hr. €5; seniors 20% discount.)*

ENTERTAINMENT

The tourist office distributes *El Giraldillo* (www.elgiraldillo.es), a free magazine with listings of music, art exhibits, theater, dance, and film.

FLAMENCO

Flamenco—traditionally consisting of dance, guitar, and song, and originally brought to Spain by gypsies—is at its best in Seville. It can be seen either in highly touristed *tablaos,* where skilled professional dancers perform, or in *tabernas,* bars where locals merrily dance *sevillanas.* Both have merit, but the *tabernas* tend to be free. The tourist office has a complete list of *tablaos* and *tabernas;* ask about student discounts. **Los Gallos,** Pl. de Santa Cruz 11, is arguably the best tourist show in Seville. Buy tickets ahead and arrive early. (☎954 21 69 81; www.tablaolosgallos.com. Shows nightly 8pm and 10:30pm. €27, includes 1 drink.) A less expensive alternative is the impressive 1hr. show at the cultural center **Casa de la Memoria Al-Andalus,** C.

THE LOCAL STORY

SEVILLE'S TRAGIC TAL

Among its many legacies, the *Jud-ería* left Seville one of its mos tragic legends: that of Susona La Hermosa Hembra (vulgar fo "beautiful woman").

During the 15th century, ever as relations between Seville's Christian and Jewish population were increasingly tense, Susona the daughter of a Jewish merchant fell in love with a Christian knight Every night, she would sneak ou the window, meet her lover by the army barracks, and make it bac home before dawn unnoticed. One night, however, she overheard he father plotting a rebellion agains the Christian government and, fear ing that she would lose her love forever, Susona warned him of the plot. The Christian army's retaliatio was swift and merciless—Susona's entire family was slaughtered, an their bodies were left to scavenger Susona's street thereafter bore the name C. Muerte.

Deeply remorseful, Susona confessed in Seville's Cathedra received baptism, and retreate into a convent. When she died she asked that her head be placed above her doorway as a symbol of redemption for all and strangely, nobody touched it fo over one-hundred years. While Susona's skull no longer can b seen on what is now C. Susona a plaque still bears testimony t her tragic story.

Ximénez de Enciso 28, in the middle of Santa Cruz. Ask at their ticket office for a schedule of performances. (Shows daily in summer are at 9pm and 10:30pm. Limited seating; buy tickets ahead. €13, students €11, under 10 €6.)

BULLFIGHTING

Seville's bullring, one of the most beautiful in Spain, hosts bullfights from *Semana Santa* through October. The cheapest place to buy tickets is at the ring on Po. Alcalde Marqués de Contadero. When there's a good *cartel* (line-up), the booths on C. Sierpes, C. Velázquez, and Pl. de Toros might be the only source of advance tickets. Ticket prices can run from €20 for a *grada de sol* (nosebleed seat in the sun) to €75 for a *barrera de sombra* (front-row seat in the shade) or more; scalpers usually add 20%. *Corridas de toros* (bull-fights) and *novilladas* (fights with apprentice bullfighters and younger bulls) are held on the 13 days around the *Feria de Abril* and into May, on Sundays April through June and September through October, more often during Corpus Cristi in June and early July, and during the *Feria de San Miguel* near the end of September. During July and August, *corridas* occasionally occur on Thursday at 9pm; check posters around town. (For current info and ticket sales, call the Plaza de Toros ticket office at ☎954 50 13 82.)

SPAIN

FESTIVALS

Seville swells with tourists during its *fiestas*, and with good reason. If you're in Spain during any of the major festivals, head straight to Seville. Reserve a room a few months in advance, and expect to pay two or three times the normal rate. Seville's world-famous **Semana Santa** lasts from Palm Sunday to Easter Sunday (Apr. 3-12, 2009). Thousands of penitents in hooded cassocks guide *pasos* (lavishly decorated floats) through the streets, illuminated by hundreds of candles. On Good Friday, the entire city turns out for the procession along the bridges and through the oldest neighborhoods. The city rewards itself for its Lenten piety with the **Feria de Abril** (Apr. 28-May 3, 2009). Begun as part of a 19th-century revolt against foreign influence, the *Feria* has grown into a massive celebration of all things Andalusian, with circuses, bullfights, and flamenco shows. At the fairgrounds at the southern end of Los Remedios, an array of flowers and lanterns decorates over 1000 kiosks, tents, and pavilions, collectively called *casetas*. Each has a small kitchen, bar, and dance floor. Most *casetas* are privately owned, so the only way to get invited is by making friends with the locals. Luckily, there are a few large public *casetas*. People-watching from the sidelines can be almost as exciting, as costumed girls dance *sevillanas* and men parade on horseback. The city holds bullfights daily during the festival; buy tickets in advance since they often sell out.

NIGHTLIFE

Seville's reputation for hoopla is tried and true—most clubs don't get going until well after midnight, and the real fun often starts only after 3am. Popular bars can be found around **Calle Mateos Gago** near the cathedral, **Calle Adriano,** and **Calle del Betis** in Triana. Gay clubs cluster around **Plaza de Armas.**

La Carbonería, C. Levies 18 (☎954 22 99 45), off C. Santa María La Blanca. Guitar-strumming Romeos abound on the outdoor stage and amid the picnic tables. Tapas

€1.50-2. Beer €1.50. *Agua de Sevilla* (champagne, cream, 4 liquors, and pineapples) €16-21. *Sangria* pitchers €8.50. Th free flamenco. Open daily 8pm-3am. Cash only.

Boss, C. del Betis (☎954 99 01 01; www.salaboss.es), knows how to get a crowd fired up. Irresistible beats and a hip atmosphere make this a wildly popular destination. Beer €3.50. Mixed drinks €6. Open fall-spring daily 9pm-5am. MC/V.

Palenque, Av. Blas Pascal (☎954 46 74 08). Cross Pte. de la Barqueta, turn left, and follow C. Materático Rey Pastor to the first big intersection. Turn left again and look for the entrance on the right. Gigantic dance club, complete with 2 dance floors and a small ice skating rink (€3; includes skate rental; closes at 4am). During the summer, the crowd consists largely of teenagers. Beer €3.50. Mixed drinks €5-6. Cover Th free, F-Sa €7. Dress to impress. Open June-Sept. Th-Sa midnight-7am. MC/V.

Alfonso, Av. la Palmera (☎954 23 37 35), adjacent to Po. de las Delicias. Avoid the longer lines elsewhere and shake it to the DJ's crazy beats in this spacious outdoor club. Palm trees and mini-bars are scattered around the dance floor. Beer €2.50-3. Mixed drinks €4.50-6. Open M-Th and Su 10pm-5am, F-Sa 10pm-7am. AmEx/MC/V.

SPAIN

DAYTRIPS FROM SEVILLE

ARCOS DE LA FRONTERA

Los Amarillos buses (☎956 32 93 47) run from C. Corregidores to Seville (2hr., 2 per day, €7.39). Transportes Generales buses go to Cádiz (1hr., 6 per day, €4.80), Costa del Sol (3-4hr., 1 per day, €10-13), and Ronda (1hr., 4 per day, €6). The tourist office is on Pl. del Cabildo. (☎956 70 22 64. Open mid-Mar. to mid-Oct. M-Sa 10am-2pm and 4-8pm, Su 10am-2pm; mid-Oct. to mid-Mar. M-Sa 10am-2pm and 3:30-7:30pm, Su 10am-2pm.)

Peaceful and romantic, Arcos (pop. 33,000) is the best of Spain's *pueblos blancos* (white towns). The **Basílica de Santa María de la Asunción,** in the town square, is a hodgepodge of Baroque, Gothic, and Renaissance styles under renovation through 2009. (Open M-F 10am-1pm and 3:30-6:30pm, Sa 10am-2pm. €1.50.) Wander through the *casco antiguo* (Old Quarter) and marvel at the view from **Plaza del Cabildo.** The Gothic **Iglesia de San Pedro** stands on the site of an Arab fortress. (Open daily 10am-2pm, 5-7pm. €1. Mass in winter 11:30am. Free.) **El Centro de Interpretacion** *"La Molinera y el Corregidor,"* C. Piedra del Molino, 50 (☎956 70 10 95), highlights the poem's influence on works by Manuel de Falla, Picasso, Dalí, and Hugo Wolf. (Open M-F 10:30am-1:30pm and 5:30-8:30pm. Free.) Cheap cafes and restaurants cluster at the bottom end of **Calle Corredera,** while *tapas* nirvana can be achieved in the *casco antiguo.* Try the *pollo a la plancha* (grilled chicken; €6.40) at **Mesón Los Murales ❷,** Pl. Boticas 1 (☎956 70 06 07. *Menú* €9. Entrees €7.50-13. Open M-W and F-Su 9am-1am. MC/V.)

To reach the *casco antiguo* from the bus station, exit left, follow the road, turn left again, and continue uphill on C. Josefa Moreno Seguro. Take a right on C. Muñoz Vásquez; upon reaching Pl. de España, veer left onto C. Debajo del Coral, which becomes C. Corredera. Manolo Blanco **buses** run every 30min. from the bus station to C. Corredera (€0.80).

RONDA

Trains (☎952 87 16 73) depart from Av. Alferez Provisional for Granada (3hr., 3 per day, €12); Madrid (4hr., 2 per day, €60); Málaga (2hr., 1 per day, €9). Buses (☎952 18 70 61) go from Pl. Concepción García Redondo 2 to: Cádiz (4hr., 2-3 per day, €13); Málaga (2hr., 8-11 per day, €9); Seville (2hr., 3-5 per day, €10).

Ancient bridges, old dungeons, and a famed bullring attract many visitors to picturesque Ronda (pop. 35,500), which has all the charm of a small, medieval town with the amenities and culture of a thriving city. A precipitous 100m gorge, carved by the Río Guadalevín, drops below the **Puente Nuevo,** opposite

Pl. España. The **views** from the **Puente Nuevo, Puente Viejo,** and **Puente San Miguel** are unparalleled. Take the first left after crossing the Puente Nuevo to Cuesta de Santo Domingo, and descend the steep stairs of the **Casa Del Rey Moro** into the 14th-century water-mine for an otherworldly view of the ravine. (☎952 18 72 00. Open daily 10am-7pm. €4, children €2.) Bullfighting aficionados charge to Ronda's **Plaza de Toros,** Spain's oldest bullring (est. 1785) as well as the cradle of the modern *corrida.* In early September, the Pl. de Toros hosts *corridas goyescas* (bullfights in traditional costumes) as part of the **Feria de Ronda.** For a selection of 50 kinds of *montaditos* (small, substantial sandwiches; €1.20), head to **Casi Ke No ❶,** C. Molino 6B. (Open Tu-Su noon-4pm and 7pm-midnight. Cash only.) **El Pataton ❶,** C. San José, 8 (☎678 87 06 26) serves great baked potatoes (€3.50-4.50) stuffed with *tapas* ingredients. (Open Tu-Su 8pm-midnight. Closed July.) The **tourist office**, Po. Blas Infante, is across from the bullring. (☎952 18 71 19. English spoken. Open June-Aug. M-F 9:30am-7:30pm, Sa-Su 10am-2pm, 3:30-6:30pm; Sept.-May M-F 9:30am-6:30pm, Sa-Su 10am-2pm, 3:30-6:30pm.)

SPAIN

GRANADA ☎958

The splendors of the Alhambra, the magnificent palace that crowns the highest point of Granada (pop. 238,000), have fascinated both prince and pauper for centuries. Legend has it that in 1492, when the Moorish ruler Boabdil fled the city, the last Muslim stronghold in Spain, his mother berated him for casting a longing look back at the Alhambra. "You do well to weep as a woman," she told him, "for what you could not defend as a man." The Albaicín, an enchanting maze of Moorish houses, is Spain's best-preserved Arab quarter. Granada has grown into a university city infused with youthful energy.

TRANSPORTATION

Trains: RENFE, Av. Andaluces (☎902 24 02 02. www.renfe.es). Take bus #3-6, 9, or 11 from Gran Vía to the Constitución (3 stops) and turn left onto Av. Andaluces. To: **Algeciras** (4-5hr., 3 per day 7:15am-5pm, €18.35); **Almería** (2hr., 4 per day 10:03am-9:06pm, €14.45); **Barcelona** (12hr.; 9:45pm; €52.10-57.40); **Madrid** (5-6hr.; 6:42am, 6pm; €61.80); **Sevilla** (4-5hr., 4 per day 8:18am-8:24pm, €21.65).

Buses: All major intercity bus routes start at the bus station (☎958 18 54 80) on the outskirts of Granada on **Ctra. de Madrid,** near C. Arzobispo Pedro de Castro. Take bus #3 or 33 from Gran Vía de Colón or a **taxi** (€6-7). Services reduced on Sundays.

ALSA (☎902 42 22 42 or 958 15 75 57; www.alsa.es) to: **Alicante** (6hr., 6 per day 2:31am-11:30pm, €26.69); **Barcelona** (14hr., 5 per day 2:31am-11:30pm, €65.96); **Valencia** (9hr., 5 per day 2:31am-11:30pm, €40.23); **Algeciras** (3hr., 6 per day 9am-8:15pm, €20.20); **Almería** (2hr., 8 per day 6:45am-7:30pm, €11.50); **Antequera** (1hr., 4 per day 9am-7pm, €7.20); **Cádiz** (5hr., 4 per day 3am-6:30pm, €29.52); **Córdoba** (3hr., 8 per day 7:30am-7pm, €12.04); **Madrid** (5-6hr., 15 per day 7am-1:30am, €15.66); **Málaga** (2hr., 16 per day 7am-9pm, €9.38); **Marbella** (2hr., 8 per day 8am-8:15pm, €14.35); **Sevill3** (3hr., 7 per day 8am-8pm, €18.57).

Public Transportation: Local **buses** (☎900 71 09 00). Pick up the bus map at the tourist office. Important buses include: "Bus Alhambra" #30 from Gran Vía de Cólon or Pl. Nueva to the Alhambra; #31 from Gran Vía or Pl. Nueva to the Albaicín; #10 from the bus station to the youth hostel, C. de Ronda, C. Recogidas, and C. Acera de Darro; #3 from the bus station to Av. de la Constitución, Gran Vía, and Pl. Isabel la Católica. €1.10, *bonobus* (9 tickets) €5.45.

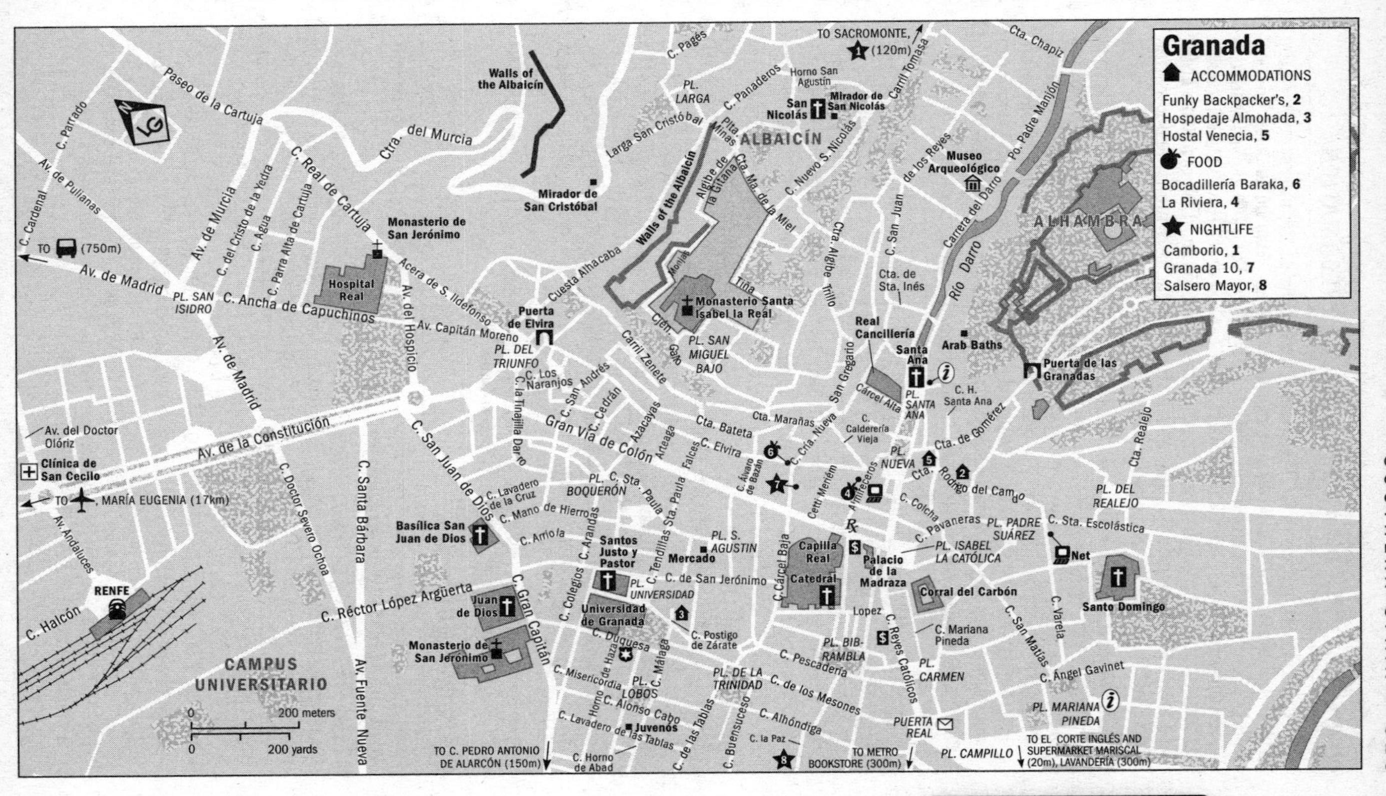
Granada
ACCOMMODATIONS
Funky Backpacker's, 2
Hospedaje Almohada, 3
Hostal Venecia, 5
FOOD
Bocadillería Baraka, 6
La Riviera, 4
NIGHTLIFE
Camborio, 1
Granada 10, 7
Salsero Mayor, 8
ALHAMBRA
ALBAICÍN
Walls of the Albaicín
Mirador de San Cristóbal
Mirador de San Nicolás
San Nicolás
Monasterio Santa Isabel la Real
Museo Arqueológico
Arab Baths
Puerta de las Granadas
Real Cancillería
Santa Ana
Capilla Real
Catedral
Palacio de la Madraza
Corral del Carbón
Santo Domingo
Mercado
Santos Justo y Pastor
Universidad de Granada
Basílica San Juan de Dios
Juan de Dios
Monasterio de San Jerónimo
Hospital Real
Puerta de Elvira
Clínica de San Cecilio
RENFE
Net
CAMPUS UNIVERSITARIO
Río Darro
Gran Vía de Colón
C. Reyes Católicos
C. San Juan de Dios
C. Gran Capitán
Av. de la Constitución
Av. de Madrid
C. Real de Cartuja
Av. del Hospicio
C. Santa Bárbara
Av. Fuente Nueva
C. Doctor Severo Ochoa
C. Réctor López Argüerta
Av. Andaluces
Paseo de la Cartuja
Av. de Pulianas
TO SACROMONTE, (120m)
TO METRO BOOKSTORE (300m)
TO EL CORTE INGLÉS AND SUPERMARKET MARISCAL (20m), LAVANDERÍA (300m)
TO C. PEDRO ANTONIO DE ALARCÓN (150m)
TO MARÍA EUGENIA (17km)
TO (750m)
0 200 meters
0 200 yards

SPAIN

ORIENTATION AND PRACTICAL INFORMATION

The center of Granada is small **Plaza Isabel la Católica,** at the intersection of the city's two main arteries, **Calle de los Reyes Católicos** and **Gran Vía de Colón.** Just off Gran Vía, you'll find the cathedral; farther down Gran Vía by Pl. de la Trinidad is the university area. Uphill from Pl. Isabel la Católica on C. Reyes Católicos sits **Plaza Nueva,** and the **Alhambra** rises on the hill above. From Pl. Nueva, **Calle Elvira,** lined with bars and eateries, runs parallel to Gran Vía. Downhill, the pedestrian streets off C. de los Reyes Católicos comprise the shopping district.

Tourist Offices: Junta de Andalucía, C. Santa Ana, 2 (☎958 57 52 02). Open M-F 9am-7:30pm, Sa 9:30am-3pm, Su 10am-2pm. Posts bus and train schedules and provides a list of accommodations. Use this office for information about all of Andalucía. **Oficina Provincial,** Pl. Mariana Pineda, 10 (☎958 24 71 28). Walk up to the left past plaza Isabel and make a right on Pineda. Walk until the square. English spoken. Great for all questions concerning Granada. Open M-F 9am-8pm, Sa 10am-7pm, Su 10am-3pm.

Currency Exchange: Banco Santander Central Hispano, Gran Vía, 3 (☎902 24 24 24). Open Apr.-Sept. M-F 8:30am-2pm.

Luggage Storage: 24hr. storage at the train and bus stations (€3). Frequently sold out.

English-Language Bookstore: Metro, C. Gracia, 31 (☎958 26 15 65), off Veronica de la Magdelana, off C. Recogidas, which begins where Reyes Católicos hits Puerta Real.. Vast foreign language section. Open M-F 10am-2pm and 56-8:30pm, Sa 11am-2pm.

Gay and Lesbian Resources: Información Homosexual Hotline (☎958 20 06 02).

Laundromat: C. de la Paz, 19., off Veronica de la Magdelena. Wash €8, dry €2 per 10min.; detergent included. Open M-F 10am-2pm and 5-8pm.

Police: C. Duquesa, 21 (☎091). English spoken.

Medical Services and Pharmacy: Hospital Universitario de San Cecilio, C. Dr. Olóriz, 16 (☎958 02 30 00). **Farmacia Gran Vía,** Gran Vía, 6 (☎958 22 29 90). Open M-F 9:30am-1:30pm and 5-8:30pm, Sa 9:30am-1:30pm and 5:30-9pm

Internet Access: Locutorio Cyber Alhambra, C. Joaquin Costa, 4 (☎958 22 43 96).. €1.20 per hour; €5 *bono* for 6hr., €10 *bono* for 13hr. Open daily 9:30am-10:30pm. Second alley to left on Reyes Católicos walking away from Plaza Isabel.

Post Office: Pta. Real (☎958 22 48 35). *Lista de Correos* and fax service. Open M-F 8:30am-8:30pm, Sa 9:30am-2pm. **Postal Code:** 18009.

ACCOMMODATIONS

Hostels line Cuesta de Gomérez, Plaza Trinidad, and Gran Vía. Be sure to call ahead during Semana Santa (Apr. 3-12, 2009).

Funky Backpacker's, Cuesta de Rodrigo del Campo, 13 (☎958 22 14 62; funky@alternativeacc.com). From Pl. Nueva, go uphill on Cuchilleros 20m to find Cuesta de Rodrigo on the right. Sizable dorms surround a central atrium over the funky lobby. Take in the view of the Alhambra, mountains, and rooftops from the bar atop the hostel. The friendly staff hangs out with travelers. Outings to nearby thermal baths (€10), tapas bars and *flamenco* shows (€21). A/C, breakfast, and lockers included. Laundry (wash, dry and fold) €7. Free internet. Dinner €4.50-6. Dorms €16.50-17; doubles €40. MC/V. ❶

Hostal Venecia, Cuesta de Gomérez, 2, 3rd fl. (☎958 22 39 87). Eccentrically decorated with bright colors and Granada paraphernalia, this small, homey hostel has the most character per square meter in town. Homemade herbal tea and conversation available any time of day. Reserve early, especially in summer, since the secret is out. Dorms €19; doubles €34; triples €45. MC/V. ❶

Hospedaje Almohada, C. Postigo de Zárate, 4 (☎958 20 74 46; www.laalmohada.com). Follow C. Trinidad out of Pl. Trinidad to the T-intersection, then make a right and walk down the short street ahead. Look for double red doors with hand-shaped knockers. Lounge in the TV area, use the kitchen to cook your own meal, and peruse the communal music collection and travel guides. Laundry (wash and hang-dry) €5 for 8kg. Four-bed dorms €15; singles €19; doubles €35; triples €50. Cash only. ❶

FOOD

North African cuisine and vegetarian options can be found around the Albaicín, while more typical *menús* await in Pl. Nueva and Pl. Trinidad. Picnickers can gather fresh fruit, vegetables, and meat for an outdoor feast at the indoor market on Pl. San Agustín. (Open M-Sa 9am-3pm.)

Bocadillería Baraka, C. Elvira, 20 (☎958 22 97 60). Stands out among many Middle Eastern eateries for being the cheapest and the tastiest. Proud that their meat is home prepared and never frozen, Baraka serves delicious traditional pitas (€2.50-4) and addictive homemade lemonade infused with *hierbabuena* (€1). Hedi, the owner, also organizes week long, all-inclusive excursions through Morocco (☎649 11 41 71). Open daily 1pm-2am. Cash only. ❶

La Riviera, C. Cetti Meriem, 7 (☎958 22 79 69), off C. Elvira. The best place to score delicious, free *tapas*. You can't go wrong with the extensive list of traditional fare. Beer or *tinto de verano* €1.80. Open daily 12:30-4pm and 8pm-midnight. ❶

SIGHTS

THE ALHAMBRA. From the streets of Granada, the Alhambra appears blocky and practical. But up close, the Alhambra is an elaborate and detailed work of architecture, one that unites water, light, wood, stucco, and ceramics to create a fortress-palace of aesthetic grandeur. The age-old saying holds true: *Si mueres sin ver la Alhambra, no has vivido.* (If you die without seeing the Alhambra, you have not lived.) Follow signs to the Palacio Nazaries to see the **Alcázar,** a 14th-century royal palace full of stalactite archways and sculpted fountains. The walls of the Patio del Cuarto Dorado are topped by the shielded windows of the harem. Off the far side of the patio, archways open onto the **Cuarto Dorado,** whose carved wooden ceiling is inlaid with ivory and mother-of-pearl. From the top of the patio, glimpse the 14th-century **Fachada de Serallo,** the palace's intricately carved facade. In the **Sala de los Abencerrajes,** Boabdil had the throats of 16 sons of the Abencerrajes family slit after one of them allegedly had amorous encounters with the sultana. Rust-colored stains in the basin are said to be traces of the massacre. *(☎902 44 12 21; www.alhambra-patronato.es; reservations ☎902 22 44 60; www.alhambra-tickets.es. Open daily Apr.-Sept. 8:30am-8pm; Oct.-Mar. 8:30am-6pm. Also open June-Sept. Tu-Sa 10-11:30pm; Oct.-May F-Sa 8-9:30pm. Audio tours are worth the €5 and are available in English, French, German, Italian, and Spanish. €12, under 12 and the disabled free. €13 if purchased online. EU students with ID and EU seniors 65+ €9.)*

THE ALBAICÍN. A labyrinth of steep, narrow alleys, the Albaicín was the only Moorish neighborhood to escape the torches of the Reconquista. After the fall of the Alhambra, a small Muslim population remained here until their expulsion in the 17th century. Today, with North African cuisine, outdoor bazaars blasting Arabic music, teahouses, and the mosque near Pl. San Nicolás, the Albaicín attests to the persistence of Islamic culture in Andalucía. The best way to explore this maze is to proceed along Carrera del Darro off Pl. Santa Ana, climb the Cuesta del Chapiz on the left, then wander through the Muslim ramparts, cisterns, and gates. On Pl. Santa Ana, the 16th-century Real Cancillería, with its arcaded patio and stalactite ceiling, was the Christians' city hall. Farther uphill are the 11th-century Arab baths. *(Carrera del Darro, 31. ☎958 22 97 38. Call ☎958 22 56 03 to confirm hours. Free.)* The **mirador,** adjacent to Iglesia de San Nicolás, affords the city's best view of the Alhambra, especially in winter when snow adorns the Sierra Nevada behind it.

CAPILLA REAL AND CATHEDRAL. Downhill from the Alhambra, the **Capilla Real** (Royal Chapel), Fernando and Isabel's private chapel, exemplifies Christian Granada. Gothic masonry and meticulously rendered figurines, as well as La Reja, the gilded iron grille of Maestro Bartolomé, grace the couple's resting place. The Sacristía houses Isabel's private art collection and the royal jewels. *(☎958 22 92 39. Capilla Real and Sacristía both open Apr.-Sept. M-Sa 10:30am-12:45pm and 4-7pm, Su 11am-12:45pm and 4-7pm; Oct.-May M-Sa 10:30am-12:45pm and 3:30-6:15pm, Su 11am-12:45pm and 3:30-6:15pm. Both sights €3.50.)* Behind the Capilla Real and the Sacristía is Granada's cathedral. After the Reconquista, construction of the cathedral began upon the smoldering embers of Granada's largest mosque. *(☎958 22 29 59. Open Apr.-Sept. M-Sa 10:45am-1:30pm and 4-8pm, Su 4-8pm; Oct.-Mar. M-Sa 10:30am-1:30pm and 4-7pm, Su 11am-1:30pm and 4-7pm. €3.50.)*

NIGHTLIFE

Granada's policy of "free *tapas* with a drink" lures students and tourists to its many pubs and bars. Great *tapas* bars can be found off the side streets near Pl. Nueva. The most boisterous nightspots belong to **Calle Pedro Antonio de Alarcón,** between Pl. Albert Einstein and Ancha de Gracia, while hip new bars and clubs line **Calle Elvira.** Gay bars are around **Carrera del Darro.**

Camborio, Camino del Sacromonte, 48 (☎958 22 12 15), a quick taxi ride or 20min. walk uphill from Pl. Nueva; bus #34 stops at midnight. DJ-spun pop music echoes through dance floors to the rooftop patio above. Striking view of the Alhambra. Beer €4. Mixed drinks €5. Cover €6, includes 1 drink. Open Tu-Sa midnight-7am. Cash only.

Salsero Mayor, C. la Paz, 20 (☎958 52 27 41). An ageless group of locals and tourists alike flocks here for crowded nights of salsa, bachata, and merengue. Beer €2-3. Mixed drinks €5. Open M-Th and Su 10pm-3am, F-Sa 1pm-4am. Cash only.

Granada 10, C. Cárcel Baja 3 (☎958 22 40 01). Movie theater by evening (shows Sept.-June at 8 and 10pm), raging dance club by night. Flashy and opulent. No sneakers or sportswear. Open M-Th and Su 12:30-4am, F-Sa 12:30-6am. Cover €10. MC/V.

COSTA DEL SOL

The Costa del Sol combines rocky beaches with chic promenades and swanky hotels. While some spots are over-developed and can be hard on the wallet, elsewhere the coast's stunning landscape has been left untouched.

MÁLAGA ☎952

Málaga (pop. 550,000) is the transportation hub of the coast, and while its beaches are known more for bars than for natural beauty, the city has much to offer. Towering high above the city, the medieval **Alcazaba** is Málaga's most imposing sight. At the east end of Po. del Parque, the 11th-century structure was originally used as both a military fortress and royal palace for Moorish kings. (Open June-Aug. Tu-Su 9:30am-8pm; Sept.-May Tu-Sa 8:30am-7pm. €2, students and seniors €0.60. Free Su after 2pm.) Málaga's breathtaking **cathedral,** C. Molina Lario 4, is nicknamed *La Manquita* (One-Armed Lady) because one of its two towers was never completed. (☎952 22 03 45. Open M-F 10am-6pm,

Sa 10am-5pm. Mass daily 9am. Entrance €3.50, includes audio tour.) **Picasso's birthplace,** Pl. de la Merced 15, is now home to the **Casa Natal y Fundación Picasso,** which organizes concerts, exhibits, and lectures. Upstairs is a permanent collection of Picasso's drawings, photographs, and pottery. (☎952 06 02 15; www.fundacionpicasso.es. Open daily 9:30am-8pm. €1; students, seniors, and under 17 free.) The **Museo Picasso,** C. San Augustin 8, details the transition of Málaga's most famous son from child prodigy to renowned master. (☎952 44 33 77; www.museopicassomalaga.org. Open Tu-Th, Su, and holidays 10am-8pm; F-Sa 10am-9pm. €6 permanent collection, €4.50 for temporary, €8 combined; students and youth €3. Free entrance last Su of every month 3-8pm.)

SPAIN

One of a few spots in Málaga just for backpackers, friendly **Picasso's Corner ❷,** C. San Juan de Letrán 9, off Pl. de la Merced, offers free Internet and top-notch bathrooms. (☎952 21 22 87; www.picassoscorner.com. Dorms €18-19; doubles €45. MC/V.) **ComoLoco ❷,** C. José Denis Belgradno, 17 specializes in salads and pitas (€4.85-10), and is one of many trendy restaurants by C. Granada. Salads are large, but you'll have to wait the typical 20-70min. for a table. (☎952 21 65 71. Open daily 1pm-1am. Cash only.)

RENFE **trains** (☎902 24 02 02) leave from Explanada de la Estación for: Barcelona (13hr., 2 per day, €58); Córdoba (2hr., 9 per day, €19); Madrid (5hr., 7 per day, €71-79); Seville (3hr., 5-6 per day, €17-33). **Buses** run from Po. de los Tilos (☎952 35 00 61), one block from the RENFE station along C. Roger de Flor, to: Barcelona (13 hr., 2 per day, €75); Cádiz (5hr., 3-6 per day, €22); Córdoba (3hr., 7 per day, €12); Granada (2hr., 17-19 per day, €9.40); Madrid (7hr., 8-12 per day, €20); Marbella (1hr., 1 per hr., €5); Ronda (3hr., 4-12 per day, €10); Seville (3hr., 11-12 per day, €15). To get to the **city center** from the bus station, take bus #3, 4, or 21 (€1) or exit right onto Callejones del Perchel, walk through the intersection with Av. de la Aurora, turn right on Av. de Andalucía, and cross Puente de Tetuán. Alameda Principal leads into Pl. de la Marina and the **tourist office.** (☎952 12 20 20. Open M-F 9am-7pm.) **Postal Code:** 29080.

TARIFA ☎956

Prepare for wind-blown hair—when the breezes pick up in the southernmost city of continental Europe, it becomes clear why Tarifa (pop. 20,000) is known as the Hawaii of Spain. World-renowned winds combined with kilometers of empty, white **beaches** make for incredible kitesurfing and windsurfing.

TRANSPORTATION AND PRACTICAL INFORMATION. From the bus station on C. Batalla del Salado 19 (☎956 68 40 38), **buses** run to Cádiz (2hr., 7 per day, €7.50) and Seville (3hr., 4 per day, €15). FRS **ferries** (☎956 68 18 30; www.frs.es) run to Tangier, MOR (35min., every 2hr., €39). For a **taxi,** call Parada Taxi (☎956 68 42 41). The **tourist office,** in Parque de la Alameda, has info on the various adventure sports available in the area. (☎956 68 09 93; www.tarifaweb.com. Open in summer M-F 10:30am-2pm and 6-8pm, Sa-Su 9am-2pm; in winter M-F 10am-2pm and 4-6pm, Sa-Su 9:30am-3pm.) The **post office,** C. Coronel Moscardó, 9, is near Pl. San Matéo. (☎956 68 42 37. Open M-F 8:30am-2:30pm, Sa 9:30am-1pm.) **Postal Code:** 11380.

ACCOMMODATIONS AND FOOD. The cheapest accommodations line **Calle Batalla del Salado** and its side streets. Prices rise significantly in summer; those visiting in August and on weekends from June to September should call ahead and arrive early. Comfortable **Hostal Villanueva ❷,** Av. de Andalucía, 11, has a restaurant and a rooftop terrace with an ocean view. Spotless rooms all have bath and TV. (☎956 68 41 49. Singles €25; doubles €45; triples €60. MC/V.)

Hostal Facundo I and II ❶, C. Batalla del Salado, 47, with its "Welcome backpackers" slogan, draws a young, budget crowd. (☎956 68 42 98; www.hostalfacundo.com. Dorms €18-22; singles €25; doubles €38-45, with bath €42-50. Cash only.) For cheap sandwiches (€1.50-3), try any one of the many *bagueterías* around C. Sancho IV el Bravo. Alternatively, C. San Francisco offers a variety of affordable, appetizing options. Take off your shoes and lounge on eclectic, pillow-covered couches in the open-air seating area of **Bamboo ❷,** Po. de la Alameda, 2, across from the castle. The lounge, which has free Wi-Fi, becomes a bar at night. (☎956 62 73 04. Fresh juices €3.50. Panini €2.80-4. F-Sa Live DJ. Open M-Th 10am-2am, F-Sa to 3am, Su to 2am. AmEx/MC/V.)

SIGHTS AND ENTERTAINMENT. Directly across the Strait of Gibraltar from Tangiers, Morocco, Tarifa boasts incomparable **views** of Africa, the Atlantic, and the Mediterranean. Next to the port and just outside the Old Town are the facade and ruins of the **Castillo de Guzmán el Bueno.** (Open Tu-Su Apr.-Oct. 11am-2pm and 6-8pm; Nov.-May 11am-2pm and 4-6pm. €1.80.) Those with something less historical in mind can head 200m south to **Playa de los Lances** for 5km of the finest sand on the Atlantic coast. Bathers should be aware of the occasional high winds and strong undertow. Adjacent to Playa de los Lances is **Playa Chica,** which is tiny but sheltered from the winds. **Tarifa Spin Out Surfbase,** 9km up the road toward Cádiz, rents windsurfing and kite-surfing boards and instructs all levels. (☎956 23 63 63 52; www.tarifaspinout.com. Book ahead. Windsurfer rental €26 per hour, €60 per day; 90min. lesson including all equipment €50. Kite and board rental €28 per hour, €58 per day; 2hr. lesson with all equipment €120.) At night, sunburnt travelers mellow out in the Old Town's many bars, which range from jazz to psychedelic to Irish. **Moskito,** C. San Francisco 11, is a combination bar-club with a Caribbean motif, dance music, and tropical cocktails. (Free salsa lessons W night 10:30pm. Beer €2.50. Mixed drinks €4.50-6. Open in summer daily 11pm-3am; in winter Th-Sa 11pm-late.) **La Tribu,** C. Nuestra Señora de la Luz, 7, a favorite among kite surfers, makes some of the most creative cocktails in town, while techno pumps energy into this otherwise mellow nightspot. (Beer €2-3. Mixed drinks €6. Shots €1.50.)

GIBRALTAR — UK/US ☎350; SPAIN ☎9567

The craggy face of the Rock of Gibraltar emerges imposingly from the mist just off the southern shore of Spain. Among history's most contested plots of land, Gibraltar today is officially a self-governing British colony, though Spain continues to campaign for its sovereignty. Gibraltar has a culture all its own—a curious mixture of not-quite-British, definitely-not-Spanish that makes it a sight worth visiting, even if it's a tourist trap.

See the titanic **Rock of Gibraltar,** even if just to say that you've seen it. About halfway up is the infamous **Apes' Den,** where Barbary macaques cavort on the sides of rocks, the tops of taxis, and the heads of tourists. At the northern tip of the Rock, facing Spain, are the **Great Siege Tunnels.** Originally used to fend off a Franco-Spanish siege in the 18th century, the underground tunnels were expanded to span 53km during WWII. Thousands of years of water erosion formed the eerie chambers of **St. Michael's Cave,** 500m from the siege tunnels. At the southern tip of Gibraltar, **Europa Point** commands a view of the straits; its lighthouse can be seen from 27km away at sea. The top of the Rock is accessible by car or cable car, or for the truly adventurous and athletic, by foot. (Cable car daily; 6 per hr. Round-trip £8/€13.50. Combined ticket to all sights, including one-way cable car ride, £16/€26.50.)

Spending the night in La Línea across the border is cheaper. In Gib, **Emile Youth Hostel Gibraltar ❷,** in Montague Bastian on Linewall Road, has bunks in cheerful rooms with clean communal baths. (☎511 06; www.emilehostel.com. Breakfast included. Lockout 10:30am-4:30pm. £1 for luggage storage and towels. Dorms £15/€20; doubles £34/€51. Cash only.) International restaurants are easy to find, but you may choke on the prices. Sample the treats of Gibraltar's thriving Hindu community at **Mumtaz ❶**, 20 Cornwalls Ln., where authentic tastes come at low prices. (☎442 57. Entrees £2.50-7, with ample vegetarian selection. Takeout available. Open daily 11am-3pm and 6pm-12:30am. Cash only.) **Marks & Spencer** on Main St. has decent prepackaged food and fresh breads. (Open M-F 9am-7pm, Sa 9:30am-5pm. AmEx/MC/V.)

Buses run from the Spanish border town of La Línea to: Cádiz (3hr., 4 per day, €13); Granada (5hr., 2 per day, €20); Madrid (7hr., 2 per day, €26); Seville (6hr., 4 per day, €21). Turner & Co., 65/67 Irish Town St. (☎783 05; fax 720 06), runs **ferries** to Tangier, MOR (1hr.; 1 per day; £18/€32, under 12 £9/€17). British Airways (☎793 00) **flights** leave from **Gibraltar Airport** (**GIB;** ☎730 26) for London, BRI (2.5hr., 2 per day, £168/€212). You must have a valid **passport** to enter Gibraltar or you'll be turned away at the border. From the bus station in La Línea, walk toward the Rock; the border is 5min. away. Once through customs and passport control, catch bus #9 or 10 or walk into town (20min.). Stay left on Av. Winston Churchill when the road forks. The **tourist office** is at Duke of Kent House, Cathedral Sq. (☎450 00. Open M-F 9am-4:30pm, Sa 10am-1pm.)

EASTERN SPAIN

Its rich soil and famous orange groves, fed by Moorish irrigation systems, have earned Eastern Spain the nickname *Huerta de España* (Spain's Orchard). Dunes, jagged promontories, and lagoons mark the coastline, while fountains grace landscaped public gardens in Valencia. The region has made a rapid transition from traditional to commercial, and continues to modernize.

ALICANTE (ALICANT) ☎965

Alicante (pop. 322,000) is a city with verve. Though its wild bars, crowded beaches, and busy streets seem decidedly modern, the looming castle-topped crag, 14th-century churches, and marble esplanades declare otherwise. Alicante is also home to the remains of a fifth-century Iberian settlement.

TRANSPORTATION AND PRACTICAL INFORMATION. RENFE **trains** (☎902 24 02 02; www.renfe.es) run from Estación Término on Av. Salamanca to Barcelona (4-6hr., 5-6 per day, €45-49), Madrid (4hr., 4-8 per day, €40), and Valencia (1hr., 3-4 per day, €12-26). **Buses** (☎965 13 07 00; www.alicante-ayto.es/trafico) leave C. Portugal 17 for: Barcelona (9hr., 8 per day, €39-44); Granada (6hr., 7 per day, €27-33); Madrid (5hr., 12-15 per day, €26.27-36); Málaga (8hr., 7 per day, €36-44); Seville (10hr., 1 per day, €46); Valencia (3hr., 14-21 per day, €17-20). The **tourist office** is by the bus station, with another branch at Rambla Méndez Núñez, 23. (☎965 92 98 02; www.alicanteturismo.com. Open M-F 9am-2pm and 5-8pm, Sa 10am-2pm.) **Internet** is available at the **Internet Cafe Xplorer,** C. San Vicente, 47, with 30 computers, printing, fax, Skype, and breakfast. (☎965 21 46 24. €0.70 per half hour. 1hr internet, *bocadillo*, and drink €2.90. Open daily, 10am-2am). **Postal Code:** 03002.

ACCOMMODATIONS AND FOOD. Hostels are plentiful but the nicest, in the *casco antiguo*, close to the port, must be booked in advance. For simple, airy rooms with A/C and views of the town's Basílica de Santa Maria, try **Hostal-**

Pension La Milagrosa ❷, C. Villa Vieja, 8. (☎965 21 69 18. Laundry €2. Internet €1.70 per 30min. Singles from €20. MC/V.) **Hostal Les Monges Palace ❸**, at the corner of C. San Agustin and C. Monjas, is in a palatial building with beautiful rooms. (☎965 21 50 46; www.lesmonges.es. Singles €30.) **Restaurante Villahelmy ❸**, C. Mayor, 37, in the Plaza Mayor, could easily go undetected. But its outrageous blue and orange interior, with folkloric murals and decorative birdcages, is a far cry from the norm. The menu offers mediterranean and Spanish cuisine, and changes frequently. Staples like *paella* and *tapas* are fixtures, however. (☎965 21 25 29; www.villahelmy.com. Salads €5-9, entrees €9-14. *Menú del día* €11. Open T-Sa 1-4pm and 8pm-midnight, Su 1-4pm. V/MC.) Buy groceries at the **Mercadona,** C. Alvarez Sereix 5. (☎965 21 58 94. Open M-Sa 9am-9pm.)

SPAIN

SIGHTS AND NIGHTLIFE. The imposing **Castell de Santa Barbara** keeps guard over Alicante's shores. The 166m high Carthaginian monument exhibits 9th- to 17th-century artifacts and offers a spectacular panorama of the city. (☎965 26 31 31. Open daily until sundown. The elevator, €2.40 on C. Jovellanos near the beach, breaks periodically, but a €2 bus leaves from the same place.) The *casco antiguo* offers an architectural window into the city's past, from the Gothic-styled **Iglesia de Santa Maria** to the Baroque **Concatedral de San Nicolas** to the twisted columns of the **Ayuntamiento.** The prize-winning **Museu Arqueológico Provincial de Alicante,** Pl. Dr. Gomez Ulls, also known as the MARQ, imaginatively showcases finds dating to prehistoric times and includes a hall dedicated to historical Alicante. (☎965 14 90 00; www.marqalicante.com. Open July-Aug. T-Sa 11am-2pm and 6pm-midnight, Su 11am-2pm. Sept.-Jun. Tu-Sa 10am-7pm, Su 10am-2pm. €3, students and seniors €1.50.) Alicante's **Playa del Postiguet,** a short walk from the *casco antigua*, attracts beach lovers, as do nearby **Playa de San Juan** (TRAM bus #21, 22, or 31) and **Playa del Mutxavista** (TRAM bus #21). Buses (€1.10) depart every 15-25min.

Nightlife in Alicante is unrelenting and unpredictable. Delightfully bizarre bars in the *casco antiguo* are the best place to start the night. **Celestial Copas,** C. San Pascual 1, fills up later than surrounding bars but the decor alone makes it worth a visit anytime. Red velvet curtains, decadent colors, and glinting gold chandeliers dominate two tiny rooms. (☎663 50 26 32. Flamenco, Spanish pop, and Latin grooves. Beer €3. Open winter Th 10pm-3am, F 10pm-4am; summer daily, 10pm-3am. Cash only.) The **Fogueres de Sant Joan** (Bonfire of Saint John; June 20-24, 2009) sets Alicante aflame for a week, celebrating the summer solstice with revelry from morning until night. *Fogueras* (giant papier-mâché structures) are erected and then burned in the street during *la Cremà*. Afterward, firefighters soak everyone during *la Banyà*.

VALENCIA ☎463

Valencia's white beaches, palm-lined avenues, and architectural treasures are noticeably less crowded than those of Spain's other major cities. Yet Valencia (pop. 807,000) possesses the energy of Madrid, the off-beat sophistication of Barcelona, and the warmth of Seville. Explore the life aquatic at L'Oceanogràfic or fulfill a quest for the Holy Grail at the stunning Catedral de Santa María.

TRANSPORTATION AND PRACTICAL INFORMATION. **Trains** arrive at Estación del Norte, C. Xàtiva 24 (☎463 52 02 02), and a slick new **metro** line runs from the Airport of Valencia to C. Colonor Xativa. **RENFE** (☎902 24 02 02) runs to: Alicante (2-3hr., 12 per day, €23.60-31.30); Barcelona (3hr., 8-16 per day, €29-37); Madrid (3hr., 12 per day, €20-39). **Buses** (☎463 46 62 66) go from Av. Menéndez Pidal 13 to: Alicante via the Costa Blanca (4hr., 10-30 per day,

€16-18); Barcelona (4hr., 19 per day, €21); Madrid (4hr., 13 per day, €21-26); Seville (11hr., 3-4 per day, €43-50). Take bus #1 or 2 from the bus station. The comprehensive **tourist office,** C. de la Paz 48, which provides information on the city and the province of Valencia, has branches at the train station and at Pl. de la Reina. (☎463 98 64 22; www.valencia.es. Open M-F 9am-8pm, Sa 10am-8pm, Su 10am-2pm.) **Ono,** C. San Vicente Mártir 22, provides **Internet** daily until 1am. (☎463 28 19 02. €1-4 per hr., depending on the time of day.) The palatial **post office** is at Pl. del Ajuntament 24. (☎463 51 23 70. Open M-F 8:30am-8:30pm, Sa 9:30am-2pm.) **Postal Code:** divided into zones, 46000-46025.

ACCOMMODATIONS AND FOOD. For the best deals and proximity to restaurants, nightlife, and architectural marvels, try hostels around Plaça del Ajuntament, Plaça del Mercat, and Plaça de la Reina. From Pl. de la Reina, turn right on C. de la Paz to reach the chic and hopping **Red Nest Youth Hostel ❷,** C. de la Paz 36, a great location for clubgoers. The hostel is spotless and smoothly operated, with a great international staff and funky, youthful decor. (☎463 42 71 68; www.nest-hostelsvalencia.net. Kitchen, dining area, and vending machines. Free luggage storage, Wi-Fi, linens, and towels (€5 deposit). Internet €1 per hr. 4-12 person dorms €18-22; doubles €41-47. AmEx/MC/V.) **The Home Youth Hostel ❶,** C. Lonja 4, is across from the Mercado Central on a side street off Pl. Dr. Collado. A couch-laden lounge, four-person dorms, and a relaxed atmosphere make this 20-room complex one of Valencia's more intimate hostels. (☎463 91 62 29; www.likeathome.net. Fully equipped kitchen. Linens included. Internet €0.50 per 15min. Singles €21; doubles €40. MC/V.)

Valencia is renowned for its *paella,* served in mammoth skillets all over town. Stuff yourself with huge portions of *paella valenciana* in the intimate courtyard outside **El Rall ❸,** by the old Gothic silk exchange monument on C. Tundidores 2. (☎463 92 20 90. *Paella* €12-21 per person, min. 2 people. Open daily 1:30-3:30pm and 8:30-11:30pm. Reserve ahead. MC/V.) **Zumeria Naturalia ❶,** C. Del Mar 12, by the Pl. de la Reina, is a sherbet-hued gem offering more than 50 fruit drinks (with and without alcohol), *bocadillos* with new and different fillings, and crepes. (Open M-W 5pm-midnight, Th 5pm-1am, F-Sa 5pm-2am, Su 5-10:30pm. Cash only.) For groceries, stop by the **Mercado Central,** where fresh fish, meat, and fruit (including Valencia's famous oranges) are sold.

SEEING RED

On the last Wednesday of every August, tens of thousands of tourists descend upon the small town of Buñol, a town in Valencia, to participate in the world's largest food fight: La Tomatina. A tradition since 1944, this tomato battle serves as the culmination of a week-long festival. Although the sloppy free-for-all is followed by a celebration of the town's patron saints, the tomato fight has no significance beyond the primal desire to get dirty and throw food.

Festivities begin when an overgrown ham is placed on a greased pole in the center of town. Locals and tourists scramble up the slippery pole, climbing on top of one another to be the captor of the prized ham. Once a winner is announced, a cannon starts the marinara blood bath.

Throngs of tourists wearing clothes destined for the dumpster crowd around the open-bed trucks that haul 240,000 lb. of tomatoes into the plaza. Over the next 2hr., Buñol becomes an every-man-for-himself battle of oozy carnage. Revelers pelt one another with tomatoes until the entire crowd is covered in tomato guts.

The origins of this food fight are unclear: some say it began as a fight between friends, while others say the original tomatoes were directed at unsatisfactory civil dignitaries. Today, no one is safe from the wrath of tomatoes hurled at friends and foreigners alike.

SIGHTS. Most sights line the **Río Turia** or cluster near **Pl. de la Reina, Pl. del Mercado,** and **Pl. de la Virgin.** EMT bus #5 is the only public bus that passes by most of Valencia's historic sites; for a guided tour, try the **Bus Turistico** from Pl. de la Reina (☎463 41 44 00; hop-on-hop-off day pass €12). The 13th-century **Catedral de Santa María** in Pl. de la Reina, which holds a chalice said to be the Holy Grail, is an impressive mix of Romanesque, Gothic, and Baroque architecture. Catch incredible views of Valencia's skyline atop the **Miguelete,** the cathedral tower. (☎463 91 01 89. Cathedral open daily 7:30am-1pm and 4:30-8:30pm. Closes earlier in winter. Tower open daily 10am-1pm and 4:30-7pm. €4 entrance fee, children and seniors €2.70. Includes audio guide.) Be sure to pass around back through the marbled **Plaza de la Virgin** and the **Basilica de la Virgin. El Palacio de los Marqueses de Dos Aguas,** C. Porta Querol 2, off C. de la Paz, is an architecturally stunning 14th-century building that recreates the home of a noble Valencian family. An incorporated ceramics museum includes works from as early as the 12th century, as well as rotating contemporary exhibits. (☎463 51 63 92; www.mnceramica.mcu.es. Open Tu-Sa 10am-2pm and 4-8pm. Tu-F €2.40, Students €1.20, Sa free.) Many museums are across the fortified bridges of what was once the Rio Turia—today, the riverbed is a lush green park that is perfect for bike rides, picnics, or walks. The blue-domed **Museu Provincial de Belles Artes,** C. Sant Pío V, displays stunning 14th- to 16th-century Valencian art and is home to El Greco's *San Juan Bautista*, Velázquez's self-portrait, and a number of works by Goya. (☎463 60 57 93; www.cult.gva.es/mbav. Open Tu-Sa 10am-8pm. Free.) Next door, pass through the eclectic **Jardines del Real,** taking in the many sculptures, fountains, and pleasant landscaping along the way.

ENTERTAINMENT AND NIGHTLIFE. To reach Valencia's two most popular beaches, **Las Arenas** and **Malvarrosa,** take bus #20, #21, or #22. If you have time to spare, take an Autocares Herca **bus** from the corner of Gran Vía de Germanias and C. Sueca (☎463 49 12 50; 30min., 1 per hr. 7am-9pm, €1-1.10) to the pristine beach of **Salér.** On Pl. de la Virgin along C. Caballeros, bars and pubs kick into action around midnight. Most dance clubs here do not have a cover. **L'Umbracle Terraza,** Av. de Saler, 5, is a worthwhile exception to this rule: located in the garden that runs parallel to the Ciudad de las Artes y las Ciencias, this is the perfect setting to view Valencia's newest architectural gems in all their illuminated splendor. (☎963 31 97 45; www.umbracleterraza.com. €15 cover. Open Apr.-Sept. M-Sa, 11:30pm-late.) In the city center, sip *agua de Valencia* (orange juice, champagne, and vodka) at the outdoor terraces in Pl. Tossal. There you will find **Bolsería Café,** C. Bolsería 41, a cafe and club packed every night with the beautiful and chic. (☎463 91 89 03; www.bolseriavalencia.com. Beer €3, free *agua de Valencia* before 12:30am. Mixed drinks €6. 'Americana' party W, T. Brazilian theme Su. Open daily 7:30pm-3:30am. MC/V.) For more info, consult the entertainment supplement *La Cartelera* (€0.50), or the free *24/7 Valencia*, available at hostels and cafes. The most famous festival in Valencia is **Las Fallas** (Mar. 12-19), in which hundreds of colossal papier-mâché puppets are paraded down the street and burned at the end of the week in celebration of spring. The nearby town of Buñol hosts the world's largest food fight during **La Tomatina** (held annually in late August; see p. 933).

BARCELONA ☎93

Barcelona is a city that has grown young as it has grown old. In the 17 years since it hosted the Olympics, this European hot-spot has drawn travelers to its beaches, clubs, and first-rate restaurants. Once home to Pablo Picasso and

Joan Miró, the city has a strong art scene, which continues the tradition of the whimsical and daring *Modernisme* architectural movement. Barcelona is a gateway—not only to Catalan art and culture, but also to the Mediterranean and the Pyrenees—and its vibrant aura lingers long after you leave.

INTERCITY TRANSPORTATION

Flights: Aeroport El Prat de Llobregat (**BCN;** ☎902 40 47 04; www.aena.es and choose Airport: Barcelona from the dropdown on the left), 13km southwest of Barcelona. To get to Pl. Catalunya, take RENFE train L10 (20-25min., 2 per hr., €2.40) or the Aerobus (☎93 415 6020; 30min., 4-10 per hr., €4).

Trains: Barcelona has 2 main train stations. **Estació Barcelona-Sants,** in Pl. Països Catalans (M: Sants-Estació), is the main terminal for domestic and international traffic. **Estació de França,** on Av. Marquès de l'Argentera (M: Barceloneta), serves regional destinations and some international arrivals. RENFE (Spain ☎902 24 02 02, international ☎902 24 34 02; www.renfe.es) trains go to: **Bilbao** (9-10hr., 12:30 and 11pm, €40-52); **Madrid** (5-9hr., 14-21 per day, €40-123); **Seville** (10-12hr., 3 per day, €57-127); **Valencia** (3-5hr., 14 per day, €32-40). 20% discount on round-trip tickets.

Buses: Most buses arrive at the **Barcelona Nord Estació d'Autobusos,** C. Alí-bei 80 (☎902 26 06 06; www.barcelonanord.com). M: Arc de Triomf or #54 bus. Buses also depart from **Estació Barcelona-Sants** and the airport. **Sarfa** (☎902 30 20 25; www.sarfa.es) goes to **Cadaqués** (2hr., 2 per day, €20). **Eurolines** (☎93 367 4400; www.eurolines.es) travels to **Paris, FRA** (15hr., M-Sa 1 per day, €69) and **Naples, ITA** (24hr; M, W, F 7pm; €122). **ALSA/Enatcar** (☎902 42 22 42; www.alsa.es) goes to: **Alicante** (8-9hr., 9 per day, €39-44); **Madrid** (8hr., 18 per day, €27); **Seville** (14-16hr., 4:30pm, €85); **Valencia** (4-5hr., 14 per day, €24-38).

Ferries: Trasmediterránea (☎902 45 46 45; www.transmediterranea.es), in Terminal Drassanes, Moll Sant Bertran. Ferries go to **Ibiza** (5-9hr., 1-2 per day, €75), **Mahón** (3-9hr., 1 per day, €75), and **Palma** (3-7hr., 1-2 per day, €75).

ORIENTATION

Imagine yourself perched on Columbus's head at the **Monument a Colom** (on Passeig de Colom, along the shore), viewing the city with the sea at your back. From the harbor, the city slopes upward to the mountains. From the Monument a Colom, **La Rambla,** a pedestrian thoroughfare, runs from the harbor to **Plaça de Catalunya** (M: Catalunya), the city center. (*Let's Go* uses "Las Ramblas" to refer to the general area and "La Rambla" in address listings.) The **Ciutat Vella** (Old City) centers around Las Ramblas and includes the neighborhoods of Barri Gòtic, La Ribera, and El Raval. The **Barri Gòtic** is to the right (with your back to the ocean) of Las Ramblas, enclosed on the other side by Vía Laietana. East of V. Laietana lies the maze-like **La Ribera,** bordered by Parc de la Ciutadella and Estació de França. Beyond La Ribera—farther east outside the Ciutat Vella—are **Poble Nou** and **Port Olímpic.** To the west of Las Ramblas is **El Raval.** Farther west rises **Montjuïc,** with sprawling gardens, museums, the 1992 Olympic grounds, and a fortress. Directly behind the Monument a Colom is the **Port Vell** (old port) development, where a wavy bridge leads across to the ultra-modern shopping and entertainment complexes Moll d'Espanya and Maremàgnum. North of the Ciutat Vella is **l'Eixample,** a gridded neighborhood created during the expansion of the 1860s, which sprawls from Pl. Catalunya toward the mountains. Gran Vía de les Corts Catalanes defines its lower edge, and the **Passeig de Gràcia,** l'Eixample's main avenue, bisects

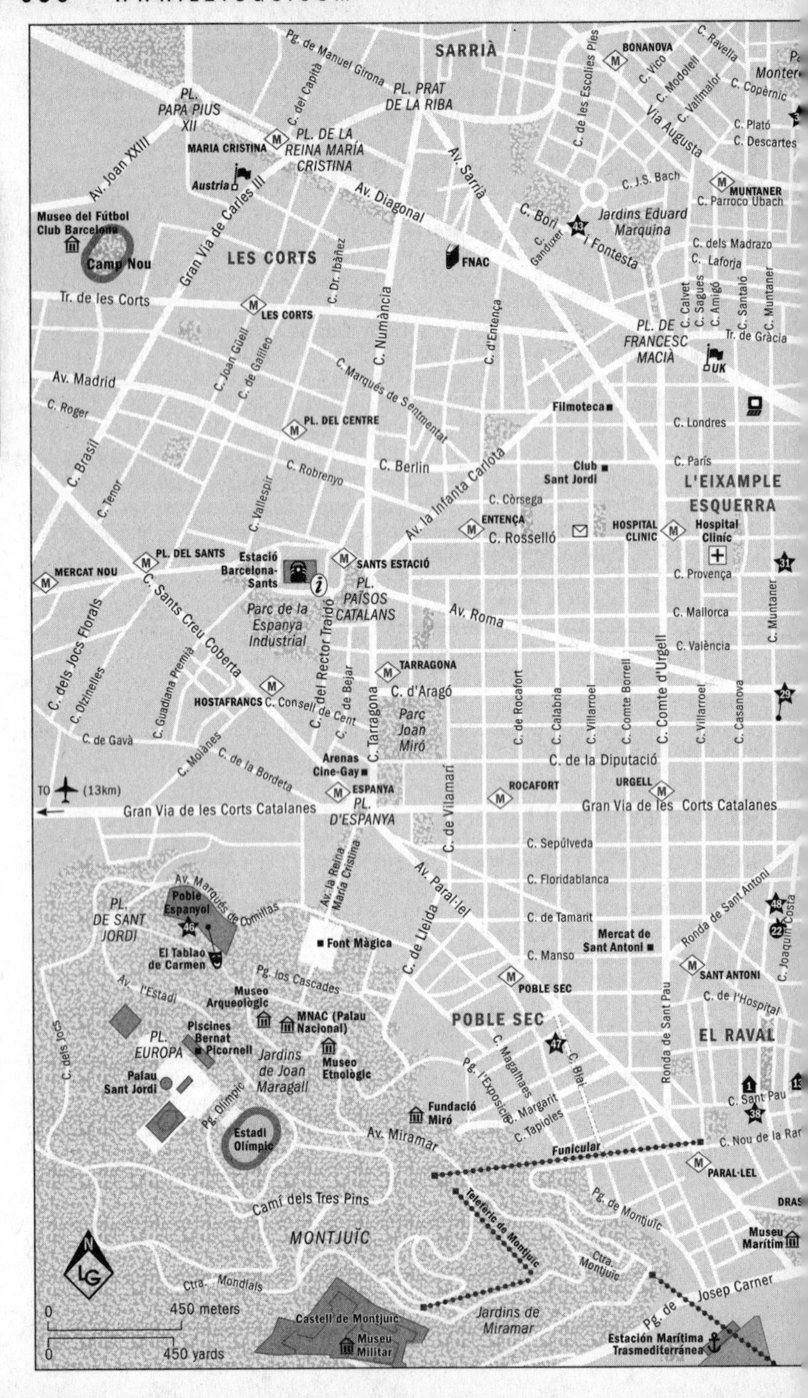
SARRIÀ
LES CORTS
L'EIXAMPLE ESQUERRA
POBLE SEC
EL RAVAL
MONTJUÏC
Camp Nou
Museo del Fútbol Club Barcelona
Estació Barcelona-Sants
Parc de la Espanya Industrial
Parc Joan Miró
PL. D'ESPANYA
Av. Diagonal
Gran Via de les Corts Catalanes
Av. Paral·lel
Av. Roma
Av. Madrid
Poble Espanyol
El Tablao de Carmen
Font Màgica
Museo Arqueològic
MNAC (Palau Nacional)
Museo Etnològic
Piscines Bernat Picornell
Palau Sant Jordi
Estadi Olímpic
Jardins de Joan Maragall
Fundació Miró
Funicular
Teleferic de Montjuïc
Castell de Montjuïc
Museu Militar
Jardins de Miramar
Estación Marítima Trasmediterránea
Museu Marítim
Mercat de Sant Antoni
Filmoteca
Club Sant Jordi
Hospital Clínic
FNAC
Austria
UK
Arenas Cine-Gay
Jardins Eduard Marquina
PL. DE FRANCESC MACIÀ
PL. PAÏSOS CATALANS
PL. DE SANT JORDI
PL. EUROPA
TO (13km)
0 450 meters
0 450 yards

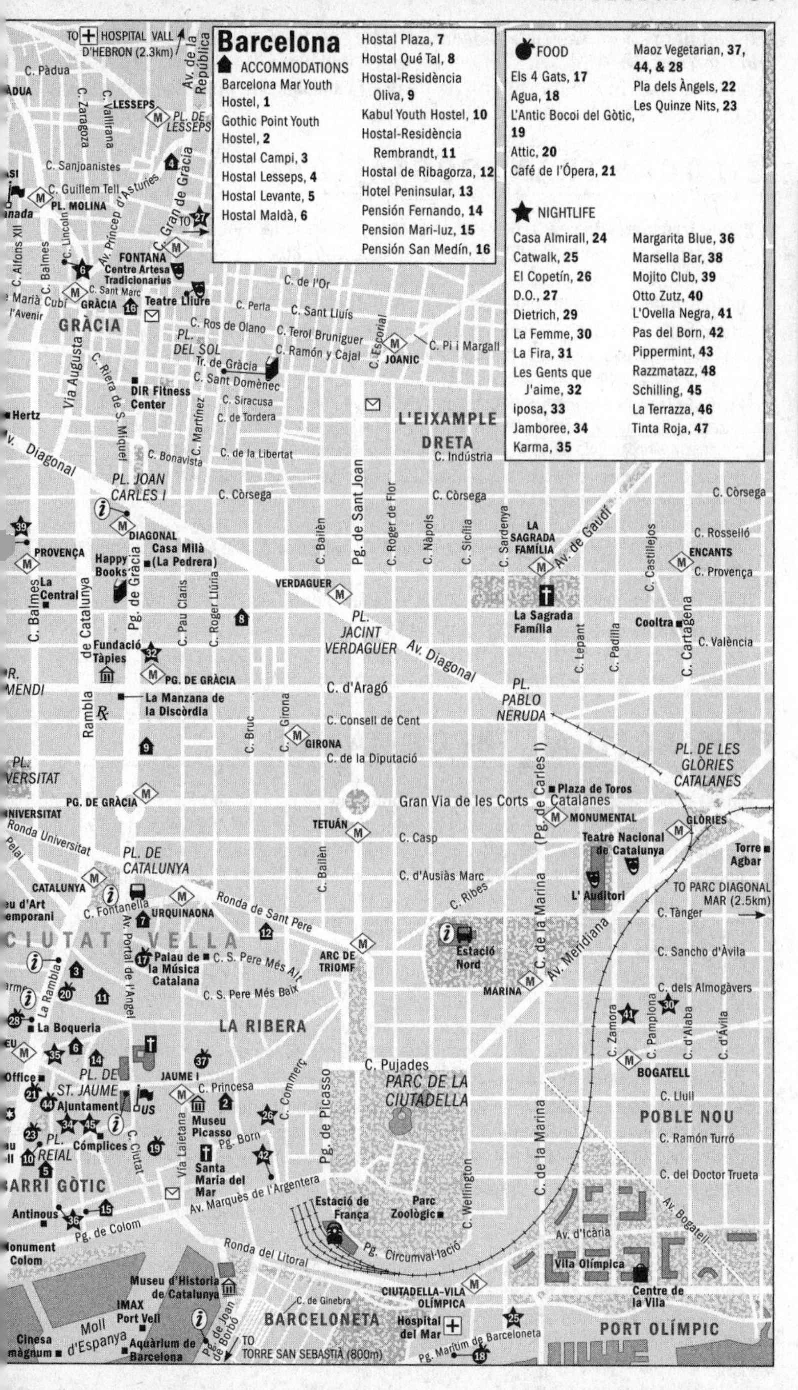
Barcelona
ACCOMMODATIONS
Barcelona Mar Youth Hostel, 1
Gothic Point Youth Hostel, 2
Hostal Campi, 3
Hostal Lesseps, 4
Hostal Levante, 5
Hostal Maldà, 6
Hostal Plaza, 7
Hostal Qué Tal, 8
Hostal-Residència Oliva, 9
Kabul Youth Hostel, 10
Hostal-Residència Rembrandt, 11
Hostal de Ribagorza, 12
Hotel Peninsular, 13
Pensión Fernando, 14
Pension Mari-luz, 15
Pensión San Medín, 16
FOOD
Els 4 Gats, 17
Agua, 18
L'Antic Bocoi del Gòtic, 19
Attic, 20
Café de l'Ópera, 21
Maoz Vegetarian, 37, 44, & 28
Pla dels Àngels, 22
Les Quinze Nits, 23
NIGHTLIFE
Casa Almirall, 24
Catwalk, 25
El Copetín, 26
D.O., 27
Dietrich, 29
La Femme, 30
La Fira, 31
Les Gents que J'aime, 32
iposa, 33
Jamboree, 34
Karma, 35
Margarita Blue, 36
Marsella Bar, 38
Mojito Club, 39
Otto Zutz, 40
L'Ovella Negra, 41
Pas del Born, 42
Pippermint, 43
Razzmatazz, 48
Schilling, 45
La Terrazza, 46
Tinta Roja, 47
TO HOSPITAL VALL D'HEBRON (2.3km)
GRÀCIA
L'EIXAMPLE DRETA
CIUTAT VELLA
LA RIBERA
BARRI GÒTIC
POBLE NOU
BARCELONETA
PORT OLÍMPIC
PARC DE LA CIUTADELLA
La Sagrada Família
Casa Milà (La Pedrera)
Fundació Tàpies
La Manzana de la Discòrdia
Palau de la Música Catalana
Teatre Nacional de Catalunya
L' Auditori
Estació Nord
Estació de França
Parc Zoològic
Museu Picasso
Santa Maria del Mar
Museu d'Història de Catalunya
Aquàrium de Barcelona
IMAX Port Vell
Vila Olímpica
Centre de la Vila
Hospital del Mar
Plaza de Toros Monumental
Torre Agbar
Happy Books
La Central
Cooltra
DIR Fitness Center
Teatre Lliure
Centre Artesa Tradicionarius
La Boqueria
Ajuntament
Antinous
Monument Colom
Cinesa Maremàgnum
Moll d'Espanya
Hertz
TO PARC DIAGONAL MAR (2.5km)
TO TORRE SAN SEBASTIÀ (800m)
Av. Diagonal
Gran Via de les Corts Catalanes
Pg. de Gràcia
Rambla de Catalunya
Pg. de Sant Joan
PL. DE CATALUNYA
PL. DE LES GLÒRIES CATALANES
PL. JOAN CARLES I
PL. JACINT VERDAGUER
PL. PABLO NERUDA
PL. DEL SOL
PL. REIAL
PL. DE ST. JAUME
LESSEPS
FONTANA
DIAGONAL
PROVENÇA
VERDAGUER
GIRONA
TETUÁN
URQUINAONA
CATALUNYA
ARC DE TRIOMF
JAUME I
MARINA
MONUMENTAL
GLÒRIES
BOGATELL
CIUTADELLA-VILA OLÍMPICA
ENCANTS
JOANIC
PG. DE GRÀCIA
Ronda de Sant Pere
Ronda Universitat
Ronda del Litoral
Av. Meridiana
Av. de Gaudí
Av. Marquès de l'Argentera
Pg. de Colom
Via Laietana
C. Pujades
C. de la Marina
Av. Bogatell
Av. d'Icària
Pg. Marítim de Barcelona

the neighborhood. **Avinguda Diagonal** marks the border between l'Eixample and the **Zona Alta** (uptown), which includes **Pedralbes, Gràcia,** and other older neighborhoods in the foothills. The peak of **Tibidabo,** the northwest border of the city, offers the best view of Barcelona.

LOCAL TRANSPORTATION

Public Transportation: ☎010. Passes *(abonos)* work for the Metro, bus, urban lines of FGC commuter trains, RENFE *cercanías,* trams, and Nitbus. A *sencillo* ticket (1 ride) costs €1.30. A **T-10 pass** (€7.20) is valid for 10 rides; a **T-Día pass** entitles you to unlimited bus and Metro travel for 1 day (€5.50) and the **T-Mes** (€46) for 1 month.

Metro: ☎93 298 7000; www.tmb.net. Vending machines and ticket windows sell passes. Hold on to your ticket until you exit or risk a €40 fine. Trains run M-Th, Su and holidays 5am-midnight; F 5am-2am; Sa non-stop service. €1.30.

Ferrocarrils de la Generalitat de Catalunya (FGC): ☎93 205 1515; www.fgc.es. Commuter trains to local destinations; main stations at Pl. de Catalunya and Pl. d'Espanya. After Tibidabo, rates increase by zone. Info office at the Pl. de Catalunya station open M-F 7am-9pm. €1.30.

Buses: Go just about anywhere, usually 5am-10pm. Most stops have maps posted. Buses run 4-6 per hr. in central locations. €1.30.

Nitbus: ☎90 151 1151, www.emt-amb.cat/links/cat/cnitbus.htm. 18 different lines run every 20-30min. 10:30pm-4:30am. Buses depart from Pl. de Catalunya, stop by most club complexes, and go through Ciutat Vella and Zona Alta.

Taxis: Try **RadioTaxi033** (☎93 303 3033; www.radiotaxi033.com. AmEx/MC/V)

Car Rental: Avis, C. Corcega 293-295 (☎93 237 5680; www.avis.com). Also at airport (☎93 298 3600) and Estació Barcelona-Sants, Pl. dels Països Catalans. (☎93 330 4193.) Open M-F 7:30am-10:30pm, Sa 8am-7pm, Su 9am-7pm.

PRACTICAL INFORMATION

Tourist Offices: ☎90 730 1282; www.barcelonaturisme.com. In addition to several tourist offices, Barcelona has numerous mobile information kiosks. **Aeroport del Prat de Llobregat,** terminals A and B (☎93 478 0565). Info and last-minute accommodation booking. Open daily 9am-9pm. **Estació Barcelona-Sants,** Pl. Països Catalans. M: Sants-Estació. Info and last-minute accommodations booking. Open June 24-Nov. 24 daily 8am-8pm; Nov. 25-June 23 M-F 8am-8pm, Sa-Su 8am-2pm. **Oficina de Turisme de Catalunya,** Pg. de Gràcia 107 (☎93 238 4000; www.gencat.es/probert). M: Diagonal. Open M-Sa 10am-7pm, Su 10am-2pm. **Plaça de Catalunya,** Pl. de Catalunya 17S. M: Catalunya. The biggest, best, and busiest tourist office. Free **maps,** brochures on sights and public transportation, booking service for accommodations, gift shop, currency exchange, and box office. Open daily 9am-9pm. **Plaça de Sant Jaume,** C. Ciutat 2. M: Jaume I. Open M-F 9am-8pm, Sa 10am-8pm, Su and holidays 10am-2pm.

Currency Exchange: ATMs give the best rates; the next-best rates are available at banks. General banking hours are M-F 8:30am-2pm. Las Ramblas has many exchange stations open late, but the rates are not as good and a commission will be taken.

Luggage Storage: Estació Barcelona-Sants. €3-4.50 per day. Open daily 5:30am-11pm. **Estació Nord.** M: Arc de Triomf. Lockers €3-5 per day, 90-day limit.

Library: Biblioteca Sant Pau, C. de l'Hospital 56 (☎93 302 0797). M: Liceu. Walk to the far end of the courtyard; the library is on the left. Do not confuse it with the Catalan library, which you'll see first and which requires permission to enter. Free Internet. Open mid-Sept. to June M-Tu and F 3:30-8:30pm, W-Th and Sa 10am-2pm.

Laundromat: Tintorería Ferrán, C. Ferran 11 (☎93 301 8730). M: Liceu. Wash, dry, and fold €15. Open M-F 9am-2pm and 4-8pm. **Lavomatic,** Pl. Joaquim Xirau (☎93 268 4768). Wash €4.75, dry €0.85 per 5min. Open M-Sa 9am-9pm.

Tourist Police: La Rambla 43 (☎93 344 1300). M: Liceu. English spoken. Open 24hr.

Late-Night Pharmacy: Rotates; check any pharmacy window for the nearest on duty.

Medical Services: Medical Emergency: ☎061. Hospital Clìnic i Provincal, C. Villarroel 170 (☎93 227 5400). M: Hospital Clìnic. Main entrance at the intersection of C. Roselló and C. Casanova.

Internet: Easy Internet Café, La Rambla 31 (☎93 301 7507). M: Liceu. Reasonable prices and 200 terminals make this Internet heaven. Digital camera, CD burning, faxing, copying, and scanning services. €2.10 per hr.; 1-day pass €7, 1-week €15, 1-month €30. Open daily 8am-2:30am. **Branch** at Ronda Universitat 35. M: Catalunya. €2 per hr.; 1-day pass €3, 1-week €7, 1-month €15. Open daily 8am-2am.

Navegaweb, La Rambla 88-94 (☎93 317 9026). M: Liceu. €0.20 per min. to USA. Internet €2 per hr. Open M-Th and Su 9am-midnight, F 9am-1am, Sa 9am-2am.

Bcnet (Internet Gallery Café), C. Barra de Ferro 3 (☎93 268 1507). M: Jaume I. €0.95 for 15 min; €2.90 per hr.; 10hr. ticket €19. Open M-F 10am-11pm, Sa-Su noon-11pm.

Post Office: Pl. d'Antoni López (☎90 219 7197, www.correos.es). M: Jaume I or Barceloneta. Fax and *Lista de Correos*. Open M-F 8:30am-9:30pm, Su (access on side street) noon-10pm. **Postal Code:** 08001.

ACCOMMODATIONS

Finding an affordable room in Barcelona can be difficult. To crash in touristy **Barri Gòtic** or **Las Ramblas** during the busier months (June-Sept. and Dec.), make reservations weeks, even months, ahead. Consider staying outside the tourist hub of *Ciutat Vella;* there are many affordable and enjoyable hostels in **l'Eixample** and **Gràcia** that tend to have more vacancies. For camping info, contact the **Associació de Càmpings i C.V. de Barcelona,** Gran Via de les Corts Catalanes 608 (☎93 412 5955; www.campingsbcn.com).

BARRI GÒTIC

Backpackers flock to these hostels to be close to the buzz of Las Ramblas.

Pensión Mari-luz, C. del Palau 4 (☎93 317 3463; www.pensionmariluz.com), up 3 flights. M: Liceu or Jaume I. Recent renovations have transformed this hostel into a modern sunny space around a historic courtyard. Free Wi-Fi. Dorms €18-24; singles €25-35; doubles €45-58; triples €57-75; quads €66€92. Hostel also offers nearby short-term apartments. MC/V. ❷

Hostal Levante, Baixada de San Miquel 2 (☎93 317 9565; www.hostallevante.com). M: Liceu. This hostel has a TV lounge and large, tastefully decorated rooms with light wood furnishings and fans. Ask for a newly renovated room; some have balconies. 4- to 8-person apartments have kitchen, living room, and laundry machine. Singles €33-45; doubles €60-70; apartments €30 per person. MC/V. ❸

Hostal Plaza, C. Fontanella 18 (☎93 301 0139; www.plazahostal.com). M: Urquinaona. Cheery rooms with colorful art, many with A/C. Free Internet and great location. Singles €35, with bath €45; doubles €55-65/65-80; triples €75-80/90-95. AmEx/MC/V. ❸

Hostal Maldà, C. Pi 5 (☎93 317 3002). M: Liceu. Enter inside the shopping center and follow signs upstairs. The friendly owner keeps these quality rooms occupied at rock-bottom prices. No reservations. Doubles €30; triples with shower €45. Cash only. ❸

Pensión Fernando, C. Ferran 31 (☎93 301 7993; www.hfernando.com). M: Liceu. This clean hostel is conveniently located. Dorms with A/C and lockers. Common kitchen with dining room and TV on 3rd fl. Towels €1.50. Dorms €17-21; singles €32-36, with bath €45-50; doubles with bath €55-70; triples with bath €70-85. MC/V. ❷

LA RIBERA AND EL RAVAL

La Ribera, while still touristed, can be calmer than the Barri Gótic. Be careful in El Raval (near the port) and farther from Las Ramblas at night.

Gothic Point Youth Hostel, C. Vigatans 5 (☎93 268 7808; www.gothicpoint.com). M: Jaume I. Hostel has a colorfully painted and highly social lounge area with TV, rooftop terrace, weekly DJ jams, and jungle-gym rooms with A/C. Breakfast included. Free Internet. Lockers free, locks €3. Linens €2, towels €2. Refrigerator and kitchen access. High-season dorms €23; mid-season €20; low-season €17.50. AmEx/MC/V; €1 fee per person per night. ❷

Hotel Peninsular, C. de Sant Pau, 34 (☎93 302 3138; www.hotelpeninsular.net). M: Liceu. 80 rooms with phone and A/C around a beautiful 4-story interior courtyard. Breakfast included. Free Internet and Wi-Fi. Singles €30, with bath €55; doubles with bath €78; triples €95; quads €120; quints €140. MC/V. ❸

Barcelona Mar Youth Hostel, C. de Sant Pau, 80 (☎93 324 8530; www.barcelonamar.es). M: Parallel. Squeezes 120 dorm-style beds into ocean-themed rooms with A/C. Breakfast included. Free Internet. All beds come with locker. Self-serve laundry €4.50 for wash and dry; laundry service available. Dorms in summer €26; in winter €16-19. Double beds €46-58, F-Sa add €2 per person. AmEx/MC/V. ❷

L'EIXAMPLE

Although L'Eixample may be far from the sights of Las Ramblas and the Barri Gòtic, it is home to Barcelona's most beautiful architecture. Accommodations here tend to be much nicer than those in *Ciutat Vella.*

Somnio Hostel, C. Diputació 251 (☎93 272 5308, www.somniohostels.com). M: Pg. de Gràcia. Clean, sun-filled, and stylish, just blocks from Pl. de Catalunya. A/C throughout, free Internet and Wi-Fi, TV in common area. Breakfast €5. Same-sex dorms with sheets, towel, comforter, pillow, and locker €23. Singles with sink and large mirror €40. Doubles €72, with bath €80. MC/V. ❷

Hostal Residència Oliva, Pg. de Gràcia 32, 4th fl. (☎93 488 0162; www.lasguias.com/hostaloliva). M: Pg. de Gràcia. Elegant wooden bureaus, mirrors, and a marble floor give this hostel a classy character. 5 of the 16 rooms look onto Pg. de Gràcia or neighboring streets, and all have high ceilings, TVs, and A/C. Singles €37; doubles €62, with bath €80; triples with bath €111. Cash only. ❸

FOOD

The restaurants on **Carrer Aragó** by Pg. de Gràcia have great lunchtime *menús*, and the **Passeig de Gràcia** has beautiful outdoor dining. Gràcia's **Plaça Sol** and the area around La Ribera's **Santa Maria del Mar** are the best *tapas* (or cheap, laid-back dinner) spots. For fruit, cheese, and wine, head to **La Boqueria** (Mercat de Sant Josep), off La Rambla outside M: Liceu. (Open M-Sa 8am-8pm.) Buy groceries at **Champion,** La Rambla 13. (M: Liceu. Open M-Sa 9am-10pm.)

BARRI GÒTIC

L'Antic Bocoi del Gòtic, Baixada de Viladecols, 3 (☎93 310 5067; www.bocoi.net). M: Jaume I. Bounded by an ancient Roman wall, this restaurant is tiny and romantic. Excellent salads (€7.20-9), *coques de recapte* (open-faced toasted sandwiches, a Catalá speciality; €6.95-8.50), and tasty cheese platters (€13-18.50) feature *jamón ibérico* (ham) and local veggies. Reserve early. Open M-Sa 8:30pm-midnight. AmEx/MC/V. ❷

Els 4 Gats, C. Montsió, 3 (☎93 302 4140; www.4gats.com). M: Catalunya. Picasso's old *Modernista* hangout, and the site of his first art exhibit (of portraits and caricatures), with plenty of bohemian character. Cuisine includes Mediterranean salad (€11) and Iberian pork with king prawns and hazelnuts (€19). Entrees €16-27. M-F lunch *menú* 1-4pm (€12) is the best deal, and comes with epic desserts; try the *crema catalana*. Live piano daily 9pm-1am. Open daily 1pm-1am. AmEx/MC/V. ❹

Les Quinze Nits, Pl. Reial 6 (☎93 317 3075; www.lesquinzenits.com). M: Liceu. Popular restaurant with nightly lines halfway through the plaza; arrive early to have a classy dinner in this happening setting. Catalan entrees at shockingly low prices. Pasta and rice €4-7. Fish €7-9. Meat €6-10. Open daily 1-3:45pm and 8:30-11:30pm. MC/V. ❶

Attic, La Rambla, 120 (☎93 302 4866; www.angrup.com). M: Liceu This chic restaurant promises surprisingly reasonable prices for touristy Las Ramblas, with an orange-and-wood-themed design. Mediterranean fusion cuisine, including their specialty ox burger (€10.35). Open daily 1-4:30pm and 7pm-12:30am. AmEx/MC/V. ❸

Maoz Vegetarian, at C. Ferran, 13 and La Rambla, 95 (www.maozvegetarian.com). A vegetarian chain and city institution with only 1 menu option—falafel, with or without hummus or feta—and an array of fresh vegetable toppings. Falafel €3.80-5.20. Open M-Th and Su 11am-2:30am, F-Sa 11am-3am. MC/V. ❶

SPAIN

ELSEWHERE IN BARCELONA

La Llavor dels Origens, C. Enric Granados, 9 (☎93 453 1120; www.lallavordelsorigens.com), C. Vidrieria, 6-8 (☎310 7531), Pg. de Born, 4 (☎932 95 66 90), and C. Ramón y Cajal, 12 (☎93 213 6031). Delectable entrees such as the beef-stuffed onion (€7) and the rabbit with chocolate and almonds (€7); a magazine-menu provides a photo of each dish with a description of ingredients and history. Small soups and vegetarian and meat dishes €5-7. Open daily noon-1am. AmEx/MC/V. ❶

Rita Rouge, Pl. Gardunya (☎93 481 3686, ritarouge@ritablue.com). M: Liceu. Just behind La Boqueria, a healthy and high-quality lunch *menù* (€11) awaits you, with plenty of vegetarian choices. Chow down on the shady, black-and-red terrace or venture inside for a cocktail (€5-8). Entrees €10-22. Salads and wok dishes €6-12. Open daily 9am-2am. Kitchen open 1pm-10pm.

Petra, C. Sombrerers, 13 (☎93 319 9199). M: Jaume I. Menus printed on wine bottles and lights made of silverware complement shockingly inexpensive, quality dishes like duck with brie and apple. Entrees €8. Salads €5. Pasta €6. Open Tu-Th 1:30-4pm and 9-11:30pm; F-Sa 1:30-4pm, 9pm-midnight; Su 1:30-4pm. MC/V. ❷

Agua, Pg. Marítim de la Barceloneta 30 (☎93 225 1272; www.grupotragaluz.com), the last building on the ocean side of Pg. Marítim before Barceloneta, near the giant copper fish. Enjoy seafood and rice dishes from the terrace on the beach. Vegetarian options. Entrees €7-21. Wheelchair-accessible. Open daily 1-3:45pm and 8-11:30pm, later on weekends. Reservations essential. AmEx/MC/V. ❸

SIGHTS AND MUSEUMS

The **Ruta del Modernisme** pass is the cheapest and most flexible option for those with an interest in seeing Barcelona's major sights. Passes give holders a 25-30% discount on attractions including Palau de la Música Catalana, the Museu de Zoología, and tours of Hospital de la Santa Creu i Sant Pau. Purchase passes at the Pl. Catalunya tourist office or at the Modernisme Centre at Hospital Santa Creu i Sant Pau, C. Sant Antoni Maria Claret 167. (☎933 17 76 52; www.

rutadelmodernisme.com. Passes free with the purchase of a €12 guidebook, €5 per additional adult, adult accompanying someone under 18 free.)

LAS RAMBLAS

This wide, tree-lined street, known in Catalan as Les Rambles, is actually six *ramblas* (promenades) that form one boulevard from the Pl. de Catalunya. According to legend, visitors who sample the water from the **Font de Canaletes** at the top of Las Ramblas will return to Barcelona. Pass the **Mirador de Colom** on your way out to Rambla del Mar for a beautiful view of the Mediterranean.

GRAN TEATRE DEL LICEU. After burning down for the second time in 1994, the Liceu was rebuilt and expanded; a tour of the building includes not just the original 1847 Sala de Espejos (Hall of Mirrors), but also the 1999 Foyer (a curvaceous bar/lecture hall/small theater). The five-level, 2292-seat theater is considered one of Europe's top stages, adorned with palatial ornamentation, gold facades, and sculptures. *(La Rambla 51-59, by C. Sant Pau. M: Liceu. ☎93 485 9913; www.liceubarcelona.com. Box office open M-F 1:30-8pm, Sa 1hr. before show. 20min. non-guided visits daily 11:30am-1pm every 30min; €4. 1hr. tours 10am by reservation only, call 9am-2pm or email visites@liceubarcelona.com; €8.50.)*

LA BOQUERIA (MERCAT DE SANT JOSEP). Just the place to pick up that hard-to-find animal part you've been looking for, La Boqueria is a traditional Catalan "*mercat*"—and the largest outdoor market in Spain—located in a giant, all-steel *Modernista* structure. Specialized vendors sell produce, fish, bread, wine, cheese, nuts, sweets, and meat from a seemingly infinite number of independent stands. *(La Rambla 89. M: Liceu. Open M-Sa 8am-8pm.)*

MUSEU DE L'ERÒTICA. Barcelona's most intrepid tourists flock to this museum, which houses an odd assortment of pictures and figurines that span human history and depict seemingly impossible **sexual acrobatics**. *(La Rambla 96b. M: Liceu. ☎93 318 98 65. Open 10am-10pm. €8, students €7.)*

BARRI GÒTIC

Brimming with cathedrals, palaces, and unabashed tourism, Barcelona's most ancient zone masks its old age with unflagging energy.

MUSEU D'HISTÒRIA DE LA CIUTAT. Buried some 20m below a seemingly innocuous old plaza lies one of the two components to the Museu d'Història de la Ciutat: the subterranean excavations of the Roman city of Barcino. This 4000-square-meter **archaeological exhibit** displays incredibly well-preserved 1st- to 6th-century ruins. Built on top of those 4th-century walls, the second part, **Palau Reial Major,** served as the residence of the Catalan-Aragonese monarchs. When restoration on the building began, the Gothic **Saló de Tinell** (Throne Room) was discovered; it is supposedly the place where Fernando and Isabel received Columbus after his journey to America. *(Pl. del Rei. M: Jaume I. ☎93 315 1111; www.museuhistoria.bcn.es. Wheelchair-accessible. Open June-Sept. Tu-Sa 10am-8pm, Su 10am-3pm; Oct.-May Tu-Sa 10am-2pm and 4-8pm, Su 10am-3pm. Palace €6, students €4. Archaeological exhibit €1.50/1. Combination ticket €6.50/4.50.)*

ESGLÉSIA CATEDRAL DE LA SANTA CREU. This cathedral is one of Barcelona's most recognizable monuments. The altar holds a cross designed by Frederic Marès in 1976 and the Crypt of Santa Eulàlia lies beneath. The museum in La Sala Capitular holds Bartolomé Bermejo's *Pietà*. *(M: Jaume I. In Pl. Seu, up C. Bisbe from Pl. St. Jaume. Cathedral open daily 8am-12:45pm and 5:15-7:30pm. Cloister open daily 9am-12:30pm and 5:15-7pm. Elevator to the roof open M-Sa 10:30am-6pm; €2. Choir area open M-F 9am-12:30pm and 5:15-7pm, Sa-Su 9am-12:30pm; €1. Guided tours daily 1-5pm; €4.)*

LA RIBERA

This neighborhood has recently evolved into an artsy nucleus, with art galleries, chic eateries, and exclusive bars.

PALAU DE LA MÚSICA CATALANA. In 1891, the Orfeó Català Choir Society commissioned *Modernista* master Luis Domènech i Montaner to design this must-see concert venue. By day, the music hall is illuminated by tall stained-glass windows and an ornate stained-glass skylight, which gleam again after dark by electric light. Sculptures of wild horses and busts of the seven muses are on the walls flanking the stage. The **Sala de Luis Millet** has a close view of the intricate "trencadis" pillars. *(C. Sant Francese de Paula, 2. ☎93 295 7200; www.palaumusica.org. M: Jaume I. Mandatory 50min. tours in English; 1 per hr. Open daily 9am-3:30pm, Aug. and Semana Santa 9am-7pm. €10, students and seniors €9. Check the Guía del Ocio for concert listings. Concert tickets €8-175. Box office open 9am-9pm. MC/V.)*

MUSEU PICASSO. Barcelona's most-visited museum traces Picasso's artistic development with the world's most comprehensive collection of work from his formative Barcelona period. Picasso donated 1700 of the museum's 3600 works. *(C. Montcada, 15-23. ☎93 256 3000; www.museupicasso.bcn.cat. M: Jaume I. Open Tu-Su 10am-8pm. Last entrance 30min. before closing. €9, 16-25 and seniors €6, temporary exhibits €2.90-5.80. Under 16 free and 1st Su of the month free.)*

MUSEU DE LA XOCOLATA (CHOCOLATE MUSEUM). The museum presents gobs of information about the history, production, and ingestion of this sensuous sweet. Chocolate sculptures include La Sagrada Família and football star Ronaldo. The cafe offers tasting and baking workshops. *(Pl. Pons i Clerch, C. Comerç 26. ☎93 268 7878; www.museudelaxocolata.com. M: Jaume I. Open M and W-Sa 10am-7pm, Su 10am-3pm. Workshops for kids from €6; reservations required. €4, under 7 free.)*

L'EIXAMPLE

The Catalan Renaissance and Barcelona's 19th-century growth pushed the city past its medieval walls and into modernity. **Ildefons Cerdà** drew up a plan for a new neighborhood where people of all social classes could live side by side; however, l'Eixample (luh-SHOMP-luh) did not thrive as a utopian community but became a playground for the bourgeoisie. Despite gentrification, L'Eixample remains an innovative neighborhood full of *Modernista* oddities.

LA SAGRADA FAMÍLIA. Antoni Gaudí's masterpiece is far from finished, which makes La Sagrada Família the world's most visited construction site. Only 8 of the 18 planned towers have been completed and the church still lacks an "interior," yet millions of people make the touristic pilgrimage to witness its work-in-progress majesty. Of the three facades, only the **Nativity Facade** was finished under Gaudí. A new team of architects led by Jordi Bonet hopes to lay the last stone by 2026 (the 100th anniversary of Gaudí's death). The affiliated museum displays plans and computer models of the fully realized structure. *(C. Mallorca, 401, across from the Pizza Hut. ☎93 207 3031; www.sagradafamilia.org. M: Sagrada Família. Open daily Apr.-Sept. 9am-8pm; Oct.-Mar. 9am-5:45pm. Elevator open Apr.-Sept. 9am-7:45pm; Oct.-Mar. 9am-5:45pm. Entrance €10, over 65, with ISIC , or in a group of 20 or more €8. Under 10 free. Combined ticket with Casa-Museu Gaudí €12, student and senior €10. Elevator €2. English language tours 11am, 1pm, 3pm and 5pm; winter 11am and 1pm. €4.)*

LA MANZANA DE LA DISCÒRDIA. A short walk from Pl. de Catalunya, the odd-numbered side of Pg. de Gràcia between C. Aragó and C. Consell de Cent has been leaving passersby scratching their heads for a century. The Spanish nickname, which translates to the "block of discord," comes from the stylistic clashing of its three most extravagant buildings. Sprouting flowers, stained glass, and legendary doorway sculptures adorn **Casa Lleó i Morera,** #35, by Domènech i Montaner, on the far left corner of the block (admire from the outside; entrance is not permitted). Two buildings down, Puig i Cadafalch's geometric, Moorish-influenced facade makes **Casa Amatller,** #41, perhaps the most beautiful building on the block *(guided tour with chocolate tasting M-F 4 per day 11am-6pm, Su at noon; €8).* The real discord comes next door at **Casa Batlló,** #43, popularly believed to represent Catalonia's patron Sant Jordi (St. George) slaying a dragon. The chimney plays the lance, the scaly roof is the dragon's back, and the bony balconies are the remains of his victims. The house was built using shapes from nature—the balconies ripple like the ocean. *(☎93 216 0306; www.casabatllo.cat. Open daily 9am-8pm. €17, students €14. Call for group discounts for 20 people or more. Free multilingual audio tour.)*

MONTJUÏC

Historically, whoever controlled Montjuïc (mon-joo-EEK; "Hill of the Jews") controlled the city. Today, the area is home to a park and **Poble Espanyol,** a recreation of famous buildings and sights from all regions of Spain.

FUNDACIÓ MIRÓ. A large collection of sculptures, drawings, and paintings from Miró's career, ranging from sketches to wall-sized canvases, engages visitors with the work of this Barcelona-born artist. His best-known pieces here include *El Carnival de Arlequín*, *La Masia*, and *L'or de l'Azuz*. The gallery also displays experimental work by young artists and pieces by Alexander Calder. *(☎93 443 9470; www.bcn.fjmiro.es. Funicular from M: Parallel or Park Montjuïc bus from Pl. Espanya. Open July-Sept. Tu-W and F-Sa 10am-8pm; Oct.-June Tu-W and F-Sa 10am-7pm; all year Th 10am-9:30pm, Su and holidays 10am-2:30pm. Last entry 15min. before closing. €7.50, students and seniors €5, under 15 free. Temporary exhibitions €4/3.)*

MUSEU NACIONAL D'ART DE CATALUNYA (PALAU NACIONAL). Designed by Enric Catà and Pedro Cendoya for the 1929 International Exposition, the magnificent Palau Nacional has housed the Museu Nacional d'Art de Catalunya (MNAC) since 1934. Its main hall is a public event space, while the wings are home to the world's finest collection of Catalan Romanesque art and a wide variety of Gothic pieces. *(☎93 622 0376; www.mnac.es. From M: Espanya, walk up Av. Reina María Cristina away from the twin brick towers. Open Tu-Sa 10am-7pm, Su and holidays 10am-2:30pm. Temporary exhibits €3-5; 2 temporary exhibits €6; all exhibits €9. 30% discount for students and seniors; under 14 and first Su of the month free. Combo ticket with Poble Espanyol €12. Audio tour included.)*

CASTELL DE MONTJUÏC. This historic fortress and its Museu Militar sit high on the hill, and from the scenic outlook, guests can enjoy a multitude of panoramic jaw-droppers and photo-ops. Taking the *telefèric*—an airborne cable-car—to and from the castle is usually half the fun. *(☎93 329 8613.From M: Parallel, take the funicular to Parc de Montjuïc and then the cable car to the castle. Funicular open M-Sa 10am-9pm, low season 10am-6pm. €6, round-trip €8, children €4.50/6. Parc de Montjuïc bus runs up the slope from in front of the telefèric. Open Mar.-Oct. Tu-Su 9:30am-8pm; Nov. Tu-F 9:30am-6:30pm, Sa-Sun 9:30am-8pm; Dec.-March Tu-F 9:30am-5pm, Sa-Sun 9:30am-7pm. Museum open Mar.-Nov. Tu-Sa 9:30am-8pm; Dec.-Feb. 9:30am-5pm. €3 for museum, fortress, Plaza de Armas, and outlook; free without museum.)*

WATERFRONT

MUSEU D'HISTÒRIA DE CATALUNYA. The last gasp of the Old City before entering the tourist trap of Barceloneta, the Museu provides an exhaustive and patriotic introduction to Catalan history, politics, and culture. There is a particularly good section devoted to Franco. Exhibits include recreations of a 1930s

Spanish bar and an 8th-century Islamic prayer tent. *(Pl. Pau Vila, 3. Near entrance to the Moll d'Espanya; to the left as you walk out toward Barceloneta. ☎93 225 4700; mhc.cultura@gencat.net. Open Tu and Th-Sa 10am-7pm, W 10am-8pm, Su 10am-2:30pm. University students €7. Under 7 and over 65 free. Free to all the first Su of the month.)*

TORRE SAN SEBASTIÀ. One of the best ways to view the city is from the cable cars spanning the Port Vell, which connect beachy Barceloneta with mountainous Montjuïc. The full ride, which takes about 10min. each way and makes an intermediate stop at the Jaume I Tower near Colom, gives a bird's-eye view of the city. *(☎93 441 5071. Pg. Joan de Borbó. M: Barceloneta. In Port Vell, as you walk down Joan de Borbó and see the beaches to the left, stay right and look for the high tower. Open daily 11am-8pm. To Montjuïc one-way €9, round-trip €12.50; elevator to the top €4.)*

L'AQUÀRIUM DE BARCELONA. This kid-friendly aquarium features sharks, exhibits on marine creatures, and a life-size model of a sperm whale. *(Moll d'Espanya. M: Drassanes or Barceloneta. ☎93 221 7474; www.aquariumbcn.com. Open daily July-Aug. 9:30am-11pm; Oct.-May M-F 9:30am-9pm, Sa-Su 9am-9:30pm, June and Sept. 9:30am-9:30pm. €17, students with ISIC €14.50, ages 4-12 €11.50, over 60 €13. AmEx/MC/V.)*

ZONA ALTA

Zona Alta (Uptown) is the section of Barcelona that lies at the top of most maps: past l'Eixample, in and around the Collserola Mountains, and away from the low-lying waterfront districts. The most visited part of Zona Alta is Gràcia, which packs a surprising number of *Modernista* buildings and parks, international cuisine, and chic shops into a relatively small area.

PARC GÜELL. This fantastical park was designed entirely by Gaudí but, in typical Gaudí fashion, was not completed until after his death. Gaudí intended Parc Güell to be a garden city, and its buildings and ceramic-mosaic stairways were designed to house the city's elite. However, only one house, now know as the **Casa-Museu Gaudí,** was built. Two staircases flank the park, leading to a towering *Modernista* pavilion originally designed as an open-air market but is now only occasionally used as a stage by street musicians. The longest park bench in the world, a multicolored serpentine wonder made of tile shards, decorates the top of the pavilion. *(Bus #24 from Pl. Catalunya stops at the upper entrance. Park open daily 10am-dusk. Museum open daily Apr.-Sept. 10am-8pm; Oct.-Mar. 10am-6pm. Park free. Museum €5, with ISIC, seniors, under 18 €4, under 10 free.)*

MUSEU DEL FÚTBOL CLUB BARCELONA. A close second to the Picasso Museum as Barcelona's most-visited museum, the FCB merits all the attention it gets from football fanatics. Fans will appreciate the storied history of the team. The high point is entering the stadium and taking in the 100,000-seat **Camp Nou.** (*Next to the stadium. ☎93 496 3608. M: Collblanc. Enter through access gate 7 or 9. Open M-Sa 10am-6:15pm, Su and holidays 10am-2pm. €8.50, students and 13 or under €7. Museum and Camp Nou tour €13/10.40. Free parking.*)

ENTERTAINMENT AND FESTIVALS

For tips on entertainment, nightlife, and food, pick up the *Guía del Ocio* (www.guiadelocio.com; €1) at any newsstand. The best shopping in the city is in the **Barri Gòtic,** but if you feel like dropping some extra cash, check out the posh **Passeig de Gràcia** in l'Eixample. The **Festa de Sant Jordi** (St. George; Apr. 23, 2009) celebrates Catalunya's patron saint with a feast. Men give women roses, and women give men books. In the last two weeks of August, city folk jam at Gràcia's **Festa Mayor;** lights blaze in *plaças* and music plays all night. The three-day **Sónar** music festival comes to town in mid-June, attracting renowned DJs and electronica enthusiasts from all over the world. Other major music festivals include **Summercase** (indie and pop) and **Jazzaldia.** Check www.mondosonoro.com or pick up the *Mondo Sonoro* festival guide for more info. In July and August, the **Grec Festival** hosts dance performances, concerts, and film screenings. The **Festa Nacional de Catalunya** (Sept. 11) brings traditional costumes and dancing. **Festa de Sant Joan** takes place the night of June 23; ceaseless fireworks will prevent any attempts to sleep. The largest celebration in Barcelona is the **Festa de Mercè,** the weeks before and after September 24. *Barceloneses* honor the patron saint of the city with fireworks, *sardana* dancing, and concerts.

NIGHTLIFE

Barcelona's wild, varied nightlife treads the line between slick and kitschy. In many ways, the city is clubbing heaven—things don't get going until late (don't bother showing up at a club before 1am), and they continue until dawn. But for every full-blown dance club, there are 100 relaxed bars, from Irish pubs to absinthe dens. Check the *Guía del Ocio* (www.guiadelocio.com) for the address of that place your hip *Barcelonese* friend just told you about.

TIP **DON'T FEAR FLYERS.** Many clubs hand out flyers, particularly in La Ribera and on La Rambla. They are far from a tourist trap—travelers can save lots of money with free admission and drink passes.

Marsella Bar, C.de Sant Pau 65. M: Liceu. Religious figurines grace the walls of Barcelona's oldest bar, first opened in 1820; perhaps they're praying for the *absenta* (absinthe; €5) drinkers. Beer €3.20. Mixed drinks €5-6. Open M-Sa 10pm-2am. Cash only.

Betty Ford, Joaquin Costa, 56 (☎93 304 1368). This hip, new local favorite is the place to be and be seen—amidst chic, simple decor and raucous conversation. Happy hour (8-10pm) offers fancy mixed drinks for €3.50; try a Manhattan or a sugar-sweetened mojito. Beer €2.50-4. Open daily 2pm-2:30am.

Mojito Club, C. Rosselló, 217 (☎93 237 6528; www.mojitobcn.com). M: Diagonal. This club lures a fun-loving crowd with Latin beats. W Brazilian party with free samba lessons at 11:30pm and R&B later. Salsa lessons Th 11:30pm and Su 9pm, free but one drink minimum; also F-Sa 11pm-1am, €10 cover including drink; full courses and intensives available, call for information. Open Tu-Su 11pm-4:30am. MC/V.

La Fira, C. Provença, 171 (☎65 085 5384). M: Hospital Clínic or FGC: Provença. A hip crowd is surrounded by carousel swings, carnival mirrors, and a fortune teller—not to mention eerie clowns painted on the walls. Variety of shows and parties, often with entrance fee. Open M-Th 7pm-2:30am, F-Sa until 3am. MC/V.

Zeltas, C. Casanova, 75 (☎93 450 8469, www.zeltas.net). This exotic bar with shimmering hangings and feather boas welcomes classy clientele—usually gay—to enjoy the palatial surroundings. Beer €4.50, mixed drinks €7. Open daily 10:30pm-3am. MC/V.

Tinta Roja, C. Creus dels Molers 17 (☎93 443 3243; www.tintaroja.net), is the best combo bar and dance floor in the city. Tango classes W 9-10:30pm, basic course 2 months (call for prices). Open M-Th, Su 8:30pm-2am, F-Sa 8:30pm-3am. Cash only.

Otto Zutz, C. Lincoln 15 (☎93 238 0722). FGC: Gracia or M: Fontana. One of Barcelona's most famous clubs, with three dance floor ambiences. Beer €6. Mixed drinks €6-12. Cover €10-15, includes 1 drink. Open Tu-Sa midnight-6am. AmEx/MC/V.

City Hall, Rambla de Catalunya, 4 (☎93 317 2177, www.cityhall-bcn.com). A popular club scene frequented by a young crowd, just a few steps from Pl. Catalunya. Has three different areas, including an outdoor patio with graffiti-style walls, and plays every type of music you can dance to. Beer €6, mixed drinks €9-11. Cover €10-12; look for discount flyers. Open M-Th and Sun midnight-5am, F-Sa midnight-6am.

Schilling, C. Ferran, 23 (☎93 317 6787). M: Liceu. One of the more laid-back and spacious wine bars in the area, with dim lighting, velvet seat cushions and bottles climbing the walls. Excellent *sangria* (pitcher €17). Wine €2-3, bottle €11-13. Serves breakfast and sandwiches (€2-6) during the day. Schilling often attracts British and gay crowds. Open M-W 10am-2:30am, Th-Sa 10am-3am, Su noon-2am.

SPAIN

DAYTRIP FROM BARCELONA

THE COSTA BRAVA: FIGUERES AND CADAQUÉS.

From Figueres, trains (☎902 24 02 02) leave Pl. de l'Estació for Barcelona (2hr., 17-22 per day, €10) and Girona (30-40min., 17-22 per day, €2.60). Buses (☎972 67 33 54) run from Pl. de l'Estació to Barcelona (2hr., 2-4 per day, €15.50), Cadaqués (1hr.,3-4 per day, €4.50), and Girona (1hr., 2-5 per day, €5). Buses from Cadaqués go to Barcelona (2hr., 2 per day, €20), Figueres (1hr., 3-4 per day, €4.50), and Girona (2hr., 1-2 per day, €8.70).

The Costa Brava's jagged **cliffs** cut into the Mediterranean Sea from Barcelona to France. Visitors here are demanding super-vacationers, which keeps the food world-class and the beaches pristine. In 1974, **Salvador Dalí** chose his native Figueres (pop. 40,000) as the site to build a museum to house his works, catapulting the city to international fame. His personal tribute is a Surrealist masterpiece, the second-most popular museum in Spain, and a prime example of ego run delightfully amok. The **Teatre-Museu Dalí** is at Pl. Gala i Salvador Dalí 5. From La Rambla, take C. Girona, which becomes C. Jonquera, and climb the steps to the left. The museum contains the artist's nightmarish landscapes and bizarre installations, as well as his tomb. (☎972 67 75 00; www.salvador-dali.org. Open daily July and Sept. 9am-7:45pm; Oct. and Mar.-May Tu-Su 9:30am-5:45pm; Jan.-Feb. and Nov.-Dec. 10:30am-7:45pm; June daily 9:30am-5:45pm. €11, students and seniors €8.)

The whitewashed houses with terracotta roofs and the small bay of **Cadaqués** (pop. 2900) have attracted artists, writers, and musicians ever since Dalí built his summer home in nearby Port Lligat. Take C. Miranda away from the ocean and follow the signs to Port Lligat and the Casa de Dalí (20min.). Alternatively, take a trolley to Port Lligat (1hr., 6 per day, €7, children €5) from Pl. Frederic Rahola. **Casa-Museu Salvador Dalí** was the home of Dalí and his wife Gala until her death in 1982. Though two of Dalí's unfinished original paintings remain in the house, the wild decorations—including a lip-shaped sofa and a Pop Art pool resembling a miniature Alhambra—are the best part. (☎972 25 10 15. Open mid-June to mid-Sept. daily 10:30am-9pm; mid-Sept. to Jan. and mid-Mar. to mid-June Tu-Su 10:30am-6pm. Tour required; make reservations 4-5 days ahead. €10; students and seniors €8, children under 9 free.) Nightlife centers on C. Miguel Rosset. With your back to the bus station, walk right along Av. Caritat Serinyana to get to Plaça Frederic Rahola. The **tourist office,** C. Cotxe 2, is to the right of the *plaça*, opposite the beach. (☎972 25 83 15. Open end of June-mid Sept. M-Sa 9am-9pm, Su 10am-1pm, 5pm-8pm; end of Sept.-mid-June M-Sa 10am-1pm and 3-6pm.) **Postal Code:** 17488.

ANDORRA

The tiny Principat d'Andorra (pop. 72,400) bills itself as *El País dels Pirineus*, the country of the Pyrenees. The natural beauty of its towering and dramatic mountainous surroundings is closely rivaled by the artificial glitz, busy highways, and gaudy billboards of its flashy capital, Andorra la Vella. According to legend, Charlemagne founded Andorra in AD 784 as a reward to the valley's inhabitants for having led his army against the Moors. For the next 12 centuries, the country was the rope in a four-sided tug-of-war between the Spanish counts of Urgell, the French counts of Foix, the Spanish bishop of Urgell, and the king of France. Not until 1990 did the country create a commission to draft a democratic constitution, adopted on March 14, 1993.

PHONE CALLS FROM ANDORRA. Collect calls to most countries—including the US—are not possible. Buy an STA (Servei Telefonica Andorra) *teletarjecta* (telecard) at the tourist office for calls within the country (€3-6). Ask for an international calling card for calls out of the country, since the domestic STA card will only get you a few minutes. To call Andorra from Spain or France, you must dial the international code (☎376) first. For directory assistance, dial ☎111 or 119 (international).

ANDORRA LA VELLA ☎376

Andorra la Vella (pop. just over 20,000), the capital, is anything but *vella* (old). However, remnants of the city's past make for quirky contrasts to shiny new electronics and sporting goods stores. After doing a little shopping, escape to the countryside for a walk in the mountains.

TRANSPORTATION. Autocars Julia/Nadal (☎902 40 50 40; www.autocaresjulia.es) runs **buses** to Barcelona (3hr.; 8 per day, 6:15am-10:15pm; €24.50/42 round trip; also stops at Barcelona Airport, €30/52). Novatel (☎376 35 20 13) has service to Barcelona (3hr.; daily 5, 8, 10am, 12:30, 3:15pm; €28/€48 round-trip). Alsina Graells has buses to downtown Barcelona (3hr., daily 9 per day 6am-7:15pm, €23). La Seu d'Urgell is accessible hourly on a La Hispano-Andorra bus (☎376 82 13 72, www.andorrabus.com; 30min.; M-Sa every hr. 8am-9pm, Su 5 per day 8:15am-7:15pm; €2.65) departing 200m from Pl. de la Rotonda. Efficient **local buses** connect the villages along the 3 major highways that converge in Andorra la Vella. The **tourist office** provides a very helpful bus schedule. Since most towns are only 10min. apart, the outlying cities can be seen in a day via public transportation (€1-5.50).

ORIENTATION AND PRACTICAL INFORMATION. There are several **tourist offices** scattered throughout Andorra la Vella, including the National Tourism Office at the junction of C. Dr. Vilanova and C. Prat de la Creu (☎376 87 57 00; open M-Sa 10am-1:30pm and 3-7pm) and the **Oficina d'Informacio i Turisme** located on the Pl. de la Rotonda (☎376 82 71 17; open Sept. 10-June 30 M-F 9am-1pm and 3-7pm, Sa 9am-1pm and 3-8pm, Su 8am-1pm). Andorra la Vella connects with the next town, Escaldes, but if you can't walk between them, the information office there will direct you to bus stops. At any one of the tourist offices, the multilingual staff offers free *Sports Activities* and *Hotels i Restaurants* guides. Local services include: **ATMs** located directly across from the information office on Pl. Rotonda; weather and ski conditions from **Ski Andorra** (☎376 80 52 00); **taxi** service (☎376 86 30 00 or 376 82 80 00); **medical emergency** (☎116); **police** (emergencies ☎110, non-emergencies 376 87 20 00); and **Hospital Nostra Senyora de Meritxell** (☎376 87 10 00). **Internet** access is available at the public library, in the Edifici Prada Casadet on the C. Prat de Creu and C. Prada Casadet (☎376 82

87 50; open Sept.-Jun. M-F 10am-8:30pm, Sa 10am-1pm; July-Aug. M-F 8:30am-7pm; €1.50 per hr). The Spanish **post office** is at C. Joan Maragall, 10. (☎376 82 02 57. Open M-F 8:30am-2:30pm, Sa 9:30am-1pm).

ACCOMMODATIONS AND FOOD. For a bargain, the quiet **Pensión Rosa ❶,** Antic C. Major 18, offers well-kept rooms with shared bathrooms. (☎376 82 18 10. Breakfast €4. Singles €18; doubles €29.50; triples €45; quads €58. MC/V.) **Hotel Viena ❸,** C. de la Vall, 32, has an open ground-floor lounge with a bar, pool table, and foosball table beneath a television. Their big rooms include bathroom, shower, TV, and telephone. (☎376 82 34 46; internet access €0.50 per 20min. Singles €30; doubles €36, triples €45, quads €50. Cash only). **Casa Teresa ❸,** C. Bonaventura Armengol, 11, has phenomenal spaghetti (€6.75) and a variety of delicious dishes, including large, creative pizzas (€6-7) and fish and meat entrees (€9-17). Try the sweet red sangria (€2.75). (☎376 82 64 76. *Menú* €9. Open daily 8am-10pm. Kitchen open 12:30-3:30pm and 8-11pm. Bar open 8am-10pm. MC/V.) **Les Alpi ❸** is convenient and distinctly modern. (☎376 80 81 00. Open daily noon-3:30pm and 8-10:30pm. Catalan meat dishes €8-18. MC/V.) **La Cantina ❷,** on Pl. Gulliemó, has a delicious vegetarian *paella* (€12), and also serves pastas and pizzas for €7-8. (☎376 82 30 65. MC/V.)

HIKING AND THE OUTDOORS. An extensive network of hiking trails traverses Andorra. The free, multilingual, and extremely helpful tourist office brochure *Mountain Activities* includes 41 hiking itineraries, 9 mountain biking itineraries, and several rock-climbing routes, as well as bike rental services and cabin and refuge locations. Most trailheads can be accessed using Andorra's public transportation system. La Massana is home to Andorra's tallest peak, **Pic Alt de la Coma Pedrosa** (2942m). For organized hiking trips, try the **La Rabassa Sports and Nature Center** (☎376 32 38 68; www.naturlandia.ad), in the parish of Sant Julía de Lòria. Vertical enthusiasts may want to try **Bosc Aventura's** treetop activities, closed in summer 2008 for renovations. Activities are €22. Call for summer 2009 hours (☎376 385 077). The **Canillo Tourist** Office, Av. Sant Joan de Caselles; ☎376 75 36 00, offers half-day canyoneering (€31) and hiking (€17) excursions, from 8:30am-3pm. **Natura I Aventura** (376 34 95 42) offers excursions for groups of 5-10 (€25-20), as well as individual guided trips (€120 per day).

SKIING. With five outstanding resorts, Andorra offers skiing opportunities galore from December to April. Lift ticket prices range €38-55, and **Ski Andorra** provides a 5-day pass to all sites (€157-168). **Vall Nord** is composed of resorts: **Pal** (☎376 878 000), 10km from La Massana, is accessible by bus from La Massana (5 per day 8:45am-7:45pm, return 9:10am-5:05pm; €1) and nearby **Arinsal** (☎376 73 70 20), which is also accessible from Andorra la Vella by bus (every hr.; 8:15am-8:45pm, return 8:25am-8:45pm; €1). On the French border, **Grand Valire** (☎376 80 10 60) is the valley's highest resort at 2050m, with 53 slopes, totaling 100km—more than any other resort. It is accessible by bus from Andorra la Vella (4 per day 9am-6:45pm, return 9:30am-7:45pm; €4.70). The more horizontal **La Rabassa** (☎376 75 97 98 or 38 75 58) is Andorra's only cross-country ski resort. If you want someone else to propel you, try taking the **sled dogs.** More recently added winter activities include snowshoeing, snowmobiling, and heli-tours. Andorra's tourist office publishes a winter edition of *Ski Andorra*, a guide to all things skiing-related. Call **SKI Andorra** (☎376 80 52 00; www.ski-andorra.ad) or the tourist offices for information on reservations, prices, and transportation. Prices at ski resorts are subject to change.

NAVARRA

From the unfathomable mayhem of Pamplona and the Running of the Bulls to the many hiking trails that wind up the peaks of the Pyrenees, there is seldom a dull moment in Navarra. Bordered by Basque Country and Aragón, the region is a mix of overlapping cultures and traditions.

PAMPLONA (IRUÑA) ☎948

El encierro, *la Fiesta de San Fermín*, the Running of the Bulls, utter debauchery: call it what you will, the outrageous festival of the city's patron saint is the principal cause of the international notoriety Pamplona (pop. 200,000) enjoys. Since the city's immortalization in Ernest Hemingway's *The Sun Also Rises*, hordes of travelers have flocked to Pamplona for one week each July to witness the daily *corridas* and ensuing chaos. The city's monuments, museums, and parks merit exploration as well.

NOT JUST A LOAD OF BULL. Although Pamplona is generally safe, crime skyrockets during San Fermín. Beware of assaults and muggings and do not walk alone at night during the festival.

TRANSPORTATION AND PRACTICAL INFORMATION. **Trains** (☎902 24 02 02) run from Estación RENFE. To travel the 2km take the #9 bus from the Po. Sarasate to the station, (20 minutes, €1, buses every 15 min., Av. de San Jorge, to Barcelona (6-8hr., 3 per day, from €36), Madrid (3hr., 4 per day, €52), and San Sebastián (1hr., 5 per day, €19). **Buses** leave from the bus station by the Ciudadela on C. Yangüas y Miranda for Barcelona (6-8hr., 4 per day, €26), Bilbao (2hr., 5-6 per day, €14), and Madrid (5hr., 6-10 per day, €28). From Pl. del Castillo, take C. San Nicolás, turn right on C. San Miguel, and walk through Pl. San Francisco to reach the **tourist office**, C. Hilarión Eslava. (☎948 42 04 20; www.turismo.navarra.es. Open during *San Fermín* daily 8am-8pm; July-Aug. M-Sa 9am-8pm, Su 10am-2pm; Sept.-June M-Sa 10am-2pm and 4-7pm, Su 10am-2pm.) **Luggage storage** is at the Escuelas de San Francisco in Pl. San Francisco during *San Fermín*. (€3.40 per day. Open 24hr. from July 4 at 8am to July 16 at 2pm.) The **biblioteca** has free Internet and Wi-Fi. (Open Sept.-June M-F 8:30am-8:45pm, Sa 8:30am-1:45pm, July-Aug. M-F 8:30am-2:45pm.) **Postal Code:** 31001.

ACCOMMODATIONS AND FOOD. Smart San Ferministas book their rooms up to a year ahead; without a reservation, it's nearly impossible to find one. Expect to pay rates up to four times the normal price. Check the tourist office for a list of official accommodations with openings or the newspaper *Diario de Navarra* for *casas particulares* (private homes that rent rooms). Many roomless backpackers are forced to fluff up their sweatshirts and sleep rough. Stay in large groups, and if you can't store your backpack, sleep on top of it. Budget accommodations line **Calle San Gregorio** and **Calle San Nicolás** off Pl. del Castillo. Deep within the *casco antiguo* (Old Town), **Pensión Eslava ❶**, C. Hilarión Eslava 13, 2nd fl., is quieter and less crowded than other *pensiones*. Older rooms have a balcony and shared bath. (☎948 22 15 58. Singles €15; doubles €20-30, during San Fermín €100. Cash only.) Small **Horno de Aralar ❸**, C. San Nicolás 12, above the restaurant, has five spotless, bright rooms with bath and TV. (☎948 22 11 16. Singles €40; doubles €50; during San Fermín all rooms €200-300. MC/V.) Look for hearty *menús* at the cafe-bars above **Plaza de San**

Francisco and around **Paseo de Ronda.** Thoroughfares **Calle Navarrería** and **Paseo de Sarasate** are home to good *bocadillo* bars. **Café-Bar Iruña ❸,** Pl. del Castillo, the former casino made famous in Hemingway's *The Sun Also Rises*, is notable for its storied past and elegant interior. The *menú* (€13) is required if eating at a table, but the restaurant serves drinks and sandwiches at the bar. (☎948 22 20 64. Open M-Th 8am-11pm, F 8am-2am, Sa 9am-2am, Su 9am-11pm. MC/V.)

SIGHTS AND NIGHTLIFE. Pamplona's rich architectural legacy is reason enough to visit during the 51 other weeks of the year. The restored 14th-century Gothic **Catedral de Santa María**, at the end of C. Navarrería is one of only four cathedrals of its kind in Europe. (☎948 22 29 90. Open M-F 10am-2pm and 4-7pm, Sa 10am-2pm. July 15-Sept. 15 M-F 10am-7pm, Sa 10am-2:30 pm. €4.40.) The walls of the pentagonal **Ciudadela** enclose free art exhibits, various summer concerts, and an amazing San Fermín fireworks display. Follow Po. de Sarasate to its end and go right on C. Navas de Tolosa, then take the next left onto C. Chinchilla and follow it to its end. (☎948 22 82 37. Open M-Sa 7:30am-9:30pm, Su 9am-9:30pm. Closed for San Fermín. Free.)

Central **Plaza del Castillo,** with outdoor seating galore, is the heart of Pamplona's social scene. A young crowd parties in the *casco antiguo*, particularly along the bar-studded **Calle San Nicolás, Calle Jarauta,** and **Calle San Gregorio.** The small plaza **Travesía de Bayona,** 600m past the Ciudela (follow Av. del Ejército as it turns into Av. de Bayona; the Travesía is just before Mo. de la Oliva branches off), has bars and *discotecas*. **Blue Shadow** (☎948 27 51 09) and **Tandem** (☎948 26 92 85), Tr. de Bayona 3 and 4, have good dancing and big crowds. (Beer €3.50. Mixed drinks €6. Both open Th-Sa 10pm-4am.)

RUNNING SCARED. So, you're going to run, and nobody's going to stop you. But because nobody—except the angry, angry bulls—wants to see you get seriously injured, here are a few words of *San Fermín* wisdom:

1. Research the *encierro* before you run; the tourist office has a pamphlet that outlines the route and offers tips for the inexperienced. Running the entire 850m course is highly inadvisable; it would mean 2-8min. of evading 6 bulls moving at 24kph (15mph). Instead, pick a 50m stretch.
2. Don't stay up all night drinking and carousing. Experienced runners get lots of sleep the night before and arrive at the course around 6:30am.
3. Take a fashion tip from the locals: wear the traditional white-and-red outfit with closed-toe shoes. Ditch the baggy clothes, backpacks, and cameras.
4. Give up on getting near the bulls and concentrate on getting to the bullring in one piece. Though some whack the bulls with rolled newspapers, runners should never distract or touch the animals.
5. Never stop in doorways, alleys, or corners; you can be trapped and killed.
6. Run in a straight line; if you cut someone off, they can easily fall.
7. Be particularly wary of isolated bulls—they seek company in the crowds. In 2007, 13 runners were seriously injured by an isolated bull.
8. If you fall, stay down. Curl up into a fetal position, lock your hands behind your head, and do not get up until the clatter of hooves has passed.

FIESTA DE SAN FERMÍN (JULY 4-15, 2009). Visitors overcrowd the city as it delivers an eight-day frenzy of bullfights, concerts, dancing, fireworks, parades, parties, and wine in what is perhaps Europe's premier party. *Pamploneses*, clad in white with red sashes and bandanas, throw themselves into the merrymaking, displaying obscene levels of both physical stamina and alcohol tolerance. *El encierro*, or "The Running of the Bulls," is the highlight of *San Fermin*; the first *encierro* takes place on July 5 at 8am and is repeated at 8am every day for the next seven days. Hundreds of bleary-eyed, hungover, hyper-adrenalized runners flee from large bulls as bystanders cheer from balconies, barricades, doorways, and windows. Both the bulls and the mob are dangerous; terrified runners react without concern for those around them. To participate in the bullring excitement without the risk of the *encierro*, onlookers should arrive at 6:45am. To watch a **bullfight,** wait in the line that forms at the bullring around 7:30pm. As one fight ends, the next day's tickets go on sale. (Tickets from €10; check www.feriadeltoro.com for details.) Tickets are incredibly hard to get at face value, as over 90% belong to season holders. Once the running ends, insanity spills into the streets and explodes at night with singing, dancing in alleyways, parades, and a no-holds-barred party in **Plaza del Castillo.**

BASQUE COUNTRY (PAÍS VASCO)

The varied landscape of Spain's Basque Country combines energetic cities, lush hills, industrial wastelands, and fishing villages. Many believe that the strongly nationalistic Basques are the native people of Iberia, as their culture and language cannot be traced to any known source.

SAN SEBASTIÁN (DONOSTIA) ☎943

Glittering on the shores of the Cantabrian Sea, coolly elegant San Sebastián (pop. 184,000) is famous for its bars, beaches, and scenery. Locals and travelers down *pintxos* (*tapas*) and drinks in the *parte vieja* (Old Town), which claims the most bars per square meter in the world. Residents, flags, and posters provide a constant reminder: you're not in Spain, you're in Basque Country.

TRANSPORTATION. RENFE **trains** (☎902 24 02 02) run from Estación del Norte, Po. de Francia, to Barcelona (8hr., 1-2 per day, €37-48); Madrid (8hr., 2 per day, €37-56); and Salamanca (6hr., 2 per day, €31-39). **Buses** leave from a platform and ticket windows at Av. de Sancho el Sabio 31-33 and Po. de Vizcaya 16. Buses to: Barcelona (7hr., 3 per day, €28); Bilbao (1hr., 1-2 per hr., €9); Madrid (6hr., 7-9 per day, €30-42); Pamplona (1hr., 6-10 per day, €6.50).

ORIENTATION AND PRACTICAL INFORMATION. The **Río Urumea** splits San Sebastián down the middle, with the **parte vieja** (Old Town) to the east and **El Centro** (the new downtown) to the west, separated by the wide walkway **Alameda del Boulevard.** The city center, most monuments, and the popular beaches **Playa de la Concha** and **Playa de Ondarreta** also line the peninsula on the western side of the river. At the tip of the peninsula rises **Monte Urgull.** The **bus platform** is south of the city center on Pl. Pío XII. To get to the *parte vieja* from the train station, cross the Puente María Cristina and turn right at the fountain. Continue four blocks north to Av. de la Libertad, make a left and follow it to the port; the *parte vieja* is to the right and Playa de la Concha is on the left.

The **tourist office** is at C. Reina Regente 3, on the edge of the *parte vieja.* (☎943 48 11 66; www.sansebastianturismo.com. Open July-Aug. M-Sa 9am-8pm, Su 10am-2pm and 3:30-7pm.) Free **Internet** is at **Biblioteca Central,** Pl Ajuntamiento. (Free; 45min. max. Free Wi-Fi. Open M-F 10am-8:30pm, Sa 10am-2pm and 4:30-8pm.) The **post office** is at C. Urdaneta, behind the cathedral. (☎902 19 71 97. Open M-F 8:30am-8:30pm, Sa 9:30am-2pm.) **Postal code:** 20006

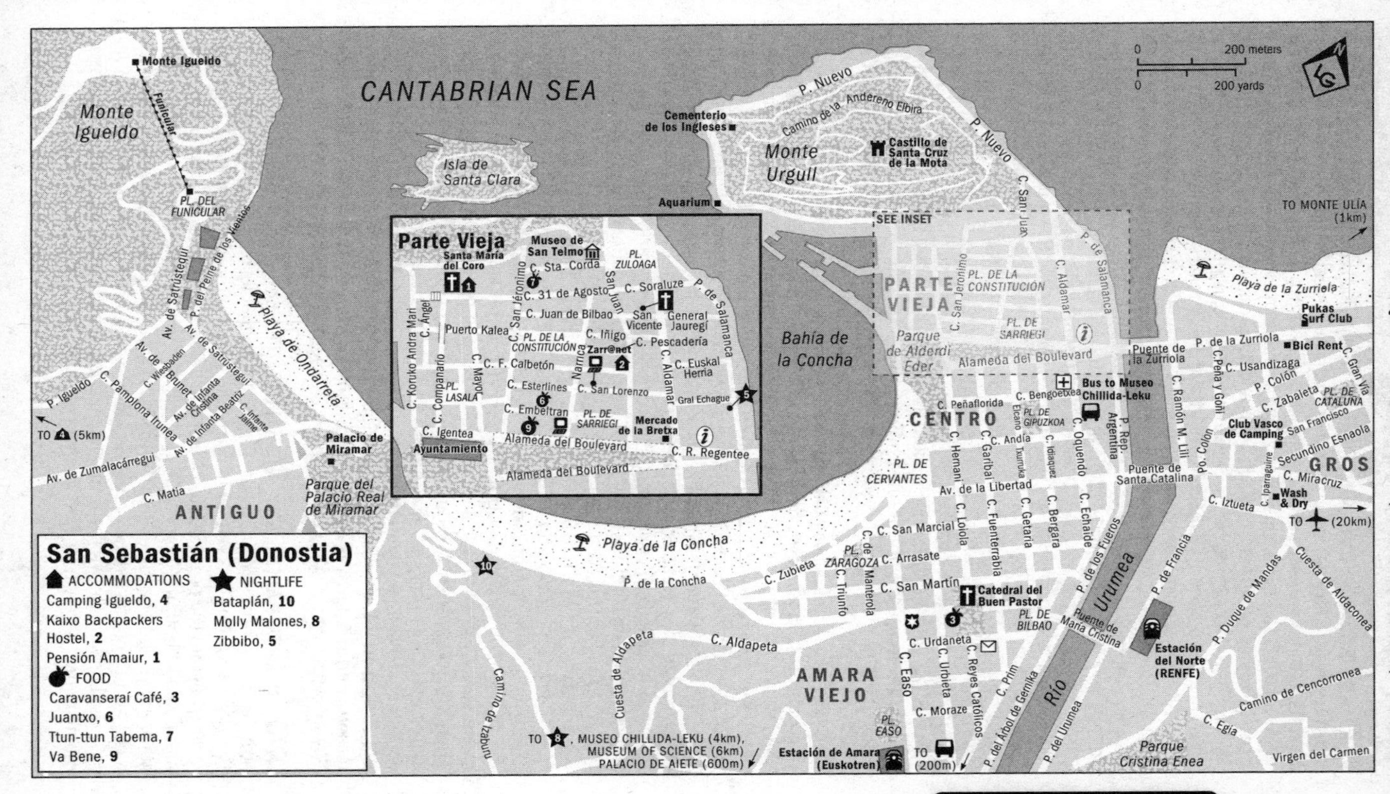
San Sebastián (Donostia)
ACCOMMODATIONS
Camping Igueldo, 4
Kaixo Backpackers Hostel, 2
Pensión Amaiur, 1
FOOD
Caravanserai Café, 3
Juantxo, 6
Ttun-ttun Tabema, 7
Va Bene, 9
NIGHTLIFE
Bataplán, 10
Molly Malones, 8
Zibbibo, 5
CANTABRIAN SEA
Monte Igueldo
Funicular
PL. DEL FUNICULAR
Isla de Santa Clara
Cementerio de los Ingleses
Monte Urgull
Castillo de Santa Cruz de la Mota
Aquarium
SEE INSET
PARTE VIEJA
Parque de Alderdi Eder
Bahía de la Concha
Playa de Ondarreta
Palacio de Miramar
Parque del Palacio Real de Miramar
ANTIGUO
Playa de la Concha
CENTRO
GROS
AMARA VIEJO
Playa de la Zurriola
Pukas Surf Club
Bici Rent
Club Vasco de Camping
Wash & Dry
Bus to Museo Chillida-Leku
Catedral del Buen Pastor
Estación del Norte (RENFE)
Estación de Amara (Euskotren)
Río Urumea
Parque Cristina Enea
TO MONTE ULÍA (1km)
TO (20km)
TO (5km)
TO (200m)
TO 8, MUSEO CHILLIDA-LEKU (4km), MUSEUM OF SCIENCE (6km) PALACIO DE AIETE (600m)
Parte Vieja
Santa María del Coro
Museo de San Telmo
Zarr@net
Mercado de la Bretxa
Ayuntamiento
200 meters
200 yards

ACCOMMODATIONS AND FOOD. Small *pensiones* are scattered throughout the streets of the noisy *parte vieja.* For a more restful night's sleep, look for hostels and *pensiones* on the outskirts of El Centro. **Pensión Amaiur ❷,** C. 31 de Agosto 44, 2nd fl., to the right of the Iglesia Santa María, offers lovely rooms in an historic house. (☎943 42 96 54; www.pensionamaiur.com. Internet €1 per 18min. Free Wi-Fi. Singles €24-37; doubles €35-60; triples €54-80; quads €65-95. 10% *Let's Go* discount. AmEx/MC/V.) **Kaixo Backpacker's Hostel ❷,** C. San Juan 9, 2nd fl. is a centrally located hostel with dorms and shared baths. The staff runs insider *tapas* tours, as well as hiking trips and surf outings. (☎659 39 38 42; reservations ☎943 42 06 51. Free laundry, Internet, and kitchen. Beds €20, June-Aug. €25. Bike rentals €2/hr. and surfboard rentals €20/day, €10 half-day for guests). *Pintxos (tapas)*, washed down with *txakoli*, the local fizzy white wine, are a religion in San Sebastián. Restaurants line the quiet, pedestrian **C. Reyes Católicos** outside the *parte vieja* below the cathedral. **Juantxo,** C. Esterlines is an authentic but unintimidating *pintxos* bar serving a selection of *bocadillos* (sandwiches; €3-3.50), *pintxos* (€1.35), and *raciones* (small dishes; €3-5). The *filete* with onions, cheese, and peppers (€3) is excellent. (☎943 42 74 05. Open M-Th 9am-11:30pm, F-Su 9am-1:45am. Cash only.) **Ttun-Ttun Taberna ❷,** C. San Jeronimo, 25, offers one choice for lunch: a superb *menú* (€9) with an assortment of authentic Basque options. (☎943 42 68 82. Open daily 1-4pm.)

SIGHTS. The **Museo Chillida-Leku** houses a large collection of the works of Eduardo Chillida, San Sebastián's contemporary art guru. His stone and steel sculptures are spread across the museum's spacious lawns. (Bo. Jauregui 66. 15min. from the city center. Autobuses Garayar, line G2, leave from C. Oquendo. 2 per hr., €1.25. ☎943 33 60 06; www.museochillidaleku.com. Open July-Aug. M-Sa 10:30am-8pm, Su 10:30am-3pm; Sept.-June M, W-Su 10:30am-3pm. €9, students and seniors €7.) The best views of San Sebastian are from the tower atop **Monte Igueldo,** ringed by an amusement park. The sidewalk from the city ends just before the base of Monte Igueldo at Chillida's sculpture *El Peine de los Vientos* (Comb of the Winds). A funicular (€1.30, 4 per hr.) runs to the summit. (☎943 21 02 11. Open July-Sept. daily 10am-10pm; Oct. and Jan.-May M-F 11am-6pm, Sa-Su 11am-8pm; June M-F 11am-8pm, Sa 11am-10pm, Su 10am-10pm. Tower admission €1.) The **Palacio de Miramar** has passed through the hands of the Spanish court, Napoleon III, and Bismarck; it is now managed by the *Ayuntamiento* (local municipality), but the adjacent **Parque de Miramar** is open. (Head up Cuesta de Aldapeta or take bus #19 or 31. Grounds open daily June-Sept. 8am-9pm, Oct.-May 8am-7pm. Free.) Sunbathers crowd the smaller and steeper **Playa de Ondarreta,** while surfers flock to **Playa de la Zurriola,** across the river from Monte Urgull. **Pukas Surf Club,** Av. de la Zurriola 24, has surfing lessons and rentals. (☎943 32 00 68. Fins €3 per hr. Surfboards €25 per day. Wetsuits €20 per 2 days. Lessons from €37 per hr. M-Sa 9am-9pm. MC/V.)

ENTERTAINMENT AND NIGHTLIFE. The *parte vieja* pulls out all the stops in the months of July and August, three blocks away from Alameda del Boulevard. During the year, when students outnumber backpackers, nightlife moves beyond the *parte vieja.* **Zibbibo,** Pl. de Sarriegi 8, has a happy hour every night 10:30-11:30pm (Open M-W 4pm-2:30am, Th-Sa 4pm-3:30am. MC/V.) **Molly Malone's,** C. San Martin, 55 (☎943 46 98 22), is a popular Irish bar that fills with a crowd of Spaniards and travelers alike. A popular pregame for the *discotecas,* the bar also draws the college-age crowd on Thursdays for international music night. (Open 4pm-4am, 5am weekends.)

BILBAO (BILBO) ☎944

The once gritty, industrial Bilbao (pop. 354,000) has risen to international cultural prominence since the creation of the shining **Guggenheim Museum.** However, this city, with its expansive parks, efficient transport, and grand architecture of all kinds, has plenty to offer beyond its oddly-shaped claim to fame.

TRANSPORTATION. To reach the **airport** (**BIO;** ☎944 86 96 64), 25km from Bilbao, take the Bizkai bus (☎902 22 22 65) marked *Aeropuerto* from the Termibús terminal or Pl. Moyúa (line A-3247; 25min., 2 per hr., €1.10). RENFE **trains** (☎902 24 02 02) leave from **Estación de Abando,** Pl. Circular 2, for Barcelona (9-10hr., 2 per day, €39-51), Madrid (5-6hr., 2 per day, €40-45), and Salamanca (5hr., 2pm, €27). Trains run between Bilboa's Estación de Atxuri and San Sebastián (2hr., 17-18 per day). FEVE trains run from **Estación de Santander,** C. Bailén, 2 (☎944 25 06 15; www.feve.es) to: León (7hr., 2:30pm, €20.55) and Santander (3hr.; 8am, 1, 7:30pm; €7.25). Most **bus** companies leave from **Termibús,** C. Gurtubay 1 (☎944 39 52 05; M: San Mamés), for: Barcelona (7hr., 4 per day, €41); Madrid (4-5hr., 10-18 per day, €26); Pamplona (2hr., 4-6 per day, €13); San Sebastián (1hr., 1-2 per hr., €8.70). Within Bilbao, a **Creditrans pass** (purchased in denominations of €5, €10, or €15) allows access to Metro, BizkaiBus, Bilbobús, and EuskoTran, the new tram-train line, at a discounted rate.

ORIENTATION AND PRACTICAL INFORMATION. The **Río de Bilbao** runs through the city, separating the historic *casco viejo* from the newer parts of town. The train stations are directly across the river to the west of the *casco viejo*. The city's major thoroughfare, **Gran Vía de Don Diego López de Haro,** connects three of Bilbao's main plazas. Heading east from Pl. de Sagrado Corazón, Gran Vía continues through the central **Pl. Moyúa** and ends at **Pl. Circular.** Past Pl. Circular, cross the Río de Bilbao on Puente del Arenal to arrive in **Plaza de Arriaga,** the entrance to the *casco viejo* and **Plaza Nueva.** The **tourist office** is at Pl. Ensanche 11. (☎944 79 57 60; www.bilbao.net/bilbaoturismo. Open M-F 9am-2pm, 4-7:30pm.), branches at Teatro Arriaga and near the Guggenheim. Free **Internet** at **Biblioteca Municipal,** C. Bidebarrieta, 4 (☎944 15 09 15; Open Sept. 16-May 31 M 2:30-8pm, Tu-F 8:30am-8:30pm, Sa 10am-1pm; July M-F 8:30am-7:30pm; Aug. M-F 8:30am-1:45pm; June Tu-F 8:30am-7:30pm, Sa 10am-2pm).

ACCOMMODATIONS AND FOOD. Plaza Arriaga and Calle Arenal have many budget accommodations, while upscale hotels are in the new city off Gran Vía. Rates climb during Semana Grande. **Pensión Méndez ❷,** C. Sta. María 13, 4th fl., provides cheery rooms with spacious balconies. (☎944 16 03 64. Singles €25; doubles €35; triples €50. MC/V.) **Hostal Méndez ❸,** on the first floor of the same building, is even more comfortable; rooms all have large windows, full bath, and TV. (Singles €38-40; doubles €50-55; triples €65-70. MC/V.) Restaurants and bars in the *casco viejo* offer a wide selection of local dishes, *pintxos (tapas)*, and *bocadillos*. The new city has even more variety. **Restaurante Peruano Ají Colorado ❸,** C. Barrenkale 5, specializes in traditional Andean *ceviche* (marinated raw fish; €10), and also serves Peruvian mountain dishes. (☎944 15 22 09. M-F lunch *menú* €12. Open M-Sa 1:30-4pm and 9-11pm, Su 1:30-4pm. MC/V.) **Restaurante Vegetariano Garibolo ❸,** C. Fernandez del Campo, 7, serves a vegetarian *menú* (€12) that lines locals up at lunchtime. (☎942 22 32 55; M-F 1-4pm, F-Sa 1-4pm and 9-11pm.)

SIGHTS AND NIGHTLIFE. Frank Gehry's **Museo Guggenheim Bilbao,** Av. Abandoibarra 2, is awe-inspiring. Lauded in the international press with every superlative imaginable, it has catapulted Bilbao straight into cultural stardom.

SPAIN

ROADTRIPPING

What do the Camino de Santiago and LSD have in common? Well... more than one might think. During the Middle Ages, thousands of pilgrims all over Europe trekked across Spain for more than enlightenment: they were afflicted by St. Anthony's Fire, a convulsive condition characterized by gangrene, hallucinations, and "possession." Along the Camino, monks would touch the afflicted with sacred scepters, and miraculously, the pilgrims would gradually be cured as they approached Santiago.

Lo and behold, what seemed like a spiritual high turned out to have a rather more mundane explanation. Their condition has a name: ergotism, a kind of intoxication brought on by consuming rye infected with ergot, a parasitic fungus that produces the same alkaloids found in the hallucinogen LSD. The illness was prevalent in Europe in those years, especially in France, where rye was abundant. As pilgrims set out on the Camino from the fields of France to the plains of Spain, they would encounter less and less rye and progressively more wheat, which was—miraculously—not susceptible to ergot. So while St. Anthony's sparks are unlikely to burn Spanish pilgrims today, send him some pilgrim love the next time you're roadtripping.

The museum hosts rotating exhibits drawn from the Guggenheim Foundation's often eccentric collection; don't be surprised if you are asked to take your shoes off, lie on the floor, or even sing throughout your visit. (☎944 35 90 80; www.guggenheim-bilbao.es. Wheelchair-accessible. Admission includes English-language audioguide, as well as guided tours Tu-Su 11am, 12:30, 4:30, 6:30pm; sign up 30min. before tour at the info desk. Open July-Aug. daily 10am-8pm; Sept.-June Tu-Su 10am-8pm. €13, students €7.50, under 12 free.) The **Museo de Bellas Artes,** Pl. del Museo 2, has an impressive collection of 12th- to 20th-century art, including excellent 15th- to 17th-century Flemish paintings, canvases by Basque artists, and works by Mary Cassatt, El Greco, Gauguin, Goya, and Velázquez. Take C. Elcano to Pl. del Museo or bus #10 from Pte. del Arenal. (☎944 39 60 60, Open Tu-Sa 10am-8pm, Su 10am-2pm. €5.50, students and seniors €4, under 12 and W free.) The best view of Bilbao's landscape is from **Monte Artxanda,** between the *casco viejo* and the Guggenheim. (Funicular 3min.; 4 per hr. M-F, June-Sept. also Sa; €0.86. Wheelchair lift €0.30.)

Mellow **Alambique,** Alda. Urquijo 37, provides elegant seating and a chance for conversation under chandeliers and photos of old Bilbao. (☎944 43 41 88. Beer €2-3. Open M-Th 8am-2am, F-Sa 8am-3am, Su 5pm-3am.) The **Cotton Club,** C. Gregorio de la Revilla 25, decorated with over 30,000 bottle caps and featuring over 100 whiskeys, draws a huge crowd on weekend nights. (☎944 10 49 51. Beer €3. Mixed drinks €6. Rum €6. Open M-Th 5pm-3:30am, F-Sa 5pm-6am, Su 6:30pm-3:30am.)

DAYTRIP FROM BILBAO: GUERNICA. On April 26, 1937, at the behest of General Franco, the Nazi "Condor Legion" dropped 29,000kg of explosives on Guernica, obliterating 70% of the city in three hours. The atrocity, which killed nearly 2000 people, is immortalized in Pablo Picasso's masterpiece, *Guernica* (p. 905). The thought-provoking **Guernica Peace Museum,** Pl. Foru 1, features a variety of multimedia exhibits. From the train station, walk two blocks up C. Adolfo Urioste and turn right on C. Artekalea. *(☎946 27 02 13. Open July-Aug. Tu-Sa 10am-8pm, Su 10am-3pm; Sept.-June Tu-Sa 10am-2pm and 4-7pm, Su 10am-2pm. English-language tours noon and 5pm. €4, students and seniors €2.)* **El Árbol,** a 300-year-old oak trunk encased in stone columns, marks the former political center of the País Vasco. At its side stands the current **Árbol,** its youngest descendant. **Trains** (☎902 54 32 10; www.euskotren.es) head to Bilbao (45min., 1-2 per hr., €2.25). Bizkai Bus (☎902 22 22 65) runs frequent, convenient buses between Guernica and Bilbao's Estación Abando; **buses** leave from Hdo. Amezaga in front of the Bilbao RENFE station. *(Lines A-3514 and A-3515; 45min., 2-4 per hr., €2.25.)* To reach the **tourist office,** C. Artekale 8, from the train station, walk up C. Adolfo Urioste, turn right on C. Barrenkale, go left at the alleyway, and look for the signs. *(☎946 25 58 92; www.gernika-lumo.net. Open July-Aug. M-Sa 10am-7pm, Su 10am-2pm; Sept.-June M-Sa 10am-2pm and 4-7pm, Su 10am-2pm.)*

GALICIA (GALIZA)

If, as the Galician saying goes, "rain is art," then there is no gallery more beautiful than the Northwest's misty skies. Often veiled in silvery drizzle, it is a province of fern-laden eucalyptus woods, slate-roofed fishing villages, and endless white beaches. Locals speak Gallego, a linguistic of Castilian and Portuguese.

SANTIAGO DE COMPOSTELA ☎981

Santiago (pop. 94,000) is a city of song; its plazas are filled with roving guitar players and outdoor operas. As the terminus of the ancient *Camino de Santiago* (Way of St. James), it is also a city of pilgrimage.

TRANSPORTATION AND PRACTICAL INFORMATION. **Trains** (☎902 24 02 02) run from R. do Hórreo to Bilbao (10hr., 1 per day, €41) via León (6hr., €29) and Madrid (8hr., 2 per day, €43-67). To reach the city, take bus #6 to Pr. de Galicia or walk up the stairs across the parking lot from the main entrance, bear right onto R. do Hórreo, and continue uphill for about 10min. **Buses** (☎981 54 24 16) run from R. de Rodríguez to Madrid (8-9hr.; 4-6 per day; €40-57) and San Sebastián (13hr., 2 per day, €55-66) via Bilbao (11hr., 2 per day, €49). To get to the Old Town from the bus station, walk 20min. or take bus #5 or 10 to Pr. de Galicia. The **tourist office** is at R. do Vilar 63. (☎981 55 51 29; www.santiagoturismo.com. Multilingual staff. Open daily June-Sept. 9am-9pm; Oct.-May 9am-2pm and 4-7pm.) **Internet** is available at CyberNova 50, R. Nova 50. (☎981 56 41 33, €1.90 per hr. Open daily 8:30am-1am) **Postal Code:** 15703.

ACCOMMODATIONS AND FOOD. Nearly every street in the *ciudad vieja* (Old Town) has at least one *pensión*. **Hospedaje Ramos ❷**, R. da Raíña 18, 2nd fl., has well-lit rooms with noise-proof windows, and private baths. Reserve ahead in summer. (☎981 58 18 59. Singles €23; doubles €36. Cash only.) The rooms of **Hospedaje Fonseca ❶**, R. de Fonseca 1, 2nd fl., are popular with students. (☎981 57 24 79. July-Aug. singles €20; doubles €30. Sept. 16-June singles €15; doubles €30; triples €45. Cash only.) Most restaurants are on R. do Vilar, R. do Franco, R. Nova, and R. da Raíña. **Restaurante Casa Manolo ❷**, Pl. Cervantes, s/n (☎981 58 29 50), is extremely popular among pilgrims and locals alike. Delight in the sizeable *menú* (€8), while lounging in a stylish atmosphere to laid-back music. (Open M-Sa 1-4pm and 8-11:30pm, Su open only during early afternoon. MC/V.) Santiago's **mercado** (market) is located between Pl. San Felix and Convento de Santo Agustín. (Open M-Sa 8am-2pm.)

SIGHTS AND ENTERTAINMENT. Each of the four facades of Santiago's **cathedral** is a masterpiece of a different era, with entrances opening onto four different plazas: Inmaculada, Obradoiro, Praterías, and Quintana. The Obradoiro is considered one of the most beautiful squares in the world. (☎981 58 35 48. Open daily 7am-9pm. Free.) Entrance to the **cathedral museums** includes a visit to the archaeology rooms, archives, chapter house, cloister, library, relics, tapestry room, and treasury. (☎981 56 93 27 Open June-Sept. M-Sa

10am-2pm and 4-8pm, Su and holidays 10am-2pm; Oct.-May M-Sa 10am-1:30pm and 4-6:30pm, Su and holidays 10am-1:30pm. €5, students €3.) The **Museo das Peregrinacións,** R. de San Miguel 4, details the history of the *Camino de Santiago.* (☎981 58 15 58; www.mdperegrinacions.com. Open Tu-F 10am-8pm, Sa 10:30am-1:30pm and 5-8pm, Su 10:30am-1:30pm. €2.40; children, students, and seniors €1.20; pilgrims free. Free in summer.)

BALEARIC ISLANDS ☎971

While all of the Islas Baleares are famous for their beautiful beaches and landscapes, each island has its own character. While Mallorca absorbs the bulk of package-tour invaders, Ibiza has perhaps the best nightlife in Europe.

TRANSPORTATION

Flying is the easiest way to reach the islands. Students with an ISIC can often get discounts from Iberia (☎902 40 05 00; www.iberia.com), which flies to Ibiza and Palma de Mallorca from Barcelona (40min., €80) and Madrid (1hr., €50). Air Europa (☎902 40 15 01; www.air-europa.com), Spanair (☎902 92 91 91; www.spanair.com), and Vueling (☎902 33 39 33; www.vueling.com) offer budget flights to and between the islands (€20-50). Ferries to the islands are less popular and take longer. Trasmediterránea (☎902 45 46 45; www.trasmediterranea.com) departs from Barcelona's Estació Marítima Moll and Valencia's Estació Marítima for Ibiza, Mallorca, and Menorca (€69-110). Fares between the islands run €28-82. Buquebus (☎902 41 42 42) has fast catamaran service between Barcelona and Palma de Mallorca (4hr., 2 per day, €11-150).

MALLORCA

A favorite destination of Spain's royal family, Mallorca has long attracted the rich and famous. The capital of the Balearics, **Palma** (pop. 383,000) is filled with Brits and Germans, but still retains genuine local flavor. In many of its cafes and traditional *tapas* bars, the native *mallorquí* is the only language heard.

Budget accommodations are scarce and must be reserved weeks ahead. **Hostal Ritzi ❸,** C. Apuntadors 6, stands a block away from Pl. de la Reina. Located in the culinary heart of the *casco antiguo*, this hostel with old-fashioned rooms is flanked by the area's best bars and eateries. (☎971 71 46 10. Breakfast included. Laundry €7. Singles €30; doubles €50, with shower €55, with bath €65. Cash only.) Palma's abundance of round-the-clock ethnic and international restaurants are an alternative to the delicious *tapas* bars. Budget travelers head to the crooked streets between Pl. de la Reina and Pl. Llotja. Those looking for local cuisine should try the *frito mallorquín* (fried lamb liver with potato, peppers, and herbs) at **Sa Premsa ❶,** Pl. Obispo, a cavernous restaurant. (☎971 72 35 29; www.cellersapremsa.com. ½ portions €3.70-6.40. Entrees €3.75-8.50. Open M-Sa noon-4pm and 7:30-11:30pm. MC/V.)

A law requiring downtown bars to close by 1am during the week and 3am on weekends has shifted the late-night action to the waterfront. **The Soho,** Av. Argentina 5, is a hip, no-frills bar that plays 80s hits, classic rock, and indie; great for anyone suffering from top-40 overload. (☎971 45 47 19. Beer €2. Cocktails from €5. Open daily from 6:30pm. MC/V.) Nearby, the swanky **Costa Galana,** Av. Argentina 45, mixes surfing videos with electronica. Head upstairs during the day for a cafe (Wi-Fi) or downstairs for an evening in a retro-style lounge. (☎695 16 86 40. Beer €1.80-2.50. Mixed drinks €5-6. Open M-Th and Su 8am-2am, F-Sa 8am-4am. MC/V.) For great live blues and jazz, head to **Blues Ville**

Cafe Bar, C. Ma des Moro 3. With rollicking music every night and no cover, this club packs in locals, though there are prettier destinations in town. (Beer €1-2. Mixed drinks €3-5. Open daily 10:30pm-4am. Cash only.) Palma's clubbers start their night in the *bares-musicales* lining the Passeig Marítim/Avinguda Gabriel Roca strip, then move on to the *discotecas* around 1am. **Tito's,** in a gorgeous Art Deco palace on Pg. Marítim, is the city's coolest club, sporting fountains, a glass elevator, and a view of the water. (Beer €3. Mixed drinks €5. Cover €15-18, includes 1 drink. High-season open daily 11pm-6am; low season open Th-Su, 11:30pm-6:00am. MC/V.) The **tourist office** is in Pl. d'Espanya (bus #1; 15min., 3 per hr., €1.10). There is also a branch at Pg. del Born 27, in the bookshop at Casa Solleric. (☎971 22 59 00; www.a-palma.es. Open daily 9am-8pm.) **Postal Code:** 07003. The tourist office distributes a list of over 40 nearby beaches.

IBIZA

Nowhere on Earth are decadence, opulence, and hedonism celebrated as religiously as on the glamorous island of Ibiza (pop. 100,000). A hippie enclave in the 1960s, Ibiza has entered a new age of debauchery and extravagance. Disco-goers, fashion gurus, movie stars, and party-hungry backpackers arrive to immerse themselves in the island's outrageous clubs and gorgeous beaches. Only one of Ibiza's beaches, **Figueretas,** is within walking distance of **Eivissa** (Ibiza City). Most, including the raucous and somewhat boozy **Platja d'en Bossa,** are a ferry or bus ride away. The best beach near the city is **Playa de ses Salinas,** where you can groove to the music of club DJs or escape to nearby **Platja des Cavallet** for some (mostly nude) peace and quiet. (Bus #11 runs to Salinas from Av. d'Isidor Macabich.) Later, crowds migrate to the bars of **Carrer de Barcelona.** The island's giant **discos** are world-famous—and outrageously expensive. Be on the lookout for publicity flyers, which list the week or night's events and often double as a coupon for a discounts. The **Discobus** runs to major hot spots (leaves Eivissa from Av. d'Isidor Macabich; hourly 12:30-6:30am, €1.75). **Amnesia,** on the road to the city of San Antoni, has a phenomenal sound system and psychedelic lights. (☎971 19 80 41. Drag performances and foam parties. Cover €20-50. Open daily midnight-8am.) World-famous **Pachá,** the only *discoteca* open year-round, is on Pg. Perimitral, a 15min. walk or 2min. cab ride from the port. (☎971 31 36 00; www.pacha.com. M "Release Yourself" night with up-and-coming DJs. Cover €35-60. Open daily midnight-7:30am.) Cap off your "night" at **Space,** on Platja d'en Bossa, which gets going around 8am and doesn't wind down until 5pm. (☎971 39 67 93; www.space-ibiza.es. Cover €30-60.)

Cheap *hostales* in town are rare, especially in summer; reserve well ahead. Rooms to rent in private homes (*casa de huéspedes*; look for the letters "CH" in doorways) are a much better deal, although they still run above €30 and can be difficult to contact. **Casa de Huespedes Vara de Rey,** Pg. Vara de Rey, 7, 3rd floor (☎971 30 13 76; www.hibiza.com), has relatively inexpensive prices given its prime location. (Singles with shared bathroom, €35; doubles, €70. Open all year. Reception open M-Sa, 9am-2pm, 7pm-10pm. MC/V.) **La Bodeguita Del Medio 1,** C. St. Cruz 15, has outdoor tables ideal for consuming beer (€3) and plates of *paella*, *tortillas* (€6.40), and *tapas*. (☎971 39 92 90. C/C accepted.) **Croissant Show,** Mercat Vell (☎971 31 76 65), on C. Antoni Palau is a bright cafe that serves creative sandwiches (€4.50-6), quiches, salads, pastries, and *platos del dia* (€7.50). Bleary-eyed punters come for "breakfast" after a hard night of clubbing. (Open daily 6am-2am. MC/V.) For groceries, try the **Spar** supermarket, near Pl. del Parque (open M-Sa 9am-9pm). **Tourist offices** are on Pg. Vara del Rey and at the airport. (☎971 30 19 00. Open June-Nov. M-F 9am-8pm, Sa 9am-7pm; schedule in winter subject to change.)

SWEDEN (SVERIGE)

With the design world cooing over bright, blocky Swedish furniture and college students donning knock-off designs from H&M, Scandinavia's largest nation has earned a reputation abroad for its chic, mass-marketable style. At home, Sweden's struggle to balance a market economy with its generous social welfare system stems from its belief that all citizens should have access to education and health care. This neutral nation's zest for spending money on butter instead of guns has also shored up a strong sense of national unity, from Sámi reindeer herders in the Lappland forests to bankers in bustling Stockholm.

DISCOVER SWEDEN: SUGGESTED ITINERARY

FOUR DAYS. Spend 3 days in the capital city of **Stockholm** (p. 965), including one sunny afternoon out on the towns and beaches of the **Skärgård Archipelago** (p. 975). Take a daytrip north to the university town of **Uppsala** (p. 976), or take an eastbound ferry to the island of **Gotland** (p. 977), where serene bike paths and medieval towns overlook the Baltic Sea.

BEST OF SWEDEN, TWO WEEKS. Begin your journey in **Stockholm** (3 days) and take a daytrip to **Uppsala** (1 day). Hop on a ferry to **Gotland** (2 days), and then head over to **Malmö** (p. 980) and **Lund** (p. 981) for bustling markets and booming student nightlife (2 days). Soak up some high culture in the museums of elegant **Gothenburg** (2 days, p. 984), and then get ready to rough it on the hiking trails of **Åre** (p. 990) and **Örnsköldsvik** (2 days, p. 991). End in mountainous **Kiruna** (2 days, p. 993), where ore miners and the indigenous Sámi share vast stretches of arctic wilderness.

ESSENTIALS

FACTS AND FIGURES

OFFICIAL NAME: Kingdom of Sweden.

CAPITAL: Stockholm.

MAJOR CITIES: Gothenburg, Malmö.

POPULATION: 9,045,000.

TIME ZONE: GMT +1.

LANGUAGE: Swedish.

RELIGION: Lutheran (87%).

LAND AREA: 450,000 sq. km.

INCOME TAX: As high as 60% for top wage-earners. Ouch.

WHEN TO GO

The most popular months to visit Sweden are July and August, when temperatures average 20°C (68°F) in the south and 16°C (61°F) in the north. Travelers who arrive in May and early June can take advantage of low-season prices and enjoy the spring flowers, but some attractions don't open until late June. The 24 hours of daylight known as the **midnight sun** are best experienced between early

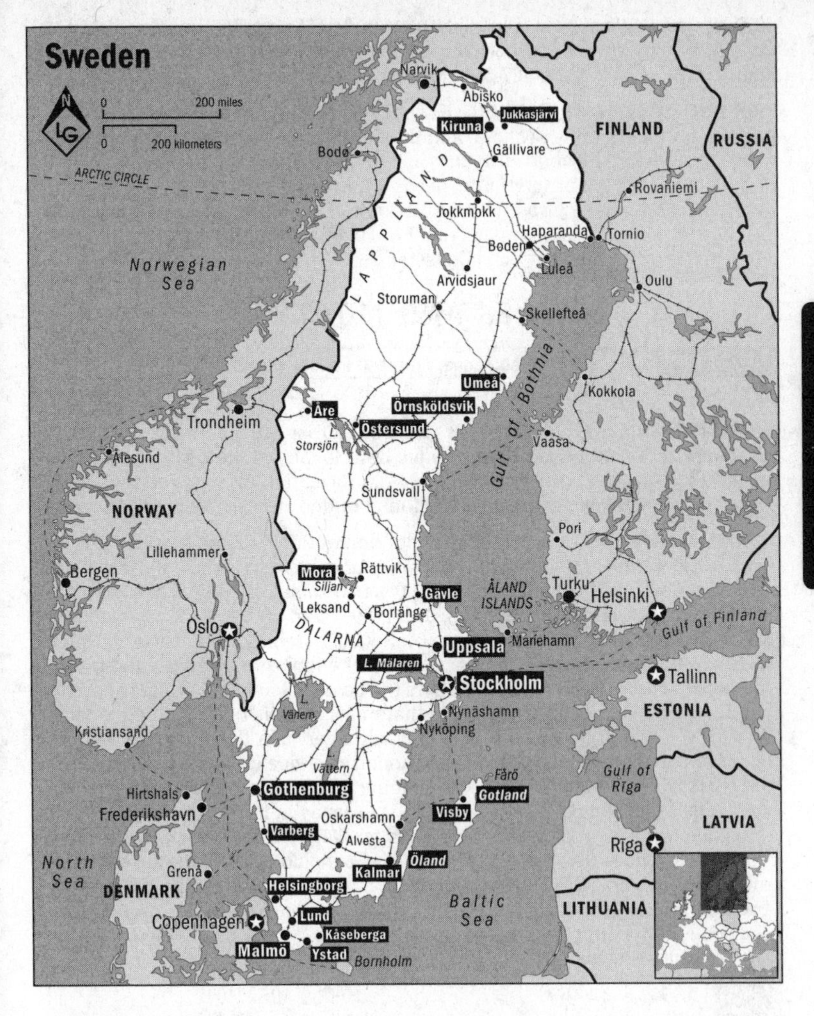

June and mid-July. In winter, keep an eye out for the **Northern Lights** and bring heavy cold-weather gear; temperatures hover around -5°C (23°F).

DOCUMENTS AND FORMALITIES

EMBASSIES AND CONSULATES. Foreign embassies to Sweden are in Stockholm (p. 968). Swedish embassies and consulates abroad include: **Australia,** 5 Turrana St., Yarralumla, Canberra, ACT, 2600 (☎2 62 70 27 00; www.swedenabroad.com/canberra); **Canada,** 377 Dalhousie St., Ottawa, ON, K1N 9N8 (☎613-244-8200; www.swedenabroad.com/ottawa); **Ireland,** 3rd Fl., Block E, Iveagh Court, Harcourt Rd., Dublin 2 (☎1 474 44 00; www.swedenabroad.com/dublin); **New Zealand,** Level 7, Molesworth House, 101 Molesworth St., Thorndon, Wellington 6011 (☎4 499

9895; www.swedenabroad.com/canberra); **UK,** 11 Montagu Pl., London, W1H 2AL (☎020 79 17 64 00; www.swedenabroad.com/london); **US,** 2900 K St., NW, Washington, D.C., 20007 (☎202-467-2600; www.swedenabroad.com/washington).

VISA AND ENTRY INFORMATION. EU citizens do not need a visa. Citizens of Australia, Canada, New Zealand, and the US do not need a visa for stays of up to 90 days, beginning upon entry into any of the countries in the EU's freedom-of-movement zone. For more info, see p. 14. For stays longer than 90 days, all non-EU citizens need visas (around US$90), available at Swedish consulates or online at www.swedenabroad.com. For US citizens, visas are usually issued a few weeks after application submission.

TOURIST SERVICES AND MONEY

EMERGENCY	**Ambulance, Fire,** and **Police:** ☎112.

TOURIST OFFICES. There are two types of tourist offices in Sweden: those marked with a yellow and blue "i" have both local and national information, while those marked with a green "i" have information only on the town they serve. The **Swedish Tourist Board** can be found online at www.visitsweden.com.

MONEY. Swedish voters rejected the adoption of the euro as the country's currency in September 2003. The Swedish unit of currency remains the **krona (kr),** plural kronor. One krona is equal to 100 **öre,** with standard denominations of 50 öre, 1kr, 5kr, and 10kr in coins, and 20kr, 50kr, 100kr, 500kr, and 1000kr in notes. Many **ATMs** do not accept non-Swedish debit cards. **Banks** and post offices exchange currency; expect a 20-35kr commission for cash and 5-15kr for **traveler's checks. Forex** generally offers the best exchange rates and has ATMs that accept foreign debit cards. Note that many Swedish ATMs do not accept PINs longer than four digits; if your PIN is longer than this, entering the first four digits of your PIN should work. Although a service charge is usually added to the bill at restaurants, **tipping** is becoming more common and a 7-10% tip is now considered standard. For more info on money in Europe, see p. 17.

Sweden has a whopping 25% **value added tax (VAT),** a sales tax applied to most goods and services. The prices given in *Let's Go* include VAT. In the airport upon exiting the EU, non-EU citizens can claim a refund on the tax paid for goods purchased at participating stores. Some stores may have minimum expenditure requirements for refunds; make sure to ask for a refund form when you pay. For more info on qualifying for a VAT refund, see p. 21.

SWEDISH KRONOR (KR)		
	AUS$1 = 5.54KR	10KR = AUS$1.81
	CDN$1 = 6.00KR	10KR = CDN$1.67
	EUR€1 = 9.39KR	10KR = EUR€1.07
	NZ$1 = 4.54KR	10KR = NZ$2.20
	UK£1= 11.88KR	10KR = UK£0.84
	US$1 = 6.37KR	10KR = US$1.57

TRANSPORTATION

BY PLANE. Most international flights land at **Arlanda Airport** in Stockholm (**ARN;** ☎797 6000; www.arlanda.com). Budget airlines, like **Ryanair,** fly out of **Västerås**

Airport (**VST;** ☎21 805 600; www.stockholmvasteras.se) and **Skavsta Airport** (see p. 47 for more info), each located 1hr. from Stockholm. Other destinations in Sweden include **Gothenburg Airport (GSE)** and **Malmö-Sturup Airport (MMX).** The main carrier in Sweden, **SAS** (☎08 797 4000, UK 4420 8990 7159, US 800-221-2350; www.scandinavian.net), offers youth fares for those under 26 on some regional flights. For more info on traveling by plane in Europe, see p. 50.

BY TRAIN. Statens Järnväger (SJ), the state railway company, runs trains throughout southern Sweden, and offers a discount up to 30% for travelers under 26 (☎0771 75 75 75; www.sj.se/english). Seat reservations (28-55kr) are required on **InterCity** and high-speed **X2000** trains; they are included in the ticket price but not in rail passes. On other routes, check to see how full the train is; don't bother with reservations on empty trains. In northern Sweden, **Connex** runs trains from Stockholm through Umeå and Kiruna to Narvik, NOR (☎0771 26 00 00; https://bokning.connex.se/connexp/index_en.html). The 35min. trip over **Öresund Bridge** connecting Malmö to Copenhagen, DEN (70kr) is the fastest way to travel from continental Europe; reserve ahead. Timetables for all SJ and Connex trains are at www.resplus.se. **Eurail Passes** are valid on all of these trains. In the south, purple **Pågatågen** trains service local traffic between Helsingborg, Lund, Malmö, and Ystad; Eurail Passes are valid. For more info on traveling by train around Europe, see p. 50.

SWEDEN

BY BUS. In the north, buses may be a better option than trains. **Swebus** (☎08 546 300 00; www.swebus.se) is the main carrier nationwide. **Swebus Express** (☎7712 182 18; www.swebusexpress.se) serves the region around Stockholm and Gothenburg. **Biljettservice** (p. 966), inside Stockholm's Cityterminalen, will reserve tickets for longer routes. Students and travelers under 26 get a 20% discount on express buses. Bicycles are not allowed on board.

BY FERRY. Ferries run from Stockholm (p. 966) to the Åland Islands, Gotland, Finland, and the Baltic states. Ystad (p. 983) sends several ferries a day to Bornholm, DEN. Ferries from Gothenburg (p. 984) serve Frederikshavn, DEN and Kiel, GER. Popular lines include **Tallinksilja** (☎08 20 21 40, international 358 60 01 57 00; www.tallinksilja.com/en), and the **Viking Line** (☎08 452 40 00, US 800-843-0602; www.vikingline.fi). On Tallinksilja, Eurail Pass holders ride for free or at reduced rates. On Viking ferries, a Eurail Pass plus a train ticket entitles holders to a free passenger fare. (Mention this discount when booking.) Additionally, Viking offers "early bird" discounts of 15-50% for those who book at least 30 days in advance within Finland or Sweden.

BY CAR. Sweden honors foreign drivers' licenses for up to one year for visitors over 18. Speed limits are 110kph on expressways, 50kph in densely populated areas, and 70-90kph elsewhere. Headlights must be used at all times. Swedish roads are uncrowded and in good condition, but take extra care in winter weather and beware of reindeer or elk in the road. Many gas stations are open until 10pm; after hours, look for cash-operated pumps marked *sedel automat.* For more info on car rental and driving in Europe, see p. 54.

BY BIKE AND THUMB. Bicycling is popular in Sweden. Paths are common, and both the **Sverigeleden** (National Route) and **Cykelspåret** (Bike Path) traverse the country. **Hitchhiking** is uncommon. *Let's Go* does not recommend hitchhiking.

KEEPING IN TOUCH

EMAIL AND THE INTERNET. There are a limited number of cybercafes in Stockholm and other big cities. Expect to pay about 20kr per hr. In smaller towns,

Internet is available for free at most tourist offices marked with the yellow and blue "i" (p. 962), as well as for a small fee at most public libraries.

TELEPHONE. Pay phones take credit cards and often accept phone cards (Telefonkort); buy them at newsstands or other shops (60kr and 100kr). Whenever possible, use a calling card for **international phone calls,** as long-distance rates for national phone services are often very high. **Mobile phones** are an increasingly popular and economical option. Major mobile carriers include Telia, Tele2, Vodafone, and 3. International access codes for calling out of Sweden include: **AT&T Direct** (☎020 79 91 11); **Canada Direct** (☎020 79 90 15); **MCI** (☎0 200 895 438); **Sprint** (☎020 79 90 11); **Telecom New Zealand** (☎020 799 064). For more info on calling home from Europe, see p. 31.

PHONE CODES	**Country code:** 46. **International dialing prefix:** 00. For more info on how to place international calls, see **Inside Back Cover.**

MAIL. From Sweden, it costs approximately 5kr to send a postcard or letter domestically, 10kr within Europe, and 10.20kr to the rest of the world. For more info, visit www.posten.se. To receive mail in Sweden, have mail delivered **Poste Restante.** Mail will go to the main post office unless you specify a subsidiary by street address. Address mail to be held according to the following example: First name, Last Name, Poste Restante, Postal Code, City, SWEDEN. Bring a passport to pick up your mail; there may also be a small fee.

LANGUAGE. Although Sweden has no official language, Swedish is universally spoken. The region around Kiruna is home to a minority of Finnish speakers, as well as 7000 speakers of the Sámi languages. Most Swedes speak English fluently. For basic Swedish words and phrases, see **Phrasebook: Swedish,** p. 1069.

ACCOMMODATIONS AND CAMPING

SWEDEN	❶	❷	❸	❹	❺
ACCOMMODATIONS	under 160kr	160-230kr	231-350kr	351-500kr	over 500kr

Youth hostels *(vandrarhem)* cost 120-200kr per night. The hostels run by the **Svenska Turistföreningen (STF)** and affiliated with HI are uniformly top-notch. Nonmembers should expect to pay 200-240kr per night; HI members receive a 45kr discount (☎08 463 21 00; www.svenskaturistforeningen.se). STF also manages **mountain huts** in the northern wilds (150-350kr). Many **campgrounds** (tent sites 80-110kr; www.camping.se) offer **cottages** *(stugor)* for 100-300kr per person. **International Camping Cards** aren't valid in Sweden; **Swedish Camping Cards,** available at all SCR campgrounds, are mandatory (one-year pass 90kr). The Swedish **right of public access** *(allemansrätten)* means travelers can camp for free in the countryside, as long as they are roughly 150m away from private homes. Tents may be pitched in one location usually for one or two days. Guidelines vary depending on the community. Visit www.allemansratten.se for more info.

FOOD AND DRINK

SWEDEN	❶	❷	❸	❹	❺
FOOD	under 50kr	50-75kr	76-100kr	101-160kr	over 160kr

Restaurant fare is usually expensive in Sweden, but **food halls** *(saluhallen)*, open-air markets, and **hot dog stands** *(varmkorv)* make budget eating easy enough. Many restaurants offer affordable **daily lunch specials** *(dagens rätt)* for 60-75kr. The Swedish palate has long been attuned to hearty meat-and-potatoes fare, but immigrant communities in Malmö and Stockholm have spiced things up for budget travelers. A league of five-star chefs in Gothenburg are tossing off increasingly imaginative riffs on herring and salmon. The Swedish love **drip coffee** (as opposed to espresso) and have institutionalized coffee breaks as a near-sacred rite of the workday. Aside from light beer containing less than 3.5% alcohol, alcohol can be purchased only at state-run **Systembolaget** liquor stores and in licensed bars and restaurants. You can buy light beer at 18, but otherwise it's 20+. Some classier bars and clubs have age restrictions as high as 25.

HOLIDAYS AND FESTIVALS

Holidays: New Year's Day (Jan. 1); Epiphany (Jan. 6); Good Friday (Apr. 10, 2009; Apr. 2, 2010); Easter (Apr. 12, 2009; Apr. 4, 2010); Ascension (May 21, 2009; May 13, 2010); May Day (May 1); Pentecost (May 31, 2009; May 23, 2010); Corpus Christi (June 14, 2009; June 6, 2010); National Day (June 6); Assumption (Aug. 15); All Saints' Day (Nov. 1); Christmas (Dec. 25); Boxing Day (Dec. 26).

Festivals: Valborgsmässoafton (Walpurgis Eve; Apr. 30) celebrates the arrival of spring with roaring bonfires in Dalarna and choral singing in Lund and Uppsala. Dalarna erects flowery maypoles in time for **Midsummer** (June 24), as young people flock to the islands of Gotland, Öland, and the Skärgård archipelago for all-night parties. Mid-July welcomes the **Stockholm Jazz Festival** (www.stockholmjazz.com) to the capital. Travelers with appetites should check out the crayfish parties in Aug. and eel parties in Sept.

BEYOND TOURISM

Summer employment is often easier to find than long-term work, since Sweden has fairly strict regulations governing the employment of foreigners. For more info on opportunities across Europe, see **Beyond Tourism,** p. 60.

The American-Scandinavian Foundation (AMSCAN), 58 Park Ave., New York, NY 10016, USA (☎212 879 9779; www.amscan.org/jobs). Internship and job opportunities throughout Scandinavia. Fellowships for study in Sweden for Americans.

Council of International Fellowship (CIF), Karlbergsvägen 80 nb. ög, SE-113 35 Stockholm (☎04 68 32 31 21; www.cif-sweden.org). Funds exchange programs for service professionals, including homestays in various Swedish cities.

Internationella Arbetslag, Tegelviksgatan 40, S-116 41 Stockholm, SWE (☎08 643 08 89; www.ial.se). Branch of Service Civil International (SCI; www.sciint.org) organizes a broad range of workcamps. Camp and SCI membership fees apply.

STOCKHOLM ☎08

The largest city in Scandinavia's biggest country, Stockholm (pop. 1,250,000) is the aptly self-titled "capital of the north." A focal point for culture and design, the elegant city exists by virtue of a latticework of bridges connecting its islands and peninsulas, uniting different neighborhoods with distinct personalities.

TRANSPORTATION

Flights: Arlanda Airport (**ARN;** ☎08 797 6000; www.arlanda.com), 42km north of the city. **Flygbussarna** shuttles (☎08 600 1000; www.flygbussarna.se) run between Arlanda and Centralstationen in Stockholm (40min.; every 15min. Station to airport 4am-10pm, airport to station 4:50am-12:30am; 95kr, students, children, and seniors 65kr; MC/V), as do **Arlanda Express** trains (☎0202 222 24; www.arlandaexpress.com. 20min.; every 15min. 5am-midnight; 200kr, students 100kr). **Bus** #583 runs to the T-bana stop Märsta (10min., 20kr); take the T-bana to T-Centralen in downtown Stockholm (40min., 20kr). Flygbussarna also operates shuttles to **Västerås Airport** (**VST;** ☎21 80 56 00; www.stockholmvasteras.se) coordinating with Ryanair departures (1hr., 100kr). **Skavsta Airport** is a major budget airline hub for the region.

Regional Hubs: Stockholm Skavsta Airport (**NYO;** ☎155 28 04 00; www.skavsta.se), 100km south of Stockholm in the town of Nyköping, is a hub for budget airlines **Ryanair** and **Wizz Air. Flybussarna** (☎08 600 1000; www.flybussarna.se) operates frequent **buses** from Stockholm (1hr., 100-200kr), coordinated with Ryanair arrivals and departures. **SJ trains** (☎0771 75 75 75; www.sj.se) also run from Stockholm (1hr., 1-2 per hr., 90-160kr). Taxis and local buses (20kr) run from Nyköping station to the airport.

Trains: Centralstationen (☎08 410 626 00). T-bana: T-Centralen. To: **Copenhagen, DEN** (5hr., 7-14 per day, 1099kr, under 26 948kr); **Gothenburg** (3-5hr., every 1-2hr., 512-1110kr, under 26 437-955kr); and **Oslo, NOR** (6-8hr., 1-5 per day, 672kr, under 26 572kr). Book up to 90 days in advance for lower fares. Fewer trains on Sa.

Buses: Cityterminalen, upstairs on the north end of Centralstationen. **Terminal Service** (☎08 762 5997) goes to the airport (95kr, 65kr students) and Gotland ferries (70kr). **Biljettservice** (☎08 762 5979) makes reservations with Sweden's bus companies for longer routes. **Swebus** (☎0771 218 218; www.swebusexpress.se), one of the largest, runs to: **Copenhagen, DEN** (9hr., 2per day, 400-500kr); **Gothenburg** (7hr., 7 per day, 250-300kr); and **Malmö** (8hr., 3 per day, 400-500kr).

Ferries: Tallinksilja, Sveavägen 14 (☎08 440 5990; www.tallinksilja.com), sails to: **Helsinki, FIN** (17hr., 1 per day at 5pm, from 75kr); **Turku, FIN** (12hr., 2 per day, from 150kr); **Tallinn, EST** (16hr., 1 per day, from 470kr, low-season 260kr). T-bana: Gärdet, follow signs to Värtahamnen, or take the Tallinksilja bus (20kr) from Cityterminalen. 50% ScanRail discount on select fares. **Viking Line** (☎08 452 4000; www.vikingline.se) sails to: **Helsinki, FIN** (17hr., 1 per day, mid-June to mid-Aug. from 430kr, low-season 300kr); **Turku, FIN** (12hr., 2 per day, mid-June to mid-Aug. from 230kr, low-season 130kr). Office in Cityterminalen (open M-Th 8am-7pm, F 7:30am-6:30pm, Sa 8am-5pm). For more info on traveling by ferry in Scandinavia, see p. 57.

Public Transportation: T-bana (Tunnelbana, Stockholm's subway; stations marked with white circular sign with blue "T") runs M-Th and Su 5am-12:30am, F-Sa 5am-3am. **Night buses** run 12:30am-5:30am. Tickets 30kr; strip of 8 tickets 180kr, sold at Pressbyrån news agents; 1hr. unlimited transfer. The **SL Tourist Card** *(Turistkort)* is valid on all public transportation. 1-day 100kr; 3-day 200kr. Office in Centralstationen (☎08 600 1000). T-bana: T-Centralen. Open M-Sa 6:30am-11:15pm, Su 7am-11:15pm. MC/V.

Taxis: Many cabs have fixed prices to certain destinations; ask when you enter the cab. Expect to pay 440-475kr from Arlanda to Centralstationen. Major companies include **Taxi 020** (☎020 202 020), **Taxi Kurir** (☎08 30 00 00; www.taxikurir.se), and **Taxi Stockholm** (☎08 15 00 00; www.taxistockholm.se).

Bike Rental: Rent-a-Bike, Strandvägen, Kajplats 24 (☎08 660 7959). From 200kr per day. Open May-Sept. daily 10am-6pm. MC/V. **Djurgårdsbrons Sjöcafé,** Galärvarvsvägen 2 (☎08 660 5757). Bikes 250kr per day, canoes 300kr per day, in-line skates 200kr per day, kayaks 500kr per day. Open June-Aug. daily 9am-9pm. AmEx/MC/V.

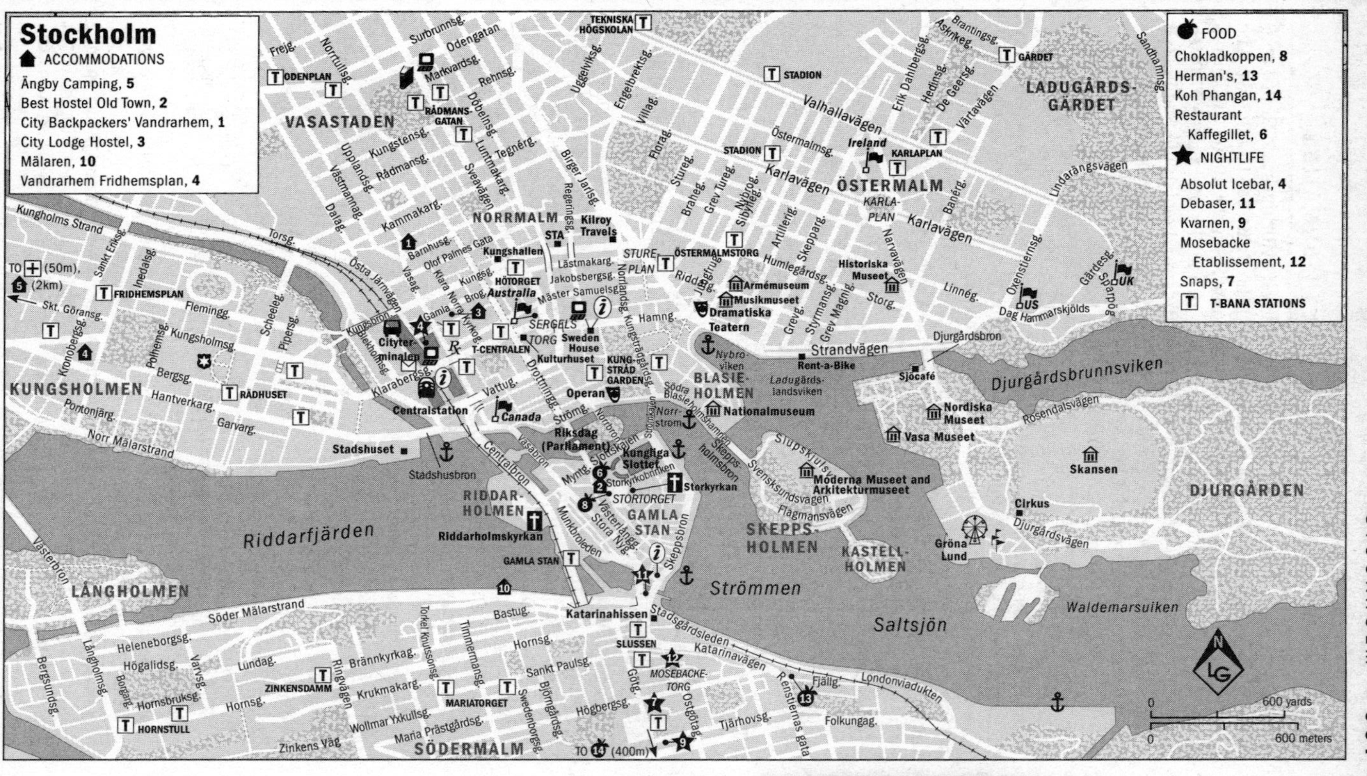
Stockholm
ACCOMMODATIONS
Ängby Camping, 5
Best Hostel Old Town, 2
City Backpackers' Vandrarhem, 1
City Lodge Hostel, 3
Mälaren, 10
Vandrarhem Fridhemsplan, 4
FOOD
Chokladkoppen, 8
Herman's, 13
Koh Phangan, 14
Restaurant Kaffegillet, 6
NIGHTLIFE
Absolut Icebar, 4
Debaser, 11
Kvarnen, 9
Mosebacke Etablissement, 12
Snaps, 7
T-BANA STATIONS
600 yards
600 meters
DJURGÅRDEN
LADUGÅRDS-GÄRDET
ÖSTERMALM
NORRMALM
VASASTADEN
KUNGSHOLMEN
SÖDERMALM
LÅNGHOLMEN
GAMLA STAN
RIDDAR-HOLMEN
SKEPPS-HOLMEN
KASTELL-HOLMEN
BLASIE-HOLMEN
Djurgårdsbrunnsviken
Riddarfjärden
Strömmen
Saltsjön
Waldemarsuiken
Skansen
Nordiska Museet
Vasa Museet
Gröna Lund
Cirkus
Moderna Museet and Arkitekturmuseet
Nationalmuseum
Historiska Museet
Armémuseum
Musikmuseet
Dramatiska Teatern
Kungliga Slottet
Storkyrkan
Riksdag (Parliament)
Riddarholmskyrkan
Stadshuset
Centralstation
Cityterminalen
Kulturhuset
Sweden House
Operan
Kilroy Travels
Sjöcafé
Rent-a-Bike
Katarinahissen
Kungshallen
UK
US
Ireland
Canada
Australia
GÄRDET
KARLAPLAN
STADION
TEKNISKA HÖGSKOLAN
ÖSTERMALMSTORG
RÅDMANSGATAN
HÖTORGET
T-CENTRALEN
GAMLA STAN
SLUSSEN
MARIATORGET
ZINKENSDAMM
HORNSTULL
RÅDHUSET
FRIDHEMSPLAN
ODENPLAN
TO (50m), (2km)
TO (400m)

ORIENTATION AND PRACTICAL INFORMATION

Stockholm spans a number of small islands (linked by bridges and the T-bana) at the junction of **Lake Mälaren** to the west and the **Baltic Sea** to the east. The large northern island is divided into two sections: **Norrmalm,** home to Centralstationen and the crowded shopping district around Drottningg., and **Östermalm,** which boasts the **Strandvägen** waterfront and upscale nightlife fanning out from Stureplan. The mainly residential western island, **Kungsholmen,** features beaches, waterside promenades, and the *Stadhuset* (city hall) on its eastern tip. The southern island of **Södermalm** retains a traditional feel in the midst of a budding cafe culture and club scene. Nearby **Långholmen** houses a nature preserve and a prison-turned-hotel and museum, while the similarly woodsy eastern island **Djurgården** hosts several popular museums on its western side. At the center of these five islands is **Gamla Stan** (Old Town). Gamla Stan's less-trafficked neighbor (via Norrmalm) is **Skeppsholmen.** Each of Stockholm's streets begins with number "1" at the end closest to the Kungliga Slottet (p. 972) in Gamla Stan; the lower the numbers, the closer you are to Old Town. Street signs also contain that block's address numbers.

Tourist Offices: Sweden House (Sverigehuset), Hamng. 27 (☎08 508 285 08; www.stockholmtown.com), entrance off Kungsträdsgården. From Centralstationen, walk up Klarabergsg. to Sergels Torg (look for the glass obelisk), bear right on Hamng., and turn right at the park. Agents sell the **SL card** and the **Stockholm Card** *(Stockholmskortet)*, which includes public transportation and admission to 75 museums and attractions. 1-day 330kr; 2-day 460kr; 3-day 580kr. Internet 1kr per min. Open M-F 9am-7pm, Sa 10am-5pm, Su 10am-4pm. AmEx/MC/V.

Budget Travel: Kilroy Travels, Kungsg. 4 (☎0771 545 769; www.kilroytravels.se). Open M-F 10am-6pm. **STA Travel,** Kungsg. 30 (☎0771 61 10 10; www.statravel.se). Open M-F 10am-6pm. AmEx/MC/V.

Embassies: Australia, Sergels Torg 12, 11th fl. (☎08 613 2900; www.sweden.embassy.gov.au). Open M-F 8:30am-4:30pm. **Canada,** Tegelbacken 4, 7th fl. (☎08 453 3000; www.canadaemb.se). Open M-F 8:30am-noon and 1-5pm. **Ireland,** Östermalmsg. 97 (☎08 661 8005). Open M-F 10am-noon and 2:30-4pm. **UK,** Skarpög. 6-8 (☎08 671 3000; www.britishembassy.se). Open M-F 9am-5pm. **US,** Daghammarskjölds väg 31 (☎08 783 5300; www.usemb.se). Open M-Th 9-11am and 1-3pm, F 9-11am.

Currency Exchange: Forex, Centralstationen (☎08 411 6734). Branch at Cityterminalen (☎08 21 42 80). 25kr commission.

Luggage Storage: Lockers at Centralstationen and Cityterminalen (30-80kr per day).

GLBT Resources: The *Queer Extra (QX)* and the *QueerMap* give info about Stockholm's GLBT hot spots. Swedish-language version available at the Sweden House tourist office or online at www.qx.se. For an English-language version, visit www.qx.se/english.

24hr. Pharmacy: Look for green-and-white Apoteket signs. **Apoteket C. W. Scheele,** Klarabergsg. 64 (☎08 454 8130), at the overpass over Vasag. T-bana: T-Centralen.

Hospitals: Karolinska (☎517 740 93), north of Norrmalm near Solnavägen. T-Bana: Skt. Eriksplan. **Sankt Göran** (☎587 010 00), on Kungsholmen. T-Bana: Fridhemsplan.

Medical Services: 24hr. hotline ☎32 01 00.

Telephones: Almost all public phones require **Telia** phone cards; buy them at Pressbyrån newsstands in increments of 50 (50kr) or 120 (100kr) units.

Internet: Stadsbiblioteket, Odeng. 53, in the annex. T-bana: Odenplan. Sign up for 2 free 30min. slots daily or drop in for 15min. Bring your passport. Open M-Th 9am-9pm, F 9am-7pm, Sa-Su noon-4pm. **Dome House,** Sveavg. 108, has almost 80 terminals.

19kr per hr. Open 24hr. **Sidewalk Express** Internet stations are located inside malls and 7-Elevens throughout the city. 19kr per hr. Open 24hr. MC/V.

Post Office: 84 Klarabergsg. (☎23 22 20). Open M-F 7am-7pm. Stamps also available at press stands and souvenir shops.

ACCOMMODATIONS AND CAMPING

Reservations are necessary in the summer. In high-season, many HI hostels limit stays to five nights. Some non-HI hostels are hotel-hostel combinations. Specify that you want to stay in a dorm-style hostel, or risk paying hotel rates. Stockholm's **botels** (boat-hotels) often make for camaraderie, but they can be cramped—request a room with harbor views. There are also various **B&B booking services,** including the **Bed and Breakfast Agency.** (☎08 643 8028; www.bba.nu. Open M 10am-noon and 1-5pm, Tu-W 9am-noon and 1-5pm.) The Sweden House **tourist office** can also help book rooms (5kr hostel booking fee, 75kr hotel booking fee). An SL or Stockholm Card is the cheapest way for campers to reach some of the more remote **campgrounds.** The right of **public access** (p. 964) does not apply within the city limits, although camping is allowed on most of the Skärgård archipelago (p. 975).

Best Hostel Old Town, Trångsund 12 (☎08 440 0004; www.besthostel.se). T-bana: Gamla Stan. With a great location in the Old Town and ample facilities, this hostel is a steal. Look out for their upcoming branch at Skeppsbron 22, which promises harbor views. 200kr per bed, 300kr per bed in twin room. Free Wi-Fi. Basic kitchen. Reception 7am-7pm, but arrivals at other times can be arranged. MC/V. ❷

City Backpackers' Vandrarhem, Upplandsg. 2A (☎08 20 69 20; www.citybackpackers.se). T-bana: T-centralen. Just north of the city center, this hostel features friendly service and free pasta, along with a relaxing courtyard for sharing travel tales. Linens 50kr. Laundry 50kr. Sauna 20kr, late-afternoon free. Free Internet and Wi-Fi. Reception 8am-2pm. Low-season dorms from 230kr; doubles 650kr. MC/V. ❷

City Lodge Hostel, Klara Norra Kyrkog. 15 (☎08 22 66 30; www.citylodge.se). T-bana: T-centralen. On a quiet street hidden in the rush of the city center, this hostel is a good place to rest. Breakfast 60kr. Linens 50kr. Towels 10kr. Laundry 50kr. Free Internet. Reception June-Aug. 8:30am-11pm, Sept.-May 8:30am-10pm. 18-bed dorms 195kr; 10-bed 225kr; doubles from 590kr. MC/V. ❷

Mälaren, Södermälarstrand, Kajplats 11 (☎08 644 4385; www.theredboat.com). T-bana: Gamla Stan. Just south of Gamla Stan, this bright red botel offers great views across the water from its compact dorms. Breakfast 65kr. Reception 8am-1am. Internet 10kr per 15min. Free Wi-Fi in reception area. Dorms 230kr; singles 450kr; doubles with bunk beds 590kr; quads 1040kr. MC/V. ❷

Vandrarhem Fridhemsplan (HI), S:t Eriksg. 20 (☎08 653 8800; www.fridhemsplan.se). T-bana: Fridhemsplan. This large hostel has modern decorations and a big kitchen. Breakfast buffet 60kr. Lockers 20kr. Linens 50kr. Laundry 50kr. Free Internet. Reception 24hr. Dorms 275kr; singles 500kr; doubles 650kr. 50kr HI discount. AmEx/MC/V. ❸

Ängby Camping, Blackebergsv. 24 (☎08 37 04 20; www.angbycamping.se), on Lake Mälaren. T-bana: Ängbyplan. Wooded campsite with swimming area. Cable TV 10kr. Stockholm Card vendor. Reception June-Aug. 8am-10pm; Sept.-May 5-8pm. 2-person tent sites 135kr; cabins 475-725kr. Electricity from 35kr. AmEx/MC/V. ❶

FOOD

Götgatan and **Folkunggatan** in Södermalm offer affordable cuisine from around the world, while pizza and kebabs are plentiful on Vasastaden's **Odengatan.** The **SoFo** (south of Folkunggatan) neighborhood offers many trendy cafe options.

TIME: 4hr., 5-6hr. with visits to the Stadhuset, Moderna Museet, or Kungliga Slottet.

DISTANCE: About 6km.

SEASON: Mid-Apr. to late Oct.

A WALKING TOUR OF STOCKHOLM

A walking tour of a city spread out over a dozen islands sounds unlikely, but both goods ar people have streamed across Stockholm's bridges since it emerged as a 13th-century tradir port. The islands are rich with fairytale lanes, green parks, and cafes where you can rest your fe in style. It's not hard to see why residents of Stockholm happily hoof it during the summer—eve though comfortable mass transit options are never far away. This tour starts at **Sweden Hous** (p. 962), Stockholm's main tourist office, and ends in the old town of **Gamla Stan.**

1. SERGELS TORG. Begin by walking west on Hamngatan past the exclusive **NK** departme store. Make for the 37m glass obelisk at the center of Sergels Torg, the plaza that was carved o of Lower Norrmalm after WWII in what the Swedes called "the great demolition wave." Moderni city planners were convinced that they could arbitrarily designate a new city center and hav civic life revolve around it, but they got more than they bargained for when a covey of drug dea ers flocked to the western side of Sergels Torg. Known as the **Plattan,** this sunken plaza shou be avoided at night. The glassy **Kulturhuset** (p. 974), on the southern side of the square, is more welcoming point of interest. Check the schedule of events posted inside Lava, a hango popular with Stockholm's university students.

2. STADHUSET. Turn left onto Drottninggatan, Norrmalm's main pedestrian thoroughfare, ar then turn right just before the bridge onto Strömgatan. Take the steps down to the quay ju before the Centralbron overpass, and go under two bridges and over one to the majestic Sta shuset (p. 968). Guided tours (45min.; 60kr, students 50kr) leave on the hour. If time or mon is short, view the city framed by the waterside arches before continuing on your way.

3. RIDDARHOLMEN. To head back to Centralbron, cross back over the bridge, take the ste up, and then turn right on the second bridge, Vasabron, onto Gamla Stan. Turn right onto Ri darhuskajen and stay on the waterfront. Peek into the lawns of Riddarhuset on your left. It w built in the 17th century for Parliament and is now occasionally used by Swedish nobility. Take right on Riddarhbron, the first bridge you come to, into the plaza on Riddarholmen (The Knigh Island). Stockholm's 17th-century elite built private palaces around the **Riddarholmskyrka** church. Parts of the church date back to the 13th century, when it was used as a Francisca monastery. Lutherans booted the Franciscans out after the Protestant Reformation and then s aside the church as the burial place for Swedish monarchs in 1807. Almost every Swedish ki from 1290 to 1950 has been buried there.

4. SKEPPSHOLMEN. Head straight out of the plaza, cross Centralbron, and make a right on charming Stora Nygatan. Turn left down any of the side streets and then left onto Västerlån gatan, lined with shops and confectionaries. Cross two bridges, cutting through the back of t Riksdag (Parliament), then turn right onto Strömgatan and turn right again back across t water, this time past the Riksdag's long east-facing facade. Turn left onto Slottskajen alongsi the royal palace of Kungliga Slottet (p. 972), and left onto the bridge toward the Grand Hot Bear right onto Södra Blasieholmshamnen and then cross the scenic Skeppsholmbron brid onto the island of Skeppsholmen. The main attraction here is the **Moderna Museet** (p. 97 home to the works of many celebrated 20th century artists.

5. KUNGLIGA SLOTTET. Retrace your steps and turn right back onto Gamla Stan, flanki the palace on Skappsbron this time. You could spend a full day wandering through the palace

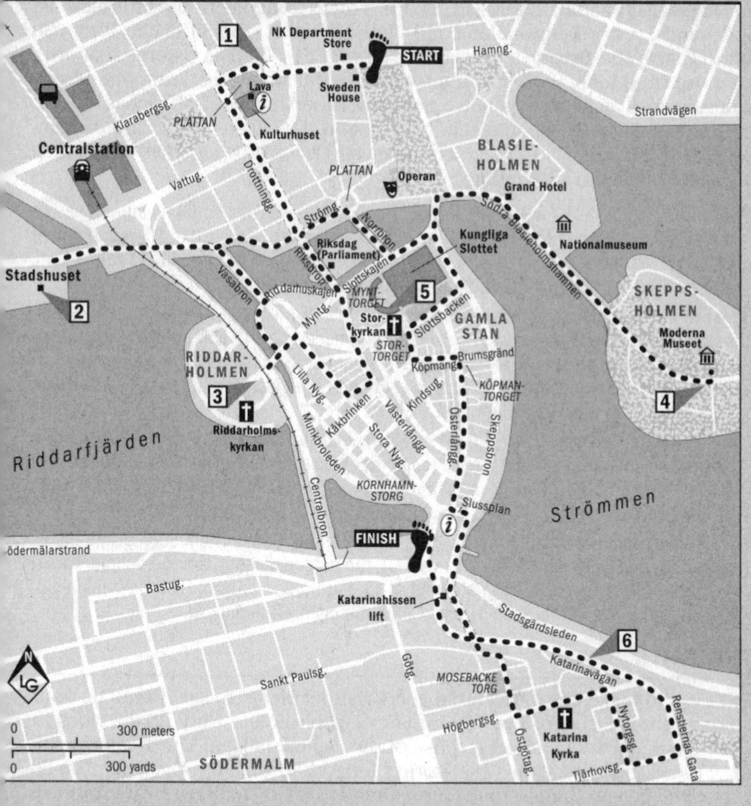

useums and courtyards, but for the sake of time, confine your visit to the **Royal Apartments.** rn into the plaza leading up to Storkyrkan; the ticket office is on the right.

SÖDERMALM. From the palace, walk straight into Stortorget, the main square of the island. ke a left and walk along its east end, and then make another left onto Köpmangatan to wander array of antique shops. At the St. George and Dragon statue, make a right along Österlång-tan. When it ends, take a left on Slussplan, then make a right on the bridge connecting Gamla an to the southern island of Södermalm. Keep to the left as you cross the bridge, hop on the **tarinahissen lift** (10 kr), and cross the bridge to the north-facing cliffs for one of the best ews of the city. You can also get the view for free by walking up the steps on the opposite side of tarinavägen. Head straight to intimate Mosebacke Torg and continue south down Östgötaga-n. Take your first left onto Högbergsgatan, passing by the octagonal tower of the **Katarina rka**—a landmark devastated by fire in 1990, but rebuilt to its former Baroque splendor. the end of Högbergsgatan, turn right onto Nytorgsgatan, left onto Tjärhovsgatan, and en left onto Renstiernas gata. As the street begins curving to the west, a beautiful ew of Stockholm's spires spreads out before you. Finish by heading down to ussen and crossing back onto Gamla Stan to rest your weary legs.

Grocery stores are easy to find around any T-bana station. Head to the outdoor fruit market at **Hötorget** for your Vitamin C fix (open M-Sa 7am-6pm), or to the **Kungshallen** food hall, Kungsg. 44, for a meal from one of the international food stands. (www.kungshallen.com. Open M-F 9am-11pm, Sa 11am-11pm, Su noon-11pm.) The **Östermalms Saluhall,** Nybrog. 31 (T-bana: Östermalmstorg), is a more traditional indoor market with fish, meat, cheese, fruit, and pastry stands, as well as more expensive restaurants serving Swedish dishes. (www. ostermalmshallen.se. Open M-Th 9:30am-6pm, F 9:30am-6:30pm, Sa 9:30am-4pm.) Take advantage of low lunch prices and track down *dagens rätt* (lunch specials; 50-80kr) to save money.

Herman's, Fjällg. 23A (☎08 643 9480). T-bana: Slussen. This small restaurant serves buffet style vegetarian fare with a grand view of the water. Lunch (88-140kr) and dinner (135-175kr) include dessert and drink combos. Open daily June-Aug. 11am-11pm, arrive by 9:30pm for full buffet; Sept.-May 11am-10pm. MC/V. ❹

Restaurant Kaffegillet, Trangsund 4 (☎08 21 39 95). T-bana: Gamla Stan. An excellent place to try classic Swedish cuisine. The reindeer roast (215kr) and the marinated herring with sour cream (135kr) are popular choices. Small dishes 105-115kr. Swedish Kitchen 145-235kr. Desserts 70-95kr. Salad and bread included. Open daily May-Sept. 9am-11pm; Oct.-Apr. 9am-6pm. AmEx/MC/V. ❹

Koh Phangan, Skåneg. 57 (☎08 642 5040). T-Bana: Skanstull. Dine on Thai food in this cozy restaurant modeled after a jungle treehouse, a welcoming sight in winter. Vegetarian entrees 139-159kr. Meat entrees 159-205kr. Seafood 180-265kr. Open M-Th 11am-11pm, F 11am-11:45pm, Sa 2-11:45pm, Su 2-11pm. AmEx/MC/V. ❺

Chokladkoppen, Stortorg. 18 (☎08 20 31 70). T-bana: Gamla Stan. Serves light meals (39-80kr) and generous desserts (23-48kr). The outdoor seating is a top people-watching spot on Stortorget. Open in summer M-Th and Su 9am-11pm, F-Sa 9am-midnight; low-season M-Th and Su 9am-10pm, F 9am-midnight. Cash only. ❷

SIGHTS

With over 75 museums, Stockholm gives visitors plenty to see. Break up your walking tour (p. 970) of the city's inner neighborhoods with T-bana rides to more remote locations to get a sense of the capital's scope. The T-bana, spanning 110km, has been called the world's longest art exhibit—over the past 50 years, the city has commissioned more than 140 artists to decorate its stations. The blue line's art is particularly notable, but the murals and sculptures of T-Centralen remain the best-recognized example of T-bana artistry.

GAMLA STAN (OLD TOWN). Stockholm was once confined to the small island of Staden. Today, the island is the center of the city. The main pedestrian street is **Västerlånggatan,** but its maze of small side streets preserves the area's historic feel. *(Tours of the island are available May-Aug. M-Tu and Th 7:30pm. Sept.-Apr. Sa-Su 1:30pm. Meet at the obelisk in front of the southern entrance to the Royal Palace. 60kr. Cash only.)* Gamla Stan is dominated by the magnificent 1754 **Kungliga Slottet** (Royal Palace), the winter home of the Swedish royal family. The **Royal Apartments** and the adjacent **Rikssalen** (State Hall) and **Slottskyrkan** (Royal Chapel) are all lavishly decorated in blue and gold, the colors of the Swedish flag. The **Skattkammaren** (Royal Treasury) houses a collection of jewel-encrusted crowns and other regal accoutrements. The statues in the **Gustav III Antikmuseum** are worth seeing, and the **Museum Tre Konor** offers an interesting look at the foundation of a 13th-century castle that once stood on the same site. *(Main ticket office and info area at the rear of the complex, near the Storkyrkan. ☎08 402 6130; www.royalcourt.se. Open Feb. to mid-May Tu-Su noon-4pm; mid-May to June 1st daily 10am-4pm; June 1st-Aug. daily 10am-5pm; Sept. 1st to mid-Sept. daily 10am-4pm; mid-Sept. to Dec. Tu-Su noon-3pm. Each* *attraction 90kr, students 35kr. Combination ticket 130/65kr. Guided tours 1 per hr. AmEx/MC/V.)* The **Livrustkammaren** (Armory) presents an extensive collection of royal clothes, weapons, and coaches. *(Slottsbacken 3. ☎08 519 555 44; www.livrustkammaren.se. Open June-Aug. daily 10am-5pm; Sept.-Apr. Tu-W and F-Su 11am-5pm, Th 11am-8pm. May daily 11am-5pm. 50kr, under 20 free. AmEx/MC/V.)* Across the street from the palace ticket office is the gilded **Storkyrkan** church. *(☎08 723 3016. Open M-Sa June-Aug. 9am-6pm; Sept.-May 9am-4pm. Church 25kr. 3 tower tours per day in summer. Cash only.)* Around the corner on **Stortorget,** the main square, the **Nobelmuseet** traces the history of the Nobel Prize and its laureates. *(☎08 534 818 00; www.nobelprize.org/nobelmuseum. Open mid-May to mid-Sept. M and W-Su 10am-5pm, Tu 10am-8pm; mid-Sept. to mid-May Tu 11am-8pm, W-Su 11am-5pm. 60kr, students 40kr. Guided English-language tours: M-F 11:15am and 3pm, Sa-Su 11:15am and 4pm. AmEx/MC/V.)* For a quirkier attraction, look for **Mårten Trotzigs Gränd,** the narrowest lane in Stockholm.

KUNGSHOLMEN. The **Stadshuset** (City Hall) has been the seat of local government since the early 20th century. The required tour of the interior takes you through the council room and the enormous **Blue Hall,** where a 10,000-pipe organ greets Nobel Prize banquet attendees. In the stunning **Golden Hall,** 18 million shimmering tiles make up a golden Art Deco mosaic. The **tower** provides the best panoramic view of the city center. *(Hantverkarg. 1. T-bana: T-Centralen. ☎08 508 290 58; www.stockholm.se/stadshuset. Tower open daily May-Sept. 10am-4pm. Call the day of your visit to make sure the building is open to visitors. 20kr. Tours daily June-Aug. 1 per hr. 10am-4pm; Sept. 10am, noon, 2pm; Oct.-May 10am, noon. 60kr, students 50kr. AmEx/MC/V.)*

SKEPPSHOLMEN AND BLASIEHOLMEN. The collection at the **Moderna Museet,** on the island of Skeppsholmen (SHEPS-hole-men), contains canvases by Dalí, Matisse, Munch, Picasso, Pollock, and Warhol. *(T-Bana: Kungsträdgården. Bus #65. ☎08 519 552 00; www.modernamuseet.se. 80kr, students 60kr, 18 and under free. Open Tu 10am-8pm, W-Su 10am-6pm. MC/V.)* In the same building, the **Arkitekturmuseet** displays the history of Swedish architecture and design using 3D models. *(T-Bana: Kungsträdgården. Bus #65. ☎08 587 270 00. Open Tu 10am-8pm, W-Su 10am-6pm. 50kr, under 19 free. F 4-6pm free. MC/V.)* Across the bridge on the Blasieholmen peninsula, the **Nationalmuseum,** Sweden's largest art museum, features pieces by Cézanne, El Greco, Monet, and Rembrandt. *(T-bana: Kungsträdgården. Bus #65. ☎08 519 544 10; www.nationalmuseum.se. Open Sept.-May Tu and Th 11am-8pm, W and F-Su 11am-5pm; June-Aug. Tu 11am-8pm, W-Su 11am-5pm. 100kr, students 80kr, under 19 free. AmEx/MC/V.)*

ÖSTERMALM. Among the dignified museums of this trendy area, the **Musikmuseet** is a quirky, fun stop. Don't miss the room in the basement where you can try a number of intriguing instruments. *(Sibylleg. 2. T-bana: Östermalmstorg, ☎08 519 554 90; www.stockholm.music.museum. Open Tu-Su July-Aug. 10am-5pm; Sept.-June noon-5pm. 40kr, students 20kr, under 19 free.)* Less than a block away, the **Armémuseum** chronicles Swedish military history. All signs are in Swedish, so be sure to pick up a language guide at the ticket desk. *(Riddarg. 13. T-bana: Östermalmstorg, exit Sibylleg. ☎08 519 563 00; www.armemuseum.se. Open Tu 11am-8pm, W-Su 11am-5pm. July-Aug. Tu 10am-8pm, W-Su 10am-5pm. 50kr, under 19 free.)* For a more complete account of Swedish history, head to the **Historiska Museet,** which plays host to famous collections of both Viking and ecclesiastical memorabilia. *(Narvav. 13-17. T-bana: Karlaplan. ☎08 519 556 00; www.historiska.se. Open May-Sept. daily 10am-5pm; Oct.-Apr. Tu-W and F-Su 11am-5pm, Th 11am-8pm. 50kr, students and seniors 40kr, under 19 free.)*

DJURGÅRDEN. This national park is a perfect summer picnic spot. The main attraction is the haunting **Vasa Museet,** home to a massive warship that sank in Stockholm's harbor during its maiden voyage in 1628; it was salvaged, fantastically preserved, three centuries later. *(From the Galärvarvet bus stop, take bus #44, 47, or 69. ☎08 519 548 00; www.vasamuseet.se. Open June-Aug. daily 8:30am-6pm; Sept.-May*

W 10am-8pm, M-Tu and Th-Su 10am-5pm. 95kr, students 50kr. AmEx/MC/V.) Next door, the **Nordiska Museet** explores Swedish cultural history from the 1500s to the present day. *(☎08 519 546 00; www.nordiskamuseet.se. Open June-Aug. daily 10am-5pm; Sept.-Aug. M-Tu and Th-F 10am-4pm, W 10am-8pm with free admission from 4pm, Sa-Su 11am-5pm. 60kr, special exhibits 60kr. AmEx/MC/V.)* The **Gröna Lund** amusement park features a handful of rides, including roller coasters. *(☎08 587 502 00; www.gronalund.se. Open daily late Apr. to late Aug., usually 11am-11pm; around Midsummer, open until 10pm; check website for detailed schedule. Prices vary throughout the year, from 65kr-120kr.)* A large portion of Djurgården is home to **Skansen,** an open-air museum established in 1891 that features 150 historical buildings, a small zoo, and an aquarium. Stroll along the hilly paths of the Old Town to find Sámi dwellings, schoolhouses, and an elk or two. Many festivals and events are held throughout the year—the Christmas market in early December is noteworthy. *(Take bus #44 or 47. ☎08 442 8000; www.skansen.se. Park and zoo open daily June-Aug. 10am-8pm; Sept.-May 10am-5pm. June-Aug. M and W-Su 90kr, Tu 110kr for concerts; Sept. 80kr; Oct.-May 60kr. AmEx/MC/V.)*

ENTERTAINMENT AND FESTIVALS

Stockholm's smaller performance venues are featured in the *What's On* pamphlet, available at the Sweden House tourist office. There are also a number of larger, more widely known performance spots. The stages of the national theater, **Dramatiska Teatern,** Nybroplan (☎08 667 0680; www.dramaten.se), feature performances of works by August Strindberg and others (60-300kr). Arrive an hour early to snatch up a 35% discount on last-minute tickets. A smaller stage behind the theater focuses on experimental material. The **Kulturhuset at Sergels Torg** (☎08 508 314 00; www.kulturhuset.se) houses art galleries, performance spaces, and cultural venues often free to the public. It also hosts **Lava** (☎08 508 314 44; www.lavaland.se; closed in July), a popular hangout with a stage, library, and cafe, that lends itself to poetry readings and other events geared toward a younger set. The **Operan,** Jakobs Torg 2, stages operas and ballets from late August through mid-June. (☎08 791 4400. Tickets 265-590kr. Student rush tickets available. AmEx/MC/V.) The imposing **Konserthuset,** Hötorg. 8, hosts the Stockholm Philharmonic and the Nobel Prize ceremony. (☎08 786 0200; www.konserthuset.se. 100-270kr. AmEx/MC/V.) Culture buffs on a budget should sample Stockholm's **Parkteatern** (☎08 506 202 99; www.stadsteatern.stockholm.se), a summer-long program of free outdoor theater, dance, and music in city parks. Call **Ticnet** (☎0771 707 070; www.ticnet.se) for tickets. The world-class **Stockholm Jazz Festival** (☎08 505 331 70; www.stockholmjazz.com) arrives in mid- to late July. Other festivals include GLBT **Stockholm Pride** (early Aug.; ☎08 33 59 55; www.stockholmpride.org), the November **Stockholm Film Festival,** (☎08 677 5000; www.filmfestival.se), and late August's **Strindberg Festival,** a celebration of Sweden's most famous morose playwright.

NIGHTLIFE

For a city with lasting summer sunlight, Stockholm knows a thing or two about nightlife. The scene varies by neighborhood, with particular social codes prevailing in each area. The posh **Stureplan** area in Östermalm (T-bana: Östermalmtorg) and **Kungsgatan** (T-bana: Hötorget) are where the beautiful people party until 5am. Expect long lines and note that many clubs honor strict guest lists. Across the river, **Södermalm's** (T-bana: Mariatorget) nightlife is less glitzy but more accessible and just as popular, with a diverse mix of bars and clubs along Götg. and around Medborgarpl. In the northern part of town, nightlife options line **Sveavägen** and the **Vasastaden** area (T-bana: Odenplan or Rådmansg.). Many bars and clubs set age limits as high as 25 to avoid crowds of drunk teenagers, but showing up early may help get you in, regardless of your age. Stockholm is compact enough to walk among all the islands, but night buses cover most of the city. The T-bana is generally safe until closing. Pick up *Queer Extra (QX)* and the *QueerMap* for gay nightlife tips.

Absolut Icebar, Vasaplan 2-4 (☎08 505 630 00; www.absoluticebar.com), in the Nordic Sea Hotel. T-bana: T-Centralen. Provided jacket and gloves keep you warm in the -5°C temperature of this bar, made completely out of natural ice. Make reservations at least 3 days ahead. Drop-in usually requires waiting. Cover 105-160kr with drink; under 18 60kr. Refills 85kr. Open June-Aug. M-W 12:45pm-midnight, Th-Sa 12:45pm-1am, Su 12:45pm-10pm; check website for details on Sept.-May hours. AmEx/MC/V.

Mosebacke Etablissement, Mosebacke Torg 3 (☎08 556 098 90). T-bana: Slussen. Take the Katarina lift (10kr) or climb the stairs to Söder Heights. Usually a large crowd inside at the bar and on the dance floor. Outside terrace is more relaxed with a great view and ample seating. Beer 48kr. Mixed drinks 74kr. 20+. Cover 80kr after 11pm. Open M-Th and Su 5pm-1am, F-Sa 5pm-2am. AmEx/MC/V.

Kvarnen, Tjärhovsg. 4 (☎08 643 0380; www.kvarnen.com). T-bana: Medborgarpl. Look for the red windmill. The mod cocktail lounge **H2O,** the energetic **Eld** dance club, and a 200-year-old **beer hall** coexist under the same roof. Beer 29-69kr. M-Th and Su 21+, F-Sa 23+. Open daily 5pm-3am. MC/V.

Debaser, Karl Johans Torg 1 (☎08 462 9860; www.debaser.se). T-bana: Slussen. Look for the plaza to your right as you cross the bridge from Södermalm to Gamla Stan. This popular rock club draws crowds with live music. 18+. Cover 60-120kr. Bar open daily 5pm-3am. Club open daily June-Aug. 10pm-3am; Sept.-May 8pm-3am. AmEx/MC/V.

Snaps, Götg. 48 (☎08 640 2868). T-bana: Medborgarpl. On the corner of Medborgarpl. Rock upstairs, house music outside, and an intimate basement dance floor that becomes more mainstream around midnight. Beer 70kr. Wine 90kr. Mixed drinks from 60kr. 23+. Cover F-Sa 60kr. Open M-W 5pm-1am, Th-Sa 5pm-3am. AmEx/MC/V.

DAYTRIPS FROM STOCKHOLM

Stockholm is situated in the center of an archipelago, where the mainland gradually crumbles into the Baltic. The islands in either direction—east toward the Baltic or west toward Lake Mälaren—are a lovely escape from the city. **Ferries** leave from in front of the Grand Hotel on the **Stromkajen** docks between Gamla Stan and Skeppsholmen or the **Nybrohamnen** docks (T-bana: Kungsträdgården). Visit the **Excursion Shop** in Sweden House (p. 969) for more info.

STOCKHOLM ARCHIPELAGO (SKÄRGÅRD)

Vaxholm is accessible by ferry (1hr., late June to late Aug. 2 per hr., 65kr) or bus #670 from T-bana: Tekniska Hogskolan (45min., 1-4 per hr., 20kr). Waxholmsbolaget runs ferries to even the tiniest islands, including Sandhamn, year-round. All ferries depart from Vaxholm. (☎08 679 5830; www.waxholmsbolaget.se. June-Aug. 1 per hr.; Sept.-May 1 per 2hr. 65kr, ages 7-19 40kr, under 7 free. AmEx/MC/V.) Sweden House sells the Båtluffarkort card, good for unlimited Waxholmsbolaget rides. (5-day 300kr; 30-day 700kr.)

The wooded islands of the Stockholm archipelago become less developed as the chain of 24,000 islands coils out into the Baltic Sea. **Vaxholm** is the de facto capital of the archipelago. Its pristine **beaches,** Eriksö and Tenö in particular, and 16th-century **fortress** have spawned pricey waterside cafes, but the rest of the streets still maintain their charm. The **tourist office** is at Torget 1. *(☎08 541 708 00; www.vaxholm.se.)* Three hours from Stockholm, **Sandhamn** is quieter, although the white sands of Trouville Beach have many devotees. The island, with its active nightlife scene, is especially popular among a younger crowd. Hikers can escape from the masses by exploring coastal trails on the **Finnhamn** group and **Tjockö** to the north. Ask at Sweden House about **hostels.** They are usually booked up months in advance, but there are alternatives—the islands are a promising place to exercise the right of public access (p. 964).

LAKE MÄLAREN

Strömma Kanalbolaget ferries (☎08 587 140 00; www.strommakanalbolaget.com) depart Stockholm from the Stadshusbron docks next to the Stadshuset for Drottningholms Slott (45min.; 1-2 per hr.; round-trip 130kr, plus admission 210kr), and Björkö (July-Aug. 9:30am and 1pm, return 2:45 and 6:15pm; May and Sept. 9:30am, return 2:45pm. 195kr. Guided tour, museum admission, and round-trip ferry 265kr. MC/V.)

Drottningholms Slott (☎08 402 60 00; www.royalcourt.se) was built for the queens of Sweden in the late 17th century and has served as the royal family's residence since 1981, when they left Kungliga Slottet (p. 972). The interior and formal Baroque gardens are impressive, but the highlight is the 1766 **Court Theater,** where the artistic director uses 18th-century sets and stage equipment to mount provocative ballets, operas, and pantomime shows. The colorful **Chinese Pavillion** was built by King Adolf Fredrick as a surprise birthday present for his queen; how the large pavillion was kept secret enough to maintain the surprise remains a mystery. *(Drottningholms Slott open daily May-Aug. 10am-4:30pm; Sept. noon-3:30pm; Sa-Su Oct.-Apr. noon-3:30pm. Palace 90kr, students 35kr; palace and pavillion 110/55kr. Court Theater tickets start at 165kr. Drottningholms Slott English tours daily June-Aug. 1 per 2hr.; Sa-Su Oct.-May noon and 2pm. Court Theater 30min. guided tours 60/40kr. AmEx/MC/V.)* The island of **Björkö** on Lake Mälaren is home to **Birka,** Sweden's largest Viking-era settlement, dated to AD 750. Though little remains at the site, amateur excavations and modern Vikings bring the island to life in July and August.

SWEDEN

UPPSALA ☎018

The footbridges and side streets of Uppsala (pop. 127,000) teem with almost 40,000 undergraduates. Archbishop Jakob Ulvsson founded **Uppsala University** in 1477, but the Reformation wrested control away from the Catholic Church and set the stage for the spirit of debate that dominates the town today. Academics aside, the city is home to **Domkyrka,** Domkyrkoplan 5-7, the largest cathedral in Scandinavia. Its red-brick facade houses a grand interior, with artwork spanning eight centuries. Many famous Swedes, ranging from scientist Carolus Linnaeus to Saint Erik, the patron saint of Stockholm, are buried within. (☎018 71 73; www.uppsaladomkyrka.se. Open May-Aug. daily 8am-6pm. For other months check website. Free.) Just across Akademig. from the church, the **Gustavianum,** Akademig. 3, takes you through the university's scientific past with physicians' tools and a reconstructed Anatomical Theater, where public dissections were conducted in the late 17th century. (☎018 471 7571. Open Tu-Su June to Aug. 10am-4pm; Sept.-May 11am-4pm. English tours Sa-Su 1pm. 40kr. AmEx/MC/V.) A walk through the center of town along the Fyrisån River is an excellent way to sample the city's gardens and cafes. Up the hill on Övre Slottsgatan lies the light pink castle, **Uppsala Slott.** Inside is the **Uppsala Konstmuseum,** with art exhibits from the university's collection. (☎018 727 2482; www.uppsala.se/konstmuseum. Museum open Tu-F noon-4pm, Sa-Su 11am-5pm, first W of the month noon-8pm. Guided tours of the castle June-Aug. 1 and 3pm. Museum 30kr, with tour 70kr, under 20 free. First W of the month 4-8pm free. AmEx/MC/V.) On the other side of the river, the **Linnéträdgården,** Svartbäcksg. 27, reconstructs Sweden's first botanical gardens (tended by Carolus Linnaeus) using his 1745 sketch. The grounds include a small, interesting museum in Linnaeus's former home. (☎018 471 2576; www.linnaeus.uu.se. Garden open May-Sept. Tu-Su 11am-8pm, museum 11am-5pm. Museum and garden 50kr, under 16 free. AmEx/MC/V.) The MS *Kung Carl Justaf* sails to **Skoklosters Slott,** a 17th-century castle with an impressive armory. (☎018 402 3060; www.skoklosterslott.se. Open May Tu-Su 11:30am-4:30pm, June Tu-Su 11:30am-5:30pm, July-Aug. 10:30am-5:30pm. For other months, check website. Admission including tour 75kr, under 19 free. Guided tour 1 per hr. Boat departs daily mid-May to mid-Aug. 11am from Islandsbron on Östra Åg. and Munkg.; departs Skokloster 2:30pm. Round-trip 200kr. Ticketing ☎018 14 48 00. AmEx/MC/V.)

STF Uppsala City Hostel (HI) ❷, S:t Persgatan 16, is the most affordable city center accommodation. (☎018 10 00 08; www.uppsalavandrarhem.se. Linens 60kr. Free Internet. Reception 4-7pm. Pets allowed in some rooms. 8-bed dorms 220kr; singles 400kr; doubles 250kr. 50kr HI discount. AmEx/MC/V.) The university is home to student organizations representing different regions in Sweden, known as **nations.** Each nation owns a house, most with their own restaurants or bars, which have lower prices than other establishments in town. However, only students are allowed in; non-Uppsalan students can pick up a guest pass at **Ubbo,** Övre Slottsg. 7. (☎018 480 3100; www.kuratorskonventet.se. Open Tu-F 5-7pm, Sa 1-3pm. 1-week pass 60kr; 2-week 80kr; 4-week 100kr; summer 200kr. Valid student ID and photo ID required. MC/V.) **Västmanlands-Dala Nation ❷,** S:t Larsgatan 13 (entrance on Sysslomangs.), serves non-students June to August. The nation restaurant offers a sizable 50-80kr dinner. (☎018 13 48 59; www.v-dala.se. Open daily 6pm-1am. AmEx/MC/V.) **Elegant Basilico ❷,** Svartbäcksgatan 24, has pizza (69-99kr), pasta (69-89kr), and other affordable lunch specials. (☎018 15 10 12. Open daily 11am-7pm. AmEx/MC/V.) Pick up groceries at **Hemköp,** Stora Torget. (Open M-F 7am-10pm, Sa-Su 9am-10pm). Bars cluster around **Stortorget,** especially on **Sysslomansgatan, Västra Ågatan,** and the pedestrian areas of **Svartbäcksgatan** and **Kungsgatan.** During the academic year, nightlife in Uppsala revolves around the nations.

Trains go to Stockholm (40min., 1-6 per hr., 64kr, students 61kr). To get to the Uppsala **tourist office,** Fyristorg 8, walk right on Kungsg. from the train station, turn left on S:t Persg., and cross the bridge. The office sells the Uppsalakortet (125kr), providing up to 50% off sight admission. (☎018 727 4800; www.uppland.nu. Open in summer M-F 10am-6pm, Sa 10am-3pm, Su 11am-3pm only in July.) The library, **Stadbiblioteket,** Svartbäcksg. 17, has free **Internet.** (☎018 727 1700. Open in summer M-F 9am-6pm, Sa 11am-2pm; Sept.-Dec. Su 1-4pm only; Jan.-Aug. M-Th 9am-8pm, F 9am-6pm, Sa 11am-4pm.) **Postal Code:** 75320.

GOTLAND ☎0498

Along the shores of Gotland, Sweden's largest island, families head to beaches in the east before returning to Visby, a town that recalls the Middle Ages with its winding alleyways and historic city wall. Each May, 30 species of orchids come into bloom, transforming the island. Even though summer is busy, visitors can leave the crowds behind to stroll along the island's cliffs and coast.

TRANSPORTATION. Destination Gotland **ferries** (☎771 22 33 00; www.destinationgotland.se) sail from Visby to Nynäshamn and Oskarshamn. (3hr., June-Aug. 2-6 per day, Oct.-May 1-4 per day. 231-519kr, students 177-390kr. Online booking discounts. AmEx/MC/V.) To get to Nynäshamn from Stockholm, take a Flygbussarna **bus** from Cityterminalen (1hr., 2-4 per day, leaves 1hr. 45min. before ferry departures. 80kr, 110kr on bus) or the Pendeltåg **train** from Centralstationen (1hr., 90kr, SL passes valid). To get to Oskarshamn from Kalmar, hop on a KLT bus (1hr., every 1-2hr., 73kr). Gotland City, Kungsg. 57A, books ferries from Stockholm. (☎08 406 1500. Open M-F 10am-6pm, phone 8am-7pm, Sa 10am-3pm. AmEx/MC/V.) Pick up a bus timetable at the ferry terminal or at the Visby **bus station,** Kung Magnusväg 1, outside the wall east of the city. (☎0498

21 41 12; www.gotland.se/kollektivtrafiken. Cash only on buses; AmEx/MC/V at station.) Buses on the island are fairly expensive (39-68kr) and only three or four cover the routes each day, so be sure to plan ahead for daytrips. **Cycling** is a good way to explore Gotland. Extensive paths and bike-friendly roads can be supplemented by strategic bus rides, as buses will carry bikes for an extra 40kr. Bike rental shops can be found in Visby and in most towns across the island.

VISBY. Passing through the medieval **Ringmuren** (Ring Wall) of Visby (pop. 22,500) is like stepping into another time. The wall encloses the ruins of churches, the most intricate of which, **S:ta Karin** (or S:ta Katarina), draws visitors with its majestic arches above a grassy floor. (☎0498 29 27 00. Open in summer M-F and Su 8am-9pm, Sa 8am-7pm. Free.) Stairs behind the **Domkyrka** lead to a scenic terrace. Follow the path along the cliff for a view of the town and sea, then walk left along the northern perimeter of the wall to visit the botanical gardens. Visby attracts thousands in the first week of August for **Medieval Week** (☎0498 29 10 70; www.medeltidsveckan.se), a festival with theater and dance performances, a jousting tournament, and wandering minstrels strumming lutes. You'll recognize **Visby Fängelse Vandrarhem ❷,** Skeppsbron 1, by the barbed wire atop its walls, remnants of the prison that preceded it. (☎0498 20 60 50. Laundry 30kr. Reception in summer 11am-noon and 5pm-9pm; low-season noon-3pm. Dorms 260kr; doubles 320kr; bed in cabin 310kr. AmEx/MC/V.) Bars and cafes line **Stora Torget, Adelsgatan,** and the harbor. Take advantage of lunch specials (60-90kr), or pick up groceries at **ICA** on Stora Torg. (Open daily 8am-10pm.) From the ferry terminal, walk left down Färjeleden, then right down Skeppsbron to the **tourist office,** Skeppsbron 4-6. (☎0498 20 17 00; www.gotland.info. Internet 2kr per min. Open mid-June to mid-Aug. daily 8am-7pm; low-season reduced hours.) **Gotlandsresor,** Färjeleden 3, near the ferry terminal, books ferries, finds private rooms, and rents bikes. (☎0498 20 12 60; www.gotlandsresor.se. Open daily June-Aug. 6am-10pm; Sept.-May 8am-6pm.) **Bike rental** shops surround the terminal; prices start at 70kr per day. **Wi-Fi** is available at the **Gotlands Bibliotek** (library), Cramerg. 5. (☎0498 29 90 00. Sept.-June free; July-Aug. 20kr per hr. Open Sept.-June M-F 10am-7pm, Sa noon-4pm; July-Aug. M-F 10am-7pm, Sa noon-4pm. Cash only.) **Postal Code:** 62101.

ELSEWHERE ON GOTLAND. Use Visby as a launchpad for visiting **Tofta** beach at the village of **Klintehamn** (bus #10, 40min.), or the cliffs of **Hoburgen,** at the island's southernmost tip (bus #11, 2hr). Bus #20 runs from Visby to Fårösund (1.5hr.), taking passengers to a free 10min. ferry ride to **Fårö,** a small island off Gotland's northern tip. Visit Gotlandsresor (see above) for help booking hostels and campgrounds outside of Visby, or you can take advantage of the right of public access (p. 964) and **camp** by the brackish waters of the Baltic Sea.

FÅRÖ. Filmmaker Ingmar Bergman came to this small island north of Gotland to scout locations and never left. Today, solitude-seekers and admirers of Bergman's art savor Fårö for its wildflowers, sheep, and calm seashore. The island is also known for **raukar,** impressive natural pillars and arches in or by the sea. They are the remains of coral reefs, left over from the island's days near the Equator. To see them, travel along the north-west coast to Digerhuvud and Langhammars. Bike up to Fårö *kyrka* (church), turn left at the sign for Lauterhorn, and follow subsequent signs. For a sandy **beach,** turn east to Sudersand. (Bus #20 from Visby. Check the bus schedule.) Ducks squawk near moss-softened rock shelves at the lonely pebbled beach near Fårö *kyrka.* There are few restaurants on the island. Two cafes are at Broa: one is near the ferry terminal, and the other is close to the church. A main road cuts across the island, and is frequented by cars as well as bikes. Since buses are widely spaced and stick to the main road, **bikes** are your best bet to zip about the island. (Bus #20 from Visby goes to Fårösund, and at certain times goes up to Skär, at the northern end of Fårö. From Fårösund, take the free 10min. **ferry** that runs every half hour until midnight. Be sure to rent a bike before boarding the ferry at Fårösund.) The **tourist information center** is by Fårö *kyrka*.

SOUTHERN SWEDEN (SKÅNE)

A fiercely contested no-man's-land during 17th-century wars between Sweden and Denmark, this region bears the marks of its martial past with well-preserved castles and forts. Today, the only invaders are the cranes and cormorants that nest alongside marshes and lakes and the flocks of vacationers who savor the region's immaculate beaches and polished cities.

KALMAR AND ÖLAND ☎0480 / 0485

An important border city when southern Sweden was part of Denmark, Kalmar (pop. 60,000) is no longer at the center of Scandinavian politics, but it still retains the dignity of its glory days. Across from downtown, the medieval **Kalmar Slott** is the town's top attraction. In 1397, the castle witnessed the birth of the Union of Kalmar, a short-lived union of Denmark, Norway, and Sweden. King Johann III gave the castle a Renaissance makeover in the 1580s, and, today, it houses lavish furnishings and exhibits. The lovely view alone makes it a worthwhile stop. (☎0480 45 14 90; www.kalmarslott.kalmar.se. Open daily July 10am-6pm; Aug. 10am-5pm; May-June and Sept. 10am-4pm; Oct.-Apr. reduced hours. 80kr, students 50kr. Free tours mid-June to mid-Aug. AmEx/MC/V.) Adjoining the castle's moat are the majority of the town's other sights: the cobblestoned **Gamla Stan** (Old Town), the tree-lined **Kyrkogarden** cemetery, the green **Stadspark,** and a handful of small museums. In the center of town, Kalmar's luminous **Domkyrkan,** the first Baroque church in Sweden, exemplifies 17th-century architecture. (Open June-Aug. M-F 8am-8pm, Sa-Su 9am-8pm.)

If you have an extra day, cross Kalmar Sound by bridge to the long, thin island of Öland. The white-sand beaches of **Böda** line the northeast shore, while the orchid-dotted steppe of Stora lies to the south. **Solliden Palace,** a summer residence for the royal family since 1906, is 40km north of Öland Bridge. (☎0485 15 356; www.sollidensslott.se. Park and exhibits open mid-May to mid-Sept. 11am-6pm. 55kr, students 45kr. MC/V.) The ruins of **Borgholms Slott** reflect eight centuries of Swedish history. (☎0485 12 333; www.borgholmsslott.se. Open daily May-Aug. 10am-6pm; Apr. and Sept. 10am-4pm. 50kr, under 18 20kr.) **Biking** is the best way to explore the island. Be aware, though, that biking is not allowed on the bridge linking Kalmar and Öland. From May 10 to Aug. 31, a **free shuttle** transports riders and their bikes across. Alternatively, rent a bike once you reach Öland. The Träffpunkt Öland **tourist office** has a list of shops that rent bikes; follow signs from the first bus stop after the Öland Bridge. (☎0485 56 06 00; www.olandsturist.se. Open May-June M-F 9am-6pm, Sa 9am-5pm, Su 9am-3pm; July-Aug. 5 M-F 9am-7pm, Sa-Su 9am-6pm; Aug. 6-19 M-F 9am-6pm, Sa 9am-5pm, Su 9am-3pm; low-season reduced hours.) Buses #103 and 106 run from Kalmar's train station to Borgholm, on the island (50min., 46kr).

Vandrarhem Svanen (SVIF) and Hotel ❷, Rappeg. 1, located 2km from the Kalmar tourist office on the island of Ängö, has polished and inviting dorms, with ensuite bath to boot. Take bus #402 toward Norrliden from the train station (14kr). To get there by foot, turn left on Larmg., right on Södra Kanalg., continue to the end, and turn left across the bridge onto Ängöleden. (☎0480 12 928; www.hotellsvanen.se. Breakfast 65kr. Linens 50kr. Laundry 25kr. Internet

1kr per min; Wi-Fi in lobby, 40kr unlimited time. Reception late June to mid-Aug. 7:30am-10pm; mid-Aug. to May 7:30am-9pm. Dorms 195kr; doubles 430kr; triples 645kr.) **Söderportshotellet ❺,** Slottsväg. 1, across from Kalmar Slott, rents spacious student apartments in summer. (☎0480 125 01; www.soderportsgarden.se. Breakfast included. Live music W-Su 9pm-1am in the cafe. Open mid-June to mid-Aug. Reception 7:30am-1am. Singles 550kr; doubles 625-735kr. MC/V.) Seaside **Stensö Camping ❶** is 3km south of Kalmar. Take bus #121 to Lanssjukhuset, turn right on Stensbergsv., and right on Stensöv. (☎0480 88 803; www.stensocamping.se. Water included. Open Apr.-Sept. Tent sites 130-170kr; cabins from 400kr. Electricity 35kr. MC/V.) Hunt for cheap eats along **Larmtorget, Larmgata,** and **Storgata,** or pick up groceries at **Coop Konsum,** Storgatan 21. (Open daily 8am-11pm.) **Trains** and **buses** arrive in Kalmar south of the center. Trains go to Gothenburg (4hr.; 1 per 2hr.; 400kr, under 26 300kr), Malmö (3hr., 1 per 2hr., 346/242kr), and Stockholm (4hr., 1 per 2hr., 1044/883kr). Buses run directly to Stockholm (6hr.; 3 per day; 263kr, students 210kr). The **tourist office,** Ölandskajen 9, offers **Internet** (10kr per 15min.). From the train station, turn right onto Stationsg. and then right onto Ölandskajen. (☎0480 41 77 00; www.kalmar.se. Open July to mid-Aug. M-F 9am-9pm, Sa-Su 10am-5pm; June and late Aug. M-F 9am-7pm, Sa-Su 10am-4pm; Sept.-May M-F 9am-5pm.) **Postal Code:** 39120.

MALMÖ ☎040

A vigorous stone's throw from Copenhagen, Malmö (pop. 276,000), Sweden's third-largest city, boasts cultural diversity unmatched elsewhere in the country. The city's proximity to the rest of Europe makes it a gateway for the thousands of immigrants who flock to the country each year. Intimate and full of outdoor cafes, Lilla Torg is a mecca for people-watching, especially as outdoor patios light up under the glow of evening lamps.

TRANSPORTATION AND PRACTICAL INFORMATION. The train station and harbor are north of the old town. **Trains** go to Copenhagen (35min., 3 per hr., 90kr), Gothenburg (3hr., 1 per hr., 500kr), and Stockholm (4hr.; 1 per hr.; 1065kr, under 26 300kr). **Bus** rides within most of the city are 16kr with 1hr. transfer, and many buses pass by the train station. The **tourist office** is in the station and offers the **Malmö Card** (1-day 130kr, 2-day 160kr, 3-day 190kr), which provides free public transportation, parking, sightseeing bus tours, and museum admission. (☎040 34 10 00; www.malmo.se/tourist. Open June-Aug. M-F 9am-7pm, Sa-Su 10am-5pm; Sept.-May reduced hours. AmEx/MC/V.) **Internet** is available in the train station. (19kr per hr.; MC/V.) **Postal Code:** 20110.

ACCOMMODATIONS AND FOOD. **STF Vandrarhem Malmö City ❷,** 3. Rönngatan 1, has roomy beds in spotless dorms near the center of town. Take bus #2 toward Lindängen to the Davidshall stop and turn right on Holmg. (☎040 611 6220; www.stfturist.se/malmocity. Breakfast 60kr. Linens 50kr. Towels 20kr. Free Internet. Wi-Fi 60kr for 24hr. Reception 24hr. Dorms 230kr; singles 380kr; doubles 270kr; triples 240kr; quads 210kr. 50kr HI discount. AmEx/MC/V.) **Vandrarhemmet Villa Hilleröd ❷,** Ängdalav. 38, fills up quickly, but a stay in this cozy house is worth the extra planning. Take bus #3 from the train station to Mellanheden, turn left on Piläkersv., then left on Ängdalav. (☎040 26 56 26; www.villahillerod.se. Kitchen available. Breakfast 50kr. Linens 50kr. Towels 25kr. Free Internet. Reception 8-10:30am and 4-8pm. Check-in 6pm. Check-out before 11am. 6-bed dorms 190kr; doubles and quads 240-280kr. MC/V.) **Vandrarhem Malmö (HI) ❶,** Backav. 18, is the cheapest option. Take bus #2 from the train station to the Vandrarhemmet stop. (☎040 822 20; www.malmohostel.se.

Breakfast 50kr. Linens 50kr. Towels 20kr. Reception mid-May to Aug. 8-10am and 4-10pm; Sept. to mid-May 8-10am and 4-8pm. Dorms 200kr; singles 350kr; doubles 480kr; triples 600kr. 50kr HI discount. AmEx/MC/V.)

Möllevångstorget, south of the city center, has a spirited open-air market, folksy local bars, and affordable ethnic eateries. For food, you can't go wrong with any of Malmö's international offerings. Restaurants with low-cost lunches (50-75kr) line **Lilla Torg,** the best square in the city for a good meal, and **Södra Förstadsg.** For Moorish cuisine, stop at **Gök Boet ❶,** Lilla Torg 3, an intimate restaurant that transforms into a popular bar at night. (☎040 611 2199. Open M-Th 11am-midnight, F-Sa 11am-2am, Su noon-11pm. AmEx/MC/V.) Next door, the massive food court **Saluhallen** has inexpensive restaurants ranging from Greek to Japanese. (Open M-F 10am-6pm, Sa 10am-4pm.) Ten minutes down Stora Nyg. is **Vegegården ❸,** Rörsjög. 23, which features all-vegetarian Chinese dishes (75-88kr) and a buffet (M-F 68kr) for the thrifty herbivore. (☎040 611 3888. Open M-W 11am-3pm, Th 11am-9pm, F 11am-10pm, Sa noon-10pm, Su noon-9pm. Buffet M-F 11am-3pm. AmEx/MC/V.) Cap off a meal by sampling one of the 48 flavors of homemade ice cream at **Lilla Glassfabriken ❶,** Holmg. 9. (☎040 611 9760. 1-6 scoops 16-60kr. Open in summer M-F 11am-6:30pm, Sa-Su noon-7pm; low-season M-F 11am-6:30pm, Sa-Su noon-6pm. MC/V.)

SIGHTS AND ENTERTAINMENT. Malmö's most famous sight is **Malmöhus Castle,** a Renaissance stronghold dating to the 15th century that today holds five museums. The **Stadsmuseet** documents the city's history. The **Konstmuseum** offers a large collection of Scandinavian art and a small **Aquarium** and **Tropicarium.** Across the moat, the **Kommendanthuset** hosts pop culture exhibits. The **Teknikens och Sjöfartens Hus** (Technology and Maritime Museum) down the road lets you ogle airplanes, cars, ships, and submarines. Most exhibit labels in the museums are in Swedish, although the castle exhibits have English translations. (☎040 34 44 37; www.malmo.se/museer. Open daily June-Aug. 10am-4pm; Sept.-May noon-4pm. Combination ticket 40kr, students 20kr. MC/V.) **Turning Torso,** Vastra Varvsg. 44, the tallest building in Sweden, is also one of the world's most unique structures—the 54-stories twist 90 degrees from bottom to top. A film in the neighboring **Turning Torso Gallery** gives a virtual tour. (☎040 17 45 39; www.turningtorso.com. Open daily noon-6pm. Virtual tour Sa-Su.) The **Form/Design Center,** Lilla Torg 9, shows off cutting-edge Swedish design for the Ikea generation. (☎040 664 5150; www.formdesigncenter.com. Open Tu-W and F 11am-5pm, Th 11am-6pm, Sa-Su 11am-4pm. Free.) The stark **Malmö Konsthall,** St. Johannesg. 7, hosts modern art exhibits and has a playground that resembles a Dr. Seuss world. (☎040 34 12 93; www.konsthall.malmo.se. Open M-Tu and Th-Su 11am-5pm, W 11am-9pm. Tours daily 2pm. Free.) After strolling through the museums, kick back at the **bars** on Lilla Torg and Möllevångstorget, or check out the **club** scene around Stortorg; some venues were once run by **"Pleasureman Günther" Mats Söderlund,** best known for the "Ding Dong Song" and other techno masterpieces.

LUND ☎046

With vibrant student life and proximity to Malmö and Copenhagen, Lund (pop. 100,500) makes a fine base for exploring Skåne. The Romanesque **Lunds Domkyrka** (cathedral) is a massive 900-year-old reminder of the city's former reign as Scandinavia's religious center. Its floor-to-ceiling, 15th-century astronomical clock rings at noon and 3pm, and the 7074-pipe organ is Sweden's largest. The popular Giant Finn column at the crypt entrance has a Rumpelstiltskin-esque tale behind it. (☎046 35 88 80; www.lundsdomkyrka.org. Open M-F 8am-6pm, Sa 9:30am-5pm, Su 9:30am-6pm. Free 30min. tours mid-June to mid-Aug. daily

2:50pm.) **Lund University's** antagonism toward its scholarly northern neighbor in Uppsala has inspired countless pranks, in addition to the drag shows and drinkfests that already enliven the city's busy streets. The **campus** is across the park from the cathedral. **Student Info,** Sandg. 2, in the Akademiska Föreningen building, has details on upcoming events. (☎046 38 49 49; www.af.lu.se. Open late Aug. to June M-W and F 9am-5pm, Th 9am-6pm.) Continue north on Sandg. to get to the **Skissernas Museum** (The Museum of Sketches), adorned from floor to ceiling with paper and sculpture studies of art from around the world. (☎046 222 7283; www.skissernasmuseum.se. Open Tu-Su noon-5pm, W noon-9pm. 50kr, students free. MC/V.) **Kulturen,** an open-air museum behind the Student Union at the end of Sankt Anneg. on Tegnerplastén, chronicles Lund's history since the Middle Ages through a series of reconstructed houses. (☎046 35 04 00; www.kulturen.com. Open mid-Apr. to Sept. daily 11am-5pm; Oct. to mid-Apr. Tu-Su noon-4pm. 50kr, students free. MC/V.)

SWEDEN

The conveniently located but cramped **Vandrarhem Tåget (HI) ❷,** Vävareg. 22, is in the sleeping compartments of a 1940s train. Take the overpass to the park side of the train station. (☎046 14 28 20; www.trainhostel.com. Breakfast 55kr. Linens 60kr. Hot water 1kr per 2min. Reception Apr.-Oct. 8-10am and 5-8pm; Nov.-Mar. 8-10am and 5-7pm. Dorms 200kr. 50kr HI discount. Cash only.) To get to **Källby Camping ❶,** next to the Källby Bad outdoor swimming pool, take bus #1 (dir.: Klostergården; 18kr) 2km south of the city center. (☎046 35 51 88. Laundry 40kr. Reception M-F 7am-9pm, Sa-Su 9am-7pm. Open mid-June to Aug. 55kr per person. Electricity 25kr. MC/V.)

Konditori Lundagård ❶, Kyrkog. 17, serves sandwiches (12-48kr) and pastries (5-29kr) in a simple and friendly environment. (☎046 211 1358. Open M-Th 7am-7pm, F 7am-6pm, Sa 9am-6pm, Su reduced hours. MC/V.) The **open-air market** at Mårtenstorg. (open daily 7am-2pm) and the adjoining turn-of-the-century **Saluhallen** (open M-F 9:30am-6pm, Sa 9am-3pm) are the best bet for budget food. As in Uppsala (p. 976), Lund's nightlife revolves around **nations,** student clubs that throw parties and serve as social centers. Stop by **Student Info,** Sandg. 2, for tips on snagging a 50kr guest pass. Another popular option is **Mejeriet,** Stora Söderg. 64, a cinema, concert venue, and bar. (☎046 211 0023; www.kulturmejeriet.se. Films Th 7pm, free. Concerts free-300kr. MC/V.)

SJ **trains** (43kr) and local Pågatågen trains (10-20min., 1-5 per hr., 39kr) run from Malmö to Lund. Trains run from Lund to Gothenburg (3hr., 1 per hr., 580kr), Kalmar (3hr., 1 per 2hr., 346kr), and Stockholm (4-5hr.; 1 per 2hr.; 1040kr, under 26 879kr). The **tourist office,** Kyrkog. 11, sells maps (130-150kr) of the nearby **Skåneleden trail.** (☎046 35 50 40; www.lund.se. Open June-Aug. M-F 10am-7pm, Sa 10am-3pm, Su 11am-3pm; May and Sept. M-F 10am-5pm, Sa 10am-2pm; Oct.-Apr. M-F 10am-5pm. MC/V.) **Internet** is available 24hr. in the **7-Eleven** across from the station. (19kr per hr. MC/V.) **Postal Code:** 22100.

KÅSEBERGA ☎0411

Most travelers would pass by Kåseberga's (pop. 150) quiet valley without giving it much notice, were it not for what lies on its coast. The riddle of **Ales Stenar** is Sweden's answer to the enigma of Stonehenge. Its 59 stones are set in the shape of a ship, with the bow and stern aligned to the position of the sun at the solstices. The stones are a popular picnic spot as well as the starting point of several trails along the surrounding cow-populated hills. The closest hostels are in Ystad, but there are a number of B&Bs in Kåseberga, including **Ales Smedja ❸,** Ales väg. 24, which also offers cabins. (☎0411 52 74 87. Breakfast 65kr. Linens 50kr. Reception 7am-6pm. Singles 420kr; doubles 690kr; cabins 800kr. MC/V.) Sample *sillamacka* (fried herring served on bread with tartar sauce) at **Kåseberga Fisk Ab ❶,** a well-known fish smokery. (☎0411 52 71 80; www.kasebergafisk.se. Open July-Aug. daily 9am-6pm. Check website for other months. MC/V.) Bus #322 from Ystad (30min., 3 per day, 27kr) is the only public transportation that serves Kåseberga from June 17 to Aug. 20. For the rest of the year, visitors must book at least 1hr. ahead for a **bus** that leaves daily at 1:30pm (☎0411 24 98 98). It is also possible to **bike** the 18km between the towns.

YSTAD ☎0411

Best known as a ferry port for trips to Bornholm, DEN, Ystad (EE-stad; pop. 27,000) is famous to Swedes as the home of fictional detective Kurt Wallander. For those not too intrigued by detective stories, be assured that Ystad's drab waterfront is no indication of its downtown, a network of well-preserved houses alongside lively shops and cafes. A few of the town's half-timbered houses date back to the 15th century; Scandinavia's oldest is at Pilgr. and Stora Österg. The **Klostret** (Monastery), on Klosterg., has engaging exhibits detailing everyday life in the Middle Ages. From the tourist office, turn left onto Lingsg., left onto Stora Österg., and right out of Stortorg. onto Klosterg. (☎0411 57 72 86; www.klostret.ystad.se. Open June-Aug. M-F 10am-5pm, Sa-Su noon-4pm; Sept.-May reduced hours. 30kr. MC/V.) In the same building as the tourist office, the **Konstmuseum** features work by Swedish and Danish artists. (☎0411 57 72 85. Open high-season M 10am-6pm, Tu-F 10am-5pm, Sa-Su noon-4pm; low-season Tu-F noon-5pm, Sa-Su noon-4pm. 30kr. AmEx/MC/V.) **Vandrarhemmet Stationen** ❷ hostel is in the train station. Look for the entrance on the side of the building facing the water. (☎0708 57 79 95. Breakfast 55kr. Linens 60kr. Reception June-Aug. daily 9-10am and 5-7pm; Oct.-May call ahead. Dorms 200kr; singles 250kr during low-season, 400kr during high-season; doubles 400kr. Cash only.) **Stora Östergatan,** a pedestrian street lined with cafes and shops, passes through the main square. For groceries, head to the **Saluhallen** market, just off Stortorg. (Open daily 8am-8pm. MC/V.) Bornholms Trafikken (☎0411 55 87 00) **ferries** go to Bornholm, DEN (1hr., up to 4 per day, 216kr). **Trains** run to Malmö (45min., 1 per hr., 72kr). The **tourist office** is across from the station. (☎0411 57 76 81; www.ystad.se. Free Internet. Open mid-June to mid-Aug. M-F 9am-7pm, Sa-Su 10am-6pm; mid-Aug. to mid-June reduced hours.) **Postal Code:** 27101.

HELSINGBORG ☎042

Warring Swedish and Danish armies passed Helsingborg (pop. 122,500) back and forth 12 times in the 17th century. By the time Magnus Stenbock captured the town for the Swedes once and for all in 1710, most of it lay in shambles. It wasn't until the 19th century that Helsingborg regained its prominence. More recently, it has transformed into an elegant cultural center. The city's showpiece, **Knutpunkten,** houses transit terminals, restaurants, and shops under one glass roof. Exit Knutpunkten and make a left on Järnvägsg. to reach **Stortorget,** a long, wide main square that branches out into shopping streets like swanky **Kullagatan.** Stortorget ends at the **Terrassen,** a series of steps leading up to the 34m high **Kärnan,** a 700 year-old remnant of the fortress that once guarded the city. The tower offers a view across the water to Helsingør, Denmark on a clear day. (☎042 10 59 91. Open June-Aug. daily 10am-6pm; low-season reduced hours. 20kr. Cash only.) Closer to sea level, the harborside **Dunkers Kulturhus,** Kungsg. 11, is the city's newest venue, with a concert hall, theater, unusual contemporary art exhibits, and a multimedia installation on city history. From the tourist office, turn right onto Drottningg. and then left onto Sundstorg. (☎042 10 74 00; www.dunkerskulturhus.se. Open Tu-W and F-Su 10am-5pm, Th 10am-8pm. 70kr, students 35kr. MC/V.) North of Helsingborg, the former royal retreat of **Sofiero Slott,** built in 1864, sits on a hill overlooking the sound. Take bus #219 (18kr) from Knutpunkten to Sofiero Huvudentréen. (☎042 13

74 00; www.sofiero.helsingborg.se. Open daily April 12-Sept. 28 10am-6pm. Grounds with castle 80kr, under 18 20kr. MC/V.)

To reach the well-kept **Helsingborgs Vandrarhem ❷,** Järnvägsg. 39, from Knutpunkten, cross Järnvägsg., turn right, and walk three blocks. (☎042 14 58 50; www.hbgturist.com. Linens 45kr. Laundry 25kr. Reception 3-5pm. Dorms 195kr; singles 295kr; doubles 420kr; triples 585kr. MC/V.) **City Wok ❷,** Järnvägsg. 27, offers Chinese and Thai dishes (52-68kr), an inexpensive relief from a sandwich diet. (☎042 18 21 30. Open daily 11am-10pm. Lunch special 42kr. Cash only.) The Knutpunkten **food court** has a wide selection. Pick up groceries at **ICA,** Drottningg. 48, past the Rådhuset. (☎042 13 15 70. Open M-Sa 8am-9pm, Su 10am-9pm. MC/V.) The harbor area has a handful of late-night bars and clubs, although the restaurants on board the Helsingør ferries (see below) can be more fun than terrestrial options during summer—stay at sea as long as you like while the ferry shuttles continuously between Denmark and Sweden.

Trains depart from Järnvägsgt. for Gothenburg (2hr.; 1 per hr.; 270-391kr, under 26 discount), Malmö (1hr., 1 per hr., 87kr), and Stockholm (4-6hr.; 2-4 per day; 1096-1107kr, under 26 discount). **Ferries** go to Helsingør, DEN, near Copenhagen; popular **Scandlines boats** depart every 20min. (☎042 18 61 00. 20min.; 28kr, round-trip 54kr. AmEx/MC/V.) Most **city buses** (15-20kr) pass Knutpunkten and include 1hr. of free transfers. For the **tourist office,** exit the station in the direction of the grand Rådhuset; the office is inside the impressive building. (☎042 10 43 50; www.helsingborg.se. Open mid-June to mid-Aug. M-F 9am-8pm, Sa 9am-5pm, Su 10am-3pm; mid-Aug. to mid-June M-F 10am-6pm, Sa 10am-2pm.) **Internet** is available in the **7-Eleven** across from the train station. (19kr per hr. MC/V.) **Postal Code:** 25189.

GOTHENBURG (GÖTEBORG) ☎031

Wrongly dismissed as Sweden's industrial center, Gothenburg (YO-teh-boree; pop. 770,000), the country's second-largest city, is a sprawling metropolis threaded with parks, strewn with museums and theaters, and intersected by the glitzy Avenyn thoroughfare that cuts through the heart of the city. While Gothenburg is often overlooked on tours of northern Europe, it has the attractions of a Scandinavian capital, but with an unapologetically youthful twist.

TRANSPORTATION

Trains run from Central Station to Malmö (2-3hr.; 1 per 1-2hr.; 362kr, under 26 307kr); Stockholm (3-5hr., every 1-2hr., 538/460kr); Oslo, NOR (4hr., 2-3 per day, 444/332kr). Stena Line **ferries** (☎031 704 0000; www.stenaline.com) sail to Frederikshavn, DEN (2-3hr.; 6-10 per day; 160-200kr, 50% Eurail discount) and Kiel, GER (13hr., daily 7:30pm, 340-810kr). Gothenburg has an extensive **tram** and **bus** system; rides are 25kr, and most trams and buses pass by the train station or through Brunnsparken, south of the Nordstan mall. A **day pass** (65kr), valid on both trams and buses, is available at kiosks throughout the city.

ORIENTATION AND PRACTICAL INFORMATION

Central Gothenburg is on the southern bank of the Göta River. The city's transportation hub is in **Nordstaden,** the northernmost part of the center. Across the Stora Hamn canal lies the busy central district of **Inom Vallgraven.** The main street, **Kungsportsavenyn** (a.k.a. "Avenyn"), begins just north of the Vallgraven canal at Kungsportsplatsen and continues south 1km to **Götaplatsen,** the main square in the Lorensberg district. Vasagatan leads west through Vasastaden to the city's oldest suburb: the trendy **Haga** district.

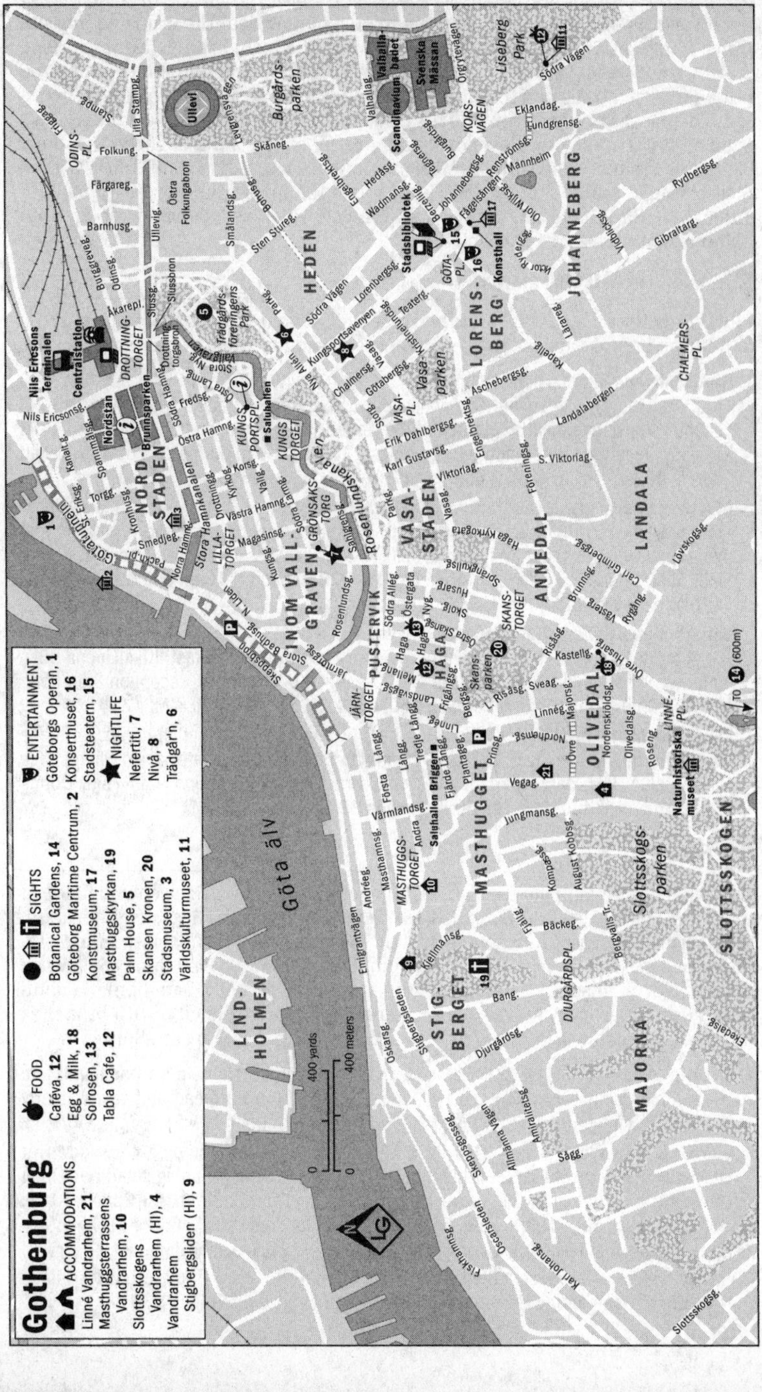

Gothenburg

ACCOMMODATIONS
- Linné Vandrarhem, 21
- Masthuggsterrassens Vandrarhem, 10
- Slottsskogens Vandrarhem (HI), 4
- Vandrarhem Stigbergsliden (HI), 9

FOOD
- Caféva, 12
- Egg & Milk, 18
- Solrosen, 13
- Tabla Cafe, 12

SIGHTS
- Botanical Gardens, 14
- Göteborg Maritime Centrum, 2
- Konstmuseum, 17
- Masthuggskyrkan, 19
- Palm House, 5
- Skansen Kronen, 20
- Stadsmuseum, 3
- Världskulturmuseet, 11

ENTERTAINMENT
- Göteborgs Operan, 1
- Konserthuset, 16
- Stadsteatern, 15

NIGHTLIFE
- Nefertiti, 7
- Nivå, 8
- Trädgår'n, 6

0 400 yards
0 400 meters

The **tourist office** has a branch in the Nordstan mall near the train and bus stations. (Open M-Sa 10am-6pm, Su noon-5pm.) The main branch, Kungsportspl. 2, sells the **Göteborg pass** (1-day 225kr, 2-day 310kr), which includes unlimited public transit, admission to many attractions, and free accommodations booking. The pass is only worthwhile for city tours or if you plan to see at least two sights. (☎031 61 25 00; www.goteborg.com. Open late June to early Aug. daily 9:30am-8:15pm; low-season M-F 9:30am-5pm, Sa 10am-2pm. AmEx/MC/V.) The **Stadsbibliotek** (public library), off Götapl., has 15min. of free **Internet.** (Open M-F 10am-8pm, Sa 11am-5pm.) There are Sidewalk Express **Internet** kiosks in train and bus stations. **Postal Code:** 40401.

ACCOMMODATIONS

Most of the city's hostels are in the West End, in and around **Masthugget;** trams and buses provide access to the city center. Reserve ahead, especially in July.

Slottsskogens Vandrarhem (HI), Vegag. 21 (☎031 42 65 20; www.sov.nu). Bus #60 (dir.: Masthugget) to Vegag. Spacious dorms and common areas with a kitchen and sauna (40kr). Breakfast 55kr. Linens 50kr. Laundry 40kr. Free Internet. Bike rental 90kr per day. Reception 8am-noon and 2pm-6am. 12- to 14-bed dorms 175kr; 3- to 6-bed dorms 195kr; singles 330kr; doubles 225kr. 50kr HI discount. MC/V. ❷

Masthuggsterrassens Vandrarhem, Masthuggsterr. 10H (☎031 42 48 20; www.mastenvandrarhem.com). Tram #3, 9, or 11 to Masthuggstorget. Classic movie posters and long hallways give this tidy hostel a college-dorm feel. TV in all private rooms. Breakfast 55kr. Linens 55kr. Laundry 45kr. Free Wi-Fi. Reception 8-10am and 5-8pm. Dorms 190kr; doubles 480kr; triples 590kr; quads 680kr. MC/V. ❷

Vandrarhem Stigbergsliden (HI), Stigbergsl. 10 (☎031 24 16 20). Tram #3, 9, or 11 to Stigbergstorget. Cozy rooms organized around a courtyard. Breakfast 60kr. Linens 50kr. Internet 1kr per min.; Wi-Fi 45kr per day. Bike rental 50kr per day. Reception 8am-noon and 4-10pm. Dorms 215kr; doubles 250kr. 50kr HI discount. AmEx/MC/V. ❷

Linné Vandrarhem, Vegag. 22 (☎031 12 10 60; www.vandrarhemmet-linne.com). Take bus #60 (dir.: Masthugget) to Vegag. Dorms turn into bright, private rooms when space is available. Breakfast 65kr, summer only. Linens 60kr. Reception 9am-7pm. Dorms 220kr; doubles 440kr; triples 660kr; quads 880kr. AmEx/MC/V. ❷

FOOD

The Avenyn is a great place for a stroll, but steer clear of its pricey eats in favor of the affordable options on **Vasagatan, Linnégatan,** and near the **Haga** neighborhood. **Saluhallen,** a food hall in Kungstorg., has the iron arches and glass ceiling of a huge train station. (Open M-Th 9am-6pm, F 8am-6pm, Sa 8am-3pm.) **Saluhallen Briggen,** Nordhemsg. 28, is in an old fire station. (Open M-F 9am-6pm, Sa 9am-2pm.) **Hemköp** grocery stores are scattered throughout the city, with branches on Andra Långatan and Vasag. (Open M-F 7am-10pm, Sa-Su 9am-8pm.)

Caféva, Haga Nyg. 5E (☎031 711 6364). Locals flock to this cafe for traditional fare with some quirky twists. You can't go wrong with fresh-baked bread and cakes, hearty soups with coffee or tea (55kr), and sandwiches (38kr). Open M-F 9am-6pm. MC/V. ❶

Solrosen, Kaponjärg. 4 (☎031 711 6697). Even carnivores come to chow down at this cozy vegetarian haven in Haga. Soup 60kr. Entrees 70kr including salad bar. Open M-Th 11:30am-11:30pm, F 11:30am-12:30am, Sa 1pm-12:30am, Su 2pm-8:30pm. Kitchen closes M-Th 10pm, F-Sa 10:30pm, Su 7:30pm. AmEx/MC/V. ❷

Tabla Cafe, Södra Vägen 54 (☎031 63 27 20). Upstairs in the Världskulturmuseet. Enjoy lavish creations for reasonable prices. Try the bread (35-40kr) or the exquisite salads (45-65kr). Open Tu and Sa-Su noon-5pm, W-F noon-9pm. AmEx/MC/V. ❷

Egg *and* **Milk,** Ovre Husarg. 23 (☎031 701 0350). This hip 50s-style diner has an English-language menu and serves generous portions of all things breakfast (pancakes 50-54kr, omelettes 54-58kr, bagel platters 43-45kr). Open daily 7am-3pm. MC/V. ❷

SIGHTS

CITY CENTER. **Göteborg Maritime Centrum,** a flotilla of 19 ships open for exploration, features a 1962 submarine and a WWII destroyer, with special effects that bring the dormant vessels to life. *(☎031 10 59 50; www.maritiman.se. Open Mar. and Nov. F-Su 10am-4pm, Apr.-May and Oct. daily 10am-4pm, June-Sept. 10am-6pm. 80kr, students 60kr. English-language tours in summer noon and 2pm. MC/V.)* **Nordstan,** Scandinavia's largest shopping center, is across from the train station. *(Open M-F 10am-7pm, Sa 10am-6pm, Su 11am-5pm.)* The **Stadsmuseum,** Norra Hamng. 12, contains the remains of the Äskekärr ship (the only preserved Viking ship exhibited in Sweden), and uses large-scale re-creations to recall the city's history. *(☎031 368 3600; www.stadsmuseum.goteborg.se. Open Tu-Su 10am-5pm, W 10am-8pm. 40kr, under 20 free; entrance fee, valid for 1 year, provides entrance to the Stadsmuseum, the Röhsska fashion, design and decorative arts museum, the Maritime museum, and the Konstmuseum. AmEx/MC/V.)* **Trädgårdsföreningens Park** is to the left as you cross the Avenyn bridge. Wind your way through the rosarium to the **Palm House.** *(☎031 365 5825; www.tradgardsforeningen.se. Park open daily Apr.-Sept. 7am-9pm; Oct.-Mar. 7am-7:30pm. Apr.-Sept. 15kr, free before 9am and after 8pm; Oct.-Mar. free. Palm House open daily 10am-5pm. Free.)* Avenyn ends at the **Götaplatsen** city square, built for the 1923 World Expo—the square is also the site of Carl Milles's famous **Poseidon fountain.** Even the sea god is dwarfed by the imposing **Konstmuseum,** which holds a spectacular sculpture and photography collection. Works by Gaugin, Monet, Picasso, and van Gogh are displayed. *(☎031 61 29 80; www.konstmuseum.goteborg.se. Open Tu and Th 11am-6pm, W 11am-9pm, F-Su 11am-5pm. 40kr, temporary exhibits 20-40kr, under 20 free. AmEx/MC/V.)*

HAGA. Westward, the Haga district offers art galleries, bookstores, and cafes, especially along the main thoroughfare, **Haga Nygata.** The flight of steps at the southern end of Kaponjärg. leads to **Skansen Kronen,** the most impressive of the hilltop towers surrounding Gothenburg. For a bird's-eye view of Gothenburg's harbor, head out to the **Masthuggskyrkan,** Storebackeg. 1, a 1914 brick church with a timber ceiling that suggests the inside of a Viking ship. Take tram #3, 9, or 11 to Masthuggstorg—it's the second church up the hill. *(☎031 731 9230. Open in summer daily 9am-6pm; low-season usually M-F 11am-4pm.)* South of the church, the vast **Slottsskogsparken** invites you to wander among its aviaries, meadows, and ponds. Take tram #1 or 6 to Linnépl. Across the highway lies Sweden's largest **Botanical Gardens,** Carl Skottsbergs G. 22A, home to orchid greenhouses, a bamboo grove, and 20,000 different flower, shrub, and tree species. Take tram #1, 2, 7, 8, or 13 to Botaniska Trädgården. *(☎031 741 1100; www.gotbot.se. Open daily 9am-sunset. Suggested donation 20kr. Greenhouses 20kr. MC/V.)*

ENTERTAINMENT AND NIGHTLIFE

The enormous **Göteborgs Operan,** at Lilla Bommen, hosts concerts, musical theater, and opera from August through May. (☎031 13 13 00; www.opera.se. Tickets from 95-540kr, students 25% off M-Th and Su. Box office open M-Sa noon-6pm. AmEx/MC/V.) Gothenburg's **Stadsteatern** (☎031 708 7000) and **Konserthuset** (☎031 726 5300) round out the music and theater scene. The event calendar at www.goteborg.com has details on performances. Gothenburg's annual **film festival** (www.filmfestival.org) draws more than 110,000 to the city (Jan. 23-Feb. 2, 2009). Mid-August brings the **Göteborg Kulturkalas,** an annual party that transforms the city with culinary masterpieces, entertainment, and music.

The chic but affordable bars that line **Linnégatan** are a good place to start or end an evening. Gothenburg's club scene is one of Scandinavia's most exclusive. Expect lines, steep covers, and strict dress codes. **Nivå,** Kungsportsavenyn 9, is the scene's standard-bearer, with three floors and an outside terrace. (☎031 701 8090. W 25+, F-Sa 27+. Cover F-Sa 120kr. Open W 8pm-3am, F 4:30pm-4am, Sa 8pm-4am. AmEx/MC/V.) For a little less attitude, head for **Trädgår'n,** Nya Allén 11. Behind the unassuming, ivy-clad exterior is a stylish restaurant, concert venue, club, and bar. (☎031 10 20 80. 20+. Cover from 100kr. Club open F-Sa 9pm-5am. AmEx/MC/V.) On a low-tempo evening, head to **Nefertiti,** Hvitfeldtspl. 6, an intimate jazz bar that reinvents itself as a dance club after 12:30am. (☎031 711 4076; www.nefertiti.se. 20+. Club cover 80kr. Tickets 80-280kr. Concerts in summer Tu-W and F-Sa 8:30 or 9pm. MC/V.)

SWEDEN

DAYTRIP FROM GOTHENBURG

VARBERG

Trains leave for Gothenburg (1hr., 93kr) and Helsingborg (1hr., 198kr). To reach the tourist office, turn right out of the train station and walk two blocks to the beginning of the pedestrian strip. (☎0340 86 800; www.turist.varberg.se. Open July M-Sa 9:30am-7pm, Su 1-6pm; May-June and Aug. M-F 10am-6pm, Sa 10am-3pm; Sept.-Apr. M-F 10am-5pm.)

This summer paradise—a classic seaside town with beaches and bath houses—lies between Gothenburg and Helsingborg. Varberg's grand **fortress** is home to a number of attractions. The **Länsmuseet Varberg** displays **Bocksten Man,** an eerily well-preserved bog corpse from 1360. To reach the fortress, turn right out of the station and right onto S. Hamnv. (☎0340 828 30; www.lansmuseet.varberg.se. Museum open June to mid-Aug. daily 10am-6pm; mid-Aug. to May M-F 10am-4pm, Sa-Su noon-4pm. June-Aug. 50kr; Sept.-May 30kr. MC/V.) Follow the boardwalk 2km south of town to the shallow **Apelviken Bay,** which has some of the best **surfing** and **windsurfing** in Northern Europe.

To escape (somewhat) from this weekend escape, go 5km north to the **Getterön Peninsula,** where rocky shores retain a calm air despite their family appeal. The area has lively campgrounds. **Getterögården ❶,** Hattviksvägen 15, has rows of beds in two rooms above the reception. (☎0340 16 806, low-season 0340 63 10 70. Shared bath in separate building close by. Dorms 120kr. Cash only.) Live like a jailbird on the fortress grounds in the former prison cells of **Fästningens Vandrarhem ❷,** Varbergs Fästning. This penitentiary-turned-hostel was once one of Sweden's largest prisons. (☎0340 868 28; www.turist.varberg.se/vandrarhem. Reception 9-11am and 4-7pm. Rooms from 205kr. MC/V.) A popular pizza and falafel joint is **Amigos Pizzeria,** Västra Vallgatan 43. (☎0340 80 850. Open M-Th 11am-9pm, F 11am-3am, Sa noon-3am, Su noon-9pm. 45-75kr.)

The Getterön Peninsula is accessible by the 15min. Getteröbåtarna **boat taxi.** (☎0703 10 13 24; www.getterobatarna.se. 1 per hr.; 30kr. Runs June-Aug. daily 10am-midnight. Cash only.) You can also take **bus** #8 from Järnvägsstationen, but service is infrequent and you must call ahead. (☎0771 33 1030. 20kr.)

CENTRAL SWEDEN

Central Sweden extends from foothills along the Norwegian border to lakeside villages in the heart of the country. Many of the region's counties are known for their handicrafts; stylized religious paintings and colorful wooden horses from the area fill homes throughout Sweden. Central Sweden is also home to some of the country's best skiing in winter and popular hiking trails in summer.

MORA ☎0250

The quiet town of Mora (pop. 22,000) sits in Europe's largest meteorite impact site: a 75km wide, 400m deep crater formed 360 million years ago. On the first Sunday in March, Mora marks the finish of the **Vasaloppet,** the world's oldest and longest cross-country ski race. The town hosts a week-long **festival** (www.vasaloppet.se) during the 90km race. The **Vasaloppet Museum** documents the history of the race with a film and serves samples of the warm blueberry soup participants drink during the competition. (☎0250 392 25. Open mid-June to mid-Aug. daily 10am-5pm; mid-Aug. to mid-June M-F 10am-5pm; closed Th at 3pm year-round. 30kr, including film and soup. MC/V.) Tucked away behind the city's church, **Zorngården,** Vasag. 37, was the 19th-century home of Anders Zorn, a renowned Swedish painter best remembered for his folk portrayals, nude paintings, and portraits. The house interior is only accessible by a 45min. tour. (Open mid-May to mid-Sept M-Sa 10am-4pm, Su 11am-4pm. Tours daily at noon, 1, 2, 3pm; call ahead for English-language tour availability. 60kr, students 50kr. AmEx/MC/V.) Hikers of any skill level can tackle the **Siljansleden** network of trails that circles the two lakes, including a well-marked 310km **bike trail.**

For comfy, cottage-style dorm rooms, head to **Vandrarhem Mora (HI) ❸,** Fredsg. 6. (☎0250 381 96; www.maalkullann.se. Breakfast 65kr. Linens 80kr. Reception M-F 5-7pm, Sa-Su 5-6pm; located at the restaurant Maalkullan, further down Vasag. Dorms 240kr; singles 370kr; doubles 600kr. 50kr HI discount on dorms and singles, 100kr on doubles. AmEx/MC/V.) **Mora Parken Camping ❶** sits on the Vasaloppet track. (☎0250 276 00; www.moraparken.se. Free showers. Breakfast 65kr. Linens 100kr. Laundry 10kr. Mid-June to mid-Aug. tent sites 150kr, with electricity 195kr; 2-person cabins 330kr, 4-person 480kr; low-season reduced rates. AmEx/MC/V.) Restaurants in Mora tend to come in two varieties: overpriced and pizzeria-kebaberies. A departure from both is **Vi På Kajen (Glassbar) ❶,** across from the tourist office on the water, which serves light meals for 35-65kr. (☎0250 177 07. Open June-Aug. daily 10am-9pm. AmEx/MC/V.) Pick up groceries at **ICA** on Kyrkog. (☎0250 103 28. Open daily 9am-9pm. MC/V.)

Trains go to Östersund (7hr., mid-June to early Aug. 1 per day, 876kr) and Stockholm (4hr., 7 per day, 351kr). **Bus** #45 (5hr., 2 per day, 182kr) runs to Östersund year-round. The **tourist office** is on Strandg.; turn left out of the station and follow Vasag. for about 15min. (☎0250 59 20 20; www.siljan.se. Open mid-June to mid-Aug. and during the ski race M-F 10am-7pm, Sa-Su 10am-5pm; mid-Aug. to mid-June M-F 10am-5pm. AmEx/MC/V.) **Internet** is available at the library, Köpmang. 4, off Kyrkog. (☎0250 267 79. 10kr per 30min. Open M-F 10am-7pm, Sa 10am-2pm; June-Aug. closed Sa. Cash only.) **Postal Code:** 79230.

ÖSTERSUND ☎063

Travelers heading to Lappland often stop for a few days in Östersund (pop. 58,000). Deep, reedy **Lake Storsjön** lines the town's western shore. Many residents believe the lake is home to the serpentine, dog-headed **Storsjöodjuret monster.** In 1894, the town called in Norwegian whalers to flush out the creature, but appeals by local Quakers and the tourist office resulted in a 1986 ban (revoked in 2005) on any monster harassment. The *SS Thomée* runs cruises and monster-spotting tours. (2-3 per day; 80-110kr.) Rent a **bike** at the tourist office, near the *Thomée* dock, and pedal 8km over the footbridge to **Frösön Island,** a getaway aptly named for the Norse god of crops and fertility. Swedish couples have taken the hint by making the island's 12th-century **Frösö kyrka** (church) one of Sweden's most popular wedding chapels. Bus #5 (20kr) from the town center also runs to the island. (☎063 16 11 50. Open daily 8am-8pm.) On the edge of the island closer to town, at the top of Frösön's highest point (468m), stands the **Frösötornet** (Frösö Tower). Norwegian mountains can be seen from the top on a clear day. (☎063 12 81 69. Open daily late June to mid-Aug. 9am-9pm; mid-Aug. to Sept. and mid-May to late June 11am-5pm. 10kr. Cash only.)

Reserve ahead for hostels in high-season. The homey **Hostel Rallaren ❶** is at Bangårdsg. 6. (☎063 13 22 32. Linens 50kr. Reception M-F 9:30am-2:30pm, Sa-Su reduced hours. Dorms 160kr; singles 210kr; doubles 360kr. Cash only.) A smattering of cozy cabins surround a 257-year-old loft-house at **Frösötornets Vandrarhem ❶,** Utsiktv. 10, Frösön. Bus #5 runs from the city center (every 1-2hr.) and stops at the bottom of a steep hill. Though the hostel is a steep climb from the bus stop, the wooded surroundings and mountain views promise a memorable stay. (☎063 51 57 67; vandrarhem@froson.com. Linens 50kr. Call for reception. Dorms 150kr; singles 190kr; doubles 300kr. Cash only.) Pick up groceries at **Hemköp,** Kyrkg. 56. (Open M-Sa 8am-10pm, Su 10am-10pm. MC/V.)

Trains run to Stockholm (6hr.; 6 per day; 554kr, under 26 461kr) and Trondheim, NOR (4hr., 2 per day, 289/202kr). From mid-June to early August, an Inlandsbanan train (☎0771 53 53 53; www.grandnordic.se) runs to Gällivare (14hr., 1 per day, from 762kr) and Mora (6hr., 1-2 per day, 379kr). The **tourist office,** Rådhusg. 44, offers **bike** rentals (100kr per day, 300kr per week) and books rooms for free. (☎063 14 40 01; www.turist.ostersund.se. Open July M-F 9am-8pm, Sa-Su 10am-7pm; early to mid-June M-Th 9am-7pm, F-Su 10am-3pm; mid-June to mid-Aug. M-F 9am-5pm, Sa-Su 10am-3pm; Sept.-May M-F 9am-5pm. AmEx/MC/V.) **Internet** is free at the tourist office or library, Rådhusg. 25-27. (Open M-Th 10am-7pm, F 10am-6pm, Sa 11am-3pm.) **Postal Code:** 83100.

ÅRE ☎0771/0647

The village of Åre (pop. 1200) is one of Sweden's top skiing destinations. The **Åre Ski Star Resort** (☎0771 84 00 00; www.skistar.com/are/english) has beginner and intermediate cross-country and downhill trails, as well as a ski school. When the snow melts, the town becomes a base for outdoor activities on and around **Åreskutan,** the region's highest peak. The **chairlift** brings you halfway up the mountain to a number of trailheads. (Lift runs daily late June-Aug. 10am-4pm. Round-trip 70kr.) For ambitious hikers, the 7km **Åreskutan trail** runs from the town square to a 1420m peak. The Kabinbanan **cable car** shortens the trip to under 1km. (Cable car runs late June-Aug. 10am-4pm. Round-trip 110kr.) The **Åre Ski Lodge ❸,** Trondheimsleden 44, is one of the cheaper accommodations in an expensive town. (☎0647 510 29. Breakfast and linens included. Laundry and lockers available. Free Wi-Fi. Reception 24hr. Reserve ahead during ski season. Summer doubles 580kr; quads 1180kr, 4760kr per week. Winter doubles 5000-9000kr per week; quads 20,000-32,000kr per week. MC/V.) Pick up groceries at the train station's **ICA.** (Open M-Sa 8am-8pm, Su 10am-8pm. MC/V.) **Trains** run from Åre to Östersund (1hr.; 2 per day; 140kr, students 118kr) and Trondheim, NOR (2hr., 2 per day, 179kr). Nabotåget (☎0771 26 00 00; www.nabotaget.nu) has the best fares to Trondheim and destinations along the way. The **tourist office** is in the train station. (☎0647 177 20; www.visitare.se. Open late June-Aug. and mid-Dec. to Apr. daily 9am-6pm; Sept. to mid-Dec. and May-late June M-F 9am-5pm, Sa-Su 10am-3pm. AmEx/MC/V.) **Postal Code:** 83013.

GULF OF BOTHNIA

Sweden's Gulf of Bothnia region is known for its dark pine forests and pristine coastline. Unlike the metropolitan centers to the south, the area's quiet cities serve as bases for wilderness excursions.

GÄVLE ☎0261/0266

Two hours north of Stockholm, Gävle (YEV-leh; pop. 90,000) is a gateway to Lappland. **Gamle Gefle** (Old Town), the only part of Gävle that survived a 19th-century fire, lies just across the canal. **Länsmuseet Gävleborg,** Södra Strandg. 20, displays contemporary art. (☎0266 556 00; www.lansmuseetgavleborg.se. Open T and Th-F 10am-4pm, W 10am-9pm, Sa-Su noon-4pm. 50kr, students free. W free. MC/V.) Farther inland, the **Gävle Konstcentrum,** Kungsbäcksv. 32, has Swedish and international contemporary art. (☎0261 794 24; www.gavle.se/konstcentrum. Open June-Aug. Tu-Su noon-4pm; Aug.-May Tu-F noon-5pm, Sa-Su noon-4pm. Free.) On the opposite bank, stroll through the city park's **sculpture garden.** The **Gävle Goat** is a giant straw Yule Goat built in Slottstorget every year since 1966. The display is famously the target of arson attacks. Protection for the goat has been amped up over the years, and finding a way to destroy it has become a pastime that draws tourists to the region.

Vandrarhem Gävle (HI) ❶, Södra Rådmansg. 1, has homey rooms around a flower-filled courtyard. (☎0266 217 45. Breakfast 55kr. Linens 80kr. Laundry 40kr. Reception 8-10am and 4:30-7pm. Dorms 210kr; singles 335kr; doubles 500kr. 50kr HI discount. MC/V.) **Cafe Spegelu ❷,** Norra Köpmang. 11, serves large, delicious sandwiches (36-40kr) in the artsy environment of a former movie theater. (☎026 12 00 12. Open daily 10:30am-5:30pm. MC/V.)

Trains run to Östersund (4-6hr., 2-4 per day, 624kr) and Stockholm (1hr., 1 per hr., 236kr). To get to the **tourist office,** Drottningg. 9, head straight out of the train station down Drottningg. to the market square; it's in the center of the Gallerian Nian shopping center. (☎0261 474 30; www.gastrikland.com. Open M-F 10am-7pm, Sa 10am-4pm, Su noon-4pm. AmEx/MC/V.) Free **Internet** is available at the library, **Stadsbiblioteket,** Slottstorget 1, for 15min. slots, usually with a short wait. (☎0261 794 29. Open in summer M-Th 9am-6pm, F 9am-5pm, Sa-Su 10am-2pm; call ahead for winter hours.) **Postal Code:** 80250.

ÖRNSKÖLDSVIK ☎0660

Although drab concrete dominates the center of Örnsköldsvik (urn-SHULDS-vik; "Ö-vik" to locals; pop. 29,000), the city is forgiven its architectural missteps thanks to popular nearby **hikes.** The 127km **Höga Kusten Leden** (High Coast Trail) winds south through **Skuleskogen National Park** as far as Veda, just north of the High Coast Bridge. Flanked by cliffs that drop into the Gulf of Bothnia, the trail is divided into 13 segments ranging in difficulty with free **mountain huts** at the end of each leg. Bring

GOAT ROAST!

Gävle had a problem. In 1966, the town center wasn't attracting many tourists. Naturally, the solution was to build a gigantic straw Yule Goat. At 13m high, 7m long, and 3 tons, it became an epic draw for the region. The dividends for Gävle have been astounding, just not in the way they expected.

When the clock struck midnight on January 1st, 1967, the new year came in with a bang: the goat exploded in flames. The arsonist was apprehended and charged with vandalism. The first Gävle goat had perished, but surely it was a mere fluke. Better luck next year. The goat survived the 1967 and 1968 holidays, but disaster struck in a 1969 inferno, again, lit by vandals. This ushered in four decades of carnage in which 50% of the goats were destroyed, be it by fireworks, flames, or cars.

It isn't easy being a goat in Gävle. As the troubles have continued, the goat has received protection worthy of a king: fences, fireproofing, military escorts, and webcams. Tourism has increased as people from around the world head to Sweden to have a crack at burning the goat to the ground, or just watch to it happen. Of course, first degree straw goatslaughter is a crime, but no one can deny that it has spurred holiday crowds in the town center, realizing the 1966 goal. Over the years, only four assailants have been caught. *Let's Go* does not recommend burning straw goats.

an insulated sleeping bag and arrive early to cut firewood. Day hikes include the 6km **Yellow Trail** loop. You'll find the trailhead on Hantverkareg. From the tourist office, walk up Centralespl., turn left on Storg., and then left again. A lift runs to the top of the mountain. (☎0660 156 92. Open M 2-4pm, Tu-Th and Sa-Su 11am-4pm, F 11am-4pm and 5:30-7pm. Round-trip 50kr. Cash only. Tickets also available at the tourist office. AmEx/MC/V.)

Örnsköldsviks Vandrarhem ❷, Viktoriaespl. 32, is a converted family manor. From the bus station, turn left onto Lasarettsg., walk four blocks, make a right onto Bergsg., then a left onto Viktoriaespl. (☎0660 29 61 11. Breakfast 50kr. Linens 50kr. Free Wi-Fi. Call for reception. Dorms 200kr; doubles 400kr. MC/V.) **Lundberg Bröd o Cafe ❷,** Nygatan 35, serves salads, crepes, and cakes. (☎0660 125 25. Meals around 50kr. Open M-F 7am-5pm. AmEx/MC/V.) Pick up groceries at **Hemköp,** Stora Torg. 3. (Open M-F 8am-8pm, Sa-Su 8am-10pm. MC/V.)

Buses run to Östersund (4hr.; M-F 2-3 per day, Sa-Su 1 per day; 275kr) and Umeå (1hr., 14 per day, 216kr). The **tourist office,** Strandg. 24, next to the station, has free **Internet.** (☎0660 881 00; www.ornskoldsvik.se. Open late June to mid-Aug. M-F 9am-6pm, Sa-Su 10am-2pm; mid-Aug. to late June M-F 10am-6pm, Sa 10am-2pm. AmEx/MC/V.) **Postal Code:** 89133.

SWEDEN

UMEÅ ☎090

In the 1970s, leftist students in Umeå (OOM-eh-oh; pop. 111,000) earned their school the nickname "red university." Today, northern Sweden's largest city is better known for its birch-lined boulevards than its Marxist leanings, although echoes of its egalitarian past live on in a slew of free attractions. At the **Gammlia** open-air museum, a 20min. walk east of the city center, visitors get a crack at 19th-century crafts they've been itching to try, like churning butter while munching on *tunnbröd* (20kr), a Swedish flatbread. (Open only in summer daily 10am-5pm. Free.) In the same complex, the **Västerbottens Museum** houses the world's oldest ski, dating back to 3200 BC. (☎090 17 18 00; www.vasterbottens-museum.se. Open mid-June to mid-Aug. daily 10am-5pm; low-season reduced hours. Free.) The **BildMuseet,** at Umeå University, displays Swedish and international contemporary art. (☎090 786 52 27; www.bildmuseet.umu.se. Open daily 10am-5pm. Free.) Umeå is also 5km away from the celebrated **Umedalen Sculpture Park,** featuring 35 pieces by leading Swedish and international artists. Take bus #1 or 61 from Vasaplan (20kr, 1hr. transfer) to Umedalen. (☎090 903 64; www.gsa.se. Free.) West of the city, the 30km **Umeleden** bike and car trail snakes past 5000-year-old rock carvings, an arboretum, and **Baggböle Herrgård,** a cafe in a 19th-century manor. (☎090 13 76 00. Open June-Aug. Tu-Su 11am-6pm. Cash only.) Pick up the trail at the **Gamla Bron** (Old Bridge) and veer across the Norvarpsbron to cut the route in half. Hikers can follow the **Tavelsjöleden** trail (30km) along a boulder ridge, or brave the **Isälvsleden** trail (60km), 80km from Umeå and carved out of the stone by melting pack ice.

YMCA Hostel (SVIF) ❷, Järvägsallen 22, offers pleasant, pastel dorms. (☎090 18 57 18; www.hostel.kfum.nu. Breakfast 50kr. Linens 65kr. Towels 25kr. Laundry 6kr. Internet 30kr per hr., 200kr per stay. Reception M-F 8am-noon and 1-6pm, Sa-Su 8-10am and 4-6pm. Dorms 160kr; singles from 330kr; doubles from 420kr. MC/V.) The city center has many cafes and *pâtisseries* (32-48kr). **Taj Mahal ❷,** Vasag. 10, serves a vegetarian-friendly lunch buffet for 79kr. (☎090 12 12 52; www.tajmahalumea.com. Open M-Th 11am-2:30pm and 4-9pm, F 11am-2:30pm and 4-10pm, Sa 4-10pm, Su 2-8pm. MC/V.) Snack on pizza and kebabs (45-65kr) near the train station, or pick up groceries at the **ICA** across from the bus station. (Open daily 8am-8pm. MC/V.) Mingle with students at the bars in **Renmarkstorget Square** or on **Västra Strandgatan** along the river.

Trains run to Gothenburg (11-15hr., 5-6 per day, 632kr). Ybuss **buses** (☎090 70 65 00) run to Stockholm (10hr., 1-3 per day, 415kr, ISIC discount available). The bus terminal is across from the train station on the right. The **tourist office,** Renmarkstorg. 15, gives free English-language tours of the city in summer and has free **Internet.** From the stations, walk to the right down Rådhusespl. and turn right on Skolg. (☎090 16 16 16; www.visitumea.se. Tours W and Su 4pm. Open mid-June to mid-Aug. M-F 8:30am-7pm, Sa 10am-4pm, Su noon-4pm; mid-Aug. to mid-June M-F 10am-5pm.) **Cykel och Mopedhandlaren,** Kungsg. 101, rents **bikes.** (☎090 14 01 70. Open M-F 9:30am-5:30pm, Sa 10am-1pm. 90kr for 1st day, 30kr per day thereafter, 250kr per week. MC/V.) **Postal Code:** 90326.

LAPPLAND (SÁPMI)

Mountains and alpine dales sprawl across Lappland, known as "Europe's last wilderness," a frontier that extends through northern Finland, Norway, Russia, and Sweden. Today, the region's indigenous Sámi people use helicopters and snowmobiles in addition to traditional dogs and lassos to tend their reindeer herds while continuing to wrangle with Stockholm over the hunting and grazing rights their ancestors enjoyed for centuries.

TRANSPORTATION

SJ runs trains along the coastal route from Stockholm through Umeå, Boden, and Kiruna to Narvik, NOR, along the iron ore railway. From late June to early August, **Inlandsbanan** trains run north from Mora (p. 989) through the country. (☎063 19 44 12; www.inlandsbanan.se.) **Buses** are the only way to reach smaller towns; call ☎020 47 00 47 or stop by Kiruna's **tourist office** for schedules.

KIRUNA ☎0980

The only large settlement in Lappland, Kiruna (pop. 18,000), 250km north of the Arctic Circle, retains the rough edges of a mining town, despite its proximity to the chic Riksgänsen ski resort. The **midnight sun** shines for 100 days beginning in late May/early June and lasts until early July.

TRANSPORTATION AND PRACTICAL INFORMATION. SJ **trains** run to Narvik, NOR (3hr., 2 per day, 149-207kr, students 105-146kr) and Luleå (4hr., 3 per day, 250-300kr, students 175-200kr). **Flights** to Stockholm (3-4 per day; from 500kr, students from 350kr) depart from **Kiruna Flygplats** (**KRN;** ☎0980 680 00). The **tourist office,** L. Janssonsgatatan 17, is in the Folkets Hus. Walk from the train station, follow the footpath through the tunnel, and go up the stairs to your right through the park to the top of the hill and cross the street. The office helps arrange **dogsled excursions** (www.kirunanature.com) and **moose safaris.** (☎0980 188 80; www.lappland.se. Internet 20kr per 30min. Open mid-June to mid-Aug. M-Sa 8:30am-6pm, Su 8:30am-5pm; mid-Aug. to mid-June M-F 8:30am-5pm, Sa 8:30am-3pm, closed Su. AmEx/MC/V.) The town **library,** Biblioteksgatan 4, offers free **Internet.** (☎0980 707 50. Open June-Aug. M-Th 1-6pm, F 1-5pm; Sept.-May M-Th 10am-7pm, F 2:30-6pm, Sa-Su 11am-3pm.) **Postal Code:** 98122.

ACCOMMODATIONS AND FOOD. The **Yellow House Hostel ❷,** Hantverkaregatan 25, has spacious rooms. Turn left from the tourist office entrance, walk uphill and turn left after the highway, walk one block and it's on the corner. (☎0980 137 50; www.yellowhouse.nu. Breakfast 50kr. Linens 50kr. Reception 2-11pm. Dorms 150-160kr; singles 300kr; doubles 400kr. MC/V.) **STF Vandrarhem**

(HI) ❷, Bergmästaregatan 7, offers standard rooms in the town center. (☎0980 666 55; www.hotellcity.se. Breakfast 70kr. Linens 50kr. Towels 15kr. Free Wi-Fi. Reception M-F 7am-10pm, Sa-Su 8am-noon and 4-8pm. Dorms 160kr; singles 320kr; doubles 400kr. AmEx/MC/V.) For a two-course lunch (9am-1:30pm, 68kr), head to the cafeteria-style **Svarta Björn,** Hjalmar Lundbohmsvägen 42. (☎0980 157 90. Open July-Aug. M-F 8am-7pm, Sa-Su 11am-3pm; Sept.-June M-F 6:30am-5pm, Sa-Su 11am-1pm. Cash only.) Get groceries at **ICA** in the central square. (Open M-F 9am-7pm, Sa 10am-4pm, Su 11am-4pm. MC/V.)

SIGHTS. While Kiruna's main appeal is its proximity to other sights, the town also has some surprisingly innovative architecture. **Kiruna Church,** Kyrkogatan 8, resembles a Sámi *goahti*, a tent-like dwelling. (☎0980 678 12. Open daily 9am-5:45pm. Free.) **City Hall,** designed by architect Arthur von Schmalensee, houses a small but worthwhile collection of modern art. (☎0980 700 00. Open M-Th June-Aug. 7am-5pm; Sept.-May 8am-5pm. Free.) The state-owned mining company, **LKAB,** was instrumental in the city's founding and development over 100 years ago, and it still hauls 20 million tons of iron ore out of the ground each year. The deposits stretch underneath the city, and recent mining has prompted the decision to move Kiruna's buildings farther north to counter **subsidence,** the downward movement of the Earth's surface. But don't worry about showing up and finding Kiruna displaced—the moving process is expected to take 30 years. LKAB offers 3hr. **InfoMine** tours, which descend 540m to a museum with exhibits on the history of the mine. (2-4 tours per day. Tickets available at the tourist office. 280kr, students 180kr. AmEx/MC/V.) Hikers take **bus** #92 from Kiruna to Nikkaluokta (1hr., 2 per day, 79kr, students 59kr). Hike 19km on the **Kungsleden trail** (King's trail) to reach Kebnekaise Fjällstation, from which you can ascend **Kebnekaise** (2104m), Sweden's highest peak. A week's trek north brings travelers into **Abisko National Park.** The STF runs **cabins** on the trail (☎0980 40 200; www.stfturist.se. Cabins mid-July to mid-Sept. 200-230kr; late Feb. to mid-July 210-240kr. 100kr HI discount. MC/V.) Day hikers can travel directly from Kiruna to Abisko on bus #91 (1hr., 2 per day, 117/return 222kr, students 88/167kr) and choose from any number of trails dotted with waterfalls.

DAYTRIP FROM KIRUNA: JUKKASJÄRVI. Nestled on the shores of the Torne River, the quiet town of Jukkasjärvi (pop. 800; dog pop. 1000; reindeer pop. 5000) transforms into one of the country's hottest tourist spots in winter. The main attraction is the **Icehotel,** which crystallizes anew each November only to melt back into the river each May. The hotel is open for tours in winter (Dec.-Apr.). Summertime visitors get to see more than just a giant puddle—the **Production Hall** offers a view of the ice block storage and cutting process. *(☎0980 668 00; www.icehotel.com. Icehotel open mid-June to Aug. daily 10am-6pm; Dec.-Apr. M-F 10am-6pm. 295kr, students 175kr. AmEx/MC/V.)* The hotel's affiliated museum, **The Homestead,** features a 19th-century family home and a small Sámi exhibit. *(☎0980 668 00. Open only to tours which, in English, leave at 11:15 and 3:15. 40kr. MC/V.)*

Budget **lodgings** do not exist in Jukkasjärvi, save for finding a good spot to pitch your tent. The only restaurants are in the Icehotel and museums. In summer, **Sámi Siida** has traditional Sámi dishes, sandwiches, and drinks (20-40kr) inside a cozy reindeer skin tent. The **Homestead Restaurant,** at the museum, has a 95kr lunch buffet 11am-2pm. *(☎0980 668 07. Open daily 11am-9pm. AmEx/MC/V.)* **Bus** #501 goes to the Kiruna (30min., 2-4 per day, round-trip 55, students 41kr). **Wi-Fi** is available at the Icehotel reception. **Postal Code:** 98191.

SWITZERLAND
(SCHWEIZ, SUISSE, SVIZZERA)

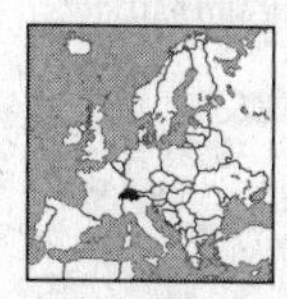

While the stereotype of Switzerland as a country of bankers, chocolatiers, and watchmakers still exists, an energetic youth culture is reviving old images of a pastoral Swiss culture. The country's gorgeous lakes and formidable peaks entice outdoor enthusiasts from around the globe. Mountains dominate about two-thirds of the country: the Jura cover the northwest region, the Alps stretch across the lower half, and the eastern Rhaetian Alps border Austria. Only in Switzerland can one indulge in decadent chocolate as a cultural experience.

DISCOVER SWITZERLAND: SUGGESTED ITINERARIES

THREE DAYS. Experience the outdoors at **Interlaken** (1 day; p. 1003). Head to **Luzern** (1 day; p. 1012) for the perfect combination of city and country before jetting to **Geneva** (1 day; p. 1021).

ONE WEEK. Begin in **Luzern** (1 day), which will fulfill your visions of a charming Swiss city. Then head to the capital, **Bern** (1 day; p. 1000), before getting your adventure thrills in **Interlaken** (1 day). Get a taste of Italian Switzerland in **Lugano** (1 day; p. 1027).

TWO WEEKS. Start in **Geneva** (3 days), then check out **Lausanne** (1 day; p. 1026). Tackle the Matterhorn in **Zermatt** (1 day) and keep hiking above **Interlaken** (1 day). Bask in **Lugano's** sun (1 day), then explore the **Swiss National Park** (1 day; p. 1019). Head to **Luzern** (1 day) and **Zürich** (2 days; p. 1007). Unwind in tiny **Stein am Rhein** (1 day; p. 1015) and visit the abbey of **St. Gallen** (1 day; p. 1014). Return to tall buildings and busy streets via **Bern** (1 day).

ESSENTIALS

FACTS AND FIGURES

OFFICIAL NAME: Swiss Confederation.

CAPITAL: Bern.

MAJOR CITIES: Basel, Geneva, Zürich.

POPULATION: 7,582,000

LAND AREA: 41,300 sq. km.

LANGUAGES: German (64%), French (20%), Italian (10%), Romansch (1%).

RELIGIONS: Roman Catholic (48%), Protestant (44%), other (8%).

TOTAL CHOCOLATE CONSUMED IN 2007: 93,501 tons.

WHEN TO GO

During ski season (Nov.-Mar.) prices double in eastern Switzerland and travelers must make reservations months ahead. The situation reverses in the summer, especially July and August, when the flatter, western half of Switzerland fills with vacationers and hikers enjoying low humidity and temperatures rarely exceeding 26°C (80°F). A good budget option is to travel during the shoulder season: May-June and September-October, when tourism lulls and the daytime temperature ranges from -2 to 7°C (46-59°F). Many mountain towns throughout Switzerland shut down completely in May and June, however, so call ahead.

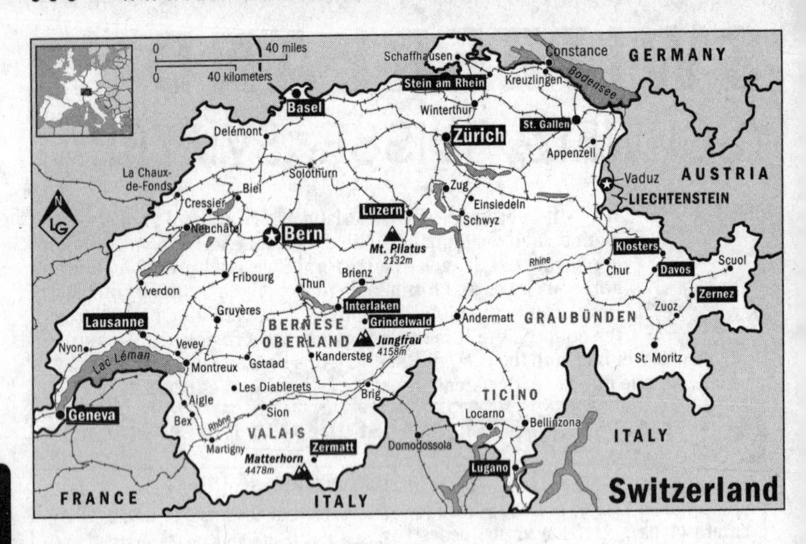

DOCUMENTS AND FORMALITIES

EMBASSIES. Most foreign embassies in Switzerland are in Bern (p. p. 1000). Swiss embassies abroad include: **Australia**, 7 Melbourne Ave., Forrest, Canberra, ACT, 2603 (☎02 6162 8400; www.eda.admin.ch/australia); **Canada**, 5 Marlborough Ave., Ottawa, ON, K1N 8E6 (☎613-235-1837; www.eda.admin.ch/canada); **Ireland,** 6 Ailesbury Rd., Ballsbridge, Dublin, 4 (☎353 12 18 63 82; www.eda.admin.ch/dublin); **New Zealand**, 22 Panama St., Wellington (☎04 472 15 93; www.eda.admin.ch/wellington); **UK,** 16-18 Montagu Pl., London, W1H 2BQ (☎020 76 16 60 00; www.eda.admin.ch/london); **US,** 2900 Cathedral Ave., NW, Washington, D.C., 20008 (☎202-745-7900; www.eda.admin.ch/washington).

VISA AND ENTRY INFORMATION. EU citizens do not need a visa. Citizens of Australia, Canada, New Zealand, and the US do not need a visa for stays of up to 90 days. For stays longer than 90 days, all visitors need visas (around US$52), available at Swiss consulates. Travelers should anticipate a processing time of about six to eight weeks.

TOURIST SERVICES AND MONEY

EMERGENCY	Ambulance: ☎144. Fire: ☎118. Police: ☎117.

TOURIST OFFICES. Branches of the **Swiss National Tourist Office,** marked by a blue "i" sign, are present in nearly every town in Switzerland; most agents speak English. The official tourism website is www.myswitzerland.com.

THE INSIDE SCOOP. If you're planning on spending a long time in Switzerland, consider the **Museum Pass** (30CHF). Available at some tourist offices and venues, it lets you into most major Swiss museums.

MONEY. The Swiss unit of currency is the **Swiss franc (CHF),** plural Swiss francs. One Swiss franc is equal to 100 centimes (called *Rappen* in German Switzerland), with standard denominations of 5, 10, 20, and 50 centimes and 1, 2, and 5CHF in coins; and 10, 20, 50, 100, 200, 500, and 1000CHF in notes. Widely accepted credit cards include American Express, MasterCard, and Visa. Euros (€) are also accepted at many museums and restaurants. Switzerland is not cheap; if you stay in hostels and prepare most of your own food, expect to spend 55-80CHF per day. Generally, it's less expensive to exchange money at home than in Switzerland. ATMs offer the best exchange rates. Although restaurant bills already include a 15% service charge, an additional tip of 1-2CHF for a modest meal or 5-10CHF for a more upscale dinner is expected. Give hotel porters and doormen about 1CHF per bag and airport porters 5CHF per bag.

Switzerland has a 7.6% **value added tax (VAT),** a sales tax applied to goods and services. The prices given in *Let's Go* include VAT. In the airport upon exiting Switzerland, non-Swiss citizens can claim a refund on the tax paid for goods purchased at participating stores. In order to qualify for a refund in a store, you must spend at least 500CHF; make sure to ask for a refund form when you pay. For more info on qualifying for a VAT refund, see p. 21.

SWISS FRANC (CHF)		
	AUS$1 = 0.95CHF	1CHF = AUS$1.05
	CDN$1 = 1.03CHF	1CHF = CDN$0.97
	EUR€1 = 1.61CHF	1CHF = EUR€0.62
	NZ$1 = 0.78CHF	1CHF = NZ$1.28
	UK£1 = 2.04CHF	1CHF = UK£0.49
	US$1 = 1.09CHF	1CHF = US$0.92

TRANSPORTATION

BY PLANE. Major international airports are in **Bern** (BRN; ☎031 960 21 11; www.alpar.ch), **Geneva** (GVA; ☎022 717 71 11; www.gva.ch), and **Zürich** (ZRH; ☎043 816 22 11; www.zurich-airport.com). From London, **easyJet** (☎0871 244 23 66; www.easyjet.com) has flights to Geneva and Zürich. **Aer Lingus** (Ireland ☎0818 365 000, Switzerland 442 86 99 33, UK 0870 876 5000; www.aerlingus.com) sells tickets from Dublin, IRE to Geneva. For info on flying to Switzerland from other locations, see p. 50.

BY TRAIN. Federal (**SBB, CFF**) and private railways connect most towns with frequent trains. For times and prices, check online (www.sbb.ch). **Eurail, Europass,** and **Inter Rail** are all valid on federal trains. The **Swiss Pass,** sold worldwide, offers four, eight, 15, 22, or 30 consecutive days of unlimited rail travel (www.swisstravelsystem.com). It also doubles as a **Swiss Museum Pass,** allowing free entry to 400 museums. (2nd-class 4-day pass US$222, 8-day US$315, 15-day US$384, 22-day US$446, 1-month US$496.)

BY BUS. PTT Post Buses, a barrage of government-run yellow coaches, connect rural villages and towns that trains don't service. Swiss Passes are valid on many buses; Eurail passes are not. Even with the Swiss Pass, you might have to pay 5-10CHF extra if you're riding certain buses.

BY CAR. Roads, generally in good condition, may become dangerous at higher altitudes in the winter. The speed limit is 50kph in towns and cities, 80kph on open roads, and 120kph on highways. Be sure to drive under the speed limit; radar traps are frequent. Many small towns forbid cars; some require special permits or restrict driving hours. US and British citizens 18 and older with a valid driver's license may drive in Switzerland for up to one year following their arrival; for stays longer than one year, drivers should contact the **Service des automobiles et de la navigation** (SAN; ☎022 388 30 30; www.geneve.ch/san) about acquiring a Swiss permit. Custom posts sell windshield stickers (US$33) required for driving on Swiss roads. Call ☎140 for roadside assistance.

BY BIKE. Cycling is a splendid way to see the country. Find bikes to rent at large train stations. The **Touring Club Suisse,** (☎022 417 22 20; www.tcs.ch), is a good source for maps and route descriptions.

KEEPING IN TOUCH

PHONE CODES	**Country code:** 41. **International dialing prefix:** 00. For more information on how to place international calls, see **Inside Back Cover.**

EMAIL AND INTERNET. Most Swiss cities, as well as a number of smaller towns, have at least one Internet cafe with web access available for about 12-24CHF per hour. Hostels and restaurants frequently offer Internet access as well, but it seldom comes for free: rates can climb as high as 12CHF per hour.

TELEPHONE. Whenever possible, use a calling card for international phone calls, as long-distance rates are often exorbitant for national phone services. For info about using mobile phones abroad, see p. 32. Most pay phones in Switzerland accept only prepaid taxcards, which are available at kiosks, post offices, and train stations. Direct access numbers include: **AT&T Direct** (☎800 89 00 11); **Canada Direct** (☎800 55 83 30); **MCI WorldPhone** (☎800 89 02 22); **Sprint** (☎800 899 777); **Telecom New Zealand** (☎800 55 64 11).

MAIL. Airmail from Switzerland averages three to 15 days to North America, although times are unpredictable from smaller towns. Domestic letters take one to three days. Bright yellow logos mark Swiss national post offices, referred to as **Die Post** in German or **La Poste** in French. Letters from Switzerland cost 1.40CHF to mail to the US, 1.20CHF to mail to the UK, and 0.85CHF mailed domestically. To receive mail in Switzerland, have mail delivered **Poste Restante.** Mail will go to the main post office unless you specify a subsidiary by street address. Address mail to be held as follows: LAST NAME, First Name, *Postlagernde Briefe*, Postal Code, City, SWITZERLAND. Bring a passport to pick up your mail; there may be a small fee.

ACCOMMODATIONS AND CAMPING

SWITZERLAND	❶	❷	❸	❹	❺
ACCOMMODATIONS	under 30CHF	30-42CHF	43-65CHF	66-125CHF	over 125CHF

There are hostels (*Jugendherbergen* in German, *Auberges de Jeunesse* in French, *Ostelli* in Italian) in all cities in Switzerland as well as in most towns. **Schweizer Jugendherbergen** (SJH; www.youthhostel.ch) runs HI hostels throughout Switzerland. Non-HI members can stay in any HI hostel, where beds are usually 30-44CHF; members typically receive a 6CHF discount. The more informal **Swiss Backpackers** (SB) organization (☎062 892 2675; www.backpacker.ch) lists over 40 hostels aimed at young, foreign travelers interested in socializing. Most **Swiss campgrounds** are not idyllic refuges but large plots glutted with RVs. Prices average 12-20CHF per tent site per night and 6-9CHF per extra person. **Hotels** and **pensions** tend to charge at least 65-80CHF for a single room and 80-120CHF for a double. The cheapest have *Gasthof*, *Gästehaus*, or *Hotel-Garni* in the name. **Privatzimmer** (rooms in a family home) run about 30-60CHF per person. Breakfast is included at most hotels, pensions, and *Privatzimmer*.

HIKING AND SKIING. Nearly every town has **hiking trails:** Interlaken (p. 1003), Grindelwald (p. 1006), Luzern (p. 1012), and Zermatt (p. 1020) offer particularly good hiking opportunities. Trails are marked with either red-white-red markers (only sturdy boots and hiking poles needed) or blue-white-blue markers (mountaineering equipment needed). **Skiing** in Switzerland is less expensive than in North America, provided you avoid pricey resorts. **Ski passes** run 40-70CHF per day, 100-300CHF per week; a week of lift tickets, equipment rental, lessons, lodging, and demi-pension (breakfast plus one other meal) averages 475CHF. **Summer skiing** is available in a few towns.

FOOD AND DRINK

SWITZERLAND	❶	❷	❸	❹	❺
FOOD	under 9CHF	9-23CHF	24-32CHF	33-52CHF	over 52CHF

Switzerland is not for the lactose intolerant. The Swiss are serious about dairy products, from rich and varied **cheeses** to decadent **milk chocolate**—even the major Swiss soft drink, **Rivella,** contains dairy. Swiss dishes vary from region to region. Bernese **rösti,** a plateful of hash-brown potatoes (sometimes flavored with bacon or cheese), is prevalent in the German regions; cheese or meat **fondue** is popular in the French regions. Try Valaisian **raclette,** made by melting cheese over a fire, scraping it onto a baked potato, and garnishing it with meat or vegetables. Supermarkets **Migros** and **Co-op** double as cafeterias; stop in for a cheap meal and groceries. Water from the fountains that adorn cities and large towns is usually safe; filling your bottle with it will save you money. *Kein Trinkwasser* or *Eau non potable* signs indicate unclean water. Each canton has its own local beer, which is often cheaper than soda.

HOLIDAYS AND FESTIVALS

Holidays: New Year's Day (Jan. 1); Epiphany (Jan. 6); Good Friday (Apr. 10); Easter (Apr. 13); Ascension (May 21); Labor Day (May 1); Whit Monday (Jun. 1); Swiss National Day (Aug. 1); All Saints' Day (Nov. 1); Christmas (Dec. 25-26).

Festivals: Two raucous festivals are the *Fasnacht* (Mar. 2-4, 2009; www.fasnacht.ch) in Basel and the *Escalade*, celebrating the invading Duke of Savoy's 1602 defeat by Geneva (Dec. 11-13, 2009; www.compagniede1602.ch). Music festivals occur throughout the summer, including Open-Air St. Gallen (late June; ☎0900 500 700; www.openairsg.ch) and the Montreux Jazz Festival (July; ☎963 8282; www.montreux.ch/mjf).

BEYOND TOURISM

Although Switzerland's volunteer opportunities are limited, a number of ecotourism and rural development organizations allow you to give back to the country. Your best bet is to go through a placement service. Look for opportunities for short-term work on websites like www.emploi.ch. For more info on opportunities across Europe, see **Beyond Tourism,** see p. 60.

Bergwald Projekt/Mountain Forest Project, Hauptstr. 24, 7014 Trin (☎081 650 40 40; www.bergwaldprojekt.ch). Organizes week-long conservation projects in Austria, Germany, and Switzerland.

Workcamp Switzerland, Komturei Tobel, Postfach 7, 9555 Tobel (☎071 917 24 86; www.workcamp.ch). Offers 2-4 week sessions during which volunteers live in a group environment and work on a community service project.

GERMAN SWITZERLAND

German Switzerland encompasses 65% of the country. While the region's intoxicating brews and industrious cities will remind visitors of Germany, the natural beauty at every turn is uniquely Swiss. Different forms of Swiss German, a dialect distinct from High German, are spoken here.

BERNESE OBERLAND

The peaks of the Bernese Oberland shelter a pristine wilderness best seen on hikes up the mountains and around the twin lakes, Thunersee and Brienzersee. Not surprisingly, the area's opportunities for paragliding, mountaineering, and whitewater rafting are unparalleled. North of the mountains lies the relaxed city of Bern, Switzerland's capital and the heart of the region.

BERN ☎031

Bern (pop. 128,000) has been Switzerland's capital since 1848, but don't expect power politics or businessmen in suits—the Bernese prefer to focus on the more leisurely things in life, like strolling through the arcades of the *Altstadt* or meandering along the banks of the serpentine Aare River.

TRANSPORTATION AND PRACTICAL INFORMATION. Bern's small **airport** (**BRN;** ☎031 960 2111) is 20min. from the city. A **bus** runs from the train station 50min. before each flight (10min., 14CHF). **Trains** run from the station at Bahnhofpl. to: Geneva (2hr., 2 per hr., 45CHF); Luzern (1hr., 2 per hr., 35CHF); St. Gallen (2hr., every hr., 65CHF); Zürich (1hr., 4 per day, 46CHF); Berlin, GER (12hr., 1-2 per hr., 95CHF); Paris, FRA (6hr., 4-5 per day, 115CHF). Local Bernmobil **buses** (departing from the left of the train station) and **trams** (departing from the front of the station) run 5:45am-midnight. (☎321 86 41; www.bernmobil.ch. Single ride 3.80CHF, day pass 12CHF.) Buses depart from the back of the station and post office. **Free bikes** are available from Bern Rollt at two locations: on Hirscheng. near the train station and on Zeugausg. near Waisenhauspl. (☎079 652 2319; www.bernrollt.ch. Passport and 20CHF deposit. Open May-Oct. daily 7:30am-9:30pm.)

Most of old Bern lies to your left as you leave the train station, along the Aare River. Bern's main train station is an often confusing tangle of essential services and extraneous shops. Take extra caution in the parks around the Parliament (Bundeshaus), especially at night. The **tourist office** is on the street level of the station. (☎031 328 1212; www.berninfo.ch. Open June-Sept. daily 9am-8:30pm; Oct.-May M-Sa 9am-6:30pm, Su 10am-5pm.) The **post office,** Schanzen-

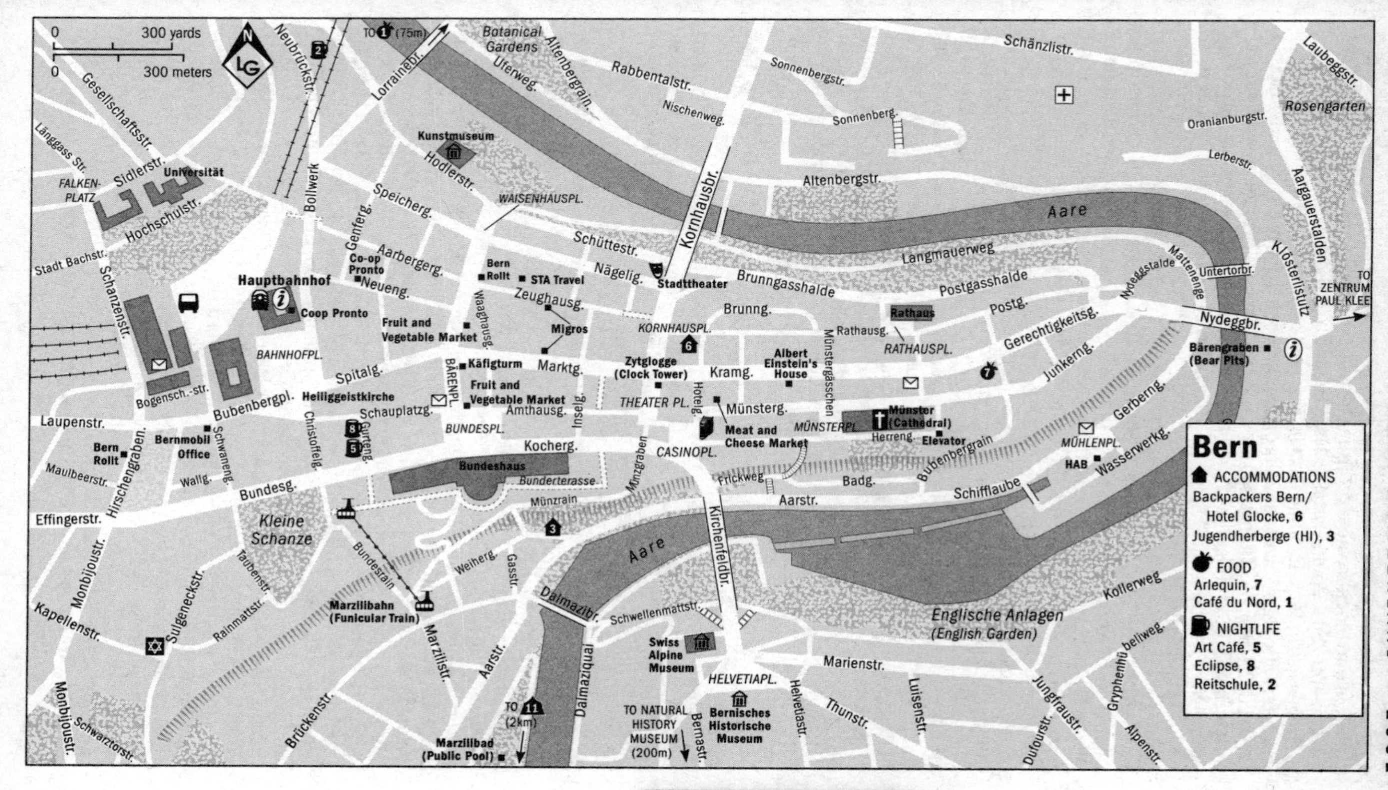

SWITZERLAND

post 1, is one block to the right from the train station. (Open M-F 7:30am-9pm, Sa 8am-4pm, Su 4-9pm.) **Postal Codes:** CH-3000 to CH-3030.

Embassies in Bern include: **Canada,** Kirchenfeldstr. 88 (☎031 357 3200; www.geo.international.gc.ca/canada-europa/switzerland); **Ireland,** Kirchenfeldstr. 68 (☎031 352 1442); **UK,** Thunstr. 50 (☎031 359 7700; www.britishembassy.gov.uk/switzerland); **US,** Jubilaumsstr. 93 (☎031 357 7011; bern.usembassy.gov). The **Australian** consulate is in Geneva (p. 1022). **New Zealanders** should contact their embassy in Berlin, GER (p. 393).

ACCOMMODATIONS AND FOOD. If Bern's cheaper hostels are full, check the tourist office for a list of private rooms. **Backpackers Bern/Hotel Glocke ❷,** Rathausg. 75, in the middle of the *Altstadt*, has friendly owners and a large common room. From the train station, cross the tram lines and turn left on Spitalg., continuing onto Marktg. Turn left at Kornhauspl., then right on Rathausg. (☎031 311 3771; www.bernbackpackers.ch. Internet 1CHF per 10min. Reception 8am-noon and 3-10pm. Dorms 33CHF; singles 69CHF; doubles 82CHF, with bath 140CHF; quads 172CHF. AmEx/MC/V.) At **Jugendherberge (HI) ❷,** Weiherg. 4 near the river, guests receive free access to a public swimming pool. (☎031 311 6316; www.youthhostel.ch/bern. Dorms 33CHF; singles 55CHF; doubles 84-98CHF; quads 148CHF. 6CHF HI discount. AmEx/MC/V.)

Markets sell produce, cheese, and meats daily at Weinhauspl. and every Tuesday and Saturday on Bundespl. and Munstergasse from May through October. A friendly couple owns **Arlequin ❷,** Gerechtigkeitsg. 51, an 80s-inspired restaurant. (☎031 311 3946. Sandwiches 6-12CHF. Meat fondue 35CHF. Open Tu-W 11am-11:30pm, Th-F 11am-1:30am, Sa 11am-11pm. AmEx/MC/V; min. 20CHF.) A diverse crowd gathers under stage lights on the terrace at **Café du Nord ❸,** Lorrainestr. 2, and enjoys an all-organic menu. (☎031 332 2328. Pasta 19-25CHF. Meat entrees 22-32CHF. Open M-W 8am-11:30pm, Th-F 8am-1:30am, Sa 9am-1:30am, Su 4pm-11:30pm. Kitchen open M-Sa 11:30am-2pm and 6:30-10pm, Su 4:30-11:30pm. MC/V.) For groceries, head to **Migros,** Marktg. 46. (Open M 9am-6:30pm, Tu 8am-6:30pm, W-F 8am-9pm, Sa 7am-4pm.)

SIGHTS. Bern's historic center *(Altstadt)*, one of the best-preserved in Switzerland, is a UNESCO World Heritage sight. Covered arcades allow for wandering and window shopping, while the wide cobblestone streets are dotted by medieval wells topped with Renaissance statues. The Swiss national parliament meets in the massive **Bundeshaus,** which rises high over the Aare; water tumbles from fountains in front of the entrance. (www.parlament.ch. One 45min. tour per hr. M-Sa 9-11am and 2-4pm. English-language tour usually 2pm. Free.) From the Bundeshaus, Kocherg. and Herreng. lead to the 15th-century Protestant **Münster** (Cathedral); above the main entrance, a golden sculpture depicts the torments of hell. For a fantastic view of the city, climb the Münster's 100m spire. (Cathedral open Easter-Oct. Tu-Sa 10am-5pm, Su. 11:30am-5pm; Nov.-Easter Tu-Sa 10am-noon, Su 11:30am-2pm. Free. Audio guide 5CHF. Tower open Easter-Oct. M-Sa 10am-4:30pm, Su 11:30am-4:30pm; Nov.-Mar. M-F 2pm-3pm, Sa 2pm-5pm, Su 11:30am-1pm. 4CHF.) For some early medieval flair, check out the **Zytglogge,** a 12th-century clock tower on Kramg. that once marked the city's western boundary. Watch the golden figure use his hammer to ring the golden bell at the top every hour. Down the road is **Albert Einstein's house,** Kramg. 49, where he conceived the theory of general relativity in 1915. His small apartment is now filled with photos and letters. (☎031 312 0091; www.einstein-bern.ch. Open Apr.-Sept. daily 10am-5pm; Feb.-Mar. Tu-F 10am-5pm, Sa 10am-4pm. 6CHF, students 4.50CHF.) Several steep walkways lead from the Bundeshaus to the **Aare River.**

A recent addition to Bern's many museums is the **Zentrum Paul Klee,** Monument im Fruchtland 3, which houses the world's largest collection of artwork by the renowned Paul Klee. (☎031 359 0101; www.zpk.org. Take bus #12 to Zentrum Paul Klee. Open Tu-Su 10am-5pm. 16CHF, students 14CHF.) Near Lorrainebrücke, the **Kunstmuseum,** Hodlerstr. 8-12, has paintings from the Middle Ages to the contemporary era and features a smattering of big 20th-century names: Giacometti, Kandinsky, Kirchner, Picasso, and Pollock. (☎031 328 0944; www.kunstmuseumbern.ch. Open Tu-Su 10am-5pm. 7CHF, students 5CHF. Special exhibits up to 18CHF.) At the east side of the river, across the Nydeggbrücke, lie the **Bärengraben** (Bear Pits), where gawking crowds observe three European brown bears—the city's namesake. (Open daily June-Sept. 9:30am-5pm; Oct.-May 10am-4pm.) The path up the hill to the left leads to the **Rosengarten** (Rose Garden), which provides visitors with a breathtaking view of Bern's *Altstadt,* especially at sunset. Anything and everything relating to Bern's long history, from technological innovations to religious art, is on display in the jam-packed **Bernisches Historische Museum,** Helvetiapl. 5. (☎031 350 7711; www.bhm.ch. Open Tu-F 10am-5pm. 13CHF, students 8CHF.)

ENTERTAINMENT AND NIGHTLIFE. Check out *Bewegungsmelder,* available at the tourist office, for events. July's **Gurten Festival** (www.gurtenfestival.ch) draws young and energetic crowds and has attracted such luminaries as Bob Dylan and Elvis Costello, while jazz-lovers arrive in early May for the **International Jazz Festival** (www.jazzfestivalbern.ch). Bern's traditional folk festival is the **Onion Market,** which brings 50 tons of onions to the city (late Nov. 2009). The orange grove at **Stadtgärtnerei Elfenau** (tram #19, dir.: Elfenau, to Luternauweg) has free Sunday concerts in the summer. From mid-July to mid-August, **Orange-Cinema** (☎0800 07 80 78; www.orangecinema.ch) screens recent films outdoors; tickets are available from the tourist office in the train station.

Find new DJs at **Art Café,** Gurteng. 6, a cafe and club with huge windows overlooking the street. (☎031 318 2070. Open M-W 7am- 1:30am, Th-F 7am-3:30am, Sa 8am-3:30am, Su 10am-3:30am. Cash only.) The Art Café crowd wanders next door to dance to funky beats at **Eclipse,** which has the same owners. (☎031 882 0888; www.eclipse-bar.ch. Open M-W 7am- 1:30am, Th-F 7am-3am, Sa 9am-3am.) Many locals gather at **Gut Gelaunt,** Shauptplatzgasse 22, just around the corner, to relax outside and enjoy the special 12-14CHF alcoholic gelato sundaes. (☎031 312 8989; www.gutgelaunt.ch. Beer 4-6CHF, and wine 6-8CHF. Open noon-midnight.) To escape the fashionable folk that gather in the *Altstadt* at night, head to the **Reitschule,** Neubrückestr. 8, a graffiti-covered center for Bern's counterculture. (Open daily 8pm-late.)

JUNGFRAU REGION

The most famous region of the Bernese Oberland, Jungfrau draws tourists with its hiking trails, glacier lakes, and snow-capped peaks. From Interlaken, the valley splits at the foot of the Jungfrau Mountain. The eastern valley contains Grindelwald, with easy access to two glaciers, while the western valley harbors many smaller towns. The two valleys are divided by an easily hikeable ridge.

INTERLAKEN ☎033

Interlaken (pop. 5,700) lies between the Thunersee and the Brienzersee at the foot of the largest mountains in Switzerland. Countless hiking trails, raging rivers,

A SAINTLY BREED

n AD 1050, the Archdeacon Ber-
ıard de Menthon founded a hos-
oice in a mountain pass in the
ungfrau region and brought with
ıim a breed of large, furry dogs of
Gallic origin. In addition to provid-
ng shelter for passing merchants,
Bernard and the monks working
ınder him would venture into bliz-
ards in search of stranded travelers. Though it is uncertain whether
he dogs accompanied the monks
on their rescue missions—early
accounts relate that dogs were used
o run an exercise wheel that turned
a cooking spit—by the time of Ber-
ıard's canonization, dogs bearing
ıis name had become famous and
egularly patrolled the pass (now
also named after Bernard).

Gifted with a fine sense of
smell, a thick coat, an amiable
manner, and a neck just made to
ie a barrel of brandy to, the St.
Bernards made a name for themselves by saving over 2000 lives
over several hundred years. In the
810s, a single dog named Barry
saved 40 lost travelers. Today, few
St. Bernards still work as rescue
dogs—smaller, lighter breeds less
iable to sink in the snow have
aken their place. The St. Bernard
s now a popular household pet,
as well as the star of popular films
ike *Cujo* and the *Beethoven* moves. But it will always have dignity
as the Alpine fixture it once was.

and peaceful lakes have turned the town into one of Switzerland's prime tourist attractions and its top adventure-sport destination.

TRANSPORTATION AND PRACTICAL INFORMATION. Westbahnhof (☎033 826 4750) and Ostbahnhof (☎033 828 7319) have **trains** to: Basel (2-3hr., 1-2 per hr., 55CHF); Bern (1hr., 1-2 per hr., 26CHF); Geneva (3hr., 1-2 per hr., 65CHF); Zürich (2hr., 1 per 2hr., 63CHF). Ostbahnhof also sends trains to Grindelwald (1-2 per hr., 10.20CHF) and Luzern (2hr., 1-2 per hr., 55CHF).

The **tourist office,** Höheweg 37, in Hotel Metropole, gives out **maps** and books accommodations for free. (☎033 826 5300; www.interlaken.ch. Open May-Oct. M-F 8am-7pm, Sa 8am-5pm, Su 10am-noon and 5pm-7pm; Nov.-Apr. M-F 8am-noon and 1:30-6pm, Sa 9am-noon.) Both train stations rent **bikes.** (33CHF per day. Open M-F 6am-8pm, Sa-Su 8am-8pm.) The **post office** is at Marktg. 1. (Open M-F 8am-noon and 1:45-6pm, Sa 8:30am-11am.) **Postal Code:** CH-3800.

ACCOMMODATIONS AND FOOD. Interlaken is a backpacking hot spot, especially in summer months, so hostels tend to fill up quickly; reserve more than a month ahead. Diagonally across the Höhenmatte from the tourist office, the friendly, low-key **Backpackers Villa Sonnenhof ❷,** Alpenstr. 16, includes admission to a nearby spa for the duration of your stay, minigolf, and free use of local buses. (☎033 826 7171; www.villa.ch. Breakfast included. Laundry 10CHF. Internet 1CHF per 8min. Free Wi-Fi. Reception 7:30-11am and 4-10pm. Dorms 35-37CHF; doubles 98CHF; triples 135CHF; quads 156CHF. AmEx/MC/V.) In contrast, **Balmer's Herberge ❶,** Hauptstr. 23, Switzerland's oldest private hostel (est. 1945), is a place to party. Services include mountain bike rental (35CHF per day), nightly movies, free sleds, and an extremely popular bar. This hostel is also right next to all the adventure companies, which makes for very convenient booking. (☎033 822 1961; www.balmers.ch. Breakfast included. Laundry 4CHF. Internet 10CHF per hr. Reception in summer 7am-9pm; in winter 6:30-10am and 4:30-10pm. Dorms 27-30CHF; doubles 74-80CHF; triples 99-105CHF; quads 132-146CHF. AmEx/MC/V.)

My Little Thai ❷, Hauptstr. 19 (right next to Balmer's Herberge), fills with hungry backpackers in the evening. (☎033 821 1017; www.mylittlethai.ch. Pad thai 16-22CHF. Vegetarian options available. Internet 8CHF per hr. Open daily 11:30am-10pm. AmEx/MC/V.) **El Azteca ❷,** Jungfraustr. 30, serves cactus salad (16CHF), fajitas (28-38CHF), and other Mexican fare. (☎033 822 7131. Open daily 7:30am-2pm and 6:30pm-11:30pm. AmEx/MC/V.) While ethnic restaurants from around the world line the streets, There are **Migros** and **Coop** supermarkets by both train stations. (Open M-Th 8am-6:30pm, F 8am-9pm, Sa 7:30am-5pm.)

OUTDOOR ACTIVITIES. With the incredible surrounding Alpine scenery, it's no wonder that many of Interlaken's tourists seem compelled to try otherwise unthinkable adventure sports. **Alpin Raft,** Hauptstr. 7 (☎033 823 4100; www.alpinraft.ch), the most established company in Interlaken, has qualified, entertaining guides and offers a wide range of activities, including paragliding (150CHF), river rafting (99-110CHF), skydiving (380-430CHF), and hang-gliding (185CHF). They also offer two different types of **bungee jumping.** At the 85m **Glacier Bungee Jump** (125CHF), thrill-seekers leap off a ledge above the Lutschine River. At the **Alpin Rush Jump** (165CHF), jumpers attached to one of the longest bungee cords in the world leap out of a gondola 134m above a lake, surrounded by the green peaks of the Simmental Valley and herds of grazing cattle. One of the most popular adventure activities at Alpin Raft is **canyoning** (110-175CHF), which involves rappelling down a series of gorge faces, jumping off cliffs into pools of churning water, and swinging—Tarzan-style—from ropes and zip cords through the canyon. All prices include transportation to and from any hostel in Interlaken and usually a beer upon completion. **Skywings Adventures** has witty professionals and a wide range of activities from paragliding (150-220CHF) to river rafting (99CHF); their booth is across the street from the tourist office (☎079 266 8228; www.skywings.ch). **Outdoor Interlaken,** Hauptstr. 15 (☎826 7719; www.outdoor-interlaken.ch), offers many of the same activities as Alpin Raft at similar prices, as well as rock-climbing lessons (half-day 89CHF) and whitewater **kayaking** tours (half-day 155CHF). At **Skydive Xdream,** you can skydive with one of the best in the world; the owner, Stefan Heuser, was on the Swiss skydiving team for 12 years and won three world championship medals. Skydivers can make their ascent over gorges and glaciers in a glass-walled helicopter, then jump from a standing position—an exhilarating option that's very different from the usual sitting take-off. (☎079 759 3483; www.justjump.ch. 380CHF per tandem plane jump; 430CHF per tandem helicopter jump. Open year-round. Pick-ups M-F 9am and 1pm, Sa-Su also 4pm. Call for winter availability.) Swiss Alpine Guide offers **ice climbing,** running full-day trips to a nearby glacier and providing all the equipment needed to scale vertical glacier walls and rappel into icy crevasses. (☎033 822 6000; www.swissalpineguides.ch. Trips May-Nov. daily, weather permitting; 160CHF.)

ADVENTURE WITH CAUTION. Interlaken's adventure sports industry is thrilling, but accidents do happen. On July 27, 1999, 21 tourists were killed by a sudden flash flood while canyoning. Be aware that you participate in all adventure sports at your own risk.

Interlaken's most-traversed trail climbs **Harder Kulm** (1310m). From the Ostbahnhof, head toward town, take the first road bridge right across the river, and follow the yellow signs that give way to white-red-white rock markings. From the top, signs lead back down to the Westbahnhof. The hike should be about 2hr. up and 1hr. down. In summer, the Harderbahn **funicular** runs from the trailhead to the top. (Open daily May to Oct. 15CHF, round-trip 25CHF. 25% Eurail and 50% SwissPass discount.) For a flatter trail, turn left from the train station and left again before the bridge; follow the canal over to the nature reserve on the shore of the **Thunersee.** The 3hr. trail winds along the Lombach River, through pastures at the base of Harder Kulm, and back toward town.

THE LOCAL STORY

ADVENTURE IN THE BLOOD

Let's Go interviewed Beat Schwiezer, an Interlaken native and founder of Skydive Interlaken, and Andrew Pfeiffer, tandem skydive instructor from Australia.

LG: Which sex jumps more frequently, male or female?

A: Among the locals, we mostly get big athletic males jumping. Among tourists our clientele is equal, maybe slightly more female.

LG: How dangerous is skydiving?

A: Tandem skydiving is actually quite safe. Skydiving starts to get dangerous when people jump by themselves and freefall for too long. More recently, skydiving has gotten even safer due to improved technology. We use the same parachutes as NASA, which have to be recycled every few years.

LG: Are there jumping age limits?

B: The lower limit is 16 for us. We don't have any upper limit though. We have this one 88 year old who comes and jumps every year.

LG: So basically, you get paid to jump out of airplanes all day. Sweet job. Your favorite part?

A: Obviously I love the jumping part—this is the best place to skydive in the world. With the helicopter, we get to jump right next to the mountains, and as you fall you get an amazing view of the two lakes, turquoise *Thunersee* and blue *Brienzersee*. But it's really wonderful to help people experience something so new and exciting.

B: So, are you ready to jump?!?

LG: Yes! Let's Go!!!

GRINDELWALD ☎033

Interlaken is frenetic center for adventure sports; Grindelwald (pop. 3,800) is its more serene counterpart, nestled right in the mountains, with more opportunities for hiking and skiing. Tucked between the Eiger and the Jungfraujoch, the village is the launching point for the only glaciers accessible by foot in the Bernese Oberland. The **Bergführerbüro** (Mountain Guide's Office), in the sports center near the tourist office, sells hiking **maps** and coordinates glacier walks, ice climbing, and mountaineering. (☎033 853 1200. Open June-Oct. M-F 9am-noon and 2-5pm.) The **Untere Grindelwaldgletscher** (Lower Glacier) hike is moderately steep (5hr.). To reach the trailhead, walk away from the station on the main street and follow the signs downhill to Pfinstegg. Hikers can either walk the first forested section of the trail (1hr.) or take a funicular. (Daily July-mid-Sept. 8am-7pm; mid-Sept. to June 9am-5:30pm. 12CHF, SwissPass 9CHF.) From there, signs lead up the glacier-filled valley to **Stiereggaße,** which sells food. Grindelwald is also the largest ski resort in the Jungfrau, with 220 km of slopes; the **Sportpass Jungfrau** gives you access to the entire region (2 days 126CHF, 3 days 173CHF, 6 days 302CHF). Grindelwald has countless **toboggan** courses, including **Europe's longest run**—during the winter, hike to Faulhorn peak (3hr.), then glide a thrilling 15km back to the village on the "Big Pintenfritz."

Pet goats greet guests at the **Jugendherberge (HI) ❷**, whose rooms have terraces that look out onto spectacular views. To reach the lodge, head left out of the train station for 400m, then cut uphill to the right and follow the steep trail all the way up the hill for 20 minutes. (☎033 853 1009; www.youthhostel.ch/grindelwald. Breakfast included. Reception 7:30-10am and 3-10pm. Dorms 29-37CHF in summer, 31-38CHF in winter; doubles 76-106CHF/78-106. 6CHF HI discount. AmEx/MC/V.) **Downtown Lodge ❶** is conveniently located to the right of the train station. It offers great views of the mountains, as well as free entrance to the public swimming pool, free Internet, and free Wi-Fi. (☎033 853 0825; www.downtown-lodge.ch. Breakfast included. Dorms 25-35CHF; doubles 70-90CHF. AmEx/MC/V.) A **Coop** supermarket is on Hauptstr., across from the tourist office. (Open M-F 8am-6:30pm, Sa 8am-6pm.)

The **Jungfraubahn train** runs to Grindelwald from Interlaken's Ostbahnhof (35min., 2 per hr., 10.20CHF). The **tourist office** is in the Sport-Zentrum 200m from the station. (☎033 854 1212. Open July-

Aug. M-F 8am-noon, 1:30-6pm, Sa 8am-noon,1:30-5pm; Sept.-June M-F 9am-noon, 2-5pm, Sa 2-5pm.) **Postal Code:** CH-3818.

DAYTRIP FROM GRINDELWALD: JUNGFRAUJOCH. It's a splurge to reach "the top of Europe," but the Jungfrau mountaintop, with Europe's highest train station and an eerie snow-filled landscape year-round, remains one of Switzerland's most popular destinations. The peak offers more than just a pretty view of the **Aletschgletscher,** the longest glacier in the Alps. Since the completion of the **Jungfrau Railway** in 1912, the building at the summit has evolved from a wood and aluminum Tourist Lodge to the present five-story complex, which includes three restaurants, two outdoor lookout points, an **Ice Palace** (tunnels of ice with ice sculptures), and an exhibition room. The **adventure center** is a fun stop, with free sleds, a Flying Fox zipline, a hole-in-one golf tee, and an all-day summer ski pass (33CHF). Follow the signs toward the Aletschgletscher. The **Jungfraubahn** runs from Grindelwald to the peak. Don't forget to bring a jacket—temperatures usually hover around 3° C. *(Open year-round. Trains 1½hr., 2 per hr., 155CHF. Last train 2:30pm. First train back from Jungafraujoch 8:37am. Good Morning ticket 135CHF; departs Grindelwald at 6:55am. Swiss Pass discounts available.)*

CENTRAL SWITZERLAND

In contrast to the unspoiled scenic vistas of the mountainous southern cantons, Central Switzerland seems to overflow with people and culture. Unique museums, majestic cathedrals, and lovely *Altstädte* (Old Towns) in Zürich and other cities are the main attractions of this vibrant region.

ZÜRICH ☎044

Battalions of executives charge daily through Zürich, Switzerland's largest city (pop. 370,000) and the world's fourth-largest stock exchange—bringing with them enough money to keep upper-crust boutiques thriving. But only footsteps away from the flashy Bahnhofstr. shopping district is the old town and city's student quarter, home to cobblestoned pieces of history and an energetic counter-culture that has inspired generations of Swiss philosophers and artists.

TRANSPORTATION

Flights: Zürich-Kloten Airport (**ZRH;** ☎044 816 2211; www.zurich-airport.com) is a major hub for Swiss International Airlines (☎084 885 2000; www.swiss.com). Daily connections to: **Frankfurt, GER; London, BRI; Paris, FRA.** Trains connect the airport to the Hauptbahnhof in the city center. 3-6 per hr., 6CHF; Eurail and SwissPass valid.

Trains: Run to: **Basel** (1hr., 2-3 per hr., 31CHF); **Bern** (1hr., 3-4 per hr., 46CHF); **Geneva** (3hr., 1-2 per hr., 88CHF); **Luzern** (1hr., 1-2 per hr., 23CHF); **St. Gallen** (30min.; 2-3 per hr.; 28CHF); **Milan, ITA** (4hr., 1 per 2hr., 72-87CHF); **Munich, GER** (5hr., 4-5 per day, 90CHF); **Paris, FRA** (5hr., 4 per day, 112-140CHF, under 26 86CHF).

Public Transportation: Trams criss-cross the city, originating at the *Hauptbahnhof.* Tickets valid for 1hr. cost 4CHF (press the blue button on automatic ticket machines); tickets (valid for 30min.) cost 2.40CHF (yellow button). Police fine riders without tickets 60CHF. If you plan to ride several times, buy a 24hr. **Tageskarte** (7.60CHF; green button), valid on trams, buses, and ferries. **Night buses** (5CHF ticket valid all night) run from the city center to outlying areas (F-Su).

Car Rental: The tourist office offers a 20% discount and free upgrade deal with **Europcar** (☎044 804 4646; www.europcar.ch). Prices from 155CHF per day with unlimited mileage. 20+. Branches at the airport (☎043 255 5656), Josefstr. 53 (☎044 271 5656), and Lindenstr. 33 (☎044 383 1747). Rent in the city; 40% tax is added at the airport.

Bike Rental: Bike loans from **Züri Rollt** (☎043 288 3400; www.zuerirollt.ch) are free for 6hr. during business hours; otherwise 5CHF per day, 20CHF per night. Pick up a bike from **Globus City,** the green hut on the edge of the garden between Bahnhofstr. and Löwenstr.; **Opernhaus**, by the opera house past Bellevuepl.; **Velogate,** across from Hauptbahnhof's tracks next to the Landesmuseum castle. Bikes must be returned to original rental station. Passport and 20CHF deposit. Open May-Oct. 7:30am-11:30pm.

ORIENTATION AND PRACTICAL INFORMATION

Zürich is in north-central Switzerland, close to the German border and on some of the lowest land in the country. The **Limmat River** splits the city down the middle on its way to the **Zürichsee** (Lake Zürich). The **Hauptbahnhof** (train station) lies on the western bank and marks the beginning of **Bahnhofstraße,** the city's main shopping street. Two-thirds of the way down Bahnhofstr. lies **Paradeplatz,** the banking center of Zürich, which marks the beginning of the last stretch of the shopping street (reserved for those with trust funds). The eastern bank of the river is dominated by the university district, which stretches above the narrow **Niederdorfstraße** and pulses with bars, clubs, and restaurants.

Tourist Office: In the **Hauptbahnhof** (☎044 215 4000; www.zuerich.com). An electronic hotel reservation board is at the front of the station. Also sells the **ZürichCARD,** which is good for unlimited public transportation, free museum admission, and discounts on sights and tours (1-day 17CHF, 3-day 34CHF). Open May-Oct. M-Sa 8am-8:30pm, Su 8:30am-6:30pm; Nov.-Apr. M-Sa 8:30am-7pm, Su 9am-6:30pm.

Currency Exchange: On the main floor of the train station. Cash advances for MC/V with photo ID; min. 200CHF, max. 1000CHF. Open daily 6:30am-9:30pm. **Crédit Suisse,** at Paradepl. 5CHF commission. Open M-F 8:15am-5pm.

Luggage Storage: Middle level of *Hauptbahnhof.* 5-8CHF. Open daily 4:15am-1:30am.

GLBT Resources: Homosexuelle Arbeitsgruppe Zürich (HAZ), on the 3rd fl. of Sihlquai 67 (☎044 271 2250; www.haz.ch), has a library and meetings. Open W 2-6pm.

24hr. Pharmacy: Bellevue Apotheke, Theaterstr. 14, on Bellevuepl. (☎044 266 6222).

Internet: Quanta Virtual Fun Space (☎044 260 7266), at the corner of Mühleg. and Niederdorfstr. 3CHF per 15min., 5CHF per 30min. Open daily 9am-midnight.

Post Office: Sihlpost, Kasernestr. 95-97, behind the station. Open M-F 6:30am-10:30pm, Sa 6:30am-8pm, Su 10am-10:30pm. **Postal Code:** CH-8021.

ACCOMMODATIONS AND CAMPING

Zürich's few budget accommodations are easily accessible by foot or public transportation. Reserve ahead, especially in summer.

Justinus Heim Zürich, Freudenbergstr. 146 (☎044 361 3806; justinuszh@bluewin.ch). Take tram #9 or 10 (dir.: Bahnhof Oerlikon) to Seilbahn Rigiblick, then take the funicular to the top (open daily 5:20am-12:40am). This hillside hostel, which hosts students during the term period, is removed from the downtown bustle but is easily accessible. Beautiful view of the city. Breakfast included. Reception 8am-noon and 5-9pm. Singles 50CHF, with shower 65CHF; doubles 90-110CHF. Rates rise July-Aug. V. ❸

The City Backpacker-Hotel Biber, Niederdorfstr. 5 (☎044 251 9015; www.city-backpacker.ch). From the Hauptbanhof, cross the bridge and Limmatquai, turn right onto Niederdorfst., and walk for 5min. With Niederdorfstr. nightlife right outside, you may not

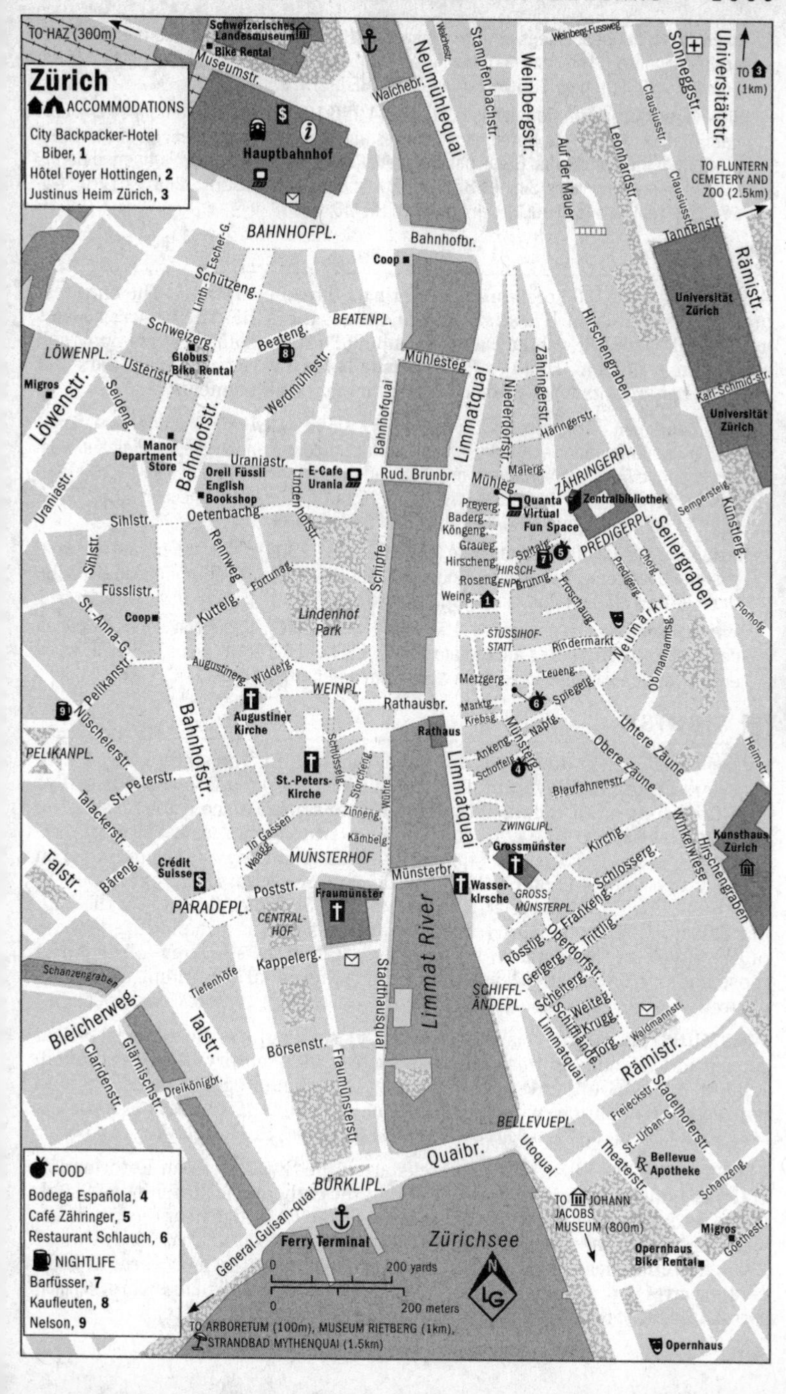
Zürich
ACCOMMODATIONS
City Backpacker-Hotel Biber, 1
Hôtel Foyer Hottingen, 2
Justinus Heim Zürich, 3
FOOD
Bodega Española, 4
Café Zähringer, 5
Restaurant Schlauch, 6
NIGHTLIFE
Barfüsser, 7
Kaufleuten, 8
Nelson, 9
TO HAZ (300m)
Schweizerisches Landesmuseum
Bike Rental
Hauptbahnhof
TO FLUNTERN CEMETERY AND ZOO (2.5km)
TO 3 (1km)
Universität Zürich
Zentralbibliothek
Quanta Virtual Fun Space
E-Cafe Urania
Orell Füssli English Bookshop
Manor Department Store
Globus Bike Rental
Lindenhof Park
Augustiner Kirche
St.-Peters-Kirche
Rathaus
Grossmünster
Wasserkirche
Fraumünster
Crédit Suisse
Limmat River
Kunsthaus Zürich
Bellevue Apotheke
TO JOHANN JACOBS MUSEUM (800m)
Opernhaus Bike Rental
Opernhaus
Ferry Terminal
Zürichsee
TO ARBORETUM (100m), MUSEUM RIETBERG (1km), STRANDBAD MYTHENQUAI (1.5km)
200 yards
200 meters

need your bunk bed. Linens and towels each 3CHF; blanket provided. Internet 6CHF per hr. Reception 8-11am and 3-10pm. Check-out 10am. Dorms 34CHF; singles 71CHF; doubles 98CHF; triples 135CHF; quads 176CHF. MC/V. ❷

Hôtel Foyer Hottingen, Hottingenstr. 31 (☎044 256 1919; www.foyer-hottingen.ch). Take tram #3 (dir.: Kluspl.) to Hottingerpl. Families and student backpackers fill this house a block from the Kunsthaus. Breakfast included. Reception 7am-11pm. Partitioned dorms (40CHF) provide privacy. Singles 85-95CHF, with bath 120-135CHF; doubles 120/160-170CHF; triples 145/190CHF; quads 180CHF. MC/V. ❷

FOOD

Zürich's has over 1300 restaurants, offering a bite of everything. The cheapest meals are available at *Würstli* (sausage) stands for 5CHF. The **farmer's markets** at Bürklipl. (Tu and F 6-11am) and Rosenhof (Th 10am-8pm, Sa 10am-5pm) sell produce and flowers. Head to **Niederdorfstraße** for a variety of snack bars and cheaper restaurants interspersed among fancier establishments.

Café Zähringer, Zähringerpl. 11 (☎044 252 0500; www.cafe-zaehringer.ch). Enjoy mainly vegetarian and vegan fare in this colorful, student-friendly cafe. Try their *Kefirwasser,* a purple, fizzy drink made from dates and mushrooms fed with sugar (4CHF). Salads 7-13CHF. Pasta 4-14CHF. Stir-fry 18.50-26.50CHF. Breakfast specials 8.50-23CHF. Open M 6pm-midnight, Tu-Su 8am-midnight. Cash only. ❷

Restaurant Schlauch, Münstergasse 20 (☎044 251 2304). Enjoy the billiard tables at this affordable downtown eatery. Soups 5-8.50CHF. Salads 7-14CHF. Entrees 8-20CHF. Open Tu-Sa 11:30am-2pm and 6-9pm. AmEx/MC/V. ❷

Bodega Española, Münstergasse 15 (☎044 251 2310). Has been serving Catalán delights since 1874. Egg-and-potato tortilla dishes 16-18CHF. Tapas 4.80CHF. Open daily 10am-midnight. Kitchen open noon-2pm and 6-10pm. AmEx/MC/V. ❷

SIGHTS

Bahnhofstraße leads into the city from the train station. The street is filled with shoppers during the day but falls dead quiet after 6pm and on weekends. At the Zürichsee end of Bahnhofstr., **Bürkliplatz** is a good place to begin walking along the lake shore. The *platz* itself hosts a Saturday **flea market** *(May-Oct. 6am-3pm).* On the other side of the Limmat River, the pedestrian zone continues on Niederdorfstr. and Münsterg. Off Niederdorfstr., **Spiegelgasse** was once home to Goethe and Lenin. **Fraumünster, Grossmünster,** and **St. Peters Kirche** grace the Limmat River. For a view of Zürich from the water, as well as a chance to see some of the towns on the banks of the Zürichsee, **boat tours** costing a fraction of those in other Swiss cities leave from the ferry terminal at Bürklipl. The shortest tour, A Kleine Rundfahrten, lasts 1hr. *(May-Sept. daily 11am-6:30pm., 7.80CHF.)*

FRAUMÜNSTER. Marc Chagall's stained glass windows depicting Biblical scenes add vibrancy to this otherwise austere 13th-century Gothic cathedral. A mural on the courtyard's archway depicts Felix and Regula (the decapitated patron saints of Zürich) with their heads in their hands. *(Off Paradepl. Open May-Nov. M-Sa 10am-6pm, Su 11:30am-6pm; Dec.-Apr. M-Sa 10am-4pm, Su 11:30am-4pm. Free.)*

GROSSMÜNSTER. Ulrich Zwingli kickstarted the Swiss German Reformation at Grossmünster in the 16th century. Today, the cathedral is Zürich's main landmark. Its defining twin towers are best viewed on the bridge near the Fraumünster. *(Towers open daily Mar.-Oct. 9:15am-5pm; Nov.-Feb. 10:15am-4:30pm. 2CHF.)* One of Zwingli's Bibles lies in a case near his pulpit. Downstairs in the cavernous 12th-century **crypt** is a menacing statue of Charlemagne and his 2m sword. *(Church open daily mid-Mar.-Oct. 9am-6pm; Nov.-mid-Mar. 10am-5pm. Free.)*

BEACHES. When the weather heats up, a visit to the beaches along the Zürichsee offers respite. The city has numerous free swimming spots, which are labeled on a map distributed by the tourist office. The convenient and popular **Arboretum** is about 100m down from the Quaibrücke. *(Tram #5 to Rentenanstalt and head to the water.)* Across the lake, **Zürichhorn** draws crowds with its peaceful gardens and a famous statue by Jean Tinguely. *(Tram #2 or 4 to Frolichst., then walk towards the lake.)* **Strandbad Mythenquai,** along the western shore, offers diving towers and a water trampoline. *(Tram #7 to Brunaustr. and walk 2min. in the same direction until you see a set of stairs. Look for signs. ☎ 044 201 0000. Check out www.sportamt.ch for info on water quality. Open daily May to early Sept. 9am-8pm. 6CHF, ages 16-20 4.50CHF.)*

MUSEUMS

MUSEUM RIETBERG. Rietberg presents an outstanding collection of Asian, African, and other non-European art, housed in three structures spread around the Rieter-Park. The basement of the new **Emerald Building** houses masterpieces from Asia and Africa; highlights include Chinese boddhisatvas and Japanese Noh masks. **Villa Wesendonck** (where Wagner wrote *Tristan and Isolde*) holds works from South Asia, Central America, and Oceania, while **Park-Villa Rieter** includes a small collection of Near Eastern art. *(Gablerstr. 15. Tram #7 to Museum Rietberg. ☎ 044 206 3131; www.rietberg.ch. Buy tickets in the Emerald building. All buildings open Apr.-Sept. Tu and F-Su 10am-5pm, W-Th 10am-8pm. 16CHF, students 12CHF. MC/V.)*

KUNSTHAUS ZÜRICH. The Kunsthaus, Europe's largest privately funded museum, houses a vast collection ranging from religious works by the Old Masters to 21st-century American Pop Art. Compositions by Chagall, Dalí, Gauguin, van Gogh, Munch, Picasso, Rembrandt, Renoir, and Rubens stretch from wall to wall in a patchwork of rich color while a Modern sculpture made of car tops adorns the entrance. *(Heimpl. 1. Take tram #3, 5, 8, or 9 to Kunsthaus. ☎ 044 253 8484; www.kunsthaus.ch. English-language audio tour and brochure. Open T and Sa-Su 10am-6pm, W-F 10am-8pm. 18CHF, students 12CHF. AmEx/MC/V.)*

ENTERTAINMENT AND NIGHTLIFE

Most English-language movies in Zürich are screened with French and German subtitles (marked "E/D/F"). Films generally cost 15CHF and up, but less on Mondays. From mid-July to mid-August, the **OrangeCinema,** an open-air cinema at Zürichhorn (tram #2 or 4 to Fröhlichstr.), attracts huge crowds to its lakefront screenings. In mid-August, the **Street Parade** brings together ravers from all over for the world's biggest techno party.

THAT EXPLAINS THE TASSELS. Beware the deceptive and common title of "night club"—it's really just a euphemism for "strip club."

For information on after-dark happenings, check **ZüriTipp** (www.zueritipp.ch) or pick up a free copy of *ZürichGuide* or *ZürichEvents* from the tourist office. On **Niederdorfstraße,** the epicenter of Zürich's *Altstadt* nightlife, bars are packed to the brim almost every night. **Kreis 5,** once the industrial area of Zürich, has recently developed into party central, with ubiquitous clubs, bars, and lounges taking over former factories. Kreis 5 lies northwest of the *Hauptbahnhof*, with Hardstr. as its axis. To get there, take tram #4 (dir.: Werdholzi) or #13 (dir.: Albisgütli) to Escher-Wyss-Pl. and follow the crowds. Closer to the Old Town, **Langstraße,** reached by walking away from the river on the city's western side, is the reputed red-light district, with many bars and clubs (some sleazier than others). Beer in Zürich is pricey (from 6CHF), but an array of cheap bars have established themselves on Niederdorfstr. near Mühleg.

Kaufleuten, Pelikanstr. 18 (☎044 225 3322; www.kaufleuten.ch). For a memorable evening, visit this former theater transformed into trendy club. Cover 10-30CHF. Hours vary, but generally open M-Th and Su 11pm-2am, F-Sa 11pm-4am. MC/V.

Nelson, Beateng. 11 (☎044 212 6016). Locals, backpackers, and businessmen chug beer (9CHF per pint) at this large Irish pub. 20+. Open M-W 11:30am-2am, Th 11:30am-3am, F 11:30am-4:30am, Sa 3pm-4:30am, Su 3pm-2am. MC/V.

Barfüsser, Spitalg. 14 (☎044 251 4064), off Zähringerpl. Freely flowing mixed drinks (14-17CHF) and wine (6-9CHF) accompany delicious sushi at this gay bar. Open M-Th noon-1am, F-Sa noon-2am, Su 5pm-1am. AmEx/MC/V.

LUZERN (LUCERNE) ☎041

Luzern (pop. 58,000) rightfully welcomes busloads of tourists each day in the summer. The streets of the *Altstadt* lead down to the placid Vierwaldstättersee (Lake Lucerne); the covered bridges over the river are among the most photographed sights in Switzerland, and the sunrise over the famous Mt. Pilatus has hypnotized artists—including Goethe, Twain, and Wagner—for centuries.

TRANSPORTATION AND PRACTICAL INFORMATION. **Trains** leave the large Bahnhof for: Basel (1hr., 2 per hr., 31CHF); Bern via Olten (1hr., 2 per hr., 31CHF); Geneva (3hr., 1-2 per hr., 69CHF); Zürich (1hr., 2 per hr., 23CHF). VBL **buses** depart in front of the train station and provide extensive coverage of Luzern. **Boats** leave from across the road to destinations all over Lake Luzern; some offer themed cruises. (☎041 612 9090; www.lakelucerne.ch. Cruises 15-60CHF.) Route maps are available at the station **tourist office,** Banhofstr. 3, also accessible from the train station, which reserves rooms for free, and holds daily guided tours at 9:45am for 18CHF. (☎041 227 1717; www.luzern.org. Open May-Oct. M-F 8:30am-6:30pm, Sa-Su 9am-6:30pm; Nov.-Apr. M-F 8:30am-5:30pm, Sa 9am-1pm.) There are two **post offices** by the train station; the older building by the bridge is the main one.

ACCOMMODATIONS AND FOOD. Inexpensive beds are limited, so call ahead to reserve. Take Bus 19 to stop Jugendherberge to reach **Youth Hostel Luzern (HI) ❹,** AmRotsee Sedelstrasse 12. (☎041 420 8800; www.youthhostel.ch/luzern. Breakfast included. Internet 6CHF per hr. Reception 7-10am and 2pm-midnight. Dorms 40-41CHF. 6CHF HI discount. AmEx/V/MC.) To reach **Backpackers Lucerne ❷,** Alpenquai 42, turn right from the station onto Inseliquai and follow it for 20min. until it turns into Alpenquai. The hostel's distance from the center of town may be inconvenient, but it has a fun, communal vibe. (☎041 360 0420; www.backpackerslucerne.ch. Laundry 9CHF. Internet 10CHF per hr. Reception 7:30-10am and 4-11pm. Dorms 31CHF; doubles 70-76CHF. Bike rental 18CHF per day. Cash only.) Overlooking the river from the *Altstadt* is the **Tourist Hotel ❷,** St. Karliquai 12, which offers plain rooms and a prime location. From the station, walk along Bahnhofstr., cross the river at the second covered bridge, and make a left onto St. Karliquai. (☎041 410 2474; www.touristhotel.ch. Breakfast included. Dorms 38-45CHF; doubles 88-120CHF; triples 129-144CHF; quads 172-188CHF. AmEx/V.) Watch trains roll by while gorging on delicious Middle Eastern fare at **Erdem Kebab ❶,** down Zentralstr. from the Banhof. (Falafel 8CHF. Kebab 8-12CHF. Open M-Th 10am-midnight, F-Sa 11am-8pm. Cash only.) Markets along the river sell fresh food on Tuesday and Saturday mornings. There's also a **Coop** supermarket at the train station. (Open M-Sa 6:30am-9pm, Su 8am-9pm.)

SIGHTS AND ENTERTAINMENT. The *Altstadt*, across the river from the station, is famous for its frescoed houses; the best examples are on Hirschenpl. and Weinmarkt. The 14th-century **Kapellbrücke,** a wooden-roofed bridge, runs from the left of the train station to the *Altstadt* and is decorated with Swiss historical scenes. Farther down the river, the **Spreuerbrücke** is adorned by Kaspar Meglinger's eerie *Totentanz* (Dance of Death) paintings. On the hills above the river, the **Museggmauer** and its towers are all that remain of the medieval city's ramparts. Three of the towers are accessible to visitors and provide panoramic views of the city; one, the **Zyt,** features the inner workings of Luzern's oldest clock, a 16th-century doozy that chimes one minute before all other city clocks. From Mühlenpl., walk up Brugglig., then head uphill to the right on Museggstr. and follow the castle signs. (Open in summer daily 8am-7pm.) To the east is the magnificent **Löwendenkmal,** the dying lion of Luzern, carved into a cliff on Denkmalstr. to honor the Swiss soldiers who died defending King Louis XVI of France during the invasion of the Tuileries in 1792. Close by is the **Gletschergarten** (Glacier Garden), which showcases an odd but interesting collection including Ice Age formations, a 19th-century Swiss house, and a hall of mirrors. (☎041 410 4340; www.gletschergarten.ch. Open daily Apr.-Oct. 9am-6pm; Nov.-Mar. 10am-5pm. 12CHF, students 9.50.)

Europe's largest transportation museum, the **Verkehrshaus der Schweiz** (Swiss Transport Museum), Lidostr. 5, has interactive displays on everything from early flying machines to cars. (☎041 370 4444; www.verkehrshaus.ch. Open daily Apr.-Oct. 10am-6pm; Nov.-Mar. 10am-5pm. 24CHF, students 22CHF, with Eurail Pass 14CHF.) The **Picasso Museum,** Am Rhyn Haus, Furreng. 21, displays some of Picasso's sketches and a large collection of photographs from his later years. (☎041 410 3533. Open daily Apr.-Oct. 10am-6pm; Nov.-Mar. 11am-1pm and 2-4pm. 8CHF, students 5CHF.)

Although Luzern's nightlife is more about relaxing than club-hopping, there are still many options for those looking to dance the night away. **The Loft,** Haldenstr. 21, hosts special DJs and theme nights. (☎041 410 9244; www.theloft.ch. Beer 9-11CHF. Open W 9pm-2am, Th-Su 10am-4am.) The mellow **Jazzkantine** club, Grabenstr. 8, is affiliated with the renowned **Lucerne School of Music.** (Sandwiches

HI-YO, SWISS INDEPENDENCE!

Everyone knows some element of the William Tell story, whether it be the famous apple-shooting scene or the ubiquitous overture from Rossini's opera (later appropriated, of course, as the theme song of The Lone Ranger). But few would guess that this tale of martial defiance originated in neutral Switzerland.

According to legend, Wilhelm Tell lived in the 14th century in the canton of Uri, just south of Zürich. The Hapsburg emperors installed an Austrian "protector," Hermann Gessler, to further their attempts to dominate the region. Gessler demanded that all citizens of Altdorf bow before a pole with his hat on it, but the stubborn Tell refused. The protector ordered Tell to shoot an apple off his son's head, or else both would be executed.

Tell, an expert marksman, had no problem with his crossbow. He then declared that if he had hit his son, he would have immediately attacked Gessler. None too happy, Gessler ordered that Tell be brought to his castle on the Vierwaldstättersee. Tell escaped his captors in a storm, waited for the Austrian in the castle, and promptly dispatched him at first sight—with a crossbow, of course. The act sparked a wave of defiance that led to the formation of the Swiss Confederation.

6-8CHF. Open mid-Aug. to mid-July M-Sa 7am-1:30am, Su 4pm-1:30am. MC/V.) Luzern attracts big names for its two jazz festivals: **Blue Balls Festival** (last week of July) and **Blues Festival** (2nd week of Nov.)

ST. GALLEN ☎071

Although it's called "the metropolis of eastern Switzerland," St. Gallen (pop. 75,000) is anything but imposing. Founded as a religious center by the Irish monk Gallus in the 7th century, the city has retained an intimate feel—especially in the historic center, where you can wander through a maze of narrow streets lined with shops, restaurants, and the occasional open-air market.

TRANSPORTATION AND PRACTICAL INFORMATION. **Trains** leave from the Hauptbanhof for: Luzern (2hr., 2 per hr., 41CHF); Zürich (1hr., 1-2 per hr., 28CHF); Bern (1hr., every hr., 65CHF); Geneva (4hr., every hr., 98CHF); Lausanne (3hr., 2 per hr., 81CHF). The **tourist office,** in front of the station, books rooms for free. (Opem May-Oct. M-F 9am-6pm, Sa 10am-3pm; Nov.-Apr. M-F 9am-3pm, Sa 10am-1pm.) **Postal Code:** CH-9000.

ACCOMMODATIONS AND FOOD. **Jugendherberge (HI) ❷,** 25 Jüchstr., has clean rooms and scenic views of the hillside; take the orange Trogenerbahn tram (dir: Trogen) from the right of the train station to the Schuleraus stop, then walk up the hill for 5min. and turn left. (☎071 245 4777. Breakfast included. Laundry 6CHF. Internet 12CHF per hr. Reception 7:30-10am and 5-10:30pm. Dorms 30-36CHF; singles 50-52CHF; doubles 39-42CHF.) There's no shortage of restaurants; for delicious, well priced Indian cuisine, drop by **Samosa,** Engelgasse 20, off of Marktplatz. (☎071 222 4321; www.samosa.ch. All you can eat lunch buffet 17CHF, vegetarian 14CHF. Curry dishes 18CHF, and a variety of samosas 5CHF. Open M-Sa 11:30am-2pm and 6-10pm.) If pious St. Gallen moves you to gluttony, indulge in a classic 70% Swiss cocoa drink (3.70CHF) at **Chocolaterie am Kosterplatz ❶,** Gallusstrasse 20, next to the Abbey Precinct. (Open M 1-6:30pm, Tu-F 9am-6:30pm, Sa 9am-5pm. AmEx/MC/V.)

SIGHTS AND ENTERTAINMENT. The **Abbey Precinct** is a grouping of remarkable Benedictine structures—some dating back to the 1400s—with UNESCO World Heritage Landmark status. The soaring towers of the Baroque **cathedral,** constructed from 1755 to 1767, dominate the scene; the ornate interior, with its majestic painted ceiling, is no less dramatic. (Open M-Tu and Th-F 9am-6pm, W 10am-6pm, Sa 9am-4pm, Su 12:15am-5:30pm.) The **Abbey Library** has a world-famous collection of over 140,000 valuable books and manuscripts, all housed in a fittingly grand Rococo hall. (☎071 227 3416; www.stiftsbibliothek.ch. Usually open M-Sa 10am-5pm, Su 10am-4pm. Check website in advance. 7CHF.) The **Lapidarium** holds ancient artifacts from the 8th century onwards. (Open M-Sa 10am-5pm, Su 10am-4pm. 3CHF.) Religious egalitarians shouldn't miss the neighboring **Church of St. Laurence,** once the hotbed of the Reformation in St. Gallen; visitors who make the long trek up to the church's viewing platform (mind those immense, oft-ringing bells) will find divine views of the city and surrounding countryside. (☎071 222 6792. Church open M 9:30-11:30am and 2-4pm, Tu-F 9:30am-6pm, Sa 9:30am-4pm. Viewing platform open M-Sa 9:30-11:30am and 2-4pm. Closed in the winter. 2CHF.)

St. Gallen isn't all worship. Museumstr., next to the **City Park (Stadtpark),** is lined by all manner of cultural institutions. Indulge a love of dinosaurs at the **Naturmuseum (National History Museum).** The **Kunstmuseum (Museum of Art),** housed in the same building, features a collection of contemporary sculpture—as you might infer from the giant fly out front. (Natural History Museum: ☎071 242 0670; www.naturmuseumsg.ch. Museum of Art: ☎071 242 0671; www.kunstmuseumsg.ch. Both museums at Museumstrasse 32 open Tu, Th-Su 10am-5pm; W 10am-8pm. Combined ticket to both museums 10CHF. AmEx/MC/V.) The **Historisches und Völkerkundemuseum (Museum of History and Ethnology)** offers exhibits on nearly every part of the world. There's a section for the *kinder* (children), too. (☎071 242 0642; www.hmsg.ch. Open Tu-Su 10am-5pm.) The **St. Gallen Theatre** is famous for its mix of musicals, drama, and dance, while the **Tonhalle,** across the street, is home to the St. Gallen Symphony Orchestra and renowned guest soloists. (☎071 242 0606. Theater: www.theatresg.ch; Tonhalle: www.sinfonieorchestersg.ch. Open daily 10am-12:30pm.) St. Gallen rocks out with its **Open Air Festival,** held annually at the end of June and featuring some of the world's biggest acts (in 2008, Lenny Kravitz and Kings of Leon).

STEIN AM RHEIN ☎052

The tiny, medieval *Altstadt* of Stein am Rhein (pop. 3190) is postcard-perfect, with traditional Swiss architecture framed by hills and the Rhine River. To reach the Old Town, walk down Bahnhofstr. from the station, turn right onto Wagenhauserstr., then go downhill and over the bridge. The buildings on the main square, the **Rathausplatz,** date back to the 15th century and feature remarkable facade paintings depicting the animal or scene for which each house is named. Ground level floors are occupied by small (and pricey) shops and restaurants. The stately **Rathaus** (town council building) is to the right upon reaching the square. Heading away from the Rathauspl., the Understadt, the main road running through the village, leads to the **Museum Lindwurm,** Understadt 18, a 19th-century house restored to its bourgeois glory, roosters and all. (☎052 741 2512; www.museum-lindwurm.ch. Open Mar.-Oct. M and W-Su 10am-5pm. 5CHF, students 3CHF.) For a look at a completely different facet of village life, visit Stein am Rhein's oldest claim to fame, the 12th-century **Kloster St. Georgen.** You can reach the tucked-away entrance to this Benedictine monastery by going through the arch across from the tourist office, behind and to the left of the Rathaus. Explore monks' dormitories, a scriptorium, preserved wall drawings, and the gorgeous **Festsaal,** a room where feet may not touch the red-green tiled floor and the sun is the only source of lighting. (☎052 741 2142. Open Apr.-Oct. Tu-Su 10am-5pm. 3CHF, students 2CHF.) The picturesque castle **Burg Hohenklingen** sits atop a hill overlooking the village; the view of the Rhine and the villages from its grounds is worth the hike. From the Rathauspl., take Brodlauberg. 30min. away from the river.

The clean, family-oriented **Jugendherberge (HI) ❷,** Hemishoferstr. 87, is a 20min. walk from the train station; cross the Rhein and walk left out of the Old Town along the main road or take bus #7349 (dir.: Singen), which runs every hour from Untertor station, to Strandbad; walk 5min. farther in the same direction. (☎052 741 1255; www.youthhostel.ch/stein. Breakfast included. Dinner 13CHF. Internet 1CHF per 10min. Reception 8-10am and 5-9pm. Open Mar.-Oct. Dorms 32-36CHF; singles 46CHF; doubles 80CHF. 6CHF HI discount. AmEx/MC/V.) The **Weinstube zum Rother Ochsen ❷,** Rathauspl. 9, built in 1466, is the oldest public house in the town. Enjoy a lovely view of the Rathausplatz with their outdoor seating on sunny days.(☎052 741 2328. Entrees 18-25CHF. Soups 8.50CHF. Appetizers 8-20CHF. Wines 4-14CHF. Open Tu-Sa 10am-11pm, Su 10am-6pm. Kitchen open 11:30am-2pm and 6-10pm.) The **Volg market** is located at Rathauspl. 17. (Open M-F 8:15am-6:30pm, Sa 8am-8pm.)

Trains connect Stein am Rhein to Constance, GER (40min., every hr., 10CHF) via Kreuzlingen, and to Zürich (1hr., 1-2 per hr., 21CHF) via Winterthur or Schaffhausen. **Boats** (☎052 634 0888; www.urh.ch) depart for Bodensee towns, including Constance (2hr., 4-6 per day, 27CHF), and Schaffhausen (1hr., 4-6 per day, 21CHF), which is within an hour's walk of the Rhine Falls, Europe's biggest waterfall. Those who want to tour the area by land can rent **bikes** from River Bike, Rathauspl. 15. (☎052 741 5541; www.riverbike.ch. 15-20CHF per 2hr., 18-28CHF per half-day, 29-35CHF per day. Open M 1:30-6:30pm, Tu-F 9am-6:30pm, Sa 9am-4pm, Su 11am-5pm.) The **tourist office,** Oberstadt. 3, on the other side of the Rathaus, has free maps for visitors, and also books rooms for free. (☎052 42 2090; www.steinamrhein.ch. Open July-Aug. M-Sa 9:30am-noon and 1:30-4pm; Sept.-June M-F 9:30am-noon and 1:30-4pm.) **Postal Code:** CH-8260.

NORTHWESTERN SWITZERLAND

Though at the junction of the French and German borders, this peaceful region remains defiantly Swiss; locals speak Swiss-German and welcome visitors with distinctive hospitality. The best part of Northwestern Switzerland is youthful Basel, Switzerland's preeminent university town.

BASEL (BÂLE) ☎061

Basel bills itself as Switzerland's "cultural capital," and though nearby Zürich might beg to differ, it's hard to argue with the city's lively medieval quarter and many museums. Basel is home to one of the oldest universities in Europe—former professors include Erasmus and Nietzsche.

TRANSPORTATION AND PRACTICAL INFORMATION. Basel has three train stations: the **French (SNCF)** and **Swiss (SBB)** stations on Centralbahnpl., near the *Altstadt*, and the **German (DB)** station across the Rhine (take tram #2 from the other train stations or connect directly from the SBB). **Trains** leave from the SBB to: Bern (1hr., 1-2 per hr., 37CHF); Geneva via Bern (3hr., every hr., 69CHF); Lausanne via Bern (2hr., every hr., 59CHF); Zürich (1hr., every 15-30min., 31CHF). The main **tourist office** is on Steinenbergstr. in the Stadt Casino building (from the SBB station, take #6, 8, 14, 16, or 17 to Barfüsserpl.). There is also a branch in the SBB station. (Both offices: ☎061 268 6868; www.baseltourismus.ch. Open M-F 8:30am-6:30pm, Sa 9am-5pm, Su 10am-4pm.) For info on **GLBT** establishments, stop by the bookstore **Arcados,** Rheing. 69. (☎061 681 3132; www.arcados.com. Open Tu-F 1-7pm, Sa noon-4pm.) To reach the **post office,** Rüdeng. 1, take tram #1 or 8 to Marktpl. and backtrack away from the river. (Open M-F 7:30am-9pm, Sa 8am-5pm, Su 2-7pm.)

ACCOMMODATIONS AND FOOD. All hostels provide free city transportation cards. Conveniently located near the train station, **YMCA Hostel Basel ❶,** Gempenstr. 6, offers great value. Exit the back entrance of the SBB station. cross the street and continue straight on Gempenstr. (☎061 361 7309; www.ymcahostelbasel.ch. Breakfast 7CHF. Free Wi-Fi. Reception 7-11am and 3:30-11:30pm. Single-sex dorms 29CHF. AmEx/MC/V.) The **Jugendherberge (HI) ❷,** St. Alban-Kirchrain 10, is located near the Rhine in a beautiful 19th-century building. To get there, take tram #2 or 15 to Kunstmuseum, turn right on St. Alban-Vorstadt, then follow the signs. (☎061 272 0572; www.youthhostel.ch/basel. Breakfast included. Laundry 7CHF. Internet 6CHF per hr. Reception Mar.-Oct. 7-10am and 2pm-midnight; Nov.-Feb. 7-10am and 2-11pm. Dorms 36-40CHF; doubles 94CHF; quads 160CHF. 6CHF HI discount. AmEx/MC/V.)

Barfüsserplatz and **Marktplatz** are full of satisfying restaurants. **Restaurant Hirscheneck ❷,** Lindenberg 23 in Klein-Basel, is popular with students, vegetarians, and Basel's alternative crowd. Take tram #2 or 15 to Wettsteinpl., then walk back towards the river and turn right on Kartausg. (☎061 692 7333; www.hirscheneck.ch. Daily menu 12-24CHF; smaller portions 9-15CHF. Su brunch 10am-4pm. Open M 2pm-midnight, Tu-Th 11am-midnight, F 11am-1am, Sa 2pm-1am, Su 10am-midnight. Cash only.) On the other bank of the Rhine off Barfüsserpl., **Café Barfi ❸**, Leonhardsberg 4, belies its name with tasty, affordable Italian meals. (☎061 261 7038. Pizza 19-23CHF. Pasta 15-20CHF. Open M-Sa 11am-11pm.) Enjoy large steaming bowls of noodles at **Namamen Japanese Ramen Bar ❷**, Steinenberg 1. (☎061 271 8068; www.namamen.ch. Ramen and Udon noodle dishes 15.50-20.50CHF. Sushi and other small entrees 4.50-9.50CHF. Bento boxes 16-17.50CHF. Open M-Th 11am-10pm, F 11am-11pm, Sa noon-10pm, Su 4pm-10pm. Cash only.)

SIGHTS. The Rhine separates **Groß-Basel (Greater Basel)** and the SBB/SNCF train stations from the **Klein-Basel (Lesser Basel).** Behind the Marktpl., the nearly 800-year-old **Mittlere Rheinbrücke** (Middle Rhine Bridge) connects the two halves of the city. To get to the Old Town from the train station, take tram #16 or 8. The very red **Rathaus** (City Hall) brightens the lively **Marktplatz** with its blinding facade and striking gold-and-green statues. Behind Marktpl. stands the red sandstone **Münster** (Cathedral), where you can see the tomb of Erasmus or climb the tower for a spectacular view of the city. (Church open Easter to mid-Oct. M-F 10am-5pm, Sa 10am-4pm, Su 11:30am-5pm; mid-Oct. to Easter M-Sa 11am-4pm, Su 11:30am-4pm. Church free. Tower 3CHF.) Get off at the Theater stop to see the spectacular **Jean Tinguely Fountain,** also known as the Fasnachtsbrunnen. The fountain's various moving metal parts spray water in all directions. From Marktpl., walk up to the **University Quarter.** Nearby looms the huge **Spalentor,** a remnant of the medieval city's fortifications.

MUSEUMS. Basel has over 30 museums; pick up a comprehensive guide at the tourist office. The **Basel Card,** also available at the tourist office, provides admission to most museums, free sightseeing tours, and other discounts. (1-day 20CHF, 2-day 27CHF, 3-day 35CHF.) The **Kunstmuseum** (Museum of Fine Arts), St. Alban-Graben 16, houses Switzerland's greatest collections of new and old masters. (Open Tu and Th-Su 10am-5pm, W 10am-7pm. 12CHF, students 5CHF. Free daily 4-5pm and 1st Su of each month.) Admission also includes access to the **Museum für Gegenwartskunst** (Museum of Modern Art), St. Alban-Rheinweg 60, which has changing exhibitions of contemporary work. Take tram #1 or 15 to the Kunstmuseum stop. (Open Tu-Su 11am-5pm.) If you thought the Jean Tinguely Fountain was intriguing, check out **Museum Tinguely,** Paul-Sacher-Anlage 1, where everything rattles in homage to the sculptor's vision of metal and movement. (☎061 681 9320; www.tinguely.ch. Open Tu-Su 11am-7pm. 15CHF, students 10CHF.) The **Fondation Beyeler,** Baselstr. 101, has one of Europe's finest private art collections. Take tram #6 to Fondation Beyeler. (☎061 645 9700; www.beyeler.com. Open M-Tu and Th-Su 10am-6pm, W 10am-8pm. 23CHF, students 12CHF. 30% discount M and W 5-8pm. AmEx/MC/V.)

FESTIVALS AND NIGHTLIFE. Basel's **Fasnacht** (Mar. 2-4, 2009, Feb. 22-24, 2010) commences the week after Lent with the *Morgestraich*, a three-day parade with a centuries-old goal—to scare away winter. Head to **Barfüsserplatz** and the adjoining **Steinenvorstadt** for an evening of bar-hopping. **Atlantis,** Klosterberg 13, is a multi-level, sophisticated bar that plays reggae, jazz, and funk. (☎061 228 9696. Cover 10-15CHF; students with ID 5CHF discount; July-Sept. no cover F. Open M 11:30am-2pm, Tu-Th 11:30am-2pm and 6pm-midnight, F 11:30am-2pm and 6pm-4am, Sa 6pm-4am. AmEx/MC/V.)

GRAUBÜNDEN

Graubünden's rugged gorges, fir forests, and eddying rivers give the region a wildness seldom found in comfortably settled Switzerland. Visitors should plan their trips carefully, especially during ski season when reservations are absolutely required, and in May and June, when nearly everything shuts down.

DAVOS ☎081

Davos (pop. 11,000) sprawls along the valley floor under mountains crisscrossed with chairlifts and cable cars. Originally a health resort, the city catered to such *fin-de-siècle* giants as Robert Louis Stevenson and Thomas Mann. Today, visitors mainly come to Davos to feel the thrill of carving down the famed, wickedly steep **ski slopes** or exploring the 700km of hiking paths. Davos provides direct access to two mountains—**Parsenn** and **Jakobshorn**—and four skiing areas. Parsenn, with long runs and fearsome vertical drops, is the mountain around which Davos built its reputation (day pass 60CHF). Jakobshorn has found a niche with the younger crowd since opening a snowboarding park with two half-pipes (day pass 55CHF). Cross-country trails cover 75km, including one lit trail. In the summer, ski lifts (½-price after 3pm) connect to hiking trails such as the **Panoramaweg** (2hr.). Europe's largest natural ice rink (18,000 sq. m) allows for curling, figure skating, hockey, ice dancing, and speed skating. (☎081 415 304. Open July-Aug. and mid-Dec. to Feb. 10am-4:30pm. 5CHF; free skating M and Th evening. Skate rental 6.50CHF.)

Davos Youthpalace (HI) ❸, Horlaubenstrasse 27, really is a palace with celestial views. From the Davos Dorf train station, turn left. Make a right at Hotel Dischma and follow the zig-zagging path up to Hohe Promenade. (☎081 410 1920; www.youthhostel.ch/davos. Breakfast and dinner included. Internet 5CHF per 30min. Dorms 46-56CHF; singles 51-140CHF. MC/V.) Avid skiers and snowboarders will also appreciate **Snowboardhotel Bolgenschanze ❸,** Skistr. 1. Dorms are sold as a package with lift passes. (☎081 413 7101; www.bolgenschanze.ch. 18+. Open mid-Dec. to mid-Mar. 1-night, 2-day ski pass 195-405CHF; 6-night, 7-day pass 650-865CHF. AmEx/MC/V.)

Davos is accessible by **train** from Klosters (25min., 2 per hr., 9.20CHF). The town is divided into two areas, Davos-Platz and Davos-Dorf, each with a train station. **Buses** frequently journey between the two stations as well as around the town. They are free with a **guest pass** available at every hotel and hostel—make sure to ask for one. Platz has the post office and the main **tourist office,** Promenade 67, which is up the hill and a ways to the right on Promenade from the station. (☎081 415 2121; www.davos.ch. Free Internet. Open Dec. to mid-Apr. and mid-June to mid-Oct. M-F 8:30am-6:30pm, Sa 9am-5pm, Su 10am-noon and 3-5:30pm; mid-Oct. to Nov. and mid-Apr. to mid-June M-F 8:30am-noon and 1:45pm-6pm, Sa 9am-noon.) **Postal Code:** CH-7260.

KLOSTERS ☎081

Although visitors choose to frequent both Klosters (pop. 3000)—a favorite ski resort of the British royals—and Davos for their natural assets, Klosters capitalizes even more on its natural serenity and cozy chalets, while Davos has a larger center with more non-outdoorsy options. **Ski passes** for the Klosters-Davos region run 121CHF for two days and 282CHF for six days, including public transportation. The **Grotschnabahn,** right behind the train station, gives access to Parsenn and Strela in Davos and Madrisa in Klosters (1-day pass 60CHF, 6-day pass 324CHF). In the summer, all guests staying in Klosters can pay just 5CHF per day for an all-inclusive Davos-Klosters mountain

transportation pass (buy one at your hostel). The **Madrisabahn** leaves from Klosters-Dorf on the other side of town (1-day pass 47CHF). **Ski rental** is also available at **Sport Gotschna,** Alte Bahnhofstr. 5, across from the tourist office. (☎081 422 1197. Skis and snowboards 28-50CHF per day plus 10% insurance. Open mid-June to late Apr. M-Sa 8am-noon and 2pm-6:30pm. AmEx/MC/V.) In summer, Klosters has access to fantastic **hiking trails.** On the lush valley floor, hikers can make a large loop from Klosters's Protestant church on Monbielstr. to Monbiel. The route continues to an elevation of 1488m and turns left, passing through Bödmerwald, Fraschmardintobel, and Monbieler Wald before climbing to its highest elevation of 1634m and returning to Klosters via Pardels. There are fourteen other local routes available. Several adventure companies offer **river rafting, canoeing, horseback riding, paragliding,** and **glacier trekking.** Summer **cable car** passes (valid on Grotschnabahn and Madrisabahn) are also available free with your Klosters transportation pass.

To get to **Jugendherberge Soldanella (HI) ❷,** Talstr. 73, from the station, go left uphill past Hotel Alpina to the church, then cross the street and head up the alleyway to the right of the Kirchpl. bus station sign. Walk 10min. uphill along the path. This massive, renovated chalet has a comfortable reading room, a flagstone terrace, and friendly, English-speaking owners. (☎081 422 1316; www.youthhostel.ch/klosters. Breakfast included. Reception 8-10am and 5-9pm. Open mid-Dec. to mid-Apr. and late June to mid-Oct. Dorms 32.50CHF; singles 46CHF; doubles 88CHF; family rooms 44CHF. HI discount 6CHF. AmEx/MC/V.) Turn right from the train station to reach the **Coop** supermarket, Bahnhofstr. 10. (Open M-F 8am-12:30pm and 2-6:30pm, Sa 8am-5pm.)

Trains run to Davos (25min., 2 per hr., 9.20CHF) and Zürich via Landquart (2hr., every hr., 45CHF). Turn right from the station and take another right on Alte Banhofstr., to reach the main **tourist office,** which has **Internet** (3CHF/15min, 5CHF/30in,10CHF/1hr.) as well as free **maps** of the area. Make sure to pick up a free copy of the helpful *Kloster-Davos from A to Z.* (☎081 410 2020; www.klosters.ch. Open M-Sa 9am-noon and 2pm-5pm.) **Postal code:** CH-7250.

SWITZERLAND

SWISS NATIONAL PARK ☎081

One of the world's best-kept nature preserves, the Swiss National Park showcases some of the Graubünden region's abundant wildlife and most stunning views. A network of 20 hiking trails, concentrated in the center, runs throughout the park. Few trails are level; most involve a lot of climbing, often into snow-covered areas. All trails are clearly marked, and it is against park rules to wander off the designated trails. Trails that require no mountaineering gear are marked with white-red-white markers. Keep in mind that every route can be tricky. However, stunning views of the surrounding mountains and unique Alpine flora, fauna, and wildlife make the effort well worth it.

Zernez is the main gateway to the park and home to its headquarters, the **National Parkhouse.** (☎081 856 1378; www.nationalpark.ch. Open June-Oct. daily 8:30am-6pm.) To reach the park itself, take a post **bus** (every hr., 4.60CHF) from the front of the train station to one of several destinations within the wilderness. Trains and buses also run to other towns in the area, including **Scuol, Samedan,** and **S-chanf.** Despite its location in ski-happy Graubünden, the park, closed November through May, is not a site for winter sports. It is one of the most strictly regulated nature reserves in the world; camping and campfires are prohibited, as is collecting flowers and plants. Wardens patrol the park at all times, so it's better not to test the rules.

VALAIS

The Valais occupies the deep glacial gorge traced by the Rhône River. The clefts of the valley divide the land linguistically: in the west, French dominates, and in the east, Swiss German is used. Though its mountain resorts can be crowded, the region's spectacular peaks make fighting the traffic worthwhile.

ZERMATT AND THE MATTERHORN ☎027

Year-round, tourists pack the trains to Zermatt (pop. 5700) where the monolithic Matterhorn (4478m) rises above the endless hotels and lodges in town. To many foreigners, the mountain is the symbol of Switzerland, and Zermatt doesn't let you forget it—you can't turn around in this resort town without glimpsing a poster or logo featuring the famously sharp peak. The area has attained mecca status with Europe's **longest ski run,** the 13km trail from Klein Matterhorn to Zermatt, and more summer ski trails than any other Alpine resort. The **Zermatt Alpin Center,** Bahnhofstr. 58, just past the post office, houses both the **Bergführerbüro** (Mountain Guide's Office; ☎027 966 2460) and the **Skischulbüro** (Ski School Office; ☎027 966 2466). The center provides ski passes (half-day 52CHF, 1-day 68CHF), four-day weather forecasts, and info on guided climbing. (www.alpincenter-zermatt.ch. Open daily July-Sept. 10am-noon and 4-6pm; late Dec. to mid-May 4-7pm.) The Bergführerbüro is also the only company to lead formal expeditions above Zermatt. Groups scale Breithorn (4164m, 3-4hr., 165CHF), Castor (4228m, 5-6hr., 319CHF), and Pollux (4091m, 5-6hr., 302CHF), and the Matterhorn itself (4478m, 4-5 hrs. 998CHF) daily in summer. Prices do not include equipment, insurance, sleeping huts, or lifts to departure points. Rental prices for skis and snowboards are standard in Zermatt (28-50CHF per day). For a new perspective on the Matterhorn, try a **tandem flight** with Paraglide Zermatt (☎027 967 6744; www.paragliding-zermatt.ch. 120-190CHF). For those who prefer to stay on the ground, the **Gornergrat Bahn rack railway,** departing from just across the train station, brings spectators 3089m above sea level to a viewing platform and Europe's highest hotel (☎027 921 4711; www.gornergrat.ch; 38CHF).

HEY, WHERE DID THE MOUNTAIN GO? The Matterhorn is a wondrous sight—when you can see it. Be sure to check the weather forecast before heading to Zermatt, even in summer. No amount of Matterhorn merchandise will cheer you up when the peak is covered with clouds.

Hotel Bahnhof ❷, on Bahnhofpl. 54, to the left of the station, provides hotel housing at hostel rates. Though small, it has a central location and mountain views. (☎027 967 2406; www.hotelbahnhof.com. Open mid-June to Oct. and mid-Dec. to mid-May. Reception 8am-8pm. Dorms 35CHF; singles 68CHF, with shower 78CHF; doubles 92-108CHF; quads 184CHF. MC/V.) A wide variety of traditional Swiss fare is available at **Walliserkanne ❷,** Bahnhofstr. 32, next to the post office. (☎027 966 4610; www.walliserkanne.ch. Raclette 8CHF. Daily specials include salad, entree, and dessert for 20-23CHF. Pasta 17-25CHF. Cheese fondues 23CHF. Kitchen open daily 11:30am-2pm and 6-10pm. Pizzeria open until 11pm. AmEx/MC/V.) Get groceries at the **Coop Center,** opposite the station. (Open M-Sa 8:15am-6:30pm.)

To preserve the alpine air, cars and buses are banned in Zermatt; the only way in is the hourly BVZ (Brig-Visp-Zermatt) **rail line,** which connects to Lausanne (3hr., 71CHF) and Bern (3hr., 78CHF) via Brig. Buy hiking **maps** (26CHF) at the **tourist office,** in the station. (☎027 966 8100; www.zermatt.ch. Open mid-June to

Sept. M-Sa 8:30am-6pm, Su 8:30am-noon and 1:30-6pm; Oct. to mid-June M-Sa 8:30am-noon and 1:30-6pm, Su 9:30am-noon and 4-6pm.) **Postal Code:** CH-3920.

FRENCH SWITZERLAND

The picturesque scenery and refined cities of French Switzerland have attracted herds of tourists for centuries, and there's no denying that the area's charm comes at a steep price. But the best experiences in French Switzerland are free: strolling down tree-lined avenues, soaking up endearing *vieilles villes*, and taking in the mountain vistas from across Lac Léman and Lac Neuchâtel.

GENEVA (GENÈVE) ☎022

Geneva (pop. 186,000) began with a tomb, blossomed into a religious center, became the "Protestant Rome," and ultimately emerged as a center for world diplomacy. Today, thanks to the presence of dozens of multinational organizations, including the United Nations and the Red Cross, the city is easily the most worldly in Switzerland. But Geneva's heritage lingers; you can sense it in the street names paying homage to Genevese patriots of old and the ubiquitous presence of the cherished cuckoo clock.

TRANSPORTATION

Flights: Cointrin Airport (**GVA;** ☎022 717 7111, flight info ☎022 717 7105) is a hub for **Swiss International Airlines** (☎0848 85 20 00) and also serves **Air France** (☎827 8787) and **British Airways** (☎0848 80 10 10). Several direct flights per day to **Amsterdam, NTH; London, BRI; New York, USA; Paris, FRA;** and **Rome, ITA.** Bus #10 runs to the Gare Cornavin (15min., 6-12 per hr., 3CHF), but the train trip is shorter (6min., 6 per hr., 3CHF).

Trains: Trains run 4:30am-1am. **Gare Cornavin,** pl. Cornavin, is the main station. To: **Basel** (2hr., 1 per 2hr., 69CHF); **Bern** (2hr., 2 per hr., 46CHF); **Lausanne** (40min., 3-4 per hr., 20.60CHF); **Zürich** (3hr., 1-2 per hr., 80CHF); **Nyon** (20 min., 8.20CHF); **St. Gallen** (4hr., 1-2 per hr., 95CHF). Ticket counter open M-F 5:15am-9:30pm, Sa-Su 5:30am-9:30pm. **Gare des Eaux-Vives** (☎022 736 1620), on av. de la Gare des Eaux-Vives (tram #12 to Amandoliers SNCF), connects to France's regional rail through **Annecy, FRA** (1hr., 6 per day, 15CHF) or **Chamonix, FRA** (2hr., 4 per day, 25CHF).

Public Transportation: Geneva has an efficient **bus and tram** network (☎022 308 3311; www.tpg.ch). Single tickets, which can be purchased in the train station, are valid for 1hr. within the "orange" city zone (which includes the airport) are 3CHF; rides of 3 stops or less 2CHF. **Day passes** (10CHF) and a **9hr. pass** (7CHF) are available for the canton of Geneva; day passes for the whole region 18CHF. MC/V. Stamp multi-use tickets before boarding at machines in the station. Buses run 5am-12:30am; **Noctambus** (F-Sa 12:30-3:45am, 3CHF) offers night service. Tram use is free with the **Geneva visitor card,** usually distributed by hotels and hostels—make sure to ask for one.

Taxis: Taxi-Phone (☎022 331 4133). 6.80CHF plus 3CHF per km. 30CHF from airport.

Bike Rental: Geneva has well-marked bike paths and special traffic signals. Behind the station, **Genève Roule,** pl. Montbrillant 17 (☎022 740 1343), has **free bikes.** (Passport and 20CHF deposit. First 4 hours free, 1CHF per hour thereafter. Fines are 60CHF for lost free bike. Mountain bikes 17CHF per day. Touring bikes 28CHF per day. May-Oct. only.) Other locations at Bains des Pâquis, Plain de Plainpalis, Place de l'Octroi, and pl.

du Rhône. Arrive before 9am, as bikes go quickly. Free **bike maps** available. Open daily May-Oct. 8am-9pm; Nov.-Apr. 8am-6pm. Cash only.

Hitchhiking: *Let's Go* does not recommend hitchhiking. Those headed to Germany or northern Switzerland take bus #4 to Jardin Botanique, where they try to catch a ride. Those headed to France take bus #4 to Palettes, then line D to St. Julien.

ORIENTATION AND PRACTICAL INFORMATION

The twisting streets and quiet squares of the historic *vieille ville* (Old Town), centered on **Cathédrale de St-Pierre,** make up the heart of Geneva. Across the **Rhône River** to the north, five-star hotels give way to lakeside promenades, **International Hill,** and rolling parks. Across the **Arve River** to the south lies the village of **Carouge,** home to bars and clubs (take tram #12 or 13 to pl. du Marché).

Tourist Office: r. du Mont-Blanc 18 (☎022 909 7000; www.geneva-tourism.ch), in the Central Post Office Building. From Cornavin, walk 5min. toward the Pont du Mont-Blanc. Staff books hotel rooms for 5CHF, gives out free city **maps,** and leads English-language walking tours (daily 10am; 15CHF). Open M 10am-6pm, Tu-Su 9am-6pm.

Consulates: Australia, chemin des Fins 2 (☎022 799 9100). **Canada,** Laurenzerberg 2 (☎531 38 3000). **New Zealand,** chemin des Fins 2 (☎022 929 0350). **UK,** r. de Vermont 37 (☎022 918 2400). **US,** r. Versonnex 7 (☎022 840 5160).

Currency Exchange: The currency exchange inside the **Gare Cornavin** has good rates with no commission on traveler's checks, makes cash advances on credit cards, and arranges **Western Union** transfers. Open M-Sa 7am-8pm, Su 8am-5:50pm.

GLBT Resources: Dialogai, r. de la Navigation 11-13, entrance Rue d. Levant 5 (☎022 906 4040). From Gare Cornavin, turn left, walk 5min. down r. de Lausanne, and turn right onto r. de la Navigation. Open M 9am-10pm, Tu-Th 9am-6pm, F 9am-5pm.

Police: R. de Berne 6 (☎117). Open M-F 9am-noon and 3-6:30pm, Sa 9am-noon.

Hospital: Geneva University Hospital, r. Micheli-du-Crest 24 (☎022 372 3311; www.hug-ge.ch). Bus #1 or 5 or tram #7, or Bus #35 from Place du Augustines. Door #2 is for emergency care; door #3 is for consultations.

Internet: Charly's Multimedia Check Point, r. de Fribourg 7 (☎022 901 1313; www.charlys.com). 4CHF per hr. Free Wi-Fi. Open M-Sa 9am-midnight, Su 1-11pm.

Post Office: Poste Centrale, r. du Mont-Blanc 18, 1 block from Gare Cornavin. Open M-F 7:30am-6pm, Sa 9am-4pm. **Postal Code:** CH-1200.

ACCOMMODATIONS AND CAMPING

The indispensable *Info Jeunes* lists about 30 budget options, and the tourist office publishes *Budget Hotels*, which stretches the definition of budget to 120CHF per person. Cheap beds are relatively scarce, so reserve ahead.

Hôme St-Pierre, Cour St-Pierre 4 (☎022 310 3707; info@homestpierre.ch). Take bus #5 to pl. Neuve, then walk up Rampe de la Treille, turn left onto R. Puits-St.-Pierre, then right on R. du Solil Levant. This 150-year-old "home" has comfortable beds and a great location beside the cathedral. Wi-Fi available. Reception M-Sa 9am-noon and 4-8pm, Su 9am-noon. Dorms 27CHF; singles 40CHF; doubles 60CHF. MC/V. ❶

City Hostel Geneva, r. Ferrier 2 (☎022 901 1500; www.cityhostel.ch). From the train station, head down r. de Lausanne. Take the 1st left on r. du Prieuré, which becomes r. Ferrier. Spotless, cozy rooms. Kitchens on each floor. Linens 3.50CHF. Internet 5CHF per hr. Reception 7:30am-noon and 1pm-midnight. 3-4 bed single-sex dorms 28.50CHF; singles 59-64CHF; doubles 72-86CHF. Reserve ahead in summer. MC/V. ❷

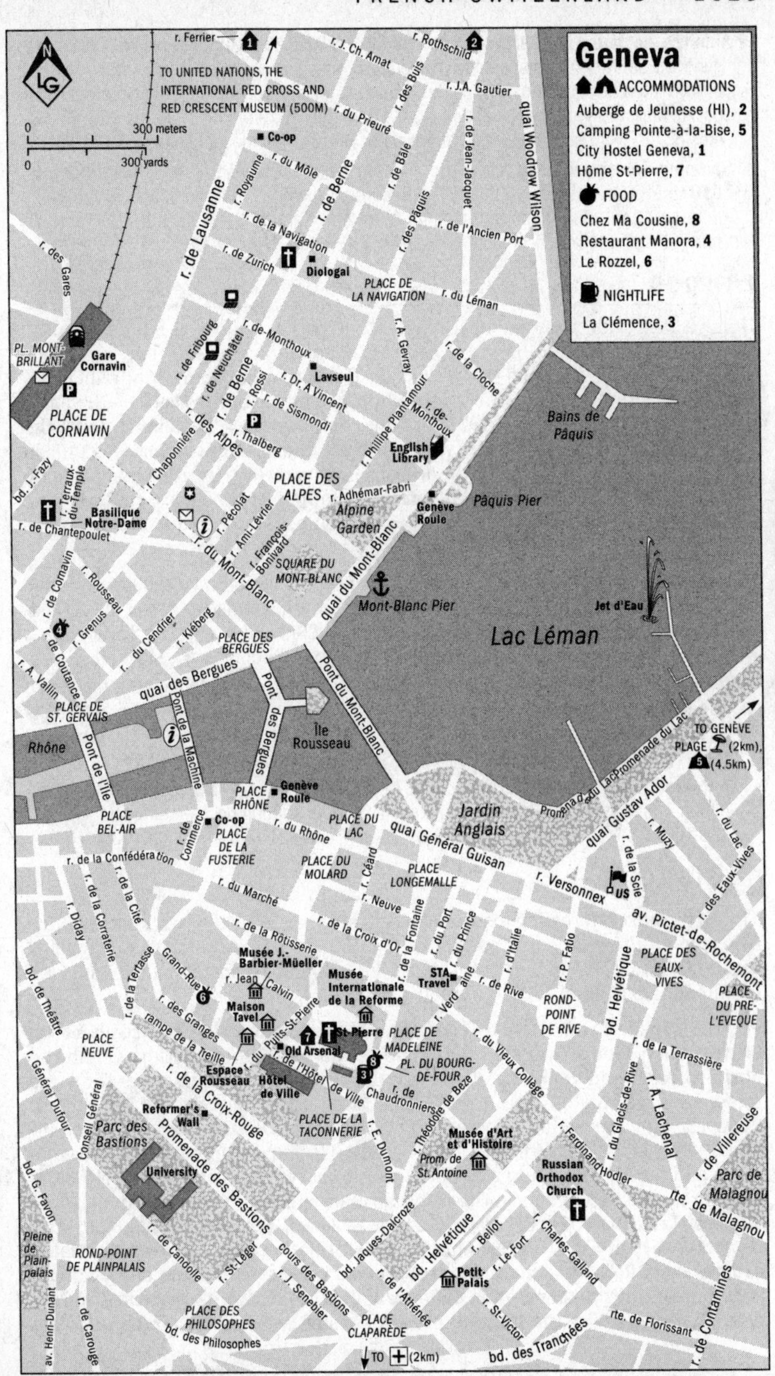
Geneva
ACCOMMODATIONS
Auberge de Jeunesse (HI), 2
Camping Pointe-à-la-Bise, 5
City Hostel Geneva, 1
Hôme St-Pierre, 7
FOOD
Chez Ma Cousine, 8
Restaurant Manora, 4
Le Rozzel, 6
NIGHTLIFE
La Clémence, 3
0
300 meters
0
300 yards
TO UNITED NATIONS, THE INTERNATIONAL RED CROSS AND RED CRESCENT MUSEUM (500M)
r. Ferrier
r. Rothschild
r. J. Ch. Amat
r. J.A. Gautier
r. des Buis
r. du Prieuré
quai Woodrow Wilson
r. de Jean-Jacquet
Co-op
r. du Môle
r. de Bâle
r. Royaume
r. de Berne
r. de Lausanne
r. des Pâquis
r. de l'Ancien Port
r. de la Navigation
r. des Gares
r. de Zurich
Diologai
PLACE DE LA NAVIGATION
r. du Léman
r. de Fribourg
r. de-Monthoux
r. A. Gevray
r. de la Cloche
PL. MONT-BRILLANT
Gare Cornavin
r. de Neuchâtel
Lavseul
r. Dr. A Vincent
r. Rossi
r. de Sismondi
r. Philippe Plantamour
r. de-Monthoux
Bains de Pâquis
PLACE DE CORNAVIN
r. des Alpes
r. Thalberg
English Library
r. Chaponnière
bd. J.-Fazy
r. Terraux-du-Temple
PLACE DES ALPES
r. Adhémar-Fabri
Alpine Garden
Genève Roule
Pâquis Pier
Basilique Notre-Dame
r. de Chantepoulet
r. Pécolat
r. Ami-Lévrier
r. François-Bonivard
r. du Mont-Blanc
SQUARE DU MONT-BLANC
quai du Mont-Blanc
r. de Cornavin
r. Rousseau
Mont-Blanc Pier
Jet d'Eau
r. Grenus
r. du Cendrier
r. Kléberg
Lac Léman
r. de Coutance
PLACE DES BERGUES
r. A. Vallin
quai des Bergues
Pont des Bergues
Pont du Mont-Blanc
PLACE DE ST. GERVAIS
Pont de la Machine
Île Rousseau
Rhône
Pont de l'Île
TO GENÈVE PLAGE (2km), (4.5km)
Promenade du Lac
PLACE RHÔNE
Genève Roule
Jardin Anglais
quai Gustav Ador
PLACE BEL-AIR
r. de Commerce
Co-op
PLACE DE LA FUSTERIE
r. du Rhône
PLACE DU LAC
quai Général Guisan
r. Muzy
r. du Lac
r. de la Confédération
r. de la Scie
r. des Eaux-Vives
PLACE DU MOLARD
r. Céard
PLACE LONGEMALLE
r. Versonnex
US
r. du Marché
r. de la Cité
r. Neuve
av. Pictet-de-Rochemont
r. de la Corraterie
r. Diday
r. de la Rôtisserie
r. de la Croix d'Or
r. de la Fontaine
r. du Port
r. du Prince
r. d'Italie
r. P. Fatio
PLACE DES EAUX-VIVES
Musée J.-Barbier-Mueller
Musée Internationale de la Reforme
STA Travel
r. de Rive
bd. de Théâtre
r. de la Tertasse
Grand-Rue
r. Jean Calvin
r. Verdaine
ROND-POINT DE RIVE
bd. Helvétique
PLACE DU PRE-L'EVEQUE
r. des Granges
Maison Tavel
St-Pierre
PLACE DE MADELEINE
PLACE NEUVE
rampe de la Treille
r. du Puits-St-Pierre
Old Arsenal
r. du Vieux Collège
r. de la Terrassière
PL. DU BOURG-DE-FOUR
Espace Rousseau
r. de l'Hôtel de Ville
Hôtel de Ville
r. de Chaudronniers
r. Théodore de Beze
r. du Glacis-de-Rive
r. A. Lachenal
r. Général Dufour
Conseil Général
r. de la Croix-Rouge
Reformer's Wall
PLACE DE LA TACONNERIE
r. E. Dumont
Musée d'Art et d'Histoire
r. Ferdinand Hodler
r. de Villereuse
Parc des Bastions
Promenade des Bastions
Prom. de St. Antoine
Russian Orthodox Church
Parc de Malagnou
University
rte. de Malagnou
bd. G. Favon
bd. Jacques-Dalcroze
bd. Helvétique
r. Bellot
r. Charles-Galland
Pleine de Plain-palais
ROND-POINT DE PLAINPALAIS
r. de Candolle
r. St-Léger
cours des Bastions
r. Le-Fort
Petit-Palais
r. J. Senebier
r. de l'Athénée
r. St-Victor
rte. de Florissant
r. de Contamines
av. Henri-Dunant
PLACE DES PHILOSOPHES
bd. des Philosophes
r. de Carouge
PLACE CLAPARÈDE
bd. des Tranchées
TO (2km)

Auberge de Jeunesse (HI), r. Rothschild 30 (☎022 732 6260; www.youthhostel.ch/geneva). Standard rooms, some of which have lake views. Chess lovers can duke it out on the life-size chess board outside. Breakfast included. Laundry 8CHF. Internet 4CHF per hr. Max. 6-night stay. Reception 6:30-10am and 2pm-midnight. Dorms 35CHF; doubles 85CHF, with shower 95CHF; quads 135CHF. 6CHF HI discount. AmEx/MC/V. ❷

Camping Pointe-à-la-Bise, chemin de la Bise (☎022 752 1296). Take bus #8 or tram #16 to Rive, then bus E north to Bise. Reception July-Aug. 8am-noon and 2-9pm; Apr.-June and Sept. 8am-noon and 4-8pm. Open Apr.-Sept. Reserve ahead. 7CHF per person, 12 CHF per tent; 4-person bungalows 98CHF. AmEx/MC/V. ❶

FOOD

Geneva has it all, from sushi to paella, but you may need a banker's salary to foot the bill. Pick up basics at *boulangeries*, *pâtisseries*, or supermarkets, which often have attached cafeterias. Try the **Coop** on the corner of r. du Commerce and r. du Rhône, in the Centre Rhône Fusterie, or the **Migros** in the basement of the Places des Cygnes shopping center on r. de Lausanne, down the street from the station. A variety of relatively cheap ethnic eateries center in the **Les Pâquis** area, bordered by r. de Lausanne and Gare Cornavin on one side and the quais Mont-Blanc and Wilson on the other. Around **place du Cirque** and **plaine de Plainpalais** are student-oriented tea rooms. To the south, the neighborhood of **Carouge** is known for its cozy pizzerias and funky brasseries.

Chez Ma Cousine, pl. du Bourg-de-Four 6 (☎022 310 9696; www.chezmacousine.ch), down the stairs behind the cathedral. This cheery cafe has perfected *poulet* with its half-chicken with salad and french fries special (14.90CHF) and a variety of chicken salads (14-15CHF). Open M-Sa 11am-11:30pm, Su 11am-10:30pm. AmEx/MC/V. ❷

Restaurant Manora, r. de Cornavin 4 (☎022 909 490), on the top floor of the Manor department store, near the train station. Offers a wide selection of entrees, fresh fruits and vegetables, and free water (a rarity in Switzerland). Entrees 5-12CHF. Open M-W 9am-7pm, Th 9am-9pm, F 9am-7:30pm, Sa 8:30am-6pm. AmEx/MC/V. ❶

Le Rozzel, Grand-Rue 18 (☎022 312 4272). Take bus #5 to pl. Neuve, then walk up the hill on r. Jean-Calvin to Grand-Rue. Pleasant outdoor seating on a winding street. Sweet and savory crepes 8-19CHF. Open M-Sa 10am-7pm, Su 10am-noon. MC/V. ❷

SIGHTS

The city's most interesting historical sights are located within walking distance from the *vieille ville* (Old Town). The tourist office has 2hr. English-language walking tours. (Mid-June to Sept. M, W, F-Sa 10am, Tu and Th at 6:30pm; Oct. to mid-June Sa 10am. 15CHF, students 10CHF.)

VIEILLE VILLE. From 1536 to 1564, Calvin preached at the **Cathédrale de St-Pierre,** which looms over the *vieille ville* from its hilltop location. Climb the north tower for an unparalleled view of the city, and the south tower for some interesting information about the bells. *(Cathedral open June-Sept. M-F 9:30-6:30, Sa 9:30am-5pm, Su 10am-6:30pm. Concert Sa 6pm; service Su 10am. Tower open June-Sept. M-F 9am-6pm, Sa 9am-4:30pm. Cathedral free, tower 4CHF.)* Ruins, including a Roman sanctuary and an AD 4th-century basilica, rest in an **archaeological site** below the cathedral; you can even see the tomb around which the city was built. *(Open June-Sept. Tu-Su 10am-5pm; Oct.-May Tu-F 2-5pm, Sa-Su 1:30-5:30pm. Last entry 4:30. 8CHF, students 4CHF.)* For a dense presentation of Reformation 101, visit the **Musée International de la Réforme,** 4 r. du Cloitre, housed on the site of the city's official acceptance of Protestantism in 1536. *(☎022 310 2431; www.musee-reforme.ch. Open [illegible] 10am-5pm. 10CHF, students 7CHF.)* At the western end of the *vieille ville* sits the 12th-century **Maison Tavel,** r. de Puits Saint Pierre 6. The oldest privately owned home in Geneva contains a wonderful scale model of the city as well a wide selection of trinkets from everyday life throughout the years. *(☎022 418 3700; www.ville-ge.ch/mah. Open Tu-Su 10am-5pm. Free.)* Across the street is the **Hôtel de Ville** (Town Hall), where world leaders met on August 22, 1864 for the first Geneva Convention. The **Grand-Rue,** beginning at the Hôtel de Ville, is lined with medieval workshops and 18th-century mansions. Plaques commemorate famous residents like **Jean-Jacques Rousseau,** who was born at #40. Visit the **Espace Rousseau** there for a short but informative audiovisual presentation of his life and work. *(☎022 310 1028; www.espace-rousseau.ch. Open Tu-Su 11am-5:30pm. 5CHF, students 3CHF.)* Below the cathedral, along r. de la Croix-Rouge, the **Parc des Bastions** stretches from pl. Neuve to pl. des Philosophes and includes **Le Mur des Réformateurs** (The Reformers' Wall), a sprawling collection of bas-relief figures depicting Protestant Reformers. The hulking **Musée d'Art et d'Histoire,** R. Charles-Galland 2, offers everything from prehistoric relics to contemporary art. *(☎022 418 2610; mah.ville-ge.ch. Open Tu-Su 10am-5pm. Free.)*

WATERFRONT. As you descend from the cathedral to the lake, medieval lanes give way to wide streets and chic boutiques. Down quai Gustave Ardor, the **Jet d'Eau,** Europe's highest fountain and Geneva's city symbol, spews a seven-ton plume of water 134m into the air. The **floral clock** in the **Jardin Anglais** pays homage to Geneva's watch industry. Possibly the city's most overrated attraction, it was once its most hazardous—the clock had to be cut back because tourists intent on taking the perfect photograph repeatedly backed into oncoming traffic. For a day on the waterfront, head up the south shore of the lake to Genève Plage, where there is a water slide and an enormous pool. *(☎022 736 2482; www.geneve-plage.ch. Open mid-May to mid-Sept. daily 10am-8pm. 7CHF, students 4.50CHF.)*

INTERNATIONAL HILL. North of the train station, the International Red Cross building contains the impressive **International Red Cross and Red Crescent Museum,** av. de la Paix 17. *(Bus #8, F, V or Z to Appia ☎022 748 9511; www.micr.org. Open M and W-Su 10am-5pm. 10CHF, students 5CHF. English-language audio tour 3CHF.)* Across the street, the European headquarters of the **United Nations,** av. de la Paix 14, is in the same building that once held the League of Nations. The constant traffic of international diplomats is entertainment in itself. *(☎022 917 4896; www.unog.ch. Mandatory 1hr. tour. English tours every hour. Open July-Aug. daily 10am-5pm; Apr.-June and Sept.-Oct. daily 10am-noon and 2-4pm; Nov.-Mar. M-F 10am-noon and 2-4pm. 10CHF, students 8CHF.)*

SWITZERLAND

ENTERTAINMENT AND NIGHTLIFE

Genève Agenda, available at the tourist office, features event listings from major festivals to movies. In late June, the **Fête de la Musique** fills the city with nearly 500 free concerts of all styles. Parc de la Grange has free **jazz concerts.** Geneva hosts the biggest celebration of **American Independence Day** outside the US (July 4), and the **Fêtes de Genève** in early August fill the city with international music and fireworks. **L'Escalade** (Dec. 2009) commemorates the successful blockade of invading Savoyard troops.

Nightlife in Geneva is divided by neighborhood. **Place Bourg-de-Four,** below the cathedral in the *vieille ville*, attracts students to its charming terraces. **Place du Molard** has loud, somewhat upscale bars and clubs. For something more frenetic, head to **Les Pâquis,** near Gare Cornavin and pl. de la Navigation. As the city's red-light district, it has a wide array of rowdy, low-lit bars and some nightclubs. This neighborhood is also home to many of the city's gay bars. Carouge, across the Arve River, is a locus of student-friendly nightlife. In the *vieille ville*, generations of students have had their share of drinks at the intimate **La Clémence,** pl. du Bourg-de-Four 20. You can count on it to be open even when the rest of the city has shut down. Try the local Calvinus beer (7.40CHF) to do your part for Protestantism. (Sandwiches 3.30-6.40CHF. Open M-Th 7am-12:30am, F-Sa 7am-1:30am. MC/V.)

LAUSANNE ☎021

The wonderfully unique museums, medieval *vieille ville*, and lazy Lac Léman waterfront of Lausanne (pop. 128,000) definitely make it worth a visit. The Gothic **Cathédrale,** with its intricate stained glass and old tombs stands as the centerpiece of the *vieille ville.* (Open May to mid-Sept. M-F 7am-7pm, Sa-Su 8am-7pm; mid-Sept. to Apr. M-F 7am-5:30pm, Sa-Su 8am-5:30pm.) Below the cathedral is the city hall, **Hôtel de Ville,** on pl. de la Palud, a meeting point for guided tours of the town. (☎021 320 1261; www.lausanne.ch/visites. Tours May-Sept. M-Sa 10am and 2:30pm. 10CHF, students free.) The **Musée Olympique,** quai d'Ouchy 1, is a high-tech shrine to modern Olympians; best of all is the extensive video collection, allowing visitors to relive almost any moment of the games. Take bus #2 to Ouchy, bus #8 to Musée Olympique, or bus #4 to Montchoisi. (☎021 621 6511; www.olympic.org. Open Apr.-Oct. daily 9am-6pm; Nov.-Mar. Tu-Su 9am-6pm. 15CHF, students 10CHF.) The fascinating **Collection de l'Art Brut,** av. Bergières 11, is filled with unusual sculptures, drawings, and paintings by fringe artists: schizophrenics, peasants, and criminals. Take bus #2 to Jomini or 3 to Beaulieu. The museum is behind the trees across from the Congress Center. (☎021 315 2570; www.artbrut.ch. Open July-Aug. daily 11am-6pm; Sept.-June Tu-Su 11am-10pm. 8CHF, students 5CHF.) The city's inhabitants descend to the lake on weekends and after work, making it one of the liveliest places in the city. In Ouchy, Lausanne's port, several booths along quai de Belgique rent **pedal boats** (13CHF per 30min., 20CHF per hr.) and offer **water skiing** or **wake boarding** (35CHF per 15min.) on Lac Léman. The gorgeous park also has a life-size chess board, a carousel (3CHF/ride), and a giant jungle gym for the young at heart. For more activity, Lausanne Roule loans **free bikes** beside pl. de la Riponne on R. du Tennel (☎021 533 0115. www.lausanneroule.ch. ID and 20CHF deposit. Open late Apr. to late Oct. daily 7:30am-9:30pm.)

Lausanne Guesthouse and Backpacker ❷, chemin des Epinettes 4, at the train tracks, manages to keep the noise out and makes the most of its location with lake views, an equipped kitchen, a cozy living room, and a rose garden with grills. Head left and downhill out of the station on W. Fraisse; take the first right on chemin des Epinettes. (☎021 601 8000; www.lausanne-guesthouse.ch. Bike rental 20CHF per day. Linens 5CHF. Laundry 5CHF. Internet 8CHF per hr. Wi-Fi free for the first 30min, 2CHF/hr thereafter. Kitchen closed from 1:30-2:30pm for cleaning. Reception daily 7:30am-noon and 3-10pm. Book ahead. Dorms 32CHF; singles 85CHF, with bath 94CHF; doubles 95/115CHF. 5% ISIC discount. MC/V.) Restaurants center around **Place St-François,** the *vieille ville*, and the lake front, while boulangeries sell sandwiches on practically every street. **Le Barbare ❶,** Escaliers du Marché 27, near the cathedral, has sandwiches (6.50CHF), omelettes (7.50-10CHF), and pizza (13-17CHF) for cheap. (☎021 312 2132. Open M-Sa 8:30am-midnight. AmEx/MC/V.)

Trains leave for: Basel (2hr., 1 per 2hr., 59CHF); Geneva (50min., 3-4 per hr., 20.60CHF); Montreux (20min., 3-4 per hr., 10.20CHF); Zürich (2½hr., 1-2 per hr., 67CHF); Paris, FRA (4hr., 4 per day, 146.20CHF). The **tourist office** by the Ouchy kefront reserves rooms for 4CHF, and gives out free maps and water. (☎021 373. Open daily 9am-7pm.) **Postal Code:** CH-1000.

SWITZERLAND

ITALIAN SWITZERLAND

Ever since Switzerland won the canton of Ticino from Italy in 1512, the region has been renowned for its mix of Swiss efficiency and Italian *dolce vita.* It's no wonder the rest of Switzerland vacations here among jasmine-laced villas painted in the muted pastels of gelato.

LUGANO

☎091

Set in a valley between sloping green mountains, Lugano (pop. 52,000) draws plenty of visitors with its mix of artistic flair and historical religious sites. The ornate frescoes filling the 16th-century **Cattedrale San Lorenzo,** located downhill from the train station and overlooking the whole city, still gleam with vivid colors. (☎091 92 28 842. Open daily 9:30am-6pm. Free.) The small, 14th-century **Chiesa San Rocco,** in P. Maghetti, two blocks left of P. della Riforma, houses an ornate altarpiece and a series of frescoes depicting the life of its patron saint. (Open daily 10:30am-12:30pm and 3:30-6:30pm. Free.) Hikers can take on the towering **Monte Brè** (933m) and **Monte San Salvatore** (912m).The **Monte Brè funicolare** (☎091 97 13 171; www.montebre.ch) is a 20min. ride down the river along Riva Albertolli from the *centro* (every 20min. 9:10am-6:45pm). An easier way is to take bus #1 (dir.: Castagnola) to the Cassarate-Monte Brè stop, or to catch the tourist train at the tourist office. (☎091 079 685 7070. Tourist train runs every 40min. daily 10am-8pm. 8CHF, children 5CHF.) During the first two weekends of July, Lugano's **Estival Jazz** (www.estivaljazz.ch) fills P. della Riforma with free nighttime concerts. In summer, the young and old trek down to the beach for **Cinema Lago,** where movies are screened lakeside for 15CHF.

Converted from a 19th-century villa, the palm-tree-enveloped **Hotel *and* Hostel Montarina ❶**, V. Montarina 1, has a large swimming pool amidst grapevines, a TV room, a kitchen, and a terrace overlooking the city. From the station, walk right 200m, cross the train tracks, then walk uphill and up the stairs to the left. (☎091 96 67 272; www.montarina.ch. Breakfast 12CHF. Linen 4CHF. Laundry 4CHF; detergent 2CHF. Internet 10CHF per hr. Reception 7:30am-11pm; after 11pm, ring buzzer. Reservations recommended. Dorms 25CHF; singles 70CHF, with bath 80CHF; doubles 100/120CHF. AmEx/MC/V.) For quick eats, the **outdoor market** in P. della Riforma sells seafood, produce, flowers, and veggie sandwiches. (Open Tu and F 8am-noon.)

Trains in Lugano (☎091 92 35 120) run from P. della Stazione to Chiasso (30min., every hr. 6:10am-1:14am, 9.60CHF), Bellinzona (30min., every 30min.-1hr. 5:26am-12:midnight, 12CHF), and Milan (45min., every hr. 6:10am-9:48pm, 27.40CHF). The **tourist office** is in the Palazzo Civico. (☎091 91 33 232; www.lugano-tourism.ch. Open Apr.-Oct. M-F 9am-7pm, Sa 9am-6pm, Su 10am-6pm; Nov.-Mar. M-F 9am-noon and 2-5:30pm, Sa 10am-noon and 1:30-5pm.) **Postal Code:** CH-6900.and 1:30-5pm.) **Postal Code:** CH-6900.

TURKEY (TÜRKİYE)

Turkey is a land rich with history and beauty. Home to some of the world's greatest civilizations, Turkey is at the intersection of two very different continents. İstanbul, on the land bridge that connects Europe and Asia, is the infinitely intricate and surprisingly seductive progeny of three thousand years of migrant history. Though resolutely secular by government decree, Turkish life is graced by the religious traditions of its 99% Muslim population. Tourists cram İstanbul and the glittering western coast, while Anatolia (the Asian portion of Turkey) remains a backpacker's paradise of alpine meadows, cliffside monasteries, and truly hospitable people.

ESSENTIALS

FACTS AND FIGURES

OFFICIAL NAME: Republic of Turkey.

FORM OF GOVERNMENT: Republican parliamentary democracy.

CAPITAL: Ankara.

MAJOR CITIES: İstanbul, Adana, Bursa, Gaziantep, İzmir.

POPULATION: 70,414,000.

TIME ZONE: GMT +2 or +3.

LANGUAGE: Turkish.

RELIGION: Muslim (99.8%).

LARGEST SKEWER OF KEBAB MEAT: Created by the Melike Döner Co. in Osmangazi-Bursa, Turkey on Nov. 6, 2005. Weighed in at 2698kg (5948 lb.).

WHEN TO GO

With mild winters and hot summers, there's no wrong time to travel to Turkey. While most tourists go in July and August, those visiting between April and June or September and October will enjoy temperate days, smaller crowds, and lower prices. The rainy season runs from November to February, so remember to bring appropriate gear if traveling during these months.

DOCUMENTS AND FORMALITIES

EMBASSIES AND CONSULATES. Foreign embassies to Turkey are in Ankara, though many nations also have consulates in İstanbul. Turkish embassies and consulates abroad include: **Australia,** 6 Moonah Pl., Yarralumla, Canberra, ACT 2600 (☎02 62 34 00 00; www.turkishembassy.org.au); **Canada,** 197 Wurtemburg St., Ottawa, ON, K1N 8L9 (☎613-789-4044; www.turkishembassy.com); **Ireland,** 11 Clyde Rd., Ballsbridge, Dublin 4 (☎353 668 52 40); **New Zealand,** 15-17 Murphy St., Level 8, Wellington 6011 (☎044 721 290; turkemşxtra.co.nz); **UK,** 43 Belgrave Sq., London SW1X 8PA (☎020 73 93 02 02; www.turkishembassylondon.org); **US,** 2525 Massachusetts Ave., N.W., Washington, D.C. 20008 (☎202-612-6700; www.turkishembassy.org).

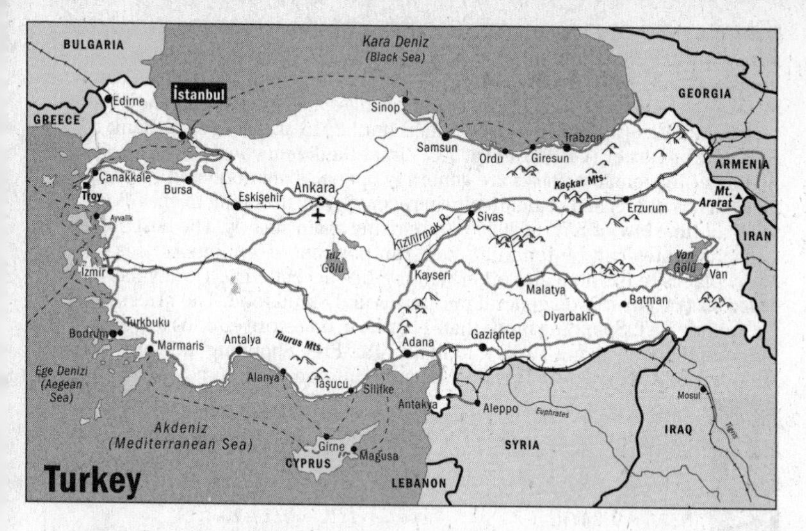

VISA AND ENTRY INFORMATION. Citizens of Canada and the US may obtain visas at entry points into Turkey for stays of less than three months (paid in cash). For longer stays, study, or work visas, and for citizens of Australia, New Zealand, and countries of the EU, it is necessary to obtain visas in advance (about US$20; Canadians, about US$60), available at Turkish consulates abroad. Travelers must apply at least one month in advance. For more info, visit www.mfa.gov.tr/mfa. If arriving by ferry, expect a port tax of at least €10.

ENTRANCE REQUIREMENTS.

Passport: Required for all travelers.

Visa: Required for citizens of Australia, Canada, some EU countries, the UK, and the US. Citizens of New Zealand do not need a visa to enter. Multiple-entry visas (€10-20), available at the border, are valid for up to 90 days.

Letter of Invitation: Not required.

Inoculations: Not required. Recommended up-to-date on DTaP (diphtheria, tetanus, and pertussis), hepatitis A, hepatitis B, MMR (measles, mumps, and rubella), polio booster, and typhoid.

Work Permit: Required for all foreigners planning to work in Turkey.

Driving Permit: Required for all those planning to drive.

TOURIST SERVICES

In big cities like İstanbul, many establishments that claim to be tourist offices are actually travel agencies. That said, **travel agencies** can often be more helpful for finding accommodations or booking transportation than the official Turkish **tourist offices.** Although it's best to shop around from agency to agency for a deal on tickets, be wary of exceptionally low prices—offices may tack on exorbitant hidden charges. The official tourism website (www.tourismturkey.org) has visa info, helpful links, and office locations.

MONEY

In response to rampant inflation and ever-confusing prices, Turkey revalued its currency in 2005, dropping 6 zeroes. One million Turkish Lira became 1 **Yeni**

Türk Lirası (New Turkish Lira; YTL). One New Turkish Lira equals 100 **New Kuruş,** with standard denominations of 5, 10, 25, and 50. 1YTL are available as both coins and bills, while denominations of 1, 5, 10, 20, 50 and 100YTL come only as banknotes. While Old Turkish Lira are no longer accepted as currency, Turkish Lira banknotes (bills) can be redeemed until 2016 at the Central Bank of the Republic of Turkey (CBRT) and at T.C. Ziraat Bank branches. Old Lira coins are no longer redeemable. **Banks** are generally open 8:30am-noon and 1:30-5:30pm. **Inflation** has decreased dramatically in recent years, dropping from 45% in 2003 to an all-time low of 7.7% in 2005 before rising again slightly. The best currency exchange rates can be found at state-run post and telephone offices (PTT). Many places in İstanbul and other major cities accept euro. Turkey has a **value added tax (VAT)** of 18% on general purchases and 8% on food. The prices in *Let's Go* include VAT. Spending more than 118YTL in one store entitles travelers to a tax refund upon leaving Turkey; look for "Tax-Free Shopping" stickers in shop windows or ask for a form inside. For more info on VAT refunds, see p. 21.

NEW TURKISH LIRA (YTL)		
	AUS$1 = 1.07YTL	1YTL = AUS$0.94
	CDN$1 = 1.12YTL	1YTL = CDN$0.90
	EUR€1 = 1.80YTL	1YTL = EUR€0.56
	NZ$1 = 0.84YTL	1YTL = NZ$1.20
	UK£1 = 2.28YTL	1YTL = UK£0.44
	US$1 = 1.17YTL	1YTL = US$0.85

HEALTH AND SAFETY

EMERGENCY **Ambulance:** ☎112. **Fire:** ☎110. **Police:** ☎155.

Medical facilities in Turkey vary greatly. In İstanbul and Ankara, high-quality hospitals for foreigners and expats provide care for all but the most serious of conditions, and most have adequate medical supplies. Outside the cities, though, it is a different story; try to avoid rural hospitals. **Pharmacies** are easy to find in major cities and are generally well stocked and have at least one professional pharmacist, as they're mandated by the government. Don't drink **water** that hasn't been boiled or filtered, and watch out for ice in drinks. Most local dairy products are safe to eat.

Petty crime is common in urban centers, especially in crowded squares, the Grand Bazaar, and on public transportation. Common schemes include distracting travelers with a staged fight while they are being robbed; drugging travelers with tea, juice, or other drinks and then robbing them; or simply presenting travelers with outrageously expensive bills. Pay attention to your valuables, never accept drinks from a stranger, and always ask in advance for prices at bars and restaurants. Though **pirated goods** are sold on the street, it is illegal to buy them; doing so can result in fines. **Drug trafficking** leads to severe jail time. It is also illegal to show disrespect to Atatürk or to insult the state.

Foreign **women,** especially those traveling alone, attract significant attention in Turkey. Unwanted catcalls and other forms of verbal harassment are common, although physical harassment is rare. Regardless of the signals a foreign woman intends to send, her foreignness alone may suggest a liberal openness to amorous advances. Smiling, regarded in the West as a sign of confidence and friendliness, is sometimes associated in Turkey with sexual attraction. As long as women expect plenty of attention and take common-sense precautions, however, even single travelers need not feel anxious.

Although **homosexuality** is legal in Turkey, religious and social norms keep most homosexual activity discreet. Homophobia can be a problem, especially in remote areas; expect authorities to be unsympathetic. Despite the close contact that Turks maintain with same-sex friends, public displays of affection between gay and lesbian travelers should be avoided. Turkey's urban centers have bars and informal cruising areas for men only, though they may not be very overt. **Lambda İstanbul**, a GLBT support group, lists guides to gay-friendly establishments on its website (www.qrd.org/qrd/www/world/europe/turkey/).

KEEPING IN TOUCH

PHONE CODES	**Country code:** 90. **International dialing prefix:** 00. From outside Turkey, dial int'l dialing prefix (see inside back cover) + 90 + city code + local number. Within Turkey, dial city code + local number.

EMAIL AND THE INTERNET. Like everything in Turkey, the availability of Internet services depends on where in the country you are. In İstanbul, Internet cafes are everywhere; in the east, they can be tough to find. Free Wi-Fi is available at hostels and cafes across the city.

TELEPHONES. Whenever possible, use a calling card for international phone calls, as long-distance rates for national phone services are often very high. **Mobile phones** are an increasingly popular and economical option. Major mobile carriers include **Turkcell, Telsim,** and **Avea.** Direct-dial access numbers for calling out of Turkey include: **AT&T Direct** (☎80 01 22 77); **British Telecom** (☎80 044 1177); **Canada Direct** (☎80 01 66 77). For info on calling from Europe, see p. 31.

MAIL. The postal system is quick and expensive in Turkey. Airmail should be marked *par avion*, and **Poste Restante** is available in most major cities.

ACCOMMODATIONS AND CAMPING

TURKEY	❶	❷	❸	❹	❺
ACCOMMODATIONS	under 20YTL	20-39YTL	40-59YTL	60-80YTL	over 80YTL

When it comes to lodging, Turkey is a budget traveler's paradise. **Hostels** are available in nearly every major city. **Pensions**—a step above hostels in both quality and price—are also generally available, as are **hotels** in every price range. **Camping** is very common throughout Turkey, especially on the Aegean coast; campgrounds are generally inexpensive (US$3-10) or free.

FOOD AND DRINK

TURKEY	❶	❷	❸	❹	❺
FOOD	under 8YTL	8-15YTL	16-20YTL	21-30YTL	over 30YTL

Turkish cuisine is as varied as Turkish culture. Strategically located on the land bridge between Europe and Asia, İstanbul is the culinary epicenter of the region, drawing from the dietary practices of many different cultures. Fish is a staple in Turkey, especially along the coast, where it is prepared with local spices according to traditional recipes. When it comes to meat, lamb and chicken are Turkish favorites, and are typically prepared as **kebab**—a term which means far more in Turkey than the dry meat cubes on a stick found in most Western restaurants. Despite its strong Muslim majority, Turkey produces good wines. More interesting, however, is the unofficial national drink: *rakı*. Translated as "lion's milk," *rakı* is Turkey's answer to French *pastis*, Italian *sambuca*, and Greek *ouzo*. An anise-flavored liquor, it turns milky white when mixed with water. The strong drink has inspired a Turkish saying: "you must drink the *rakı*, and not let the *rakı* drink you."

PEOPLE AND CULTURE

LANGUAGE. Turkish *(Türkçe)*, the official language of Turkey, is spoken by approximately 65 million people domestically and a few million more abroad. It is the most prominent member of the Turkic language family, which also includes Azerbaijani, Kazakh, Kyrgyz, Uighur, and Uzbek. Turkish was originally written in Arabic script and exhibited strong Arabic and Persian influences. In 1928, however, Atatürk reformed the language, purging foreign influences. This linguistic standardization was not absolute, and common Arabic and Persian words such as *merhaba* (hello) remain.

Visitors who speak little or no Turkish should not be intimidated. Though Turks appreciate attempts at conversing in their language, English is widely spoken wherever tourism is big business—mainly in the major coastal towns. Especially in İstanbul, a small phrasebook will help greatly. For in-depth study, consult *Teach Yourself Turkish* by Pollard and Pollard (New York, 2004; $17).

DEMOGRAPHICS. Over 99% of the Turkish population is **Muslim.** Jews and Orthodox Christians of Armenian, Greek, and Syrian backgrounds comprise the remainder. While Turkey does not have an official state religion, every Turkish citizen's national identification card states his or her faith. Although Atatürk's reforms aimed to secularize the nation, Islam continues to play a key role in the country's politics and culture.

CUSTOMS AND ETIQUETTE. Turks value **hospitality** and will frequently go out of their way to welcome travelers, commonly offering to buy visitors a meal or a cup of *çay* (tea). Try not to refuse tea unless you have very strong objections; accepting the offer provides a friendly, easy way to converse with locals. If you are invited to a Turkish house as a guest, it is customary to bring a small gift, often pastries or chocolates, and to remove your shoes before entering. A pair of slippers will usually be provided. Always treat elders with special respect. When chatting with Turks, do not speak with any disrespect or skepticism about **Atatürk,** as this is illegal, and avoid other sensitive subjects. In particular, avoid discussing the Kurdish issue, the PKK (the Kurdistan Workers' Party), Northern Cyprus, or Turkey's human rights record.

Many of Turkey's greatest architectural monuments, including **tombs** and **mosques,** have religious significance. Visitors are welcome but should show respect by dressing and acting appropriately. Shorts and skimpy clothing are forbidden inside mosques. Women must cover their arms, heads, and legs, and both sexes should take off their shoes and carry them inside. There are usually shoe racks in the back of the mosques; otherwise, caretakers will provide plastic bags for carrying shoes. Do not take flash photos, never photograph people in prayer, and avoid visits on Fridays (Islam's holy day). Also forgo visiting during prayer times, which are announced by the *müezzin's* call to prayer from the mosque's minarets. Donations are sometimes expected.

If **bargaining** is a fine art, then İstanbul is its cultural center. Never pay full price at the Grand Bazaar; start out by offering less than 50% of the asking price. For that matter, bargain just about everywhere—even when stores list prices, they'll usually take around 60-70%. If you're not asked to pay a service charge when paying by credit card, you're probably paying too much for your purchase. Tipping isn't required in Turkey: at bathhouses, hairdressers, hotels, and restaurants, a tip of 5-15% is common, but taxis and *dolmuş* drivers do not expect tips—just try to round up to the nearest YTL.

BODY VIBES. In Turkey, **body language** often matters as much as the spoken word. When a Turk raises his chin and clicks his tongue, he means *hayır* (no); this gesture is sometimes accompanied by a shutting of the eyes or the raising of eyebrows. A sideways shake of the head means *anlamadım* (I don't understand), and *evet* (yes) may be signaled by a sharp downward nod. If a Turk waves a hand up and down at you, palm toward the ground, he is signaling you to come, not bidding you farewell. In Turkey, the idle habit of snapping the fingers of one hand and then slapping the top of the other fist is considered obscene; so too is the hand gesture made by bringing thumb and forefinger together (the Western sign for "OK"). However, bringing all fingers toward the thumb is a compliment, generally meaning that something is "good." It is also considered rude to point your finger or the sole of your shoe toward someone. Though public displays of affection are considered inappropriate, Turks of both sexes greet each other with a kiss on both cheeks, and often touch or hug one another during conversation. Turks also tend to stand close to one another while talking.

DRESS. Wearing shorts will single you out as a tourist, as most Turks—particularly women—prefer pants or skirts. Women will probably find a **head scarf** or a bandana handy, perhaps essential, in more conservative regions. Even in İstanbul and the resort towns of the Aegean and Mediterranean coasts where casual, beachy dress is more widely accepted, revealing clothing sends a flirtatious message. More acceptable knee-length skirts and lightweight pants are also comfortable and practical, especially in summer. T-shirts are generally appropriate, though you should always cover your arms when entering mosques or traveling into the more religious regions of the country. Topless bathing is common in some areas along the Aegean and Mediterranean coasts but is severely inappropriate in a number of other regions.

BEYOND TOURISM

Finding work in Turkey is tough, as the government tries to restrict employment primarily to Turkish citizens. Foreigners seeking jobs must obtain a **work visa,** which in turn requires a **permit** issued by the Ministry of the Interior. An excellent option for work in Turkey is to **teach English.** Since English is the language of instruction at many Turkish universities, it's also possible to enroll directly as a special student, which might be less expensive than enrolling in an American university program. For more information on opportunities across Europe, see **Beyond Tourism, p. 60**.

Buğday Ekolojik Yaşam Kapısı İletişim Bilgileri, Kemankeş Cad. Akçe Sok. 14, Karaköy, İstanbul (☎212 252 5255; www.bugday.org/eng). Support sustainable agriculture by living or working on an *Ekolojik TaTuTa* (organic farm), or volunteer at the national organic farm association.

Gençtur Turizm ve Seyahat Ac. Ltd., İstiklal Cad. 212, Aznavur Pasajı, Kat: 5, Galatasaray, İstanbul 80080 (☎212 244 62 30; www.genctur.com). A tourism-travel agency that sets up various workshops, nannying jobs, volunteer camps, and year-round study tours.

Volunteers for Peace, 1034 Tiffany Rd., Belmont, VT 05730, USA (☎802-259-2759; www.vfp.org). Arranges placement in volunteer camps. Registration fee US$250.

İSTANBUL

İstanbul is the heart of Turkey. In this giant city that straddles Europe and Asia on two intercontinental bridges, the "East meets West" refrain of fusion restaurants, trendy boutiques, and yoga studios returns to its semantic roots. The huge, Western-style suburbs on the Asian side are evidence of rampant modernization, while across the Bosphorus the sprawling ancient city of mosques and bazaars—Old İstanbul—brims with cafes, bars, and people, day or night. As taxis rush by at mind-boggling speeds, shop owners sip tea with potential customers and tourists mingle with devout Muslims at the entrances to magnificent mosques. İstanbul is a turbulent city, full of history yet charged with a dynamism that makes it one of the most exciting cities in Europe—or Asia.

INTERCITY TRANSPORTATION

Flights: Atatürk Havaalanı (**IST;** ☎663 6400), is 30km from the city. Buses (3 per hr. 6am-11pm) connect domestic and international terminals. To get to Sultanahmet from the airport, take the HAVAS bus or the metro to the Aksaray stop at the end of the line. From there catch a tram to Sultanahmet. A direct taxi to Sultanahmet costs 25YTL. Most hostels and hotels in Sultanahmet arrange airport shuttles several times a day.

Trains: Haydarpaşa Garı (☎21 63 36 04 75 or 336 2063), on the Asian side, sends trains to Anatolia. To get to the station, take the ferry from Karaköy pier #7 (every 20min. 6am-midnight), halfway between Galata Bridge and the Karaköy tourist office. Rail tickets for Anatolia can be bought in advance at the TCDD office upstairs or at any of the travel agencies in Sultanahmet; many of these offices also offer free transportation to the station. Trains go to **Ankara** (6-9hr., 6 per day, from 22YTL) and **Kars** (11-13hr., 1 per day, from 35YTL). Sirkeci Garı (☎527 0050 or 527 0051), in Eminönü, sends trains to Europe via **Athens, GCE** (24hr., 1 per day, 110YTL); **Bucharest, ROM** (17hr., 1 per day, 65YTL); and **Budapest, HUN** (40hr., 1 per day, 185YTL).

Buses: Modern, comfortable buses run to all major destinations in Turkey and are the cheapest and most convenient way to get around. If you arrange your tickets with any travel agency in Sultanahmet, a free ride is included from the agency to the bus station. To reach **Esenler Otobüs Terminal** (☎658 0036), take the tram to Yusufpaşa (1.30YTL); then, walk to the Aksaray Metro and take it to the *otogar* (bus station; 15min., 1.30YTL). Most companies have courtesy buses, called *servis,* that run to the *otogar* from Eminönü, Taksim, and other city points (free with bus ticket purchase). From İstanbul, buses travel to every city in Turkey. Buses run to: **Ankara** (8hr., 6-8 per day, 30YTL); **Antalya** (11hr., 2 per day, 40YTL); **Bodrum** (15hr., 2 per day, 45YTL); **İzmir** (10hr., 4 per day, 35YTL); **Kappadokia** (8hr., 2 per day, 30YTL). International buses run to: **Amman, JOR** (28hr., daily noon, 100YTL); **Athens, GCE** (19hr.; daily 10am; 130YTL, students 135YTL); **Damascus, SYR** (25hr., daily 1:30pm and 7:30pm, 50YTL); **Sofia, BUL** (15hr., daily 10am and 9pm, 65YTL); **Tehran, IRAN** (40hr., M-Sa 1:30pm, 70YTL). To get to Sultanahmet from the *otogar,* catch the metro to the Aksaray stop at the end of the line. From there, catch one of the trams that head to Sultanahmet.

TURKISH ROUTE-LETTE. Be wary of bus companies offering ludicrously low prices. Unlicensed companies have been known to offer discounts to Western European destinations and then ditch passengers somewhere en route. To ensure that you're on a legitimate bus, make sure to reserve your tickets with a travel agency in advance.

Ferries: Turkish Maritime Lines (reservations ☎252 1700, info 21 22 49 92 22), near pier #7 at Karaköy, to the left of the Haydarpaşa ferry terminal (blue awning marked Denizcilik İşletmeleri). To **İzmir** (16hr., every 2 days, 65YTL) and other destinations on the coast. Many travel agencies don't know much about ferry connections, so you're better off going to the pier by the Galata Bridge, where you can pick up a free schedule. For more info, call ☎444 4436 or visit www.ido.com.tr. **To and from Greece:** One of the most popular routes into Turkey is from the Greek Dodecanese and Northern Aegean islands, whose proximity to the Turkish coast makes for an easy and inexpensive way into Asia. There are 5 main crossing points from Greece to Turkey: Rhodes to Marmaris, Kos to Bodrum, Samos to Kusadasi, Chios to Çeşme, and Lesvos to Ayvalik. Ferries run 1-2 times per day in summer, the ride takes under 2hr., and the tickets are usually €25-34, plus €10 port tax when entering Turkey and a €10-20 visa (see p. 14). If you are visiting a Greek island as a daytrip from Turkey, port taxes are usually waived.

ORIENTATION

Waterways divide İstanbul into three sections. The **Bosphorus Strait** (Boğaz) separates **Asya** (Asia) from **Avrupa** (Europe). The **Golden Horn,** a sizeable river originating just outside the city, splits Avrupa into northern and southern parts. Directions in İstanbul are usually further specified by neighborhood. On the European side, **Sultanahmet,** home to the major sights, is packed with tourists and has plenty of parks and benches and many monuments, shops, and cafes. In Sultanahmet, backpackers congregate in **Akbıyık Cad.,** while **Divan Yolu** is the main street. Walk away from **Aya Sofya** and the **Blue Mosque** to reach the **Grand Bazaar.** As you walk out of the covered Bazaar on the northern side, you'll reach more streets of outdoor markets that lead uphill to the massive **Suleymaniye Mosque** and the gardens of İstanbul's **University.** To the right, descend through the **Spice Bazaar** to reach the well-lit **Galata Bridge,** where street vendors and seafood restaurants keep the night lively. Across the two-level bridge, narrow, warehouse-filled streets lead to the panoramic **Galata Tower.** Past the tower is the broad main shopping drag **İstiklâl Cad.,** which takes you directly to **Taksim Square,** modern İstanbul's pulsing center. Sultanahmet and Taksim (on the European side), and **Kadıköy** (on the Asian side) are the most relevant for sightseers. Asya is primarily a residential area.

TRANSPORTATION

PUBLIC TRANSPORTATION. AKBİL is an electronic ticket system that saves you 15-50% on fares for municipal ferries, buses, trams, water taxis, and subways (but not *dolmuş*). Cards (6YTL) are sold at tram stations or ticket offices and can be recharged in 1YTL increments at the white IETT public bus booths, marked **AKBİL satılır.**

Buses: Run 6am-midnight, arriving every 10min. at most stops, less frequently after 10:30pm. 1-2YTL. Hubs are Eminönü, Aksaray (Yusuf Paşa tram stop), Beyazıt, Taksim, Beşiktaş, and Üsküdar. Signs on the front of buses indicate destination, and signs on the right side list major stops. **Dolmuş** (shared taxi vans) are more comfortable but less frequent than buses. Most *dolmuş* gather on the side streets north of Taksim Sq.

Tram: The *Tramvay* runs from Eminönü to Zeytinburnu every 5min. Make sure to be on the right side of the street, as the carriage follows the traffic. Get tokens at any station and toss them in at the turnstile to board (1.30YTL). The old-fashioned carriages of the **his-**

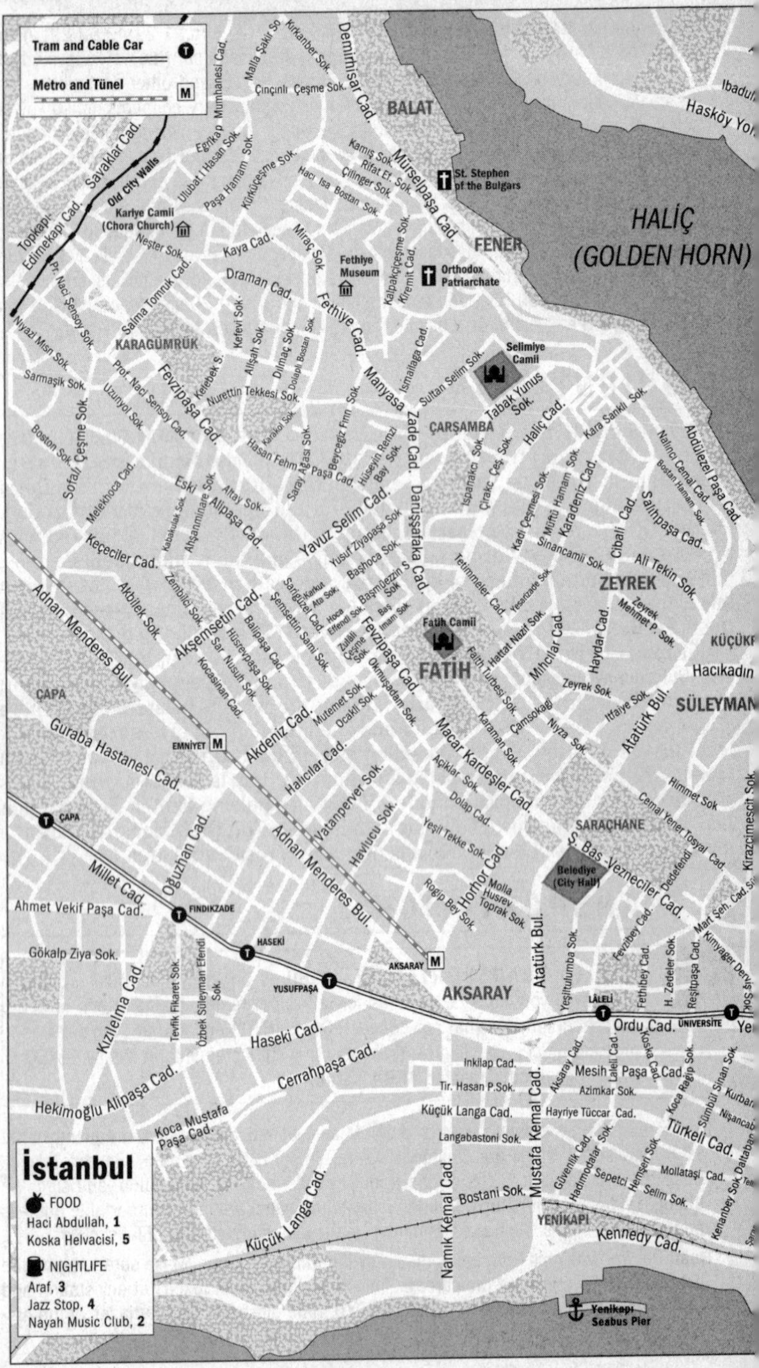

Tram and Cable Car
Metro and Tünel

İstanbul

FOOD
Haci Abdullah, **1**
Koska Helvacisi, **5**

NIGHTLIFE
Araf, **3**
Jazz Stop, **4**
Nayah Music Club, **2**

TAKSİM
Taksim Buses
Esmet İnönü Cad.
Tarlabaşı Bul.
Çeşme Sok.
Zambak Sok.
Kurabiye
Kulluğu Cad.
Kurdele Cad.
Hayam Cad.
Hammalbaşı Cad.
Kalyoncu
BEYOĞLU
İstiklal Cad.
Akarcası Sok.
Bayramyeri Sok.
Keramet Sok.
Camii
Aynalıçeşme
Emin
Asian Cad.
Bahriye Cad.
Nalıncıbayırı Sok.
Mutfakkapısı Cad.
Sipahinini Sok.
Aşiklar Meydanı Sok.
Meşrutiyet Cad.
Ministry of Tourism
TEPEBAŞI
Tepebaşı Cad.
Turabı Baba Sok.
Çivici Sok.
KASIMPAŞA
Alyon Sok.
Turnacıbaşı Sok.
Turnacıbaşı Sok.
Billurca Sok.
Sıraselviler Cad.
Kazan Sok.
Sormagir Sok.
Cihangir Sok.
Ağa Çırağı Sok.
Saraykas Sok.
Hatun Camii Sok.
Mebusan Y.
Alcakdan Sok.
DOLMABAHÇE
Kabataş Seabus Terminal
GALATASARAY
Yeniçarşı Cad.
Çukurcuma Cad.
Bakraç Sok.
Yeniçarşı Cad.
Kurular Sok.
Hevvar Sok.
Coşkun Sok.
Cihangir Y.
CİHANGİR
KABATAŞ
Adahamam Sok.
Kadirler Yolu
Defterdar Yokuşu
Boğazkesen Cad.
Meclisi Mebusan Cad.
Tomtom Kaptan Sok.
Refik Saydam Cad.
Meşrutiyet Cad.
Lobut Sok.
Evliya Çelebi Cad.
TÜNEL
Galipdede Cad.
Tünel Metro Terminal
Kumbaraç Yokuşu
Ali Hoca Sok.
Lüleciherdek Cad.
Yolcuzade Cad.
Okçumusa Cad.
Şair Ziya Paşa Cad.
Galata Tower
Yüksek Kaldırım Cad.
Kemeraltı Cad.
Necatibey Cad.
Galata Mumhane Cad.
Kemankeş Cad.
TOPHANE
Atatürk Köprüsü
Tersane Cad.
Fütuhat Sok.
Hediye Sok.
Voyvoda Cad.
Söğüt Sok.
Maliye Sok.
Tünel Metro Terminal
KARAKÖY
Karaköy Maritime Terminal
Rıhtım Cad.
Karaköy Seabus Pier
İSTANBUL BOĞAZI (BOSPHORUS)
Yeni Galata Köprüsü
Rüstem Paşa Camii
Eminönü Otogar
EMİNÖNÜ
Hasırcılar Cad.
Tahtakale Cad.
Süleymaniye Camii & Türbesi
Mısır Çarşısı (Egyptian Spice Bazaar)
Yeni Camii
Yalı Köşkü Cad.
SİRKECİ
Sirkeci Gar
Kennedy Cad.
İstasyon Arkası Sok.
Şahinde Sok.
Uzun Çarşı Cad.
Onar Cad.
Fuatpaşa Cad.
Fıncılar Yokuşu
Havanc Sok.
Yeni Postane Cad.
Hamidiye Cad.
Aşirefendi Cad.
Cemal
Hoca Hanı
İbni Kemal Cad.
Ebussuut Cad.
Hüdavendigâr Cad.
GÜLHANE
Gülhane Park
Topkapı Palace
BEYAZIT
Çakmakçılar Sok.
Mahmut Paşa Yokuşu
Saka Mehmet Sok.
Tereke Sok.
Nadir Cad.
Alemdar Cad.
Archeological Complex
Sult. Mektebi Sok.
Yerebatan Cad.
Ankara Cad.
KAPALI ÇARI (GRAND BAZAAR)
Nuruosmaniye Camii
Şeretefendi Sok.
M. Fenari Sok.
Alayköşkü Cad.
SULTANAHMET
AHIRKAPI
Beyazıt Camii
BEYAZIT
Bileyciler Sok.
Vezirhanı Cad.
ÇEMBERLİTAŞ
Museum of Islamic and Turkish Art
Divan Yolu
Aya Sofia
İshakpaşa Cad.
Gedikpaşa Camii Sok.
Emin Sinan Hamamı Sok.
Peykhane Sok.
Hippodrome
Atmeydanı
Tülcü Cad.
Piyerloti Cad.
Gedik Paşa Cad.
Terzihane Sok.
Sultanahmet Camii (Blue Mosque)
Mimar Mehmet Ağa Cad.
Tevfikhane Sok.
Cankurtaran İst.
Kadırga Limanı Cad.
Dizdariye Sok.
Tavukhane Sok.
Kasap Osman Sok.
Şair Sermet
Şeyhsuvar Cad.
Küçük Ayasofya Cad.
Kabasakal Cad.
KUMKAPI
Sahil Yolu
Cankurtaran Cad.
ÇATLADIKAPI
Küçük Aya Sofia
SEE SULTANAHMET & SÜLEYMANIYE MAP p. 1046
0 300 yards
0 300 meters
LG

TURKEY

torical tram run 1km uphill from Tunnel (by the Galata Bridge) through İstiklâl Cad. and up to Taksim Sq. They're the same ones that made the trip in the early 20th century.

Metro: İstanbul operates two metro lines (☎568 9970): one from Aksaray to the Esenler Bus Terminal and the other from Taksim Sq. to 4th Levent. A funicular connects the tram stop Cabatas to Taksim Sq. The metro runs daily every 5min. 5:40am-11:15pm.

Commuter Rail: A slow commuter rail *(tren)* runs 6am-11pm between Sirkeci Gar and the far western suburbs, as well as the Asian side. The stop in Bostanci is near the ferry to the Princes Islands. Keep your ticket until the end of the journey.

Taxis: Taxi drivers are even more reckless and speed-crazed than other İstanbul drivers, but the city's more than 20,000 taxis offer an undoubtedly quick way to get around. Don't ask the driver to fix a price before getting in; instead, make sure he restarts the meter. Night fares, usually starting at midnight, are double. Rides from Sultanahmet to Taksim Sq. should be around 15YTL, and to the airport around 25YTL.

GETTING A FARE PRICE. While most İstanbul taxis are metered, some cabdrivers have a tendency to drive circles around the city before bringing you to your destination. Watch the roads and look out for signs pointing to where you're going. To avoid the risk altogether, take taxis only as far as the Galata Bridge, and walk from there to Sultanahmet or Taksim.

PRACTICAL INFORMATION

TURKEY

Tourist Office: 3 Divan Yolu (☎/fax 518 8754), at the north end of the Hippodrome in Sultanahmet. Open daily 9am-5pm. Branches in Taksim's Hilton Hotel Arcade on Cumhuriyet Cad., Sirkeci train station, Atatürk Airport, and Karaköy Maritime Station.

Budget Travel: İstanbul has many travel agencies; almost all speak English, and most hostels and hotels have started running their own travel services as well. Though most are trustworthy, there are some scams. Always check that the agency is licensed. If anything happens, make sure you have your agent's info and report it to the tourist police.

Fez Travel, 15 Akbıyık Cad. (☎212 516 9024; www.feztravel.com). İstanbul's most efficient and well informed agency, Fez's English-speaking staff organizes everything from accommodations to ferries, flights, and buses, as well as their own backpacker-tailored tours of Turkey and Greece. STA-affiliated. Open daily 9am-7pm. MC/V.

Hassle Free, 10 Akbıyık Cad. (☎212 458 9500; www.anzachouse.com), right next to New Backpackers. The name is self-explanatory, and the young, friendly staff provides great deals and tips. Books local buses or boat cruises of southern Turkey. Open daily 9am-11pm.

Barefoot Travel, 1 Cetinkaya Sok. (☎212 517 0269; www.barefoot-travel.com), just off Akbıyık Cad. The English-speaking staff is helpful and offers good deals on airfare, as well as free maps of İstanbul and Turkey. Open daily in summer 8am-8pm; in winter 8am-6pm. AmEx/MC/V.

Consulates: Australia, 15 Asker Ocaği Cad., Elmadag Sisli (☎212 257 7050; fax 212 243 1332). **Canada,** 373/5 İstiklâl Cad. (☎212 251 9838; fax 212 251 9888). **Ireland,** 26 Cumhuriyet Cad., Mobil Altı, Elmadağ (☎212 246 6025). **NZ,** Inonu Caddesi No:48/3. (☎212 244 0272; fax 212 251 4004.) **UK,** 34 Meşrutiyet Cad., Beyoğlu/Tepebaşı (☎212 252 6436). **US,** 2 Kaplicalar Mevkii Sok., Istinye (☎212 335 9000).

Currency Exchange: *Bureaux de change* around the city are open M-F 8:30am-noon and 1:30-5pm. Most don't charge commission. **ATMs** generally accept all international cards. Most banks exchange **traveler's checks.** Exchanges in Sultanahmet have poor rates but are open late and on weekends. There is a yellow **PTT** kiosk between the Aya Sofya and the Blue Mosque that changes currency for no commission. **Western Union** offices are located in many banks throughout Sultanahmet and Taksim; they operate M-F 8:30am-noon and 1:30-5pm.

English-Language Bookstores: English-language books are all over the city. In Sultanahmet, *köşk* (kiosks) at the Blue Mosque, on Aya Sofya Meydanı, and on Divan Yolu sell international papers. **Galeri Kayseri,** 58 Divan Yolu (☎512 0456), caters to tourists with informational books on Turkish and Islamic history and literature, as well as a host of guidebooks. Open daily 9am-9pm. MC/V.

Laundromat: Star Laundry, 18 Akbıyık Cad., between New Backpackers and Hassle Free. Wash, dry, and iron 4YTL per kg. Min. 2kg. Ready in 3hr. Open daily 9am-8pm.

Tourist Police: In Sultanahmet, at the beginning of Yerebatan Cad. (24hr. hotline ☎527 4503 or 528 5369). Tourist police speak excellent English, and their mere presence causes hawkers to scatter. In an emergency, call from any phone.

Hospitals: American Hospital, Admiral Bristol Hastanesi, 20 Güzelbahçe Sok., Nişantaşı (☎231 4050), is applauded by locals and tourists. Has many English-speaking doctors. **German Hospital,** 119 Sıraselviler Cad., Taksim (☎293 2150), also has a multilingual staff and is conveniently located for Sultanahmet hostelers. **International Hospital,** 82 İstanbul Cad., Yesilköy (☎663 3000).

Internet: Internet in İstanbul is everywhere from hotels to barber shops, and connections are usually cheap and decently fast—notwithstanding the frequent power cuts. Most hostels have free Internet, though many impose a 15min. limit. Some hostels now offer Wi-Fi, as do more upscale hotels and eateries; signs are usually posted on the door. Rates at travel agencies are usually 1YTL per 15min., 3YTL per hr.

Post and Telephone Offices: Known as **PTTs.** All accept packages. **Main branch** in Sirkeci, 25 Büyük Postane Sok. Stamp and currency exchange services open daily 8:30am-midnight. 24hr. phones. Phone cards available for 5-10YTL. There is a yellow PTT kiosk in Sultanahmet between the Aya Sofya and the Blue Mosque, which exchanges currency and sells stamps. Open daily 9am-5pm.

PHONE CODES. The code is **212** on the European side and **216** on the Asian side. All numbers listed here begin with 212 unless otherwise specified. For more on how to place international calls, see **Inside Back Cover.**

TURKEY

ACCOMMODATIONS

Budget accommodations are concentrated in **Sultanahmet** (a.k.a. Türist Şeğntral). As Turkey has become a backpacker's must, there has been an explosion of cheap places to stay, turning Akbıyık Cad. into a virtually uninterrupted line of hostels. The side streets around **Sirkeci** railway station and **Aksaray** have dozens of dirt-cheap, run-down hotels, while more expensive options are in more touristy districts. All accommodations listed below are in Sultanahmet and, despite their number, they fill up quickly in high-season. Though you will always find a bed somewhere, reserve ahead to get the hostel of your choice. Hotels in **Lâleli** are in İstanbul's center of prostitution and should be avoided. Rates can increase up to 20% in July and August.

Big Apple Hostel, 12 Bayram Fırını Sok. (☎517 7931; www.hostelbigapple.com), down the road from Akbıyık Cad., next to Barefoot Travel. On a quieter side street off of Akbiyik Cad., this hostel offers one of the most fun and relaxing atmospheres in İstanbul for both individuals and groups. Has a large downstairs common room and an upstairs terrace with beanbag chairs, beach loungers, and a swing, not to mention some of the friendliest staff around. Breakfast (8:30-10:30am), towels, and linens included. Internet. Dorms €10; singles €22; doubles €25. MC/V. ❷

Metropolis, 24 Terbıyık Sok. (☎212 518 1822; www.metropolishostel.com), removed from the hustle of Akbıyık, on a central yet quieter back street. This beautifully kept hostel has comfortable, stylish rooms, friendly staff, and a peaceful location. Guests get a 10% discount at the Metropolis Restaurant and Downunder Bar around the corner. Breakfast included. Free Internet. Single-sex dorms 23YTL; doubles 60YTL. MC/V. ❷

Bahaus Guesthouse, 11-13 Akbıyık Cad. (☎212 638 6534; www.travelinistanbul.com), across the street from Big Apple. Though its dorm rooms are simple, Bahaus's cozy Anatolian-themed closed terrace and couch-filled open terrace are comfortable and lively. Travelers rave about this place, and the rooms are usually full. Book in advance. Airport pickup available. Free Internet. Breakfast included. Dorms €9; doubles €44. MC/V. ❶

Sultan Hostel, 21 Akbiyik Cad. (☎212 9260; www.sultanhostel.com). Right in the middle of backpacker land, this happening hostel is İstanbul's most famous. Streetside, rooftop restaurant and comfortable, clean dorms make it a great place to meet new, fun, fellow travelers. Breakfast included. Free safes. Free Internet. Reserve ahead. Dorms with bathroom €14; doubles €19, with bathroom €22; quads €15/17. Rates per person, but rooms booked as a unit. MC/V. ❷

Sydney Hostel, 42 Akbıyık Cad. (☎212 518 6671; fax 518 6672), in the middle of Akbıyık. Calm, with cheerful sky-blue walls, modern rooms and bathrooms, and much-coveted in-room A/C. Rooftop terrace. Free safes. Free Internet. Breakfast included. Dorms €10; singles and doubles €35. V. ❶

Terrace Guesthouse, 39 Kutlugün Sok. (☎212 638 9733; www.terracehotelistanbul.com), behind Akbıyık Cad. Housed in a narrow carpet shop, this elegant hotel has beautifully decorated rooms for affordable prices. The 2 upstairs terraces have spectacular views. Breakfast included. Free Wi-Fi. Singles €60; doubles €70; triples €80. V. ❺

Zeugma Hostel, 35 Akbıyık Cad. (☎212 517 4040; www.zeugmahostel.net). This clean, 1-room hostel has a huge basement dorm with comfortable wooden bunks separated by colorful curtains, giving it a bedouin camp feel. Though there is no common space, the dorm has A/C and a quiet, relaxed vibe. Airport pick-up available. Linens included. Free Internet. Reception 24hr. Rooms €9-12, with breakfast €11-13. V. ❶

FOOD

İstanbul's restaurants often demonstrate the golden rule: if it's well advertised or easy to find, it's not worth a visit. Great meals can be found across the **Galata Bridge** and around **Taksim Square.** Small Bosphorus suburbs such as **Arnavutköy** and Sariyer (on the European side) and **Çengelköy** (on the Asian side) are the best places for fresh fish. For a cheaper meal, **İstiklâl Caddesi** has all the major Western chains, as well as quick and tasty Turkish fast food. Vendors in Ottoman dress sell *Vişne suyu* (sour cherry juice), and on any street you'll find dried fruit and nuts for sale, as well as the omnipresent stalls of sesame bagels (1YTL). The best open-air **market** is open daily in **Beşiktaş,** near Barbaros Cad., while at the Egyptian Spice Bazaar *(Mısır Çarşısı)* you can find almonds, fruit, and—of course—**kebab,** which range from shawarma-type meat to Western-style meat-on-a-stick.

Doy-Doy, 13 Şifa Hammamı Sok. (☎517 1588). The best in Sultanahmet, 3-story Doy-Doy's rooftop tables are right under the Blue Mosque. On the lower levels are cushioned floors and plenty of *nargilas (hookahs)*. Try the *kebab* (5-10YTL) or shepherd salads with *cacik* (yogurt and cucumber; 4YTL). Open daily 8am-11pm. MC/V. ❷

Trabzon Lokantasi, 10 Dervisler Sok, near Sirkeci. Tucked in an alleyway off the tram tracks, this small cafe-restaurant features real Turkish homecooking in cheap, plentiful servings, with several vegetarian options. The lentil soup (1.50YTL) is exceptional. Be sure to check out the colorful guestbook, filled with notes from visitors from around the world. Entrees 3-6YTL. Open 11am-11pm. Cash only. ❶

Muhammed Said Baklavaci, 88 Divan Yolu Cad. (☎212 526 9666; www.baklavacimuhammedsaid.com). Specializing in homemade *baklava* and Turkish delights, this small, locally-owned bakery is a wonderland of sweets. Prices are reasonable and the food is amazing. 1 kilo 20-29YTL. Open daily 9am-10pm. Cash only. ❸

Hacı Abdullah, 17 Sakizağacı Cad. (☎293 8561; www.haciabdullah.com.tr), down the street from Ağa Camii, in Taksim Sq. This family-style restaurant, going strong since 1888, features huge vases of preserved fruit, as well as high-tech bathrooms. Their homemade grapefruit juice is fantastic. Soups and salads 3-7YTL. Entrees 10-20YTL. No alcohol served. Open daily noon-11pm. Kitchen closes 10:30pm. MC/V. ❷

Koska Helvacısı, İstiklâl Cad. 238 (☎212 244 0877; www.koskahelvacisi.com.tr). This confectionery superstore, which celebrated its 100th anniversary in 2007, is a sugar-lover's dream. Fantastic take-out *baklava* trays (3YTL) and boxed assortments of sweets (6-20YTL) in all colors and flavors. Open daily 9am-11:30pm. V. ❷

SIGHTS

İstanbul's array of churches, mosques, palaces, and museums can keep an ardent tourist busy for weeks. Most first time travelers to İstanbul spend a lot of time in Sultanahmet, the area around the Aya Sofya south of and uphill from Sirkeci. Merchants crowd the district between the enormous Grand Bazaar, east of the university, and the less touristy Egyptian Spice Bazaar, just southeast of Eminönü. Soak in the city's sights and hop on one of the small boats near the Galata Bridge and go for a relaxing and panoramic **Bosphorus tour.**

BARGAINING FOR BEGINNERS. İstanbul bargaining doesn't end at carpets: it's acceptable to bargain for almost anything, including tours. For the best deals on boat trips, bargain with boat owners at the port. Trips shouldn't be more than 20YTL for a few hours down the Bosphorus.

AYA SOFYA (HAGIA SOPHIA). When Aya Sofya (Divine Wisdom) was built in AD 537, it was the biggest building in the world. Built as a church, it fell to the Ottomans in 1453 and was converted into a mosque; it remained such until 1932, when Atatürk declared it a museum. The nave is overshadowed by the gold-leaf mosaic dome, lined with hundreds of circular windows that make it seem as though the dome is floating on a bed of luminescent pearls. Throughout the building, Qur'anic inscriptions and mosaics of Mary and the angels intertwine in a fascinating symmetry. The gallery contains Byzantine mosaics uncovered from beneath a thick layer of Ottoman plaster, as well as the famed **sweating pillar,** sheathed in bronze. The pillar has a hole big enough to stick a finger in and collect the odd drop of water, believed to possess healing powers. *(Open daily 9am-7:30pm. Upper gallery open 9:30am-6:45pm. 10YTL.)*

BLUE MOSQUE (SULTANAHMET CAMİİ). Named for the beautiful blue İznik tiles covering the interior, the extravagant Blue Mosque and its six **minarets** were Sultan Ahmet's 1617 claim to fame. At the time of construction, only the mosque at Mecca had as many minarets, and the thought of rivaling that sacred edifice was considered heretical. The crafty Sultan circumvented this difficulty by financing the construction of a seventh minaret at Mecca. The interior was originally lit with candles, the chandelier structure intended to create the illusion of tiny starlights floating freely in the air. The small, square,

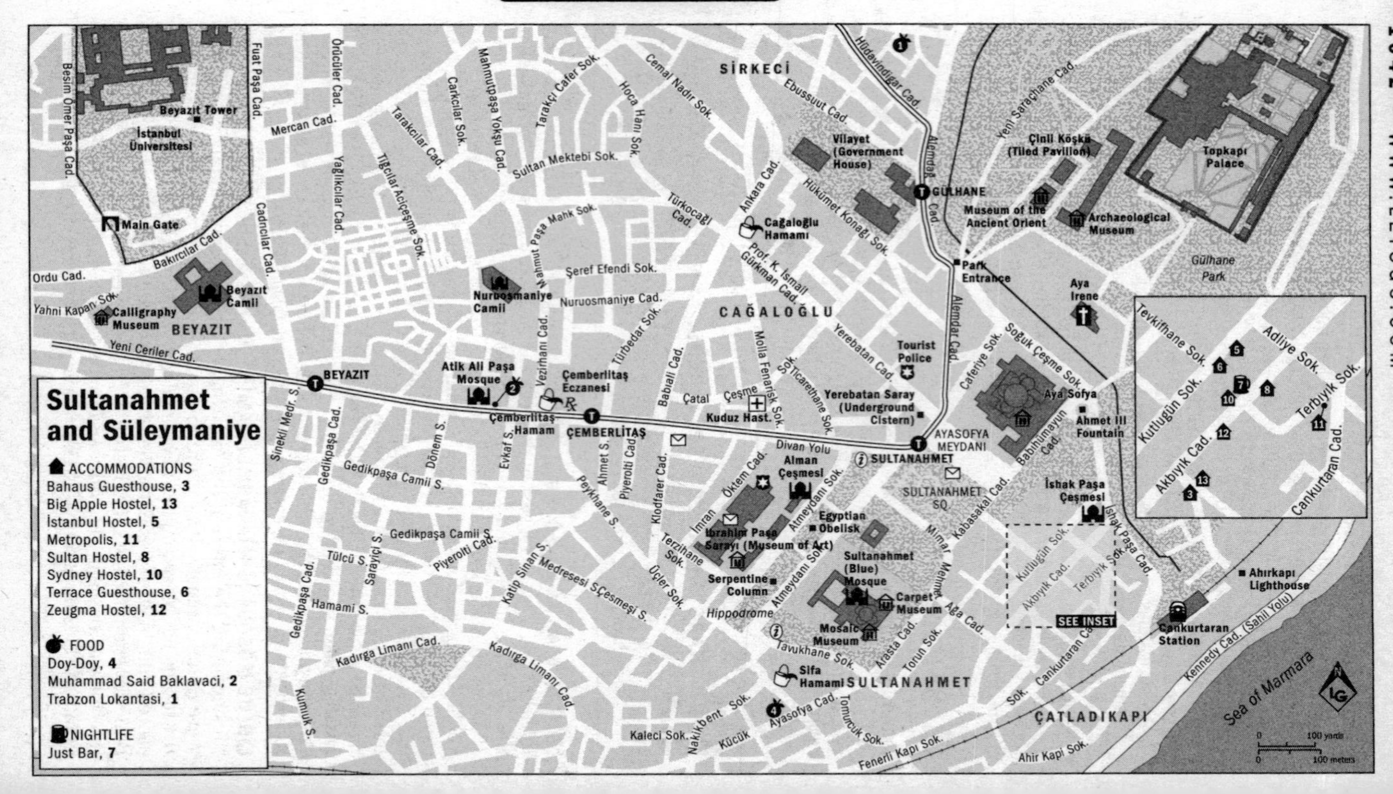
Sultanahmet and Süleymaniye
ACCOMMODATIONS
Bahaus Guesthouse, 3
Big Apple Hostel, 13
İstanbul Hostel, 5
Metropolis, 11
Sultan Hostel, 8
Sydney Hostel, 10
Terrace Guesthouse, 6
Zeugma Hostel, 12
FOOD
Doy-Doy, 4
Muhammad Said Baklavaci, 2
Trabzon Lokantasi, 1
NIGHTLIFE
Just Bar, 7
SİRKECİ
CAĞALOĞLU
BEYAZIT
SULTANAHMET
ÇATLADIKAPI
Topkapı Palace
Çinli Köşkü (Tiled Pavilion)
Museum of the Ancient Orient
Archaeological Museum
Gülhane Park
Park Entrance
Aya Irene
Aya Sofya
Ahmet III Fountain
Vilayet (Government House)
GÜLHANE
Cağaloğlu Hamamı
Tourist Police
Yerebatan Saray (Underground Cistern)
Kuduz Hast.
AYASOFYA MEYDANI
SULTANAHMET
SULTANAHMET SQ.
İshak Paşa Çeşmesi
SEE INSET
Alman Çeşmesi
Egyptian Obelisk
İbrahim Paşa Sarayı (Museum of Art)
Serpentine Column
Hippodrome
Sultanahmet (Blue) Mosque
Carpet Museum
Mosaic Museum
Sifa Hamamı
Ahırkapı Lighthouse
Cankurtaran Station
Sea of Marmara
Kennedy Cad. (Sahil Yolu)
Beyazıt Tower
İstanbul Üniversitesi
Main Gate
Beyazıt Camii
Calligraphy Museum
Nurbosmaniye Camii
Atik Ali Paşa Mosque
Çemberlitaş Eczanesi
Çemberlitaş Hamam
ÇEMBERLİTAŞ
BEYAZIT
Divan Yolu
Alemdar Cad.
Hüdavendigar Cad.
Ebussuut Cad.
Yeni Saraçhane Cad.
Hükümet Konağı Sok.
Ankara Cad.
Türkocağı Cad.
Prof. K. İsmail Gürkman Cad.
Yerebatan Cad.
Molla Fenarisk Sok.
Ticarethane Sok.
Çatal Çeşme
Babıali Cad.
Klodfarer Cad.
Piyerolti Cad.
Ahmet S.
Peykhane S.
Türbedar Sok.
Nuruosmaniye Cad.
Şeref Efendi Sok.
Mahmut Paşa Mahk Sok.
Vezirhanı Cad.
Evkaf S.
Dönem S.
Gedikpaşa Camii S.
Gedikpaşa Cad.
Sinekli Medr. S.
Yeni Ceriler Cad.
Ordu Cad.
Yahni Kapan Sok.
Bakırcılar Cad.
Besim Ömer Paşa Cad.
Fuat Paşa Cad.
Cadırcılar Cad.
Mercan Cad.
Örücüler Cad.
Yağlıkcılar Cad.
Tığcılar Aciçeşme Sok.
Tarakcılar Cad.
Carkcılar Sok.
Mahmutpaşa Yokşu Cad.
Sultan Mektebi Sok.
Tarakçı Cafer Sok.
Hoca Hanı Sok.
Cemal Nadır Sok.
Caferiye Sok.
Soğuk Çeşme Sok.
Babıhümayun Cad.
Kabasakal Cad.
Mimar Mehmet Ağa Cad.
İshak Paşa Cad.
Kutlugün Sok.
Akbıyık Cad.
Terbıyık Sok.
Cankurtaran Cad.
Arasta Cad.
Torun Sok.
Tavukhane Sok.
Atmeydanı Sok.
Öktem Cad.
Imran
Terzihane Sok.
Üçler Sok.
Medresesi S.Çesmeşi S.
Katip Sinan S.
Tülcü S.
Sarayiçi S.
Hamami S.
Kadırga Limanı Cad.
Kumuk S.
Kaleci Sok.
Nakikbent Sok.
Küçük Ayasofya Cad.
Tomurcuk Sok.
Fenerli Kapı Sok.
Ahir Kapı Sok.
Tevkifhane Sok.
Adliye Sok.
100 yards
100 meters

single-domed structure in front of the Blue Mosque is **Sultanahmet'in Türbesi,** or Sultan Ahmet's Tomb, which contains the sultan's remains. The reliquary in the back contains strands of the Prophet Muhammad's beard. *(Open M-Th and Sa-Su 9am-12:30pm, 1:45-4:40pm and 5:40-6:30pm, F noon-2:20pm. The Blue Mosque is a working religious facility and closes to the public for prayer 5 times a day. Scarves are provided at the entrance; women should cover their knees, hair, and shoulders. Inside the mosque, behave respectfully and don't cross into the sections limited to prayer. Donations are welcome on the way out. See p. 1032 for more details on appropriate mosque etiquette.)*

TOPKAPI PALACE (TOPKAPI SARAYI). Towering from the high ground at the tip of the old city and hidden behind walls up to 12m high, Topkapı was the nerve center of the Ottoman Empire. Built by Mehmet the Conqueror in 1458-1465, the palace became an imperial residence during the reign of Süleyman the Magnificent. The palace is divided into a series of courtyards. The **first courtyard** was the popular center of the palace, where the general public could enter to watch executions and other displays of imperial might. The **second courtyard** leads to displays of wealth, including collections of porcelain, silver, gold, and torture instruments—not to mention crystal staircases. The Gate of Felicity leads to the **third courtyard,** which houses imperial clothing and the awesome **Palace Treasury.** The **fourth courtyard** is the pleasure center of the palace—it was among these pavilions, gardens, and fountains that the Ottomans really got their mojo working. The most interesting part of Topkapı is the 400-plus-room **harem.** Tours begin at the Blap. 1032ck Eunuchs' Dormitory and continue into the chambers of the Valide Sultan, the sultan's mother and the harem's most powerful woman. Surrounding the room of the queen mum are the chambers of the concubines. If a particular woman attracted the sultan's affections or if the sultan spent a night with her, she would be promoted to "odalisque" status, which meant that she had to stay in İstanbul forever, but got nicer quarters in exchange for her undying ministrations. *(Palace open M and W-Su 9am-7pm. 10YTL. Harem open 10am-5pm. 10YTL. Audio tour of palace 5YTL. Harem can only be visited on guided tours, which leave every 30min. Lines for tours can be long; arrive early.)*

UNDERGROUND CISTERN (YEREBATAN SARAYI). This underground "palace" is a vast cavern whose shallow water reflects the images of its 336 supporting columns. The columns are all illuminated by colored ambient lighting, making the cistern slightly resemble a horror-movie set. Underground walkways originally linked the cistern to Topkapı Palace but were blocked to curb rampant trafficking in stolen goods and abducted women. At the far end of the cistern, two huge Medusa heads lie upside down in the water. Legend has it that looking at them directly turns people to stone. The cistern's overpriced cafe, in a dark corner, is a cross between creepy and romantic. *(The entrance lies 175m from the Aya Sofya in the small stone kiosk on the left side of Yerebatan Cad. Open daily 9am-6:30pm. 10YTL.)*

ARCHAEOLOGICAL MUSEUM COMPLEX. The Archaeological Museum Complex encompasses four distinct museums. The **Tiled Pavilion** explains more than you ever wanted to know about the omnipresent İznik tiles. The smaller, adjacent building is the **Ancient Orient Museum.** It houses an excellent collection of 3000-year-old stone artifacts from the ancient Middle East and the Treaty of Kadesh, the world's oldest known written treaty, drafted after a battle between Ramses II of Egypt and the Hittite King Muvatellish. The immense **Archaeology Museum** has one of the world's greatest collections of Classical and Hellenistic art but is surprisingly bereft of visitors. The highlight is the famous Alexander Sarcophagus. The superb **Museum of Turkish and Islamic Art**

features a large collection of Islamic art, organized by period. *(150m downhill from the Topkapı Palace's 1st courtyard. All museums open Tu-Su 8:30am-5pm. 5YTL.)*

GRAND BAZAAR. Through banter, barter, and haggle, **Kapalı Çarşısı** (Grand Bazaar) operates on a scale unmatched by even the most frenetic of markets elsewhere in Europe. The largest, oldest covered bazaar in the world, the Grand Bazaar began in 1461 as a modest affair during the reign of Mehmet the Conqueror. Today, the enormous Kapalı Çarşısı combines the best and worst of shopping in Turkey to form the massive mercantile sprawl that starts at Çemberlitaş and covers the hill down to Eminönü, ending at the more authentic and less claustrophobic **Mısır Çarşısı** (Egyptian Spice Bazaar) and the Golden Horn waterfront. Rule number one in bargaining: never settle for more than half the first price asked; the place is touristy and shop owners know their tricks. Most wares in the Grand Bazaar are available for less in the Spice Bazaar or in shops. And don't worry about getting lost—there are directional arrows from virtually any spot, so relax and enjoy the ride. *(From Sultanahmet, follow the tram tracks toward Aksaray until you see the Nuruosmanıye Camii on the right. Walk down Vezirhanı Cad. for one block, keeping the mosque on your left. Otherwise, follow the crowds. www.grandbazaar.com. Open M-Sa 9am-7pm.)*

SÜLEYMANİYE COMPLEX. To the north of İstanbul University stands the elegant **Süleymaniye Camii,** one of Ottoman architect Sinan's great masterpieces. This mosque is part of a larger **külliye** (complex), which includes **tombs,** an **imaret** (soup kitchen), and several **madrasas** (Islamic schools). After walking through the cemetery to see the **royal tombs** of Süleyman I and his wife, proceed inside the vast and perfectly proportioned mosque—the height of the dome (53m) is exactly twice the measurement of each side of the square base. The **stained-glass windows** are the sobering work of the master Sarhoş İbrahim (İbrahim the Drunkard). The İznik tile İnzanity all started here: the area around the **mihrab** showcases Sinan's first experiment in blue tiles. *(From Sultanahmet, take the tramvay to the Üniversite stop, walk across the square, and take Besim Ömer Paşa Cad. past the walls of the university to Süleymaniye Cad. Open daily except during prayer. Leave your shoes at the entrance. Women need to cover their shoulders; men and women should cover their heads. Scarves are available at the entrance.)*

TURKEY

HAMMAMS (TURKISH BATHS)

In the past, a man found in a women's bath was sentenced to death, but today customs have relaxed and it's not rare to find co-ed baths where both genders strip beyond their skivvies. Most baths have separate women's sections or hours, but only some have designated female attendants. If you'd rather have a masseuse of your same sex, make sure to ask at the entrance.

Cağaloğlu Hamami, on Yerebatan Cad. at Babiali Cad. (☎212 522 2424; www.cagaloğluhamami.com.tr), near Cağaloğlu Sq. in Sultanahmet. Donated to İstanbul in 1741 by Sultan Mehmet I, this luxurious white-marble bath is one of the city's most illustrious. Self-service bath 20YTL, bath with scrub 30YTL, complete bath and massage 40YTL, luxury treatment with hand-knit Oriental washcloth 60YTL. Slippers, soap, and towels included. Open daily for women 8am-8pm, for men 8am-10pm. V.

Çemberlitaş Hamamı, 8 Vezirhan Cad. (☎212 522 7974; www.cemberlitashamami.com.tr). Just a soap-slide away from the Çemberlitaş tram stop. Built in 1584, the marble interiors make this place downright regal. Vigorous "towel service" after the bath; guests are welcome to lounge around the relaxing, hot marble rooms afterward. Open daily 6am-midnight. Am/Ex/MC/V.

NIGHTLIFE

Locals and travelers alike pour into the streets to savor intense nightlife, which falls into three categories. The first includes male-only *çay* (tea) houses, backgammon parlors, and dancing shows. Women are not prohibited but are unwelcome and should avoid these places, which are often unsafe for male travelers as well. *Let's Go* does not endorse patronage of these establishments. The second category includes the local youth **cafe-bars, rock bars,** and **backpacker bars.** In **Sultanahmet,** pubs are crammed within 10m of one another, usually on the rooftop or front tables of the hostels. They have standardized beer prices (5YTL) and are usually Australian-dominated; **Orient,** the most popular hostel bar, is open to all. **Clubs** and **discos** comprise the third nightlife category. Even taxi drivers can't keep up with the ever-fluctuating club scene. The Beşiktaş end of **Ortaköy** is a maze of upscale hangouts. The cheerful **Nevizade** is a virtually uninterrupted row of wine shops and *tapas* bars, parallel to İstiklâl Cad. İstanbul's local specialty is *balyoz* (sledgehammer/wrecking ball). Getting wrecked won't be difficult: *balyoz* consists of *rakı*, whiskey, vodka, and gin with orange juice.

Just Bar, 18 Akbıyık Cad. (☎01 23 45 67 89). This bar has become almost as much of a must-see as the Aya Sofya. Outdoor wooden pub tables, rock/funk/R&B music, and free-flowing beer make for a typical backpacker's night, every night. Beer 5YTL. Mixed drinks 7-10YTL. Open daily 11am-4am. It's hard to tell where Just Bar stops and **Cheers,** next door, begins. Cheers is equally popular, friendly, and laid-back. Beer 4-5YTL. Mixed drinks and shots 7-10YTL. Open daily noon-late. MC/V.

Jazz Stop, at the end of Büyük Parmakkapı Sok., in Taksim (☎292 5314). A mixed group of music lovers sit in this large underground tavern while live bands lay the funk, blues, and jazz on thick. The owner, the drummer from one of Turkey's oldest and most respected rock groups, occasionally takes part in the jams. A late-night hangout where the crowds don't build until 2 or 3am. Beer 5YTL. Mixed drinks 7-20YTL. Live music daily 2am. Cover F-Sa 10YTL; includes 1 drink. Open daily 7pm-6am. V.

Araf, İstiklâl Cad. and 32 Balo Sok. (☎244 8301), across from the entrance to Nevizade. Take the elevator to the 4th fl., then walk upstairs to reach this funky rooftop veranda with international music and freestyle dancing in a birthday-party atmosphere. No cover. Beer 4YTL. Mixed drinks 7-20YTL. Open daily 5pm-2am. Cash only.

Nayah Music Club, Kurabiye Sok. 23 (☎212 244 1183; www.myspace.com/nayahmusicclub), in Beyoglu. From İstiklâl Cad., take a right onto Mis Sok.; Nayah is one block down, on the corner with Kurabiye Sok. This reggae bar is small and relaxed, with rasta bartenders. Customers sit and groove to the music with subtle head bobs. Beer 4YTL. Mixed drinks 7-14YTL. Open M-Th 6pm-2am, F-Sa 6pm-4am. Cash only.

UKRAINE (УКРАЇНА)

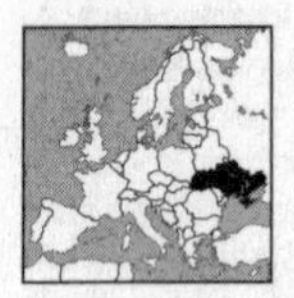

In late 2004, Ukraine's Orange Revolution brought international attention to the country. President Viktor Yushchenko and his administration have since enacted important reforms; however, a muddled Ukrainian political climate has slowed the rate of change. Today, Ukrainians are divided over their own identity: this internal struggle to reinvent and yet retain traditions can make Ukrainian culture confusing to navigate. Don't be surprised if a desk clerk and a website provide two different prices for a room, and don't expect anyone outside Kyiv to speak much English. Despite these inconveniences, Ukraine is captivating. Whole cities are under renovation, and the energy of revitalization spills over into the streets. If you can get past the almost complete lack of tourist infrastructure, Ukraine can be a beautiful and adventurous place to travel.

DISCOVER UKRAINE: SUGGESTED ITINERARIES

THREE DAYS. Stick to **Kyiv**, the epicenter of the Orange Revolution. Check out **Independence Square,** stop by **Shevchenko Park** to enjoy real Ukrainian fare at **O'Panas,** and ponder your mortality among the mummified monks of the **Kyiv-Cave Monastery** (p. 1055).

ONE WEEK. After three days in **Kyiv,** take a train to **Lviv** (2 days; p. 1056), the cultural capital of Ukraine. Spend your last two days in **Odessa** (p. 1057) soaking up the sun on the beach and experiencing high culture for cheap at the **Theater of Opera and Ballet.**

ESSENTIALS

FACTS AND FIGURES

OFFICIAL NAME: Ukraine.

CAPITAL: Kyiv.

MAJOR CITIES: Lviv, Odessa, Sevastopol, Simferopol, Yalta.

POPULATION: 45,994,000.

LAND AREA: 603,700 sq. km.

TIME ZONE: GMT + 2.

LANGUAGE: Ukrainian.

RELIGIONS: Ukrainian Orthodox (29%), Orthodox (16%), other (55%).

THE HEART OF IT ALL: Some measurements have placed the geographic center of Europe in Dilove, UKR.

WHEN TO GO

Ukraine is a huge country with a diverse climate. Things heat up from June to August in Odessa and Crimea, which are just barely subtropical. It is best to reserve accommodations in advance at these times. Kyiv enjoys a moderate climate, while the more mountainous west remains cool even in summer. Winter tourism is popular in the Carpathians, but unless you're skiing, spring and summer are probably the best times to visit the country. Book accommodations early around the May 1 holiday.

DOCUMENTS AND FORMALITIES

EMBASSIES AND CONSULATES. Foreign embassies to Ukraine are in Kyiv (p. 1053). Ukrainian embassies and consulates abroad include: **Australia,** Level 12, St. George Centre, 60 Marcus Clarke St., Canberra, ACT 2601 (☎02 62 30 57 89; www.ukremb.info); **Canada,** 310 Somerset St., West Ottawa, ON K2P 0J9 (☎613-230-2400; www.mfa.gov.ua/canada); **Ireland,** refer to UK embassy; **New Zealand,** 48, Ayton Drive, Glenfield, Auckland (☎94 01 94 93; http://ukraine.visahq.com/embassy/New-Zealand); **UK,** 60 Holland Park, London, W11 3SJ (☎020 77 27 63 12, visas ☎020 72 43 89 23; www.ukremb.org.uk); **US,** 3350 M St., NW, Washington, DC 20007 (☎202-333-0606; www.mfa.gov.ua/usa).

ENTRANCE REQUIREMENTS.

Passport: Required for all travelers.

Visa: Not required for citizens of Canada, the EU, or the US, but mandatory for citizens of Australia and New Zealand.

Letter of Invitation: Required for citizens of Australia and New Zealand.

Inoculations: Recommended up-to-date on DTaP (diphtheria, tetanus, and pertussis), Hepatitis A, Hepatitis B, MMR (measles, mumps, and rubella), polio booster, rabies (if you'll be in rural areas for long periods of time), and typhoid.

Work Permit: Required of all foreigners planning to work in Ukraine.

International Driving Permit: Required for all those planning to drive.

VISA AND ENTRY INFORMATION. Ukraine's visa requirements have changed rapidly since 2005 as the new government works to encourage tourism. Visas are no longer required for American or Canadian citizens or citizens of the EU for stays of up to 90 days. All visas are valid for 90 days. Citizens of Australia and New Zealand require a **letter of invitation** (available from Ukrainian or Australian/New Zealand travel agencies) but citizens of Canada, the EU, and the US do not. Travelers should allow three weeks for processing. You can extend your visa in Ukraine, at the Ministry of Foreign Affairs, (Velyka Zhitomirska st., 2, Kyiv) or at the local **Office of Visas and Registration** (ОВИ; OVYR), often located at the police station. **Do not lose the paper given to you when entering the country to supplement your visa.** Make sure to carry your passport and visa at all times.

TOURIST SERVICES AND MONEY

EMERGENCY	Ambulance: ☎03. Fire: ☎01. Police: ☎02.

TOURIST OFFICES. Lviv's tourist office is helpful, but it is the only official tourist office in Ukraine. The remains of the Soviet giant **Intourist** have offices in hotels, but staff often doesn't speak English. The official tourist website, **www.traveltoukraine.org,** has a list of "reliable travel agents." Local travel agencies can be helpful, but are sometimes overly pushy.

MONEY. The Ukrainian unit of currency is the *hryvnya* (*hv*), and *Obmin Valyut* (Обмшн Валт) kiosks in most cities offer the best rates for currency exchange. **Traveler's checks** can be changed for a small commission in many cities. **ATMs** are everywhere. Most **banks** will give MasterCard and Visa **cash advances** for a high commission. The lobbies of upscale hotels usually exchange US dollars at

lousy rates. **Private money changers** lurk near kiosks, ready with brilliant schemes for scamming you, but exchanging money with them is illegal.

UKRANHIAN HRYVNIA (HV)		
	AUS$1 = 3.85HV	1HV = AUS$0.26
	CDN$1 = 4.58HV	1HV = CDN$0.22
	EUR€1 = 6.47HV	1HV = EUR€0.15
	NZ$1 = 3.23HV	1HV = NZ$0.31
	UK£1 = 9.45HV	1HV = UK£0.11
	US$1 = 5.05HV	1HV = US$0.20

HEALTH AND SAFETY

Hospital facilities in Ukraine are limited and do not meet American or Western European standards. Patients may be required to bring their own medical supplies (e.g., bandages). When in doubt, it is advisable to seek aid from your local embassy. Medical evacuations to Western Europe cost US$25,000 and upwards of US$50,000 to the US. **Pharmacies** (Аптеки; Apteky) are quite common and carry basic Western products. **Boil all water** or learn to love brushing your teeth with soda water. **Peel or wash fruits and vegetables** from open markets. Meat purchased at public markets should be checked carefully and cooked thoroughly; refrigeration is infrequent and insects run rampant. Avoid the tasty-looking hunks of meat for sale out of buckets on the Kyiv metro. Embassy officials declare that Chernobyl-related radiation poses minimal risk to short-term travelers. **Public restrooms** range from disgusting to frightening. **Pay toilets** (платн; *platni*) are cleaner and might provide toilet paper, but bring your own.

While Ukraine is politically stable, it is poor. Pickpocketing and wallet scams are the most common **crimes** against tourists; however, instances of armed robbery and assault have been reported. Do not accept drinks from strangers, as this could result in your being drugged. Credit card and ATM fraud are rampant; only use ATMs inside banks and hotels, and avoid using credit cards when possible. Also use caution when crossing the street—drivers do not stop for pedestrians. It's wise to register with your embassy once you get to Ukraine.

Women traveling alone may receive catcalls by men anywhere they go, but usually will be safe otherwise. Ukrainian women rarely go to restaurants alone, so expect to feel conspicuous if you do. Women may request to ride in female-only compartments during long train rides, though most do not. Although non-Caucasians may experience **discrimination,** the biggest problems stem from the militia, who frequently stop people who appear non-Slavic. **Homosexuality** is not yet accepted in Ukraine; it's best to be discreet.

TRANSPORTATION

BY PLANE. It is expensive to travel to Ukraine by plane, and few budget airlines fly in or out of the country. Ground transportation tends to be safer and more pleasant, but it can take a long time to traverse the great distances between cities. Most international flights land at **Borispol International Airport** (KPB, www.airport-borispol.kiev.ua, ☎490 47 77). Air Ukraine flies to Kyiv, Lviv, and Odessa from many European capitals. **Aerosvit, Air France, British Airways, SA, Delta, Lufthansa, LOT,** and **Malev** fly to Kyiv.

BY TRAIN. Trains run frequently and are the best way to travel. Ukraine's system is generally safe, although *Let's Go* discourages the use of **night trains** in the region. When coming from a non-ex-Soviet country, expect a 2hr. stop at the border. To purchase tickets, you must present a passport or student ID. Once on board, you must present both your ticket and ID to the *konduktor*. On most Ukrainian trains, there are three classes: плацкарт, or *platskart*, where you'll be crammed in with *babushki* (little old ladies) and baskets of strawberries; купе, or *kupe*, a clean, more private, four-person compartment; and first class, referred to as CB, or SV (for *Spalny Wagon*), which is twice as roomy and expensive as *kupe*. Unless you're determined to live like a local, pay the extra two dollars for *kupe*. Then again, women traveling alone may want to avoid the smaller, enclosed compartments of *kupe*; in that case, *platskart* may be the safer option. The *kasa* will sell you a kupe seat unless you specify otherwise. Except in larger cities, where platform numbers are posted on the electronic board, the only way to figure out which platform your train leaves from is by listening to the distorted announcement. In large cities, trains arrive well before they are scheduled to depart, so you'll have a few minutes to show your ticket to cashiers or fellow passengers and ask "plaht-FORM-ah?"

BY BUS, TAXI, AND THUMB. Buses cost about the same as trains, but are often much shabbier. For long distances, the train is usually more comfortable, although on some routes the bus proves considerably faster. One exception is **AutoLux** (АвтоЛкс, www.autolux.ua), which runs buses with A/C, snacks, and movies. Bus schedules are generally reliable, but low demand can cause cancellations. Buy tickets at the *kasa*; if they're sold out, try going directly to the driver, who might just magically find you a seat and pocket the money. Navigating the bus system can be tough for those who do not speak Ukrainian or Russian. **Taxi** drivers love to rip off foreigners, so negotiate the price beforehand. Few Ukrainians **hitchhike,** but those who do hold a sign with their destination or just wave an outstretched hand. *Let's Go* does not recommend hitchhiking.

DON'T MESS WITH TRANSNISTRIA. If you're planning a trip from Western Ukraine to the Crimea, make sure that your train or bus route doesn't pass through Moldova on the way. Much of eastern Moldova is part of the unrecognized breakaway territory of Transnistria; border guards in Transnistria have been known to demand bribes, confiscate expensive items like laptops and cameras, or simply throw unlucky travelers off of the train. To make sure this doesn't happen to you, check at the ticket counter before buying to make sure your ticket won't take you for an unpleasant ride.

KEEPING IN TOUCH

PHONE CODES	**Country code**: 380. **International dialing prefix:** 8, await a second tone, then 10. For more info on placing international calls, see **Inside Back Cover.**

TELEPHONE AND INTERNET. **Telephone services** are stumbling toward modernity. The easiest way to make **international calls** is with Utel. Buy an Utel **phonecard** (sold at most Utel phone locations) and dial the number of your international operator (counted as a local call). International access codes include: **AT&T Direct** (☎8 100 11); **Canada Direct** (☎8 100 17); and **MCI WorldPhone** (☎8 100 13). Alternatively, call at the **central telephone office**; estimate the length of your call and pay at the counter, and they'll direct you to a booth. Calling can be expensive, but you can purchase a 30min. international calling card for 15hv. Local calls from gray **payphones** generally cost 10-30hv. For an English-speaking operator, dial ☎8192. Cell phones are everywhere; to get one, stop at any kiosk or corner store. **Internet cafes** can be found in every major city and typically charge 4-12hv per hour of use. Major cities typically have 24hr. Internet cafes.

MAIL. Mail is cheap, reliable, and extremely user-friendly, taking about 8-10 days to reach North America. Sending a postcard or a letter of less than 20g internationally costs 0.66hv. Address **Poste Restante** (mail held at the post office for collection, до запитання; do zapytannya) as follows: First name LAST NAME, post office address, Postal Code, city, ГЛКФШТУ.

LANGUAGE. Traveling in Ukraine is much easier if you know some Ukrainian or Russian. Ukrainian is an East Slavic language written in the Cyrillic alphabet. For basic Russian words and phrases see **Phrasebook** (p. 1068). In Kyiv, Odessa, and Crimea, Russian is more commonly spoken than Ukrainian (although all official signs are in Ukrainian). If you're trying to get by with Russian in western Ukraine, you may run into some difficulty: everyone understands Russian, but some people will answer in Ukrainian out of habit or nationalist sentiment. *Let's Go* provides city names in Ukrainian for Kyiv and western Ukraine, while Russian names are used for Crimea and Odessa.

ACCOMMODATIONS AND CAMPING

UKRAINE	❶	❷	❸	❹	❺
ACCOMMODATIONS	under 75hv	75-150hv	151-250hv	251-350hv	over 350hv

The **hostel** scene in Ukraine is quickly establishing itself, though hostels are uncommon outside Lviv, Kyiv, and Odessa. Budget accommodations are often in unrenovated Soviet-era buildings, though they are rapidly improving. More expensive lodgings aren't necessarily nicer. Not all hotels accept foreigners, and overcharging tourists is common. Though room prices in Kyiv are astronomical, singles run anywhere from 65-110hv in the rest of the country. Standard hotel rooms include TVs, phones, and refrigerators. You will be given a *vizitka* (hotel card) to show to the hall monitor (*dezhurnaya*) to get a key; return it each time you leave. Hot water doesn't necessarily come with a bath—ask before checking in. Private rooms are the best bargain and run 20-50hv. These can be arranged through overseas agencies or bargained for at the train station. Big cities have camping facilities—usually a remote spot with trailers. Camping outside designated areas is illegal, and enforcement is strict.

FOOD AND DRINK

UKRAINE	❶	❷	❸	❹	❺
FOOD	under 15hv	15-35hv	36-55hv	56-75hv	over 75hv

New, fancy restaurants accommodate tourists and the few Ukrainians who can afford them, while *stolovayas* (cafeterias)—remnants of Soviet times—serve cheap, hot food. Pierogi-like dumplings called *vavenyky* are ubiquitous and delicious. **Vegetarians** beware: meat has a tendency to show up in so-called "vegetarian" dishes. Finding **kosher** foods can be daunting, but it helps to eat non-meat items. Fruits and veggies are sold at markets; bring your own bag. State food stores are classified by content: *hastronom* (packaged goods); *moloko* (milk products); *ovochi-frukty* (fruits and vegetables); *myaso* (meat); *khlib* (bread); *kolbasy* (sausage); and *ryba* (fish). *Kvas* is a popular, barely-alcoholic, fermented bread drink. Grocery stores are often simply labeled *mahazyn* (store). Beer can be drunk publicly but hard liquor can't. The distinction is telling—"I drink beer," goes one Ukrainian saying, "and I also drink alcohol."

HOLIDAYS AND FESTIVALS

Holidays: Orthodox Christmas (Jan. 7); Orthodox New Year (Jan. 14); International Women's Day (Mar. 8); Easter (Apr. 19th, 2009; Apr. 4th, 2010); Labor Day (May 1-2); Victory Day (May 9); Holy Trinity Day (June 16); Constitution Day (June 28); Independence Day (Aug. 24).

Festivals: One of the most widely celebrated festivals is the **Donetsk Jazz Festival**, usually held in March. The **Chervona Ruta Festival,** which occurs in different Ukrainian cities each year, celebrating both modern Ukrainian pop and traditional music. The **Molodist Kyiv International Film Festival,** held in the last week of October, offers a platform for student films and up-and-coming film directors.

BEYOND TOURISM

For more info on opportunities across Europe, see **Beyond Tourism,** p. 60.

Jewish Volunteer Corps, American Jewish World Service, 45 W. 36th St., New York City, NY 10018, USA (☎+1 212-792-2919, www.ajws.org). Places volunteers at summer camps and Jewish community centers in Russia Ukraine.

Odessa Language Center (☎+380 482 345 058; www.studyrus.com). Spend a few weeks or up to a year in Ukraine learning Russian and studying history and culture.

KYIV (КИЇВ) ☎8044

Since becoming the capital of the Kyivan Rus empire over a millennium ago, Kyiv (pop. 2,700,000) has been a social and economic center for the region. No stranger to foreign control, the city was razed by the Nazi army only to be rebuilt with extravagant Stalinist pomp by the Soviets. Since Ukraine gained its independence from the USSR in 1991, Kyiv has reemerged as a proud capital and cultural center. One can find a legion of gilded towers and buildings reminiscent of mother Russia strewn along its hilly streets. However, the open squares, countless cafes, and shaded paths add a distinct western flavor to this Eastern European capital. The new government—elected beneath the international spotlight during the 2004 Orange Revolution—struggles to institute promised reforms as the cost of living rises.

TRANSPORTATION

Flights: **Boryspil International Airport** (Бориспіль, **KBP**, ☎8044 281 7498) 30km southeast of the capital. Polit (Політ; ☎8044 296 7367), just right of the main entrance, sends **minibuses** called *marshrutkis* to Ploshcha Peremohi, the train station, and Boryspilska, the metro stop. Buy tickets on board (1-2 per hr., 17-22hv). Expect to be hassled by an army of **taxi** drivers upon exiting the airport. A taxi to the center costs 80-100hv. Negotiate with drivers near the Polit bus stop; those stationed outside customs will take you for a ride.

Trains: Kyiv-Pasazhyrskyy (Київ-Пасажирський), Vokzalna pl. (☎005 or 8044 465 4895). MR: Vokzalna (Вокзальна). Purchase tickets for **domestic trains** in the main hall. For international tickets, go to window #40 or 41 in the newest section of the train station, across the tracks. For the *elektrychka* **commuter rail** (електричка), go to Prymiskyy Vokzal (Примский Вокзал; Suburban Station), next to the Metro station. **Information windows** (довідка; dovidka) are located in each section of the train station; some stay open 24hr. However, assistance is entirely in Ukrainian or Russian. Look for a large departure board in the main hall that posts platform numbers and any last-minute changes. There is an **Advance Ticket Office** next to Hotel Express at Shevchenka 38. Train tickets are divided into 4 classes, and trains usually have beds rather than seats. 1st class seats hold 2 beds to a room, while 2nd class has 4 beds and shabbier conditions, but is considerably less expensive. Trains to: **Lviv** (10hr., 5-6 per day, 65-100hv); **Odessa** (11hr., 4-5 per day, 80-105hv); **Sevastopol** (20hr., 2 per day, 75-180hv); **Bratislava, SLK** (21hr., 1 per day, 700hv); **Budapest, HUN** (24hr., 1 per day, 800hv); **Moscow, RUS** (14-17hr., 12-15 per day, 350hv); **Prague, CZR** (35hr., 1 per day, 600hv); **Warsaw, POL** (19hr., 2 per day, 450hv). Check prices before purchasing train tickets, as train ticket prices in Ukraine change frequently.

Buses: Tsentralny Avtovokzal (Центральний Автовокзал), Moskovska pl. 3 (Московська; ☎8044 264 5774). MR: Libydska. Take trolley #1 or 11 from the Libydska metro station. Open 5am-10pm. Buses to: **Lviv** (7-12hr., 4 per day, 70hv); **Odessa** (8-10hr., 9 per day, 75hv); **Moscow, RUS** (18hr., 1 per day, 150hv).

Public Transportation: 3 **metro** lines–blue (MB), green (MG), and red (MR)–cover the city center. Purchase tokens (житон; zhyton; 0.50hv) at the kasa (каса). "Вхід" (vkhid) indicates an entrance, "перехід" (perekhid) a walkway to another station, and "вихід

UKRAINE

у місто" (vykhid u misto) an exit onto the street. **Trolleys, buses,** and **marshrutki** (private vans) go where the metro doesn't. Bus tickets sold at kiosks or by the driver; punch your ticket using the manual lever on board or face a fine. *Marshrutki* tickets (1-3hv) are sold on board; pay attention and request stops from the driver. Public transport runs approx. 5:45am-12:15am. The *elektrychka* (електричка) **commuter rail** leaves from Prymiskyy Vokzal (Примский Вокзал), MR: Vokzalna.

Taxis: Taxis are everywhere. A ride to the center of town should cost about 20hv. Always agree on the price before getting in.

ORIENTATION AND PRACTICAL INFORMATION

Most attractions and services lie on the west bank of the Dniper River. Three metro stops from the train station is the main avenue, **vulitsa Khreshchatyk** (Хрещатик; MR line). The center of Kyiv is vul. Khreshchatyk's **Independence Square** (Майдан Незалежност; Maidan Nezalezhnosti; MB line), which is home to six fountains, an underground mall, and the 16m high **Independence Column.**

Tourist Offices: Kyiv lacks official tourist services. Various agencies at the airport offer vouchers, excursion packages, hotel arrangements, and other services. Travel agencies also organize **tours.** Carlson Wagonlit Travel, Khnoelnistkiy 33/34, 2nd fl. (☎8044 238 6156). Open daily 9am-9pm. Has branch at the US Embassy. For tours, accommodation, and **visa assistance,** go to Yana Travel Group, Saksahanskoho 42 (Саксаганського; ☎490 7373; www.yana.kiev.ua). Open M-F 10am-7pm, Sa 10am-5pm.

Embassies: Australia, Kominterna 18/137 (комінтерне; ☎8044 246 4223; fax 244 3597). Open M-Th 10am-1pm. **Canada,** Yaroslaviv Val. 31 (Ярославів; ☎8044 464 1144; fax 464 0598). Open M-F 8:30am-1pm and 2-5pm; visa section open M-Th. **Ireland,** 44 Shchorsa St. (☎8044 285 5902. Open M-Th 10am-1pm.) Citizens of **New Zealand** should refer to the Australian embassy. **UK,** Desyatynna 9 (Десятинна; ☎8044 490 3660; fax 8044 490 3662). Consular section at Glybochytska 4 (Глибоицька; ☎8044 494 3400; fax 8044 494 3418). Open M-Th 9am-1pm and 2pm-5:30pm, F 9am-1pm and 2pm-4pm. **US,** Yu. Kotsyubynskoho 10 (Коцбинського; ☎8044 490 4000; http://kyiv.usembassy.gov). Open M-F 9am-6pm. Consular section at Pymonenka 6 (Пимоненка; ☎8044 490 4422 or 8044 490 4445; fax 8044 490 4040). From the corner of Maidan Nezalezhnosti and Sofievska (Софіевска), take trolley #16 or 18 for 4 stops. Continue on bul. Artyoma (Артема) until it curves to the right, then take the 1st right, Pymonenka.

Medical Services: American Medical Center, Berdychivska 1 (Бердиерска; ☎8044 490 7600; www.amcenters.com). English-speaking doctors will take patients without documents or insurance. Open 24hr. MC/V.

Telephones: English operator (☎81 92.) **Telephone-Telegraph** (Телефон-Телеграф; telefon-telehraf) around the corner of the post office (enter on Khreshchatyk). The main post-office, located in independence square, also has **phone booths** where you can call destinations like the US for about $0.10/min. Open daily 8am-10pm. Buy cards for **public telephones** (тфксофон; taksofon) at any post office. Less widespread than Taksofon phones, **Utel** phones and cards are in the post office, train station, and hotels.

Internet: C-Club, Bessarabskaye pl. 1 (Бессарабскає; ☎8044 238 6446), in the underground mall (globus shopping center) between Bessarabskiy market and the Lenin statue has over 100 computers. 12hv per hr. 9am-8am. **Vault 13,** Bolshaya Vasilkovskaya 19. Also a bar, so feel free to surf the web with a gin and tonic in hand.

Post Office: Khreshchatyk 22 (☎8044 278 1167; www.poshta.kiev.ua). **Poste Restante** at counters #28 and 30. For packages, enter on Maidan Nezalezhnosti. Copy, fax, and photo services available. Open M-Sa 8am-9pm, Su 9am-7pm. **Postal Code:** 01001.

RADIOACTIVE TOURISM

The year 2006 marked the 20th anniversary of the world's worst nuclear accident. Controversy still exists about the overall effect of the explosion at Chernobyl. Independent studies contest the UN's estimate of 4000-9000 cancer deaths; some even suggest a staggering figure of 93,000.

Today, a new trade is beginning in the ghost-towns of Chernobyl: tourism. Although radiation levels remain extremely high in the "Dead Zone," several travel agencies have begun leading tours (which cost US$100-400), to look at the fateful reactor 4, visit towns in the Dead Zone, and check out radiation-filled tanks.

Despite the influx of tourism, Chernobyl is still not considered safe. Geiger counters have found over 50 times normal radiation. And to make matters worse, the ruins of reactor 4—still filled with nuclear material—are showing signs of breaking down, prompting Ukraine to propose the building of a new steel facility in 2008. Tour agencies press ahead, leading over 500 tourists every year, insising that the danger lies in long-term radiation, not in a one-day encounter. Others feel that the name "the Dead Zone" speaks for itself.

For info on tours, visit www.tourkiev.com/chernobyl.php, or call ☎405 35 00. Solo East Tours is located at Travneva St. 12.

ACCOMMODATIONS

Hotels in Kyiv tend to be expensive; the **Kyiv Post** (www.kyivpost.com) lists short-term apartment rentals, as do most English-language publications and websites about Kyiv. People at train stations offer cheaper rooms (from US$5), though English speakers are rare and the quality of rooms varies. Another way to find lodging is through the commission-free telephone service **Okean-9.** (☎8044 443 6167. Open M-F 9am-5pm, Sa 9am-3pm.)

International Youth Hostel Yaroslav (Ярослав), vul. Yaroslavska 10 (Ярославська; ☎8066 417 3189), in the historic Podil district; MB: Kontraktova Ploshcha. Enter through courtyard; it's the 1st door on the right. Press the numbers 4 and 7 simultaneously on the keypad to enter. 12-bed hostel with warm English-speaking staff. Free lockers for every bed, recently renovated 2nd floor. Spacious rooms. Kitchen. (Internet next door 9hv per hr. Doubles 250hv; 4- to 5-bed dorms 130hv, 120 with ISIC. MC/V.) ❸

International Hostel Tatarka, vul. Lukjanivska 77, (MB: Kontraktova Ploscha; ☎8044 417 3393) has large 5-bed rooms (some with balconies) and views of the city. Staff does not speak English, but if you can put together a few Ukrainian sentences this hostel is a real find. Bathrooms leave a little to be desired, however. Uphill from station, so from, consider a taxi (around 20hv). Rooms 80hv. Cash only. ❶

Youth Hostel Kiev, 52-A Artema #2, 5th floor. vul Artema. (MB: Lukjanivska; ☎8044 481 3838) Go past the new complex (which is also labeled 52-A) to the 2nd building with a garden in front. Calm, well-kept hostel with 30 beds, popular with families and groups. English speaking staff. Singles, doubles, triples available; all beds 125 hv. 24 hr reception. Laundry 10 hv. Towels, linen free. Cash only.) ❷

FOOD

Kyiv has a myriad of Western and Eastern restaraunts, with plenty of Chinese, Italian, and Russian restaraunts all over town. The most popular are traditional Ukrainian cafeteria-style eateries—these are usually quite cheap. When you go in, point at your food, get a big glass of beer, and enjoy.

O'Panas, (О'Панас), Tereshchenkivska vul. 10 (Терещенківська; ☎8044 235 2132), is located in the Taras Shevchenko Park. Serves local dishes in traditional Ukrainian decor. Known for delectable traditional Ukrainian pancakes; order them out of the front of the restaraunt. Entrees 40-120hv. Business lunch noon-3pm. Open M-F 8am-1am, Sa-Su 10am-1am. MC/V. ❸

Puzata Hata, vul Sahaidachnoho 24 (Сагайдачного; ☎8044 391 4699; www.puzatahata.kiev.us) MB: Poshtova Poloscha. Food served in a beautiful 2-story restaraunt popular with youth and families alike. When coming in, go up the stairs, grab a tray, and point at the food you want. Soups and salads, to begin, followed by meat and potatoes, moving on to *piroshikis* and desserts. Pay by weight; the average hearty meal costs about 20-30hv. Open daily 8am-11pm. Cash only. ❶

Antresol, (Антресоль), bul. T. Shevchenka 2 (☎8044 235 8347), has a hip bookstore-cafe downstairs and a restaurant upstairs. Large selection of coffee and good wine produces a relaxed ambiance, ideal for grabbing a book and enjoying a latte. English-language menu. Salads 25-50hv. Entrees 29-110hv. Tu and Su live piano 8-10pm. Open daily 9am-late. MC/V. ❸

SIGHTS

KYIV-CAVE MONASTERY. Also known as *Kyiv-Pechersk Lavra*, the Kyiv-Cave Monastery is Kyiv's oldest holy site, and a major pilgrimage site for Orthodox Christians. It houses the **Refectory Church,** the 12th-century **Holy Trinity Gate Church,** and caves where monks lie mummified (though they are hidden by decorative shrouds). The **Great Lavra Bell Tower** offers great views. *(Києво-Печерська Лавра; Kyivo-Pecherska Lavra. MR: Arsenalna; Арсенальна. ☎8044 255 1109. Turn left out of the metro and walk down vul. Sichnevoho Povstaniya to #25. Open daily May-Aug. 9am-7pm; Sept.-Apr. 9:30am-6pm. Upper lavra, which is state-run, will cost about 24hv. The lower section requires only the purchase of a candle as an entrance free. Monastery 10hv, students 5hv. Photography 12hv.)*

ST. SOPHIA CATHEDRAL. Once the religious center of Kyivan Rus, the 11th century St. Sophia Cathedral—with its ornamented facades and Byzantine mosaics—offers a look into the religious history of Ukraine. It was originally designed to rival Constantinople's Hagia Sofia. *(vul. Volodymyrska. MG: Zoloti Vorota or trolley #16 from Maidan Nezalezhnosti. Grounds open daily 10am-7pm. Museums open M-Tu and F-Su 10am-6pm, W 10am-5pm. Grounds 5hv. Museums 20hv, students 8hv. Bell tower 5/3hv.)*

VUL. KHRESHCHATYK. Kyiv's central road, vul. Khreshchatyk (Хрещатик), is where locals go to see and be seen. It begins at bul. T. Shevchenka and extends to **Independence Square** (Майдан Незалежности; Maidan Nezalezhnosti), which hosted a massive tent city during the Orange Revolution. **Khreshchatyk Park,** past the **Friendship of the Peoples Arch,** contains a monument to Prince Volodymyr, who converted the Kyivan Rus to Christianity. (MR: Khreshchatyk; Хрещатик.) Full of cafes and galleries, the cobblestone district of **Andriy's Descent** (Андрівский Узвз; Andriyivskyy uzviz) can be reached by walking down Desyatynna from Mikhaylivska Sq. *(MB: Poshtova Ploshcha; Поштова Площа.)*

MUSEUM OF ONE STREET. Bizarrely, this museum recounts the history of Kyiv's most famous street, Andriy's Descent. *(Andriyivskyy uzviz 2B. Open Tu-Su noon-6pm. 10hv. 45min. English-language tour 100hv.)*

ST. ANDREW'S CHURCH. At the corner of Volodymyrska and Andriyivskyy uzviz is the beautiful St. Andrew's Church. Its ornate exterior makes it one of Ukraine's most significant pieces of architecture. *(Open daily 10am-5pm.)*

THE CHERNOBYL MUSEUM. Artifacts and testimonies from the disaster's aftermath as well as a poster exhibit commemorating its 20th anniversary. *(1 Khoryvyj Pereulok Street. Open M-Sa 10am-6pm. Closed last M of each month. 8hv, with ISIC 4hv.)*

ENTERTAINMENT AND NIGHTLIFE

The last weekend in May brings the **Kyiv Days,** attracting thousands of spectators with art and music performances all over the city. During the rest of the year, the **National Philharmonic,** Volodymyrska 2, holds concerts most nights at 7pm. (☎8044 278 1697; www.filharmonia.com.ua. Kasa open Tu-Su noon-2pm and 3-7pm. 10-50hv.) While you're in town don't miss **Dynamo Kyiv,** Ukraine's top football team. (*Kasa* in front of stadium.) Check out *What's On* magazine (www.whatson-kiev.com) and the *Kyiv Post* (www.kyivpost.com) for nightlife listings. Kyiv's popular jazz club, **Artclub 44,** vul. Khreshchatyk 44, has live music nightly starting at 10pm; it attracts a diverse crowd ranging from students to businessmen. (☎8044 279 4137. Cover 10-20hv. Open daily 11am-2 am.)

LVIV (ЛЬВІВ) ☎80322

Lviv's star is rising. While Kyiv is the political and economic capital of Ukraine, many consider Lviv (pop. 1,000,000) to be the cultural and patriotic center of the country. Lviv's cobblestone streets and picturesque churches, packed with architecture of every imaginable style, still manage to feel lived-in rather than on display. The modern city, which stretches beyond the historic center, is bustling, chock-full of cafes, and close to the beautiful Carpathian mountains

Climb up the **High Castle Hill** (Високий Замок; Vysokyy Zamok), the former site of the Galician King's Palace, for a stunning panoramic view of Lviv. **Ploshcha Rynok,** the historic market square, is surrounded by richly decorated homes and numerous Baroque churches. The **History Museum** (сторичний Музей; Istorichnyy Muzey) complex is at pl. Rynok #4, 6, and 24. Exhibits at #4 recount the history of Ukraine's struggle for liberation during WWI and WWII; some are accompanied by English translations. (☎80322 72 06 71. Open Mar.-Nov. M-Tu and Th-Su 10am-6pm, Dec.-Feb. M-Tu and Th-Su 10am-5pm. Each museum 3-7hv, some student discounts.) Walk up to the end of vul. Staroyevreiska (Old Jewish St.), and on your left at Arsenalna Square you'll see the ruins of the 16th-century **Golden Rose Synagogue,** a center of Jewish culture before its destruction by the Nazis. A number of new hostels are opening up in Lviv to accommodate the city's growing tourism industry. **Lviv Backpackers' Hostel,** Kolyaretskoho 37, Apt. 2 (Котляреценького), offers more amenities than most backpackers will ever need, among them a hot tub, free Wi-Fi, a patio, satellite TV, and a DVD collection. Book in advance.(☎80322 37 20 53. English spoken. Dorms US$16-22; special offers available. AmEx/MC/V.) **Veronika ❶** (Веронка), pr. Shevchenka Prospect 21, serves pastries (5hv) and mouth-watering cakes (10-24hv) in its upstairs cafe, as well as classic European dishes (35-175hv) in the small, dark restaurant downstairs. (☎80322 97 81 28. Open daily 10am-11pm. MC/V.) For nightlife, check out the expansive **Millennium,** vul. Chornovola 2. (☎80322 40 35 91. Beer 5hv. Cover up to 50hv. Open Tu-Su 9pm-4am.)

LOCAL PHONE CALLS. From a landline, dial "2" before numbers that begin with "9."

Trains go from pl. Vokzalna (Вокзальна) to: Kyiv (9hr., 3 per day, 50-100hv); Odessa (12hr., 1 per day, 60-110hv); Budapest, HUN (13hr., 1 per day, 400hv); Krakow, POL (8hr., 1 per day, 250hv); Moscow, RUS (25hr., 3 per day, 250hv); Prague, CZR (32hr., 1 per day, 400hv); Warsaw, POL (14hr., every other day, 400hv). Tickets can be bought at the railway *kasa* at Hnatyuka 20. (☎80322 26 11 76. Open M-Sa 8am-2pm and 3-8pm, Su 8am-2pm and 3-6pm.) **Taxis** from the

UKRAINE

train station into town cost about 25hv. **Buses** run from the main station, vul. Stryyska 189 (Стрийська; ☎294 9817); to Krakow, POL (10hr., 1 per day, 103hv) and Warsaw, POL (10hr., 3 per day, 150hv). **Trolleys** in town cost 0.50hv. The **Lviv Tourist Info Center,** vul. Pidvalna 3, has a helpful English-speaking staff. (☎80322 97 57 51; www.tourism.lviv.ua. Open M-F 10am-6pm.) **Internet Club,** vul. Dudaeva 12, offers Internet and international calling at reasonable rates. (☎80322 72 27 38; www.ic.lviv.ua. Open 24hr. Internet 4hv per hr.) **Postal Code:** 79000.

ODESSA (ОДЕСА) ☎80482

Odessa (pop. 1,000,000) has been blessed with prosperity (and cursed with corruption) since its founding by Catherine the Great in 1794. Beneath the city lies the world's longest series of **catacombs.** The tunnels were the base of resistance during the Nazi occupation. The labyrinth is only legally accessible with a private guide. FGT and Eugenia travel agencies (see below), as well as most hotels, organize **excursions** for about 20hv. The **Odessa Art Museum** (Художний Музей; Khudozhiy Muzei), ul. Sofiyevskaya 5A, houses a diverse collection of 19th-century art, as well as an underground grotto of secret passageways. (☎80482 25 10 34. Open M and W-Su 10:30am-5:30pm. 3hv for each of the 3 exhibits.) The crowds on **ul. Deribasovskaya** guarantee an animated scene at any time of day, and the fashion stores and cafes provide entertainment for all. The **Pushkin Museum and Memorial** (Литературно-мемориальний Музей Пушкина; Literaturno-memorialniy Muzey Pushkina) at #13 was the hotel where Pushkin lived during his 1823-1824 exile from St. Petersburg. (Open M-Sa 10am-5pm. 5hv, students 2hv.) The city's crowded **beaches** are easily accessible, though their quality varies. To reach nearby **Lanzheron** (Ланжерон) beach, walk through Shevchenko park or take *marshrutka* 253 or 233. Tram #5 goes to **Arkadiya** (Аркадия), the city's most popular beach. The **Potemkin Staircase** (Потьомкинськи сходи), as made famous by Sergei Eisenstein's 1925 film *Battleship Potemkin*, also known as the **Maritime Stairs,** has 192 steps, and is a must-see for film and history buffs alike.

Private rooms (from 30hv) are the cheapest accommodation options; hosts solicit customers at the train station. Hostels, however, rival private rooms in price and often trump them in comfort. **Black Sea Backpackers' Hostel ❸,** Yekaterinskaya 25, 2nd fl., has a bar, free breakfast, computer access, jacuzzi, kitchen, and Wi-Fi, along with a great location. (☎80482 25 22 00 or ☎80482 24 55 67; www.blackseahostels.com. Dorms US$25 May-Oct, $20 per night Nov.-Apr.) **Tavriya** (Таврія), Ploshcha Grechevskaya, in the basement of Galeria Afena, has a huge selection of cheap Ukrainian food, pizzas, crepes, and desserts, with live music. (Drinks 4-10hv. Soups 4-6hv. Entrees 6-20hv. Desserts 3-5hv. Open daily 8am-11pm. Cash only.) On summer nights, the crowds head to **Arkadiya,** where a strip of nightclubs blasts everything from electronica to hip hop with an emphasis on Russian pop. Tram #5 goes to Arkadiya but stops running around midnight; taxis back from the clubs cost 25-40hv.

Trains run from pl. Privokzalnaya 2 (Привокзальная), at the northern end of ul. Pushkinskaya, to: Kyiv (10hr., 5 per day, 60-90hv); Lviv (12hr., 2 per day, 70-90hv); Moscow, RUS (23-27hr., 1-3per day, 180-290hv); Simferopol (12hr., 70-90hv); Warsaw, POL (24hr., 1 per 2 days, 400hv). To reach the bus station, take tram #5 to the last stop. **Buses** run from ul. Kolontayevskaya 58 (Колонтаевская) to Kyiv (10-12hr., 8 per day, 66-88hv). **FGT Travel,** ul. Deribasovskaya 13, in Hotel Frapolli, provides tourist information. (☎80482 37 52 01; www.odessapassage.com. Open daily 8:30am-7pm.) **Postal Code:** 65001.

APPENDIX

CLIMATE

AVG. TEMP. (LOW/ HIGH), PRECIP.	JANUARY			APRIL			JULY			OCTOBER		
	°C	°F	mm	°C	°F	mm	°C	°F	mm	°C	°F	mm
Amsterdam	1/5	33/41	69	4/12	40/54	53	12/20	54/68	76	7/13	45/56	74
Athens	6/13	43/55	46	11/20	52/68	28	22/32	72/90	5	14/23	58/73	48
Berlin	-3/2	26/35	43	4/13	39/55	43	13/23	55/73	53	6/13	42/55	36
Budapest	-3/2	27/35	41	7/17	45/62	41	16/27	61/80	46	8/16	46/61	33
Copenhagen	-2/2	28/36	53	2/10	36/49	43	13/20	55/69	74	7/12	44/54	58
Dublin	3/8	37/46	69	4/12	40/53	51	12/19	53/66	51	8/14	46/57	71
İstanbul	3/8	37/47	99	8/17	46/62	48	18/28	65/82	20	12/19	53/67	71
Kraków	-7/-1	19/31	33	3/13	37/56	48	12/23	54/73	86	4/13	39/56	46
London	2/7	35/45	51	5/13	41/56	46	13/22	55/71	33	8/14	46/58	71
Madrid	0/11	32/51	46	6/17	42/63	46	16/32	61/90	10	8/20	47/68	46
Moscow	-10/-5	14/23	42	0/9	32/48	44	13/23	56/74	94	1/7	34/44	59
Paris	1/6	34/43	7	6/14	42/57	33	14/24	58/75	8	8/15	46/59	17
Prague	-4/1	24/34	20	2/12	36/54	36	12/22	54/72	66	4/12	39/54	31
Reykjavík	-3/2	27/35	86	1/5	33/41	56	8/13	47/55	51	2/7	36/44	89
Rome	2/12	35/53	84	7/19	44/66	69	17/31	62/88	23	10/22	50/72	107
Stockholm	-1/-5	23/30	38	1/8	34/47	31	13/22	56/71	71	5/9	41/49	51
Vienna	-3/2	27/36	38	5/14	41/57	51	15/25	59/77	64	6/14	43/57	41

MEASUREMENTS

Like the rest of the rational world, Europe uses the metric system. The basic unit of length is the meter (m), which is divided into 100 centimeters (cm) or 1000 millimeters (mm). One thousand meters make up one kilometer (km). Fluids are measured in liters (L), each divided into 1000 milliliters (mL). A liter of pure water weighs one kilogram (kg), the unit of mass that is divided into 1000 grams (g). One metric ton is 1000kg.

MEASUREMENT CONVERSIONS	
1 inch (in.) = 25.4mm	1 millimeter (mm) = 0.039 in.
1 foot (ft.) = 0.305m	1 meter (m) = 3.28 ft.
1 yard (yd.) = 0.914m	1 meter (m) = 1.094 yd.
1 mile (mi.) = 1.609km	1 kilometer (km) = 0.621 mi.
1 ounce (oz.) = 28.35g	1 gram (g) = 0.035 oz.
1 pound (lb.) = 0.454kg	1 kilogram (kg) = 2.205 lb.
1 fluid ounce (fl. oz.) = 29.57mL	1 milliliter (mL) = 0.034 fl. oz.
1 gallon (gal.) = 3.785L	1 liter (L) = 0.264 gal.

Britain uses the metric system, although its longtime conversion to the metric system is still in progress—road signs indicate distance in miles. Gallons in the US and those in Britain are not identical: one US gallon equals 0.83 Imperial gallons. Pub aficionados will note that an Imperial pint (20 oz.) is larger than its US counterpart (16 oz.).

LANGUAGE PHRASEBOOK

CYRILLIC ALPHABET

Bulgaria and **Ukraine** use variations of the Russian Cyrillic alphabet.

CYRILLIC	ENGLISH	PRONOUNCED	CYRILLIC	ENGLISH	PRONOUNCED
А а	a	*ah* as in Pr**a**gue	Р р	r	*r* as in **r**evolution
Б б	b	*b* as in **B**osnia	С с	s	*s* as in **S**erbia
В в	v	*v* as in **V**olga	Т т	t	*t* as in **t**ank
Г г	g	*g* as in **G**lasnost	У у	u	*oo* as in B**u**dapest
Д д	d	*d* as in **d**ictatorship	Ф ф	f	*f* as in **f**ormer USSR
Е е	e	*yeh* as in **Ye**ltsin	Х х	kh	*kh* as in Ba**ch**
Ё ё	yo	*yo* as in **yo!**	Ц ц	ts	*ts* as in **ts**ar
Ж ж	zh, ž	*zh* as in mira**ge**	Ч ч	ch, \	*ch* as in Gorba**ch**ev
З з	z	*z* as in communi**s**m	Ш ш	sh, š	*sh* as in Bol**sh**evik
И и	i	*ee* as in Gr**ee**k	Щ щ	shch	*shch* in Khru**shch**ev
Й й	y	*y* as in Tolsto**y**	Ъ ъ	(hard sign)	(not pronounced)
К к	k	*k* as in **K**remlin	Ы ы	i	*i* as in s**i**lver
Л л	l	*l* as in **L**enin	Ь ь	(soft sign)	(not pronounced)
М м	m	*m* as in **M**oscow	Э э	e	*eh* as in **E**stonia
Н н	n	*n* as in **n**uclear	Ю ю	yu	*yoo* as in **U**kraine
О о	o	*o* as in Cr**o**atia	Я я	ya	*yah* as in **Ya**lta
П п	p	*p* as in **P**oland			

GREEK ALPHABET

SYMBOL	NAME	PRONOUNCED	SYMBOL	NAME	PRONOUNCED
Α α	alpha	*a* as in f**a**ther	Ν ν	nu	*n* as in **n**et
Β β	beta	*v* as in **v**elvet	Ξ ξ	xi	*x* as in mi**x**
Γ γ	gamma	*y* or *g* as in **y**oga	Ο ο	omicron	*o* as in r**o**w
Δ δ	delta	*th* as in **th**ere	Π π	pi	*p* as in **p**eace
Ε ε	epsilon	*e* as in j**e**t	Ρ ρ	rho	*r* as in **r**oll
Ζ ζ	zeta	*z* as in **z**ebra	Σ σ/ς	sigma	*s* as in **s**ense
Η η	eta	*ee* as in qu**ee**n	Τ τ	tau	*t* as in **t**ent
Θ θ	theta	*th* as in **th**ree	Υ υ	upsilon	*ee* as in gr**ee**n
Ι ι	iota	*ee* as in tr**ee**	Φ φ	phi	*f* as in **f**og
Κ κ	kappa	*k* as in **k**ite	Χ χ	chi	*h* as in **h**orse
Λ λ	lambda	*l* as in **l**and	Ψ ψ	psi	*ps* as in oo**ps**
Μ μ	mu	*m* as in **m**oose	Ω ω	omega	*o* as in Let's G**o**

CROATIAN

ENGLISH	CROATIAN	PRONOUNCED	ENGLISH	CROATIAN	PRONOUNCED
Yes/No	Da/Ne	dah/neh	**Train/Bus**	Vlak/Autobus	vlahk/OW-toh-bus
Please	Molim	MOH-leem	**Station**	Kolodvor	KOH-loh-dvor
Thank you	Hvala lijepa	HVAH-la lee-yee-pah	**Airport**	Zračna Luka	ZRA-chna LU-kah
Good morning	Dobro jutro	DOH-broh YOO-tro	**Ticket**	Karta	KAHR-tah
Goodbye	Bog	Bog	**Taxi**	Taksi	TAH-ksee
Sorry/Excuse me	Oprostite	oh-PROH-stee-teh	**Hotel**	Hotel	HOH-tel
Help!	U pomoć!	OO poh-mohch	**Bathroom**	zahod	ZAH-hod

ENGLISH	CROATIAN	PRONOUNCED	ENGLISH	CROATIAN	PRONOUNCED
I'm lost.	Izgubljen sam.	eez-GUB-lye-n sahm	**Open/Closed**	Otvoreno/Zatvoreno	OHT-voh-reh-noh/ZAHT-voh-reh-noh
Police	Policija	po-LEE-tsee-ya	**Left/Right**	Lijevo/Desno	lee-YEH-voh/DEHS-noh
Embassy	Ambasada	ahm-bah-SAH-da	**Bank**	Banka	BAHN-kah
Passport	Putovnica	POO-toh-vnee-tsah	**Exchange**	Mjenjačnica	myehn-YAHCH-nee-tsah
Doctor/Hospital	Liječnik/Bolnica	lee-YECH-neek/BOHL-neet-sa	**Grocery/Market**	Trgovina	TER-goh-vee-nah
Pharmacy	Ljekarna	lye-KHAR-na	**Post Office**	Pošta	POSH-tah

ENGLISH	CROATIAN	PRONUNCIATION
Where is the...?	Gdje je...?	GDYE yeh
How much does this cost?	Koliko to košta?	KOH-lee-koh toh KOH-shtah
When is the next...?	Kada polazi sljedeći...?	ka-DA po-LA-zee SLYE-de-tchee
Do you have (a vacant room)?	Imate li (slobodne sobe)?	ee-MAH-teh lee (SLOH-boh-dneh SOH-beh)
Do you speak English?	Govorite li engleski?	GO-vohr-ee-teh lee ehn-GLEH-skee

CROATIAN CARDINAL NUMBERS										
0	**1**	**2**	**3**	**4**	**5**	**6**	**7**	**8**	**9**	**10**
nula	jedan	dva	tri	četiri	pet	šest	sedam	osam	devet	sto

CZECH

ENGLISH	CZECH	PRONOUNCED	ENGLISH	CZECH	PRONOUNCED
Yes/No	Ano/Ne	AH-no/neh	**Train/Bus**	Vlak/Autobus	vlahk/OW-toh-boos
Please	Prosím	PROH-seem	**Station**	Nádraží	NA-drah-zhee
Thank you	Děkuji	DYEH-koo-yee	**Airport**	Letiště	LEH-teesh-tyeh
Hello	Dobrý den	DOH-bree den	**Ticket**	Lístek	LIS-tek
Goodbye	Nashledanou	NAS-kleh-dah-noh	**Taxi**	Taxi	TEHK-see
Sorry/Excuse me	Promiňte	PROH-meen-teh	**Hotel**	Hotel	HOH-tel
Help!	Pomoc!	POH-mots	**Bathroom**	WC	VEE-TSEE
I'm lost. (m/f)	Zabloudil(a) jsem.	ZAH-bloh-dyeel-(ah) sem	**Open/Closed**	Otevřeno/Zavřeno	O-te-zheno/ZAV-rzhen-o
Police	Policie	POH-leets-ee-yeh	**Left/Right**	Vlevo/Vpravo	VLE-voh/VPRAH-voh
Embassy	Velvyslanectví	VEHL-vee-slah-nehts-vee	**Bank**	Banka	BAN-ka
Passport	Cestovní pas	TSEH-stohv-nee pahs	**Exchange**	Směnárna	smyeh-NAR-na
Doctor	Lékař	LEK-arzh	**Grocery**	Potraviny	PO-tra-vee-nee
Pharmacy	Lékárna	LEE-khaar-nah	**Post Office**	Pošta	POSH-tah

ENGLISH	CZECH	PRONUNCIATION
Where is the...?	Kde je...?	gdeh yeh
How much does this cost?	Kolik to stojí?	KOH-lihk STOH-yee
When is the next...?	Kdy jede příští...?	gdi YEH-deh przh-EESH-tyee
Do you have (a vacant room)?	Máte (volný pokoj)?	MAA-teh (VOHL-nee POH-koy)
I would like...	Prosím...	PROH-seem

CZECH CARDINAL NUMBERS										
0	**1**	**2**	**3**	**4**	**5**	**6**	**7**	**8**	**9**	**10**
nula	jeden	dva	tøi	ètyøi	pìt	šest	sedm	osm	devìt	deset

FINNISH

ENGLISH	FINNISH	PRONOUNCED	ENGLISH	FINNISH	PRONOUNCED
Yes/No	Kyllä/Ei	KEW-la/ay	**Ticket**	Lippu	LIP-ooh
Please	Olkaa hyvä	OHL-ka HEW-va	**Train/Bus**	Juna/Bussi	YU-nuh/BUS-see
Thank you	Kiitos	KEE-tohss	**Boat**	Vene	VEH-nay
Hello	Hei	hey	**Departures**	Lähtevät	lah-teh-VAHT
Goodbye	Näkemiin	NA-keh-meen	**Market**	Tori	TOH-ree
Sorry/Excuse me	Anteeksi	ON-take-see	**Hotel**	Hotelli	HO-tehl-lee
Help!	Apua!	AH-poo-ah	**Hostel**	Retkeilymaja	reht-kayl-oo-MAH-yuh
Police	Poliisi	POH-lee-see	**Bathroom**	Vessa	VEHS-sah
Embassy	Suurlähetystö	SOOHR-la-heh-toos-ter	**Telephone**	Puhelin	POO-heh-leen
I'm lost!	Olen kadok-sissa!	OH-lehn cou-doc-sissa	**Open/Closed**	Avoinna/Suljettu	a-VOH-een-ah/sool-JET-too
Railway station	Rautatieasema	ROW-tah-tiah-ah-seh-ma	**Hospital**	Sairaala	SAIH-raah-lah
Bank	Pankki	PAHNK-kih	**Left/Right**	Vasen/Oikea	VAH-sen/OY-kay-uh
Currency exchange	Rahanvaihto-piste	RAA-han-vyeh-tow-pees-teh	**Post Office**	Posti	PAUS-teeh
Airport	lentokenttä	LEH-toh-kehnt-tah	**Pharmacy**	Apteekki	UHP-take-kee

ENGLISH	FINNISH	PRONUNCIATION
Where is the...?	Missä on..?	MEE-sah ohn
How do I get to...?	Miten pääsen...?	MEE-ten PA-sen
How much does this cost?	Paljonko se maksaa?	PAHL-yon-ko seh MOCK-sah
I'd like to buy...	Haluaisin ostaa...	HUH-loo-ay-sihn OS-tuh
Do you speak English?	Puhutteko englantia?	POO-hoot-teh-kaw ENG-lan-tee-ah
When is the next...?	Milloin on seuraava...?	MEEHL-loyhn OHN SEUH-raah-vah
I'm allergic to/I cannot eat...	En voi syödä...	ehn voy SEW-dah

FINNISH CARDINAL NUMBERS										
0	**1**	**2**	**3**	**4**	**5**	**6**	**7**	**8**	**9**	**10**
nolla	yksi	kaksi	kolme	neljä	viisi	kuusi	seitsemän	kahdeksan	yhdeksän	kymmenen

FRENCH

ENGLISH	FRENCH	PRONOUNCED	ENGLISH	FRENCH	PRONOUNCED
Hello	Bonjour	bohn-zhoor	**Exchange**	L'échange	lay-shanzh
Please	S'il vous plaît	see voo pley	**Grocery**	L'épicerie	lay-pees-ree
Thank you	Merci	mehr-see	**Market**	Le marché	leuh marzh-chay
Excuse me	Excusez-moi	ex-ku-zey mwah	**Police**	La police	la poh-lees
Yes/No	Oui/Non	wee/nohn	**Embassy**	L'ambassade	lahm-ba-sahd
Goodbye	Au revoir	oh ruh-vwahr	**Passport**	Le passeport	leuh pass-por
Help!	Au secours!	oh seh-coor	**Post Office**	La poste	la pohst
I'm lost.	Je suis perdu.	zhe swee pehr-doo	**One-way**	Le billet simple	leuh bee-ay samp
Train/Bus	Le train/Le bus	leuh tran/leuh boos	**Round-trip**	Le billet aller-retour	leuh bee-ay a-lay-re-toor
Station	La gare	la gahr	**Ticket**	Le billet	leuh bee-ay
Airport	L'aéroport	la-ehr-o-por	**Single room**	Une chambre simple	oon shahm-br samp
Hotel	L'hôtel	lo-tel	**Double room**	Une chambre pour deux	oon shahm-br poor duh

ENGLISH	FRENCH	PRONOUNCED	ENGLISH	FRENCH	PRONOUNCED
Hostel	L'auberge	lo-berzhe	**With shower**	Avec une douche	ah-vec une doosh
Bathroom	La salle de bain	la sal de bahn	**Taxi**	Le taxi	leuh tax-ee
Open/Closed	Ouvert/Fermé	oo-ver/fer-may	**Ferry**	Le bac	leuh bak
Doctor	Le médecin	leuh mehd-sen	**Tourist office**	Le bureau de tourisme	leuh byur-oh de toor-eesm
Hospital	L'hôpital	loh-pee-tal	**Town hall**	L'hôtel de ville	lo-tel de veel
Pharmacy	La pharmacie	la far-ma-see	**Vegetarian**	Végétarien	vay-jay-ta-ree-ehn
Left/Right	À gauche/À droite	a gohsh/a dwat	**Kosher/Halal**	Kascher/Halal	ka-shey/ha-lal
Straight	Tout droit	too dwa	**Newsstand**	Le tabac	leuh ta-bac

ENGLISH	FRENCH	PRONUNCIATION
Do you speak English?	Parlez-vous anglais?	par-leh voo ahn-gleh
Where is...?	Où se trouve...?	oo seh-trhoov
When is the next...?	À quelle heure part le prochain..?	ah kel ur par leuh pro-chan
How much does this cost?	Ça fait combien?	sah f com-bee-en?
Do you have rooms available?	Avez-vous des chambres disponibles?	av-eh voo deh shahm-br dees-pon-eeb-bl?
I would like...	Je voudrais...	zhe voo-dreh
I'm allergic to...	Je suis allergique à...	zhe swee al-ehr-zheek a
I love you.	Je t'aime.	zhe tem

FRENCH CARDINAL NUMBERS										
0	1	2	3	4	5	6	7	8	9	10
zéro	un	deux	trois	quatre	cinq	six	sept	huit	neuf	dix

GERMAN

ENGLISH	GERMAN	PRONOUNCED	ENGLISH	GERMAN	PRONOUNCED
Yes/No	Ja/Nein	yah/nein	**Train/Bus**	Zug/Bus	tsoog/boos
Please	Bitte	BIH-tuh	**Station**	Bahnhof	BAHN-hohf
Thank you	Danke	DAHNG-kuh	**Airport**	Flughafen	FLOOG-hah-fen
Hello	Hallo	HAH-lo	**Taxi**	Taxi	TAHK-see
Goodbye	Auf Wiedersehen	owf VEE-der-zehn	**Ticket**	Fahrkarte	FAR-kar-tuh
Excuse me	Entschuldigung	ent-SHOOL-dih-gung	**Departure**	Abfahrt	AHB-fart
Help!	Hilfe!	HIL-fuh	**One-way**	Einfache	AYHN-fah-kuh
I'm lost.	Ich habe mich verlaufen.	eesh HAH-buh meesh fer-LAU-fun	**Round-trip**	Hin und zurück	hin oond tsuh-RYOOK
Police	Polizei	poh-lee-TSAI	**Reservation**	Reservierung	reh-zer-VEER-ung
Embassy	Botschaft	BOAT-shahft	**Ferry**	Fährschiff	FAYHR-shiff
Passport	Reisepass	RYE-zeh-pahss	**Bank**	Bank	bahnk
Doctor/Hospital	Arzt/Krankenhaus	ahrtst/KRANK-en-house	**Exchange**	Wechseln	VEHK-zeln
Pharmacy	Apotheke	AH-po-TAY-kuh	**Grocery**	Lebensmittelgeschäft	LAY-bens-miht-tel-guh-SHEFT
Hotel/Hostel	Hotel/Jugendherberge	ho-TEL/YOO-gend-air-BAIR-guh	**Tourist office**	Touristbüro	TU-reest-byur-oh
Single room	Einzellzimmer	EIN-tsel-tsihm-meh	**Post Office**	Postamt	POST-ahmt
Double room	Doppelzimmer	DOP-pel-tsihm-meh	**Old Town/City Center**	Altstadt	AHLT-shtat

APPENDIX

ENGLISH	GERMAN	PRONOUNCED	ENGLISH	GERMAN	PRONOUNCED
Dorm	Schlafsaal	SHLAF-zahl	**Vegetarian**	Vegetarier	Feh-geh-TAYR-ee-er
With shower	Mit dusche	mitt DOO-shuh	**Vegan**	Veganer	FEH-gan-er
Bathroom	Badezimmer	BAH-deh-tsihm-meh	**Kosher/Halal**	Koscher/Halaal	KOH-shehr/hah-LAAL
Open/Closed	Geöffnet/Geschlossen	geh-UHF-net/geh-SHLOS-sen	**Nuts/Milk**	Nüsse/Milch	NYOO-seh/mihlsh
Left/Right	Links/Rechts	lihnks/rekhts	**Bridge**	Brücke	BRUKE-eh
Straight	Geradeaus	geh-RAH-de-OWS	**Castle**	Schloß	shloss
(To) Turn	Drehen	DREH-ehn	**Square**	Platz	plahtz

ENGLISH	GERMAN	PRONUNCIATION
Where is...?	Wo ist...?	vo ihst
How do I get to...?	Wie komme ich nach...?	vee KOM-muh eesh NAHKH
How much does that cost?	Wieviel kostet das?	VEE-feel KOS-tet das
Do you have...?	Haben Sie...?	HOB-en zee
I would like...	Ich möchte...	eesh MERSH-teh
I'm allergic to...	Ich bin zu...allergisch.	eesh bihn tsoo...ah-LEHR-gish
Do you speak English?	Sprechen sie Englisch?	SHPREK-en zee EHNG-lish
I'm waiting for my boyfriend/husband	Ich warte auf meinen Freund/Mann.	eesh VAHR-tuh owf MYN-en froynd/mahn

GERMAN CARDINAL NUMBERS										
0	**1**	**2**	**3**	**4**	**5**	**6**	**7**	**8**	**9**	**10**
null	eins	zwei	drei	vier	fünf	sechs	sieben	acht	neun	zehn

GREEK

For an introduction to the Greek alphabet, see p. 1059.

ENGLISH	GREEK	PRONOUNCED	ENGLISH	GREEK	PRONOUNCED
Yes/No	Ναι/Οχι	neh/OH-hee	**Train/Bus**	Τραίνο/Λεωφορείο	TREH-no/leh-o-fo-REE-o
Please	Παρακαλώ	pah-rah-kah-LO	**Ferry**	Πλοίο	PLEE-o
Thank you	Ευχαριστώ	ef-hah-ree-STO	**Station**	Σταθμός	stath-MOS
Hello/Goodbye	Γειά σας	YAH-sas	**Airport**	Αεροδρόμιο	ah-e-ro-DHRO-mee-o
Sorry/Excuse me	Συγνόμη	sig-NO-mee	**Taxi**	Ταξί	tah-XEE
Help!	Βοήθειά!	vo-EE-thee-ah	**Hotel/Hostel**	Ξενοδοχείο	kse-no-dho-HEE-o
I'm lost.	Εχω χαθεί.	EH-o ha-THEE	**Rooms to let**	Δωμάτια	do-MA-tee-ah
Police	Αστυνομία	as-tee-no-MEE-a	**Bathroom**	Τουαλέττα	tou-ah-LET-ta
Embassy	Πρεσβεία	prez-VEE-ah	**Open/Closed**	Ανοικτό/Κλειστό	ah-nee-KTO/klee-STO
Passport	Διαβατήριο	dhee-ah-vah-TEE-ree-o	**Left/Right**	Αριστερά/Δεξία	aris-te-RA/de-XIA
Doctor	Γιατρός	yah-TROSE	**Bank**	Τράπεζα	TRAH-peh-zah
Pharmacy	Φαρμακèιο	fahr-mah-KEE-o	**Exchange**	Ανταλλάσσω	an-da-LAS-so
Post Office	Ταχυδρομείο	ta-hi-dhro-MEE-o	**Market**	Αγορά	ah-go-RAH

ENGLISH	GREEK	PRONUNCIATION
Where is...?	Που είναι...?	poo-EE-neh
How much does this cost?	Πόσο κάνει?	PO-so KAH-nee
Do you have (a vacant room)?	Μηπώς έχετε (ελέυθερα δωμάτια)?	mee-POSE EK-he-teh (e-LEF-the-ra dho-MA-tee-a)
Do you speak English?	Μιλατε αγγλικά?	mee-LAH-teh ahn-glee-KAH

GREEK CARDINAL NUMBERS										
0	1	2	3	4	5	6	7	8	9	10
ουδέν	ενα	δυο	τρια	τεσσερα	πρια	εξι	επτα	οκτω	εννεα	δεκα

HUNGARIAN

ENGLISH	HUNGARIAN	PRONOUNCED	ENGLISH	HUNGARIAN	PRONOUNCED
Yes/No	Igen/Nem	EE-ghen/nehm	**Train/Bus**	Vonat/Autóbusz	VAW-noht/AU-OO-toh-boos
Please	Kérem	KEH-rehm	**Train Station**	Pályaudvar	pah-yoh-OOT-vahr
Thank you	Köszönöm	KUH-suh-nuhm	**Airport**	Repülőtér	rep-oo-loo-TAYR
Hello	Szervusz	SAYHR-voose	**Ticket**	Jegyet	YEHD-eht
Goodbye	Viszontlátásra	VEE-sohnt-laht-ah-shrah	**Bus Station**	Buszmegálló	boos-mehg-AH-loh
Excuse me	Elnézést	EHL-neh-zaysht	**Hotel**	Szálloda	SAH-law-dah
Help!	Segítség!	she-GHEET-sheg	**Toilet**	WC	VEH-tseh
I'm lost.	Eltévedtem.	el-TEH-ved-tem	**Open/Closed**	Nyitva/Zárva	NYEET-vah/ZAHR-vuh
Police	Rendőrség	REN-dur-shayg	**Left/Right**	Bal/Jobb	bol/yowb
Embassy	Követséget	ker-vet-SHE-get	**Bank**	Bank	bohnk
Passport	Az útlevelemet	ahz oot-leh-veh-leh-meht	**Exchange**	Pénzaváltó	pehn-zah-VAHL-toh
Doctor/Hospital	Orvos/Kórház	OR-vosh/kohr-HAAZ	**Grocery**	Élelmiszerbolt	EH-lehl-meh-sehr-bawlt
Pharmacy	Gyógyszertár	DYAW-dyser-tar	**Post Office**	Posta	PAWSH-tuh

ENGLISH	HUNGARIAN	PRONUNCIATION
Where is...?	Hol van...?	haul vahn
How much does this cost?	Mennyibe kerül?	MEHN-yee-beh KEH-rool
When is the next...?	Mikor indul a következő...?	mee-KOR in-DUL ah ker-VET-ke-zoer
Do you have (a vacant room)?	Van üres (szoba)?	vahn ew-REHSH (SAH-bah)
Can I have...?	Kaphatok...?	KAH-foht-tohk
I do not eat...	Nem eszem...	nem EH-sem
Do you speak English?	Beszél angolul?	BESS-ayl AHN-gawl-ool

HUNGARIAN CARDINAL NUMBERS										
0	1	2	3	4	5	6	7	8	9	10
nulla	egy	kettő	három	négy	öt	hat	hét	nyolc	kilenc	tíz

ITALIAN

ENGLISH	ITALIAN	PRONOUNCED	ENGLISH	ITALIAN	PRONOUNCED
Hello (informal/formal)	Ciao/Buongiorno	chow/bwohn-JOHR-noh	**Bank**	La banca	lah bahn-KAH
Please	Per favore/Per piacere	pehr fah-VOH-reh/pehr pyah-CHEH-reh	**Supermarket**	Il Supermercato	eel soo-pair-mehr-CAHT-oh
Thank you	Grazie	GRAHT-see-yeh	**Exchange**	Il cambio	eel CAHM-bee-oh
Sorry/Excuse me	Mi dispiace/Scusi	mee dees-PYAH-cheh/SKOO-zee	**Police**	La Polizia	lah po-LEET-ZEE-ah
Yes/No	Sì/No	see/no	**Embassy**	L'Ambasciata	lahm-bah-SHAH-tah
Help!	Aiuto!	ah-YOO-toh	**Goodbye**	Arrivederci/Arrivederla	ah-ree-veh-DAIR-chee/ah-ree-veh-DAIR-lah

ENGLISH	ITALIAN	PRONOUNCED	ENGLISH	ITALIAN	PRONOUNCED
I'm lost.	Sono perso.	SO-noh PERH-so	**One-way**	Solo andata	SO-lo ahn-DAH-tah
Train/Bus	Il treno/ l'autobus	eel TREH-no/ laow-toh-BOOS	**Round-trip**	Andata e ritorno	ahn-DAH-tah eh ree-TOHR-noh
Station	La stazione	lah staht-see-YOH-neh	**Ticket**	Il biglietto	eel beel-YEHT-toh
Airport	L'aeroporto	LAYR-o-PORT-o	**Single room**	Una camera singola	OO-nah CAH-meh-rah SEEN-goh-lah
Hotel/Hostel	L'albergo/ L'ostello	lal-BEHR-go/los-TEHL-loh	**Left/Right**	Sinistra/destra	see-NEE-strah/ DEH-strah
Bathroom	Un gabinetto/Un bagno	oon gah-bee-NEHT-toh/oon BAHN-yoh	**Double room**	Una camera doppia	OO-nah CAH-meh-rah DOH-pee-yah
Open/Closed	Aperto/Chiuso	ah-PAIR-toh/ KYOO-zoh	**Tourist office**	L'Ufficio Turistico	loof-FEETCH-o tur-EES-tee-koh
Doctor	Il medico	eel MEH-dee-koh	**Ferry**	Il traghetto	eel tra-GHEHT-toh
Hospital	L'ospedale	lohs-sped-DAL-e	**Tip**	La mancia	lah MAHN-cha
Vegetarian	Vegetariano	veh-jeh-tar-ee-AN-oh	**Kosher/Halal**	Kasher/Halal	KA-sher/HA-lal
Turn	Gira a	JEE-rah ah	**Bill**	Il conto	eel COHN-toh

ENGLISH	ITALIAN	PRONUNCIATION
Do you speak English?	Parla inglese?	PAHR-lah een-GLAY-zeh
Where is...?	Dov'è...?	doh-VEH
When is the next...?	A che ora è il prossimo...?	AH keh OH-rah eh eel pross-EE-moh
How much does this cost?	Quanto costa?	KWAN-toh CO-stah
Do you have rooms available?	Ha camere libere?	ah CAH-mer-reh LEE-ber-eh
I would like...	Vorrei...	VOH-re
Not even if you were the last man on Earth!	Neanche se tu fossi l'unico uomo sulla terra!	neh-AHN-keh seh too FOH-see LOO-nee-koh WOH-moh soo-LAH TEH-rah

ITALIAN CARDINAL NUMBERS										
0	1	2	3	4	5	6	7	8	9	10
zero	uno	due	tre	quattro	cinque	sei	sette	otto	nove	dieci

NORWEGIAN

ENGLISH	NORWEGIAN	PRONOUNCED	ENGLISH	NORWEGIAN	PRONOUNCED
Yes/No	Ja/Nei	yah/neh	**Ticket**	Billett	bee-LEHT
Please	Vær så snill	vah sho SNEEL	**Train/Bus**	Toget/Buss	TOR-guh/buhs
Thank you	Takk	tahk	**Airport**	Lufthavn	LUFT-hahn
Hello	Goddag	gud-DAHG	**Departures**	Avgang	AHV-gahng
Goodbye	Ha det bra	HAH deh BRAH	**Market**	Torget	TOHR-geh
Sorry/Excuse me	Unnskyld	UHRN-shuhrl (UHN-shuhl)	**Hotel/Hostel**	Hotell/Vandrerhjem	hoo-TEHL/VAN-drair-yaim
Help!	Hjelp!	yehlp	**Pharmacy**	Apotek	ah-pu-TAYK
Police	politiet	poh-lih-TEE-eh	**Toilets**	Toalettene	tuah-LEHT-tuh-nuh
Embassy	Ambassade	ahm-bah-SAH-duh	**City center**	Sentrum	SEHN-trum
I'm lost.	Jeg har gått meg bort	yai har goht mai boort	**Open/Closed**	Åpen/Stengt	OH-pen/Stengt
Bank	Bank	banhk	**Left/Right**	Venstre/Høyre	VEHN-stre/ HUHR-uh
Currency exchange	Vekslingskontor	VEHK-shlings-koon-toohr	**Post Office**	Postkontor	POST-koon-toohr

APPENDIX

ENGLISH	NORWEGIAN	PRONUNCIATION
Where is...?	Hvor er...?	VORR ahr
How do I get to...?	Hvordan kommer jeg til...?	VOOR-dan KOH-mer yai teel
How much is...?	Hvor mye koster...?	voor MEE-uh KOH-ster
Do you speak English?	Snakker du engelsk?	SNA-koh dew EHNG-olsk

NORWEGIAN CARDINAL NUMBERS										
0	1	2	3	4	5	6	7	8	9	10
null	en	to	tre	fire	fem	seks	syv	åtte	ni	ti

POLISH

ENGLISH	POLISH	PRONOUNCED	ENGLISH	POLISH	PRONOUNCED
Yes/No	Tak/Nie	tahk/nyeh	Train/Bus	Pociąg/Autobus	POH-chawnk/ ow-TOH-booss
Please	Proszę	PROH-sheh	Train Station	Dworzec	DVOH-zhets
Thank you	Dziękuję	jen-KOO-yeh	Airport	Lotnisko	loht-NEE-skoh
Hello	Cześć	cheshch	Ticket	Bilet	BEE-leht
Goodbye	Do widzenia	doh veed-ZEHN-yah	Hostel	Schronisko młodzieżowe	sroh-NEE-skoh mwo-jeh-ZHO-veh
Sorry/Excuse me	Przepraszam	psheh-PRAH-shahm	Bathroom	Toaleta	toh-ah-LEH-tah
Help!	Pomocy!	poh-MOH-tsih	Open/Closed	Otwarty/ Zamknięty	ot-FAHR-tih/ zahmk-NYENT-ih
I'm lost.	Zgubiłem się.	zgoo-BEE-wem sheh	Left/Right	Lewo/Prawo	LEH-voh/PRAH-voh
Police	Policja	poh-LEETS-yah	Bank	Bank	bahnk
Embassy	Ambasada	am-ba-SA-da	Exchange	Kantor	KAHN-tor
Doctor/ Hospital	Lekarz/Szpital	LEH-kazh/ SHPEE-tal	Grocery/Market	Sklep spożywczy	sklehp spoh-ZHIV-chih
Pharmacy	Apteka	ahp-TEH-ka	Post Office	Poczta	POHCH-tah

ENGLISH	POLISH	PRONUNCIATION
Where is...?	Gdzie jest...?	g-JEH yest
How much does this cost?	Ile to kosztuje?	EE-leh toh kohsh-TOO-yeh
When is the next...?	O której jest następny...?	o KTOO-rey yest nas-TEMP-nee
Do you have (a vacant room)?	Czy są (jakieś wolne pokoje)?	chih SAWN (yah-kyesh VOHL-neh poh-KOY-eh)
I'd like to order...	Chciałbym zamówić...	kh-CHOW-bihm za-MOOV-eech
Do you (m/f) speak English?	Czy pan(i) mówi po angielsku?	chih PAHN(-ee) MOO-vee poh ahn-GYEL-skoo

POLISH CARDINAL NUMBERS										
0	1	2	3	4	5	6	7	8	9	10
zero	jeden	dwa	trzy	cztery	pięć	sześć	siedem	osiem	dziewięć	dziesięć

PORTUGUESE

ENGLISH	PORTUGUESE	PRONOUNCED	ENGLISH	PORTUGUESE	PRONOUNCED
Hello	Olá/Oi	oh-LAH/oy	Hotel	Pousada	poh-ZAH-dah
Please	Por favor	pohr fah-VOHR	Bathroom	Banheiro	bahn-YEH-roo
Thank you (m/f)	Obrigado/ Obrigada	oh-bree-GAH-doo/dah	Open/Closed	Aberto/Fechado	ah-BEHR-toh/ feh-CHAH-do
Sorry/ Excuse me	Desculpe	dish-KOOLP-eh	Doctor	Médico	MEH-dee-koo

ENGLISH	PORTUGUESE	PRONOUNCED	ENGLISH	PORTUGUESE	PRONOUNCED
Yes/No	Sim/Não	seem/now	**Pharmacy**	Farmácia	far-MAH-see-ah
Goodbye	Adeus	ah-DEH-oosh	**Left/Right**	Esquerda/ Direita	esh-KER-dah/ dee-REH-tah
Help!	Socorro!	soh-KOO-roh	**Bank**	Banco	BAHN-koh
I'm lost.	Estou perdido.	ish-TOW per-DEE-doo	**Exchange**	Câmbio	CAHM-bee-yoo
Ticket	Bilhete	beel-YEHT	**Market**	Mercado	mer-KAH-doo
Train/Bus	Comboio/ Autocarro	kom-BOY-yoo/ OW-to-KAH-roo	**Police**	Polícia	po-LEE-see-ah
Station	Estação	eh-stah-SAO	**Embassy**	Embaixada	ehm-bai-SHAH-dah
Airport	Aeroporto	aye-ro-POR-too	**Post Office**	Correio	coh-REH-yoh

ENGLISH	PORTUGUESE	PRONUNCIATION
Do you speak English?	Fala inglês?	FAH-lah een-GLAYSH
Where is...?	Onde é...?	OHN-deh eh
How much does this cost?	Quanto custa?	KWAHN-too KOOSH-tah
Do you have rooms available?	Tem quartos disponíveis?	teng KWAHR-toosh dish-po-NEE-veysh
I want/would like...	Eu quero/gostaria de...	eh-oo KER-oh/gost-ar-EE-ah deh
Another round, please.	Mais uma rodada, por favor.	maish OO-mah roh-DAH-dah pohr fah-VOHR

PORTUGUESE CARDINAL NUMBERS										
0	**1**	**2**	**3**	**4**	**5**	**6**	**7**	**8**	**9**	**10**
zero	um	dois	três	quatro	cinco	seis	sete	oito	nove	dez

ROMANIAN

ENGLISH	ROMANIAN	PRONOUNCED	ENGLISH	ROMANIAN	PRONOUNCED
Yes/No	Da/Nu	dah/noo	**Train/Bus**	Trenul/Autobuz	TREH-nuhl/au-toh-BOOZ
Please/ Thank you	Vă rog/ Mulțumesc	vuh rohg/ mool-tsoo-MESK	**Station**	Gară	GAH-ruh
Hello	Bună ziua	BOO-nuh ZEE-wah	**Airport**	Aeroportul	ai-roh-POHR-tool
Goodbye	La revedere	lah reh-veh-DEH-reh	**Ticket**	Bilet	bee-LEHT
Sorry	Îmi pare rău	uhm PAH-reh ruh-oo	**Taxi**	Taxi	tak-SEE
Excuse me	Scuzați-mă	skoo-ZAH-tsee muh	**Hotel**	Hotel	ho-TEHL
Help!	Ajutor!	ah-zhoo-TOHR	**Bathroom**	Toaletă	toh-ah-LEH-tah
I'm lost.	Sînt pierdut.	sunt PYER-dut	**Open/Closed**	Deschis/închis	DESS-kees/ un-KEES
Police	Poliție	poh-LEE-tsee-eh	**Left/Right**	Stânga/Dreapta	STUHN-gah/ drahp-TAH
Embassy	Ambasada	ahm-bah-SAH-da	**Bank**	Banca	BAHN-cah
Passport	Pașaport	pah-shah-PORT	**Exchange**	Birou de schimb	bee-ROW deh skeemb
Doctor/ Hospital	Doctorul/ spitalul	DOK-toh-rul/ SPEE-ta-lul	**Grocery**	Alimentară	a-lee-men-TAH-ruh
Pharmacy	Farmacie	fahr-ma-CHEE-eh	**Post Office**	Poșta	POH-shta

ENGLISH	ROMANIAN	PRONUNCIATION
Where is...?	Unde e...?	OON-deh YEH
How much does this cost?	Cât costă?	kuht KOH-stuh
When is the next...?	Cînd este următorul...?	kuhnd es-te ur-muh-TOH-rul

APPENDIX

ENGLISH	ROMANIAN	PRONUNCIATION
Do you have (a vacant room?)	Aveţi (camere libere)?	a-VETS (KAH-meh-reh LEE-beh-reh)
I would like...	Aş vrea...	ahsh vreh-AH
Do you speak English?	Vorbiţi englezeşte?	vohr-BEETS ehng-leh-ZEHSH-teh

ROMANIAN CARDINAL NUMBERS										
0	1	2	3	4	5	6	7	8	9	10
zero	unu	doi	trei	patru	cinci	şase	şapte	opt	nouă	zece

RUSSIAN

For the Cyrillic alphabet, see p. 1059.

ENGLISH	RUSSIAN	PRONOUNCED	ENGLISH	RUSSIAN	PRONOUNCED
Yes/No	Да/нет	dah/nyet	**Train/Bus**	Поезд/ автобус	POH-yihzt/av-TOH-boos
Please	Пожалуйста	pah-ZHAHL-uy-stah	**Station**	вокзал	vak-ZAL
Thank you	Спасибо	spa-SEE-bah	**Airport**	аэропрт	ai-roh-PORT
Hello	Здравствуйте	ZDRAHV-zvuht-yeh	**Ticket**	билет	bil-YET
Goodbye	До свидания	da svee-DAHN-yah	**Hotel**	гостиница	gahs-TEE-nee-tsah
Sorry/ Excuse me	Извините	eez-vee-NEET-yeh	**Dorm/Hostel**	общежитие	ob-sheh-ZHEE-tee-yeh
Help!	Помогите!	pah-mah-GEE-tyeh	**Bathroom**	туалет	TOO-ah-lyet
I'm lost.	Я потерен.	ya po-TYE-ren	**Open/Closed**	открыт/ закрыт	ot-KRIHT/ za-KRIHT
Police	милиция	mee-LEE-tsee-ya	**Left/Right**	налево/нап-раво	nah-LYEH-vah/ nah-PRAH-vah
Embassy	посольство	pah-SOHL-stva	**Bank**	банк	bahnk
Passport	паспорт	PAS-pahrt	**Exchange**	обмен валюты	ab-MYEHN val-ee-YU-tee
Doctor/ Hospital	Врач/ больница	vrach/bol-NEE-tsa	**Grocery/Market**	гастроном/ рынок	gah-stroh-NOM/ REE-nohk
Pharmacy	аптека	ahp-TYE-kah	**Post Office**	Почта	POCH-ta

ENGLISH	RUSSIAN	PRONUNCIATION
Where is...?	Где...?	gdyeh
How much does this cost?	Сколько это стоит?	SKOHL-ka EH-ta STOY-iht
When is the next...?	Когда будет следуший...?	kog-DAH BOOD-yet SLYED-ooshee
Do you have a vacancy?	У вас етсь свободный номер?	oo vahs yehst svah-BOHD-neey NOH-myehr
I'd like (m/f)...	Я хотел(а) бы...	ya khah-TYEL(a) bwee
Do you speak English?	Вы говорите по-английски?	vy gah-vah-REE-tyeh pah ahn-GLEE-skee

RUSSIAN CARDINAL NUMBERS										
0	1	2	3	4	5	6	7	8	9	10
ноль	один	два	три	четыре	пять	шесть	семь	восемь	девять	десять

SPANISH

ENGLISH	SPANISH	PRONOUNCED	ENGLISH	SPANISH	PRONOUNCED
Hello	Hola	O-lah	**Hotel/Hostel**	Hotel/Hostal	oh-TEL/ohs-TAHL
Please	Por favor	pohr fah-VOHR	**Bathroom**	Baño	BAHN-yoh
Thank you	Gracias	GRAH-see-ahs	**Open/Closed**	Abierto(a)/ Cerrado(a)	ah-bee-EHR-toh/ sehr-RAH-doh
Sorry/Excuse me	Perdón	pehr-DOHN	**Doctor**	Médico	MEH-dee-koh

APPENDIX

ENGLISH	SPANISH	PRONOUNCED	ENGLISH	SPANISH	PRONOUNCED
Yes/No	Sí/No	see/no	**Pharmacy**	Farmacia	far-MAH-see-ah
Goodbye	Adiós	ah-DYOYS	**Left/Right**	Izquierda/ Derecha	ihz-kee-EHR-da/ deh-REH-chah
Help!	¡Ayuda!	ay-YOOH-dah	**Bank**	Banco	BAHN-koh
I'm lost.	Estoy perdido (a).	ess-TOY pehr-DEE-doh (dah)	**Exchange**	Cambio	CAHM-bee-oh
Ticket	Boleto	boh-LEH-toh	**Grocery**	Supermercado	soo-pehr-mer-KAH-doh
Train/Bus	Tren/Autobús	trehn/ow-toh-BOOS	**Police**	Policía	poh-lee-SEE-ah
Station	Estación	es-tah-SYOHN	**Embassy**	Embajada	em-bah-HA-dah
Airport	Aeropuerto	ay-roh-PWER-toh	**Post Office**	Oficina de correos	oh-fee-SEE-nah deh coh-REH-ohs

ENGLISH	SPANISH	PRONUNCIATION
Do you speak English?	¿Habla inglés?	AH-blah een-GLEHS?
Where is...?	¿Dónde está?	DOHN-deh eh-STA?
How much does this cost?	¿Cuánto cuesta?	KWAN-toh KWEHS-tah?
Do you have rooms available?	¿Tiene habitaciones libres?	tee-YEH-neh ah-bee-tah-see-YOH-nehs LEE-brehs?
I want/would like...	Quiero/Me gustaría...	kee-YEH-roh/meh goo-tah-REE-ah

SPANISH CARDINAL NUMBERS										
0	1	2	3	4	5	6	7	8	9	10
cero	uno	dos	tres	cuatro	cinco	seis	siete	ocho	nueve	diez

SWEDISH

ENGLISH	SWEDISH	PRONOUNCED	ENGLISH	SWEDISH	PRONOUNCED
Yes/No	Ja/Nej	yah/nay	**Ticket**	Biljett	bihl-YEHT
Please	Va så snäll	VAH sahw snel	**Train/Bus**	Tåget/Buss	TOH-get/boos
Thank you	Tack	tahk	**Ferry**	Färjan	FAR-yuhn
Hello	Hej	hay	**Departure**	Avgångar	uhv-GONG-er
Goodbye	Hejdå	HAY-doh	**Market**	Torget	TOHR-yet
Excuse me	Ursäkta mig	oor-SHEHK-tuh MAY	**Hotel/Hostel**	Hotell/Vandrar-hem	hoo-TEHL/vun-DRAR-huhm
Help!	Hjälp!	yehlp	**Pharmacy**	Apotek	uh-poo-TEEK
Police	Polisen	poo-LEE-sehn	**Toilets**	Toaletten	too-uh-LEHT-en
Embassy	Ambassad	uhm-bah-SAHD	**Post Office**	Posten	POHS-tehn
I'm lost.	Jag har kommit bort.	yuh hahr KUM-met borht	**Open/Closed**	Öppen/Stängd	UH-pen/staingd
Railway station	Järnvägssta-tionen	yairn-vas-gues-stah-SHO-nen	**Hospital**	Sjukhus	SHUHK-huhs
Currency exchange	Växel kontor	vai-xil KOON-toohr	**Left/Right**	Vänster/Höger	VAIN-ster/ HUH-ger

ENGLISH	SWEDISH	PRONUNCIATION
Where is...?	Var finns...?	vahr FIHNS
How much does this cost?	Hur mycket kostar det?	hurr MUEK-keh KOS-tuhr deh
I'd like to buy...	Jag skulle vilja köpa...	yuh SKOO-leh vihl-yuh CHEU-pah
Do you speak English?	Talar du engelska?	TAH-luhr du EHNG-ehl-skuh
I'm allergic to/I cannot eat...	Jag är allergisk mot/Jag kan inte ata...	yuh air ALLEHR-ghihsk moot/yuh kahn intuh aitah
Do you have rooms available?	Har Ni fria rum?	harh nih freeah ruhm

SWEDISH CARDINAL NUMBERS										
0	1	2	3	4	5	6	7	8	9	10
noll	ett	två	tre	fyra	fem	sex	sju	åtta	nio	tio

INDEX

Symbols

Ærø, DEN 271
Þingvellir National Park, ICE 525
Þórsmörk, ICE 528

A

Aachen, GER 418
Aalborg, DEN 273
Aalsmeer, NTH 722
accommodations 33
  bed & breakfasts 35
  camping 36
  guesthouses 35
  home exchange 36
  hostels 33
  hotels 35
  pensions 35
  university dorms 35
Aeolian Islands, ITA 654
Aix-en-Provence, FRA 370
Ajaccio, FRA 381
Akureyri, ICE 528
alcohol 23
Ålesund, NOR 759
Algarve, POR 819
Alghero, ITA 656
Alicante, SPA 931
Allinge, DEN 269
Alsace-Lorraine, FRA 346
Amalfi Coast, ITA 651
Amalfi, ITA 652
Amsterdam, NTH 705
Ancona, ITA 645
Åndalsnes, NOR 760
Andalucía, SPA 914
Andorra, SPA 947
Annecy, FRA 356
Å, NOR 765
Antibes, FRA 379
Antwerp, BEL 111
Appendix 1058
  climate 1058
  language phrasebook 1059
  measurements 1058
Aquitaine, FRA 360
Aran Islands, IRE 558
architecture 3
Arcos de la Frontera, SPA 923
Ardennes, LUX 689
Åre, SWE 990
Århus, DEN 271
Arnhem, NTH 729
Assisi, ITA 643
Athens, GCE 458
ATMs 17
Atrani, ITA 652
au pair work 68
Aurland, NOR 753
Auschwitz-Birkenau, POL 787
Austria 69
  Graz 96
  Hohe Tauern National Park 91
  Innsbruck 92
  Linz 85
  Salzburg 86
  Salzburger Land 85
  Styria 96
  Tyrol 92
  Vienna 73
  Zell am See 90
Avebury, BRI 152
Avignon, FRA 371

B

Bachkovo Monastery, BUL 208
Bakewell, BRI 169
Balearic Islands, SPA 958
Balestrand, NOR 755
Baradla Caves, HUN 508
Barcelona, SPA 934
Barentsburg, NOR 766
bargaining 21
Basel, SWI 1016
Basque Country, SPA 951
Bastia, FRA 381
Bath, BRI 152
Bavaria, GER 436
Bayeux, FRA 341
Bay of Naples, ITA 650
Bayonne, FRA 361
bed & breakfasts 35
Belfast, BRI 561
Belgium 98
  Antwerp 111
  Bruges 107
  Brussels 102
  Dinant 116
  Flanders 107
  Ghent 112
  Liège 114
  Mechelen 107
  Namur 116
  Tournai 115
  Wallonie 114
  Ypres 114
Ben Nevis, BRI 196
Bergamo, ITA 602
Bergen, NOR 748
Berlin, GER 389
Bernese Oberland, SWI 1000
Bern, SWI 1000
Besançon, FRA 349
Beyond Tourism 60
  au pair work 68
  community development 61
  conservation 61
  humanitarian and social services 62
  language schools 64
  long-term work 66
  short-term work 68
  study abroad 62
  teaching English 66
  volunteering abroad 60
Bilbao, SPA 955
Billund, DEN 272
Birgu, MTA 698
Birmingham, BRI 160
Birzebugga, MTA 698
Björkö, SWE 976
Black Forest, GER 435
Blarney, IRE 552
Bled, SLN 886
Bloemendaal aan Zee, NTH 723
Blois, FRA 336
Blue Lagoon, ICE 526
boats 57
Bodø, NOR 764
Bol, CRO 226
Bologna, ITA 609
Bolzano, ITA 614
Bonifacio, FRA 382
Bonn, GER 423
Bordeaux, FRA 360
Bornholm, DEN 268
Borromean Islands, ITA 604

Bourges, FRA 358
Brač Island, CRO 226
Braga, POR 816
Bran, ROM 836
Braşov, ROM 835
Bratislava, SLK 871
Britain 117
 Avebury 152
 Bakewell 169
 Bath 152
 Ben Nevis 196
 Birmingham 160
 Buxton 170
 Caernarfon 181
 Callander 194
 Cambridge 162
 Canterbury 150
 Cardiff 178
 Castleton 170
 Chepstow 180
 Conwy 182
 Cornish Coast 154
 Douglas 176
 East Anglia and the Midlands 155
 Edale 169
 Edinburgh 183
 England 123
 Fort William 196
 Glasgow 190
 Glastonbury 153
 Hadrian's Wall 174
 Harlech 181
 Inverness 195
 Isle of Man 175
 Liverpool 167
 Loch Lomond 195
 Loch Ness 195
 London 123
 Manchester 165
 Newcastle-upon-Tyne 173
 Northern England 165
 Oxford 155
 Peak District National Park 169
 Penzance 154
 Salisbury 151
 Scotland 182
 Snowdonia National Park 180
 Southern England 150
 Stirling 193
 Stonehenge 152
 Stratford-upon Avon 159
 Tintern 180
 Trossachs 193
 Wales 178
 Wye Valley 179
 York 170
Brittany, FRA 338
Brno, CZR 251
Bruges, BEL 107
Brussels, BEL 102
Bucharest, ROM 827
Bucovina, ROM 837
Budapest, HUN 494
budget airlines 48
Bulduri, LAT 666
Bulgaria 197
 Bachkovo Monastery 208
 Plovdiv 207
 Rila Monastery 207
 Sofia 202
 Varna 208
 Veliko Turnovo 208
Burgundy, FRA 343
Burren, IRE 556
buses 53
Buxton, BRI 170

C

Cáceres, SPA 913
Cadaqués, SPA 947
Caen, FRA 340
Caernarfon, BRI 181
Cagliari, ITA 656
Cahersiveen, IRE 554
Calais, FRA 343
Callander, BRI 194
Cambridge, BRI 162
Camogli, ITA 607
Campania, ITA 645
camping 36
Cannes, FRA 379
Canterbury, BRI 150
Cape Sounion, GCE 466
Capri, ITA 651
Carcassonne, FRA 364
Cardiff, BRI 178
cars 53
Cascais, POR 813
Cashel, IRE 548
Castilla la Mancha, SPA 907
Castilla y León, SPA 910
Castleton, BRI 170
Cauterets, FRA 362
Central Germany, GER 417
Central Greece, GCE 470
Central Portugal, POR 818
Central Spain, SPA 907
Central Sweden, SWE 988
Central Switzerland, SWI 1007
Cēsis, LAT 667
České Budějovice, CZR 249
Český Krumlov, CZR 250
Český Ráj National Preserve, CZR 248
Chamonix, FRA 357
Champagne, FRA 343
Chania, GCE 485
Chartres, FRA 335
Chepstow, BRI 180
Cinque Terre, ITA 608
Clifden, IRE 558
Cliffs of Moher, IRE 556
climate 1058
Cluj-Napoca, ROM 834
Coimbra, POR 817
Colmar, FRA 348
Cologne, GER 419
community development 61
Como, ITA 603
Connemara, IRE 558
Connemara National Park, IRE 558
conservation 61
Constance, GER 435
Constanta, ROM 838
consulates 14
Conwy, BRI 182
Copenhagen, DEN 258
Córdoba, SPA 914
Corfu, GCE 478
Cork, IRE 549
Cornish Coast, BRI 154
Corsica, FRA 380
Costa Brava, SPA 947
Costa del Sol, SPA 928
credits cards 17
Crete, GCE 483
Croatia 210
 Bol 226
 Brač Island 226
 Dalmatian Coast 223
 Dubrovnik 226
 Krk Town 221
 Lopud Island 229
 Northern Coast 220
 Plitvice Lakes National Park 219
 Pula 222
 Rijeka 220
 Rovinj 223
 Split 224
 Zadar 224
 Zagreb 215
Curonian Spit, LIT 681
currency exchange 17
Cyclades, GCE 479

INDEX

Cyrillic alphabet 1059
Czech Republic 230
Brno 251
České Budějovice 249
Český Krumlov 250
Český Ráj National Preserve 248
Karlovy Vary 248
Moravia 251
Olomouc 252
Plzeň 249
Prague 235
South Bohemia 248
Terezín 247
West Bohemia 248

D

Dalmatian Coast, CRO 223
Danube Bend, HUN 505
Davos, SWI 1018
D-Day Beaches, FRA 341
debit cards 17
De Hoge Veluwe National Park, NTH 729
Delft, NTH 726
Delphi, GCE 475
Denmark 253
Aalborg 273
Ærø 271
Allinge 269
Århus 271
Billund 272
Bornholm 268
Copenhagen 258
Frederikshavn 273
Funen 269
Helsingør 266
Hillerød 266
Humlebæk 267
Jutland 271
Kværndrup 270
Møn 267
Odense 269
Rønne 269
Roskilde 267
Rungsted 267
Sandvig 269
Skagen 274
Derry/Londonderry, BRI 567
Desenzano, ITA 604
Dinan, FRA 339
Dinant, BEL 116
Dingle Peninsula, IRE 554
Dingle Town, IRE 555
Discover
architecture 3
festivals 5
museums 2
outdoors 4
documents and formalities 14
Donegal Town, IRE 560
Dordogne, FRA 358
Douglas, BRI 176
Dresden, GER 447
Dublin, IRE 537
Dubrovnik, CRO 226
Dubulti, LAT 666
Dunquin, IRE 555
Düsseldorf, GER 417

E

East Anglia and the Midlands, BRI 155
Eastern Aegean Islands, GCE 487
Eastern Germany, GER 445
Eastern Spain, SPA 931
Echternach, LUX 689
Edale, BRI 169
Edinburgh, BRI 183
Eger, HUN 506
Eidfjord, NOR 754
Eisenach, GER 446
El Escorial, SPA 907
embassies 14
Emilia-Romagna, ITA 609
England, BRI 123
Epernay, FRA 344
Epidavros, GCE 469
Esch-sur-Sûre, LUX 690
Essentials
accommodations 33
consulates 14
documents and formalities 14
embassies 14
keeping in touch 30
money 17
outdoors 37
packing 21
passports 14
safety and health 23
specific concerns 40
Estonia 275
Estonian Islands 284
Hiiumaa 285
Kärdla 285
Kassari 285
Kuressaare 284
Pärnu 283
Saaremaa 284
Tallinn 279
Tartu 283
Viljandi 284
Estonian Islands, EST 284
Esztergom, HUN 506
Ettelbrück, LUX 689
Évora, POR 818
exchange rates 17
Extremadura, SPA 913

F

Faro, POR 819
Fårö, SWE 978
Ferrara, ITA 613
festivals 5
Figueres, SPA 947
Finale Ligure, ITA 607
Finland 286
Helsinki 290
Kuopio 303
Lahti 298
Pori 300
Porvoo 298
Rauma 300
Rovaniemi 304
Savonlinna 302
Tampere 301
Turku 298
Finnhamn, SWE 975
Finse, NOR 753
Fjærland, NOR 756
Fjærlandsfjord, NOR 756
Fjords, NOR 748
Flåm, NOR 753
Flanders, BEL 107
Flanders, FRA 342
Florence, ITA 630
Fort William, BRI 196
France 305
Aix-en-Provence 370
Ajaccio 381
Alsace-Lorraine 346
Annecy 356
Antibes 379
Aquitaine 360
Avignon 371
Bastia 381
Bayeux 341
Bayonne 361
Besançon 349
Blois 336
Bonifacio 382
Bordeaux 360
Bourges 358
Brittany 338
Burgundy 343
Caen 340
Calais 343
Cannes 379
Carcassonne 364
Cauterets 362
Chamonix 357
Champagne 343
Chartres 335

Colmar 348
Corsica 380
D-Day Beaches 341
Dinan 339
Dordogne 358
Epernay 344
Flanders 342
Franche-Comté 346
French Riviera 372
Grenoble 355
Languedoc-Roussillon 363
Le Mont-Dore 358
Lille 343
Limousin 358
Loire Valley 335
Lyon 350
Marseille 365
Massif Central 350
Monaco 377
Monte-Carlo 377
Montpellier 365
Mont-St-Michel 342
Nancy 349
Nantes 339
Nice 372
Nîmes 371
Normandy 340
Orléans 335
Parc National des Pyrénées 362
Paris 311
Pas de Calais 342
Pays Basque 360
Périgueux 359
Provence 365
Pyrénées 362
Reims 344
Rennes 338
Rhône-Alpes 350
Rouen 340
Route du Vin 347
Sélestat 348
St-Malo 338
Strasbourg 346
St-Tropez 380
Toulouse 363
Tours 337
Troyes 345
Versailles 334
Vézères Valley 359
Franche-Comté, FRA 346
Frankfurt am Main, GER 425
Frederikshavn, DEN 273
Fredrikstad, NOR 745
French Riviera, FRA 372
French Switzerland, SWI 1021
Friuli-Venezia Giulia, ITA 628
Frösön Island, SWE 989
Funen, DEN 269
Füssen, GER 444

G

Galicia, SPA 957
Galway, IRE 557
Gävle, SWE 991
Gdańsk, POL 794, 796
Geirangerfjord, NOR 757
Geiranger, NOR 757
Geneva, SWI 1021
Genoa, ITA 605
German Switzerland, SWI 1000
Germany 383
Aachen 418
Bavaria 436
Berlin 389
Black Forest 435
Bonn 423
Central Germany 417
Cologne 419
Constance 435
Dresden 447
Düsseldorf 417
Eastern Germany 445
Eisenach 446
Frankfurt am Main 425
Füssen 444
Hamburg 410
Hanover 416
Heidelberg 431
Kassel 424
Königsschlößer 444
Leipzig 451
Lorelei 430
Lübeck 410
Mainz 429
Munich 436
Northern Germany 409
Oktoberfest 442
Rhine Valley 429
Romantic Road 443
Rothenburg ob der Tauber 444
Sachsenhausen 409
Southwestern Germany 428
St. Goar 430
St. Goarhausen 430
Stuttgart 434
Triberg 435
Trier 428
Weimar 445
Western Germany 417
Wittenberg 447
Getterön Peninsula, SWE 988
Geysir, ICE 525
Ghent, BEL 112
Giant's Causeway, BRI 568
Gibraltar, SPA 930
Glasgow, BRI 190
Glastonbury, BRI 153
Goðafoss, ICE 530
Gothenburg, SWE 984
Gotland, SWE 977
Granada, SPA 924
Graubünden, SWI 1018
Graz, AUT 96
Greece 453
Athens 458
Cape Sounion 466
Central Greece 470
Chania 485
Corfu 478
Crete 483
Cyclades 479
Delphi 475
Eastern Aegean Islands 487
Epidavros 469
Heraklion 484
Ioannina 477
Ionian Islands 478
Ios 482
Kalambaka 475
Knossos 485
Lesvos 487
Meteora 475
Monemvasia 468
Mount Olympus 474
Mykonos 479
Mystras 468
Nafplion 469
Naxos 482
Northern Greece 470
Olympia 467
Paros 480
Patras 466
Peloponnese 466
Rethymno 486
Rhodes 487
Samothraki 488
Santorini 483
Sparta 468
Thessaloniki 470
Zagorohoria 476
Zakynthos 479
Greek alphabet 1059
Grenoble, FRA 355
Grindelwald, SWI 1006
Groningen, NTH 729
Guernica, SPA 956
guesthouses 35
Gult of Bothnia, SWE 990
Győr, HUN 508

H

Haarlem, NTH 723
Hadrian's Wall, BRI 174
Hamburg, GER 410
Hanover, GER 416
Hardangerjøkulen Glacier, NOR 754
Harlech, BRI 181
Heidelberg, GER 431
Hellesylt, NOR 758
Helsingborg, SWE 983

INDEX

Helsingør, DEN 266
Helsinki, FIN 290
Heraklion, GCE 484
Herculaneum, ITA 649
Hiiumaa, EST 285
Hillerød, DEN 266
hitchhiking 59
Hoburgen, SWE 978
Hohe Tauern National Park, AUT 91
home exchange 36
hostels 33
hotels 35
humanitarian and social services 62
Humlebæk. DEN 267
Hungary 489
- Baradla Caves 508
- Budapest 494
- Danube Bend 505
- Eger 506
- Esztergom 506
- Győr 508
- Keszthely 509
- Lake Balaton 509
- Pannonhalma 508
- Pécs 510
- Siófok 509
- Szentendre 505
- Tihany 510
- Visegrád 506

Húsavík, ICE 530
Hvaler Islands, NOR 745

I

Ibiza, SPA 959
Iceland 512
- Akureyri 528
- Blue Lagoon 526
- Geysir 525
- Goðafoss 530
- Gullfoss 525
- Húsavík 530
- Jökulsárgljúfur National Park 531
- Landmannalaugar 528
- Mývatn 530
- Nesjavelliri 526
- Reykjavík 518, 519
- Westman Islands 526
- Þingvellir National Park 525
- Þórsmörk 528

Innsbruck, AUT 92
Interlaken, SWI 1003
Inverness, BRI 195
Ioannina, GCE 477
Ionian Islands, GCE 478
Ios, GCE 482
Isle of Man, BRI 175
İstanbul, TUR 1034
Italian Riviera, ITA 605
Italian Switzerland, SWI 1027
Italy 569
- Aeolian Islands 654
- Alghero 656
- Amalfi 652
- Amalfi Coast 651
- Ancona 645
- Assisi 643
- Atrani 652
- Bay of Naples 650
- Bergamo 602
- Bologna 609
- Bolzano 614
- Borromean Islands 604
- Cagliari 656
- Camogli 607
- Campania 645
- Capri 651
- Cinque Terre 608
- Como 603
- Desenzano 604
- Emilia-Romagna 609
- Ferrara 613
- Finale Ligure 607
- Florence 630
- Friuli-Venezia Giulia 628
- Genoa 605
- Herculaneum 649
- Italian Riviera 605
- Lake Como 603
- Lake Country 603
- Lake Garda 604
- Lake Maggiore 604
- Limone 604
- Lipari 654
- Lombardy 596
- Maddalena Archipelago 657
- Mantua 602
- Marches 644
- Menaggio 603
- Milan 596
- Naples 645
- Orvieto 644
- Padua 626
- Palau 656
- Palermo 653
- Parma 611
- Perugia 642
- Piedmont 628
- Pisa 641
- Pompeii 650
- Positano 652
- Ravello 652
- Ravenna 611
- Razzoli 657
- Rimini 612
- Riva del Garda 604
- Rome 574
- Santa Margherita Ligure 607
- Sardinia 655
- Sicily 653
- Siena 640
- Sirmione 604
- Sorrento 650
- Stresa 604
- Syracuse 654
- Tivoli 595
- Trent 614
- Trentino-Alto Adige 614
- Trieste 628
- Turin 628
- Tuscany 630
- Umbria 642
- Urbino 644
- Vatican City 590
- Veneto 615
- Venice 615
- Verona 626
- Vulcano 655

J

Jaskyňa Domica, SLK 878
Jökulsárgljúfur National Park, ICE 531
Jotunheimen National Park, NOR 758
Jukkasjärvi, SWE 994
Jungfraujoch, SWI 1007
Jungfrau Region, SWI 1003
Jūrmala, LAT 666
Jutland, DEN 271

K

Kalambaka, GCE 475
Kalmar, SWE 979
Kärdla, EST 285
Karlovy Vary, CZR 248
Kåseberga, SWE 982
Kassari, EST 285
Kassel, GER 424
Kaunas, LIT 679
keeping in touch 30
Keszthely, HUN 509
Kilkenny, IRE 547
Killarney, IRE 552
Killarney National Park, IRE 552
Kiruna, SWE 993
Klaipėda, LIT 680
Klintehamn, SWE 978
Klosters, SWI 1018
Knossos, GCE 485
Königsschlößer, GER 444
Košice, SLK 877
Kraków, POL 781, 782
Kristiansand, NOR 746

Krk Town, CRO 221
Kuopio, FIN 303
Kuressaare, EST 284
Kuźnice, POL 790
Kværndrup, DEN 270
Kyiv, UKR 1052

L

Lagos, POR 820
Lahti, FIN 298
Lake Balaton, HUN 509
Lake Bohinj, SLN 887
Lake Como, ITA 603
Lake Country, ITA 603
Lake Garda, ITA 604
Lake Maggiore, ITA 604
Lake Mälaren, SWE 976
Landmannalaugar, ICE 528
language phrasebook 1059
- Croatian 1059
- Cyrillic alphabet 1059
- Czech 1060
- Finnish 1061
- French 1061
- German 1062
- Greek 1063
- Greek alphabet 1059
- Hungarian 1064
- Italian 1064
- Norwegian 1065
- Polish 1066
- Portuguese 1066
- Romanian 1067
- Russian 1068
- Spanish 1068
- Swedish 1069

language schools 64
Languedoc-Roussillon, FRA 363
Lappland, SWE 993
Latvia 658
- Bulduri 666
- Cēsis 667
- Dubulti 666
- Jūrmala 666
- Majori 666
- Rīga 662
- Sigulda 666
- Ventspils 667

Lausanne, SWI 1026
Leiden, NTH 724
Leipzig, GER 451
Leknes, NOR 765
Le Mont-Dore, FRA 358
Lesvos, GCE 487
Lichtenstein 668
- Vaduz 669

Liège, BEL 114
Lille, FRA 343
Lillehammer, NOR 745
Limone, ITA 604
Limousin, FRA 358
Linz, AUT 85
Lipari, ITA 654
Liptovský Mikuláš, SLK 876
Lisbon, POR 804
Lithuania 671
- Curonian Spit 681
- Kaunas 679
- Klaipėda 680
- Nida 681
- Palanga 681
- Vilnius 675

Liverpool, BRI 167
Ljubljana, SLN 882
Loch Lomond, BRI 195
Loch Ness, BRI 195
Łódź, POL 793
Lofoten Islands, NOR 764
Loire Valley, FRA 335
Lombardy, ITA 596
Lom, NOR 758
London, BRI 123
long-term work 66
Lopud Island, CRO 229
Lorelei, GER 430
Lübeck, GER 410
Lublin, POL 788
Lucca, ITA 641
Lugano, SWI 1027
Lund, SWE 981
Luxembourg 682
- Ardennes 689
- Echternach 689
- Esch-sur-Sûre 690
- Ettelbrück 689
- Luxembourg City 684
- Vianden 690

Luxembourg City, LUX 684
Luzern, SWI 1012
Lviv, UKR 1056
Lyon, FRA 350

M

Maastricht, NTH 730
Maddalena Archipelago, ITA 657
Madrid, SPA 896
Mainz, GER 429
Majori, LAT 666
Málaga, SPA 928
Mallorca, SPA 958
Malmö, SWE 980
Malta 691
- Birgu 698
- Birzebugga 698
- Marsaxlokk 698
- Mdina 698
- Paola 697
- Rabat 698
- Sleima 699
- St. Julian's 699
- Valletta 694

Manchester, BRI 165
Mantua, ITA 602
Marches, ITA 644
Maribor, SLN 888
Marsaxlokk, MTA 698
Marseille, FRA 365
Massif Central, FRA 350
Matterhorn, The SWI 1020
Mdina, MTA 698
measurements 1058
Mechelen, BEL 107
Menaggio, ITA 603
Meteora, GCE 475
Milan, ITA 596
Moldavia, ROM 836
Monaco, FRA 377
Møn, DEN 267
Monemvasia, GCE 468
money 17
- ATMs 17
- bargaining 21
- credit cards 17
- currency exchange 17
- debit cards 17
- exchange rates 17
- taxes 21
- tipping 21
- traveler's checks 18
- wiring money 20

Monte-Carlo, FRA 377
Montpellier, FRA 365
Mont-St-Michel, FRA 342
mopeds 58
Mora, SWE 989
Moravia, CZR 251
Moscow, RUS 846
Moskenes, NOR 764
Moskenesøya, NOR 764
motorcycles 58

INDEX

Mount Olympus, GCE 474
Munich, GER 436
museums 2
Mykonos, GCE 479
Myrdal, NOR 753
Mystras, GCE 468
Mývatn, ICE 530

N

Nafplion, GCE 469
Namur, BEL 116
Nancy, FRA 349
Nantes, FRA 339
Naples, ITA 645
Navarra, SPA 950
Naxos, GCE 482
Nesjavelliri, ICE 526
Netherlands 700
- Aalsmeer 722
- Amsterdam 705
- Arnhem 729
- Bloemendaal aan Zee 723
- De Hoge Veluwe National Park 729
- Delft 726
- Groningen 729
- Haarlem 723
- Leiden 724
- Maastricht 730
- Rotterdam 726
- The Hague 725
- Utrecht 728
- Zandvoort aan Zee 723

Newcastle-upon-Tyne, BRI 173
Nice, FRA 372
Nida, LIT 681
Nîmes, FRA 371
Nordfjord, NOR 757
Normandy, FRA 340
Northern Coast, CRO 220
Northern England, BRI 165
Northern Germany, GER 409
Northern Greece, GCE 470
Northern Ireland 561
- Belfast 561
- Derry/Londonderry 567
- Giant's Causeway 568

Northern Norway, NOR 762
Northern Portugal, POR 814
Northwestern Ireland, IRE 560
Northwestern Switzerland, SWI 1016
Norway 731
- Å 765
- Ålesund 759
- Åndalsnes 760
- Aurland 753
- Balestrand 755
- Barentsburg 766
- Bergen 748
- Bodø 764
- Eidfjord 754
- Finse 753
- Fjærland 756
- Fjærlandsfjord 756
- Fjords 748
- Flåm 753
- Fredrikstad 745
- Geiranger 757
- Geirangerfjord 757
- Hardangerjøkulen Glacier 754
- Hellesylt 758
- Hvaler Islands 745
- Jotunheimen National Park 758
- Kristiansand 746
- Leknes 765
- Lillehammer 745
- Lofoten Islands 764
- Lom 758
- Moskenes 764
- Moskenesøya 764
- Myrdal 753
- Nordfjord 757
- Northern Norway 762
- Oslo 737
- Oslo-Bergen Rail Line 753
- Posebyen 746
- Pyramiden 766
- Reinheimen National Park 758
- Romsdal 759
- Sogndal 756
- Sognefjord 755
- Southern Norway 746
- Stamsund 766
- Stavanger 747
- Stryn 757
- Tromsø 762
- Trøndelag 759
- Trondheim 761
- Vestvågøy 765
- Voss 754
- West Norway 748

Nyköping, SWE 966

O

Odense, DEN 269
Odessa, UKR 1057
Oktoberfest 442
Öland, SWE 979
Olomouc, CZR 252
Olympia, GCE 467
Orléans, FRA 335
Örnsköldsvik, SWE 991
Orvieto, ITA 644
Oslo-Bergen Rail Line, NOR 753
Oslo, NOR 737
Östersund, SWE 989
outdoors 4, 37
Oxford, BRI 155

P

packing 21
Padua, ITA 626
Palanga, LIT 681
Palau, ITA 656
Palermo, ITA 653
Palma, SPA 958
Pamplona, SPA 950
Pannonhalma, HUN 508
Paola, MTA 697
Parc National des Pyrénées, FRA 362
Paris, FRA 311
Parma, ITA 611
Pärnu, EST 283
Paros, GCE 480
Pas de Calais, FRA 342
passports 14
Patras, GCE 466
Pays Basque, FRA 360
Peak District National Park, BRI 169
Pécs, HUN 510
Peloponnese, GCE 466
pensions 35
Penzance, BRI 154
Périgueux, FRA 359
Perugia, ITA 642
Peterhof, RUS 866
Piedmont, ITA 628
Piran, SLN 885
Pisa, ITA 641
planes 46
Plitvice Lakes National Park, CRO 219
Plovdiv, BUL 207
Plzeň, CZR 249
Poland 767
- Auschwitz-Birkenau 787
- Gdańsk 794, 796
- Kraków 781, 782
- Kuźnice 790
- Łódź 793
- Lublin 788
- Sopot 798
- Warsaw 772
- Wieliczka 788

Wrocław 790
Zakopane 789
Pompeii, ITA 650
Pori, FIN 300
Porto, POR 814
Portugal 799
Algarve 819
Braga 816
Cascais 813
Central Portugal 818
Coimbra 817
Évora 818
Faro 819
Lagos 820
Lisbon 804
Northern Portugal 814
Porto 814
Sagres 821
Sintra 813
Porvoo, EST 298
Posebyen, NOR 746
Positano, ITA 652
Poste Restante 33
Prague, CZR 235
Provence, FRA 365
Pula, CRO 222
Pyramiden, NOR 766
Pyrénées, FRA 362

R

Rabat, MTA 698
rail passes 51
Râşnov, ROM 836
Rauma, FIN 300
Ravello, ITA 652
Ravenna, ITA 611
Razzoli, ITA 657
Reims, FRA 344
Reinheimen National Park, NOR 758
Rennes, FRA 338
Republic of Ireland 532
Aran Islands 558
Blarney 552
Burren 556
Cahersiveen 554
Cashel 548
Clifden 558
Cliffs of Moher 556
Connemara 558
Connemara National Park 558
Cork 549
Dingle Peninsula 554
Dingle Town 555
Donegal Town 560
Dublin 537
Dunquin 555
Galway 557
Kilkenny 547
Killarney 552
Killarney National Park 552
Northwestern Ireland 560
Ring of Kerry 554
Rosslare Harbour 546
Slea Head 555
Sligo 559
Southeastern Ireland 546
Southwestern Ireland 548
Ventry 555
Waterford 547
Western Ireland 555
Wicklow Mountains 546
Rethymno, GCE 486
Reykjavík, ICE 518, 519
Rhine Valley, GER 429
Rhodes, GCE 487
Rhône-Alpes, FRA 350
Rīga, LAT 662
Rijeka, CRO 220
Rila Monastery, BUL 207
Rimini, ITA 612
Ring of Kerry, IRE 554
Riva del Garda, ITA 604
Romania 822
Bran 836
Braşov 835
Bucharest 827
Bucovina 837
Cluj-Napoca 834
Constanta 838
Moldavia 836
Râşnov 836
Sighișoara 835
Sinaia 833
Suceava 837
Transylvania 834
Romantic Road, GER 443
Rome, ITA 574
Romsdal, NOR 759
Ronda, SPA 923
Rønne, DEN 269
Roskilde, DEN 267
Rosslare Harbour, IRE 546
Rothenburg ob der Tauber, GER 444
Rotterdam, NTH 726
Rouen, FRA 340
Route du Vin, FRA 347
Rovaniemi, FIN 304
Rovinj, CRO 223
Rungsted, DEN 267
Russia 839
Moscow 846
Peterhof 866
St. Petersburg 857

S

Saaremaa, EST 284
Sachsenhausen, GER 409
safety and health 23
Sagres, POR 821
Salamanca, SPA 911
Salisbury, BRI 151
Salzburg, AUT 86
Salzburger Land, AUT 85
Samothraki, GCE 488
Sandhamn, SWE 975
Sandvig, DEN 269
San Sebastián, SPA 952
Santa Margherita Ligure, ITA 607
Santiago de Compostela, SPA 957
Santorini, GCE 483
Sardinia, ITA 655
Savonlinna, FIN 302
Scotland, BRI 182
Segovia, SPA 910
Sélestat, FRA 348
self defense 24
Seville, SPA 917
short-term work 68
Sicily, ITA 653
Siena, ITA 640
Sighișoara, ROM 835
Sigulda, LAT 666
Sinaia, ROM 833
Sintra, POR 813
Siófok, HUN 509
Sirmione, ITA 604
Skagen, DEN 274
Slea Head, IRE 555
Sleima, MTA 699
Sligo, IRE 559
Slovakia 867
Bratislava 871
Jaskyňa Domica 878
Košice 877
Liptovský Mikuláš 876
Starý Smokovec 876
Tatra Mountains 876
Slovenia 879
Bled 886
Lake Bohinj 887
Ljubljana 882
Maribor 888
Piran 885

Snowdonia National Park, BRI 180
Sofia, BUL 202
Sogndal, NOR 756
Sognefjord, NOR 755
Sopot, POL 798
Sorrento, ITA 650
South Bohemia, CZR 248
Southeastern Ireland, IRE 546
Southern England, BRI 150
Southern Norway, NOR 746
Southern Spain, SPA 914
Southern Sweden, SWE 979
Southwestern Germany, GER 428
Southwestern Ireland, IRE 548
Spain 890
- Alicante 931
- Andalucía 914
- Andorra 947
- Arcos de la Frontera 923
- Balearic Islands 958
- Barcelona 934
- Bilbao 955
- Cáceres 913
- Cadaqués 947
- Castilla la Mancha 907
- Castilla y León 910
- Central Spain 907
- Córdoba 914
- Costa Brava 947
- Costa del Sol 928
- Eastern Spain 931
- El Escorial 907
- Extremadura 913
- Figueres 947
- Galicia 957
- Gibraltar 930
- Granada 924
- Guernica 956
- Ibiza 959
- Madrid 896
- Málaga 928
- Mallorca 958
- Navarra 950
- Palma 958
- Pamplona 950
- Ronda 923
- Salamanca 911
- San Sebastián 952
- Santiago de Compostela 957
- Segovia 910
- Seville 917
- Southern Spain 914
- Tarifa 929
- Toledo 907
- Valencia 932

Sparta, GCE 468
specific concerns 40
Split, CRO 224
Stamsund, NOR 766
Starý Smokovec, SLK 876
Stavanger, NOR 747
Stein am Rhein, SWI 1015
St. Gallen, SWI 1014
St. Goar, GER 430
St. Goarhausen, GER 430
Stirling, BRI 193
St. Julian's, MTA 699
St-Malo, FRA 338
Stockholm Archipelago, SWE 975
Stockholm, SWE 965
Stonehenge, BRI 152
St. Petersburg, RUS 857
Strasbourg, FRA 346
Stratford-upon-Avon, BRI 159
Stresa, ITA 604
Stryn, NOR 757
St-Tropez, FRA 380
study abroad 62
Stuttgart, GER 434
Styria, AUT 96
Suceava, ROM 837
Sweden 960
- Åre 990
- Björkö 976
- Central Sweden 988
- Fårö 978
- Finnhamn 975
- Frösön Island 989
- Gävle 991
- Getterön Peninsula 988
- Gothenburg 984
- Gotland 977
- Gulf of Bothnia 990
- Helsingborg 983
- Hoburgen 978
- Jukkasjärvi 994
- Kalmar 979
- Kåseberga 982
- Kiruna 993
- Klintehamn 978
- Lake Mälaren 976
- Lappland 993
- Lund 981
- Malmö 980
- Mora 989
- Nyköping 966
- Öland 979
- Örnsköldsvik 991
- Östersund 989
- Sandhamn 975
- Southern Sweden 979
- Stockholm 965
- Stockholm Archipelago 975
- Tjockö 976
- Umeå 992
- Uppsala 976
- Varberg 988
- Vaxholm 975
- Visby 978
- Ystad 983

Swiss National Park, SWI 1019
Switzerland 995
- Basel 1016
- Bern 1000
- Bernese Oberland 1000
- Central Switzerland 1007
- Davos 1018
- French Switzerland 1021
- Geneva 1021
- German Switzerland 1000
- Graubünden 1018
- Grindelwald 1006
- Interlaken 1003
- Italian Switzerland 1027
- Jungfraujoch 1007
- Jungfrau Region 1003
- Klosters 1018
- Lausanne 1026
- Lugano 1027
- Luzern 1012
- Matterhorn, The 1020
- Northwestern Switzerland 1016
- Stein am Rhein 1015
- St. Gallen 1014
- Swiss National Park 1019
- Valais 1020
- Zermatt 1020
- Zernez 1019
- Zürich 1007

Syracuse, ITA 654
Szentendre, HUN 505

T

Tallinn, EST 279
Tampere, FIN 301
Tarifa, SPA 929
Tartu, EST 283
Tatra Mountains, SLK 876
taxes 21
teaching English 66
Terezín, CZR 247
The Hague, NTH 725
Thessaloniki, GCE 470
Tihany, HUN 510
Tintern, BRI 180
tipping 21
Tivoli, ITA 595
Tjockö, SWE 976
Toledo, SPA 907
Toulouse, FRA 363
Tournai, BEL 115
Tours, FRA 337
trains 50

Transportation 46
- boats 57
- budget airlines 48
- buses 53
- cars 53
- hitchhiking 59
- mopeds 58
- motorcycles 58
- planes 46
- rail passes 51
- trains 50
- travel agencies 46

Transylvania, ROM 834
travel agencies 46
traveler's checks 18
Trentino-Alto Adige, ITA 614
Trent, ITA 614
Triberg, GER 435
Trier, GER 428
Trieste, ITA 628
Tromsø, NOR 762
Trøndelag, NOR 759
Trondheim, NOR 761
Trossachs, BRI 193
Troyes, FRA 345
Turin, ITA 628
Turkey 1028
- İstanbul 1034

Turku, FIN 298
Tuscany, ITA 630
Tyrol, AUT 92

U

Ukraine 1046
- Kyiv 1052
- Lviv 1056
- Odessa 1057

Umbria, ITA 642
Umeå, SWE 992
university dorms 35
Uppsala, SWE 976
Urbino, ITA 644
Utrecht, NTH 728

V

Vaduz, LCH 669
Valais, SWI 1020
Valencia, SPA 932
Valletta, MTA 694
Varberg, SWE 988
Varna, BUL 208
Vatican City, ITA 590
Vaxholm, SWE 975
Veliko Turnovo, BUL 208
Veneto, ITA 615
Venice, ITA 615
Ventry, IRE 555
Ventspils, LAT 667
Verona, ITA 626
Versailles, FRA 334
Vestvågøy, NOR 765
Vézères Valley, FRA 359
Vianden, LUX 690
Vienna, AUT 73
Viljandi, EST 284
Vilnius, LIT 675
Visby, SWE 978
Visegrád, HUN 506
volunteering abroad 60
Voss, NOR 754
Vulcano, ITA 655

W

Wales, BRI 178
Wallonie, BEL 114
Warsaw, POL 772
Waterford, IRE 547
Weimar, GER 445
West Bohemia, CZR 248
Western Germany, GER 417
Western Ireland, IRE 555
Westman Islands, ICE 526
West Norway, NOR 748
Wicklow Mountains, IRE 546
Wieliczka, POL 788
wiring money 20
Wittenberg, GER 447
Wrocław, POL 790
Wye Valley, BRI 179

Y

York, BRI 170
Ypres, BEL 114
Ystad, SWE 983

Z

Zadar, CRO 224
Zagorohoria, GCE 476
Zagreb, CRO 215
Zakopane, POL 789
Zakynthos, GCE 479
Zandvoort aan Zee, NTH 723
Zell am See, AUT 90
Zermatt, SWI 1020
Zernez, SWI 1019
Zürich, SWI 1007